Customs Duties Handbook 2007

Customs Duties Handbook 2007

Consultant Editor

JEREMY WHITE, *Barrister, Pump Court Tax Chambers*

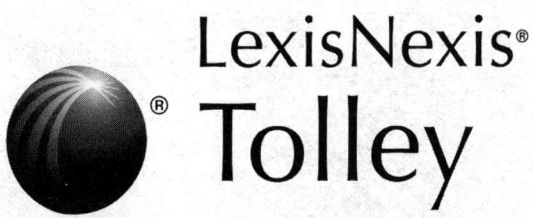

Members of the LexisNexis Group worldwide

United Kingdom	LexisNexis Butterworths, a Division of Reed Elsevier (UK) Ltd, Halsbury House, 35 Chancery Lane, London, WC2A 1EL, and RSH, 1–3 Baxter's Place, Leith Walk Edinburgh EH1 3AF
Argentina	LexisNexis Argentina, Buenos Aires
Australia	LexisNexis Butterworths, Chatswood, New South Wales
Austria	LexisNexis Verlag ARD Orac GmbH & Co KG, Vienna
Benelux	LexisNexis Benelux, Amsterdam
Canada	LexisNexis Canada, Markham, Ontario
Chile	LexisNexis Chile Ltda, Santiago
China	LexisNexis China, Beijing and Shanghai
France	LexisNexis SA, Paris
Germany	LexisNexis Deutschland GmbH, Munster
Hong Kong	LexisNexis Hong Kong, Hong Kong
India	LexisNexis India, New Delhi
Italy	Giuffrè Editore, Milan
Japan	LexisNexis Japan, Tokyo
Malaysia	Malayan Law Journal Sdn Bhd, Kuala Lumpur
Mexico	LexisNexis Mexico, Mexico
New Zealand	LexisNexis NZ Ltd, Wellington
Poland	Wydawnictwo Prawnicze LexisNexis Sp, Warsaw
Singapore	LexisNexis Singapore, Singapore
South Africa	LexisNexis Butterworths, Durban
USA	LexisNexis, Dayton, Ohio

© Reed Elsevier (UK) Ltd 2007

Published by LexisNexis Butterworths

A CIP Catalogue record for this book is available from the British Library.

ISBN: 9781405725163

Printed and bound in Great Britain by William Clowes Limited, Beccles, Suffolk

Visit LexisNexis Butterworths at www.lexisnexis.co.uk

Preface

Tolley's Customs Duties Handbook 2007 is designed to complement *Tolley's Yellow and Orange Tax Handbooks* and the *Excise Duties Handbook* as an indispensable source of the tax legislation currently in force. The Handbook covers customs duties, the product-based excise duties and air passenger duty. It is particularly aimed at practitioners in the VAT and duties tribunals.

The Handbook is intended to provide busy practitioners and other persons working in the area of Customs and Excise with a useful collection of highly relevant materials.

Community Customs Code

The book is of particular benefit to practitioners because it reproduces the Community Customs Code and Implementing Code (Council Regulation (EEC) No 2913/92 and Commission Regulation (EEC) No 2454/93) as amended.

Amendments to the Customs Code and Implementing Code

The security amendments to the Customs Code (Council Regulation 2913/92) made by Regulation (EC) No 648/2005 of the European Parliament and Council of 13 April 2005 have now been consolidated in the text. Together with Commission Regulation (EC) No 1875/2006 of 18 December 2006, the Regulations provide the following—

- Since early 2007, a common risk management framework to support improved risk-based controls by customs authorities.
- From 1 January 2008 the provisions for the Authorised Economic Operator programme (AEO) will enter into force. The AEO programme will strike a balance between increasing security requirements and facilitation for compliant traders.
- From 1 July 2009 it will become mandatory for traders to provide customs authorities with advance information on goods brought into, or out of, the customs territory of the European Community.

The Regulations also envisage the exchange and sharing of the information between the member states' administrations, when possible.

Provisions relating to the definition of data requirements and the electronic lodging of pre-arrival and pre-departure information, which are to apply from

1 July 2009, are reproduced in full at the end of Part III to this work (see Commission Regulation (EC) No 1875/2006).

Modernised Customs Code

Political agreement was reached by the EU Council of Ministers on 25 June 2007 on a modernised Community Customs Code which will simplify legislation and streamline customs process and procedures for the benefit of both customs authorities and traders. The agreement now needs to be confirmed by the European Parliament The modernised Customs Code will—

– introduce the electronic lodging of customs declarations as the rule;
– provide for the exchange of electronic information between the national customs and other competent authorities;
– promote the concept of "centralised clearance"; and
– offer bases for the development of the "Single Window" and "One-Stop-Shop" concepts.

Finance Act 2007

Tobacco products duty

The rates of excise duty charged under the Tobacco Products Duty Act 1979 are increased on all tobacco products by around 3.4 per cent, in line with retail prices inflation. The ad valorem rate of duty on cigarettes remains unchanged at 22 per cent.

Alcoholic liquor duties

The rates of duty charged under the Alcoholic Liquor Duties Act 1979 on beer, cider and wine, in most cases rise by 3.4 per cent, in line with the increase in retail prices inflation. There is no increase in the rate of duty on spirits. As a consequence of the rise in beer duty, the duty on small-brewery beer under FA 2002 s 4, Sch 1 also rises.

Hydrocarbon oil duties

The rates of excise duty on hydrocarbon oils used as main road fuels are increased by 2p per litre (equivalent to an increase of 4.14 per cent). The effective rates of duty (ie duty minus rebate) for non-road fuels are also increased by 2p per litre.

Further increases maintain the existing differentials with the duties on main road fuels, with the exception of road fuel gas other than natural gas, where the duty differential is reduced by 1p per litre. The increases take effect from 1 October 2007 and are not negated by statutory instrument, as has been the case in recent years.

Air passenger duty

The rates of APD are doubled. Within the EEA and other qualifying territories, the rates are increased to £10 per passenger in standard class, and £20 per passenger in other classes of travel. For other destinations, the rates are £40 and £80 respectively. The increases took effect from 1 February 2007.

As announced in the 2007 Pre-Budget Report, the class of travel definition will be amended so that business class only flights attract the standard rate of duty, rather than the reduced rate as at present. The Government also proposes, from 1 November 2009, to replace APD with a tax payable per plane rather than per passenger.

How to use this book

The Handbook is divided into four parts:

I Statutes;

II Statutory Instruments;

III European Community legislation; and

IV Extra-statutory concessions.

The book contains the text of the relevant statutes, statutory instruments, and Community instruments as amended together with the current texts of extra-statutory concessions. Within each part, items are printed in chronological order.

Scope

Community customs duties, alcoholic liquor duties, hydrocarbon oil duties, tobacco products duty and air passenger duty are covered. While product excise duties are included within the *Customs Duties Handbook*, the *Excise Duties Handbook* contains the comprehensive European legislation that would not fit in the *Customs Duties Handbook*.

Betting and gaming duties are not covered (the reader is referred to the *Excise Duties Handbook*). VAT chargeable on importation in so far as it is treated as a duty of customs is covered (in other respects the reader is referred to *Tolley's Orange Tax Handbook*).

The Handbook concentrates on materials that relate to civil liability. General customs management provisions and the main offence provisions are included. However particular materials relating to import and export prohibitions and restrictions are not included (the reader is referred to *Archbold* and *Stone's Justices Manual* for this material).

Even within the customs field, in order to keep the book to a manageable size, certain arcane legislation in respect of ECSC matters and Shipbuilders' Relief has been excluded. Also appointment of ports orders and designation of free zone orders have not been reproduced.

Generally, legislation that applies to Scotland or Northern Ireland only is omitted.

The contents are reproduced as amended to 1 November 2007, although later developments have been included where practicable.

Jeremy White

Pump Court Tax Chambers

1 November 2007

Contents

Contents

Part II
Statutory instruments

Contents

Contents

Part III
European community materials

Contents

Part I

Statutes

FINANCE ACT 1901

(1 Edw c 7)

*An Act to grant certain duties of Customs and Inland Revenue, to alter other duties,
and to amend the Law relating to Customs and Inland Revenue . . .*

[26 July 1901]

NOTES

Words omitted repealed by the Statute Law Revision Act 1927.

PART I
CUSTOMS AND EXCISE

1–9

*(Ss 1, 2(1), 4, 6 repealed by the Statute Law Revision Act 1927; s 2(2) repealed by the
Import Duties Act 1958, s 16(3), (4), Sch 7; s 3 repealed by the Finance Act 1906, s 58(1), Sch
2; ss 5, 7–9 repealed by the Customs and Excise Act 1952, s 320, Sch 12, Pt I.)*

10 Addition or deduction of new or altered duties in the case of contract

(1) Where any new [customs duty] or new excise duty is imposed, or where any
[customs duty] or excise duty is increased, and any goods in respect of which the duty
is payable are delivered after the day on which the new or increased duty takes effect
in pursuance of a contract made before that day, the seller of the goods may, in the
absence of agreement to the contrary, recover, as an addition to the contract price, a
sum equal to any amount paid by him in respect of the goods on account of the new
duty or the increase of duty, as the case may be.

(2) Where any [customs duty] or excise duty is repealed or decreased, and any
goods affected by the duty are delivered after the day on which the duty ceases or the
decrease in the duty takes effect in pursuance of a contract made before that day, the
purchaser of the goods, in the absence of agreement to the contrary, may, if the seller
of the goods has had in respect of those goods the benefit of the repeal or decrease of
the duty, deduct from the contract price a sum equal to the amount of the duty or
decrease of duty, as the case may be.

(3) Where any addition to, or deduction from, the contract price may be made
under this section on account of any new or repealed duty, such sum as may be agreed
upon or in default of agreement determined by the Commissioners of Customs . . ., as
representing in the case of a new duty any new expenses incurred, and in the case of a
repealed duty any expenses saved, may be included in the addition to or deduction
from the contract price, and may be recovered or deducted accordingly.

(4) . . .

NOTES

Sub-ss (1), (2): words in square brackets substituted by the Customs and Excise
Management Act 1979, s 177(1), Sch 4, para 12, Table, Pt I.

Sub-s (3): words omitted repealed by the Statute Law (Repeals) Act 1989.

Sub-s (4): repealed by the Statute Law (Repeals) Act 1989.

11–14

((Pts II–IV) S 11 repealed by the Finance Act 1959, s 37(5), Sch 8, Pt II; ss 12, 14 repealed by the Statute Law Revision Act 1927; s 13 repealed by the Finance Act 1924, ss 20, 41(4), Sch 3.)

PART V
GENERAL

15 Short title and construction

(1)   This Act may be cited as the Finance Act 1901.

(2)   Part I of this Act, so far as it relates to duties of customs, shall be construed together with the Customs Consolidation Act 1876 and the Acts amending that Act (in this Act referred to as the Customs Acts), and so far as it relates to duties of excise shall be construed together with the Acts which relate to the duties of excise and the management of those duties.

(Schs 1–3 repealed by the Statute Law Revision Act 1927; Sch 4 repealed by the Finance Act 1906, s 8(1), Sch 2.)

POST OFFICE ACT 1953

(1953 c 36)

An Act to consolidate certain enactments relating to the Post Office with corrections and improvements made under the Consolidation of Enactments (Procedure) Act 1949

[31 July 1953]

General provisions as to transmission of postal packets

16 Application of customs Acts to postal packets

[(1)   Subject to the provisions of this section, the enactments for the time being in force relating to [customs or excise] shall apply in relation to goods contained in postal packets to which this section applies brought into or sent out of the United Kingdom by post from or to any place outside the United Kingdom as they apply in relation to goods otherwise imported, exported or removed into or out of the United Kingdom from or to any such place.]

(2)   The Treasury, on the recommendation of the Commissioners of Customs and Excise and [the Secretary of State], may by statutory instrument make regulations—

    (a)   for specifying the postal packets to which this section applies;

    (b)   for making modifications or exceptions in the application of the said enactments to such packets;

    (c)   for enabling [persons engaged in the business of the Post Office] to perform for the purposes of the said enactments and otherwise all or any of the duties of the importer, exporter or person removing the goods;

    (d)   for carrying into effect any arrangement with the government or postal administration of any other country with respect to foreign postal packets;

(e)   *for securing the observance of the said enactments and, without prejudice to any liability of any person under those enactments, for punishing any contravention of the regulations;*

and different regulations may be made for foreign and inland postal packets respectively.

(3), (4) . . .

NOTES

Whole Act repealed by the Postal Services Act 2000, s 127(6), Sch 9 with effect from 26 March 2001 subject to transitional provisions and savings.

Sub-s (1): substituted by the Postal Services (Isle of Man Consequential Provisions) Order 1973, SI 1973/960, art 11(1); words in square brackets substituted by the Customs and Excise Management Act 1979, s 177(1), Sch 4, para 12, Table, Pt I.

Sub-s (2): words in first pair of square brackets substituted by virtue of the Post Office Act 1969, ss 76, 88, 139, Sch 4, para 2(1) and by the Ministry of Posts and Telecommunications (Dissolution) Order 1974, SI 1974/691, arts 2, 3(3); words in second pair of square brackets substituted by virtue of the Post Office Act 1969, ss 76, 88, 139, Sch 4, para 2(1).

Sub-s (3): repealed by the Post Office Act 1969, s 141, Sch 11, Pt II.

Sub-s (4): repealed by the Finance Act 1987, s 72(7), Sch 16, Pt XI.

Regulations: the Postal Packets (Customs and Excise) (Amendment) Regulations 1986, SI 1986/1019; the Postal Packets (Customs and Excise) (Amendment) Regulations 1992, SI 1992/3224. The following warrants have effect, by virtue of s 91(2), as if made under this section and the regulations mentioned as follows were made under sub-s (2) above: the Jersey Parcels (Customs) Warrant 1901, SR & O 1901/1024; the Guernsey Parcels (Customs) Warrant 1902, SR & O 1902/812; the Alderney Parcels (Customs) Warrant 1949, SI 1949/1356; the Postal Packets (Customs and Excise) Regulations 1986, SI 1986/260, as amended by SI 1986/1019, SI 1992/3224. Note that regulations under this section may make special provision in relation to value added tax; see the Value Added Tax Act 1994, s 16(2).

17 Power to detain postal packets containing contraband

(1) Without prejudice to the last foregoing section, [the Post Office] may detain any postal packet suspected to contain any goods chargeable with any [duty charged on imported goods (whether a customs or an excise duty)] which has not been paid or secured or any goods in the course of importation, exportation or removal into or out of the United Kingdom, . . . contrary to any prohibition or restriction for the time being in force with respect thereto under or by virtue of any enactment and may forward the packet to the Commissioners of Customs and Excise.

(2) Where any postal packet has been forwarded to the said Commissioners under this section they may—

(a)   *in the presence of the person to whom the packet is addressed; or*

(b)   *if, after notice in writing from them requiring his attendance left at or forwarded by post to the address on the packet, the addressee fails to attend, or if the address on the packet is outside the British postal area, then in his absence,*

open and examine the packet.

(3) Where the said Commissioners open and examine a postal packet under this section, then—

(a)   *if they find any such goods as aforesaid they may detain the packet and its contents for the purpose of taking proceedings with respect thereto;*

(b)   *if they find no such goods, they shall either deliver the packet to the addressee upon his paying any postage and other sums chargeable thereon or, if he is absent, forward the packet to him by post.*

NOTES

Whole Act repealed by the Postal Services Act 2000, s 127(6), Sch 9 with effect from 26 March 2001 subject to transitional provisions and savings.

Sub-s (1): words in first pair of square brackets substituted by virtue of the Post Office Act 1969, ss 76, 88, 139, Sch 4, paras 1, 2(6); words in second pair of square brackets substituted by the Customs and Excise Management Act 1979, s 177(1), Sch 4, para 12, Table, Pt I; words omitted repealed by the Postal Services (Channel Islands Consequential Provisions) Order 1969, SI 1969/1368, art 10, and the Postal Services (Isle of Man Consequential Provisions) Order 1973, SI 1973/960, art 12.

Miscellaneous and General

92 Short title

(1)   This Act may be cited as the Post Office Act 1953.

(2)   This Act shall come into force one month after the passing thereof.

NOTES

Whole Act repealed by the Postal Services Act 2000, s 127(6), Sch 9 with effect from 26 March 2001 subject to transitional provisions and savings.

(Sch 1 repealed by the Post Office Act 1969, s 141, Sch 11, Pt II; Sch 2 outside the scope of this work; Sch 3 repealed by the Statute Law (Repeals) Act 1974.)

DIPLOMATIC PRIVILEGES ACT 1964

(1964 c 81)

ARRANGEMENT OF SECTIONS

An Act to amend the law on diplomatic privileges and immunities by giving effect to the Vienna Convention on Diplomatic Relations; and for purposes connected therewith

[31 July 1964]

1 Replacement of existing law

The following provisions of this Act shall, with respect to the matters dealt with therein, have effect in substitution for any previous enactment or rule of law.

Application of Vienna Convention

(1) Subject to section 3 of this Act, the Articles set out in Schedule 1 to this Act (being Articles of the Vienna Convention on Diplomatic Relations signed in 1961) shall have the force of law in the United Kingdom and shall for that purpose be construed in accordance with the following provisions of this section.

(2) In those Articles—

"agents of the receiving State" shall be construed as including any constable and any person exercising a power of entry to any premises under any enactment (including any enactment of the Parliament of Northern Ireland);

"national of the receiving State" shall be construed as meaning citizen of the United Kingdom and Colonies;

"Ministry for Foreign Affairs or such other ministry as may be agreed" shall be construed as meaning the department of the Secretary of State concerned;

and, in the application of those Articles to Scotland, any reference to attachment or execution shall be construed as a reference to the execution of diligence, and any reference to the execution of a judgment as a reference to the enforcement of a decree by diligence.

(3) For the purposes of Article 32 a waiver by the head of the mission of any State or any person for the time being performing his functions shall be deemed to be a waiver by that State.

(4) The exemption granted by Article 33 with respect to any services shall be deemed to except those services from any class of employment [in respect of which contributions or premiums are payable under the enactments relating to . . . social security, including enactments in force in Northern Ireland, but not so as to render any person liable to any contribution or premium] which he would not be required to pay if those services were not so excepted.

(5) Articles 35, 36 and 40 shall be construed as granting any privilege or immunity which they require to be granted.

[(5A) The reference in Article 36 to customs duties shall be construed as including a reference to excise duties chargeable on goods imported into the United Kingdom [and to value added tax charged in accordance with section [10 or 15 of the Value Added Tax Act 1994] (acquisitions from other member States and importations from outside the European Community)].]

(6) The references in Articles 37 and 38 to the extent to which any privileges and immunities are admitted by the receiving State and to additional privileges and immunities that may be granted by the receiving State shall be construed as referring respectively to the extent to which any privileges and immunities may be specified by Her Majesty by Order in Council, and to any additional privileges and immunities that may be so specified.

NOTES

Sub-s (4): words in square brackets substituted by the Social Security Act 1973, ss 100, 101, Sch 27, para 24 (but note that the words "or premiums" and "or premium" have not yet been bought into force); words omitted repealed by the Social Security (Consequential Provisions) Act 1975, ss 1(2), 5, Sch 1, Pt I.

Sub-s (5A): inserted by the Customs and Excise Management Act 1979, s 177(1), Sch 4, para 3; words in first (outer) pair of square brackets inserted by the Finance (No 2) Act 1992, s 14, Sch 3, para 87; words in second (inner) pair of square brackets substituted by the Value Added Tax Act 1994, s 100(1), Sch 14, para 1.

Orders in Council: the Diplomatic Privileges (British Nationals) Order 1999, SI 1999/670 (made under sub-s (6)).

3 Restriction of privileges and immunities

(1)   If it appears to Her Majesty that the privileges and immunities accorded to a mission of Her Majesty in the territory of any State, or to persons connected with that mission, are less than those conferred by this Act on the mission of that State or on persons connected with that mission, Her Majesty may by an Order in Council withdraw such of the privileges and immunities so conferred from the mission of that State or from such persons connected with it as appears to Her Majesty to be proper.

[(2)   An Order in Council under this section shall be disregarded for the purposes of section 50(4) of the British Nationality Act 1981 (circumstances in which certain persons entitled to exemption under section 8(3) of the Immigration Act 1971 are to be regarded for the purposes of section 1(1) of the said Act of 1981 as settled in the United Kingdom).]

NOTES

Sub-s (2): substituted by the British Nationality Act 1981, s 52(6), Sch 7.

4 Evidence

If in any proceedings any question arises whether or not any person is entitled to any privilege or immunity under this Act a certificate issued by or under the authority of the Secretary of State stating any fact relating to that question shall be conclusive evidence of that fact.

5

(Sub-s (1) amended the Aliens Restriction (Amendment) Act 1919, s 14(1) (repealed); sub-s (2) repealed by the British Nationality Act 1981, s 52(8), Sch 9.)

6 Orders in Council

(1)   No recommendation shall be made to Her Majesty in Council to make an Order under section 2 of this Act unless a draft thereof has been laid before Parliament and approved by resolution of each House of Parliament; and any statutory instrument containing an Order under section 3 of this Act shall be subject to annulment in pursuance of a resolution of either House of Parliament.

(2)   Any power to make an Order conferred by the foregoing provisions of this Act includes power to vary or revoke an Order by a subsequent Order.

7 Saving for certain bilateral arrangements

(1)   Where any special agreement or arrangement between the Government of any State and the Government of the United Kingdom in force at the commencement of this Act provides for extending—

(a)   such immunity from jurisdiction and from arrest or detention, and such inviolability of residence, as are conferred by this Act on a diplomatic agent; or

(b)   such exemption from [duties (whether of customs or excise) chargeable on imported goods], taxes and related charges as is conferred by this Act in respect of articles for the personal use of a diplomatic agent;

to any class of person, or to articles for the personal use of any class of person, connected with the mission of that State, that immunity and inviolability or exemption shall so extend, so long as that agreement or arrangement continues in force.

(2)   The Secretary of State shall publish in the London, Edinburgh and Belfast Gazettes a notice specifying the States with which and the classes of person with respect to which such an agreement or arrangement as is mentioned in subsection (1)

of this section is in force and whether its effect is as mentioned in paragraph (a) or paragraph (b) of that subsection, and shall whenever necessary amend the notice by a further such notice; and the notice shall be conclusive evidence of the agreement or arrangement and the classes of person with respect to which it is in force.

NOTES

Sub-s (1): words in square brackets in para (b) substituted by the Customs and Excise Management Act 1979, s 177(1), Sch 4, para 12, Table, Pt I.

8 Short title, interpretation, commencement, repeal and saving

(1) This Act may be cited as the Diplomatic Privileges Act 1964.

(2) . . .

(3) This Act shall come into force on such day as Her Majesty may by Order in Council appoint.

(4) . . .

(5) Any Order in Council under the Diplomatic Immunities Restriction Act 1955 which is in force immediately before the commencement of this Act shall, so far as it could have been made under section 3 of this Act, have effect as if so made.

NOTES

Sub-s (2): repealed by the Zimbabwe Act 1979, s 6(3), Sch 3.

Sub-s (4): repealed by the Statute Law (Repeals) Act 1974.

SCHEDULES

SCHEDULE 1

ARTICLES OF VIENNA CONVENTION HAVING THE FORCE OF LAW IN
THE UNITED KINGDOM

(Section 2)

ARTICLE 1

For the purpose of the present Convention, the following expressions shall have the meanings hereunder assigned to them:

(a)   the "head of the mission" is the person charged by the sending State with the duty of acting in that capacity;

(b)   the "members of the mission" are the head of the mission and the members of the staff of the mission;

(c)   the "members of the staff of the mission" are the members of the diplomatic staff, of the administrative and technical staff and of the service staff of the mission;

(d)   the "members of the diplomatic staff" are the members of the staff of the mission having diplomatic rank;

(e)   a "diplomatic agent" is the head of the mission or a member of the diplomatic staff of the mission;

(f)   the "members of the administrative and technical staff" are the members of the staff of the mission employed in the administrative and technical service of the mission;

(g)   the "members of the service staff" are the members of the staff of the mission in the domestic service of the mission;

(h)   a "private servant" is a person who is in the domestic service of a member of the mission and who is not an employee of the sending State;

(i)   the "premises of the mission" are the buildings or parts of buildings and the land ancillary thereto, irrespective of ownership, used for the purposes of the mission including the residence of the head of the mission.

ARTICLE 22

1. The premises of the mission shall be inviolable. The agents of the receiving State may not enter them, except with the consent of the head of the mission.

2. The receiving State is under a special duty to take all appropriate steps to protect the premises of the mission against any intrusion or damage and to prevent any disturbance of the peace of the mission or impairment of its dignity.

3. The premises of the mission, their furnishings and other property thereon and the means of transport of the mission shall be immune from search, requisition, attachment or execution.

ARTICLE 23

1. The sending State and the head of the mission shall be exempt from all national, regional or municipal dues and taxes in respect of the premises of the mission, whether owned or leased, other than such as represent payment for specific services rendered.

2. The exemption from taxation referred to in this Article shall not apply to such dues and taxes payable under the law of the receiving State by persons contracting with the sending State or the head of the mission.

ARTICLE 24

The archives and documents of the mission shall be inviolable at any time and wherever they may be.

ARTICLE 27

1. The receiving State shall permit and protect free communication on the part of the mission for all official purposes. In communicating with the Government and other missions and consulates of the sending State, wherever situated, the mission may employ all appropriate means, including diplomatic couriers and messages in code or cipher. However, the mission may install and use a wireless transmitter only with the consent of the receiving State.

2. The official correspondence of the mission shall be inviolable. Official correspondence means all correspondence relating to the mission and its functions.

3. The diplomatic bag shall not be opened or detained.

4. The packages constituting the diplomatic bag must bear visible external marks of their character and may contain only diplomatic documents or articles intended for official use.

5. The diplomatic courier, who shall be provided with an official document indicating his status and the number of packages constituting the diplomatic bag, shall be protected by the receiving State in the performance of his functions. He shall enjoy personal inviolability and shall not be liable to any form of arrest or detention.

6. The sending State or the mission may designate diplomatic couriers ad hoc. In such cases the provisions of paragraph 5 of this Article shall also apply, except that the immunities therein mentioned shall cease to apply when such a courier has delivered to the consignee the diplomatic bag in his charge.

7. A diplomatic bag may be entrusted to the captain of a commercial aircraft scheduled to land at an authorised port of entry. He shall be provided with an official document indicating the number of packages constituting the bag but he shall not be

considered to be a diplomatic courier. The mission may send one of its members to take possession of the diplomatic bag directly and freely from the captain of the aircraft.

ARTICLE 28

The fees and charges levied by the mission in the course of its official duties shall be exempt from all dues and taxes.

ARTICLE 29

The person of a diplomatic agent shall be inviolable. He shall not be liable to any form of arrest or detention. The receiving State shall treat him with due respect and shall take all appropriate steps to prevent any attack on his person, freedom or dignity.

ARTICLE 30

1.   The private residence of a diplomatic agent shall enjoy the same inviolability and protection as the premises of the mission.

2.   His papers, correspondence and, except as provided in paragraph 3 of Article 31, his property, shall likewise enjoy inviolability.

ARTICLE 31

1.   A diplomatic agent shall enjoy immunity from the criminal jurisdiction of the receiving State. He shall also enjoy immunity from its civil and administrative jurisdiction, except in the case of:

   (a)   a real action relating to private immovable property situated in the territory of the receiving State, unless he holds it on behalf of the sending State for the purposes of the mission;

   (b)   an action relating to succession in which the diplomatic agent is involved as executor, administrator, heir or legatee as a private person and not on behalf of the sending State;

   (c)   an action relating to any professional or commercial activity exercised by the diplomatic agent in the receiving State outside his official functions.

2.   A diplomatic agent is not obliged to give evidence as a witness.

3.   No measures of execution may be taken in respect of a diplomatic agent except in the cases coming under sub-paragraphs (a), (b) and (c) of paragraph 1 of this Article, and provided that the measures concerned can be taken without infringing the inviolability of his person or of his residence.

4.   The immunity of a diplomatic agent from the jurisdiction of the receiving State does not exempt him from the jurisdiction of the sending State.

ARTICLE 32

1.   The immunity from jurisdiction of diplomatic agents and of persons enjoying immunity under Article 37 may be waived by the sending State.

2.   The waiver must always be express.

3.   The initiation of proceedings by a diplomatic agent or by a person enjoying immunity from jurisdiction under Article 37 shall preclude him from invoking immunity from jurisdiction in respect of any counter-claim directly connected with the principal claim.

4.   Waiver of immunity from jurisdiction in respect of civil or administrative proceedings shall not be held to imply waiver of immunity in respect of the execution of the judgment, for which a separate waiver shall be necessary.

ARTICLE 33

1.   Subject to the provisions of paragraph 3 of this Article, a diplomatic agent shall with respect to services rendered for the sending State be exempt from social security provisions which may be in force in the receiving State.

2.   The exemption provided for in paragraph 1 of this Article shall also apply to private servants who are in the sole employ of a diplomatic agent, on condition:

(a)   that they are not nationals of or permanently resident in the receiving State; and

(b)   that they are covered by the social security provisions which may be in force in the sending State or a third State.

3.   A diplomatic agent who employs persons to whom the exemption provided for in paragraph 2 of this Article does not apply shall observe the obligations which the social security provisions of the receiving State impose upon employers.

4.   The exemption provided for in paragraphs 1 and 2 of this Article shall not preclude voluntary participation in the social security system of the receiving State provided that such participation is permitted by that State.

5.   The provisions of this Article shall not affect bilateral or multilateral agreements concerning social security concluded previously and shall not prevent the conclusion of such agreements in the future.

ARTICLE 34

A diplomatic agent shall be exempt from all dues and taxes, personal or real, national, regional or municipal, except;

(a)   indirect taxes of a kind which are normally incorporated in the price of goods or services;

(b)   dues and taxes on private immovable property situated in the territory of the receiving State, unless he holds it on behalf of the sending State for the purposes of the mission;

(c)   estate, succession or inheritance duties levied by the receiving State, subject to the provisions of paragraph 4 of Article 39;

(d)   dues and taxes on private income having its source in the receiving State and capital taxes on investments made in commercial undertakings in the receiving State;

(e)   charges levied for specific services rendered;

(f)   registration, court or record fees, mortgage dues and stamp duty, with respect to immovable property, subject to the provisions of Article 23.

ARTICLE 35

The receiving State shall exempt diplomatic agents from all personal services, from all public service of any kind whatsoever, and from military obligations such as those connected with requisitioning, military contributions and billeting.

ARTICLE 36

1.   The receiving State shall, in accordance with such laws and regulations as it may adopt, permit entry of and grant exemption from all customs duties, taxes, and related charges other than charges for storage, cartage and similar services on:

(a)   articles for the official use of the mission;

(b)   articles for the personal use of a diplomatic agent or members of his family forming part of his household, including articles intended for his establishment.

2.   The personal baggage of a diplomatic agent shall be exempt from inspection, unless there are serious grounds for presuming that it contains articles not covered by the exemptions mentioned in paragraph 1 of this Article, or articles the import or

export of which is prohibited by the law or controlled by the quarantine regulations of the receiving State. Such inspection shall be conducted only in the presence of the diplomatic agent or of his authorised representative.

ARTICLE 37

1.   The members of the family of a diplomatic agent forming part of his household shall, if they are not nationals of the receiving State, enjoy the privileges and immunities specified in Articles 29 to 36.

2.   Members of the administrative and technical staff of the mission, together with members of their families forming part of their respective households, shall, if they are not nationals of or permanently resident in the receiving State, enjoy the privileges and immunities specified in Articles 29 to 35, except that the immunity from civil and administrative jurisdiction of the receiving State specified in paragraph 1 of Article 31 shall not extend to acts performed outside the course of their duties. They shall also enjoy the privileges specified in Article 36, paragraph 1, in respect of articles imported at the time of first installation.

3.   Members of the service staff of the mission who are not nationals of or permanently resident in the receiving State shall enjoy immunity in respect of acts performed in the course of their duties, exemption from dues and taxes on the emoluments they receive by reason of their employment and the exemption contained in Article 33.

4.   Private servants of members of the mission shall, if they are not nationals of or permanently resident in the receiving State, be exempt from dues and taxes on the emoluments they receive by reason of their employment. In other respects, they may enjoy privileges and immunities only to the extent admitted by the receiving State. However, the receiving State must exercise its jurisdiction over those persons in such a manner as not to interfere unduly with the performance of the functions of the mission.

ARTICLE 38

1.   Except in so far as additional privileges and immunities may be granted by the receiving State, a diplomatic agent who is a national of or permanently resident in that State shall enjoy only immunity from jurisdiction, and inviolability, in respect of official acts performed in the exercise of his functions.

2.   Other members of the staff of the mission and private servants who are nationals of or permanently resident in the receiving State shall enjoy privileges and immunities only to the extent admitted by the receiving State. However, the receiving State must exercise its jurisdiction over those persons in such a manner as not to interfere unduly with the performance of the functions of the mission.

ARTICLE 39

1.   Every person entitled to privileges and immunities shall enjoy them from the moment he enters the territory of the receiving State on proceedings to take up his post or, if already in its territory, from the moment when his appointment is notified to the Ministry for Foreign Affairs or such other ministry as may be agreed.

2.   When the functions of a person enjoying privileges and immunities have come to an end, such privileges and immunities shall normally cease at the moment when he leaves the country, or on expiry of a reasonable period in which to do so, but shall subsist until that time, even in case of armed conflict. However, with respect to acts performed by such a person in the exercise of his functions as a member of the mission, immunity shall continue to subsist.

3.   In case of the death of a member of the mission, the members of his family shall continue to enjoy the privileges and immunities to which they are entitled until the expiry of a reasonable period in which to leave the country.

4. In the event of the death of a member of the mission not a national of or permanently resident in the receiving State or a member of his family forming part of his household, the receiving State shall permit the withdrawal of the movable property of the deceased, with the exception of any property acquired in the country the export of which was prohibited at the time of his death. Estate, succession and inheritance duties shall not be levied on movable property the presence of which in the receiving State was due solely to the presence there of the deceased as a member of the mission or as a member of the family of a member of the mission.

ARTICLE 40

1. If a diplomatic agent passes through or is in the territory of a third State, which has granted him a passport visa if such visa was necessary, while proceeding to take up or to return to his post, or when returning to his own country, the third State shall accord him inviolability and such other immunities as may be required to ensure his transit or return. The same shall apply in the case of any members of his family enjoying privileges or immunities who are accompanying the diplomatic agent, or travelling separately to join him or to return to their country.

2. In circumstances similar to those specified in paragraph 1 of this Article, third States shall not hinder the passage of members of the administrative and technical or service staff of a mission, and of members of their families, through their territories.

3. Third States shall accord to official communications in transit, including messages in code or cipher, the same freedom and protection as is accorded by the receiving State. They shall accord to diplomatic couriers, who have been granted a passport visa if such visa was necessary, and diplomatic bags in transit the same inviolability and protection as the receiving State is bound to accord.

4. The obligations of third States under paragraphs 1, 2 and 3 of this Article shall also apply to the persons mentioned respectively in those paragraphs, and to official communications and diplomatic bags, whose presence in the territory of the third State is due to *force majeure*.

[ARTICLE 45

If diplomatic relations are broken off between two States, or if a mission is permanently or temporarily recalled:

  (a)   the receiving State must, even in case of armed conflict, respect and protect the premises of the mission, together with its property and archives;

  (b)   the sending State may entrust the custody of the premises of the mission, together with its property and archives, to a third State acceptable to the receiving State;

  (c)   the sending State may entrust the protection of its interests and those of its nationals to a third State acceptable to the receiving State.]

NOTES

Article 45: added by the Diplomatic and Consular Premises Act 1987, s 6, Sch 2, para 1.

By the Arms Control and Disarmament (Privileges and Immunities) Act 1988, s 1(1), references to a diplomatic agent include references to any person designated by a state other than the UK as an observer or inspector under the Stockholm Document as defined in s 1(4) of that Act.

(Sch 2 repealed by the Statute Law (Repeals) Act 1974.)

PROVISIONAL COLLECTION OF TAXES ACT 1968

(1968 c 2)

ARRANGEMENT OF SECTIONS

An Act to consolidate the Provisional Collection of Taxes Act 1913 and certain other enactments relating to the provisional collection of taxes or matters connected therewith

[1 February 1968]

1 Temporary statutory effect of House of Commons resolutions affecting income tax, purchase tax or customs or excise duties

(1) This section applies only to income tax, [corporation tax. . .] [value added tax][, climate change levy,] [insurance premium tax] [landfill tax,] [aggregates levy,] [. . .] [petroleum revenue tax] [stamp duty reserve tax] [supplementary petroleum duty] [selective employment tax] . . . and duties of customs and excise.

[(1A) . . .]

(2) Subject to that, and to the provisions of subsections (4) to (8) below, where the House of Commons passes a resolution which—

(a)   provides for the renewal for a further period of any tax in force or imposed during the previous financial year (whether at the same or a different rate, and whether with or without modifications) or for the variation or abolition of any existing tax, and

(b)   contains a declaration that it is expedient in the public interest that the resolution should have statutory effect under the provisions of this Act,

the resolution shall, for the period specified in the next following subsection, have statutory effect as if contained in an Act of Parliament and, where the resolution provides for the renewal of a tax, all enactments which were in force with reference to that tax as last imposed by Act of Parliament shall during that period have full force and effect with respect to the tax as renewed by the resolution.

In this section references to the renewal of a tax include references to its reimposition, and references to the abolition of a tax include references to its repeal.

(3) The said period is—

(a)   in the case of a resolution passed in [November or December] in any year, one expiring with [5th May in the next calendar year];

[(aa)   in the case of a resolution passed in February or March in any year, one expiring with 5th August in the same calendar year; and]

(b)   in the case of any other resolution, one expiring at the end of four months after the date on which it is expressed to take effect or, if no such date is expressed, after the date on which it is passed.

(4)   A resolution shall cease to have statutory effect under this section unless within the next [thirty] days on which the House of Commons sits after the day on which the resolution is passed—

    (a)   a Bill renewing, varying or, as the case may be, abolishing the tax is read a second time by the House, or

    (b)   a Bill is amended by the House [in Committee or on Report, or by any [Public Bill Committee] of the House] so as to include provision for the renewal, variation or, as the case may be, abolition of the tax.

(5)   A resolution shall also cease to have statutory effect under this section if—

    (a)   the provisions giving effect to it are rejected during the passage of the Bill containing them through the House, or

    (b)   an Act comes into operation renewing, varying or, as the case may be, abolishing the tax, or

    (c)   Parliament is dissolved or prorogued.

(6)   Where, in the case of a resolution providing for the renewal or variation of a tax, the resolution ceases to have statutory effect by virtue of subsection (4) or (5) above, or the period specified in subsection (3) above terminates, before an Act comes into operation renewing or varying the tax, any money paid in pursuance of the resolution shall be repaid or made good, and any deduction made in pursuance of the resolution shall be deemed to be an unauthorised deduction.

(7)   Where any tax as renewed or varied by a resolution is modified by the Act renewing or varying the tax, any money paid in pursuance of the resolution which would not have been payable under the new conditions affecting the tax shall be repaid or made good, and any deduction made in pursuance of the resolution shall, so far as it would not have been authorised under the new conditions affecting the tax, be deemed to be an unauthorised deduction.

(8)   When during any session a resolution has had statutory effect under this section, statutory effect shall not be again given under this section in the same session to the same resolution or to a resolution having the same effect.

NOTES

Sub-s (1): words in first pair of square brackets inserted and words omitted in the second place (inserted by the Car Tax Act 1983, s 10(1)) repealed, in relation to resolutions passed after 27 July 1993, by the Finance Act 1993, ss 205(1), (2), 213, Sch 23, Pt VI; words in second pair of square brackets inserted by the Value Added Tax Act 1983, s 50(1), Sch 9, para 1; words in third pair of square brackets inserted by the Finance Act 2000, s 30, Sch 7, para 1; words in fourth pair of square brackets inserted by the Finance Act 1994, s 67, Sch 7, Pt VI, para 33; words in fifth pair of square brackets inserted, and words omitted in the first place repealed, in relation to distributions made on or after 6 April 1999, by the Finance Act 1998, ss 31(5), 148(1), 165, Sch 3, para 1, Sch 27, Pt III(2); words in sixth pair of square brackets inserted by the Oil Taxation Act 1975, s 11; words in seventh pair of square brackets inserted by the Finance Act 1986, 86(3); words in eighth pair of square brackets inserted by the Finance Act 1981, s 128(2); words in ninth pair of square brackets added by the Finance Act 1968, s 51(2); words omitted in the third place repealed by the Finance Act 1972, s 54(8), Sch 28, Pt I, words "aggregates levy" inserted by the Finance Act 2001, s 49(1).

Sub-s (1A): inserted by the Finance Act 1985, s 97 and repealed, in relation to resolutions passed after 27 July 1993, by the Finance Act 1993, ss 205(1), (3), 213, Sch 23, Pt VI.

Sub-s (3): words in square brackets in para (a) substituted, in relation to resolutions passed after 27 July 1993, by the Finance Act 1993, s 205(1), (4); para (aa) inserted, in relation to resolutions passed after 31 July 1997, by the Finance (No 2) Act 1997, s 50(1).

Sub-s (4): word in first pair of square brackets substituted, in relation to resolutions passed after 27 July 1993, by the Finance Act 1993, s 205(1), (5); words in square brackets in para (b) inserted by the Finance Act 1968, s 60; words in inner square brackets in para (b) substituted by the Finance Act 2007, s 112.

Income and Corporation Taxes Act 1988, ss 476, 479: repealed by the Finance Act 1990, ss 30, 132, Sch 5, paras 1, 2, 5, Sch 19, Pt IV.

2 Payments and deductions made on account, and before renewal, of any temporary tax within s 1

(1) Any payment or deduction made on account of a temporary tax to which section 1 above applies and within one month after the date of its expiry shall, if the payment or deduction would have been a legal payment or deduction if the tax had not expired, be deemed to be a legal payment or deduction, subject to the condition that—

(a) if a resolution for the renewal or reimposition of the tax is not passed by the House of Commons within that month, or such a resolution is passed within that month but ceases to have statutory effect under the said section 1, any money so paid or deducted shall be repaid or made good, and

(b) if the tax is ultimately renewed or reimposed at a different rate, or with modifications, any amount paid or deducted which could not properly have been paid or deducted under the new conditions affecting the tax shall be repaid or made good.

(2) In this section "temporary tax" means a tax which has been imposed, or renewed or reimposed, for a limited period not exceeding eighteen months, and was in force or imposed during the previous financial year.

3 Customs and excise: provisions for securing duties under resolutions not having statutory effect

(1) The following provisions of this section shall have effect where the House of Commons passes a resolution providing for the imposition as from a specified date of any duty of customs or excise, not being a resolution to which statutory effect can be given under section 1 of this Act.

(2) If the duty so imposed is a duty of customs, the Commissioners may require any person who, on or after the specified date, imports or clears from warehouse any goods to which the resolution applies to give security that he will, if and when an Act giving effect to the resolution comes into operation, pay the duty chargeable in respect of the goods under that Act.

[(2A) Subsection (2) above shall apply for the purposes of a duty of excise imposed as mentioned in subsection (1) above to the extent that the duty is charged on goods imported into the United Kingdom, as it applies for the purposes of a duty of customs so imposed.]

(3) If the duty is a duty of excise, [then—

(a) where it is a duty of excise charged otherwise than on goods; or

(b) where it is a duty of excise charged on goods, to the extent that it is charged on goods produced or manufactured in the United Kingdom,]

the Commissioners may make regulations for the purpose of securing the payment of such duty as may by law become chargeable in the event of an Act giving effect to the resolution coming into operation, and may by those regulations apply to the duty and to any trade or business in connection with which the duty may become chargeable and to any person carrying on, or premises used for the purpose of, that trade or business any provision of [the revenue trade provisions of the customs and excise Acts].

(4) If any person contravenes or fails to comply with regulations made under this section, he shall be liable to a penalty of [level 3 on the standard scale], and any goods in respect of which the offence was committed shall be liable to forfeiture.

(5) This and the next following section shall be construed as one with [the Customs and Excise Management Act 1979].

NOTES

Sub-s (2A): inserted by the Customs and Excise Management Act 1979, s 177(1), Sch 4, para 4.

Sub-s (3): words in first pair of square brackets inserted and words in second pair of square brackets substituted by the Customs and Excise Management Act 1979, s 177(1), Sch 4, paras 5, 12.

Sub-s (4): reference to a level on the standard scale substituted by virtue of the Criminal Justice Act 1982, ss 38, 46.

Sub-s (5): words in square brackets substituted by the Customs and Excise Management Act 1979, s 177(1), Sch 4, para 12.

4 Customs and excise: alteration of rate of drawback where rate of duty altered by resolution having statutory effect

Where the rate of any [duty of excise] is altered by any resolution of the House of Commons having statutory effect, and any Bill which has been introduced into the House to give effect to that resolution provides for an alteration of the rate of drawback to be allowed in respect of that duty, then, so long as the resolution continues to have statutory effect, drawback shall be allowed in accordance with the rate provided in the Bill, subject to any necessary adjustment in case the rate of drawback as enacted by Parliament differs from the rate provided in the Bill.

NOTES

Words in square brackets substituted by the Customs and Excise Management Act 1979, s 177(1), Sch 4, para 12, Table, Pt I.

5 House of Commons resolution giving provisional effect to motions affecting taxation

(1) This section shall apply if the House of Commons resolves that provisional statutory effect shall be given to one or more motions to be moved by the Chancellor of the Exchequer, or some other Minister, and which, if agreed to by the House, would be resolutions—

    (a)   to which statutory effect could be given under section 1 of this Act, or

    (b)   to which section 3 of this Act could be applied . . .

    (c)   . . .

(2) Subject to subsection (3) below, on the passing of the resolution under subsection (1) above, sections 1 to 3 of this Act [[and section 822 of the Income and Corporation Taxes Act 1988] (over-deductions from preference dividends before passing of annual Act] shall apply as if each motion to which the resolution applies had been agreed to by a resolution of the House.

(3) Subsection (2) above shall cease to apply to a motion if that motion, or a motion containing the same proposals with modifications, is not agreed to by a resolution of the House (in this section referred to as "a confirmatory resolution") within the next ten days on which the House sits after the resolution under subsection (1) above is passed, and, if it ceases to apply, all such adjustments, whether by way of discharge or repayment of tax, or discharge of security, or otherwise, shall be made as may be necessary to restore the position to what it would have been if subsection (2) above had never applied to that motion, and to make good any deductions which have become unauthorised deductions.

(4) The enactments specified in subsection (2) above shall have effect as if—

(a)   any confirmatory resolution passed within the said period of ten sitting days had been passed when the resolution under subsection (1) above was passed, and

(b)   everything done in pursuance of the said subsection (2) by reference to the motion to which the confirmatory resolution relates had been done by reference to the confirmatory resolution,

but any necessary adjustments shall be made, whether by way of discharge or repayment of tax, or modification of the terms of any security, or further assessment, or otherwise, where the proposals in the confirmatory resolution are not the same as those in the original motion to which that resolution relates.

NOTES

Sub-s (1): words omitted repealed, in relation to resolutions passed after 27 July 1993, by the Finance Act 1993, ss 205(1), (6)(a), 213, Sch 23, Pt VI.

Sub-s (2): words in first (outer) pair of square brackets substituted by the Income and Corporation Taxes Act 1988, s 844, Sch 29, para 32; words in second (inner) pair of square brackets substituted, in relation to resolutions passed after 27 July 1993, by the Finance Act 1993, s 205(1), (6)(b).

6 Short title, repeals and saving as respects Northern Ireland

(1)   This Act may be cited as the Provisional Collection of Taxes Act 1968.

(2), (3) . . .

NOTES

Sub-s (2): introduces Schedule to this Act (not reproduced in this work).

Sub-s (3): repealed by the Northern Ireland Constitution Act 1973, s 41(1)(a), Sch 6, Pt I.

(Schedule (Repeals) outside the scope of this work.)

FINANCE ACT 1972

(1972 c 41)

An Act to grant certain duties, to alter other duties, and to amend the law relating to the National Debt and the Public Revenue, and to make further provision in connection with Finance

[27 July 1972]

PART VII
MISCELLANEOUS

127 Disclosure of information between revenue departments

. . .

NOTES

Section 127 repealed by the Commissioners for Revenue and Customs Act 2005 s 50, Sch 4 para 16.

134 Citation, interpretation, construction, extent and repeals

(1)   This Act may be cited as the Finance Act 1972.

(2)　In this Act "the Taxes Act" means the Income and Corporation Taxes Act [1988].

(3)　In this Act—

(a)–(d) . . .

(4)　Except so far as the context otherwise requires, any reference in this Act to any enactment shall be construed as a reference to that enactment as amended, and as including a reference to that enactment as applied, by or under any other enactment, including this Act.

(5) . . .

(6)　If the Parliament of Northern Ireland passes provisions amending or replacing any enactment of that Parliament referred to in this Act the reference shall be construed as a reference to the enactment as so amended or, as the case may be, as a reference to those provisions.

(7) . . .

NOTES

Sub-s (2): figure in square brackets substituted by the Income and Corporation Taxes Act 1988, s 844(1), Sch 29, para 32.

Sub-s (3): para (a) repealed by the Customs and Excise Management Act 1979, s 177(3), Sch 6, Pt I; para (b) outside the scope of this work; para (c) repealed by the Capital Gains Tax Act 1979, s 158(1), Sch 8; para (d) repealed by the Finance Act 1975, ss 52(2), 59(5), Sch 13, Pt I.

Sub-s (5): repealed by the Finance Act 1991, s 123, Sch 19, Pt VII.

Sub-s (7): outside the scope of this work.

EUROPEAN COMMUNITIES ACT 1972

(1972 c 68)

ARRANGEMENT OF SECTIONS

An Act to make provision in connection with the enlargement of the
European Communities to include the United Kingdom, together with (for certain
purposes) the Channel Islands, the Isle of Man and Gibraltar

[17 October 1972]

PART I
GENERAL PROVISIONS

1 Short title and interpretation

(1) This Act may be cited as the European Communities Act 1972.

(2) In this Act . . . —

"the Communities" means the European Economic Community, the European Coal and Steel Community and the European Atomic Energy Community;

"the Treaties" or "the Community Treaties" means, subject to subsection (3) below, the pre-accession treaties, that is to say, those described in Part I of Schedule 1 to this Act, taken with—

(a) the treaty relating to the accession of the United Kingdom to the European Economic Community and to the European Atomic Energy Community, signed at Brussels on the 22nd January 1972; and

(b) the decision, of the same date, of the Council of the European Communities relating to the accession of the United Kingdom to the European Coal and Steel Community; [and

(c) the treaty relating to the accession of the Hellenic Republic to the European Economic Community and to the European Atomic Energy Community, signed at Athens on 28th May 1979; and

(d) the decision, of 24th May 1979, of the Council relating to the accession of the Hellenic Republic to the European Coal and Steel Community;] [and

(e) the decisions of the Council of 7th May 1985, 24th June 1988, 31st October 1994 and 29th September 2000, on the Communities' system of own resources; and] [

(g) the treaty relating to the accession of the Kingdom of Spain and the Portuguese Republic to the European Economic Community and to the European Atomic Energy Community, signed at Lisbon and Madrid on 12th June 1985; and

(h) the decision, of 11th June 1985, of the Council relating to the accession of the Kingdom of Spain and the Portuguese Republic to the European Coal and Steel Community;] [and

(j) the following provisions of the Single European Act signed at Luxembourg and The Hague on 17th and 28th February 1986, namely Title II (amendment of the treaties establishing the Communities) and, so far as they relate to any of the Communities or any Community institution, the preamble and Titles I (common provisions) and IV (general and final provisions);] [and

(k) Titles II, III and IV of the Treaty on European Union signed at Maastricht on 7th February 1992, together with the other provisions of the Treaty so far as they relate to those Titles, and the Protocols adopted at Maastricht on that date and annexed to the Treaty establishing the European Community with the exception of the Protocol on Social Policy on page 117 of Cm 1934] [and

(l) the decision, of 1st February 1993, of the Council amending the Act concerning the election of the representatives of the European Parliament by direct universal suffrage annexed to Council Decision 76/787/ECSC, EEC, Euratom of 20th September 1976] [and

(m) the Agreement on the European Economic Area signed at Oporto on 2nd May 1992 together with the Protocol adjusting that Agreement signed at Brussels on 17th March 1993] [and

(n) the treaty concerning the accession of the Kingdom of Norway, the Republic of Austria, the Republic of Finland and the Kingdom of Sweden to the European Union, signed at Corfu on 24th June 1994;] [and

(o) the following provisions of the Treaty signed at Amsterdam on 2nd October 1997 amending the Treaty on European Union, the Treaties establishing the European Communities and certain related Acts—
  (i) Articles 2 to 9,
  (ii) Article 12, and
  (iii) the other provisions of the Treaty so far as they relate to those Articles,
  and the Protocols adopted on that occasion other than the Protocol on Article J.7 of the Treaty on European Union] [and

(p) the following provisions of the Treaty signed at Nice on 26th February 2001 amending the Treaty on European Union, the Treaties establishing the European Communities and certain related Acts—
  (i) Articles 2 to 10, and
  (ii) the other provisions of the Treaty so far as they relate to those Articles,
  and the Protocols adopted on that occasion;] [and

(q) the treaty concerning the accession of the Czech Republic, the Republic of Estonia, the Republic of Cyprus, the Republic of Latvia, the Republic of Lithuania, the Republic of Hungary, the Republic of Malta, the Republic of Poland, the Republic of Slovenia and the Slovak Republic to the European Union, signed at Athens on 16th April 2003;] [and

(r) the treaty concerning the accession of the Republic of Bulgaria and Romania to the European Union, signed at Luxembourg on 25th April 2005;]

and any other treaty entered into by any of the Communities, with or without any of the member States, or entered into, as a treaty ancillary to any of the Treaties, by the United Kingdom;
and any expression defined in Schedule 1 to this Act has the meaning there given to it.

(3) If Her Majesty by Order in Council declares that a treaty specified in the Order is to be regarded as one of the Community Treaties as herein defined, the Order shall be conclusive that it is to be so regarded; but a treaty entered into by the United Kingdom after the 22nd January 1972, other than a pre-accession treaty to which the United Kingdom accedes on terms settled on or before that date, shall not be so regarded unless it is so specified, nor be so specified unless a draft of the Order in Council has been approved by resolution of each House of Parliament.

(4) For purposes of subsections (2) and (3) above, "treaty" includes any international agreement, and any protocol or annex to a treaty or international agreement.

NOTES

Sub-s (2): words omitted repealed by the Interpretation Act 1978, s 25(1), Sch 3; in definition "the Treaties" or the "Community Treaties" paras (c), (d) and the word "and" preceding them added by the European Communities (Greek Accession) Act 1979, s 1, para (e) originally inserted, together with para (f), by the European Communities (Finance) Act 1985, s 1, substituted, for paras (e), (f), by the European Communities (Finance) Act 1995, s 1, para (e) further substituted by the European Communities (Finance) Act 2001, s 1, paras (g), (h) and the word "and" preceding them added by the European Communities (Spanish and Portuguese Accession) Act 1985, s 1, para (j) and the word "and" preceding it added by the European Communities (Amendment) Act 1986, s 1, para (k) and the word "and" preceding it added by the European Communities (Amendment) Act 1993, s 1(1), para (l) and the word "and" preceding it added by the European Parliamentary Elections Act 1993, s 3(2), para (m) and the word "and" preceding it added by the European Economic Area Act 1993, s 1, para (n) and the word "and" preceding it added by the European Union (Accessions) Act 1994, s 1 para (o) and the word "and" preceding it added by the European Communities (Amendment) Act 1998, s 1; and para (p) and the word "and" preceding it inserted by the European Communities (Amendment) Act 2002 s 1; para (q) and word "and" preceding it inserted by the European Union (Accessions) Act 2003 s 1(1); para (r) inserted by the European Union (Accessions) Act 2006 s 1(1).

Orders in Council: the Orders in Council listed below are "designation orders" for the purposes of sub-s (2) above:

Order in Council	Command paper; Official Journal
1972/1993	5131, 5150, 5151, 5152, 5155
1973/1314	5347, 5159, 5180, 5181; OJ L59, 5.2.73, p 29
1973/2154	5472, 5479, 5480, 5490, 5491; OJ L171, 27.6.73, p 2, L244, 31.8.73, p 7
1974/1263	5624; OJ L352, 21.12.73, p 192, L358, 28.12.73, p 192
1975/408	5876; OJ L313, 25.11.74, pp 55, 57, L195, 18.7.74, p 24
1975/2162	6037, 6220
1976/217*	6252, 6253
1976/218	6265, 6289, 6304, 6331
1977/822	5548, 6632, 6640
1977/823	6646; OJ L176, 1.7.76, p 99, L367, 31.12.76, p 35
1977/2144	6781
1977/2145*	6894, 6920, 6938
1977/2146	6907, 6955, 6957, 6958
1977/2147*	6917, 6981
1978/617	6940, 6959, 6968, 6995
1978/618	6940, 6959, 6968, 6995
1978/619	6894, 6920, 6938
1978/781	6623
1978/1032	7255
1978/1103	7256
1978/1104	7240
1979/292	7464
1979/932	7584
1979/1446*	OJ L152, 20.6.79, p 10
1980/191*	7657, 7658, 7660, 7661, 7662, 7663, 7664, 7668, 7774
1980/1077*	7895
1980/1090	7936

Order in Council	Command paper; Official Journal
1980/1094	5891, 5892, 6258; OJ L315, 11.12.79, p 17
1981/835*	8150, 8151, 8219
1981/1125*	8088
1982/341	8490
1982/707	5891, 5892
1984/1820*	9283
1985/1198*	9511
1985/1772	9488
1987/2040	9666, 109
1990/236	596
1991/758*	1364
1992/2871*	2056
1992/2872*	2059
1993/944	5891, 5892
1993/1783	2078
1994/758*	2336
1994/759*	2437
1994/760*	2292
1994/761*	2435
1995/265*	2556
1995/1618*	2701
1995/1619*	2667
1996/267	2712
1996/1290*	2972
1996/1291*	2966
1996/1292	2969
1996/1293*	2863
1996/1639	2952
1996/1931*	3159
1997/269	3187
1997/270	3238
1997/271	3228
1997/863	3239
1997/2576	3511
1997/2577	3532
1997/2603	3342
1997/2972*	3767
1998/1059	3472
1998/1060	3452
1998/1061	3456
1998/1062	3571
1998/1063	3463
1999/279	4265
1999/1738*	4097
1999/1739*	3946
1999/1740*	3770.

The Orders indicated by asterisks make reference to treaties some or all of which are to be recognised as Community treaties as from certain days to be notified in the London Gazette.

2 General implementation of Treaties

(1) All such rights, powers, liabilities, obligations and restrictions from time to time created or arising by or under the Treaties, and all such remedies and procedures from time to time provided for by or under the Treaties, as in accordance with the Treaties are without further enactment to be given legal effect or used in the United Kingdom shall be recognised and available in law, and be enforced, allowed and followed accordingly; and the expression "enforceable Community right" and similar expressions shall be read as referring to one to which this subsection applies.

(2) Subject to Schedule 2 to this Act, at any time after its passing Her Majesty may by Order in Council, and any designated Minister or department may [by order, rules, regulations or scheme], make provision—

    (a)   for the purpose of implementing any Community obligation of the United Kingdom, or enabling any such obligation to be implemented, or of enabling any rights enjoyed or to be enjoyed by the United Kingdom under or by virtue of the Treaties to be exercised; or

    (b)   for the purpose of dealing with matters arising out of or related to any such obligation or rights or the coming into force, or the operation from time to time, of subsection (1) above;

and in the exercise of any statutory power or duty, including any power to give directions or to legislate by means of orders, rules, regulations or other subordinate instrument, the person entrusted with the power or duty may have regard to the objects of the Communities and to any such obligation or rights as aforesaid.

In this subsection "designated Minister or department" means such Minister of the Crown or government department as may from time to time be designated by Order in Council in relation to any matter or for any purpose, but subject to such restrictions or conditions (if any) as may be specified by the Order in Council.

(3) There shall be charged on and issued out of the Consolidated Fund or, if so determined by the Treasury, the National Loans Fund the amounts required to meet any Community obligation to make payments to any of the Communities or member States, or any Community obligation in respect of contributions to the capital or reserves of the European Investment Bank or in respect of loans to the Bank, or to redeem any notes or obligations issued or created in respect of any such Community obligation; and, except as otherwise provided by or under any enactment,—

    (a)   any other expenses incurred under or by virtue of the Treaties or this Act by any Minister of the Crown or government department may be paid out of moneys provided by Parliament; and

    (b)   any sums received under or by virtue of the Treaties or this Act by any Minister of the Crown or government department, save for such sums as may be required for disbursements permitted by any other enactment, shall be paid into the Consolidated Fund or, if so determined by the Treasury, the National Loans Fund.

(4) The provision that may be made under subsection (2) above includes, subject to Schedule 2 to this Act, any such provision (of any such extent) as might be made by Act of Parliament, and any enactment passed or to be passed, other than one contained in this Part of this Act, shall be construed and have effect subject to the foregoing provisions of this section; but, except as may be provided by any Act passed after this Act, Schedule 2 shall have effect in connection with the powers conferred by this and the following sections of this Act to make Orders in Council [or orders, rules, regulations or schemes].

(5) . . . and the references in that subsection to a Minister of the Crown or government department and to a statutory power or duty shall include a Minister or department of the Government of Northern Ireland and a power or duty arising under or by virtue of an Act of the Parliament of Northern Ireland.

(6) A law passed by the legislature of any of the Channel Islands or of the Isle of Man, or a colonial law (within the meaning of the Colonial Laws Validity Act 1865) passed or made for Gibraltar, if expressed to be passed or made in the implementation of the Treaties and of the obligations of the United Kingdom thereunder, shall not be void or inoperative by reason of any inconsistency with or repugnancy to an Act of Parliament, passed or to be passed, that extends to the Island or Gibraltar or any provision having the force and effect of an Act there (but not including this section), nor by reason of its having some operation outside the Island or Gibraltar; and any such Act or provision that extends to the Island or Gibraltar shall be construed and have effect subject to the provisions of any such law.

NOTES

Sub-s (2): functions conferred on a Minister of the Crown shall, so far as they are exercisable by him in or as regards Scotland, be exercisable by the Scottish Ministers concurrently with the Minister of the Crown. These functions are so exercisable only in so far as they relate to food (including drink) including the primary production of food (Scotland Act 1998 (Transfer of Functions to the Scottish Ministers etc) Order, SI 2005/849 art 3(1), (2)).

Despite the transfer to the Scottish Ministers of functions, any function of a Minister of the Crown in relation to any matter shall continue to be exercisable by him as regards Scotland for the purposes specified in sub-s (2) (Scotland Act 1998 (Transfer of Functions to the Scottish Ministers etc) Order, SI 2005/849 art 6).

Sub-ss (2), (4): Words in square brackets substituted by the Legislative and Regulatory Reform Act 2006 s 27(1).

Sub-s (5): words omitted repealed by the Northern Ireland Constitution Act 1973, s 41(1), Sch 6, Pt I.

Modification: this section is modified by the Scotland Act 1998, s 125, Sch 8, para 15.

Orders in Council: the European Communities (Designation) Order 1973, SI 1973/1889; the European Communities (Designation) Order 1975, SI 1975/427; the European Communities (Designation) (No 2) Order 1975, SI 1975/1707; the European Communities (Designation) Order 1976, SI 1976/897; the European Communities (Designation) (No 2) Order 1976, SI 1976/2141; the European Communities (Designation) Order 1977, SI 1977/980; the European Communities (Designation) (No 2) Order 1977, SI 1977/1718; the European Communities (Designation) Order 1980, SI 1980/865; the European Communities (Designation) Order 1981, SI 1981/206; the European Communities (Designation) (No 2) Order 1981, SI 1981/833; the European Communities (Designation) (No 3) Order 1981, SI 1981/1536; the European Communities (Designation) Order 1982, SI 1982/529; the European Communities (Designation) (No 2) Order 1982, SI 1982/847; the European Communities (Designation) (No 3) Order 1982, SI 1982/1675; the European Communities (Designation) (No 2) Order 1983, SI 1983/1706; the European Communities (Designation) Order 1984, SI 1984/353; the European Communities (Designation) Order 1985, SI 1985/749; the European Communities (Designation) (No 2) Order 1985, SI 1985/956; the European Communities (Designation) (No 3) Order 1985, SI 1985/1195; the European Communities (Designation) Order 1986, SI 1986/947; the European Communities (Designation) Order 1987, SI 1987/448, as amended by SI 1995/3207; the European Communities (Designation) (No 2) Order 1987, SI 1987/926, as amended by SI 1995/751; the European Communities (Designation) Order 1988, SI 1988/785; the European Communities (Designation) (No 2) Order 1988, SI 1988/2240; the European Communities (Designation) Order 1989, SI 1989/1327; the European Communities (Designation) (No 2) Order 1989, SI 1989/2393; the European Communities (Designation) Order 1990, SI 1990/600; the European Communities (Designation) (No 2) Order 1990, SI 1990/1304; the European Communities (Designation) (No 2) Order 1991, SI 1991/755, as amended by SI 1999/2788; the European Communities (Designation) (No 3) Order 1991, SI 1991/2289, as amended by SI 1995/262; the European Communities (Designation) (No 2) Order 1992, SI 1992/1711; the European Communities (Designation) (No 3) Order 1992, SI

1992/2661, as amended by SI 1999/2788; the European Communities (Designation) (No 4) Order 1992, SI 1992/2870, partially superseded by SI 1994/757 and amended by SI 1995/2983; the European Communities (Designation) (No 5) Order 1992, SI 1992/3197; the European Communities (Designation) Order 1993, SI 1993/595; the European Communities (Designation) (No 2) Order 1993, SI 1993/1571; the European Communities (Designation) (No 3) Order 1993, SI 1993/2661, as amended by SI 1997/2563; the European Communities (Designation) Order 1994, SI 1994/757; the European Communities (Designation) (No 2) Order 1994, SI 1994/1327; the European Communities (Designation) (No 3) Order 1994, SI 1994/1887, as amended by SI 1999/2788; the European Communities (Designation) (No 4) Order 1994, SI 1994/2791, as amended by SI 1995/3207; the European Communities (Designation) Order 1995, SI 1995/262; the European Communities (Designation) (No 3) Order 1995, SI 1995/2983; the European Communities (Designation) (No 4) Order 1995, SI 1995/3207; the European Communities (Designation) Order 1996, SI 1996/266, as amended by SI 1999/2788; the European Communities (Designation) (No 2) Order 1996, SI 1996/1912; the European Communities (Designation) (No 3) Order 1996, SI 1996/3155; the European Communities (Designation) Order 1997, SI 1997/1174; the European Communities (Designation) (No 2) Order 1997, SI 1997/1742; the European Communities (Designation) (No 3) Order 1997, SI 1997/2563, as amended by SI 1999/2788; the European Communities (Designation) Order 1998, SI 1998/745; the European Communities (Designation) (No 2) Order 1998, SI 1998/1750; the European Communities (Designation) (No 3) Order 1998, SI 1998/2793; the European Communities (Designation) Order 1999, SI 1999/654; the European Communities (Designation) (No 2) Order 1999, SI 1999/2027; the European Communities (Designation) (No 3) Order 1999, SI 1999/2788.

Regulations: the Anti-dumping and Countervailing Duties (Postponement of Collection) Regulations 1978, SI 1978/77, as amended by SI 1978/598; the Customs and Excise (Positive Monetary Compensatory Amounts) Regulations 1980, SI 1980/927; the Customs and Excise (Repayment of Customs Duties) Regulations 1980, SI 1980/1825; the Customs Duty Regulations 1982, SI 1982/1324; Control of Trade in Endangered Species (Designation of Ports of Entry) Regulations 1985, SI 1985/1154; the Excise Duties (Small Non-Commercial Consignments) Relief Regulations 1986, SI 1986/938, as amended by SI 1987/149, SI 1989/2253, SI 1992/1821; the Inward Processing Relief (Revocation) Regulations 1986, SI 1986/2141; the Inward Processing Relief Arrangements (Customs Duties and Agricultural Levies) Regulations 1986, SI 1986/2148; the Foreign Prison-made Goods Act 1897 (Amendment) Regulations 1988, SI 1988/1772; the Outward Processing Relief (Revocation) Regulations 1989, SI 1989/116; the Customs Controls on Importation of Goods Regulations 1991, SI 1991/2724, as amended by SI 1992/3095, SI 1993/3014; the Customs Warehousing Regulations 1991, SI 1991/2725, as amended by SI 1993/3014; the Free Zone Regulations 1991, SI 1991/2727, as amended by SI 1993/3014; the Statistics of Trade (Customs and Excise) Regulations 1992, SI 1992/2790, as amended by SI 1993/541, SI 1993/3015, SI 1994/2914, SI 1995/2946, SI 1996/2968, SI 1997/2864, SI 1999/3269; the Customs and Excise (Single Market etc) Regulations 1992, SI 1992/3095; the Excise Duties (Deferred Payment) Regulations 1992, SI 1992/3152, as amended by SI 1996/2537; the Excise Duty (Amendment of the Alcoholic Liquor Duties Act 1979 and the Hydrocarbon Oil Duties Act 1979) Regulations 1992, SI 1992/3158, as amended by the Finance Act 1995, s 162, Sch 1, Pt I(2); the Customs and Excise (Transit) Regulations 1993, SI 1993/1353, as amended by SI 1993/3014; the Dual-Use and Related Goods (Export Control) Regulations 1995, SI 1995/271 (which came into force in accordance with reg 1(1) thereof, SI 1995/441 and SI 1995/1151), as amended by SI 1995/1424, SI 1995/3298; the Endangered Species (Import and Export) Act 1976 (Amendment) Regulations 1996, SI 1996/2684; the Import of Seal Skins Regulations 1996, SI 1996/2686; the Dual-Use and Related Goods (Export Control) Regulations 1996, SI 1996/2721, as amended by SI 1997/324, SI 1997/ 1007, SI 1997/1694, SI 1997/1912, SI 1997/2759, SI 1998/272, SI 1998/899, SI 1999/894; the Control of Trade in Endangered Species (Enforcement) Regulations 1997, SI 1997/1372; the Federal Republic of Yugoslavia (Supply and Sale of Equipment) (Penalties and Licences) Regulations 1998, SI 1998/1531, as amended by SI 1999/1775; the Federal Republic of Yugoslavia (Supply, Sale and Export of Petroleum and Petroleum Products) (No 2) Regulations 1999, SI 1999/1516; the Excise Goods (Sales on Board Ships and Aircraft) Regulations 1999, SI 1999/1565; the Goods Infringing Intellectual Property Rights (Customs) Regulations 1999, SI 1999/1601; Federal Republic of Yugoslavia (Supply, Sale and Export of Petroleum and Petroleum Products) (Penalties and Licences) (No 3) Regulations 1999, SI 1999/2821; Indonesia (Supply,

Sale, Export and Shipment of Equipment) (Penalties and Licences) Regulations 1999, SI 1999/2822.

3 Decisions on, and proof of, Treaties and Community instruments, etc

(1) For the purposes of all legal proceedings any question as to the meaning or effect of any of the Treaties, or as to the validity, meaning or effect of any Community instrument, shall be treated as a question of law (and, if not referred to the European Court, be for determination as such in accordance with the principles laid down by and any relevant [decision of the European Court or any court attached thereto)].

(2) Judicial notice shall be taken of the Treaties, of the Official Journal of the Communities and of any decision of, or expression of opinion by, the European Court [or any court attached thereto] on any such question as aforesaid; and the Official Journal shall be admissible as evidence of any instrument or other act thereby communicated of any of the Communities or of any Community institution.

(3) Evidence of any instrument issued by a Community institution, including any judgment or order of the European Court [or any court attached thereto], or of any document in the custody of a Community institution, or any entry in or extract from such a document, may be given in any legal proceedings by production of a copy certified as a true copy by an official of that institution; and any document purporting to be such a copy shall be received in evidence without proof of the official position or handwriting of the person signing the certificate.

(4) Evidence of any Community instrument may also be given in any legal proceedings—

    (a)   by production of a copy purporting to be printed by the Queen's Printer;

    (b)   where the instrument is in the custody of a government department (including a department of the Government of Northern Ireland), by production of a copy certified on behalf of the department to be a true copy by an officer of the department generally or specially authorised so to do;

and any document purporting to be such a copy as is mentioned in paragraph (b) above of an instrument in the custody of a department shall be received in evidence without proof of the official position or handwriting of the person signing the certificate, or of his authority to do so, or of the document being in the custody of the department.

(5) In any legal proceedings in Scotland evidence of any matter given in a manner authorised by this section shall be sufficient evidence of it.

NOTES

Sub-s (1): words in square brackets substituted by the European Communities (Amendment) Act 1986, s 2(a).

Sub-ss (2), (3): words in square brackets inserted by the European Communities (Amendment) Act 1986, s 2(b).

Modification: this section is modified so as to have effect as if references to a government department include any part of the Scottish administration, by virtue of the Scotland Act 1998, s 125, Sch 8, para 15(4).

By the European Economic Area Act 1993, s 4, sub-ss (2)–(5) above have effect in relation to the EFTA Court and the EFTA Surveillance Authority as they have effect in relation to the European Court and a Community institution other than the European Court.

PART II
AMENDMENT OF LAW

4 General provision for repeal and amendment

(1)   The enactments mentioned in Schedule 3 to this Act (being enactments that are superseded or to be superseded by reason of Community obligations and of the provision made by this Act in relation thereto or are not compatible with Community obligations) are hereby repealed, to the extent specified in column 3 of the Schedule, with effect from the entry date or other date mentioned in the Schedule; and in the enactments mentioned in Schedule 4 to this Act there shall, subject to any transitional provision there included, be made the amendments provided for by that Schedule.

(2)   Where in any Part of Schedule 3 to this Act it is provided that repeals made by that Part are to take effect from a date appointed by order, the orders shall be made by statutory instrument, and an order may appoint different dates for the repeal of different provisions to take effect, or for the repeal of the same provision to take effect for different purposes; and an order appointing a date for a repeal to take effect may include transitional and other supplementary provisions arising out of that repeal, including provisions adapting the operation of other enactments included for repeal but not yet repealed by that Schedule, and may amend or revoke any such provisions included in a previous order.

(3)   Where any of the following sections of this Act, or any paragraph of Schedule 4 to this Act, affects or is construed as one with an Act or Part of an Act similar in purpose to provisions having effect only in Northern Ireland, then—

(a)   unless otherwise provided by Act of the Parliament of Northern Ireland, the Governor of Northern Ireland may by Order in Council make provision corresponding to any made by the section or paragraph, and amend or revoke any provision so made; and

(b)   . . .

(4)   Where Schedule 3 or 4 to this Act provides for the repeal or amendment of an enactment that extends or is capable of being extended to any of the Channel Islands or the Isle of Man, the repeal or amendment shall in like manner extend or be capable of being extended thereto.

NOTES

Sub-s (3): para (b) repealed by the Northern Ireland Constitution Act 1973, s 41(1), Sch 6, Pt I.

The following orders have been made under sub-s (2) above for the purpose of bringing into effect the repeals in Sch 3 post.

In relation to Pt I: the Import Duties Act 1958 (Repeals) (Appointed Day) Order 1973, SI 1973/2176 (providing for the repeal of the Import Duties Act 1958, ss 5(2), (3), (6), 9(4) and 9(5) from "and" onwards; on 1 January 1974); the Customs Duties (Repeals) (Appointed Day) Order 1976, SI 1976/1304 (providing for the repeal of the Import Duties Act 1958, ss 5(5), 7(1)(c) with the preceding "and", s 16(3), Schs 2, 6, the European Free Trade Association Act 1960, the Finance Act 1965, s 2, except sub-s (5), and the Finance Act 1966, ss 1(6), 9; on 1 September 1976); the Customs Duties (Repeals) (Appointed Day) Order 1977, SI 1977/2028, as amended by SI 1987/2106 (providing for the repeal of the Import Duties Act 1958, ss 1–3, 11, 12 (save as provided by Sch 3, Pt I to this Act), Sch 1, Sch 4, para 1, and the Finance Act 1971, ss 1(1)–(3); on 1 January 1978, with a saving for the operation of the Origin of Goods (Petroleum Products) Regulations 1977, SI 1977/972 and any direction under s 6 of the 1958 Act (note that this provision was revoked by SI 1987/2106)). By virtue of those orders and other repealing enactments the repeals provided for by Pt I have been carried into effect.

In relation to Pt II: the Sugar Act 1956 (Repeals) (Appointed Day) (No 1) Order 1973, SI 1973/135 (providing for the repeal of the Sugar Act 1956, ss 3(2)(b), 4(2), (3); in s 17, sub-s (1) from the beginning to "this section" and sub-ss (3)–(5); s 18(3), (4); ss 21 and 22, except as regards advances made and guarantees given before 1 February 1973; ss 24–32; in s 33, in sub-s (2) the words from "except" to "subsection", and sub-ss (3), (5); Sch 4, the South Africa Act 1962, Sch 2, para 5; the Finance Act 1968, s 58; on 1 February 1973); the Sugar Act 1956 (Repeals) (Appointed Day) (No 2) Order 1973, SI 1973/1019 (providing for the repeal of the Sugar Act 1956, ss 7–16, 20(6); in s 33, in sub-s (1) the words "regulations or", in sub-s (2) the words "Every instrument containing any such regulations, and,"; in s 34, "or the Commissioners"; in s 35(2) the definitions of "the Commissioners", "composite sugar products", "distribution payments", "distribution repayments", "manufacture", "refiner", "surcharge" and "surcharge repayment", s 35(4)–(6); s 36(2); the Finance Act 1962, in s 3(6) the words from "the Sugar Act 1956" onwards, Sch 5, Pt II; the Finance Act 1964, s 22; the Finance Act 1966, s 52; on 1 July 1973); the Sugar Act 1956 (Repeals) (Appointed Day) (No 3) Order 1975, SI 1975/1164 (providing for the repeal of the Sugar Act 1956, s 17(2), (6), (7), Sch 3, paras 2, 3; the Agriculture Act 1957, s 4, and in s 36(2) the words "and to sugar beet"; the Agriculture (Miscellaneous Provisions) Act 1963, s 25; on 1 August 1975); the Sugar Act 1956 (Repeals) (Appointed Day) (No 4) Order 1976, SI 1976/548 (providing for the repeal of the Sugar Act 1956, ss 3(1) (from "including" onwards), 19, 20(1)–(5), (7), (8), in s 35(2) the definitions of "the Consolidated Fund" and "refined sugar", Sch 3, para 4; on 5 May 1976); the Sugar Act 1956 (Repeals) (Appointed Day) (No 5) Order 1976, SI 1976/2016 (providing for the repeal of the Sugar Act 1956, ss 5 (except as regards advances made before the repeal takes effect), 23(5), in s 35(2) the definition of "the Minister", and the entry for the Sugar Act 1956 in the National Loans Act 1968, Sch 1, (except as regards advances made before this repeal takes effect); on 1 December 1976); the Sugar Act 1956 (Repeals) (Appointed Day) (No 6) Order 1981, SI 1981/1192 (providing for the repeal of the Sugar Act 1956, s 23(1)–(3)(but without prejudice to the modification made by sub-s (2) in the articles of association of the British Sugar Corporation); on 1 September 1981). The whole of the Sugar Act 1956 was repealed by the Food Act 1984, s 134, Sch 11, subject to transitional and savings provisions in Sch 9, para 6, to that Act. S 134 of, and Schs 9, 11 to, the 1984 Act were repealed by the Food Safety Act 1990, s 59(4), Sch 5.

In relation to Pt III: the Plant Varieties and Seeds Act 1964 (Repeals) (Appointed Day) Order 1978, SI 1978/1003 (providing for the repeal of the Plant Varieties and Seeds Act 1964, s 32, and the Trade Descriptions Act 1968, s 2(4)(a) on 1 September 1978); the Plant Varieties and Seeds Act 1964 (Repeals) (Appointed Day) Order 1982, SI 1982/1048 (bringing the remainder of Sch 3, Pt III to this Act, into force on 16 August 1982).

Orders under sub-s (3) above: the Companies (European Communities) Order (Northern Ireland) 1972, SR & O (NI) 1972/277; the European Communities (Agriculture) Order (Northern Ireland) 1972, SR & O (NI) 1972/351, as amended by SR & O (NI) 1973/17; the European Communities (Road Traffic and Transport) Order (Northern Ireland) 1972, SR & O (NI) 1972/359; the European Communities (Food and Drugs) Order (Northern Ireland) 1972, SR & O (NI) 1972/363; the European Communities (Food and Drugs) Order (Northern Ireland) 1975, SR & O (NI) 1975/373; the Statistics of Trade and Employment (Northern Ireland) Order 1988, SI 1988/595.

5 Customs duties

(1) Subject to subsection (2) below, on and after the relevant date there shall be charged, levied, collected and paid on goods imported into the United Kingdom such Community customs duty, if any, as is for the time being applicable in accordance with the Treaties or, if the goods are not within the common customs tariff of the Economic Community and the duties chargeable are not otherwise fixed by any directly applicable Community provision, such duty of customs, if any, as the Treasury, on the recommendation of the Secretary of State, may by order specify.

For this purpose "the relevant date", in relation to any goods, is the date on and after which the duties of customs that may be charged thereon are no longer affected under the Treaties by any temporary provision made on or with reference to the accession of the United Kingdom to the Communities.

(2) Where as regards goods imported into the United Kingdom provision may, in accordance with the Treaties, be made in derogation of the common customs tariff or of the exclusion of customs duties as between member States, the Treasury may by order make such provision as to the customs duties chargeable on the goods, or as to

exempting the goods from any customs duty, as the Treasury may on the recommendation of the Secretary of State determine.

[(3)   Schedule 2 to this Act shall also have effect in connection with the powers to make orders conferred by subsections (1) and (2) above.]

(4)–(9)   . . .

NOTES

Sub-s (3): substituted by the Customs and Excise Duties (General Reliefs) Act 1979, s 19(1), (2), Sch 2, para 3.

Sub-ss (4), (7)–(9): repealed, subject to a saving in relation to sub-s (4), by the Customs and Excise Management Act 1979, s 177(3), (4), Sch 6, Pt I, Sch 7, para 5.

Sub-ss (5), (6), (6A): repealed by the Customs and Excise Duties (General Reliefs) Act 1979, s 19(2), Sch 3, Pt I.

Orders: the Customs Duties (ECSC) Anti-Dumping (No 16) Order 1978, SI 1978/698, as amended by SI 1979/155; the Customs Duties (ECSC) Anti-Dumping (No 17) Order 1978, SI 1978/765; the Customs Duties (ECSC) Anti-Dumping (No 18) Order 1978, SI 1978/1142, as amended by SI 1978/1143; the Customs Duties (ECSC) Order 1987, SI 1987/2184, as amended by SI 1991/2583, SI 1992/792, SI 1992/2623 (all made under sub-ss (1) and (3) above); and the Customs Duties (Greece) Order 1984, SI 1984/1754; the Customs Duties (Portugal) Order 1988, SI 1988/1260; and the Customs Duties (Spain) Order 1988, SI 1988/1262.

6 The common agricultural policy

(1)   . . .

(2)   . . .

(3)   Sections 5 and 7 of the Agriculture Act 1957 (which make provision for the support of arrangements under section 1 of that Act for providing guaranteed prices or assured markets) shall apply in relation to any Community arrangements for or related to the regulation of the market for any agricultural produce as if references, in whatever terms, to payments made by virtue of section 1 were references to payments made by virtue of the Community arrangements by or on behalf of [the relevant Minister and as if for every reference in section 5 to the Minister there were substituted a reference to the relevant Minister.]

(4)   Agricultural levies of the Economic Community, so far as they are charged on goods exported from the United Kingdom or shipped as stores, shall be paid to and recoverable by [the relevant Minister]; and the power of [the relevant Minister] to make orders under section 5 of the Agriculture Act 1957, as extended by this section, shall include power to make such provision supplementary to any directly applicable Community provision as [the relevant Minister considers] necessary for securing the payment of any agricultural levies so charged, including provision for the making of declarations or the giving of other information in respect of goods exported, shipped as stores, warehoused or otherwise dealt with.

[(4A)   Section 9 of the Agriculture Act 1957 shall apply in relation to an order made under section 5 of that Act as extended by this section as if—

    (a)   in the case of an order made by the Scottish Ministers—

         (i)   for the references in subsection (3) of section 9 to Parliament and each House of Parliament there were substituted references to the Scottish Parliament; and

         (ii)   for the reference in that subsection to section 7(1) of the Statutory Instruments Act 1946 there were substituted a reference to article 13(1) of the Scotland Act 1998 (Transitory and Transitional Provisions) (Statutory Instruments) Order 1999;

    (b)   in the case of an order made by the National Assembly for Wales, subsection (3) of section 9 were omitted;

(c) in the case of an order made by the Department of Agriculture and Rural Development, for subsection (3) of section 9 there were substituted the following subsection—

"(3) Any order under any provision of this Part of this Act shall be laid before the Northern Ireland Assembly as soon as may be after it is made, and shall cease to have effect (without prejudice to anything previously done thereunder or to the making of a new order) on the expiration of the period of forty days beginning with the day on which it comes into force unless within that period it has been approved by resolution passed by the Northern Ireland Assembly."

; and

(d) in subsection (4) of section 9 for the reference to the Minister there were substituted a reference to the relevant Minister.]

[(4B) Section 35(2) of the Agriculture Act 1957 shall not apply in relation to an order made by the Department of Agriculture and Rural Development under section 5 of that Act as extended by this section.]

[(4C) Section 3(2) of the Agriculture Act 1967 shall apply in relation to section 5(1)(d) of the Agriculture Act 1957 as extended by this section as if the references in section 3(2) of the Act of 1967 to the Minister were references to the relevant Minister.]

(5) Except as otherwise provided by or under any enactment, agricultural levies of the Economic Community, so far as they are charged on goods imported into the United Kingdom, shall be levied, collected and paid, and the proceeds shall be dealt with, as if they were Community customs duties, and in relation to those levies the following enactments shall apply as they would apply in relation to Community customs duties, that is to say:—

[(a) the Customs and Excise Management Act 1979 (as for the time being amended by any later Act) and any other statutory provisions for the time being in force relating generally to customs or excise duties on imported goods; and]

[(b) sections 1, 3, 4, 5, 6 (including Schedule 1), 7, 8, 9, 12, 13, 15, 17 and 18 of the Customs and Excise Duties (General Reliefs) Act 1979 but so that—

(i) any references in section 1, 3 and 4 to the Secretary of State shall include the Ministers; and

(ii) the reference in section 15 to an application for an authorisation under regulations made under section 2 of that Act shall be read as a reference to an application for an authorisation under regulations made under section 2(2) of this Act;]

and if, in connection with any such Community arrangements as aforesaid, the Commissioners of Customs and Excise are charged [or entrusted] with the performance . . . or otherwise, of any duties in relation to the payment of refunds or allowances on goods exported or to be exported from the United Kingdom, then in relation to any such refund or allowance [section 133 (except subsection (3) and the reference to that subsection in subsection (2)) and section 159 of the Customs and Excise Management Act 1979 shall apply as they apply in relation to a drawback of excise duties], and other provisions of that Act shall have effect accordingly.

(6) The enactments applied by subsection (5)(a) above shall apply subject to such exceptions and modification, if any, as the Commissioners of Customs and Excise may by regulations prescribe, and shall be taken to include section 10 of the Finance Act 1901 (which relates to changes in customs import duties in their effect on contracts), but shall not include [section 126 of the Customs and Excise Management Act 1979] (charge of duty on manufactured or composite articles).

(7) . . .

(8)   Expressions used in this section shall be construed as if contained in Part I of the Agriculture Act 1957; and in this section "agricultural levy" shall include any tax not being a customs duty, but of equivalent effect, that may be chargeable in accordance with any such Community arrangements as aforesaid, and "statutory provision" includes any provision having effect by virtue of any enactment and, in subsection (2), any enactment of the Parliament of Northern Ireland or provision having effect by virtue of such an enactment.

[(9)   In this section "the relevant Minister" means—

(a)   in relation to England, the Secretary of State;

(b)   in relation to Scotland, the Scottish Ministers;

(c)   in relation to Wales, the National Assembly for Wales; and

(d)   in relation to Northern Ireland, the Department of Agriculture and Rural Development;

and, in the case of goods exported or to be exported from the United Kingdom or shipped or to be shipped as stores, the identity of the relevant Minister is determined by reference to the territory from which the goods are, or are to be, exported or shipped.]

NOTES

Sub-ss (1), (2): revoked by the Intervention Board for Agricultural Produce (Abolition) Regulations, SI 2001/3686, reg 3(a).

Sub-s (3): words substituted by the Intervention Board for Agricultural Produce (Abolition) Regulations, SI 2001/3686, reg 3(b).

Sub-s (4): words substituted by the Intervention Board for Agricultural Produce (Abolition) Regulations, SI 2001/3686, reg 3(c).

Sub-ss (4A)–(4C): inserted by the Intervention Board for Agricultural Produce (Abolition) Regulations, SI 2001/3686, reg 3(d).

Sub-s (5): para (a) and words in fourth pair of square brackets substituted by the Customs and Excise Management Act 1979, s 177(1), Sch 4, para 12, Table, Pt I; para (b) substituted by the Customs and Excise Duties (General Reliefs) Act 1979, s 19(1), Sch 2, para 4; words in third pair of square brackets inserted, and words revoked, by the Intervention Board for Agricultural Produce (Abolition) Regulations, SI 2001/3686, reg 3(e).

Sub-s (6): words in square brackets substituted by the Customs and Excise Management Act 1979, s 177(1), Sch 4.

Sub-s (7): repealed by the Agriculture Act 1993, s 64(1), Sch 5.

Sub-s (9: added by the Intervention Board for Agricultural Produce (Abolition) Regulations, SI 2001/3686, reg 3(f).

Transfer of functions: functions of the Ministers, so far as exercisable in relation to Wales, transferred to the National Assembly for Wales, by the National Assembly for Wales (Transfer of Functions) Order 1999, SI 1999/672, art 2, Sch 1.

Transfer of functions in relation to the Board: the Scotland Act 1998 (Cross-Border Public Authorities) (Adaptation of Functions etc) Order 1999, SI 1999/1747, art 3, Sch 15, Pt II, para 2 provides that any function exercisable in relation to the Board, which is exercisable either by the Secretary of State for Scotland acting alone, or the Secretary of State acting jointly with other Ministers of the Crown, shall instead be exercisable by the Scottish Ministers, or as the case may be, the Scottish Ministers and those other Ministers acting jointly. It further provides that no written direction shall be given under sub-s (2)(a) above, and no regulations shall be made under para (a) or (b) of that sub-section, except with the agreement of the Scottish Ministers.

Orders and regulations. the Intervention Board for Agricultural Produce Order 1972, SI 1972/1578 (made under sub-s (2) above); the Intervention Functions (Delegation) Regulations 1972, SI 1972/1679, as amended by SI 1988/1000 (made under sub-s (2)(a) above as read with sub-s (8) above); the Common Agricultural Policy (Termination of Guarantee Arrangements) (Fat Cattle and Rye) Order 1973, SI 1973/351; the Common Agricultural Policy (Termination of Guarantee Arrangements) (Wheat, Barley and Oats) Order 1976, SI 1976/918 (made under sub-s (7) above as read with sub-s (8) above); the Common Agricultural Policy (Termination of Guarantee Arrangements) (Milk) Order 1977, SI

1977/2053 (made under sub-ss (7) and (8) above); the Intervention Functions (Delegation) (Hops) Regulations 1979, SI 1979/433; the Common Agricultural Policy (Termination of Guarantee Managements) (Fat Sheep) Order 1980, SI 1980/1564 (made under sub-ss (7) and (8) above); the Intervention Functions (Delegation) (Milk) Regulations 1982, SI 1982/1502 (made under sub-s (2)(a) above as read with sub-s (8) above).

7 – 10

(S 7(1), (2) repealed by the Agriculture (Miscellaneous Provisions) Act 1976, s 26(3), Sch 4, Pt I; s 7(3), (4) repealed by the Food Act 1984, s 134, Sch 11; s 8 repealed by the Films Act 1985, s 7(1), Sch 2; s 9 repealed by the Companies Consolidation (Consequential Provisions) Act 1985, s 29, Sch 1; s 10 repealed by the Restrictive Trade Practices Act 1976, s 44(6), Sch 6.)

11 Community offences

(1) A person who, in sworn evidence before the European Court [or any court attached thereto], makes any statement which he knows to be false or does not believe to be true shall, whether he is a British subject or not, be guilty of an offence and may be proceeded against and punished—

(a)   in England and Wales as for an offence against section 1(1) of the Perjury Act 1911; or

(b)   in Scotland as for an offence against [section 44(1) of the Criminal Law (Consolidation) (Scotland) Act 1995]; or

(c)   in Northern Ireland as for an offence against [Article 3(1) of the Perjury (Northern Ireland) Order 1979].

Where a report is made as to any such offence under the authority of the European Court [or any court attached thereto], then a bill of indictment for the offence may, . . . in Northern Ireland, be preferred as in a case where a prosecution is ordered under . . . or [Article 13 of the Perjury (Northern Ireland) Order 1979], but the report shall not be given in evidence on a person's trial for the offence.

(2) Where a person (whether a British subject or not) owing either—

(a)   to his duties as a member of any Euratom institution or committee, or as an officer or servant of Euratom; or

(b)   to his dealings in any capacity (official or unofficial) with any Euratom institution or installation or with any Euratom joint enterprise;

has occasion to acquire, or obtain cognisance of, any classified information, he shall be guilty of a misdemeanour if, knowing or having reason to believe that it is classified information, he communicates it to any unauthorised person or makes any public disclosure of it, whether in the United Kingdom or elsewhere and whether before or after the termination of those duties or dealings; and for this purpose "classified information" means any facts, information, knowledge, documents or objects that are subject to the security rules of a member State or of any Euratom institution.

This subsection shall be construed, and the Official Secrets Acts 1911 to 1939 shall have effect, as if this subsection were contained in the Official Secrets Act 1911, but so that in that Act sections 10 and 11, except section 10(4), shall not apply.

(3) This section shall not come into force until the entry date.

NOTES

Sub-s (1): words in first and fourth pairs of square brackets inserted by the European Communities (Amendment) Act 1986, s 2(b); words in second pair of square brackets substituted by the Criminal Procedure (Consequential Provisions) (Scotland) Act 1995, s 5, Sch 4, para 8; words in third and final pairs of square brackets substituted by the

Perjury (Northern Ireland) Order 1979, SI 1979/1714, art 19(1), Sch 1, para 24; words omitted repealed by the Prosecution of Offences Act 1985, s 31(6), Sch 2.

12 Furnishing of information to Communities

Estimates, returns and information that may under section 9 of the Statistics of Trade Act 1947 or section [3 of the Agricultural Statistics Act 1979] be disclosed to a government department[, the Scottish Ministers] or Minister in charge of a government department may, in like manner, be disclosed in pursuance of a Community obligation to a Community institution.

NOTES

Words in first pair of square brackets substituted by the Agricultural Statistics Act 1979, s 7(1), Sch 1, para 4; words in second pair of square brackets inserted by the Scotland Act 1998 (Consequential Modifications) (No 2) Order 1999, SI 1999/1820, art 4, Sch 2, Pt I, para 52.

SCHEDULES

SCHEDULE 1

DEFINITIONS RELATING TO COMMUNITIES

Section 1

PART I
THE PRE-ACCESSION TREATIES

1. The "ECSC Treaty", that is to say, the Treaty establishing the European Coal and Steel Community, signed at Paris on the 18th April 1951.

2. The "EEC Treaty", that is to say, the Treaty establishing the European Economic Community, signed at Rome on the 25th March 1957.

3. The "Euratom Treaty", that is to say, the Treaty establishing the European Atomic Energy Community, signed at Rome on the 25th March 1957.

4. The Convention on certain Institutions common to the European Communities, signed at Rome on the 25th March 1957.

5. The Treaty establishing a single Council and a single Commission of the European Communities, signed at Brussels on the 8th April 1965.

6. The Treaty amending certain Budgetary Provisions of the Treaties establishing the European Communities and of the Treaty establishing a single Council and a single Commission of the European Communities, signed at Luxembourg on the 22nd April 1970.

7. Any treaty entered into before the 22nd January 1972 by any of the Communities (with or without any of the member States) or, as a treaty ancillary to any treaty included in this Part of this Schedule, by the member States (with or without any other country).

PART II
OTHER DEFINITIONS

"Economic Community", "Coal and Steel Community" and "Euratom" mean respectively the European Economic Community, the European Coal and Steel Community and the European Atomic Energy Community.

"Community customs duty" means, in relation to any goods, such duty of customs as may from time to time be fixed for those goods by directly applicable Community provision as the duty chargeable on importation into member States.

"Community institution" means any institution of any of the Communities or common to the Communities; and any reference to an institution of a particular Community shall include one common to the Communities when it acts for that Community, and similarly with references to a committee, officer or servant of a particular Community.

"Community instrument" means any instrument issued by a Community institution.

"Community obligation" means any obligation created or arising by or under the Treaties, whether an enforceable Community obligation or not.

"Enforceable Community right" and similar expressions shall be construed in accordance with section 2(1) of this Act.

"Entry date" means the date on which the United Kingdom becomes a member of the Communities.

"European Court" means the Court of Justice of the European Communities [or the Court of First Instance, and any reference to a court attached to the European Court is a reference to a judicial panel attached to the Court of First Instance].

"Member", in the expression "member State", refers to membership of the Communities.

NOTES

Words in definition of "European Court" inserted by the European Communities (Amendment) Act 2002 s 2.

SCHEDULE 2
PROVISIONS AS TO SUBORDINATE LEGISLATION

Section 2

1.—(1)   The powers conferred by section 2(2) of this Act to make provision for the purposes mentioned in section 2(2)(a) and (b) shall not include power—

(a)   to make any provision imposing or increasing taxation; or

(b)   to make any provision taking effect from a date earlier than that of the making of the instrument containing the provision; or

(c)   to confer any power to legislate by means of orders, rules, regulations or other subordinate instrument, other than rules of procedure for any court or tribunal; or

(d)   to create any new criminal offence punishable with imprisonment for more than two years or punishable on summary conviction with imprisonment for more than *three months* or with a fine of more than [level 5 on the standard scale] (if not calculated on a daily basis) or with a fine of more than [£100 a day].

(2)   Sub-paragraph (1)(c) above shall not be taken to preclude the modification of a power to legislate conferred otherwise than under section 2(2), or the extension of any such power to purposes of the like nature as those for which it was conferred; and a power to give directions as to matters of administration is not to be regarded as a power to legislate within the meaning of sub-paragraph (1)(c).

[1A.—(1)   Where—

(a)   subordinate legislation makes provision for a purpose mentioned in section 2(2) of this Act,

(b)   the legislation contains a reference to a Community instrument or any provision of a Community instrument, and

(c)   it appears to the person making the legislation that it is necessary or expedient for the reference to be construed as a reference to that instrument or that provision as amended from time to time, the subordinate legislation may make express provision to that effect.

(2) In this paragraph "subordinate legislation" means any Order in Council, order, rules, regulations, scheme, warrant, byelaws or other instrument made after the coming into force of this paragraph under any Act, Act of the Scottish Parliament[, Measure or Act of the National Assembly for Wales] or Northern Ireland legislation passed or made before or after the coming into force of this paragraph.]

2.—(1) Subject to paragraph 3 below, where a provision contained in any section of this Act confers power to make [any order, rules, regulations or scheme] (otherwise than by modification or extension of an existing power), the power shall be exercisable by statutory instrument.

(2) Any statutory instrument containing an Order in Council or [any order, rules, regulations or scheme] made in the exercise of a power so conferred, if made without a draft having been approved by resolution of each House of Parliament, shall be subject to annulment in pursuance of a resolution of either House.

[2A.—(1) This paragraph applies where, pursuant to paragraph 2(2) above, a draft of a statutory instrument containing provision made in exercise of the power conferred by section 2(2) of this Act is laid before Parliament for approval by resolution of each House of Parliament and—

(a) the instrument also contains provision made in exercise of a power conferred by any other enactment; and

(b) apart from this paragraph, any of the conditions in sub-paragraph (2) below applies in relation to the instrument so far as containing that provision.

(2) The conditions referred to in sub-paragraph (1)(b) above are that—

(a) the instrument, so far as containing the provision referred to in sub-paragraph (1)(a) above, is by virtue of any enactment subject to annulment in pursuance of a resolution of either House of Parliament;

(b) the instrument so far as containing that provision is by virtue of any enactment required to be laid before Parliament after being made and to be approved by resolution of each House of Parliament in order to come into or remain in force;

(c) in a case not falling within paragraph (a) or (b) above, the instrument so far as containing that provision is by virtue of any enactment required to be laid before Parliament after being made;

(d) the instrument or a draft of the instrument so far as containing that provision is not by virtue of any enactment required at any time to be laid before Parliament.

(3) Where this paragraph applies in relation to the draft of a statutory instrument—

(a) the instrument, so far as containing the provision referred to in sub-paragraph (1)(a) above, may not be made unless the draft is approved by a resolution of each House of Parliament;

(b) in a case where the condition in sub-paragraph (2)(a) above is satisfied, the instrument so far as containing that provision is not subject to annulment in pursuance of a resolution of either House of Parliament;

(c) in a case where the condition in sub-paragraph (2)(b) above is satisfied, the instrument is not required to be laid before Parliament after being made (and accordingly any requirement that the instrument be approved by each House of Parliament in order for it to come into or remain in force does not apply); and

(d)   in a case where the condition in sub-paragraph (2)(c) above is satisfied, the instrument so far as containing that provision is not required to be laid before Parliament after being made.

(4) In this paragraph, references to an enactment are to an enactment passed or made before or after the coming into force of this paragraph.

2B.—(1) This paragraph applies where, pursuant to paragraph 2(2) above, a statutory instrument containing provision made in exercise of the power conferred by section 2(2) of this Act is laid before Parliament under section 5 of the Statutory Instruments Act 1946 (instruments subject to annulment) and—

(a)   the instrument also contains provision made in exercise of a power conferred by any other enactment; and

(b)   apart from this paragraph, either of the conditions in sub-paragraph (2) below applies in relation to the instrument so far as containing that provision.

(2) The conditions referred to in sub-paragraph (1)(b) above are that—

(a)   the instrument so far as containing the provision referred to in sub-paragraph (1)(a) above is by virtue of any enactment required to be laid before Parliament after being made but—

(i)   is not subject to annulment in pursuance of a resolution of either House of Parliament; and

(ii)   is not by virtue of any enactment required to be approved by resolution of each House of Parliament in order to come into or remain in force;

(b)   the instrument or a draft of the instrument so far as containing that provision is not by virtue of any enactment required at any time to be laid before Parliament.

(3) Where this paragraph applies in relation to a statutory instrument, the instrument, so far as containing the provision referred to in sub-paragraph (1)(a) above, is subject to annulment in pursuance of a resolution of either House of Parliament.

(4) In this paragraph, references to an enactment are to an enactment passed or made before or after the coming into force of this paragraph.

2C. Paragraphs 2A and 2B above apply to a Scottish statutory instrument containing provision made in the exercise of the power conferred by section 2(2) of this Act (and a draft of any such instrument) as they apply to any other statutory instrument containing such provision (or, as the case may be, any draft of such an instrument), but subject to the following modifications—

(a)   references to Parliament and to each or either House of Parliament are to be read as references to the Scottish Parliament;

(b)   references to an enactment include an enactment comprised in, or in an instrument made under, an Act of the Scottish Parliament; and

(c)   the reference in paragraph 2B(1) to section 5 of the Statutory Instruments Act 1946 is to be read as a reference to article 11 of the Scotland Act 1998 (Transitory and Transitional Provisions) (Statutory Instruments) Order 1999 (SI 1999/1096).]

3. Nothing in paragraph 2 above shall apply to any Order in Council made by the Governor of Northern Ireland or to any [order, rules, regulations or scheme] made by a Minister or department of the Government of Northern Ireland; but where a provision contained in any section of this Act confers power to make such an Order in Council or [order, rules, regulations or scheme], then any Order in Council or [order, rules, regulations or scheme] made in the exercise of that power, if made without a draft having been approved by resolution of each House of the Parliament of Northern Ireland, shall be subject to negative resolution within the meaning of

section 41(6) of the Interpretation Act (Northern Ireland) 1954 as if the Order or [order, rules, regulations or scheme] were a statutory instrument within the meaning of that Act.

[4.—(1) The power to make orders under section 5(1) or (2) of this Act shall be exercisable in accordance with the following provisions of this paragraph.

(2) The power to make such orders shall be exercisable by statutory instrument and includes power to amend or revoke any such order made in the exercise of that power.

(3) Any statutory instrument containing any such order shall be subject to annulment in pursuance of a resolution of the House of Commons except in a case falling within sub-paragraph (4) below.

(4) Subject to sub-paragraph (6) below, where an order imposes or increases any customs duty, or restricts any relief from customs duty under the said section 5, the statutory instrument containing the order shall be laid before the House of Commons after being made and, unless the order is approved by that House before the end of the period of 28 days beginning with the day on which it was made, it shall cease to have effect at the end of that period, but without prejudice to anything previously done under the order or to the making of a new order.

In reckoning the said period of 28 days no account shall be taken of any time during which Parliament is dissolved or prorogued or during which the House of Commons is adjourned for more than 4 days.

(5) Where an order has the effect of altering the rate of duty on any goods in such a way that the new rate is not directly comparable with the old, it shall not be treated for the purposes of sub-paragraph (4) above as increasing the duty on those goods if it declares the opinion of the Treasury to be that, in the circumstances existing at the date of the order, the alteration is not calculated to raise the general level of duty on the goods.

(6) Sub-paragraph (4) above does not apply in the case of an instrument containing an order which states that it does not impose or increase any customs duty or restrict any relief from customs duty otherwise than in pursuance of a Community obligation.

5. As soon as may be after the end of each financial year the Secretary of State shall lay before each House of Parliament a report on the exercise during that year of the powers conferred by section 5(1) and (2) of this Act with respect to the imposition of customs duties and the allowance of exemptions and reliefs from duties so imposed (including the power to amend or revoke orders imposing customs duties or providing for any exemption or relief from duties so imposed).]

NOTES

Para 1: words in first pair of brackets in sub-para (d) substituted by virtue of the Criminal Justice Act 1982, ss 40, 46; words in second pair of square brackets in sub-para (d) substituted by the Criminal Law Act 1977, ss 32(3), 65(10). In sub-para (d), words substituted for the words "three months" by the Criminal Justice Act 2003 s 283, Sch 27 para 3(1), (2) with effect from a date to be appointed. Sub-para (3) to be inserted by the Criminal Justice Act 2003 s 283, Sch 27 para 3(1), (3). with effect from a date to be appointed. Sub-para (3) to read as follows—

(3) In sub-paragraph (1)(d), "the prescribed term" means—

    (a)   in relation to England and Wales, where the offence is a summary offence, 51 weeks;

    (b)   in relation to England and Wales, where the offence is triable either way, twelve months;

    (c)   in relation to Scotland and Northern Ireland, three months.

Para 1A: added by the Legislative and Regulatory Reform Act 2006 s 28; words in sub-para (2) in square brackets added by the Government of Wales Act 2006 (Consequential Modifications and Transitional Provisions) Order, SI 2007/1388, art 3, Sch 1 para 1.

Paras 2, 3: words in square brackets substituted by the Legislative and Regulatory Reform Act 2006 s 27(2).

Paras 2A–2C added by the Legislative and Regulatory Reform Act 2006 s 29

Paras 4, 5: added by the Customs and Excise Duties (General Reliefs) Act 1979, s 19(1), Sch 2, para 5.

(Sch 3 (Repeals) and Sch 4 (Enactments amended) outside the scope of this work.)

FINANCE ACT 1977

(1977 c 36)

An Act to grant certain duties, to alter other duties, and to amend the law relating to the National Debt and the Public Revenue, and to make further provision in connection with Finance

[29 July 1977]

PART I

CUSTOMS AND EXCISE

1–10

(S 1(1)–(5), (8), (9) repealed by the Alcoholic Liquor Duties Act 1979, s 92(2), Sch 4, Pt I; ss 1(6), (7), 2(1), (3) repealed by s 59(5) of, and Sch 9, Pt II to, this Act; ss 2(2), (4)–(8), 3(1), (5) repealed by the Tobacco Products Duty Act 1979, s 11(1), Sch 2; ss 3(2)–(4), 7, 10 repealed by the Finance Act 1996, ss 24, 205, Sch 41, Pt III; s 4 repealed by the Hydrocarbon Oil Duties Act 1979, s 28(2), Sch 7; s 5(1) (5) repealed by the Vehicle Excise and Registration Act 1994, s 65, Sch 5, Pt I; s 5(2), (3) repealed by the Finance Act 1980, s 122(4), Sch 20, Pt III; s 5(4) repealed by the Finance Act 1985, s 98(6), Sch 27, Pt II; s 6 repealed by the Finance Act 1991, s 123, Sch 19, Pt IV; ss 8, 9 repealed by the Customs and Excise Management Act 1979, s 177(3), Sch 6, Pt I.)

---

11 Recovery of duty etc due in other member States

(1) This section applies where, in accordance with the Directive of the Council of the European Communities dated 15th March 1976 No 76/308/EEC, an authority in a member State makes a request for the recovery in the United Kingdom of any sum claimed by that authority in that State.

(2) Subject to the following provisions, where this section applies the Commissioners or [—

(a)   in relation to England, the Secretary of State;

(b)   in relation to Scotland, the Scottish Ministers;

(c)   in relation to Wales, the National Assembly for Wales;

(d)   in relation to Northern Ireland, the Department of Agriculture and Rural Development,

may] recover the sum specified in the request as if it were a debt due to the Crown.

(3) Proceedings for the recovery of any sum under this section shall be stayed if the defendant satisfies the court that proceedings relevant to his liability on the claim in relation to which the request has been made are pending, or are about to be instituted, before a court, tribunal or other competent body in the member State in question; but any such stay may be removed if the proceedings in the member State are not prosecuted or instituted with reasonable expedition.

(4) It shall be a defence to proceedings under this section for the defendant to show that a final decision on the claim has been given in his favour by a court, tribunal or other competent body in the member State in question; and if he shows that such a decision has been given in respect of part of the claim it shall be a defence to the proceedings in so far as they relate to that part.

(5) For the purposes of subsection (3) above proceedings shall be regarded as pending so long as an appeal may be brought against any decision in the proceedings; and for the purposes of subsection (4) above a final decision is one against which no appeal lies or against which an appeal lies within a period which has expired without an appeal having been brought.

(6) In proceedings under this section any averment in the pleadings that a request has been made as mentioned in subsection (1) above for the recovery of the sum which is the subject of the proceedings shall be conclusive evidence of that fact; and except as provided in subsection (4) above no question shall be raised in any such proceedings as to the defendant's liability on the claim in relation to which the request has been made.

(7) In relation to proceedings under this section in Scotland—

    (a)   the reference in subsection (3) above—

        (i)   to proceedings being stayed shall be construed as a reference to their being sisted;

        (ii)   to a stay being removed shall be construed as a reference to a sist being recalled; and

    (b)   the references in subsections (3), (4) and (6) above to a defendant shall be construed as references to a defender.

(8) This section shall not have effect in relation to a request for the recovery of any sum which became due before 15th March 1976.

NOTES

Sub-s (2): words substituted by the Intervention Board for Agricultural Produce (Abolition) Regulations, SI 2001/3686 reg 6(6).

12, 13

(S 12 repealed by the Customs and Excise Duties (General Reliefs) Act 1979, s 19(2), Sch 3, Pt I; s 13, repealed by the Finance Act 1978, s 80(5), Sch 13, Pts I–IV.)

PART V
MISCELLANEOUS AND SUPPLEMENTARY

59 Citation, interpretation, construction and repeals

(1) This Act may be cited as the Finance Act 1977.

(2) . . .

(3) In this Act—

    (a)   Part I (except sections 5 and 6) shall be construed as one with [such of the Customs and Excise Acts 1979 as the provision in question requires.]

    (b)–(d) . . .

(4) Except so far as the context otherwise requires, any reference in this Act to any enactment shall be construed as a reference to that enactment as amended, and as including a reference to that enactment as applied, by or under any other enactment, including this Act.

(5) The enactments mentioned in Schedule 9 to this Act (which include spent enactments) are hereby repealed to the extent specified in the third column of that Schedule, but subject to any provision at the end of any Part of that Schedule.

NOTES

Sub-s (2): outside the scope of this work.

Sub-s (3): words in square brackets in para (a) substituted by the Customs and Excise Management Act 1979, s 177(1), Sch 4, para 12; para (b) repealed by the Value Added Tax Act 1983, s 50(2), Sch 11; para (c) outside the scope of this work; para (d) repealed by the Capital Transfer Tax Act 1984, s 277, Sch 9.

(Schs 1, 2 repealed by the Alcoholic Liquor Duties Act 1979, s 92(2), Sch 4, Pt I; Schs 3, 9 outside the scope of this work; Schs 4, 5, repealed by the Finance Act 1980, s 122(4), Sch 20, Pt III; Sch 6 repealed by the Value Added Tax Act 1983, s 50(2), Sch 11; Schs 7, 8 repealed by the Income and Corporation Taxes Act 1988, s 844(4), Sch 31.)

FINANCE ACT 1978

(1978 c 42)

An Act to grant certain duties, to alter other duties, and to amend the law relating to the National Debt and the Public Revenue, and to make further provision in connection with Finance

[31 July 1978]

PART V
MISCELLANEOUS AND SUPPLEMENTARY

77 Disclosure of information to tax authorities in other member States

(1) No obligation as to secrecy imposed by statute or otherwise shall preclude the Commissioners of Inland Revenue or an authorised officer of those Commissioners from disclosing to the competent authorities of another member State any information required to be so disclosed by virtue of the Directive of the Council of the European Communities dated 19th December 1977 No 77/799/EEC.

(2) Neither the Commissioners nor an authorised officer shall disclose any information in pursuance of the said Directive unless satisfied that the competent authorities of the other State are bound by, or have undertaken to observe, rules of confidentiality with respect to the information which are not less strict than those applying to it in the United Kingdom.

(3) Nothing in this section shall permit the Commissioners of Inland Revenue or an authorised officer of those Commissioners to authorise the use of information disclosed by virtue of the said Directive other than for the purposes of taxation or to facilitate legal proceedings for failure to observe the tax laws of the receiving State.

NOTES

Directive of the Council of the European Communities No 77/799/EEC: OJ L336, 27.12.77, p 15.

78, 79

(S 78 repealed by the Finance Act 1984, s 128(6), Sch 23, Pt XIV; s 79 repealed by the Customs and Excise Management Act 1979, s 177(3), Sch 6, Pt I.)

80 Short title, interpretation, construction and repeals

(1) This Act may be cited as the Finance Act 1978.

(2) . . .

(3) In this Act—

 (a) Part I (except sections 8 and 9) shall be construed as one with [the Customs and Excise Management Act 1979];

 (b)–(d) . . .

(4) Except so far as the context otherwise requires, any reference in this Act to any enactment shall be construed as a reference to that enactment as amended, and as including a reference to that enactment as applied, by or under any other enactment, including this Act.

(5) The enactments mentioned in Schedule 13 to this Act (which include spent enactments) are hereby repealed to the extent specified in the third column of that Schedule, but subject to any provision at the end of any Part of that Schedule.

NOTES

Sub-s (2): outside the scope of this work.

Sub-s (3): words in square brackets in para (a) substituted by the Customs and Excise Management Act 1979, s 177(1), Sch 14, para 12; para (b) repealed by the Value Added Tax Act 1983, s 50(2), Sch 11; para (c) outside the scope of this work; para (d) repealed by the Capital Transfer Tax Act 1984, ss 274, 277, Sch 9.

INTERPRETATION ACT 1978

(1978 c 30)

ARRANGEMENT OF SECTIONS

An Act to consolidate the Interpretation Act 1889 and certain other enactments relating to the construction and operation of Acts of Parliament and other instruments, with amendments to give effect to recommendations of the Law Commission and the Scottish Law Commission

[20 July 1978]

General provisions as to enactment and operation

1 Words of enactment

Every section of an Act takes effect as a substantive enactment without introductory words.

2 Amendment or repeal in same Session

Any Act may be amended or repealed in the Session of Parliament in which it is passed.

3 Judicial notice

Every Act is a public Act to be judicially noticed as such, unless the contrary is expressly provided by the Act.

4 Time of commencement

An Act or provision of an Act comes into force—

(a)   where provision is made for it to come into force on a particular day, at the beginning of that day;

(b)   where no provision is made for its coming into force, at the beginning of the day on which the Act receives the Royal Assent.

Interpretation and construction

5 Definitions

In any Act, unless the contrary intention appears, words and expressions listed in Schedule 1 to this Act are to be construed according to that Schedule.

6 Gender and number

In any Act, unless the contrary intention appears,—

    (a)   words importing the masculine gender include the feminine;

    (b)   words importing the feminine gender include the masculine;

    (c)   words in the singular include the plural and words in the plural include the singular.

7 References to service by post

Where an Act authorises or requires any document to be served by post (whether the expression "serve" or the expression "give" or "send" or any other expression is used) then, unless the contrary intention appears, the service is deemed to be effected by properly addressing, pre-paying and posting a letter containing the document and, unless the contrary is proved, to have been effected at the time at which the letter would be delivered in the ordinary course of post.

8 References to distance

In the measurement of any distance for the purposes of an Act, that distance shall, unless the contrary intention appears, be measured in a straight line on a horizontal plane.

9 References to time of day

Subject to section 3 of the Summer Time Act 1972 (construction of references to points of time during the period of summer time), whenever an expression of time occurs in an Act, the time referred to shall, unless it is otherwise specifically stated, be held to be Greenwich mean time.

10 References to the Sovereign

In any Act a reference to the Sovereign reigning at the time of the passing of the Act is to be construed, unless the contrary intention appears, as a reference to the Sovereign for the time being.

11 Construction of subordinate legislation

Where an Act confers power to make subordinate legislation, expressions used in that legislation have, unless the contrary intention appears, the meaning which they bear in the Act.

Statutory powers and duties

12 Continuity of powers and duties

    (1)   Where an Act confers a power or imposes a duty it is implied, unless the contrary intention appears, that the power may be exercised, or the duty is to be performed, from time to time as occasion requires.

    (2)   Where an Act confers a power or imposes a duty on the holder of an office as such, it is implied, unless the contrary intention appears, that the power may be exercised, or the duty is to be performed, by the holder for the time being of the office.

13 Anticipatory exercise of powers

Where an Act which (or any provision of which) does not come into force immediately on its passing confers power to make subordinate legislation, or to make appointments, give notices, prescribe forms or do any other thing for the purposes of the Act, then, unless the contrary intention appears, the power may be exercised, and any instrument made thereunder may be made so as to come into force, at any time after the passing of the Act so far as may be necessary or expedient for the purpose—

    (a)   of bringing the Act or any provision of the Act into force; or

(b)   of giving full effect to the Act or any such provision at or after the time when it comes into force.

14 Implied power to amend

Where an Act confers power to make—

(a)   rules, regulations or byelaws; or

(b)   Orders in Council, orders or other subordinate legislation to be made by statutory instrument,

it implies, unless the contrary intention appears, a power, exercisable in the same manner and subject to the same conditions or limitations, to revoke, amend or re-enact any instrument made under the power.

Repealing enactments

15 Repeal of repeal

Where an Act repeals a repealing enactment, the repeal does not revive any enactment previously repealed unless words are added reviving it.

16 General savings

(1)   Without prejudice to section 15, where an Act repeals an enactment, the repeal does not, unless the contrary intention appears,—

(a)   revive anything not in force or existing at the time at which the repeal takes effect;

(b)   affect the previous operation of the enactment repealed or anything duly done or suffered under that enactment;

(c)   affect any right, privilege, obligation or liability acquired, accrued or incurred under that enactment;

(d)   affect any penalty, forfeiture or punishment incurred in respect of any offence committed against that enactment;

(e)   affect any investigation, legal proceeding or remedy in respect of any such right, privilege, obligation, liability, penalty, forfeiture or punishment;

and any such investigation, legal proceeding or remedy may be instituted, continued or enforced, and any such penalty, forfeiture or punishment may be imposed, as if the repealing Act had not been passed.

(2)   This section applies to the expiry of a temporary enactment as if it were repealed by an Act.

17 Repeal and re-enactment

(1)   Where an Act repeals a previous enactment and substitutes provisions for the enactment repealed, the repealed enactment remains in force until the substituted provisions come into force.

(2)   Where an Act repeals and re-enacts, with or without modification, a previous enactment then, unless the contrary intention appears,—

(a)   any reference in any other enactment to the enactment so repealed shall be construed as a reference to the provision re-enacted;

(b)   in so far as any subordinate legislation made or other thing done under the enactment so repealed, or having effect as if so made or done, could have been made or done under the provision re-enacted, it shall have effect as if made or done under that provision.

Part I

Miscellaneous

18 Duplicated offences

Where an act or omission constitutes an offence under two or more Acts, or both under an Act and at common law, the offender shall, unless the contrary intention appears, be liable to be prosecuted and punished under either or any of those Acts or at common law, but shall not be liable to be punished more than once for the same offence.

19 Citation of other Acts

(1) Where an Act cites another Act by year, statute, session or chapter, or a section or other portion of another Act by number or letter, the reference shall, unless the contrary intention appears, be read as referring—

(a) in the case of Acts included in any revised edition of the statutes printed by authority, to that edition;

(b) in the case of Acts not so included but included in the edition prepared under the direction of the Record Commission, to that edition;

(c) in any other case, to the Acts printed by the Queen's Printer, or under the superintendence or authority of Her Majesty's Stationery Office.

(2) An Act may continue to be cited by the short title authorised by any enactment notwithstanding the repeal of that enactment.

20 References to other enactments

(1) Where an Act describes or cites a portion of an enactment by referring to words, sections or other parts from or to which (or from and to which) the portion extends, the portion described or cited includes the words, sections or other parts referred to unless the contrary intention appears.

(2) Where an Act refers to an enactment, the reference, unless the contrary intention appears, is a reference to that enactment as amended, and includes a reference thereto as extended or applied, by or under any other enactment, including any other provision of that Act.

[20A References to Community instruments

Where an Act passed after the commencement of this section refers to a Community instrument that has been amended, extended or applied by another such instrument, the reference, unless the contrary intention appears, is a reference to that instrument as so amended, extended or applied.]

NOTES

Inserted by the Legislative and Regulatory Reform Act 2006 s 25(1).

Supplementary

21 Interpretation etc

(1) In this Act "Act" includes a local and personal or private Act; and "subordinate legislation" means Orders in Council, orders, rules, regulations, schemes, warrants, byelaws and other instruments made or to be made under any Act.

(2) This Act binds the Crown.

22 Application to Acts and Measures

(1) This Act applies to itself, to any Act passed after the commencement of this Act [(subject, in the case of section 20A, to the provision made in that section)] and, to

the extent specified in Part I of Schedule 2, to Acts passed before the commencement of this Act.

(2)   In any of the foregoing provisions of this Act a reference to an Act is a reference to an Act to which that provision applies; but this does not affect the generality of references to enactments or of the references in section 19(1) to other Acts.

(3)   This Act applies to Measures of the General Synod of the Church of England (and, so far as it relates to Acts passed before the commencement of this Act, to Measures of the Church Assembly passed after 28th May 1925) as it applies to Acts.

NOTES

Words in square brackets in sub-s (1) inserted by the Legislative and Regulatory Reform Act 2006 s 25(2).

23   Application to other instruments

(1)   The provisions of this Act, except sections 1 to 3 and 4(b), apply, so far as applicable and unless the contrary intention appears, to subordinate legislation made after the commencement of this Act and, to the extent specified in Part II of Schedule 2, to subordinate legislation made before the commencement of this Act, as they apply to Acts.

(2)   In the application of this Act to Acts passed or subordinate legislation made after the commencement of this Act, all references to an enactment include an enactment comprised in subordinate legislation whenever made, and references to the passing or repeal of an enactment are to be construed accordingly.

(3)   Sections 9 and 19(1) also apply to deeds and other instruments and documents as they apply to Acts and subordinate legislation; and in the application of section 17(2)(a) to Acts passed or subordinate legislation made after the commencement of this Act, the reference to any other enactment includes any deed or other instrument or document.

(4)   Subsections (1) and (2) of this section do not apply to Orders in Council made under section 5 of the Statutory Instruments Act 1946, section 1(3) of the Northern Ireland (Temporary Provisions) Act 1972 or Schedule 1 to the Northern Ireland Act 1974.

[23A   Acts of the Scottish Parliament etc

(1)   This Act applies in relation to an Act of the Scottish Parliament and an instrument made under such an Act only to the extent provided in this section.

(2)   Except as provided in subsection (3) below, sections 15 to 18 apply to—

(a)   an Act of the Scottish Parliament as they apply to an Act,

(b)   an instrument made under an Act of the Scottish Parliament as they apply to subordinate legislation.

(3)   In the application of those sections to an Act and to subordinate legislation—

(a)   references to an enactment include an enactment comprised in, or in an instrument made under, an Act of the Scottish Parliament, and

(b)   the reference in section 17(2)(b) to subordinate legislation includes an instrument made under an Act of the Scottish Parliament.

(4)   In the application of section 20 to an Act and to subordinate legislation, references to an enactment include an enactment comprised in, or in an instrument made under, an Act of the Scottish Parliament.]

NOTES

Inserted by the Scotland Act 1998, s 125, Sch 8, para 16(1), (2).

[23B Measures and Acts of the National Assembly for Wales etc

    (1)   Subject as follows, the provisions of this Act—

        (a)   apply to a Measure or Act of the National Assembly for Wales as they apply to an Act, and

        (b)   apply to an instrument made under a Measure or Act of the National Assembly for Wales as they apply to other subordinate legislation.

    (2)   Sections 1 to 3 do not apply to a Measure or Act of the National Assembly for Wales.

    (3)   In this Act references to an enactment include an enactment comprised in, or in an instrument made under, a Measure or Act of the National Assembly for Wales.

    (4)   In the application of this Act to a Measure or Act of the National Assembly for Wales, references to the passing of an Act or an enactment are to be read as references to the enactment of the Measure or Act.

    (5)   Section 4(b) does not apply to a Measure of the National Assembly for Wales; but where such a Measure makes no provision for the coming into force of a provision contained in it, that provision comes into force at the beginning of the day on which the Measure is approved by Her Majesty in Council.]

NOTES

    Inserted by the Government of Wales Act 2006, s 160, Sch 10, para 11.

24

(Applies to Northern Ireland only.)

25 Repeals and savings

    (1)   The enactments described in Schedule 3 are repealed to the extent specified in the third column of that Schedule.

    (2)   Without prejudice to section 17(2)(a), a reference to the Interpretation Act 1889, to any provision of that Act or to any other enactment repealed by this Act, whether occurring in another Act, in subordinate legislation, in Northern Ireland legislation or in any deed or other instrument or document, shall be construed as referring to this Act, or to the corresponding provision of this Act, as it applies to Acts passed at the time of the reference.

    (3)   The provisions of this Act relating to Acts passed after any particular time do not affect the construction of Acts passed before that time, though continued or amended by Acts passed thereafter.

26 Commencement

This Act shall come into force on 1st January 1979.

27 Short title

This Act may be cited as the Interpretation Act 1978.

SCHEDULES

SCHEDULE 1

WORDS AND EXPRESSIONS DEFINED

Section 5

Note: *The years or dates which follow certain entries in this Schedule are relevant for the purposes of paragraph 4 of Schedule 2 (application to existing enactments).*

Definitions

["Act" means an Act of Parliament.]

"Associated state" means a territory maintaining a status of association with the United Kingdom in accordance with the West Indies Act 1967. [16th February 1967]

"Bank of England" means, as the context requires, the Governor and Company of the Bank of England or the bank of the Governor and Company of the Bank of England.

"Bank of Ireland" means, as the context requires, the Governor and Company of the Bank of Ireland or the bank of the Governor and Company of the Bank of Ireland.

"British Islands" means the United Kingdom, the Channel Islands and the Isle of Man. [1889]

["British overseas territory" has the same meaning as in the British Nationality Act 1981;]

"British possession" means any part of Her Majesty's dominions outside the United Kingdom; and where parts of such dominions are under both a central and a local legislature, all parts under the central legislature are deemed, for the purposes of this definition, to be one British possession. [1889]

. . .

"Building regulations", in relation to England and Wales, [has the meaning given by section 122 of the Building Act 1984].

"Central funds", in an enactment providing in relation to England and Wales for the payment of costs out of central funds, means money provided by Parliament.

["Charity Commission" means the Charity Commission for England and Wales established by section 1A of the Charities Act 1993.]

"Church Commissioners" means the Commissioners constituted by the Church Commissioners Measure 1947.

["Civil partnership" means a civil partnership which exists under or by virtue of the Civil Partnership Act 2004 (and any reference to a civil partner is to be read accordingly).]

"Colonial legislature", and "legislature" in relation to a British possession, mean the authority, other than the Parliament of the United Kingdom or Her Majesty in Council, competent to make laws for the possession. [1889]

"Colony" means any part of Her Majesty's dominions outside the British Islands except—

- (a) countries having fully responsible status within the Commonwealth;
- (b) territories for whose external relations a country other than the United Kingdom is responsible;
- (c) associated states;

and where parts of such dominions are under both a central and a local legislature, all parts under the central legislature are deemed for the purposes of this definition to be one colony. [1889]

"Commencement", in relation to an Act or enactment, means the time when the Act or enactment comes into force.

"Committed for trial" means—

- (a) *in relation to England and Wales, committed in custody or on bail by a magistrates' court pursuant to [section 6 of the Magistrates' Courts Act 1980] or by any judge or other authority having power to do so, with a view to trial before a judge and jury; [1889]*
- (b) in relation to Northern Ireland, committed in custody or on bail by a magistrates' court pursuant to [Article 37 of the Magistrates' Courts (Northern Ireland) Order 1981], or by a court, judge, resident magistrate, . . . or other authority having power to do so, with a view to trial on indictment. [1st January 1979]

"The Communities", "the Treaties" or "the Community Treaties" and other expressions defined by section 1 of and Schedule 1 to the European Communities Act 1972 have the meanings prescribed by that Act.

"Comptroller and Auditor General" means the Comptroller-General of the receipt and issue of Her Majesty's Exchequer and Auditor-General of Public Accounts appointed in pursuance of the Exchequer and Audit Departments Act 1866.

"Consular officer" has the meaning assigned by Article 1 of the Vienna Convention set out in Schedule 1 to the Consular Relations Act 1968.

["The Corporation Tax Acts" means the enactments relating to the taxation of the income and chargeable gains of companies and of company distributions (including provisions relating to income tax);]

"County court" means—

(a) in relation to England and Wales, a court held for a district under [the County Courts Act 1984], [1846]

(b) in relation to Northern Ireland, a court held for a division under the County Courts [(Northern Ireland) Order 1980]. [1889]

"Court of Appeal" means—

(a) in relation to England and Wales, Her Majesty's Court of Appeal in England;

(b) in relation to Northern Ireland, Her Majesty's Court of Appeal in Northern Ireland.

["Court of Judicature" means the Court of Judicature of Northern Ireland.]

"Court of summary jurisdiction", "summary conviction" and "Summary Jurisdiction Acts", in relation to Northern Ireland, have the same meanings as in Measures of the Northern Ireland Assembly and Acts of the Parliament of Northern Ireland.

"Crown Court" means—

(a) in relation to England and Wales, the Crown Court constituted by section 4 of the Courts Act 1971;

(b) in relation to Northern Ireland, the Crown Court constituted by section 4 of the Judicature (Northern Ireland) Act 1978.

"Crown Estate Commissioners" means the Commissioners referred to in section 1 of the Crown Estate Act 1961.

["EEA agreement" means the agreement on the European Economic Area signed at Oporto on 2nd May 1992, together with the Protocol adjusting that Agreement signed at Brussels on 17th March 1993, as modified or supplemented from time to time. [The date of the coming into force of this paragraph.]

"EEA state", in relation to any time, means—

(a) a state which at that time is a member State; or

(b) any other state which at that time is a party to the EEA agreement. [The date of the coming into force of this paragraph.]]

["Enactment" does not include an enactment comprised in, or in an instrument made under, an Act of the Scottish Parliament.]

"England" means, subject to any alteration of boundaries under Part IV of the Local Government Act 1972, the area consisting of the counties established by section 1 of that Act, Greater London and the Isles of Scilly. [1st April 1974]

"Financial year" means, in relation to matters relating to the Consolidated Fund, the National Loans Fund, or moneys provided by Parliament, or to the Exchequer or to central taxes or finance, the twelve months ending with 31st March. [1889]

"Governor-General" includes any person who for the time being has the powers of the Governor-General, and "Governor", in relation to any British possession, includes the officer for the time being administering the government of that possession. [1889]

["Her Majesty's Revenue and Customs" has the meaning given by section 4 of the Commissioners for Revenue and Customs Act 2005.]

"High Court" means—

(a)   in relation to England and Wales, Her Majesty's High Court of Justice in England;

(b)   in relation to Northern Ireland, Her Majesty's High Court of Justice in Northern Ireland.

"The Income Tax Acts" means all enactments relating to income tax, including any provisions of the Corporation Tax Acts which relate to income tax.

"Land" includes buildings and other structures, land covered with water, and any estate, interest, easement, servitude or right in or over land. [1st January 1979].

"Lands Clauses Acts" means—

(a)   in relation to England and Wales, the Lands Clauses Consolidation Act 1845 and the Lands Clauses Consolidation Acts Amendment Act 1860, and any Acts for the time being in force amending those Acts; [1889]

(b)   in relation to Scotland, the Lands Clauses Consolidation (Scotland) Act 1845 and the Lands Clauses Consolidation Acts Amendment Act 1860, and any Acts for the time being in force amending those Acts; [1889]

(c)   in relation to Northern Ireland, the enactments defined as such by section 46(1) of the Interpretation Act (Northern Ireland) 1954. [1889]

"Local land charges register", in relation to England and Wales, means a register kept pursuant to section 3 of the Local Land Charges Act 1975, and "the appropriate local land charges register" has the meaning assigned by section 4 of that Act.

"London borough" means a borough described in Schedule 1 to the London Government Act 1963, "inner London borough" means one of the boroughs so described and numbered from 1 to 12 and "outer London borough" means one of the boroughs so described and numbered from 13 to 32, subject (in each case) to any alterations made under Part IV of the Local Government Act 1972 [or Part II of the Local Government Act 1992].

"Lord Chancellor" means the Lord High Chancellor of Great Britain.

"Magistrates' court" has the meaning assigned to it—

(a)   in relation to England and Wales, by [section 148 of the Magistrates' Courts Act 1980];

(b)   in relation to Northern Ireland, by [Article 2(2) of the Magistrates' Courts (Northern Ireland) Order 1981].

"Month" means calendar month. [1850]

"National Debt Commissioners" means the Commissioners for the Reduction of the National Debt.

"Northern Ireland legislation" has the meaning assigned by section 24(5) of this Act. [1st January 1979]

"Oath" and "affidavit" include affirmation and declaration, and "swear" includes affirm and declare.

["Officer of Revenue and Customs" has the meaning given by section 2(1) of the Commissioners for Revenue and Customs Act 2005.]

"Ordnance Map" means a map made under powers conferred by the Ordnance Survey Act 1841 or the Boundary Survey (Ireland) Act 1854.

"Parliamentary Election" means the election of a Member to serve in Parliament for a constituency. [1889]

["PAYE income" has the meaning given by section 683 of the Income Tax (Earnings and Pensions) Act 2003.

"PAYE regulations" means regulations under section 684 of that Act.]

"Person" includes a body of persons corporate or unincorporate. [1889]

"Police area", "police authority" and other expressions relating to the police have the meaning or effect described—

 (a) in relation to England and Wales, by [section 101(1) of the Police Act 1996];

 (b) in relation to Scotland, by sections 50 and 51(4) of the Police (Scotland) Act 1967.

["Police Service of Northern Ireland" and "Police Service of Northern Ireland Reserve" have the same meaning as in the Police (Northern Ireland) Act 2000;]

"The Privy Council" means the Lords and others of Her Majesty's Most Honourable Privy Council.

["Registered" in relation to nurses and midwives, means registered in the register maintained under article 5 of the [Nursing and Midwifery Order 2001] by virtue of qualifications in nursing or midwifery, as the case may be.]

"Registered medical practitioner" means a fully registered person within the meaning of [the Medical Act 1983]. [1st January 1979]

"Rules of Court" in relation to any court means rules made by the authority having power to make rules or orders regulating the practice and procedure of that court, and in Scotland includes Acts of Adjournal and Acts of Sederunt; and the power of the authority to make rules of court (as above defined) includes power to make such rules for the purpose of any Act which directs or authorises anything to be done by rules of court. [1889]

"Secretary of State" means one of Her Majesty's Principal Secretaries of State.

["Senior Courts" means the Senior Courts of England and Wales.]

["Sent for trial" means, in relation to England and Wales, sent by a magistrates' court to the Crown Court for trial pursuant to section 51 or 51A of the Crime and Disorder Act 1998.]

["Sewerage undertaker", in relation to England and Wales, shall be construed in accordance with [section 6 of the Water Industry Act 1991].]

"Sheriff", in relation to Scotland, includes sheriff principal.

["The standard scale", with reference to a fine or penalty for an offence triable only summarily,—

 (a) in relation to England and Wales, has the meaning given by section 37 of the Criminal Justice Act 1982;

 (b) in relation to Scotland, has the meaning given by section 289G of the Criminal Procedure (Scotland) Act 1975;

 (c) in relation to Northern Ireland, has the meaning given by Article 5 of the Fines and Penalties (Northern Ireland) Order 1984.]

"Statutory declaration" means a declaration made by virtue of the Statutory Declarations Act 1835.

["Statutory maximum", with reference to a fine or penalty on summary conviction for an offence,—

 (a) in relation to England and Wales, means the prescribed sum within the meaning of section 32 of the Magistrates' Courts Act 1980;

 (b) in relation to Scotland, means the prescribed sum within the meaning of section 289B(6) of the Criminal Procedure (Scotland) Act 1975; and

 (c) in relation to Northern Ireland, means the prescribed sum within the meaning of Article 4 of the Fines and Penalties (Northern Ireland) Order 1984.]

["Supreme Court" means the Supreme Court of the United Kingdom.]

["The Tax Acts" means the Income Tax Acts and the Corporation Tax Acts.]

"The Treasury" means the Commissioners of Her Majesty's Treasury.

["Trust of land" and "trustees of land", in relation to England and Wales, have the same meanings as in the Trusts of Land and Appointment of Trustees Act 1996.]

"United Kingdom" means Great Britain and Northern Ireland. [12th April 1927]

"Wales" means, subject to any alteration of boundaries made under Part IV of the Local Government Act 1972, the area consisting of the counties established by section 20 of that Act. [1st April 1974]

["Water undertaker", in relation to England and Wales, shall be construed in accordance with [section 6 of the Water Industry Act 1991].]

"Writing" includes typing, printing, lithography, photography and other modes of representing or reproducing words in a visible form, and expressions referring to writing are construed accordingly.

. . .

Construction of certain expressions relating to offences

In relation to England and Wales—

(a) "indictable offence" means an offence which, if committed by an adult, is triable on indictment, whether it is exclusively so triable or triable either way;

(b) "summary offence" means an offence which, if committed by an adult, is triable only summarily;

(c) "offence triable either way" means an offence[, other than an offence triable on indictment only by virtue of Part V of the Criminal Justice Act 1988] which, if committed by an adult, is triable either on indictment or summarily;

and the terms "indictable", "summary" and "triable either way", in their application to offences, are to be construed accordingly.

In the above definitions references to the way or ways in which an offence is triable are to be construed without regard to the effect, if any, of [section 22 of the Magistrates' Courts Act 1980] on the mode of trial in a particular case.

[Construction of certain references to relationships

In relation to England and Wales—

(a) references (however expressed) to any relationship between two persons;

(b) references to a person whose father and mother were or were not married to each other at the time of his birth; and

(c) references cognate with references falling within paragraph (b) above,

shall be construed in accordance with section 1 of the Family Law Reform Act 1987. [The date of the coming into force of that section].]

NOTES

Definitions "Act" and "Enactment" inserted by the Scotland Act 1998, s 125(1), Sch 8, para 16(1), (3); definitions omitted in the first place repealed by the British Nationality Act 1981, s 52(8), Sch 9; words in square brackets in definition "Building regulations" substituted by the Building Act 1984, s 133(1), Sch 6, para 19; definition "Charity Commission" substituted by the Charities Act 2006, s 75, Sch 8, para 61; definition "Civil partnership" inserted by the Civil Partnership Act 2004 s 261(1), Sch 27 para 59; in definition "Committed for trial" words in square brackets in para (a) substituted by the Magistrates' Courts Act 1980, s 154, Sch 7, para 169(a); para (a) to be repealed by the Criminal Justice Act 2003 ss 41, 332, Sch 3 para 49(a), Sch 37, Pt 4 with effect from a date to be appointed; words in square brackets in para (b) substituted by the Magistrates' Courts (Northern Ireland) Order 1981, SI 1981/1675 (NI 26), art 170(2), Sch 6, Pt I, para 56(a); words omitted from para (b) repealed by the Justice (Northern Ireland) Act 2002 s 86, Sch 13; definition "the Corporation Tax Acts" substituted by the Finance Act 1987, s 71, Sch 15, para 12; in definition "County Court" words in square brackets in para (a) substituted by the County Courts Act 1984, s 148(1), Sch 2, Pt V, para 68, words in square brackets in para (b) substituted by the County Courts (Northern Ireland) Order 1980, SI 1980/397 (NI 3), art 68(2), Sch 1, Pt II; definition "Court of Judicature" inserted by the Constitutional Reform Act 2005, s 59, Sch 11, para 24(b); definitions "EEA agreement" and "EEA state" inserted by the Legislative and Regulatory Reform Act 2006, s 26(1); definition "Her Majesty's Revenue and Customs" inserted by the Commissioners for Revenue and Customs Act 2005 s 4(3); words in square brackets in definition "London borough" inserted by the Local Government Act 1992, s 27(1), Sch 3, para 21; in definition "Magistrates' court" words in square brackets in para (a) substituted by the Magistrates' Courts Act 1980, s 154, Sch 7, para 169(b), words in square brackets in para (b) substituted by the Magistrates' Courts (Northern Ireland) Order 1981, SI 1981/1675 (NI 26), art 170(2), Sch 6, Pt I, para 56(b); definition "Officer of Revenue and Customs" inserted by the Commissioners for Revenue and Customs Act 2005 s 2(7); definitions "PAYE income" and "PAYE regulations" inserted by the Income Tax (Earnings and Pensions) Act 2003, s 722, Sch 6, Pt 2, para 148; in definition "police area" words in square brackets substituted by the Police Act 1996, s 103(1), Sch 7, Pt II, para 32; definition "Police Service of Northern Ireland" inserted by the Police (Northern Ireland) Act 2000 s 78(1), Sch 6 para 5; definition "Registered" in relation to nurses and midwives substituted by the Nursing and Midwifery Order, SI 2002/253 art 54, Sch 5 para 7, words in square brackets therein substituted by the Health Act 1999 (Consequential Amendments) (Nursing and Midwifery) Order 2004, SI 2004/1771 art 3, Schedule para 7; in definition "Registered medical practitioner" words in square brackets substituted by the Medical Act 1983, s 56(1), Sch 5, para 18; definition "Senior Courts" inserted by the Constitutional Reform Act 2005, s 59, Sch 11, para 24(b); definition "Sent for trial" inserted by the Criminal Justice Act 2003 s 41, Sch 3 para 49(b) in relation to cases sent for trial under sections 51 or 51A(3)(d) of the Crime and Disorder Act 1998 (sending cases to the Crown Court); definition "Sewerage undertaker" inserted by the Water Act 1989, s 190(1), Sch 25, para 55(1), (2), words in square brackets therein substituted by the Water Consolidation (Consequential Provisions) Act 1991, s 2(1), Sch 1, para 32; definitions of "The standard scale" and "Statutory maximum" inserted by the Criminal Justice Act 1988, s 170(1), Sch 15, para 58; definition of "Supreme Court" substituted by the Constitutional Reform Act 2005, s 59, Sch 11 para 24(a); definition "The Tax Acts" substituted by the Finance Act 1987, s 71, Sch 15, para 12; definition "Trusts of land" and "trustees of land" inserted with savings by the Trusts of Land and Appointment of Trustees Act 1996, s 25(1), (4), (5), Sch 3, para 16; definition "Water undertaker" substituted (for the definitions of "Water Authority" and "water authority area") by the Water Act 1989, s 190(1), Sch 25, para 55(1), (3), words in square brackets therein substituted by the Water Consolidation (Consequential Provisions) Act 1991, s 2(1), Sch 1, para 32; definition omitted in the second place repealed by the Children Act 1989, s 108(7), Sch 15; words in square brackets in definition of "offence triable either way" inserted by the Criminal Justice Act 1988, s 170(1), Sch 15, para 59; words in square brackets in third paragraph of entry about expressions relating to offences substituted by the Magistrates' Courts Act 1980, s 154, Sch 7, para 169(c); final paragraph, and the cross-heading preceding it, added by the Family Law Reform Act 1987, s 33(1), Sch 2, para 73; definition "British overseas territory" inserted by the British Overseas Territories Act 2002, s 1(3).

Definition "Court of Judicature" to be inserted by the Constitutional Reform Act 2005 s 59, Sch 11 Part 4 para 24(b), with effect from a day to be appointed. The definition as substituted to read as follows—

'Court of Judicature' means the Court of Judicature of Northern Ireland.

Definitions "Officer of a provider of probation services" and "Provider of probation services" to be inserted by the Offender Management Act 2007, s 39, Sch 3, para 2 with effect from a date to be appointed. Those definitions as inserted to read as follows—

"Officer of a provider of probation services" in relation to England and Wales, has the meaning given by section 9(1) of the Offender Management Act 2007;

"Provider of probation services", in relation to England and Wales, has the meaning given by section 3(6) of the Offender Management Act 2007;

Definition "Registered medical practitioner" to be substituted by the Medical Act 1983 (Amendment) Order, SI 2002/3135, art 16(1), Sch 1, Pt I, para 10 with effect from a date to be appointed. The definition as substituted to read as follows—

"Registered medical practitioner" means a fully registered person within the meaning of the Medical Act 1983 who holds a licence to practise under that Act.

Definition "Senior Courts" to be inserted by the Constitutional Reform Act 2005 s 59, Sch 11 Part 4 para 24(b), with effect from a day to be appointed. The definition as substituted to read as follows—

"Senior Courts" means the Senior Courts of England and Wales.

Definition "Supreme Court" to be substituted by the Constitutional Reform Act 2005 s 59, Sch 11 Part 4 para 24(a), with effect from a day to be appointed. The definition as substituted to read as follows—

"Supreme Court" means the Supreme Court of the United Kingdom.

SCHEDULE 2
APPLICATION OF ACT TO EXISTING ENACTMENTS
Sections 22, 23

PART I
ACTS

1. The following provisions of this Act apply to Acts whenever passed:—
Section 6(a) and (c) so far as applicable to enactments relating to offences punishable on indictment or on summary conviction
Section 9
Section 10
Section 11 so far as it relates to subordinate legislation made after the year 1889
Section 18
Section 19(2).

2. The following apply to Acts passed after the year 1850:—
Section 1
Section 2
Section 3
Section 6(a) and (c) so far as not applicable to such Acts by virtue of paragraph 1
Section 15
Section 17(1).

3. The following apply to Acts passed after the year 1889:—
Section 4
Section 7
Section 8
Section 12
Section 13
Section 14 so far as it relates to rules, regulations or byelaws
Section 16(1)
Section 17(2)(a)
Section 19(1)
Section 20(1).

4.—(1) Subject to the following provisions of this paragraph—
  (a)   paragraphs of Schedule 1 at the end of which a year or date . . . is specified [or described] apply, so far as applicable, to Acts passed on or after the date, or after the year, so specified [or described]; and
  (b)   paragraphs of that Schedule at the end of which no year or date is specified [or described] apply, so far as applicable, to Acts passed at any time.

(2) The definition of "British Islands", in its application to Acts passed after the establishment of the Irish Free State but before the commencement of this Act, includes the Republic of Ireland.

(3) The definition of "colony", in its application to an Act passed at any time before the commencement of this Act, includes—

(a) any colony within the meaning of section 18(3) of the Interpretation Act 1889 which was excluded, but in relation only to Acts passed at a later time, by any enactment repealed by this Act;

(b) any country or territory which ceased after that time to be part of Her Majesty's dominions but subject to a provision for the continuation of existing law as if it had not so ceased;

and paragraph (b) of the definition does not apply.

(4) The definition of "Lord Chancellor" does not apply to Acts passed before 1st October 1921 in which that expression was used in relation to Ireland only.

(5) The definition of "person", so far as it includes bodies corporate, applies to any provision of an Act whenever passed relating to an offence punishable on indictment or on summary conviction.

(6) This paragraph applies to . . . the Water Act 1973 as if they were passed after 1st April 1974.

5. The following definitions shall be treated as included in Schedule 1 for the purposes specified in this paragraph—

(a) in any Act passed before 1st April 1974, a reference to England includes Berwick upon Tweed and Monmouthshire and, in the case of an Act passed before the Welsh Language Act 1967, Wales;

(b) in any Act passed before the commencement of this Act and after the year 1850, "land" includes messuages, tenements and hereditaments, houses and buildings of any tenure;

(c) in any Act passed before the commencement of the Criminal Procedure (Scotland) Act 1975, "the Summary Jurisdiction (Scotland) Acts" means Part II of that Act.

NOTES

Para 4: words omitted from sub-para (1) repealed, and words in square brackets inserted, by the Family Law Reform Act 1987, s 33(1), (4), Sch 2, para 74, Sch 4; in sub-para (6) words omitted repealed by the Health Authorities Act 1995, s 5(1), Sch 3.

PART II
SUBORDINATE LEGISLATION

6. Sections 4(a), 9 and 19(1), and so much of Schedule 1 as defines the following expressions, namely—

. . .

England;

Local land charges register and appropriate local land charges register;

Police area (and related expressions) in relation to Scotland.

United Kingdom;

Wales,

apply to subordinate legislation made at any time before the commencement of this Act as they apply to Acts passed at that time.

7. The definition in Schedule 1 of "county court", in relation to England and Wales, applies to Orders in Council made after the year 1846.

NOTES

Para 6: words omitted in the first place repealed by the British Nationality Act 1981, s 52(8), Sch 9.

(Sch 3 (Enactments repealed) outside the scope of this work).

customs and excise airport at which it is cleared before departing for a destination outside the United Kingdom.

(6)   Goods imported by means of a pipe-line shall be treated as imported at the time when they are brought within the limits of a port or brought across the boundary into Northern Ireland.

(7)   Goods exported by means a of pipe-line shall be treated as exported at the time when they are charged into that pipe-line for exportation.

(8)   A ship shall be deemed to have arrived at or departed from a port at the time when the ship comes within or, as the case may be, leaves the limits of that port.

NOTES

Sub-s (3): words in square brackets substituted by the Customs and Excise (Single Market etc) Regulations 1992, SI 1992/3095, reg 10(1), Sch 1, para 3.

Postal packets: see note at the beginning of this Act.

PART II
ADMINISTRATION

Appointment and duties of Commissioners, officers, etc

6

(Repealed by the Commissioners for Revenue and Customs Act 2005 s 50, Sch 4 para 21, s 52, Sch 5.)

7

(Repealed by the Commissioners for Revenue and Customs Act 2005 s 50, Sch 4 para 21, s 52, Sch 5.)

8 Exercise of powers and performance of duties

(1)   . . .

(2)   Any person, whether an officer or not, engaged by the orders or with the concurrence of the Commissioners (whether previously or subsequently expressed) in the performance of any act or duty relating to an assigned matter which is by law required or authorised to be performed by or with an officer, shall be deemed to be the proper officer by or with whom that act or duty is to be performed.

(3)   Any person deemed by virtue of subsection (2) above to be the proper officer shall have all the powers of an officer in relation to the act or duty performed or to be performed by him as mentioned in that subsection.

NOTES

Sub-s (1) repealed by the Commissioners for Revenue and Customs Act 2005 s 50, Sch 4 para 21, s 52, Sch 5.

Sub-ss (2), (3) shall not apply to a person engaged in connection with a function relating to a matter to which Commissioners for Revenue and Customs Act 2005 s 7 applies (CRCA 2005 ss 16, 17, Sch 2 para 4).

9 General duties of Commissioners in relation to customs matters concerning the European Communities

For the purpose of implementing Community obligations the Commissioners shall co-operate with other customs services on matters of mutual concern and (without prejudice to the foregoing) may for that purpose—

(a) give effect, in accordance with such arrangements as they may direct or by regulations prescribe, to any Community requirement or practice as to the movement of goods between countries, including any rules requiring payment to be made in connection with the exportation of goods to compensate for any relief from customs duty allowed or to be allowed (and may recover any such payment as if it were an amount of customs duty unpaid); and

(b) give effect to any reciprocal arrangements made between member States (with or without other countries or territories) for securing by the exchange of information or otherwise, the due administration of their customs laws and the prevention or detection of fraud or evasion.

10 Disclosure by Commissioners of certain information as to imported goods

(1) On being notified at any time by the Treasury that they are satisfied that it is in the national interest that the information in question should be disclosed to persons other than the Commissioners, the Commissioners may disclose through such person as may be specified in the notification such information to which this section applies, in respect of imported goods of such descriptions, as may be so specified.

(2) The information to which this section applies is information contained in any document with which the Commissioners have been provided in pursuance of the Customs and Excise Acts 1979 for the purpose of making entry of any goods on their importation, being information of the following descriptions only, namely—

(a) the description of the goods, including any maker's catalogue number;

(b) the quantities of the goods imported in a particular period, so, however, that if any quantity is given by value it shall not also be given in any other form;

(c) the name of the maker of the goods;

(d) the country of origin of the goods;

(e) the country from which the goods were consigned.

(3) Without prejudice to paragraph 10 of Schedule 7 to this Act, this section also applies to information of any of those descriptions contained in any document with which the Commissioners have been provided for that purpose after 7th March 1967 in pursuance of the Customs and Excise Act 1952.

(4) The Treasury may by order add to the descriptions of information to which this section applies any further description of information contained in any document such as is mentioned in subsection (2) or (3) above other than the price of the goods or the name of the importer of the goods.

(5) The power to make orders under subsection (4) above shall be exercisable by statutory instrument subject to annulment in pursuance of a resolution of either House of Parliament.

11 Assistance to be rendered by police, etc

It shall be the duty of every constable and every member of Her Majesty's armed forces or coastguard to assist in the enforcement of the law relating to any assigned matter.

NOTES

Section 11 does not apply in connection with a function relating to a matter to which Commissioners for Revenue and Customs Act 2005 s 7 applies (CRCA 2005 ss 16, 17,

Sch 2 para 5(1)). For the purposes of this section, a person may rely on a statement (written or oral) of an officer of Revenue and Customs that a function does not relate to a matter to which CRCA 2005 s 7 applies (CRCA 2005 ss 16, 17, Sch 2 para 5(2)).

12

(Repealed by the Commissioners for Revenue and Customs Act 2005 s 52(1)(a)(i), Sch 5.)

Offences in connection with Commissioners, officers, etc

13, 14

(Repealed by the Commissioners for Revenue and Customs Act 2005 s 50, Sch 4 para 21, s 52, Sch 5.)

15

(Repealed by the Commissioners for Revenue and Customs Act 2005 s 52(1)(a)(ii), Sch 5.)

16, 17, 18

(Repealed by the Commissioners for Revenue and Customs Act 2005 s 50, Sch 4 para 21, s 52, Sch 5.)

PART III
CUSTOMS AND EXCISE CONTROL AREAS

19 Appointment of ports, etc

(1) The Commissioners may by order made by statutory instrument appoint and name as a port for the purposes of customs and excise any area in the United Kingdom specified in the order.

(2) The appointment of any port for those purposes made before 1st August 1952 may be revoked, and the name or limits of any such port may be altered, by an order under subsection (1) above as if the appointment had been made by an order under that subsection.

(3) The Commissioners may in any port from time to time appoint boarding stations for the purpose of the boarding of or disembarkation from ships by officers.

[20 Approval of wharves

(1) The Commissioners may approve, for such periods and subject to such conditions and restrictions as they think fit, places for the loading or unloading of goods or of any class or description of goods.

(2) The Commissioners may at any time for reasonable cause revoke or vary the terms of any approval given under this section.

(3) This section shall not apply in relation to goods imported on or after 1st January 1992 from a place outside the customs territory of the Community [or to any goods which are moving under the procedure specified in [Article 165 of Council Regulation (EEC) No 2913/92 and Article 311 of Commission Regulation (EEC) No 2454/93] (transit procedures).]]

NOTES

Substituted together with s 20A for original s 20 by the Customs Controls on Importation of Goods Regulations 1991, SI 1991/2724, reg 6(1), (3).

Sub-s (3): words in first (outer) pair of square brackets inserted by the Customs and Excise (Single Market etc) Regulations 1992, SI 1992/3095, reg 3(2), words in second (inner) pair of square brackets substituted by the Community Customs Code (Consequential Amendment of References) Regulations 1993, SI 1993/3014, reg 2(1), (2).

Council Regulation (EEC) No 2913/92: OJ L302, 19.10.92, p 1.

Commission Regulation (EEC) No 2454/93: OJ L253, 11.10.93, p 1.

[20A Approved wharves

(1) In this Act, references to an approved wharf are to—

    (a)   a place approved under section 20 above; or

    (b)   a place specified or approved under [Article 46 of Council Regulation (EEC) No 2913/92] (equivalent provision for goods imported on or after 1st January 1992 from a place outside the customs territory of the Community), other than an examination station.

(2) Any person contravening or failing to comply with any condition or restriction attaching to an approval by virtue of which a place is an approved wharf shall be liable on summary conviction to a penalty of level 3 on the standard scale.

(3) An officer may at any time enter an approved wharf and inspect it and any goods for the time being at the wharf.]

NOTES

Substituted as noted to s 20.

Sub-s (1): words in square brackets substituted by the Community Customs Code (Consequential Amendment of References) Regulations 1993, SI 1993/3014, reg 2(1), (3).

Council Regulation (EEC) No 2913/92: OJ L302, 19.10.92, p 1.

21 Control of movement of aircraft, etc into and out of the United Kingdom

(1) Save as permitted by the Commissioners, the commander of an aircraft entering the United Kingdom from a place outside the United Kingdom shall not cause or permit the aircraft to land—

    (a)   for the first time after its arrival in the United Kingdom; or

    (b)   at any time while it is carrying passengers or goods brought in that aircraft from a place outside the United Kingdom and not yet cleared,

at any place other than a customs and excise airport.

[(1A) Subsection (1) above shall not apply by virtue only of the fact that the aircraft is carrying goods brought in it from a place outside the customs territory of the Community.]

(2) Save as permitted by the Commissioners, no person importing [from a place within the customs territory of the Community] or concerned in [so] importing any goods in any aircraft shall bring the goods into the United Kingdom at any place other than a customs and excise airport.

(3) Save as permitted by the Commissioners—

    (a)   no person shall depart on a flight to a place or area outside the United Kingdom from any place in the United Kingdom other than a customs and excise airport; and

    (b)   the commander of any aircraft engaged in a flight from a customs and excise airport to a place or area outside the United Kingdom shall not cause or permit it to land at any place in the United Kingdom other than a customs and excise airport specified in the application for clearance for that flight.

(4) Subsections (1) to (3) above shall not apply in relation to any aircraft flying from or to any place or area outside the United Kingdom to or from any place in the United Kingdom which is required by or under any enactment relating to air navigation, or is compelled by accident, stress of weather or other unavoidable cause, to land at a place other than a customs and excise airport; but, subject to subsection (5) below,—

(a)   the commander of any such aircraft—

(i)   shall immediately report the landing to an officer or constable and shall on demand produce to him the journey log book belonging to the aircraft,

(ii)   shall not without the consent of an officer permit any goods carried in the aircraft to be unloaded from, or any of the crew or passengers to depart from the vicinity of, the aircraft, and

(iii)   shall comply with any directions given by an officer with respect to any such goods; and

(b)   no passenger or member of the crew shall without the consent of an officer or constable leave the immediate vicinity of any such aircraft.

[(4A) Subsection 4(a)(ii) and (iii) above shall not apply in relation to goods brought in the aircraft from a place outside the customs territory of the Community.]

(5) Nothing in subsection (4) above shall prohibit—

(a)   the departure of passengers or crew from the vicinity of an aircraft; or

(b)   the removal of goods from an aircraft,

where that departure or removal is necessary for reasons of health, safety or the preservation of life or property.

(6) Any person contravening or failing to comply with any provision of this section shall be liable on summary conviction to a penalty of [level 4 on the standard scale], or to imprisonment for a term not exceeding *3 months*, or to both.

(7) In this Act "customs and excise airport" means an aerodrome for the time being designated as a place for the landing or departure of aircraft for the purposes of the customs and excise Acts by an order made by the Secretary of State with the concurrence of the Commissioners which is in force under an Order in Council made in pursuance of [section 60 of the Civil Aviation Act 1982].

[(8) References in this section to a place or area outside the United Kingdom do not include references to a place or area in the Isle of Man and in subsection (3)(b) above the reference to a place in the United Kingdom includes a reference to a place in the Isle of Man.]

NOTES

Sub-ss (1A), (4A): inserted by the Customs Controls on Importation of Goods Regulations 1991, SI 1991/2724, reg 6(1), (4)(a), (5).

Sub-s (2): words in square brackets inserted by SI 1991/2724, reg 6(1), (4)(b).

Sub-s (6): reference to a level on the standard scale substituted by virtue of the Criminal Justice Act 1982, ss 38, 46. Words "51 weeks" to be substituted for "3 months" by the Criminal Justice Act 2003 s 280(2), (3), Sch 26 para 26(1), (2) with effect from a date to be appointed.

Sub-s (7): words in square brackets substituted by the Civil Aviation Act 1982, s 109(2), Sch 15, para 23.

Sub-s (8): added by the Isle of Man Act 1979, s 13, Sch 1.

[22 Approval of examination stations at customs and excise airports

(1) The Commissioners may approve, for such periods and subject to such conditions and restrictions as they think fit, a part of, or a place at, any customs and excise airport for the loading and unloading of goods and the embarkation and disembarkation of passengers.

(2) The Commissioners may at any time for reasonable cause revoke or vary the terms of any approval given under this section.

(3) This section shall not apply in relation to goods imported on or after 1st January 1992 from a place outside the customs territory of the Community [or to any goods which are moving under the procedure specified in [Article 165 of Council Regulation (EEC) No 2913/92 and Article 311 of Commission Regulation (EEC) No 2454/93] (transit procedures).]]

NOTES

Substituted together with s 22A for original s 22 by the Customs Controls on Importation of Goods Regulations 1991, SI 1991/2724, reg 6(1), (6).

Sub-s (3): words in first (outer) pair of square brackets inserted by the Customs and Excise (Single Market etc) Regulations 1992, SI 1992/3095, reg 3(2), words in second (inner) pair of square brackets substituted by the Community Customs Code (Consequential Amendment of References) Regulations 1993, SI 1993/3014, reg 2(1), (2).

Council Regulation (EEC) No 2913/92: OJ L302, 19.10.92, p 1.

Commission Regulation (EEC) No 2454/93: OJ L253, 11.10.93, p 1.

[22A Examination stations

(1) In this Act, references to an examination station are to—

    (a)   a part of, or a place at, a customs and excise airport approved under section 22 above; or

    (b)   a place at such an airport specified or approved under [Article 46 of Council Regulation (EEC) No 2913/92] (equivalent provision for goods imported on or after 1st January 1992 from a place outside the customs territory of the Community).

(2) Any person contravening or failing to comply with any condition or restriction attaching to an approval by virtue of which a part of, or a place at, a customs and excise airport is an examination station shall be liable on summary conviction to a penalty of level 3 on the standard scale.]

NOTES

Substituted as noted to s 22.

Sub-s (1): words in square brackets substituted by the Community Customs Code (Consequential Amendment of References) Regulations 1993, SI 1993/3014, reg 2(1), (3).

Council Regulation (EEC) No 2913/92: OJ L302, 19.10.92, p 1.

23 Control of movement of hovercraft

(1) The Commissioners may by regulations impose conditions and restrictions as respects the movement of hovercraft and the carriage of goods by hovercraft, and in particular—

    (a)   may prescribe the procedure to be followed by hovercraft proceeding to or from a port or any customs and excise airport or customs and excise station, and authorise the proper officer to give directions as to their routes; and

    (b)   may make provision for cases where by reason of accident, or in any other circumstance, it is impracticable to comply with any conditions or restrictions imposed or directions given as respects hovercraft.

(2)   Subsection (1) above shall apply to hovercraft proceeding to or from any approved wharf or transit shed which is not in a port as if it were a port.

(3)   If any person contravenes or fails to comply with any regulation made under subsection (1) above, or with any direction given by the Commissioners of the proper officer in pursuance of any such regulation, he shall be liable on summary conviction to a penalty of [level 3 on the standard scale] and any goods in respect of which the offence was committed shall be liable to forfeiture.

NOTES

Sub-s (3): reference to a level on the standard scale substituted by virtue of the Criminal Justice Act 1982, ss 38, 46.

24 Control of movement of goods by pipe-line

(1)   Goods shall not be imported or exported by means of a pipe-line that is not for the time being approved by the Commissioners for the purposes of this section.

(2)   Uncleared goods, that is to say—

(a)   imported goods, whether or not chargeable with duty, which have not been cleared out of charge, and in particular goods which are, or are to be, moved under section 30 below; or

(b)   dutiable goods moved from warehouse without payment of duty,

shall not be moved by means of a pipe-line that is not for the time being approved by the Commissioners for the purposes of this section.

(3)   The Commissioners may give their approval under this section for such period and subject to such conditions as they think fit, and may at any time for reasonable cause—

(a)   vary the terms of their approval; and

(b)   (if they have given to the owner of the pipe-line not less than 3 months' written notice of their intention so to do) revoke their approval.

(4)   Section 49 of the Pipe-lines Act 1962 (procedure for service of documents under that Act) shall apply to a notice required by subsection (3)(b) above to be served on the owner of a pipe-line as it applies to a document required by that Act to be so served.

(5)   A person who—

(a)   contravenes subsection (1) or (2) above, or contravenes or fails to comply with a condition imposed by the Commissioners under subsection (3) above; or

(b)   except with the authority of the proper officer or for just and sufficient cause, obtains access to goods which are in, or in course of conveyance by, a pipe-line approved under this section,

shall be guilty of an offence under this section and may be [arrested]; and any goods in respect of which the offence was committed shall be liable to forfeiture.

(6)   A person guilty of an offence under this section shall be liable—

(a)   on summary conviction, to a penalty of the prescribed sum, or to imprisonment for a term not exceeding 6 months, or to both; or

(b)   on conviction on indictment, to a penalty of any amount, or to imprisonment for a term not exceeding 2 years, or to both.

(7)   In the application of subsection (4) above to Northern Ireland, the reference to the Pipe-lines Act 1962 shall have effect as if that Act extended to Northern Ireland.

Sub-s (5): word in square brackets substituted by the Police and Criminal Evidence Act 1984, s 114(1).

[25 Approval of transit sheds

(1) The Commissioners may approve, for such periods and subject to such conditions and restrictions as they think fit, places for the deposit of goods imported and not yet cleared out of charge, including goods not yet reported and entered [under regulation 5 of the Customs Controls on Importation of Goods Regulations 1991].

(2) The Commissioners may at any time for reasonable cause revoke or vary the terms of any approval given under this section.

(3) Subsection (1) above shall not apply in relation to goods imported on or after 1st January 1992 from a place outside the customs territory of the Community [or to any goods which are moving under the procedure specified in [Article 165 of Council Regulation (EEC) No 2913/92 and Article 311 of Commission Regulation (EEC) No 2454/93] (transit procedures).]

(4) Where, by any local Act, provision is made for the landing of goods without entry for deposit in transit sheds authorised thereunder, the provisions of this Act relating to goods deposited in transit sheds approved under this section shall have effect in relation to goods deposited in transit sheds authorised under that Act.]

NOTES
Substituted together with s 25A for original s 25 by the Customs Controls on Importation of Goods Regulations 1991, SI 1991/2724, reg 6(7).

Sub-s (1): words in square brackets substituted by the Customs and Excise (Single Market etc) Regulations 1992, SI 1992/3095, reg 10(1), Sch 1, para 4.

Sub-s (3): words in first (outer) pair of square brackets inserted by SI 1992/3095, reg 3(2), words in (second) pair of square brackets substituted by the Community Customs Code (Consequential Amendment of References) Regulations 1993, SI 1993/3014, reg 2(1), (2).

Council Regulation (EEC) No 2913/92: OJ L302, 19.10.92, p 1.

Commission Regulation (EEC) No 2454/93: OJ L253, 11.10.93, p 1.

[25A Transit sheds

(1) In this Act, references to a transit shed are to a place approved—
    (a)   under section 25 above; or
    (b)   under [Article 51 of Council Regulation (EEC) No 2913/92] (equivalent provision for goods imported on or after 1st January 1992 from a place outside the customs territory of the Community).

(2) Any person contravening or failing to comply with any condition or restriction attaching to an approval by virtue of which a place is a transit shed shall be liable on summary conviction to a penalty of level 3 on the standard scale.

(3) An officer may at any time enter a transit shed and inspect it and any goods for the time being in the transit shed.]

NOTES
Substituted as noted to 25.

Sub-s (1): words in square brackets substituted by the Community Customs Code (Consequential Amendment of References) Regulations 1993, SI 1993/3014, reg 2(1), (4).

Council Regulation (EEC) No 2913/92: OJ L302, 19.10.92, p 1.

26 Power to regulate movements of goods into and out of Northern Ireland by land

(1)   The Commissioners may, for the purpose of safeguarding the revenue and for the better enforcement of any prohibition or restriction for the time being in force under or by virtue of any enactment with respect to the importation or exportation of any goods, make regulations—

    (a)   . . .

    (b)   appointing places for the examination and entry of any payment of any duty chargeable on any goods being imported or exported by land (referred to in this Act as "customs and excise stations")

[and any such regulations may make different provision in relation to different classes or descriptions of goods and, in particular, in relation to different classes or descriptions of vehicles].

[(1A)   In such cases and subject to compliance with such conditions as appear to the Commissioners to be appropriate, the Commissioners may dispense with any requirement of a regulation made under subsection (1) above.]

(2)   If any person contravenes or fails to comply with any regulation made under subsection (1) above [or such condition of a dispensation given under subsection (1A) above] he shall be liable on summary conviction to a penalty of [level 3 on a standard scale], and any goods in respect of which the offence was committed shall be liable to forfeiture.

NOTES

Sub-s (1): para (a) repealed by the Customs and Excise (Single Market etc) Regulations 1992, SI 1992/3095, regs 3(3), 10(2), Sch 2; words in square brackets added by the Finance Act 1983, s 7(1)(b).

Sub-s (1A): inserted by the Finance Act 1983, s 7(2).

Sub-s (2): words in first pair of square brackets added by the Finance Act 1983, s 7(3); reference to a level on the standard scale substituted by virtue of the Criminal Justice Act 1982, ss 38, 46.

Regulations: by virtue of the Interpretation Act 1978, s 17(2)(b), in conjunction with s 177(5) of this Act, the Customs and Excise (Single Market etc) Regulations 1992, SI 1992/3095.

---

27 Officers' powers of boarding

(1)   At any time while a ship is within the limits of a port, or an aircraft is at [an aerodrome], or [a vehicle is—

    (a)   entering, leaving or about to leave the United Kingdom,

    (b)   within the prescribed area,

    (c)   within the limits of or entering or leaving a port or any land adjacent to a port and occupied wholly or mainly for the purpose of activities carried on at the port,

    (d)   at, entering or leaving an aerodrome,

    (e)   at, entering or leaving an approved wharf, transit shed, customs warehouse or free zone, or

    (f)   at, entering or leaving any such premises as are mentioned in subsection (1) of section 112 below,

any officer] and any other person duly engaged in the prevention of smuggling may board the ship, aircraft or vehicle and remain therein and rummage and search any part thereof.

[(1A)   For the purposes of subsection (1) above "customs warehouse" means a victualling warehouse or a place approved by the Commissioners under [Article 98 of Council Regulation (EEC) No 2913/92 or Article 505 of Commission Regulation (EEC) No 2454/93].]

(2) The Commissioners may station officers in any ship at any time while it is within the limits of a port, and if the master of any ship neglects or refuses to provide—

    (a)   reasonable accommodation below decks for any officer stationed therein; or

    (b)   means of safe access to and egress from the ship in accordance with the requirements of any such officer,

the master shall be liable on summary conviction to a penalty of [level 2 on the standard scale].

NOTES

Sub-s (1): words in first pair of square brackets substituted by the Finance (No 2) Act 1992, s 10(1), (2); words in final pair of square brackets substituted by the Finance Act 1987, s 7(1).

Sub-s (1A): inserted by the Customs Warehousing Regulations 1991, SI 1991/2725, reg 3(1), (3); words in square brackets substituted by the Community Customs Code (Consequential Amendment of References) Regulations 1993, SI 1993/3014, reg 2(1), (5).

Sub-s (2): reference to a level on the standard scale substituted by virtue of the Criminal Justice Act 1982, s 46.

Council Regulation (EEC) No 2913/92: OJ L302, 19.10.92, p 1.

Commission Regulation (EEC) No 2454/93: OJ L253, 11.10.93, p 1.

---

28 Officers' powers of access, etc

(1) Without prejudice to section 27 above, the proper officer shall have free access to every part of any ship or aircraft at a port or [aerodrome] and of any vehicle [which falls within paragraph (a) to (f) of subsection (1) of section 27 above or is] brought to a customs and excise station, and may—

    (a)   cause any goods to be marked before they are unloaded from that ship, aircraft or vehicle;

    (b)   lock up, seal, mark or otherwise secure any goods carried in the ship, aircraft or vehicle or any place or container in which they are so carried; and

    (c)   break open any place or container which is locked and of which the keys are withheld.

(2) Any goods found concealed on board any such ship, aircraft or vehicle shall be liable to forfeiture.

NOTES

Sub-s (1): word in first pair of square brackets substituted by the Finance (No 2) Act 1992, s 10(1), (3); words in second pair of square brackets inserted by the Finance Act 1987, s 7(2).

---

29 Officers' powers of detention of ships, etc

(1) Where, in the case of a ship, aircraft or vehicle of which due report has been made under section 35 below, any goods are still on board that ship, aircraft or vehicle at the expiration of the relevant period, the proper officer may detain that ship, aircraft or vehicle until there have been repaid to the Commissioners—

    (a)   any expenses properly incurred in watching and guarding the goods beyond the relevant period, except, in the case of a ship or aircraft, in respect of the day of clearance inwards; and

    (b)   where the goods are removed by virtue of any provision of the Customs and Excise Acts 1979 from the ship, aircraft or vehicle to a Queen's warehouse, the expenses of that removal.

(2)   In subsection (1) above, "the relevant period" means—

(a)   in the case of a ship or vehicle, 21 clear days from the date of making due report of the ship or vehicle under section 35 below or such longer period as the Commissioners may in any case allow;

(b)   in the case of an aircraft, 7 clear days from the date of making due report of the aircraft under that section or such longer period as the Commissioners may in any case allow.

(3)   Where, in the case of—

(a)   any derelict or other ship or aircraft coming, driven or brought into the United Kingdom under legal process, by stress of weather or for safety; or

(b)   any vehicle in Northern Ireland which suffers any mishap,

it is necessary for the protection of the revenue to station any officer in charge thereof, whether on board or otherwise, the proper officer may detain that ship, aircraft or vehicle until any expenses thereby incurred by the Commissioners have been repaid.

30 Control of movement of uncleared goods within or between port or airport and other places

(1)   The Commissioners may from time to time give general or special directions as to the manner in which, and the conditions under which, goods to which this section applies, or any class or description of such goods, may be moved within the limits of any port or customs and excise airport or between any port or customs and excise airport and any other place.

(2)   This section applies to goods chargeable with any duty which has not been paid, to drawback goods, and to any other goods which have not been cleared out of charge.

(3)   Any directions under subsection (1) above may require that any goods to which this section applies shall be moved only—

(a)   by persons licensed by the Commissioners for that purpose;

(b)   in such ships, aircraft or vehicles or by such other means as may be approved by the Commissioners for that purpose;

and any such licence or approval may be granted for such period and subject to such conditions and restrictions as the Commissioners think fit and may be revoked at any time by the Commissioners.

(4)   Any person contravening or failing to comply with any direction given or condition or restriction imposed, or the terms of any licence granted, by the Commissioners under this section shall be liable on summary conviction to a penalty of [level 2 on the standard scale].

NOTES

Sub-s (4): reference to a level on the standard scale substituted by virtue of the Criminal Justice Act 1982, s 46.

31 Control of movement of goods to and from inland clearance depot, etc

(1)   The Commissioners may by regulations impose conditions and restrictions as respects—

(a)   the movement of imported goods between the place of importation and a place approved by the Commissioners for the clearance out of charge of such goods[, a free zone] [or the place of exportation of such goods]; and

[(aa)   the movement of goods between—

(i)   a free zone and a place approved by the Commissioners for the clearance out of charge of such goods,

   (ii) such a place and a free zone, and

   (iii) a free zone and another free zone;]

 (b) the movement of goods intended for export between a place approved by the Commissioners for the examination of such goods[, or a place designated by the proper officer under section 53(4) or 58(3) below,] and the place of exportation.

(2) Regulations under subsection (1) above may in particular—

 (a) require the goods to be moved within such period and by such route as may be specified by or under the regulations;

 (b) require the goods to be carried in a vehicle or container complying with such requirements and secured in such manner as may be so specified;

 (c) prohibit, except in such circumstances as may be so specified, any unloading or loading of the vehicle or container or any interference with its security.

[(2A) Any documents required to be made or produced as a result of regulations made under subsection (1) above shall be made or produced in such form and manner and contain such particulars as the Commissioners may direct; but the Commissioners may relax any requirement imposed under the regulations that any specific document be made or produced and if they do so may impose substituted requirements.]

(3) If any person contravenes or fails to comply with any regulation under subsection (1) above or any requirement imposed by or under any such regulation [or a direction made under subsection (2A) above or any requirement imposed under that subsection], that person and the person then in charge of the goods shall each be liable on summary conviction to a penalty of [level 4 on the standard scale] and any goods in respect of which the offence was committed shall be liable to forfeiture.

NOTES

Sub-s (1): words in first pair of square brackets and para (aa) inserted by the Finance Act 1984, s 8, Sch 4, Pt II, para 2; words in second pair of square brackets in para (a) and words in square brackets in para (b) inserted by the Finance Act 1981, s 10(2), (4), Sch 7, Pt II, para 1(1), (2), except in relation to goods exported before 1 October 1981.

Sub-s (2A): inserted by the Finance Act 1981, s 10(2), (4), Sch 7, Pt II, para 1(1), (3), except in relation to goods exported before 1 October 1981.

Sub-s (3): first words in square brackets added by the Finance Act 1981, s 10(2), (4), Sch 7, Pt II, para 1(1), (4), except in relation to goods exported before 1 October 1981; reference to a level on the standard scale substituted by virtue of the Criminal Justice Act 1982, s 46.

Regulations: the Control of Movement of Goods Regulations 1984, SI 1984/1176.

32

(Repealed by the Commissioners for Revenue and Customs Act 2005 s 52(1)(a)(iii), Sch 5.)

33 Power to inspect aircraft, aerodromes, records, etc

(1) The commander of an aircraft shall permit an officer at any time to board the aircraft and inspect—

 (a) the aircraft and any goods loaded therein; and

 (b) all documents relating to the aircraft or to goods or persons carried therein;

and an officer shall have the right of access at any time to any place to which access is required for the purpose of any such inspection.

(2) The person in control of any aerodrome shall permit an officer at any time to enter upon and inspect the aerodrome and all buildings and goods thereon.

(3)   The person in control of an aerodrome licensed under any enactment relating to air navigation and, if so required by the Commissioners, the person in control of any other aerodrome shall—

    (a)   keep a record in such form and manner as the Commissioners may approve of all aircraft arriving at or departing from the aerodrome;

    (b)   keep that record available and produce it on demand to any officer, together with all other documents kept on the aerodrome which relate to the movement of aircraft; and

    (c)   permit any officer to make copies of and take extracts from any such record or document.

(4)   If any person contravenes or fails to comply with any of the provisions of this section he shall be liable on summary conviction to a penalty of [level 4 on the standard scale] or to imprisonment for a term not exceeding 3 *months*, or to both.

NOTES

Sub-s (4): reference to a level on the standard scale substituted by virtue of the Criminal Justice Act 1982, ss 38, 46. Words "51 weeks" to be substituted for "3 months" by the Criminal Justice Act 2003 s 280(2), (3), Sch 26 para 26(1), (3) with effect from a date to be appointed.

34 Power to prevent flight of aircraft

(1)   If it appears to any officer or constable that an aircraft is intended or likely to depart for a destination outside the United Kingdom [and the Isle of Man] from—

    (a)   any place other than a customs and excise airport; or

    (b)   a customs and excise airport before clearance outwards is given,

he may give such instructions and take such steps by way of detention of the aircraft or otherwise as appear to him necessary in order to prevent the flight.

(2)   Any person who contravenes any instructions given under subsection (1) above shall be liable on summary conviction to a penalty of [level 4 on the standard scale], or to imprisonment for a term not exceeding 3 *months*, or to both.

(3)   If an aircraft flies in contravention of any instruction given under subsection (1) above or notwithstanding any steps taken to prevent the flight, the owner and the commander thereof shall, without prejudice to the liability of any other person under subsection (2) above, each be liable on summary conviction to a penalty of [level 4 on the standard scale], or to imprisonment for a term not exceeding 3 *months*, or to both, unless he proves that the flight took place without his consent or connivance.

NOTES

Sub-s (1): words in square brackets inserted by the Isle of Man Act 1979, s 13, Sch 1.

Sub-s (2), (3): references to a level on the standard scale substituted by virtue of the Criminal Justice Act 1982, ss 38, 46. Words "51 weeks" to be substituted for "3 months" by the Criminal Justice Act 2003 s 280(2), (3), Sch 26 para 26(1), (4) with effect from a date to be appointed.

PART IV

CONTROL OF IMPORTATION

Inward entry and clearance

35 Report inwards

(1) Report shall be made in such form and manner and containing such particulars as the Commissioners may direct of every ship and aircraft to which this section applies . . .

(2) This section applies to every ship arriving at a port—

(a)   from any place outside the United Kingdom; or

(b)   carrying any goods brought in that ship from some place outside the United Kingdom and not yet cleared on importation.

(3) This section applies to every aircraft arriving at any place in the United Kingdom—

(a)   from any place or area outside the United Kingdom; or

(b)   carrying passengers or goods taken on board that aircraft at a place outside the United Kingdom, being passengers or goods either—

(i)   bound for a destination in the United Kingdom and not already cleared at a customs and excise airport; or

(ii)   bound for a destination outside the United Kingdom.

(4) The Commissioners may make regulations prescribing the procedure for making report under this section.

(5) If the person by whom the report should be made fails to make report as required by or under this section—

(a)   he shall be liable on summary conviction to a penalty of [level 3 on the standard scale]; and

(b)   any goods required to be reported which are not duly reported may be detained by any officer until so reported or until the omission is explained to the satisfaction of the Commissioners, and may in the meantime be deposited in a Queen's warehouse.

(6) The person making the report shall at the time of making it answer all such questions relating to the ship, [or aircraft], to the goods carried therein, to the crew and to the voyage, [or flight] as may be put to him by the proper officer; and if he refuses to answer he shall be liable on summary conviction to a penalty of [level 3 on the standard scale].

(7) If at any time after a ship or aircraft carrying goods brought therein from any place outside the United Kingdom arrives [in or over United Kingdom waters], . . . and before report has been made in accordance with this section—

(a)   bulk is broken; or

(b)   any alteration is made in the stowage of any goods carried so as to facilitate the unloading of any part thereof before due report has been made; or

(c)   any part of the goods is staved, destroyed or thrown overboard or any container is opened,

and the matter is not explained to the satisfaction of the Commissioners, the master of the ship or commander of the aircraft . . . shall be liable on summary conviction to a penalty of [level 3 on the standard scale].

(8) . . .

[(9) References in this section to a place, area or destination outside the United Kingdom do not include references to a place, area or destination in the Isle of Man and in subsection (3)(b)(i) above the reference to a destination in the United Kingdom includes a reference to a destination in the Isle of Man.]

NOTES

Sub-s (1): words omitted repealed by the Customs and Excise (Single Market etc) Regulations 1992, SI 1992/3095, regs 3(4)(a), 10(2), Sch 2.

Sub-s (5): reference to a level on the standard scale substituted by virtue of the Criminal Justice Act 1982, ss 38, 46.

Sub-s (6): words in first pair of square brackets substituted by SI 1992/3095, reg 3(4)(b); reference to a level on the standard scale substituted by virtue of the Criminal Justice Act 1982, ss 38, 46.

Sub-s (7): words in first pair of square brackets substituted by the Territorial Sea Act 1987, s 3(1), Sch 1, para 4(2); words omitted repealed by SI 1992/3095, regs 3(4)(c), 10(2), Sch 2; reference to a level on the standard scale substituted by virtue the Criminal Justice Act 1982, ss 38, 46.

Sub-s (8): repealed by SI 1992/3095, regs 3(4)(d), 10(2), Sch 2.

Sub-s (9): added by the Isle of Man Act 1979, s 13, Sch 1.

Regulations: the following regulations have been made partly under sub-s (4) above: the Aircraft (Customs and Excise) Regulations 1981, SI 1981/1259, as amended by SI 1992/3095; the Ship's Report, Importation and Exportation by Sea Regulations 1981, SI 1981/1260, as amended by SI 1986/1819, SI 1992/3095; the Customs and Excise (Single Market etc) Regulations 1992, SI 1992/3095; the Pleasure Craft (Arrival and Report) Regulations 1996, SI 1996/1406.

Sub-ss (2), (3): words ", or expected to arrive," to be inserted after "arriving" by the Immigration, Asylum and Nationality Act 2006, s 35 with effect from a date to be appointed.

36 Provisions as to Her Majesty's ships, etc

(1) The person in command of any ship having a commission from Her Majesty or any foreign State which has on board any goods loaded in any place outside the United Kingdom [and the Isle of Man] shall, before any such goods are unloaded, or at any time when called upon to do so by the proper officer, deliver to the proper officer an account of the goods in accordance with subsection (2) below, and if he fails so to do he shall be liable on summary conviction to a penalty of [level 3 on the standard scale].

(2) An account of goods under subsection (1) above shall be in such form, and shall contain to the best of the knowledge of the person delivering the account such particulars, and shall be delivered in such manner, as the Commissioners may direct.

(3) The person delivering such an account shall when delivering it answer all such questions relating to the goods as may be put to him by the proper officer and if he refuses to answer he shall be liable on summary conviction to a penalty of [level 3 on the standard scale].

(4) Subject in the case of ships having a commission from Her Majesty to any regulations made by the Treasury, the provisions of Parts III to VII of this Act as to the boarding and search of ships shall have effect in relation to such a ship as aforesaid as they have effect in relation to any other ship, and any officer may remove to a Queen's warehouse any goods loaded as aforesaid found on board the ship.

NOTES

Sub-s (1): words in first pair of square brackets added by the Isle of Man Act 1979, s 13, Sch 1; reference to a level on the standard scale substituted by virtue of the Criminal Justice Act 1982, ss 38, 46.

Sub-s (3): reference to a level on the standard scale substituted by virtue of the Criminal Justice Act 1982, ss 38, 46.

37

(Repealed by the Customs and Excise (Single Market etc) Regulations 1992, SI 1992/3095, regs 3(5), 10(2), Sch 2.)

[37A Initial and supplementary entries

[(1) The Commissioners may—

(a) give such directions as they think fit for enabling an entry under regulation 5 of the Customs Controls on Importation of Goods Regulations 1991 to consist of an initial entry and a supplementary entry where the importer is authorised for the purposes of this section in accordance with the directions; and

(b) include in the directions such supplementary provision in connection with entries consisting of initial and supplementary entries as they think fit.]

[(1A) Without prejudice to section 37 above, a direction under that section may—

(a) provide that where the importer is not authorised for the purposes of this section but a person who is so authorised is appointed as his agent for the purpose of entering the goods, the entry may consist of an initial entry made by the person so appointed and a supplementary entry so made; and

(b) make such supplementary provision in connection with entries consisting of initial and supplementary entries made as mentioned in paragraph (a) above as the Commissioners think fit.]

[(2) Where—

(a) an initial entry made under subsection (1) above has been accepted and the importer has given security by deposit of money or otherwise to the satisfaction of the Commissioners for payment of the unpaid duty, or

(b) an initial entry made under subsection (1A) above has been accepted and the person making the entry on the importer's behalf has given such security as is mentioned in paragraph (a) above,

the goods may] be delivered without payment of any duty chargeable in respect of the goods, but any such duty shall be paid within such time as the Commissioners may direct.

(3) An importer who makes an initial entry [under subsection (1) above] shall complete the entry by delivering the supplementary entry within such time as the Commissioners may direct.

[(3A) A person who makes an initial entry under subsection (1A) above on behalf of an importer shall complete the entry by delivering the supplementary entry within such time as the Commissioners may direct.]

(4) For the purposes of the customs and excise Acts an entry of goods shall be taken to have been delivered when an initial entry of the goods has been delivered, and accepted when an initial entry has been accepted.]

NOTES

Inserted by the Finance Act 1984, s 9, Sch 5, para 2.

Sub-s (1): substituted by the Customs and Excise (Single Market etc) Regulations 1992, SI 1992/3095, reg 10(1), Sch 1, para 5.

Sub-ss (1A), (3A): inserted, in relation to goods imported on or after 26 July 1990, by the Finance Act 1990, s 7, Sch 3, para 2.

Sub-s (2): words in square brackets substituted, in relation to goods imported on or after 26 July 1990, by the Finance Act 1990, s 7, Sch 3, para 2.

Sub-s (3): words in square brackets inserted, in relation to goods imported on or after 26 July 1990, by the Finance Act 1990, s 7, Sch 3, para 2.

[37B Postponed entry

(1) The Commissioners may, if they think fit, direct that where—

  (a)   such goods as may be specified in the direction are imported by an importer authorised for the purposes of this subsection;

  (b)   the importer has delivered a document relating to the goods to the proper officer, in such form and manner, containing such particulars and accompanied by such documents as the Commissioners may direct; and

  (c)   the document has been accepted by the proper officer,

the goods may be delivered before an entry of them has been delivered or any duty chargeable in respect of them has been paid.

[(1A)   The Commissioners may, if they think fit, direct that where—

  (a)   such goods as may be specified in the direction are imported by an importer who is not authorised for the purposes of this subsection;

  (b)   a person who is authorised for the purposes of this subsection is appointed as his agent for the purpose of entering the goods;

  (c)   the person so appointed has delivered a document relating to the goods to the proper officer, in such form and manner, containing such particulars and accompanied by such documents as the Commissioners may direct; and

  (d)   the document has been accepted by the proper officer,

the goods may be delivered before an entry of them has been delivered or any duty chargeable in respect of them has been paid.]

(2) The Commissioners may, if they think fit, direct that where—

  (a)   such goods as may be specified in the direction are imported by an importer authorised for the purposes of this subsection;

  (b)   the goods have been removed from the place of importation to a place approved by the Commissioners for the clearance out of charge of such goods; and

  (c)   the conditions mentioned in subsection (3) below have been satisfied,

the goods may be delivered before an entry of them has been delivered or any duty chargeable in respect of them has been paid.

(3) The conditions are that—

  (a)   on the arrival of the goods at the approved place the importer delivers to the proper officer a notice of the arrival of the goods in such form and containing such particulars as may be required by the directions;

  (b)   within such time as may be so required the importer enters such particulars of the goods and such other information as may be so required in a record maintained by him at such place as the proper officer may require; and

  (c)   the goods are kept secure in the approved place for such period as may be required by the directions.

[(3A)   The Commissioners may, if they think fit, direct that where—

  (a)   such goods as may be specified in the direction are imported by an importer who is not authorised for the purposes of this subsection;

  (b)   a person who is authorised for the purposes of this subsection is appointed as his agent for the purpose of entering the goods;

  (c)   the goods have been removed from the place of importation to a place approved by the Commissioners for the clearance out of charge of such goods; and

(d) the conditions mentioned in subsection (3B) below have been satisfied,
the goods may be delivered before an entry of them has been delivered or any duty
chargeable in respect of them has been paid.

(3B) The conditions are that—

(a) on the arrival of the goods at the approved place the person appointed
as the agent of the importer for the purpose of entering the goods
delivers to the proper officer a notice of the arrival of the goods in such
form and containing such particulars as may be required by the
directions;

(b) within such time as may be so required the person appointed as the
agent of the importer for the purpose of entering the goods enters such
particulars of the goods and such other information as may be so
required in a record maintained by him at such place as the proper
officer may require; and

(c) the goods are kept secure in the approved place for such period as may
be required by the directions.]

(4) The Commissioners may direct that the condition mentioned in subsection
(3)(a) [or (3B)(a)] above shall not apply in relation to any goods specified in the
direction and such a direction may substitute another condition.

(5) No goods shall be delivered under [subsection (1) or (2) above] unless the
importer gives security by deposit of money or otherwise to the satisfaction of
the Commissioners for the payment of any duty chargeable in respect of the goods
which is unpaid.

[(5A) No goods shall be delivered under subsection (1A) or (3A) above unless the
person appointed as the agent of the importer for the purpose of entering the goods
gives security by deposit of money or otherwise to the satisfaction of
the Commissioners for the payment of any duty chargeable in respect of the goods
which is unpaid.]

(6) Where goods of which no entry has been made have been delivered under
[subsection (1) or (2) above], the importer shall deliver an entry of the goods under
[regulation 5 of the Customs Controls on Importation of Goods Regulations 1991]
within such time as the Commissioners may direct.

[(6A) Where goods of which no entry has been made have been delivered under
subsection (1A) or (3A) above, the person appointed as the agent of the importer for
the purpose of entering the goods shall deliver an entry of the goods, under
section 37(1) above within such time as the Commissioners may direct.]

(7) For the purposes of section 43(2)(a) below such an entry shall be taken to have
been accepted—

(a) in the case of goods delivered by virtue of a direction under subsection
(1) [or (1A)] above, on the date on which the document mentioned in
that subsection was accepted; and

(b) in the case of goods delivered by virtue of a direction under subsection
(2) above, on the date on which particulars of the goods were entered as
mentioned in subsection (3)(b) above [and

(c) in the case of goods delivered by virtue of a direction under subsection
(3A) above, on the date on which particulars of the goods were entered
as mentioned in subsection (3B)(b) above.]

NOTES

Inserted as noted to s 37A.

Sub-ss (1A), (3A), (3B), (5A), (6A): inserted, in relation to goods imported on or after
26 July 1990, by the Finance Act 1990, s 7, Sch 3, paras 1, 3.

Sub-ss (4), (7): words in square brackets inserted, in relation to goods imported on or after 26 July 1990, by the Finance Act 1990, s 7, Sch 3, paras 1, 3.

Sub-s (5): words in square brackets substituted, in relation to goods imported on or after 26 July 1990, by the Finance Act 1990, s 7, Sch 3, paras 1, 3.

Sub-s (6): words in first pair of square brackets substituted, in relation to goods imported on or after 26 July 1990, by the Finance Act 1990, s 7, Sch 3, para 3; words in second pair of square brackets substituted by the Customs and Excise (Single Market etc) Regulations 1992, SI 1992/3095, reg 10(1), Sch 1, para 6.

[37C Provisions supplementary to ss 37A and 37B

(1)   The Commissioners may, if they think fit—

   (a)   authorise any [person] for the purposes of sections 37A, or 37B(1)[, (1A), (2) or (3A)] above; and

   (b)   suspend or cancel the authorisation of any [person] where it appears to them that he has failed to comply with any requirement imposed on him by or under this Part of this Act or that there is other reasonable cause for suspension or cancellation.

(2)   The Commissioners may give directions—

   (a)   imposing such requirements as they think fit on any [person] authorised under this section; or

   (b)   varying any such requirements previously imposed.

(3)   If any person without reasonable excuse contravenes any requirement imposed by or under section 37A, 37B or this section he shall be liable on summary conviction to a penalty of level 4 on the standard scale.]

NOTES

Inserted as noted to s 37A.

Sub-ss (1), (2): words in square brackets substituted, in relation to goods imported on or after 26 July 1990, by the Finance Act 1990, s 7, Sch 3, paras 1, 4.

38, 38A

(Repealed by the Customs and Excise (Single Market etc) Regulations 1992, SI 1992/3095, s 3(5), 10(2), Sch 2 (s 38A originally inserted by the Finance Act 1981, s 10(1), Sch 6, para 4).)

[38B Correction and cancellation of entry

(1)   Where goods have been entered for home use or for free circulation the importer may correct any of the particulars contained in an entry of the goods after it has been accepted if—

   (a)   the goods have not been cleared from customs and excise charge;

   (b)   he has not been notified by an officer that the goods are to be examined; and

   (c)   the entry has not been found by an officer to be incorrect.

(2)   The proper officer may permit or require any correction allowed by subsection (1) above to be made by the delivery of a substituted entry.

(3)   An entry of goods may at the request of the importer be cancelled at any time before the goods are cleared from customs and excise charge if the importer proves to the satisfaction of the Commissioners that the entry was delivered by mistake or that the goods cannot be cleared for free circulation.]

NOTES

Inserted by the Finance Act 1981, s 10(1), Sch 6, para 4.

39 Entry of surplus stores

(1) With the permission of the proper officer, surplus stores of any ship or aircraft—

    (a)   if intended for private use and in quantities which do not appear to him to be excessive, may be entered and otherwise treated as if they were goods imported in the ship or aircraft; or

    (b)   in any other case may, subject to subsection (2) below, be entered for warehousing notwithstanding that they could not lawfully be imported as merchandise.

(2) Goods entered for warehousing by virtue of subsection (1)(b) above shall not, except with the sanction of the Commissioners, be further entered, or be removed from the warehouse, otherwise than for use as stores.

40 Removal of uncleared goods to Queen's warehouse

(1) Where in the case of any imported goods—

    (a)   entry has not been made thereof by the expiration of the relevant period; or

    [(b)   at the expiration of 21 clear days from the date when they were presented at the proper office of customs and excise they have not been produced for examination and clearance and the failure to produce them is attributable to an act or omission for which the importer is responsible; or]

    (c)   being goods imported by sea and not being in large quantity, they are at any time after the arrival of the importing ship at the port at which they are to be unloaded the only goods remaining to be unloaded from that ship at that port,

the proper officer may cause the goods to be deposited in a Queen's warehouse.

(2) Where any small package or consignment of goods is imported, the proper officer may at any time after the relevant date cause that package or consignment to be deposited in a Queen's warehouse to await entry.

(3) Without prejudice to section 99(3) below, if any goods deposited in a Queen's warehouse by the proper officer under this section are not cleared by the importer thereof—

    (a)   in the case of goods which are in the opinion of the Commissioners of a perishable nature, forthwith; or

    (b)   in any other case, within 3 months after they have been so deposited or such longer time as the Commissioners may in any case allow,

the Commissioners may sell them.

(4) In this section—

    (a)   "the relevant period" means a period of, in the case of goods imported by air, 7 or, in any other case, 14 clear days from the relevant date; and

    (b)   "the relevant date" means, subject to subsection (5) below, the date when report was made of the importing ship, aircraft or vehicle or of the goods under section 35 above, or, where no such report was made, the date when it should properly have been made.

(5) Where any restriction is placed upon the unloading of goods from any ship or aircraft by virtue of any enactment relating to the prevention of epidemic and

infectious diseases, then, in relation to that ship or aircraft, "the relevant date" in this section means the date of the removal of the restriction.

NOTES

Sub-s (1): para (b) substituted by the Finance Act 1981, s 10(1), Sch 6, para 5.
Postal packets: see note at the beginning of this Act.

41 Failure to comply with provisions as to entry

Without prejudice to any liability under any other provision of the Customs and Excise Acts 1979, any person making entry of goods on their importation who fails to comply with any of the requirements of this Part of this Act in connection with that entry shall be liable on summary conviction to a penalty of [level 2 on the standard scale], and the goods in question shall be liable to forfeiture [but this section shall not apply to—

    (a)   any failure which has been or may be remedied by virtue of section 38B(1); or

    (b)   any failure in respect of an entry which by virtue of section 38B(3) has been or may be cancelled at his request.]

NOTES

Reference to a level on the standard scale substituted by virtue of the Criminal Justice Act 1982, s 46; words in square brackets added by the Finance Act 1981, s 10(1), Sch 6, para 6.

42 Power to regulate unloading, removal, etc of imported goods

    (1)   The Commissioners may make regulations—

    (a)   prescribing the procedure to be followed by a ship arriving at a port, an aircraft arriving at a customs and excise airport, or a person conveying goods into Northern Ireland by land;

    (b)   regulating the unloading, landing, movement and removal of goods on their importation;

and different regulations may be made with respect to importation by sea, air or land respectively.

    (2)   If any person contravenes or fails to comply with any regulation made under this section or with any direction given by the Commissioners or the proper officer in pursuance of any such regulation, he shall be liable on summary conviction to a penalty of [level 3 on the standard scale] and any goods in respect of which the offence was committed shall be liable to forfeiture.

    [(3)   Subsection (1)(b) above shall not apply in relation to goods imported on or after 1st January 1992 from a place outside the customs territory of the Community [or to any goods which are moving under the procedure specified in [Article 165 of Council Regulation (EEC) No 2913/92 and Article 311 of Commission Regulation (EEC) No 2454/93] (transit procedures).]]

NOTES

Sub-s (2): reference to a level on the standard scale substituted by virtue of the Criminal Justice Act 1982, ss 38, 46.
Sub-s (3): added by the Customs Controls on Importation of Goods Regulations 1991, SI 1991/2724, reg 6(1), (9); words in first (outer) pair of square brackets added by the Customs and Excise (Single Market etc) Regulations 1992, SI 1992/3095, reg 3(2), words in second (inner) square brackets substituted by the Community Customs Code (Consequential Amendment of References) Regulations 1993, SI 1993/3014, reg 2(1), (2).
Council Regulation (EEC) No 2913/92: OJ L302, 19.10.92, p 1.

Commission Regulation (EEC) No 2454/93: OJ L253, 11.10.93, p 1.

Regulations: the following regulations have been made partly under sub-s (1) above: the Aircraft (Customs and Excise) Regulations 1981, SI 1981/1259, as amended by SI 1992/3095; the Ship's Report, Importation and Exportation by Sea Regulations 1981, SI 1981/1260, as amended by SI 1986/1819, SI 1992/3095; the Customs and Excise (Single Market etc) Regulations 1992, SI 1992/3095; the Pleasure Craft (Arrival and Report) Regulations 1996, SI 1996/1406.

Provisions as to duty on imported goods

43 Duty on imported goods

(1)   Save as permitted by or under the customs and excise Acts or section 2(2) of the European Communities Act 1972 or any Community regulation or other instrument having the force of law, no imported goods shall be delivered or removed on importation until the importer has paid to the proper officer any duty chargeable thereon, and that duty shall, in the case of goods of which entry is made, be paid on making the entry.

(2)   [Subject to subsections (2A),(2B) [(2C) and (2D)] below,] the duties of customs or excise and the rates thereof chargeable on imported goods—

    [(a)   if entry is made thereof, except where the entry is for warehousing, or if they are declared under section 78 below, shall be those in force with respect to such goods at the time when the entry is accepted or the declaration is made;]

    (b)   if entry *or, in the case of goods entered by bill of sight, perfect entry* is made thereof for warehousing, shall be ascertained in accordance with warehousing regulations;

    [(c)   if no entry is made thereof and the goods are not declared under section 78 below shall be—

        (i)   as respects Community customs duties, those in force with respect to such goods at the time of their entry into the customs territory of the Community; and

        (ii)   as respects other duties, those in force with respect to such goods at the time of their importation.]

[(2A)   Where the Commissioners require a duty of customs to be paid because of a failure to comply with a condition or other obligation imposed under section 47 or 48 below (not being a condition or obligation required to be complied with before the goods were allowed to be removed or delivered) the duty shall be charged as if entry of the goods had been accepted at the time when the non-compliance occurred.

(2B)   Where any duties of customs are chargeable in respect of waste or debris resulting from the destruction of imported goods in free circulation, those duties and their rates shall be those in force at the time when the goods were destroyed.

(2C)   As respects goods which have been unlawfully removed from customs charge, subsection (2)(c) above shall have effect with respect to any duties of customs as if they had entered the customs territory of the Community, or, as the case may be, had been imported at the time of their removal.]

[(2D)   Nothing in the provisions of subsections (1) and (2) above or of subsection (6) below or in any exception to any of those provisions made by or under any of sections 44 to 48 below shall have effect for the purposes of any duty of excise chargeable on any goods for which—

    (a)   the excise duty point is fixed by regulations under section 1 of the Finance (No 2) Act 1992; and

    (b)   the applicable rate of duty is determined in accordance with subsection (2) of that section.]

(3)   Any goods brought or coming into the United Kingdom by sea otherwise than as cargo, stores or baggage carried in a ship shall be chargeable with the like duty, if any, as would be applicable to those goods if they had been imported as merchandise; and if any question arises as to the origin of the goods they shall, unless that question is determined under section 120 below, section 14 of the Customs and Excise Duties (General Reliefs) Act 1979 (produce of the sea or continental shelf) or under a Community regulation or other instrument having the force of law, be deemed to be the produce of such country as the Commissioners may on investigation determine.

(4)   Where, in accordance with approval given by the Commissioners, entry of goods is made by any method involving the use of a computer, subsection (2) above shall have effect as if the reference in paragraph (a) to the time of the delivery of the entry were a reference to the time when particulars contained in the entry are accepted by the computer.

(5)   Subject to sections 10 and 11 of the Customs and Excise Duties (General Reliefs) Act 1979 (reliefs for re-imported goods) and save as provided by or under any such enactments or instruments as are mentioned in subsection (1) above, any goods which are re-imported into the United Kingdom [after exportation from the United Kingdom or the Isle of Man], whether they were manufactured or produced in or outside the United Kingdom and whether or not any duty was paid thereon at a previous importation, shall be treated for the purpose of charging duty—

(a)   as if they were being imported for the first time; and

(b)   in the case of goods manufactured or produced in the United Kingdom, as if they had not been so manufactured or produced.

[(6)   Where entry of goods is made otherwise than for warehousing and there is a reduction in the rate of duty of customs or excise chargeable on the goods between—

(a)   the time mentioned in subsection (2)(a) above; and

(b)   the time when the goods are cleared from customs and excise charge,

the rate of the duty chargeable on the goods shall, if the importer so requests, be that in force at the time mentioned in paragraph (b) above unless clearance of the goods has been delayed by reason of any act or omission for which the importer is responsible.

(7)   Notwithstanding section 6(5) of the European Communities Act 1972 "duty of customs" in subsection (6) above does not include any agricultural levy.

(8)   Where samples are taken of goods under section 38A above and the quantity of the goods covered by the entry which is subsequently delivered does not include the samples the duties of customs and the rates of those duties chargeable on the samples shall be those in force at the time when the application under subsection (1) of that section was made and shall be determined by reference to the particulars contained in the application.

(9)   Where a substituted entry is delivered under section 38(2) or 38B(2) above the entry referred to in subsection (2)(a) above is the original entry.]

NOTES

Sub-s (2): words in first (outer) pair of square brackets inserted, and para (c) substituted, by the Customs Duty Regulations 1982, SI 1982/1324, reg 2(2), words in second (inner) pair of square brackets substituted by the Finance (No 2) Act 1992, s 1, Sch 1, para 2(a); para (a) substituted by the Finance Act 1981, s 10(1), Sch 6, para 7(1), (2); words in italics in para (b) repealed by the Finance Act 1981, s 139, Sch 19, Pt I, with effect from a day to be appointed.

Sub-ss (2A)–(2C): inserted by SI 1982/1324, reg 2(4).

Sub-s (2D): inserted by the Finance (No 2) Act 1992, s 1, Sch 1, para 2(b).

Sub-s (4): repealed by the Finance Act 1981, s 139, Sch 19, Pt I, with effect from a day to be appointed.

Sub-s (5): words in square brackets substituted by the Isle of Man Act 1979, s 13, Sch 1.

Sub-ss (6)–(9): added by the Finance Act 1981, s 10(1), Sch 6, para 7(1), (4).

Postal packets: see note at the beginning of this Act.

44 Exclusion of s 43(1) for importers etc keeping standing deposits

Where the Commissioners so direct, section 43(1) above shall not apply if and so long as the importer or his agent pays to, and keeps deposited with, the Commissioners a sum by way of standing deposit sufficient in their opinion to cover any duty which may become payable in respect of goods entered by that importer or agent, and if the importer or agent complies with such other conditions as the Commissioners may impose.

45 Deferred payment of customs duty

(1) The Commissioners may by regulations provide for the payment of customs duty to be deferred in such cases as may be specified by the regulations and subject to such conditions as may be imposed by or under the regulations; and duty of which payment is deferred under the regulations shall be treated, for such purposes as may be specified thereby, as if it had been paid.

(2) Regulations under this section may make different provision for goods of different descriptions or for goods of the same description in different circumstances.

NOTES

Regulations: the Customs and Excise (Deferred Payment) (RAF Airfields and Offshore Installations) (No 2) Regulations 1988, SI 1988/1898. By virtue of the Interpretation Act 1978, s 17(2)(b), in conjunction with s 177(5) of this Act, the Customs Duties (Deferred Payment) Regulations 1976, SI 1976/1223, as amended by SI 1978/1725, have effect under this section.

46 Goods to be warehoused without payment of duty

Any goods which are on their importation permitted to be entered for warehousing shall be allowed, subject to such conditions or restrictions as may be imposed by or under warehousing regulations, to be warehoused without payment of duty.

47 Relief from payment of duty of goods entered for transit or transhipment

Where any goods are entered for transit or transhipment, the Commissioners may allow the goods to be removed for that purpose, subject to such conditions and restrictions as they see fit, without payment of duty.

48 Relief from payment of duty of goods temporarily imported

In such cases as the Commissioners may by regulations prescribe, where the Commissioners are satisfied that goods are imported only temporarily with a view to subsequent re-exportation, they may permit the goods to be delivered on importation, subject to such conditions as they see fit to impose, without payment of duty.

NOTES

Regulations: the Customs Duties (Temporary Importation) (Revocation) Regulations 1987, SI 1987/1781. By virtue of the Interpretation Act 1978, s 17(2)(b), in conjunction with s 177(5) of this Act, the Temporary Importation (Commercial Vehicles and Aircraft) Regulations 1961, SI 1961/1523, have effect as if made under this section.

Forfeiture, offences, etc in connection with importation

49 Forfeiture of goods improperly imported

(1) Where—

    (a)   except as provided by or under the Customs and Excise Acts 1979, any imported goods, being goods chargeable on their importation with customs or excise duty, are, without payment of that duty—

        (i)   unshipped in any port,

        (ii)   unloaded from any aircraft in the United Kingdom,

        (iii) unloaded from any vehicle in, or otherwise brought across the boundary into, Northern Ireland, or

        (iv) removed from their place of importation or from any approved wharf, examination station or transit shed; or

    (b)   any goods are imported, landed or unloaded contrary to any prohibition or restriction for the time being in force with respect thereto under or by virtue of any enactment; or

    (c)   any goods, being goods chargeable with any duty or goods the importation of which is for the time being prohibited or restricted by or under any enactment, are found, whether before or after the unloading thereof, to have been concealed in any manner on board any ship or aircraft or, while in Northern Ireland, in any vehicle; or

    (d)   any goods are imported concealed in a container holding goods of a different description; or

    (e)   any imported goods are found, whether before or after delivery, not to correspond with the entry made thereof; or

    (f)   any imported goods are concealed or packed in any manner appearing to be intended to deceive an officer,

those goods shall, subject to subsection (2) below, be liable to forfeiture.

    (2)   Where any goods, the importation of which is for the time being prohibited or restricted by or under any enactment, are on their importation either—

    (a)   reported as intended for exportation in the same ship, aircraft or vehicle; or

    (b)   entered for transit or transhipment; or

    (c)   entered to be warehoused for exportation or for use as stores,

the Commissioners may, if they see fit, permit the goods to be dealt with accordingly.

NOTES

Postal packets: see note at the beginning of this Act.

50 Penalty for improper importation of goods

    (1)   Subsection (2) below applies to goods of the following descriptions, that is to say—

    (a)   goods chargeable with a duty which has not been paid; and

    (b)   goods the importation, landing or unloading of which is for the time being prohibited or restricted by or under any enactment.

    (2)   If any person with intent to defraud Her Majesty of any such duty or to evade any such prohibition or restriction as is mentioned in subsection (1) above—

    (a)   unships or lands in any port or unloads from any aircraft in the United Kingdom or from any vehicle in Northern Ireland any goods to which this subsection applies, or assists or is otherwise concerned in such unshipping, landing or unloading; or

    (b)   removes from their place of importation or from any approved wharf, examination station, transit shed or customs and excise station any goods to which this subsection applies or assists or is otherwise concerned in such removal,

he shall be guilty of an offence under this subsection and may be [arrested].

(3) If any person imports or is concerned in importing any goods contrary to any prohibition or restriction for the time being in force under or by virtue of any enactment with respect to those goods, whether or not the goods are unloaded, and does so with intent to evade the prohibition or restriction, he shall be guilty of an offence under this subsection and may be [arrested].

(4) Subject to subsection [(5), (5A) or (5B)] below, a person guilty of an offence under subsection (2) or (3) above shall be liable—

    (a)   on summary conviction, to a penalty of the prescribed sum or of three times the value of the goods, whichever is the greater, or to imprisonment for a term not exceeding 6 months, or to both; or

    (b)   on conviction on indictment, to a penalty of any amount, or to imprisonment for a term not exceeding [7 years], or to both.

(5) In the case of an offence under subsection (2) or (3) above in connection with a prohibition or restriction on importation having effect by virtue of section 3 of the Misuse of Drugs Act 1971, subsection (4) above shall have effect subject to the modifications specified in Schedule 1 to this Act.

[(5A) In the case of—

    (a)   an offence under subsection (2) or (3) above committed in Great Britain in connection with a prohibition or restriction on the importation of any weapon or ammunition that is of a kind mentioned in section 5(1)(a), (ab), (aba), (ac), (ad), (ae), (af) or (c) or (1A)(a) of the Firearms Act 1968,

    (b)   any such offence committed in Northern Ireland in connection with a prohibition or restriction on the importation of any weapon or ammunition that is of a kind mentioned in [Article 45(1)(a), (b), (c), (d), (e) or (g) or (2)(a)] of the Firearms (Northern Ireland) Order [2004], or

    (c)   any such offence committed in connection with the prohibition contained in section 20 of the Forgery and Counterfeiting Act 1981,

subsection (4)(b) above shall have effect as if for the words "7 years" there were substituted the words "10 years".]

[(5B) In the case of an offence under subsection (2) or (3) above in connection with the prohibition contained in regulation 2 of the Import of Seal Skins Regulations 1996, subsection (4) above shall have effect as if—

    (a)   for paragraph (a) there were substituted the following—

        "(a) on summary conviction, to a fine not exceeding the statutory maximum or to imprisonment for a term not exceeding three months, or to both"; and

    (b)   in paragraph (b) for the words "7 years" there were substituted the words "2 years".]

(6) If any person—

    (a)   imports or causes to be imported any goods concealed in a container holding goods of a different description; or

    (b)   directly or indirectly imports or causes to be imported or entered any goods found, whether before or after delivery, not to correspond with the entry made thereof,

he shall be liable on summary conviction to a penalty of three times the value of the goods or [level 3 on the standard scale], whichever is the greater.

(7) In any case where a person would, apart from this subsection, be guilty of—

    (a)   an offence under this section in connection with the importation of goods contrary to a prohibition or restriction; and

    (b)   a corresponding offence under the enactment or other instrument imposing the prohibition or restriction, being an offence for which a fine or other penalty is expressly provided by that enactment or other instrument,

he shall not be guilty of the offence mentioned in paragraph (a) of this subsection.

NOTES

Sub-ss (2), (3): words in square brackets substituted by the Police and Criminal Evidence Act 1984, s 114(1).

Sub-s (4): words in first pair of square brackets substituted by the Import of Seal Skins Regulations 1996, SI 1996/2686, reg 4(1); words in second pair of square brackets substituted, in relation to offences committed after 29 July 1988, by the Finance Act 1988, s 12(1)(a), (6).

Sub-s (5A): substituted by the Criminal Justice Act 2003 s 293(1), (2). In para (b), words in square brackets substituted by the Firearms (Northern Ireland) Order 2004, SI 2004/702 art 82(1), Sch 7 para 3.

Sub-s (5B): inserted by SI 1996/2686, reg 4(1).

Sub-s (6): reference to a level on the standard scale substituted by virtue of the Criminal Justice Act 1982, ss 38, 46.

---

51 Special provisions as to proof in Northern Ireland

(1) If goods of any class or description chargeable with duty on their importation from the Republic of Ireland are found in the possession or control of any person . . . in Northern Ireland, any officer or any person having by law in Northern Ireland the powers of an officer may require that person to furnish proof that the goods have not been imported from the Republic of Ireland or that the duty chargeable on their importation has been paid.

(2) If proof of any matter is required to be furnished in relation to any goods under subsection (1) above but is not furnished to the satisfaction of the Commissioners, the goods shall, for the purposes of proceedings under the customs and excise Acts, be deemed to have been unlawfully imported from the Republic of Ireland without payment of duty, unless the contrary is proved.

NOTES

Sub-s (1): words omitted repealed by the Finance Act 1983, ss 7(5), 48(5), Sch 10, Pt I.

PART V
CONTROL OF EXPORTATION

Outward entry and clearance of goods

52 Meaning for this Part of "dutiable or restricted goods"

[(1)] For the purposes of this Part of this Act "dutiable or restricted goods" are goods of the following descriptions, that is to say—

(a) goods from warehouse, other than goods which have been kept, without being warehoused, in a warehouse by virtue of section 92(4) below;

(b) transit goods;

(c) any other goods chargeable with any duty which has not been paid;

(d) drawback goods;

(e) goods with respect to the exportation of which any restriction is for the time being in force under or by virtue of any enactment;

(f) any goods required by or under any provision of this Act other than a provision of this Part or by or under a provision of any other Act to be entered before exportation or before shipment for exportation or as stores.

[(g) goods incorporating or resulting from the use of inward processing goods or any goods which, following a determination by the Commissioners, are to be treated for customs purposes as inward processing goods in substitution for such goods.]

[(2) In this section "inward processing goods" means goods imported for the purpose of being worked on, processed or used in any process or repaired and on the importation of which relief from import duty or agricultural levy was given on condition that goods incorporating or resulting from the use of them would be exported outside the Community; and in this subsection "agricultural levy" means any tax or charge, not being a customs duty, provided for under the common agricultural policy or under any special arrangements which, pursuant to Article 235 of the EEC Treaty are applicable to goods resulting from the processing of agricultural products.]

NOTES

Sub-s (1): numbered as such, and para (g) added, by the Finance Act 1981, s 10(2), (4), Sch 7, Pt II, para 2(1), (2), except in relation to goods exported before 1 October 1981.

Sub-s (2): added by the Finance Act 1981, s 10(2), (4), Sch 7, Pt II, para 2(1), (3), except in relation to goods exported before 1 October 1981.

[53 Entry outwards of goods

(1) Subject to the provisions of this Part of this Act, before any goods other than Community transit goods are exported or shipped as stores for use on a voyage or flight to an eventual destination outside the United Kingdom and the Isle of Man there shall be delivered by the exporter to the proper officer an entry outwards of the goods in such form and manner, containing such particulars and accompanied by such documents as the Commissioners may direct.

(2) Except with the permission of the Commissioners no entry shall be delivered before the goods have been presented to the proper officer.

(3) Where the Commissioners permit an entry to be delivered before presentation of the goods, the goods must be presented to the proper officer within such time as the Commissioners may allow; and if the goods are not so presented the entry shall be treated as not having been delivered.

(4) Goods may be treated as presented to the proper officer if notice is given, in such form and manner as the Commissioners may direct, to the proper officer of the presence of the goods at a place designated by him.

(5) An entry in respect of dutiable or restricted goods shall not be accepted unless security is given to the satisfaction of the Commissioners that the goods will, within such time as the Commissioners think reasonable, be exported and discharged at the destination for which they are entered or which is otherwise specified by the exporter or, in the case of goods for use as stores, that they will be duly so used or otherwise accounted for to the satisfaction of the Commissioners.

(6) Acceptance of an entry by the proper officer shall be signified in such manner as the Commissioners may direct; and once acceptance of an entry in respect of any goods has been signified, the goods shall not be removed from the place where they were at the time of acceptance without the permission of the proper officer.

(7) The Commissioners may relax all or any of the requirements imposed by this section as they think fit in relation to any goods and, if they do so, may impose substituted requirements.

(8) If any dutiable or restricted goods of which entry is required under this section are shipped for exportation or as stores or are waterborne for such shipment before entry has been delivered and accepted, the goods shall be liable to forfeiture

and where the shipping or making waterborne is done with fraudulent intent any person concerned therein with knowledge of that intent shall be guilty of an offence under this subsection and may be [arrested].

(9) A person guilty of an offence under subsection (8) above shall be liable—

(a) on summary conviction, to a penalty of the prescribed sum or of three times the value of the goods, whichever is the greater, or to imprisonment for a term not exceeding six months, or to both; or

(b) on conviction on indictment, to a penalty of any amount, or to imprisonment for a term not exceeding [seven years], or to both.

(10) If any goods which are not dutiable or restricted goods and of which entry is required under this section are exported or shipped for exportation or as stores before entry has been delivered and accepted, the exporter shall be liable on summary conviction to a penalty of [level 4 on the standard scale].

(11) Any person who removes any goods in contravention of subsection (6) above or contravenes or fails to comply with any requirement imposed under subsection (7) above shall be liable on summary conviction to a penalty of [level 4 on the standard scale].

(12) If any dutiable or restricted goods are found not to correspond with any entry in respect of them delivered under this section, they shall be liable to forfeiture.]

NOTES

Substituted together with ss 54–58E for original ss 53–58 by the Finance Act 1981, s 10(2), (4), Sch 7, Pt I, except in relation to goods exported before 1 October 1981.

Sub-s (8): word in square brackets substituted by the Police and Criminal Evidence Act 1984, s 114(1).

Sub-s (9): words in square brackets substituted, in relation to offences committed after 29 July 1988, by the Finance Act 1988, s 12(1)(a), (6).

Sub-ss (10), (11): references to levels on the standard scale substituted by virtue of the Criminal Justice Act 1982, s 46.

Postal packets: see note at the beginning of this Act.

[54 Acceptance of incomplete entry

(1) The proper officer may, if he thinks fit, accept an entry which does not in every respect comply with section 53 above, but he shall not do so in a case in which the goods have not been presented.

(2) Where an entry is accepted under this section the exporter shall, within such time as the Commissioners may allow, deliver to the proper officer such of the particulars or documents as were required to be, but were not, contained in or delivered with the entry or, if the proper officer so permits, deliver to him a substituted entry complying in all respects with section 53 above.

(3) If any person fails to comply with subsection (2) above he shall be liable on summary conviction to a penalty of [level 4 on the standard scale].]

NOTES

Substituted as noted to s 53.

Sub-s (3): reference to a level on the standard scale substituted by virtue of the Criminal Justice Act 1982, s 46.

[55 Correction and cancellation of entry

(1) The exporter may correct any of the particulars contained in an entry of goods under section 53 above after it has been accepted if—

(a) the appropriate authority has not been given for the removal of the goods; and

(b) the exporter has not been notified by an officer that the goods are to be examined; and

(c) the entry has not been found by an officer to be incorrect;

and in paragraph (a) above "the appropriate authority" means—

(i) in the case of goods which have been presented to the proper officer at a place approved by the Commissioners under section 31(1)(b) above or at a place designated by the proper officer under section 53 above, any authority to remove the goods from the place where they were presented to the proper officer which is required under section 31 above or permission under section 53(6) above, and

(ii) in any other case, the authority to load the goods which is required under section 57(4) or section 66 below.

(2) Particulars in an entry may be corrected after the giving of such authority as is mentioned in subsection (1)(a) above if they relate to a matter which can be established in the absence of the goods.

(3) The proper officer may permit or require any correction allowed by subsection (1) above to be made by the delivery of a substituted entry.

(4) Subject to subsection (5) below, an entry which has been accepted may be cancelled at the request of the exporter if he delivers to the proper officer all copies of the entry and such other documents delivered to him on or in connection with the entry as the Commissioners may require and shows to the satisfaction of the Commissioners that—

(a) the goods are in the United Kingdom and the arrangements for exporting them have been cancelled; and

(b) any payment to which he is entitled from the Commissioners or under a Community instrument by virtue of exporting the goods has been repaid or will not be paid.

(5) An entry shall not be cancelled under subsection (4) above—

(a) in a case where the exporter is informed by an officer that the goods are to be examined, until the examination has taken place; and

(b) until the exporter has complied with any requirements imposed by the Commissioners as to the movement of the goods in respect of which the entry was made to such places as they may specify.

(6) Where an entry in respect of goods which are not dutiable or restricted goods is cancelled under subsection (4) above, the exporter shall within such period as may be specified by directions given by the Commissioners furnish them with such information and such documents relating to the goods as may be specified in the directions.

(7) Any person who contravenes or fails to comply with subsection (6) above shall be liable on summary conviction to a penalty of [level 4 on the standard scale].]

NOTES

Substituted as noted to s 53.

Sub-s (7): reference to a level on the standard scale substituted by virtue of the Criminal Justice Act 1982, s 46.

[56 Failure to export

(1) Where any goods in respect of which an entry has been accepted have not been shipped or exported by land, an officer may by notice given to the exporter require the

goods to be exported within such time as is specified in the notice; and if the notice is not complied with the entry shall be treated as cancelled.

(2)   Where, in the case of any such goods as are mentioned in subsection (1) above which are due to be loaded into a ship or aircraft specified in the entry or by the person having charge of them at the port or customs and excise airport of intended shipment, no notice has been served under that subsection and the goods have not been shipped by the time the ship or aircraft departs from the port or airport at which it has been cleared by the proper officer, then—

(a)   the entry shall be treated as cancelled at that time; and

(b)   if the goods are dutiable or restricted goods, they shall be liable to forfeiture unless notice of the failure to export them is given to the proper officer immediately after that time.

(3)   Where an entry in respect of dutiable or restricted goods is treated as cancelled by virtue of this section—

(a)   if the exporter would have been entitled to a payment of any sum from the Commissioners or under a Community instrument by virtue of exporting the goods, he shall take such steps as the Commissioners may direct to ensure that the sum is not paid to him or, if it has already been paid, he shall (unless the Commissioners agree to his retaining it) repay it within seven days or such longer period as the Commissioners may allow;

(b)   the exporter shall within such period as may be specified by directions given by the Commissioners furnish them with such information and such documents as may be specified in the directions; and

(c)   if the goods have not been forfeited under subsection (2)(b) above, they shall be warehoused or, if the Commissioners so require, shall be moved to such place as the Commissioners may specify.

(4)   Where an entry in respect of goods which are not dutiable or restricted goods is treated as cancelled by virtue of this section, the exporter shall within such period as may be specified by directions given by the Commissioners furnish them with such information and such documents relating to the goods as may be specified in the directions.

(5)   Any person who contravenes or fails to comply with subsection (3) above shall be liable on summary conviction to a penalty of [level 5 on the standard scale] and the goods shall be liable to forfeiture.

(6)   Any person who contravenes or fails to comply with subsection (4) above shall be liable on summary conviction to a penalty of [level 4 on the standard scale].]

NOTES

Substituted as noted to s 53.

Sub-ss (5), (6): references to levels on the standard scale substituted by virtue of the Criminal Justice Act 1982, s 46.

Postal packets: see note at the beginning of this Act.

[57 Delivery of entry by owner of exporting ship etc

(1)   The Commissioners may direct that any entry required to be delivered under section 53 above in respect of any goods which are to be shipped or exported in a ship or aircraft and the documents which are required to accompany it shall, instead of being delivered by the exporter be delivered by the loader (that is to say the owner of the ship or aircraft or a person appointed by him) and such delivery shall be treated as delivery by the exporter for the purposes of this Part of this Act.

Part I

(2)   The proper officer shall not accept an entry which is delivered in pursuance of subsection (1) above unless the goods in respect of which the entry is made are under the control of the loader at the time of the delivery.

(3)   Directions under this section may impose on the loader requirements as to—

(a)   the place, time and manner in which entries and any documents required by virtue of section 31 above are to be delivered;

(b)   the production to the proper officer of such documents as may be specified in the directions; and

(c)   the information to be supplied to the proper officer and the form and manner in which the information is to be supplied.

(4)   Directions under this section may also require that the goods in respect of which the entry is to be made shall not be loaded into the ship or aircraft in which they are to be exported without the authority of the proper officer.

(5)   Directions under this section may authorise an officer to relax all or any of the requirements imposed by the directions and, if he does so, to impose substituted requirements.

(6)   If a person without reasonable excuse fails to comply with any requirement imposed on him under this section he shall be liable on summary conviction to a penalty of [level 4 on the standard scale] or in the case of a failure to comply with a requirement imposed by virtue of subsection (4) above to a penalty of [level 5 on the standard scale].

(7)   For the purposes of this section a ship subject to charter by demise shall be treated as owned by the charterer.]

NOTES

Substituted as noted to s 53.

Sub-s (6): references to levels on the standard scale substituted by virtue of the Criminal Justice Act 1982, s 46.

[58 Simplified clearance procedure

(1)   If the Commissioners think fit so to direct, goods which are not dutiable or restricted goods may be shipped for exportation without entry under section 53 above if—

(a)   the exporter is registered in a register of exporters maintained by the Commissioners for the purposes of this section; and

(b)   before the goods are shipped the conditions mentioned in subsection (3) below are satisfied.

(2)   The Commissioners may for the purposes of this section—

(a)   enter in a register maintained by them any person applying for registration and appearing to them to be concerned in the exportation of goods and to satisfy such requirements for registration as they may think fit to impose;

(b)   give directions imposing requirements on registered persons including, in particular, requirements as to the keeping of records and accounts and the giving of access to them;

(c)   assign to registered persons numbers for use under this section; and

(d)   suspend or cancel the registration of any person if it appears to them that he has failed to comply with any direction under this section or with section 58B(1) or (2) below or that there is other reasonable cause for suspension or cancellation.

(3)   The conditions referred to in subsection (1) above are—

(a)   that the goods are presented to the proper officer;

(b)   that the exporter delivers to the proper officer and the proper officer accepts such document relating to the goods as the directions may require bearing an endorsement which contains a number assigned to the exporter under this section; and

(c)   that the exporter complies with such other requirements as the directions may impose,

and goods may be treated as presented to the proper officer if notice is given, in such form and manner as the Commissioners may direct, to the proper officer of the presence of the goods at a place designated by him.

(4) The document referred to in subsection (3)(b) above shall be delivered in such manner as the directions may require and acceptance of that document by the proper officer shall be signified in such manner as the Commissioners may direct; and once acceptance of a document relating to any goods has been signified, the goods shall not be removed from the place they were at the time of acceptance without the permission of the proper officer.

(5) Directions under this section may contain provision enabling the Commissioners to exclude shipments of goods from their operation in such cases as the Commissioners think fit by giving notice to that effect in accordance with the directions.

(6) The Commissioners may relax any requirement imposed under this section as they think fit in relation to any goods and, if they do so, may impose substituted requirements.

(7) Sections 55 and 57 above and section 58D(3) below shall apply in relation to a document required to be delivered under subsection (3)(b) above as they apply in relation to an entry and section 56 above shall apply in relation to goods in respect of which such a document has been accepted under that subsection as it applies to goods in respect of which an entry has been accepted.]

NOTES

Substituted as noted to s 53.

Postal packets: see note at the beginning of this Act.

[58A Local export control

(1) If the Commissioners think fit so to direct, goods may be shipped for exportation or exported by land without entry under section 53 above if—

(a)   the exporter is registered in a register maintained by the Commissioners for the purposes of this section; and

(b)   the conditions mentioned in subsection (3) below are satisfied

[and, subject to and to such modifications as may be specified in the directions, this section and section 58D below shall apply in relation to goods which, for the purposes of any Community regulation relating to export refunds or monetary compensatory amounts, are treated as exports as if the supply of the goods were their exportation or, as the case may require, their shipping for exportation].

(2) The Commissioners may for the purposes of this section—

(a)   maintain a register of exporters whose premises are approved by the Commissioners under section 31 above for the examination of goods intended for export;

(b)   enter in the register any such persons applying for registration who satisfy such requirements for registration as the Commissioners may think fit to impose;

(c)   give directions imposing requirements on registered persons including, in particular, requirements as to the keeping of records and accounts and the giving of access to them;

(d)   assign to registered persons numbers for use under this section; and

(e)   suspend or cancel the registration of any person if it appears to them that he has failed to comply with any direction under this section or with section 58B(1) or (2) below or that there is other reasonable cause for suspension or cancellation.

(3)   The conditions referred to in subsection (1) above are—

(a)   that before the goods are removed from the approved premises—

    (i)   the exporter delivers to the proper officer, at such time and place as he may require, a notice of the intention to remove the goods, being a notice in such form and containing such particulars as may be required by the directions; and

    (ii)   on such day as the proper officer may appoint (not being earlier than the day that notice is delivered or later than the day the goods are removed) the exporter enters such particulars of the goods and of such other matters as may be required by the directions in a record maintained by him at such place as the proper officer may require; and

(b)   that before the goods are shipped [for exportation or exported by land], the exporter delivers to the proper officer such document relating to the goods as the directions may require bearing an endorsement which contains a number assigned to the exporter under this section and complies with such other requirements as the directions may impose.

(4)   The directions may impose requirements as to—

(a)   the manner in which the notice referred to in paragraph (a)(i) of subsection (3) above shall be delivered and the form it should take;

(b)   the manner and form in which the record referred to in paragraph (a)(ii) of that subsection should be maintained; and

(c)   the place at which and the manner in which the document referred to in paragraph (b) of that subsection should be delivered,

and the conditions mentioned in that subsection shall not be treated as satisfied unless any requirements which are so imposed are complied with.

(5)   The Commissioners may, in addition to any exporter within subsection (2)(a) above, enter in the register any person who applies to them to be registered and satisfies them—

(a)   that the exporter is a company under the applicant's control; or

(b)   that the exporter has agreed to the registration of the applicant in addition to the exporter.

(6)   Where in pursuance of subsection (5) above both an exporter and another person are registered—

(a)   the proper officer shall direct which of them shall do the things mentioned in subsection (3) above and section 58B(1) below; and

(b)   the registration of both of them may be cancelled or suspended under subsection (2)(e) above if it appears to the Commissioners that either of them has failed as mentioned in that subsection.

(7)   The Commissioners may relax any requirement imposed under this section as they think fit in relation to any goods and, if they do so, may impose substituted requirements.

[(7A) Without prejudice to the powers of the Commissioners under subsection (7) above, they may direct that, in relation to goods of a description specified in the directions which are shipped for exportation or exported by land by an exporter of a description so specified, paragraph (a) of subsection (3) above shall have effect as if—

(a)   in sub-paragraph (i) the words "time and" were omitted; and

(b)   for sub-paragraph (ii) there were substituted—

"(ii) at the time that notice is delivered or immediately thereafter, the exporter enters such particulars of the goods and of such other matters as may be required by the directions in a record maintained by him at such place as the proper officer may require; and

(iii) the proper officer informs the exporter that he consents to the removal of the goods; and".]

(8) Section 56 above shall apply in relation to goods in respect of which particulars have been entered in a record under subsection (3)(a) above as it applies in relation to goods in respect of which an entry has been accepted.]

NOTES

Substituted as noted to s 53.

Sub-ss (1), (3): words in square brackets added or inserted by the Finance Act 1987, s 8(1), (2).

Sub-s (7A): inserted by the Finance Act 1987, s 8(3).

Postal packets: see note at the beginning of this Act.

[58B Provisions supplementary to ss 58 and 58A

(1) Where by virtue of section 58 or 58A above goods have been shipped for exportation or exported by land without entry under section 53 above, the exporter shall deliver to the proper officer a specification of the goods containing, as the Commissioners may direct, either the particulars that would have been required to be contained in the entry or such other particulars as may be so directed.

(2) The specification referred to in subsection (1) above may, if the Commissioners permit, be a single specification relating to the goods exported during a particular period and shall be delivered at such place and manner and by such time as the Commissioners may allow.

(3) If any person fails to deliver a specification in accordance with the foregoing provisions of this section or delivers a specification which is incorrect and does not correct it within a period of fourteen days following delivery, he shall be liable on summary conviction to a penalty of [level 4 on the standard scale].

(4) In connection with any arrangements approved by the Commissioners for recording particulars of exported goods by computer they may relax the requirements of subsections (1) and (2) above by suspending the obligation to deliver the specifications there mentioned on condition that—

(a) the particulars which should otherwise be contained in the specifications, or such of those particulars as the Commissioners may specify, are recorded by computer in accordance with the arrangements; and

(b) the particulars so recorded are subsequently delivered to the proper officer within such time as the Commissioners may specify;

but subject to such other conditions as they may impose.

(5) If any person without reasonable excuse fails to comply with a requirement imposed on him by or under section 58 or 58A above he shall be liable on summary conviction to a penalty of [level 4 on the standard scale].

(6) If any person for the purpose of enabling goods to be shipped in accordance with either of those sections furnishes any documents bearing a number assigned under that section which is not one for the time being assigned to him or to another person who has consented to his furnishing the document bearing that number, he shall be liable on summary conviction to a penalty of [level 4 on the standard scale].

(7) In sections 58 and 58A above references to a person registered under either of those sections do not include references to a person whose registration is for the time

being suspended; and for the purposes of subsection (6) above a person whose registration is for the time being suspended shall be regarded as not having any number assigned to him.]

NOTES

Substituted as noted to s 53.

Sub-ss (3), (5), (6): references to levels on the standard scale substituted by virtue of the Criminal Justice Act 1982, s 46.

Postal packets: see note at the beginning of this Act.

[58C Pipe-lines and export of ships and aircraft

(1)   For the purposes of this Part of this Act goods which are to be exported by means of a pipe-line shall be treated as having been presented to the proper officer when notice of the goods to be exported has been given to the proper officer and accepted by him.

(2)   Notice under subsection (1) above shall be given by such person and in such form and manner and shall contain such particulars as the Commissioners may direct.

(3)   A ship or aircraft departing from the United Kingdom which—

(a)   is within the definition of dutiable or restricted goods in section 52 above; or

(b)   is a ship built, or aircraft manufactured, in the United Kingdom departing for the first time for a voyage or flight to a place outside the United Kingdom for the purpose of its delivery to a consignee outside the United Kingdom,

shall be treated for the purposes of this Part of this Act both as goods shipped for exportation and as the exporting ship or aircraft and, in the case of a ship or aircraft within paragraph (b) above, the owner of the ship or aircraft or, where the owner is outside the United Kingdom, the builder of the ship or the manufacturer of the aircraft shall be deemed to be the exporter.]

NOTES

Substituted as noted to s 53.

[58D Operative date for Community purposes

(1)   Except as provided by any Community regulation or other instrument having the force of law and subject to subsection (3) below, the operative date for determining whether any, and if so what, levy or other charge provided for under any Community provision governing the exportation of goods is due in respect of the goods and for applying any other such provision including, in particular, any provision whereby any refund or relief is due in respect of the goods shall be such date as is mentioned in subsection (2) below.

(2)   The date referred to in subsection (1) above is—

(a)   in a case where an entry or a document such as is mentioned in section 58(3)(b) above is delivered, the date of acceptance of the entry or document;

(b)   in the case of goods particulars of which are entered in a record in accordance with section 58A(3)(a)(ii) above [as set out in section 58A(7A)(b) above the day entry is made];

(c)   in the case of goods in relation to which substituted requirements are imposed under section 53(7) or 58(6) above, such date as the Commissioners may specify;

(d)   in any other case, the date on which the goods are shipped or exported by land or, if that date cannot be established to the Commissioners' satisfaction, such date as they may specify.

(3)   At the time when the proper officer accepts an entry delivered in pursuance of section 57(1) above he may direct that the operative date for the purposes of this section shall be the date on which the entry was furnished by the exporter to the loader.

(4)   Where a substituted entry is delivered under section 54(2) or 55(3) above the entry referred to in subsections (2)(a) and (3) above is the original entry.]

NOTES

Substituted as noted to s 53.

Sub-s (2): words in square brackets substituted by the Finance Act 1987, s 8(4).

[58E Authentication of Community customs documents

(1)   In such cases as the Commissioners may direct, an officer shall not authenticate any Community customs document unless—

(a)   there is presented with the document—

     (i)   an entry relating to the goods in question and complying with section 53; or

     (ii)   a document relating to the goods and complying with section 58(3)(b) above; or

     (iii) a document to be used instead of an entry or such a document as aforesaid by virtue of substituted requirements imposed under section 53(7) or 58(6) above; and

(b)   the officer marks the Community customs document and the entry or other document referred to in paragraph (a) above with a registration number allocated by the Commissioners for that purpose.

(2)   Subject to subsections (3) and (4) below, a person who has obtained an authenticated Community customs document in respect of any goods shall surrender it at the office at which it was obtained, together with the entry or other document marked under subsection (1)(b) above ("the marked export document"), unless—

(a)   the goods are shipped, or cleared by the proper officer for export by land, before the end of such period as may be specified by directions given by the Commissioners; and

(b)   the marked export document is delivered to the proper officer as required by or under the provisions mentioned in subsection (1)(a) above.

(3)   The proper officer may, on an application made to him before the end of the period mentioned in subsection (2) above, permit the retention of the authenticated Community customs document and the marked export document.

(4)   The proper officer may at any time require a person who has obtained an authenticated Community customs document in respect of any goods to surrender to him that document and the marked export document.

(5)   If a person without reasonable excuse fails to comply with subsection (2) above he shall be liable on summary conviction to a penalty of [level 4 on the standard scale]; and if a person without reasonable excuse fails to comply with a requirement imposed under subsection (4) above he shall be liable on summary conviction to a penalty of [level 5 on the standard scale].

(6)   In this section "Community customs document" means a document which in accordance with any Community instrument or any agreement permitted under such

an instrument or in accordance with any arrangements made between the Commissioners and any other customs authority—

(a) is used to indicate whether or not the goods are Community goods or are subject to duty at a preferential rate in any country with which the Community has an agreement of association; and

(b) is required to be authenticated by the customs authorities of the member State from which they are exported.

(7) In subsection (6) above "Community goods" means—

(a) goods which satisfy the conditions laid down in Articles 9 and 10 of the EEC Treaty; and

(b) goods to which the ECSC. Treaty applies and which under the terms of that Treaty are in free circulation within the European Coal and Steel Community.]

NOTES

Substituted as noted to s 53.

Sub-s (5); references to levels on the standard scale substituted by virtue of the Criminal Justice Act 1982, s 46.

59 Restrictions on putting export goods alongside for loading

(1) This section applies to all goods which are required to be entered outwards before shipment for exportation, [under section 53 above].

(2) The Commissioners may make regulations—

(a) prohibiting, as from such date as is specified in the regulations, the putting of any goods to which this section applies alongside any ship or aircraft for loading for exportation, except under a written authority in that behalf obtained in accordance with, and in such form as is specified in, the regulations; and

(b) requiring any person putting goods alongside a ship or aircraft under one or more such authorities to endorse the authority or each of the authorities with such particulars as are specified in the regulations, and to deliver the endorsed authority or authorities, together with a written statement of the number of authorities delivered, to the proper officer within such period as is so specified.

(3) Regulations under subsection (2) above may make different provision for different circumstances.

(4) Without prejudice to section 3 above, subsection (2) above shall apply to the charging of goods into a pipe-line for exportation as it applies to the putting of goods alongside a ship or aircraft for loading for exportation.

(5) The Commissioners may relax any requirement imposed under subsection (2) above as they think fit in relation to any goods.

(6) Any person who contravenes or fails to comply with any regulation under subsection (2) above shall be liable on summary conviction to a penalty of [level 3 on the standard scale].

(7) This section shall not come into force until such day as the Commissioners may appoint by order made by statutory instrument.

NOTES

Commencement: to be appointed.

Sub-s (1): words in square brackets substituted by the Finance Act 1981, s 10(2), (4), Sch 7, Pt II, para 3, except in relation to goods exported before 1 October 1981.

Sub-s (6): reference to a level on the standard scale substituted by virtue of the Criminal Justice Act 1982, ss 38, 46.

60 Additional restrictions as to certain export goods

(1) No person shall export any dutiable or restricted goods falling within paragraphs (a) to (d) of section 52 above, or enter any such goods for exportation, in any ship of less than 40 tons register.

(2) Subsection (1) above shall not apply to hovercraft, but dutiable or restricted goods shall only be exported in a hovercraft if it is of a class or description for the time being approved by the Commissioners and subject to such conditions and restrictions as they may impose.

(3) Any goods shipped or entered contrary to subsection (1) or (2) above shall be liable to forfeiture.

(4) A person contravening or failing to comply with subsection (2) above, or with any condition or restriction imposed thereunder, shall be liable on summary conviction to a penalty of three times the value of the goods or [level 3 on the standard scale], whichever is the greater.

(5)–(7) . . .

NOTES

Sub-s (4): reference to a level on the standard scale substituted by virtue of the Criminal Justice Act 1982, ss 38, 46.

Sub-ss (5)–(7): repealed by the Finance Act 1981, s 139, Sch 19, Pt II, except in relation to goods exported before 1 October 1981.

61 Provisions as to stores

(1) The Commissioners may give directions—

(a) as to the quantity of any goods which may be carried in any ship or aircraft as stores for use on a voyage or flight to an eventual destination outside the United Kingdom;

[(aa) as to the descriptions of vessel on which goods carried as stores may be used in port without payment of duty in accordance with section 103(1) of the Finance (No 2) Act 1987;

(ab) as to the quantity of any goods which may be carried as stores for use in port as mentioned in paragraph (aa) above as to the time within which such goods or any specified quantities of them may be so used; and]

(b) as to the authorisation to be obtained for the supply and carriage of, and the procedure to be followed in supplying, any goods as stores for use as mentioned in paragraph (a) [or paragraph (aa)] above, whether or not any duty is chargeable or has been paid, or any drawback is payable, in respect of those goods.

(2) Save as provided in subsection (3) below . . . and notwithstanding anything in the customs and excise Acts, goods shall not be permitted to be shipped as stores without payment of duty or on drawback except in a ship of not less than 40 tons register or in an aircraft departing for a voyage or flight [to a country outside the United Kingdom].

(3) The Commissioners may, in such cases and subject to such conditions and restrictions as they see fit, permit goods to be shipped as mentioned in subsection (2) above in

[(a) any ship departing from the United Kingdom, being either a ship of not less than 40 tons register departing for a voyage not falling within subsection (2) above or a ship of less than 40 tons register; or

(b)   any aircraft departing from the United Kingdom for a flight not falling within that subsection].

(4) For the purposes of subsections (2) and (3) above, all hovercraft (of whatever size) shall be treated as ships of less than 40 tons register.

(5) If any goods shipped or carried as stores for use on a voyage or flight to an eventual destination outside the United Kingdom [or for use in port without payment of duty] are without the authority of the proper officer landed or unloaded at any place in the United Kingdom—

(a)   the goods shall be liable to forfeiture; and

(b)   the master or commander and the owner of the ship or aircraft shall each be liable on summary conviction to a penalty of three times the value of the goods or [level 3 on the standard scale], whichever is the greater.

(6) The proper officer may lock up, mark, seal or otherwise secure any goods entered, shipped or carried as stores for use as mentioned in subsection (5) above or any place or container in which such goods are kept or held.

(7) If any ship or aircraft which has departed from any port or customs and excise airport for a destination outside the United Kingdom carrying stores fails to reach the destination for which it was cleared outwards and returns to any place within the United Kingdom, then—

(a)   if the failure was not due to stress of weather, mechanical defect or any other unavoidable cause and any deficiency is discovered in the said goods; or

(b)   if the failure was due to any such cause as is mentioned in paragraph (a) above and any deficiency is discovered in the said goods which, in the opinion of the Commissioners, exceeds the quantity which might fairly have been consumed having regard to the length of time between the ship's or aircraft's departure and return as aforesaid,

the master of the ship or the commander of the aircraft shall be liable on summary conviction to a penalty of [level 2 on the standard scale], and shall also pay on the deficiency or, as the case may be, on the excess deficiency any duty chargeable on the importation of such goods.

[(7A) No amount of excise duty shall be payable under subsection (7) above unless the Commissioners have assessed that amount as being excise duty due from the master of the ship or the commander of the aircraft and notified him or his representative accordingly.]

(8) Any duty[, other than excise duty,] payable under subsection (7) above shall be recoverable summarily as a civil debt.

[(8A) An amount of excise duty assessed as being due under subsection (7A) above shall, unless, or except to the extent that, the assessment has subsequently been withdrawn or reduced and subject to any appeal under section 16 of the Finance Act 1994, be recoverable summarily as a civil debt.]

[(9) References in this section to a country or destination outside the United Kingdom do not include references to, or to a destination in, the Isle of Man; and subsection (5) above applies whether the goods were shipped in the United Kingdom or the Isle of Man.]

NOTES

Sub-s (1): paras (aa), (ab) and words in square brackets in para (b) inserted by the Finance (No 2) Act 1987, s 103(4).

Sub-s (2): words in square brackets substituted by the Finance Act 1981, s 10(2), (4), Sch 7, Pt II, para 4(1), (2), except in relation to goods exported before 1 October 1981; words omitted repealed by the Finance Act 1996, ss 8(2), 205, Sch 41, Pt I.

Sub-s (3): words in square brackets substituted by the Finance Act 1981, s 10(2), (4), Sch 7, Pt II, para 4(1), (3), except in relation to goods exported before 1 October 1981.

Sub-s (5): words in first pair of square brackets inserted by the Finance (No 2) Act 1987, s 103(5); reference to a level on the standard scale substituted by virtue of the Criminal Justice Act 1982, ss 38, 46.

Sub-s (7): reference to a level on the standard scale substituted by virtue of the Criminal Justice Act 1982, s 46.

Sub-ss (7A), (8A): inserted by the Finance Act 1997, s 50(2), Sch 6, paras 2(1), (3), 7.

Sub-s (8): words in square brackets inserted by the Finance Act 1997, s 50(2), Sch 6, paras 2(2), 7.

Sub-s (9): added by the Isle of Man Act 1979, s 13, Sch 1; substituted by the Finance Act 1981, s 10(2), (4), Sch 7, Pt II, para 4(1), (4), except in relation to goods exported before 1 October 1981.

62 Information, documentation, etc as to export goods

(1) The Commissioners may give directions under this subsection imposing on persons specified in the directions requirements as to the giving of information with respect to, or the furnishing of documents in connection with, goods exported, or intended to be exported, in any such vehicle or container as is specified in the directions, or by such other means, or in accordance with any such commercial procedure, as is so specified.

(2) The Commissioners may give directions under this subsection providing that, before any goods are shipped for exportation, a number identifying the goods in compliance with the directions is to be given in accordance with the directions by and to such persons as are specified in the directions.

This subsection shall not come into force until such day as the Commissioners may appoint by order made by statutory instrument.

(3) The Commissioners may relax any requirement imposed under subsection (1) or (2) above as they think fit in relation to any goods.

(4) Any person who contravenes or fails to comply with any direction given under subsection (1) or (2) above shall be liable on summary conviction to a penalty of [level 3 on the standard scale].

NOTES

Commencement: 1 April 1979 (sub-ss (1), (3), (4)); to be appointed (sub-s (2)).

Sub-s (4): reference to a level on the standard scale substituted by virtue of the Criminal Justice Act 1982, ss 40, 46.

Outward entry and clearance of ships, etc

63 Entry outwards of exporting ships

(1) Where a ship is to load any goods at a port for exportation [to a place outside the member States] or as stores for use on a voyage to an eventual destination outside [those States], the master of the ship shall, before any goods are taken on board that ship at that port, other than goods for exportation loaded in accordance with a stiffening order issued by the proper officer, deliver to the proper officer—

    (a)   an entry outwards of the ship in such form and manner and containing such particulars as the Commissioners may direct; and

    (b)   a certificate from the proper officer of the clearance inwards or coastwise of the ship of her last voyage with cargo; and

    (c)   if the ship has already loaded goods at some other port for exportation or as stores for use as aforesaid or has been cleared in ballast from some other port, the clearance outwards of the ship from that other port.

(2)   If, on the arrival at any port of a ship carrying goods coastwise from one place in the United Kingdom to another such place, it is desired that the ship shall proceed with those goods or any of them to a place outside the [member States], entry outwards shall be made of that ship (whether or not any other goods are to be loaded at that port) and of any of those goods which are dutiable or restricted goods as if the goods were to be loaded for exportation at that port, but any such entry may, subject to such conditions as the Commissioners see fit to impose, be made without the goods being first discharged.

(3)   A ship may, subject to subsection (4) below, be entered outwards from a port under this section notwithstanding that before departing for any place outside the United Kingdom the ship is to go to another port.

(4)   A ship carrying cargo brought in that ship from some place outside the United Kingdom and intended to be discharged in the United Kingdom may only be entered outwards by virtue of subsection (3) above subject to such conditions as the Commissioners see fit to impose.

(5)   If, when a ship is required by this section to be entered outwards from any port, any goods are taken on board that ship at that port, except in accordance with such a stiffening order as is mentioned in subsection (1) above, before the ship is so entered, the goods shall be liable to forfeiture and the master of the ship shall be liable on summary conviction to a penalty of [level 3 on the standard scale].

(6)   Where goods are taken on board a ship as mentioned in subsection (5) above or made waterborne for that purpose with fraudulent intent, any person concerned therein with knowledge of that intent may be [arrested] and shall be liable—

(a)   on summary conviction, to a penalty of the prescribed sum or of three times the value of the goods, whichever is the greater, or to imprisonment for a term not exceeding 6 months, or to both; or

(b)   on conviction on indictment, to a penalty of any amount, or to imprisonment for a term not exceeding [7 years], or to both.

[(7)   References in this section to a destination or place outside the United Kingdom [or the member States] do not include references to a destination or place in the Isle of Man and in subsections (2) and (4) above references to a place in the United Kingdom and to discharge in the United Kingdom include references to a place in the Isle of Man and to discharge in the Island.]

NOTES

Sub-s (1): words in first pair of square brackets inserted and words in second pair of square brackets substituted by the Customs and Excise (Single Market etc) Regulations 1992, SI 1992/3095, reg 3(6)(a).

Sub-s (2): words in square brackets substituted by SI 1992/3095, reg 3(6)(b).

Sub-s (5): reference to a level on the standard scale substituted by virtue of the Criminal Justice Act 1982, ss 40, 46.

Sub-s (6): word in first pair of square brackets substituted by the Police and Criminal Evidence Act 1984, s 114(1); words in second square brackets substituted, in relation to offences committed after 29 July 1988, by the Finance Act 1988, s 12(1)(a), (6).

Sub-s (7): added by the Isle of Man Act 1979, s 13, Sch 1; words in square brackets inserted by SI 1992/3095, reg 3(6)(c).

64 Clearance outwards of ships and aircraft

(1)   Save as permitted by the Commissioners, no ship or aircraft shall depart from any port or customs and excise airport from which it commences, or at which it touches during, a voyage or flight to an eventual destination outside the [member States] [and the Isle of Man] until clearance of the ship or aircraft for that departure has been obtained from the proper officer at that port or airport.

(2)   The Commissioners may give directions—

(a) as to the procedure for obtaining clearance under this section;

(b) as to the documents to be produced and the information to be furnished by any person applying for such clearance.

(3) Where clearance is sought under this section for any ship which is in ballast or has on board no goods other than stores, the baggage of passengers carried in that ship, chalk, slate, or empty returned containers upon which no freight or profit is earned, the proper officer in granting clearance thereof shall, on the application of the master, clear the ship as in ballast.

(4) Any officer may board any ship which is cleared outwards from a port at any time while the ship is [in United Kingdom waters] and require the production of the ship's clearance, and if the master refuses to produce it or to answer such questions as the officer may put to him concerning the ship, cargo and intended voyage, he shall be liable on summary conviction to a penalty of [level 1 on the standard scale].

(5) Every ship departing from a port shall, if so required for the purpose of disembarking an officer or of further examination, bring to at the boarding station, and if any ship fails to comply with any such requirement the master shall be liable on summary conviction to a penalty of [level 2 on the standard scale].

(6) If any ship or aircraft required to be cleared under this section departs from any port or customs and excise airport without a valid clearance, the master or commander shall be liable on summary conviction to a penalty of [level 3 on the standard scale].

(7) If, where any aircraft is required to obtain clearance from any customs and excise airport under this section, any goods are loaded, or are waterborne for loading, into that aircraft at that airport before application for clearance has been made, the goods shall be liable to forfeiture and, where the loading or making waterborne is done with fraudulent intent, any person concerned therein with knowledge of that intent shall be guilty of an offence under this subsection and may be [arrested].

(8) A person guilty of an offence under subsection (7) above shall be liable—

(a) on summary conviction, to a penalty of the prescribed sum or of three times the value of the goods, whichever is the greater, or to imprisonment for a term not exceeding 6 months, or to both, or

(b) on conviction on indictment, to a penalty of any amount, or to imprisonment for a term not exceeding 2 years, or to both.

NOTES

Sub-s (1): words in first pair of square brackets substituted by the Customs and Excise (Single Market etc) Regulations 1992, SI 1992/2095, reg 3(7); words in second pair of square brackets inserted by the Isle of Man Act 1979, s 13, Sch 1.

Sub-s (4): words in square brackets substituted by the Territorial Sea Act 1987, s 3(1), Sch 1, para 4(3)(a); reference to a level on the standard scale substituted by virtue of the Criminal Justice Act 1982, s 46.

Sub-ss (5), (6): references to levels on the standard scale substituted by virtue of the Criminal Justice Act 1982, ss 38, 46.

Sub-s (7): word in square brackets substituted by the Police and Criminal Evidence Act 1984, s 114(1).

65 Power to refuse or cancel clearance of ship or aircraft

(1) For the purpose of the detention thereof in pursuance of any power or duty conferred or imposed by or under any enactment, or for the purpose of securing compliance with any provision of the Customs and Excise Acts 1979 or of any other enactment or of any instrument made thereunder, being a provision relating to the importation or exportation of goods—

(a)   the proper officer may at any time refuse clearance of any ship or aircraft; and

(b)   where clearance has been granted to a ship or aircraft, any officer may at any time while the ship is within the limits of any port or the aircraft is at any customs and excise airport demand that the clearance shall be returned to him.

(2)   Any such demand may be made either orally or in writing on the master of the ship or commander of the aircraft, and if made in writing may be served—

(a)   by delivering it to him personally;

(b)   by leaving it at his last known place of abode; or

(c)   by leaving it on board the ship or aircraft with the person appearing to be in charge or command thereof.

(3)   Where a demand for the return of a clearance is made as aforesaid—

(a)   the clearance shall forthwith become void; and

(b)   if the demand is not complied with, the master of the ship or the commander of the aircraft shall be liable on summary conviction to a penalty of [level 3 on the standard scale].

NOTES

Sub-s (3): reference to a level on the standard scale substituted by virtue of the Criminal Justice Act 1982, ss 38, 46.

General regulation of exportation, etc

66 Power to make regulations as to exportation, etc

(1)   The Commissioners may make regulations—

(a)   regulating with respect to ships and aircraft respectively the loading and making waterborne for loading of goods for exportation or as stores and the embarking of passengers for a destination outside the United Kingdom [and the Isle of Man];

(b)   prescribing the procedure to be followed and the documents to be produced and information to be furnished by any person conveying goods out of Northern Ireland by land;

(c)   requiring delivery of a manifest containing such particulars as the Commissioners may direct of all cargo carried in an exporting ship and, if the Commissioners so direct, such other documents relating to the cargo as are specified in the direction;

(d)   requiring delivery of a certificate of the fuel shipped in any ship departing from a port for a place outside the United Kingdom [and the Isle of Man].

(2)   If any person contravenes or fails to comply with any regulation made under this section, he shall be liable on summary conviction to [a penalty of [level 4 on the standard scale], or in the case of a contravention of or a failure to comply with a regulation made under subsection (1)(b) above a penalty of [level 5 on the standard scale],] and any goods in respect of which the offence was committed shall be liable to forfeiture.

NOTES

Sub-s (1): words in square brackets in para (a) added and words in square brackets in para (d) inserted by the Isle of Man Act 1979, s 13, Sch 1.

Sub-s (2): words in first (outer) pair of square brackets substituted by the Finance Act 1981, s 10(2), (4), Sch 7, Pt II, para 5, except in relation to goods exported before 1 October 1981; references to levels on the standard scale therein substituted by virtue of the Criminal Justice Act 1982, s 46.

Regulations: the Aircraft (Customs and Excise) Regulations 1981, SI 1981/1259, as amended by SI 1992/3095; the Ship's Report, Importation and Exportation by Sea Regulations 1981, SI 1981/1260, as amended by SI 1986/1819, SI 1992/3095; the Customs and Excise (Single Market etc) Regulations 1992, SI 1992/3095.

Offences in relation to exportation

67 Offences in relation to exportation of goods

(1)   If any goods which have been loaded or retained on board any ship or aircraft for exportation are not exported to and discharged at a place outside the United Kingdom but are unloaded in the United Kingdom, then, unless—

(a)   the unloading was authorised by the proper officer; and

(b)   except where that officer otherwise permits, any duty chargeable and unpaid on the goods is paid and any drawback or allowance paid in respect thereof is repaid,

the master of the ship or the commander of the aircraft and any person concerned in the unshipping, relanding, landing, unloading or carrying of the goods from the ship or aircraft without such authority, payment or repayment shall each be guilty of an offence under this section.

(2)   The Commissioners may impose such conditions as they see fit with respect of any goods loaded or retained as mentioned in subsection (1) above which are permitted to be unloaded in the United Kingdom.

(3)   If any person contravenes or fails to comply with, or is concerned in any contravention of or failure to comply with, any condition imposed under subsection (2) above he shall be guilty of an offence under this section.

(4)   Where any goods loaded or retained as mentioned in subsection (1) above or brought to a customs and excise station for exportation by land are—

(a)   goods from warehouse, other than goods which have been kept, without being warehoused, in a warehouse by virtue of section 92(4) below;

(b)   transit goods;

(c)   other goods chargeable with a duty which has not been paid; or

(d)   drawback goods,

then if any container in which the goods are held is without the authority of the proper officer opened, or any mark, letter or device on any such container or on any lot of the goods is without that authority cancelled, obliterated or altered, every person concerned in the opening, cancellation, obliteration or alteration shall be guilty of an offence under this section.

(5)   Any goods in respect of which an offence under this section is committed shall be liable to forfeiture and any person guilty of an offence under this section shall be liable on summary conviction to a penalty of three times the value of the goods or [level 3 on the standard scale], whichever is the greater.

NOTES

Sub-s (5): reference to a level on the standard scale substituted by virtue of the Criminal Justice Act 1982, ss 38, 46.

68 Offences in relation to exportation of prohibited or restricted goods

(1)   If any goods are—

> (a)   exported or shipped as stores; or
>
> (b)   brought to any place in the United Kingdom for the purpose of being exported or shipped as stores,

and the exportation or shipment is or would be contrary to any prohibition or restriction for the time being in force with respect to those goods under or by virtue of any enactment, the goods shall be liable to forfeiture and the exporter or intending exporter of the goods and any agent of his concerned in the exportation or shipment or intended exportation or shipment shall each be liable on summary conviction to a penalty of three times the value of the goods or [level 3 on the standard scale], whichever is the greater.

(2)   Any person knowingly concerned in the exportation or shipment as stores, or in the attempted exportation or shipment as stores, of any goods with intent to evade any such prohibition or restriction as is mentioned in subsection (1) above shall be guilty of an offence under this subsection and may be [arrested].

(3)   Subject to subsection (4) [or (4A)] below, a person guilty of an offence under subsection (2) above shall be liable—

> (a)   on summary conviction, to a penalty of the prescribed sum or of three times the value of the goods, whichever is the greater, or to imprisonment for a term not exceeding 6 months, or to both; or
>
> (b)   on conviction on indictment, to a penalty of any amount, or to imprisonment for a term not exceeding [7 years], or to both.

(4)   In the case of an offence under subsection (2) above in connection with a prohibition or restriction on exportation having effect by virtue of section 3 of the Misuse of Drugs Act 1971, subsection (3) above shall have effect subject to the modifications specified in Schedule 1 to this Act.

[(4A)   In the case of—

> (a)   an offence under subsection (2) or (3) above committed in Great Britain in connection with a prohibition or restriction on the exportation of any weapon or ammunition that is of a kind mentioned in section 5(1)(a), (ab), (aba), (ac), (ad), (ae), (af) or (c) or (1A)(a) of the Firearms Act 1968,
>
> (b)   any such offence committed in Northern Ireland in connection with a prohibition or restriction on the exportation of any weapon or ammunition that is of a kind mentioned in [Article 45(1)(a), (b), (c), (d), (e) or (g) or (2)(a)] of the Firearms (Northern Ireland) Order [2004], or
>
> (c)   any such offence committed in connection with the prohibition contained in section 21 of the Forgery and Counterfeiting Act 1981,

subsection (3)(b) above shall have effect as if for the words "7 years" there were substituted the words "10 years".]

(5)   If by virtue of any such restriction as is mentioned in subsection (1) above any goods may be exported only when consigned to a particular place or person and any goods so consigned are delivered to some other place or person, the ship, aircraft or vehicle in which they were exported shall be liable to forfeiture unless it is proved to the satisfaction of the Commissioners that both the owner of the ship, aircraft or vehicle and the master of the ship, commander of the aircraft or person in charge of the vehicle—

> (a)   took all reasonable steps to secure that the goods were delivered to the particular place to which or person to whom they were consigned, and
>
> (b)   did not connive at or, except under duress, consent to the delivery of the goods to that other place or person.

(6)   In any case where a person would, apart from this subsection, be guilty of—

> (a)   an offence under subsection (1) or (2) above; and

(b)   a corresponding offence under the enactment or instrument imposing the prohibition or restriction in question, being an offence for which a fine or other penalty is expressly provided by that enactment or other instrument,

he shall not be guilty of the offence mentioned in paragraph (a) of this subsection.

NOTES

Sub-s (1): reference to a level on the standard scale substituted by virtue of the Criminal Justice Act 1982, ss 38, 46.

Sub-s (2): word in square brackets substituted by the Police and Criminal Evidence Act 1984, s 114(1).

Sub-s (3): words in first pair of square brackets inserted by the Forgery and Counterfeiting Act 1981, s 23(2); words in second pair of square brackets substituted, in relation to offences committed after 29 July 1988, by the Finance Act 1988, s 12(1)(a), (6).

Sub-s (4A): substituted by the Criminal Justice Act 2003 s 293(1), (3). In para (b), references in square brackets substituted by the Firearms (Northern Ireland) Order, SI 2004/702 art 82(1), Sch 7 para 4.

Modification: modified, in relation to drugs, by the Controlled Drugs (Substances Useful for Manufacture) Regulations 1991, SI 1991/1285, reg 6.

Modification: modified, in relation to exportation of any controlled radioactive source, by the Export of Radioactive Sources (Control) Order SI 2006/1846.

[68A Offences in relation to agricultural levies

(1)   Without prejudice to section 11(1) of the Finance Act 1982, if any person is, in relation to any goods, in any way knowingly concerned in any fraudulent evasion or attempt at evasion of any agricultural levy chargeable on the export of the goods, he shall be guilty of an offence and may be [arrested].

[(2)   A person guilty of an offence under this section shall be liable—

(a)   on summary conviction, to a penalty of the prescribed sum or of three times the value of the goods, whichever is the greater, or to imprisonment for a term not exceeding 6 months, or to both; or

(b)   on conviction on indictment, to a penalty of any amount, or to imprisonment for a term not exceeding 7 years, or to both.]

(3)   Any goods in respect of which an offence under this section is committed shall be liable to forfeiture.

(4)   In this section "agricultural levy" has the same meaning as in section 6 of the European Communities Act 1972 and the provisions of this section apply notwithstanding that any such levy may be payable to [the Secretary of State, the Scottish Ministers, the National Assembly for Wales or (in relation to Northern Ireland) the Department of Agriculture and Rural Development, as the case may be].]

NOTES

Inserted by the Finance Act 1982, s 11(2).

Sub-s (1): word in square brackets substituted by the Police and Criminal Evidence Act 1984, s 114(1).

Sub-s (2): substituted, in relation to offences committed after 29 July 1988, by the Finance Act 1988, s 12(2), (6).

Sub-s (4): words substituted by the Intervention Board for Agricultural Produce (Abolition) Regulations, SI 2001/3686 reg 6(7)(a).

[68B

(Applies to Northern Ireland only.)

PART VI
CONTROL OF COASTWISE TRAFFIC

69 Coasting trade

(1) Subject to section 70 below, any ship for the time being engaged in the trade of carrying goods coastwise between places in the United Kingdom [or between a place in the United Kingdom and a place in the Isle of Man] shall for the purposes of the Customs and Excise Acts 1979 be a coasting ship.

(2) Subject to that section, no goods not yet entered on importation and no goods for exportation shall be carried in a ship engaged in the trade of carrying goods coastwise.

(3) The Commissioners may from time to time give directions as to what trade by water between places in the United Kingdom [or between a place in the United Kingdom and a place in the Isle of Man] is or is not to be deemed to be carrying goods coastwise.

NOTES

Sub-ss (1), (3): words in square brackets inserted by the Isle of Man Act 1979, s 13, Sch 1.

70 Coasting trade—exceptional provisions

(1) The Commissioners may, subject to such conditions and restrictions as they see fit to impose, permit a ship to carry goods coastwise notwithstanding that the ship is carrying goods brought therein from some place outside the United Kingdom and not yet entered on importation; but a ship so permitted to carry goods coastwise shall not for the purposes of the Customs and Excise Acts 1979 be a coasting ship.

(2) The Commissioners may, subject to such conditions and restrictions as they see fit to impose, permit goods brought by an importing ship to some place in the United Kingdom but consigned to and intended to be delivered at some other such place to be transhipped before due entry of the goods has been made to another ship for carriage coastwise to that other place.

(3) Where any ship has begun to load goods at any place in the United Kingdom for exportation or as stores for use on a voyage to an eventual destination outside the United Kingdom and is to go to any other such place to complete loading, the Commissioners may, subject to such conditions as they see fit to impose, permit that ship to carry other goods coastwise until she has completed her loading.

(4) If, where any goods are permitted to be carried coastwise in any ship under this section, the goods are loaded, unloaded, carried or otherwise dealt with contrary to any condition or restriction imposed by the Commissioners, the goods shall be liable to forfeiture and the master of the ship shall be liable on summary conviction to a penalty of [level 2 on the standard scale].

[(5) References in this section to a place or destination outside the United Kingdom do not include references to a place or destination in the Isle of Man and in subsection (2) the reference to some other place in the United Kingdom includes a reference to a place in the Isle of Man.]

NOTES

Sub-s (4): reference to a level on the standard scale substituted by virtue of the Criminal Justice Act 1982, s 46.

Part I

Sub-s (5): added by the Isle of Man Act 1979, s 13, Sch 1.

71 Clearance of coasting ship and transire

(1) Subject to the provisions of this section and save as permitted by the Commissioners, before any coasting ship departs from any port the master thereof shall deliver to the proper officer an account in such form and manner and containing such particulars as the Commissioners may direct; and that account when signed by the proper officer shall be the transire, that is to say, the clearance of the ship from that port and the pass for any goods to which the account relates.

(2) The Commissioners may, subject to such conditions as they see fit to impose, grant a general transire in respect of any coasting ship and any goods carried therein.

(3) Any such general transire may be revoked by the proper officer by notice in writing delivered to the master or the owner of the ship or to any member of the crew on board the ship.

(4) If a coasting ship departs from any port without a correct account having been delivered, except as permitted by the Commissioners or under and in compliance with any conditions imposed on the grant of a general transire, the master shall be liable on summary conviction to a penalty of [level 2 on the standard scale].

NOTES

Sub-s (4): reference to a level on the standard scale substituted by virtue of the Criminal Justice Act 1982, s 46.

72 Additional powers of officers in relation to coasting ships

(1) The proper officer may examine any goods carried or to be carried in a coasting ship—

    (a)   at any time while they are on board the ship; or

    (b)   at any place in the United Kingdom to which the goods have been brought for shipment in, or at which they have been unloaded from, the ship.

(2) For the purpose of examining any goods in pursuance of subsection (1) above, the proper officer may require any container to be opened or unpacked; and any such opening or unpacking and any repacking shall be done by or at the expense of the proprietor of the goods.

(3) The proper officer—

    (a)   may board and search a coasting ship at any time during its voyage;

    (b)   may at any time require any document which should properly be on board a coasting ship to be produced or brought to him for examination;

and if the master of the ship fails to produce or bring any such document to the proper officer when required, he shall be liable on summary conviction to a penalty of [level 2 on the standard scale].

NOTES

Sub-s (3): reference to a level on the standard scale substituted by virtue of the Criminal Justice Act 1982, s 46.

73 Power to make regulations as to carriage of goods coastwise, etc

(1) The Commissioners may make regulations as to the carriage of goods coastwise—

(a)   regulating the loading and unloading and the making waterborne for loading of the goods;

(b)   requiring the keeping and production by the master of a coasting ship of such record of the cargo carried in that ship as may be prescribed by the regulations.

(2)   If any person contravenes or fails to comply with any regulation made under this section, he shall be liable on summary conviction to a penalty of [level 3 on the standard scale] and any goods in respect of which the offence was committed shall be liable to forfeiture.

NOTES

Sub-s (2): reference to a level on the standard scale substituted by virtue of the Criminal Justice Act 1982, ss 38, 46.

Regulations: by virtue of the Interpretation Act 1978, s 17(2)(b), in conjunction with s 177(5) of this Act, the Carriage of Goods Coastwise Regulations 1952, SI 1952/2223, have effect as it made under this section.

74 Offences in connection with carriage of goods coastwise

(1)   If in the case of any coasting ship

(a)   any goods are taken on board or removed therefrom at sea or at any place outside the United Kingdom; or

(b)   except for some unavoidable cause, the ship touches at any place outside the United Kingdom or deviates from her voyage; or

(c)   the ship touches at any place outside the United Kingdom and the master does not report that fact in writing to the proper officer at the first port at which the ship arrives thereafter,

the master of the ship shall be liable on summary conviction to a penalty of [level 3 on the standard scale].

(2)   Any goods which are shipped and carried coastwise, or which, having been carried coastwise, are unloaded in any place in the United Kingdom, otherwise than in accordance with the provisions of sections 69 to 71 above or of any regulations made under section 73 above, or which are brought to any place for the purpose of being so shipped and carried coastwise, shall be liable to forfeiture.

(3)   If any goods—

(a)   are carried coastwise or shipped as stores in a coasting ship contrary to any prohibition or restriction for the time being in force with respect thereto under or by virtue of any enactment; or

(b)   are brought to any place in the United Kingdom for the purpose of being so carried or shipped,

then those goods shall be liable to forfeiture and the shipper or intending shipper of the goods shall be liable on summary conviction to a penalty of [level 3 on the standard scale].

(4)   In any case where a person would, apart from this subsection, be guilty of—

(a)   an offence under subsection (3) above; and

(b)   a corresponding offence under the enactment or other instrument imposing the prohibition or restriction in question, being an offence for which a fine or other penalty is expressly provided by that enactment or other instrument,

he shall not be guilty of the offence mentioned in paragraph (a) of this subsection.

[(5) References in this section to a place outside the United Kingdom do not include references to a place in the Isle of Man.]

NOTES

Sub-ss (1), (3): references to levels on the standard scale substituted by virtue of the Criminal Justice Act 1982, ss 38, 46.

Sub-s (5): added by the Isle of Man Act 1979, s 13, Sch 1.

PART VII
CUSTOMS AND EXCISE CONTROL: SUPPLEMENTARY PROVISIONS

Special requirements as to movement of certain goods

75 Explosives

(1) No goods which are explosives within the meaning of [the Manufacture and Storage of Explosives Regulations 2005] shall be loaded into any ship or aircraft for exportation, exported by land or shipped for carriage coastwise as cargo, until due entry has been made of the goods in such form and manner and containing such particulars as the Commissioners may direct.

(2) Without prejudice to sections 53 and 60 above, any goods required to be entered under this section which are loaded, exported or shipped as mentioned in subsection (1) above without being entered under this section shall be liable to forfeiture, and the exporter or, as the case may be, shipper shall be liable on summary conviction to a penalty of [level 3 on the standard scale].

NOTES

Sub-s (1): words in square brackets substituted by the Manufacture and Storage of Explosives Regulations, SI 2005/1082 regs 1, 28(1), Sch 5 para 16.

Sub-s (2): reference to a level on the standard scale substituted by virtue of the Criminal Justice Act 1982, ss 38, 46.

[Keeping and preservation of records

75A Records relating to importation and exportation

(1) Every person who is concerned (in whatever capacity) in the importation or exportation of goods of which [for that purpose an entry is required by regulation 5 of the Customs Controls on Importation of Goods Regulations 1991 or an entry or specification is required by or under this Act] shall keep such records as the Commissioners may require.

(2) The Commissioners may require any records kept in pursuance of this section to be preserved for such period not exceeding four years as they may require.

(3) The duty under this section to preserve records may be discharged by the preservation of the information contained therein by such means as the Commissioners may approve; and where that information is so preserved a copy of any document forming part of the records shall, subject to the following provisions of this section, be admissible in evidence in any proceedings, whether civil or criminal, to the same extent as the records themselves.

(4) The Commissioners may, as a condition of an approval under subsection (3) above of any means of preserving information, impose such reasonable requirements as appear to them necessary for securing that the information will be as readily available to them as if the records themselves had been preserved.

(5) The Commissioners may at any time for reasonable cause revoke or vary the conditions of any approval given under subsection (3) above.

(6) A statement contained in a document produced by a computer shall not by virtue of subsection (3) above be admissible in evidence—

(a)–(c) . . .;

(d) *in criminal proceedings in Northern Ireland, except in accordance with [Article 68 of the Police and Criminal Evidence (Northern Ireland) Order 1989 and Part II of the Criminal Justice (Evidence, Etc) (Northern Ireland) Order 1988.]*

NOTES

Inserted, together with preceding cross-heading, by the Finance Act 1987, s 9.

Sub-s (1): words in square brackets substituted by the Customs and Excise (Single Market etc) Regulations 1992, SI 1992/3095, reg 10(1), Sch 1, para 7.

Sub-s (6): para (a) repealed by the Civil Evidence Act 1995, s 15(2), Sch 2; para (b) repealed by the Youth Justice and Criminal Evidence Act 1999, s 67(3), Sch 6, as from 14 April 2000 (by virtue of SI 2000/1034); para (c) repealed, and words in square brackets in para (d) substituted, by the Civil Evidence (Northern Ireland) Order 1997, SI 1997/2983 (NI 21), art 13, Sch 1, para 3, Sch 2, subject to savings; para (d) repealed by the Criminal Evidence (Northern Ireland) Order 1999, SI 1999/2789, art 40(3), Sch 3, as from a day to be appointed.

Person who is concerned in the importation or preservation of goods: by the Finance Act 1994, s 20(5), any power under this section or s 75B or 75C of this Act to require a person importing or exporting goods to keep or preserve records, ceases to be exercisable in relation to a person to the extent that the goods in question are "customs goods".

[75B Records relating to firearms

(1) Every person who is concerned (in whatever capacity) in the importation or exportation of weapons or firearms within the meaning of Council Directive 91/477/EEC (control of acquisition and possession of such goods) shall keep such records as the Commissioners may require for the purposes of that Directive.

(2) Subsections (2) to (6) of section 75A above shall apply in relation to any requirement under this section and to the records kept in pursuance of this section as they apply in relation to any requirement under that section and to the records kept in pursuance of that section.]

NOTES

Inserted by the Customs and Excise (Single Market etc) Regulations 1992, SI 1992/3095, reg 3(8).

Person who is concerned in the importation or preservation of goods: see note to s 75A.

[75C Records relating to goods subject to certain transit arrangements

(1) Every person who is concerned (in whatever capacity) in the importation or exportation of goods which are subject to the transit arrangements set out in [Title II of Part II of Commission Regulation (EEC) No 2454/93] shall keep such records as the Commissioners may require for the purposes of [Article 324] of that Regulation (verification of procedures and documents).

(2) Subsections (2) to (6) of section 75A above shall apply in relation to any requirement under this section and to the records kept in pursuance of this section as they apply in relation to any requirement under that section and to the records kept in pursuance of that section.]

NOTES

Inserted as noted to s 75B.

Sub-s (1): words in square brackets substituted by the Community Customs Code (Consequential Amendment of References) Regulations 1993, SI 1993/3014, reg 2(1), (6).

Person who is concerned in the importation or preservation of goods: see note to s 75A.

Commission Regulation (EEC) No 2454/93: OJ L253, 11.10.93, p 1.

76

(Repealed by the Finance Act 1981, s 139, Sch 19, Pt II, except as respects goods exported before 1 October 1981.)

Additional provisions as to information

77 Information in relation to goods imported or exported

(1) An officer may require any person—

    (a)   concerned with the . . . shipment for carriage coastwise of goods of which [for that purpose an entry is required by regulation 5 of the Customs Controls on Importation of Goods Regulations 1991 or an entry or specification is required by or under this Act]; or

    (b)   concerned in the carriage, unloading, landing or loading of goods which are being or have been imported or exported,

to furnish in such form as the officer may require any information relating to the goods and to produce and allow the officer to inspect and take extracts from or make copies of any invoice, bill of lading or other book or document whatsoever relating to the goods.

(2) If any person without reasonable cause fails to comply with a requirement imposed on him under subsection (1) above he shall be liable on summary conviction to a penalty of [level 3 on the standard scale].

(3) Where any prohibition or restriction to which this subsection applies, that is to say, any prohibition or restriction under or by virtue of any enactment with respect to—

    (a)   the exportation of goods to any particular destination; or

    (b)   the exportation of goods of any particular class or description to any particular destination,

is for the time being in force, then, if any person about to ship for exportation or to export any goods or, as the case may be, any goods of that class or description, in the course of making entry thereof before shipment or exportation makes a declaration as to the ultimate destination thereof, and the Commissioners have reason to suspect that the declaration is untrue in any material particular, the goods may be detained until the Commissioners are satisfied as to the truth of the declaration, and if they are not so satisfied the goods shall be liable to forfeiture.

(4) Any person concerned in the exportation of any goods which are subject to any prohibition or restriction to which subsection (3) above applies shall, if so required by the Commissioners, satisfy the Commissioners that those goods have not reached any destination other than that mentioned in the entry delivered in respect of the goods.

(5) If any person required under subsection (4) above to satisfy the Commissioners as mentioned in that subsection fails to do so, then, unless he proves—

    (a)   that he did not consent to or connive at the goods reaching any destination other than that mentioned in the entry delivered in respect of the goods; and

(b)   that he took all reasonable steps to secure that the ultimate destination of the goods was not other than that so mentioned,

he shall be liable on summary conviction to a penalty of three times the value of the goods or [level 3 on the standard scale], whichever is the greater.

NOTES

Sub-s (1): words omitted repealed by the Finance Act 1987, ss 10, 72(7), Sch 16, Pt III; words in square brackets substituted by the Customs and Excise (Single Market etc) Regulations 1992, SI 1992/3095, reg 10(1), Sch 1, para 7.

Sub-ss (2), (5): references to levels on the standard scale substituted by virtue of the Criminal Justice Act 1982, ss 38, 46.

Postal packets: see note at the beginning of this Act.

[**77A Information powers**

(1) Every person who is concerned (in whatever capacity) in the importation or exportation of goods for which [for that purpose an entry is required by regulation 5 of the Customs Controls on Importation of Goods Regulations 1991 or an entry or specification is required by or under this Act] shall—

(a)   furnish to the Commissioners, within such time and in such form as they may reasonably require, such information relating to the goods or to the importation or exportation as the Commissioners may reasonably specify; and

(b)   if so required by an officer, produce or cause to be produced for inspection by the officer—

(i)   at the principal place of business of the person upon whom the demand is made or at such other place as the officer may reasonably require, and

(ii)   at such time as the officer may reasonably require,

any documents relating to the goods or to the importation or exportation.

(2) Where, by virtue of subsection (1) above, an officer has power to require the production of any documents from any such person as is referred to in that subsection, he shall have the like power to require production of the documents concerned from any other person who appears to the officer to be in possession of them; but where any such other person claims a lien on any document produced by him, the production shall be without prejudice to the lien.

(3) An officer may take copies of, or make extracts from, any document produced under subsection (1) or subsection (2) above.

(4) If it appears to him to be necessary to do so, an officer may, at a reasonable time and for a reasonable period, remove any document produced under subsection (1) or subsection (2) above and shall, on request, provide a receipt for any document so removed; and where a lien is claimed on a document produced under subsection (2) above, the removal of the document under this subsection shall not be regarded as breaking the lien.

(5) Where a document removed by an officer under subsection (4) above is reasonably required for the proper conduct of a business, the officer shall, as soon as practicable, provide a copy of the document, free of charge, to the person by whom it was produced or caused to be produced.

(6) Where any documents removed under the powers conferred by this section are lost or damaged, the Commissioners shall be liable to compensate their owner for any expenses reasonably incurred by him in replacing or repairing the documents.

(7) If any person fails to comply with a requirement under this section, he shall be liable on summary conviction to a penalty of level 3 on the standard scale.]

NOTES

Inserted by the Finance Act 1987, s 10.

Sub-s (1): words in square brackets substituted by the Customs and Excise (Single Market etc) Regulations 1992, SI 1992/3095, reg 10(1), Sch 1, para 7.

Person who is concerned in the importation or preservation of goods: by the Finance Act 1994, s 20(5), any power under this section or s 77B or 77C of this Act to require a person importing or exporting goods to keep or preserve records, ceases to be exercisable in relation to a person to the extent that the goods in question are "customs goods".

References in this section to exportation shall be read as including any activity requiring a licence under the Trade in Goods (Control) Order, SI 2003/2765 (SI 2003/2765 art 12(5)).

[77B Information powers relating to firearms

(1) Every person who is concerned (in whatever capacity) in the importation or exportation of weapons or firearms within the meaning of the Directive mentioned in section 75B(1) above shall—

> (a) furnish to the Commissioners, within such time and in such form as they may reasonably require, such information relating to such goods or to the importation or exportation as the Commissioners may specify for the purposes of that Directive; and
>
> (b) if so required by an officer for such purposes, produce or cause to be produced for inspection by the officer—
>
> > (i) at the principal place of business of the person upon whom the demand is made or at such other place as the officer may reasonably require, and
> >
> > (ii) at such time as the officer may reasonably require, any documents relating to such goods or to the importation or exportation.

(2) Subsections (2) to (7) of section 77A above shall apply in relation to any requirement under this section as they apply in relation to any requirement under that section.]

NOTES

Inserted by the Customs and Excise (Single Market etc) Regulations 1992, SI 1992/3095, reg 3(9).

Person who is concerned in the importation or preservation of goods: see note to s 77A.

[77C Information powers relating to goods subject to certain transit arrangements

(1) Every person who is concerned (in whatever capacity) in the importation or exportation of goods which are subject to the transit arrangements set out in the Commission Regulation mentioned in section 75C(1) above shall—

> (a) furnish to the Commissioners, within such time and in such form as they may reasonably require, such information relating to the goods or to the importation or exportation as the Commissioners may specify for the purposes of [Article 324] of that Regulation (verification of procedures and documents); and
>
> (b) if so required by an officer for such purposes, produce or cause to be produced for inspection by the officer—
>
> > (i) at the principal place of business of the person upon whom the demand is made or at such other place as the officer may reasonably require, and
> >
> > (ii) at such time as the officer may reasonably require, any documents relating to such goods or to the importation or exportation.

(2) Subsections (2) to (7) of section 77A above shall apply in relation to any requirement under this section as they apply in relation to any requirement under that section.]

NOTES

Inserted as noted to s 77B.

Sub-s (1): words in square brackets substituted by the Community Customs Code (Consequential Amendment of References) Regulations 1993, SI 1993/3014, reg 2(1), (7).

Person who is concerned in the importation or preservation of goods: see note to s 77A.

Commission Regulation: Commission Regulation (EEC) No 2454/93, OJ L253, 11.10.93, p 1.

78 Customs and excise control of persons entering or leaving the United Kingdom

(1) Any person entering the United Kingdom shall, at such place and in such manner as the Commissioners may direct, declare any thing contained in his baggage or carried with him which—

    (a)   he has obtained outside the United Kingdom; or

    (b)   being dutiable goods or chargeable goods, he has obtained in the United Kingdom without payment of duty or tax,

and in respect of which he is not entitled to exemption from duty and tax by virtue of any order under section 13 of the Customs and Excise Duties (General Reliefs) Act 1979 [personal reliefs).

In this subsection "chargeable goods" means goods on the importation of which value added tax is chargeable or goods obtained in the United Kingdom before 1st April 1973 which are chargeable goods within the meaning of the Purchase Tax Act 1963; and "tax" means value added tax or purchase tax.

[(1A) Subsection (1) above does not apply to a person entering the United Kingdom from the Isle of Man as respects anything obtained by him in the Island unless it is chargeable there with duty or value added tax and he has obtained it without payment of the duty or tax.]

[(1B) Subsection (1) above does not apply to a person entering the United Kingdom from another member State, except—

    (a)   where he arrives at a customs and excise airport in an aircraft in which he began his journey in a place outside the member States; or

    (b)   as respects such of his baggage as—

        (i)   is carried in the hold of the aircraft in which he arrives at a customs and excise airport, and

        (ii)   notwithstanding that it was transferred on one or more occasions from aircraft to aircraft at an airport in a member State, began its journey by air from a place outside the member States.]

(2) Any person entering or leaving the United Kingdom shall answer such questions as the proper officer may put to him with respect to his baggage and any thing contained therein or carried with him, and shall, if required by the proper officer, produce that baggage and any such thing for examination at such place as the Commissioners may direct.

[(2A) Subject to subsection (1A) above, where the journey of a person arriving by air in the United Kingdom is continued or resumed by air to a destination in the United Kingdom which is not the place where he is regarded for the purposes of this section as entering the United Kingdom, subsections (1) and (2) above shall apply in relation to that person on his arrival at that destination as they apply in relation to a person entering the United Kingdom.]

(3) Any person failing to declare any thing or to produce any baggage or thing as required by this section shall be liable on summary conviction to a penalty of three

times the value of the thing not declared or of the baggage or thing not produced, as the case may be, or [level 3 on the standard scale], whichever is the greater.

(4) Any thing chargeable with any duty or tax which is found concealed, or is not declared, and any thing which is being taken into or out of the United Kingdom contrary to any prohibition or restriction for the time being in force with respect thereto under or by virtue of any enactment, shall be liable to forfeiture.

NOTES

Sub-s (1A): inserted by the Isle of Man Act 1979, s 13, Sch 1.

Sub-s (1B): inserted by the Customs and Excise (Single Market etc) Regulations 1992, SI 1992/3095, reg 3(10).

Sub-s (2A): inserted by the Finance (No 2) Act 1992, s 5.

Sub-s (3): reference to a level on the standard scale substituted by virtue of the Criminal Justice Act 1982, ss 38, 46.

79 Power to require evidence in support of information

(1) The Commissioners may, if they consider it necessary, require evidence to be produced to their satisfaction in support of any information required by or under Parts III to VII of this Act to be provided in respect of goods imported or exported.

(2) Without prejudice to subsection (1) above, where any question as to the duties chargeable on any imported goods, or the operation of any prohibition or restriction on importation, depends on any question as to the place from which the goods were consigned, or any question where they or other goods are to be treated as grown, manufactured or produced, or any question as to payments made or relief from duty allowed in any country or territory, then—

    (a)   the Commissioners may require the importer of the goods to furnish to them, in such form as they may prescribe, proof of—

        (i)   any statement made to them as to any fact necessary to determine that question, or

        (ii)   the accuracy of any certificate or other document furnished in connection with the importation of the goods and relating to the matter in issue,

        and if such proof is not furnished to their satisfaction, the question may be determined without regard to that statement or to that certificate or document; and

    (b)   if in any proceedings relating to the goods or to the duty chargeable thereon the accuracy of any such certificate or document comes in question, it shall be for the person relying on it to furnish proof of its accuracy.

80 Power to require information or production of documents where origin of goods exported is evidenced under Community law or practice

(1) Where on the exportation of any goods from the United Kingdom there has been furnished for the purpose of any Community requirement or practice any certificate or other evidence as to the origin of those goods, or as to payments made or relief from duty allowed in any country or territory, then, for the purpose of verifying or investigating that certificate or evidence, the Commissioners or an officer may require the exporter, or any other person appearing to the Commissioners or officer to have been concerned in any way with the goods, or with any goods from which, directly or indirectly, they have been produced or manufactured, or to have been concerned with the obtaining or furnishing of the certificate or evidence—

    (a)   to furnish such information, in such form and within such time, as the Commissioners or officer may specify in the requirement; or

(b)   to produce for inspection, and to allow the taking of copies or extracts from, such invoices, bills of lading, books or documents as may be so specified.

(2)   Any person who, without reasonable cause, fails to comply with a requirement imposed on him under subsection (1) above shall be liable on summary conviction to a penalty of [level 3 on the standard scale].

NOTES

Sub-s (2): reference to a level on the standard scale substituted by virtue of the Criminal Justice Act 1982, ss 38, 46.

Prevention of smuggling

81 Power to regulate small craft

(1)   In this section "small ships" means—
    (a)   ships not exceeding 100 tons register; and
    (b)   hovercraft, of whatever size.

(2)   The Commissioners may make general regulations with respect to small ships and any such regulations may in particular make provision as to the purposes for which and the limits within which such ships may be used.

(3)   Different provision may be made by regulations under this section for different classes or descriptions of small ships.

(4)   The Commissioners may, in respect of any small ship, grant a licence exempting that ship from all or any of the provisions of any regulations made under this section.

(5)   Any such licence may be granted for such period, for such purposes and subject to such conditions and restrictions as the Commissioners see fit, and may be revoked at any time by the Commissioners.

(6)   Any small ship which, except under and in accordance with the terms of a licence granted under this section, is used contrary to any regulation made under this section, and any ship granted such a licence which is found not to have that licence on board, shall be liable to forfeiture.

(7)   Every boat belonging to a British ship and every other vessel not exceeding 100 tons register, [not being a fishing vessel registered under Part II of the Merchant Shipping Act 1995], and every hovercraft, shall be marked in such manner as the Commissioners may direct, and any such boat, vessel or hovercraft which is not so marked shall be liable to forfeiture.

NOTES

Sub-s (7): words in square brackets substituted by the Merchant Shipping Act 1995, s 314(2), Sch 13, para 53(3).

82 Power to haul up revenue vessels, patrol coasts, etc

(1)   The person in command or charge of any vessel in the service of Her Majesty which is engaged in the prevention of smuggling—
    (a)   may haul up and leave that vessel on any part of the coast or of the shore or bank of any river or creek; and
    (b)   may moor that vessel at any place below high water mark on any part of the coast or of any such shore or bank.

(2)   Any officer and any person acting in aid of an officer or otherwise duly engaged in the prevention of smuggling may for that purpose patrol upon and pass

freely along and over any part of the coast or of the shore or bank of any river or creek, over any railway or aerodrome or land adjoining any aerodrome, and over any land in Northern Ireland within the prescribed area.

(3) Nothing in this section shall authorise the use of or entry into any garden or pleasure ground.

83 Penalty for removing seals, etc

(1) Where, in pursuance of any power conferred by the customs and excise Acts or of any requirement imposed by or under those Acts, a seal, lock or mark is used to secure or identify any goods for any of the purposes of those Acts and—

(a) at any time while the goods are in the United Kingdom or within the limits of any port or on passage between ports in the United Kingdom [or between a port in the United Kingdom and a port in the Isle of Man], the seal, lock or mark is wilfully and prematurely removed or tampered with by any person; or

(b) at any time before the seal, lock or mark is lawfully removed, any of the goods are wilfully removed by any person,

that person and the person then in charge of the goods shall each be liable on summary conviction to a penalty of [level 4 on the standard scale].

(2) For the purposes of subsection (1) above, goods in a ship or aircraft shall be deemed to be in the charge of the master of the ship or commander of the aircraft.

(3) Where, in pursuance of any Community requirement or practice which relates to the movement of goods between countries or of any international agreement to which the United Kingdom is a party and which so relates,—

(a) a seal, lock or mark is used (whether in the United Kingdom or elsewhere) to secure or identify any goods for customs or excise purposes; and

(b) at any time while the goods are in the United Kingdom, the seal, lock or mark is wilfully and prematurely removed or tampered with by any person,

that person and the person then in charge of the goods shall each be liable on summary conviction to a penalty of [level 4 on the standard scale].

NOTES

Sub-s (1): words in first pair of square brackets inserted by the Isle of Man Act 1979, s 13, Sch 1; reference to a level on the standard scale substituted by virtue of the Criminal Justice Act 1982, s 46.

Sub-s (3): reference to a level on the standard scale substituted by virtue of the Criminal Justice Act 1982, s 46.

84

(Repealed by the Commissioners for Revenue and Customs Act 2005 s 52(1)(a)(iv), Sch 5.)

85 Penalty for interfering with revenue vessels, etc

(1) Any person who save for just and sufficient cause interferes in any way with any ship, aircraft, vehicle, buoy, anchor, chain, rope or mark which is being used for the purposes of any functions of the Commissioners under Parts III to VII of this Act shall be liable on summary conviction to a penalty of [level 1 on the standard scale].

(2) Any person who fires upon any vessel, aircraft or vehicle in the service of Her Majesty while that vessel, aircraft or vehicle is engaged in the prevention of smuggling shall be liable on conviction on indictment to imprisonment for a term not exceeding 5 years.

NOTES

Sub-s (1): reference to a level on the standard scale substituted by virtue of the Criminal Justice Act 1982, s 46.

86

(Repealed by the Commissioners for Revenue and Customs Act 2005 s 52(1)(a)(v), Sch 5.)

87 Penalty for offering goods for sale as smuggled goods

If any person offers any goods for sale as having been imported without payment of duty, or as having been otherwise unlawfully imported, then, whether or not the goods were so imported or were in fact chargeable with duty, the goods shall be liable to forfeiture and the person so offering them for sale shall be liable on summary conviction to a penalty of three times the value of the goods or [level 3 on the standard scale], whichever is the greater, and may be [arrested].

NOTES

Reference to a level on the standard scale substituted by virtue of the Criminal Justice Act 1982, ss 40, 46; words in second pair of square brackets substituted by the Police and Criminal Evidence Act 1984, s 114(1).

Forfeiture of ships, etc for certain offences

88 Forfeiture of ship, aircraft or vehicle constructed, etc for concealing goods

Where—

(a)   a ship is or has been [in United Kingdom waters]; or

(b)   an aircraft is or has been at any place, whether on land or on water, in the United Kingdom; or

(c)   a vehicle is or has been within the limits of any port or at any aerodrome or, while in Northern Ireland, within the prescribed area,

while constructed, adapted, altered or fitted in any manner for the purpose of concealing goods, that ship, aircraft or vehicle shall be liable to forfeiture.

NOTES

Words in square brackets substituted by the Territorial Sea Act 1987, s 3(1), Sch 1, para 4(3)(b).

89 Forfeiture of ship jettisoning cargo, etc

(1) If any part of the cargo of a ship is thrown overboard or is staved or destroyed to prevent seizure—

(a)   while the ship is [in United Kingdom waters]; or

(b)   where the ship, having been properly summoned to bring to by any vessel in the service of Her Majesty, fails so to do and chase is given, at any time during the chase,

the ship shall be liable to forfeiture.

(2) For the purposes of this section a ship shall be deemed to have been properly summoned to bring to—

(a)   if the vessel making the summons did so by means of an international signal code or other recognised means and while flying her proper ensign; and

(b)   in the case of a ship which is not a British ship, if at the time when the summons was made the ship was [in United Kingdom waters].

NOTES

Words in square brackets substituted by the Territorial Sea Act 1987, s 3(1), Sch 1, para 4(3)(c).

90 Forfeiture of ship or aircraft unable to account for missing cargo

Where a ship has been within the limits of any port [in the United Kingdom or the Isle of Man], or an aircraft has been in the United Kingdom [or the Isle of Man], with a cargo on board and a substantial part of that cargo is afterwards found [in the United Kingdom] to be missing, then, if the master of the ship or commander of the aircraft fails to account therefor to the satisfaction of the Commissioners, the ship or aircraft shall be liable to forfeiture.

NOTES

Words in square brackets inserted by the Isle of Man Act 1979, s 13, Sch 1.

91 Ships failing to bring to

(1)   If, save for just and sufficient cause, any ship which is liable to forfeiture or examination under or by virtue of any provision of the Customs and Excise Acts 1979 does not bring to when required to do so, the master of the ship shall be liable on summary conviction to a penalty of [level 2 on the standard scale].

(2)   Where any ship liable to forfeiture or examination as aforesaid has failed to bring to when required to do so and chase has been given thereto by any vessel in the service of Her Majesty and, after the commander of that vessel has hoisted the proper ensign and caused a gun to be fired as a signal, the ship still fails to bring to, the ship may be fired upon.

NOTES

Sub-s (1): reference to a level on the standard scale substituted by virtue of the Criminal Justice Act 1982, s 46.

PART VIII
WAREHOUSES AND QUEEN'S WAREHOUSES AND RELATED PROVISIONS ABOUT PIPE-LINES

92 Approval of warehouses

(1)   The Commissioners may approve, for such periods and subject to such conditions as they think fit, places of security for the deposit, keeping and securing—

(a)   of imported goods chargeable as such with excise duty (whether or not also chargeable with customs duty) without payment of the excise duty;

(b)   of goods for exportation or for use as stores, being goods not eligible for home use;

(c)   of goods manufactured or produced in the United Kingdom [or the Isle of Man] and permitted by or under the customs and excise Acts to be warehoused without payment of any duty of excise chargeable thereon;

(d) of goods imported into or manufactured or produced in the United Kingdom [or the Isle of Man] and permitted by or under the customs and excise Acts to be warehoused on drawback,

subject to and in accordance with warehousing regulations; and any place of security so approved is referred to in this Act as an "excise warehouse".

[(2) Functions with respect to the approval of warehouses for the purposes of Article 38 of Commission Regulation (EEC) No 3665/87 shall be exercised by the Commissioners; and a warehouse approved by them for such purposes is referred to in this Act as a "victualling warehouse".]

(3) The same place may be approved under this section both as a [victualling] and as an excise warehouse.

(4) Notwithstanding subsection (2) above and the terms of the approval of the warehouse but subject to directions under subsection (5) below, goods of the following descriptions, not being goods chargeable with excise duty which has not been paid, that is to say—

(a) goods originating in member States;

(b) goods which are in free circulation in member States; and

(c) goods placed on importation under a customs procedure (other than warehousing) involving the suspension of, or the giving of relief from, customs duties,

may be kept, without being warehoused, in a [victualling warehouse].

(5) The Commissioners may from time to time give directions—

(a) as to the goods which may or may not be deposited in any particular warehouse or class of warehouse;

(b) as to the part of any warehouse in which any class or description of goods may be kept or secured.

(6) If, after the approval of a warehouse as an excise warehouse, the occupier thereof makes without the previous consent of the Commissioners any alteration therein or addition thereto, [the making of the alteration or addition shall attract a penalty under section 9 of the Finance Act 1994 (civil penalties)].

(7) The Commissioners may at any time for reasonable cause revoke or vary the terms of their approval of any warehouse under this section.

[(8) Where any person contravenes or fails to comply with any condition imposed or direction given by the Commissioners under this section, his contravention or failure to comply shall attract a penalty under section 9 of the Finance Act 1994 (civil penalties).]

NOTES

Sub-s (1): words in square brackets in paras (c), (d) inserted by the Isle of Man Act 1979, s 13, Sch 1.

Sub-s (2): substituted by the Customs Warehousing Regulations 1991, SI 1991/2725, reg 3(1), (4)(a).

Sub-ss (3), (4): words in square brackets substituted by SI 1991/2725, reg 3(1), (4)(b), (c).

Sub-s (6): words in square brackets substituted by the Finance Act 1994, s 9, Sch 4, paras 1, 2(1).

Sub-s (8): substituted by the Finance Act 1994, s 9, Sch 4, paras 1, 2(2).

---

93 Regulation of warehouses and warehoused goods

[(1) The Commissioners may by regulations under this section (referred to in this Act as "warehousing regulations")—

(a) prohibit the deposit or keeping of goods in a warehouse except where the occupier of the warehouse has been approved by the Commissioners in accordance with the regulations and where such conditions as may be prescribed in relation to that occupier are satisfied;

(b) otherwise regulate the deposit, keeping, securing and treatment of goods in a warehouse;

(c) make provision with respect to goods which are required to be deposited in a warehouse;

(d) regulate the removal of goods from a warehouse and make provision with respect to goods which have lawfully been permitted to be removed from a warehouse without payment of duty; and

(e) make provision, in relation to goods which have been warehoused or are required to be deposited in a warehouse with respect to the keeping, preservation and production of records and the furnishing of information.]

(2) Warehousing regulations may, without prejudice to the generality of subsection (1) above, include provisions—

(a) imposing or providing for the imposition under the regulations of conditions and restrictions subject to which goods may be deposited in [secured in], kept in or removed from warehouse or made available there to their owner for any prescribed purpose;

(b) requiring goods deposited in warehouse to be produced to or made available for inspection by an officer on request by him;

(c) permitting the carrying out on warehoused goods of such operations . . . as may be prescribed by or allowed under the regulations in such manner and subject to such conditions and restrictions as may be imposed by or under the regulations;

(d) for determining, for the purpose of charging or securing the payment of duty, the duties of customs or excise and the rates thereof to be applied to warehoused goods (other than goods falling within section 92(2)(b) above) and in that connection—

(i) for determining the time by reference to which warehoused goods are to be classified;

(ii) for determining the time at which warehoused goods are to be treated as having been removed from warehouse;

(iii) for ascertaining the quantity which is to be taken as the quantity of warehoused goods;

[(da) providing for all or any prescribed purposes of the customs and excise Acts—

(i) for goods to be treated as warehoused where in a prescribed case they are in the custody or under the control of an approved occupier of a warehouse; and

(ii) for goods to be treated, at such times before the excise duty point for those goods as may be prescribed or as may be determined under the regulations, as goods which are required to be deposited in a warehouse;

(db) providing for the revocation of the approval under regulations of any occupier of a warehouse and applying, with modifications, any of the provisions of section 98 below in relation to such a revocation or to cases where such an approval is not renewed;]

(e) enabling the Commissioners to allow goods to be removed from warehouse without payment of duty in such circumstances and subject to such conditions as they may determine;

[(ee) providing that goods which are [required to be deposited in a warehouse], or which have been lawfully permitted to be removed from a warehouse without payment of duty, are to be treated as if, for all or any prescribed purposes of the customs and excise Acts, they were warehoused;]

(f) permitting goods to be destroyed or abandoned to the Commissioners without payment of customs duty in such circumstances and subject to such conditions as they may determine;

[(fa) requiring goods which are required to be deposited in a warehouse or which have lawfully been permitted to be removed from a warehouse without payment of duty to be accompanied by such documents in such form and containing such particulars as may be prescribed;

(fb) imposing or providing for the imposition under the regulations of requirements on persons concerned in any prescribed respect with the carriage of such goods to keep and preserve the documents that are required to accompany the goods;

(fc) imposing or providing for the imposition under the regulations of requirements on a person so concerned to produce or cause to be produced any documents which are required to accompany any goods by virtue of paragraph (fa) above to an officer when required to do so for the purpose of allowing the officer to inspect them, to copy or take extracts from them or to remove them at a reasonable time and for a reasonable period;]

[(g) imposing or providing for the imposition under the regulations of requirements on the occupier of a warehouse or the proprietor of goods in a warehouse or goods which have been in or are [required] to be deposited in a warehouse to keep and preserve such records as may be prescribed relating to his occupation of the warehouse or proprietorship of the goods;

(h) imposing or providing for the imposition under the regulations of requirements on such an occupier or proprietor to preserve all other records kept by him for the purposes of any relevant business or activity, except any records which (or records of a class which) the Commissioners specify as not needing preservation;

(j) imposing or providing for the imposition under the regulations of requirements on such an occupier or proprietor to produce or cause to be produced any records which he has been required to preserve by virtue of paragraph (g) or (h) above to an officer when required to do so for the purpose of allowing the officer to inspect them, to copy or take extracts from them or to remove them at a reasonable time and for a reasonable period;

(k) imposing or providing for the imposition under the regulations of requirements on such an occupier or proprietor to furnish the Commissioners with any information relating to any relevant business or activity which they specify as information which they think it is necessary or expedient for them to be given for the protection of the revenue;

(l) allowing a requirement to preserve any records which has been imposed by virtue of paragraph (h) above to be discharged by the preservation in a form approved by the Commissioners of the information contained in the records],

and may contain such incidental or supplementary provisions as the Commissioners think necessary or expedient for the protection of the revenue.

[In this subsection "relevant business or activity" means, in relation to an occupier or proprietor, any business or activity of his which includes occupation of a warehouse or (as the case may be) proprietorship of goods in a warehouse or goods which have been in or are [required] to be deposited in a warehouse, where the goods are of a kind in which the proprietor trades or deals.]

[(2A) Where any documents [or records] removed under the powers conferred by subsection [(2)(fc) or (j)] above are lost or damaged the Commissioners shall be liable to compensate their owner for any expenses reasonably incurred by him in replacing or repairing the documents [or records].]

(3) Warehousing regulations may make different provision for [different cases, including different provision for different occupiers or descriptions of occupier, for] warehouses or parts of warehouses of different descriptions or for goods of different classes or descriptions or of the same class or description in different circumstances.

(4) Warehousing regulations may make provision about the removal of goods from one warehouse to another or from one part of a warehouse to another part or for treating goods remaining in a warehouse as if, for all or any prescribed purposes of the customs and excise Acts, they had been so removed; and regulations about the removal of goods may, for all or any prescribed purposes of those Acts, include provision for treating the goods as having been warehoused or removed from warehouse (where they would not otherwise be so treated).

(5) Warehousing regulations made by virtue of paragraph (a) or (c) of subsection (2) above may also provide for the forfeiture of goods in the event of non-compliance with any condition or restriction imposed by virtue of that paragraph or in the event of the carrying out of any operation on warehoused goods which is not by virtue of the said paragraph (c) permitted to be carried out in the warehouse.

[(5A) Warehousing regulations made by virtue of any of paragraphs (fa) to (fc) or (g) to (j) of subsection (2) above may also provide for the forfeiture of the goods in question in the event of any contravention of, or non-compliance with, any requirements imposed by or under the regulations with respect to any documents or records relating to prescribed goods.]

(6) If any person fails to comply with any warehousing regulation or with any condition [restriction or requirement] imposed under a warehousing regulation [his failure to comply shall attract a penalty under section 9 of the Finance Act 1994 (civil penalties).]

[(7) In this section—
  (a)   "prescribed" means prescribed by warehousing regulations;
  (b)   references to goods which are [required to be deposited in a warehouse] are references to goods which have been entered for warehousing on importation, which have been removed from a producer's premises for warehousing without payment of duty [which are to be warehoused on drawback or which are otherwise to be treated by virtue of subsection (2)(da)(ii) above as goods which are required to be deposited in a warehouse].]

NOTES

Sub-s (1): substituted by the Finance (No 2) Act 1992, s 3, Sch 2, para 2(1).

Sub-s (2): words in square brackets in para (a) inserted by the Finance Act 1981, s 11(1), Sch 8, Pt I, para 2(a); words omitted from para (c) repealed by the Finance Act 1988, ss 9(2), 148, Sch 14, Pt I; paras (da), (db), (fa), (fb), (fc) inserted, and in definition "relevant business or activity" words in square brackets inserted, by the Finance (No 2) Act 1992, s 3, Sch 2, para 2(2); para (ee) inserted by the Finance Act 1986, s 5, Sch 3, paras 1, 3, 4, words in square brackets substituted by the Finance (No 2) Act 1992, s 3, Sch 2, para 2(2); paras (g)–(l) substituted for original para (g) (as added by the Finance Act 1981, ss 11(1), Sch 8, Pt I, para 2(b)) by the Finance Act 1986, s 5, Sch 3, paras 1, 4, words in square brackets in para (g) substituted by the Finance (No 2) Act 1992, s 3, Sch 2, para 2(2); words in final pair of square brackets added by the Finance Act 1986, s 5, Sch 3.

Sub-s (2A): inserted by the Finance Act 1981, s 11(1), Sch 8, Pt I, para 2(c); words in first and final pairs of square brackets inserted, and second words in square brackets substituted, by the Finance (No 2) Act 1992, s 3, Sch 2, para 2(3).

Sub-s (3): words in square brackets inserted by the Finance (No 2) Act 1992, s 3, Sch 2, para 2(4).

Sub-s (5A): inserted by the Finance (No 2) Act 1992, s 3, Sch 2, para 2(5).

Sub-s (6): words in square brackets substituted with savings by the Finance Act 1994, s 9, Sch 4, para 3, in accordance with s 19 thereof, for savings see SI 1994/2679, art 4(3).

Sub-s (7): added by the Finance Act 1981, s 11(1), Sch 8, Pt I, para 2, substituted by the Finance Act 1986, s 5, Sch 3, paras 1, 7; words in square brackets substituted, by the Finance (No 2) Act 1992, s 3, Sch 2, para 2(7).

Regulations: the Excise Warehousing (Etc) Regulations 1988, SI 1988/809, as amended by SI 1995/1046; the Spirits (Rectifying, Compounding and Drawback) Regulations 1988, SI 1988/1760, as amended by SI 1991/2564; the Spirits Regulations 1991, SI 1991/2564; the Customs Warehousing (Victualling) Regulations 1991, SI 1991/2726; the Excise Goods (Holding, Movement, Warehousing and REDS) Regulations 1992, SI 1992/3135, as amended by SI 1993/1228, SI 1999/1278, SI 1999/1565; the Excise Duties (Deferred Payment) Regulations 1992, SI 1992/3152, as amended by SI 1996/2537; the Beer Regulations 1993, SI 1993/1228, as amended by SI 1995/3059, SI 2000/3213; the Excise Goods (Drawback) Regulations 1995, SI 1995/1046, as modified by SI 1999/1565; the Warehousekeepers and Owners of Warehoused Goods Regulations 1999, SI 1999/1278.

94 Deficiency in warehoused goods

(1)   . . . this section applies where goods have been warehoused and, before they are lawfully removed from warehouse in accordance with a proper clearance thereof, they are found to be missing or deficient.

(2)   . . .

(3)   In any case where this section applies, unless it is shown to the satisfaction of the Commissioners that the absence of or deficiency in the goods can be accounted for by natural waste or other legitimate cause, the Commissioners may—

[(a)   require the occupier of the warehouse or the proprietor of the goods to pay immediately any duty, other than excise duty, chargeable or deemed under warehousing regulations to be chargeable on the relevant goods or, in the case of goods warehoused on drawback which could not lawfully be entered for home use, an amount equal to any drawback or allowance of such duty paid in respect of the relevant goods;

(b)   assess, as being excise duty due from the occupier of the warehouse or the proprietor of the goods, the excise duty chargeable or deemed under warehousing regulations to be chargeable on the relevant goods or, in the case of goods warehoused on drawback which could not lawfully be entered for home use, an amount equal to any drawback or allowance of excise duty paid in respect of the relevant goods.]

[(3A)   Where the Commissioners make an assessment under subsection (3)(b) above they shall notify the person assessed or his representative accordingly.]

(4)   If, on the written demand of an officer, the occupier of the warehouse or the proprietor of the goods refuses to pay any sum which he is required to pay under subsection [(3)(a)] above he shall in addition be liable on summary conviction to a penalty of double that sum.

[(4A)   If—

(a)   the occupier of the warehouse or the proprietor of the goods refuses to pay any amount of excise duty to which he has been assessed under subsection (3)(b) above, and

(b)   the conditions set out in subsection (4B) below are fulfilled,

he shall be liable on summary conviction to a penalty of double that amount.

(4B)   The conditions are that—

    (a)   the period of forty-five days referred to in section 14(3) of the Finance Act 1994 (period during which review may be required) has expired;

    (b)   on any review under Chapter II of Part I of that Act the Commissioners' decision ("the original decision") in relation to the assessment has been confirmed (or treated as confirmed by virtue of section 15(2) of that Act), or confirmed subject only to a reduction in the amount of duty due under the assessment; and

    (c)   the final result of any further appeal is that the original decision has been confirmed, subject only to any reduction in the amount of duty due under the assessment; and "final result" means the result of the last of any such appeals, against which no appeal may be made (whether because of expiry of time or for any other reason).

(4C) Where the amount of excise duty due under subsection (3)(b) above is reduced in consequence of a review or appeal, the penalty to which the person assessed is liable under subsection (4A) above shall be a penalty of double the reduced amount.]

(5) This section has effect without prejudice to any penalty or forfeiture incurred under any other provision of the customs and excise Acts.

[(5A) In this section "the relevant goods" means the missing goods or the whole or any part of the deficiency, as the Commissioners see fit.]

[(6) The preceding provisions of this section so far as they have effect for—

    (a)   fixing the excise duty point for any goods chargeable with a duty of excise; or

    (b)   determining the person on whom any liability to pay any such duty is to fall,

shall have effect subject to the provisions of any regulations under section 1 of the Finance (No 2) Act 1992; and accordingly, the power to make regulations under that section shall include power, for the purposes of, or in connection with, the making of any provision falling within paragraph (a) or (b) above, to modify any of the preceding provisions of this section and the provisions of section 95 below.]

NOTES

Sub-s (1): words omitted repealed by the Finance Act 1981, ss 11(1), 139, Sch 8, Pt I, para 3, Sch 19, Pt III.

Sub-s (2): repealed by the Finance Act 1981, s 139, Sch 19, Pt III.

Sub-ss (3), (4): words in square brackets substituted by the Finance Act 1997, s 50(2), Sch 6, paras 3(1), (2), (4), 7.

Sub-ss (3A), (4A)–(4C), (5A): inserted by the Finance Act 1997, s 50(2), Sch 6, paras 3(1), (3), (5), (6), 7.

Sub-s (6): added by the Finance (No 2) Act 1992, s 1, Sch 1, para 3.

95 Deficiency in goods occurring in course of removal from warehouse without payment of duty

(1) Where any goods have been lawfully permitted to be taken from a warehouse without payment of duty for removal to another warehouse or to some other place, section 94 above shall, subject to subsection (2) below [and to any such regulations as are mentioned in subsection (6) of that section], have effect in relation to those goods in the course of that removal as if those goods were still in warehouse.

(2) In its application in relation to any goods by virtue of subsection (1) above, section 94 above shall have effect as if the following provisions were omitted, namely—

    (a)   . . .

    (b)   the references in subsections (3)[, (4) and (4A)] to the occupier of the warehouse.

NOTES

Sub-s (1): words in square brackets inserted by the Finance (No 2) Act 1992, s 1, Sch 1, para 4.

Sub-s (2): para (a) repealed by the Finance Act 1981, s 139, Sch 19, Pt III; words in square brackets in para (b) substituted by the Finance Act 1997, s 50(2), Sch 6, paras 3(1), (7), 7.

96 Deficiency in certain goods moved by pipe-line

(1) This section applies where goods of any of the following descriptions, that is to say—

    (a)   goods which are chargeable with a duty which has not been paid;

    (b)   goods on which duty has been repaid or remitted in whole or in part; and

    (c)   goods on which drawback has been paid,

are moved by pipe-line, or notified to the proper officer as being goods to be moved by pipe-line, and are at any time thereafter found to be missing or deficient.

(2) In any case where this section applies, unless it is shown to the satisfaction of the Commissioners that the absence of or deficiency in the goods can be accounted for by natural waste or other legitimate cause, the Commissioners may—

    [(a)   require the owner of the pipe-line or the proprietor of the goods to pay immediately any duty, other than excise duty, unpaid or repaid on the relevant goods or, as the case may be, an amount equal to any drawback of such duty paid on the relevant goods;

    (b)   assess, as being excise duty due from the owner of the pipe-line or the proprietor of the goods, the excise duty unpaid or repaid on the relevant goods or, as the case may be, an amount equal to any drawback of excise duty paid on the relevant goods.]

[(2A) Where the Commissioners make an assessment under subsection (2)(b) above they shall notify the person assessed or his representative accordingly.]

(3) If, on the written demand of an officer, any person refuses to pay any sum which he is required to pay under subsection [(2)(a)] above he shall in addition be liable on summary conviction to a penalty of double that sum.

[(3A) If—

    (a)   any person refuses to pay any amount of excise duty to which he has been assessed under subsection (2)(b) above, and

    (b)   the conditions set out in paragraphs (a) to (c) of section 94(4B) above (exhaustion of opportunities for review and appeal) are fulfilled,

he shall be liable on summary conviction to a penalty of double that amount.

(3B) Where the amount of excise duty due under subsection (2)(b) above is reduced in consequence of a review or appeal, the penalty to which the person assessed is liable under subsection (3A) above shall be a penalty of double the reduced amount.]

(4) For the purposes of this section any absence or deficiency in the case of goods moved by a pipe-line used for the importation or exportation of goods shall be deemed to have taken place within the United Kingdom unless the contrary is shown.

(5) This section has effect without prejudice to any penalty or forfeiture incurred under any other provision of the customs and excise Acts.

[(5A) In this section "the relevant goods" means the missing goods or the whole or any part of the deficiency, as the Commissioners see fit.]

[(6) The preceding provisions of this section so far as they have effect for—

Part I

    (a)   fixing the excise duty point for any goods chargeable with a duty of excise; or

    (b)   determining the person on whom any liability to pay any such duty is to fall,

shall have effect subject to the provisions of any regulations under section 1 of the Finance (No 2) Act 1992; and, accordingly, the power to make regulations under that section shall include power, for the purposes of, or in connection with, the making of any provision falling within paragraph (a) or (b) above, to modify any of the preceding provisions of this section.]

NOTES

Sub-ss (2), (3): words in square brackets substituted by the Finance Act 1997, s 50(2), Sch 6, paras 4(1), (2), (4), 7.

Sub-ss (2A), (3A)–(3C), (5A): inserted by the Finance Act 1997, s 50(2), Sch 6, paras 4(1), (3), (5), (6), 7.

Sub-s (6): added by the Finance (No 2) Act 1992, s 1, Sch 1, para 5.

97 Restriction on compensation for loss or damage to goods in, or for removal of goods from, warehouse or pipe-line

(1) This section applies to—

    (a)   any loss or damage caused to goods while in a warehouse or pipe-line; and

    (b)   any unlawful removal of goods from a warehouse or pipe-line.

(2) Subject to subsection (3) below, no compensation shall be payable by, and no action shall lie against, the Commissioners or any officer acting in the execution of his duty for any loss or damage to which this section applies or for any unlawful removal to which this section applies.

(3) If any goods in a warehouse or pipe-line are destroyed, stolen or unlawfully removed by or with the assistance or connivance of an officer and that officer is convicted of the offence, then, except where the proprietor of the goods or the occupier of the warehouse or, as the case may be, the owner of the pipe-line was a party to the offence, the Commissioners shall pay compensation for any loss caused by any such destruction, theft or removal.

(4) Where compensation is payable by virtue of subsection (3) above then, notwithstanding any provision of the Customs and Excise Acts 1979, no duty shall be payable on the goods by the proprietor of the goods or by the occupier of the warehouse or, as the case may be, the owner of the pipe-line, and any sum paid by way of duty on those goods by any of those persons before the conviction shall be repaid.

98 Procedure on warehouse ceasing to be approved

(1) Where the Commissioners intend to revoke or not to renew their approval of a warehouse, they shall, not later than the beginning of the prescribed period ending with the date when the revocation is to take effect or the approval is due to expire, as the case may be, give notice of their intention, specifying therein the said date [and, unless the notice has been withdrawn or extended, the warehouse shall cease to be approved on that date].

(2) The notice shall be given in writing and shall be deemed to have been served on all persons interested in any goods then deposited in that warehouse, or permitted under the Customs and Excise Acts 1979 to be so deposited between the date of the giving of the notice and the date specified therein, if addressed to the occupier of, and left at, the warehouse.

[(3) If after the date on which the warehouse ceases to be approved any goods not duly cleared still remain in the former warehouse—

    (a)   they may be taken by an officer to a Queen's warehouse and, without prejudice to section 99(3) below, if they are not cleared from it within one month may be sold; or

    (b)   if the Commissioners so allow, they may remain in the former warehouse and if they are not cleared from it within one month may be sold.

(3A) Where in accordance with paragraph (b) above goods remain in the warehouse after the revocation or expiry of the Commissioners' approval—

    (a)   subsections (6) and (7) of section 99 below shall apply to them as if they were deposited in a Queen's warehouse under the Customs and Excise Acts 1979; and

    (b)   sections 93, 94, 95 and 97 above and section 100 below shall apply and any security given by bond or otherwise and any condition imposed by or under the customs and excise Acts shall continue to have effect as if the former warehouse were still a warehouse.]

(4)   In this section "the prescribed period" means—

    (a)   in the case of a warehouse which is a [victualling warehouse] but not also an excise warehouse, such period as may be prescribed by warehousing regulations;

    (b)   in the case of a warehouse which is or is also an excise warehouse, 3 months.

NOTES

Sub-s (1): words in square brackets inserted by the Finance Act 1981, s 11(1), Sch 8, Pt I, para 4(a).

Sub-ss (3), (3A): substituted for original sub-s (3) by the Finance Act 1981, s 11(1), Sch 8, Pt I, para 4(b).

Sub-s (4): words in square brackets substituted by the Customs Warehousing Regulations 1991, SI 1991/2725, reg 3(5).

99 Provisions as to deposit in Queen's warehouse

(1)   The following provisions of this section shall have effect in relation to any goods which are deposited in a Queen's warehouse under or by virtue of any provision of the Customs and Excise Acts 1979.

(2)   Such rent shall be payable while the goods are deposited as may be fixed by the Commissioners.

(3)   If the goods are of a combustible or inflammable nature or otherwise of such a character as to require special care or treatment—

    (a)   they shall, in addition to any other charges payable thereon, be chargeable with such expenses for securing, watching and guarding them as the Commissioners see fit;

    (b)   neither the Commissioners nor any officer shall be liable to make good any damage which the goods may have sustained; and

    (c)   if the proprietor of the goods has not cleared them within a period of 14 days from the date of deposit, they may be sold by the Commissioners;

but, in the case of goods deposited by virtue of section 40(2) above, paragraph (c) above shall only apply if the goods are of a combustible or inflammable nature.

(4)   Save as permitted by or under the Customs and Excise Acts 1979, the goods shall not be removed from the warehouse until—

    (a)   any duty chargeable thereon; and

    (b)   any charges in respect thereof—

        (i)   for their removal to the warehouse, and

(ii) under subsections (2) and (3) above,

have been paid and, in the case of goods requiring entry and not yet entered, until entry has been made thereof.

(5) The officer having the custody of the goods may refuse to allow them to be removed until it is shown to his satisfaction that any freight charges due thereon have been paid.

(6) If the goods are sold under or by virtue of any provision of the Customs and Excise Acts 1979, the proceeds of sale shall be applied—

(a) first, in paying any duty chargeable on the goods;

(b) secondly, in defraying any such charges as are mentioned in subsection (4) above; and

(c) thirdly, in defraying any charges for freight;

and if the person who was immediately before the sale the proprietor of the goods makes application in that behalf the remainder, if any, shall be paid over to him.

(7) When the goods are authorised to be sold under or by virtue of any provision of the Customs and Excise Acts 1979 but cannot be sold—

(a) if the goods are to be exported, for a sum sufficient to make the payment mentioned in paragraph (b) of subsection (6) above; or

(b) in any other case, for a sum sufficient to make the payments mentioned in paragraphs (a) and (b) of that subsection,

the Commissioners may destroy the goods.

NOTES

Postal packets: see note at the beginning of this Act.

---

100 General offences relating to warehouses and warehoused goods

(1) Any person who, except with the authority of the proper officer or for just and sufficient cause, opens any of the doors or locks of a warehouse or Queen's warehouse or makes or obtains access to any such warehouse or to any goods warehoused therein shall be liable on summary conviction to a penalty of [level 5 on the standard scale] and may be [arrested].

(2) Where—

(a) any goods which have been entered for warehousing [or are otherwise required to be deposited in a warehouse] are taken into the warehouse without the authority of, or otherwise than in accordance with any directions given by, the proper officer; or

(b) save as permitted by the Customs and Excise Acts 1979 or by or under warehousing regulations, any goods which have been entered for warehousing [or are otherwise required to be deposited in a warehouse] are removed without being duly warehoused or are otherwise not duly warehoused; or

(c) any goods which have been deposited in a warehouse or Queen's warehouse are unlawfully removed therefrom or are unlawfully loaded into any ship, aircraft or vehicle for removal or for exportation or use as stores; or

[(d) any goods are concealed at a time before they are warehoused when they have been entered for warehousing or are otherwise required to be deposited in a warehouse or when they are required to be in the custody or under the control of the occupier of a warehouse; or]

(e) any goods which have been lawfully permitted to be removed from a warehouse or Queen's warehouse without payment of duty for any purpose are not duly delivered at the destination to which they should have been taken in accordance with that permission,

those goods shall be liable to forfeiture.

(3) If any person who took, removed, loaded or concealed any goods as mentioned in subsection (2) above did so with intent to defraud Her Majesty of any duty chargeable thereon or to evade any prohibition or restriction for the time being in force with respect thereto under or by virtue of any enactment, he shall be guilty of an offence under this subsection and may be [arrested].

(4) A person guilty of an offence under subsection (3) above shall be liable—

    (a)   on summary conviction, to a penalty of the prescribed sum or of three times the value of the goods, whichever is the greater, or to imprisonment for a term not exceeding 6 months, or to both; or

    (b)   on conviction on indictment, to a penalty of any amount, or to imprisonment for a term not exceeding [7 years], or to both.

NOTES

Sub-s (1): reference to a level on the standard scale substituted by virtue of the Criminal Justice Act 1982, ss 38, 46; word in second pair of square brackets substituted by the Police and Criminal Evidence Act 1984, s 114(1).

Sub-s (2): words in square brackets in paras (a), (b), inserted, and para (d) substituted, by the Finance (No 2) Act 1992, s 3, Sch 2, para 3.

Sub-s (3): word in square brackets substituted by the Police and Criminal Evidence Act 1984, s 114(1).

Sub-s (4): words in square brackets in para (b) substituted, in relation to offences committed after 29 July 1988, by the Finance Act 1988, s 12(1)(a), (6).

[PART VIIIA
FREE ZONES

100A Designation of free zones

(1) The Treasury may by order designate any area in the United Kingdom as a special area for customs purposes.

(2) An area so designated shall be known as a "free zone".

(3) An order under subsection (1) above—

    (a)   shall have effect for such period as shall be specified in the order;

    (b)   may be made so as to take effect, in relation to the area or any part of the area designated by a previous order under this section, on the expiry of the period specified in the previous order;

    (c)   shall appoint one or more persons as the responsible authority or authorities for the free zone;

    (d)   may impose on any responsible authority such conditions or restrictions as may be specified; and

    (e)   may be revoked if the Commissioners are satisfied that there has been a failure to comply with any condition or restriction.

(4) The Treasury may by order—

    (a)   from time to time vary—

        (i)   the conditions or restrictions imposed by a designation order; or

        (ii)   with the agreement of the responsible authority, the area designated; or

    (b)   appoint one or more persons as the responsible authority or authorities for a free zone either in addition to or in substitution for any person appointed as such by a designation order.

(5) In this Act "designation order" means an order made under subsection (1) above.

(6) Any order under this section shall be made by statutory instrument.]

NOTES

Part VIIIA (ss 100A–100F) inserted by the Finance Act 1984, s 8, Sch 4, Pt I.

Orders: the Free Zone (Belfast Airport) Designation Order 1984, SI 1984/1206, as amended by SI 1986/1643; the Free Zone (Cardiff) Designation Order 1984, SI 1986/1208; the Free Zone (Birmingham Airport) Designation Order 1991, SI 1991/1737, as amended by SI 1994/2509; the Free Zone (Liverpool) Designation Order 1991, SI 1991/1738, as amended by SI 1999/3122; the Free Zone (Prestwick Airport) Designation Order 1991, SI 1991/1739; the Free Zone (Southampton) Designation Order 1991, SI 1991/1740, as amended by SI 1994/1410, SI 1996/2615; the Free Zone (Port of Tilbury) Designation Order 1992, SI 1992/1282, as amended by SI 1994/2216; the Free Zone (Port of Sheerness) Designation Order 1994, SI 1994/2898, as amended by SI 1997/994; the Free Zone (Humberside) Designation Order 1994, SI 1994/144, as amended by SI 1995/1067.

100B–100E

(Inserted by the Finance Act 1984, s 8, Sch 4, Pt I; ss 100B, 100C repealed, subject to transitional provisions, by the Value Added Tax Act 1994, s 100(1), (2), Schs 13, 15; ss 100D, 100E repealed by the Free Zone Regulations 1991, SI 1991/2727, reg 3(1).)

[100F Powers of search

(1) Any person entering or leaving a free zone shall answer such questions as any officer may put to him with respect to any goods and shall, if required by the officer, produce those goods for examination at such place as the Commissioners may direct.

(2) At any time while a vehicle is entering or leaving a free zone, any officer may board the vehicle and search any part of it.

(3) Any officer may at any time enter upon and inspect a free zone and all buildings and goods within the zone.]

NOTES

Inserted as noted to s 100A.

[PART VIIIB
REGISTERED EXCISE DEALERS AND SHIPPERS

100G Registered excise dealers and shippers

(1) For the purpose of administering, collecting or protecting the revenues derived from duties of excise, the Commissioners may by regulations under this section (in this Act referred to as "registered excise dealers and shippers regulations")—

    (a)   confer or impose such powers, duties, privileges and liabilities as may be prescribed in the regulations upon any person who is or has been a registered excise dealer and shipper; and

    (b)   impose on persons other than registered excise dealers and shippers, or in respect of any goods of a class or description specified in the regulations, such requirements or restrictions as may by or under the regulations be prescribed with respect to registered excise dealers and shippers or any activities carried on by them.

(2) The Commissioners may approve, and enter in a register maintained by them for the purpose, any revenue trader who applies for registration under this section and

who appears to them to satisfy such requirements for registration as they may think fit to impose.

(3) In the customs and excise Acts "registered excise dealer and shipper" means a revenue trader approved and registered by the Commissioners under this section.

(4) The Commissioners may approve and register a person under this section for such periods and subject to such conditions or restrictions as they may think fit or as they may by or under the regulations prescribe.

(5) The Commissioners may at any time for reasonable cause revoke or vary the terms of their approval or registration of any person under this section.

(6) The regulations may make provision for treating revenue traders as approved and registered under this section in cases where they are members of a group of companies (within the meaning of the regulations) which is approved and registered in accordance with the regulations.]

NOTES

Part VIIIB (ss 100G–100J) inserted by the Finance Act 1991, s 11(3), Sch 4.

Regulations: the Excise Goods (Holding, Movement, Warehousing and REDS) Regulations 1992, SI 1992/3135, as amended by SI 1993/1228, SI 1999/1278, SI 1999/1565; the Beer Regulations 1993, SI 1993/1228, as amended by SI 1995/3059, SI 2000/3213; the Excise Duty Point (External and Internal Community Transit Procedure) Regulations 1998, SI 1998/202, as amended by SI 1998/3110; the Warehousekeepers and Owners of Warehoused Goods Regulations 1999, SI 1999/1278; the Excise Goods (Sales on Board Ships and Aircraft) Regulations 1999, SI 1999/1565.

[**100H Registered excise dealers and shippers regulations**

(1) Without prejudice to the generality of section 100G above, registered excise dealers and shippers regulations may, in particular, make provision—

(a) regulating the approval and registration of persons as registered excise dealers and shippers and the variation or revocation of any such approval or registration or of any condition or restriction to which such an approval or registration is subject;

(b) regulating any activities carried on by or for a registered excise dealer and shipper and, in particular, the importation, exportation, buying, selling, loading, unloading, delivery, movement, holding, deposit, security, treatment or removal of, or the carrying out of operations on, or the effecting of any other transaction relating to, any goods of a class or description subject to a duty of excise;

(c) authorising a registered excise dealer and shipper to carry out or arrange for the carrying out of any prescribed activity falling within paragraph (b) above in relation to goods chargeable with a duty of excise which has not been paid, but subject to prescribed conditions or restrictions and to prescribed requirements for the payment of the unpaid duty;

(d) exempting registered excise dealers and shippers from compliance with such provisions made by or under the customs and excise Acts as may be prescribed, or applying such provisions in relation to registered excise dealers and shippers with prescribed modifications or adaptations, or applying in relation to registered excise dealers and shippers such substitute provisions as may be prescribed in place of any such provisions;

(e) requiring, except as otherwise permitted by the Commissioners, goods which are subject to a duty of excise that has not been paid and which are not consigned to an excise warehouse—

>   (i)   to be consigned to a registered excise dealer and shipper; and
>
>   (ii)   to be accompanied by such documents in such form and such manner and containing such particulars as may be prescribed;
>
> (f)   . . .
>
> (g)   for securing and collecting any duty of excise [on goods which have been or may be the subject of a transaction involving a registered excise dealer and shipper];
>
> [(h)   for determining, in relation to goods which are the subject of a transaction involving a registered excise dealer and shipper, the duties of excise chargeable on those goods and the rates of those duties and, in that connection, the method of charging the duties;]
>
> (j)   permitting payment of excise duty by a registered excise dealer and shipper to be deferred, subject to compliance with prescribed conditions;
>
> (k)   for relieving registered excise dealers and shippers from liability to pay excise duty on goods in prescribed circumstances;
>
> (l)   for cases where a registered excise dealer and shipper acts as agent for some other person (whether a registered excise dealer and shipper or not);
>
> (m)   requiring registered excise dealers and shippers to keep and make available for inspection such records relating to their activities as such as may be prescribed;
>
> [(ma)   imposing requirements with respect to, or to the production of, the documents required to accompany goods which are the subject of a transaction involving a registered excise dealer and shipper on any person concerned in any prescribed respect with the carriage of those goods, or providing for the imposition under the regulations of any such requirements;]
>
> (n)   for goods in the United Kingdom which are liable to a duty of excise which has not been paid to be subject to forfeiture for any breach of—
>
>   (i)   registered excise dealers and shippers regulations, so far as relating to goods chargeable with a duty of excise which has not been paid, or
>
>   (ii)   any condition or restriction imposed by or under any such regulations so far as so relating.
>
> [(p)   authorised by section 24AA of the Hydrocarbon Oil Duties Act 1979 (regulation of traders in controlled oil).]

(2) Registered excise dealers and shippers regulations may make different provision for persons or goods of different classes or descriptions, for different circumstances and for different cases.

(3) In this section "prescribed" means prescribed in registered excise dealers and shippers regulations or prescribed by the Commissioners under any such regulations.]

NOTES

Inserted as noted to s 100G.

Sub-s (1): para (f) repealed, words in square brackets in para (g) substituted, para (h) substituted, and para (ma) inserted, by the Finance (No 2) Act 1992, ss 1, 3, 82, Sch 1, para 6, Sch 2, para 4, Sch 18, Pt I; para (p) added by the Finance Act 2002, s 6, Sch 3 para 2.

[100J Contravention of regulations etc

If any person contravenes any provision of registered excise dealers and shippers regulations or fails to comply with any condition or restriction which the Commissioners impose upon him under section 100G above or by or under any such regulations, [his contravention or failure to comply shall attract a penalty under section 9 of the Finance Act 1994 (civil penalties), and any goods in respect of which any person contravenes any provision of any such regulations, or fails to comply with any such condition or restriction, shall be liable to forfeiture.]]

NOTES

Inserted as noted to s 100G.

Words in square brackets substituted by the Finance Act 1994, s 9, Sch 4, Pt I, paras 1, 4.

See the Channel Tunnel (Alcoholic Liquor and Tobacco Products) Order, SI 2003/2758 art 4(d): this section applies, for the purposes of SI 2003/2758, in corresponding manner to events involving goods in a control zone in the same way that it applies to events involving goods in the United Kingdom.

PART IX
CONTROL OF EXCISE LICENCE TRADES AND REVENUE TRADERS

Excise licences—general provisions

101 Excise licences

(1) An excise licence shall be in such form and contain such particulars as the Commissioners may direct and, subject to the provisions of any enactment relating to the licence or trade in question, may be granted by the proper officer on payment of [any appropriate duty].

(2) An excise licence for the carrying on of a trade shall be granted in respect of one set of premises only, but a licence for the same trade may be granted to the same person in respect of each of two or more sets of premises.

(3) Where an excise licence trade is carried on at any set of premises by two or more persons in partnership, then, subject to the provisions of any enactment relating to the licence or trade in question, not more than one licence shall be required to be [held] by those persons in respect of those premises [at any one time].

(4) Without prejudice to any other requirement as to the production of licences contained in the Customs and Excise Acts 1979, if any person who is the holder of an excise licence to carry on any trade or to manufacture or sell any goods fails to produce his licence for examination within [one month] after being so requested by an officer [his failure shall attract a penalty under section 9 of the Finance Act 1994 (civil penalties).]

NOTES

Sub-ss (1), (3): words in square brackets substituted by the Finance Act 1986, s 8(6), Sch 5, para 1.

Sub-s (4): words in square brackets substituted by the Finance Act 1994, s 9, Sch 4, Pt I, paras 1, 5.

102 Payment for excise licences by cheque

(1) Any government department or local authority having power to grant an excise licence may, if they think fit, grant the licence upon receipt of a cheque for the amount of [any duty] payable thereon.

(2) Where a licence is granted to any person on receipt of a cheque and the cheque is subsequently dishonoured, the licence shall be void as from the time when it was granted, and the department or authority who granted it shall send to that person, by letter sent by registered post or the recorded delivery service and addressed to him at

the address given by him when applying for the licence, a notice requiring him to deliver up the licence within the period of 7 days from the date when the notice was posted.

(3) If a person who has been required under subsection (2) above to deliver up a licence fails to comply with the requirement within the period mentioned in that subsection he shall be liable on summary conviction to a penalty of the following amount, that is to say—

(a) where the licence is a gaming licence or [an amusement machine licence], a penalty of [level 5 on the standard scale];

[(aa) where the licence is a licence under [the Vehicle Excise and Registration Act 1994], a penalty of whichever is the greater of—

(i) level 3 on the standard scale, or

(ii) an amount equal to five times the annual rate of duty that was payable on the grant of the licence or would have been so payable if it had been taken out for a period of twelve months]

(b) in any other case, a penalty of [level 3 on the standard scale].

NOTES

Sub-s (1): words in square brackets substituted by virtue of the Finance Act 1986, s 8(6), Sch 5, para 2.

Sub-s (3): words in square brackets in para (a) substituted by the Finance Act 1995, s 14, Sch 3, para 12 (for transitional provision see s 14(2) thereof); reference in para (a) to a level on the standard scale substituted by virtue of the Criminal Justice Act 1982, ss 38, 46; para (aa) inserted by the Finance Act 1987, s 2(1), (6), (8)(c), Sch 1, Pt III, para 20, words in square brackets therein substituted by the Vehicle Excise and Registration Act 1994, s 63, Sch 3, para 15; reference in para (b) to a level on the standard scale substituted by virtue of the Criminal Justice Act 1982, ss 38, 46.

103 Renewal of excise licences

(1) Subject to subsection (2) below, where a person who has taken out an excise licence issuable annually in respect of any trade takes out a fresh licence in respect of that trade for the next following licence year, then, subject to the provisions of any enactment relating to the licence or trade in question, the fresh licence shall bear the date of the day immediately following that on which the previous licence expires.

(2) Where an application for the fresh licence is made after the day on which the previous licence expires or such later day as the Commissioners may in any case allow, the licence shall bear the date of the day when the application is made.

104 Transfer and removal of excise licence trades and licences

(1) Subject to any provision of the Customs and Excise Acts 1979 or of any other enactment relating to the licence or trade in question, where the holder of an excise licence to carry on any trade dies, or where the holder of such a licence in respect of premises specified therein leaves those premises, the proper officer may transfer that licence in such manner as the Commissioners may direct, without any additional payment, to some other person for the remainder of the period for which the licence was granted.

(2) Subject to any such provision as aforesaid, where any person who holds an excise licence in respect of any premises removes his trade to other premises on which it may be lawfully carried on, the proper officer may authorise in such manner as the Commissioners may direct the carrying on, without any additional payment other than any required to be paid by subsection (3) below, of that trade on those other premises for the remainder of the period for which the licence was granted.

(3) Where, in a case falling within subsection (2) above, the amount of [any duty] payable on the grant of the licence was determined by reference to the annual value of

the premises in respect of which it was granted and would have been greater if the licence had originally been granted in respect of the premises to which the trade is removed, such additional sum shall be payable as bears the same proportion to the difference as the remainder of the period for which the licence was granted bears to a year.

(4)   Notwithstanding anything in subsections (1) to (3) above, where by any other enactment relating to the licence or trade in question the authorisation of any court or other authority or the production of any certificate is required for such a transfer or removal of an excise licence trade as is mentioned in this section, no transfer or removal of an excise licence to carry on that trade shall be granted unless it is shown to the satisfaction of the proper officer that the authorisation or certificate has been granted.

NOTES

Sub-s (3): words in square brackets substituted by the Finance Act 1986, s 8(6), Sch 5, para 2.

105, 106

(Repealed by the Finance Act 1981, ss 11, 139(6), Sch 8, Pt I, para 5, Sch 19, Pt III.)

107 Power to require person carrying on excise licence trade to display sign

(1)   The Commissioners may require any person holding an excise licence to carry on any trade to affix to and maintain on the premises in respect of which the licence is granted, in such form and manner and containing such particulars as they may direct, a notification of the person to whom and the purpose for which the licence is granted.

(2)   If any person contravenes or fails to comply with any requirement made or direction given under this section [his contravention or failure to comply shall attract a penalty under section 9 of the Finance Act 1994 (civil penalties).]

(3)   If any person not duly licensed to carry on an excise licence trade affixes to any premises any sign or notice purporting to show that he is so licensed [his doing so shall attract a penalty under section 9 of the Finance Act 1994 (civil penalties).]

NOTES

Sub-ss (2), (3): words in square brackets substituted by the Finance Act 1994, s 9, Sch 4, Pt I, paras 1, 6.

General provisions as to entries of premises, etc

108 Making of entries

(1)   Where by or under the revenue trade provisions of the customs and excise Acts any person is required to make entry of any premises or article—

(a)   the entry shall be made in such form and manner and contain such particulars; and

(b)   the premises or article shall be, and be kept, marked in such manner, as the Commissioners may direct.

(2)   No entry shall be valid unless the person by whom it was made—

(a)   had at the time of its making attained the age of 18 years; and

(b)   was at that time and is for the time being a true and real owner of the trade in respect of which the entry was made.

(3)   Where any person required to make entry is a body corporate—

(a)   the entry shall be signed by a director, general manager, secretary or other similar officer of the body and, except where authority for that person to sign has been given under the seal of the body, shall be made under that seal; and

(b)   both the body corporate and the person by whom the entry is signed shall be liable for all duties charged in respect of the trade to which the entry relates.

(4)   If any person making entry of any premises or article contravenes or fails to comply with any direction of the Commissioners given under this section with respect thereto, [his contravention or failure to comply shall attract a penalty under section 9 of the Finance Act 1994 (civil penalties).]

NOTES

Sub-s (4): words in square brackets substituted with savings by the Finance Act 1994, s 9, Sch 4, Pt I, paras 1, 7.

109 New or further entries of same premises

(1)   The Commissioners may at any time, by notice in writing to the person by whom any existing entry was signed addressed to him at any premises entered by him, require a new entry to be made of any premises or article to which the existing entry relates, and the existing entry shall, without prejudice to any liability incurred, become void at the expiration of 14 days from the delivery of the notice.

(2)   Save as permitted by the Commissioners and subject to such conditions as they may impose, no premises or article of which entry has been made by any person shall, while that entry remains in force, be entered by any other person for any purpose of the revenue trade provisions of the customs and excise Acts, and any entry made in contravention of this subsection shall be void.

(3)   Where the person by whom entry has been made of any premises absconds or quits possession of the premises and discontinues the trade in respect of which the entry was made, and the Commissioners permit a further entry to be made of the premises by some other person, the former entry shall be deemed to have been withdrawn and shall be void.

110 Proof as to entries

For the purpose of any proceedings before any court, if any question arises as to whether or not entry under the revenue trade provisions of the customs and excise Acts has been made by any person, or of any premises or article, or for any purpose, then—

(a)   if a document purporting to be an original entry made by the person, or of the premises or article, or for the purpose, in question is produced to the court by an officer, that document shall, until the contrary is proved, be sufficient evidence that the entry was so made; and

(b)   if the officer in whose custody any such entry, if made, would be gives evidence that the original entries produced by him to the court constitute all those in his custody and that no such entry as is in question is among them, it shall be deemed, until the contrary is proved, that no such entry has been made.

111 Offences in connection with entries

(1)   If any person uses for any purpose of his trade any premises or article required by or under the revenue trade provisions of the customs and excise Acts to be entered for that purpose without entry having been duly made thereof, [his use of the premises

or article shall attract a penalty under section 9 of the Finance Act 1994 (civil penalties), and any] such article and any goods found on any such premises or in any such article shall be liable to forfeiture.

(2) . . .

NOTES

Sub-s (1): words in square brackets substituted by the Finance Act 1994, s 9, Sch 4, Pt I, paras 1, 8(1).

Sub-s (2): repealed by the Finance Act 1994, ss 9, 258, Sch 4, para 8(2), Sch 26, Pt II.

General provisions as to revenue traders

112 Power of entry upon premises, etc of revenue traders

(1) An officer may, subject to subsection (2) below, at any time enter upon any premises of which entry is made, or is required by or under the revenue trade provisions of the customs and excise Acts to be made, or any other premises owned or used by a revenue trader for the purposes of his trade and may inspect the premises and search for, examine and take account of any machinery, [vehicles], vessels, utensils, goods or materials belonging to or in any way connected with that trade.

(2) Except in the case of such traders as are mentioned in subsection (3) below, no officer shall exercise the powers conferred on him by subsection (1) above by night unless he is accompanied by a constable.

(3) Where any such premises as are mentioned in subsection (1) above are those of a distiller, rectifier, compounder, [registered brewer], producer of wine, producer of made-wine[, maker of cider or occupier of an excise warehouse], and an officer, after having demanded admission into the premises and declared his name and business at the entrance thereof, is not immediately admitted, that officer and any person acting in his aid may, subject to subsection (4) below, break open any door or window of the premises or break through any wall thereof for the purpose of obtaining admission.

(4) No officer or person acting in his aid shall exercise the powers conferred on him by subsection (3) above by night unless he is accompanied by a constable.

(5) Subsection (1) above applies to vehicles, vessels, aircraft, hovercraft or structures in or from which tobacco products are sold or dealt in or dutiable alcoholic liquors are sold by retail as it applies to premises.

(6) This section applies to the occupier of a refinery as it applies to a distiller, whether or not the occupier is a revenue trader.

NOTES

Sub-s (1): word in square brackets inserted by the Finance Act 1981, s 11(1), Sch 8, Pt I, para 6.

Sub-s (3): words in first pair of square brackets substituted by the Finance Act 1991, s 7(4), Sch 2, para 1; words in second pair of square brackets substituted by the Finance Act 1981, s 11(1), Sch 8, Pt I, para 6.

113 Power to search for concealed pipes, etc

(1) If an officer has reasonable grounds to suspect that any secret pipe or other means of conveyance, cock, vessel or utensil is kept or used by a revenue trader to whom this section applies, that officer may, subject to subsection (2) below, at any time, break open any part of the premises of that trader and forcibly enter thereon and so far as is reasonably necessary break up the ground in or adjoining those premises or any wall thereof to search for that pipe or other means of conveyance, cock, vessel or utensil.

(2)   No officer shall exercise the powers conferred on him by subsection (1) above by night unless he is accompanied by a constable.

(3)   If the officer finds any such pipe or other form of conveyance leading to or from the trader's premises, he may enter any other premises from or into which it leads, and so far as is reasonably necessary break up any part of those other premises to trace its course, and may cut it away and turn any cock thereon, and examine whether it conveys or conceals any goods chargeable with a duty of excise, or any materials used in the manufacture of such goods, in such manner as to prevent a true account thereof from being taken.

(4)   Every such pipe or other means of conveyance, cock, vessel or utensil as aforesaid, and all goods chargeable with a duty of excise or materials for the manufacture of such goods found therein, shall be liable to forfeiture . . .

(5)   If any damage is done in any such search as aforesaid and the search is unsuccessful, the Commissioners shall make good the damage.

(6)   The revenue traders to whom this section applies are distillers, rectifiers, compounders, [registered brewers], producers of wine, producers of made-wine and makers of cider.

(7)   This section also applies to the occupier of a refinery as it applies to the traders mentioned in subsection (6) above, whether or not the occupier is a revenue trader.

NOTES

Sub-s (4): words omitted repealed by the Finance Act 1994, s 258, Sch 26, Pt III.

Sub-s (6): words in square brackets substituted by the Finance Act 1991, s 7, Sch 2, para 1.

114   Power to prohibit use of certain substances in exciseable goods

(1)   If it appears to the satisfaction of the Commissioners that any substance or liquor is used, or is capable of being used, in the manufacture or preparation for sale of any goods chargeable, as goods manufactured or produced in the United Kingdom, with a duty of excise, and that that substance or liquor is of a noxious or detrimental nature or, being a chemical or artificial extract or product, may affect prejudicially the interests of the revenue, the Commissioners may by regulations prohibit the use of that substance or liquor in the manufacture or preparation for sale of any goods specified in the regulations.

(2)   If while any such regulations are in force any person knowingly uses a substance or liquor thereby prohibited in the manufacture or preparation for sale of any goods specified in the regulations [his use of that substance or liquor in that manner shall attract a penalty under section 9 of the Finance Act 1994 (civil penalties); but section 10 of that Act (exception for cases of reasonable excuse) shall not apply in relation to conduct attracting a penalty by virtue of this subsection.]

(3)   Any substance or liquor the use of which is for the time being prohibited by any such regulations found in the possession of any person licensed for the manufacture or sale of any goods specified in the regulations, and any goods in the manufacture or preparation of which any substance or liquid has been used contrary to any such prohibition, shall be liable to forfeiture.

NOTES

Sub-s (2): words in square brackets substituted by the Finance Act 1994, s 9, Sch 4, Pt I, paras 1, 9.

115 Power to keep specimen on premises of revenue traders

(1) The proper officer may place and leave on the premises of a revenue trader a specimen, that is to say, a document in which may be entered any particulars relating to the trader's trade from time to time recorded by that or any other officer.

(2) Any such specimen shall be deposited at some place on premises entered by the trader where convenient access may be had thereto at any time by the trader and by any officer, and any officer may at any time remove the specimen and deposit a new one in its place.

(3) Where any charge of duty made by an officer upon a trader is not recorded in a specimen, the officer shall, if so required in writing by the trader at the time when the officer takes his account for the purpose of charging duty, give to the trader a copy of the charge in writing under his hand.

(4) If [the revenue trader] removes, conceals, withholds, damages or destroys a specimen, or alters, defaces, or obliterates any entry therein, [his doing so shall attract a penalty under section 9 of the Finance Act 1994 (civil penalties).]

[(5) For the purposes of subsection (4) above and without prejudice to section 10(1) of the Finance Act 1994 (exception for cases of reasonable excuse), conduct by an employee of the revenue trader or by any other person entitled to act on the trader's behalf in connection with his trade shall be deemed to be conduct by that trader except in so far as he took all reasonable steps to prevent it.]

NOTES
Sub-s (4): words in square brackets substituted by the Finance Act 1994, s 9, Sch 4, Pt I, paras 1, 10(1).

Sub-s (5): added by the Finance Act 1994, s 9, Sch 4, Pt I, paras 1, 10(2).

116 Payment of excise duty by revenue traders

(1) Every revenue trader shall pay any duty of excise payable in respect of his trade at or within such time, at such place and to such person as the Commissioners may direct whether or not payment of that duty has been secured by bond or otherwise.

(2) If any duty payable is not paid in accordance with subsection (1) above, it shall be paid on demand made by the Commissioners either to the trader personally or by delivering the demand in writing at his place of abode or business.

(3) If any duty is not paid on demand made under subsection (2) above [the trader's failure to pay the duty on demand shall attract a penalty under section 9 of the Finance Act 1994 (civil penalties) which shall be calculated by reference to the amount of the duty demanded and shall also attract daily penalties.]

NOTES
Sub-s (3): words in square brackets substituted by the Finance Act 1994, s 9, Sch 4, Pt I, paras 1, 11.

116A

(Inserted by the Finance Act 1981, s 11(1), Sch 8, Pt I, para 7 and repealed by the Finance Act 1994, s 258, Sch 26, Pt III.)

117 Execution and distress against revenue traders

(1) Where any sum is owing by a revenue trader in respect of any . . . excise duty or of any relevant penalty, all the following things which are in the possession or

custody of that trader or of any agent of his or of any other person on his behalf shall be liable to be taken in execution in default of the payment of that sum, that is to say—

  (a)   all goods liable to [any] excise duty, whether or not that duty has been paid;

  (b)   all materials for manufacturing or producing any such goods; and

  (c)   all apparatus, equipment, machinery, tools, vessels and utensils for, or for preparing any such materials for, such manufacture or production, or by which the trade in respect of which the duty is imposed is carried on.

[(1A)   In subsection (1) above as it applies in relation to a sum owing by a revenue trader in respect of lottery duty or of a relevant penalty—

  (a)   references to goods liable to any excise duty include lottery tickets on the taking of which lottery duty will be chargeable, and

  (b)   "the trade in respect of which the duty is imposed" includes any trade or business carried on by the revenue trader that consists of or includes the buying, selling, importation, exportation, dealing in or handling of tickets or chances on the taking of which lottery duty is or will be chargeable.]

(2)   Subsection (1) above shall also apply in relation to things falling within paragraph (a), (b) or (c) of that subsection which, although they are not still in the possession or custody of the trader, an agent of his or other person on his behalf, were in such possession or custody—

  (a)   at the time when the . . . . excise duty was charged or became chargeable or at any time while it was owing; or

  (b)   at the time of the commission of the offence for which the penalty was incurred.

(3)   Notwithstanding anything in subsection (1) or (2) above, but subject to subsection (4) below, where the proper officer has taken account of and charged any goods chargeable with [any] excise duty and those goods are in the ordinary course of trade sold for full and valuable consideration to a bona fide purchaser and delivered into his possession before the issue of any warrant or process for distress or seizure of the goods, those goods shall not be liable to be seized under this section.

(4)   Where any goods have been seized under this section, the burden of proof that the goods are by virtue of subsection (3) above not liable to be so seized shall lie upon the person claiming that they are not so liable.

[(4A)   This section does not apply for the purposes of levying distress in accordance with regulations under section 51 of the Finance Act 1997 or for the purposes of any execution under section 52 of that Act by diligence.]

(5)–(7A)   . . .

(8)   In this section—

    . . . .

    "relevant penalty" means a penalty incurred under the revenue trade provisions of the customs and excise Acts.

[(9)   This section shall apply to Scotland subject to the following modifications—

  (a)   in subsection (3) for the words from "issue" to the end there shall be substituted the words "granting of a warrant for the recovery of a sum owing by the revenue trader, those goods shall not be liable to be taken in execution under this section.";

  (b)   in subsection (4) for the word "seized" in both places where it occurs there shall be substituted the words "taken in execution";

  (c)–(f)   . . . .

(10)   . . .]

NOTES

Sub-s (1): word omitted repealed and word in square brackets substituted by the Finance (No 2) Act 1992, ss 3, 82, Sch 2, para 5, Sch 18, Pt I.

Sub-s (1A): inserted by the Finance Act 1993, s 30(4).

Sub-ss (2), (8): words omitted repealed by the Finance (No 2) Act 1992, ss 3, 82, Sch 2, para 5, Sch 18, Pt I.

Sub-s (3): word in square brackets substituted by the Finance (No 2) Act 1992, s 3, Sch 2, para 5.

Sub-s (4A): inserted by the Finance Act 1997, s 53(1).

Sub-ss (5)–(7A), (10): repealed by the Finance Act 1997, s 113, Sch 18, Pt V(2) (sub-s (7A) originally inserted by the Finance Act 1981, s 11(1), Sch 8, Pt I, para 8).

Sub-s (9): substituted, together with sub-s (10) (repealed), for original sub-s (9) by the Debtors (Scotland) Act 1987, s 108(1), Sch 6, para 21; paras (c)–(f) repealed by the Finance Act 1997, s 113, Sch 18, Pt V(2).

118 Liability of ostensible owner or principal manager

Any person who acts ostensibly as the owner or who is a principal manager of the business of a revenue trader in respect of which entry of any premises or article has been made or who occupies or uses any entered premises or article shall, notwithstanding that he is under full age, be liable in like manner as the real and true owner of the business for all duties charged and all penalties incurred in respect of that business.

[PART IXA

PROTECTION OF THE REVENUES DERIVED FROM EXCISE DUTIES

118A Duty of revenue traders to keep records

(1)   The Commissioners may by regulations require every revenue trader—

    (a)   to keep such records as may be prescribed in the regulations; and

    (b)   to preserve those records for such period not exceeding six years as may be prescribed in the regulations or for such lesser period as the Commissioners may require.

(2)   Regulations under this section—

    (a)   may make different provision for different cases; and

    (b)   may be framed by reference to such records as may be specified in any notice published by the Commissioners in pursuance of the regulations and not withdrawn by a further notice.

(3)   Any duty imposed under this section to preserve records may be discharged by the preservation of the information contained therein by such means as the Commissioners may approve.

(4)   Where any information is preserved in accordance with subsection (3) above, a copy of any document forming part of the records in question shall, subject to the following provisions of this section, be admissible in evidence in any proceedings, whether civil or criminal, to the same extent as the records themselves.

(5)   The Commissioners may, as a condition of approving under subsection (3) above any means of preserving information contained in any records, impose such reasonable requirements as appear to them necessary for securing that the information will be as readily available to them as if the records themselves had been preserved.

(6)   A statement contained in a document produced by a computer shall not by virtue of subsection (4) above be admissible in evidence—

    (a)   . . .;

    (b)   in criminal proceedings in England and Wales, except in accordance with . . . Part II of the Criminal Justice Act 1988;

(c)   in criminal proceedings in Scotland, except in accordance with [sections 5 and 6 of the Civil Evidence (Scotland) Act 1988];

(d)   in criminal proceedings in Scotland, [except in accordance with Schedule 3 to the Prisoners and Criminal Proceedings (Scotland) Act 1993];

(e)   . . .; and

(f)   in criminal proceedings in Northern Ireland, except in accordance with *Article 68 of the Police and Criminal Evidence (Northern Ireland) Order 1989* and Part II of the Criminal Justice (Evidence Etc) (Northern Ireland) Order 1988.

(7)   . . .]

NOTES

Part IXA (ss 118A–118G) inserted by the Finance Act 1991, s 12, Sch 5.

Sub-s (6): para (a) repealed by the Civil Evidence Act 1995, s 15(2), Sch 2; words in para (b) repealed by the Youth Justice and Criminal Evidence Act 1999, s 67(3), Sch 6, as from 14 April 2000; words in square brackets in paras (c), (d) substituted by the Finance Act 1994, s 256(3); para (e) repealed by the Civil Evidence (Northern Ireland) Order 1997, SI 1997/2983 (NI 21), art 13(2), Sch 2, subject to savings; words in italics in para (f) repealed by the Criminal Evidence (Northern Ireland) Order 1999, SI 1999/2789 (NI 8), art 40(3), Sch 3, as from a day to be appointed.

Sub-s (7): repealed by the Finance Act 1994, ss 256(4), 258, Sch 26, Pt VIII.

Regulations: the Revenue Traders (Accounts and Records) Regulations 1992, SI 1992/3150, as amended by SI 1998/62; the Beer Regulations 1993, SI 1993/1228, as amended by SI 1995/3059, SI 2000/3213; the Tobacco Products (Amendment) Regulations 1993/2167; the Aircraft Operators (Accounts and Records) Regulations 1994, SI 1994/1737, as amended by SI 1998/63; the Cider and Perry (Amendment) Regulations 1996, SI 1996/2287; the Wine and Made-wine (Amendment) Regulations 1996, SI 1996/2752; the Excise Goods (Sales on Board Ships and Aircraft) Regulations 1999, SI 1999/1565.

[118B Duty of revenue traders and others to furnish information and produce documents

(1)   Every revenue trader shall—

(a)   furnish to the Commissioners, within such time and in such form as they may reasonably require, such information relating to—

(i)   any goods or services supplied by or to him in the course or furtherance of a business, or

(ii)   any goods in the importation or exportation of which he is concerned in the course or furtherance of a business, [or

(iii)   any transaction or activity effected or taking place in the course or furtherance of a business,]

as they may reasonably specify; and

(b)   upon demand made by an officer, produce or cause to be produced for inspection by that officer—

(i)   at the principal place of business of the revenue trader or at such other place as the officer may reasonably require, and

(ii)   at such time as the officer may reasonably require,

any documents relating to the goods or services or to the supply, importation or exportation [or to the transaction or activity].

(2)   Where, by virtue of subsection (1) above, an officer has power to require the production of any documents from a revenue trader—

(a)   he shall have the like power to require production of the documents concerned from any other person who appears to the officer to be in possession of them; but

(b)   if that other person claims a lien on any document produced by him, the production shall be without prejudice to the lien.

(3) For the purposes of this section, the documents relating to the supply of goods or services, or the importation or exportation of goods, in the course or furtherance of any business[, or to any transaction or activity effected or taking place in the course or furtherance of any business,] shall be taken to include—

(a)   any profit and loss account and balance sheet, and

(b)   any records required to be kept by virtue of section 118A above,

relating to that business.

(4) An officer may take copies of, or make extracts from, any document produced under subsection (1) or (2) above.

(5) If it appears to an officer to be necessary to do so, he may, at a reasonable time and for a reasonable period, remove any document produced under subsection (1) or (2) above and shall, on request, provide a receipt for any document so removed.

(6) Where a lien is claimed on a document produced under subsection (2) above, the removal of the document under subsection (5) above shall not be regarded as breaking the lien.

(7) Where a document removed by an officer under subsection (5) above is reasonably required for the proper conduct of a business he shall, as soon as practicable, provide a copy of the document, free of charge, to the person by whom it was produced or caused to be produced.

(8) Where any documents removed under the powers conferred by this section are lost or damaged, the Commissioners shall be liable to compensate their owner for any expenses reasonably incurred by him in replacing or repairing the documents.]

NOTES

Inserted as noted to s 118A.

Sub-ss (1), (3): words in square brackets inserted or added by the Finance Act 1997, s 13(2), Sch 2, Pt I, paras 1, 3.

[118C Entry and search of premises and persons

(1) For the purpose of exercising any powers under the customs and excise Acts an officer may at any reasonable time enter premises used in connection with the carrying on of a business.

(2) Where an officer has reasonable cause to believe that any premises are used in connection with the supply, importation or exportation of goods of a class or description chargeable with a duty of excise and that any such goods are on those premises, he may at any reasonable time enter and inspect those premises and inspect any goods found on them.

[(2A) Where an officer has reasonable cause to believe that any premises are premises where gaming to which section 10 of the Finance Act 1997 (gaming duty) applies is taking place, has taken place or is about to take place, he may at any reasonable time enter and inspect those premises and inspect any relevant materials found on them.

(2B) In subsection (2A) above "relevant materials" means—

(a)   any accounts, records or other documents found on the premises in the custody or control of any person who is engaging, or whom the officer reasonably suspects of engaging—

(i)   in any such gaming, or

   (ii)   in any activity by reason of which he is or may become liable to
         gaming duty, and
  (b)   any equipment which is being, or which the officer reasonably suspects
         of having been or of being intended to be, used on the premises for or in
         connection with any such gaming.]

(3)   If a justice of the peace or, in Scotland, a justice (within the meaning of
[section 307 of the Criminal Procedure (Scotland) Act 1995]) is satisfied on
information on oath—

  (a)   that there is reasonable ground for suspecting that a fraud offence
         which appears to be of a serious nature is being, has been or is about to
         be committed on any premises, or
  (b)   that evidence of the commission of such an offence is to be found there,
         [or
  (c)   that there is reasonable ground for suspecting—
         (i)   that gaming to which section 10 of the Finance Act 1997 applies is
                taking place, has taken place or is about to take place on any
                premises, or
         (ii)   that evidence of the commission of a gaming duty offence is to be
                found there,]

he may issue a warrant in writing authorising, subject to subsections (6) and (7) below,
any officer to enter those premises, if necessary by force, at any time within the period
of one month beginning with the date of the issue of the warrant and search them.

(4)   Any officer who enters premises under the authority of a warrant under
subsection (3) above may—

  (a)   take with him such other persons as appear to him to be necessary;
  (b)   seize and remove any documents or other things whatsoever found on
         the premises which he has reasonable cause to believe may be required
         as evidence for the purposes of proceedings in respect of a fraud offence
         which appears to him to be of a serious nature [or in respect of a gaming
         duty offence]; and
  (c)   search or cause to be searched any person found on the premises whom
         he has reasonable cause to believe to be in possession of any such
         documents or other things;

but no woman or girl shall be searched by virtue of this subsection except by a
woman.

(5)   In subsections (3) and (4) above "a fraud offence" means an offence under any
provision of section 167(1), 168 or 170 below [and "a gaming duty offence" means an
offence under paragraph 12(2) of Schedule 1 to the Finance Act 1997 (offences in
connection with gaming duty)].

(6)   The powers conferred by a warrant under this section shall not be
exercisable—

  (a)   by more than such number of officers as may be specified in the
         warrant; nor
  (b)   outside such times of day as may be so specified; nor
  (c)   if the warrant so provides, otherwise than in the presence of a constable
         in uniform.

(7)   An officer seeking to exercise the powers conferred by a warrant under this
section or, if there is more than one such officer, that one of them who is in charge of
the search shall provide a copy of the warrant endorsed with his name as follows—

  (a)   if the occupier of the premises concerned is present at the time the
         search is to begin, the copy shall be supplied to the occupier;

(b)　　if at the time the occupier is not present but a person who appears to the officer to be in charge of the premises is present, the copy shall be supplied to that person; and

(c)　　if neither paragraph (a) nor paragraph (b) above applies, the copy shall be left in a prominent place on the premises.]

NOTES

Inserted as noted to s 118A.

Sub-ss (2A), (2B): inserted by the Finance Act 1997, s 13(2), Sch 2, Pt I, paras 1, 4(1), (2).

Sub-s (3): words in first pair of square brackets substituted by the Criminal Procedure (Consequential Provisions) (Scotland) Act 1995, s 5, Sch 4, para 18(3); para (c), and word "or" preceding it, inserted by the Finance Act 1997, s 13(2), Sch 2, Pt I, paras 1, 4(1), (3).

Sub-ss (4), (5): words in square brackets inserted or added by the Finance Act 1997, s 13(2), Sch 2, Pt I, paras 1, 4(1), (4), (5).

Sub-s (3)(c) and preceding word "or", in sub-s (4)(b) words "or in respect of a gaming duty offence", and in sub-s (5), words from "and "a gaming duty offence"" to the end, to be repealed by the Finance Act 2007, s 114, Sch 27, Pt 5 with effect from a date to be appointed.

[118D　Order for access to recorded information, etc

(1)　Where, on an application by an officer, a justice of the peace or, in Scotland, a justice (within the meaning of [section 307 of the Criminal Procedure (Scotland) Act 1995]) is satisfied that there are reasonable grounds for believing—

(a)　　that an offence in connection with a duty of excise is being, has been or is about to be committed, and

(b)　　that any recorded information (including any document of any nature whatsoever) which may be required as evidence for the purpose of any proceedings in respect of such an offence is in the possession of any person,

he may make an order under this section.

(2)　An order under this section is an order that the person who appears to the justice to be in possession of the recorded information to which the application relates shall—

(a)　　give an officer access to it, and

(b)　　permit an officer to remove and take away any of it which he reasonably considers necessary,

not later than the end of the period of seven days beginning with the date of the order or the end of such longer period as the order may specify.

(3)　The reference in subsection (2)(a) above to giving an officer access to the recorded information to which the application relates includes a reference to permitting the officer to take copies of it or to make extracts from it.

(4)　Where the recorded information consists of information [stored in any electronic form], an order under this section shall have effect as an order to produce the information in a form in which it is visible and legible [or from which it can readily be produced in a visible and legible form] and, if the officer wishes to remove it, in a form in which it can be removed.

(5)　This section is without prejudice to sections 118B and 118C above.]

NOTES

Inserted as noted to s 118A.

Sub-s (1): words in square brackets substituted by the Criminal Procedure (Consequential Provisions) (Scotland) Act 1995, s 5, Sch 4, para 18(4).

Sub-s (4): words substituted and inserted by the Criminal Justice and Police Act 2001, s 70, Sch 2, Pt 2, para 13(1), (2)(e).

[118E Procedure when documents etc are removed

(1) An officer who removes anything in the exercise of a power conferred by or under section 118C or 118D above shall, if so requested by a person showing himself—

(a)　　to be the occupier of premises from which it was removed, or

(b)　　to have had custody or control of it immediately before the removal,

provide that person with a record of what he removed.

(2) The officer shall provide the record within a reasonable time from the making of the request for it.

(3) Subject to subsection (7) below, if a request for permission to be granted access to anything which—

(a)　　has been removed by an officer, and

(b)　　is retained by the Commissioners for the purposes of investigating an offence,

is made to the officer in overall charge of the investigation by a person who had custody or control of the thing immediately before it was so removed or by someone acting on behalf of such a person, the officer shall allow the person who made the request access to it under the supervision of an officer.

(4) Subject to subsection (7) below, if a request for a photograph or copy of any such thing is made to the officer in overall charge of the investigation by a person who had custody or control of the thing immediately before it was so removed, or by someone acting on behalf of such a person, the officer shall—

(a)　　allow the person who made the request access to it under the supervision of an officer for the purpose of photographing it or copying it, or

(b)　　photograph or copy it, or cause it to be photographed or copied.

(5) Where anything is photographed or copied under subsection (4)(b) above, the photograph or copy shall be supplied to the person who made the request.

(6) The photograph or copy shall be supplied within a reasonable time from the making of the request.

(7) There is no duty under this section to grant access to, or to supply a photograph or copy of, anything if the officer in overall charge of the investigation for the purposes of which it was removed has reasonable grounds for believing that to do so would prejudice—

(a)　　that investigation;

(b)　　the investigation of an offence other than the offence for the purposes of the investigation of which the thing was removed; or

(c)　　any criminal proceedings which may be brought as a result of—

(i)　　the investigation of which he is in charge; or

(ii)　　any such investigation as is mentioned in paragraph (b) above.

(8) Any reference in this section to the officer in overall charge of the investigation is a reference to the person whose name and address are endorsed on the warrant or order concerned as being the officer so in charge.]

NOTES

Inserted as noted to s 118A.

[118F Failure of officer to comply with requirements under section 118E

(1)   Where, on an application made as mentioned in subsection (2) below, the appropriate judicial authority is satisfied that a person has failed to comply with a requirement imposed by section 118E above, the authority may order that person to comply with the requirement within such time and in such manner as may be specified in the order.

(2)   An application under subsection (1) above shall be made—

(a)   in the case of a failure to comply with any of the requirements imposed by subsections (1) and (2) of section 118E above, by the occupier of the premises from which the thing in question was removed or by the person who had custody or control of it immediately before it was so removed, and

(b)   in any other case, by the person who has such custody or control.

(3)   In this section "the appropriate judicial authority" means—

(a)   in England and Wales, a magistrates' court;

(b)   in Scotland, the sheriff; and

(c)   in Northern Ireland, a court of summary jurisdiction, as defined in Article 2(2)(a) of the Magistrates' Courts (Northern Ireland) Order 1981.

(4)   Any application for an order under this section—

(a)   in England and Wales, shall be made by way of complaint; or

(b)   in Northern Ireland, shall be made by way of civil proceedings on complaint.

(5)   Sections 21 and 42(2) of the Interpretation Act (Northern Ireland) 1954 (rules and orders regulating procedure of courts etc and assignment of business to particular courts) shall apply as if any reference in those provisions to any enactment included a reference to this section.]

NOTES
Inserted as noted to s 118A.

[118G Offences under Part IXA]
If any person fails to comply with any requirement imposed under section 118A(1) or section 118B above, [his failure to comply shall attract a penalty under section 9 of the Finance Act 1994 (civil penalties) and, in the case of any failure to keep records, shall also attract daily penalties.]]

NOTES
Inserted as noted to s 118A.
Words in square brackets substituted by the Finance Act 1994, s 9, Sch 4, Pt I, paras 1, 12.

PART X

DUTIES AND DRAWBACKS—GENERAL PROVISIONS

General provisions relating to imported goods

119 Delivery of imported goods on giving of security for duty

(1)   Where it is impracticable immediately to ascertain whether any or what duty is payable in respect of any imported goods which are entered for home use [or for free circulation], whether on importation or from warehouse [or free zone], the Commissioners may, if they think fit and notwithstanding any other provision of

the Customs and Excise Acts 1979, allow those goods to be delivered upon the importer giving security by deposit of money or otherwise to their satisfaction for payment of any amount unpaid which may be payable by way of duty.

(2)   The Commissioners may for the purposes of subsection (1) above treat goods as entered for home use notwithstanding that the entry does not contain all the particulars required for perfect entry if it contains as many of those particulars as are then known to the importer, and in that event the importer shall supply the remaining particulars as soon as may be to the Commissioners.

(3)   Where goods are allowed to be delivered under this section, the Commissioners shall, when they have determined the amount of duty which in their opinion is payable, give to the importer a notice specifying that amount.

(4)   On the giving of a notice under subsection (3) above the amount specified in the notice or, where any amount has been deposited under subsection (1) above, any difference between those amounts shall forthwith be paid or repaid as the case may require.

(5)   Subject to subsection (6) below, if the importer disputes the correctness of the amount specified in a notice given to him under subsection (3) above he may at any time within 3 months of the date of the notice make such a requirement for reference to arbitration or such an application to the court as is provided for by section 127 below, and that section shall have effect accordingly.

(6)   No requirement or application shall be made by virtue of subsection (5) above until any sum falling to be paid by the importer under subsection (4) above has been paid, and where any sum so falls to be paid no interest shall be paid under section 127(2) below in respect of any period before that sum is paid.

NOTES

Sub-s (1): words in first pair of square brackets inserted by the Finance Act 1981, s 10(1), Sch 6, para 8; words in second pair of square brackets inserted by the Finance Act 1984, s 8, Sch 4, Pt II, para 4.

Sub-s (2): repealed by the Finance Act 1981, s 139, Sch 19, Pt I, with effect from a day to be appointed.

120 Regulations for determining origin of goods

(1)   The Secretary of State may by regulations make provision for determining, for the purposes of any duty of customs or excise, the origin of any goods in cases where it does not fall to be determined under a Community regulation or any Act or other instrument having the force of law.

(2)   Regulations under this section may—

(a)   make provision as to the evidence which is to be required or is to be sufficient for the purpose of showing that goods are of a particular origin; and

(b)   make different provision for different purposes and in relation to goods of different descriptions.

(3)   Subject to the provisions of any regulations under this section, where in connection with a duty of customs or excise chargeable on any goods any question arises as to the origin of the goods, the Commissioners may require the importer of the goods to furnish to them, in such form as they may prescribe, proof of any statement made to them as to any fact necessary to determine that question; and if such proof is not furnished to their satisfaction, the question may be determined without regard to that statement.

NOTES

Regulations: the Origin of Goods (Petroleum Products) Regulations 1988, SI 1988/1, as amended by SI 1992/3289.

121 Power to impose restrictions where duty depends on certain matters other than use

Where any question as to the duties of customs or excise chargeable on any imported goods depends on any matter (other than the use to be made of the goods) not reasonably ascertainable from an examination of the goods, and that question is not in law conclusively determined by the production of any certificate or other document, then, on the importation of those goods, the Commissioners may impose such conditions as they see fit for the prevention of abuse or the protection of the revenue (including conditions requiring security for the observance of any conditions so imposed).

122 Regulations where customs duty depends on use

(1) The Commissioners may, in accordance with subsection (2) below, make regulations applying in cases where any question as to the duties of customs chargeable on any goods depends on the use to be made of them.

(2) In cases in which a Community instrument makes provision for the purpose of securing that the relevant use is made of the goods, regulations under this section may make provision for any matter which under the instrument is required or authorised to be dealt with by the authorities of member States or which otherwise arises out of the instrument; and in other cases regulations under this section may make such provision for that purpose as appears to the Commissioners to be necessary or expedient.

NOTES

Regulations: by virtue of the Interpretation Act 1978, s 17(2)(b), in conjunction with s 177(5) of this Act, the Import Duties (End-Use Goods) Regulations 1977, SI 1977/2042, have effect as if made under this section.

123 Repayment of duty where goods returned or destroyed by importer

(1) Subject to such conditions as the Commissioners see fit to impose, where it is shown to the satisfaction of the Commissioners—

    (a)   that goods were imported in pursuance of a contract of sale and that the description, quality, state or condition of the goods was not in accordance with the contract or that the goods were damaged in transit; and

    (b)   that the importer with the consent of the seller either—

        (i)   returned the goods unused to the seller and for that purpose complied with the provisions of section 53 above as to entry in like manner as if they had been dutiable or restricted goods for the purposes of Part V of this Act; or

        (ii)   destroyed the goods unused,

the importer shall be entitled to obtain from the Commissioners repayment of any [excise duty] paid on the importation of the goods.

(2) Nothing in this section shall apply to goods imported on approval, or on sale or return, or on other similar terms.

NOTES

Sub-s (1): words in square brackets substituted by the Customs and Excise (Repayment of Customs Duties) Regulations 1980, SI 1980/1825, reg 2.

124 Forfeiture for breach of certain conditions

(1) Where—

   (a)   any imported goods have been relieved from customs or excise duty chargeable on their importation or have been charged with duty at a reduced rate; and

   (b)   any condition or other obligation required to be complied with in connection with the relief or with the charge of duty at that rate is not complied with,

the goods shall be liable to forfeiture.

(2) The provisions of this section shall apply whether or not any undertaking or security has been given for compliance with the condition or obligation or for the payment of the duty payable apart therefrom, and the forfeiture of any goods under this section shall not affect any liability of any person who has given any such undertaking or security.

125 Valuation of goods for purpose of ad valorem duties

(1) For the purposes of any duty for the time being chargeable on any imported goods by reference to their value (whether a Community customs duty or not), the value of the goods shall, subject to subsection (2) below, be taken according to the rules applicable in the case of Community customs duties, and duty shall be paid on that value.

(2) In relation to an importation in the course of trade within the Communities the value of any imported goods for the purposes mentioned in subsection (1) above shall be determined on the basis of a delivery to the buyer at the port or place of importation into the United Kingdom.

(3) The Commissioners may make regulations for the purpose of giving effect to the foregoing provisions of this section, and in particular for requiring any importer or other person concerned with the importation of goods—

   (a)   to furnish to the Commissioners in such form as they may require, such information as is in their opinion necessary for a proper valuation of the goods; and

   (b)   to produce any books of account or other documents of whatever nature relating to the purchase, importation or sale of the goods by that person.

(4) If any person contravenes or fails to comply with any regulation made under subsection (3) above he shall be liable on summary conviction to a penalty of [level 3 on the standard scale].

NOTES

Sub-s (4): reference to a level on the standard scale substituted by virtue of the Criminal Justice Act 1982, ss 38, 46.

Regulations: the Free Zone Regulations 1984, SI 1984/1177, as amended by SI 1988/710 (made partly under sub-s (3) above); by virtue of the Interpretation Act 1978, s 17(2)(b), in conjunction with s 177(5) of this Act, the Import Duties (Valuation of Goods) Regulations 1935, SR & O 1935/689, also have effect as if made under sub-s (3) above.

126 Charge of excise duty on manufactured or composite imported articles

(1) Subject to subsections (2) to (4) below, if any imported goods contain as a part or ingredient thereof any article chargeable with excise duty, excise duty shall be chargeable on the goods in respect of each such article according to the quantity thereof appearing to the Commissioners to be used in the manufacture or preparation of the goods.

(2) Where, in the opinion of the Treasury, it is necessary for the protection of the revenue, such imported goods shall be chargeable with the amount of excise duty with which they would be chargeable if they consisted wholly of the chargeable article or, if the goods contain more than one such article, of that one of the chargeable articles which will yield the highest amount of excise duty.

(3) Schedule 2 to this Act shall have effect with respect to the excise duties to be charged, and the excise drawbacks to be allowed, on imported composite goods containing a dutiable part or ingredient and with respect to rebates and drawbacks of excise duties charged in accordance with that Schedule.

(4) Subsections (1) and (2) above do not apply where other provision is made by any other enactment relating to excise duties on imported goods.

(5) Any rebate which can be allowed by law on any article when separately charged shall be allowed in charging goods under subsection (1) or (2) above in respect of any quantity of that article used in the manufacture or preparation of the goods.

127

(Repealed by the Finance Act 1994, ss 18(3), 258, Sch 26, Pt III.)

[Deferred payment of excise duty on goods

127A Deferred payment of excise duty on goods

(1) The Commissioners may by regulations make provision for the payment [(in accordance, where any requirement to pay the duty takes effect, with that requirement)] of any excise duty on goods of a prescribed kind to be deferred, in prescribed cases, subject to such conditions or requirements as may be imposed—

    (a)   by the regulations; or

    (b)   where the regulations so provide, by the Commissioners.

(2) Any duty payment of which is deferred under the regulations shall be treated, for prescribed purposes, as it if had been paid.

(3) Where—

    (a)   any excise duty to which an application for deferment of duty made under the regulations relates is payable on goods on their removal from an excise warehouse; and

    (b)   the Commissioners are not satisfied—

        (i)   that the conditions imposed under section 92(1) above in relation to the warehouse have been complied with by the occupier of the warehouse; or

        (ii)   that the warehousing regulations made by virtue of section 93(2)(g) above have been complied with by the occupier or by the proprietor of the goods;

the Commissioners may, notwithstanding any provision of the regulations, refuse the application or refuse it in so far as it relates to those goods.

Nothing in this subsection shall be taken to prejudice the power of the Commissioners to prescribe the cases in which excise duty may be deferred.

(4) Regulations under this section may make different provision for goods of different descriptions or for goods of the same description in different circumstances.

(5) In this section "prescribed" means prescribed by regulations made under this section.]

NOTES

Inserted, together with the preceding cross-heading, by the Finance Act 1983, s 6.

Sub-s (1): words in square brackets inserted by the Finance (No 2) Act 1992, s 1, Sch 1, para 7.

Regulations: the Customs and Excise (Deferred Payment) (RAF Airfields and Offshore Installations) (No 2) Regulations 1988, SI 1988/1898; the Excise Duties (Deferred Payment) Regulations 1992, SI 1992/3152, as amended by SI 1996/2537; the Excise Goods (Holding, Movement, Warehousing and REDS) Regulations 1992, SI 1992/3135, as amended by SI 1992/3154, SI 1993/1228, SI 1999/1278, SI 1999/1565; the Tobacco Products (Amendment) Regulations 1992, SI 1992/3154; the Beer Regulations 1993, SI 1993/1228, as amended by SI 1995/3059, SI 2000/3213; the Hydrocarbon Oil Duties (Marine Voyages Reliefs) Regulations 1996, SI 1996/2537.

General provisions relating to charge of duty on and delivery of goods

128 Restriction of delivery of goods

(1) During any period not exceeding 3 months specified at any time by order of the Commissioners for the purposes of this section, the Commissioners may refuse to allow the removal for home use on payment of duty, or the sending out for home use after the charging of duty, of goods of any class or description chargeable with a duty of . . . excise, notwithstanding payment of that duty, in quantities exceeding those which appear to the Commissioners to be reasonable in the circumstances.

(2) Where the Commissioners have during any such period exercised their powers under this section with respect to goods of any class or description, then, in the case of any such goods which are removed or sent out for home use after the end of that period, the duties of . . . excise and the rates thereof chargeable on those goods shall, notwithstanding any other provision of the customs and excise Acts relating to the determination of those duties and rates, be those in force at the date of the removal or sending out of the goods.

NOTES

Words omitted repealed by the Finance Act 1981, ss 10(1), 139, Sch 6, para 9, Sch 19, Pt I.

129 Power to remit or repay duty on denatured goods

(1) Subject to subsection (2) below, where any goods—

    (a)   which have been imported but not yet cleared for any purpose for which they may be entered on importation; or

    (b)   which are [chargeable with a duty the requirement to pay which has not yet taken effect],

have by reason of their state or condition ceased to be worth the full duty chargeable thereon and have been denatured in such manner as the Commissioners may direct and in accordance with such conditions as they see fit to impose, the Commissioners may remit or repay the whole or part of any duty chargeable or paid thereon, or waive repayment of the whole or part of any drawback paid on their warehousing, upon the delivery of the goods for use for such purposes as the Commissioners may allow.

[(1A) The reference in subsection (1) above to goods which are chargeable with a duty the requirement to pay which has not yet taken effect shall be construed as a reference to any goods which are warehoused or, in the application of that section in relation to a duty of excise, to any goods at a time, before the excise duty point for those goods, when they are chargeable with such a duty.]

(2)   Subsection (1) above does not apply in relation to spirits.

(3)   Where, whether under subsection (1) above or otherwise, any goods chargeable with duty have gone into home use after having been denatured by mixture with some other substance, any person who separates the goods from that other substance shall be guilty of an offence under this subsection and may be [arrested], and the goods shall be liable to forfeiture.

(4)   A person guilty of an offence under subsection (3) above shall be liable—

(a)   on summary conviction, to a penalty of the prescribed sum or of three times the value of the goods, whichever is the greater, or to imprisonment for a term not exceeding 6 months, or to both; or

(b)   on conviction on indictment, to a penalty of any amount, or to imprisonment for a term not exceeding 2 years, or to both.

[(5)   Subsection (1)(a) above shall not apply in relation to goods imported on or after 1st January 1992 from a place outside the customs territory of the Community.]

NOTES

Sub-s (1): words in square brackets substituted by the Finance (No 2) Act 1992, s 3, Sch 2, para 6(a).

Sub-s (1A): inserted by the Finance (No 2) Act 1992, s 3, Sch 2, para 6(b).

Sub-s (3): word in square brackets substituted by the Police and Criminal Evidence Act 1984, s 114(1).

Sub-s (5): added by the Customs Controls on Importation of Goods Regulations 1991, SI 1991/2724, reg 6(10).

---

130 Power to remit or repay duty on goods lost or destroyed, etc

(1)   Where it is shown to the satisfaction of the Commissioners that any goods chargeable with any duty have been lost or destroyed by unavoidable accident—

(a)   after importation but before clearance for any purpose for which they might be entered on importation; or

(b)   in the case of goods chargeable with a duty of excise on their manufacture or production or on their removal from the place of their manufacture or production, at any time before their removal from that place; or

(c)   while in a warehouse or Queen's warehouse; or

(d)   at any time while that duty is otherwise lawfully unpaid, except when payment of that duty has become due but has been allowed by the Commissioners to be deferred; or

(e)   at any time after drawback of that duty has been paid,

the Commissioners may remit or repay any duty chargeable or paid thereon or waive repayment of any drawback paid on their warehousing.

(2)   The Commissioners may, at the request of the proprietor of the goods in question and subject to compliance with such conditions as the Commissioners see fit to impose, permit the destruction of, and waive payment of duty or repayment of drawback on—

(a)   any part of any warehoused goods which becomes damaged or surplus by reason of the carrying out of any permitted operation on those goods in warehouse, and any refuse resulting from any such operation; and

(b)   any imported goods not yet cleared for any purpose for which they might be entered on importation or any warehoused goods, being in either case goods which have by reason of their state or condition ceased to be worth the full duty chargeable thereon.

131 Enforcement of bond in respect of goods removed without payment of duty

If any goods which have been lawfully permitted to be removed for any purpose without payment of duty are unlawfully taken from any ship, aircraft, vehicle or place before that purpose is accomplished, the Commissioners may if they see fit enforce any bond given in respect thereof notwithstanding that any time prescribed in the bond for accomplishing that purpose has not expired.

Drawback, allowances, duties, etc—general

132 Extension of drawback

(1) Without prejudice to any other provision of the Customs and Excise Acts 1979 or any other Act, where drawback is allowable on the shipment of any goods as stores, the like drawback shall, subject to such conditions and restrictions as the Commissioners see fit to impose, be allowed on the warehousing in an excise warehouse of those goods for use as stores.

(2) Without prejudice to any other provision of the Customs and Excise Acts 1979 or any other Act, where drawback would be payable on the exportation of any goods, or on the warehousing of any goods for exportation, then, subject to such conditions and restrictions as the Commissioners see fit, the like drawback shall be payable on the shipment of any such goods as stores or, as the case may be, on their warehousing in an excise warehouse for use as stores.

NOTES

Repealed by the Finance Act 1999, ss 11(3), (4), 139, Sch 20, Pt I(2), as from a day to be appointed.

133 General provisions as to claims for drawback

(1) Any claim for drawback shall be made in such form and manner and contain such particulars as the Commissioners may direct.

(2) Where drawback has been claimed in the case of any goods [subsections (4) to (6)] below shall apply in relation to the claim.

(3) . . .

(4) No drawback shall be paid until the person entitled thereto or his agent has made a declaration in such form and manner and containing such particulars as the Commissioners may direct that the conditions on which the drawback is payable have been fulfilled.

(5) The Commissioners may require any person who has been concerned at any stage with the goods or article—

    (a)   to furnish such information as may be reasonably necessary to enable the Commissioners to determine whether duty has been duly paid and not drawn back and for enabling a calculation to be made of the amount of drawback payable; and

    (b)   to produce any book of account or other document of whatever nature relating to the goods or article.

(6) If any person fails to comply with any requirement made under subsection (5) above, he shall be liable on summary conviction to a penalty of [level 3 on the standard scale].

NOTES

Sub-s (2): words in square brackets substituted by the Finance Act 2002, 21(1).

Sub-s (3): repealed by the Finance Act 2002, 21(1).

Sub-s (6): reference to a level on the standard scale substituted by virtue of the Criminal Justice Act 1982, ss 38, 46.

134 Drawback and allowance on goods damaged or destroyed after shipment

(1)   Where it is proved to the satisfaction of the Commissioners that any goods after being duly shipped for exportation have been destroyed by accident on board the exporting ship or aircraft, any amount payable in respect of the goods by way of drawback, allowance or repayment of duty shall be payable in the same manner as if the goods had been exported to their destination.

(2)   Where it is proved to the satisfaction of the Commissioners that any goods, after being duly shipped for exportation, have been materially damaged by accident on board the exporting ship or aircraft, and the goods are with the consent of and in accordance with any conditions imposed by the Commissioners relanded or unloaded again in or brought back into the United Kingdom and either abandoned to the Commissioners or destroyed, any amount payable in respect of the goods by way of drawback, allowance or repayment of duty shall be paid as if they had been duly exported and not so relanded, unloaded or brought back.

(3)   Notwithstanding any provision of the Customs and Excise Acts 1979 or any other Act relating to the reimportation of exported goods, the person to whom any amount is payable or has been paid under subsection (2) above shall not be required to pay any duty in respect of any goods relanded, unloaded or brought back under that subsection.

135 Time limit on payment of drawback or allowance

No payment shall be made in respect of any drawback or allowance unless the debenture or other document authorising payment is presented for payment within 2 years from the date of the event on the happening of which the drawback or allowance became payable.

136 Offences in connection with claims for drawback, etc

[(1)   If any person, with intent to defraud Her Majesty, obtains or attempts to obtain, or does anything whereby there might be obtained by any person, any amount by way of drawback, allowance, remission or repayment of, or any rebate from, any duty in respect of any goods which—

    (a)   is not lawfully payable or allowable in respect thereof; or

    (b)   is greater than the amount so payable or allowable,

he shall be guilty of an offence under this subsection.

(1A)   If any person, without such intent as is mentioned in subsection (1) above, does any of the things there mentioned, he shall be guilty of an offence under this subsection.

(2)   A person guilty of an offence under subsection (1) above shall be liable—

    (a)   on summary conviction, to a penalty of the prescribed sum or of three times the value of the goods, whichever is the greater, or to imprisonment for a term not exceeding 6 months, or to both; or

    (b)   on conviction on indictment, to a penalty of any amount, or to imprisonment for a term not exceeding 7 years, or to both;

and a person guilty of an offence under subsection (1A) above shall be liable on summary conviction to a penalty of level 3 on the standard scale or three times the amount which was or might have been improperly obtained or allowed, whichever is the greater.]

(3) Any goods in respect of which an offence under subsection (1) [or (1A)] above is committed shall be liable to forfeiture; but in the case of a claim for drawback, the Commissioners may, if they see fit, instead of seizing the goods either refuse to allow any drawback thereon or allow only such drawback as they consider proper.

(4) Without prejudice to the foregoing provisions of this section, if, in the case of any goods upon which a claim for drawback, allowance, remission or repayment of duty has been made, it is found that those goods do not correspond with any entry made thereof in connection with that claim, the goods shall be liable to forfeiture and any person by whom any such entry or claim was made shall be liable on summary conviction to a penalty of three times the amount claimed or [level 3 on the standard scale], whichever is the greater.

(5) Subsection (4) above applies in the case of any goods upon which a claim for drawback, allowance, remission or repayment of duty has been made where it is found that the goods, if sold for home use, would realise less than the amount claimed as it applies where the finding specified in that subsection is made except that it does not apply by virtue of this subsection to any claim under—

(a) section 123 or 134(2) above; or

(b) section 46, 61 or 64 of the Alcoholic Liquor Duties Act 1979 (remission or repayment of duty on certain spoilt liquors).

[(6) Without prejudice to section 6(5) of the European Communities Act 1972 (which provides for the application of certain enactments, including this section, if the Commissioners are charged or entrusted with the performance of certain duties in relation to the payment of refunds or allowances on goods exported or to be exported from the United Kingdom)—

(a) references in this section to amounts by way of drawback include amounts payable by or on behalf of the Secretary of State, the Scottish Ministers, the National Assembly for Wales or (in relation to Northern Ireland) the Department of Agriculture and Rural Development by virtue of Community arrangements to which section 6(3) of the European Communities Act 1972 applies; and

(b) in relation to such amounts, subsection (3) above shall have effect with the omission of the words from "but in the case" onwards.]

NOTES

Sub-ss (1), (1A), (2): substituted for original sub-ss (1), (2), in relation to offences committed after 29 July 1988, by the Finance Act 1988, s 12(3), (6).

Sub-s (3): words in square brackets inserted by the Finance Act 1988, s 12(3), (6).

Sub-s (4): reference to a level on the standard scale substituted by virtue of the Criminal Justice Act 1982, ss 38, 46.

Sub-s (6): substituted by the Intervention Board for Agricultural Produce (Abolition) Regulations, SI 2001/3686 reg 6(7)(b).

137 Recovery of duties and calculation of duties, drawbacks, etc

(1) Without prejudice to any other provision of the Customs and Excise Acts 1979, any amount due by way of customs or excise duty may be recovered as a debt due to the Crown.

(2) Any duty, drawback, allowance or rebate the rate of which is expressed by reference to a specified quantity or weight of any goods shall, subject to subsection (3) below, be chargeable or allowable on any fraction of that quantity or weight of the goods, and the amount payable or allowable on any such fraction shall be calculated proportionately.

(3)   The Commissioners may for the purposes of subsection (2) above determine the fractions to be taken into account in the case of any weight or quantity.

(4)   For the purpose of calculating any amount due from or to any person under the customs and excise Acts by way of duty, drawback, allowance, repayment or rebate any fraction of a penny in that amount shall be disregarded.

[137A Recovery of overpaid excise duty

(1)   Where a person pays to the Commissioners an amount by way of excise duty which is not due to them, the Commissioners are liable to repay that amount.

(2)   The Commissioners shall not be required to make any such repayment unless a claim is made to them in such form, and supported by such documentary evidence, as may be prescribed by them by regulations; and regulations under this subsection may make different provision for different cases.

(3)   It is a defence to a claim for repayment that the repayment would unjustly enrich the claimant.

[(4)   The Commissioners shall not be liable, on a claim made under this section, to repay any amount paid to them more than three years before the making of the claim.]

(5)   Except as provided by this section the Commissioners are not liable to repay an amount paid to them by way of excise duty by reason of the fact that it was not due to them.]

[(6)   This section does not apply in a case where the Commissioners are—

    (a)   entitled to pay an amount under Part I of Schedule 3 to the Finance Act 2001, or

    (b)   required to repay an amount under Part III of that Schedule.]

NOTES

Commencement: 1 December 1995.

Inserted, in relation to payments made on or after 1 December 1995, by the Finance Act 1995, s 20(1), (5).

Sub-s (4): substituted by the Finance Act 1997, s 50(1), Sch 5, Pt II, para 5(1).

Sub-s (6) inserted by the Finance Act 2001, s 15, Sch 3 paras 15, 21(1).

Regulations: the Revenue Traders (Accounts and Records) (Amendment) Regulations 1995, SI 1995/2893; Finance Act 2001 (Commencement No 2 and Saving Provision) Order 2001.

PART XI
[ARREST] OF PERSONS, FORFEITURE AND LEGAL PROCEEDINGS

[Arrest] of persons

NOTES

Headings: word in square brackets substituted by the Police and Criminal Evidence Act 1984, s 114(1).

138 Provisions as to [arrest] of persons

(1)   Any person who has committed, or whom there are reasonable grounds to suspect of having committed, any offence for which he is liable to be [arrested] under the customs and excise Acts may be [arrested] by any officer . . . or any member of Her Majesty's armed forces or coastguard at any time within [20 years] from the date of the commission of the offence.

(2)   Where it was not practicable [to arrest] any person so liable at the time of the commission of the offence, or where any such person having been then or

subsequently [arrested] for that offence has escaped, he may be [arrested] by any officer . . . or any member of Her Majesty's armed forces or coastguard at any time and may be proceeded against in like manner as if the offence had been committed at the date when he was finally [arrested].

(3) Where any person who is a member of the crew of any ship in Her Majesty's employment or service is [arrested] by an officer for an offence under the customs and excise Acts, the commanding officer of the ship shall, if so required by the [arresting] officer, keep that person secured on board that ship until he can be brought before a court and shall then deliver him up to the proper officer.

[(4) Where any person has been arrested by a person who is not an officer—

(a)   by virtue of this section; or

(b)   by virtue of section 24 [or 24A] of the Police and Criminal Evidence Act 1984 in its application to offences under the customs and excise Acts, [or

(c)   by virtue of Article 26 of the Police and Criminal Evidence (Northern Ireland) Order 1989 in its application to such offences]

the person arresting him shall give notice of the arrest to an officer at the nearest convenient office of customs and excise.]

NOTES

Section heading: word in square brackets substituted by the Police and Criminal Evidence Act 1984, s 114(1).

Sub-s (1): words in first and second pairs of square brackets substituted, words omitted repealed by the Police and Criminal Evidence Act 1984, ss 114(1), 119(2), Sch 7, Pt I; words in third pair of square brackets substituted, in relation to offences committed after 29 July 1988, by the Finance Act 1988, s 11(1), (3).

Sub-s (2): words omitted repealed and words in square brackets substituted by the Police and Criminal Evidence Act 1984, ss 114(1), 119(2), Sch 7, Pt I.

Sub-s (3): words in square brackets substituted by the Police and Criminal Evidence Act 1984, s 114(1).

Sub-s (4): substituted by the Police and Criminal Evidence Act 1984, s 119, Sch 6, para 37; words in square brackets therein added by the Police and Criminal Evidence (Northern Ireland) Order 1989, SI 1989/1341, art 90(1), Sch 6, para 9.

Sub-s (4)(b): words in square brackets inserted by the Serious Organised Crime and Police Act 2005 s 111, Sch 7 para 54.

Forfeiture

139 Provisions as to detention, seizure and condemnation of goods, etc

(1) Any thing liable to forfeiture under the customs and excise Acts may be seized or detained by any officer or constable or any member of Her Majesty's armed forces or coastguard.

(2) Where any thing is seized or detained as liable to forfeiture under the customs and excise Acts by a person other than an officer, that person shall, subject to subsection (3) below, either—

(a)   deliver that thing to the nearest convenient office of customs and excise; or

(b)   if such delivery is not practicable, give to the Commissioners at the nearest convenient office of customs and excise notice in writing of the seizure or detention with full particulars of the thing seized or detained.

(3) Where the person seizing or detaining any thing as liable to forfeiture under the customs and excise Acts is a constable and that thing is or may be required for use in connection with any proceedings to be brought otherwise than under those Acts it

may, subject to subsection (4) below, be retained in the custody of the police until either those proceedings are completed or it is decided that no such proceedings shall be brought.

(4) The following provisions apply in relation to things retained in the custody of the police by virtue of subsection (3) above, that is to say—

(a)   notice in writing of the seizure or detention and of the intention to retain the thing in question in the custody of the police, together with full particulars as to that thing, shall be given to the Commissioners at the nearest convenient office of customs and excise;

(b)   any officer shall be permitted to examine that thing and take account thereof at any time while it remains in the custody of the police;

(c)   nothing in the Police (Property) Act 1897 shall apply in relation to that thing.

(5) Subject to subsections (3) and (4) above and to Schedule 3 to this Act, any thing seized or detained under the customs and excise Acts shall, pending the determination as to its forfeiture or disposal, be dealt with, and, if condemned or deemed to have been condemned or forfeited, shall be disposed of in such manner as the Commissioners may direct.

(6) Schedule 3 to this Act shall have effect for the purpose of forfeitures, and of proceedings for the condemnation of any thing as being forfeited, under the customs and excise Acts.

(7) If any person, not being an officer, by whom any thing is seized or detained or who has custody thereof after its seizure or detention, fails to comply with any requirement of this section or with any direction of the Commissioners given thereunder, he shall be liable on summary conviction to a penalty of [level 2 on the standard scale].

(8) Subsections (2) to (7) above shall apply in relation to any dutiable goods seized or detained by any person other than an officer notwithstanding that they were not so seized as liable to forfeiture under the customs and excise Acts.

NOTES

Sub-s (4): for the words "the Police (Property) Act 1897" in para (c) there are substituted the words "section 31 of the Police (Northern Ireland) Act 1998", in relation to Northern Ireland, by the Police (Northern Ireland) Act 1998, s 74(1), Sch 4, para 14.

Sub-s (7): reference to a level on the standard scale substituted by virtue of the Criminal Justice Act 1982, s 46.

140 Forfeiture of spirits

Where, by any provision of, or of any instrument made under, the Customs and Excise Acts 1979, any spirits become liable to forfeiture by reason of some offence committed by a revenue trader, then—

(a)   where that provision specifies the quantity of those spirits but does not specify the spirits so liable, the Commissioners may seize the equivalent of that quantity . . . from any spirits in the stock of that trader; and

(b)   where that provision specifies the spirits so liable the Commissioners may, if they think fit, seize instead of the spirits so specified an equivalent quantity . . . of any other spirits in the stock of that trader.

NOTES

Words omitted repealed by the Alcoholic Liquors (Amendment of Enactments Relating to Strength and to Units of Measurement) Order 1979, SI 1979/241, arts 39, 41.

141 Forfeiture of ships, etc used in connection with goods liable to forfeiture

(1)   Without prejudice to any other provision of the Customs and Excise Acts 1979, where any thing has become liable to forfeiture under the customs and excise Acts—

(a)   any ship, aircraft, vehicle, animal, container (including any article of passengers' baggage) or other thing whatsoever which has been used for the carriage, handling, deposit or concealment of the thing so liable to forfeiture, either at a time when it was so liable or for the purposes of the commission of the offence for which it later became so liable; and

(b)   any other thing mixed, packed or found with the thing so liable,

shall also be liable to forfeiture.

(2)   Where any ship, aircraft, vehicle or animal has become liable to forfeiture under the customs and excise Acts, whether by virtue of subsection (1) above or otherwise, all tackle, apparel or furniture thereof shall also be liable to forfeiture.

(3)   Where any of the following, that is to say—

(a)   any ship not exceeding 100 tons register;

(b)   any aircraft; or

(c)   any hovercraft,

becomes liable to forfeiture under this section by reason of having been used in the importation, exportation or carriage of goods contrary to or for the purpose of contravening any prohibition or restriction for the time being in force with respect to those goods, or without payment having been made of, or security given for, any duty payable thereon, the owner and the master or commander shall each be liable on summary conviction to a penalty equal to the value of the ship, aircraft or hovercraft or [level 5 on the standard scale], whichever is the less.

NOTES

Sub-s (3): reference to a level on the standard scale substituted by virtue of the Criminal Justice Act 1982, ss 38, 46.

142 Special provision as to forfeiture of larger ships

(1)   Notwithstanding any other provision of the Customs and Excise Acts 1979, a ship of 250 or more tons register shall not be liable to forfeiture under or by virtue of any provision of the Customs and Excise Acts 1979, except under section 88 above, unless the offence in respect of or in connection with which the forfeiture is claimed—

(a)   was substantially the object of the voyage during which the offence was committed; or

(b)   was committed while the ship was under chase by a vessel in the service of Her Majesty after failing to bring to when properly summoned to do so by that vessel.

(2)   For the purposes of this section, a ship shall be deemed to have been properly summoned to bring to—

(a)   if the vessel making the summons did so by means of an international signal code or other recognised means and while flying her proper ensign; and

(b)   in the case of a ship which is not a British ship, if at the time when the summons was made the ship was [in United Kingdom waters].

(3)   For the purposes of this section, all hovercraft (of whatever size) shall be treated as ships of less than 250 tons register.

(4)   The exemption from forfeiture of any ship under this section shall not affect any liability to forfeiture of goods carried therein.

NOTES

Sub-s (2): words in square brackets substituted by the Territorial Sea Act 1987, s 3(1), Sch 1, para 4(3)(d).

143 Penalty in lieu of forfeiture of larger ship where responsible officer implicated in offence

(1) Where any ship of 250 or more tons register would, but for section 142 above, be liable to forfeiture for or in connection with any offence under the customs and excise Acts and, in the opinion of the Commissioners, a responsible officer of the ship is implicated either by his own act or by neglect in that offence, the Commissioners may fine that ship such sum not exceeding £50 as they see fit.

(2) For the purposes of this section, all hovercraft (of whatever size) shall be treated as ships of less than 250 tons register.

(3) Where any ship is liable to a fine under subsection (1) above but the Commissioners consider that fine an inadequate penalty for the offence, they may take proceedings in accordance with Schedule 3 to this Act, in like manner as they might but for section 142 above have taken proceedings for the condemnation of the ship if notice of claim had been given in respect thereof, for the condemnation of the ship in such sum not exceeding £500 as the court may see fit.

(4) Where any fine is to be imposed or any proceedings are to be taken under this section, the Commissioners may require such sum as they see fit, not exceeding £50 or, as the case may be, £500, to be deposited with them to await their final decision or, as the case may be, the decision of the court, and may detain the ship until that sum has been so deposited.

(5) No claim shall lie against the Commissioners for damages in respect of the payment of any deposit or the detention of any ship under this section.

(6) For the purposes of this section—

(a) "responsible officer", in relation to any ship, means the master, a mate or an engineer of the ship and, in the case of a ship carrying a passenger certificate, the purser or chief steward and, in the case of a ship manned wholly or partly by Asiatic seamen, the serang or other leading Asiatic officer of the ship;

(b) without prejudice to any other grounds upon which a responsible officer of any ship may be held to be implicated by neglect, he may be so held if goods not owned to by any member of the crew are discovered in a place under that officer's supervision in which they could not reasonably have been put if he had exercised proper care at the time of the loading of the ship or subsequently.

144 Protection of officers, etc in relation to seizure and detention of goods, etc

(1) Where, in any proceedings for the condemnation of any thing seized as liable to forfeiture under the customs and excise Acts, judgment is given for the claimant, the court may, if it sees fit, certify that there were reasonable grounds for the seizure.

(2) Where any proceedings, whether civil or criminal, are brought against the Commissioners, a law officer of the Crown or any person authorised by or under the Customs and Excise Acts 1979 to seize or detain any thing liable to forfeiture under the customs and excise Acts on account of the seizure or detention of any thing, and judgment is given for the plaintiff or prosecutor, then if either—

(a) a certificate relating to the seizure has been granted under subsection (1) above; or

(b) the court is satisfied that there were reasonable grounds for seizing or detaining that thing under the customs and excise Acts, the plaintiff or prosecutor shall not be entitled to recover any damages or costs and the defendant shall not be liable to any punishment.

(3) Nothing in subsection (2) above shall affect any right of any person to the return of the thing seized or detained or to compensation in respect of any damage to the thing or in respect of the destruction thereof.

(4) Any certificate under subsection (1) above may be proved by the production of either the original certificate or a certified copy thereof purporting to be signed by an officer of the court by which it was granted.

General provisions as to legal proceedings

145 Institution of proceedings

(1) Subject to the following provisions of this section, no proceedings for an offence under the customs and excise Acts or for condemnation under Schedule 3 to this Act shall be instituted [except—

 (a) by or with the consent of the Director of Revenue and Customs Prosecutions, or

 (b) by order of, or with the consent of, the Commissioners for Her Majesty's Revenue and Customs.

(2) Subject to the following provisions of this section, any proceedings under the customs and excise Acts instituted [by order of the Commissioners] in a magistrates' court, and any such proceedings instituted [by order of the Commissioners] in a court of summary jurisdiction in Northern Ireland, shall be commenced in the name of an officer [of Revenue and Customs].

(3) Subsections (1) and (2) above shall not apply to proceedings on indictment in Scotland.

(4) . . .

(5) Nothing in the foregoing provisions of this section shall prevent the institution of proceedings for an offence under the customs and excise Acts by order and in the name of a law officer of the Crown in any case in which he thinks it proper that proceedings should be so instituted.

(6) Notwithstanding anything in the foregoing provisions of this section, where any person has been [arrested] for any offence for which he is liable to be [arrested] under the customs and excise Acts, any court before which he is brought may proceed to deal with the case although the proceedings have not been instituted [in accordance with this section.]

NOTES

Sub-s (1): words in square brackets substituted by the Commissioners for Revenue and Customs Act 2005 s 50, Sch 4 para 23(a).

Sub-s (2): words in square brackets substituted by the Commissioners for Revenue and Customs Act 2005 s 50, Sch 4 para 23(b).

Sub-s (4) repealed by the Commissioners for Revenue and Customs Act 2005 s 50, Sch 4 para 23(c), s 52, Sch 5.

Sub-s (6): word "arrested" in square brackets substituted by the Police and Criminal Evidence Act 1984, s 114(1); words "in accordance with this section." substituted by the Commissioners for Revenue and Customs Act 2005 s 50, Sch 4 para 23(d).

146 Service of process

(1) Any summons or other process issued anywhere in the United Kingdom for the purpose of any proceedings under the customs and excise Acts may be served on the person to whom it is addressed in any part of the United Kingdom without any further endorsement, and shall be deemed to have been duly served—

(a)   if delivered to him personally; or

(b)   if left at his last known place of abode or business or, in the case of a body corporate, at their registered or principal office; or

(c)   if left on board any vessel or aircraft to which he may belong or have lately belonged.

(2)   Any summons, notice, order or other document issued for the purposes of any proceedings under the customs and excise Acts, or of any appeal from the decision of the court in any such proceedings, may be served by an officer.

In this subsection "appeal" includes an appeal by way of case stated.

(3)   This section shall not apply in relation to proceedings instituted in the High Court or Court of Session.

[146A Time limits for proceedings

(1)   Except as otherwise provided in the customs and excise Acts, and notwithstanding anything in any other enactment, the following provisions shall apply in relation to proceedings for an offence under those Acts.

(2)   Proceedings for an indictable offence shall not be commenced after the end of the period of 20 years beginning with the day on which the offence was committed.

(3)   Proceedings for a summary offence shall not be commenced after the end of the period of 3 years beginning with that day but, subject to that, may be commenced at any time within 6 months from the date on which sufficient evidence to warrant the proceedings came to the knowledge of the prosecuting authority.

(4)   For the purposes of subsection (3) above, a certificate of the prosecuting authority as to the date on which such evidence as is there mentioned came to that authority's knowledge shall be conclusive evidence of that fact.

(5)   In the application of this section to Scotland—

(a)   in subsection (2), "proceedings for an indictable offence" means proceedings on indictment;

(b)   in subsection (3), "proceedings for a summary offence" means summary proceedings.

(6)   In the application of this section to Northern Ireland—

(a)   "indictable offence" means an offence which, if committed by an adult, is punishable on conviction on indictment (whether only on conviction on indictment, or either on conviction on indictment or on summary conviction);

(b)   "summary offence" means an offence which, if committed by an adult, is punishable only on summary conviction.

(7)   In this section, "prosecuting authority"—

[(a)   in England and Wales, means the Director of Revenue and Customs Prosecutions,

(b)   in Scotland, means the Commissioners or the procurator fiscal, and

(c)   in Northern Ireland, means the Commissioners.]]

NOTES

Inserted, in relation to offences committed on or after 27 July 1989, by the Finance Act 1989, s 16(1), (4).

Sub-s (7): words in square brackets substituted by the Commissioners for Revenue and Customs Act 2005 s 50, Sch 4 para 24.

147 Proceedings for offences

(1)   . . .

(2) Where, in England or Wales, a magistrates' court has begun to inquire into an information charging a person with an offence under the customs and excise Acts as examining justices the court shall not proceed under [section 25(3) of the Magistrates' Courts Act 1980] to try the information summarily without the consent of—

   (a)   the Attorney General, in a case where the proceedings were instituted by his order and in his name; or
   (b)   the Commissioners, in any other case.

(3) In the case of proceedings in England or Wales, without prejudice to any right to require the statement of a case for the opinion of the High Court, the prosecutor may appeal to the Crown Court against any decision of a magistrates' court in proceedings for an offence under the customs and excise Acts.

(4) In the case of proceedings in Northern Ireland, without prejudice to any right to require the statement of a case for the opinion of the High Court, the prosecutor may appeal to the county court against any decision of a court of summary jurisdiction in proceedings for an offence under the customs and excise Acts.

(5) . . .

NOTES

Sub-s (1): repealed, in relation to offences committed on or after 27 July 1989, by the Finance Act 1989, ss 16(2), (4), 187(1), Sch 17, Pt I.

Sub-s (2): words in square brackets substituted by the Magistrates' Courts Act 1980, s 154, Sch 7, para 176. This sub-section to be repealed (except in relation to Northern Ireland) by the Criminal Justice Act 2003 ss 41, 332, Sch 3 Pt 2 para 50, Sch 37 Pt 4 with effect from a date to be appointed.

Sub-s (5): repealed by the Criminal Justice Act 1982, s 78, Sch 16.

148 Place of trial for offences

(1) Proceedings for an offence under the customs and excise Acts may be commenced—

   (a)   in any court having jurisdiction in the place where the person charged with the offence resides or is found; or
   (b)   if any thing was detained or seized in connection with the offence, in any court having jurisdiction in the place where that thing was so detained or seized or was found or condemned as forfeited; or
   (c)   in any court having jurisdiction anywhere in that part of the United Kingdom, namely—
       (i)   England and Wales,
       (ii)   Scotland, or
       (iii) Northern Ireland,

   in which the place where the offence was committed is situated.

(2) Where any such offence was committed at some place outside the area of any commission of the peace, the place of the commission of the offence shall, for the purposes of the jurisdiction of any court, be deemed to be any place in the United Kingdom where the offender is found or to which he is first brought after the commission of the offence.

(3) The jurisdiction under subsection (2) above shall be in addition to and not in derogation of any jurisdiction or power of any court under any other enactment.

149 Non-payment of penalties, etc: maximum terms of imprisonment

(1) Where, in any proceedings for an offence under the customs and excise Acts, a magistrates' court in England or Wales or a court of summary jurisdiction in Scotland, in addition to ordering the person convicted to pay a penalty for the offence—

     (a)   orders him to be imprisoned for a term in respect of the same offence; and

     (b)   further (whether at the same time or subsequently) orders him to be imprisoned for a term in respect of non-payment of that penalty or default of a sufficient distress to satisfy the amount of that penalty,

the aggregate of the terms for which he is so ordered to be imprisoned shall not exceed 15 months.

(2) . . .

(3) Where, under any enactment for the time being in force in Northern Ireland, a court of summary jurisdiction has power to order a person to be imprisoned in respect of the non-payment of a penalty, or of the default of a sufficient distress to satisfy the amount of that penalty, for a term in addition and succession to a term of imprisonment imposed for the same offence as the penalty, then in relation to a sentence for an offence under the customs and excise Acts the aggregate of those terms of imprisonment may, notwithstanding anything in any such enactment, be any period not exceeding 15 months.

NOTES

Sub-s (2): repealed by the Criminal Justice (Scotland) Act 1980, s 83(3), Sch 8.

New sub-s (1A) to be inserted by the Tribunals, Courts and Enforcement Act 2007, s 62(3), Sch 13, para 44, with effect from a date to be appointed. Sub-s (1A) as inserted to read as follows—

(1A) In subsection (1)(b) as it applies to a magistrates' court in England or Wales the reference to default of sufficient distress to satisfy the amount of the penalty is a reference to want of sufficient goods to satisfy the amount, within the meaning given by section 79(4) of the Magistrates' Courts Act 1980.

150 Incidental provisions as to legal proceedings

(1) Where liability for any offence under the customs and excise Acts is incurred by two or more persons jointly, those persons shall each be liable for the full amount of any pecuniary penalty and may be proceeded against jointly or severally as [the Director of Revenue and Customs Prosecutions (in relation to proceedings instituted in England and Wales) or the Commissioners (in relation to proceedings instituted in Scotland or Northern Ireland)] may see fit.

(2) In any proceedings for an offence under the customs and excise Acts instituted in England, Wales or Northern Ireland, any court by whom the matter is considered may mitigate any pecuniary penalty as they see fit.

(3) In any proceedings for an offence or for the condemnation of any thing as being forfeited under the customs and excise Acts, the fact that security has been given by bond or otherwise for the payment of any duty or for compliance with any condition in respect of the non-payment of which or non-compliance with which the proceedings are instituted shall not be a defence.

NOTES

Sub-s (1): words in square brackets substituted by the Commissioners for Revenue and Customs Act 2005 s 50, Sch 4 para 25.

151 Application of penalties

The balance of any sum paid or recovered on account of any penalty imposed under the customs and excise Acts, after paying any such compensation or costs as are mentioned in [section 139 of the Magistrates' Courts Act 1980] to persons other than the Commissioners shall, notwithstanding any local or other special right or privilege of whatever origin, be accounted for and paid to the Commissioners or as they direct.

NOTES

Words in square brackets substituted by the Magistrates' Courts Act 1980, s 154, Sch 7, para 177.

152 Power of Commissioners to mitigate penalties, etc

The Commissioners may, as they see fit—

(a)   . . . [compound an offence (whether or not proceedings have been instituted in respect of it) and compound proceedings] or for the condemnation of any thing as being forfeited under the customs and excise Acts; or

(b)   restore, subject to such conditions (if any) as they think proper, any thing forfeited or seized under those Acts; or

(c)   . . .

(d)   . . .

but paragraph (a) above shall not apply to proceedings on indictment in Scotland.

NOTES

Para (a): omitted words "stay, sist or" repealed by the Commissioners for Revenue and Customs Act 2005 s 52, Sch 5; words in square brackets substituted by the Commissioners for Revenue and Customs Act 2005 s 50, Sch 4 para 26.

Para (c) repealed by the Commissioners for Revenue and Customs Act 2005 s 52(1)(a)(vi), Sch 5.

Para (d) repealed by the Commissioners for Revenue and Customs Act 2005 s 52(1)(a)(vii), Sch 5.

153

(Repealed by the Commissioners for Revenue and Customs Act 2005 s 50, Sch 4 para 21, s 52, Sch 5.)

154 Proof of certain other matters

(1) An averment in any process in proceedings under the customs and excise Acts—

(a)   that those proceedings were instituted by the order of the Commissioners; or

(b)   that any person is or was a Commissioner, officer or constable, or a member of Her Majesty's armed forces or coastguard; or

(c)   that any person is or was appointed or authorised by the Commissioners to discharge, or was engaged by the orders or with the concurrence of the Commissioners in the discharge of, any duty; or

(d)   that the Commissioners have or have not been satisfied as to any matter as to which they are required by any provision of those Acts to be satisfied; or

(e)   that any ship is a British ship; or

(f)   that any goods thrown overboard, staved or destroyed were so dealt with in order to prevent or avoid the seizure of those goods,

shall, until the contrary is proved, be sufficient evidence of the matter in question.

(2)   Where in any proceedings relating to customs or excise any question arises as to the place from which any goods have been brought or as to whether or not—

(a)   any duty has been paid or secured in respect of any goods; or

(b)   any goods or other things whatsoever are of the description or nature alleged in the information, writ or other process; or

(c)   any goods have been lawfully imported or lawfully unloaded from any ship or aircraft; or

(d)   any goods have been lawfully loaded into any ship or aircraft or lawfully exported or were lawfully water-borne; or

(e)   any goods were lawfully brought to any place for the purpose of being loaded into any ship or aircraft or exported; or

(f)   any goods are or were subject to any prohibition of or restriction on their importation or exportation,

then, where those proceedings are brought by or against the Commissioners, a law officer of the Crown or an officer, or against any other person in respect of anything purporting to have been done in pursuance of any power or duty conferred or imposed on him by or under the customs and excise Acts, the burden of proof shall lie upon the other party to the proceedings.

155 Persons who may conduct proceedings

[An officer of Revenue and Customs or other person authorised by the Commissioners may conduct criminal proceedings relating to an assigned matter before a court of summary jurisdiction in Scotland or Northern Ireland.]

. . .

NOTES

Words in square brackets substituted for sub-s (1) by the Commissioners for Revenue and Customs Act 2005 s 50, Sch 4 para 27.

Sub-s (2) repealed by the Commissioners for Revenue and Customs Act 2005 s 50, Sch 4 para 21, s 52, Sch 5.

Saving for outlying enactments of certain general provisions as to offences

156 Saving for outlying enactments of certain general provisions as to offences

(1)   In subsections (2), (3) and (4) below (which reproduce certain enactments not required as general provisions for the purposes of the enactments re-enacted in the Customs and Excise Acts 1979) "the outlying provisions of the customs and excise Acts" [means the provisions] of the customs and excise Acts, as for the time being amended, which were passed before the commencement of this Act and are not re-enacted in the Customs and Excise Acts 1979 [or the Betting and Gaming Duties Act 1981].

(2)   It is hereby declared that any act or omission in respect of which a pecuniary penalty (however described) is imposed by any of the outlying provisions of the customs and excise Acts is an offence under that provision; and accordingly in this Part of this Act any reference to an offence under the customs and excise Acts includes a reference to such an act or omission.

(3)   Subject to any express provision made by the enactment in question, an offence under any of the outlying provisions of the customs and excise Acts—

(a)   where it is punishable with imprisonment for a term of 2 years, with or without a pecuniary penalty, shall be punishable either on summary conviction or on conviction on indictment;

(b)   in any other case, shall be punishable on summary conviction.

[(4) The maximum term of imprisonment which may be imposed on summary conviction in the sheriff court of an offence under any of the outlying provisions of the customs and excise Acts shall be 6 months.

(5) Where, in Scotland, an offence under any of the outlying provisions of the customs and excise Acts is triable only summarily by virtue of subsection (3)(b) above, the penalty for the offence shall be that to which a person was liable on summary conviction of the offence immediately before 29th July 1977 (the date of the passing of the Criminal Law Act 1977) subject to any increase by virtue of section 289C(5) of the Criminal Procedure (Scotland) Act 1975 or Part IV of the Criminal Justice Act 1982.]

NOTES

Sub-s (1): words in square brackets substituted by the Betting and Gaming Duties Act 1981, s 34(1), Sch 5, para 5(b).

Sub-s (3): words omitted repealed by the Criminal Justice Act 1982, ss 77, 78, Sch 14, para 43, Sch 16.

Sub-ss (4), (5): substituted for original sub-s (4) by the Criminal Justice Act 1982, s 77, Sch 14, para 43.

PART XII
GENERAL AND MISCELLANEOUS

General powers, etc

157 Bonds and security

(1) Without prejudice to any express requirement as to security contained in the customs and excise Acts, the Commissioners may, if they see fit, require any person to give security [(or further security) by bond, guarantee] or otherwise for the observance of any condition in connection with customs or excise.

[(1A) For the purposes of this section "condition in connection with excise" includes a condition in connection with excise duty charged, under the law of a member State other than the United Kingdom, on—

  (a) manufactured tobacco,

  (b) alcohol or alcoholic beverages, or

  (c) mineral oils.

The expressions used in paragraphs (a) to (c) above have the same meaning as in Council Directive 92/12/EEC.]

(2) Any bond[, guarantee or other security] taken for the purposes of any assigned matter—

  (a) shall be taken [either on behalf of Her Majesty or on behalf of Her Majesty and the tax authorities of each member State other than the United Kingdom]; and

  (b) shall be valid notwithstanding that it is entered into by a person under full age; and

  (c) may be cancelled at any time by or by order of the Commissioners.

[In this subsection "assigned matter" includes any excise duty charged as mentioned in subsection (1A) above.]

NOTES

Sub-s (1): words in square brackets substituted by the Finance Act 2000, s 27(1), (2).

Sub-s (1A): inserted by the Finance Act 2000, s 27(1), (3).

Sub-s (2): words in square brackets inserted and substituted by the Finance Act 2000, s 27(1), (4)–(6).

Council Directive 92/12/EEC.

158 Power to require provision of facilities

(1) A person to whom this section applies, that is to say, a revenue trader and any person required by the Commissioners under the Customs and Excise Acts 1979 to give security in respect of any premises or place to be used for the examination of goods by an officer, shall—

(a) provide and maintain such appliances and afford such other facilities reasonably necessary to enable an officer to take any account or make any examination or search or to perform any other of his duties on the premises of that trader or at the bonded premises or place as the Commissioners may direct;

(b) keep any appliances so provided in a convenient place approved by the proper officer for that purpose; and

(c) allow the proper officer at any time to use anything so provided and give him any assistance necessary for the performance of his duties.

(2) Any person who contravenes or fails to comply with any provision of subsection (1) above shall be liable on summary conviction to a penalty of [level 3 on the standard scale].

(3) A person to whom this section applies shall provide and maintain any fitting required for the purpose of affixing any lock which the proper officer may require to affix to the premises of that person or any part thereof or to any vessel, utensil or other apparatus whatsoever kept thereon, and in default—

(a) the fitting may be provided or any work necessary for its maintenance may be carried out by the proper officer, and any expenses so incurred shall be paid on demand by that person; and

(b) if that person fails to pay those expenses on demand, he shall in addition be liable on summary conviction to a penalty of [level 3 on the standard scale].

(4) If any person to whom this section applies or any servant of his—

(a) wilfully destroys or damages any such fitting as is mentioned in subsection (3) above or any lock or key provided for use therewith, or any label or seal placed on any such lock; or

(b) improperly obtains access to any place or article secured by any such lock; or

(c) has any such fitting or any article intended to be secured by means thereof so constructed that that intention is defeated,

he shall be liable on summary conviction to a penalty of [level 5 on the standard scale] and may be [arrested].

NOTES

Sub-ss (2), (3): references to levels on the standard scale substituted by virtue of the Criminal Justice Act 1982, ss 38, 46.

Sub-s (4): reference to a level on the standard scale substituted by virtue of the Criminal Justice Act 1982, ss 38, 46; word in second pair of square brackets substituted by the Police and Criminal Evidence Act 1984, s 114(1).

159 Power to examine and take account of goods

(1) Without prejudice to any other power conferred by the Customs and Excise Acts 1979, an officer may examine and take account of any goods—

(a)   which are imported; or

(b)   which are in a warehouse or Queen's warehouse; or

[(bb)   which are in a free zone; or]

(c)   which have been loaded into any ship or aircraft at any place in the United Kingdom [or the Isle of Man]; or

(d)   which are entered for exportation or for use as stores; or

(e)   which are brought to any place in the United Kingdom for exportation or for shipment for exportation or as stores; or

(f)   in the case of which any claim for drawback, allowance, rebate, remission or repayment of duty is made;

and may for that purpose require any container to be opened or unpacked.

(2)   Any examination of goods by an officer under the Customs and Excise Acts 1979 shall be made at such place as the Commissioners appoint for the purpose.

(3)   In the case of such goods as the Commissioners may direct, and subject to such conditions as they see fit to impose, an officer may permit goods to be skipped on the quay or bulked, sorted, lotted, packed or repacked before account is taken thereof.

(4)   Any opening, unpacking, weighing, measuring, repacking, bulking, sorting, lotting, marking, numbering, loading, unloading, carrying or landing of goods or their containers for the purposes of, or incidental to, the examination by an officer, removal or warehousing thereof shall be done, and any facilities or assistance required for any such examination shall be provided, by or at the expense of the proprietor of the goods.

(5)   If any imported goods which an officer has power under the Customs and Excise Acts 1979 to examine are without the authority of the proper officer removed from customs and excise charge before they have been examined, those goods shall be liable to forfeiture.

(6)   If any goods falling within subsection (5) above are removed by a person with intent to defraud Her Majesty of any duty chargeable thereon or to evade any prohibition or restriction for the time being in force with respect thereto under or by virtue of any enactment, that person shall be guilty of an offence under this subsection and may be [arrested].

(7)   A person guilty of an offence under subsection (6) above shall be liable—

(a)   on summary conviction, to a penalty of the prescribed sum or of three times the value of the goods, whichever is the greater, or to imprisonment for a term not exceeding 6 months, or to both; or

(b)   on conviction on indictment, to a penalty of any amount, or to imprisonment for a term not exceeding [7 years], or to both.

(8)   Without prejudice to the foregoing provisions of this section, where by this section or by or under any other provision of the Customs and Excise Acts 1979 an account is authorised or required to be taken of any goods for any purpose by an officer, the Commissioners may, with the consent of the proprietor of the goods, accept as the account of those goods for that purpose an account taken by such other person as may be approved in that behalf by both the Commissioners and the proprietor of the goods.

NOTES

Sub-s (1): para (bb) inserted by the Finance Act 1984, s 8, Sch 4, Pt II, para 5; words in square brackets in para (c) inserted by the Isle of Man Act 1979, s 13, Sch 1.

Sub-s (6): word in square brackets substituted by the Police and Criminal Evidence Act 1984, s 114(1).

Sub-s (7): words in square brackets substituted, in relation to offences committed after 29 July 1988, by the Finance Act 1988, s 12(1)(a), (6).

160 Power to take samples

(1) An officer may at any time take samples of any goods—

    (a)   which he is empowered by the Customs and Excise Acts 1979 to examine; or

    (b)   which are on premises where goods chargeable with any duty are manufactured, prepared or subjected to any process; or

    (c)   which, being dutiable goods, are held by any person as stock for his business or as materials for manufacture or processing.

(2) Where an officer takes from any vessel, pipe or utensil on the premises of any of the following revenue traders, that is to say, a distiller, [registered brewer], producer of wine, producer of made-wine or maker of cider, a sample of any product of, or of any materials for, the manufacture of that trader—

    (a)   the trader may, if he wishes, stir up and mix together the contents of that vessel, pipe or utensil before the sample is taken; and

    (b)   the sample taken by the officer shall be deemed to be representative of the whole contents of that vessel, pipe or utensil.

(3) Any sample taken under this section shall be disposed of and accounted for in such manner as the Commissioners may direct.

(4) Where any sample is taken under this section from any goods chargeable with a duty of customs or excise after that duty has been paid, other than—

    (a)   a sample taken when goods are first entered on importation; or

    (b)   a sample taken from goods in respect of which a claim for drawback, allowance, rebate, remission or repayment of that duty is being made,

and the sample so taken is to be retained, the officer taking it shall, if so required by the person in possession of the goods, pay for the sample on behalf of the Commissioners such sum as reasonably represents the wholesale value thereof.

NOTES

Sub-s (2): words in square brackets substituted by the Finance Act 1991, s 7(4), Sch 2, para 1.

[161 Power to search premises: writ of assistance

(1) The powers conferred by this section are exercisable by an officer having a writ of assistance if there are reasonable grounds to suspect that anything liable to forfeiture under the customs and excise Acts—

    (a)   is kept or concealed in any building or place, and

    (b)   is likely to be removed, destroyed or lost before a search warrant can be obtained and executed.

(2) The powers are—

    (a)   to enter the building or place at any time, whether by day or night, on any day, and search for, seize, and detain or remove any such thing, and

    (b)   so far as is necessary for the purpose of such entry, search, seizure, detention or removal, to break open any door, window or container and force and remove any other impediment or obstruction.

(3) An officer shall not exercise the power of entry conferred by this section by night unless accompanied by a constable.

(4) A writ of assistance shall continue in force during the reign in which it is issued and for six months thereafter.]

NOTES

Substituted, together with s 161A (for original s 161) by the Finance Act 2000, s 25.

[161A Power to search premises: search warrant

(1)   If a justice of the peace is satisfied by information upon oath given by an officer that there are reasonable grounds to suspect that anything liable to forfeiture under the customs and excise Acts is kept or concealed in any building or place, he may by warrant under his hand authorise any officer, and any person accompanying an officer, to enter and search the building or place named in the warrant.

(2)   An officer or other person so authorised has power—

    (a)   to enter the building or place at any time, whether by day or night, on any day, and search for, seize, and detain or remove any such thing, and

    (b)   so far as is necessary for the purpose of such entry, search, seizure, detention or removal, to break open any door, window or container and force and remove any other impediment or obstruction.

(3)   Where there are reasonable grounds to suspect that any still, vessel, utensil, spirits or materials for the manufacture of spirits is or are unlawfully kept or deposited in any building or place, subsections (1) and (2) above apply in relation to any constable as they would apply in relation to an officer.

(4)   The powers conferred by a warrant under this section are exercisable until the end of the period of one month beginning with the day on which the warrant is issued.

(5)   A person other than a constable shall not exercise the power of entry conferred by this section by night unless accompanied by a constable.]

NOTES

Substituted, together with s 161 (for original s 161) by the Finance Act 2000, s 25.

---

162 Power to enter land for or in connection with access to pipe-lines

Where any thing conveyed by a pipe-line is chargeable with a duty of customs or excise which has not been paid, an officer may enter any land adjacent to the pipe-line in order to get to the pipe-line for the purpose of exercising in relation to that thing any power conferred by or under the Customs and Excise Acts 1979 or to get from the pipe-line after an exercise of any such power.

This section does not extend to Northern Ireland.

163 Power to search vehicles or vessels

(1)   Without prejudice to any other power conferred by the Customs and Excise Acts 1979, where there are reasonable grounds to suspect that any vehicle or vessel is or may be carrying any goods which are—

    (a)   chargeable with any duty which has not been paid or secured; or

    (b)   in the course of being unlawfully removed from or to any place; or

    (c)   otherwise liable to forfeiture under the customs and excise Acts,

any officer or constable or member of Her Majesty's armed forces or coast-guard may stop and search that vehicle or vessel.

(2)   If when so required by any such officer, constable or member the person in charge of any such vehicle or vessel refuses to stop or to permit the vehicle or vessel to be searched, he shall be liable on summary conviction to a penalty of [level 3 on the standard scale].

[(3)   This section shall apply in relation to aircraft as it applies in relation to vehicles or vessels but the power to stop and search in subsection (1) above shall not be available in respect of aircraft which are airborne.]

NOTES

Sub-s (2): reference to a level on the standard scale substituted by virtue of the Criminal Justice Act 1982, ss 38, 46.

Sub-s (3): added by the Finance (No 2) Act 1992, s 10(1), (4).

[163A Power to search articles

(1) Without prejudice to any other power conferred by the Customs and Excise Acts 1979, where there are reasonable grounds to suspect that a person in the United Kingdom (referred to in this section as "the suspect") has with him, or at the place where he is, any goods to which this section applies, an officer may—

(a)   require the suspect to permit a search of any article that he has with him or at that place, and

(b)   if the suspect is not under arrest, detain him (and any such article) for so long as may be necessary to carry out the search.

(2) The goods to which this section applies are dutiable alcoholic liquor, or tobacco products, which are—

(a)   chargeable with any duty of excise, and

(b)   liable to forfeiture under the customs and excise Acts.

(3) Notwithstanding anything in subsection (4) of section 24 of the Criminal Law (Consolidation) (Scotland) Act 1995 (detention and questioning by customs officers), detention of the suspect under subsection (1) above shall not prevent his subsequent detention under subsection (1) of that section.]

NOTES

Inserted by the Finance Act 2000, s 26.

---

164 Power to search persons

(1) Where there are reasonable grounds to suspect that any person to whom this section applies [(referred to in this section as "the suspect")] is carrying any article—

(a)   which is chargeable with any duty which has not been paid or secured; or

(b)   with respect to the importation or exportation of which any prohibition or restriction is for the time being in force under or by virtue of any enactment,

[an officer may exercise the powers conferred by subsection (2) below and, if the suspect is not under arrest, may detain him for so long as may be necessary for the exercise of those powers and (where applicable) the exercise of the rights conferred by subsection (3) below].

[(2) The officer may require the suspect—

(a)   to permit such a search of any article which he has with him; and

(b)   subject to subsection (3) below, to submit to such searches of his person, whether rub-down, strip or intimate,

as the officer may consider necessary or expedient; but no such requirement may be imposed under paragraph (b) above without the officer informing the suspect of the effect of subsection (3) below.

(3) If the suspect is required to submit to a search of his person, he may require to be taken—

(a)   except in the case of a rub-down search, before a justice of the peace or a superior of the officer concerned; and

(b)   in the excepted case, before such a superior;

and the justice or superior shall consider the grounds for suspicion and direct accordingly whether the suspect is to submit to the search.

(3A) A rub-down or strip search shall not be carried out except by a person of the same sex as the suspect; and an intimate search shall not be carried out except by a suitably qualified person.]

(4) This section applies to the following persons, namely—

(a)   any person who is on board or has landed from any ship or aircraft;

(b)   any person entering or about to leave the United Kingdom;

(c)   any person within the dock area of a port;

(d)   any person at a customs and excise airport;

(e)   any person in, entering or leaving any approved wharf or transit shed which is not in a port;

[(ee)   any person in, entering or leaving a free zone;]

(f)   in Northern Ireland, any person travelling from or to any place which is on or beyond the boundary.

[(5) In this section—

"intimate search" means any search which involves a physical examination (that is, an examination which is more than simply a visual examination) of a person's body orifices;

"rub-down search" means any search which is neither an intimate search nor a strip search;

"strip search" means any search which is not an intimate search but which involves the removal of an article of clothing which—

(a)   is being worn (wholly or partly) on the trunk; and

(b)   is being so worn either next to the skin or next to an article of underwear;

"suitably qualified person" means a registered medical practitioner or a registered nurse.

(6) Notwithstanding anything in subsection (4) of section 48 of the Criminal Justice (Scotland) Act 1987 (detention and questioning by customs officers), detention of the suspect under subsection (1) above shall not prevent his subsequent detention under subsection (1) of that section.

NOTES

Sub-s (1): words in first pair of square brackets inserted, words in second pair of square brackets substituted by the Finance Act 1988, s 10(1).

Sub-ss (2), (3), (3A): substituted for original sub-ss (2), (3) by the Finance Act 1988, s 10(2).

Sub-s (4): para (ee) inserted by the Finance Act 1984, s 8, Sch 4, Pt II, para 6.

Sub-ss (5), (6): added by the Finance Act 1988, s 10(3).

165

(Repealed by the Commissioners for Revenue and Customs Act 2005 s 50, Sch 4 para 21, s 52, Sch 5.)

---

166 Agents

(1) If any person requests an officer or a person appointed by the Commissioners to transact any business relating to an assigned matter with him on behalf of another person, the officer or person so appointed may refuse to transact that business with him unless written authority from that other person is produced in such form as the Commissioners may direct.

(2)   Subject to subsection (1) above, anything required by the Customs and Excise Acts 1979 to be done by the importer or exporter of any goods may, except where the Commissioners otherwise require, be done on his behalf by an agent.

General offences

167   Untrue declarations, etc

(1)   If any person either knowingly or recklessly—

(a)   makes or signs, or causes to be made or signed, or delivers or causes to be delivered to the Commissioners or an officer, any declaration, notice, certificate or other document whatsoever; or

(b)   makes any statement in answer to any question put to him by an officer which he is required by or under any enactment to answer,

being a document or statement produced or made for any purpose of any assigned matter, which is untrue in any material particular, he shall be guilty of an offence under this subsection and may be [arrested]; and any goods in relation to which the document or statement was made shall be liable to forfeiture.

(2)   Without prejudice to subsection (4) below, a person who commits an offence under subsection (1) above shall be liable—

(a)   on summary conviction, to a penalty of the prescribed sum, or to imprisonment for a term not exceeding 6 months, or to both; or

(b)   on conviction on indictment, to a penalty of any amount, or to imprisonment for a term not exceeding 2 years, or to both.

(3)   If any person—

(a)   makes or signs, or causes to be made or signed, or delivers or causes to be delivered to the Commissioners or an officer, any declaration, notice, certificate or other document whatsoever; or

(b)   makes any statement in answer to any question put to him by an officer which he is required by or under any enactment to answer,

being a document or statement produced or made for any purpose of any assigned matter, which is untrue in any material particular, then, without prejudice to subsection (4) below, he shall be liable on summary conviction to a penalty of [level 4 on the standard scale].

(4)   Where by reason of any such document or statement as is mentioned in subsection (1) or (3) above the full amount of any duty payable is not paid or any overpayment is made in respect of any drawback, allowance, rebate or repayment of duty, the amount of the duty unpaid or of the overpayment shall be recoverable as a debt due to the Crown or may be summarily recovered as a civil debt.

[(5)   An amount of excise duty, or the amount of an overpayment in respect of any drawback, allowance, rebate or repayment of any excise duty, shall not be recoverable as mentioned in subsection (4) above unless the Commissioners have assessed the amount of the duty or of the overpayment as being excise duty due from the person mentioned in subsection (1) or (3) above and notified him or his representative accordingly.]

NOTES

Sub-s (1): word in square brackets substituted by the Police and Criminal Evidence Act 1984, s 114(1).

Sub-s (3): reference to a level on the standard scale substituted by virtue of the Criminal Justice Act 1982, ss 38, 46.

Sub-s (5): added by the Finance Act 1997, s 50(2), Sch 6, paras 5, 7.

Modification: modified, in relation to the application of sub-s (2)(a) above, by the Statistics of Trade (Customs and Excise) Regulations 1992, SI 1992/2790, reg 12.

This section shall not apply in relation to a declaration, document or statement in respect of a function relating to a matter to which the Commissioners for Revenue and Customs Act 2005 s 7 applies (CRCA 2005 ss 16, 17, Sch 2 para 6).

168 Counterfeiting documents, etc

(1) If any person—

(a) counterfeits or falsifies any document which is required by or under any enactment relating to an assigned matter or which is used in the transaction of any business relating to an assigned matter; or

(b) knowingly accepts, receives or uses any such document so counterfeited or falsified; or

(c) alters any such document after it is officially issued; or

(d) counterfeits any seal, signature, initials or other mark of, or used by, any officer for the verification of such a document or for the security of goods or for any other purpose relating to an assigned matter,

he shall be guilty of an offence under this section and may be [arrested].

(2) A person guilty of an offence under this section shall be liable—

(a) on summary conviction, to a penalty of the prescribed sum, or to imprisonment for a term not exceeding 6 months, or to both; or

(b) on conviction on indictment, to a penalty of any amount, or to imprisonment for a term not exceeding 2 years, or to both.

NOTES

Sub-s (1): word in square brackets substituted by the Police and Criminal Evidence Act 1984, s 114(1).

Modified, in relation to the application of sub-s (2)(a) above, by the Statistics of Trade (Customs and Excise) Regulations 1992, SI 1992/2790, reg 12.

This section shall not apply in relation to a declaration, document or statement in respect of a function relating to a matter to which the Commissioners for Revenue and Customs Act 2005 s 7 applies (CRCA 2005 ss 16, 17, Sch 2 para 6).

169

(Repealed by the Commissioners for Revenue and Customs Act 2005 s 52(1)(a)(viii), Sch 5.)

170 Penalty for fraudulent evasion of duty, etc

(1) Without prejudice to any other provision of the Customs and Excise Acts 1979, if any person—

(a) knowingly acquires possession of any of the following goods, that is to say—

(i) goods which have been unlawfully removed from a warehouse or Queen's warehouse;

(ii) goods which are chargeable with a duty which has not been paid;

(iii) goods with respect to the importation or exportation of which any prohibition or restriction is for the time being in force under or by virtue of any enactment; or

(b) is in any way knowingly concerned in carrying, removing, depositing, harbouring, keeping or concealing or in any manner dealing with any such goods,

and does so with intent to defraud Her Majesty of any duty payable on the goods or to evade any such prohibition or restriction with respect to the goods he shall be guilty of an offence under this section and may be [arrested].

(2)   Without prejudice to any other provision of the Customs and Excise Acts 1979, if any person is, in relation to any goods, in any way knowingly concerned in any fraudulent evasion or attempt at evasion—

(a)   of any duty chargeable on the goods;

(b)   of any prohibition or restriction for the time being in force with respect to the goods under or by virtue of any enactment; or

(c)   of any provision of the Customs and Excise Acts 1979 applicable to the goods,

he shall be guilty of an offence under this section and may be [arrested].

(3)   Subject to subsection [(4), (4A) or (4B)] below, a person guilty of an offence under this section shall be liable—

(a)   on summary conviction, to a penalty of the prescribed sum or of three times the value of the goods, whichever is the greater, or to imprisonment for a term not exceeding 6 months, or to both; or

(b)   on conviction on indictment, to a penalty of any amount, or to imprisonment for a term not exceeding [7 years], or to both.

(4)   In the case of an offence under this section in connection with a prohibition or restriction on importation or exportation having effect by virtue of section 3 of the Misuse of Drugs Act 1971, subsection (3) above shall have effect subject to the modifications specified in Schedule 1 to this Act.

[(4A)   In the case of—

(a)   an offence under subsection (2) or (3) above committed in Great Britain in connection with a prohibition or restriction on the importation or exportation of any weapon or ammunition that is of a kind mentioned in section 5(1)(a), (ab), (aba), (ac), (ad), (ae), (af) or (c) or (1A)(a) of the Firearms Act 1968,

(b)   any such offence committed in Northern Ireland in connection with a prohibition or restriction on the importation or exportation of any weapon or ammunition that is of a kind mentioned in [Article 45(1)(a), (b), (c), (d), (e) or (g) or (2)(a)] of the Firearms (Northern Ireland) Order [2004], or

(c)   any such offence committed in connection with the prohibitions contained in sections 20 and 21 of the Forgery and Counterfeiting Act 1981,

subsection (3)(b) above shall have effect as if for the words "7 years" there were substituted the words "10 years".]

[(4B)   In the case of an offence under subsection (1) or (2) above in connection with the prohibition contained in regulation 2 of the Import of Seal Skins Regulations 1996, subsection (3) above shall have effect as if—

(a)   for paragraph (a) there were substituted the following—

"(a)   on summary conviction, to a fine not exceeding the statutory maximum or to imprisonment for a term not exceeding three months, or to both"; and

(b)   in paragraph (b) for the words "7 years" there were substituted the words "2 years".]

(5)   In any case where a person would, apart from this subsection, be guilty of—

(a)   an offence under this section in connection with a prohibition or restriction; and

(b)   a corresponding offence under the enactment or other instrument imposing the prohibition or restriction, being an offence for which a fine or other penalty is expressly provided by that enactment or other instrument, he shall not be guilty of the offence mentioned in paragraph (a) of this subsection.

[(6) Where any person is guilty of an offence under this section, the goods in respect of which the offence was committed shall be liable to forfeiture.]

NOTES

Sub-ss (1), (2): words in square brackets substituted by the Police and Criminal Evidence Act 1984, s 114(1).

Sub-s (3): words in first pair of square brackets substituted by the Import of Seal Skins Regulations 1996, SI 1996/2686, reg 4(2); words in second pair of square brackets substituted, in relation to offences committed after 29 July 1988, by the Finance Act 1988, s 12(1)(a), (6).

Sub-s (4A): substituted by the Criminal Justice Act 2003 s 293(1), (4). In para (b), references in square brackets substituted by the Firearms (Northern Ireland) Order, SI 2004/702 art 82(1), Sch 7 para 5.

Sub-s (4B): inserted by SI 1996/2686, reg 4(2).

Sub-s (6): added by the Finance (No 2) Act 1992, s 3, Sch 2, para 7.

Modification: modified, in relation to exportation of any controlled radioactive source, by the Export of Radioactive Sources (Control) Order SI 2006/1846.

[170A Offence of handling goods subject to unpaid excise duty

(1) Subject to subsection (2) below, if—

    (a)   after the excise duty point for any goods which are chargeable with a duty of excise, a person acquires possession of those goods or is concerned in carrying, removing, depositing, keeping or otherwise dealing with those goods; and

    (b)   at the time when he acquires possession of those goods or is so concerned, [a payment of duty on the goods is outstanding and] has not been deferred,

[the conduct of that person falling within paragraph (a) above shall attract a penalty under section 9 of the Finance Act 1994 (civil penalties) which shall be calculated by reference to the amount of the unpaid duty.]

[(2) Section 10 of the Finance Act 1994 (exception to civil penalty in cases of reasonable excuse) shall not apply in relation to conduct attracting a penalty by virtue of subsection (1) above; but such conduct shall not give rise to any liability to a penalty under section 9 of that Act if the person whose conduct it is satisfies the Commissioners or, on appeal, a VAT and duties tribunal, that he—]

    (a)   acted in accordance with the directions of, or with the consent of, the proper officer; or

    (b)   was not himself the person, or one of the persons, liable to pay the unpaid duty and at the time when he acted either—

        (i)   had no grounds for suspecting that the goods were chargeable with a duty of excise that had not yet been paid; or

        (ii)   believed on reasonable grounds that the duty had been paid or its payment deferred or that the liability to pay the duty had not yet taken effect.]

NOTES

Inserted by the Finance (No 2) Act 1992, s 3, Sch 2, para 8.

Sub-ss (1), (2): words in square brackets substituted by the Finance Act 1994, s 9, Sch 4, Pt I, paras 1, 13.

Modification of this section by the Channel Tunnel (Alcoholic Liquor and Tobacco Products) Order 2003, SI 2003/2758, art 3, Schedule, in the application of this section to goods in a control zone.

170B Offence of taking preparatory steps for evasion of excise duty

(1) If any person is knowingly concerned in the taking of any steps with a view to the fraudulent evasion, whether by himself or another, of any duty of excise on any goods, he shall be liable—

    (a)   on summary conviction, to a penalty of the prescribed sum or of three times the amount of the duty, whichever is the greater, or to imprisonment for a term not exceeding six months or to both; and

    (b)   on conviction on indictment, to a penalty of any amount or to imprisonment for a term not exceeding seven years or to both.

(2) Where any person is guilty of an offence under this section, the goods in respect of which the offence was committed shall be liable to forfeiture.]

NOTES

Inserted as noted to s 170A.

---

171 General provisions as to offences and penalties

(1) Where—

    (a)   by any provision of any enactment relating to an assigned matter a punishment is prescribed for any offence thereunder or for any contravention of or failure to comply with any regulation, direction, condition or requirement made, given or imposed thereunder; and

    (b)   any person is convicted in the same proceedings of more than one such offence, contravention or failure,

that person shall be liable to that punishment for each such offence, contravention or failure of which he is so convicted.

(2) In this Act the "prescribed sum", in relation to the penalty provided for an offence, means—

    (a)   if the offence was committed in England [or Wales], the prescribed sum within the meaning of [section 32 of the Magistrates' Courts Act 1980 (£1,000 or other sum substituted by order under section 143(1) of that Act)]

    (b)   if the offence was committed in Scotland, the prescribed sum within the meaning of section 289B of the Criminal Procedure (Scotland) Act 1975 (£1,000 or other sum substituted by order under section 289D(1) of that Act);

    [(c)   if the offence was committed in Northern Ireland, the prescribed sum within the meaning of Article 4 of the Fines and Penalties (Northern Ireland) Order 1984 ([£5,000] or other sum substituted by order under Article 17 of that Order);]

and in subsection (1)(a) above, the reference to a provision by which a punishment is prescribed includes a reference to a provision which makes a person liable to a penalty of the prescribed sum within the meaning of this subsection.

[(2A) . . .]

(3) Where a penalty for an offence under any enactment relating to an assigned matter is required to be fixed by reference to the value of any goods, that value shall be taken as the price which those goods might reasonably be expected to have fetched, after payment of any duty or tax chargeable thereon, if they had been sold in the open market at or about the date of the commission of the offence for which the penalty is imposed.

(4) Where an offence under any enactment relating to an assigned matter which has been committed by a body corporate is proved to have been committed with the consent or connivance of, or to be attributable to any neglect on the part of, any

director, manager, secretary or other similar officer of the body corporate or any person purporting to act in any such capacity, he as well as the body corporate shall be guilty of that offence and shall be liable to be proceeded against and punished accordingly.

In this subsection "director", in relation to any body corporate established by or under any enactment for the purpose of carrying on under national ownership any industry or part of an industry or undertaking, being a body corporate whose affairs are managed by the members thereof, means a member of that body corporate.

[(4A)   Subsection (4) shall not apply to an offence which relates to a matter listed in Schedule 1 to the Commissioners for Revenue and Customs Act 2005 (former Inland Revenue matters).]

(5)   Where in any proceedings for an offence under the customs and excise Acts any question arises as to the duty or the rate thereof chargeable on any imported goods, and it is not possible to ascertain the relevant time specified in section 43 above [or the relevant excise duty point], that duty or rate shall be determined as if the goods had been imported without entry at the time when the proceedings were commenced [or, as the case may be, as if the time when the proceedings were commenced was the relevant excise duty point].

NOTES

Sub-s (2): words in first pair of square brackets in para (a) substituted, and para (c) added, by the Fines and Penalties (Northern Ireland) Order 1984, SI 1984/703, art 19(1), Sch 6, para 7; words in second pair of square brackets in para (a) substituted by the Magistrates' Courts Act 1980, s 154, Sch 7, para 178; sum in square brackets in para (c) substituted by virtue of the Criminal Justice (Northern Ireland) Order 1994, SR 1994/2795 (NI 15), art 3(1).

Sub-s (2A): inserted by the Finance Act 1984, s 9, Sch 5, para 3; repealed by the Statute Law (Repeals) Act 1993.

Sub-s (4A) inserted by the Commissioners for Revenue and Customs Act 2005 s 50, Sch 4 para 28.

Sub-s (5): words in square brackets inserted by the Finance (No 2) Act 1992, s 3, Sch 2, para 9.

Miscellaneous

172 Regulations

(1)   Any power to make regulations under this Act shall be exercisable by statutory instrument.

(2)   Subject to subsection (3) below, a statutory instrument containing regulations made under this Act shall be subject to annulment in pursuance of a resolution of either House of Parliament.

(3)   A statutory instrument containing regulations made under section 120 above shall be subject to annulment in pursuance of a resolution of the House of Commons.

NOTES

Regulations: the Aircraft Operators (Accounts and Records) Regulations 1994, SI 1994/1737.

173 Directions

Directions given under any provision of this Act may make different provision for different circumstances and may be varied or revoked by subsequent directions thereunder.

174

(Repealed by the Isle of Man Act 1979, s 14(5), Sch 2.)

175 Scotland—special provisions

(1) In the application of this Act to Scotland—

(a)   any reference to costs shall be construed as a reference to expenses;

(b)   any provision that any amount shall be recoverable summarily as a civil debt shall be construed as if the word "summarily" were omitted;

(c)   any reference to a plaintiff shall be construed as a reference to a pursuer;

(d)   any reference to a magistrates' court shall be construed as a reference to the sheriff court.

(2) . . .

NOTES

Sub-s (2): repealed by the Law Reform (Miscellaneous Provisions) (Scotland) Act 1980, s 28(2), Sch 3.

176 Game licences

. . .

NOTES

Section 176 repealed by the Regulatory Reform (Game) Order, SI 2007/2007, art 6, Sch 1, para 1(n). Section 176 applied only in relation to England and Wales. Consequently, the repeal in this Order does not extend to Scotland (SI 2007/2007 art 1(2)).

177 Consequential amendments, repeals and saving and transitional provisions

(1) The enactments specified in Schedule 4 to this Act shall be amended in accordance with the provisions of that Schedule.

(2) . . .

(3) The enactments specified in Schedule 6 to this Act are hereby repealed to the extent specified in the third column of that Schedule.

(4) The saving and transitional provisions contained in Schedule 7 to this Act shall have effect.

(5) The provisions of Schedules 4, 5 and 7 to this Act shall not be taken as prejudicing the operation of sections 15 to 17 of the Interpretation Act 1978 (which relate to the effect of repeals).

NOTES

Sub-s (2): repealed by the Statute Law (Repeals) Act 1986.

178 Citation and commencement

(1) This Act may be cited as the Customs and Excise Management Act 1979.

(2) This Act, the Customs and Excise Duties (General Reliefs) Act 1979, the Alcoholic Liquor Duties Act 1979, the Hydrocarbon Oil Duties Act 1979, . . . and the Tobacco Products Duty Act 1979 may be cited together as the Customs and Excise Acts 1979.

(3) This Act shall come into operation on 1st April 1979.

SCHEDULES

SCHEDULE 1
CONTROLLED DRUGS: VARIATION OF PUNISHMENTS FOR CERTAIN OFFENCES UNDER THIS ACT

Sections 50(5), 68(4), 170(4)

1.   Section 50(4), 68(3), and 170(3) of this Act shall have effect in a case where the goods in respect of which the offence referred to in that subsection was committed were a Class A drug or a Class B drug as if for the words from "shall be liable" onwards there were substituted the following words, that is to say—

"shall be liable—

  (a)   on summary conviction, to a penalty of the prescribed sum or of three times the value of the goods, whichever is the greater, or to imprisonment for a term not exceeding 6 months, or to both;

  [(b)   on conviction on indictment—

  (i)   where the goods were a Class A drug, to a penalty of any amount, or to imprisonment for life, or to both; and

  (ii)   where they were a Class B drug, to a penalty of any amount, or to imprisonment for a term not exceeding 14 years, or to both"].

2.   Section 50(4), 68(3) and 170(3) of this Act shall have effect in a case where the goods in respect of which the offence referred to in that subsection was committed were a Class C drug as if for the words from "shall be liable" onwards there were substituted the following words, that is to say—

"shall be liable—

  (a)   on summary conviction . . ., to a penalty of three times the value of the goods or [level 5 on the standard scale], whichever is the greater, or to imprisonment for a term not exceeding 3 months, or to both;

  (b)   . . .

  (c)   on conviction on indictment, to a penalty of any amount, or to imprisonment for a term not exceeding [14 years], or to both.".

3.   In this Schedule "Class A drug", "Class B drug" and "Class C drug" have the same meanings as in the Misuse of Drugs Act 1971.

SCHEDULE 2
COMPOSITE GOODS: SUPPLEMENTARY PROVISIONS AS TO EXCISE DUTIES AND DRAWBACKS
Section 126(3)

Duties

1.—(1) Where under subsection (1) of the principal section imported goods of any class or description are chargeable with a duty of excise in respect of any article contained in the goods as a part or ingredient of them and it appears to the Treasury on the recommendation of the Commissioners that to charge the duty according to the quantity of the article used in the manufacture or preparation of the goods (as provided by the principal section) is inconvenient and of no material advantage to the revenue or to importers of goods of that class or description, then the Treasury may by order give a direction in relation to goods of that class or description under and in accordance with this paragraph.

(2) An order under this paragraph may direct that in the case of goods of the class or description to which it applies the duty shall be calculated in such of the following ways as may be provided by the order, that is to say—

(a) at a rate specified in the order by reference to the weight, quantity or value of the goods; or

(b) by reference to a quantity so specified of the article, and (where material) on the basis that the article is of such value, type or quality as may be so specified.

(3) If it appears to the Treasury on the recommendation of the Commissioners that, in the case of goods of any class or description, the net amounts payable in the absence of any direction under this paragraph are insignificant, the order may direct that any such goods shall be treated for the purpose of the duty as not containing the article in respect of which the duty is chargeable.

(4) If it appears to the Treasury on the recommendation of the Commissioners that goods of any class or description are substantially of the same nature and use as if they consisted wholly of the article in respect of which the duty is chargeable, the order may direct that any such goods shall be treated for the purpose of the duty as consisting wholly of that article.

(5) In making an order under this paragraph the Treasury shall have regard to the quantity and (where material) the type or quality of the article in question appearing to them, on the advice of the Commissioners, to be ordinarily used in the manufacture or preparation of goods of the class or description to which the order applies which are imported into the United Kingdom.

2. Where a direction given by virtue of paragraph 1 above is in force as regards goods of any class or description and any article contained in them, and goods of that class or description are imported into the United Kingdom containing a quantity of that article such as, in the opinion of the Commissioners, to suggest that advantage is being taken of the direction for the purpose of evading duty chargeable on the article, the Commissioners may, notwithstanding the direction, require that on those goods the duty in question shall be calculated as if they consisted wholly of that article or (if the Commissioners see fit) shall be calculated according to the quantity of the article actually contained in the goods.

3. Nothing in paragraphs 1 and 2 above shall affect the powers of the Treasury under subsection (2) of the principal section; and any goods as regards which a direction under that subsection is for the time being in force shall be deemed to be excepted from any order under paragraph 1 above.

Drawbacks

4.   Where a direction is given by virtue of paragraph 1 above as regards imported goods of any class or description, the Treasury may by order provide that for the purpose of allowing any drawback of excise duties there shall, in such cases and subject to such conditions (if any) as may be specified in the order, be treated as paid on imported goods of that class or description the same duties as would be chargeable apart from the direction.

5.—(1)   Where, in the case of imported goods of any class or description which contain as a part or ingredient any article chargeable with a duty of excise, drawback of the duty may be allowed in respect of the article according to the quantity contained in the goods or the quantity used in their preparation or manufacture, and it appears to the Treasury on the recommendation of the Commissioners that to allow the drawback according to that quantity is inconvenient and of no material advantage to the revenue or to the persons entitled to the drawback, then the Treasury may by order give the like directions as to the manner in which the drawback is to be calculated, or in which the goods are to be treated for the purposes of the drawback, as by virtue of paragraph 1 above they may give in relation to charging duty.

(2)   For the purposes of this paragraph, the reference in paragraph 1(5) above to goods imported into the United Kingdom shall be taken as a reference to goods in the case of which the drawback may be allowed.

Supplementary

6.   Where any order under paragraph 1 or 5 above directs that, for the purpose of any duty or of any drawback, goods are to be treated as not containing or as consisting wholly of a particular article, the goods shall be so treated also for the purpose of determining whether any other duty is chargeable or any other drawback may be allowed, as the case may be; but any duty or drawback which is charged or allowed shall, notwithstanding the direction, be calculated by reference to the actual quantity and value of the goods and, except for the duty or drawback to which the direction relates, by reference to their actual composition.

7.   Where a resolution passed by the House of Commons has statutory effect under the Provisional Collection of Taxes Act 1968 in relation to any duty of excise charged on imported goods, and any provision about that duty contained in an order under paragraph 1 above is expressed to be made in view of the resolution, then that provision may be varied or revoked retrospectively by an order made not later than one month after the resolution ceases to have statutory effect, and that order may include provision for repayment of any duty overpaid or for other matters arising from its having retrospective effect; but no such order shall have retrospective effect for the purpose of increasing the duty chargeable on any goods.

8.   The power to make orders under this Schedule shall be exercisable by statutory instrument subject to annulment in pursuance of a resolution of the House of Commons.

Interpretation

9.   In this Schedule "the principal section" means section 126 of this Act.

SCHEDULE 3
PROVISIONS RELATING TO FORFEITURE
Sections 139, 143, 145

Notice of seizure

1.—(1) The Commissioners shall, except as provided in sub-paragraph (2) below, give notice of the seizure of any thing as liable to forfeiture and of the grounds therefor to any person who to their knowledge was at the time of the seizure the owner or one of the owners thereof.

(2) Notice need not be given under this paragraph if the seizure was made in the presence of—

    (a)   the person whose offence or suspected offence occasioned the seizure; or

    (b)   the owner or any of the owners of the thing seized or any servant or agent of his; or

    (c)   in the case of anything seized in any ship or aircraft, the master or commander.

2. Notice under paragraph 1 above shall be given in writing and shall be deemed to have been duly served on the person concerned—

    (a)   if delivered to him personally; or

    (b)   if addressed to him and left or forwarded by post to him at his usual or last known place of abode or business or, in the case of a body corporate, at their registered or principal office; or

    (c)   where he has no address within the United Kingdom [or the Isle of Man], or his address is unknown, by publication of notice of the seizure in the London, Edinburgh or Belfast Gazette.

Notice of claim

3. Any person claiming that any thing seized as liable to forfeiture is not so liable shall, within one month of the date of the notice of seizure or, where no such notice has been served on him, within one month of the date of the seizure, give notice of his claim in writing to the Commissioners at any office of customs and excise.

4.—(1) Any notice under paragraph 3 above shall specify the name and address of the claimant and, in the case of a claimant who is outside the United Kingdom [and the Isle of Man], shall specify the name and address of a solicitor in the United Kingdom who is authorised to accept service of process and to act on behalf of the claimant.

(2) Service of process upon a solicitor so specified shall be deemed to be proper service upon the claimant.

Condemnation

5. If on the expiration of the relevant period under paragraph 3 above for the giving of notice of claim in respect of any thing no such notice has been given to the Commissioners, or if, in the case of any such notice given, any requirement of paragraph 4 above is not complied with, the thing in question shall be deemed to have been duly condemned as forfeited.

6. Where notice of claim in respect of any thing is duly given in accordance with paragraphs 3 and 4 above, the Commissioners shall take proceedings for the condemnation of that thing by the court, and if the court finds that the thing was at the time of seizure liable to forfeiture the court shall condemn it as forfeited.

7. Where any thing is in accordance with either of paragraphs 5 or 6 above condemned or deemed to have been condemned as forfeited, then, without prejudice to any delivery up or sale of the thing by the Commissioners under paragraph 16 below, the forfeiture shall have effect as from the date when the liability to forfeiture arose.

Proceedings for condemnation by court

8. Proceedings for condemnation shall be civil proceedings and may be instituted—

(a)   in England or Wales either in the High Court or in a magistrates' court;

(b)   in Scotland either in the Court of Session or in the sheriff court;

(c)   in Northern Ireland either in the High Court or in a court of summary jurisdiction.

9. Proceedings for the condemnation of any thing instituted in a magistrates' court in England or Wales, in the sheriff court in Scotland or in a court of summary jurisdiction in Northern Ireland may be so instituted—

(a)   in any such court having jurisdiction in the place where any offence in connection with that thing was committed or where any proceedings for such an offence are instituted; or

(b)   in any such court having jurisdiction in the place where the claimant resides or, if the claimant has specified a solicitor under paragraph 4 above, in the place where that solicitor has his office; or

(c)   in any such court having jurisdiction in the place where that thing was found, detained or seized or to which it is first brought after being found, detained or seized.

10.—(1) In any proceedings for condemnation instituted in England, Wales or Northern Ireland, the claimant or his solicitor shall make oath that the thing seized was, or was to the best of his knowledge and belief, the property of the claimant at the time of the seizure.

(2) In any such proceedings instituted in the High Court, the claimant shall give such security for the costs of the proceedings as may be determined by the Court.

(3) If any requirement of this paragraph is not complied with, the court shall give judgment for the Commissioners.

11.—(1) In the case of any proceedings for condemnation instituted in a magistrates' court in England or Wales, without prejudice to any right to require the statement of a case for the opinion of the High Court, either party may appeal against the decision of that court to the Crown Court.

(2) In the case of any proceedings for condemnation instituted in a court of summary jurisdiction in Northern Ireland, without prejudice to any right to require the statement of a case for the opinion of the High Court, either party may appeal against the decision of that court to the county court.

12. Where an appeal, including an appeal by way of case stated, has been made against the decision of the court in any proceedings for the condemnation of any thing, that thing shall, pending the final determination of the matter, be left with the Commissioners or at any convenient office of customs and excise.

Provisions as to proof

13. In any proceedings arising out of the seizure of any thing, the fact, form and manner of the seizure shall be taken to have been as set forth in the process without any further evidence thereof, unless the contrary is proved.

14.   In any proceedings, the condemnation by a court of any thing as forfeited may be proved by the production either of the order or certificate of condemnation or of a certified copy thereof purporting to be signed by an officer of the court by which the order or certificate was made or granted.

Special provisions as to certain claimants

15.   For the purposes of any claim to, or proceedings for the condemnation of, any thing, where that thing is at the time of seizure the property of a body corporate, of two or more partners or of any number of persons exceeding five, the oath required by paragraph 10 above to be taken and any other thing required by this Schedule or by any rules of the court to be done by, or by any person authorised by, the claimant or owner may be taken or done by, or by any other person authorised by, the following persons respectively, that is to say—

(a)   where the owner is a body corporate, the secretary or some duly authorised officer of that body;

(b)   where the owners are in partnership, any one of those owners;

(c)   where the owners are any number of persons exceeding five not being in partnership, any two of those persons on behalf of themselves and their co-owners.

Power to deal with seizures before condemnation, etc.

16.   Where any thing has been seized as liable to forfeiture the Commissioners may at any time if they see fit and notwithstanding that the thing has not yet been condemned, or is not yet deemed to have been condemned, as forfeited—

(a)   deliver it up to any claimant upon his paying to the Commissioners such sum as they think proper, being a sum not exceeding that which in their opinion represents the value of the thing, including any duty or tax chargeable thereon which has not been paid;

(b)   if the thing seized is a living creature or is in the opinion of the Commissioners of a perishable nature, sell or destroy it.

17.—(1)   If, where any thing is delivered up, sold or destroyed under paragraph 16 above, it is held in proceedings taken under this Schedule that the thing was not liable to forfeiture at the time of its seizure, the Commissioners shall, subject to any deduction allowed under sub-paragraph (2) below, on demand by the claimant tender to him—

(a)   an amount equal to any sum paid by him under sub-paragraph (a) of that paragraph; or

(b)   where they have sold the thing, an amount equal to the proceeds of sale; or

(c)   where they have destroyed the thing, an amount equal to the market value of the thing at the time of its seizure.

(2)   Where the amount to be tendered under sub-paragraph (1)(a), (b) or (c) above includes any sum on account of any duty or tax chargeable on the thing which had not been paid before its seizure the Commissioners may deduct so much of that amount as represents that duty or tax.

(3)   If the claimant accepts any amount tendered to him under sub-paragraph (1) above, he shall not be entitled to maintain any action on account of the seizure, detention, sale or destruction of the thing.

(4)   For the purposes of sub-paragraph (1)(c) above, the market value of any thing at the time of its seizure shall be taken to be such amount as the Commissioners and the claimant may agree or, in default of agreement, as may be determined by a referee appointed by the Lord Chancellor (not being an official of any government

department [or an office-holder in, or a member of the staff of, the Scottish Administration]), whose decision shall be final and conclusive; and the procedure on any reference to a referee shall be such as may be determined by the referee.

[(5) The Lord Chancellor may make an appointment under sub-paragraph (4) only with the concurrence—

(a) where the proceedings referred to in sub-paragraph (1) were taken in England and Wales, of the Lord Chief Justice of England and Wales;

(b) where those proceedings were taken in Scotland, of the Lord President of the Court of Session;

(c) where those proceedings were taken in Northern Ireland, of the Lord Chief Justice of Northern Ireland.

(6) The Lord Chief Justice of England and Wales may nominate a judicial office holder (as defined in section 109(4) of the Constitutional Reform Act 2005) to exercise his functions under this paragraph.

(7) The Lord President of the Court of Session may nominate a judge of the Court of Session who is a member of the First or Second Division of the Inner House of that Court to exercise his functions under this paragraph.

(8) The Lord Chief Justice of Northern Ireland may nominate any of the following to exercise his functions under this paragraph—

(a) the holder of one of the offices listed in Schedule 1 to the Justice (Northern Ireland) Act 2002;

(b) a Lord Justice of Appeal (as defined in section 88 of that Act).]

NOTES

Paras 2, 4: words in square brackets added by the Isle of Man Act 1979, s 13, Sch 1.

Para 17: words in square brackets inserted by the Scotland Act 1998 (Consequential Modifications) (No 2) Order 1999, SI 1999/1820, art 4, Sch 2, Pt I, para 59. New sub-paras (5)–(8) inserted by the Constitutional Reform Act 2005 s 15, Sch 4 para 97, with effect from 3 April 2006.

Postal packets: see note at the beginning of this Act.

Modification: any reference to solicitor(s) etc modified to include references to bodies recognised under the Administration of Justice Act 1985, s 9, by the Solicitors' Incorporated Practices Order 1991, SI 1991/2684, arts 4, 5, Sch 1.

SCHEDULE 4

CONSEQUENTIAL AMENDMENTS

Section 177(1)

Construction of references in Acts passed before 1st April 1909 and in instruments made thereunder

1. Save where the context otherwise requires, any reference in, or in any instrument made under, any enactment relating to customs or excise passed before 1st April 1909 to any of the persons mentioned in column 1 of the following Table shall be construed as a reference to the persons respectively specified in relation thereto in column 2.

Original reference	*To be construed as reference to—*
Commissioners of Customs	
Commissioners of Inland Revenue	Commissioners of Customs and Excise.
Commissioners of Excise	
Solicitor for The Customs	Solicitor for the Customs and Excise

Original reference	*To be construed as reference to—*
Solicitor of Inland Revenue	
Secretary for the Customs	Secretary to the Commissioners of Customs and Excise.
Secretary of the Commissioners of Inland Revenue	
Accountant and Comptroller General of Customs	Accountant and Comptroller General of the Customs and Excise.
Accountant and Comptroller General of Inland Revenue	
Collector of Customs	
Collector of Inland Revenue	Collector of Customs and Excise
Collector of Excise	
Officer of Customs	
Officer of Inland Revenue	Officer of Customs and Excise.
Officer of Excise	
2–12 . . .	

NOTES

Para 2: repealed by the Isle of Man Act 1979, s 14(5), Sch 2.

Para 3: inserts the Diplomatic Privileges Act 1964, s 2(5A).

Paras 4, 5: amend the Provisional Collection of Taxes Act 1968, s 3.

Paras 6, 7: amend the Consular Relations Act 1968, ss 1, 5.

Para 8: amends the Misuse of Drugs Act 1971, s 12(1)(b).

Paras 9–11: repealed by the Value Added Tax Act 1983, s 50(2), Sch 11.

Para 12, Table, Pt I: insofar as unrepealed, contains amending material only. Where amendments affect legislation contained in this book, they are noted to that legislation.

(Sch 5 repealed by the Finance Act 1972, ss 54(8), 134(7), Sch 28, Pt II; Sch 6 contains repeals.)

SCHEDULE 7
SAVING AND TRANSITIONAL PROVISIONS

Section 177(4)

1. Notwithstanding the repeal by this Act of section 258 of the Customs and Excise Act 1952, of paragraph 5 of Schedule 2 to the Finance Act 1970, and of paragraph 2(8) of Schedule 4 to the European Communities Act 1972, that section (together with Schedule 6) as it had effect immediately before the entry date within the meaning of the said Act of 1972, shall continue to have effect for cases in which the value of goods falls to be determined as at a time before that date.

2. . . .

3. Notwithstanding the repeal by this Act of section 308(3) of the Customs and Excise Act 1952, section 277 of the Customs Consolidation Act 1876 does not apply in relation to any Act passed after 1st January 1953.

4. . . .

5. The repeal by this Act of section 5(4) of the European Communities Act 1972 (which, so far as it relates to enactments contained in this Act, is re-enacted by section 1(7) of this Act) shall not affect the application of any law not contained in this Act which relates to customs duties.

6.   The repeal by this Act of any enactment already repealed by section 75(5) of the Finance (No 2) Act 1975 and specified in Part I of Schedule 14 to that Act shall not affect the operation of the saving in paragraph 2 in that Part in relation to that enactment.

7.   The repeal by this Act of section 8(4) of the Finance (No. 2) Act 1975 and the repeal by any of the Customs and Excise Acts 1979 of any provision of Part I of Schedule 3 to that Act shall not affect the right to any drawback or other relief under any enactment amended by that provision in respect of customs duty charged before the end of 1975.

8.   Any such reference as is specified in paragraph 1 of Schedule 3 to the Finance (No. 2) Act 1975 ("customs duty", "excise duty" and associated references), being a reference in—

(a)   any instrument of a legislative character made under the customs and excise Acts which was in force at the end of 1975; or

(b)   any local and personal or private Act which was then in force,

shall continue to be construed as provided by that paragraph notwithstanding the repeal of that paragraph by this Act.

9.   Any such reference as is specified in sub-paragraph (2), (6) or (8) of paragraph 19 of Schedule 12 to the Finance Act 1978 ("customs Acts", "excise Acts", "excise trade", "excise trader", "customs airport" and "customs station"), being a reference in—

(a)   any instrument in force immediately before the commencement of this Act; or

(b)   any local and personal or private Act then in force,

shall continue to be construed as provided by the said sub-paragraph (2), (6) or (8), as the case may be, notwithstanding the repeal of that sub-paragraph by this Act.

10.—(1)   Any provision of this Act relating to anything done or required or authorised to be done under or in pursuance of the Customs and Excise Acts 1979 shall have effect as if any reference to those Acts included a reference to the Customs and Excise Act 1952.

(2)   Any provision of this Act relating to anything done or required or authorised to be done under, in pursuance of or by reference to that provision or any other provision of this Act shall have effect as if any reference to that provision, or that other provision, as the case may be, included a reference to the corresponding provision of the enactments repealed by this Act.

11.   Any functions which, immediately before the commencement of this Act, fall to be performed on behalf of any other person by the Commissioners or by officers or by any person appointed by the Commissioners shall continue to be so performed by them unless and until other arrangements are made, notwithstanding that those functions are not expressly mentioned in this Act.

12.—(1)   The repeal by this Act of subsection (4) of section 316 of the Customs and Excise Act 1952 shall not affect any such right or privilege as is referred to in that subsection.

(2)   Where by any enactment, grant or other instrument, any right or privilege not relating to customs or excise has at any time been granted by reference to the then existing limits of any port or approved wharf appointed or approved for the purposes of customs and excise, then, subject to any provision contained in that instrument, nothing in any order made or other thing done under section 19 or 20 of this Act shall affect that right or privilege.

NOTES

Para 2: repealed so far as it related to car tax by the Car Tax Act 1983, s 10(4), Sch 3; repealed so far as it related to value added tax by the Value Added Tax Act 1983, s 50(2), Sch 11.

Para 4: repealed by the Isle of Man Act 1979, s 14(5), Sch 2.

CUSTOMS AND EXCISE DUTIES (GENERAL RELIEFS) ACT 1979

(1979 c 3)

ARRANGEMENT OF SECTIONS

An Act to consolidate certain enactments relating to reliefs and exemptions from customs and excise duties, section 7 of the Finance Act 1968 and certain other related enactments

[22 February 1979]

Principal reliefs from customs duties

1 Reliefs from customs duty for conformity with Community obligations and other international obligations, etc

(1)   The Secretary of State may, in accordance with subsections (2) to (6) below, by order provide for relieving goods from the whole or part of any customs duty chargeable on goods imported into the United Kingdom.

(2)   Goods of any description may be relieved from customs duty if and in so far as the relief appears to the Secretary of State to be necessary or expedient with a view to—

    (a)   conforming with any Community obligations; or

    (b)   otherwise affording relief provided for by or under the Community Treaties or any decisions of the representatives of the governments of the member States of the Coal and Steel Community meeting in Council.

(3)   Goods of any description may be relieved from customs duty if and in so far as the relief appears to the Secretary of State to be necessary or expedient with a view to conforming with an international agreement relating to matters other than commercial relations.

(4)   Exposed cinematograph film may be relieved from customs duty if certified as provided by the order to be of an educational character.

(5)   Relief given by virtue of subsection (4) above may be restricted with a view to securing reciprocity in countries or territories outside the United Kingdom.

(6)   Articles recorded with sound, other than exposed cinematograph film, may be relieved from customs duty (other than duty chargeable on similar articles not so recorded) if the articles are not produced in quantity for general sale as so recorded.

NOTES

Orders: by virtue of the Interpretation Act 1978, s 17(2)(b), the following orders have effect as it made under this section: the Import Duty Reliefs Order 1963, SI 1963/2013; the Import Duty Reliefs (No 1) Order 1965, SI 1965/1664; the Import Duty Reliefs (No 2) Order 1965, SI 1965/1665; the Import Duties Reliefs (No 2) Order 1970, SI 1970/1497; the Import Duties Reliefs (No 3) Order 1970, SI 1970/1617.

2 Reliefs from customs duty referable to Community practices

(1)   The Secretary of State may by regulations make such provision as regards reliefs from customs duty chargeable on goods imported into the United Kingdom as appears to him to be expedient having regard to the practices adopted or to be adopted in other member States, whether by law or administrative action and whether or not for conformity with Community obligations.

(2)   Regulations under this section may amend or repeal accordingly any of sections 1, 3, 4 and 15 of this Act.

NOTES

Regulations: the Customs Duties (Standard Exchange Relief and Outward Processing Relief) (Revocation) Regulations 1989, SI 1989/116.

Part I

3 Power to exempt particular importations of certain goods from customs duty

(1)   Subject to the provisions of this section, the Secretary of State may direct that payment shall not be required of the whole or part of any customs duty which is chargeable on any goods imported or proposed to be imported into the United Kingdom if he is satisfied—

(a)   that the goods qualify for relief under this section; and

(b)   that in all the circumstances it is expedient for the relief to be given.

(2)   The following goods qualify for relief under this section, that is to say, articles intended and reasonably required—

(a)   for the purpose of subjecting the articles, or any material or component in the articles, to examination or tests with a view to promoting or improving the manufacture in the United Kingdom of goods similar to those articles or to that material or component, as the case may be; or

(b)   for the purpose of subjecting goods capable of use with those or similar articles (including goods which might be used as materials or components in such articles or in which such articles might be used as materials or components) to examination or tests with a view to promoting or improving the manufacture in the United Kingdom of those or similar goods.

(3)   Any direction of the Secretary of State under this section may be given subject to such conditions as he thinks fit.

(4)   Where a direction given by the Secretary of State under this section is subject to any conditions, and it is proposed to use or dispose of the goods in any manner for which the consent of the Secretary of State is required by the conditions, the Secretary of State may consent to the goods being so used or disposed of subject to payment of the duty which would have been payable but for the direction or such part of the duty as the Secretary of State thinks appropriate in the circumstances.

(5)   The Secretary of State shall not give a direction under this section except on a written application made by the importer, and a direction under this section shall have effect to such extent (if any) as the Commissioners may allow if the goods have been released from customs and excise control without the importer having given to the Commissioners notice of the direction or of his application or intention to apply for it.

(6)   Any notice to the Commissioners under subsection (5) above shall be in such form as they may require, and the Commissioners on receiving any such notice or at any time afterwards may impose any such conditions as they see fit for the protection of the revenue (including conditions requiring security for the observance of any conditions subject to which relief is granted).

(7)   A direction of the Secretary of State under this section shall have effect only if and so long as any conditions of the relief, including any conditions imposed by the Commissioners under subsection (6) above, are complied with; but where any customs duty is paid on the importation of any goods, and the Commissioners are satisfied that by virtue of a direction subsequently given and having effect under this section payment of the duty is not required, then the duty shall be repaid.

4 Administration of reliefs under section 1 and administration or implementation of similar Community reliefs

(1)   The Secretary of State may by order make provision for the administration of any relief under section 1 above or for the implementation or administration of any like relief provided for by any Community instrument.

(2)   An order under this section may in particular—

(a)   impose or authorise the imposition of conditions for securing that goods relieved from duty as being imported for a particular purpose are used for that purpose or such other conditions as appear expedient to secure the object or prevent abuse of the relief;

(b) where the relief is limited to a quota of imported goods, provide for determining the allocation of the quota or for enabling it to be determined by the issue of certificates or licences or otherwise;

(c) confer on a government department or any other authority or person functions in connection with the administration of the relief or the enforcement of any condition of relief;

(d) authorise any government department having any such functions to make payments (whether for remuneration or for expenses) to persons advising the department or otherwise acting in the administration of the relief;

(e) require the payment of fees by persons applying for the relief or applying for the registration of any person or premises in connection with the relief;

(f) authorise articles for which relief is claimed to be sold or otherwise disposed of if the relief is not allowed and duty is not paid.

(3) Any expenses incurred by a government department by virtue of any order under this section shall be defrayed out of money provided by Parliament, and any fees received by a government department by virtue of any such order shall be paid into the Consolidated Fund.

NOTES

Orders: the Customs Duties Quota Relief (Administration) Order 1986, SI 1986/2174; the Agricultural Levy Reliefs (Frozen Beef and Veal) Order 1989, SI 1989/154; by virtue of the Interpretation Act 1978, s 17(2)(b), the Import Duty Reliefs (Administration) Order 1958, SI 1958/1965, as restricted by SI 1986/2174, has effect as if made under this section.

Reliefs from duties for Channel Islands or Isle of Man goods

5 Relief from customs duty of certain goods from Channel Islands

(1) Subject to subsection (2) below, any goods which are the produce or growth of any of the Channel Islands or which have been manufactured in any of those islands from—

(a) materials which are such produce or growth; or

(b) materials not chargeable with any duty in the United Kingdom; or

(c) materials so chargeable upon which that duty has been paid and not drawn back,

may be imported without payment of any customs duty chargeable thereon.

(2) Subsection (1) above shall not apply in relation to any goods unless the master of the ship or commander of the aircraft in which the goods are imported produces to the proper officer at the place of importation a certificate from the Lieutenant-Governor or other proper authority of the island from which the goods are imported that a declaration in such form and containing such particulars as the Commissioners may direct has been made before a magistrate of that island by the person exporting the goods therefrom that the goods are goods to which this section applies.

(3) Directions under subsection (2) above may make different provision for different circumstances and may be varied or revoked by subsequent directions thereunder.

6

(Repealed by the Isle of Man Act 1979, s 14(5), Sch 2.)

Miscellaneous reliefs from customs and excise duties

[7 Power to provide for reliefs from duty and value added tax in respect of imported legacies

(1) The Commissioners may by order make provision for conferring reliefs from duty and value added tax in respect of goods imported into the United Kingdom by or for any person who has become entitled to them as legatee.

(2) Any such relief may take the form either of an exemption from payment of duty and tax or of a provision whereby the sum payable by way of duty or tax is less than it would otherwise be.

(3) The Commissioners may by order make provision supplementing any Community relief, in such manner as they think necessary or expedient.

(4) An order under this section—

    (a)   may make any relief for which it provides or any Community relief subject to conditions, including conditions which are to be complied with after the importation of the goods to which the relief applies;

    (b)   may, in relation to any relief conferred by order made under this section, contain such incidental and supplementary provisions as the Commissioners think necessary or expedient; and

    (c)   may make different provision for different cases.

(5) In this section—

"Community relief" means any relief which is conferred by a Community instrument and is of a kind, or of a kind similar to that, which could otherwise be conferred by order made under this section;

"duty" means customs or excise duty chargeable on goods imported into the United Kingdom and, in the case of excise duty, includes any addition to the duty by virtue of section 1 of the Excise Duties (Surcharges or Rebates) Act 1979;

"legatee" means any person taking under a testamentary disposition or donatio mortis causa or on an intestacy; and

"value added tax" means value added tax chargeable on the importation of goods.]

NOTES

Substituted with effect from 1 July 1984 by the Finance Act 1984, s 4(1), (3).

Orders: the Customs and Excise Duties (Personal Reliefs for Goods Permanently Imported) Order 1992, SI 1992/3193.

8 Relief from customs or excise duty on trade samples, labels, etc

The Commissioners may allow the delivery without payment of customs or excise duty on importation, subject to such conditions and restrictions as they see fit—

    (a)   of trade samples of such goods as they see fit, whether imported as samples or drawn from the goods on their importation;

    (b)   of labels or other articles supplied without charge for the purpose of being re-exported with goods manufactured or produced in, and to be exported from, the United Kingdom [or the Isle of Man].

NOTES

Words in square brackets added by the Isle of Man Act 1979, s 13, Sch 1.

9 Relief from customs or excise duty on antiques, prizes, etc

The Commissioners may allow the delivery without payment of customs or excise duty on importation—

    (a)   of any goods (other than spirits or wine) which are proved to the satisfaction of the Commissioners to have been manufactured or produced more than 100 years before the date of importation;

    (b)   of articles which are shown to the satisfaction of the Commissioners to have been awarded abroad to any person for distinction in art, literature, science or sport, or for public service, or otherwise as a record of meritorious achievement or conduct, and to be imported by or on behalf of that person.

Reliefs from excise duties

10 Relief from excise duty on certain United Kingdom goods re-imported

(1) Without prejudice to any other enactment relating to excise, the following provisions of this section shall have effect in relation to goods manufactured or produced in the United Kingdom [or the Isle of Man] which are re-imported into the United Kingdom after exportation therefrom.

(2) If the goods are at the date of their re-importation excise goods, they may on re-importation be delivered for home use without payment of excise duty if it is shown to the satisfaction of the Commissioners—

    (a)   that at the date of their exportation the goods were not excise goods or, if they were then excise goods, that the excise duty had been paid before their exportation; and

    (b)   that no drawback in respect of the excise duty and no allowance has been paid on their exportation or that any such drawback or allowance so paid has been repaid to the Consolidated Fund; and

    (c)   that the goods have not undergone any process outside the United Kingdom since their exportation.

(3) If the goods both are at the date of their re-importation and were at the date of their exportation excise goods, but they were exported without the excise duty having been paid from a warehouse or from the place where they were manufactured or produced, then, where the following conditions are satisfied, that is to say—

    (a)   it is shown to the satisfaction of the Commissioners that they have not undergone any process outside the United Kingdom since their exportation; and

    (b)   any allowance paid on their exportation is repaid to the Consolidated Fund,

the goods may on their re-importation, subject to such conditions and restrictions as the Commissioners may impose, be entered and removed without payment of excise duty for re-warehousing or for return to the place where they were manufactured or produced, as the case may be.

(4) Nothing in this section shall authorise the delivery for home use of any goods not otherwise eligible therefor.

(5) In this section—

    "excise goods" means goods—

        (a)   of a class or description chargeable at the time in question with a duty of excise; or

        (b)   in the manufacture or preparation of which any goods of such a class or description have been used;

    "the excise duty" means the duty by virtue of which the goods are or were at the time in question excise goods.

NOTES

Sub-s (1): words in square brackets inserted by the Isle of Man Act 1979, s 13, Sch 1.

11 Relief from excise duty on certain foreign goods re-imported

(1) Without prejudice to any other enactment relating to excise but subject to subsection (2) below, goods manufactured or produced outside the United Kingdom [and the Isle of Man] which are re-imported into the United Kingdom after exportation therefrom may on their re-importation be delivered without payment of excise duty for home use, where so eligible, if it is shown to the satisfaction of the Commissioners—

    (a)   that no excise duty was chargeable thereon at their previous importation or that any excise duty so chargeable was then paid; and

    (b)   that no drawback has been paid or excise duty refunded on their exportation or that any drawback so paid or excise duty so refunded has been repaid to the Consolidated Fund; and

    (c)   that the goods have not undergone any process outside the United Kingdom since their exportation.

(2) For the purposes of this section goods which on their previous importation were entered for transit or transhipment or were permitted to be delivered without payment of excise duty as being imported only temporarily with a view to subsequent re-exportation and which were re-exported accordingly shall on their re-importation be deemed not to have been previously imported.

NOTES

Sub-s (1): words in square brackets inserted by the Isle of Man Act 1979, s 13, Sch 1.

[11A Relief from excise duty on goods imported for testing etc

(1) The Commissioners may by order provide that, in such cases and subject to such exceptions as may be specified in the order, goods imported into the United Kingdom for the sole or main purpose—

    (a)   of being examined, analysed or tested; or

    (b)   of being used to test other goods,

shall be relieved from excise duty chargeable on importation; and any such relief may take the form either of an exemption from payment of duty or of a provision whereby the sum payable by way of duty is less than it otherwise would be.

(2) An order under this section—

    (a)   may make any relief for which it provides subject to conditions specified in or under the order, including conditions to be complied with after the importation of the goods to which the relief applies;

    (b)   may contain such incidental and supplementary provisions as the Commissioners think necessary or expedient; and

    (c)   may make different provision for different cases.

(3) In this section, references to excise duty include any additions to such duty by virtue of section 1 of the Excise Duties (Surcharges or Rebates) Act 1979.]

NOTES

Inserted by the Finance Act 1988, s 5(1).

Orders: the Excise Duties (Goods Imported for Testing, etc) Relief Order 1991, SI 1991/2089.

Relief for goods for Her Majesty's ships

12 Supply of duty-free goods to Her Majesty's ships

(1) The Treasury may by regulations provide that, subject to any prescribed conditions, goods of any description specified in the regulations which are supplied either—

(a) to any ship of the Royal Navy in commission of a description so specified, for the use of persons serving in that ship, being persons borne on the books of that or some other ship of the Royal Navy or a naval establishment; or

(b) to the Secretary of State, for the use of persons serving in ships of the Royal Navy or naval establishments,

shall for all or any purposes of any excise duty or drawback in respect of those goods be treated as exported, and a person supplying or intending to supply goods as mentioned in paragraph (a) or (b) above shall be treated accordingly as exporting or intending to export them.

(2) Regulations made under this section with respect to goods of any description may regulate or provide for regulating the quantity allowed to any ship or establishment, the manner in which they are to be obtained and their use or distribution.

(3) The regulations may—

(a) contain such other incidental or supplementary provisions as appear to the Treasury to be necessary for the purposes of this section, including any adaptations of the customs and excise Acts; and

(b) make different provision in relation to different cases, and in particular in relation to different classes or descriptions of goods or of ships or establishments.

(4) In subsection (1) above "prescribed" means prescribed by regulations under this section or, in pursuance of any such regulations, by the Commissioners after consultation with the Secretary of State.

(5) Before making any regulations under this section, the Treasury shall consult with the Secretary of State and with the Commissioners.

(6) The powers conferred by this section shall apply for the purposes of customs duty as they apply for the purposes of excise duty but shall not so apply after such day as the Commissioners may by order appoint.

NOTES

Regulations: by virtue of the Interpretation Act 1978, s 17(2)(b), the Duty-Free Supplies for the Royal Navy Regulations 1954, SI 1954/1406, have effect as if made under sub-s (1) above.

Personal reliefs

13 Power to provide, in relation to persons entering the United Kingdom, for reliefs from duty and value added tax and for simplified computation of duty and tax

(1) The Commissioners may by order make provision for conferring on persons entering the United Kingdom reliefs from duty and value added tax; and any such relief may take the form either of an exemption from payment of duty and tax or of a provision whereby the sum payable by way of duty or tax is less than it would otherwise be.

[(1A) The Commissioners may by order make provision supplementing any Community relief, in such manner as they think necessary or expedient.]

(2) Without prejudice to subsection (1) above, the Commissioners may by order make provision whereby, in such cases and to such extent as may be specified in the order, a sum calculated at a rate specified in the order is treated as the aggregate amount payable by way of duty and tax in respect of goods imported by a person entering the United Kingdom; but any order making such provision shall enable the person concerned to elect that duty and tax shall be charged on the goods in question at the rate which would be applicable apart from that provision.

(3) An order under this section—

    (a)   may make any relief for which it provides[, or any Community relief] subject to conditions, including conditions which are to be complied with after the importation of the goods to which the relief applies [and conditions with respect to the conduct in relation to the goods of persons other than the person on whom the relief is conferred and of persons whose identity cannot be ascertained at the time of importation];

    (b)   may[, in relation to any relief conferred by order made under this section,] contain such incidental and supplementary provisions as the Commissioners think necessary or expedient, including [provisions requiring any person to whom a condition of the relief at any time relates to notify the Commissioners of any non-compliance with the condition and] provisions for the forfeiture of goods in the event of non-compliance with any condition subject to which they have been relieved from duty or tax; and

    (c)   may make different provision for different cases.

[(3A) An order under this section may provide, in relation to any relief which under such an order is made subject to a condition, for there to be a presumption that, in such cases as may be described in the order by reference—

    (a)   to the quantity of goods in question; or

    (b)   to any other factor which the Commissioners consider appropriate,

the condition is to be treated, unless the Commissioners are satisfied to the contrary, as not being complied with.

(3B) An order under this section may provide, in relation to any requirement of such an order for the Commissioners to be notified of non-compliance with a condition to which any relief from payment of any duty of excise is made subject, for goods to be exempt from forfeiture under section 124 of the Customs and Excise Management Act 1979 (forfeiture for breach of certain conditions) in respect of non-compliance with that condition if—

    (a)   the non-compliance is notified to the Commissioners in accordance with that requirement;

    (b)   any duty which becomes payable on those goods by virtue of the non-compliance is paid; and

    (c)   the circumstances are otherwise such as may be described in the order.

(3C) If any person fails to comply with any requirement of an order under this section to notify the Commissioners of any non-compliance with a condition to which any relief is made subject—

    (a)   he shall be liable, on summary conviction, to a penalty of an amount not exceeding level 5 on the standard scale; and

    (b)   the goods in respect of which the offence was committed shall be liable to forfeiture.]

(4) In this section—

["Community relief" means any relief which is conferred by a Community instrument and is of a kind, or of a kind similar to that, which could otherwise be conferred by order made under this section;]

["conduct", in relation to any person who has or may acquire possession or control of any goods, includes that person's intentions at any time in relation to those goods;]

"duty" means customs or excise duty chargeable on goods imported into the United Kingdom and, in the case of excise duty, includes any addition thereto by virtue of section 1 of the Excise Duties (Surcharges or Rebates) Act 1979; and

"value added tax" or "tax" means value added tax chargeable on the importation of goods [from places outside the member States or on the acquisition of goods from the member States other than the United Kingdom].

(5) Nothing in any order under this section shall be construed as authorising any person to import any thing in contravention of any prohibition or restriction for the time being in force with respect thereto under or by virtue of any enactment.

NOTES

Sub-s (1A): inserted with effect from 31 March 1984 by the Finance Act 1984, s 15(1), (2).

Sub-s (3): words in first and third pairs of square brackets inserted with effect from 31 March 1984 by the Finance Act 1984, s 15(1), (3), (4); words in second and fourth pairs of square brackets inserted by the Finance (No 2) Act 1992, s 1, Sch 1, para 8(1).

Sub-ss (3A)–(3C): inserted by the Finance (No 2) Act 1992, s 1, Sch 1, para 8(2).

Sub-s (4): definition "Community relief" inserted with effect from 31 March 1984 by the Finance Act 1984, s 15(1), (5); definition "conduct" and words in square brackets in definition "value added tax" inserted by the Finance (No 2) Act 1992, ss 1, 14, Sch 1, para 8(3), Sch 3, Pt III, para 93.

Orders: the Customs Duties (Community Reliefs) Order 1984, SI 1984/719; the Excise Duties (Personal Reliefs) (Fuel and Lubricants Imported in Vehicles) Order 1989, SI 1989/1898, as amended by SI 1995/1777; the Excise Duties (Personal Reliefs) Order 1992, SI 1992/3155, as amended by SI 1999/1617; the Customs and Excise Duties (Personal Reliefs for Goods Permanently Imported) Order 1992, SI 1992/3193; the Travellers' Allowances Order 1994, SI 1994/955; the Traveller's Reliefs (Fuel and Lubricants) Order 1995, SI 1995/1777.

[13A Reliefs from duties and taxes for persons enjoying certain immunities and privileges

(1) The Commissioners may by order make provision for conferring in respect of any persons to whom this section applies reliefs, by way of remission or repayment, from payment by them or others of duties of customs or excise, value added tax or car tax.

(2) An order under this section may make any relief for which it provides subject to such conditions binding the person in respect of whom the relief is conferred and, if different, the person liable apart from the relief for payment of the tax or duty (including conditions which are to be complied with after the time when, apart from the relief, the duty or tax would become payable) as may be imposed by or under the order.

(3) An order under this section may include any of the provisions mentioned in subsection (4) below for cases where—

(a)   relief from payment of any duty of customs or excise, value added tax or car tax chargeable on any goods, or on the supply of any goods or services or the importation of any goods has been conferred (whether by virtue of an order under this section or otherwise) in respect of any person to whom this section applies, and

(b)   any condition required to be complied with in connection with the relief is not complied with.

(4) The provisions referred to in subsection (3) above are—

(a)   provision for payment to the Commissioners of the tax or duty by—
(i)   the person liable, apart from the relief, for its payment, or

(ii)   any person bound by the condition, or

(iii) any person who is or has been in possession of the goods or has received the benefit of the services,

or for two or more of those persons to be jointly and severally liable for such payment, and

(b)   in the case of goods, provision for forfeiture of the goods.

(5) An order under this section—

(a)   may contain such incidental and supplementary provisions as the Commissioners think necessary or expedient, and

(b)   may make different provision for different cases.

(6) In this section and section 13C of this Act—

"duty of customs" includes any agricultural levy within the meaning of section 6 of the European Communities Act 1972 chargeable on goods imported into the United Kingdom, and

"duty of excise" means any duty of excise chargeable on goods and includes any addition to excise duty by virtue of section 1 of the Excise Duties (Surcharges or Rebates) Act 1979.

(7) For the purposes of this section and section 13C of this Act, where in respect of any person to whom this section applies relief is conferred (whether by virtue of an order under this section or otherwise) in relation to the use of goods by any persons or for any purposes, the relief is to be treated as conferred subject to a condition binding on him that the goods will be used only by those persons or for those purposes.

(8) Nothing in any order under this section shall be construed as authorising a person to import any thing in contravention of any prohibition or restriction for the time being in force with respect to it under or by virtue of any enactment.]

NOTES

Inserted, together with s 13B, by the Finance Act 1989, s 28(1).

Orders: the Customs and Excise (Personal Reliefs for Special Visitors) Order 1992, SI 1992/3156.

[13B Persons to whom section 13A applies

(1)   The persons to whom section 13A of this Act applies are—

(a)   any person who, for the purposes of any provision of the Visiting Forces Act 1952 or the International Headquarters and Defence Organisations Act 1964 is—

(i)   a member of a visiting force or of a civilian component of such a force or a dependant of such a member, or

(ii)   a headquarters, a member of a headquarters or a dependant of such a member,

(b)   any person enjoying any privileges or immunities under or by virtue of—

(i)   the Diplomatic Privileges Act 1964,

(ii)   the Commonwealth Secretariat Act 1966,

(iii) the Consular Relations Act 1968,

(iv) the International Organisations Act 1968, or

[(v)   the International Development Act 2002.]

(c)   any person enjoying, under or by virtue of section 2 of the European Communities Act 1972, any privileges or immunities similar to those enjoyed under or by virtue of the enactments referred to in paragraph (b) above.

(2)   The Secretary of State may by order amend subsection (1) above to include any persons enjoying any privileges or immunities similar to those enjoyed under or by virtue of the enactments referred to in paragraph (b) of that subsection.

(3)   No order shall be made under this section unless a draft of the order has been laid before and approved by resolution of each House of Parliament.]

NOTES

Inserted as noted to s 13A.

Sub-s (1): para (b)(v) substituted by the International Development Act 2002, s 19, Sch 3 para 7.

[13C Offence where relieved goods used, etc, in breach of condition

(1)   Subsection (2) below applies where—

- (a)   any relief from payment of any duty of customs or excise, value added tax or car tax chargeable on, or on the supply or importation of, any goods has been conferred (whether by virtue of an order under section 13A of this Act or otherwise) in respect of any person to whom that section applies subject to any condition as to the persons by whom or the purposes for which the goods may be used, and
- (b)   if the tax or duty has subsequently become payable, it has not been paid.

(2)   If any person—

- (a)   acquires the goods for his own use, where he is not permitted by the condition to use them, or for use for a purpose that is not permitted by the condition or uses them for such a purpose, or
- (b)   acquires the goods for use, or causes or permits them to be used, by a person for a purpose that is not permitted by the condition or disposes of them to a person not permitted by the condition to use them,

with intent to evade payment of any tax or duty that has become payable or that, by reason of the disposal, acquisition or use, becomes or will become payable, he is guilty of an offence.

(3)   For the purposes of this section—

- (a)   in the case of a condition as to the persons by whom goods may be used, a person is not permitted by the condition to use them unless he is a person referred to in the condition as permitted to use them, and
- (b)   in relation to a condition as to the purposes for which goods may be used, a purpose is not permitted by the condition unless it is a purpose referred to in the condition as a permitted purpose,

and in this section "dispose" includes "lend" and "let on hire", and "acquire" shall be interpreted accordingly.

(4)   A person guilty of an offence under this section may be detained and shall be liable—

- (a)   on summary conviction, to a penalty of the statutory maximum or of three times the value of the goods (whichever is the greater), or to imprisonment for a term not exceeding six months, or to both, or
- (b)   on conviction on indictment, to a penalty of any amount, or to imprisonment for a term not exceeding seven years, or to both.

[(5)   Where any person is guilty of an offence under this section, the goods in respect of which the offence was committed shall be liable to forfeiture.]]

Part I

Inserted, in cases where relief is conferred on or after 27 July 1989, by the Finance Act 1989, s 28(1), (2).

Sub-s (5): added by the Finance (No 2) Act 1992, s 3, Sch 2, para 10.

Produce of the sea or continental shelf

14 Produce of the sea or continental shelf

(1)   Fish, whales or other natural produce of the sea, or goods produced or manufactured therefrom at sea, if brought direct to the United Kingdom, shall—

(a)   in the case of goods which, under any enactment or instrument having the force of law, are to be treated as originating in the United Kingdom, be deemed for the purposes of any charge to customs duty not to be imported; and

(b)   in the case of goods which, under any enactment or instrument having the force of law, are to be treated as originating in any other country or territory, be deemed to be consigned to the United Kingdom from that country.

(2)   Any goods brought into the United Kingdom which are shown to the satisfaction of the Commissioners to have been grown, produced or manufactured in any area for the time being designated under section 1(7) of the Continental Shelf Act 1964 and to have been so brought direct from that area shall be deemed for the purposes of any charge to customs duty not to be imported.

(3)   The Secretary of State may by regulations prescribe cases in which, with a view to exempting any goods from any duty, or charging any goods with duty at a reduced or preferential rate, under any of the enactments relating to duties of customs the continental shelf of any country prescribed by the regulations, or of any country of a class of countries so prescribed, shall be treated for the purposes of such of those enactments or of any instruments made thereunder as may be so prescribed as if that shelf formed part of that country and any goods brought from that shelf were consigned from that country.

(4)   In subsection (3) above "continental shelf", in relation to any country means—

(a)   if that country is the United Kingdom, any area for the time being designated under section 1(7) of the Continental Shelf Act 1964;

(b)   in any other case, the seabed and sub-soil of the submarine areas adjacent to the coast, but outside the seaward limits of the territorial waters, of that country over which the exercise by that country of sovereign rights in accordance with international law is recognised or authorised by Her Majesty's Government in the United Kingdom.

False statements etc in connection with reliefs from customs duties

15 False statements etc in connection with reliefs from customs duties

(1)   If a person—

(a)   for the purpose of an application for relief from customs duty under section 1 or 3 above or under a Community instrument; or

(b)   for the purpose of an application for an authorisation under regulations made under section 2 above,

makes any statement or furnishes any document which is false in a material particular to any government department or to any authority or person on whom functions are conferred by or under section 1, 3 or 4 above or a Community instrument, then—

> (i)   any decision allowing the relief or granting the authorisation applied for shall be of no effect; and
>
> (ii)   if the statement was made or the document was furnished knowingly or recklessly, that person shall be guilty of an offence under this section.

(2)   A person guilty of an offence under this section shall be liable—

> (a)   on summary conviction, to a fine not exceeding the prescribed sum, or to imprisonment for a term not exceeding 3 months, or to both; or
>
> (b)   on conviction on indictment, to a fine of any amount or to imprisonment for a term not exceeding 2 years, or to both.

(3)   In subsection (2)(a) above "the prescribed sum" means—

> (a)   if the offence was committed in England [or Wales], the prescribed sum within the meaning of [section 32 of the Magistrates' Courts Act 1980 (£1,000 or other sum substituted by order under section 143(1) of that Act)]
>
> (b)   if the offence was committed in Scotland, the prescribed sum within the meaning of section 289B of the Criminal Procedure (Scotland) Act 1975 (£1,000 or other sum substituted by order under section 289D(1) of that Act).
>
> [(c)   if the offence was committed in Northern Ireland, the prescribed sum within the meaning of Article 4 of the Fines and Penalties (Northern Ireland) Order 1984 ([£5,000] or other sum substituted by order under Article 17 of that Order).]

(4)   References in Parts XI and XII of the Customs and Excise Management Act 1979 to an offence under the customs and excise Acts shall not apply to an offence under this section.

NOTES

Sub-s (3): words in first pair of square brackets in para (a) substituted and para (c) added, by the Fines and Penalties (Northern Ireland) Order 1984, SI 1984/703, art 19(1), Sch 6, para 8; words in second pair of square brackets in para (a) substituted by the Magistrates' Courts Act 1980, s 154, Sch 7, para 179; sum in square brackets in para (c) substituted by virtue of the Criminal Justice (Northern Ireland) Order 1994, SI 1994/279, art 3(1).

Supplementary provisions

16 Annual reports to Parliament

As soon as may be after the end of each financial year the Secretary of State shall lay before each House of Parliament a report on the exercise during that year of the powers conferred by sections 1, 3 and 4 above with respect to the allowance of exemptions and reliefs from customs duties (including the power to amend or revoke orders providing for any exemption or relief from customs duties).

17 Orders and regulations

(1)   Any power to make orders or regulations under this Act shall be exercisable by statutory instrument.

(2)   Any statutory instrument containing regulations under section 2 or 12 above shall be subject to annulment in pursuance of a resolution of either House of Parliament except where, in the case of regulations under section 2, a draft of the regulations has been approved by resolution of each House of Parliament.

(3)   Any statutory instrument containing an order under section 1, 4 [7][, 11A] [13 or 13A] above or regulations under section 14(3) above shall be subject to annulment in pursuance of a resolution of the House of Commons except in a case falling within subsection (4) below.

(4)   Subject to subsection (5) below, where an order under section 1, 4[, 11A] [13(1) or 13A] above restricts any relief from duty or tax the statutory instrument containing the order shall be laid before the House of Commons after being made and, unless the order is approved by that House before the end of the period of 28 days beginning with the day on which it was made, it shall cease to have effect at the end of that period but without prejudice to anything previously done under the order or to the making of a new order.

In reckoning the said period of 28 days no account shall be taken of any time during which Parliament is dissolved or prorogued or during which the House of Commons is adjourned for more than 4 days.

(5)   Subsection (4) above does not apply in the case of an instrument containing an order under section 1[, 4 or 11A] above which states that it does not restrict any relief otherwise than in pursuance of a Community obligation.

(6)   For the purposes of this section restricting any relief includes removing or reducing any relief previously conferred.

NOTES

Sub-s (3): figure in first pair of square brackets inserted with effect from 1 July 1984 by the Finance Act 1984, s 14(2), (3); figure in second pair of square brackets inserted by the Finance Act 1988, s 5(2); figures in third pair of square brackets substituted by the Finance Act 1989, s 28(3).

Sub-s (4): figure in first pair of square brackets inserted by the Finance Act 1988, s 5(2); figures in second pair of square brackets substituted by the Finance Act 1989, s 28(3).

Sub-s (5): words in square brackets inserted by the Finance Act 1988, s 5(2).

18 Interpretation

(1)   This Act and the other Acts included in the Customs and Excise Acts 1979 shall be construed as one Act but where a provision of this Act refers to this Act that reference is not to be construed as including a reference to any of the others.

(2)   Any expression used in this Act or in any instrument made under this Act to which a meaning is given by any other Act included in the Customs and Excise Acts 1979 has, except where the context otherwise requires, the same meaning in this Act or in any such instrument as in that Act; and for ease of reference the Table below indicates the expressions used in this Act to which a meaning is given by any other such Act—

Customs and Excise Management Act 1979

"the Commissioners"
"the Customs and Excise Acts 1979"
"the customs and excise Acts"
"customs and excise airport"
"goods"
"hovercraft"
"importer"
"master"
"officer" and "proper" in relation to an officer
"port"
"ship"

"transit and transhipment"

"warehouse"

Alcoholic Liquor Duties Act 1979

"spirits"

"wine"

(3) This Act applies as if references to ships included references to hovercraft.

19 Consequential amendments, repeals and transitional provision

(1) The enactments specified in Schedule 2 to this Act shall be amended in accordance with the provisions of that Schedule.

(2) The enactments specified in Part I of Schedule 3 to this Act are hereby repealed to the extent specified in the third column of that Schedule and the regulations specified in Part II of that Schedule are hereby revoked to the extent so specified.

(3) References to import duties in instruments in force at the commencement of this Act shall, on and after that commencement, be construed—

    (a)   in the case of references in orders under section 5 or directions under section 6 of the Import Duties Act 1958, as references to customs duties charged under section 5(1) or (2) of the European Communities Act 1972;

    (b)   in the case of references in such orders or directions made by virtue of section 5(1A) of the said Act of 1958 or in regulations under section 5(6) of the European Communities Act 1972, as references to customs duties (whether so charged or charged under the Customs Duties (Dumping and Subsidies) Act 1969 or section 6(1) of the Finance Act 1978).

20 Citation and commencement

(1) This Act may be cited as the Customs and Excise Duties (General Reliefs) Act 1979 and is included in the Acts which may be cited as the Customs and Excise Acts 1979.

(2) This Act shall come into operation on 1st April 1979.

(Sch 1 repealed by the Isle of Man Act 1979, s 14(5), Sch 2; Sch 2: para 1 repealed by the Statute Law (Repeals) Act 1993; para 2 repealed by the Value Added Tax Act 1983, s 50, Sch 11; paras 3–5 amend the European Communities Act 1972, ss 5, 6(5), Sch 2; para 6 amends the Finance Act 1977, s 10(4); Sch 3 (Repeals and revocations) outside the scope of this work).

ALCOHOLIC LIQUOR DUTIES ACT 1979

(1979 c 4)

ARRANGEMENT OF SECTIONS

PART I

PRELIMINARY

An Act to consolidate the enactments relating to the excise duties on spirits, beer, wine, made-wine and cider together with certain other enactments relating to excise
[22 February 1979]

PART I
PRELIMINARY

1 The alcoholic liquors dutiable under this Act

(1) Subsections (2) to (8) below define for the purposes of this Act the alcoholic liquors which are subject to excise duty under this Act, that is to say—

    (a)   spirits,

    (b)   beer,

    (c)   wine,

    (d)   made-wine, and

    (e)   cider;

and in this Act "dutiable alcoholic liquor" means any of those liquors and "duty" means excise duty.

    [(2)   "Spirits" means, subject to subsections (7) to (9) below—

    (a)   spirits of any description which are of a strength exceeding 1.2 per cent

    (b)   any such mixture, compound or preparation made with spirits as is of a strength exceeding 1.2 per cent or

    (c)   liquors contained, with any spirits, in any mixture which is of a strength exceeding 1.2 per cent,

. . .]

    (3)   "Beer" includes ale, porter, stout and any other description of beer, and any liquor which is made or sold as a description of beer or as a substitute for beer and which [is] of a strength exceeding [0.5 per cent], but does not include—

    (a)   black beer the worts whereof before fermentation were of a specific gravity of 1200° or more, . . .

    (b)   . . .

    (4)   "Wine" means any liquor [which is of a strength exceeding 1.2 percent and which is] obtained from the alcoholic fermentation of fresh grapes or of the must of fresh grapes, whether or not the liquor is fortified with spirits or flavoured with aromatic extracts.

    (5)   "Made-wine" means [subject to subsection (10) [and section 55B(1)] below] any liquor [which is of a strength exceeding 1.2 per cent and which is] obtained from the alcoholic fermentation of any substance or by mixing a liquor so obtained or derived from a liquor so obtained with any other liquor or substance but does not include wine, beer, black beer, spirits or cider.

    (6)   "Cider" means[, subject to section 55B(1) below,] cider (or perry) of a strength [exceeding 1.2 per cent but] [less than 8.5 per cent] . . . obtained from the fermentation of apple or pear juice without the addition at any time of any alcoholic liquor or of any liquor or substance which communicates colour or flavour other than such as the Commissioners may allow as appearing to them to be necessary to make cider (or perry).

    (7)   Angostura bitters, that is to say, the aromatic flavouring essence commonly known as angostura bitters, shall be deemed not to be spirits, but this subsection does not apply for the purposes of sections 2, 5, 6 and 27 to 30 below.

    (8)   Methyl alcohol, notwithstanding that it is so purified or prepared as to be drinkable, shall not be deemed to be spirits nor shall naphtha or any mixture or preparation containing naphtha or methyl alcohol and not containing spirits as defined in subsection (2) above.

    (9)   . . .

    (10) The Treasury may by order made by statutory instrument provide that any beverage of an alcoholic strength exceeding 1.2 per cent but not exceeding 5.5 per cent which is made with beer or cider and is of a description specified in the order shall be deemed to be beer or, as the case may be, cider, and not to be made-wine.]

NOTES

    Sub-s (2): substituted by the Excise Duty (Amendment of the Alcoholic Liquor Duties Act 1979 and the Hydrocarbon Oil Duties Act 1979) Regulations 1992, SI 1992/3158, reg 2(1), (2); words omitted are repealed by the Finance Act 1995, s 162, Sch 29, Pt I(3).

    Sub-s (3): word in first pair of square brackets substituted, and words omitted repealed, by the Finance Act 1991, ss 7(4), 123, Sch 2, para 2, Sch 19, Pt II; words in second pair of square brackets substituted by the Finance Act 1993, s 3(1), (3), in relation to liquor produced in, or imported into, the United Kingdom, or removed into the United Kingdom from the Isle of Man, on or after 27 July 1993.

Sub-s (4): words in square brackets inserted by the Finance Act 1995, s 1(1), (2), (5), in relation to liquor imported into, or produced in, the United Kingdom, or removed to the United Kingdom from the Isle of Man, on or after 1 January 1995.

Sub-s (5): words in first (outer) pair of square brackets inserted by the Finance Act 1988, s 1(5), Sch 1, Pt II, para 1(3); words in second (inner) pair of square brackets inserted by the Finance Act 1997, s 5(2), (5), with retrospective effect as from 1 January 1997; words in third pair of square brackets inserted by the Finance Act 1995, s 1(1), (2), (5), in relation to liquor imported into, or produced in, the United Kingdom, or removed to the United Kingdom from the Isle of Man, on or after 1 January 1995.

Sub-s (6): words in first pair of square brackets inserted by the Finance Act 1997, s 5(2), (5), with retrospective effect as from 1 January 1997; words in second pair of square brackets inserted by the Finance Act 1995, s 1(1), (3), (6), in relation to liquor imported into, or made in, the United Kingdom on or after 1 January 1995; words in third pair of square brackets substituted by the Finance Act 1984, s 1(5); words omitted repealed by the Alcoholic Liquors (Amendment of Enactments Relating to Strength and to Units of Measurement) Order 1979, SI 1979/241, art 5.

Sub-s (9): repealed by the Finance Act 2002, s 3, Sch 39 Pt 1(1).

Sub-s (10): added by the Finance Act 1988, s 1(5), Sch 1, Pt II, para 1(4).

Orders: the Alcoholic Liquor Duties (Beer-based Beverages) Order 1994, SI 1994/2904; the Finance Act 1995 (Denatured Alcohol) (Appointed Day and Savings) Order, SI 2005/1523.

[2 Ascertainment of strength, volume and weight of alcoholic liquors

(1) Subject to subsections (5) and (6) below, this section applies to spirits, [anything that would be spirits if it were of a strength exceeding 1.2 per cent,] . . . and any fermented liquor other than wash, and "liquor" shall be construed accordingly.

(2) For all purposes of this Act—

   (a) except where some other measure of quantity is specified, any computation of the quantity of any liquor or of the alcohol contained in any liquor shall be made in terms of the volume of the liquor or alcohol, as the case may be;

   (b) any computation of the volume of any liquor or of the alcohol contained in any liquor shall be made in litres as at 20°C; and

   (c) the alcoholic strength of any liquor is the ratio of the volume of the alcohol contained in the liquor to the volume of the liquor (inclusive of the alcohol contained in it);

and in this Act, unless the context otherwise requires—

"alcohol" means ethyl alcohol; and

   "strength" in relation to any liquor, means its alcoholic strength computed in accordance with this section, the ratio referred to in paragraph (c) above being expressed as a percentage.

(3) The Commissioners may make regulations prescribing the means to be used for ascertaining for any purpose the strength, weight or volume of any liquor, and any such regulations may provide that in computing for any purpose the strength of any liquor any substance contained therein which is not alcohol or distilled water may be treated as if it were.

[(3A) Without prejudice to the generality of subsection (3) above, regulations under that subsection may provide that for the purpose of charging duty on any spirits, [beer,] [cider,] wine or made-wine contained in any bottle or other container, the strength, weight or volume of the [liquor in that bottle or other container] may be ascertained by reference to any information given on the bottle or other container by means of a label or otherwise or to any documents relating to the bottle or other container.]

(4) Different regulations may be made under subsection (3) above for different purposes.

(5) Nothing in this section shall prevent the strength, weight or volume of [beer,] wine, made-wine or cider from being computed for the purpose of charging duty thereon by methods other than that provided in this section.

(6) . . .

(7) Except as provided in subsection (8) below, where the quantity of alcohol contained in any spirits . . . falls to be computed in accordance with this section on or after 1st January 1980 and the quantity of those spirits . . . was last computed in accordance with this section before that date the following conversion factor shall be applied in making the first-mentioned computation, that is to say, one gallon of spirits at proof shall be taken to be equivalent to 2.595 litres of alcohol.

(8) The Commissioners may, if they think fit in any particular case, require the quantity of alcohol contained in any spirits . . . falling within subsection (7) above to be computed in accordance with this section without applying the conversion factor specified in that subsection.]

NOTES

Substituted by the Alcoholic Liquors (Amendment of Enactments Relating to Strength and to Units of Measurement) Order 1979, SI 1979/241, art 6.

Sub-s (1): words in square brackets inserted by the Excise Duty (Amendment of the Alcoholic Liquor Duties Act 1979 and the Hydrocarbon Oil Duties Act 1979) Regulations 1992, SI 1992/3158, reg 2(1), (3); words omitted are repealed by the Finance Act 1995 s 162, Sch 29 Pt I(3).

Sub-s (3A): inserted by the Finance Act 1981, s 11(1), Sch 8, Pt II, para 10; words in first pair of square brackets inserted by the Finance Act 1991, s 7(4), Sch 2, para 3(1); words in second pair of square brackets inserted, and those in third pair of square brackets substituted, by the Finance Act 1997, s 5(3).

Sub-s (5): word in square brackets inserted by the Finance Act 1991, s 7(4), Sch 2, para 3(2).

Sub-s (6): repealed by the Finance Act 1991, ss 7(4), 123, Sch 2, para 3(3), Sch 19, Pt II.

Sub-ss (7), (8): words omitted are repealed by the Finance Act 1995 s 162, Sch 29 Pt I(3).

Regulations: the Excise Warehousing (Etc) Regulations 1988, SI 1988/809, as amended by the Excise Goods (Drawback) Regulations 1995, SI 1995/1046; the Spirits Regulations 1991, SI 1991/2564; the Beer Regulations 1993, SI 1993/1228, as amended by SI 1995/3059, 2000/3213.

Orders: the Finance Act 1995 (Denatured Alcohol) (Appointed Day and Savings) Order, SI 2005/1523.

---

3 Meaning of and method of ascertaining gravity of liquids

(1) For the purposes of the Customs and Excise Acts 1979—

(a) "gravity", in relation to any liquid, means the ratio of the weight of a volume of the liquid to the weight of an equal volume of distilled water, the volume of each liquid being computed as at [20°C];

(b) where the gravity of any liquid is expressed as a number of degrees that number shall be the said ratio multiplied by 1,000; and

(c) "original gravity", in relation to any liquid in which fermentation has taken place, means its gravity before fermentation.

(2) The gravity of any liquid at any time shall be ascertained by such means as the Commissioners may approve, and the gravity so ascertained shall be deemed to be the true gravity of the liquid.

(3) . . . where for any purposes of the Customs and Excise Acts 1979 it is necessary to ascertain the original gravity of worts in which fermentation has commenced or of any liquid produced from such worts, that gravity shall be determined in such manner as the Commissioners may by regulations prescribe.

(4) Different regulations may be made under subsection (3) above in relation to different liquids.

(5) . . .

NOTES

Sub-s (1): words in square brackets substituted by the Alcoholic Liquors (Amendment of Enactments Relating to Strength and to Units of Measurement) Order 1979, SI 1979/241, art 7.

Sub-s (3): words omitted repealed by the Finance Act 1991, ss 7(4), 123, Sch 2, para 4, Sch 19, Pt II.

Sub-s (5): repealed by the Finance Act 1991, ss 7(4), 123, Sch 2, para 4, Sch 19, Pt II.

Regulations: the Spirits Regulations 1991, SI 1991/2564.

4 Interpretation

(1) In this Act, unless the context otherwise requires,—

["alcohol" has the meaning given by section 2 above;]

["authorised denaturer" means a person authorised under section 75(1) below to denature dutiable alcoholic liquor;]

"beer" has the meaning given by section 1 above;

"black beer" means beer of the description called or similar to black beer, mum, spruce beer or Berlin white beer, and any other preparation (whether fermented or not) of a similar character;

. . .

"British compounded spirits" means spirits which have, in the United Kingdom, had any flavour communicated thereto or ingredient or material mixed therewith, not being [denatured alcohol];

"case", in relation to dutiable alcoholic liquor, means 1 dozen units each consisting of a container holding not less than [65 nor more than 80 centilitres], or the equivalent of that number of such units made up wholly or partly of containers of a larger or smaller size;

"cider" has the meaning given by section 1 above;

"compounder" means a person holding a licence as a compounder under section 18 below;

["denatured alcohol" means denatured alcohol within the meaning of section 5 of the Finance Act 1995, and references to denaturing a liquor are references to subjecting it to any process by which it becomes denatured alcohol;]

"distiller", means a person holding a distiller's licence under section 12 below;

"distiller's licence" has the meaning given by section 12(1) below;

"distiller's warehouse" means a place of security provided by a distiller and approved by the Commissioners under section 15(1) below;

"distillery" means premises where spirits are manufactured, whether by distillation of a fermented liquor or by any other process;

"dutiable alcoholic liquor" has the meaning given by section 1(1) above;

"duty" has the meaning given by section 1(1) above and "duty-paid", "duty-free" and references to drawback shall be construed accordingly;

"gravity" and "original gravity" have the meanings given by section 3 above;

"justices' licence" and "justices' on-licence"—

(a) . . .

(b) in the application of this Act to Northern Ireland mean a licence corresponding to the relevant licence such as is mentioned in paragraph (a) of this definition;

"licensed", in relation to a producer of wine or of made-wine, means a producer who holds a licence to produce wine or made-wine respectively under subsection (2) of section 54 or 55 below;

"licensed methylator" means a person holding a licence under section 75(2) below;

. . .

"made-wine" has the meaning given by section 1 above;

"the Management Act" means the Customs and Excise Management Act 1979;

. . .

["package", in relation to beer, means to put beer into tanks, casks, kegs, cans, bottles or any other receptacles of a kind in which beer is distributed to wholesalers or retailers;

"packager", in relation to beer, means a person carrying on the business of packaging beer;]

"the prescribed sum", in relation to the penalty provided for an offence, means—

(a) if the offence was committed in England or Wales . . ., the prescribed sum within the meaning of [section 32 of the Magistrates' Courts Act 1980 (£1,000 or other sum substituted by order under section 143(1) of that Act)];

(b) if the offence was committed in Scotland, the prescribed sum within the meaning of section 289B of the Criminal Procedure (Scotland) Act 1975 (£1,000 or other sum substituted by order under section 289D(1) of that Act);

[(c) if the offence was committed in Northern Ireland, the prescribed sum within the meaning of Article 4 of the Fines and Penalties (Northern Ireland) Order 1984 ([£5,000] or other sum substituted by order under Article 17 of that Order);]

"producer of made-wine" includes a person who renders made-wine sparkling, and "produce", in relation to made-wine, shall be construed accordingly;

"producer of wine" includes a person who renders wine sparkling, and "produce", in relation to wine, shall be construed accordingly;

. . .

"rectifier" means a person holding a licence as a rectifier under section 18 below;

["registered brewer" has the meaning given by section 47(1) below;]

"registered club" means a club . . . which is for the time being a registered club within the meaning of the Licensing (Scotland) Act 1976 or which is for the time being a registered club within the meaning of the [Registration of Clubs (Northern Ireland) Order 1996];

"retailer" means—

(a) in relation to dutiable alcoholic liquor, a person who sells such liquor by retail;

(b) . . .

"Scottish licence" includes a licence of a type described in Schedule 1 to the Licensing (Scotland) Act 1976 (other than an off-sale licence), an occasional licence granted in terms of section 33 of the said Act, an occasional permission granted in terms of section 34 of the said Act, and a licence granted in terms of section 40 of the said Act;

"spirits" has the meaning given by section 1 above;

. . .

"spirits of wine" means plain spirits of a strength of not less than [80 per cent] manufactured in the United Kingdom;

["strength", in relation to any liquor has the meaning given by section 2 above;]

["wholesale", in relation to dealing in dutiable alcoholic liquor, means the sale at any one time to any one person of quantities not less than the following, namely—

    (a) in the case of spirits, wine or made-wine, 9 litres or 1 case; or

    (b) in the case of beer or cider, 20 litres or 2 cases;

"wholesaler" means a person who deals wholesale in dutiable alcoholic liquor;]

"wine" has the meaning given by section 1 above.

(2) This Act and the other Acts included in the Customs and Excise Acts 1979 shall be construed as one Act but where a provision of this Act refers to this Act that reference is not to be construed as including a reference to any of the others.

(3) Any expression used in this Act or in any instrument made under this Act to which a meaning is given by any other Act included in the Customs and Excise Acts 1979 has, except where the context otherwise requires, the same meaning in this Act or in any such instrument as in that Act; and for ease of reference the Table below indicates the expressions used in this Act to which a meaning is given by any other such Act—

Management Act

"the Commissioners"

"container"

"the Customs and Excise Acts 1979"

"excise warehouse"

"goods"

"hovercraft"

"importer"

. . .

"night"

"occupier"

"officer" and "proper" in relation to an officer

"ship" and "British ship"

"shipped"

"shipment"

"stores"

"tons register"

["United Kingdom waters"]

"warehouse"

"warehousing regulations".

(4) For the purposes of this Act, selling by retail, in relation to dutiable alcoholic liquor, means the sale at any one time to any one person of quantities not exceeding the following, that is to say—

    (a) in the case of spirits, wine or made-wine, [9 litres] or 1 case;

    (b) in the case of beer or cider, [21 litres] or 2 cases.

NOTES

Sub-s (1): definitions "alcohol" and "strength" inserted, words in square brackets in definitions "case" and "spirits of wine" substituted, and definition omitted in the third place repealed, by the Alcoholic Liquors (Amendment of Enactments Relating to Strength and to

Units of Measurement) Order 1979, SI 1979/241, art 8; definition "authorised methylator" substituted by the Finance Act 1995, s 5(5), Sch 2, para 1(a).

Definitions omitted in the first and second places repealed, and definitions "package", "packager" and "registered brewer" inserted, by the Finance Act 1991, ss 7(4), 123, Sch 2, para 5, Sch 19, Pt II.

In definition "British compounded spirits" words in square brackets substituted, definition "denatured alcohol" inserted and definition "licensed methylator" substituted by the Finance Act 1995 s 5(5), Sch 2 para 1(b)–(d).

In definition "justices' licence" and "justices' on-licence", para (a) repealed by the Licensing Act 2003, ss 198, 199, Sch 6 para 72(a), Sch 7; definition "methylated spirits" repealed by the Finance Act 1995 s 162, Sch 29 Pt I(3); in definition "the prescribed sum" words omitted in the first place repealed, and para (c) added, by the Fines and Penalties (Northern Ireland) Order 1984, SI 1984/703 (NI 3), art 19(1), (2), Sch 6, para 9, Sch 7, words in first pair of square brackets substituted by the Magistrates' Courts Act 1980, s 154, Sch 7, para 180, and sum in square brackets in para (c) substituted by virtue of the Criminal Justice (Northern Ireland) Order 1994, SI 1994/2795 (NI 15), art 3(1); in definition "registered club", words in square brackets substituted by the Registration of Clubs (Northern Ireland) Order 1996, SI 1996/3159 (NI 23), art 52(2), Sch 7, para 1, and words in italics repealed by the Licensing Act 2003, ss 198, 199, Sch 6 para 72(b), Sch 7; para (b) of definition "retailer" and definition omitted from the final place repealed, and definitions "wholesale" and "wholesaler" substituted, by the Finance Act 1981, ss 11(1), 139(6), Sch 8, Pt II, para 11, Sch 19, Pt III.

Sub-s (3): definition "licence year" repealed by the Finance Act 1986, s 114(6), Sch 23, Pt IV; definition "nautical mile" repealed, and definition "United Kingdom waters" inserted, by the Territorial Sea Act 1987, s 3(1), (4), Sch 1, para 5(1), Sch 2.

Sub-s (4): words in square brackets substituted by the Alcoholic Liquors (Amendment of Enactments Relating to Strength and to Units of Measurement) Order 1979, SI 1979/241, art 8.

Orders: the Finance Act 1995 (Denatured Alcohol) (Appointed Day and Savings) Order, SI 2005/1523.

PART II
SPIRITS

Charge of excise duty

5 Spirits: charge of excise duty

There shall be charged on spirits—

(a)   imported into the United Kingdom; or

(b)   distilled, or manufactured by any other process whatsoever, in the United Kingdom,

a duty of excise [at the rate of [£19.56] per litre of alcohol in the spirits].

NOTES

Words in first (outer) pair of square brackets substituted by the Finance Act 1982, s 1; sum in second (inner) pair of square brackets substituted by the Finance (No 2) Act 1997, s 7, with effect from 1 January 1998 (sum previously substituted by the Finance Act 1996, s 1 and the Finance Act 1997, s 1(1), (3)).

Reliefs from excise duty

6 Power to exempt angostura bitters from duty

On the importation of the aromatic flavouring essence commonly known as angostura bitters, the Commissioners may, subject to such conditions as they see fit to impose, direct the bitters to be treated for the purposes of the charge of duty on spirits as not being spirits.

[6A

(Inserted by the Excise Duty (Amendment of the Alcoholic Liquor Duties Act 1979 and the Hydrocarbon Oil Duties Act 1979) Regulations 1992, SI 1992/3158, reg 2(1), (4), and repealed by the Finance Act 1995, s 162, Sch 29, Pt I(2).)

7 Exemption from duty of spirits in articles used for medical purposes

Duty shall not be payable on any spirits contained in an article imported or delivered from warehouse which is recognised by the Commissioners as being used for medical purposes.

[8 Remission of duty in respect of spirits used for medical or scientific purposes

(1) Where a person proposes to use spirits—

    (a)   in the manufacture or preparation of any article recognised by the Commissioners as being an article used for medical purposes; or

    (b)   for scientific purposes,

the Commissioners may, if they think fit and subject to such conditions as they see fit to impose, authorise that person to receive, and permit the delivery from warehouse to that person of, spirits for that use without payment of the duty chargeable thereon.

(2) If any person contravenes or fails to comply with any condition imposed under this section [his contravention or failure to comply shall attract a penalty under section 9 of the Finance Act 1994 (civil penalties).]]

[(3) Subsection (4) below applies if—

    (a)   spirits are received and delivered in accordance with subsection (1) above,

    (b)   they are not used as proposed, and

    (c)   it is not shown to the satisfaction of the Commissioners that they can be accounted for by natural waste or other legitimate cause.

(4) In such a case the Commissioners—

    (a)   may assess as being excise duty due from the person concerned an amount equal to the duty that would have been chargeable on the spirits if, at the time of delivery from warehouse, they had been delivered for home use and otherwise than in accordance with subsection (1) above, and

    (b)   may notify him or his representative accordingly.]

NOTES

Substituted by the Finance Act 1988, s 6(1).

Sub-s (2): words in square brackets substituted by the Finance Act 1994, s 9, Sch 4, Pt II, paras 14, 15.

Sub-ss (3), (4): added by the Finance Act 1998, s 20, Sch 2, paras 1, 12.

9

(Repealed by the Finance Act 1995 ss 5(5), 162, Sch 2 para 2, Sch 29 Pt I(3).)

10 Remission of duty on spirits for use in art or manufacture

(1) Where, in the case of any art or manufacture carried on by any person in which the use of spirits is required, it is proved to the satisfaction of the Commissioners that the use of [denatured alcohol] is unsuitable or detrimental, the Commissioners may, if they think fit and subject to such conditions as they see fit

to impose, authorise that person to receive, and permit the delivery from warehouse to that person of, spirits for use in that art or manufacture without payment of the duty chargeable thereon.

(2) If any person contravenes or fails to comply with any condition imposed under this section [his contravention or failure to comply shall attract a penalty under section 9 of the Finance Act 1994 (civil penalties).]

[(3) Subsection (4) below applies if—

(a) spirits are received and delivered in accordance with subsection (1) above,

(b) they are not used as proposed, and

(c) it is not shown to the satisfaction of the Commissioners that they can be accounted for by natural waste or other legitimate cause.

(4) In such a case the Commissioners—

(a) may assess as being excise duty due from the person concerned an amount equal to the duty that would have been chargeable on the spirits if, at the time of delivery from warehouse, they had been delivered for home use and otherwise than in accordance with subsection (1) above, and

(b) may notify him or his representative accordingly.]

NOTES

Sub-s (1): words in square brackets substituted by the Finance Act 1995 s 5(5), Sch 2 para 3.

Sub-s (2): words in square brackets substituted by the Finance Act 1994, s 9, Sch 4, Pt II, paras 14, 16.

Sub-ss (3), (4): added by the Finance Act 1998, s 20, Sch 2, paras 2, 12.

---

11 Relief from duty on imported goods not for human consumption containing spirits

[(1)] On the importation of goods not for human consumption containing spirits as a part or ingredient thereof, the Commissioners may, subject to such conditions as they may think fit to impose, direct the goods to be treated for the purposes of the charge of duty on spirits (and in particular the charge under section 126 of the Management Act) as not containing spirits.

[(2) Subsection (3) below applies if—

(a) the Commissioners make a direction under subsection (1) above, but

(b) it turns out that the goods were for human consumption.

(3) In such a case the Commissioners—

(a) may assess as being excise duty due from the relevant person an amount equal to the duty that would have been chargeable on the goods if the direction had not been made, and

(b) may notify him or his representative accordingly.

(4) The reference in subsection (3) above to the relevant person is to the importer or (if different) the person who sought the direction.]

NOTES

Sub-s (1): numbered as such by the Finance Act 1998, s 20, Sch 2, paras 3, 12.

Sub-ss (2)–(4): added by the Finance Act 1998, s 20, Sch 2, paras 3, 12.

Manufacture of spirits

12 Licence to manufacture spirits

(1) No person shall manufacture spirits, whether by distillation of a fermented liquor or by any other process, unless he holds an excise licence for that purpose under this section (referred to in this Act as a "distiller's licence").

(2), (3) . . .

(4) . . .

(5) Where the largest still to be used on any premises in respect of which a distiller's licence is sought for the manufacture of spirits by distillation of a fermented liquor is of less than [18 hectolitres] capacity, the Commissioners may refuse to grant the licence or may grant it only subject to such conditions as they see fit to impose [and where the largest still so used on any premises in respect of which a licence is held is of less than that capacity, the Commissioners may revoke the licence or attach to it such conditions as they see fit to impose].

(6), [(6A)], (7)–(9) . . .

NOTES

Sub-ss (2), (3): repealed by the Finance Act 1986, ss 8(2), 114(6), Sch 23, Pt IV.

Sub-s (4): repealed by the Finance Act 2006, ss 5(1)(a), 178, Sch 26, Pt 1(1).

Sub-s (5): words in first pair of square brackets substituted by the Alcoholic Liquors (Amendment of Enactments Relating to Strength and to Units of Measurement) Order 1979, SI 1979/241, art 10; words in second pair of square brackets added by the Finance Act 1986, s 8(6), Sch 5, para 3(1), (3).

Sub-ss (6)–(9): inserted (in the case of sub-s (6A)) by the Finance Act 1986, s 8(6), Sch 5, para 3(1), (4) and repealed by the Finance Act 1990, ss 9, 132, Sch 19, Pt I.

13 Power to make regulations relating to manufacture of spirits

(1) The Commissioners may, with a view to the protection of the revenue, make regulations—

(a) regulating the manufacture of spirits, whether by distillation of a fermented liquor or by any other process;

(b) for securing and collecting the duty on spirits manufactured in the United Kingdom; and

(c) regulating the removal of spirits from a distillery;

and different regulations may be made in respect of manufacture for different purposes or by different processes.

[(1A) Without prejudice to the generality of subsection (1) above, regulations under that subsection may—

(a) provide for the imposition under the regulations of conditions and restrictions relating to the matters mentioned in that subsection; and

(b) impose or provide for the imposition of requirements on a manufacturer of spirits to keep and preserve records relating to his business as such a manufacturer and to produce them to an officer when required to do so for the purpose of allowing him to inspect them, to copy or take extracts from them or to remove them at a reasonable time and for a reasonable period.

(1B) Where any documents removed under the powers conferred by subsection (1A)(b) above are lost or damaged the Commissioners shall be liable to compensate their owner for any expenses reasonably incurred by him in replacing or repairing the documents.]

(2) Where—

(a)   the Commissioners are satisfied that any process of manufacture carried on by any person involving the manufacture of spirits is primarily directed to the production of some article other than spirits; or

(b)   the Commissioners see fit in the case of any person manufacturing spirits by any process other than distillation of a fermented liquor,

they may direct that, subject to compliance with such conditions as they think proper to impose, such of the provisions of this Act relating to the manufacture of, or manufacturers of, spirits or such of any regulations made under this section as may be specified in the direction shall not apply in the case of that person.

[(2A)   If the Commissioners so direct, spirits manufactured by a process to which a direction under subsection (2) above applies shall be treated as not being within the charge of duty on spirits under section 5 above.]

(3)   If, save as provided in subsection (2) above, any person contravenes or fails to comply with any regulation made under subsection (1) above [or with any condition, restriction or requirement imposed under such a regulation] [his contravention or failure to comply shall attract a penalty under section 9 of the Finance Act 1994 (civil penalties)], and any spirits, and any vessels, utensils and materials used for distilling or otherwise manufacturing or for preparing spirits, [in respect of which any person contravenes any such regulation, or fails to comply with any such regulation, condition, restriction or requirement, shall be liable to forfeiture.]

(4) . . .

(5)   If any person in whose case a direction is given by the Commissioners under subsection (2) above acts in contravention of or fails to comply with any condition imposed under that subsection which is applicable in his case, [his contravention or failure to comply shall attract a penalty under section 9 of the Finance Act 1994 (civil penalties), and any spirits in respect of which any person contravenes or fails to comply with any such condition shall be liable to forfeiture.]

NOTES

Sub-ss (1A), (1B): inserted by the Finance Act 1981, s 11(1), Sch 8, Part II, para 11.

Sub-s (2A): inserted by the Finance Act 1985, s 6, Sch 3, para 1.

Sub-s (3): words in first pair of square brackets inserted by the Finance Act 1981, s 11(1), Sch 8, Pt II, para 12; words in second and third pairs of square brackets substituted by the Finance Act 1994, s 9, Sch 4, Pt II, paras 14, 17(1).

Sub-s (4): repealed by the Finance Act 1994, ss 9, 258, Sch 4, Pt II, paras 14, 17(2), Sch 26, Pt III.

Sub-s (5): words in square brackets substituted by the Finance Act 1994, s 9, Sch 4, Pt II, paras 14, 17(3).

Regulations: the Spirits Regulations 1991, SI 1991/2564; the Excise Duties (Deferred Payment) Regulations 1992, SI 1992/3152, as amended by SI 1996/2537.

14

((Repealed by Finance Act 2006, ss 5(1)(b), 178, Sch 26, Pt 1(1)).

15 Distiller's warehouse

(1)   A distiller may provide in association with his distillery a place of security for the deposit of spirits manufactured at that distillery and, if that place is approved by the Commissioners and entry is made thereof by the distiller, may deposit therein without payment of duty any spirits so manufactured.

[(2) The Commissioners may approve such a place of security for such periods and subject to such conditions as they think fit.]

(3)   A place of security for the time being approved by the Commissioners under subsection (1) above is referred to in this Act as a "distiller's warehouse".

(4) . . .

[(5) Where, after the approval of a distiller's warehouse, the distiller by whom it is provided makes, without the previous consent of the Commissioners, an alteration in or addition to that warehouse, the making of the alteration or addition shall attract a penalty under section 9 of the Finance Act 1994 (civil penalties).]

(6) The Commissioners may make regulations—

(a) regulating the warehousing of spirits in a distiller's warehouse;

(b) permitting, in so far as it appears to them necessary in order to meet the circumstances of any special case and subject to such conditions as they see fit to impose, the deposit by a distiller in his distiller's warehouse without payment of duty of spirits other than spirits manufactured at the distillery associated with that warehouse;

(c) for securing the duties on spirits so warehoused;

and subject to any such regulations, the provisions of Parts VIII and X of the Management Act, except sections 92 and 96, shall apply in relation to a distiller's warehouse and spirits warehoused therein as they apply in relation to an excise warehouse approved under subsection (1) of section 92 of that Act and goods warehoused therein.

(6A), (6B) . . .

(7) If any person contravenes or fails to comply with any regulation made under subsection (6) above [or with any condition, . . . imposed under such a regulation] [his contravention or failure to comply shall attract a penalty under section 9 of the Finance Act 1994 (civil penalties), and any spirits in respect of which any person contravenes any such regulation, or fails to comply with any such regulation or condition, shall be liable to forfeiture.]

(8) . . .

(9) The Commissioners may at any time for reasonable cause revoke or vary the terms of their approval of a distiller's warehouse.

NOTES

Sub-s (2): substituted by the Finance Act 1981, s 11(1), Sch 8, Pt II, para 14.

Sub-s (4): repealed by Finance Act 2006, ss 5(1)(c), 178, Sch 26, Pt 1(1).

Sub-s (5): substituted by the Finance Act 1994, s 9, Sch 4, Pt II, paras 14, 18(2).

Sub-ss (6A), (6B): inserted by the Finance Act 1981, s 11(1), Sch 8, Pt II, para 14, and repealed by the Finance Act 1986, ss 5, 114(6), Sch 3, para 8, Sch 23, Pt I.

Sub-s (7): words in first pair of square brackets inserted by the Finance Act 1981, s 11(1), Sch 8, Pt II, para 14; words omitted repealed by the Finance Act 1986, ss 5, 114(6), Sch 3, para 8, Sch 23, Pt I; words in second pair of square brackets substituted by the Finance Act 1994, s 9, Sch 4, Pt II, paras 14, 18(3).

Sub-s (8): repealed by the Finance Act 1994, ss 9, 258, Sch 4, Pt II, paras 14, 18(4), Sch 26, Pt III.

Regulations: the Excise Warehousing (Etc) Regulations 1988, SI 1988/809, as amended by SI 1995/1046; the Spirits Regulations 1991, SI 1991/2564; the Excise Duties (Deferred Payment) Regulations 1992, SI 1992/3152, as amended by SI 1996/2537.

16 Racking of duty-paid spirits at distillery

(1) The Commissioners may, with a view to the protection of the revenue, make regulations regulating the racking at a distillery of duty-paid spirits.

(2) If any person contravenes or fails to comply with any regulation made under this section, [his contravention or failure to comply shall attract a penalty under section 9 of the Finance Act 1994 (civil penalties), and any spirits in respect of which any person contravenes or fails to comply with any such regulation shall be liable to forfeiture.]

[(3) If on an officer's taking stock of duty-paid spirits racked at a distillery, a greater quantity of alcohol is found at the place of racking than ought to be there according to any accounts required by regulations made under this section to be kept thereof then—

   (a)   duty shall be charged on the excess; and

   (b)   if the excess amounts to more than 1 per cent of the quantity of alcohol lawfully brought into the place of racking since stock was last taken, such quantity of spirits as contains an amount of alcohol equal to that excess shall be liable to forfeiture, and [there shall be deemed to have been conduct by the distiller attracting a penalty under section 9 of the Finance Act 1994 (civil penalties).]

   (4) Paragraph (b) of subsection (3) above shall not apply where the excess of alcohol is less than 3 litres.]

NOTES

Sub-s (2): words in square brackets substituted by the Finance Act 1994, s 9, Sch 4, Pt II, paras 14, 19(1).

Sub-ss (3), (4): substituted by the Alcoholic Liquors (Amendment of Enactments Relating to Strength and to Units of Measurement) Order 1979, SI 1979/241, art 12; words in square brackets in sub-s (3) substituted by the Finance Act 1994, s 9, Sch 4, Pt II, paras 14, 19(2).

17 Offences in connection with removal of spirits from distillery, etc

   (1)   If any person—

   (a)   conceals in or without the consent of the proper officer removes from a distillery any wort, wash, low wines, feints or spirits; or

   (b)   knowingly buys or receives any wort, wash, low wines, feints or spirits so concealed or removed; or

   (c)   knowingly buys or receives or has in his possession any spirits which have been removed from the place where they ought to have been charged with duty before the duty payable thereon has been charged and either paid or secured, not being spirits which have been condemned or are deemed to have been condemned as forfeited,

he shall be guilty of an offence under this section and may be [arrested], and the goods shall be liable to forfeiture.

   (2)   A person guilty of an offence under this section shall be liable—

   (a)   on summary conviction, to a penalty of the prescribed sum or three times the value of the goods, whichever is the greater, or to imprisonment for a term not exceeding 6 months, or to both; or

   (b)   on conviction on indictment, to a penalty of any amount, or to imprisonment for a term not exceeding 2 years, or to both.

NOTES

Sub-s (1): word in square brackets substituted by the Police and Criminal Evidence Act 1984, s 114(1).

Rectifying and compounding of spirits

18 Rectifier's and compounder's licences

   (1)   No person shall rectify or compound spirits and keep a still for that purpose unless he holds an excise licence under this section as a rectifier.

(2) Except as permitted by the Commissioners and subject to such conditions as they see fit to impose, no other person shall compound spirits unless he holds an excise licence under this section as a compounder.

(3), (4) . . .

(5) . . .

(6) Without prejudice to section 25 below and except as provided by this section, if any person rectifies or compounds spirits otherwise than under and in accordance with an excise licence under this Act so authorising him, [his doing so shall attract a penalty under section 9 of the Finance Act 1994 (civil penalties).]

NOTES

Sub-ss (3), (4): repealed by the Finance Act 1986, ss 8(2), 114(6), Sch 23, Pt IV.

Sub-s (5): repealed by the Finance Act 2006, ss 5(1)(d), 178, Sch 26, Pt 1(1).

Sub-s (6): words in square brackets substituted by the Finance Act 1994, s 9, Sch 4, Pt II, paras 14, 20.

19 Regulation of rectifying and compounding

(1) The Commissioners may, with a view to the protection of the revenue, make regulations—

    (a)   regulating the rectifying and compounding of spirits;

    (b)   regulating the receipt, storage, removal and delivery of spirits by rectifiers and compounders;

and different regulations may be made under this section for rectifiers and compounders.

[(1A) Without prejudice to the generality of subsection (1) above, regulations under that subsection may—

    (a)   provide for the imposition under the regulations of conditions and restrictions relating to the matters mentioned in that subsection; and

    (b)   impose or provide for the imposition under the regulations of requirements on rectifiers and compounders of spirits to keep and preserve records relating to their business as such and to produce them to an officer when required to do so for the purpose of allowing him to inspect them, to copy or take extracts from them or to remove them at a reasonable time and for a reasonable period.

(1B) Where any documents removed under the powers conferred by subsection (1A)(b) above are lost or damaged the Commissioners shall be liable to compensate their owner for any expenses reasonably incurred by him in replacing or repairing the documents.]

(2) If any person contravenes or fails to comply with any regulation made under this section [or with any condition, restriction or requirement imposed under any such regulation], [his contravention or failure to comply shall attract a penalty under section 9 of the Finance Act 1994 (civil penalties), and any spirits and any other article in respect of which any person contravenes any such regulation, or fails to comply with any such regulation, condition, requirement or restriction, shall be liable to forfeiture.]

(3) . . .

NOTES

Sub-ss (1A), (1B): inserted by the Finance Act 1981, s 11(1), Sch 8, Pt II, para 15.

Sub-s (2): words in first pair of square brackets inserted by the Finance Act 1981, s 11(1), Sch 8, Pt II, para 15; words in second pair of square brackets substituted by the Finance Act 1994, s 9, Sch 4, Pt II, paras 14, 21(1).

Sub-s (3): repealed by the Finance Act 1994, ss 9, 258, Sch 4, Pt II, paras 14, 21(2), Sch 26, Pt III.

Regulations: the Spirits (Rectifying, Compounding and Drawback) Regulations 1988, SI 1988/1760, as amended by SI 1991/2564.

20 Penalty for excess or deficiency in rectifier's stock

[(1) If at any time when an account is taken by an officer and a balance struck of the spirits in the stock of a rectifier any excess of alcohol is found, such a quantity of spirits as contains an amount of alcohol equal to the excess shall be liable to forfeiture and [there shall be deemed to have been conduct by the rectifier attracting a penalty under section 9 of the Finance Act 1994 (civil penalties).]

(2) If at any time when an account is taken and a balance struck as aforesaid any deficiency of alcohol is found which cannot be accounted for to the satisfaction of the Commissioners and which exceeds 5 per cent of the aggregate of—

(a) the quantity of alcohol in the balance of spirits struck when an account was last taken; and

(b) the quantity of alcohol contained in any spirits since lawfully received by the rectifier,

[there shall be deemed to have been conduct by the rectifier attracting a penalty under section 9 of the Finance Act 1994 (civil penalties).]]

(3) For the purposes of any such account and of this section—

(a) spirits used by a rectifier in warehouse in pursuance of warehousing regulations shall be deemed not to be spirits in his stock as a rectifier; and

(b) where a rectifier also carries on the trade of a wholesaler of spirits on the same premises, all spirits in his possession (other than spirits so used) shall be deemed to be spirits in his stock as a rectifier.

NOTES

Sub-ss (1), (2): substituted by the Alcoholic Liquors (Amendment of Enactments Relating to Strength and to Units of Measurement) Order 1979, SI 1979/241, art 13; words in square brackets substituted by the Finance Act 1994, s 9, Sch 4, Pt II, paras 14, 22.

21

(Repealed by Finance Act 2006, ss 5(1)(e), 178, Sch 26, Part 1(1)).

22 Drawback on British compounds and spirits of wine

(1) Subject to the provisions of this section and to such conditions and restrictions as the Commissioners may by regulations impose, a rectifier or compounder may warehouse in an excise warehouse on drawback any British compounded spirits or spirits of wine rectified or compounded by him from duty-paid spirits and not containing any methyl alcohol or any wine, made-wine or other fermented liquor.

(2) British compounded spirits may be warehoused under this section for exportation [or removal to the Isle of Man], for use in any permitted operation in warehouse, for use as stores or, except in the case of tinctures other than perfumed spirits, for home use.

(3) Spirits of wine may be warehoused under this section—

(a) for exportation [or removal to the Isle of Man], for use in any permitted operation in warehouse, or for use as stores; or

(b) if of a strength of not less than [85 per cent], for delivery for use in art or manufacture under section 10 above; or

(c) if of a strength of not less than [99 per cent], for home use.

[(3A)   The Commissioners may, subject to such conditions and restrictions as they may by regulations impose, allow drawback to any person on any British compounded spirits or spirits of wine rectified or compounded by him from duty-paid spirits and not containing any methyl alcohol or any wine, made-wine or other fermented liquor if they are exported direct from his premises.]

(4)   The Commissioners may, subject to such conditions and restrictions as they may by regulations impose, allow drawback on tinctures or spirits of wine exported or, except in the case of spirits of wine, shipped as stores by a rectifier or compounder direct from his premises.

[(5)   Subject to subsection (6) below, the amount of any drawback payable under this section shall be calculated by reference to the quantity of alcohol contained in the British compounded spirits or spirits of wine and shall be an amount equal to the duty at the appropriate rate chargeable on spirits containing an equal quantity of alcohol and so chargeable at the date when duty was paid on the spirits from which the British compounded spirits or spirits of wine were rectified or compounded.]

(6), (7)   . . .

(8)   British compounded spirits warehoused under this section for home use shall upon delivery from warehouse for that purpose be chargeable with the same rate of duty as spirits warehoused by a distiller.

(9)   If any person contravenes or fails to comply with any regulation made under this section [his contravention or failure to comply shall attract a penalty under section 9 of the Finance Act 1994 (civil penalties), and any article in respect of which any person contravenes or fails to comply with any such regulation shall be liable to forfeiture.]

(10)   In this section "tinctures" means medicinal spirits, flavouring essences, perfumed spirits and such other articles containing spirits as the Commissioners may by regulations specify as tinctures.

NOTES

Sub-s (2): words in square brackets inserted by the Isle of Man Act 1979, s 13, Sch 1.

Sub-s (3): words in first pair of square brackets inserted by the Isle of Man Act 1979, s 13, Sch 1; words in second and third pairs of square brackets substituted by the Alcoholic Liquors (Amendment of Enactments Relating to Strength and to Units of Measurement) Order 1979, SI 1979/241, art 15.

Sub-s (3A): inserted by the Finance Act 1981, s 11(1), Sch 8, Pt II, para 16.

Sub-s (5): substituted by the Alcoholic Liquors (Amendment of Enactments Relating to Strength and to Units of Measurement) Order 1979, SI 1979/241, art 15.

Sub-s (6): repealed by the Finance Act 1996, ss 24(b), 205, Sch 41, Pt III.

Sub-s (7): repealed by the Finance Act 1988, ss 6(2), 148, Sch 14, Pt I.

Sub-s (9): words in square brackets substituted by the Finance Act 1994, s 9, Sch 4, Pt II, paras 14, 24.

Regulations: the Spirits (Rectifying, Compounding and Drawback) Regulations 1988, SI 1988/1760, as amended by SI 1991/2564.

23

(Repealed by the Finance Act 1996, ss 24(c), 205, Sch 41, Pt III.)

General provisions relating to manufacture of spirits and British compounds

24

(Repealed by Finance Act 2006, ss 5(1)(f), 178, Sch 26, Pt 1(1)).

25 Penalty for unlawful manufacture of spirits, etc

(1) Save as provided by or under this Act, any person who, otherwise than under and in accordance with an excise licence under this Act so authorising him—

(a)   manufactures spirits, whether by distillation of a fermented liquor or by any other process; or

(b)   . . . uses a still for distilling, rectifying or compounding spirits; or

(c)   distils or has in his possession any low wines or feints; or

(d)   not being a vinegar-maker, [produces] or makes or has in his possession any wort or wash fit for distillation,

shall be liable on summary conviction to a penalty [not exceeding level 5 on the standard scale].

(2) Where there is insufficient evidence to convict a person of an offence under subsection (1) above, but it is proved that such an offence has been committed on some part of premises belonging to or occupied by that person in such circumstances that it could not have been committed without his knowledge, that person shall be liable on summary conviction to a penalty [not exceeding level 3 on the standard scale].

(3) Any person found on premises on which spirits are being unlawfully manufactured or on which a still is being unlawfully used for rectifying or compounding spirits may be [arrested].

(4) All spirits and stills, vessels, utensils, wort, wash and other materials for manufacturing, distilling or preparing spirits—

(a)   found in the possession of any person who commits an offence under subsection (1) above; or

(b)   found on any premises on which such an offence has been committed,

shall be liable to forfeiture.

(5) Notwithstanding any other provision of the Customs and Excise Acts 1979 relating to goods seized as liable to forfeiture, any officer by whom any thing is seized as liable to forfeiture under subsection (4) above may at his discretion forthwith spill, break up or destroy that thing.

(6) Without prejudice to any other power conferred by the Customs and Excise Acts 1979, if any officer has reasonable grounds for suspecting that any thing liable to forfeiture under this section is in or upon any land or other premises in Northern Ireland, he may enter upon those premises, if need be by force, and search them and seize and remove any thing which he has reasonable grounds to believe to be so liable.

NOTES

Sub-s (1): words omitted repealed by the Finance Act 1986, s 114(6), Sch 23, Pt IV; word in first pair of square brackets substituted by virtue of the Finance Act 1991, s 7(4), Sch 2, para 1; words in second pair of square brackets substituted by virtue of the Criminal Justice Act 1982, ss 37, 46.

Sub-s (2): words in square brackets substituted by virtue of the Criminal Justice Act 1982, ss 37, 38, 46.

Sub-s (3): word in square brackets substituted by the Police and Criminal Evidence Act 1984, s 114(1).

General provisions relating to spirits

26

(Repealed by Finance Act 2006, ss 5(1)(g), 178, Sch 26, Pt 1(1)).

27–31

(Sections 27–30 repealed by the Finance Act 1981, ss 11(1), 139, Sch 8, Pt II, para 18, Sch 19, Pt III; s 31 repealed by the Alcoholic Liquor Duties Act 1979 (Repeal of Section 31) Order 1989, SI 1989/2098.)

32

(Repealed by Finance Act 2006, ss 5(1)(h), 178, Sch 26, Pt 1(1)).

33 Restrictions on use of certain goods relieved from spirits duty

(1)   If any person uses otherwise than for a medical or scientific purpose—

    (a)   any mixture which has on importation been relieved to any extent of the duty chargeable in respect of the spirits contained in it or used in its preparation or manufacture by reason of being a mixture which is recognised by the Commissioners as being used for medical purposes; or

    (b)   any article containing spirits which were exempted from duty under section 7 above; or

    (c)   any article manufactured or prepared from spirits in respect of which [remission] of duty has been obtained under section 8 above; . . .

    (d)   . . .

[his doing so shall, unless he has complied with the requirements specified in subsection (2) below, attract a penalty under section 9 of the Finance Act 1994 (civil penalties)], and any article in his possession in the preparation or manufacture of which the mixture or the article has been used shall be liable to forfeiture.

(2)   The requirements with which a person must comply to avoid incurring liability under subsection (1) above are that—

    (a)   he must obtain the consent of the Commissioners in writing to the use of the mixture or article otherwise than for a medical or scientific purpose; and

    (b)   he must pay to the Commissioners an amount equal to the difference between the duty charged on the mixture and the duty which would have been chargeable if it had not been a mixture recognised as mentioned in subsection (1)(a) above, or to the amount of the duty [remitted], as the case may be.

(3)   The Commissioners may make regulations for the purpose of enforcing the provisions of this section.

(4)   Regulations under subsection (3) above may in particular require any person carrying on any trade in which spirits, or mixtures or articles containing or prepared or manufactured with spirits, are in the opinion of the Commissioners likely to be or to have been used—

    (a)   to give and verify particulars of the materials which he is using or has used and of any such mixtures or articles which he has sold; and

    (b)   to produce any books of account or other documents of whatever nature relating to any such materials, mixtures or articles.

(5)   If any person contravenes or fails to comply with any regulation made under subsection (3) above [his contravention or failure to comply shall attract a penalty under section 9 of the Finance Act 1994 (civil penalties).]

(6)   In this section "mixture" includes a preparation and a compound, and any reference to a mixture or article includes a reference to any part thereof.

NOTES

Sub-s (1): word in first pair of square brackets substituted, and para (d) and word "or" immediately preceding it repealed, by the Finance Act 1988, s 6(4)(a), (b); words in second pair of square brackets substituted by the Finance Act 1994, s 9, Sch 4, Pt II, paras 14, 26(1).

Sub-s (2): word in square brackets substituted by the Finance Act 1988, s 6(4)(c).

Sub-s (5): words in square brackets substituted by the Finance Act 1994, s 9, Sch 4, Pt II, paras 14, 26(2).

34 Prohibition of grogging
(1) No person shall—
- (a)   subject any cask to any process for the purpose of extracting any spirits absorbed in the wood thereof; or
- (b)   have on his premises any cask which is being subjected to any such process or any spirits extracted from the wood of any cask.

[(2)   A contravention of this section shall attract a penalty under section 9 of the Finance Act 1994 (civil penalties).]

(3)   All spirits extracted contrary to this section and every cask which is being subjected to any such process or which, being upon premises upon which spirits so extracted are found, has been subjected to any such process shall be liable to forfeiture.

NOTES
Sub-s (2): substituted by the Finance Act 1994, s 9, Sch 4, Pt II, paras 14, 27.

35
(Repealed by Finance Act 2006, ss 5(1)(i), 178, Sch 26, Pt 1(1)).

PART III
BEER

Charge of excise duty

[36 Beer: charge of excise duty
(1)   There shall be charged on beer—
- (a)   imported into the United Kingdom, or
- (b)   produced in the United Kingdom,

a duty of excise [at the rates specified in subsection (1AA) below].

[(1AA)   The rates at which the duty shall be charged are—
- (a)   in the case of beer that is not small brewery beer, [£13.71] per hectolitre per cent of alcohol in the beer;
- (b)   in the case of small brewery beer produced in a singleton brewery, the rate per hectolitre per cent of alcohol in the beer that is given by section 36D below;
- (c)   in the case of small brewery beer produced in a co-operated brewery, the rate per hectolitre per cent of alcohol in the beer that is given by section 36F below.]

[(1A)   No duty shall be chargeable under subsection (1) above on beer which is of a strength of 1.2 per cent or less; but any such beer shall in all other respects be treated as if it were chargeable with a duty of excise.]

(2)   Subject to the provisions of this Act—
- (a)   the duty on beer produced in, or imported into, the United Kingdom shall be charged and paid, and
- (b)   the amount chargeable in respect of any such duty shall be determined and become due,

in accordance with regulations under section 49 below [and with any regulations under section 1 of the Finance (No 2) Act 1992].]

NOTES

Substituted by the Finance Act 1991, s 7(1).

Sub-s (1): sum in square brackets substituted by the Finance Act 2000, s 1, with effect from 1 April 2000; words substituted by the Finance Act 2002, s 4, Sch 1 para 1(1), (2).

Sub-s (1AA): inserted by the Finance Act 2002, s 4, Sch 1 para 1(1), (3). Figure substituted by the Finance Act 2007, s 5(1), (2).

Sub-s (1A): inserted by the Finance Act 1993, s 3(2), in relation to liquor produced in or imported into the United Kingdom, or removed into the United Kingdom from the Isle of Man, on or after 27 July 1993.

Sub-s (2): words in square brackets added by the Finance (No 2) Act 1992, s 1, Sch 1, para 9.

[Reduced rates of excise duty

36A Beer from small breweries: introductory

(1)   For the purposes of section 36(1AA) above (but subject to subsection (2) below)—

> (a)   whether beer produced in a singleton brewery is "small brewery beer" is determined in accordance with section 36C below, and
>
> (b)   whether beer produced in a co-operated brewery is "small brewery beer" is determined in accordance with section 36E below.

(2)   Beer is not small brewery beer if it is produced by a person on any premises in circumstances in which he is required to be, but is not, registered under section 47 below in respect of those premises.]

NOTES

Inserted by the Finance Act 2002, s 4, Sch 1 para 2.

[36B Interpretation of provisions relating to small brewery beer

(1)   The following provisions of this section have effect for the purposes of section 36(1AA) above, section 36A above, this section and sections 36C to 36F below.

(2)   A brewery is a "singleton brewery" at any particular time in a calendar year if it is not a co-operated brewery at that time.

(3)   A brewery is a "co-operated brewery" at any particular time in a calendar year if—

> (a)   a person who produces beer in the brewery at that time or any earlier time in that year, or
>
> (b)   a person connected with such a person,

also produces beer in any other brewery at that time or any earlier time in that year.

(4)   "Brewery" means premises (whether or not in the United Kingdom) on which beer is produced and that are situated physically apart from any other premises on which beer is produced.

(5)   "The standard beer duty rate" means the rate of duty specified by section 36(1AA)(a) above.

(6)   References to "the grossed-up amount" of an estimate of the amount of a brewery's production in a calendar year are to the amount given by—

$$\frac{E}{(365-N)} \times 365$$

where—

E is the amount of the estimate, and

N is the number of days (if any) in the calendar year before the brewery begins to be used as beer-production premises.

(7) References to a brewery being used as beer-production premises are, in the case of a brewery in the United Kingdom, to there being at least one person who is required to be registered under section 47 below in respect of the brewery.

(8) Any question whether a person is connected with another shall be determined in accordance with section 839 of the Income and Corporation Taxes Act 1988 (c 1).]

NOTES

Inserted by the Finance Act 2002, s 4, Sch 1 para 2.

[36C Meaning of "small brewery beer": beer from singleton breweries

(1) This section applies to beer produced in a brewery at a time in a calendar year ("the current year") when the brewery is a singleton brewery.

(2) The beer is "small brewery beer" if the following conditions are satisfied; but this is subject to subsections (9) and (10) below.

(3) The first condition is that either—

    (a)   no beer was produced in the brewery in the previous calendar year ("the previous year"), or

    (b)   the amount of beer produced in the brewery in the previous year was not more than [60,000 hectolitres].

(4) For the purposes of subsection (3)(b) above, where the brewery was in use as beer-production premises during part only of the previous year, the amount of beer produced in the previous year in the brewery shall be taken to have been—

$$\frac{A}{D} \times 365$$

where—

A is the amount of beer actually produced in the previous year in the brewery, and

D is the number of days in that part of the previous year.

(5) The second condition is that the amount of the estimate under subsection (9) below of the brewery's production in the current year is not more than [60,000 hectolitres].

(6) The third condition is that if the brewery begins to be used as beer-production premises part-way through the current year, the grossed-up amount of that estimate is not more than [60,000 hectolitres].

(7) The fourth condition is that less than half of the beer produced in the brewery in the previous year was produced under licence.

(8) The fifth condition is that the beer is not produced under licence.

(9) Beer produced in the brewery in the current year before the person who first produces beer in the brewery in that year has made a reasonable estimate of the amount of beer that will be produced in the brewery in that year is not small brewery beer.

(10) Beer produced in the brewery in the current year after the amount of beer produced in the brewery in the current year has reached [60,000 hectolitres] is not small brewery beer.

(11) Subsection (10) above is without prejudice to section 167(4) of the Customs and Excise Management Act 1979 (recovery of duty unpaid by reason of untrue document or statement).]

NOTES

Inserted by the Finance Act 2002, s 4, Sch 1 para 2.

Sub-ss (3), (5), (6), (10): words substituted by the Beer from Small Breweries (Extension of Reduced Rates of Excise Duty) Order 2004, SI 2004/1296 art 3(1), (2).

[36D Rate of duty for small brewery beer from singleton breweries

(1) This section applies to small brewery beer produced in a brewery at a time in a calendar year ("the current year") when the brewery is a singleton brewery.

(2) The rate of duty in the case of that beer ("the brewery rate") is determined in accordance with this section.

(3) Subsection (4) below applies if—

    (a)   beer was produced in the brewery in the previous calendar year ("the previous year") and the amount produced in the brewery in that year was not more than 5,000 hectolitres, or

    (b)   no beer was produced in the brewery in the previous year and the grossed-up amount of the estimate under section 36C(9) above of the brewery's production in the current year is not more than 5,000 hectolitres.

(4) If this subsection applies, "the brewery rate" is 50% of the standard beer duty rate at the time concerned; but this is subject to rounding under subsection (7) below.

(5) Subsection (6) below applies if—

    (a)   beer was produced in the brewery in the previous year and the amount produced in the brewery in that year was more than 5,000 hectolitres but not more than 30,000 hectolitres, or

    (b)   no beer was produced in the brewery in the previous year and the grossed-up amount of the estimate under section 36C(9) above of the brewery's production in the current year is more than 5,000 hectolitres but not more than 30,000 hectolitres.

(6) If this subsection applies, "the brewery rate" is, subject to rounding under subsection (7) below, given by—

$$\frac{P - 2,500}{P} \times \text{the standard beer duty rate at the time concerned}$$

where—

if this subsection applies by reason of subsection (5)(a) above, P is the amount, in hectolitres, of beer produced in the brewery in the previous year, and

if this subsection applies by reason of subsection (5)(b) above, P is the grossed-up amount (expressed in hectolitres) mentioned in subsection (5)(b).

[(6A) Subsection (6B) below applies if—

    (a)   beer was produced in the brewery in the previous year and the amount produced in the brewery in that year was more than 30,000 hectolitres but not more than 60,000 hectolitres, or

    (b)   no beer was produced in the brewery in the previous year and the grossed-up amount of the estimate under section 36C(9) above of the brewery's production in the current year is more than 30,000 hectolitres but not more than 60,000 hectolitres.]

[(6B) If this subsection applies, "the brewery rate" is, subject to rounding under subsection (7) below, given by—

$$((P - (2500 - 8.33\% \text{ of } P \text{ in excess of } 30,000 \text{ hectolitres})) / P) \times \text{the standard beer duty}$$
rate at the time concerned

where—

if this subsection applies by reason of subsection (6A)(a) above, P is the amount, in hectolitres, of beer produced in the brewery in the previous year, and

if this subsection applies by reason of subsection (6A)(b) above, P is the grossed-up amount (expressed in hectolitres) mentioned in subsection (6A)(b).]

(7)   Where a rate given by subsection (4)[, (6) or (6B)] above would (apart from this subsection) not be a whole number of pennies, the rate given by that subsection shall be taken to be the rate actually given by that subsection rounded up to the nearest penny.

(8)   Where the brewery was in use as beer-production premises during part only of the previous year, for the purposes of subsections (3)(a), (5)(a)[, (6), (6A)(a) and (6B)] above the amount of beer produced in the brewery in the previous year shall be taken to have been—

$$\frac{A}{D} \times 365$$

where—

A is the amount of beer actually produced in the previous year in the brewery, and

D is the number of days in that part of the previous year.]

NOTES

Inserted by the Finance Act 2002, s 4, Sch 1 para 2.

Sub-ss (6A), (6B): inserted by the Beer from Small Breweries (Extension of Reduced Rates of Excise Duty) Order 2004, SI 2004/1296 art 3(1), (3).

Sub-ss (7), (8): references substituted by SI 2004/1296 art 3(1), (4), (5).

[36E   Meaning of "small brewery beer": beer from co-operated breweries

(1)   This section applies to beer produced in a brewery at a time in a calendar year ("the current year") when the brewery is a co-operated brewery.

(2)   The beer is "small brewery beer" if the following conditions are satisfied; but this is subject to subsections (10) and (11) below.

(3)   In this section—

"the group" means the group of breweries consisting of—

(a)   the co-operated brewery, and

(b)   every brewery (other than the co-operated brewery) in which beer is produced at the time mentioned in subsection (1) above, or at any earlier time in the current year, by—

(i)   a person who produces beer in the co-operated brewery at the time so mentioned or at any earlier time in the current year, or

(ii)   a person connected with such a person;

"group brewery" means a brewery that is in the group;

"the previous year" means the calendar year immediately preceding the current year.

(4)   The first condition is that either—

(a)   no beer was produced in the previous year in the group, or

(b)   the amount given by PY + GE is not more than [60,000 hectolitres], where—

PY is the amount of beer produced in the previous year in the group, and

GE is the aggregate of the grossed-up amount of each estimate that—

(i)   is an estimate for the purposes of subsection (10) below of the amount of the production in the current year in a group brewery in which no beer was produced in the previous year, and

(ii) is made no later than the time mentioned in subsection (1) above.

(5) For the purposes of subsection (4)(b) above, where a group brewery was in use as beer-production premises during part only of the previous year, the amount of beer produced in the previous year in that brewery shall be taken to have been—

$$\frac{A}{D} \times 365$$

where—

A is the amount of beer actually produced in the previous year in that brewery, and

D is the number of days in that part of the previous year.

(6) The second condition is that the aggregate of each estimate that—

(a) is an estimate for the purposes of subsection (10) below of the amount of a group brewery's production in the current year, and

(b) is made no later than the time mentioned in subsection (1) above, is not more than [60,000 hectolitres].

(7) The third condition is that if any group brewery begins to be used as beer-production premises part-way through the current year, the aggregate of the grossed-up amount of each estimate that—

(a) is an estimate for the purposes of subsection (10) below of the amount of a group brewery's production in the current year, and

(b) is made no later than the time mentioned in subsection (1) above, is not more than [60,000 hectolitres].

(8) The fourth condition is that less than half of the beer produced in the previous year in each group brewery was produced under licence.

(9) The fifth condition is that the beer is not produced under licence.

(10) Beer produced in the co-operated brewery at an unestimated time is not small brewery beer; and here "unestimated time" means a time in the current year when there is a group brewery for which there does not exist a reasonable estimate, made by the person who first produces beer in that brewery in that year, of the amount of beer that will be produced in that brewery in that year.

(11) Beer produced in the co-operated brewery in the current year after the amount of beer produced in the group in the current year has reached [60,000 hectolitres] is not small brewery beer.

(12) Subsection (11) above is without prejudice to section 167(4) of the Customs and Excise Management Act 1979 (recovery of duty unpaid by reason of untrue document or statement).]

NOTES

Inserted by the Finance Act 2002, s 4, Sch 1 para 2.

Sub-ss (4), (6), (7), (11): words substituted by the Beer from Small Breweries (Extension of Reduced Rates of Excise Duty) Order 2004, SI 2004/1296 art 3(1), (6).

[36F Rate of duty for small brewery beer from co-operated breweries

(1) This section applies to small brewery beer produced in a brewery at a time in a calendar year ("the current year") when the brewery is a co-operated brewery.

(2) The rate of duty in the case of that beer ("the brewery rate") is determined in accordance with this section.

(3) In this section—

"the group" means the group of breweries consisting of—

    (a)   the co-operated brewery, and

    (b)   every brewery (other than the co-operated brewery) in which beer is produced at the time mentioned in subsection (1) above, or at any earlier time in the current year, by—

        (i)   a person who produces beer in the co-operated brewery at the time so mentioned or at any earlier time in the current year, or

        (ii)   a person connected with such a person;

"group brewery" means a brewery that is in the group;

"the previous year" means the calendar year immediately preceding the current year;

"the notional previous year's production" has the meaning given by subsection (4) below.

(4) In this section "the notional previous year's production" means the amount, in hectolitres, given by PY + GE where—

PY is the amount of beer produced in the group in the previous year, and

GE is the aggregate of the grossed-up amount of each estimate that—

    (a)   is an estimate for the purposes of section 36E(10) above of the amount of the production in the current year in a group brewery in which no beer was produced in the previous year, and

    (b)   is made no later than the time mentioned in subsection (1) above.

(5) Where a group brewery was in use as beer-production premises during part only of the previous year, in calculating PY for the purposes of subsection (4) above the amount of beer produced in that brewery in the previous year shall be taken to have been—

$$\frac{A}{D} \times 365$$

where—

A is the amount of beer actually produced in the previous year in that brewery, and

D is the number of days in that part of the previous year.

(6) Subsection (7) below applies if—

    (a)   beer was produced in at least one group brewery in the previous year and the notional previous year's production is not more than 5,000 hectolitres, or

    (b)   no beer was produced in the group in the previous year and the aggregate of each estimate that—

        (i)   is an estimate for the purposes of section 36E(10) above of the amount of a group brewery's production in the current year, and

        (ii)   is made no later than the time mentioned in subsection (1) above,

is not more than 5,000 hectolitres.

(7) If this subsection applies, "the brewery rate" is 50% of the standard rate at the time mentioned in subsection (1) above; but this is subject to rounding under subsection (10) below.

(8) Subsection (9) below applies if—

    (a)   beer was produced in at least one group brewery in the previous year and the notional previous year's production is more than 5,000 hectolitres but not more than 30,000 hectolitres, or

(b)   no beer was produced in the group in the previous year and the aggregate mentioned in subsection (6)(b) above is more than 5,000 hectolitres but not more than 30,000 hectolitres.

(9) If this subsection applies, "the brewery rate" is, subject to rounding under subsection (10) below, given by—

$$\frac{P - 2,500}{P} \times \textit{the standard rate}$$

where—

if this subsection applies by reason of subsection (8)(a) above, P is the previous year's notional production,

if this subsection applies by reason of subsection (8)(b) above, P is the amount, in hectolitres, of the aggregate mentioned in subsection (6)(b) above, and

"the standard rate" means the standard beer duty rate at the time mentioned in subsection (1) above.

[(9A) Subsection (9B) below applies if—

(a)   beer was produced in at least one group brewery in the previous year and the notional previous year's production is more than 30,000 hectolitres but not more than 60,000 hectolitres, or

(b)   no beer was produced in the group in the previous year and the aggregate mentioned in subsection (6)(b) above is more than 30,000 hectolitres but not more than 60,000 hectolitres.]

[(9B) If this subsection applies, "the brewery rate" is, subject to rounding under subsection (10) below, given by—

((P − (2500 − 8.33% of P in excess of 30,000 hectolitres)) / P) × the standard rate

where—

if this subsection applies by reason of subsection (9A)(a) above, P is the previous year's notional production,

if this subsection applies by reason of subsection (9A)(b) above, P is the amount, in hectolitres, of the aggregate mentioned in subsection (6)(b) above, and

"the standard rate" means the standard beer duty rate at the time mentioned in subsection (1) above.]

(10) Where a rate given by subsection (7)[, (9) or (9B)] above would (apart from this subsection) not be a whole number of pennies, the rate given by that subsection shall be taken to be the rate actually given by that subsection rounded up to the nearest penny.]

NOTES

Inserted by the Finance Act 2002, s 4, Sch 1 para 2.

Sub-ss (9A), (9B): inserted by the Beer from Small Breweries (Extension of Reduced Rates of Excise Duty) Order 2004, SI 2004/1296 art 3(1), (7).

Sub-s (10): references substituted by SI 2004/1296 art 3(1), (8).

[36G Assessments where incorrectly low rate of duty applied

(1) Subsection (3) below applies if—

(a)   duty is charged by section 36 above on any beer, and

(b)   it appears at the excise duty point that the beer is small brewery beer for the purposes of section 36(1AA) above, but

(c)   it turns out that the beer was not small brewery beer for those purposes (because, for example, circumstances were not as they appeared at that point or they subsequently changed).

(2) Subsection (3) below also applies if—

Part I

(a)   duty is charged by section 36 above on any beer that is small brewery beer for the purposes of section 36(1AA) above, and

(b)   the rate of duty that at the excise duty point appeared to be the correct rate turns out to have been lower than the correct rate (because, for example, circumstances were not as they appeared at that point or they subsequently changed).

(3)   In any such case the Commissioners—

(a)   may assess the amount that is the difference between—

   (i)   the actual amount of the duty charged on the beer by section 36 above, and

   (ii)   the lower amount that, at the excise duty point, appeared to be the amount charged,

as being excise duty due from the person liable to pay the duty charged on the beer by section 36 above, and

(b)   may notify him or his representative accordingly.

(4)   Where two or more persons are liable to pay the duty charged on the beer—

(a)   the reference in subsection (3)(a) above to the person liable to pay the duty is to any one or more of those persons, and

(b)   the reference in subsection (3)(b) above to notifying the person liable or his representative is to notifying each person assessed or his representative.]

NOTES

Inserted by the Finance Act 2002, s 4, Sch 1 para 2.

[36H Power to vary reduced rate provisions

(1)   The Treasury may by order made by statutory instrument make provision amending this Act for the purpose of causing excise duty to be charged on a description of beer—

(a)   at a reduced rate instead of at the standard rate;

(b)   at the standard rate instead of at a reduced rate;

(c)   at a different reduced rate.

(2)   In this section—

"reduced rate" means a rate lower than the standard rate, and

"the standard rate" means the rate specified by section 36(1AA)(a) above.

(3)   An order under subsection (1) above may—

(a)   make different provision for different cases;

(b)   make such consequential amendments in this Act and other enactments as appear to the Treasury to be necessary or expedient;

(c)   make such other consequential provision, and such incidental and transitional provision, as appears to the Treasury to be necessary or expedient.

(4)   A statutory instrument by which there is made an order under subsection (1) above shall be laid before the House of Commons after being made.

Unless the instrument is approved by the House of Commons before the expiration of 28 days beginning with the date on which the instrument was made, the order shall cease to have effect on the expiration of that period.

Where the order so ceases to have effect, that does not prejudice—

(a)   anything previously done under the order, or

(b)   the making of a new order.

In reckoning any such period of 28 days, no account shall be taken of any time during which Parliament is dissolved or prorogued or during which the House of Commons is adjourned for more than 4 days.]

NOTES

Inserted by the Finance Act 2002, s 4, Sch 1 para 2.

37–40

(Repealed by the Finance Act 1991, ss 7(4), 123, Sch 2, paras 6, 7, Sch 19, Pt II.)

Reliefs from excise duty

[41 Exemption from duty of beer produced for private consumption

The duty on beer produced in the United Kingdom shall not be chargeable on beer produced by a person who produces beer only for his own domestic use.]

NOTES

Substituted by the Finance Act 1991, s 7(4), Sch 2, para 8.

[41A Suspension of duty: registration of persons and premises

(1) A person registered by the Commissioners under this section may hold, on premises so registered in relation to him, any beer of a prescribed class or description—

(a) which has been produced in, or imported into, the United Kingdom, and

(b) which is chargeable as such with excise duty,

without payment of that duty.

(2) A person entitled under subsection (1) above to hold beer on premises without payment of duty may also without payment of duty carry out on those premises such operations as may be prescribed on, or in relation to, such of the beer as may be prescribed.

(3) No person shall be registered under this section unless—

(a) he is a registered brewer or a packager of beer;

(b) he appears to the Commissioners to satisfy such requirements for registration as they may think fit to impose.

(4) No premises shall be registered under this section unless—

(a) they are used for the production or packaging of beer, or

(b) they are adjacent to, and occupied by the same person as, premises falling within paragraph (a) above which are registered under this section,

and they appear to the Commissioners to satisfy such requirements for registration as the Commissioners may think fit to impose.

(5) The Commissioners may register a person or premises under this section for such periods and subject to such conditions as they think fit.

(6) The Commissioners may at any time for reasonable cause—

(a) revoke or vary the terms of their registration of any person or premises under this section; or

(b) restrict the premises which are so registered.

(7) As respects beer chargeable with a duty of excise that has not been paid, regulations under section 49 below may, without prejudice to the generality of that section, make provision—

Part I

(a)   regulating the holding or packaging of, or the carrying out of other operations on or in relation to, any such beer on registered premises without payment of the duty;

(b)   for securing and collecting the duty on any such beer held on registered premises;

(c)   permitting the removal of any such beer from registered premises without payment of duty in such circumstances and subject to such conditions as may be prescribed;

(d)   . . .

(8)   If any person contravenes or fails to comply with any condition of registration under this section [his contravention or failure to comply shall attract a penalty under section 9 of the Finance Act 1994 (civil penalties), and any beer in respect of which any person contravenes or fails to comply with any such condition shall be liable to forfeiture.]

(9)   In this section—

"prescribed" means specified in, or determined in accordance with, regulations made by the Commissioners under section 49 below;

"registered premises" means premises registered under this section.]

NOTES

Inserted by the Finance Act 1991, s 7(2).

Sub-s (7): para (d) repealed by the Finance (No 2) Act 1992, ss 1, 82, Sch 1, para 10, Sch 18, Pt I.

Sub-s (8): words in square brackets substituted by the Finance Act 1994, s 9, Sch 4, Pt II, paras 14, 29.

Regulations: the Beer Regulations 1993, SI 1993/1228, as amended by SI 1995/3059, SI 2000/3213.

42 Drawback on exportation, removal to warehouse, shipment as stores, etc

(1) This section applies to—

(a)   beer which has been [produced] by a [registered brewer]; and

(b)   beer which has been imported, or which has been removed into the United Kingdom from the Isle of Man.

(2) Subject to the provisions of this section and to such conditions as the Commissioners see fit to impose, drawback shall be allowable—

(a)   . . .

(b)   on the exportation . . . by any person of [any beer to which this section applies]; or

(c)   on the shipment as stores by any person of any such beer;

and shall also be allowable, subject as aforesaid, in the case of any beer to which this section applies which it is shown to the satisfaction of the Commissioners is being [exported or shipped] as mentioned in paragraph (b) or (c) above as an ingredient of other goods.

[(3) In the case of beer produced in the United Kingdom, the person intending to . . . export or ship the beer shall produce to the proper officer a declaration made by the person who paid the duty on the beer, in such form and manner as the Commissioners may direct, stating the strength of the beer and the date on which the duty became payable.]

(4) In the case of beer [produced] outside the United Kingdom, the person intending to . . . export or ship the beer shall produce to the proper officer in such form and manner as the Commissioners may direct a declaration that the proper duty has been charged and paid thereon.

(5) The amount of the drawback payable under this section in respect of any duty paid shall be calculated according to the rate of drawback applicable during the period of currency of the rate at which the duty was paid to like beer charged with that rate of duty during that period.

(6) Drawback under this section shall, where it is shown to the satisfaction of the Commissioners that duty has been paid, be allowed at the same rate as the rate at which the duty is charged, . . .

NOTES

Repealed by the Finance Act 1998, ss 5, 165, Sch 27, Pt I(1), as from a day to be appointed.

Sub-s (1): words in square brackets substituted by virtue of the Finance Act 1991, s 7(4), Sch 2, para 1.

Sub-s (2): words omitted repealed, and words in square brackets substituted, by the Finance Act 1993, ss 4(1), (2), (7), (8), 213, Sch 23, Pt I(1).

Sub-s (3): substituted by the Finance Act 1991, s 7(4), Sch 2, para 9; word omitted repealed by the Finance Act 1993, ss 4(1), (3), (8), 213, Sch 23, Pt I(1).

Sub-s (4): word in square brackets substituted by the Finance Act 1991, s 7(4), Sch 2, para 1; word omitted repealed by the Finance Act 1993, ss 4(1), (3), (8), 213, Sch 23, Pt I(1).

Sub-s (6): words omitted repealed by the Finance Act 1988, ss 1(2), 148, Sch 14, Pt I.

43

(Repealed by the Finance Act 1993, ss 4(1), (4), (7), 213, Sch 23, Pt I(1).)

44 Remission or repayment of duty on beer used for purposes of research or experiment

(1) Where it is proved to the satisfaction of the Commissioners that any beer [produced] in the United Kingdom which is chargeable with duty is to be used only for the purposes of research or of experiments in [the production of beer], the Commissioners may, if they think fit and subject to such conditions as they see fit to impose, remit or repay the duty chargeable on that beer.

(2) If any person contravenes or fails to comply with any condition imposed under subsection (1) above, [his contravention or failure to comply shall attract a penalty under section 9 of the Finance Act 1994 (civil penalties).]

NOTES

Sub-s (1): words in square brackets substituted by the Finance Act 1991, s 7(4), Sch 2, paras 1, 11.

Sub-s (2): words in square brackets substituted by the Finance Act 1994, s 9, Sch 4, Pt II, paras 14, 30.

45

(Repealed by the Finance Act 1995, s 162, Sch 29, Pt I(2).)

[46 Remission or repayment of duty on spoilt beer

(1) Where it is shown to the satisfaction of the Commissioners that any beer which has been removed from any premises of a registered brewer in respect of which he is registered under section 47 below has become spoilt or otherwise unfit for use and, in the case of beer delivered to another person, has been returned to the registered brewer as so spoilt or unfit, the Commissioners shall, subject to compliance with such conditions as they may by regulations impose, remit or repay any duty charged or paid in respect of the beer.

(2)   If any person contravenes or fails to comply with any regulation made under subsection (1) above, [his contravention or failure to comply shall attract a penalty under section 9 of the Finance Act 1994 (civil penalties).]]

NOTES

Substituted by the Finance Act 1991, s 7(4), Sch 2, para 13.

Sub-s (2): words in square brackets substituted by the Finance Act 1994, s 9, Sch 4, Pt II, paras 14, 31.

Regulations: the Beer Regulations 1993, SI 1993/1228, as amended by SI 1995/3059, SI 2000/3213.

[[Producing] of beer

47 Registration of producers of beer

(1)   A person who produces beer on any premises in the United Kingdom must be registered with the Commissioners under this section in respect of those premises; and in this Act "registered brewer" means a person registered under this section in respect of any premises.

(2)   A person who produces beer on any premises shall not be required to be registered under this section in respect of those premises if the beer is produced solely for his own domestic use or solely for the purposes of research or experiments in the production of beer.

(3)   An application for the registration under this section of any person required to be so registered in respect of any premises—

(a)   shall be made at least fourteen days before the day on which he begins production of beer on those premises; and

(b)   shall be in such form and manner as the Commissioners may by or under regulations prescribe.

(4)   If any person fails to apply for registration under this section in circumstances where he is required by subsection (3)(a) above to do so, [his failure shall attract a penalty under section 9 of the Finance Act 1994 (civil penalties)]; and any beer or worts produced in contravention of that provision shall be liable to forfeiture.

(5)   If any person produces beer on any premises in circumstances in which he is required to be, but is not, registered under this section in respect of those premises, [his doing so shall attract a penalty under section 9 of the Finance Act 1994 (civil penalties) which shall be calculated by reference to the amount of duty charged on the beer produced, and the beer produced and any worts found on those premises shall be liable to forfeiture.]]

NOTES

Substituted, together with the preceding cross heading, for original ss 47, 48 by the Finance Act 1991, s 7(3).

Cross-heading: word in square brackets substituted by virtue of the Finance Act 1991, s 7(4), Sch 2, para 1.

Sub-s (4): words in square brackets substituted by the Finance Act 1994, s 9, Sch 4, Pt II, paras 14, 32(1).

Sub-s (5): words in square brackets substituted by the Finance Act 1994, s 9, Sch 4, Pt II, paras 14, 32(2).

Regulations: the Beer Regulations 1993, SI 1993/1228, as amended by SI 1995/3059, SI 2000/3213.

[49 Beer regulations

(1) The Commissioners may, with a view to managing, securing and collecting the duty on beer produced in, or imported into, the United Kingdom or to the protection of the revenues derived from the duty of excise on beer, make regulations—

(a)   regulating the production, packaging, keeping and storage of beer produced in the United Kingdom and the packaging, keeping and storage of beer imported into the United Kingdom;

(b)   regulating the registration of persons and premises under section 41A or 47 above and the revocation or variation of any such registration;

(c)   for determining under or in accordance with the regulations when the production of beer begins and when it is completed;

(d)   for securing and collecting the duty;

[(e)   for determining the duty and the rate thereof and, in that connection, prescribing the method of charging the duty;]

(f)   for charging the duty, in such circumstances as may be prescribed in the regulations, by reference to a strength which the beer might reasonably be expected to have, or the rate of duty in force, at a time other than that at which the beer becomes chargeable;

(g)   for relieving beer from the duty in such circumstances and to such extent as may be prescribed in the regulations;

(h)   regulating and, in such circumstances as may be prescribed in the regulations, prohibiting the addition of substances to, the mixing of, or the carrying out of other operations on or in relation to, beer;

(j)   regulating the transportation of beer in such circumstances as may be prescribed in the regulations.

[(k)   requiring the production of certificates as to matters relating to beer imported into the United Kingdom and the beer's production and producer, whether as alternative conditions for charging the duty on the beer at a rate lower than that specified by section 36(1AA)(a) above or as evidence that conditions for charging the duty at such a rate are satisfied.]

(2) Regulations under this section may make different provision for persons, premises or beer of different classes or descriptions, for different circumstances and for different cases.

[(3) Where any person contravenes or fails to comply with any regulation made under this section, his contravention or failure to comply shall attract a penalty under section 9 of the Finance Act 1994 (civil penalties), and any article or substance in respect of which any person contravenes or fails to comply with any such regulation shall be liable to forfeiture.]]

NOTES

Substituted by the Finance Act 1991, s 7(4), Sch 2, para 14.

Sub-s (1): para (e) substituted by the Finance (No 2) Act 1992, s 1, Sch 1, para 11(1); para (k) added by the Finance Act 2002, s 4, Sch 1 para 3.

Sub-s (3): substituted by the Finance Act 1994, s 9, Sch 4, Pt II, paras 14, 33.

See the Channel Tunnel (Alcoholic Liquor and Tobacco Products) Order, SI 2003/2758 art 4(b): sub-s (3) above applies, for the purposes of SI 2003/2758, in corresponding manner to events involving goods in a control zone in the same way that it applies to events involving goods in the United Kingdom.

[49A Drawback allowable to [registered brewer]

(1) For the purpose of any claim for drawback by a [registered brewer or person registered under section 41A above] in respect of duty charged on beer, duty which has

been determined in accordance with regulations under [section 49(1)(e)] above shall be deemed to be duty which has been paid (whether or not it is in fact paid by the time the claim is made).

(2) Subject to such conditions as the Commissioners see fit to impose, drawback allowable to a [registered brewer or person registered under section 41A above] in respect of beer may be set against any amount to which [he] is chargeable [in respect of the excise duty on beer] and, in relation to a [registered brewer or person registered under section 41A above], any reference in this Act or the Management Act to drawback payable shall be construed accordingly.]

NOTES

Inserted by the Finance Act 1986, s 4(2).

Section heading: words in square brackets substituted by virtue of the Finance Act 1991, s 7(4), Sch 2, para 1.

Sub-ss (1), (2): words in square brackets substituted by the Finance Act 1991, s 7(4), Sch 2, paras 15.

50–53

(Ss 50, 53 repealed by the Finance Act 1991, ss 7(4), 123, Sch 2, paras 16, 18, Sch 19, Pt II; s 51 repealed by the Finance Act 1993, ss 4(1), (6), (7), 213, Sch 23, Pt I(1); s 52 repealed by the Finance (No 2) Act 1992, s 82, Sch 18, Pt I.)

PART IV
WINE AND MADE-WINE

54 Wine: charge of excise duty

(1) There shall be charged on wine—

(a)   imported into the United Kingdom; or

(b)   produced in the United Kingdom by a person who is required by subsection (2) below to be licensed to produce wine for sale,

a duty of excise at the rates shown in Schedule 1 to this Act and the duty shall, in so far as it is chargeable on wine produced in the United Kingdom, be charged and paid in accordance with regulations under section 56 below [and with any regulations under section 1 of the Finance (No 2) Act 1992].

(2) Subject to subsection (4) below, a person who, on any premises in the United Kingdom, produces wine for sale must hold an excise licence under this subsection in respect of those premises for that purpose.

(3) . . . .

[(3A) For the purposes of this Act, the process of blending or otherwise mixing two or more wines (in this subsection referred to as "the constituent wines") constitutes the production of wine if—

(a)   the rate of duty applicable to one of the constituent wines is different from that applicable to the other or, as the case may be, at least one of the others; and

(b)   the rate of duty applicable to the wine which is the product of the blending or other mixing is higher than that which is applicable to at least one of the constituent wines; and

(c)   the blending or other mixing is with a view to dealing wholesale in the wine which is the product thereof;

and for the purposes of this subsection the rate of duty applicable to any wine is that which is or would be chargeable under subsection (1) above on its importation into the United Kingdom or, as the case may be, on its production as mentioned in paragraph (b) of that subsection.

(3B)   Where, by virtue of subsection (3A) above, wine is produced in the United Kingdom, duty shall be chargeable on that wine by virtue of paragraph (b) of subsection (1) above whether or not duty was previously charged on all or any of the constituent wines by virtue of paragraph (a) or paragraph (b) of that subsection; but nothing in this subsection shall affect the operation of any regulations under section 56 below giving relief from duty on wine so produced by reference to duty charged on all or any of the constituent wines.]

(4)   A person who, in warehouse, produces wine for sale by rendering it sparkling in accordance with warehousing regulations need not hold an excise licence under subsection (2) above in respect of those premises.

[(4A)   A person who, on any premises, produces [wine of a strength not exceeding 5.5 per cent] by rendering it sparkling, need not on that account hold an excise licence under subsection (2) above in respect of those premises.]

(5)   If any person who is required by subsection (2) above to hold a licence under that subsection in respect of any premises produces wine on those premises without being the holder of a licence under that subsection in respect of those premises [his doing so shall attract a penalty under section 9 of the Finance Act 1994 (civil penalties) which shall be calculated by reference to the amount of duty charged on the wine produced, and the wine] and all vessels, utensils and materials for producing wine found in his possession shall be liable to forfeiture.

NOTES

Sub-s (1): words in square brackets added by the Finance (No 2) Act 1992, s 1, Sch 1, para 12.

Sub-s (3): repealed by the Finance Act 1986, s 114(6), Sch 23, Pt IV.

Sub-ss (3A), (3B): inserted by the Finance Act 1985, s 5, with effect in relation to the blending or otherwise mixing of wines on or after 26 March 1985.

Sub-s (4A): inserted by the Finance Act 1988, s 1(5), Sch 1, Pt II, para 4; words in square brackets inserted by the Finance Act 2006, s 5(2), (3).

Sub-s (5): words in square brackets substituted by the Finance Act 1994, s 9, Sch 4, para 34.

55 Made-wine: charge of excise duty

(1)   There shall be charged on made-wine—

    (a)   imported into the United Kingdom; or

    (b)   produced in the United Kingdom by a person who is required by subsection (2) below to be licensed to produce made-wine for sale,

a duty of excise at the rates shown in [Schedule 1] to this Act and the duty shall, in so far as it is chargeable on made-wine produced in the United Kingdom, be charged and paid in accordance with regulations under section 56 below [and with any regulations under section 1 of the Finance (No 2) Act 1992].

(2)   Subject to subsections (4) and (5) below, a person who, on any premises in the United Kingdom, produces made-wine for sale must hold an excise licence under this subsection in respect of those premises for that purpose.

(3)   . . .

(4)   A person who, in warehouse, produces made-wine for sale by rendering it sparkling in accordance with warehousing regulations need not hold an excise licence under subsection (2) above in respect of those premises.

[(4A)   A person who, on any premises, produces [made-wine of a strength not exceeding 5.5 per cent] by rendering it sparkling, need not on that account hold an excise licence under subsection (2) above in respect of those premises.]

(5)   A person need not hold an excise licence under subsection (2) above in respect of premises on which he produces made-wine for sale so long as all the following

conditions are satisfied in relation to the production of made-wine by him on those premises, that is to say—

[(aa)   he does not blend or otherwise mix two or more alcoholic liquors to which paragraphs (a) and (b) of section 66A(1) below or paragraphs (a) and (b) of section 66A(2) below apply;]

(a)   the duty chargeable on each alcoholic ingredient used by him has become payable before he uses it;

(b)   the ingredients he uses do not include cider or black beer;

(c)   he does not increase by fermentation the alcoholic strength of any liquor or substance used by him; and

(d)   he does not [render sparkling any made-wine other than [made-wine of a strength not exceeding 5.5 per cent]]; [. . .

(e)   . . .]

[(5A) . . .]

(6) If any person who is required by subsection (2) above to hold a licence under that subsection in respect of any premises produces made-wine on those premises without being the holder of a licence under that subsection in respect of those premises [his doing so shall attract a penalty under section 9 of the Finance Act 1994 (civil penalties) which shall be calculated by reference to the amount of duty charged on the made-wine produced, and the made-wine] and all vessels, utensils and materials for producing made-wine found in his possession shall be liable to forfeiture.

NOTES

Sub-s (1): words in first pair of square brackets substituted by the Finance Act 1984, s 1(4); words in second pair of square brackets added by the Finance (No 2) Act 1992, s 1, Sch 1, para 13.

Sub-s (3): repealed by the Finance Act 1986, s 114(6), Sch 23, Pt IV.

Sub-s (4A): inserted by the Finance Act 1988, s 1, Sch 1, Part II, para 5(1); words in square brackets substituted by the Finance Act 2006, s 5(2), (4).

Sub-s (5): para (aa) inserted by the Finance Act 1993, s 5(2), (4), in relation to the blending or other mixing of alcoholic liquors on or after 27 July 1993; para (d): words in outer square brackets substituted by the Finance Act 1988, s 1(5), Sch 1, Pt II, para 5(2); words in inner square brackets substituted by the Finance Act 2006, s 5(2), (4); para (e) and the word immediately preceding it added by the Finance Act 1989, s 4, in relation to the blending or other mixing of made-wines, or of made-wines and wines, on or after 27 July 1989, and repealed by the Finance Act 1993, ss 5(3)(a), (4), 213, Sch 23, Pt I(2), in relation to the blending or other mixing of alcoholic liquors on or after 27 July 1993.

Sub-s (5A): inserted by the Finance Act 1989, s 4, in relation to the blending or other mixing of made-wines, or of made-wines and wines, on or after 27 July 1989, and repealed by the Finance Act 1993, ss 5(3)(b), (4), 213, Sch 23, Pt I(2), in relation to the blending or other mixing of alcoholic liquors on or after 27 July 1993.

Sub-s (6): words in square brackets substituted by the Finance Act 1994, s 9, Sch 4, Pt II, paras 14, 35.

[55A

(Repealed by Finance Act 2006, ss 5(1)(j), 178, Sch 26, Pt 1(1)).

[55B Cider labelled as made-wine

(1) For the purposes of this Act, any liquor which would apart from this section be cider and which—

(a)   is in an up-labelled container, or

(b)   has, at any time after 31st December 1996 when it was in the United Kingdom, been in an up-labelled container,

shall be deemed to be made-wine, and not cider.

(2)   Accordingly, references in this Act to producing made-wine include references to—

(a)   putting cider in an up-labelled container; or

(b)   causing a container in which there is cider to be up-labelled.

(3)   For the purposes of this Act, where any liquor is deemed by this section to be made-wine, it shall be deemed—

(a)   if it is in an up-labelled container, to be made-wine of the strength that the labelling for the container states or tends to suggest; and

(b)   if it is no longer in an up-labelled container, to be made-wine of the strength stated or suggested by the labelling for the up- labelled container in which it was contained when it was first deemed by this section to be made-wine.

(4)   Subsection (3)(a) above has effect subject to any provision that may be made by regulations under section 2(3) above.

(5)   Where, by virtue of this section, any duty is charged under section 55 above on any liquor, a rebate shall be allowed in respect of the amount of any duty charged on that liquor under section 62 below.

(6)   For the purposes of this section a container is up-labelled if the labelling for the container states or tends to suggest that the strength of any liquor in that container is or exceeds 8.5 per cent.

(7)   In this section references to the labelling for any container are references to anything on—

(a)   the container itself,

(b)   a label or leaflet attached to or used with the container, or

(c)   any packaging used for or in association with the container.]

NOTES

Inserted by the Finance Act 1997, s 5(1), (5), with retrospective effect as from 1 January 1997.

56 Power to regulate making of wine and made-wine and provide for charging duty thereon

(1)   The Commissioners may with a view to managing the duties on wine and made-wine produced in the United Kingdom for sale make regulations—

(a)   regulating the production of wine and made-wine for sale, and the issue, . . . and cancellation of excise licences therefor;

(b)   for determining the duty and the rates thereof and in that connection prescribing the method of charging the duty;

(c)   prohibiting or restricting the use of wine [or cider] in the production of made-wine;

(d)   for securing and collecting the duty;

(e)   for relieving wine or made-wine from the duty in such circumstances and to such extent as may be prescribed in the regulations.

(2)   If any person contravenes or fails to comply with any regulation made under this section, [his contravention or failure to comply shall attract a penalty under section 9 of the Finance Act 1994 (civil penalties), and any article in respect of which any person contravenes or fails to comply with any such regulation shall be liable to forfeiture.]

NOTES

Sub-s (1): words omitted repealed by the Finance Act 1986, s 114(6), Sch 23, Pt IV; word in square brackets inserted by the Finance Act 1997, s 5(4).

Sub-s (2): words in square brackets substituted by the Finance Act 1994, s 9, Sch 4, Pt II, paras 14, 37.

Regulations: the Excise Duty (Relief on Alcoholic Ingredients) Regulations 1978, SI 1978/1786, as amended by SI 1979/1146, SI 1992/3157; the Excise Duty (Wine) (Temporary Relief) Regulations 1985, SI 1985/403; the Excise Warehousing (Etc) Regulations 1988, SI 1988/809, as amended by SI 1995/1046; the Cider and Perry Regulations 1989, SI 1989/1355, as amended by SI 1996/2287, SI 1997/659; the Wine and Made-Wine Regulations 1989, SI 1989/1356, as amended by SI 1996/2752, SI 1997/658; the Excise Duties (Deferred Payment) Regulations 1992, SI 1992/3152, as amended by SI 1996/2537; the Excise Duty (Relief on Alcoholic Ingredients) (Amendment) Regulations 1992, SI 1992/3157.

57 Mixing of made-wine and spirits in warehouse

The Commissioners may, subject to such conditions as they see fit to impose, permit the mixing in an excise warehouse with made-wine (whether imported into or produced in the United Kingdom [or removed to the United Kingdom from the Isle of Man]) of duty-free spirits in a proportion not exceeding [12 litres of alcohol to 1 hectolitre of made-wine]; so, however, that the mixture shall not by virtue of this section be raised to a greater strength than [22 per cent].

NOTES

Words in first pair of square brackets inserted by the Isle of Man Act 1979, s 13, Sch 1; words in second pair of square brackets substituted by the Alcoholic Liquors (Amendment of Enactments Relating to Strength and to Units of Measurement) Order 1979, SI 1979/241, art 23; words in third pair of square brackets substituted by the Excise Duty (Amendment of the Alcoholic Liquor Duties Act 1979 and the Hydrocarbon Oil Duties Act 1979) Regulations 1992, SI 1992/3158, reg 2(1), (6).

58 Mixing of wine and spirits in warehouse

(1) The Commissioners may, subject to such conditions as they see fit to impose, permit the mixing in an excise warehouse with wine (whether imported into or produced in the United Kingdom [or removed to the United Kingdom from the Isle of Man]) of duty-free spirits in a proportion not exceeding [[12 litres] of alcohol to 1 hectolitre of wine], so, however, that the mixture shall not, [by virtue of this section], be raised to a greater strength than [22 per cent].

(2) . . .

NOTES

Sub-s (1): words in first pair of square brackets inserted by the Isle of Man Act 1979, s 13, Sch 1; words in second (outer) pair of square brackets substituted by the Alcoholic Liquors (Amendment of Enactments Relating to Strength and to Units of Measurement) Order 1979, SI 1979/241, art 24; words in third (inner), fourth and fifth pairs of square brackets substituted by the Finance Act 1993, s 6(1), (3), in relation to mixing done on or after 27 July 1993.

Sub-s (2): repealed by the Finance Act 1993, ss 6(1)–(3), 213, Sch 23, Pt I(3), in relation to mixing done on or after 27 July 1993.

59 Rendering imported wine or made-wine sparkling in warehouse

[(1) Wine or made-wine which—

    (a)   is imported or is removed to the United Kingdom from the Isle of Man; and

[(b)   is wine or made-wine of a strength exceeding 5.5 per cent],

shall not be rendered sparkling, whether by aeration, fermentation or any other process, except in warehouse in accordance with warehousing regulations.]

[(2)   Where any person contravenes subsection (1) above or is concerned in such a contravention, his contravention or, as the case may be, his being so concerned shall attract a penalty under section 9 of the Finance Act 1994 (civil penalties).]

(3)   All imported wine and imported made-wine rendered or being rendered sparkling in contravention of subsection (1) above, and all machinery, utensils, bottles and materials (including wine or made-wine) used or intended to be used in any process for rendering any wine or made-wine sparkling in contravention of that subsection shall be liable to forfeiture.

NOTES

Sub-s (1): substituted by the Finance Act 1988, s 1(5), Sch 1, Pt II, para 7; para (b) substituted by the Finance Act 1995, s 1(1), (4), (5), in relation to liquor imported into, or produced in, the United Kingdom, or removed to the United Kingdom from the Isle of Man, on or after 1 January 1995.

Sub-s (2): substituted by the Finance Act 1994, s 9, Sch 4, Pt II, paras 14, 38.

60

(Sub-ss (1), (2) repealed by the Finance Act 1995, s 162, Sch 29, Pt I(2); sub-s (1A) inserted. by the Finance Act 1988, s 1(5), Sch 1, Pt II, para 8, and repealed by s 162 of, and Sch 29, Pt I(1) to, the 1995 Act, in relation to liquor imported into, or produced in, the United Kingdom, or removed to the United Kingdom from the Isle of Man, on or after 1 January 1995.)

61   Remission or repayment of duty on spoilt wine or made-wine

(1)   Where it is shown to the satisfaction of the Commissioners that any wine or made-wine which has been removed from the entered premises of a licensed producer of wine or of made-wine has accidentally become spoilt or otherwise unfit for use and, in the case of wine or made-wine delivered to another person, has been returned to the producer as so spoilt or unfit, the Commissioners shall, subject to compliance with such conditions as they may by regulations impose, remit or repay any duty charged or paid in respect of the wine or made-wine.

(2)   If any person contravenes or fails to comply with any regulation made under subsection (1) above, [his contravention or failure to comply shall attract a penalty under section 9 of the Finance Act 1994 (civil penalties).]

NOTES

Sub-s (2): words in square brackets substituted by the Finance Act 1994, s 9, Sch 4, Pt II, paras 14, 39.

Regulations: the Wine and Made-Wine Regulations 1989, SI 1989/1356, as amended by SI 1996/2752, SI 1997/658;

PART V
CIDER

62   Excise duty on cider

(1)   There shall be charged on cider—

    (a)   imported into the United Kingdom; or

    (b)   made in the United Kingdom by a person who is required by subsection (2) below to be registered as a maker of cider,

a duty of excise at the [rates shown in subsection (1A) below].

[(1A)   The rates at which the duty shall be charged are—

    (a)   [£172.33] per hectolitre in the case of sparkling cider of a strength exceeding 5.5 per cent;

[(b)   [£39.73] per hectolitre in the case of cider of a strength exceeding 7.5 per cent which is not sparkling cider; and

(c)   [£26.48] per hectolitre in any other case.]

(2)   Subject to subsection (3) below, a person who, on any premises in the United Kingdom, makes cider for sale must be registered with the Commissioners in respect of those premises.

(3)   The Treasury may by order made by statutory instrument provide for exempting from subsection (2) above makers of cider whose production does not exceed such limit as is specified in the order and who comply with such other conditions as may be so specified.

(4)   If any person who is required by subsection (2) above to be registered in respect of any premises makes cider on those premises without being registered in respect of them, [his doing so shall attract a penalty under section 9 of the Finance Act 1994 (civil penalties) which shall be calculated by reference to the amount of duty charged on the cider made, and the cider] and all vessels, utensils and materials for making cider found in his possession shall be liable to forfeiture.

(5)   The Commissioners may with a view to managing the duty on cider made in the United Kingdom make regulations—

(a)   regulating the making of cider for sale and the registration and cancellation of registration of makers of cider;

(b)   for determining the duty and the rate thereof and in that connection prescribing the method of charging the duty;

(c)   for securing and collecting the duty;

(d)   for relieving cider from the duty in such circumstances and to such extent as may be prescribed in the regulations.

[(e)   regulating and, in such circumstances as may be prescribed in the regulations, prohibiting the addition of substances to, the mixing of, or the carrying out of other operations on or in relation to, cider.]

(6)   If any person contravenes or fails to comply with any regulation made under subsection (5) above, [his contravention or failure to comply shall attract a penalty under section 9 of the Finance Act 1994 (civil penalties), and any article in respect of which any person contravenes or fails to comply with any such regulation shall be liable to forfeiture.]

[(7)   References in this section to making cider shall be construed as including references to producing sparkling cider by rendering cider sparkling; and references in this section to cider made in the United Kingdom, to makers of cider and to making cider for sale shall be construed accordingly.]

NOTES

Sub-s (1): words in square brackets substituted by the Finance Act 1996, s 3(1), (3).

Sub-s (1A): inserted by the Finance Act 1996, s 3(2), (3); substituted by the Finance (No 2) Act 1997, s 10; sums in square brackets in paras (a)–(c) substituted by the Finance Act 2007, s 5(1), (3).

Sub-ss (4), (6): words in square brackets substituted by the Finance Act 1994, s 9, Sch 4, Pt II, paras 14, 40(1), (2).

Sub-s (5)(e) added by the Finance Act 2001, 5.

Sub-s (7): added by the Finance Act 1997, s 3(2), (5).

Orders: the Cider and Perry (Exemption from Registration) Order 1976, SI 1976/1206, as amended by SI 1979/1218.

Regulations: the Excise Duty (Relief on Alcoholic Ingredients) Regulations 1978, SI 1978/1786, as amended by SI 1979/1146, SI 1992/3157; the Cider and Perry Regulations 1989, SI 1989/1355, as amended by SI 1996/2287, SI 1997/659; the Wine and Made-Wine Regulations 1989, SI 1989/1356, as amended by SI 1996/2752, SI 1997/658; the Excise Duties

(Deferred Payment) Regulations 1992, SI 1992/3152; the Excise Duty (Relief on Alcoholic Ingredients) (Amendment) Regulations 1992, SI 1992/3157.

[62A Meaning of "sparkling" etc in section 62

(1)   This section applies for the purposes of section 62 above.

(2)   Cider which is for the time being in a closed bottle is sparkling if, due to the presence of carbon dioxide, the pressure in the bottle, measured at a temperature of 20 degrees C, is not less than 3 bars in excess of atmospheric pressure.

(3)   Cider which is for the time being in a closed bottle is sparkling regardless of the pressure in the bottle if the bottle has a mushroom-shaped stopper (whether solid or hollow) held in place by a tie or fastening.

(4)   Cider which is not for the time being in a closed container is sparkling if it has characteristics similar to those of cider which has been removed from a closed bottle and which, before removal, fell within subsection (2) above.

(5)   Cider shall be regarded as having been rendered sparkling if, as a result of aeration, fermentation or any other process, it either–

   (a)   falls within subsection (2) above; or

   (b)   takes on characteristics similar to those of cider which has been removed from a closed bottle and which, before removal, fell within subsection (2) above.

(6)   Cider which has not previously been rendered sparkling by virtue of subsection (5) above shall be regarded as having been rendered sparkling if it is transferred into a closed bottle which has a mushroom-shaped stopper (whether solid or hollow) held in place by a tie or fastening.

(7)   Cider which is in a closed bottle and has not previously been rendered sparkling by virtue of subsection (5) or (6) above shall be regarded as having been rendered sparkling if the stopper of its bottle is exchanged for a stopper of a kind mentioned in subsection (6) above.]

NOTES
Inserted by the Finance Act 1997, s 3(3), (5).

[62B Cider labelled as strong cider

(1)   For the purposes of this Act, any liquor which would apart from this section be standard cider and which—

   (a)   is in an up-labelled container, or

   (b)   has, at any time after 31st December 1996 when it was in the United Kingdom, been in an up-labelled container,

shall be deemed to be strong cider, and not standard cider.

(2)   Accordingly, references in this Act to making cider include references to—

   (a)   putting standard cider in an up-labelled container; or

   (b)   causing a container in which there is standard cider to be up- labelled.

(3)   Where, by virtue of this section, any duty is charged under section 62 above on any cider, a rebate shall be allowed in respect of the amount of any duty charged on that cider under that section otherwise than by virtue of this section.

(4)   For the purposes of this section—

   (a)   "standard cider" means cider which is not sparkling and is of a strength not exceeding 7.5 per cent; and

   (b)   "strong cider" means cider which is not sparkling and is of a strength exceeding 7.5 per cent.

(5) For the purposes of this section a container is up-labelled if there is anything on—

(a)   the container itself,

(b)   a label or leaflet attached to or used with the container, or

(c)   any packaging used for or in association with the container,

which states or tends to suggest that the strength of any liquor in that container falls within the strong cider strength range.

(6) For the purposes of subsection (5) above, a strength falls within the strong cider strength range if it exceeds 7.5 per cent but is less than 8.5 per cent.]

NOTES

Inserted by the Finance Act 1997, s 4, with retrospective effect as from 1 January 1997.

63

(Sub-s (1) repealed by the Finance Act 1995, s 162, Sch 29, Pt I(2); sub-s (2) added by the Finance Act 1988, s 1(5), Sch 1, Pt II, para 9 and repealed by s 162 of, and Sch 29, Pt I(1) to, the 1995 Act, in relation to liquor imported into, or made in, the United Kingdom on or after 1 January 1995.)

64 Remission or repayment of duty on spoilt cider

(1)   Where it is shown to the satisfaction of the Commissioners that any cider which has been removed from the entered premises of a registered maker of cider has accidentally become spoilt or otherwise unfit for use and, in the case of cider delivered to another person, has been returned to the maker as so spoilt or unfit, the Commissioners shall, subject to compliance with such conditions as they may by regulations impose, remit or repay any duty charged or paid in respect of the cider.

[(1A)   In subsection (1) above the references to a maker of cider include references to any person who is taken for the purposes of section 62 above to be a maker of cider.]

(2)   If any person contravenes or fails to comply with any regulation made under subsection (1) above, [his contravention or failure to comply shall attract a penalty under section 9 of the Finance Act 1994 (civil penalties).]

NOTES

Sub-s (1A): inserted by the Finance Act 1997, s 3(4), (5), with retrospective effect as from 1 January 1997.

Sub-s (2): words in square brackets substituted by the Finance Act 1994, s 9, Sch 4, Pt II, paras 14, 41.

Regulations: the Cider and Perry Regulations 1989, SI 1989/1355, as amended by SI 1996/2287, SI 1997/659.

PART VI
GENERAL CONTROL PROVISIONS

Sale of dutiable alcoholic liquors

[64A Retail containers of certain alcoholic liquors to be stamped
Schedule 2A to this Act (duty stamps) has effect.]

NOTES

Inserted by the Finance Act 2004, s 4(1) with effect in relation to retail containers containing alcoholic liquor if the excise duty point for the alcoholic liquor falls on or after

22 February 2006. For definition of "excise duty point" see the Finance (No 2) Act 1992, s 1.

65, 66

(Repealed by the Finance Act 1981, ss 11(1), 139(6), Sch 8, Pt II, para 20, Sch 19, Pt III.)

[66A Blending of alcoholic liquors

(1) Subject to subsections (4) to (6) below, a person shall not blend two or more alcoholic liquors—

    (a)   each of which is of a kind mentioned in paragraphs (a) to (e) of section 1(1) above, but

    (b)   not all of which fall within the same one of those paragraphs,

except in an excise warehouse or on premises which, in relation to the liquors blended, are for the time being permitted premises.

(2) Subject to subsections (4) to (6) below, a person shall not blend two or more alcoholic liquors which—

    (a)   fall within the same paragraph of section 1(1) above, but

    (b)   are not all of the same alcoholic strength,

except in an excise warehouse or on premises which, in relation to the liquors blended, are for the time being permitted premises.

(3) In relation to the blending of particular alcoholic liquors—

    (a)   if the liquor which is the product of the blending is beer, permitted premises are premises which are registered under section 41A above and premises in respect of which a person is registered under section 47 above;

    (b)   if the liquor which is the product of the blending is wine, permitted premises are premises in respect of which a licence under section 54(2) above is held;

    (c)   if the liquor which is the product of the blending is made-wine, permitted premises are premises in respect of which a licence under section 55(2) above is held;

    (d)   if the liquor which is the product of the blending is cider, permitted premises are premises in respect of which a person is registered under section 62 above.

(4) Subsections (1) and (2) above do not apply unless the blending is done with a view to offering for sale the liquor which is the product of the blending.

(5) Subsections (1) and (2) above do not apply where the liquor which is the product of the blending is intended for consumption on the premises on which the blending takes place.

(6) The Commissioners may direct that subsections (1) and (2) above shall not apply to the blending of alcoholic liquors in such circumstances as are specified in the direction.

(7) Where a person contravenes subsection (1) or (2) above, the following shall be liable to forfeiture—

    (a)   the liquor which is the product of the blending;

    (b)   all such vessels, utensils and materials for the blending of alcoholic liquors as are found in his possession.

(8) In this section any reference to blending liquors includes a reference to otherwise mixing them.]

NOTES

Inserted by the Finance Act 1993, s 5(1), (4), in relation to the blending or mixing of alcoholic liquors on or after 27 July 1993.

67

(Repealed by Finance Act 2006, ss 5(1)(k), 178, Sch 26, Pt 1(1)).

68

(Repealed by the Finance Act 1981, ss 11(1), 139(6), Sch 8, Pt II, para 20, Sch 19, Pt III.)

69

Repealed by Finance Act 2006, ss 5(1)(l), 178, Sch 26, Pt 1(1)).

70

(Repealed by the Finance Act 1981, ss 11(1), 139(6), Sch 8, Pt II, para 20, Sch 19, Pt III.)

71

(Repealed by the Finance Act 2006, ss 5(1)(m), 178, Sch 26, Pt 1(1)).

[71A]–73

(Ss 71A, 72 (inserted in the case of s 71A by the Finance Act 1985, s 6, Sch 3, para 4(2)) repealed by the Finance Act 1991, ss 7(4), 123, Sch 2, paras 19, 20, Sch 19, Pt II; s 72 repealed by the Finance Act 1989, ss 5, 187(1), Sch 17, Pt I.)

74

(Repealed by the Finance Act 2006, ss 5(1)(n), 178, Sch 26, Pt 1(1)).

Methylated spirits

75 Licence or authority to manufacture and deal wholesale in [denatured alcohol]

(1) The Commissioners may authorise any distiller, rectifier or compounder to [denature] [dutiable alcoholic liquor], and any person so authorised is referred to in this Act as an "authorised [denaturer]".

(2) No person other than an authorised [denaturer] shall [denature] [dutiable alcoholic liquor] or deal wholesale in [denatured alcohol] unless he holds an excise licence as a [denaturer] under this section.

(3), (4) . . .

(5) [Where any person], not being an authorised [denaturer], [denatures] [dutiable alcoholic liquor] otherwise than under and in accordance with a licence under this section [his doing so shall attract a penalty under section 9 of the Finance Act 1994 (civil penalties).]

(6) The Commissioners may at any time revoke or suspend any authorisation or licence granted under this section.

(7) For the purposes of this section, dealing wholesale means the sale at any one time to any one person of a quantity of [denatured alcohol] of not less than [20 litres] or such smaller quantity as the Commissioners may by regulations specify.

NOTES

Section heading substituted by the Finance Act 1995 s 5(5), Sch 2 para 5.

Sub-ss (1), (2): words in square brackets substituted by the Finance Act 1995 s 5(5), Sch 2 para 5.

Sub-ss (3), (4): repealed by the Finance Act 1986, ss 8(2), 114(6), Sch 23, Pt IV.

Sub-s (5): words in first pair of square brackets substituted by the Finance Act 1994, s 9, Sch 4, Pt II, paras 14, 45; words in subsequent square brackets substituted by the Finance Act 1995 s 5(5), Sch 2 para 5.

Sub-s (7): words in first pair of square brackets substituted by the Finance Act 1995 s 5(5), Sch 2 para 5; words in second pair of square brackets substituted by the Alcoholic Liquors (Amendment of Enactments Relating to Strength and to Units of Measurement) Order 1979, SI 1979/241, art 33.

Orders: the Finance Act 1995 (Denatured Alcohol) (Appointed Day and Savings) Order, SI 2005/1523.

76

(Repealed by the Finance Act 1981, ss 11(1), 139(6), Sch 8, Pt II, para 22, Sch 19, Pt III.)

77 Power to make regulations relating to [denatured alcohol]

(1) The Commissioners may with a view to the protection of the revenue make regulations—

(a) regulating the [denaturing] of [dutiable alcoholic liquor] and the supply, storage, removal, sale, delivery, receipt, use and exportation or shipment as stores of [denatured alcohol];

(b) . . .

(c) permitting [dutiable alcoholic liquor] to be [denatured] in warehouse;

(d) permitting [dealing wholesale (within the meaning of section 75 above) without a licence in] such [denatured alcohol] as may be specified in the regulations;

(e) regulating the importation, receipt, removal, storage and use of [dutiable alcoholic liquor] for [denaturing];

(f) regulating the storage and removal of substances to be used in [denaturing] [dutiable alcoholic liquor];

(g) prescribing the manner in which account is to be kept of stocks of [denatured alcohol] in the possession of authorised or licensed [denaturer] and of retailers of [denatured alcohol];

(h) for securing any duty chargeable in respect of [denatured alcohol] of any class.

(2) Different regulations may be made under this section with respect to different classes of [denatured alcohol] or different kinds of [denatured alcohol] of any class [and, without prejudice to the generality of subsection (1) above, regulations under this section may—

(a) provide for the imposition under the regulations of conditions and restrictions relating to the matters mentioned in that subsection; and

[(aa) frame any provision of the regulations with respect to the supply, receipt or use of denatured alcohol by reference to matters to be contained from time to time in a notice published in accordance with the regulations by the Commissioners and having effect until withdrawn in accordance with the regulations; and]

(b) impose or provide for the imposition by regulations of requirements on authorised or licensed [denaturers] and on retailers of [denatured alcohol] to keep and preserve records relating to their businesses as such and to produce them to an officer when required to do so for the purpose of allowing him to inspect them, to copy or take extracts from them or to remove them at a reasonable time and for a reasonable period.]

[(2A)   Where any documents removed under the powers conferred by subsection (2)(b) above are lost or damaged the Commissioners shall be liable to compensate their owner for any expenses reasonably incurred by him in replacing or repairing the documents.]

(3)   If any person contravenes or fails to comply with any regulation under this section, [or with any condition, restriction or requirement imposed under such a regulation, [his contravention or failure to comply shall attract a penalty under section 9 of the Finance Act 1994 (civil penalties).]]

(4)   If, save as permitted by any regulation under this section, any person [deals wholesale (within the meaning of section 75 above) in] [denatured alcohol] otherwise than under and in accordance with a licence under section 75 . . . above, [his doing so shall attract a penalty under section 9 of the Finance Act 1994 (civil penalties).]

(5)   Any [dutiable alcoholic liquor] or [denatured alcohol] in respect of which [there is such a contravention or failure to comply as is mentioned in subsection (3) above or any such dealing as is mentioned in subsection (4) above] shall be liable to forfeiture.

(6)   . . .

NOTES

Section heading: words in square brackets substituted by the Finance Act 1995 s 5(5), Sch 2 para 5.

Sub-s (1): words in square brackets substituted by the Finance Act 1995 s 5(5), Sch 2 para 5; para (b) repealed by the Finance Act 1995 s 162, Sch 29 Pt I; words in first pair of square brackets in para (d) substituted by the Finance Act 1981, s 11(1), Sch 8, Pt II, para 23(a).

Sub-s (2): words "denatured alcohol" and "denaturers", and para (aa) inserted by the Finance Act 1995 s 5(5), Sch 2 paras 5, 6; words from "and, without prejudice" to "a reasonable period" in square brackets inserted by the Finance Act 1981, s 11(1), Sch 8, Pt II, para 23(b).

Sub-s (2A): inserted by the Finance Act 1981, s 11(1), Sch 8, Pt II, para 23.

Sub-s (3): words in first (outer) pair of square brackets substituted by the Finance Act 1981, s 11(1), Sch 8, Pt II, para 23(c); words in second (inner) pair of square brackets substituted by the Finance Act 1994, s 9, Sch 4, Pt II, paras 14, 46(1).

Sub-s (4): words in first pair of square brackets substituted, and words omitted repealed, by the Finance Act 1981, s 11(1), 139(6), Sch 8, Pt II, para 23(d), Sch 19, Pt III; words in second pair of square brackets substituted by the Finance Act 1995 s 5(5), Sch 2 para 5; words in third pair of square brackets substituted by the Finance Act 1994, s 9, Sch 4, Pt II, paras 14, 46(2).

Sub-s (5): words in first two pairs of square brackets substituted by the Finance Act 1995 s 5(5), Sch 2 para 5; words in third pair of square brackets substituted by the Finance Act 1994, s 9, Sch 4, Pt II, paras 14, 46(3).

Sub-s (6) repealed by the Licensing (Scotland) Act 2005 s 149, Sch 7.

Orders: the Finance Act 1995 (Denatured Alcohol) (Appointed Day and Savings) Order, SI 2005/1523.

[78 Defaults in respect of denatured alcohol

(1)   This subsection applies if, at any time when an account is taken and a balance struck of the quantity of any kind of denatured alcohol in the possession of an authorised or licensed denaturer, there is a difference between—

(a)   the quantity ("the actual amount") of the dutiable alcoholic liquor of any description in the denatured alcohol in his possession; and

(b)   the quantity ("the proper amount") of dutiable alcoholic liquor of that description which, according to any such accounts as are required to be kept by virtue of any regulations under section 77 above, ought to be in the denatured alcohol in his possession.

(2) Subsection (1) above shall not apply if the difference constitutes—

(a) an excess of the actual amount over the proper amount of not more than 1 per cent of the aggregate of—

    (i) the quantity of dutiable alcoholic liquor of the description in question in the balance of dutiable alcoholic liquor struck when an account was last taken; and

    (ii) the quantity of dutiable alcoholic liquor of that description which has since been lawfully added to the denaturer's stock;

or

(b) a deficiency such that the actual amount is less than the proper amount by not more than 2 per cent of that aggregate.

(3) If, where subsection (1) above applies, the actual amount exceeds the proper amount, the relevant amount of any dutiable alcoholic liquor of the description in question which is in the possession of the denaturer shall be liable to forfeiture; and for this purpose the relevant amount is the amount corresponding to the amount of the excess or such part of that amount as the Commissioners consider appropriate.

(4) If, where subsection (1) above applies, the actual amount is less than the proper amount, the denaturer shall, on demand by the Commissioners, pay on the amount of the deficiency, or on such part of it as the Commissioners may specify in the demand, the duty payable on dutiable alcoholic liquor of the description comprised in the deficiency.

(5) If any person—

(a) supplies to another, in contravention of any regulations under section 77 above, any denatured alcohol containing dutiable alcoholic liquor of any description, or

(b) uses any such denatured alcohol in contravention of any such regulations,

that person shall, on demand by the Commissioners, pay on the amount of dutiable alcoholic liquor of that description comprised, at the time of its supply or use, in the denatured alcohol that is so supplied or used, or on such part of it as the Commissioners may specify, the duty payable on dutiable alcoholic liquor of that description.

(6) Any supply of denatured alcohol to a person who—

(a) by virtue of any regulations under section 77 above is prohibited from receiving it unless authorised to do so by or under the regulations, and

(b) is not so authorised in the case of the denatured alcohol supplied to him,

shall be taken for the purposes of subsection (5) above to be a supply in contravention of those regulations.

(7) A demand made for the purposes of subsection (4) or (5) above shall be combined, as if there had been a default such as is mentioned in that section, with an assessment and notification under section 12 of the Finance Act 1994 (assessments to excise duty) of the amount of duty due in consequence of the making of the demand.]

NOTES

Whole of section 78 substituted by the Finance Act 1995 s 5(5), Sch 2 para 7.

79 Inspection of premises, etc

Without prejudice to any other power conferred by the Customs and Excise Acts 1979, an officer may in the daytime enter and inspect the premises of any person authorised by regulations made under section 77 above to receive [denatured alcohol], and may inspect and examine any [denatured alcohol] thereon and take samples of any [denatured alcohol] or of any goods containing [denatured alcohol], paying a reasonable price for each sample.

NOTES
Words in square brackets substituted by the Finance Act 1995 s 5(5), Sch 2 para 5.

80 Prohibition of use of [denatured alcohol], etc as a beverage or medicine

(1) If any person—

(a) prepares or attempts to prepare any liquor to which this section applies for use as a beverage or as a mixture with a beverage; or

(b) sells any such liquor, whether so prepared or not, as a beverage or mixed with a beverage; or

(c) uses any such liquor or any derivative thereof in the preparation of any article capable of being used wholly or partially as a beverage or internally as a medicine; or

(d) sells or has in his possession any such article in the preparation of which any such liquor or any derivative thereof has been used; or

(e) except as permitted by the Commissioners and in accordance with any conditions imposed by them, purifies or attempts to purify any such liquor or, after any such liquor has once been used, recovers or attempts to recover the spirit or alcohol contained therein by distillation or condensation or in any other manner,

he shall be liable on summary conviction to a penalty [not exceeding level 3 on the standard scale] and the liquor in respect of which the offence was committed shall be liable to forfeiture.

(2) Nothing in this section shall prohibit the use of any liquor to which this section applies or any derivative thereof—

(a) in the preparation for use as a medicine of sulphuric ether, chloroform, or any other article which the Commissioners may by order specify; or

(b) in the making for external use only of any article sold or supplied in accordance with regulations made by the Commissioners under section 77 above; or

(c) in any art or manufacture,

or the sale or possession of any article permitted to be prepared or made by virtue of paragraph (a) or (b) above where the article is sold or possessed for use as mentioned in that paragraph.

(3) The liquors to which this section applies are [denatured alcohol], methyl alcohol, and any mixture containing [denatured alcohol] or methyl alcohol.

NOTES
Section heading: words in square brackets substituted by the Finance Act 1995 s 5(5), Sch 2 para 5.

Sub-s (1): words in square brackets substituted by virtue of the Criminal Justice Act 1982, ss 37, 38, 46.

Sub-s (3): words in square brackets substituted by the Finance Act 1995 s 5(5), Sch 2 para 5.

Still licences

81

(Repealed by the Finance Act 1986, ss 8(2), 114(6), Sch 23, Pt IV.)

82

(Repealed by the Finance Act 2006, ss 5(1)(o), 178, Sch 26, Pt 1(1)).

83–88

(S 83 repealed by the Finance Act 1986, ss 8(2), 114(6), Sch 23, Pt IV; ss 84–88 repealed by the Finance Act 1981, ss 11(1), 139(6), Sch 8, Pt II, para 20, Sch 19, Pt III.)

PART VII
MISCELLANEOUS

General

89

(Repealed by the Finance Act 1981, ss 11(1), 139(6), Sch 8, Pt II, para 20, Sch 19, Pt III.)

90 Regulations

(1)   Any power to make regulations conferred by this Act shall be exercisable by statutory instrument.

(2)   A statutory instrument containing regulations under this Act shall be subject to annulment in pursuance of a resolution of either House of Parliament.

91 Directions

Directions given under any provision of this Act may make different provision for different circumstances and may be varied or revoked by subsequent directions thereunder.

92 Consequential amendments, repeals and saving and transitional provisions

(1)   The enactments specified in Schedule 3 to this Act shall be amended in accordance with the provisions of that Schedule.

(2)   The enactments specified in Parts I and II of Schedule 4 to this Act are hereby repealed to the extent specified in the third column of that Schedule and the instrument specified in Part III of that Schedule is hereby revoked to the extent so specified.

(3)   Any provision of this Act relating to anything done or required or authorised to be done under or by reference to that provision or any other provision of this Act shall have effect as if any reference to that provision, or that other provision, as the case may be, included a reference to the corresponding provision of the enactments repealed by this Act.

(4)   Where an offence has been committed under section 129 of the Customs and Excise Act 1952 proceedings may be taken under section 51 of this Act in respect of the continuance of the offence under section 129 after the commencement of this Act in the same manner as if the offence had been committed under section 51 of this Act.

(5)   Where an offence has been committed under section 102 of the Customs and Excise Act 1952 before the commencement of this Act subsection (4) of section 21 of this Act shall apply on a conviction of an offence under that section as it would apply had the earlier offence been committed under section 21.

(6)   . . .

(7) The repeal by this Act of section 243 of the Customs and Excise Act 1952 and section 3(4) of the Finance Act 1960 shall not affect the operation of the saving in relation to spirits distilled before 1st August 1969 contained in paragraph 1 of Schedule 7 to the Finance Act 1969 (which repealed subsection (1)(b) of that section except in relation to spirits distilled before that date).

(8)   Nothing in this section shall be taken as prejudicing the operation of sections 15 to 17 of the Interpretation Act 1978 (which relate to the effect of repeals).

NOTES

Sub-s (6): repealed by the Finance Act 1996, ss 24(d), 205, Sch 41, Pt III.

Sub-s (7): repealed by the Finance Act 1983, ss 9(2), 48(5), Sch 10, Pt I, as from a day to be appointed.

93   Citation and commencement

(1)   This Act may be cited as the Alcoholic Liquor Duties Act 1979 and is included in the Acts which may be cited as the Customs and Excise Acts 1979.

(2)   This Act shall come into operation on 1st April 1979.

SCHEDULES

[SCHEDULE 1
WINE AND MADE-WINE

Section 54

[TABLE OF RATES OF DUTY ON WINE AND MADE-WINE

[PART 1
WINE AND MADE-WINE OF A STRENGTH NOT EXCEEDING 22 PER CENT

Description of wine or made-wine	Rates of duty per hectolitre
	£
Wine or made-wine of a strength not exceeding 4 per cent	54.85
Wine or made-wine of a strength exceeding 4 per cent but not exceeding 5.5 per cent	75.42
Wine or made-wine of a strength exceeding 5.5 per cent but not exceeding 15 per cent and not sparkling	177.99
Sparkling wine or sparkling made-wine of a strength exceeding 5.5 per cent but less than 8.5 per cent	172.33
Sparkling wine or sparkling made-wine of a strength of 8.5 per cent or of a strength exceeding 8.5 per cent but not exceeding 15 per cent	227.99
Wine or made-wine of a strength exceeding 15 per cent but not exceeding 22 per cent	237.31]

NOTES

Substituted by the Finance Act 2007, s 5(1), (4).

PART II
WINE OR MADE-WINE OF A STRENGTH EXCEEDING 22 PER CENT

Description of wine or made-wine	*Rates of duty per litre of alcohol in the wine or made-wine*
Wine or made-wine of a strength exceeding 15 per cent but not exceeding 22 per cent	223.62]

[1. Paragraphs 2 and 3 below apply for the purposes of this Act.

2.—(1) Wine or made-wine which is for the time being in a closed container is sparkling if, due to the presence of carbon dioxide or any other gas, the pressure in the container, measured at a temperature of 20 degrees C, is not less than 3 bars in excess of atmospheric pressure.

(2) Wine or made-wine which is for the time being in a closed container is sparkling regardless of the pressure in the container if the container has a mushroom-shaped stopper (whether solid or hollow) held in place by a tie or fastening.

(3) Wine or made-wine which is not for the time being in a closed container is sparkling if it has characteristics similar to those of wine or made-wine which has been removed from a closed container and which, before removal, fell within sub-paragraph (1) above.

3.—(1) Wine or made-wine shall be regarded as having been rendered sparkling if, as a result of aeration, fermentation or any other process, it either falls within paragraph 2(1) above or takes on such characteristics as are referred to in paragraph 2(3) above.

(2) Wine or made-wine which has not previously been rendered sparkling by virtue of sub-paragraph (1) above shall be regarded as having been rendered sparkling if it is transferred into a closed container which has a mushroom-shaped stopper (whether solid or hollow) held in place by a tie or fastening.

(3) Wine or made-wine which is in a closed container and has not previously been rendered sparkling by virtue of sub-paragraph (1) or (2) above shall be regarded as having been rendered sparkling if the stopper of its container is exchanged for a stopper of a kind mentioned in sub-paragraph (2) above.]]

NOTES

Schedule 1 substituted by the Finance Act 1984, s 1(3), Sch 1.

Table of rates of duty: Pt II substituted by the Finance (No 2) Act 1997, s 9.

Paras 1–3: substituted for original paras 1, 2 by the Finance Act 1993, s 7, in relation to wine and made-wine produced in or imported into the United Kingdom, or removed into the United Kingdom from the Isle of Man, on or after 27 July 1993.

(Sch 2 repealed by the Finance Act 1984, s 128(6), Sch 23, Pt I)

[SCHEDULE 2A
DUTY STAMPS

Section 64A

Retail containers to be stamped

1.—(1) Retail containers of alcoholic liquors to which this Schedule applies shall be stamped—

(a) in such cases and circumstances, and with a duty stamp of such a type, as may be prescribed; but

(b) subject to such exceptions as may be prescribed.

(2) In this Schedule "retail container", in relation to an alcoholic liquor, means a container—

(a)   of a capacity of 35 centilitres or more, and

(b)   in which, or from which, the liquor is intended to be sold by retail.

(3)   This Schedule applies to the following alcoholic liquors—

(a)   spirits [of a strength of 30 per cent or more];

(b)   wine or made-wine of a strength [of 30 per cent or more].

(4)   For the purposes of this Schedule a retail container is "stamped" if—

(a)   it carries a duty stamp of a type mentioned in sub-paragraph (5)(a) below which has been affixed to the container in a way that complies with the requirements of regulations under this Schedule, or

(b)   it carries a label which has been so affixed to the container and the label incorporates a duty stamp of a type mentioned in sub-paragraph (5)(b) below.

(5)   In this Schedule "duty stamp" means any of the following—

(a)   a document (a "type A stamp") issued by or on behalf of the Commissioners which—

(i)   is designed to be affixed to a retail container of alcoholic liquor, and

(ii)   indicates that the appropriate duty, or an amount representing some or all of the appropriate duty, has been (or is to be) paid;

(b)   a part of a label for a retail container of alcoholic liquor (a "type B stamp") which—

(i)   is incorporated in the label under the authority of the Commissioners, and

(ii)   indicates that the appropriate duty, or an amount representing some or all of the appropriate duty, has been (or is to be) paid.

(6)   In sub-paragraph (5) above "the appropriate duty" means the duty chargeable on the quantity and description of alcoholic liquor contained, or to be contained, in the retail container to which the stamp, or the label incorporating the stamp, is, or is to be, affixed.

NOTES

Para 1(3): words inserted in para (a) and words in para (b) substituted by the Duty Stamps (Amendment of paragraph 1(3) of Schedule 2A to the Alcoholic Liquor Duties Act 1979) Order SI 2006/144, art 2.

Power to alter liquors, and capacity of container, to which this Schedule applies

2.—(1)   The Treasury may by order made by statutory instrument amend paragraph (a) of paragraph 1(2) above for the purpose of varying the capacity from time to time specified in that paragraph.

(2)   The Treasury may by order made by statutory instrument amend paragraph 1(3) above for the purpose of causing this Schedule—

(a)   to apply to any description of alcoholic liquor to which it does not apply, or

(b)   to cease to apply to any description of alcoholic liquor to which it does apply.

(3)   A statutory instrument containing an order under this paragraph shall not be made unless a draft of the instrument has been laid before, and approved by a resolution of, the House of Commons.

Acquisition of and payment for duty stamps

3.—(1) The Commissioners may by regulations make provision as to the terms and conditions on which a person may obtain—

(a)   a type A stamp,

(b)   authority to incorporate in a label a type B stamp,

(c)   authority to obtain a label incorporating a type B stamp,

(d)   authority to affix such a label to a retail container of alcoholic liquor.

(2) Regulations under sub-paragraph (1) above may in particular make provision for or in connection with—

(a)   requiring a person in prescribed cases or circumstances to pay, or agree to pay, the prescribed amount to the Commissioners or to a person authorised by the Commissioners for this purpose;

(b)   requiring a person in prescribed cases or circumstances to provide to the Commissioners such security as they may require in respect of payment of the appropriate duty.

(3) An amount prescribed for the purposes of sub-paragraph (2)(a) above must not exceed the aggregate of—

(a)   an amount representing the appropriate duty, and

(b)   in the case of a type A stamp, the cost of issuing the stamp.

(4) Regulations under sub-paragraph (1) above may also in particular make provision for or in connection with requiring or enabling the Commissioners to bear, in prescribed circumstances, in the case of a type B stamp, all or part of so much of the cost of producing the label as is attributable to the incorporation in it of the stamp.

(5) The whole of an amount payable for a duty stamp shall be treated for the purposes of the Customs and Excise Acts 1979 as an amount due by way of excise duty.

(6) In this paragraph "the appropriate duty" means the duty chargeable on the quantity and description of alcoholic liquor contained, or to be contained, in the retail container to which the stamp, or the label incorporating the stamp, is to be affixed.

Regulations

4.—(1) The Commissioners may by regulations make provision as to such matters relating to duty stamps as appear to them to be necessary or expedient.

(2) Regulations under this Schedule may in particular make provision about—

(a)   the times at which a retail container must bear a duty stamp;

(b)   the type of duty stamp (see paragraph 1(5)) with which a retail container is to be stamped in any particular case or circumstances;

(c)   the design and appearance of a duty stamp (including the production of a label incorporating a type B stamp);

(d)   the information that is to appear on a duty stamp;

(e)   the cost of issuing a type A stamp for the purposes of paragraph 3(3)(b) above;

(f)   the procedure for obtaining—

(i)   a type A stamp,

(ii)   authority to incorporate in a label a type B stamp,

(iii) authority to obtain a label incorporating a type B stamp,

(iv) authority to affix such a label to a retail container of alcoholic liquor,

(including provision setting periods of notice);

(g)   where on the container a type A stamp, or a label incorporating a type B stamp, is to be affixed;

(h)   repayment of, or credit for, in prescribed circumstances and subject to such conditions as may be prescribed, all or part of a payment made under or by virtue of this Schedule to the Commissioners or to a person authorised by the Commissioners;

(i)   liability to forfeiture in prescribed circumstances of some or all of a payment made, or security provided, under or by virtue of this Schedule to the Commissioners or to a person authorised by the Commissioners.

(3)   Regulations under this Schedule may also, in particular, make provision for or in connection with preventing a type A stamp, or a label incorporating a type B stamp, from being used by a person other than—

(a)   in the case of a type A stamp, the person to or for whom the stamp was issued or a person authorised by that person to affix the stamp to a retail container of alcoholic liquor,

(b)   in the case of a type B stamp, the person to or for whom authority to obtain the label incorporating the stamp, or to affix that label to a retail container of alcoholic liquor, was given by the Commissioners.

(4)   Regulations under this Schedule may also, in particular, make provision—

(a)   for or in connection with requiring a person who is not established, and does not have any fixed establishment, in the United Kingdom, in prescribed circumstances, to appoint another person (a "duty stamps representative") to act on his behalf in relation to duty stamps, and

(b)   as to the rights, obligations or liabilities of duty stamps representatives.

(5)   The Commissioners may, with a view to the protection of the revenue, make regulations for securing and collecting duty payable in accordance with this Schedule.

(6)   Regulations under this Schedule may make different provision for different cases.

Offences of possession, sale etc of unstamped containers

5.—(1)   Except in such cases as may be prescribed, a person commits an offence if he—

(a)   is in possession of, transports or displays, or

(b)   sells, offers for sale or otherwise deals in,

unstamped retail containers containing alcoholic liquor to which this Schedule applies.

(2)   It is a defence for a person charged with an offence under this paragraph to prove that the retail containers in question were not required to be stamped.

(3)   A person who commits an offence under this paragraph is liable on summary conviction to a fine not exceeding level 5 on the standard scale.

(4)   A retail container in relation to which an offence under this paragraph is committed is liable to forfeiture (together with its contents).

Offence of using premises for sale of liquor in or from unstamped containers

6.—(1)   A manager of premises commits an offence if—

(a)   he suffers the premises to be used for the sale of liquor in an unstamped retail container, or for the sale of liquor that is from an unstamped retail container; and

(b)   the liquor is alcoholic liquor to which this Schedule applies.

(2)   It is a defence for a person charged with an offence under this paragraph to prove that the retail container in question was not required to be stamped.

(3)   A person who commits an offence under this paragraph is liable on summary conviction to a fine not exceeding level 5 on the standard scale.

(4) Where an offence is committed under this paragraph, all unstamped retail containers of alcoholic liquor to which this Schedule applies that are on the premises at the time of the offence are liable to forfeiture (together with their contents).

(5) For the purposes of this Schedule a person is a "manager" of premises if he—

(a)   is entitled to control their use,

(b)   is entrusted with their management, or

(c)   is in charge of them.

Alcohol sales ban following conviction for offence under paragraph 6

7.—(1) A court by or before which a person is convicted of an offence under paragraph 6 above may make an order prohibiting the use of the premises in question for the sale of alcoholic liquors during a period specified in the order.

(2) The period specified in an order under this paragraph shall not exceed six months; and the first day of the period shall be the day specified as such in the order.

(3) If a manager of premises suffers the premises to be used in breach of an order under this paragraph, he commits an offence and is liable on summary conviction to a fine not exceeding level 5 on the standard scale.

Penalty for altering duty stamps

8.—(1) This paragraph applies where a person—

(a)   alters a type A stamp, otherwise than in accordance with regulations under this Schedule, after it has been issued, or

(b)   so alters a type B stamp after the label in which it is incorporated has been produced.

(2) His conduct attracts a penalty under section 9 of the Finance Act 1994 (civil penalties).

(3) The stamp, or the label in which it is incorporated, is liable to forfeiture.

Penalty for affixing wrong, altered or forged stamps, or over-labelling

9.—(1) This paragraph applies where a person affixes to a retail container that is required to be stamped any of the items mentioned in sub-paragraphs (2) to (5) below.

(2) The first is—

(a)   a type A stamp, or

(b)   a label incorporating a type B stamp,

if the stamp is not a correct stamp for that container in accordance with regulations under this Schedule.

(3) The second is—

(a)   a type A stamp that has been altered, otherwise than in accordance with regulations under this Schedule, after it has been issued, or

(b)   a label incorporating a type B stamp if the stamp has been so altered after the label has been produced.

(4) The third is an item that purports to be, but is not,—

(a)   a type A stamp, or

(b)   a label incorporating a type B stamp.

(5) The fourth is any label or other item affixed in such a way as to cover up all or part of—

(a)   a type A stamp affixed to the container, or

(b)   a type B stamp incorporated in a label affixed to the container,

except where the label or other item is so affixed in accordance with regulations under this Schedule.

(6) The person's conduct attracts a penalty under section 9 of the Finance Act 1994 (civil penalties).

(7) The container is liable to forfeiture (together with its contents).

Penalty for failing to comply with regulations

10.—(1) If a person fails to comply with a requirement imposed by or under regulations under this Schedule—

(a) his conduct attracts a penalty under section 9 of the Finance Act 1994 (civil penalties);

(b) any article in respect of which he fails to comply with the requirement is liable to forfeiture (including, in the case of a container, its contents).

(2) Regulations under this Schedule may make provision as to the amount by reference to which the penalty under sub-paragraph (1)(a) above is to be calculated.

Forfeiture of forged, altered or stolen duty stamps

11.—(1) The following items are liable to forfeiture.

(2) The first is an item that purports to be, but is not,—

(a) a type A stamp, or

(b) a label incorporating a type B stamp.

(3) The second is—

(a) a type A stamp that has been altered, otherwise than in accordance with regulations under this Schedule, after it has been issued, or

(b) a label incorporating a type B stamp if the stamp has been so altered after the label has been produced.

(4) The third is—

(a) a type A stamp, or

(b) a label incorporating a type B stamp,

that is in a person's possession unlawfully.

Interpretation

12. In this Schedule—

"duty stamp" has the meaning given by paragraph 1(5) above;

"prescribed" means prescribed in regulations made by the Commissioners;

"retail container" has the meaning given by paragraph 1(2) above;

"stamped" and "unstamped" are to be read in accordance with paragraph 1(4) above;

"type A stamp" has the meaning given by paragraph 1(5)(a) above;

"type B stamp" has the meaning given by paragraph 1(5)(b) above.]

NOTES

Schedule inserted by the Finance Act 2004, s 4(2) with effect in relation to retail containers containing alcoholic liquor if the excise duty point for the alcoholic liquor falls on or after 22 February 2006. For definition of "excise duty point" see the Finance (No 2) Act 1992, s 1.

(Sch 3, in so far as unrepealed, contains consequential amendments; Sch 4 contains repeals.)

HYDROCARBON OIL DUTIES ACT 1979

(1979 c 5)

ARRANGEMENT OF SECTIONS

An Act to consolidate the enactments relating to the excise duties on hydrocarbon oil, petrol substitutes, power methylated spirits and road fuel gas

[22 February 1979]

The dutiable commodities

1 Hydrocarbon oil

(1)   Subsections [(2) to (7)] below define the various descriptions of oil referred to in this Act.

(2)   "Hydrocarbon oil" means petroleum oil, coal tar and oil produced from coal, shale, peat or any other bituminous substance, and all liquid hydrocarbons, but does not include such hydrocarbons or bituminous or asphaltic substances as are—

(a)   solid or semi-solid at a temperature of 1°C, or

(b)   gaseous at a temperature of 15°C and under a pressure of 1013.25 millibars.

(3)   "Light oil" means hydrocarbon oil—

(a)   of which not less than 90° by volume distils at a temperature not exceeding 21°C, or

(b)   which gives off an inflammable vapour at a temperature of less than 2°C when tested in the manner prescribed by the Acts relating to petroleum.

[(3A) "Ultra low sulphur petrol" means unleaded petrol—

(a)   the sulphur content of which does not exceed 0.005 per cent by weight,

(b)   the aromatics content of which does not exceed 35 per cent by volume, and

(c)   which is not sulphur-free petrol.]

[(3B) "Sulphur-free petrol" means unleaded petrol the sulphur content of which does not exceed 0.001 per cent by weight (or is nil).]

[(3C) "Unleaded petrol" means petrol that contains not more than 0.013 grams of lead per litre of petrol; and petrol is "leaded petrol" if it is not unleaded petrol.]

(4) "Heavy oil" means hydrocarbon oil other than light oil.

[(5) "Gas oil" means heavy oil of which not more than 50 per cent by volume distils at a temperature not exceeding 240°C and of which more than 50 per cent by volume distils at a temperature not exceeding 340°C.]

[(6) "Ultra low sulphur diesel" means gas oil—

(a)   the sulphur content of which does not exceed 0.005 per cent by weight,

(b)   the density of which does not exceed 835 kilograms per cubic metre at a temperature of 15°C,

(c)   of which not less than 95 per cent by volume distils at a temperature not exceeding 345°C, and

(d)   which is not sulphur-free diesel.]

[(7) "Sulphur-free diesel" means gas oil the sulphur content of which does not exceed 0.001 per cent by weight (or is nil).]

NOTES

Sub-s (1): words in square brackets substituted by the Finance Act 2004, s 7(3).

Sub-ss (3A)–(3C): substituted for sub-ss (3A), (3B) by the Finance Act 2004, s 7(1).

Sub-s (5): added by the Finance Act 1997, s 7(1)(b), (10).

Sub-s (6): substituted for sub-ss (6), (7) by the Finance Act 2004, s 7(2).

2 Provisions supplementing s 1

(1) The method of testing oil for the purpose of ascertaining its classification in accordance with section 1 above shall, subject to subsection (3)(b) of that section, be such as the Commissioners may direct.

(1A) . . .

(2) Subject to subsection (3) below, the Treasury may from time to time direct that, for the purposes of any duty of excise for the time being chargeable on hydrocarbon oil, any specified description of light oil shall be treated as being heavy oil.

(3) The Treasury shall not give a direction under subsection (2) above in relation to any description of oil unless they are satisfied that the description is one which should, according to its use, be classed with heavy oil.

(4) For the purposes of the Customs and Excise Acts 1979, the production of hydrocarbon oil includes—

(a)   the obtaining of one description of hydrocarbon oil from another description of hydrocarbon oil; and

(b)   the subjecting of hydrocarbon oil to any process of purification or blending,

as well as the obtaining of hydrocarbon oil from other substances or from any natural source.

(5) . . .

NOTES

Sub-s (1A): repealed by the Finance Act 2001, s 110, Sch 33 Pt 1(1).

Sub-s (5): repealed by the Finance Act 1993, ss 12(7)(a), 213, Sch 23, Pt I(5).

[2AA Biodiesel

(1) In this Act "biodiesel" means diesel quality liquid fuel that—

    (a)   is produced from biomass or waste cooking oil,

    (b)   the ester content of which is not less than 96.5% by weight, and

    (c)   the sulphur content of which does not exceed 0.005% by weight or is nil.

(2) In subsection (1)—

    (a)   "diesel quality" means capable of being used for the same purposes as heavy oil;

    (b)   "liquid" does not include any substance that is gaseous at a temperature of 15°C and under a pressure of 1013.25 millibars;

    (c)   "biomass" means vegetable and animal substances constituting the biodegradable fraction of—

         (i)   products, wastes and residues from agriculture, forestry and related activities, or

         (ii)   industrial and municipal waste.]

NOTES

Inserted by the Finance Act 2002, s 5(1), (2).

[2AB Bioethanol

(1) In this Act "bioethanol" means a liquid fuel—

    (a)   consisting of ethanol produced from biomass, and

    (b)   capable of being used for the same purposes as light oil.

(2) In subsection (1)—

    (a)   "liquid" does not include any substance that is gaseous at a temperature of 15°C and under a pressure of 1013.25 millibars, and

    (b)   "biomass" means vegetable and animal substances constituting the biodegradable fraction of—

         (i)   products, wastes and residues from agriculture, forestry and related activities, or

         (ii)   industrial and municipal waste.

(3) A substance shall be treated as falling within subsection (1)(a) if it—

    (a)   is denatured alcohol for the purposes of section 5 of the Finance Act 1995 (c 4), and

    (b)   would fall within subsection (1)(a) above (without reliance on this subsection) but for the presence of a component introduced—

         (i)   for the purpose of rendering the substance denatured alcohol, and

         (ii)   in the minimum proportion necessary for that purpose.]

NOTES

Inserted by the Finance Act 2004, s 10(1) with effect from 1 January 2005: see the Finance Act 2004, s 10(10).

[2A Power to amend definitions

[(1) The Treasury may by order made by statutory instrument amend the definition for the purposes of this Act of—

    (a)   sulphur-free diesel;

    (b)   sulphur-free petrol;

    (c)   ultra low sulphur diesel;

(d)   ultra low sulphur petrol;

(e)   unleaded petrol and leaded petrol.]

[(1A)   The Treasury may by order made by statutory instrument amend the definition for the purposes of this Act of "biodiesel".]

[(1B)   The Treasury may by order made by statutory instrument amend the definition for the purposes of this Act of "bioethanol".]

[(1C)   The Treasury may by order made by statutory instrument amend the definition for the purposes of section 11 of "fuel oil".]

(2)   An order under this section may contain such incidental, supplementary and transitional provision as appears to the Treasury to be appropriate.

(3)   No order shall be made under this section unless a draft of it has been laid before and approved by a resolution of the House of Commons.]

NOTES

Inserted by the Finance Act 2000, s 7.

Sub-s (1): substituted by the Finance Act 2004, s 7(4).

Sub-s (1A): inserted by the Finance Act 2002, s 5(1), (3).

Sub-s (1B): inserted by the Finance Act 2004, s 10(2) with effect from 1 January 2005: see the Finance Act 2004, s 10(10).

Sub-s (1C): inserted by the Finance Act 2004, s 8.

3 Hydrocarbon oil as ingredient of imported goods

Where imported goods contain hydrocarbon oil as a part or ingredient thereof, the oil shall be disregarded in the application to the goods of section 126 of the Management Act (charge of duty on manufactured or composite imported articles) unless in the opinion of the Commissioners the goods should, according to their use, be classed with hydrocarbon oil.

NOTES

Cross reference: see the Biofuels and Other Fuel Substitutes (Payment of Excise Duties etc) Regulations 2004, SI 2004/2065 reg 3(2) (the references to hydrocarbon oil above are to be construed as including references to bioblend and bioethanol blend).

4

(Repealed by the Finance Act 1993, ss 11(2), (5) 213, Sch 23, Pt I(4).)

5 Road fuel gas

[(1)]   In this Act "road fuel gas" means any substance which is gaseous at a temperature of 15°C and under a pressure of 1013.25 millibars, and which is for use as fuel in road vehicles.

[(2)   In this Act "natural road fuel gas" is road fuel gas with a methane content of not less than 80%.]

NOTES

Sub-s (1): numbered as such by the Finance Act 2004, s 6(1) with effect from 1 September 2004.

Sub-s (2): inserted by the Finance Act 2004, s 6(1) with effect from 1 September 2004.

Charging provisions

6 Excise duty on hydrocarbon oil

(1) Subject to [*subsections (2) [. . .] and (3)*] below, there shall be charged on hydrocarbon oil—

    (a)   imported into the United Kingdom; or

    (b)   produced in the United Kingdom *and delivered for home use from a refinery or from other premises used for the production of hydrocarbon oil or from any bonded storage for hydrocarbon oil, not being hydrocarbon oil chargeable with duty under paragraph (a) above,*

[a duty of excise at [the rates specified in subsection (1A) below.]]

    [(1A)   The rates at which the duty shall be charged are—

    (a)   [£0.5035] a litre in the case of ultra low sulphur petrol;

    [(aa)   [£0.5035] a litre in the case of sulphur-free petrol;]

    (b)   [£0.6007] a litre in the case of light oil other than ultra low sulphur petrol [and sulphur-free petrol];

    (c)   [£0.5035] a litre in the case of ultra low sulphur diesel; and

    [(ca)   [£0.5035] a litre in the case of sulphur-free diesel;]

    (d)   [£0.5694] a litre in the case of heavy oil other than ultra low sulphur diesel [and sulphur-free diesel].]

(2) *Where imported hydrocarbon oil is removed to a refinery, the duty chargeable under subsection (1) above shall, instead of being charged at the time of the importation of that oil, be charged on the delivery of any goods from the refinery for home use and shall be the same as that which would be payable on the importation of like goods.*

[(2A) . . .]

[(3) In the case of aviation gasoline, the duty of excise charged under subsection (1) above shall be at one half of the rate specified in [subsection [(1A)(b) above]] in relation to light oil.

(4) In this Act "aviation gasoline" means light oil which—

    (a)   is specially produced as fuel for aircraft; and

    (b)   is not normally used in road vehicles; and

    (c)   is delivered for use solely as fuel for aircraft.]

NOTES

Sub-s (1): words in first pair of square brackets substituted by the Finance Act 1982, s 4(1), (2), (7); for the words "subsections (2) and" in italics there is substituted the word "subsection", and words in italics in para (b) repealed by the Finance Act 1998, s 6(1), (3), 165, Sch 27, Pt I(2) as from a day to be appointed; words omitted (inserted by the Finance Act 1989, s 1) repealed by the Finance Act 1990, s 132, Sch 19, Pt I; words in second (outer) pair of square brackets substituted by the Finance Act 1981, s 4(1); words in third (inner) pair of square brackets substituted by the Finance Act 1997, s 7(2). Paras (aa), (ca) inserted, words "and sulphur-free petrol" in para (b) and "and sulphur-free diesel" in para (d) inserted by the Finance Act 2004 s 7(5).

Sub-s (1A): substituted by the Finance Act 2000, s 5(3). Figures in square brackets substituted by the Finance Act 2007, s 10(1), (2), with effect from 1 October 2007.

Sub-s (2): substituted by new sub-ss (2), (2A), (2B) by the Finance Act 1998, s 6(2), (3) as from a day to be appointed as follows—

    (2)   Where—

        (a)   imported hydrocarbon oil is removed to relevant premises,

        (b)   the oil undergoes a production process at those premises or any other relevant premises, and

(c)   any duty charged on the importation of the oil has not become payable at any time before the production time,

the duty charged on importation shall not become payable at any time after the production time.

(2AA)In subsection (2) above—

"the production time" means the time at which the oil undergoes the production process; and

"relevant premises" means—

(a)   a refinery;

(b)   other premises used for the production of hydrocarbon oil; or

(c)   premises of such other description as may be specified in regulations made by the Commissioners.

(2AB)For the purposes of subsection (2) above, oil undergoes a production process if—

(a)   hydrocarbon oil of another description is obtained from it, or

(b)   it is subjected to any process of purification or blending.

Sub-s (2A): inserted by the Finance Act 1989, s 1, and repealed by the Finance Act 1990, ss 3(1)(b), (6), 132, Sch 19, Pt I, with effect from 20 March 1990.

Sub-s (3): added by the Finance Act 1982, s 4(1), (2), (7); word "subsection" in first (outer) square brackets substituted by the Finance Act 1997, s 7(4), (10); words in second (inner) square brackets substituted by the Finance Act 2005 s 4(3).

Sub-s (4): added by the Finance Act 1982, s 4(1), (2), (7).

[6AA Excise duty on biodiesel

(1)   A duty of excise shall be charged on the setting aside for a chargeable use by any person, or (where it has not already been charged under this section) on the chargeable use by any person, of biodiesel.

(2) In subsection (1) "chargeable use" means use—

(a)   as fuel for any engine, motor or other machinery, . . .

(b)   as an additive or extender in any substance so used

[(c)   for the production of bioblend.]

(3)   The rate of duty under this section shall be [£0.3035 a litre.]

NOTES

Inserted by the Finance Act 2002, s 5(1), (4).

Sub-s (2): sub-para (c) inserted by the Finance Act 2004, s 11 with effect from 1 January 2005. Word repealed by the Finance Act 2004, s 326, Sch 42 Pt 1(1).

Sub-s (3): figure substituted by the Finance Act 2007, s 10(1), (3) with effect from 1 October 2007.

[6AB Excise duty on blends of biodiesel and heavy oils

(1)   A duty of excise shall be charged on bioblend—

(a)   imported into the United Kingdom, or

(b)   produced in the United Kingdom and delivered for home use from a refinery or from other premises used for the production of hydrocarbon oil or from any bonded storage for hydrocarbon oil, not being bioblend chargeable with duty under paragraph (a) above.

This is subject to subsection (6) below.

(2) In this Act "bioblend" means any mixture that is produced by mixing—

(a)   biodiesel, and

(b)   heavy oil not charged with the excise duty on hydrocarbon oil.

(3)   The rate at which the duty shall be charged on any bioblend shall be a composite rate representing—

    (a)   in respect of the proportion of the bioblend that is hydrocarbon oil, the rate that would be applicable to the bioblend if it consisted entirely of heavy oil of the description that went into producing the bioblend, and

    (b)   in respect of the proportion of the bioblend that is biodiesel, the rate that would be applicable to the bioblend if it consisted entirely of biodiesel.

  (4) The references in subsection (3) above to the proportions of—

    (a)   hydrocarbon oil, and

    (b)   biodiesel,

are to the proportions by volume to the nearest 0.001%.

  (5) If the Commissioners are not satisfied as to the proportion of biodiesel in any bioblend, the rate of duty chargeable shall be the rate that would be applicable to the bioblend if it consisted entirely of heavy oil of the description that went into producing the bioblend.

  (6) Where imported bioblend is removed to a refinery, the duty chargeable under subsection (1) above shall, instead of being charged at the time of the importation of the bioblend, be charged on the delivery of any goods from the refinery for home use and shall be the same as that which would be payable on the importation of like goods.]

NOTES

Inserted by the Finance Act 2002, s 5(1), (4).

Sub-s (1): words "and delivered" to the end to be repealed by the Finance Act 2002, s 5, Sch 2, para 7(1), Sch 39 Pt 1(2). See the Finance Act 2002, s 5(8)(c) for provisions as to the commencement of this amendment.

Sub- (6): Sub-ss (6)–(8) to be substituted for sub-s (6) by the Finance Act 2002, s 5, Sch 2, para 7(2). See Finance Act 2002, s 5(8)(c) for provisions as to the commencement of this amendment. Sub-ss (6)–(8) as substituted to read as follows—

  (6) Where—

    (a)   imported bioblend is removed to relevant premises,

    (b)   the bioblend undergoes a production process at those premises or any other relevant premises, and

    (c)   any duty charged on the importation of the bioblend has not become payable at any time before the production time,

the duty charged on importation shall not become payable at any time after the production time.

  (7) In subsection (6) above—

      "the production time" means the time at which the bioblend undergoes the production process; and

      "relevant premises" means—

        (a)   a refinery,

        (b)   other premises used for the production of hydrocarbon oil, or

        (c)   premises of such description as may be specified in regulations made by the Commissioners.

  (8) For the purposes of subsection (6) above, bioblend undergoes a production process if—

    (a)   hydrocarbon oil, or bioblend, of any description, or biodiesel, is obtained from it, or

    (b)   it is subjected to any process of purification or blending.

[6AC Application to biodiesel and bioblend of provisions relating to hydrocarbon oil

  (1) The Commissioners may by regulations provide for—

(a) references in this Act, or specified references in this Act, to hydrocarbon oil to be construed as including references to—

(i) biodiesel;

(ii) bioblend;

(b) references in this Act, or specified references in this Act, to duty on hydrocarbon oil to be construed as including references to duty under—

(i) section 6AA above;

(ii) section 6AB above;

(c) biodiesel, or bioblend, to be treated for the purposes of such of the following provisions of this Act as may be specified as if it fell within a specified description of hydrocarbon oil.

(2) Where the effect of provision made under subsection (1) above is to extend any power to make regulations, provision made in exercise of the power as extended may be contained in the same statutory instrument as the provision extending the power.

(3) In this section "specified" means specified by regulations under this section.

(4) Regulations under this section may make different provision for different cases.

(5) Paragraph (b) of subsection (1) above shall not be taken as prejudicing the generality of paragraph (a) of that subsection.]

NOTES

Inserted by the Finance Act 2002, s 5(1), (4).

[6AD Excise duty on bioethanol

(1) A duty of excise shall be charged on the setting aside for a chargeable use by any person, or (where it has not already been charged under this section) on the chargeable use by any person, of bioethanol.

(2) In subsection (1) "chargeable use" means use—

(a) as fuel for any engine, motor or other machinery,

(b) as an additive or extender in any substance so used, or

(c) for the production of bioethanol blend.

(3) The rate of duty under this section shall be [£0.3035] a litre.]

NOTES

Inserted by the Finance Act 2004, s 10(3) with effect from 1 January 2005: see the Finance Act 2004, s 10(10). For transitional provisions see the Finance Act 2004, s 10(11).

Sub-s (3): figure substituted by the Finance Act 2007, s 10(1), (4) with effect from 1 October 2007.

[6AE Excise duty on blends of bioethanol and hydrocarbon oil

(1) A duty of excise shall be charged on bioethanol blend—

(a) imported into the United Kingdom, or

(b) produced in the United Kingdom and delivered for home use from a refinery or other premises used for the production of hydrocarbon oil or from any bonded storage for hydrocarbon oil, not being bioethanol blend chargeable with duty under paragraph (a) above.

(2) In this Act "bioethanol blend" means any mixture that is produced by mixing—

(a) bioethanol, and

(b) hydrocarbon oil not charged with excise duty.

(3)   The rate at which the duty shall be charged on any bioethanol blend shall be a composite rate representing—

(a)   in respect of the proportion of the blend that is hydrocarbon oil, the rate that would be applicable to the blend if it consisted entirely of hydrocarbon oil of the description that went into producing the blend, and

(b)   in respect of the proportion of the blend that is bioethanol, the rate that would be applicable to the blend if it consisted entirely of bioethanol.

(4)   A reference in subsection (3) to a proportion is to a proportion by volume to the nearest 0.001%.

(5)   If the Commissioners are not satisfied as to the proportion of bioethanol in any bioethanol blend, the rate of duty chargeable shall be the rate that would be applicable to the blend if it consisted entirely of hydrocarbon oil of the description that went into producing the blend.

(6)   Where imported bioethanol blend is removed to a refinery, the duty chargeable under subsection (1) above shall, instead of being charged at the time of the importation of the blend, be charged on the delivery of any goods from the refinery for home use and shall be the same as that which would be payable on the importation of like goods.]

NOTES

Inserted by the Finance Act 2004, s 10(3) with effect from 1 January 2005: see the Finance Act 2004, s 10(10). For transitional provisions see the Finance Act 2004, s 10(11).

[6AF Application to bioethanol and bioethanol blend of provisions relating to hydrocarbon oil

(1)   The Commissioners may by regulations provide for—

(a)   references in this Act, or specified references in this Act, to hydrocarbon oil to be construed as including references to—

(i)   bioethanol;

(ii)   bioethanol blend;

(b)   references in this Act, or specified references in this Act, to duty on hydrocarbon oil to be construed as including references to duty under—

(i)   section 6AD above;

(ii)   section 6AE above;

(c)   bioethanol, or bioethanol blend, to be treated for the purposes of such of the following provisions of this Act as may be specified as if it fell within a specified description of hydrocarbon oil.

(2)   Where the effect of provision made under subsection (1) above is to extend any power to make regulations, provision made in exercise of the power as extended may be contained in the same statutory instrument as the provision extending the power.

(3)   In this section "specified" means specified by regulations under this section.

(4)   Regulations under this section may make different provision for different cases.

(5)   Paragraph (b) of subsection (1) above shall not be taken as prejudicing the generality of paragraph (a) of that subsection.]

NOTES

Inserted by the Finance Act 2004, s 10(3) with effect from 1 January 2005: see the Finance Act 2004, s 10(10).

[6A Fuel substitutes

(1) A duty of excise shall be charged on the setting aside for a chargeable use by any person, or (where it has not already been charged under this section) on the chargeable use by any person, of any liquid [which is not—

(a)   hydrocarbon oil,

(b)   biodiesel,

(c)   bioblend,

(d)   bioethanol, or

(e)   bioethanol blend.]

(2)   In this section "chargeable use" in relation to any substance means the use of that substance—

(a)   as fuel for any engine, motor or other machinery; or

[(b)   as an additive or extender in any substance so used.]

[(2A)   But the use of water is not a chargeable use if—

(a)   the water is comprised in an emulsion of water in gas oil, and

(b)   the emulsion is stabilised by additives.]

(3)   The rate of the duty under this section shall be prescribed by order made by the Treasury.

(4)   In the following provisions of this Act references to hydrocarbon oil shall be construed as including references to any substance on which duty is charged under this section; and, accordingly, references to duty on hydrocarbon oil shall be construed, where a substance is to be treated as such oil, as including references to duty under this section.

(5)   The Treasury may by order provide for any substance on which duty is charged under this section to be treated for the purposes of such of the following provisions of this Act as may be specified in the order as if it fell within [such description of hydrocarbon oil as may be so specified.]

(6)   In exercising their powers under this section, the Treasury shall so far as practicable secure—

(a)   that a substance set aside for use or used as mentioned in subsection (2)(a) above is—

(i)   charged with duty at the same rate as, and

(ii)   otherwise treated for the purposes of the following provisions of this Act as if it were,

[hydrocarbon oil of the description] to which, when put to that use, it is most closely equivalent; and

(b)   that a substance set aside for use or used as an additive or extender in any substance is—

(i)   charged with duty at the same rate as, and

(ii)   otherwise treated for the purposes of the following provisions of this Act as if it were,

the substance in which it is an additive or extender.

(7)   For the purposes of this section "liquid" does not include any substance which is gaseous at a temperature of 15°C and under a pressure of 1013.25 millibars.

(8)   The power of the Treasury to make an order under this section shall be exercisable by statutory instrument subject to annulment in pursuance of a resolution of the House of Commons.

(9)   An order under this section—

(a)   may make different provision for different cases and for different substances;

(b)   may prescribe the rate of duty under this section in respect of any substance by reference to the rate of duty under this Act in respect of any other substance; and

(c)   in making different provision for different substances, may define a substance by reference to the use for which it is set aside or the use to which it is put.]

NOTES

Commencement: 1 December 1995.

Inserted by the Finance Act 1993, s 11(1), (5).

Sub-s (1): words substituted by the Finance Act 2004, s 10(4) with effect from 1 January 2005: see the Finance Act 2004, s 10(10).

Sub-s (2): para (b) substituted by the Finance Act 2004, s 12.

Sub-s (2A): inserted by the Finance Act 2000, s 11 in relation to duty charged after 27 July 2000.

Sub-s (5): words in square brackets substituted by the Finance Act 2002, s 7(1)(a).

Sub-s (6): words in para (a) substituted by the Finance Act 2002, s 7(1)(b).

Orders: the Other Fuel Substitutes (Rates of Excise Duty etc) Order 1995, SI 1995/2716.

7

(Repealed by the Finance Act 1993, ss 11(2), (5) 213, Sch 23, Pt I(4).)

8 Excise duty on road fuel gas

(1) A duty of excise shall be charged on road fuel gas which is sent out from the premises of a person producing or dealing in road fuel gas and on which the duty charged by this section has not been paid.

(2) The like duty of excise shall be charged on the setting aside for use, or on the use, by any person, as fuel in a road vehicle, of road fuel gas on which the duty charged by this section has not been paid.

[(3) The rate of the duty under this section shall be—

(a)   in the case of natural road fuel gas, [£0.1370] a kilogram, and

(b)   in any other case, [£0.1649] a kilogram.]

(6) For the purposes of this Act, so far as it relates to the excise duty chargeable under this section, road fuel gas shall be deemed to be used as fuel in a road vehicle if, but only if, it is used as fuel for the engine provided for propelling the vehicle, or for an engine which draws its fuel from the same supply as that engine.

(7) . . .

NOTES

Sub-s (3): substituted by the Finance Act 2004, s 6(2); figures in square brackets substituted by the Finance Act 2007, s 10(1), (5) with effect from 1 October 2007.

Sub-s (7): repealed by the Finance Act 1995, ss 9, 162, Sch 29, Pt II.

Delivery of oil without payment of duty

9 Oil delivered for home use for certain industrial purposes

(1) The Commissioners may permit hydrocarbon oil to be delivered for home use to an approved person, without payment of excise duty on the oil, where—

(a)   it is to be put by him to a use qualifying for relief under this section; or

(b)   it is to be supplied by him in the course of a trade of supplying oil for any such use.

[(2)   The uses of hydrocarbon oil qualifying for relief under this section are all uses which do not consist in either—

    (a)   the use of the oil as fuel for any engine, motor or other machinery; or

    (b)   the use of the oil as heating fuel.]

(4)   Where the Commissioners are authorised to give permission under subsection (1) above in the case of any oil, but the permission is for any reason not given, they shall, if satisfied that the oil has been put by an approved person to a use qualifying for relief under this section, repay to him the amount of the excise duty paid on the oil, less any rebate allowed in respect of the duty.

(5)   In this section—

    (a)   "an approved person" means a person for the time being approved in accordance with regulations made for any of the purposes of subsection (1) or (4) above under section 24(1) below; . . .

    (b)   . . .

NOTES

Sub-s (2): substituted for original sub-ss (2), (3), by the Excise Duty (Amendment of the Alcoholic Liquor Duties Act 1979 and the Hydrocarbon Oil Duties Act 1979) Regulations 1992, SI 1992/3158, reg 3(1).

Sub-s (5): para (b) and word immediately preceding it repealed by SI 1992/3158, reg 3(2).

---

10 Restrictions on the use of duty-free oil

(1)   Except with the consent of the Commissioners, no oil in whose case delivery without payment of duty has been permitted under section 9 above shall—

    (a)   be put to a use not qualifying for relief under that section; or

    (b)   be acquired or taken into any vehicle, appliance or storage tank in order to be put to such a use.

(2)   In giving their consent for the purposes of subsection (1) above, the Commissioners may impose such conditions as they think fit.

(3)   [Where any person]—

    (a)   uses or acquires oil in contravention of subsection (1) above; or

    (b)   is liable for oil being taken into a vehicle, appliance or storage tank in contravention of that subsection,

[his use or acquisition of the oil or, as the case may be, his becoming so liable shall attract a penalty under section 9 of the Finance Act 1994 (civil penalties)]; and the Commissioners may [assess an amount equal to the excise duty on like oil at the rate in force at the time of the contravention as being excise duty due from him, and notify him or his representative accordingly.]

(4)   [Where any person] supplies oil having reason to believe that it will be put to a use not qualifying for relief under section 9 above [and] that use without the consent of the Commissioners would contravene subsection (1) above [his supplying the oil shall attract a penalty under section 9 of the Finance Act 1994 (civil penalties)].

(5)   A person who, with the intent that the restrictions imposed by subsection (1) above should be contravened—

    (a)   uses or acquires oil in contravention of that subsection; or

    (b)   supplies oil having reason to believe that it will be put to a use not qualifying for relief under section 9 above, being a use which, without the consent of the Commissioners, would contravene that subsection,

shall be guilty of an offence under this subsection.

(6)   A person who is liable for oil being taken into a vehicle, appliance or storage tank in contravention of subsection (1) above shall be guilty of an offence under this

subsection where the oil was taken in with the intent by him that the restrictions imposed by that subsection should be contravened.

(7) A person guilty of an offence under subsection (5) or (6) above shall be liable—

    (a)   on summary conviction, to a penalty of the prescribed sum or of three times the value of the oil in question, whichever is the greater, or to imprisonment for a term not exceeding 6 months, or to both;

    (b)   on conviction on indictment, to a penalty of any amount or to imprisonment for a term not exceeding [7 years], or to both.

(8) For the purposes of this section, a person is liable for oil being taken into a vehicle, appliance or storage tank in contravention of subsection (1) above if he is at the time the person having the charge of the vehicle, appliance or tank, or is its owner, except that if a person other than the owner is, or is for the time being, entitled to possession of it, that person and not the owner is liable.

(9) Any oil acquired, or taken into a vehicle, appliance or storage tank as mentioned in subsection (1) above, or supplied as mentioned in subsection (4) or (5) above, shall be liable to forfeiture.

NOTES

Sub-s (3): words in first and second pairs of square brackets substituted by the Finance Act 1994, s 9, Sch 4, Pt III, paras 49, 50(1); words in third pair of square brackets substituted by the Finance Act 1997, s 50(2), Sch 6, paras 6(1), 7.

Sub-s (4): words in first and second pairs of square brackets substituted and words in final pair of square brackets added by the Finance Act 1994, s 9, Sch 4, Pt III, paras 49, 50(2).

Sub-s (7): words in square brackets in para (b) substituted by the Finance Act 1988, s 12(1)(b), (6), in relation to offences committed after 29 July 1988.

Rebate of duty

11 Rebate on heavy oil

(1) Subject to sections 12 [13, 13AA and 13AB] below, where heavy oil charged with the excise duty on hydrocarbon oil is delivered for home use, there shall be allowed on the oil at the time of delivery a rebate of duty at a rate—

    [(a)   in the case of fuel oil, of [£0.0929] a litre less than the rate at which the duty is for the time being chargeable;

    (b)   in the case of gas oil [which is not ultra low sulphur diesel], of [£0.0969] a litre less than the rate at which the duty is for the time being chargeable; . . .

    [(ba)   in the case of ultra low sulphur diesel oil, of [£0.0969] a litre less than the rate at which the duty is for the time being chargeable; and]

    (c)   in the case of heavy oil [which is neither fuel oil nor] gas oil, equal to the rate at which the duty is for the time being chargeable.]

[(2) In this section—

"fuel oil" means heavy oil which contains in solution an amount of asphaltenes of not less than 0.5 per cent or which contains less than 0.5 per cent but not less than 0.1 per cent of asphaltenes and has a closed flash point not exceeding 150°C;

. . .

. . .]

[(3) This subsection applies in any case where—

    (a)   oil is delivered for home use,

(b)   regulations under section 24 below require, as a condition of allowing a rebate on the oil under subsection (1) above, that a marker prescribed by regulations under that section shall have been added to the oil, and

(c)   the marker is present at the time of delivery for home use but in such a proportion that its presence falls to be disregarded by virtue of provision made by regulations under that section.

(4)   In any case where subsection (3) above applies, a rebate may be allowed on the oil at the time it is delivered for home use if it appears to the Commissioners to be appropriate to allow it.

(5)   Where a rebate is allowed under subsection (4) above, the rate at which the rebate is allowed—

(a)   shall be such rate as appears to the Commissioners to be appropriate, but

(b)   shall not be less than 95 per cent of, and shall not exceed, the rate of rebate specified in the relevant paragraph of subsection (1) above.]

[(6)   No rebate shall be allowed under this section in respect of bioblend [or bioethanol blend].]

NOTES

Sub-s (1): words in first pair of square brackets substituted by the Finance Act 1996, s 5(1), (2); paras (a)–(c) substituted for original paras (a), (b) by the Finance Act 1986, s 2(2), (4); in para (b) words in first pair of square brackets inserted, and word omitted repealed, para (ba) inserted, and words in square brackets in para (c) substituted, by the Finance Act 1997, s 7(5). Figures in square brackets substituted by the Finance Act 2007, s 10(1), (6) with effect from 1 October 2007.

Sub-s (2): substituted by the Finance Act 1986, s 2(3), (4); definition and word "and" preceding it repealed by the Finance Act 1997, ss 7(10), 113(1), Sch 18, Pt I.

Sub-s (3)–(5): added by the Finance Act 2000, s 10(1), (2).

Sub-s (6): added by the Finance Act 2002, s 5, Sch 2, paras 1, 3. Words inserted by the Finance Act 2004, s 10(5) with effect from 1 January 2005: see the Finance Act 2004, s 10(10).

12 Rebate not allowed on fuel for road vehicles

(1)   If, on the delivery of heavy oil for home use, it is intended to use the oil as fuel for a road vehicle, a declaration shall be made to that effect in the entry for home use and thereupon no rebate [under section 11 above] shall be allowed in respect of that oil.

(2)   No heavy oil on whose delivery for home use rebate has been allowed [(whether under [section 11] above or 13AA(1) below)] shall—

(a)   be used as fuel for a road vehicle; or

(b)   be taken into a road vehicle as fuel,

unless an amount equal to the amount for the time being allowable in respect of rebate on like oil has been paid to the Commissioners in accordance with regulations made under section 24(1) below for the purposes of this section.

(3)   For the purposes of this section and section 13 below—

(a)   heavy oil shall be deemed to be used as fuel for a road vehicle if, but only if, it is used as fuel for the engine provided for propelling the vehicle or for an engine which draws its fuel from the same supply as that engine; and

(b)   heavy oil shall be deemed to be taken into a road vehicle as fuel if, but only if, it is taken into it as part of that supply.

NOTES

Sub-s (1): words in square brackets inserted by the Finance Act 2002, s 6(1), Sch 3, paras 5, 6.

Sub-s (2): words in square brackets inserted by the Finance Act 1996, s 5(1), (3), in relation to cases where kerosene is used as a fuel or taken into a fuel supply; reference in square brackets within square brackets substituted by the Finance Act 2002, s 6(1), Sch 3, paras 5, 7.

13 Penalties for misuse of rebated heavy oil

(1) [Where any person]—

    (a)   uses heavy oil in contravention of section 12(2) above; or

    (b)   is liable for heavy oil being taken into a road vehicle in contravention of that subsection,

[his use of the oil [or his becoming so liable (or, where his conduct includes both, each of them)] shall attract a penalty under section 9 of the Finance Act 1994 (civil penalties)]; . . .

[(1A) Where oil is used, or is taken into a road vehicle, in contravention of section 12(2) above, the Commissioners may—

    (a)   assess an amount equal to the rebate on like oil at the rate in force at the time of the contravention as being excise duty due from any person who used the oil or was liable for the oil being taken into the road vehicle, and

    (b)   notify him or his representative accordingly.]

(2) [Where any person] supplies heavy oil having reason to believe that it will be put to a particular use [and] that use would, if a payment under subsection (2) of section 12 above were not made in respect of the oil, contravene that subsection [his supplying the oil shall attract a penalty under section 9 of the Finance Act 1994 (civil penalties).]

(3) A person who, with the intent that the restrictions imposed by section 12 above should be contravened—

    (a)   uses heavy oil in contravention of subsection (2) of that section; or

    (b)   supplies heavy oil having reason to believe that it will be put to a particular use, being a use which would, if a payment under that subsection were not made in respect of the oil, contravene that subsection,

shall be guilty of an offence under this subsection.

(4) A person who is liable for heavy oil being taken into a road vehicle in contravention of subsection (2) of section 12 above shall be guilty of an offence under this subsection where the oil was taken in with the intent by him that the restrictions imposed by that section should be contravened.

(5) A person guilty of an offence under subsection (3) or (4) above shall be liable—

    (a)   on summary conviction, to a penalty of the prescribed sum or of three times the value of the oil in question, whichever is the greater, or to imprisonment for a term not exceeding 6 months, or to both, or

    (b)   on conviction on indictment, to a penalty of any amount, or to imprisonment for a term not exceeding [7 years], or to both.

(6) Any heavy oil—

    (a)   taken into a road vehicle as mentioned in section 12(2) above or supplied as mentioned in subsection (2) or (3) above; or

(b)   taken as fuel into a vehicle at a time when it is not a road vehicle and remaining in the vehicle as part of its fuel supply at a later time when it becomes a road vehicle,

shall be liable to forfeiture.

(7) For the purposes of this section, a person is liable for heavy oil being taken into a road vehicle in contravention of section 12(2) above if he is at the time the person having the charge of the vehicle or is its owner, except that if a person other than the owner is, or is for the time being, entitled to possession of it, that person and not the owner is liable.

NOTES

Sub-s (1): words in first and second (outer) pairs of square brackets substituted by the Finance Act 1994, s 9, Sch 4, Pt III, paras 49, 51(1); words in third (inner) pair of square brackets substituted and words repealed by FA 2000, ss 8(1), (2), 156, Sch 40 Pt I.

Sub-s (1A): inserted by FA 2000, ss 8(1), (3).

Sub-s (2): words in first and second pairs of square brackets substituted and words in third pair of square brackets added by the Finance Act 1994, s 9, Sch 4, Pt III, paras 49, 51(2).

Sub-s (5): words in square brackets substituted by the Finance Act 1988, s 12(1)(b), (6), in relation to offences committed after 29 July 1988.

[13AA Restrictions on use of rebated kerosene

(1) If, on the delivery of kerosene for home use, it is intended to use the kerosene as fuel for—

(a)   an engine provided for propelling an excepted vehicle, or

(b)   an engine which is used neither for propelling a vehicle nor for heating,

a declaration shall be made to that effect and thereupon rebate shall be allowed at the rate [then in force under paragraph (b) of subsection (1) of section 11, instead of at the rate then in force under paragraph (c) of that subsection].

(2) Subject to subsection (3) below, no kerosene on whose delivery for home use a rebate at the rate given by section 11(1)(c) above has been allowed shall—

(a)   be used as fuel for an engine provided for propelling an excepted vehicle;

(b)   be used as fuel for an engine which is used neither for propelling a vehicle nor for heating; or

(c)   be taken into the fuel supply of an engine falling within paragraph (a) or (b) above.

(3) Subsection (2) above does not apply to any quantity of kerosene in respect of which there has been paid to the Commissioners an amount equal to duty on the same quantity of gas oil at the rate for rebated gas oil which is in force at the time of the payment.

(4) A payment under subsection (3) above shall be made in accordance with regulations made under section 24(1) below for the purposes of this section.

(5) For the purposes of this section and section 13AB below—

"excepted vehicle" means a vehicle which is an excepted vehicle under any provision of Schedule 1 to this Act; and

"kerosene" means heavy oil of which more than 50 per cent by volume distils at a temperature of 240

(6) For the purposes of this section and section 13AB below the rate for rebated gas oil which is in force at any time is the rate of duty which at that time is in force under [section 6(1A) above in the case of heavy oil which is not ultra low sulphur diesel [or sulphur-free diesel],] as reduced by the rate of rebate allowable at that time under section 11(1)(b) above.]

[(7) Nothing in this section has the effect of allowing a rebate on bioblend or bioethanol blend.]

NOTES

Inserted by the Finance Act 1996, s 5(1), (4), in relation to cases where kerosene is used as a fuel or taken into a fuel supply.

Sub-s (1): words in square brackets substituted by the Finance Act 2005 s 4(8).

Sub-s (6): words in square brackets substituted by the Finance Act 1997, s 7(6), (10). Words "or sulphur-free diesel" inserted by the Finance Act 2004, s 7(6).

Sub-s (7): inserted by the Finance Act 2004, s 10(6) with effect from 1 January 2005: see the Finance Act 2004, s 10(10).

[13AB Penalties for misuse of kerosene

(1) If a person uses kerosene in contravention of section 13AA(2) above—

    [(a)   in respect of the quantity of kerosene used the Commissioners may assess as being excise duty due from him an amount equal to duty on the same quantity of gas oil at the rate for rebated gas oil which is in force at the time of the contravention, and they may notify him or his representative accordingly;]

    (b)   his use of the kerosene shall attract a penalty under section 9 of the Finance Act 1994 (civil penalties); and

    (c)   if he uses the kerosene with the relevant intent, he shall be guilty of an offence.

(2) If a person is liable for kerosene being taken into a fuel supply of an engine in contravention of section 13AA(2) above—

    [(a)   in respect of the quantity of kerosene taken into the fuel supply the Commissioners may assess as being excise duty due from him an amount equal to duty on the same quantity of gas oil at the rate for rebated gas oil which is in force at the time of the contravention, and they may notify him or his representative accordingly;]

    (b)   his becoming so liable shall attract a penalty under section 9 of the Finance Act 1994 (civil penalties); and

    (c)   if he has the relevant intent in relation to the kerosene being taken into the fuel supply, he shall be guilty of an offence.

(3) For the purposes of subsection (2) above, a person is liable for kerosene being taken into a fuel supply of an engine if at the time—

    (a)   he has the charge of the engine; or

    (b)   subject to subsection (4) below, he is the owner of the engine.

(4) If a person other than the owner is for the time being entitled to possession of the engine, that other person and not the owner is liable.

(5) If—

    (a)   a person supplies kerosene having reason to believe that it will be put to a particular use, and

    (b)   that use is one which, if a payment is not made under subsection (3) of section 13AA above, will contravene subsection (2) of that section,

his supplying the kerosene shall attract a penalty under section 9 of the Finance Act 1994 (civil penalties) and, if he makes the supply with the relevant intent, he shall be guilty of an offence.

(6) In this section "the relevant intent" means the intent that the restrictions imposed by section 13AA(2) above shall be contravened.

(7) A person guilty of an offence under this section shall be liable—

    (a)   on summary conviction, to a penalty of the statutory maximum, or to imprisonment for a term not exceeding 6 months, or to both;

    (b)   on conviction on indictment, to a penalty of any amount, or to a term of imprisonment not exceeding 7 years, or to both.

(8) Any kerosene falling within subsection (9) or (10) below is liable to forfeiture.

(9) Kerosene falls within this subsection if it is taken into a fuel supply in contravention of section 13AA(2) above.

(10) Kerosene falls within this subsection if—

    (a)   it has been supplied in circumstances in which there is reason to believe that it will be put to a particular use; and

    (b)   that use is one which, if payment is not made under subsection (3) of section 13AA above, will contravene subsection (2) of that section."

NOTES

Inserted by the Finance Act 1996, s 5(1), (4), in relation to cases where kerosene is used as a fuel or taken into a fuel supply.

Sub-s (1): para (a) substituted by the Finance Act 1998, s 20, Sch 2, paras 4(2).

Sub-s (2): para (a) substituted by the Finance Act 1998, s 20, Sch 2, paras 4(3).

[13A Rebate on unleaded petrol

(1) On unleaded petrol, other than ultra low sulphur petrol [and sulphur-free petrol], charged with the excise duty on hydrocarbon oil and delivered for home use there shall be allowed at the time of delivery a rebate of duty at the rate of [£0.0642] a litre.

(2) Rebate is not allowed under this section in a case where a rebate is allowed under section 14 below.]

NOTES

This section is substituted by the Finance Act 2001, s 2.

Sub-s (1): words inserted by the Finance Act 2004, s 7(7); figure substituted by the Finance Act 2007, s 10(1), (7) with effect from 1 October 2007.

14 Rebate on light oil for use as furnace fuel

(1) On light oil charged with the excise duty on hydrocarbon oil, and delivered for home use as furnace fuel for burning in vaporised or atomised form by a person for the time being approved in accordance with regulations made for the purposes of this subsection under section 24(1) below, there shall be allowed at the time of delivery a rebate of duty at a rate of [£0.0929] a litre less than the rate at which the duty is charged.

[(1A) No rebate shall be allowed under this section in respect of bioethanol blend.]

(2) Except with the consent of the Commissioners, no oil in whose case rebate has been allowed under this section shall—

    (a)   be put to a use otherwise than as mentioned in subsection (1) above; or

    (b)   be acquired or taken into any vehicle, appliance or storage tank in order to be put to such a use.

(3) In giving their consent for the purposes of subsection (2) above, the Commissioners may impose such conditions as they think fit.

(4) [Where any person]—

    (a)   uses or acquires oil in contravention of subsection (2) above; or

    (b)   is liable for oil being taken into a vehicle, appliance or storage tank in contravention of that subsection, [his use or acquisition of the oil or, as the case may be, his becoming so liable shall attract a penalty under section 9 of the Finance Act 1994 (civil penalties)]; and the Commissioners may [assess the amount of rebate allowed on the oil as being excise duty due from him, and notify him or his representative accordingly.]

(5) [Where any person] supplies oil having reason to believe that it will be used otherwise than as mentioned in subsection (1) above [and] that use without the consent of the Commissioners would contravene subsection (2) above [his supplying the oil shall attract a penalty under section 9 of the Finance Act 1994 (civil penalties).]

(6) A person who, with the intent that the restrictions imposed by subsection (2) above should be contravened—

    (a)   uses or acquires oil in contravention of that subsection; or

    (b)   supplies oil having reason to believe that it will be put to a use otherwise than as mentioned in subsection (1) above, being a use which, without the consent of the Commissioners, would contravene subsection (2) above,

shall be guilty of an offence under this subsection.

(7) A person who is liable for oil being taken into a vehicle, appliance or storage tank in contravention of subsection (2) above shall be guilty of an offence under this subsection where the oil was taken in with the intent by him that the restrictions imposed by that subsection should be contravened.

(8) A person guilty of an offence under subsection (6) or (7) above shall be liable—

    (a)   on summary conviction, to a penalty of the prescribed sum or of three times the value of the oil in question, whichever is the greater, or to imprisonment for a term not exceeding 6 months, or to both; or

    (b)   on conviction on indictment, to a penalty of any amount, or to imprisonment for a term not exceeding [7 years], or to both.

(9) For the purposes of this section, a person is liable for oil being taken into a vehicle, appliance or storage tank in contravention of subsection (2) above if he is at the time the person having the charge of the vehicle, appliance or tank, or is its owner, except that if a person other than the owner is, or is for the time being, entitled to possession of it, that person and not the owner is liable.

(10) Any oil acquired, or taken into a vehicle, appliance or storage tank, as mentioned in subsection (2) above, or supplied as mentioned in subsection (5) or (6) above, shall be liable to forfeiture.

NOTES

Sub-s (1): figure substituted by the Finance Act 2007, s 10(1), (8) with effect from 1 October 2007.

Sub-s (1A): inserted by the Finance Act 2004, s 10(7) with effect from 1 January 2005: see the Finance Act 2004, s 10(10).

Sub-s (4): words in first and second pairs of square brackets substituted by the Finance Act 1994, s 9, Sch 4, Pt III, paras 49, 52(1); words in third pair of square brackets substituted by the Finance Act 1997, ss 6(4), (5), 50(2), Sch 6, paras 6(3), 7.

Sub-s (5): words in first and second pairs of square brackets substituted and words in third pair of square brackets added by the Finance Act 1994, s 9, Sch 4, Pt III, paras 49, 52(2).

Sub-s (8): words in square brackets substituted by the Finance Act 1988, s 12(1)(b), (6), in relation to offences committed after 29 July 1988.

Drawback

15 Drawback of duty on exportation etc of certain goods

(1) A drawback equal to any amount . . . . paid in respect of the goods in question by way of the excise duty on hydrocarbon oil shall be allowed on the . . ., shipment as stores or warehousing in an excise warehouse for use as stores of—

(a) any hydrocarbon oil; or

(b) any article in which there is contained any hydrocarbon oil which was used, or which formed a component of any article used, as an ingredient in the manufacture or preparation of the article.

(2) The Treasury may by order direct as respects articles of any class or description specified in the order that, subject to the provisions of the order, drawback shall be allowed under subsection (1) above in respect of hydrocarbon oil (or goods containing it) used as a material, solvent, extractant, preservative or finish in the manufacture or preparation of the articles.

(3) On the making of an order under subsection (2) above this Act shall have effect, subject to the provisions of the order and of this section, as if the reference in subsection (1)(b) above to an article in which there is contained any hydrocarbon oil used as an ingredient in the manufacture or preparation of the article included a reference to an article of the class or description specified in the order.

(4) An order made under subsection (2) above as respects articles of any class or description—

(a) may provide for drawback to be allowed in respect of hydrocarbon oil (or goods containing it) used as a material, solvent, extractant, preservative or finish in the manufacture or preparation not directly of articles of that class or description but of articles incorporated in them; and

(b) may provide that the quantity of hydrocarbon oil as respects duty on which drawback is to be allowed shall be determined by reference to average quantities or otherwise.

(5) The power to make orders under subsection (2) above shall be exercisable by statutory instrument, and any statutory instrument by which the power is exercised shall be subject to annulment in pursuance of a resolution of the House of Commons.

NOTES

Sub-s (1): words omitted in the first place repealed by the Finance Act 1993, ss 12(7)(b), 213, Sch 23. Pt I(5); word omitted in the second place repealed by the Finance Act 1999, ss 4, 139, Sch 20, Pt I(1) in relation to any exportation after 26 July 1999.

Cross references: see the Biofuels and Other Fuel Substitutes (Payment of Excise Duties etc) Regulations 2004, SI 2004/2065 reg 3(1) (the reference to hydrocarbon oil in sub-s (1) above to be construed as including references to biodiesel and bioethanol).

SI 2004/2065 reg 3(2) (the references to hydrocarbon oil in sub-s (1) above are to be construed as including references to bioblend and bioethanol blend).

SI 2004/2065 reg 3(3) (the reference to the duty on hydrocarbon oil in sub-s (1) above is to be construed as including reference to biodiesel duty, the duty under section 6AB above, bioethanol duty, and the duty under section 6AE above).

Modification: this section and ss 17–19A modified by the Finance Act 1993, s 12(3).

16

(Repealed by the Finance Act 1993, ss 11(2), (5), 213, Sch 23, Pt I(4).)

Miscellaneous reliefs

17 Heavy oil used by horticultural producers

(1) If, on an application made for the purposes of this section by a horticultural producer, it is shown to the satisfaction of the Commissioners that within the period for which the application is made any quantity of heavy oil has been used by the applicant as mentioned in subsection (2) below, then, subject as provided below, the applicant shall be entitled to obtain from the Commissioners repayment of the amount of any excise duty which has been paid in respect of the quantity so used [less any rebate allowed in respect of the duty] . . .

(2) A horticultural producer shall be entitled to repayment under this section in respect of oil used by him—

    (a)   in the heating, for the growth of horticultural produce primarily with a view to the production of horticultural produce for sale, of any building or structure, or of the earth or other growing medium in it; or

    (b)   in the sterilisation of the earth or other growing medium to be used for the growth of horticultural produce as mentioned in paragraph (a) above in any building or structure.

(3) Where any quantity of oil is used partly for any such purpose as is mentioned in subsection (2) above and partly for another purpose, such part of that quantity shall be treated as used for each purpose as may be determined by the Commissioners.

(4) . . .

(5) The Commissioners may require an applicant for repayment under this section—

    (a)   to state such facts concerning the hydrocarbon oil delivered to or used by him, or concerning the production of horticultural produce by him, as they may think necessary to deal with the application;

    (b)   to furnish them in such form as they may require with proof of any statement so made; and

    (c)   to permit an officer to inspect any premises or plant used by him for the production of horticultural produce or in or for which any such oil was used.

(6) If—

    (a)   the facts required by the Commissioners under subsection (5)(a) above are not stated; or

    (b)   proof of the matters referred to in subsection (5)(b) above is not furnished to the satisfaction of the Commissioners; or

    (c)   an applicant fails to permit inspection of premises or plant as required under the subsection (5)(c) above,

the facts shall be deemed for the purposes of this section to be such as the Commissioners may determine.

(7) In this section—

    (a)   "horticultural produce" has the meaning assigned to it by Schedule 2 to this Act; and

    (b)   "horticultural producer" means a person growing horticultural produce primarily for sale.

NOTES

Sub-s (1): words in square brackets substituted and words omitted repealed by the Finance Act 1981, ss 6(4), 139(6), Sch 19, Pt III.

Sub-s (4): repealed by the Finance Act 1981, s 139(6), Sch 19, Pt III.

Modification: modified as noted to s 15.

[17A Biodiesel used otherwise than as road fuel

(1) If, on an application made for the purposes of this section, it is shown to the satisfaction of the Commissioners that within the period for which the application is made any quantity of biodiesel has been used by the applicant as mentioned in subsection (2) below, then, subject as provided below, the applicant shall be entitled to obtain from the Commissioners repayment of the amount specified below.

(2) A person is entitled to repayment under this section in respect of biodiesel used by him—

    (a)   otherwise than as road fuel,

    (b)   otherwise than by mixing the biodiesel with—

        (i)   hydrocarbon oil, or

        (ii)   a mixture containing hydrocarbon oil, and

    (c)   otherwise than in the form of a mixture containing biodiesel and hydrocarbon oil.

(3) For the purposes of subsection (2)(a) above, use "as road fuel" means use—

    (a)   as fuel for the engine provided for propelling a road vehicle or for an engine that draws its fuel from the same supply as such an engine, or

    (b)   as an additive or extender in any substance so used.

(4) The amount of the repayment is the amount of the excise duty which has been paid in respect of the quantity of biodiesel used less the amount of £0.0313 a litre.

(5) The Commissioners may require an applicant for repayment under this section—

    (a)   to state such facts concerning the biodiesel that is the subject of the claim, or the use to which it was put, as they may think necessary to deal with the application;

    (b)   to furnish them in such form as they may require with proof of any statement so made;

    (c)   to retain such records as the Commissioners may require relating to the use of biodiesel; and

    (d)   to permit an officer to inspect any premises, plant or vehicle on or in which the biodiesel in respect of which repayment is claimed is used.

(6) If the applicant fails to comply with any such requirement, the Commissioners may reject the claim.]

NOTES

Inserted by the Finance Act 2002, s 5, Sch 2, paras 1, 4(1).

18

(Repealed by the Finance Act 1996, s 8(2)(a).)

19 Fuel used in fishing boats, etc

(1) Subsection (3) below shall have effect in the case of—

    (a)   . . .

    (b)   any lifeboat owned by the Royal National Lifeboat Institution (in this subsection called "the Institution"); or

    (c)   any tractor or gear owned by the Institution and used for the purpose of launching or hauling in any lifeboat owned by it,

in respect of which an application is made to the Commissioners for the purposes of this section . . ., by the Institution.

(2) Paragraphs (b) and (c) of subsection (1) above shall apply to hovercraft as if hovercraft were boats or vessels.

(3)   Subject to the provisions of this section, if it appears to the satisfaction of the Commissioners that the applicant has . . ., used any quantity of hydrocarbon oil on board that boat or for the purposes of that tractor or gear, the applicant shall be entitled to obtain from the Commissioners repayment of any excise duty which has been paid in respect of the oil so used [less any rebate allowed in respect of the duty].

(4)–(6)   . . .

NOTES

Sub-s (1): words omitted repealed by the Finance Act 1996, s 8(2)(b).

Sub-s (3): words omitted repealed and words in square brackets substituted by the Finance Act 1981, ss 6(4), 139(6), Sch 19, Pt III.

Sub-ss (4), (5): repealed by the Finance Act 1981, s 139(6), Sch 19, Pt III.

Sub-s (6): repealed by the Finance Act 1993, s 213, Sch 23, Pt I(4).

Cross reference: see the Biofuels and Other Fuel Substitutes (Payment of Excise Duties etc) Regulations 2004, SI 2004/2065 reg 3(1) (the reference to hydrocarbon oil in sub-s (3) above to be construed as including references to biodiesel and bioethanol).

SI 2004/2065 reg 3(2) (the references to hydrocarbon oil in sub-s (3) above to be construed as including references to bioblend and bioethanol blend).

Modification: modified as noted to s 15.

[19A Fuel for producing energy for refineries etc

(1)   If on an application made for the purposes of this section by an approved person it is shown to the satisfaction of the Commissioners—

(a)   that any quantity of rebated hydrocarbon oil has been used by him, otherwise than at a refinery or other premises used for the production of hydrocarbon oil, as fuel for producing energy; and

(b)   that not less than one-sixth or more than one-third of that energy was used in the treatment of hydrocarbon oil at a refinery or in the production of hydrocarbon oil at other premises used for the production of such oil,

the applicant shall be entitled to obtain from the Commissioners repayment of one-third of the amount of excise duty which has been paid in respect of the quantity so used less the rebate allowed in respect of the duty.

(2)   In this section "an approved person" means a person for the time being approved in accordance with regulations made for the purposes of this section under section 24(1) below.]

NOTES

Inserted by the Finance Act 1981, s 5(2), (5).

Modification: modified as noted to s 15.

[20 Contaminated or accidentally mixed oil

(1)   This   section   applies   where   it   is   shown   to   the   satisfaction   of the Commissioners—

(a)   that hydrocarbon oil has been delivered for home use, that since it was so delivered it has become contaminated, and that at the time it became contaminated it was oil on which the appropriate duty of excise had been paid, or

(b)   that hydrocarbon oils of different descriptions have been delivered for home use, that since they were so delivered they have become accidentally mixed with each other, and that at the time of mixing they were oils on which the appropriate duty of excise had been paid.

(2)   Subject to any conditions which the Commissioners see fit to impose for the protection of the revenue, they may make to such person as they see fit a payment in accordance with subsection (3) below.

(3)   The payment shall be of an amount appearing to the Commissioners to be equal to the excise duty which would have been payable if—

(a)   the oil had been delivered for home use (uncontaminated) at the time it became contaminated (where subsection (1)(a) above applies), or

(b)   the oils had been delivered for home use (unmixed) at the time they became mixed (where subsection (1)(b) above applies).]

[(4)   The power to make a payment to a person under subsection (2) above in relation to oils that have become accidentally mixed does not apply in relation to a mixture in respect of which he is liable to pay duty under section 20AA below.]

NOTES

Substituted by the Finance Act 1985, s 7, Sch 4, para 1.

Sub-s (4): added by the Finance Act 1996, s 6(1), (2), in relation to the production of a mixture which is leaded or unleaded petrol and to the supply of a mixture of heavy oils.

Cross reference: see the Biofuels and Other Fuel Substitutes (Payment of Excise Duties etc) Regulations 2004, SI 2004/2065 reg 3(2) (the references to hydrocarbon oil in sub-s (1)(a) and (3)(a) above to be construed as including references to bioblend and bioethanol blend).

[Mixing: adjustment of duty

20A Mixing: adjustment of duty

(1)   In this section "new oil" means hydrocarbon oil which after it has been charged under section 6 above as oil of one description becomes oil of a different description as a result of approved mixing in a pipe-line with other hydrocarbon oil which has been so charged; and "approved mixing" has the meaning given by subsection (5) below.

(2)   Where the Commissioners are of opinion that, if the new oil had fallen to be charged under section 6 above as oil of the different description, the amount of duty would have been greater or less than that actually charged, then—

(a)   if in their opinion the amount would have been greater, they may charge under this section a duty of excise on the oil of an amount equal to the difference, and

(b)   if in their opinion the amount would have been less, they may make under this section an allowance equal to the difference.

(3)   In determining the amount of duty which would have been charged if the new oil had fallen to be charged under section 6 above as oil of the different description, the rates to be applied are those effective at the time when in the Commissioners' opinion the oil became oil of the different description.

(4)   Where the Commissioners have made a charge or allowance under subsection (2) above, then, for the purposes of this Act, any relief or rebate which was permitted or allowed at the time of the charge under section 6 above shall be disregarded.

(5)   The Commissioners may make regulations—

(a)   enabling them to grant to persons (whether individually or of a specified class) permission to mix in a pipe-line different descriptions of hydrocarbon oil (whether generally or in the case of specified descriptions only), and to withdraw permission for reasonable cause;

(b)   enabling permission to be granted subject to conditions and conditions to be varied for reasonable cause, and in this section "approved mixing" means mixing in accordance with permission under the regulations.

    (6)   The Commissioners may make regulations—

        (a)   for prescribing the method of charging the duty under this section;

        (b)   for determining the form of the allowance under this section (which may be by way of repayment or otherwise) and the time of the allowance may be made.

    (7)   Regulations under this section may make different provision for different circumstances.]

NOTES

Inserted, together with the preceding cross-heading, by the Finance Act 1985, s 7, Sch 4, para 2.

Regulations: the Hydrocarbon Oil (Mixing of Oils) Regulations 1985, SI 1985/1450.

[20AAA Mixing of rebated oil

    (1)   A duty of excise shall be charged on a mixture which is—

        (a)   produced by mixing fully rebated heavy oil with heavy oil which is not fully rebated, and

        (b)   supplied for use as fuel for any engine, motor or other machinery.

    (2)   A duty of excise shall be charged on a mixture which is—

        (a)   produced by mixing partially rebated heavy oil with heavy oil which is not partially rebated, and

        (b)   supplied for use as fuel for any engine, motor or other machinery;

but a mixture on which duty is charged under subsection (1) shall not be charged under this subsection.

    (3)   A duty of excise shall be charged on a mixture which is produced by mixing—

        (a)   fully or partially rebated heavy oil, with

        (b)   biodiesel or a substance containing biodiesel.

    (4)   The rate of duty on a mixture under subsection (1) or (2) shall be—

        (a)   in the case of a mixture supplied for use as fuel for a road vehicle, the rate of duty specified in section 6(1A)(d) (general rate for heavy oil), and

        (b)   in any other case, equivalent to the rate of rebate specified in section 11(1)(b) (general rate for gas oil).

    (5)   The rate of duty on a mixture under subsection (3) shall be the rate of duty specified in section 6(1A)(d).

    (6)   For the purposes of this section—

        (a)   oil is fully rebated if a rebate has been allowed in respect of it under section 11(1)(c) (general rebate for heavy oil),

        (b)   oil is partially rebated if a rebate has been allowed in respect of it under any other provision of section 11 or under section 13AA, and

        (c)   a reference to mixing is a reference to non-approved mixing (within the meaning given by section 20A(5)).

    (7)   The person liable to pay duty charged under this section on supply or production of a mixture is the person supplying or producing the mixture.

    (8)   Where duty under a provision of this Act has been paid on an ingredient of a mixture, the duty charged under this section shall be reduced by the amount of any duty that the Commissioners are satisfied has been paid on the ingredient (but not to a negative amount).

    (9)   The Commissioners may exempt a person from liability to pay duty under any provision of this Act in respect of production or supply of a mixture of a kind described in subsection (1)(a), (2)(a) or (3) if satisfied that—

(a)   the liability was incurred accidentally, and
(b)   in the circumstances the person should be exempted.]

NOTES

Substituted by the Finance Act 2004, s 9(1). For commencement provisions see the Finance Act 2004, s 9(4), (5).

[**20AAB Mixing of rebated oil: supplementary**
[(1)   A person who supplies or produces a mixture on which duty is charged under section 20AAA above must notify the Commissioners of the supply or production—
(a)   in advance, or
(b)   within the period of seven days beginning with the date of supply or production.]
(3)   Notification under subsection (1) . . . above must be given in such form and in such manner, and must contain such particulars, as the Commissioners may direct.
(4)   Subject to subsection (7) below, where it appears to the Commissioners—
(a)   that a person has produced or supplied a mixture on which duty is charged under section 20AAA above, and
(b)   that he is the person liable to pay the duty,
they may assess the amount of duty due from him to the best of their judgement and notify that amount to him or his representative.
(5)   An assessment under subsection (4) above shall be treated as if it were an assessment under section 12(1) of the Finance Act 1994.
(6)   The Commissioners may give a direction that a person who is, or expects to be, liable to pay duty charged under section 20AAA above—
(a)   shall account for duty charged under that section by reference to such periods ("accounting periods") as may be determined by or under the direction;
(b)   shall make, in relation to accounting periods, returns in such form and at such times and containing such particulars as may be so determined;
(c)   shall pay duty charged under that section at such times and in such manner as may be so determined.
(7)   The power to make an assessment under subsection (4) above does not apply in relation to a person who is for the time being subject to a direction under subsection (6) above.
(8)   Where any person—
(a)   fails to give a notification which he is required to give under subsection (1) above, or
(b)   fails to comply with a direction under subsection (6) above,
his failure shall attract a penalty under section 9 of the Finance Act 1994 (civil penalties).]

NOTES

Inserted by the Finance Act 1996, s 6(1), (3), in relation to the production of a mixture which is leaded or unleaded petrol and to the supply of a mixture of heavy oils.

Sub-s (1): substituted for sub-ss (1), (2) by the Finance Act 2004, s 9(2)(a). For commencement provisions see the Finance Act 2004, s 9(4), (5).

Sub-s (3): words repealed by the Finance Act 2004, ss 9(2)(b), 326, Sch 42 Pt 1(1). For commencement provisions see the Finance Act 2004, s 9(4), (5).

[20AA Power to allow reliefs

(1)   The Commissioners may make regulations allowing reliefs as regards—

(a)   any duty of excise which has been charged in respect of hydrocarbon oil, . . ., or road fuel gas;

(b)   any amount which has been paid to the Commissioners under section 12(2) above;

(c)   any amount which would (apart from the regulations) be payable to the Commissioners under section 12(2) above.

(2)   The regulations may include such provision as the Commissioners think fit in connection with allowing reliefs, and in particular may—

(a)   provide for relief to take the form of a repayment or remission [or an allowance to be set off against duty payable to the Commissioners by the person claiming relief];

(b)   provide for relief to be allowed in cases or classes of case set out in the regulations;

(c)   provide for relief to be allowed to the extent set out in the regulations;

(d)   provide for relief to be allowed subject to conditions imposed by the regulations;

(e)   provide for relief to be allowed subject to such conditions as the Commissioners may impose on the person claiming relief;

(f)   provide for the taking of samples of hydrocarbon oil in order to ascertain whether relief should be allowed or has been properly allowed;

(g)   make provision as to administration (which may include provision requiring the making of applications for relief);

[(ga) provide for oil on which relief is allowed to be treated for the purposes of this Act as oil on which a rebate has been allowed;]

(h)   make different provision in relation to different cases or classes of case;

(i)   include such supplementary, incidental, consequential or transitional provisions as appear to the Commissioners to be necessary or expedient.

(3)   The conditions which may be imposed as mentioned in subsection (2)(d) or (e) above may include conditions as to the physical security of premises, the provision (by bond or otherwise) of security for payment, or such other matters as the Commissioners think fit.

(4)   Where a person contravenes or fails to comply with any regulation made under this section or any condition imposed by or under such a regulation—

[(a)   his contravention or failure to comply shall attract a penalty under section 9 of the Finance Act 1994 (civil penalties); and]

(b)   any goods in respect of which the contravention or failure occurred shall be liable to forfeiture.

(5)   A reference in this section to a duty of excise includes a reference to any addition to such duty by virtue of section 1 of the Excise Duties (Surcharges or Rebates) Act 1979.

(6)   Schedule 5 to this Act shall have effect with respect to any sample of hydrocarbon oil taken in pursuance of regulations made under this section.]

NOTES

Inserted by the Finance Act 1989, s 2(1).

Sub-s (1): words omitted repealed by the Finance Act 1993, s 213, Sch 23, Pt I(4).

Sub-s (2): words in para (a) and whole of para (ga) inserted by the Finance Act 2000, s 10(1), (3).

Sub-s (4): para (a) substituted by the Finance Act 1994, s 9, Sch 4, Pt III, paras 49, 54.

Cross references: see the Biofuels and Other Fuel Substitutes (Payment of Excise Duties etc) Regulations 2004, SI 2004/2065 reg 3(1) (the reference to hydrocarbon oil in sub-s (1)(a) above to be construed as including references to biodiesel and bioethanol).

SI 2004/2065 reg 3(1) (the references to the duty on hydrocarbon oil in sub-s (1) above are to be construed as including references to biodiesel duty and bioethanol duty).

Regulations: the Excise Duties (Hydrocarbon Oil) (Travelling Showmen) Relief Regulations 1989, SI 1989/2439; the Hydrocarbon Oil Duties (Marine Voyages Reliefs) Regulations 1996, SI 1996/2537.

[**20AB Power to allow reliefs for fuel testing etc**

(1) The Commissioners may by regulations make provision allowing reliefs as regards excise duty charged in respect of experimental fuel where—

(a)   the fuel is, or is to be, used for the purposes of a fuel-testing project that is approved by the Commissioners,

(b)   the project is approved for the purposes of the development of the fuel (see subsection (8)(a) below), and

(c)   the use takes place, or is to take place, during the period that, for the purposes of the project, is the relief period for the fuel (see subsection (8)(b) below).

(2) In this section "experimental fuel" means a substance of a description specified in regulations made by the Commissioners.

(3) For each experimental fuel, the Commissioners shall by regulations make provision specifying—

(a)   the beginning and end of the period that is the experimental period for that fuel; and

(b)   the form that (subject to any directions under subsection (9)(a) below) is to be taken by relief under this section as regards excise duty chargeable on that fuel.

(4) A form of relief specified under subsection (3)(b) above must be an authorised form; and for the purposes of this section "an authorised form" is—

(a)   a repayment, or

(b)   a rebate (or extra rebate).

(5) Relief under this section shall be allowed—

(a)   to the extent specified in, or determined in accordance with, regulations under subsection (1) above, and

(b)   subject to—

(i)   such conditions as the Commissioners may impose, and

(ii)   any directions under subsection (9)(b) below.

(6) The conditions that may be imposed under subsection (5)(b)(i) above include, in particular, conditions in connection with—

(a)   the collection, keeping, compilation or analysis, or

(b)   the supply to the Commissioners or other persons,

of data, or information, relating to the production, use or performance of an experimental fuel.

(7) Subsections (8) and (9) below apply where the Commissioners have approved a fuel-testing project.

(8) The Commissioners shall give directions specifying—

(a)   each experimental fuel for the purposes of whose development the project is approved;

(b)   for each fuel specified under paragraph (a) above, the beginning and end of the period that, for the purposes of the project, is (in accordance with subsection (10) below) the relief period for the fuel; and

    (c)   any conditions imposed under subsection (5)(b)(i) above that apply to the allowance under this section of relief as regards excise duty chargeable in respect of an experimental fuel used, or to be used, for the purposes of the project.

(9) The Commissioners may give directions—

    (a)   providing for relief as regards excise duty chargeable in respect of an experimental fuel used, or to be used, for the purposes of the project to take an authorised form different to the form specified under subsection (3)(b) above;

    (b)   as to administration in connection with allowing reliefs under this section as regards excise duty chargeable in respect of an experimental fuel used, or to be used, for the purposes of the project.

(10) For the purposes of subsection (8)(b) above—

    (a)   the beginning of the relief period for a fuel may not be earlier than the beginning of the experimental period for that fuel; and

    (b)   the end of the relief period for a fuel may not be later than the end of the experimental period for that fuel.

(11) In this section—

"excise duty" means—

    (a)   excise duty chargeable by virtue of this Act, or

    (b)   any addition to such duty by virtue of section 1 of the Excise Duties (Surcharges or Rebates) Act 1979;

"fuel-testing project" means a pilot project connected with the technological development of environment-friendly fuels.

(12) Regulations under this section may make different provision for different cases.]

NOTES

Inserted by the Finance Act 2001, s 3.

Administration and enforcement

21 Regulations with respect to hydrocarbon oil, petrol substitutes and road fuel gas

(1) The Commissioners may, with a view to the protection of the revenue, make regulations—

    (a)   for any of the purposes specified in Part I of Schedule 3 to this Act (which relates to hydrocarbon oil);

    (b)   . . .;

    (c)   for any of the purposes specified in Part III of that Schedule (which relates to road fuel gas).

(2) In the case of regulations made for the purposes mentioned in subsection (1)(a) above, different regulations may be made for different classes of hydrocarbon oil; and the power to make such regulations shall include power to make regulations—

    (a)   regulating the allowance and payment of drawback under or by virtue of section 15 above; and

    (b)   for making the allowance and payment of drawback by virtue of an order under subsection (2) of that section subject to such conditions as the Commissioners see fit to impose for the protection of the revenue.

[(2A) In the case of regulations made for the purposes mentioned in subsection (1)(c) above, different regulations may be made for different classes of road fuel gas.]

(3) [Where any person] contravenes or fails to comply with any regulation made under this section [his contravention or failure to comply shall attract a penalty under section 9 of the Finance Act 1994 (civil penalties), and any goods in respect of which any person contravenes or fails to comply with any such regulation shall be liable to forfeiture.]

NOTES

Sub-s (1): para (b) repealed by the Finance Act 1993, s 213, Sch 23, Pt I(4).

Sub-s (2A): inserted by the Finance Act 2004, s 6(3) with effect from 1 September 2004.

Sub-s (3): words in square brackets substituted by the Finance Act 1994, s 9, Sch 4, Pt III, paras 49, 55.

Cross reference: see the Biofuels and Other Fuel Substitutes (Payment of Excise Duties etc) Regulations 2004, SI 2004/2065 reg 3(1) (the reference to hydrocarbon oil in sub-s (2) above to be construed as including references to biodiesel and bioethanol).

Regulations: the Gas (Road Fuel) Regulations 1972, SI 1972/846, as amended by SI 1977/1869, and the Hydrocarbon Oil Regulations 1973, SI 1973/1311, as amended by SI 1976/443, SI 1977/1868, SI 1981/1868, SI 1981/1134, SI 1985/1033, SI 1985/1450, SI 1992/3149, SI 1993/2267, SI 1994/694, SI 1996/2313, SI 1996/2537 (which both have effect under this section by virtue of the Interpretation Act 1978, s 17(2)(b), as read with s 28(6) of this Act); the Hydrocarbon Oil (Amendment) Regulations 1981, SI 1981/1134, as amended by SI 1996/2313, SI 1996/2537; the Hydrocarbon Oil (Mixing of Oils) Regulations 1985, SI 1985/1450; the Excise Duties (Deferred Payments) Regulations 1992, SI 1992/3152, as amended by SI 1996/2537; the Hydrocarbon Oil (Amendment) Regulations 1993, SI 1993/2267; the Hydrocarbon Oil Duties (Marine Voyages Reliefs) Regulations 1996, SI 1996/2537.

22 Prohibition on use of petrol substitutes on which duty has not been paid

(1) [[Where any person]—

(a)   puts to a chargeable use (within the meaning of section 6A above) any liquid which is not hydrocarbon oil; and

(b)   knows or has reasonable cause to believe that there is duty charged under section 6A above on that liquid which has not been paid and is not lawfully deferred,]

[his putting the liquid to that use shall attract a penalty under section 9 of the Finance Act 1994 (civil penalties), and any goods in respect of which any person contravenes this subsection shall be liable to forfeiture.]

[(1AA)   Where any person—

(a)   puts any biodiesel to a chargeable use (within the meaning of section 6AA above), and

(b)   knows or has reasonable cause to believe that there is duty charged under section 6AA above on that biodiesel which has not been paid and is not lawfully deferred,

his putting the biodiesel to that use shall attract a penalty under section 9 of the Finance Act 1994 (civil penalties), and any goods in respect of which any person contravenes this subsection shall be liable to forfeiture.]

[(1AB)   Where any person—

(a)   puts any bioethanol to a chargeable use (within the meaning of section 6AD above), and

(b)   knows or has reasonable cause to believe that there is duty charged under section 6AD above on that bioethanol which has not been paid and is not lawfully deferred,

his putting the bioethanol to that use shall attract a penalty under section 9 of the Finance Act 1994 (c 9) (civil penalties), and any goods in respect of which a person contravenes this section shall be liable to forfeiture.]

[(1A) Section 10 of the Finance Act 1994 (exception for cases of reasonable excuse) shall not apply in relation to conduct attracting a penalty by virtue of [subsection (1), (1AA) or (1AB) above.]]

(2) In subsection (1) above, "liquid" does not include any substance which is gaseous at a temperature of 15 degrees C and under a pressure of 1013.25 millibars.

NOTES

Sub-s (1): words in first (outer) pair of square brackets substituted by the Finance Act 1993, s 11(3), (5); words second (inner) pair of square brackets substituted by the Finance Act 1994, s 9, Sch 4, Pt III, paras 49, 56(1)(a)); words in final pair of square brackets substituted by the Finance Act 1994, s 9, Sch 4, para 56(1)(b).

Sub-s (1AA): inserted by the Finance Act 2002, s 5, Sch 1, paras 1, 5(7).

Sub-s (1AB): inserted by the Finance Act 2004, s 10(8)(a) with effect from 1 January 2005: see the Finance Act 2004, s 10(10).

Sub-s (1A): inserted by the Finance Act 1994, s 9, Sch 4, para 56(2); words substituted by the Finance Act 2004, s 10(8)(b) with effect from 1 January 2005: see the Finance Act 2004, s 10(10).

23 Prohibition on use etc of road fuel gas on which duty has not been paid

(1) [Where any person]—

    (a)   uses as fuel in; or

    (b)   takes as fuel into,

a road vehicle any road fuel gas on which he knows or has reasonable cause to believe that the excise duty chargeable under section 8 above has not been paid [his use of the road fuel gas or, as the case may be, his taking it as fuel into that vehicle shall attract a penalty under section 9 of the Finance Act 1994 (civil penalties), and any goods in respect of which a person contravenes this subsection shall be liable to forfeiture.]

[(1A) Section 10 of the Finance Act 1994 (exception for cases of reasonable excuse) shall not apply in relation to conduct attracting a penalty by virtue of subsection (1) above.]

[(1B) Where any person—

    (a)   uses as fuel in, or

    (b)   takes as fuel into,

a road vehicle any road fuel gas on which the excise duty chargeable under section 8 above has not been paid, the Commissioners may assess the amount of that duty as being excise duty due from that person any notify him or his representative accordingly.]

(2) For the purposes of [subsections (1)(b) and (1B)(b)] above, road fuel gas shall be deemed to be taken into a road vehicle as fuel if, but only if, it is taken into it as part of the supply of fuel for the engine provided for propelling the vehicle or for an engine which draws its fuel from the same supply as that engine.

NOTES

Sub-s (1): words in square brackets substituted by the Finance Act 1994, s 9, Sch 4, Pt III, paras 49, 57(1).

Sub-s (1A): inserted by the Finance Act 1994, s 9, Sch 4, Pt III, paras 49, 57(2).

Sub-s (1B): inserted by the Finance Act 1997, s 50(2), Sch 6, paras 6(4), 7.

Sub-s (2): words in square brackets substituted by the Finance Act 1997, s 50(2), Sch 6, paras 6(5), 7.

[23A Regulation of traders in controlled oil

(1) If a revenue trader who is not a registered excise dealer and shipper—

    (a)   buys or sells controlled oil in the course of a trade or business, or

(b)   in the course of a trade or business deals in controlled oil,

his buying or selling, or dealing in, the oil shall attract a penalty under section 9 of the Finance Act 1994 (civil penalties).

(2)   Subsection (1) above does not apply to the buying of oil by a revenue trader if—

(a)   the oil is for use by the trader, and

(b)   that use does not involve selling or dealing in hydrocarbon oil.

(3)   Subsection (1) above does not apply to the selling of oil by a revenue trader if—

(a)   that oil was for use by the trader,

(b)   that use did not involve selling or dealing in hydrocarbon oil,

(c)   that use came to an end before the oil was used, and

(d)   the oil is sold after the use ends.

(4)   Where a revenue trader who is not a registered excise dealer and shipper is entitled to the possession of any controlled oil, the oil is liable to forfeiture.

(5)   Subsection (4) above does not apply to oil if—

(a)   that oil is for use by the revenue trader, and

(b)   that use does not involve selling or dealing in hydrocarbon oil.

(6)   Subsection (4) above does not apply to oil if—

(a)   the oil was for use by the revenue trader,

(b)   that use did not involve selling or dealing in hydrocarbon oil,

(c)   that use has come to an end,

(d)   that use came to an end before the oil was used, and

(e)   the oil is being held pending sale or other disposal.

(7)   Where oil is liable to forfeiture by virtue of subsection (4) above—

(a)   anything mixed with the oil,

(b)   any container in which the oil (and anything mixed with it) is kept, and

(c)   any equipment kept for dispensing the contents of any such container, is liable to forfeiture.]

NOTES

Inserted by the Finance Act 2002, s 6, Sch 3, para 1.

[23B Power to provide for exceptions to Section 23A

(1)   The Commissioners may by regulations make provision for—

(a)   exceptions to section 23A(1) above in addition to those allowed by section 23A(2) and (3) above;

(b)   exceptions to section 23A(4) above in addition to those allowed by section 23A(5) and (6) above;

(c)   exceptions to section 23A(7) above.

(2)   Regulations under subsection (1) above may provide for exceptions allowed by such regulations to have effect subject to conditions—

(a)   specified by such regulations;

(b)   specified by the Commissioners under such regulations.]

NOTES

Inserted by the Finance Act 2002, s 6, Sch 3, para 1.

[23C Warehousing

(1) For the purposes of Part VIII of the Customs and Excise Management Act 1979 (c 2) (warehousing) the substances specified in subsection (4) shall be treated as if they were chargeable with duty (and therefore within the scope of section 92(1)(a) or (c) of that Act) whether or not duty is in fact chargeable.

(2) The Commissioners may make regulations under section 93 of that Act (warehousing regulations) that relate to a substance specified in subsection (4).

(3) In respect of a substance specified in subsection (4) which has been or is to be deposited in an excise warehouse by virtue of subsection (2), the Commissioners may—

    (a)   treat the substance, or make provision by regulations for treating the substance, as if duty were chargeable in relation to it by virtue of a specified enactment;

    (b)   make any regulations, or do any other thing, of a kind that they could make or do (whether or not by virtue of a provision of Part VIII of that Act) in respect of a substance deposited in an excise warehouse under Part VIII of that Act.

(4) The substances referred to in subsection (1) are—

    (a)   petroleum gas,

    (b)   animal fat set aside for use as motor fuel or heating fuel,

    (c)   vegetable fat set aside for use as motor fuel or heating fuel,

    (d)   non-synthetic methanol set aside for use as motor fuel or heating fuel,

    (e)   biodiesel,

    (f)   a mixture of two or more substances specified in paragraphs (a) to (e), and

    (g)   any other substance specified for the purposes of this section in regulations made by the Commissioners.

(5) In subsection (4)—

    (a)   "petroleum gas" means any hydrocarbon which—

        (i)   is gaseous at a temperature of 15°C and under a pressure of 1013.25 millibars, and

        (ii)   is not natural gas (as defined in paragraph (b) below),

    (b)   "natural gas" means gas with a methane content of not less than 80%,

    (c)   "animal fat" means a triglyceride of animal origin,

    (d)   "vegetable fat" means a triglyceride of vegetable origin, and

    (e)   "non-synthetic methanol" means methyl alcohol of non-synthetic origin.

(6) Regulations under subsection (4)(g)—

    (a)   may make provision only if the Commissioners think it necessary or expedient for a purpose connected with Council Directive 92/12/EEC on the general arrangements for products subject to excise duty and on the holding, movement and monitoring of such products,

    (b)   may, in particular, make provision by reference to that Directive or any other Community instrument, and

    (c)   may, in particular, make provision by reference to the purpose for which a substance is intended to be used.]

NOTES

Inserted by the Finance Act 2004, s 13.

24 Control of use of duty-free and rebated oil

(1) The Commissioners may make regulations for any of the purposes of [section 6(3),] section 9(1) or (4), [section 11,] section 12, [section 13A] [or section 13AA][, section 14(1), section 17, . . ., section 19[, section 19A[, section 20AB] or section 24A of this Act], and in particular for the purposes specified in Schedule 4 to this Act.

(2) Regulations made for the purposes of section 12 [or section 13AA] above may provide for restricting (whether by reference to locality, the obtaining of a licence from the Commissioners or other matters) the cases in which payments to the Commissioners [under subsection (2) of section 12, or subsection (3) of section 13AA,] are to be effective for the purposes of that subsection.

(3) For the purposes of the Customs and Excise Acts 1979, the presence in any hydrocarbon oil of a marker which, in regulations made under this section, is prescribed in relation to—

(a) oil delivered without payment of duty under section 9 above; or

(b) rebated heavy oil or rebated light oil,

shall be conclusive evidence that that oil has been so delivered or, as the case may be, that the rebate in question has been allowed.

(4) [Where any person] contravenes or fails to comply with any regulation made under this section [his contravention or failure to comply shall attract a penalty under section 9 of the Finance Act 1994 (civil penalties), and any goods in respect of which any person contravenes or fails to comply with any such regulation shall be liable to forfeiture.]

[(4A) Where—

(a) a rebate of duty is allowed on any oil, and

(b) a person contravenes or fails to comply with any requirement which, by virtue of any regulations made under this section, is a condition of allowing the rebate,

the Commissioners may assess an amount equal to the rebate as being excise duty due from that person, and notify him or his representative accordingly.

(4B) Where—

(a) any oil is delivered without payment of duty, and

(b) a person contravenes or fails to comply with any requirement which, by virtue of any regulations made under this section, is a condition of allowing the oil to be delivered without payment of duty,

the Commissioners may assess an amount equal to the excise duty on like oil at the rate in force at the time of the contravention or failure to comply as being excise duty due from that person, and notify him or his representative accordingly.]

[(4C) In a case where subsection (4D) below applies, the power of the Commissioners under subsection (4A) above includes power, if it appears to them to be appropriate, to assess (and notify) an amount less than the amount of the rebate concerned.

(4D) This subsection applies in any case where—

(a) the Commissioners have power to assess (and notify) an amount under subsection (4A) above by virtue of a contravention of, or failure to comply with, a requirement such as is mentioned in paragraph 5 of Schedule 4 to this Act, and

(b) the marker whose addition is required by the requirement is present at the time of the contravention or failure but in such a proportion that its presence falls to be disregarded by virtue of provision made by regulations under this section for the purpose mentioned in paragraph 7 of that Schedule.]

(5)   Schedule 5 to this Act shall have effect with respect to any sample of hydrocarbon oil taken in pursuance of regulations made under this section.

NOTES

Sub-s (1): words in first pair of square brackets inserted by the Finance Act 1982, s 4(3); words in second pair of square brackets inserted by the Finance Act 1997, s 7(7); words in third pair of square brackets inserted by the Finance Act 1987, s 1(2), (4); words in fourth pair of square brackets inserted by the Finance Act 1996, s 5(1), (5), in relation to cases where kerosene is used as a fuel or taken into a fuel supply; words in fifth (outer) pair of square brackets substituted by the Finance Act 1981, s 6(2); words in sixth (inner) pair of square brackets substituted by the Finance Act 1996, s 7(2); words omitted repealed by the Finance Act 1996, s 205, Sch 41, Pt I, words ", section 20AB" inserted by the Finance Act 2001, s 3(2).

Sub-s (2): words in first pair of square brackets inserted by the Finance Act 1996, s 5(1), (5); words in second pair of square brackets substituted by the Finance Act 2002, s 6(1), Sch 3, paras 5, 8.

Sub-s (4): words in square brackets substituted by the Finance Act 1994, s 9, Sch 4, Pt III, paras 49, 58.

Sub-ss (4A), (4B): inserted by the Finance Act 1997, s 50(2), Sch 6, paras 6(6), 7.

Sub-ss (4C), (4D): inserted by the Finance Act 2000, s 10(1), (4).

Regulations: the Hydrocarbon Oil Regulations 1973, SI 1973/1311, as amended by SI 1976/443, SI 1977/1868, SI 1981/1868, SI 1981/1134, SI 1985/1033, SI 1985/1450, SI 1992/3149, SI 1993/2267, SI 1994/694, as amended by SI 1996/2313, SI 1996/2537 (which have effect under this section by virtue of the Interpretation Act 1978, s 17(2)(b), as read with s 28(6) of this Act); the Hydrocarbon Oil (Amendment) Regulations 1981, SI 1981/1134 as amended by SI 1996/2313, SI 1996/2537; the Hydrocarbon Oils (Amendment) Regulations 1985, SI 1985/1033; the Hydrocarbon Oil (Mixing of Oils) Regulations 1985, SI 1985/1450; the Hydrocarbon Oils (Amendment) Regulations 1992, SI 1992/3149; the Excise Duties (Deferred Payments) Regulations 1992, SI 1992/3152, as amended by SI 1996/2537; the Hydrocarbon Oil (Amendment) Regulations 1993, SI 1993/2267; the Hydrocarbon Oils (Amendment) (No 2) Regulations 1994, SI 1994/694; the Hydrocarbon Oil (Payment of Rebates) Regulations 1996, SI 1996/2313.

[24AA Registered excise dealers and shippers regulations: special provision for traders in controlled oil

(1)   For the purposes of section 100H(1)(p) of the Management Act (registered excise dealers and shippers regulations may, in particular, make provision authorised by this section), this section authorises provision—

(a)   requiring traders in controlled oil to notify prescribed information;

(b)   requiring traders in controlled oil to make prescribed returns;

(c)   authorising a trader in controlled oil to carry out or arrange for the carrying out of any prescribed activity falling within section 100H(1)(b) of the Management Act in relation to controlled oil, but subject to prescribed conditions or restrictions;

(d)   requiring a trader in controlled oil to give security by prescribed means for amounts that may become due from him by way of repayment of rebate;

(e)   for taking into account, in determining whether a trader in controlled oil has—

(i)   contravened any provision of registered excise dealers and shippers regulations, or

(ii)   failed to comply with any prescribed condition, restriction or requirement,

the   extent   to   which   the   trader   has   followed   guidance   issued   by the Commissioners (including guidance issued after the making of provision under this paragraph referring to it).

(2)   In this section—

"prescribed" has the meaning given by section 100H(3) of the Management Act;

"trader in controlled oil" means a registered excise dealer and shipper carrying on a trade or business that consists of or includes the dealing in, buying or selling of controlled oil.]

NOTES

Inserted by the Finance Act 2002, s 6(1), Sch 3, para 3.

[24A Penalties for misuse of marked oil

(1)   Marked oil shall not be used as fuel for a road vehicle.

(2)   For the purposes of this section marked oil is any hydrocarbon oil in which a marker is present which is for the time being designated by regulations made by the Commissioners under subsection (3) below.

(3)   The Commissioners may for the purposes of this section designate any marker which appears to them to be used for the purposes of the law of any place (whether within or outside the United Kingdom) for identifying hydrocarbon oil that is not to be used as fuel for road vehicles, or for road vehicles of a particular description.

(4)   For the purposes of this section marked oil shall be taken to be used as fuel for a road vehicle if, but only if, it is used as fuel for the engine provided for propelling the vehicle or for an engine which draws its fuel from the same supply as that engine.

(5)   Where a person uses any hydrocarbon oil in contravention of subsection (1) above, his use of the oil shall attract a penalty under section 9 of the Finance Act 1994 (civil penalties).

(6)   If a person who uses any marked oil in contravention of subsection (1) above does so in the knowledge that the oil he is using is marked oil, he shall be guilty of an offence and liable—

(a)   on summary conviction, to a penalty of the statutory maximum, or to imprisonment for a term not exceeding 6 months, or to both;

(b)   on conviction on indictment, to a penalty of any amount, or to a term of imprisonment not exceeding 7 years, or to both.

(7)   Any marked oil which is in a road vehicle as part of the fuel supply for the engine which propels the vehicle shall be liable to forfeiture.

(8)   Where in any proceedings relating to this section a question arises as to the nature of any substance present at any time in any hydrocarbon oil—

(a)   a certificate of the Commissioners to the effect that that substance is or was a marker designated for the purposes of this section shall be sufficient, unless the contrary is shown, for establishing that fact; and

(b)   any document purporting to be such a certificate shall be taken to be one unless it is shown not to be.]

NOTES

Inserted by the Finance Act 1996, s 7(1).

Regulations: the Hydrocarbon (Designated Markers) Regulations 1996, SI 1996/1251.

Supplementary

25 Regulations

Any power to make regulations under this Act shall be exercisable by statutory instrument, and any statutory instrument by which the power is exercised shall be subject to annulment in pursuance of a resolution of either House of Parliament.

26 Directions

Directions given under any provision of this Act may make different provision for different circumstances and may be varied or revoked by subsequent directions thereunder.

27 Interpretation

(1) In this Act—

["aviation gasoline" has the meaning given by section 6(4) above;]

["bioblend" has the meaning given by section 6AB(2) above;]

["biodiesel" has the meaning given by section 2AA above;]

["bioethanol" has the meaning given by section 2AB above;]

["bioethanol blend" has the meaning given by section 6AE(2) above;]

["controlled oil" means hydrocarbon oil in respect of which a rebate has been allowed under section 11(1)(b), (ba) or (c) or 13AA;]

["gas oil" has the meaning given by section 1(5) above;]

"heavy oil" has the meaning given by section 1(4) above;

"hydrocarbon oil" has the meaning given by section 1(2) above;

"light oil" has the meaning given by section 1(3) above;

"the Management Act" means the Customs and Excise Management Act 1979;

. . .

"the prescribed sum", in relation to the penalty provided for an offence, means—

(a) if the offence was committed in England [or Wales], the prescribed sum within the meaning of [section 32 of the Magistrates' Courts Act 1980 (£1000 or other sum substituted by order under section 143(1) of that Act)];

(b) if the offence was committed in Scotland, the prescribed sum within the meaning of section 289B of the Criminal Procedure (Scotland) Act 1975 (£1,000 or other sum substituted by order under section 289D(1) of that Act);

[(c) if the offence was committed in Northern Ireland, the prescribed sum within the meaning of Article 14 of the Fines and Penalties (Northern Ireland) Order 1984 ([£5,000] or other sum substituted by order under Article 17 of that Order);]

"rebate" means rebate of duty under section 11, [13AA,] [13A] [, 14 or 20AB] above, and "rebated" has a corresponding meaning;

["refinery" means any premises which—

(a) are approved by the Commissioners for the treatment of hydrocarbon oil; or

(b) are approved by them for the production of energy for use in the treatment of hydrocarbon oil at premises approved under paragraph (a) above or in the production of hydrocarbon oil at other premises used for the production of such oil;

and the Commissioners may approve any premises under paragraph (b) above if it appears to them that more than one-third of the energy will be produced

for such use as is mentioned in that paragraph;]
"road fuel gas" has the meaning given by section 5 above; . . .

"road vehicle" means a vehicle constructed or adapted for use on roads, but does not include any vehicle [which is an excepted vehicle within the meaning given by Schedule 1 to this Act.]

["sulphur-free diesel" has the meaning given by section 1(7) above;]

["sulphur-free petrol" has the meaning given by section 1(3B) above;]

["ultra low sulphur diesel" has the meaning given by section 1(6) above.]

["ultra low sulphur petrol" has the meaning given by section 1(3A) above;]

["unleaded petrol" and "leaded petrol" have the meaning given by [section 1(3C) above.]]

[(1A)   If in the case of any premises which the Commissioners can approve under paragraph (b) of the definition of "refinery" in subsection (1) above it appears to them appropriate to do so, they may direct that the provisions of this Act (other than that definition) shall apply to them as if, instead of being a refinery, they were other premises used for the production of hydrocarbon oil.]

[(1B)   The Treasury may by order made by statutory instrument amend Schedule 1 to this Act so as to—

(a)   add a class of excepted vehicle,

(b)   remove a class of excepted vehicle, or

(c)   redefine a class of excepted vehicle.

(1C)   Section 2A(2) and (3) above shall apply to an order under subsection (1B).]

(2)   This Act and the other Acts included in the Customs and Excise Acts 1979 shall be construed as one Act but where a provision of this Act refers to this Act that reference is not to be construed as including a reference to any of the others.

(3)   Any expression used in this Act or in any instrument made under this Act to which a meaning is given by any other Act included in the Customs and Excise Acts 1979 has, except where the context otherwise requires, the same meaning in this Act or in any such instrument as in that Act; and for ease of reference the Table below indicates the expressions used in this Act to which a meaning is given by any other such Act—

Management Act

"the Commissioners"
"container"
"the Customs and Excise Acts 1979"
"excise warehouse"
"goods"
"hovercraft"
"occupier"
"officer" and "proper" in relation to an officer
["pipe-line"]
"port"
["registered excise dealer and shipper"]
["revenue trader"]
["representative"]
"ship"
"shipment"
"stores"
"warehouse"

Alcoholic Liquor Duties Act 1979

. . .
"spirits".

NOTES

Sub-s (1): definition "aviation gasoline" inserted by the Finance Act 1982, s 4(4); definitions "bioblend" and "biodiesel" inserted by the Finance Act 2002, s 5, Sch 2, paras 1, 6. Definitions "bioethanol" and "bioethanol blend" inserted by the Finance Act 2004, s 10(9) with effect from 1 January 2005: see the Finance Act 2004, s 10(10). Definition "controlled oil" inserted by the Finance Act 2002, s 6(1), Sch 3, para 4(1), (2); definitions "gas oil" and "ultra low sulphur diesel" inserted by the Finance Act 1997, s 7(8), (10); definitions "higher octane unleaded petrol", "ultra low sulphur petrol" and "unleaded petrol" and "leaded petrol" inserted by the Finance Act 2000, s 5(5), (6); definition "higher octane unleaded petrol" repealed by the Finance Act 2001, s 110, Sch 33 Pt 1(1), definitions "petrol substitute" and "power methylated spirits" repealed by the Finance Act 1993, s 213, Sch 23, Pt I(4); in definition "the prescribed sum" words in square brackets in para (a) substituted and whole of para (c) added by the Fines and Penalties (Northern Ireland) Order 1984, SI 1984/703, art 19(1), Sch 6, para 10, words in second pair of square brackets substituted by the Magistrates' Courts Act 1980, s 154, Sch 7, para 181, sum in square brackets in para (c) substituted by virtue of the Criminal Justice (Northern Ireland) Order 1994, SI 1994/2795, art 3(1); in definition "rebate", figure in first pair of square brackets inserted by the Finance Act 2002, s 6(1), Sch 3, paras 5, 9; figure in second pair of square brackets inserted by the Finance Act 1987, s 1(3), (4), figure in third pair of square brackets substituted by the Finance Act 2001, s 3(3); definition "refinery" substituted by the Finance Act 1981, s 5(3); words omitted in definition "road fuel gas" repealed by the Finance Act 1997, s 113, Sch 18, Pt I; words in square brackets in definition "road vehicle" substituted by the Finance Act 1995, s 8(1), (3). Definitions "sulphur-free diesel" and "sulphur-free petrol" inserted by the Finance Act 2004, s 7(8)(a). Words substituted in definition "unleaded petrol" and "leaded petrol" by the Finance Act 2004, s 7(8)(b).

Sub-s (1A): inserted by the Finance Act 1981, s 5(4).

Sub-ss (1A), (1B): inserted by the Finance Act 2006, s 8.

Sub-s (3): first entry in square brackets inserted by the Finance Act 1985, s 7, Sch 4, para 3; entry "methylated spirits" repealed by the Finance Act 1995, s 162, Sch 29, Pt I(3); second and third entries in square brackets inserted by the Finance Act 2002 s 6, Sch 3 para 4(1), (3); fourth entry in square brackets inserted by the Finance Act 1997, s 50(2), Sch 6, paras 6(7), 7.

28 Consequential amendments, repeals, savings and transitional provisions

(1)   The enactments and order specified in Schedule 6 to this Act shall be amended in accordance with the provisions of that Schedule.

(2)   The enactments specified in Schedule 7 to this Act are hereby repealed to the extent specified in the third column of that Schedule.

(3)   Any provision of this Act relating to anything done or required or authorised to be done under or by reference to that provision or any other provision of this Act shall have effect as if any reference to that provision, or that other provision, as the case may be, included a reference to the corresponding provision of the enactments repealed by this Act.

(4)   The repeal by subsection (2) above of the Hydrocarbon Oil (Customs and Excise) Act 1971 shall not affect the operation of the saving in paragraph 2 in Part I of Schedule 14 to the Finance (No 2) Act 1975 in relation to the provisions of the said Act of 1971 repealed by section 75(5) of the said Act of 1975 and specified in that Part.

(5)   The Amendment of Units of Measurement (Hydrocarbon Oil, etc.) Order 1977 is hereby revoked.

(6)   Nothing in this section shall be taken as prejudicing the operation of sections 15 to 17 of the Interpretation Act 1978 (which relate to the effect of repeals).

29 Citation and commencement

(1) This Act may be cited as the Hydrocarbon Oil Duties Act 1979 and is included in the Acts which may be cited as the Customs and Excise Acts 1979.

(2) This Act shall come into operation on 1st April 1979.

SCHEDULES

[SCHEDULE 1
EXCEPTED VEHICLES

Section 27(1)

Unlicensed vehicles not used on public roads

1.   —(1) A vehicle is an excepted vehicle while—

(a)   it is not used on a public road, . . .

(b)   no licence under the Vehicle Excise and Registration Act 1994 is in force in respect of it[, and

(c)   it is kept by a person who has furnished such particulars and made such declarations as may be prescribed by regulations under section 22(1D) of that Act.]

(2) A vehicle in respect of which there is current a certificate or document in the form of a licence issued under regulations under section 22(2) of the Vehicle Excise and Registration Act 1994 shall be treated for the purposes of sub-paragraph (1) above as a vehicle in respect of which a licence under that Act is in force.

Tractors

2.   —(1) A vehicle is an excepted vehicle if it is—

(a)   an agricultural tractor, . . .

(b)   . . .

[(2) In sub-paragraph (1) above "agricultural tractor" means a tractor which—

(a)   is designed and constructed primarily for use otherwise than on roads, and

(b)   is used on public roads solely for—

(i)   purposes relating to agriculture, horticulture or forestry;

(ii)   cutting verges bordering public roads; or

(iii)   cutting hedges or trees bordering public roads or bordering verges which border public roads.]

(4) . . .

Light agricultural vehicles

3.—(1) A vehicle is an excepted vehicle if it is a light agricultural vehicle.

(2) In sub-paragraph (1) above "light agricultural vehicle" means a vehicle which—

(a)   has a revenue weight not exceeding 1,000 kilograms,

(b)   is designed and constructed so as to seat only the driver,

(c)   is designed and constructed primarily for use otherwise than on roads, and

(d)   is used solely for purposes relating to agriculture, horticulture or forestry.

(3) In sub-paragraph (2)(a) above "revenue weight" has the meaning given by section 60A of the Vehicle Excise and Registration Act 1994.

[Agricultural material handlers

3A.—(1) An agricultural material handler is an excepted vehicle.

(2) In sub-paragraph (1) above an "agricultural material handler" means a vehicle which is

(a) designed and constructed primarily for use otherwise than on roads,

(b) designed to lift goods or burden, and

(c) used on public roads solely for

(i) purposes relating to agriculture, horticulture or forestry;

(ii) cutting verges bordering public roads; or

(iii) cutting hedges or trees bordering public roads or bordering verges which border public roads.]

Agricultural engines

4.—[(1)] An agricultural engine is an excepted vehicle.

[(2) In sub-paragraph (1) above "agricultural engine" means a vehicle which—

(a) is designed and constructed primarily for use otherwise than on roads,

(b) is designed, and used, solely for purposes relating to agriculture, horticulture or forestry,

(c) is used on public roads only for proceeding to and from the place where it is to be or has been used for those purposes, and

(d) when so proceeding does not carry any load except such as is necessary for its propulsion or for the operation of any machinery built-in or permanently attached to the vehicle.]

[Agricultural processing vehicles

4A.—(1) An agricultural processing vehicle is an excepted vehicle.

(2) In sub-paragraph (1) above an agricultural processing vehicle means a vehicle which

(a) is used for the conveyance of built-in processing machinery,

(b) is used on public roads only for proceeding to and from the place where that processing machinery is to be used, and

(c) when so proceeding does not carry any load except such as is necessary for its propulsion or for the operation of the processing machinery.

(3) Built-in processing machinery means machinery built in as part of, or permanently attached to, the vehicle that is used for the processing of agricultural, horticultural or forestry produce whilst the vehicle is stationary.]

Vehicles used between different parts of land

5.—(1) A vehicle is an excepted vehicle if—

(a) it is used only for purposes relating to agriculture, horticulture or forestry,

(b) it is used on public roads only in passing between different areas of land occupied by the same person, . . .

(c) the distance it travels on public roads in passing between any two such areas does not exceed 1.5 kilometres[, and.

(d) a nil licence is in force in respect of it.

(2) In sub-paragraph (1) above nil licence has the meaning given by section 62 of the Vehicle Excise and Registration Act 1994.]

Mowing machines

6.   A mowing machine is an excepted vehicle.

Snow clearing vehicles

7.   A vehicle is an excepted vehicle when it is—
(a)   being used, or
(b)   going to or from the place where it is to be or has been used,
for the purpose of clearing snow from public roads by means of a snow plough or similar device (whether or not forming part of the vehicle).

Gritters

8.   A vehicle is an excepted vehicle if it is constructed or adapted, and used, solely for the conveyance of machinery for spreading material on roads to deal with frost, ice or snow (with or without articles or material used for the purposes of the machinery).

Mobile cranes

9.—(1)   A mobile crane is an excepted vehicle.
(2)   In sub-paragraph (1) above "mobile crane" means a vehicle which is designed and constructed as a mobile crane and which—
(a)   is used on public roads only as a crane in connection with work carried on at a site in the immediate vicinity or for the purpose of proceeding to and from a place where it is to be or has been used as a crane, . . .
(b)   when so proceeding does not carry any load except such as is necessary for its propulsion or [the operation of built-in lifting apparatus, and
(c)   has a revenue weight exceeding 3,500 kilograms.
(3)   In sub-paragraph (2)(c) above revenue weight has the meaning given by section 60A of the Vehicle Excise and Registration Act 1994.]

[Mobile pumping vehicles

9A.—(1)   A mobile pumping vehicle is an excepted vehicle.
(2)   In sub-paragraph (1) above a mobile pumping vehicle means a vehicle
(a)   which is constructed or adapted for use, and used, for the conveyance of a pump and a jib satisfying the requirements specified in sub-paragraph (3),
(b)   which is used on public roads only
(i)   when the vehicle is stationary and the pump is being used to pump material from a point in the immediate vicinity to another such point, or
(ii)   for the purpose of proceeding to and from a place where the pump is to be or has been used, and
(c)   which when so proceeding, does not carry
(i)   the material that is to be or has been pumped, or
(ii)   any other load except such as is necessary for the propulsion or equipment of the vehicle or for the operation of the pump.
(3)   The requirements referred to in sub-paragraph (2)(a) are that each of the pump and the jib is
(a)   built in as part of the vehicle, and
(b)   designed so that material pumped by the pump is delivered to a desired height or depth through piping that
(i)   is attached to the pump and the jib, and

(ii)   is raised or lowered to that height or depth by operation of the jib.]

Digging machines

10.—(1)   A digging machine is an excepted vehicle.

(2)   In sub-paragraph (1) above "digging machine" means a vehicle which is designed, constructed and used for the purpose of trench digging, or any kind of excavating or shovelling work, and which—

(a)   is used on public roads only for that purpose or for the purpose of proceeding to and from the place where it is to be or has been used for that purpose, and

(b)   when so proceeding does not carry any load except such as is necessary for its propulsion or equipment.

Works trucks

11.—(1)   A works truck is an excepted vehicle.

(2)   In sub-paragraph (1) above "works truck" means a goods vehicle which is designed for use in private premises and is used on public roads only—

(a)   for carrying goods between private premises and a vehicle on a road within one kilometre of those premises,

(b)   in passing from one part of private premises to another,

(c)   in passing between private premises and other private premises in a case where the premises are within one kilometre of each other, or

(d)   in connection with road works at the site of the works or within one kilometre of the site of the works.

(3)   In sub-paragraph (2) above "goods vehicle" means a vehicle constructed or adapted for use and used for the conveyance of goods or burden of any description, whether in the course of trade or not.

Road construction vehicles

12.—(1)   A vehicle is an excepted vehicle if it is—

(a)   a road construction vehicle, and

(b)   used or kept solely for the conveyance of built-in road construction machinery (with or without articles or material used for the purposes of the machinery).

(2)   In sub-paragraph (1) above "road construction vehicle" means a vehicle—

(a)   which is constructed or adapted for use for the conveyance of built-in road construction machinery, and

(b)   which is not constructed or adapted for the conveyance of any other load except articles and material used for the purposes of such machinery.

(3)   In sub-paragraphs (1) and (2) above "built-in road construction machinery", in relation to a vehicle, means road construction machinery built in as part of, or permanently attached to, the vehicle.

(4)   In sub-paragraph (3) above "road construction machinery" means a machine or device suitable for use for the construction or repair of roads and used for no purpose other than the construction or repair of roads.

Road rollers

13.   A road roller is an excepted vehicle.

[Road surfacing vehicles

13A.—(1)   A road surfacing vehicle is an excepted vehicle.

(2)   In sub-paragraph (1) above road surfacing vehicle means a vehicle which

   (a)   is designed and constructed to perform an operation necessary to construct or restore the surface of a road,

   (b)   does not carry any load on a public road except such as is necessary for its propulsion or for the operation of any machinery built-in or permanently attached to the vehicle, and

   (c)   has a maximum speed not exceeding 20 kilometres per hour.

Tar Sprayers

13B.—(1)   A tar sprayer is an excepted vehicle.

(2)   In sub-paragraph (1) above a tar sprayer means a vehicle which is constructed or permanently adapted, and used, solely for spraying tar on to the road or for proceeding to and from the place where it is to be or has been used for that purpose.]

Interpretation

14.   In this Schedule "public road" means a road which is repairable at the public expense.]

NOTES

Substituted by the Finance Act 1995, s 8(2), (3).

Para 1: sub-para (1)(c) and preceding word "and" inserted by the Excepted Vehicles (Amendment of Schedule 1 to the Hydrocarbon Oil Duties Act 1979) Order, SI 2007/93, art 3.

Para 2: sub-para (1)(b) and the word preceding it and sub-para (4) repealed by the Finance Act 2000, ss 9, 156, Sch 40, Pt I, with effect in relation to the use of rebated heavy oil as fuel after 30 April 2000; sub-para (2) substituted for previous sub-paras (2), (3) by the Excepted Vehicles (Amendment of Schedule 1 to the Hydrocarbon Oil Duties Act 1979) Order, SI 2007/93, art 4.

Para 3A: inserted by the Excepted Vehicles (Amendment of Schedule 1 to the Hydrocarbon Oil Duties Act 1979) Order, SI 2007/93, art 5.

Para 4: Sub-para (1) renumbered as such, and sub-para (2) inserted, by the Excepted Vehicles (Amendment of Schedule 1 to the Hydrocarbon Oil Duties Act 1979) Order, SI 2007/93, art 6.

Para 4A: inserted by the Excepted Vehicles (Amendment of Schedule 1 to the Hydrocarbon Oil Duties Act 1979) Order, SI 2007/93, art 7.

Para 5: sub-para (1) renumbered as such, word "and" omitted from sub-para (1)(b) repealed, and sub-para (1)(d) and preceding word "and", and sub-para (2), inserted, by the Excepted Vehicles (Amendment of Schedule 1 to the Hydrocarbon Oil Duties Act 1979) Order, SI 2007/93, art 8.

Para 9: in sub-para (2)(a) omitted word "and" repealed, in sub-para (2)(b) words substituted, and sub-paras (2)(c), (3) inserted, by the Excepted Vehicles (Amendment of Schedule 1 to the Hydrocarbon Oil Duties Act 1979) Order, SI 2007/93, art 9.

Para 9A: inserted by the Excepted Vehicles (Amendment of Schedule 1 to the Hydrocarbon Oil Duties Act 1979) Order, SI 2007/93, art 10.

Para 12: repealed by the Excepted Vehicles (Amendment of Schedule 1 to the Hydrocarbon Oil Duties Act 1979) Order, SI 2007/93, art 11 with effect from 1 April 2008.

Paras 13A, 13B: inserted by the Excepted Vehicles (Amendment of Schedule 1 to the Hydrocarbon Oil Duties Act 1979) Order, SI 2007/93, art 12 with effect from 1 April 2008.

SCHEDULE 2

MEANING OF "HORTICULTURAL PRODUCE" FOR PURPOSES OF RELIEF UNDER SECTION 17

Section 17(7)

In section 17 of this Act "horticultural produce" means—

    (a)   fruit;

    (b)   vegetables of a kind grown for human consumption, including fungi, but not including maincrop potatoes or peas grown for seed, for harvesting dry or for vining;

    (c)   flowers, pot plants and decorative foliage;

    (d)   herbs;

    (e)   seeds other than pea seeds, and bulbs and other material, being seeds, bulbs or material for sowing or planting for the production of—

        (i)   fruit,

        (ii)   vegetables falling within paragraph (b) above,

        (iii)   flowers, plants or foliage falling within paragraph (c) above, or

        (iv)   herbs,

    or for reproduction of the seeds, bulbs or other material planted; or

    (f)   trees and shrubs, other than trees grown for the purpose of afforestation;

but does not include hops.

(Sch 2A repealed by the Finance Act 2004, ss 9(3), 326, Sch 42 Pt 1(1). For commencement provisions see the Finance Act 2004, s 9(4), (5))

SCHEDULE 3

SUBJECTS FOR REGULATIONS UNDER SECTION 21

Section 21(1)

PART I
HYDROCARBON OIL

1.   Prohibiting the production of hydrocarbon oil or any description of hydrocarbon oil except by a person holding a licence.

2.   [Specifying the circumstances in which any such licence may be surrendered or revoked].

3.   Regulating the production, storage and warehousing of hydrocarbon oil or any description of hydrocarbon oil and the removal of any such oil to or from premises used for the production of any such oil.

4.   Prohibiting the refining of hydrocarbon oil elsewhere than in a refinery.

5.   Prohibiting the incorporation of gas in hydrocarbon oil elsewhere than in a refinery.

6.   Regulating the use and storage of hydrocarbon oil in a refinery.

7.   Regulating or prohibiting the removal to a refinery of hydrocarbon oil in respect of which any rebate has been allowed.

8.   Regulating the removal of imported hydrocarbon oil to a refinery without payment of the excise duty on such oil.

9.   Making provision for securing payment of the excise duty on any imported hydrocarbon oil received into a refinery.

10.   Relieving from the excise duty chargeable on hydrocarbon oil produced in the United Kingdom any such oil intended for exportation or shipment as stores.

[[10A.   Amending the definition of "aviation gasoline" in subsection (4) of section 6 of this Act.]

10B. Conferring power to require information relating to the supply or use of aviation gasoline to be given by producers, dealers and users.

10C. Requiring producers and users of and dealers in aviation gasoline to keep and produce records relating to aviation gasoline.]

11. Generally for securing and collecting the excise duty chargeable on hydrocarbon oil . . .

NOTES

Para 2: words in square brackets substituted by the Finance Act 1986, s 8(6), Sch 5, para 4.

Paras 10A–10C: inserted by the Finance Act 1982, s 4(5), and substituted, in the case of para 10A, by the Finance Act 1990, s 3(5).

Para 11: words omitted repealed by the Finance Act 1985, ss 7, 98(6), Sch 4, para 4, Sch 27, Pt I.

Cross reference: see the Biofuels and Other Fuel Substitutes (Payment of Excise Duties etc) Regulations 2004, SI 2004/2065 reg 3(1) (the reference to hydrocarbon oil in paras 3, 11 above to be construed as including references to biodiesel and bioethanol).

(Pt II repealed by the Finance Act 1993, s 213, Sch 23, Pt I(4).)

PART III
ROAD FUEL GAS

17. Prohibiting the production of gas, and dealing in gas on which the excise duty has not been paid, except by persons holding a licence.

18. [Specifying the circumstances in which any such licence may be surrendered or revoked].

19. Regulating the production, dealing in, storage and warehousing of gas and the removal of gas to and from premises used therefor.

20. Requiring containers for gas to be marked in the manner prescribed by the regulations.

21. Conferring power to require information relating to the supply or use of gas and containers for gas to be given by producers of and dealer in gas, and by the person owning or possessing or for the time being in charge of any road vehicle which is constructed or adapted to use gas as fuel.

22. Requiring a person owning or possessing a road vehicle which is constructed or adapted to use gas as fuel to keep such accounts and records in such manner as may be prescribed by the regulations, and to preserve such books and documents relating to the supply of gas to or by him, or the use of gas by him, for such period as may be so prescribed.

23. Requiring the production of books or documents relating to the supply or use of gas or the use of any road vehicle.

24. Authorising the entry and inspection of premises (other than private dwelling-houses) and the examination of road vehicles, and authorising, or requiring the giving of facilities for, the inspection of gas found on any premises entered or on or in any road vehicle.

25. Generally for securing and collecting the excise duty.

In this Part of this Schedule "the excise duty" means the excise duty chargeable under section 8 of this Act on gas, and "gas" means road fuel gas.

NOTES

Para 18: words in square brackets substituted by the Finance Act 1986, s 8(6), Sch 5, para 4.

SCHEDULE 4
SUBJECTS FOR REGULATIONS UNDER SECTION 24
Section 24(1)

As to grant of relief . . .

1. Regulating the approval of persons for purposes of section 9(1) or (4) or 14(1) of this Act, whether individually or by reference to a class, and whether in relation to particular descriptions of oil or generally; enabling approval to be granted subject to conditions and providing for the conditions to be varied, or the approval revoked, for reasonable cause.

2. Enabling permission under section 9(1) of this Act to be granted subject to conditions as to the giving of security and otherwise.

[3. Requiring claims or applications for repayment under section 9(4), 17, [17A,]. . ., 19 or 19A of this Act to be made at such times and in respect of such periods as are prescribed; providing that no such claim or application shall lie where the amount to be paid is less than the prescribed minimum; and preventing, where a claim or application can be made under section 9(4) or 19, the payment of drawback.]

As to mixing of oil

4. Imposing restrictions on the mixing with other oil of any rebated oil or oil delivered without payment of duty.

As to marking of oil

5. Requiring as a condition of allowing rebate on, or delivery without payment of duty of, any oil (subject to any exceptions provided by or under the regulations) that there shall have been added to that oil, at such times, in such manner and in such proportions as may be prescribed, one or more prescribed markers, with or without a prescribed colouring substance (not being a prescribed marker), and that a declaration to that effect is furnished.

6. Prescribing the substances which are to be used as markers.

7. Providing that the presence of a marker shall be disregarded if the proportion in which it is present is less than that prescribed for the purposes of this paragraph.

8. Prohibiting the addition to any oil of any prescribed marker or prescribed colouring substance except in such circumstances as may be prescribed.

9. Prohibiting the removal from any oil of any prescribed marker or prescribed colouring substance.

10. Prohibiting the addition to oil of any substance, not being a prescribed marker, which is calculated to impede the identification of a prescribed marker.

11. Regulating the storage or movement of prescribed markers.

12. Requiring any person who adds a prescribed marker to any oil to keep in such manner and to preserve for such period as may be prescribed such accounts and records in connection with his use of that marker as may be prescribed, and requiring the production of the accounts and records.

13. Requiring, in such circumstances or subject to such exceptions as may be prescribed, that any drum, storage tank, delivery pump or other container or outlet which contains any oil in which a prescribed marker is present shall be marked in the prescribed manner to indicate that the oil is not to be used as road fuel or for any other prohibited purpose.

14. Requiring any person who supplies oil in which a prescribed marker is present to deliver to the recipient a document containing a statement in the prescribed form to the effect that the oil is not to be used as road fuel or for any other prohibited purpose.

15. Prohibiting the sale of any oil the colour of which would prevent any prescribed colouring substance from being readily visible if present in the oil.

16. Prohibiting the importation of oil in which any prescribed marker, or any other substance which is calculated to impede the identification of a prescribed marker, is present.

As to control of storage, supply etc of oil, entry of premises etc

17. Regulating the storage or movement of oil.

18. Restricting the supplying of oil in respect of which rebate has been allowed and not repaid or on which excise duty has not been paid.

[18A. Prohibiting the use of aviation gasoline otherwise than as a fuel for aircraft.

18B. Prohibiting the taking of aviation gasoline into fuel tanks for engines other than aircraft engines.]

19. Requiring a person owning or possessing a road vehicle which is constructed or adapted to use heavy oil as fuel to keep such accounts and records in such manner as may be prescribed, and to preserve such books and documents relating to the supply of heavy oil to or by him, or the use of heavy oil by him, for such period as may be prescribed.

20. Requiring the production of books or documents relating to the supply or use of oil or the use of any vehicle.

21. Authorising the entry and inspection of premises (other than private dwelling-houses) and the examination of vehicles, and authorising, or requiring the giving of facilities for, the inspection of oil found on any premises entered or on or in any vehicle and the taking of samples of any oil inspected.

Interpretation

22. In this Schedule—
"oil" means hydrocarbon oil;
   "prescribed" means prescribed by regulations made under section 24 of this Act; and section 12(3)(a) of this Act shall apply for the purposes of paragraph 19 above as it applies for the purposes of that section.

NOTES
   Heading to paras 1–3: words omitted repealed by the Finance Act 1981, s 139(6), Sch 19, Pt III.
   Para 3: substituted by the Finance Act 1981, s 6(3); figure omitted repealed by the Finance Act 1996, s 205, Sch 41, Pt I; figures in square brackets inserted by the Finance Act 2002, s 5, Sch 2, paras 1, 4(2).
   Paras 18A, 18B: inserted by the Finance Act 1982, s 4(6).
   Cross reference: see the Biofuels and Other Fuel Substitutes (Payment of Excise Duties etc) Regulations 2004, SI 2004/2065 reg 3(1) (the reference to hydrocarbon oil in paras 17, 21 above to be construed as including references to biodiesel and bioethanol).

SCHEDULE 5
SAMPLING

Section 24(5)

1. The person taking a sample—
   (a)   if he takes it from a motor vehicle, shall if practicable do so in the presence of a person appearing to him to be the owner or person for the time being in charge of the vehicle;

(b)   if he takes the sample on any premises but not from a motor vehicle, shall if practicable take it in the presence of a person appearing to him to be the occupier of the premises or for the time being in charge of the part of the premises from which it is taken.

2.—(1) The result of an analysis of a sample shall not be admissible—

(a)   in criminal proceedings under the Customs and Excise Acts 1979; or

(b)   on behalf of the Commissioners in any civil proceedings under those Acts,

unless the analysis was made by an authorised analyst and the requirements of paragraph 1 above (where applicable) and of the following provisions of this paragraph have been complied with.

(2) The person taking a sample must at the time have divided it into three parts (including the part to be analysed), marked and sealed or fastened up each part, and—

(a)   delivered one part to the person in whose presence the sample was taken in accordance with paragraph 1 above, if he requires it; and

(b)   retained one part for future comparison.

(3) Where it was not practicable to comply with the relevant requirements of paragraph 1 above, the person taking the sample must have served notice on the owner or person in charge of the vehicle or, as the case may be, the occupier of the premises informing him that the sample has been taken and that one part of it is available for delivery to him, if he requires it, at such time and place as may be specified in the notice.

3.—(1) Subject to sub-paragraph (2) below, in any such proceedings as are mentioned in paragraph 2(1) above a certificate purporting to be signed by an authorised analyst and certifying the presence of any substance in any such sample of oil as may be specified in the certificate shall be evidence, and in Scotland sufficient evidence, of the facts stated in it.

(3) Without prejudice to the admissibility of the evidence of the analyst (which shall be sufficient in Scotland as well as in England), such a certificate shall not be admissible as evidence—

(a)   unless a copy of it has, not less than 7 days before the hearing, been served by the prosecutor or, in the case of civil proceedings, the Commissioners on all other parties to the proceedings; or

(b)   if any of those other parties, not less than 3 days before the hearing or within such further time as the court may in special circumstances allow, serves notice on the prosecutor or, as the case may be, the Commissioners requiring the attendance at the hearing of the person by whom the analysis was made.

4.—(1) Any notice required or authorised to be given under this Schedule shall be in writing.

[(1A) Any decision which is made under or for the purposes of any regulations made under section 20AA of the Hydrocarbon Oil Duties Act 1979 and is a decision as to whether or not relief is to be allowed.]

(2) Any such notice shall be deemed, unless the contrary is shown, to have been received by a person if it is shown to have been left for him at his last-known residence or place of business in the United Kingdom.

(3) Any such notice may be given by post, and the letter containing the notice may be sent to the last-known residence or place of business in the United Kingdom of the person to whom it is directed.

(4) Any such notice given to the secretary or clerk of a company or body of persons (incorporated or unincorporated) on behalf of the company or body shall be deemed to have been given to the company or body; and for the purpose of the foregoing provisions of this paragraph any such company or body of persons having

an office in the United Kingdom shall be treated as resident at that office or, if it has more than one, at the registered or principal office.

(5)   Where any such notice is to be given to any person as the occupier of any land, and it is not practicable after reasonable inquiry to ascertain—

(a)   what is the name of any person being the occupier of the land; or

(b)   whether or not there is a person being the occupier of the land,

the notice may be addressed to the person concerned by any sufficient description of the capacity in which it is given to him.

(6)   In any case to which sub-paragraph (5) above applies, and in any other case where it is not practicable after reasonable inquiry to ascertain an address in the United Kingdom for the service of a notice to be given to a person as being the occupier of any land, the notice shall be deemed to have been received by the person concerned on being left for him on the land, either in the hands of a responsible person or conspicuously affixed to some building or object on the land.

(7)   Sub-paragraphs (2) to (6) above shall not affect the validity of any notice duly given otherwise than in accordance with those sub-paragraphs.

5.   In this Schedule "authorised analyst" means—

(a)   the Government Chemist or a person acting under his direction;

(b)   the Government Chemist for Northern Ireland or a person acting under his direction;

(c)   any chemist authorised by the Treasury to make analyses for the purposes of this Schedule; or

(d)   any other person appointed as a public analyst or deputy public analyst under—

[section 27 of the Food Safety Act 1990], or

[article 27(1) of the Food Safety (Northern Ireland) Order 1991].

6.   References in this Schedule to the taking of a sample or to a sample shall be construed respectively as references to the taking of a sample in pursuance of regulations under section [20AA or] 24 of this Act and to a sample so taken.

7.   This Schedule shall have effect in its application to a vehicle of which a person other than the owner is, or is for the time being, entitled to possession as if for references to the owner there were substituted references to the person entitled to possession.

NOTES

Para 4: Sub-para (1A) inserted by the Finance Act 2000, s 10(5).

Para 5: words in first pair of square brackets substituted by the Food Safety Act 1990, s 59(1), Sch 3, para 22; words in second pair of square brackets substituted by the Food Safety (Northern Ireland) Order 1991, SI 1991/762, Sch 2.

Para 6: words in square brackets inserted by the Finance Act 1989, s 2(2).

(Sch 6: para 1 superseded; para 2 repealed by the Goods Vehicles (Licensing of Operators) Act 1995, s 60(2), Sch 8; paras 3–5, 7 repealed by the Value Added Tax Act 1983, s 50, Sch 11; para 6 outside the scope of this work; Sch 7 contains repeals only.)

TOBACCO PRODUCTS DUTY ACT 1979

(1979 c 7)

ARRANGEMENT OF SECTIONS

An Act to consolidate the enactments relating to the excise duty on tobacco products

[22 February 1979]

1 Tobacco products

(1) In this Act "tobacco products" means any of the following products, namely—

  (a)   cigarettes;

  (b)   cigars;

  (c)   hand-rolling tobacco;

  (d)   other smoking tobacco; and

  (e)   chewing tobacco,

which are manufactured wholly or partly from tobacco or any substance used as a substitute for tobacco, but does not include herbal smoking products.

(2) . . .

(2A) . . .

(3) The Treasury may by order made by statutory instrument provide that in this Act references to cigarettes, cigars, hand-rolling tobacco, other smoking tobacco and chewing tobacco shall or shall not include references to any product of a description specified in the order, being a product manufactured as mentioned in subsection (1) above but not including herbal smoking products; and any such order may amend or repeal subsection (2) [or (2A)] above.

(4) Subject to subsection (5) below, a statutory instrument by which there is made an order under subsection (3) above shall be laid before the House of Commons after being made; and unless the order is approved by that House before the expiration of 28 days beginning with the date on which it was made, it shall cease to have effect on the expiration of that period, but without prejudice to anything previously done under it or to the making of a new order.

In reckoning any such period no account shall be taken of any time during which Parliament is dissolved or prorogued or during which the House of Commons is adjourned for more than 4 days.

(5) Subsection (4) above shall not apply to any order containing a statement by the Treasury that the order does not extend the incidence of the duty or involve a greater charge to duty or a reduction of any relief; and a statutory instrument by which any such order is made shall be subject to annulment in pursuance of a resolution of the House of Commons.

(6) In this section "herbal smoking products" means products commonly known as herbal cigarettes or herbal smoking mixtures.

NOTES

Sub-ss (2), (2A): repealed by the Tobacco Products (Description of Products) Order, SI 2003/1471, art 3(1).

Sub-s (3): words in square brackets inserted by the Finance Act 1993, s 14(1), (5).

2 Charge and remission or repayment of tobacco products duty

(1) There shall be charged on tobacco products imported into or manufactured in the United Kingdom a duty of excise at the rates shown, . . ., in the Table in Schedule 1 to this Act.

(2) Subject to such conditions as they see fit to impose, the Commissioners shall remit or repay the duty charged by this section where it is shown to their satisfaction [that—

    (a)   the products in question have been—

            (i)   exported or shipped as stores, or

            (ii)   used solely for the purposes of research or experiment; and

    (b)   any fiscal marks carried by the products have been obliterated;]

and the Commissioners may by regulations provide for the remission or repayment of the duty in such other cases as may be specified in the regulations and subject to such conditions as they see fit to impose.

NOTES

Sub-s (1): words omitted repealed by the Finance Act 1981, s 139(6), Sch 19, Pt III.

Sub-s (2): words in square brackets substituted by the Finance Act 2000, s 15(1), (2).

Regulations: the Tobacco Products Regulations 1979, SI 1979/904, as amended by SI 1980/992, SI 1982/964, SI 1990/544, SI 1992/3154, SI 1993/2167; the Excise Warehousing Regulations 1979, etc (Amendment) Regulations 1980, SI 1980/992; the Tobacco Products Regulations 1979 (Amendment) Regulations 1990, SI 1990/544.

3

(Repealed by the Finance Act 1981, ss 2(2), 139(6), Sch 19, Pt III.)

4 Calculation of duty in case of cigarettes more than 9cm long

For the purposes of the references to a thousand cigarettes in paragraph 1 in the Table in Schedule 1 to this Act . . . any cigarette more than 9 cm long (excluding any filter or mouthpiece) shall be treated as if each 9 cm or part thereof were a separate cigarette.

NOTES

Words omitted repealed by the Finance Act 1981, s 139(6), Sch 19, Pt III.

5 Retail price of cigarettes

(1) For the purposes of the duty chargeable at any time under section 2 above in respect of cigarettes of any description, the retail price of the cigarettes [shall be taken to be—

    (a)   the higher of—

        (i)   the recommended price for the sale by retail at that time in the United Kingdom of cigarettes of that description, and

        (ii)   any (or, if more than one, the highest) retail price shown at that time on the packaging of the cigarettes in question,

    or

    (b)   if there is no such price recommended or shown, the highest price at which cigarettes of that description are normally sold by retail at that time in the United Kingdom.]

[(1A) In subsection (1) above "recommended price"—

    (a)   in relation to a case in which cigarettes of the applicable description are manufactured by a manufacturer in a member State, means any price recommended by that manufacturer; and

    (b)   in relation to a case which does not fall within paragraph (a) above, means any price recommended by an importer of cigarettes of the applicable description.]

(2) The duty in respect of any number of cigarettes shall be charged by reference to the price which, in accordance with subsection (1) above, is applicable to cigarettes sold in packets of 20 or of such other number as the Commissioners may determine in relation to cigarettes of the description in question; and the whole of the price of a packet shall be regarded as referable to the cigarettes it contains notwithstanding that it also contains a coupon, token, card or other additional item.

(3) In any case in which duty is chargeable in accordance with [paragraph (b) of subsection (1)] above—

    (a)   the question as to what price is applicable under that paragraph shall, subject to subsection (4) below, be determined by the Commissioners; and

    (b)   the Commissioners may require security (by deposit of money or otherwise to their satisfaction) for the payment of duty to be given pending their determination.

(4) Any person who has paid duty in accordance with a determination of the Commissioners under subsection (3)(a) above and is dissatisfied with their determination may require the question of what price was applicable under [subsection (1)(b)] above to be referred to the arbitration of a referee appointed [in accordance with subsections (7) to (9)].

(5) If, on a reference to him under subsection (4) above, the referee determines that the price was lower than that determined by the Commissioners, they shall repay the duty overpaid together with interest on the overpaid duty from the date of the overpayment as such rate as the referee may determine.

(6) The procedure on any reference under subsection (4) above shall be such as may be determined by the referee; and the referee's decision on any such reference shall be final and conclusive.

[(7) The Lord Chancellor is to appoint the referee.

(8) The appointment is to be made only with the concurrence of—

    (a)   the Lord Chief Justice of England and Wales, if the determination of the Commissioners was made in relation to England and Wales;

    (b)   the Lord President of the Court of Session, if the determination was made in relation to Scotland; or

(c)   the Lord Chief Justice of Northern Ireland, if the determination was made in relation to Northern Ireland.

(9)   None of the following may be appointed—

(a)   an official of any government department;

(b)   an office holder in, or a member of the staff of, the Scottish Administration.

(10)   The Lord Chief Justice of England and Wales may nominate a judicial office holder (as defined in section 109(4) of the Constitutional Reform Act 2005) to exercise his functions under this section.

(11)   The Lord President of the Court of Session may nominate a judge of the Court of Session who is a member of the First or Second Division of the Inner House of that Court to exercise his functions under this section.

(12)   The Lord Chief Justice of Northern Ireland may nominate any of the following to exercise his functions under this section—

(a)   the holder of one of the offices listed in Schedule 1 to the Justice (Northern Ireland) Act 2002;

(b)   a Lord Justice of Appeal (as defined in section 88 of that Act).]

NOTES

Sub-s (1), (3): words in square brackets substituted by the Finance Act 2000, s 13(1)–(3).

Sub-s (1A): inserted by the Finance (No 2) Act 1992, s 8(b).

Sub-s (4): words in first pair of square brackets substituted by the Finance Act 2000, s 13(1), (4); words in second pair of square brackets substituted by the Constitutional Reform Act 2005, s 15(1), Sch 4, Pt 1, para 98(1), (2).

Sub-ss (7)–(12): inserted by the Constitutional Reform Act 2005 s 15, Sch 4 para 98.

6 Alteration of rates of duty

(1)   The Treasury may by order made by statutory instrument increase or decrease any of the rates of duty for the time being in force under the Table in Schedule 1 to this Act by such percentage of the rate, not exceeding 10 per cent., as may be specified in the order, but any such order shall cease to be in force at the expiration of a period of one year from the date on which it takes effect unless continued in force by a further order made under this subsection.

(2)   In relation to any order made under subsection (1) above to continue, vary or replace a previous order so made, the reference in that subsection to the rate for the time being in force is a reference to the rate that would be in force if no order under that subsection had been made.

(3)   A statutory instrument under subsection (1) above by which there is made an order increasing the rate in force at the time of making the order shall be laid before the House of Commons after being made; and unless the order is approved by that House before the expiration of 28 days beginning with the date on which it was made, it shall cease to have effect on the expiration of that period, but without prejudice to anything previously done under it or to the making of a new order.

In reckoning any such period no account shall be taken of any time during which Parliament is dissolved or prorogued or during which the House of Commons is adjourned for more than 4 days.

(4)   A statutory instrument made under subsection (1) above to which subsection (3) above does not apply shall be subject to annulment in pursuance of a resolution of the House of Commons.

(5)   For the purposes of this section—

(a)   the percentage and the amount per thousand cigarettes in paragraph 1 in the Table in Schedule 1 to this Act shall be treated as separate rates of duty; . . .

(b)   . . .

NOTES

Sub-s (5): words omitted repealed by the Finance Act 1981, s 139(6), Sch 19, Pt III.

7 Regulations for management of duty

(1) The Commissioners may with a view to managing the duty charged by section 2 above make regulations—

(a)   prescribing the method of charging the duty and for securing and collecting the duty;

[(aa)   for charging the duty, in such circumstances as may be specified in the regulations, by reference to the weight of the tobacco products at a time specified in the regulations or by the Commissioners (whether the time at which the products become chargeable or that at which the duty becomes payable or any other time);]

(b)   for the registration of premises for the safe storage of tobacco products and for requiring the deposit of tobacco products in, and regulating their [storage and] treatment in and removal from, premises so registered;

[(ba)   for the registration of premises for the manufacture of tobacco products, for restricting or prohibiting the manufacture of tobacco products otherwise than in premises so registered and for regulating their storage and treatment in, and removal from, such premises;]

(c)   for the registration of premises where—

      (i)   . . .;

      (ii)   materials for the manufacture of tobacco products are grown, produced, stored or treated; or

      (iii)   refuse from the manufacture of tobacco products is stored or treated,

and for regulating the storage and treatment in, and removal from, premises so registered of such materials and refuse;

(d)   for requiring the keeping and preservation of such records, [the notification of such information, and the making of such returns, as may be specified in the regulations or required by the Commissioners]; and

(e)   for the inspection of goods, documents and premises.

[(1A) Regulations under subsection (1) above may, in particular, include provision—

(a)   imposing, or providing for the imposition under the regulations of, conditions and restrictions relating to any of the matters mentioned in that subsection;

(b)   enabling the Commissioners to dispense with compliance with any provision contained in the regulations in such circumstances and subject to such conditions (if any) as they may determine.]

(2) If any person fails to comply with any regulation made under subsection (1) above [his failure to comply shall attract a penalty under section 9 of the Finance Act 1994 (civil penalties), and any article in respect of which any person fails to comply with any such regulation, or which is found on premises in respect of which any person has failed to comply with any such regulation, shall be liable to forfeiture.]

NOTES

Sub-s (1): paras (aa), (ba) and words in square brackets in para (b) inserted, para (c)(i) repealed and words in square brackets in para (d) substituted by the Finance Act 2000, ss 15(1), (3)–(8), 156, Sch 40, Pt I.

Sub-s (1A): inserted by the Finance Act 2000, s 15(1), (9).

Sub-s (2): words in square brackets substituted by the Finance Act 1994, s 9, Sch 4, Pt IV, para 59.

See the Channel Tunnel (Alcoholic Liquor and Tobacco Products) Order, SI 2003/2758 art 4(c): sub-s (2) above applies, for the purposes of SI 2003/2758, in corresponding manner to events involving goods in a control zone in the same way that it applies to events involving goods in the United Kingdom.

[7A Duty not to facilitate smuggling

(1) A manufacturer of cigarettes or hand-rolling tobacco shall so far as is reasonably practicable avoid—

(a)   supplying cigarettes or hand-rolling tobacco to persons who are likely to smuggle them into the United Kingdom,

(b)   supplying cigarettes or hand-rolling tobacco where the nature or circumstances of the supply makes it likely that they will be resupplied to persons who are likely to smuggle them into the United Kingdom, or

(c)   otherwise facilitating the smuggling into the United Kingdom of cigarettes or hand-rolling tobacco.

(2)   In particular, a manufacturer—

(a)   in supplying cigarettes or hand-rolling tobacco to persons carrying on business in or in relation to a country other than the United Kingdom, shall consider whether the size or nature of the supply suggests that the products may be required for smuggling into the United Kingdom,

(b)   shall maintain a written policy about steps to be taken for the purpose of complying with the duty under subsection (1), and

(c)   shall provide a copy of the policy to the Commissioners on request.

(3)   In this section a reference to smuggling products into the United Kingdom is a reference to importing them into the United Kingdom without payment of duty which is—

(a)   chargeable under section 2, and

(b)   payable by virtue of section 1(1) of the Finance (No 2) Act 1992 (c 48) (power to fix excise duty point).

(4)   The Commissioners may notify a manufacturer in writing that they think the risk of smuggling into the United Kingdom is particularly great in relation to—

(a)   products marketed under a specified brand name;

(b)   products supplied to persons carrying on business in or in relation to a specified country or place.

(5)   The Commissioners may by notice in writing require a manufacturer of cigarettes or hand-rolling tobacco to provide, within a specified period of time, specified information about—

(a)   supply of products marketed under a brand name specified under subsection (4)(a);

(b)   supply to persons carrying on business in or in relation to a country or place specified under subsection (4)(b);

(c)   demand for cigarettes or hand-rolling tobacco in a country or place specified under subsection (4)(b).

(6)   The Commissioners may issue guidance about the content of policies under subsection (2)(b).

(7)   The Commissioners may make regulations—

    (a)   under which they are required to notify manufacturers of cigarettes or hand-rolling tobacco where products of a kind specified in the regulations are seized under section 139 of the Customs and Excise Management Act 1979 (c 2) in circumstances specified in the regulations,

    (b)   specifying the procedure for notification,

    (c)   including provision about access to seized products for the purpose of determining who manufactured them, and

    (d)   requiring manufacturers to provide the Commissioners with information or documents, of a kind specified in the regulations or determined by the Commissioners, in relation to notified seizures.]

NOTES

Section inserted by Finance Act 2006, s 2(1).

Regulations: Tobacco Products (Amendment) Regulations, SI 2006/2368 (made under sub-s (7)).

[7B Penalty for facilitating smuggling: initial notice

[(1)   Where the Commissioners think that a manufacturer has without reasonable excuse failed to comply with the duty under section 7A(1) they may give him written notice that they are considering requiring him to pay a penalty.

(2)   In determining whether to give notice to a manufacturer under subsection (1) the Commissioners shall have regard to—

    (a)   the content of the manufacturer's policy under section 7A(2)(b),

    (b)   compliance with that policy,

    (c)   action taken pursuant to any notice under section 7A(4),

    (d)   compliance by the manufacturer with any notice under section 7A(5),

    (e)   the number, size and nature of seizures of which the manufacturer has been given notice by virtue of section 7A(7)(a),

    (f)   compliance by the manufacturer with any requirement by virtue of section 7A(7)(d),

    (g)   evidence about the level of demand for the manufacturer's products for consumption outside the United Kingdom, and

    (h)   any other matter that they think relevant.

(3)   A notice must specify the matters to which the Commissioners have had regard in determining to give it.

(4)   After the end of the period of six months beginning with the date on which a notice is given to a manufacturer, the Commissioners shall give him notice in writing either—

    (a)   that they require payment of a penalty, or

    (b)   that they do not require payment of a penalty.

(5)   The Commissioners shall comply with subsection (4) during the period of 45 days beginning with the end of the period specified in that subsection; and for that purpose they shall consider—

    (a)   any representations made by the manufacturer during that period in such form and manner as the Commissioners may direct, and

    (b)   action taken by the manufacturer during that period.]

NOTES

Section inserted by Finance Act 2006, s 2(1).

[7C Penalty for facilitating evasion: penalty notice

[(1) A notice under section 7B(4)(a) (a "penalty notice") must—

- (a)   specify the amount of the penalty which the manufacturer is required to pay, and

- (b)   state the grounds on which the Commissioners think that the manufacturer has failed to comply with the duty under section 7A(1).

(2) The amount specified under subsection (1)(a) must not exceed £5 million; and in determining the amount to specify the Commissioners shall have regard to—

- (a)   the nature or extent of the manufacturer's failure to comply with the duty under section 7A(1),

- (b)   action taken by the manufacturer to secure compliance with that duty,

- (c)   the content of the manufacturer's policy under section 7A(2)(b),

- (d)   compliance with that policy,

- (e)   action taken pursuant to any notice under section 7A(4),

- (f)   compliance by the manufacturer with any notice under section 7A(5),

- (g)   the number, size and nature of seizures of which the manufacturer has been given notice by virtue of section 7A(7)(a),

- (h)   the loss of revenue by way of duty under section 2, or VAT, in respect of the products seized, and

- (i)   any other matter that they think relevant.

(3) A manufacturer who is given a penalty notice may require the Commissioners to review the decision to issue the notice; and—

- (a)   a requirement must be imposed by notice in writing given to the Commissioners before the end of the period of 45 days beginning with the date of the penalty notice,

- (b)   the Commissioners shall comply with a requirement given in accordance with paragraph (a),

- (c)   the Commissioners shall confirm, vary or withdraw the penalty notice, and

- (d)   the Commissioners shall be taken to have confirmed the penalty notice unless, within the period of 45 days beginning with the

date of the requirement to conduct the review, they have varied or withdrawn it by notice in writing to the manufacturer.

(4) If following a requirement under subsection (3) the Commissioners confirm or vary the notice (or are taken to have confirmed it) the manufacturer may appeal to a VAT and duties tribunal.

(5) The tribunal may—

- (a)   cancel the penalty notice,

- (b)   reduce the penalty, or

- (c)   confirm the penalty notice.]

NOTES

Section inserted by Finance Act 2006, s 2(1).

[7D Sections 7A to 7C: supplemental

[(1) Payment of a penalty imposed under section 7B(4)(a) shall not be allowed as a deduction in computing income, profits or losses for purposes of income tax or corporation tax.

(2) A penalty may be enforced as a debt due to the Commissioners.

(3) In sections 7A to 7C and this section a reference to a manufacturer of cigarettes or hand-rolling tobacco includes a reference to a person who, in the opinion of the Commissioners—

    (a)   arranges to have cigarettes or hand-rolling tobacco manufactured, and

    (b)   is wholly or partly responsible for the initial supply of the products after manufacture.

(4) Where a manufacturer is a parent undertaking or a subsidiary undertaking (within the meaning of section 258 of the Companies Act 1985 (c 6)) the Commissioners may—

    (a)   treat the parent and its subsidiaries as a single undertaking for the purpose of sections 7A to 7C and this section, and

    (b)   in particular, enforce a penalty imposed on the single undertaking as a debt owed by—

        (i)   the single undertaking,

        (ii)   the parent, or

        (iii)   any of the subsidiaries.

(5) A notice or guidance under section 7A(4) to (6)—

    (a)   may be issued to manufacturers generally or to one or more manufacturers or classes of manufacturer,

    (b)   may be expressed to apply to or in respect of manufacturers generally or only to or in respect of one or more specified manufacturers or classes of manufacturer,

    (c)   may make provision generally or only in relation to specified cases or circumstances,

    (d)   may make different provision in relation to different cases or circumstances, and

    (e)   may be varied, replaced or revoked.

(6) The Treasury may by order—

    (a)   amend the list in section 7B(2) or 7C(2) so as to—

        (i)   add an entry,

        (ii)   remove an entry, or

        (iii)   amend an entry;

    (b)   amend sections 7A to 7C and this section so as to alter the class of tobacco products in relation to which they apply.

(7) An order under subsection (6)—

    (a)   may include transitional, consequential or incidental provision,

    (b)   shall be made by statutory instrument,

    (c)   shall be laid before the House of Commons, and

    (d)   shall cease to have effect unless approved by resolution of the House of Commons within the period of 28 days beginning with the date on which it is laid (disregarding any period of dissolution or prorogation or of adjournment for more than four days).]

NOTES

Section inserted by Finance Act 2006, s 2(1).

8 Charge in cases of default

(1) Where the records or returns kept or made by any person in pursuance of regulations under section 2 or 7 above show that any tobacco product or materials for their manufacture are or have been in his possession or under his control, the Commissioners may from time to time require him to account for those products or materials.

(2) Unless a person required under subsection (1) above to account for any products or materials proves—

(a)   that duty has been paid or secured under section 7 above in respect of the products or, as the case may be, products manufactured from the materials; or

(b)   that the products or materials are being or have been otherwise dealt with in accordance with regulations under section 2 or 7 above,

the Commissioners may [assess an amount as duty due from him] under section 2 above in respect of those products or, as the case may be, in respect of such products as in their opinion might reasonably be expected to be manufactured from those materials[, and they may notify him or his representative accordingly].

(3) . . .

___

NOTES

Sub-s (2): words in first pair of square brackets substituted and words in second pair of square brackets added, by the Finance Act 1998 s 20, Sch 2, para 5.

Sub-s (3): repealed by the Finance Act 1994, s 258, Sch 26, Pt III.

___

[8A Fiscal marks: introductory

Fiscal marking applies to tobacco products that are—

(a)   cigarettes, or

(b)   hand-rolling tobacco.]

___

NOTES

Inserted by the Finance Act 2000 s 14.

___

[8B Power to alter range of products to which fiscal marking applies

(1) The Commissioners may by order made by statutory instrument amend section 8A above for the purpose of causing fiscal marking—

(a)   to apply to any description of tobacco products to which it does not apply, or

(b)   to cease to apply to any description of tobacco products to which it does apply.

(2) Where fiscal marking applies to any description of tobacco products, the Commissioners may by regulations provide that fiscal marking does not apply to such products of that description as are of a description specified in the regulations.

(3) A statutory instrument containing (whether alone or with other provisions) an order under subsection (1)(a) above shall not be made unless a draft of the instrument has been laid before, and approved by a resolution of, each House of Parliament.

(4) A statutory instrument that—

(a)   contains (whether alone or with other provisions) an order under subsection (1) above, and

(b)   is not subject to any requirement that a draft of the instrument be laid before and approved by a resolution of each House of Parliament, shall be subject to annulment in pursuance of a resolution of either House of Parliament.]

NOTES

Inserted by the Finance Act 2000 s 14.

[8C Fiscal mark regulations

(1)   The Commissioners may make provision by regulations—

(a)   requiring the carrying of fiscal marks by tobacco products to which fiscal marking applies, and

(b)   as to such matters relating to fiscal marks as appear to the Commissioners to be necessary or expedient.

(2)   In this Act "fiscal mark" means a mark carried by tobacco products indicating all or any of the following—

(a)   that excise duty has been paid on the products;

(b)   the rate at which excise duty was paid on the products;

(c)   the amount of excise duty paid on the products;

(d)   when excise duty was paid on the products;

(e)   that sale of the products—

(i)   is only permissible on dates ascertainable from the mark;

(ii)   is not permissible after (or on or after) a date so ascertainable;

(iii)   is not permissible before (or before or on) a date so ascertainable.

(3)   Regulations under this section may, in particular, make provision about—

(a)   the contents of a fiscal mark;

(b)   the appearance of a fiscal mark;

(c)   in the case of tobacco products that have more than one layer of packaging, which of the layers is (or are) to carry a fiscal mark;

(d)   the positioning of a fiscal mark on the packaging of any tobacco products;

(e)   when tobacco products are required to carry a fiscal mark.

(4)   Regulations under this section may make different provision for different cases.]

NOTES

Inserted by the Finance Act 2000 s 14.

[8D Fiscal marks: public notices

(1)   The Commissioners may by notices published by them regulate any of the matters mentioned in paragraphs (a) to (d) of section 8C(3) above.

(2)   A notice under this section may provide for provision made by regulations under section 8C above to have effect subject to provisions of the notice.

(3)   A notice under this section may make different provision for different cases.]

NOTES

Inserted by the Finance Act 2000 s 14.

[8E Failure to comply with fiscal mark regulations and public notices

(1)   This section applies if a person fails to comply with any requirement imposed by or under—

(a)   regulations made under section 8C above, or

(b)   a notice published under section 8D above.

(2)   Any article in respect of which the person fails to comply with the requirement shall be liable to forfeiture.

(3)   The person's failure to comply shall attract a penalty under section 9 of the Finance Act 1994 (civil penalties).

(4)   The Commissioners may by regulations make such provision as is mentioned in subsection (5) below about the calculation of the penalty in a case where the failure involves post-dating of any tobacco products.

For this purpose "post-dating" means that the products carry a fiscal mark ("the later period mark") that—

(a)   is not one they are required to carry by virtue of this Act, and

(b)   is one they would be required to carry by virtue of this Act if the requirement to pay the duty charged on them under section 2 above took effect at a time later than that at which it in fact takes effect.

(5)   The provision that may be made by regulations under subsection (4) above is for the penalty to be calculated by reference to the duty currently charged on the products.

For this purpose "the duty currently charged" on the products is the amount of the duty charged under section 2 above that would be payable on the products if the requirement to pay the duty took effect at the time of the failure.]

NOTES

Inserted by the Finance Act 2000 s 14.

[8F Sale of marked tobacco when not permitted: penalties

(1)   This section applies if provision made by or under—

(a)   regulations made under section 8C above, or

(b)   a notice published under section 8D above,

provides for any tobacco products to carry a period of sale mark.

(2)   In this section—

"a period of sale mark" means a fiscal mark indicating any of the matters mentioned in subsection (2)(e) of section 8C above; and

"prohibited time", in relation to tobacco products that carry a period of sale mark, means a time when, according to the mark, sale of the products is not permissible.

(3)   If—

(a)   a person sells by way of retail sale, or exposes for retail sale, any tobacco products that carry a period of sale mark, and

(b)   he so sells or exposes the products at a prohibited time,

his so selling or exposing the products shall attract a penalty under section 9 of the Finance Act 1994 (civil penalties) and the products are liable to forfeiture.]

NOTES

Inserted by the Finance Act 2000 s 14.

[8G Offences: possession and sale etc of unmarked tobacco

(1)   In this section "unmarked products" means tobacco products that are subject to fiscal marking but do not carry a compliant duty-paid fiscal mark.

---

(2)   For the purposes of this section "duty-paid fiscal mark" means a fiscal mark carried by tobacco products indicating that excise duty has been paid on the products.

(3)   For the purposes of this section a duty-paid fiscal mark carried by tobacco products of any description is "compliant" if it complies with all relevant requirements for any duty-paid fiscal mark that by virtue of this Act is required to be carried by such tobacco products of that description as are by virtue of this Act required to carry such a mark.

For this purpose "relevant requirement" means a requirement, imposed by virtue of this Act, as to any of the matters mentioned in paragraphs (a) to (d) of section 8C(3) above (contents, appearance and positioning etc of fiscal marks).

(4)   If a person—

(a)   is in possession of, transports or displays, or

(b)   sells, offers for sale or otherwise deals in,

unmarked products then, except in such cases as may be prescribed in regulations made by the Commissioners, that person commits an offence and the products are liable to forfeiture.

(5)   It is a defence for a person charged with an offence under subsection (4) above to prove that the unmarked products were not required by virtue of this Act to carry a duty paid fiscal mark.

(6)   A person guilty of an offence under subsection (4) above shall be liable on summary conviction to a fine not exceeding level 5 on the standard scale.]

NOTES

Inserted by the Finance Act 2000 s 14.

[8H Offences: use of premises for sale of unmarked tobacco

(1)   A manager of premises commits an offence if he suffers the premises to be used for the sale of unmarked products.

In this section "unmarked products" has the same meaning as in section 8G above.

(2)   It is a defence for a person charged with an offence under subsection (1) above to prove that the unmarked products were not required by virtue of this Act to carry a duty-paid fiscal mark.

For this purpose "duty-paid fiscal mark" has the same meaning as in section 8G above.

(3)   A person guilty of an offence under subsection (1) above shall be liable on summary conviction to a fine not exceeding level 5 on the standard scale.

(4)   A court by or before which a person is convicted of an offence under subsection (1) above may make an order prohibiting the use of the premises in question for the sale of tobacco products during a period specified in the order.

(5)   The period specified in an order under subsection (4) above shall not exceed six months; and the first day of the period shall be the day specified as such in the order.

(6)   A manager of premises commits an offence if he suffers the premises to be used in breach of an order under subsection (4) above.

(7)   A person guilty of an offence under subsection (6) above shall be liable on summary conviction to a fine not exceeding level 5 on the standard scale.

(8)   For the purposes of this section a person is a manager of premises if he—

(a)   is entitled to control their use,

(b)   is entrusted with their management, or

(c)   is in charge of them.]

NOTES

Inserted by the Finance Act 2000 s 14.

[8J Interfering with fiscal marks: penalties

(1)   This section applies where a person—

(a)   alters or overprints any fiscal mark carried by any tobacco products in compliance with any provision made under this Act, or

(b)   causes any such mark to be altered or overprinted.

(2)   His altering or overprinting of the mark, or his causing it to be altered or overprinted, shall attract a penalty under section 9 of the Finance Act 1994 (civil penalties).

(3)   The products that carried the mark shall be liable to forfeiture.

(4)   The penalty under subsection (2) above shall be calculated by reference to the duty currently charged on the products.

For this purpose "the duty currently charged" on the products is the amount of the duty charged under section 2 above that would be payable on the products if the requirement to pay the duty took effect at the time of the conduct attracting the penalty.]

NOTES

Inserted by the Finance Act 2000 s 14.

9 Regulations

[(1)]   Any power to make regulations under this Act shall be exercisable by statutory instrument and any statutory instrument by which the power is exercised shall be subject to annulment in pursuance of a resolution of either House of Parliament.

[(2)   Regulations under this Act—

(a)   may enable the Commissioners to dispense with compliance with a provision of the regulations (whether absolutely or conditionally),

(b)   may make provision generally or only in relation to specified cases or circumstances,

(c)   may make different provision in relation to different cases or circumstances, and

(d)   may include transitional, consequential or incidental provision.]

NOTES

Sub-s (1): numbered as such by the Finance Act 2006, s 2(2).

Sub-s (2): inserted by the Finance Act 2006, s 2(2).

10 Interpretation

(1)   In this Act—

"hand-rolling tobacco" has the meaning given by section 1(2) above; and

"tobacco products" has the meaning given by section 1(1) above.

(2)   This Act and the other Acts included in the Customs and Excise Acts 1979 shall be construed as one Act but where a provision of this Act refers to this Act that reference is not to be construed as including a reference to any of the others.

(3) Any expression used in this Act or in any instrument made under this Act to which a meaning is given by any other Act included in the Customs and Excise Acts 1979 has, except where the context otherwise requires, the same meaning in this Act or in any such instrument as in that Act; and for ease of reference the Table below indicates the expressions used in this Act to which a meaning is given by any other Act—

Customs and Excise Management Act 1979

"the Commissioners"
"the Customs and Excise Acts 1979"
"goods"
"importer"
"shipped"
"stores".

11 Repeals, savings and transitional and consequential provisions

(1) The enactments specified in Schedule 2 to this Act are hereby repealed to the extent specified in the third column of that Schedule, but subject to the provision at the end of that Schedule.

(2) Any provision of this Act relating to anything done or required or authorised to be done under or by reference to that provision or any other provision of this Act shall have effect as if any reference to that provision, or that other provision, as the case may be, included a reference to the corresponding provision of the enactments repealed by this Act.

(3) . . .

(4) Nothing in this section shall be taken as prejudicing the operation of sections 15 to 17 of the Interpretation Act 1978 (which relate to the effect of repeals).

NOTES

Sub-s (3): repealed by the Finance Act 1996, s 205, Sch 41, Pt III.

12 Citation and commencement

(1) This Act may be cited as the Tobacco Products Duty Act 1979 and is included in the Acts which may be cited as the Customs and Excise Acts 1979.

(2) This Act shall come into operation on 1st April 1979.

SCHEDULES

SCHEDULE 1

Section 2(1)

[TABLE

1	Cigarettes	An amount equal to 22 per cent of the retail price plus £108.65 per thousand cigarettes.
2	Cigars	£158.24 per kilogram.
3	Hand-rolling tobacco	£113.74 per kilogram.
4	Other smoking tobacco and chewing tobacco	£69.57 per kilogram.]

NOTES

This table is substituted by the Finance Act 2007, s 6(1).

(Sch 2 contains repeals.)

EXCISE DUTIES (SURCHARGES OR REBATES) ACT 1979

(1979 c 8)

An Act to consolidate the provisions of section 9 of and Schedules 3 and 4 to the Finance Act 1961 with the provisions amending them

[22 February 1979]

1 Surcharges or rebates of amounts due for excise duties

(1) This section applies to the following groups of excise duties, namely—

    (a)   those chargeable in respect of spirits . . ., beer, wine, made-wine and cider;

    [(b)   those chargeable by virtue of the Hydrocarbon Oil Duties Act 1979;]

    (c)   all other duties of excise except—

        (i)   that chargeable on tobacco products;

        (ii)   those payable on a licence; and

        (iii)   those with respect to which the Parliament of Northern Ireland would, if the Northern Ireland Constitution Act 1973 had not been passed, have had power to make laws.

(2) [The Treasury may, by an order applying to one or more of the [duties to which this section applies, provide for an adjustment—

    (a)   of any liability to such a duty; and

    (b)   of any right]] to a drawback, rebate or allowance in connection with such a duty,

by the addition to or deduction from the amount payable or allowable of such percentage, not exceeding 10 per cent, as may be specified in the order.

(3) The adjustment under this section of a liability to duty shall be made where the duty becomes due while the order is in force with respect to it . . .

(4) The adjustment under this section of a right to any drawback, rebate or allowance in respect of a duty or goods charged with a duty shall be made where the right arises while the order is in force with respect to the duty (whenever the duty became due); but in calculating the amount to be adjusted any adjustment under this section of the liability to the duty shall be disregarded.

(5) A repayment of any duty within a group to which this section applies or of drawback or allowance in respect of such a duty or goods chargeable with such a duty shall be calculated by reference to the amount actually paid or allowed (after effect was given to any adjustment falling to be made under this section) but save as aforesaid this section does not require the adjustment of any such repayment.

(6) Subsection (5) above shall apply to any payment under section 94 or 95 of the Customs and Excise Management Act 1979 (deficiency in goods in or from warehouse) in the case of goods warehoused on drawback which could not lawfully be entered for home use (being a payment of an amount equal to the drawback and any allowance paid in respect of the goods) as if it were a repayment of drawback or allowance.

(7) The preceding provisions of this section shall apply to repayments of duty under the following provisions of the Hydrocarbon Oil Duties Act 1979—

    (a)   section 9(4) (repayment of duty on oil put to an industrial use which would have qualified it for duty-free delivery);

    (b)   section 17 (relief for heavy oil used by horticultural producers);

    (c)   . . .;

    (d)   section 19 (relief for oil etc used in . . ., lifeboats and lifeboat launching gear).

as if the repayments were drawbacks and not repayments.

NOTES

Sub-s (1): words omitted from para (a) repealed, and para (b) substituted, by the Finance Act 1993, ss 11 (4), (5), 213, Sch 23, Pt I(4).

Sub-s (2): words in first (outer) pair of square brackets substituted by the Finance Act 1980, s 10(2); words in second (inner) pair of square brackets substituted by the Finance Act 1982, s 10(1).

Sub-s (3): words omitted repealed by the Finance Act 2002, ss 12(1), 141, Sch 4, Pt 2, para 11, Sch 40, Pt 1(4).

Sub-s (7): para (c) and words omitted in para (d) repealed by the Finance Act 1996, s 205, Sch 41, Pt I.

2 Orders under s 1

(1) The following provisions of this section shall have effect with respect to orders under section 1 above.

[(2) An order shall cease to be in force at the expiration of a period of one year from the date on which it takes effect unless continued in force by a further order.]

[(3) An order—

    (a)   may specify different percentages for different cases; but

    (b)   may not provide for both an addition to any amount payable and a deduction from any other amount payable.]

(5) An order may be made so as to come into operation at different times of day for different duties, whether or not within the same group.

(6) The power to make an order shall be exercisable by statutory instrument.

[(7) A statutory instrument containing an order which, [—

    (a)   specifies a percentage by way of addition to any amount payable or increases a percentage so specified; or

    (b)   withdraws or reduces a percentage specified by way of deduction from any amount payable,]

shall be laid before the House of Commons after being made; and unless the order is approved by that House before the expiration of twenty-eight days beginning with the date on which it was made, it shall cease to have effect on the expiration of that period, but without prejudice to anything previously done under it or to the making of a new order.

In reckoning any such period no account shall be taken of any time during which Parliament is dissolved or prorogued or during which the House of Commons is adjourned for more than four days.

(8) A statutory instrument containing an order to which subsection (7) above does not apply shall be subject to annulment in pursuance of a resolution of the House of Commons.]

NOTES

Sub-s (2): substituted by the Finance Act 1980, s 10(3).

Sub-s (3): substituted for the original sub-ss (3), (4) by the Finance Act 1982, s 10(2).

Sub-s (7), (8): substituted for the original sub-ss (7)–(9) by the Finance Act 1980, s 10(4); words in square brackets in sub-s (7) substituted by the Finance Act 1982, s 10(3).

3 Application of certain enactments

(1)   The enactments relating to the collection or recovery or otherwise to the management of any duty within a group to which section 1 above applies shall apply to the amount of any adjustment under that section as if it were duty, drawback, rebate or allowance, as the case may be.

(2)   For the purposes of subsections (1) and (2) of section 10 of the Finance Act 1901 (adjustment of contract prices and variation of duties) the beginning or ending of a period during which an order under section 1 above is in force with respect to any duty, or the variation of a percentage specified in such an order, shall be treated as an increase or decrease (as the case may require) of that duty; and references in those subsections to an amount paid on account of an increase of duty, to having had the benefit of a decrease of duty, and to the amount of the decrease of duty shall be construed accordingly.

(3)   . . .

NOTES

Sub-s (3): repealed by the Isle of Man Act 1979, s 14(5), Sch 2.

4 Interpretation, consequential amendments, repeals and saving

(1)   Any expression used in this Act and in any Act included in the Customs and Excise Acts 1979 has the same meaning in this Act as in that Act.

(2)   The enactments specified in Schedule 1 to this Act shall be amended in accordance with the provisions of that Schedule.

(3)   The enactments specified in Schedule 2 to this Act are hereby repealed to the extent specified in the third column of that Schedule.

(4)   If at the commencement of this Act an order under section 9 of the Finance Act 1961 is in force, the order shall have effect as if made under this Act.

5 Citation and commencement

(1)   This Act may be cited as the Excise Duties (Surcharges or Rebates) Act 1979.

(2)   This Act shall come into operation on 1st April 1979.

(Sch 1: para 1 repealed by the Statute Law (Repeals) Act 1986; paras 2, 3 outside the scope of this work; Sch 2 contains repeals.)

ISLE OF MAN ACT 1979

(1979 c 58)

ARRANGEMENT OF SECTIONS

An Act to make such amendments of the law relating to customs and excise, value added tax, car tax and the importation and exportation of goods as are required for giving effect to an Agreement between the government of the United Kingdom and the government of the Isle of Man signed on 15th October 1979; to make other amendments as respects the Isle of Man in the law relating to those matters; to provide for the transfer of functions vested in the Lieutenant Governor of the Isle of Man or, as respects that Island, in the Commissioners of Customs and Excise; and for purposes connected with those matters

[20 December 1979]

1 Common duties

(1)   Subject to subsection (2) below, in this Act "common duties" means—

(a)   customs duties chargeable on goods imported into the United Kingdom or the Isle of Man;

(b)   excise duties chargeable on goods . . . imported into or produced in the United Kingdom or the Isle of Man;

(c)   pool betting duty chargeable under the law of the United Kingdom or the Isle of Man;

[(ca)   lottery duty chargeable under the law of the United Kingdom or the Isle of Man;]

(d)   value added tax chargeable under the law of the United Kingdom or the Isle of Man except tax chargeable in accordance with [section [23 of the Value Added Tax Act 1994]] (gaming machines);

(e)   . . .

(2)   The Treasury may by order amend subsection (1) above by adding or deleting any duty or tax which is under the care and management of the Commissioners of Customs and Excise (in this Act referred to as "the Commissioners") or any corresponding duty or tax chargeable under the law of the Isle of Man; and any such order may apply to a duty or tax generally or in such cases or subject to such restrictions as may be specified in the order.

(3)   The power to make orders under subsection (2) above shall be exercisable by statutory instrument subject to annulment in pursuance of a resolution of the House of Commons.

NOTES

Sub-s (1): words omitted from para (b) repealed by the Excise Duty (Amendment of the Isle of Man Act 1979) Order 1994, SI 1994/3041; para (ca) inserted by the Excise Duty (Amendment of the Isle of Man Act 1979) Order 1999, SI 1999/2925, art 2; words in first (outer) pair of square brackets in para (d) substituted by the Value Added Tax Act 1983, s 50(1), Sch 9, para 3(a); words in second (inner) pair of square brackets substituted by the Value Added Tax Act 1994, s 100(1), Sch 14, para 7(1); para (e) repealed by Statute Law (Repeals) Act 2004 s 1(1), Sch 1 Part 9.

Orders: the Excise Duty (Amendment of the Isle of Man Act 1979) Order 1994, SI 1994/3041.

---

2 Isle of Man share of common duties

(1)   Of the moneys standing to the credit of the General Account of the Commissioners an amount ascertained for each financial year in accordance with

subsection (2) below shall be paid by the Commissioners, at such times and in such manner as they may determine, to the Treasurer of the Isle of Man.

(2) There shall be calculated in such manner as the Treasury may direct—

(a) the amount of common duties, whether collected in the United Kingdom or the Isle of Man, which is attributable to goods consumed or used in the Island, to services supplied in the Island or (as respects pool betting duty) to bets placed by persons in the Island;

(b) the cost incurred by the Commissioners in collecting the amount so attributable together with the amount of any drawback or repayment referable to that amount;

and the amount arrived at by deducting from the amount calculated under paragraph (a) above the amount calculated under paragraph (b) above shall be known as the net Isle of Man share of common duties; and the amount mentioned in subsection (1) above shall be the excess of the net Isle of Man share of common duties over the common duties collected in the Island.

(3) For the purposes of this section the amount of common duties collected in the Isle of Man and the United Kingdom, or in the Isle of Man, shall be calculated by reference to the amount so collected in respect of such duties after giving effect to any addition or deduction provided for under section 1 of the Excise Duties (Surcharges or Rebates) Act 1979 or any Isle of Man equivalent.

(4) The Commissioners shall for each financial year prepare, in such form and manner as the Treasury may direct, an account showing the payments made by them under this section and shall send it, not later than the end of November in the following financial year, to the Comptroller and Auditor General, who shall examine and certify the account.

(5) The Comptroller and Auditor General shall send every account examined and certified by him under this section and his report thereon to the Treasury and a copy of every such account and report to the Treasurer of the Isle of Man; and the Treasury shall lay copies of the account and report before Parliament.

3 Recovery of common duties chargeable in Isle of Man

(1) Any liability to pay an amount on account of a common duty chargeable under the law of the Isle of Man shall, to the extent to which it has not been discharged or enforced there, be enforceable in the United Kingdom as if it were a liability to pay an amount on account of the corresponding common duty chargeable under the law of the United Kingdom.

(2) Any amount recoverable by the Commissioners from any person under subsection (1) above may be set off against any amount recoverable by him from the Commissioners on account of a common duty chargeable under the law of the United Kingdom.

4 Enforcement of Isle of Man judgments for common duties

(1) Subject to subsection (2) below, the provisions of sections 2 to 5 of the Foreign Judgments (Reciprocal Enforcement) Act 1933 shall have effect in relation to any judgment or order given or made by the High Court of Justice of the Isle of Man under which an amount is payable on account of—

(a) a common duty chargeable under the law of the Island; or

(b) a fine or penalty imposed in connection with such a duty,

as if the judgment or order were a judgment to which Part I of that Act applied.

(2) Subsection (1) above does not apply to a judgment or order given or made on appeal from a lower court but, except when given or made in criminal proceedings, applies notwithstanding that it is subject to appeal or that an appeal against it is pending.

(3) In their application by virtue of subsection (1) above the provisions there mentioned shall have effect—

    (a)   with the omission of so much of section 2(1) as imposes a time-limit for applications for registration;

    (b)   with the omission of section 4(1)(a)(v) and (vi); and

    (c)   as if the Commissioners were the judgment creditor and any criminal proceedings in which the judgment or order was given or made were an action.

(4) The reference in subsection (1) above to sections 2 to 5 of the said Act of 1933 includes a reference to so much of sections 11 to 13 of that Act as is relevant to those sections and the definition of "appeal" in section 11 shall apply for the purposes of subsection (2) above.

(5) The reference in subsection (1) above to the High Court of Justice of the Isle of Man includes a reference to the Court of General Gaol Delivery.

5 Offences relating to common duties etc

(1) Any summons or other process requiring a person in the Isle of Man to appear before a court in the United Kingdom—

    (a)   to answer a charge that he has committed an offence relating to a common duty chargeable under the law of the United Kingdom or to the importation or exportation of anything into or from the United Kingdom; or

    (b)   to give evidence or to produce any document or thing in proceedings for any such offence,

may be served by being sent to him by registered post or the recorded delivery service.

(2) In relation to proceedings for any such offence as is mentioned in subsection (1) above—

    (a)   [section 97 of the Magistrates' Courts Act 1980] (summons to witness and warrant for his arrest) shall have effect as if the reference in subsection (1) of that section to a person in England and Wales included a reference to a person in the Isle of Man;

    (b)   in Scotland a warrant for the citation of accused persons and witnesses shall include a warrant to cite accused persons and witnesses in the Isle of Man.

(3) In relation to proceedings for any such offence as is mentioned in subsection (1) above—

    (a)   [section 9 of the Criminal Justice Act 1967 and section 102 of the Magistrates' Courts Act 1980] (admission of written statements) shall apply also to written statements made in the Isle of Man but with the omission of subsections (2)(b) and (3A) of [section 102] and subsections (2)(b) and (3A) of section 9;

    (b)   section 1 of the Criminal Justice (Miscellaneous Provisions) Act (Northern Ireland) 1968 and section 3 of the Criminal Procedure (Committal for Trial) Act (Northern Ireland) 1968 (which contain corresponding provisions) shall apply also to written statements made in the Isle of Man but with the omission of subsection (2)(b) of section 1 and subsection (2)(c) of section 3.

(4) Subject to subsection (5) below, a warrant issued in the Isle of Man for the arrest of—

    (a)   a person charged with an offence relating to a common duty chargeable under the law of the Isle of Man or to the importation or exportation of anything into or from the Island; or

(b)   a person required to give evidence or to produce any document or thing in proceedings for any such offence,

may be executed in England and Wales by any constable acting within his police area, in Scotland by any officer of law as defined in [section 307(1) of the Criminal Procedure (Scotland) Act 1995] and in Northern Ireland by any member of the Royal Ulster Constabulary or the Royal Ulster Constabulary Reserve.

(5)   A warrant, other than one for the arrest of a person charged with an offence punishable with at least two years' imprisonment, shall not be executed under subsection (4) above unless it has been endorsed for execution under that subsection by a justice of the peace in England, Wales, Scotland or Northern Ireland, as the case may be; and any warrant which purports to have been issued as mentioned in that subsection may be so endorsed without further proof.

(6)   A warrant for the arrest of a person charged with an offence may be executed by a constable under subsection (4) above notwithstanding that it is not in his possession at the time; but the warrant shall, on demand of that person, be shown to him as soon as practicable.

(7)   Subsections (1) and (4) above are without prejudice to any other enactment enabling any process to be served or executed otherwise than as provided in those subsections.

(8)   References in this section to a warrant for the arrest of any person include references to any process for that purpose available under the law of the Isle of Man; and references to an offence relating to a common duty or to importation or exportation include references to any offence which relates to any of those matters whether or not it is an offence under a provision dealing specifically with that matter.

NOTES

Sub-ss (2), (3): words in square brackets substituted by the Magistrates' Courts Act 1980, s 154, Sch 7, para 198.

Sub-s (4): words in square brackets substituted by the Criminal Procedure (Consequential Provisions) (Scotland) Act 1995, ss 4, 5, Sch 3, Sch 4, para 25, subject to transitional provisions and savings.

6 Value added tax

(1)   For the purpose of giving effect to any Agreement between the government of the United Kingdom and the government of the Isle of Man whereby both countries are to be treated as a single area for the purposes of value added tax charged under [the Value Added Tax Act [1994]] and value added tax charged under the corresponding Act of Tynwald, Her Majesty may by Order in Council make provision for securing that tax is charged under [the Act of [1994]] as if all or any of the references in it to the United Kingdom included both the United Kingdom and the Isle of Man but so that tax is not charged under both Acts in respect of the same transaction.

(2)   An Order in Council under this section may make provision—

(a)   for determining, or enabling the Commissioners to determine, under which Act a person is to be registered and for transferring a person registered under one Act to the register kept under the other;

(b)   for treating a person who is a taxable person for the purposes of the Act of Tynwald as a taxable person for all or any of the purposes of [the Act of [1994]];

(c)   for extending any reference in [the Act of [1994]] to tax under that Act so as to include tax under the Act of Tynwald;

(d)   for treating any requirement imposed by or under either Act as a requirement imposed by or under the other;

(e)   for treating any permission, direction, notice, determination or other thing given, made or done under the Act of Tynwald by the Isle of Man authority corresponding to the Commissioners as given, made or done by the Commissioners under [the Act of [1994]];

(f)   for enabling the Commissioners to determine for the purposes of [section [43]] of [the Act of [1994]] (groups of companies) which member of a group is to be the representative member in cases where supplies are made both in the United Kingdom and the Isle of Man;

(g)   for modifying or excluding, as respects goods removed from the Isle of Man to the United Kingdom or from the United Kingdom to the Isle of Man, any provision relating to importation or exportation contained in [the Act of [1994]] or in the customs and excise Acts as applied by that Act;

(h)   for any supplementary, incidental or transitional matter.

(3) An Order in Council under this section may make such modifications of any provision contained in or having effect under any Act of Parliament relating to value added tax as appears to Her Majesty to be necessary or expedient for the purposes of the Order.

(4) While an Order in Council under this section is in force and without prejudice to the powers conferred by the foregoing provisions—

(a)   [section [30(10)]] of [the Act of [1994]] (forfeiture of zero-rated goods) shall have effect as if the reference to goods zero-rated under the regulations there mentioned included a reference to goods zero-rated under any corresponding regulations made under the Act of Tynwald;

(b)   [paragraph 10(3) of [Schedule 11] to] [the Act of [1994]] (search of premises where offence is suspected) shall have effect as if the references to an offence in connection with the tax included references to an offence in connection with the tax charged under the Act of Tynwald;

(c)   [section [72(8)]] of [the Act of [1994]] (course of conduct involving offences) shall have effect as if the reference to offences under the provisions there mentioned included a reference to offences under the corresponding provisions of the Act of Tynwald.

(5) Provision may be made by or under an Act of Tynwald for purposes corresponding to those of this section and of any Order in Council made under it.

NOTES

Sub-s (1): words in first and third (outer) pairs of square brackets substituted by the Value Added Tax Act 1983, s 50, Sch 9, para 3; words in second and fourth (inner) pairs of square brackets substituted by the Value Added Tax Act 1994 s 100(1), Sch 14, para 7(2)(a).

Sub-s (2): words in first (outer) pair of square brackets in paras (b), (c), (g), and words in first and third (outer) pairs of square brackets in para (f), substituted by the Value Added Tax Act 1983, s 50, Sch 9, para 3; words in second (inner) pair of square brackets in paras (b), (c), (g), and words in second and fourth (inner) pairs of square brackets in para (f), substituted by the Value Added Tax Act 1994 s 100(1), Sch 14, para 7(2)(a), (b).

Sub-s (4): words in first and third (outer) pairs of square brackets in paras (a)–(c) substituted by the Value Added Tax Act 1983, s 50, Sch 9, para 3; words in second and fourth (inner) pairs of square brackets in paras (a)–(c) substituted by the Value Added Tax Act 1994 s 100(1), Sch 14, para 7(2)(a), (c)–(e).

Orders in Council: the Value Added Tax (Isle of Man) Order 1982, SI 1982/1067; the Value Added Tax (Isle of Man) (No 2) Order 1982, SI 1982/1068.

7 Car Tax

(1) For the purpose of giving effect to any Agreement between the government of the United Kingdom and the government of the Isle of Man whereby both countries are to be treated as a single area for the purposes of the car tax charged under the Finance Act 1972 [or the Car Tax Act 1983] and the car tax charged under the corresponding Act of Tynwald, Her Majesty may by Order in Council make provision for securing that tax is charged under [the Act of 1983] as if all or any of the references in it to the United Kingdom included both the United Kingdom and the Isle of Man but so that tax is not charged under both Acts in respect of the same vehicle.

(2) An Order in Council under this section may make provision—

(a) for determining, or enabling the Commissioners to determine, under which Act a person is to be registered and for transferring a person registered under one Act to the register kept under the other;

(b) for treating a person who is registered for the purposes of the Act of Tynwald as registered for all or any of the purposes of [the Act of 1983];

(c) for extending any reference in [the Act of 1983] to tax under that Act so as to include tax under the Act of Tynwald;

(d) for treating any requirement imposed by or under either Act as a requirement imposed by or under the other;

(e) for treating any permission, direction, notice, determination or other thing given, made or done under the Act of Tynwald by the Isle of Man authority corresponding to the Commissioners as given, made or done by the Commissioners under [the Act of 1983];

(f) for modifying or excluding, as respects a vehicle removed from the Isle of Man to the United Kingdom or from the United Kingdom to the Isle of Man, any provision of [the Act of 1983] which relates to importation or exportation;

(g) for any supplementary, incidental or transitional matter.

(3) An Order in Council under this section may make such modifications of any provision contained in or having effect under any Act of Parliament relating to car tax as appears to Her Majesty to be necessary or expedient for the purposes of the Order.

(4) While an Order in Council under this section is in force and without prejudice to the powers conferred by the foregoing provisions—

(a) [paragraph 7(3) of Schedule 1 to the Act of 1983] (search of premises where offence is suspected) shall have effect as if the references to an offence in connection with the tax included references to an offence in connection with the tax charged under the Act of Tynwald;

(b) [paragraph 9] of that Schedule (forfeiture of chargeable vehicle if not registered or tax not paid etc.) shall have effect as if references to chargeable vehicles, the registration of a vehicle and tax included references to a chargeable vehicle, the registration of a vehicle and tax within the meaning of the Act of Tynwald.

(5) Provision may be made by or under an Act of Tynwald for purposes corresponding to those of this section and of any Order in Council made under it.

NOTES

Sub-ss (1), (2), (4): words in square brackets inserted or substituted by the Car Tax Act 1983, s 10(2).

Orders in Council: the Car Tax (Isle of Man) Order 1983, SI 1983/140.

8 Removal of goods from Isle of Man to United Kingdom

(1) Except as provided in subsection (2) below, goods removed to the United Kingdom from the Isle of Man shall be deemed for the purposes of the customs and excise Acts not to be imported into the United Kingdom.

(2) Subsection (1) above does not apply to—

(a) goods imported into or produced in the Isle of Man which are of a class or description chargeable with customs or excise duty under the law of the United Kingdom and which have not borne a corresponding duty under the law of the Isle of Man;

(b) goods which were imported into the Isle of Man in contravention of any prohibition or restriction and which are of a class or description the importation of which into the United Kingdom is for the time being subject to a corresponding prohibition or restriction; . . .

(c) any explosives within the meaning of the Explosives Act 1875 on the unloading or landing of which any restriction is for the time being in force under or by virtue of that Act.

(3) The goods referred to in subsection (2)(a) above do not include goods which have been wholly or partly exempted from duty under any Isle of Man equivalent to section 48 of the Customs and Excise Management Act 1979 (relief for goods temporarily imported) or section 13 of the Customs and Excise Duties (General Reliefs) Act 1979 (personal reliefs for imported goods) [or under any Community instrument] but where—

(a) any such exemption was subject to conditions required to be complied with after importation of the goods into the Isle of Man; and

(b) the goods are removed to the United Kingdom,

the customs and excise Acts shall apply to the goods as if they had been imported into the United Kingdom when they were imported into the Isle of Man and as if corresponding conditions had then been imposed under the said section 48 or 13 [or under the Community instrument in question].

(4) For the purposes of subsection (2)(a) above goods of any class or description shall be treated as having borne a corresponding duty under the law of the Isle of Man if they have borne duty under that law at a rate not less than that at which duty was then chargeable under the law of the United Kingdom in respect of goods of that class or description; and where goods have borne duty under the law of the Isle of Man at a lower rate, the duty charged on their importation into the United Kingdom shall be reduced by an amount equal to the duty borne under that law.

NOTES

Sub-s (2): final word "or" in para (b) repealed by Manufacture and Storage of Explosives Regulations, SI 2005/1082 reg 28(1), Sch 5 para 17.

Sub-s (3): words in first pair of square brackets inserted and words in second pair of square brackets added by the Finance Act 1984, s 15(7)(a).

9 Removal of goods from United Kingdom to Isle of Man

(1) Except as provided in . . . [. . . section 21(2) of the Forgery and Counterfeiting Act 1981], goods removed to the Isle of Man from the United Kingdom shall be deemed for the purposes of the customs and excise Acts not to be exported from the United Kingdom.

(2), (3) . . .

(4) Where goods imported into or produced in the United Kingdom have not borne customs or excise duty and would be chargeable with customs or excise duty if

imported into the Isle of Man, the goods shall not be removed from the United Kingdom to the Isle Man until—

    (a)   they have been cleared for that purpose by the proper officer; and

    (b)   security has been given to the satisfaction of the Commissioners for the due delivery of the goods at some port, airport or place of security in the Isle of Man approved for customs and excise purposes under the law of the Island;

but paragraph (b) above shall not apply if the goods are reported on arrival in the United Kingdom for removal to the Isle of Man in the same ship or aircraft and in continuance of the same voyage or flight.

(5)   The goods referred to in subsection (4) above do not include passengers' baggage or goods that have been relieved or exempted from duty under any of the provisions of sections 7 to 11 or 13 of the Customs and Excise Duties (General Reliefs) Act 1979 [or under any Community instrument].

(6)   Any goods removed from the United Kingdom contrary to subsection (4) above shall be liable to forfeiture and any person concerned in the removal of the goods shall be liable on summary conviction to a penalty of [level 3 on the standard scale].

NOTES

Sub-s (1): words in square brackets inserted by the Forgery and Counterfeiting Act 1981, s 21(3); words omitted repealed by the Finance Act 1996, s 205, Sch 41, Pt III.

Sub-ss (2), (3): repealed by the Finance Act 1996, ss 24(e), 205, Sch 41, Pt III.

Sub-s (5): words in square brackets added by the Finance Act 1984, s 15(7)(b).

Sub-s (6): words in square brackets substituted by virtue of the Criminal Justice Act 1982, s 46.

Regulations: the Spirits (Rectifying, Compounding and Drawback) Regulations 1988, SI 1988/1760, as amended by SI 1991/2564.

10 Exchange of information

No obligation as to secrecy or other restriction on the disclosure of information imposed by statute or otherwise shall prevent the Commissioners or any officer of the Commissioners from disclosing information to the Isle of Man customs and excise service for the purpose of facilitating the proper administration of common duties and the enforcement of prohibitions or restrictions on importation or exportation into or from the Isle of Man or the United Kingdom.

11 Transfer of functions to Isle of Man authorities

(1)   Her Majesty may by Order in Council make such modifications in any provision contained in or having effect under any Act of Parliament extending to the Isle of Man as appear to Her Majesty to be appropriate for the purpose of transferring to any authority or person constituted by or having functions under the law of the Island—

    (a)   any functions under that provision of the Lieutenant Governor of the Isle of Man (whether referred to by that title or otherwise) or of a deputy governor of the Island;

    (b)   any functions under that provision, so far as exercisable in relation to the Island, of the Commissioners or an officer of the Commissioners.

(2)   Any statutory instrument made by virtue of this section shall be subject to annulment in pursuance of a resolution of either House of Parliament.

NOTES

Orders in Council: the Isle of Man (Transfer of Functions) Order 1980, SI 1980/399.

12 Proof of Acts of Tynwald etc

(1) Without prejudice to the Evidence (Colonial Statutes) Act 1907, any Act of Tynwald or other instrument forming part of the law of the Isle of Man may, in any proceedings in the United Kingdom relating to a common duty or to importation or exportation into or from the United Kingdom or the Isle of Man, be proved by producing a copy of the Act or instrument authenticated by a certificate purporting to be signed by or on behalf of the Attorney General for the Island.

(2) Any provision contained in or having effect under an Act of Tynwald which—

(a) prescribes the mode or burden of proof with respect to any matter in proceedings relating to a common duty chargeable under the law of the Isle of Man; and

(b) corresponds to a provision of United Kingdom law for similar purposes, shall apply to any proceedings in the United Kingdom relating to that duty.

(3) For the purposes of any proceedings in the United Kingdom relating to a common duty an order may be made under the Bankers' Books Evidence Act 1879 in respect of books and persons in the Isle of Man.

13

(Introduces Sch 1 to this Act.)

14 Short title, interpretation, repeals, commencement and extent

(1) This Act may be cited as the Isle of Man Act 1979.

(2) In this Act—

"the Commissioners" means the Commissioners of Customs and Excise;

"common duties" has the meaning given in section 1 above and "common duty" shall be construed accordingly;

"customs duty" includes any levy or other charge which is treated as a customs duty by section 6 of the European Communities Act 1972.

(3) Any other expression used in this Act which is also used in the Customs and Excise Management Act 1979 has the same meaning as in that Act.

(4) Without prejudice to section 2(3) above,—

(a) any addition to an excise duty by virtue of section 1 of the Excise Duties (Surcharges or Rebates) Act 1979 or any Isle of Man equivalent; and

(b) any sum recoverable as a debt due to the Crown under [paragraph 5(3) of Schedule 11 to the Value Added Tax Act 1994] (sums shown in invoices as value added tax) or any Isle of Man equivalent,

shall be treated for the purposes of this Act as an amount of excise duty or value added tax chargeable under the law of the United Kingdom or, as the case may be, the Isle of Man.

(5) The enactments mentioned in Schedule 2 to this Act (which include spent provisions) are hereby repealed to the extent specified in the third column of that Schedule.

(6) Subject to subsection (7) below, this Act shall come into force on 1st April 1980.

(7) Sections 6, 7, 10 and 11 above shall come into force on the passing of this Act but no Order in Council shall be made under section 6, 7 or 11, and no provision shall

by virtue of section 6(5) or 7(5) be made by or under an Act of Tynwald, so as to come into force before 1st April 1980.

(8)   Except for sections 6, 7, 11 and this section, this Act does not extend to the Isle of Man as part of the law of the Island.

NOTES

Sub-s (4): words in square brackets in para (b) substituted by the Value Added Tax Act 1994, s 100(1), Sch 14, para 7(3).

(Sch 1: para 1 repealed by the Value Added Tax Act 1983, s 50(2), Sch 11; paras 2–8, 12–24 amend the Customs and Excise Management Act 1979, ss 1, 17, 21, 34–36, 43, 63, 64, 66, 69, 70, 74, 78, 83, 90, 92, 159, Sch 3; paras 9–11 repealed with savings by the Finance Act 1981, s 139, Sch 19, Pt II; paras 25–28 amend the Customs and Excise Duties (General Reliefs) Act 1979, ss 7, 8, 10, 11; paras 29, 31–33 amend the Alcoholic Liquor Duties Act 1979, ss 22, 43, 57–59; para 30 repealed by the Finance Act 1993, s 213, Sch 23, Pt I(1); paras 34, 35 repealed by the Finance (No 2) Act 1992, s 82, Sch 18, Pt II; Sch 2 contains repeals.)

FINANCE ACT 1985

(1985 c 54)

An Act to grant certain duties, to alter other duties, and to amend the law relating to the National Debt and the Public Revenue, and to make further provision in connection with Finance

[25 July 1985]

PART I
CUSTOMS AND EXCISE AND VALUE ADDED TAX

CHAPTER I
Customs and Excise

1–4

(Ss 1, 3 superseded; s 2 repealed by the Finance Act 1986, s 114(6), Sch 2, Pt I; s 4(1)–(3), (5)–(8) repealed by the Vehicle and Excise Registration Act 1994, s 65, Sch 5, Pt I; s 4(4) repealed by the Finance Act 1994, s 258, Sch 26, Pt I(1), in relation to licences taken out after 30 November 1993.)

Other provisions

5–9

(Ss 5–8 outside the scope of this work; s 9 repealed by the Vehicle Excise and Registration Act 1994, s 65, Sch 5, Pt I.)

10 Computer records etc

(1)   Any provision made by or under any enactment which requires a person, in connection with any assigned matter,—

   (a)   to produce, furnish or deliver any document, or cause any document to be produced, furnished or delivered, or

   (b)   to permit the Commissioners of Customs and Excise (in this section referred to as "the Commissioners") or a person authorised by them—

      (i)   to inspect any document, or

      (ii)   to make or take the extracts from or copies of or remove any document,

shall have effect as if any reference in that provision to a document [were a reference to anything in which information of any description is recorded and any reference to a copy of a document were a reference to anything onto which information is recorded in the document has been copied, by whatever means and whether directly or indirectly].

(2) In connection with any assigned matter, a person authorised by the Commissioners to exercise the powers conferred by this subsection—

    (a)   shall be entitled at any reasonable time to have access to, and inspect and check the operation of, any computer and any associated apparatus or material which is or has been in use in connection with any document to which this subsection applies; and

    (b)   may require—

      (i)   the person by whom or on whose behalf the computer is or has been so used, or

      (ii)   any person having charge of, or otherwise concerned with the operation of, the computer, apparatus or material,

to afford him such reasonable assistance as he may require for the purposes of paragraph (a) above.

(3) Subsection (2) above applies to any document[, within the meaning given by subsection (1) above,] which, in connection with any assigned matter, a person is or may be required by or under any enactment—

    (a)   to produce, furnish or deliver, or cause to be produced, furnished or delivered; or

    (b)   to permit the Commissioners or a person authorised by them to inspect, make or take extracts from or copies of or remove.

(4) Any person who—

    (a)   obstructs a person authorised under subsection (2) above in the exercise of his powers under paragraph (a) of that subsection, or

    (b)   without reasonable excuse fails to comply within a reasonable time with a requirement under paragraph (b) of that subsection,

shall be liable on summary conviction to a penalty of level 4 on the standard scale . . .

(5) In each of the enactments mentioned in subsection (6) below (which create offences in relation, among other matters, to false documents) "document" shall have [the meaning given by subsection (1) above].

(6) The enactments referred to in subsection (5) above are—

    (a)   paragraph 4(1) of Schedule 1 to the Miscellaneous Transferred Excise Duties Act (Northern Ireland) 1972 (false statements and documents in connection with pool betting duty);

    (b)   paragraph 8(1) of Schedule 2 to that Act (false statements and documents in connection with general betting duty);

    (c)   section 167 of the Customs and Excise Management Act 1979 (untrue declarations etc);

    (d)   section 168 of that Act (counterfeit documents etc.);

    (e)   section 15 of the Customs and Excise Duties (General Reliefs) Act 1979 (false statements and documents in connection with reliefs);

    (f)   paragraph 13(3) of Schedule 1 to the Betting and Gaming Duties 1981 (false statements and documents in connection with betting duty);

    (g)   paragraph 7(3) of Schedule 2 to that Act (false statements and documents in connection with gaming licence duty);

(h)   . . .

(7) . . .

(8)   In this section "assigned matter" means any matter which is an assigned matter for the purposes of the Customs and Excise Management Act 1979.

NOTES

Sub-s (4): words omitted repealed by the Statute Law (Repeals) Act 1993.

Sub-ss (1), (3), (5): words in square brackets substituted by the Civil Evidence Act 1995, s 15(1), Sch 1, para 11(2)–(4).

Sub-s (6): para (h) repealed by the Statute Law (Repeals) Act 2004 s 1(1), Sch 1 Part 9.

Sub-s (7): repealed by the Civil Evidence Act 1995, s 15(1), (2), Sch 1, para 11(5), Sch 2.

Modification: section 10 shall not apply in connection with a function relating to a matter to which Commissioners for Revenue and Customs Act 2005 s 7 applies (CRCA 2005 ss 16, 17, Sch 2 para 8).

PART V
MISCELLANEOUS AND SUPPLEMENTARY

98 Short title, interpretation, construction and repeals

(1)   This Act may be cited as the Finance Act 1985.

(2)–(6) . . .

NOTES

Sub-ss (2)–(6): outside the scope of this work.

Part I

EUROPEAN COMMUNITIES (AMENDMENT) ACT 1986

(1986 c 58)

An Act to amend the European Communities Act 1972 so as to include in the definition of "the Treaties" and "the Community Treaties" certain provisions of the Single European Act signed at Luxembourg and The Hague on 17th and 28th February 1986 and extend certain provisions relating to the European Court to any court attached thereto; and to amend references to the Assembly of the European Communities and approve the Single European Act

[7 November 1986]

1, 2

(Amend the European Communities Act 1972, ss 1, 3, 11.)

3 Provisions relating to European Assembly

(1) Subject to subsection (2) below and to the repeals and revocations made by section 4(3) below, any enactment or instrument passed or made before the day on which the Single European Act enters into force shall have effect on and after that day with the substitution—

(a) of a reference to the (or, as the case may be, a) European Parliament for any reference (however worded) to the (or an) Assembly of the European Communities; and

(b) of the words "European Parliamentary" for the word "Assembly" and for the words "European Assembly" wherever that word or those words are used adjectivally with reference to the European Assembly (together with, where necessary) the consequential substitution of "a" for "an").

(2) The provisions on which subsection (1) above operates do not include that subsection itself or subsection (3) below or the long title of this Act but, subject to those exceptions, include—

(a) the long titles of Acts passed before the day mentioned in subsection (1) above;

(b) any provision of an Act or instrument passed or made before that day specifying how that Act or instrument may be cited; and

(c) so much of any Act or instrument so passed or made as uses a mode of citation authorised by another such Act or instrument to refer to that other Act or instrument.

(3) On and after the day mentioned in subsection (1) above the enactments and instruments amended by this section shall have effect as if the Assembly of the European Communities has always been named the European Parliament.

(4) For the purpose of section 6 of the European Assembly Act 1978 the Single European Act is hereby approved.

4 Short title, interpretation and repeals

(1) This Act may be cited as the European Communities (Amendment) Act 1986.

(2) In this Act "the Single European Act" means the Single European Act signed at Luxembourg and The Hague on 17th and 28th February 1986,

(3) . . .

NOTES

Sub-s (3): outside the scope of this work.

FINANCE ACT 1988

(1988 c 39)

An Act to grant certain duties, to alter other duties, and to amend the law relating to the National Debt and the Public Revenue, and to make further provision in connection with Finance

[29 July 1988]

PART I
CUSTOMS AND EXCISE

1–7

(Ss 5–7 outside the scope of this work; ss 2, 3 superseded; s 4(1), (3)(b)–(d), (4), (6)–(9) repealed by the Vehicle Excise and Registration Act 1994, s 65, Sch 5, Pt I; s 4(2) repealed by the Finance Act 1993, s 213, Sch 23, Pt I(6); s 4(3)(a) repealed by the Finance Act 1989, s 187(1), Sch 17, Pt II; s 4(5) repealed by the Finance Act 1991, s 123, Sch 19, Pt IV.)

Management

8 Disclosure of information as to imports

(1) The Commissioners may, for the purpose of supplementing the information as to imported goods which may be made available to persons other than the Commissioners, disclose information to which this section applies to such persons as they think fit.

(2) Such information may be so disclosed on such terms and conditions (including terms and conditions as to the payment of fees or charges to the Commissioners and the making of the information available to other persons) as the Commissioners think fit.

(3) This section applies to information consisting of the names and addresses of persons declared as consignees in entries of imported goods, arranged by reference to such classifications of imported goods as the Commissioners think fit.

(4) This section shall be construed as if it were contained in the Customs and Excise Management Act 1979.

NOTES

Entries: by the Customs and Excise (Single Market etc) Regulations 1992, SI 1992/3095, reg 10(1), Sch 1, para 1, reference in sub-s (3) above to entries of imported goods is to be treated as including an entry of such goods under the Customs Controls on Importation of Goods Regulations 1991, SI 1991/2724, reg 5, as amended by SI 1992/3095, SI 1993/3014.

PART IV
MISCELLANEOUS AND GENERAL

Miscellaneous

149 Short title

This Act may be cited as the Finance Act 1988.

FINANCE ACT 1989

(1989 c 26)

An Act to grant certain duties, to alter other duties, and to amend the law relating to the National Debt and the Public Revenue, and to make further provision in connection with Finance

[27 July 1989]

PART III
MISCELLANEOUS AND GENERAL

Miscellaneous

182 Disclosure of information

(1) A person who discloses any information which he holds or has held in the exercise of tax functions . . . is guilty of an offence if it is information about any matter relevant, for the purposes of [any of those functions—

    (a)   to tax or duty in the case of any identifiable person,

. . .

(2) In this section "tax functions" means functions relating to tax or duty—

    (a)   of the Commissioners, the Board and their officers,

    (b)   of any person carrying out the administrative work of any tribunal mentioned in subsection (3) below, and

    (c)   of any other person providing, or employed in the provision of, services to any person mentioned in paragraph (a) or (b) above.

. . .

(3) The tribunals referred to in subsection (2)(b) above are—

    (a)   the General Commissioners and the Special Commissioners,

    (b)   any value added tax tribunal,

    (c)   . . .

    (d)   any tribunal established under section 463 of the Taxes Act 1970 or section 706 of the Taxes Act 1988 [or section 704 of the Income Tax Act 2007].

(4) A person who discloses any information which—

    (a)   he holds or has held in the exercise of functions—

        (i)   of the Comptroller and Auditor General and any member of the staff of the National Audit Office, . . .

        (ii)   of the Parliamentary Commissioner for Administration and his officers,

        [(iii)   of the Auditor General for Wales and any member of his staff, . . .

        [(iv)   of the Public Services Ombudsman for Wales and any member of his staff, or]

        (v)   of the Scottish Public Services Ombudsman and any member of his staff,]

    (b)   is, or is derived from, information which was held by any person in the exercise of tax functions . . ., and

    (c)   is information about any matter relevant, for the purposes of [tax functions . . .—

        (i)   to tax or duty in the case of any identifiable person,

        . . .

is guilty of an offence.

(5)   Subsections (1) and (4) above do not apply to any disclosure of information—

(a)   with lawful authority,

(b)   with the consent of any person in whose case the information is about a matter relevant to tax or duty . . ., or

(c)   which has been lawfully made available to the public before the disclosure is made.

(6)   For the purposes of this section a disclosure of any information is made with lawful authority if, and only if, it is made—

(a)   by a Crown servant in accordance with his official duty,

(b)   by any other person for the purposes of the function in the exercise of which he holds the information and without contravening any restriction duly imposed by the person responsible,

(c)   to, or in accordance with an authorisation duly given by, the person responsible,

(d)   in pursuance of any enactment or of any order of a court, or

(e)   in connection with the institution of or otherwise for the purposes of any proceedings relating to any matter within the general responsibility of the Commissioners or, as the case requires, the Board,

and in this subsection, "the person responsible" means the Commissioners, the Board, the Comptroller[, the Parliamentary Commissioner, the Auditor General for Wales[, [the Public Services Ombudsman for Wales]] or the Scottish Public Services Ombudsman], as the case requires.

(7)   It is a defence for a person charged with an offence under this section to prove that at the time of the alleged offence—

(a)   he believed that he had lawful authority to make the disclosure in question and had not reasonable cause to believe otherwise, or

(b)   he believed that the information in question had been lawfully made available to the public before the disclosure was made and had no reasonable cause to believe otherwise.

(8)   A person guilty of an offence under this section is liable—

(a)   on conviction on indictment, to imprisonment for a term not exceeding two years or a fine or both, and

(b)   on summary conviction, to imprisonment for a term not exceeding six months or a fine not exceeding the statutory maximum or both.

(9)   No prosecution for an offence under this section shall be instituted in England and Wales or in Northern Ireland except—

(a)   by the Commissioners or the Board, as the case requires, or

(b)   by or with the consent of the Director of Public Prosecutions or, in Northern Ireland, the Director of Public Prosecutions for Northern Ireland.

(10)   In this section—

"the Board" means the Commissioners of Inland Revenue,

"the Commissioners" means the Commissioners of Customs and Excise,

"Crown servant" has the same meaning as in the Official Secrets Act 1989, . . . and

"tax or duty" means any tax or duty within the general responsibility of the Commissioners or the Board.

[(10A)   In this section, in relation to the disclosure of information "identifiable person" means a person whose identity is specified in the disclosure or can be deduced from it.]

(11)   In this section—

(a)   references to the Comptroller and Auditor General include the Comptroller and Auditor General for Northern Ireland,

(b)   references to the National Audit Office include the Northern Ireland Audit Office, and

(c)   references to the Parliamentary Commissioner for Administration include the Health Service Commissioner for England. . ., . . . the Northern Ireland Parliamentary Commissioner for Administration and the Northern Ireland Commissioner for Complaints.

. . .

(12)   This section shall come into force on the repeal of section 2 of the Official Secrets Act 1911.

NOTES

Sub-ss (2ZA), (2A), (11A), and words omitted in sub-ss (1), (4), (5) and (10) are outside the scope of this publication.

Sub-s (1): words s substituted, by the Social Security Contributions (Transfer of Functions, etc) Act 1999, s 6, Sch 6, para 9(1), (2) (subject to savings contained in Sch 8 to that Act).

Sub-s (3): para (c) repealed by the Statute Law (Repeals) Act 2004 s 1(1), Sch 1 Part 5; in para (d), words in square brackets inserted by the Income Tax Act 2007, s 1027, Sch 1, Pt 2, paras 278, 282. This amendment has effect, for the purposes of income tax for the year 2007–08 and subsequent tax years, and for the purposes of corporation tax for accounting periods ending after 5 April 2007.

Sub-s (4): word omitted from para (a)(i) repealed, and words in first pair of square brackets inserted, by the Government of Wales Act 1998, ss 125, 152, Sch 12, para 31(1), (2), Sch 18, Pt I. In para (a)(iii) word omitted by the Scottish Public Services Ombudsman Act 2002 (Consequential Provisions and Modifications) Order, SI 2004/1823 art 10(a). Para (a)(iv) substituted by the Public Services Ombudsman (Wales) Act 2005, s 39(1), Sch 6, para 22(a). Para (a)(v) inserted by the Scottish Public Services Ombudsman Act 2002 (Consequential Provisions and Modifications) Order, SI 2004/1823 art 10(b). In para (c), words inserted by the Social Security Contributions (Transfer of Functions, etc) Act 1999, s 6, Sch 6, para 9(1), (4)(b).

Sub-s (6): words in outer square brackets substituted by the Government of Wales Act 1998, ss 125, Sch 12, para 31(1), (3). Words in inner square brackets substituted by the Scottish Public Services Ombudsman Act 2002 (Consequential Provisions and Modifications) Order, SI 2004/1823 art 10(c). Words "the Public Services Ombudsman for Wales" substituted by the Public Services Ombudsman (Wales) Act 2005 s 39, Sch 6 para 22(b).

Sub-s (10A) inserted by the Commissioners for Revenue and Customs Act 2005 s 50, Sch 4 para 39.

Sub-s (11): in para (c) first words omitted repealed by the Public Services Ombudsman (Wales) Act 2005, s 39, Sch 6, para 22(c), Sch 7; in para (c) final words omitted repealed by the Scottish Public Services Ombudsman Act 2002 (Consequential Provisions and Modifications) Order, SI 2004/1823, art 10(d).

General

188   Short title

This Act may be cited as the Finance Act 1989.

FINANCE (NO 2) ACT 1992

(1992 c 48)

An Act to grant certain duties, to alter other duties, and to amend the law relating to the National Debt and the Public Revenue, and to make further provision in connection with Finance

[16 July 1992]

PART I

CUSTOMS AND EXCISE, VALUE ADDED TAX AND CAR TAX

CHAPTER I
CUSTOMS AND EXCISE
Abolition of fiscal frontiers etc

1 Powers to fix excise duty point

(1) Subject to the following provisions of this section, the Commissioners may by regulations make provision, in relation to any duties of excise on goods, for fixing the time when the requirement to pay any duty with which goods become chargeable is to take effect ("the excise duty point").

(2) Where regulations under this section fix an excise duty point for any goods, the rate of duty for the time being in force at that point shall be the rate used for determining the amount of duty to be paid in pursuance of the requirement that takes effect at that point.

(3) Regulations under this section may provide for the excise duty point for any goods to be such of the following times as may be prescribed in relation to the circumstances of the case, that is to say—

(a) the time when the goods become chargeable with the duty in question;

(b) the time when there is a contravention of any prescribed requirements relating to any suspension arrangements applying to the goods;

(c) the time when the duty on the goods ceases, in the prescribed manner, to be suspended in accordance with any such arrangements;

(d) the time when there is a contravention of any prescribed condition subject to which any relief has been conferred in relation to the goods;

(e) such time after the time which, in accordance with regulations made by virtue of any of the preceding paragraphs, would otherwise be the excise duty point for those goods as may be prescribed;

and regulations made by virtue of any of paragraphs (b) to (e) above may define a time by reference to whether or not at that time the Commissioners have been satisfied as to any matter.

(4) Where regulations under this section prescribe an excise duty point for any goods, such regulations may also make provision—

(a) specifying the person or persons on whom the liability to pay duty on the goods is to fall at the excise duty point (being the person or persons having the prescribed connection with the goods at that point or at such other time, falling no earlier than when the goods become chargeable with the duty, as may be prescribed); and

(b) where more than one person is to be liable to pay the duty, specifying whether the liability is to be both joint and several.

(5) Schedule 1 to this Act (which contains minor and consequential amendments and savings for purposes connected with the other provision made by this section) shall have effect.

(6) The power of the Commissioners to make regulations under this section shall be exercisable by statutory instrument subject to annulment in pursuance of a resolution of either House of Parliament and shall include power—

(a)   to make different provision for different cases, including different provision for different duties and different goods; and

(b)   to make such incidental, supplemental, consequential and transitional provision as the Commissioners think necessary or expedient.

(7) In this section—

"the Commissioners" means the Commissioners of Customs and Excise;

"contravention" includes a failure to comply;

"customs and excise Acts" and "goods" have the same meanings as in the Customs and Excise Management Act 1979; and

"prescribed" means prescribed by regulations under this section;

and references in this section to suspension arrangements are references to any provision made by or under the customs and excise Acts for enabling goods to be held or moved without payment of duty or any provision made by or under those Acts in connection with any provision enabling goods to be so held or moved.

(8) This section and Schedule 1 to this Act shall come into force on such day as the Commissioners may by order made by statutory instrument appoint, and different days may be appointed under this subsection for different provisions and for different purposes.

NOTES

Orders: the Finance (No 2) Act 1992 (Commencement No 2 and Transitional Provisions) Order 1992, SI 1992/2979, the Finance (No 2) Act 1992 (Commencement No 4 and Transitional Provisions) Order 1992, SI 1992/3261, the Finance (No 2) Act 1992 (Commencement No 5) Order 1993, SI 1993/1341.

Regulations: the Excise Goods (Holding, Movement, Warehousing and REDS) Regulations 1992, SI 1992/3135, as amended by SI 1993/1228, SI 1999/1278, SI 1999/1565; the Beer Regulations 1993, SI 1993/1228; the Cider and Perry (Amendment) Regulations 1996, SI 1996/2287; the Hydrocarbon Oil Duties (Marine Voyages Reliefs) Regulations 1996, SI 1996/2537; the Wine and Made-wine (Amendment) Regulations 1996, SI 1996/2752; the Excise Duty Point (External and Internal Community Transit Procedure) Regulations 1998, SI 1998/202, as amended by SI 1998/3110; the Warehousekeepers and Owners of Warehoused Goods Regulations 1999, SI 1999/1278; the Excise Goods (Sales on Board Ships and Aircraft) Regulations 1999, SI 1999/1565; Excise Goods (Export Shops) Regulations 2000, SI 2000/645; Tobacco Products Regulations 2001, SI 2001/1712; Excise Duty Points (Duty Suspended Movements of Excise Goods) Regulations 2001, SI 2001/3022; Excise Goods (Accompanying Documents) Regulations 2002, SI 2002/501; Excise Goods, Beer and Tobacco Products (Amendment) Regulations 2002, SI 2002/2692. Excise Duty Points (etc) (New Member States) Regulations 2004, SI 2004/1003. Biofuels and Other Fuel Substitutes (Payment of Excise Duties etc) Regulations 2004, SI 2004/2065 (made under sub-ss (1), (3), (4)(a), (6)). Denatured Alcohol Regulations 2005, SI 2005/1524. Tobacco Products and Excise Goods (Amendment) Regulations 2006, SI 2006/1787.

2 Power to provide for drawback of excise duty

(1) Subject to the following provisions of this section, the Commissioners may, in relation to any duties of excise, by regulations make provision—

[(a)]   conferring an entitlement to drawback of duty in prescribed cases where the Commissioners are satisfied that goods chargeable with duty have not been, and will not be, consumed in the United Kingdom[; and

(b)   conferring an entitlement to drawback of duty, in prescribed cases, on the shipment as stores, or warehousing in an excise warehouse for use as stores, of goods chargeable with duty].

(2)   The power of the Commissioners to make regulations under this section shall include power—

   (a)   to provide for, or for the imposition of, the conditions to which an entitlement to drawback under the regulations is to be subject;

   (b)   to provide for the determination of the person on whom any such entitlement is conferred;

   (c)   to make different provision for different cases, including different provision for different duties and different goods; and

   (d)   to make such incidental, supplemental, consequential and transitional provision as the Commissioners think necessary or expedient.

(3)   Without prejudice to the generality of subsection (2)(d) above, the power of the Commissioners to make regulations under this section shall include power, in relation to any drawback of duty to which any person is entitled by virtue of regulations under this section, to provide—

   (a)   for entitlement to the drawback to be cancelled at any time after it has been conferred if there is a contravention of any conditions to which it is subject or in such other circumstances as may be prescribed; *and*

   (b)   for such persons as may be prescribed to be liable to the Commissioners for sums paid or credited to any person in respect of any drawback that has been cancelled in accordance with any such regulations.

[(3A)   If entitlement to drawback is cancelled under any provision contained in regulations by virtue of subsection (3) above the Commissioners—

   (a)   may assess as being excise duty due from the prescribed person an amount equal to sums paid or credited to any person in respect of the drawback, and

   (b)   may notify the prescribed person or his representative accordingly.]

[(3B)   The reference in subsection (3A) above to the prescribed person is to such person as may be prescribed for the purposes of the subsection by regulations under this section.]

(4)   The power of the Commissioners to make regulations under this section shall be exercisable by statutory instrument subject to annulment in pursuance of a resolution of either House of Parliament.

(5)   In this section—

   "the Commissioners" means the Commissioners of Customs and Excise;

   "contravention" includes a failure to comply;

   ["excise warehouse", "goods", "shipment", "stores" and "warehousing" have the same meanings] as in the Customs and Excise Management Act 1979; and

   "prescribed" means prescribed by regulations under this section.

(6)   This section shall come into force on such day as the Commissioners may by order made by statutory instrument appoint, and different days may be appointed under this subsection for different provisions and for different purposes.

NOTES

Sub-s (2): words in square brackets inserted by the Finance Act 1999, s 11(1).

Sub-s (3): para (b) and word "and" preceding it repealed by the Finance Act 1998, ss 20, 165, Sch 2, paras 6(1), (2), 12, Sch 27, Pt I(5), as from a day to be appointed.

Sub-ss (3A), (3B): inserted by the Finance Act 1998, s 20, Sch 2, paras 6(1), (3), 12, as from a day to be appointed.

Sub-s (5): words in square brackets substituted by the Finance Act 1999, s 11(2).

Orders: the Finance (No 2) Act 1992 (Commencement No 2 and Transitional Provisions) Order 1992, SI 1992/2979.

Regulations: the Excise Goods (Holding, Movement, Warehousing and REDS) Regulations 1992, SI 1992/3135, as amended by SI 1993/1228, SI 1999/1278, SI 1999/1565; the Beer

Regulations 1993, SI 1993/1228, as amended by SI 1995/3059, SI 2000/3213; the Excise Goods (Drawback) Regulations 1995, SI 1995/1046. Excise Duty Points (etc) (New Member States) Regulations 2004, SI 2004/1003.

3 Protection of revenues derived from excise duties

(1)   Schedule 2 to this Act (which makes additional provision for purposes connected with the protection of the revenues derived from excise duties) shall have effect.

(2)   This section and Schedule 2 to this Act shall come into force on such day as the Commissioners of Customs and Excise may by order made by statutory instrument appoint, and different days may be appointed under this subsection for different provisions and for different purposes.

NOTES

Orders: the Finance (No 2) Act 1992 (Commencement No 3) Order 1992, SI 1992/3104; the Finance (No 2) Act 1992 (Commencement No 5) Order 1993, SI 1993/1341.

4 Enforcement powers

(1)   Except in a case falling within subsection (2) below, the powers to which this section applies shall not be exercisable in relation to any person or thing entering or leaving the United Kingdom so as to prevent, restrict or delay the movement of that person or thing between different member States.

(2)   The cases in which a power to which this section applies may be exercised as mentioned in subsection (1) above are those where it appears to the person on whom the power is conferred that there are reasonable grounds for believing that the movement in question is not in fact between different member States or that it is necessary to exercise the power for purposes connected with—

   (a)   securing the collection of any Community customs duty or giving effect to any Community legislation relating to any such duty;

   (b)   the enforcement of any prohibition or restriction for the time being in force by virtue of any Community legislation with respect to the movement of goods into or out of the member States; or

   (c)   the enforcement of any prohibition or restriction for the time being in force by virtue of any enactment with respect to the importation or exportation of goods into or out of the United Kingdom.

(3)   Subject to subsection (4) below, this section applies to any power which is conferred on the Commissioners of Customs and Excise or any officer or constable under any of the following provisions of the Customs and Excise Management Act 1979, that is to say—

   (a)   section 21 (control of movement of aircraft into and out of the United Kingdom);

   (b)   section 26 (power to regulate movement by land into and out of Northern Ireland);

   (c)   section 27 (officers' powers of boarding);

   (d)   section 28 (officers' powers of access);

   (e)   section 29 (officers' powers to detain ships);

   (f)   section 34 (power to prevent flight of aircraft);

   (g)   section 78 (questions as to baggage of person entering or leaving the United Kingdom);

   (h)   section 164 (powers of search).

(4)   The Treasury may by order made by statutory instrument add any power conferred by any enactment contained in the customs and excise Acts to the powers to

which this section applies; and a statutory instrument containing an order under this subsection shall be subject to annulment in pursuance of a resolution of either House of Parliament.

(5) In this section—

"Community customs duty" includes any agricultural levy of the Economic Community; and

"the customs and excise Acts" and "goods" have the same meanings as in the Customs and Excise Management Act 1979;

and for the purposes of this section a power shall be taken to be exercised otherwise than in relation to a person or thing entering or leaving the United Kingdom in any case where the power is exercisable irrespective of whether the person or thing in question is entering or leaving the United Kingdom.

(6) This section shall come into force on 1st January 1993.

PART III
MISCELLANEOUS AND GENERAL

General

83 Short title
This Act may be cited as the Finance (No 2) Act 1992.

EUROPEAN COMMUNITIES (AMENDMENT) ACT 1993

(1993 c 32)

An Act to make provision consequential on the Treaty on European Union signed at Maastricht on 7th February 1992

[20 July 1993]

1 Treaty on European Union

(1) . . .

(2) For the purpose of section 6 of the European Parliamentary Elections Act 1978 (approval of treaties increasing the Parliament's powers) the Treaty on European Union signed at Maastricht on 7th February 1992 is approved.

NOTES

Sub-s (1): amends the European Communities Act 1972, s 1(2).

2 Economic and monetary union

No notification shall be given to the Council of the European Communities that the United Kingdom intends to move to the third stage of economic and monetary union (in accordance with the Protocol on certain provisions relating to the United Kingdom adopted at Maastricht on 7th February 1992) unless a draft of the notification has first been approved by Act of Parliament and unless Her Majesty's Government has reported to Parliament on its proposals for the co-ordination of economic policies, its role in the European Council of Finance Ministers (ECOFIN) in pursuit of the objectives of Article 2 of the Treaty establishing the European Community as provided for in Articles 103 and 102a, and the work of the European Monetary Institute in preparation for economic and monetary union.

3 Annual report by Bank of England

In implementing Article 108 of the Treaty establishing the European Community, and ensuring compatibility of the statutes of the national central bank, Her Majesty's Government shall, by order, make provision for the Governor of the Bank of England to make an annual report to Parliament, which shall be subject to approval by a Resolution of each House of Parliament.

4 Information for Commission

In implementing the provisions of Article 103(3) of the Treaty establishing the European Community, information shall be submitted to the Commission from the United Kingdom indicating performance on economic growth, industrial investment, employment and balance of trade, together with comparisons with those items of performance from other member States.

5 Convergence criteria: assessment of deficits

Before submitting the information required in implementing Article 103(3) of the Treaty establishing the European Community, Her Majesty's Government shall report to Parliament for its approval an assessment of the medium term economic and budgetary position in relation to public investment expenditure and to the social, economic and environmental goals set out in Article 2, which report shall form the basis of any submission to the Council and Commission in pursuit of their responsibilities under Articles 103 and 104c.

6 Committee of the Regions

A person may be proposed as a member or alternate member for the United Kingdom of the Committee of the Regions constituted under Article 198a of the Treaty establishing the European Community only if, at the time of the proposal, he is [a member of the Northern Ireland Assembly] [a member of the Scottish Parliament] [a member of the National Assembly for Wales or][, the Mayor of London, a member of the London Assembly] an elected member of a local authority.

NOTES

Words in first pair of square brackets inserted by the Northern Ireland Act 1998 (Amendment of Enactment) Order, SI 2001/3675 art 2; words in second pair of square brackets inserted by the Scotland Act 1998, s 125, Sch 8, para 28; words in third pair of square brackets inserted by the Government of Wales Act 1998, s 125, Sch 12, para 34; words in fourth pair of square brackets inserted by the Greater London Authority (Miscellaneous Amendments) (No 2) Order, SI 2001/3719 Schedule para 5.

---

7 Commencement (Protocol on Social Policy)

This Act shall come into force only when each House of Parliament has come to a Resolution on a motion tabled by a Minister of the Crown considering the question of adopting the Protocol on Social Policy.

8 Short title

This Act may be cited as the European Communities (Amendment) Act 1993.

FINANCE ACT 1993

(1993 c 34)

An Act to grant certain duties, to alter other duties, and to amend the law relating to the National Debt and the Public Revenue, and to make further provision in connection with Finance

[27 July 1993]

PART I
CUSTOMS AND EXCISE AND VALUE ADDED TAX

CHAPTER I
GENERAL
Alcoholic liquor duties

1–7

(Amend the Alcoholic Liquor Duties Act 1979, ss 1, 36, 42, 43, 45, 51, 62, Sch 1 and insert s 66A of that Act.)

8 Denatured alcohol

_____

NOTES

Repealed by the Finance Act 1995, s 162, Sch 29, Pt I(3), as from 1 July 2005 (see SI 2005/1523, art 2(b)).

Hydrocarbon oil duties

9

(Amends the Hydrocarbon Oil Duties Act 1979, ss 6, 11, 13A, 14.)

10 [Extension of Hydrocarbon Oil Duties Act 1979 to energy products]

(1) The Hydrocarbon Oil Duties Act 1979 ("the 1979 Act") shall have effect in relation to such cases as may be specified in an order made by the Treasury as if references in that Act to hydrocarbon oil or to road fuel gas included references to any [energy product] which is designated by that order as a substance which is to be treated for the purposes of that Act as the equivalent of hydrocarbon oil or, as the case may be, of road fuel gas.

(2) The Treasury may by order provide, in relation to any substance which by virtue of this section is to be treated for the purposes of the 1979 Act as the equivalent of hydrocarbon oil [or road fuel gas], for that substance to be treated for the purposes of such of the provisions of that Act as may be specified in the order [[as if it fell within such class or description of substance] as may be so specified.]

(3) In exercising their powers under this section, the Treasury shall so far as practicable secure that [an energy product] which is intended for, or capable of being put to, a particular use is treated for the purposes of the 1979 Act as if it were [the substance] to which, when put to that use, it is most closely equivalent.

[(4) In this section "energy product" means a substance which—

(a)   is an energy product for the purposes of Council Directive 2003/96/EC restructuring the Community framework for the taxation of energy products and electricity, and

(b)   is not (apart from as a result of this section) hydrocarbon oil or road fuel gas within the meaning of the 1979 Act.]

(5) The power of the Treasury to make an order under this section shall be exercisable by statutory instrument subject to annulment in pursuance of a resolution of the House of Commons; and any such order may make different provision for different cases and different substances.

[(6) Where a duty of excise is charged on a substance under a provision of the 1979 Act by virtue of an order under this section, no duty shall be charged on the substance under any other provision of that Act.]

NOTES

Heading: substituted by the Finance Act 2004, s 14(2), (7).

Sub-s (1): words substituted by the Finance Act 2004, s 14(1), (2).

Sub-s (2): words in first pair of square brackets inserted, and words in inner pair of square brackets substituted, by the Finance Act 2004, s 14(1), (3) and words in outer pair of square brackets substituted by the Finance Act 2002, s 7(2)(a).

Sub-s (3): words in square brackets substituted by the Finance Act 2004, s 14(1), (4).

Sub-s (4): substituted by the Finance Act 2004, s 14(1), (5).

Sub-s (6): substituted by the Finance Act 2004, s 14(1), (6).

11

(inserts the Hydrocarbon Oil Duties Act 1979, s 6A, and amends the Excise Duties (Surcharges or Rebates) Act 1979, s 1.)

12 Measurement of volume

(1) In ascertaining for the purposes of the Hydrocarbon Oil Duties Act 1979—

    (a)   the amount of any duty of excise chargeable on any liquid by virtue of that Act; or

    (b)   the amount of any rebate allowable on any such liquid by virtue of that Act,

the volume of that liquid shall be taken (if it would not otherwise be so taken) to be what would be its volume, calculated in accordance with regulations under subsection (2) below, at a temperature of 15°C.

(2) The Commissioners of Customs and Excise may by regulations make such provision as they think fit as to the method by which, in ascertaining any amount mentioned in subsection (1) above—

    (a)   the volume of any liquid is to be measured; or

    (b)   the volume as at a temperature of 15°C of any amount of a liquid is to be determined,

and that provision may include provision made by reference to any internationally recognised conversion tables.

(3) Any reference in sections 15 and 17 to 19A of that Act (drawback and relief) to the amount of any duty of excise which has been paid in respect of any substance, or to the amount of any rebate that has been allowed in respect of any substance, shall be construed as a reference—

    (a)   to such amount as is shown to the satisfaction of the Commissioners of Customs and Excise to have been paid or, as the case may be, allowed in respect of that substance; or

    (b)   where regulations made by those Commissioners so provide, to such amount as is calculated on such assumptions as to the volume of the substance in question as may be determined in accordance with any such regulations.

(4) The power of the Commissioners of Customs and Excise to make regulations under this section shall be exercisable by statutory instrument subject to annulment in pursuance of a resolution of either House of Parliament; and any such regulations—

(a)   may make different provision for different cases and for different substances; and

(b)   may contain such transitional, supplemental and incidental provision as those Commissioners think fit.

(5) Provision made under this section by any regulations may provide for any determination or measurement under the regulations to be made, or any description of a case or substance to be framed, by reference to such circumstances or other factors, or to the opinion of such persons, as the Commissioners think fit.

(6) For the purposes of this section "liquid" does not include any substance which is gaseous at a temperature of 15°C and under a pressure of 1013.25 millibars.

(7) . . .

(8) This section shall come into force on such day as the Commissioners of Customs and Excise may by order made by statutory instrument appoint, and different days may be appointed under this subsection for different provisions and for different purposes.

NOTES

Sub-s (7): amends the Hydrocarbon Oil Duties Act 1979, ss 2(5), 15(1).
Orders: the Finance Act 1993, section 12 (Appointed Day) Order 1993, SI 1993/2215.
Regulations: the Hydrocarbon Oil (Amendment) Regulations 1993, SI 1993/2267.

PART VI
MISCELLANEOUS AND GENERAL

General

214 Short title
This Act may be cited as the Finance Act 1993.

FINANCE ACT 1994

(1994 c 9)

ARRANGEMENT OF SECTIONS

PART I
CUSTOMS AND EXCISE

CHAPTER II
APPEALS AND PENALTIES

Schedule 6—Air passenger duty: administration and enforcement

An Act to grant certain duties, to alter other duties, and to amend the law relating to the National Debt and the Public Revenue, and to make further provision in connection with Finance

[[3 May 1994]

PART I
CUSTOMS AND EXCISE

1–6

((Ch I) S 1 superseded; s 2 amends the Tobacco Products Act 1979, Sch 1; s 3 amends the Hydrocarbon Oil Duties Act 1979, ss 6, 11, 14; s 4 repealed by the Vehicle Excise and Registration Act 1994, s 65, Sch 5, Pt I; s 5 introduces Sch 2 to this Act; s 6 outside the scope of this work.)

CHAPTER II
APPEALS AND PENALTIES

NOTES

See the Channel Tunnel (Alcoholic Liquor and Tobacco Products) Order, SI 2003/2758 art 4(a): this Chapter applies, for the purposes of SI 2003/2758, in corresponding manner to events involving goods in a control zone in the same way that it applies to events involving goods in the United Kingdom.

VAT and duties tribunals

7 VAT and duties tribunals

(1), (2) . . .

(3)   In the following provisions of this Chapter references to an appeal tribunal are references to a VAT and duties tribunal.

(4)   Sections [85 and 87 of the Value Added Tax Act 1994] (settling of appeals by agreement and enforcement of decisions of tribunal) shall have effect as if—

    (a)   the references to section [83 of that Act] included references to this Chapter; and

    (b)   references to value added tax included references to any relevant duty.

(5)   Without prejudice to the generality of the power conferred by paragraph 9 of Schedule [12 to the Value Added Tax Act 1994] (rules of procedure for tribunals), rules under that paragraph may provide for costs awarded against an appellant on an appeal by virtue of this Chapter to be recoverable, and for any directly applicable Community legislation relating to any relevant duty or any enactment so relating to apply, as if the amount awarded were an amount of duty which the appellant is required to pay.

(6), (7) . . .

NOTES

Sub-ss (1), (2): repealed subject to transitional provisions by the Value Added Tax Act 1994, s 100(1), (2), Schs 13, 15.

Sub-s (4): words in square brackets substituted by the Value Added Tax Act 1994, s 100(1), Sch 14, para 13 (as amended with retrospective effect by the Finance Act 1995, s 33(1), (5)).

Sub-s (5): words in square brackets substituted by the Value Added Tax Act 1994, s 100(1), Sch 14, para 13(b).

Sub-ss (6), (7): amend the Tribunals and Inquiries Act 1992, Sch 1, Pts I, II.

Civil penalties

8 Penalty for evasion of excise duty

(1)   Subject to the following provisions of this section, in any case where—

   (a)   any person engages in any conduct for the purpose of evading any duty of excise, and

   (b)   his conduct involves dishonesty (whether or not such as to give rise to any criminal liability),

that person shall be liable to a penalty of an amount equal to the amount of duty evaded or, as the case may be, sought to be evaded.

(2)   References in this section to a person's evading a duty of excise shall include references to his obtaining or securing, without his being entitled to it—

   (a)   any repayment, rebate or drawback of duty;

   (b)   any relief or exemption from or any allowance against duty; or

   (c)   any deferral or other postponement of his liability to pay any duty or of the discharge by payment of any such liability,

and shall also include references to his evading the cancellation of any entitlement to, or the withdrawal of, any such repayment, rebate, drawback, relief, exemption or allowance.

(3)   In relation to any such evasion of duty as is mentioned in subsection (2) above, the reference in subsection (1) above to the amount of duty evaded or sought to be evaded shall be construed as a reference to the amount of the repayment, rebate, drawback, relief, exemption or allowance or, as the case may be, the amount of the payment which, or the liability to make which, is deferred or otherwise postponed.

(4)   Where a person is liable to a penalty under this section—

   (a)   the Commissioners or, on appeal, an appeal tribunal may reduce the penalty to such amount (including nil) as they think proper; and

   (b)   an appeal tribunal, on an appeal relating to a penalty reduced by the Commissioners under this subsection, may cancel the whole or any part of the reduction made by the Commissioners.

(5)   Neither of the following matters shall be a matter which the Commissioners or any appeal tribunal shall be entitled to take into account in exercising their powers under subsection (4) above, that is to say—

   (a)   the insufficiency of the funds available to any person for paying any duty of excise or for paying the amount of the penalty;

   (b)   the fact that there has, in the case in question or in that case taken with any other cases, been no or no significant loss of duty.

(6)   Statements made or documents produced by or on behalf of a person shall not be inadmissible in—

   (a)   any criminal proceedings against that person in respect of any offence in connection with or in relation to any duty of excise, or

   (b)   any proceedings against that person for the recovery of any sum due from him in connection with or in relation to any duty of excise,

by reason only that any of the matters specified in subsection (7) below has been drawn to his attention and that he was, or may have been, induced by that matter having been brought to his attention to make the statements or produce the documents.

(7)   The matters mentioned in subsection (6) above are—

   (a)   that the Commissioners have power, in relation to any duty of excise, to assess an amount due by way of a civil penalty, instead of instituting criminal proceedings;

   (b)   that it is the Commissioners' practice, without being able to give an undertaking as to whether they will make such an assessment in any case, to be influenced in determining whether to make such an assessment by the fact (where it is the case) that a person has made a full confession of any dishonest conduct to which he has been a party and has given full facilities for an investigation;

(c)   that the Commissioners or, on appeal, an appeal tribunal have power to reduce a penalty under this section, as provided in subsection (4) above; and

(d)   that, in determining the extent of such a reduction in the case of any person, the Commissioners or tribunal will have regard to the extent of the co-operation which he has given to the Commissioners in their investigation.

(8)   Where, by reason of conduct falling within subsection (1) above, a person is convicted of an offence, that conduct shall not also give rise to liability to a penalty under this section.

9 Penalties for contraventions of statutory requirements

(1)   This section applies, subject to section 10 below, to any conduct in relation to which any enactment (including an enactment contained in this Act or in any Act passed after this Act) provides for the conduct to attract a penalty under this section.

(2)   Any person to whose conduct this section applies shall be liable—

(a)   in the case of conduct in relation to which provision is made by subsection (4) below[, or by or under any other enactment,] for the penalty attracted to be calculated by reference to an amount of, or an amount payable on account of, any duty of excise, to a penalty of whichever is the greater of 5 per cent of that amount and £250; and

(b)   in any other case, to a penalty of £250.

(3)   Subject to section 13(3) and (4) below, in the case of any conduct to which this section applies which is conduct in relation to which provision is made by subsection (4) or (5) below or any other enactment for that conduct to attract daily penalties, the person whose conduct it is—

(a)   shall be liable, in addition to an initial penalty under subsection (2) above, to a penalty of £20 for every day, after the first, on which the conduct continues, but

(b)   shall not, in respect of the continuation of that conduct, be liable to further penalties under subsection (2) above.

(4)   Where any conduct to which this section applies consists in a failure, in contravention of any subordinate legislation, to pay any amount of any duty of excise or an amount payable on account of any such duty, then, in so far as that would not otherwise be the case—

(a)   the penalty attracted to that contravention shall be calculated by reference to the amount unpaid; and

(b)   the contravention shall also attract daily penalties.

(5)   Where—

(a)   a contravention of any provision made by or under any enactment consists in or involves a failure, before such time as may be specified in or determined in accordance with that provision, to send a return to the Commissioners showing the amount which any person is or may become required to pay by way of, or on account of, any duty of excise, and

(b)   that contravention attracts a penalty under this section,

that contravention shall also attract daily penalties.

(6)   Where, by reason of any conduct to which this section applies, a person is convicted of an offence, that conduct shall not also give rise to liability to a penalty under this section.

(7)   If it appears to the Treasury that there has been a change in the value of money since the passing of this Act or, as the case may be, the last occasion when the power conferred by this subsection was exercised, they may by order substitute for any sum for the time being specified in subsection (2) or (3) above such other sum as appears to them to be justified by the change.

(8)   The power to make an order under subsection (7) above—

(a)   shall be exercisable by statutory instrument subject to annulment in pursuance of a resolution of the House of Commons; but

(b)   shall not be exercisable so as to vary the penalty for any conduct occurring before the coming into force of the order.

(9)   Schedule 4 to this Act (which provides for the conduct to which this section applies, repeals the summary offences superseded by this section and makes related provision with respect to forfeiture) shall have effect.

NOTES

Words in square brackets substituted by the Finance Act 2000, s 28.

10   Exceptions to liability under section 9

(1)   Subject to subsection (2) below and to any express provision to the contrary made in relation to any conduct to which section 9 above applies, such conduct shall not give rise to any liability to a penalty under that section if the person whose conduct it is satisfies the Commissioners or, on appeal, an appeal tribunal that there is a reasonable excuse for the conduct.

(2)   Where it appears to the Commissioners or, on appeal, an appeal tribunal that there is no reasonable excuse for a continuation of conduct for which there was at first a reasonable excuse, liability for a penalty under section 9 above shall be determined as if the conduct began at the time when there ceased to be a reasonable excuse for its continuation.

(3)   For the purposes of this section—

(a)   an insufficiency of funds available for paying any duty or penalty due shall not be a reasonable excuse; and

(b)   where reliance is placed by any person on another to perform any task, then neither the fact of that reliance nor the fact that any conduct to which section 9 above applies was attributable to the conduct of that other person shall be a reasonable excuse.

[10A   Breaches of controlled goods agreements

(1)   This section applies where an enforcement agent acting under the power conferred by section 51(A1) of the Finance Act 1997 (power to use the procedure in Schedule 12 to the Tribunals, Courts and Enforcement Act 2007) has entered into a controlled goods agreement with the person against whom the power is exercisable ("the person in default").

(2)   In this section, "controlled goods agreement" has the meaning given by paragraph 13(4) of that Schedule.

(3)   Subject to subsection (4) below, if the person in default removes or disposes of goods (or permits their removal or disposal) in breach of the controlled goods agreement, he is liable to a penalty equal to half of the unpaid duty or other amount recoverable under section 51(A1) of the Finance Act 1997.

(4)   The person in default shall not be liable to a penalty under subsection (3) above if he satisfies the Commissioners or, on appeal, an appeal tribunal that there is a reasonable excuse for the breach in question.

(5)   This section extends only to England and Wales.]

NOTES

Section 10A to be inserted by the Tribunals, Courts and Enforcement Act 2007, s 62(3), Sch 13, paras 113, 114 with effect from a date to be appointed.

11   Breaches of walking possession agreements

(1)   This section applies where—

(a)   [in accordance with regulations under section 51 of the Finance Act 1997 (enforcement by distress)], a person ("the person levying the distress") is empowered or authorised to distrain any property of another person ("the person in default") [who has refused or neglected to pay any amount of relevant duty or any amount recoverable as if it were an amount of relevant duty due from him]; and

(b)   the person levying the distress and the person in default have entered into a walking possession agreement.

(2)   In this section a "walking possession agreement" means an agreement under which, in consideration of the property distrained upon being allowed to remain in the custody of the person in default and of the delaying of its sale, the person in default—

(a)   acknowledges that the property specified in the agreement is under distraint and held in walking possession; and

(b)   undertakes that, except with the consent of the Commissioners and subject to such conditions as they may impose, he will not remove or allow the removal of any of the specified property from the premises named in the agreement.

(3)   Subject to subsection (4) below, if the person in default is in breach of the undertaking contained in a walking possession agreement, he shall be liable to a penalty equal to one-half of the unpaid duty or penalty which gives rise to the distraint.

(4)   The person in default shall not be liable to a penalty under subsection (3) above if he satisfies the Commissioners or, on appeal, an appeal tribunal that there is a reasonable excuse for the breach in question.

(5)   This section does not extend to Scotland.

NOTES

Sub-s (1): words in first pair of square brackets substituted, and words in second pair of square brackets inserted, by the Finance Act 1997, s 53(2), (9).

Sub-s (5): to be substituted by the Tribunals, Courts and Enforcement Act 2007, s 62(3), Sch 13, paras 113, 115, with effect from a date to be appointed. Substituted sub-s (5) to read as follows—

"(5) This section extends only to Northern Ireland.".

Assessments to excise duty or to penalties

12   Assessments to excise duty

(1)   Subject to subsection (4) below, where it appears to the Commissioners—

(a)   that any person is a person from whom any amount has become due in respect of any duty of excise; and

(b)   that there has been a default falling within subsection (2) below, the Commissioners may assess the amount of duty due from that person to the best of their judgement and notify that amount to that person or his representative.

[(1A)   Subject to subsection (4) below, where it appears to the Commissioners—

  (a)   that any person is a person from whom any amount has become due in respect of any duty of excise; and

  (b)   that the amount due can be ascertained by the Commissioners,

the Commissioners may assess the amount of duty due from that person and notify that amount to that person or his representative.]

(2)   The defaults falling within this subsection are—

  (a)   any failure by any person to make, keep, preserve or produce as required or directed by or under any enactment any returns, accounts, books, records or other documents;

  (b)   any omission from or inaccuracy in any returns, accounts, books, records or other documents which any person is required or directed by or under any enactment to make, keep, preserve or produce;

  (c)   any failure by any person to take or permit to be taken any step which he is required under Schedule 1 or 3 to the Betting and Gaming Duties Act 1981 [or Schedule 1 to the Finance Act 1997] to take or to permit to be taken;

  [(ca)   any failure by any person to comply with a requirement to which he is made subject by or under Schedule 2A to the Alcoholic Liquor Duties Act 1979 (duty stamps);]

  (d)   any unreasonable delay in performing any obligation the failure to perform which would be a default falling within this subsection.

[(2A)   In subsection (2)(a) and (b) above "enactment" includes directly applicable Community provision.]

(3)   Where an amount has been assessed as due from any person and notified in accordance with this section, it shall, subject to any appeal under section 16 below, be deemed to be an amount of the duty in question due from that person and may be recovered accordingly, unless, or except to the extent that, the assessment has subsequently been withdrawn or reduced.

(4)   An assessment of the amount of any duty of excise due from any person shall not be made under this section at any time after whichever is the earlier of the following times, that is to say—

  (a)   subject to subsection (5) below, the end of the period of [three years] beginning with the time when his liability to the duty arose; and

  (b)   the end of the period of one year beginning with the day on which evidence of facts, sufficient in the opinion of the Commissioners to justify the making of the assessment, comes to their knowledge;

but this subsection shall be without prejudice, where further evidence comes to the knowledge of the Commissioners at any time after the making of an assessment under this section, to the making of a further assessment within the period applicable by virtue of this subsection in relation to that further assessment.

(5)   Subsection (4) above shall have effect as if the reference in paragraph (a) to [three years] were a reference to twenty years in the case of any assessment to any amount of duty the assessment or payment of any of which has been postponed or otherwise affected by—

  (a)   conduct in respect of which any person (whether or not the person assessed)—

      (i)   has become liable to a penalty under section 8 above, or

      (ii)   has been convicted of an offence of fraud or dishonesty; or

  (b)   any conduct in respect of which proceedings for an offence of fraud or dishonesty would have been commenced or continued against any person (whether or not the person assessed), but for their having been compounded under section 152(a) of the Management Act.

(6)   The reference in subsection (4) above to the time when a person's liability to a duty of excise arose are references—

(a)   in the case of a duty of excise on goods, to the excise duty point; and

(b)   in any other case, to the time when the duty was charged.

(7)   In this section references to an offence of fraud or dishonesty include references to an offence under any of the following provisions, that is to say—

(a)   sections 100(3), 136(1), 159(6), 167(1), 168(1), 170(1) and (2) and 170B(1) of the Management Act,

(b)   section 24(6) of the Betting and Gaming Duties Act 1981 and paragraph 13(3) of Schedule 1 . . . and paragraph 16(1) of Schedule 3 to that Act,

(c)   section 31(1) and (3) of the Finance Act 1993, and

(d)   section 41(1) and (3) below,

and also include references to attempting or conspiring to commit an offence of fraud or dishonesty and to inciting the commission of such an offence.

(8)   In this section "representative", in relation to a person appearing to the Commissioners to be a person from whom any amount has become due in respect of any duty of excise, means his personal representative[, trustee in bankruptcy or interim or permanent trustee] any receiver or liquidator appointed in relation to that person or any of his property or any other person acting in a representative capacity in relation to that person.

NOTES

Sub-s (1A): inserted by the Finance Act 1998, s 20, Sch 2, para 7.

Sub-s (2): in para (c) words in square brackets inserted by the Finance Act 1997, s 13, Sch 2, para 7. Para (ca) inserted by the Finance Act 2004, s 4(3) with effect in relation to retail containers containing alcoholic liquor if the excise duty point for the alcoholic liquor falls on or after 22 February 2006. For definition of "excise duty point" see the Finance (No 2) Act 1992, s 1.

Sub-s (2A): inserted by the Excise Duty Points (Duty Suspended Movements of Excise Goods) Regulations, SI 2001/3022 reg 9.

Sub-ss (4), (5), (8): words in square brackets substituted by the Finance Act 1997, s 50, Sch 5, para 6, Sch 6, paras 1(3), 7.

Sub-s (7): in para (b) words omitted repealed, in relation to any gaming on or after 1 October 1997, by the Finance Act 1997, s 113, Sch 18, Part II.

[12A Other assessment relating to excise duty matters

(1)   This subsection applies where any relevant excise duty relief other than an excepted relief—

(a)   has been given but ought not to have been given, or

(b)   would not have been given had the facts been known or been as they later turn out to be.

(2)   Where subsection (1) above applies, the Commissioners may assess the amount of the relief given as being excise duty due from the liable person and notify him or his representative accordingly.

(3)   Where an amount has been assessed as due from any person under—

(a)   subsection (2) above,

(b)   section 94 or 96 of the Management Act, . . .

[(bb)   section 8, 10[,11 or 36G] of the Alcoholic Liquor Duties Act 1979,]

(c)   section 10, 13, [13AB,] 14, 23 or 24 of the Hydrocarbon Oil Duties Act 1979, [(d)   section 8 of the Tobacco Products Duty Act 1979, or

(e)   section 2 of the Finance (No 2) Act 1992,]

and notice has been given accordingly, that amount shall, subject to any appeal under section 16 below, be deemed to be an amount of excise duty due from that person and may be recovered accordingly, unless, or except to the extent that, the assessment has subsequently been withdrawn or reduced.

(4)   No assessment under any of the provisions referred to in subsection (3) above, or under section 61 or 167 of the Management Act, shall be made at any time after whichever is the earlier of the following times, that is to say—

(a)   subject to subsection (6) below, the end of the period of three years beginning with the relevant time; and

(b)   the end of the period of one year beginning with the day on which evidence of facts, sufficient in the opinion of the Commissioners to justify the making of the assessment, comes to their knowledge.

(5)   Subsection (4) above shall be without prejudice, where further evidence comes to the knowledge of the Commissioners at any time after the making the assessment concerned, to the making of a further assessment within the period applicable by virtue of that subsection in relation to that further assessment.

(6)   Subsection (4) above shall have effect as if the reference in paragraph (a) to three years were a reference to twenty years in any case where the assessment has been postponed or otherwise affected by, or the power to make the assessment arises out of, conduct falling within subsection (5)(a) or (b) of section 12 above (construed in accordance with subsection (7) of that section).]

NOTES

Inserted by the Finance Act 1997, s 50, Sch 6, paras 1(1), 7.

Sub-s (3): word "or" at the end of para (b) repealed, paras (bb), (d) and word in para (c) inserted by the Finance Act 1998, ss 20, 165, Sch 2, para 8, Sch 27, Pt I(5); para (e) inserted by the Finance Act 1998, s 20, Sch 2, para 8(3), as from a day to be appointed. References in para (bb) substituted by the Finance Act 2002, s 4, Sch 1 para 4(1), (2).

[12B   Section 12A: supplementary provisions

(1)   For the purposes of section 12A above and this section, relevant excise duty relief has been given if (and only if)—

(a)   an amount of excise duty which a person is liable to pay has been remitted or payment of an amount of excise duty which a person is liable to pay has been waived;

(b)   an amount of excise duty has been repaid to a person;

(c)   an amount by way of drawback of excise duty has been paid to a person;

(d)   an allowance of excise duty in any amount has been made to a person;

(e)   an amount by way of rebate has been allowed to a person;

(f)   the liability of a person to repay an amount paid by way of drawback of excise duty has been waived;

(g)   an amount has been paid to a person under section 20(3) of the Hydrocarbon Oil Duties Act 1979 (payments in respect of contaminated or accidentally mixed oil); or

(h)   an amount of relief has been allowed to a person by virtue of section 20AA [or 20AB] of that Act (power to allow reliefs), or in accordance with paragraph 10 of Schedule 3 to that Act (power to make regulations for the purpose of relieving from excise duty oil intended for exportation or shipment as stores);

and the amount of the relief is the amount mentioned in relation to the relief in this subsection.

(2) For the purposes of section 12A above the relevant time is—

    (a)   in the case of an assessment under section 61 of the Management Act, the time when the ship or aircraft in question returned to a place within the United Kingdom;

    (b)   in the case of an assessment under section 94 of that Act, the time at which the goods in question were warehoused;

    (c)   in the case of an assessment under that section as it has effect by virtue of section 95 of that Act, the time when the goods in question were lawfully taken from the warehouse;

    (d)   in the case of an assessment under section 96 of that Act, the time when the goods in question were moved by pipe-line or notified as goods to be moved by pipe-line;

    (e)   in the case of an assessment under section 167 of that Act—

        (i)   if the assessment relates to unpaid duty, the time when the duty became payable or, if later, the time when the document in question was delivered or the statement in question was made; and

        (ii)   if the assessment relates to an overpayment, the time when the overpayment was made;

    [(ea)   in the case of an assessment under section 8 or 10 of the Alcoholic Liquor Duties Act 1979, the time of delivery from warehouse;

    (eb)   in the case of an assessment under section 11 of that Act, the time when the direction was made;]

    [(ec)   in the case of an assessment under section 36G of that Act, the time at which the requirement to pay the duty took effect (which time, in a case where there was an excise duty point for the beer fixed under section 1 of the Finance (No 2) Act 1992, is that excise duty point);]

    (f)   in the case of an assessment under section 10, 13, [13AB,] 14 or 23 of the Hydrocarbon Oil Duties Act 1979, the time of the action which gave rise to the power to assess;

    (g)   in the case of an assessment under section 24(4A) or (4B) of that Act, the time when the rebate was allowed or the oil was delivered without payment of duty (as the case may be);

    [(ga)   in the case of an assessment under section 8 of the Tobacco Products Duty Act 1979, the time when the Commissioners are satisfied of a failure to prove as mentioned in subsection (2)(a) or (b) of that section;

    (gb)   in the case of an assessment under section 2 of the Finance (No 2) Act 1992, the time when the sums were paid or credited in respect of the drawback;]

    (h)   in the case of an assessment under section 12A(2) above, the time when the relevant excise duty relief in question was given.

(3) In section 12A above "the liable person" means—

    (a)   in the case of excise duty which has been remitted or repaid under section 130 of the Management Act on the basis that goods were lost or destroyed while in a warehouse, the proprietor of the goods or the occupier of the warehouse;

    (b)   in the case of a rebate which has been allowed on any oil under section 11 of the Hydrocarbon Oil Duties Act 1979, the person to whom the rebate was allowed or the occupier of any warehouse from which the oil was delivered for home use;

(c)   in the case of a rebate allowed on any petrol under section 13A of that Act, the person to whom the rebate was allowed or the occupier of any warehouse from which the petrol was delivered for home use;

(d)   in any other case, the person mentioned in subsection (1) above to whom the relief in question was given.

(4)   In section 12A above—

"excepted relief" means any relief which is given by the making of a repayment on a claim made under section 137A of the Management Act;

"representative", in relation to any person from whom the Commissioners assess an amount as being excise duty due, means his personal representative, trustee in bankruptcy or interim or permanent trustee, any receiver or liquidator appointed in relation to him or any of his property or any other person acting in a representative capacity in relation to him.]

NOTES

Inserted by the Finance Act 1997, s 50, Sch 6, paras 1(1), 7.

Sub-s (1): words in para (h) inserted by the Finance Act 2001, s 3(4).

Sub-s (2): paras (ea), (eb), (ga) and words in square brackets in para (f), inserted by the Finance Act 1998, s 20, Sch 2, para 9; para (gb) inserted by the Finance Act 1998, s 20, Sch 2, para 9(4), as from a day to be appointed. Para (ec) added by the Finance Act 2002, s 4, Sch 1 para 4(1), (3).

13 Assessments to penalties

(1)   Where any person is liable to a penalty under this Chapter, the Commissioners may assess the amount due by way of penalty and notify that person, or his representative, accordingly.

(2)   An assessment under this section may be combined with an assessment under section 12 above, but any notification for the purposes of any such combined assessment shall separately identify any amount assessed by way of a penalty.

(3)   In the case of any amount due from any person by way of a penalty under section 9 above for conduct consisting in a contravention which attracts daily penalties—

(a)   a notification of an assessment under this section shall specify a date, being a date no later than the date of the notification, to which the penalty as assessed is to be calculated; and

(b)   if the contravention continues after that date, a further assessment, or (subject to this subsection) further assessments, may be made under this section in respect of any continuation of the contravention after that date.

(4)   If—

(a)   a person is assessed to a penalty in accordance with paragraph (a) of subsection (3) above, and

(b)   the contravention to which that penalty relates is remedied within such period after the date specified for the purposes of that subsection in the notification of assessment as may for the purposes of this subsection be notified to that person by the Commissioners,

that contravention shall be treated for the purposes of this Chapter as having been remedied, and accordingly the conduct shall be deemed to have ceased, immediately before that date.

(5)   If an amount has been assessed as due from any person and notified in accordance with this section, then unless, or except to the extent that, the assessment

has subsequently been withdrawn or reduced, that amount shall, subject to any appeal under section 16 below, be recoverable as if it were an amount due from that person as an amount of the appropriate[duty.

(6) In subsection (5) above "the appropriate duty" means—

    (a)   the [relevant duty] (if any) by reference to an amount of which the penalty in question is calculated; or

    (b)   where there is no such duty, the [relevant duty] the provisions relating to which are contravened by the conduct giving rise to the penalty or, if those provisions relate to more than one duty, such of the duties as appear to the Commissioners and are certified by them to be relevant in the case in question.

(7) In this section "representative", in relation to a person liable to a penalty under this Chapter, means his personal representative[, trustee in bankruptcy or interim or permanent trustee,] any receiver or liquidator appointed in relation to that person or any of his property or any other person acting in a representative capacity in relation to that person.

NOTES

Sub-ss (6), (7): words in square brackets substituted by the Finance Act 1997, ss 50(2), 53(3), Sch 6, paras 1(3), 7.

Customs and excise reviews and appeals

14 Requirement for review of a decision

(1) This section applies to the following decisions, not being decisions under this section or section 15 below, that is to say—

    (a)   any decision by the Commissioners, in relation to any customs duty or to any agricultural levy of the European Community, as to—

        (i)   whether or not, and at what time, anything is charged in any case with any such duty or levy;

        (ii)   the rate at which any such duty or levy is charged in any case, or the amount charged;

        (iii)   the person liable in any case to pay any amount charged, or the amount of his liability; or

        (iv)   whether or not any person is entitled in any case to relief or to any repayment, remission or drawback of any such duty or levy, or the amount of the relief, repayment, remission or drawback to which any person is entitled;

    (b)   so much of any decision by the Commissioners that a person is liable to any duty of excise, or as to the amount of his liability, as is contained in any assessment under section 12 above;

    [(ba)   any decision by the Commissioners to assess any person to excise duty under section 12A(2) above, section 61, 94, 96 or 167 of the Management Act[, section 8, 10[,11 or 36G] of the Alcoholic Liquor Duties Act 1979,] section 10, 13, [13AB,] 14, 23 or 24 of the Hydrocarbon Oil Duties Act 1979, [section 8 of the Tobacco Products Duty Act 1979, section 2 of the Finance (No 2) Act 1992,] or as to the amount of duty to which a person is to be assessed under any of those provisions;]

    [(bb)   any decision of the Commissioners on a claim under section 137A of the Customs and Excise Management Act 1979 for repayment of excise duty;]

[(bc)   any decision by the Commissioners as to whether or not any person is entitled to any drawback of excise duty by virtue of regulations under section 2 of the Finance (No 2) Act 1992, or the amount of the drawback to which any person is so entitled;]

[(bd)   any decision by the Commissioners as to whether or not any person is entitled to any repayment or credit by virtue of regulations under paragraph 4(2)(h) of Schedule 2A to the Alcoholic Liquor Duties Act 1979 (duty stamps), or the amount of the repayment or credit to which any person is so entitled;]

[(be)   any decision by the Commissioners made by virtue of regulations under paragraph 4(2)(i) of that Schedule that some or all of a payment made, or security provided, is forfeit, or the amount which is so forfeit;]

(c)   so much of any decision by the Commissioners that a person is liable to any penalty under any of the provisions of this Chapter, or as to the amount of his liability, as is contained in any assessment under section 13 above;

[(ca)   any decision as to whether or not—

    (i)   an amount due in respect of customs duty or agricultural levy, or

    (ii)   any repayment by the Commissioners of an amount paid by way of customs duty or agricultural levy,

is to carry interest, or as to the rate at which, or period for which, any such amount is to carry interest;]

(d)   any decision by the Commissioners or any officer which is of a description specified in Schedule 5 to this Act.

(2)   Any person who is—

(a)   a person whose liability to pay any relevant duty or penalty is determined by, results from or is or will be affected by any decision to which this section applies,

(b)   a person in relation to whom, or on whose application, such a decision has been made, or

(c)   a person on or to whom the conditions, limitations, restrictions, prohibitions or other requirements to which such a decision relates are or are to be imposed or applied,

may by notice in writing to the Commissioners require them to review that decision.

(3)   The Commissioners shall not be required under this section to review any decision unless the notice requiring the review is given before the end of the period of forty-five days beginning with the day on which written notification of the decision, or of the assessment containing the decision, was first given to the person requiring the review.

(4)   For the purposes of subsection (3) above it shall be the duty of the Commissioners to give written notification of any decision to which this section applies to any person who—

(a)   requests such a notification;

(b)   has not previously been given written notification of that decision; and

(c)   if given such a notification, will be entitled to require a review of the decision under this section.

(5)   A person shall be entitled to give a notice under this section requiring a decision to be reviewed for a second or subsequent time only if—

(a)   the grounds on which he requires the further review are that the Commissioners did not, on any previous review, have the opportunity to consider certain facts or other matters; and

(b)   he does not, on the further review, require the Commissioners to consider any facts or matters which were considered on a previous review except in so far as they are relevant to any issue to which the facts or matters not previously considered relate.

(6)   If it appears to the Commissioners that there is any description of decisions falling to be made for the purposes of any provision of—

(a)   the Community Customs Code,

(b)   any Community legislation made for the purpose of implementing that Code, or

(c)   any enactment or subordinate legislation so made,

which are not decisions to which this section otherwise applies, the Commissioners may by regulations provide for this section to apply to decisions of that description as it applies to the decisions mentioned in subsection (1) above.

(7)   The power to make regulations under subsection (6) above shall be exercisable by statutory instrument subject to annulment in pursuance of a resolution of either House of Parliament and shall include power—

(a)   to provide, in relation to any description of decisions to which this section is applied by any such regulations, that section 16(4) below shall have effect as if those decisions were of a description specified in Schedule 5 to this Act; and

(b)   to make such other incidental, supplemental, consequential and transitional provision as the Commissioners think fit.

NOTES

Sub-s (1): para (ba) inserted by the Finance Act 1997, s 50(2), Sch 6, paras 1(2), 7, words within first pair of square brackets substituted by the Finance Act 2002, s 4, Sch 1 para 4(1), (4); words in first and second pairs of square brackets substituted by the Finance Act 1998, s 20, Sch 2, paras 10(a), (b), 12, words in third pair of square brackets inserted by the Finance Act 1998, s 20, Sch 2, paras 10(c), (b), 12 (this amendment is not yet in force insofar as it relates to the Finance (No 2) Act 1992); para (bb) inserted by the Finance Act 1995, s 20(4), in relation to payments made on or after 1 December 1995; para (bc) inserted by the Finance Act 2002, s 21(2) (this amendment does not apply in relation to decisions made before the day the Finance Act 2002 comes into force). Paras (bd), (be) inserted by the Finance Act 2004, s 4(4) with effect in relation to retail containers containing alcoholic liquor if the excise duty point for the alcoholic liquor falls on or after 22 February 2006. For definition of "excise duty point" see the Finance (No 2) Act 1992, s 1. Para (ca) substituted for word "and" at the end of para (c) by the Finance Act 1999, s 130(1), (4), with effect in relation to decisions made on or after 27 July 1999.

Community Customs Code: Regulation of the Council of the European Communities dated 12 October 1992 (EEC) No 2913/92, OJ No L302, 19.10.92, p 1.

Regulations: the Customs Reviews and Appeals (Tariff and Origin) Regulations 1997, SI 1997/534.

Note: ss 14–16 apply in relation to liability to pay remote gaming duty (BGDA 1981 s 26M, as inserted by FA 2007, s 8, Sch 1, para 2).

---

15 Review procedure

(1)   Where the Commissioners are required in accordance with this Chapter to review any decision, it shall be their duty to do so and they may, on that review, either—

(a)   confirm the decision; or

(b)   withdraw or vary the decision and take such further steps (if any) in consequence of the withdrawal or variation as they may consider appropriate.

(2)   Where—

(a) it is the duty of the Commissioners in pursuance of a requirement by any person under section 14 above to review any decision; and

(b) they do not, within the period of forty-five days beginning with the day on which the review was required, give notice to that person of their determination on the review,

they shall be assumed for the purposes of this Chapter to have confirmed the decision.

(3) The Commissioners shall not by virtue of any requirement under this Chapter to review a decision have any power, apart from their power in pursuance of section 8(4) above, to mitigate the amount of any penalty imposed under this Chapter.

NOTES

Note: ss 14–16 apply in relation to liability to pay remote gaming duty (BGDA 1981 s 26M, as inserted by FA 2007, s 8, Sch 1, para 2).

16 Appeals to a tribunal

(1) Subject to the following provisions of this section, an appeal shall lie to an appeal tribunal with respect to any of the following decisions, that is to say—

(a) any decision by the Commissioners on a review under section 15 above (including a deemed confirmation under subsection (2) of that section); and

(b) any decision by the Commissioners on such review of a decision to which section 14 above applies as the Commissioners have agreed to undertake in consequence of a request made after the end of the period mentioned in section 14(3) above.

(2) An appeal under this section shall not be entertained unless the appellant is the person who required the review in question.

(3) An appeal which relates to, or to any decision on a review of, any decision falling within any of paragraphs (a) to (c) of section 14(1) above shall not be entertained if any amount is outstanding from the appellant in respect of any liability of the appellant to pay any relevant duty to the Commissioners (including an amount of any such duty which would be so outstanding if the appeal had already been decided in favour of the Commissioners) unless—

(a) the Commissioners have, on the application of the appellant, issued a certificate stating either—

(i) that such security as appears to them to be adequate has been given to them for the payment of that amount; or

(ii) that, on the grounds of the hardship that would otherwise be suffered by the appellant, they either do not require the giving of security for the payment of that amount or have accepted such lesser security as they consider appropriate;

or

(b) the tribunal to which the appeal is made decide that the Commissioners should not have refused to issue a certificate under paragraph (a) above and are satisfied that such security (if any) as it would have been reasonable for the Commissioners to accept in the circumstances has been given to the Commissioners.

[(3A) Subsection (3) above shall not apply if the appeal arises out of an assessment under section 8, 10 or 11 of the Alcoholic Liquor Duties Act 1979.]

(4) In relation to any decision as to an ancillary matter, or any decision on the review of such a decision, the powers of an appeal tribunal on an appeal under this section shall be confined to a power, where the tribunal are satisfied that

the Commissioners or other person making that decision could not reasonably have arrived at it, to do one or more of the following, that is to say—

(a)   to direct that the decision, so far as it remains in force, is to cease to have effect from such time as the tribunal may direct;

(b)   to require the Commissioners to conduct, in accordance with the directions of the tribunal, a further review of the original decision; and

(c)   in the case of a decision which has already been acted on or taken effect and cannot be remedied by a further review, to declare the decision to have been unreasonable and to give directions to the Commissioners as to the steps to be taken for securing that repetitions of the unreasonableness do not occur when comparable circumstances arise in future.

(5)   In relation to other decisions, the powers of an appeal tribunal on an appeal under this section shall also include power to quash or vary any decision and power to substitute their own decision for any decision quashed on appeal.

(6)   On an appeal under this section the burden of proof as to—

(a)   the matters mentioned in subsection (1)(a) and (b) of section 8 above,

(b)   the question whether any person has acted knowingly in using any substance or liquor in contravention of section 114(2) of the Management Act, and

(c)   the question whether any person had such knowledge or reasonable cause for belief as is required for liability to a penalty to arise under section 22(1) or 23(1) of the Hydrocarbon Oil Duties Act 1979 (use of fuel substitute or road fuel gas on which duty not paid),

shall lie upon the Commissioners; but it shall otherwise be for the appellant to show that the grounds on which any such appeal is brought have been established.

(7)   An appeal tribunal shall not, by virtue of anything contained in this section, have any power, apart from their power in pursuance of section 8(4) above, to mitigate the amount of any penalty imposed under this Chapter.

(8)   [Subject to subsection (9) below] references in this section to a decision as to an ancillary matter are references to any decision of a description specified in Schedule 5 to this Act which is not comprised in a decision falling within section 14(1)(a) to (c) above.

[(9)   References in this section to a decision as to an ancillary matter do not include a reference to a decision of a description specified in [the following paragraphs of Schedule 5—

(a)   paragraph 3(4);

(b)   paragraph 4(3);

(c)   paragraph 9(e);

(d)   paragraph 9A.]

(10)   Nothing in this section shall be taken to confer on an appeal tribunal any power to vary an amount of interest specified in an assessment under paragraph 11A of Schedule 6 to this Act except in so far as it is necessary to reduce it to the amount which is appropriate under paragraph 7 of that Schedule.]

NOTES

Commencement: 1 May 1995 (sub-ss (9), (10)); 1 January 1995 (sub-ss (1)–(5), (7), (8) (for certain purposes), sub-s (6) (in part)); 1 November 1994 (sub-ss (1)–(5), (7), (8) (for remaining purposes), sub-s (6) (remainder)).

Sub-s (3A): inserted by the Finance Act 1998, s 20, Sch 2, para 11.

Sub-s (8): words in square brackets inserted by the Finance Act 1995, s 16(3), (4), in relation to accounting periods ending on or after 1 January 1995.

Sub-ss (9), (10): added by the Finance Act 1995, s 16(3), (4), in relation to accounting periods ending on or after 1 January 1995

Sub-s (9), words in square brackets substituted by the Finance Act 2001, s 15, Sch 3, Pt 4, paras 16, 21.

Regulations: Finance Act 2001 (Commencement No 2 and Saving Provision) Order 2001, SI 2001/3300.

Note: ss 14–16 apply in relation to liability to pay remote gaming duty (BGDA 1981 s 26M, as inserted by FA 2007, s 8, Sch 1, para 2).

Supplemental provisions

17 Interpretation

(1)   Subject to the following provisions of this section, expressions used in this Chapter and in the Management Act have the same meanings in this Chapter as in that Act.

(2)   In this Chapter—

"appeal tribunal" shall be construed in accordance with section 7(3) above;

"conduct" includes any act, omission or statement;

"contravention" includes a failure to comply, and cognate expressions shall be construed accordingly;

"the Community Customs Code" means the Regulation of the Council of the European Communities dated 12 October 1992 (EEC) No 2913/92 for establishing the Community Customs Code;

"the Management Act" means the Customs and Excise Management Act 1979;

"relevant duty" means any Community customs duty or agricultural levy of the European Community or any duty of excise; and

"subordinate legislation" has the same meaning as in the Interpretation Act 1978.

(3)   For the purposes of this Chapter a contravention consisting in a failure to do something at or before a particular time shall be taken to continue after that time until the thing is done, and references in this Chapter to the remedying of such a contravention shall be construed accordingly.

(4)   References in this Chapter to a duty of excise do not include references to [vehicle] excise duty.

NOTES

Sub-s (4): word in square brackets substituted by the Vehicle Excise and Registration Act 1994, s 63, Sch 3, para 32.

Regulation of the Council of the European Communities dated 12 October 1992 (EEC) No 2913/92: OJ L302, 19.10.92, p 1.

18 Consequential modifications of enactments

(1)   Subject to subsection (2) below, references in the Management Act to a penalty shall not include references to a penalty under this Chapter.

(2)   Section 117 of the Management Act (execution and distress against revenue traders) shall have effect—

(a)   as if any amount assessed as due from any person by way of a penalty under this Chapter. . ., were an amount of excise duty payable by that person; . . .

(b)   . . .

(3)–(7)   . . .

(8) Subsections (1) [and (2)] above shall be without prejudice to section 13(5) above; and subsection (7) above shall have effect in relation to any chargeable period ending after the coming into force of the provision which provides for the imposition of the penalty in question.

NOTES

Sub-s (2): words omitted repealed by the Finance Act 1997, ss 113, Sch 18, Pt V(2); para (b) amends the Customs and Excise Management Act 1979, s 117(7A).

Sub-s (3): partly repeals the Customs and Excise Management Act 1979, s 127, and remainder repealed by the Value Added Tax Act 1994, s 100(2), Sch 15.

Sub-s (4): repealed by the Finance Act 1997, s 113, Sch 18, Pt V(2).

Sub-s (5): amends the Betting and Gaming Duties Act 1981, s 29A(1).

Sub-s (6): amends the Finance Act 1993, s 35(1).

Sub-s (7): adds the Income and Corporation Taxes Act 1988, s 827(1A).

Sub-s (8): words in square brackets substituted by the Finance Act 1997, ss 53(4), (9).

19 Commencement of Chapter

(1) Subject to section 18(8) above, this Chapter shall come into force on such day as the Commissioners may by order made by statutory instrument appoint, and different days may be appointed under this subsection for different provisions and for different purposes.

(2) An order under this section may make such transitional provision and savings as appear to the Commissioners to be appropriate in connection with the bringing into force by such an order of any provision of this Chapter.

(3) Nothing in any provision of this Chapter shall, in respect of conduct occurring before the coming into force of that provision, impose or affect any liability to any civil or criminal penalty or any liability of goods to forfeiture.

NOTES

Orders: the Finance Act 1994, section 7, (Appointed Day) Order 1994, SI 1994/1690; the Finance Act 1994, section 7, (Appointed Day) (No 2) Order 1994, SI 1994/2143; the Finance Act 1994, Part I, (Appointed Day etc) Order 1994, SI 1994/2679.

CHAPTER III
CUSTOMS
Enforcement Powers

20 Interpretation, etc

(1) This Chapter applies to any person carrying on a trade or business which consists of or includes any of the following activities—

 (a) importing or exporting any goods of a class or description subject to a duty of customs (whether or not in fact chargeable with that duty);

 (b) producing, manufacturing or applying a process to them;

 (c) buying, selling or dealing in them;

 (d) handling or storing them;

 (e) financing or facilitating any activity mentioned in paragraphs (a) to (d) above.

(2) In subsection (1) above "duty of customs" includes any agricultural levy of the European Community.

(3) In this Chapter—

 (a) "*customs goods*" means any goods mentioned in paragraph (a) of subsection (1) above; and (b)　　any reference to the business of a person to whom this Chapter applies is a reference to the trade or business carried on by him as mentioned in that subsection.

(4)　This Chapter shall have effect and be construed as if it were contained in the Customs and Excise Management Act 1979.

(5)　In consequence of the provision made by sections 21 to 27 below, any power under—

(a)　　section 75A, 75B or 75C of the Customs and Excise Management Act 1979 to require a person importing or exporting goods to keep or preserve records, or

(b)　　section 77A, 77B or 77C of that Act to require a person to furnish information or produce documents relating to imported or exported goods,

shall cease to be exercisable in relation to a person to the extent that the goods in question are customs goods.

21 Requirements about keeping records

(1)　The Commissioners may by regulations require any person to whom this Chapter applies—

(a)　　to keep such records as may be prescribed in the regulations; and

(b)　　to preserve those records—

(i)　　for such period not exceeding four years as may be prescribed in the regulations, or

(ii)　　for such lesser period as the Commissioners may require.

(2)　The Commissioners may also require any person mentioned in subsection (3) below—

(a)　　to keep such records as they may specify; and

(b)　　to preserve those records for such period not exceeding four years as they may require.

(3)　The person referred to is any person who—

(a)　　is not carrying on a trade or business which consists of or includes the importation or exportation of customs goods, but

(b)　　is concerned in some other capacity in such importation or exportation.

(4)　A duty imposed under subsection (1)(b) or (2)(b) above to preserve records may be discharged by the preservation of the information contained in them by such means as the Commissioners may approve.

(5)　On giving approval under subsection (4) above, the Commissioners may impose such reasonable requirements as appear to them necessary for securing that the information will be as readily available to them as if the records themselves had been preserved.

(6)　Regulations under this section may—

(a)　　make different provision for different cases; and

(b)　　be framed by reference to such records as may be specified in any notice published by the Commissioners in pursuance of the regulations and not withdrawn by a further notice.

(7)　Any person who fails to comply with a requirement imposed by virtue of this section shall be liable on summary conviction to a penalty not exceeding level 3 on the standard scale.

NOTES

Regulations: the Customs Traders (Accounts and Records) Regulations 1995, SI 1995/1203.

---

22 Records and rules of evidence

(1) Where any information is preserved by approved means as mentioned in section 21(4) above, a copy of any document in which it is contained shall, subject to subsection (2) below, be admissible in evidence in any proceedings, whether civil or criminal, to the same extent as the records themselves.

(2) A statement contained in a document produced by a computer shall not by virtue of subsection (1) above be admissible in evidence—

(a)   . . .;

(b)   . . .;

(c)   in civil proceedings in Scotland, except in accordance with sections 5 and 6 of the Civil Evidence (Scotland) Act 1988;

(d)   in criminal proceedings in Scotland, except in accordance with [Schedule 8 to the Criminal Procedure (Scotland) Act 1995];

(e)   . . .; and

(f)   . . .

NOTES

Sub-s (2): para (a) repealed by the Civil Evidence Act 1995, s 15(2), Sch 2, words in para (b) repealed by the Youth Justice and Criminal Evidence Act 1999, s 67(3), Sch 6, as from 14 April 2000 (by virtue of SI 2000/1034), para (b) repealed by the Criminal Justice Act 2003, s 332, Sch 37 Pt 6, in para (d) words in square brackets substituted by the Criminal Procedure (Consequential Provisions) (Scotland) Act 1995, s 5, Sch 4, para 89(2), para (e) repealed by the Civil Evidence (Northern Ireland) Order 1997, SI 1997/2983 (NI 21), art 13(2), Sch 2, subject to savings; para (f) repealed by the Criminal Justice (Evidence) (Northern Ireland) Order, SI 2004/1501 art 46(2), Sch 2, subject to savings (see art 43 thereof).

---

23 Furnishing of information and production of documents

(1) Every person to whom this Chapter applies shall furnish the Commissioners, within such time and in such form as they may reasonably require, with such information relating to his business as they may reasonably specify.

(2) Every person to whom this Chapter applies shall, if required to do so by an officer, produce or cause to be produced for inspection by the officer—

(a)   at that person's principal place of business or at such other place as the officer may reasonably require, and

(b)   at such time as the officer may reasonably require,

any documents which relate to his business.

(3) Where it appears to an officer that any documents which relate to a business of a person to whom this Chapter applies are in the possession of another person, the officer may require that other person, at such time and place as the officer may reasonably require, to produce those documents or cause them to be produced.

(4) For the purposes of this section, the documents which relate to a business of a person to whom this Chapter applies shall be taken to include—

(a)   any profit and loss account and balance sheet, and

(b)   any documents required to be kept by virtue of section 21(1) above.

(5) Every person mentioned in section 21(3) above shall furnish the Commissioners, within such time and in such form as they may reasonably require, with such information relating to the importation or exportation of customs goods in which he is concerned as they may reasonably specify.

(6) Every person mentioned in section 21(3) above shall, if required to do so by an officer, produce or cause to be produced for inspection by the officer at such time and place as the officer may reasonably require, any documents which relate to the importation or exportation of customs goods in which he is concerned.

(7)   An officer may take copies of, or make extracts from, any document produced under this section.

(8)   If it appears to an officer to be necessary to do so, he may, at a reasonable time and for a reasonable period, remove any document produced under this section.

(9)   Where a document is removed under subsection (8) above—

   (a)   if the person from whom the document is removed so requests, he shall be given a record of what was removed;

   (b)   if the document is reasonably required for the proper conduct of any business, the person by whom the document was produced or caused to be produced shall be provided as soon as practicable with a copy of the document free of charge;

   (c)   if the document is lost or damaged, the Commissioners shall be liable to compensate the owner of it for any expenses reasonably incurred by him in replacing or repairing it.

(10)   If a person claims a lien on any document produced by him under subsection (3) or (6) above—

   (a)   the production of the document shall be without prejudice to the lien; and

   (b)   the removal of the document under subsection (8) above shall not be regarded as breaking the lien.

(11)   Any person who fails to comply with a requirement imposed under this section shall be liable on summary conviction to a penalty not exceeding level 3 on the standard scale.

24 Power of entry

Where an officer has reasonable cause to believe that—

   (a)   any premises are used in connection with a business of a person to whom this Chapter applies, and

   (b)   any customs goods are on those premises,

he may at any reasonable time enter and inspect those premises and inspect any goods found on them.

25 Order for production of documents

(1)   Where, on an application by an officer, a justice is satisfied that there are reasonable grounds for believing—

   (a)   that an offence in connection with a duty of customs is being, has been or is about to be committed, and

   (b)   that any information or documents which may be required as evidence for the purpose of any proceedings in respect of such an offence is in the possession of any person,

he may make an order under this section.

(2)   An order under this section is an order that the person who appears to the justice to be in possession of the information or documents to which the application relates shall—

   (a)   furnish an officer with the information or produce the document,

   (b)   permit an officer to take copies of or make extracts of any document produced, and

   (c)   permit an officer to remove any document which he reasonably considers necessary,

not later than the end of the period of seven days beginning with the date of the order or the end of such longer period as the order may specify.

(3) In this section "justice" means a justice of the peace or, in relation to Scotland, a justice within the meaning of [section 308 of the Criminal Procedure (Scotland) Act 1995].

NOTES

Sub-s (3): words in square brackets substituted by the Criminal Procedure (Consequential Provisions) (Scotland) Act 1995, s 5, Sch 4, para 89(3).

26 Procedure when documents are removed

(1) An officer who removes any document in the exercise of a power conferred under section 25 above shall, if so requested by a person showing himself—

    (a)   to be the occupier of premises from which it was removed, or

    (b)   to have had custody or control of it immediately before the removal,

provide that person with a record of what he removed.

(2) The officer shall provide the record within a reasonable time from the making of the request for it.

(3) Subject to subsection (7) below, if a request for permission to be granted access to any document which—

    (a)   has been removed by an officer, and

    (b)   is retained by the Commissioners for the purposes of investigating an offence,

is made to the officer in charge of the investigation by a person who had custody or control of the document immediately before it was so removed or by someone acting on behalf of such a person, the officer shall allow the person who made the request access to it under the supervision of an officer.

(4) Subject to subsection (7) below, if a request for a photograph or copy of any such document is made to the officer in charge of the investigation by a person who had custody or control of the document immediately before it was so removed, or by someone acting on behalf of such a person, the officer shall—

    (a)   allow the person who made the request access to it under the supervision of an officer for the purpose of photographing it or copying it, or

    (b)   photograph or copy it, or cause it to be photographed or copied.

(5) Where any document is photographed or copied under subsection (4)(b) above, the photograph or copy shall be supplied to the person who made the request.

(6) The photograph or copy shall be supplied within a reasonable time from the making of the request.

(7) There is no duty under this section to grant access to, or to supply a photograph or copy of, any document if the officer in charge of the investigation for the purposes of which it was removed has reasonable grounds for believing that to do so would prejudice—

    (a)   that investigation;

    (b)   the investigation of an offence other than the offence for the purposes of the investigation of which the document was removed; or

    (c)   any criminal proceedings which may be brought as a result of—

        (i)   the investigation of which he is in charge; or

        (ii)   any such investigation as is mentioned in paragraph (b) above.

(8) Any reference in this section to the officer in charge of the investigation is a reference to the person whose name and address are endorsed on the order concerned as being the officer in charge of it.

27 Failure of officer to comply with requirements under section 26

(1) Where, on an application made as mentioned in subsection (2) below, the appropriate judicial authority is satisfied that a person has failed to comply with a requirement imposed by section 26 above, the authority may order that person to comply with the requirement within such time and in such manner as may be specified in the order.

(2) An application under subsection (1) above shall be made—

    (a)   in the case of a failure to comply with any of the requirements imposed by subsections (1) and (2) of section 26 above, by the occupier of the premises from which the document in question was removed or by the person who had custody or control of it immediately before it was so removed, and

    (b)   in any other case, by the person who has such custody or control.

(3) In this section "the appropriate judicial authority" means—

    (a)   in England and Wales, a magistrates' court;

    (b)   in Scotland, the sheriff; and

    (c)   in Northern Ireland, a court of summary jurisdiction, as defined in Article 2(2)(a) of the Magistrates' Courts (Northern Ireland) Order 1981.

(4) Any application for an order under this section—

    (a)   in England and Wales, shall be made by way of complaint; or

    (b)   in Northern Ireland, shall be made by way of civil proceedings upon complaint.

(5) Sections 21 and 42(2) of the Interpretation Act (Northern Ireland) 1954 (rules and orders regulating procedure of courts etc and assignment of business to particular courts) shall apply as if any reference in those provisions to any enactment included a reference to this section.

CHAPTER IV
AIR PASSENGER DUTY
The duty

28 Air passenger duty

(1) A duty to be known as air passenger duty shall be charged in accordance with this Chapter on the carriage on a chargeable aircraft of any chargeable passenger.

(2) Subject to the provisions of this Chapter about accounting and payment, the duty in respect of any carriage on an aircraft of a chargeable passenger—

    (a)   becomes due when the aircraft first takes off on the passenger's flight, and

    (b)   shall be paid by the operator of the aircraft.

(3) Subject to section 29 below, every aircraft designed or adapted to carry persons in addition to the flight crew is a chargeable aircraft for the purposes of this Chapter.

(4) Subject to sections 31 and 32 below, every passenger on an aircraft is a chargeable passenger for the purposes of this Chapter if his flight begins at an airport in the United Kingdom.

(5) In this Chapter, "flight", in relation to any person, means his carriage on an aircraft; and for the purposes of this Chapter, a person's flight is to be treated as beginning when he first boards the aircraft and ending when he finally disembarks from the aircraft.

29 Chargeable aircraft

(1) Where—

    (a)   the authorised take-off weight in respect of an aircraft is less than ten tonnes, or

    (b)   an aircraft is not authorised to seat twenty or more persons (excluding members of the flight crew and cabin attendants),

the aircraft is not a chargeable aircraft for the purposes of this Chapter.

(2)   In this section "take-off weight", in relation to an aircraft, means the total weight of the aircraft and its contents when taking off; and for the purposes of this section the authorised take-off weight of an aircraft is less than ten tonnes if—

    (a)   there is a certificate of airworthiness in force in respect of the aircraft showing that the maximum authorised take-off weight (assuming the most favourable circumstances for take-off) is less than ten tonnes, or

    (b)   the Commissioners are satisfied that the aircraft is not designed or adapted to take off when its take-off weight is ten tonnes or more (assuming the most favourable circumstances for take-off) or the aircraft belongs to a class or description of aircraft in respect of which the Commissioners are so satisfied.

(3)   For the purposes of this section an aircraft is not authorised as mentioned in subsection (1)(b) above if—

    (a)   there is a certificate of airworthiness in force in respect of the aircraft showing that the maximum number of persons who may be seated on the aircraft (excluding members of the flight crew and cabin attendants) is less than twenty, or

    (b)   the Commissioners are satisfied that the aircraft is not designed or adapted to seat twenty or more persons (excluding members of the flight crew and cabin attendants) or the aircraft belongs to a class or description of aircraft in respect of which the Commissioners are so satisfied.

(4)   In this section "certificate of airworthiness" has the same meaning as in the Air Navigation Order.

30 The rate of duty

(1)   Air passenger duty shall be charged on the carriage of each chargeable passenger at the rate [determined in accordance with subsections (2) to (4) below].

[(2)   [If the place where the passenger's journey ends] is in the area specified in subsection (3) below and in—

    (a)   the United Kingdom or another EEA State, . . .

    (b)   any territory for whose external relations the United Kingdom or another member State is responsible] [or

    (c)   any qualifying territory (so long as not falling within paragraph (a) above),]

[the rate shall be determined in accordance with subsection (3A) below.]

(3)   The area referred to in subsection (2) above is the area bounded by the meridians of longitude 32 degrees W and [45 degrees E] and the parallels of latitude 26 degrees N and 81 degrees N.

[(3A)   In a case falling within subsection (2) above—

    (a)   if the passenger's agreement for carriage provides for standard class travel in relation to every flight on his journey, the rate is [£10];

    (b)   in any other case, the rate is [£20].]

[(4)   In a case not falling within subsection (2) above—

    (a)   if the passenger's agreement for carriage provides for standard class travel in relation to every flight on his journey, the rate is [£40];

    (b)   in any other case, the rate is [£80].]

Part I

(5) Subject to subsection (6) below, the journey of a passenger whose agreement for carriage is evidenced by a ticket ends for the purposes of this section at his final place of destination.

(6) Where in the case of such a passenger—

(a)   his journey includes two or more flights, and

(b)   any of those flights is not followed by a connected flight,

his journey ends for those purposes where the first flight not followed by a connected flight ends.

(7) The journey of any passenger whose agreement for carriage is not evidenced by a ticket ends for those purposes where his flight ends.

(8) For the purposes of this Chapter, successive flights are connected if (and only if) they are treated under an order as connected.

[(9) In this section "EEA State" means a State which is a Contracting Party to the EEA Agreement but until the EEA Agreement comes into force in relation to Liechtenstein does not include the State of Liechtenstein; and "EEA Agreement" here means the Agreement on the European Economic Area signed at Oporto on 2nd May 1992 as adjusted by the Protocol signed at Brussels on 17th March 1993.]

[(9A) In this section "qualifying territory" means each of the following territories—

[Albania]	Estonia	Malta	Slovenia
[Bosnia and Herzegovina]	Former Yugoslav Republic of Macedonia	Montenegro	Switzerland
Bulgaria	Hungary	Poland	Turkey.]
Croatia	Kosovo under the Interim Administration of the United Nations Mission	Romania	
Cyprus	Latvia	Serbia	
[Czech Republic]	Lithuania	Slovak Republic	

[(9B) The Treasury may by order amend the definition of "qualifying territory" in subsection (9A) above by adding, removing, or varying the description of, any territory.]

[(10) In this section "standard class travel", in relation to carriage on an aircraft, means—

(a)   in the case of an aircraft on which only one class of travel is available, that class of travel;

(b)   in any other case, the lowest class of travel available on the aircraft.]

NOTES

Sub-s (1): words in square brackets substituted by the Finance Act 2000 s 18 (1), (2), (8) with effect for any carriage of a passenger on an aircraft which begins after 31 March 2001. Words previously read "appropriate for the place where the passenger's journey ends".

Sub-s (2): substituted with retrospective effect to 1 November 1994 by the Finance Act 1995, s 15(1), (2); sum in square brackets substituted by the Finance Act 1997, s 9, in relation to cases where, in accordance with s 28(2)(a), duty becomes due on or after 1 November 1997; words in square brackets substituted and added by the Finance Act 2000, s 18(1), (3), (8) with effect for any carriage of a passenger on an aircraft which begins after 31 March 2001. Words substituted previously read "The rate is £10 if that place". Word in para (a) repealed, and para (c) inserted by the Finance Act 2002, s 118(1), (2).

Sub-s (3): words substituted by the Finance Act 2002, s 118(1), (3).

Sub-ss (3A), (10): inserted by the Finance Act 2000 s 18(1), (4), (6), (8) with effect for any carriage of a passenger on an aircraft which begins after 31 March 2001; references in sub-s (3A) substituted by the Finance Act 2007 s 12(3) with effect for any carriage of a passenger on an aircraft which begins on or after 1st February 2007. If the amount of duty due from any operator in the accounting period ending before 21 March 2007 increased as a result of these amendments, the operator is to pay the amount of that increase as if it became due in the first accounting period ending after that day (FA 2007 s 12(5)).

Sub-s (4): substituted by the Finance Act 2000 s 18(1), (5), (8) with effect for any carriage of a passenger on an aircraft which begins after 31 March 2001; references substituted by the Finance Act 2007 s 12(3) with effect for any carriage of a passenger on an aircraft which begins on or after 1st February 2007. If the amount of duty due from any operator in the accounting period ending before 21 March 2007 increased as a result of these amendments, the operator is to pay the amount of that increase as if it became due in the first accounting period ending after that day (FA 2007 s 12(5)).

Sub-s (9): added with retrospective effect to 1 November 1994 by the Finance Act 1995, s 15(1), (3).

Sub-ss (9A), (B): inserted by the Finance Act 2002, s 118(1), (4).

Sub-s (9A) entry "Croatia" inserted by the Air Passenger Duty (Rate) (Qualifying Territories) Order, SI 2006/2693 art 2; entries "Albania", "Bosnia and Herzegovina", "Former Yugoslav Republic of Macedonia", Kosovo under the Interim Administration of the United Nations Mission", "Montenegro" and "Serbia" inserted by the Air Passenger Duty (Rate) (Qualifying Territories) Order, SI 2007/22.

Orders: the Air Passenger Duty (Connected Flights) Order 1994, SI 1994/1821, as amended by SI 2001/809.

---

31 Passengers: exceptions

(1), (2) . . .

(3) A passenger whose agreement for carriage is evidenced by a ticket is not a chargeable passenger in relation to a flight which is the second or a subsequent flight on his journey if—

    (a)   the prescribed particulars of the flight are shown on the ticket, and

    (b)   that flight and the previous flight are connected.

(4) A child who—

    (a)   has not attained the age of two years, and

    (b)   is not allocated a separate seat before he first boards the aircraft,

is not a chargeable passenger.

[(4A) A passenger is not a chargeable passenger in relation to a flight if under his agreement for carriage (whether or not it is evidenced by a ticket)—

    (a)   the flight is to depart from and return to the same airport, and

    (b)   the duration of the flight (excluding any period during which the aircraft's doors are open for boarding or disembarkation) is not to exceed 60 minutes.]

[(4B) A passenger is not a chargeable passenger in relation to a flight if under his agreement for carriage (whether or not it is evidenced by a ticket) the flight is to depart from an airport which is in a region of the United Kingdom designated by order.

(4C) An order may be made for the purposes of subsection (4B) above in respect of any region which has a population density of not more than 12.5 persons per square kilometre.

(4D) In subsections (4B) and (4C) above, references to a region are references to an area which is determined by the Treasury to constitute a region for the purposes of those subsections.]

(5) A passenger not carried for reward is not a chargeable passenger if he is carried—

    (a)   in pursuance of any requirement imposed under any enactment, or

   (b)   for the purpose only of inspecting matters relating to the aircraft or the flight crew.

(6) . . .

NOTES

Sub-ss (1), (2), (6): repealed by FA 2000 ss 19(1), (2), (4), 156, Sch 40, Pt I, with effect for any carriage of a passenger on an aircraft which begins after 31 March 2001. Sub-ss previously read—

  (1)   Where in the case of a passenger whose agreement for carriage is evidenced by a return ticket—

     (a)   he is a chargeable passenger in relation to a flight on his outward journey, and

     (b)   his final place of destination in relation to that journey is in the United Kingdom,

he is not a chargeable passenger in relation to a flight on his return journey.

  (2)   Subsection (1) above does not apply if—

     (a)   either his outward journey or his return journey includes two or more flights, and

     (b)   in relation to any of those flights (other than the first) on the journey in question, he would (apart from that subsection) be a chargeable passenger.

  (6)   Regulations may provide for subsection (1) above to have effect as if the reference in paragraph (a) to a person who is a chargeable passenger in relation to a flight on his outward journey included a person whose outward journey began at an airport in the Isle of Man.

Sub-s (4A): inserted by the Finance Act 1996, s 13(1).

Sub-ss (4B)–(4D): inserted by FA 2000 s 19(1), (3) with effect for any carriage of a passenger on an aircraft which begins after 31 March 2001.

Regulations: the Air Passenger Duty Regulations 1994, SI 1994/1738; Air Passenger Duty (Designated Region of the United Kingdom) Order 2001, SI 2001/808.

32 Change of circumstances after ticket issued etc

  (1)   [Subsections (2) and (3) below apply] in the case of a person whose agreement for carriage is evidenced by a ticket.

  (2)   Where—

     (a)   at the time the ticket is issued or, if it is altered, at the time it is last altered, he would not (assuming there is no change of circumstances) be a chargeable passenger in relation to any flight in the course of his journey, and

     (b)   by reason only of a change of circumstances not attributable to any act or default of his, he arrives at or departs from an airport in the course of that journey on a flight the prescribed particulars of which were not shown on his ticket at that time,

he shall not by reason of the change of circumstances be treated as a chargeable passenger in relation to that flight.

  (3)   Where—

     (a)   at the time the ticket is issued or, if it is altered, at the time it is last altered, he would (assuming there is no change of circumstances) be a chargeable passenger in relation to one or more flights ("the proposed chargeable flights") in the course of his journey,

     (b)   by reason only of a change of circumstances not attributable to any act or default of his, he arrives at or departs from an airport in the course of that journey on a flight the prescribed particulars of which were not shown on his ticket at that time, and

    (c)   but for this subsection he would by reason of the change be a chargeable passenger in relation to a number of flights exceeding the number of the proposed chargeable flights,

he shall not by reason of the change of circumstances be treated as a chargeable passenger in relation to that flight.

  [(4) Where—

    (a)   at the time a passenger's flight begins, by virtue of section 31(4A) above he would not (assuming there is no change of circumstances) be a chargeable passenger in relation to the flight, and

    (b)   by reason only of a change of circumstances not attributable to any act or default of his, the flight does not return to the airport from which it departed or exceeds 60 minutes in duration (excluding any period during which the aircraft's doors are open for boarding or disembarkation),

he shall not by reason of the change of circumstances be treated as a chargeable passenger in relation to that flight.]

NOTES

Sub-s (1): words in square brackets substituted by the Finance Act 1996, s 13(2)(a).
Sub-s (4): inserted by the Finance Act 1996, s 13(2)(b).
Regulations: the Air Passenger Duty Regulations 1994, SI 1994/1738.

Persons liable for the duty

33 Registration of aircraft operators

(1)   The Commissioners shall under this section keep a register of aircraft operators.

(2)   The operator of a chargeable aircraft becomes liable to be registered under this section if the aircraft is used for the carriage of any chargeable passengers.

(3)   A person who has become liable to be registered under this section ceases to be so liable if the Commissioners are satisfied at any time—

    (a)   that he no longer operates any chargeable aircraft, or

    (b)   that no chargeable aircraft which he operates will be used for the carriage of chargeable passengers.

(4)   A person who is not registered and has not given notice under this subsection shall, if he becomes liable to be registered at any time, give written notice of that fact to the Commissioners not later than the end of the prescribed period beginning with that time.

(5)   Notice under subsection (4) above shall be in such form, be given in such manner and contain such information as the Commissioners may direct.

(6)   If a person who is required to give notice under subsection (4) above fails to do so, his failure shall attract a penalty under section 9 above which, if any amount of duty is then due from him and unpaid, shall be calculated by reference to that amount.

(7)   Regulations may make provision as to the information to be included in, and the correction of, the register kept under this section.

(8)   In particular, the regulations may provide—

    (a)   for the inclusion in the register of persons who have not given notice under this section but appear to the Commissioners to be liable to be registered,

    (b)   for persons who are liable to be registered—

          (i)   not to be included in, or

     (ii)   to be removed from,

the register in prescribed circumstances,

    (c)   for the removal from the register of persons who have ceased to be so liable, and

    (d)   for the time from which an entry in the register is to be effective (which may be earlier than the time when the entry is first made in the register).

NOTES

Regulations: the Air Passenger Duty Regulations 1994, SI 1994/1738.

34 Fiscal representatives

(1) An aircraft operator who—

    (a)   is or is liable to be registered, and

    (b)   does not meet the requirements of subsection (3) below,

is required to have a fiscal representative.

(2) In this Chapter "fiscal representative", in relation to an aircraft operator, means a person who meets those requirements and stands appointed by the operator for the purposes of this section.

(3) A person meets the requirements of this subsection if—

    (a)   he has any business establishment or other fixed establishment in the United Kingdom, or

    (b)   if he is an individual, he has his usual place of residence in the United Kingdom.

(4) Where any person is appointed under this section to be the fiscal representative of any aircraft operator (in this section referred to as his "principal"), then, subject to subsection (5) [and section 34A] below, the fiscal representative—

    (a)   shall be entitled to act on his principal's behalf for any of the purposes of the enactments relating to duty,

    (b)   shall, subject to such provisions as may be made by regulations, secure (where appropriate by acting on his principal's behalf) his principal's compliance with and discharge of the obligations and liabilities to which his principal is subject by virtue of those enactments, and

    (c)   shall be personally liable in respect of any failure of his principal to comply with or discharge any such obligation or liability as if the obligations and liabilities imposed on his principal were imposed jointly and severally on the fiscal representative and his principal.

(5) A fiscal representative shall not be liable by virtue of subsection (4) above himself to be registered under section 33 above, but regulations may—

    (a)   require the names of fiscal representatives to be shown in such manner as may be prescribed against the names of their principals in the register kept under that section, and

    (b)   make it the duty of a fiscal representative, for the purposes of registration, to notify the Commissioners, within such period as may be prescribed, that his appointment has taken effect or has ceased to have effect.

NOTES

Sub-s (4): words in square brackets inserted by the Finance Act 1998, s 15(2).
Regulations: the Air Passenger Duty Regulations 1994, SI 1994/1738.

[34A Administrative representatives

(1)   Subject to the following provisions of this section, where—

(a)   the appointment of any person to be the fiscal representative of an aircraft operator contains a statement that the appointment is made for administrative purposes only,

(b)   the operator has complied with any obligations for the provision of security imposed, in relation to appointments containing such statements, by any general directions given by the Commissioners, and

(c)   the operator is not for the time being in contravention of any requirement to provide any security that he is required to provide under section 36 below,

that appointment shall have effect in accordance with subsection (2) below.

(2)   Where the appointment of any person as a fiscal representative has effect in accordance with this subsection section 34(4)(b) and (c) above shall be taken, in the case of that person—

(a)   not to impose any requirement on the representative to secure the payment of amounts of duty which are or may become due from his principal, and

(b)   not to make him personally liable either to pay any such amounts or in respect of any failure by his principal to pay them.

(3)   The security that may be required by general directions given by the Commissioners for the purposes of this section is any such security for the payment of amounts of duty which are or may become due from the person providing the security as may be determined in accordance with the directions.

(4)   The power of the Commissioners under section 36 below to require the provision of security shall not include any power to require a fiscal representative of an aircraft operator whose appointment has effect in accordance with subsection (2) above to provide any security for the payment of amounts of duty which are or may become due from his principal.

(5)   In this section references to an amount of duty include references to any penalty or interest that is recoverable as if it were an amount of duty, but only in so far as the penalty or interest is in respect of a failure by an aircraft operator to pay an amount of duty, or to pay such an amount before a certain time.]

NOTES

Commencement: 31 July 1998.

Inserted by the Finance Act 1998, s 15(1).

35   Fiscal representatives: supplementary

(1)   Regulations may make provision about—

(a)   the manner in which a person is to be appointed as a fiscal representative, and

(b)   the circumstances in which a person is to be treated as having ceased to be a fiscal representative.

(2)   If any aircraft operator who is required to have a fiscal representative fails to appoint such a representative before the prescribed time, his failure shall attract a penalty under section 9 above.

(3)   Any failure of a fiscal representative to give any notice which he is required to give by regulations under section 34(5)(b) above shall attract a penalty under section 9 above.

NOTES

Regulations: the Air Passenger Duty Regulations 1994, SI 1994/1738.

36 Security for payment of duty

(1) The Commissioners may require—

(a)   any operator of an aircraft who is or is liable to be registered, or

(b)   any fiscal representative,

to provide such security, or further security, as they may think appropriate for the payment of any duty which is or may become due from the operator.

(2) Any failure by a person to provide any security which he is required by the Commissioners to provide under subsection (1) above shall attract a penalty under section 9 above.

(3) For the purposes of this section, a person shall not be treated as having been required to provide security under subsection (1) above unless the Commissioners have either—

(a)   served notice of the requirement on him, or

(b)   taken all such other steps as appear to them to be reasonable for bringing the requirement to his attention.

37 Handling agents

(1) Where any amount of duty becomes payable at any time by the operator of an aircraft and, within the period of ninety days beginning with that time, that amount, or any other amount which becomes payable by him within the period, is not paid, the Commissioners may give notice under this section to any handling agent of his.

(2) If any operator of an aircraft who is required to have a fiscal representative fails to appoint such a representative before the prescribed time, the Commissioners may give notice under this section to any handling agent of his.

(3) In this Chapter "handling agent", in relation to the operator of an aircraft ("the principal"), means any person (other than an individual) who, under an agreement with the principal, makes arrangements for—

(a)   the allocation of seats to passengers on aircraft operated by the principal, or

(b)   the supervision of the boarding of such aircraft by passengers.

(4) A notice under this section—

(a)   may be given on the ground referred to in subsection (1) above only if the Commissioners consider it necessary to do so for the protection of the revenue, and

(b)   may at any time be withdrawn by the Commissioners.

(5) A notice under this section shall become effective on the date stated in it or, if later, the time when the notice is received by the handling agent and shall continue to be effective until withdrawn.

(6) If, where a notice given to a handling agent under this section is effective—

(a)   the allocation of seats to passengers on aircraft operated by his principal, or the supervision of the boarding of such aircraft by passengers, is carried out in pursuance of arrangements made by him under any agreement with his principal, and

(b)   any duty payable in respect of those passengers is not paid,

the handling agent shall be liable jointly and severally with his principal for the payment of the duty.

38 Accounting for and payment of duty

(1) Regulations shall require aircraft operators who are registered or liable to be registered—

    (a)   to keep accounts for the purposes of duty in such form and manner as may be prescribed, and

    (b)   to make returns in respect of duty—

        (i)   by reference to such periods as may be prescribed or as may be allowed by the Commissioners, in relation to a particular operator, in accordance with regulations, and

        (ii)   at such time and in such manner as may be prescribed or specified.

(2) Any person from whom any duty is due shall pay the duty at such time and in such manner as may be prescribed or specified.

(3) In this section "specified" means specified in a notice published, and not withdrawn, by the Commissioners.

(4) Any failure by any person to comply with regulations under this section shall, unless he is complying with the corresponding provisions of such a notice, attract a penalty under section 9 above and, in the case of any failure to keep accounts, daily penalties.

NOTES

Regulations: the Air Passenger Duty Regulations 1994, SI 1994/1738, as amended by SI 2001/836.

---

39 Schemes for simplifying operation of reliefs etc

(1) If in the opinion of the Commissioners it is expedient to do so in the light of difficulties encountered or expected to be encountered by any registered operator in obtaining and recording information about passengers and their journeys, they may in accordance with the provisions of this section prepare a scheme for the registered operator.

(2) Any scheme so prepared shall specify the period for which it is to have effect.

[(2A) A scheme may be either a standard scheme or an extended scheme.]

(3) [A standard scheme] for a registered operator shall relate only to passengers—

    (a)   who are carried on chargeable aircraft operated by that operator,

    (b)   whose flights begin in the United Kingdom, and

    (c)   who are not passengers of a description mentioned in section 31(4) or (5) above;

and in this section any reference to the relevant passengers of a registered operator is a reference to passengers who fall within this subsection in relation to him.

(4) [A standard scheme] for a registered operator shall provide, in relation to passengers who are relevant passengers of his in the period specified in the scheme, for methods of calculating—

    (a)   how many of those relevant passengers may be treated as passengers who are not chargeable passengers, and

    (b)   how many of them may be treated as passengers on the carriage of whom duty shall be charged *at the rate mentioned in section 30(2) above*.

[(4A) An extended scheme for a registered operator shall relate to all persons who are carried—

    (a)   on chargeable aircraft operated by that operator, and

    (b)   in circumstances where the aircraft take off in the United Kingdom;

and in this section any reference to persons travelling with a registered operator is a reference to persons who fall within this subsection in relation to him.

(4B)   An extended scheme for a registered operator shall provide, in relation to persons travelling with him in the period specified in the scheme, for methods of calculating—

    (a)   how many of them may be treated as persons who are not passengers,

    (b)   how many of them may be treated as passengers who are not chargeable passengers, and

    (c)   how many of them may be treated as passengers on the carriage of whom duty shall be charged[—

        (i)   at the rate mentioned in paragraph (a) of section 30(3A) above, and

        (ii)   at the rate mentioned in paragraph (b) of that provision].

(5)   A calculation provided for by the scheme may be provided by reference to such factors as appear to the Commissioners to be expedient in the circumstances, including in particular information—

    (a)   derived from surveys of [persons] carried on chargeable aircraft operated by the operator for whom the scheme is prepared, or

    (b)   relating to airports and routes used by that operator,

whether obtained before or during the specified period.

(6)   No scheme prepared in accordance with this section shall be of any effect unless the registered operator for whom it is prepared elects in writing to be bound by it for the specified period.

(7)   If the registered operator makes such an election the scheme shall have effect for the specified period . . .

(8)   [Where a standard scheme has effect for the specified period, this Chapter shall have effect for that period] as if, except in accordance with provision made to the contrary by the scheme (by virtue of subsection (4) above)—

    (a)   each of the passengers who are relevant passengers of the registered operator were chargeable passengers, and

    (b)   duty were charged[—

        (i)   on the carriage of each of those falling within paragraph (a) of section 30(4) above at the rate mentioned in that paragraph, and

        (ii)   on the carriage of each of those falling within paragraph (b) of section 30(4) above at the rate mentioned in that paragraph].

[(8A)   Where an extended scheme has effect for the specified period, this Chapter shall have effect for that period as if, except in accordance with provision made to the contrary by the scheme (by virtue of subsection (4B) above)—

    (a)   each of the persons travelling with the registered operator were passengers of his,

    (b)   each of those passengers were chargeable passengers, and

    (c)   duty were charged[—

        (i)   on the carriage of each of those falling within paragraph (a) of section 30(4) above at the rate mentioned in that paragraph, and

        (ii)   on the carriage of each of those falling within paragraph (b) of section 30(4) above at the rate mentioned in that paragraph.]

(9)   Regulations may make further provision with respect to schemes under this section, including in particular provision amending this section.

NOTES

Sub-ss (2A), (4A), (4B), (8A): inserted by the Air Passenger Duty (Extended Schemes) Regulations 1995, SI 1995/1216, reg 2(2), (5), (9).

Sub-ss (3), (5): words in square brackets substituted by SI 1995/1216, reg 2(3), (6).

Sub-s (4): words in square brackets substituted by SI 1995/1216, reg 2(5); words in para (b) substituted by the Finance Act 2000, s 18(1), (7)(a), (8) with effect for any carriage of a passenger on an aircraft which begins after 31 March 2001. Words in square brackets in para (b) previously read "on the carriage of each of them at the rate mentioned in section 30(4) above".

Sub-s (4B): words in square brackets in para (c) substituted by the Finance Act 2000, s 18(1), (7)(b), (8) with effect for any carriage of a passenger on an aircraft which begins after 31 March 2001. Words previously read "at the rate mentioned in section 30(2) above".

Sub-s (7): words omitted repealed by SI 1995/1216, reg 2(7).

Sub-s (8): words in square brackets substituted by SI 1995/1216, reg 2(5); words in square brackets in para (b) substituted by the Finance Act 2000, s 18(1), (7)(c), (8) with effect for any carriage of a passenger on an aircraft which begins after 31 March 2001. Words previously read "on the carriage of each of them at the rate mentioned in section 30(4) above".

Sub-s (8A): words in square brackets substituted by the Finance Act 2000, s 18(1), (7)(d), (8) with effect for any carriage of a passenger on an aircraft which begins after 31 March 2001. Words previously read "on the carriage of each of them at the rate mentioned in section 30(4) above".

Regulations: the Air Passenger Duty (Extended Schemes) Regulations 1995, SI 1995/1216.

Administration and enforcement

40 Administration and enforcement

(1)   Air passenger duty shall be a duty of excise and, accordingly, shall be under the care and management of the Commissioners.

(2)   Schedule 6 to this Act (administration and enforcement) shall have effect.

41 Offences

(1)   A person who is knowingly concerned—

(a)   in the fraudulent evasion (by him or another person) of duty, or

(b)   in taking steps with a view to such fraudulent evasion,

is guilty of an offence.

(2)   A person guilty of an offence under subsection (1) above is liable—

(a)   on summary conviction, to a penalty of—

(i)   the statutory maximum, or

(ii)   if greater, treble the amount of the duty evaded or sought to be evaded,

or to imprisonment for a term not exceeding six months, or to both, or

(b)   on conviction on indictment, to a penalty of any amount or to imprisonment for a term not exceeding seven years, or to both.

(3)   A person who in connection with duty—

(a)   makes a statement that he knows to be false in a material particular or recklessly makes a statement that is false in a material particular, or

(b)   with intent to deceive, produces or makes use of a book, account, return or other document that is false in a material particular,

is guilty of an offence.

(4)   A person guilty of an offence under subsection (3) above is liable—

(a)   on summary conviction, to a penalty of the statutory maximum or to imprisonment for a term not exceeding six months, or to both, or

(b)   on conviction on indictment, to a penalty of any amount or to imprisonment for a term not exceeding two years, or to both.

Supplementary

42 Regulations and orders

(1)   In this Chapter "regulations" means regulations made by the Commissioners and "order" means an order made by the Treasury.

(2)   Regulations and orders may make different provision for different cases or circumstances and make incidental, supplemental, saving or transitional provision.

(3)   Any power to make regulations or an order is exercisable by statutory instrument.

(4)   No order which appears to the Treasury to extend the circumstances in which passengers are to be treated as chargeable passengers shall be made unless a draft of the order has been laid before and approved by the House of Commons.

(5)   Any other order, and any regulations, shall be subject to annulment in pursuance of a resolution of the House of Commons.

Orders: the Air Passenger Duty (Connected Flights) Order 1994, SI 1994/1821, as amended by SI 2001/809.

---

43 Interpretation

(1)   In this Chapter—

"accounting period" means any period prescribed or allowed for the purposes of section 38 above,

"agreement for carriage", in relation to the carriage of any person, means the agreement or arrangement under which he is carried, whether the carriage is by a single carrier or successive carriers,

"Air Navigation Order" has the same meaning as in the Civil Aviation Act 1982,

"airport" means any aerodrome (within the meaning of that Act),

"carriage" means carriage wholly or partly by air, and "carried" is to be read accordingly,

"connected", in relation to any flights, has the meaning given by section 30(8) above,

"document" includes information recorded in any form,

"duty" means air passenger duty,

"fiscal representative" has the meaning given by section 34(2) above,

"flight" has the meaning given by section 28(5) above,

"operator", in relation to any aircraft, means the person having the management of the aircraft for the time being,

"passenger", in relation to any aircraft, means—

(a)   where the operator is an air transport undertaking (within the meaning of the Air Navigation Order), any person carried on the aircraft other than—

(i)   a member of the flight crew,

(ii)   a cabin attendant, or

(iii)   a person who is not carried for reward, who is an employee of any aircraft operator and who satisfies such other requirements as may be prescribed, and

(b)   in any other case, any person carried on the aircraft for reward,

"prescribed" means prescribed by regulations,

"reward", in relation to the carriage of any person, includes any form of consideration received or to be received wholly or partly in connection with the carriage, irrespective of the person by whom or to whom the consideration has been or is to be given, and "ticket" means a document or documents evidencing an agreement (wherever made) for the carriage of any person.

(2) . . . In this Chapter, in relation to a passenger whose agreement for carriage is evidenced by a ticket—

"journey" means the journey from his original place of departure to his final place of destination, and

"original place of departure" and "final place of destination" mean the original place of departure and the final place of destination indicated on his ticket.

(3) . . .

(4) Subject to the preceding provisions of this section, expressions used in this Chapter and in the Customs and Excise Management Act 1979 have the same meaning as in that Act.

NOTES

Sub-s (2): words repealed by FA 2000 ss 19(1), (2), (5), 156, Sch 40, Pt I, with effect for any carriage of a passenger on an aircraft which begins after 31 March 2001. Words previously read "Subject to subsection (3) below,".

Sub-s (3):repealed by FA 2000 ss 19(1), (2), (5), 156, Sch 40, Pt I, with effect for any carriage of a passenger on an aircraft which begins after 31 March 2001. Sub-s (3) previously read—

"(3) For the purposes of this Chapter, where the agreement for carriage of a passenger by air is evidenced by a ticket, the ticket is a return ticket if (and only if) it covers his return by air to the airport from which he originally departed; and, in such a case, there is both an outward and a return journey and the return journey is the journey from the final place of destination on the outward journey to that airport.".

44 Commencement

(1) This Chapter applies to any carriage of a passenger on an aircraft which begins after 31st October 1994.

(2) For the purpose of determining whether or not a person is a chargeable passenger in relation to any carriage on an aircraft beginning after that date, the provisions of section 31 above and any order made by virtue of that section shall be treated as having applied to any such carriage of that person which began on or before that date as they would apply to any such carriage of that person beginning after that date.

45–248

((Pts II–VII) Ss 45, 47 repealed subject to transitional provisions by the Value Added Tax Act 1994, s 100(1), (2), Schs 13, 15; s 46 amends the Finance Act 1985, s 20; ss 48–110, 112–123, 125–142, 144–170, 172–197, 199–248 outside the scope of this work; s 111 repealed, with effect from the year 1996–1997; ss 124, 131 repealed, in relation to accounting periods beginning on or after 31 March 1996, subject to savings and transitional provisions, by the Finance Act 1996, ss 105, 205, Sch 41, Pt V(1), (3), (21); s 143 repealed by the Finance Act 1995, s 162, Sch 29, Pt VIII(5), in relation to accounting periods beginning on or after 1 January 1995; s 198 repealed by the Finance Act 1995, ss 116(2), 162, Sch 29, Pt VIII(14).)

PART VIII

MISCELLANEOUS AND GENERAL

249–256

(Outside the scope of this work.)

Part I

General

257, 258

(Outside the scope of this work.)

259 Short title

This Act may be cited as the Finance Act 1994.

SCHEDULES

NOTES

Schs 1–3, in so far as unrepealed, outside the scope of this work; Sch 4: Pt I amends the Customs and Excise Management Act 1979; Pt II amends the Alcoholic Liquor Duties Act 1979; Pt III repealed by the Finance Act 1996, ss 8(2), 205, Sch 41, Pt I; Pt IV amends the Tobacco Products Duty Act 1979; Pt V amends the Betting and Gaming Duties Act 1981; Pt VI amends the Finance Act 1993.

SCHEDULE 5

DECISIONS SUBJECT TO REVIEW AND APPEAL

Section 14

The Community Customs Code etc

1. The following decisions, so far as they are made for the purposes of the Community Customs Code and are decisions the authority for which is not contained in provisions outside that Code and any directly applicable Community legislation made for the purpose of implementing that Code, that is to say—

(a) any decision in relation to any goods as to whether or not the entry, unloading or transhipment of the goods, or their release by or to any person or for any purpose, is to be allowed or otherwise permitted;

(b) any decision as to whether or not permission for the examination of, or the taking of samples from, any goods presented to the Commissioners is to be granted;

(c) any decision as to the route to be used for the movement of any goods;

(d) any other decision as to whether or not the requirements of any procedure for goods which are to be or have been presented to the Commissioners, or any other formalities in relation to any such goods, have been satisfied or complied with or are to be waived, or as to the measures to be taken, including any requirements to be imposed, in consequence of the inability or other failure of any person to comply with the required procedure;

(e) any decision in relation to any place or area as to whether or not it is to be, or to continue to be, designated or approved for any purpose;

(f) any decision, in any particular case, as to whether or not the carrying out of any processing or other operations or the use of any procedure is to be, or to continue to be, authorised or approved;

(g) any decision in relation to—

(i) the establishment or operation of any warehouse or other facility, or

(ii) the construction of any building,

as to whether or not its establishment, operation or construction or the person by whom it is to be established, operated or constructed, is to be, or to continue to be, authorised or approved for any purpose;

(h)   any decision consisting in the imposition of a requirement to supply information or assistance, or to furnish any document or other evidence, to the Commissioners or any officer or of a requirement to be present or represented when anything is done in relation to any goods;

(i)   any decision to take or retain samples of any goods or as to the examination or analysis to which any goods or samples are to be subjected;

(j)   any decision as to whether or not any person is to bear any of the expenses of the supply of any information by or on behalf of the Commissioners or as to the amount of any such expenses to be borne by any person;

[(k)   any decision as to whether or not collection of interest on arrears of customs duty or agricultural levy is to be waived;]

(l)   any decision, in relation to a decision mentioned in any of the preceding sub-paragraphs, as to the conditions subject to which the decision so mentioned is made or, as the case may be, the matters to which that decision relates have effect;

(m)   any decision as to whether or not any person is to be required to give any security for the fulfilment, in whole or in part, of—

(i)   any obligation to pay any customs duty or any agricultural levy of the European Community; or

(ii)   any obligation to comply with a condition of any permission, designation, approval, authorisation or requirement mentioned in any of the preceding sub-paragraphs or with any provision for the purposes of which any decision falling within any of those sub-paragraphs is made,

or as to the form or amount of, or the conditions of, any such security;

(n)   any decision as to the time at which or the period within which any obligation to pay any customs duty or agricultural levy of the European Community or to do any other thing required by virtue of the Community Customs Code is to be complied with;

(o)   any decision as to whether or not a decision falling within this paragraph is to be varied or revoked, including a decision as to whether or not the time at which any such decision is to take effect is to be deferred.

The Management Act

2.—(1)   The following decisions under or for the purposes of the Management Act, that is to say—

(a)   any decision for the purposes of section 20, 22 or 25 as to whether or not an approval of a place as an approved wharf, as an examination station or as a transit shed is to be given or withdrawn or as to the conditions subject to which any such approval is given;

(b)   any decision as to whether or not any permission for any of the purposes of section 21 (control of movement of aircraft) is to be given or withdrawn or as to the conditions subject to which any such permission is given;

(c)   any decision as to whether or not approval of a pipe-line for the purposes of section 24 (control of movement of goods by pipe-line) is to be given or withdrawn or as to the conditions subject to which any such approval is given;

(d)   any decision as to whether or not expenses incurred by the Commissioners are to be borne by any person by virtue of section 29(3) (expenses of detention etc of ships, aircraft and vehicles) or as to the amount of the expenses to be so borne;

(e)   any decision consisting in the giving of a direction under section 30(1) (control of uncleared goods);

(f)   any decision by virtue of subsection (2A) of section 31 (control of movement of goods) as to whether or not the requirements of any regulations under subsection (1) of that section are to be relaxed, as to whether or not substituted requirements are to be imposed or as to the terms of any such substituted requirements;

(g)   any decision consisting in the imposition of a requirement by virtue of subsection (3) of section 33 (requirements as to record keeping) on a person in control of an aerodrome who is not licensed under any enactment relating to air navigation or as to what is or is not to be approved (whether or not in relation to such a requirement) for the purposes of paragraph (a) of that subsection;

(h)   any decision as to whether or not permission is to be given to any person for the purposes of section 39 (entry of surplus stores);

(i)   any decision for the purposes of section 40 that any goods are to be deposited in a Queen's warehouse;

(j)   any decision for the purposes of section 47 as to whether or not goods are allowed to be removed for transit or transhipment or as to the conditions subject to which they are removed;

(k)   any decision as to the conditions subject to which any permission is given for the purposes of section 48 (temporary importation);

(l)   any decision for the purposes of section 63 (entry outwards) as to whether or not entry outwards is to be made of any ship or goods or as to the conditions subject to which any such entry outwards is to be made;

(m)   any decision consisting in the imposition of a requirement under section 77, 79 or 80 to produce or furnish any document or other evidence or information;

(n)   any decision for the purposes of section 92 (approval of warehouses)—

    (i)   as to whether or not any approval is to be given to any place as a warehouse or any consent is to be given to any alteration in or addition to any warehouse;

    (ii)   as to the conditions subject to which any approval or consent is given for the purposes of that section; or

    (iii)   for the withdrawal of any such approval or consent;

(o)   any decision as to whether or not any amount is payable to the Commissioners in pursuance of section 99 (provision as to deposit in Queen's warehouse) or as to the amount to be so paid by any person;

(p)   any decision for the purposes of section 100G (registered excise dealers and shippers) as to whether or not, and in which respects, any person is to be, or to continue to be, approved and registered or as to the conditions subject to which any person is approved and registered;

(q)   any decision as to the conditions subject to which any drawback is allowed or payable under section 132 or 134;

(r)   any decision under section 152(b) as to whether or not anything forfeited or seized under the customs and excise Acts is to be restored to any person or as to the conditions subject to which any such thing is so restored;

(s)   any decision under section 157 as to whether or not any person is to be required to give any security for the observance of any condition, as to the form or amount of, or the conditions of, any such security or as to the cancellation of any bond;

(t)   any decision consisting in the giving or imposition of a direction or requirement for the purposes of section 158 (power to require the provision of facilities) or any decision as to whether or not an approval is to be given for the purposes of any such direction.

(2)   Any decision which is made under or for the purposes of any regulations under any of sections 3, 31 or 93 of the Management Act (application to pipe-lines, control of movement of goods and warehousing regulations) and is—

(a)   a decision in relation to any goods as to whether or not they may be moved, deposited, kept, secured, treated in any manner, removed or made available to any person or as to the conditions subject to which they are moved, deposited, kept, secured, treated in any manner, removed or made available to any person;

(b)   a decision as to whether or not any person or place is to be, or to continue to be, authorised or approved in any respect for any purpose or as to the conditions subject to which any person or place is so authorised or approved; or

(c)   a decision as to whether or not any person is to be required to give any security for the fulfilment of any obligation or as to the form or amount of, or the conditions of, any such security.

(3)   Any decision which is made under or for the purposes of any regulations under section 35(4), 42 or 66 of the Management Act (report inwards, procedure in relation to goods on arrival etc or in relation to goods for exportation) and is—

(a)   a decision as to whether or not any permission is to be given for the purpose of dispensing with any of the requirements of any such regulations;

(b)   a decision consisting in the imposition or variation of any requirement in exercise of any power conferred by any such regulations; or

(c)   a decision as to whether or not any approval, authority or permission is to be given or granted for the purpose of determining the manner in which any requirement imposed by or under any such regulations is to be performed.

(4)   Any decision which is made under or for the purposes of any regulations under section 127A of the Management Act (deferment of duty) and is—

(a)   a decision as to whether or not any person or place is to be, or to continue to be, approved for any purpose connected with the deferment of duty or as to the conditions subject to which any person or place is so approved;

(b)   a decision as to the amount of duty that may be deferred in any case; or

(c)   a decision as to whether or not any person is to be required to give any security for the fulfilment of any obligation or as to the form or amount of, or the conditions of, any such security.

The Alcoholic Liquor Duties Act 1979

3.—(1)   The following decisions under or for the purposes of the Alcoholic Liquor Duties Act 1979, that is to say—

(a)   any decision for the purposes of section 6 (power to exempt angostura bitters) as to whether or not to give a direction that any bitters are to be treated as not being spirits or as to the conditions subject to which any such direction is given;

(b)   any decision for the purposes of section 7 (exemption of spirits used for medical purposes) as to whether or not to recognise any article as used for medical purposes;

(c)   any decision for the purposes of section 8 (remission of duty on spirits used for medical purposes etc)—

    (i)   as to the use to which any article is or is to be put or as to the purposes for which it is or is to be used; or

    (ii)   as to the conditions subject to which the receipt and delivery of any spirits is permitted as mentioned in that section;

(d)   any decision for the purposes of [section 10 (remission of duty on spirits] or for use in art or manufacture) as to whether or not permission or authorisation for any person to receive, or for the delivery of, any spirits without payment of duty is to be granted or withdrawn or as to the conditions subject to which any such permission or authorisation is granted;

(e)   any decision as to whether or not any goods are to be directed under section 11 (goods not for human consumption) to be treated as not containing spirits or as to the conditions subject to which any goods are directed to be so treated;

(f)   any decision for the purposes of section 12 (licences to manufacture spirits) as to whether or not a licence under that section is to be granted or as to the suspension or revocation of such a licence or as to the conditions subject to which such a licence is granted;

(g)   any decision for the purposes of section 15 (distillers' warehouses)—

    (i)   as to whether or not any approval is to be given to any place as a warehouse or any consent is to be given to any alteration in or addition to any warehouse;

    (ii)   as to the conditions subject to which any approval or consent is given for the purposes of that section; or

    (iii)   for the withdrawal of any such approval or consent;

(h)   any decision for the purposes of section 18 (licences for rectifiers and compounders)—

    (i)   as to whether or not any person is to be granted a licence as a rectifier or compounder or permission to compound spirits without a licence;

    (ii)   as to the conditions subject to which any such licence or permission is granted; or

    (iii)   as to the revocation or withdrawal of any such licence or permission;

(i)   any decision for the purposes of section 32 (transfer of spirits in a distiller's warehouse) as to whether or not any person is to be required to give any security for the payment of any duty or as to the form or amount of, or the conditions of, any such security;

(j)   any decision as to whether or not drawback is to be allowed in any case under section 42 (drawback on exportation etc) or as to the conditions subject to which drawback is so allowed;

(k)   any decision as to whether or not any duty is to be remitted or repaid under section 44 (remission or repayment of duty on beer used for the purposes of research or experiment) or as to the conditions subject to which any duty is so remitted or repaid;

(l)   any decision for the purposes of section 49A as to whether or not any drawback is to be set against an amount chargeable in respect of excise duty on beer or as to the conditions subject to which any drawback is set against any such amount;

(m)   any decision as to whether or not any permission for the purposes of section 57 or 58 (mixing of made-wine or wine with spirits) is to be given or withdrawn or as to the conditions subject to which any such permission is given;

(n)   any decision as to whether or not any permission for the purposes of subsection (1) or (2) of section 69 (restrictions applying to wholesalers and retailers of spirits) is to be given or withdrawn or as to the conditions subject to which any such permission is given;

(o)   any decision as to whether or not an authorisation or licence for the purposes of section 75 (. . . denatured alcohol) is to be granted to any person or as to the revocation or suspension of any such authorisation or licence.

(2)   Any decision which is made under or for the purposes of any regulations under section 13 or 77 of the Alcoholic Liquor Duties Act 1979 (regulation of the manufacture of spirits, . . . and denatured alcohol) and is a decision as to whether or not any premises, plant or process is to be, or to continue to be, approved for any purpose or as to the conditions subject to which any premises, plant or process is so approved.

(3)   Any decision which is made under or for the purposes of section 55, or any regulations under section 56, of the Alcoholic Liquor Duties Act 1979 (regulation of the making of wine and made-wine) and is a decision as to whether or not a licence under that section is to be granted or cancelled.

[(4)   Any decision which—

(a)   is made under paragraph 1 of Schedule 3 to the Finance Act 2001, and

(b)   relates to the Alcoholic Liquor Duties Act 1979.]

The Hydrocarbon Oil Duties Act 1979

4.—(1)   The following decisions under or for the purposes of the Hydrocarbon Oil Duties Act 1979—

(a)   any decision under section 9 (delivery of oil for home use etc) as to whether or not permission is to be given for the delivery of anything without payment of duty or as to the conditions subject to which any such permission is given;

(b)   any decision as to whether or not a consent is to be given for the purposes of section 10(1) (consent to certain uses of oil delivered for home use) or as to the conditions subject to which any such consent is given;

(c)   any decision as to whether or not a consent is to be given for the purposes of section 14(2) (consent to certain uses of rebated oil) or as to the conditions subject to which any such consent is given;

(d)   any decision consisting in a determination for the purposes of section 17(3) (determination of use of oil etc for different purposes);

(e)   any decision as to the conditions subject to which any payment is to be made to any person in accordance with section 20(3) (payments in respect of contaminated or mixed substances).

[(1A)   Any decision which is made under or for the purposes of any regulations made under section 20AA of the Hydrocarbon Oil Duties Act 1979 and is a decision as to whether or not relief is to be allowed.]

(2)   Any decision which is made under or for the purposes of any regulations made or having effect as if made under section 21 or 24 of the Hydrocarbon Oil Duties Act 1979 and is—

(a)   a decision as to whether or not any person is to be required to give any security for any duty which is or may become due, or as to the form or amount of, or the conditions of, any such security; or

(b)   a decision as to whether or not any person is to be, or to continue to be, approved for the purposes of section 9(1) or (4), 14(1) or 19A(1) of that Act or as to the conditions subject to which any person is so approved.

[(3)   Any decision which—

(a)   is made under paragraph 1 or 2 of Schedule 3 to the Finance Act 2001, and

(b)   relates to the Hydrocarbon Oil Duties Act 1979.]

The Tobacco Products Duty Act 1979

5.   Any decision which is made under or for the purposes of any regulations made under section 2 or 7 of the Tobacco Products Duty Act 1979 and is—

(a)   a decision as to whether or not any duty is remitted or repaid or as to the conditions subject to which it is remitted or repaid; or

(b)   a decision as to whether or not any premises are to be, or to continue to be, registered for any purpose or as to the conditions subject to which any premises are so registered.

The Betting and Gaming Duties Act 1981

6.—(1)   The following decisions under or for the purposes of the Betting and Gaming Duties Act 1981, that is to say—

(a)   any decision as to whether or not a permit under paragraph 5 of Schedule 1 (permit for carrying on pool betting business) is to be granted to any person or as to the revocation of such a permit;

(b)   any decision under paragraph 10(2) of Schedule 3 (registration of bingo promoters) as to the conditions subject to which any person is to be, or to continue to be, registered as a bingo-promoter.

(2)   Any decision which is made under or for the purposes of—

(a)   any regulations under paragraph 2 of Schedule 1 to the Betting and Gaming Duties Act 1981 (regulations in relation to general betting duty), or

(b)   paragraph 10(2) of Schedule 3 to that Act,

and is a decision as to whether or not any person is to be required to give any security for any duty which is or may become due, or as to the form or amount of, or the conditions of, any such security.

The Finance Act 1993

7.   Any decision as to whether or not any person is to be or to continue to be registered under section 29 of the Finance Act 1993 (registration for the purposes of lottery duty) and any decision which is made under or for the purposes of any regulations under that section and is a decision as to whether or not any person is to be required to give any security for the payment of any lottery duty that may become due, or as to the form or amount of, or the conditions of, any such security.

Chapter III of Part I of this Act

8.—(1)   Any decision made under or for the purposes of any regulations under section 21 of this Act or for the purposes of subsection (2) of that section which is—

(a)   a decision consisting in the imposition or variation of any requirement as to the records which are to be kept by any person;

(b)   a decision as to the manner in which any record or information is to be preserved or is to be made available to the Commissioners; or

(c)   a decision as to the period for which any record or information is to be preserved.

(2) Any decision for the purposes of section 23 of this Act which is—

(a)   a decision consisting in the imposition or variation of any requirement as to the information or documents which are to be furnished or produced by any person, including any decision as to the time or place at which, period within which or form in which anything is to be furnished or produced in pursuance of that section; or

(b)   a decision as to the removal of any document produced under that section or as to the period for which such a document may be removed.

Chapter IV of Part I of this Act

9. The following decisions under or for the purposes of Chapter IV of Part I of this Act, that is to say—

(a)   any decision under regulations made by virtue of section 33 to register, or not to register, any person as an aircraft operator in the register kept under that section or to remove a person so registered from the register;

(b)   any decision under such regulations to show, or not to show, the name of any person as a fiscal representative in that register or to remove a name from the register;

(c)   any decision under section 36 to require a person to provide security, including any decision as to the form or amount of the security; . . .

(d)   any decision to give a person a notice under section 37

[(e)   any decision with respect to the amount of any interest specified in an assessment under paragraph 11A of Schedule 6;]

[The Finance Act 2001

9A. Any decision under or for the purposes of Part II of Schedule 3 to the Finance Act 2001 (interest).]

Interpretation of Schedule

10.—(1) In this Schedule references to any decision as to the conditions subject to which any other decision (whether or not specified in this Schedule) is made include references to—

(a)   any decision as to whether the other decision should be made subject to or to the imposition of any conditions, limitations, restrictions, prohibitions or other requirements, either from the time when the other decision takes effect or in exercise of any power to impose them subsequently;

(b)   any decision as to the terms of any conditions, limitations, restrictions, prohibitions or other requirements imposed or applied in relation to that other decision;

(c)   any decision as to the period for which any licence, approval, permission or other authorisation to which the other decision relates is to have effect or as to any variation of that period; and

(d)   any decision as to whether any conditions, limitations, restrictions, prohibitions or other requirements so imposed or applied are to be revoked, suspended or cancelled or as to whether or in what respect their terms are at any time to be varied;

but those references do not include references to any decision as to the enforcement of any condition, restriction or prohibition in criminal proceedings, by the seizure or forfeiture of goods or, for purposes connected with any duty of excise, by any other means.

(2) References in this Schedule to decisions as to the exercise of any power to require security for the fulfilment of any obligation, the observance of any conditions or the payment of any duty shall be without prejudice to any reference to decisions as to the exercise of any general power in the case in question to impose conditions in connection with the making of any other decision and shall include references to the exercise of any power to require further security for the fulfilment of that obligation, the observance of those conditions or, as the case may be, the payment of that duty.

NOTES

Para 1: sub-para (k) substituted by the Finance Act 1999, s 130(2), (4), with effect in relation to decisions made on or after 27 July 1999.

Para 3: words in sub-para (1)(d) substituted and words omitted from sub-paras (1)(o), (2) repealed, by the Finance Act 1995, ss 5(5), 162, Sch 2, para 8, Sch 29, Pt I(3); sub-para (4) added by the Finance Act 2001, s 15, Sch 3 paras 17(1), (2), 21.

Para 4: sub-para (1A) inserted by the Finance Act 2000, s 10; sub-para (3) added by the Finance Act 2001, s 15, Sch 3 paras 17(1), (3),.

Para 9: word omitted repealed and sub-para (e) added by the Finance Act 1995, ss 16(2), (4), 162, Sch 29, Pt IV, in relation to accounting periods ending on or after 1 January 1995.

Para 9A: added by the Finance Act 2001, s 15, Sch 3 paras 17(1), (4), 21.

Regulations: the Finance Act 2001 (Commencement No 2 and Saving Provision) Order 2001.

SCHEDULE 6
AIR PASSENGER DUTY: ADMINISTRATION AND ENFORCEMENT
Section 40

Application of excise enactments

1.—(1) The Customs and Excise Management Act 1979 shall have effect for the purposes of Chapter IV of Part I of this Act in relation to—

  (a)   any person who is or is liable to be registered,

  (b)   any fiscal representative, and

  (c)   any handling agent where a notice given to him under section 37 of this Act is effective,

as it has effect in relation to revenue traders, but with the modifications mentioned in sub-paragraph (2), and paragraphs 3 and 4, below.

(2) That Act shall have effect, in relation to any person to whom sub-paragraph (1) above applies, as if—

  (a)   the reference in section 112(1) (power of entry) to vehicles included aircraft,

  (b)   section 116 (payment of duty) were omitted,

  (c)   in section 117 (execution and distress)—

    (i)   the references to goods liable to any excise duty included tickets, and

    (ii)   the references to the trade in respect of which duty is imposed were to the trade or business by virtue of which sub-paragraph (1) above applies to him, and

  (d)   any power under section 118B(1)(b) to require any person who is or is liable to be registered to produce or cause to be produced any such documents as are referred to in that subsection included power to require his fiscal representative to produce them.

2. Section 118B of that Act shall have effect for the purposes of Chapter IV of Part I of this Act in relation to any person who, in the course of a trade or business carried on by him, issues or arranges for the issue of tickets as if—

    (a)   he were a revenue trader, and

    (b)   the references to services supplied by or to him in the course or furtherance of a business were to services supplied by or to him in the course of issuing or arranging for the issue of tickets.

3.—(1) A notice may require any person to whom paragraph 1 above applies to furnish, at specified times and in the specified form, any such information to the Commissioners as he could be required by the Commissioners to furnish under subsection (1) of section 118B; and any such requirement shall have effect as a requirement under that subsection.

(2) A notice may require any person to whom paragraph 1 or 2 above applies to produce or cause to be produced for inspection by an officer, at specified places and times, any such documents as he could be required by the officer to produce under that subsection; and any such requirement shall have effect as a requirement under that subsection.

(3) In this paragraph—

"notice" means a notice published, and not withdrawn, by the Commissioners, and

    "specified" means specified in such a notice.

4. In relation to any person to whom paragraph 1 or 2 above applies—

    (a)   that Act shall have effect as if "document" had the same meaning as in Chapter IV of Part I of this Act, and

    (b)   that Act and this Schedule shall have effect as if any reference to the production of any document, in the case of information recorded otherwise than in legible form, were to producing a copy of the information in legible form.

Information

5.—(1) Any person having the management of an airport shall, if required to do so by the Commissioners—

    (a)   give notice to the Commissioners, within such time and in such form as they may reasonably require, stating whether or not he holds or has at any time held any information relating to the matters mentioned in sub-paragraph (3) below and, if he does or has done, stating the general nature of the information, and

    (b)   furnish to the Commissioners, within such time and in such form as they may reasonably require, such information relating to such matters as they may reasonably specify.

(2) Any such person shall, if required to do so by an officer, produce any documents relating to those matters, or cause them to be produced, for inspection by that officer.

(3) The matters referred to in sub-paragraphs (1) and (2) above are—

    (a)   whether or not any aircraft is a chargeable aircraft,

    (b)   who is the operator of any aircraft,

    (c)   whether or not any person is a handling agent of the operator of any aircraft, and

    (d)   whether or not any duty is payable on the carriage of any person and, if so, the amount of duty.

(4) Documents produced under sub-paragraph (2) above shall be produced, at such time as the officer may reasonably require, at the principal place of business of the person required to produce them or cause them to be produced or at such other place as the officer may reasonably require.

(5) An officer may take copies of, or make extracts from, any document produced under this paragraph.

(6) If it appears to an officer to be necessary to do so, he may, at a reasonable time and for a reasonable period, remove any document produced under this paragraph.

(7) Where an officer removes a document under sub-paragraph (6) above, then—

(a) if the person from whom it is removed so requests, the officer shall give him a receipt for the document,

(b) if the document is reasonably required for the proper conduct of any business, the officer shall, as soon as practicable, provide a copy of the document, free of charge, to the person by whom it was produced or caused to be produced, and

(c) if the document is lost or damaged, the Commissioners shall be liable to compensate the owner for any expenses reasonably incurred by him in replacing or repairing it.

(8) Any reference in this paragraph to the production of a document, in the case of information recorded otherwise than in legible form, is to producing a copy of the information in legible form.

(9) Any failure by a person having the management of an airport to comply with a requirement imposed under this paragraph shall attract a penalty under section 9 of this Act.

Application of Chapter II

6. An appeal which relates to duty shall not be entertained under section 16 of this Act at any time if any return which the appellant is required by regulations made by virtue of section 38 of this Act to make has not at that time been made.

Interest payable to Commissioners

7.—(1) Where an assessment of duty due from any person ("the person assessed") is made under section 12 of this Act and any of the conditions in sub-paragraph (2) below is fulfilled, the whole of the amount assessed shall, subject to paragraph 8 below, carry interest at [the rate applicable under section 197 of the Finance Act 1996] from the reckonable date until payment.

(2) The conditions are—

(a) that the assessment relates to an accounting period in respect of which either a return has previously been made or an earlier assessment has already been notified to the person assessed, or

(b) that the assessment relates to an accounting period which exceeds one month and begins on the date on which the person assessed was, or became liable to be, registered.

(3) In a case where—

(a) the circumstances are such that an assessment of duty due from any person could have been made and, if it had been made, the conditions in sub-paragraph (2) above would have been fulfilled, but

(b) before such an assessment was made the duty was paid (so that no such assessment was necessary),

the whole of the amount paid shall carry interest at [the rate applicable under section 197 of the Finance Act 1996] from the reckonable date until the date on which it was paid.

(4) In this paragraph and paragraph 8 below the "reckonable date" means the latest date on which a return is required to be made under Chapter IV of Part I of this Act for the accounting period to which the amount assessed or paid relates; and interest under this paragraph shall run from the reckonable date even if that date is a non-business day, within the meaning of section 92 of the Bills of Exchange Act 1882.

(5) Interest under this paragraph shall be paid without any deduction of income tax.

8.—(1) Where on an appeal by any person ("the appellant") to a tribunal under section 16 of this Act against an assessment of duty—

> (a)   it is found that the whole or any part of the duty was due from him, and
>
> (b)   the amount due, or any part of that amount, has not been paid and no cash security has been given for it,

that amount or, as the case may be, that part of it shall carry interest at such rate as the tribunal may determine from the reckonable date until payment.

(2) In sub-paragraph (1) above, "cash security" means such adequate security as enables the Commissioners to place the amount in question on deposit.

(3) Interest under this paragraph shall be paid without any deduction of income tax.

Interest payable by the Commissioners

9. . . .

10. . . .

11. . . .

[Assessment of interest

11A.—(1) Where by virtue of paragraph 7 above duty due from any person for an accounting period carries interest, the Commissioners may assess that person to an amount of interest in accordance with this paragraph.

(2) Notice of the assessment shall be given to the person liable for the interest or a representative of his.

(3) The amount of the interest shall be calculated by reference to a period ending on a date ("the due date") no later than the date of the notice.

(4) The notice shall specify—

> (a)   the amount of the duty which carries the interest assessed ("the specified duty");
>
> (b)   the amount of the interest assessed ("the specified interest");
>
> (c)   the due date; and
>
> (d)   a date by which that amount is required to be paid ("the payment date").

(5) Sub-paragraphs (6) and (7) below apply where the specified duty or any part of it is unpaid on the date of the notice.

(6) If the unpaid amount or any part of it is paid by the payment date, the payment shall be treated for the purposes of paragraph 7 above as made on the due date.

(7) To the extent that the unpaid amount is not paid by the payment date, an assessment may be made under this paragraph in respect of any interest on the unpaid amount which accrues after the due date.

(8) For the purposes of sub-paragraphs (6) and (7) above, a payment—

> (a)   which purports to be a payment of the unpaid amount or any part of it, but

(b)   which is insufficient to discharge both the liability to pay the unpaid amount and the liability to pay the specified interest,

shall be treated as made in discharge (or partial discharge) of the liability to pay the specified interest before it is treated as discharging to any extent the liability to pay the unpaid amount.

(9)   A notice of interest assessed under this paragraph may be combined in one document with notification of an assessment under section 12 of this Act which relates to the specified duty.

(10)   A notice which is so combined must comply with the requirements of this paragraph which relate to a notice which is not so combined.

(11)   The specified interest shall be recoverable as if it were duty due from the person assessed to that interest.

(12)   For the purposes of this paragraph a person is a representative of another if—

(a)   he is that other's personal representative;

(b)   he is that other's trustee in bankruptcy or is a receiver or liquidator appointed in relation to that other or in relation to any of his property; or

(c)   he is a person acting in some other representative capacity in relation to that other.]

Evidence by certificate

12.—(1)   A certificate of the Commissioners—

(a)   that a person was or was not, on any date specified in the certificate, registered or liable to be registered under section 33 of this Act,

(b)   that the name of any person was or was not, on any date so specified, shown as the fiscal representative of any person in the register kept under that section,

(c)   that any aircraft was or was not, on any date so specified, a chargeable aircraft,

(d)   that any return required to be made under regulations made by virtue of section 38 of this Act had not, on any date so specified, been made, or

(e)   that any duty shown as due in such a return, or in an assessment under section 12 of this Act, had not, on any date so specified, been paid,

shall be sufficient evidence of that fact until the contrary is proved.

(2)   A photograph of any document furnished to the Commissioners for the purposes of Chapter IV of Part I of this Act and certified by them to be such a photograph shall be admissible in any proceedings, whether civil or criminal, to the same extent as the document itself.

(3)   Any document purporting to be a certificate under sub-paragraph (1) or (2) above shall be taken to be such a certificate until the contrary is proved.

13.   . . .

NOTES

Para 7: words in square brackets substituted by the Finance Act 1996, s 197(6)(a), (7), with effect from 1 April 1997.

Paras 9, 10: repealed by the Finance Act 2001, ss 15, 110, Sch 3 paras 20, 21 Sch 33 Pt 1 (4) with effect in accordance with provision made by the Commissioners by order.

Para 11: repealed by the Finance Act 1996, s 205, Sch 41, Part VIII(1), with effect from 1 April 1997.

Para 11A: inserted, in relation to accounting periods ending on or after 1 January 1995, by the Finance Act 1995, s 16(1), (4).

Para 13: adds the Insolvency Act 1986, Sch 6, para 5C and the Insolvency (Northern Ireland) Order 1989, SI 1989/2405, Sch 4, para 5C, and amends the Bankruptcy (Scotland) Act 1985, Sch 3, para 2. Sub-paras (1), (2) hereof repealed by the Enterprise Act 2002 s 278, Sch 26.

Orders: the Air Passenger (Prescribed Rates of Interest) Order 1994, SI 1994/1820, as amended by SI 1996/164; the Finance Act 2001 (Commencement No 2 and Saving Provision) Order 2001.

Regulations: the Aircraft Operators (Accounts and Records) Regulations 1994, SI 1994/1737 as amended by SI 1998/63.

(Schs 7–26, in so far as unrepealed, outside the scope of this work.)

VALUE ADDED TAX ACT 1994

(1994 c 23)

ARRANGEMENT OF SECTIONS

An Act to consolidate the enactments relating to value added tax, including certain enactments relating to VAT tribunals

[5 July 1994]

PART I
THE CHARGE TO TAX

Importation of goods from outside the member States

15 General provisions relating to imported goods

(1)   For the purposes of this Act goods are imported from a place outside the member States where—

(a)   having been removed from a place outside the member States, they enter the territory of the Community;

(b)   they enter that territory by being removed to the United Kingdom or are removed to the United Kingdom after entering that territory; and

(c)   the circumstances are such that it is on their removal to the United Kingdom or subsequently while they are in the United Kingdom that any Community customs debt in respect of duty on their entry into the territory of the Community would be incurred.

(2)   Accordingly—

(a)   goods shall not be treated for the purposes of this Act as imported at any time before a Community customs debt in respect of duty on their entry into the territory of the Community would be incurred, and

(b)   the person who is to be treated for the purposes of this Act as importing any goods from a place outside the member States is the person who would be liable to discharge any such Community customs debt.

(3)   Subsections (1) and (2) above shall not apply, except in so far as the context otherwise requires or provision to the contrary is contained in regulations under section 16(1), for construing any references to importation or to an importer in any enactment or subordinate legislation applied for the purposes of this Act by section 16(1).

NOTES

This section contains provisions formerly in the Value Added Tax Act 1983, s 2B(2)–(4) as inserted by the Finance (No 2) Act 1992, s 14, Sch 3, Part I, para 3.

16 Application of customs enactments

(1)   Subject to such exceptions and adaptations as the Commissioners may by regulations prescribe and except where the contrary intention appears—

(a)   the provision made by or under the Customs and Excise Acts 1979 and the other enactments and subordinate legislation for the time being having effect generally in relation to duties of customs and excise charged on the importation of goods into the United Kingdom; and

(b)   the Community legislation for the time being having effect in relation to Community customs duties charged on goods entering the territory of the Community,

shall apply (so far as relevant) in relation to any VAT chargeable on the importation of goods from places outside the member States as they apply in relation to any such duty of customs or excise or, as the case may be, Community customs duties.

(2)   Regulations under [section 105 of the Postal Services Act 2000] (which provides for the application of customs enactments to postal packets) may make special provision in relation to VAT.

NOTES

Words in square brackets in sub-s (2) substituted by the Postal Services Act 2000 s 127(4), Sch 8 para 22(1), (2) as from 26 March 2001 (by virtue of SI 2000/2957). Words previously read "section 16 of the Post Office Act 1953".

This section contains provisions formerly in the Value Added Tax Act 1983, s 24 as amended by the Finance (No 2) Act 1992, s 14, Sch 3, Part I, para 25.

17 Free zone regulations

(1)   This section applies in relation to VAT chargeable on the importation of goods from places outside the member States; and in this section "free zone" has the meaning given by section 100A(2) of the Management Act.

(2)   Subject to any contrary provision made by any directly applicable Community provision, goods which are chargeable with VAT may be moved into a free zone and may remain as free zone goods without payment of VAT.

(3)   The Commissioners may by regulations ("free zone regulations") make provision with respect to the movement of goods into, and the removal of goods from, any free zone and the keeping, securing and treatment of goods which are within a free zone, and subject to any provision of the regulations, "free zone goods" means goods which are within a free zone.

(4)   Without prejudice to the generality of subsection (3), free zone regulations may make provision—

  (a)   for enabling the Commissioners to allow goods to be removed from a free zone without payment of VAT in such circumstances and subject to such conditions as they may determine;

  (b)   for determining where any VAT becomes payable in respect of goods which cease to be free zone goods—

    (i)   the rates of any VAT applicable; and

    (ii)   the time at which those goods cease to be free zone goods;

  (c)   for determining for the purpose of enabling VAT to be charged in respect of free zone goods in a case where a person wishes to pay that VAT notwithstanding that the goods will continue to be free zone goods, the rate of VAT to be applied; and

  (d)   permitting free zone goods to be destroyed without payment of VAT in such circumstances and subject to such conditions as the Commissioners may determine.

(5)   The Commissioners, with respect to free zone goods or the movement of goods into any free zone, may by regulations make provision—

  (a)   for relief from the whole or part of any VAT chargeable on the importation of goods into the United Kingdom in such circumstances as they may determine;

  (b)   in place of, or in addition to, any provision made by section 6 or any other enactment, for determining the time when a supply of goods which are or have been free zone goods is to be treated as taking place for the purposes of the charge to VAT; and

  (c)   as to the treatment, for the purposes of VAT, of goods which are manufactured or produced within a free zone from other goods or which have other goods incorporated in them while they are free zone goods.

NOTES

Sub-s (1) contains provisions formerly in the Value Added Tax Act 1983, s 24(1) as substituted by the Finance (No 2) Act 1992, s 14, Sch 3, Part I, para 25; sub-ss (2), (4)

contains provisions formerly in the Customs and Excise Management Act 1979, s 100C(1), (3), as inserted by the Finance Act 1984, s 8, Sch 4, Part I and as read with the Free Zone Regulations 1991, SI 1991/2727, reg 3; sub-s (3) contains provisions formerly in the Customs and Excise Management Act 1979, s 100B as inserted by the Finance Act 1984, s 8, Sch 4, Part I, and from the Customs and Excise Management Act 1979, s 100C(4)(d) as inserted by the Free Zone Regulations 1991, SI 1991/2727, reg 5(b); sub-s (5) contains provisions formerly in the Customs and Excise Management Act 1979, s 100C(4) as inserted by the Finance Act 1984, s 8, Sch 4, Part I, and as amended by the Free Zone Regulations 1991, SI 1991/2727, reg 5(b).

Goods subject to a warehousing regime

18 Place and time of acquisition or supply

(1) Where—

   (a) any goods have been removed from a place outside the member States and have entered the territory of the Community;

   (b) the material time for any acquisition of those goods from another member State or for any supply of those goods is while they are subject to a warehousing regime and before the duty point; and

   (c) those goods are not mixed with any dutiable goods which were produced or manufactured in the United Kingdom or acquired from another member State,

then the acquisition or supply mentioned in paragraph (b) above shall be treated for the purposes of this Act as taking place outside the United Kingdom.

[(1A) The Commissioners may by regulations prescribe circumstances in which subsection (1) above shall not apply.]

(2) Subsection (3) below applies where—

   (a) any dutiable goods are acquired from another member State; or

   (b) any person makes a supply of—

      (i) any dutiable goods which were produced or manufactured in the United Kingdom or acquired from another member State; or

      (ii) any goods comprising a mixture of goods falling within sub-paragraph (i) above and other goods.

(3) Where this subsection applies and the material time for the acquisition or supply mentioned in subsection (2) above is while the goods in question are subject to a warehousing regime and before the duty point, that acquisition or supply shall be treated for the purposes of this Act as taking place outside the United Kingdom if the material time for any subsequent supply of those goods is also while the goods are subject to the warehousing regime and before the duty point.

(4) Where the material time for any acquisition or supply of any goods in relation to which subsection (3) above applies is while the goods are subject to a warehousing regime and before the duty point but the acquisition or supply nevertheless falls, for the purposes of this Act, to be treated as taking place in the United Kingdom—

   (a) that acquisition or supply shall be treated for the purposes of this Act as taking place at the earlier of the following times, that is to say, the time when the goods are removed from the warehousing regime and the duty point; and

   (b) in the case of a supply, any VAT payable on the supply shall be paid (subject to any regulations under subsection (5) below)—

      (i) at the time when the supply is treated as taking place under paragraph (a) above; and

(ii)   by the person by whom the goods are so removed or, as the case may be, together with the duty or agricultural levy, by the person who is required to pay the duty or levy.

[(5)   The Commissioners may by regulations make provision for enabling a taxable person to pay the VAT he is required to pay by virtue of paragraph (b) of subsection (4) above at a time later than that provided for by that paragraph.

(5A)   Regulations under subsection (5) above may in particular make provision for either or both of the following—

(a)   for the taxable person to pay the VAT together with the VAT chargeable on other supplies by him of goods and services;

(b)   for the taxable person to pay the VAT together with any duty of excise deferment of which has been granted to him under section 127A of the Customs and Excise Management Act 1979;

and they may make different provision for different descriptions of taxable person and for different descriptions of goods.]

(6)   In this section—

"dutiable goods" means any goods which are subject—

(a)   to a duty of excise; or

(b)   in accordance with any provision for the time being having effect for transitional purposes in connection with the accession of any State to the European Communities, to any Community customs duty or agricultural levy of the European Community;

"the duty point", in relation to any goods, means—

(a)   in the case of goods which are subject to a duty of excise, the time when the requirement to pay the duty on those goods takes effect; and

(b)   in the case of goods which are not so subject, the time when any Community customs debt in respect of duty on the entry of the goods into the territory of the Community would be incurred or, as the case may be, the corresponding time in relation to any such duty or levy as is mentioned in paragraph (b) of the definition of dutiable goods;

"material time"—

(a)   in relation to any acquisition or supply the time of which is determined in accordance with regulations under section 6(14) or 12(3), means such time as may be prescribed for the purpose of this section by those regulations;

(b)   in relation to any other acquisition, means the time of the event which, in relation to the acquisition, is the first relevant event for the purposes of taxing it; and

(c)   in relation to any other supply, means the time when the supply would be treated as taking place in accordance with subsection (2) of section 6 if paragraph (c) of that subsection were omitted;

"warehouse" means any warehouse where goods may be stored in any member State without payment of any one or more of the following, that is to say—

(a)   Community customs duty;

(b)   any agricultural levy of the European Community;

(c)   VAT on the importation of the goods into any member State;

(d)   any duty of excise or any duty which is equivalent in another member State to a duty of excise.

(7)   References in this section to goods being subject to a warehousing regime is a reference to goods being kept in a warehouse or being transported between

warehouses (whether in the same or different member States) without the payment in a member State of any duty, levy or VAT; and references to the removal of goods from a warehousing regime shall be construed accordingly.

NOTES

This section contains provisions formerly in the Value Added Tax Act 1983, s 35 as substituted by the Finance (No 2) Act 1992, s 14, Sch 3, Part I, para 35.

Sub-s (1A): inserted by the Finance (No 2) Act 2005 s 1.

Sub-ss (5), (5A): substituted, for sub-s (5) as originally enacted, by the Finance Act 1995, s 29.

Regulations: the Value Added Tax Regulations 1995, SI 1995/2518.

[18A Fiscal warehousing

(1) The Commissioners may, if it appears to them proper, upon application approve any registered person as a fiscal warehousekeeper; and such approval shall be subject to such conditions as they shall impose.

(2) Subject to those conditions and to regulations made under section 18F such a person shall be entitled to keep a fiscal warehouse.

(3) "Fiscal warehouse" means such place in the United Kingdom in the occupation or under the control of the fiscal warehousekeeper, not being retail premises, as he shall notify to the Commissioners in writing; and such a place shall become a fiscal warehouse on receipt by the Commissioners of that notification or on the date stated in it as the date from which it is to have effect, whichever is the later, and, subject to subsection (6) below, shall remain a fiscal warehouse so long as it is in the occupation or under the control of the fiscal warehousekeeper or until he shall notify the Commissioners in writing that it is to cease to be a fiscal warehouse.

(4) The Commissioners may in considering an application by a person to be a fiscal warehousekeeper take into account any matter which they consider relevant, and may without prejudice to the generality of that provision take into account all or any one or more of the following—

(a) his record of compliance and ability to comply with the requirements of this Act and regulations made hereunder;

(b) his record of compliance and ability to comply with the requirements of the customs and excise Acts (as defined in the Management Act) and regulations made thereunder;

(c) his record of compliance and ability to comply with Community customs provisions;

(d) his record of compliance and ability to comply with the requirements of other member States relating to VAT and duties equivalent to duties of excise;

(e) if the applicant is a company the records of compliance and ability to comply with the matters set out at (a) to (d) above of its directors, persons connected with its directors, its managing officers, any shadow directors or any of those persons, and, if it is a close company, the records of compliance and ability to comply with the matters set out at (a) to (d) above of the beneficial owners of the shares of the company or any of them; and

(f) if the applicant is an individual the records of compliance and ability to comply with the matters set out at (a) to (d) above of any company of which he is or has been a director, managing officer or shadow director or, in the case of a close company, a shareholder or the beneficial owner of shares,

Part I

and for the purposes of paragraphs (e) and (f) "connected" shall have the meaning given by section 24(7), "managing officer" the meaning given by section 61(6), "shadow director" the meaning given by [section 251 of the Companies Act 2006] and "close company" the meaning given by the Taxes Act.

NOTES

Section inserted, in relation to any acquisition of goods from another member State and any supply taking place on or after 1 June 1996, by the Finance Act 1996, s 26, Sch 3, para 5.

Sub-s (4): words in square brackets substituted by SI 2007/2194, art 10(1), (2), Sch 4, Pt 3, para 85 with effect from 1 October 2007.

[18B Fiscally warehoused goods: relief

(1) Subsections (3) and (4) below apply where—
    (a)   there is an acquisition of goods from another member State;
    (b)   those goods are eligible goods;
    (c)   either—
        (i)   that supply takes place while the goods are subject to a fiscal warehousing regime; or
        (ii)   after the acquisition but before the supply, if any, of those goods which next occurs, the acquirer causes the goods to be placed in a fiscal warehousing regime; and
    (d)   the acquirer, not later than the time of the acquisition, prepares and keeps a certificate that the goods are subject to a fiscal warehousing regime, or (as the case may be) that he will cause paragraph (c)(ii) above to be satisfied; and the certificate shall be in such form and be kept for such period as the Commissioners may by regulations specify.

(2) Subsections (3) and (4) below also apply where—
    (a)   there is a supply of goods;
    (b)   those goods are eligible goods;
    (c)   either—
        (i)   that supply takes place while the goods are subject to a fiscal warehousing regime; or
        (ii)   after that supply but before the supply, if any, of those goods which next occurs, the person to whom the former supply is made causes the goods to be placed in a fiscal warehousing regime;
    (d)   in a case falling within paragraph (c)(ii) above, the person to whom the supply is made gives the supplier, not later than the time of the supply, a certificate in such form as the Commissioners may by regulations specify that he will cause paragraph (c)(ii) to be satisfied; and
    (e)   the supply is not a retail transaction.

(3) The acquisition or supply in question shall be treated for the purposes of this Act as taking place outside the United Kingdom if any subsequent supply of those goods is while they are subject to the fiscal warehousing regime.

(4) Where subsection (3) does not apply and the acquisition or supply in question falls, for the purposes of this Act, to be treated as taking place in the United Kingdom, that acquisition or supply shall be treated for the purposes of this Act as taking place when the goods are removed from the fiscal warehousing regime.

(5) Where—
    (a)   subsection (4) above applies to an acquisition or a supply,
    (b)   the acquisition or supply is taxable and not zero-rated, and

(c)   the acquirer or supplier is not a taxable person but would be were it not for paragraph 1(9) of Schedule 1, paragraph 1(7) of Schedule 2 and paragraph 1(6) of Schedule 3, or any of those provisions, VAT shall be chargeable on that acquisition or supply notwithstanding that the acquirer or the supplier is not a taxable person.

(6)   In this section "eligible goods" means goods—

    (a)   of a description falling within Schedule 5A;

    (b)   upon which any import duties, as defined in article 4(10) of the Community Customs Code of 12th October 1992 (Council Regulation (EEC) No 2913/92), either have been paid or have been deferred under article 224 of that Code or regulations made under section 45 of the Management Act;

    (c)   (in the case of goods imported from a place outside the member States) upon which any VAT chargeable under section 1(1)(c) has been either paid or deferred in accordance with Community customs provisions, and

    (d)   (in the case of goods subject to a duty of excise) upon which that duty has been either paid or deferred under section 127A of the Management Act.

(7)   For the purposes of this section, apart from subsection (4), an acquisition or supply shall be treated as taking place at the material time for the acquisition or supply.

(8)   The Treasury may by order vary Schedule 5A by adding to or deleting from it any goods or varying any description of any goods.]

NOTES

Section inserted, in relation to any acquisition of goods from another member state and any supply taking place on or after 1 June 1996, by the Finance Act 1996, s 26, Sch 3, para 5.

[18C Warehouses and fiscal warehouses: services

(1)   Where—

    (a)   a taxable person makes a supply of specified services;

    (b)   those services are wholly performed on or in relation to goods while those goods are subject to a warehousing or fiscal warehousing regime;

    (c)   (except where the services are the supply by an occupier of a warehouse or a fiscal warehousekeeper of warehousing or fiscal warehousing the goods) the person to whom the supply is made gives the supplier a certificate, in such a form as the Commissioners may by regulations specify, that the services are so performed;

    (d)   the supply of services would (apart from this section) be taxable and not zero-rated; and

    (e)   the supplier issues to the person to whom the supply is made an invoice of such a description as the Commissioners may by regulations prescribe,

his supply shall be zero-rated.

(2)   If a supply of services is zero-rated under subsection (1) above ("the zero-rated supply of services") then, unless there is a supply of the goods in question the material time for which is—

    (a)   while the goods are subject to a warehousing or fiscal warehousing regime, and

    (b)   after the material time for the zero-rated supply of services,

subsection (3) below shall apply.

(3) Where this subsection applies—

   (a) a supply of services identical to the zero-rated supply of services shall be treated for the purposes of this Act as being, at the time the goods are removed from the warehousing or fiscal warehousing regime or (if earlier) at the duty point, both made (for the purposes of his business) to the person to whom the zero-rated supply of services was actually made and made by him in the course or furtherance of his business,

   (b) that supply shall have the same value as the zero-rated supply of services,

   (c) that supply shall be a taxable (and not a zero-rated) supply, and

   (d) VAT shall be charged on that supply even if the person treated as making it is not a taxable person.

(4) In this section "specified services" means—

   (a) services of an occupier of a warehouse or a fiscal warehousekeeper of keeping the goods in question in a warehousing or fiscal warehousing regime;

   (b) in relation to goods subject to a warehousing regime, services of carrying out on the goods operations which are permitted to be carried out under Community customs provisions or warehousing regulations as the case may be; and

   (c) in relation to goods subject to a fiscal warehousing regime, services of carrying out on the goods any physical operations (other than any prohibited by regulations made under section 18F), for example, and without prejudice to the generality of the foregoing words, preservation and repacking operations.]

NOTES

Section inserted, in relation to any acquisition of goods from another member state and any supply taking place on or after 1 June 1996, by the Finance Act 1996, s 26, Sch 3, para 5.

[18D Removal from warehousing: accountability

(1) This section applies to any supply to which section 18B(4) or section 18C(3) applies (supply treated as taking place on removal or duty point) and any acquisition to which section 18B(5) applies (acquisition treated as taking place on removal where acquirer not a taxable person).

(2) Any VAT payable on the supply or acquisition shall (subject to any regulations under subsection (3) below) be paid—

   (a) at the time when the supply or acquisition is treated as taking place under the section in question; and

   (b) by the person by whom the goods are removed or, as the case may be, together with the excise duty, by the person who is required to pay that duty.

(3) The Commissioners may by regulations make provision for enabling a taxable person to pay the VAT he is required to pay by virtue of subsection (2) above at a time later than that provided by that subsection; and they may make different provisions for different descriptions of taxable persons and for different descriptions of goods and services.]

NOTES

Section inserted, in relation to any acquisition of goods from another member state and any supply taking place on or after 1 June 1996, by the Finance Act 1996, s 26, Sch 3, para 5.

[18E Deficiency in fiscally warehoused goods

(1) This section applies where goods have been subject to a fiscal warehousing regime and, before being lawfully removed from the fiscal warehouse, they are found to be missing or deficient.

(2) In any case where this section applies, unless it is shown to the satisfaction of the Commissioners that the absence of or deficiency in the goods can be accounted for by natural waste or other legitimate cause, the Commissioners may require the fiscal warehousekeeper to pay immediately in respect of the missing goods or of the whole or any part of the deficiency, as they see fit, the VAT that would have been chargeable.

(3) In subsection (2) "VAT that would have been chargeable" means VAT that would have been chargeable on a supply of the missing goods, or the amount of goods by which the goods are deficient, taking place at the time immediately before the absence arose or the deficiency occurred, if the value of that supply were the open market value; but where that time cannot be ascertained to the Commissioners' satisfaction, that VAT shall be the greater of the amounts of VAT which would have been chargeable on a supply of those goods—

    (a)   if the value of that supply were the highest open market value during the period (the relevant period) commencing when the goods were placed in the fiscal warehousing regime and ending when the absence or deficiency came to the notice of the Commissioners, or

    (b)   if the rate of VAT chargeable on that supply were the highest rate chargeable on a supply of such goods during the relevant period and the value of that supply were the highest open market value while that rate prevailed

(4) This section has effect without prejudice to any penalty incurred under any other provision of this Act or regulations made under it.]

NOTES

Section inserted, in relation to any acquisition of goods from another member state and any supply taking place on or after 1 June 1996, by the Finance Act 1996, s 26, Sch 3, para 5.

[18F Sections 18A to 18E: supplementary

(1) In sections 18A to 18E and this section—

"duty point" has the meaning given by section 18(6);

"eligible goods" has the meaning given by section 18B(6);

"fiscal warehouse" means a place notified to the Commissioners under section 18A(3) and from which such status has not been withdrawn;

"fiscal warehousekeeper" means a person approved under section 18A(1);

"material time"—

    (a)   in relation to any acquisition or supply the time of which is determined in accordance with regulations under section 6(14) or 12(3), means such time as may be prescribed for the purpose of this section by those regulations;

    (b)   in relation to any other acquisition, means the time when the goods reach the destination to which they are despatched from the member State in question;

    (c)   in relation to any other supply of goods, means the time when the supply would be treated as taking place in accordance with subsection (2) of section 6 if paragraph (c) of that subsection were omitted; and

    (d)   in relation to any other supply of services, means the time when the services are performed;

"warehouse", except in the expression "fiscal warehouse", has the meaning given by section 18(6);

"warehousing regulations" has the same meaning as in the Management Act.

(2)   Any reference in sections 18A to 18E or this section to goods being subject to a fiscal warehousing regime is, subject to any regulations made under subsection (8)(e) below, a reference to eligible goods being kept in a fiscal warehouse or being transferred between fiscal warehouses in accordance with such regulations; and any reference to the removal of goods from a fiscal warehousing regime shall be construed accordingly.

(3)   Subject to subsection (2) above, any reference in sections 18C and 18D to goods being subject to a warehousing regime or to the removal of goods from a warehousing regime shall have the same meaning as in section 18(7).

(4)   Where as a result of an operation on eligible goods subject to a fiscal warehousing regime they change their nature but the resulting goods are also eligible goods, the provisions of sections 18B to 18E and this section shall apply as if the resulting goods were the original goods.

(5)   Where as a result of an operation on eligible goods subject to a fiscal warehousing regime they cease to be eligible goods, on their ceasing to be so sections 18B to 18E shall apply as if they had at that time been removed from the fiscal warehousing regime; and for that purpose the proprietor of the goods shall be treated as if he were the person removing them.

(6)   Where—

(a)   any person ceases to be a fiscal warehousekeeper; or

(b)   any premises cease to have fiscal warehouse status,

sections 18B to 18E and this section shall apply as if the goods of which he is the fiscal warehousekeeper, or the goods in the fiscal warehouse, as the case may be, had at that time been removed from the fiscal warehousing regime; and for that purpose the proprietor of the goods shall be treated as if he were the person removing them.

(7)   The Commissioners may make regulations governing the deposit, keeping, securing and treatment of goods in a fiscal warehouse, and the removal of goods from a fiscal warehouse.

(8)   Regulations may, without prejudice to the generality of subsection (7) above, include provisions—

in relation to—

(i)   goods which are, have been or are to be subject to a fiscal warehousing regime,

(ii)   other goods which are, have been or are to be kept in fiscal warehouses,

(iii)   fiscal warehouse premises, and

(iv)   fiscal warehousekeepers and their businesses, as to the keeping, preservation and production of records and the furnishing of returns and information by fiscal warehousekeepers and any other persons;

(b)   requiring goods deposited in a fiscal warehouse to be produced to or made available for inspection by an authorised person on request by him;

(c)   prohibiting the carrying out on fiscally warehoused goods of such operations as they may prescribe;

(d)   regulating the transfer of goods from one fiscal warehouse to another;

(e)   concerning goods which, though kept in a fiscal warehouse, are not eligible goods or are not intended by a relevant person to be goods in respect of which reliefs are to be enjoyed under sections 18A to 18E and this section;

(f)   prohibiting the fiscal warehousekeeper from allowing goods to be
        removed from the fiscal warehousing regime without payment of any
        VAT payable under section 18D on or by reference to that removal and,
        if in breach of that prohibition he allows goods to be so removed,
        making him liable for the VAT jointly and severally with the remover,

and may contain such incidental or supplementary provisions as the Commissioners
think necessary or expedient.

(9)   Regulations may make different provision for different cases, including
different provision for different fiscal warehousekeepers or descriptions of fiscal
warehousekeeper, for fiscal warehouses of different descriptions or for goods of
different classes or descriptions or of the same class or description in different
circumstances.]

NOTES

Section inserted, in relation to any acquisition of goods from another member state and any
supply taking place on or after 1 June 1996, by the Finance Act 1996, s 26, Sch 3, para 5.

PART V
APPEALS

82 Appeal tribunals

(1)   Any reference in this Act to a tribunal is a reference to a tribunal constituted in
accordance with Schedule 12, and that Schedule shall have effect generally with
respect to appointments to and the procedure and administration of the tribunals.

(2)   The tribunals shall continue to have jurisdiction in relation to matters relating
to VAT conferred upon them by this Part of this Act and jurisdiction in relation to
matters relating to customs and excise conferred by Chapter II of Part I of the Finance
Act 1994.

(3)   Officers and staff may be appointed under [section 2(1) of the Courts Act
2003] (court staff) for carrying out the administrative work of the tribunals in
England and Wales.

(4)   The Secretary of State may make available such officers and staff as he may
consider necessary for carrying out the administrative work of the tribunals in
Scotland.

NOTES

Sub-ss (1), (2) contain provisions formerly in the Value Added Tax Act 1983, s 40(1) (in
part), Sch 8, para 1, the Finance Act 1985, s 30(1), and from the Finance Act 1994, s 7(1) (in
part); sub-ss (3), (4) contain provisions formerly in Sch 8, para 6 to the 1985 Act.

Sub-s (3): words in square brackets substituted by the Courts Act 2003 s 109(1), Sch 8
para 363.

Modification of this section in respect of appeals to a VAT and duties tribunal made under
the Money Laundering Regulations, SI 2007/2157, reg 44, Sch 5, para 1.

83 Appeals

Subject to section 84, an appeal shall lie to a tribunal with respect to any of the
following matters—

(a)   the registration or cancellation of registration of any person under this
        Act;
(b)   the VAT chargeable on the supply of any goods or services, on the
        acquisition of goods from another member State or, subject to
        section 84(9), on the importation of goods from a place outside the
        member States;

(c)   the amount of any input tax which may be credited to a person;

(d)   any claim for a refund under any regulations made by virtue of section 13(5);

[(da)   a decision of the Commissioners under section 18A—

(i)   as to whether or not a person is to be approved as a fiscal warehouse keeper or the conditions from time to time subject to which he is so approved;

(ii)   for the withdrawal of any such approval; or

(iii)   for the withdrawal of fiscal warehouse status from any premises;]

(e)   the proportion of input tax allowable under section 26;

(f)   a claim by a taxable person under section 27;

[(fza) a decision of the Commissioners—

(i)   refusing or withdrawing authorisation for a person's liability to pay VAT (or entitlement to credit for VAT) to be determined as mentioned in subsection (1) of section 26B;

(ii)   as to the appropriate percentage or percentages (within the meaning of that section) applicable in a person's case;]

[(fa)   a decision contained in a notification under paragraph (4) of article 12A of the Value Added Tax (Payments on Account) Order 1993 that an election under paragraph (1) of that article shall cease to have effect;]

(g)   the amount of any refunds under section 35;

(h)   a claim for a refund under section 36 or section 22 of the 1983 Act;

(j)   the amount of any refunds under section 40;

[(k)   the refusal of an application such as is mentioned in section 43B(1) or (2);]

[(ka)   the giving of a notice under section 43C(1) or (3);]

(l)   the requirement of any security under section 48(7) or [paragraph 4(1A) or (2)] of Schedule 11;

(m)   any refusal or cancellation of certification under section 54 or any refusal to cancel such certification;

(n)   any liability to a penalty or surcharge by virtue of any of sections [59 to [69B]];

(o)   a decision of the Commissioners under section 61 (in accordance with section 61(5));

(p)   an assessment—

(i)   under section 73(1) or (2) in respect of a period for which the appellant has made a return under this Act; or

(ii)   under [subsections (7), (7A) or (7B)] of that section; or

(iii)   under section 75;

or the amount of such an assessment;

(q)   the amount of any penalty, interest or surcharge specified in an assessment under section 76;

(r)   the making of an assessment on the basis set out in section 77(4);

[(ra)   any liability arising by virtue of section 77A;]

(s)   any liability of the Commissioners to pay interest under section 78 or the amount of interest so payable;

[(sa)   an assessment under section 78A(1) or the amount of such an assessment;]

(t)   a claim for the [crediting or] repayment of an amount under section 80[, an assessment under subsection (4A) of that section or the amount of such an assessment;]

[(ta)   an assessment under section 80B(1) or the amount of such an assessment;]

(u)   any direction or supplementary direction made under paragraph 2 of Schedule 1;

(v)   any direction under paragraph 1[, 1A] or 2 of Schedule 6 or under paragraph 2 of Schedule 4 to the 1983 Act;

(w)   any direction under paragraph 1 of Schedule 7;

[(wa)   any direction or assessment under Schedule 9A;]

(x)   any refusal to permit the value of supplies to be determined by a method described in a notice published under paragraph 2(6) of Schedule 11;

(y)   any refusal of authorisation or termination of authorisation in connection with the scheme made under paragraph 2(7) of Schedule 11;

[(z)   any conditions imposed by the Commissioners in a particular case by virtue of paragraph 2B(2)(c) or 3(1) of Schedule 11;]

[(zza)   a direction under paragraph 6A of Schedule 11;]

[(za)   a direction under paragraph 8 of Schedule 11A,]

[(zb)   any liability to a penalty under paragraph 10(1) of Schedule 11A, any assessment under paragraph 12(1) of that Schedule or the amount of such an assessment;]

[(zc)   a decision of the Commissioners about the application of regulations under section 135 of the Finance Act 2002 (mandatory electronic filing of returns) in connection with VAT (including, in particular, a decision as to whether a requirement of the regulations applies and a decision to impose a penalty);]]

(zz)   . . .

NOTES

This section contains provisions formerly in the Value Added Tax Act 1983, s 40(1), as amended by the Finance Act 1985, s 24(1), the Finance Act 1986, s 10(2), the Finance Act 1987, s 19(2), Sch 2, para 4, the Value Added Tax (Cash Accounting) Regulations 1991, SI 1991/1427, reg 11, the Finance Act 1989, s 24(9), the Finance Act 1990, s 11(11)(b), the Finance Act 1991, s 17(1), and the Finance (No 2) Act 1992, ss 14, 16(2), Sch 3, Pt I, paras 1, 40.

Paras (da), (wa) inserted, and words in square brackets in para (p)(ii) substituted, by the Finance Act 1996, ss 26(1), 31(3), Sch 3, para 12, para (fza) inserted by the Finance Act 2002, s 23(4), para (fa) inserted by the Value Added Tax (Payments on Account) (Appeals) Order, SI 1997/2542, paras (k), (ka) substituted for original para (k) by the Finance Act 1999, s 16, Sch 2, para 3, subject to transitional provisions, words in para (l) substituted by the Finance Act 2003, s 17(6), words in outer square brackets in para (n) substituted by FA 2000 s 137(1), (5), with effect from 28 July 2000, reference in inner square brackets in para (n) substituted by the Finance Act 2006, s 21(1), (4)(a); para (ra) inserted by the Finance Act 2003, s 18(2), para (sa) inserted by the Finance Act 1997, s 45(2), and deemed to have come into force on 4 December 1996 in relation to assessments made on or after that date, words in square brackets in para (t) and whole of para (ta) inserted by FA 1997 ss 46(3), 47(7); words "crediting or" in para (t) inserted by the Finance (No 2) Act 2005 s 4(5)(a) with effect in any case where a claim under VATA 1994 s 80(2) is made on or after 26th May 2005, whenever the event occurred in respect of which the claim is made; reference in para (v) inserted by the Finance Act 2004, s 22(1), (3) with effect from a date to be appointed, para (z) substituted by the Finance Act 2002, s 24(4)(b); para (zza) inserted by the Finance Act 2006, s 21(1), (4)(b); paras (za), (zb) inserted by the Finance Act 2004, s 19(1), Sch 2 para 4; para (zb) inserted by the Finance Act 2007, s 93(8); para (zz) repealed by the Money Laundering Regulations, SI 2007/2157, reg 51, Sch 6, para 1, with effect from 15 December 2007.

Transitional provision: see s 100 of, and Sch 13, para 22 to, this Act.

Modification of this section in respect of appeals to a VAT and duties tribunal made under the Money Laundering Regulations, SI 2007/2157, reg 44, Sch 5, para 1.

84 Further provisions relating to appeals

(1) References in this section to an appeal are references to an appeal under section 83.

(2) An appeal shall not be entertained unless the appellant has made all the returns which he was required to make under paragraph 2(1) of Schedule 11 and . . . has paid the amounts shown in those returns as payable by him.

(3) Where the appeal is against a decision with respect to any of the matters mentioned in section 83(b), (n), (p) [, (q)[, (ra) or (zb)]] it shall not be entertained unless—

    (a)   the amount which the Commissioners have determined to be payable as VAT has been paid or deposited with them; or

    (b)   on being satisfied that the appellant would otherwise suffer hardship the Commissioners agree or the tribunal decides that it should be entertained notwithstanding that that amount has not been so paid or deposited.

[(3A) An appeal against an assessment which is a recovery assessment for the purposes of this subsection, or against the amount of such an assessment, shall not be entertained unless–

    (a)   the amount notified by the assessment has been paid or deposited with the Commissioners; or

    (b)   on being satisfied that the appellant would otherwise suffer hardship, the Commissioners agree, or the tribunal decides, that the appeal should be entertained notwithstanding that that amount has not been so paid or deposited.]

(4) Subject to subsection (11) below, where—

    (a)   there is an appeal against a decision of the Commissioners with respect to, or to so much of any assessment as concerns, the amount of input tax that may be credited to any person or the proportion of input tax allowable under section 26, and

    (b)   that appeal relates, in whole or in part, to any determination by the Commissioners—

          (i)   as to the purposes for which any goods or services were or were to be used by any person, or

          (ii)   as to whether or to what extent the matters to which any input tax was attributable were or included matters other than the making of supplies within section 26(2), and

    (c)   VAT for which, in pursuance of that determination, there is no entitlement to a credit is VAT on the supply, acquisition or importation of something in the nature of a luxury, amusement or entertainment,

the tribunal shall not allow the appeal or, as the case may be, so much of it as relates to that determination unless it considers that the determination is one which it was unreasonable to make or which it would have been unreasonable to make if information brought to the attention of the tribunal that could not have been brought to the attention of the Commissioners had been available to be taken into account when the determination was made.

[(4A) Where an appeal is brought against the refusal of an application such as is mentioned in section 43B(1) or (2) on the grounds stated in section 43B(5)(c)—

    (a)   the tribunal shall not allow the appeal unless it considers that the Commissioners could not reasonably have been satisfied that there were grounds for refusing the application,

    (b)   the refusal shall have effect pending the determination of the appeal, and

    (c)   if the appeal is allowed, the refusal shall be deemed not to have occurred.

(4B) Where an appeal is brought against the giving of a notice under section 43C(1) or (3)—

    (a)   the notice shall have effect pending the determination of the appeal, and

    (b)   if the appeal is allowed, the notice shall be deemed never to have had effect.

(4C) Where an appeal is brought against the giving of a notice under section 43C(1), the tribunal shall not allow the appeal unless it considers that the Commissioners could not reasonably have been satisfied that there were grounds for giving the notice.

(4D) Where—

    (a)   an appeal is brought against the giving of a notice under section 43C(3), and

    (b)   the grounds of appeal relate wholly or partly to the date specified in the notice,

the tribunal shall not allow the appeal in respect of the date unless it considers that the Commissioners could not reasonably have been satisfied that it was appropriate.]

[(4E) Where an appeal is brought against a requirement imposed under paragraph 4(2)(b) of Schedule 11 that a person give security, the tribunal shall allow the appeal unless the Commissioners satisfy the tribunal that—

    (a)   there has been an evasion of, or an attempt to evade, VAT in relation to goods or services supplied to or by that person, or

    (b)   it is likely, or without the requirement for security it is likely, that VAT in relation to such goods or services will be evaded.]

[(4F) A reference in subsection (4E) above to evading VAT includes a reference to obtaining a VAT credit that is not due or a VAT credit in excess of what is due.]

(5) Where, on an appeal against a decision with respect to any of the matters mentioned in section 83(p)—

    (a)   it is found that the amount specified in the assessment is less than it ought to have been, and

    (b)   the tribunal gives a direction specifying the correct amount,

the assessment shall have effect as an assessment of the amount specified in the direction, and that amount shall be deemed to have been notified to the appellant.

(6) Without prejudice to section 70, nothing in section 83(q) shall be taken to confer on a tribunal any power to vary an amount assessed by way of penalty, interest or surcharge except in so far as it is necessary to reduce it to the amount which is appropriate under sections 59 to 70; and in this subsection "penalty" includes an amount assessed by virtue of section 61(3) or (4)(a).

[(6A) Without prejudice to section 70, nothing in section 83(zb) shall be taken to confer on a tribunal any power to vary an amount assessed by way of penalty except in so far as it is necessary to reduce it to the amount which is appropriate under paragraph 11 of Schedule 11A.]

[(6B) Nothing in section 83(zc) shall be taken to confer on a tribunal any power to vary an amount assessed by way of penalty except in so far as it is necessary to reduce it to the amount which is appropriate under regulations made under section 135 of the Finance Act 2002.]

(7) Where there is an appeal against a decision to make such a direction as is mentioned in section 83(u), the tribunal shall not allow the appeal unless it considers that the Commissioners could not reasonably have been satisfied [that there were grounds for making the direction].

[(7A) Where there is an appeal against a decision to make such a direction as is mentioned in section 83(wa), the cases in which the tribunal shall allow the appeal shall include (in addition to the case where the conditions for the making of the direction were not fulfilled) the case where the tribunal are satisfied, in relation to the relevant event by reference to which the direction was given, that—

  (a)   the change in the treatment of the body corporate, or
  (b)   the transaction in question,

had as its main purpose or, as the case may be, as each of its main purposes a genuine commercial purpose unconnected with the fulfilment of the condition specified in paragraph 1(3) of Schedule 9A.]

[(7B)   Where there is an appeal against a decision to make such a direction as is mentioned in section 83(zza)—

  (a)   the tribunal shall not allow the appeal unless it considers that the Commissioners could not reasonably have been satisfied that there were grounds for making the direction;
  (b)   the direction shall have effect pending the determination of the appeal.]

  (8)   Where on an appeal it is found—

  (a)   that the whole or part of any amount paid or deposited in pursuance of subsection (3) above is not due; or
  (b)   that the whole or part of any VAT credit due to the appellant has not been paid,

so much of that amount as is found not to be due or not to have been paid shall be repaid (or, as the case may be, paid) with interest at such rate as the tribunal may determine; and where the appeal has been entertained notwithstanding that an amount determined by the Commissioners to be payable as VAT has not been paid or deposited and it is found on the appeal that that amount is due, the tribunal may, if it thinks fit, direct that that amount shall be paid with interest at such rate as may be specified in the direction.

  (9)   No appeal shall lie under this section with respect to the subject-matter of any decision which by virtue of section 16 is a decision to which section 14 of the Finance Act 1994 (decisions subject to review) applies unless the decision—

  (a)   relates exclusively to one or both of the following matters, namely whether or not section 30(3) applies in relation to the importation of the goods in question and (if it does not) the rate of tax charged on those goods; and
  (b)   is not one in respect of which notice has been given to the Commissioners under section 14 of that Act requiring them to review it.

  (10)   Where an appeal is against a decision of the Commissioners which depended upon a prior decision taken by them in relation to the appellant, the fact that the prior decision is not within section 83 shall not prevent the tribunal from allowing the appeal on the ground that it would have allowed an appeal against the prior decision.

  (11)   Subsection (4) above shall not apply in relation to any appeal relating to the input tax that may be credited to any person at the end of a prescribed accounting period beginning before 27th July 1993.

NOTES

  Sub-s (1) is a drafting provision; sub-ss (2), (3) contain provisions formerly in the Value Added Tax Act 1983, s 40(2), (3), as amended by the Finance Act 1985, s 24(3), (4); sub-s (4) contains provisions formerly in s 40(3ZA) of the 1983 Act, as inserted by the Finance Act 1993, s 46(1); sub-s (5) contains provisions formerly in s 40(3B) of the 1983 Act, as inserted by the Finance Act 1985, s 24(5) and as amended by the Finance Act 1986, s 10(3); sub-s (6) contains provisions formerly in s 40(1A) of the 1983 Act, as inserted by s 24(2) of the 1985 Act and as amended by s 49 of, and Sch 2, para 3(2)(b) to, the 1993 Act, and formerly in s 14(6) of the 1983 Act (in part); sub-s (7) contain provisions formerly in s 40(3A) of the 1983 Act, as inserted by s 10(3) of the 1986 Act; sub-ss (8), (10) contain provisions formerly in s 40(4), (6) of the 1983 Act; sub-s (9) contain provisions formerly in s 40(5) of the 1983 Act, as substituted by the Finance Act 1994, s 18(3); sub-s (11) contain provisions formerly in s 46(2) of the 1993 Act.

Sub-s (2): words omitted repealed by the Finance Act 1995, ss 31, 162, Sch 29, Pt VI(4), in relation to appeals brought after 1 May 1995.

Sub-s (3): references substituted by the Finance Act 2003, s 18(3), and the Finance Act 2004, s 19(1), Sch 2 para 5(1), (2).

Sub-s (3A): inserted by the Finance Act 1997, s 45(3), (5) and deemed to have come into force on 4 December 1996 in relation to assessments made on or after that date.

Sub-ss (4A), (4B), (4C), (4D): inserted by the Finance Act 1999, s 16, Sch 2, para 4, subject to transitional provisions.

Sub-ss (4E), (4F): inserted by the Finance Act 2003, s 17(7).

Sub-s (6A): inserted by the Finance Act 2004, s 19(1), Sch 2, Pt 2, para 5(1), (3).

Sub-s (6B): inserted by the Finance Act 2007, s 93(9).

Sub-s (7): words in square brackets substituted by the Finance Act 1997, s 31(3), in relation to directions made on or after 19 March 1997.

Sub-s (7A): inserted by the Finance Act 1996, s 31(4).

Sub-s (7B): inserted by the Finance Act 2006, s 21(1), (5).

Transitional provision: see s 100 of, and Sch 13, para 22 to, this Act.

Modification of this section in respect of appeals to a VAT and duties tribunal made under the Money Laundering Regulations, SI 2007/2157, reg 44, Sch 5, para 1.

---

85 Settling appeals by agreement

(1) Subject to the provisions of this section, where a person gives notice of appeal under section 83 and, before the appeal is determined by a tribunal, the Commissioners and the appellant come to an agreement (whether in writing or otherwise) under the terms of which the decision under appeal is to be treated—

    (a)   as upheld without variation, or

    (b)   as varied in a particular manner, or

    (c)   as discharged or cancelled,

the like consequences shall ensue for all purposes as would have ensued if, at the time when the agreement was come to, a tribunal had determined the appeal in accordance with the terms of the agreement (including any terms as to costs).

(2) Subsection (1) above shall not apply where, within 30 days from the date when the agreement was come to, the appellant gives notice in writing to the Commissioners that he desires to repudiate or resile for the agreement.

(3) Where an agreement is not in writing—

    (a)   the preceding provisions of this section shall not apply unless the fact that an agreement was come to, and the terms agreed, are confirmed by notice in writing given by the Commissioners to the appellant or by the appellant to the Commissioners, and

    (b)   references in those provisions to the time when the agreement was come to shall be construed as references to the time of the giving of that notice of confirmation.

(4) Where—

    (a)   a person who has given a notice of appeal notifies the Commissioners, whether orally or in writing, that he desires not to proceed with the appeal; and

    (b)   30 days have elapsed since the giving of the notification without the Commissioners giving to the appellant notice in writing indicating that they are unwilling that the appeal should be treated as withdrawn,

the preceding provisions of this section shall have effect as if, at the date of the appellant's notification, the appellant and the Commissioners had come to an agreement, orally or in writing, as the case may be, that the decision under appeal should be upheld without variation.

(5) References in this section to an agreement being come to with an appellant and the giving of notice or notification to or by an appellant include references to an agreement being come to with, and the giving of notice or notification to or by, a person acting on behalf of the appellant in relation to the appeal.

NOTES

This section contains provisions formerly in the Finance Act 1985, s 25.

Modification of this section in respect of appeals to a VAT and duties tribunal made under the Money Laundering Regulations, SI 2007/2157, reg 44, Sch 5, para 1.

86 Appeals to Court of Appeal

(1) The Lord Chancellor may by order provide that—
  (a)   in such classes of appeal as may be prescribed by the order, and
  (b)   subject to the consent of the parties and to such other conditions as may be so prescribed,
an appeal from a tribunal shall lie to the Court of Appeal.

(2) An order under this section may provide that section 11 of the Tribunals and Inquiries Act 1992 (which provides for appeals to the High Court from a tribunal) shall have effect, in relation to any appeal to which the order applies, with such modifications as may be specified in the order.

[(2A) Before making an order under this section that relates to England and Wales, the Lord Chancellor must consult the Lord Chief Justice of England and Wales.

(2B) Before making an order under this section that relates to Northern Ireland, the Lord Chancellor must consult the Lord Chief Justice of Northern Ireland.

(2C) The Lord Chief Justice of England and Wales may nominate a judicial office holder (as defined in section 109(4) of the Constitutional Reform Act 2005) to exercise his functions under this section.

(2D) The Lord Chief Justice of Northern Ireland may nominate any of the following to exercise his functions under this section—
  (a)   the holder of one of the offices listed in Schedule 1 to the Justice (Northern Ireland) Act 2002;
  (b)   a Lord Justice of Appeal (as defined in section 88 of that Act).]

(3) This section does not extend to Scotland.

NOTES

Sub-ss (1), (3) contains provisions formerly in the Finance Act 1985, s 26(1), (3); sub-s (2) contains provisions formerly in s 26(2)(a) of the 1985 Act, as amended by the Tribunals and Inquiries Act 1992, s 18(1), Sch 3, para 17.

Sub-ss (2A)–(2D) inserted by the Constitutional Reform Act 2005 s 15, Sch 4 para 236, with effect from 3 April 2006.

Orders: by virtue of the Interpretation Act 1978, s 17(2)(b), the Value Added Tax Tribunals Appeals Order 1986, SI 1986/2288, the Value Added Tax Tribunals Appeals (Northern Ireland) Order 1994, SI 1994/1978 have effect as if made under this section.

Modification of this section in respect of appeals to a VAT and duties tribunal made under the Money Laundering Regulations, SI 2007/2157, reg 44, Sch 5, para 1.

87 Enforcement of registered or recorded tribunal decisions etc

(1) If the decision of a tribunal in England and Wales on an appeal under section 83 is registered by the Commissioners in accordance with rules of court, payment of—

(a)   any amount which, as a result of the decision, is, or is recoverable as, VAT due from any person, and

(b)   any costs awarded to the Commissioners by the decision,

may be enforced by the High Court as if that amount or, as the case may be, the amount of those costs were an amount due to the Commissioners in pursuance of a judgment or order of the High Court.

(2)   If the decision of a tribunal in Scotland on an appeal under section 83—

(a)   confirms or varies an amount which is, or is recoverable as, VAT due from any person, or

(b)   awards costs to the Commissioners,

the decision may be recorded for execution in the Books of Council and Session and shall be enforceable accordingly.

(3)   Subsection (4) below shall apply in relation to the decision of a tribunal in Northern Ireland on an appeal under section 83 where—

(a)   any amount is, or is recoverable as, VAT due from any person, as a result of the decision, whether with or without an award of costs to the Commissioners; or

(b)   any costs are awarded to the Commissioners by the decision.

(4)   Where this subsection applies—

(a)   payment of the amount mentioned in paragraph (a) of subsection (3) above or, as the case may be, the amount of the costs mentioned in paragraph (b) of that subsection may be enforced by the Enforcement of Judgments Office; and

(b)   a sum equal to any such amount shall be deemed to be payable under a money judgment within the meaning of Article 2(2) of the Judgments Enforcement (Northern Ireland) Order 1981, and the provisions of that Order shall apply accordingly.

(5)   Any reference in this section to a decision of a tribunal includes a reference to an order (however described) made by a tribunal for giving effect to a decision.

NOTES

This section contains provisions formerly in the Finance Act 1985, s 29.

Rules of court: by virtue of the Interpretation Act 1978, s 17(2)(b), the Rules of the Supreme Court (Revision) 1965, SI 1965/1776, Ord 45, r 14, has effect as if made under this section.

Modification of this section in respect of appeals to a VAT and duties tribunal made under the Money Laundering Regulations, SI 2007/2157, reg 44, Sch 5, para 1.

PART VI
SUPPLEMENTARY PROVISIONS

Supplementary provisions

97 Orders, rules and regulations

(1)   Any order made by the Treasury or the Lord Chancellor under this Act and any regulations or rules under this Act shall be made by statutory instrument.

(2)   A statutory instrument containing an order under section 86 or rules under paragraph 9 of Schedule 12 shall be subject to annulment in pursuance of a resolution of either House of Parliament.

(3)   An order to which this subsection applies shall be laid before the House of Commons; and unless it is approved by that House before the expiration of a period of 28 days beginning with the date on which it was made, it shall cease to have

effect on the expiration of that period, but without prejudice to anything previously done thereunder or to the making of a new order.

In reckoning any such period no account shall be taken of any time during which Parliament is dissolved or prorogued or during which the House of Commons is adjourned for more that 4 days.

(4) . . .

(5)   A statutory instrument made under any provision of this Act except—

(a)   an order made under section 79, or

(b)   an instrument as respects which any other Parliamentary procedure is expressly provided, or

(c)   an instrument containing an order appointing a day for the purposes of any provision of this Act, being a day as from which the provision will have effect, with or without amendments, or will cease to have effect,

shall be subject to annulment in pursuance of a resolution of the House of Commons.

NOTES

Sub-ss (1), (2) contain provisions formerly in the Value Added Tax Act 1983, s 45(1), and in the Finance Act 1985, ss 18(8)(c) (in part), 26(2)(b), 27(3)(c); sub-s (3) contains provisions formerly in s 45(3) of the 1983 Act; sub-s (5) contains provisions formerly in s 45(2) of the 1983 Act, in ss 15(8), 17(8), 18(8) (in part) of the 1985 Act and in s 17A(9) of the 1985 Act (as inserted by the Finance (No 2) Act 1992, s 14, Sch 3, Pt II, paras 76, 82, and is partly a drafting provision.

Sub-s (4): outside the scope of this work.

[97A   Place of supply orders: transitional provision.

(1)   This section shall have effect for the purpose of giving effect to any order made on or after 17th March 1998 under section 7(11), if—

(a)   the order provides for services of a description specified in the order to be treated as supplied in the United Kingdom;

(b)   the services would not have fallen to be so treated apart from the order;

(c)   the services are not services that would have fallen to be so treated under any provision re-enacted in the order; and

(d)   the order is expressed to come into force in relation to services supplied on or after a date specified in the order ("the commencement date").

(2)   Invoices and other documents provided to any person before the commencement date shall be disregarded in determining the time of the supply of any services which, if their time of supply were on or after the commencement date, would be treated by virtue of the order as supplied in the United Kingdom.

(3)   If there is a payment in respect of any services of the specified description that was received by the supplier before the commencement date, so much (if any) of that payment as relates to times on or after that date shall be treated as if it were a payment received on the commencement date.

(4)   If there is a payment in respect of services of the specified description that is or has been received by the supplier on or after the commencement date, so much (if any) of that payment as relates to times before that date shall be treated as if it were a payment received before that date.

(5)   Subject to subsection (6) below, a payment in respect of any services shall be taken for the purposes of this section to relate to the time of the performance of those services.

(6)   Where a payment is received in respect of any services the performance of which takes place over a period a part of which falls before the commencement date and a part of which does not—

(a)   an apportionment shall be made, on a just and reasonable basis, of the extent to which the payment is attributable to so much of the performance of those services as took place before that date;

(b)   the payment shall, to that extent, be taken for the purposes of this section to relate to a time before that date; and

(c)   the remainder, if any, of the payment shall be taken for those purposes to relate to times on or after that date.]

NOTES

Commencement: 17 March 1998.

Inserted by the Finance Act 1998, s 22(1), (3).

100   Savings and transitional provisions, consequential amendments and repeals

(1)   Schedule 13 (savings and transitional provisions) and Schedule 14 (consequential amendments) shall have effect.

(2)   . . .

(3)   This section is without prejudice to the operation of sections 15 to 17 of the Interpretation Act 1978 (which relate to the effect of repeals).

NOTES

This section is a drafting provision.

Sub-s (2): outside the scope of this work.

101   Commencement and extent

(1)   This Act shall come into force on 1st September 1994 and Part I shall have effect in relation to the charge to VAT on supplies, acquisitions and importations in prescribed accounting periods ending on or after that date.

(2), (3)   . . .

(4)   Paragraph 23 of Schedule 13 and paragraph 7 of Schedule 14 shall extend to the Isle of Man but no other provision of this Act shall extend there.

NOTES

This section is a drafting provision.

Sub-ss (2), (3): outside the scope of this work.

102   Short title

This Act may be cited as the Value Added Tax Act 1994.

SCHEDULES

SCHEDULE 12

CONSTITUTION AND PROCEDURE OF TRIBUNALS

Section 61

Establishment of tribunals

1.—(1)   There shall continue to be tribunals for England and Wales, Scotland and Northern Ireland respectively known as VAT tribunals.

(2) If section 7(1) and (2) of the Finance Act 1994 have come into force before this Schedule comes into force then for any reference in this Schedule to VAT tribunals there shall, as from the commencement of this Schedule, be substituted a reference to VAT and duties tribunals.

(3) If sub-paragraph (2) above does not apply, then, as from a day to be appointed by order made by the Commissioners by statutory instrument for the purposes of this paragraph, for any reference in this Schedule to VAT tribunals there shall be substituted a reference to VAT and duties tribunals.

(4) Any reference in any enactment or any subordinate legislation to a value added tax tribunal (or to a VAT tribunal) shall be construed in accordance with paragraphs (1) to (3) above, and cognate expressions shall be construed similarly.

The President

2.—(1) There shall continue to be a President of VAT tribunals, who shall perform the functions conferred on him by the following provisions of this Schedule in relation to VAT tribunals in any part of the United Kingdom.

(2) The President shall be appointed by the Lord Chancellor after consultation with the [Secretary of State] and shall be—

- (a) a person who has a 10 year general qualification, within the meaning of section 71 of the Courts and Legal Services Act 1990;
- (b) an advocate or solicitor in Scotland of at least *10* years' standing; or
- (c) a member of the Bar of Northern Ireland or solicitor of the Supreme Court of Northern Ireland of at least *10* years' standing.

(3) Subject to paragraph 3 below, the appointment of the President shall be for such term and subject to such conditions as may be determined by the Lord Chancellor, after consultation with the Lord Advocate, and a person who ceases to hold the office of President shall be eligible for re-appointment thereto.

3.—(1) The President may resign his office at any time and shall vacate his office—

- (a) at the end of the completed year of service in which he attains the age of 72, or
- (b) if sub-paragraph (2) below applies, on the date on which he attains the age of 75.

This sub-paragraph shall cease to have effect on the day appointed under section 31 of the Judicial Pensions and Retirement Act 1993 ("the 1993 Act") for the coming into force of section 26 of that Act.

(2) If the Lord Chancellor, after consultation with the Lord Advocate, considers it desirable in the public interest to do so he may authorise the President to continue in office after the end of the completed year of service mentioned in sub-paragraph (1)(a) above.

(3) The President—

- (a) may resign his office at any time; and
- (b) shall vacate his office on the day on which he attains the age of 70;

but sub-paragraph (b) above is subject to section 26(4) to (6) of the 1993 Act (power to authorise continuance in office up to the age of 75).

This sub-paragraph shall come into force on the day appointed under section 31 of the 1993 Act for the coming into force of section 26 of that Act.

(4) The Lord Chancellor may, if he thinks fit and after consultation with the Lord Advocate, remove the President from office on the ground of incapacity or misbehaviour.

(5)   The functions of the President may, if he is for any reason unable to act or his office is vacant, be discharged by a person nominated for the purpose by the Lord Chancellor after consultation with the Lord Advocate.

[(5A)   The Lord Chancellor may remove a person from office under sub-paragraph (4), or nominate a person under sub-paragraph (5), only with the concurrence of all of the following—

    (a)   the Lord Chief Justice of England and Wales;

    (b)   the Lord President of the Court of Session;

    (c)   the Lord Chief Justice of Northern Ireland.]

(6)   There shall be paid to the President such salary or fees and there may be paid to or in respect of a former President such pension, allowance or gratuity as the Lord Chancellor may with the approval of the Treasury determine.

(7)   Sub-paragraph (6) above, so far as relating to pensions allowances and gratuities, shall not have effect in relation to a person to whom Part I of the 1993 Act applies, except to the extent provided under or by that Act.

(8)   If a person ceases to be President of VAT tribunals and it appears to the Lord Chancellor that there are special circumstances which make it right that he should receive compensation, there may be paid to that person a sum of such amount as the Lord Chancellor may with the approval of the Treasury determine.

[(9)   The Lord Chief Justice of England and Wales may nominate a judicial office holder (as defined in section 109(4) of the Constitutional Reform Act 2005) to exercise his functions under sub-paragraph (5A) in relation to the nomination of a person under sub-paragraph (5).

(10)   The Lord President of the Court of Session may nominate a judge of the Court of Session who is a member of the First or Second Division of the Inner House of that Court to exercise his functions under sub-paragraph (5A) in relation to the nomination of a person under sub-paragraph (5).

(11)   The Lord Chief Justice of Northern Ireland may nominate any of the following to exercise his functions under sub-paragraph (5A) in relation to the nomination of a person under sub-paragraph (5)—

    (a)   the holder of one of the offices listed in Schedule 1 to the Justice (Northern Ireland) Act 2002;

    (b)   a Lord Justice of Appeal (as defined in section 88 of that Act).]

Sittings of tribunals

4.—[(1)]   Such number of VAT tribunals shall be established as the Lord Chancellor or, in relation to Scotland, the Secretary of State may from time to time determine, and they shall sit at such times and at such places as the Lord Chancellor or, as the case may be, the Secretary of State may from time to time determine.

[(2)   The powers of the Lord Chancellor under sub-paragraph (1) may be exercised—

    (a)   in relation to England and Wales only after consulting the Lord Chief Justice of England and Wales;

    (b)   in relation to Northern Ireland only after consulting the Lord Chief Justice of Northern Ireland.

(3)   The Lord Chief Justice of England and Wales may nominate a judicial office holder (as defined in section 109(4) of the Constitutional Reform Act 2005) to exercise his functions under this paragraph.

(4)   The Lord Chief Justice of Northern Ireland may nominate any of the following to exercise his functions under this paragraph—

    (a)   the holder of one of the offices listed in Schedule 1 to the Justice (Northern Ireland) Act 2002;

(b)   a Lord Justice of Appeal (as defined in section 88 of that Act).]

Composition of tribunals

5.—(1) A VAT tribunal shall consist of a chairman sitting either with two other members or with one other member or alone.

(2) If the tribunal does not consist of the chairman sitting alone, its decisions may be taken by a majority of votes and the chairman, if sitting with one other member, shall have a casting vote.

Membership of tribunals

6. For each sitting of a VAT tribunal the chairman shall be either the President or if so authorised by the President, a member of the appropriate panel of chairmen constituted in accordance with paragraph 7 below; and any other member of the tribunal shall be a person selected from the appropriate panel of other members so constituted, the selection being made either by the President or by a member of the panel of chairmen, authorised by the President to make it.

7.—(1) There shall be a panel of chairmen and a panel of other members of VAT tribunals for England and Wales, Scotland and Northern Ireland respectively.

(2) One member of each panel of chairmen shall be known as Vice-President of VAT tribunals.

(3) Appointments to a panel of chairmen shall be made by the appropriate authority, that is to say—

(a)   for England and Wales, the Lord Chancellor;

(b)   for Scotland, the Lord President of the Court of Session; and

(c)   for Northern Ireland, the [Lord Chancellor];

and appointments to a panel of other members shall be made by the Treasury.

(4) No person may be appointed to a panel of chairmen of tribunals for England and Wales or Northern Ireland unless he is—

(a)   a person who has a 7 year general qualification, within the meaning of section 71 of the Courts and Legal Services Act 1990; or

(b)   a member of the Bar of Northern Ireland or solicitor of the Supreme Court of Northern Ireland of at least 7 years' standing,

and no person may be appointed to a panel of chairmen of tribunals for Scotland unless he is an advocate or solicitor of not less than 7 years' standing.

(5) Subject to the following provisions of this paragraph, the appointment of a chairman of VAT tribunals shall be for such term and subject to such conditions as may be determined by the appropriate authority, and a person who ceases to hold the office of chairman shall be eligible for re-appointment thereto.

(6) A chairman of VAT tribunals—

(a)   may resign his office at any time; and

(b)   shall vacate his office on the day on which he attains the age of 70 years; but paragraph (b) above is subject to section 26(4) to (6) of the Judicial Pensions and Retirement Act 1993 (power to authorise continuance in office up to the age of 75).

[(7A) The Lord Chancellor may, with the concurrence of the Lord Chief Justice of England and Wales, remove from office on the ground of incapacity or misbehaviour a chairman of VAT Tribunals appointed under sub-paragraph (3)(a).

(7B) The Lord President of the Court of Session may remove from office on the ground of incapacity or misbehaviour a chairman of VAT Tribunals appointed under sub-paragraph (3)(b).]

(8) There shall be paid to a chairman of VAT tribunals such salary or fees, and to other members such fees, as the Lord Chancellor may with the approval of the Treasury determine; and there may be paid to or in respect of a former chairman of

VAT tribunals such pension, allowance or gratuity as the Lord Chancellor may with the approval of the Treasury determine.

(9) Sub-paragraph (8) above, so far as relating to pensions allowances and gratuities, shall not have effect in relation to a person to whom Part I of the Judicial Pensions and Retirement Act 1993 applies, except to the extent provided under or by that Act.

(10) If a person ceases to be a chairman of VAT tribunals and it appears to the Lord Chancellor that there are special circumstances which make it right that he should receive compensation, there may be paid to that person a sum of such amount as the Lord Chancellor may with the approval of the Treasury determine.

Exemption from jury service

8. No member of a VAT tribunal shall be compelled to serve on any jury in Scotland or Northern Ireland.

Rules of procedure

9. The Lord Chancellor after consultation with the [Secretary of State] may make rules with respect to the procedure to be followed on appeals to and in other proceedings before VAT tribunals and such rules may include provisions—

(a) for limiting the time within which appeals may be brought;

(b) for enabling hearings to be held in private in such circumstances as may be determined by or under the rules;

(c) for parties to proceedings to be represented by such persons as may be determined by or under the rules;

(d) for requiring persons to attend to give evidence;

(e) for discovery and for requiring persons to produce documents;

(f) for the payment of expenses and allowances to persons attending as witnesses or producing documents;

(g) for the award and recovery of costs;

(h) for authorising the administration of oaths to witnesses; and

(j) with respect to the joinder of appeals brought by different persons where a notice is served under section 61 and the appeals relate to, or to different portions of, the basic penalty referred to in the notice.

10.—(1) A person who fails to comply with a direction or summons issued by a VAT tribunal under rules made under paragraph 9 above shall be liable to a penalty not exceeding £1,000.

(2) A penalty for which a person is liable by virtue of sub-paragraph (1) above may be awarded summarily by a tribunal notwithstanding that no proceedings for its recovery have been commenced.

(3) An appeal shall lie to the High Court or, in Scotland, the Court of Session as the Court of Exchequer in Scotland, from the award of a penalty under this paragraph, and on such an appeal the court may either confirm or reverse the decision of the tribunal or reduce or increase the sum awarded.

(4) A penalty awarded by virtue of this paragraph shall be recoverable as if it were VAT due from the person liable for the penalty.

NOTES

Para 1 contains provisions formerly in the Value Added Tax Act 1983, Sch 8, para 1, and the Finance Act 1994, s 7; para 2 contains provisions formerly Sch 8, para 2 to the 1983 Act, as amended by the Finance Act 1985, s 30, Sch 8, para 2 and the Courts and Legal Services Act 1990, s 71(2), Sch 10, para 52; para 3 contains provisions formerly in Sch 8, para 3 to the 1983 Act, as amended by s 30 of, and Sch 8. para 3 to, the 1985 Act and the Judicial Pensions and Retirement Act 1993, ss 26, 31, Sch 6, para 35, Sch 8, para 16; para 4 contains provisions formerly in Sch 8, para 4 to the 1983 Act, as amended by s 30 of, and Sch 8, para 4 to, the 1985 Act; paras 5, 6, 8 contains provisions formerly in Sch 8, paras 5, 6, 8 to the 1983 Act; para 7 contains provisions formerly in Sch 8, para 7 to the 1983 Act, as amended by s 30 of, and Sch 8, para 5 to, the 1985 Act, the Courts and Legal Services Act 1990, s 71(2), Sch 10, para 52, and the Judicial Pensions and Retirement Act 1993, ss 26, 31, Sch 6, para 35, Sch 8, para 16; para 9 contains provisions formerly in Sch 8, para 9 to the 1983 Act, as amended by s 27(2) of the 1985 Act, and from the Finance Act 1986, s 14(7); para 10 contains provisions formerly in Sch 8, para 10 to the 1983 Act, as added by s 28 of the 1985 Act.

Para 2: words substituted by virtue of the Transfer of Functions (Lord Advocate and Secretary of State) Order, SI 1999/678, art 2(1), Schedule; sub-para (2)(a) to be substituted by the Tribunals, Courts and Enforcement Act 2007, s 50, Sch 10, para 24, with effect from a date to be appointed. Para (a) as substituted to read as follows—

(a) a person who satisfies the judicial-appointment eligibility condition on a 7-year basis;

In sub-paras (2)(b), (c) "7" to be substituted for "10" by the Tribunals, Courts and Enforcement Act 2007, s 50, Sch 10, para 24, with effect from a date to be appointed.

Para 3: sub-para (5A) inserted by the Constitutional Reform Act 2005 s 15, Sch 4 para 237(2)(a); sub-paras (9)–(11) inserted by the Constitutional Reform Act 2005 s 15, Sch 4 para 237(2)(b).

Para 4: existing para 4 renumbered as sub-para (1) and new sub-paras (2)–(4) inserted by the Constitutional Reform Act 2005 s 15, Sch 4 para 237(3).

Para 7: in sub-para (3)(c) words in square brackets substituted by the Constitutional Reform Act 2005 s 15, Sch 4 para 237(4)(a); sub-para (4)(a) to be substituted by the Tribunals, Courts and Enforcement Act 2007, s 50, Sch 10, para 24, with effect from a date to be appointed. Sub-para (4)(a) as substituted to read as follows—

(a) a person who satisfies the judicial-appointment eligibility condition on a 5-year basis; or

In sub-para (4)(b), and in the words after that paragraph, "5" to be substituted for "7" by the Tribunals, Courts and Enforcement Act 2007, s 50, Sch 10, para 24, with effect from a date to be appointed.

New sub-paras (7A) and (7B) substituted for sub-para 7 by the Constitutional Reform Act 2005 s 15, Sch 4 para 237(4)(b);

Para 9: words in square brackets substituted by virtue of the Transfer of Functions (Lord Advocate and Secretary of State) Order, SI 1999/678, art 2(1), Schedule.

Rules: by virtue of the Interpretation Act 1978, s 17(2)(b), the Value Added Tax Tribunal Rules 1986, SI 1986/590, as modified by SI 1982/1068, and as modified by SI 1986/2290, SI 1991/186, SI 1994/2617, SI 1997/255.

Transitional provisions: see s 100 of, and Sch 13 para 5 to, this Act.

SCHEDULE 13

TRANSITIONAL PROVISIONS AND SAVINGS

Section 100

1.   . . .

Validity of subordinate legislation

2.   So far as this Act re-enacts any provision contained in a statutory instrument made in exercise of powers conferred by any Act, it shall be without prejudice to the validity of that provision, and any question as to its validity shall be determined as if the re-enacted provision were contained in a statutory instrument made under those powers.

3, 4.   . . .

President, chairmen etc of tribunals

5.—(1) Any appointment to a panel of chairmen of the tribunals current at the commencement of this Act and made by the Treasury before the passing of the 1983 Act shall not be affected by the repeal by this Act of paragraph 8 of Schedule 10 to that Act.

(2) The terms of appointment of any person who was appointed to the office of President of the tribunal or chairman or other member of the tribunals before 1st April 1986 and holds that office on the coming into force of this Act shall continue to have effect notwithstanding the re-enactment, as Schedule 12 to this Act, of Schedule 8 to the 1983 Act as amended by Schedule 8 to the Finance Act 1985.

Overseas suppliers accounting through their customers

6–21. . . . .

VAT tribunals

22.—(1) Without prejudice to paragraph 1 above, section 83 applies to things done or omitted to be done before the coming into force of this Act and accordingly references in Part V to any provision of this Act includes a reference to the corresponding provision of the enactments repealed by this Act or by any enactment repealed by such an enactment.

(2) Section 84 shall have effect before such day as may be appointed for the purposes of section 18(3) of the Finance Act 1994 with the substitution for subsection (5) of the following subsection—

"(5) No appeal shall lied with respect to any matter that has been or could have been referred to arbitration under s 127 of the Management Act as applied by section 16.".

23. . . . .

NOTES

Paras 1, 3, 4, 6, 8–21, 23: outside the scope of this work.

Para 7: repealed by the Finance Act 1995, ss 21(5), (6), 162, Sch 29, Pt VI(1), in relation to any supply made on or after 1st April 1995 and any acquisition or importation taking place on or after that date.

FINANCE ACT 1995

(1995 c 4)

An Act to grant certain duties, to alter other duties, and to amend the law relating to the National Debt and the Public Revenue, and to make further provision in connection with Finance

[1 May 1995]

PART I
DUTIES OF EXCISE

Alcoholic liquor duties

1–3

(Amend the Alcoholic Liquor Duties Act 1979, ss 1, 5, 36, 62, 59, Sch 1.)

4 Alcoholic ingredients relief

(1)   Subject to the following provisions of this section, where any person proves to the satisfaction of the Commissioners that any dutiable alcoholic liquor on which duty has been paid has been—

    (a)   used as an ingredient in the production or manufacture of a product falling within subsection (2) below, or

    (b)   converted into vinegar,

he shall be entitled to obtain from the Commissioners the repayment of the duty paid thereon.

(2)   The products falling within this subsection are—

    (a)   any beverage of an alcoholic strength not exceeding 1.2 per cent,

    (b)   chocolates for human consumption which contain alcohol such that 100 kilograms of the chocolates would not contain more than 8.5 litres of alcohol, or

    (c)   any other food for human consumption which contains alcohol such that 100 kilograms of the food would not contain more than 5 litres of alcohol.

(3)   A repayment of duty shall not be made under this section in respect of any liquor except to a person who—

    (a)   is the person who used the liquor as an ingredient in a product falling within subsection (2) above or, as the case may be, who converted it into vinegar;

    (b)   carries on a business as a wholesale supplier of products of the applicable description falling within that subsection or, as the case may be, of vinegar;

    (c)   produced or manufactured the product or vinegar for the purposes of that business;

    (d)   makes a claim for the repayment in accordance with the following provisions of this section; and

    (e)   satisfies the Commissioners as to the matters mentioned in paragraphs (a) to (c) above and that the repayment claimed does not relate to any duty which has been repaid or drawn back prior to the making of the claim.

(4)   A claim for repayment under this section shall take such form and be made in such manner, and shall contain such particulars, as the Commissioners may direct, either generally or in a particular case.

(5)   Except so far as the Commissioners otherwise allow, a person shall not make a claim for a repayment under this section unless—

    (a)   the claim relates to duty paid on liquor used as an ingredient or, as the case may be, converted into vinegar in the course of a period of three months ending not more than one month before the making of the claim; and

    (b)   the amount of the repayment which is claimed is not less than £250.

(6)   The Commissioners may by order made by statutory instrument increase the amount for the time being specified in subsection (5)(b) above; and a statutory instrument containing an order under this subsection shall be subject to annulment in pursuance of a resolution of the House of Commons.

(7)   There may be remitted by the Commissioners any duty charged either—

    (a)   on any dutiable alcoholic liquor imported into the United Kingdom at a time when it is contained as an ingredient in any chocolates or food falling within subsection (2)(b) or (c) above; or

(b) on any dutiable alcoholic liquor used as an ingredient in the manufacture or production in an excise warehouse of any such chocolates or food.

(8) This section shall be construed as one with the Alcoholic Liquor Duties Act 1979, and references in this section to chocolates or food do not include references to any beverages.

5 Denatured alcohol

(1) The liquors on which duty is charged under the Alcoholic Liquor Duties Act 1979 shall not include any denatured alcohol; and any duty so charged on liquor which has become denatured alcohol before the requirement to pay the duty takes effect shall be remitted.

(2) In this section—

"denatured alcohol" means any dutiable alcoholic liquor which has been subjected to the process of being mixed in the prescribed manner with a prescribed substance; and

"prescribed" means prescribed by the Commissioners by regulations made by statutory instrument.

(3) The power of the Commissioners to make regulations defining denatured alcohol for the purposes of this section shall include—

(a) power, in prescribing any substance or any manner of mixing a substance with a liquor, to do so by reference to such circumstances or other factors, or to the approval or opinion of such persons (including the authorities of another member State), as they may consider appropriate;

(b) power to make different provision for different cases; and

(c) power to make such supplemental, incidental, consequential and transitional provision as the Commissioners think fit;

and a statutory instrument containing any regulations under this section shall be subject to annulment in pursuance of a resolution of either House of Parliament.

(4) Sections 14 to 16 of the Finance Act 1994 (review and appeals) shall have effect in relation to any decision which—

(a) is made under or for the purposes of any regulations under this section, and

(b) is a decision given to any person as to whether a manner of mixing any substance with any liquor is to be, or to continue to be, approved in his case, or as to the conditions subject to which it is so approved,

as if that decision were a decision specified in Schedule 5 to that Act.

(5) Schedule 2 to this Act (which contains amendments for or in connection with the application to all denatured alcohol of provisions of the Alcoholic Liquor Duties Act 1979 relating to methylated spirits and also makes a consequential amendment of the Finance Act 1994) shall have effect.

(6) This section and Schedule 2 to this Act shall come into force on such day as the Commissioners may by order made by statutory instrument appoint, and different days may be appointed under this subsection for different purposes.

(7) An order under subsection (6) above may make such transitional provisions and savings as appear to the Commissioners to be appropriate in connection with the bringing into force by such an order of any provision for any purposes.

(8) This section shall be construed as one with the Alcoholic Liquor Duties Act 1979.

NOTES

Commencement: 1 July 2005.

Denatured Alcohol Regulations, SI 2005/1524.

PART VI
MISCELLANEOUS AND GENERAL

General

163 Short title

This Act may be cited as the Finance Act 1995.

SCHEDULES

(Schs 1, 2 amend the Alcoholic Liquor Duties Act 1979, ss 4, 10, 24, 75, 77–80, Sch 1, repeal s 9 thereof, and amend the Finance Act 1994, Sch 5, para 3; Schs 3–29 outside the scope of this work.)

CIVIL EVIDENCE ACT 1995

(1995 c 38)

ARRANGEMENT OF SECTIONS

An Act to provide for the admissibility of hearsay evidence, the proof of certain documentary evidence and the admissibility and proof of official actuarial tables in civil proceedings; and for connected purposes

[8 November 1995]

Admissibility of hearsay evidence

1 Admissibility of hearsay evidence

(1) In civil proceedings evidence shall not be excluded on the ground that it is hearsay.

(2) In this Act—

(a) "hearsay" means a statement made otherwise than by a person while giving oral evidence in the proceedings which is tendered as evidence of the matters stated; and

(b) references to hearsay include hearsay of whatever degree.

(3) Nothing in this Act affects the admissibility of evidence admissible apart from this section.

(4) The provisions of sections 2 to 6 (safeguards and supplementary provisions relating to hearsay evidence) do not apply in relation to hearsay evidence admissible apart from this section, notwithstanding that it may also be admissible by virtue of this section.

NOTES

Commencement: 31 January 1997.

Safeguards in relation to hearsay evidence

2 Notice of proposal to adduce hearsay evidence

(1) A party proposing to adduce hearsay evidence in civil proceedings shall, subject to the following provisions of this section, give to the other party or parties to the proceedings—

(a) such notice (if any) of that fact, and

(b) on request, such particulars of or relating to the evidence,

as is reasonable and practicable in the circumstances for the purpose of enabling him or them to deal with any matters arising from its being hearsay.

(2) Provision may be made by rules of court—

(a) specifying classes of proceedings or evidence in relation to which subsection (1) does not apply, and

(b) as to the manner in which (including the time within which) the duties imposed by that subsection are to be complied with in the cases where it does apply.

(3) Subsection (1) may also be excluded by agreement of the parties; and compliance with the duty to give notice may in any case be waived by the person to whom notice is required to be given.

(4) A failure to comply with subsection (1), or with rules under subsection (2)(b), does not affect the admissibility of the evidence but may be taken into account by the court—

(a) in considering the exercise of its powers with respect to the course of proceedings and costs, and

(b) as a matter adversely affecting the weight to be given to the evidence in accordance with section 4.

NOTES

Commencement: 31 January 1997.

Rules: the Magistrates' Courts (Hearsay Evidence in Civil Proceedings) Rules 1999, SI 1999/681.

3 Power to call witness for cross-examination on hearsay statement

Rules of court may provide that where a party to civil proceedings adduces hearsay evidence of a statement made by a person and does not call that person as a witness, any other party to the proceedings may, with the leave of the court, call that person as a witness and cross-examine him on the statement as if he had been called by the first-mentioned party and as if the hearsay statement were his evidence in chief.

NOTES

Commencement: 31 January 1997.

Rules: the Magistrates' Courts (Hearsay Evidence in Civil Proceedings) Rules 1999, SI 1999/681.

4 Considerations relevant to weighing of hearsay evidence

(1) In estimating the weight (if any) to be given to hearsay evidence in civil proceedings the court shall have regard to any circumstances from which any inference can reasonably be drawn as to the reliability or otherwise of the evidence.

(2) Regard may be had, in particular, to the following—

(a) whether it would have been reasonable and practicable for the party by whom the evidence was adduced to have produced the maker of the original statement as a witness;

(b) whether the original statement was made contemporaneously with the occurrence or existence of the matters stated;

(c) whether the evidence involves multiple hearsay;

(d) whether any person involved had any motive to conceal or misrepresent matters;

(e) whether the original statement was an edited account, or was made in collaboration with another or for a particular purpose;

(f) whether the circumstances in which the evidence is adduced as hearsay are such as to suggest an attempt to prevent proper evaluation of its weight.

NOTES

Commencement: 31 January 1997.

Supplementary provisions as to hearsay evidence

5 Competence and credibility

(1) Hearsay evidence shall not be admitted in civil proceedings if or to the extent that it is shown to consist of, or to be proved by means of, a statement made by a person who at the time he made the statement was not competent as a witness.

For this purpose "not competent as a witness" means suffering from such mental or physical infirmity, or lack of understanding, as would render a person incompetent as a witness in civil proceedings; but a child shall be treated as competent as a witness if he satisfies the requirements of section 96(2)(a) and (b) of the Children Act 1989 (conditions for reception of unsworn evidence of child).

(2)   Where in civil proceedings hearsay evidence is adduced and the maker of the original statement, or of any statement relied upon to prove another statement, is not called as a witness—

    (a)   evidence which if he had been so called would be admissible for the purpose of attacking or supporting his credibility as a witness is admissible for that purpose in the proceedings; and

    (b)   evidence tending to prove that, whether before or after he made the statement, he made any other statement inconsistent with it is admissible for the purpose of showing that he had contradicted himself.

Provided that evidence may not be given of any matter of which, if he had been called as a witness and had denied that matter in cross-examination, evidence could not have been adduced by the cross-examining party.

NOTES

Commencement: 31 January 1997.

6 Previous statements of witnesses

(1)   Subject as follows, the provisions of this Act as to hearsay evidence in civil proceedings apply equally (but with any necessary modifications) in relation to a previous statement made by a person called as a witness in the proceedings.

(2)   A party who has called or intends to call a person as a witness in civil proceedings may not in those proceedings adduce evidence of a previous statement made by that person, except—

    (a)   with the leave of the court, or

    (b)   for the purpose of rebutting a suggestion that his evidence has been fabricated.

This shall not be construed as preventing a witness statement (that is, a written statement of oral evidence which a party to the proceedings intends to lead) from being adopted by a witness in giving evidence or treated as his evidence.

(3)   Where in the case of civil proceedings section 3, 4 or 5 of the Criminal Procedure Act 1865 applies, which make provision as to—

    (a)   how far a witness may be discredited by the party producing him,

    (b)   the proof of contradictory statements made by a witness, and

    (c)   cross-examination as to previous statements in writing,

this Act does not authorise the adducing of evidence of a previous inconsistent or contradictory statement otherwise than in accordance with those sections.

This is without prejudice to any provision made by rules of court under section 3 above (power to call witness for cross-examination on hearsay statement).

(4)   Nothing in this Act affects any of the rules of law as to the circumstances in which, where a person called as a witness in civil proceedings is cross-examined on a document used by him to refresh his memory, that document may be made evidence in the proceedings.

(5)   Nothing in this section shall be construed as preventing a statement of any description referred to above from being admissible by virtue of section 1 as evidence of the matters stated.

NOTES

Commencement: 31 January 1997.

7 Evidence formerly admissible at common law

(1)   The common law rule effectively preserved by section 9(1) and (2)(a) of the Civil Evidence Act 1968 (admissibility of admissions adverse to a party) is superseded by the provisions of this Act.

(2)   The common law rules effectively preserved by section 9(1) and (2)(b) to (d) of the Civil Evidence Act 1968, that is, any rule of law whereby in civil proceedings—

(a)   published works dealing with matters of a public nature (for example, histories, scientific works, dictionaries and maps) are admissible as evidence of facts of a public nature stated in them,

(b)   public documents (for example, public registers, and returns made under public authority with respect to matters of public interest) are admissible as evidence of facts stated in them, or

(c)   records (for example, the records of certain courts, treaties, Crown grants, pardons and commissions) are admissible as evidence of facts stated in them,

shall continue to have effect.

(3)   The common law rules effectively preserved by section 9(3) and (4) of the Civil Evidence Act 1968, that is, any rule of law whereby in civil proceedings—

(a)   evidence of a person's reputation is admissible for the purpose of proving his good or bad character, or

(b)   evidence of reputation or family tradition is admissible—

(i)   for the purpose of proving or disproving pedigree or the existence of a marriage, or

(ii)   for the purpose of proving or disproving the existence of any public or general right or of identifying any person or thing,

shall continue to have effect in so far as they authorise the court to treat such evidence as proving or disproving that matter.

Where any such rule applies, reputation or family tradition shall be treated for the purposes of this Act as a fact and not as a statement or multiplicity of statements about the matter in question.

(4)   The words in which a rule of law mentioned in this section is described are intended only to identify the rule and shall not be construed as altering it in any way.

NOTES

Commencement: 31 January 1997.

Other matters

8 Proof of statements contained in documents

(1)   Where a statement contained in a document is admissible as evidence in civil proceedings, it may be proved—

(a)   by the production of that document, or

(b)   whether or not that document is still in existence, by the production of a copy of that document or of the material part of it,

authenticated in such manner as the court may approve.

(2)   It is immaterial for this purpose how many removes there are between a copy and the original.

NOTES

Commencement: 31 January 1997.

9 Proof of records of business or public authority

(1) A document which is shown to form part of the records of a business or public authority may be received in evidence in civil proceedings without further proof.

(2) A document shall be taken to form part of the records of a business or public authority if there is produced to the court a certificate to that effect signed by an officer of the business or authority to which the records belong.

For this purpose—

(a) a document purporting to be a certificate signed by an officer of a business or public authority shall be deemed to have been duly given by such an officer and signed by him; and

(b) a certificate shall be treated as signed by a person if it purports to bear a facsimile of his signature.

(3) The absence of an entry in the records of a business or public authority may be proved in civil proceedings by affidavit of an officer of the business or authority to which the records belong.

(4) In this section—

"records" means records in whatever form;

"business" includes any activity regularly carried on over a period of time, whether for profit or not, by any body (whether corporate or not) or by an individual;

"officer" includes any person occupying a responsible position in relation to the relevant activities of the business or public authority or in relation to its records; and

"public authority" includes any public or statutory undertaking, any government department and any person holding office under Her Majesty.

(5) The court may, having regard to the circumstances of the case, direct that all or any of the above provisions of this section do not apply in relation to a particular document or record, or description of documents or records.

NOTES

Commencement: 31 January 1997.

10 Admissibility and proof of Ogden Tables

(1) The actuarial tables (together with explanatory notes) for use in personal injury and fatal accident cases issued from time to time by the Government Actuary's Department are admissible in evidence for the purpose of assessing, in an action for personal injury, the sum to be awarded as general damages for future pecuniary loss.

(2) They may be proved by the production of a copy published by Her Majesty's Stationery Office.

(3) For the purposes of this section—

(a) "personal injury" includes any disease and any impairment of a person's physical or mental condition; and

(b) "action for personal injury" includes an action brought by virtue of the Law Reform (Miscellaneous Provisions) Act 1934 or the Fatal Accidents Act 1976.

NOTES

Commencement: to be appointed.

Repealed, in relation to Northern Ireland, by the Civil Evidence (Northern Ireland) Order 1997, SI 1997/2983 (NI 21), art 13(2), subject to savings, as from a day to be appointed.

Sub-s (3) is modified, in relation to Northern Ireland, by s 16(5)(b) of this Act.

General

11 Meaning of "civil proceedings"

In this Act "civil proceedings" means civil proceedings, before any tribunal, in relation to which the strict rules of evidence apply, whether as a matter of law or by agreement of the parties.

References to "the court" and "rules of court" shall be construed accordingly.

NOTES

Commencement: 31 January 1997.

12 Provisions as to rules of court

(1)   Any power to make rules of court regulating the practice or procedure of the court in relation to civil proceedings includes power to make such provision as may be necessary or expedient for carrying into effect the provisions of this Act.

(2)   Any rules of court made for the purposes of this Act as it applies in relation to proceedings in the High Court apply, except in so far as their operation is excluded by agreement, to arbitration proceedings to which this Act applies, subject to such modifications as may be appropriate.

Any question arising as to what modifications are appropriate shall be determined, in default of agreement, by the arbitrator or umpire, as the case may be.

NOTES

Commencement: 31 January 1997.

Rules: the Magistrates' Courts (Hearsay Evidence in Civil Proceedings) Rules 1999, SI 1999/681.

13 Interpretation

In this Act—

"civil proceedings" has the meaning given by section 11 and "court" and "rules of court" shall be construed in accordance with that section;

"document" means anything in which information of any description is recorded, and "copy", in relation to a document, means anything onto which information recorded in the document has been copied, by whatever means and whether directly or indirectly;

"hearsay" shall be construed in accordance with section 1(2);

"oral evidence" includes evidence which, by reason of a defect of speech or hearing, a person called as a witness gives in writing or by signs;

"the original statement", in relation to hearsay evidence, means the underlying statement (if any) by—

(a)   in the case of evidence of fact, a person having personal knowledge of that fact, or

(b)   in the case of evidence of opinion, the person whose opinion it is; and

"statement" means any representation of fact or opinion, however made.

NOTES
Commencement: 31 January 1997.

14 Savings

(1)   Nothing in this Act affects the exclusion of evidence on grounds other than that it is hearsay.

This applies whether the evidence falls to be excluded in pursuance of any enactment or rule of law, for failure to comply with rules of court or an order of the court, or otherwise.

(2)   Nothing in this Act affects the proof of documents by means other than those specified in section 8 or 9.

(3)   Nothing in this Act affects the operation of the following enactments—

    (a)   section 2 of the Documentary Evidence Act 1868 (mode of proving certain official documents);

    (b)   section 2 of the Documentary Evidence Act 1882 (documents printed under the superintendence of Stationery Office);

    (c)   section 1 of the Evidence (Colonial Statutes) Act 1907 (proof of statutes of certain legislatures);

    (d)   section 1 of the Evidence (Foreign, Dominion and Colonial Documents) Act 1933 (proof and effect of registers and official certificates of certain countries);

    (e)   section 5 of the Oaths and Evidence (Overseas Authorities and Countries) Act 1963 (provision in respect of public registers of other countries).

NOTES
Commencement: 31 January 1997.

16 Short title, commencement and extent

(1)   This Act may be cited as the Civil Evidence Act 1995.

(2)   The provisions of this Act come into force on such day as the Lord Chancellor may appoint by order made by statutory instrument, and different days may be appointed for different provisions and for different purposes.

[(3)   Subject to subsection (3A), the provisions of this Act shall not apply in relation to proceedings begun before commencement.]

[(3A)   Transitional provisions for the application of the provisions of this Act to proceedings begun before commencement may be made by rules of court or practice directions.]

(4)   This Act extends to England and Wales.

(5)   Section 10 (admissibility and proof of Ogden Tables) also extends to Northern Ireland.

As it extends to Northern Ireland, the following shall be substituted for subsection (3)(b)—

    "(b)   "action for personal injury" includes an action brought by virtue of the Law Reform (Miscellaneous Provisions) (Northern Ireland) Act 1937 or the Fatal Accidents (Northern Ireland) Order 1977."

(6)   The provisions of Schedules 1 and 2 (consequential amendments and repeals) have the same extent as the enactments respectively amended or repealed.

NOTES

Commencement: 31 January 1997 (sub-ss (1)–(4), (6)); to be appointed (remainder).

Sub-s (3): substituted by the Civil Procedure (Modification of Enactments) Order 1999, SI 1999/1217, art 4(a).

Sub-s (3A): inserted by SI 1999/1217, art 4(b).

Sub-s (5): repealed, in relation to Northern Ireland, by the Civil Evidence (Northern Ireland) Order 1997, SI 1997/2983 (NI 21), art 13(2), subject to savings, as from a day to be appointed.

Orders: the Civil Evidence Act 1995 (Commencement No 1) Order 1996, SI 1996/3217.

FINANCE ACT 1996

(1996 c 8)

An Act to grant certain duties, to alter other duties, and to amend the law relating to the National Debt and the Public Revenue, and to make further provision in connection with Finance

[29th April 1996]

PART VII
MISCELLANEOUS AND SUPPLEMENTAL

Miscellaneous: indirect taxation

197 Setting of rates of interest

(1) The rate of interest applicable for the purposes of an enactment to which this section applies shall be the rate which for the purposes of that enactment is provided for by regulations made by the Treasury under this section.

(2) This section applies to—

[(a) paragraph 7 of Schedule 6 to the Finance Act 1994 (interest payable to the Commissioners of Customs and Excise in connection with air passenger duty);]

(b) paragraphs 21 and 22 of Schedule 7 to that Act (interest on amounts of insurance premium tax and on amounts payable by the Commissioners in respect of that tax);

(c) sections 74 and 78 of the Value Added Tax Act 1994 (interest on VAT recovered or recoverable by assessment and interest payable in cases of official error); . . .

(d) paragraphs 26 and 29 of Schedule 5 to this Act (interest payable to or by the Commissioners in connection with landfill tax) [. . .

(e) paragraph 17 of Schedule 5 to the Finance Act 1997 (interest on amounts repayable in respect of overpayments by the Commissioners in connection with excise duties, insurance premium tax and landfill tax).]

[(f) sections 126 and 127 of the Finance Act 1999 (interest on overdue customs duty and on repayments of amounts paid by way of customs duty).]

[(g) the following provisions of Schedule 6 to the Finance Act 2000 (interest payable to or by the Commissioners in connection with climate change levy), that is to say, paragraphs 41(2)(f), 62(3)(f), 66, 70(1)(b) and 81(3).]

[(h)   the following provisions of the Finance Act 2001 (interest payable to or by the Commissioners in connection with aggregates levy), that is to say—

(i)   sections 25(2)(f) and 30(3)(f);

(ii)   [paragraphs 6 and 8(3)(a)] of Schedule 5; and

(iii)   paragraphs 2 and 6(1)(b) of Schedule 8.]

[(i)   Parts II and III of Schedule 3 to the Finance Act 2001 (interest payable on repayments etc).]

(3)   Regulations under this section may—

(a)   make different provision for different enactments or for different purposes of the same enactment,

(b)   either themselves specify a rate of interest for the purposes of an enactment or make provision for any such rate to be determined, and to change from time to time, by reference to such rate or the average of such rates as may be referred to in the regulations,

(c)   provide for rates to be reduced below, or increased above, what they otherwise would be by specified amounts or by reference to specified formulae,

(d)   provide for rates arrived at by reference to averages or formulae to be rounded up or down,

(e)   provide for circumstances in which changes of rates of interest are or are not to take place, and

(f)   provide that changes of rates are to have effect for periods beginning on or after a day determined in accordance with the regulations in relation to interest running from before that day, as well as in relation to interest running from, or from after, that day.

(4)   The power to make regulations under this section shall be exercisable by statutory instrument subject to annulment in pursuance of a resolution of the House of Commons.

(5)   Where—

(a)   regulations under this section provide, without specifying the rate determined in accordance with the regulations, for a new method of determining the rate applicable for the purposes of any enactment, or

(b)   the rate which, in accordance with regulations under this section, is the rate applicable for the purposes of any enactment changes otherwise than by virtue of the making of regulations specifying a new rate,

the Commissioners of Customs and Excise shall make an order specifying the new rate and the day from which, in accordance with the regulations, it has effect.

(6)   . . .

(7)   Subsections (1) and (6) above shall have effect for periods beginning on or after such day as the Treasury may by order made by statutory instrument appoint and shall have effect in relation to interest running from before that day, as well as in relation to interest running from, or from after, that day; and different days may be appointed under this subsection for different purposes.

NOTES

Commencement: 1 April 1997 (sub-ss (1), (6)); 29 April 1996 (remainder).

Sub-s (2): word omitted from para (c) repealed, and para (e) and word immediately preceding it added, by the Finance Act 1997, s 50(1), Sch 5, Pt V, para 21; word omitted from para (d) repealed, para (f) inserted by the Finance Act 1999, ss 130(3), 139, Sch 20, Pt VI and para (g) inserted by the Finance Act 2000, s 30, Sch 7, para 6; para (h) added by the Finance Act 2001, s 49(2); words substituted by the Finance Act 2002, s 132(2); para (a) substituted, and para (i) added by the Finance Act 2001, s 15, Sch 3 paras 18(1), (2).

Sub-s (6): amends the Finance Act 1994, Sch 6, paras 7(1), (3), 9(1), Sch 7, paras 21(1), (3), 22(2), and the Value Added Tax Act 1994, ss 74(1), (2), (4), 78(3).

Orders: the Finance Act 1996, section 197 (Appointed Day) Order 1997, SI 1997/1015; the Finance Act 2001 (Commencement No 2 and Saving Provision) Order 2001.

Regulations: the Air Passenger Duty and Other Indirect Taxes (Interest Rate) Regulations 1998, SI 1998/1461, as amended. Air Passenger Duty and Other Indirect Taxes (Interest Rate) (Amendment) Regulations, SI 2000/631. Air Passenger Duty and Other Indirect Taxes (Interest Rate) (Amendment) Regulations, SI 2001/3337. Air Passenger Duty and Other Indirect Taxes (Interest Rate) (Amendment) Regulations, SI 2003/230.

Supplemental

206 Short title

This Act may be cited as the Finance Act 1996.

FINANCE ACT 1997

(1997 c 16)

An Act to grant certain duties, to alter other duties, and to amend the law relating to the National Debt and the Public Revenue, and to make further provision in connection with Finance

[19th March 1997]

PART IV
PAYMENTS AND OVERPAYMENTS IN RESPECT OF INDIRECT TAXES

Excise duties and other indirect taxes

50 Overpayments, interest, assessments, etc

(1)   Schedule 5 to this Act (which makes provision in relation to excise duties, insurance premium tax and landfill tax which corresponds to that made for VAT by sections 44 to 48 above) shall have effect.

(2)   . . .

NOTES

Commencement: 19 March 1997.

Sub-s (2): outside the scope of this work.

Enforcement of payment

51 Enforcement by distress

(1)   The Commissioners may by regulations make provision—

(a)   for authorising distress to be levied on the goods and chattels of any person refusing or neglecting to pay—

(i)   any amount of relevant tax due from him, or

(ii)   any amount recoverable as if it were relevant tax due from him;

(b)   for the disposal of any goods or chattels on which distress is levied in pursuance of the regulations; and

(c)   for the imposition and recovery of costs, charges, expenses and fees in connection with anything done under the regulations.

(2) The provision that may be contained in regulations under this section shall include, in particular—

    (a)   provision for the levying of distress, by any person authorised to do so under the regulations, on goods or chattels located at any place whatever (including on a public highway); and

    (b)   provision authorising distress to be levied at any such time of the day or night, and on any such day of the week, as may be specified or described in the regulations.

(3) Regulations under this section may—

    (a)   make different provision for different cases, and

    (b)   contain any such incidental, supplemental, consequential or transitional provision as the Commissioners think fit;

and the transitional provision that may be contained in regulations under this section shall include transitional provision in connection with the coming into force of the repeal by this Act of any other power by regulations to make provision for or in connection with the levying of distress.

(4) The power to make regulations under this section shall be exercisable by statutory instrument subject to annulment in pursuance of a resolution of the House of Commons.

(5) The following are relevant taxes for the purposes of this section, that is to say—

    (a)   any duty of customs or excise, other than vehicle excise duty;

    (b)   value added tax;

    (c)   insurance premium tax;

    (d)   landfill tax;

    [(da)   aggregates levy;]

    (e)   any agricultural levy of the European Community.

    [(f)   climate change levy.]

(6) In this section "the Commissioners" means the Commissioners of Customs and Excise.

(7) *Regulations made under this section shall not have effect in Scotland.*

NOTES

Commencement: 19 March 1997.

Sub-s (5): para (da) inserted by the Finance Act 2001, s 27, Sch 5, para 14; para (f) inserted by the Finance Act 2000, s 30, Sch 7, para 7.

Regulations: the Distress for Customs and Excise Duties and Other Indirect Taxes Regulations 1997, SI 1997/1431.

New sub-s (A1) to be inserted by the Tribunals, Courts and Enforcement Act 2007, s 62(3), Sch 13, para 126, with effect from a date to be appointed. That sub-para to read as follows—

(A1) The Commissioners may, in England and Wales, use the procedure in Schedule 12 to the Tribunals, Courts and Enforcement Act 2007 (taking control of goods) to recover any of these that a person refuses or neglects to pay—

(a) any amount of relevant tax due from him;

(b) any amount recoverable as if it were relevant tax due from him.

In sub-s (1), words "not having effect in England and Wales or Scotland" to be inserted after words "by regulations" by the Tribunals, Courts and Enforcement Act 2007, s 62(3), Sch 13, para 126, with effect from a date to be appointed.

Sub-s (7) to be repealed by the Tribunals, Courts and Enforcement Act 2007, ss 62(3), 146, Sch 13, para 126, Sch 23, Pt 3, with effect from a date to be appointed.

52 Enforcement by diligence

(1)   Where any amount of relevant tax or any amount recoverable as if it were relevant tax is due and has not been paid, the sheriff, on an application by the Commissioners accompanied by a certificate by them—

  (a)   stating that none of the persons specified in the application has paid the amount due from him;

  (b)   stating that payment of the amount due from each such person has been demanded from him; and

  (c)   specifying the amount due from and unpaid by each such person,

shall grant a summary warrant in a form prescribed by Act of Sederunt authorising the recovery, by any of the diligences mentioned in subsection (2) below, of the amount remaining due and unpaid.

(2)   The diligences referred to in subsection (1) above are—

  [(a)   an attachment;]

  (b)   an earnings arrestment;

  (c)   an arrestment and action of forthcoming or sale.

(3)   Subject to subsection (4) below and without prejudice to [section 39(1) of the Debt Arrangement and Attachment (Scotland) Act 2002 (asp 17) (expenses of attachment)] the sheriff officer's fees, together with the outlays necessarily incurred by him, in connection with the execution of a summary warrant shall be chargeable against the debtor.

(4)   No fees shall be chargeable by the sheriff officer against the debtor for collecting, and accounting to the Commissioners for, sums paid to him by the debtor in respect of the amount owing.

(5)   The following are relevant taxes for the purposes of this section, that is to say—

  (a)   any duty of customs or excise, other than vehicle excise duty;

  (b)   value added tax;

  (c)   insurance premium tax;

  (d)   landfill tax;

  [(da)   aggregates levy;]

  (e)   any agricultural levy of the European Community.

  [(f)   climate change levy.]

(6)   In this section "the Commissioners" means the Commissioners of Customs and Excise.

(7)   This section shall come into force on such day as the Commissioners of Customs and Excise may by order made by statutory instrument appoint, and different days may be appointed under this subsection for different purposes.

(8)   This section extends only to Scotland.

NOTES

Commencement: 1 July 1997.

Sub-s (2): para (a) substituted by the Debt Arrangement and Attachment (Scotland) Act 2002, s 61, Sch 3 para 26(a).

Sub-s (3): words substituted by the Debt Arrangement and Attachment (Scotland) Act 2002, s 61, Sch 3 para 26(b).

Sub-s (5): para (da) inserted by the Finance Act 2001, s 27, Sch 5 para 16; para (f) inserted by the Finance Act 2000, s 30, Sch 7, para 7.

PART VIII

MISCELLANEOUS AND SUPPLEMENTAL

Supplemental

114 Short title

This Act may be cited as the Finance Act 1997.

NOTES

Commencement: 19 March 1997.

SCHEDULE 5

INDIRECT TAXES: OVERPAYMENTS ETC

Section 50

PART I

UNJUST ENRICHMENT

Application of Part I

1.—(1) This Part of this Schedule has effect for the purposes of the following provisions (which make it a defence to a claim for repayment that the repayment would unjustly enrich the claimant), namely—

    (a)   section 137A(3) of the Customs and Excise Management Act 1979 (excise duties);

    (b)   paragraph 8(3) of Schedule 7 to the Finance Act 1994 (insurance premium tax); and

    (c)   paragraph 14(3) of Schedule 5 to the Finance Act 1996 (landfill tax).

(2) Those provisions are referred to in this Part of this Schedule as unjust enrichment provisions.

(3) In this Part of this Schedule—

"the Commissioners" means the Commissioners of Customs and Excise;

    "relevant repayment provision" means—

    (a)   section 137A of the Customs and Excise Management Act 1979 (recovery of overpaid excise duty);

    (b)   paragraph 8 of Schedule 7 to the Finance Act 1994 (recovery of overpaid insurance premium tax); or

    (c)   paragraph 14 of Schedule 5 to the Finance Act 1996 (recovery of overpaid landfill tax);

"relevant tax" means any duty of excise, insurance premium tax or landfill tax; and

"subordinate legislation" has the same meaning as in the Interpretation Act 1978.

Disregard of business losses

2.—(1) This paragraph applies where—

    (a)   there is an amount paid by way of relevant tax which (apart from an unjust enrichment provision) would fall to be repaid under a relevant repayment provision to any person ("the taxpayer"), and

    (b)   the whole or a part of the cost of the payment of that amount to the Commissioners has, for practical purposes, been borne by a person other than the taxpayer.

(2) Where, in a case to which this paragraph applies, loss or damage has been or may be incurred by the taxpayer as a result of mistaken assumptions made in his case about the operation of any provisions relating to a relevant tax, that loss or damage shall be disregarded, except to the extent of the quantified amount, in the making of any determination—

(a) of whether or to what extent the repayment of an amount to the taxpayer would enrich him; or

(b) of whether or to what extent any enrichment of the taxpayer would be unjust.

(3) In sub-paragraph (2) above "the quantified amount" means the amount (if any) which is shown by the taxpayer to constitute the amount that would appropriately compensate him for loss or damage shown by him to have resulted, for any business carried on by him, from the making of the mistaken assumptions.

(4) The reference in sub-paragraph (2) above to provisions relating to a relevant tax is a reference to any provisions of—

(a) any enactment, subordinate legislation or Community legislation (whether or not still in force) which relates to that tax or to any matter connected with it; or

(b) any notice published by the Commissioners under or for the purposes of any such enactment or subordinate legislation.

(5) This paragraph has effect for the purposes of making any repayment on or after the day on which this Act is passed, even if the claim for that repayment was made before that day.

Reimbursement arrangements

3.—(1) The Commissioners may by regulations make provision for reimbursement arrangements made by any person to be disregarded for the purposes of any or all of the unjust enrichment provisions except where the arrangements—

(a) contain such provision as may be required by the regulations; and

(b) are supported by such undertakings to comply with the provisions of the arrangements as may be required by the regulations to be given to the Commissioners.

(2) In this paragraph "reimbursement arrangements" means any arrangements for the purposes of a claim under a relevant repayment provision which—

(a) are made by any person for the purpose of securing that he is not unjustly enriched by the repayment of any amount in pursuance of the claim; and

(b) provide for the reimbursement of persons who have for practical purposes borne the whole or any part of the cost of the original payment of that amount to the Commissioners.

(3) Without prejudice to the generality of sub-paragraph (1) above, the provision that may be required by regulations under this paragraph to be contained in reimbursement arrangements includes—

(a) provision requiring a reimbursement for which the arrangements provide to be made within such period after the repayment to which it relates as may be specified in the regulations;

(b) provision for the repayment of amounts to the Commissioners where those amounts are not reimbursed in accordance with the arrangements;

(c) provision requiring interest paid by the Commissioners on any amount repaid by them to be treated in the same way as that amount for the purposes of any requirement under the arrangements to make reimbursement or to repay the Commissioners;

    (d)   provision requiring such records relating to the carrying out of the arrangements as may be described in the regulations to be kept and produced to the Commissioners, or to an officer of theirs.

(4) Regulations under this paragraph may impose obligations on such persons as may be specified in the regulations—

    (a)   to make the repayments to the Commissioners that they are required to make in pursuance of any provisions contained in any reimbursement arrangements by virtue of sub-paragraph (3)(b) or (c) above;

    (b)   to comply with any requirements contained in any such arrangements by virtue of sub-paragraph (3)(d) above.

(5) Regulations under this paragraph may make provision for the form and manner in which, and the times at which, undertakings are to be given to the Commissioners in accordance with the regulations; and any such provision may allow for those matters to be determined by the Commissioners in accordance with the regulations.

(6) Regulations under this paragraph may—

    (a)   contain any such incidental, supplementary, consequential or transitional provision as appears to the Commissioners to be necessary or expedient; and

    (b)   make different provision for different circumstances.

(7) Regulations under this paragraph may have effect (irrespective of when the claim for repayment was made) for the purposes of the making of any repayment by the Commissioners after the time when the regulations are made; and, accordingly, such regulations may apply to arrangements made before that time.

(8) Regulations under this paragraph shall be made by statutory instrument subject to annulment in pursuance of a resolution of the House of Commons.

Contravention of requirement to repay Commissioners

4.—(1) Where any obligation is imposed by regulations made by virtue of paragraph 3(4) above, a contravention or failure to comply with that obligation shall, to the extent that it relates to amounts repaid under section 137A of the Customs and Excise Management Act 1979, attract a penalty under section 9 of the Finance Act 1994 (penalties in connection with excise duties).

(2) For the purposes of Schedule 7 to the Finance Act 1994 (insurance premium tax), a contravention or failure to comply with an obligation imposed by regulations made by virtue of paragraph 3(4) above shall be deemed, to the extent that it relates to amounts repaid under paragraph 8 of that Schedule (recovery of overpaid insurance premium tax), to be a failure to comply with a requirement falling within paragraph 17(1)(c) of that Schedule (breach of regulations).

(3) Paragraph 23 of Schedule 5 to the Finance Act 1996 (power to provide for penalty) shall have effect as if an obligation imposed by regulations made by virtue of paragraph 3(4) above were, to the extent that it relates to amounts repaid under paragraph 14 of that Schedule (recovery of overpaid landfill tax), a requirement imposed by regulations under Part III of that Act; and the provisions of that Schedule in relation to penalties under Part V of that Schedule shall have effect accordingly.

NOTES

Commencement: 19 March 1997.

Paras 5, 6(Pt II) amend the Customs and Excise Management Act 1979, s 137A(4), the Finance Act 1994, s 12, Sch 7, paras 8, 26, the Finance Act 1996, Sch 5, paras 14, 33; paras 7–12 (Pt III) amend the Finance Act 1994, Sch 6, para 9, the Finance Act 1996, Sch 5, para 29; para 13 (Pt IV) amends the Finance Act 1996, Sch 5, paras 42, 43.

PART V
RECOVERY OF EXCESS PAYMENTS BY THE COMMISSIONERS

Assessment for excessive repayment

14.—(1) Where—

    (a)   any amount has been paid at any time to any person by way of a repayment under a relevant repayment provision, and

    (b)   the amount paid exceeded the amount which the Commissioners were liable at that time to repay to that person,

the Commissioners may, to the best of their judgement, assess the excess paid to that person and notify it to him.

(2) Where any person is liable to pay any amount to the Commissioners in pursuance of an obligation imposed by virtue of paragraph 3(4)(a) above, the Commissioners may, to the best of their judgement, assess the amount due from that person and notify it to him.

(3) In this paragraph "relevant repayment provision" means—

    (a)   section 137A of the Customs and Excise Management Act 1979 (recovery of overpaid excise duty);

    (b)   paragraph 8 of Schedule 7 to the Finance Act 1994 (recovery of overpaid insurance premium tax); . . .

    (c)   paragraph 14 of Schedule 5 to the Finance Act 1996 (recovery of overpaid landfill tax) [or

    (d)   Part I of Schedule 3 to the Finance Act 2001 (payments made and rebates disallowed in error)].

Assessment for overpayments of interest

15.—(1) Where—

    (a)   any amount has been paid to any person by way of interest under a relevant interest provision, but

    (b)   that person was not entitled to that amount under that provision,

the Commissioners may, to the best of their judgement, assess the amount so paid to which that person was not entitled and notify it to him.

(2) In this paragraph "relevant interest provision" means—

    (a)   *paragraph 9 of Schedule 6 to the Finance Act 1994 (interest payable by the Commissioners on overpayments of air passenger duty);*

    (b)   paragraph 22 of Schedule 7 to that Act (interest payable by the Commissioners on overpayments etc of insurance premium tax); . . .

    (c)   paragraph 29 of Schedule 5 to the Finance Act 1996 (interest payable by the Commissioners on overpayments etc of landfill tax) [or

    (d)   Part II of Schedule 3 to the Finance Act 2001 (interest)].

Assessments under paragraphs 14 and 15

16.—(1) An assessment under paragraph 14 or 15 above shall not be made more than two years after the time when evidence of facts sufficient in the opinion of the Commissioners to justify the making of the assessment comes to the knowledge of the Commissioners.

(2) Where an amount has been assessed and notified to any person under paragraph 14 or 15 above, it shall be recoverable (subject to any provision having effect in accordance with paragraph 19 below) as if it were relevant tax due from him.

(3) Sub-paragraph (2) above does not have effect if, or to the extent that, the assessment in question has been withdrawn or reduced.

Interest on amounts assessed

17.—(1) Where an assessment is made under paragraph 14 or 15 above, the whole of the amount assessed shall carry interest at the rate applicable under section 197 of the Finance Act 1996 from the date on which the assessment is notified until payment.

(2) Where any person is liable to interest under sub-paragraph (1) above the Commissioners may assess the amount due by way of interest and notify it to him.

(3) Without prejudice to the power to make assessments under this paragraph for later periods, the interest to which an assessment under this paragraph may relate shall be confined to interest for a period of no more than two years ending with the time when the assessment under this paragraph is made.

(4) Interest under this paragraph shall be paid without any deduction of income tax.

(5) A notice of assessment under this paragraph shall specify a date, being not later than the date of the notice, to which the amount of interest is calculated; and, if the interest continues to accrue after that date, a further assessment or assessments may be made under this paragraph in respect of amounts which so accrue.

(6) If, within such period as may be notified by the Commissioners to the person liable for interest under sub-paragraph (1) above, the amount referred to in that sub-paragraph is paid, it shall be treated for the purposes of that sub-paragraph as paid on the date specified as mentioned in sub-paragraph (5) above.

(7) Where an amount has been assessed and notified to any person under this paragraph it shall be recoverable as if it were relevant tax due from him.

(8) Sub-paragraph (7) above does not have effect if, or to the extent that, the assessment in question has been withdrawn or reduced.

Supplementary assessments

18. If it appears to the Commissioners that the amount which ought to have been assessed in an assessment under paragraph 14, 15 or 17 above exceeds the amount which was so assessed, then—

    (a)   under the same paragraph as that assessment was made, and

    (b)   on or before the last day on which that assessment could have been made,

the Commissioners may make a supplementary assessment of the amount of the excess and shall notify the person concerned accordingly.

Review of decisions and appeals

19.—(1) Sections 14 to 16 of the Finance Act 1994 (review and appeals) shall have effect in relation to any decision which—

    (a)   is contained in an assessment under paragraph 14, 15 or 17 above,

    (b)   is a decision about whether any amount is due to the Commissioners or about how much is due, and

    (c)   is made in a case in which the relevant repayment provision is section 137A of the Customs and Excise Management Act 1979 or [Part I of Schedule 3 to the Finance Act 2001 or the relevant interest provision is Part II of that Schedule],

as if that decision were such a decision as is mentioned in section 14(1)(b) of that Act of 1994.

(2) Sections 59 and 60 of that Act of 1994 (review and appeal in the case of insurance premium tax) shall have effect in relation to any decision which—

    (a)   is contained in an assessment under paragraph 14, 15 or 17 above,

    (b)   is a decision about whether any amount is due to the Commissioners or about how much is due, and

    (c)   is made in a case in which the relevant repayment provision is paragraph 8 of Schedule 7 to that Act or the relevant interest provision is paragraph 22 of that Schedule,

as if that decision were a decision to which section 59 of that Act applies.

(3) Sections 54 to 56 of the Finance Act 1996 (review and appeal in the case of landfill tax) shall have effect in relation to any decision which—

    (a)   is contained in an assessment under paragraph 14, 15 or 17 above,

    (b)   is a decision about whether any amount is due to the Commissioners or about how much is due, and

    (c)   is made in a case in which the relevant repayment provision is paragraph 14 of Schedule 5 to that Act or the relevant interest provision is paragraph 29 of that Schedule,

as if that decision were a decision to which section 54 of that Act applies.

Interpretation of Part V

20.—(1) In this Part of this Schedule "the Commissioners" means the Commissioners of Customs and Excise.

(2) In this Part of this Schedule "relevant tax", in relation to any assessment, means—

    (a)   a duty of excise if the assessment relates to—

        (i)   a repayment of an amount paid by way of such a duty,

        (ii)   an overpayment of interest under [Part II of Schedule 3 to the Finance Act 2001] or

        (iii)   interest on an amount specified in an assessment in relation to which the relevant tax is a duty of excise;

    (b)   insurance premium tax if the assessment relates to–

        (i)   a repayment of an amount paid by way of such tax,

        (ii)   an overpayment of interest under paragraph 22 of Schedule 7 to the Finance Act 1994, or

        (iii)   interest on an amount specified in an assessment in relation to which the relevant tax is insurance premium tax;

    and

    (c)   landfill tax if the assessment relates to—

        (i)   a repayment of an amount paid by way of such tax,

        (ii)   an overpayment of interest under paragraph 29 of Schedule 5 to the Finance Act 1996, or

        (iii)   interest on an amount specified in an assessment in relation to which the relevant tax is landfill tax.

(3) For the purposes of this Part of this Schedule notification to a personal representative, trustee in bankruptcy, interim or permanent trustee, receiver, liquidator or person otherwise acting in a representative capacity in relation to another shall be treated as notification to the person in relation to whom he so acts.

21. . . .

NOTES

Commencement: 19 March 1997.

Para 14: word in sub-para (3)(b) repealed, and sub-para (3)(d) added, by the Finance Act 2001, s 15, Sch 3 para 19(1), (2), 21.

Para 15: sub-para (2)(a), word in sub-para (2)(b) repealed, and sub-para (2)(d) added, by the Finance Act 2001, s 15, Sch 3 para 19(1), (3), 21.

Para 19: words in square brackets substituted by the Finance Act 2001, s 15, Sch 3 para 19(1), (4).

Para 20: words in square brackets substituted by the Finance Act 2001, s 15, Sch 3 para 19(1), (5), 21.

Para 21: amends the Finance Act 1996, s 197(2).

Orders: the Finance Act 2001 (Commencement No 2 and Saving Provision) Order 2001.

HUMAN RIGHTS ACT 1998

(1998 c 42)

ARRANGEMENT OF SECTIONS

An Act to give further effect to rights and freedoms guaranteed under the European Convention on Human Rights; to make provision with respect to holders of certain judicial offices who become judges of the European Court of Human Rights; and for connected purposes

[9th November 1998]

Introduction

1 The Convention Rights

(1) In this Act "the Convention rights" means the rights and fundamental freedoms set out in—

    (a)   Articles 2 to 12 and 14 of the Convention,

    (b)   Articles 1 to 3 of the First Protocol, and

    (c)   [Article 1 of the Thirteenth Protocol],

as read with Articles 16 to 18 of the Convention.

(2) Those Articles are to have effect for the purposes of this Act subject to any designated derogation or reservation (as to which see sections 14 and 15).

(3) The Articles are set out in Schedule 1.

(4) The Secretary of State may by order make such amendments to this Act as he considers appropriate to reflect the effect, in relation to the United Kingdom, of a protocol.

(5) In subsection (4) "protocol" means a protocol to the Convention—

    (a)   which the United Kingdom has ratified; or

    (b)   which the United Kingdom has signed with a view to ratification.

(6) No amendment may be made by an order under subsection (4) so as to come into force before the protocol concerned is in force in relation to the United Kingdom.

NOTES

Sub-s (1): words in para (c) substituted by the Human Rights Act 1998 (Amendment) Order 2004, SI 2004/1574 art 2(1).

2 Interpretation of Convention rights

(1) A court or tribunal determining a question which has arisen in connection with a Convention right must take into account any—

    (a)   judgment, decision, declaration or advisory opinion of the European Court of Human Rights,

    (b)   opinion of the Commission given in a report adopted under Article 31 of the Convention,

    (c)   decision of the Commission in connection with Article 26 or 27(2) of the Convention, or

    (d)   decision of the Committee of Ministers taken under Article 46 of the Convention, whenever made or given, so far as, in the opinion of the court or tribunal, it is relevant to the proceedings in which that question has arisen.

(2)   Evidence of any judgment, decision, declaration or opinion of which account may have to be taken under this section is to be given in proceedings before any court or tribunal in such manner as may be provided by rules.

(3)   In this section "rules" means rules of court or, in the case of proceedings before a tribunal, rules made for the purposes of this section—

  (a)   by . . .[the Lord Chancellor or] the Secretary of State, in relation to any proceedings outside Scotland;

  (b)   by the Secretary of State, in relation to proceedings in Scotland; or

  (c)   by a Northern Ireland department, in relation to proceedings before a tribunal in Northern Ireland—

    (i)   which deals with transferred matters; and

    (ii)   for which no rules made under paragraph (a) are in force.

NOTES

Rules: Act of Sederunt (Rules of the Court of Session Amendment No 6) (Human Rights Act 1998) 2000, SSI 2000/316.

Sub-s (3): in para (a), words repealed by the Secretary of State for Constitutional Affairs Order 2003, SI 2003/1887 art 9, Sch 2 para 10(2); in para (a) words inserted by the Transfer of Functions (Lord Chancellor and Secretary of State) Order SI 2005/3429, art 8, Sch, para 3.

Legislation

3 Interpretation of legislation

(1)   So far as it is possible to do so, primary legislation and subordinate legislation must be read and given effect in a way which is compatible with the Convention rights.

(2)   This section—

  (a)   applies to primary legislation and subordinate legislation whenever enacted;

  (b)   does not affect the validity, continuing operation or enforcement of any incompatible primary legislation; and

  (c)   does not affect the validity, continuing operation or enforcement of any incompatible subordinate legislation if (disregarding any possibility of revocation) primary legislation prevents removal of the incompatibility.

4 Declaration of incompatibility

(1)   Subsection (2) applies in any proceedings in which a court determines whether a provision of primary legislation is compatible with a Convention right.

(2)   If the court is satisfied that the provision is incompatible with a Convention right, it may make a declaration of that incompatibility.

(3)   Subsection (4) applies in any proceedings in which a court determines whether a provision of subordinate legislation, made in the exercise of a power conferred by primary legislation, is compatible with a Convention right.

(4)   If the court is satisfied—

  (a)   that the provision is incompatible with a Convention right, and

  (b)   that (disregarding any possibility of revocation) the primary legislation concerned prevents removal of the incompatibility,

it may make a declaration of that incompatibility.

(5)   In this section "court" means—

  (a)   *the House of Lords;*

(b) the Judicial Committee of the Privy Council;

(c) the *Courts-Martial Appeal Court*;

(d) in Scotland, the High Court of Justiciary sitting otherwise than as a trial court or the Court of Session;

(e) in England and Wales or Northern Ireland, the High Court or the Court of Appeal.

(6) A declaration under this section ("a declaration of incompatibility")—

(a) does not affect the validity, continuing operation or enforcement of the provision in respect of which it is given; and

(b) is not binding on the parties to the proceedings in which it is made.

NOTES

Sub-s (5): para (a) substituted by the Constitutional Reform Act 2005 s 40, Sch 9 para 66(1), (2) with effect from a day to be appointed. That para as substituted to read as follows—

"(a) the Supreme Court;".

Words in para (c) in italics to be substituted by words "Court Martial Appeal Court" by the Armed Forces Act 2006, s 378, Sch 16, para 156, with effect from a date to be appointed.

New para (f) to be inserted by the Mental Capacity Act 2005 s 67(1), Sch 6 para 43 from a day to be appointed. That para as inserted to read as follows—

"(f) the Court of Protection, in any matter being dealt with by the President of the Family Division, the Vice-Chancellor or a puisne judge of the High Court.".

5 Right of Crown to intervene

(1) Where a court is considering whether to make a declaration of incompatibility, the Crown is entitled to notice in accordance with rules of court.

(2) In any case to which subsection (1) applies—

(a) a Minister of the Crown (or a person nominated by him),

(b) a member of the Scottish Executive,

(c) a Northern Ireland Minister,

(d) a Northern Ireland department,

is entitled, on giving notice in accordance with rules of court, to be joined as a party to the proceedings.

(3) Notice under subsection (2) may be given at any time during the proceedings.

(4) A person who has been made a party to criminal proceedings (other than in Scotland) as the result of a notice under subsection (2) may, with leave, appeal to the *House of Lords* against any declaration of incompatibility made in the proceedings.

(5) In subsection (4)—

"criminal proceedings" includes all proceedings before the *Courts-Martial Appeal Court*; and

"leave" means leave granted by the court making the declaration of incompatibility or by the *House of Lords*.

NOTES

Sub-ss (4), (5): words "Supreme Court" substituted for words in italics by the Constitutional Reform Act 2005 s 40, Sch 9 para 66(1), (3) with effect from a day to be appointed.

Sub-s (5): words in italics to be substituted by words "Court Martial Appeal Court" by the Armed Forces Act 2006, s 378, Sch 16, para 156, with effect from a date to be appointed.

Transfer of Functions: see the National Assembly for Wales (Transfer of Functions) (No 2) Order 2000, SI 2000/1830, art 2.

Rules: Criminal Appeal (Amendment) Rules 2000, SI 2000/2036; Act of Sederunt (Rules of the Court of Session Amendment No 6) (Human Rights Act 1998) 2000, SSI 2000/316.

Public authorities

6 Acts of public authorities

(1)   It is unlawful for a public authority to act in a way which is incompatible with a Convention right.

(2)   Subsection (1) does not apply to an act if—

(a)   as the result of one or more provisions of primary legislation, the authority could not have acted differently; or

(b)   in the case of one or more provisions of, or made under, primary legislation which cannot be read or given effect in a way which is compatible with the Convention rights, the authority was acting so as to give effect to or enforce those provisions.

(3)   In this section "public authority" includes—

(a)   a court or tribunal, and

(b)   any person certain of whose functions are functions of a public nature, but does not include either House of Parliament or a person exercising functions in connection with proceedings in Parliament.

(4)   *In subsection (3) "Parliament" does not include the House of Lords in its judicial capacity.*

(5)   In relation to a particular act, a person is not a public authority by virtue only of subsection (3)(b) if the nature of the act is private.

(6)   "An act" includes a failure to act but does not include a failure to—

(a)   introduce in, or lay before, Parliament a proposal for legislation; or

(b)   make any primary legislation or remedial order.

NOTES

Sub-s (4) repealed by the Constitutional Reform Act 2005 s 40, Sch 9 para 66(1), (4) with effect from a day to be appointed.

7 Proceedings

(1)   A person who claims that a public authority has acted (or proposes to act) in a way which is made unlawful by section 6(1) may—

(a)   bring proceedings against the authority under this Act in the appropriate court or tribunal, or

(b)   rely on the Convention right or rights concerned in any legal proceedings,

but only if he is (or would be) a victim of the unlawful act.

(2)   In subsection (1)(a) "appropriate court or tribunal" means such court or tribunal as may be determined in accordance with rules; and proceedings against an authority include a counterclaim or similar proceeding.

(3)   If the proceedings are brought on an application for judicial review, the applicant is to be taken to have a sufficient interest in relation to the unlawful act only if he is, or would be, a victim of that act.

(4)   If the proceedings are made by way of a petition for judicial review in Scotland, the applicant shall be taken to have title and interest to sue in relation to the unlawful act only if he is, or would be, a victim of that act.

(5)   Proceedings under subsection (1)(a) must be brought before the end of—

    (a)   the period of one year beginning with the date on which the act complained of took place; or

    (b)   such longer period as the court or tribunal considers equitable having regard to all the circumstances,

but that is subject to any rule imposing a stricter time limit in relation to the procedure in question.

    (6)   In subsection (1)(b) "legal proceedings" includes—

    (a)   proceedings brought by or at the instigation of a public authority; and

    (b)   an appeal against the decision of a court or tribunal.

    (7)   For the purposes of this section, a person is a victim of an unlawful act only if he would be a victim for the purposes of Article 34 of the Convention if proceedings were brought in the European Court of Human Rights in respect of that act.

    (8)   Nothing in this Act creates a criminal offence.

    (9)   In this section "rules" means—

    (a)   in relation to proceedings before a court or tribunal outside Scotland, rules made by . . . [the Lord Chancellor or] the Secretary of State for the purposes of this section or rules of court,

    (b)   in relation to proceedings before a court or tribunal in Scotland, rules made by the Secretary of State for those purposes,

    (c)   in relation to proceedings before a tribunal in Northern Ireland—

         (i)   which deals with transferred matters; and

         (ii) for which no rules made under paragraph (a) are in force,

      rules made by a Northern Ireland department for those purposes,

and includes provision made by order under section 1 of the Courts and Legal Services Act 1990.

    (10) In making rules, regard must be had to section 9.

    (11) The Minister who has power to make rules in relation to a particular tribunal may, to the extent he considers it necessary to ensure that the tribunal can provide an appropriate remedy in relation to an act (or proposed act) of a public authority which is (or would be) unlawful as a result of section 6(1), by order add to—

    (a)   the relief or remedies which the tribunal may grant; or

    (b)   the grounds on which it may grant any of them.

    (12) An order made under subsection (11) may contain such incidental, supplemental, consequential or transitional provision as the Minister making it considers appropriate.

    (13) "The Minister" includes the Northern Ireland department concerned.

NOTES

Rules: Proscribed Organisations Appeal Commission (Human Rights Act Proceedings) Rules 2001, SI 2001/127 (made under sub-s 7(9)(a), (b)).

Sub-s (9): in para (a) words inserted by the Transfer of Functions (Lord Chancellor and Secretary of State) Order SI 2005/3429, art 8, Sch, para 3; in para (a), words repealed by the Secretary of State for Constitutional Affairs Order 2003, SI 2003/1887 art 9, Sch 2 para 10(2).

8 Judicial remedies

    (1)   In relation to any act (or proposed act) of a public authority which the court finds is (or would be) unlawful, it may grant such relief or remedy, or make such order, within its powers as it considers just and appropriate.

    (2)   But damages may be awarded only by a court which has power to award damages, or to order the payment of compensation, in civil proceedings.

(3)   No award of damages is to be made unless, taking account of all the circumstances of the case, including—

(a)   any other relief or remedy granted, or order made, in relation to the act in question (by that or any other court), and

(b)   the consequences of any decision (of that or any other court) in respect of that act,

the court is satisfied that the award is necessary to afford just satisfaction to the person in whose favour it is made.

(4)   In determining—

(a)   whether to award damages, or

(b)   the amount of an award,

the court must take into account the principles applied by the European Court of Human Rights in relation to the award of compensation under Article 41 of the Convention.

(5)   A public authority against which damages are awarded is to be treated—

(a)   in Scotland, for the purposes of section 3 of the Law Reform (Miscellaneous Provisions) (Scotland) Act 1940 as if the award were made in an action of damages in which the authority has been found liable in respect of loss or damage to the person to whom the award is made;

(b)   for the purposes of the Civil Liability (Contribution) Act 1978 as liable in respect of damage suffered by the person to whom the award is made.

(6)   In this section—

"court" includes a tribunal;

"damages" means damages for an unlawful act of a public authority; and

"unlawful" means unlawful under section 6(1).

9 Judicial acts

(1)   Proceedings under section 7(1)(a) in respect of a judicial act may be brought only—

(a)   by exercising a right of appeal;

(b)   on an application (in Scotland a petition) for judicial review; or

(c)   in such other forum as may be prescribed by rules.

(2)   That does not affect any rule of law which prevents a court from being the subject of judicial review.

(3)   In proceedings under this Act in respect of a judicial act done in good faith, damages may not be awarded otherwise than to compensate a person to the extent required by Article 5(5) of the Convention.

(4)   An award of damages permitted by subsection (3) is to be made against the Crown; but no award may be made unless the appropriate person, if not a party to the proceedings, is joined.

(5)   In this section—

"appropriate person" means the Minister responsible for the court concerned, or a person or government department nominated by him;

"court" includes a tribunal;

"judge" includes a member of a tribunal, a justice of the peace [(or, in Northern Ireland, a lay magistrate)] and a clerk or other officer entitled to exercise the jurisdiction of a court;

"judicial act" means a judicial act of a court and includes an act done on the instructions, or on behalf, of a judge; and

"rules" has the same meaning as in section 7(9).

NOTES

Sub-s (5): words in square brackets inserted by the Justice (Northern Ireland) Act 2002 s 10(6), Sch 4 para 39.

Rules: Human Rights Act 1998 (Jurisdiction) (Scotland) Rules 2000, SSI 2000/301.

Remedial action

10 Power to take remedial action

(1) This section applies if—

   (a)   a provision of legislation has been declared under section 4 to be incompatible with a Convention right and, if an appeal lies—

     (i)   all persons who may appeal have stated in writing that they do not intend to do so;

     (ii)   the time for bringing an appeal has expired and no appeal has been brought within that time; or

     (iii)   an appeal brought within that time has been determined or abandoned; or

   (b)   it appears to a Minister of the Crown or Her Majesty in Council that, having regard to a finding of the European Court of Human Rights made after the coming into force of this section in proceedings against the United Kingdom, a provision of legislation is incompatible with an obligation of the United Kingdom arising from the Convention.

(2) If a Minister of the Crown considers that there are compelling reasons for proceeding under this section, he may by order make such amendments to the legislation as he considers necessary to remove the incompatibility.

(3) If, in the case of subordinate legislation, a Minister of the Crown considers—

   (a)   that it is necessary to amend the primary legislation under which the subordinate legislation in question was made, in order to enable the incompatibility to be removed, and

   (b)   that there are compelling reasons for proceeding under this section,

he may by order make such amendments to the primary legislation as he considers necessary.

(4) This section also applies where the provision in question is in subordinate legislation and has been quashed, or declared invalid, by reason of incompatibility with a Convention right and the Minister proposes to proceed under paragraph 2(b) of Schedule 2.

(5) If the legislation is an Order in Council, the power conferred by subsection (2) or (3) is exercisable by Her Majesty in Council.

(6) In this section "legislation" does not include a Measure of the Church Assembly or of the General Synod of the Church of England.

(7) Schedule 2 makes further provision about remedial orders.

Other rights and proceedings

11 Safeguard for existing human rights

A person's reliance on a Convention right does not restrict—

   (a)   any other right or freedom conferred on him by or under any law having effect in any part of the United Kingdom; or

   (b)   his right to make any claim or bring any proceedings which he could make or bring apart from sections 7 to 9.

12 Freedom of expression

(1)   This section applies if a court is considering whether to grant any relief which, if granted, might affect the exercise of the Convention right to freedom of expression.

(2)   If the person against whom the application for relief is made ("the respondent") is neither present nor represented, no such relief is to be granted unless the court is satisfied—

(a)   that the applicant has taken all practicable steps to notify the respondent; or

(b)   that there are compelling reasons why the respondent should not be notified.

(3)   No such relief is to be granted so as to restrain publication before trial unless the court is satisfied that the applicant is likely to establish that publication should not be allowed.

(4)   The court must have particular regard to the importance of the Convention right to freedom of expression and, where the proceedings relate to material which the respondent claims, or which appears to the court, to be journalistic, literary or artistic material (or to conduct connected with such material), to—

(a)   the extent to which—

(i)   the material has, or is about to, become available to the public; or

(ii)   it is, or would be, in the public interest for the material to be published;

(b)   any relevant privacy code.

(5)   In this section—

"court" includes a tribunal; and

"relief" includes any remedy or order (other than in criminal proceedings).

13 Freedom of thought, conscience and religion

(1)   If a court's determination of any question arising under this Act might affect the exercise by a religious organisation (itself or its members collectively) of the Convention right to freedom of thought, conscience and religion, it must have particular regard to the importance of that right.

(2)   In this section "court" includes a tribunal.

Derogations and reservations

14 Derogations

(1)   In this Act "designated derogation" means . . . any derogation by the United Kingdom from an Article of the Convention, or of any protocol to the Convention, which is designated for the purposes of this Act in an order made by the [Secretary of State].

(2)   . . .

(3)   If a designated derogation is amended or replaced it ceases to be a designated derogation.

(4)   But subsection (3) does not prevent the [Secretary of State] from exercising his power under subsection (1) . . . to make a fresh designation order in respect of the Article concerned.

(5)   The [Secretary of State] must by order make such amendments to Schedule 3 as he considers appropriate to reflect—

(a)   any designation order; or

(b)   the effect of subsection (3).

(6)   A designation order may be made in anticipation of the making by the United Kingdom of a proposed derogation.

NOTES

Sub-ss (1), (4): words omitted repealed by the Human Rights Act (Amendment) Order 2001, SI 2001/1216, art 2(a), (c). Words substituted by the Secretary of State for Constitutional Affairs Order 2003, SI 2003/1887 art 9, Sch 2.

Sub-s (2): repealed by SI 2001/1216, art 2(b).

Sub-s (5): words substituted by the Secretary of State for Constitutional Affairs Order 2003, SI 2003/1887 art 9, Sch 2 para 10(1).

15 Reservations

(1) In this Act "designated reservation" means—

(a)   the United Kingdom's reservation to Article 2 of the First Protocol to the Convention; and

(b)   any other reservation by the United Kingdom to an Article of the Convention, or of any protocol to the Convention, which is designated for the purposes of this Act in an order made by the [Secretary of State].

(2) The text of the reservation referred to in subsection (1)(a) is set out in Part II of Schedule 3.

(3) If a designated reservation is withdrawn wholly or in part it ceases to be a designated reservation.

(4) But subsection (3) does not prevent the [Secretary of State] from exercising his power under subsection (1)(b) to make a fresh designation order in respect of the Article concerned.

(5) The [Secretary of State] must by order make such amendments to this Act as he considers appropriate to reflect—

(a)   any designation order; or

(b)   the effect of subsection (3).

NOTES

Sub-ss (1), (4), (5): words substituted by the Secretary of State for Constitutional Affairs Order 2003, SI 2003/1887 art 9, Sch 2 para 10(1).

16 Period for which designated derogations have effect

(1) If it has not already been withdrawn by the United Kingdom, a designated derogation ceases to have effect for the purposes of this Act . . ., at the end of the period of five years beginning with the date on which the order designating it was made.

(2) At any time before the period—

(a)   fixed by subsection (1) . . ., or

(b)   extended by an order under this subsection,

comes to an end, the [Secretary of State] may by order extend it by a further period of five years.

(3) An order under section 14(1) . . . ceases to have effect at the end of the period for consideration, unless a resolution has been passed by each House approving the order.

(4) Subsection (3) does not affect—

(a)   anything done in reliance on the order; or

(b)   the power to make a fresh order under section 14(1) . . .

(5) In subsection (3) "period for consideration" means the period of forty days beginning with the day on which the order was made.

(6) In calculating the period for consideration, no account is to be taken of any time during which—

(a)   Parliament is dissolved or prorogued; or

(b)   both Houses are adjourned for more than four days.

(7) If a designated derogation is withdrawn by the United Kingdom, the [Secretary of State] must by order make such amendments to this Act as he considers are required to reflect that withdrawal.

NOTES

Sub-ss (1)–(4): words omitted repealed by the Human Rights Act (Amendment) Order 2001, SI 2001/1216, art 3.

Sub-ss (2), (7): words substituted by the Secretary of State for Constitutional Affairs Order 2003, SI 2003/1887 art 9, Sch 2 para 10(1).

17 Periodic review of designated reservations

(1) The appropriate Minister must review the designated reservation referred to in section 15(1)(a)—

(a)   before the end of the period of five years beginning with the date on which section 1(2) came into force; and

(b)   if that designation is still in force, before the end of the period of five years beginning with the date on which the last report relating to it was laid under subsection (3).

(2) The appropriate Minister must review each of the other designated reservations (if any)—

(a)   before the end of the period of five years beginning with the date on which the order designating the reservation first came into force; and

(b)   if the designation is still in force, before the end of the period of five years beginning with the date on which the last report relating to it was laid under subsection (3).

(3) The Minister conducting a review under this section must prepare a report on the result of the review and lay a copy of it before each House of Parliament.

Judges of the European Court of Human Rights

18 Appointment to European Court of Human Rights

(1) In this section "judicial office" means the office of—

(a)   Lord Justice of Appeal, Justice of the High Court or Circuit judge, in England and Wales;

(b)   judge of the Court of Session or sheriff, in Scotland;

(c)   Lord Justice of Appeal, judge of the High Court or county court judge, in Northern Ireland.

(2) The holder of a judicial office may become a judge of the European Court of Human Rights ("the Court") without being required to relinquish his office.

(3) But he is not required to perform the duties of his judicial office while he is a judge of the Court.

(4) In respect of any period during which he is a judge of the Court—

(a)   a Lord Justice of Appeal or Justice of the High Court is not to count as a judge of the relevant court for the purposes of section 2(1) or 4(1) of the Supreme Court Act 1981 (maximum number of judges) nor as a judge of the *Supreme Court* for the purposes of section 12(1) to (6) of that Act (salaries etc);

    (b)   a judge of the Court of Session is not to count as a judge of that court for the purposes of section 1(1) of the Court of Session Act 1988 (maximum number of judges) or of section 9(1)(c) of the Administration of Justice Act 1973 ("the 1973 Act") (salaries etc);

    (c)   a Lord Justice of Appeal or judge of the High Court in Northern Ireland is not to count as a judge of the relevant court for the purposes of section 2(1) or 3(1) of the Judicature (Northern Ireland) Act 1978 (maximum number of judges) nor as a judge of the *Supreme Court* of Northern Ireland for the purposes of section 9(1)(d) of the 1973 Act (salaries etc);

    (d)   a Circuit judge is not to count as such for the purposes of section 18 of the Courts Act 1971 (salaries etc);

    (e)   a sheriff is not to count as such for the purposes of section 14 of the Sheriff Courts (Scotland) Act 1907 (salaries etc);

    (f)   a county court judge of Northern Ireland is not to count as such for the purposes of section 106 of the County Courts Act (Northern Ireland) 1959 (salaries etc).

(5)   If a sheriff principal is appointed a judge of the Court, section 11(1) of the Sheriff Courts (Scotland) Act 1971 (temporary appointment of sheriff principal) applies, while he holds that appointment, as if his office is vacant.

(6)   Schedule 4 makes provision about judicial pensions in relation to the holder of a judicial office who serves as a judge of the Court.

(7)   The Lord Chancellor or the Secretary of State may by order make such transitional provision (including, in particular, provision for a temporary increase in the maximum number of judges) as he considers appropriate in relation to any holder of a judicial office who has completed his service as a judge of the Court.

[(7A)   The following paragraphs apply to the making of an order under subsection (7) in relation to any holder of a judicial office listed in subsection (1)(a)—

    (a)   before deciding what transitional provision it is appropriate to make, the person making the order must consult the Lord Chief Justice of England and Wales;

    (b)   before making the order, that person must consult the Lord Chief Justice of England and Wales.

(7B)   The following paragraphs apply to the making of an order under subsection (7) in relation to any holder of a judicial office listed in subsection (1)(c)—

    (a)   before deciding what transitional provision it is appropriate to make, the person making the order must consult the Lord Chief Justice of Northern Ireland;

    (b)   before making the order, that person must consult the Lord Chief Justice of Northern Ireland.

(7C)   The Lord Chief Justice of England and Wales may nominate a judicial office holder (within the meaning of section 109(4) of the Constitutional Reform Act 2005) to exercise his functions under this section.

(7D)   The Lord Chief Justice of Northern Ireland may nominate any of the following to exercise his functions under this section—

    (a)   the holder of one of the offices listed in Schedule 1 to the Justice (Northern Ireland) Act 2002;

    (b)   a Lord Justice of Appeal (as defined in section 88 of that Act).]

NOTES

Sub-s (4): in para (a) words "Supreme Court" substituted for words in italics by the Constitutional Reform Act 2005 s 59, Sch 11 para 4 with effect from a day to be appointed; in para (c) words "Court of Judicature" substituted for words in italics by the Constitutional Reform Act 2005 s 59, Sch 11 para 6 with effect from a day to be appointed.

Sub-ss (7A)–(7D) inserted by the Constitutional Reform Act 2005 s 15, Sch 4 para 278 with effect from 3 April 2006.

Parliamentary procedure

19 Statements of compatibility

(1)   A Minister of the Crown in charge of a Bill in either House of Parliament must, before Second Reading of the Bill—

(a)   make a statement to the effect that in his view the provisions of the Bill are compatible with the Convention rights ("a statement of compatibility"); or

(b)   make a statement to the effect that although he is unable to make a statement of compatibility the government nevertheless wishes the House to proceed with the Bill.

(2)   The statement must be in writing and be published in such manner as the Minister making it considers appropriate.

Supplemental

20 Orders etc under this Act

(1)   Any power of a Minister of the Crown to make an order under this Act is exercisable by statutory instrument.

(2)   The power of . . . [the Lord Chancellor or] the Secretary of State to make rules (other than rules of court) under section 2(3) or 7(9) is exercisable by statutory instrument.

(3)   Any statutory instrument made under section 14, 15 or 16(7) must be laid before Parliament.

(4)   No order may be made by . . . [the Lord Chancellor or] the Secretary of State under section 1(4), 7(11) or 16(2) unless a draft of the order has been laid before, and approved by, each House of Parliament.

(5)   Any statutory instrument made under section 18(7) or Schedule 4, or to which subsection (2) applies, shall be subject to annulment in pursuance of a resolution of either House of Parliament.

(6)   The power of a Northern Ireland department to make—

(a)   rules under section 2(3)(c) or 7(9)(c), or

(b)   an order under section 7(11),

is exercisable by statutory rule for the purposes of the Statutory Rules (Northern Ireland) Order 1979.

(7)   Any rules made under section 2(3)(c) or 7(9)(c) shall be subject to negative resolution; and section 41(6) of the Interpretation Act (Northern Ireland) 1954 (meaning of "subject to negative resolution") shall apply as if the power to make the rules were conferred by an Act of the Northern Ireland Assembly.

(8)   No order may be made by a Northern Ireland department under section 7(11) unless a draft of the order has been laid before, and approved by, the Northern Ireland Assembly.

NOTES

Sub-ss (2), (4): words repealed by the Secretary of State for Constitutional Affairs Order 2003, SI 2003/1887 art 9, Sch 2 para 10(2); words inserted by the Transfer of Functions (Lord

Chancellor and Secretary of State) Order SI 2005/3429, art 8, Sch, para 3.

21 Interpretation, etc

(1)   In this Act—

"amend" includes repeal and apply (with or without modifications);

"the appropriate Minister" means the Minister of the Crown having charge of the appropriate authorised government department (within the meaning of the Crown Proceedings Act 1947);

"the Commission" means the European Commission of Human Rights;

"the Convention" means the Convention for the Protection of Human Rights and Fundamental Freedoms, agreed by the Council of Europe at Rome on 4th November 1950 as it has effect for the time being in relation to the United Kingdom;

"declaration of incompatibility" means a declaration under section 4;

"Minister of the Crown" has the same meaning as in the Ministers of the Crown Act 1975;

"Northern Ireland Minister" includes the First Minister and the deputy First Minister in Northern Ireland;

"primary legislation" means any—

    (a)   public general Act;

    (b)   local and personal Act;

    (c)   private Act;

    (d)   Measure of the Church Assembly;

    (e)   Measure of the General Synod of the Church of England;

    (f)   Order in Council—

        (i)   made in exercise of Her Majesty's Royal Prerogative;

        (ii)   made under section 38(1)(a) of the Northern Ireland Constitution Act 1973 or the corresponding provision of the Northern Ireland Act 1998; or

        (iii)   amending an Act of a kind mentioned in paragraph (a), (b) or (c);

and includes an order or other instrument made under primary legislation (otherwise than by the [Welsh Ministers, the First Minister for Wales, the Counsel General to the Welsh Assembly Government,], a member of the Scottish Executive, a Northern Ireland Minister or a Northern Ireland department) to the extent to which it operates to bring one or more provisions of that legislation into force or amends any primary legislation;

"the First Protocol" means the protocol to the Convention agreed at Paris on 20th March 1952;

. . .

"the Eleventh Protocol" means the protocol to the Convention (restructuring the control machinery established by the Convention) agreed at Strasbourg on 11th May 1994;

["the Thirteenth Protocol" means the protocol to the Convention (concerning the abolition of the death penalty in all circumstances) agreed at Vilnius on 3rd May 2002;]

"remedial order" means an order under section 10;

"subordinate legislation" means any—

    (a)   Order in Council other than one—

        (i)   made in exercise of Her Majesty's Royal Prerogative;

        (ii)   made under section 38(1)(a) of the Northern

Ireland Constitution Act 1973 or the corresponding provision of the Northern Ireland Act 1998; or

    (iii)   amending an Act of a kind mentioned in the definition of primary legislation;

  (b)   Act of the Scottish Parliament;

[(ba) Measure of the National Assembly for Wales;

 (bb) Act of the National Assembly for Wales;]

  (c)   Act of the Parliament of Northern Ireland;

  (d)   Measure of the Assembly established under section 1 of the Northern Ireland Assembly Act 1973;

  (e)   Act of the Northern Ireland Assembly;

  (f)   order, rules, regulations, scheme, warrant, byelaw or other instrument made under primary legislation (except to the extent to which it operates to bring one or more provisions of that legislation into force or amends any primary legislation);

  (g)   order, rules, regulations, scheme, warrant, byelaw or other instrument made under legislation mentioned in paragraph (b), (c), (d) or (e) or made under an Order in Council applying only to Northern Ireland;

  (h)   order, rules, regulations, scheme, warrant, byelaw or other instrument made by a member of the Scottish Executive[, Welsh Ministers, the First Minister for Wales, the Counsel General to the Welsh Assembly Government,] a Northern Ireland Minister or a Northern Ireland department in exercise of prerogative or other executive functions of Her Majesty which are exercisable by such a person on behalf of Her Majesty;

"transferred matters" has the same meaning as in the Northern Ireland Act 1998; and

"tribunal" means any tribunal in which legal proceedings may be brought.

(2)   The references in paragraphs (b) and (c) of section 2(1) to Articles are to Articles of the Convention as they had effect immediately before the coming into force of the Eleventh Protocol.

(3)   The reference in paragraph (d) of section 2(1) to Article 46 includes a reference to Articles 32 and 54 of the Convention as they had effect immediately before the coming into force of the Eleventh Protocol.

(4)   The references in section 2(1) to a report or decision of the Commission or a decision of the Committee of Ministers include references to a report or decision made as provided by paragraphs 3, 4 and 6 of Article 5 of the Eleventh Protocol (transitional provisions).

(5)   Any liability under the Army Act 1955, the Air Force Act 1955 or the Naval Discipline Act 1957 to suffer death for an offence is replaced by a liability to imprisonment for life or any less punishment authorised by those Acts; and those Acts shall accordingly have effect with the necessary modifications.

NOTES

Sub-s (1): definition of "the Sixth Protocol" revoked, and definition of "the Thirteenth Protocol" inserted, by the Human Rights Act 1998 (Amendment) Order 2004, SI 2004/1574 art 2(2); in the definition of "primary legislation", words substituted by the Government of Wales Act 2006, s 160, Sch 10, para 56, with effect from 4 May 2007; in the definition of "subordinate legislation", new paras (ba) and (bb) inserted by the Government of Wales Act 2006, s 160, Sch 10, para 5 with effect from 4 May 2007; in the definition of "subordinate legislation, words inserted by the Government of Wales Act 2006, s 160, Sch 10, para 56, with effect from 4 May 2007.

Sub-s (5): to be repealed by the Armed Forces Act 2006, s 378, Sch 17, with effect from a date to be appointed.

22 Short title, commencement, application and extent

(1)   This Act may be cited as the Human Rights Act 1998.

(2)   Sections 18, 20 and 21(5) and this section come into force on the passing of this Act.

(3)   The other provisions of this Act come into force on such day as the Secretary of State may by order appoint; and different days may be appointed for different purposes.

(4)   Paragraph (b) of subsection (1) of section 7 applies to proceedings brought by or at the instigation of a public authority whenever the act in question took place; but otherwise that subsection does not apply to an act taking place before the coming into force of that section.

(5)   This Act binds the Crown.

(6)   This Act extends to Northern Ireland.

(7)   *Section 21(5), so far as it relates to any provision contained in the Army Act 1955, the Air Force Act 1955 or the Naval Discipline Act 1957, extends to any place to which that provision extends.*

NOTES

Sub-s (7): to be repealed by the Armed Forces Act 2006, s 378, Sch 17, with effect from a date to be appointed.

SCHEDULE 1
THE ARTICLES

Section 1(3)

PART I
THE CONVENTION
RIGHTS AND FREEDOMS

ARTICLE 2
Right to life

1.   Everyone's right to life shall be protected by law. No one shall be deprived of his life intentionally save in the execution of a sentence of a court following his conviction of a crime for which this penalty is provided by law.

2.   Deprivation of life shall not be regarded as inflicted in contravention of this Article when it results from the use of force which is no more than absolutely necessary—

(a)   in defence of any person from unlawful violence;

(b)   in order to effect a lawful arrest or to prevent the escape of a person lawfully detained;

(c)   in action lawfully taken for the purpose of quelling a riot or insurrection.

ARTICLE 3
Prohibition of torture

No one shall be subjected to torture or to inhuman or degrading treatment or punishment.

ARTICLE 4
Prohibition of slavery and forced labour

1. No one shall be held in slavery or servitude.

2. No one shall be required to perform forced or compulsory labour.

3. For the purpose of this Article the term "forced or compulsory labour" shall not include—

(a)   any work required to be done in the ordinary course of detention imposed according to the provisions of Article 5 of this Convention or during conditional release from such detention;

(b)   any service of a military character or, in case of conscientious objectors in countries where they are recognised, service exacted instead of compulsory military service;

(c)   any service exacted in case of an emergency or calamity threatening the life or well-being of the community;

(d)   any work or service which forms part of normal civic obligations.

ARTICLE 5
Right to liberty and security

1. Everyone has the right to liberty and security of person. No one shall be deprived of his liberty save in the following cases and in accordance with a procedure prescribed by law—

(a)   the lawful detention of a person after conviction by a competent court;

(b)   the lawful arrest or detention of a person for non-compliance with the lawful order of a court or in order to secure the fulfilment of any obligation prescribed by law;

(c)   the lawful arrest or detention of a person effected for the purpose of bringing him before the competent legal authority on reasonable suspicion of having committed an offence or when it is reasonably considered necessary to prevent his committing an offence or fleeing after having done so;

(d)   the detention of a minor by lawful order for the purpose of educational supervision or his lawful detention for the purpose of bringing him before the competent legal authority;

(e)   the lawful detention of persons for the prevention of the spreading of infectious diseases, of persons of unsound mind, alcoholics or drug addicts or vagrants;

(f)   the lawful arrest or detention of a person to prevent his effecting an unauthorised entry into the country or of a person against whom action is being taken with a view to deportation or extradition.

2. Everyone who is arrested shall be informed promptly, in a language which he understands, of the reasons for his arrest and of any charge against him.

3. Everyone arrested or detained in accordance with the provisions of paragraph 1(c) of this Article shall be brought promptly before a judge or other officer authorised by law to exercise judicial power and shall be entitled to trial within a reasonable time or to release pending trial. Release may be conditioned by guarantees to appear for trial.

4. Everyone who is deprived of his liberty by arrest or detention shall be entitled to take proceedings by which the lawfulness of his detention shall be decided speedily by a court and his release ordered if the detention is not lawful.

5. Everyone who has been the victim of arrest or detention in contravention of the provisions of this Article shall have an enforceable right to compensation.

ARTICLE 6
Right to a fair trial

1.   In the determination of his civil rights and obligations or of any criminal charge against him, everyone is entitled to a fair and public hearing within a reasonable time by an independent and impartial tribunal established by law. Judgment shall be pronounced publicly but the press and public may be excluded from all or part of the trial in the interest of morals, public order or national security in a democratic society, where the interests of juveniles or the protection of the private life of the parties so require, or to the extent strictly necessary in the opinion of the court in special circumstances where publicity would prejudice the interests of justice.

2.   Everyone charged with a criminal offence shall be presumed innocent until proved guilty according to law.

3.   Everyone charged with a criminal offence has the following minimum rights—

(a)   to be informed promptly, in a language which he understands and in detail, of the nature and cause of the accusation against him;

(b)   to have adequate time and facilities for the preparation of his defence;

(c)   to defend himself in person or through legal assistance of his own choosing or, if he has not sufficient means to pay for legal assistance, to be given it free when the interests of justice so require;

(d)   to examine or have examined witnesses against him and to obtain the attendance and examination of witnesses on his behalf under the same conditions as witnesses against him;

(e)   to have the free assistance of an interpreter if he cannot understand or speak the language used in court.

ARTICLE 7
No punishment without law

1.   No one shall be held guilty of any criminal offence on account of any act or omission which did not constitute a criminal offence under national or international law at the time when it was committed. Nor shall a heavier penalty be imposed than the one that was applicable at the time the criminal offence was committed.

2.   This Article shall not prejudice the trial and punishment of any person for any act or omission which, at the time when it was committed, was criminal according to the general principles of law recognised by civilised nations.

ARTICLE 8
Right to respect for private and family life

1.   Everyone has the right to respect for his private and family life, his home and his correspondence.

2.   There shall be no interference by a public authority with the exercise of this right except such as is in accordance with the law and is necessary in a democratic society in the interests of national security, public safety or the economic well-being of the country, for the prevention of disorder or crime, for the protection of health or morals, or for the protection of the rights and freedoms of others.

ARTICLE 9
Freedom of thought, conscience and religion

1.   Everyone has the right to freedom of thought, conscience and religion; this right includes freedom to change his religion or belief and freedom, either alone or in community with others and in public or private, to manifest his religion or belief, in worship, teaching, practice and observance.

2. Freedom to manifest one's religion or beliefs shall be subject only to such limitations as are prescribed by law and are necessary in a democratic society in the interests of public safety, for the protection of public order, health or morals, or for the protection of the rights and freedoms of others.

ARTICLE 10
Freedom of expression

1. Everyone has the right to freedom of expression. This right shall include freedom to hold opinions and to receive and impart information and ideas without interference by public authority and regardless of frontiers. This Article shall not prevent States from requiring the licensing of broadcasting, television or cinema enterprises.

2. The exercise of these freedoms, since it carries with it duties and responsibilities, may be subject to such formalities, conditions, restrictions or penalties as are prescribed by law and are necessary in a democratic society, in the interests of national security, territorial integrity or public safety, for the prevention of disorder or crime, for the protection of health or morals, for the protection of the reputation or rights of others, for preventing the disclosure of information received in confidence, or for maintaining the authority and impartiality of the judiciary.

ARTICLE 11
Freedom of assembly and association

1. Everyone has the right to freedom of peaceful assembly and to freedom of association with others, including the right to form and to join trade unions for the protection of his interests.

2. No restrictions shall be placed on the exercise of these rights other than such as are prescribed by law and are necessary in a democratic society in the interests of national security or public safety, for the prevention of disorder or crime, for the protection of health or morals or for the protection of the rights and freedoms of others. This Article shall not prevent the imposition of lawful restrictions on the exercise of these rights by members of the armed forces, of the police or of the administration of the State.

ARTICLE 12
Right to marry

Men and women of marriageable age have the right to marry and to found a family, according to the national laws governing the exercise of this right.

ARTICLE 14
Prohibition of discrimination

The enjoyment of the rights and freedoms set forth in this Convention shall be secured without discrimination on any ground such as sex, race, colour, language, religion, political or other opinion, national or social origin, association with a national minority, property, birth or other status.

ARTICLE 16
Restrictions on political activity of aliens

Nothing in Articles 10, 11 and 14 shall be regarded as preventing the High Contracting Parties from imposing restrictions on the political activity of aliens.

ARTICLE 17
Prohibition of abuse of rights

Nothing in this Convention may be interpreted as implying for any State, group or person any right to engage in any activity or perform any act aimed at the destruction of any of the rights and freedoms set forth herein or at their limitation to a greater extent than is provided for in the Convention.

ARTICLE 18
Limitation on use of restrictions on rights

The restrictions permitted under this Convention to the said rights and freedoms shall not be applied for any purpose other than those for which they have been prescribed.

PART II
THE FIRST PROTOCOL

ARTICLE 1
Protection of property

Every natural or legal person is entitled to the peaceful enjoyment of his possessions. No one shall be deprived of his possessions except in the public interest and subject to the conditions provided for by law and by the general principles of international law. The preceding provisions shall not, however, in any way impair the right of a State to enforce such laws as it deems necessary to control the use of property in accordance with the general interest or to secure the payment of taxes or other contributions or penalties.

ARTICLE 2
Right to education

No person shall be denied the right to education. In the exercise of any functions which it assumes in relation to education and to teaching, the State shall respect the right of parents to ensure such education and teaching in conformity with their own religious and philosophical convictions.

ARTICLE 3
Right to free elections

The High Contracting Parties undertake to hold free elections at reasonable intervals by secret ballot, under conditions which will ensure the free expression of the opinion of the people in the choice of the legislature.

[PART 3
ARTICLE 1 OF THE THIRTEENTH PROTOCOL

Abolition of the Death Penalty

The death penalty shall be abolished. No one shall be condemned to such penalty or executed.]

NOTES

Part 3: this Part substituted by the Human Rights Act 1998 (Amendment) Order 2004, SI 2004/1574 art 2(3).

SCHEDULE 2
REMEDIAL ORDERS

Section 10

Orders

1.—(1) A remedial order may—

(a)   contain such incidental, supplemental, consequential or transitional provision as the person making it considers appropriate;

(b)   be made so as to have effect from a date earlier than that on which it is made;

(c)   make provision for the delegation of specific functions;

(d)   make different provision for different cases.

(2) The power conferred by sub-paragraph (1)(a) includes—

(a)   power to amend primary legislation (including primary legislation other than that which contains the incompatible provision); and

(b)   power to amend or revoke subordinate legislation (including subordinate legislation other than that which contains the incompatible provision).

(3) A remedial order may be made so as to have the same extent as the legislation which it affects.

(4) No person is to be guilty of an offence solely as a result of the retrospective effect of a remedial order.

Procedure

2. No remedial order may be made unless—

(a)   a draft of the order has been approved by a resolution of each House of Parliament made after the end of the period of 60 days beginning with the day on which the draft was laid; or

(b)   it is declared in the order that it appears to the person making it that, because of the urgency of the matter, it is necessary to make the order without a draft being so approved.

Orders laid in draft

3.—(1) No draft may be laid under paragraph 2(a) unless—

(a)   the person proposing to make the order has laid before Parliament a document which contains a draft of the proposed order and the required information; and

(b)   the period of 60 days, beginning with the day on which the document required by this sub-paragraph was laid, has ended.

(2) If representations have been made during that period, the draft laid under paragraph 2(a) must be accompanied by a statement containing—

(a)   a summary of the representations; and

(b)   if, as a result of the representations, the proposed order has been changed, details of the changes.

Urgent cases

4.—(1) If a remedial order ("the original order") is made without being approved in draft, the person making it must lay it before Parliament, accompanied by the required information, after it is made.

(2) If representations have been made during the period of 60 days beginning with the day on which the original order was made, the person making it must (after the end of that period) lay before Parliament a statement containing—
- (a)   a summary of the representations; and
- (b)   if, as a result of the representations, he considers it appropriate to make changes to the original order, details of the changes.

(3) If sub-paragraph (2)(b) applies, the person making the statement must—
- (a)   make a further remedial order replacing the original order; and
- (b)   lay the replacement order before Parliament.

(4) If, at the end of the period of 120 days beginning with the day on which the original order was made, a resolution has not been passed by each House approving the original or replacement order, the order ceases to have effect (but without that affecting anything previously done under either order or the power to make a fresh remedial order).

Definitions

5. In this Schedule—

"representations" means representations about a remedial order (or proposed remedial order) made to the person making (or proposing to make) it and includes any relevant Parliamentary report or resolution; and

"required information" means—
- (a)   an explanation of the incompatibility which the order (or proposed order) seeks to remove, including particulars of the relevant declaration, finding or order; and
- (b)   a statement of the reasons for proceeding under section 10 and for making an order in those terms.

Calculating periods

6. In calculating any period for the purposes of this Schedule, no account is to be taken of any time during which—
- (a)   Parliament is dissolved or prorogued; or
- (b)   both Houses are adjourned for more than four days.

[7.—(1) This paragraph applies in relation to—
- (a)   any remedial order made, and any draft of such an order proposed to be made,—
  - (i)   by the Scottish Ministers; or
  - (ii)   within devolved competence (within the meaning of the Scotland Act 1998) by Her Majesty in Council; and
- (b)   any document or statement to be laid in connection with such an order (or proposed order).

(2) This Schedule has effect in relation to any such order (or proposed order), document or statement subject to the following modifications.

(3) Any reference to Parliament, each House of Parliament or both Houses of Parliament shall be construed as a reference to the Scottish Parliament.

(4) Paragraph 6 does not apply and instead, in calculating any period for the purposes of this Schedule, no account is to be taken of any time during which the Scottish Parliament is dissolved or is in recess for more than four days.]

NOTES

Para 7: inserted by SI 2000/2040, art 2(1), Schedule, Pt I, para 21.

SCHEDULE 3
DEROGATION AND RESERVATION
Sections 14 and 15

[PART 1
DEROGATION

NOTES

Part I repealed by the Human Rights Act 1998 (Amendment) Order, SI 2005/1071 art 2.

PART II
RESERVATION

At the time of signing the present (First) Protocol, I declare that, in view of certain provisions of the Education Acts in the United Kingdom, the principle affirmed in the second sentence of Article 2 is accepted by the United Kingdom only so far as it is compatible with the provision of efficient instruction and training, and the avoidance of unreasonable public expenditure.

Dated 20 March 1952. Made by the United Kingdom Permanent Representative to the Council of Europe.

SCHEDULE 4
JUDICIAL PENSIONS
Section 18(6)

Duty to make orders about pensions

1.—(1) The appropriate Minister must by order make provision with respect to pensions payable to or in respect of any holder of a judicial office who serves as an ECHR judge.

(2) A pensions order must include such provision as the Minister making it considers is necessary to secure that—

(a)   an ECHR judge who was, immediately before his appointment as an ECHR judge, a member of a judicial pension scheme is entitled to remain as a member of that scheme;

(b)   the terms on which he remains a member of the scheme are those which would have been applicable had he not been appointed as an ECHR judge; and

(c)   entitlement to benefits payable in accordance with the scheme continues to be determined as if, while serving as an ECHR judge, his salary was that which would (but for section 18(4)) have been payable to him in respect of his continuing service as the holder of his judicial office.

Contributions

2. A pensions order may, in particular, make provision—

(a)   for any contributions which are payable by a person who remains a member of a scheme as a result of the order, and which would otherwise be payable by deduction from his salary, to be made otherwise than by deduction from his salary as an ECHR judge; and

(b)   for such contributions to be collected in such manner as may be determined by the administrators of the scheme.

Amendments of other enactments

3. A pensions order may amend any provision of, or made under, a pensions Act in such manner and to such extent as the Minister making the order considers necessary or expedient to ensure the proper administration of any scheme to which it relates.

Definitions

4. In this Schedule—

"appropriate Minister" means—

    (a)   in relation to any judicial office whose jurisdiction is exercisable exclusively in relation to Scotland, the Secretary of State; and

    (b)   otherwise, the Lord Chancellor;

"ECHR judge" means the holder of a judicial office who is serving as a judge of the Court;

"judicial pension scheme" means a scheme established by and in accordance with a pensions Act;

"pensions Act" means—

    (a)   the County Courts Act (Northern Ireland) 1959;

    (b)   the Sheriffs' Pensions (Scotland) Act 1961;

    (c)   the Judicial Pensions Act 1981; or

    (d)   the Judicial Pensions and Retirement Act 1993; and

"pensions order" means an order made under paragraph 1.

FINANCE ACT 1999

(1999 c 16)

An Act to grant certain duties, to alter other duties, and to amend the law relating to the National Debt and the Public Revenue, and to make further provision in connection with Finance

[27 July 1999]

PART VII
OTHER TAXES

Customs duties

126 Interest on unpaid customs debts

(1) This section applies for the determination and recovery of the amount of any interest charged in accordance with Article 232 of the Community Customs Code (interest on duty not paid within the prescribed period) on arrears of customs duty payable to the Commissioners.

(2) Subject to subsection (3) below, the interest shall be charged on the amount in arrears at the rate applicable under section 197 of the Finance Act 1996 (power to fix rates of interest applicable in the case of indirect taxes) for the period which—

    (a)   begins with the latest time for payment of that amount; and

    (b)   ends with the day before that on which payment of that amount is actually made.

(3) Regulations made for the purposes of this section under section 197 of the Finance Act 1996 may provide that, where the amount of interest computed in any case in accordance with subsection (2) above is less than such minimum amount as

may be specified in or determined in accordance with the regulations, the amount of interest charged in that case is (instead of being the amount so computed) to be taken to be equal to that minimum amount.

(4) Subsections (2) and (3) above have effect subject to Article 232(2) of the Community Customs Code (power to waive interest in certain cases).

(5) Any interest the amount of which falls to be determined in accordance with this section shall be recoverable by the Commissioners as if it were customs duty; but nothing in this subsection shall be taken to impose any liability to interest on an amount so determined.

(6) Interest on an amount of customs duty shall not be recoverable from any person at any time more than three years after the latest time for payment of that amount unless a written notice that arrears of customs duty attract interest was given to that person by the Commissioners at a time falling—

(a)   at or after the time when that amount first became payable; and

(b)   before the end of that three years.

(7) In this section—

"the Commissioners" means the Commissioners of Customs and Excise;

"the Community Customs Code" means Council Regulation (EEC) No 2913/92 establishing the Community Customs Code;

"customs duty" includes any agricultural levy of the European Community; and

"the latest time for payment", in relation to an amount of customs duty, means the end of the period prescribed by the Community Customs Code for the payment of that amount.

(8) The preceding provisions of this section—

(a)   shall have effect for periods beginning on or after such day as the Treasury may by order made by statutory instrument appoint; and

(b)   shall so have effect in relation to interest running from before that day, as well as in relation to interest running from, or from after, that day;

and different days may be appointed under this subsection for different purposes.

NOTES

The appointed day, for the purposes of sub-s (8) above, is 1 April 2000 (by virtue of SI 2000/632).

Regulations: Recovery of Duties and Taxes etc Due in Other Member States (Corresponding UK Claims, Procedure and Supplementary) Regulations, SI 2004/674, reg 22, Sch 2, paras 1, 2.

---

127 Interest on repayments

(1) Subject to the following provisions of this section, where the Commissioners are liable to repay an amount to any person in consequence of—

(a)   the payment to them by way of customs duty of an amount that was not due from that person, or

(b)   any requirement to repay an amount of customs duty in accordance with the Community Customs Code or [Commission Regulation (EEC) No 2454/93],

then, if and to the extent that they would not be liable to do so apart from this section, the Commissioners shall pay interest to him on that amount for the applicable period.

(2) The amounts that carry interest under subsection (1) above—

(a)   include only so much of any amount mentioned in that subsection as is the subject of a claim that the Commissioners are required to satisfy or have satisfied; and

(b)   do not include any amount of interest under this section.

Part I

[(3)   Subject to section 128 below, in relation to any amount that carries interest under subsection (1) above, the applicable period for the purposes of this section is the period which—

(a)   begins with the thirty-first working day after the making of the claim for repayment of that amount; and

(b)   ends with the date on which the Commissioners issue the repayment of that amount,

and in paragraph (a) above "working day" means any day other than a non-business day within the meaning of section 92 of the Bills of Exchange Act 1882.]

(4)   The Commissioners shall not be liable to pay interest under this section except on the making of a claim for that purpose.

(5)   A claim under this section must be in writing and must be made not more than three years after the end of the applicable period to which it relates.

(6)   Any reference in this section to the issue by the Commissioners of any repayment of any amount includes a reference to the discharge by way of set-off of the Commissioners' liability to repay that amount.

(7)   Interest under this section shall be payable at the rate applicable under section 197 of the Finance Act 1996.

(8)   In this section and section 128 below—

"the Commissioners" means the Commissioners of Customs and Excise;

"the Community Customs Code" means Council Regulation (EEC) No 2913/92 establishing the Community Customs Code; and

"customs duty" includes any agricultural levy of the European Community.

(9)   The Commissioners may by order modify subsection (3) above so as to provide for interest under this section to begin to run from a time before the sixty-first day after the making of the claim for repayment.

(10)   The power of the Commissioners to make an order under subsection (9) above shall be exercisable by statutory instrument subject to annulment in pursuance of a resolution of the House of Commons.

(11)   This section has effect in relation only to a repayment the claim for which is made on or after such day as the Treasury may by order made by statutory instrument appoint; and different days may be appointed under this subsection for different purposes.

NOTES

The appointed day, for the purposes of sub-s (11) above, is 1 April 2000 (by virtue of SI 2000/632).

Sub-s (1): words in square brackets in para (b) substituted by the Finance Act 2000, s 29 and deemed always to have had effect.

Sub-s (3): substituted by the Interest on Repayments of Customs Duty (Applicable Period) Order 2000, SI 2000/633, art 2.

Commission Regulation (EEC) No 2454/93.

128   Periods to be disregarded in determining interest under s 127

(1)   In determining the applicable period for the purposes of section 127 above in the case of interest on the amount of any repayment there shall be left out of account any period by which the Commissioners' issue of the repayment is delayed as a result of circumstances beyond their control.

(2)   The reference in subsection (1) above to a period by which the Commissioners' issue of a repayment is delayed as a result of circumstances beyond their control includes, in particular, any period which is referable to any one or more of the matters mentioned in subsections (3) to (5) below.

(3)   The first of those matters is any unreasonable delay in the making of any claim for the repayment of the amount on which interest is claimed.

(4)   The second of those matters is any failure by any person to provide the Commissioners—

    (a)   at or before the time of the making of any such claim, or

    (b)   subsequently in response to a request for information by the Commissioners,

with all the information required by them to enable the existence and amount of the claimant's entitlement to a repayment to be determined.

(5)   The third of those matters is the making, as part of or in association with such a claim, of a claim to anything to which the person making the claim has no entitlement.

(6)   In determining for the purposes of subsection (4) above whether any period of delay is referable to a failure by any person to provide information in response to a request by the Commissioners, there shall be taken to be so referable any period which—

    (a)   begins with the date on which the Commissioners request that person to provide information which they reasonably consider relevant to the matter to be determined; and

    (b)   ends with the earliest date on which it would be reasonable for the Commissioners to conclude—

        (i)   that they have received a complete answer to their request for information;

        (ii)   that they have received all that they need in answer to that request; or

        (iii)   that it is unnecessary for them to be provided with any information in answer to that request.

NOTES

Commencement: 27 July 1999.

129 Repayment of overpaid interest etc

(1)   Where—

    (a)   the Commissioners have issued an amount to any person by way of—

        (i)   a payment of interest under section 127 above, or

        (ii)   a repayment of customs duty or of interest on arrears of customs duty,

    (b)   that person was not entitled to that amount, and

    (c)   the Commissioners are entitled to recover it,

the amount shall be recoverable by the Commissioners as if it were customs duty.

(2)   An amount shall not be recoverable from any person in accordance with subsection (1) above at any time more than three years after the payment or repayment was issued unless a written notice that the amount is recoverable was given to that person by the Commissioners before the end of those three years.

(3)   Any reference in this section to the issue by the Commissioners of any payment or repayment of any amount includes a reference to the discharge by way of set-off of the Commissioners' liability to pay or, as the case may be, to repay that amount.

(4)   Nothing in this section shall be taken to impose any liability to interest on an amount to which subsection (1) above applies.

(5)   In this section—

    "*the Commissioners*" means the Commissioners of Customs and Excise; and

    "customs duty" includes any agricultural levy of the European Community.

(6) This section shall have effect in relation to amounts issued on or after such day as the Treasury may by order made by statutory instrument appoint; and different days may be appointed under this subsection for different purposes.

NOTES

The appointed day, for the purposes of sub-s (6) above, is 1 April 2000 (by virtue of SI 2000/632).

ELECTRONIC COMMUNICATIONS ACT 2000

(2000 c 7)

ARRANGEMENT OF SECTIONS

An Act to make provision to facilitate the use of electronic communications and electronic data storage; to make provision about the modification of licences granted under section 7 of the Telecommunications Act 1984; and for connected purposes.

[25 May 2000]

PART I
CRYPTOGRAPHY SERVICE PROVIDERS

NOTES

If no order for bringing this Part into force has been made before 25 May 2005, this section shall be repealed as from that date by virtue of s 16(4) hereof.

1 Register of approved providers

(1) It shall be the duty of the Secretary of State to establish and maintain a register of approved providers of cryptography support services.

(2) The Secretary of State shall secure that the register contains particulars of every person who is for the time being approved under any arrangements in force under section 2.

(3) The particulars that must be recorded in every entry in the register relating to an approved person are—

    (a)   the name and address of that person;

    (b)   the services in respect of which that person is approved; and

    (c)   the conditions of the approval.

(4)   It shall be the duty of the Secretary of State to ensure that such arrangements are in force as he considers appropriate for—

> (a)   allowing members of the public to inspect the contents of the register; and
>
> (b)   securing that such publicity is given to any withdrawal or modification of an approval as will bring it to the attention of persons likely to be interested in it.

2   Arrangements for the grant of approvals

(1)   It shall be the duty of the Secretary of State to secure that there are arrangements in force for granting approvals to persons who—

> (a)   are providing cryptography support services in the United Kingdom or are proposing to do so; and
>
> (b)   seek approval in respect of any such services that they are providing, or are proposing to provide, whether in the United Kingdom or elsewhere.

(2)   The arrangements must—

> (a)   allow for an approval to be granted either in respect of all the services in respect of which it is sought or in respect of only some of them;
>
> (b)   ensure that an approval is granted to a person in respect of any services only if the condition for the grant of an approval to that person is fulfilled in accordance with subsection (3);
>
> (c)   provide for an approval granted to any person to have effect subject to such conditions (whether or not connected with the provision of the services in respect of which the approval is granted) as may be contained in the approval;
>
> (d)   enable a person to whom the Secretary of State is proposing to grant an approval to refuse it if the proposal is in different terms from the approval which was sought;
>
> (e)   make provision for the handling of complaints and disputes which—
>
>> (i)   are required by the conditions of an approved person's approval to be dealt with in accordance with a procedure maintained by him in pursuance of those conditions; but
>>
>> (ii)   are not disposed of by the application of that procedure;
>
> (f)   provide for the modification and withdrawal of approvals.

(3)   The condition that must be fulfilled before an approval is granted to any person is that the Secretary of State is satisfied that that person—

> (a)   will comply, in providing the services in respect of which he is approved, with such technical and other requirements as may be prescribed;
>
> (b)   is a person in relation to whom such other requirements as may be prescribed are, and will continue to be, satisfied;
>
> (c)   is, and will continue to be, able and willing to comply with any requirements that the Secretary of State is proposing to impose by means of conditions of the approval; and
>
> (d)   is otherwise a fit and proper person to be approved in respect of those services.

(4)   Regulations made by virtue of paragraph (a) or (b) of subsection (3) may frame a requirement for the purposes of that subsection by reference to the opinion of a person specified in the regulations, or of a person chosen in a manner determined in accordance with the regulations.

(5)   The requirements which (subject to subsection (6)) may be imposed by conditions contained in an approval in accordance with the arrangements include—

(a)   requirements to provide information to such persons, in such form, at such times and in response to such requests as may be specified in or determined under the terms of the condition;

(b)   requirements that impose obligations that will continue or recur notwithstanding the withdrawal (in whole or in part) of the approval;

(c)   requirements framed by reference to the opinion or directions of a person specified in or chosen in accordance with provision contained in the conditions.

(6) Nothing in the arrangements shall authorise the imposition, by conditions contained in an approval, of any requirements for—

(a)   the provision of information, or

(b)   the maintenance of a procedure for handling complaints or disputes,

in relation to any matter other than one appearing to the Secretary of State to be relevant to the matters mentioned in subsection (3)(a) to (d).

(7) Any requirement to provide information that is imposed in accordance with the arrangements on any person by the conditions of his approval shall be enforceable at the suit or instance of the Secretary of State.

(8) Where any arrangements under this section so provide, a person who—

(a)   seeks an approval under the arrangements,

(b)   applies for a modification of such an approval,

(c)   is for the time being approved under the arrangements, or

(d)   has his approval under the arrangements modified wholly or partly in consequence of an application made by him,

shall pay to the Secretary of State, at such time or times as may be prescribed, such fee or fees as may be prescribed in relation to that time or those times.

(9) Sums received by the Secretary of State by virtue of subsection (8) shall be paid into the Consolidated Fund.

(10) For the purposes of subsection (1) cryptography support services are provided in the United Kingdom if—

(a)   they are provided from premises in the United Kingdom;

(b)   they are provided to a person who is in the United Kingdom when he makes use of the services; or

(c)   they are provided to a person who makes use of the services for the purposes of a business carried on in the United Kingdom or from premises in the United Kingdom.

3 Delegation of approval functions

(1) The Secretary of State may appoint any person to carry out, in his place, such of his functions under the preceding provisions of this Part (other than any power of his to make regulations) as may be specified in the appointment.

(2) An appointment under this section—

(a)   shall have effect only to such extent, and subject to such conditions, as may be set out in the appointment; and

(b)   may be revoked or varied at any time by a notice given by the Secretary of State to the appointed person.

(3) A person appointed under this section shall, in the carrying out of the functions specified in his appointment, comply with all such general directions as may be given to him from time to time by the Secretary of State.

(4) Subject to any order under subsection (5) and to any directions given by the Secretary of State, where a body established by or under any enactment or the holder of any office created by or under any enactment is appointed to carry out any functions of the Secretary of State under this Part—

    (a)   *the enactments relating to the functions of that body or office shall have effect as if the functions of that body or office included the functions specified in the appointment; and*

    (b)   *the body or office-holder shall be taken to have power to do anything which is calculated to facilitate, or is incidental or conducive to, the carrying out of the functions so specified.*

  (5) *The Secretary of State may, by order made by statutory instrument, provide for enactments relating to any such body or office as is mentioned in subsection (4) to have effect, so far as appears to him appropriate for purposes connected with the carrying out of functions that have been or may be conferred on the body or office-holder under this section, with such modifications as may be provided for in the order.*

  (6) *An order shall not be made under subsection (5) unless a draft of it has first been laid before Parliament and approved by a resolution of each House.*

  (7) *It shall be the duty of the Secretary of State to secure—*

    (a)   *that any appointment made under this section is published in such manner as he considers best calculated to bring it to the attention of persons likely to be interested in it;*

    (b)   *that any variation or revocation of such an appointment is also so published; and*

    (c)   *that the time fixed for any notice varying or revoking such an appointment to take effect allows a reasonable period after the giving of the notice for the making of any necessary incidental or transitional arrangements.*

  (8) *Nothing in this section, or in anything done under this section, shall prejudice—*

    (a)   *any power of the Secretary of State, apart from this Act, to exercise functions through a Minister or official in his department;*

    (b)   *any power of any person by virtue of subsection (4), or by virtue of an order under subsection (5), to act on behalf of a body or office-holder in connection with the carrying out of any function;*

    (c)   *any provision by virtue of section 2(4) or (5)(c) that imposes a requirement by reference to the opinion of any person or determines the manner of choosing a person whose opinion is to be referred to.*

4 Restrictions on disclosure of information

  (1) *Subject to the following provisions of this section, no information which—*

    (a)   *has been obtained under or by virtue of the provisions of this Part, and*

    (b)   *relates to the private affairs of any individual or to any particular business,*

shall, during the lifetime of that individual or so long as that business continues to be carried on, be disclosed without the consent of that individual or the person for the time being carrying on that business.

  (2) *Subsection (1) does not apply to any disclosure of information which is made—*

    (a)   *for the purpose of facilitating the carrying out of any functions under this Part, or any prescribed functions, of the Secretary of State or a person appointed under section 3;*

    (b)   *for the purpose of facilitating the carrying out of any functions of a local weights and measures authority in Great Britain;*

    (c)   *for the purpose of facilitating the carrying out of prescribed public functions of any person;*

    (d)   *in connection with the investigation of any criminal offence or for the purposes of any criminal proceedings;*

(e)   for the purposes of any civil proceedings which—
> (i)   relate to the provision of cryptography support services; and
> (ii)   are proceedings to which a person approved in accordance with
>   arrangements under section 2 is a party;

[(ea)   for the purposes of any proceedings before the tribunal established
        under section 65 of the Regulation of Investigatory Powers Act 2000;
        or]

(f)   in pursuance of a Community obligation.

(3)   In subsection (2)(a) the reference to functions under this Part does not include
a reference to any power of the Secretary of State to make regulations.

(4)   In subsection (2)(c) "public functions" includes any function conferred by or
in accordance with any provision contained in or made under any enactment
or Community legislation.

(5)   If information is disclosed to the public in circumstances in which the
disclosure does not contravene this section, this section shall not prevent its further
disclosure by any person.

(6)   Any person who discloses any information in contravention of this
section shall be guilty of an offence and liable—

(a)   on summary conviction, to a fine not exceeding the statutory maximum;
(b)   on conviction on indictment, to imprisonment for a term not exceeding
        two years or a fine, or to both.

NOTES

Sub-s (2): para (ea) substituted by the Regulation of Investigatory Powers Act 2000,
s 82(1), Sch 4, para 10, with effect from 2 October 2000.

---

5   Regulations under Part I

(1)   In this Part "prescribed" means prescribed by regulations made by the
Secretary of State, or determined in such manner as may be provided for in any such
regulations.

(2)   The powers of the Secretary of State to make regulations under this Part shall
be exercisable by statutory instrument, which (except in the case of the initial
regulations) shall be subject to annulment in pursuance of a resolution of either House
of Parliament.

(3)   The initial regulations shall not be made unless a draft of them has been laid
before Parliament and approved by a resolution of each House.

(4)   In this section "the initial regulations" means the regulations made on the first
occasion on which the Secretary of State exercises his powers to make regulations
under this Part.

(5)   Before making any regulations by virtue of section 2(3)(a) or (b) the Secretary
of State shall consult—

(a)   such persons appearing to him to be likely to be affected by those
        regulations, and
(b)   such persons appearing to him to be representative of persons likely to
        be so affected,

as he thinks fit.

(6)   Regulations made by the Secretary of State under any provision of this Part—

(a)   may make different provision for different cases; and
(b)   may contain such incidental, supplemental, consequential and
        transitional provision as the Secretary of State thinks fit.

6 Provision of cryptography support services

(1) *In this Part "cryptography support service" means any service which is provided to the senders or recipients of electronic communications, or to those storing electronic data, and is designed to facilitate the use of cryptographic techniques for the purpose of—*

    (a)   *securing that such communications or data can be accessed, or can be put into an intelligible form, only by certain persons; or*

    (b)   *securing that the authenticity or integrity of such communications or data is capable of being ascertained.*

(2) *References in this Part to the provision of a cryptography support service do not include references to the supply of, or of any right to use, computer software or computer hardware except where the supply is integral to the provision of cryptography support services not consisting in such a supply.*

PART II
FACILITATION OF ELECTRONIC COMMERCE, DATA STORAGE, ETC

7 Electronic signatures and related certificates

(1) In any legal proceedings—

    (a)   an electronic signature incorporated into or logically associated with a particular electronic communication or particular electronic data, and

    (b)   the certification by any person of such a signature,

shall each be admissible in evidence in relation to any question as to the authenticity of the communication or data or as to the integrity of the communication or data.

(2) For the purposes of this section an electronic signature is so much of anything in electronic form as—

    (a)   is incorporated into or otherwise logically associated with any electronic communication or electronic data; and

    (b)   purports to be so incorporated or associated for the purpose of being used in establishing the authenticity of the communication or data, the integrity of the communication or data, or both.

(3) For the purposes of this section an electronic signature incorporated into or associated with a particular electronic communication or particular electronic data is certified by any person if that person (whether before or after the making of the communication) has made a statement confirming that—

    (a)   the signature,

    (b)   a means of producing, communicating or verifying the signature, or

    (c)   a procedure applied to the signature,

is (either alone or in combination with other factors) a valid means of establishing the authenticity of the communication or data, the integrity of the communication or data, or both.

NOTES

    Commencement: 25 July 2000: see SI 2000/1798, art 2.

8 Power to modify legislation

(1) Subject to subsection (3), the appropriate Minister may by order made by statutory instrument modify the provisions of—

    (a)   any enactment or subordinate legislation, or

    (b)   any scheme, licence, authorisation or approval issued, granted or given by or under any enactment or subordinate legislation, in such manner as he may think fit for the purpose of authorising or facilitating the use of electronic communications or electronic storage (instead of other forms of communication or storage) for any purpose mentioned in subsection (2).

(2) Those purposes are—

(a) the doing of anything which under any such provisions is required to be or may be done or evidenced in writing or otherwise using a document, notice or instrument;

(b) the doing of anything which under any such provisions is required to be or may be done by post or other specified means of delivery;

(c) the doing of anything which under any such provisions is required to be or may be authorised by a person's signature or seal, or is required to be delivered as a deed or witnessed;

(d) the making of any statement or declaration which under any such provisions is required to be made under oath or to be contained in a statutory declaration;

(e) the keeping, maintenance or preservation, for the purposes or in pursuance of any such provisions, of any account, record, notice, instrument or other document;

(f) the provision, production or publication under any such provisions of any information or other matter;

(g) the making of any payment that is required to be or may be made under any such provisions.

(3) The appropriate Minister shall not make an order under this section authorising the use of electronic communications or electronic storage for any purpose, unless he considers that the authorisation is such that the extent (if any) to which records of things done for that purpose will be available will be no less satisfactory in cases where use is made of electronic communications or electronic storage than in other cases.

(4) Without prejudice to the generality of subsection (1), the power to make an order under this section shall include power to make an order containing any of the following provisions—

(a) provision as to the electronic form to be taken by any electronic communications or electronic storage the use of which is authorised by an order under this section;

(b) provision imposing conditions subject to which the use of electronic communications or electronic storage is so authorised;

(c) provision, in relation to cases in which any such conditions are not satisfied, for treating anything for the purposes of which the use of such communications or storage is so authorised as not having been done;

(d) provision, in connection with anything so authorised, for a person to be able to refuse to accept receipt of something in electronic form except in such circumstances as may be specified in or determined under the order;

(e) provision, in connection with any use of electronic communications so authorised, for intermediaries to be used, or to be capable of being used, for the transmission of any data or for establishing the authenticity or integrity of any data;

(f) provision, in connection with any use of electronic storage so authorised, for persons satisfying such conditions as may be specified in or determined under the regulations to carry out functions in relation to the storage;

(g) provision, in relation to cases in which the use of electronic communications or electronic storage is so authorised, for the determination of any of the matters mentioned in subsection (5), or as to the manner in which they may be proved in legal proceedings;

(h) provision, in relation to cases in which fees or charges are or may be imposed in connection with anything for the purposes of which the use of electronic communications or electronic storage is so authorised, for different fees or charges to apply where use is made of such communications or storage;

(i) provision, in relation to any criminal or other liabilities that may arise (in respect of the making of false or misleading statements or otherwise) in connection with anything for the purposes of which the use of electronic communications or electronic storage is so authorised, for corresponding liabilities to arise in corresponding circumstances where use is made of such communications or storage;

(j) provision requiring persons to prepare and keep records in connection with any use of electronic communications or electronic storage which is so authorised;

(k) provision requiring the production of the contents of any records kept in accordance with an order under this section;

(l) provision for a requirement imposed by virtue of paragraph (j) or (k) to be enforceable at the suit or instance of such person as may be specified in or determined in accordance with the order;

(m) any such provision, in relation to electronic communications or electronic storage the use of which is authorised otherwise than by an order under this section, as corresponds to any provision falling within any of the preceding paragraphs that may be made where it is such an order that authorises the use of the communications or storage.

(5) The matters referred to in subsection (4)(g) are—

(a) whether a thing has been done using an electronic communication or electronic storage;

(b) the time at which, or date on which, a thing done using any such communication or storage was done;

(c) the place where a thing done using such communication or storage was done;

(d) the person by whom such a thing was done; and

(e) the contents, authenticity or integrity of any electronic data.

(6) An order under this section—

(a) shall not (subject to paragraph (b)) require the use of electronic communications or electronic storage for any purpose; but

(b) may make provision that a period of notice specified in the order must expire before effect is given to a variation or withdrawal of an election or other decision which—

(i) has been made for the purposes of such an order; and

(ii) is an election or decision to make use of electronic communications or electronic storage.

(7) The matters in relation to which provision may be made by an order under this section do not include any matter under the care and management of the Commissioners of Inland Revenue or any matter under the care and management of the Commissioners of Customs and Excise.

(8) In this section references to doing anything under the provisions of any enactment include references to doing it under the provisions of any subordinate legislation the power to make which is conferred by that enactment.

NOTES
Commencement: 25 May 2000.
Orders: Local Government and Housing Act 1989 (Electronic Communications) (England) Order 2000, SI 2000/3056; Companies Act 1985 (Electronic Communications) Order 2000, SI 2000/3373.

9 Section 8 orders

(1)   In this Part "the appropriate Minister" means (subject to subsections (2) and (7) and section 10(1))—

(a)   in relation to any matter with which a department of the Secretary of State is concerned, the Secretary of State;

(b)   in relation to any matter with which the Treasury is concerned, the Treasury; and

(c)   in relation to any matter with which any Government department other than a department of the Secretary of State or the Treasury is concerned, the Minister in charge of the other department.

(2)   Where in the case of any matter—

(a)   that matter falls within more than one paragraph of subsection (1),

(b)   there is more than one such department as is mentioned in paragraph (c) of that subsection that is concerned with that matter, or

(c)   both paragraphs (a) and (b) of this subsection apply,

references, in relation to that matter, to the appropriate Minister are references to any one or more of the appropriate Ministers acting (in the case of more than one) jointly.

(3)   Subject to subsection (4) and section 10(6), a statutory instrument containing an order under section 8 shall be subject to annulment in pursuance of a resolution of either House of Parliament.

(4)   Subsection (3) does not apply in the case of an order a draft of which has been laid before Parliament and approved by a resolution of each House.

(5)   An order under section 8 may—

(a)   provide for any conditions or requirements imposed by such an order to be framed by reference to the directions of such persons as may be specified in or determined in accordance with the order;

(b)   provide that any such condition or requirement is to be satisfied only where a person so specified or determined is satisfied as to specified matters.

(6)   The provision made by such an order may include—

(a)   different provision for different cases;

(b)   such exceptions and exclusions as the person making the order may think fit; and

(c)   any such incidental, supplemental, consequential and transitional provision as he may think fit;

and the provision that may be made by virtue of paragraph (c) includes provision modifying any enactment or subordinate legislation or any scheme, licence, authorisation or approval issued, granted or given by or under any enactment or subordinate legislation.

(7)   In the case of any matter which is not one of the reserved matters within the meaning of the Scotland Act 1998 or in respect of which functions are, by virtue of section 63 of that Act, exercisable by the Scottish Ministers instead of by or concurrently with a Minister of the Crown, this section and section 8 shall apply to Scotland subject to the following modifications—

(a)   subsections (1) and (2) of this section are omitted;

(b)   any reference to the appropriate Minister is to be read as a reference to the Secretary of State;

(c)   any power of the Secretary of State, by virtue of paragraph (b), to make an order under section 8 may also be exercised by the Scottish Ministers with the consent of the Secretary of State; and

(d)   where the Scottish Ministers make an order under section 8—

    (i)   any reference to the Secretary of State (other than a reference in this subsection) shall be construed as a reference to the Scottish Ministers; and

    (ii)   any reference to Parliament or to a House of Parliament shall be construed as a reference to the Scottish Parliament.

NOTES

Commencement: 25 May 2000.

Orders: Companies Act 1985 (Electronic Communications) Order 2000, SI 2000/3373.

10 Modifications in relation to Welsh matters

(1) For the purposes of the exercise of the powers conferred by section 8 in relation to any matter the functions in respect of which are exercisable by the National Assembly for Wales, the appropriate Minister is the Secretary of State.

(2) Subject to the following provisions of this section, the powers conferred by section 8, so far as they fall within subsection (3), shall be exercisable by the National Assembly for Wales, as well as by the appropriate Minister.

(3) The powers conferred by section 8 fall within this subsection to the extent that they are exercisable in relation to—

(a)   the provisions of any subordinate legislation made by the National Assembly for Wales;

(b)   so much of any other subordinate legislation as makes provision the power to make which is exercisable by that Assembly;

(c)   any power under any enactment to make provision the power to make which is so exercisable;

(d)   the giving, sending or production of any notice, account, record or other document or of any information to or by a body mentioned in subsection (4); or

(e)   the publication of anything by a body mentioned in subsection (4).

(4) Those bodies are—

(a)   the National Assembly for Wales;

(b)   any body specified in Schedule 4 to the Government of Wales Act 1998 (Welsh public bodies subject to reform by that Assembly);

(c)   any other such body as may be specified for the purposes of this section by an order made by the Secretary of State with the consent of that Assembly.

(5) The National Assembly for Wales shall not make an order under section 8 except with the consent of the Secretary of State.

(6) Section 9(3) shall not apply to any order made under section 8 by the National Assembly for Wales.

(7) Nothing in this section shall confer any power on the National Assembly for Wales to modify any provision of the Government of Wales Act 1998.

(8) The power of the Secretary of State to make an order under subsection (4)(c)—

(a)   shall include power to make any such incidental, supplemental, consequential and transitional provision as he may think fit; and

    (b)   shall be exercisable by statutory instrument subject to annulment in pursuance of a resolution of either House of Parliament.

NOTES

Commencement: 25 May 2000.

PART III
MISCELLANEOUS AND SUPPLEMENTAL

Telecommunications licences

11, 12
(Amend the Telecommunications Act 1984, ss 12, 46B; repealed by the Communications Act 2003 s 406(7), Sch 19(1)).

Supplemental

13 Ministerial expenditure etc
There shall be paid out of money provided by Parliament—

    (a)   any expenditure incurred by the Secretary of State for or in connection with the carrying out of his functions under this Act; and

    (b)   any increase attributable to this Act in the sums which are payable out of money so provided under any other Act.

NOTES

Commencement: 25 May 2000.

14 Prohibition on key escrow requirements
  (1) Subject to subsection (2), nothing in this Act shall confer any power on any Minister of the Crown, on the Scottish Ministers, on the National Assembly for Wales or on any person appointed under section 3—

    (a)   by conditions of an approval under Part I, or

    (b)   by any regulations or order under this Act,

to impose a requirement on any person to deposit a key for electronic data with another person.

  (2) Subsection (1) shall not prohibit the imposition by an order under section 8 of—

    (a)   a requirement to deposit a key for electronic data with the intended recipient of electronic communications comprising the data; or

    (b)   a requirement for arrangements to be made, in cases where a key for data is not deposited with another person, which otherwise secure that the loss of a key, or its becoming unusable, does not have the effect that the information contained in a record kept in pursuance of any provision made by or under any enactment or subordinate legislation becomes inaccessible or incapable of being put into an intelligible form.

  (3) In this section "key", in relation to electronic data, means any code, password, algorithm, key or other data the use of which (with or without other keys)—

    (a)   allows access to the electronic data, or

    (b)   facilitates the putting of the electronic data into an intelligible form;

and references in this section to depositing a key for electronic data with a person include references to doing anything that has the effect of making the key available to that person.

NOTES

Commencement: 25 May 2000.

15 General interpretation

(1)   In this Act, except in so far as the context otherwise requires—

"document" includes a map, plan, design, drawing, picture or other image;

"communication" includes a communication comprising sounds or images or both and a communication effecting a payment;

"electronic communication" means a communication transmitted (whether from one person to another, from one device to another or from a person to a device or vice versa)—

   (a)   by means of [an electronic communications network]; or

   (b)   by other means but while in an electronic form;

"enactment" includes—

   (a)   an enactment passed after the passing of this Act,

   (b)   an enactment comprised in an Act of the Scottish Parliament, and

   (c)   an enactment contained in Northern Ireland legislation,

but does not include an enactment contained in Part I or II of this Act;

"modification" includes any alteration, addition or omission, and cognate expressions shall be construed accordingly;

"record" includes an electronic record; and

"subordinate legislation" means—

   (a)   any subordinate legislation (within the meaning of the Interpretation Act 1978);

   (b)   any instrument made under an Act of the Scottish Parliament; or

   (c)   any statutory rules (within the meaning of the Statutory Rules (Northern Ireland) Order 1979).

(2)   In this Act—

   (a)   references to the authenticity of any communication or data are references to any one or more of the following—

      (i)   whether the communication or data comes from a particular person or other source;

      (ii)   whether it is accurately timed and dated;

      (iii)   whether it is intended to have legal effect;

   and

   (b)   references to the integrity of any communication or data are references to whether there has been any tampering with or other modification of the communication or data.

(3)   References in this Act to something's being put into an intelligible form include references to its being restored to the condition in which it was before any encryption or similar process was applied to it.

NOTES

Commencement: 25 May 2000.

Sub-s (1): in definition "electronic communication", in para (a), words substituted by the Communications Act 2003, s 406(1), Sch 17 para 158.

16 Short title, commencement, extent

(1)   This Act may be cited as the Electronic Communications Act 2000.

(2)   Part I of this Act and sections 7, 11 and 12 shall come into force on such day as the Secretary of State may by order made by statutory instrument appoint; and different days may be appointed under this subsection for different purposes.

(3)   An order shall not be made for bringing any of Part I of this Act into force for any purpose unless a draft of the order has been laid before Parliament and approved by a resolution of each House.

(4)   If no order for bringing Part I of this Act into force has been made under subsection (2) by the end of the period of five years beginning with the day on which this Act is passed, that Part shall, by virtue of this subsection, be repealed at the end of that period.

(5)   This Act extends to Northern Ireland.

NOTES

Commencement: 25 May 2000.

Orders: Electronic Communications Act 2000 (Commencement No 1) Order 2000, SI 2000/1798.

POSTAL SERVICES ACT 2000

(2000 Chapter 26)

An Act to establish the Postal Services Commission and the Consumer Council for Postal Services; to provide for the licensing of certain postal services and for a universal postal service; to provide for the vesting of the property, rights and liabilities of the Post Office in a company nominated by the Secretary of State and for the subsequent dissolution of the Post Office; to make further provision in relation to postal services; and for connected purposes

[28th July 2000]

PART VII
MISCELLANEOUS AND SUPPLEMENTARY

Inviolability of mails etc

105 Application of customs and excise enactments to certain postal packets

(1)   Subject as follows, the enactments for the time being in force in relation to customs or excise shall apply in relation to goods contained in postal packets to which this section applies which are brought into or sent out of the United Kingdom by post from or to any place outside the United Kingdom as they apply in relation to goods otherwise imported, exported or removed into or out of the United Kingdom from or to any such place.

(2)   The Treasury, on the recommendation of the Commissioners of Customs and Excise and the Secretary of State, may make regulations for—

(a)   specifying the postal packets to which this section applies,

(b)   making modifications or exceptions in the application of the enactments mentioned in subsection (1) to such packets,

(c)   enabling persons engaged in the business of a postal operator to perform for the purposes of those enactments and otherwise all or any of the duties of the importer, exporter or person removing the goods,

(d)   carrying into effect any arrangement with the government or postal administration of any country or territory outside the United Kingdom with respect to foreign postal packets,

(e)   securing the observance of the enactments mentioned in subsection (1),

(f)   without prejudice to any liability of any person under those enactments, punishing any contravention of the regulations.

(3)   Duties (whether of customs or excise) charged on imported goods or other charges payable in respect of postal packets to which this section applies (whether payable to a postal operator or to a foreign administration) may be recovered by the postal operator concerned and in England and Wales and Northern Ireland may be so recovered as a civil debt due to him.

(4)   In any proceedings for the recovery of any charges payable as mentioned in subsection (3), a certificate of the postal operator concerned of the amount of the charges shall be evidence (and, in Scotland, sufficient evidence) of that fact.

(5)   In this section "foreign postal packet" means any postal packet either posted in the United Kingdom and sent to a place outside the United Kingdom, or posted in a place outside the United Kingdom and sent to a place within the United Kingdom, or in transit through the United Kingdom to a place outside the United Kingdom.

NOTES

Commencement: 26 Feb 2001 (sub-s (2)); 26 March 2001 (remainder).

Regulations: Postal Packets (Revenue and Customs) Regulations, SI 2007/2195.

106 Power to detain postal packets containing contraband

(1)   A postal operator may—

(a)   detain any postal packet if he suspects that it may contain relevant goods,

(b)   forward any packet so detained to the Commissioners of Customs and Excise.

(2)   In this section "relevant goods" means—

(a)   any goods chargeable with any duty charged on imported goods (whether a customs or an excise duty) which has not been paid or secured, or

(b)   any goods in the course of importation, exportation or removal into or out of the United Kingdom contrary to any prohibition or restriction for the time being in force by virtue of any enactment.

(3)   Subsection (1) is without prejudice to section 105.

(4)   The Commissioners may open and examine any postal packet forwarded to them under this section—

(a)   in the presence of the person to whom the packet is addressed, or

(b)   where the address on the packet is outside the United Kingdom or where subsection (5) applies, in the absence of that person.

(5)   This subsection applies where—

(a)   the Commissioners have—

(i)   left at the address on the packet notice requiring the attendance of the person concerned, or

(ii)   forwarded such notice by post to that address, and

(b)   the addressee fails to attend.

(6)   If the Commissioners find any relevant goods on opening and examining a postal packet under this section, they may detain the packet and its contents for the purpose of taking proceedings in relation to them.

Part I

(7) If the Commissioners do not find any relevant goods on opening and examining a postal packet under this section, they shall—

(a)   deliver the packet to the addressee upon his paying any postage and other sums chargeable on it, or

(b)   if he is absent, forward the packet to him by post.

NOTES

Commencement: 26 March 2001.

107 Conditions of transit of postal packets

(1) If a postal operator knows or reasonably suspects that a postal packet is being sent by post in contravention of section 85, he may—

(a)   refuse the transmission of the packet,

(b)   detain the packet and open it,

(c)   subject to any requirements as to additional postage or charges, return the packet to its sender or forward it to its destination,

(d)   destroy or otherwise dispose of the packet.

(2) Subsection (1) is without prejudice to any other powers which the postal operator may have in relation to the packet (whether under the terms and conditions applicable to its transmission by post or otherwise).

(3) The detention or disposal by a postal operator of any postal packet on the grounds of a contravention of section 85 or of any terms and conditions applicable to its transmission by post shall not exempt the sender from any proceedings which might have been taken if the packet had been delivered in due course of post.

NOTES

Commencement: 26 March 2001.

FINANCE ACT 2001

(2001 c 9)

ARRANGEMENT OF SECTIONS

*An Act to grant certain duties, to alter other duties, and to amend the law relating
to the National Debt and the Public Revenue, and to make further provision in
connection with Finance.*

[11 May 2001]

PART 1
EXCISE DUTIES

Hydrocarbon oil duties

1 Rates of duty on hydrocarbon oil

(1)–(3)   (*Amend the Hydrocarbon Oil Duties Act 1979*)

(4)   This section shall be deemed to have come into force at 6 o'clock in the
evening of 7th March 2001.

2 Rebate on unleaded petrol

(1)   (*Substitutes the Hydrocarbon Oil Duties Act 1979, s 13A*)

(2)–(4)   (*Amend the Hydrocarbon Oil Duties Act 1979, Sch 2A*)

(5)   This section shall be deemed to have come into force at 6 o'clock in the
evening of 7th March 2001.

3 Fuel-testing pilot projects

(1)   (*Inserts the Hydrocarbon Oil Duties Act 1979, s 20AA*)

(2), (3)   (*Amend the Hydrocarbon Oil Duties Act 1979, ss 24(1), 27(1)*).

(4)   (*Amends the Finance Act 1994, s 12B(1)*)

Tobacco products duty

4 Rates of tobacco products duty

(1)   (*Substitutes the Tobacco Products Duty Act 1979 Schedule 1 Table*)

(2)   This section shall be deemed to have come into force at 6 o'clock in the
evening of 7th March 2001.

Alcoholic liquor duties

5 Dilution etc of cider

(*Inserts the Alcoholic Liquor Duties Act 1979, s 62(5)(e)*)

General

15 Payments by Commissioners in case of error or delay

Schedule 3 to this Act (which allows or requires the Commissioners of Customs and
Excise to make payments in cases of error or delay in relation to excise duty) has
effect.

SCHEDULE 3
EXCISE DUTY: PAYMENTS BY COMMISSIONERS IN CASE OF ERROR OR DELAY

Section 15

PART 1
PAYMENTS

Duty paid in error

1.—(1) This paragraph applies if—

    (a)   the first condition set out below is satisfied, and

    (b)   either the second or the third condition set out below is satisfied.

(2) The first condition is that, due to an error on the part of the Commissioners, any of the following occurs at any time—

    (a)   a person is refused authorisation for the purposes of section 8(1) or 10(1) of the Alcoholic Liquor Duties Act 1979;

    (b)   a person is refused a direction for the purposes of section 11(1) of that Act;

    (c)   a person is refused approval for the purposes of section 9(1) or 14(1) of the Hydrocarbon Oil Duties Act 1979;

    (d)   a person is refused consent for the purposes of section 10(1) of that Act.

(3) The second condition is that on or after the commencement day a person pays to the Commissioners an amount by way of excise duty which would not have been paid but for the error.

(4) The third condition is that on or after the commencement day the person refused pays for goods an amount which includes an amount which—

    (a)   represents a payment by way of excise duty, and

    (b)   would not have been included but for the error.

(5) If the second condition is satisfied the Commissioners may pay to the person refused an amount equal to the duty which would not have been paid.

(6) If the third condition is satisfied the Commissioners may pay to the person refused an amount which appears to them to be equal to the payment by way of excise duty.

(7) The person refused is the person refused an authorisation, direction, approval or consent.

Error relating to rebate

2.—(1) This paragraph applies if the following two conditions are satisfied.

(2) The first condition is that a person is entitled to use rebated heavy oil in particular circumstances.

(3) The second condition is that—

    (a)   due to an error on the part of the Commissioners he is unable to use rebated heavy oil in those circumstances,

    (b)   he uses unrebated heavy oil instead in those circumstances, and

    (c)   the use occurs on or after the commencement day.

(4) The Commissioners may pay to the person an amount equal to the rebate which would have been allowable under section 11 of the Hydrocarbon Oil Duties Act 1979 if—

    (a)   the heavy oil used by him in those circumstances had (at the time of that use) been delivered for home use, and

    (b)   the other conditions for allowing rebate had been satisfied at that time.

(5) Rebated heavy oil is heavy oil on whose delivery for home use a rebate has been allowed under section 11 of the Hydrocarbon Oil Duties Act 1979, and unrebated heavy oil is other heavy oil.

Claims

3. No payment may be made to a person under this Part of this Schedule unless—

  (a)   he makes a claim in such form and manner, and containing such matters, as the Commissioners may prescribe by regulations, and

  (b)   he satisfies such other conditions as the Commissioners may impose by regulations.

PART 2
INTEREST

Commissioners' delay

4.—(1) This paragraph applies if—

  (a)   a person is entitled to obtain an amount by way of repayment or drawback in respect of excise duty paid to the Commissioners,

  (b)   on or after the commencement day he makes a claim for the repayment or drawback, and

  (c)   the Commissioners fail to authorise it within the allowable period.

(2) The Commissioners must pay interest to the person on the amount for the applicable period.

(3) The allowable period is the period of 30 days starting with the day on which the Commissioners receive the claim.

(4) The applicable period is the period which—

  (a)   starts with the day after the allowable period ends, and

  (b)   ends with the day when the Commissioners authorise the repayment or drawback.

(5) Sub-paragraph (4) is subject to paragraph 6.

5.—(1) This paragraph applies if—

  (a)   a person is entitled to obtain an amount by way of repayment or drawback in respect of excise duty paid to the Commissioners,

  (b)   on or after the commencement day he makes a claim for the repayment or drawback,

  (c)   the Commissioners set off the amount against an assessment,

  (d)   the assessment is withdrawn, and

  (e)   the Commissioners authorise the repayment or drawback.

(2) The Commissioners must pay interest to the person on the amount for the applicable period.

(3) The applicable period is the period which—

  (a)   starts with the earlier of the days referred to in sub-paragraph (4), and

  (b)   ends with the day when the Commissioners authorise the repayment or drawback.

(4) The days are—

  (a)   the day the amount is set off;

  (b)   the day after the end of the period of 30 days starting with the day on which the Commissioners receive the claim.

(5) Sub-paragraphs (3) and (4) are subject to paragraph 6.

6.—(1) In deciding the applicable period for the purposes of paragraphs 4 and 5 any period by which the Commissioners' authorisation of the repayment or drawback is delayed by circumstances beyond their control must be ignored.

(2) In applying sub-paragraph (1) account must be taken in particular of any period referable to—

    (a)   any failure by any person to provide the Commissioners with information requested by them to enable the existence and amount of the claimant's entitlement to a repayment or drawback to be determined;

    (b)   the making (in connection with the claim for repayment or drawback) of a claim to anything to which the claimant is not entitled.

(3) In deciding for the purposes of sub-paragraph (2)(a) whether a period of delay is referable to a failure by a person to provide information requested, the period mentioned in sub-paragraph (4) must be taken to be so referable (except so far as may be prescribed by the Commissioners by regulations).

(4) The period is that which—

    (a)   starts with the day when the Commissioners request the person to provide information they reasonably consider relevant to the matter to be determined, and

    (b)   ends with the earliest day when it would be reasonable for them to conclude that they have received a complete answer to their request or all they need to answer it, or to conclude that it is unnecessary for them to be provided with information in answer to their request.

Commissioners' error

7.—(1) This paragraph applies if—

    (a)   due to an error on the part of the Commissioners a person pays to them an amount by way of excise duty,

    (b)   the person is entitled to obtain repayment of the amount,

    (c)   he makes a claim (at any time) for the repayment and the Commissioners authorise it on or after the commencement day, and

    (d)   he makes a claim for interest under this paragraph before the end of the period of three years starting with the day when the Commissioners authorise the repayment.

(2) The Commissioners must pay interest to the person on the amount concerned for the applicable period.

(3) The applicable period is the period which—

    (a)   starts with the day when the payment is received by the Commissioners, and

    (b)   ends with the day when they authorise repayment.

(4) Sub-paragraph (3) is subject to paragraph 11.

8.—(1) This paragraph applies if—

    (a)   a person pays to the Commissioners an amount by way of excise duty,

    (b)   he is entitled to obtain an amount by way of repayment, remission, rebate or drawback in respect of the duty,

    (c)   due to an error on the part of the Commissioners he fails to claim the amount when he would (apart from the error) have done so,

    (d)   the person makes a claim (at any time) for the repayment, remission, rebate or drawback and the Commissioners authorise it on or after the commencement day, and

    (e)   he makes a claim for interest under this paragraph before the end of the period of three years starting with the day when the Commissioners authorise the repayment, remission, rebate or drawback.

(2)   The Commissioners must pay interest to the person on the amount concerned for the applicable period.

(3)   The applicable period is the period which—

    (a)   starts with the day when (apart from the error) the Commissioners might reasonably have been expected to authorise repayment, remission, rebate or drawback, and

    (b)   ends with the day when they authorise it.

(4)   Sub-paragraph (3) is subject to paragraph 11.

9.—(1)   This paragraph applies if—

    (a)   a person pays to the Commissioners an amount by way of excise duty,

    (b)   he is entitled to obtain an amount by way of repayment, remission, rebate or drawback in respect of the duty,

    (c)   he makes a claim (at any time) for the repayment, remission, rebate or drawback and the Commissioners authorise it,

    (d)   due to an error on the part of the Commissioners their authorisation is delayed,

    (e)   the Commissioners authorise the repayment, remission, rebate or drawback on or after the commencement day,

    (f)   neither paragraph 4 nor paragraph 5 applies in relation to the person, and

    (g)   the person makes a claim for interest under this paragraph before the end of the period of three years starting with the day when the Commissioners authorise the repayment, remission, rebate or drawback.

(2)   The Commissioners must pay interest to the person on the amount concerned for the applicable period.

(3)   The applicable period is the period which—

    (a)   starts with the day when (apart from the error) the Commissioners might reasonably have been expected to authorise repayment, remission, rebate or drawback, and

    (b)   ends with the day when they authorise it.

(4)   Sub-paragraph (3) is subject to paragraph 11.

10.—(1)   This paragraph applies if—

    (a)   a person makes a claim for a payment under paragraph 1 or 2 of this Schedule and the Commissioners authorise it, and

    (b)   he makes a claim for interest under this paragraph before the end of the period of three years starting with the day when the Commissioners authorise the payment.

(2)   The Commissioners must pay interest to the person on the amount concerned for the applicable period.

(3)   The applicable period is the period which—

    (a)   starts with the day when the second or third condition in paragraph 1 or the second condition in paragraph 2 (as the case may be) is satisfied in relation to that person, and

    (b)   ends with the day when the Commissioners authorise the payment under that paragraph.

(4)   Sub-paragraph (3) is subject to paragraph 11.

11.—(1)   In deciding the applicable period for the purposes of paragraphs 7 to 10 any period by which the Commissioners' authorisation of the repayment, remission, rebate, drawback or payment is delayed by circumstances beyond their control must be ignored.

(2)   In applying sub-paragraph (1) account must be taken in particular of any period referable to—

(a)   any unreasonable delay in claiming repayment, remission, rebate, drawback or payment;

(b)   any failure by any person to provide the Commissioners with information requested by them to enable the existence and amount of a claimant's entitlement to repayment, remission, rebate, drawback, payment or interest to be determined;

(c)   the making (in connection with the claim for repayment, remission, rebate, drawback or payment) of a claim to anything to which the claimant is not entitled.

(3)   In deciding for the purposes of sub-paragraph (2)(b) whether a period of delay is referable to a failure by a person to provide information requested, the period mentioned in sub-paragraph (4) must be taken to be so referable (except so far as may be prescribed by the Commissioners by regulations).

(4)   The period is that which—

(a)   starts with the day when the Commissioners request the person to provide information they reasonably consider relevant to the matter to be determined, and

(b)   ends with the earliest day when it would be reasonable for them to conclude that they have received a complete answer to their request or all they need to answer it, or to conclude that it is unnecessary for them to be provided with information in answer to their request.

Claims

12.—(1)   A claim for interest under a relevant paragraph must be made in such form and manner, and contain such matters, as the Commissioners may prescribe by regulations.

(2)   If a person makes a claim under a relevant paragraph for interest on an amount, he may not make a claim under another relevant paragraph for interest on that amount.

(3)   The relevant paragraphs are paragraphs 7 to 10.

Rate of interest

13.   In the case of interest under this Part of this Schedule, the rate is that applicable under section 197 of the Finance Act 1996 (rates of interest).

PART 3
APPEALS

14.—(1)   This paragraph applies if—

(a)   a person (the appellant) appeals to a tribunal under section 16 of the Finance Act 1994 in relation to an assessment to excise duty,

(b)   the appellant pays, or gives cash security for, the whole or any part of that duty, and

(c)   the tribunal finds that the whole or any part of the amount paid or secured is not due.

(2)   The Commissioners must repay to the appellant an amount equal to—

(a)   so much of the duty paid as is found not to be due, or

(b)   so much of the cash security as relates to the duty found not to be due.

(3)   The Commissioners must pay interest to the appellant on the amount referred to in sub-paragraph (2) for the period which—

(a)   starts with the day when the duty is paid or the cash security is given, and

(b)   ends with the day when the Commissioners authorise the repayment.

(4)   The rate of interest is—

(a)   such rate as the tribunal determines, or

(b)   if it does not determine a rate, the rate applicable under section 197 of the Finance Act 1996.

(5)   In this paragraph "cash security" means such adequate security as enables the Commissioners to place the amount in question on deposit.

PART 4

GENERAL

Amendments

(The amendments made by paras 15–20 are already in force and these provisions have therefore been omitted)

General

21.—(1)   This Schedule shall come into force in accordance with provision made by the Commissioners by order.

(2)   A reference in a provision of this Schedule to the commencement day is to such day as the Commissioners appoint by such order for the purposes of that provision.

22.—(1)   A power to make an order or regulations under this Schedule is exercisable by statutory instrument.

(2)   An order or regulations under this Schedule—

(a)   may make different provision for different purposes;

(b)   may make incidental, supplemental, saving or transitional provision.

(3)   Regulations under this Schedule are subject to annulment in pursuance of a resolution of either House of Parliament.

23.   References in this Schedule to the Commissioners are to the Commissioners of Customs and Excise.

NOTES

Orders: the Finance Act 2001 (Commencement No 2 and Saving Provision) Order 2001, SI 2001/3300 (made under paras 21, 22).

Regulations: the Excise Duty (Payments in case of Error or Delay) Regulations 2001, SI 2001/3299 (made under para 22).

SCHEDULE 33
REPEALS

Section 110

PART 1
EXCISE DUTIES

(This Part contains repeals)

CRIMINAL JUSTICE AND POLICE ACT 2001

(2001 c 16)

An Act to make provision for combatting crime and disorder; to make provision about the disclosure of information relating to criminal matters and about powers of search and seizure; to amend the Police and Criminal Evidence Act 1984, the Police and Criminal Evidence (Northern Ireland) Order 1989 and the Terrorism Act 2000; to make provision about the police, the National Criminal Intelligence Service and the National Crime Squad; to make provision about the powers of the courts in relation to criminal matters; and for connected purposes

[11 May 2001]

PART 2
POWERS OF SEIZURE

Additional powers of seizure

50 Additional powers of seizure from premises

(1) Where—

    (a)   a person who is lawfully on any premises finds anything on those premises that he has reasonable grounds for believing may be or may contain something for which he is authorised to search on those premises,

    (b)   a power of seizure to which this section applies or the power conferred by subsection (2) would entitle him, if he found it, to seize whatever it is that he has grounds for believing that thing to be or to contain, and

    (c)   in all the circumstances, it is not reasonably practicable for it to be determined, on those premises—

        (i)   whether what he has found is something that he is entitled to seize, or

        (ii)   the extent to which what he has found contains something that he is entitled to seize,

    that person's powers of seizure shall include power under this section to seize so much of what he has found as it is necessary to remove from the premises to enable that to be determined.

(2) Where—

    (a)   a person who is lawfully on any premises finds anything on those premises ("the seizable property") which he would be entitled to seize but for its being comprised in something else that he has (apart from this subsection) no power to seize,

(b)   the power under which that person would have power to seize the seizable property is a power to which this section applies, and

(c)   in all the circumstances it is not reasonably practicable for the seizable property to be separated, on those premises, from that in which it is comprised,

that person's powers of seizure shall include power under this section to seize both the seizable property and that from which it is not reasonably practicable to separate it.

(3)   The factors to be taken into account in considering, for the purposes of this section, whether or not it is reasonably practicable on particular premises for something to be determined, or for something to be separated from something else, shall be confined to the following—

(a)   how long it would take to carry out the determination or separation on those premises;

(b)   the number of persons that would be required to carry out that determination or separation on those premises within a reasonable period;

(c)   whether the determination or separation would (or would if carried out on those premises) involve damage to property;

(d)   the apparatus or equipment that it would be necessary or appropriate to use for the carrying out of the determination or separation; and

(e)   in the case of separation, whether the separation—

    (i)   would be likely, or

    (ii)   if carried out by the only means that are reasonably practicable on those premises, would be likely,

to prejudice the use of some or all of the separated seizable property for a purpose for which something seized under the power in question is capable of being used.

(4)   Section 19(6) of the 1984 Act and Article 21(6) of the Police and Criminal Evidence (Northern Ireland) Order 1989 (SI 1989/1341 (NI 12)) (powers of seizure not to include power to seize anything that a person has reasonable grounds for believing is legally privileged) shall not apply to the power of seizure conferred by subsection (2).

(5)   This section applies to each of the powers of seizure specified in Part 1 of Schedule 1.

(6)   Without prejudice to any power conferred by this section to take a copy of any document, nothing in this section, so far as it has effect by reference to the power to take copies of documents under section 28(2)(b) of the Competition Act 1998 (c 41), shall be taken to confer any power to seize any document.

51 Additional powers of seizure from the person

(1)   Where—

(a)   a person carrying out a lawful search of any person finds something that he has reasonable grounds for believing may be or may contain something for which he is authorised to search,

(b)   a power of seizure to which this section applies or the power conferred by subsection (2) would entitle him, if he found it, to seize whatever it is that he has grounds for believing that thing to be or to contain, and

(c)   in all the circumstances it is not reasonably practicable for it to be determined, at the time and place of the search—

    (i)   whether what he has found is something that he is entitled to seize, or

    (ii)   the extent to which what he has found contains something that he is entitled to seize, that person's powers of seizure shall include power under this section to seize so much of what he has found as it is necessary to remove from that place to enable that to be determined.

(2) Where—

    (a) a person carrying out a lawful search of any person finds something ("the seizable property") which he would be entitled to seize but for its being comprised in something else that he has (apart from this subsection) no power to seize,

    (b) the power under which that person would have power to seize the seizable property is a power to which this section applies, and

    (c) in all the circumstances it is not reasonably practicable for the seizable property to be separated, at the time and place of the search, from that in which it is comprised,

that person's powers of seizure shall include power under this section to seize both the seizable property and that from which it is not reasonably practicable to separate it.

(3) The factors to be taken into account in considering, for the purposes of this section, whether or not it is reasonably practicable, at the time and place of a search, for something to be determined, or for something to be separated from something else, shall be confined to the following—

    (a) how long it would take to carry out the determination or separation at that time and place;

    (b) the number of persons that would be required to carry out that determination or separation at that time and place within a reasonable period;

    (c) whether the determination or separation would (or would if carried out at that time and place) involve damage to property;

    (d) the apparatus or equipment that it would be necessary or appropriate to use for the carrying out of the determination or separation; and

    (e) in the case of separation, whether the separation—

        (i) would be likely, or

        (ii) if carried out by the only means that are reasonably practicable at that time and place, would be likely,

to prejudice the use of some or all of the separated seizable property for a purpose for which something seized under the power in question is capable of being used.

(4) Section 19(6) of the 1984 Act and Article 21(6) of the Police and Criminal Evidence (Northern Ireland) Order 1989 (SI 1989/1341 (NI 12)) (powers of seizure not to include power to seize anything a person has reasonable grounds for believing is legally privileged) shall not apply to the power of seizure conferred by subsection (2).

(5) This section applies to each of the powers of seizure specified in Part 2 of Schedule 1.

52 Notice of exercise of power under s 50 or 51

(1) Where a person exercises a power of seizure conferred by section 50, it shall (subject to subsections (2) and (3)) be his duty, on doing so, to give to the occupier of the premises a written notice—

    (a) specifying what has been seized in reliance on the powers conferred by that section;

    (b) specifying the grounds on which those powers have been exercised;

    (c) setting out the effect of sections 59 to 61;

(d)   specifying the name and address of the person to whom notice of an application under section 59(2) to the appropriate judicial authority in respect of any of the seized property must be given; and

(e)   specifying the name and address of the person to whom an application may be made to be allowed to attend the initial examination required by any arrangements made for the purposes of section 53(2).

(2)   Where it appears to the person exercising on any premises a power of seizure conferred by section 50—

(a)   that the occupier of the premises is not present on the premises at the time of the exercise of the power, but

(b)   that there is some other person present on the premises who is in charge of the premises,

subsection (1) of this section shall have effect as if it required the notice under that subsection to be given to that other person.

(3)   Where it appears to the person exercising a power of seizure conferred by section 50 that there is no one present on the premises to whom he may give a notice for the purposes of complying with subsection (1) of this section, he shall, before leaving the premises, instead of complying with that subsection, attach a notice such as is mentioned in that subsection in a prominent place to the premises.

(4)   Where a person exercises a power of seizure conferred by section 51 it shall be his duty, on doing so, to give a written notice to the person from whom the seizure is made—

(a)   specifying what has been seized in reliance on the powers conferred by that section;

(b)   specifying the grounds on which those powers have been exercised;

(c)   setting out the effect of sections 59 to 61;

(d)   specifying the name and address of the person to whom notice of any application under section 59(2) to the appropriate judicial authority in respect of any of the seized property must be given; and

(e)   specifying the name and address of the person to whom an application may be made to be allowed to attend the initial examination required by any arrangements made for the purposes of section 53(2).

(5)   The Secretary of State may by regulations made by statutory instrument, after consultation with the Scottish Ministers, provide that a person who exercises a power of seizure conferred by section 50 shall be required to give a notice such as is mentioned in subsection (1) of this section to any person, or send it to any place, described in the regulations.

(6)   Regulations under subsection (5) may make different provision for different cases.

(7)   A statutory instrument containing regulations under subsection (5) shall be subject to annulment in pursuance of a resolution of either House of Parliament.

Return or retention of seized property

53 Examination and return of property seized under s 50 or 51

(1)   This section applies where anything has been seized under a power conferred by section 50 or 51.

(2)   It shall be the duty of the person for the time being in possession of the seized property in consequence of the exercise of that power to secure that there are arrangements in force which (subject to section 61) ensure—

(a)   that an initial examination of the property is carried out as soon as reasonably practicable after the seizure;

(b)   that that examination is confined to whatever is necessary for determining how much of the property falls within subsection (3);

(c)   that anything which is found, on that examination, not to fall within subsection (3) is separated from the rest of the seized property and is returned as soon as reasonably practicable after the examination of all the seized property has been completed; and

(d)   that, until the initial examination of all the seized property has been completed and anything which does not fall within subsection (3) has been returned, the seized property is kept separate from anything seized under any other power.

(3)   The seized property falls within this subsection to the extent only—

    (a)   that it is property for which the person seizing it had power to search when he made the seizure but is not property the return of which is required by section 54;

    (b)   that it is property the retention of which is authorised by section 56; or

    (c)   that it is something which, in all the circumstances, it will not be reasonably practicable, following the examination, to separate from property falling within paragraph (a) or (b).

(4)   In determining for the purposes of this section the earliest practicable time for the carrying out of an initial examination of the seized property, due regard shall be had to the desirability of allowing the person from whom it was seized, or a person with an interest in that property, an opportunity of being present or (if he chooses) of being represented at the examination.

(5)   In this section, references to whether or not it is reasonably practicable to separate part of the seized property from the rest of it are references to whether or not it is reasonably practicable to do so without prejudicing the use of the rest of that property, or a part of it, for purposes for which (disregarding the part to be separated) the use of the whole or of a part of the rest of the property, if retained, would be lawful.

54 Obligation to return items subject to legal privilege

(1)   If, at any time after a seizure of anything has been made in exercise of a power of seizure to which this section applies—

    (a)   it appears to the person for the time being having possession of the seized property in consequence of the seizure that the property—

        (i)   is an item subject to legal privilege, or

        (ii)   has such an item comprised in it,

   and

    (b)   in a case where the item is comprised in something else which has been lawfully seized, it is not comprised in property falling within subsection (2),

it shall be the duty of that person to secure that the item is returned as soon as reasonably practicable after the seizure.

(2)   Property in which an item subject to legal privilege is comprised falls within this subsection if—

    (a)   the whole or a part of the rest of the property is property falling within subsection (3) or property the retention of which is authorised by section 56; and

    (b)   in all the circumstances, it is not reasonably practicable for that item to be separated from the rest of that property (or, as the case may be, from that part of it) without prejudicing the use of the rest of that property, or that part of it, for purposes for which (disregarding that item) its use, if retained, would be lawful.

(3)   Property falls within this subsection to the extent that it is property for which the person seizing it had power to search when he made the seizure, but is not property which is required to be returned under this section or section 55.

(4)   This section applies—

(a)   to the powers of seizure conferred by sections 50 and 51;

(b)   to each of the powers of seizure specified in Parts 1 and 2 of Schedule 1; and

(c)   to any power of seizure (not falling within paragraph (a) or (b)) conferred on a constable by or under any enactment, including an enactment passed after this Act.

55 Obligation to return excluded and special procedure material

(1)   If, at any time after a seizure of anything has been made in exercise of a power to which this section applies—

(a)   it appears to the person for the time being having possession of the seized property in consequence of the seizure that the property—

(i)   is excluded material or special procedure material, or

(ii)   has any excluded material or any special procedure material comprised in it,

(b)   its retention is not authorised by section 56, and

(c)   in a case where the material is comprised in something else which has been lawfully seized, it is not comprised in property falling within subsection (2) or (3),

it shall be the duty of that person to secure that the item is returned as soon as reasonably practicable after the seizure.

(2)   Property in which any excluded material or special procedure material is comprised falls within this subsection if—

(a)   the whole or a part of the rest of the property is property for which the person seizing it had power to search when he made the seizure but is not property the return of which is required by this section or section 54; and

(b)   in all the circumstances, it is not reasonably practicable for that material to be separated from the rest of that property (or, as the case may be, from that part of it) without prejudicing the use of the rest of that property, or that part of it, for purposes for which (disregarding that material) its use, if retained, would be lawful.

(3)   Property in which any excluded material or special procedure material is comprised falls within this subsection if—

(a)   the whole or a part of the rest of the property is property the retention of which is authorised by section 56; and

(b)   in all the circumstances, it is not reasonably practicable for that material to be separated from the rest of that property (or, as the case may be, from that part of it) without prejudicing the use of the rest of that property, or that part of it, for purposes for which (disregarding that material) its use, if retained, would be lawful.

(4)   This section applies (subject to subsection (5)) to each of the powers of seizure specified in Part 3 of Schedule 1.

(5)   In its application to the powers of seizure conferred by—

(a)   . . .

(b)   section 56(5) of the Drug Trafficking Act 1994 (c. 37), . . .

(c)   Article 51(5) of the Proceeds of Crime (Northern Ireland) Order 1996 (SI 1996/1299 (NI 6)), [and

(d)   section 352(4) of the Proceeds of Crime Act 2002,]

this section shall have effect with the omission of every reference to special procedure material.

(6) In this section, except in its application to—

(a)   the power of seizure conferred by section 8(2) of the 1984 Act,

(b)   the power of seizure conferred by Article 10(2) of the Police and Criminal Evidence (Northern Ireland) Order 1989 (SI 1989/1341 (NI 12)),

(c)   each of the powers of seizure conferred by the provisions of paragraphs 1 and 3 of Schedule 5 to the Terrorism Act 2000 (c 11), and

(d)   the power of seizure conferred by paragraphs 15 and 19 of Schedule 5 to that Act of 2000, so far only as the power in question is conferred by reference to paragraph 1 of that Schedule,

"special procedure material" means special procedure material consisting of documents or records other than documents.

NOTE

Sub-s (5): para (a) repealed; word in para (b) repealed; and para (d) and word preceding it inserted, by the Proceeds of Crime Act 2002, ss 456, 457, Sch 11 paras 1, 40(1), (2), Sch 12.

---

56 Property seized by constables etc

(1) The retention of—

(a)   property seized on any premises by a constable who was lawfully on the premises,

(b)   property seized on any premises by a relevant person who was on the premises accompanied by a constable, and

(c)   property seized by a constable carrying out a lawful search of any person,

is authorised by this section if the property falls within subsection (2) or (3).

(2) Property falls within this subsection to the extent that there are reasonable grounds for believing—

(a)   that it is property obtained in consequence of the commission of an offence; and

(b)   that it is necessary for it to be retained in order to prevent its being concealed, lost, damaged, altered or destroyed.

(3) Property falls within this subsection to the extent that there are reasonable grounds for believing—

(a)   that it is evidence in relation to any offence; and

(b)   that it is necessary for it to be retained in order to prevent its being concealed, lost, altered or destroyed.

(4) Nothing in this section authorises the retention (except in pursuance of section 54(2)) of anything at any time when its return is required by section 54.

[(4A) Subsection (1)(a) includes property seized on any premises—

(a)   by a person authorised under section 16(2) of the 1984 Act to accompany a constable executing a warrant, or

(b)   by a person accompanying a constable under section 2(6) of the Criminal Justice Act 1987 in the execution of a warrant under section 2(4) of that Act.]

(5) In subsection (1)(b) the reference to a relevant person's being on any premises accompanied by a constable is a reference only to a person who was so on the premises under the authority of—

(a)   a warrant under section 448 of the Companies Act 1985 (c 6) authorising him to exercise together with a constable the powers conferred by subsection (3) of that section;

(b)   a warrant under Article 441 of the Companies (Northern Ireland) Order 1986 (SI 1986/1032 (NI 6)) authorising him to exercise together with a constable the powers conferred by paragraph (3) of that Article;

(c)–(e) . . .

NOTES

Sub-s (4A): inserted by the Criminal Justice Act 2003, s 12, Sch 1 para 14.

Sub-s (5): paras (c)–(e) repealed by the Financial Services and Markets Act 2000 (Consequential Amendments and Repeals) Order, SI 2001/3649 art 364(a).

57 Retention of seized items

(1)   This section has effect in relation to the following provisions (which are about the retention of items which have been seized and are referred to in this section as "the relevant provisions")—

(a)   section 22 of the 1984 Act;

(b)   Article 24 of the Police and Criminal Evidence (Northern Ireland) Order 1989 (SI 1989/1341 (NI 12));

(c)   *section 20CC(3) of the Taxes Management Act 1970 (c 9);*

(d)   paragraph 4 of Schedule 9 to the Weights and Measures (Northern Ireland) Order 1981 (SI 1981/231 (NI 10));

(e)   . . .

(f)   section 448(6) of the Companies Act 1985 (c 6);

(g)   paragraph 4 of [Schedule 7 to the Weights and Measures (Packaged Goods) Regulations 2006];

(h)   . . .

(i)   Article 441(6) of the Companies (Northern Ireland) Order 1986;

(j)   . . .

(k)   section 40(4) of the Human Fertilisation and Embryology Act 1990 (c 37);

(l)   section 5(4) of the Knives Act 1997 (c 21);

(m)   paragraph 7(2) of Schedule 9 to the Data Protection Act 1998 (c 29);

(n)   section 28(7) of the Competition Act 1998 (c 41);

(o)   section 176(8) of the Financial Services and Markets Act 2000 (c 8);

(p)   paragraph 7(2) of Schedule 3 to the Freedom of Information Act 2000 (c 36);

[(pa)   section 227F of the Enterprise Act 2002;]

[(q)   paragraph 5(4) of Schedule 5 to the Human Tissue Act 2004;]

[(r)   paragraph 12(3) of Schedule 2 to the Animal Welfare Act 2006].

(2)   The relevant provisions shall apply in relation to any property seized in exercise of a power conferred by section 50 or 51 as if the property had been seized under the power of seizure by reference to which the power under that section was exercised in relation to that property.

(3)   Nothing in any of sections 53 to 56 authorises the retention of any property at any time when its retention would not (apart from the provisions of this Part) be authorised by the relevant provisions.

(4)   Nothing in any of the relevant provisions authorises the retention of anything after an obligation to return it has arisen under this Part.

NOTES

Sub-s (1): paras (e), (h), (j) repealed by the Financial Services and Markets Act 2000 (Consequential Amendments and Repeals) Order, SI 2001/3649 art 364(b); words in para (g) substituted by the Weights and Measures (Packaged Goods) Regulations SI 2006/659, reg 1(2), Sch 1, Pt 2, paras (24), (25); para (pa) inserted by the Enterprise Act 2002 (Amendment) Regulations, SI 2006/3363, regs 24, 25; new para (q) inserted by the Human Tissue Act 2004 s 56, Sch 6 para 5; para (r) inserted by the Animal Welfare Act 2006, s 64, Sch 3, para 14(1) in relation to England and Wales (in relation to Scotland and Northern Ireland from a date to be appointed).

Sub-s (1)(c) to be repealed by the Finance Act 2007, ss 84(4), 114, Sch 22, paras 3, 13(1)(a), Sch 27, Pt 5(1) with effect from a date to be appointed.

58 Person to whom seized property is to be returned

(1) Where—
- (a) anything has been seized in exercise of any power of seizure, and
- (b) there is an obligation under this Part for the whole or any part of the seized property to be returned,

the obligation to return it shall (subject to the following provisions of this section) be an obligation to return it to the person from whom it was seized.

(2) Where—
- (a) any person is obliged under this Part to return anything that has been seized to the person from whom it was seized, and
- (b) the person under that obligation is satisfied that some other person has a better right to that thing than the person from whom it was seized,

his duty to return it shall, instead, be a duty to return it to that other person or, as the case may be, to the person appearing to him to have the best right to the thing in question.

(3) Where different persons claim to be entitled to the return of anything that is required to be returned under this Part, that thing may be retained for as long as is reasonably necessary for the determination in accordance with subsection (2) of the person to whom it must be returned.

(4) References in this Part to the person from whom something has been seized, in relation to a case in which the power of seizure was exercisable by reason of that thing's having been found on any premises, are references to the occupier of the premises at the time of the seizure.

(5) References in this section to the occupier of any premises at the time of a seizure, in relation to a case in which—
- (a) a notice in connection with the entry or search of the premises in question, or with the seizure, was given to a person appearing in the occupier's absence to be in charge of the premises, and
- (b) it is practicable, for the purpose of returning something that has been seized, to identify that person but not to identify the occupier of the premises,

are references to that person.

Remedies and safeguards

59 Application to the appropriate judicial authority

(1) This section applies where anything has been seized in exercise, or purported exercise, of a relevant power of seizure.

(2)   Any person with a relevant interest in the seized property may apply to the appropriate judicial authority, on one or more of the grounds mentioned in subsection (3), for the return of the whole or a part of the seized property.

(3)   Those grounds are—

(a)   that there was no power to make the seizure;

(b)   that the seized property is or contains an item subject to legal privilege that is not comprised in property falling within section 54(2);

(c)   that the seized property is or contains any excluded material or special procedure material which—

(i)   has been seized under a power to which section 55 applies;

(ii)   is not comprised in property falling within section 55(2) or (3); and

(iii) is not property the retention of which is authorised by section 56;

(d)   that the seized property is or contains something seized under section 50 or 51 which does not fall within section 53(3);

and subsections (5) and (6) of section 55 shall apply for the purposes of paragraph (c) as they apply for the purposes of that section.

(4)   Subject to subsection (6), the appropriate judicial authority, on an application under subsection (2), shall—

(a)   if satisfied as to any of the matters mentioned in subsection (3), order the return of so much of the seized property as is property in relation to which the authority is so satisfied; and

(b)   to the extent that that authority is not so satisfied, dismiss the application.

(5)   The appropriate judicial authority—

(a)   on an application under subsection (2),

(b)   on an application made by the person for the time being having possession of anything in consequence of its seizure under a relevant power of seizure, or

(c)   on an application made—

(i)   by a person with a relevant interest in anything seized under section 50 or 51, and

(ii)   on the grounds that the requirements of section 53(2) have not been or are not being complied with,

may give such directions as the authority thinks fit as to the examination, retention, separation or return of the whole or any part of the seized property.

(6)   On any application under this section, the appropriate judicial authority may authorise the retention of any property which—

(a)   has been seized in exercise, or purported exercise, of a relevant power of seizure, and

(b)   would otherwise fall to be returned,

if that authority is satisfied that the retention of the property is justified on grounds falling within subsection (7).

(7)   Those grounds are that (if the property were returned) it would immediately become appropriate—

(a)   to issue, on the application of the person who is in possession of the property at the time of the application under this section, a warrant in pursuance of which, or of the exercise of which, it would be lawful to seize the property; or

(b)   to make an order under—

(i)   paragraph 4 of Schedule 1 to the 1984 Act,

    (ii)   paragraph 4 of Schedule 1 to the Police and Criminal Evidence (Northern Ireland) Order 1989 (SI 1989/1341 (NI 12)),

    (iii)   section 20BA of the Taxes Management Act 1970 (c 9), or

    (iv)   paragraph 5 of Schedule 5 to the Terrorism Act 2000 (c 11),

under which the property would fall to be delivered up or produced to the person mentioned in paragraph (a).

(8) Where any property which has been seized in exercise, or purported exercise, of a relevant power of seizure has parts ("part A" and "part B") comprised in it such that—

    (a)   it would be inappropriate, if the property were returned, to take any action such as is mentioned in subsection (7) in relation to part A,

    (b)   it would (or would but for the facts mentioned in paragraph (a)) be appropriate, if the property were returned, to take such action in relation to part B, and

    (c)   in all the circumstances, it is not reasonably practicable to separate part A from part B without prejudicing the use of part B for purposes for which it is lawful to use property seized under the power in question,

the facts mentioned in paragraph (a) shall not be taken into account by the appropriate judicial authority in deciding whether the retention of the property is justified on grounds falling within subsection (7).

(9) If a person fails to comply with any order or direction made or given by a judge of the Crown Court in exercise of any jurisdiction under this section—

    (a)   the authority may deal with him as if he had committed a contempt of the Crown Court; and

    (b)   any enactment relating to contempt of the Crown Court shall have effect in relation to the failure as if it were such a contempt.

(10) The relevant powers of seizure for the purposes of this section are—

    (a)   the powers of seizure conferred by sections 50 and 51;

    (b)   each of the powers of seizure specified in Parts 1 and 2 of Schedule 1; and

    (c)   any power of seizure (not falling within paragraph (a) or (b)) conferred on a constable by or under any enactment, including an enactment passed after this Act.

(11) References in this section to a person with a relevant interest in seized property are references to—

    (a)   the person from whom it was seized;

    (b)   any person with an interest in the property; or

    (c)   any person, not falling within paragraph (a) or (b), who had custody or control of the property immediately before the seizure.

(12) For the purposes of subsection (11)(b), the persons who have an interest in seized property shall, in the case of property which is or contains an item subject to legal privilege, be taken to include the person in whose favour that privilege is conferred.

60 Cases where duty to secure arises

(1) Where property has been seized in exercise, or purported exercise, of any power of seizure conferred by section 50 or 51, a duty to secure arises under section 61 in relation to the seized property if—

    (a)   a person entitled to do so makes an application under section 59 for the return of the property;

    (b)   in relation to England, Wales and Northern Ireland, at least one of the conditions set out in subsections (2) and (3) is satisfied;

    (c)   in relation to Scotland, the condition set out in subsection (2) is satisfied; and

    (d)   notice of the application is given to a relevant person.

(2)   The first condition is that the application is made on the grounds that the seized property is or contains an item subject to legal privilege that is not comprised in property falling within section 54(2).

(3)   The second condition is that—

    (a)   the seized property was seized by a person who had, or purported to have, power under this Part to seize it by virtue only of one or more of the powers specified in subsection (6); and

    (b)   the application—

        (i)   is made on the ground that the seized property is or contains something which does not fall within section 53(3); and

        (ii)   states that the seized property is or contains special procedure material or excluded material.

(4)   In relation to property seized by a person who had, or purported to have, power under this Part to seize it by virtue only of one or more of the powers of seizure conferred by—

    (a)   . . .

    (b)   section 56(5) of the Drug Trafficking Act 1994 (c 37), . . .

    (c)   Article 51(5) of the Proceeds of Crime (Northern Ireland) Order 1996 (SI 1996/1299 (NI 6)), [or

    (d)   section 352(4) of the Proceeds of Crime Act 2002,]

the second condition is satisfied only if the application states that the seized property is or contains excluded material.

(5)   In relation to property seized by a person who had, or purported to have, power under this Part to seize it by virtue only of one or more of the powers of seizure specified in Part 3 of Schedule 1 but not by virtue of—

    (a)   the power of seizure conferred by section 8(2) of the 1984 Act,

    (b)   the power of seizure conferred by Article 10(2) of the Police and Criminal Evidence (Northern Ireland) Order 1989 (SI 1989/1341 (NI 12)),

    (c)   either of the powers of seizure conferred by paragraphs 1 and 3 of Schedule 5 to the Terrorism Act 2000 (c 11), or

    (d)   either of the powers of seizure conferred by paragraphs 15 and 19 of Schedule 5 to that Act of 2000 so far as they are conferred by reference to paragraph 1 of that Schedule,

the second condition is satisfied only if the application states that the seized property is or contains excluded material or special procedure material consisting of documents or records other than documents

(6)   The powers mentioned in subsection (3) are—

    (a)   the powers of seizure specified in Part 3 of Schedule 1;

    (b)   the powers of seizure conferred by the provisions of Parts 2 and 3 of the 1984 Act (except section 8(2) of that Act);

    (c)   the powers of seizure conferred by the provisions of Parts 3 and 4 of the Police and Criminal Evidence (Northern Ireland) Order 1989 (except Article 10(2) of that Order);

    (d)   the powers of seizure conferred by the provisions of paragraph 11 of Schedule 5 to the Terrorism Act 2000; and

    (e)   the powers of seizure conferred by the provisions of paragraphs 15 and 19 of that Schedule so far as they are conferred by reference to paragraph 11 of that Schedule.

Part I

(7) In this section "a relevant person" means any one of the following—

    (a)   the person who made the seizure;

    (b)   the person for the time being having possession, in consequence of the seizure, of the seized property;

    (c)   the person named for the purposes of subsection (1)(d) or (4)(d) of section 52 in any notice given under that section with respect to the seizure.

NOTES

Sub-s (4): para (a) repealed; word in para (b) repealed, and para (d) and word preceding it inserted, by the Proceeds of Crime Act 2002, ss 456, 457, Sch 11 paras 1, 40(1), (3), Sch 12.

61 The duty to secure

(1) The duty to secure that arises under this section is a duty of the person for the time being having possession, in consequence of the seizure, of the seized property to secure that arrangements are in force that ensure that the seized property (without being returned) is not, at any time after the giving of the notice of the application under section 60(1), either—

    (a)   examined or copied, or

    (b)   put to any use to which its seizure would, apart from this subsection, entitle it to be put,

except with the consent of the applicant or in accordance with the directions of the appropriate judicial authority.

(2) Subsection (1) shall not have effect in relation to any time after the withdrawal of the application to which the notice relates.

(3) Nothing in any arrangements for the purposes of this section shall be taken to prevent the giving of a notice under section 49 of the Regulation of Investigatory Powers Act 2000 (c 23) (notices for the disclosure of material protected by encryption etc) in respect of any information contained in the seized material; but subsection (1) of this section shall apply to anything disclosed for the purpose of complying with such a notice as it applies to the seized material in which the information in question is contained.

(4) Subsection (9) of section 59 shall apply in relation to any jurisdiction conferred on the appropriate judicial authority by this section as it applies in relation to the jurisdiction conferred by that section.

62 Use of inextricably linked property

(1) This section applies to property, other than property which is for the time being required to be secured in pursuance of section 61, if—

    (a)   it has been seized under any power conferred by section 50 or 51 or specified in Part 1 or 2 of Schedule 1, and

    (b)   it is inextricably linked property.

(2) Subject to subsection (3), it shall be the duty of the person for the time being having possession, in consequence of the seizure, of the inextricably linked property to ensure that arrangements are in force which secure that that property (without being returned) is not at any time, except with the consent of the person from whom it was seized, either—

    (a)   examined or copied, or

    (b)   put to any other use.

(3) Subsection (2) does not require that arrangements under that subsection should prevent inextricably linked property from being put to any use falling within subsection (4).

(4) A use falls within this subsection to the extent that it is use which is necessary for facilitating the use, in any investigation or proceedings, of property in which the inextricably linked property is comprised.

(5) Property is inextricably linked property for the purposes of this section if it falls within any of subsections (6) to (8).

(6) Property falls within this subsection if—

  (a)   it has been seized under a power conferred by section 50 or 51; and

  (b)   but for subsection (3)(c) of section 53, arrangements under subsection (2) of that section in relation to the property would be required to ensure the return of the property as mentioned in subsection (2)(c) of that section.

(7) Property falls within this subsection if—

  (a)   it has been seized under a power to which section 54 applies; and

  (b)   but for paragraph (b) of subsection (1) of that section, the person for the time being having possession of the property would be under a duty to secure its return as mentioned in that subsection.

(8) Property falls within this subsection if—

  (a)   it has been seized under a power of seizure to which section 55 applies; and

  (b)   but for paragraph (c) of subsection (1) of that section, the person for the time being having possession of the property would be under a duty to secure its return as mentioned in that subsection.

Construction of Part 2

63 Copies

(1) Subject to subsection (3)—

  (a)   in this Part, "seize" includes "take a copy of", and cognate expressions shall be construed accordingly;

  (b)   this Part shall apply as if any copy taken under any power to which any provision of this Part applies were the original of that of which it is a copy; and

  (c)   for the purposes of this Part, except sections 50 and 51, the powers mentioned in subsection (2) (which are powers to obtain hard copies etc of information which is stored in electronic form) shall be treated as powers of seizure, and references to seizure and to seized property shall be construed accordingly.

(2) The powers mentioned in subsection (1)(c) are any powers which are conferred by—

  (a)   section 19(4) or 20 of the 1984 Act;

  (b)   Article 21(4) or 22 of the Police and Criminal Evidence (Northern Ireland) Order 1989 (SI 1989/1341 (NI 12));

  (c)   section 46(3) of the Firearms Act 1968 (c 27);

  (d)   . . .

  (e)   *section 20C(3A) of the Taxes Management Act 1970 (c 9);*

  (f)   section 32(6)(b) of the Food Safety Act 1990 (c 16);

  (g)   Article 34(6)(b) of the Food Safety (Northern Ireland) Order 1991 (SI 1991/762 (NI 7));

  [(ga) Criminal Law (Consolidation) (Scotland) Act 1995;]

  (h)   section 28(2)(f) of the Competition Act 1998 (c 41); or

  (i)   *section 8(2)(c) of the Nuclear Safeguards Act 2000 (c 5).*

(3) Subsection (1) does not apply to section 50(6) or 57.

NOTES

Sub-s (2): para (d) repealed by the Gambling Act 2005, s 356(4), Sch 17; para (e) to be repealed by the Finance Act 2007, ss 84(4), 114, Sch 22, Pt 2, paras 3, 13(1)(b), Sch 27, Pt 5(1), with effect from a date to be appointed; para (ga) to be inserted by the Finance Act 2007, s 85, Sch 23, paras 11, 12, with effect from a date to be appointed.

64 Meaning of "appropriate judicial authority"

(1)   Subject to subsection (2), in this Part "appropriate judicial authority" means—

    (a)   in relation to England and Wales and Northern Ireland, a judge of the Crown Court;

    (b)   in relation to Scotland, a sheriff.

(2)   In this Part "appropriate judicial authority", in relation to the seizure of items under any power mentioned in subsection (3) and in relation to items seized under any such power, means—

    (a)   in relation to England and Wales and Northern Ireland, the High Court;

    (b)   in relation to Scotland, the Court of Session.

(3)   Those powers are—

    (a)   the powers of seizure conferred by—

        (i)   section 448(3) of the Companies Act 1985 (c 6);

        (ii)   Article 441(3) of the Companies (Northern Ireland) Order 1986 (SI 1986/1032 (NI 6)); and

        (iii)   section 28(2) of the Competition Act 1998; . . .

    [(aa)   the power of seizure conferred by section 352(4) of the Proceeds of Crime Act 2002, if the power is exercisable for the purposes of a civil recovery investigation (within the meaning of Part 8 of that Act);]

    (b)   any power of seizure conferred by section 50, so far as that power is exercisable by reference to any power mentioned in paragraph (a).

NOTES

Sub-s (3): para (a)(iii) repealed, and para (aa) and word preceding it inserted, by the Proceeds of Crime Act 2002, ss 456, 457, Sch 11 paras 1, 40(1), (4), Sch 12.

65 Meaning of "legal privilege"

(1)   Subject to the following provisions of this section, references in this Part to an item subject to legal privilege shall be construed—

    (a)   for the purposes of the application of this Part to England and Wales, in accordance with section 10 of the 1984 Act (meaning of "legal privilege");

    (b)   for the purposes of the application of this Part to Scotland, in accordance with section [412 of the Proceeds of Crime Act 2002] (interpretation); and

    (c)   for the purposes of the application of this Part to Northern Ireland, in accordance with Article 12 of the Police and Criminal Evidence (Northern Ireland) Order 1989 (SI 1989/1341 (NI 12)) (meaning of "legal privilege").

(2)   In relation to property which has been seized in exercise, or purported exercise, of—

    (a)   the power of seizure conferred by section 28(2) of the Competition Act 1998, or

    (b)   so much of any power of seizure conferred by section 50 as is exercisable by reference to that power,

references in this Part to an item subject to legal privilege shall be read as references to a privileged communication within the meaning of section 30 of that Act.

    (3) *In relation to property which has been seized in exercise, or purported exercise, of—*

    (a)   *the power of seizure conferred by section 20C of the Taxes Management Act 1970 (c 9), or*

    (b)   *so much of any power of seizure conferred by section 50 as is exercisable by reference to that power,*

references in this Part to an item subject to legal privilege shall be construed in accordance with section 20C(4A) of that Act.

    [(3A) In relation to property which has been seized in exercise, or purported exercise, of—

    (a)   the power of seizure conferred by section 352(4) of the Proceeds of Crime Act 2002, or

    (b)   so much of any power of seizure conferred by section 50 as is exercisable by reference to that power,

references in this Part to an item subject to legal privilege shall be read as references to privileged material within the meaning of section 354(2) of that Act.]

    (4) An item which is, or is comprised in, property which has been seized in exercise, or purported exercise, of the power of seizure conferred by section 448(3) of the Companies Act 1985 (c 6) shall be taken for the purposes of this Part to be an item subject to legal privilege if, and only if, the seizure of that item was in contravention of section 452(2) of that Act (privileged information).

    (5) An item which is, or is comprised in, property which has been seized in exercise, or purported exercise, of the power of seizure conferred by Article 441(3) of the Companies (Northern Ireland) Order 1986 (SI 1986/1032 (NI 6)) shall be taken for the purposes of this Part to be an item subject to legal privilege if, and only if, the seizure of that item was in contravention of Article 445(2) of that Order (privileged information).

    (6) An item which is, or is comprised in, property which has been seized in exercise, or purported exercise, of the power of seizure conferred by sub-paragraph (2) of paragraph 3 of Schedule 2 to the Timeshare Act 1992 (c 35) shall be taken for the purposes of this Part to be an item subject to legal privilege if, and only if, the seizure of that item was in contravention of sub-paragraph (4) of that paragraph (privileged documents).

    (7) An item which is, or is comprised in, property which has been seized in exercise, or purported exercise, of the power of seizure conferred by paragraph 1 of Schedule 9 to the Data Protection Act 1998 (c 29) shall be taken for the purposes of this Part to be an item subject to legal privilege if, and only if, the seizure of that item was in contravention of paragraph 9 of that Schedule (privileged communications).

    (8) An item which is, or is comprised in, property which has been seized in exercise, or purported exercise, of the power of seizure conferred by paragraph 1 of Schedule 3 to the Freedom of Information Act 2000 (c 36) shall be taken for the purposes of this Part to be an item subject to legal privilege if, and only if, the seizure of that item was in contravention of paragraph 9 of that Schedule (privileged communications).

    [(8A) An item which is, or is comprised in, property which has been seized in exercise, or purported exercise, of the power of seizure conferred by section 227C of the Enterprise Act 2002 (c 40) shall be taken for the purposes of this Part to be an item subject to legal privilege if, and only if, the seizure of that item was in contravention of section 227B(4) of that Act (privileged items).]

(9)   An item which is, or is comprised in, property which has been seized in exercise, or purported exercise, of so much of any power of seizure conferred by section 50 as is exercisable by reference to a power of seizure conferred by—

- (a)   section 448(3) of the Companies Act 1985,
- (b)   Article 441(3) of the Companies (Northern Ireland) Order 1986,
- (c)   paragraph 3(2) of Schedule 2 to the Timeshare Act 1992,
- (d)   paragraph 1 of Schedule 9 to the Data Protection Act 1998 . . .
- (e)   paragraph 1 of Schedule 3 to the Freedom of Information Act 2000, [or
- (f)   section 227C of the Enterprise Act 2002,]

shall be taken for the purposes of this Part to be an item subject to legal privilege if, and only if, the item would have been taken for the purposes of this Part to be an item subject to legal privilege had it been seized under the power of seizure by reference to which the power conferred by section 50 was exercised.

NOTES

Sub-s (1): words in para (b) substituted by the Proceeds of Crime Act 2002, s 456, Sch 11 paras 1, 40(1), (5)(a).

Sub-s (3): to be repealed by the Finance Act 2007, ss 84(4), 114, Sch 22, Pt 2, paras 3, 13(1)(c), Sch 27, Pt 5(1) with effect from a date to be appointed.

Sub-s (3A): inserted by the Proceeds of Crime Act 2002, s 456, Sch 11 paras 1, 40(1), (5)(b).

Sub-s (8A): inserted by the Enterprise Act 2002 (Amendment) Regulations, SI 2006/3363, regs 24, 26(1).

Sub-s (9): in para (d) word repealed by the Enterprise Act 2002 (Amendment) Regulations, SI 2006/3363, regs 24, 26(2); para (f) and word "or" immediately preceding it inserted by the Enterprise Act 2002 (Amendment) Regulations, SI 2006/3363, regs 24, 26(3).

66   General interpretation of Part 2

(1)   In this Part—

"appropriate judicial authority" has the meaning given by section 64;

"documents" includes information recorded in any form;

"item subject to legal privilege" shall be construed in accordance with section 65;

"premises" includes any vehicle, stall or moveable structure (including an offshore installation) and any other place whatever, whether or not occupied as land;

"offshore installation" has the same meaning as in the Mineral Workings (Offshore Installations) Act 1971 (c 61);

"return", in relation to seized property, shall be construed in accordance with section 58, and cognate expressions shall be construed accordingly;

"seize", and cognate expressions, shall be construed in accordance with section 63(1) and subsection (5) below;

"seized property", in relation to any exercise of a power of seizure, means (subject to subsection (5)) anything seized in exercise of that power; and

"vehicle" includes any vessel, aircraft or hovercraft.

(2)   In this Part references, in relation to a time when seized property is in any person's possession in consequence of a seizure ("the relevant time"), to something for which the person making the seizure had power to search shall be construed—

- (a)   where the seizure was made on the occasion of a search carried out on the authority of a warrant, as including anything of the description of things the presence or suspected presence of which provided grounds for the issue of the warrant;
- (b)   where the property was seized in the course of a search on the occasion of which it would have been lawful for the person carrying out the

search to seize anything which on that occasion was believed by him to be, or appeared to him to be, of a particular description, as including—

    (i)   anything which at the relevant time is believed by the person in possession of the seized property, or (as the case may be) appears to him, to be of that description; and

    (ii)   anything which is in fact of that description;

(c)   where the property was seized in the course of a search on the occasion of which it would have been lawful for the person carrying out the search to seize anything which there were on that occasion reasonable grounds for believing was of a particular description, as including—

    (i)   anything which there are at the relevant time reasonable grounds for believing is of that description; and

    (ii)   anything which is in fact of that description;

(d)   where the property was seized in the course of a search to which neither paragraph (b) nor paragraph (c) applies, as including anything which is of a description of things which, on the occasion of the search, it would have been lawful for the person carrying it out to seize otherwise than under section 50 and 51; and

(e)   where the property was seized on the occasion of a search authorised under section 82 of the Terrorism Act 2000 (c 11) (seizure of items suspected to have been, or to be intended to be, used in commission of certain offences), as including anything—

    (i)   which is or has been, or is or was intended to be, used in the commission of an offence such as is mentioned in subsection (3)(a) or (b) of that section; or

    (ii)   which at the relevant time the person who is in possession of the seized property reasonably suspects is something falling within sub-paragraph (i).

(3)   For the purpose of determining in accordance with subsection (2), in relation to any time, whether or to what extent property seized on the occasion of a search authorised under section 9 of the Official Secrets Act 1911 (c 28) (seizure of evidence of offences under that Act having been or being about to be committed) is something for which the person making the seizure had power to search, subsection (1) of that section shall be construed—

(a)   as if the reference in that subsection to evidence of an offence under that Act being about to be committed were a reference to evidence of such an offence having been, at the time of the seizure, about to be committed; and

(b)   as if the reference in that subsection to reasonable ground for suspecting that such an offence is about to be committed were a reference to reasonable ground for suspecting that at the time of the seizure such an offence was about to be committed.

(4)   References in subsection (2) to a search include references to any activities authorised by virtue of any of the following—

(a)   section 28(1) of the Trade Descriptions Act 1968 (c 29) (power to enter premises and to inspect and seize goods and documents);

(b)   section 29(1) of the Fair Trading Act 1973 (c 41) (power to enter premises and to inspect and seize goods and documents);

(c)   paragraph 9 of the Schedule to the Prices Act 1974 (c 24) (powers of entry and inspection);

(d)   section 162(1) of the Consumer Credit Act 1974 (c 39) (powers of entry and inspection);

(e) *section 11(1) of the Estate Agents Act 1979* (c 38) (powers of entry and inspection);

(f) Schedule 9 to the Weights and Measures (Northern Ireland) Order 1981 (SI 1981/231 (NI 10));

[(g) section 79 of the Weights and Measures Act 1985 (c 72) or Schedule 7 to the Weights and Measures (Packaged Goods) Regulations 2006 (powers of entry and inspection etc);]

(h) section 29 of the Consumer Protection Act 1987 (c 43) (powers of search etc);

(i) Article 22 of the Consumer Protection (Northern Ireland) Order 1987 (SI 1987/2049 (NI 20));

(j) section 32(5) of the Food Safety Act 1990 (c 16) (power to inspect records relating to a food business);

(k) paragraph 3 of the Schedule to the Property Misdescriptions Act 1991 (c 29) (powers of seizure etc);

(l) Article 33(6) of the Food Safety (Northern Ireland) Order 1991 (SI 1991/762 (NI 7));

(m) paragraph 3 of Schedule 2 to the Timeshare Act 1992 (c 35) (powers of officers of enforcement authority);

[(ma) section 227C of the Enterprise Act 2002 (power to enter premises with warrant)]

[(n) paragraph 2 of Schedule 5 to the Human Tissue Act 2004 (entry and inspection of licensed premises);]

[(o) regulation 22 of the General Product Safety Regulations 2005 (powers of entry and search etc)]

[(p) sections 26(1), 27(1), 28(1) and 29(1) of the Animal Welfare Act 2006 (inspection in connection with licences, inspection in connection with registration, inspection of farm premises and inspection relating to Community obligations)]

(5) References in this Part to a power of seizure include references to each of the powers to take possession of items under—

(a) . . .

(b) section 448(3) of the Companies Act 1985 (c 6);

(c) . . .

(d) Article 441(3) of the Companies (Northern Ireland) Order 1986 (SI 1986/1032 (NI 6));

(e) . . .

(f) section 2(5) of the Criminal Justice Act 1987 (c 38);

(g) section 40(2) of the Human Fertilisation and Embryology Act 1990 (c 37);

(h) section 28(2)(c) of the Competition Act 1998 (c 41); and

(i) section 176(5) of the Financial Services and Markets Act 2000 (c 8);

and references in this Part to seizure and to seized property shall be construed accordingly.

(6) In this Part, so far as it applies to England and Wales—

(a) references to excluded material shall be construed in accordance with section 11 of the 1984 Act (meaning of "excluded material"); and

(b) references to special procedure material shall be construed in accordance with section 14 of that Act (meaning of "special procedure material").

(7) In this Part, so far as it applies to Northern Ireland—

(a)   references to excluded material shall be construed in accordance with Article 13 of the Police and Criminal Evidence (Northern Ireland) Order 1989 (SI 1989/1341 (NI 12)) (meaning of "excluded material"); and

(b)   references to special procedure material shall be construed in accordance with Article 16 of that Order (meaning of "special procedure material").

(8)   References in this Part to any item or material being comprised in other property include references to its being mixed with that other property.

(9)   In this Part "enactment" includes an enactment contained in Northern Ireland legislation.

NOTES

Sub-s (4): in para (e) words "section 11(1) to (1C) of the Estate Agents Act 1979" to be substituted for words in italics by the Consumers, Estate Agents and Redress Act 2007, s 63(1), Sch 7, para 22(a) with effect from a date to be appointed.

Sub-s (4): para (g) substituted by the Weights and Measures (Packaged Goods) Regulations, SI 2006/659, reg 1(2), Sch 1, Pt 2, paras (24), (26); para (ma) inserted by the Enterprise Act 2002 (Amendment) Regulations, SI 2006/3363, regs 24, 27; para (n) inserted by Human Tissue Act 2004 s 56, Sch 6 para 5; para (o) inserted by the General Product Safety Regulations, SI 2005/1803 reg 47(2), (3); para (p) inserted by the Animal Welfare Act 2006, s 64, Sch 3, para 14(2) in relation to England and Wales (in relation to Scotland and Northern Ireland from a date to be appointed).

Sub-s (5): paras (a), (c), (e) repealed by the Financial Services and Markets Act 2000 (Consequential Amendments and Repeals) Order, SI 2001/3649 art 364(c).

Supplemental provisions of Part 2

67 Application to *customs officers*

The powers conferred by section 114(2) of the 1984 Act and Article 85(1) of the Police and Criminal Evidence (Northern Ireland) Order 1989 (application of provisions relating to police officers to *customs officers*) shall have effect in relation to the provisions of this Part as they have effect in relation to the provisions of that Act or, as the case may be, that Order.

NOTES

Section heading: words "officers of Revenue and Customs" to be substituted for words "customs officers", by the Finance Act 2007, s 84(4), Sch 22, Pt 1, para 2 with effect from a date to be appointed.

Words "officers of Revenue and Customs" to be substituted for words "customs officers", by the Finance Act 2007, s 84(4), Sch 22, Pt 1, para 2 with effect from a date to be appointed.

68 Application to Scotland

(1)   In the application of this Part to Scotland—

(a)   subsection (4) of section 54 and subsection (10) of section 59 shall each have effect with the omission of paragraph (c) of that subsection;

(b)   section 55 and subsection (3)(c) of section 59 shall be omitted; and

(c)   Schedule 1 shall have effect as if the powers specified in that Schedule did not include any power of seizure under any enactment mentioned in that Schedule, so far as it is exercisable in Scotland by a constable, except a power conferred by an enactment mentioned in subsection (2).

(2)   Those enactments are—

(a)   section 43(5) of the Gaming Act 1968 (c 65);

(b)   . . .

    (c)   section 448(3) of the Companies Act 1985 (c 6);

    (d)   . . .

    (e)   . . .

    (f)   section 176(5) of the Financial Services and Markets Act 2000 (c 8).

NOTES

Sub-s (2): paras (b), (d), (e) repealed by the Financial Services and Markets Act 2000 (Consequential Amendments and Repeals) Order, SI 2001/3649 art 364(d).

---

69 Application to powers designated by order

(1)   The Secretary of State may by order—

    (a)   provide for any power designated by the order to be added to those specified in Schedule 1 or section 63(2);

    (b)   make any modification of the provisions of this Part which the Secretary of State considers appropriate in consequence of any provision made by virtue of paragraph (a);

    (c)   make any modification of any enactment making provision in relation to seizures, or things seized, under a power designated by an order under this subsection which the Secretary of State considers appropriate in consequence of any provision made by virtue of that paragraph.

(2)   Where the power designated by the order made under subsection (1) is a power conferred in relation to Scotland, the Secretary of State shall consult the Scottish Ministers before making the order.

(3)   The power to make an order under subsection (1) shall be exercisable by statutory instrument; and no such order shall be made unless a draft of it has been laid before Parliament and approved by a resolution of each House.

(4)   In this section "modification" includes any exclusion, extension or application.

70 Consequential applications and amendments of enactments

Schedule 2 (which applies enactments in relation to provision made by this Part and contains minor and consequential amendments) shall have effect.

PART 6
MISCELLANEOUS AND SUPPLEMENTAL

Supplemental

136 General interpretation

In this Act—

"the 1984 Act" means the Police and Criminal Evidence Act 1984;

"the 1996 Act" means the Police Act 1996; and

"the 1997 Act" means the Police Act 1997.

NOTES

Commencement: 19 June 2001, by virtue of SI 2001/2223.

---

138 Short title, commencement and extent

(1)   This Act may be cited as the Criminal Justice and Police Act 2001.

(2)   The provisions of this Act, other than this section and sections 42 and 43, 81 to 85, 109, 116(7) and 119(7), shall come into force on such day as the Secretary

of State may by order made by statutory instrument appoint; and different days may be appointed under this subsection for different purposes.

(3)   An order under subsection (2) may contain such savings as the Secretary of State thinks fit.

(4)   Section 85 comes into force at the end of the period of two months beginning with the day on which this Act is passed.

(5)   Subject to subsections (6) to (12), this Act extends to England and Wales only.

(6)   The following provisions of this Act extend to the United Kingdom—

    (a)   sections 33 to 38;

    (b)   Part 2;

    (c)   section 86(1) and (2);

    (d)   . . .

    (e)   section 127; and

    (f)   section 136 and this section.

(7)   Except in so far as it contains provision relating to the matters mentioned in section 745(1) of the Companies Act 1985 (c 6) (companies registered or incorporated in Northern Ireland or outside Great Britain), section 45 extends to Great Britain only.

(8)   Section 126 extends to Great Britain only.

(9)   Sections 29, 39 to 41, 72, 75, 84 and 134 extend to England and Wales and Northern Ireland only.

(10)   Section 83 extends to Northern Ireland only.

(11)   Section 86(3) has the same extent as section 27 of the Petty Sessions (Ireland) Act 1851 (c 93).

(12)   An amendment, repeal or revocation contained in Schedule 4, 6 or 7 has the same extent as the enactment or instrument to which it relates.

NOTES

Sub-s (6): para (d) repealed by the Serious Organised Crime and Police Act 2005 s 59, Sch 4 para 167.

SCHEDULE 1
POWERS OF SEIZURE

Sections 50, 51 & 55

PART 1
POWERS TO WHICH SECTION 50 APPLIES

. . .

Customs and Excise Management Act 1979 (c 2)

23.

The power of seizure conferred by section 118C(4) of the Customs and Excise Management Act 1979 (seizure of evidence of fraud offences).

. . .

NOTES

Provisions omitted are outside the scope of this work.

SCHEDULE 2
APPLICATIONS AND MINOR AND CONSEQUENTIAL AMENDMENTS
Section 70

PART 1
APPLICATION OF ENACTMENTS

. . .

Disclosure of information

11

Any provision which—

(a) restricts the disclosure, or permits the disclosure only for limited purposes or in limited circumstances, of information obtained through the exercise of a power of seizure specified in Part 1 or 2 of Schedule 1, or

(b) confers power to make provision which does either or both of those things,

shall apply in relation to information obtained under section 50 or 51 in reliance on the power in question as it applies in relation to information obtained through the exercise of that power.

Interpretation

12

For the purposes of this Part of this Schedule, an item is seized, or information is obtained, under section 50 or 51 in reliance on a power of seizure if the item is seized, or the information obtained, in exercise of so much of any power conferred by that section as is exercisable by reference to that power of seizure.

NOTES

Provisions omitted are outside the scope of this work.

ANTI-TERRORISM, CRIME AND SECURITY ACT 2001

(2001 c 24)

ARRANGEMENT OF SECTIONS

PART 3
DISCLOSURE OF INFORMATION

PART 14
SUPPLEMENTAL

An Act to amend the Terrorism Act 2000; to make further provision about terrorism and security;. . . and for connected purposes.

[14 December 2001]

PART 3
DISCLOSURE OF INFORMATION

17 Extension of existing disclosure powers

(1) This section applies to the provisions listed in Schedule 4, so far as they authorise the disclosure of information.

(2) Each of the provisions to which this section applies shall have effect, in relation to the disclosure of information by or on behalf of a public authority, as if the purposes for which the disclosure of information is authorised by that provision included each of the following—

(a)   the purposes of any criminal investigation whatever which is being or may be carried out, whether in the United Kingdom or elsewhere;

(b)   the purposes of any criminal proceedings whatever which have been or may be initiated, whether in the United Kingdom or elsewhere;

(c)   the purposes of the initiation or bringing to an end of any such investigation or proceedings;

(d)   the purpose of facilitating a determination of whether any such investigation or proceedings should be initiated or brought to an end.

(3)   The Treasury may by order made by statutory instrument add any provision contained in any subordinate legislation to the provisions to which this section applies.

(4)   The Treasury shall not make an order under subsection (3) unless a draft of it has been laid before Parliament and approved by a resolution of each House.

(5)   No disclosure of information shall be made by virtue of this section unless the public authority by which the disclosure is made is satisfied that the making of the disclosure is proportionate to what is sought to be achieved by it.

(6)   Nothing in this section shall be taken to prejudice any power to disclose information which exists apart from this section.

(7)   The information that may be disclosed by virtue of this section includes information obtained before the commencement of this section.

18 Restriction on disclosure of information for overseas purposes

(1)   Subject to subsections (2) and (3), the Secretary of State may give a direction which—

(a)   specifies any overseas proceedings or any description of overseas proceedings; and

(b)   prohibits the making of any relevant disclosure for the purposes of those proceedings or, as the case may be, of proceedings of that description.

(2)   In subsection (1) the reference, in relation to a direction, to a relevant disclosure is a reference to a disclosure authorised by any of the provisions to which section 17 applies which—

(a)   is made for a purpose mentioned in subsection (2)(a) to (d) of that section; and

(b)   is a disclosure of any such information as is described in the direction.

(3)   The Secretary of State shall not give a direction under this section unless it appears to him that the overseas proceedings in question, or that overseas proceedings of the description in question, relate or would relate—

(a)   to a matter in respect of which it would be more appropriate for any jurisdiction or investigation to be exercised or carried out by a court or other authority of the United Kingdom, or of a particular part of the United Kingdom;

    (b)   to a matter in respect of which it would be more appropriate for any jurisdiction or investigation to be exercised or carried out by a court or other authority of a third country; or

    (c)   to a matter that would fall within paragraph (a) or (b)—

        (i)   if it were appropriate for there to be any exercise of jurisdiction or investigation at all; and

        (ii)   if (where one does not exist) a court or other authority with the necessary jurisdiction or functions existed in the United Kingdom, in the part of the United Kingdom in question or, as the case may be, in the third country in question.

(4)   A direction under this section shall not have the effect of prohibiting—

    (a)   the making of any disclosure by a Minister of the Crown or by the Treasury; or

    (b)   the making of any disclosure in pursuance of a Community obligation.

(5)   A direction under this section—

    (a)   may prohibit the making of disclosures absolutely or in such cases, or subject to such conditions as to consent or otherwise, as may be specified in it; and

    (b)   must be published or otherwise issued by the Secretary of State in such manner as he considers appropriate for bringing it to the attention of persons likely to be affected by it.

(6)   A person who, knowing of any direction under this section, discloses any information in contravention of that direction shall be guilty of an offence and liable—

    (a)   on conviction on indictment, to imprisonment for a term not exceeding two years or to a fine or to both;

    (b)   on summary conviction, to imprisonment for a term not exceeding three months or to a fine not exceeding the statutory maximum or to both.

(7)   The following are overseas proceedings for the purposes of this section—

    (a)   criminal proceedings which are taking place, or will or may take place, in a country or territory outside the United Kingdom;

    (b)   a criminal investigation which is being, or will or may be, conducted by an authority of any such country or territory.

(8)   References in this section, in relation to any proceedings or investigation, to a third country are references to any country or territory outside the United Kingdom which is not the country or territory where the proceedings are taking place, or will or may take place or, as the case may be, is not the country or territory of the authority which is conducting the investigation, or which will or may conduct it.

(9)   In this section "court" includes a tribunal of any description.

19 Disclosure of information held by revenue departments

(1)   This section applies to information which is held by or on behalf of the Commissioners of Inland Revenue or by or on behalf of the Commissioners of Customs and Excise, including information obtained before the coming into force of this section.

(2)   No obligation of secrecy imposed by statute or otherwise prevents the disclosure, in accordance with the following provisions of this section, of information to which this section applies if the disclosure is made—

    (a)   for the purpose of facilitating the carrying out by any of the intelligence services of any of that service's functions;

(b)   for the purposes of any criminal investigation whatever which is being or may be carried out, whether in the United Kingdom or elsewhere;

(c)   for the purposes of any criminal proceedings whatever which have been or may be initiated, whether in the United Kingdom or elsewhere;

(d)   for the purposes of the initiation or bringing to an end of any such investigation or proceedings; or

(e)   for the purpose of facilitating a determination of whether any such investigation or proceedings should be initiated or brought to an end.

(3)   No disclosure of information to which this section applies shall be made by virtue of this section unless the person by whom the disclosure is made is satisfied that the making of the disclosure is proportionate to what is sought to be achieved by it.

(4)   Information to which this section applies shall not be disclosed by virtue of this section except by the Commissioners by or on whose behalf it is held or with their authority.

(5)   Information obtained by means of a disclosure authorised by subsection (2) shall not be further disclosed except—

(a)   for a purpose mentioned in that subsection; and

(b)   with the consent of the Commissioners by whom or with whose authority it was initially disclosed;

and information so obtained otherwise than by or on behalf of any of the intelligence services shall not be further disclosed (with or without such consent) to any of those services, or to any person acting on behalf of any of those services, except for a purpose mentioned in paragraphs (b) to (e) of that subsection.

(6)   A consent for the purposes of subsection (5) may be given either in relation to a particular disclosure or in relation to disclosures made in such circumstances as may be specified or described in the consent.

(7)   Nothing in this section authorises the making of any disclosure which is prohibited by any provision of the Data Protection Act 1998.

(8)   References in this section to information which is held on behalf of the Commissioners of Inland Revenue or of the Commissioners of Customs and Excise include references to information which—

(a)   is held by a person who provides services to the Commissioners of Inland Revenue or, as the case may be, to the Commissioners of Customs and Excise; and

(b)   is held by that person in connection with the provision of those services.

(9)   In this section "intelligence service" has the same meaning as in the Regulation of Investigatory Powers Act 2000.

(10)   Nothing in this section shall be taken to prejudice any power to disclose information which exists apart from this section.

20 Interpretation of Part 3

(1)   In this Part—

"criminal investigation" means an investigation of any criminal conduct, including an investigation of alleged or suspected criminal conduct and an investigation of whether criminal conduct has taken place;

"information" includes—

(a)   documents; and

(b)   in relation to a disclosure authorised by a provision to which section 17 applies, anything that falls to be treated as information for the purposes of that provision;

"public authority" has the same meaning as in section 6 of the Human Rights Act 1998; and

"subordinate legislation" has the same meaning as in the Interpretation Act 1978.

(2) Proceedings outside the United Kingdom shall not be taken to be criminal proceedings for the purposes of this Part unless the conduct with which the defendant in those proceedings is charged is criminal conduct or conduct which, to a substantial extent, consists of criminal conduct.

(3) In this section—

"conduct" includes acts, omissions and statements; and

"criminal conduct" means any conduct which—

(a)   constitutes one or more criminal offences under the law of a part of the United Kingdom; or

(b)   is, or corresponds to, conduct which, if it all took place in a particular part of the United Kingdom, would constitute one or more offences under the law of that part of the United Kingdom.

PART 14
SUPPLEMENTAL

127 Commencement

(1) Except as provided in subsections (2) to (4), this Act comes into force on such day as the Secretary of State may appoint by order.

(2) The following provisions come into force on the day on which this Act is passed—

(a)   Parts 2 to 6,

(b)–(h) . . .

(i)   this Part, except section 125 and Schedule 8 so far as they relate to the entries—

(i)   in Part 1 of Schedule 8,

(ii)   in Part 5 of Schedule 8, in respect of the Nuclear Installations Act 1965,

(iii)   in Part 6 of Schedule 8, in respect of the British Transport Commission Act 1962 and the Ministry of Defence Police Act 1987, so far as those entries extend to Scotland,

(iv)   in Part 7 of Schedule 8, in respect of Schedule 5 to the Terrorism Act 2000.

(3), (4) . . .

(5) Different days may be appointed for different provisions and for different purposes.

(6) An order under this section—

(a)   must be made by statutory instrument, and

(b)   may contain incidental, supplemental, consequential or transitional provision.

NOTE

Sub-ss (2)(b)–(h), (3), (4) are outside the scope of this work.

---

129 Short title

This Act may be cited as the Anti-terrorism, Crime and Security Act 2001.

EUROPEAN COMMUNITIES (AMENDMENT) ACT 2002

(2002 c 3)

An Act to make provision consequential on the Treaty signed at Nice on 26th February 2001 amending the Treaty on European Union, the Treaties establishing the European Communities and certain related Acts.

[26 February 2002]

1 Incorporation of provisions of the Treaty of Nice

(1) *(Amends the European Communities Act 1972)*

(2) Her Majesty may by Order in Council amend the definition referred to in subsection (1) so as to add to it provisions adopted by the Council of the European Communities under Article 229a of the Treaty establishing the European Community (provisions conferring jurisdiction on the European Court in connection with Community industrial property rights).

(3) No recommendation may be made to Her Majesty to make an Order in Council under subsection (2) unless a draft of the Order has been laid before and approved by a resolution of each House of Parliament.

2 References to the European Court etc

(Amends the European Communities Act 1972 Sch 1 Pt 2)

3 Approval of increase in powers of European Parliament

For the purpose of section 6 of the European Parliamentary Elections Act 1978 (c 10) (approval of treaties increasing the Parliament's powers) the Treaty signed at Nice on 26th February 2001 amending the Treaty on European Union, the Treaties establishing the European Communities and certain related Acts is approved.

4 Short title

This Act may be cited as the European Communities (Amendment) Act 2002.

FINANCE ACT 2002

(2002 c 23)

ARRANGEMENT OF SECTIONS

PART 1
EXCISE DUTIES

An Act to grant certain duties, to alter other duties, and to amend the law relating to National Debt and the Public Revenue, and to make further provision in connection with Finance.

[24 July 2002]

PART 1
EXCISE DUTIES

Tobacco products duty

1 Rates of tobacco products duty

(1)   (*Substitutes Tobacco Products Duty Act 1979 Sch 1 Table of rates of duty*)

(2)   This section shall be deemed to have come into force at 6 o'clock in the evening of 17th April 2002.

Alcoholic liquor duties

2 Rates of duty on cider

(1)   (*Amends the Alcoholic Liquor Duties Act 1979 s 62(1A)*)

(2)   This section shall be deemed to have come into force on 28th April 2002.

3 Duty on beverages made with spirits to be at spirits rate

(1)   (*Repeals the Alcoholic Liquor Duties Act 1979 s 1(9)*)

(2)   This section shall be deemed to have come into force on 28th April 2002.

4 Reduced rates of duty on beer from small breweries

(1)   Schedule 1 to this Act (which makes provision for the excise duty on beer to be charged at reduced rates on beer produced in small breweries) has effect.

(2)   Subject to subsection (3), subsection (1) shall be deemed to have come into force on 1st June 2002.

(3)   So far as relating to—

    (a)   the insertion by paragraph 2 of that Schedule of the new section 36H of the Alcoholic Liquor Duties Act 1979, and

    (b)   paragraph 3 of that Schedule, subsection (1) comes into force on the day on which this Act is passed.

Hydrocarbon oil duties

5 Biodiesel

(1)   The Hydrocarbon Oil Duties Act 1979 (c 5) is amended as follows.

(2)   (*Inserts s 2AA*)

(3)   (*Inserts s 2A(1A)*)

(4)   (*Inserts ss 6AA–6AC*)

(5)   Schedule 2 to this Act contains minor and consequential amendments of the Hydrocarbon Oil Duties Act 1979 (c 5).

(6)   Subsection (4), and subsection (5) so far as relating to paragraphs 2 and 4(1) of that Schedule, have effect in relation to biodiesel that—

(a)   is set aside for chargeable use (as defined in the section 6AA inserted by subsection (4)) after such date as the Commissioners of Customs and Excise may by order made by statutory instrument appoint, or

(b)   not having been so set aside, is the subject of such chargeable use after that date,

and has not been set aside for chargeable use under section 6A of that Act (fuel substitutes) on or before that date.

(7)   Subsection (4), and subsection (5) so far as relating to paragraph 2 of that Schedule, have effect in relation to bioblend that—

(a)   is imported into the United Kingdom after the date appointed under subsection (6)(a), or

(b)   not having been so imported—

(i)   is produced in the United Kingdom and delivered for home use after that date, and

(ii)   has not been set aside for chargeable use under section 6A of that Act (fuel substitutes) on or before that date.

(8)   Subsection (5)—

(a)   so far as relating to paragraph 3 of that Schedule, comes into force on the day after the date appointed under subsection (6)(a),

(b)   so far as relating to paragraph 5 of that Schedule, applies to mixtures produced after the date appointed under subsection (6)(a), and

(c)   so far as relating to paragraph 7 of that Schedule, comes into force on such day as the Commissioners of Customs and Excise may by order made by statutory instrument appoint.

6 Regulating trade in rebated heavy oil etc

(1)   Schedule 3 to this Act has effect.

(2)   In that Schedule—

Part 1 makes provision for regulating trade in certain heavy oil on which rebate of excise duty has been allowed, and

Part 2 amends provisions of the Hydrocarbon Oil Duties Act 1979 relating to rebates.

(3)   Subject to subsection (4), subsection (1) so far as relating to paragraph 1 of that Schedule shall not come into force until such day as the Commissioners of Customs and Excise may appoint by order made by statutory instrument.

(4)   For the purpose of the exercise of any power to make regulations, subsection (1) so far as relating to that paragraph comes into force on the day on which this Act is passed.

7 Fuel substitutes

(1)   (*Amends the Hydrocarbon Oil Duties Act 1979 s 6A(5), (6)(a)*)

(2)   (*Amends the Finance Act 1993 s 10(2), (3)*)

General

21 Drawback of excise duty

(1)   (*Amends the Customs and Excise Management Act 1979 s 133*)

(2)   In section 14(1) of the Finance Act 1994 (c 9) (reviewable decisions) after paragraph (bb) insert—

"(bc) any decision by the Commissioners as to whether or not any person is entitled to any drawback of excise duty by virtue of regulations under section 2 of the Finance (No 2) Act 1992, or the amount of the drawback to which any person is so entitled;".

(3)   The amendment made by subsection (2) does not apply in relation to decisions made before the day on which this Act comes into force.

Air passenger duty

121 Air passenger duty: extension of area to which EEA rates apply

(1)–(4)   (*Amend the Finance Act 1994, s 30*)

(5)   This section applies to any carriage of a passenger on an aircraft which begins on or after 1st November 2002.

Supplementary

138 Repeals

(1)   The enactments mentioned in Schedule 39 to this Act (which include provisions that are spent or of no practical utility) are repealed to the extent specified.

(2)   The repeals specified in that Schedule have effect subject to the commencement provisions and savings contained or referred to in the notes set out in that Schedule.

140 Short title
This Act may be cited as the Finance Act 2002.

SCHEDULES

SCHEDULE 1

BEER FROM SMALL BREWERIES: REDUCED RATE OF DUTY

Section 4

(Amends the Alcoholic Liquor Duties Act 1979 s 36, inserts ss 36A–36H; adds the Alcoholic Liquor Duties Act 1979 s 49(1)(k), amends the Finance Act 1994 ss 12A(3)(bb), 12B(2), 14(1)(ba))

SCHEDULE 2

HYDROCARBON OIL DUTIES: MINOR AND CONSEQUENTIAL
AMENDMENTS RELATING TO BIODIESEL

Section 5

(Amends the Hydrocarbon Oil Duties Act 1979 s 6A, 6AB, 20AAA(3), 20AAB(1), 22(1A), 27, Sch 2A paras 9, 10, Sch 4, para 3, inserts ss 11(6), 17A, 20AAA(2B), 22(1AA), Sch 2A Pt 2B)

SCHEDULE 3
HYDROCARBON OIL DUTIES: REBATED HEAVY OIL ETC
Section 6
PART 1
REGULATING TRADERS IN REBATED HEAVY OIL

(Inserts the Hydrocarbon Oil Duties Act 1979 ss 23A, 23B, 24AA, Customs and Excise Management Act 1979 s 100H(1)(p); amends the Hydrocarbon Oil Duties Act 1979 s 27)

PART 2
MINOR AMENDMENTS RELATING TO REBATES

(Amends the Hydrocarbon Oil Duties Act 1979 ss 12, 24, 27)

SCHEDULE 39
REPEALS
Section 138
PART 1
EXCISE DUTIES

(1)
ALCOHOLIC LIQUOR DUTIES

Short title and chapter	Extent of repeal
Alcoholic Liquor Duties Act 1979 (c 4)	Section 1(9).

This repeal shall be deemed to have come into force on 27th April 2002.

(2)
HYDROCARBON OIL DUTIES

Short title and chapter	Extent of repeal
Hydrocarbon Oil Duties Act 1979 (c 5)	In section 6AB(1), the words from "and delivered" to the end.
Finance Act 1998 (c 36)	Section 9(2) and (3).

1. The repeal in the Hydrocarbon Oil Duties Act 1979 has effect in accordance with section 5(8)(c) of this Act.

2. The repeals in the Finance Act 1988 have effect in accordance with section 5(8)(b) of this Act.

(b)   engages in any conduct by which he contravenes a duty, obligation, requirement or condition imposed by or under legislation relating to any relevant tax or duty.

(2) For the purposes of this Part "relevant tax or duty" means any of the following—

(a)   customs duty;

(b)   Community export duty;

(c)   Community import duty;

(d)   import VAT;

(e)   customs duty of a preferential tariff country.

(3) In this Part—

"appeal tribunal" means a VAT and duties tribunal;

"the Commissioners" means the Commissioners of Customs and Excise;

"the Community Customs Code" means Council Regulation 2913/92/EEC establishing the Community Customs Code;

"Community export duty" means any of the duties, charges or levies which are export duties within the meaning of the Community Customs Code (as at 9th April 2003, see the definition of "export duties" in Article 4(11) of that Code);

"Community import duty" means any of the duties, charges or levies which are import duties within the meaning of the Community Customs Code (as at 9th April 2003, see the definition of "import duties" in Article 4(10) of that Code);

"contravene" includes fail to comply with;

"customs duty of a preferential tariff country" includes a reference to any charge imposed by a preferential tariff country and having an equivalent effect to customs duty payable on the importation of goods into the territory of that country;

"demand notice" means a demand notice within the meaning of section 30;

"import VAT" means value added tax chargeable by virtue of section 1(1)(c) of the Value Added Tax Act 1994 (c 23) (importation of goods from places outside the member States);

"notice" means notice in writing;

"preferential tariff country" means a country outside the European Community which is, or is a member of a group of countries which is, party to an agreement falling within Article 20(3)(d) of the Community Customs Code (preferential tariff agreements with the Community);

"prescribed" means specified in, or determined in accordance with, regulations made by the Treasury;

"relevant rule", in relation to any relevant tax or duty, has the meaning given by subsection (8) of section 26 (as read with subsection (9) of that section);

"representative", in relation to any person, means—

(a)   his personal representative,

(b)   his trustee in bankruptcy or interim or permanent trustee,

(c)   any receiver or liquidator appointed in relation to that person or any of his property,

or any other person acting in a representative capacity in relation to that person.

(4) References in this Part to the Community Customs Code are references to that Code as from time to time amended, whether before or after the coming into force of this Part.

(5) The Treasury may by order amend this Part for the purpose of replacing any reference to, or to a provision of,—

(a)   the Community Customs Code, or

(b) any instrument referred to in this Part by virtue of an order under this subsection,

with a reference to, or (as the case may be) to a provision of, a different instrument.

(6) A statutory instrument containing an order under subsection (5) may not be made unless a draft of the instrument has been laid before, and approved by a resolution of, the House of Commons.

(7) Except for this subsection and section 41 (which accordingly come into force on the passing of this Act), this Part comes into force on such day as the Treasury may by order appoint.

The penalties

25 Penalty for evasion

(1) In any case where—

(a) a person engages in any conduct for the purpose of evading any relevant tax or duty, and

(b) his conduct involves dishonesty (whether or not such as to give rise to any criminal liability),

that person is liable to a penalty of an amount equal to the amount of the tax or duty evaded or, as the case may be, sought to be evaded.

(2) Subsection (1) is subject to the following provisions of this Part.

(3) Nothing in this section applies in relation to any customs duty of a preferential tariff country.

(4) Any reference in this section to a person's "evading" any relevant tax or duty includes a reference to his obtaining or securing, without his being entitled to it,—

(a) any repayment, rebate or drawback of any relevant tax or duty,

(b) any relief or exemption from, or any allowance against, any relevant tax or duty, or

(c) any deferral or other postponement of his liability to pay any relevant tax or duty or of the discharge by payment of any such liability,

and also includes a reference to his evading the cancellation of any entitlement to, or the withdrawal of, any such repayment, rebate, drawback, relief, exemption or allowance.

(5) In relation to any such evasion of any relevant tax or duty as is mentioned in subsection (4), the reference in subsection (1) to the amount of the tax or duty evaded or sought to be evaded is a reference to the amount of—

(a) the repayment, rebate or drawback,

(b) the relief, exemption or allowance, or

(c) the payment which, or the liability to make which, is deferred or otherwise postponed,

as the case may be.

(6) Where, by reason of conduct falling within subsection (1) in the case of any relevant tax or duty, a person—

(a) is convicted of an offence,

(b) is given, and has not had withdrawn, a demand notice in respect of a penalty to which he is liable under section 26, or

(c) is liable to a penalty imposed upon him under any other provision of the law relating to that relevant tax or duty,

that conduct does not also give rise to liability to a penalty under this section in respect of that relevant tax or duty.

26 Penalty for contravention of relevant rule

(1) If, in the case of any relevant tax or duty, a person of a prescribed description engages in any conduct by which he contravenes—

    (a)   a prescribed relevant rule, or

    (b)   a relevant rule of a prescribed description,

he is liable to a penalty under this section of a prescribed amount.

(2) Subsection (1) is subject to the following provisions of this Part.

(3) The power conferred by subsection (1) to prescribe a description of person includes power to prescribe any person (without further qualification) as such a description.

(4) Different penalties may be prescribed under subsection (1) for different cases or different circumstances.

(5) Any amount prescribed under subsection (1) as the amount of a penalty must not be more than £2,500.

(6) The Treasury may by order amend subsection (5) by substituting a different amount for the amount for the time being specified in that subsection.

(7) A statutory instrument containing an order under subsection (6) may not be made unless a draft of the instrument has been laid before, and approved by a resolution of, the House of Commons.

(8) In this Part "relevant rule", in relation to any relevant tax or duty, means any duty, obligation, requirement or condition imposed by or under any of the following—

    (a)   the Customs and Excise Management Act 1979, as it applies in relation to the relevant tax or duty;

    (b)   any other Act, or any statutory instrument, as it applies in relation to the relevant tax or duty;

    (c)   in the case of customs duty, Community export duty or Community import duty, Community customs rules;

    (d)   in the case of import VAT, Community customs rules as they apply in relation to import VAT;

    (e)   any directly applicable Community legislation relating to the relevant tax or duty;

    (f)   any relevant international rules applying in relation to the relevant tax or duty.

(9) In subsection (8)—

"Community customs rules" means customs rules, as defined in Article 1 of the Community Customs Code;

"relevant international rules" means international agreements so far as applying in relation to a relevant tax or duty and having effect as part of the law of any part of the United Kingdom by virtue of—

    (a)   any Act or statutory instrument, or

    (b)   any directly applicable Community legislation.

27 Exceptions from section 26

(1) A person is not liable to a penalty under section 26 if he satisfies—

    (a)   the Commissioners, or

    (b)   on appeal, an appeal tribunal,

that there is a reasonable excuse for his conduct.

(2) For the purposes of subsection (1) none of the following is a reasonable excuse—

    (a)   an insufficiency of funds available to any person for paying any relevant tax or duty or any penalty due;

    (b)   that reliance was placed by any person on another to perform any task;

(c)   that the contravention is attributable, in whole or in part, to the conduct of a person on whom reliance to perform any task was so placed.

(3) Where, by reason of conduct falling within subsection (1) of section 26 in the case of any relevant tax or duty, a person—

(a)   is prosecuted for an offence,

(b)   is given, and has not had withdrawn, a demand notice in respect of a penalty to which he is liable under section 25, or

(c)   is liable to a penalty imposed upon him under any other provision of the law relating to that relevant tax or duty,

that conduct does not also give rise to liability to a penalty under section 26 in respect of that relevant tax or duty.

(4) A person is not liable to a penalty under section 26 in respect of any conduct, so far as relating to import VAT, if in respect of that conduct—

(a)   he is liable to a penalty under any of sections 62 to 69A of the Value Added Tax Act 1994 (penalty for contravention of statutory requirements as to VAT), or

(b)   he would be so liable but for section 62(4), 63(11), 64(6), 67(9), 69(9) or 69A(7) of that Act (conduct resulting in conviction, different penalty etc).

28 Liability of directors etc where body corporate liable to penalty for evasion

(1) Where it appears to the Commissioners—

(a)   that a body corporate is liable to a penalty under section 25, and

(b)   that the conduct giving rise to the penalty is, in whole or in part, attributable to the dishonesty of a person who is, or at the material time was, a director or managing officer of the body corporate (a "relevant officer"),

the Commissioners may give a notice under this section to the body corporate (or its representative) and to the relevant officer (or his representative).

(2) A notice under this section must state—

(a)   the amount of the penalty referred to in subsection (1)(a) (the "basic penalty"), and

(b)   that the Commissioners propose, in accordance with this section, to recover from the relevant officer such portion (which may be the whole) of the basic penalty as is specified in the notice.

(3) If a notice is given under this section, this Part shall apply in relation to the relevant officer as if he were personally liable under section 25 to a penalty which corresponds to that portion of the basic penalty specified in the notice.

(4) If a notice is given under this section—

(a)   the amount which may be recovered from the body corporate under this Part is limited to so much (if any) of the basic penalty as is not recoverable from the relevant officer by virtue of subsection (3), and

(b)   the body corporate is to be treated as discharged from liability for so much of the basic penalty as is so recoverable from the relevant officer.

(5) In this section "managing officer", in relation to a body corporate, means—

(a)   a manager, secretary or other similar officer of the body corporate, or

(b)   a person purporting to act in any such capacity or as a director.

(6) Where the affairs of a body corporate are managed by its members, this section applies in relation to the conduct of a member in connection with his functions of management as if he were a director of the body corporate.

Reduction of amount of penalty

29 Reduction of penalty under section 25 or 26

(1)   Where a person is liable to a penalty under section 25 or 26—

(a)   the Commissioners (whether originally or on review) or, on appeal, an appeal tribunal may reduce the penalty to such amount (including nil) as they think proper; and

(b)   the Commissioners on a review, or an appeal tribunal on an appeal, relating to a penalty reduced by the Commissioners under this subsection may cancel the whole or any part of the reduction previously made by the Commissioners.

(2)   In exercising their powers under subsection (1), neither the Commissioners nor an appeal tribunal are entitled to take into account any of the matters specified in subsection (3).

(3)   Those matters are—

(a)   the insufficiency of the funds available to any person for paying any relevant tax or duty or the amount of the penalty,

(b)   the fact that there has, in the case in question or in that case taken with any other cases, been no or no significant loss of any relevant tax or duty,

(c)   the fact that the person liable to the penalty, or a person acting on his behalf, has acted in good faith.

Demand notices

30 Demands for penalties

(1)   Where a person is liable to a penalty under this Part, the Commissioners may give to that person or his representative a notice in writing (a "demand notice") demanding payment of the amount due by way of penalty.

(2)   An amount demanded as due from a person or his representative in accordance with subsection (1) is recoverable as if it were an amount due from the person or, as the case may be, the representative as an amount of customs duty.

This subsection is subject to—

(a)   any appeal under section 36 (appeals to tribunal); and

(b)   subsection (3).

(3)   An amount so demanded is not recoverable if or to the extent that—

(a)   the demand has subsequently been withdrawn; or

(b)   the amount has been reduced under section 29.

31 Time limits for demands for penalties

(1)   A demand notice may not be given—

(a)   in the case of a penalty under section 25, more than 20 years after the conduct giving rise to the liability to the penalty ceased, or

(b)   in the case of a penalty under section 26, more than 3 years after the conduct giving rise to the liability to the penalty ceased.

(2)   A demand notice may not be given more than 2 years after there has come to the knowledge of the Commissioners evidence of facts sufficient in the opinion of the Commissioners to justify the giving of the demand notice.

(3)   A demand notice—

(a)   may be given in respect of a penalty to which a person was liable under section 25 or 26 immediately before his death, but

(b)   in the case of a penalty to which the deceased was so liable under section 25, may not be given more than 3 years after his death.

32 No prosecution after demand notice for penalty under section 26

Where a demand notice is given demanding payment of an amount due by way of penalty under section 26 in respect of any conduct of a person, no proceedings may be brought against that person for any offence constituted by that conduct (whether or not the demand notice is subsequently withdrawn).

Reviews

33 Right to review of certain decisions

(1) If, in the case of any relevant tax or duty, the Commissioners give a person or his representative a notice informing him—

- (a) that they have decided that the person has engaged in conduct by which he contravenes a relevant rule, and
- (b) that the person is, in consequence, liable to a penalty under section 26, but
- (c) that they do not propose to give a demand notice in respect of the penalty,

the person or his representative may give a notice to the Commissioners requiring them to review the decision mentioned in paragraph (a).

(2) Where the Commissioners give a demand notice to a person or his representative, the person or his representative may by notice require the Commissioners to review—

- (a) their decision that the person is liable to a penalty under section 25 or 26, or
- (b) their decision as to the amount of the liability.

(3) Where the Commissioners give a notice under section 28 to a body corporate and to a relevant officer—

- (a) subsection (2) does not apply to any demand notice given in respect of the liability of either of them to a penalty under this Part in respect of the conduct in question, but
- (b) subsections (4) and (5) have effect instead in relation to any such demand notice.

(4) Where the Commissioners give a demand notice to the relevant officer or his representative for a penalty which corresponds to the portion of the basic penalty specified in the notice under section 28, the relevant officer or his representative may by notice require the Commissioners to review—

- (a) their decision that the conduct of the body corporate referred to in section 28(1)(b) is, in whole or in part, attributable to the relevant officer's dishonesty, or
- (b) their decision as to the portion of the basic penalty which the Commissioners are seeking to recover from the relevant officer or his representative.

(5) Where the Commissioners give a demand notice to the body corporate or its representative for so much of the basic penalty as is not recoverable from the relevant officer by virtue of section 28(3), the body corporate or its representative may by notice require the Commissioners to review—

- (a) their decision that the body corporate is liable to a penalty under section 25, or
- (b) their decision as to amount of the basic penalty as if it were the amount specified in the demand notice.

(6) A person may not under this section require a review of a decision under section 35 (decision on review).

34 Time limit and right to further review

(1) The Commissioners are not required under section 33 to review any decision unless the notice requiring the review is given before the end of the permitted period.

(2) For the purposes of this section the "permitted period" is the period of 45 days beginning with the day on which the relevant notice is given.

(3) For the purposes of subsection (2) the "relevant notice" is—

    (a)   in the case of a review by virtue of subsection (1) of section 33, the notice mentioned in that subsection; or

    (b)   in any other case, the demand notice in question.

(4) Nothing in subsection (1) prevents the Commissioners from agreeing on request to review a decision in a case where the notice required by that subsection is not given within the permitted period.

(5) A person may give notice under section 33 requiring a decision to be reviewed a second or subsequent time only if—

    (a)   the grounds on which he requires the further review are that the Commissioners did not, on any previous review, have the opportunity to consider any particular facts or matters; and

    (b)   he does not, on the further review, require the Commissioners to consider any facts or matters which were considered on a previous review of the decision, except in so far as they are relevant to any issue to which the facts or matters not previously considered relate.

35 Powers of Commissioners on a review

(1) Where the Commissioners—

    (a)   are required in accordance with section 33 to review a decision, or

    (b)   agree to do so on such a request as is mentioned in section 34(4),

the following provisions of this section apply.

(2) On any such review, the Commissioners may—

    (a)   confirm the decision,

    (b)   withdraw the decision, or

    (c)   vary the decision.

(3) Where the Commissioners withdraw or vary the decision, they may also take such further steps (if any) in consequence of the withdrawal or variation as they may consider appropriate.

(4) If the Commissioners do not within the permitted period give notice of their determination on the review to the person who required the review or his representative, they shall be taken for the purposes of this Part to have confirmed the decision.

(5) For the purposes of subsection (4), the "permitted period" is the period of 45 days beginning with the day on which the review—

    (a)   is required by the person or his representative in accordance with section 33, or

    (b)   is agreed to by the Commissioners as mentioned in section 34(4).

Appeals

36 Appeals to a tribunal

(1) Where the Commissioners—

    (a)   are required in accordance with section 33 to review a decision, or

    (b)   agree to do so on such a request as is mentioned in section 34(4),

an appeal lies to an appeal tribunal against any decision by the Commissioners on the review (including any confirmation under section 35(4)).

(2)   An appeal lies under this section only if the appellant is one of the following persons—

    (a)   the person who required the review in question,

    (b)   where the person who required the review in question did so as representative of another person, that other person, or

    (c)   a representative of a person falling within paragraph (a) or (b).

(3)   The powers of an appeal tribunal on an appeal under this section include—

    (a)   power to quash or vary a decision; and

    (b)   power to substitute the tribunal's own decision for any decision so quashed.

(4)   On an appeal under this section—

    (a)   the burden of proof as to the matters mentioned in section 25(1) or 26(1) lies on the Commissioners; but

    (b)   it is otherwise for the appellant to show that the grounds on which any such appeal is brought have been established.

37   Appeal tribunals

(1)   Sections 85 and 87 of the Value Added Tax Act 1994 (settling of appeals by agreement and enforcement of decisions of tribunal) have effect as if—

    (a)   any reference to section 83 of that Act included a reference to section 36 above, and

    (b)   any reference to VAT included a reference to any relevant tax or duty.

(2)   The provision that may be made by rules under paragraph 9 of Schedule 12 to the Value Added Tax Act 1994 (rules of procedure for tribunals) includes provision for costs awarded against an appellant on an appeal by virtue of this Part to be recoverable as if the amount awarded were an amount of customs duty which the appellant is required to pay.

Evidence

38   Admissibility of certain statements and documents

(1)   Statements made or documents produced by or on behalf of a person are not inadmissible in—

    (a)   any criminal proceedings against that person in respect of any offence in connection with or in relation to any relevant tax or duty, or

    (b)   any proceedings against that person for the recovery of any sum due from him in connection with or in relation to any relevant tax or duty,

by reason only that any of the matters specified in subsection (2) has been drawn to his attention and that he was, or may have been, induced by that matter having been brought to his attention to make the statements or produce the documents.

(2)   The matters mentioned in subsection (1) are—

    (a)   that the Commissioners have power, in relation to any relevant tax or duty, to demand by means of a written notice an amount by way of a civil penalty, instead of instituting criminal proceedings;

    (b)   that it is the Commissioners' practice, without being able to give an undertaking as to whether they will make such a demand in any case, to be influenced in determining whether to make such a demand by the fact (where it is the case) that a person has made a full confession of any dishonest conduct to which he has been a party and has given full facilities for an investigation;

    (c)   that the Commissioners or, on appeal, an appeal tribunal have power to reduce a penalty under section 25, as provided in subsection (1) of section 29; and

(d)   that, in determining the extent of such a reduction in the case of any person, the Commissioners or tribunal will have regard to the extent of the co-operation which he has given to the Commissioners in their investigation.

(3)   References in this section to a relevant tax or duty do not include a reference to customs duty of a preferential tariff country.

Miscellaneous and supplementary

39 Service of notices

Any notice to be given to any person for the purposes of this Part may be given by sending it by post in a letter addressed to that person or his representative at the last or usual residence or place of business of that person or representative.

40 Penalties not to be deducted for income tax or corporation tax purposes

(*inserts* TA 1988 s 827(1E))

41 Regulations and orders

(1)   Any power conferred on the Treasury by this Part to make regulations or an order includes power—

    (a)   to make different provision for different cases, and

    (b)   to make incidental, consequential, supplemental or transitional provision or savings.

(2)   Any power conferred on the Treasury by this Part to make regulations or an order shall be exercisable by statutory instrument.

(3)   Any statutory instrument containing regulations under this Part shall be subject to annulment in pursuance of a resolution of the House of Commons.

FINANCE ACT 2004

(2004 c 12)

ARRANGEMENT OF SECTIONS

PART 1
EXCISE DUTIES

An Act to grant certain duties, to alter other duties, and to amend the law relating to the National Debt and the Public Revenue, and to make further provision in connection with finance.

[22 July 2004]

PART 1
EXCISE DUTIES

Tobacco products duty

1 Rates of tobacco products duty

(1)   *(Substitutes Tobacco Products Duty Act 1979, Sch 1, Table).*

(2)   This section shall be deemed to have come into force at 6 o'clock in the evening of 17th March 2004.

Alcoholic liquor duties

2 Rate of duty on beer

(1)   *(Amends Alcoholic Liquor Duties Act 1979, s 36(1AA)(a)).*

(2)   This section shall be deemed to have come into force at midnight on 21st March 2004.

3 Rates of duty on wine and made-wine

(1)   *(Amends Alcoholic Liquor Duties Act 1979, Sch 1, Table, Part 1).*

(2)   This section shall be deemed to have come into force at midnight on 21st March 2004.

4 Duty stamps for spirits etc

(1)   *(Inserts Alcoholic Liquor Duties Act 1979, s 64A).*

(2)   Before Schedule 3 to that Act insert the Schedule 2A set out in Schedule 1 to this Act.

(3), (4)   *(Insert FA 1994 ss 12(2)(ca), 14(1)(bd), (be)).*

(5)   The amendments made by this section have effect in relation to retail containers containing alcoholic liquor if the excise duty point for the alcoholic liquor falls on or after such day as the Treasury may by order made by statutory instrument appoint.

(6)   An order under subsection (5) may contain such supplemental and transitional provision and savings as the Treasury think fit in connection with the coming into effect of those amendments.

(7)   In subsection (5) "excise duty point" has the meaning given by section 1 of the Finance (No 2) Act 1992 (c 48).

Hydrocarbon oil etc duties

5 Rates
(1)–(5)   (Amend Hydrocarbon Oil Duties Act 1979 ss 6, 6AA(3), 11(1), 13A(1), 14(1)).

(6)   This section shall come into force on 1st September 2004.

6 Road fuel gas
(1)–(3)   (Amend Hydrocarbon Oil Duties Act 1979 ss 5, 8(3), 21).

(4)   This section shall come into force on 1st September 2004.

7 Sulphur-free fuel
(1)–(8)   *(Amend Hydrocarbon Oil Duties Act 1979 ss 1, 2A, 6, 13AA, 13A, 27).*

(9)   This section shall come into force on 1st September 2004.

8 Definition of "fuel oil"
(Inserts Hydrocarbon Oil Duties Act 1979 s 2A(1C)).

9 Mixing of rebated oil
(1)–(3)   *(Amend Hydrocarbon Oil Duties Act 1979 ss 20AAA, 20AAB, Sch 2A)).*

(4)   This section—

    (a)   in so far as it imposes or relates to the charge specified in section 20AAA(1) or (2) of that Act (as substituted by subsection (1) above), shall have effect in relation to anything supplied on or after the date on which this Act is passed,

    (b)   in so far as it imposes or relates to the charge specified in section 20AAA(3) of that Act (as substituted by subsection (1) above), shall have effect in relation to anything produced on or after the date on which this Act is passed, and

    (c)   in so far as it causes sections 20AAA and 20AAB(1) and (2) of, and Schedule 2A to, that Act to cease to have effect in their present form, shall come into force on the day on which this Act is passed.

(5)   But no duty shall be charged on the supply of a mixture under section 20AAA(1) or (2) of that Act (as substituted by subsection (1) above) if duty was charged on the production of the mixture under section 20AAA as it had effect before the date on which this Act is passed.

10 Bioethanol
(1)–(9)   *(Amend Hydrocarbon Oil Duties Act 1979, ss 2AB, 2A, 6A, 6AD–6AF, 11, 13A, 14, 22, 27).*

(10)   This section shall come into force on 1st January 2005.

(11)   But no duty shall be charged under section 6AD or 6AE of that Act (inserted by subsection (3) above) in respect of the chargeable use of any goods, or the setting aside of any goods for a chargeable use, if before 1st January 2005—

    (a)   the goods were used or set aside for a chargeable use within the meaning of section 6A of that Act, and

    (b)   a duty of excise was charged under that section on that use or setting aside.

11 Biodiesel

(1)   *(Inserts Hydrocarbon Oil Duties Act 1979 s 6AA(2)(c)).*

(2)   This section shall come into force on 1st January 2005.

12 Fuel substitutes

(1)   (Substituted Hydrocarbon Oil Duties Act 1979 s 6A(2)(b)).

(2)   This section shall have effect in relation to anything done on or after the date on which this Act is passed.

13 Warehousing

(Inserts Hydrocarbon Oil Duties Act 1979 s 23C).

14 Treatment of certain energy products

(1)   Section 10 of the Finance Act 1993 (c 34) (application of Hydrocarbon Oil Duties Act 1979 to certain substances) shall be amended as follows.

(2)–(7)   *(Amend FA 1993 s 10).*

PART 9
SUPPLEMENTARY PROVISIONS

326 Repeals

(1)   The enactments mentioned in Schedule 42 to this Act (which include provisions that are spent or of no practical utility) are repealed to the extent specified.

(2)   The repeals specified in that Schedule have effect subject to the commencement provisions and savings contained or referred to in the notes set out in that Schedule.

328 Short title

This Act may be cited as the Finance Act 2004.

SCHEDULES

SCHEDULE 1
NEW SCHEDULE 2A TO THE ALCOHOLIC LIQUOR DUTIES ACT 1979
Section 4

(Inserts Alcoholic Liquor Duties Act 1979 Sch 2A).

SCHEDULE 42
REPEALS

Section 326

PART 1
EXCISE DUTIES

(1)
HYDROCARBON OIL ETC DUTIES

Short title and chapter	Extent of repeal
Hydrocarbon Oil Duties Act 1979 (c 5)	In section 6AA(2), the word "or" preceding paragraph (b). In section 20AAB(3), "or (2)". Schedule 2A.

1.   The repeal in section 6AA(2) of the Hydrocarbon Oil Duties Act 1979 has effect in accordance with section 11(2) of this Act.

2. The other repeals have effect in accordance with section 9(4) of this Act.

FINANCE ACT 2005

(2005 c 7)

ARRANGEMENT OF SECTIONS

An Act to Grant certain duties, to alter other duties, and to amend the law relating to the National Debt and the Public Revenue, and to make further provision in connection with finance.

[7 April 2005]

PART 1
EXCISE DUTIES
Tobacco products duty

1 Rates of tobacco products duty

(1) *(Substitutes Tobacco Products Duty Act 1979, Sch 1, Table).*

(2) This section shall be deemed to have come into force at 6 o'clock in the evening of 16th March 2005.

Alcoholic liquor duties

2 Rate of duty on beer

(1) *(Amends Alcoholic Liquor Duties Act 1979, s 36(1AA)(a)).*

(2) This section shall be deemed to have come into force at midnight on 20th March 2005.

3 Rates of duty on wine and made-wine

(1) *(Substitutes Alcoholic Liquor Duties Act 1979, Sch 1, Table, Part 1).*

(2) This section shall be deemed to have come into force at midnight on 20th March 2005.

Hydrocarbon oil etc duties

4 Consolidation of current rates of hydrocarbon oil duties etc.

(1) HODA 1979 is amended as follows.

(2)–(10) *(Amend Hydrocarbon Oil Duties Act 1979, ss 6(1A), (3), 6AA(3), 6AD(3), 8(3), 11(1), 13AA(1), 13A(1), 14(1)).*

(11) In consequence of the preceding provisions the following instruments are revoked—

    (a)   the Excise Duties (Surcharges or Rebates) (Hydrocarbon Oils etc.) Order 2004 (SI 2004/2063),

    (b)   the Excise Duties (Road Fuel Gas) (Reliefs) Regulations 2004 (SI. 2004/2069),

    (c)   the Excise Duties (Surcharges or Rebates) (Hydrocarbon Oils etc.) (Amendment) Order 2004 (SI 2004/3160), and

    (d)   the Excise Duties (Surcharges or Rebates) (Bioethanol) Order 2004 (SI 2004/3162).

(12) This section comes into force on the day on which this Act is passed.

5 Rates of hydrocarbon oil duties etc. from 1st September 2005

(1) HODA 1979 is amended as follows.

(2)–(8) *(Amend Hydrocarbon Oil Duties Act 1979, ss 6(1A), 6AA(3), 6AD(3), 8(3), 11(1), 13A(1), 14(1)).*

(9) This section comes into force on 1st September 2005.

PART 7
SUPPLEMENTARY PROVISIONS

106 Short title
This Act may be cited as the Finance Act 2005.

COMMISSIONERS FOR REVENUE AND CUSTOMS ACT 2005

(2005 c 11)

ARRANGEMENT OF SECTIONS

An Act to make provision for the appointment of Commissioners to exercise functions presently vested in the Commissioners of Inland Revenue and the Commissioners of Customs and Excise; for the establishment of a Revenue and Customs Prosecutions Office; and for connected purposes.

[7th April 2005]

Commissioners and officers

1 The Commissioners

(1)   Her Majesty may by Letters Patent appoint Commissioners for Her Majesty's Revenue and Customs.

(2)   The Welsh title of the Commissioners shall be Comisynwyr Cyllid a Thollau Ei Mawrhydi.

(3)   A Commissioner—

    (a)   may resign by notice in writing to the Treasury, and

    (b)   otherwise, shall hold office in accordance with the terms and conditions of his appointment (which may include provision for dismissal).

(4)   In exercising their functions, the Commissioners act on behalf of the Crown.

(5)   Service as a Commissioner is service in the civil service of the State.

2 Officers of Revenue and Customs

(1)   The Commissioners may appoint staff, to be known as officers of Revenue and Customs.

(2)   A person shall hold and vacate office as an officer of Revenue and Customs in accordance with the terms of his appointment (which may include provision for dismissal).

(3)   An officer of Revenue and Customs shall comply with directions of the Commissioners (whether he is exercising a function conferred on officers of Revenue and Customs or exercising a function on behalf of the Commissioners).

(4)   Anything (including anything in relation to legal proceedings) begun by or in relation to one officer of Revenue and Customs may be continued by or in relation to another.

(5)   Appointments under subsection (1) may be made only with the approval of the Minister for the Civil Service as to terms and conditions of service.

(6)   Service in the employment of the Commissioners is service in the civil service of the State.

(7)   (*Amends Interpretation Act 1978, Sch 1*)

3 Declaration of confidentiality

(1)   Each person who is appointed under this Act as a Commissioner or officer of Revenue and Customs shall make a declaration acknowledging his obligation of confidentiality under section 18.

(2)   A declaration under subsection (1) shall be made—

    (a)   as soon as is reasonably practicable following the person's appointment, and

    (b)   in such form, and before such a person, as the Commissioners may direct.

(3) For the purposes of this section, the renewal of a fixed term appointment shall not be treated as an appointment.

4 "Her Majesty's Revenue and Customs"

(1) The Commissioners and the officers of Revenue and Customs may together be referred to as Her Majesty's Revenue and Customs.

(2) The Welsh title of the Commissioners and the officers of Revenue and Customs together shall be Cyllid a Thollau Ei Mawrhydi.

(3) (*Amends Interpretation Act 1978, Schedule 1*).

Functions

5 Commissioners' initial functions

(1) The Commissioners shall be responsible for—

(a) the collection and management of revenue for which the Commissioners of Inland Revenue were responsible before the commencement of this section,

(b) the collection and management of revenue for which the Commissioners of Customs and Excise were responsible before the commencement of this section, and

(c) the payment and management of tax credits for which the Commissioners of Inland Revenue were responsible before the commencement of this section.

(2) The Commissioners shall also have all the other functions which before the commencement of this section vested in—

(a) the Commissioners of Inland Revenue (or in a Commissioner), or

(b) the Commissioners of Customs and Excise (or in a Commissioner).

(3) This section is subject to section 35.

(4) In this Act "revenue" includes taxes, duties and national insurance contributions.

6 Officers' initial functions

(1) A function conferred by an enactment (in whatever terms) on any of the persons listed in subsection (2) shall by virtue of this subsection vest in an officer of Revenue and Customs.

(2) Those persons are—

(a) an officer as defined by section 1(1) of the Customs and Excise Management Act 1979 (c 2),

(b) a person acting under the authority of the Commissioners of Customs and Excise,

(c) an officer of the Commissioners of Customs and Excise,

(d) a customs officer,

(e) an officer of customs,

(f) a customs and excise officer,

(g) an officer of customs and excise, and

(h) a collector of customs and excise.

(3) This section is subject to sections 7 and 35.

8 Power to transfer functions

(1) (*Amends Ministers of the Crown Act 1975, s 5*)

(2) For the purposes of sections 63 and 108 of the Scotland Act 1998 (c 46) (transfer of functions)—

(a) the Commissioners shall be treated as a Minister of the Crown, and

    (b)   the officers of Revenue and Customs shall be treated as a Minister of the Crown.

(3)   An Order in Council under section 63 or 108 of that Act—

    (a)   may not make provision about a function specified in section 5(1) of this Act, and

    (b)   if it transfers a function to the Commissioners or to officers of Revenue and Customs—

        (i)   may restrict or prohibit the exercise of specified powers in relation to that function, and

        (ii)   may provide that the function may be exercised only with the consent of a specified member of the Scottish Executive.

(4)   For the purposes of section 22 of and Schedule 3 to the Government of Wales Act 1998 (c 38) (transfer of functions)—

    (a)   the Commissioners shall be treated as a Minister of the Crown, and

    (b)   the officers of Revenue and Customs shall be treated as a Minister of the Crown.

(5)   An Order in Council under section 22 of that Act may not make provision about a function specified in section 5(1) of this Act.

9 Ancillary powers

(1)   The Commissioners may do anything which they think—

    (a)   necessary or expedient in connection with the exercise of their functions, or

    (b)   incidental or conducive to the exercise of their functions.

(2)   This section is subject to section 35.

Exercise of functions

11 Treasury directions

In the exercise of their functions the Commissioners shall comply with any directions of a general nature given to them by the Treasury.

12 Commissioners' arrangements

(1)   The Commissioners shall make arrangements for—

    (a)   the conduct of their proceedings, and

    (b)   the conduct of the proceedings of any committee established by them.

(2)   Arrangements under subsection (1) may, in particular—

    (a)   make provision for a quorum at meetings;

    (b)   provide that a function of the Commissioners—

        (i)   may be exercised by two Commissioners, or

        (ii)   may be exercised by a specified number of Commissioners (greater than two).

(3)   A decision to make arrangements under subsection (1) must be taken with the agreement of more than half of the Commissioners holding office at the time.

13 Exercise of Commissioners' functions by officers

(1)   An officer of Revenue and Customs may exercise any function of the Commissioners.

(2)   But subsection (1)—

    (a)   does not apply to the functions specified in subsection (3), and

    (b)   is subject to directions under section 2(3) and arrangements under section 12.

(3)   The non-delegable functions mentioned in subsection (2)(a) are—

(a)   making, by statutory instrument, regulations, rules or an order,

(b)   *approving an application for a warrant to search premises under section 20C of the Taxes Management Act 1970 (c 9),*

(c)   *approving an application for a warrant to enter premises under Part 7 of Schedule 13 to the Finance Act 2003 (c 14), and*

(d)   giving instructions for the disclosure of information under section 20(1)(a), except that an officer of Revenue and Customs may give an instruction under section 20(1)(a) authorising disclosure of specified information relating to—

     (i)   one or more specified persons,

     (ii)   one or more specified transactions, or

     (iii) specified goods.

NOTES

Sub-s (3): paras (b), (c) repealed by the Finance Act 2007, ss 84(4), 114, Sch 22, Pt 2, paras 3, 17(a), Sch 27, Pt 5(1) with effect in accordance with provision made by the Treasury by order: see the Finance Act 2007, s 84(5).

14 Delegation

(1)   Arrangements under section 12 may, in particular, enable the Commissioners, or a number of Commissioners acting in accordance with arrangements by virtue of section 12(2)(b), to delegate a function of the Commissioners, other than a function specified in subsection (2) below—

(a)   to a single Commissioner,

(b)   *to a committee established by the Commissioners (which may include persons who are neither Commissioners nor staff of the Commissioners nor officers of Revenue and Customs), or*

(c)   *to any other person.*

(2)   The non-delegable functions mentioned in subsection (1) are—

(a)   making, by statutory instrument, regulations, rules or an order,

(b)   approving an application for a warrant to search premises under section 20C of the Taxes Management Act 1970 (c 9), and

(c)   approving an application for a warrant to enter premises under Part 7 of Schedule 13 to the Finance Act 2003 (c 14).

(3)   The Commissioners may not delegate the function under section 20(1)(a) except to a single Commissioner.

(4)   The delegation of a function by virtue of subsection (1) by the Commissioners or a number of Commissioners—

(a)   shall not prevent the exercise of the function by the Commissioners or those Commissioners, and

(b)   shall not, subject to express provision to the contrary in directions under section 2(3) or arrangements under section 12, prevent the exercise of the function by an officer of Revenue and Customs.

(5)   Where the Commissioners or a number of Commissioners delegate a function to a person by virtue of subsection (1)(c)—

(a)   the Commissioners or those Commissioners shall monitor the exercise of the function by that person, and

(b)   in the exercise of the function the delegate shall comply with any directions of the Commissioners or of those Commissioners.

NOTES

Sub-s (2): paras (b), (c) repealed by the Finance Act 2007, ss 84(4), 114, Sch 22, Pt 2, paras 3, 17(b), Sch 27, Pt 5(1) with effect in accordance with provision made by the Treasury by order: see the Finance Act 2007, s 84(5).

15 Agency: Scotland and Northern Ireland

(1) For the purposes of section 93 of the Scotland Act 1998 (c 46) (agency)—

(a)   the Commissioners shall be treated as a Minister of the Crown, and

(b)   the officers of Revenue and Customs shall be treated as a Minister of the Crown.

(2) For the purposes of section 28 of the Northern Ireland Act 1998 (c 47) (agency)—

(a)   the Commissioners shall be treated as a Minister of the Crown, and

(b)   the officers of Revenue and Customs shall be treated as a Minister of the Crown.

16 Restrictions, etc

Part 1 of Schedule 2 (which restricts, or makes other provision in connection with, the exercise of certain functions) shall have effect.

Information

17 Use of information

(1) Information acquired by the Revenue and Customs in connection with a function may be used by them in connection with any other function.

(2) Subsection (1) is subject to any provision which restricts or prohibits the use of information and which is contained in—

(a)   this Act,

(b)   any other enactment, or

(c)   an international or other agreement to which the United Kingdom or Her Majesty's Government is party.

(3) In subsection (1) "the Revenue and Customs" means—

(a)   the Commissioners,

(b)   an officer of Revenue and Customs,

(c)   a person acting on behalf of the Commissioners or an officer of Revenue and Customs,

(d)   a committee established by the Commissioners,

(e)   a member of a committee established by the Commissioners,

(f)   the Commissioners of Inland Revenue (or any committee or staff of theirs or anyone acting on their behalf),

(g)   the Commissioners of Customs and Excise (or any committee or staff of theirs or anyone acting on their behalf), and

(h)   a person specified in section 6(2) or 7(3).

(4) In subsection (1) "function" means a function of any of the persons listed in subsection (3).

(5) In subsection (2) the reference to an enactment does not include—

(a)   an Act of the Scottish Parliament or an instrument made under such an Act, or

(b)   an Act of the Northern Ireland Assembly or an instrument made under such an Act.

(6)   Part 2 of Schedule 2 (which makes provision about the supply and other use of information in specified circumstances) shall have effect.

18 Confidentiality

(1)   Revenue and Customs officials may not disclose information which is held by the Revenue and Customs in connection with a function of the Revenue and Customs.

(2)   But subsection (1) does not apply to a disclosure—

(a)   which—

(i)   is made for the purposes of a function of the Revenue and Customs, and

(ii)   does not contravene any restriction imposed by the Commissioners,

(b)   which is made in accordance with section 20 or 21,

(c)   which is made for the purposes of civil proceedings (whether or not within the United Kingdom) relating to a matter in respect of which the Revenue and Customs have functions,

(d)   which is made for the purposes of a criminal investigation or criminal proceedings (whether or not within the United Kingdom) relating to a matter in respect of which the Revenue and Customs have functions,

(e)   which is made in pursuance of an order of a court,

(f)   which is made to Her Majesty's Inspectors of Constabulary, the Scottish inspectors or the Northern Ireland inspectors for the purpose of an inspection by virtue of section 27,

(g)   which is made to the Independent Police Complaints Commission, or a person acting on its behalf, for the purpose of the exercise of a function by virtue of section 28, or

(h)   which is made with the consent of each person to whom the information relates.

(3)   Subsection (1) is subject to any other enactment permitting disclosure.

(4)   In this section—

(a)   a reference to Revenue and Customs officials is a reference to any person who is or was—

(i)   a Commissioner,

(ii)   an officer of Revenue and Customs,

(iii)   a person acting on behalf of the Commissioners or an officer of Revenue and Customs, or

(iv)   a member of a committee established by the Commissioners,

(b)   a reference to the Revenue and Customs has the same meaning as in section 17,

(c)   a reference to a function of the Revenue and Customs is a reference to a function of—

(i)   the Commissioners, or

(ii)   an officer of Revenue and Customs,

(d)   a reference to the Scottish inspectors or the Northern Ireland inspectors has the same meaning as in section 27, and

(e)   a reference to an enactment does not include—

(i)   an Act of the Scottish Parliament or an instrument made under such an Act, or

(ii)   an Act of the Northern Ireland Assembly or an instrument made under such an Act.

19 Wrongful disclosure

(1)   A person commits an offence if he contravenes section 18(1) or 20(9) by disclosing revenue and customs information relating to a person whose identity—

    (a)   is specified in the disclosure, or

    (b)   can be deduced from it.

(2)   In subsection (1) "revenue and customs information relating to a person" means information about, acquired as a result of, or held in connection with the exercise of a function of the Revenue and Customs (within the meaning given by section 18(4)(c)) in respect of the person; but it does not include information about internal administrative arrangements of Her Majesty's Revenue and Customs (whether relating to Commissioners, officers or others).

(3)   It is a defence for a person charged with an offence under this section of disclosing information to prove that he reasonably believed—

    (a)   that the disclosure was lawful, or

    (b)   that the information had already and lawfully been made available to the public.

(4)   A person guilty of an offence under this section shall be liable—

    (a)   on conviction on indictment, to imprisonment for a term not exceeding two years, to a fine or to both, or

    (b)   on summary conviction, to imprisonment for a term not exceeding 12 months, to a fine not exceeding the statutory maximum or to both.

(5)   A prosecution for an offence under this section may be instituted in England and Wales only—

    (a)   by the Director of Revenue and Customs Prosecutions, or

    (b)   with the consent of the Director of Public Prosecutions.

(6)   A prosecution for an offence under this section may be instituted in Northern Ireland only—

    (a)   by the Commissioners, or

    (b)   with the consent of the Director of Public Prosecutions for Northern Ireland.

(7)   In the application of this section to Scotland or Northern Ireland the reference in subsection (4)(b) to 12 months shall be taken as a reference to six months.

(8)   This section is without prejudice to the pursuit of any remedy or the taking of any action in relation to a contravention of section 18(1) or 20(9) (whether or not this section applies to the contravention).

20 Public interest disclosure

(1)   Disclosure is in accordance with this section (as mentioned in section 18(2)(b)) if—

    (a)   it is made on the instructions of the Commissioners (which may be general or specific),

    (b)   it is of a kind—

        (i)   to which any of subsections (2) to (7) applies, or

        (ii)   specified in regulations made by the Treasury, and

    (c)   the Commissioners are satisfied that it is in the public interest.

(2)   This subsection applies to a disclosure made—

    (a)   to a person exercising public functions (whether or not within the United Kingdom),

    (b)   for the purposes of the prevention or detection of crime, and

    (c)   in order to comply with an obligation of the United Kingdom, or Her Majesty's Government, under an international or other agreement relating to the movement of persons, goods or services.

(3) This subsection applies to a disclosure if—
- (a)   it is made to a body which has responsibility for the regulation of a profession,
- (b)   it relates to misconduct on the part of a member of the profession, and
- (c)   the misconduct relates to a function of the Revenue and Customs.

(4) This subsection applies to a disclosure if—
- (a)   it is made to a constable, and
- (b)   either—
  - (i)   the constable is exercising functions which relate to the movement of persons or goods into or out of the United Kingdom, or
  - (ii)   the disclosure is made for the purposes of the prevention or detection of crime.

(5) This subsection applies to a disclosure if it is made—
- (a)   to the National Criminal Intelligence Service, and
- (b)   for a purpose connected with its functions under section 2(2) of the Police Act 1997 (c 50) (criminal intelligence).

(6) This subsection applies to a disclosure if it is made—
- (a)   to a person exercising public functions in relation to public safety or public health, and
- (b)   for the purposes of those functions.

(7) This subsection applies to a disclosure if it—
- (a)   is made to the [National Policing Improvement Agency] for the purpose of enabling information to be entered in a computerised database, and
- (b)   relates to—
  - (i)   a person suspected of an offence,
  - (ii)   a person arrested for an offence,
  - (iii)   the results of an investigation, or
  - (iv)   anything seized.

(8) Regulations under subsection (1)(b)(ii)—
- (a)   may specify a kind of disclosure only if the Treasury are satisfied that it relates to—
  - (i)   national security,
  - (ii)   public safety,
  - (iii)   public health, or
  - (iv)   the prevention or detection of crime;
- (b)   may make provision limiting or restricting the disclosures that may be made in reliance on the regulations; and that provision may, in particular, operate by reference to—
  - (i)   the nature of information,
  - (ii)   the person or class of person to whom the disclosure is made,
  - (iii)   the person or class of person by whom the disclosure is made,
  - (iv)   any other factor, or
  - (v)   a combination of factors;
- (c)   shall be made by statutory instrument;
- (d)   may not be made unless a draft has been laid before and approved by resolution of each House of Parliament.

(9) Information disclosed in reliance on this section may not be further disclosed without the consent of the Commissioners (which may be general or specific); (but the Commissioners shall be taken to have consented to further disclosure by use of the computerised database of information disclosed by virtue of subsection (7)).

NOTES

Sub-s (7): in para (a) words "National Policing Improvement Agency" in square brackets substituted by the Police and Justice Act 2006, s 1(3), Sch 1, Pt 7, para 91.

21 Disclosure to prosecuting authority

(1)   Disclosure is in accordance with this section (as mentioned in section 18(2)(b)) if made—

    (a)   to a prosecuting authority, and

    (b)   for the purpose of enabling the authority—

          (i)   to consider whether to institute criminal proceedings in respect of a matter considered in the course of an investigation conducted by or on behalf of Her Majesty's Revenue and Customs, or

          (ii)   to give advice in connection with a criminal investigation (within the meaning of section 35(5)(b)) or criminal proceedings.

(2)   In subsection (1) "prosecuting authority" means—

    (a)   the Director of Revenue and Customs Prosecutions,

    (b)   in Scotland, the Lord Advocate or a procurator fiscal, and

    (c)   in Northern Ireland, the Director of Public Prosecutions for Northern Ireland.

(3)   Information disclosed to a prosecuting authority in accordance with this section may not be further disclosed except—

    (a)   for a purpose connected with the exercise of the prosecuting authority's functions, or

    (b)   with the consent of the Commissioners (which may be general or specific).

(4)   A person commits an offence if he contravenes subsection (3).

(5)   It is a defence for a person charged with an offence under this section to prove that he reasonably believed—

    (a)   that the disclosure was lawful, or

    (b)   that the information had already and lawfully been made available to the public.

(6)   A person guilty of an offence under this section shall be liable—

    (a)   on conviction on indictment, to imprisonment for a term not exceeding two years, to a fine or to both, or

    (b)   on summary conviction, to imprisonment for a term not exceeding 12 months, to a fine not exceeding the statutory maximum or to both.

(7)   A prosecution for an offence under this section may be instituted in England and Wales only—

    (a)   by the Director of Revenue and Customs Prosecutions, or

    (b)   with the consent of the Director of Public Prosecutions.

(8)   A prosecution for an offence under this section may be instituted in Northern Ireland only—

    (a)   by the Commissioners, or

    (b)   with the consent of the Director of Public Prosecutions for Northern Ireland.

(9)   In the application of this section to Scotland or Northern Ireland the reference in subsection (6)(b) to 12 months shall be taken as a reference to six months.

22 Data protection, etc

Nothing in sections 17 to 21 authorises the making of a disclosure which—

    (a)   contravenes the Data Protection Act 1998 (c 29), or

(b)   is prohibited by Part 1 of the Regulation of Investigatory Powers Act 2000 (c 23).

23 Freedom of information

(1)   Revenue and customs information relating to a person, the disclosure of which is prohibited by section 18(1), is exempt information by virtue of section 44(1)(a) of the Freedom of Information Act 2000 (c 36) (prohibitions on disclosure) if its disclosure—

(a)   would specify the identity of the person to whom the information relates, or

(b)   would enable the identity of such a person to be deduced.

(2)   Except as specified in subsection (1), information the disclosure of which is prohibited by section 18(1) is not exempt information for the purposes of section 44(1)(a) of the Freedom of Information Act 2000.

(3)   In subsection (1) "revenue and customs information relating to a person" has the same meaning as in section 19.

Proceedings

24 Evidence

(1)   A document that purports to have been issued or signed by or with the authority of the Commissioners—

(a)   shall be treated as having been so issued or signed unless the contrary is proved, and

(b)   shall be admissible in any legal proceedings.

(2)   A document that purports to have been issued by the Commissioners and which certifies any of the matters specified in subsection (3) shall (in addition to the matters provided for by subsection (1)(a) and (b)) be treated as accurate unless the contrary is proved.

(3)   The matters mentioned in subsection (2) are—

(a)   that a specified person was appointed as a commissioner on a specified date,

(b)   that a specified person was appointed as an officer of Revenue and Customs on a specified date,

(c)   that at a specified time or for a specified purpose (or both) a function was delegated to a specified Commissioner,

(d)   that at a specified time or for a specified purpose (or both) a function was delegated to a specified committee, and

(e)   that at a specified time or for a specified purpose (or both) a function was delegated to another specified person.

(4)   A photographic or other copy of a document acquired by the Commissioners shall, if certified by them to be an accurate copy, be admissible in any legal proceedings to the same extent as the document itself.

(5)   Section 2 of the Documentary Evidence Act 1868 (c 37) (proof of documents) shall apply to a Revenue and Customs document as it applies in relation to the documents mentioned in that section.

(6)   In the application of that section to a Revenue and Customs document the Schedule to that Act shall be treated as if—

(a)   the first column contained a reference to the Commissioners, and

(b)   the second column contained a reference to a Commissioner or a person acting on his authority.

(7)   In this section—

(a)   "Revenue and Customs document" means a document issued by or on behalf of the Commissioners, and

(b)   a reference to the Commissioners includes a reference to the Commissioners of Inland Revenue and to the Commissioners of Customs and Excise.

25 Conduct of civil proceedings

(1) An officer of Revenue and Customs or a person authorised by the Commissioners may conduct civil proceedings, in a magistrates' court or in the sheriff court, relating to a function of the Revenue and Customs.

(2) A solicitor member of the Commissioners' staff may act as a solicitor in connection with civil proceedings relating to a function of the Revenue and Customs.

(3) A legally qualified member of the Commissioners' staff may conduct county court proceedings relating to a matter specified in section 7.

(4) A court shall grant any rights of audience necessary to enable a person to exercise a function under this section.

(5) In this section—

(a)   a reference to a function of the Revenue and Customs is a reference to a function of—
    (i)   the Commissioners, or
    (ii)   an officer of Revenue and Customs,

(b)   a reference to civil proceedings is a reference to proceedings other than proceedings in respect of an offence,

(c)   a reference to county court proceedings is a reference to civil proceedings in a county court,

(d)   the reference to a legally qualified member of the Commissioners' staff is a reference to a member of staff who has been admitted as a solicitor, or called to the Bar, whether or not he holds a practising certificate, and

(e)   the reference to a solicitor member of the Commissioners' staff—
    (i)   except in relation to Scotland, is a reference to a member of staff who has been admitted as a solicitor, whether or not he holds a practising certificate,
    (ii)   in relation to Scotland, is a reference to a member of staff who has been admitted as a solicitor and who holds a practising certificate.

26 Rewards

The Commissioners may pay a reward to a person in return for a service which relates to a function of—

(a)   the Commissioners, or

(b)   an officer of Revenue and Customs.

Inspection and complaints

27 Inspection

(1) The Treasury may make regulations conferring functions on Her Majesty's Inspectors of Constabulary, the Scottish inspectors or the Northern Ireland inspectors in relation to—

(a)   the Commissioners for Her Majesty's Revenue and Customs, and

(b)   officers of Revenue and Customs.

(2) Regulations under subsection (1)—

(a)   may—
    (i)   in relation to Her Majesty's Inspectors of Constabulary, apply (with or without modification) or make provision similar to any

provision of sections 54 to 56 of the Police Act 1996 (c 16) (inspection);

(ii) in relation to the Scottish inspectors, apply (with or without modification) or make provision similar to any provision of section 33 or 34 of the Police (Scotland) Act 1967 (c 77) (inspection);

(iii) in relation to the Northern Ireland inspectors, apply (with or without modification) or make provision similar to any provision of section 41 or 42 of the Police (Northern Ireland) Act 1998 (c 32) (inspection);

(b) may enable a Minister of the Crown or the Commissioners to require an inspection to be carried out;

(c) shall provide for a report of an inspection to be made and, subject to any exceptions required or permitted by the regulations, published;

(d) shall provide for an annual report by Her Majesty's Inspectors of Constabulary;

(e) may make provision for payment by the Commissioners to or in respect of Her Majesty's Inspectors of Constabulary, the Scottish inspectors or the Northern Ireland inspectors.

(3) An inspection carried out by virtue of this section may not address a matter of a kind which the Comptroller and Auditor General may examine under section 6 of the National Audit Act 1983 (c 44).

(4) An inspection carried out by virtue of this section shall be carried out jointly by Her Majesty's Inspectors of Constabulary and the Scottish inspectors—

(a) if it is carried out wholly in Scotland, or

(b) in a case where it is carried out partly in Scotland, to the extent that it is carried out there.

(5) Regulations under subsection (1)—

(a) shall be made by statutory instrument, and

(b) shall be subject to annulment in pursuance of a resolution of either House of Parliament.

(6) In this section—

(a) "the Scottish inspectors" means the inspectors of constabulary appointed under section 33(1) of the Police (Scotland) Act 1967, and

(b) "the Northern Ireland inspectors" means the inspectors of constabulary appointed under section 41(1) of the Police (Northern Ireland) Act 1998.

NOTES

Regulations: the Revenue and Customs (Inspections) Regulations 2005, SI 2005/1133.

28 Complaints and misconduct: England and Wales

(1) The Treasury may make regulations conferring functions on the Independent Police Complaints Commission in relation to—

(a) the Commissioners for Her Majesty's Revenue and Customs, and

(b) officers of Revenue and Customs.

(2) Regulations under subsection (1)—

(a) may apply (with or without modification) or make provision similar to any provision of or made under Part 2 of the Police Reform Act 2002 (c 30) (complaints);

    (b)   may confer on the Independent Police Complaints Commission, or on a person acting on its behalf, a power of a kind conferred by this Act or another enactment on an officer of Revenue and Customs;

    (c)   may make provision for payment by the Commissioners to or in respect of the Independent Police Complaints Commission.

(3) The Independent Police Complaints Commission and the Parliamentary Commissioner for Administration may disclose information to each other for the purposes of the exercise of a function—

    (a)   by virtue of this section, or

    (b)   under the Parliamentary Commissioner Act 1967 (c 13).

(4) The Independent Police Complaints Commission and the Parliamentary Commissioner for Administration may jointly investigate a matter in relation to which—

    (a)   the Independent Police Complaints Commission has functions by virtue of this section, and

    (b)   the Parliamentary Commissioner for Administration has functions by virtue of the Parliamentary Commissioner Act 1967.

(5) Regulations under subsection (1)—

    (a)   shall be made by statutory instrument, and

    (b)   shall be subject to annulment in pursuance of a resolution of either House of Parliament.

(6) Regulations under subsection (1) shall relate to the Commissioners or officers of Revenue and Customs only in so far as their functions are exercised in or in relation to England and Wales.

29 Confidentiality, &c

(1) Where Her Majesty's Inspectors of Constabulary, the Scottish inspectors or the Northern Ireland inspectors obtain information in the course of exercising a function by virtue of section 27—

    (a)   they may not disclose it without the consent of the Commissioners, and

    (b)   they may not use it for any purpose other than the exercise of the function by virtue of section 27.

(2) A report of an inspection by virtue of section 27 may not include information relating to a specified person without his consent.

(3) Where the Independent Police Complaints Commission or a person acting on its behalf obtains information from the Commissioners or an officer of Revenue and Customs, or from the Parliamentary Commissioner for Administration, in the course of exercising a function by virtue of section 28—

    (a)   the Commission or person shall comply with any restriction on disclosure imposed by regulations under that section (and those regulations may, in particular, prohibit disclosure generally or only in specified circumstances or only without the consent of the Commissioners), and

    (b)   the Commission or person may not use the information for any purpose other than the exercise of the function by virtue of that section.

(4) A person commits an offence if he contravenes a provision of this section.

(5) It is a defence for a person charged with an offence under this section of disclosing or using information to prove that he reasonably believed—

    (a)   that the disclosure or use was lawful, or

    (b)   that the information had already and lawfully been made available to the public.

(6) A person guilty of an offence under this section shall be liable—

(a)   on conviction on indictment, to imprisonment for a term not exceeding two years, to a fine or to both, or

(b)   on summary conviction, to imprisonment for a term not exceeding 12 months, to a fine not exceeding the statutory maximum or to both.

(7)   A prosecution for an offence under this section may be instituted in England and Wales only—

(a)   by the Director of Revenue and Customs Prosecutions, or

(b)   with the consent of the Director of Public Prosecutions.

(8)   A prosecution for an offence under this section may be instituted in Northern Ireland only—

(a)   by the Commissioners, or

(b)   with the consent of the Director of Public Prosecutions for Northern Ireland.

(9)   In the application of this section to Scotland or Northern Ireland the reference in subsection (6)(b) to 12 months shall be taken as a reference to six months.

(10)   In this section a reference to the Scottish inspectors or the Northern Ireland inspectors has the same meaning as in section 27.

Offences

30 Impersonation

(1)   A person commits an offence if he pretends to be a Commissioner or an officer of Revenue and Customs with a view to obtaining—

(a)   admission to premises,

(b)   information, or

(c)   any other benefit.

(2)   A person guilty of an offence under this section shall be liable on summary conviction to—

(a)   imprisonment for a period not exceeding 51 weeks,

(b)   a fine not exceeding level 5 on the standard scale, or

(c)   both.

(3)   In the application of this section to Scotland or Northern Ireland the reference in subsection (2)(a) to 51 weeks shall be taken as a reference to six months.

31 Obstruction

(1)   A person commits an offence if without reasonable excuse he obstructs—

(a)   an officer of Revenue and Customs,

(b)   a person acting on behalf of the Commissioners or an officer of Revenue and Customs, or

(c)   a person assisting an officer of Revenue and Customs.

(2)   A person guilty of an offence under this section shall be liable on summary conviction to—

(a)   imprisonment for a period not exceeding 51 weeks,

(b)   a fine not exceeding level 3 on the standard scale, or

(c)   both.

(3)   In the application of this section to Scotland or Northern Ireland the reference in subsection (2)(a) to 51 weeks shall be taken as a reference to six months.

32 Assault

(1)   A person commits an offence if he assaults an officer of Revenue and Customs.

(2)   A person guilty of an offence under this section shall be liable on summary conviction to—

(a)   imprisonment for a period not exceeding 51 weeks,

(b)   a fine not exceeding level 5 on the standard scale, or

(c)   both.

(3)   In the application of this section to Scotland or Northern Ireland the reference in subsection (2)(a) to 51 weeks shall be taken as a reference to six months.

33 Power of arrest

(1)   An authorised officer of Revenue and Customs may arrest a person without warrant if the officer reasonably suspects that the person—

(a)   has committed an offence under section 30, 31 or 32,

(b)   is committing an offence under any of those sections, or

(c)   is about to commit an offence under any of those sections.

(2)   In subsection (1) "authorised" means authorised by the Commissioners.

(3)   Authorisation for the purposes of this section may be specific or general.

(4)   In Scotland or Northern Ireland, a constable may arrest a person without warrant if the constable reasonably suspects that the person—

(a)   has committed an offence under this Act,

(b)   is committing an offence under this Act, or

(c)   is about to commit an offence under this Act.

Prosecutions

34 The Revenue and Customs Prosecutions Office

(1)   The Attorney General shall appoint an individual as Director of Revenue and Customs Prosecutions.

(2)   The Director may, with the approval of the Minister for the Civil Service as to terms and conditions of service, appoint staff.

(3)   The Director and his staff may together be referred to as the Revenue and Customs Prosecutions Office.

(4)   Schedule 3 (which makes provision about the Office) shall have effect.

35 Functions

(1)   The Director—

(a)   may institute and conduct criminal proceedings in England and Wales relating to a criminal investigation by the Revenue and Customs, and

(b)   shall take over the conduct of criminal proceedings instituted in England and Wales by the Revenue and Customs.

(2)   The Director shall provide such advice as he thinks appropriate, to such persons as he thinks appropriate, in relation to—

(a)   a criminal investigation by the Revenue and Customs, or

(b)   criminal proceedings instituted in England and Wales relating to a criminal investigation by the Revenue and Customs.

(3)   In this section a reference to the Revenue and Customs is a reference to—

(a)   the Commissioners,

(b)   an officer of Revenue and Customs, and

(c)   a person acting on behalf of the Commissioners or an officer of Revenue and Customs.

(4)   The Attorney General may by order assign to the Director a function of—

(a)   instituting criminal proceedings,

(b)   assuming the conduct of criminal proceedings, or

(c)   providing legal advice.

(5)   In this section—

(a)   a reference to the institution of criminal proceedings shall be construed in accordance with section 15(2) of the Prosecution of Offences Act 1985 (c 23), and

(b)   "criminal investigation" means any process—

    (i)   for considering whether an offence has been committed,

    (ii)   for discovering by whom an offence has been committed, or

    (iii) as a result of which an offence is alleged to have been committed.

36 Functions: supplemental

(1)   The Director shall discharge his functions under the superintendence of the Attorney General.

(2)   The Director or an individual designated under section 37 or 39 or appointed under section 38 must have regard to the Code for Crown Prosecutors issued by the Director of Public Prosecutions under section 10 of the Prosecution of Offences Act 1985 (c 23)—

(a)   in determining whether proceedings for an offence should be instituted,

(b)   in determining what charges should be preferred,

(c)   in considering what representations to make to a magistrates' court about mode of trial, and

(d)   in determining whether to discontinue proceedings.

(3)   Sections 23 and 23A of the Prosecution of Offences Act 1985 (power to discontinue proceedings) shall apply (with any necessary modifications) to proceedings conducted by the Director under this Act as they apply to proceedings conducted by the Director of Public Prosecutions.

(4)   A power of the Director under an enactment to institute proceedings may be exercised to institute proceedings in England and Wales only.

37 Prosecutors

(1)   The Director may designate a member of the Office (to be known as a "Revenue and Customs Prosecutor") to exercise any function of the Director under or by virtue of section 35.

(2)   An individual may be designated as a Prosecutor only if he has a general qualification within the meaning of section 71 of the Courts and Legal Services Act 1990 (c 41) (qualification for judicial appointments).

(3)   A Prosecutor shall act in accordance with any instructions of the Director.

38 Conduct of prosecutions on behalf of the Office

(1)   An individual who is not a member of the Office may be appointed by the Director to exercise any function of the Director under or by virtue of section 35 in relation to—

(a)   specified criminal proceedings, or

(b)   a specified class or description of criminal proceedings.

(2)   An individual may be appointed under this section only if he has a general qualification within the meaning of section 71 of the Courts and Legal Services Act 1990 (qualifications for judicial appointments).

(3)   An individual appointed under this section shall act in accordance with any instructions of—

(a)   the Director, or

(b)   a Prosecutor.

39 Designation of non-legal staff

(1)   The Director may designate a member of the Office—

(a)   to conduct summary bail applications, and

(b)   to conduct other ancillary magistrates' criminal proceedings.

(2) In carrying out a function for which he is designated under this section an individual shall have the same powers and rights of audience as a Prosecutor.

(3) In subsection (1)—

    (a)   "summary bail application" means an application for bail made in connection with an offence—

        (i)   which is not triable only on indictment, and

        (ii)   in respect of which the accused has not been sent to the Crown Court for trial, and

    (b)   "ancillary magistrates' criminal proceedings" means criminal proceedings other than trials in a magistrates' court.

(4) An individual designated under this section shall act in accordance with any instructions of—

    (a)   the Director, or

    (b)   a Prosecutor.

40 Confidentiality

(1) The Revenue and Customs Prosecutions Office may not disclose information which—

    (a)   is held by the Prosecutions Office in connection with any of its functions, and

    (b)   relates to a person whose identity is specified in the disclosure or can be deduced from it.

(2) But subsection (1)—

    (a)   does not apply to a disclosure which—

        (i)   is made for the purposes of a function of the Prosecutions Office, and

        (ii)   does not contravene any restriction imposed by the Director,

    (b)   does not apply to a disclosure made to Her Majesty's Revenue and Customs in connection with a function of the Revenue and Customs (within the meaning of section 25),

    (c)   does not apply to a disclosure made for the purposes of a criminal investigation or criminal proceedings (whether or not within the United Kingdom),

    (d)   does not apply to a disclosure which in the opinion of the Director is desirable for the purpose of safeguarding national security,

    (e)   does not apply to a disclosure made in pursuance of an order of a court,

    (f)   does not apply to a disclosure made with the consent of each person to whom the information relates, and

    (g)   is subject to any other enactment.

(3) A person commits an offence if he contravenes subsection (1).

(4) Subsection (3) does not apply to the disclosure of information about internal administrative arrangements of the Revenue and Customs Prosecutions Office (whether relating to a member of the Office or to another person).

(5) It is a defence for a person charged with an offence under this section of disclosing information to prove that he reasonably believed—

    (a)   that the disclosure was lawful, or

    (b)   that the information had already and lawfully been made available to the public.

(6) In this section a reference to the Revenue and Customs Prosecutions Office includes a reference to—

    (a)   former members of the Office, and

    (b)   persons who hold or have held appointment under section 38.

(7) A person guilty of an offence under this section shall be liable—

(a)   on conviction on indictment, to imprisonment for a term not exceeding two years, to a fine or to both, or

(b)   on summary conviction, to imprisonment for a term not exceeding 12 months, to a fine not exceeding the statutory maximum or to both.

(8) A prosecution for an offence under this section may be instituted in England and Wales only—

(a)   by the Director of Revenue and Customs Prosecutions, or

(b)   with the consent of the Director of Public Prosecutions.

(9) A prosecution for an offence under this section may be instituted in Northern Ireland only—

(a)   by the Commissioners, or

(b)   with the consent of the Director of Public Prosecutions for Northern Ireland.

(10) In the application of this section to Scotland or Northern Ireland the reference in subsection (7)(b) to 12 months shall be taken as a reference to six months.

(11) In subsection (2) the reference to an enactment does not include—

(a)   an Act of the Scottish Parliament or an instrument made under such an Act, or

(b)   an Act of the Northern Ireland Assembly or an instrument made under such an Act.

41 Disclosure of information to Director of Revenue and Customs Prosecutions

(1) A person specified in subsection (2) may disclose information held by him to the Director for a purpose connected with a specified investigation or prosecution.

(2) Those persons are—

(a)   a constable,

(b)   the Director General of the National Criminal Intelligence Service,

(c)   the Director General of the National Crime Squad,

(d)   the Director of the Serious Fraud Office,

(e)   the Director of Public Prosecutions,

(g)   the Director of Public Prosecutions for Northern Ireland, and

(h)   such other persons as the Attorney General may specify by order.

(3) An order under subsection (2)(h)—

(a)   may specify a person only if, or in so far as, he appears to the Attorney General to be exercising public functions,

(b)   may include transitional or incidental provision,

(c)   shall be made by statutory instrument, and

(d)   shall not be made unless a draft has been laid before, and approved by resolution of, each House of Parliament.

(4) In relation to a person if or in so far as he exercises functions in respect of Northern Ireland subsections (2)(h) and (3)(a) shall have effect as if a reference to the Attorney General were a reference to—

(a)   the Advocate General for Northern Ireland, or

(b)   before the commencement of section 27(1) of the Justice (Northern Ireland) Act 2002 (c 26), the Attorney General for Northern Ireland.

(5) In the application of this section to Scotland, references to the Attorney General are to be read as references to a Minister of the Crown (including the Treasury).

(6) Nothing in this section authorises the making of a disclosure which—

(a)   contravenes the Data Protection Act 1998 (c 29), or

(b)   is prohibited by Part 1 of the Regulation of Investigatory Powers Act 2000 (c 23).

42 Inspection

Section 2 of the Crown Prosecution Service Inspectorate Act 2000 (c 10) shall apply to the Revenue and Customs Prosecutions Office as it applies to the Crown Prosecution Service.

Money and property

43 Expenditure

Expenditure of the Commissioners in connection with the exercise of their functions shall be paid out of money provided by Parliament.

44 Payment into Consolidated Fund

(1) The Commissioners shall pay money received in the exercise of their functions into the Consolidated Fund—

(a)   at such times and in such manner as the Treasury directs,

(b)   with the exception of receipts specified in subsection (2), and

(c)   after deduction of the disbursements specified in subsection (3).

(2) The exceptions mentioned in subsection (1)(b) are—

(a)   contributions under Part I of the Social Security Contributions and Benefits Act 1992 (c 4),

(b)   contributions under Part I of the Social Security Contributions and Benefits (Northern Ireland) Act 1992 (c 7),

(c)   any other sums payable, under or by virtue of an enactment, into the National Insurance Fund or the Northern Ireland National Insurance Fund,

(d)   sums required under or by virtue of an enactment to be paid into the National Loans Fund,

(e)   sums required to be paid to a Minister of the Crown by virtue of an enactment relating to financial support for students,

(f)   penalties under section 21 of the National Minimum Wage Act 1998 (c 39) (non-compliance), and

(g)   sums required under or by virtue of an enactment to be paid into the Scottish Consolidated Fund.

(3) The disbursements mentioned in subsection (1)(c) are—

(a)   payments in connection with drawback, repayments and discounts,

(b)   payments under section 77 of the Scotland Act 1998 (c 46) (additional tax),

(c)   payments under section 2 of the Isle of Man Act 1979 (c 58) (Isle of Man share of common duties), and

(d)   tax credits.

(4) In subsection (3)(a) "repayments" includes—

(a)   payments in respect of actual or deemed credits relating to any tax or duty, and

(b)   payments of interest (or repayment supplement) on—

(i)   repayments, or

(ii) payments treated as repayments.

45 Remuneration, etc

(1) The Commissioners shall be paid, out of money provided by Parliament, such remuneration, expenses and other allowances as may be determined by the Minister for the Civil Service.

(2) The Commissioners may incur expenditure in respect of staff (whether in respect of remuneration, allowances, pensions, gratuities or otherwise).

(3) The Commissioners shall pay to the Minister for the Civil Service, at such times as the Minister may direct, such sums as the Minister may determine in respect of any increase attributable to this Act in the sums payable under the Superannuation Act 1972 (c 11) out of money provided by Parliament.

46 Accounts

(1) The Commissioners shall provide to the Comptroller and Auditor General, in such form as the Treasury shall direct, a daily account of—

    (a)   the amount of revenue received, and

    (b)   the disposal of revenue received.

(2) The Commissioners shall provide to the Comptroller and Auditor General, in such form and at such times as the Treasury shall direct, an account of liabilities satisfied by the acceptance of property in satisfaction of tax under—

    (a)   section 230 of the Inheritance Tax Act 1984 (c 51), or

    (b)   any other enactment.

47 Payment out of Consolidated Fund

(1) This section applies if the Treasury think that the funds available to the Commissioners may be insufficient to make, under or by virtue of an enactment—

    (a)   a payment into the National Insurance Fund,

    (b)   a payment into the Northern Ireland National Insurance Fund,

    (c)   a payment of a kind specified in section 44(2)(c) to (g), or

    (d)   a disbursement of a kind specified in section 44(3).

(2) Where this section applies the Treasury may pay money to the Commissioners out of the Consolidated Fund to enable them to make a payment or disbursement.

(3) This section applies whether or not the reason for a deficiency is or may be that an amount has been paid or retained on the basis of an estimate that has proved or may prove to be inaccurate.

48 Transfer of property, etc: general

(1) Upon commencement the property, rights and liabilities of any of the old commissioners shall by virtue of this section vest in the new commissioners.

(2) Anything done by, on behalf of or in relation to any of the old commissioners which has effect immediately before commencement shall continue to have effect as if done by, on behalf of or in relation to the new commissioners.

(3) Anything (including any legal proceedings) which immediately before commencement is in the process of being done by, on behalf of or in relation to any of the old commissioners may be continued by, on behalf of or in relation to the new commissioners.

(4) Upon commencement the property, rights and liabilities of any of the old officers shall by virtue of this section vest in the officers of Revenue and Customs.

(5) Anything done by, on behalf of or in relation to any of the old officers which has effect immediately before commencement shall continue to have effect as if done by, on behalf of or in relation to an officer of Revenue and Customs.

(6) Anything (including any legal proceedings) which immediately before commencement is in the process of being done by, on behalf of or in relation to any of the old officers may be continued by, on behalf of or in relation to an officer of Revenue and Customs.

(7)   So far as is necessary or appropriate in consequence of section 5 or the preceding provisions of this section, on and after commencement—

- (a)   a reference to any of the old commissioners in an agreement (whether written or not), instrument or other document shall be treated as a reference to the new commissioners, and
- (b)   a reference in an agreement (whether written or not), instrument or other document to any of the old officers shall be treated as a reference to an officer of Revenue and Customs.

(8)   This section shall operate in relation to property, rights or liabilities—

- (a)   whether or not they would otherwise be capable of being transferred,
- (b)   without any instrument or other formality being required, and
- (c)   irrespective of any requirement for consent that would otherwise apply.

(9)   In this section—

"commencement" means the time appointed under section 53 for the commencement of section 5,

"rights and liabilities" includes rights and liabilities relating to employment,

"the old commissioners" means—

- (a)   the Commissioners of Inland Revenue, and
- (b)   the Commissioners of Customs and Excise,

"the old officers" means any of the persons listed in section 6(2) or 7(3), and

"the new commissioners" means the Commissioners for Her Majesty's Revenue and Customs.

(10)   This section is subject to section 49.

49 Transfer of property, etc: Prosecutions Office

(1)   The Treasury may make a scheme identifying property, rights and liabilities of the old commissioners which shall on commencement vest not in the new commissioners but in the Director of Revenue and Customs Prosecutions.

(2)   A scheme shall have effect—

- (a)   in so far as it excludes anything from the operation of section 48, on the coming into force of that section, and
- (b)   in so far as it vests anything in the Director of Revenue and Customs Prosecutions, upon the coming into force of section 35.

(3)   A scheme may include consequential and incidental provision and may, in particular—

- (a)   apply (with or without modification) or make provision similar to any provision of section 48;
- (b)   modify the effect of section 48(2), (3), (5), (6) or (7);
- (c)   make provision for shared ownership, use or access.

(4)   The Treasury may require the new commissioners to transfer specified property, rights and liabilities to the Director of Revenue and Customs Prosecutions (and the commissioners shall comply).

(5)   In relation to any matter that becomes a function of the Director of Revenue and Customs Prosecutions under section 35, section 48(2), (3), (5), (6) and (7) shall have effect with—

- (a)   the substitution of a reference to the Director for any reference to the new commissioners or to an officer of Revenue and Customs (or officers of Revenue and Customs), and
- (b)   the substitution of a reference to this section and anything done under it for a reference to section 48.

(6)   In this section the following expressions have the same meaning as in section 48—

(a)   "commencement",

(b)   "the old commissioners", and

(c)   "the new commissioners".

General

50 Consequential amendments, etc

(1)   In so far as is appropriate in consequence of section 5 a reference in an enactment, instrument or other document to the Commissioners of Customs and Excise, to customs and excise or to the Commissioners of Inland Revenue (however expressed) shall be taken as a reference to the Commissioners for Her Majesty's Revenue and Customs.

(2)   In so far as is appropriate in consequence of sections 6 and 7 a reference in an enactment, instrument or other document to any of the persons specified in section 6(2) or 7(3) (however expressed) shall be taken as a reference to an officer of Revenue and Customs.

(3)   In so far as is appropriate in consequence of this Act a reference in an enactment, instrument or other document to the Valuation Office of the Inland Revenue (however expressed) shall be taken as a reference to the Valuation Office of Her Majesty's Revenue and Customs.

(4)   The Treasury may by regulations make such provision as they think appropriate in consequence of section 5, 6 or 7 in respect of a reference in an enactment (however expressed) to—

(a)   the Commissioners of Inland Revenue (or to a Commissioner),

(b)   the Commissioners of Customs and Excise (or to a Commissioner),

(c)   customs,

(d)   customs and excise,

(e)   Inland Revenue, or

(f)   any of the persons specified in section 6(2) or 7(3).

(5)   Regulations under subsection (4) in respect of a reference in an enactment—

(a)   may amend an enactment,

(b)   may make incidental and consequential provision,

(c)   shall be made by statutory instrument, and

(d)   shall not be made unless a draft has first been laid before, and approved by resolution of, each House of Parliament.

(6)   Schedule 4 (consequential amendments, etc) shall have effect (and is without prejudice to the generality of subsections (1) to (4)).

(7)   Subsections (1) to (4) shall, subject to any express provision to the contrary, have effect in relation to enactments passed or made, and instruments and documents issued, whether before or after the passing of this Act.

51 Interpretation

(1)   In this Act—

except where otherwise expressly provided, "enactment" includes—

(a)   an Act of the Scottish Parliament,

(b)   an instrument made under an Act of the Scottish Parliament,

(c)   Northern Ireland legislation, and

(d)   an instrument made under Northern Ireland legislation,

"officer of Revenue and Customs" means a person appointed under section 2, and

"revenue" has the meaning given by section 5(4).

(2)   In this Act—

(a)   "function" means any power or duty (including a power or duty that is ancillary to another power or duty), and

(b)   a reference to the functions of the Commissioners or of officers of Revenue and Customs is a reference to the functions conferred—

(i)   by or by virtue of this Act, or

(ii)   by or by virtue of any enactment passed or made after the commencement of this Act.

(3)   A reference in this Act, in an enactment amended by this Act or, subject to express provision to the contrary, in any future enactment, to responsibility for collection and management of revenue has the same meaning as references to responsibility for care and management of revenue in enactments passed before this Act.

(4)   In this Act a reference to information acquired in connection with a matter includes a reference to information held in connection with that matter.

52 Repeals

(1)   *(Repeals the Customs and Excise Management Act 1979, ss 12, 15, 32, 84, 86, 152(c)(d), 169 and the Taxes Management Act 1970, s 111(2)).*

(2)   The enactments specified in Schedule 5 are hereby repealed to the extent specified.

53 Commencement

(1)   This Act shall come into force in accordance with provision made by order of the Treasury.

(2)   An order under subsection (1)—

(a)   may make provision generally or only in relation to specified provisions or purposes,

(b)   may include transitional, consequential or incidental provision or savings, and

(c)   shall be made by statutory instrument.

NOTES

Orders: Commissioners for Revenue and Customs Act 2005 (Commencement) Order 2005, SI 2005/1126.

54 Transitional: general

(1)   In the application of section 5—

(a)   a reference to responsibility before commencement of that section includes a reference to responsibility under an enactment passed or made, but not yet in force, before commencement, and

(b)   a reference to a function vesting includes a reference to a function which is to vest under an enactment passed or made, but not yet in force, before commencement of that section.

(2)   In the application of section 6 or 7 a reference to a function conferred by an enactment includes a reference to a function conferred by an enactment passed or made, but not yet in force, before commencement of that section.

(3)   Where immediately before the commencement of section 6 a person holds appointment as a member of the staff of the Commissioners of Inland Revenue or of the Commissioners of Customs and Excise, his appointment shall have effect on commencement as if made by the Commissioners for Her Majesty's Revenue and Customs under section 2.

(4)   The following shall be treated as being included in the list in Schedule 1—

(a)   development land tax,

(b)   disabled person's tax credit,

(c)   estate duty,

(d)   the national defence contribution under Part III of the Finance Act 1937 (c 54),

(e)   the special tax on banking deposits under section 134 of the Finance Act 1981 (c 35), and

(f)   working families tax credit.

(5)   The Treasury may by order made by statutory instrument add to the list in subsection (4) an item relating to a matter for which the Commissioners of Inland Revenue or a person listed in section 7(3) had responsibility before the commencement of section 5, if it appears to the Treasury that the law relating to that matter has lapsed or ceased to have effect but that transitional matters may continue to arise in respect of it.

(6)   An order under subsection (5)—

(a)   may include consequential, transitional or incidental provision,

(b)   shall be made by statutory instrument, and

(c)   shall be subject to annulment in pursuance of a resolution of either House of Parliament.

(7)   A reference in this Act to anything done by, on behalf of or in relation to a specified person or class of person includes a reference to anything treated as if done by, on behalf of or in relation to that person by virtue of transitional provision of an enactment passed or made before this Act.

55 Transitional: penalties

(1)   In relation to an offence under section 19 committed before the commencement of section 282 of the Criminal Justice Act 2003 (c 44) (short sentences) the reference in section 19(4)(b) to 12 months shall have effect as if it were a reference to six months.

(2)   In relation to an offence under section 21 committed before the commencement of section 282 of the Criminal Justice Act (short sentences), the reference in section 21(6)(b) to 12 months shall have effect as if it were a reference to six months.

(3)   In relation to an offence under section 29 committed before the commencement of section 282 of the Criminal Justice Act 2003 (c 44) (short sentences) the reference in section 29(6)(b) to 12 months shall have effect as if it were a reference to six months.

(4)   In relation to an offence under section 30 committed before the commencement of section 281(4) and (5) of the Criminal Justice Act 2003 (51 week maximum term of sentences) the reference in section 30(2)(a) to 51 weeks shall have effect as if it were a reference to six months.

(5)   In relation to an offence under section 31 committed before the commencement of section 281(4) and (5) of the Criminal Justice Act 2003 (51 week maximum term of sentences) the reference in section 31(2)(a) to 51 weeks shall have effect as if it were a reference to one month.

(6)   In relation to an offence under section 32 committed before the commencement of section 281(4) and (5) of the Criminal Justice Act 2003 (51 week maximum term of sentences) the reference in section 32(2)(a) to 51 weeks shall have effect as if it were a reference to six months.

(7)   In relation to an offence under section 40 committed before the commencement of section 282 of the Criminal Justice Act 2003 (short sentences) the reference in section 40(7)(b) to 12 months shall have effect as if it were a reference to six months.

56 Extent

(1)   This Act extends to the United Kingdom.

(2)   But an amendment, modification or repeal effected by this Act has the same extent as the enactment (or the relevant part of the enactment) to which it relates.

57 Short title

This Act may be cited as the Commissioners for Revenue and Customs Act 2005.

SCHEDULE 2
FUNCTIONS OF COMMISSIONERS AND OFFICERS: RESTRICTIONS, ETC
Sections 16 and 17

PART 1
GENERAL

. . .

Customs and Excise Management Act 1979 (c 2)

4.

Section 8(2) and (3) of the Customs and Excise Management Act 1979 (person acting deemed to be proper officer) shall not apply to a person engaged in connection with a function relating to a matter to which section 7 above applies.

5.—

(1)   Section 11 of that Act (assistance to be rendered by police, &c) shall not apply in connection with a function relating to a matter to which section 7 above applies.

(2)   A person may rely for the purposes of section 11 of that Act on a statement (written or oral) of an officer of Revenue and Customs that a function does not relate to a matter to which section 7 above applies.

6.—

(1)   Sections 167 (untrue declarations, &c) and 168 (counterfeiting documents, &c) of that Act shall not apply in relation to a declaration, document or statement in respect of a function relating to a matter to which section 7 above applies.

. . .

Finance Act 1985 (c 54)

8.

Section 10 of the Finance Act 1985 (computer records &c) shall not apply in connection with a function relating to a matter to which section 7 above applies.

. . .

PART 2
USE OF INFORMATION

. . .

NOTES

   Paras omitted are outside the scope of this work

SCHEDULE 3
REVENUE AND CUSTOMS PROSECUTIONS OFFICE

Section 34

Appointment of Director

1.

The Director must have a ten year general qualification within the meaning of section 71 of the Courts and Legal Services Act 1990 (c 41) (qualification for judicial appointments).

2.

The Director shall hold and vacate office in accordance with the terms of his appointment (which may include provision for dismissal).

Money

3.

The Director shall be paid such remuneration, expenses and other allowances as the Attorney General shall determine with the approval of the Minister for the Civil Service.

4.

In incurring expenditure the Director shall comply with any directions given to him by the Attorney General with the consent of the Treasury.

5.

Expenditure of the Director shall be paid out of money provided by Parliament.

Annual report

6.—

(1)   As soon as is reasonably practicable after the end of each financial year the Director shall send to the Attorney General a report on the exercise of the Director's functions during that year.

(2)   A report shall, in particular, give details of—
   (a)   the nature and outcomes of prosecutions undertaken,
   (b)   the criteria used to determine whether to designate individuals under section 39, and
   (c)   the arrangements for training individuals designated under that section.

(3)   Where the Attorney General receives a report under sub-paragraph (1) he shall—
   (a)   lay a copy before Parliament, and
   (b)   arrange for it to be published.

Financial year

7.—

(1)   The financial year of the Office shall begin with 1st April and end with 31st March.

(2)   But the first financial year of the Office shall—
   (a)   begin with the date on which section 34 comes into force, and
   (b)   end with the following 31st March.

Status

8.

Service as the Director or a member of the Office is service in the civil service of the State.

SCHEDULE 4

CONSEQUENTIAL AMENDMENTS, ETC

Section 50

. . .

16.

(Repeals Finance Act 1972, s 127)

. . .

Customs and Excise Management Act 1979 (c 2)

20.

The Customs and Excise Management Act 1979 shall be amended as follows.

21.

(Repeals CEMA 1979, ss 6, 7, 8(1), 13, 14, 16, 17, 18, 153, 155(2), 165).

22.

(Amends CEMA 1979, s 1(1)).

23.

(Amends CEMA 1979, s 145).

24.

(Amends CEMA 1979, s 146A(7)).

25.

(Amends CEMA 1979, s 150(1)).

26.

(Amends CEMA 1979, s 152(a)).

27.

(Amends CEMA 1979, s 155(1)).

28.

(Amends CEMA 1979, s 171).

. . .

Finance Act 1989 (c 26)

39.

(Amends FA 1989, s 182).

. . .

NOTES

    Paras omitted are outside the scope of this work

SCHEDULE 5

REPEALS

Section 52

Short title and chapter	Extent of repeal
. . .	. . .
Finance Act 1972 (c 41)	Section 127.
. . .	. . .
Customs and Excise Management Act 1979 (c 2)	Sections 6 and 7.
	Section 8(1).
	Sections 12 to 18.
	Section 32.
	Section 84.
	Section 86.
	Section 145(4).
	In section 152(a), the words "stay, sist or".
	Paragraphs (c) and (d) of section 152.
	Section 153.
	Section 155(2).
	Section 165.
	Section 169.
. . .	

NOTES

Words omitted are outside the scope of this work.

FINANCE (NO 2) ACT 2005

(2005 c 22)

An Act to Grant certain duties, to alter other duties, and to amend the law relating to the National Debt and the Public Revenue, and to make further provision in connection with finance.

[20 July 2005]

PART 1

VALUE ADDED TAX

1 Goods subject to warehousing regime: place of acquisition or supply
(Inserts VATA 1994 s 18(1A)).

4 Section 3: consequential and supplementary provision
(1) In consequence of the amendments made by section 3, VATA 1994 is amended as follows.
(2)–(4) . . .
(5) *(Amends VATA 1994 s 83).*

(6)   The amendments made by section 3 and this section have effect in any case where a claim under section 80(2) of VATA 1994 is made on or after 26th May 2005, whenever the event occurred in respect of which the claim is made.

NOTE

Subsections omitted are beyond the scope of this work.

72 Short title

This Act may be cited as the Finance (No 2) Act 2005.

FINANCE ACT 2006

(2006 c 25)

ARRANGEMENT OF SECTIONS

An Act to Grant certain duties, to alter other duties, and to amend the law relating to the National Debt and the Public Revenue, and to make further provision in connection with finance.

[19 July 2006]

1 Rates of tobacco products duty

(1)   (*substitutes Table of rates of duty in TPDA 1979 Schedule 1*)

(2)   This section shall be deemed to have come into force at 6 o'clock in the evening of 22nd March 2006.

2 Tobacco products duty: evasion

(1)   (*inserts TPDA 1979 ss 7A–7D*)

(2)   (*inserts TPDA 1979 s 9(2)*)

(3)   This section shall come into force in accordance with provision made by the Treasury by order.

(4)   An order under subsection (3)—

(a)   may include transitional, consequential or incidental provision, and

(b)   shall be made by statutory instrument.

NOTE

Commencement: 1 October 2006: see SI 2006/2367, art 2.

Orders: Finance Act 2006 (Tobacco Products Duty: Evasion) (Appointed Day) Order, SI 2006/2367 (made under sub-s (3)).

Alcoholic liquor duties

3 Rate of duty on beer

(1)   (*substitutes figure in ALDA 1979 s 36(1AA)*)

(2)   This section shall be deemed to have come into force at midnight on 26th March 2006.

4 Rates of duty on wine and made-wine

(1)   (*substitutes Table in ALDA 1979 Sch 1 Pt 1*)

(2)   This section shall be deemed to have come into force at midnight on 26th March 2006.

5 Repeal of provisions of ALDA 1979 of no practical utility etc

(1)   (*repeals ALDA 1979 ss 12(4), 14, 15(4), 18(5), 21, 24, 26, 32, 35, 55A, 67, 69, 71, 74, 82*)

(2)   In consequence of the repeal of section 55A of ALDA 1979, that Act is amended as follows.

(3)   (*amends ALDA 1979 s 54(4A)*)

(4)   (*amends ALDA 1979 s 55(4A), (5)(d)*)

Hydrocarbon oil duties

6 Rates until 1st September 2006

(1)–(6)   (*amend HODA 1979 ss 6(1A), 6AA(3), 6AD(3), 8(3), 13A(1)*)

(7)   (*revokes SIs 2005/1978, 2005/1979 and 2005/3330*)

NOTES

Orders: Excise Duties (Surcharges or Rebates) (Hydrocarbon Oils etc) Order, SI 2006/1979.

7 Rates from 1st September 2006

(1)–(8)   (*amend HODA 1979 ss 6(1A), 6AA(3), 6AD(3), 8(3), 11(1), 13A(1), 14(1)*)

(9)   This section comes into force on 1st September 2006.

NOTES

Orders: Excise Duties (Surcharges or Rebates) (Hydrocarbon Oils etc) Order, SI 2006/1979.

8 Road vehicles
(*inserts HODA 1979 s 27(1A)*)

PART 10
SUPPLEMENTARY PROVISIONS

178 Repeals

(1) The enactments mentioned in Schedule 26 (which include provisions that are spent or of no practical utility) are repealed to the extent specified.

(2) The repeals specified in that Schedule have effect subject to the commencement provisions and savings contained or referred to in the notes set out in that Schedule.

179 Interpretation
In this Act—

"ALDA 1979" means the Alcoholic Liquor Duties Act 1979 (c 4);

"CAA 2001" means the Capital Allowances Act 2001 (c 2);

"FA", followed by a year, means the Finance Act of that year;

"F(No 2)A", followed by a year, means the Finance (No 2) Act of that year;

"HODA 1979" means the Hydrocarbon Oil Duties Act 1979 (c 5);

"ICTA" means the Income and Corporation Taxes Act 1988 (c 1);

"IHTA 1984" means the Inheritance Tax Act 1984 (c 51);

"ITEPA 2003" means the Income Tax (Earnings and Pensions) Act 2003 (c 1);

"ITTOIA 2005" means the Income Tax (Trading and Other Income) Act 2005 (c 5);

"OTA 1975" means the Oil Taxation Act 1975 (c 22);

"TCGA 1992" means the Taxation of Chargeable Gains Act 1992 (c 12);

"TMA 1970" means the Taxes Management Act 1970 (c 9);

"VATA 1994" means the Value Added Tax Act 1994 (c 23);

"VERA 1994" means the Vehicle Excise and Registration Act 1994 (c 22).

180 Short title
This Act may be cited as the Finance Act 2006.

SCHEDULES

SCHEDULE 26
REPEALS
Section 178

PART 1
EXCISE DUTIES

(1) PROVISIONS OF ALDA 1979 OF NO PRACTICAL UTILITY ETC

Short title and chapter	Extent of repeal
Alcoholic Liquor Duties Act 1979 (c 4)	Section 12(4).
	Section 14.
	Section 15(4).
	Section 18(5).
	Section 21.
	Section 24.
	Section 26.

Short title and chapter	Extent of repeal
	Section 32.
	Section 35.
	Section 55A.
	Section 67.
	Section 69.
	Section 71.
	Section 74.
	Section 82.
Finance Act 1981 (c 35)	In Schedule 8, paragraphs 13, 17 and 21.
Finance Act 1985 (c 54)	In Schedule 3, paragraph 2.
Finance Act 1986 (c 41)	In Schedule 5, paragraph 3(2).
Territorial Sea Act 1987 (c 49)	In Schedule 1, paragraph 5(2).
Finance Act 1988 (c 39)	In Schedule 1, paragraphs 6 and 10.
Finance Act 1994 (c 9)	In Schedule 4, in paragraph 18(1), the words from "(offence" to the end, and paragraphs 23, 25, 28, 36, 42 to 44 and 48.
	In Schedule 5, paragraph 3(1)(i) and (n).
Finance Act 1995 (c 4)	In Schedule 2, paragraph 4.
Licensing Act 2003 (c 17)	In Schedule 6, paragraph 73.

FINANCE ACT 2007

(2007 c 11)

An Act to grant certain duties, to alter other duties, and to amend the law relating to the National Debt and the Public Revenue, and to make further provision in connection with finance.

[19th July 2007]

PART 1
CHARGES, RATES, THRESHOLDS ETC

Alcohol and tobacco

5 Rates of duty on alcoholic liquor

(1)   The Alcoholic Liquor Duties Act 1979 (c 4) is amended as follows.

(2)   In section 36(1AA)(a) (standard rate of duty on beer), for "£13.26" substitute "£13.71".

(3)   In section 62(1A) (rates of duty on cider)—

   (a)   in paragraph (a) (rate of duty per hectolitre in the case of sparkling cider of a strength exceeding 5.5 per cent), for "£166.70" substitute "£172.33",

   (b)   in paragraph (b) (rate of duty per hectolitre in the case of cider of a strength exceeding 7.5 per cent which is not sparkling cider), for "£38.43" substitute "£39.73", and

   (c)   in paragraph (c) (rate of duty per hectolitre in any other case), for "£25.61" substitute "£26.48".

(4)   For Part 1 of the Table in Schedule 1 substitute—

"PART 1
WINE AND MADE-WINE OF A STRENGTH NOT EXCEEDING 22 PER CENT

Description of wine or made-wine	Rates of duty per hectolitre
	£
Wine or made-wine of a strength not exceeding 4 per cent	54.85
Wine or made-wine of a strength exceeding 4 per cent but not exceeding 5.5 per cent	75.42
Wine or made-wine of a strength exceeding 5.5 per cent but not exceeding 15 per cent and not sparkling	177.99
Sparkling wine or sparkling made-wine of a strength exceeding 5.5 per cent but less than 8.5 per cent	172.33
Sparkling wine or sparkling made-wine of a strength of 8.5 per cent or of a strength exceeding 8.5 per cent but not exceeding 15 per cent	227.99
Wine or made-wine of a strength exceeding 15 per cent but not exceeding 22 per cent	237.31"

(5)   The amendments made by this section are deemed to have come into force on 26th March 2007.

6 Rates of tobacco products duty

(1)   For the Table in Schedule 1 to the Tobacco Products Duty Act 1979 (c 7) substitute—

> "Table

1 Cigarettes	An amount equal to 22 per cent of the retail price plus £108.65 per thousand cigarettes.
2 Cigars	£158.24 per kilogram.
3 Hand-rolling tobacco	£113.74 per kilogram.
4 Other smoking tobacco and chewing tobacco	£69.57 per kilogram."

(2)   The amendment made by subsection (1) is deemed to have come into force at 6pm on 21st March 2007.

Environment

10 Fuel duty rates and rebates

(1)   The Hydrocarbon Oil Duties Act 1979 (c 5) is amended as follows.

(2)   In section 6(1A) (hydrocarbon oil: rates of duty)—

   (a)   in paragraph (a) (ultra low sulphur petrol), for "£0.4835" substitute "£0.5035",

   (b)   in paragraph (aa) (sulphur-free petrol), for "£0.4835" substitute "£0.5035",

   (c)   in paragraph (b) (light oil other than ultra low sulphur petrol and sulphur-free petrol), for "£0.5768" substitute "£0.6007",

   (d)   in paragraph (c) (ultra low sulphur diesel), for "£0.4835" substitute "£0.5035",

   (e)   in paragraph (ca) (sulphur-free diesel), for "£0.4835" substitute "£0.5035", and

   (f)   in paragraph (d) (heavy oil other than ultra low sulphur diesel and sulphur-free diesel), for "£0.5468" substitute "£0.5694".

(3)   In section 6AA(3) (biodiesel), for "£0.2835" substitute "£0.3035".

(4)   In section 6AD(3) (bioethanol), for "£0.2835" substitute "£0.3035".

(5)   In section 8(3) (road fuel gas)—

   (a)   in paragraph (a) (natural road fuel gas), for "£0.1081" substitute "£0.1370", and

   (b)   in paragraph (b) (other road fuel gas), for "£0.1221" substitute "£0.1649".

(6)   In section 11(1) (rebate on heavy oil)—

   (a)   in paragraph (a) (fuel oil), for "£0.0729" substitute "£0.0929",

   (b)   in paragraph (b) (gas oil which is not ultra low sulphur diesel), for "£0.0769" substitute "£0.0969", and

   (c)   in paragraph (ba) (ultra low sulphur diesel), for "£0.0769" substitute "£0.0969".

(7)   In section 13A(1) (rebate on unleaded petrol), for "£0.0617" substitute "£0.0642".

(8)   In section 14(1) (rebate on light oil for use as furnace oil), for "£0.0729" substitute "£0.0929".

(9)   The amendments made by this section come into force on 1st October 2007.

12 Rates of air passenger duty

(1) Section 30 of FA 1994 (rates of air passenger duty) is amended as follows.

(2) In subsection (3A) (destinations in EEA States and qualifying territories etc)—

    (a)   in paragraph (a) (standard class travel), for "£5" substitute "£10", and

    (b)   in paragraph (b) (any other case), for "£10" substitute "£20".

(3) In subsection (4) (other destinations)—

    (a)   in paragraph (a) (standard class travel), for "£20" substitute "£40", and

    (b)   in paragraph (b) (any other case), for "£40" substitute "£80".

(4) The amendments made by this section have effect in relation to any carriage of a passenger on an aircraft which begins on or after 1st February 2007.

(5) But if the amount of duty due from any operator in the accounting period ending before 21st March 2007 increased as a result of those amendments, the operator is to pay the amount of that increase as if it became due in the first accounting period ending after that day.

(6) Expressions which are used in subsection (5) and in the Air Passenger Duty Regulations 1994 (SI 1994/1738) have the same meaning in that subsection as in those regulations.

PART 6
INVESTIGATION, ADMINISTRATION ETC

Investigation etc

84 Sections 82 and 83: supplementary

(1)–(3) ...

(4) Schedule 22 contains amendments and repeals consequential on extension of police powers to Revenue and Customs.

...

PART 8
FINAL PROVISIONS

113 Interpretation

(1) In this Act—

"BGDA 1981" means the Betting and Gaming Duties Act 1981 (c 63),

"CAA 2001" means the Capital Allowances Act 2001 (c 2),

"CEMA 1979" means the Customs and Excise Management Act 1979 (c 2),

"CRCA 2005" means the Commissioners for Revenue and Customs Act 2005 (c 11),

"ICTA" means the Income and Corporation Taxes Act 1988 (c 1),

...

"VATA 1994" means the Value Added Tax Act 1994 (c 23), and

"VERA 1994" means the Vehicle Excise and Registration Act 1994 (c 22).

(2) In this Act—

"FA", followed by a year, means the Finance Act of that year, and

"F(No 2)A", followed by a year, means the Finance (No 2) Act of that year.

114 Repeals

Schedule 27 contains repeals.

115 Short title
This Act may be cited as the Finance Act 2007.

SCHEDULES

SCHEDULE 22
AMENDMENTS AND REPEALS CONSEQUENTIAL ON EXTENSION OF
HMRC POWERS
Section 84

PART 1
AMENDMENTS
2.   In section 67 of the Criminal Justice and Police Act 2001 (c 16) and the heading
of that section, for "customs officers" substitute "officers of Revenue and Customs".

PART 2
REPEALS
5.   In CEMA 1979—
  (a)   section 118C(3)(c) (gaming duty), and
  (b)   the references to a gaming duty offence in section 118C(4)(b) and (5).
. . .
  13.—(1)   In the Criminal Justice and Police Act 2001—
  (a)   section 57(1)(c) (section 20CC of TMA 1970),
  (b)   section 63(2)(e) (section 20C of TMA 1970), and
  (c)   section 65(3) (section 20C of TMA 1970).
  (2)   In Schedule 1 to that Act—
  (a)   paragraph 13 (section 20C of TMA 1970),
  (b)   paragraph 28 (paragraph 17(2) of Schedule 3 to BGDA 1981),
  (c)   paragraph 29 (paragraph 17(2) of Schedule 4 to BDGA 1981),
  (d)   paragraph 57 (paragraph 4(3) of Schedule 7 to FA 1994),
  (e)   paragraph 58 (paragraph 10(3) of Schedule 11 to VATA 1994),
  (f)   paragraph 61 (paragraph 5(2) of Schedule 5 to FA 1996), and
  (g)   paragraph 72 (paragraph 130(2) of Schedule 6 to FA 2000).
. . .

Part II

Statutory Instruments

Statutory Instruments

ISO-PROPYL ALCOHOL REGULATIONS 1927

(SI 1927/783)

NOTES

Made: 16 August 1927.

Authority: Finance Act 1927, s 16 (see now the Alcoholic Liquor Duties Act 1979, s 35).

Commencement: 1 September 1927.

These Regulations revoked by the Denatured Alcohol Regulations, SI 2005/1524 reg 3, with effect from 1 July 2005.

...

IMPORT DUTIES (VALUATION OF GOODS) REGULATIONS 1935

(SI 1935/689)

NOTES

Made: 10 July 1935.

Authority: Import Duties Act, 1932, s 15(3) (see now the Customs and Excise Management Act 1979, s 177(5)).

Commencement: 10 July 1935.

1

The importer of any goods liable to duty under any enactment whereunder a duty of customs is chargeable on any goods by reference to their value shall at the time of making entry, or within such period thereafter as the Commissioners may in special cases allow, produce a declaration in respect of the goods duly completed in such form as the Commissioners may require, and shall give such further particulars as the Commissioners may think necessary for a proper valuation of the goods in such form as the Commissioners may direct.

NOTES

Entry on the importation of goods: by the Customs and Excise (Single Market etc) Regulations 1992, SI 1992/3095, reg 10(1), Sch 1, para 1, the reference to an entry on the importation of goods is to be treated as including an entry of such goods under the Customs Controls on Importation of Goods Regulations 1991, SI 1991/2724, reg 5, as amended by SI 1992/3095 and SI 1993/3014.

2

The importer shall produce at his premises or elsewhere, as the Commissioners may appoint, to an Officer upon demand any books of account or other documents of whatever nature relating to the purchase, importation, or sale of the goods.

3

Nothing in these Regulations shall affect the powers of the Commissioners or of their Officers under any Act relating to the Customs.

4—

(1) These Regulations may be cited as the Import Duties (Valuation of Goods) Regulations 1935.

(2)   In these Regulations unless the context otherwise requires, the following expressions shall have the meanings hereinafter respectively attached to them, that is to say—

"Commissioners" means Commissioners of Customs and Excise.

"Officer" means any official of the Customs and Excise authorised by the Commissioners.

"Importer" includes an agent of the importer making entry and any other person concerned with the importation of the goods into the United Kingdom.

(3)   The Interpretation Act, 1889, applies for the purpose of the interpretation of these Regulations in like manner as it applies for the purpose of the interpretation of an Act of Parliament and as if these Regulations were an Act of Parliament.

5—

(1)   . . .

(2)   These Regulations shall come into force on the tenth day of July, 1935.

NOTES

Para (1): revokes the Import Duties (Valuation of Goods) Regulations 1934, SR & O 1934/731.

CARRIAGE OF GOODS COASTWISE REGULATIONS 1952

(SI 1952/2225)

NOTES

Made: 22 December 1952.

Authority: Customs and Excise Act, 1952, s 61(1) (see now the Customs and Excise Management Act 1979, s 73(1)).

Commencement: 1 January 1953.

1

No person shall unload goods from any ship arriving coastwise or load or make waterborne for loading goods for carriage coastwise—

(a)   outside such hours as the Commissioners may appoint,

(b)   except at an approved wharf,

(c)   without the authority of the proper officer of customs and excise, or

(d)   on a Sunday or a holiday, save as permitted by the Commissioners.

2

Within twenty-four hours after the arrival at the port or place of discharge of any ship carrying goods coastwise, and before any goods are unloaded, the master shall, by himself or his agent, deliver to the collector or other proper officer the transire or other prescribed document giving particulars of the goods carried in the ship.

3

(Spent.)

4

No person shall unload any imported goods which have been transhipped and carried coastwise by virtue of subsection (2) of section fifty-eight of the said Act before due entry thereof has been made, except where the goods are unloaded for deposit in a transit shed and duly deposited therein.

NOTES

Entry on the importation of goods: by the Customs and Excise (Single Market etc) Regulations 1992, SI 1992/3095, reg 10(1), Sch 1, para 1, the reference to an entry on the importation of goods is to be treated as including an entry of such goods under the Customs Controls on Importation of Goods Regulations 1991, SI 1991/2724, reg 5, as amended by SI 1992/3095, SI 1993/3014.

5

The master of every coasting ship shall keep or cause to be kept a cargo book, shall produce the same on demand to any officer, and shall permit him to make any note therein.

6

The master shall enter in the cargo book the names of the ship, the master and the port to which the ship belongs, and unless the Commissioners otherwise direct shall also enter therein—

(a)   the name of the port to which the ship is bound on each voyage,

(b)   at every port of loading, the name of such port and an account of all goods there taken on board, stating—

(i)   the description of the packages and the quantities and descriptions of the goods therein,

(ii)   the quantities and descriptions of any goods stowed loose,

(iii)   which of any such goods are foreign, and

(iv)   the names of the respective shippers and consignees,

(c)   at every port of unloading, the name of such port, an account of all goods delivered out of the said ship stating the particulars specified in sub-paragraphs (i) to (iv) of paragraph (b) of this Regulation and the date of such delivery, and

(d)   the respective times of departure from every port of loading and of arrival at every port of unloading.

7

These Regulations may be cited as the Carriage of Goods Coastwise Regulations, 1952, and shall come into operation on the first day of January, 1953.

DUTY-FREE SUPPLIES FOR THE ROYAL NAVY REGULATIONS 1954

(SI 1954/1406)

NOTES

Made: 26 October 1954.

Authority: Customs and Excise Act, 1952, s 272(1) (see now the Customs and Excise Duties (General Reliefs) Act 1979, s 12(1)).

Commencement: 1 November 1954.

ARRANGEMENT OF REGULATIONS

1   Goods to which the Regulations apply

2   Ships and naval establishments to which these Regulations apply

3   Scale of supply of tobacco

Part II

1 Goods to which the Regulations apply

These Regulations shall apply to dutiable food and drink, tobacco and matches which are supplied to any of HM Ships specified in paragraphs (a) and (b) of Regulation 2, or (with the exception of matches) to the Admiralty at a naval victualling yard, depot or sub-depot, for distribution to any of HM Ships specified in paragraphs (a), (b) or (c) of Regulation 2 for the use of persons living in that ship (being persons borne on the books of that or of another of HM Ships or of a naval establishment) or to the Admiralty as aforesaid for distribution to any naval establishment for the use of officers and men of the Royal Navy and Royal Marines living in that establishment, and borne on the books of that or of some other naval establishment or of one of HM Ships.

2 Ships and naval establishments to which these Regulations apply

The goods specified in Regulation 1 may be supplied in accordance with these Regulations for consumption in the following classes of ships and naval establishments—

(a)   HM Ships in commission which are normally required in the ordinary course of their duty to be absent from United Kingdom territorial waters for periods of more than six days continuously in each year;

(b)   HM Ships in commission which are normally required in the ordinary course of their duty to be absent from United Kingdom territorial waters but not for periods as long as six days continuously and HM Ships in commission belonging to classes I and II (state of readiness) of the Reserve Fleet in which only officers and men serving in the Reserve Fleet are living;

(c)   HM Ships other than those aforementioned and naval establishments.

3 Scale of supply of tobacco

The quantity of tobacco to be supplied under the terms of these Regulations in each month for the use of each person or officer or man mentioned in Regulation 1 who is an habitual user of tobacco and who is living in a ship or establishment specified in Regulation 2 hereof shall not exceed in the case of—

(a)   HM Ships designated in paragraph (a) of Regulation 2, save when undergoing a refit exceeding 28 days .... 1½lb.

(b)   HM Ships designated in paragraph (b) of Regulation 2, save when undergoing a refit exceeding 28 days .... 1¼lb.

(c)   HM Ships designated in paragraph (c) of Regulation 2, and naval establishments (other than such establishments as the Admiralty may from time to time exclude) .... ¾lb.

(d)   HM Ships designated in paragraphs (a) and (b) of Regulation 2 during any refit which exceeds 28 days .... ¾lb.

and no such person or officer or man shall during any month receive any quantity of such tobacco in excess of the amount as aforesaid properly applicable to him.

Provided that any tobacco taken on board any of HM Ships at any place outside the United Kingdom, shall, if it is supplied after the return of the ship to the Home Station for the use of any person, officer or man mentioned in this Regulation, be taken into account in calculating the quantities to be supplied for the purposes of this Regulation.

4 Supply of tobacco in certain cases

The tobacco supplied in accordance with paragraphs (c) and (d) of Regulation 3 shall be provided by the Admiralty from a naval victualling yard, depot or sub-depot.

5 Control of tobacco

The marking, supply and distribution of tobacco supplied under the terms of these Regulations shall be in accordance with such conditions as may from time to time be prescribed by the Commissioners after consultation with the Admiralty.

6 Control of dutiable liquor

The supply and distribution of dutiable liquor supplied under the terms of these Regulations shall be controlled by the Admiralty subject to the agreement of the Commissioners.

7 Goods to be treated as exported

The goods specified in and supplied in accordance with Regulation 1 shall for all or any purposes of any customs or excise duty, drawback or allowance in respect of those goods be treated as exported, and a person supplying or intending to supply goods as aforesaid shall be treated accordingly as exporting or intending to export them, provided that all the conditions which may from time to time be prescribed by the Commissioners after consultation with the Admiralty in pursuance of section two hundred and seventy-two of the Customs and Excise Act, 1952, are duly complied with.

8 Time of exportation

The time of exportation of goods specified in Regulation 1 shall be deemed to be—

    (a)   in the case of goods supplied direct to any of HM Ships of the classes specified in paragraphs (a) and (b) of Regulation 2, the time when the said goods are first received on board such ship, and

    (b)   in the case of goods supplied to the Admiralty, the time when the said goods are received for the first time in any naval victualling yard, depot or sub-depot in the United Kingdom.

9 Adaptation of the customs and excise enactments

The provisions of the Customs and Excise Act, 1952, so far as they are applicable, shall apply to goods supplied to HM Ships or to the Admiralty in accordance with these Regulations, with the following adaptations, namely—

    (a)   In subsection (1) of section forty-seven, for the reference to goods to be shipped for exportation or as stores, or brought to any customs station for exportation, there shall be substituted a reference to goods supplied to HM Ships in accordance with regulations made under section two hundred and seventy-two, the expression "exporter" shall include a person so supplying such goods, and in sub-paragraph (b) of the said subsection the security to be given by the exporter to the satisfaction of the Commissioners shall, in lieu of the security mentioned in the said sub-paragraph, be security to the satisfaction of the Commissioners that all goods entered for supply to HM Ships shall be duly delivered to these ships, or that they will be otherwise accounted for to the satisfaction of the Commissioners;

    (b)   In section fifty-five, subsection (1) shall be adapted to read as follows—

"(1)   If any goods supplied to any of HM Ships or to the Admiralty in accordance with regulations made under section two hundred and seventy-two of this Act are relanded, unloaded or carried from any of HM Ships or removed from a naval establishment, naval victualling yard, depot, or sub-depot in the United Kingdom, except to another of HM Ships or to another such establishment, yard, depot or sub-depot as aforementioned, for use therein in accordance with regulations made under section two hundred and seventy-two of this Act, then, unless such relanding, unloading, carriage or removal was authorised by the proper officer and, except where that officer otherwise permits, unless any duty chargeable and unpaid on the goods is paid and any drawback or allowance paid in respect thereof is repaid, any person concerned in the relanding, unloading, carriage or removal of the goods from the ship, naval establishment, naval victualling yard, depot or sub-depot without such authority, payment or repayment shall be guilty of an offence under this section."

(c)   In subsection (2) of the said section fifty-five, for the words "loaded or retained as aforesaid" there shall be substituted the words "supplied to any of HM Ships or to the Admiralty in accordance with such regulations as aforesaid", and for the words "unloaded in the United Kingdom" there shall be substituted the words "relanded, unloaded, carried or removed as aforesaid".

(d)   In subsection (3) of the said section fifty-five, for the words "loaded or retained as aforesaid or brought to a customs station for exportation by land" there shall be substituted the words "supplied to any of HM Ships or to the Admiralty in accordance with such regulations as aforesaid".

10 Definitions

In these Regulations unless the context otherwise requires each of the following expressions shall have the meaning hereby assigned to it—

"Commissioners" means the Commissioners of Customs and Excise;

"food and drink" means any article used as food or drink for human consumption other than drugs;

"tobacco" means manufactured tobacco of every description;

"HM Ship" means a ship of the Royal Navy on the Home Station (other than a naval establishment);

"Naval establishment" means any naval establishment ashore in the United Kingdom manned by officers and men of the Royal Navy;

"Officers and men of the Royal Navy" means serving officers and ratings of the Royal Navy and officers and ratings of the Royal Naval Reserve, Royal Naval Volunteer Reserve or other naval reserve when in actual service;

"Officers and men of the Royal Marines" means serving officers and men of the Royal Marines and officers and men of the Royal Marine Forces Volunteer Reserve or other Royal Marine reserve when in actual service.

11

The Interpretation Act 1889 shall apply for the interpretation of these Regulations as it applies for the interpretation of an Act of Parliament.

NOTES

Interpretation Act 1889: see now the Interpretation Act 1978.

12

(Revokes the Duty-Free Supplies for the Royal Navy Regulations, 1951, SI 1951/803.)

13

These Regulations may be cited as the Duty-Free Supplies for the Royal Navy Regulations 1954 and shall come into operation on the first day of November, 1954.

IMPORT DUTY RELIEFS (ADMINISTRATION) ORDER 1958

(SI 1958/1965)

NOTES

Made: 24 November 1958.

Authority: Import Duties Act, 1958, s 5 (see now the Customs and Excise Duties (General Reliefs) Act 1979, s 4).

Commencement: 1 January 1959.

1

The following provisions of this Order shall have effect with respect to the administration of any relief from import duty under section five of the Import Duties Act, 1958, in so far as those provisions are appropriate and are not excluded or modified by any Order under that section conferring or relating to the relief.

2—

(1) Applications for the relief to be allowed in the case of any goods shall be made by the importer to the Commissioners of Customs and Excise (unless otherwise provided by any Order conferring or relating to the relief), and shall be in such form, and verified in such manner, as may be required by the authority or person to whom the application is to be made; and the importer shall furnish such information as may be so required for the purpose of the application.

(2) Where the application for relief is not made before the time when the goods are released from customs control, or is not made to the Commissioners of Customs and Excise, the importer shall before that time give notice to the Commissioners, in such form as they may require, of his intention to make the application or of his having made it.

(3) The Commissioners at any time after receiving any such application or notice as aforesaid may impose such conditions as they think fit for the protection of the revenue, and in particular—

(a)   may, where the relief depends on goods being imported for a particular purpose, impose such conditions as they think fit to secure that the goods are used for that purpose and that any relief allowed may be withdrawn if the goods are not so used or are used for any other purpose; and

(b)   may, in any case, require the keeping of such records and the giving of such security for the payment of any duty which is or may become chargeable or for the observance of any conditions, as the Commissioners consider appropriate having regard to the nature of the relief and other circumstances.

NOTES

Exclusion: this article and art 3 at are not to apply to the administration of any relief from duty with regard to which the Customs Duties Quota Relief (Administration) Order 1986, SI 1986/2174 applies.

3—

(1) Applications for any premises or person to be registered for the purposes of the relief shall be made to the registering authority named in the Order conferring or relating to the relief by the occupier of the premises to be registered or by the person to be registered, as the case may be.

(2)   Any such application shall be in such form, and verified in such manner, as the registering authority may require; and the applicant shall furnish the registering authority with such information as the registering authority may require for the purposes of the application.

(3)   On application being duly made for the registration of any premises or person, and on payment of any fee required in connection with the application, the registering authority, if satisfied that the premises or person qualifies for registration, shall register the premises or person accordingly.

(4)   On an application for any premises or person to be registered for the purposes of the relief there shall be paid to the registering authority a fee of one pound.

(5)   The registering authority may cancel the registration of any premises or person for the purpose of the relief, if after reasonable inquiry the registering authority are no longer satisfied that the premises or person qualifies for registration, or if the occupier of the premises or the person registered applies for the registration to be cancelled.

NOTES

Exclusion: see the note to art 2.

4—

(1)   This Order may be cited as the Import Duty Reliefs (Administration) Order, 1958.

(2)   The Interpretation Act, 1889, shall apply for the interpretation of this Order as it applies for the interpretation of an Act of Parliament.

(3)   This Order shall come into operation on the first day of January, nineteen hundred and fifty-nine.

NOTES

Interpretation Act 1889: see now the Interpretation Act 1978.

TEMPORARY IMPORTATION (COMMERCIAL VEHICLES AND AIRCRAFT) REGULATIONS 1961

(SI 1961/1523)

NOTES

Made: 3 August 1961.

Authority: Customs and Excise Act 1952, s 40 (see now the Customs and Excise Management Act 1979, s 48).

Commencement: 14 August 1961.

PART I

1

If any vehicle or aircraft is imported into any part of the United Kingdom other than the Isle of Man and the importer satisfies the Commissioners that—

    (a)   his principal place of business is outside the United Kingdom,

    (b)   the vehicle or aircraft is registered outside the United Kingdom,

    (c)   the vehicle or aircraft is owned and operated by a person whose principal place of business is outside the United Kingdom,

(d)   the importation is taking place in the course of a journey which has begun and will end outside the United Kingdom,

(e)   the purpose of the journey is to use the vehicle or aircraft either—

      (i)   for the transport of passengers for remuneration or for the industrial or commercial transport of goods from or to a place outside the United Kingdom, or

      (ii)   for such other purpose as the Commissioners may in special circumstances allow, and

(f)   the following provisions of this Part of these Regulations, and such other conditions as may be imposed by the Commissioners, are and will be complied with,

such vehicle or aircraft may be delivered without payment of duty, and duty shall not be payable so long as the Commissioners continue to be so satisfied:

Provided that no vehicle or aircraft may be so delivered without payment of duty if the vehicle or aircraft is principally kept in the United Kingdom or if the importer principally keeps in the United Kingdom any vehicle or aircraft so delivered.

2

The importer shall at the time of importation—

(a)   produce the vehicle or aircraft to the officer for examination.

(b)   produce to the officer all documents in his possession which relate to the ownership or foreign registration of the vehicle or aircraft or which in the opinion of the officer might affect the entitlement to delivery of the vehicle or aircraft without payment of duty,

(c)   if, and as, the Commissioners require, give security for payment of the duty and for compliance with these regulations either—

      (i)   by producing a carnet for the vehicle or aircraft issued either to the importer by name, or to another person whose principal place of business is outside the United Kingdom, or

      (ii)   by entering into a bond with sureties acceptable to the officer, or

      (iii) by depositing such sum of money or giving such other security as the officer may require,

(d)   furnish to the officer such documents in such form and containing such particulars as the officer may require.

3

Save as the Commissioners may allow, the vehicle or aircraft while in the United Kingdom—

(a)   shall not be (or be offered to be) lent, sold, pledged, hired, given away, exchanged or otherwise disposed of, and shall not be used for the purpose of picking up passengers or goods at any place within the United Kingdom for conveyance to another place within the United Kingdom,

(b)   shall be operated and used only by or on behalf of the owner or operator of the vehicle or aircraft or other person in charge thereof at the time of its importation or by other persons whose principal place of business is outside the United Kingdom who are expressly authorised in writing by the owner or operator of the vehicle or aircraft to operate and use the vehicle or aircraft,

(c)   shall not be operated or used by, or in the service of, any other person and in particular any person whose principal place of business is in the United Kingdom.

4

The vehicle or aircraft shall be re-exported from the United Kingdom either—

(a) in the case of a vehicle or aircraft delivered on importation on production of a carnet, before the expiration of the period of validity of the carnet, or

(b) before the expiration of three months from the date of importation, or

(c) as soon as the purpose referred to in paragraph (e) of Regulation 1 of these Regulations has been served,

whichever is the earliest date, or, in any case,

(d) within such period as the Commissioners may allow.

5

The importer shall at the time of re-exportation—

(a) produce the vehicle or aircraft and any relevant import documents to the officer, and

(b) give such additional information and make such declaration relating to the vehicle or aircraft and the circumstances of its use in the United Kingdom as the officer may require.

PART II

6

If any spare parts or accessories of a vehicle are imported into any part of the United Kingdom other than the Isle of Man by or on behalf of a person whose principal place of business is outside the United Kingdom, and the importer satisfies the Commissioners that—

(a) the spare parts or accessories—

(i) are imported solely for the purpose of being incorporated in, or used with, a vehicle which has been delivered without payment of duty under the provisions of Part I of these Regulations or under Part I of the Commercial Vehicles (Temporary Importation) Regulations, 1952, and

(ii) will be re-exported in, or with, the vehicle before the expiration of the period specified in Regulation 4 of these Regulations which is applicable to that vehicle, and

(b) the following provisions of this Part of these Regulations and such other conditions as may be imposed by the Commissioners are and will be complied with,

such spare parts or accessories may be delivered without payment of duty, and duty shall not be payable so long as the Commissioners continue to be so satisfied.

7

The importer shall—

(a) at the time of importation of such parts or accessories, if the Commissioners so require, deposit in accordance with the officer's directions such sum of money for securing the duty and compliance with these Regulations, and produce such documents and give such information, as the officer may require,

(b) use the spare parts or accessories solely for incorporation in, or with, the vehicle,

(c) re-export the spare parts or accessories in, or with, the vehicle before the expiration of the period specified in Regulation 4 of these Regulations which is applicable to that vehicle, and

(d)   at the time of re-exportation, unless the Commissioners otherwise permit, produce to the officer all used or defective parts or accessories as have been displaced during the incorporation in, or use with, the vehicle by the imported spare parts or accessories, and—

(i)   re-export such displaced parts or accessories, or

(ii) destroy them under such conditions as the Commissioners may specify, or

(iii) if the Commissioners so permit, abandon them to the Crown.

PART III

8

If any goods of the following descriptions are imported into any part of the United Kingdom other than the Isle of Man for the purposes hereinafter mentioned—

(a)   spare parts or equipment imported solely for the purpose of being incorporated in, or used with, any aircraft which is—

(i)   registered outside the United Kingdom,

(ii) owned and operated by a person whose principal place of business is outside the United Kingdom, and

(iii) used in international air transport services and in compliance with the provisions of Regulation 3 of these Regulations;

(b)   aircraft, special tools, spare parts and equipment imported solely for the purpose of being used in the search for, or in the rescue, examination, repair or salvage of, an aircraft which is of the kind referred to in paragraph (a) of this Regulation and which has been accidentally lost or damaged;

and if the importer satisfies the Commissioners that the goods will be re-exported as soon as the purpose for which they were imported has been served or before the expiration of such period as may be allowed by the Commissioners, whichever is the earlier, and that the provisions of this Part of these Regulations and such other conditions as may be imposed by the Commissioners are and will be complied with, the goods may be delivered without payment of duty, and duty shall not be payable so long as the Commissioners continue to be so satisfied.

PART IV

9

For the purposes of these Regulations—

(a)   the principal place of business of a person shall be deemed to be the place from which in the opinion of the Commissioners the control of the business is exercised;

(b)   a vehicle or aircraft shall be deemed to be not principally kept in the United Kingdom if during the two years immediately preceding the date of importation of the vehicle or aircraft it has been present in the United Kingdom for less than either—

(i)   a total of 365 days, or

(ii) such greater number of days as the Commissioners may in special circumstances allow;

(c)   an importer shall be deemed not to keep a vehicle or aircraft principally in the United Kingdom if he has kept in the United Kingdom during the two years immediately preceding the date of importation of the vehicle or aircraft in question any other vehicle or aircraft which has been delivered without payment of duty under these Regulations or under the Commercial Vehicles (Temporary Importation) Regulations, 1952, for an aggregate period of less than either—

(i)   a total of 365 days, or

(ii)   such greater number of days as the Commissioners may in special
circumstances allow.

10

In these Regulations unless the context otherwise requires—

"aircraft" means any aeroplane, airship, balloon, flying machine or glider which
is designed for the transport of persons for remuneration or the industrial or
commercial transport of goods and also includes any accessories or component
parts of any aircraft required for and imported in, or forming part of, such
aircraft but does not include any accessories or component parts imported
separately;

"carnet" means a carnet de passages en douane or a triptyque which is issued by
an association belonging to the Federation Internationale de l'Automobile, the
Alliance Internationale de Tourisme or the Federation Aeronautique
Internationale, and which is covered by a guarantee given to the Commissioners
by an approved association established in the United Kingdom;

"officer" means the proper officer of Customs and Excise;

"United Kingdom" means the United Kingdom including the Isle of Man;

"vehicle" means any motor road vehicle (including a trailer) which is designed for
the transport of persons for remuneration or for the industrial or commercial
transport of goods and also includes any accessories or component parts of such
vehicle required for and imported in, or forming part of, such vehicle, but does
not include any accessories or component parts imported separately.

11

The Interpretation Act, 1889, shall apply for the interpretation of these Regulations as
it applies for the interpretation of an Act of Parliament.

NOTES

Interpretation Act 1889: see now the Interpretation Act 1978.

12

*(Revokes the Commercial Vehicles (Temporary Importation) Regulations, 1952, SI
1952/2222.)*

13

These Regulations may be cited as the Temporary Importation (Commercial Vehicles
and Aircraft) Regulations 1961 and shall come into operation on the 14th day of
August, 1961.

EXCISE DUTIES (GAS AS ROAD FUEL) ORDER 1972
(SI 1972/567)

NOTES

Made: 11 April 1972.

Authority: Finance Act 1971, s 3 (see now the Hydrocarbon Oil Duties Act 1979, s 8(3)).

Commencement: 3 July 1972.

1—

(1)   This Order may be cited as the Excise Duties (Gas as Road Fuel) Order 1972.

(2)   The Interpretation Act 1889 shall apply for the interpretation of this Order as it applies for the interpretation of an Act of Parliament.

(3)   This Order shall come into operation on 3rd July 1972.

NOTES

Interpretation Act 1889: see now the Interpretation Act 1978.

2

Section 3 of the Finance Act 1971 shall come into force on 3rd July 1972.

3

The rate of duty of excise under that section shall be such rate per liquid [litre] as is equal to one half of the rate for the time being of excise duty charged on [light oil].

NOTES

Word in first pair of square brackets substituted by the Excise Duties (Gas as Road Fuel) Order 1977, SI 1977/1867; words in second pair of square brackets substituted by the Hydrocarbon Oil Duties Act 1979, s 28(1), Sch 6, para 6, and the Finance Act 1981, s 4(2)(a).

GAS (ROAD FUEL) REGULATIONS 1972
(SI 1972/846)

NOTES

Made: 2 June 1972.

Authority: Finance Act 1971, s 3 (see now the Hydrocarbon Oil Duties Act 1979, s 21(1)).

Commencement: 3 July 1972.

1

These Regulations may be cited as the Gas (Road Fuel) Regulations 1972 and shall come into operation on the 3rd July 1972.

2

In these Regulations—

"Authorised person" means any person acting under the authority of the Commissioners;

"gas" means any substance which is gaseous [at a temperature of 15°C and under a pressure of 1013.25 millibars] and which is for use as fuel in road vehicles.

NOTES

Words in square brackets substituted by the Gas (Road Fuel) (Amendment) Regulations 1977, SI 1977/1869, reg 2.

3

The Interpretation Act 1889 shall apply for the interpretation of these Regulations as it applies for the interpretation of an Act of Parliament.

NOTES

Interpretation Act 1889: see now the Interpretation Act 1978.

4—

(1) Any person who intends to send out, set aside or supply gas shall notify the Commissioners in such form and manner as they may require not later than 7 days before such gas is first sent out, set aside or supplied.

(2) A person who has notified the Commissioners in accordance with sub-paragraph (1), shall, within 7 days of any variation arising in such notification, give the Commissioners particulars in writing of that variation.

5

Every person required by Regulation 4 to give a notification shall, unless the Commissioners otherwise require, furnish, not later than the 15th day of each month, to the Collector of Customs and Excise in whose Collection that person's premises are situated, on forms provided by the Commissioners, a return of the quantities of gas upon which excise duty has not been paid, which have been sent out, set aside or used as fuel in a road vehicle during the preceding month and at the same time pay to that Collector the excise duty chargeable on the said gas.

6

No person shall mix or cause to be mixed gas upon which the duty has been charged with gas upon which the duty has not been charged or with any other substance, save with the authority of the Commissioners and subject to such conditions as they impose.

7

Every person required by Regulation 4 to give a notification shall keep books and documents in which are recorded the date, quantity and description of the gas which on each occasion he produces, deals in, supplies, sends out or sets aside.

8

A person who owns or possesses any road vehicle constructed or adapted to use gas as fuel for its propulsion shall, if the Commissioners so require, keep books and documents showing in respect of each such vehicle—

(a) the description, registration mark and number of the vehicle;

(b) the date, quantity and description of all gas taken into the vehicle as fuel for its propulsion;

(c) the date of, and the distance travelled by the vehicle on, each journey or where the vehicle is used otherwise than in making a journey from place to place, the date and nature of such use,

and shall retain such books and documents for not less than 12 months from the date of the last entry therein, and produce them on demand to an authorised person at all reasonable times for his inspection.

9

Save with the permission of the Commissioners, no person shall within 12 months from the date of the last entry therein cancel, obliterate, alter or destroy any book or document required by these Regulations to be kept.

10

Every person concerned with the supply or use of gas shall on demand at all reasonable times produce to an authorised person any book or other document relating thereto.

11

An authorised person may, at any reasonable time, enter and inspect any premises (other than a private dwelling house) and may examine any gas and may require the occupier of such premises to give such facilities as may be necessary for that purpose.

12

An authorised person may at any time examine any road vehicle constructed or adapted to use gas as fuel for its propulsion.

13

Every person concerned with the production of, or dealing in gas or owning, possessing, or for the time being in charge of a road vehicle constructed or adapted to use gas as fuel for its propulsion shall on demand by an authorised person furnish such information relating to the supply or use of gas or containers for gas as that authorised person may require.

HYDROCARBON OIL REGULATIONS 1973

(SI 1973/1311)

NOTES

Made: 27 July 1973.

Authority: Hydrocarbon Oil (Customs and Excise) Act 1971, ss 16, 19, 20, 21 (see now the Hydrocarbon Oil Duties Act 1979, ss 18(6)(b), 21(1), 24).

Commencement: 1 September 1973.

ARRANGEMENT OF REGULATIONS

Preliminary

1 Short title, etc

(1) These Regulations may be cited as the Hydrocarbon Oil Regulations 1973 and shall come into operation on 1st September 1973.

(2) The Interpretation Act 1889 applies for the interpretation of these Regulations as it applies for the interpretation of an Act of Parliament.

(3) The Regulations specified in the Schedule to these Regulations are hereby revoked.

(4) Where any document used or required for the purpose of any assigned matter refers to a provision of a regulation revoked by these Regulations, such reference shall, unless the contrary intention appears, be construed as referring to the corresponding provision of these Regulations.

NOTES

Interpretation Act 1889: see now the Interpretation Act 1978.

2 Definitions

In these Regulations—

"the Act" means the Hydrocarbon Oil (Customs & Excise) Act 1971;

"the Act of 1952" means the Customs and Excise Act 1952;

"approved" means approved by the Commissioners;

. . .

. . .

"authorised person" means a person authorised by the Commissioners;

"Collector" means Collector of Customs and Excise;

"Colour Index" means Colour Index, [3rd Edition (1971)] compiled by the Society of Dyers and Colourists and the American Association of Textile Chemists and Colorists;

. . .

. . .

["the mixing Regulations" means the Hydrocarbon Oil (Mixing of Oils) Regulations 1985;]

"entered premises" means premises and plant . . . thereon entered pursuant to Regulation 3;

"fuel oil" means heavy oil which contains in solution an amount of asphaltenes of not less than 0.5% or which contains less than 0.5% but not less than 0.1% of asphaltenes and has a closed flash point not exceeding 150°C;

"gas" means hydrocarbon gas and includes all hydrocarbons which are gaseous [at a temperature of 15°C and under a pressure of 1013.25 millibars];

"gas oil" means heavy oil of which not more than 50% by volume distils at a temperature not exceeding 240°C and of which more than 50% by volume distils at a temperature not exceeding 340°C;

. . ...

"heavy oil vehicle" means a vehicle to which section 10 of the Act applies;

["liquid" does not include any substance which is gaseous at a temperature of 15°C and under a pressure of 1013.25 millibars;]

"kerosene" means heavy oil of which more than 50% by volume distils at a temperature not exceeding 240°C;

"oil" means hydrocarbon oil;

"plant" includes any machinery, apparatus, equipment[,pipe] or vessel;

["standard litre" shall mean a litre of any liquid at a temperature of 15°C;]

"vessel" includes any tank or container for storing oil and any still or utensil in which oil may be processed.

NOTES

Definitions "approved furnace operator" and "approved repayment user" revoked by the Hydrocarbon Oil (Industrial Reliefs) Regulations, SI 2002/1471 reg 11(a); definitions "dark oil" and, "the duty deferment Regulations" revoked by the Hydrocarbon Oil (Marking) Regulations, SI 2002/1773 reg 18(1), (2); definition "the mixing Regulations" inserted by the Hydrocarbon Oil (Mixing of Oils) Regulations 1985, SI 1985/1450, reg 10(1), (2); words in square brackets in definitions "Colour Index" and "plant" substituted and inserted and words omitted from definition "entered premises" revoked by the Hydrocarbon Oil (Amendment) Regulations 1981, SI 1981/1134, reg 3(a); words in square brackets in definition "gas" substituted by the Hydrocarbon Oil (Amendment) Regulations 1977, SI 1977/1868, reg 2(a)(i); definition omitted revoked and definitions "liquid" and "standard litre" inserted by the Hydrocarbon Oil (Amendment) Regulations 1993, SI 1993/2267, reg 3.

Excise production

3 Entry of premises, security and warehouse

(1) No person shall begin production of oil until he has made entry of the premises and of every building, and all plant, . . . on those premises which he intends to use for that purpose.

Provided that the foregoing provision shall not apply to production in a refinery, nor to production in the course of use of oil delivered under section 7 or section 12 of the Act.

(2) Every person who makes entry of any premises pursuant to paragraph (1) of this Regulation shall, if so required by the Commissioners, give security by bond or otherwise to the satisfaction of the Commissioners for the payment of duty on oil produced or stored on the entered premises.

(3) Every person who makes entry of any premises pursuant to paragraph (1) of this Regulation shall, if so required by the Commissioners in respect of any particular description of oil, set aside, subject to their approval under section 80 of the Act of 1952, a part of the entered premises to be a warehouse, and upon production by him of oil of that description, and before such oil is delivered or removed from the entered premises, shall deposit it in such warehouse.

NOTES

Para (1): words omitted revoked by the Hydrocarbon Oil (Amendment) Regulations 1981, SI 1981/1134, reg 3(b).

The Act: see now the Hydrocarbon Oil Duties Act 1979, ss 9, 14.

Removal of oil

4 Removal of oil to and from entered premises and refineries

The provisions of [regulations 15, 16 and 17 of the Excise Warehousing (Etc) Regulations 1988] shall apply to entered premises and to refineries as though they were warehouses approved under [section 92 of the Customs and Excise Management Act 1979].

NOTES

Words in square brackets substituted by the Hydrocarbon Oil Duties (Marine Voyages Reliefs) Regulations 1996, SI 1996/2537, reg 13(a).

5 Refineries Refinery operations and warehousing

(1)   No person shall elsewhere than in a refinery—

    (a)   produce oil from imported oil;

    (b)   refine imported oil, or

    (c)   incorporate gas in oil.

Provided that the foregoing provisions of this Regulation shall not apply to persons approved [for the purposes of sections 9 or 14(1) of the Hydrocarbon Oil Duties Act 1979].

(2)   If a refinery does not include a warehouse approved by the Commissioners under section 80 of the Act of 1952 for the deposit of any particular description of oil, the occupier of the refinery shall, if so required by the Commissioners, provide such a warehouse in relation to that refinery, and on production and removal of oils of such descriptions as the Commissioners specify from the refinery, deposit them in such warehouse.

NOTES

Para (1): words in square brackets substituted by the Hydrocarbon Oil (Industrial Reliefs) Regulations, SI 2002/1471 reg 11(b).

6 Entry of imported oil

Imported oil intended to be removed to a refinery shall on importation be entered for warehousing.

7 Setting oil aside for use in a refinery

Before any oil is taken for use in a refinery, the occupier of the refinery shall, if so required by the Commissioners, set aside such oil for such use, and oil so set aside shall not, save as the Commissioners allow, be diverted to any other use nor for any other purpose.

8 Security for duty at a refinery

The occupier of a refinery shall, if so required by the Commissioners, give security by bond or otherwise to the satisfaction of the Commissioners for the payment of duty on oil produced at, or received into, that refinery.

Storage and warehousing

9 Commissioners' approval of plant, etc

The occupier of a warehouse shall not in that warehouse—

(a)   use any place or plant unless the same has been approved by the Commissioners and bears conspicuous distinguishing marks, or

(b)   add to, alter, demolish or remove any place or plant which has been approved by the Commissioners unless he has given two days' previous notice thereof in writing to the authorised person.

10 Restriction on operations

Save as the Commissioners may otherwise allow, the occupier of a warehouse not approved as a refinery shall not in the warehouse mix light oil with any other oil so as to produce an oil which is not a light oil.

11 Certificates of receipt

The occupier of entered premises, of a refinery or of a warehouse shall furnish to the authorised person within 7 days of the receipt of any oil into the entered premises, refinery or warehouse a certificate showing the quantity and description of oil received and the name of the person and the place whence received.

12 Delivery notes

(1)   The occupier of entered premises, of a refinery or of a warehouse shall, within such time as the Commissioners may allow, issue to the consignee, in respect of any oil which he removes or allows to be removed from the entered premises, refinery or warehouse, a delivery note showing—

(a)   the address of the premises from which that oil is removed;

(b)   the date of that removal;

(c)   the description and quantity in [standard litres] of that oil . . .;

(d)   the name and address of the consignee;

(e)   identifying particulars of the conveying ship or vehicle or other means of transport; and

(f)   [if the oil is required by the Hydrocarbon Oil (Marking) Regulations 2002 to be marked, the statements required by regulation 13 of those Regulations].

(2)   The occupier of entered premises, of a refinery or of a warehouse shall, unless the authorised person otherwise allows, cause oil at the time of its removal from the entered premises, refinery or warehouse, by a ship or vehicle, to be accompanied by the delivery note required by the foregoing paragraph of this Regulation, or by a copy thereof or by a document which shows—

(a)   the description and quantity in [standard litres] of the oil at the time of its removal from the entered premises, refinery or warehouse;

(b)   [if the oil is required by the Hydrocarbon Oil (Marking) Regulations 2002 to be marked, the statements required by regulation 13 of those Regulations];

(c)   identifying particulars of the conveying ship or vehicle;

(d)   particulars sufficient to identify the delivery note required as aforesaid in respect of the oil in question; and

(e)   the name and address of the person who holds the delivery note as aforesaid or record of the particulars required to be shown on such delivery note.

NOTES

Para (1): words in square brackets in sub-para (c) substituted and words omitted revoked by the Hydrocarbon Oil (Amendment) Regulations 1993, SI 1993/2267, reg 4; para (f) substituted by the Hydrocarbon Oil (Marking) Regulations, SI 2002/1773 reg 18(3).

Paras (2): words in square brackets in sub-para (a) substituted by SI 1993/2267, reg 4; para (b) substituted by the Hydrocarbon Oil (Marking) Regulations, SI 2002/1773 reg 18(3).

13

(Revoked by the Hydrocarbon Oil (Amendment) Regulations 1993, SI 1993/2267, reg 5.)

14 Method of measurement

Where the authorised person requires the use of a particular method of measurement or of calibration or of conversion tables to ascertain any quantity of oil at or received into, used at or delivered from entered premises, a refinery or warehouse, the occupier of the entered premises, the refinery or the warehouse shall comply with such requirement.

15, 16

(Revoked by the Hydrocarbon Oil (Amendment) Regulations 1993, SI 1993/2267, reg 5.)

Marking

17–30A

(Revoked by the Hydrocarbon Oil (Marking) Regulations 2002, SI 2002/1773 reg 18(4))

31–36

(Regs 31–33 revoked by the Hydrocarbon Oil (Payment of Rebates) Regulations 1996, SI 1996/2313, reg 2(a); regs 34–36 revoked by the Hydrocarbon Oil Duties (Marine Voyages Reliefs) Regulations 1996, SI 1996/2537, reg 13(b).)

Industrial reliefs

37–42

(Regs 37–42 revoked by Hydrocarbon Oil (Industrial Reliefs) Regulations, SI 2002/1471.)

Mixing

43 Licence required

No person shall mix—

    (a)   any fuel oil, gas oil, kerosene or light oil in respect of which a rebate of duty has been allowed; or

    (b)   any oil which has been delivered for home use without payment of duty—

with any oil on which no rebate of duty has been allowed except under and in accordance with the terms of [either an approval granted by the Commissioners under the mixing Regulations or] a licence granted by the Commissioners and, where they so require [in relation to such a licence], after paying an amount equal to—

    (i)   in the case of oil on which rebate has been allowed, the rebate allowable on like oil at the rate for the time being in force, and

(ii) in the case of oil delivered without payment of duty, the duty chargeable on like oil at the rate for the time being in force.

NOTES

Words in square brackets substituted by the Hydrocarbon Oil (Mixing of Oils) Regulations 1985, SI 1985/1450, reg 10(1), (3).

44, 45

(Lapsed on repeal of the Hydrocarbon Oil Duties Act 1979, s 21(1)(b) by the Finance Act 1993, s 213, Sch 23, Pt I(4).)

Provision of facilities

46 Means of measurement

The occupier of entered premises, of a refinery, or of a warehouse and any person approved, individually or as a member of a class, for any of the purposes of section 7 or section 12 of the Act, shall, to the satisfaction of the Commissioners, provide such measuring appliance, gauges, calibration and conversion tables and shall afford such facilities and assistance as may be required by an authorised person for the examination, taking account of or sampling any oil on the premises of such occupier or such approved person.

47 Authorised person's rights of access

(1) An authorised person may enter and inspect any premises, other than a private dwelling house, and may inspect, test or sample any oil on those premises, or any oil in or on or forming part of the fuel supply of any vehicle on those premises, whether or not such vehicle is in the same ownership as those premises, and the right of entry afforded to an authorised person by this Regulation shall extend to any vehicle for the time being used by him for carrying out the provisions of this Regulation.

(2) Any person occupying or for the time being in charge of any premises entered by an authorised person in accordance with the preceding provision shall, when required by the authorised person, give facilities for inspecting, testing or sampling any oil found on those premises or in or on or forming part of the fuel supply of any vehicle on those premises.

(3) An authorised person may examine any vehicle and may inspect, test or sample any oil in or on or forming part of the fuel supply of any vehicle.

(4) A person owning or for the time being in charge of a vehicle shall, when required by an authorised person so to do, and for the purpose of enabling him to search for, inspect, test or sample any oil forming part of the fuel supply of the vehicle, open or cause to be opened the fuel tank or other source of fuel supply and remove or cause to be removed any device or obstruction which might hinder the authorised person from inspecting or taking a sample of such oil.

(5) The person in charge of any vehicle shall produce to an authorised person on demand all books or documents of whatsoever nature carried by him or on the vehicle, relating to the vehicle or to any oil in or on or forming part of the fuel supply of the vehicle.

48 Production of records

A person concerned with the supply or use of any oil shall, at all reasonable times, produce to an authorised person on demand all relevant books and other documents relating thereto.

49 Retention of records

No person shall cancel, obliterate, alter or destroy any books or documents required to be kept by or under these Regulations, or the Act, save with the permission of an authorised person.

50 Where records to be kept

The occupier of entered premises, of a refinery or of a warehouse and any person approved individually or as a member of a class for any of the purposes of section 7 or section 12 of the Act, shall keep at the premises where he receives, stores, uses or carries on the production or treatment of oil, all books and documents required by these Regulations to be kept or which relate to oil at those premises, including such books as have been filled up or taken out of use within the preceding twelve months or such less period as the authorised person may allow, and such occupier or person shall on demand produce such books and documents to an authorised person.

[51 Measurement of Volume

(1) Where pursuant to section 12 of the Finance Act 1993 the volume of any liquid is to be calculated in accordance with regulations made under that section its volume shall be calculated in the following manner—

(a)   subject to any requirement made by the authorised person in accordance with regulation 14 above, its volume, density and temperature shall be measured; and

(b)   its volume in standard litres shall then be determined by means of reference to such internationally recognised conversion tables as, in the opinion of the Commissioners, are suitable for this purpose.

(2)   In ascertaining for the purposes of the Hydrocarbon Oil Duties Act 1979—

(a)   the amount of any duty of excise chargeable on any liquid by virtue of that Act; or

(b)   the amount of any rebate allowable on any such liquid by virtue of that Act,

except as otherwise provided for in this regulation, the volume of that liquid shall be taken (if it would not otherwise be so taken) to be what would be its volume in standard litres.

(3)   Where any hydrocarbon oil is imported or removed for home use in a quantity or in circumstances where, in the opinion of the authorised person, it is inexpedient to measure the temperature of that oil the temperature shall be assumed to be 15°C.]

NOTES

Added by the Hydrocarbon Oil (Amendment) Regulations 1993, SI 1993/2267, reg 6.

CIDER AND PERRY (EXEMPTION FROM REGISTRATION) ORDER 1976

(SI 1976/1206)

NOTES

Made: 29 July 1976.

Authority: Finance Act 1976, s 2(3) (see now the Alcoholic Liquor Duties Act 1979, s 62(3)).

Commencement: 20 August 1976.

1—

(1)   This Order may be cited as the Cider and Perry (Exemption from Registration) Order 1976 and shall come into operation on 20th August 1976.

(2)   In this Order—

"cider" means cider (or perry) as defined in section 2(8) of the Finance Act 1976;

"claim" means a claim to exemption from registration as a maker of cider pursuant to Article 2 of this Order;

"Collector" means Collector of Customs and Excise for the area in which are situate the premises on which cider is made.

(3)   The Interpretation Act 1889 shall apply for the interpretation of this Order as it applies for the interpretation of an Act of Parliament.

NOTES

Interpretation Act 1889: see now the Interpretation Act 1978.

2—

(1)   Subject to Articles 3 and 4 of this Order, a person who makes cider for sale whose production of cider does not exceed [70 hectolitres] in a period of 12 consecutive months shall be exempt from the requirement in section 2(2) of the Finance Act 1976 in respect of the premises on which such production takes place.

(2)   Save as the Commissioners otherwise allow, no more than one maker of cider shall be exempt at any one time in respect of the same premises.

NOTES

Para (1): words in square brackets substituted by the Cider and Perry (Exemption from Registration) (Amendment) Order 1979, SI 1979/1218, art 2.

3

Every maker of cider claiming exemption shall notify the Collector in writing of such claim and shall specify the premises in respect of which he claims exemption.

4

A person exempt under Article 2 of this Order shall furnish to the Commissioners on request such records of or information about his production of cider as may be necessary to establish that the conditions of Article 2 of this Order are or have been complied with.

CUSTOMS DUTIES (DEFERRED PAYMENT) REGULATIONS 1976

(SI 1976/1223)

NOTES

Made: 2 August 1976.

Authority: Finance (No 2) Act 1975, s 16(2), Finance Act 1976, s 15 (see now the Customs and Excise Management Act 1979, s 45).

Commencement: 1 September 1976.

ARRANGEMENT OF REGULATIONS

Part II

1 Citation and commencement

These Regulations may be cited as the Customs Duties (Deferred Payment) Regulations 1976 and shall come into operation on 1st September 1976.

2 Interpretation

(1)   In these Regulations—

"approved" means approved by the Commissioners [to apply for deferment of payment of duty on behalf of himself or another and "approve" and "approval" shall be construed accordingly];

"deferment" means deferment of payment of customs duty granted under these Regulations and "deferred" shall be construed accordingly;

["payment day" means the 15th day of the month next following that in which the amount of duty deferred is entered into the Commissioners' accounts, or in the case of import entries scheduled periodically, the 15th day of the period following that in which deferment is granted (save that where that day in either case falls on a non-working day it shall be the next working day thereafter);]

["period" means a period commencing on the 16th day of any month and ending on the 15th day of the month next following].

(2)   The Interpretation Act 1889 shall apply for the interpretation of these Regulations as it applies for the interpretation of an Act of Parliament.

(3)   Where any document used or required for the purpose of deferment refers to a provision of the Customs Duties (Deferred Payment) Regulations 1972 such reference shall, unless the contrary intention appears, be construed as referring to the corresponding provision of these Regulations.

(4)   Any approval granted by a Collector under the Customs Duties (Deferred Payments) Regulations 1972 and in force immediately before the commencement of these Regulations shall have effect as if granted under these Regulations.

NOTES

Para (1): words in square brackets in definition "approved" and whole definition "period" added and definition "payment day" substituted by the Customs Duties (Deferred Payment) Regulations 1978, SI 1978/1725, reg 4.

Interpretation Act 1889: see now the Interpretation Act 1978.

3 Application

These Regulations apply in the case of customs duty . . . payable, apart from these Regulations, on the making of entry of goods chargeable therewith.

NOTES

Words omitted revoked by the Customs Duties (Deferred Payment) Regulations 1978, SI 1978/1725, reg 5.

4 Approval

(1)   A person who wishes to be approved for the purposes of these Regulations shall apply to the Commissioners [in such form and manner as they shall determine],

furnish security for payment on payment day of the amount of customs duty in respect of which he seeks deferment, and make arrangements with the Commissioners for the payment of that duty on payment day.

(2)   If satisfied with the security and arrangements as aforesaid, the Commissioners shall in writing approve the applicant with respect to an amount of customs duty not exceeding that for which he has furnished security;

Provided that such approval may be limited to the deferment of customs duty payable, apart from these Regulations, on the making of entry within any named Collection.

(3)   The Commissioners may, for reasonable cause, at any time vary or revoke any approval granted under this Regulation.

(4)   A person to whom approval has been granted under this Regulation shall forthwith notify the Commissioners of any change in the particulars furnished, the security given, or the arrangements for payment provided for in paragraph (1) above.

NOTES

Para (1): words in square brackets substituted by the Customs Duties (Deferred Payment) Regulations 1978, SI 1978/1725, reg 6.

Modifications: see the VAT Regulations 1995, SI 1995/2518 reg 121A (modification of this regulation in relation to any VAT chargeable on the importation of goods from places outside the member state).

5 Grant of deferment

Subject to Regulations 3, 4, 6 and 7, the Commissioners shall, upon application by an approved person [in such form and manner as they shall determine], grant deferment of customs duty until payment day.

NOTES

Words in square brackets substituted by the Customs Duties (Deferred Payment) Regulations 1978, SI 1978/1725, reg 7.

6 Payment

On each payment day an approved person shall pay to the Commissioners in accordance with the arrangements referred to in Regulation 4(1) the total amount of customs duty of which he has been granted deferment until that payment day.

7

If at any time after entry has been made the Commissioners are satisfied that—

(a)   the full amount of customs duty payable has not been shown on the entry [or periodic schedule] then, save as the Commissioners otherwise allow, the balance shall forthwith be paid by the person making entry of the goods and no deferment in respect thereof shall be permitted;

(b)   customs duty in excess of the amount payable has been shown on the entry [or periodic schedule], the Commissioners shall repay the excess, but the total amount shown shall nevertheless be paid on payment day.

NOTES

Words in square brackets inserted by the Customs Duties (Deferred Payment) Regulations 1978, SI 1978/1725, reg 8.

[8

Without prejudice to Regulation 6, for the purposes of—

    (a)   sections 34(1) and 260(1) of the Customs and Excise Act 1952 and the Warehousing Regulations 1975; and

    (b)   any relief by way of repayment or suspension of customs duty, or agricultural levy falling to be treated as such, under—

        (i)   the Inward Processing Relief Regulations 1977,

        (ii)   The Customs Duties and Agricultural Levies (Goods for Free Circulation) Regulations 1977,

        (iii)   Regulation 4 of the Import Duties (Outward Processing Relief) Regulations 1976, and

        (iv)   Article 4 of the Agricultural Levies (Outward Processing Relief) Order 1976

duty shall be deemed to have been paid at the time when deferment thereof was granted.]

NOTES

Substituted by the Customs Duties (Deferred Payment) Regulations 1978, SI 1978/1725, reg 9.

Modifications: see the VAT Regulations 1995, SI 1995/2518 reg 121A (modification of this regulation in relation to any VAT chargeable on the importation of goods from places outside the member state).

9

(Revoked by the Customs Duties (Deferred Payment) Regulations 1978, SI 1978/1725, reg 10.)

CUSTOMS DUTIES AND AGRICULTURAL LEVIES (GOODS FOR FREE CIRCULATION) REGULATIONS 1977

(SI 1977/1404)

NOTES

Made: 12 August 1977.

Authority: Finance Act 1977, s 10.

Commencement: 12 September 1977.

1

These Regulations may be cited as the Customs Duties and Agricultural Levies (Goods for Free Circulation) Regulations 1977. They shall come into operation on 12th September 1977 and have effect in relation to goods imported into the United Kingdom on or after 1st July 1977.

2—

    (1) In these Regulations—

    "Community transit external procedure" means the procedure for external Community transit laid down by Regulation (EEC) 222/77;

    "outside the Community" means outside the Customs territory of the European Economic Community, or in the case of goods covered by the ECSC Treaty or the Euratom Treaty, outside the territories to which the Treaty constituting the Community in question applies, as the case may be.

(2) The Interpretation Act 1889 shall apply for the interpretation of these Regulations as it applies for the interpretation of an Act of Parliament.

NOTES

Interpretation Act 1889: see now the Interpretation Act 1978.

3

These Regulations shall apply to goods not in free circulation and in respect of which inward processing relief had been granted by the competent authorities of another member State, and which were imported into the United Kingdom from that or another member State with a view to exportation outside the Community, whether or not any further processing was to take place in the United Kingdom, and which

    (a)   were entered in the United Kingdom for—

        (i)   inward processing, or

        (ii)   warehousing, or

        (iii)   transit or transhipment, or

    (b)   remained under the Community transit external procedure,

and which are subsequently allowed by the Commissioners to be put on the market in the United Kingdom or destroyed, or otherwise cease to be subject to special arrangements involving the suspension of, or the giving of relief from, customs duties or agricultural levies in another member State.

4

Duties of customs and levies shall be chargeable on goods to which these Regulations apply and the amounts thereof shall be calculated by reference to either—

    (a)   the duties and levies from which inward processing relief was granted in another member State; or

    (b)   in the case of goods specified in Regulation 3(a)(ii), (iii) and (b) and which are removed from warehouse in the United Kingdom or withdrawn from exportation, the rates applicable to those goods at the time they are put on the market or destroyed, provided that the Commissioners are satisfied that the amount thereof is at least equal to the amount ascertained in accordance with paragraph (a) hereof.

5

In the case of goods described in Regulation 3(a)(i) the provisions of the Inward Processing Relief Regulations 1977 shall apply, except that for the basis of calculation set out in Regulation 5(2) of those Regulations and any references thereto there shall be substituted the basis set out in Regulation 4(a) of these Regulations.

6

Where at any time any goods to which these Regulations apply are not produced or accounted for to the Commissioners on request, duties of customs and levies in respect of the goods shall be payable in accordance with these Regulations as if they had been put on the market.

7

Notwithstanding the previous provisions of these Regulations, where goods to which these Regulations apply are destroyed with the permission of the Commissioners, or are in their opinion destroyed accidentally or by force majeure, and are deprived of all value, no duties of customs or levies shall be charged.

Part II

TOBACCO PRODUCTS (CIGARETTES AND CIGARS) ORDER 1977

(SI 1977/1979)

NOTES

This Order revoked by the Tobacco Products (Description of Products) Order 2003, SI 2003/1471 art 3(2).

IMPORT DUTIES (END-USE GOODS) REGULATIONS 1977

(SI 1977/2042)

NOTES

Made: 8 December 1977.

Authority: Finance Act 1977, s 8 (see now the Customs and Excise Management Act 1979, s 122).

Commencement: 1 January 1978.

PART I
PRELIMINARY

1 Citation and commencement

These Regulations may be cited as the Import Duties (End-Use Goods) Regulations 1977 and shall come into operation on 1st January 1978.

2 Interpretation

(1) The Interpretation Act 1889 shall apply for the interpretation of these Regulations as it applies for the interpretation of an Act of Parliament.

(2) In these Regulations—

"authorised person" means a person authorised by the Commissioners to import or receive end-use goods;

"end-use goods" means goods in relation to which the import duties chargeable depend on the use to be made of them;

"import duties" includes customs duties and any charge or levy chargeable under Community arrangements on agricultural products or on products which are processed from agricultural products and are the subject of arrangements under Article 235 of the EEC Treaty;

"outside the Community" means outside the Customs territory of the European Economic Community or, in the case of goods covered by the ECSC Treaty, outside the territories to which that Treaty applies;

"prescribed use" means the use prescribed for end-use goods;

"uncollected import duties" means the difference between the amount of import duties chargeable on end-use goods and the amount chargeable on like goods not intended to be put to a prescribed use.

(3) References to a tariff heading or subheading are references to a heading or subheading of the Common Customs Tariff of the European Communities.

NOTES

Interpretation Act 1889: see now the Interpretation Act 1978.

PART II
IMPLEMENTATION OF COMMUNITY PROVISIONS

3

This Part of these Regulations shall apply for the implementation of the system for the control of end-use goods provided by Regulations (EEC) 1535/77, (EEC) 1775/77, and (EEC) 2695/77.

NOTES

Regulations (EEC) 1535/77, (EEC) 1775/77 and (EEC) 2695/77: see now Regulations (EEC) 4142/87, 4139/87 and 4141/87.

4

Save as the Commissioners may otherwise allow an authorised person shall allocate a serial number to each consignment of end-use goods imported or received by him.

5—

(1)   An authorised person shall keep records containing particulars of—

    (a)   importation,

    (b)   receipt,

    (c)   disposal, and

    (d)   use

by him of end-use goods, and provide such other information as the Commissioners may require to check the use to which end-use goods have been put.

(2)   The records required by paragraph (1) hereof to be kept by an authorised person shall be—

    (a)   produced for inspection by the proper officer at any reasonable time, and

    (b)   preserved for a period of one year from the date on which the end-use goods to which they refer were either put to the prescribed use or transferred to another person.

6

An authorised person shall permit the proper officer at any reasonable time to examine and take account of end-use goods imported or received by him and shall provide such assistance as the officer may require for those purposes.

7

Where an authorised person transfers end-use goods to another person before the said goods have been put to the prescribed use, he shall notify the proper officer without delay of such transfer in such form and manner as the Commissioners may require.

8

Save as the Commissioners may otherwise allow, an authorised person shall without delay notify the proper officer in writing of—

    (a)   the date of arrival of end-use goods at his premises;

    (b)   particulars of any end-use goods lost or damaged in transit;

    (c)   completion of the prescribed use;

    (d)   particulars of any end-use goods which he has not put to the prescribed use within the respective periods laid down by the said EEC Regulations from—

           (i)   the making of entry, or

           (ii)   removal from warehouse, or

           (iii) the date of receipt thereof;

Part II

  (e)   particulars of any end-use goods which he cannot put to the prescribed use on account of—

  (i)   reasons relating to his circumstances or to the goods, and

  (ii)   in the case of goods of a description contained in the Schedule hereto, economic reasons justified to the satisfaction of the Commissioners; and

  (f)   the delivery of end-use goods to a vessel not berthed at his premises.

NOTES

Entry on the importation of goods: by the Customs and Excise (Single Market etc) Regulations 1992, SI 1992/3095, reg 10(1), Sch 1, para 1, the reference in this regulation and in reg 15 to an entry on the importation of goods is to be treated as including an entry of such goods under the Customs Controls on Importation of Goods Regulations 1991, SI 1991/2724, reg 5, as amended by SI 1992/3095, SI 1993/3014.

9—

(1)   Save as the Commissioners may otherwise allow, an authorised person shall each year on a date agreed with the proper officer take stock of all end-use goods at his premises and shall forthwith furnish a return thereof to the proper officer.

(2)   The return of stock required by this Regulation shall include—

  (a)   the consignment serial number referred to in Regulation 4 hereof for each consignment or part thereof of end-use goods; and

  (b)   the quantity and description of the goods to which each consignment serial number relates.

(3)   Every return required under this Regulation shall be dated and signed by the authorised person as being correct and complete.

PART III

ECSC GOODS

10

This Part of these Regulations and Regulations 4 to 9 of Part II of these Regulations shall apply to end-use goods covered by the Treaty establishing the European Coal and Steel Community.

11

A person wishing to become an authorised person shall—

  (a)   apply to the Commissioners and furnish such information as they may require for the purposes of the application; and

  (b)   if the Commissioners so require, furnish security for the payment of any import duties which are or may become payable.

12—

(1)   No person shall import or receive end-use goods except under and in accordance with an authorisation in that behalf issued to him by the Commissioners.

(2)   The Commissioners may limit the period of validity of an authorisation issued under this Regulation.

13

The Commissioners may revoke the authorisation of any authorised person who does not observe or fails to comply with any obligation or condition imposed by or under these Regulations.

14

An authorised person may transfer end-use goods before they have been put to the prescribed use provided the transferee is also an authorised person, and the transferee shall be responsible for the observance of all obligations and conditions imposed by or under these Regulations as from the date of transfer.

15

An authorised person shall put end-use goods to their prescribed use within one year (or, in the case of goods of a description contained in the Schedule hereto, five years) from the making of entry, or removal from warehouse, or, if he is not the importer, the date of receipt thereof from another authorised trader, or within such further period as the Commissioners may allow on account of unavoidable accident, force majeure or reasons inherent in the processing of the goods within the said periods.

NOTES

Entry on the importation of goods: see the note to reg 8.

16

Except with the approval of the proper officer, an authorised person shall not—

(a)   deliver end-use goods of a description contained in the Schedule hereto to a vessel not berthed at his premises, or

(b)   export end-use goods outside the Community, or

(c)   destroy end-use goods, or

(d)   otherwise put end-use goods to a use which is not prescribed.

17—

(1)   Where an authorised person is unable to put end-use goods (other than goods of a description contained in the Schedule hereto) to the prescribed use on account of reasons relating to his circumstances or to the goods, the Commissioners may permit him to export the said goods outside the Community or to destroy him under the supervision of the proper officer.

(2)   Where such goods are permitted to be exported or destroyed the uncollected import duties shall not be payable.

(3)   Where such goods are permitted to be destroyed, import duties shall be chargeable on any products resulting from the destruction thereof at the rates applicable thereto on the date of destruction.

18—

(1)   In the case of goods of a description contained in the Schedule hereto, the Commissioners may permit an authorised person—

(a)   to export such goods outside the Community or to put them to a use other than that prescribed if they consider such permission justified by economic reasons; and

(b)   to destroy such goods where he is unable to put them to the prescribed use on account of reasons relating to his circumstances or to the goods.

(2)   Where such goods—

(a)   are permitted to be destroyed, import duties shall be chargeable on any products resulting from the destruction thereof at the rates applicable thereto on the date of destruction; and

(b)   are permitted to be exported, the uncollected import duties shall not be payable.

19

An authorised person shall pay immediately upon demand the amount of uncollected import duties payable on end-use goods when—

    (a)   the said goods have not been put to the prescribed use within the required period, or

    (b)   his authorisation is revoked before the said goods have been put to the prescribed use, or

    (c)   the said goods are transferred to an unauthorised person, or

    (d)   except in cases where Regulations 17(2) or 18(2) hereof apply, the said goods are put to a use other than that prescribed.

20

Waste and scrap necessarily resulting from the normal working or processing of end-use goods together with losses resulting from natural causes shall be regarded as goods which have been put to the prescribed use.

21

The Commissioners, where satisfied that it is necessary, may permit an authorised person to store end-use goods in common with other goods of the same kind and quality and having the same technical and physical characteristics, and in such cases his obligations in respect of end-use goods will be complied with when he has put to the prescribed use a quantity of the goods so stored which is equivalent to the quantity of the end-use goods.

PART IV

IMPLEMENTATION OF COMMUNITY PROVISIONS FOR FROZEN BEEF

22

This Part of these Regulations shall apply for the implementation of the system of control provided by Regulation (EEC) 597/77 as amended by Regulation (EEC) 1384/77 in relation to certain types of frozen beef intended for processing in respect of which total or partial suspension of levy has been claimed, and "beef" in this Part of these Regulations shall be construed accordingly.

NOTES

    Regulation (EEC) 597/77: see now Regulation (EEC) 1136/79.

23

Save as the Commissioners may otherwise allow, an importer of beef shall allocate a serial number to each assignment of beef imported or received by him.

24—

    (1)   An importer or processor of beef shall keep records containing particulars of—

        (a)   importation,

        (b)   receipt, and

        (c)   processing

by him thereof, and shall provide such other information as may be necessary to prove that the beef has been processed into the prescribed product within the period prescribed by the said EEC Regulation.

    (2)   The records required by paragraph (1) hereof to be kept by an importer or processor of beef shall—

        (a)   be produced for inspection by the proper officer at any reasonable time, and

them and containing such particulars as they may require, being a day occurring at least one month after the day on which the notice was furnished;

(b)   Where, as a consequence of an application (containing such particulars as the Commissioners may require) by the owner of a ship to be used as an exporting ship, or, in the case where such a ship will be subject to a charter by demise at the time of a clearance outwards of it, by the person who will be the charterer at the time, the Commissioners permit him in their discretion to be subject to sub-paragraph (c) below, paragraph (2) of this regulation shall not apply in respect of the clearance outwards of the aforementioned ship occurring on or after the day appointed by the Commissioners for these purposes and not later than any terminating day;

(c)   In the case of the clearance outwards of an exporting ship which occurs on or after the day appointed by the Commissioners for these purposes and not later than any terminating day, the person permitted by the Commissioners to be subject to this sub-paragraph, shall by himself or his agent deliver a manifest to the proper officer within 7 days, or such longer period as may be permitted by the Commissioners, after a demand for it is made by the proper officer on him within 6 months after the aforementioned clearance outwards.

[12—

(1) The Commissioners and the proper officer shall exercise their powers under regulations 8 to 11 above so as to secure that the obligations imposed by those regulations do not, except in a case falling within paragraph (2) below, prevent, restrict or delay the movement between different member States of any goods or ship entering or leaving the United Kingdom.

(2) The cases mentioned in paragraph (1) above are those where it appears to the Commissioners or the proper officer that there are reasonable grounds for believing that the movement in question is not in fact between different member States or that compliance with an obligation imposed by those regulations is required for purposes connected with—

(a)   securing the collection of any Community customs duty or giving effect to any Community legislation relating to any such duty;

(b)   the enforcement of any prohibition or restriction for the time being in force by virtue of any Community legislation with respect to the movement of goods into or out of the member States; or

(c)   the enforcement of any prohibition or restriction for the time being in force by virtue of any enactment with respect to the importation or exportation of goods into or out of the United Kingdom.]

NOTES

Added by the Customs and Excise (Single Market etc) Regulations 1992, SI 1992/3095, reg 4.

CUSTOMS DUTY (COMMUNITY RELIEFS) ORDER 1984

(SI 1984/719)

NOTES

Made: 22 May 1984.

Authority: Customs and Excise Duties (General Reliefs) Act 1979, ss 13(1A), (3), 17(3).

Commencement: 1 July 1984.

ARRANGEMENT OF ARTICLES

1	Citation, commencement and extent
2	Interpretation
3	Rules for determining normal residence
4	Exclusion of goods obtained duty or tax free abroad
5	Goods to be produced for examination
6	Fulfilment of intention to be a condition

1 Citation, commencement and extent

(1) This Order may be cited as the Customs Duty (Community Reliefs) Order 1984 and shall come into operation on 1st July 1984.

(2) Nothing in this Order shall apply for the purposes of relief from excise duty or value added tax.

2 Interpretation

In this Order—

"Community instrument" means Chapter 1 of Council Regulation (EEC) No. 918/83;

"customs duty" means Community customs duty and, except where the context otherwise requires, includes any agricultural levy, tax or charge provided for under the common agricultural policy or under any special arrangements which, pursuant to Article 235 of the EEC Treaty, are applicable to goods resulting from the processing of agricultural products;

"occupational ties" shall not include attendance by a pupil or student at a school, college or university;

"personal ties" means family or social ties to which a person devotes most of his time not devoted to occupational ties.

3 Rules for determining normal residence

(1) For the purposes of relief from customs duty conferred by Titles I, II, IV or XVII of the Community instrument, a person's normal place of residence shall be the country where, in accordance with the provisions of this article, he is treated as being normally resident.

(2) A person shall be treated as being normally resident in the country where he usually lives—

(a) for a period of, or periods together amounting to, at least 185 days in a period of twelve months;

(b) because of his occupational ties; and

(c) because of his personal ties.

(3) In the case of a person with no occupational ties, paragraph (2) above shall apply with the omission of sub-paragraph (b), provided his personal ties show close links with that country.

Para (2): number omitted revoked by SI 1996/2537, reg 14(b).

8

No drawback shall be allowed on any oil for which a claim for repayment of duty lies under section 19 of the Act of 1979.

9

Regulation 46 (provision of facilities) and regulation 50 (keeping and production of documents) of the principal Regulations shall apply to a person approved for the purposes of section 19A of the Act of 1979 as those regulations apply to the persons mentioned therein.

AIRCRAFT (CUSTOMS AND EXCISE) REGULATIONS 1981

(SI 1981/1259)

NOTES

Made: 28 August 1981.

Authority: Customs and Excise Management Act 1979, ss 35(4), 42(1), 66(1)(a).

Commencement: 1 October 1981.

ARRANGEMENT OF REGULATIONS

1 Citation, commencement, interpretation and revocation

These Regulations may be cited as the Aircraft (Customs and Excise) Regulations 1981 and shall come into operation on 1st October 1981.

2

In these Regulations—

"the Act" means the Customs and Excise Management Act 1979;

"aircraft" includes all balloons, kites, gliders, airships and flying machines;

"Community transit document" means a document which is being used in accordance with a Community Regulation governing Community transit requiring, amongst other matters or conditions, that the goods which are to be moved under the external or internal Community transit procedure be covered by that document;

"loader" means the owner of an aircraft into which goods are to be loaded, or a person appointed by him; and

"loading pass" means a document relating to goods which a proper officer in his discretion may issue indicating the existence of a Community transit document relating to those goods and containing such other information as he considers appropriate.

3

(Revokes the Aircraft (Customs) Regulations 1971, SI 1971/848 and the Aircraft (Customs) Regulations 1971, SI 1971/1299.)

4 Duties of the commander of an aircraft arriving in the United Kingdom

(1)   Save as the Commissioners otherwise permit, the commander of an aircraft arriving in the United Kingdom of which report is required under section 35(1) of the Act shall immediately—

    (a)   take the aircraft or cause it to be taken to the examination station at the customs and excise airport at which the aircraft has arrived;

    (b)   make report of the aircraft by delivering to the proper officer in such form as the Commissioners direct—

        (i)   a General Declaration;

        (ii)   particulars of the goods on board the aircraft; and

        (iii)   a list in duplicate of the stores on board the aircraft;

    (c)   produce to the proper officer such other documents relating to the flight as the officer may require;

    (d)   produce to the proper officer all goods in the aircraft except such as are to be carried on to another customs and excise airport or to a foreign destination and are permitted by the proper officer to remain in the aircraft;

    (e)   unload, subject to regulation 5 below, all goods in the aircraft except such as are to be carried on to another customs and excise airport or to a foreign destination and are permitted by the proper officer to remain in the aircraft; and

    (f)   unless the proper officer otherwise permits, deposit all goods unloaded from the aircraft in a transit shed at the customs and excise airport.

(2)   If through circumstances over which the commander has no control an aircraft is prevented from being taken to the examination station as required by paragraph (1)(a) above the commander shall—

    (a)   immediately make report of the aircraft as required by paragraph (1)(b) above; and

    (b)   remove all goods in the aircraft to a transit shed or other place as required by the proper officer.

(3)   With the exception of the requirement contained in paragraph (1)(a) above, any act required to be performed by the commander of an aircraft by virtue of this regulation may, subject to such conditions as the Commissioners see fit, be carried out on his behalf by a responsible person authorised for the purpose by the owner of the aircraft.

NOTES

Modification: paras (1)(e), (f), (2)(b) above and regs 5, 6 below modified by the Customs Controls on Importation of Goods Regulations 1991, SI 1991/2724 so as to disapply them to goods imported into the United Kingdom from outside the EC.

---

5 Unloading of goods imported by air

No person shall unload, or permit the unloading of, any goods imported by air from the importing aircraft—

    (a)   except during such hours as the Commissioners may approve for the purpose;

    (b)   without the authority of the proper officer; and

(c)   unless the unloading is done for the purpose of a removal pursuant to the provisions of paragraph (2) of regulation 4, at any place other than an examination station or such other place as the Commissioners may permit.

NOTES

Modification: modified as noted to reg 4 above.

6 Removal of unloaded goods imported by air

(1) Save as the Commissioners may otherwise permit, no person shall remove or permit to be removed goods imported by air from an examination station or from such other place as the Commissioners may permit under sub-paragraph (c) of regulation 5—

(a)   except to a transit shed;

(b)   unless, in the case of goods entered under section 37 of the Act, the proper officer authorises the removal from the examination station or from the other place mentioned above; or

(c)   except in accordance with any special permission granted by the Commissioners and in compliance with any conditions attached to the grant of such permission.

(2) Save as the Commissioners may otherwise permit, goods imported by air situated in a transit shed or at any other place to which they were removed as required by the proper officer under paragraph (2)(b) of regulation 4 shall not be removed therefrom—

(a)   until, in the case of goods of which entry is required by section 37 of the Act, the entry is made; and

(b)   without the authority of the proper officer.

NOTES

Modification: modified as noted to reg 4 above.

7 Loading of goods on a departing aircraft

(1) Subject to paragraph (2) of this regulation, no person shall load on an aircraft about to depart on a flight to an eventual destination outside the United Kingdom and the Isle of Man goods for exportation or as stores—

(a)   except at the examination station at a customs and excise airport, or such other place as the Commissioners may permit; and

(b)   without the authority of the proper officer, save as may be permitted by him.

(2) Paragraph (1)(b) of this regulation shall not apply to a loader if, in relation to the goods due to be loaded by him, he is acting under a direction of the Commissioners pursuant to subsection (4) or (5) of section 57 of the Act (directions that certain goods should not be loaded without authority of a proper officer, and directions relaxing such requirements and substituting other requirements).

(3) Where the goods are said to be moving under the external or internal Community transit procedure the proper officer may withhold his authority required by paragraph (1)(b) of this regulation until the person applying for his authority either, produces to him the Community transit document or, instead of it, furnishes him with a loading pass which satisfies him that the goods are being moved under one of the aforementioned procedures.

8 Embarkation of passengers

No passenger shall embark or be permitted by any person to embark on a flight to an eventual destination outside the United Kingdom and the Isle of Man unless—

(a)   he is authorised by the proper officer to embark; and

(b)   he embarks at the examination station at a customs and excise airport or at such other place as the Commissioners may permit.

[9—

(1)   The Commissioners and the proper officer shall exercise their powers under regulations 4 to 8 above so as to secure that the obligations imposed by those regulations do not, except in a case falling within paragraph (2) below, prevent, restrict or delay the movement between different member States of any goods or passenger entering or leaving the United Kingdom.

(2)   The cases mentioned in paragraph (1) above are those where it appears to the Commissioners or the proper officer that there are reasonable grounds for believing that the movement in question is not in fact between different member States or that compliance with an obligation imposed by those regulations is required for purposes connected with—

(a)   securing the collection of any Community customs duty or giving effect to any Community legislation relating to any such duty;

(b)   the enforcement of any prohibition or restriction for the time being in force by virtue of any Community legislation with respect to the movement of goods into or out of the member States; or

(c)   the enforcement of any prohibition or restriction for the time being in force by virtue of any enactment with respect to the importation or exportation of goods into or out of the United Kingdom.]

NOTES

Added by the Customs and Excise (Single Market etc) Regulations 1992, SI 1992/3095, reg 5.

SHIP'S REPORT, IMPORTATION AND EXPORTATION BY SEA REGULATIONS 1981

(SI 1981/1260)

NOTES

Made: 28 August 1981.

Authority: Customs and Excise Management Act 1979, ss 35(4), 42(1), 66(1)(a), (c).

Commencement: 1 October 1981.

ARRANGEMENT OF REGULATIONS

1 Citation, commencement, application, interpretation and revocation

(1) These Regulations may be cited as the Ship's Report, Importation and Exportation by Sea Regulations 1981 and shall come into operation on 1st October 1981.

(2) These Regulations shall not apply to pleasure craft as defined in the Pleasure Craft (Arrival and Report) Regulations 1979.

(3) In these Regulations "the Act" means the Customs and Excise Management Act 1979.

(4) . . .

NOTES

Para (4): revokes the Ship's Report, Importation and Exportation by Sea Regulations 1981, SI 1965/1993, the Ship's Report, Importation and Exportation by Sea (Amendment) Regulations 1971, SI 1971/1300 and the Ship's Report Regulations 1979, SI 1979/565.

[PART I

PROCEDURE FOR SHIP'S REPORT REQUIRED UNDER SECTION 35(1) OF
THE ACT

2 Report procedure

Subject to regulation 6 below, the procedure for making report of a ship of which report is required under section 35(1) of the Act shall be in accordance with regulations 3 and 4 below.]

NOTES

Regs 2–6 (Pt I) substituted by the Ship's Report, Importation and Exportation by Sea (Amendment) Regulations 1986, SI 1986/1819, reg 3.

[3

The forms directed by the Commissioners under section 35(1) of the Act shall be completed by the master or, where the Commissioners so permit, a person authorised by him.]

NOTES

Substituted as noted to reg 2.

[4

The forms duly completed in accordance with regulation 3 above shall be delivered by the master or a person authorised by him—

  (a) in the case of a ship boarded by an officer, to the officer immediately, if so requested by him,

(b)   in any other case, to the proper place designated at the port of arrival—

        (i)   within 3 hours of the ship having reached its place of loading or unloading; or

        (ii)   on the expiration of 24 hours following the arrival of the ship within the limits of that port if by then the ship has not reached a place of loading or unloading.]

NOTES

Substituted as noted to reg 2.

[5 Copies of report documents

(1)   The master shall ensure that a copy of each of the forms referred to in regulation 3 above is retained on board ship for inspection by an officer as long as the ship remains within the limits of the port.

(2)   At the request of an officer either the master or any person authorised by him shall furnish the officer with an additional copy of any such form.]

NOTES

Substituted as noted to reg 2.

[6 Modified procedure for report

The Commissioners may relax all or any of the requirements of regulations 3 to 5 above as they see fit in relation to any ship arriving at any port in the United Kingdom.]

NOTES

Substituted as noted to reg 2.

PART II
PROCEDURE FOR SHIP ARRIVING AT A PORT AND FOR THE UNLOADING, LANDING AND REMOVAL OF GOODS IMPORTED BY SEA
PROCEDURE FOR SHIP ARRIVING AT A PORT

7—

(1)   On the arrival of a ship at a port the master shall—

      (a)   where a boarding station has been appointed at that port, immediately bring the ship to at that boarding station;

      (b)   thereafter, or where no boarding station has been appointed at that port, bring the ship as quickly up to the proper mooring or unloading place as the nature of the port will permit without touching at any other place except as may be necessary for the safe navigation of the ship:

Provided always that nothing in this regulation shall affect the provisions of any regulations made under the powers conferred by the enactments relating to public health in force respectively in England and Wales, Scotland and Northern Ireland with respect to ships which are to be taken to mooring stations within the meaning of those regulations.

(2)   The ship shall not be moved from the said mooring or unloading place—

      (a)   except directly to some other mooring or unloading place; and

      (b)   unless the proper officer has been informed of such movement.

8 Unloading, landing and removal of goods imported by sea

Goods imported by sea shall not be landed except at an approved wharf, and shall not be unloaded, landed or removed from the place of landing or from a transit shed—

    (a)   outside such hours as the Commissioners may appoint;

    (b)   without the authority of the proper officer;

    (c)   until . . . report of the importing ship has been made, save as permitted by the Commissioners;

    (d)   until due entry of the goods has been made, save as permitted by the Commissioners; or

    (e)   on a Sunday or a holiday, save as permitted by the Commissioners:

  Provided that—

    (i)   paragraphs (a), (c), (d) and (e) of this regulation shall not apply in relation to whales and fresh fish (including shellfish) of British taking brought by British ships;

    (ii)   paragraphs (c) and (d) shall not apply in relation to the unloading or landing of goods for deposit in a transit shed; and

    (iii)   paragraph (d) shall not apply in relation to passengers' baggage.

NOTES

Para (c): words omitted revoked by the Ship's Report, Importation and Exportation by Sea (Amendment) Regulations 1986, SI 1986/1819, reg 4.

Modification: this regulation and reg 9 below modified by the Customs Controls on Importation of Goods Regulations 1991, SI 1991/2724 so as to disapply them to goods imported into the United Kingdom from outside the EC.

9 Transfer of imported goods from one ship to another for landing

Goods unloaded from an importing ship into another ship for landing at an approved wharf shall not, except with the permission of the proper officer, be again removed into another ship before being so landed, but shall forthwith be taken to and landed at that wharf.

NOTES

Modification: modified as noted to reg 8 above.

PART III

LOADING OF GOODS INTO AND EXPORTING SHIP AND MANIFESTS

LOADING OF GOODS INTO AN EXPORTING SHIP

10—

(1)(a) In paragraph (3) of this regulation "loader" means the owner of the ship into which goods are to be shipped, or a person appointed by him, except that, where the ship is subject to charter by demise, "loader" means the charterer or a person appointed by him;

    (b)   In paragraph (4) of this regulation—

        (i)   and in sub-paragraph (ii) below, "Community transit document" means a document which is being used in accordance with a Community Regulation governing Community transit requiring, amongst other matters or conditions, that the goods which are to be moved under the external or internal Community transit procedure be covered by that document, and

        (ii)   "loading pass" means a document relating to goods which a proper officer in his discretion may issue indicating the existence

Part II

of a Community transit document relating to those goods and containing such other information as the proper officer considers appropriate.

(2)   Subject to paragraph (3) of this regulation, no person shall load into a ship or make waterborne for loading any goods for exportation or as stores—

(a)   outside such hours as the Commissioners may appoint;

(b)   except at an approved wharf;

(c)   without the authority of the proper officer, save as permitted by him;

(d)   before entry outwards of the ship; or

(e)   on a Sunday or a holiday, save as permitted by the Commissioners.

(3)   Paragraph (2)(c) of this regulation shall not apply to a loader if, in relation to the goods due to be loaded by him, he is acting under a direction of the Commissioners pursuant to subsection (4) or (5) of section 57 of the Act (directions that certain goods should not be loaded without authority of a proper officer, and directions relaxing such requirements and substituting other requirements).

(4)   Where the goods are said to be moving under the external or internal Community transit procedure the proper officer may withhold his authority required by paragraph (2)(c) of this regulation until the person applying for his authority either, produces to him the Community transit document or, instead of it, furnishes him with a loading pass which satisfies him that the goods are being moved under one of the aforementioned procedures.

11 Delivery of manifest and contingent manifest facility

(1)   The manifest due to be delivered pursuant to paragraph (2), or (3)(c), of this regulation shall—

(a)   contain such particulars as the Commissioners direct of all goods shipped as cargo into the exporting ship which has been cleared outwards;

(b)   be accompanied by such other documents relating to the cargo as the Commissioners direct; and

(c)   be accompanied by a declaration, made by the person discharging the obligation to deliver the manifest, that the manifest contains a true account of the cargo of the exporting ship which has been cleared outwards.

(2)   Subject to paragraph (3)(b) of this regulation and save as may be permitted otherwise by the Commissioners, the owner or master of every exporting ship, or in the case of the exporting ship being subject to a charter by demise at the time of its clearance outwards, the charterer or master of that ship shall by himself or his agent deliver a manifest to the proper officer within 14 days after the clearance outwards of the ship.

(3)(a)   In sub-paragraphs (b) and (c) below the expression "any terminating day" means such day, if any, which is the first to be specified by the Commissioners or the person who has been permitted by them to be subject to sub-paragraph (c) below in accordance with respectively the first or the second of the following procedures—

(i)   a day specified by the Commissioners in a notice served on the person permitted by them to be subject to sub-paragraph (c) below or deposited at the address given for these purposes in the application described in sub-paragraph (b) below, being a day occurring at least one month after the day of the service or deposit of the notice, and

(ii)   a day specified by the person permitted by the Commissioners to be subject to sub-paragraph (c) below in a notice furnished to

(4)   Where a person has his occupational ties in one country and his personal ties in another country, he shall be treated as being normally resident in the latter country provided that either—

(a)   his stay in the former country is in order to carry out a task of a definite duration, or

(b)   he returns regularly to the country where he has his personal ties.

(5)   Notwithstanding paragraph (4) above, a United Kingdom citizen whose personal ties are in the United Kingdom but whose occupational ties are abroad may be treated as normally resident in the country of his occupational ties, provided he has lived there for a period of, or periods together amounting to, at least 185 days in a period of twelve months.

4 Exclusion of goods obtained duty or tax free abroad

Relief from customs duty conferred by Titles I, II or IV of the Community instrument shall be subject to the condition that the Commissioners are satisfied that the goods in respect of which any such relief is claimed have borne, in their country of origin or exportation, the customs or other duties and taxes to which goods of that class or description are normally liable and have not been subject, by reason of their exportation, to any exemption from, or refund of, such duties and taxes as aforesaid, or any turnover tax, excise duty or other consumption tax.

5 Goods to be produced for examination

Relief from customs duty conferred by Titles I, II, IV V, XVII or XVIII of the Community instrument shall be subject to the condition that when any such relief is claimed on importation of the goods, or on their removal from another customs procedure, the goods are produced to the proper officer for examination.

6 Fulfilment of intention to be a condition

Where relief from customs duty is conferred by Titles I, II, IV, V, XVII or XVIII of the Community instrument in terms which require, whether expressly or by implication, a particular intention on the part of a person in relation to the establishment of his normal place of residence, or the use of any goods in respect of which relief is conferred, it shall be a condition of the relief that such intention be fulfilled.

CONTROL OF MOVEMENT OF GOODS REGULATIONS 1984

(SI 1984/1176)

NOTES

Made: 1 August 1984.

Authority: Customs and Excise Management Act 1979, s 31.

Commencement: 6 August 1984.

ARRANGEMENT OF REGULATIONS

1 Citation and Commencement

These Regulations may be cited as the Control of Movement of Goods Regulations 1984 and shall come into operation on 6th August 1984.

2

(Revokes the Control of Movement of Goods Regulations 1981, SI 1981/1257

3 Interpretation

In these Regulations—

"the Act" means the Customs and Excise Management Act 1979;

"approved place"—

(a) in relation to imported goods means a place approved by the Commissioners under section 20 or 25 of the Act for the clearance out of charge of such goods, and

(b) in relation to goods intended for export means a place appointed under section 159 of the Act for the examination of goods which is approved by the Commissioners under section 31 of the Act for the examination of such goods before their movement to a place of exportation;

"the loader" shall have the same meaning as in section 57 of the Act; that is to say the owner of the ship or aircraft in which the goods are to be exported or a person appointed by him;

"place of importation" and "place of exportation" shall, where appropriate, include a free zone;

"removal" means a movement of goods which is authorised under these Regulations and "remove" and "removed" shall be construed accordingly;

"removal document" means a document to be obtained from or approved by the Commissioners made in such form and containing such particulars as the Commissioners may direct under section 31(2A) of the Act and for the purpose of regulation 16 shall include a copy of the application referred to in regulations 5, 6 and 7 stamped by the proper officer.

4—

(1) These Regulations shall not apply where any goods are moved under the internal or external Community transit procedure.

(2) The application of regulations 11 and 13 of these Regulations to goods carried under the provisions of an international convention having effect in the United Kingdom shall be without prejudice to any such provisions.

5 Restrictions on the movement of goods

Subject to regulation 10, no imported goods not yet cleared from customs and excise charge shall be moved between their place of importation and either an approved place or a free zone and, in the case of transit goods, between their place of exportation unless the movement is authorised by the proper officer upon application made to him.

6

Subject to regulation 10, no goods shall be moved between—

(a) a free zone and a place approved for the clearance out of charge of such goods,

(b)   such a place and a free zone, and

(c)   a free zone and another free zone,

unless the movement is authorised by the proper officer upon application made to him.

7

Subject to regulations 9 and 10, no goods intended for export and made available at an approved place or a place designated by the proper officer under sections 53(4) or 58(3) of the Act for the purposes of examination shall be moved between any such place and a place of exportation unless the movement is authorised by the proper officer upon application made to him.

8

Save as the Commissioners may otherwise allow, the applications referred to in regulations 5, 6 and 7 above shall be made in writing on a document obtained from or approved by the Commissioners for that purpose and shall be made—

(a)   in the case of imported goods, by the importer or the person in charge of the goods,

(b)   in the case of goods intended for export, by the exporter or the person in charge of the goods, and

(c)   in any other case, by the proprietor of the goods or the person in charge of the goods.

9 Local export control

(1)   Where a notice under section 58A(3)(a)(i) of the Act is delivered by the exporter such notice shall replace the application required under regulation 7.

(2)   Where the notice is for a single movement of goods, if the authority of the proper officer, required under regulation 7, is neither given nor refused by the date and time for the movement specified in that notice, it shall be deemed to be given on the date and immediately before the time so specified.

(3)   Where the notice is for more than one movement of goods, if the authority of the proper officer, required under regulation 7, is neither given nor refused, it shall be deemed to be given immediately before each movement commences.

10 Standing permission to remove

Where the Commissioners so permit, during a period specified by them, goods may be moved as contemplated in regulations 5, 6 and 7 without an application to the proper officer; and, unless the proper officer previously gives or refuses his authority, it shall be deemed to be given immediately before the movement commences.

11 Requirement for removal document

Before any removal commences the person by whom, or on whose behalf, the goods are being moved shall be in possession of a removal document.

12 Specification of vehicles etc

(1)   The Commissioners may, in respect of any class or description of goods, require that vehicles or containers in which goods of a particular class or description are removed shall be of a type specified by them for the removal of such goods.

(2)   Save as provided by paragraph (3) below, no person shall remove any goods in respect of which a requirement under paragraph (1) above has been imposed unless the vehicle or container in which they are carried conforms to such requirement.

(3)   The proper officer, upon application made to him by the person in charge of goods to be removed, may for the purposes of the removal in question relax any requirement imposed under paragraph (1) above.

13 Specification of routes

Vehicles and containers proceeding under a removal shall be moved by such routes as the Commissioners may specify.

14 Security of goods, vehicles and containers

(1) Before any goods are removed they or the vehicle or container carrying them shall be secured or identified by any such seals, locks or marks as the Commissioners may specify.

(2) Where in the United Kingdom, seals, locks or marks are affixed for any customs or excise purpose in order to secure or identify the goods to be removed or the vehicles or containers carrying the goods, they shall be so affixed by the proper officer or by such other person as the Commissioners may authorise.

15—

(1) Save in the circumstances hereunder mentioned, no person shall at any time during a removal—

    (a)   wilfully break, open or remove any seal, lock or mark affixed for any customs or excise purpose on any goods or to a vehicle or container; or

    (b)   load or unload or assist in the loading or unloading of a vehicle or container.

(2) The circumstances referred to in paragraph (1) above are—

    (a)   where authorisation has been given by the proper officer; or

    (b)   in accordance with any general or special permission given by the Commissioners; or

    (c)   in an emergency in order to safeguard the goods or to protect life or property.

16 Completion of removals, time limits and accidents

(1) Save as the Commissioners otherwise allow, the person in charge of goods proceeding under a removal shall complete the removal by producing the goods, together with the vehicle or container in which they are carried if such vehicle or container has been secured or identified, and delivering a removal document to the proper officer at the approval place or, in the case of goods intended for export, at the place of exportation.

(2) The Commissioners may allow the removal of goods intended for export to be completed by the person in charge of the goods placing them, together with any container in which they are carried if such container has been secured or identified, under the control of the loader and delivering the removal document to him.

17

The person in charge of goods proceeding under a removal shall complete the removal within such period as the Commissioners may specify.

18

Where as a result of an accident or other occurrence arising during a removal a vehicle or container is delayed or diverted from a specified route the person in charge of the goods shall as soon as practicable give sufficient notification of the accident or occurrence as required by the Commissioners to the local office of customs and excise.

FREE ZONE REGULATIONS 1984

(SI 1984/1177)

NOTES

Made: 1 August 1984.

Authority: Customs and Excise Management Act 1979, ss 100B(1), 100C(3), (4), 100D(1), (2), 125(3), the Value Added Tax Act 1983, s 24 (see now Value Added Tax Act 1994, s 17).

Commencement: 6 August 1984.

ARRANGEMENT OF REGULATIONS

PART I
PRELIMINARY

1 Citation and commencement
These Regulations may be cited as the Free Zone Regulations 1984 and shall come into operation on 6th August 1984.

2 Interpretation
In these Regulations—

"chargeable operation" means any operation carried out on Community goods to which are free zone goods where, because of Commission Regulation (EEC) 1371/81 and the nature of the operation, agricultural levy becomes chargeable or a negative monetary compensatory amount payable;

"Community goods" means goods which fulfil the conditions of Article 9(2) of the EEC Treaty, and goods covered by the Treaty establishing the European Coal and Steel Community which are in free circulation in the Community in accordance with that Treaty;

"tax" means value added tax;

"transfer to another customs procedure providing for suspension of, or relief from, customs duty or agricultural levy" in regulation 11 (requirement for entry) shall not be taken to include the removal of free zone goods from one free zone to another or from a free zone to a place for the clearance out of charge of imported goods.

NOTES
Entry on the importation of goods: by the Customs and Excise (Single Market etc) Regulations 1992, SI 1992/3095, reg 10(1), Sch 1, para 1, the reference to an entry on the importation of goods is to be treated as including an entry of such goods under the Customs Controls on Importation of Goods Regulations 1991, SI 1991/2724, reg 5, as amended by SI 1992/3095, SI 1993/3014.

PART II
SECURITY OF FREE ZONES

3 Security and recovery of expenditure by Commissioners
The Commissioners may by direction impose obligations on the responsible authority for a free zone to ensure the security of that free zone; and where the responsible authority fails to comply with such direction and the Commissioners thereby incur any expenditure, such expenditure shall be recoverable on demand by the Commissioners as a civil debt from that responsible authority.

4 Residence in free zones not permitted
The responsible authority shall not permit any person to take up residence within a free zone.

PART III
GOODS CHARGEABLE WITH EXCISE DUTY

5 Excise goods which may became free zone goods without payment of excise duty

Goods chargeable with excise duty may be moved into a free zone in accordance with these Regulations without payment of that duty and remain as free zone goods; provided that they are goods which, by or under the customs and excise Acts, the Commissioners may allow to be removed or delivered without payment of excise duty and which have been allowed to be so removed or delivered.

PART IV
MOVEMENT OF GOODS INTO FREE ZONE

6 Goods to become free zone goods

(1) Goods moved into a free zone shall not be free zone goods unless, within [such time as the Commissioners may direct], such particulars as the Commissioners may direct have been entered in a record to be kept by the occupier of the premises at which the goods are received or, if the Commissioners so direct, by the responsible authority.

(2) . . .

NOTES

Para (1): words in square brackets substituted by the Free Zone (Amendment) Regulations 1988, SI 1988/710, reg 3(a).

Para (2): revoked by SI 1988/710, reg 3(b).

---

7 Acknowledgement of Community status of free zone goods

(1) Where the proprietor of free zone goods wishes to obtain in acknowledgement that the goods are Community goods he shall deliver to the proper officer, within the relevant period, a document in such form and containing such particulars as the Commissioners may direct together with such supporting evidence as will enable the officer to establish to his satisfaction that they are Community goods, and, if so satisfied, the proper officer shall provide a written acknowledgement of such Community status.

(2) The written acknowledgement referred to in paragraph (1) above shall consist of a copy of the document containing particulars of the goods, endorsed by the proper officer.

(3) In this regulation "relevant period" shall mean a period not exceeding 7 days from the time the goods become free zone goods or from the time an entry for free circulation under regulation 17(2) is accepted.

8 Goods from another customs procedure

Goods moved into a free zone which are subject to another customs procedure shall not be free zone goods until the proprietor of the goods has presented them to the proper officer and that procedure has been discharged.

PART V
OPERATIONS

9 Operations on free zone goods

(1) Operations on free zone goods shall only be permitted in accordance with this regulation and subject to any prohibition or restriction imposed by or under any enactment for the time being in force.

(2) Any operation is prohibited in which goods that are not free zone goods are mixed with or incorporated into free zone goods.

(3)   The Commissioners shall allow, subject to such conditions as they may impose, operations to be carried out on free zone goods as follows:—

   (a)   where only Community goods are involved, any operation;

   (b)   where any other goods are involved—

       (i)   the usual forms of handling listed in Article 1.1 of Council Directive 71/235/EEC,

       (ii)   processing under customs control for free circulation in accordance with Council Regulation (EEC) 2763/83, or

       (iii) any operation carried out in accordance with the Inward Processing Relief Regulations 1977.

(4)   A person intending to carry out any operation shall—

   (a)   before commencing an operation referred to in paragraph (3)(a) above, inform the proper officer of his intention and, in addition, where the operation is a chargeable operation enter such particulars as the Commissioners may require in a record to be kept by him,

   (b)   before commencing an operation referred to in paragraph (3)(b)(i) above, notify the proper officer of his intention, and

   (c)   before commencing any other operation, make a declaration by entering such particulars as the Commissioners may require in a record to be kept by him.

(5)   A person intending to carry out an operation referred to in paragraph (3)(b)(i) above may, at the time he notifies the proper officer of his intention to carry out the operation, apply for a written acknowledgement that the operation is to commence and the application shall be in such form as the Commissioners may direct and contain such particulars as the Commissioners may require to enable them to apply regulation 25(4).

(6)   The written acknowledgement referred to in paragraph (5) above, shall consist of a copy of the application endorsed by the proper officer.

(7)   Save as provided by this regulation, free zone goods shall not be used or consumed in a free zone unless they are entered in accordance with regulation 17(1).

(8)   Notwithstanding paragraph (3) above, free zone goods chargeable with excise duty which have been removed or delivered without payment of that duty by or under the customs and excise Acts before becoming free zone goods may only be used or consumed in the free zone without payment of that duty where such use or consumption does not affect the relief from excise duty under the requirements of those Acts applicable to the relief; and paragraph (7) above shall only apply to such goods if they are also chargeable with a duty of customs or agricultural levy which has not been paid.

(9)   Where an operation is carried out on free zone goods otherwise than in accordance with this regulation, they shall cease to be free zone goods, and shall be liable to forfeiture.

PART VI
ENTRY, REMOVAL AND PAYMENT OF DUTY ETC

10 Procedure for entering free zone goods

(1)   Free zone goods, required by these Regulations to be entered, shall be entered by the proprietor of the goods delivering to the proper officer an entry thereof in such form and manner, containing such particulars and accompanied by such documents as the Commissioners may direct.

(2)   Acceptance of an entry by the proper officer shall be signified in such manner as the Commissioners may direct.

(3)   Where free zone goods are required to be entered under regulation 17, the Commissioners may direct that if the proprietor of the goods—

(a)   enters such particulars as the Commissioners may direct in a record to be kept by him, and

(b)   furnishes a schedule to the proper officer at such place and at such intervals as the Commissioners may direct containing such particulars extracted from the record and accompanied by such documents as the Commissioners may direct,

an entry of the goods shall be taken to have been delivered and accepted when the particulars are entered in the record.

11 Entry required before removal for home use etc

Subject to regulation 12, before any free zone goods are removed from a free zone for—

(a)   home use, or

(b)   transfer to another customs procedure providing for suspension of, or relief from, customs duty or agricultural levy,

the goods shall be entered for such purpose.

12 Removal without entry

(1) Upon application by the proprietor of free zone goods, the Commissioners may allow the goods to be removed from the free zone for the purposes set out in regulation 11 without the goods being entered, if such particulars as the Commissioners may direct are entered in a record to be kept by the proprietor of the goods.

(2) Where goods are allowed to be removed from the free zone in accordance with paragraph (1) above, the proprietor of the goods shall comply with such conditions as the Commissioners may impose.

13 Goods to be removed after entry etc

Subject to regulations 15 and 16, free zone goods which have been entered under regulation 11 or in respect of which the particulars required under regulation 12 have been entered in the record, shall be removed, forthwith, from the free zone.

14 Removal of goods for export etc

Part V of the Customs and Excise Management Act 1979 (procedures for the export of goods) and any prohibition or restriction on the export of goods or their shipment as stores, imposed by or under any enactment for the time being in force, shall apply to goods removed from a free zone for export or shipment as stores.

15 Restriction on removal of goods

No goods shall be removed from a free zone except with the authority of and in accordance with any requirement made by the proper officer.

16 Payment of duty before removal of goods

Save as the Commissioners may otherwise allow and subject to such conditions as they may impose, no goods shall be removed from a free zone until any customs duty and agricultural levy chargeable thereon has been paid; and where the goods have been entered under regulation 11(a), such duty and levy shall be paid at the time the entry is delivered.

17 Entry of goods which are to remain in free zone

(1) Free zone goods to be used or consumed in a free zone, as provided in regulation 9(7), shall be entered for home use.

(2) Where the proprietor of free zone goods wishes to pay any customs duty or agricultural levy chargeable on the goods and for the goods to remain as free zone goods, the goods shall be entered for free circulation.

18 Payment of duty etc on goods to remain in free zone after entry

(1) Where goods are entered under regulation 17, any customs duty and agricultural levy chargeable thereon shall be paid at the time the entry is delivered.

(2) As an exception to paragraph (1) above, where the goods are entered for free circulation, tax on importation shall not be paid at the time customs duty is paid.

NOTES

Entry on the importation of goods: by the Customs and Excise (Single Market etc) Regulations 1992, SI 1992/3095, reg 10(1), Sch 1, para 1, the reference to an entry on the importation of goods is to be treated as including an entry of such goods under the Customs Controls on Importation of Goods Regulations 1991, SI 1991/2724, reg 5, as amended by SI 1992/3095, SI 1993/3014.

19 Agricultural levy chargeable because of chargeable operation

Where agricultural levy becomes chargeable or a negative monetary compensatory amount payable, because of a chargeable operation, a schedule in such form and containing such particulars of the goods and the operation as the Commissioners may direct shall be furnished by the proprietor of the goods to the proper officer at such place and at such intervals as the Commissioners may direct, and any agricultural levy so chargeable shall be paid at the time the schedule is furnished.

20 Customs duty etc deemed to have been paid

For the purposes of these Regulations, customs duty and agricultural levy shall be deemed to have been paid if payment thereof has been deferred under the Customs Duties (Deferred Payment) Regulations 1976, secured to the satisfaction of the Commissioners or otherwise accounted for.

21 Destruction of free zone goods

Subject to such conditions as the Commissioners may impose, free zone goods may be destroyed and no customs duty or agricultural levy shall be payable on them: Provided that where any scrap or waste resulting from their destruction is entered for removal for home use, duty and levy shall be chargeable thereon in accordance with regulation 25.

PART VII

CONTROLS

22 Production of goods

Goods in a free zone shall be produced to the proper officer for examination on request.

23 Segregation etc of goods

The proper officer may require any goods in a free zone to be segregated and marked or otherwise identified.

24 Keeping of records and provision of information

(1) In addition to any requirement in that regard imposed by or under these Regulations, the Value Added Tax Act 1983 or the Inward Processing Relief Regulations 1977, the occupier of any premises upon which free zone goods are kept or, where the Commissioners so direct, the responsible authority on his behalf, shall keep such records relating to the goods as the Commissioners may direct.

(2) Any records required to be kept under these Regulations shall be kept in the free zone or such other place as the Commissioners may allow and be kept in such form and be preserved for such time, not exceeding three years from the date the goods are removed from the zone, as the Commissioners may direct.

(3) The person keeping the record shall—

(a) furnish to the Commissioners, within such time and in such form as they may require, such information relating to the goods as the Commissioners may direct, and

(b) upon demand made by the proper officer produce to him any records and any document relating to the goods for inspection by the proper officer and permit him to take copies of or to make extracts from them or remove them at a reasonable time and for a reasonable purpose: Provided that if the information that would otherwise be contained in any record or document is not made or preserved in a form which is easily readable or which is not readable without the aid of equipment, the person keeping the record or document, shall, at the request of the proper officer produce the information contained in the record or document in the form of a transcript or other permanent legible reproduction.

PART VIII
CUSTOMS DUTY ETC CHARGEABLE ON FREE ZONE GOODS

25 Customs duty chargeable on free zone goods

(1) Except as provided in paragraph (5) of this regulation (compensating products from inward processing), the customs duty and agricultural levy and the rate thereof chargeable, or the negative monetary compensatory amount and the rate thereof payable, on free zone goods—

(a) removed from a free zone for home use, or

(b) remaining in a free zone after being entered for home use or free circulation;

shall be those in force for goods of that class or description at the time of acceptance of the entry or, where the goods are allowed to be removed without entry, those in force at the time the particulars required under regulation 12 are entered in the record.

(2) The agricultural levy and the rate thereof chargeable or the negative monetary compensatory amount and the rate thereof payable on free zone goods because of a chargeable operation thereon shall be those in force for goods of that class or description at the time the operation commenced.

(3) Except as provided in paragraph (4) below, the value for customs purposes of free zone goods of any class or description shall be that ascertained or accepted by the Commissioners at the time of the acceptance of the entry for home use or free circulation.

(4) Where goods which are removed from a free zone have undergone any of the usual forms of handling referred to in regulation 9(3)(b)(i), provided that the proprietor of the goods—

(a) if the goods are entered, produces with the entry, or

(b) in any other case, produces to the proper officer at such time as the Commissioners may direct,

the written acknowledgement referred to in regulation 9(5), the quantity of goods, their class or description and value shall, at his option, be those accepted or ascertained at the date of the acknowledgement.

(5) Notwithstanding any other provision of this regulation, where any goods imported into the United Kingdom are granted an authorisation, or have been granted in another Member State an authorisation, for inward processing relief and the Commissioners have allowed compensating products, derived from such goods which have become free zone goods, to be entered for home use or free circulation, the customs duty and agricultural levy chargeable shall be either—

(a) the amount calculated in accordance with the Inward processing Relief Regulations 1977, or

(b) at the option of the proprietor of the goods and provided that the Commissioners are satisfied that the amount is at least equal to the amount ascertainable under sub-paragraph (a) above, the amount calculated in accordance with paragraph (1) above.

(6) In this regulation, "compensating products" shall have the same meaning as in the Inward Processing Relief Regulations 1977.

NOTES

Entry on the importation of goods: by the Customs and Excise (Single Market etc) Regulations 1992, SI 1992/3095, reg 10(1), Sch 1, para 1, the reference to an entry on the importation of goods is to be treated as including an entry of such goods under the Customs Controls on Importation of Goods Regulations 1991, SI 1991/2724, reg 5, as amended by SI 1992/3095, SI 1993/3014.

PART IX
VALUE ADDED TAX

26

(Revoked by the Free Zone (Amendment) Regulations 1988, SI 1988/710, reg 4.)

27 Relief from import tax following supply to non-registered person

Where free zone goods have been supplied whilst in the free zone to a person who is neither registered nor liable to be registered for tax and he enters the goods for home use, the amount of tax payable shall be reduced by the amount of tax paid on the supply.

HYDROCARBON OIL (MIXING OF OILS) REGULATIONS 1985

(SI 1985/1450)

NOTES

Made: 16 September 1985.
Authority: Hydrocarbon Oil Duties Act 1979, ss 20A(5), (6), (7), 21, 24.
Commencement: 15 October 1985.

ARRANGEMENT OF REGULATIONS

1	Citation and commencement
2	Interpretation
3	Application
4	Approval
5	Security
6	Charge to duty and allowance
7	Furnishing of returns
8	Payment of duty
9	Allowances

1 Citation and commencement

These Regulations may be cited as the Hydrocarbon Oil (Mixing of Oils) Regulations 1985 and shall come into operation on 15th October 1985.

Part II

2 Interpretation

(1)   In these Regulations:—

"the Act" means the Hydrocarbon Oil Duties Act 1979;

"the 1973 Regulations" means the Hydrocarbon Oil Regulations 1973;

"the duty deferment Regulations" means the Excise Duties (Hydrocarbon Oils) (Deferred Payment) Regulations 1985;

"approved mixer" means a person approved by the Commissioners for the purposes of section 20A of the Act;

"business day" means a day which is a business day within the meaning of the Bills of Exchange Act 1882;

"mixing" means the mixing of different descriptions of hydrocarbon oil so as to produce new oil in accordance with section 20A of the Act and "mix" and its cognate expressions shall be construed accordingly.

(2)   Any expression used in these Regulations to which a meaning is given by the 1973 Regulations has, except where the context otherwise requires, the same meaning in these Regulations.

3 Application

These Regulations apply to oil which has been either charged with excise duty under section 6 of the Act or which would have been charged but for a relief or rebate allowed in respect of that oil.

4 Approval

(1)   Save where the Commissioners otherwise permit, a person seeking approval as a mixer shall apply to the Commissioners in writing and give such particulars as they may require.

(2)   Approval of persons as mixers, whether individually or by reference to a class, and whether in relation to particular descriptions of oil or generally may be:—

(a)   limited as to the mixture stated in the approval;

(b)   granted subject to conditions; and

(c)   revoked for reasonable cause.

(3)   Where conditions are imposed under this regulation they may be varied for reasonable cause.

(4)   Any person who has applied to be approved or who has been approved under paragraph (2) above shall notify the Commissioners immediately of any change in circumstances which materially affects any application for approval or approval given by the Commissioners or security given by him under these Regulations.

5 Security

An approved mixer shall provide security in such amount and in such form as the Commissioners may require for:—

(a)   the observance of any conditions imposed under regulation 4(2) above; and

(b)   the furnishing of returns as required by regulation 7 below.

6 Charge to duty and allowance

(1)   New oil subject to a charge of duty under section 20A of the Act shall be charged at the time it is mixed and that duty shall be paid in accordance with regulation 8 below.

(2)   Where new oil is subject to an allowance under section 20A of the Act that allowance shall be determined at the time it is mixed and it shall be made in accordance with regulation 9 below.

7 Furnishing of returns

(1)   An approved mixer shall furnish to the Commissioners a return—

(a)   on the last business day of each month, or,

(b)   where the approved mixer is also approved under the duty deferment Regulations, on the appropriate payment day of each month which is prescribed in regulation 5 of the said Regulations—

of all new oil mixed in the month preceding that in which the return is rendered, save that the Commissioners may allow a return to be rendered on a day and for a period different from the aforesaid.

(2)   The return shall be in such form and manner and containing such particulars as the Commissioners may require.

8 Payment of duty

(1)   At the time of furnishing a return under regulation 7 above an approved mixer shall pay to the Commissioners, or account for, the amount of duty appearing by the return to be due from him for the period to which it relates, and any duty which may be due from him for an earlier period.

(2)   The duty deferment Regulations shall not apply to the payment of duty under paragraph (1) above.

9 Allowances

Where it appears by a return furnished under regulation 7 above that an allowance under section 20A of the Act is due to an approved mixer, that allowance, unless the Commissioners otherwise allow, shall be in the form of a credit which he shall set off against excise duty on oil otherwise due from him to the Commissioners at the time of furnishing the return.

10

(Amends the Hydrocarbon Oil Regulations 1973, SI 1973/1311, regs 2, 43.)

POLICE AND CRIMINAL EVIDENCE ACT 1984 (APPLICATION TO CUSTOMS AND EXCISE) ORDER 1985

(SI 1985/1800)

NOTES

Made: 20 November 1985.

Authority: Police and Criminal Evidence Act 1984, s 114(2).

Commencement: 1 January 1986.

1

This Order may be cited as the Police and Criminal Evidence Act 1984 (Application to Customs and Excise) Order 1985 and shall come into operation on 1st January 1986.

2—

(1)   In this Order, unless the context otherwise requires—

"the Act" means the Police and Criminal Evidence Act 1984;

"assigned matter" has the meaning given to it by section 1 of the Customs and Excise Management Act 1979;

"the customs and excise Acts" has the meaning given to it by section 1 of the Customs and Excise Management Act 1979;

"customs office" means a place for the time being occupied by Her Majesty's Customs and Excise;

"officer" means a person commissioned by the Commissioners of Customs and Excise under section 6(3) of the Customs and Excise Management Act 1979.

(2)   A person is in customs detention for the purpose of this Order if—

(a)   he has been taken to a customs office after being arrested for an offence; or

(b)   he is arrested at a customs office after attending voluntarily at the office or accompanying an officer to it,

and is detained there or is detained elsewhere in the charge of an officer, and nothing shall prevent a detained person from being transferred between customs detention and police detention.

3—

(1)   Subject to the modifications in paragraphs (2) and (3) of this article, in [articles 4 to 12] below and in Schedule 2 to this Order, the provisions of the Act contained in Schedule 1 to this Order which relate to investigations of offences conducted by police officers or to persons detained by the police shall apply to investigations conducted by officers of Customs and Excise of offences which relate to assigned matters, and to persons detained by such officers.

(2)   The Act shall have effect as if the words and phrases in Column 1 of Part 1 of Schedule 2 to this Order were replaced by the substitute words and phrases in Column 2 of that Part.

(3)   Where in the Act any act or thing is to be done by a constable of a specified rank, that act or thing shall be done by an officer of at least the grade specified in Column 2 of Part 2 of Schedule 2 to this Order, and the Act shall be interpreted as if the substituted grade were specified in the Act.

NOTES

Para (1): words in square brackets substituted by the Police and Criminal Evidence Act 1984 (Application to Customs and Excise) (Amendment) Order 1995, SI 1995/3217, art 2(a).

4

Nothing in the application of the Act to Customs and Excise shall be construed as conferring upon an officer any power—

(a)   to charge a person with any offence;

(b)   to release a person on bail;

(c)   to detain a person for an offence after he has been charged with that offence.

5—

(1)   Where in the Act a constable is given power to seize and retain any thing found upon a lawful search of person or premises, an officer shall have the same power notwithstanding that the thing found is not evidence of an offence in relation to an assigned matter.

(2)   Nothing in the application of the Act to Customs and Excise shall be construed to prevent any thing lawfully seized by a person under any enactment from being accepted and retained by an officer.

(3)   Section 21 of the Act (access and copying) shall not apply to any thing seized as liable to forfeiture under the customs and excise Acts.

6

In its application by virtue of article 3 above the Act shall have effect as if the following section were inserted after section 14—

"**14A**

Material in the possession of a person who acquired or created it in the course of any trade, business, profession or other occupation or for the purpose of any paid or unpaid office and which relates to an assigned matter, as defined in section 1 of the Customs and Excise Management Act 1979, is neither excluded material nor special procedure material for the purposes of any enactment such as is mentioned in section 9(2) above.".

7

Section 18(1) of the Act shall be modified as follows:—

"**18—**

(1) Subject to the following provisions of this section, an officer of Customs and Excise may enter and search any premises occupied or controlled by a person who is under arrest for any [indictable] offence which relates to an assigned matter, as defined in section 1 of the Customs and Excise Management Act 1979, if he has reasonable grounds for suspecting that there is on the premises evidence, other than items subject to legal privilege, that relates—

    (a)   to that offence; or

    (b)   to some other [indictable] offence which is connected with or similar to that offence.".

NOTES

Para (1), as set out: words in square brackets substituted by the Serious Organised Crime and Police Act 2005 (Powers of Arrest) (Consequential Amendments) Order, SI 2005/3389, art 2(1), (2).

8—

(1) The Commissioners of Customs and Excise shall keep on an annual basis the written records mentioned in subsection (1) of section 50 of the Act.

(2) The Annual Report of the Commissioners of Her Majesty's Customs and Excise shall contain information about the matters mentioned in subsection (1) of section 50 of the Act in respect of the period to which it relates.

9—

(1) Section 55 of the Act shall have effect as if it related only to things such as are mentioned in subsection (1)(a) of that section.

(2) The Annual Report of the Commissioners of Her Majesty's Customs and Excise shall contain the information mentioned in subsection (15) of section 55 of the Act about searches made under that section.

10

Section 77(3) of the Act shall be modified to the extent that the definition of "independent person" shall, in addition to the persons mentioned therein, also include an officer or any other person acting under the authority of the Commissioners of Customs and Excise.

11

Where any provision of the Act as applied to Customs and Excise—

    (a)   confers a power on an officer, and

    (b)   does not provide that the power may only be exercised with the consent of some person other than an officer,

the officer may use reasonable force, if necessary, in the exercise of the power.

[12

[Section 24(2)] of the Act shall apply without prejudice to section 138(1) of the Customs and Excise Management Act 1979, section 72(9) of the Value Added Tax Act 1994, section 20 of and paragraph 4 of Schedule 3 to the Criminal Justice (International Co-operation) Act 1990, or any other enactment, including any enactment contained in subordinate legislation, for the time being in force which confers upon officers of Customs and Excise the power to arrest or detain persons.]

NOTES

Commencement: 1 January 1996.

Inserted by the Police and Criminal Evidence Act 1984 (Application to Customs and Excise) (Amendment) Order 1995, SI 1995/3217, art 2(c).

Opening words in square brackets inserted by the Serious Organised Crime and Police Act 2005 (Powers of Arrest) (Consequential Amendments) Order, SI 2005/3389, art 2(1), (3).

SCHEDULES

SCHEDULE 1
PROVISIONS OF THE ACT APPLIED TO CUSTOMS AND EXCISE

Article 3
Section 8
Section 9 and Schedule 1
Section 15
Section 16
Section 17(1)(b), (2), (4)
Section 18 subject to the modification in article 7 hereof
Section 19
Section 20
Section 21 subject to the modifications in article 5 hereof
Section 22(1) to (4)
[[Section 24(2)], subject to the modification in article 12 hereof]
Section 28
Section 29
Section 30(1) to (4)(a) and (5) to (11)
Section 31
Section 32(1) to (9) subject to the modifications in article 5 hereof
Section 34(1) to (5)
Section 35
Section 36
Section 37
Section 39
Section 40
Section 41
Section 42
Section 43
Section 44
Section 50 subject to the modification in article 8 hereof
Section 51(d)
Section 52
Section 54

Part II

Section 55 subject to the modifications in articles 5 and 9 hereof
Section 56(1) to (9)
Section 57(1) to (9)
Section 58(1) to (11)
Section 62
Section 63
Section 64(1) to (6)
[Section 107]

NOTES

Para (1): entry relating to "Section 24(2)" (originally "Section 24(6)") inserted by the Police and Criminal Evidence Act 1984 (Application to Customs and Excise) (Amendment) Order, SI 1995/3217, art 2(b). In entry relating to "Section 24(2)" words "Section 24(2)" in square brackets substituted by the Serious Organised Crime and Police Act 2005 (Powers of Arrest) (Consequential Amendments) Order, SI 2005/3389.

Words in final pair of square brackets added by the Police and Criminal Evidence Act 1984 (Application to Customs and Excise) Order 1987, SI 1987/439, art 3.

SCHEDULE 2

(Article 3)

PART 1

Substitution of equivalent words and phrases in the Act.

Where in the Act a word or phrase specified in Column 1 below is used, in the application of the Act to Customs and Excise, there shall be substituted the equivalent word or phrase in Column 2 below—

Column 1	*Column 2*
WORDS AND PHRASES USED IN THE ACT	SUBSTITUTED WORDS AND PHRASES
Area	Collection
chief officer	Collector
Constable	Officer
designated police station	designated customs office
officer of a force maintained by a police authority	Officer
police area	Collection
police detention (except in section 118 and in section 39(1)(a) the second time the words occur)	customs detention
police force	HM Commissioners of Customs and Excise
police officer	Officer
police station	customs office
Rank	[title]
Station	customs office
the police	HM Customs and Excise

NOTES

Words in square brackets substituted by the Police and Criminal Evidence Act 1984 (Application to Customs and Excise) (Amendment) Order 1996, SI 1996/1860, art 2.

[PART 2

Equivalent titles of officers

Where in the Act an act or thing is to be done by a constable of the rank specified in Column 1 below, that same act or thing shall, in the application of the Act to Customs and Excise, be done by an officer of at least an equivalent title specified in Column 2 below—

Column 1	Column 2
Rank of constable	*Title of officer*
Sergeant	Anti-Smuggling Officer (2);
	Cargo Team Leader (1);
	Cargo Team Member (3);
	Drug Dog Unit Team Leader;
	EFIT Team Member;
	EVO (2);
	LVOIT Officer (1);
	PSD Team Member (1);
	Road Fuel Testing Officer;
	Specialist Investigator (1); or
	any other officer within job bands 5 or 6
inspector	Anti-Smuggling Team Leader;
	Cargo Team Leader (2);
	EFIT Team Leader;
	EVU Team Leader;
	LVOIT Officer (2);
	PSD Team Manager;
	Road Fuel Control Officer;
	Specialist Investigator (2);
	Specialist Investigator (3); or
	any other officer within job bands 7 or 8
superintendent	Anti-Smuggling Manager;
	Cargo Operational Manager;
	Investigation Team Leader;
	PSD Operations Manager; or
	any other officer within job band 9
[Chief Inspector	Anti-Smuggling Team Leader;
	Cargo Team Leader (2);

Column 1	Column 2
Rank of constable	Title of officer
	EFIT Team Leader;
	EVU Team Leader;
	LVOIT Officer (2);
	PSD Team Manager;
	Road Fuel Control Officer;
	Specialist Investigator (2);
	Specialist Investigator (3); or
	any other officer within job bands 7 or 8]

The abbreviations used in Column 2 above shall have the following meaning:—

"PSD" shall mean "Passenger Services Division"

"EFIT" shall mean "Excise Fraud Investigation Team"

"EVO" shall mean "Excise Verification Officer"

"EVU" shall mean "Excise Verification Unit"

"LVOIT" shall mean "Local Value Added Tax Office Investigation Team".

The job bands referred to in Column 2 above are set from time to time by the Commissioners of Customs and Excise.]

NOTES

Substituted by the Police and Criminal Evidence Act 1984 (Application to Customs and Excise) (Amendment) Order 1996, SI 1996/1860, art 2. Entries in square brackets inserted by the Police and Criminal Evidence Act 1984 (Application to Customs and Excise) Order 1987, SI 1987/439, art 4 (as substituted by SI 1996/1860, art 3).

Definitions of the abbreviations used in Column 2 in SI 1996/1860, art 3 are omitted as they are defined above.

POSTAL PACKETS (CUSTOMS AND EXCISE) REGULATIONS 1986
(SI 1986/260)

NOTES

Made: 14 February 1986.

Authority: Post Office Act 1953, s 16(2).

Commencement: 1 March 1986.

1

These Regulations may be cited as the Postal Packets (Customs and Excise) Regulations 1986 and shall come into force on 1st March 1986.

2—

(1) In these Regulations—

"Act of 1979" means the Customs and Excise Management Act 1979;

"Commissioners" means Commissioners of Customs and Excise;

"the customs and excise Acts" has the meaning given by section 1(1) of the Act of 1979;

. . .

"dutiable goods" has the meaning given by section 1(1) of the Act of 1979 but includes goods chargeable with value added tax and goods subject to any other charge on importation;

"duty" and "duty of customs or excise" include value added tax and any other charge on imported goods;

"exporter" and "importer" have the meanings assigned to them by section 1(1) of the Act of 1979;

["post office", "postal operator" and "registered post service" have the same meaning as in the Postal Services Act 2000;

"postal packet" means a letter, parcel, packet or other article transmissible by post, conveyed by a universal service provider (within the meaning of the Postal Services Act 2000) in connection with the provision of a universal postal service (within the meaning of that Act);]

. . .

"prescribed" means prescribed by the provisions of the Universal Postal Convention and Detailed Regulations made thereunder which are for the time being in force;

"proper" in relation to an officer means appointed or authorised by the Commissioners or the [postal operator] to perform any duty in relation to a postal packet.

(2), (3) . . .

NOTES

Definitions "post office", "postal operator" and "registered post service" and "postal packet" inserted, and words in square brackets in definition of "proper" substituted and definitions "datapost packet", "inland post" and "letter packet" revoked by the Postal Services Act 2000 (Consequential Modifications No 1) Order 2001, SI 2001/1149, arts 3(2), 66(1), (2), Sch 2.

Paras (2), (3): revoked by SI 2001/1149, art 66(1), (2).

3

(Revokes the Postal Packets (Customs and Excise) Regulations 1975, SI 1975/1992.)

4

Section 16 of the Post Office Act 1953 shall apply to all postal packets, other than postcards, which are posted in the United Kingdom for transmission to any place outside it or which are brought by post into the United Kingdom.

5

In their application to goods contained in such postal packets, the following provisions of the Act of 1979 shall be subject to the following modifications and exceptions:—

(a)   In the application of section 5, subsection (3) shall be omitted and subsection (4) shall apply with the modification that the time of exportation of goods shall be the time when they are posted (or redirected) in the United Kingdom for transmission to a place outside it.

(b)   . . .

(c)   Section 40 shall apply only where the Commissioners have required entry to be made, and, where they have so required, shall apply only to the extent, and with the modification, set out in Regulation 14 of these Regulations.

[(d)   In the application of section 43, subsection (1) shall not apply, and paragraph (c) of subsection (2) shall apply with the substitution for sub-paragraphs (i) and (ii) of the words "those in force at the time when, the packet containing the goods having been presented to the proper officer of customs and excise, the amount of duty appearing to be due is assessed by him".]

(e)   In the application of section 49 subsection (1)(a) shall be omitted.

(f)   For references in—

    (i)   section 53 to "exported", "shipped for exportation", and "exported or shipped for exportation";

    (ii)   section 56 to "shipped or exported by land", "exported", and "shipped";

    (iii)   section 58 to "shipped for exportation", and "shipped";

    (iv)   section 58A to "shipped for exportation or exported by land", and "shipped",

there shall be substituted references to "posted in the United Kingdom for transmission to any place outside it".

(g)   Section 58B shall apply only in any cases, or class of cases, in which the Commissioners require a specification to be delivered.

(h)   Section 77(1) shall apply to goods brought by post into the United Kingdom or posted in the United Kingdom for transmission to any place outside it, if an entry or specification is required of such goods when they are imported or exported otherwise than by post.

(ij)   Section 99 shall apply to any goods deposited in a Queen's Warehouse under Regulation 14 of these Regulations as it applies to goods so deposited under or by virtue of any provision of the Act of 1979.

(k)   Paragraph 1 of Schedule 3 shall, in the case of a thing brought by post into the United Kingdom, apply with the substitution, for the words "to any person who to their knowledge was at the time of seizure the owner or one of the owners thereof", of the following:—

"to any person:

    (a)   who to their knowledge was at the time of the seizure the owner or one of the owners of the postal packet containing the thing; or

    (b)   who appears to them to be the sender of the postal packet containing the thing; or

    (c)   to whom the postal packet containing the thing was addressed"

and paragraph 10(1) shall not apply.

NOTES

Para (b): revoked by the Postal Packets (Customs and Excise) (Amendment) Regulations 1992, SI 1992/3224, reg 3(a).

Para (d): substituted by the Postal Packets (Customs and Excise) (Amendment) Regulations 1986, SI 1986/1019, reg 2.

Entry on the importation of goods: by the Customs and Excise (Single Market etc) Regulations 1992, SI 1992/3095, reg 10(1), Sch 1, para 1, the reference to an entry on the importation of goods is to be treated as including an entry of such goods under the Customs Controls on Importation of Goods Regulations 1991, SI 1991/2724, reg 5, as amended by SI 1992/3095, SI 1993/3014.

[5A

In its application to goods contained in postal packets brought into the United Kingdom, Regulation 5 of the Customs Controls on Importation of Goods

Regulations 1991 shall apply only in any case, or class of cases, in which the Commissioners require an entry to be made in accordance with that Regulation.]

NOTES

Inserted by the Postal Packets (Customs and Excise) (Amendment) Regulations 1992, SI 1992/3224, reg 3(b).

6

Dutiable goods shall not be brought by post into the United Kingdom from a place situated outside the United Kingdom and the Isle of Man for delivery in the United Kingdom or the Isle of Man except [in a postal packet].

(a), (b) . . .

NOTES

Words in square brackets inserted and sub-paras (a), (b) revoked by the Postal Services Act 2000 (Consequential Modifications No 1) Order 2001, SI 2001/1149, arts 3(2), 66(1), (2), Sch 2.

[7—

(1) Subject to paragraphs (2) to (6) below, every postal packet brought into the United Kingdom containing dutiable goods shall have affixed to it, or be accompanied by, a customs declaration fully stating the nature, quantity and value of the goods which it contains or of which it consists, and such other particulars as the Commissioners or the postal operator may require.

(2) The Commissioners may, at the request of the postal operator, relax the requirements of paragraph (1) above by allowing the bringing in by post into the United Kingdom of any number of postal packets accompanied by a single customs declaration containing the particulars described in paragraph (1) above if they are brought in together, sent by or on behalf of the same person and addressed to a single addressee.

(3) Subject to paragraph (5) below, every postal packet brought into the United Kingdom the value of which exceeds £270, shall in additional to the requirements contained in paragraph (1) above, bear on the outside the top portion of a green label in the prescribed form.

(4) Subject to paragraph (6) below, every postal packet brought into the United Kingdom the value of which does not exceed £270, shall either—

(a) bear on the outside a green label in the prescribed form, in which the declaration as to the description, net weight and value of the contents shall be fully and correctly completed; or

(b) bear on the outside the top portion of a green label in the prescribed form and, in addition, have attached to it a full and correct customs declaration of the kind prescribed in paragraph (1) above.

(5) Any postal packet falling within paragraph (3) above which contains any article of value and is brought into the United Kingdom by a registered post service, may have the customs declaration referred to in paragraph (3) above enclosed in it.

(6) Any postal packet falling within paragraph (4) above which contains any article of value and is brought into the United Kingdom by registered post service, may have the customs declaration referred to in paragraph (4)(b) above enclosed in it.]

NOTES

Substituted by the Postal Services Act 2000 (Consequential Modifications No 1) Order 2001, SI 2001/1149, art 66(1), (4).

[8—

(1)   Subject to paragraphs (2) to (6) below, every postal packet posted into the United Kingdom for transmission to any place outside it containing dutiable goods shall have affixed to it, or be accompanied by, a customs declaration fully stating the nature, quantity and value of the goods which it contains or of which it consists, and such other particulars as the Commissioners or the postal operator may require.

(2)   The Commissioners may, at the request of the postal operator, relax the requirements of paragraph (1) above by allowing the exportation by post of any number of postal packets accompanied by a single customs declaration containing the particulars described in paragraph (1) above if they are brought in together, sent by or on behalf of the same person and addressed to a single addressee.

(3)   Subject to paragraph (5) below every postal packet posted in the United Kingdom for transmission to any place outside it the value of which exceeds £270, shall bear on the outside the top portion of a green label in the prescribed form and, in addition, shall have attached to it, or, if the postal administration of the country of destination so requires, enclosed in it, a full and correct customs declaration of the kind described in paragraph (1) above.

(4)   Subject to paragraph (6) below, every postal packet posted in the United Kingdom for transmission to any place outside it the value of which does not exceed £270, shall either—

(a)   bear on the outside on the outside a green label in the prescribed form, in which the declaration as to the description, net weight and value of the contents shall be fully and correctly completed; or, if the sender so prefers,

(b)   bear on the outside the top portion of a green label in the prescribed form and, in addition, have attached to it or, if the postal administration of the country of destination so requires, enclosed in it, a full and correct customs declaration of the kind prescribed in paragraph (1) above.

(5)   Any postal packet falling within paragraph (3) above which contains any article of value and is exported by registered post service, may have the customs declaration referred to in paragraph (3) above enclosed in it if the sender so prefers.

(6)   Any postal packet falling within paragraph (4) above which contains any article of value and is exported by registered post service may have the customs declaration referred to in paragraph (4)(b) above enclosed in it if the sender so prefers.]

NOTES

Substituted by the Postal Services Act 2000 (Consequential Modifications No 1) Order 2001, SI 2001/1149, art 66(1), (5).

9—

[(1)   Every mail bag containing postal packets containing or consisting of goods which are dutiable in the country of destination, brought by post into the United Kingdom or posted in the United Kingdom for transmission to any place outside it by a universal service provider (within the meaning of the Postal Services Act 2000) in connection with the provision of a universal postal service (within the meaning of that Act), shall have affixed to the bag label a green label in the prescribed form.]

[(2) Regulations 7 and 8 of these regulations and paragraph (1) of this Regulation shall not apply to a postal packet or mail bag which—

    (a)   contains only Community goods, and

        (i)   having been posted elsewhere in the territory of the Community, is brought by post to the United Kingdom for delivery there, or

        (ii)   is posted in the United Kingdom for delivery elsewhere in the territory of the Community; or

    (b)   is posted in a place situated outside the United Kingdom for delivery in another place so situated.]

NOTES

Para (1): substituted by the Postal Services Act 2000 (Consequential Modifications No 1) Order 2001, SI 2001/1149, art 66(1), (6).

Para (2): substituted by the Postal Packets (Customs and Excise) (Amendment) Regulations 1992, SI 1992/3224, reg 3(c).

10

Without prejudice to the provisions of Regulations 7, 8 and 9 of these Regulations, every postal packet containing goods to be exported by post without payment of any duty of customs or excise to which they are subject, or on drawback or repayment of such duty, shall on its removal to the post office—

    (a)   be accompanied by such shipping bill, declaration or other document containing such particulars as the Commissioners may require; and

    (b)   have affixed to its outer cover in the form and manner so required a label having printed thereon the words "Exported by Post under Customs and Excise Control", or be distinguished in such other manner as may be so required.

11

The proper officer of the [postal operator] is hereby authorised to perform in relation to any postal packet or the goods which it contains such of the duties required by virtue of the customs and excise Acts to be performed by the importer or exporter of goods as the Commissioners may require.

NOTES

Words in square brackets substituted by the Postal Services Act 2000 (Consequential Modifications No 1) Order 2001, SI 2001/1149, art 66(1), (7).

12

In such cases or classes of case as the Commissioners may so require, the proper officer of the [postal operator] shall produce to the proper officer of customs and excise postal packets arriving in the United Kingdom or about to be despatched from the United Kingdom and, if the proper officer of customs and excise so requires, shall open for customs examination any packets so produced.

NOTES

Words in square brackets substituted by the Postal Services Act 2000 (Consequential Modifications No 1) Order 2001, SI 2001/1149, art 66(1), (7).

13

The proper officer of the [postal operator] accepting any outgoing packet in respect of which the requirements of paragraph (b) of Regulation 10 of these Regulations have been duly complied with shall endorse a certificate of the posting of the packet on the appropriate document and shall give it to the sender.

NOTES

Words in square brackets substituted by the Postal Services Act 2000 (Consequential Modifications No 1) Order 2001, SI 2001/1149, art 66(1), (7).

14—

(1) If goods are brought by post into the United Kingdom, and an officer of customs and excise sends to the addressee of the packet in which they are contained, or to any other person who is for the time being the importer of the goods, a notice requiring entry to be made of them or requiring a full and accurate account of them to be delivered to the proper officer of customs and excise but entry is not made or such account is not delivered within 28 days of the date of such notice or within such longer period as the Commissioners may allow, then unless the Commissioners have required the packet to be delivered to them under Regulation 17 of these Regulations the [postal operator] shall—

(a)   return the goods to the sender of the packet in which they were contained, or otherwise export them from the United Kingdom in accordance with any request or indication appearing on the packet; or

(b)   deliver the goods to the proper officer of customs and excise; or

(c)   with the permission of the Commissioners, and under the supervision of the proper officer of customs and excise, destroy them.

(2) Where goods have been delivered to him in accordance with paragraph 1(b) of this Regulation, the proper officer of customs and excise may cause the goods to be deposited in a Queen's Warehouse and section 40(3) of the Act of 1979 shall apply to the goods as it applies to goods so deposited under the said Section 40.

NOTES

Words in square brackets substituted by the Postal Services Act 2000 (Consequential Modifications No 1) Order 2001, SI 2001/1149, art 66(1), (7).

Entry on the importation of goods: by the Customs and Excise (Single Market etc) Regulations 1992, SI 1992/3095, reg 10(1), Sch 1, para 1, the reference to an entry on the importation of goods is to be treated as including an entry of such goods under the Customs Controls on Importation of Goods Regulations 1991, SI 1991/2724, reg 5, as amended by SI 1992/3095, SI 1993/3014.

15—

(1) On delivering a postal packet the proper officer of the [postal operator] may demand payment of any duty or other sum due to the Commissioners in respect of it, and any sum so received shall be paid over to the Commissioners by the Post Office.

(2) If payment is not made of any duty so demanded, then, subject to paragraph (3) of this Regulation, the [postal operator] may, with the agreement of the Commissioners, dispose of the goods contained in the packet as it sees fit.

(3) If any amount demanded in accordance with paragraph (1) of this Regulation, but not paid, is an amount other than duty, the [postal operator] shall deliver the packet to the proper officer of customs and excise.

NOTES

Words in square brackets substituted by the Postal Services Act 2000 (Consequential Modifications No 1) Order 2001, SI 2001/1149, art 66(1), (7).

16

If dutiable goods are brought by post into the United Kingdom in any postal packet contrary to Regulation 6 of these Regulations, or if any postal packet or mail bag to which Regulations 7, 8 and 9 of these Regulations or any of them apply does not contain, does not have affixed or attached to it, or is not accompanied by, the declaration, or does not bear the green label, required by those Regulations or any of them, or if the contents of any postal packet do not agree with the green label or customs declaration affixed or attached to the packet, or by which it is accompanied, or if the other requirements of these Regulations or any of them are not complied with in every material respect, then in every such case the postal packet or mail bag and all its contents shall be liable to forfeiture.

17

If the Commissioners require any postal packet to be delivered to them on the ground that any goods contained in it are liable to forfeiture under the customs and excise Acts (including these Regulations) the proper officer of the [postal operator] shall deliver the packet to the proper officer of Customs and Excise.

NOTES

Words in square brackets substituted by the Postal Services Act 2000 (Consequential Modifications No 1) Order 2001, SI 2001/1149, art 66(1), (7).

18

Nothing in these Regulations shall authorise the sending or bringing of any article out of or into the United Kingdom by post contrary to any provisions of [the Postal Services Act 2000].

NOTES

Words in square brackets substituted by the Postal Services Act 2000 (Consequential Modifications No 1) Order 2001, SI 2001/1149, art 66(1), (7).

VALUE ADDED TAX TRIBUNALS RULES 1986

(SI 1986/590)

NOTES

Made: 26 March 1986.

Authority: Value Added Tax Act 1983, Sch 8, para 9 (see now the Value Added Tax Act 1994, Sch 12, para 9).

Modifications: references to "value added tax tribunals" modified by the Finance Act 1994, s 7, and by the Value Added Tax Act 1994, Sch 12, para 1.

Commencement: 1 May 1986.

ARRANGEMENT OF RULES

1 Citation, commencement, revocation and savings

(1) These rules may be cited as the Value Added Tax Tribunals Rules 1986 and shall come into operation on 1st May 1986.

(2) . . .

(3) Anything begun under or for the purpose of any rules revoked by these rules may be continued under or, as the case may be, for the purpose of the corresponding provision of these rules.

(4) Where any document in any appeal to, or other proceedings before, a tribunal refers to a provision of any rules revoked by these rules, such reference shall, unless a contrary intention appears, be construed as referring to the corresponding provision of these rules.

NOTES

Para (2): revokes the Value Added Tax Tribunals Rules 1972, SI 1972/1344, the Value Added Tax Tribunals (Amendment) Rules 1974, SI 1974/1934, the Value Added Tax Tribunals (Amendment) Rules 1977, SI 1977/1017, and the Value Added Tax Tribunals (Amendment) Rules 197, SI 1977/1760.

2 Interpretation

In these rules, unless the context otherwise requires,—

"the Act" means the Value Added Tax Act [1994];

["the 1985 Act" means the Finance Act 1985;]

["the 1994 Act" means the Finance Act 1994;

"the 1996 Act" means the Finance Act 1996;]

["the 2000 Act" means the Finance Act 2000;]

["the 2001 Act" means the Finance Act 2001;]

["the 2003 Act" means the Finance Act 2003;]

["appellant" means a person who, being entitled to do so under any enactment for the time being in force, brings an appeal to a VAT and duties tribunal;]

"the appropriate tribunal centre" means the tribunal centre for the time being appointed by the President for the area in which is situated the address to which the disputed decision was sent by the Commissioners or the tribunal centre to which the appeal against the disputed decision may be transferred under these rules;

"chairman" has the same meaning as in Schedule [12] to the Act, and includes the President and any Vice-President;

"the Commissioners" means the Commissioners [for Revenue and Customs];

"costs" includes fees, charges, disbursements, expenses and remuneration;

["date of notification", in relation to any document, means the date on which a proper officer sends that document, or [a] copy of that document, to any person under these rules;]

"disputed decision" means the decision of the Commissioners against which an appellant or intending appellant appeals or desires to appeal to a tribunal;

["evasion penalty appeal" means an appeal against an assessment to a penalty under section 60 or section 61 of the Act, or section 8 of or paragraph 12 of Schedule 7 to [the 1994 Act or paragraph 18 or 19 of Schedule 5 to the 1996 Act] [or paragraph 98 [or 99] of Schedule 6 to the 2000 Act] [or paragraph 7 or 8 of Schedule 6 to the 2001 Act][, or section 25 or 28 of the 2003 Act,] which is not solely a mitigation appeal and any accompanying appeal by the appellant against an assessment for the amount of tax alleged to have been evaded by the same conduct as that in the appeal against the assessment to a penalty;]

["the Export (Penalty) Regulations" means the Export (Penalty) Regulations 2003;]

["hardship direction" means a direction that an appeal or an intended appeal should be entertained notwithstanding that the amount which the Commissioners have determined to be payable as tax has not been paid or deposited with them;]

"mitigation appeal" means an appeal which, according to the notice of appeal or other document received from the appellant at the appropriate tribunal centre, is against a decision of the Commissioners with respect to the amount of a penalty [on grounds confined to those set out in section 13(4) of the 1985 Act (in respect of penalties imposed before 27th July 1993), or with respect to the amount of a penalty or (as the case may be) interest solely under section 70 of the Act, section 8(4) of or paragraph 13 of Schedule 7 to the 1994 Act or paragraph 25 or

28 of Schedule 5 to the 1996 Act] [or paragraph 104 of Schedule 6 to the 2000 Act] [or section 46(1) of the 2001 Act] [or section 29 of the 2003 Act] [or regulation 5 of the Export (Penalty) Regulations];

"the President" means the President of [the VAT and [Duties] Tribunals] or the person nominated by the Lord Chancellor to discharge for the time being the functions of the President;

"proper officer" means a member of the administrative staff of the [VAT and duties tribunals] appointed by a chairman to perform the duties of a proper officer under these rules;

["reasonable excuse appeal" means an appeal which, according to the notice of appeal or other document received from the appellant at the appropriate tribunal centre, is against a decision of the Commissioners with respect to [any liability to or the amount of any] penalty or surcharge on grounds confined to those set out in sections 59(7), 62(3), 63(10), 64(5), [65(3)], [66(7)], 67(8), 68(4), or 69(8) of the Act or [[section 10(1)] or 11(4) of or any of paragraphs 14(3), 15(5), 16(4), 17(3), 18(2) or 19(4) of Schedule 7 to the 1994 Act]; [or any of paragraphs 41(4), 55(5), 90(4), 100(4), 101(4), 114(4), 124(4), 125(7), 127(5) of Schedule 6 to the 2000 Act] [or section 25(4) or 33(4) of or any of paragraphs 1(5) of Schedule 4, 15(4) of Schedule 5, 9(4) of Schedule 6, 1(4)(a) or (b), 2(7) or 4(5)(a) or (b) of Schedule 7 to the 2001 Act] [or section 27 of the 2003 Act] [or regulation 4 of the Export (Penalty) Regulations]]

"the Registrar" means the Registrar of the [VAT and [Duties] tribunals] or any member of the administrative staff of the [VAT and duties tribunals] authorised by the [President] to perform for the time being all or any of the duties of a Registrar under these rules;

["tax" in relation to an appeal or application, means any tax, duty, levy or security to which that appeal or application relates;]

. . .

"tribunal centre" means an administrative office of the [VAT and duties tribunals];

"Vice-President" means a Vice-President of [the VAT and Duties Tribunals].

NOTES

Definitions "date of notification" and "hardship direction" inserted by the Value Added Tax Tribunals (Amendment) Rules 1991, SI 1991/186, r 3; definition "reasonable excuse appeal", words in first (inner) pair of square brackets in definitions "appellant" and "the President" substituted, and words in square brackets in definition "the Act", "proper officer", "the Registrar" and "tribunal centre" substituted, definitions "the 1985 Act", "evasion penalty appeal" and "tax" inserted, and definition omitted revoked, by the Value Added Tax Tribunals (Amendment) Rules 1994, SI 1994/2617, r 4; definitions "the 1994 Act" and "the 1996 Act" inserted, words in second (inner) pairs of square brackets in definitions "appellant" and "the President" substituted, and words in square brackets in definitions "chairman", "date of notification", "evasion penalty appeal", mitigation appeal", "reasonable excuse appeal" and "Vice-President" substituted, by the Value Added Tax Tribunals (Amendment) Rules 1997, SI 1997/255, r 4. Definition "the 2000 Act" inserted, words in second (inner) pair of square brackets in definition "evasion penalty appeal" inserted, words in second pair of square brackets in definition "mitigation appeal" inserted, and words in square brackets in definition "reasonable excuse appeal" inserted, by the Value Added Tax Tribunals (Amendment) Rules 2001, SI 2001/3073 r 3. Definition "the 2001 Act" inserted, words in square brackets in definition of "evasion penalty appeal" inserted, words in third pair of square brackets in definition "mitigation appeal" inserted, and words in final square brackets in definition "reasonable excuse appeal" inserted, by the Value Added Tax Tribunals (Amendment) Rules 2002, SI 2002/2851 rr 2, 3. Definition "the 2003 Act" inserted, and definitions "evasion penalty appeal", "mitigation appeal", and "reasonable excuse appeal" amended by the Value Added Tax Tribunals (Amendment) Rules 2003, SI 2003/2757 r 2. Definition "the Export (Penalty) Regulations" inserted, and definitions "mitigation appeal", and "reasonable excuse appeal" amended, by the Value Added Tax Tribunals (Amendment) Rules 2004, SI 2004/1032 r 2. Definition of "appellant" substituted, and words in definition "the Commissioners" in square brackets inserted, by the Value Added Tax Tribunals (Amendment) Rules, SI 2007/2351 r 2(1), (2).

3 Method of appealing

(1)   An appeal to a tribunal shall be brought by a notice of appeal served at the appropriate tribunal centre.

(2)   A notice of appeal shall be signed by or on behalf of the appellant and shall—

(a)   state the name and address of the appellant;

[(aa)   state the date (if any) with effect from which the appellant was registered for tax and the nature of his business;]

(b)   state the address of the office of the Commissioners from which the disputed decision was sent;

(c)   state the date of the document containing the disputed decision and the address to which it was sent;

(d)   . . . have attached thereto a copy of the document containing the disputed decision; and

(e)   set out, or have attached thereto a document containing, the grounds of the appeal, including in a reasonable excuse appeal, particulars of the excuse relied upon.

(3)   A notice of appeal shall have attached thereto a copy of any letter from the Commissioners extending the appellant's time to appeal against the disputed decision and of any further letter from the Commissioners notifying him of a date from which his time to appeal against the disputed decision shall run.

(4)   Subject to any direction made under rule 13, the parties to an appeal shall be the appellant and the Commissioners.

NOTES

Para (2): sub-para (aa) inserted, and words omitted from sub-para (d) revoked, by the Value Added Tax Tribunals (Amendment) Rules 1994, SI 1994/2617, r 5.

4 Time for appealing

(1)   Subject to [paragraphs (2) and (3)] of this rule . . ., a notice of appeal shall be served at the appropriate tribunal centre before the expiration of 30 days after the date of the document containing the disputed decision of the Commissioners.

(2)   If, during the period of 30 days after the date of the document containing the disputed decision, the Commissioners shall have notified the appellant by letter that his time to appeal against the disputed decision is extended until the expiration of 21 days after a date set out in such letter, or to be set out in a further letter to him, a notice of appeal against that disputed decision may be served at the appropriate tribunal centre at any time before the expiration of the period of 21 days set out in such letter or further letter.

[(3)   Where a decision is deemed to have been confirmed by the Commissioners under [section 7C(3)(d) of the Tobacco Products Duty Act 1979,] section 15(2) of the 1994 Act, section 54(8) of the 1996 Act, paragraph 121(8) of Schedule 6 to the 2000 Act[, section 40(8) of the 2001 Act[, section 35(4) of the 2003 Act [regulation 11(4) of the Export (Penalty) Regulations, or regulation 4(5) of the Control of Cash (Penalties) Regulations 2007]], a notice of appeal shall be served at the appropriate tribunal centre before the expiration of 75 days after the day on which the review was required.]

NOTES

Para (1): words in square brackets substituted, and words revoked, by the Value Added Tax Tribunals (Amendment) Rules 2002, SI 2002/2851 rr 2, 4(a).

Para (3): inserted by SI 2002/2851 rr 2, 4(b). Words inserted by the Value Added Tax Tribunals (Amendment) Rules 2004, SI 2004/1032 r 3. Words in square brackets beginning "section 7C(3)(d)" inserted, and words in square brackets beginning "regulation 11(4)" substituted, by the Value Added Tax Tribunals (Amendment) Rules, SI 2007/2351 r 2(1), (3).

5 Acknowledgement and notification of an appeal

A proper officer shall send—

(a)   an acknowledgement of the service of a notice of appeal at the appropriate tribunal centre to the appellant; and

(b)   a copy of the notice of appeal and of any accompanying document or documents to the Commissioners;

and the acknowledgement and such copy of the notice of appeal shall state the date of service [and the date of notification] of the notice of appeal.

NOTES

Words in square brackets inserted by the Value Added Tax Tribunals (Amendment) Rules 1991, SI 1991/186, r 4.

6 Notice that an appeal does not lie or cannot be entertained

(1)   Where the Commissioners contend that an appeal does not lie to, or cannot be entertained by, a tribunal they shall serve a notice to that effect at the appropriate tribunal centre containing the grounds for such contention and applying for the appeal to be struck out or dismissed, as the case may be, as soon as practicable after the receipt by them of the notice of appeal.

(2)   Any notice served by the Commissioners under this rule shall be accompanied by a copy of the disputed decision unless a copy thereof has been served previously at the appropriate tribunal centre by either party to the appeal.

(3)   In a reasonable excuse or a mitigation appeal the hearing of any application made by the Commissioners under the provisions of this rule may immediately precede the hearing of the substantive appeal.

(4)   A proper officer shall send a copy of any notice or certificate served under this rule and of any document or documents accompanying the same to the appellant.

7 Statement of case, defence and reply in [an evasion] penalty appeal

(1)   Unless a tribunal shall otherwise direct, in [an evasion penalty appeal]—

(a)   the Commissioners shall within 42 days of the date of [notification] of the notice of appeal or the withdrawal or dismissal of any application made by them under rule 6 hereof (whichever shall be the later) serve at the appropriate tribunal centre a statement of case in the appeal setting out the matters and facts on which they rely for the making of the penalty assessment [or, as the case may be, the ascertainment of the penalty] and (where also disputed) the making of the assessment for[, or, as the case may be, the ascertainment of,] the tax alleged to have been evaded by the same conduct;

[(aa)   a statement of case served by the Commissioners in accordance with (a) above shall include full particulars of the alleged dishonesty and shall state the statutory provision under which the penalty or tax is assessed or the decision is made;]

(b)   the appellant shall within 42 days of the date of [notification] of such statement of case serve at the appropriate tribunal centre a defence thereto setting out the matters and facts on which he relies for his defence; and

(c)   the Commissioners may within 21 days of the date of [notification] of such defence serve at the appropriate tribunal centre a reply to a defence and shall do so if it is necessary thereby to set out specifically any matter or any fact showing illegality, or

    (i)   which they allege makes the defence not maintainable; or

    (ii) which, if not specifically set out, might take the appellant by surprise; or

    (iii) which raises any issue of fact not arising out of the statement of case.

(2)   At any hearing of [an evasion penalty appeal] the Commissioners shall not be required to prove, or to bring evidence relating to, any matter or fact which is admitted by the appellant in his defence.

(3)   Every statement of case, defence and reply hereunder shall be divided into paragraphs numbered consecutively, each allegation being so far as convenient contained in a separate paragraph.

(4)   Each such document shall contain in summary form a brief statement of the matters and facts on which the party relies but not the evidence by which those facts are to be proved.

(5)   A party may raise a point of law in such documents.

NOTES

Rule heading: words in square brackets substituted by the Value Added Tax Tribunals (Amendment) Rules 1997, SI 1997/255, r 5.

Para (1): words in first pair of square brackets substituted, and sub-para (aa) inserted, by SI 1994/2617, r 6; words in square brackets in sub-paras (a), (b), (c) substituted by the Value Added Tax Tribunals (Amendment) Rules 1991, SI 1991/186, r 5. Words in sub-para (a) inserted by the Value Added Tax Tribunals (Amendment) Rules 2003, SI 2003/2757 r 4.

Para (2): words in square brackets substituted by SI 1994/2617, r 6.

8 Statement of case in an appeal other than [an evasion] penalty appeal and reasonable excuse and mitigation appeals

Unless a tribunal otherwise directs, in appeals other than reasonable excuse and mitigation appeals and [evasion penalty appeals] the Commissioners shall [within the period of 30 days after—

(a)   the date of notification of the notice of appeal; or

(b)   the date of notification of the notice of withdrawal of any application under rule 6 in the appeal; or

(c)   the date on which a direction dismissing any application under rule 6 in the appeal is released in accordance with rule 30;

whichever shall be the latest] serve at the appropriate tribunal centre a statement of case in the appeal setting out the matters and facts on which they rely to support the disputed decision [and the statutory provision under which the tax or penalty is assessed [or, as the case may be, demanded] or the decision is made].

NOTES

Rule heading: words in square brackets substituted by the Value Added Tax Tribunals (Amendment) Rules 1997, SI 1997/255, r 5.

Words in first pair of square brackets substituted and words in third pair of square brackets inserted by SI 1994/2617, r 7; words in second pair of square brackets substituted by the Value Added Tax Tribunals (Amendment) Rules 1991, SI 1991/186, r 6. Words "or as the case may be, demanded" inserted by the Value Added Tax Tribunals (Amendment) Rules 2003, SI 2003/2757 r 5.

[8A Further provisions about statements of case

Where on an appeal against a decision with respect to an assessment [or a demand notice (as defined by section 30(1) of the 2003 Act)] [or regulation 6(1) of the Export (Penalty) Regulations] or the amount of an assessment the Commissioners wish to contend that an amount specified in the assessment [or, as the case may be, demand notice] is less than it ought to have been, they shall so state in their statement of case in that appeal, indicating the amount of the alleged deficiency and the manner in which it has been calculated.]

NOTES

Commencement: 1 March 1997.

Inserted by the Value Added Tax Tribunals (Amendment) Rules 1997, SI 1997/255, r 6. Words inserted by the Value Added Tax Tribunals (Amendment) Rules 2003, SI 2003/2757 r 6. Words in second square brackets inserted by the Value Added Tax Tribunals (Amendment) Rules 2004, SI 2004/1032 r 4.

9 Further and better particulars

. . . A tribunal may at any time direct a party to an appeal to serve further particulars of his case at the appropriate tribunal centre for the appeal within such period from the date of such direction (not being less than 14 days from the date thereof) as it may specify therein.

(2) . . .

NOTES

Para (1): numbering revoked by the Value Added Tax Tribunals (Amendment) Rules 1997, SI 1997/255, r 7(1).

Para (2): revoked by SI 1997/255, r 7(2).

10 Acknowledgement and notification of service of formal documents served in an appeal

(1) Any statement of case served by the Commissioners under rule 7 or rule 8 of these rules shall be accompanied by a copy of the disputed decision unless a copy of the disputed decision has been served previously at the appropriate tribunal centre by either party to the appeal.

(2) In a reasonable excuse or a mitigation appeal the Commissioners shall serve a copy of the disputed decision at the appropriate tribunal centre as soon as practicable after the receipt by them of the copy of the notice of appeal unless a copy of the disputed decision has been so served previously by the appellant.

(3) A proper officer shall send—

   (a)   an acknowledgement of the service at the appropriate tribunal centre of any statement of case, defence, reply or particulars in any appeal to the party serving the same; and

   (b)   a copy of such document or particulars and any other document accompanying the same to the other party to the appeal.

11 Method of applying for a direction

(1)   An application to a tribunal, made otherwise than at a hearing, for

[(a)   the issue of a witness summons; or

(b)   a direction (including a hardship direction or a direction for the setting aside of a witness summons)

shall be made by notice served at the appropriate tribunal centre.]

(2)   A notice under this rule shall—

(a)   state the name and address of the applicant;

(b)   state the direction sought or details of the witness summons sought to be issued or set aside; and

(c)   set out, or have attached thereto a document containing, the grounds of the application.

(3)   In addition to the requirement of paragraph (2) hereof, any notice of application by an intending appellant shall—

(a)   state the address of the office of the Commissioners from which the disputed decision was sent;

(b)   state the date of the disputed decision and the address to which it was sent;

(c)   set out shortly the disputed decision or have attached thereto a copy of the document containing the same; and

(d)   have attached thereto a copy of any letter from the Commissioners extending the applicant's time to appeal against the disputed decision and of any letter from the Commissioners notifying him of a date from which his time of appeal against the disputed decision shall run.

(4)   A notice of application for [a hardship direction] shall be served at the appropriate tribunal centre within the period for the service of a notice of appeal.

(5)   Except as provided by rule 22, the parties to an application shall be the parties to the appeal or intended appeal.

(6)   Except as provided by rule 22, a proper officer shall send—

(a)   an acknowledgement of the service of a notice of application at the appropriate tribunal centre to the applicant; and

(b)   a copy of such notice of application and of accompanying document or documents to the other party to the application (if any);

and the acknowledgement and copy of the notice of application shall state the date of service [and date of notification] of the notice of application.

(7)   Within 14 days of the date of [notification] of a notice of application the other party to the application (if any) shall indicate whether or not he consents thereto and, if he does not consent thereto, the reason therefor.

NOTES

Para (1): words in square brackets substituted by the Value Added Tax Tribunals (Amendment) Rules 1991, SI 1991/186, r 7.

Para (4): words in square brackets substituted by SI 1991/186, r 8.

Para (6): words in square brackets added by SI 1991/186, r 9.

Para (7): word in square brackets substituted by SI 1991/186, r 10.

12 Partners

[One or more partners] in a firm which is not a legal person distinct from the partners of whom it is composed may appeal against a decision of the Commissioners relating to the firm or its business, or apply to a tribunal in an appeal or intended appeal, in the name of the firm and, unless a tribunal shall otherwise direct, the proceedings shall be carried on in the name of the firm, but with the same consequences as would have ensued if the appeal or application had been brought in the names of the partners.

NOTES

Words in square brackets substituted by the Value Added Tax Tribunals (Amendment) Rules 1994, SI 1994/2617, r 8.

[13 Death or bankruptcy of an appellant or applicant

(1) This rule applies where, in the course of proceedings, the liability or interest of the applicant or appellant passes to another person ("the successor") by reason of death insolvency or otherwise.

(2) The tribunal may direct, on the application of the Commissioners or the successor, and with the written consent of the successor, that the successor shall be substituted for the applicant or appellant in the proceedings.

(3) Where the tribunal is satisfied that there is no person interested in the application or appeal, or the successor fails to give written consent for his substitution in the proceedings within a period of two months after being requested to do so by the tribunal it may, of its own motion or on application by the Commissioners and after giving prior written notice to the successor, dismiss the application or appeal.]

NOTES

Substituted by the Value Added Tax Tribunals (Amendment) Rules 1994, SI 1994/2617, r 9.

14 Amendments

(1) For the purposes of determining the issues in dispute or of correcting an error or defect in an appeal or application or intended appeal, a tribunal may at any time, either of its own motion or on the application of any party to the appeal or application, or any other person interested, direct that a notice of appeal, notice of application, statement of case, defence, reply, particulars or other document in the proceedings be amended in such manner as may be specified in such direction on such terms as it may think fit.

(2) This rule shall not apply to a decision or direction of a tribunal.

15 Transfers between tribunal centres

A tribunal on the application of a party to an appeal may direct that the appeal and all proceedings in the appeal be transferred to such tribunal centre as may be specified in such direction whereupon, for the purposes of these rules, the tribunal centre specified in such direction shall become the appropriate tribunal centre for such appeal and all proceedings therein, without prejudice to the power of a tribunal to give a further direction relating thereto under this rule.

16 Withdrawal of an appeal or application

(1) An appellant or applicant may at any time withdraw his appeal or application by serving at the appropriate tribunal centre a notice of withdrawal signed by him or on his behalf, and a proper officer shall send a copy thereof to [the other parties to the appeal].

(2) The withdrawal of an appeal or application under this rule shall not prevent a party to such appeal or application from applying under rule 29 for an award or direction as to his or their costs or under [section 84(8)] of the Act [or under section 56(3), (4) or (5) of the 1996 Act] [or under paragraph 123(4)[, (5) or (6)] of Schedule 6 to the 2000 Act] [or under section 42(4), (5) or (6) of the 2001 Act] for a direction for the payment or repayment of a sum of money with interest or prevent a tribunal from making such an award or direction if it thinks fit so to do.

NOTES

Para (1): words in square brackets substituted by the Value Added Tax Tribunals (Amendment) Rules 1994, SI 1994/2617, r 10.

Para (2): words in first pair of square brackets substituted by the Value Added Tax Tribunals (Amendment) Rules 1994, SI 1994/2617, r 10; words in second pair of square brackets inserted by the Value Added Tax Tribunals (Amendment) Rules 1997, SI 1997/255, r 8; words in third pair of square brackets inserted by the Value Added Tax Tribunals (Amendment) Rules 2001, SI 2001/3073 r 4; words in pair of square brackets within third pair of square brackets inserted by the Value Added Tax Tribunals (Amendment) Rules 2002, SI 2002/2851 rr 2, 5.

17 Appeal or application allowed by consent

Where the parties to an appeal or application have agreed upon the terms of any decision or direction to be given by a tribunal, a tribunal may give a decision or make a direction in accordance with those terms without a hearing.

18 Power of a tribunal to strike out or dismiss an appeal

(1) A tribunal shall—

    (a)   strike out an appeal where no appeal against the disputed decision lies to a tribunal; and

    (b)   dismiss an appeal where the appeal cannot be entertained by a tribunal.

(2) A tribunal may dismiss an appeal for want of prosecution where the appellant or the person to whom the interest or liability of the appellant has been assigned or transmitted, or upon whom such interest or liability has devolved, has been guilty of inordinate and inexcusable delay.

(3) Except in accordance with rule 17, no appeal shall be struck out or dismissed under this rule without a hearing.

19 Power of a tribunal to extend time and to give directions

(1) A tribunal may of its own motion or on the application of any party to an appeal or application extend the time within which a party to the appeal or application or any other person is required or authorised by these rules or any decision or direction of a tribunal to do anything in relation to the appeal or application (including the time for service for a notice of appeal or notice of application) upon such terms as it may think fit.

(2) A tribunal may make a direction under paragraph (1) of this rule of its own motion without prior notice or reference to any party or other person and without a hearing.

(3) Without prejudice to the preceding provisions of this rule a tribunal may [of its own motion or] on the application of a party to an appeal or application or other person interested give or make any direction as to the conduct of or as to any matter or thing in connection with the appeal or application which it may think necessary or expedient to ensure the speedy and just determination of the appeal [including the joining of other persons as parties to the appeal].

[(3A) Where a notice is served under section 61 of the Act [or paragraph 19 of Schedule 5 to the 1996 Act] [or paragraph 99 of Schedule 6 to the 2000 Act] [or paragraph 8 of Schedule 6 to the 2001 Act] [or section 28 of the 2003 Act] and appeals are brought by different persons which relate to, or to different portions of, the basic penalty referred to in the notice, the tribunal may, of its own motion or on the application of any party to any such appeal, give any direction it thinks fit as to the joinder of the appeals.]

(4) If any party to an appeal or application or other person fails to comply with any direction of a tribunal, a tribunal may allow or dismiss the appeal or [application].

(5) A tribunal may, of its own motion or on the application of any party to an appeal or application, waive any breach or non-observance of any provision of these rules or of any decision or direction of a tribunal upon such terms as it may think just.

NOTES

Para (3): words in square brackets inserted by the Value Added Tax Tribunals (Amendment) Rules 1994, SI 1994/2617, r 11.

Para (3A): inserted by SI 1994/2617, r 12; words in first pair of square brackets inserted by the Value Added Tax Tribunals (Amendment) Rules 1997, SI 1997/255, r 9; words in second pair of square brackets inserted by the Value Added Tax Tribunals (Amendment) Rules 2001, SI 2001/3073 r 5; words in third pair of square brackets inserted by the Value Added Tax Tribunals (Amendment) Rules 2002, SI 2002/2851 rr 2, 6. Words "or section 28 of the 2003 Act" inserted by the Value Added Tax Tribunals (Amendment) Rules 2003, SI 2003/2757 r 7.

Para (4): word in square brackets substituted by the Value Added Tax Tribunals (Amendment) Rules 1991, SI 1991/186, r 11.

20 Disclosure, inspection and production of documents

(1) [Each of the parties] to an appeal other than a reasonable excuse or a mitigation appeal and [each of the parties] to an application for [a hardship direction] shall, before the expiration of the time set out in paragraph (2) of this rule, serve at the appropriate tribunal centre a list of the documents in his possession, custody or power which he proposes to produce at the hearing of the appeal or application.

[(1A) The list of documents to be served by the Commissioners in accordance with paragraph (1) shall contain a reference to the documents relied upon in reaching a decision on a review under section 15 or 59 of [the 1994 Act or section 54 of the 1996 Act] [or paragraph 121 of Schedule 6 to the 2000 Act] [or section 40 of the 2001 Act] [or section 33 of the 2003 Act] [or regulation 9 of the Export (Penalty) Regulations] [or regulation 4(5) of the Control of Cash (Penalties) Regulations 2007].]

(2) The time within which a list of documents shall be served under paragraph (1) of this rule shall be—

    (a)   in [an evasion penalty appeal], a period of 15 days after the last day for the service by the Commissioners of any reply pursuant to rule 7(1)(c) hereof;

    [(b)   in any other appeal except a reasonable excuse appeal or a mitigation appeal, a period of 30 days after—

        (i)   the date of notification of the notice of appeal; or

        (ii)   the date of notification of the notice of withdrawal of any application under rule 6 in the appeal; or

        (iii)   the date on which a direction dismissing any application under rule 6 in the appeal is released in accordance with rule 30;

    whichever shall be the latest;

    (c)   in an application for a hardship direction, a period of 30 days after the date of notification of the application.]

(3) In addition, and without prejudice to the foregoing provisions of this rule, a tribunal may, where it appears necessary for disposing fairly of the proceedings, on the application of a party to an appeal direct that the other party to the appeal shall serve at the appropriate tribunal centre for the appeal within such period as it may specify a list of the documents or any class of documents which are or have been in his possession, custody or power relating to any question in issue in the appeal, and may at the same time or subsequently order him to make and serve an affidavit verifying such list.

(4)   If a party desires to claim that any document included in a list of documents served by him in pursuance of a direction made under paragraph (3) of this rule is privileged from production in the appeal, that claim must be made in the list of documents with a sufficient statement of the grounds of privilege.

(5)   A proper officer shall send a copy of any list of documents and affidavit served under paragraph (1) or paragraph (3) of this rule to the other party to the appeal or application and such other party shall be entitled to inspect and take copies of the documents set out in such list which are in the possession, custody or power of the party who made the list and are not privileged from production in the appeal at such time and place as he and the party who served such list of documents may agree or a tribunal may direct.

(6)   At the hearing of an appeal or application a party shall produce any document included in a list of documents served by him in relation to such appeal or application under paragraph (1) or paragraph (3) of this rule which is in his possession, custody or power and is not privileged from production when called upon so to do by the other party to the appeal or application.

NOTES

Para (1): words in square brackets substituted by the Value Added Tax Tribunals (Amendment) Rules 1991, SI 1991/186, r 12.

Para (1A): inserted by the Value Added Tax Tribunals (Amendment) Rules 1994, SI 1994/2617, r 14; words in first pair of square brackets substituted by the Value Added Tax Tribunals (Amendment) Rules 1997, SI 1997/255, r 10; words in second pair of square brackets inserted by the Value Added Tax Tribunals (Amendment) Rules 2001, SI 2001/3073 r 6; words in third pair of square brackets inserted by the Value Added Tax Tribunals (Amendment) Rules 2002, SI 2002/2851 rr 2, 7. Words "or section 33 of the 2003 Act" inserted by the Value Added Tax Tribunals (Amendment) Rules 2003, SI 2003/2757 r 8. Words "or regulation 9 of the Export (Penalty) Regulations" inserted by the Value Added Tax Tribunals (Amendment) Rules 2004, SI 2004/1032 r 5. Words "or regulation 4(5) of the Control of Cash (Penalties) Regulations 2007" inserted by the Value Added Tax Tribunals (Amendment) Rules, SI 2007/2351 r 2(1), (4).

Para (2): words in square brackets in sub-para (a) substituted by SI 1994/2617, r 14; sub-paras (b), (c) substituted for original sub-para (b) by SI 1991/186, r 13.

21 Witness statements

(1)   A party to an appeal may, within the time specified in paragraph (6) of this rule, serve at the appropriate tribunal centre a statement in writing (in these rules called "a witness statement") containing evidence proposed to be given by any person at the hearing of the appeal.

(2)   A witness statement shall contain the name, address and description of the person proposing to give the evidence contained therein and shall be signed by him.

(3)   A proper officer shall send a copy of a witness statement served at the appropriate tribunal centre to the other party to the appeal and such copy shall state the date of service [and the date of notification of the witness statement] and shall contain or be accompanied by a note to the effect that unless a notice of objection thereto is served in accordance with paragraph (4) of this rule, the witness statement may be read at the hearing of the appeal as evidence of the facts stated therein without the person who made the witness statement giving oral evidence thereat.

(4)   If a party objects to a witness statement being read at the hearing of the appeal as evidence of any fact stated therein he shall serve a notice of objection to such witness statement at the appropriate tribunal centre not later than 14 days after the date of [notification] of such witness statement . . . whereupon a proper officer shall send a copy of the notice of objection to the other party and the witness statement

shall not be read or admitted in evidence at such hearing but the person who signed such witness statement may give evidence orally at the hearing.

(5)   Subject to paragraph (4) of this rule, unless a tribunal shall otherwise direct, a witness statement signed by any person and duly served under this rule shall be admissible in evidence at the hearing of the appeal as evidence of any fact stated therein of which oral evidence by him at that hearing would be admissible.

(6)   The time within which a witness statement may be served under this rule shall be—

> (a)   in the case of [an evasion penalty appeal], before the expiration of 21 days after the last day for the service by the Commissioners of a reply pursuant to paragraph (1)(c) of rule 7;
>
> (b)   in the case of a mitigation appeal or a reasonable excuse appeal, before the expiration of 21 days after the date of [notification] of the Notice of Appeal; and
>
> (c)   in the case of any other appeal, before the expiration of 21 days after the date of [notification of the Commissioners' statement of case.]

NOTES

Para (3): words in square brackets inserted by the Value Added Tax Tribunals (Amendment) Rules 1991, SI 1991/186, r 14(a).

Para (4): word in square brackets substituted by SI 1991/186, r 14(b); words omitted revoked by the Value Added Tax Tribunals (Amendment) Rules 1997, SI 1997/255, r 11.

Para (6): words in square brackets in sub-para (a) substituted by the Value Added Tax Tribunals (Amendment) Rules 1994, SI 1994/2617, r 15; words in square brackets in sub-paras (b), (c) substituted by SI 1991/186, r 14(c), (d).

[21A   Affidavits and depositions made in other legal proceedings

(1)   If—

> (a)   an affidavit or deposition made in other legal proceedings (whether civil or criminal) is specified as such in a list of documents served under rule 20(1) by a party to an appeal or application or (in the case of an appeal or application to which rule 20(1) does not apply) in a notice served by such a party at the appropriate tribunal centre, and
>
> (b)   it is stated in that list or notice that the party serving the list or notice proposes to give that affidavit or deposition in evidence at the hearing of the appeal or application and that the person who made that affidavit or deposition is dead, or outside the United Kingdom or unfit by reason of his bodily or mental condition to attend as a witness or (as the case may be) that despite the exercise of reasonable diligence it has not been possible to find him,

then, subject to the following paragraphs of this rule, the affidavit or deposition shall be admissible at the hearing of the appeal or application as evidence of any fact stated therein of which oral evidence by the person who made the affidavit or deposition would be admissible.

(2)   The time within which a notice may be served under paragraph (1) of this rule shall be before the expiration of 21 days after the date of notification of the notice of appeal or notice of application.

(3)   When a proper officer sends a copy of any such list or notice as is mentioned in paragraph (1) of this rule to any person pursuant to rule 20(5) or rule 11(6)(b), he shall also send to that person a copy of this rule.

(4)   If a party objects to an affidavit or deposition being read and admitted as evidence under paragraph (1) of this rule, he shall serve a notice of application for

directions with regard to that affidavit or deposition at the appropriate tribunal centre not later than 21 days after the date of notification of the list of documents or notice (as the case may be).

(5) At the hearing of an application under paragraph (4) of this rule a tribunal may give directions as to whether, and if so how and on what conditions, the affidavit or deposition may be admitted as evidence and (where applicable) as to the manner in which the affidavit or deposition is to be proved, and the affidavit or deposition shall be admissible as evidence to the extent and on the conditions (if any) specified in the direction but not further or otherwise.

(6) The members of the tribunal hearing an application under paragraph (4) of this rule shall not sit on the hearing of the appeal or application to which the first-mentioned application relates.]

NOTES

Inserted by the Value Added Tax Tribunals (Amendment) Rules 1991, SI 1991/186, r 15(1).

22 Witness summonses and summonses to third parties

(1) Where a witness is required by a party to an appeal or application to attend the hearing of an appeal or application to give oral evidence or to produce any document in his possession, custody or power necessary for the purpose of that hearing, a chairman or the Registrar shall, upon the application of such party, issue a summons requiring the attendance of such witness at such hearing or the production of the document, wherever such witness may be in the United Kingdom or the Isle of Man.

(2) Where a party to an appeal or application desires to inspect any document necessary for the purpose of the hearing thereof which is in the possession, custody or power of any other person in the United Kingdom or the Isle of Man (whether or not such other person is a party to that appeal or application) a chairman or the Registrar shall, upon the application of such party, issue a summons requiring either—

    (a)   the attendance of such other person at such date, time and place as the chairman or the Registrar may direct and then and there to produce such document for inspection by such party or his representative and to allow such party or his representative then and there to peruse such document and to take a copy thereof; or

    (b)   such other person to post the document by ordinary post to an address in the United Kingdom or Isle of Man by First Class Mail in an envelope duly prepaid and properly addressed to the party requiring to inspect the same.

(3) A chairman or the Registrar may issue a summons under this rule without prior notice or reference to the applicant or any other person and without a hearing and the only party to the application shall be the applicant.

(4) [A summons issued under this rule shall be signed by a chairman or the Registrar and must be served—

    (a)   where the witness or third party is an individual, by leaving a copy of the summons with him and showing him the original thereof,

    (b)   where the witness or third party is a body corporate, by sending a copy of the summons by post to, or leaving it at, the registered or principal office [in the United Kingdom or the Isle of Man] of the body to be served,

not less than 4 days before the day on which the attendance of the witness or third party or the posting of the document is thereby required] A summons issued under this rule shall contain a statement, or be accompanied by a note, to the effect that the witness or third party may apply, by a notice served at the tribunal centre from which the summons was issued, for a direction that the summons be set aside.

(5)   A witness summons issued under this rule for the purpose of a hearing and duly served shall have effect until the conclusion of the hearing at which the attendance of the witness is thereby required.

(6)   No person shall be required to attend to give evidence or to produce any document at any hearing or otherwise under paragraph (2) of this rule which he could not be required to give or produce on the trial of an action in a court of law.

(7)   No person shall be bound to attend any hearing or to produce or post any document for the purpose of a hearing or for inspection and perusal in accordance with a summons issued under this rule unless a reasonable and sufficient sum of money to defray the expenses of coming to, attending at and returning from such hearing or place of inspection and perusal was tendered to him at the time when the summons was served on him.

(8)   A tribunal may, upon the application of any person served at the appropriate tribunal centre, set aside a summons served upon him under this rule.

(9)   The parties to an application to set aside a summons issued under this rule shall be the applicant and the party who obtained the issue of the summons.

NOTES

Para (4): words in first (outer) pair of square brackets substituted by the Value Added Tax Tribunals (Amendment) Rules 1991, SI 1991/186, r 16; words in second (inner) pair of square brackets inserted by the Value Added Tax Tribunals (Amendment) Rules 1994, SI 1994/2617, r 16.

23   Notice of hearings

(1)   A proper officer shall send a notice stating the date and time when, and [the] place where, an appeal will be heard to the parties to the appeal which, unless the parties otherwise agree, shall be not earlier than 14 days after the date on which the notice is sent.

(2)   Unless a tribunal otherwise directs, an application made at a hearing shall be heard forthwith, and no notice thereof shall be sent to the parties thereto.

(3)   Subject to paragraph (2) of this rule, a proper officer shall send a notice stating the date and time when, and the place where, an application will be heard which, unless the parties shall otherwise agree, shall be not earlier than 14 days after the date on which the notice is sent—

    (a)   in the case of an application for the issue of a witness summons, to the applicant;

    (b)   in the case of an application to set aside the issue of a witness summons, to the applicant and the party who obtained the issue of the witness summons;

    (c)   in the case of any other application, to the parties to the application.

[(4)   A proper officer shall send a notice stating the date and time when, and the place where, a hearing for the purpose of giving directions relating to an appeal will take place to the parties to the appeal which, unless the parties otherwise agree, shall be not earlier than 14 days after the date on which the notice is sent.]

NOTES

Para (1): words in square brackets inserted by the Value Added Tax Tribunals (Amendment) Rules 1997, SI 1997/255, r 12(1).

Para (4): added by the Value Added Tax Tribunals (Amendment) Rules 1997, SI 1997/255, r 12(2).

24 Hearings in public or in private

(1) The hearing of an appeal shall be in public unless a tribunal, on the application of a party thereto, directs that the hearing or any part of the hearing shall take place in private.

(2) Unless a tribunal otherwise directs, the hearing of any application made otherwise than at or subsequent to the hearing of an appeal shall take place in private.

(3) Any member of the Council on Tribunals or the Scottish Committee of the Council on Tribunals in his capacity as such a member may attend the hearing of any appeal or application notwithstanding that the appeal or application takes place in private.

25 Representation at a hearing

At the hearing of an appeal or application—

(a) any party to the appeal or application (other than the Commissioners) may conduct his case himself or may be represented by any person whom he may appoint for the purpose; and

(b) the Commissioners may be represented at any hearing at which they are entitled to attend by any person whom they may appoint for the purpose.

26 Failure to appear at a hearing

(1) If, when an appeal or application is called on for hearing no party thereto appears in person or by his representative, a tribunal may dismiss or strike out the appeal or application, but a tribunal may, on the application of any such party or of any person interested served at the appropriate tribunal centre within 14 days after the date when the decision [or direction] of the tribunal was released in accordance with rule 30, reinstate such appeal or application on such terms as it may think just.

(2) If, when an appeal or application is called on for hearing, a party does not appear in person or by his representative, the tribunal may proceed to consider the appeal or application in the absence of that party . . ..

[(3) Subject to paragraph (4) below, the tribunal may set aside any decision or direction given in the absence of a party on such terms as it thinks just, on the application of that party or of any other person interested served at the appropriate tribunal centre within 14 days after the date when the decision or direction of the tribunal was released.

(4) Where a party makes an application under paragraph (3) above and does not attend the hearing of that application, he shall not be entitled to apply to have a decision or direction of the tribunal on the hearing of that application set aside.]

NOTES

Para (1): words in square brackets inserted by the Value Added Tax Tribunals (Amendment) Rules 1991, SI 1991/186, r 17.

Para (2): words omitted revoked by the Value Added Tax Tribunals (Amendment) Rules 1994, SI 1994/2617, r 17(a).

Paras (3), (4): added by SI 1994/2617, r 17(b).

27 Procedure at a hearing

(1) At the hearing of an appeal or application other than [an evasion penalty appeal] the tribunal shall allow—

(a) the appellant or applicant or his representative to open his case;

(b) the appellant or applicant to give evidence in support of the appeal or application and to produce documentary evidence;

(c)   the appellant or applicant or his representative to call other witnesses to give evidence in support of the appeal [or application] or to produce documentary evidence, and to re-examine any such witness following his cross-examination;

(d)   the other party to the appeal or application or his representative to cross-examine any witness called to give evidence in support of the appeal or application (including the appellant or applicant if he gives evidence);

(e)   the other party to the appeal or application or his representative to open his case;

(f)   the other party to the appeal or application to give evidence in opposition to the appeal or application and to produce documentary evidence;

(g)   the other party to the appeal or application or his representative to call other witnesses to give evidence in opposition to the appeal or application or to produce documentary evidence and to re-examine any such witness following his cross-examination;

(h)   the appellant or applicant or his representative to cross-examine any witness called to give evidence in opposition to the appeal or application (including the other party to the appeal or application if he gives evidence);

(i)   the other party to the appeal or application or his representative to make a second address closing his case; and

(j)   the appellant or applicant or his representative to make a final address closing his case.

[(2) At the hearing of an evasion penalty appeal, or an appeal against a penalty imposed under section 114(2) of the Customs and Excise Management Act 1979 or section 22 or section 23 of the Hydrocarbon Oil Duties Act 1979, the tribunal shall follow the same procedure as is set out in paragraph (1) of this rule for the hearing of an appeal or application, but as if there were substituted—

(a)   "the Commissioners" for "the appellant or applicant";

(b)   "their" for "his" in sub-paragraphs (a), (c), (h) and (j);

(c)   "in opposition to" for "in support of" in sub-paragraphs (b), (c) and (d); and

(d)   "in support of" for "in opposition to" in sub-paragraphs (f), (g) and (h).]

(3) At the hearing of an appeal or application the chairman and any other member of the tribunal may put any question to any witness called to give evidence thereat (including a party to the appeal or application if he gives evidence).

(4) Subject to the foregoing provisions of this rule, a tribunal may regulate its own procedure as it may think fit [and in particular may determine the order in which the matters mentioned in paragraphs (1) and (2) are to take place].

(5) A chairman or the Registrar may postpone the hearing of any appeal or application.

(6) A tribunal may adjourn the hearing of any appeal or application on such terms as it may think just.

NOTES

Para (1): words in first pair of square brackets substituted, and words in square brackets in sub-para (c) added, by the Value Added Tax Tribunals (Amendment) Rules 1994, SI 1994/2617, r 18.

Para (2): substituted by SI 1994/2617, r 19.

Para (4): words in square brackets added by SI 1994/2617, r 20.

---

28 Evidence at a hearing

(1)   Subject to paragraph (4) and (5) of rule 21 [and to rule 21A] a tribunal may direct or allow evidence of any fact to be given in any manner it may think fit and shall not refuse evidence tendered to it on the grounds only that such evidence would be inadmissible in a court of law.

(2)   A tribunal may require oral evidence of a witness (including a party to an appeal or application) to be given on oath or affirmation and for that purpose a chairman and any member of the administrative staff of the tribunals on the direction of a chairman shall have power to administer oaths or take affirmations.

(3)   At the hearing of an appeal or application the tribunal shall allow a party to produce any document set out in his list of documents served under rule 20 and unless a tribunal otherwise directs—

    (a)   any document contained in such a list of documents which appears to be an original document shall be deemed to be an original document printed, written, signed or executed as it respectively appears to have been; and

    (b)   any document contained in such list of documents which appears to be a copy shall be deemed to be a true copy.

NOTES

Para (1): words in square brackets inserted by the Value Added Tax Tribunals (Amendment) Rules 1991, SI 1991/186, r 15(2).

---

29 Award and direction as to costs

(1)   A tribunal may direct that a party or applicant shall pay to the other party to the appeal or application—

    (a)   within such period as it may specify such sum as it may determine on account of the costs of such other party of and incidental to and consequent upon the appeal or application; or

    (b)   the costs of such other party of and incidental to and consequent upon the appeal or application to be [assessed by a Taxing Master of the Supreme Court or a district judge of the High Court of Justice in England and Wales by way of detailed assessment or taxed] (by) the Auditor of the Court of Session in Scotland or by the Taxing Master of the Supreme Court of Northern Ireland or by the Taxing Master of the High Court of Justice of the Isle of Man on such basis as it shall specify.

(2)   Where a tribunal gives a direction under paragraph 1(b) of this rule in proceedings in England and Wales the provisions of [Part 47 of the Civil Procedure Rules 1998 and any practice directions supplementing that Part] shall apply, with the necessary modifications, to the taxation of the costs as if the proceedings in the tribunal were a cause or matter in the Supreme Court of Judicature in England.

(3)   Where a tribunal gives a direction under paragraph 1(b) of this rule in proceedings in Scotland the provisions of [Chapter 42 of the Act of Sederunt (Rules of the Court of Session 1994)] shall apply, with the necessary modifications, to the taxation of the costs as if those proceedings were a cause or matter in the Court of Session in Scotland.

(4)   Where a tribunal gives a direction under paragraph 1(b) of this rule in proceedings in Northern Ireland the [provisions] of Order 62 of the Rules of the Supreme Court (Northern Ireland) 1980 shall apply, with the necessary modifications,

to the taxation of the costs as if those proceedings were a cause or matter in the High Court of Northern Ireland.

(5) Any costs awarded under this rule shall be recoverable as a civil debt.

NOTES

Para (1): words substituted by the Value Added Tax Tribunals (Amendment) Rules 2003, SI 2003/2757 r 9(1). Word (by) appears to have been omitted in error in the legislation.

Para (2): words substituted by SI 2003/2757 r 9(2).

Paras (3), (4): words substituted by the Value Added Tax Tribunals (Amendment) Rules 1994, SI 1994/2617, rr 21, 22.

30 Decisions and directions

(1) At the conclusion of the hearing of an appeal the chairman may give or announce the decision of the tribunal but [subject to paragraph (8) of this rule] the decision shall be recorded in a written document containing the findings of fact by the tribunal and its reasons for the decision which shall be signed by a chairman; provided that if a party to the appeal shall so request by notice in writing served at the appropriate tribunal centre within one year of the [date on which the decision is released in accordance with this rule] the outcome of the appeal and any award and direction as to costs or for the payment or repayment of any sum of money with or without interest given or made by the tribunal during or at the conclusion of the hearing of the appeal shall be recorded in a written direction which shall be signed by a chairman or the Registrar.

(2) At the conclusion of the hearing of an application the chairman may give or announce the decision of the tribunal but in any event the outcome of the application and any award or direction given or made by the tribunal during or at the conclusion of the hearing shall be recorded in a written direction which shall be signed by a chairman or the Registrar; provided that if a party to the application shall so request by notice in writing served at the appropriate tribunal centre within 14 days of the [date on which the direction is released in accordance with this rule] the decision of the tribunal on the application shall be recorded in a written document containing the findings of fact by the tribunal and its reasons for the decision which shall be signed by a chairman.

(3) A proper officer shall send a copy of the decision and of any direction in an appeal to each party to the appeal and a duplicate of the direction and of any decision in an application to each party to the application.

(4) Every decision in an appeal shall bear the date when the copies thereof are released to be sent to the parties and such copies and any direction, and all copies of any direction, recording the outcome of the appeal shall state that date.

(5) Every direction on an application shall bear the date when the copies thereof are released to be sent to the parties and such copies and any decision on that application given or made under the proviso to paragraph (2) of this rule and all copies thereof shall state that date.

(6) A chairman or the Registrar may correct any clerical mistake or other error in expressing his manifest intention in a decision or direction signed by him but if a chairman or the Registrar corrects any such document after a copy thereof has been sent to a party, a proper officer shall as soon as practicable thereafter send a copy of the corrected document, or the page or pages which have been corrected, to that party.

(7) Where a copy of a decision or a direction dismissing an appeal or application or containing a decision or direction given or made in the absence of a party is sent to a party or other person entitled to apply under rule 26 to apply to have the appeal or application reinstated [or the decision or direction set aside], the copy shall contain or be accompanied by a note to that effect.

[(8) If, at the conclusion of the hearing of a mitigation appeal or a reasonable excuse appeal the chairman gives or announces the decision of the tribunal, he may ask the parties present at the hearing whether they require the decision to be recorded in a written document in accordance with paragraph (1) of this rule, and if none of the parties present requires this the provisions of this rule shall apply as if the appeal had been an application.]

NOTES

Paras (1), (2): words in square brackets substituted by the Value Added Tax Tribunals (Amendment) Rules 1991, SI 1991/186, rr 19, 20.

Para (7): words in square brackets inserted by SI 1991/186, r 21.

Para (8): added by SI 1991/186, r 22, and substituted by the Value Added Tax Tribunals (Amendment) Rules 1994, SI 1994/2617, r 23.

[30A Appeals from tribunal

A party who wishes to appeal from a decision of the tribunal direct to the Court of Appeal shall apply to the tribunal in accordance with rule 11 for a certificate under Article 2(b) of the Value Added Tax Tribunals Appeals Order 1986 [or Article 2(b) of the Value Added Tax Tribunals Appeals (Northern Ireland) Order 1994, as appropriate,] at the conclusion of the hearing or within 21 days after the date when the decision of the tribunal was released in accordance with rule 30.]

NOTES

Inserted by the Value Added Tax Tribunals (Amendment) Rules 1986, SI 1986/2290, art 2.

Words in square brackets inserted by the Value Added Tax Tribunals (Amendment) Rules 1994, SI 1994/2617, r 24.

31 Service at a tribunal centre

(1) Service of a notice of appeal, notice of application or other document shall be effected by the same being handed to a proper officer at the appropriate tribunal centre or by the same being received by post at the appropriate tribunal [centre or by a facsimile of the same being received at the appropriate tribunal centre by facsimile transmission process [or telex or other means of electronic communication which produces a text of the document, in which event the document shall be regarded as sent when the text of it is received in legible form]].

[(2) Any notice of appeal, notice of application or other document (including a facsimile of a document received by facsimile transmission process or telex or other means of electronic communication which produces a text of the document) [handed in or received at a tribunal centre other than the appropriate tribunal centre] may be—

(a) sent by post in a letter addressed to a proper officer at the appropriate tribunal centre; or

(b) handed back to the person from whom it was received; or

(c) sent by post in a letter addressed to the person from whom it appears to have been received or by whom it appears to have been sent; or

(d) if a facsimile of a document is received by facsimile transmission process or telex or other means of electronic communication which produces a text of the document, sent by the means by which it was received, either to a proper officer at the appropriate tribunal centre or to the person from whom it appears to have been received or by whom it appears to have been sent.]

Part II

NOTES

Para (1): words in first square brackets substituted by the Value Added Tax Tribunals (Amendment) Rules 1991, SI 1991/186, r 23(a). Words in second square brackets inserted by the Value Added Tax Tribunals (Amendment) Rules 2003, SI 2003/2757 r 10(1).

Para (2): substituted by SI 2003/2757 r 10(2). Words inserted by the Value Added Tax Tribunals (Amendment) Rules 2004, SI 2004/1032 r 6.

32 Sending of documents to the parties

(1) Any document authorised or required to be sent to the Commissioners may be sent to them by post in a letter addressed to them at the address of their office from which the disputed decision appears to have been sent, or handed or sent to them by post or in such manner and at such address as the Commissioners may from time to time request by a general notice served at the appropriate tribunal centre.

(2) Any document authorised or required to be sent to any party to an appeal or application other than the Commissioners may be sent by post in a letter addressed to him at his address stated in his notice of appeal or application, or sent by post in a letter addressed to any person named in his notice of appeal or application as having been instructed to act for him in connection therewith at the address therein stated, or sent by post in a letter addressed to such person and at such address as he may specify from time to time by notice served at the appropriate tribunal centre; provided that where partners appeal or apply to a tribunal in the name of their firm, any document sent by post in a letter addressed to the firm at the address of the firm stated in the notice of appeal or notice of application or to any person named in the notice of appeal or application as having been instructed to act for the firm at the address therein stated or to such other address as such partners may from time to time specify by notice served at the appropriate tribunal centre, shall be deemed to have been duly sent to all such partners.

(3) Subject to the foregoing provisions of this rule any document authorised or required to be sent to any party to an appeal or application or other person may be sent by post in a letter addressed to him at his usual or last known address or addressed to him or to such other person at such address as he may from time to time specify by notice served at the appropriate tribunal centre.

[(4) Any reference in this rule to the sending of any document to any party to an appeal or application or to any other person by post shall be construed as including a reference to the transmission of a facsimile of such document by facsimile transmission process [or telex or other means of electronic communication which produces a text of the document, in which event the document shall be regarded as sent when the text of it is received in legible form].]

NOTES

Para (4): inserted by the Value Added Tax Tribunals (Amendment) Rules 1991, SI 1991/186, r 24. Words inserted by the Value Added Tax Tribunals (Amendment) Rules 2003, SI 2003/2757 r 11.

33 Delegation of powers to the Registrar

(1) All or any of the following powers of a tribunal or a chairman under these rules shall be exercisable by the Registrar, that is to say—

(a)   power to give or make any direction by consent of the parties to the appeal or application;

(b)   power to give or make any direction on the application of one party which is not opposed by the other party to the application;

    (c)   power to issue a witness summons;

    (d)   power to postpone any hearing; and

    (e)   power to extend the time for the service of any notice of appeal, notice of application or other document at the appropriate tribunal centre for a period not exceeding one month without prior notice or reference to any party or other person and without a hearing.

(2)   The Registrar shall have power to sign a direction recording the outcome of an appeal and any award or direction given or made by the tribunal during or at the conclusion of the hearing of an appeal as provided by rule 30(1) and to sign any document recording any direction given or made by him under this rule.

EXCISE DUTIES (SMALL NON-COMMERCIAL CONSIGNMENTS) RELIEF REGULATIONS 1986

(SI 1986/938)

NOTES

These Regulations were revoked by the Finance Act 2007, s 111(1) with effect in relation to goods consigned on or after 19 July 2007.

Commencement: 1 July 1986.

. . .

INWARD PROCESSING RELIEF ARRANGEMENTS (CUSTOMS DUTIES AND AGRICULTURAL LEVIES) REGULATIONS 1986

(SI 1986/2148)

NOTES

Made: 4 December 1986.

Authority: European Communities Act 1972, s 2(2).

Commencement: 1 January 1987.

1

These Regulations may be cited as the Inward Processing Relief Arrangements (Customs Duties and Agricultural Levies) Regulations 1986 and shall come into operation on 1st January 1987.

2

In these Regulations—

    "Commissioners" means the Commissioners of Customs and Excise;

    "agricultural levies" means any taxes or charges, not being customs duties, provided for under the common agricultural policy or under any special arrangements which, pursuant to Article 235 of the EEC Treaty, are applicable to goods resulting from the processing of agricultural products;

    "inward processing authorisation" and "inward processing relief arrangements", for the purposes of Regulation 3, have the same meaning as in Council Regulation (EEC) No 1999/85.

3

Where in the case of any imported goods which are chargeable with customs duties or agricultural levies and are subject to an inward processing authorisation issued by the Commissioners—

(a)   there has been a contravention of, or failure to comply with, any requirement contained in the authorisation other than one which, to the satisfaction of the Commissioners, had no significant effect; or

(b)   the goods are unlawfully removed from customs charge; or

(c)   an entry thereof for home use or free circulation is accepted,

the customs duties and agricultural levies—

(i)   in respect of which relief was available by virtue of the inward processing relief arrangements, and

(ii)   payable in pursuance of, and in accordance with, Council Regulation (EEC) 1999/85,

shall be paid forthwith.

NOTES

Entry on the importation of goods: by the Customs and Excise (Single Market etc) Regulations 1992, SI 1992/3095, reg 10(1), Sch 1, para 1, the reference to an entry on the importation of goods is to be treated as including an entry of such goods under the Customs Controls on Importation of Goods Regulations 1991, SI 1991/2724, reg 5, as amended by SI 1992/3095, SI 1993/3014.

CUSTOMS DUTIES QUOTA RELIEF (ADMINISTRATION) ORDER 1986

(SI 1986/2174)

NOTES

Made: 8 December 1986.

Authority: Customs and Excise Duties (General Reliefs) Act 1979, s 4.

Commencement: 1 January 1987.

1 Citation, commencement and interpretation

This Order may be cited as the Customs Duties Quota Relief (Administration) Order 1986 and shall come into operation on 1st January 1987.

2 Implementation and Administration of Relief

(1)   The following provisions of this Order shall have effect with regard to—

(a)   the administration of any relief from customs duty under section 1 of the Customs and Excise Duties (General Reliefs) Act 1979 where the relief is limited to a quota of imported goods;

(b)   the implementation or administration of any like relief provided for by any Community instrument;

in so far as those provisions are not excluded or modified by any statutory instrument or any directly applicable Community provision conferring or relating to such relief.

(2)   The provisions of Articles 2 and 3 of the Import Duty Reliefs (Administration) Order 1958 shall not apply to the administration of any relief from duty with regard to which the provisions of this Order apply.

3

Relief from duty shall not be allowed in the case of any goods unless an entry has been made in respect of the goods and unless at the time of delivery of such entry, or such later time as the Commissioners of Customs and Excise may in any case allow, application for the relief is made by the importer to the Commissioners in such form, at such place and verified in such manner as may be required by them before the quota is exhausted; and the importer shall furnish such information as may be required for the purpose of the application.

4—

(1) Subject as hereinafter provided, goods shall be treated as forming part of a quota in the order in which an entry thereof is accepted on or after the date of the opening of the quota, being an entry—

    (a)   under section 37(3)(a) of the Customs and Excise Management Act 1979; or

    (b)   under Regulation 13(2) of the Customs Warehousing Regulations 1979

containing an application for relief from duty made in accordance with this Order.

(2) The Commissioners may delay the acceptance of an application for relief from duty in respect of any goods for the purposes of paragraph (1) of this Article for any period not exceeding 7 days from the date of the opening of the quota, and in such a case may, if the amount of the quota is smaller than the total amount of the goods in respect of which applications are made in accordance with this Order during that period, allocate the quota proportionally among all the applicants whose applications are accepted.

(3) Goods shall not be treated as forming part of a quota if customs duty would not otherwise be chargeable or would not be chargeable at a higher rate than that applying within the quota.

5

(Revokes the Customs Duties Quota Relief (Administration) Order 1976, SI 1976/2105.)

VALUE ADDED TAX TRIBUNALS APPEALS ORDER 1986

(SI 1986/2288)

NOTES

Made: 18 December 1986.

Authority: Finance Act 1985, s 26 (see now the Value Added Tax Act 1994, s 86).

Modifications: references to "value added tax tribunals" modified by the Finance Act 1994, s 7, and by the Value Added Tax Act 1994, Sch 12, para 1.

Commencement: 12 January 1987.

1

This Order may be cited as the Value Added Tax Tribunals Appeals Order 1986 and shall come into operation on 12th January 1987.

2

If any party to proceedings before a value added tax tribunal is dissatisfied in point of law with a decision of the tribunal he may, notwithstanding section 13 of the Tribunals and Inquiries Act 1971, appeal from the tribunal direct to the Court of Appeal if—

    (a)   the parties consent;

(b) the tribunal endorses its decision with a certificate that the decision involves a point of law relating wholly or mainly to the construction of an enactment, or of a statutory instrument, or of any of the Community Treaties or of any Community Instrument, which has been fully argued before it and fully considered by it; and

(c) the leave of a single judge of the Court of Appeal has been obtained pursuant to section 54(6) of the Supreme Court Act 1981.

METHYLATED SPIRITS REGULATIONS 1987

(SI 1987/2009)

NOTES

Made: 25 November 1987.

Authority: Alcoholic Liquor Duties Act 1979, s 77.

Commencement: 28 December 1987.

These Regulations revoked by the Denatured Alcohol Regulations, SI 2005/1524 reg 3 with effect from 1 July 2005.

. . .

EXCISE WAREHOUSING (ETC) REGULATIONS 1988

(SI 1988/809)

NOTES

Made: 29 April 1988.

Authority: Customs and Excise Management Act 1979, s 93; Alcoholic Liquor Duties Act 1979, ss 2(3A), 15, 56(1).

Commencement: 1 June 1988 (see reg 1).

ARRANGEMENT OF REGULATIONS

PART I
PRELIMINARY

PART II
PROCEDURES FOR EXCISE WAREHOUSES AND WAREHOUSED GOODS

PART I
PRELIMINARY

1 Citation and commencement

These Regulations may be cited as the Excise Warehousing (Etc) Regulations 1988 and shall come into force on 1st June 1988, but the Commissioners may give consent and agree conditions, restrictions or requirements under regulation 5 (variation of provisions at request of occupier or proprietor) before that date.

2 Interpretation

In these Regulations, unless the context otherwise requires—

"duty" means excise duty;

"occupier" means the occupier of an excise warehouse, and in the case of a distiller's warehouse means the distiller;

"package" includes any bundle, case, carton, cask, or other container whatsoever;

"proprietor" means the proprietor of goods in an excise warehouse or of goods which have been in, or are to be deposited in, or are treated as being in, an excise warehouse, and "proprietorship" shall be construed accordingly;

"warehoused" means warehoused or rewarehoused in an excise warehouse, and "warehousing" and "rewarehousing" shall be construed accordingly.

3 Application

(1)   Except as provided by or under the Hydrocarbon Oil Duties Act 1979, Parts I to IV of these Regulations apply to all goods chargeable with a duty of excise.

(2)   Part V of these Regulations applies for all purposes of the Alcoholic Liquor Duties Act 1979.

4 Designated file

(1)   For the purposes of these Regulations delivery to the proper officer of anything in writing—

(a)   shall be effected by placing it in the relevant designated file; and

(b)   the time of such delivery shall be when it is placed in that designated file, but the proper officer may direct that delivery shall be effected in another manner.

(2)   Nothing in a designated file shall be removed without the permission of the proper officer.

(3)   Nothing in a designated file shall be altered in any way, and an amendment to anything in it shall be made by depositing a notice of amendment in the designated file.

(4)   The designated file shall be kept at such place as the Commissioners direct and, if kept at the excise warehouse, shall be provided by the occupier.

(5)   The designated file shall be a receptacle approved by the Commissioners for the secure keeping of written material, and different files may be approved for different purposes.

(6)   For the purposes of these Regulations delivery to the proper officer of anything not in writing shall be effected in such manner, and be subject to such conditions, as the Commissioners direct.

5 Variation of provisions at request of occupier or proprietor

(1)   The Commissioners may, if they see fit, consent in writing to an application by an occupier or proprietor for variation of any condition, restriction or requirement contained in or arising under regulations 11 to 24 below, and may make that consent subject to compliance with such other condition, restriction or requirement (as the case may be) as may be agreed by them and the applicant in writing.

(2)   Where under paragraph (1) above any condition or restriction is varied or another is substituted for it, then, if the varied or substituted condition or restriction is one—

(a)   subject to which goods may be deposited in, secured in, kept in or removed from an excise warehouse or made available there to their owner for any prescribed purpose; or

(b)   subject to which an operation may be carried out on goods in an excise warehouse,

breach of the varied or substituted condition or restriction shall give rise to forfeiture of those goods, provided that breach of the original condition or restriction would have given rise to forfeiture.

6

(Revoked by the Excise Goods (Drawback) Regulations 1995, SI 1995/1046, reg 15(a).)

7 Manner of Commissioners' directions etc

(1)   Where, by or under these Regulations, it is provided that the Commissioners may—

(a)   make a direction or requirement;

(b)   give their permission or consent;

(c)   grant approval; or

    (d)   impose a condition or restriction,

then they may do so only in writing; and they may make a direction or requirement or impose a condition or restriction by means of a public notice.

(2)   Any request for the proper officer to give his permission or grant approval under these Regulations shall, if he or the Commissioners direct, be made in writing.

(3)   Any right granted to the Commissioners or the proper officer by these Regulations to—

    (a)   make a direction or requirement;

    (b)   give permission or consent;

    (c)   grant approval; or

    (d)   impose a condition or restriction,

shall include a right to revoke, vary or replace any such direction, requirement, permission, consent, approval, condition or restriction.

8 Form of entries etc

(1)   Except as the Commissioners otherwise allow, and subject to paragraph (2) below, any entry, account, notice, specification, record or return required by or under these Regulations shall be in writing.

(2)   This regulation does not apply to the records referred to in regulation 22(3) and (4) below (records kept for the purposes of any relevant business or activity).

9

(Revokes the Excise Warehousing (Etc) Regulations 1982, SI 1982/612, and the Excise Warehousing (Etc) (Amendment) Regulations 1986, SI 1986/79.)

PART II
PROCEDURES FOR EXCISE WAREHOUSES AND WAREHOUSED GOODS

10 Time of warehousing

Goods brought to an excise warehouse for warehousing shall be deemed to be warehoused when they are put in the excise warehouse.

[10A Goods to which section 46 of the Customs and Excise Management Act 1979 applies

(1)   This regulation applies to goods other than hydrocarbon oil that have been imported from a place outside the Communities ("section 46 goods").

(2)   Section 46 goods may be entered for warehousing and moved from their place of importation to an excise warehouse without payment of excise duty if, but only if, the following conditions are complied with—

    (a)   any customs duty charged on the goods is paid or otherwise accounted for to the satisfaction of the Commissioners, and

    (b)   at all times during the movement the goods are accompanied by a copy of copy 6 of the single administrative document that was used to make the customs declaration for those goods.

(3)   In this regulation the references to copy 6 of the single administrative document and the customs declaration have the same meaning as in Commission Regulation (EEC) No 2454/93.]

NOTES

Inserted by the Excise Goods (Accompanying Documents) Regulations, SI 2002/501 reg 27(1), (2).

11 Receipt of goods into warehouse

(1) Subject to paragraph (6) below, when goods are warehoused the occupier shall immediately deliver to the proper officer an entry of the goods in such form and containing such particulars as the Commissioners direct.

(2) When goods are warehoused the occupier shall take account of the goods and deliver a copy of that account to the proper officer by the start of business on the next day after warehousing that the warehouse is open.

(3) The occupier shall, if there is any indication that the goods may have been subject to loss or tampering in the course of removal to the excise warehouse, immediately inform the proper officer and retain the goods intact for his examination.

(4) Except as the proper officer may otherwise allow, the occupier shall, within 5 days of goods being warehoused, send a certificate of receipt for the goods to the person from whom they were received identifying the goods and stating the quantity which has been warehoused.

[(4A) Where goods are warehoused in circumstances where duty may be drawn back the certificate of receipt mentioned in paragraph (4) above shall—

    (a)   be in such form and contain such particulars as the Commissioners may require, and

    (b)   be endorsed on one of the copies of the warehousing advice note that accompanied the goods,

and in this paragraph "warehousing advice note" means a document (in such form and containing such particulars as the Commissioners may require) drawn up by the person to whom the certificate of receipt will be sent.]

(5) Except as the proper officer otherwise allows the occupier shall give only one receipt required by paragraph (4) above for each lot or parcel of goods warehoused.

(6) In the case of spirits warehoused at the distillery where they were produced satisfaction of the requirements of regulation 21 of the Spirits Regulations 1982 shall be deemed to be compliance with the requirements of entry and account in paragraphs (1) and (2) above.

(7) Should the occupier fail to comply with any condition or restriction imposed by or under paragraphs (1), (2), (3) or (6) above any goods in respect of which the failure occurred shall be liable to forfeiture.

NOTES

Para (4A): inserted by the Excise Goods (Drawback) Regulations 1995, SI 1995/1046, reg 15(b).

12 Securing, marking and taking stock of warehoused goods

(1) The occupier shall take all necessary steps to ensure that no access is had to warehoused goods other than as allowed by or under these Regulations.

(2) Goods shall be warehoused in the packages and lots in which they were first entered for warehousing.

(3) The occupier shall—

    (a)   legibly and uniquely mark and keep marked warehoused goods so that at any time they can be identified in the stock records; and

    (b)   stow warehoused goods so that safe and easy access may be had to each package or lot.

(4) The occupier shall, when required by the proper officer to do so, promptly produce to him any warehoused goods which have not lawfully been removed from the warehouse.

(5) The occupier shall take stock of all goods in the warehouse—

    (a)   monthly in the case of bulk goods in vats or in storage tanks; and

(b)   annually in the case of all other goods,

and shall take stock at such other times and to such extent as the Commissioners may for reasonable cause require.

(6)   In accordance with the Commissioners' directions the occupier shall—

(a)   balance his stock accounts and reconcile the quantities of those balances with his Excise Warehouse Returns; and

(b)   balance his stock accounts so that they can be compared with the result of any stock-taking.

(7)   The occupier shall notify the proper officer immediately in writing of any deficiency, surplus or other discrepancy concerning stocks or records of stocks whenever or however discovered.

(8)   Any goods—

(a)   found not to be marked in accordance with paragraph (3) above; or

(b)   found to be in excess of the relevant stock account and not immediately notified to the proper officer,

shall be liable to forfeiture.

13 Proprietor's examination of goods

The proprietor of warehoused goods may, provided that the occupier has first given his consent and has given at least 6 hours' notice to the proper officer—

(a)   examine the goods and their packaging;

(b)   take any steps necessary to prevent any loss therefrom; or

(c)   display them for sale.

14 Operations

(1)   Except as provided by or under this regulation or by or under sections 57 and 58 of the Alcoholic Liquor Duties Act 1979 (mixing of spirits with made-wine or wine), no operation shall be carried out on warehoused goods.

(2)   The Commissioners may allow the operations described in Schedule 1 to these Regulations to be carried out on warehoused goods, and may allow other operations if they are satisfied that the control of the goods and the security and collection of the revenue will not be prejudiced.

(3)   Save as the proper officer may allow in cases of emergency for the preservation of the goods, no operation shall be commenced unless the occupier has delivered to the proper officer a notice of the proposed operation with a specification of the goods involved, and 24 hours have elapsed following the delivery of that notice.

(4)   Before commencing any operation on goods the occupier shall ensure that an account is taken of those goods and that immediately after completion of the operation an account is taken of the out-turn quantities.

(5)   The occupier shall deliver to the proper officer a notice containing such detail of the accounts required by paragraph (4) above as the proper officer requires.

(6)   The occupier shall ensure that—

(a)   any operation is carried out in a part of the warehouse approved by the Commissioners for that purpose, or in such other part as the proper officer allows; and

(b)   such other requirements as the proper officer may impose in any particular circumstances are observed.

(7)   Any goods in respect of which this regulation is not observed shall be liable to forfeiture.

(8)   Nothing in paragraph (2) above shall permit the mixing of spirits with wine or made-wine while that operation is excluded from the provisions of section 93(2)(c) of the Customs and Excise Management Act 1979.

Part II

15 Removal from warehouse—occupier's responsibilities

The occupier shall ensure that—

(a)   notice of intention to remove the goods is given to the proper officer in accordance with any directions made by the Commissioners;

(b)   an entry of the goods is delivered to the proper officer in such form and containing such particulars as the Commissioners may direct;

(c)   no goods are removed until any duty chargeable has been paid, secured, or otherwise accounted for;

(d)   no goods are removed contrary to any condition or restriction imposed by the proper officer;

(e)   an account of the goods is taken in such manner and to such extent as the proper officer requires and a copy of the account is delivered to the proper officer; and

(f)   when goods are removed other than for home use, a certificate of receipt is obtained showing that all the goods arrived at the place to which they were entered on removal and, if no such receipt is obtained within 21 days of the removal, notice of that fact is given to the proper officer for the excise warehouse from which the goods were removed.

16 Removal from warehouse—entry

(1)   Goods may be entered for removal from warehouse for—

(a)   home use, if so eligible;

(b)   exportation;

(c)   shipment as stores; or

(d)   removal to the Isle of Man[;

provided that, where goods are warehoused in circumstances where duty may be drawn back they may not, under this paragraph, be entered for removal from warehouse for any purpose that may result in their being consumed in the United Kingdom or the Isle of Man.]

(2)   The Commissioners may allow goods to be entered for removal from warehouse for—

(a)   rewarehousing in another excise warehouse;

(b)   temporary removal for such purposes and such periods as they may allow;

(c)   scientific research and testing;

(d)   removal to premises where goods of the same class or description may, by or under the customs and excise Acts, be kept without payment of excise duty;

(e)   denaturing or destruction; or

(f)   such other purpose as they permit,

and may by direction impose conditions and restrictions on the entry of goods or classes of goods for any of the above purposes.

(3)   Save as the Commissioners direct no goods may be removed from warehouse unless they have been entered in accordance with this regulation.

(4)   Goods entered for home use may be removed from warehouse only if—

(a)   the duty has been paid to the Commissioners;

(b)   the removal is in accordance with provisions of, or under, the customs and excise Acts, allowing payment of the duty to be deferred; or

(c)   the removal is permitted under an arrangement approved by the Commissioners for the payment of duty on the day the goods are removed.

(5)   Goods entered for a purpose other than home use may be removed from warehouse without payment of duty only if security for that duty is given (by bond or

otherwise) to the satisfaction of the Commissioners and the security is such as to remain in force until the accomplishment of the purpose for which entry is made.

NOTES

Para (1): words in square brackets added by the Excise Goods (Drawback) Regulations 1995, SI 1995/1046, reg 15(c).

17 Removal from warehouse—general

(1) Any goods removed from an excise warehouse without payment of duty as samples or for scientific research and testing and which are no longer required for the purpose for which they were removed shall be—

(a) destroyed to the satisfaction of the proper officer;

(b) rewarehoused in an excise warehouse; or

(c) diverted to home use on payment of the duty chargeable thereon.

(2) The proper officer may require any goods entered for removal from an excise warehouse for any purpose, other than home use, to be secured or identified by the use of a seal, lock or mark, and any such requirement may continue after the goods have been removed.

(3) In such cases as the Commissioners may direct the proper officer may impose conditions and restrictions on the removal of goods from an excise warehouse in addition to those imposed elsewhere in these Regulations.

(4) Any goods in respect of which any of the provisions of these Regulations relating to removal of goods from an excise warehouse (other than regulation 15(f) is contravened shall be liable to forfeiture.

(5) The Commissioners may direct that any provision of these Regulations relating to removal of goods from an excise warehouse shall not apply in the case of hydrocarbon oils.

[(6) Subject to paragraph (7) below, goods entered for removal from an excise warehouse for any of the purposes set out in regulation 16 above shall be accompanied by an accompanying document that has been completed and is used in accordance with the instructions for completion and use set out on the reverse of copy 1 of that document.

(7) Paragraph (6) above does not apply to—

(a) goods entered for removal for home use, shipment as stores or denaturing;

(b) goods entered for removal for use by a person to whom section 13A of the Customs and Excise Duties (General Reliefs) Act 1979 (reliefs from duties and taxes for persons enjoying certain immunities and privileges) applies;

(c) goods entered for removal that are, in accordance with regulations made under section 12(1) of the Customs and Excise Duties (General Reliefs) Act 1979 (supply of duty-free goods to Her Majesty's ships), to be treated as exported;

(d) spirits entered for removal for use by a person authorised to receive them in accordance with section 8 of the Alcoholic Liquor Duties Act 1979 (remission of duty in respect of spirits used for medical or scientific purposes);

(e) goods entered for removal for exportation in circumstances to which Part II of the Excise Goods (Accompanying Documents) Regulations 2002 apply;

(f) goods that are being lawfully moved under the cover of a single administrative document; or

Part II

(g)   any goods that are entered for removal from an excise warehouse for any of the purposes set out in regulation 16 above before 1st October 2002 if those goods are accompanied by a document that has been approved by the Commissioners for that purpose.

(8)   If there is a contravention of, or failure to comply with, paragraph (6) above, the excise duty point for excise goods that are required by this regulation to be accompanied by an accompanying document is the time those goods were removed from the excise warehouse.

(9)   The person liable to pay the excise duty at the excise duty point is—

(a)   the person who arranged for the security required by regulation 16(5) above, or

(b)   if regulation 16(5) above was not complied with, the authorized warehousekeeper.

(10)   Any person whose conduct caused a contravention of, or failure to comply with, paragraph (6) above is jointly and severally liable to pay the excise duty with the person specified in paragraph (9) above.

(11)   Any excise duty that any person is liable to pay by virtue of this regulation must be paid immediately.

(12)   In this regulation—

"single administrative document" has the same meaning as in Commission Regulation (EEC) No 2454/93;

"accompanying document" means the document set out in Schedule 4 below.]

NOTES

Paras (6)–(12): inserted by the Excise Goods (Accompanying Documents) Regulations, SI 2002/501 reg 27(1), (3).

18 Entry of goods not in warehouse

Except in such cases as the Commissioners direct, goods which are to be warehoused and goods which have been lawfully removed from an excise warehouse without payment of duty may, with the permission of the proper officer, be entered or further entered by their proprietor for any of the purposes referred to in paragraphs (1) and (2) of regulation 16 above as if they were to be removed from the excise warehouse:

Provided that where any such goods are packaged and part only is to be further entered, that part shall consist of one or more complete packages.

19 Samples

(1)   The Commissioners may make directions—

(a)   allowing the proprietor of warehoused goods to draw samples thereof for such purposes and subject to such conditions as they specify; and

(b)   allowing the removal of samples from an excise warehouse with or without payment of duty,

and no sample shall be drawn or removed except as allowed by, and in accordance with directions and conditions under, this regulation.

(2)   Any samples drawn or removed in breach of this regulation shall be liable to forfeiture.

PART III
RETURNS AND RECORDS

20 Returns

(1) The occupier shall complete and sign an Excise Warehouse Return and shall deliver such return to the proper officer within 14 days of the end of the stock period to which it relates.

(2) A return shall be in such form and contain such particulars of goods received into, stored in and delivered from an excise warehouse as the Commissioners direct, and different provisions may be made for goods of different classes or descriptions.

(3) The Commissioners may direct that separate returns be made in respect of goods of different classes or descriptions.

(4) The occupier shall support each return with such schedules and further information relating to the goods as the Commissioners may require.

(5) "Stock period" means one calendar month or such other period, not exceeding 5 weeks, as the proper officer, at the request of the occupier, allows.

21 Records to be kept

(1) The occupier shall, in relation to goods in an excise warehouse, keep the records prescribed by Schedule 2 to these Regulations.

(2) The proprietor of goods in an excise warehouse, or of goods which have been removed from an excise warehouse without payment of duty, or which are to be warehoused, may be required by the proper officer to keep the records prescribed by Schedule 3 to these Regulations in so far as they relate to his proprietorship of the goods.

(3) In addition to the other records required by this regulation the occupier shall, in relation to his occupation of the warehouse, keep such records of the receipt and use of goods received into the excise warehouse other than for warehousing therein as the proper officer requires.

(4) Records required by or under this regulation shall—

    (a)   be entered up promptly;

    (b)   identify the goods to which they relate;

    (c)   in the case of an occupier be kept at the warehouse;

    (d)   in the case of a proprietor be kept at his principal place of business in the United Kingdom, or at such other place as the proper officer allows; and

    (e)   be kept in such form and manner and contain such information as the Commissioners direct.

22 Preservation of records

(1) The occupier shall preserve, for not less than 3 years from the lawful removal of the goods or such shorter period as the Commissioners direct, all records which he is required to keep by virtue of regulation 21(1) above, but no record shall be destroyed until the relevant stock accounts have been balanced and any discrepancy reconciled.

(2) The proprietor shall preserve, for not less than 3 years from when he ceased to be the proprietor of the goods, or for such shorter period as the Commissioners direct, all records which he is required to keep by virtue of regulation 21(2) above.

(3) Each occupier and proprietor shall preserve all records (other than those referred to in paragraphs (1) and (2) above) kept by him for the purposes of any relevant business or activity for not less than 3 years from the events recorded in them, except that such records need not be preserved if they are records which (or records of a class which) the Commissioners have directed as not needing preservation.

(4)   The requirements to preserve records imposed by paragraph (3) above may be discharged by the preservation in a form approved by the Commissioners of the information contained in those records.

23 Production of records

(1)   The occupier or the proprietor shall, when required by the Commissioners, produce or cause to be produced to the proper officer any records, copy records or information which he was required by these Regulations to preserve.

(2)   Production under paragraph (1) above shall—

- (a)   take place at such reasonable time as the proper officer requires; and
- (b)   take place at the excise warehouse or at such other place as the proper officer may reasonably require.

(3)   The proper officer may inspect, copy or take extracts from and may remove at a reasonable time and for a reasonable period any record produced or required to be produced to him under this regulation, and the occupier and proprietor shall permit such inspection, copying, extraction and removal.

(4)   Where the records required to be produced by this regulation are preserved in a form which is not readily legible, or which is legible only with the aid of equipment, the occupier or proprietor shall, if the proper officer so requires, produce a transcript or other permanently legible reproduction of the records and shall permit the proper officer to retain that reproduction.

24 Information for the protection of the revenue

(1)   The occupier or the proprietor shall furnish the Commissioners with any information relating to any relevant business or activity of his which they specify as information which they think it is necessary or expedient for them to be given for the protection of the revenue.

(2)   Such information shall be furnished to the Commissioners within such time, and at such place and in such form as they may reasonably require.

25 Further provision as to records

For the purposes of regulations 21 to 24 above, in relation to a proprietor—

- (a)   goods which are to be warehoused shall be treated as if they were warehoused in the warehouse to which they are being removed; and
- (b)   goods which have been removed from warehouse without payment of duty shall be treated as if they were warehoused in the warehouse from which they have been removed.

PART IV
DUTY CHARGEABLE ON WAREHOUSED GOODS

26 Duty chargeable on goods removed for home use

[(1)]   The duty and the rate thereof chargeable on any warehoused goods removed from an excise warehouse for home use shall be those in force for goods of that class or description at the time of their removal.

[(2)   Where the removal for home use of any tobacco product takes place on a day upon which an increase in the rate of duty chargeable on that product takes effect then if that removal takes place after 11.59 am on that day the time of removal is deemed to be the time at which that increase takes effect.]

NOTES

Para (1): numbered as such by the Tobacco Products Regulations 2001, SI 2001/1712, reg 27(1).

Para (2): added by SI 2001/1712, reg 27(2).

27 Duty chargeable on goods diverted to home use after removal without payment of duty

(1) The duty and the rate thereof chargeable on any goods removed from an excise warehouse without payment of duty and in respect of which duty is payable under regulation 17(1)(c) above shall be those in force for goods of that class or description at the time of payment of the duty.

(2) The duty and the rate thereof chargeable on any goods which have been entered for home use under regulation 18 above shall be those in force for goods of that class or description—

(a)   where removal for home use is allowed under section 119 of the Customs and Excise Management Act 1979 on the giving of security for the duty chargeable thereon, at the time of giving of the security, or

(b)   in any other case, at the time of payment.

28 Duty chargeable on missing or deficient goods

The duty and the rate thereof chargeable on any goods found to be missing or deficient and upon which duty is payable under section 94 of the Customs and Excise Management Act 1979, shall be those in force for goods of that class or description at the time the loss or deficiency occurred:

Provided that where that time cannot be ascertained to the proper officer's satisfaction, the rate of duty chargeable on such goods shall be the highest rate applicable thereto from the time of their deposit in the excise warehouse, or, where appropriate, from the time that the last account of them was taken, until the loss or deficiency came to the notice of the proper officer.

29 Calculation of duty

(1) Where duty is charged on any such goods as are referred to in regulation 26 above, the quantity of those goods shall be ascertained by reference to any account taken in accordance with these Regulations at the time of their removal from the excise warehouse or, if no account is taken, the quantity declared to and accepted by the proper officer as the quantity of goods being removed or, if greater, the actual quantity of goods being removed.

(2) Where duty is charged on any such goods as are referred to in regulations 27 or 28 above the quantity of such goods shall be ascertained by reference to the last account taken in accordance with these Regulations, or, if no account has been taken, the quantity declared to and accepted by the proper officer as the quantity of goods on which duty is to be charged, or, if greater, the actual quantity of goods.

30 Ascertainment of quantity by taking an account

(1) Where the quantity of warehoused goods is to be ascertained by taking an account thereof, it shall be ascertained for the purposes of these Regulations by reference to weight, measure, strength, original gravity or number as the case may require.

(2) Where under these Regulations an occupier is required to deliver a copy of an account of goods he shall deliver to the proper officer a notice giving such details of the account as the proper officer requires, and the taking of the account shall not be complete until that notice has been delivered.

PART V

ASCERTAINMENT OF DUTY BY REFERENCE TO LABELS ETC

31 Ascertainment of duty by reference to labels etc

(1) Subject to paragraph (2) of this regulation, for the purpose of charging duty on any spirits, wine or made-wine contained in any bottle or other container the strength, weight and volume of the spirits, wine or made-wine shall be ascertained conclusively

by reference to any information given on the bottle or other container by means of a label, or otherwise, or by reference to any documents relating to the bottle or other container, notwithstanding any other legal provision.

(2) The method of ascertaining the strength, weight or volume, or any of them, referred to in paragraph (1) above shall not be used if another method would produce a result upon which a greater amount of duty would be charged than would be the case if the method in paragraph (1) above were used.

SCHEDULE 1

OPERATIONS WHICH MAY BE PERMITTED ON WAREHOUSED GOODS

Regulation 14(2)

1. Sorting, separating, packing or repacking and such other operations as are necessary for the preservation, sale, shipment or disposal of the goods.
2. The rectifying and compounding of spirits.
3. The rendering sparkling of wine and made-wine.
4. The mixing of a fermented liquor or a liquor derived from a fermented liquor with any other liquor or substance so as to produce made-wine.
5. The mixing of lime or lemon juice with spirits for shipment as stores or for exportation.
6. Denaturing.
7. Reducing.
8. Marrying.
9. Blending.

SCHEDULE 2

RECORDS TO BE KEPT BY THE OCCUPIER

Regulation 21(1)

Records of—

(a) goods deposited in the excise warehouse, from where and from whom received, and date of warehousing;

[(aa) any certificate or other document that accompanied beer that contained a statement of the amount of beer produced in the brewery where the beer was produced;]

(b) goods removed from the excise warehouse, the purpose of the removal, date of removal and (if the purpose of the removal is other than for home use) the place to which the goods are removed;

(c) stock of warehoused goods;

(d) deficiencies and increases in stock;

(e) operations performed;

(f) deficiencies and increases in operation;

(g) accounts taken of goods deposited in the excise warehouse, removed from the excise warehouse, put into operation, received from operation, and of stocks in the excise warehouse;

(h) samples drawn from warehoused goods, samples removed from warehouse, and the person to whom samples are delivered;

(i) the manner in which duty is paid or accounted for when goods chargeable with duty are removed for home use;

(j) the manner in which security is given when goods chargeable with duty are removed for purposes other than home use, and the dates when certificates of receipt or shipment are received;

(k) notices delivered to the proper officer and of the manner and time of delivery;

 (l) times when the excise warehouse is opened and closed;

 (m) names and titles of keyholders to the excise warehouse;

 (n) the name and address of the proprietor of each lot or parcel of goods, and of changes of proprietorship.

NOTES

Para (aa): inserted by the Beer and Warehousing (Amendment) Regulations 2002, SI 2002/1265 reg 3(1), (2).

SCHEDULE 3

RECORDS WHICH THE PROPRIETOR MAY BE REQUIRED TO KEEP

Regulation 21(2)

Records of—

 (a) goods which are to be warehoused in an excise warehouse;

 (b) goods which have been warehoused in an excise warehouse;

 (c) goods which have been removed from an excise warehouse otherwise than for home use on payment of the duty chargeable, and all movements of such goods;

 (d) his stock of goods in each excise warehouse;

 (e) operations performed;

 (f) samples drawn, removed from warehouse and, where that removal is other than on payment of the duty chargeable, their use, location and disposal;

 (g) the time and manner in which the duty chargeable on goods to which regulation 21(2) relates is paid, secured or accounted for.

[SCHEDULE 4]

UNITED KINGDOM INTERNAL ACCOMPANYING DOCUMENT PRODUCTS SUBJECT TO EXCISE DUTY

This Form, as inserted by the Excise Goods (Accompanying Documents) Regulations, SI 2002/501 reg 27(4), Schedule, and amended by the Beer and Warehousing (Amendment) Regulations 2002, SI 2002/1265 reg 3(1), (3), has not been reproduced).

Part II

SPIRITS (RECTIFYING, COMPOUNDING AND DRAWBACK) REGULATIONS 1988

(SI 1988/1760)

NOTES

Made: 14 October 1988.

Authority: Alcoholic Liquor Duties Act 1979, ss 19(1), (1A), 22(1), (3A), (4), (10); Customs and Excise Management Act 1979, s 93(2)(a); Isle of Man Act 1979, s 9(2).

Commencement: 1 December 1988.

ARRANGEMENT OF REGULATIONS

PART I
PRELIMINARY

1 Citation, commencement and interpretation

(1)   These Regulations may be cited as the Spirits (Rectifying, Compounding and Drawback) Regulations 1988 and shall come into force on 1st December 1988.

(2)   In these Regulations, unless the context otherwise requires—

"compounder" means a person holding a licence as a compounder under section 18 of the Alcoholic Liquor Duties Act 1979;

"officer" means the proper officer of Customs and Excise;

"rectifier" means a person holding a licence as a rectifier under section 18 of the Alcoholic Liquor Duties Act 1979.

(3)   For the purposes of section 22(4) and (6) of the Alcoholic Liquor Duties Act 1979, "tinctures" means medicinal spirits, flavouring essences, perfumed spirits and British compounded spirits prepared as toilet waters, toilet vinegars, dentifrices, hairwashes and brilliantines.

2

(Revoked in part by the Spirits Regulations 1991, SI 1991/2564, reg 1(2), Sch 1; remainder revokes the Spirits (Removal and Stock Books) Regulations 1967, SI

1967/1094, and the Spirits (Removal and Stock Books) Regulations 1967, etc (Amendment) Regulations 1981, SI 1981/1258.)

3 Application

(1)   Part II of these Regulations applies to all rectifiers and compounders, except in respect of operations carried out in an excise warehouse [or where the rectifier or compounder is authorised as described in section 8(1) or section 10(1) of the Alcoholic Liquor Duties Act 1979].

(2)   Part III of these Regulations applies only in respect of claims for drawback on spirits.

NOTES

Para (1): words in square brackets inserted by the Beer, Cider and Perry, Spirits, and Wine and Made-wine (Amendment) Regulations, SI 2006/1058.

PART II
RECTIFIERS AND COMPOUNDERS

4 Entry

No person shall begin to carry on the business of a rectifier or of a compounder until he has made entry of the premises, rooms, places, fixed vessels and plant which he intends to use for keeping, rectifying or compounding spirits.

5 Changes not in accordance with existing entry

A rectifier or compounder—

    (a)   shall not alter, move or add to any entered premises, rooms, places, fixed vessels and plant in any way not in accordance with the entry thereof, unless he has given to the Commissioners 7 clear days' notice of his intention to do so; and

    (b)   shall make entry of any premises, rooms, places, fixed vessels and plant which have been altered, moved, added or added to, which he intends to use for keeping, rectifying or compounding spirits before he uses them for that purpose.

6 Marking

A rectifier or compounder shall, if so required by the officer, legibly mark on every vessel in the entered premises the capacity of the vessel in litres and the quantity and strength of spirits contained therein.

7 Stock account

A rectifier or compounder shall—

    (a)   keep at his premises a stock account in a form approved by the officer;

    (b)   on receiving or sending out any spirits, enter in the stock account such particulars as the officer may require, and those particulars shall be entered at or within such time as the officer may require;

    (c)   retain the stock account for not less than 2 years from the date of the last entry in it; and

    (d)   produce the stock account when required to do so by the officer, and permit him to make notes in it or take copies or extracts from it.

8 Account of spirits

A rectifier or compounder shall permit the officer to take an account of the spirits in stock at any time.

PART III
DRAWBACK

9 Records

A rectifier or compounder shall in respect of his business as such—

    (a)   keep such records as the officer may require, and preserve all records for not less than 2 years at his trade premises or such other premises as the officer may approve;

    (b)   produce the records to the officer at such place and time as the officer may reasonably require, and allow the officer to inspect, copy, or take extracts from the records, and to remove the records at a reasonable time and for a reasonable period.

10 Notices, declarations and packing

A rectifier or compounder intending to warehouse, export, ship as stores, or remove to the Isle of Man, any British compounded spirits or spirits of wine on drawback shall—

    (a)   give to the officer 24 hours' notice in writing, specifying the place and time at which he intends to pack the goods;

    (b)   produce them for examination by an officer at the place and time specified in the notice before they are packed; and

    (c)   ensure that the vessels and containers in which the goods are packed are secured and marked in such manner as the officer may require.

11 Representative sample

Before a sample is taken by an officer from any vessel containing British compounded spirits or spirits of wine, the rectifier or compounder shall be given an opportunity to stir up and mix the contents of that vessel.

12 Conditions in respect of payment of drawback

Where drawback is allowed on any British compounded spirits or spirits of wine, it shall be on condition that—

    (a)   if requested to do so by the officer the rectifier or compounder shall provide proof of the warehousing, exportation, shipment as stores or removal to the Isle of Man of the goods in respect of which drawback has been claimed; and

    (b)   where it appears to the Commissioners that the amount of drawback paid in response to a claim was greater than the amount payable, the rectifier or compounder shall repay on demand the amount which appears to the Commissioners to have been overpaid.

CUSTOMS AND EXCISE (DEFERRED PAYMENT) (RAF AIRFIELDS AND OFFSHORE INSTALLATIONS) (NO 2) REGULATIONS 1988

(SI 1988/1898)

NOTES

Made: 2 November 1988.

Authority: Customs and Excise Management Act 1979, ss 45(1), 127A.

Commencement: 21 November 1988.

1

These Regulations may be cited as the Customs and Excise (Deferred Payment) (RAF Airfields and Offshore Installations) (No 2) Regulations 1988 and shall come into force on 21st November 1988.

2

In these Regulations "the Act" shall mean the Customs and Excise Management Act 1979.

3

Subject to the following conditions, a passenger of an aircraft entering the United Kingdom from an offshore gas or oil installation or arriving at a Royal Air Force airfield shall be granted deferment of any customs or excise duties payable immediately, apart from these Regulations, on goods contained in his baggage or carried with him—

    (a)   directions made by the Commissioners under section 78 of the Act as to the form and manner of his declaration of the goods shall be complied with;

    (b)   he shall pay to the Commissioners any duty so deferred by the 15th day of the month following his arrival from the installation or at the airfield but, where an earlier time is specified in a notice of demand served on him by the Commissioners, he shall pay such duty by such earlier time; and

    (c)   the owner or operator of the gas or oil installation shall provide the Commissioners with such security as the Commissioners consider adequate for the purposes of these Regulations.

4

In order, solely, to enable the passenger to remove the goods without payment of duty, for the purposes of section 43(1) of the Act duty deferred in accordance with these Regulations shall be treated as paid at the time the goods are landed.

5

These Regulations shall not apply to a person approved for duty deferment purposes under any Regulations made by the Commissioners under sections 45(1) or 127A of the Act other than these Regulations.

6

(Revokes the Customs and Excise (Deferred Payment) (RAF Airfields and Offshore Installations) Regulations 1988, SI 1988/1810.)

AGRICULTURAL LEVY RELIEFS (FROZEN BEEF AND VEAL) ORDER 1989

(SI 1989/154)

NOTES

    Made: 6 February 1989.

    Authority: Customs and Excise Duties (General Reliefs) Act 1979, s 4.

    Commencement: 28 February 1989.

1

This Order may be cited as the Agricultural Levy Reliefs (Frozen Beef and Veal) Order 1989 and shall come into force on 28th February 1989.

2

In this Order, unless the context otherwise requires—

"the Board" means the Intervention Board for Agricultural Produce established under section 6 of the European Communities Act 1972;

"entered for home use" means entered for home use within the meaning of the Customs and Excise Management Act 1979 or regulation 13 of the Customs Warehousing Regulations 1979;

"international organisations established in the Economic Community" means the following:—

> Delegation of the Commission of European Communities;
> International Coffee Organisation;
> International Labour Organisation;
> International Sugar Council;
> International Wheat Council;
> United Nations International Children's Emergency Fund;
> United Nations Information Centre;
> United Nations High Commission for Refugees;
> Western European Union;
> Commonwealth Secretariat;

"intervention agencies" means the Board or any other agency designated by a Member State of the Economic Community for the purposes of Article 6 of Council Regulation (EEC) No 805/68 on the common organisation of the market in beef and veal;

"licence" means an import licence issued by the Board under the provisions of Council Regulation (EEC) No 805/68. Commission Regulation (EEC) No 3719/88 laying down common detailed rules for the application of the system of import and export licences and advance fixing certificates for agricultural products, and Commission Regulation (EEC) No 2377/80 on special detailed rules for the application of the system of import and export licences in the beef and veal sector;

"local authorities" means—

> (a) in Greater London the Inner London Education Authority, the councils of London boroughs and the Common Council of the City of London,
> (b) in England and Wales outside Greater London the county and metropolitan district councils,
> (c) in Scotland the councils of islands areas and regions,
> (d) in Northern Ireland Education and Library Boards;

"the Minister" means the Minister of Agriculture, Fisheries and Food;

"the quota" means the Community quota for the levy-free importation of frozen beef and veal provided for by Council Regulation (EEC) No 4076/88 opening, allocating and providing for the administration of a Community tariff quota for frozen meat of bovine animals falling within CN code 0202 and products falling within CN code 0206 29 91;

"the reference period" means the period from 1st October 1986 to 30th September 1988;

"the Third Lomé Convention" means the third ACP-EEC Convention signed at Lomé on 8th December 1984 between the African, Caribbean and Pacific States of the one part and the Economic Community and its Member States of the other part as set out in Council and Commission Decision 86/125/EEC/ECSC;

3—

(1) The Minister shall determine the allocation of the United Kingdom's share of the quota.

(2) The determination mentioned in paragraph (1) of this article shall be made by the Minister by allocating an amount not exceeding one third of the United Kingdom's share to local authorities and government departments (including Northern Ireland departments) and allocating the remainder to persons established within the United Kingdom as follows:—

    (a)   as to 70% thereof to importers of frozen beef and veal by reference to the amounts of frozen beef and veal which such importers have imported from outside the Economic Community and entered for home use during the reference period, other than amounts imported free of duty pursuant to the Third Lomé Convention;

    (b)   as to 20% thereof to exporters of fresh, chilled or frozen beef and veal by reference to the amounts of fresh, chilled or frozen beef and veal which such exporters have exported during the reference period from the United Kingdom to countries outside the Economic Community or to one of the following destinations:—

        (i)   seagoing vessels, or aircraft serving on international routes, including routes between Member States of the Economic Community;

        (ii)   international organisations established in the Economic Community;

        (iii)   armed forces stationed in the territory of a Member State but not serving under its flag;

        (iv)   drilling or extraction platforms, including workpoints providing support services for such operations, situated within the area of the European continental shelf, or within the area of the continental shelf of the non-European part of the Community, but beyond a three mile zone starting from the base line used to determine the width of the territorial sea of a Member State of the Economic Community; and

    (c)   as to the remaining 10% thereof to purchasers of frozen beef and veal from intervention agencies by reference to the amounts of frozen beef and veal which they have purchased from such agencies during the reference period, other than frozen beef and veal sold on condition that it should be exported from the Economic Community.

(3) For the purposes of this article, the amounts of beef and veal imported, exported or purchased by a person during the reference period shall include any amounts so imported, exported or purchased during that period by any other person whose business relating to such import, export or purchase has been transferred to the first mentioned person.

(4) An allocation under this article shall be made subject to such conditions as appear to the Minister to be expedient to secure the object, or prevent abuse, of the relief.

4

Any entitlement to relief under the United Kingdom's share of the quota shall be subject to—

(a)   the production of the licence in respect of the goods on which relief is sought appropriately endorsed by the Board with a statement that the amount of frozen beef or veal appearing in the licence may be imported free of levy under the quota;

(b)   the entry for home use of such goods on or before 30th September 1989; and

(c)   the observance by the importer of any conditions subject to which the allocation was made.

NOTES

Entry on the importation of goods: by the Customs and Excise (Single Market etc) Regulations 1992, SI 1992/3095, reg 10(1), Sch 1, para 1, the reference to an entry on the importation of goods is to be treated as including an entry of such goods under the Customs Controls on Importation of Goods Regulations 1991, SI 1991/2724, reg 5, as amended by SI 1992/3095, SI 1993/3014.

5

A licence endorsed with the statement referred to in article 4(a) of this Order shall not be issued to an importer unless the Board is satisfied, after taking into account any levy-free imports of beef or veal authorised under previous licences issued to that importer, that the amount of levy-free beef or veal allocated to him in pursuance of this Order will not be exceeded by the import of beef or veal under that licence.

6

Goods shall be treated as forming part of the quota when they are entered for home use under the authority of a licence endorsed with the statement referred to in article 4(a) of this Order.

WINE AND MADE-WINE OF A STRENGTH EXCEEDING 1.2 PER CENT AND NOT EXCEEDING 5.5 PER CENT (PROHIBITION OF FORTIFICATION) REGULATIONS 1989

(SI 1989/916)

NOTES

Revoked by the Beer, Cider and Perry, Spirits, and Wine and Made-wine (Amendment) Regulations, SI 2006/1058.

. . .

CIDER AND PERRY REGULATIONS 1989

(SI 1989/1355)

NOTES

Made: 3 August 1989.

Authority: Alcoholic Liquor Duties Act 1979, ss 56(1), 62(5), 64(1).

Commencement: 1 September 1989.

ARRANGEMENT OF REGULATIONS

PART I
PRELIMINARY

1 Citation and commencement

These Regulations may be cited as the Cider and Perry Regulations 1989 and shall come into force on 1st September 1989.

2

(Revokes the Cider and Perry Regulations 1976, SI 1976/1207.)

3 Application

[(1)]   These Regulations apply to cider produced in the United Kingdom for sale.

[(2)   Regulation 11A and the Schedule below also apply to imported cider.]

NOTES

Para (1): numbered as such and words inserted by the Beer and Cider and Perry (Amendment) Regulations 2000, SI 2000/3213, reg 3(1), (2), with effect from 1 January 2001.

Para (2): added by SI 2000/3213, reg 2(1), (2), with effect from 1 January 2001.

4 Interpretation

In these Regulations—

"accounting period" means a calendar month or any period of 4 or, as the case may be, 5 weeks allowed by the Commissioners for the purpose of accounting for duty;

"the Act" means the Alcoholic Liquor Duties Act 1979;

"approved" means approved by the Commissioners;

"business day" means a day which is a business day within the meaning of the Bills of Exchange Act 1882 for the purposes of the General Account of the Commissioners of Customs and Excise at the Bank of England in London;

"cider" has the meaning given by section 1(6) but subject to section 1(10) of the Act;

"cider premises" means the premises, rooms, places and vessels entered by a registered maker for use by him in his trade as a maker [and any other premises on which cider is made by a maker for use by him in his trade as a maker];

. . .

"duty" means the duty of excise charged on cider under section 62 of the Act;

"excise warehouse" has the meaning given by section 1(1) of the Customs and Excise Management Act 1979;

["large pack" means a container that is intended to contain a volume of more than 10 litres but not more than 400 litres;]

"made-wine" has the meaning given by section 1(5) but subject to section 1(10) of the Act;

"maker" means a maker of cider who is or is required to be registered;

"officer" means the proper officer of Customs and Excise;

"registered" means registered as a maker of cider under section 62(2) of the Act, and "registration" shall be construed accordingly;

"strength" in relation to any liquor means its alcoholic strength computed in accordance with section 2 of the Act;

"wine" has the meaning given by section 1(4) of the Act.

NOTES

In definition "cider premises" words in square brackets inserted by the Beer, Cider and Perry, Spirits, and Wine and Made-wine (Amendment) Regulations, SI 2006/1058, reg 4(1), (3)(ii).

Definition "the Collector" revoked by the Beer, Cider and Perry, Spirits, and Wine and Made-wine (Amendment) Regulations, SI 2006/1058, reg 4(1), (3)(i).

Definition "large pack" inserted by the Beer and Cider and Perry (Amendment) Regulations 2000, SI 2000/3213, reg 3(1), (3), with effect from 1 January 2001.

PART II
REGISTRATION

5 Application for registration

(1) Every person required to be registered shall make application to the Commissioners for registration in respect of his premises.

(2) A separate application shall be made in respect of each of the premises on which the applicant makes or intends to make cider.

6 Registration

(1) The Commissioners may register the applicant in respect of each of the premises in respect of which application is made, and may issue a separate certificate of registration in respect of each of those premises.

(2) The certificate of registration shall remain the property of the Commissioners.

7 Certificate of registration

(1) Every certificate of registration shall be kept at all times on the premises to which it relates, and shall be produced for inspection to an officer on demand.

(2) A maker shall notify the Commissioners of his intention to stop making cider at any of his cider premises.

(3) A maker shall notify the Commissioners of the discontinuance of trade in cider at any of his cider premises.

8 Cancellation of registration

(1) Where the Commissioners are satisfied that a maker has ceased to trade at his cider premises, or that cider is not being made on premises in respect of which he is registered for that purpose, they may cancel the relevant registration at any time.

(2) Without prejudice to paragraph (1) above the Commissioners may, for reasonable cause, cancel the registration in respect of the premises of any maker, provided that the Commissioners shall give three months' notice in writing of such cancellation.

PART III
ENTRIES

9 Entries

A maker shall not begin to make cider on any premises in respect of which he is registered until he has made entry of all rooms, places and vessels intended to be used by him thereon for that purpose.

10 Withdrawal of entry

Save as the Commissioners may otherwise allow, a maker shall not withdraw his entry in respect of cider premises while there remains in any place specified therein any cider on which duty has not been paid or remitted or any materials for making cider.

PART IV
DETERMINATION OF DUTY AND THE RATES THEREOF

11 Charge to duty

(1) Subject to regulations 12 and 13 below, cider in cider premises shall be charged with duty at [the time it is made and the excise duty point shall be] [the earlier of the following times—

(i)   the time it is consumed at those premises; or

(ii)   the time it is sent out from those premises;] . . .;

Provided that—

(a)   where any cider is sent out to other cider premises in accordance with regulation 12(c)(i) below, those other cider premises shall be treated as being the cider premises in which the cider was made and the maker registered in respect of those other cider premises shall be treated accordingly;

(b)   where any cider is sent out of cider premises at a strength not exceeding 1.2 per cent the duty charged thereon shall be [remitted;]

[(c)   where the time of consumption of cider at cider premises cannot be established to the Commissioners' satisfaction (for the purposes of determining the appropriate rate of duty in relation to the excise duty point specified by subparagraph (i) above), the rate of duty shall be taken to be the highest rate in force during the preceding 12 calendar months ending on the day before the time when the Commissioners can, for the first time, make an assessment of the excise duty due (as governed by section 12 of the Finance Act 1994) in respect of that consumption.]

(2) Duty charged under paragraph (1) above shall be accounted for and paid in accordance with the provisions of regulation 23 below.

NOTES

Para (1): words in first pair of square brackets inserted, and words omitted revoked, by the Cider and Perry (Amendment) Regulations 1996, SI 1996/2287, reg 2(1), (2); words in second and third pairs of square brackets substituted, and sub-para (c) inserted, by the Cider and Perry (Amendment) Regulations 1997, SI 1997/659, reg 2(1), (2).

[11A The amount of cider in a large pack

The amount of cider in a large pack may be ascertained by reference to any information on the label of that pack or any information in any invoice, delivery note or similar document indicating the amount of cider in that pack and, except in a case where the tolerance requirements set out in the Schedule below are not met, any cider in excess of that amount is relieved from duty at the excise duty point.]

NOTES

Inserted by the Beer and Cider and Perry (Amendment) Regulations 2000, SI 2000/3213, reg 3(1), (4), with effect from 1 January 2001.

---

12 Removal without payment of duty

Subject to such conditions as the Commissioners may impose, including any condition that security shall be given to their satisfaction, a maker may send cider chargeable with duty out from cider premises without payment of the duty for any of the following purposes—

(a)   exportation, shipment as stores or removal to the Isle of Man;

    (b)   deposit in an excise warehouse for—
           (i)   mixing with spirits;
           (ii) exportation or shipment as stores or removal to the Isle of Man;
           (iii) use as ingredients of goods permitted to be produced in an excise warehouse and intended for exportation or shipment as stores or removal to the Isle of Man; or
           (iv) such other purposes as the Commissioners may allow;
    (c)   removal, subject to the prior approval of the officer—
           (i)   to other cider premises;
           (ii) to the premises of a vinegar maker for use in the production of vinegar; or
           (iii) to premises in respect of which any person is licensed in accordance with section 55(2) of the Act as a producer of made-wine, for use as an ingredient in the production of made-wine on those premises;
    (d)   such use as trade samples as the Commissioners may allow; or
    (e)   such other purposes (except home use) as the Commissioners may allow.

Provided that if any cider which has been sent out of cider premises under the foregoing provisions of this regulation is applied to some purpose other than one therein mentioned, [the time of that occurrence shall be the excise duty point]; and the duty shall be paid in accordance with regulation 23(2) below.

NOTES

Words in square brackets substituted by the Cider and Perry (Amendment) Regulations 1996, SI 1996/2287, reg 2(1), (3).

12A Constructive removal

[(1) Where cider is held on any cider premises to which this regulation applies it shall be deemed to have been sent out from those premises for home use at the time of its constructive removal or, if earlier, the time it actually left them.

(2) This regulation applies to cider premises where the records relating to cider sent out from the premises are kept by means approved for this purpose by the Commissioners; and the Commissioners may at any time revoke such approval upon giving fourteen days' notice in writing.

(3) The maker from whose cider premises constructive removal may take place shall keep the records specified in a notice published by the Commissioners and not withdrawn by a further notice.

(4) Constructive removal shall mean the making of an entry in the records specified in accordance with paragraph (3) above which identifies the cider that is the subject of that entry as having been sent out from the cider premises for home use notwithstanding that it remains on those premises.

(5) An entry showing the constructive removal of any cider shall not be cancelled, amended or altered.]

NOTES

Commencement: 30 September 1996.

Inserted by the Cider and Perry (Amendment) Regulations 1996, SI 1996/2287, reg 2(1), (4).

---

13 Deficiencies and discontinuance of trade

Where either—

(a)   the business of making cider is discontinued at cider premises having cider therein; or

(b)   a certificate of registration held under regulation 6 above in respect of premises having cider therein is surrendered or cancelled; or

(c)   any cider is found to be deficient or missing from cider premises [for any reason (other than the reason that the cider was consumed at those premises)] and the maker is unable to account for the deficiency to the Commissioners' satisfaction,

the [excise duty point shall be] the time of discontinuance or at the time of the surrender or cancellation of the certificate of registration or at the time the deficiency occurred, as the case may be . . .; and the duty shall be paid in accordance with regulation 23(2) below.

Provided that where the time that any deficiency occurred cannot be established to the Commissioners' satisfaction, the rate of duty shall be taken to be the highest rate in force between the time of the latest stocktaking . . . before the discovery of the deficiency and the time of that recovery.

NOTES

Words in first pair of square brackets inserted by the Cider and Perry (Amendment) Regulations 1997, SI 1997/659, reg 2(1), (3); words in second pair of square brackets substituted, and words omitted revoked, by the Cider and Perry (Amendment) Regulations 1996, SI 1996/2287, reg 2(1), (5). In the proviso words revoked by the Beer, Cider and Perry, Spirits, and Wine and Made-wine (Amendment) Regulations, SI 2006/1058, reg 4(1), (4).

PART V
PRODUCTION, STORAGE AND REMOVAL

14 Production

Save as the Commissioners may otherwise allow—

(a)   cider for the making of which registration is not required may not be made in cider premises;

(b)   wine and made-wine may not be produced in cider premises.

[14A Protection of the revenue derived from excise duty on cider

(1)   After the excise duty point no person may carry out any operation on or in relation to cider before it is sold by way of retail (or otherwise supplied for consumption) if that operation would, had it been carried out before the excise duty point, have resulted in a greater amount of duty being payable than was actually payable at the excise duty point.

(2)   In this regulation "operation" includes the mixing of cider and the addition of substances (including water) to cider.]

NOTES

Inserted by the Cider and Perry (Amendment) Regulations, SI 2001/2449 reg 2.

15 Use

The Commissioners may allow the use in cider premises of cider in the preparation of, or as ingredients for, goods intended for exportation, shipment as stores or removal to the Isle of Man.

16

Revoked by the Beer, Cider and Perry, Spirits, and Wine and Made-wine (Amendment) Regulations, SI 2006/1058, reg 4(1), (2).

Part II

17 Storage

A maker shall keep stock entered for payment or remission of duty under regulation 11(1)(b) above segregated from stock which has neither been entered for payment nor for remission of duty.

18 Removal by pipe-line

Save as approved by the Commissioners, a maker shall not send out cider from cider premises by pipe-line.

PART VI
RECORDS, ACCOUNTS AND PAYMENT OF DUTY

19–21

(Revoked by the Beer, Cider and Perry, Spirits, and Wine and Made-wine (Amendment) Regulations, SI 2006/1058, reg 4(1), (2).)

22

(Revoked by the Cider and Perry Wine and Made-wine (Amendment) Regulations, SI 2007/4, reg 2(1), (2).)

23 Furnishing of returns and payment of duty

(1)   Save as the Commissioners otherwise allow, every . . . maker shall—

    (a)   not later than the fifteenth day of every accounting period furnish to . . . the Commissioners . . ., a return in approved form of all cider sent out from his cider premises for home use during the preceding accounting period and of the duty charged thereon;

    (b)   . . .

Provided that where the last day for furnishing a return . . . would, if determined in accordance with the foregoing provisions of this paragraph, fall on a day which is not a business day the return shall be furnished . . . not later than the last business day before that date.

[(2)   Unless payment of the duty is deferred, it must be paid at or before the excise duty point prescribed by regulation 11(1).

(3)   A registered maker is approved for the purpose of deferring payment of the duty for so long as he complies with the conditions imposed by or under this regulation.

(4)   A registered maker who is approved may defer payment of duty that is payable by him until the fifteenth day of the accounting period following that in which the excise duty point fell. But if that day is not a business day, payment may only be deferred until the last business day before that day.

(5)   As a condition of his being approved (or continuing to be approved), the Commissioners may require a registered maker to provide security, or further security, for duty.

(6)   It is a condition of approval that any security must be given in the form and amount that the Commissioners require.]

NOTES

Para (1): introductory text: word omitted revoked by the Beer, Cider and Perry, Spirits, and Wine and Made-wine (Amendment) Regulations, SI 2006/1058, reg 4(1), (5); sub-para (a): words omitted revoked by the Beer, Cider and Perry, Spirits, and Wine and Made-wine (Amendment) Regulations, SI 2006/1058, reg 4(1), (6); sub-para (b): revoked by the Cider and Perry Wine and Made-wine (Amendment) Regulations, SI 2007/4, reg 2(1), (3).

Para (1): words in proviso text revoked by the Cider and Perry Wine and Made-wine (Amendment) Regulations, SI 2007/4, reg 2(1), (4).

Paras (2)–(6): substituted for previous para (2) by the Cider and Perry Wine and Made-wine (Amendment) Regulations, SI 2007/4, reg 2(1), (5).

PART VII
RELIEF FROM DUTY

24 Grower's domestic consumption relief

Cider made from fruit grown in the United Kingdom by the maker may be sent out from his cider premises, in such quantity as the Commissioners may on application by him allow, without payment of duty for his own domestic consumption or for consumption free of charge in the course of their employment by agricultural workers employed by him, and regulation 23 above shall not apply to any such cider.

NOTES

Para (1): words in first (outer) pair of square brackets substituted by the Cider and Perry (Amendment) Regulations 1996, SI 1996/2287, reg 2(1), (6); word in second (inner) pair of square brackets substituted by the Cider and Perry (Amendment) Regulations 1997, SI 1997/659, reg 2(1), (4).

Para (2): word in square brackets substituted by SI 1996/2287, reg 2(1), (7).

25 Conditions for relief from duty on spoilt cider

Remission or repayment of duty under section 64(1) of the Act in respect of cider which has accidentally become spoilt or unfit for use shall be subject to the conditions that—

    (a)   the cider has not been subjected to any process of production or dilution since it was sent out from the cider premises; and

    (b)   the maker has complied with the requirements of regulation 26 below.

26 Claim for relief on spoilt cider

A maker claiming remission or repayment of duty in respect of cider which has been sent out or removed from his cider premises and which has accidentally become spoilt or otherwise unfit for use shall—

    (a)   notify the officer immediately any such cider has been returned to the cider premises;

    (b)   retain such cider in the vessels in which it was returned to the cider premises, and without making any addition thereto, for a period of forty-eight hours after its return or until such earlier time as the officer authorises the disposal or other processing thereof;

    (c)   make his claim for relief in writing; and

    (d)   provide the officer with proof that the duty which was due on the cider when it was sent out or removed from the cider premises was paid, and with such other particulars as are necessary to substantiate the claim.

[SCHEDULE
THE TOLERANCE REQUIREMENTS

Regulation 11A

1. If a large pack is filled with a metered or weighed amount of cider the amount of cider in the pack must not exceed the amount ascertained by reference to any information on the label of that pack or any information in any invoice, delivery note or similar document indicating the amount of cider in that pack by more than—

    (a)   in the case of a pack intended to contain a volume exceeding 100 litres, 0.5 per cent of that volume, or

    (b)   in any other case, 0.5 litres.

2.   If paragraph 1 above does not apply the amount of cider in a large pack must not exceed the amount ascertained by reference to any information on the label of that pack or any information in any invoice, delivery note or similar document indicating the amount of cider in that pack by more than—

(a)   in the case of a pack intended to contain a volume exceeding 200 litres, 3 litres,

(b)   in the case of a pack intended to contain a volume exceeding 100 litres, but not exceeding 200 litres, 2 litres, or

(c)   in any other case, 1 litre.]

NOTES

Schedule inserted by the Beer and Cider and Perry (Amendment) Regulations 2000, SI 2000/3213, reg 3(1), (5), with effect from 1 January 2001.

WINE AND MADE-WINE REGULATIONS 1989

(SI 1989/1356)

NOTES

Made: 3 August 1989.

Authority: Alcoholic Liquor Duties Act 1979, ss 56(1), 61(1), 62(5).

Commencement: 1 September 1989.

ARRANGEMENT OF REGULATIONS

PART I
PRELIMINARY

1 Citation and commencement

These Regulations may be cited as the Wine and Made-wine Regulations 1989 and shall come into force on 1st September 1989.

2

(Revokes the Wine and Made-wine Regulations 1989, SI 1979/1240.)

3 Application

These Regulations apply to wine and made-wine produced in the United Kingdom for sale.

4 Interpretation

In these Regulations—

"accounting period" means a calendar month or any period of 4 or, as the case may be, 5 weeks allowed by the Commissioners for the purpose of accounting for duty;

"the Act" means the Alcoholic Liquor Duties Act 1979;

"approved" means approved by the Commissioners;

"business day" means a day which is a business day within the meaning of the Bills of Exchange Act 1882 for the purposes of the General Account of the Commissioners of Customs and Excise at the Bank of England in London;

"cider" has the meaning given by section 1(6), but subject to section 1(10), of the Act;

. . .

"duty" means the duty of excise charged on wine or made-wine under sections 54(1) and 55(1) of the Act respectively;

"excise warehouse" has the meaning given by section 1(1) of the Customs and Excise Management Act 1979;

"licence" means a licence issued under section 54(2) or 55(2) of the Act, and "licensed" shall be construed accordingly;

"made-wine" has the meaning given by section 1(5), but subject to section 1(10) of the Act;

"officer" means the proper officer of Customs and Excise;

"producer" means a producer of wine or of made-wine who is or is required to be licensed;

"sparkling" has the meaning given to it by paragraphs 1 and 2 of Schedule 1 to the Act;

"still wine" and "still made-wine" mean any wine or made-wine, as the case may be, which is not sparkling;

"strength" in relation to any liquor means its alcoholic strength computed in accordance with section 2 of the Act;

"wine" has the meaning given by section 1(4) of the Act;

"winery" means the premises, rooms, places and vessels entered by a licensed producer for use by him in his trade as a producer [and any other premises on which wine or made-wine is made by a producer for use by him in his trade as a producer].

Definition "the Collector" revoked by the Beer, Cider and Perry, Spirits, and Wine and Made-wine (Amendment) Regulations, SI 2006/1058, reg 7(1), (3)(i).

In definition "winery", words in square brackets inserted by the Beer, Cider and Perry, Spirits, and Wine and Made-wine (Amendment) Regulations, SI 2006/1058, reg 7(1), (3)(ii).

PART II
LICENSING

5 Application for a licence

(1) Every person required to hold a licence shall make application to the Commissioners to be licensed in respect of his premises.

(2) A separate application shall be made in respect of each of the premises on which the applicant produces or intends to produce wine or made-wine.

6 Licensing

(1) The Commissioners may license the applicant in respect of each of the premises in respect of which application is made, and may issue a separate licence in respect of each of those premises.

(2) The licence shall remain the property of the Commissioners.

7 Licences

(1) Every licence shall be kept at all times on the premises to which it relates, and shall be produced for inspection to an officer on demand.

(2) A producer shall notify the Commissioners of his intention to stop production of wine or of made-wine at any of his wineries.

(3) A producer shall notify the Commissioners of the discontinuance of trade in wine or in made-wine at any of his wineries.

8 Cancellation of licence

(1) Where the Commissioners are satisfied that a producer has ceased to trade at a winery, or that either wine or made-wine is not being produced on premises in respect of which he is licensed for that purpose, they may cancel the relevant licence at any time.

(2) Without prejudice to paragraph (1) above, the Commissioners may, for reasonable cause, cancel the licence in respect of the premises of any producer, provided that the Commissioners shall give three months' notice in writing of such cancellation.

PART III
ENTRIES

9 Entries

A producer shall not begin to produce wine or made-wine on any premises in respect of which he is licensed until he has made entry of all rooms, places and vessels intended to be used by him thereon for that purpose.

10 Withdrawal of entry

Save as the Commissioners may otherwise allow, a producer shall not withdraw his entry in respect of a winery while there remains in any place specified therein any wine or made-wine on which duty has not been paid or remitted or any materials for making wine or made-wine.

PART IV
DETERMINATION OF DUTY AND THE RATES THEREOF

11 Charge to duty

(1) Subject to regulations 12 and 13 below, wine or made-wine in a winery shall be charged with duty at [the time it is made and the excise duty point shall be] [the earlier of the following times—

    (i)   the time it is consumed at that winery; or

    (ii)   the time it is sent out from that winery;] . . .;

Provided that—

    (a)   where any wine or made-wine is sent out to another winery in accordance with regulation 12(c)(i) below, that other winery shall be treated as being the winery in which the wine or made-wine was produced and the producer licensed in respect of that other winery shall be treated accordingly;

    (b)   where any wine or made-wine is sent out of a winery at a strength not exceeding 1.2 per cent the duty charged thereon shall be [remitted;]

    [(c)   where the time of consumption of the wine or the made-wine at a winery cannot be established to the Commissioners' satisfaction (for the purposes of determining the appropriate rate of duty in relation to the excise duty point specified by subparagraph (i) above), the rate of duty shall be taken to be the highest rate in force during the preceding 12 calendar months ending on the day before the time when the Commissioners can, for the first time, make an assessment of the excise duty due (as governed by section 12 of the Finance Act 1994) in respect of that consumption.]

(2) Duty charged under paragraph (1) above shall be accounted for and paid in accordance with the provisions of regulation 23 below.

NOTES

Para (1): words in first pair of square brackets inserted, and words omitted revoked, by the Wine and Made-wine (Amendment) Regulations 1996, SI 1996/2752, reg 2(1), (2); words in second pair of square brackets and sub-para (c) inserted, and word in third pair of square brackets substituted, by the Wine and Made-wine (Amendment) Regulations 1997, SI 1997/658, reg 2(1), (2).

12 Removal without payment of duty

Subject to such conditions as the Commissioners may impose, including any condition that security shall be given to their satisfaction, a producer may send wine or made-wine chargeable with duty out from a winery without payment of the duty for any of the following purposes—

    (a)   exportation, shipment as stores or removal to the Isle of Man;

    (b)   deposit in an excise warehouse for—

           (i)   mixing with spirits;

           (ii)   exportation or shipment as stores or removal to the Isle of Man;

           (iii) use as ingredients of goods permitted to be produced in an excise warehouse and intended for exportation or shipment as stores or removal to the Isle of Man; or

           (iv) such other purposes as the Commissioners may allow;

    (c)   removal, subject to the prior approval of the officer—

           (i)   to another winery;

           (ii)   to the premises of a vinegar maker for use in the production of vinegar; or

           (iii) in the case of made-wine only, to premises in respect of which any person is registered in accordance with section 62(2) of the Act as a maker of cider, for use as an ingredient in the making of cider on those premises;

    (d)   such use as trade samples as the Commissioners may allow; or

    (e)   such other purposes (except home use) as the Commissioners may allow.

Provided that if any wine or made-wine which has been sent out of a winery under the foregoing provisions of this regulation is applied to some purpose other than one therein mentioned, [the time of that occurrence shall be the excise duty point]; and the duty shall be paid in accordance with regulation 23(2) below.

NOTES

Words in square brackets substituted by the by the Wine and Made-wine (Amendment) Regulations 1996, SI 1996/2752, reg 2(1), (3).

[12A Constructive removal

(1) Where wine or made-wine is held in any winery to which this regulation applies it shall be deemed to have been sent out from that that winery for home use at the time of its constructive removal or, if earlier, the time it actually left that winery.

(2) This regulation applies to a winery where the records relating to wine or made-wine sent out from the winery are kept by means approved for this purpose by the Commissioners; and the Commissioners may at any time revoke such approval upon giving fourteen days' notice in writing.

(3) The producer from whose winery constructive removal may take place shall keep the records specified in a notice published by the Commissioners and not withdrawn by a further notice.

(4) Constructive removal shall mean the making of an entry in the records specified in accordance with paragraph (3) above which identifies the wine or made-wine that is the subject of that entry as having been sent out from the winery for home use notwithstanding that it remains in that winery.

(5) An entry showing the constructive removal of any wine or made-wine shall not be cancelled, amended or altered.]

NOTES

Commencement: 30 November 1996.

Inserted by the Wine and Made-wine (Amendment) Regulations 1996, SI 1996/2752, reg 2(1), (4).

13 Deficiencies and discontinuance of trade

Where either—

   (a)   the business of producing wine or made-wine is discontinued at a winery having wine or made-wine therein; or

   (b)   a licence held under regulation 6 above in respect of a winery having wine or made-wine therein is surrendered or cancelled; or

   (c)   any wine or made-wine is found to be deficient or missing from a winery [for any reason (other than the reason that the cider was consumed at those premises)] and the producer is unable to account for the deficiency to the Commissioners' satisfaction,

the [excise duty point shall be] the time of discontinuance or at the time of the surrender or cancellation of the licence or at the time the deficiency occurred, as the case may be . . .; and the duty shall be paid in accordance with regulation 23(2) below.

Provided that where the time that any deficiency occurred cannot be established to the Commissioners' satisfaction, the rate of duty shall be taken to be the highest rate in force between the time of the latest stocktaking . . . before the discovery of the deficiency and the time of that discovery.

NOTES

Words in first pair of square brackets inserted by the Wine and Made-wine (Amendment) Regulations 1997, SI 1997/658, reg 2(1), (3); words in second pair of square brackets substituted, and words omitted revoked, by the Wine and Made-wine (Amendment) Regulations 1996, SI 1996/2752, reg 2(1), (2).

Words omitted from the proviso revoked by the Beer, Cider and Perry, Spirits, and Wine and Made-wine (Amendment) Regulations, SI 2006/1058, reg 7(1), (4).

PART V
PRODUCTION, STORAGE AND REMOVAL

14 Production

Save as the Commissioners may otherwise allow—

   (a)   wine or made-wine for the production of which a licence is not required may not be produced in a winery;

   (b)   cider may not be [made] in a winery.

NOTES

Words in square brackets by the Wine and Made-wine (Amendment) Regulations 1997, SI 1997/658, reg 2(1), (4).

15 Use

The Commissioners may allow the use in a winery of wine or made-wine in the preparation of, or as ingredients for, goods intended for exportation, shipment as stores or removal to the Isle of Man.

16

Revoked by the Beer, Cider and Perry, Spirits, and Wine and Made-wine (Amendment) Regulations, SI 2006/1058, reg 7(1), (2).

17 Storage

A producer shall keep stock entered for payment or for remission of duty under regulation 11(1)(b) above segregated from stock which has neither been entered for payment nor for remission of duty.

18 Removal by pipe-line

Save as approved by the Commissioners, a producer shall not send out wine or made-wine from a winery by pipe-line.

PART VI
RECORDS, ACCOUNTS AND PAYMENT OF DUTY

19–21

(Revoked by the Beer, Cider and Perry, Spirits, and Wine and Made-wine (Amendment) Regulations, SI 2006/1058, reg 7(1), (2).)

22

(Revoked by the Cider and Perry and Wine and Made-wine (Amendment) Regulations, SI 2007/4, reg 3(1), (2).)

23 Furnishing of returns and payment of duty

  (1)   Save as the Commissioners otherwise allow, every . . . producer shall—

  (a)   not later than the fifteenth day of every accounting period furnish to . . . the Commissioners . . ., a return in approved form of all wine and made-wine sent out from his winery for home use during the preceding accounting period and of the duty charged thereon;

  (b)   . . .

Provided that where the last day for furnishing a return . . . would, if determined in accordance with the foregoing provisions of this paragraph, fall on a day which is not a business day the return shall be furnished . . . not later than the last business day before that date.

  [(2)   Unless payment of the duty is deferred, it must be paid at or before the excise duty point prescribed by regulation 11(1).

  (3)   A registered maker is approved for the purpose of deferring payment of the duty for so long as he complies with the conditions imposed by or under this regulation.

  (4)   A registered maker who is approved may defer payment of duty that is payable by him until the fifteenth day of the accounting period following that in which the excise duty point fell. But if that day is not a business day, payment may only be deferred until the last business day before that day.

  (5)   As a condition of his being approved (or continuing to be approved), the Commissioners may require a registered maker to provide security, or further security, for duty.

  (6)   It is a condition of approval that any security must be given in the form and amount that the Commissioners require.]

NOTES

In opening words, word revoked by the Beer, Cider and Perry, Spirits, and Wine and Made-wine (Amendment) Regulations, SI 2006/1058, reg 7(1), (5).

Para (1)(a): words repealed by the Beer, Cider and Perry, Spirits, and Wine and Made-wine (Amendment) Regulations, SI 2006/1058, reg 7(1), (6).

Para (1)(b): revoked by the Cider and Perry and Wine and Made-wine (Amendment) Regulations, SI 2007/4, reg 3(1), (3).

Para 1: in the proviso text words revoked by the Cider and Perry and Wine and Made-wine (Amendment) Regulations, SI 2007/4, reg 3(1), (4).

Paras (2)–(6):substituted for previous para (2), by the Cider and Perry and Wine and Made-wine (Amendment) Regulations, SI 2007/4, reg 3(1), (5).

PART VII
RELIEF FROM DUTY

24 Grower's domestic consumption relief

(1) Wine and made-wine produced from ingredients grown in the United Kingdom may be sent out from a winery without payment of duty for the domestic consumption of the grower of the ingredients in such quantity as the Commissioners may on application from him allow.

(2) In this regulation, "grower" includes bee-keeper and "grown" shall be construed accordingly.

25 Conditions for relief from duty on spoilt wine and made-wine

Remission or repayment of duty under section 61(1) of the Act in respect of wine or made-wine which has accidentally become spoilt or unfit for use shall be subject to the conditions that—

(a)   the wine or made-wine has not been subjected to any process of production or dilution since it was sent out from the winery; and

(b)   the producer has complied with the requirements of regulation 26 below.

26 Claim for relief on spoilt wine and made-wine

A producer claiming remission or repayment of duty in respect of wine or made-wine which has been sent out or removed from his winery and which has accidentally become spoilt or otherwise unfit for use shall—

(a)   notify the officer immediately any such wine or made-wine has been returned to the winery;

(b)   retain such wine or made-wine in the vessels in which it was returned to the winery, and without making any addition thereto, for a period of forty-eight hours after its return or until such earlier time as the officer authorises the disposal or other processing thereof;

(c)   make his claim for relief in writing; and

(d)   provide the officer with proof that the duty which was due on the wine or made-wine when it was sent out or removed from the winery was paid, and with such other particulars as are necessary to substantiate the claim.

EXCISE DUTIES (PERSONAL RELIEFS) (FUEL AND LUBRICANTS IM-PORTED IN VEHICLES) ORDER 1989

(SI 1989/1898)

NOTES

Made: 16 October 1989.

Authority: Customs and Excise Duties (General Reliefs) Act 1979, ss 13, 17(1).

Commencement: 13 November 1989.

1

This Order may be cited as the Excise Duties (Personal Reliefs) (Fuel and Lubricants Imported in Vehicles) Order 1989 and shall come into force on 13th November 1989.

[1A Application

(1)   Except for fuel and lubricants taken into a vehicle outside the European Union, where a person entering the United Kingdom has travelled from another member State, the reliefs afforded by this Order shall not apply to fuel and lubricants in a commercial vehicle he has with him.

(2)   In this article "commercial vehicle" means any road vehicle that—

    (a)   by its type of construction and equipment, is designed for and capable of transporting goods or more than 9 persons, including the driver; or

    (b)   is being used or is intended for use to carry passengers for reward; or

    (c)   is being used or is intended for use for a purpose other than transport.]

NOTES

Commencement: 1 August 1995.

Inserted by the Travellers' Reliefs (Fuel and Lubricants) Order 1995, SI 1995/1777, art 5.

2

In this Order—

    "private vehicle" means any road vehicle other than one which—

        (a)   by its type of construction and equipment, is designed for and capable of transporting goods or more than 9 persons, including the driver; or

        (b)   is for a special purpose other than transport;

    "standard fuel tank" means—

        (a)   the tank, permanently fitted by the manufacturer to a vehicle and to all vehicles of that type, supplying fuel directly for propulsion and, where appropriate, refrigeration; and

        (b)   a gas tank fitted to a vehicle designed for the direct use of gas as a fuel;

    "vehicle" means any motor vehicle.

3

A person entering the United Kingdom shall not be required to pay any excise duty chargeable on the importation of fuel and lubricants contained in a vehicle imported by and with him on condition that—

    (a)   the fuel is contained in the standard fuel tank of the vehicle; and

    (b)   the fuel and lubricants are used only in the vehicle and are not removed from the vehicle except—

        (i)   temporarily, in order to facilitate repair; or

        (ii)   permanently, in order to be destroyed; and

    (c)   the lubricants are of a type and quantity necessary for the normal operation of the vehicle during its journey.

4

A person entering the United Kingdom shall not be required to pay any excise duty chargeable on the importation of fuel contained in a portable tank carried in a private vehicle imported by and with him on condition that—

    (a)   the total quantity of fuel carried in such a tank in the vehicle does not exceed ten litres; and

    (b)   the fuel is used only in the vehicle.

5

The relief granted by this Order is without prejudice to any other relief.

EXCISE DUTIES (HYDROCARBON OIL) (TRAVELLING SHOWMEN) RELIEF REGULATIONS 1989

(SI 1989/2439)

NOTES

Made: 21 December 1989.

Authority: Hydrocarbon Oil Duties Act 1979, s 20AA(1)(c).

Commencement: 5 February 1990.

1 Citation and commencement

These Regulations may be cited as the Excise Duties (Hydrocarbon Oil) (Travelling Showmen) Relief Regulations 1989, and shall come into force on 5th February 1990.

2 Relief

A travelling showman who uses as fuel for a road vehicle heavy oil on whose delivery for home use rebate has been allowed, shall not be required to pay the amount which would (apart from these Regulations) be payable to the Commissioners under section 12(2) of the Hydrocarbon Oil Duties Act 1979 provided that—

(a) the road vehicle is immobilised by disconnection of the propeller shaft; and

(b) the heavy oil is drawn—

    (i) from a tank which is not permanently attached to the vehicle and which is separate from the tank from which fuel is drawn for propelling the vehicle; and

    (ii) through a fuel pipe which is not permanently attached to the engine of the vehicle.

CHANNEL TUNNEL (CUSTOMS AND EXCISE) ORDER 1990

(SI 1990/2167)

NOTES

Made: 1 November 1990.

Authority: Channel Tunnel Act 1987, ss 11(1)(a), (c), (d), (g), (h), (2), (3)(a), (d), 13(1), (2).

Commencement: 1 December 1990.

ARRANGEMENT OF ARTICLES

1 Citation and commencement

This Order may be cited as the Channel Tunnel (Customs and Excise) Order 1990 and shall come into force on 1st December 1990.

Part II

2 Interpretation

    (1)   In this Order—

       "the Act of 1979" means the Customs and Excise Management Act 1979;

       "the Act of 1987" means the Channel Tunnel Act 1987;

       "customs approved area" has the meaning given by article 3(1) below;

       "the tunnel" except in the expression "tunnel system" means that part of the tunnel system comprising the tunnels specified in section 1(7)(a) of the Act 1987 or any of those tunnels.

    (2)   In this Order the following expressions have the meanings assigned to them by section 1 of the Act of 1979:

       "approved wharf";

       "the boundary";

       "commander";

       "the Commissioners";

       "the customs and excise Acts";

       "customs and excise airport";

       "goods";

       "officer";

       "owner";

       "port";

       ["proper";]

       "ship";

       "shipped" and cognate expressions.

    [(3)   In this Order the following expressions have the same meaning as in the Channel Tunnel (International Arrangements) Order 1993—

       "Concessionaires";

       ["the international articles"]

       "control zone";

       "international service";

       "shuttle train";

       "terminal control point";

       "through train";

       "train manager".]

    [(4)   In this Order—

       "control zone" includes, subject to paragraph (5), a control zone within the meaning of the Channel Tunnel (International Arrangements) Order 1993 ("the 1993 Order") and a control zone within the meaning of the Channel Tunnel (Miscellaneous Provisions) Order 1994 ("the 1994 Order"); and

       "the Part II provisions" has the meaning as in the 1994 Order.

    (5)   In the first place in which it occurs in article 5(2)(a), and in the Schedule to this Order—

       (a)   in paragraph 7(b)(iii),

       (b)   in the second place in which it occurs in paragraph 17C, and

       (c)   in paragraph 22,

"control zone" has the same meaning as in the 1993 Order.]

NOTES

    Commencement: to be appointed (paras (4), (5)); 2 August 1993 (para (3)); 1 December 1990 (remainder).

    Para (2): word in square brackets inserted by the Channel Tunnel (International Arrangements) Order 1993, SI 1993/1813, art 8, Sch 5, Pt II, para 8(a).

Para (3): added by SI 1993/1813, art 8, Sch 5, Pt II, para 8(b); words in square brackets inserted and words in italics revoked by the Channel Tunnel (Miscellaneous Provisions) Order 1994, SI 1994/1405, art 8, Sch 4, para 5(a), as from a day to be appointed.

Paras (4), (5): added by SI 1994/1405, art 8, Sch 4, para 5(b), as from a day to be appointed.

3 Channel tunnel customs approved areas

(1) The Commissioners may approve, for such periods and subject to such conditions [and restrictions] as they think fit, places [in the United Kingdom, and in France in a control zone within the tunnel system,] for the customs and excise control of persons, goods or vehicles in relation to the construction, operation or use of the tunnel or any part of it[, and may also so approve all or any through trains while they are within any area in the United Kingdom specified in the approval or while they constitute a control zone, and any place or train] so approved is referred to in this Order as a "customs approved area".

(2) Without prejudice to the generality of paragraph (1) above, the conditions and restrictions mentioned in that paragraph may include such as relate to—

(a)   the security of a customs approved area;

(b)   the access and egress of persons, goods and vehicles to and from it;

(c)   the giving of notice to the Commissioners of the arrival of persons at it through the tunnel from France;

(d)   the provision of accommodation for the use of the Commissioners and the costs of and incidental to such provision;

(e)   the processing of goods in it;

(f)   the keeping of records.

(3) Different conditions and restrictions may be imposed in respect of different parts of a customs approved area.

(4) The Commissioners may at any time for reasonable cause revoke or vary the terms of any approval given under paragraph (1).

(5) An officer may at any time enter a customs approved area and inspect it and any buildings and goods in it.

[(6) Subject to paragraphs (6A) and (6B) below—

(a)   goods imported through the tunnel shall not be unloaded from the importing vehicle, and

(b)   goods to be exported through the tunnel shall not be loaded onto the exporting vehicle,

except at a place which is a customs approved area.

(6A) Paragraph (6) above does not apply, except in a case falling within paragraph (6B) below, so as to prevent, restrict or delay the movement between different member States of any goods entering or leaving the United Kingdom.

(6B) The cases mentioned in paragraph (6A) above are those where it appears to the Commissioners or the proper officer that there are reasonable grounds for believing that compliance with paragraph (6) above is required for purposes connected with—

(a)   securing the collection of any Community customs duty or giving effect to any Community legislation relating to any such duty;

(b)   the enforcement of any prohibition or restriction for the time being in force by virtue of any Community legislation with respect to the movement of goods into or out of the member States; or

(c)   the enforcement of any prohibition or restriction for the time being in force by virtue of any enactment with respect to the importation or exportation of goods into or out of the United Kingdom.]

(7)   Any person contravening or failing to comply with paragraph (6) above or with any condition or restriction imposed by the Commissioners under paragraph (1) above shall be liable on summary conviction to a penalty not exceeding level 3 on the standard scale.

NOTES

Para (1): words in first pair of square brackets inserted, and words in second and third pairs of square brackets substituted, by the Channel Tunnel (International Arrangements) Order 1993, SI 1993/1813, art 8, Sch 5, Pt II, para 9(a).

Paras (6), (6A), (6B): substituted for original para (6) by SI 1993/1813, art 8, Sch 5, Pt II, para 9(b).

4 Modification of the Act of 1979

The Act of 1979 shall be modified in accordance with the provisions of the Schedule to this Order.

5 Time of importation, exportation, etc

(1)   The provisions of this article shall have effect for the purposes of the customs and excise Acts [and of any enactment under or by virtue of which any prohibition or restriction with respect to the importation or exportation of any goods is for the time being in force].

[(2)   Goods intended to be brought into the United Kingdom through the tunnel shall be treated as being imported into the United Kingdom—]

  [(a)   in the case of goods intended to be carried in a shuttle train, when they are taken into a control zone in France within the tunnel system,

  (b)   in the case of goods carried, while the train constitutes a control zone in France or Belgium, in a through train carrying passengers on a journey intended to end at a place in Great Britain other than London, at the time when officers become authorised under Article 12 of the international Articles or, as the case may be, under Article 5 of the Part II provisions, to begin to carry out controls, and

  (c)   in any other case, when they cross the frontier.]

(5)   Subject to paragraph (6) below, where any goods are exported through the tunnel the time of exportation of any goods so exported shall be deemed to be the time when they are loaded onto the exporting vehicle.

(6)   In the case of goods of a class or description with respect to the exportation of which any prohibition or restriction is for the time being in force under or by virtue of any enactment and which are exported by vehicle through the tunnel, the time of exportation shall be deemed to be the time when the exporting vehicle departs from the last customs approved area at which goods were loaded onto it for exportation.

(7)   . . .

NOTES

Para (1): words in square brackets inserted by the Channel Tunnel (International Arrangements) Order 1993, SI 1993/1813, art 8, Sch 5, Pt II, para 10(a).

Para (2): substituted for original paras (2)–(4) by SI 1993/1813, arts 8, 9, Sch 5, Pt II, para 10(b), Sch 6, Pt II; sub-paras (a)–(c) substituted for original paras (a) and (b) by the Channel Tunnel (Miscellaneous Provisions) Order 1994, SI 1994/1405, art 8, Sch 4, para 6.

Para (7): revoked by SI 1993/1813, art 9, Sch 6, Pt II.

SCHEDULE

MODIFICATIONS OF THE ACT OF 1979

Article 4

[Part II of the Act of 1979: Administration

A1.   In section 17(1) (disposal of duties, etc) the reference to Great Britain shall be construed as including a reference to a control zone in France [or Belgium].]

Part III of the Act of 1979: Customs and Excise Control Areas

A2.

- (1)   For the purposes of section 21 (control of movement of aircraft, etc, into and out of the United Kingdom) references to an aircraft shall be treated as including references to a through train, and in relation to such trains section 21 shall be construed in accordance with sub-paragraphs (2) to (5).
- (2)   References to a customs and excise airport shall be construed as references to a terminal control point or a place which is a customs approved area.
- (3)   References to a flight shall be construed as references to a journey, and the reference in section 21(4) to flying shall be construed accordingly.
- (4)   References to landing shall be construed as references to stopping for the purpose of enabling passengers or crew to board or leave the train or goods to be loaded onto or unloaded from it.
- (5)   References to the commander of an aircraft shall be construed as references to the train manager of a train.]

1.   Sections 27 and 28 (officers' powers of boarding and access, etc) shall have effect as if a vehicle at, entering or leaving a customs approved area fell within paragraphs (a) to (f) of subsection (1) of section 27 [and as if a through train fell within those paragraphs while it constituted a control zone in France [or Belgium]].

2.   Section 29(3) (officers' powers of detention of ships, etc) shall have effect as if any vehicle that has arrived from France through the tunnel were a vehicle in Northern Ireland.

3.   For the purposes of section 30(1) (control of movement of uncleared goods within or between port or airport and other places) a customs approved area shall be treated as being within the limits of a port, whether or not it is.

[3A.   In section 31(1) (control of movement of goods to and from inland clearance depot, etc) the reference to the place of importation shall be construed as including a reference to a customs approved area in France.]

4.   In section 32(1) (penalty for carrying away officers) the reference to [a ship or aircraft departing from any place shall be construed as including a reference to a vehicle which departs from a place which is a customs approved area.]

[4A.—(1)   For the purposes of section 33 (power to inspect aircraft, aerodromes, records, etc) references to an aircraft shall be treated as including references to a through train and to a shuttle train, and in relation to such trains section 33—

- (a)   shall have effect as if in section 33(3) the words from "licensed" to "other aerodrome" had not been enacted, and
- (b)   shall be construed in accordance with sub-paragraphs (2) and (3).

(2)   The reference in section 33(1) to the commander of an aircraft shall be construed as a reference to the train manager of a train.

(3)   References to an aerodrome shall be construed as references to a place which is a customs approved area.

4B.—(1)   For the purposes of section 34 (power to prevent flight of aircraft) references to an aircraft shall be treated as including references to a through train, and in relation to such trains section 34 shall be construed in accordance with sub-paragraphs (2) to (4).

(2)   References to a customs and excise airport shall be construed as references to a place which is a customs approved area.

(3)   References to a flight shall be construed as references to a journey, and any cognate expression shall be construed accordingly.

(4)   The reference in section 34(3) to the commander of an aircraft shall be construed as a reference to the train manager of a train.]

Part IV of the Act of 1979: Control of Importation

5.—(1)   Section 35(1) (report inwards) shall have effect as if any [through train] entering the United Kingdom through the tunnel were [a ship arriving at a port from a place outside the United Kingdom].

(2)   For the purposes of section 35(7) any [through train] which arrives in the United Kingdom through the tunnel shall be treated as [a ship carrying goods arriving in or over United Kingdom waters, and in relation to such a vehicle the reference to the master of such a ship shall be construed as a reference to the person in charge of the vehicle].

[5A.   In section 40(5) (removal of uncleared goods to Queen's warehouse) the references to a ship or aircraft shall be construed as including references to a through train.]

6.   In section 42(1)(a) (power to regulate the unloading, removal, etc of imported goods) the reference to a ship arriving at a port shall be construed as including a reference to a vehicle arriving [at a place which is a customs approved area either in France or through the tunnel from France].

[7.   In section 49(1) (forfeiture of goods improperly imported)—

(a)   the reference in paragraph (a)(ii) to goods unloaded from any aircraft in the United Kingdom shall be construed as including a reference to goods unloaded from a through train or shuttle train which has brought them into the United Kingdom and a reference to goods otherwise brought through the tunnel into the United Kingdom; and

(b)   the reference in paragraph (c) to goods found to have been concealed on board any aircraft shall be construed as including references to goods found concealed—

(i)   on a through train or shuttle train which has brought them into the United Kingdom,

(ii)   on a through train while it constitutes a control zone in France [or Belgium], or

(iii)   in a road vehicle in a control zone in France within the tunnel system.]

8.   Section 50(2) (penalty for improper importation of goods) shall have effect as if—

(a)   any person who unloads or assists or is otherwise concerned in the unloading of those goods mentioned in section 50(1) from any vehicle which has arrived from France through the tunnel[, or who brings or assists or is otherwise concerned in the bringing of such goods into a control zone in France [or Belgium],] were a person who unships such goods in a port; and

(b)   any person who removes or assists or is otherwise concerned in the removal of such goods from any customs approved area were a person who removes such goods from an approved wharf.

Part V of the Act of 1979: Control of Exportation

9. In sections 53 (entry outwards of goods), 58D (operative date for Community purposes) and 58E (authentication of Community customs documentation) [and in section 62 (information, documentation, etc as to export goods]) any reference to goods shipped or shipped for exportation shall be construed as including a reference to goods loaded onto a vehicle for exportation through the tunnel.

10.—(1) Section 56(1) (failure to export) shall have effect as if goods in respect of which an entry has been accepted and which have not been loaded onto a vehicle for exportation through the tunnel were goods in respect of which an entry has been accepted and which have not been shipped.

(2) Section 56(2) shall have effect as if goods in respect of which paragraphs (a) and (b) of that section apply include goods—

(a)   in respect of which an entry has been accepted;

(b)   which are due to be loaded for exportation through the tunnel onto a vehicle specified in the entry or by the person having charge of them at the customs approved area of intended loading;

(c)   in respect of which no notice has been served under section 56(1); and

(d)   which have not been loaded by the time the vehicle departs from the customs approved area at which it has been cleared for departure.

11.—(1) In section 57(1) (delivery of entry by owner of exporting ship, etc) the reference to goods which are to be exported in an aircraft shall be construed as including a reference to goods which are to be exported through the tunnel in a vehicle and the reference to the owner of the aircraft shall be construed as including a reference to the owner or person in charge of the vehicle.

(2) For the purposes of section 57(4) a vehicle shall be treated as an aircraft.

12.—(1) Subject to subparagraph (2) below, section 58C(3) (export of ships and aircraft) shall have effect as if a vehicle departing on a journey from the United Kingdom through the tunnel were a ship departing for a voyage from the United Kingdom and the reference to the owner of the ship shall be construed as including a reference to the owner of the vehicle.

(2) In its application to a vehicle so departing section 58C(3) shall have effect as if the words "or, where" to "aircraft" had not been enacted.

[12A. In section 59 (restrictions on putting export goods alongside for loading)—

(a)   in construing the references in section 59(1) to shipment for exportation and in section 59(2)(a) to loading for exportation regard shall be had to paragraph 9 above; and accordingly

(b)   references in section 59(2) to a ship or aircraft shall be construed as including references to a vehicle.]

13. Section 64(1), (6) and (7) (clearance outwards of ships and aircraft) shall have effect as if a vehicle departing from [a place which is] a customs approved area on a journey to an eventual destination outside the [member States] through the tunnel were an aircraft departing from a customs and excise airport on a flight to an eventual destination outside the [member States] and Isle of Man and—

(a)   the reference in subsection (6) to the commander of an aircraft shall be construed as including a reference to the [train manager];

(b)   for the purposes of subsection (7) goods loaded onto such a vehicle shall be treated as goods loaded into an aircraft.

14.—(1) Section 65(1) (power to refuse or cancel clearance of ship or aircraft) shall have effect as if a vehicle departing to France through the tunnel were an aircraft and the reference in paragraph (b) of that section to a customs and excise airport shall be construed as including a reference to a customs approved area.

Part II

(2)   In section 65(2) and (3) any reference to the commander of an aircraft shall be construed as including a reference to the [train manager] and for the purposes of subsection (2) a written demand left on board a vehicle with the person appearing to be [the train manager] shall be treated as left on board an aircraft with the person appearing to be in charge thereof.

15.   In section 66(1) (power to make regulations as to exportation, etc) the reference to aircraft shall be construed as including a reference to vehicles leaving the United Kingdom through the tunnel.

16.   Section 67(1) (offences in relation to exportation of goods) shall have effect as if goods which have been loaded or retained on any vehicle for exportation through the tunnel were goods loaded or retained on board an aircraft for exportation and the references to the aircraft and to the commander of the aircraft shall be construed respectively as including references to the vehicle and to the [train manager].

Part VII of the Act of 1979: Customs and Excise Control: Supplementary Provisions

17.   In section 75(1) (explosives) the reference to goods loaded into a ship for exportation shall be construed as including a reference to goods loaded onto a vehicle for exportation through the tunnel.

[17A.   For the purposes of section 77 (information in relation to goods imported or exported) goods about to be loaded onto a vehicle for exportation through the tunnel shall be treated as goods about to be shipped for exportation, and the reference in subsection (3) to shipment shall be construed accordingly.

17B.   For the purposes of section 78 (customs and excise control of persons entering or leaving the United Kingdom)—

(a)   a person intending to travel to the United Kingdom through the tunnel who has entered a control zone in France [or Belgium] shall be treated as a person entering the United Kingdom,

(b)   a person who has travelled from the United Kingdom through the tunnel and is in such a control zone shall be treated as still being a person leaving the United Kingdom, and

(c)   concealment shall be taken to include concealment in such a control zone.

17C.   For the purposes of section 83(1) (penalty for removing seals, etc)—

(a)   goods which are in a control zone in France [or Belgium] shall be treated as being in the United Kingdom, and

(b)   goods in a through train shall be deemed to be in the charge of the person operating the international service on which the train is engaged,

and for the purposes of section 83(3)(b) goods which are in a control zone in France [or Belgium] shall be treated as being in the United Kingdom.]

18.   In section 84(2) (penalty for signalling to smugglers) any reference to a ship shall be construed as including a reference to a vehicle anywhere within the tunnel system (whether in England or in France) [and a reference to a through train, and the reference to the United Kingdom shall be construed as including a reference to a control zone in France].

[18A.   In section 86 (special penalty where offender armed or disguised) the reference to the United Kingdom shall be construed as including a reference to a control zone in France [or Belgium].]

19.   For the purposes of section 88 (forfeiture of ship, aircraft or vehicle constructed, etc for concealing goods) a vehicle which is or has been in a customs approved area, whether or not such area is within the limits of a port, shall be treated as if it is or has been within the limits of a port.

Part X of the Act of 1979: Duties and Drawbacks—General Provisions

20.   Section 134 (drawback and allowance on goods damaged or destroyed after shipment) shall have effect as if goods which have been loaded onto a vehicle for exportation through the tunnel were goods which had been shipped for exportation and as if such vehicle were an exporting ship.

Part XI of the Act of 1979: Detention of Persons, Forfeiture and Legal Proceedings

[20A.   The power conferred by section 139(1) to seize or detain any thing liable to forfeiture shall be taken to include a power for any officer or constable to seize or detain any such thing in a control zone in France [or Belgium].]

21.   Section 141(3) (forfeiture of ships, etc used in connection with goods liable to forfeiture) shall have effect as if a vehicle which has been used in the importation, exportation or carriage of goods through the tunnel were an aircraft and the references to the owner and the commander of an aircraft shall be construed respectively as including references to the owner of a vehicle and the [train manager].

22.   In section 146(1) (service of process) the reference in paragraph (c) to an aircraft shall be construed as including a reference to a vehicle which has arrived from or is departing to France through the tunnel[, and in relation to such a vehicle the second reference to the United Kingdom shall be construed as including a reference to a control zone in France within the tunnel system].

23.   In section 154(2) (proof of certain other matters) any reference to goods loaded or to be loaded into or unloaded from an aircraft shall be construed respectively as including references to goods loaded or to be loaded onto or unloaded from a vehicle which is departing to or has arrived from France through the tunnel.

24.   In section 159(1) (power to examine and take account of goods) the reference in paragraph (c) to goods which have been loaded into a ship shall be construed as including a reference to goods which have been loaded onto a vehicle for exportation through the tunnel.

[25.   The persons to whom section 164 (search of persons) applies shall be taken to include any person who is—

(a)   in the tunnel system in the United Kingdom;

(b)   in a through train in the United Kingdom;

(c)   in, entering or leaving a customs approved area in the United Kingdom; or

(d)   in a control zone in France [or Belgium].]

NOTES

Para A1: inserted, together with preceding cross-heading, by the Channel Tunnel (International Arrangements) Order 1993, SI 1993/1813, art 8, Sch 5, Pt II, para 11; words in square brackets added by the Channel Tunnel (Miscellaneous Provisions) Order 1994, SI 1994/1405, art 8, Sch 4, para 7, as from a day to be appointed.

Paras A2, 3A, 4A, 4B, 5A, 12A, 17A: inserted by SI 1993/1813, art 8, Sch 5, Pt II, paras 12, 14, 16, 18, 23.

Para 1: words in first (outer) pair of square brackets added by SI 1993/1813, art 8, Sch 5, Pt II, para 13, words in second (inner) pair of square brackets added by SI 1994/1405, art 8, Sch 4, para 7, as from a day to be appointed.

Paras 4, 5, 6, 14, 16, 21: words in square brackets substituted by SI 1993/1813, art 8, Sch 5, Pt II, paras 15, 17, 19, 25, 26, 31.

Para 7: substituted by SI 1993/1813, art 8, Sch 5, Pt II, para 20; words in square brackets inserted by SI 1994/1405, art 8, Sch 4, para 7, as from a day to be appointed.

Para 8: words in first (outer) pair of square brackets inserted by SI 1993/1813, art 8, Sch 5, Pt II, para 21, words in second (inner) pair of square brackets inserted by SI 1994/1405, art 8, Sch 4, para 7, as from a day to be appointed.

Part II

Paras 9, 18, 22: words in square brackets inserted or added by SI 1993/1813, art 8, Sch 5, Pt II, paras 22, 28, 32.

Para 13: words in first pair of square brackets inserted and words in remaining pairs of square brackets substituted by SI 1993/1813, art 8, Sch 5, Pt II, para 24.

Paras 17B, 18A, 20A: inserted by SI 1993/1813, art 8, Sch 5, Pt II, paras 27, 29, 30; words in square brackets inserted or added by SI 1994/1405, art 8, Sch 4, para 7, as from a day to be appointed.

Para 17C: inserted by SI 1993/1813, art 8, Sch 5, Pt II, para 27; words in first pair of square brackets inserted as from a day to be appointed, and words in second pair of square brackets substituted, by SI 1994/1405, art 8, para 8.

Para 25: substituted by SI 1993/1813, arts 8, 9, Sch 5, Pt II, para 33, Sch 6, Pt II; words in square brackets added by SI 1994/1405, art 8, Sch 4, para 7, as from a day to be appointed.

Entry on the importation of goods: by the Customs and Excise (Single Market etc) Regulations 1992, SI 1992/3095, reg 10(1), Sch 1, para 1, the reference to an entry on the importation of goods is to be treated as including an entry of such goods under the Customs Controls on Importation of Goods Regulations 1991, SI 1991/2724, reg 5, as amended by SI 1992/3095, SI 1993/3014.

CRIMINAL JUSTICE (INTERNATIONAL CO-OPERATION) ACT 1990 (EXERCISE OF POWERS) ORDER 1991

(SI 1991/1297)

NOTES

Revoked by the Crime (International Co-operation) Act 2003 (Exercise of Functions) Order, SI 2005/425 art 13.

. . .

EXCISE DUTIES (GOODS IMPORTED FOR TESTING, ETC) RELIEF ORDER 1991

(SI 1991/2089)

NOTES

Made: 16 September 1991.

Authority: Customs and Excise Duties (General Reliefs) Act 1979, s 11A.

Commencement: 1 November 1991.

ARRANGEMENT OF ARTICLES

10   Records and information]
11   Transfer of goods
12   Notification at end of test etc

1 Citation

This Order may be cited as the Excise Duties (Goods Imported for Testing, etc) Relief Order 1991 and shall come into force on 1st November 1991.

2 Scope of relief

(1)   Subject to the following provisions of this Order, where goods are imported into the United Kingdom for the sole or main purpose of being—

(a)   examined, analysed or tested, or

(b)   used to test equipment to establish whether that equipment can process such imported goods in a manner which may be specified by a potential buyer of that equipment,

payment of excise duty chargeable on those imported goods shall not be required.

(2)   Paragraph (1) above does not apply—

(a)   to goods exceeding the quantities which the Commissioners may determine are necessary for the purpose of the examination, analysis or test;

(b)   to goods which are consumed by a person in the examination, analysis or test; or

(c)   to petrol or any petrol substitute.

(3)   This Order shall apply without prejudice to any other relief from payment of excise duty chargeable on the importation of goods.

(4)   Nothing in this Order shall permit goods to be imported contrary to any prohibition or restriction on their importation.

(5)   In this Order "petrol substitute" has the same meaning as in section 4 of the Hydrocarbon Oil Duties Act 1979.

3 Excepted cases

(1)   Relief shall not be afforded by this Order in respect of goods imported for the purpose of any examination, analysis or test which itself constitutes a sales promotion.

(2)   Relief shall not be afforded by this Order in respect of heavy oil imported for the purpose of being used as fuel for a road vehicle.

(3)   In this Order "heavy oil" has the same meaning as in section 1 of the Hydrocarbon Oil Duties Act 1979.

4 Notice before importation

(1)   A person intending to import goods eligible for relief under this Order shall give the Commissioners notice of the importation in writing, containing such particulars as the Commissioners may direct, of his intentions with respect to that importation by him of such goods.

(2)   Where the goods referred to in paragraph (1) above are to form part of a series of similar importations the Commissioners may regard the requirements of that paragraph as being satisfied by a single notice.

5 Entry etc

An importer of goods who intends to claim relief under this Order shall make such entry and declaration relating to the importation as the Commissioners may direct.

NOTES

Entry on the importation of goods: by the Customs and Excise (Single Market etc) Regulations 1992, SI 1992/3095, reg 10(1), Sch 1, para 1, the reference to an entry on the importation of goods is to be treated as including an entry of such goods under the Customs Controls on Importation of Goods Regulations 1991, SI 1991/2724, reg 5, as amended by SI 1992/3095, SI 1993/3014.

6 Security

Security shall be provided to the Commissioners in respect of the amount of excise duty which is to be relieved from payment by this Order, and such security shall be in such form as the Commissioners may require.

7 Conditions

Articles 8 to 12 below set out the conditions subject to which relief under this Order is granted, and if any such condition is not complied with the excise duty shall immediately become payable.

8 Purpose to be fulfilled

(1) The purpose for which the goods were imported shall be fulfilled—

    (a)   in the United Kingdom; and

    (b)   within such time as the Commissioners may require.

(2) Without prejudice to the generality of paragraph (1) above, the goods shall not be used for any purpose excepted from relief under this Order by article 3 above.

9 Goods remaining

Any goods not completely used up or destroyed in the course of, or as a result of, the examination, analysis or test, and any products resulting from those operations, shall be—

    (a)   destroyed or otherwise rendered commercially worthless;

    (b)   exported; or

    (c)   put to other use on payment of duty.

10 Records and information

(1) The importer shall keep such records as the Commissioners may require relating to the importation of the goods, the use to which the goods are put, and to any remaining or resulting goods, and shall preserve the records for such period, not exceeding 2 years from the completion of the goods' use in the examination, analysis or test, as the Commissioners may require.

(2) The importer shall, at any reasonable time, permit the Commissioners to—

    (a)   inspect; and

    (b)   take extracts from, copy, or remove for a reasonable period the records required under paragraph (1) above.

(3) Where the records required under paragraph (1) above are in a form which is not readily legible, or which is legible only with the aid of equipment, the importer shall, if the Commissioners so require, furnish to them a transcript or other permanently legible reproduction of those records.

(4) Records required under paragraph (1) above shall be kept at the importer's principal place of business or such other place as the Commissioners may direct.

(5) The importer shall provide the Commissioners with such information relating to—

    (a)   the examination, analysis or test; and

    (b)   any goods remaining after or resulting from such operation, as the Commissioners may require.

11 Transfer of goods

The importer shall, before goods relieved from excise duty by this Order are transferred to another person not employed by him, notify the Commissioners of his intention in writing and, on receiving the goods, the recipient shall comply with the conditions of the relief as if he were the importer.

12 Notification at end of test etc

The importer shall, as soon as the examination, analysis or test is finished—

- (a) notify the Commissioners in writing of the date it was finished; and
- (b) supply the Commissioners with details in writing of any goods not completely used up in, and of any goods resulting from, that operation, together with written notice of how he proposes to dispose of them in accordance with article 9 above.

SPIRITS REGULATIONS 1991

(SI 1991/2564)

NOTES

Made: 11 November 1991.

Authority: Customs and Excise Management Act 1979, s 93; Alcoholic Liquor Duties Act 1979, ss 2, 3, 13, 15.

Commencement: 1 January 1992.

ARRANGEMENT OF REGULATIONS

PART I
PRELIMINARY

1 Citation, commencement and revocation

(1)   These Regulations may be cited as the Spirits Regulations 1991 and shall come into force on 1st January 1992.

(2)   The statutory instruments specified in column (1) of Schedule 1 to these Regulations (the references to which are specified in column (2) of that Schedule) are hereby revoked to the extent specified in column (3) of that Schedule.

2 Application

These Regulations apply to the manufacture of spirits by any process, except where by their nature or context they apply only to the manufacture of spirits by distillation of a fermented liquor.

3 Interpretation

In these Regulations, unless the context otherwise requires—

"the Act" means the Alcoholic Liquor Duties Act 1979;

"approved" means approved by the Commissioners. . .;

. . .

"class of spirits" means one of the classes of spirits specified from time to time for the purpose of these Regulations in a notice published by the Commissioners;

"the Contents by Weight Table", "the Laboratory Alcohol Table" and "the Practical Alcohol Tables" mean respectively a set of tables of which a copy, signed by the Chairman of the Commissioners and identifying the tables as being ones to which these Regulations relate, has been deposited in the office of the Queen's Remembrancer at the Royal Courts of Justice;

"distillation period" means the period prescribed by regulation 10 below in respect of each class of spirits;

"distiller" means a person holding a distiller's licence under section 12 of the Act;

"distiller's warehouse" has the meaning given by section 4(1) of the Act;

"distillery" means premises where spirits are manufactured, whether by distillation of a fermented liquor or by any other process;

. . .

"feints" means spirits conveyed into a feints receiver;

"low wines" means spirits of the first extraction conveyed into a low wines receiver;

. . .

"plant" means [the vessels] used for the manufacture of spirits, or for the storage or processing of materials for the manufacture of spirits or for the storage of spirits after their manufacture;

"process" includes an operation carried on in order to manufacture spirits, and an operation on spirits after their manufacture;

. . .

"still" includes part of a still;

. . .

"warehouse" means a place of security approved by the Commissioners under subsection (1) (whether or not it is also approved under subsection (2)) of section 92 of the Customs and Excise Management Act 1979 and also includes a distiller's warehouse;

"warehouse vat" means a vessel which forms the whole or a part of a distiller's warehouse;

"wash" means wort in which fermentation has begun;

"wort" means any infusion, solution or mixture intended for fermentation as part of the process of manufacturing spirits.

NOTES

In definition of "approved" words revoked by the Beer, Cider and Perry, Spirits, and Wine and Made-wine (Amendment) Regulations, SI 2006/1058, reg 5(1), (4)(ii).

Definitions of "approved saccharometer", "document", "hydrometer", "officer", "records", "sugar", and "thermometer", revoked by the Beer, Cider and Perry, Spirits, and Wine and Made-wine (Amendment) Regulations, SI 2006/1058, reg 5(1), (4)(i).

In definition of "plant" words substituted by the Beer, Cider and Perry, Spirits, and Wine and Made-wine (Amendment) Regulations, SI 2006/1058, reg 5(1), (4)(iii).

PART II
APPROVAL OF PLANT AND PROCESSES AND ENTRY OF PREMISES

4 Approval of plant and processes

(1) Before a distiller manufactures spirits he shall make [application in writing or by means of an electronic communication] to the [Commissioners] for approval of the plant and processes he intends to use.

(2) Any application made under paragraph (1) above shall be accompanied by a description of the processes referred to in it, and a [description of] the plant referred to in it, together with such additional information as the Commissioners may require.

(3) No distiller shall begin to manufacture spirits until he has received the approval of the Commissioners of the plant and processes referred to in his application under paragraph (1) above, and any such approval may be given subject to conditions.

(4) The Commissioners may for reasonable cause at any time vary or add to any conditions imposed on the approval of any plant or process, or withdraw any such approval.

NOTES

Para (1): words in first square brackets substituted by the Beer, Cider and Perry, Spirits, and Wine and Made-wine (Amendment) Regulations, SI 2006/1058, reg 5(1), (5); word in second square brackets substituted by the Beer, Cider and Perry, Spirits, and Wine and Made-wine (Amendment) Regulations, SI 2006/1058, reg 5(1), (3).

Para (2): words in square brackets substituted by the Beer, Cider and Perry, Spirits, and Wine and Made-wine (Amendment) Regulations, SI 2006/1058, reg 5(1), (6).

5

Revoked by the Beer, Cider and Perry, Spirits, and Wine and Made-wine (Amendment) Regulations, SI 2006/1058, reg 5(1), (2).

6 Variations to plant or processes

(1)   A distiller receiving approval under regulation 4 above shall ensure that any plant or process so approved is not [significantly] varied, altered or changed unless the variation, alteration or change is first approved by the Commissioners, and any such approval may be given subject to conditions.

(2)   Application for the approval of any variation, alteration or change to any plant or process shall be in such form and manner and shall provide such details, including a written description, drawing or model, as the Commissioners may require.

(3)   The Commissioners may for reasonable cause at any time vary or add to any conditions imposed on the approval of any variation, alteration or change of any plant or process, or withdraw any such approval.

NOTES

Para (1): word in square brackets substituted by the Beer, Cider and Perry, Spirits, and Wine and Made-wine (Amendment) Regulations, SI 2006/1058, reg 5(1), (7).

7, 8

Revoked by the Beer, Cider and Perry, Spirits, and Wine and Made-wine (Amendment) Regulations, SI 2006/1058, reg 5(1), (2).

PART III
CONDUCT OF PROCESSES

9

Revoked by the Beer, Cider and Perry, Spirits, and Wine and Made-wine (Amendment) Regulations, SI 2006/1058, reg 5(1), (2).

10 Distillation periods

(1)   A distiller shall conduct his operations in separate distillation periods for each class of spirits . . .

(2)   A distiller may conduct his operations so that more than one distillation period is in progress at any one time.

(3)   In respect of each batch of wort which he makes, the distiller shall specify to which distillation period it belongs, and a distillation period shall commence at the date when production of the earliest of the wort included in it commences.

(4)   Each distillation period shall end when all the wort specified to belong to it has been distilled and the feints and spirits produced therefrom have been conveyed into their receivers and account has been taken of them.

(5)   Save as the [Commissioners] may otherwise allow, a distiller shall conduct his operations so that no distillation period exceeds one month in length.

NOTES

Para (1): words omitted revoked by the Beer, Cider and Perry, Spirits, and Wine and Made-wine (Amendment) Regulations, SI 2006/1058, reg 5(1), (8).

Para (5): word in square brackets substituted by the Beer, Cider and Perry, Spirits, and Wine and Made-wine (Amendment) Regulations, SI 2006/1058, reg 5(1), (3).

11 Produce of distillation periods

(1) Save as the Commissioners may otherwise allow, a distiller shall ensure that the produce of any distillation period is not mixed with any other matter until account of that produce has been taken in such manner and to such an extent as the [Commissioners] may require.

(2) Notwithstanding paragraph (1) above, before account is taken of the produce of any distillation period it may be mixed with feints of which account has been taken in an earlier distillation period.

NOTES

Para (1): word in square brackets substituted by the Beer, Cider and Perry, Spirits, and Wine and Made-wine (Amendment) Regulations, SI 2006/1058, reg 5(1), (3).

12–16

Revoked by the Beer, Cider and Perry, Spirits, and Wine and Made-wine (Amendment) Regulations, SI 2006/1058, reg 5(1), (2).

PART IV
TAKING ACCOUNT OF SPIRITS PRODUCED

17

Revoked by the Beer, Cider and Perry, Spirits, and Wine and Made-wine (Amendment) Regulations, SI 2006/1058, reg 5(1), (2).

18 Ascertainment of strength of spirits

(1) Subject to paragraph (2) below, the strength of spirits may be ascertained—

   (a)   by means of a hydrometer, a thermometer and the table entitled "The Practical Alcohol Tables Volume 2"; or

   (b)   by determining the density of the spirits in air at 20° Celsius and taking the strength of the spirits to be the percentage of alcohol by volume corresponding to that density in the table entitled "Laboratory Alcohol Table", provided that where the density of any spirits determined as aforesaid falls between any two consecutive numbers in that table the strength shall be determined by linear interpolation; [or

   (c)   by a method set out in the Annex to Commission Regulation (EC) No 2870/2000.]

(2) Where spirits contain any substance other than alcohol and water the Commissioners may either—

   (a)   require that the strength of the spirits be ascertained by any of the means prescribed by this Part of these Regulations after removing from the spirits any such substance to the extent which they consider necessary by distillation or such other process as they direct and adding water to replace the volume so removed; or

   (b)   allow the strength of the spirits to be ascertained, as though they contained alcohol and water only, by any of the means prescribed by this Part of these Regulations.

NOTES

Para (1): sub-para (c) and preceding word "or" inserted by the Beer, Cider and Perry, Spirits, and Wine and Made-wine (Amendment) Regulations, SI 2006/1058, reg 5(1), (9).

19 Ascertainment of volume of spirits

(1) The volume of spirits contained in any container may be ascertained for any purpose by such method involving weight, measure or gauge as the Commissioners may approve.

(2) Where the Commissioners under paragraph (1) of this Regulation approve ascertainment by weighing, the volume shall be calculated by means of a hydrometer and the table entitled "Contents by Weight Table".

20 Application of regulations 18 and 19

Regulations 18 and 19 above shall apply to spirits, . . . and any fermented liquor other than wash.

NOTES

Words omitted revoked by the Denatured Alcohol Regulations, SI 2005/1524 reg 19, with effect from 1 July 2005.

PART V
DISTILLERS' RECORDS

21–24

Revoked by the Beer, Cider and Perry, Spirits, and Wine and Made-wine (Amendment) Regulations, SI 2006/1058, reg 5(1), (2).

25 Quarterly distillery returns

Within 14 days of the end of each calendar quarter the distiller shall furnish to the [Commissioners] a return in respect of that quarter, which shall be made in such form and manner and shall contain such particulars as the Commissioners may from time to time direct.

NOTES

Word in square brackets substituted by the Beer, Cider and Perry, Spirits, and Wine and Made-wine (Amendment) Regulations, SI 2006/1058, reg 5(1), (3).

PART VI
WAREHOUSING

26 Warehousing

(1) A distiller shall not warehouse any spirits until he has taken account of them in such manner and to such extent as the [Commissioners] may require. . ..

(2) Save as the Commissioners may otherwise allow, when spirits of which account has been taken are contained in a spirit receiver which is not also approved as a warehouse vat the distiller shall remove them to a warehouse immediately . . .

(3) When spirits of which account has been taken are contained in a spirit receiver which is also approved as a warehouse vat those spirits shall be deemed to be warehoused as soon as account of them has been [taken].

(4) . . .

(5) Where spirits remain in a warehouse vat which is also approved as a spirit receiver, the distiller shall take account of such spirits before the warehouse vat is used as a spirit receiver . . .

NOTES

Para (1): word in square brackets substituted by the Beer, Cider and Perry, Spirits, and Wine and Made-wine (Amendment) Regulations, SI 2006/1058, reg 5(1), (3); words omitted revoked by the Beer, Cider and Perry, Spirits, and Wine and Made-wine (Amendment) Regulations, SI 2006/1058, reg 5(1), (10).

Para (2): words revoked by the Beer, Cider and Perry, Spirits, and Wine and Made-wine (Amendment) Regulations, SI 2006/1058, reg 5(1), (11).

Para (3): word substituted by the Beer, Cider and Perry, Spirits, and Wine and Made-wine (Amendment) Regulations, SI 2006/1058, reg 5(1), (12).

Para (4): revoked by the Beer, Cider and Perry, Spirits, and Wine and Made-wine (Amendment) Regulations, SI 2006/1058, reg 5(1), (2).

Para (5): words revoked by the Beer, Cider and Perry, Spirits, and Wine and Made-wine (Amendment) Regulations, SI 2006/1058, reg 5(1), (13).

SCHEDULES

NOTES

Schedule 1 revokes the Spirits Regulations 1952, SI 1952/2229, Pts IV, IX, the Alcoholic Liquors (Amendment of Units and Methods of Measurement) Regulations 1979, SI 1979/1146, reg 2, the Spirits Regulations 1982, SI 1982/611, and the Spirits (Rectifying, Compounding and Drawback) Regulations 1988, SI 1988/1760, reg 2 (in part).

Schedule 2 revoked by the Beer, Cider and Perry, Spirits, and Wine and Made-wine (Amendment) Regulations, SI 2006/1058, reg 5(1), (2).

CUSTOMS CONTROLS ON IMPORTATION OF GOODS REGULATIONS 1991

(SI 1991/2724)

NOTES

Made: 4 December 1991.

Authority: European Communities Act 1972, s 2(2).

Commencement: 1 January 1992.

ARRANGEMENT OF REGULATIONS

Part II

1 Citation and commencement

These Regulations may be cited as the Customs Controls on Importation of Goods Regulations 1991 and shall come into force on 1st January 1992.

2 Interpretation

In these Regulations—

"the Act" means the Customs and Excise Management Act 1979;

"the Commissioners" means the Commissioners of Customs and Excise;

"the Council Regulation" means [Council Regulation (EEC) No 2913/92];

["the Commission Regulation" means the Commission Regulation (EEC) No 2454/93]

"the customs and excise Acts" has the same meaning as in section 1(1) of the Act.

NOTES

Words in first pair of square brackets substituted and definition "the Commission Regulation" inserted by the Community Customs Code (Consequential Amendment of References) Regulations 1993, SI 1993/3014, reg 4(2).

3 Presentation

(1) Notification to the Commissioners of the arrival of goods [when presentation of the goods is required by Article 40] of the Council Regulation shall be made in the form prescribed in Schedule 1 or a form to the like effect approved by the Commissioners.

(2) Where a computerised inventory system has been approved by the Commissioners presentation may consist in a computerised record capable of being printed out.

(3) Within three hours of its arrival at the wharf or airport at which a ship or aircraft carrying the goods is to unload them, notification of such arrival, as required by [Article 40], of the Council Regulation shall be made at the customs office for the wharf or airport; should such notification be impossible due to the office being closed during that period, the period shall end at the expiration of one hour following the reopening of the office.

NOTES

Paras (1), (3): words in square brackets substituted by the Community Customs Code (Consequential Amendment of References) Regulations 1993, SI 1993/3014, reg 4(3), (4).

4 Summary declaration

The summary declaration required under [Article 43] of the Council Regulation shall be in the form prescribed in Schedule 2 or a form to the like effect approved by the Commissioners.

NOTES

Words in square brackets substituted by the Community Customs Code (Consequential Amendment of References) Regulations 1993, SI 1993/3014, reg 4(5).

5 Entry

(1) For the purposes of [Article 49] of the Council Regulation the goods shall be entered not later than—

    (a)   [forty-five] days from the date on which the summary declaration is lodged in the case of goods carried by sea; or

(b)   [twenty] days from the date on which the summary declaration is lodged in the case of goods carried otherwise than by sea.

(2)   The entry shall be delivered by the importer to the proper officer . . ..

(3)   Except with the permission of the Commissioners no entry shall be delivered before the goods have been presented at the proper office of customs and excise.

(4)   Where the Commissioners permit an entry to be delivered before presentation of the goods, the goods must be presented to the proper office of customs and excise within such time as the Commissioners may allow; and if the goods are not so presented the entry shall be treated as not having been delivered.

(5)   Acceptance of an entry by the proper officer shall be signified in such manner as the Commissioners may direct.

NOTES

Para (1): words in first pair of square brackets substituted by the Community Customs Code (Consequential Amendment of References) Regulations 1993, SI 1993/3014, reg 4(6); words in second and third pairs of square brackets substituted by the Customs and Excise (Single Market etc) Regulations 1992, SI 1992/3095, reg 7(a)(i).

Para (2): words omitted revoked by SI 1992/3095, reg 7(a)(ii).

Entry on the importation of goods: by the Customs and Excise (Single Market etc) Regulations 1992, SI 1992/3095, reg 10(1), Sch 1, para 1, the reference to an entry on the importation of goods is to be treated as including an entry of such goods under the Customs Controls on Importation of Goods Regulations 1991, SI 1991/2724, reg 5, as amended by SI 1992/3095, SI 1993/3014.

6

(Amends the Customs and Excise Management Act 1979, ss 1(1), 21(2), substitutes ss 20, 20A for the original s 20, substitutes ss 22, 22A for the original s 22, substitutes ss 25, 25A for the original s 25, and adds ss 21(1A), (4A), 37(10), 42(3), 129(5) of that Act.)

7 Provisions of statutory instruments disapplied to certain goods
The Statutory Instruments specified in Schedule 3, to the extent indicated in that Schedule, shall not have effect for or in respect of any goods imported into the United Kingdom from a place outside the customs territory of the Community [or which are moving under the procedure specified in [Article 165 of the Council Regulation and Article 311 of the Commission Regulation] (transit procedures)].

NOTES

Words in first (outer) pair of square brackets added by the Customs and Excise (Single Market etc) Regulations 1992, SI 1992/3095, reg 7(b), words in second (inner) pair of square brackets substituted by the Community Customs Code (Consequential Amendment of References) Regulations 1993, SI 1993/3014, reg 4(7).

8 Offences, penalty and forfeiture
In the event of any contravention or failure to comply with—

(a)   any provision of the Council Regulation [or any provision of the Commission Regulation] as specified in Schedule 4; or

(b)   any requirement or condition imposed by or under any such provision; or

(c)   any undertaking given pursuant to any such provision or requirement; or

(d)   regulations 3, 4 or 5 above,

Part II

the person responsible for the contravention or failure shall be liable on summary conviction to a penalty of level 3 on the standard scale and any goods in respect of which the offence was committed shall be liable to forfeiture.

NOTES

Words in square brackets inserted by the Community Customs Code (Consequential Amendment of References) Regulations 1993, SI 1993/3014, reg 4(8).

9

(Repeals the Finance Act 1987, s 6.)

10 Supplementary

(1) Section 139 of and Schedule 3 to the Act (detention, seizure and condemnation of goods) shall apply to any goods liable to forfeiture under regulation 8 above as if the goods were liable to forfeiture under the customs and excise Acts.

(2) Sections 144 to 148 and 150 to 155 of the Act (proceedings for offences, mitigation of penalties, proof and other matters) shall apply in relation to offences and penalties under regulation 8 above and proceedings for such offences or for condemnation of any thing being forfeited under that regulation as they apply in relation to offences and penalties and proceedings for offences or for condemnation under the customs and excise Acts.

SCHEDULES

SCHEDULE 1

FORM OF PRESENTATION

Regulation 3(1)

Presentation of Third Country Goods

I hereby notify customs that the goods listed on . . . .
(document reference)

attached/not attached*

Arrived at . . . .
(name of wharf, airport, etc)

on . . . . (date) at . . . . (time)

I present the goods under [Article 40 of the Council Regulation].

      Signature . . . .
      Name . . . .
      Company . . . .
      Status . . . .
      Date . . . .
      * Delete as appropriate

C 1600A

NOTES

Words in square brackets substituted by the Community Customs Code (Consequential Amendment of References) Regulations 1993, SI 1993/3014, reg 2(9).

(Sch 2 contains the form of Summary Declaration.)

SCHEDULE 3
DISAPPLICATION OF ENACTMENTS TO GOODS FROM OUTSIDE EC
Regulation 7

Ship's Report, Importation and Exportation by Sea Regulations 1981
Regulations to be disapplied

Regulation 8	Landing, unloading, removal
Regulation 9	Transhipment

The Aircraft (Customs and Excise) Regulations 1981
Regulations to be disapplied

Regulation 4(1)(e)	Unloading
Regulation 4(1)(f)	Transit sheds
Regulation 4(2)(b)	Failure to arrive at examination stations
Regulation 5	Conditions of unloading
Regulation 6	Removal of unloaded goods

[SCHEDULE 4
OFFENCES
Regulation 8

Provisions of the Council Regulation

Article 38(1)	Imported goods to be conveyed to a customs office or a free zone by a specified route.
Article 39(1)	Importer to notify the customs authorities where unable to comply with Article 38(1).
Article 39(2)	Person in charge of ship or aircraft forced into United Kingdom to notify the customs authorities when he cannot comply with the provisions of Article 38(1).
Article 39(3)	Goods to be brought under customs control.
Article 40	Imported goods to be presented.
Article 42	Authorised sampling of goods.
Article 43	Summary declaration to be lodged for all goods presented.
Article 44(1)	Summary declaration to be in prescribed form.
Article 46(1)	Unloading or transhipment by permission and at approved places; notification of unauthorised unloading due to imminent danger.
Article 46(2)	Goods to be unloaded as required.
Article 47	Unauthorised removal of goods.
Articles 49(1) and 59	Goods to be entered within prescribed period.

Article 51(1)   Goods in temporary storage to be stored
                                       in approved places.
Article 52   Forms of handling of goods in tempo-
                                       rary storage.

Provisions of the Commission Regulation

Article 183(1)   Summary declaration to be signed by
                                       person making it.
Article 184(1)   Re-presentation of goods not unloaded.
Article 184(2)   Re-presentation of unloaded goods.
Article 186   Special declaration to be lodged when
                                       required for goods in temporary
                                       storage."

NOTES

Substituted by the Community Customs Code (Consequential Amendment of References) Regulations 1993, SI 1993/3014, reg 4(10), Sch 2.

CUSTOMS WAREHOUSING REGULATIONS 1991

(SI 1991/2725)

NOTES

Made: 4 December 1991.

Authority: European Communities Act 1972, s 2(2).

Commencement: 1 January 1992.

ARRANGEMENT OF REGULATIONS

1   Citation and commencement
2   Interpretation
4   Value Added Tax
5   Offences, penalty and forfeiture
6   Supplementary
           Schedule—Relevant Community Provisions

1 Citation and commencement

These Regulations may be cited as the Customs Warehousing Regulations 1991 and shall come into force on 1st January 1992.

2 Interpretation

In these Regulations—

"the Act" means the Customs and Excise Management Act 1979;

"the customs and excise Acts" has the same meaning as in section 1(1) of the Act;

"relevant Community provision" means any provision of a Community Regulation specified in the first and second columns of the Schedule.

3

(Amends the Customs and Excise Management Act 1979, ss 1, 27, 92, 98.)

4 Value Added Tax

The amendments made to the Act by regulation 3 above shall not have effect in relation to the application of the Act by virtue of section 24(1) of the Value Added Tax Act 1983.

5 Offences, penalty and forfeiture

In the event of any contravention or failure to comply with—

(a)   any relevant Community provision; or

(b)   any requirement or condition imposed by or under any such provision; or

(c)   any undertaking given pursuant to any such provision or requirement,

the person responsible for the contravention or failure shall be liable on summary conviction to a penalty of level 3 on the standard scale together with a penalty of £40 for each day on which such contravention or failure continues; and any goods in respect of which such offence was committed shall be liable to forfeiture.

6 Supplementary

(1)   Section 139 of and Schedule 3 to the Act (detention, seizure and condemnation of goods) shall apply to any goods liable to forfeiture under regulation 5 above as if the goods were liable to forfeiture under the customs and excise Acts.

(2)   Sections 144 to 148 and 150 to 155 of the Act (proceedings for offences, mitigation of penalties, proof and other matters) shall apply in relation to offences and penalties under regulation 5 above and proceedings for such offences or for condemnation of any thing as being forfeited under that regulation as they apply in relation to offences and penalties and proceedings for offences or for condemnation under the customs and excise Acts.

SCHEDULE

RELEVANT COMMUNITY PROVISIONS

Regulation 2

[(1) Community Regulation	(2) Relevant Provision	(3) Subject Matter of Provision
Council Regulation (EEC) No 2913/92	Article 59	All goods intended to be placed under a customs procedure shall be covered by a declaration for that customs procedure.
	Article 101(a)	Warehousekeeper to ensure that goods in warehouse are not removed from customs supervision.
	Article 101(b)	Warehousekeeper to fulfil obligations arising from storage of goods.
	Article 101(c)	Warehousekeeper to comply with conditions of authorisation.
	Article 105	Designated person to keep stock records in approved form.
	Article 110	Temporary removal requires authorisation.

[(1) Community Regulation	(2) Relevant Provision	(3) Subject Matter of Provision
	Article 111	Transfer requires authorisation.
Commission Regulation (EEC) No 2454/93	Article 513	Failure to make presentation of goods and lodge declaration.
	Article 269	Authorised use of simplified procedures.
	Article 517	Stock records to be made available to the supervising office.
	Articles 522, 523 and 532	Authorisation for usual forms of handling.
	Article 527	Inventory to be furnished when required.
	Articles 223, 528 and 864	Treatment without customs approved formalities.
	Articles 529–534	Requirement for export declaration.
	Article 536	Customs status and identification of Community goods.]

NOTES

Substituted by the Community Customs Code (Consequential Amendment of References) Regulations 1993, SI 1993/3014, reg 6, Sch 4.

CUSTOMS WAREHOUSING (VICTUALLING) REGULATIONS 1991

(SI 1991/2726)

NOTES

Made: 4 December 1991.

Authority: Customs and Excise Management Act 1979, s 93.

Commencement: 1 January 1992.

ARRANGEMENT OF REGULATIONS

PART I
PRELIMINARY

PART II
CONTROL OF VICTUALLING WAREHOUSES AND WAREHOUSED GOODS

PART III
REVOCATION

PART I
PRELIMINARY

1 Citation and commencement

These Regulations may be cited as the Customs Warehousing (Victualling) Regulations 1991 and shall come into force on 1st January 1992.

2 Interpretation

In these Regulations—

"the Act" means the Customs and Excise Management Act 1979;

"the Commission Regulation" means Commission Regulation (EEC) No 3665/87;

"computer" has the same meaning as, by virtue of section 10 of the Civil Evidence Act 1968, it has in Part I of that Act;

"occupier" means the person who has given security to the Crown in respect of a victualling warehouse;

"package" includes any bundle and any box, cask or other receptacle whatsoever;

"proprietor" means the proprietor of goods in a victualling warehouse;

"victualling warehouse" means a place of security approved by the Commissioners under section 92(2) of the Act.

3 Application

These Regulations shall apply to all victualling warehouses and to all goods warehoused therein.

PART II
CONTROL OF VICTUALLING WAREHOUSES AND WAREHOUSED GOODS

4 Time of warehousing

Goods brought to a victualling warehouse for warehousing or rewarehousing shall be deemed to be warehoused or rewarehoused, as the case may be, when they are put in the victualling warehouse for that purpose.

5 Receipt of goods

Save as the proper officer may otherwise allow, when any goods are brought to a victualling warehouse for warehousing or rewarehousing, the occupier shall without delay notify the proper officer in writing of any deficiency, surplus or other discrepancy between the particulars of the goods shown on the receipt documents and the goods received.

6 Records

(1) The occupier shall keep a register in such form and manner as the proper officer shall approve.

(2)   At such times as the proper officer shall require, the occupier shall enter in the register the following particulars of goods which are warehoused or rewarehoused which have been removed from the victualling warehouse—

(a)   the date on which the goods were brought to the victualling warehouse;

(b)   the number of any customs document accompanying the goods and the name and address of the issuing customs office;

(c)   the information specified in Article 3.5 of the Commission Regulation;

(d)   the date on which the goods were removed from the victualling warehouse;

(e)   where the goods have been transferred to another victualling warehouse, the name and address of such other warehouse;

(f)   where the goods have been loaded on board a vessel or aircraft—

(i)   the registration number and name of such vessel or aircraft, and

(ii)   the date of such loading; and

(g)   where the goods have been supplied to a rig or workpoint of a kind specified in Article 42.1(a) of the Commission Regulation, the name of such rig or workpoint.

(3)   The occupier shall keep the register at the victualling warehouse unless the proper officer consents to it being kept at some other place.

(4)   The occupier shall retain the register for at least three years from the end of the calendar year in which the goods were removed from the victualling warehouse.

(5)   The occupier shall, if so required by the proper officer, produce the register and shall permit the proper officer to take copies thereof or to make notes therein:

Provided that if the information which would otherwise be contained in the register is—

(a)   stored in a computer; or

(b)   contained on a film (including microfilm), negative, tape or other device in which one or more visual images are embodied so as to be capable (with or without the aid of some other equipment) of being reproduced therefrom,

the occupier shall, on request, produce that information in the form of a transcript or other legible reproduction.

(6)   The occupier shall keep in such manner as the proper officer shall approve the certificates of delivery on board produced for the purposes of Article 42 of the Commission Regulation; and paragraphs (3), (4) and (5) above shall apply to such certificates as if they formed part of the register kept in accordance with this Regulation.

7 Stocktaking

(1)   The occupier shall permit the proper officer at any reasonable time to take stock of warehoused goods and shall afford such facilities as the officer may reasonably require for this purpose.

(2)   The occupier shall take stock of warehoused goods when the proper officer may for reasonable cause so require.

(3)   When the occupier takes stock of the goods deposited in the warehouse, whether or not in pursuance of a requirement under paragraph (2) above, he shall notify the proper officer forthwith in writing of any deficiency, surplus or any discrepancy revealed thereby, and if so required by the proper officer shall provide him with a copy of the stocktaking account.

8 Warehousing and marking of packages and lots

(1)   Save as the proper officer may otherwise allow, goods shall be warehoused in the packages or lots in which they were first entered for warehousing and their

proprietor shall mark and keep marked those packages or lots as the proper officer may require.

(2)   No alteration shall be made to warehoused goods or to their packaging or marking except with the authority of the proper officer.

(3)   Any goods in respect of which this regulation is contravened shall be liable to forfeiture.

9 Stowage and production of goods

Save as the proper officer may otherwise allow, the occupier shall so stow every package or lot of warehoused goods that safe and easy access may be had thereto and shall produce to the proper officer on request any such goods which have not been lawfully removed from the victualling warehouse.

10 Operations on warehoused goods

(1)   Operations by way of marking, airing, chilling, freezing and packaging and those specified in Article 36 of the Commission Regulation may be carried out in accordance with any requirement made by the proper officer.

(2)   A requirement made under paragraph (1) above may relate to the parts of victualling warehouses in which operations may be carried out.

(3)   The person intending to carry out any operation mentioned in this regulation shall first obtain an authorisation from the proper officer.

(4)   The proper officer may for reasonable cause revoke or vary any requirements imposed under this regulation.

(5)   Any goods upon which any operation is carried out in breach of this regulation shall be liable to forfeiture.

11 Removal of goods from victualling warehouse

(1)   Save as the proper officer may otherwise allow, before any goods are removed from a victualling warehouse for rewarehousing in another victualling warehouse, their proprietor shall deliver to the proper officer an entry thereof in such form and manner and containing such particulars as the proper officer may direct.

(2)   Warehoused goods shall not be removed from a victualling warehouse as supplies of the kind and for the purposes mentioned in Article 38 of the Commission Regulation, except with the authority of and in accordance with any requirement made by the proper officer.

(3)   Where goods are entered under this regulation they shall forthwith be removed from the victualling warehouse; but if the proper officer allows those goods to remain therein they shall for warehousing purposes be treated as having been removed at the time of entry.

12 Goods not sent to an entitled destination

Where it is found that goods warehoused in a victualling warehouse have not reached the destination referred to in regulation 11(2) above or, due to the operation of Article 13 of the Commission Regulation, no longer qualify for a refund, the occupier shall notify the proper officer forthwith in writing.

PART III
REVOCATION

13 Revocation of approvals of victualling warehouses

The period prescribed by the Commissioners at the end of which the revocation of their approval of a victualling warehouse is to take effect shall be two working days ending with the date specified in their notice of intention to revoke or such longer period as they may, upon application by the occupier, allow.

14

(Revokes the Customs Warehousing Regulations 1979, SI 1979/207.)

FREE ZONE REGULATIONS 1991

(SI 1991/2727)

NOTES

Made: 4 December 1991.

Authority: European Communities Act 1972, s 2(2).

Commencement: 1 January 1992.

ARRANGEMENT OF REGULATIONS

1 Citation and commencement

These Regulations may be cited as the Free Zone Regulations 1991 and shall come into force on 1st January 1992.

2 Interpretation

In these Regulations—

"the Act" means the Customs and Excise Management Act 1979;

"the customs and excise Acts" has the same meaning as in section 1(1) of the Act;

"relevant Community provision" means any provision of a Community Regulation specified in the first and second columns of the Schedule.

3 Repeals

(1) Subject to paragraph (2) . . .

(2) This regulation shall not have effect in relation to the application of the following provisions of the Act by virtue of section 24(1) of the Value Added Tax Act 1983—

section 100B (free zone regulations),

section 100C(1) (free zone goods) insofar as the subsection purports to apply to goods chargeable with customs duty, and

section 100C(3) (scope of free zone regulations).

NOTES

It should be noted that the Customs and Excise Management Act 1979, ss 100B, 100C have been repealed, subject to transitional provisions, by the Value Added Tax Act 1994, s 100(1), (2), Schs 13, 15 and have been replaced by s 17 of the 1994 Act.

Para (1): words omitted repeal the Customs and Excise Management Act 1979, ss 100B–100E.

4, 5

(Reg 4 amends the Customs and Excise Management Act 1979, s 1(1); reg 5 spent.)

6 Offences, penalty and forfeiture

In the event of any contravention or failure to comply with—

    (a)   any relevant Community provision; or

    (b)   any requirement or condition imposed by or under any such provision; or

    (c)   any undertaking given pursuant to any such provision or requirement; or

    (d)   any regulation made under section 100B of the Act in its continued application by virtue of regulation 3(2) above; or

    (e)   any regulation made under section 100C(4) of the Act,

the person responsible for the contravention or failure shall be liable on summary conviction to a penalty of level 3 on the standard scale together with a penalty of £40 for each day on which the contravention or failure continues and any goods in respect of which the offence was committed shall be liable to forfeiture.

NOTES

It should be noted that the Customs and Excise Management Act 1979, ss 100B, 100C have been repealed, subject to transitional provisions, by the Value Added Tax Act 1994, s 100(1), (2), Schs 13, 15 and have been replaced by s 17 of the 1994 Act.

7 Supplementary

(1) Section 139 of and Schedule 3 to the Act (detention, seizure and condemnation of goods) shall apply to any goods where liable to forfeiture under regulation 6 above as if the goods were liable to forfeiture under the customs and excise Acts.

(2) Sections 144 to 148 and 150 to 155 of the Act (proceedings for offences, mitigation of penalties, proof and other matters) shall apply in relation to offences and penalties under regulation 6 above and proceedings for such offences or for condemnation of any thing as being forfeited under that regulation as they apply in relation to offences and penalties and proceedings for offences or for condemnation under the customs and excise Acts.

[SCHEDULE

RELEVANT COMMUNITY PROVISIONS

Regulation 2

(1) Community Regulation	(2) Relevant Provision	(3) Subject Matter of Provision
Council Regulation (EEC) No 2913/92	Article 167(4)	Construction of a building requires authorisation.
	Article 172	Activities require authorisation.
	Article 176(1)	Stock records to be kept in approved form and at the disposal of the customs authorities; goods to be identified and movements recorded.
	Article 176(2)	Transhipment documents to be kept at the disposal of the customs authorities.
Commission Regulation (EEC) No 2454/93	Article 805	Advance notification of activities.

Part II

(1)	(2)	(3)
Community Regulation	**Relevant Provision**	**Subject Matter of Provision**
	Article 807	Activities commenced before approval of stock records.
	Article 811	Entry of goods into premises to be recorded immediately in stock records.
	Article 820	Removal of goods from premises to be recorded immediately in stock records.
	Article 823(1)	Prefinanced goods to be presented and declaration lodged.
	Article 823(2)	Form of declaration.
	Article 825	Permitted forms of handling for prefinanced goods.]

NOTES

Substituted by the Community Customs Code (Consequential Amendment of References) Regulations 1993, SI 1993/3014, reg 3, Sch 1.

STATISTICS OF TRADE (CUSTOMS AND EXCISE) REGULATIONS 1992

(SI 1992/2790)

NOTES

Made: 6 November 1992.

Authority: European Communities Act 1972, s 2(2).

Commencement: 1 December 1992.

ARRANGEMENT OF REGULATIONS

1 Citation, commencement and interpretation

(1) These Regulations may be cited as the Statistics of Trade (Customs and Excise) Regulations 1992 and shall come into force on 1st December 1992.

(2) In these Regulations—

"the Act" means the Customs and Excise Management Act 1979;
[. . .]

. . .

. . .

"authorised person" means any person acting under the authority of the Commissioners;
[. . .]

. . .

"document" includes in addition to a document in writing—

(a) any photograph;

(b) any disc, tape, sound track or other device in which sounds or other data (not being visual images) are recorded so as to be capable (with or without the aid of some other equipment) of being reproduced therefrom; and

(c) any film, negative, tape or other device in which one or more visual images are recorded so as to be capable (as aforesaid) of being reproduced therefrom;

"film" includes a microfilm;

. . .

["Intrastat" refers to the data collection system established and implemented by—

(a) Council and European Parliament Regulation (EC) No 638/2004 ("establishing Regulation"); and

(b) Commission Regulation (EC) No 1982/2004 ("implementing Regulation");]

["periodic declaration" refers to the means of providing the simplified information in regulations 3(1) and 3(2) (VAT return) or to a supplementary declaration in regulation 4;]

. . .

. . .

. . .

[. . .]

(3) In these Regulations, unless defined above, words and expressions shall have the meanings assigned to them by section 1 of the Act [or have the same meaning as in the establishing or implementing Regulation].

NOTES

Para (2): definitions "ancillary costs sample survey", "business day", "commodity code" and "supplementary units" omitted revoked by the Statistics of Trade (Customs and Excise) (Amendment) Regulations 1997, SI 1997/2864, regs 2, 3 (previously inserted by the Statistics of Trade (Customs and Excise) (Amendment) Regulations 1993, SI 1993/541, reg 3); definitions "arrival stage", "assimilation threshold", "dispatch stage", "goods", "Member State", "Principal Regulation", "reference period", "register of intra-Community operators", "supplementary declaration" and "Threshold Regulation" revoked by the Statistics of Trade (Customs and Excise) (Amendment) Regulations, SI 2004/3284 reg 5, Schedule; definitions "intrastat" and "periodic declaration" substituted by the Statistics of Trade (Customs and Excise) (Amendment) Regulations, SI 2004/3284 reg 2(1), (2), with effect from 1 January 2005; definitions "Principal Regulation" and "Threshold Regulation" substituted by the Statistics of Trade (Customs and Excise) (Amendment) Regulations 2000, SI 2000/3227, regs 2, 3, with effect from 1 January 2001.

Para (3): words in square brackets inserted by the Statistics of Trade (Customs and Excise) (Amendment) Regulations, SI 2004/3284 reg 2(3).

2 [Application of Intrastat

(1) For the purposes of the United Kingdom's statistical territory (see Article 4(1) of the establishing Regulation), Intrastat is under the care and management of the Commissioners of Customs and Excise (the "Commissioners").

(2) For the purposes mentioned in paragraph (1), the Commissioners are—

(a) "customs" within Article 5(2) of the establishing Regulation (provision to national authority of statistical information on other goods at least once a month);

(b) the "national authority" within—

(i) Articles 5(2), 8(1), 8(2), 9(1) and 11 of the establishing Regulation (other goods, etc; register of intra-Community operators; identification of parties responsible for providing information; information that must be collected; statistical confidentiality); and

(ii) Articles 5, 13(4), 17(4), 21(4), 22(4) and 23(2) of the implementing Regulation (identification of persons who have declared goods for fiscal purposes; simplification for certain individual transactions; access to additional data sources in the case of vessels and aircraft, sea products, spacecraft and electricity);

(c) the "tax administration" within—

(i) Articles 8(2) and 8(3) of the establishing Regulation (duty to furnish lists of persons who have declared that they have supplied goods to or acquired goods from other Member States; duty to furnish information provided for fiscal purposes which could improve quality of statistics; duty to bring the Intrastat obligations to the attention of VAT-registered traders); and

(ii) Article 5 of the implementing Regulation (duty to provide specified information to identify persons who have declared goods for fiscal purposes).

(3) Also, for the purposes mentioned in paragraph (1), the duties or discretions expressed in the following Articles as those of the "Member States" must be performed or exercised by the Commissioners—

(a) Articles 10(6), 12 and 13 of the establishing Regulation (sending information on thresholds to Commission; transmission of that data; quality of that data and yearly quality report to Commission); and

(b) Articles 10, 16(2), 18, 19(3), 20(3), 23(3), 24(2), 25(2), 25(4) to 25(7) and 26(1) of the implementing Regulation (reporting nature of transaction; application of specific rules for staggered consignments, motor vehicle and aircraft parts, goods delivered to vessels and aircraft, offshore installations, electricity, military goods; transmission of data to Commission; yearly quality report to Commission).

(4) The Commissioners may do anything necessary for and reasonably incidental to any Article mentioned in paragraphs (2) and (3).
This paragraph is additional to any other basis for their doing so.

(5) For the purposes of Article 9 of the establishing Regulation (information that must or may be collected), the Commissioners must only collect information in accordance with Regulations 3, 4 and 4A (simplified information and supplementary declaration).]

NOTES

Reg 2 substituted by the Statistics of Trade (Customs and Excise) (Amendment) Regulations, SI 2004/3284 reg 3.

3 [[Information collected on the value added tax return]

(1) The Commissioners may treat the following information collected in accordance with regulations made under section 58 of, and Schedule 11 paragraphs 2(1) and 2(11) to, the Value Added Tax Act 1994 (information collected on the VAT return) for Intrastat purposes (see Article 10(1) of the establishing Regulation)—

(a)   information about the value of supplies of goods and related costs to other Member States;

(b)   information about the value of acquisitions of goods and related costs from other Member States.

(2)   If a party's annual value of intra-Community trade is at or below £260,000, that party may be treated as exempt from providing Intrastat information and is not subject to regulation 4 (supplementary declarations) (and see Article 10(1) of the establishing Regulation).]

(3)   The threshold in paragraph (2) separately applies to a party's responsibilities for providing information about "dispatches" and "arrivals" (see Articles 3, 7 and 10(2) of the establishing Regulation).]

NOTES

Reg 3 substituted by the Statistics of Trade (Customs and Excise) (Amendment) Regulations, SI 2004/3284 reg 3.

Heading substituted by the Statistics of Trade (Customs and Excise) (Amendment) Regulations, SI 2006/3216, regs 2, 3(1).

Paras (1), (2): substituted by the Statistics of Trade (Customs and Excise) (Amendment) Regulations, SI 2006/3216, regs 2, 3(2).

4 [Supplementary declarations

[(1)   A party that in relation to the United Kingdom is responsible for providing the information (see Article 7 of the establishing Regulation) must, save as otherwise directed by the Commissioners under paragraph (6A), provide it to the Commissioners in the appropriate form set out in the Schedule to these Regulations ("supplementary declaration" for "arrivals" or "dispatches").

That party must provide all the information sought by the appropriate form, in accordance with the establishing and implementing Regulations.]

That party must provide all the information sought by the appropriate form, in accordance with the establishing and implementing Regulations.

(2)   But that party need provide the "delivery terms" information sought by the appropriate form only if that party's annual value of intra-Community trade relevant to that form (namely, value of "arrivals" or value of "dispatches") exceeds [£14,500,000].

That party must use the coding mentioned in Article 11 of the implementing Regulation in providing any "delivery terms" information pursuant to paragraph (1) and this paragraph (and see also Article 9(2)(d) of the establishing Regulation).

(3)   That party must deliver the completed supplementary declaration to the Commissioners no later than the final day of the month following the end of the reference period to which it relates.

Only the reference period in Article 6(1) of the establishing Regulation applies in relation to the supplementary declaration ("calendar month of dispatch or arrival of the goods").

But the reference periods in Article 3 of the implementing Regulation may be used instead if a current Commissioners' direction so permits in the interests of better administration ("calendar month" of "chargeable event" or in which "declaration is accepted").

(4)   That party must deliver that supplementary declaration—

    (a)   to a place specified in a current Commissioners' direction, or

    (b)   by means of electronic communication.

(5)   A supplementary declaration sent by post is not presumed to have been delivered without proof of its posting.

(6)   That party may only deliver the supplementary declaration by means of electronic communication—

    (a)   if the party applies to do so and the Commissioners approve the application, or

    (b)   in accordance with any current Commissioners' direction permitting that party to do so in such circumstances as the direction may specify.

[(6A)   A party that delivers the supplementary declaration by means of electronic communication must do so in the appropriate form as directed from time to time by the Commissioners.]

(7)   The Commissioners may at any time for reasonable cause revoke or vary any approval under paragraph (6)(a).

(8)   A direction under paragraph (6)(b) may include any conditions the Commissioners deem necessary or expedient for the purpose.

(9)   A direction under paragraph (3), (4)(a)[, (6)(b) or (6A)] is not current for the purposes of the relevant paragraph to the extent that it is varied, replaced or revoked by another Commissioners' direction.]

NOTES

Reg 4 substituted by the Statistics of Trade (Customs and Excise) (Amendment) Regulations, SI 2004/3284 reg 3.

Para (1): substituted by the Statistics of Trade (Customs and Excise) (Amendment) Regulations, SI 2006/3216, regs 2, 4.

Para (2): reference in square brackets substituted by the Statistics of Trade (Customs and Excise) (Amendment) Regulations, SI 2006/3216, regs 2, 5.

Para (6A): inserted by the Statistics of Trade (Customs and Excise) (Amendment) Regulations, SI 2006/3216, regs 2, 6.

Para (9): words in square brackets substituted by the Statistics of Trade (Customs and Excise) (Amendment) Regulations, SI 2006/3216, regs 2, 7.

4A [Administration of rules concerning specific goods and movements

(1)   The Commissioners must give directions as to matters of administration for the proper application of these Regulations in the case of the rules set out in Articles 16, 17, 19, 20, 21, 22, 23 and 24 of the implementing Regulation (rules concerning specific goods and movements – staggered consignments, vessels and aircraft, goods delivered to vessels and aircraft, offshore installations, sea products, spacecraft, electricity, military goods).

(2)   The Commissioners may give such a direction in the case of the rules set out in Articles 15 and 18 of that Regulation (industrial plant, motor vehicle and aircraft parts).

---

(3) Regulation 4 (supplementary declarations) is subject to every current direction under this regulation.

(4) A direction is not current for the purposes of paragraph (3) to the extent that it is varied, replaced or revoked by another such direction.]

NOTES

Reg 4A inserted by the Statistics of Trade (Customs and Excise) (Amendment) Regulations, SI 2004/3284 reg 3. Original section 4A revoked by the Statistics of Trade (Customs and Excise) (Amendment) Regulations 1997, SI 1997/2864, regs 2, 5 (previously inserted by the Statistics of Trade (Customs and Excise) (Amendment) Regulations 1993, SI 1993/541, reg 4.)

5 Duty to keep and retain records

(1) Every person who is mentioned in the register of intra-Community operators, shall—

  (a) keep a copy of every periodic declaration [. . .] he makes [or delivers or which is made or delivered] on his behalf;

  (b) keep copies of all documents which he or anyone acting on his behalf used for the purpose of compiling [his periodic declarations];

  (c) produce or cause to be produced [periodic declarations and documents] mentioned in paragraphs (a) and (b) above when required to do so by an authorised person;

  (d) permit an authorised person exercising the powers mentioned in paragraph (c) above to make [copies or extracts of those periodic declarations and documents] or to remove them for a reasonable period.

(2) The Commissioners may require [periodic declarations and documents] mentioned in paragraph (1) above to be preserved for such period not exceeding six years as they may require.

(3) For the purpose of exercising any powers granted by this regulation an authorised person may at any reasonable time enter premises used in connection with the carrying on of a business by a person mentioned in the register of intra-Community operators or another person compiling periodic declarations on his behalf.

NOTES

Para (1): in sub-para (a) words in square brackets revoked, and in sub-paras (b)–(d) words in square brackets substituted, by the Statistics of Trade (Customs and Excise) (Amendment) Regulations 1997, SI 1997/2864, regs 2, 6 (words previously inserted and substituted by the Statistics of Trade (Customs and Excise) (Amendment) Regulations 1993, SI 1993/541, reg 5(1)); words in second pair of square brackets substituted by the Statistics of Trade (Customs and Excise) (Amendment) Regulations, SI 2004/3284 reg 4.

Para (2): words in square brackets substituted by SI 1997/2864, reg 6(2) (previously substituted by SI 1993/541, reg 5(2)).

6 Offences and evidence

(1) If any person required to [deliver] a supplementary declaration in accordance with [these Regulations] fails to do so he shall be liable on summary conviction to a penalty not exceeding level 4 on the standard scale.

(2) Any failure to [deliver] a supplementary declaration includes a failure to [provide] such supplementary declaration in the form and manner required by these Regulations. . .

(3) Subject to paragraph (4) below, for the purpose of the rules against charging more than one offence in the same information—

(a) failure to [deliver] one or more supplementary declarations of trade in goods dispatched to other Member States for any given reference period shall constitute one offence; and

(b) failure to [deliver] one or more supplementary declarations of trade in goods [arriving] from other Member States for any given reference period shall constitute one offence.

(4) If the failure in respect of which a person is convicted under paragraph (1) above is continued after the conviction he shall be guilty of a further offence and may on summary conviction thereof be punished accordingly.

(5) . . .

[(5A) . . .]

(6) . . .

(7) In any proceedings for an offence mentioned in this regulation it shall be a defence for the accused to prove that he took all reasonable precautions and exercised all due diligence to avoid the commission of such an offence by himself, any person under his control or any person to whom he transferred the task of providing information in accordance with [and subject to Article 7(2) of the establishing Regulation].

NOTES

Paras (1)–(3): words in square brackets substituted by the Statistics of Trade (Customs and Excise) (Amendment) Regulations, SI 2004/3284 reg 4(1)–(5).

Para (2): words omitted revoked by the Statistics of Trade (Customs and Excise) (Amendment) Regulations, SI 2004/3284 reg 5, Schedule.

Para (5A): revoked by the Statistics of Trade (Customs and Excise) (Amendment) Regulations 1997, SI 1997/2864, regs 2, 7(a) (previously inserted by the Statistics of Trade (Customs and Excise) (Amendment) Regulations 1993, SI 1993/541, reg 6(a)).

Paras (5), (6): revoked by the Statistics of Trade (Customs and Excise) (Amendment) Regulations, SI 2004/3284 reg 5, Schedule.

Para (7): words in square brackets substituted by the Statistics of Trade (Customs and Excise) (Amendment) Regulations, SI 2004/3284 reg 4(6).

7—

(1) In any legal proceedings, whether civil or criminal, where any question arises concerning a document furnished[, provided, delivered] or created for the purposes of the Intrastat system this regulation shall apply.

(2) Where any document does not consist of legible visual images its . . . content may be proved in any proceedings by production of a copy of the information in the form of legible visual images.

NOTES

Para (1): words in square brackets inserted by the Statistics of Trade (Customs and Excise) (Amendment) Regulations, SI 2004/3284 reg 4(7).

Para (2): words omitted revoked by the Statistics of Trade (Customs and Excise) (Amendment) Regulations 1993, SI 1993/541, reg 7.

8—

(1) A certificate of the Commissioners—

(a) that a person was or was not a party responsible for providing information in accordance with the Intrastat system;

(b)   that a person was or was not mentioned in the register of intra-Community operators;

(c)   that any information required for purposes connected with the Intrastat system has not been given or had not been given at any date;

(d)   that a copy produced in accordance with paragraph (2) of regulation 7 above is, both as to form and content, identical to that received by electronic means in accordance with [regulations 4(4)(b) and 4(6)] above

shall be sufficient evidence of that fact until the contrary is proved.

(2)   A photograph of any document furnished[, provided or delivered] to the Commissioners for the purposes of these Regulations and certified by them to be such a photograph shall be admissible in any proceedings, whether civil or criminal, to the same extent as the document itself.

(3)   Any document purporting to be a certificate under paragraph (1) or (2) above shall be deemed to be such a certificate until the contrary is proved.

NOTES

Para (1): in sub-para (1)(d), words in square brackets substituted by the Statistics of Trade (Customs and Excise) (Amendment) Regulations, SI 2004/3284 reg 4(8).

Para (2): words in square brackets inserted by the Statistics of Trade (Customs and Excise) (Amendment) Regulations, SI 2004/3284 reg 4(9).

9 Access to recorded information

(1)   Where, on an application by an authorised person, a justice of the peace or, in Scotland, a justice (within the meaning of section 462 of the Criminal Procedure (Scotland) Act 1975) is satisfied that there are reasonable grounds for believing—

(a)   that an offence in connection with the Intrastat system is being, has been or is about to be committed, and

(b)   that any recorded information (including any document of any nature whatsoever) which may be required as evidence for the purpose of any proceedings in respect of such an offence is in the possession of any person,

he may make an order in accordance with this regulation.

(2)   An order made in accordance with this regulation is an order that the person who appears to the justice to be in possession of the recorded information to which the application relates shall—

(a)   give an authorised person access to it, and

(b)   permit an authorised person to remove and take away any of it which he reasonably considers necessary,

not later than the end of the period of seven days beginning on the date of the order or the end of such longer period as the order may specify.

(3)   The reference in sub-paragraph (2)(a) above to giving an authorised person access to the recorded information to which the application relates includes a reference to permitting the authorised person to take copies of it or to make extracts from it.

(4)   Where the recorded information consists of information contained in a computer, an order made in accordance with this regulation shall have effect as an order to produce the information in a form in which it is visible and legible and, if the authorised person wishes to remove it, in a form in which it can be removed.

10—

(1)   An authorised person who removes anything in the exercise of a power conferred by or under regulation 9 above shall, if so requested by a person showing himself—

(a)   to be the occupier of premises from which it was removed, or

(b)   to have had custody or control of it immediately before the removal,

provide that person with a record of what he removed.

(2)   The authorised person shall provide the record within a reasonable time from the making of the request for it.

(3)   Subject to paragraph (7) below, if a request for permission to be granted access to anything which—

(a)   has been removed by an authorised person, and

(b)   is retained by the Commissioners for the purpose of investigating an offence,

is made to the officer in overall charge of the investigation by a person who had custody or control of the thing immediately before it was so removed or by someone acting on behalf of such a person, the officer shall allow the person who made the request access to it under the supervision of an authorised person.

(4)   Subject to paragraph (7) below, if a request for a photograph or copy of any such thing is made to the officer in overall charge of the investigation by a person who had custody or control of the thing immediately before it was so removed, or by someone acting on behalf of such a person, the officer shall—

(a)   allow the person who made the request access to it under the supervision of an authorised person for the purpose of photographing it or copying
it; or

(b)   photograph or copy it, or cause it to be photographed or copied.

(5)   Where anything is photographed or copied under sub-paragraph (4)(b) above the photograph or copy shall be supplied to the person who made the request.

(6)   The photograph or copy shall be supplied within a reasonable time from the making of the request.

(7)   There is no duty under this regulation to grant access to, or to supply a photograph or copy of, anything if the officer in overall charge of the investigation for the purposes of which it was removed has reasonable grounds for believing that to do so would prejudice—

(a)   that investigation;

(b)   the investigation of an offence other than the offence for the purposes of the investigation of which the thing was removed; or

(c)   any criminal proceedings which may be brought as a result of—

     (i)   the investigation of which he is in charge, or

    (ii)   any such investigation as is mentioned in sub-paragraph (b) above.

(8)   Any reference in this regulation to the officer in overall charge of the investigation is a reference to the person whose name and address are endorsed on the order concerned as being the officer so in charge.

11—

(1)   Where, on an application made as mentioned in paragraph (2) below, the appropriate judicial authority is satisfied that a person has failed to comply with a requirement imposed by regulation 10 above, the authority may order that person to comply with the requirement within such time and in such manner as may be specified in the order.

(2)   An application under paragraph (1) above shall be made

(a)   in the case of a failure to comply with any of the requirements imposed by paragraphs (1) and (2) of regulation 10 above, by the occupier of the premises from which the thing in question was removed or by the person who had custody or control of it immediately before it was so removed, and

(b)   in any other case, by the person who has such custody or control.

(3)   In this regulation "the appropriate judicial authority" means—

(a)   in England and Wales, a magistrates' court;

(b)   in Scotland, the sheriff; and

(c)   in Northern Ireland, a court of summary jurisdiction, as defined in Article 2(2)(a) of the Magistrates' Court (Northern Ireland) Order 1981.

(4)   In England and Wales and Northern Ireland, an application for an order under this regulation shall be made by way of complaint; and sections 21 and 42(2) of the Interpretation Act (Northern Ireland) 1954 shall apply as if any reference in those provisions to any enactment included a reference to this regulation.

12 Supplementary

Where in connection with the operation of the Intrastat system a person is convicted of an offence contrary to section 167(1) or section 168(1) of the Act, section 167(2)(a) and section 168(2)(a) of the Act shall have effect as if, in each case, for the words "6 months" there were substituted the words "3 months".

[13

The following provisions of the Act shall apply to these Regulations as they apply to the customs and excise Acts—

Sections 145 to 148 (proceedings for offences, etc);

Sections 150 to 154 (incidental provisions as to legal proceedings, mitigation of penalties, proof and other matters).]

NOTES

Added by the Statistics of Trade (Customs and Excise) (Amendment No 2) Regulations 1993,
SI 1993/3015, reg 4.

(Schedule contains the forms of Supplementary Declaration.)

CUSTOMS AND EXCISE (SINGLE MARKET ETC) REGULATIONS 1992

(SI 1992/3095)

NOTES

Made: 8 December 1992.

Authority: Customs and Excise Management Act 1979, ss 26, 35, 42, 66; European Communities Act 1972, s 2(2).

Commencement: 1 January 1993.

1 Citation and commencement

These Regulations may be cited as the Customs and Excise (Single Market etc) Regulations 1992 and shall come into force on 1st January 1993.

2 Interpretation

In these Regulations "the 1979 Act" means the Customs and Excise Management Act 1979.

3–9

(Reg 3 amends the Customs and Excise Management Act 1979, ss 1, 20, 22, 25, 26, 35, 42, 63, 64, repeals ss 37, 38, 38A of that Act, and adds ss 75B, 75C, 77B, 77C, 78(1B) of that Act; reg 4 amends the Ship's Report, Importation and Exportation by Sea Regulations 1981, SI 1981/1260; reg 5 amends the Aircraft (Customs and Excise) Regulations 1981, SI 1981/1259; reg 6 amends the Pleasure Craft (Arrival and Report) Regulations 1990, SI 1990/1169; reg 7 amends the Customs Controls on Importation of Goods Regulations 1991, SI 1991/2724; reg 8 applies to Northern Ireland only; reg 9 revokes the Customs (Land Boundary) Regulations 1953, SI 1953/1532 and the Customs (Land Boundary) Regulations 1965, SI 1965/1031.)

10—

(1)   The enactments mentioned in Schedule 1 to these Regulations shall have effect subject to the amendments there specified (being amendments consequential on regulation 3(5)).

(2)   The enactments mentioned in Schedule 2 to these Regulations are hereby repealed to the extent specified in the third column of that Schedule.

SCHEDULES

SCHEDULE 1

AMENDMENTS IN CONNECTION WITH REPEAL OF SECTION 37 OF THE 1979 ACT

Regulation 10(1)

General modification of enactments

1.   Any reference in any enactment, or subordinate legislation within the meaning of section 21(1) of the Interpretation Act 1978, to an entry on the importation of goods shall, unless the context otherwise requires, be treated as including an entry of such goods under regulation 5 of the Customs Controls on Importation of Goods Regulations 1991.

2–8.   . . .

NOTES

Paras 2–7: amend the Customs and Excise Management Act 1979, ss 1, 5, 25, 37A, 37B, 75A.

Para 8: amends the Value Added Tax Act 1983, Sch 5, Group 15.

(Sch 2 repeals the Customs and Excise Management Act 1979, ss 1(1) (in part), 26(1)(a), 35 (in part), 37, 38, 38A, the Finance Act 1981, Sch 6, paras 1–3, and the Finance Act 1984, Sch 4, Pt II, para 3, Sch 5, para 1.)

EXCISE GOODS (HOLDING, MOVEMENT, WAREHOUSING AND REDS) REGULATIONS 1992

(SI 1992/3135)

NOTES

Made: 10 December 1992.

Authority: Customs and Excise Management Act 1979, ss 93, 100G, 100H, 127A; Finance (No 2) Act 1992, ss 1, 2.

Commencement: 1 January 1993.

Modification of these regulations by the Channel Tunnel (Alcoholic Liquor and Tobacco Products) Order 2003, SI 2003/2758, art 2(a), Schedule, in their application to a control zone.

ARRANGEMENT OF REGULATIONS

PART I
PRELIMINARY

1 Citation and commencement

These Regulations may be cited as the Excise Goods (Holding, Movement, Warehousing and REDS) Regulations 1992 and shall come into force on 1 January 1993.

2 Interpretation

(1) In these Regulations except where the context requires—

"the Management Act" means the Customs and Excise Management Act 1979;

"the 1992 Act" means the Finance (No 2) Act 1992;

["accompanying document" means the accompanying administrative document set out in the Annex to Commission Regulation (EEC) No 2719/92 or, as the case may require, the simplified accompanying document set out in the Annex to Commission Regulation (EEC) No 3649/92;]

"approved" means approved by the Commissioners;

["authorised warehousekeeper" means the occupier of an excise warehouse or a person who is registered under section 41A of the Alcoholic Liquor Duties Act 1979;]

["certificate of receipt" means the certificate of receipt set out on the reverse of one or more of the copies of the accompanying document;]

. . .

"Community excise goods" means excise goods imported into the United Kingdom from another member State and which have been produced or are in free circulation in the European Community at that importation;

"duty"[, except in regulation 4(1B)(d) below,] means a duty of excise which becomes chargeable on excise goods by virtue of the enactments specified below in the definition of excise goods;

"excise duty point" (the time when the duty is payable by a person, whether or not payment may be deferred) has the meaning given by section 1 of the 1992 Act;

"excise goods" means a good . . . that is chargeable with a duty of excise by or under the Alcoholic Liquor Duties Act 1979, the Hydrocarbon Oil Duties Act 1979 or the Tobacco Products Duty Act 1979;

"excise warehouse" has the meaning given by section 1(1) of the Management Act;

"occasional importer" means a person approved under regulation 15 below;

[REDS means a registered excise dealer and shipper who is authorized, in the course of his business, to import without payment of excise duty excise goods from other member States, but who is not authorized to hold or consign those goods without first paying that duty;]

["shuttle train goods" has the meaning given in article 2 of the Channel Tunnel (Alcoholic Liquors and Tobacco Products) Order 2000;]

"tax representative" means a person who is a REDS and who agrees to be appointed, or accepts the appointment, and is appointed by a vendor pursuant to the requirements of regulation 13 below;

"tax warehouse" means an excise warehouse [and any premises registered under section 41A of the Alcoholic Liquor Duties Act 1979] [and any premises registered for the safe storage of tobacco products in accordance with regulations made under section 7(1)(b) of the Tobacco Products Duty Act 1979]; and

"vendor" means the person referred to as the vendor in subparagraph (a) of paragraph (3) below.

(2)   References in these Regulations to suspension arrangements are references to the provisions made by Part IV of these Regulations or to any provision made by or under the customs and excise Acts for enabling goods to be held or moved without payment of duty or any provisions made by or under those Acts in connection with any provision enabling goods to be so held or moved.

(3)   For the purpose of these Regulations there is a distance selling arrangement where:

(a)   a person ("the vendor"), in another member State, sells or agrees to sell goods, in that State, to a person ("the purchaser") in the United Kingdom;

(b)   those goods are dispatched by or to the order of the vendor to the purchaser or a person nominated by the purchaser and consigned to an address in the United Kingdom;

(c)   those goods will be excise goods on their importation into the United Kingdom;

(d)   the purchaser is not a revenue trader;

and "distance selling arrangements" in these Regulations shall be construed accordingly.

(4)   "UK distance selling arrangements" means a distance selling arrangement except that the vendor is in the United Kingdom (and is referred to in these Regulations as the "UK vendor"), the purchaser is in another member State, and the address to which the goods are consigned is in a member State other than the United Kingdom; and the goods that are the subject of that UK distance selling arrangement are excise goods, and will be charged with the equivalent of a duty in the member State to which they are consigned by the law of that State (and in these Regulations those goods are referred to as "excise products" and that duty is referred to as "the other member State's charge").

(5)   In these Regulations the expression "European Community" means the European Communities and the expressions "member State" and "European Communities" respectively have the meaning given to those expressions in the European Communities Act 1972; and "another member State" means a member State other than the United Kingdom, and cognate expressions shall be construed accordingly.

(6)   For the purposes of these Regulations—

(a)   excise goods being imported into the United Kingdom shall be deemed to be moved under the instructions of—

(i)   the authorised warehousekeeper who arranged the importation or to whose tax warehouse the excise goods are consigned;

(ii)   the REDS who arranged the importation;

(iii)   the occasional importer who arranged the importation; or

(iv)   the consignee if there was no such arrangement; and

(b)   in any other case excise goods shall be deemed to be moved under the instructions of the consignor.

NOTES

Para (1): definitions "accompanying document" and "certificate of receipt" substituted by the Excise Goods (Accompanying Documents) Regulations, SI 2002/501 reg 28(1), (2); definition "authorised warehousekeeper" substituted by the Warehousekeepers and Owners of Warehoused Goods Regulations 1999, SI 1999/1278, reg 23(1), (2); definition "chewing tobacco" revoked by the Tobacco Products and Excise Goods (Amendment) Regulations, SI 2006/1787, reg 2(1), (2); in definition "duty", words inserted by the Excise Goods, Beer and Tobacco Products (Amendment) Regulations, SI 2002/2692 reg 2(1) (2); in definition "excise goods" words repealed by the Tobacco Products and Excise Goods (Amendment) Regulations, SI 2006/1787, reg 2(1), (3); definition "REDS" substituted by the Hydrocarbon Oil

Part II

(Registered Remote Markers) Regulations, SI 2005/3472, reg 14; definition "shuttle train goods" inserted by virtue of the Channel Tunnel (Alcoholic Liquor and Tobacco Products) Order 2000, SI 2000/426, art 3, Sch 1, para 2; words in first pair of square brackets in definition "tax warehouse" inserted by the Beer Regulations 1993, SI 1993/1228, reg 34(a); words in second pair of square brackets added by the Tobacco Products Regulations 2001, SI 2001/1712, reg 28(2)(a).

3 Particular application of regulations and transitional arrangements for Community excise goods

(1)   With regard to Community excise goods imported into the United Kingdom ("those goods") these Regulations apply as follows.

(2)   These Regulations apply in respect of those goods imported into the United Kingdom after 31st December 1992.

(3)   Save as the Commissioners may otherwise allow, these Regulations apply in respect of those goods which were imported before 1st January 1993 and which, being required to be entered, were not entered before that date.

[(4)   Save in the case of tobacco products that were at the time of the excise duty point or immediately before that time in an excise warehouse, Part II and (except for the case of UK distance selling arrangements) Part III of these Regulations do not apply to tobacco products.]

NOTES

Para (4): added by the Tobacco Products Regulations 2001, SI 2001/1712, reg 28(2)(b).

PART II
DETERMINATION OF THE DUTY

4 Excise duty point

(1)   Except in the cases specified in paragraphs [(1A)] to (6) below, the excise duty point in relation to any Community excise goods shall be the time when the goods are charged with duty at importation.

[(1A)   In the case of excise goods acquired by a person in another member State for his own use and transported by him to the United Kingdom, the excise duty point is the time when those goods are held or used for a commercial purpose by any person.]

[(1B)   For the purposes of paragraph (1A) above—

(a)   "member State" includes the Principality of Monaco[, San Marino and the United Kingdom Sovereign Base Areas of Akrotiri and Dhekelia], but does not include the Island of Heligoland and the territory of Büsingen in the Federal Republic of Germany, Livigno, Campione d'Italia and the waters of Lake Lugano in the Italian Republic, Ceuta, Melilla and the Canary Islands in the Kingdom of Spain, or the overseas departments of the French Republic,

(b)   "own use" includes use as a personal gift,

(c)   if the goods in question are—

(i)   transferred to another person for money or money's worth (including any reimbursement of expenses incurred in connection with obtaining them), or

(ii)   the person holding them intends to make such a transfer,

those goods are to be regarded as being held for a commercial purpose,

(d)   if the goods are not duty and tax paid in the member State at the time of acquisition, or the duty and tax that was paid will be or has been reimbursed, refunded or otherwise dispensed with, those goods are to be regarded as being held for a commercial purpose,

(e) without prejudice to sub-paragraphs (c) and (d) above, in determining whether excise goods are held or used for a commercial purpose by any person regard shall be taken of—

    (i) that person's reasons for having possession or control of those goods,

    (ii) whether or not that person is a revenue trader (as defined in section 1(1) of the Customs and Excise Management Act 1979),

    (iii) that person's conduct, including his intended use of those goods or any refusal to disclose his intended use of those goods,

    (iv) the location of those goods,

    (v) the mode of transport used to convey those goods,

    (vi) any document or other information whatsoever relating to those goods,

    (vii) the nature of those goods including the nature and condition of any package or container,

    (viii) the quantity of those goods, and in particular, whether the quantity exceeds any of the following quantities—
10 litres of spirits,
20 litres of intermediate products (as defined in Article 17(1) of Council Directive 92/83/EEC),
90 litres of wine,

    (ix) whether that person personally financed the purchase of those goods,

    (x) any other circumstance that appears to be relevant,

(f) "excise goods" do not include any goods chargeable with excise duty by virtue of any provision of the Hydrocarbon Oil Duties Act 1979 or of any order made under section 10 of the Finance Act 1993.]

(2) If any duty suspension arrangements apply to any excise goods, the excise duty point shall be the earlier of—

(a) the time when the excise goods are delivered for home use from a tax warehouse or are otherwise made available for consumption, including consumption in a warehouse;

(b) the time when the excise goods are consumed;

(c) the time when the excise goods are received by a REDS or by an occasional importer or by an importer for whom the REDS is acting, or when the duty ceases to be suspended in accordance with those duty suspension arrangements;

(d) the time when the premises on which the excise goods are deposited cease to be a tax warehouse;

(e) . . .;

(f) the time when the excise goods leave any tax warehouse unless—

    (i) the goods are consigned to another tax warehouse in respect of which the authorised warehousekeeper has been approved in relation to the deposit and keeping of those goods, and the goods are moved in accordance with requirements prescribed in regulations 9 and 10 below;

    (ii) the goods are delivered for export, shipment as stores, removal to the Isle of Man; or

    (iii) any relief is conferred in relation to the goods by or under the customs and excise Acts.

(3)   If duty suspension arrangements do not apply in respect of Community excise goods consigned, in accordance with these Regulations, to a REDS or to an occasional importer or to an importer for whom a REDS is acting, the excise duty point shall be the time when those goods are received by that person.

(4)   If . . . or perfumed spirits are imported into the United Kingdom having been consigned from another member State and are charged with duty at that importation the excise duty point shall, unless those goods are deposited in a tax warehouse approved for the purpose, be the time when they are received by the importer, owner or person beneficially interested in the goods.

(5)   [Where duty suspension arrangements do not apply in respect of Community excise goods consigned to a REDS or to an occasional importer or to an importer for whom a REDS is acting and, after importation, those goods do not arrive so that the excise duty point provided by paragraph (3) above does not occur, the excise duty point provided by paragraph (1) above shall apply.]

(6)   If excise goods have been relieved from payment of duty and there is a contravention of any condition subject to which the relief was conferred, the excise duty point shall be the time of that contravention.

(7)   In this regulation "contravention" includes a failure to comply.

(8)   . . .

(9)   This regulation—

(a)   shall apply to fix an excise duty point with respect to any Community excise goods imported into the United Kingdom from another member State; and

(b)   shall not apply to fix an excise duty point with respect to any other excise goods unless and until those goods are deposited in a tax warehouse under duty suspension arrangements.

[(10)   Paragraph (9) above shall not apply in relation to shuttle train goods.]

NOTES

Para (1): figure substituted by the Excise Goods, Beer and Tobacco Products (Amendment) Regulations, SI 2002/2692 reg 2(1), (3).

Paras (1A), (1B): inserted by the Excise Goods, Beer and Tobacco Products (Amendment) Regulations, SI 2002/2692 reg 2(1), (3).

Para (1B): words substituted by the Excise Duty Points (Etc) (New Member States) Regulations 2004, SI 2004/1003 reg 8.

Para (2): sub-para (e) revoked by the Warehousekeepers and Owners of Warehoused Goods Regulations 1999, SI 1999/1278, reg 23(1), (3).

Para (4): words revoked by the Tobacco Products Regulations 2001, SI 2001/1712, reg 28(2)(c).

Para (5): words substituted by the Excise Duty Points (Duty Suspended Movements of Excise Goods) Regulations 2001, SI 2001/3022 reg 10.

Para (8): revoked by the Excise Duty Points (Duty Suspended Movements of Excise Goods) Regulations 2001, SI 2001/3022 reg 11.

Para (10): inserted by virtue of the Channel Tunnel (Alcoholic Liquor and Tobacco Products) Order 2000, SI 2000/426, art 3, Sch 1, para 3.

This regulation does not apply to the internal Community transit procedure by the Excise Duty Point (External and Internal Community Transit Procedure) Regulations 1998, SI 1998/202, reg 3.

[**4A   Excise duty point—shuttle train goods**

The excise duty point in relation to shuttle train goods shall be treated as being the time when the goods became shuttle train goods.]

NOTES

Reg 4A inserted by virtue of the Channel Tunnel (Alcoholic Liquor and Tobacco Products) Order 2000, SI 2000/426, art 3, Sch 1, para 4.

PART III
PAYMENT OF THE DUTY

5 Person liable to pay the duty

(1)   The person liable to pay the duty in the case of an importation of excise goods from another member State shall be the importer of the excise goods.

(2)   Each of the persons specified in paragraph (3) below having the specified connection with the excise goods at the excise duty point, shall be jointly and severally liable to pay the duty with the person specified in paragraph (1) above of this regulation.

(3)   The persons specified in this paragraph are—

 (a)   any authorised warehousekeeper or REDS acting on behalf of [an] importer of the excise goods in respect of the importation of those goods;

 (b)   any other person acting on behalf of the importer of the excise goods in respect of the importation of those goods;

 (c)   any vendor of the excise goods consigned to the United Kingdom under a distance selling arrangement;

 (d)   any tax representative of the vendor in subparagraph (c) above;

 (e)   any consignee of the excise goods which have been imported into the United Kingdom; and

 (f)   any other person who causes or has caused the imported goods to reach an excise duty point.

[(3A)   In the case of shuttle train goods, the following persons shall be treated as jointly and severally liable to pay the duty—

 (a)   any person who caused the goods to become shuttle train goods;

 (b)   any owner of the goods; and

 (c)   any person beneficially interested in the goods.]

(4)   The person liable to pay the duty when the excise duty point specified in paragraph 2(a) of regulation 4 above occurs, shall be the authorised warehousekeeper.

(5)   Each of the persons specified in paragraph (6) below having the specified connection with the excise goods at the excise duty point, shall be jointly and severally liable to pay the duty with the person specified in paragraph (4) above.

(6)   The persons specified (for the purposes of paragraph (5) above) are—

 (a)   any owner of those excise goods or other person beneficially interested in those goods; and

 (b)   any other person who causes or has caused those goods to reach an excise duty point.

[(6A)   The person liable to pay the duty when the excise duty point specified in paragraph (1A) or (2)(b) of regulation 4 above occurs is the person holding the excise goods at the excise duty point.]

(7)   . . .

(8)   In the UK distance selling arrangements the person liable to pay the other member State's charge in respect of the excise products shall be the UK vendor.

(9)   In this regulation "importer of the excise goods" includes any owner of those excise goods or any person beneficially interested in those excise goods.

NOTES

Para 3: word substituted by the Excise Goods (Accompanying Documents) Regulations, SI 2002/501 reg 28(1), (3)(a).

Para (3A): inserted by virtue of the Channel Tunnel (Alcoholic Liquor and Tobacco Products) Order 2000, SI 2000/426, art 3, Sch 1, para 5.

Para (6A): inserted by the Excise Goods, Beer and Tobacco Products (Amendment) Regulations, SI 2002/2692 reg 2(1), (4).

Para 7: revoked by the Excise Goods (Accompanying Documents) Regulations, SI 2002/501 reg 28(1), (3)(b).

This regulation does not apply to the internal Community transit procedure by the Excise Duty Point (External and Internal Community Transit Procedure) Regulations 1998, SI 1998/202, reg 3.

6 Time and method of payment of the duty

(1) Subject to paragraph (2) below and save as the Commissioners may otherwise direct, duty shall be paid on or before an excise duty point.

(2) In a duty deferment arrangement, and save as the Commissioners may otherwise direct, the time when the duty is to be paid shall be the time specified by that arrangement.

(3) In this regulation "duty deferment arrangement" means any provision made by or under the customs and excise Acts that permits the payment of excise duty to be deferred.

NOTES

This regulation does not apply to the internal Community transit procedure by the Excise Duty Point (External and Internal Community Transit Procedure) Regulations 1998, SI 1998/202, reg 3.

PART IV
HOLDING AND MOVEMENT

7 Movement requirements

Save as the Commissioners may otherwise allow, no person may import Community excise goods of a certain class or description into the United Kingdom unless—

    (a)   he is a REDS who has been registered in relation to excise goods of that class or description;

    (b)   . . .

    (c)   the goods are consigned to a tax warehouse which has been approved in relation to goods of that class or description; or

    (d)   he is in relation to the goods an occasional importer who has complied with the requirements of regulation 15 below.

NOTES

Para (b): revoked by the Excise Goods (Accompanying Documents) Regulations, SI 2002/501 reg 28(1), (4).

8 Holding excise goods in duty suspension and approval of the occupier etc of a tax warehouse

(1) Excise goods may be deposited and kept under duty suspension arrangements only in a tax warehouse.

(2), (3) . . .

NOTES

Paras (2), (3): revoked by the Warehousekeepers and Owners of Warehoused Goods Regulations 1999, SI 1999/1278, reg 23(1), (4).

This regulation does not apply to the internal Community transit procedure by the Excise Duty Point (External and Internal Community Transit Procedure) Regulations 1998, SI 1998/202, reg 3.

9 Moving excise goods in duty suspension

(1) Subject to regulations 10 and 11 below, Community excise goods may be moved in duty suspension from the place of importation to—

    (a)   a tax warehouse, provided that the excise goods are of a class or description specified in the Commissioners' approval of that tax warehouse;

    (b)   any other premises provided that the excise goods are moved under the instructions of—

        (i)   a REDS who is registered in respect of excise goods of the same class or description as the imported Community excise goods and who has complied with the requirements imposed by regulation 12 below; or

        (ii)   an occasional importer who has complied with the requirements imposed by regulation 15 below.

(2) Subject to regulations 10 and 11 below [and to Part V of the Beer Regulations 1993] excise goods of any class or description may be moved in duty suspension from a tax warehouse—

    (a)   to any other tax warehouse, in respect of which an authorised warehousekeeper has been approved to hold excise goods of the same class or description; or

    (b)   for export, shipment as stores or removal to the isle of Man.

(3) Excise goods in relation to which any relief is conferred by or under the customs and excise Acts may be removed from a tax warehouse without payment of duty subject to any conditions relating to that relief.

NOTES

Para (2): words in square brackets inserted by the Beer Regulations 1993, SI 1993/1228, reg 34(b).

This regulation does not apply to the internal Community transit procedure by the Excise Duty Point (External and Internal Community Transit Procedure) Regulations 1998, SI 1998/202, reg 3.

10 Movement conditions

(1) Save as the Commissioners may otherwise allow or require and except for movements between excise warehouses which the Commissioners may specify in a notice, a consignment of excise goods may not be moved under duty suspension arrangements unless—

    (a)   the duty chargeable on the excise goods, and any charge described in paragraph (4) below, is secured as provided for in that paragraph;

    (b)   the excise goods are accompanied by an [accompanying] document issued by the consignor;

    (c)   the excise goods are transported in containers or packages;

    (d)   the consignment is retained intact until one hour or such lesser period as the Commissioners may allow after the time of arrival of the excise

Part II

goods at their destination when any approved seal (referred to in subparagraph (e) below) may be broken or removed; and

(e) except as the Commissioners may allow, the containers or the packages referred to in subparagraph (c) above are secured by a seal, the form of which has been approved by the Commissioners.

(2) Except as the Commissioners otherwise allow, imported Community excise goods which are subject to a duty of excise that has not been paid and which are not consigned to a tax warehouse shall upon their importation be consigned to a REDS.

(3) In a UK distance selling arrangement the UK vendor shall—

(a) before the excise products are consigned to the address in another member State, enter into a guarantee (containing such terms and particulars as that member State may specify) for the payment of the other member State's charge;

(b) at or before the importation of the excise products into the other member State, pay or arrange the payment of the other member State's charge (and that obligation to pay or of arranging the payment shall be considered, for the purpose of this paragraph, to be discharged only if that payment is made);

(c) keep and preserve a record of each UK distance selling arrangement.

(4) The duty mentioned in subparagraph (a) of paragraph (1) above shall be secured by an approved guarantee or bond; and any charge of a similar nature to duty that may arise in another member State in respect of those excise goods, when consigned to any of the other member States, shall also be secured by such a guarantee or bond.

(5) Where excise goods which are not in duty suspension are supplied, other than by way of UK distance selling arrangements, to a relevant person and those goods are to be removed to another member State, the consignor prior to the movement of the goods, shall ensure—

(a) that the tax authorities in the member State of destination have been informed of the pending importation; and

(b) that, before those goods are imported into that other member State, the latter's charge in respect of those goods has been paid or arrangements have been made for its payment.

(6) In paragraph (5) above "relevant person" means any person acquiring, other than for private purposes, excise goods that are not in duty suspension, and "charge" means the equivalent of a duty which will be charged by the law of the other member State.

NOTES

Para (1): word in sub-para (b) substituted by the Excise Goods (Accompanying Documents) Regulations, SI 2002/501 reg 28(1), (5).

This regulation does not apply to the internal Community transit procedure by the Excise Duty Point (External and Internal Community Transit Procedure) Regulations 1998, SI 1998/202, reg 3.

---

11 Accompanying document and certificate of receipt

(1) As specified in paragraph (2) below any person who consigns excise goods from the United Kingdom in the circumstances specified therein to an address in another member State shall—

(a) issue [an accompanying document];

(b) keep a record of every accompanying document issued by him and the receipt of every certificate of receipt received by him.

(2) The persons specified in this paragraph are—

(a)   an authorised warehousekeeper who consigns excise goods under duty suspension arrangements to any person;

(b)   a trader who consigns duty-paid excise goods to himself or another trader;

(c)   . . .

(d)   a trader who consigns duty-paid excise goods to any person when the trader is entitled to claim drawback of duty by or under the customs and excise Acts in respect of those excise goods.

(3)   Any trader who receives any excise goods by way of trade shall issue [a certificate of receipt.]

(4)   The certificate of receipt shall be delivered to the consignor of the excise goods by the 15th day of the month next following the month in which the excise goods were received.

(5)   [Except in the case of any excise goods to which the Excise Goods (Accompanying Documents) Regulations 2002 apply, if] the excise goods are not received or if there is any material difference between excise goods and the description of those excise goods in any accompanying document issued to any consignee of those goods then the consignee shall—

(a)   furnish the Commissioners with a statement that the goods have not been received, or containing full particulars of that difference; and

(b)   furnish the consignor of the goods with a copy of that statement.

(6)   Upon receipt of a request made by any person concerned with the movement of any excise goods, the person who issued any accompanying document shall issue the person making the request with a certified copy of that accompanying document.

(7)   [Except in the case of any excise goods to which the Excise Goods (Accompanying Documents) Regulations 2002 apply, the] carrier of any excise goods in relation to which any accompanying document has been issued shall while carrying the goods—

(a)   keep and preserve that document; and

(b)   produce it or cause it to be produced to an officer when required to do so for the purpose of allowing the officer to inspect it, copy or take extracts from it or to remove it at a reasonable time and for a reasonable period.

(8)   In this regulation—

"trader" means any person carrying on a trade or business which consists of or includes the buying, selling, dealing or handling of excise goods; and

"duty-paid excise goods" means excise goods which have been charged with a duty of excise which has been paid or otherwise accounted for to the satisfaction of the Commissioners.

NOTES

Para 1: words in sub-para (a) substituted by the Excise Goods (Accompanying Documents) Regulations, SI 2002/501 reg 28(1), (6)(a).

Para 2: revoked by SI 2002/501 reg 28(1), (6)(b).

Para 3: words substituted by SI 2002/501 reg 28(1), (6)(c).

Para 5: words substituted by SI 2002/501 reg 28(1), (6)(d).

Para 7: words substituted by SI 2002/501 reg 28(1), (6)(e).

This regulation does not apply to the internal Community transit procedure by the Excise Duty Point (External and Internal Community Transit Procedure) Regulations 1998, SI 1998/202, reg 3.

PART V

REGISTERED EXCISE DEALERS AND SHIPPERS

12 Conditions of registration as a REDS

(1)   It shall be a condition of a REDS registration pursuant to Section 100G of the Management Act that he shall notify the Commissioners immediately in writing of any change to the particulars contained in any application that he made in discharge of a requirement imposed by the Commissioners for the purposes of obtaining that registration.

(2)   REDS may not hold or consign any excise goods under duty suspension arrangements.

(3)   A REDS who has arranged the importation of excise goods from another member State shall enter in a record the date of arrival of those excise goods on the territory of the United Kingdom, and the quantity and description of those goods, and shall do so immediately after that arrival.

13 Acting as a tax representative

Except as the Commissioners may allow, excise goods may not be consigned to an address in the United Kingdom under distance selling arrangements unless a REDS has been appointed to act as the vendor's tax representative for the purpose of accounting for the duty.

14 Accounting for duty

(1)   Subject to the provisions of this regulation a REDS shall each month furnish the Commissioners with a return (to be known as a REDS return) which has been issued to him.

(2)   A REDS shall furnish his REDS return by delivering it to the Commissioners (at the REDS central accounting centre specified on the issued REDS return) within the following period ("the critical period"), that is to say—

(a)   the critical period shall be the four consecutive days immediately following the end of the calendar month, specified in the issued REDS return, when each of those days is a business day; and

(b)   if any of those days is not a business day the critical period shall be the three consecutive business days immediately following the end of that calendar month.

(3)   Subject to any duty deferment arrangements, a REDS shall pay to the Commissioners by the end of each critical period the duty which—

(a)   is entered on a REDS return as being due from him; or

(b)   is due from him and has not been paid by him or by any other person;

and in this paragraph the duty that is due from him includes that duty for which a REDS, who is required by this Regulation to furnish a REDS return, is severally or jointly liable to pay by virtue of these Regulations, or any other provision made by or under the customs and excise Acts; and it includes any duty that should have been paid by the end of a previous critical period.

(4)   The Commissioners may impose a requirement which is different from, or is a variation of a requirement imposed by this regulation; and the paragraphs of this regulation that impose a requirement include a reference to such a different or varied requirement.

(5)   In this regulation "business day" means a day which is a business day within the meaning of section 92 of the Bills of Exchange Act 1892.

PART VI
OCCASIONAL IMPORTERS

15 Approval and requirements

(1) The Commissioners may approve a person as an occasional importer to import in the course of his business a consignment of excise goods under duty suspension arrangements.

(2) Occasional importers may not hold or consign any excise goods under duty suspension arrangements.

(3) Every occasional importer, in respect of each consignment of excise goods imported by him whether or not those goods are under duty suspension arrangements shall—

    (a)   before the excise goods are dispatched to him—

        (i)   inform the Commissioners that he is expecting the above-mentioned goods and shall supply such further particulars with respect to the consignment as the Commissioners may require;

        (ii)   pay the duty or provide a guarantee satisfactory to the Commissioners securing payment of the duty; and

        (iii)   furnish the consignor with a certificate stating that the duty has been paid or otherwise accounted for, or that the payment of duty has been secured to the satisfaction of the Commissioners.

    (b)   as soon as the excise goods have been received by him, inform the Commissioners of the arrival of the goods;

    (c)   retain the consignment intact with any seals unbroken for one hour or such other period as the Commissioners may allow or require; and

    (d)   pay any duty that has not been paid in such manner as the Commissioners may direct.

(4) . . .

(5) The Commissioners may permit a requirement which is different from or a variation of a requirement imposed by this regulation; and the paragraphs of this regulation that impose a requirement include a reference to any such different or varied requirement.

(6) In this regulation "business day" has the same meaning given by paragraph (5) of regulation 14 above.

NOTES

Para 4: revoked by the Excise Goods (Accompanying Documents) Regulations, SI 2002/501 reg 28(1), (7).

PART VII
FORFEITURE

16 Forfeiture of excise goods on which the duty has not been paid

Excise goods, in respect of which duty has not been paid, shall be liable to forfeiture where a breach of regulation 6 above or of any regulation contained in Part IV, V or VI of these Regulations, or of any condition or restriction imposed by or under such a regulation, relates to those excise goods.

REVENUE TRADERS (ACCOUNTS AND RECORDS) REGULATIONS 1992

(SI 1992/3150)

NOTES

Made: 10 December 1992.

Authority: Customs and Excise Management Act 1979, s 118A.

Commencement: 1 January 1993.

ARRANGEMENT OF REGULATIONS

1 Citation and commencement

These Regulations may be cited as the Revenue Traders (Accounts and Records) Regulations 1992 and shall come into force on 1st January 1993.

2 Interpretation

(1) In these Regulations—

"accounting period" means any period for accounting for duty allowed or prescribed by or under the customs and excise Acts;

"adjustment" means such adjustment of the duty payable in any accounting period as is allowed or prescribed by or under the customs and excise Acts with respect to errors in accounting for the duty made in any previous accounting period;

"duty" means any duty of excise;

"duty payable" means duty which is due and payable by a person whether or not payment of the duty may be deferred;

"excise duty account" is the account described in regulation 5;

"excise duty point" (the time when the duty is payable by a person whether or not payment may be deferred) has the meaning given by section 1 of the Finance (No 2) Act 1992;

"excise goods" means any goods of a class or description which is subject to a duty of excise (whether or not duty is chargeable on the goods).

(2)(a) The records, excise duty account or the copy specified in paragraph (b) below may be kept or preserved, but without prejudice to the provisions of section 118A(3) and (5) of the Customs and Excise Management Act 1979, in any form, and in particular they may be in documentary or other written form, or be in the form of anything that is commonly called or referred to as an account or a report; and the information which they contain or are to contain may be contained in or be in the form of an item described in Schedule 4 to these Regulations; and

(b) the records and other items referred to in sub-paragraph (a) above, as being specified in this sub-paragraph, are—

(i) the record and other information required by regulation 4 of these Regulations;

(ii) the excise duty account required by regulation 5 of these Regulations;

(iii) the record described in regulation 6 of these Regulations;

(iv) the record containing the information specified in paragraph (b) of regulation 7 of these Regulations; and

(v) the copy of an item required by regulation 3 of these Regulations.

(3) Schedule 1 to these Regulations shall be interpreted in accordance with the notes contained therein (called therein "Notes of interpretation").

3 Items and records (including an excise duty account) to be kept and preserved
A revenue trader who receives, prepares, maintains or issues an item described in Schedule 1 to these Regulations shall—

(a) in the case of a received item, keep and preserve the item;

(b) in the case of an issued item, keep and preserve a copy of the item; and

(c) in the case of an item that is prepared or maintained and which has not been received or which is not issued, preserve the item.

4—

(1) A revenue trader shall keep and preserve a record of—

(a) the production, buying, selling, importation, exportation, dealing in or handling of any excise goods carried on by him;

(b) the goods (whether or not they are excise goods) or services received by him in connection with or to enable him to undertake a transaction or activity described in sub-paragraph (a) of this paragraph; and

(c) the financing or the facilitation, made or effected by him, of a transaction or activity described in sub-paragraph (a) of this paragraph (whether or not that transaction or activity was carried on by him).

(2) The record, required of a revenue trader by paragraph (1) of this Regulation, shall include—

(a) in the case of a receipt by him of excise goods, the date of receipt, and the name and address of the supplier of those goods to him;

(b) in the case of the disposal by him of excise goods, the name and address, except where disposed of by a retail sale, of the person who acquires them, and the date of that disposal; and

(c) in the case of a transaction described in sub-paragraph (c) of paragraph (1) of this regulation (financing or facilitation)—

(i) the date of receipt and the name and address of the person making or effecting that transaction, where the revenue trader (keeping and preserving a record as required by paragraph (1) of this regulation) is the recipient of that transaction; and

   (ii) the date of making or effecting that transaction and the name and address of the recipient of it, where the revenue trader (keeping and preserving a record as required by paragraph (1) of this regulation) is making or effecting that transaction.

(3) The record, required of a revenue trader by paragraph (1) of this regulation, shall contain sufficient information, by way of cross referencing or otherwise, to enable an officer to trace readily any payments, made or received by that trader in respect of any excise goods or of any financing or facilitation described in sub-paragraph (c) of paragraph (1) of this regulation.

5—

(1) Subject to paragraph (2) of this regulation, a revenue trader who, in an accounting period, is liable to pay an amount of duty shall keep and preserve a record, to be known as the excise duty account, containing the particulars specified in Schedule 2 to these regulations (and this requirement to keep and preserve an excise duty account is called "the obligation" in paragraph (2) of this regulation).

(2) Where two or more revenue traders are liable jointly and severally to pay an amount of duty (called below "the debt"), and one of them (called below "the responsible revenue trader"), with the understanding of the other or, as the case may be, the others, agrees to take on the responsibility as between all of those revenue traders, to pay the debt or a portion of it, the obligation of that other or those others shall be considered, for the purposes of this regulation, to be discharged to the extent, having regard to the amount of the debt, that the debt is discharged through any payment made by the responsible revenue trader.

6

A revenue trader shall keep and preserve such records as the Commissioners may specify for any case or cases, in a notice published by them and not withdrawn by a further notice.

7 Time of recording and period of preservation of items and records (including an excise duty account)

A revenue trader required by or under these Regulations to keep a record (including an item or copy of an item governed by regulation 3 of these Regulations) or an excise duty account shall—

 (a) do so at the time of or as soon as possible after—

  (i) the happening of the event that is required by these Regulation to be recorded; and

  (ii) in any other case, the moment when the information, that is by virtue of these Regulations to be recorded, is first known to him; and

 (b) include in the record or the excise duty account sufficient information, by way of cross referencing or otherwise, to enable an officer to ascertain readily the particulars specified in Schedule 3 to these Regulations.

8

Anything that is required by or under these Regulations to be preserved by a revenue trader shall be preserved for a period of six years, or such lesser period as the Commissioners may allow, starting, on the day that the obligation to preserve arises.

[9 Claims for recovery of overpaid excise duty

Any claim under section 137A of the Customs and Excise Management Act 1979 shall be made in writing to the Commissioners and shall, by reference to such documentary evidence as is in the possession of the claimant, state the amount of the claim and the method by which that amount was calculated.]

NOTES

Added by the Revenue Traders (Accounts and Records) (Amendment) Regulations 1995, SI 1995/2893, reg 3.

[10 Interpretation of regulations 10 to 17

In this regulation and in regulations 11 to 17 below—

"claim" means a claim made (irrespective of when it was made) under section 137A of the Customs and Excise Management Act 1979 for repayment of an amount paid to the Commissioners by way of excise duty which was not due to them; and "claimed" and "claimant" shall be construed accordingly;

"reimbursement arrangements" means any arrangements (whether made before, on or after 30th January 1998) for the purposes of a claim which—

 (a) are made by a claimant for the purpose of securing that he is not unjustly enriched by the repayment of any amount in pursuance of the claim; and

 (b) provide for the reimbursement of persons (consumers) who have, for practical purposes, borne the whole or any part of the cost of the original payment of that amount to the Commissioners;

"relevant amount" means that part (which may be the whole) of the amount of a claim which the claimant has reimbursed or intends to reimburse to consumers.]

NOTES

Commencement: 11 February 1998.

Inserted, together with regs 11–17, by the Revenue Traders (Accounts and Records) (Amendment) Regulations 1998, SI 1998/62, reg 2.

[11 Reimbursement arrangements—general

Without prejudice to regulation 17 below, for the purposes of section 137A(3) of the Customs and Excise Management Act 1979 (defence by the Commissioners that repayment by them of an amount claimed would unjustly enrich the claimant) reimbursement arrangements made by a claimant shall be disregarded except where they—

 (a) include the provisions described in regulation 12 below; and

 (b) are supported by the undertakings described in regulation 16 below.]

NOTES

Commencement: 11 February 1998.

Inserted, together with regs 10, 12–17, by the Revenue Traders (Accounts and Records) (Amendment) Regulations 1998, SI 1998/62, reg 2.

[12 Reimbursement arrangements—provisions to be included

The provisions referred to in regulation 11(a) above are that—

 (a) reimbursement for which the arrangements provide will be completed by no later than 90 days after the repayment to which it relates;

 (b) no deduction will be made from the relevant amount by way of fee or charge (howsoever expressed or effected);

 (c) reimbursement will be made only in cash or by cheque;

(d)   any part of the relevant amount that is not reimbursed by the time mentioned in paragraph (a) above will be repaid by the claimant to the Commissioners;

(e)   any interest paid by the Commissioners on any relevant amount repaid by them will also be treated by the claimant in the same way as the relevant amount falls to be treated under paragraphs (a) and (b) above; and

(f)   the records described in regulation 14 below will be kept by the claimant and produced by him to the Commissioners, or to an officer of theirs in accordance with regulation 15 below.]

NOTES

Commencement: 11 February 1998.

Inserted, together with regs 10, 11, 13–17, by the Revenue Traders (Accounts and Records) (Amendment) Regulations 1998, SI 1998/62, reg 2.

[13 Repayments to the Commissioners
The claimant shall, without prior demand, make any repayment to the Commissioners that he is required to make by virtue of regulation 12(d) and (e) above within 14 days of the expiration of the period of 90 days referred to in regulation 12(a) above.]

NOTES

Commencement: 11 February 1998.

Inserted, together with regs 10–12, 14–17, by the Revenue Traders (Accounts and Records) (Amendment) Regulations 1998, SI 1998/62, reg 2.

[14 Records
The claimant shall keep records of the following matters—

(a)   the names and addresses of those consumers whom he has reimbursed or whom he intends to reimburse;

(b)   the total amount reimbursed to each such consumer;

(c)   the amount of interest included in each total amount reimbursed to each consumer;

(d)   the date that each reimbursement is made.]

NOTES

Commencement: 11 February 1998.

Inserted, together with regs 10–13, 15–17, by the Revenue Traders (Accounts and Records) (Amendment) Regulations 1998, SI 1998/62, reg 2.

[15 Production of records
(1)   Where a claimant is given notice in accordance with paragraph (2) below, he shall, in accordance with such notice produce to the Commissioners, or to an officer of theirs, the records that he is required to keep pursuant to regulation 14 above.

(2)   A notice given for the purposes of paragraph (1) above shall—

(a)   be in writing;

(b)   state the place and time at which, and the date on which the records are to be produced; and

(c)   be signed and dated by the Commissioners, or by an officer of theirs, and may be given before or after, or both before and after the Commissioners have paid the relevant amount to the claimant.]

NOTES

Commencement: 11 February 1998.

Inserted, together with regs 10–14, 16, 17, by the Revenue Traders (Accounts and Records) (Amendment) Regulations 1998, SI 1998/62, reg 2.

[16 Undertakings

(1) Without prejudice to regulation 17(b) below, the undertakings referred to in regulation 11(b) above shall be given to the Commissioners by the claimant no later than the time at which he makes the claim for which the reimbursement arrangements have been made.

(2) The undertakings shall be in writing, shall be signed and dated by the claimant, and shall be to the effect that—

(a) at the date of the undertakings he is able to identify the names and addresses of those consumers whom he has reimbursed or whom he intends to reimburse;

(b) he will apply the whole of the relevant amount repaid to him, without any deduction by way of fee or charge or otherwise, to the reimbursement in cash or by cheque, of such consumers by no later than 90 days after his receipt of that amount (except insofar as he has already so reimbursed them);

(c) he will apply any interest paid to him on the relevant amount repaid to him wholly to the reimbursement of such consumers by no later than 90 days after his receipt of that interest;

(d) he will repay to the Commissioners without demand the whole or such part of the relevant amount repaid to him or of any interest paid to him as he fails to apply in accordance with the undertakings mentioned in sub-paragraphs (b) and (c) above;

(e) he will keep the records described in regulation 14 above; and

(f) he will comply with any notice given to him in accordance with regulation 15 above concerning the production of such records.]

NOTES

Commencement: 11 February 1998.

Inserted, together with regs 10–15, 17, by the Revenue Traders (Accounts and Records) (Amendment) Regulations 1998, SI 1998/62, reg 2.

[17 Reimbursement arrangements made before 11th February 1998

Reimbursement arrangements made by a claimant before 11th February 1998 shall not be disregarded for the purposes of section 137A(3) of the Customs and Excise Management Act 1979 if, not later than 11th March 1998—

(a) he includes in those arrangements (if they are not already included) the provisions described in regulation 12 above; and

(b) gives the undertakings described in regulation 16 above.]

NOTES

Commencement: 11 February 1998.

Inserted, together with regs 10–16, by the Revenue Traders (Accounts and Records) (Amendment) Regulations 1998, SI 1998/62, reg 2.

SCHEDULES

SCHEDULE 1

RECEIVED, PREPARED, MAINTAINED OR ISSUED ITEMS

Regulation 3

1. An invoice.
2. A credit note.
3. A debit note.
4. A record relating to an importation or to an exportation.
5. A statement of account.
6. A record of payment or of receipt.
7. A journal or a ledger.
8. A profit and loss account, trading account, management account, management report or balance sheet.
9. An internal or an external auditor's report.
10. A record relating to any drawback, repayment or reimbursement of duty.
11. A record required, other than by virtue of these Regulations, by or under the customs and excise Acts.
12. Any other record maintained for a trading or business purpose.

NOTES OF INTERPRETATION

1. In paragraph 1 to 12 above the item, described therein, includes anything in any form that it may take when the information, to which the item relates, is received, or, as the case may be, when that information is dealt with for the purpose of preparing, maintaining or issuing an item, and which it may take subsequently whilst it is being preserved by the revenue trader who received it or, as the case may be, prepared or maintained it or issued it.

2. In note (1) above "anything" includes—
   (a) an item described in Schedule 4 to these Regulations containing the information which is expressly or impliedly described in paragraph 1 to 12 above or which is obtained for a purpose described in those paragraphs; and
   (b) anything which is commonly called or referred to as an account or a report.

3. In note 1 above "form" includes documentary or other written form.

4. In paragraph 4, 6 and 10 above "record" means anything containing the information expressly or impliedly described, respectively, in those paragraphs, irrespective of its form.

5. In paragraph 11 above "record" means anything containing information which is required by or under the legislation specified therein, irrespective of its form.

6. In paragraph 12 above "record" means anything that is maintained for the purposes specified therein, irrespective of its form.

SCHEDULE 2

PARTICULARS OF THE EXCISE DUTY ACCOUNT

Regulation 5

1. The amount, before adjustment, of any duty payable by the revenue trader in each accounting period.
2. The amount of any adjustment in each accounting period.

3. The amount, after any adjustment, of any duty payable by the revenue trader in each accounting period.

4. The amount, date and method of payment of any duty paid by the revenue trader.

SCHEDULE 3
PARTICULARS TO BE READILY ASCERTAINABLE
Regulation 7

1. The particulars specified at paragraph 2 below are to be kept by reference to each accounting period of the revenue trader, and in respect of each transaction, involving excise goods, that gives rise to a joint or several liability on the part of that revenue trader to pay (and the amount of duty for which the revenue trader is liable jointly or severally is called in paragraph 2 below "the amount of duty").

2.—(1) Particulars showing how the amount of duty was calculated, including the nature, quantity and value of the excise goods for the purpose of that calculation, and the applicable rate of that duty.

(2) Particulars of the circumstances and of the reasons relied on by the revenue trader for the making of an adjustment.

(3) Particulars of the excise duty point.

SCHEDULE 4
Regulation 2(2), Schedule 1

1. A drawing, graph, map or plan.

2. A photocopy.

3. A disc, sound track, tape, or other device in which sounds or other data (not being visual images) are recorded so as to be capable (with or without the aid of some other equipment) of being reproduced therefrom.

4. Any film, microfilm, negative, tape or other device in which one or more visual images are recorded so as to be capable (as aforesaid) of being reproduced therefrom.

5. A transcript or reproduction.

EXCISE DUTIES (DEFERRED PAYMENT) REGULATIONS 1992
(SI 1992/3152)

NOTES

Made: 10 December 1992.

Authority: Customs and Excise Management Act 1979, ss 93, 127A; Alcoholic Liquor Duties Act 1979, ss 13, 15, 56, 62(5); Hydrocarbon Oil Duties Act 1979, ss 21, 24; European Communities Act 1972, s 2(2).

ARRANGEMENT OF REGULATIONS

PART I
PRELIMINARY

PART I
PRELIMINARY

1 Citation, commencement and revocation

(1)   These Regulations may be cited as the Excise Duties (Deferred Payment) Regulations 1992 and shall come into force on 1st January 1993.

(2)   . . .

NOTES

Para (2): revokes the Excise Duties (Deferred Payment) Regulations 1983, SI 1983/947, the Excise Duties (Hydrocarbon Oils) (Deferred Payment) Regulations 1985, SI 1985/1032, the Excise Duties (Deferred Payment) (Amendment) Regulations 1986, SI 1986/910, the Excise Duties (Deferred Payment) (Amendment) Regulations 1989, SI 1989/1368.

---

2 Interpretation

In these Regulations—

"approved person" means a person approved by the Commissioners under regulation 4 below;

["biofuels" means a liquid that is charged with excise duty under section 6AA(2) (biodiesel), 6AD(2) (bioethanol) or 6A(2) (other liquid fuel substitutes) of the Hydrocarbon Oil Duties Act 1979;]

"business day" means a day which is a business day within the meaning of section 92 of the Bills of Exchange Act 1882;

"hydrocarbon oils" means goods ([except biofuels and road fuel gas]) chargeable with excise duty by virtue of the Hydrocarbon Oil Duties Act 1979 and includes composite goods containing hydrocarbon oils on which goods excise duty is chargeable;

"imported by a registered excise dealer and shipper" includes any importation where goods are moved under the instructions of a registered excise dealer and shipper or are, in accordance with registered excise dealers and shippers regulations, deemed to be so moved;

"made-wine" includes composite goods containing made-wine on which goods excise duty is chargeable;

"spirits" includes composite goods containing spirits on which goods excise duty is chargeable;

"payment day" has the meaning given by regulation 5 below;

"wine" includes composite goods containing wine on which goods excise duty is chargeable.

NOTES

Definition "biofuels" inserted, and definition "hydrocarbon oil" amended, by the Biofuels and Other Fuel Substitutes (Payment of Excise Duties etc) Regulations 2004, SI 2004/2065 reg 5(1), (2).

3 Application

These Regulations shall apply to goods on which excise duty would, but for deferment granted by these Regulations, be payable on or after 1st January 1993; being goods of any of the following descriptions—

(a) wine, made-wine, cider, spirits, [biofuels,] hydrocarbon oils; and

(b) beer imported by a registered excise dealer and shipper.

NOTES

Word in para (a) inserted by the Biofuels and Other Fuel Substitutes (Payment of Excise Duties etc) Regulations 2004, SI 2004/2065 reg 5(1), (3).

PART II
DEFERMENT OF EXCISE DUTY

4 Approved persons

(1) A person who wishes to be granted excise duty deferment under these Regulations shall apply to be approved for excise duty deferment purposes.

(2) When approving a person under this regulation the Commissioners may specify the maximum amount of excise duty which may be deferred by that person at any time under that approval.

(3) When approving a person under this regulation the Commissioners may limit the approval to deferment in respect of goods which are at specified places.

(4) A person may be approved separately under this regulation in respect of different places.

(5) The Commissioners may, for reasonable cause, at any time vary or revoke any approval granted under this regulation.

5 Deferment

(1) Deferment shall be granted upon the giving of notice by an approved person that he wishes excise duty in respect of any goods to be deferred until a day, to be known as "payment day", provided that the notice is given in such form and manner and contains such particulars as the Commissioners may require and provided that the provisions of these Regulations are complied with.

(2) Subject to regulation 6 below, on each payment day an approved person shall pay to the Commissioners the total amount of excise duty of which he has been granted deferment until that payment day.

(3) Payment day shall be—

(a) in the case of beer imported by a registered excise dealer and shipper, the 25th day of the month following the month in which the duty would, but for deferment granted by these Regulations, be payable;

(b) in the case of any goods other than beer imported by a registered excise dealer and shipper, the 15th day of the month following the month in which the duty on those goods would, but for deferment granted by these Regulations, be payable;

[(ba)   in the case of biofuels on which the duty would, but for deferment granted by these Regulations, be payable on or after the 15th day of one month and not later than the 14th day of the next month, the last business day of that next month;]

(c)   in the case of hydrocarbon oils delivered for home use from a refinery or other premises used for the production of hydrocarbon oil or from an excise warehouse on or after the 15th day of one month and not later than the 14th day of the next month, the last business day of that next month; and

(d)   in any other case, where the duty on those goods would, but for deferment granted by these Regulations, be payable on or after the 15th day of one month and not later than the 14th day of the next month, either—

     (i)   the 29th day of that next month; or

     (ii)   where that next month has only 28 days, the 28th day of that month;

provided that where the payment day would, if determined in accordance with the foregoing provisions of this paragraph, fall on a day upon which the Bank of England is closed, the payment day shall be, in the case mentioned in sub-paragraph (b) above the next business day following that day and, in any other case, the last business day preceding that day.

NOTES

Para 3: sub-para (ba) inserted by the Biofuels and Other Fuel Substitutes (Payment of Excise Duties etc) Regulations 2004, SI 2004/2065 reg 5(1), (4).

---

6 Set-offs

(1) Subject to paragraph (2) below an approved person shall set-off all sums to which he is entitled as rebate under section 11 of the Hydrocarbon Oil Duties Act 1979 all sums to which he is entitled to repayment under section 15 of that Act [all sums to which he is entitled as relief in accordance with regulations made under section 20AA of that Act, all sums to which he is entitled to repayment under] [, regulation 3(1)(b) of the Hydrocarbon Oil Duties (Marine Voyages Reliefs) Regulations 1996][, all sums to which he is entitled to relief under regulation 21 of the Biofuels and Other Fuel Substitutes (Payment of Excise Duties etc) Regulations 2004] and such other sums as the Commissioners may allow against excise duty required to be paid by him on payment day under regulation 5 above.

(2) An approved person shall not set-off those sums referred to in paragraph (1) above unless on or before the said payment day he submits to the Commissioners a claim for set-off in such form and manner and containing such particulars as they may require.

(3) Rebate shall not be set-off under paragraph (1) above at a payment day earlier than that on which duty deferred under these Regulations, in respect of which the rebate exists, would have been due.

NOTES

Para (1): words in first square brackets inserted by the Hydrocarbon Oil (Registered Remote Markers) Regulations, SI 2005/3472, reg 15; words in second square brackets inserted by the Hydrocarbon Oil Duties (Marine Voyages Reliefs) Regulations 1996, SI 1996/2537, reg 15(a). Words in third square brackets inserted by the Biofuels and Other Fuel Substitutes (Payment of Excise Duties etc) Regulations 2004, SI 2004/2065 reg 5(1), (5).

---

7 Adjustments

(1)   If a notice has been given under regulation 5 above or any other document has been submitted to the Commissioners in respect of excise duty deferment and the Commissioners are satisfied that the full amount of excise duty payable has not been shown then, save as the Commissioners may otherwise allow, the balance of excise duty shall be paid forthwith.

(2)   If a notice has been given under regulation 5 above or any other document has been submitted to the Commissioners in respect of excise duty deferment and the Commissioners are satisfied that excise duty in excess of the amount payable has been shown other than by reason of a set-off under regulation 6 above, the Commissioners shall repay or give credit for that excess, but the total amount shown shall nonetheless be paid on payment day.

PART III
REQUIREMENTS TO BE OBSERVED

8 Security

A person who is approved for the purpose of applying for deferment of excise duty shall provide such security for that duty in such form and manner and in such amount as the Commissioners may require.

9 Conditions

The Commissioners may make any approval of a person or any grant of deferment of duty subject to any condition or requirement and conditions or requirements may be added to or varied at any time by the Commissioners.

10 Change of circumstances

Any person who has applied to be approved or has been approved under regulation 4 above shall notify the Commissioners immediately of any change in circumstances which materially affects any application for approval or for deferment of duty or any security given by him under these Regulations.

PART IV
RELATIONSHIP TO OTHER ENACTMENTS

11 Purposes for which excise duty is treated as paid

Without prejudice to regulation 5 above for the purposes of the following enactments excise duty shall be deemed to have been paid at the time when deferment was granted—

(a)   sections 24(2)(b), [43(1), 49(1)(a)], 51, 67(1)(b), 96(1)(a), 127 and 162 of the Customs and Excise Management Act 1979;

(b)   sections 10(2)(a) and 11(1)(a) of the Customs and Excise Duties (General Reliefs) Act 1979;

(c)   sections 16, 21, 22(1), 22(3A), 22(5), 42 and 43 of the Alcoholic Liquor Duties Act 1979;

(d)   sections 9(4), 15(1), 17(1), . . . 19(3), 19A(1) and 20(1) of the Hydrocarbon Oils Duties Act 1979;

[(e)   regulation 3(1)(b) of the Hydrocarbon Oil Duties (Marine Voyages Reliefs) Regulations 1996][;

(f)   regulation 21 of the Biofuels and Other Fuel Substitutes (Payment of Excise Duties etc) Regulations 2004.]

NOTES

Figures in square brackets substituted, figures omitted revoked, and para (e) inserted, by the Hydrocarbon Oil Duties (Marine Voyages Reliefs) Regulations 1996, SI 1996/2537, reg 15(b)–(d). Para (f) inserted by the Biofuels and Other Fuel Substitutes (Payment of Excise Duties etc) Regulations 2004, SI 2004/2065 reg 5(1), (6).

12 Savings for requirements of other Regulations

Nothing in these Regulations shall be taken to remove any obligation placed upon any person to comply with the requirements or conditions imposed by or under any other Regulations relating to the goods in respect of which payment of duty is deferred under these Regulations, except in so far as those other Regulations relate to the date for payment of duty and deferment of that payment is granted under these Regulations.

EXCISE DUTIES (PERSONAL RELIEFS) ORDER 1992

(SI 1992/3155)

NOTES

These Regulations revoked by the Excise Duties (Personal Reliefs) (Revocation) Order, SI 2002/2691 with effect from 1 December 2002.

CUSTOMS AND EXCISE (PERSONAL RELIEFS FOR SPECIAL VISITORS) ORDER 1992

(SI 1992/3156)

NOTES

Made: 10 December 1992.

Authority: Customs and Excise Duties (General Reliefs) Act 1979, s 13A.

PART I
PRELIMINARY

1

This Order may be cited as the Customs and Excise (Personal Reliefs for Special Visitors) Order 1992 and shall come into force on 1st January 1993.

PART II
INTERPRETATION

2

In this Order—

"acquisition" means an acquisition of goods from another member State within the meaning of section 2A of the Value Added Tax Act 1983, and "acquired" shall be construed accordingly;

"duty" means any duty of customs or duty of excise;

"importation" means an importation from a place outside the member States, and "imported" shall be construed accordingly;

"relief" means the remission of any duty or tax which is chargeable and which a person, whether the person upon whom the relief is conferred or some other person, would be liable to pay were it not for the relief conferred;

"supply" means a supply within the meaning of section 3 of the Value Added Tax Act 1983 and "supplied" shall be construed accordingly;

"tax" means value added tax;

"United Kingdom national" means a British citizen, a British Dependent Territories citizen, a British National (Overseas) or a British Overseas citizen;

"used", in relation to a person's use of consumable property, includes having the property at his disposal;

"warehouse" means a warehouse within the meaning of section 1(1) of the Customs and Excise Management Act 1979, [the premises in respect of which a person is registered under section 41A, 47, or 62(2) of the Alcoholic Liquor Duties Act 1979, the premises in respect of which a person holds an excise licence under section 54(2) or 55(2) of that Act, or premises registered for the safe storage of tobacco products in accordance with regulations made under section 7(1)(b) of the Tobacco Products Duty Act 1979;] and "removal from warehouse" shall be construed accordingly.

NOTES

In definition of "warehouse", words in square brackets inserted by the Customs and Excise (Personal Reliefs for Special Visitors) (Amendment) Order, SI 2007/5, art 2.

PART III
CONDITIONS ATTACHING TO PART VI RELIEFS

3

In this Part—

"entitled person" means an entitled person for the purposes of Part VI.

4

It shall be a condition of the relief conferred under article 16 below that the entitled person deliver or cause to be delivered to the supplier of the motor vehicle a certificate in the form numbered 1 in the Schedule to this Order—

    (a)   containing full information in respect of the matters specified therein; and

    (b)   signed—

        (i)   as to Part A, by the entitled person upon whom the relief is conferred;

        (ii)   as to Part B, by the head of the mission or other body or organisation of which the entitled person is a member;

        (iii)   as to Part C, by the Secretary of State or a person authorised to sign on his behalf; and

        (iv)   as to Part D, by the supplier,

before the supply is made.

PART IV
CONDITIONS ATTACHING TO PART VII RELIEFS

5—

(1) In this Part—

"entitled person" means an entitled person for the purposes of Part VII.

(2) For the purposes of articles 6 and 7 below, any reference to a certificate shall be construed as including a reference to a copy of such a certificate.

6—

(1) It shall be a condition of relief conferred under article 19 below that the entitled person deliver or cause to be delivered in accordance with paragraph (2) below five certificates in the form numbered 2 in the Schedule to this Order—

    (a)   containing full information in respect of the matters specified therein; and

    (b)   signed—

        (i)   as to Part A, by the entitled person upon whom the relief is conferred; and

        (ii)   as to Part B, by the officer commanding the visiting force or other body or organisation of which the entitled person is a member or by a person authorised to sign on his behalf.

(2) The certificates referred to in paragraph (1) above shall be delivered before the supply is made as follows:

    (a)   two certificates shall be delivered to the visiting force or other body or organisation of which the entitled person is a member;

    (b)   two certificates shall be delivered to the proper officer; and

    (c)   one certificate shall be delivered to the supplier of the motor vehicle.

7—

(1) It shall be a condition of relief conferred under article 20 below in respect of a motor vehicle that the entitled person deliver or cause to be delivered in accordance with paragraph (2) below four certificates in the form numbered 3 in the Schedule to this Order—

    (a)   containing full information in respect of the matters specified therein; and

    (b)   signed—

        (i)   as to Part A, by the entitled person upon whom the relief is conferred; and

        (ii)   as to Part B, by the officer commanding the visiting force or other body or organisation of which the entitled person is a member or by a person authorised to sign on his behalf.

(2) The certificates referred to in paragraph (1) above shall be delivered before the goods are removed by or on behalf of the entitled person as follows:

    (a)   one certificate shall be delivered to the visiting force or other body or organisation of which the entitled person is a member; and

    (b)   three certificates shall be delivered to the proper officer.

PART V
CONDITIONS ATTACHING TO ALL RELIEFS

8

In this Part—

    "entitled person" means an entitled person for the purposes of either part VI or Part VII of this Order.

9

An entitled person upon whom any relief is conferred under any Part of this Order shall be bound by the conditions described in the following provisions of this Part and in Part III or IV above, as the case may be.

10—

(1) It shall be a condition of the relief that the goods shall not be lent, hired-out, given as security or transferred by the entitled person or any other person without the prior authorisation in writing of the Commissioners.

(2) Where the Commissioners authorise such disposal as is mentioned in paragraph (1) above, they may discharge the relief and the entitled person to whom the relief was afforded shall forthwith pay the duty or tax at the rate then in force,

provided that where a lower rate was in force when relief was afforded the amount payable shall be determined by reference to the lower rate.

11

It shall be a condition of the relief that the goods are used exclusively by the entitled person or members of his family forming part of his household.

12

Where relief has been afforded and subsequently the Commissioners are not satisfied that any condition attaching to such relief, whether by virtue of a provision of this Order or otherwise, has been complied with, then, unless the Commissioners sanction the non-compliance in writing, the duty or tax shall become payable forthwith and the goods shall be liable to forfeiture.

13

Where relief has been afforded, but any duty or tax subsequently becomes payable by virtue of article 12 above, the following persons shall be jointly and severally liable to pay it—

    (a)   the entitled person upon whom the relief was conferred;

    (b)   any person who, at or after the time of the non-compliance with the condition which has caused the duty or tax to become payable, has been in possession of the goods.

PART VI

DIPLOMATS ETC

14

In this Part—

    "entitled person" means—

        (a)   any person enjoying any privilege or immunity by virtue or his being—

            (i)   a diplomatic agent for the purposes of the Diplomatic Privileges Act 1964,

            (ii)   a senior officer of the Commonwealth Secretariat for the purposes of the Commonwealth Secretariat Act 1966,

            (iii)   a consular officer for the purposes of the Consular Relations Act 1968,

            (iv)   a representative or a person recognised as holding a rank equivalent to a diplomatic agent for the purposes of the International Organisations Act 1968, or

        (b)   any person enjoying, under or by virtue of section 2 of the European Communities Act 1972, any privilege or immunity similar to those enjoyed under or by virtue of the enactments referred to in paragraph (a) above by the persons therein specified,

who is neither a United Kingdom national nor a permanent resident of the United Kingdom.

15

Where any tobacco product or beverage containing alcohol is removed from warehouse in the course of its being supplied to an entitled person, payment of any duty or tax chargeable in respect of the removal from warehouse or supply shall not be required.

Part II

16—

(1)   Subject to the following provisions of this article, where an entitled person purchases a motor vehicle which has been manufactured in a country, other than the United Kingdom, which is—

(a)   a member State; or

(b)   a member of the European Free Trade Association,

payment of any tax chargeable in respect of the supply shall not be required.

(2)   No relief shall be afforded under paragraph (1) above if the entitled person has previously been afforded relief in respect of any other motor vehicle, whether under paragraph (1) above or otherwise, unless he has disposed of all previous motor vehicles in respect of which relief has been so afforded and paid any duty or tax which was required to be paid under article 10(2) above.

(3)   Where the spouse [or civil partner] of the entitled person is present in the United Kingdom, paragraph (2) above shall apply as if the words "(or all but one)" were inserted after the words "motor vehicles".

NOTES

Para (3): words in square brackets inserted by the Civil Partnership Act 2004 (Amendments to Subordinate Legislation) Order, SI 2005/2114 art 2(1), Sch 1 para 5, with effect from 5 December 2005.

17

Nothing in this Part of this Order shall be taken as conferring relief in respect of any duty or tax which is subject to remission or refund by or under any of the enactments referred to in article 14 above.

PART VII

VISITING FORCES AND HEADQUARTERS

18

In this Part—

"entitled person" means a person who is—

(a)   for the purposes of any provision of the Visiting Forces Act 1952, a serving member of a visiting force of a country, other than the United Kingdom, which is a party to the North Atlantic Treaty, or a person recognised by the Secretary of State as a member of a civilian component of such a force, or

(b)   a person who is a military or civilian member of a headquarters or organisation designated for the purposes of any provision of the International Headquarters and Defence Organisations Act 1964,

who is neither a United Kingdom national nor a permanent resident of the United Kingdom.

19

Subject to article 22 below, where an entitled person purchases a motor vehicle which has been manufactured in a country which is—

(a)   a member State; or

(b)   a member of the European Free Trade Association,

payment of any tax in respect of the supply shall not be required.

20

Subject to article 22 below, where an entitled person imports, acquires or removes from warehouse any goods, payment of any duty or tax chargeable in respect of the importation, acquisition or removal from warehouse shall not be required.

21

Subject to article 22 below, where a gift of goods, other than tobacco products or beverages containing alcohol, is made to an entitled person by dispatching them to him from a place outside the United Kingdom, payment of any duty or tax chargeable in respect of their acquisition or importation shall not be required.

22—

(1)   No relief shall be afforded under this Part of this Order in respect of a motor vehicle if the entitled person has previously been afforded relief under this Order in respect of any other motor vehicle, unless he has disposed of all previous motor vehicles in respect of which relief has been so afforded and paid any duty or tax which was required to be paid under article 10(2) above.

(2)   Where the spouse [or civil partner] of the entitled person is present in the United Kingdom, paragraph (1) above shall apply as if the words "(or all but one)" were inserted after the words "motor vehicles".

NOTES

Para (2): words in square brackets inserted by the Civil Partnership Act 2004 (Amendments to Subordinate Legislation) Order, SI 2005/2114 art 2(1), Sch 1 para 5, with effect from 5 December 2005.

SCHEDULE

Article 4

FORM 1

**Certificate for use in Connection with the Purchase of an EC (not UK) or
EFTA Origin Vehicle free of Value Added Tax**

Part A: To be completed by entitled person		
Surname	Forenames	Rank or status
Embassy/High Commission/International Organisation		
Signature of entitled person.		Date

Part B: Certificate by Head of Mission	
	Official Stamp
Signature	
Name	
(BLOCK LETTERS)	

Part C: Certificate by Foreign & Commonwealth Office

This is to certify that the above named is entitled to purchase an EC or EFTA origin vehicle at a VAT exclusive price.

Signature .... Department .... Date ....

Part D: Particular of Vehicle (to be completed by supplier)		
Make and model	Engine number	Chassis number
Vehicle registration mark	Year of manufacture	

Name of supplier ....

Signature of supplier .... Date ....

C 428   CD3433/N3(12/92)   F 8860(   )

HM Customs and Excise

Visiting Forces' Certificate of Entitlement to Relief from Value Added Tax on the purchase of a New Means of Transport

Please complete five copies

Part A: To be completed by entitled person

Surname	Forenames	Rank and Service No.

Base in the UK to which assigned

Private address in the UK

*Particulars of vehicle/ship/aircraft

Make and model		Engine number	Chassis/Hull/Airframe number

Registration mark			Year of manufacture

Name and address
of supplier ....
....

Declaration

I declare that:-

I am a member of *the civilian component of/the.. visiting forces
and that the details given above are true and complete.

Signature of entitled person. .... Date ....

Part B Certificate by Visiting Force

I certify that .... is a member of *the civilian
component of/the visiting forces serving in the United Kingdom.

Signature .... Date ....

Name and rank (in BLOCK LETTERS) ....

For official use

Date stamp

* delete as necessary

C&E 941A   PCU (October 1997)
© Crown Copyright. Reproduced by permission of the Controller of Her Majesty's Stationery Office. Published by LexisNexis Butterworths.

Part II

HM Customs and Excise

Visiting Forces' Certificate of Entitlement to Relief from Duty and Value Added Tax on the Import/Withdrawal from Warehouse of a Motor Vehicle or on the Acquisition of a New Means of Transport

Please complete four copies.

Part A: To be completed by entitled person

Surname	Forenames	Rank and Service No.

Base in the UK to which assigned

Private address in the UK

*Particulars of vehicle/new means of transport

Make and model	Engine number	Chassis/Hull/Airframe number
Registration mark		Year of manufacture

Declaration

I declare that:-

I am a member of *the civilian component of/the .... visiting forces and that the details given above are true and complete.

Signature of entitled person. .... Date ....

Part B Certificate by Visiting Force

I certify that .... is a member of *the civilian component of/the visiting forces serving in the United Kingdom.

Signature .... Date ....

Name and rank (in BLOCK LETTERS) ....

For official use

Date stamp

* delete as necessary

C&E 941

PCU (October 1997)

CUSTOMS AND EXCISE DUTIES (PERSONAL RELIEFS FOR GOODS PERMANENTLY IMPORTED) ORDER 1992

(SI 1992/3193)

NOTES

Made: 16 December 1992.

Authority: Customs and Excise Duties (General Reliefs) Act 1979, ss 7, 13.

ARRANGEMENT OF ARTICLES

PART I
PRELIMINARY

1 Citation and commencement

This Order may be cited as the Customs and Excise Duties (Personal Reliefs for Goods Permanently Imported) Order 1992 and shall come into force on 1st January 1993.

2 Interpretation

In this Order—

"declared for relief" has the meaning assigned to it by article 8 below;

"household effects" means furnishings and equipment for personal household use;

"motor vehicle" shall include a trailer;

"normal residence" means a person's principal place of abode situated in the country where he is normally resident;

"normally resident" has the meaning assigned to it by article 3 below;

"occupational ties" shall not include attendance by a pupil or student at a school, college or university;

"personal ties" shall mean family or social ties to which a person devotes most of his time not devoted to occupational ties;

"property" means any personal property intended for personal use or for meeting household needs and shall include household effects, household provisions, household pets and riding animals, cycles, motor vehicles, caravans, pleasure boats and private aircraft, provided that there shall be excluded any goods which, by their nature or quantity, indicate that they are being imported for a commercial purpose;

"third country", shall have the meaning given by Article 3.1 of Council Directive 77/388/EEC;

"used", in relation to a person's use of consumable property, shall include having the property at his disposal.

3 Rules for determining where a person is normally resident

(1) This article shall apply for the purpose of determining, in relation to this Order, where a person is normally resident.

(2) A person shall be treated as being normally resident in the country where he usually lives—

(a)   for a period of, or periods together amounting to, at least 185 days in a period of twelve months;

(b)   because of his occupational ties; and

(c)   because of his personal ties.

(3) In the case of a person with no occupational ties, paragraph (2) above shall apply with the omission of sub-paragraph (b), provided his personal ties show close links with that country.

(4) Where a person has his occupational ties in one country and his personal ties in another country, he shall be treated as being normally resident in the latter country provided that either—

(a)   his stay in the former country is in order to carry out a task of a definite duration, or

(b)   he returns regularly to the country where he has his personal ties.

(5) Notwithstanding paragraph (4) above, a United Kingdom citizen whose personal ties are in the United Kingdom but whose occupational ties are in a third country may for the purposes of relief under this Order be treated as normally resident in the country of his occupational ties, provided he has lived there for a period of, or periods together amounting to, at least 185 days in a period of twelve months.

4 Supplementary

For the purposes of this Order—

(a)   any reference to a person who has been normally resident in a third country and who intends to become normally resident in the United Kingdom shall be taken as a reference to a person who intends to comply with the requirements of paragraphs (2), (3) or (4) of article 3 above, as the case may be, for being treated as normally resident in the United Kingdom;

(b)   the date on which a person becomes normally resident in the United Kingdom shall be the date when having given up his normal residence in a third country he is in the United Kingdom for the purpose of fulfilling such intention as is mentioned in paragraph (a) above.

PART II
PROVISIONS COMMON TO CERTAIN RELIEFS

5 Property may be in separate consignments

Except as otherwise provided by this Order, where property in respect of which relief is afforded is permitted to be imported over a period it may be imported in more than one consignment during such period.

6 Condition as to security for certain importations

Where any goods are declared for relief under this Order—

(a)   before the date on which a person becomes normally resident in the United Kingdom, or

(b)   if he intends to become so resident on the occasion of his marriage before such marriage has taken place,

the relief shall be subject to the condition that there is furnished to the Commissioners such security as they may require.

7 Restriction on disposal without authorisation

(1)   Except as provided by or under this Order, where relief is afforded under any Part of this Order, it shall be a condition of the relief that the goods are not lent, hired-out, given as security or transferred in the United Kingdom within a period of twelve months from the date on which relief was afforded, unless such disposal is authorised by the Commissioners.

(2)   Where the Commissioners authorise any such disposal as is mentioned in paragraph (1) above, they may discharge the relief and the person to whom the relief was afforded shall forthwith pay tax at the rate then in force, provided that where a lower rate was in force when relief was afforded the amount payable shall be determined by reference to the lower rate.

PART III
PROVISIONS COMMON TO ALL RELIEFS

8 Goods to be declared for relief

(1)   A person shall not be entitled to relief from payment of duty or tax in respect of any goods under any Part of this Order unless the goods are declared for relief to the proper officer.

(2)   For the purposes of this Order, the expression "declared for relief" shall refer to the act by which a person applies for relief on importation of the goods or on their removal from another customs procedure and includes, as the case may be, any declaration under section 78 of the Customs and Excise Management Act 1979, or any entry under the Postal Packets (Customs and Excise) Regulations 1986, the Excise Warehousing (Etc) Regulations 1988, or regulation 5 of the Customs Controls on

Importation of Goods Regulations 1991, or any entry required by Article 40 of Commission Regulation (EEC) No 2561/90.

9 Fulfilment of intention to be a condition

Where relief from payment of duty or tax is afforded under any Part of this Order subject to a specified intention on the part of a person in relation to his becoming normally resident in the United Kingdom, or the use of the goods in respect of which relief is afforded, it shall be a condition of the relief that such intention be fulfilled.

10 Enforcement

Where relief from payment of duty or tax has been afforded under any Part of this Order and subsequently the Commissioners are not satisfied that any condition subject to which such relief was afforded has been complied with, then, unless the Commissioners sanction the non-compliance, the duty or tax shall become payable forthwith by the person to whom relief was afforded (except to the extent that the Commissioners may see fit to waive payment of the whole or any part thereof) and the goods shall be liable to forfeiture.

PART IV
PERSONS TRANSFERRING THEIR NORMAL RESIDENCE FROM A THIRD COUNTRY

11—

(1)   Subject to the provisions of this Part, a person entering the United Kingdom shall not be required to pay any duty or tax chargeable in respect of property imported into the United Kingdom on condition that—

    (a)   he has been normally resident in a third country for a continuous period of at least twelve months;

    (b)   he intends to become normally resident in the United Kingdom;

    (c)   the property has been in his possession and used by him in the country where he has been normally resident, for a period of at least six months before its importation;

    (d)   the property is intended for his personal or household use in the United Kingdom; and

    (e)   the property is declared for relief—

        (i)   not earlier than six months before the date on which he becomes normally resident in the United Kingdom, and

        (ii)   not later than twelve months following that date.

(2)   A person shall not be afforded relief under this Part unless the Commissioners are satisfied that the goods have borne, in their country of origin or exportation, the customs or other duties and taxes to which goods of that class or description are normally liable and that such goods have not, by reason of their exportation, been subject to any exemption from, or refund of, such duties and taxes as aforesaid, or any turnover tax, excise duty or other consumption tax.

(3)   For the purposes of this Part, "property" shall not include—

    (a)   beverages containing alcohol;

    (b)   tobacco products;

    (c)   any motor road vehicle which by its type of construction and equipment is designed for and capable of transporting more than nine persons including the driver, or goods, or any special purpose vehicle or mobile workshop; and

    (d)   articles for use in the exercise of a trade or profession, other than portable instruments of the applied or liberal arts.

12 Supplementary

Where the Commissioners are satisfied that a person has given up his normal residence in a third country but is prevented by occupational ties from becoming normally resident in the United Kingdom immediately, they may allow property to be declared for relief earlier than as prescribed in article 11(1)(e)(i) above, subject to such conditions and restrictions as they think fit.

PART V
ADDITIONAL RELIEF FOR PROPERTY IMPORTED ON MARRIAGE FROM A THIRD COUNTRY

13 Relief

(1)   Subject to the provisions of this article, in addition to the relief afforded by Part IV, a person entering the United Kingdom shall not be required to pay any duty or tax chargeable in respect of property imported into the United Kingdom on condition that—

(a)   he has been normally resident in a third country for a continuous period of at least twelve months;

(b)   he intends to become normally resident in the United Kingdom on the occasion of his marriage; and

(c)   the property is declared for relief within the period provided by article 15 below.

(2)   In this article "property" shall be limited to household effects and trousseaux, other than tobacco products and beverages containing alcohol.

14 Wedding gifts

(1)   Subject to the provisions of this article, a person to whom article 13(1) above applies shall not be required to pay any duty or tax chargeable in respect of any wedding gift imported into the United Kingdom by him or on his behalf on condition that such wedding gift is—

(a)   given or intended to be given to him on the occasion of his marriage by a person who is normally resident in a third country;

(b)   declared for relief within the period provided by article 15 below.

(2)   Relief shall not be afforded under this article in respect of any wedding gift the value of which exceeds £800.

(3)   For the purpose of affording relief from any duty or tax under this article, a wedding gift shall be treated as if it were liable to Community customs duty and valued in accordance with the rules applicable to such duty.

(4)   In this article "wedding gift" means any property customarily given on the occasion of a marriage, other than tobacco products or beverages containing alcohol.

15 Time limit for relief

The property to which this Part applies shall be declared for relief—

(a)   not earlier than two months before the date fixed for the solemnisation of the marriage; and

(b)   not later than four months following the date of the marriage.

PART VI
PUPILS AND STUDENTS

16 Relief for scholastic equipment

(1)   Without prejudice to relief afforded under any other Part of this Order and subject to the provisions of this article, a person entering the United Kingdom shall not be required to pay any duty or tax chargeable in respect of scholastic equipment imported into the United Kingdom on condition that—

(a)   he is a pupil or student normally resident in a third country who has been accepted to attend a full-time course at a school, college or university in the United Kingdom; and

(b)   such equipment belongs to him and is intended for his personal use during the period of his studies.

(2)   For the purposes of this article, "scholastic equipment" shall mean household effects which represent the normal furnishings for the room of a pupil or student, clothing, uniforms, and articles or instruments normally used by pupils or students for the purpose of their studies, including calculators or typewriters.

(3)   The provisions of article 7 above shall not apply to relief afforded under this Part.

PART VII
HONORARY DECORATIONS, AWARDS AND GOODWILL GIFTS

17 Relief for honorary decorations and awards
Subject to article 20 below, a person entering the United Kingdom shall not be required to pay any duty or tax chargeable on the importation into the United Kingdom of any goods on condition that—

(a)   he is normally resident in the United Kingdom; and

(b)   such goods comprise—

(i)   any honorary decoration which has been conferred on him by a government in a third country or

(ii)   any cup, medal or similar article of an essentially symbolic nature which has been awarded to him in a third country as a tribute to his activities in the arts, sciences, sport or the public service, or in recognition of merit at a particular event.

18 Relief for gifts received by official visitors in a third country
Subject to article 20 below, a person entering the United Kingdom shall not be required to pay any duty or tax chargeable on the importation into the United Kingdom of any goods on condition that—

(a)   he is normally resident in the United Kingdom;

(b)   he is returning from an official visit to a third country;

(c)   the goods were given to him by the host authorities of such country on the occasion of his visit; and

(d)   the goods are not intended for a commercial purpose.

19 Relief for gifts brought by official visitors
Subject to article 20 below, a person entering the United Kingdom shall not be required to pay any duty or tax chargeable on the importation into the United Kingdom of any goods on condition that—

(a)   he is normally resident in a third country;

(b)   he is paying an official visit to the United Kingdom;

(c)   the goods are in the nature of an occasional gift which he intends to offer to the host authorities during his visit; and

(d)   the goods are not intended for a commercial purpose.

20 Supplementary
(1)   Part II shall not apply to relief afforded under this Part.

(2)   No relief shall be afforded under this Part in respect of beverages containing alcohol, tobacco products or importations having a commercial character.

PART VIII
PERSONAL PROPERTY ACQUIRED BY INHERITANCE

21 Relief for legacies imported from a third country

(1)   Without prejudice to relief afforded under any other Part of this Order and subject to the provisions of this article, a person who has become entitled as a legatee to property situated in a third country shall not be required to pay any duty or tax chargeable on the importation thereof into the United Kingdom, on condition that—

(a)   he is either—

    (i)   normally resident in the United Kingdom or the Isle of Man; or

    (ii)   a secondary resident who is not normally resident in a third country; or

    (iii)   an eligible body;

(b)   he furnishes proof to the officer of his entitlement as legatee to the property; and

(c)   save as the Commissioners otherwise allow, the property is imported by or for such person not later than two years from the date on which his entitlement as legatee is finally determined.

(2)   No relief shall be afforded under paragraph (1) above in respect of goods specified in the Schedule to this Order.

(3)   For the purposes of this Part—

"eligible body" means a body solely concerned with carrying on a non-profit making activity and which is incorporated in the United Kingdom or the Isle of Man;

"secondary resident" means a person who, without being normally resident in the United Kingdom or the Isle of Man has a home situated in the United Kingdom which he owns or is renting for at least twelve months.

22

(Revokes the Customs and Excise Duties (Personal Reliefs for Goods Permanently Imported) Order 1983, SI 1983/1828, the Customs and Excise Duties (Relief for Imported Legacies) Order 1984, SI 1984/895, the Customs and Excise Duties (Relief for Imported Legacies) Order 1984 (Amendment) Order 1985, SI 1985/1378 and the Customs and Excise Duties (Personal Reliefs for Goods Permanently Imported) (Amendment) Order 1991, SI 1991/1287.)

SCHEDULE

Article 21(2)

1.   Beverages containing alcohol.

2.   Tobacco products.

3.   Any motor road vehicle which, by its type of construction and equipment, is designed for and capable of transporting more than nine persons including the driver, or goods, or any special purpose vehicle or mobile workshop.

4.   Articles, other than portable instruments of the applied or liberal arts, used in the exercise of a trade or profession before his death by the person from whom the legatee has acquired them.

5.   Stocks of new materials and finished or semi-finished products.

6.   Livestock and stocks of agricultural products exceeding the quantities appropriate to normal family requirements.

BEER REGULATIONS 1993

(SI 1993/1228)

NOTES

Made: 6 May 1993.

Authority: Alcoholic Liquor Duties Act 1979, ss 2, 41A, 46, 47, 49, 67; Customs and Excise Management Act 1979, ss 93, 100G, 100H, 118A, 127A; Finance (No 2) Act 1992, ss 1, 2.

Modification of Pts I, VI and VII hereof by the Channel Tunnel (Alcoholic Liquor and Tobacco Products) Order 2003, SI 2003/2758, art 2(b), Schedule, in their application to a control zone.

ARRANGEMENT OF REGULATIONS

PART I
PRELIMINARY

NOTES

Modification of this Part by the Channel Tunnel (Alcoholic Liquor and Tobacco Products) Order 2003, SI 2003/2758, art 2(b), Schedule, in its application to a control zone.

1 Citation and commencement

These Regulations may be cited as the Beer Regulations 1993 and shall come into force on 1st June 1993.

2 Revocation and saving provisions

(1)   Subject to paragraph (2) below . . .

(2)   The Spoilt Beer (Remission and Repayment of Duty) Regulations 1987 shall continue to have effect in relation to any beer which is not eligible for relief under article 7 of the Finance Act 1991 (Commencement and Transitional Provisions) Order 1993 and which was removed from the entered premises of a brewer for sale before 1st June 1993 and, for the purposes of this paragraph, "entered premises of a brewer for sale" has the same meaning as it has in regulation 4 of those Regulations.

NOTES

Para (1): words omitted revoke the Beer Regulations 1985, SI 1985/1627 and the Spoilt Beer (Remission and Repayment of Duty) Regulations 1987, SI 1987/314.

3 Application

These Regulations apply to beer produced in or imported into the United Kingdom, or removed into the United Kingdom from the Isle of Man.

4 Interpretation

In these Regulations except where the context otherwise requires—

"the Act" means the Alcoholic Liquor Duties Act 1979;

"accounting period" means one month or such other period as the Commissioners may in any particular case determine;

"approved guarantee" means a guarantee to pay duty in the event of default by the person who is liable to pay the duty ("the payer"), that is approved by the Commissioners, and is given by a person, other than the payer, who is satisfactory to the Commissioners for these purposes;

"beer" has the meaning given by section 1(3), but subject to section 1(10) of the Act;

"brewery" includes any premises on which the production of beer is begun;

"class or description" in relation to beer includes its strength and the following classes or descriptions—

   (a)   beer held at the registered brewery at which it was produced;

   (b)   beer held on registered premises adjacent to the registered brewery at which it was produced;

   (c)   beer held otherwise than at the registered brewery at which it was produced or on registered premises adjacent to that brewery;

   (d)   packaged beer (that is to say any beer which is in a container in which, or from which, it will be sold by retail or otherwise supplied for consumption after the duty point);

   (e)   packaged beer held on the registered premises at which it was packaged or on registered premises adjacent to those premises; and

   (f)   bulk beer (that is to say any beer which is not packaged beer);

"duty", [except in regulation 15(1B)(d) below,] means the duty of excise charged on any beer by section 36(1) of the Act;

"duty point" means the time when the duty is payable by a person, whether or not payment may be deferred;

"excise warehouse" means a place of security for the keeping of beer approved by the Commissioners under section 92(1) of the Customs and Excise Management Act 1979 (whether or not it is also approved for the keeping of other goods);

["large pack" means a container that is intended to contain a volume of more than 10 litres but not more than 400 litres;]

"package" and "packager" have the meanings given by section 4(1) of the Act;

"registered brewer" has the meaning given by section 47(1) of the Act;

"registered brewery" means any premises in respect of which a registered brewer is registered under section 47 of the Act;

"registered holder" means a packager of beer or a registered brewer registered under section 41A of the Act in relation to any registered premises;

"registered holder certificate" means a certificate of registration issued in accordance with regulation 10 below;

"registered premises" means any premises registered under section 41A of the Act on which a registered holder may hold beer without payment of duty;

"registered store" means any store registered under section 41A of the Act;

"return of duty" means the return prepared pursuant to regulation 21 below;

"spoilt beer record" means the record maintained pursuant to regulation 33 below;

"strength" in relation to any beer has the meaning given in section 2 of the Act;

"unfinished" in relation to any beer means beer in any stage of production before it has reached that state of maturity at which it is fit for consumption,

and references in these Regulations to suspension arrangements are references to the provisions made by Part V of these Regulations or to any provision made by or under the customs and excise Acts for enabling goods to be held or moved without payment of duty or any provisions made by or under the customs and excise Acts for enabling goods to be held or moved without payment of duty or any provisions made by or under those Acts in connection with any provision enabling goods to be so held or moved.

NOTES

Words in definition "duty" inserted by the Excise Goods, Beer and Tobacco Products (Amendment) Regulations, SI 2002/2692 reg 3(1), (2); definition "large pack" inserted by the Beer and Cider and Perry (Amendment) Regulations 2000, SI 2000/3213, reg 2(1), (2).

PART II
REGISTRATION OF PRODUCERS OF BEER

5 Application for registration by producers of beer

(1) Every person required to be registered under section 47 of the Act ("the applicant") shall make application to the Commissioners for registration in respect of the premises on which he produces or intends to produce beer.

(2) A separate application shall be made in respect of each of the premises on which the applicant produces or intends to produce beer.

(3) Save as the Commissioners may otherwise allow, each application shall contain the particulars specified in Schedule 1 and shall be in such form and manner as the Commissioners may prescribe in any notice published by them in pursuance of these Regulations and not withdrawn by a further notice.

6 Registration of producers of beer

(1) The Commissioners may register the applicant in respect of each of the premises in respect of which application is made, and may issue a separate certificate of registration in respect of each of those premises.

(2) Without prejudice to regulation 10 below, where the applicant is or will also be registered under section 41A of the Act a certificate of registration issued in accordance with this regulation may, in such circumstances as the Commissioners think fit, be issued in one document serving both as a certificate of registration under section 47 of the Act and as a registered holder certificate.

(3) The certificate of registration shall remain the property of the Commissioners.

(4) Every certificate of registration shall be kept at all times on the premises to which it relates, and shall be produced for inspection to the proper officer on demand.

(5) Subject to paragraph (6) below, a registered brewer shall notify the Commissioners of any change to the particulars contained in any application made pursuant to regulation 5 above and the Commissioners may vary the registration accordingly.

(6) A registered brewer is not required to notify the Commissioners of any change in his estimate of the quantity of beer to be produced each year.

(7) The Commissioners may, for reasonable cause, vary the registration of a registered brewer with respect to any registered brewery, provided that the Commissioners shall give 14 days notice in writing of such variation.

7 Revocation of registration of producers of beer

(1)   A registered brewer shall notify the Commissioners of his intention to cease production of beer at any of his registered breweries.

(2)   A registered brewer shall notify the Commissioners of the cessation of production of beer at any of his registered breweries.

(3)   Where the Commissioners are satisfied that a registered brewer has failed to produce any beer or has ceased to produce beer at any registered brewery, they may revoke his registration as a registered brewer with respect to that registered brewery at any time.

PART III
PRODUCTION

8 When the production of beer begins and when it is completed

(1)   For the purposes of section 47 of the Act (registration of producers of beer) and these Regulations, the production of beer begins when the mash is made.

(2)   For the purposes of section 36 of the Act (the charge of excise duty) and these Regulations, beer shall be deemed to have been produced at the time determined in accordance with any direction given by the Commissioners or in the absence of any such direction at the earlier of—

(a)   the time when the beer is put into any package;

(b)   the time when the beer is removed from the brewery;

(c)   the time when the beer is consumed;

(d)   the time when the beer is lost;

(e)   the time when the beer reaches that state of maturity at which it is fit for consumption.

(3)   In this regulation "beer" includes unfinished beer.

PART IV
SUSPENSION OF DUTY

Registration of persons and premises

9 Application for registration for duty suspension

(1)   Every application by a packager of beer or a brewer ("the applicant") to be registered under section 41A of the Act in relation to any premises shall be made to the Commissioners.

(2)   A separate application shall be made in respect of each of the premises on which the applicant intends to hold beer without payment of the duty.

(3)   Save as the Commissioners may otherwise allow, each application shall contain the particulars specified in Schedule 2.

(4)   Every application shall be made at least 14 days before the day on which the applicant intends to hold beer without payment of the duty.

10 Registration for duty suspension

(1)   The Commissioners may register the applicant in respect of each of the premises in respect of which application is made, and may issue a separate registered holder certificate in respect of each of those premises.

(2)   The Commissioners may specify in the registered holder certificate each class or description of beer that the applicant may hold without payment of duty on the premises to which the certificate relates.

(3)   The registered holder certificate shall remain the property of the Commissioners.

[(1A) In the case of beer acquired by a person in another member State for his own use and transported by him to the United Kingdom, the duty point is the time when that beer is held or used for a commercial purpose by any person.]

[(1B) For the purposes of paragraph (1A) above—

(a)   "member State" includes the Principality of Monaco[, San Marino and the United Kingdom Sovereign Base Areas of Akrotiri and Dhekelia], but does not include the Island of Heligoland and the territory of Büsingen in the Federal Republic of Germany, Livigno, Campione d'Italia and the waters of Lake Lugano in the Italian Republic, Ceuta, Melilla and the Canary Islands in the Kingdom of Spain, or the overseas departments of the French Republic,

(b)   "own use" includes use as a personal gift,

(c)   if the beer in question is—

(i)   transferred to another person for money or money's worth (including any reimbursement of expenses incurred in connection with obtaining them), or

(ii)   the person holding it intends to make such a transfer,

that beer is to be regarded as being held for a commercial purpose,

(d)   if the beer is not duty and tax paid in the member State at the time of acquisition, or the duty and tax that was paid will be or has been reimbursed, refunded or otherwise dispensed with, that beer is to be regarded as being held for a commercial purpose,

(e)   without prejudice to sub-paragraphs (c) and (d) above, in determining whether beer is held or used for a commercial purpose by any person regard shall be taken of—

(i)   that person's reasons for having possession or control of that beer,

(ii)   whether or not that person is a revenue trader (as defined in section 1(1) of the Customs and Excise Management Act 1979),

(iii)   that person's conduct, including his intended use of that beer or any refusal to disclose his intended use of that beer,

(iv)   the location of that beer,

(v)   the mode of transport used to convey that beer,

(vi)   any document or other information whatsoever relating to that beer,

(vii)   the nature of that beer including the nature and condition of any package or container,

(viii) the quantity of that beer, and in particular, whether the quantity exceeds 110 litres,

(ix)   whether that person personally financed the purchase of that beer,

(x)   any other circumstance that appears to be relevant.]

(2) If any duty suspension arrangements apply to the beer, the duty point shall be the earlier of—

(a)   the time when the duty ceases to be suspended in accordance with those arrangements;

(b)   the time when there is any contravention of any requirement relating to those arrangements; and

(c)   the time when the duty ceases to be suspended by virtue of paragraph (3) below.

(3) The duty ceases to be suspended when—

(a)   the premises on which the beer is held cease to be registered premises under Part IV of these Regulations;

(b) the person holding the beer ceases to be registered under Part IV of these Regulations;

(c) the beer is consumed; or

(d) the beer leaves any registered premises unless—

(i) the beer is consigned to other registered premises or an excise warehouse in accordance with requirements prescribed in Part V of these Regulations and Part IV of the Excise Goods (Holding, Movement, Warehousing and REDS) Regulations 1992; or

(ii) the beer is delivered for export, shipment as stores or removal to the Isle of Man.

(4) In this regulation "contravention" includes a failure to comply.

NOTES

Para (1): words inserted by the Excise Goods, Beer and Tobacco (Amendment) Regulations 2002, SI 2002/2692 reg 3(1), (3)(a).

Paras (1A), (1B): inserted by the Excise Goods, Beer and Tobacco (Amendment) Regulations 2002, SI 2002/2692 reg 3(1), (3)(b).

Para (1B): words substituted by the Excise Duty Points (Etc) (New Member States) Regulations 2004, SI 2004/1003 reg 9.

[15A Constructive removal

(1) Where beer is held on any registered premises to which this regulation applies it shall be deemed to have left those premises at the time of its constructive removal or, if earlier, the time it actually left them.

(2) This regulation applies to registered premises where the records relating to removal are kept by means approved for this purpose by the Commissioners; and the Commissioners may at any time revoke such approval upon giving fourteen days' notice in writing.

(3) The registered holder from whose registered premises constructive removal may take place shall keep such records as may be specified in a notice published by the Commissioners and not withdrawn by a further notice.

(4) Constructive removal shall mean the making of an entry in the records specified in accordance with paragraph (3) above which identifies the beer that is the subject of that entry as having left the registered premises (so that duty ceases to be suspended) notwithstanding that it remains on those premises.

(5) An entry showing the constructive removal of any beer shall not be cancelled, amended or altered.]

NOTES

Commencement: 1 January 1996.

Inserted by the Beer (Amendment) Regulations 1995, SI 1995/3059, reg 2.

16 Rate of duty

The duty shall be paid at the rate in force at the duty point.

17 The amount of beer in any container

[(1) Except in the case of beer to which paragraph (2) below applies] the amount of beer in any container shall be deemed to be the greater of—

(a) the amount determined in accordance with section 2 of the Act;

(b) the amount ascertained by reference to information on the label of the container of the beer; and

(c)   the amount ascertained by reference to information on any invoice, delivery note or similar document issued in relation to the beer.

[(2)   The amount of beer in a large pack may be ascertained by reference to any information on the label of that pack or any information in any invoice, delivery note or similar document indicating the amount of beer in that pack and, except in a case where the tolerance requirements set out in Schedule 6 below are not met, any beer in excess of that amount is relieved from duty at the duty point.]

NOTES

Para (1): numbered as such and words inserted by the Beer and Cider and Perry (Amendment) Regulations 2000, SI 2000/3213, reg 2(1), (3), with effect from 1 January 2001.

Para (2): added by SI 2000/3213, reg 2(1), (4), with effect from 1 January 2001.

18 The strength of the beer

Save as the Commissioners otherwise allow, the strength of the beer shall be deemed to be the greater of—

(a)   the strength determined by the method described in Schedule 4 to these Regulations;

(b)   the strength ascertained by reference to information on the label of the container of the beer;

(c)   the strength ascertained by reference to information on any invoice, delivery note or similar document issued in relation to the beer; and

(d)   the strength which any cask or bottle conditioned beer or any other unfinished beer is reasonably expected to have when sold by way of retail or otherwise supplied for consumption.

PART VII
PAYMENT OF THE DUTY AND RETURNS

NOTES

Modification of this Part by the Channel Tunnel (Alcoholic Liquor and Tobacco Products) Order 2003, SI 2003/2758, art 2(b), Schedule, in its application to a control zone.

19 Person liable to pay the duty

(1)   The person liable to pay the duty shall be the person holding the beer at the duty point.

(2)   Any person (not being the person specified in paragraph (1) above) who imported the beer, who produced the beer or who held the beer under duty suspension arrangements at any time before the duty point and who does not hold a certificate of receipt for the beer with respect to every holding of the beer by him shall be jointly and severally liable to pay the duty with the person specified in paragraph (1) of this regulation; provided that—

(a)   no person shall be so liable before the 30th day following the day of despatch of the beer in question; and

(b)   a person shall cease to be so liable upon his receiving the certificate of receipt in question or upon his satisfying the Commissioners that the beer in question was received by the consignee in circumstances where a valid certificate of receipt could and should have been issued.

(3)   For the purposes of this regulation "certificate of receipt" means—

(a)   a certificate issued in accordance with regulation 13(3)(d) above;

(b) a certificate issued in accordance with regulation 11(3) of the Excise Goods (Holding, Movement, Warehousing and REDS) Regulations 1992; or

(c) a certificate issued in accordance with regulation 11(4) of the Excise Warehousing (Etc) Regulations 1988.

20 Time and method of payment

(1) Subject to paragraph (2) and save as the Commissioners may allow, the duty shall be paid at the duty point.

(2) Where the person liable to pay the duty is a registered brewer or registered holder, save as the Commissioners otherwise direct, the duty shall be paid not later than the 25th day of the month next following the month containing the duty point in relation to the duty provided that—

(a) where the last day for making payment would, if determined in accordance with the foregoing provision of this paragraph, fall on a day which is not a business day, the duty shall be paid not later than the last business day before that day; and

(b) save as the Commissioners otherwise agree, the duty is secured by an approved guarantee.

(3) Save as the Commissioners otherwise allow, the duty shall be paid by direct debit.

(4) The duty shall be paid to the Commissioners.

(5) In this regulation "business day" means a day which is a business day within the meaning of section 92 of the Bills of Exchange Act 1882 for the purposes of the General Account of the Commissioners of Customs and Excise at the Bank of England in London.

21 Furnishing of returns

(1) Save, in the case of a registered holder, as the Commissioners may otherwise direct, every person who is registered or was or is required to be registered in accordance with these Regulations shall, in respect of every period of a month furnish the Commissioners, not later than the 15th day of the month next following the end of the period to which it relates, with a return on a form approved by the Commissioners showing the amount of duty payable by him and containing full information in respect of the other matters specified in the form and a declaration signed by him that the return is true and complete.

(2) Returns shall be furnished at such place as the Commissioners may direct and, unless furnished in person when that place is open to the public for business, may be furnished in such other manner as the Commissioners may allow.

PART VIII
OPERATIONS ON BEER

22 Mixing

(1) This regulation does not apply to beer in relation to which any personal relief has been conferred.

(2) Beer to which any suspension arrangements apply shall not be mixed with any beer to which no such arrangements apply.

(3) Unless and until the beer is sold by way of retail or otherwise supplied for consumption, beer shall not be mixed with any beer of a different strength unless the mixing takes place—

(a) before the duty point; and

(b) at a registered store or a registered brewery.

[(4)   Beer to which any duty suspension arrangements apply must not be mixed with any beer that would, had the duty been charged immediately before the time of mixing, have been charged with a different rate of duty [unless the resulting mixture is charged with the rate of duty specified in section 36(1AA)(a) of the Act].]

NOTES
Para 4: added by the Beer and Warehousing (Amendment) Regulations 2002, SI 2002/1265 reg 2(1), (3); words in square brackets inserted by the Beer, Cider and Perry, Spirits, and Wine and Made-wine (Amendment) Regulations, SI 2006/1058 reg 2(1), (3).

23 Addition of substances

(1)   Save as the Commissioners otherwise allow, unless and until the beer is sold by way of retail or otherwise supplied for consumption, no relevant operation with respect to any beer shall be carried out by any person, except by a registered brewer at a registered brewery or by a registered holder at a registered store.

(2)   Every registered brewer and registered holder shall keep a record containing the particulars specified in Schedule 5 below of all relevant operations carried out by him.

(2A)   . . .

(3)   In this regulation "relevant operation" means the addition of any substance to any beer which causes or is likely to cause the beer to be chargeable with a greater amount of duty than would be chargeable if the operation had not taken place.

NOTES
Para (2A): revoked by the Beer, Cider and Perry, Spirits, and Wine and Made-wine (Amendment) Regulations, SI 2006/1058 reg 2(1), (4).

24 Dilution of beer

[(1)   Without prejudice to paragraph (3), after small brewery beer has left the brewery where its production began water must not be added to it before the duty point.

(2)   Paragraph (1) does not prohibit any operation that is reasonably necessary to make small brewery beer fit for packaging in a package that is not a large pack.]

[(3)]   Save as the Commissioners otherwise allow, no water shall be added to any beer after the duty point with respect to the beer unless and until the time that the beer is sold by way of retail or otherwise supplied for consumption.

NOTES
Paras (1), (2) inserted, and para (3) numbered as such, by the Beer, Cider and Perry, Spirits, and Wine and Made-wine (Amendment) Regulations, SI 2006/1058 reg 2(1), (5).

25 Protection of the revenue derived from excise duty on beer

Unless and until the beer is sold by way of retail or otherwise supplied for consumption, after the duty point no person may carry out any operation on, or in relation to, beer of any description if that operation would, had it been carried out before the duty point, have resulted in a greater amount of duty being payable than was actually payable at the duty point.

PART IX
SPOILT BEER

26 Introduction

(1) Remission of duty charged or repayment of duty paid in respect of beer which has been removed from any registered brewery and which has become spoilt or otherwise unfit for use, is subject to compliance with the conditions set out in this part of these Regulations.

(2) Where any beer has been removed from the registered store of a registered holder and the beer has become spoilt or otherwise unfit for use and the Commissioners are satisfied that the beer has not been and will not be consumed in the United Kingdom the registered holder shall be entitled to drawback of duty in respect of the beer subject to compliance with the conditions set out in this part of these Regulations.

(3) The claimant shall, save as the Commissioners may otherwise allow, satisfy the Commissioners that he was the person who actually paid the duty in respect of the spoilt beer which is the subject of his claim.

(4) Only one claim for remission or repayment of duty or drawback of duty may be made in respect of any spoilt beer.

(5) A claim for remission or repayment of duty or drawback of duty shall not be made in respect of any spoilt beer which has been adulterated or diluted except that such a claim may be made in respect of spoilt beer which was diluted before the duty point.

(6) In this part of these Regulations "claimant" means the registered brewer claiming remission or repayment of duty or the registered holder claiming drawback of duty as the case may be.

27 Return to the registered brewery or registered premises

(1) Save as the Commissioners otherwise allow, spoilt beer shall be returned to the claimant's premises.

(2) Where a claimant claims remission or repayment of duty or a drawback of duty, except in the case of cellar tank beer, spoilt beer shall be returned in the container in which it left the claimant's premises.

(3) In this regulation and in regulation 28 below, "claimant's premises" means the claimant's registered brewery or, as the case may be, the claimant's registered premises.

28 Ascertainment of the amount of duty charged or paid

(1) Except as the Commissioners otherwise allow, the amount of duty charged or paid shall be ascertained by reference to—

    (a)   the quantity of the spoilt beer (determined in accordance with paragraph (2) below);

    (b)   its strength (determined in accordance with paragraph (3) below); and

    (c)   the rate of duty charged upon it.

(2) The quantity of the spoilt beer shall be—

    (a)   in the case of beer which is returned in the same containers in which it left the claimant's premises and from which no beer has been removed, the amount upon which the duty was charged; and

    (b)   in any other case, the quantity of beer upon which the duty was charged which is returned.

(3) The strength of the spoilt beer shall be—

    (a)   in the case of beer which is returned in the same container in which it left the claimant's premises and from which no beer has been removed, the strength by reference to which the duty was charged; and

(b)   in any other case, the lesser of the actual strength ascertained in accordance with regulation 18 above and the strength by reference to which the duty was charged.

29 Destruction etc

(1)   Subject to paragraph (2) below, spoilt beer shall be destroyed so that it is rendered unsaleable as a beverage to the satisfaction of the Commissioners.

(2)   A registered brewer may reprocess spoilt beer in a manner which is satisfactory to the Commissioners and if he does so reprocess any spoilt beer regulation 30 below shall apply as if—

(a)   for the words "destroying" and "destruction" in that regulation there were substituted the word "reprocessing";

(b)   for the word "destroyed" in that regulation there were substituted "reprocessed"; and

(c)   paragraph (3) of that regulation were omitted;

provided that no claim for remission or repayment of duty shall be made for any spoilt beer to which this paragraph applies unless and until the reprocessing of that beer has commenced.

30 Procedure

(1)   If the proper officer so requires, the claimant shall, at least 24 hours before destroying spoilt beer—

(a)   enter the date and time of the proposed destruction in the spoilt beer record; and

(b)   notify the proper officer of the date and time of the proposed destruction.

(2)   Except as the proper officer otherwise allows, the claimant shall, before destroying the spoilt beer—

(a)   enter in the spoilt beer record the quantity of spoilt beer;

(b)   determine the strength of the beer in accordance with regulation 28 and enter the result in the spoilt beer record when it is known to him.

(3)   Except as the proper officer otherwise allows, within one hour of the completion of destruction the claimant shall enter the date and time of the completion in the spoilt beer record.

(4)   If the claimant transfers spoilt beer from the container in which it was returned to his premises to another container otherwise than for immediate destruction, he shall enter in the spoilt beer record such particulars relating to the transfer, the spoilt beer and the containers as would be required by these Regulations if the spoilt beer was destroyed.

31 Remission, repayment or drawback

No claim for remission or repayment of duty or for drawback of duty shall be made unless, taken together with any other claim being made at the same time, the total quantity of spoilt beer in respect of which the claim is made amounts to not less than 10 hectolitres; provided that if during the six months immediately preceding the date upon which the claim is made the quantity of spoilt beer upon which remission or repayment of duty or drawback of duty could be claimed by the claimant amounts in total to less than 10 hectolitres this paragraph shall operate as if the reference to not less than 10 hectolitres were a reference to not less than such quantity of beer as would result in a claim for remission or repayment of duty or for drawback of duty of at least £50.

32 Claims

The claimant shall make a claim for remission or repayment of duty or drawback of duty to the Commissioners on his return of duty; provided that, where by virtue of his

Part II

being registered in respect of more than one brewery or premises, he makes more than one return for the same accounting period he shall, except as the Commissioners may otherwise allow, make his claim on his return relating to the brewery or premises in respect of which the return of duty was made.

33 Records

(1)   In support of his claims for remission or repayment of duty or drawback of duty the claimant shall keep—

(a)   a spoilt beer record containing such particulars as the Commissioners may specify in a notice published by them and not withdrawn by a further notice; and

(b)   records for the purposes of establishing that duty has been charged or paid on the spoilt beer and the amount of that charge or payment.

(2)   The claimant shall retain the records required under paragraph (1) above for at least 6 years (or such lesser period as the Commissioners may otherwise allow) from the date of the claim on the return of duty and shall allow the proper officer to inspect, copy and take extracts from them at any reasonable time.

(3)   Where the records required under paragraph (1) above are preserved in a form which is not readily legible or which is legible only with the aid of equipment the claimant shall, at the proper officer's request, produce a transcript or other permanently legible reproduction of the records and shall permit the proper officer to retain that reproduction.

34

(Amends the Excise Goods (Holding, Movement, Warehousing and REDS) Regulations 1992, SI 1992/3135, regs 2(1), 9(2).)

SCHEDULES

SCHEDULE 1

PARTICULARS OF A REGISTERED BREWER APPLICATION

Regulation 5

(a)   the name of the applicant;

(b)   the status (sole proprietor, partnership, limited company or other status) of the applicant's business;

[(ba)   the name and address of any co-operated brewery;]

(c)   the address of the premises to be registered;

(d)   a plan of the premises to be registered;

(e)   the date the applicant intends to begin the production of beer;

(f)   the name and number of a bank account held by the applicant and the name and branch of the bank providing that account; and

(g)   an estimate of the quantity of beer to be produced by the applicant each year.

[In this Schedule "co-operated brewery" means a brewery (other than the one that is the subject of the application) at which—

(a)   the applicant produces beer, or

(b)   a person connected with the applicant produces beer.

Any question whether a person is connected with another shall be determined in accordance with section 839 of the Income and Corporation Taxes Act 1988.]

NOTES

Para (ba): inserted by the Beer and Warehousing (Amendment) Regulations 2002, SI 2002/1265 reg 2(1), (5).

Words in second pair of square brackets added by the Beer and Warehousing (Amendment) Regulations 2002, SI 2002/1265 reg 2(1), (5).

SCHEDULE 2
PARTICULARS OF A REGISTERED HOLDER APPLICATION
Regulation 9

- (a)   the name of the applicant;
- (b)   the status (sole proprietor, partnership, limited company or other status) of the applicant's business;
- (c)   the address of the premises to be registered;
- (d)   a plan of the premises to be registered;
- (e)   the date the applicant intends to begin the packaging of beer;
- (f)   the name and number of a bank account held by the applicant and the name and branch of the bank providing that account; and
- (g)   particulars of each class or description of beer to be held.

SCHEDULE 3
PARTICULARS OF THE RECORD OF BEER IN DUTY SUSPENSION
Regulation 14

- (a)   the name and address of the person from whom the beer was received or to whom the beer was delivered;
- [(aa)   if the amount of beer produced in the brewery where the beer was produced is relevant for the purpose of determining the duty charged on the beer, a record of that production;]
- (b)   the place from which the beer was received or to which it was delivered;
- (c)   the date of receipt or delivery;
- (d)   unless the beer is in bottles or cans, the numbers and size of each container in which the beer is contained, the quantity in litres name and strength of the beer in each container or tanker;
- (e)   if the beer is in bottles or cans, the total number of bottles or cans, the number of bottles or cans according to each size of bottle or can the name and strength of the beer, and the total quantity in litres.

NOTES
Para (aa): inserted by the Beer and Warehousing (Amendment) Regulations 2002, SI 2002/1265 reg 2(1), (6).

SCHEDULE 4
METHOD OF DETERMINING THE STRENGTH OF BEER
Regulation 18

1.—(1) Subject to sub-paragraph (2) below, the strength of beer shall be determined in the following manner—

- (a)   a representative sample is to be taken and, after first being cleared of sediment and gas by filtration in an approved manner, a definite quantity thereof by measure at the temperature of 20 degrees Celsius shall be distilled;
- (b)   the distillate shall be made up at the temperature of 20 degrees Celsius with distilled water to the original measure of the quantity before distillation;

(c)   the strength of the distillate made up in accordance with paragraph (b) above shall be ascertained by determining its density in air at the temperature of 20 degrees Celsius by means of an approved pycnometer used in an approved manner; and

(d)   the strength of beer shall be taken to be the percentage of alcohol by volume in the table entitled "Laboratory Alcohol Table" which corresponds to the density determined in accordance with paragraph (c) above except that where the density so determined is between two consecutive numbers in the table aforesaid the strength shall be determined by linear interpolation.

(2)   Where the result ascertained by the method specified in sub-paragraph (1) above is rendered inaccurate by the presence of substances other than alcohol that method shall be adjusted in such manner as may be approved for the purpose of producing an accurate result.

2.   In this Schedule—

"approved" means approved by the Commissioners; and

"Laboratory Alcohol Table" means a table of which a copy, signed by the Chairman of the Commissioners and identifying it as relating to the Spirits Regulations 1991, has been deposited in the office of the Queen's Remembrancer at the Royal Courts of Justice.

SCHEDULE 5
PARTICULARS OF THE ADDITIONS OF SUBSTANCES RECORD
Regulation 23

(a)   the place where the operation took place;

(b)   the date and time of the operation;

(c)   the class and description of the beer used in the operation;

(d)   the quantity and strength of the beer used in the operation;

(e)   the description of the substance added to the beer;

(f)   the quantity of the substance added to the beer;

(g)   the quantity and strength of the resultant product.

[SCHEDULE 6
THE TOLERANCE REQUIREMENTS
Regulation 17

1.   If a large pack is filled with a metered or weighed amount of beer the amount of beer in the pack must not exceed the amount ascertained by reference to any information on the label of that pack or any information in any invoice, delivery note or similar document indicating the amount of beer in that pack by more than—

(a)   in the case of a pack intended to contain a volume exceeding 100 litres, 0.5 per cent of that volume, or

(b)   in any other case, 0.5 litres.

2.   If paragraph 1 above does not apply the amount of beer in a large pack must not exceed the amount ascertained by reference to any information on the label of that pack or any information in any invoice, delivery note or similar document indicating the amount of beer in that pack by more than—

(a)   in the case of a pack intended to contain a volume exceeding 200 litres, 3 litres,

(b)   in the case of a pack intended to contain a volume exceeding 100 litres but not exceeding 200 litres, 2 litres, or

(c)   in any other case, 1 litre.]

NOTES

Sch 6 inserted by the Beer and Cider and Perry (Amendment) Regulations 2000, SI 2000/3213, reg 2(1), (5), with effect from 1 January 2001.

CUSTOMS AND EXCISE (TRANSIT) REGULATIONS 1993

(SI 1993/1353)

NOTES

Made: 26 May 1993.

Authority: European Communities Act 1972, s 2(2).

ARRANGEMENT OF REGULATIONS

1 Citation, commencement and interpretation

These Regulations may be cited as the Customs and Excise (Transit) Regulations 1993 and shall come into force on 23rd June 1993.

2

In these Regulations—

"Consignment Note CIM" and "TR transfer note"—

    (a)   in relation to Community transit, have the same meanings as in [Articles 413 and 427 respectively of Commission Regulation (EEC) No 2454/93];

    (b)   in relation to common transit, have the same meanings as in Articles 72 and 86 respectively of Appendix II to the Convention;

"the Convention" means the Convention of 20th May 1987 on a common transit procedure entered into by the Economic Community, Austria, Finland, Iceland, Norway, Sweden and the Swiss Confederation;

"the customs and excise Acts" has the same meaning as in section 1 of the Customs and Excise Management Act 1979;

"relevant Community provision" means—

    (a)   in relation to Community transit, any provision of a Community Regulation specified in the [first or second] columns of the Schedule to these Regulations and shall include any such provisions as applied by—

        (i)   [Article 163(3) of Council Regulation (EEC) No 2913/92 and Article 381(2) of Commission Regulation (EEC) No 2454/93];

        (ii)   [Articles 422(1) and 437(1) of Commission Regulation (EEC) No 2454/93];

    (b)   in relation to common transit, any provision of the Convention specified in the [third or fourth] columns of the Schedule to these Regulations and shall include any such provisions as applied by—

(i)   Article 37(3) of Appendix I to the Convention;

(ii)   Articles 81(1) and 96(1) of Appendix II to the Convention.

NOTES

Words in square brackets in definitions "Consignment Note CIM" and "TR transfer note" and "relevant Community provision" substituted by the Community Customs Code (Consequential Amendment of References) Regulations 1993, SI 1993/3014, reg 5(2), (3).

3 Offences, penalty and forfeiture

In the event of any contravention or failure to comply with—

(a)   any relevant Community provision, or

(b)   any requirement or condition imposed by or under any such provision,

the person responsible for the contravention or failure and the person then in charge of the goods shall each be liable on summary conviction to a penalty of level 5 on the standard scale and any goods in respect of which the offence was committed shall be liable to forfeiture.

4 Supplementary

(1)   Section 139 of and Schedule 3 to the Customs and Excise Management Act 1979 (detention, seizure and condemnation of goods) shall apply to any goods liable to forfeiture under regulation 3 above as if the goods were liable to forfeiture under the customs and excise Acts.

(2)   Sections 144 to 148 and 150 to 155 of the Customs and Excise Management Act 1979 (proceedings for offences, mitigation of penalties, proof and other matters) shall apply in relation to offences and penalties under regulation 3 above and proceedings for such offences or for condemnation of anything as being forfeited under that regulation as they apply in relation to offences and penalties and proceedings for offences or for condemnation under the customs and excise Acts.

5 Revocation

(1)

(2)   Notwithstanding their revocation, the Regulations mentioned in paragraph 1 of this regulation shall continue to have effect—

(a)   until 1st July 1993, to the extent that they create offences for the contravention of Articles 35 and 37 of Commission Regulation (EEC) No 1062/87 and Articles 35 and 37 of the Convention in the application of those Articles to the carriage of goods under cover of an International Express Parcels Consignment Note;

(b)   in relation to carriage begun, in accordance with the provisions of Council Regulation (EEC) No 222/77 and Commission Regulation (EEC) No 1062/87, on or before 31st December 1992.

NOTES

Para (1): revokes the Customs and Excise (Community Transit) (No 2) Regulations 1987, SI 1987/2105 and the Customs and Excise (Common Transit) Regulations 1988, SI 1988/1476.

[SCHEDULE
RELEVANT COMMUNITY PROVISIONS

Regulation 2

EC REGULATIONS (COMMUNITY TRANSIT)		THE CONVENTION (COMMON TRANSIT)		
(1) COUNCIL REGULATION (EEC) No 2913/92	(2) COMMISSION REGULATION (EEC) No 2454/93	(3) APPENDIX I	(4) APPENDIX II	SUBJECT MATTER OF PROVISIONS
Article 96(1)	Article 356(1)	Article 11(1)(a) and (b)		Principal's responsibility for production of goods and T1 document at office of destination and for observance of time limits, identification measures and provisions relating, as the case may be, to Community transit or common transit.
Article 96(2)		Article 11(2)		Responsibility of carrier and recipient for production of goods at office of destination and for observance of time limits and identification measures.
	Article 350	Article 15(1)		Copies of T1 document to accompany the goods.
	Article 352(1)	Article 18(1)		Consignment and copies of T1 document to be produced at each office of transit.
	Article 352(2)	Article 18(2)		Carrier to give each office of transit a transit advice note.
	Article 354(1) 1st sentence	Article 20(1) 1st sentence		Transfer of goods under supervision of customs authorities.
Article 94(1)	Article 359	Article 24(1) 1st sub-paragraph		Principal to furnish guarantee.
	Article 219(2)		Article 20(1)	Document for dispatch or export of goods to be presented to office of departure together with declaration to which it relates.

EC REGULATIONS (COMMUNITY TRANSIT)		THE CONVENTION (COMMON TRANSIT)		
(1) COUNCIL REGULATION (EEC) No 2913/92	(2) COMMISSION REGULATION (EEC) No 2454/93	(3) APPENDIX I	(4) APPENDIX II	SUBJECT MATTER OF PROVISIONS
	Article 464			Restriction etc on exportation from Community to be stated on Community transit document.
	Article 465(1)			When restricted etc goods placed under a transit procedure other than the Community transit procedure Control Copy T5 to be endorsed with statement of restriction on export.
	Article 419(1)		Article 78(1)	Consignment Note CIM to be produced at office of departure.
	Article 421(1)		Article 80(1)	Railway authority to forward to office of destination sheets of Consignment Note CIM.
	Article 434(1)		Article 93(1)	TR transfer note to be produced at office of departure.
	Article 434(7)		Article 93(10)	TR transfer note to be produced at office of destination.
	Article 436(1)		Article 95(1)	Transport undertaking to deliver to office of destination sheets of TR transfer note.
	Article 405(1)(a)		Article 110(1)(a)	Authorised consignor to comply with simplified formalities applicable at the office of departure and conditions of authorisation.
	Article 409(1)		Article 114(1)	Authorised consignee to notify excess quantities, shortages etc, and to send documents to office of destination.

EC REGULATIONS (COMMUNITY TRANSIT)		THE CONVENTION (COMMON TRANSIT)		
(1) COUNCIL REGULATION (EEC) No 2913/92	(2) COMMISSION REGULATION (EEC) No 2454/93	(3) APPENDIX I	(4) APPENDIX II	SUBJECT MATTER OF PROVISIONS
	Article 395(1)(a)		Article 125(1)(a)	Formalities to be complied with by authorised consignor under T2L simplified procedure.
	Article 472(2)			Goods to be put to declared use and dispatched to a declared destination.
	Article 493(1)			Authorised consignor to comply with simplified formalities applicable at office of departure and conditions of authorisation.]

NOTES

Substituted by the Community Customs Code (Consequential Amendment of References) Regulations 1993, SI 1993/3014, reg 5(4), Sch 3.

CHANNEL TUNNEL (INTERNATIONAL ARRANGEMENTS) ORDER 1993

(SI 1993/1813)

NOTES

Made: 16 July 1993.

Authority: Channel Tunnel Act 1987, s 11.

Commencement: see art 1.

ARRANGEMENT OF ARTICLES

1   Citation and commencement
2   Interpretation
3   Application of international articles
4   Application of enactments
5   Application of criminal law
6   Powers of officers and supplementary controls
    SCHEDULES:
    Schedule 1—Expressions Defined
    Schedule 2—International Articles
    Schedule 2A—Supplementary Articles

Schedule 3
Part I—Powers of Officers
Part II—Supplementary Controls Over Animals

1 Citation and commencement

This Order may be cited as the Channel Tunnel (International Arrangements) Order 1993 and shall come into force on the date on which the Protocol between the Government of the United Kingdom of Great Britain and Northern Ireland and the Government of the French Republic Concerning Frontier Controls and Policing, Co-operation in Criminal Justice, Public Safety and Mutual Assistance Relating to the Channel Fixed Link enters into force. That date will be notified in the London, Edinburgh and Belfast Gazettes.

NOTES

Date notified in the London, Edinburgh and Belfast Gazettes for the commencement of this Order was 2 August 1993.

2 Interpretation

(1) In this Order, except for the purpose of construing the international articles [or the supplementary articles], and in any enactment as applied by it with modifications, any expression for which there is an entry in the first column of Schedule 1 has the meaning given against it in the second column.

(2) In this Order "the authorised purposes" means—

(a)   purposes for which provision is authorised by any of paragraphs (a), (d) and (g), and

(b)   purposes connected with any matter in relation to or with respect to or for regulating which provision is authorised by any of paragraphs (c), (e), (f) and (h),

of section 11(1) of the Channel Tunnel Act 1987.

(3) In this Order "the international articles" means the provisions set out in Schedule 2 (being Articles or parts of Articles of the Protocol mentioned in article 1 above); and in the international articles the expression "the Fixed Link" shall for the purposes of this Order be taken to have the same meaning as is given to "the tunnel system" by section 1(7) of the Channel Tunnel Act 1987.

[(4) In this Order "the supplementary articles" means the provisions set out in Schedule 2A (being Articles of the Additional Protocol between the Government of the United Kingdom of Great Britain and Northern Ireland and the Government of the French Republic), and in the supplementary articles "the Protocol signed at Sangatte" and "the Sangatte Protocol" mean the Protocol mentioned in article 1 above.

(5) In paragraph (4) and in the supplementary articles, "Additional Protocol" means the Additional Protocol to the Sangatte Protocol on the Establishment of Bureaux Responsible for Controls on Persons Travelling by Train between France and the United Kingdom, signed at Brussels on 29th May 2000.]

NOTES

Para (1): words in square brackets inserted by the Channel Tunnel (International Arrangements) (Amendment No 3) Order 2001, SI 2001/1544, arts 2, 3(1), as from 25 May 2001.

Paras (4), (5): inserted by SI 2001/1544, arts 2, 3(1), as from 25 May 2001.

3 Application of international articles

(1) The international articles shall have the force of law in the United Kingdom—

(a)   within the tunnel system,

(b)   within a control zone, and

(c)   elsewhere for the authorised purposes only.

(2) Without prejudice to paragraph (1) officers belonging to the French Republic shall to the extent specified in the international articles have rights and obligations and powers to carry out functions in the United Kingdom.

(3) For the purpose of giving full effect to Article 34 of the international articles (accommodation, etc, for authorities of adjoining State) the appropriate Minister may by written notice require any occupier or person concerned with the management of a terminal control point to provide [free of charge] such accommodation, installations and equipment as may be necessary to satisfy requirements determined under Article 33 of the Protocol mentioned in article 1 above (which requires the competent authorities of the two States to determine their respective requirements in consultation with one another).

NOTES

Para 3: words inserted by the Channel Tunnel (International Arrangements) (Amendment No 4) Order, SI 2001/3707 art 3(1).

[3A Application of supplementary articles

(1) The supplementary articles shall have the force of law in the United Kingdom within a supplementary control zone.

(2) Without prejudice to paragraph (1), officers belonging to the French Republic who are responsible for immigration controls shall to the extent specified in the supplementary articles have rights and obligations and powers to carry out functions in the United Kingdom.

(3) [For the purpose of enabling the authorities of the French Republic to make use in the United Kingdom of the accommodation, installations and equipment necessary for the performance of their functions under the supplementary articles, the Secretary of State for the Home Department may by written notice require any occupier or person concerned with the management of a terminal control point to provide free of charge such accommodation, installations and equipment as may be necessary to satisfy requirements determined by the authorities of the French Republic in consultation with the authorities of the United Kingdom.]]

NOTES

Inserted by the Channel Tunnel (International Arrangements) (Amendment No 3) Order 2001, SI 2001/1544, arts 2, 3(3), as from 25 May 2001.

Para 3: substituted by the Channel Tunnel (International Arrangements) (Amendment No 4) Order, SI 2001/3707 art 3(2).

4 Application of enactments

(1) All frontier control enactments [except those relating to transport and road traffic controls] shall for the purpose of enabling officers belonging to the United Kingdom to carry out frontier controls extend to France within a control zone.

[(1A) All frontier control enactments relating to transport and road traffic controls shall for the purpose of enabling officers belonging to the United Kingdom to carry out such controls extend to France within the control zone in France within the tunnel system.]

[(1B) All immigration control enactments shall, for the purpose of enabling immigration officers to carry out immigration controls, extend to France within a supplementary control zone.]

855

[(1C) The Race Relations Act 1976 shall apply to the carrying out by immigration officers of their functions in a control zone or a supplementary control zone outside the United Kingdom as it applies to the carrying out of their functions within the United Kingdom.]

[(2) For the purposes of section 5 of the Data Protection Act 1998 ("the 1998 Act"), data which are—

    (a)   processed within a control zone in France in connection with the carrying out of frontier controls by an officer belonging to the United Kingdom, or

    (b)   processed within a supplementary control zone in France in connection with the carrying out of immigration controls by an immigration officer,

shall be treated as processed by a data controller established in the United Kingdom in the context of that establishment (and the 1998 Act shall accordingly apply in respect of such data).]

[(3) For the purposes of section 5 of the 1998 Act, data which are—

    (a)   processed within a control zone in the United Kingdom in connection with the carrying out of frontier controls by an officer belonging to the French Republic, or

    (b)   processed within a supplementary control zone in the United Kingdom in connection with the carrying out of immigration controls by such an officer,

shall be treated as processed by a data controller established in France in the context of that establishment (and the 1998 Act shall accordingly not apply in respect of such data).]

NOTES

Para (1): words in square brackets inserted by the Channel Tunnel (International Arrangements) (Amendment) Order 1996, SI 1996/2283, art 2(b).

Para (1A): inserted by SI 1996/2283, art 2(b).

Para (1B): inserted by the Channel Tunnel (International Arrangements) (Amendment No 3) Order 2001, SI 2001/1544, arts 2, 3(4), as from 25 May 2001.

Para (1C): inserted by the Channel Tunnel (International Arrangements) (Amendment No 4) Order, SI 2001/3707 art 4.

Paras (2), (3): substituted by SI 2001/1544, arts 2, 3(5), (6), as from 25 May 2001.

5 Application of criminal law

(1) Any act or omission which—

    (a)   takes place outside the United Kingdom in a control zone, and

    (b)   would, if taking place in England, constitute an offence under a frontier control enactment,

[or any act or omission which—

    (c)   takes place outside the United Kingdom in a supplementary control zone, and

    (d)   would, if taking place in England, constitute an offence under an immigration control enactment,]

shall be treated for the purposes of that enactment as taking place in England.

[(1A) Summary proceedings for anything that is by virtue of paragraph (1) an offence triable summarily or triable either way may be taken, and the offence may for all incidental purposes be treated as having been committed, in the county of Kent or in the inner London area as defined in section 2(1)(a) of the Justices of the Peace Act 1979.]

(2)   Any jurisdiction conferred by virtue of [paragraphs (1) and (1A)] on any court is without prejudice to any jurisdiction exercisable apart from this article by that or any other court.

(3)   Where it is proposed to institute proceedings in respect of an alleged offence in any court and a question as to the court's jurisdiction arises under Article 38(2)(a) of the international articles, it shall be presumed, unless the contrary is proved, that the court has jurisdiction by virtue of that Article.

NOTES

Para (1): words in square brackets inserted by the Channel Tunnel (International Arrangements) (Amendment No 3) Order 2001, SI 2001/1544, arts 2, 3(7), as from 25 May 2001.

Para (1A): inserted by the Channel Tunnel (Miscellaneous Provisions) Order 1994, SI 1994/1405, art 8, Sch 4, para 9(a).

Para (2): words in square brackets substituted by SI 1994/1405, art 8, Sch 4, para 9(b).

[5A   Persons boarding a through train
For the purposes of the exercise of any power of an immigration officer in a supplementary control zone in France, any person who seeks to board a through train shall be deemed to be seeking to arrive in the United Kingdom through the tunnel system.]

NOTES

Inserted by the Channel Tunnel (International Arrangements) (Amendment No 3) Order 2001, SI 2001/1544, arts 2, 3(8), as from 25 May 2001.

6   Powers of officers and supplementary controls
Schedule 3 (which contains in Part I provision as to powers exercisable by constables and other officers and in Part II provision for meeting obligations under Article 25 of the Protocol mentioned in article 1 above concerning the prevention of animals from straying into the Fixed Link) shall have effect.

7, 8, 9
(Ss 7–9 relate to Schs 4–6 of this Act (not reproduced in this work).)

SCHEDULES

SCHEDULE 1
EXPRESSIONS DEFINED

Article 2(1)

Expression	*Meaning*
"The Concession-aires"	The meaning given by section 1(8) (read with section 3(3)) of the Channel Tunnel Act 1987.
"Control zone"	A control zone within the meaning of the international articles.
"Frontier controls"	So far as they constitute frontier controls within the meaning of the international articles and are controls in relation to persons or goods, police, immigration, customs, health, veterinary and phytosanitary[, and transport and road traffic] controls.

Expression	Meaning
"Frontier control enactment"	An Act, or an instrument made under an Act, for the time being in force, which contains provision relating to frontier controls.
["Immigration control enactment"	An Act, or an instrument made under an Act, for the time being in force, which contains provision relating to immigration controls.
"Immigration officer"	The same meaning as in the Immigration Act 1971.]
"The international articles"	The meaning given by article 2(3) above.
"International service"	The meaning given in section 13(6) of the Channel Tunnel Act 1987.
"Shuttle train"	The meaning given in section 1(9) of the Channel Tunnel Act 1987.
["State of arrival"	The meaning given by the supplementary articles.]
["State of departure"	The meaning given by the supplementary articles.]
["The supplementary articles"	The meaning given by article 2(4) above.
"Supplementary control zone"	[The part of the territory of the State of departure, determined by mutual agreement between the Governments of the State of departure and the State of arrival, within which the officers of the State of arrival are empowered to effect controls under the supplementary articles.]]
"Terminal control point"	A place which is an authorised terminal control point for international services for the purposes of sections 11 and 12 of the Channel Tunnel Act 1987.
"Through train"	A train, other than a shuttle train, which for the purposes of sections 11 and 12 of the Channel Tunnel Act 1987 is engaged on an international service.
"Train manager"	In relation to a through train or shuttle train, the person designated as train manager by the person operating the international service on which the train is engaged.
"The tunnel system"	The meaning given by section 1(7) of the Channel Tunnel Act 1987.

NOTES

Words in square brackets in definition "Frontier controls" inserted by the Channel Tunnel (International Arrangements) (Amendment) Order 1996, SI 1996/2283, art 2(a); definitions "Immigration control enactment", "Immigration officer", "The supplementary articles" and "Supplementary control zone" inserted by the Channel Tunnel (International Arrangements) (Amendment No 3) Order 2001, SI 2001/1544, arts 2, 4(1), as from 25 May 2001; definition "supplementary control zone" substituted, definitions "State of arrival" and "State of departure" inserted, by the Channel Tunnel (International Arrangements) (Amendment No 4) Order, SI 2001/3707 art 5.

SCHEDULE 2
INTERNATIONAL ARTICLES
Article 2(3)

ARTICLE 1
DEFINITIONS

(1) Any term defined in the Treaty shall have the same meaning in this Protocol.

(2) Otherwise for the purposes of this Protocol the expression—

(a)   "frontier controls" means police, immigration, customs, health, veterinary and phytosanitary, consumer protection, and transport and road traffic controls, as well as any other controls provided for in national or European Community laws and regulations;

(b)   "host State" means the State in whose territory the controls of the other State are effected;

(c)   "adjoining State" means the other State;

(d)   "officers" means persons responsible for policing and frontier controls who are under the command of the persons or authorities designated in accordance with Article 2(1);

(e)   "rescue services" means the authorities and organisations whose functions are provided for in the emergency arrangements referred to in Part VII of this Protocol who are under the command of the persons or authorities designated in accordance with Article 2(1);

(g)   "control zone" means the part of the territory of the host State determined by mutual agreement between the two Governments within which the officers of the adjoining State are empowered to effect controls;

(h)   "restricted zone" means the part of the Fixed Link situated in each State subject to special protective security measures;

(i)   "through trains" means trains travelling the Fixed Link but originating and terminating outside it, as opposed to "shuttle trains" which are trains travelling solely within the Fixed Link.

PART I
AUTHORITIES AND GENERAL PRINCIPLES OF CO-OPERATION
ARTICLE 2

(1)   Each of the Governments shall designate the authorities or the persons having charge of the services which in its territory have responsibility for the exercise of frontier controls, the maintenance of law and order and fire fighting and rescue within the Fixed Link.

PART II
FRONTIER CONTROLS AND POLICE: GENERAL

ARTICLE 5

(1)   In order to simplify and speed up the formalities relating to entry into the State of arrival and exit from the State of departure, the two Governments agree to establish juxtaposed national control bureaux in the terminal installations situated at Frethun in French territory and at Folkestone in British territory. These bureaux shall be so arranged that, for each direction of travel, the frontier controls shall be carried out in the terminal in the State of departure.

(2)   Supplementary frontier controls may exceptionally be carried out in the Fixed Link by officers of the State of arrival on its own territory.

ARTICLE 6

The competence of those juxtaposed national control bureaux shall extend to all cross-frontier movements with the exception of customs clearance of commercial traffic.

ARTICLE 7

(1)   For through trains, each state may carry out its frontier controls during the journey and may authorise the officers of the other State to carry out their frontier controls in its territory.

Part II

(2)   The two States may agree to an extension of the control zones for through trains, as far as London and Paris, respectively.

ARTICLE 8

Within the Fixed Link, each Government shall permit officers of the other State to carry out their functions in its own territory in application of their powers relating to frontier controls.

ARTICLE 9

The laws and regulations relating to frontier controls of the adjoining State shall be applicable in the control zone situated in the host State and shall be put into effect by the officers of the adjoining State in the same way as in their own territory.

ARTICLE 10

(1)   The officers of the adjoining State shall, in exercise of their national powers, be permitted in the control zone situated in the host State to detain or arrest persons in accordance with the laws and regulations relating to frontier controls of the adjoining State or persons sought by the authorities of the adjoining State. These officers shall also be permitted to conduct such persons to the territory of the adjoining State.

(2)   However, except in exceptional circumstances, no person may be held more than 24 hours in the areas reserved, in the host State, for the frontier controls of the adjoining State. Any such detention shall be subject to the requirements and procedures laid down by the legislation of the adjoining State.

(3)   In exceptional circumstances the 24 hour period of detention may be extended for a further period of 24 hours in accordance with the legislation of the adjoining State. The extension of the period of detention shall be notified to the authorities of the host State.

ARTICLE 11

Breaches of the laws and regulations relating to frontier controls of the adjoining State which are detected in the control zone situated in the host State shall be subject to the laws and regulations of the adjoining State, as if the breaches had occurred in the latter's own territory.

ARTICLE 12

(1)   The frontier controls of the State of departure shall normally be effected before those of the State of arrival.

(2)   The officers of the State of arrival are not authorised to begin to carry out such controls before the end of controls of the State of departure. Any form of relinquishment of such controls shall be considered as a control.

(3)   The officers of the State of departure may no longer carry out their controls when the officers of the State of arrival have begun their own operations except with the consent of the competent officers of the State of arrival.

(4)   If exceptionally, in the course of the frontier controls, the sequence of operations provided for in paragraph (1) of this Article is modified, the officers of the State of arrival may not proceed to detentions, arrests or seizures until the frontier controls of the State of departure are completed. In such a case, these officers shall escort the persons, vehicles, merchandise, animals or other goods, for which the frontier controls of the State of departure are not yet completed, to the officers of that State. If these latter then wish to proceed to detentions, arrests or seizures, they shall have priority.

ARTICLE 14

The detailed plans for the Fixed Link and its means of access, shall, in accordance with the relevant provisions of the Concession, delimit among other things—

(a)   the control zones;

(b)   the restricted zones and their sub-divisions;

(c)   railway lines and their means of access included in the control zones;

(d)   the area of the frontier control installations and their means of access.

ARTICLE 16

Where investigations and proceedings concern offences committed in the Fixed Link or having a connection with the Fixed Link, the authorities of the host State shall, at the request of the authorities of the adjoining State, undertake official enquiries, the examination of witnesses and experts and the notification to accused persons of summonses and administrative decisions.

ARTICLE 17

The assistance provided for in Article 16 shall be furnished in accordance with the laws, regulations and procedures in force in the State providing the assistance, and with international agreements to which that State is a party.

ARTICLE 18

If the State of arrival refuses admission to persons, vehicles, animals or goods, or if persons decide not to pass through the frontier controls of the State of arrival, or send or take back any vehicles, animals or goods which are accompanying them, the authorities of the State of departure may not refuse to accept back such persons, vehicles, animals or goods. However, the authorities of the State of departure may take any measures to deal with them in accordance with national law and in a way which does not impose obligations on the other State.

ARTICLE 19

(2)   In an emergency, the local representatives of the authorities concerned may by mutual agreement, provisionally bring into effect alterations to the delimitation of the control zones which may prove necessary. Any arrangement so reached shall come into effect immediately.

PART III
HEALTH, VETERINARY AND PHYTOSANITARY CONTROLS

ARTICLE 20

Controls on persons for the purpose of safeguarding public health shall be carried out in the control zone situated in the host State by the competent authorities of the adjoining State in conformity with the regulations applicable in that State.

ARTICLE 21

The bringing into each of the two States of living animals, animal products, plants, plant products and foodstuffs for human or animal consumption shall be subject to controls by the competent authorities of the importing State in conformity with the regulations applicable in that State.

ARTICLE 22

The frontier controls referred to in Article 21 shall be carried out by the competent authorities of the two States either before or during Customs clearance.

Article 23

(1)   The frontier controls referred to in Article 21 shall include—

> (a)   inspection of certificates or accompanying documents, termed documentary inspection;
>
> (b)   physical examination, including where necessary the taking of samples;
>
> (c)   inspection of means of transport.

(2)   Such controls may be limited to documentary inspection, while physical examination may be undertaken as considered necessary.

ARTICLE 24

Veterinary inspection of living animals shall be without prejudice to any subsequent quarantine measures which may be imposed by the importing State.

PART IV
OFFICERS

ARTICLE 26

Officers of both States shall be permitted to circulate freely in the whole of the Fixed Link for official purposes. In carrying out their functions they shall be authorised to pass through the frontier controls simply by producing appropriate evidence of their identity and status.

ARTICLE 28

(1)   Officers of the adjoining State may wear their national uniform or visible distinctive insignia in the host State.

(2)   In accordance with the laws, regulations and procedures governing the carriage and use of firearms in the host State, the competent authorities of that State will issue permanent licences to carry arms—

> (a)   to officers of the adjoining State exercising their official functions on board trains within the Fixed Link; and
>
> (b)   to an agreed number of specified officers of the adjoining State exercising their functions within the control zone of the host State.

ARTICLE 29

(1)   The authorities of the host State shall grant the same protection and assistance to officers of the adjoining State, in the exercise of their functions, as they grant to their own officers.

(2)   The provisions of the criminal law in force in the host State for the protection of officers in the exercise of their functions shall be equally applicable to the punishment of offences committed against officers of the adjoining State in the exercise of their functions.

ARTICLE 30

(1)   Without prejudice to the application of the provisions of Article 46, claims for compensation for loss, injury or damage caused by or to officers of the adjoining State in the exercise of their functions in the host State shall be subject to the law and jurisdiction of the adjoining State as if the circumstance giving rise to the claim had occurred in that State.

(2)   Officers of the adjoining State may not be prosecuted by authorities of the host State for any acts performed in the control zone or within the Fixed Link whilst in the exercise of their functions. In such a case, they shall come under the jurisdiction of the adjoining State, as if the act had been committed in that State.

(3)   The judicial authorities or the police of the host State, having taken steps to record the complaint and to assemble the facts relating thereto, shall communicate all the particulars and evidence thereof to the competent authorities of the other State for the purposes of a possible prosecution according to the laws in force in the latter.

ARTICLE 31

(1) Officers of the adjoining State shall be permitted freely to transfer to that State sums of money levied on behalf of their Government in the control zone situated in the host State, as well as merchandise and other goods seized there.

(2) They may equally sell such merchandise and other goods in the host State in conformity with the provisions in force in the host State, and transfer the proceeds to the adjoining State.

PART V
FACILITIES

ARTICLE 34

The authorities of the adjoining State shall be able to make use in the host State of the accommodation, installations and equipment necessary for the performance of their functions.

ARTICLE 35

(1) The officers of the adjoining State are empowered to keep order within the accommodation appointed for their exclusive use in the host State.

(2) The officers of the host State shall not have access to such accommodation, except at the request of the officers of the adjoining State or in accordance with the laws of the host State applicable to entry into and searches of private premises.

ARTICLE 36

All goods which are necessary to enable the officers of the adjoining State to carry out their functions in the host State shall be exempt from all taxes and dues on entry and exit.

ARTICLE 37

(1) The officers of the adjoining State whilst exercising their functions in the host State shall be authorised to communicate with their national authorities.

PART VI
CO-OPERATION IN CRIMINAL JUSTICE

ARTICLE 38

(1) Without prejudice to the provisions of Articles 11 and 30(2), when an offence is committed in the territory of one of the two States, including that lying within the Fixed Link up to its frontier, that State shall have jurisdiction.

(2)
- (a) Within the Fixed Link, each State shall have jurisdiction and shall apply its own law—
  - (i) when it cannot be ascertained with certainty where an offence has been committed; or
  - (ii) when an offence committed in the territory of one State is related to an offence committed on the territory of the other State; or
  - (iii) when an offence has begun in or has been continued into its own territory;
- (b) however, the State which first receives the person suspected of having committed such an offence (in this Article referred to as "the receiving State") shall have priority in exercising jurisdiction.

(3)   When the receiving State decides not to exercise its priority jurisdiction under paragraph (2) of this Article it shall inform the other State without delay. If the latter decides not to exercise its jurisdiction, the receiving State shall be obliged to exercise its jurisdiction in accordance with its own national law.

ARTICLE 39

Where an arrest has been made for an offence in respect of which a State has jurisdiction under Article 38, that arrest shall not be affected by the fact that it continues in the territory of the other State.

ARTICLE 40

Without prejudice to the application of Article 3 of the Treaty and of Part II of this Protocol, the police and customs officers of one State may in accordance with their own national laws make arrests on the territory of the other State in cases where a person is found committing, attempting to commit, or just having committed an offence—

(a)   on board any train which has commenced its journey from one State to the other and is within the Fixed Link; or

(b)   within any tunnel described in Article 1(2) of the Treaty.

ARTICLE 41

In the case of arrests covered by Articles 39 and 40—

(a)   the person arrested shall be presented without delay to the competent authorities of the State of arrival for that State to be responsible for determining the exercise of jurisdiction as required by Article 38; and

(b)   where jurisdiction shall be exercised by the other State in accordance with Article 38, the person arrested may be transferred to the territory of that State. However, any such transfer shall take place within 48 hours of the presentation under paragraph (a) of this Article. Moreover, each State reserves the right not to transfer its nationals.

PART VII
PUBLIC SAFETY AND RESCUE

ARTICLE 42

(1)   In case of need the rescue services of the two countries may be committed to joint interventions within the Fixed Link; the rescue services of the adjoining State shall in that case be placed at the disposal of the competent authorities of the host State.

(2)   The rescue services so committed shall however remain under their own internal command.

ARTICLE 43

(1)   In the case of a joint intervention, the competent authorities of each State shall be responsible for the costs incurred by their own rescue services. Any costs which may be recovered from any person or organisation shall be shared in proportion to their actual costs incurred by the rescue services of the two countries.

(2)   The conditions under which the rescue services of the two countries may intervene shall be determined by the emergency arrangements established jointly by the competent authorities of the two States.

ARTICLE 44

(1)   Without prejudice to the application of the provisions of Article 46, if, during a rescue operation in the territory of the host State, damage is caused to a third party by a member of the rescue services of the adjoining State, the competent authorities of

the host State shall make reparations in respect of the damage according to the arrangements which would have applied had the damage been caused by its own rescue services.

(2)   In the case of the death of, or personal injury to, the personnel of the rescue services of the adjoining State, that State shall waive any claim against the host State.

(3)   Whilst in the exercise of their official functions, members of the rescue services shall—

(a)   benefit in the same way as officers from the provisions of Articles 28(1), 29 and 30(2);

(b)   in the case of a joint intervention, be permitted to circulate freely in the whole of the Fixed Link;

(c)   except in circumstances provided for in sub-paragraph (b) and after agreement by the competent authorities of the two States, be granted access where necessary to that part of the Fixed Link lying within the territory of the adjoining State.

PART VIII
FINAL CLAUSES

ARTICLE 46

(1)   Without prejudice to the application of Articles 15 and 16 of the Treaty in any case covered by those two Articles, in the case of claims for compensation resulting from the application of this Protocol the following provisions shall apply—

(a)   each State shall waive any claim which it may have against the other State for compensation in respect of damage caused to its officers or its property;

(b)   claims by the Concessionaires shall be dealt with in accordance with the provisions of the Concession.

(2)   The provisions of this Article do not affect in any way the rights of third parties under the laws of each State.

ARTICLE 47

The procedures for the implementation of this Protocol may, as far as necessary, be the subject of technical or administrative arrangements between the competent authorities of the two States.

[SCHEDULE 2A
SUPPLEMENTARY ARTICLES

Article 2(4)

ARTICLE 1

Any terms defined in Article 1 of the Protocol signed at Sangatte have the same meaning in this Additional Protocol. For the purposes of this Additional Protocol, the following definitions shall be added—

"State of departure" means the State in which the persons board the train;

"State of arrival" means the State in which the persons alight from the train.

ARTICLE 2

The authorities of the two States shall jointly put in place control bureaux, for persons using through trains and wishing to travel to the State of arrival, in the stations of London–Waterloo, London–St Pancras and Ashford on British territory, and the stations of Paris–Gare du Nord, Calais, and Lille–Europe on French territory.

The provisions of the Protocol signed at Sangatte concerning the officers of the adjoining State shall be applicable, under the same conditions, to the officers of the State of arrival who are on duty in the stations mentioned in the preceding paragraph.

ARTICLE 3

The purpose of the controls carried out by the authorities of the State of departure shall be to check whether the person can leave its territory.

The purpose of the controls carried out by the authorities of the State of arrival shall be to check whether the person is in possession of the necessary travel documents and fulfils the other conditions for entry to its territory. If this is not the case, the person shall be immediately handed over to the authorities of the State of departure who shall apply their domestic law procedures.

The authorities of the State of departure and of the State of arrival shall carry out their controls in accordance with this Additional Protocol, with their laws and regulations and with their international obligations.

The controls mentioned in the preceding paragraphs are without prejudice to customs and security controls.

ARTICLE 4

Notwithstanding the third paragraph of Article 3 of this Additional Protocol, when a person submits a request for refugee status or any other kind of protection provided for in international law or in the domestic law of the State of departure during a control carried out at the station of the State of departure by the officers of the State of arrival, this request shall be examined by the authorities of the State of departure in accordance with the rules and procedures of its domestic law.

The same provisions shall be applicable when the request is submitted after the person has passed through this control and before the train doors close at the last scheduled stop at a station located in the territory of the State of departure. If such a request is made after the train doors have closed, it shall be processed by the State of arrival in accordance with the rules and procedures of its domestic law.

ARTICLE 5

The controls referred to in Article 3 of this Additional Protocol shall be carried out in accordance with Article 12 of the Sangatte Protocol.

ARTICLE 6

The procedures for the implementation of this Additional Protocol may, as far as necessary, be the subject of technical or administrative arrangements between the competent authorities of the two States.]

NOTES

Inserted by the Channel Tunnel (International Arrangements) (Amendment No 3) Order 2001, SI 2001/1544, arts 2, 4(2), as from 25 May 2001.

SCHEDULE 3

Article 6

PART I
POWERS OF OFFICERS
Power to assist French authorities

1.—(1) Where—

(a)   an officer belonging to the French Republic has in a control zone in the United Kingdom [or in a supplementary control zone in the United Kingdom] arrested or detained a person as permitted by Article 10(1) of the international articles [and Article 2 of the supplementary articles], and

(b)   such an officer so requests,

a constable or an officer commissioned by the Commissioners of Customs and Excise under section 6(3) of the Customs and Excise Management Act 1979(a) (in this Schedule referred to as a "customs officer") may make arrangements for the person to be taken into temporary custody.

(2)   A person taken into temporary custody under sub-paragraph (1)—

(a)   shall be treated for all purposes as being in lawful custody, and

(b)   may be taken to a police station or such other place as may be appropriate in the circumstances, and shall in that case be treated as being a person in whose case sections 36(7) and (8), 54 to 56 and 58 of the Police and Criminal Evidence Act 1984 (in this Schedule referred to as "the 1984 Act"), and in the case of a child or young person section 34(2) to (7), (8) and (9) of the Children and Young Persons Act 1933, apply, and

(c)   must be returned, before the end of the period for which he could in the circumstances be detained in the United Kingdom under Article 10 of the international articles [or Article 2 of the supplementary articles], to a place where detention under that Article could be resumed.

[(3)   Where a person falls to be treated as mentioned in sub-paragraph (2)(b) section 56 of the 1984 Act shall be taken to apply as if he were detained for a serious arrestable offence.]

Powers of arrest outside United Kingdom

2.—(1)   A constable may in a control zone in France—

(a)   exercise any power of arrest conferred by a frontier control enactment or conferred by the 1984 Act in respect of an offence under such an enactment,

(b)   make any arrest authorised by a warrant issued by a court in the United Kingdom, and

(c)   arrest any person whose name or description or both, together with particulars of an [indictable offence] of which there are reasonable grounds for suspecting him to be guilty, have been made available by a chief officer of police to other such officers.

(2)   For the purposes of sub-paragraph (1)(a) the reference in sub-paragraph (1) to a constable shall be construed—

(a)   in relation to the powers of arrest conferred by [section 28A(1) and (3)] of and paragraph 17(1) of Schedule 2 to the Immigration Act 1971, as including a reference both—

     (i)   to an immigration officer appointed for the purposes of that Act under paragraph 1 of that Schedule, and

     (ii)   to an officer of customs and excise who is the subject of arrangements for the employment of such officers as immigration officers made under that paragraph by the Secretary of State,

[and where this sub-paragraph applies, the reference in sub-paragraph (1) to a control zone in France shall be construed as including a reference to a supplementary control zone in France,]

(b)   . . .

(c)   in relation to any arrest that may be made by a customs officer by virtue of section 138 of the Customs and Excise Management Act 1979 and an arrest for a drug trafficking offence as defined in section 38(1) of the Drug Trafficking Offences Act 1986, as including a reference to a customs officer.

(3) A customs officer may in a control zone in France arrest any person whose name or description or both, together with particulars of an arrestable offence (within the meaning of section 24 of the 1984 Act) which is an offence in relation to an assigned matter as defined in section 1(1) of the Customs and Excise Management Act 1979 and of which there are reasonable grounds for suspecting him to be guilty, have been made available to customs officers generally under the authority of the Commissioners of Customs and Excise.

(4) For the purpose of enabling constables to make arrests in France in the cases described in Article 40 of the international articles sections 24 and 25 of the 1984 Act shall extend to France.

(5) Where—

(a)   an arrest has been made for an offence of the kind mentioned in Article 39 of the international articles, and

(b)   it falls to the competent authorities in France to determine the exercise of jurisdiction in accordance with Article 38,

the person arrested shall be treated as continuing to be under arrest while in France until he is presented to those authorities as required by Article 41(a).

(6) Where—

(a)   an arrest falling within sub-paragraph (4) or (5) above has been made, and

(b)   the competent authorities in France determine under Article 4I of the international articles that jurisdiction is to be exercised by the United Kingdom,

the person arrested shall be treated as having continued to be under arrest throughout, even if he was for some period in the custody of those authorities, and sections 30 and 41 of the 1984 Act shall apply accordingly.

(7) Any power conferred by an enactment to search an arrested person may be exercised following an arrest authorised by this paragraph as if the person had been arrested in the United Kingdom.

Arrested persons held in France

3.—(1) Where—

(a)   an arrest of any kind authorised by paragraph 2 above has been made in a control zone in France [or in a supplementary control zone in France], or

(b)   an arrest of any such kind has been made in the United Kingdom and the person arrested enters such a control zone while under arrest,

the person arrested may be held in France for a period of not more than 24 hours and, if there are exceptional circumstances and an officer belonging to the French Republic is notified of the extension, for a further such period.

(2) Subject to sub-paragraphs (3) and (4), the person arrested shall be treated as if the place where he is held were for the purposes of the provisions mentioned in paragraph 1(2)(b) above and those of sections 61 to 63 of the 1984 Act a police station, or where the arrest was made by a customs officer, a customs office, in England, not being a police station or customs office designated under section 35 of the 1984 Act.

(3) Where—

(a)   an arrest falling within paragraph 2(1)(a) or (3) above has been made by a customs officer, and

(b)   the person arrested is held in France in a place within the tunnel system which would if it were in England be a customs office within the meaning of the 1984 Act,

sections 34(1) to (5), 36, 37, 39 to 42, 50, 54, 55, 56(1) to (9), 58 (1) to (11), 62, 63 and 64(1) to (6) of the 1984 Act and in the case of a child or young person section 34(2) to (7), (8) and (9) of the Children and Young Persons Act 1933, shall apply as if the place where he is held were a customs office in England designated under section 35 of the 1984 Act.

(4) . . .

[Arrested persons arriving in the United Kingdom]

4.—[(1)   Where—

(a)   an arrest falling within Article 39 or 40 of the international articles has been made, and

(b)   the person arrested enters the United Kingdom while under arrest,

the person arrested shall be taken to a police station.]

(2)   The custody officer at the police station to which the person is taken shall determine—

(a)   whether the offence is one over which the United Kingdom has jurisdiction by virtue of Article 38(1), and

(b)   if he determines that it is not, whether it is one over which the United Kingdom may exercise jurisdiction by virtue of Article 38(2) and if so whether jurisdiction is to be exercised,

and may for the purpose of determining those questions detain the person at the police station for not longer than the permitted period.

(3)   The permitted period is the period of 48 hours beginning at the time at which the person arrives at the police station.

(4)   Subject to sub-paragraph (6), the person shall be treated—

(a)   as not being detained at the police station for the purposes of section 37 of the 1984 Act, and

(b)   as not being in police detention for the purposes of sections 40 to 43 of the 1984 Act.

(5)   Where the custody officer determines that the United Kingdom does not have jurisdiction by virtue of Article 38(1) and—

(a)   that jurisdiction is not exercisable by virtue of Article 38(2), or

(b)   that jurisdiction is exercisable by virtue of Article 38(2) but is not to be exercised,

he shall immediately inform the competent French authorities of his determination and shall arrange for the person to be transferred to France within the permitted period.

(6)   Where the custody officer determines that the United Kingdom has jurisdiction by virtue of Article 38(1) or that jurisdiction is exercisable by virtue of Article 38(2) and is to be exercised—

(a)   he shall immediately inform the person of his determination,

(b)   the person shall be treated as being in police detention for all purposes of Part IV of the 1984 Act, and

(c)   that Part shall have effect in relation to him as if the relevant time mentioned in section 41(1) were the time at which he is informed of the determination.

(7)   Where the police station to which the person is taken is not a police station designated under section 35 of the 1984 Act, references in this paragraph to the custody officer are to be construed as references to an officer not below the rank of sergeant.

Arrests of French officers

5.—(1)   This paragraph applies where an officer belonging to the French Republic ("the officer") is arrested for an act performed in the United Kingdom in the tunnel system or a control zone [or supplementary control zone].

(2)   If the officer enters France while under arrest—

(a)   he shall without delay be handed over for custody to the competent French authorities and shall be treated as continuing to be under arrest until he has been handed over, and

(b)   if after consultation with those authorities it is then determined that the act was not performed by the officer whilst in the exercise of his functions and he accordingly does not by virtue of Article 30(2) of the international articles come under French jurisdiction, he shall be treated as having continued to be under arrest until sub-paragraph (3) has been complied with.

(3)   Where—

(a)   sub-paragraph (2)(b) applies, or

(b)   the officer does not enter France while under arrest,

he shall be taken to a police station designated under section 35 of the 1984 Act.

(4)   Sub-paragraphs (5) to (9) apply in a case falling within sub-paragraph (3)(b).

(5)   The custody officer at the police station to which the officer is taken shall after consultation with the competent French authorities determine whether the act was performed by the officer whilst in the exercise of his functions, and may for the purpose of determining that question detain the officer at the police station for not longer than the permitted period.

(6)   The permitted period is the period of 48 hours beginning at the time at which the officer arrives at the police station.

(7)   Subject to sub-paragraph (9), the officer shall be treated—

(a)   as not being detained at the police station for the purposes of section 37 of the 1984 Act, and

(b)   as not being in police detention for the purposes of sections 40 to 43 of the 1984 Act.

(8)   Where the custody officer determines that the act was performed by the officer whilst in the exercise of his functions and the officer accordingly comes under French jurisdiction by virtue of Article 30(2), he shall immediately inform the competent French authorities and shall arrange for the officer to be transferred to France within the permitted period.

(9)   In any other case—

(a)   the custody officer shall immediately inform the officer of his determination,

(b)   the officer shall be treated as being in police detention for all purposes of Part IV of the 1984 Act, and

(c)   that Part shall have effect in relation to him as if the relevant time mentioned in section 41(1) were the time at which he is informed of the determination.

Arrests of United Kingdom officers

6.—(1) This paragraph applies where an officer belonging to the United Kingdom ("the officer") is arrested for an act performed in France in the tunnel system or a control zone [or supplementary control zone].

(2) If—

(a) the officer does not enter the United Kingdom while under arrest, and

(b) the competent French authorities determine that the act was performed by the officer whilst in the exercise of his functions and he accordingly comes under United Kingdom jurisdiction by virtue of Article 30(2) of the international articles,

he shall on being handed over by those authorities to a constable be treated as having been arrested by the constable.

(3) Where—

(a) sub-paragraph (2)(b) applies, or

(b) the officer enters the United Kingdom while under the original arrest,

he shall be taken to a police station designated under section 35 of the 1984 Act.

(4) Sub-paragraphs (5) to (9) apply in a case falling within sub-paragraph (3)(b).

(5) The custody officer at the police station to which the officer is taken shall—

(a) immediately invite the competent French authorities to determine whether the act was performed by the officer whilst in the exercise of his functions, and

(b) afford those authorities any assistance they may require in determining that question, and may for the purpose of enabling that question to be determined detain the officer at the police station for not longer than the permitted period.

(6) The permitted period is the period of 48 hours beginning at the time at which the officer arrives at the police station.

(7) Subject to sub-paragraph (9), the officer shall be treated—

(a) as not being detained at the police station for the purposes of section 37 of the 1984 Act, and

(b) as not being in police detention for the purposes of sections 40 to 43 of the 1984 Act.

(8) Where the competent French authorities determine that the act was not performed by the officer whilst in the exercise of his functions and the officer accordingly does not by virtue of Article 30(2) come under United Kingdom jurisdiction, the custody officer shall arrange for the officer to be transferred to France within the permitted period.(9) In any other case—

(a) the custody officer shall immediately inform the officer of the determination,

(b) the officer shall be treated as being in police detention for all purposes of Part IV of the 1984 Act, and

(c) that Part shall have effect in relation to him as if the relevant time mentioned in section 41(1) were the time at which he is informed of the determination.

NOTES

Para 1: words in paras (1)(a), (2)(c) inserted by the Channel Tunnel (International Arrangements) (Amendment No 3) Order 2001, SI 2001/1544, arts 2, 5(1)–(3), as from 25 May 2001; sub-para (3) inserted by the Channel Tunnel (Miscellaneous Provisions) Order 1994, SI 1994/1405, art 8, Sch 4, para 10(a).

Para 2: words substituted, and words at end of that para inserted by SI 2001/1544, arts 2, 5(4); in sub-para (1)(c) words substituted by the Serious Organised Crime and Police Act 2005

(Powers of Arrest) (Consequential Amendments) Order, SI 2005/3389, art 5; sub-para (2)(b) repealed by the Channel Tunnel (International Arrangements) (Amendment) Order 2001, SI 2001/178, art 3(a).

Para 3: words in para (1)(a) inserted by SI 2001/1544, arts 2, 5(5); sub-para (4) repealed by SI 2001/178, art 3(b).

Para 4: paragraph heading and sub-para (1) substituted by SI 1994/1405, art 8, Sch 4, para 10(b), (c).

Paras 5, 6: words in para (1) inserted by SI 2001/1544, arts 2, 5(6).

PART II
SUPPLEMENTARY CONTROLS OVER ANIMALS

Extent

1. This Part does not extend to France.

Interpretation

2. In this Part "animal" means a four-footed mammal capable of carrying the rabies virus, except one which—

    (a)   is lawfully being transported through the tunnel system, or

    (b)   enters the tunnel system for purposes connected with law enforcement or security and is under the control of a person approved in writing by the appropriate Minister,

and "tunnel", except in the expression "tunnel system", means a tunnel mentioned in section 1(7)(a) of the Channel Tunnel Act 1987.

Duties of Concessionaires

3. The Concessionaires shall—

    [(a)   construct and maintain fencing around the entrance to each tunnel, except at places where gaps are necessary to allow the passage of vehicles through the tunnel, of such material and of such a height above and depth below the surface of the ground as to ensure, so far as is practicable, that an animal cannot cross it, and]

    (b)   comply with the requirements imposed by paragraph 5.

Installations

4. . . .

Requirements

5. The requirements mentioned in paragraph 3(b) are—

    (a)   to ensure, so far as is practicable, that any animal which has entered a tunnel is removed from the tunnel system,

    (b)   to operate a system of surveillance that will ensure, so far as is practicable, that the passage of any animal through a tunnel is detected,

    (c)   to take effective measures for the control of rodents, including monitoring each tunnel for the presence of rodents and laying poisoned bait for them,

    (d)   so far as is practicable, to keep each tunnel free of waste food, urine, faeces and every other substance likely to attract animals,

    (e)   to ensure that all points of access to a tunnel, other than the entrance to the tunnel and any ventilation shafts, are sealed when not in use,

(f)   to ensure that all tunnel ventilation shafts are so constructed as effectively to deter animals from passing through them, and

(g)   to keep records of the taking of any bait laid as mentioned in sub-paragraph (c) and of the detection of the presence of any animal in a tunnel or within the fencing [described in paragraph 3(a)].

Unauthorised interference

6. Unless authorised in writing by the Concessionaires, no person shall intentionally—

(a)   remove or in any way impair the effectiveness of [the fencing described in paragraph 3(a)], or

(b)   do anything which might in any way impair the effectiveness of any measures taken to comply with the requirements described in paragraph 5.

Enforcement

7. A person authorised by the appropriate Minister may, on producing, if required to do so, some duly authenticated document showing his authority—

(a)   enter any part of the tunnel system for the purpose of ascertaining whether there is or has been any breach of a requirement or prohibition imposed by this Part, and

(b)   for that purpose inspect any relevant document or computer record.

Offences

8. A person who contravenes any of paragraphs 3 to 6 or obstructs the exercise of powers by an authorised person under paragraph 7 shall be guilty of an offence and shall be liable—

(a)   on conviction on indictment to a fine, and

(b)   on summary conviction to a fine not exceeding the statutory maximum.

NOTES

Para 3: sub-para (a) substituted by the Channel Tunnel (International Arrangements) (Amendment) Order 2003, SI 2003/2799 art 2(1), (2).

Para (4): revoked by SI 2003/2799 art 2(1), (3).

Para (5): in sub-para (g), words substituted by SI 2003/2799 art 2(1), (4).

Para (6): in sub-para (a), words substituted by SI 2003/2799 art 2(1), (5).

(Sch 4 modifies enactments not reproduced in this work; Schs 5, 6 contain amendments and repeals only.)

Part II

TRAVELLERS' ALLOWANCES ORDER 1994

(SI 1994/955)

NOTES

Made: 28 March 1994.

Authority: Customs and Excise Duties (General Reliefs) Act 1979, s 13(1), (3).

Commencement: 1 April 1994.

1

This Order may be cited as the Travellers' Allowances Order 1994 and shall come into force on 1st April 1994.

2—

(1)   Subject to the following provisions of this Order a person who has travelled from a third country shall on entering the United Kingdom be relieved from payment of value added tax and excise duty on goods of the descriptions and in the quantities shown in the Schedule to this Order obtained by him in a third country and contained in his personal luggage.

(2)   For the purposes of this article—

(a)   goods shall be treated as contained in a person's personal luggage where they are carried with or accompanied by the person or, if intended to accompany him, were at the time of his departure for the United Kingdom consigned by him as personal luggage to the transport operator with whom he travelled;

(b)   a person shall not be treated as having travelled from a third country by reason only of his having arrived from its territorial waters or air space;

(c)   "third country", in relation to relief from excise duties, shall mean a place to which Council Directive 92/12/EEC of 25th February 1992 does not apply; and, in relation to relief from value added tax, shall have the meaning given by Article 3(1) of Council Directive 77/388/EEC of 17th May 1977 (as substituted by Article 1.1 of Council Directive 91/680/EEC of 16th December 1991).

3

The reliefs afforded under this Order are subject to the condition that the goods in question, as indicated by their nature or quantity or otherwise, are not imported for a commercial purpose nor are used for such purpose; and if that condition is not complied with in relation to any goods, those goods shall, unless the non-compliance was sanctioned by the Commissioners, be liable to forfeiture.

4

No relief shall be afforded under this Order to any person under the age of 17 in respect of tobacco products or alcoholic beverages.

5

(Revokes the Customs Duty (Personal Reliefs) (No 1) Order 1968, SI 1968/1558, the Customs Duty (Personal Reliefs) (No 1) Order 1968 (Amendment) Order 1972, SI 1972/1770, the Customs Duty (Personal Reliefs) (No 1) Order 1968 (Amendment) Order 1978, SI 1978/1883, the Customs Duty (Personal Reliefs) (No 1) Order 1968 (Amendment) Order 1979, SI 1979/1551, the Customs Duty (Personal Reliefs) (No 1) Order 1968 (Amendments) Order 1982, SI 1982/1591, the Customs Duty (Personal Reliefs) (No 1) Order 1968 (Amendment) Order 1984, SI 1984/718, the Customs Duty (Personal Reliefs) (No 1) Order 1968 (Amendment) Order 1985, SI 1985/1375, the Customs Duty (Personal Reliefs) (No 1)

Order 1968 (Amendment) Order 1986, SI 1986/2105, the Customs Duty (Personal Reliefs) (Amendment) Order 1989, SI 1989/2252, the Customs Duty (Personal Reliefs) (Amendment) Order 1991, SI 1991/1286, and the Customs Duty (Personal Reliefs) (Amendment) Order 1992, SI 1992/3192.)

SCHEDULE
GOODS OBTAINED IN THIRD COUNTRIES
Article 2

ALCOHOLIC BEVERAGES

(a) with an alcoholic strength of more than 22% by volume	a total of 1 litre
OR	
with an alcoholic strength of not more than 22% by volume; fortified wines, sparkling wines (including made wines)	a total of 2 litres
(b) still wines (including made wines)	a total of 2 litres

PERFUME AND TOILET WATER

Perfume	60 ml
Toilet Water	250 ml

TOBACCO

Cigarettes	200
OR	
Cigarillos	100
OR	
Cigars	50
OR	
Smoking tobacco	250 grammes

OTHER GOODS

An article of any other description the value of which does not exceed [£145] or several such articles the combined values of which do not exceed that amount.

NOTES

Sum in square brackets substituted by the Travellers' Allowances Amendment Order 1995, SI 1995/3044, art 2.

AIRCRAFT OPERATORS (ACCOUNTS AND RECORDS) REGULATIONS 1994

(SI 1994/1737)

NOTES

Made: 1 July 1994.

Authority: Customs and Excise Management Act 1979, ss 118A, 172.

Commencement: 1 November 1994.

ARRANGEMENT OF REGULATIONS

1 Citation and commencement

These Regulations may be cited as the Aircraft Operators (Accounts and Records) Regulations 1994 and shall come into force on 1st November 1994.

2 Application

(1) These Regulations shall apply to every operator who operates chargeable aircraft for the carriage of chargeable passengers.

(2) Where, in relation to air passenger duty, the Revenue Traders (Accounts and Records) Regulations 1992 would apply to any operator or fiscal representative, these Regulations shall apply to him and those Regulations shall not apply to him.

3 Interpretation

(1) In these Regulations—

"the Act" means the Finance Act 1994;

"Air Passenger Duty Account" has the meaning given in regulation 4;

"operator" means the operator of an aircraft;

"scheme" means a scheme prepared for a registered operator in accordance with the provisions of section 39 of the Act.

(2) Except as provided in paragraph (1) above, expressions used in these Regulations bear the meaning which they bear in Chapter IV of Part I of the Act.

4 Air Passenger Duty Account

(1) Every operator shall keep and preserve a record to be known as an Air Passenger Duty Account.

(2) Except in the case of operators to whom regulation 5 applies, an Air Passenger Duty Account shall contain the particulars set out in Schedule 1.

5 Schemes

(1) This regulation shall apply to an operator ("relevant operator") for so long as a scheme has effect in relation to him.

(2) An Air Passenger Duty Account kept by a relevant operator shall contain the particulars set out in Part I of Schedule 2.

(3) Every relevant operator shall keep and preserve the items described in Part II of Schedule 2.

6 Other records

Every operator shall keep and preserve such other records as the Commissioners may specify in a notice published by them and not withdrawn by a further notice.

7 Time for making records

Where an operator is required by or under these Regulations to keep any record, he shall do so at the time—

    (a)   of the happening of the event recorded; or

    (b)   as the case may be, when the information recorded is first known to him,

or as soon as possible thereafter.

8 Content and preservation of records

(1) Where an operator is required by or under these Regulations to keep any record he shall include in it sufficient information (by way of cross referencing or otherwise) to enable the Commissioners to ascertain readily that every return he makes is true and accurate.

(2) Except as otherwise provided by a scheme, where an operator is required by or under these Regulations to preserve any record, he shall preserve that record—

    (a)   for six years; or

    (b)   for such lesser period as the Commissioners may specify for any case or cases in a notice published by them and not withdrawn by a further notice.

[9 Interpretation of regulations 9 to 16

In this regulation and in regulations 10 to 16 below—

    "claim" means a claim made (irrespective of when it was made) under section 137A of the Customs and Excise Management Act 1979 for repayment of an amount paid to the Commissioners by way of excise duty which was not due to them; and "claimed" and "claimant" shall be construed accordingly;

    "reimbursement arrangements" means any arrangements (whether made before, on or after 30th January 1998) for the purposes of a claim which—

        (a)   are made by a claimant for the purpose of securing that he is not unjustly enriched by the repayment of any amount in pursuance of the claim; and

        (b)   provide for the reimbursement of persons (consumers) who have, for practical purposes, borne the whole or any part of the cost of the original payment of that amount to the Commissioners;

    "relevant amount" means that part (which may be the whole) of the amount of a claim which the claimant has reimbursed or intends to reimburse to consumers.]

NOTES

Commencement: 15 February 1999.

Inserted, together with regs 10–16, by the Aircraft Operators (Accounts and Records) (Amendment) Regulations 1998, SI 1998/63, reg 2.

[10 Reimbursement arrangements—general
Without prejudice to regulation 16 below, for the purposes of section 137A(3) of the Customs and Excise Management Act 1979 (defence by the Commissioners that repayment by them of an amount claimed would unjustly enrich the claimant) reimbursement arrangements made by a claimant shall be disregarded except where they—

(a)   include the provisions described in regulation 11 below; and

(b)   are supported by the undertakings described in regulation 15 below.]

NOTES

Commencement: 15 February 1999.

Inserted, together with regs 9, 11–16, by the Aircraft Operators (Accounts and Records) (Amendment) Regulations 1998, SI 1998/63, reg 2.

[11 Reimbursement arrangements—provisions to be included
The provisions referred to in regulation 10(a) above are that—

(a)   reimbursement for which the arrangements provide will be completed by no later than 90 days after the repayment to which it relates;

(b)   no deduction will be made from the relevant amount by way of fee or charge (howsoever expressed or effected);

(c)   reimbursement will be made only in cash or by cheque;

(d)   any part of the relevant amount that is not reimbursed by the time mentioned in paragraph (a) above will be repaid by the claimant to the Commissioners;

(e)   any interest paid by the Commissioners on any relevant amount repaid by them will also be treated by the claimant in the same way as the relevant amount falls to be treated under paragraphs (a) and (b) above; and

(f)   the records described in regulation 13 below will be kept by the claimant and produced by him to the Commissioners, or to an officer of theirs in accordance with regulation 14 below.]

NOTES

Commencement: 15 February 1999.

Inserted, together with regs 9, 10, 12–16, by the Aircraft Operators (Accounts and Records) (Amendment) Regulations 1998, SI 1998/63, reg 2.

[12 Repayments to the Commissioners
The claimant shall, without prior demand, make any repayment to the Commissioners that he is required to make by virtue of regulation 11(d) and (e) above within 14 days of the expiration of the period of 90 days referred to in regulation 11(a) above.]

NOTES

Commencement: 15 February 1999.

Inserted, together with regs 9–11, 13–16, by the Aircraft Operators (Accounts and Records) (Amendment) Regulations 1998, SI 1998/63, reg 2.

[13 Records
The claimant shall keep records of the following matters—

(a)   the names and addresses of those consumers whom he has reimbursed or whom he intends to reimburse;

(b)   the total amount reimbursed to each such consumer;

(c)   the amount of interest included in each total amount reimbursed to each consumer;

(d)   the date that each reimbursement is made.]

NOTES

Commencement: 15 February 1999.

Inserted, together with regs 9–12, 14–16, by the Aircraft Operators (Accounts and Records) (Amendment) Regulations 1998, SI 1998/63, reg 2.

[14 Production of records

(1)   Where a claimant is given notice in accordance with paragraph (2) below, he shall, in accordance with such notice produce to the Commissioners, or to an officer of theirs, the records that he is required to keep pursuant to regulation 13 above.

(2)   A notice given for the purposes of paragraph (1) above shall—

(a)   be in writing;

(b)   state the place and time at which, and the date on which the records are to be produced; and

(c)   be signed and dated by the Commissioners, or by an officer of theirs, and may be given before or after, or both before and after the Commissioners have paid the relevant amount to the claimant.]

NOTES

Commencement: 15 February 1999.

Inserted, together with regs 9–13, 15, 16, by the Aircraft Operators (Accounts and Records) (Amendment) Regulations 1998, SI 1998/63, reg 2.

[15 Undertakings

(1)   Without prejudice to regulation 16(b) below, the undertakings referred to in regulation 10(b) above shall be given to the Commissioners by the claimant no later than the time at which he makes the claim for which the reimbursement arrangements have been made.

(2)   The undertakings shall be in writing, shall be signed and dated by the claimant, and shall be to the effect that—

(a)   at the date of the undertakings he is able to identify the names and addresses of those consumers whom he has reimbursed or whom he intends to reimburse;

(b)   he will apply the whole of the relevant amount repaid to him, without any deduction by way of fee or charge or otherwise, to the reimbursement in cash or by cheque, of such consumers by no later than 90 days after his receipt of that amount (except insofar as he has already so reimbursed them);

(c)   he will apply any interest paid to him on the relevant amount repaid to him wholly to the reimbursement of such consumers by no later than 90 days after his receipt of that interest;

(d)   he will repay to the Commissioners without demand the whole or such part of the relevant amount repaid to him or of any interest paid to him as he fails to apply in accordance with the undertakings mentioned in sub-paragraphs (b) and (c) above;

(e)   he will keep the records described in regulation 13 above; and

(f)   he will comply with any notice given to him in accordance with regulation 14 above concerning the production of such records.]

NOTES

Commencement: 15 February 1999.

Inserted, together with regs 9–14, 16, by the Aircraft Operators (Accounts and Records) (Amendment) Regulations 1998, SI 1998/63, reg 2.

[16   Reimbursement arrangements made before 11th February 1998

Reimbursement arrangements made by a claimant before 11th February 1998 shall not be disregarded for the purposes of section 137A(3) of the Customs and Excise Management Act 1979 if, not later than 11th March 1998—

(a)   he includes in those arrangements (if they are not already included) the provisions described in regulation 11 above; and

(b)   gives the undertakings described in regulation 15 above.]

NOTES

Commencement: 15 February 1999.

Inserted, together with regs 9–15, by the Aircraft Operators (Accounts and Records) (Amendment) Regulations 1998, SI 1998/63, reg 2.

SCHEDULES

SCHEDULE 1

PARTICULARS OF AN AIR PASSENGER DUTY ACCOUNT

Regulation 4

For each accounting period—

(a)   the amount, before adjustment, of any duty payable;

(b)   the amount of any adjustment;

(c)   the amount, after adjustment, of any duty payable;

(d)   the amount, date and method of payment of any duty paid;

(e)   the number of passengers carried—

(i)   chargeable at the [rates set out in section 30(3A)(a) and (b)] of the Act; and

(ii)   chargeable at the [rates set out in section 30(4)(a) and (b)] of the Act;

(f)   the number of passengers who were not chargeable passengers by virtue of each of subsections . . ., (3), (4) and (5) of section 31 of the Act;

(g)   the number of persons carried who, but for the exceptions provided for by the definition of "passenger" in section 43(1) of the Act, would be chargeable passengers;

(h)   . . .

NOTES

Words in square brackets in para (e) substituted and words in para (f) and whole of para (h) revoked by the Aircraft Operators (Accounts and Records) (Amendment) Regulations 2001, SI 2001/837, reg 3.

SCHEDULE 2
RELEVANT OPERATORS

Regulation 5

PART I
PARTICULARS OF AN AIR PASSENGER DUTY ACCOUNT KEPT BY RELEVANT OPERATORS

1. For each accounting period—
   (a)   the amount, before adjustment, of any duty payable;
   (b)   the amount, of any adjustment;
   (c)   the amount, after adjustment, of any duty payable;
   (d)   the amount, the calculations used in ascertaining this amount, date and method of payment of any duty paid;
   (e)   the number of passengers who were not chargeable passengers by virtue of each of subsections (4) and (5) of section 31 of the Act;
   (f)   the number of persons carried who, but for the exceptions provided for by the definition of "passenger" in section 43(1) of the Act, would be chargeable passengers;
   (g)   such other particulars as the Commissioners may specify in a notice published by them and not withdrawn by a further notice.

PART II
OTHER ITEMS TO BE KEPT BY RELEVANT OPERATORS

2.—(1)   A copy of the scheme prepared for him by the Commissioners.

(2)   A copy of the surveys of passengers by reference to which the calculations provided for by the scheme will be made.

(3)   Such other documents as appear to the Commissioners to be relevant to the calculations provided for by the scheme and which are specified in a notice published by them and not withdrawn by a further notice.

AIR PASSENGER DUTY REGULATIONS 1994
(SI 1994/1738)

NOTES

Made: 1 July 1994.

Authority: Finance Act 1994, ss 31(3), (6), 32(2), (3), 33(4), (7), (8), 34(5), 35(1), (2), 38(1), (2), 42, 43(1).

Commencement: 1 August 1994.

ARRANGEMENT OF REGULATIONS

PART I
PRELIMINARY

PART II
REGISTRATION

PART I
PRELIMINARY

1 Citation and commencement

These Regulations may be cited as the Air Passenger Duty Regulations 1994 and shall
come into force on 1st August 1994.

2 Interpretation

(1)   In these Regulations—

"accounting period" means either—

(a)   a period ending on the last day of each month; or

(b)   such other period as, in any particular case, the Commissioners
      allow;

"the Act" means the Finance Act 1994;

"business day" means a day which is a business day within the meaning of
section 92 of the Bills of Exchange Act 1882;

"operator" means the operator of an aircraft;

"the register" means the register of operators which the Commissioners are
required to keep by virtue of section 33(1) of the Act.

(2)   Any notice given to the Commissioners pursuant to these Regulations must be
given at the place at which notice pursuant to section 33(4) of the Act must be given.

PART II
REGISTRATION

3 Time for giving notice of liability to register

Where an operator is required to give notice under section 33(4) of the Act, he shall do
so no later than the seventh day following that on which he became liable to be
registered.

4 Registration of operators

(1)   The register shall contain the information set out in Schedule 1.

(2)   Where an operator is included in the register, that entry shall be effective from
the first day of the month in which he became liable to be registered.

(3) Where—

(a) an operator has not given notice of his liability to be registered, but

(b) it appears to the Commissioners that he is liable to be registered,

they shall include him in the register.

(4) Where an operator is included in the register the Commissioners shall furnish him with a certificate of registration.

(5) A certificate of registration shall contain the information included in the entry in the register relating to the operator to whom it is furnished ("relevant information").

(6) A registered operator shall give notice of any change in any relevant information within thirty days of the change by returning his certificate of registration to the Commissioners with the change recorded on it.

(7) Where, in accordance with paragraph (6) above, a certificate of registration is returned to them, the Commissioners shall—

(a) correct the register, and

(b) furnish the registered operator with a new certificate of registration.

5 Removal from the register

(1) Subject to paragraph (2) below, where—

(a) a registered operator gives the Commissioners notice in writing that he has ceased to operate chargeable aircraft; or

(b) a registered operator—

(i) has not within the preceding six months operated chargeable aircraft, and

(ii) it appears to the Commissioners that he will not within the next twelve months operate chargeable aircraft,

he shall be removed from the register.

(2) A registered operator shall not be removed from the register if he owes any duty to the Commissioners.

PART III

FISCAL REPRESENTATIVES

6 Appointment

(1) An operator who is required to have a fiscal representative shall appoint such a representative—

(a) within seven days of the day on which he is required by section 34(1) of the Act to have a fiscal representative; or

(b) where—

(i) a fiscal representative ("his representative") ceases to act for him, and

(ii) he continues to be required by section 34(1) of the Act to have a fiscal representative,

within seven days of the day on which his representative ceased to act for him.

(2) A fiscal representative shall give to the Commissioners written notice of his appointment, within seven days of his being appointed.

(3) A notice given in accordance with paragraph (2) above shall contain the information set out in Schedule 2.

7 Ceasing to act as a fiscal representative

(1) Where a person ceases to act as a fiscal representative for an operator he shall, within seven days, give written notice of that fact to the Commissioners.

(2) A person shall be treated as having ceased to act as a fiscal representative if—

(a)   he gives notice in accordance with paragraph (1) above;

(b)   his principal gives the Commissioners notice that his appointment is terminated;

(c)   he is imprisoned in pursuance of the order of any court whether in the United Kingdom or elsewhere;

(d)   he becomes bankrupt or insolvent whether in the United Kingdom or elsewhere [or is the subject of a bankruptcy restrictions order or an interim order]; or

(e)   he ceases to meet the requirements of section 34(3) of the Act.

NOTES

Para (2): words in sub-para (d) inserted by the Enterprise Act 2002 (Disqualification from Office: General) Order, SI 2006/1722, art 2(2), Sch 2, para 10.

8 Inclusion of particulars in register of operators

Where the Commissioners receive notice that a person has been appointed as the fiscal representative of an operator they shall include his name in the entry in the register relating to that operator.

PART IV

RETURNS AND PAYMENT

9 Returns

(1)   Subject to paragraph (2) below, every operator who is liable to be registered and every registered operator shall, not later than the twenty-second day following the end of each accounting period, furnish to the Commissioners a return on the form set out in Schedule 3.

(2)   Where the last day for furnishing a return would (if determined in accordance with paragraph (1) above) fall on a day which is not a business day the return shall be furnished not later than the last business day before that day.

(3)   Returns shall be furnished to the Commissioners at such place as, in accordance with section 38(1)(b) of the Act, they have specified.

10 Payment

(1)   Subject to paragraph (2) below, every operator shall pay the duty which becomes due from him in any accounting period—

(a)   in the case of a registered operator who has made arrangements with the Commissioners for duty to be paid by means of direct debit or credit transfer, not later than the twenty-ninth day following the end of that accounting period; or

(b)   in any other case, not later than the twenty-second day following the end of that accounting period.

(2)   Where the last day for making payment would (if determined in accordance with paragraph (1) above) fall on a day which is not a business day the payment shall be made not later than the last business day before that day.

(3)   Where payment is not made by means of direct debit or credit transfer, it shall be made to the Commissioners at such place as, in accordance with section 38(1)(b) of the Act, they have specified.

PART V

FLIGHTS AND PASSENGERS

11 Particulars of flights

(1)   For the purposes of section 31(3) of the Act the following particulars of a second or subsequent flight are prescribed—

    (a)   the airport from which the passenger intends to depart;

    (b)   the date and time of his intended departure; and

    (c)   the airport at which he intends to arrive.

(2)   For the purposes of section 32(2)(b) and (3)(b) of the Act the following particulars of a flight are prescribed—

    (a)   the airport from which the passenger intends to depart;

    (b)   the date and time of his intended departure; and

    (c)   the airport at which he intends to arrive.

12 Passengers

(1)   For the purposes of paragraph (a)(iii) of the definition of "passenger" in section 43(1) of the Act the following requirements are prescribed—

    (a)   the employee is—

        (i)   engaged in relevant duties, or

        (ii)   performing on board services,

    at the time he is carried;

    (b)   the employee will within the seventy-two hours next following the end of his flight—

        (i)   act as a member of a flight crew,

        (ii)   act as a cabin attendant,

        (iii)   be engaged in relevant duties, or

        (iv)   perform on board services,

    on, or in respect of, any aircraft; or

    (c)   the employee is returning to his base and has within the seventy-two hours immediately preceding the beginning of his flight—

        (i)   acted as a member of a flight crew,

        (ii)   acted as a cabin attendant,

        (iii)   been engaged in relevant duties, or

        (iv)   performed on board services,

    on, or in respect of, any aircraft.

(2)   In this regulation—

"base" means the place from which the employee ordinarily operates or at which he is ordinarily stationed;

"on board services" means escorting a passenger or goods;

"relevant duties" means—

    (a)   repair, maintenance, safety or security work; or

    (b)   ensuring the hygienic preparation and handling of food and drink.

13 Outward journey of an Isle of Man return passenger

(1)   Subject to paragraph (2) below, section 31(1) of the Act shall have effect as if the reference in paragraph (a) thereof to a person who is a chargeable passenger in relation to a flight on his outward journey included a person whose outward journey began at an airport in the Isle of Man.

(2)   Paragraph (1) above only applies in the case of a person—

(a) whose outward journey in question begins at an airport in the Isle of Man; and

(b) who, by virtue of an act of Tynwald charging a duty equivalent to air passenger duty, is the equivalent of a chargeable passenger in relation to that outward journey.

SCHEDULES

SCHEDULE 1
INFORMATION TO BE INCLUDED IN THE REGISTER
(reg 4)

(a) a unique reference number assigned to the operator by the Commissioners;

(b) the name and (if different) the trading name of the operator;

(c) the address of the operator's principal, or only place of business (including any postcode)—

(i) in the United Kingdom, or

(ii) if he does not have any place of business in the United Kingdom, elsewhere;

(d) if he has one, the operator's telephone number and (if different) his telephone number for facsimile transmissions;

(e) the date on which the Commissioners received any notice given pursuant to section 33(4) of the Act and the time from which the operator's entry in the register was effective;

(f) if required by regulation 8, the name and (if different) the trading name of any fiscal representative appointed to act for the operator in accordance with section 34 of the Act.

SCHEDULE 2
INFORMATION TO BE INCLUDED IN A NOTICE OF APPOINTMENT AS A FISCAL REPRESENTATIVE
(reg 6)

(a) the name and (if different) the trading name of the fiscal representative;

(b) the address of the fiscal representative's principal, or only place of business in the United Kingdom (including his postcode);

(c) if he has one, the fiscal representative's telephone number and (if different) his telephone number for facsimile transmissions;

(d) the name and (if different) the trading name of the operator for whom he is acting ("his principal");

(e) the date on which he was appointed to act for his principal.

SCHEDULE 3
(reg 9)

Regulation 2

Air Passenger Duty Return

For the period
to

For Official Use

APD Registration number   Period Number

You could be liable to a financial penalty if
your completed return is not received by the
due date and all duty due for the period is not paid
in not paid in full by the payment due date.

Due date:

D O R
only

Before you complete this form please read the enclosed general notes. Both sides should be completed.
Do not enter more than one amount in any box, fill in all boxes clearly and write "None" where necessary.

A. Passenger and Duty Details

		Passengers	£	p
1	Total number of chargeable passengers flown in chargeable aircraft at the lower EEA Rate			00
2	Total number of chargeable passengers flown in chargeable aircraft at the standard EEA Rate			00
3	Total number of chargeable passengers flown in chargeable aircraft at the lower non EEA Rate			00
4	Total number of chargeable passengers flown in chargeable aircraft at the standard non EEA Rate			00
5	Total number of Exempt Passengers			
6	Total number of Passengers flown in this period			
7	Underdeclarations from previous periods (Must not exceed £2000. see general notes)			00
8	Overdeclarations from previous periods (no limit)			00
	TOTAL DUTY DUE			00

For Official Use

APD 2

B. Special Accounting Schemes

**For further information please refer to Notice 551 'Special Accounting Schemes for APD'.
This is available from your local Air Passenger Duty Office. Look under Customs and Excise in your phone book.**

Please tick this box (   ) if you are using a Special Accounting Scheme

---

C. Declaration

I,

(Full name in BLOCK LETTERS)

declare that the information given above is true and complete. Remittance for the full duty* is enclosed/is paid by
direct debit/is paid by credit transfer.

Signature

Date   Status

(Managing Director, Company Secretary, Financial Director,
Fiscal Representative or other authorised signatory)

* *delete as appropriate*

WARNING: A false declaration may result in prosecution

Data Protection Act 1998

HM Customs and Excise collects information in order to administer the taxes for which it is responsible (such as VAT,
insurance premium tax, excise duties, air passenger duty, landfill tax), and for detecting and preventing crime.

Where the law permits we may also get information about you from third parties, or give information to them, for example in
order to check accuracy, prevent or detect crime or protect public funds in other ways. These third parties may include the
police, other government departments and agencies.

APD 2 (Reverse)

NOTES

Form substituted by the Air Passenger Duty (Amendment) Regulations 2001, SI 2001/836,
reg 2, Schedule.

AIR PASSENGER DUTY (PRESCRIBED RATES OF INTEREST) ORDER 1994

(SI 1994/1820)

NOTES

Made: 8 July 1994.

Authority: Finance Act 1994, Sch 6, para 11.

Commencement: 1 November 1994.

1

This Order may be cited as the Air Passenger Duty (Prescribed Rates of Interest) Order 1994 and shall come into force on 1st November 1994.

2

For the purposes of Schedule 6 to the Finance Act 1994 the prescribed rates shall be—

    (a)   in the case of paragraph 7 (interest payable to the Commissioners of Customs and Excise), [6.25 per cent per annum]; and

    (b)   in the case of paragraph 9 (interest payable by the Commissioners of Customs and Excise), 8 per cent per annum.

NOTES

    Words in square brackets in para (b) substituted by the Air Passenger Duty (Prescribed Rates of Interest) (Amendment) Order 1996, SI 1996/164, art 2.

AIR PASSENGER DUTY (CONNECTED FLIGHTS) ORDER 1994

(SI 1994/1821)

NOTES

Made: 8 July 1994.

Authority: Finance Act 1994, ss 30, 42.

Commencement: 1 November 1994.

1 Citation and commencement

This Order may be cited as the Air Passenger Duty (Connected Flights) Order 1994 and shall come into force on 1st November 1994.

2 Interpretation

The provisions of the Schedule to this Order, including the Notes next mentioned, shall be interpreted and applied in accordance with the notes contained therein.

3 Rules for determining whether successive flights are connected

The provisions of the Schedule to this Order shall be used, in respect of the transfer of a passenger as described therein, for determining whether successive flights are treated as connected for the purpose of section 30(6), or section 31(3), of the Finance Act 1994.

SCHEDULE
RULES FOR DETERMINING WHETHER SUCCESSIVE FLIGHTS IN QUESTION ARE CONNECTED FLIGHTS FOR THE PURPOSES OF AIR PASSENGER DUTY
Article 3

Case A Rule, governing a transfer to a domestic flight

1. The following rule (the "Case A Rule") applies in the case of a passenger who transfers to an aircraft on which he is carried domestically.

CASE A RULE

The passenger's previous flight ("Flight A"), and the next flight after it on his journey ("Flight B") on which he is carried domestically, are connected if the booked time of departure of Flight B is by or at the time or within the period in column 3 of the following Table specified opposite to the period of time (specified in column 2 of that Table) into which the scheduled time of arrival of Flight A falls on the scheduled day of arrival.

TABLE

Col 1 Category Number	Col 2 Scheduled time of arrival of Flight A falls in the period:—	Col 3 Qualifying booked departure time for Flight B
1	after midnight to 0400 hours	by or at 1000 hours on the scheduled day of arrival of Flight A
2	after 0400 to 1700 hours	within the period of 6 hours of the scheduled time of arrival of Flight A
3	after 1700 to midnight	by or at 1000 hours on the day following the scheduled day of arrival of Flight A

Notes of interpretation for the Case A Rule and for these Notes

(1) "Booked", in relation to a time or an airport, means the time or the airport that is specified expressly and correctly on the passenger's ticket at the time it is issued or last amended, by reference to the journey to be undertaken by the passenger constituted wholly or partly by Flight A and Flight B.

(2) If the ticket does not specify correctly and expressly the time or the airport in question, having regard to the journey undertaken by the passenger which is constituted wholly or partly by Flight A and Flight B (so that the flights in question are not connected), then those flights shall nevertheless be connected where the aircraft operator who would be liable, but for this Note, for the air passenger duty in question satisfies the Commissioners that, had the ticket in question been correctly and expressly specified with the time or the airport in question, the two Flights A and B in question would have been connected by virtue of this Rule.

(3) A passenger is carried domestically where the booked airport for the beginning and ending of his flight is in the United Kingdom . . .

(4) "Scheduled" means:—

    (a)   in relation to a time, the time indicated in the operator's timetable for the flight in question at the time the passenger's ticket is issued or last amended; and

Part II

     (b)   in relation to "the day of arrival", the day of arrival indicated in the operator's timetable for the flight in question at the time the passenger's ticket is issued or last amended.

(5)   Notwithstanding the effect of this Rule that, but for this Note, would result, Flight A and Flight B are not connected:—

     (a)   where the booked airport of departure of Flight A is the same airport as the booked airport of arrival of Flight B; or

     (b)   where the ticket for Flight A and the ticket for Flight B are not conjunction tickets.

(6)   For the purposes of paragraph (b) of Note (5) the two tickets in question are only conjunction tickets at the time of issue or when last amended:—

     (a)   if those tickets are contained in one booklet of tickets; or

     (b)   in the case of each of those tickets being contained in a separate booklet of tickets, if:—

          (i)   each of those booklets is referable to the other by virtue of a statement on each to the effect that each is to be read in conjunction with the other; or

          (ii)   each booklet or each ticket in question has as a part of it a summary of the flights of the passenger constituting his journey, which includes the flights in question.

(7)   "Ticket", for the purposes of this Rule, means the ticket in the form of a coupon, or the coupon (as it is sometimes called in the airline industry), issued for the passenger in relation to his intended flight specifying the time of and the airport of departure for that flight.

Case B Rule, governing a transfer to an international flight

2.   The following rule (the "Case B Rule") applies in the case of a passenger who transfers to an aircraft on which he is carried internationally.

CASE B RULE

The passenger's previous flight ("Flight A"), and the next flight after it on his journey ("Flight B") on which he is carried internationally, are connected if the booked time of departure of Flight B falls within the period of 24 hours starting at the scheduled time of arrival of Flight A.

Notes of interpretation for the Case B Rule and these Notes

(1)   The Notes of Interpretation for the Case A Rule and its Notes (set out above) numbered (1), (2), (4) limited to its sub-paragraph (a), (5) limited to its sub-paragraph (b), (6) and (7) shall be used for the interpretation and application of this Rule and its Notes.

(2)   A passenger is carried internationally where his flight begins at an airport in one country and ends at an airport in another country; and for the purposes of this Note the United Kingdom, subject to the provisions of Note (4), is a country.

(3)   Notwithstanding the effect of this Rule that, but for this Note, would result, Flight A and Flight B are not connected where the airport at which the passenger first boards the aircraft for Flight A is in the same country as that at which the passenger finally disembarks from the aircraft for Flight B.

(4)   . . .

NOTES

   Case A: words in Note (3) revoked by the Air Passenger Duty (Connected Flights) (Amendment) Order 2001, SI 2001/809, arts 2, 3.

   Case B: Note (4) revoked by SI 2001/809, arts 2, 4.

TRADE MARKS (CUSTOMS) REGULATIONS 1994

(SI 1994/2625)

NOTES

Made: 11 October 1994.

Authority: Trade Marks Act 1994, s 90(1), (2), (3).

Commencement: 31 October 1994.

1

These Regulations may be cited as the Trade Marks (Customs) Regulations 1994 and shall come into force on 31st October 1994.

2

If notice is given under section 89(1) of The Trade Marks Act 1994 by the proprietor or licensee of a registered trade mark in respect of certain goods it shall be in the form set out in the Schedule to these Regulations or a form to the like effect approved by the Commissioners; and separate notices shall be given in respect of each arrival of such goods.

3

A fee of £30 (plus value added tax) in respect of each notice shall be paid to the Commissioners at the time it is given.

4

The person giving the notice shall give to the Commissioners such security or further security within such time and in such manner, whether by deposit of a sum of money or guarantee, as the Commissioners may require, in respect of any liability or expense which they may incur in consequence of the notice by reason of the detention of any goods or anything done to goods so detained: and if such security or further security is not given within the time specified by the Commissioners, then (but without prejudice to the operation of regulation 5 below) the notice shall have no effect.

5

In every case, whether any security or further security is given or not, the person who has given the notice shall keep the Commissioners indemnified against all such liability and expense as is mentioned in regulation 4 above.

6

(1) The person giving the notice shall, either on giving notice or when the goods are imported, furnish the Commissioners with the certificate of registration (or a copy of it) issued by the Registrar of Trade Marks on the registration of the trade mark specified in the notice, together with evidence that such registration was duly renewed at all such times as it may have expired.

(2) If such a certificate or copy and, where applicable, evidence of renewal is not furnished in accordance with paragraph (1) above then the goods shall not be detained, or, if detained, shall be released, and (but without prejudice to the operation of regulation 5 above) any notice given in respect of them shall have no effect.

7

(Revokes the Trade Marks (Customs) Regulations 1970, SI 1970/212.)

SCHEDULE
NOTICE UNDER SECTION 89 TRADE MARKS ACT 1994 REQUESTING INFRINGING GOODS, MATERIAL OR ARTICLES TO BE TREATED AS PROHIBITED GOODS

Regulation 2

PLEASE READ THESE NOTES BEFORE COMPLETING THIS NOTICE

1. This notice may only be given by the proprietor of a registered trade mark, or a licensee. A separate notice must be given in respect of each consignment.

2. Please note that in Part 3 it is not mandatory to provide details other than the time and place of expected arrival of infringing goods but it will greatly increase the prospect of intercepting the consignment concerned if all the details requested are given.

3. A fee of £30 (plus VAT) is payable for each notice given. Please enclose a cheque for the required amount, made payable to "Commissioners of Customs and Excise".

4. A copy of the certificate of registration for the trade mark, as well as the certificate of renewal (where applicable), is to be enclosed with the notice, or submitted when the goods are imported.

5. The person who has given notice shall keep the Commissioners of Customs and Excise indemnified against any liability or expense which they may incur in consequence of the notice by reason of the detention of any goods or anything done to goods detained. The person giving the notice may be required to provide a security to cover this indemnity.

---

1 Person giving notice
* I/We ....
Full name of signatory in BLOCK LETTERS
give notice to the Commissioners of Customs and Excise that
....
Name and address of proprietor or licensee in BLOCK LETTERS
....
is the * proprietor/licensee of a trade mark registered in the United Kingdom and that infringing goods, material or articles are expected to arrive in the United Kingdom, and* I/we request that they be treated as prohibited goods.
(Delete as necessary)

2 Details of infringing goods, material or articles
Trade mark ....
Infringing goods, material or articles ....
Quantity ....
Commodity Code(s) ....

3 Details of expected importation
Place of importation ....
Method of importation ....
Please include details of ship, aircraft or vehicle, where known
Expected date of arrival ....
Country of origin ....
Country of consignment ....
Importer's details ....
Please include VAT number, if known
Consignor's details ....

4 Declaration
I declare that the information given by me in this notice is true.
Signature ....
(* Sole Proprietor/Partner/Director/Company Secretary/Duly Authorised Person)
Date ....
* Delete as necessary

5 Submission of notice
Please send the completed notice, fee and copies of relevant certificates to:
HM Customs and Excise
CD3A
New King's Beam House
22 Upper Ground
London SE1 9PJ

ALCOHOLIC LIQUOR DUTIES (BEER-BASED BEVERAGES) ORDER 1994

(SI 1994/2904)

NOTES

Made: 29 November 1994.

Authority: Alcoholic Liquor Duties Act 1979, s 1(10).

Commencement: 30 November 1994.

1 Citation
This Order may be cited as the Alcoholic Liquor Duties (Beer-based Beverages) Order 1994 and shall come into force on 30th November 1994.

2
(Revokes the Alcoholic Liquor Duties (Beer-based Beverages) Order 1988, SI 1988/1684.)

3 Beverages to which this Order applies
This Order applies to any beverage of an alcoholic strength exceeding 1.2 per cent but not exceeding 5.5 per cent which is made with beer and is made-wine, and which falls within any one or more of the descriptions specified in any one or more of the paragraphs of the schedule to this Order.

4 Made-wine beer based beverages deemed to be beer
A beverage to which this Order applies shall be deemed to be beer and not made-wine.

SCHEDULE
DESCRIPTIONS OF BEVERAGES
Article 3

1. Shandy made with lemonade, or a mixture of beer and lemonade, lemon cordial, lemon flavouring, lemon juice, or lemon squash.

2. Lager-and-lime, or a mixture of beer and lime cordial, lime flavouring, lime juice, lime squash, or limeade.

3. Ginger beer shandy, shandygaff, or a mixture of beer and ginger, ginger cordial, ginger flavouring, ginger squash, or unfermented ginger beer.

4. A mixture of beer and:—

    (a)   fruit cordial, fruit flavourings, fruit flavoured carbonated water, fruit juice or fruit squash; or

    (b)   any alcoholic liquor or other alcoholic substance.

EXCISE GOODS (DRAWBACK) REGULATIONS 1995

(SI 1995/1046)

NOTES

Made: 2 May 1995.

Authority: Customs and Excise Management Act 1979, s 93(1), (2)(a), (3); Finance (No 2) Act 1992, s 2.

Commencement: 1 June 1995.

Modification: These regulations are modified for the purposes of claims for drawback of excise duty by registered mobile operators by the Excise Duties (Personal Reliefs) (Amendment) Order 1999, SI 1999/1617.

ARRANGEMENT OF REGULATIONS

PART I
PRELIMINARY

1 Citation and commencement

These Regulations may be cited as the Excise Goods (Drawback) Regulations 1995 and shall come into force on 1st June 1995.

2

(Revokes the Excise Goods (Drawback) Regulations 1992, SI 1992/3151.)

3 Application
These Regulations apply to goods chargeable with a duty of excise provided that those goods have not been, and will not be, consumed in the United Kingdom or the Isle of Man.

4 Interpretation
In these Regulations—

"the Act" means the Customs and Excise Management Act 1979;

"accompanying document" means the document which in accordance with registered excise dealers and shippers regulations or, as the case may be, warehousing regulations will accompany the goods and will be endorsed with the certificate of receipt;

"business day" has the meaning given in section 92 of the Bills of Exchange Act 1882;

"certificate of receipt" means the certificate of receipt issued by the consignee;

"dispatch" means any export of goods where, at the time of their exportation, they are consigned to a place to which Council Directive 92/12/EEC applies;

"drawback" means drawback of duty, and cognate expressions shall be construed accordingly;

"duty" means duty of excise;

"eligible claimant" has the meaning given in regulation 6 below;

"eligible goods" has the meaning given in regulation 5 below;

"planned destruction"—

    (a)   means the destruction of goods which, by reason of faulty manufacture or subsequent deterioration or contamination, were at the time of their destruction not of satisfactory quality provided that, save as the Commissioners may otherwise allow, that destruction was carried out in accordance with the provisions of Schedule 1 to these Regulations, and

    (b)   includes denaturing to the satisfaction of the Commissioners;

"satisfactory quality" has the meaning given in section 14 of the Sale of Goods Act 1979;

"single administrative document" and references to "copy 3" of the single administrative document have the meanings they bear in Commission Regulation (EEC) No 2454/93;

"warehouse" means an excise warehouse.

PART II
ENTITLEMENT TO DRAWBACK

5 Eligible goods
(1) A claim for drawback may only be made in relation to eligible goods.

(2) Subject to paragraphs (3) and (4) below, goods are eligible goods if duty has been paid and has not been remitted, repaid or drawn back and those goods have been—

    (a)   exported,

    (b)   warehoused for export, or

    (c)   destroyed.

(3) Goods shall not be eligible goods if they are destroyed either—

    (a)   accidentally, unless—

        (i)   the goods were being removed to a warehouse for export,

        (ii)   the goods were being exported and destruction took place within the United Kingdom but after leaving the premises at which they were available for inspection before export, or

        (iii) the destruction was occasioned in any of the circumstances set out in Schedule 2 to these Regulations; or

  (b)   otherwise than accidentally, unless that destruction was a planned destruction.

(4) In the case of dispatch, chewing tobacco shall not be eligible goods.

6 Eligible claimants

(1) A claim for drawback may only be made by an eligible claimant.

(2) A claimant is an eligible claimant if he is a revenue trader—

  (a)   in the course of whose business the export, removal to warehouse for export or, as the case may be, destruction took place; and

  (b)   in the case of planned destruction—

        (i)   who (except as the Commissioners may otherwise allow) paid the duty to be drawn back, and

        (ii)   whose business is not wholly or mainly the destruction of goods on which duty has been charged.

PART III
CLAIMS, CONDITIONS AND CANCELLATION OF DRAWBACK

7 General conditions

(1) Subject to paragraph (2) below and without prejudice to any condition imposed by, or in accordance with section 133 of the Act, every eligible claimant shall—

  (a)   save as the Commissioners may otherwise allow, comply with the conditions imposed by these Regulations; and

  (b)   in addition to those conditions, comply with such other conditions as the Commissioners see fit to impose in a notice published by them and not withdrawn by a further notice.

(2) If the Commissioners consider it necessary for the protection of the revenue they may, by a notice in writing delivered to a revenue trader, require him to comply with such additional conditions as they think fit to impose.

(3) Sections 14 to 16 of the Finance Act 1994 shall have effect in relation to any decision of the Commissioners to impose additional conditions under paragraph (2) above as if that decision were a decision of a description specified in Schedule 5 to that Act.

(4) Subject to paragraph (5) below, no claim for drawback shall be made unless, taken together with any other claim being made at the same time, the total amount of duty to be drawn back is at least £500.

(5) If—

  (a)   during the six months immediately preceding the date upon which the claim for drawback is made the amounts of drawback which could be claimed by the eligible claimant amount in total to less than £500, and

  (b)   the eligible claimant has not made any other claim for drawback during that period, paragraph (4) above shall operate as if the reference to at least £500 were a reference to at least £50.

(6) No claim for drawback shall be made if the event giving rise to the claim occurred more than three years after the duty on the goods in question was paid.

8 Conditions to be complied with before export

(1) Where an eligible claimant intends to claim drawback on eligible goods warehoused for export he shall comply with the following conditions—

    (a)   before removal to warehouse, he shall deliver to the Commissioners at such address as they shall specify a notice in writing stating that he intends to claim drawback and containing the following particulars—

        (i)   his name and address,

        (ii)   the address of the premises at which the goods may be inspected prior to their removal to warehouse,

        (iii) the description of the goods, including their nature and quantity,

        (iv) the amount of duty paid in respect of the goods, and

        (v)   the address of the warehouse to which the goods are being removed;

    (b)   before removal to warehouse, he shall draw up a document ("warehousing advice note") in such form and containing such particulars as the Commissioners may require;

    (c)   before removal to warehouse, the goods and the warehousing advice note shall be available for inspection by the Commissioners, at any reasonable time, for not less than two clear business days following the day upon which the notice mentioned in sub-paragraph (a) above was received by the Commissioners; and

    (d)   he shall ensure that, when the goods are removed to warehouse they are accompanied by two copies of the warehousing advice note.

(2) where an eligible claimant intends to claim drawback after export he shall, before export, comply with the following conditions—

    (a)   he shall deliver to the Commissioners at such address as they shall specify a notice in writing stating that he intends to claim drawback and containing the following particulars—

        (i)   his name and address,

        (ii)   the address of the premises at which the goods may be inspected prior to their export,

        (iii) the description of the goods, including their nature and quantity,

        (iv) the amount of duty paid in respect of the goods, and

        (v)   the address of the premises to which the goods are being exported;

    (b)   if the export is a dispatch he shall complete an accompanying document;

    (c)   if the export is not a dispatch he shall complete a single administrative document; and

    (d)   the goods and the accompanying document or single administrative document shall be available for inspection by the Commissioners, at any reasonable time, for not less than two clear business days following the day upon which the notice mentioned in sub-paragraph (a) above was received by the Commissioners.

9 Conditions to be complied with after warehousing for export

Where an eligible claimant claims drawback after warehousing for export the following conditions shall be complied with—

    (a)   the eligible claimant shall include with his claim the certificate of receipt; and

    (b)   the eligible claimant shall ensure that the goods are exported within six months of making his claim for drawback.

Part II

10 Conditions to be complied with after export

Where an eligible claimant claims drawback after export he shall comply with the following conditions—

(a)   if the export is a dispatch, he shall include with his claim—

    (i)   unless duty is not payable on that description of goods in the place to which they have been exported, the document evidencing payment of duty in that place, and

    (ii)   the copy of the accompanying document which is endorsed with the certificate of receipt; or

(b)   if the export is not a dispatch, he shall include with his claim copy 3 of the single administrative document endorsed as described in Article 793 of Commission Regulation (EEC) No 2454/93.

11 Conditions to be complied with where goods are accidentally destroyed

Where an eligible claimant claims drawback in relation to goods which have been accidentally destroyed he shall comply with the following conditions—

(a)   he shall notify the Commissioners forthwith at such address as they shall specify that goods have been accidentally destroyed in circumstances where a claim for drawback may be made;

(b)   notification given in accordance with sub-paragraph (a) above shall include particulars of the goods and the amount of duty paid in respect of those goods or, if that amount cannot immediately be ascertained, an estimate of the amount of the duty so paid; and

(c)   he shall prove to the satisfaction of the Commissioners that the goods have been accidentally destroyed.

12 Payment of claim

(1)   No drawbacks shall be payable unless it is shown to the satisfaction of the Commissioners that the claimant is an eligible claimant and that the goods are eligible goods.

(2)   Without prejudice to section 133 of the Act, where the Commissioners are satisfied that duty may be drawn back in accordance with these Regulations they may set-off the amount due against any other debt then due to them from the eligible claimant.

(3)   If the Commissioners are not satisfied that the amount of duty claimed may be drawn back but are satisfied that some lesser amount of duty may be drawn back they may, in such circumstances as they see fit, permit the drawback of that lesser sum.

13 Cancellation of drawback

(1)   The Commissioners may at any time cancel drawback granted in accordance with these Regulations where they are satisfied that a contravention of any conditions (whether imposed by or under these Regulations or by or under section 133 of the Act) has taken place.

(2)   Without prejudice to section 116 of the Act, where drawback has been cancelled in accordance with paragraph (1) above the person to whom drawback was paid or credited shall on demand made by the Commissioners be liable to repay to the Commissioners the sum so paid or credited.

PART IV
CIVIL PENALTIES

14 Conduct attracting a civil penalty

(1)   If any person who is not an eligible claimant makes a claim for drawback his conduct shall attract a penalty under section 9 of the Finance Act 1994 which shall be calculated by reference to the amount of the drawback claimed.

(2) If any eligible claimant makes a claim for drawback in respect of goods that are not eligible goods his conduct shall attract a penalty under section 9 of the Finance Act 1994 which shall be calculated by reference to the amount of the drawback claimed.

15

(Revokes the Excise Warehousing (Etc) Regulations 1988, SI 1988/809, reg 6, adds reg 11(4A) and amends reg 16(1).)

SCHEDULES

SCHEDULE 1
PLANNED DESTRUCTION: CONDITIONS

Regulation 4

Conditions to be complied with before destruction

1. The eligible claimant shall deliver to the Commissioners at such address as they shall specify notice in writing of his intention to carry out a planned destruction of goods.

2. A notice delivered in accordance with paragraph 1 above shall contain the following particulars—

    (a)   the name and address of the eligible claimant;

    (b)   the address of the premises at which the goods to be destroyed may be inspected prior to destruction;

    (c)   the description of the goods to be destroyed including their nature and amount;

    (d)   the amount of duty paid in respect of those goods;

    (e)   the date and time when destruction will take place; and

    (f)   the method of destruction which is to be employed.

3. The goods shall be available for inspection by the Commissioners at any reasonable time for not less than two clear business days following the day upon which the notice mentioned in paragraph 1 above was received by the Commissioners provided that if the place where the goods are available for inspection is different from the address mentioned in sub-paragraph (a) of paragraph 2 above, for the reference to two clear business days in this paragraph there shall be substituted a reference to five clear business days.

Conditions to be complied with at the time of destruction

4. Destruction shall take place on the day and at the time appointed.

5. Destruction shall take place at the address mentioned in sub-paragraph (b) of paragraph 2 above; provided that the Commissioners may, on the application of the eligible claimant, permit, subject to such conditions as they deem necessary or expedient, destruction to take place at a different address.

6. The eligible claimant shall permit the Commissioners to attend the destruction.

7. The goods shall be destroyed in accordance with the method specified in the notice mentioned in paragraph 1 above save that if the Commissioners give notice that such method is not in their opinion satisfactory, the goods shall be destroyed in accordance with such other method as the Commissioners may approve.

SCHEDULE 2
ACCIDENTAL DESTRUCTION: CIRCUMSTANCES IN WHICH GOODS MAY BE ELIGIBLE FOR DRAWBACK

Regulation 5

Where the goods are destroyed by, or as a result of—

(a)   civil commotion;

(b)   riot;

(c)   terrorism;

(d)   war;

(e)   explosion;

(f)   earthquake;

(g)   any other fortuitous event; provided that, in the opinion of the Commissioners, it would not have been reasonable to insure the goods against the risk of destruction by or as a result of that event.

CUSTOMS TRADERS (ACCOUNTS AND RECORDS) REGULATIONS 1995

(SI 1995/1203)

NOTES

Made: 2 May 1995.

Authority: Finance Act 1994, s 21(1), (6).

Commencement: 1 June 1995.

ARRANGEMENT OF REGULATIONS

1   Citation and Commencement
2   Interpretation
3   Customs trader's records to be kept and preserved
4   Specific records in the case of certain traders
5   Records specified in public notices
6   Records relating to customs declarations
7   Form of records
8   Time of recording
9   Period of preservation of records
           Schedules:
           Schedule 1—Received, Prepared, Maintained or Issued Items
           Schedule 2

1 Citation and Commencement

These Regulations may be cited as the Customs Traders (Accounts and Records) Regulations 1995 and shall come into force on 1st June 1995.

2 Interpretation

(1)   In these Regulations—

"the Act" means the Finance Act 1994;

"the Commission Regulation" means Commission Regulation (EEC) No 2454/93;

"customs trader" means any person carrying on a trade or business which consists of or includes any of the activities mentioned in section 20(1) of the Act.

(2) Schedule 1 shall be interpreted in accordance with the notes contained therein.

3 Customs trader's records to be kept and preserved

A customs trader who receives, prepares, maintains or issues a record consisting of an item described in Schedule 1 relating to a business within the meaning of section 20(3)(b) of the Act shall—

(a) in the case of a received record, keep and preserve it;

(b) in the case of an issued record, keep and preserve a copy of it; and

(c) in the case of a record that is prepared or maintained and which has not been received or which is not issued, preserve it.

4 Specific records in the case of certain traders

(1) Subject to paragraph (2) below, a customs trader required by Article 76(2) of Council Regulation (EEC) No 2913/92 to furnish a supplementary declaration shall keep and preserve a copy of every such supplementary declaration made by him or on his behalf and a copy of every simplified declaration so made.

(2) The trader referred to in paragraph (1) above may instead keep and preserve a record of all the information set out in the declarations referred to in that paragraph.

(3) For the purposes of paragraph (2) above, in cases where the declarations are made using a data-processing technique, the information shall consist of all data sent by him or on his behalf for that purpose.

(4) In this regulation—

"data-processing technique" has the meaning given by Article 4a of the Commission Regulation;

"simplified declaration" is a declaration within the meaning of Article 253(2) of the Commission Regulation.

5 Records specified in public notices

A customs trader shall keep and preserve such other records as the Commissioners may specify for any case or cases in a notice published by them in pursuance of these Regulations and not withdrawn by a further notice.

6 Records relating to customs declarations

(1) Where any record (including a copy of a record) is kept or preserved by a customs trader under a duty imposed by or under these Regulations and that record relates to a customs declaration made by him or on his behalf, it shall be so kept or preserved as to be readily apparent that it does relate to that particular declaration.

(2) In this regulation "customs declaration" has the meaning given by Article 4(17) of Council Regulation (EEC) No 2913/92.

7 Form of records

(1) Except for the records specified in paragraph (2) below and without prejudice to the provisions of section 21(4) and (5) of the Act, records (including copies of records) required to be kept or preserved by or under these Regulations may be kept or preserved in any form, and in particular they may be in documentary or other written form, or be in the form of anything that is commonly called or referred to as an account or a report; and the information which they contain or are to contain may be contained in or be in the form of an item described in Schedule 2.

(2) The excepted records referred to are—

(a) records required to be kept and preserved by regulation 3(a) and (c) above; and

(b) such records as may be required to be kept and preserved under regulation 5 above which are—

(i) received by a customs trader; or

(ii) prepared or maintained by him which he has neither received nor issued.

8 Time of recording

Where a customs trader is required by or under these Regulations to keep a record, he shall do so at the time when any information that is by virtue of these Regulations to be recorded is first known to him or as soon as possible thereafter.

9 Period of preservation of records

Any record (including a copy of a record) required by or under these Regulations to be preserved shall be preserved for a period of four years or such lesser period as the Commissioners may require, starting on the day that the obligation to preserve arises.

SCHEDULES

SCHEDULE 1
RECEIVED, PREPARED, MAINTAINED OR ISSUED ITEMS

Regulation 3

1. An order.
2. An invoice.
3. A delivery note.
4. A credit note.
5. A debit note.
6. A record relating to an importation or an exportation.
7. A statement of account.
8. A record of payment or of receipt.
9. A journal or ledger.
10. A profit and loss account, trading account, management account, management report or balance sheet.
11. An internal or an external auditor's report.
12. A record relating to any drawback, remission, repayment or reimbursement of, or relief from, duty.
13. A record required, other than by virtue of these Regulations, by or under the customs and excise Acts.
14. A stock record.
15. Any other record maintained for a trading or business purpose.

Notes of interpretation

1. In paragraphs 1 to 15 above an item described therein includes anything in any form that it may take when the information, to which the item relates, is received, or, as the case may be, when that information is dealt with for the purpose of preparing, maintaining or issuing an item, and which it may take subsequently whilst it is being preserved by the customs trader who received it or, as the case may be, prepared, maintained or issued it.

2. In note 1 above "anything" includes—

(a) an item described in Schedule 2 to these Regulations containing the information which is expressly or impliedly described in paragraphs 1 to 15 above or which is obtained for a purpose described in those paragraphs; and

(b) anything which is commonly called or referred to as an account or a report.

3. In note 1 above "form" includes documentary or other written form.

4. In paragraphs 6, 8 and 12 above "record" means anything containing information expressly or impliedly described respectively in those paragraphs, irrespective of its form.

5. In paragraph 12 above "duty" means any duty of customs and includes any agricultural levy of the European Community.

6. In paragraph 13 above "record" means anything containing information which is required by or under the legislation specified therein, irrespective of its form.

7. In paragraph 15 above "record" means anything that is maintained for the purposes specified therein, irrespective of its form.

SCHEDULE 2

Regulation 7(1), Sch 1

1. A drawing, graph, map or plan.

2. A photocopy.

3. A disc, sound track, tape, or other device in which sounds or other data (not being visual images) are recorded so as to be capable (with or without the aid of some other equipment) of being reproduced therefrom.

4. Any film, microfilm, negative, tape or other device in which one or more visual images are recorded so as to be capable (as aforesaid) of being reproduced therefrom.

5. A transcript or reproduction.

TRAVELLERS' RELIEFS (FUEL AND LUBRICANTS) ORDER 1995

(SI 1995/1777)

NOTES

Made: 13 July 1995.

Authority: Customs and Excise Duties (General Reliefs) Act 1979, s 13(1), (3).

Commencement: 1 August 1995.

1 Citation and commencement

This Order may be cited as the Travellers' Reliefs (Fuel and Lubricants) Order 1995 and shall come into force on 1st August 1995.

2 Interpretation

In this Order—

"commercial vehicle" means any road vehicle that—

    (a) by its type of construction and equipment, is designed for and capable of transporting goods or more than 9 persons, including the driver; or

    (b) is being used or is intended for use to carry passengers for reward; or

    (c) is being used or is intended for use for a purpose other than transport;

"standard tanks" has the meaning given in Article 8a of Council Directive 92/81/EEC.

3 Relief for fuel and lubricants contained in a commercial vehicle

(1) Subject to the provisions of this Order, a person who has travelled from another member State shall on entering the United Kingdom be relieved from payment

of excise duty on the fuel and lubricants contained in a commercial vehicle that he has with him.

(2) The reliefs afforded by this Order apply only to fuel that—

(a)   is contained in the vehicle's standard tanks; and

(b)   is being used or is intended for use by that vehicle.

(3) The reliefs afforded by this Order apply only to fuel on which–

(a)   excise duty has been paid in the member State in which the fuel was acquired at a rate that is appropriate to the use to which that fuel is being or is intended to be put; and

(b)   the excise duty paid on that fuel has not been remitted, repaid or drawn back.

(4) The reliefs afforded by this Order apply only to fuel and lubricants that were taken into the vehicle within the European Union and are of a type and quantity necessary for the normal operation of the vehicle during its journey.

4 Conditions

(1) The reliefs afforded by this Order are subject to the following conditions; and if any condition is not complied with the fuel and lubricants shall, unless that non-compliance was sanctioned by the Commissioners, be liable to forfeiture.

(2) The fuel and lubricants are used only in the vehicle and are not removed from the vehicle except—

(a)   temporarily, to facilitate repair; or

(b)   permanently, to be destroyed.

(3) The fuel and lubricants are used only for purposes appropriate to the rate of excise duty paid in the member State in which the fuel was acquired.

(4) The excise duty paid on the fuel and lubricants is not remitted, repaid or drawn back.

5

(Inserts the Excise Duties (Personal Reliefs) (Fuel and Lubricants Imported in Vehicles) Order 1989, art 1A.)

VALUE ADDED TAX REGULATIONS 1995

(SI 1995/2518)

NOTES

Made: 27 September 1995.

Authority: Value Added Tax Act 1994, ss 3(4), 6(14), 7(9), 8(4), 12(3), 14(3), 16(1), (2), 18(5), (5A), 24(3), (4), (6), 25(1), (4), (6), 26(1), (3), (4), 28(3)–(5), 30(8), 35(2), 36(5), 37(3), (4), 38, 39(1), 40(3), 46(2), (4), 48(3)(b), (4), (6), 49(2), (3), 52, 54(1)–(3), (6), 58, 79(3), 80(6), 88(3), (5), 92(4), 93(1), (2), 95(5), 97(1). Sch 1, para 17, Sch 2, para 9, Sch 3, para 10, Sch 7, para 2(1), (2), Sch 11, paras 2(1)–(12), 5(4), (9), 6(1), (2), 7(1).

Commencement: 20 October 1995.

ARRANGEMENT OF REGULATIONS

PART I
PRELIMINARY

4   Requirement, direction, demand or permission

PART I
PRELIMINARY

1 Citation and commencement

These Regulations may be cited as the Value Added Tax Regulations 1995 and shall come into force on 20th October 1995.

2 Interpretation—general

(1)   In these Regulations unless the context otherwise requires—

"the Act" means the Value Added Tax Act 1994 and any reference to a Schedule to the Act includes a reference to a Schedule as amended from time to time by Order of the Treasury;

["alphabetical code" means the alphabetical prefix as set out below which shall be used to identify the member State—

Austria—AT

        Belgium—BE

        [Bulgaria—BG]

        Cyprus—CY

        Czech Republic—CZ

        Denmark—DK

        Estonia—EE

        Finland—FI

        France—FR

        Germany—DE

        Greece—EL

        Hungary—HU

        Ireland—IE

        Italy—IT

        Latvia—LV

Part II

Lithuania—LT
Luxembourg—LU
Malta—MT
Netherlands—NL
Poland—PL
Portugal—PT
[Romania—RO]
Slovakia—SK
Slovenia—SI
Spain—ES
Sweden—SE
United Kingdom—GB]

"Collector" includes Deputy Collector and Assistant Collector;

"the Community" means the European Community;

"continental shelf" means a designated area within the meaning of the Continental Shelf Act 1964;

"Controller" means the Controller, Customs and Excise Value Added Tax Central Unit;

"datapost packet" means a postal packet containing goods which is posted in the United Kingdom as a datapost packet for transmission to a place outside the United Kingdom in accordance with the terms of a contract entered into between [the Post Office company] and the sender of the packet; or which is received at a post office [of the Post Office company] in the United Kingdom from a place outside the United Kingdom for transmission and delivery in the United Kingdom [by that company] as if it were a datapost packet;

["fiscal or other warehousing regime" means "fiscal warehousing regime or warehousing regime";]

"prescribed accounting period", subject to regulation 99(1), means a period such as is referred to in regulation 25;

["the Post Office" company has the same meaning as in Part IV of the Postal Services Act 2000;]

"proper officer" means the person appointed or authorised by the Commissioners to act in respect of any matter in the course of his duties;

"registered person" means a person registered by the Commissioners under [Schedule 1, 2, 3 or 3A] to the Act;

"registration number" means the number allocated by the Commissioners to a taxable person in the certificate of registration issued to him;

"return" means a return which is required to be made in accordance with regulation 25;

"specified date" means the date specified in a person's application for registration for the purpose of VAT as that on which he expects to make his first taxable supply.

(2) A reference in these Regulations to "this Part" is a reference to the Part of these Regulations in which that reference is made.

(3) In these Regulations any reference to a form prescribed in Schedule 1 to these Regulations shall include a reference to a form which the Commissioners are satisfied is a form to the like effect.

NOTES

Para (1): definition "alphabetical code" substituted by the VAT (Amendment) (No 2) Regulations 2004, SI 2004/1082 regs 2, 3. In definition "alphabetical code" entries "Bulgaria–BG" and "Romania–RO" inserted by the VAT (Amendment) (No 3) Regulations,

SI 2006/3292, regs 2, 3(2). In definition "datapost packet" words "the Post Office company" and "of the Post Office company" in square brackets substituted, and words "by that company" inserted, by the Postal Services Act 2000, s 127(4), Sch 8, Pt II, para 23; definition "fiscal or other warehousing regime" inserted by the VAT (Amendment) (No 3) Regulations 1996, SI 1996/1250, reg 4; definition "the Post Office" inserted by the Postal Services Act 2000 (Consequential Modifications No 1) Order 2001, SI 2001/1149, art 108; words in square brackets in definition "registered person" substituted by the VAT (Amendment) (No 3) Regulations 2000, SI 2000/794, regs 2, 3.

4 Requirement, direction, demand or permission

Any requirement, direction, demand or permission by the Commissioners, under or for the purposes of these Regulations, may be made or given by a notice in writing, or otherwise.

PART XVI
IMPORTATIONS, EXPORTATIONS AND REMOVALS

117 Interpretation of Part XVI

(1) In regulation 127 "approved inland clearance depot" means any inland premises approved by the Commissioners for the clearance of goods for customs and excise purposes.

(2) For the purposes of regulation 128 "container" means an article of transport equipment (lift-van, moveable tank or other similar structure)—

(a)   fully or partially enclosed to constitute a compartment intended for containing goods,

(b)   of a permanent character and accordingly strong enough to be suitable for repeated use,

(c)   specially designed to facilitate the carriage of goods, by one or more modes of transport, without intermediate reloading,

(d)   designed for ready handling, particularly when being transferred from one mode of transport to another,

(e)   designed to be easy to fill and to empty, and

(f)   having an internal volume of one cubic metre or more,

and the term "container" shall include the accessories and equipment of the container, appropriate for the type concerned, provided that such accessories and equipment are carried with the container, but shall not include vehicles, accessories or spare parts of vehicles, or packaging.

(3) . . .

[(4) In [regulation] 131 "goods" does not include—

(a)   a motor-vehicle, or

(b)   a boat intended to be exported under its own power.]

(5), (6) . . .

(7) For the purposes of regulation 129 "overseas authority" means any country other than the United Kingdom or any part of or place in such a country or the government of any such country, part or place.

[(7A) In [regulation] 131 the words "overseas visitor" refer to a traveller who is not established within the member States.

(7B) For the purposes of paragraph (7A) above, a traveller is not established within the member States only if that traveller's domicile or habitual residence is situated outside the member States.

(7C) Solely for the purposes of paragraph (7B) above, the traveller's domicile or habitual residence is the place entered as such in a valid—

(a)   identity document,

(b)   identity card, or

(c) passport.

(7D) A document referred to in sub-paragraph (a), (b) or (c) of paragraph (7C) above is valid for the purposes of that paragraph only if—

(a) it is so recognised by the Commissioners; and

(b) it is not misleading as to the traveller's true place of domicile or habitual residence.]

(8) In [regulation 132] "overseas visitor" means a person who, during the 2 years immediately preceding . . . the date of the application mentioned in regulation 132, has not been in the member States for more than 365 days, or who, . . . during the 6 years immediately preceding the date of the application has not been in the member States for more than 1,095 days.

(9) . . .

(10) In regulations 140 and 144 "customs territory of the Community" has the same meaning as it has for the purposes of Council Regulation (EEC) No 2913/92.

[(11) In this Part references to Council Regulation (EEC) No 2913/92 (the Community Customs Code) and Commission Regulation (EEC) No 2454/93 (which contains provisions implementing the Community Customs Code) shall be read as references to those instruments as—

(a) amended by the Act concerning the accession of the Czech Republic, the Republic of Estonia, the Republic of Cyprus, the Republic of Latvia, the Republic of Lithuania, the Republic of Hungary, the Republic of Malta, the Republic of Poland, the Republic of Slovenia and the Slovak Republic, signed at Athens on 16th April 2003,

(b) amended, modified or otherwise affected by the Act concerning the conditions of Accession of the Republic of Bulgaria and Romania and the adjustments to the Treaties on which the European Union is founded, signed at Luxembourg on 25th April 2005 and Council Regulation (EC) No 1791/2006 (which contains consequential amendments to the Customs Code).]

NOTES

Para (3): revoked by the VAT (Amendment) Regulations 1999, SI 1999/438, reg 10(1).

Para (4): substituted by the VAT (Amendment) Regulations 1996, SI 1996/210, reg 8; words substituted by the VAT (Amendment) (No 4) Regulations 2003, SI 2003/1485 reg 5(a).

Paras (5), (6): revoked by SI 1996/210, reg 9.

Paras (7A), (7B), (7C), (7D): inserted by SI 1999/438, reg 10(2).

Para (7A): words substituted by the VAT (Amendment) (No 4) Regulations 2003, SI 2003/1485 reg 5(b).

Para (8): words in square brackets substituted, and words omitted revoked, by SI 1999/438, reg 10(3)(a), (b).

Para (9): revoked by the VAT (Amendment) (No 4) Regulations 2003, SI 2003/1485 reg 5(c).

Para (11) (as inserted by SI 2004/1082, regs 2, 4): substituted by the VAT (Amendment) (No 3) Regulations, SI 2006/3292, regs 2, 4.

118 Enactments excepted

There shall be excepted from the enactments which are to apply as mentioned in section 16(1) of the Act—

(a) the Alcoholic Liquor Duties Act 1979—

(i) section 7 (exemption from duty on spirits in articles used for medical purposes),

(ii) section 8 (repayment of duty on spirits for medical or scientific purposes),

(iii) section 9 (remission of duty on spirits for methylation),

(iv) section 10 (remission of duty on spirits for use in art or manufacture),

(v) section 22(4) (drawback on exportation of tinctures or spirits of wine), and

(vi) sections 42 and 43 (drawback on exportation and warehousing of beer),

(b) the Hydrocarbon Oil Duties Act 1979—

(i) section 9 (relief for certain industrial uses),

(ii) section 15 (drawback of duty on exportation etc of certain goods),

(iii) section 16 (drawback of duty on exportation etc of power methylated spirits),

(iv) section 17 (repayment of duty on heavy oil used by horticultural producers),

(v) section 18 (repayment of duty on fuel for ships in home waters),

(vi) section 19 (repayment of duty on fuel used in fishing boats etc),

(vii) section 20 (relief from duty on oil contaminated or accidentally mixed in warehouse), and

(viii) section 20AA (power to allow reliefs),

(c) the Customs and Excise Management Act 1979—

(i) section 43(5) (provisions as to duty on re-imported goods),

(ii) section 125(1) and (2) (valuation of goods for the purpose of ad valorem duties),

(iii) section 126 (charge of excise duty on manufactured or composite imported articles), and

(iv) section 127(1)(b) (determination of disputes as to duties on imported goods),

(d) the Customs and Excise Duties (General Reliefs) Act 1979 other than sections 8 and 9(b),

(e) the Isle of Man Act 1979, sections 8 and 9 (removal of goods from Isle of Man to United Kingdom), . . .

(f) the Tobacco Products Duty Act 1979, section 2(2) (remission or repayment of duty on tobacco products)[, and

(g) the Finance Act 1999, sections 126 and 127 (interest on unpaid customs debts and on certain repayments relating to customs duty).]

NOTES

Word at end of para (e) revoked and para (g) and word preceding it added by the Value Added Tax (Amendment) (No 2) Regulations 2000, SI 2000/634, regs 2, 3.

[**119 Regulations excepted**

The provision made by or under the following subordinate legislation shall be excepted from applying as mentioned in section 16(1) of the Act—

(a) regulations 16(4) and (5) and 19(1)(b) of the Excise Warehousing (Etc) Regulations 1988 (certain removals from warehouse);

(b) any regulations made under section 197(2)(f) of the Finance Act 1996 (rate of interest on overdue customs duty and on repayments of amounts paid by way of customs duty).]

NOTES

Commencement: 1 April 2000.

Substituted by the Value Added Tax (Amendment) (No 2) Regulations 2000, SI 2000/634, regs 2, 4.

120 Community legislation excepted

(1)   Council Regulation (EEC) No 918/83 on conditional reliefs from duty on the final importation of goods, and any implementing Regulations made thereunder shall be excepted from the Community legislation which is to apply as mentioned in section 16(1) of the Act.

(2)   The following Articles shall be excepted from the Community legislation which is to apply as mentioned in section 16(1) of the Act—

    (a)   in Council Regulation (EEC) No 2913/92 establishing the Community Customs Code—

         (i)   Articles 126 to 128 (drawback system of inward processing relief),

         (ii)   . . .

         (iii)   Article 137 so far as it relates to partial relief on temporary importation, and Article 142,

         (iv)   Articles 145 to 160 (outward processing),

         (v)   . . .

         (vi)   Article 229(b) (interest payable on a customs debt),

        [(vii) Articles 232(1)(b), (2) and (3) (interest on arrears of duty), and

        (viii) Article 241, second and third sentences only (interest on certain repayments by the authorities),]

    [(b)   in Commission Regulation (EEC) No 2454/93 which contains provisions implementing the Community Customs Code—

         (i)   Articles 496 to 523, Articles 536 to 544 and Article 550 (but only to the extent that these Articles apply to the drawback system of inward processing relief),

         (ii)   Article 519 (compensatory interest),

         (iii)   Articles 585 to 592 (outward processing) (and Articles 496 to 523 to the extent that they are relevant to outward processing),

         (iv) . . .]

(3)   Council Regulation (EEC) No 2658/87 on the tariff and statistical nomenclature and on the Common Customs Tariff and implementing Regulations made thereunder (end use relief), save and in so far as the said Regulations apply to goods admitted into territorial waters—

    (a)   in order to be incorporated into drilling or production platforms, for purposes of the construction, repair, maintenance, alteration or fitting-out of such platforms, or to link such drilling or production platforms to the mainland of the United Kingdom, or

    (b)   for the fuelling and provisioning of drilling or production platforms,

shall be excepted from the Community legislation which is to apply as mentioned in section 16(1) of the Act.

NOTES

Para (2)(a)(v) revoked by the VAT (Amendment) Regulations, SI 2006/587, regs 1(5), 4; para (2)(a)(vii), (viii), added by the Value Added Tax (Amendment) (No 2) Regulations 2000, SI 2000/634, regs 2, 5; para (2)(a)(ii), revoked by the VAT (Amendment) Regulations 2001, SI 2001/630, regs 2–4, with effect in relation to goods which are imported on or after 1st April 2001. Para (2)(b) substituted by the VAT (Amendment) (No 5) Regulations 2003, SI 2003/2318 reg 5 with effect from 1 October 2003; para (2)(b)(iv) revoked by the VAT (Amendment) Regulations, SI 2006/587, regs 1(5), 5.

[121 Adaptations

(1) The provision made by the following enactments shall apply, as mentioned in section 16(1) of the Act, subject to the adaptations prescribed by this regulation.

(2) Section 125(3) of the Customs and Excise Management Act 1979 (valuation of goods) shall have effect as if the reference to the preceding subsections of that section included a reference to section 21 of the Act.

(3) Section 129 of the Finance Act 1999 (recovery of certain amounts by the Commissioners) shall be regarded as providing for the recovery of a repayment of any relevant VAT (import VAT).]

NOTES

Commencement: 1 April 2000.

Substituted by the Value Added Tax (Amendment) (No 2) Regulations 2000, SI 2000/634, regs 2, 6.

[121A—

(1) The application of the Customs Duties (Deferred Payment) Regulations 1976 in relation to any VAT chargeable on the importation of goods from places outside the member States is subject to the following prescribed adaptations.

(2) In regulation 4(1) (application for approval), regard "security" as being "appropriate security (which may be nil if there is no risk to the payment)".

(3) In regulation 4(2) (security and payment arrangements), regard there being a second sub-paragraph as follows—

"Provided that the amount in question may exceed that of the security in the case of nil security.".

(4) For regulation 4(3) (variations and revocations of approval), regard any Commissioners' variation consequent on the adaptations prescribed by this regulation as only being able to have effect after 30th November 2003.

(5) Before "and" at the end of regulation 8(a) (deemed payment for certain purposes at time deferment granted), regard there being—

"(aa)   Article 74(1) of Council Regulation (EEC) No 2913/92 (Community Customs Code) (no release of goods unless customs debt paid or secured);".]

NOTES

Inserted by the VAT (Amendment) (No 5) Regulations 2003, SI 2003/2318 reg 6.

[121B—

(1) The application of Council Regulation (EEC) No 2913/92 (Community Customs Code) in relation to any VAT chargeable on the importation of goods from places outside the member States is subject to the following prescribed adaptations.

(2) But the adaptation in paragraph (5) only applies to the extent that the Commissioners grant deferment of payment of the relevant VAT with nil security.

(3) In Article 218(1) second sub-paragraph (single entry in the accounts), after "secured" regard there being "if required".

(4) In Article 225 first sub-paragraph (deferment of payment conditional on security), after "applicant" regard there being " (but the customs authorities may waive this condition if there is no risk to the payment)".

(5) Regard Article 225 as not being subject to Article 192 (fixing amount of security).]

NOTES

Inserted by the VAT (Amendment) (No 5) Regulations 2003, SI 2003/2318 reg 6.

[121C—

(1) The application of Commission Regulation (EEC) No 2454/93 (implementation of Community Customs Code) in relation to any VAT chargeable on the importation of goods from places outside the member States is subject to the following prescribed adaptations.

(2) But the adaptations in paragraphs (3) and (4) only apply to the extent that the Commissioners grant deferment of payment of the relevant VAT with nil security.

(3) Regard Articles 244, 248(1), 257(3), 257(4), 258, 262(1) and 876a(1) (circumstances in which duties have to be or are taken as having to be secured) as providing that the provision of security is at the discretion of the customs authorities.

(4) Regard Articles 244, 248(1), 257(3), 257(4) and 876a(1) (circumstances in which duties have to be secured) as not being subject to Article 192 of Council Regulation (EEC) No 2913/92 (Community Customs Code) (fixing amount of security).]

NOTES

Inserted by the VAT (Amendment) (No 5) Regulations 2003, SI 2003/2318 reg 6.

[121D Adaptations and exceptions for the application of returned goods relief

(1) The application of Council Regulation (EEC) No 2913/92 (Community Customs Code) and Commission Regulation (EEC) No 2454/93 (implementation Regulation) in relation to any VAT chargeable on the importation of goods from places outside the member States is subject to the following prescribed adaptations.

(2) Regard—

(a) Articles 185 to 187 of the Community Customs Code (returned Community goods and returned compensating products), and

(b) Articles 844 to 856 and Article 882 of the implementation Regulation (returned Community goods and returned compensating products),

as only applying in the case and to the extent of a reimportation to the United Kingdom by the person who originally exported or re-exported the relevant Community goods or compensating products from the VAT territory of the Community.

That VAT territory is the territorial application of Council Directive 77/388/EEC in accordance with Title III of that Directive (territorial application).

(3) Regard the amount of the relief mentioned in Article 186 of the Community Customs Code (returned Community goods) as reduced by the amount of any unpaid VAT.

(4) Regard the amount legally owed in Article 187 of the Community Customs Code (returned compensating products) as reduced by the amount of any paid VAT.

(5) For the purposes of paragraphs (3) and (4)—

(a) "VAT" includes value added tax charged in accordance with the law of another member State (see sections 92(1), 92(2) and 96(1) of the Act);

(b) "unpaid" refers to any part of the VAT charged and due on—

(i) a supply or acquisition of the goods in a member State before the reimportation, or

      (ii)   an importation of the goods from outside the member States before the reimportation,

but repaid, remitted or otherwise not paid;

(c)   "paid" refers to any part of the VAT charged, due and paid on—

      (i)   a supply or acquisition of the goods in a member State before the reimportation, or

      (ii)   an importation of the goods from outside the member States before the reimportation,

and without any actual, or prospect of, repayment or remission;

(d)   a sum for which there is or was under the law of a member State an entitlement or right to a deduction or refund within Article 17 of Council Directive 77/388/EEC (origin and scope of the right to deduct) is neither "unpaid" nor "paid".

(6)   In the circumstances described by paragraph (7) or (8)—

(a)   Articles 185 to 187 of the Community Customs Code (returned goods), and

(b)   Articles 844 to 856 and Article 882 of the implementation Regulation (returned goods),

are excepted from the Community legislation which is to apply as mentioned in section 16(1) of the Act (application of customs legislation in relation to import VAT).

(7)   These circumstances are that—

(a)   the reimporter contemplated by those Articles makes a supply of, or concerning, the goods whilst under the inward processing procedure or in the course of, or after, the relevant exportation, re-exportation or reimportation,

(b)   the place of that supply for the purposes of VAT is determined by or under section 7 of the Act (place of supply) as being outside the United Kingdom, and

(c)   the goods nevertheless are or may be stored or physically used in the United Kingdom by or under the direction of that reimporter or the person to whom that supply is made ("recipient").

For these purposes, "reimporter" and "recipient" include someone connected with either person or both persons as determined in accordance with section 839 of the Taxes Act.

(8)   These circumstances are that the goods in question were supplied at any time to any person pursuant to regulations 131 to 133 (supplies to persons departing from the member States) or pursuant to any corresponding provision of the Isle of Man.

(9)   For the purposes of the Articles of the Community Customs Code and implementation Regulation mentioned in paragraph (2)—

(a)   regard the description of the customs territory of the Community in Article 3 of the Community Customs Code as being substituted with a description of the VAT territory (see paragraph (2));

(b)   regard the following references as including a reference to the completion of the formalities referred to in Article 33a(1)(a) of Council Directive 77/388/EEC (formalities relating to entry of goods into VAT territory from territory considered a third territory)—

      (i)   "released for free circulation" in the definition of "Community goods" in Article 4(7), second indent and Article 185(1) of the Community Customs Code;

      (ii)   "entered" and "declared" for "release for free circulation" in, or for the purposes of, Articles 844(4), 848(1), 848(2), 849(1) and 849(5) of the implementation Regulation;

    (c)   regard the following references as including a reference to the completion of the formalities referred to in Article 33a(2)(a) of Council Directive 77/388/EEC (or to a declaration under those formalities) (formalities relating to dispatch or transport of goods from Member State to territory considered a third territory)—

        (i)   "customs export formalities" in Articles 844(1), 849(1), 849(2) and 849(3) of the implementation Regulation;

        (ii)   "export declaration" in Article 848(1) of that Regulation;

        (iii)   "customs formalities relating to their exportation" in Articles 844(4) and 849(1) of that Regulation;

    (d)   regard—

        (i)   the definition of "import duties" in Article 4(10) of the Community Customs Code as defining instead VAT charged on the importation of goods from places outside the member States in accordance with the Act; and

        (ii)   the references to "import duty" and "duty" in Article 185(1), second sub-paragraph, second indent and Article 187 of the Community Customs Code as references to such VAT.

(10) The references to Council Directive 77/388/EEC in paragraphs (2), (5)(d), (9)(b) and (9)(c) embrace relevant amendments up to and including 6th April 2006 only.]

NOTES
Inserted by the VAT (Amendment) Regulations 2006, SI 2006/587, regs 1(5), 4.

122 Postal importations by registered persons in the course of business

Goods imported by post from places outside the member States, other than by datapost packet, not exceeding £2,000 in value, or such greater sum as is determined for the time being by the Commissioners, by a registered person in the course of a business carried on by him may, with the authority of the proper officer, be delivered without payment of VAT if—

    (a)   the registered person has given such security as the Commissioners may require, and

    (b)   his registration number is shown on the customs declaration attached to or accompanying the package,

and save as the Commissioners may otherwise allow he shall account for VAT chargeable on the goods on their importation together with any VAT chargeable on the supply of goods or services by him or on the acquisition of goods by him from another member State in a return furnished by him in accordance with these Regulations for the prescribed accounting period during which the goods were imported.

123 Temporary importations

(1) Subject to such conditions as the Commissioners may impose, the VAT chargeable on the importation of goods from a place outside the member States shall not be payable where—

    (a)   a taxable person makes a supply of goods which is to be zero-rated in accordance with sub-paragraphs (a)(i) and (ii), and (b) of section 30(8) of the Act,

    (b)   the goods so imported are the subject of that supply, and

    (c)   the Commissioners are satisfied that—

        (i)   the importer intends to remove the goods to another member State, and

(ii)   the importer is importing the goods in the course of a supply by him of those goods in accordance with the provisions of sub-paragraphs (a)(i) and (ii), and (b) of section 30(8) of the Act and any Regulations made thereunder.

(2)   As a condition of granting the relief afforded by paragraph (1) above the Commissioners may require the deposit of security, the amount of which shall not exceed the amount of VAT chargeable on the importation.

(3)   The relief afforded by paragraph (1) above shall continue to apply provided that the importer—

(a)   removes the goods to another member State within one month of the date of importation or within such longer period as the Commissioners may allow, and

(b)   supplies the goods in accordance with sub-paragraphs (a)(i) and (ii), and (b) of section 30(8) of the Act and any Regulations made thereunder,

124, 125

Revoked by the VAT (Amendment) Regulations, SI 2006/587, regs 1(5), 5.

126 Reimportation of goods exported for treatment or process

Subject to such conditions as the Commissioners may impose, VAT chargeable on the importation of goods from a place outside the member States which have been temporarily exported from the member States and are reimported after having undergone repair, process or adaptation outside the member States, or after having been made up or reworked outside the member States, shall be payable as if such treatment or process had been carried out in the United Kingdom, if the Commissioners are satisfied that—

(a)   at the time of exportation the goods were intended to be reimported after completion of the treatment or process outside the member States, and

(b)   the ownership in the goods was not transferred to any other person at exportation or during the time they were abroad.

127

(Revoked by the Value Added Tax (Amendment) Regulations 1999, SI 1999/438, reg 11.)

128 Export of freight containers

Where the Commissioners are satisfied that a container is to be exported to a place outside the member States, its supply, subject to such conditions as they may impose, shall be zero-rated.

129 Supplies to overseas persons

(1)   Where the Commissioners are satisfied that—

(a)   goods intended for export to a place outside the member States have been supplied, otherwise than to a taxable person, to—

(i)   a person not resident in the United Kingdom,

(ii)   a trader who has no business establishment in the United Kingdom from which taxable supplies are made, or

(iii) an overseas authority, and

(b)   the goods were exported to a place outside the member States,

the supply, subject to such conditions as they may impose, shall be zero-rated.

(2) . . .

NOTES
Para 2: repealed by the Value Added Tax (Amendment) (No 4) Regulations 2003, SI 2003/1485, regs 2, 6.

Supplies to persons departing from the member States

130

(Repealed by Value Added Tax (Amendment) (No 4) Regulations 2003, SI 2003/1485, regs 2, 6)

131—

(1)   Where the Commissioners are satisfied that—

(a)   goods have been supplied to a person who is an overseas visitor and who, at the time of the supply, intended to depart from the member States [before the end of the third month following that in which the supply is effected] and that the goods should accompany him,

(b)   save as they may allow, the goods were produced to the competent authorities for the purposes of the common system of VAT in the member State from which the goods were finally exported to a place outside the member States, and

(c)   the goods were exported to a place outside the member States,

the supply, subject to such conditions as they may impose, shall be zero-rated.

(2)   . . .

NOTES
Para (1): words in square brackets substituted by the *Value Added Tax (Amendment) Regulations 1995*, SI 1995/3147, reg 6.

132

The Commissioners may, on application by an overseas visitor who intends to depart from the member States within 15 months and remain outside the member States for a period of at least 6 months, permit him within 12 months of his intended departure to purchase, from a registered person, a . . . motor vehicle without payment of VAT, for subsequent export, and its supply, subject to such conditions as they may impose, shall be zero-rated.

NOTES
Word omitted revoked by the Value Added Tax (Amendment) Regulations 2000, SI 2000/258 reg 6.

133

The Commissioners may, on application by any person who intends to depart from the member States within 9 months and remain outside the member States for a period of at least 6 months, permit him within 6 months of his intended departure to purchase, from a registered person, a . . . motor vehicle without payment of VAT, for subsequent export, and its supply, subject to such conditions as they may impose, shall be zero-rated.

NOTES

Word omitted revoked by the Value Added Tax (Amendment) Regulations 2000, SI 2000/258 reg 6.

134 Supplies to persons taxable in another member State

Where the Commissioners are satisfied that—

(a)   a supply of goods by a taxable person involves their removal from the United Kingdom,

(b)   the supply is to a person taxable in another member State,

(c)   the goods have been removed to another member State, and

(d)   the goods are not goods in relation to whose supply the taxable person has opted, pursuant to section 50A of the Act, for VAT to be charged by reference to the profit margin on the supply,

the supply, subject to such conditions as they may impose, shall be zero-rated.

135 Supplies of goods subject to excise duty to persons who are not taxable in another member State

Where the Commissioners are satisfied that—

(a)   a supply by a taxable person of goods subject to excise duty involves their removal from the United Kingdom to another member State,

(b)   that supply is other than to a person taxable in another member State and the place of supply is not, by virtue of section 7(5) of the Act, treated as outside the United Kingdom,

(c)   the goods have been removed to another member State in accordance with the provisions of the Excise Goods (Holding, Movement, Warehousing and REDS) Regulations 1992, and

(d)   the goods are not goods in relation to whose supply the taxable person has opted, pursuant to section 50A of the Act, for VAT to be charged by reference to the profit margin on the supply,

the supply, subject to such conditions as they may impose, shall be zero-rated.

Territories to be treated as excluded from or included in the territory of the Community and of the member States

136

For the purposes of the Act the following territories shall be treated as excluded from the territory of the Community—

(a)   the Channel Islands,

(b)   Andorra,

(c)   San Marino, and

(d)   the Aland Islands.

137

For the purposes of the Act the following territories shall be treated as excluded from the territory of the member States and the territory of the Community—

(a)   the Canary Islands (Kingdom of Spain),

(b)   the overseas departments of the French Republic (Guadeloupe, Martinique, Reunion, St Pierre and Miquelon and French Guiana), and

(c)   Mount Athos (Hellenic Republic).

138

[(1) For the purposes of the Act the territory of the Community shall be treated as excluding—

    (a)   Austria, Finland and Sweden ("the 1995 acceding States"),

    (b)   the Czech Republic, Estonia, Cyprus, Latvia, Lithuania, Hungary, Malta, Poland, Slovakia and Slovenia ("the 2004 acceding States"), and

    (c)   Bulgaria and Romania ("the 2007 acceding states")

in relation to goods to which this regulation applies.]

(2) Subject to [paragraph (4)] below, the goods to which this regulation applies are—

    (a)   goods which are the subject of a supply made in an acceding State before [the date specified in paragraph (5)] and which in pursuance of that supply are removed to the United Kingdom on or after [the date specified in paragraph (6)] being goods in the case of which provisions of the law of the acceding State in question having effect for purposes corresponding to those of subsection (6)(a) or (so far as it applies to exportations) subsection (8) of section 30 of the Act have prevented VAT from being charged on that supply, and

    (b)   goods which were subject to a suspension regime before [the date specified in paragraph (5)], which by virtue of any Community legislation were to remain, for VAT purposes only, subject to that regime for a period beginning with that date and which cease to be subject to that regime on or after [the date specified in paragraph (6)].

(3) For the purposes of paragraph (2)(b) above, goods shall be treated as having become subject to a suspension regime if—

    (a)   on their entry into the territory of the Community—

        (i)   they were placed under a temporary admission procedure with full exemption from import duties, in temporary storage, in a free zone, or under customs warehousing arrangements or inward processing arrangements, or

        (ii)   they were admitted into the territorial waters of the United Kingdom for the purpose of being incorporated into drilling or production platforms, for the purposes of the construction, repair, maintenance, alteration or fitting-out of such platforms, for the purpose of linking such platforms to the mainland of the United Kingdom, or for the purpose of fuelling or provisioning such platforms, or

    (b)   they were placed under any customs transit procedure in pursuance of a supply made in the course of a business,

and (in the case in question) the time that any Community customs debt in relation to the goods would be incurred in the United Kingdom if the accession to the European Union of the acceding States were disregarded would fall to be determined by reference to the matters mentioned in sub-paragraph (a) or (b) above.

(4) This regulation does not apply to the following goods—

    (a)   goods which are exported on or after [the date specified in paragraph (6)] to a place outside the member States,

    (b)   goods which are not means of transport and are removed on or after [the date specified in paragraph (6)] from a temporary admission procedure such as is referred to in paragraph (3)(a)(i) above, in order to be returned to the person in an acceding State who had exported them from that State,

(c)   means of transport which are removed on or after [the date specified in paragraph (6)] from a temporary admission procedure such as is referred to in paragraph (3)(a)(i) above and which—

    (i)   were first brought into service before [the date specified in paragraph (7)], or

    (ii)   have a value not exceeding £4,000, or

    (iii)   have been charged in an acceding State with VAT which has not been remitted or refunded by reason of their exportation and to such other tax (if any) to which means of transport of that class or description are normally chargeable.

[(5) For the purposes of paragraphs (2) and (4) the specified date—

    (a)   in relation to the 1995 acceding states is 1st January 1995;

    (b)   in relation to the 2004 acceding states is 1st May 2004; and

    (c)   in relation to the 2007 acceding states is 1st January 2007.

(6) For the purposes of paragraphs (2) and (4) the specified date—

    (a)   in relation to the 1995 acceding states is 20th October 1995;

    (b)   in relation to the 2004 acceding states 1st May 2004; and

    (c)   in relation to the 2007 acceding states 1st January 2007.

(7) For the purposes of paragraph (4)(c)(i) the specified date—

    (a)   in relation to the 1995 acceding states is 1st January 1987;

    (b)   in relation to the 2004 acceding states is 1st May 2006; and

    (c)   in relation to the 2007 acceding states is 1st January 1999.]

NOTES

Para (1): substituted by the VAT (Amendment) (No 3) Regulations, SI 2006/3292 regs 2, 5(1), (2).

Para (2):words in square brackets substituted by the VAT (Amendment) (No 3) Regulations, SI 2006/3292, regs 2, 5(1), (3)(i), (ii). In sub-paras (a), (b) words in square brackets substituted by the VAT (Amendment) (No 3) Regulations, SI 2006/3292, regs 2, 5(1), (3)(ii).

Para (4): in sub-paras (a), (b), (c) words in square brackets substituted by the VAT (Amendment) (No 3) Regulations, SI 2006/3292, regs 2, 5(1), (4)(i), (ii).

Paras (5)–(7): substituted, for para (5) (as inserted by SI 2004/1082, regs 2, 5(1), (4)), by the VAT (Amendment) (No 3) Regulations, SI 2006/3292, regs 2, 5(1), (5).

139

For the purposes of the Act the following territories shall be treated as included in the territory of the member States and the territory of the Community—

    (i)   the Principality of Monaco (French Republic), . . .

    (ii)   the Isle of Man (United Kingdom)[, and

    [(iii)   the United Kingdom Sovereign Base Areas of Akrotiri and Dhekelia (Cyprus).]

NOTES

Word in para (I) revoked, and para (iii) inserted, by the VAT (Amendment) (No 2) Regulations 2004, SI 2004/1082 regs 2, 6.

140 Entry and exit formalities

(1) Where goods enter the United Kingdom from the territories prescribed in regulation 136 or 137 the formalities relating to the entry of goods into the customs territory of the Community contained in Council Regulation (EEC) No

2913/92, Commission Regulation (EEC) No 2454/93 and the Customs Controls on Importation of Goods Regulations 1991, shall be completed.

(2) Where goods are exported from the United Kingdom to the territories prescribed in regulation 136 or 137 the formalities relating to the export of goods to a place outside the customs territory of the Community contained in Council Regulation (EEC) No 2913/92 and Commission Regulation (EEC) No 2454/93 shall be completed.

141 Use of the internal Community transit procedure
Where goods enter the United Kingdom from the territories prescribed in regulation 136 or 137 and the said goods are intended for another member State, or other destination outside the United Kingdom transport of the goods to which destination involves their passage through another member State, the internal Community transit procedure described in Council Regulation (EEC) No 2913/92 and Commission Regulation (EEC) No 2454/93 shall apply.

Customs and excise legislation to be applied

142
Subject to regulation 143, where goods are imported into the United Kingdom from the territories prescribed in regulation 136 or 137 customs and excise legislation shall apply (so far as relevant) in relation to any VAT chargeable upon such importation with the same exception and adaptations as are prescribed in regulations 118, 119, 120 and 121 in relation to the application of section 16(1) of the Act.

143
Where goods are imported into the United Kingdom from the territories prescribed in regulation 137, section 4 of the Finance (No 2) Act 1992 (enforcement powers) shall apply in relation to any VAT chargeable upon such importation as if references in that section to "member States" excluded the territories prescribed in regulation 137.

144
Where goods are exported from the United Kingdom to the territories prescribed in regulation 136 or 137 the provisions relating to the export of goods to a place outside the customs territory of the Community contained in Council Regulation (EEC) No 2913/92 and Commission Regulation (EEC) No 2454/93 shall apply for the purpose of ensuring the correct application of the zero rate of VAT to such goods.

145—
(1) Subject to paragraph (2) below, where goods are exported from the United Kingdom to the territories prescribed in regulation 136 or 137 the provisions made by or under the Customs and Excise Management Act 1979 in relation to the exportation of goods to places outside the member States shall apply (so far as relevant) for the purpose of ensuring the correct application of the zero rate of VAT to such goods.

(2) Where goods are being exported from the United Kingdom to the territories prescribed in regulation 137, section 4 of the Finance (No 2) Act 1992 (enforcement powers) shall apply to such goods as if references in that section to "member States" excluded the territories prescribed in regulation 137.

OTHER FUEL SUBSTITUTES (RATES OF EXCISE DUTY ETC) ORDER 1995

(SI 1995/2716)

NOTES

Made: 9 November 1995.

Authority: Hydrocarbon Oil Duties Act 1979, s 6A.

Commencement: 1 December 1995.

ARRANGEMENT OF ARTICLES

1 Citation and commencement

This Order may be cited as the Other Fuel Substitutes (Rates of Excise Duty etc) Order 1995 and shall come into force on 1st December 1995.

2 Interpretation

(1)   In this Order—

(a)   "the Act" means the Hydrocarbon Oil Duties Act 1979;

(b)   "additive or extender" means additive or extender comprised in section 6A of the Act;

(c)   "the charge to duty" means the charge to duty imposed by section 6A of the Act;

(d)   "diesel engine" means an engine which is designed or adapted to be powered by diesel fuel;

(e)   "duty" means excise duty;

(f)   "engine" means an engine, motor or other machinery comprised in section 6A of the Act; and, in relation to an aircraft, which is designed or adapted to be a part of an aircraft and to give it motive power;

(g)   . . .

(h)   . . .

(i)   "liquid" means a liquid or substance comprised in section 6A of the Act;

(j)   "petrol engine" means an engine which is designed or adapted to be powered by leaded or unleaded petrol; and

[(k)   "record" means the motor fuels record governed by regulation 13 of the Biofuels and Other Fuel Substitutes (Payment of Excise Duties etc) Regulations 2004.]

(2)   Where in this Order a rate of duty or a rebate is described as a rate or rebate specified in or by a section of the Act, that rate or rebate is the rate or rebate specified or having statutory effect for the time being when the liquid became the subject of the charge to duty by virtue of section 6A of the Act.

Paras (g), (h) revoked, and para (k) substituted, by the Other Fuel Substitutes (Rates of Excise Duty etc) (Amendment) Order 2004, SI 2004/2062 arts 2, 3.

3 Determination of appropriate rate of duty

Subject to the proviso mentioned herein, the rate of the duty charged by virtue of section 6A of the Act on the setting aside or on the use of a liquid—

    (a)   as fuel for any engine; or

    (b)   as an additive or extender,

shall be determined, in the case of a liquid falling within subparagraph (a) above, in accordance with the provisions of article 4 below, and, in the case of a liquid falling within subparagraph (b) above, in accordance with the provisions of article 5 below; provided that in any case not provided for by this Order the rate of duty in respect of the aforementioned liquid which is the subject of the charge to duty shall be that which is specified by [section 6] of the Act for light oil [other than ultra low sulphur petrol and sulphur-free petrol].

NOTES

Words substituted by the Other Fuel Substitutes (Rates of Excise Duty etc) Order 2002, SI 2002/3042 arts 2, 3.

Words inserted by the Other Fuel Substitutes (Rates of Excise Duty etc) (Amendment) Order 2004, SI 2004/2062 arts 2, 4.

4 Rates of duty for fuel substitutes

(1) Paragraphs (2) to (4) below apply where, within the meaning of section 6A of the Act, a liquid as a fuel is set aside for a chargeable use with the consequence that a duty of excise is charged by virtue of that section, and paragraph (5) below applies where, within the meaning of that section, a liquid as a fuel is put to a chargeable use, not already having been charged under that section with a duty of excise, with the consequence that a duty of excise is charged on that use under that section.

[(2) Where a liquid is entered in the record as being suitable only as fuel for—

    (a)   a diesel engine, or an engine, other than a piston engine, of an aircraft, the rate of duty shall be that specified by section 6 of the Act for [sulphur-free diesel];

    (b)   a petrol engine powered by leaded petrol, the rate of duty shall be that specified by section 6 of the Act for light oil [other than ultra low sulphur petrol and sulphur-free petrol]; and

    (c)   a petrol engine powered by unleaded petrol, the rate of duty shall be that specified by section 6 of the Act for [sulphur-free petrol]; and]

(3) Where a liquid is not entered in the record as being suitable only as fuel for one of the categories of engine described in the preceding paragraph, the rate of duty shall be the rate specified by [section 6] of the Act for light oil [other than ultra low sulphur petrol and sulphur-free petrol], unless in respect of that liquid paragraph (4) applies.

(4) Where the liquid mentioned at the end of the preceding paragraph is entered in the record as being specially produced as fuel for the piston engine of an aircraft and is delivered for use solely as fuel for the piston engine of an aircraft, the rate of duty shall be . . . the rate specified by [section 6 of the Act for aviation gasoline.].

(5) Where a liquid is used as fuel in an engine described in subparagraph (a), (b) or of paragraph (2) above, the rate of duty shall be that which is specified in that

subparagraph; and, if the liquid is used in the piston engine of an aircraft, the rate of duty shall be that which is specified in paragraph (4) above.

NOTES

Para 2: substituted by the Other Fuel Substitutes (Rates of Excise Duty etc) Order 2002, SI 2002/3042 arts 2, 4(a). Words in para (b) inserted by the Other Fuel Substitutes (Rates of Excise Duty etc) (Amendment) Order 2004, SI 2004/2062 arts 2, 4. Words in paras (a), (c) substituted by SI 2004/2062 arts 2, 5.

Para 3: words substituted by SI 2002/3042 arts 2, 3. Words inserted by SI 2004/2062 arts 2, 4.

Para 4: words substituted by SI 2002/3042 arts 2, 4.(b). Words revoked by SI 2004/2062 arts 2, 5.

5 Rates of duty for additives or extenders

(1)   Paragraphs (2) to (4) below apply where, within the meaning of section 6A of the Act, a liquid as an additive or extender is set aside for a chargeable use with the consequence that a duty of excise is charged by virtue of that section, and paragraph (5) applies where, within the meaning of that section, a liquid as an additive or extender is put to a chargeable use, not already having been charged under that section with a duty of excise, with the consequence that a duty of excise is charged on that use under that section.

(2)   Where a liquid is entered in the record as being suitable only as an additive or extender in fuel for one of categories of engine described in subparagraphs (a) to (c) of paragraph (2) of article 4 above, the rate of duty shall be that which is specified in the subparagraph describing that category.

[(3)   Subject to paragraph (6) below, where a liquid is entered in the record as a multi-purpose additive or extender, the rate of duty shall be that which is specified by section 6 of the Act for [sulphur-free petrol]; and]

(4)   Where a liquid is not entered in the record under paragraph (2) and paragraph (3) above, the rate of duty shall be the rate specified by [section 6] of the Act for light oil [other than ultra low sulphur petrol and sulphur-free petrol].

(5)   Where a liquid is used as an additive or extender in fuel used in:—

(a)   one of the categories of engine described in subparagraphs (a) to (c) of paragraph (2) of article 4 above, the rate of duty shall be that specified in the subparagraph describing that engine; or

(b)   in an engine described in paragraph (4) of article 4 above, the rate of duty shall be that specified by that paragraph.

(6)   For the purposes of paragraph (3) above a liquid only constitutes a multi-purpose additive or extender if, at the time it is set aside, within the meaning of section 6A of the Act, as a multi-purpose additive or extender, the liquid has been designated, made and prepared as being for acceptable use as an additive or extender in [any] light oil fuels for an engine.

NOTES

Para 3: substituted by the Other Fuel Substitutes (Rates of Excise Duty etc) Order 2002, SI 2002/3042 arts 2, 5(a). Words substituted by the Other Fuel Substitutes (Rates of Excise Duty etc) (Amendment) Order 2004, SI 2004/2062 arts 2, 6.

Para 4: words substituted by SI 2002/3042 arts 2, 3. Words inserted SI 2004/2062 arts 2, 4.

Para 6: word substituted by SI 2002/3042 arts 2, 5(b).

6 Treatment of fuel substitutes etc, as heavy oil etc
(Revoked by the Other Fuel Substitutes (Rates of Excise Duty etc) Order 2002, SI 2002/3042 arts 2, 6)

OTHER FUEL SUBSTITUTES (PAYMENT OF EXCISE DUTY ETC) REGULATIONS 1995

(SI 1995/2717)

NOTES

Revoked by the Biofuels and Other Fuel Substitutes (Payment of Excise Duties etc) Regulations 2004, SI 2004/2065 reg 4(1).

. . .

HYDROCARBON OIL (DESIGNATED MARKERS) REGULATIONS 1996

(SI 1996/1251)

NOTES

Made: 8 May 1996.

Authority: Hydrocarbon Oil Duties Act 1979, s 24A(3).

Commencement: 1 June 1996.

1 Citation and commencement

These Regulations may be cited as the Hydrocarbon Oil (Designated Markers) Regulations 1996 and shall come into force on 1st June 1996.

2 Designation of markers

(1)   It appears to the Commissioners that the markers designated by paragraph (2) below are used for the purposes of the law of the United Kingdom (except for 2-Furaldehyde) and for the purposes of the law of places outside the United Kingdom for identifying hydrocarbon oil that is not to be used as fuel for road vehicles.

(2)   For the purposes of section 24A of the Hydrocarbon Oil Duties Act 1979 the following markers are hereby designated—

1,4-dihydroxanthraquinone;

[N-Ethyl-N-[2-(1-isobutoxyethoxy)ethyl]-4-(phenylazo)aniline]

. . .

Coumarin.

NOTES

Para (2): second designated marker substituted, and third designated marker revoked, by the Hydrocarbon Oil (Marking) Regulations 2002, SI 2002/1773 reg 19.

PLEASURE CRAFT (ARRIVAL AND REPORT) REGULATIONS 1996

(SI 1996/1406)

NOTES

Made: 29 May 1996.

Authority: Customs and Excise Management Act 1979, ss 35(4), 42(1)(a).

Commencement: 28 June 1996.

PART I
PRELIMINARY

1 Citation and commencement

These Regulations may be cited as the Pleasure Craft (Arrival and Report) Regulations 1996 and shall come into force on 28th June 1996.

2 Interpretation

In these Regulations—

"arrival" means the anchoring, berthing or mooring of a vessel within the limits of a port and "arrive" and cognate expressions shall be construed accordingly;

"notification of arrival" means notification of arrival as referred to in regulation 6(2);

"pleasure craft" means a vessel which, at the time of its arrival in the United Kingdom, is being used for private recreational purposes;

"the person responsible" means the person on board a vessel under whose command or subject to whose personal direction it has arrived or is intended to arrive as a pleasure craft;

"the prescribed form" means the form prescribed by the Commissioners for the purposes of these Regulations in directions made under section 35(1) of the Customs and Excise Management Act 1979.

3 Application

These Regulations shall apply to a pleasure craft which arrives in the United Kingdom from a place outside the customs territory of the European Community or from a territory listed in the Schedule.

PART II
GENERAL

4 The flying of the signal flag "Q"

The person responsible shall cause a yellow flag (the signal flag for "Q" in the International Code of Signals) to be flown on a vessel which it is intended shall arrive as a pleasure craft at all times between the crossing of the limits of a port in the United Kingdom and the making of report of that vessel in accordance with regulation 6.

5 Movement of vessels and persons

(1) Subject to paragraph (3) below, no person, after the arrival of a pleasure craft in the United Kingdom, shall move the vessel until report of the vessel has been made in accordance with regulation 6.

(2) Subject to paragraph (4) below, no person who is on board a pleasure craft at the time of its arrival in the United Kingdom shall disembark from the vessel until report of the vessel has been made in accordance with regulation 6, save that such a person may disembark for the purpose of giving notification of arrival and may remain away from the vessel for as long as is reasonable in connection with that purpose.

(3) By way of exception to paragraph (1) above, where a person giving notification of arrival is told that an officer is not to board the vessel, the vessel may be moved as soon as the person giving such notification has been so told.

(4) By way of exception to paragraph (2) above, where a person giving notification of arrival is told that an officer is not to board the vessel, persons may disembark as soon as the person giving such notification has been so told.

(5) Nothing in this regulation shall affect any Act or subordinate legislation relating to public health, having effect in the United Kingdom or any part thereof. In this paragraph, "Act" and "subordinate legislation" have the same respective meanings as in the Interpretation Act 1978.

PART III
PROCEDURE FOR REPORT ON ARRIVAL

6—

(1) The procedure for making report of a pleasure craft which has arrived in the United Kingdom shall be as set out in paragraphs (2) to (7) below.

(2) Subject to paragraph (3) below, the person responsible, or a person acting on his behalf, shall notify arrival of the vessel to an officer, either in person or by telephone.

(3) Where an officer boards the vessel after its arrival and before notification of arrival has been given, such notification shall not be required with effect from the moment of such boarding.

(4) Notification of arrival, where it is required, shall be given as soon as practicable after the arrival of the vessel.

(5) Where a person giving notification of arrival is told that an officer is to board the vessel, the person responsible shall, when the officer boards, deliver to the officer the prescribed form, duly completed.

(6) Where a person giving notification of arrival is told that an officer is not to board the vessel, the person responsible shall put the prescribed form, duly completed, in a Customs and Excise post box where one is provided for that purpose or deliver it to an officer, or to the Customs and Excise office for the port of arrival.

(7) Where an officer boards the vessel after its arrival but before notification of arrival has been given, the person responsible shall deliver the prescribed form, duly completed, to the officer who has boarded.

7

((Pt IV) revokes the Pleasure Craft (Arrival and Report) Regulations 1990, SI 1990/1169.)

SCHEDULE
THE TERRITORIES REFERRED TO

Regulation 3

Mount Athos (Hellenic Republic).

The Aland Islands.

The Canary Islands (Kingdom of Spain).

The Channel Islands.

The overseas departments of the French Republic (Guadeloupe, Martinique, Réunion, St Pierre and Miquelon and French Guiana).

HYDROCARBON OIL (PAYMENT OF REBATES)
REGULATIONS 1996

(SI 1996/2313)

NOTES

Made: 9 September 1996.

Authority: Hydrocarbon Oil Duties Act 1979, s 24.

Part II

Commencement: 1 October 1996.

ARRANGEMENT OF REGULATIONS

1 Citation and commencement

These Regulations may be cited as the Hydrocarbon Oil (Payment of Rebates) Regulations 1996 and shall come into force on 1st October 1996.

2

(*Revokes the Hydrocarbon Oil Regulations 1973, SI 1973/1311, regs 31–33 and the Hydrocarbon Oil (Amendment) Regulations 1981, SI 1981/1134, reg 3(c), (d).*)

3 Interpretation

(1) In these Regulations—

"Act" means the Hydrocarbon Oil Duties Act 1979;

"annual rebate payment person" means a rebate payment person permitted by the Commissioners in the licence issued by them to him as a rebate payment person to furnish an estimate (as required by these Regulations) in relation to any year commencing 1st January after the issue of the licence;

"business days" means days which are business days within the meaning of section 92 of the Bills of Exchange Act 1882;

"Collector for the Oils Accounting Centre" means the Collector of Customs and Excise responsible for the Oils Accounting Centre at HM Customs and Excise, Dorset House, Stamford Street, London SE1 9PY or at such other address which may be specified in directions made by the Commissioners under section 116 of the Customs and Excise Management Act 1979;

"Event A" is the event described in regulation 6(2)(a) below;

"Event B(1)", "Event B(2)" and "Event B(3)" is, in each case, the event described in regulation 6(2)(b) below in association with the consequence described by the following subparagraphs ((a) to (c)) of regulation 6(3) below—

(i) subparagraph (a) in the case of Event B(1);

(ii) subparagraph (b) in the case of Event B(2); and

(iii) subparagraph (c) in the case of Event B(3);

"gas oil" has the meaning given by section 11(2) of the Act;

"his accounting period" means—

(a) in relation to a quarterly rebate payment person, any quarter in any year commencing 1st January, 1st April, 1st July and 1st October; and

(b) in relation to an annual rebate payment person, any year commencing 1st January following the issue of the licence to him, in which the Commissioners permit him to furnish an estimate in relation to a year commencing on that date;

"licensed user" means an annual rebate payment person or a quarterly rebate payment person;

"quarterly rebate payment person" means a rebate payment person permitted by the Commissioners, in the licence issued by them to him as a rebate payment person, to furnish an estimate (governed by these Regulations) in relation to any quarterly period in any year commencing 1st January, 1st April, 1st July and 1st October;

"rebated heavy oil activity" means, in relation to heavy oil described in section 12(2) of the Act (which includes gas oil and section 12 kerosene), the use of that heavy oil as fuel for a road vehicle (falling within that section) or the taking of that heavy oil into that vehicle as fuel;

"rebated kerosene activity" means, in relation to section 13AA kerosene, either of the two uses of that kerosene as fuel for engines, or the taking of that kerosene into the fuel supply of an engine, which engines and engine fall respectively within paragraph 5(a), (b) and (c) of section 13AA(2) of the Act;

"rebate payment person" means, subject to paragraph (3) below of this regulation, a person—

(a) who applies in writing to the Commissioners for a licence authorising him to make payments in accordance with the provisions of these Regulations for the purposes of section 12(2) or section 13AA(3) and (4) of the Act, as specified in his application; and

(b) to whom such a licence is issued by the Commissioners;

"section 12 kerosene" means heavy oil of the description given by paragraph (c) of section 11(1) of the Act; and

"section 13AA kerosene" means kerosene of the description given by section 13AA(5) of the Act for the purposes of sections 13AA and 13AB of the Act.

(2) In regulation 6(3)(c) below "the rate of net excise duty per litre of section 13AA kerosene" means the rate, expressed as pence per litre, calculated in accordance with the formula provided by paragraph 2 of, and by paragraph 3 of Schedule 2 to these Regulations for the purpose of effecting the comparison (required by regulation 6(3)(c) below) in accordance with the provisions of Schedule 2.

(3) "Rebate payment person" does not include a person, in relation to any period after the withdrawal of the following licence takes effect, whose licence, issued to him as a rebate payment person, has been withdrawn for reasonable cause by the Commissioners (in a notice of withdrawal issued to him at his address appearing in his written application for the licence) with effect from the end of the quarter commencing 1st January, 1st April, 1st June or 1st October (in any year) in which the notice of withdrawal is issued.

4 Effective rebate payments for the purposes of section 12(2) or 13AA(2) of the Act

A payment made for the purposes of section 12(2) or 13AA(2) of the Act shall not be effective unless it is made by a licensed user in accordance with the provisions of regulation 5 or, as the case may be, regulation 6 below in respect of any rebated heavy oil activity or rebated kerosene activity carried out by him.

5 Estimates and payments

(1) A licensed user shall comply with the requirements of paragraphs (2) and (3) below before he begins for the first time in his accounting period to carry out any rebated heavy oil activity or any rebated kerosene activity.

(2) The licensed user shall furnish the Collector for the Oils Accounting Centre an estimate, relating to his accounting period in which he intends to begin for the first time in that period to carry out the activities mentioned in paragraph (1) above, of the

volumes of fuel (described in the following form) which he estimates he will use in carrying out those activities during that accounting period, on the form numbered 1 in Schedule 1 to these Regulations, containing full information in respect of all other matters specified in the form.

(3)   The licensed user shall, at the same time as he furnishes the estimate (required by paragraph 2 above), pay the Commissioners—

(a)   in the case of any rebated heavy oil activities, relating to gas oil, dealt with in the estimate at Part 2, an amount equal to the amount which would, at the time the estimate is furnished, be allowed as a rebate of excise duty under section 11(1)(b) of the Act on a quantity of gas oil (if delivered at that time for home use), being of the same volume as that specified at Part 2(a) in the estimate;

(b)   in the case of rebated heavy oil activities, relating to section 12 kerosene, dealt with in the estimate at Part 3, an amount equal to the amount which would, at the time the estimate is furnished, be allowed as a rebate of excise duty under section 11(1)(c) of the Act on a quantity of section 12 kerosene (if delivered at that time for home use), being of the same volume as that specified at Part 3(a) in the estimate; and

(c)   in the case of any rebated kerosene activities, relating to section 13AA kerosene, dealt with in the estimate at Part 4, an amount calculated in accordance with the formula A — B, where—

(i)   A is the amount of excise duty that would be charged, at the legally effective rate at the time the estimate is furnished, by section 6(1) of the Act on a quantity of heavy oil (if imported or produced, as described in section 6(1), at that time), being of the same volume as that specified at Part 4(c) in the estimate in relation to section 13AA kerosene; and

(ii)   B is the amount of rebate of excise duty on heavy oil allowable in the case of gas oil under section 11(1)(b) of the Act, at the legally effective rate at the same time as that specified in paragraph (i) above, on a quantity of gas oil (if delivered for home use as envisaged by section 11), being of the same volume as that used in the calculation for the purposes of paragraph (i) above.

6 Supplementary estimates, Events A, B(1), B(2) and B(3), and additional rebate payments and forms

(1)   Paragraph (4) below applies to a licensed user—

(a)   who furnished an estimate (required by regulation 5(2) above); and

(b)   where, subsequently in relation to him and his accounting period and the estimate, and to any rebated heavy oil activities or rebated kerosene activities carried out by him by the time of the following occurrence, there is an occurrence of an event described in paragraph (2) and (3) below (referred to in these Regulations respectively as Event A, Event B(1), Event B(2) and Event B(3)).

(2)   For the purposes of these Regulations the events are—

(a)   Event A—at any time during his accounting period, to which the estimate relates, the amounts of fuel used by that time by the licensed user for carrying out any rebated heavy activity, or any rebated kerosene activity (which activity, respectively, is the subject of an entry in Part 2 or Part 3, or Part 4 of the estimate) is equal to the estimated volume of fuel specified in that Part of the estimate;

(b)   Event B(1), B(2) and B(3)—on a day, in his accounting period to which the licensed user's estimate relates, a change of either or both—

    (i)   the legally effective rate of excise duty in the case of heavy oil (charged by section 6(1) of the Act); and

    (ii)   the legally effective rate of rebate of the heavy oil excise duty in the case of gas oil (allowed under section 11(1)(b) of the Act),

takes legal effect, which is associated with any one or more of the three consequences described in paragraph (3) below.

(3)   For the purposes of paragraph (2)(b) above the consequences are as follows: where the licensed user has furnished an estimate (required by regulation 5(2) above)—

    (a)   (Event B(1)) in which there is an entry in Part 2 (for estimated gas oil consumption), the consequence is that the amount of rebate allowable under section 11(1)(b) of the Act on a quantity of gas oil, when the change takes legal effect, would be greater than it would have been immediately before the change takes legal effect;

    (b)   (Event B(2)) in which there is an entry in Part 3 (for estimated section 12 kerosene consumption), the consequence is that the amount of rebate allowable under section 11(1)(c) of the Act on a quantity of section 12 kerosene, when the change takes legal effect, would be greater than it would have been immediately before the change takes legal effect; and

    (c)   (Event B(3)) in which there is an entry in Part 4 (for estimated section 13AA kerosene consumption), the consequence is that a comparison (effected in accordance with the provisions of Schedule 2 to those Regulations) of—

        (i)   the rate, immediately before the change takes legal effect, of the net excise duty per litre of section 13AA kerosene calculated in accordance with the formula provided by paragraph 2 of Schedule 2 (called in this sub-paragraph "the paragraph (i) rate"); with

        (ii)   the rate, when the change takes legal effect, of the net excise duty per litre of section 13AA kerosene calculated in accordance with the formula provided by paragraph 3 of Schedule 2 (called in this sub-paragraph "the paragraph (ii) rate"),

indicates that the paragraph (ii) rate is greater than the paragraph (i) rate.

(4)   The licensed user, to whom this paragraph applies, shall, in respect of that part of any rebated heavy oil activity or of any rebated kerosene activity (called in this paragraph the "relevant part-activity") to which Event A, Event B(1), Event B(2) or Event B(3) relates (called in this paragraph the "related Event"), cease to carry out the relevant part-activity upon the occurrence of the related Event; and he may again carry out the relevant ceased part-activity only if, before doing so—

    (a)   in the case of the related Event being Event A, he furnishes the Collector for the Oils Accounting Centre a supplementary estimate of the volumes of fuel (described in the following form) estimated to be used in carrying out the relevant part-activity, on the form numbered 2 in Schedule 1 to those Regulations, containing full information in respect of all other matters specified on the form, and only if he complies with the requirements specified in paragraph (5) below; and

    (b)   in the case of Event B(1), B(2) or B(3) occurring, he furnishes the Collector for the Oils Accounting Centre with an additional rebate payment form in the form numbered 3 in Schedule 1 to these Regulations (called below in this sub-paragraph the "form") showing the additional amount payable (correctly calculated in accordance with the provisions of the form) in the following parts of the form in relation to the occurring event (that is to say Part 2(e) in relation to Event B(1),

Part 3(e) in relation to Event B(2) and Part 4(a) in relation to Event B(3)), containing full information in respect of all other matters specified in the form, and containing a declaration, signed by him, that the information given in the form is true and complete; and only if he pays to the Commissioners the additional amount payable, at the same time as he furnishes the form.

(5) A licensed user shall comply, when furnishing a supplementary estimate under paragraph 4(a) above, with the requirements of paragraph (3) of regulation 5 above (requiring payments to be made to the Commissioners when furnishing an estimate), as if the supplementary estimate was the estimate mentioned therein.

7 Application of regulation 6 provisions to supplementary estimates

(1) The provisions of paragraphs (4) and (5) of regulation 6 above shall apply to a licensed user who has furnished a supplementary estimate under that regulation in respect of his accounting period, or has furnished another supplementary estimate or further supplementary estimates, in respect of that accounting period, by virtue of operation of this regulation in relation to it or them—

   (a)   as if the supplementary estimate was the estimate mentioned in regulation 6 or, as the case may be, each of those supplementary estimates was such an estimate; and

   (b)   where there is an occurrence of Event A, Event B(1), Event B(2) or Event B(3) in relation to that supplementary estimate or, as the case may be, those supplementary estimates, to the licensed user, to the period of his accounting period dealt with by that supplementary estimate or supplementary estimates, and to any rebated heavy oil activities or rebated kerosene activities carried out by him in the above first-mentioned period by the time of that occurrence.

8 Returns

(1) A person, who furnished an estimate (as required by paragraph 2 of regulation 5 above) as a licensed user, shall furnish, within 10 business days after the end of the period determined in accordance with paragraph 2 below, the Collector for the Oils Accounting Centre a return, relating to the accounting period specified in Part 1 of that estimate, in the form numbered 4 in Schedule 1 to these Regulations, containing full information in respect of the matters specified in the form, and containing a declaration, signed by him, that the information given in the return is true and complete.

(2) (a) Unless subparagraph (b) below applies, the period is the accounting period specified in Part 1 of the estimate or, in the absence of sufficient specification in Part 1, is the accounting period which the licensed user ought to have specified as his accounting period;

   (b)   This subparagraph applies in the case of a person (falling within paragraph (1) above) who—

      (i)   furnishes the estimate (referred to in paragraph (1) above) for an annual accounting period of a particular year; and

     (ii)   ceases to be a rebate payment person with effect, as the case may be, from the end of one of the three quarters commencing in that particular year 1st January, 1st April or 1st July, by reason of the Commissioners withdrawing, under paragraph (3) of regulation 3 above, the licence issued to him as a rebate payment person;

in such a case, and having regard to those three quarters, the period is the quarter from the end of which the withdrawal takes effect.

(3) A person furnishing a return under this Regulation may, at the same time, claim any amount which he may have overpaid to the Commissioners in the accounting period to which the return relates.

9 Records to be kept by a licensed user

(1) Paragraphs (2) and (4) below apply to a licensed user who uses a road vehicle falling within section 12 of the Act for any rebated heavy oil activity or any rebated kerosene activity, and to a person who has ceased to be such a licensed user during the period of 12 months (defined in paragraph (2) below) with effect from a time falling within that period, by reason of the withdrawal by the Commissioners (as envisaged by paragraph (3) of regulation 2 above) of the licence issued to him as a rebate payment person.

(2) A licensed user, and a person, to whom, in either case, this paragraph applies by virtue of paragraph (1) above shall—

    (a)   keep a record of all fuel used by him respectively, for any rebated heavy oil activity or rebated kerosene activity carried out by way of a road vehicle falling within section 12 of the Act, in which shall be entered, on the day of the use of the fuel (and by reference to its date), the particulars specified in paragraph (3) below; and

    (b)   preserve that record—

        (i)   at the premises at which the aforementioned road vehicle is usually kept, or at such other place as may be agreed between the aforementioned licensed user or person and the proper officer; and

        (ii)   for not less than the period of 12 months from the date on which the last entry was made in it.

(3) The particulars in relation to the road vehicle falling within paragraph 2(a) above are—

    (a)   the registration number of the road vehicle or other identification mark in the case of an unregistered vehicle;

    (b)   the date of each journey, or, where the road vehicle is employed otherwise than in making a journey from place to place, the place of that employment;

    (c)   the quantities of, and the fuel (by reference to the classification of whether it is gas oil, section 12 kerosene or section 13AA kerosene) supplied into the road vehicle; and

    (d)   the number of miles travelled by the road vehicle on any journey (falling within paragraph (b) above), and the number of hours the vehicle is used in employment falling within paragraph (b) above.

(4) A licensed user, and a person, to whom, in either case, this paragraph applies by virtue of paragraph 1 above, shall, on demand by the proper officer, produce to the proper officer at all reasonable times the record which he is required by paragraph (2) above to keep.

SCHEDULE 1

CONTENTS OF SCHEDULE 1

Form No	Title	Regulation	Page
1	HO72: Rebated Heavy Oil to be used as Fuel: Estimate of volumes of fuel and statements of amounts payable.	5(2)	8, 9 and 10

Part II

Form No	Title	Regulation	Page
2	HO73: Rebated Heavy Oil to be used as Fuel: Supplementary estimate of volumes of fuel and statements of amounts payable.	6(4)(a)	11, 12 and 13
3	HO74: Rebated Heavy Oil to be used as Fuel: Additional Rebate Payment Form (Event B).	6(4)(b)	14, 15 and 16
4	HO75: Rebated Heavy Oil to be used as Fuel: Return of Rebate due (and paid) to the Commissioners.	8(1)	17, 18 and 19

Form No. 1

HO72

Rebated Heavy Oil to be used as Fuel:
Estimate of volumes of fuel and statements of amounts payable

Before completing this form please read the Notes on completion

A Name and address of licensed user	B Address at which stock of fuels is kept (if different from A)
Postcode:	Postcode:

Part 1 This estimate, signed by me at the end, is for the quarterly/annual* accounting period ending

(Note 1) .... of the above named licensed person.

The estimates of volumes involved and the related payable amounts are shown in Parts 2,3 and 4*.

Part 2 Estimated volumes of gas oil: usage governed by section 12 of the Act (road vehicle use)

(a) volume of gas oil to be used for a road vehicle (Note 2: ⌷ litres

(b) gas oil rebates rate (Note 3): £ 0 . ⌷ per litre

(c) amount payable under this Part with the estimate (Note 4): £ ⌷

Part 3 Estimated volume of section 12 kerosene: usage governed by Section 12 of the Act (road vehicle use)

(a) volume of section 12 kerosene to be used for a road vehicle (Note 5): ⌷ litres

(b) kerosene rebate rate applicable (tax type 541) (Note 6): £ 0 . ⌷ per litre

(c) amount payable under this Part with the estimate (Note 7): £ ⌷

*Delete as necessary

HO72

PCU(September 1996)

(Substitute)(LexisNexis Butterworths)

937

Date received at Accounting Centre

The Collector
HM Customs and Excise
Oils Accounting Centre
Dorset House
Stamford Street
London SE1 9PJ

Fold Here

Part 4 Estimated volume of section 13AA kerosene: usage governed by Section 13AA of the Act

(a) volume of kerosene to propel excepted vehicles (Note 8): ⬚ litres

(b) volume of kerosene to be used in other engines
not falling in (a) (Note 9): ⬚ litres

(c) total of subparagraphs (a) and (b) (Note 10): ⬚ litres

(d) rate of net excise duty applicable (tax type 542) (Note 11): £ 0 . ⬚ per litre

(e) net excise duty payable under this Part with the estimate (Note 12): £ ⬚

Part 5 Total amount payable with this estimate (Note 13): £ ⬚

On behalf of/As* the licensed user I sign this estimate and include the total sum due

Signature: ....
(Proprietor/Partner/Director/Company Secretary/Duly Authorised signatory)

Name in capital letters: ....

*Delete as necessary

For Official Use

<u>Accounting Centre Cost Code 16245</u>:

Received by BD/C/GC/N/PO/PRT the sum of £ ⬚

Placed on MCD against Deposit Number ....

Input keyed in by .... (Intls)

HO72   reverse (09/96)

NOTES ON COMPLETION

PART 1

1.   Accounting periods end 31 March, 30 June, 30 September and 31 December in each year. In some instances the Commissioners may licence a user to use an annual accounting period, which will end on 31 December. Complete Part 1 with the quarterly or annual period-end date, as shown in your licence.

PART 2:
REBATED GAS OIL (USED AS DERV)

2. In Part 2(a) show number of litres of gas oil which you estimate will be used (in the accounting period specified in Part 1) in your "road vehicle". ("Road vehicle" means a diesel engined vehicle which is not entitled to use gas oil, or kerosene, under section 12, unless the rebate is paid in advance with this estimate.)

3. In Part 2(b) show current rate of gas oil rebate shown in the Tariff, Volume 1, Part 12, as may be updated by a Budget Notice with a change of rate (these may be examined at any Excise Advice Centre—address in local phone book).

4. To obtain this amount multiply the figure entered in 2(a) by the figure entered in 2(b). The result should be shown in 2(c).

PART 3:
FULLY-REBATED KEROSENE (USED AS DERV)

5. In Part 3(a) show number of litres of kerosene which you estimate will be used (in the accounting period specified in Part 1) in your "road vehicle" ("road vehicle" is explained in Note 2 above).

6. In Part 3(b) show current rate of kerosene rebate shown in the Tariff, Volume 1, Part 12, as may be updated by a Budget Notice with a change of rate (these may be examined at any Excise Advice Centre—address in local phone book).

7. To obtain this amount multiply the figure entered in 3(a) by the figure entered in 3(b). The result should be shown in 3(c).

PART 4:
FULLY-REBATED KEROSENE (USED AS REBATED GAS OIL IN 'EXCEPTED VEHICLES' ETC)

8. In Part 4(a) show number of litres of kerosene which you estimate will be used in the accounting period specified in Part 1 in your "excepted vehicle". ("Excepted vehicle" means any vehicle listed in Schedule 1 to the Act.)

9. In Part 4(b) show number of litres of kerosene which you estimate will be used to fuel an engine which is neither for propelling an "excepted vehicle" (see Note 8 above) nor for heating.

10. Add together the figure at 4(a) and the figure at 4(b), and enter that total at 4(c).

11. In Part 4(d) show current rate of net excise duty shown in the Tariff, Volume 1, Part 12, against tax type 542, as may be updated by a Budget Notice with a change of rate (these may be examined at any Excise Advice Centre—address in local phone book).

12. Multiply the figure at 4(c) by the rate of 4(d) to obtain the amount payable and enter that amount in 4(e).

PART 5:
TOTAL AMOUNT PAYABLE WITH THIS ESTIMATE

13. Add together any amount shown at 2(c), 3(c) and 4(e) and enter that total in Part 5. Your cheque for the total amount entered in Part 5 should be made payable to **HM Customs and Excise** and be crossed account payee.

WARNING: Use of rebated oil as fuel contrary to the Regulations is an offence for which penalties may be imposed by the Commissioners of Customs and Excise, in addition to recovery of the rebate. If you have any doubt about your position under the Law you should consult your local Excise Advice Centre immediately.

Form No. 2   **H073**

Rebated Heavy Oil to be used as Fuel:
Supplementary estimate of volumes of fuel and statements
of amounts payable

Before completing this form please read the Notes on completion

A Name and address of licensed user	**B** Address at which stock of fuels is kept (if different from A)
Postcode:	Postcode:

Part 1   This supplementary estimate, signed by me at the end, is for the quarterly/annual* accounting period ending

(Note 1) - - - - - - - - - - - - - of the above named licensed person.

The estimates of volumes involved and the related payable amounts are shown in Parts 2, 3 and 4*.

Part 2   Estimated volume of gas oil: usage governed by section 12 of the Act (road vehicle use)

(a) volume of gas oil to be used for a road vehicle (Note 2):   [   ] litres

(b) gas oil rebate rate (Note 3):   [£ 0 *] per litre

(c) amount payable under this Part with the estimate (Note 4):   [£ *]

Part 3   Estimated volume of section 12 kerosene: usage governed by Section 12 of the Act (road vehicle use)

(a) volume of section 12 kerosene to be used for a road vehicle (Note 5):   [   ] litres

(b) kerosene rebate rate applicable (tax type 541) (Note 6):   [£ 0 *] per litre

(c) amount payable under this Part with the estimate (Note 7):   [£ *]

Delete as necessary

HO73   PCU(September 1996)   **(Substitute)(LexisNexis Butterworths)**

Date received at Accounting Centre

The Collector
HM Customs and Excise
Oils Accounting Centre
Dorset House
Stamford Street
London SE1 9PJ

Part 4   Estimated volume of section 13AA kerosene: usage governed by Section 13AA of the Act

(a) volume of section 13AA kerosene to propel excepted vehicles (Note 8): ⎣   ⎦ litres

(b) volume of section 13AA kerosene to be used in other engines not falling in (a) (Note 9): ⎣   ⎦ litres

(c) total of subparagraphs (a) and (b) (Note 10): ⎣   ⎦ litres

(d) rate of net excise duty applicable (tax type 542) (Note 11): £ 0 . ⎣   ⎦ per litre

(e) net excise duty payable under this Part with the estimate (Note 12): £ ⎣   . ⎦

Part 5   Total amount payable with this estimate (Note 13): £ ⎣   . ⎦

On behalf of/As* the licensed user I sign this supplementary estimate and include the total sum due

Signature: ....
(Proprietor/Partner/Director/Company Secretary/Duly Authorised signatory)

Name in capital letters: ....

*Delete as necessary

For Official Use

Accounting Centre Cost Code 16245:

Received by BD/C/GC/N/PO/PRT the sum of   £ ⎣   . ⎦

Placed on MCD against Deposit Number ....

Input keyed in by... (Intls)

HO73   reverse (09/96)

NOTES ON COMPLETION

PART 1

1. Accounting periods end 31 March, 30 June, 30 September and 31 December in each year. In some instances the Commissioners may licence a user to use an annual accounting period, which will end on 31 December. Complete Part 1 with the quarterly or annual period-end date, as shown in your licence.

PART 2:
REBATED GAS OIL (USED AS DERV)

2.   In Part 2(a) show number of litres of gas oil which you estimate will be used (in the accounting period specified in Part 1, on and after furnishing this supplementary estimate) in your "road vehicle". ("Road vehicle" means a diesel engined vehicle which is not entitled to use gas oil, or kerosene, under section 12, unless the rebate is paid in advance with the supplementary estimate.)

3.   In Part 2(b) show current rate of gas oil rebate shown in the Tariff, Volume 1, Part 12, as may be updated by a Budget Notice with a change of rate (these may be examined at any Excise Advice Centre—address in local phone book).

4.   To obtain this amount multiply the figure entered in 2(a) by the figure entered in 2(b). The result should be shown in 2(c).

PART 3:
FULLY-REBATED KEROSENE (USED AS DERV)

5.   In Part 3(a) show number of litres of kerosene which you estimate will be used (in the accounting period specified in Part 1, on and after furnishing this supplementary estimate) in your "road vehicle" ("road vehicle" is explained in Note 2 above).

6.   In Part 3(b) show current rate of kerosene rebate shown in the Tariff, Volume 1, Part 12, as may be updated by a Budget Notice with a change of rate (these may be examined at any Excise Advice Centre—address in local phone book).

7.   To obtain this amount multiply the figure entered in 3(a) by the figure entered in 3(b). The result should be shown in 3(c).

PART 4:
FULLY-REBATED KEROSENE (USED AS REBATED GAS OIL IN 'EXCEPTED VEHICLES' ETC)

8.   In Part 4(a) show number of litres of kerosene which you estimate will be used (in the accounting period, specified in Pt 1, on and after furnishing this supplementary estimate) in your "excepted vehicle". ("Excepted vehicle" means any vehicle listed in Schedule 1 to the Act.)

9.   In Part 4(b) show number of litres of kerosene which you estimate will be used (in the accounting period, specified in Part 1, on and after furnishing this supplementary estimate) to fuel an engine which is neither for propelling an "excepted vehicle" (see Note 8 above) nor for heating.

10.   Add together the figure at 4(a) and the figure at 4(b), and enter that total at 4(c).

11.   In Part 4(d) show current rate of net excise duty shown in the Tariff, Volume 1, Part 12, against tax type 542, as may be updated by a Budget Notice with a change of rate (these may be examined at any Excise Advice Centre—address in local phone book).

12.   Multiply the figure at 4(c) by the rate of 4(d) to obtain the amount payable and enter that amount in 4(e).

PART 5:
TOTAL AMOUNT PAYABLE WITH THIS ESTIMATE

13.   Add together any amount shown at 2(c), 3(c) and 4(e) and enter that total in Part 5. Your cheque for the total amount entered in Part 5 should be made payable to **HM Customs and Excise** and be crossed account payee.

WARNING: Use of rebated oil as fuel contrary to the Regulations is an offence for which penalties may be imposed by the Commissioners of Customs and Excise, in addition to recovery of the rebate. If you have any doubt about your position under the Law you should consult your local Excise Advice Centre immediately.

Form No. 3

Rebated Heavy Oil used as Fuel:
Additional Rebate Payment Form (Event B(1), (2) & (3))

Before completing this form please read the Notes on completion

HO74

A Name and address of licensed user	B Address at which stock of fuel is kept (if different from A)
Postcode:	Postcode:

Part 1 This is the additional rebate payment form for the quarterly/annual* accounting period ending

(Note 1) .... of the above named licenced user.

Event B (Note 2) occurred on .... and as a consequence a further amount is payable.

Part 2 Volume of gas oil: usage governed by section 12 of the Act (road fuel usage) (Event B(1))
(Note 3 deals with (a) to (e) below)

(a) volume of gas oil shown in Part 2 of the estimate and any
supplementary estimate made in this accounting period ☐☐☐☐☐☐☐☐☐☐ litres

(b) volume of gas oil used in this accounting period as road fuel
up to the date, shown in Part 1 above, of Event B(1) ☐☐☐☐☐☐☐☐☐☐ litres

(c) volume of gas oil remaining unused (difference between
figures at (a) and (b) above) ☐☐☐☐☐☐☐☐☐☐ litres

(d) amount rate of rebate per litre of fuel currently upon
Event B(1)(as published for this purpose by the
Commissioners of Customs and Excise in a Notice) £ 0 . ☐☐☐☐☐ per litre

(e) additional amount payable (multiply the figure at (c) above
by the figure at (c) above) £ ☐☐☐☐☐.☐☐

Part 3 Volume of section 12 kerosene: usage governed by Section 12 of the Act (road fuel usage) (Event B(2))
(Note 4 deals with (a) to (e) below)

(a) volume of section 12 kerosene shown in Part 3 of the estimate
and any supplementary estimate made in this accounting period ☐☐☐☐☐☐☐☐☐☐ litres

(b) volume of section 12 kerosene used in this accounting period as
road fuel up to the date, shown in Part 1 above, of Event B(2) ☐☐☐☐☐☐☐☐☐☐ litres

(c) volume of section 12 kerosene remaining unused (difference
between figures at (a) and (b) above) ☐☐☐☐☐☐☐☐☐☐ litres

(d) additional rate of rebate per litre of fuel consequent upon
Event B(2)(as published for this purpose by the
Commissioners of Customs and Excise in a Notice) £ 0 . ☐☐☐☐☐ per litre

(e) additional amount payable (multiply figure at (d) above
by the figure at (c) above) £ ☐☐☐☐☐.☐☐

Delete as necessary

HO74

PCU(September 1996)

(Substitute)(LexisNexis Butterworths)

Date received at Accounting Centre

The Collector
HM Customs and Excise
Oils Accounting Centre
Dorset House
Stamford Street
London SE1 9PJ

Fold here

Part 4 Volume of section 13AA kerosene: usage governed by Section 13AA of the Act (Event B(3))
(Notes 5 deals with (a) to (g) below)

(a) volume of section 13AA kerosene shown in Part 4(a) of the estimate and any supplementary estimate and made in this period — litres

(b) volume of section 13AA kerosene shown in Part 4(b) of the estimate and any supplementary estimate made in this period — litres

(c) total of (a) and (b) above — litres

(d) volume of section 13AA kerosene used in this period (either to propel excepted vehicles or in other engines) up to the date, shown in Part 1 above, of Event B(3) — litres

(e) volume of section 13AA kerosene remaining unused (difference between figure at (c) and figure at (d) above) — litres

(f) additional rate of net excise duty per litre of section 13AA kerosene consequent upon Event B(3)(as published for this purpose by the Commissioners of Customs and Excise in a Notice) £ 0 . per litre

(g) additional amount payable (multiply the figure at (e) above by the figure at (f) above) £ .

Part 5 Total amount now payable with this form (being the sum of amounts shown at 2(e), 3(e) and 4(g) above) (Note 6) £ .

Declaration

I, ... declare that the information given in this return is true and complete.

Signature... Date ....
(Proprietor/Partner/Director/Company Secretary/Duly authorised signatory)

Name in capital letters ....

A false declaration can result in prosecution
*Delete as necessary

For Official Use

__Accounting Centre Cost Code 16245__:

Received by BD/C/GC/N/PO/PRT the sum of £ .

Placed on MCD against Deposit Number ....

Input keyed in by .... (Intls)

HO74   reverse (09/96)

NOTES ON COMPLETION

PART 1:

1. Accounting periods end on 31 March, 30 June, 30 September and 31 December in each year. In some instances the Commissioners may licence a user to use an annual accounting period, which will end on 31 December. Complete Part 1 with the quarterly or annual period-end date, as shown in your licence.

2.   Event B is either or both (a) an increase in the full rate of duty due on heavy oil by section 6(1) of the Act, or (b) an increase in the rate of rebate allowed on heavy oil by section 11(1)(b) of the Act, with the consequence that an insufficient amount of rebate has been paid in the accounting period shown in Part 1.

It is expected that such event will only take place on Budget day, and that date (which should lie within the current accounting period) is to be entered in Part 1.

PART 2:
REBATED GAS OIL (USED AS DERV)

3.—(a)   The figures entered in this Part are to reflect figures entered in Part 2 of the estimate and any supplementary estimate **in respect of this accounting period.**

(b)   Enter the volume of rebated gas oil actually used in this accounting period as road fuel up to the time of event B(1), when the amount of rebate on gas oil increased (usually from 6pm on Budget Day).

(c)   Subtract the figure 2(b) from the total at 2(a) and enter the difference at 2(c).

(d)   Enter the published additional rate.

(e)   Enter the additional amount payable.

PART 3:
FULLY-REBATED KEROSENE (USED AS DERV)

4.—(a)   The figures entered in this Part are to reflect figures entered in Part 3 of the estimate and any supplementary estimate **in respect of this accounting period.**

(b)   Enter the volume of fully-rebated kerosene actually used in this accounting period as road fuel (other than in an 'excepted vehicle' — see Part 4) up to the time of event B(2), when the amount of rebate on kerosene increased (usually from 6pm on Budget Day).

(c)   Subtract the figure 3(b) from the total at 3(c) and enter the difference at 3(c).

(d)   Enter the published additional rate.

(e)   Enter the additional amount payable.

PART 4:
FULLY-REBATED KEROSENE (USED AS REBATED GAS OIL IN 'EXCEPTED VEHICLES' ETC)

5.—(a)   and (b) The figures entered in this Part are to reflect figures entered in Part 4 of the estimate and any supplementary estimate in respect of this accounting period.

(c)   Sum total of (a) and (b) to be entered here.

(d)   Enter the volume of fully-rebated kerosene actually used in this accounting period as fuel for an 'excepted vehicle' or in an engine not used for heating, up to the time of event B(3).

(e)   Subtract the figure at 4(d) from the sum total at 4(c) and enter the difference at 4(e).

(f)   Enter the published additional rate. The rate of net duty due is given in the Tariff, Volume 1 Part 12 against tax type 542; a Budget Notice may amend that rate with immediate effect. The Commissioners will publish the additional rate.

(g)   Enter the additional amount payable.

Part II

PART 5:
TOTAL AMOUNT PAYABLE WITH THIS FORM

6. Add together any amount shown at 2(e), 3(e) and 4(g) and enter that total in Part 5. Your cheque for the total amount entered in Part 5 should be made payable to **HM Customs and Excise** and be crossed account payee.

WARNING: Use of rebated oil as fuel contrary to the Regulations is an offence for which penalties may be imposed by the Commissioners of Customs and Excise, in addition to recovery of the rebate. If you have any doubt about your position under the Law you should consult your local Excise Advice Centre immediately.

Form No. 4

HO75

Rebated Heavy Oil used as Fuel:
Return of Rebate due (and paid) to the Commissioners

Before completing this form please read the Notes on completion

Note: This return must be completed and sent to the Accounting Centre within 10 business days of the period ending shown in your licence.

A Name and address of licensed user	B Address at which stock of fuel is kept (if different from A)
Postcode:	Postcode:

Part 1 This is the return for the quarterly/annual* accounting period ending (Note 1) .... of the above named licensed user. It takes account of the initial estimate and any supplementary estimates and additional payments made in this period.

Part 2 Volume of gas oil: usage governed by section 12 of the Act (road fuel usage) (Note 2 deals with (a) to (e) below)

(a) volume of gas oil shown in Part 2(a) of the estimate and any supplementary estimate made in this accounting period   litres

(b) volume of gas oil actually used in this accounting period as road fuel   litres

(c) volume of gas oil remaining unused (if any) at the end of this period (difference between figures at (a) and (b) above)   litres

(d) amount of rebate per litre of fuel currently payable (as shown in a Notice published for this purpose by the Commissioners of Customs and Excise)   £ 0 ·   per litre

(e) amount overpaid if any and due to be refunded in this period (multiply the figure at (c) above by the figure at (d) above)   £

Part 3 Volume of section 12 kerosene: usage governed by Section 12 of the Act (road fuel usage) (Note 3 deals with (a) to (e) below)

(a) volume of section 12 kerosene shown in Part 3(a) of the estimate and any supplementary estimate made in this accounting period   litres

(b) volume of section 12 kerosene actually used in this accounting period as road fuel   litres

(c) volume of section 12 kerosene remaining unused (if any) at the end of this period (difference between figures at (a) and (b) above)   litres

(d) amount of rebate per litre of fuel currently payable (as shown in a Notice published for this purpose by the Commissioners of Customs and Excise)   £ 0 ·   per litre

(e) amount overpaid (if any) and due to be refunded in this period (multiply figure at (c) above by the figure at (d) above)   £

*Delete as necessary

HO75   PCU(September 1996)   **(Substitute)(LexisNexis Butterworths)**

Part II

Date received at Accounting Centre

The Collector
HM Customs and Excise
Oils Accounting Centre
Dorset House
Stamford Street
London SE1 9PJ

Fold here

Part 4 Volume of section 13AA kerosene: usage governed by Section 13AA of the Act
(Notes 4 and 5 deal with (a) to (g) below)

(a) volume of section 13AA kerosene shown in Part 4(a) of the estimate and any supplementary estimate and made in this accounting period .... litres

(b) volume of section 13AA kerosene shown in Part 4(b) of the estimate and any supplementary estimate made in this period .... litres

(c) total of (a) and (b) above .... litres

(d) volume of section 13AA kerosene actually used in this period (either to propel excepted vehicles or in other engines) .... litres

(e) volume of section 13AA kerosene remaining unused (if any) at the end of this period (difference between figure at (c) and figure at (d) above) .... litres

(f) rate of net excise duty per litre of section 13AA kerosene currently applicable (as shown in a Notice published for this purpose by the Commissioners of Customs and Excise) £ 0 . per litre

(g) amount overpaid (if any) and due to be refunded in this period (multiply the figure at (e) above by the figure at (f) above) £ .

Part 5 Total amount overpaid in this period (being the sum of amounts shown at 2(e), 3(e) and 4(g) above) (Note 6) £ .

Declaration

I, ... declare that the information given in this return is true and complete.

Signature.. Date ....

*(Proprietor/Partner/Director/Company Secretary/Duly authorised signatory)

Name in capital letters ....

A false declaration can result in prosecution

*Delete as necessary

For Official Use

Accounting Centre Cost Code 16245:

MCD number(s) .... dated .... brought to account against this return, to the following account codes

33541: .... litres and duty of £ .

33542: .... litres and duty of £ .

33556: .... litres and duty of £ .

Total £ . : Balance repaid £ .

Input keyed in by ....(Intls) Date .... (Intls) ....

HO75 reverse (09/96)

948

NOTES ON COMPLETION

PART 1:

1.   Accounting periods end on 31 March, 30 June, 30 September and 31 December in each year. In some instances the Commissioners may licence a user to use an annual accounting period, which will end on 31 December. Complete Part 1 with the quarterly or annual period-end date, as shown in your licence.

PART 2:
REBATED GAS OIL (USED AS DERV)

2.   The figures entered in this Part are to reflect figures entered in Part 2 of the estimate, any supplementary estimate, and any additional payment form **in respect of this accounting period.**

(a)	Enter the sum of all the volumes declared in Part 2 of the estimate etc.
(b)	Enter the volume of rebated gas oil actually used in this accounting period as road fuel.
(c)	Subtract the figure at 2(b) from the total at 2(a) and enter the difference at 2(c).
(d)	Enter the current rate of rebate (as shown in the latest relative Budget Notice).
(e)	Enter the amount of rebate overpaid in this accounting period.

PART 3:
FULLY-REBATED KEROSENE (USED AS DERV)

3.   The figures entered in this Part are to reflect figures entered in Part 3 of the estimate, any supplementary estimate, and any additional payment form **in respect of this accounting period.**

(a)	Enter the sum of all the volumes declared in Part 3 of the estimate etc.
(b)	Enter the volume of fully-rebated kerosene actually used in this accounting period as road fuel (other than in an 'excepted vehicle' — see Part 4).
(c)	Subtract the figure at 3(b) from the total at 3(c) and enter the difference at 3(c).
(d)	Enter the current rate of rebate (as shown in the latest relative Budget Notice).
(e)	Enter the amount of rebate overpaid in this accounting period.

PART 4:
FULLY-REBATED KEROSENE (USED AS REBATED GAS OIL IN 'EXCEPTED VEHICLES' ETC)

4.   The figures entered in this Part are to reflect figures entered in Part 4 of the estimate, any supplementary estimate, and any additional payment form in respect of this accounting period.

(a)	Enter the sum of all the volumes declared in Part 4(a) of the estimate etc.
(b)	Enter the sum of all the volumes declared in Part 4(b) of the estimate etc.
(c)	Sum total of (a) and (b) to be entered here.
(d)	Enter the volume of fully-rebated kerosene actually used in this accounting period as fuel for an 'excepted vehicle' or in an engine not used for heating. 'Excepted vehicle' Schedule 1 of the Hydrocarbon Oil Duties Act 1979. Enter the whole volume of such kerosene in Part 4(d).
(e)	Subtract the figure at 4(d) from the sum total at 4(c) and enter the difference at 4(e).

(f)   Enter the current rate of net excise duty, shown in the Tariff Volume 1 Part 12 against tax type 542.

(g)   Enter the amount of rebate overpaid in this accounting period.

PART 5:
TOTAL AMOUNT PAYABLE WITH THIS FORM

5.   Add together any amount shown at 2(e), 3(e) and 4(g) and enter that total in Part 5. Your cheque for the total amount entered in Part 5 should be made payable to HM Customs and Excise and be crossed account payee.

WARNING: Use of rebated oil as fuel contrary to the Regulations is an offence for which penalties may be imposed by the Commissioners of Customs and Excise, in addition to recovery of the rebate. If you have any doubt about your position under the Law you should consult your local Excise Advice Centre immediately.

SCHEDULE 2

PROCEDURE AND FORMULAS FOR EFFECTING THE COMPARISON REQUIRED BY REGULATION 6(3)(C) IN RESPECT OF THE RATE OF NET EXCISE DUTY PER LITRE OF SECTION 13AA KEROSENE (CALLED BELOW THE "RATE OF NET EXCISE DUTY")

Regulation 6(3)(c)

1.   The comparison shall be effected by the following steps—

(a)   determine the rate of net excise duty (expressed as pence per litre), immediately before the change takes legal effect, in accordance with the formula provided by paragraph 2 below;

(b)   determine the rate of net excise duty (expressed as pence per litre), applicable when the change takes legal effect, in accordance with the formula provided by paragraph 3 below; and

(c)   compare the correctly determined results of those calculations to see whether or not the paragraph 3 rate of net excise duty (for the purposes of regulation 6(3)(c) of these Regulations) is greater than the paragraph 2 rate of net excise duty, expressed in both cases as pence per litre.

2.   The rate of net excise duty (for the purposes of paragraph 1(a) and (c) above) shall be calculated in accordance with the formula C − D where—

(a)   C is the rate of excise duty charged by section 6(1) of the Act on a litre of heavy oil, immediately before a change (envisaged by regulation 6(2)(b) of these Regulations) takes legal effect, expressed as pence per litre; and

(b)   D is the rate of rebate of the excise duty allowed on a litre of gas oil (in accordance with the rebate section of section 11 of the Act for gas oil), immediately before the above-mentioned change takes legal effect, expressed as pence per litre.

3.   The rate of net excise duty (for the purposes of paragraph 1(b) and (c) above) shall be calculated in accordance with the formula F − G where—

(a)   F is the rate of excise duty charged by section 6(1) of the Act on a litre of heavy oil when the change (envisaged by regulation 6(2)(b) of these Regulations) takes legal effect, expressed as pence per litre; and

(b)   G is the rate of rebate of the excise duty allowed on a litre of gas oil (in accordance with the rebate scheme of section 11 of the Act for gas oil) when the above-mentioned change takes legal effect, expressed as pence per litre.

HYDROCARBON OIL DUTIES (MARINE VOYAGES RELIEFS) REGULATIONS 1996

(SI 1996/2537)

NOTES

Made: 4 October 1996.

Authority: Customs and Excise Management Act 1979, s 127A; Hydrocarbon Oil Duties Act 1979, ss 20AA, 21(1)(a), (2), Sch 3, Pt I; Finance (No 2) Act 1992, s 1.

Commencement: 1 November 1996.

ARRANGEMENT OF REGULATIONS

PART I
PRELIMINARY

1 Citation and commencement

These Regulations may be cited as the Hydrocarbon Oil Duties (Marine Voyages Reliefs) Regulations 1996 and shall come into force on 1st November 1996.

2 Interpretation

In these Regulations—

"approved person" means a person approved under regulation 4 of the deferment Regulations in respect of heavy oil for use by ships making marine voyages;

"contravention" includes a failure to comply;

"the deferment Regulations" means the Excise Duties (Deferred Payment) Regulations 1992;

"marine voyage" means a voyage in which the ship is at all times—

(a)   within the limits of a port, or

(b)   outside the United Kingdom.

"private pleasure craft" has the meaning given in Article 8(1) of Council Directive 92/81/EEC;

"qualified claimant" means—

(a)   the owner of the ship on which the hydrocarbon oil was, or will be, used;

(b)   the charterer to whom that ship is, or was at the time of the marine voyage, demised;

(c)   a person appointed by the person mentioned in sub-paragraph (a) or (b) above to act as sole agent for that ship;

(d)   if he is authorised to do so by the person mentioned in sub-paragraph (a) or (b) above, the master of that ship; and

(e)   where the claim relates to hydrocarbon oil used on that ship while undergoing trials for the purpose of testing her hull or machinery, the builder or other person conducting the trials.

PART II

RELIEFS FROM EXCISE DUTY

3 Reliefs

(1)   Subject to the provisions of these Regulations—

(a)   where hydrocarbon oil has been used as fuel for the machinery of a ship that has been engaged on a marine voyage the Commissioners shall, in respect of that fuel, repay any excise duty that has been charged and paid; or

(b)   where heavy oil is delivered for use as fuel for the machinery of a ship that will be engaged on a marine voyage the Commissioners shall, in respect of that fuel, repay any excise duty that has been charged and paid; or

(c)   where heavy oil is delivered for use as fuel for the machinery of a ship that will be engaged on a marine voyage the Commissioners shall, in respect of that fuel, remit the payment of any excise duty that has been charged.

(2)   No relief shall be allowed in the case of a ship that is a private pleasure craft.

(3)   No relief shall be allowed otherwise than upon the written application of a qualified claimant.

(4)   No relief shall be allowed by paragraph (1)(a) or (b) above in the case of drawback goods.

(5)   No relief shall be allowed by paragraph (1)(b) above unless the heavy oil is supplied by an approved person.

(6)   No relief shall be allowed by paragraph (1)(b) or (c) above unless the heavy oil is delivered directly from a warehouse or refinery to the ship that will be engaged on a marine voyage.

4 Amount

(1)   Where the relief is allowed by regulation 3(1)(a) or (b) above the amount that may be repaid shall be the amount of duty charged and paid less any rebate or other repayment that has been allowed.

(2)   Where the relief is allowed by regulation 3(1)(c) above the amount that may be remitted shall be the amount of duty charged.

PART III
REPAYMENT OF DUTY

5 Application of Part III

This Part applies to relief allowed by regulation 3(1)(a) or (b) above.

6 Repayment

(1)   Except where paragraph (2) below applies repayment shall be made to the qualified claimant.

(2)   Where the relief is allowed by regulation 3(1)(b) above and an approved person supplied the heavy oil at a price reduced by an amount equal to the duty on that oil that approved person shall be treated as entitled to the repayment.

(3)   If in relation to any application for relief it appears to the Commissioners that the relief applied for exceeds the amount repayable under regulation 4(1) above they may, in such circumstances as they see fit and notwithstanding the provisions of regulations 8(1) and 11(2) below, repay such lesser sum as appears to them to be repayable.

(4)   If two or more qualified claimants make application for relief relating to the same hydrocarbon oil the Commissioners may make repayment to any of them (or, where paragraph (2) above applies, to the approved person) and that repayment shall be deemed to satisfy all the applications.

7 Set-off

(1)   Except where paragraph (2) below applies the Commissioners may set-off the amount of any repayment against any other debt then due to them from any person who is a qualified claimant in relation to the application.

(2)   Where regulation 6(2) above applies the approved person shall set-off the repayment in accordance with regulation 6 of the deferment Regulations.

8 Cancellation of relief

(1)   Where there is a contravention of any condition imposed by or under Part V below the relief allowed shall be cancelled.

(2)   Where any relief is cancelled any person who is a qualified claimant in relation to the application for relief shall, on demand, be liable to repay the amount of the repayment.

PART IV
REMISSION OF PAYMENT

9 Application of Part IV

This Part applies to relief allowed by regulation 3(1)(c) above.

10 Excise duty point

(1)   Where there is a contravention of any condition imposed by or under Part V below the excise duty point shall be the time of that contravention.

(2)   The following persons shall be jointly and severally liable to pay the duty at the excise duty point—

(a)   any person who is a qualified claimant in relation to the application for relief, and

(b)   any person who supplied the heavy oil to the qualified claimant.

PART V
CONDITIONS SUBJECT TO WHICH RELIEF IS ALLOWED

11 General conditions

(1)   Relief is allowed subject to the following conditions.

(2) The amount of relief applied for shall not exceed the amount of relief that may be allowed by regulation 4 above.

(3) Where relief is allowed by regulation 3(1)(a) above—

(a) the qualified claimant must, on being so required by the Commissioners, furnish to their satisfaction evidence that the duty that is the subject of the application for relief has been paid and has not been repaid, remitted or drawn back,

(b) the hydrocarbon oil must not have been used otherwise than as fuel for the machinery of the ship specified in the application for relief while engaged on a marine voyage, and

(c) the duty that is the subject of the application for relief must not be the subject of any other application or claim for repayment, remission or drawback.

(4) Where relief is allowed by regulation 3(1)(b) or (c) above—

(a) the qualified claimant (or someone authorised to act on his behalf) shall, upon delivery of the hydrocarbon oil to the ship, provide the supplier of that oil with an acknowledgement of receipt in such form as the supplier may require,

(b) the hydrocarbon oil must not be used otherwise than as fuel for the machinery of the ship to which it was delivered while that ship is engaged on a marine voyage,

(c) the hydrocarbon oil must not be relanded at any place in the United Kingdom, and

(d) the duty that is the subject of the application for relief must not be the subject of any other application or claim for repayment, remission or drawback.

(5) The master of a ship on which there is hydrocarbon oil in respect of which relief has been or may be allowed must, at any time that the ship is within the limits of a port—

(a) permit an officer to board the ship for the purpose of taking samples of hydrocarbon oil in order to ascertain whether relief should be allowed or has been properly allowed,

(b) give such assistance as the officer may reasonably require to enable him to safely take such samples of hydrocarbon oil, and

(c) provide such equipment (and if the case so requires conversion tables) as the officer may reasonably require to enable him to ascertain the volume, at a temperature of 15°C, of the hydrocarbon oil on board the ship.

12 Conditions imposed by the Commissioners

Relief is allowed subject to such conditions (if any) as the Commissioners impose on qualified claimants in a notice published by the Commissioners and not withdrawn by a further notice.

13–15

((Pt VI) *amend the Hydrocarbon Oil Regulations 1973, SI 1973/1311, reg 4 and revokes regs 34–36 of the 1973 Regulations; the Hydrocarbon Oil (Amendment) Regulations 1981, SI 1981/1134, reg 7; and the Excise Duties (Deferred Payment) Regulations 1992, SI 1992/3152, regs 6, 11.)*

CUSTOMS REVIEWS AND APPEALS (TARIFF AND ORIGIN) REGULATIONS 1997

(SI 1997/534)

NOTES

Made: 27 February 1997.

Authority: Finance Act 1994, s 14(6), (7).

Commencement: 24 March 1997.

1

These Regulations may be cited as the Customs Reviews and Appeals (Tariff and Origin) Regulations 1997 and shall come into force on 24th March 1997.

NOTES

Commencement: 24 March 1997.

2

In these Regulations—

"the Act" means the Finance Act 1994;

"the Commissioners" means the Commissioners of Customs and Excise.

NOTES

Commencement: 24 March 1997.

3—

(1) Section 14 of the Act, as it applies to the decisions mentioned in section 14(1) of the Act, shall apply to the following decisions of the Commissioners, so far as they are made for the purposes of the Community provisions relating to binding tariff information or the Community provisions relating to binding origin information—

(a)   any decision as to the tariff classification or determination of the origin of any goods;

(b)   any decision as to whether or not binding tariff information or binding origin information is to be supplied;

(c)   any decision as to whether or not any binding tariff information or binding origin information is to be annulled, withdrawn or revoked.

(2) In this regulation—

"binding tariff information" and "tariff classification" have the same meaning as in the Community provisions relating to binding tariff information;

"binding origin information" and "determination of the origin" have the same meanings as in the Community provisions relating to binding origin information;

"the Community provisions relating to binding tariff information" and "the Community provisions relating to binding origin information" mean Article 12 of Council Regulation (EEC) No 2913/92 establishing the Community Customs Code and Title II of Part I of Commission Regulation (EEC) No 2454/93 laying down provisions for the implementation of Council Regulation (EEC) No 2913/92.

NOTES

Commencement: 24 March 1997.

4

Section 16(4) of the Act (review jurisdiction) shall have effect as if decisions (b) and (c) mentioned in regulation 3(1) above were of a description specified in paragraph 1 of Schedule 5 to the Act.

NOTES

Commencement: 24 March 1997.

5—

(1)   Section 14 of the Act, as it applies to the decisions mentioned in section 14(1) of the Act, shall apply to the following decisions of the Commissioners, so far as they are made for the purposes of preferential tariff measures applicable to the exportation of goods and are not decisions falling within regulation 3 above—

   (a)   any decision as to the determination of the origin of any goods;
   (b)   any decision as to whether there is sufficient evidence to determine the origin of any goods.

(2)   In this regulation—
   "preferential tariff measures" means the preferential tariff measures mentioned in Article 20(3)(d) and (e) of the Community Customs Code.

NOTES

Commencement: 24 March 1997.

6

Section 16(4) of the Act (review jurisdiction) shall have effect as if decision (b) mentioned in regulation 5(1) above was of a description specified in paragraph 1 of Schedule 5 to the Act.

NOTES

Commencement: 24 March 1997.

7

(Revokes the Customs Reviews and Appeals (Binding Tariff Information) Regulations 1995, SI 1995/2351.

EXCISE DUTY POINT (EXTERNAL AND INTERNAL COMMUNITY TRANSIT PROCEDURE) REGULATIONS 1998

(SI 1998/202)

NOTES

Made: 2 February 1998.

Authority: Customs and Excise Management Act 1979, ss100G, 100H; Finance (No 2) Act 1992, s 1.

Commencement: 25 February 1998.

ARRANGEMENT OF REGULATIONS

1	Citation and commencement
2	Interpretation
3	Non-application of the REDS Regulations to the external and internal Community transit procedure
4	Excise duty point for breaches of the external Community transit procedure
5	Excise duty point for breaches of the internal Community transit procedure
6–8	Person liable to pay the excise duty
9	Payment of excise duty

1 Citation and commencement

These Regulations may be cited as the Excise Duty Point (External and Internal Community Transit Procedure) Regulations 1998 and shall come into force on 25th February 1998.

NOTES

Commencement: 25 February 1998.

2 Interpretation

In these Regulations—

(a) "Community Customs Code" means Council Regulation (EEC) No 2913/92 dated 12 October 1992;

(b) "excise duty point" has the meaning given by section 1 of the Finance Act (No 2) Act 1992;

(c) "excise goods" means goods charged with excise duty by or under an enactment;

(d) "external Community transit procedure" means the movement referred to in article 91(2) at subparagraph (a) of the Community Customs Code, in respect of which articles 91 to 97 of that Code and articles 341 to 380 and 382 to 388 of the Implementing Regulation make provision;

(e) "Implementing Regulation" means Commission Regulation (EEC) No 2454/93 dated 2 July 1993; and

(f) "internal Community transit procedure" means the movement referred to in article 163(2) at subparagraph (a) of the Community Customs Code, in respect of which article 163(3) of that Code and article 381, and articles 382 to 388 of the Implementing Regulation make provision.

NOTES

Commencement: 25 February 1998.

3 Non-application of the REDS Regulations to the external and internal Community transit procedure

Regulations 4 to 6 and 8 to 11 of the Excise Goods (Holding, Movement, Warehousing and REDS) Regulations 1992 shall not apply in respect of excise goods which are subject to the external or internal Community transit procedure.

NOTES

Commencement: 25 February 1998.

4 Excise duty point for breaches of the external Community transit procedure

(1) Paragraph (2) below applies if—

(a) excise goods are subject to the external Community transit procedure; and

(b) in respect of those goods;

(i) a customs debt is incurred, as determined by article 203 or, in cases other than those referred to in that article, 204 of the Community Customs Code; and

(ii) the place where the events from which that customs debt arises occur is in the United Kingdom, as determined by article 215 of that Code and article 378 of the Implementing Regulation.

(2) The excise duty point shall be the time, as determined by article 203, or, as the case may be, article 204, specified by paragraph (1)(b)(i) above and which governs the time of the incurrence of the customs debt, when the customs debt mentioned in that paragraph is incurred.

NOTES

Commencement: 25 February 1998.

5 Excise duty point for breaches of the internal Community transit procedure

(1) In this Regulation—

(a) "action" means any act or omission, in relation to the goods described in paragraph (2)(a) below and to the performance and discharge of the obligation to present those goods to the office of destination designated for the particular internal Community transit procedure movement of the goods, which is inconsistent with the performance and discharge of that obligation; and

(b) "relevant time" means—

(i) the time when the office of departure in the United Kingdom accepted the declaration for the internal Community transit procedure; or

(ii) as the case may be, the time when a transit advice note was given to an office of transit in the United Kingdom.

(2) Paragraph (3) below applies if—

(a) excise goods are subject to the internal Community transit procedure; and

(b) an action occurs in the United Kingdom provided that—

(i) the evidence appertaining to the action establishes that the place of the action is in the United Kingdom; or

(ii) where that evidence does not establish the place of the action, the provisions of article 378(1) of the Implementing Regulation are used, for the purposes of this regulation, to determine the place of the action as if the reference in that article to "offence or irregularity" is a reference to "action", and the action is deemed by virtue of using the article in that way to have been committed or to have occurred in the United Kingdom.

(3)   The excise duty point shall be—

(a)   the time when the action occurs in the United Kingdom where the evidence, described in paragraph 2(b)(i) above, establishes the place of the action as being in the United Kingdom; or

(b)   the relevant time where the provisions of article 378(1) are used in the circumstances specified by and required by paragraph 2(b)(ii) above.

NOTES

Commencement: 25 February 1998.

6   Person liable to pay the excise duty

(1)   This regulation applies if there is an excise duty point by virtue of regulation 4 above.

(2)   A person specified by subparagraph (a) or (b) of paragraph (3) below, having the specified connection with the excise goods, shall be liable to pay the excise duty relating to the excise duty point.

(3)   For the purposes of paragraph (2) above, the person is—

(a)   any person who is a debtor in respect of the customs debt, giving rise to the excise duty point, as determined by the article of the Community Customs Code specified by regulation 4(1)(b)(i) above which governs that customs debt;

(b)   any other person who, in relation to the excise goods that are the subject of the excise duty point, at any time in the period:

(i)   starting with the charging of those goods with excise duty; and

(ii)   ending with the incurrence of the customs debt specified by subparagraph (a) above,

brings about, or assists in bringing about, that customs debt.

NOTES

Commencement: 25 February 1998.

7—

(1)   This regulation applies if there is an excise duty point by virtue of regulation 5 above.

(2)   A person specified by subparagraph (a) or (b) of paragraph (3) below, having the specified connection with the excise goods, shall be liable to pay the excise duty relating to the excise duty point.

(3)   For the purposes of paragraph (2) above, the person is—

(a)   any person who, in respect of the particular internal Community transit procedure in relation to which there is an excise duty point by virtue of regulation 5 above, is the principal for that particular procedure, as governed by article 96 and article 163(3) of the Community Customs Code;

(b)   any other person who, in relation to the excise goods that are the subject of the excise duty point, at any time in the period—

(i)   starting with the charging of those goods with excise duty; and

>   (ii)   ending with the time of the occurrence of the action described by
>   paragraph (2)(b) of regulation 5 above,
>
>   brings about, or assists in bringing about, that action.

NOTES

Commencement: 25 February 1998.

8

Where more than one person is liable to pay the excise duty by virtue of regulation 6 above, or 7 above, each person shall be jointly and severally liable to pay the excise duty with the other person or, as the case may be, with each of the others.

NOTES

Commencement: 25 February 1998.

[9 Payment of excise duty

A person liable to pay excise duty relating to an excise duty point specified by regulation 4 or 5 above shall pay the excise duty to the Commissioners upon the occurrence of that excise duty point.]

NOTES

Commencement: 25 February 1998.

Substituted by the Excise Duty Point (External and Internal Community Transit Procedure) (Amendment) Regulations 1998, SI 1998/3110, reg 2.

AIR PASSENGER DUTY AND OTHER INDIRECT TAXES (INTEREST RATE) REGULATIONS 1998

(SI 1998/1461)

NOTES

Made: 15 June 1998.

Authority: Finance Act 1996, s 197.

1 Citation and commencement

These Regulations may be cited as the Air Passenger Duty and Other Indirect Taxes (Interest Rate) Regulations 1998 and shall come into force on 6th July 1998.

NOTES

Commencement: 6 July 1998.

2 Interpretation

(1)   In these Regulations unless the context otherwise requires—
        "established rate" means—
                (a)   on the coming into force of these Regulations, [6 per cent] per
                       annum; and

(b)　in relation to any day after the first reference day after the coming into force of these Regulations, the reference rate found on the immediately preceding reference day;

"operative day" means the sixth day of each month;

　"reference day" means the twelfth working day before the next operative day;

　"section 197" means section 197 of the Finance Act 1996;

　the "relevant enactments" are those referred to in regulations 4(1) and 5(1) below;

　"working day" means any day other than a non-business day within the meaning of section 92 of the Bills of Exchange Act 1882.

(2)　In these Regulations the reference rate found on a reference day is the percentage per annum found by averaging the base lending rates at close of business on that day of—

(a)　Bank of Scotland,

(b)　Barclays Bank plc,

(c)　Lloyds Bank plc,

(d)　[HSBC Bank plc],

(e)　National Westminster Bank plc, and

(f)　The Royal Bank of Scotland plc,

and, if the result is not a whole number, rounding the result to the nearest such number, with any result midway between two whole numbers rounded down.

NOTES

　Commencement: 6 July 1998.

　Word in square brackets substituted by the Air Passenger Duty and Other Indirect Taxes (Interest Rate) (Amendment) Regulations 2000, SI 2000/631, regs 2, 3.

3

(Revokes the Air Passenger Duty and Other Indirect Taxes (Interest Rate) Regulations 1997, SI 1997/1016.)

[4 Applicable rate of interest payable to the Commissioners of Customs and Excise in connection with excise duties, insurance premium tax, VAT, landfill tax, and customs duty

(1)　For the purposes of—

(a)　paragraph 7 of Schedule 6 to the Finance Act 1994,

(b)　paragraph 21 of Schedule 7 to that Act,

(c)　section 74 of the Value Added Tax Act 1994,

(d)　paragraph 26 of Schedule 5 to the Finance Act 1996,

(e)　paragraph 17 of Schedule 5 to the Finance Act 1997, . . .

(f)　section 126 of the Finance Act 1999, [. . .

(g)　paragraphs 41(2)(f), 70(1)(b) and 81(3) of Schedule 6 to the Finance Act 2000 (climate change levy),] [and

(h)　sections 25(2)(f) and 30(3)(f) of, and paragraphs 6 and 8(3)(a) of Schedule 5 to, the Finance Act 2001 (aggregates levy),]

the rate applicable under section 197 shall, subject to paragraph (2) below, be 8.5 per cent per annum.

(2)　Where, on any reference day after the coming into force of these Regulations, the reference rate found on that day differs from the established rate, the rate applicable under section 197 of the Finance Act 1996 for the purposes of the enactments referred to in paragraph (1) above shall, from the next operative day, be the percentage per annum determined in accordance with the formula specified in paragraph (3) below.

(3)   The formula specified in this paragraph is—

RR + 2.5,

where RR is the reference rate referred to in paragraph (2) above.]

[(4)With effect from 1st November 2001 the rate of interest prescribed in paragraph (1) above for the purposes of paragraph 17 of Schedule 5 to the Finance Act 1997 also applies in the application of that paragraph to assessments under paragraph 14 or 15 of that Schedule as amended by paragraph 19 of Schedule 3 to the Finance Act 2001.]

NOTES

Commencement: 1 April 2000.

Substituted by the Air Passenger Duty and Other Indirect Taxes (Interest Rate) (Amendment) Regulations 2000, SI 2000/631, regs 2, 4.

Para (1): word in sub-para (e) revoked, and sub-para (g) added, by the Air Passenger Duty and Other Indirect Taxes (Interest Rate) (Amendment) Regulations 2001, SI 2001/3337 art 2(1), (2); word in para (f) revoked, and para (h) inserted, by the Air Passenger Duty and Other Indirect Taxes (Interest Rate) (Amendment) Regulations 2003, SI 2003/230 regs 2, 3.

Para (4): added by SI 2001/3337 art 2(3).

[5 Applicable rate of interest payable by the Commissioners of Customs and Excise in connection with air passenger duty, insurance premium tax, VAT, landfill tax, and customs duty

(1)   For the purposes of—

(a)   [Parts 2 and 3 of Schedule 3 to the Finance Act 2001 (interest payable on repayments etc),]

(b)   paragraph 22 of Schedule 7 to that Act,

(c)   section 78 of the Value Added Tax Act 1994,

(d)   paragraph 29 of Schedule 5 to the Finance Act 1996, . . .

(e)   section 127 of the Finance Act 1999, [. . .,

(f)   paragraphs 62(3)(f) and 66 of Schedule 6 to the Finance Act 2000 (climate change levy)][, and

(g)   paragraphs 2 and 6(1)(b) of Schedule 8 to the Finance Act 2001 (aggregates levy),]

the rate applicable under section 197 of the Finance Act 1996 shall be 5 per cent per annum.

(2)   Where, on a reference day after the coming into force of these Regulations, the reference rate found on that date differs from the established rate, the rate applicable under section 197 for the purposes of the enactments referred to in paragraph (1) above shall, from the next operative day, be the percentage per annum determined in accordance with the formula specified in paragraph (3) below.

(3)   The formula specified in this paragraph is—

RR – 1,

where RR is the reference rate referred to in paragraph (2) above.]

NOTES

Commencement: 1 April 2000.

Substituted by the Air Passenger Duty and Other Indirect Taxes (Interest Rate) (Amendment) Regulations 2000, SI 2000/631, regs 2, 5.

Para (1): words in sub-para (a) substituted, word in sub-para (d) revoked, sub-para (f) added, by the Air Passenger Duty and Other Indirect Taxes (Interest Rate) (Amendment) Regulations, SI 2001/3337 art 3; word in para (e) revoked, and para (g) inserted, by the Air Passenger Duty and Other Indirect Taxes (Interest Rate) (Amendment) Regulations 2003, SI 2003/230 regs 2, 4.

6 Effect of change in applicable rate

Where the rate applicable under section 197 for the purposes of any of the relevant enactments changes on an operative day by virtue of these Regulations, that change shall have effect for periods beginning on or after the operative day in relation to interest running from before that day as well as in relation to interest running from, or from after that day.

NOTES

Commencement: 6 July 1998.

7

Where the rate applicable under section 197 for the purposes of any of the relevant enactments changes on an operative day by virtue of these Regulations, the rate in force immediately prior to any change shall continue to have effect for periods immediately prior to the change and so on in the case of any number of successive changes.

NOTES

Commencement: 6 July 1998.

8 Applicable rate of interest prior to the coming into force of these Regulations

The rate applicable under section 197 for interest running from before the date these Regulations come into force in relation to periods prior to that date shall be that specified for the relevant enactments in the following Tables—

TABLE 1
PARAGRAPH 7 OF SCHEDULE 6 TO THE FINANCE ACT 1994

Interest for any period	Rate
from 1st November 1994 and before 6th February 1996	5.5 per cent
after 5th February 1996 and before 6th July 1998	6.25 per cent

TABLE 2
PARAGRAPH 21 OF SCHEDULE 7 TO THE FINANCE ACT 1994

Interest for any period	Rate
from 1st October 1994 and before 6th February 1996	5.5 per cent
after 5th February 1996 and before 6th July 1998	6.25 per cent

TABLE 3
SECTION 74 OF THE VALUE ADDED TAX ACT 1994

Interest for any period	Rate
from 1st April 1990 and before 6th November 1990	13 per cent
after 5th November 1990 and before 6th March 1991	12.25 per cent
after 5th March 1991 and before 6th May 1991	11.5 per cent
after 5th May 1991 and before 6th July 1991	10.75 per cent

Interest for any period	Rate
after 5th July 1991 and before 6th October 1991	10 per cent
after 5th October 1991 and before 6th November 1992	9.25 per cent
after 5th November 1992 and before 6th December 1992	7.75 per cent
after 5th December 1992 and before 6th March 1993	7 per cent
after 5th March 1993 and before 6th January 1994	6.25 per cent
after 5th January 1994 and before 6th October 1994	5.5 per cent
after 5th October 1994 and before 6th March 1995	6.25 per cent
after 5th March 1995 and before 6th February 1996	7 per cent
after 5th February 1996 and before 6th July 1998	6.25 per cent

TABLE 4
PARAGRAPH 26 OF SCHEDULE 5 TO THE FINANCE ACT 1996

Interest for any period	Rate
from 1st April 1997 and before 6th July 1998	6.25 per cent

TABLE 5
PARAGRAPH 9 OF SCHEDULE 6 TO THE FINANCE ACT 1994

Interest for any period	Rate
from 1st November 1994 and before 1st April 1997	8 per cent
from 31st March 1997 and before 6th July 1998	6 per cent

TABLE 6
PARAGRAPH 22 OF SCHEDULE 7 TO THE FINANCE ACT 1994

Interest for any period	Rate
after 1st October 1994 and before 1st April 1997	8 per cent
after 31st March 1997 and before 6th July 1998	6 per cent

TABLE 7
SECTION 78 OF THE VALUE ADDED TAX ACT 1994

Interest for any period	Rate
from 1st April 1973 and before 1st March 1974	8 per cent
after 28th February 1974 and before 1st February 1977	9 per cent
after 31st January and before 1st March 1979	10 per cent
after 28th February 1979 and before 1st January 1980	12.5 per cent
after 31st December 1979 and before 1st January 1981	15 per cent
after 31st December 1980 and before 1st December 1981	12.5 per cent
after 30th November 1981 and before 1st March 1982	15 per cent
after 28th February 1982 and before 1st July 1982	14 per cent
after 30th June 1982 and before 1st April 1983	13 per cent
after 31st March 1983 and before 1st April 1984	12.5 per cent
after 31st March 1984 and before 1st August 1986	12 per cent
after 31st July 1986 and before 1st January 1987	11.5 per cent
after 31st December 1986 and before 1st April 1987	12.25 per cent
after 31st March 1987 and before 1st November 1987	11.75 per cent
after 31st October 1987 and before 1st December 1987	11.25 per cent
after 30th November 1987 and before 1st May 1988	11 per cent

Interest for any period	Rate
after 30th April 1988 and before 1st August 1988	9.5 per cent
after 31st July 1988 and before 1st November 1988	11 per cent
after 31st October 1988 and before 1st January 1989	12.25 per cent
after 31st December 1988 and before 1st November 1989	13 per cent
after 31st October 1989 and before 1st April 1991	14.25 per cent
after 31st March 1991 and before [16th October 1991]	12 per cent
after 15th October 1991 and before 6th February 1993	10.25 per cent
after 5th February 1993 and before 1st April 1997	8 per cent
after 31st March 1997 and before 6th July 1998	6 per cent

TABLE 8

PARAGRAPH 29 OF SCHEDULE 5 TO THE FINANCE ACT 1996

Interest for any period	Rate
from 1st April 1997 and before 6th July 1998	6 per cent

NOTES

Words in square brackets in table 7 substituted by the Air Passenger Duty and Other Indirect Taxes (Interest Rate) (Amendment) Regulations 2000, SI 2000/631, regs 2, 6.

[9 **Minimum amount of interest payable in connection with customs duty**
Where interest charged on arrears of customs duty payable to the Commissioners of Customs and Excise is computed in accordance with section 126(2) of the Finance Act 1999 and, in any case, is less than £25 the amount of interest charged in that case is (instead of being the amount so computed) to be taken to be £25.]

NOTES

Commencement: 1 April 2000.

Substituted by the Air Passenger Duty and Other Indirect Taxes (Interest Rate) (Amendment) Regulations 2000, SI 2000/631, regs 2, 7.

WAREHOUSEKEEPERS AND OWNERS OF WAREHOUSED GOODS REGULATIONS 1999

(SI 1999/1278)

NOTES

Made: 4 May 1999.

Authority: Customs and Excise Management Act 1979, ss 93(1), (2)(a), (db), (3), (5), 100G(1), (4), 100H(1)(a), (b), (c), (g), (k), (l), (n), (2); Finance (No 2) Act 1992, s 1.

ARRANGEMENT OF REGULATIONS

PART I

PRELIMINARY

PART I
PRELIMINARY

1 Citation and commencement
These regulations may be cited as the Warehousekeepers and Owners of Warehoused Goods Regulations 1999 and shall come into force on 1st October 1999.

NOTES
    Commencement: 1 October 1999.

2 Interpretation
In these Regulations—
    "the Act" means the Customs and Excise Management Act 1979;
    "authorized warehousekeeper" has the meaning given in regulation 3 below;
    "duty representative" has the meaning given in regulation 6 below;

"the initial period" means a period of seventy-two hours but, for the purpose of calculating seventy-two hours, hours comprised in any day that is a Saturday, Sunday, Christmas Day, Boxing Day, New Year's Day, Good Friday or Easter Monday shall not be counted;

"occupier" means the occupier of an excise warehouse;

"operations" means operations that are permitted to be carried out on warehoused goods by or under warehousing regulations;

"registered owner" has the meaning given in regulation 5 below;

["relevant goods" means dutiable goods, other than—

    (a)   hydrocarbon oil,

    (b)   bioethanol within the meaning of section 2AB of the Hydrocarbon Oil Act, and

    (c)   special energy product,

on which excise duty has not been paid;]

"relevant revenue trader" means any authorized warehousekeeper, registered owner, or duty representative;

["special energy product" has the meaning given by regulation 2 of the Excise Warehousing (Energy Products) Regulations 2004.]

NOTES

Commencement: 1 October 1999.

Definition "relevant goods" substituted, and definition "special energy product" inserted, by the Excise Warehousing (Energy Products) Regulations 2004, SI 2004/2064 reg 7(1)–(3).

PART II
APPROVAL AND REGISTRATION OF WAREHOUSEKEEPERS

3 Authorized warehousekeepers

(1)   For the purposes of sections 93(1) and 100G of the Act the Commissioners may approve occupiers of excise warehouses in accordance with the provisions of this Part of these regulations and register them as registered excise dealers and shippers in accordance with section 100G(2) of the Act.

(2)   An occupier who has been so approved and registered shall be known as an authorized warehousekeeper.

(3)   An authorized warehousekeeper may be approved and registered in respect of all the excise warehouses he occupies.

NOTES

Commencement: 1 October 1999.

4 Revocation

If the Commissioners exercise their power to revoke their approval and registration of an occupier as an authorized warehousekeeper in accordance with section 100G(5) of the Act they shall also revoke his approval for the purposes of section 93(1) of the Act.

NOTES

Commencement: 1 October 1999.

PART III
APPROVAL AND REGISTRATION OF OWNERS AND DUTY REPRESENTATIVES

5 Registered owners

(1)   For the purposes of section 100G of the Act, the Commissioners may approve revenue traders who wish to deposit relevant goods that they own in an excise warehouse and register them as registered excise dealers and shippers in accordance with section 100G(2) of the Act.

(2)   A revenue trader who has been so approved and registered shall be known as a registered owner.

NOTES

Commencement: 1 October 1999.

6 Duty representatives

(1)   For the purposes of section 100G of the Act, and subject to paragraph (3) below, the Commissioners may approve revenue traders who wish to act as the agent of revenue traders who deposit relevant goods that they own in an excise warehouse and register them as registered excise dealers and shippers in accordance with section 100G(2) of the Act.

(2)   A revenue trader who has been so approved and registered shall be known as a duty representative.

(3)   The Commissioners shall not approve a revenue trader as a duty representative unless he—

(a)   has a business establishment or other fixed establishment in the United Kingdom, or

(b)   if he is an individual, has his usual place of residence in the United Kingdom.

NOTES

Commencement: 1 October 1999.

PART IV
APPROVAL AND REGISTRATION: SUPPLEMENTARY PROVISIONS

7 Registration

(1)   The Commissioners shall furnish every relevant revenue trader with a certificate of registration.

(2)   When a person ceases to be a relevant revenue trader he shall immediately destroy his certificate of registration.

(3)   Every relevant revenue trader shall give notice in writing to the Commissioners of any change in the information contained in his certificate of registration within seven days of the change.

(4)   Where—

(a)   any relevant revenue trader gives the Commissioners notice in writing of any change in the information contained in his certificate of registration, or

(b)   without any such notice having been given it appears to the Commissioners that his certificate of registration requires correction, they shall, unless they revoke his approval and registration in accordance with section 100G(5) of the Act, furnish him with a corrected certificate of registration.

(5)   Where in accordance with paragraph (4) above the Commissioners furnish any relevant revenue trader with a corrected certificate of registration he shall upon receiving that certificate destroy the original certificate that required correction.

NOTES
Commencement: 1 October 1999.

8 Certificates of registration

Every certificate of registration shall contain the following particulars—

- (a) a unique reference number assigned to the relevant revenue trader by the Commissioners;
- (b) the name and (if different) the trading name of the relevant revenue trader;
- (c) the address of the relevant revenue trader's principal, or only place of business (including any postcode)—
    - (i) in the United Kingdom, or
    - (ii) in the case of a registered owner, if he does not have any place of business in the United Kingdom, elsewhere;
- (d) any conditions or restrictions imposed by the Commissioners in the exercise of their discretion under section 100G(4) of the Act;
- (e) if the relevant revenue trader is an authorized warehousekeeper, the address of every excise warehouse to which his approval and registration applies.

NOTES
Commencement: 1 October 1999.

PART V
WAREHOUSING

9 Holding dutiable goods

(1)   Dutiable goods shall not be deposited in an excise warehouse or kept in an excise warehouse unless the occupier of that warehouse—

- (a) is an authorized warehousekeeper, and
- (b) is permitted by the terms of his approval to hold dutiable goods of that class or description.

(2)   Relevant goods shall not be kept in an excise warehouse for more than the initial period beginning with their deposit in that warehouse unless the owner of those goods—

- (a) is not a revenue trader, or
- (b) is the authorized warehousekeeper, or
- (c) is a registered owner who resides or has a business establishment or other fixed establishment in the United Kingdom, or
- (d) has a duty representative acting as his agent in respect of those goods.

(3)   Relevant goods shall not be sold whilst they are being kept in an excise warehouse unless the seller, or if the seller has a duty representative that representative, gives notice of the sale to the authorized warehousekeeper.

NOTES
Commencement: 1 October 1999.

10 Application of section 98 of the Act

If the Commissioners revoke their approval of an occupier as an authorized warehousekeeper for the purposes of section 93(1)(a) of the Act section 98(3) and (3A) of the Act shall apply as if—

(a)   in subsection (3), for the words "the warehouse ceases to be approved" there were substituted "the Commissioners notified the authorized warehousekeeper that they have revoked his approval",

(b)   in both subsections, as if the word "former" (in every place at which it occurs) were omitted, and

(c)   in subsection (3A)(b) for the words "warehouse were still a warehouse" there were substituted "occupier were still approved".

NOTES
Commencement: 1 October 1999.

PART VI
PRIVILEGES

11 Privileges of an authorized warehousekeeper

(1)   Subject to regulation 14 below, an authorized warehousekeeper shall be afforded the following privileges in respect of dutiable goods.

(2)   An authorized warehousekeeper may—

(a)   receive dutiable goods at his excise warehouse and keep them there;

[(aa)   consign—

(i)   relevant goods, or

(ii)   special energy product,

to other member States;]

(b)   carry out operations on dutiable goods in his excise warehouse; and

(c)   remove dutiable goods from his excise warehouse.

(3)   An authorized warehousekeeper may exercise these privileges in relation to both dutiable goods that he owns and dutiable goods that are owned by others.

NOTES
Commencement: 1 October 1999.
Para 2: sub-para (aa) substituted by the Excise Warehousing (Energy Products) Regulations 2004, SI 2004/2064 reg 7(1), (4).

12 Privileges of a registered owner

(1)   Subject to regulation 14 below, a registered owner shall be afforded the following privileges in respect of relevant goods.

(2)   A registered owner may—

(a)   hold relevant goods that he owns in an excise warehouse; and

(b)   buy relevant goods that are held in an excise warehouse.

NOTES
Commencement: 1 October 1999.

13 Privileges of a duty representative

(1) Subject to regulation 14 below, a duty representative shall be afforded the following privileges as agent for the owner or buyer of relevant goods.

(2) A duty representative may—

(a)   on behalf of his principal, arrange for relevant goods to be held in an excise warehouse; and

(b)   act as agent for the buyer of relevant goods that are held in an excise warehouse.

NOTES
Commencement: 1 October 1999.

14 Exceptions

(1) Regulation 11 above does not confer on any authorized warehousekeeper any privilege that would cause him to be in breach of—

(a)   any condition of approval that applies to his excise warehouse;

(b)   any condition or restriction imposed by or under warehousing regulations;

(c)   any condition or restriction imposed by or under registered excise dealers and shippers regulations;

(d)   any condition or restriction imposed under section 100G(4) of the Act; or

(e)   any condition or restriction imposed by or under Part VII of these regulations.

(2) Regulations 12 and 13 above do not confer on any registered owner or duty representative any privilege that would cause the breach of—

(a)   any condition of approval that applies to the excise warehouse in which relevant goods are or will be held;

(b)   any condition or restriction imposed by or under warehousing regulations;

(c)   any condition or restriction imposed by or under registered excise dealers and shippers regulations;

(d)   any condition or restriction imposed under section 100G(4) of the Act; or

(e)   any condition or restriction imposed by or under Part VII of these regulations.

NOTES
Commencement: 1 October 1999.

PART VII
CONDITIONS AND RESTRICTIONS

15 General conditions and restrictions

The approval and registration of relevant revenue traders shall, in addition to any conditions or restrictions imposed on them by the Commissioners under section 100G(4) of the Act, be subject to the conditions and restrictions imposed by or under this Part of these regulations.

NOTES

Commencement: 1 October 1999.

16 Security

The Commissioners may require any relevant revenue trader to provide such security, or further security, as they may think appropriate for the payment of any excise duty that is or may become due from him.

NOTES

Commencement: 1 October 1999.

17 Conditions and restrictions that apply to authorized warehousekeepers

(1) The approval and registration of every authorized warehousekeeper shall be subject to the conditions and restrictions prescribed in a notice published by the Commissioners and not withdrawn by a further notice.

(2) Subject to paragraph (3) below, if at the time when relevant goods are deposited in an excise warehouse either the owner of those goods is not a registered owner or the owner does not have a duty representative acting as his agent, an authorized warehousekeeper—

    (a)   shall not keep those goods at his excise warehouse for longer than the initial period, and

    (b)   shall not permit those goods to be entered for removal from his warehouse in accordance with regulation 16 of the Excise Warehousing (Etc) Regulations 1988 for any purpose other than home use.

(3) The restrictions imposed by paragraph (2) above shall not apply if—

    (a)   the authorized warehousekeeper is the owner of the relevant goods, or

    (b)   the relevant goods are owned by a person who is not a revenue trader, or

    (c)   before the expiration of the initial period from the time when relevant goods are deposited in an excise warehouse—

        (i)   the owner of those goods is registered as a registered owner, or

        (ii)   the owner has a duty representative acting as his agent in respect of those goods.

NOTES

Commencement: 1 October 1999.

18 Conditions and restrictions that apply to registered owners

(1) The approval and registration of every registered owner shall be subject to the conditions and restrictions prescribed in a notice published by the Commissioners and not withdrawn by a further notice.

(2) Every registered owner shall, before arranging for relevant goods to be deposited in an excise warehouse, provide the authorized warehousekeeper with a copy of his certificate of registration.

(3) Every registered owner shall, before buying relevant goods that are in an excise warehouse, provide the authorized warehousekeeper with a copy of his certificate of registration.

(4)   Where in accordance with regulation 7(4) above the Commissioners have furnished a registered owner with a corrected certificate of registration that owner shall, within seven days of his receiving it, provide a copy of it to every authorized warehousekeeper in whose excise warehouse his goods are deposited.

(5)   Every registered owner whose registration is revoked shall immediately give written notice of that revocation to every authorized warehousekeeper in whose excise warehouse his goods are deposited.

NOTES

Commencement: 1 October 1999.

19 Conditions and restrictions that apply to duty representatives

(1)   The approval and registration of every duty representative shall be subject to the conditions and restrictions prescribed in a notice published by the Commissioners and not withdrawn by a further notice.

(2)   Every duty representative shall, before arranging for relevant goods to be deposited in an excise warehouse, provide the authorized warehousekeeper with a copy of his certificate of registration.

(3)   Every duty representative shall, when acting for the buyer of relevant goods that are in an excise warehouse and before those goods are bought by his principal, provide the authorized warehousekeeper with a copy of his certificate of registration.

(4)   Where in accordance with regulation 7(4) above the Commissioners have furnished a duty representative with a corrected certificate of registration that representative shall, within seven days of his receiving it, provide a copy of it to every authorized warehousekeeper in whose excise warehouse his principal's goods are deposited.

(5)   Every duty representative whose registration is revoked shall immediately give written notice of that revocation to every authorized warehousekeeper in whose excise warehouse his principal's goods are deposited.

(6)   A duty representative shall not act as agent for the owner or buyer of relevant goods if his principal—

(a)   has any business establishment or other fixed establishment in the United Kingdom, or

(b)   if he is an individual, has his usual place of residence in the United Kingdom.

NOTES

Commencement: 1 October 1999.

PART VIII
EXCISE DUTY POINTS AND FORFEITURE

20 Excise duty points—warehoused goods

(1)   If dutiable goods are deposited in an excise warehouse in contravention of regulation 9(1) above, the time that they were deposited shall be the excise duty point for those goods.

(2)   If dutiable goods are kept in an excise warehouse in contravention of regulation 9(1) above, the time when the occupier of that warehouse ceases to be an authorized warehousekeeper permitted by the terms of his approval to hold dutiable goods of that class or description shall be the excise duty point for those goods.

(3)   If relevant goods are kept in an excise warehouse in contravention of regulation 17(2)(a) above, or are entered for removal in contravention of

regulation 17(2)(b) above, the time that they were deposited shall be the excise duty point for those goods.

(4) The person liable to pay the duty at the excise duty point shall be the occupier of the excise warehouse in which the goods were deposited or kept.

(5) If more than one person occupies the excise warehouse in which the goods were deposited or kept, all the occupiers shall be jointly and severally liable to pay the duty at the excise duty point.

(6) Where relevant goods are kept in an excise warehouse in contravention of regulation 17(2)(a) above and in accordance with this regulation an authorized warehousekeeper is liable for the duty he shall be relieved from liability to pay that duty if, immediately following the excise duty point, he abandons those goods to the Commissioners.

(7) Where relevant goods are abandoned to the Commissioners in accordance with paragraph (6) above the person liable to pay the duty at the excise duty point shall be the owner of those goods at that excise duty point.

NOTES
Commencement: 1 October 1999.

21 Excise duty points—ownership of goods

(1) Subject to paragraph (2) below, if at anytime after relevant goods are deposited in an excise warehouse either—

(a) those goods cease to be owned by a registered owner, or

(b) there is no duty representative acting as the owner's agent,

the time when those goods ceased to be owned by a registered owner or there ceased to be a duty representative acting as the owner's agent shall be the excise duty point for those goods.

(2) Paragraph (1) above shall not apply if—

(a) the authorized warehousekeeper is the owner of the relevant goods, or

(b) the relevant goods are owned by a person who is not a revenue trader.

(3) The persons jointly and severally liable to pay the duty at the excise duty point shall be—

(a) the authorized warehousekeeper for the excise warehouse in which the goods were kept,

(b) the owner of the goods immediately before the excise duty point,

(c) if different, the owner of the goods immediately after the excise duty point, and

(d) the duty representative of the owner of the goods immediately before the excise duty point.

[(4) Where—

(a) the excise duty point for relevant goods is prescribed by paragraph (1),

(b) the registered owner did not comply with paragraph (3) or (5) of regulation 18, or, as the case may have required, the duty representative did not comply with paragraph (3) or (5) of regulation 19, and

(c) the authorized warehousekeeper is liable to pay the duty,

he is relieved from liability to pay that duty if, immediately following the excise duty point, he abandons those goods to the Commissioners.".

NOTES
Commencement: 1 October 1999.

19 Deferred payment—payment of duty

On each payment day the person whose arrangements have been approved under regulation 18 must—

(a)   pay the amount due to the Commissioners in accordance with those arrangements, or

(b)   where those arrangements involve the collection of the amount due to the Commissioners by means of a direct debit, ensure that he has sufficient funds in his account to satisfy the claim for payment.

20 Returns

The occupier of registered premises must make such returns at such time, in such form and manner and containing such particulars as the Commissioners may require.

PART IV

FISCAL MARKS

21 Application of Part IV

(1)   This Part of these Regulations applies to specified tobacco products.

(2)   In these Regulations "specified tobacco products" means tobacco products that are—

(a)   cigarettes, or

(b)   hand-rolling tobacco other than hand-rolling tobacco intended for retail sale in loose form that is supplied by the manufacturer or importer in packets that each contain not less than 500 grams.

22 When specified tobacco products are required to carry a fiscal mark

(1)   Subject to regulation 23 below, specified tobacco products—

(a)   that are manufactured in, imported into or removed to home use within the United Kingdom on or after 1st June 2001, or

(b)   whenever manufactured in, imported into or removed to home use within the United Kingdom, that are held by a person who is a revenue trader on or after 1st July 2001,

are required to carry a fiscal mark.

(2)   Specified tobacco products that are required to carry a fiscal mark must not be packaged otherwise than in packets that, in conformity with requirements imposed under section 8C(3) or section 8D of the Act, carry a fiscal mark.

(3)   Imported specified tobacco products that are required to carry a fiscal mark must carry a fiscal mark at the time they are imported.

23 Exceptions to the requirement to carry a fiscal mark

(1)   Specified tobacco products are not required to carry a fiscal mark if—

(a)   they are not intended for home use and are not delivered to home use or otherwise made available for home use;

[(aa)   they were acquired by a person in another member State for his own use and transported by him to the United Kingdom.]

(b)   in accordance with an Order made under section 13(1) or section 13A(1) of the Customs and Excise Duties (General Reliefs) Act 1979 relief from duty is afforded and the conditions (if any) subject to which that relief was afforded are complied with; or

(c)   they are intended for supply to, or have been supplied to, entitled passengers in an export shop.

[(1A)   Specified tobacco products acquired by private individuals for their own use and transported by them to the United Kingdom are not required to carry a fiscal mark if—

(a) relief from duty would have been afforded by an Order made under section 13(1) of the Customs and Excise Duties (General Reliefs) Act 1979, but for the fact that the quantity of those products exceeds any limit on quantity specified in the Order, and

(b) those products are declared as required by section 78(1) of the Customs and Excise Management Act 1979, and

(c) the duty on those products is paid.]

(2) Specified tobacco products are not required to carry a fiscal mark if, having been removed to home use upon payment of excise duty in the Isle of Man—

(a) they carry a mark prescribed for fiscal purposes in conformity with the requirements of the law of the Isle of Man, and

(b) the excise duty paid in the Isle of Man has not been and will not be repaid, remitted or drawn back.

[(2A) Specified tobacco products are not required to carry a fiscal mark if those products are not sold or offered for sale and are, upon being removed to home use, supplied by the occupier of the registered premises from which they were removed to a person who will use them solely for one or both of the following purposes—

(a) testing quality, or

(b) testing products that are being developed.

Paragraph (3) does not apply to specified tobacco products to which this paragraph applies.]

(3) Specified tobacco products that are not required to carry a fiscal mark must not carry a fiscal mark.

(4) In this regulation "entitled passengers" and "export shop" have the meanings given in regulation 3 of the Excise Goods (Export Shops) Regulations 2000.

NOTE

Para (1): para (aa) inserted by the Excise Goods, Beer and Tobacco Products (Amendment) Regulations 2002, SI 2002/2692 reg 4(1). (4).

Para (1A): inserted by the Tobacco Products and Excise Goods (Amendment) Regulations, SI 2006/1787, reg 3(1), (7).

Para (2A): inserted by the Tobacco Products and Excise Goods (Amendment) Regulations, SI 2006/1787, reg 3(1), (8).

---

24 Removal of products that are required to carry a fiscal mark

(1) Without prejudice to regulation 9 above (removal) and subject to such conditions as the Commissioners see fit to impose, specified tobacco products that carry a fiscal mark may be removed without payment of duty—

(a) from a registered factory to a registered store, or

(b) from a registered store to another registered store.

(2) Specified tobacco products that carry a fiscal mark that are in registered premises and that are not removed to home use may only be—

(a) removed in accordance with paragraph (1) above,

(b) destroyed or disposed of within the United Kingdom to the satisfaction of the Commissioners,

(c) with the Commissioners' consent—

(i) recycled, or

(ii) repackaged,

within the United Kingdom, or

(d) with the Commissioners' consent and following the obliteration or destruction of the fiscal mark to their satisfaction, used solely for the purpose of research or experiment.

(3) Specified tobacco products that carry a fiscal mark that are in an excise warehouse and that are not removed to home use may only be—

(a) removed to—

(i) a registered store, or

(ii) another excise warehouse for rewarehousing,

in accordance with an entry made for that purpose under regulation 16(2) of the Excise Warehousing (Etc) Regulations 1988,

(b) destroyed or disposed of to the satisfaction of the Commissioners, or

(c) following the obliteration or destruction of the fiscal mark to the satisfaction of the Commissioners—

(i) exported, or

(ii) with the Commissioners' consent, used solely for the purpose of research or experiment.

(4) During any period specified by order of the Commissioners in accordance with section 128 of the Customs and Excise Management Act 1979 specified tobacco products that carry a fiscal mark must not be removed to home use in quantities exceeding those that the Commissioners have specified as appearing to them to be reasonable in the circumstances.

25 Offences—supplementary provisions

(1) A person is not guilty of an offence contrary to section 8G(4) of the Act in relation to any conduct that took place before 1st July 2001.

(2) A person afforded relief from duty in accordance with an Order made under section 13(1) or section 13A(1) of the Customs and Excise Duties (General Reliefs) Act 1979 [(or a person who would have been afforded relief by an Order made under section 13(1) but for the fact that the quantity of the specified tobacco products exceeded any limit on quantity specified in the Order and who declared those products as required by section 78(1) of the Customs and Excise Management Act 1979 and paid the duty on them)] is not guilty of an offence contrary to section 8G(4) of the Act unless his conduct occasioned the excise duty point prescribed by regulation 12(4) above.

(3) Where any person is, in accordance with section 13 of the Finance Act 1994, the subject of an assessment to a penalty for conduct falling within paragraph (a) of section 170A(1) of the Customs and Excise Management Act 1979 he is not, in relation to that conduct, guilty of an offence contrary to section 8G(4) of the Act.

NOTE

Para (2): words in square brackets inserted by the Tobacco Products and Excise Goods (Amendment) Regulations, SI 2006/1787, reg 3(1), (9).

PART V

REPAYMENT AND DRAWBACK OF DUTY

26 Returned products

(1) Where any tobacco products are returned to registered premises within three years of their removal to home use and are—

(a) recycled;

(b) repackaged; or

(c) otherwise disposed of to the satisfaction of the Commissioners,

the Commissioners may, subject to such conditions as they may impose under section 2(2) of the Act, allow credit for the duty charged on those products.

(2) For the purposes of any claim for drawback to which the Excise Goods (Drawback) Regulations 1995 apply specified tobacco products are not eligible goods unless the Commissioners are satisfied that any fiscal marks carried by the products have been obliterated or destroyed.

[26A

Subject to compliance with any conditions imposed by the Commissioners under section 2(2) of the Act, duty payable on tobacco products is remitted if those products are not smoked by human beings and are used solely for one or both of the following purposes—

(a)   testing quality, or

(b)   testing products that are being developed.]

NOTE

Inserted by the Tobacco Products and Excise Goods (Amendment) Regulations, SI 2006/1787, reg 3(1), (10).

PART VI
APPLICATION AND AMENDMENT OF OTHER REGULATIONS

NOTES

Modification of this Part by the Channel Tunnel (Alcoholic Liquor and Tobacco Products) Order 2003, SI 2003/2758, art 2(c), Schedule, in its application to a control zone.

27

(amends SI 1988/809, reg 26.)

28 The Excise Goods (Holding, Movement, Warehousing and REDS) Regulations 1992

(1) Save in the case of tobacco products that were at the time of the excise duty point or immediately before that time in an excise warehouse, Part II and (except for the case of UK distance selling arrangements) Part III of the Excise Goods (Holding, Movement, Warehousing and REDS) Regulations 1992 do not apply to tobacco products.

(2)   *(Amends SI 1992/3135.)*

[PART VII
DUTY NOT TO FACILITATE SMUGGLING]

NOTES

Inserted by the Tobacco Products (Amendment) Regulations, SI 2006/2368, regs 2, 4.

[29—

(1) The Commissioners shall provide written notification of a seizure of cigarettes or hand-rolling tobacco under section 139 of the Customs and Excise Management Act 1979 ("the seized products") to a manufacturer in the circumstances specified in paragraph (2).

(2)   The circumstances referred to in paragraph (1) are—

(a)   the seized products consist of at least 100,000 cigarettes or 50 kilogrammes of hand-rolling tobacco; and

(b) the Commissioners believe that the seized products were manufactured by, or that manufacture was arranged by, the manufacturer on or after 1st October 2006.]

NOTES

Inserted by the Tobacco Products (Amendment) Regulations, SI 2006/2368, regs 2, 4.

[30—

(1) The written notification shall be accompanied by a sample of the seized products.

(2) The remaining seized products shall be available for inspection by the manufacturer at any reasonable time for a period of one month beginning with the day on which written notification was given to that manufacturer.

(3) A manufacturer who wishes to inspect the remaining seized products shall notify the Commissioners of that fact in such form and manner as the Commissioners may specify.]

NOTES

Inserted by the Tobacco Products (Amendment) Regulations, SI 2006/2368, regs 2, 4.

[31—

(1) A manufacturer shall provide the Commissioners with the information specified in the Schedule.

(2) The information shall be provided—

(a) before the end of the period of one month beginning with the day on which written notification was given to the manufacturer, or

(b) at such other time as the Commissioners may allow.

(3) The Commissioners may dispense with the requirement to provide any information specified in the Schedule where they are satisfied that a manufacturer is unable to provide that information despite taking reasonable steps to do so.]

NOTES

Inserted by the Tobacco Products (Amendment) Regulations, SI 2006/2368, regs 2, 4.

SCHEDULE

Regulation 31

1.

Where the seized products were—

(a) manufactured by the manufacturer, or

(b) manufactured by a person with whom the manufacturer had arranged to have cigarettes or hand-rolling tobacco manufactured,

the manufacturer shall provide the information specified in paragraphs 4 to 10 below.

2.

Where it appears the seized products were manufactured on premises occupied by—

(a) the manufacturer, or

(b) a person falling within paragraph 1(b),

other than in accordance with instructions given by, or with the agreement of, the manufacturer the manufacturer shall provide the address of those premises, the name of the undertaking occupying those premises and, if that undertaking is a subsidiary undertaking, the name of the parent undertaking.

Part II

3.

Where the seized products do not fall within paragraphs 1 or 2 the manufacturer shall notify the Commissioners of that fact.

Information to be provided

4.

The name of the undertaking who manufactured the seized products and, if that undertaking is a subsidiary undertaking, the name of the parent undertaking.

5.

The address of the premises on which the seized products were manufactured.

6.

The date the seized products were manufactured.

7.

The total quantity of cigarettes or hand rolling tobacco bearing the same manufacturer's coding as the seized products.

8.

The name of the country to which the seized products were, or were to be, supplied.

9.

The name and address of the first customer to whom the seized products were, or were to be, supplied.

10.

The date of the invoice issued to the first customer and the total invoiced quantity of cigarettes or hand-rolling tobacco.

Interpretation

11.

For the purposes of this Schedule "subsidiary undertaking", "parent undertaking", and "undertaking" shall have the meaning given by sections 258 and 259 of the Companies Act 1985]

NOTES

Schedule inserted by the Tobacco Products (Amendment) Regulations, SI 2006/2368, regs 2, 4.

EXCISE DUTY POINTS (DUTY SUSPENDED MOVEMENTS OF EXCISE GOODS) REGULATIONS 2001

(SI 2001/3022)

NOTES

Made: 5 September 2001.

Authority: Customs and Excise Management Act 1979, ss 100G, 100H, the Finance (No 2) Act 1992 s 1.

Commencement: 28 September 2001.

Modification of these regulations, in their application to a control zone, by the Channel

Tunnel (Alcoholic Liquor and Tobacco Products) Order 2003, SI 2003/2758, art 2(d), Schedule.

ARRANGEMENT OF REGULATIONS

PART I
PRELIMINARY

1 Citation and commencement

These Regulations may be cited as the Excise Duty Points (Duty Suspended Movements of Excise Goods) Regulations 2001 and shall come into force on 28th September 2001.

2 Interpretation

In these Regulations—

"accompanying administrative document" means

(a) the document specified in Annex 1 to Commission Regulation (EEC) No 2719/92 or any document that in accordance with Article 2 of that Regulation replaces that document; and

(b) in any case where, under an exemption granted in accordance with Article 29 of the Directive, a person is entitled to use, and uses, a document specified by Commission Regulation (EEC) No 2238/93 in substitution for an accompanying administrative document, that document as so specified;

"authorized warehousekeeper" has the same meaning as in Article 4(a) of the Directive;

"the Directive" means Council Directive 92/12/EEC of 25 February 1992;

"duty suspended movement" means

(a) a movement of excise goods which:

    (1)   starts at a tax warehouse in one member State and is intended to finish by the arrival of those goods with either:

       (i)   the authorized warehousekeeper at a tax warehouse or a registered or non-registered trader in another member State; or

      (ii)   the authorized warehousekeeper at a tax warehouse in the same member State having passed through at least one other member State during the course of the movement; and

    (2)   in respect of which the excise duty to which those goods are subject by virtue of Article 5 of the Directive is suspended pursuant to suspension arrangements as defined in Article 4(c) of the Directive; and

  (b)   does not include any movement that has been discharged as described in Article 19(3) of the Directive;

"excise duty" means:

  (a)   in relation to the United Kingdom, a duty of excise charged by or under an enactment on excise goods falling within Article 3(1) of the Directive; and

  (b)   in relation to a member State other than the United Kingdom, a similar charge, imposition or levy;

"excise goods" means goods (other than chewing tobacco) of a class or description subject to any excise duty;

"guarantee" means the guarantee provided in accordance with the provisions of Article 15(3) of the Directive;

"irregularity" means an irregularity or offence within the meaning of Article 20 of the Directive;

"non-registered trader" has the meaning given in Article 4(e) of the Directive, and, in relation to the United Kingdom, is an "occasional importer" within the meaning of regulation 2(1) of the Excise Goods (Holding, Movement, Warehousing and REDS) Regulations 1992;

"registered trader" has the meaning given in Article 4(d) of the Directive and, in relation to the United Kingdom, is a "REDS" within the meaning of regulation 2(1) of the Excise Goods (Holding, Movement, Warehousing and REDS) Regulations 1992;

"tax warehouse" has the same meaning as in Article 4(b) of the Directive.

PART II
EXCISE DUTY POINTS

3 Irregularity occurring or detected in the United Kingdom

(1) This regulation applies where:

  (a)   excise goods are:

     (i)   subject to a duty suspended movement that started in the United Kingdom; or

    (ii)   imported into the United Kingdom during a duty suspended movement; and

  (b)   in relation to those goods and that movement, there is an irregularity which occurs or is detected in the United Kingdom.

(2) Where the Commissioners are satisfied that the irregularity occurred in the United Kingdom, the excise duty point shall be the time of the occurrence of the irregularity or, where it is not possible to establish when the irregularity occurred, the time when the irregularity first comes to the attention of the Commissioners.

(3) Where it is not possible to establish in which member State the irregularity occurred, the excise duty point shall be the time of the detection of the irregularity or, where it is not possible to establish when the irregularity was detected, the time when the irregularity first comes to the attention of the Commissioners.

(4) For the purposes of this regulation, detection has the same meaning as in Article 20(2) of the Directive.

4 Failure of excise goods to arrive at their destination

(1) This regulation applies where:

(a)   there is a duty suspended movement that started in the United Kingdom; and

(b)   within four months of the date of removal, the duty suspended movement is not discharged by the arrival of the excise goods at their destination; and

(c)   there is no excise duty point as prescribed by regulation 3 above; and

(d)   there has been an irregularity.

(2) Where this regulation applies and subject to paragraph (3) below, the excise duty point shall be the time when the goods were removed from the tax warehouse in the United Kingdom.

(3) The excise duty point as prescribed by paragraph (2) above shall not apply where, within four months of the date of removal, the authorized warehousekeeper accounts for the excise goods to the satisfaction of the Commissioners.

PART III
ADMINISTRATIVE PROVISIONS

5 Repayment of excise duty

(1) This regulation applies where:

(a)   there has been an excise duty point as prescribed by either regulation 3(3) or 4 above; and

(b)   within three years of either:

(i)   the date on which the accompanying administrative document for the particular duty suspended movement of excise goods was drawn up; or

(ii)   in the absence of such a document, the date when that movement started;

the Commissioners ascertain that the member State in which the irregularity actually occurred is a member State other than the United Kingdom; and

(c)   either excise duty in relation to that irregularity has been paid in the member State where the irregularity actually occurred or no excise duty was due under the laws of that member State.

(2) Where this regulation applies, the person who paid the excise duty at the excise duty point shall be entitled to claim a repayment of that duty from the Commissioners.

(3) For the purposes of paragraph (2) above, such a claim shall be made in writing to the Commissioners and include full particulars, including evidence to satisfy the Commissioners that either the excise duty has been paid in the member State in which the irregularity actually occurred or that no excise duty was due under the laws of that member State.

6

For the purposes of regulation 5(2) above, section 137A(1) of the Customs and Excise Management Act 1979 shall be modified so as to apply to any amounts paid by way of excise duty and not be limited to excise duty which is not due to the Commissioners.

PART IV
PAYMENT OF EXCISE DUTY

7 Payment

(1) Subject to paragraph (2) below, where there is an excise duty point as prescribed by regulation 3 or 4 above, the person liable to pay the excise duty on the occurrence of that excise duty point shall be the person shown as the consignor on the accompanying administrative document or, if someone other than the consignor is shown in Box 10 of that document as having arranged for the guarantee, that other person.

(2) Any other person who causes or has caused the occurrence of an excise duty point as prescribed by regulation 3 or 4 above, shall be jointly and severally liable to pay the duty with the person specified in paragraph (1) above.

8 Time for payment

Any excise duty that any person is liable to pay by virtue of this Part shall be paid by that person at or before the excise duty point.

PART V
CONSEQUENTIAL AMENDMENTS

9

(inserts the Finance Act 1994 s 12(2A))

The Excise Goods (Holding, Movement, Warehousing and REDS) Regulations 1992

10, 11

(amend the Excise Goods (Holding, Movement, Warehousing and REDS) Regulations 1992, SI 1992/3135)

EXCISE DUTY (PAYMENTS IN CASE OF ERROR OR DELAY) REGULATIONS 2001

(SI 2001/3299)

NOTES

Made: 2 October 2001.

Authority: Finance Act 2001, Sch 3 paras 3, 12, 22.

Commencement: 1 November 2001.

1 Citation and commencement

These Regulations may be cited as the Excise Duty (Payments in Case of Error or Delay) Regulations 2001 and come into force on 1st November 2001.

2 Claim for payment

(1) Any claim for a payment under Part 1 of Schedule 3 to the Finance Act 2001 must be made in the form and manner and contain the matters prescribed by this *regulation*.

(2) A claim must be made in writing to the Commissioners.

(3)   A claim must, by reference to documents that are in the possession of the claimant, state the amount of the claim and the method by which that amount was calculated.

(4)   A claim must include a statement setting out the full particulars of the error on the part of the Commissioners that the claimant relies on to satisfy the first condition in paragraph 1 of Schedule 3 to the Finance Act 2001 or, as the case may be, the second condition in paragraph 2 of that Schedule.

3   Claim for interest

(1)   Any claim for interest under paragraphs 7 to 10 of Schedule 3 to the Finance Act 2001 must be made in the form and manner and contain the matters prescribed by this regulation.

(2)   A claim must be made in writing to the Commissioners.

(3)   A claim must identify—

(a)   the paragraph of Schedule 3 to the Finance Act 2001 under which it is made, and

(b)   the claim for payment, repayment, remission, rebate or drawback to which it relates.

(4)   A claim for interest under paragraphs 7 to 10 of Schedule 3 to the Finance Act 2001 may be combined with the claim for payment, repayment, remission, rebate or drawback to which it relates but each claim must be separately identified within the document that constitutes the combined claim.

FINANCE ACT 2001 (COMMENCEMENT NO 2 AND SAVING PROVISION) ORDER 2001

(SI 2001/3300)

NOTES

Made: 2 October 2001.

Authority: Finance Act 2001, Sch 3 paras 21, 22.

1

This Order may be cited as the Finance Act 2001 (Commencement No 2 and Saving Provision) Order 2001.

2

Schedule 3 to the Finance Act 2001 comes into force on 1st November 2001.

3

The provision made by paragraph 20 of Schedule 3 to the Finance Act 2001 shall not prejudice a person's right to be paid interest for a period before 1st November 2001 where that right accrues on or after that date in relation to a payment that he made before that date.

EXCISE GOODS (ACCOMPANYING DOCUMENTS) REGULATIONS 2002

(SI 2002/501)

NOTES

Made: 6 March 2002.

Authority: Customs and Excise Management Act 1979 ss 93(1), (2)(a), (e), (fa), (fb), (g), (h), (j), (k), (3), (4) and (5), 100G, 100H and 118A(1), (2); Finance (No 2) Act 1992 s 1.

Commencement: 1 April 2002.

Modification of these regulations, in their application to a control zone, by the Channel Tunnel (Alcoholic Liquor and Tobacco Products) Order 2003, SI 2003/2758, art 2(e), Schedule.

PART I
PRELIMINARY

1 Citation and commencement

These Regulations may be cited as the Excise Goods (Accompanying Documents) Regulations 2002 and come into force on 1st April 2002.

2 Interpretation

(1) In these Regulations—

"accompanying administrative document" means, subject to paragraph (2) below, the document specified in Annex I to Commission Regulation (EEC) No 2719/92 or any document that in accordance with Article 2 of that Regulation replaces that document;

"authorized warehousekeeper", except in regulation 7 below, has the meaning given in regulation 2 of the Warehousekeepers and Owners of Warehoused Goods Regulations 1999;

"certificate of payment" means a document drawn up in compliance with the requirements of the member State to which the excise goods are consigned (including, where the context so requires, the United Kingdom) that certifies that excise duty has been paid in respect of those goods in that State;

"Community provisions" means, subject to paragraph (2) below—

    (a) in the case of accompanying administrative documents the provisions set out in Articles 1, 2 and 2a of Commission Regulation (EEC) No 2719/92 including the instructions concerning completion and the procedures for use mentioned in Article 1,

    (b) in the case of simplified accompanying documents the provisions set out in Articles 1, 2, 3, 4 and 5 of Commission Regulation (EEC) No 3649/92 and the explanatory notes set out on the reverse of copy 1 in the Annex;

"excise goods" means goods (other than chewing tobacco) of a class or description subject to any duty of excise;

"non-registered trader" has the meaning given in Article 4(e) of Council Directive 92/12/EEC;

"occasional importer" has the meaning given in regulation 2(1) of the Excise Goods (Holding, Movement, Warehousing and REDS) Regulations 1992;

"own use" does not include use for the purposes of any trade or business;

"REDS" means a registered excise dealer and shipper who is authorized, in the course of his business, to import without payment of excise duty excise goods from other member States but who is not authorized to hold or export such goods without first paying that duty;

"simplified accompanying document" means, subject to paragraph (2) below, the document specified in the Annex to Commission Regulation (EEC) No 3649/92 or any document that in accordance with Article 2 of that Regulation replaces that document;

"transporter" means the person shown as the transporter in the accompanying administrative document or simplified accompanying document.

(2)   In any case where, under an exemption granted in accordance with Article 29 of Council Directive 92/12/EEC, a person is entitled to use, and uses, a document specified by Commission Regulation (EEC) No 2238/93 in substitution for an accompanying administrative document or simplified accompanying document—

(a)   references in these Regulations to an accompanying administrative document or simplified accompanying document are to be treated as references to a document specified by that Regulation, and

(b)   references in these Regulations to Community provisions are to be treated as references to the provisions set out in Articles 3(1) and (4), 5(2) and (3), 6(1), (2), (3), (4) and (7), 8(1), (2) and (3), 9 and 10 of, and Annex II to, that Regulation.

3   Application

(1)   These Regulations do not apply to any excise goods that are being lawfully moved—

(a)   under the cover of a single administrative document;

(b)   from or to premises registered under section 41A(1) of the Alcoholic Liquor Duties Act 1979 (registered beer stores);

(c)   from or to premises in respect of which a person is registered under section 47(1) of the Alcoholic Liquor Duties Act 1979 (breweries);

(d)   from premises licensed under section 54(2) or section 55(2) of the Alcoholic Liquor Duties Act 1979 (wineries);

(e)   from premises in respect of which a person is registered under section 62(2) of the Alcoholic Liquor Duties Act 1979 (cider maker's premises);

(f)   from or to premises registered in accordance with regulations made under section 7(1) of the Tobacco Products Duty Act 1979 (registered tobacco factories and stores);

(g)   for the use of, and to the order of, a person to whom section 13A of the Customs and Excise Duties (General Reliefs) Act 1979 (reliefs from duties and taxes for persons enjoying certain immunities and privileges) applies; or

(h)   in circumstances where, in accordance with regulations made under section 12(1) of the Customs and Excise Duties (General Reliefs) Act 1979 (supply of duty-free goods to Her Majesty's ships), they are to be treated as exported.

(2)   In this regulation single administrative document has the same meaning as in Commission Regulation (EEC) No 2454/93.

PART II
EXPORTS UNDER DUTY SUSPENSION ARRANGEMENTS

4 Application of Part II

This Part does not apply to excise goods exported in accordance with the arrangements described in Article 10 of Council Directive 92/12/EEC (distance sales).

5 Completion of accompanying administrative documents

(1) Excise goods entered for removal from an excise warehouse for exportation to another member State must not be removed from that warehouse unless—

    (a)   the authorized warehousekeeper is the consignor for the purpose of complying with the Community provisions concerning accompanying administrative documents, and

    (b)   the authorized warehousekeeper and any person authorized by him to act on his behalf ensure that the Community provisions are complied with when the accompanying administrative document is completed.

(2) These requirements also apply to excise goods exported to another member State in the course of a movement to an ultimate destination within the United Kingdom.

6 Accompanying administrative documents for exports—supplementary provisions

(1) Subject to paragraphs (4) and (5) below, an accompanying administrative document—

    (a)   must not be amended, and

    (b)   must accompany the excise goods to which it relates at all times until those goods arrive at their ultimate destination.

(2) If the consignee of the excise goods is a non-registered trader, a certificate of payment must accompany the accompanying administrative document and the excise goods at all times until those goods arrive at their ultimate destination.

(3) The authorized warehousekeeper from whose warehouse any excise goods have been removed for exportation to another member State must ensure, so far as it is in his power to do so, that the Community provisions are complied with at all times until the goods reach their ultimate destination.

(4) For the purpose of complying with the Community provisions concerning changes in the destination of goods only the authorized warehousekeeper who completed the accompanying administrative document, or a person authorized by him to act on his behalf, may amend that document or enter information in Box B of that document to show a new consignee or place of delivery.

(5) Where there is a new consignee or place of delivery—

    (a)   any amendment made to the accompanying administrative document must comply with Article 15(5) of Council Directive 92/12/EEC, and

    (b)   the authorized warehousekeeper must immediately give notice of the amendment to the Commissioners.

(6) In this regulation where the ultimate destination of the goods is a place outside the Communities references to the ultimate destination of the goods are references to the place at which the goods finally leave the Communities.

7 Consignees

(1) The person shown as the consignee in any accompanying administrative document must be—

    (a)   an authorized warehousekeeper, or

    (b)   a registered trader who is not a REDS, or

    (c)   a non-registered trader who is not an occasional importer,

in a member State.

(2) Paragraph (1) above does not apply in the case of goods consigned to an ultimate destination outside the Communities.

(3) In this regulation authorized warehousekeeper and registered trader have the meanings given in Article 4 of Council Directive 92/12/EEC.

PART III
EXPORTS NOT UNDER DUTY SUSPENSION ARRANGEMENTS

8 Application of Part III

(1) Subject to paragraph (2) below, this Part applies to excise goods in respect of which excise duty has been paid.

(2) This Part does not apply—

    (a)   to excise goods exported in accordance with the arrangements described in Article 10 of Council Directive 92/12/EEC (distance sales), or

    (b)   in any case to which Part VII of the Excise Goods (Sales on Board Ships and Aircraft) Regulations 1999 applies, or

    (c)   to excise goods exported by a person for his own use.

9 Completion of simplified accompanying documents

(1) Excise goods must not be exported to another member State unless—

    (a)   the exporter completes a simplified accompanying document showing that he is the supplier, and

    (b)   when he completes that document he complies with the Community provisions.

(2) These requirements also apply to excise goods exported to another member State in the course of a movement to an ultimate destination within the United Kingdom.

10 Simplified accompanying documents for exports—supplementary provisions

(1) A simplified accompanying document—

    (a)   must not be amended, and

    (b)   must accompany the excise goods to which it relates at all times until those goods arrive at their ultimate destination.

(2) A certificate of payment must accompany the simplified accompanying document and the excise goods at all times until those goods arrive at their ultimate destination.

(3) The exporter must ensure, so far as it is in his power to do so, that the Community provisions are complied with at all times until the goods reach their ultimate destination.

PART IV
IMPORTS UNDER COMMUNITY DUTY SUSPENSION ARRANGEMENTS

11 Application of Part IV

(1) Subject to paragraph (2) below, this Part applies to imported excise goods.

(2) This Part does not apply to excise goods—

    (a)   to which Part V below applies (imports not under Community duty suspension arrangements), or

    (b)   to which Part VII of the Excise Goods (Sales on Board Ships and Aircraft) Regulations 1999 applies (simplified procedures), or

    (c)   imported in accordance with the arrangements described in Article 10 of Council Directive 92/12/EEC (distance sales), or

    (d)   to excise goods imported by a person for his own use.

Part II

12 Accompanying administrative documents for imports

Imported excise goods must be consigned to—

    (a)   an authorized warehousekeeper, or

    (b)   a REDS, or

    (c)   an occasional importer, or

    (d)   an ultimate destination outside the United Kingdom,

and must at all times be accompanied by an accompanying administrative document that complies with the Community provisions.

13 Accompanying administrative documents for imports—supplementary provisions

(1)   Except as provided in paragraph (4) below, an accompanying administrative document must not be amended.

(2)   If the consignee of the excise goods is a non-registered trader, a certificate of payment must accompany the accompanying administrative document and the excise goods at all times until those goods arrive at their ultimate destination.

(3)   The person to whom any excise goods are consigned from another member State must ensure, so far as it is in his power to do so, that the Community provisions are complied with at all times.

(4)   For the purpose of complying with the Community provisions concerning changes in the destination of goods only the consignor who completed the accompanying administrative document, or a person authorized by him to act on his behalf, may amend that document or enter information in Box B of that document to show a new consignee or place of delivery.

14 Receipt of goods under Community duty suspension arrangements

(1)   The consignee must, upon receipt of the excise goods, complete the certificates on the reverse of copies 2, 3 and 4 of the accompanying administrative document in accordance with the Community provisions.

(2)   If the quantity of excise goods received is less than the consigned quantity shown on the accompanying administrative document—

    (a)   the consignee must, no later than the third day after that on which he received the excise goods, send copy 3 of the accompanying administrative document to the Commissioners together with such other documents and such information as may be necessary to enable the Commissioners to determine whether the shortage was attributable to fortuitous events or *force majeure* or to losses inherent in the nature of the excise goods, and

    (b)   the Commissioners must, no later than the fifth day after that on which they received the documents and information supplied to them in accordance with this regulation, return copy 3 of the accompanying administrative document to the consignee.

This paragraph does not apply to hydrocarbon oil brought by sea where the consigned quantity shown on the accompanying administrative document exceeds 50,000 litres and any shortage does not exceed 0.5 per cent of that quantity.

(3)   The Commissioners are not required to comply with paragraph (2)(b) above in any case where they—

    (a)   require further documents or information in order to determine whether the shortage was attributable to fortuitous events or force *majeure* or to losses inherent in the nature of the excise goods, or

    (b)   have reasonable grounds to suspect that any document or information supplied to them in accordance with this regulation is inaccurate or untrue.

(4)   Except where paragraph (3) above applies, the consignee must, no later than the fifteenth day of the month following that in which he received the excise goods,

send copy 3 of the accompanying administrative document, with the completed certificate on the reverse, to the person shown as the consignor in that document.

(5) Where paragraph (3) above applies and the Commissioners return copy 3 of the accompanying administrative document to the consignee he must send that copy to the person shown as the consignor in that document no later than either—

(a)   the fifteenth day of the month following that in which he received the excise goods, or

(b)   the third day after that on which he received that copy from the Commissioners,

whichever is the later.

(6) For the purpose of calculating a number of days mentioned in paragraphs (2) and (5)(b) above any day that is a Saturday, Sunday, Christmas Day, Boxing Day, New Year's Day, Good Friday or Easter Monday is not to be counted.

(7) In this regulation and in regulation 21(3) below "consignee" means the person who is shown as the consignee in the accompanying administrative document.

PART V
IMPORTS NOT UNDER COMMUNITY DUTY
SUSPENSION ARRANGEMENTS

15 Application of Part V

(1) Subject to paragraph (2) below, this Part applies to imported excise goods consigned from another member State in respect of which that member State's excise duty has been paid and has not, at the time of importation, been remitted, refunded or drawn back.

(2) This Part does not apply—

(a)   to excise goods imported in accordance with the arrangements described in Article 10 of Council Directive 92/12/EEC (distance sales), or

(b)   in any case to which Part VII of the Excise Goods (Sales on Board Ships and Aircraft) Regulations 1999 applies (simplified procedures), or

(c)   to excise goods imported by a person for his own use.

16 Simplified accompanying documents for imports

Imported excise goods must be consigned—

(a)   to the person shown on the simplified accompanying document as the recipient, or

(b)   if the recipient is not in the United Kingdom, to an ultimate destination outside the United Kingdom,

and must at all times be accompanied by a simplified accompanying document that complies with the Community provisions.

17 Simplified accompanying documents for imports—supplementary provisions

(1) A simplified accompanying document must not be amended.

(2) A certificate of payment must accompany the simplified accompanying document and the excise goods at all times until those goods arrive at their ultimate destination.

(3) The person to whom any excise goods are consigned from another member State must ensure, so far as it is in his power to do so, that the Community provisions are complied with at all times.

18 Receipt of excise goods

(1) The recipient must, upon receipt of the excise goods, complete the certificates on the reverse of copies 2 and 3 of the simplified accompanying document in accordance with the Community provisions.

(2) Except where the supplier does not require it, the recipient must, no later than the fifteenth day of the month following that in which he received the excise goods, send copy 3 of the simplified accompanying document to the person shown as the supplier in that document.

(3) In this regulation and in regulation 21(4) below "recipient" means the person who is shown as the recipient in the simplified accompanying document.

PART VI

OBLIGATIONS, CONDITIONS AND RESTRICTIONS

19 General conditions and restrictions

(1) The Commissioners may in a notice published by them and not withdrawn by a further notice impose on authorized warehousekeepers conditions and restrictions subject to which excise goods to which these Regulations apply may be deposited in or removed from excise warehouses.

(2) The Commissioners may in a notice published by them and not withdrawn by a further notice prescribe conditions and restrictions subject to which excise goods to which these Regulations apply and in respect of which excise duty has not been paid may be imported by REDS and occasional importers.

(3) A certificate of payment that relates to excise goods imported by an occasional importer must be in such form and conform with such other requirements as are prescribed by the Commissioners in a notice published by them and not withdrawn by a further notice.

(4) The Commissioners may in a notice published by them and not withdrawn by a further notice impose on transporters and on persons undertaking the carriage of excise goods requirements concerning the keeping and preservation of accompanying administrative documents and simplified accompanying documents.

20 Obligations of owners and transporters

(1) Every owner and every transporter of excise goods to which these Regulations apply must ensure, so far as it is in his power to do so, that the Community provisions are complied with at all times.

(2) Every transporter of excise goods to which these Regulations apply must, whilst the goods remain in his custody or under his control, produce or cause to be produced to an officer any accompanying administrative document or simplified accompanying document and any certificate of payment that is required to accompany the goods when required to do so.

(3) This regulation also applies to—

> (a)   any person who undertakes the carriage of excise goods who is not shown as the transporter in the accompanying administrative document or simplified accompanying document, and
>
> (b)   the driver of any vehicle in which the goods are being carried,

as it applies to the transporter.

PART VII
EXCISE DUTY POINT, PAYMENT OF EXCISE DUTY, FORFEITURE AND CIVIL PENALTIES

21 Excise duty point

(1)   The excise duty point for excise goods to which these Regulations apply and in respect of which there has been a contravention described in paragraph (2), (3), or (4) below is the time specified in paragraph (5) below.

(2)   For excise goods to which Part II above applies (exports under duty suspension arrangements) the contraventions are—

    (a)   removal of the goods from an excise warehouse in contravention of regulation 5 above (completion of accompanying administrative documents); and

    (b)   whilst the goods are in the United Kingdom—

        (i)   contravention of or failure to comply with regulation 6(1) or (2) or (4) or (5) above (accompanying administrative documents for exports—supplementary provisions);

        (ii)   after removal of the goods from an excise warehouse, contravention of or failure to comply with the Community provisions; and

        (iii)   contravention of or failure to comply with regulation 7 above (consignees).

(3)   For excise goods to which Part IV above applies (imports under Community duty suspension arrangements) the contraventions are—

    (a)   contravention of or failure to comply with regulation 12 above (accompanying administrative documents for imports);

    (b)   contravention of or failure to comply with regulation 13(1) or (3) above (accompanying administrative documents for imports—supplementary provisions);

    (c)   contravention of or failure to comply with the Community provisions;

    (d)   delivery of the goods to a place other than the place for delivery specified in the accompanying administrative document; and

    (e)   except where the failure is occasioned by action or inaction on the part of the Commissioners, failure by the consignee to comply with regulation 14 above (receipt of goods under Community duty suspension arrangements).

(4)   For the excise goods to which Part V above applies (imports not under Community duty suspension arrangements) the contraventions are—

    (a)   contravention of or failure to comply with regulation 16 above (simplified accompanying documents for imports);

    (b)   contravention of or failure to comply with regulation 17(1) above (simplified accompanying documents for imports—supplementary provisions);

    (c)   contravention of or failure to comply with the Community provisions;

    (d)   delivery of the goods to a place other than the place for delivery specified in the simplified accompanying document; and

    (e)   failure by the recipient to comply with regulation 18 above (receipt of excise goods).

(5)   The excise duty point is—

    (a)   for excise goods to which Part II above applies, the time the goods were removed from the excise warehouse;

    (b)   in any other case, the time the excise goods were imported.

22 Payment

(1)   Subject to paragraphs (2) to (4) below, the person liable to pay the excise duty at the excise duty point is—

(a)   for excise goods to which Part II above applies (exports under duty suspension arrangements), the authorized warehousekeeper;

(b)   for excise goods to which Part IV above applies (imports under Community duty suspension arrangements), the person shown as consignor on the accompanying administrative document or, if someone other than the consignor is shown in Box 10 of that document as having arranged for the guarantee, that other person; or

(c)   for excise goods to which Part V above applies (imports not under Community duty suspension arrangements), the person shown as the recipient in the simplified accompanying document.

(2)   The authorized warehousekeeper is not the person liable to pay the excise duty in accordance with paragraph (1)(a) above in any case where—

(a)   the contravention that occasioned the excise duty point was not caused by the authorized warehousekeeper and occurred after the goods had been removed from the excise warehouse, and

(b)   the authorized warehousekeeper did not provide security for the export, and

(c)   the transporter or the owner of the goods did provide security for the export.

(3)   In any case where paragraph (2) above applies, the person liable to pay the excise duty due at the excise duty point is the transporter or the owner of the goods who provided security for the export.

(4)   Any person whose conduct caused a contravention described in regulation 21 above so that there was an excise duty point is jointly and severally liable to pay the excise duty at that excise duty point with the person specified in paragraph (1) or (3) above.

23 Time for payment

Any excise duty that any person is liable to pay by virtue of this Part must be paid immediately.

24 Forfeiture

If in relation to any excise goods that are liable to a duty of excise that has not been paid there is—

(a)   a contravention of any provision of these Regulations, or

(b)   a contravention of any condition or restriction imposed by or under these Regulations,

those goods shall be liable to forfeiture.

25 Civil penalties

(1)   In the case of any contravention of or failure to comply with any relevant regulation or any Community provision, section 100J of the Customs and Excise Management Act 1979 (contravention of registered excise dealers and shippers regulations) applies for the purpose of attracting civil penalties under section 9 of the Finance Act 1994 in the following manner.

(2)   Any contravention of any relevant regulation is treated as if it were a contravention of a provision of registered excise dealers and shippers regulations.

(3)   In so far as the contravention or failure is not included in paragraph (2) above, any contravention of or failure to comply with any Community provision is treated as if it were a failure to comply with a condition or restriction imposed by or under registered excise dealers and shippers regulations.

(4)   In this regulation "relevant regulation" means the following regulations—

5(1)(b)	(completion of accompanying administrative documents);
6	(accompanying administrative documents for exports—supplementary provisions);
7	(consignees);
9	(completion of simplified accompanying documents);
10	(simplified accompanying documents for exports—supplementary provisions);
12	(accompanying administrative documents for imports);
13	(accompanying administrative documents for imports- supplementary provisions);
14	(receipt of goods under Community duty suspension arrangements);
16	(simplified accompanying documents for imports);
17	(simplified accompanying documents for imports- supplementary provisions);
18	(receipt of excise goods);
20(1)	(obligations of owners and transporters).

PART VIII
ADMINISTRATIVE PROVISION AND CONSEQUENTIAL AMENDMENTS

26 Administrative provision—imports

(1)   This regulation applies to excise goods to which Part IV above applies (imports under Community duty suspension arrangements).

(2)   Where, in accordance with regulation 14 above the Commissioners receive an accompanying administrative document they must endorse that document to indicate that they have seen it.

(3)   The Commissioners must consider whether a shortage shown on the certificate of receipt on the reverse of the accompanying administrative document was attributable to fortuitous events or force majeure or to losses inherent in the nature of the excise goods and annotate the certificate of receipt accordingly.

(4)   The annotation required by paragraph (3) above must indicate whether the Commissioners have granted exemption, partial exemption or no exemption from excise duty in respect of the shortage.

27

(Amends the Excise Warehousing (Etc) Regulations, SI 1988/809).

28

(Amends the Excise Goods (Holding, Movement, Warehousing and REDS) Regulations, SI 1992/3135).

29

(Amends the Beer Regulations, SI 1993/1228)

30

(Amends the Warehousekeepers and Owners of Warehoused Goods Regulations, SI 1999/1278)

HYDROCARBON OIL (INDUSTRIAL RELIEFS) REGULATIONS 2002

(SI 2002/1471)

Made: 5 June 2002.

Authority: Customs and Excise Management Act 1979 s 24(1), Sch 4

Commencement: For the purposes of regs 5, 6, 1 July 2002. For all other purposes, 1 September 2002.

1 Citation

These Regulations may be cited as the Hydrocarbon Oil (Industrial Reliefs) Regulations 2002.

2 Commencement

These Regulations come into force for the purposes of regulations 5 and 6 on 1st July 2002 and for all other purposes on 1st September 2002.

3 Interpretation

In these Regulations—

"approved furnace operator" means a person approved by the Commissioners for the purposes of section 14(1) of the Oil Act (rebate of duty on light oil delivered for home use for use as furnace fuel);

"approved repayment user" means a person approved by the Commissioners for the purposes of section 9(4) of the Oil Act (repayment of duty where duty paid hydrocarbon oil put to qualifying use);

"approved tied oil trader" means a person approved by the Commissioners for the purposes of section 9(1) of the Oil Act (delivery for home use of hydrocarbon oil without payment of duty);

"duty" means the excise duty charged on hydrocarbon oil by section 6(1) of the Oil Act;

"the Oil Act" means the Hydrocarbon Oil Duties Act 1979.

4 Approvals

(1) The Commissioners may approve a person as an approved furnace operator, an approved repayment user or an approved tied oil trader—

    (a)   individually or by reference to a class,

    (b)   in relation to particular descriptions of hydrocarbon oil or generally, and

    (c)   subject to conditions.

(2) Any such approval may be revoked, or the conditions varied, for reasonable cause.

5 Applications for approval

(1) The Commissioners may not approve any person individually as an—

    (a)   approved furnace operator,

    (b)   approved repayment user, or

    (c)   approved tied oil trader,

unless he makes application on a form, or forms, provided by the Commissioners for the purpose.

(2) The applicant must fully and accurately complete the form of application and deliver it to the Commissioners at the address stated in the form.

6 Certificates of approval

(1) The Commissioners must furnish every person approved individually as an—

(a)   approved furnace operator,

(b)   approved repayment user, or

(c)   approved tied oil trader,

with a certificate of approval.

(2)   Every certificate of approval must contain the following particulars—

(a)   the name and (if different) the trading name of the person;

(b)   a unique reference number assigned to the person by the Commissioners;

(c)   a statement of the approval, or approvals, which the person holds;

(d)   particulars of the descriptions of hydrocarbon oil to which the approval, or approvals, relates.

(3)   If the Commissioners revoke an individual approval of a person, he must immediately return his certificate of approval to the Commissioners.

7 Restriction on supply of rebated and duty free oil

(1)   Tied oil may be supplied only to an approved tied oil trader.

(2)   "Tied oil" means hydrocarbon oil that the Commissioners permit to be delivered for home use to an approved tied oil trader, without payment of duty in accordance with section 9(1) of the Oil Act.

(3)   Light oil in respect of which rebate has been allowed under section 14(1) of the Oil Act and not repaid may be supplied only to an approved furnace operator.

8 Security

The Commissioners may grant permission under section 9(1) of the Oil Act subject to conditions as to the giving of security or otherwise.

9 Claims for repayment

Claims by an approved repayment user for repayment of duty—

(a)   must be made no later than 3 months after the period to which they relate, and that period must not be shorter than 2 months nor longer than 3 years, and

(b)   shall not lie where the amount to be paid is less than £250.

10 No drawback allowable where repayment permitted

No drawback of duty shall be allowed on any hydrocarbon oil for which a claim for repayment of duty lies under section 9(4) of the Oil Act.

11

(Amends the Hydrocarbon Oil Regulations, SI 1973/1311)

HYDROCARBON OIL (MARKING) REGULATIONS 2002

(SI 2002/1773)

Made: 16 July 2002

Authority: Hydrocarbon Oil Duties Act 1979 ss 24(1), 24A(3), Sch 4

Commencement: 1 August 2002

Part II

PART I
PRELIMINARY

1 Citation and commencement

These Regulations may be cited as the Hydrocarbon Oil (Marking) Regulations 2002 and come into force on 1st August 2002.

2 Interpretation

(1)   In these Regulations—

"the Act" means the Hydrocarbon Oil Duties Act 1979;

"ASTM" means American Society for Testing and Materials;

"Colour Index" means the Colour Index, compiled by the Society of Dyers and Colourists and the American Association of Textile Chemists and Colorists, published 1997, ISBN 0 90195 671 6;

"the common fiscal marker" means N-Ethyl-N-[2-(1-isobutoxyethoxy)ethyl]-4-(phenylazo)aniline together with CI Solvent Yellow 124 as described in the Colour Index;

"coumarin" means 1:2 benzopyrone;

"dark oil" means heavy oil that is darker than ASTM colour 3.0 in the Table of Glass Colour Standards included in "Standard method of Test for ASTM Colour of Petroleum Products" adopted as a joint ASTM-IP standard with ASTM designation D 1500–98 and IP designation IP 196/97, which appears in "IP Standard Methods", when the heavy oil and ASTM Colour 3.0 are compared in the manner described in that publication for that method of test;

"duty" means the excise duty charged on hydrocarbon oil by section 6(1) of the Act;

"heavy oil vehicle" means a vehicle to which section 12 of the Act (rebate not allowed on fuel for road vehicles) applies;

"IP" means Institute of Petroleum;

"IP Standard Methods" means "IP Standard Methods for Analysis and Testing of Petroleum and Related Products and British Standard 2000 Parts 2002", 61st edition, May 2002, published by the Institute of Petroleum, ISBN 0 85293 348 7;

"kerosene" means heavy oil of which more than 50% by volume distils at a temperature not exceeding 240°C;

"marker" means, except where the context requires otherwise, a marker or colouring substance prescribed by these Regulations and includes, in regulation 10, a composite solution of the type referred to in regulation 9;

"oil" means hydrocarbon oil;

"quinizarin" means 1,4-dihydroxyanthraquinone;

"solvent red" means CI Solvent Red 24 as described in the Colour Index.

(2)   Any reference in these Regulations to marked oil means oil to which a marker has been added and related expressions must be construed accordingly.

PART II
REQUIREMENT TO WORK

3 Prescribed markers and colouring substance

(1)   The following markers and colouring substance are prescribed by these Regulations—

    (a)   for gas oil and light oil, the markers described in paragraph (2)(a) and (b) and the colouring substance described in paragraph (3);

    (b)   for kerosene, the markers described in paragraph (2)(a) and (c).

(2)   The markers are—

(a) the common fiscal marker added in the proportion of not less than 6 kilograms [, and not more than 9 kilograms,] per 1,000,000 litres of oil;

(b) quinizarin added in the proportion of not less than 1.75 kilograms per 1,000,000 litres of oil;

(c) coumarin added in the proportion of not less than 2 kilograms per 1,000,000 litres of oil.

(3) The colouring substance is solvent red added in the proportion of not less than 4 kilograms per 1,000,000 litres of oil.

NOTES

Para (2): words in square brackets inserted by the Hydrocarbon Oil (Marking) (Amendment) Regulations, SI 2007/1416, regs 2, 3.

4 Marking required for rebate

Subject to Part III (Exceptions to marking requirements), no rebate of duty on the delivery for home use of—

(a) gas oil under section 11(1)(b) or (ba) of the Act; or

(b) kerosene under section 11(1)(c) or 13AA(1) of the Act; or

(c) light oil under section 14(1) of the Act;

may be allowed unless there is added to the oil, in accordance with these Regulations, the markers and, [except in the case of kerosene], the colouring substance, prescribed by regulation 3.

NOTES

Words in square brackets substituted by the Hydrocarbon Oil (Marking) (Amendment) Regulations, SI 2007/1416, regs 2, 4.

5 Marking required for delivery of oil without payment of duty

Subject to Part III (Exceptions to marking requirements), the Commissioners may not permit any gas oil or kerosene to be delivered for home use without payment of duty on that oil under section 9 of the Act, unless there is added to the oil, in accordance with these Regulations, the markers and, in the case of gas oil, the colouring substance, prescribed by regulation 3.

PART III
EXCEPTIONS TO MARKING REQUIREMENTS

6 Commissioners' power to waive marking

The Commissioners may waive the requirements of regulation 4 (marking required for rebate) and regulation 5 (marking required for delivery of oil without payment of duty) only where they are satisfied that it is necessary for technical reasons or for reasons of public health or safety.

PART IV
TIME AND MANNER OF MARKING

7 Application

This Part applies for the purpose of determining the time and manner in which any oil required to be marked by these Regulations is to be marked.

8 Time of marking

Except as otherwise provided in regulations made by the Commissioners, oil must be marked before delivery for home use of that oil.

Part II

9 Use of composite solution

Any oil may be marked by the addition to it of a solution containing the markers.

PART V

STORAGE, LABELLING ETC

10 Storage of markers

(1) The occupier of any premises where marking occurs must keep any marker—

  (a) separately from all other substances; and

  (b) except when removed for immediate use, in containers bearing a description of their contents.

(2) At the end of each month, the occupier of any premises where marking occurs must—

  (a) take stock of the markers that he stores for use or that are in use at those premises;

  (b) make a written record of that stocktake;

  (c) preserve that written record for not less than 6 years.

11 Storage of marked oil

Marked oil must be stored separately from unmarked oil.

12 Labelling of delivery points for marked oil

Any drum, storage tank or other container or any delivery pump or pipe must bear an indelible notice to the effect that—

  (a) where it contains, or is an outlet for, any gas oil or kerosene marked under regulation 4 (marking required for rebate), such oil is not to be used as road fuel;

  (b) where it contains, or is an outlet for, any light oil marked under regulation 4 (marking required for rebate), such oil is to be used only as furnace fuel;

  (c) where it contains, or is an outlet for, any oil marked under regulation 5 (marking required for delivery without payment of duty), such oil is not to be used as fuel for any engine, motor or other machinery or as heating fuel.

13 Particulars to be recorded on delivery notes

(1) Any person who supplies—

  (a) gas oil marked under regulation 4 (marking required for rebate); or

  (b) a quantity . . . exceeding two hundred and fifty litres of kerosene, marked under regulation 4 (marking required for rebate);

must provide to the recipient a delivery note bearing a statement to the effect that such oil is not to be used as road fuel.

(2) Any person who supplies light oil marked under regulation 4 (marking required for rebate) must provide to the recipient a delivery note bearing a statement to the effect that such oil is only to be used as furnace fuel.

(3) Any person who supplies oil marked under regulation 5 (marking required for delivery for home use without payment of duty) must supply to the recipient a delivery note bearing a statement to the effect that such oil is not to be used as fuel for any engine, motor or other machinery or as heating fuel.

NOTES

  Para (1): in sub-para (b) word revoked by the Hydrocarbon Oil (Marking) (Amendment) Regulations, SI 2007/1416, regs 2, 5.

PART VI
PROHIBITIONS

14 Prohibitions relating to prescribed markers

(1) No oil may be marked except in the circumstances prescribed by these Regulations.

(2) No marker may be removed from any oil.

(3) No substance calculated to impede the identification of any marker may be added to any oil.

15 Prohibition relating to other markers

(1) No person may add any chemical identifier or dye other than a marker to any gas oil or kerosene required by these Regulations to be marked (other than gas oil or kerosene to which regulation 6 applies).

(2) Where any person contravenes this regulation, his contravention shall attract a penalty under section 9 of the Finance Act 1994 (civil penalties) and any oil to which such a chemical identifier or dye has been added shall be liable to forfeiture.

16 Prohibition on importation of certain oil

No oil of a description required by these Regulations to be marked may be imported where there has been added any substance calculated to impede the identification of any marker.

17 Prohibition on the sale of dark oil

No dark oil may be sold as fuel for a heavy oil vehicle.

PART VII
AMENDMENTS, OMISSIONS AND REVOCATIONS

18

(Amends the Hydrocarbon Oil Regulations, SI 1973/1311 regs 2, 12; revokes regs 17–30A)

19

(Amends the Hydrocarbon Oil (Designated Markers) Regulations, SI 1996/1251 reg 2)

20 Revocations

(1) Revoke the Hydrocarbon Oil (Amendment) Regulations 1985.

(2) Revoke the Hydrocarbon Oil (Amendment) (No 2) Regulations 1994.

BIODIESEL AND BIOBLEND REGULATIONS 2002

(SI 2002/1928)

NOTES

Revoked by the Biofuels and Other Fuel Substitutes (Payment of Excise Duties etc) Regulations 2004, SI 2004/2065 reg 4(2).

CUSTOMS (PRESENTATION OF GOODS FOR EXPORT) REGULATIONS 2003

(SI 2003/467)

NOTES

Made: 3 March 2003.

Authority: European Communities Act 1972 s 2(2).

Commencement: 26 March 2003

1 Citation and commencement

These Regulations may be cited as the Customs (Presentation of Goods for Export) Regulations 2003 and shall come into force on 26th March 2003.

2 Interpretation

In these Regulations—

"the Commissioners" mean the Commissioners of Customs and Excise;

"the Council Regulation" means the Council Regulation (EEC) 2913/92 establishing the Community Customs Code;

"customs declaration" has the meaning given by Article 4(17) of the Council Regulation;

"electronic communication" means a communication transmitted (whether from one person to another, from one device to another or from a person to a device or vice versa)—

    [(a)   by means of electronic communications network, or]

    (b)   by other means but while in an electronic form;

"export" means the customs procedure for export described in Articles 4(16), 161 and 162 of the Council Regulation;

"official system" means a system operated by the Commissioners for the acceptance of an electronic communication containing information in connection with the completion of a customs procedure.

NOTES

In definition "electronic communications", para (a) substituted by the Communications Act 2003 (Consequential Amendments) Order 2003, SI 2003/2155 reg 3(1), Sch 1 para 52.

3 Presentation of goods for export by documentary means

For the purposes of Article 4(19) of the Council Regulation (presentation of goods to Customs), presentation of goods to the Commissioners for export shall be made by delivering to them—

    (a)   the form prescribed in Schedule 1, or a form to the like effect approved by the Commissioners, containing the information required in relation to those goods by that form; and

    (b)   a document containing the information required in relation to those goods by Schedule 2.

4 Presentation of goods for export using an electronic communication

(1)   Subject to paragraph (2), the requirements concerning presentation of goods described in regulation 3 may be satisfied by delivery, to an official system by means of an electronic communication, of information concerning the place at which those goods are situated.

(2)   Information shall be taken to have been delivered to an official system by means of an electronic communication only if it is accepted by the official system to which it is delivered and is in a form intelligible to the Commissioners.

5 Evidence of contents of an electronic communication

(1)   A document certified by the Commissioners to be a printed-out version of any information delivered by means of an electronic communication shall be evidence, unless the contrary is proved, of the authenticity and entirety of the information delivered on that occasion.

(2)   A document purporting to be a certificate given in accordance with paragraph (1) shall be presumed to be such a certificate unless the contrary is proved.

SCHEDULE 1

PRESENTATION OF GOODS FOR EXPORT

Regulation 3(a)

I hereby notify Customs that goods listed on
_____

(document reference)
attached
Arrived at
_____

(name of wharf, port, airport, together with
transit shed reference)
On
_____
(date) at
_____
(time)

I present the goods under Article 161 of
the Council Regulation (EEC) No 2913/92.

Signature	
Name	
Company	
Status	
Date	

C1601

SCHEDULE 2

PARTICULARS

Regulation 3(b)

1.   The number of packages containing goods in respect of which a customs declaration for export will be made.

2.   The marks and numbers affixed to each such package.

3.   A description of the goods in each such package sufficient to enable an officer of customs and excise to identify them.

4.   The expected date of export of each such package.

5.   The final destination of each such package.

6.   The name of the ship, the flight number of the aircraft or the number of the train by means of which each such package will be exported.

Part II

Note: For goods carried in a freight container or vehicle, items 4, 5 and 6 may be omitted provided the appropriate container or vehicle manifest showing the details required by those items and the identifying number of the container or the registration number of the vehicle is attached to the form prescribed in Schedule 1 or the form to like effect approved by the Commissioners.

TOBACCO PRODUCTS (DESCRIPTIONS OF PRODUCTS) ORDER 2003

(SI 2003/1471)

NOTES

Made: 5 June 2003.

Authority: Tobacco Products Duty Act 1979, s 1(3).

Commencement: 1 August 2003.

1 Citation and commencement

This Order may be cited as the Tobacco Products (Descriptions of Products) Order 2003 and comes into force on 1st August 2003.

2 Interpretation

In this Order "the Act" means the Tobacco Products Duty Act 1979.

3 Repeal and revocation

(1)   Subsections (2) and (2A) of section 1 of the Act are repealed.

(2)   The Tobacco Products (Cigarettes and Cigars) Order 1977 is revoked.

4 Cigarettes

(1)   Subject to paragraph (2) below, references to cigarettes in the Act include any product that comprises—

      (a)   rolls of tobacco capable of being smoked as they are and that are not cigars, or

      (b)   rolls of tobacco that, by simple non-industrial handling, are—

           (i)   inserted into cigarette-paper tubes, or

           (ii)   wrapped in cigarette paper.

(2)   References to cigarettes in the Act include products consisting in whole or in part of substances other than tobacco that otherwise conform to a description in paragraph (1) above, unless they are herbal smoking products.

5 Cigars

References to cigars in the Act include any product that is described in the Schedule below and do not include tobacco products of any other description.

6 Hand-rolling tobacco

(1)   References to hand-rolling tobacco in the Act include any product that would, but for the reference to hand-rolling tobacco in article 7(1) below, be other smoking tobacco and—

      (a)   in which more than 25% by weight of the tobacco particles have a cut width of less than 1 millimetre, or

      (b)   that is sold or intended to be sold for making into cigarettes by hand, or

      (c)   that is of a kind used for making into cigarettes by hand.

(2)   In this regulation—

(a)   the references to "making into cigarettes by hand" in paragraph (1)(b) and (c) above include making into cigarettes by hand with the aid of a mechanical device, and

(b)   the use for making into cigarettes referred to in paragraph (1)(c) above must amount to more than occasional use but need not amount to common use.

7 Other smoking tobacco

(1)   Subject to paragraph (2) below, references to other smoking tobacco in the Act include any product that is not cigarettes, cigars, or hand-rolling tobacco and comprises—

(a)   tobacco that has been cut or otherwise split, twisted or pressed into blocks, and is capable of being smoked without further industrial processing, or

(b)   tobacco refuse put up for retail sale that can be smoked.

(2)   References to other smoking tobacco in the Act include products consisting in whole or in part of substances other than tobacco that otherwise conform to a description in paragraph (1) above, unless they are herbal smoking products.

8 Chewing tobacco

(1)   Subject to paragraph (2) below, references to chewing tobacco in the Act include any product that—

(a)   is not cigarettes, cigars, hand-rolling tobacco, or other smoking tobacco,

(b)   consists of or includes tobacco, and

(c)   has been prepared so that it can be chewed.

(2)   References to chewing tobacco in the Act include any product prepared for chewing that does not include tobacco but consists in whole or in part of a substitute for tobacco, except for such a product that is intended solely as an aid to persons to give up smoking.

SCHEDULE
DESCRIPTIONS OF CIGARS

Article 5

1

Cigars made entirely of natural tobacco. Cigars do not fall within this description if they contain substances other than natural tobacco.

2

Cigars with an outer wrapper of natural tobacco. Cigars falling within this description include cigars containing a mixture of tobacco and other substances; provided that they have an outer wrapper of natural tobacco. A cigar containing only substances other than tobacco does not fall within this description.

3

Cigars with a threshed blend filler and with an outer wrapper that has the normal colour of a cigar. The outer wrapper must cover the cigar in full, including where appropriate the filter but not (in the case of cigars with a mouthpiece) the mouthpiece. The cigar must have a binder (which holds the filler together before the outer wrapper is applied). Both the outer wrapper and the binder must be made of reconstituted tobacco. Each cigar must have a unit weight of not less than 1.2 grams (excluding the weight of any filter or mouthpiece). The outer wrapper must be fitted in spiral form with an acute angle of at least 30 degrees to the longitudinal axis of the cigar. A cigar containing only substances other than tobacco does not fall within this description.

4

Cigars with a threshed blend filler and with an outer wrapper that has the normal colour of a cigar. The outer wrapper must be made of reconstituted tobacco and must cover the cigar in full, including where appropriate the filter, but not (in the case of cigars with a mouthpiece) the mouthpiece. If the filler is held together with a binder, the binder may be made of a material other than tobacco or reconstituted tobacco. Each cigar must have a unit weight of not less than 2.3 grams (excluding the weight of any filter or mouthpiece). The circumference over at least one third of the length of the cigar must not be less than 34 mm. A cigar containing only substances other than tobacco does not fall within this description.

5

A product that is described as a cigarillo but falls within one of the above descriptions is a cigar.

CHANNEL TUNNEL (ALCOHOLIC LIQUOR AND TOBACCO PRODUCTS) ORDER 2003

(SI 2003/2758)

NOTES

Made: 29 October 2003.

Authority: Channel Tunnel Act 1987 ss 11(1), 11(2), 11(3), 13(1), 13(2), 34(1), 34(2) and 34(4).

Commencement: 24 November 2003.

1 Citation and commencement

This Order may be cited as the Channel Tunnel (Alcoholic Liquor and Tobacco Products) Order 2003 and comes into force on 24 November 2003.

2 Controls

The following Regulations [and Order] apply in a control zone with the modifications indicated in the Schedule—

(a)	the Excise Goods (Holding, Movement, Warehousing and REDS) Regulations 1992;
(b)	the Beer Regulations 1993 Parts I, VI and VII (determination of the duty, payment of duty and returns);
(c)	the Tobacco Products Regulations 2001 Parts I, III and VI (excise duty points, security and payment of duty, and application of other regulations);
(d)	the Excise Duty Points (Duty Suspended Movements of Excise Goods) Regulations 2001;
(e)	the Excise Goods (Accompanying Documents) Regulations 2002.
[(f)	the Excise Duty Points (Etc.)(New Member States) Regulations 2004;]
[(g)	the Customs and Excise Duties (Travellers' Allowances and Personal Reliefs)(New Member States) Order 2004.]

NOTES

Words inserted by the Channel Tunnel (Alcoholic Liquor and Tobacco Products) (Amendment) Order 2004, SI 2004/1004 arts 2, 3.

Paras (f), (g) inserted by SI 2004/1004 arts 2, 3.

3 Penalties, assessments and appeals

Section 170A of the Customs and Excise Management Act 1979 (civil penalty for handling goods subject to unpaid excise duty) applies to goods in a control zone with the modifications indicated in the Schedule.

4

The following enactments apply, for the purposes of this Order, in corresponding manner to events involving goods in a control zone in the same way that they apply to events involving goods in the United Kingdom—

(a) Part I Chapter II of the Finance Act 1994 (appeals and penalties);

(b) section 49(3) of the Alcoholic Liquor Duties Act 1979 (civil penalty and forfeiture for contravention of or failure to comply with beer regulations);

(c) section 7(2) of the Tobacco Products Duty Act 1979 (civil penalty and forfeiture for contravention of or failure to comply with regulations for management of duty);

(d) section 10OJ of the Customs and Excise Management Act 1979 (civil penalty and forfeiture for contravention of or failure to comply with registered excise dealers and shippers regulations).

5 Interpretation

For the purposes of this Order, "control zone" bears the same meaning as in article 5(2)(a) of the Channel Tunnel (Customs and Excise) Order 1990.

6

(Revokes the Channel Tunnel (Alcoholic Liquor and Tobacco Products) Order 2000, SI 2000/426 and the Channel Tunnel (Alcoholic Liquor and Tobacco Products) (Amendment) Order 2002, SI 2002/2693)

SCHEDULE

Regulations 2 and 3

The Excise Goods (Holding, Movement, Warehousing and REDS) Regulations 1992, the Beer Regulations 1993 and the Tobacco Products Regulations 2001

1.

In regulation 2(1) of the Excise Goods (Holding, Movement, Warehousing and REDS) Regulations 1992, regard the meaning given for "excise goods" as omitting the expression ", the Hydrocarbon Oil Duties Act 1979".

2.

After regulation 2(1) of those Regulations, regard there as being—

"(1A) Any reference in these Regulations to "import", "importation", "imported" or "importer" includes such reference as is appropriate for their application to, or in the case of, goods or products that are treated as being imported into the United Kingdom by article 5(2)(a) of the Channel Tunnel (Customs and Excise) Order 1990.".

3.

In regulation 4(1A) of those Regulations, regulation 15(1A) of the Beer Regulations 1993 and regulation 12(1A) of the Tobacco Products Regulations 2001, regard—

(a) the words "another member State" as being followed by " (including the French Republic)";

(b) the words "United Kingdom" as being followed by "or a control zone to which article 5(2)(a) of the Channel Tunnel (Customs and Excise) Order 1990 refers".

The Excise Duty Points (Duty Suspended Movements of Goods) Regulations 2001

4.

In regulation 2 of the Excise Duty Points (Duty Suspended Movements of Goods) Regulations 2001, after the meaning given for "authorized warehousekeeper", regard there as being—

" "control zone" means a control zone to which article 5(2)(a) of the Channel Tunnel (Customs and Excise) Order 1990 refers;".

5.

In regulation 2 of those Regulations, regard the meaning given for "excise duty" as—

"(a)   in relation to the United Kingdom, a duty of excise charged by or under an enactment on excise goods (except mineral oils) falling within Article 3(1) of the Directive; and

(b)   in relation to a member State other than the United Kingdom, a similar charge, imposition or levy;".

6.

In Part I and after regulation 2 of those Regulations, regard there as being—

"2A   For the purposes of regulations 3(1)(a)(ii), 3(1)(b), 3(2) and 5(1), "United Kingdom" includes a control zone.".

The Excise Goods (Accompanying Documents) Regulations 2002

7.

In regulation 2(1) of the Excise Goods (Accompanying Documents) Regulations 2002, after the meaning given for "Community provisions", regard there as being—

" "control zone" means a control zone to which article 5(2)(a) of the Channel Tunnel (Customs and Excise) Order 1990 refers;".

8.

In regulation 2(1) of those Regulations, regard the meaning given for "excise goods" as being—

"goods (other than chewing tobacco or hydrocarbon oil) of a class or description subject to any duty of excise;".

9.

After regulation 2(1) of those Regulations, regard there as being—

"(1A) References in these Regulations to "imported excise goods" include references to goods that are treated as being imported into the United Kingdom by article 5(2)(a) of the Channel Tunnel (Customs and Excise) Order 1990.".

10.

In regulations 15(1) and 17(3) of those Regulations, regard the words "another member State" as being followed by " (including the French Republic)".

11.

In regulation 21(2)(b) of those Regulations, regard the words "United Kingdom" as being followed by "or a control zone".

12.

In regulation 21(5)(b) of those Regulations, regard the word "imported" as being followed by "or were treated as being imported into the United Kingdom by article 5(2)(a) of the Channel Tunnel (Customs and Excise) Order 1990".

[The Excise Duty Points (Etc.) (New Member States) Regulations 2004 and the Customs and Excise Duties (Travellers' Allowances and Personal Reliefs) (New Member States) Order 2004

12A.
In regulations 3(2) and 6 of the Excise Duty Points (Etc.)(New Member States) Regulations 2004, and article 3 of the Customs and Excise Duties (Travellers' Allowances and Personal Reliefs)(New Member States) Order 2004, regard each reference to the words "United Kingdom" as being followed by "or a control zone to which article 5(2)(a) of the Channel Tunnel (Customs and Excise) Order 1990 refers."]

NOTES
Inserted by SI 2004/1004 arts 2, 4.

The Customs and Excise Management Act 1979

13.
After section 170A(2) of the Customs and Excise Management Act 1979, regard there as being—

"(2A)   In relation to a case involving goods that are treated as being imported into the United Kingdom by virtue of an order made under sections 11 and 13 of the Channel Tunnel Act 1987, subsections (1) and (2) above shall apply and be construed as if—

    (a)   the excise duty point for those goods has been passed, and

    (b)   those goods are chargeable with a duty of excise.

(2B)   Subsection (2A) does not apply to goods meeting the description of anything chargeable with duty under the Hydrocarbon Oil Duties Act 1979.".

EXPORT (PENALTY) REGULATIONS 2003

(SI 2003/3102)

NOTES
Made: 2 December 2003.
Authority: European Communities Act 1972 s 2(2).
Commencement: 23 December 2003.

1 Citation and Commencement
These regulations may be cited as the Export (Penalty) Regulations 2003 and shall come into force on 23 December 2003.

2 Interpretation
In these regulations—
    "the Act" means the Customs and Excise Management Act 1979;
    "appeal tribunal" means a VAT and duties tribunal;
    "the Commissioners" means the Commissioners of Customs and Excise;
    "the Code" means Council Regulation 2913/92/EEC;
    "Community customs rules" means customs rules, as defined in Article 1 of the Code;

Part II

"Community export duty" means any of the duties, charges or levies which are export duties within the meaning of the Code (see the definition of "export duties" in Article 4(11) of that Code);

"contravene" includes fail to comply with;

"declaration" in relation to export has the meaning assigned by Article 4(17) of the Code;

"demand notice" means a demand notice within the meaning of regulation 6;

"export" means that "customs procedure" within the meaning of Article 4(16)(h) of the Code;

"exporter" has the meaning assigned to it by Article 788 of the Implementing Regulation;

"the Implementing Regulation" means Commission Regulation 2454/93/EEC;

"notice" means notice in writing;

"person" means a person, of a description specified in Column 2 of the Schedule to these Regulations to whom that provision referred to in Column 1 applies;

"penalty" shall mean a penalty up to the maximum amount specified in Column 3 of the schedule to these Regulations;

"relevant export rule" shall mean any Community imposed duty, obligation, requirement, or condition in relation to export imposed or implemented by or under any of the following provisions or combination of provisions in any case where Community export duty is not chargeable or payable in application of the rule—

(a)   Community customs rules in relation to export;

(b)   the Act, as it applies in implementation of Community customs rules in relation to export from the Community;

(c)   any other Act, or statutory instrument, as it applies in implementation of Community customs rules in relation to export from the Community;

(d)   any directly applicable Community legislation as it applies in application of Community customs rules in relation to export;

(e)   any relevant international rules applying in relation to export;

specified in Column 1 of the Schedule to these Regulations;

"relevant international rules" means international agreements so far as applying in relation to export from the Community and having effect as part of the law of the United Kingdom by virtue of—

(a)   any directly applicable Community legislation, or

(b)   any Act or statutory instrument implementing such agreement.

"representative", in relation to any person, means—

(a)   his personal representative,

(b)   his trustee in bankruptcy or interim or permanent trustee,

(c)   any receiver or liquidator appointed in relation to that person or any of his property,

or any other person acting in a representative capacity in relation to that person.

3 Penalty for contravention of a relevant export rule

(1)   If a person engages in any conduct by which he contravenes a relevant export rule specified he shall be liable to a penalty under this regulation.

(2)   The Schedule to these regulations shall have effect.

(3)   Column 1 of the Schedule specifies a relevant export rule a contravention of which gives rise to a penalty under paragraph (1) above.

(4)   Column 2 of the Schedule specifies the person whose conduct in contravening a relevant export rule gives rise to liability under paragraph (1) above.

(5)   Column 3 of the Schedule specifies the maximum penalty for contravention of a relevant export rule for which a person is liable under paragraph (1) above.

4 Exceptions from regulation 3

(1)   A person is not liable to a penalty under regulation 3 if he satisfies—

    (a)   the Commissioners, or

    (b)   on appeal, an appeal tribunal,

that there is a reasonable excuse for his conduct.

(2)   For the purposes of paragraph (1) above none of the following is a reasonable excuse—

    (a)   An insufficiency of funds available to any person for paying any penalty due;

    (b)   That reliance was placed by any person on another to perform any task;

    (c)   That the contravention is attributable, in whole or in part, to the conduct of a person on whom reliance to perform any task was so placed.

(3)   Where, by reason of conduct falling within regulation 3(1) a person is prosecuted for an offence that conduct does not also give rise to liability to a penalty.

5 Reduction of penalty under regulation 3

(1)   Where a person is liable to a penalty under regulation 3—

    (a)   the Commissioners (whether originally or on review) or, on appeal, an appeal tribunal may reduce the penalty to such amount (including nil) as they think proper; and

    (b)   the Commissioners on a review, or an appeal tribunal on an appeal, relating to a penalty reduced by the Commissioners under this regulation may cancel the whole or any part of the reduction previously made by the Commissioners.

(2)   In exercising their powers under paragraph (1) above, neither the Commissioners nor an appeal tribunal are entitled to take into account any of the matters specified in paragraph (3) below.

(3)   Those matters are—

    (a)   The insufficiency of the funds available to any person for paying the amount of the penalty,

    (b)   The fact that the person liable to the penalty, or a person acting on his behalf, has acted in good faith.

6 Demands for penalties

(1)   Where a person is liable to a penalty under regulation 3, the Commissioners may give to that person or his representative a notice in writing (a "demand notice") demanding payment of the amount due by way of penalty.

(2)   An amount demanded as due from a person or his representative in accordance with subsection (1) is recoverable as if it were an amount due from the person or, as the case may be, the representative as an amount of customs duty.

This paragraph is subject to—

    (a)   any appeal under regulation 12 (appeals to tribunal); and

    (b)   paragraph (3) below.

(3)   An amount so demanded is not recoverable if or to the extent that—

    (a)   The demand has subsequently been withdrawn; or

    (b)   The amount has been reduced under regulation 5.

7 Time limits for demands for penalties

(1)   A demand notice may not be given in relation to a penalty under regulation 3 more than 3 years after the conduct giving rise to the penalty ceased.

(2)   A demand notice may not be given more than 2 years after there has come to the knowledge of the Commissioners evidence of facts sufficient in the opinion of the Commissioners to justify the giving of the demand notice.

(3)   A demand notice may be given in respect of a penalty under regulation 3 to which a person was liable immediately before his death.

8 No prosecution after demand notice for penalty under regulation 3

(1)   Where a demand notice is given demanding payment of an amount due by way of penalty under regulation 3 in respect of any conduct of a person, no proceedings may be brought against that person for any offence constituted by that conduct (whether or not the demand notice is subsequently withdrawn).

9 Right to review of certain decisions

(1)   If the Commissioners give a person or his representative a notice informing him—

(a)   that they have decided that the person has engaged in conduct by which he contravenes a relevant export rule, and

(b)   that the person is, in consequence, liable to a penalty under regulation 3, but

(c)   that they do not propose to give a demand notice in respect of the penalty,

the person or his representative may give a notice to the Commissioners requiring them to review the decision mentioned in sub-paragraph(a) above.

(2)   Where the Commissioners give a demand notice to a person or his representative, the person or his representative may by notice require the Commissioners to review—

(a)   their decision that the person is liable to a penalty under regulation 3, or

(b)   their decision as to the amount of the liability.

(3)   A person may not under this regulation require a review of a decision under regulation 11 (decision on review).

10 Time limit and right to further review

(1)   The Commissioners are not required under regulation 9 to review any decision unless the notice requiring the review is given before the end of the permitted period.

(2)   For the purposes of this regulation the "permitted period" is the period of 45 days beginning with the day on which the relevant notice is given.

(3)   For the purposes of paragraph (2) above the "relevant notice" is—

(a)   in the case of a review by virtue of paragraph (1) of regulation 9, the notice mentioned in that paragraph; or

(b)   in any other case, the demand notice in question.

(4)   Nothing in paragraph (1) prevents the Commissioners from agreeing on request to review a decision in a case where the notice required by that paragraph is not given within the permitted period.

(5)   A person may give notice under regulation 9 requiring a decision to be reviewed a second or subsequent time only if—

(a)   the grounds on which he requires the further review are that the Commissioners did not, on any previous review, have the opportunity to consider any particular facts or matters; and

(b)   he does not, on the further review, require the Commissioners to consider any facts or matters which were considered on a previous review of the decision, except insofar as they are relevant to any issue to which the facts or matters not previously considered relate.

11 Powers of the Commissioners on a review

(1) Where the Commissioners—

    (a)   are required in accordance with regulation 9 to review a decision, or

    (b)   agree to do so on such a request as is mentioned in regulation 10(4)

the following provisions of this regulation apply.

(2) On any such review, the Commissioners may—

    (a)   confirm the decision,

    (b)   withdraw the decision, or

    (c)   vary the decision.

(3) Where the Commissioners withdraw or vary the decision, they may also take such further steps (if any) in consequence of the withdrawal or variation as they consider appropriate.

(4) If the Commissioners do not within the permitted period give notice of their determination on the review to the person who required the review or his representative, they shall be taken to have confirmed the decision.

(5) For the purposes of paragraph(4), the "permitted period" is the period of 45 days beginning with the day on which the review—

    (a)   is required by the person or his representative in accordance with regulation 9, or

    (b)   is agreed to by the Commissioners as mentioned in regulation 10(4).

12 Appeals to a tribunal

(1) Where the Commissioners—

    (a)   are required in accordance with regulation 9 to review a decision, or

    (b)   agree to do so on such a request as is mentioned in regulation 10(4),

an appeal lies to an appeal tribunal against any decision by the Commissioners on the review (including any confirmation under regulation 11(4)).

(2) An appeal lies under this regulation only if the appellant is one of the following persons—

    (a)   the person who required the review in question,

    (b)   where the person who required the review in question did so as representative of another person, that other person, or

    (c)   a representative of a person falling within paragraph (a) or (b).

(3) The powers of an appeal tribunal on an appeal under this section include—

    (a)   power to quash or vary a decision; and

    (b)   power to substitute the tribunal's own decision for any decision so quashed.

(4) On an appeal under this regulation—

    (a)   the burden of proof as to the matters mentioned in regulation 3(1) lies on the Commissioners; but

    (b)   it is otherwise for the appellant to show that the grounds on which any such appeal is brought have been established.

13 Appeal Tribunals

(1) Sections 85 and 87 of the Value Added Tax Act 1994 (c 23) (settling of appeals by agreement and enforcement of decisions of tribunals) have effect as if—

    (a)   any reference to section 83 of that Act included a reference to regulation 12, and

    (b)   any reference to VAT included a reference to any relevant export rule.

(2) The provision that may be made by rules under paragraph 9 of Schedule 12 to the Value Added Tax Act 1984 (rules of procedure for tribunals) includes provision for costs awarded against an appellant on an appeal by virtue of these Regulations to be recoverable as if the amount awarded were an amount of customs duty which the appellant is required to pay.

14 Service of notices

Any notice to be given to any person for the purposes of these Regulations may be given by sending it by post in a letter addressed to that person or his representative at the last or usual residence or place of business of that person or representative.

SCHEDULE

Column 1 *Relevant Export Rule*	Column 2 *Description of Person liable*	Column 3 *Maximum Penalty*
Article 161(2) of the Code All Community goods intended for export to be placed under the export procedure, except goods to be placed under the outward processing procedure or transit procedure.	Any person intending to send goods outside the Community.	£1000
Article 183 of the Code And Articles 793, 794 and 795 of the Implementing Regulation Goods leaving the customs territory of the Community subject to customs supervision shall:	The exporter.	£2500
(a) be presented to customs authorities in accordance with the provisions in force in order that checks may be carried out; and	Approved exporter. Any person.	£2500 £2500
(b) leave the territory of the Community using, where appropriate, the route determined by the customs authorities.		
Articles 59(1) of the Code Goods shall be covered by a declaration for the customs procedure of export.	A person who is able to present the goods in question or to have them presented to the competent customs authority together with all the documents required to be produced.	£1000
	A specific person (where acceptance of a declaration imposes particular obligations on that person).	£1000

Column 1 *Relevant Export Rule*	Column 2 *Description of Person liable*	Column 3 *Maximum Penalty*
	By an agent on his behalf.	£1000
	By a direct agent in the case of a specific person.	£1000
Article 59(2) of the Code		
Community goods declared for export subject to customs supervision from acceptance of the declaration until they leave the customs territory of the Community.	The declarant The exporter.	£1000 £1000
Article 62 of the Code and Article 199 of the Implementing Regulation and Sections 167(3) 168(1) of the Act		
Declarations shall be: (a) made on a form corresponding to the official specimen prescribed for the purpose;	Any person who is able to present the goods in question together with the documents required for the application of the rules governing the procedure.	£2500
(b) signed and contain all the particulars necessary for implementation of the provisions of the customs procedure for export; and	A specific person (where acceptance of a declaration imposes particular obligations on that specific person).	£2500
(c) be accompanied by all the documents required for implementation of the customs procedure of export.	By an agent on his behalf. By a direct agent in the case of a specific person.	£2500 £2500
Article 161(5) of the Code and Articles 789 and 790 of the Implementing Regulation		
Export declaration to be lodged at: The customs office responsible for supervising:	Any person who is able to present the goods in question together with the documents required for the application of the rules governing the procedure.	£1000
(a) the place where the exporter is established; or (b) the place where the goods are packed or loaded for export shipment; or	A specific person (where acceptance of the declaration imposes particular obligations on that specific person).	£1000

Column 1 *Relevant Export Rule*	Column 2 *Description of Person liable*	Column 3 *Maximum Penalty*
(c) the place where the sub-contractor is established (as permitted pursuant to Article 789); and, any customs office competent for the operation in question (permitted pursuant to Article 790).	By an agent on his behalf. By a direct agent in the case of a specific person.	£1000 £1000
Article 793 of the Implementing Regulation Goods released for export to be presented at the customs office of exit together with copy three of the Single Administrative Document.	The exporter. Any person who is able to present the goods in question together with the documents required for the application of the rules governing the procedure. A specific person (where acceptance of the declaration imposes particular obligations on that specific person).	£1000 £1000 £1000
Article 795 of the Implementing Regulation Declaration for export to be lodged retrospectively by the exporter at the competent customs office where goods leave the customs territory of the Community without an export declaration.	By an agent on his behalf. By a direct agent in the case of a specific person. The exporter. Any person who is able to present the goods in question together with the documents required for the application of the rules governing the procedure.	£1000 £1000 £1000 £1000
	A specific person (where acceptance of the declaration imposes particular obligations on that specific person). By an agent on his behalf. By a direct agent in the case of a specific person	£1000 £1000
Article 796 of the Implementing Regulation		

Column 1 *Relevant Export Rule*	Column 2 *Description of Person liable*	Column 3 *Maximum Penalty*
The exporter to immediately inform the customs office of Export and return copy 3 of the export declaration where goods released for export do not leave the customs territory of the Community.	The exporter. Any person who is able to present the goods in question together with the documents required for the application of the rules governing the procedure.	£1000 £1000
	A specific person (where acceptance of the declaration imposes particular obligations on that specific person).	£1000
	By an agent on his behalf.	£1000
	By a direct agent in the case of a specific person.	£1000
Article 798 of the Implementing Regulation Export declaration in the specified form to be presented to the customs office of export where goods which left the customs territory of the Community under cover of an ATA carnet are no longer intended to be re-imported.	The exporter. Any person who is able to present the goods in question together with the documents required for the application of the rules governing the procedure.	£1000 £1000
	A specific person (where acceptance of the declaration imposes particular obligations on that specific person).	£1000
	By an agent on his behalf.	£1000
	By a direct agent in the case of a specific person.	£1000
Article 162 of the Code Condition that goods granted release for export leave the customs territory of the Community in the same condition as when the export declaration was accepted.	The exporter.	£1000
Simplified Procedure		
Articles 6 and 7 and 76 of the Code and Articles 282 and 261 and 262 of the Implementing Regulation		

Column 1 *Relevant Export Rule*	Column 2 *Description of Person liable*	Column 3 *Maximum Penalty*
To comply with a condition of an immediately enforceable binding decision of the customs authorities, in respect of an authorisation to make the declaration for export in a simplified form.	The exporter. The person authorised.	£2500 £2500
Local Clearance		
Articles 283, 284 and 264 of the Implementing Regulation Maintain records sufficient to enable the customs authority to carry out effective checks, in particular, retrospective checks.	Approved exporter.	£2500
Articles 6 and 7 of the Code and Articles 283, 286 and 287 of the Implementing Regulation To comply with a condition of an immediately enforceable binding decision of the customs authorities, in respect of an authorisation referred to in Article 283 of the Implementing Regulation.	Approved exporter.	£2500

CUSTOMS (CONTRAVENTION OF A RELEVANT RULE) REGULATIONS 2003

(SI 2003/3113)

NOTES

Made: 2 December 2003.

Authority: Finance Act 2003, ss 26(1)–(4), 41

Commencement: 23 December 2003.

1 Citation and Commencement

These Regulations may be cited as the Customs (Contravention of a Relevant Rule) Regulations 2003 and shall come into force on 23rd December 2003.

2 Interpretation

In these Regulations—

"the Act" means the Customs and Excise Management Act 1979;

"the Accounts and Records Regulations" means the Customs Traders (Accounts and Records) Regulations 1995;

"the Aircraft Report Regulations" means the Aircraft (Customs and Excise) Regulations 1981;

"the 1994 Act" means the Finance Act 1994;

"the Code" means Council Regulation 2913/92/EEC;

"Customs" means the customs authority of the United Kingdom;

"Customs authority of the United Kingdom" has the meaning "the Commissioners" as defined in section 1 of the Act;

for the purpose of the Code and the Implementing Regulation customs authority of the United Kingdom is one of the "customs authorities" defined in Article 4(3) with responsibility for *inter alia* applying customs rules within the territory of the United Kingdom;

"contravene" has the meaning assigned to it by section 24(3) of the Finance Act 2003;

"customs approved treatment or use" has the meaning assigned to it by Article 4(15) of the Code;

"customs procedure" has the meaning assigned to it by Article 4(16) of the Code;

"customs procedure with economic impact" has the meaning assigned to it by Article 84(1)(b) of the Code;

"declaration" has the meaning assigned to it by Article 4(17) of the Code;

"the Implementing Regulation" means Commission Regulation 2454/93/EEC as it implements the Code;

"the Importation Regulations" means the Customs Controls on Importation of Goods Regulations 1991;

"officer" has the meaning assigned to it by section 1 of the Act;

"the Personal Reliefs Order" means the Customs and Excise Duties (Personal Reliefs for Goods Permanently Imported) Order 1992;

"the Postal Packets Regulations" means the Postal Packets (Customs and Excise) Regulations 1986;

"products remaining" has the meaning as defined in Article 104(2) of Council Regulation 918/83/EEC;

"proper officer" means in relation to the person by, with or to whom anything is to be done, the person appointed or authorised in that behalf by the Commissioners;

"relevant rule" has the meaning assigned to it by section 24(3) of the Finance Act 2003;

"relevant tax or duty" has the meaning assigned to it by section 24(2) of the Finance Act 2003;

"the Relief Regulation" means Council Regulation 918/83/EEC;

"the Ship's Report Regulations" means the Ship's Report, Importation and Exportation by Sea Regulations 1981;

"the Transit Regulations" means the Customs and Excise (Transit) Regulations 1993.

3 Relevant Rule and Amount of Penalty

(1)   The Schedule to these regulations shall have effect.

(2)   An entry in Column 1 of the Schedule specifies the relevant rule or the description of a relevant rule in the case of any relevant tax or duty to which it applies for the purposes of section 26(1) of the Finance Act 2003 (Penalty for contravention of relevant rule).

(3)   An entry in Column 2 of the Schedule adjacent to an entry in Column 1 specifies a person, of the description there laid out, who shall be liable to a penalty under section 26 of the Finance Act 2003 (where his conduct contravenes the relevant rule or a relevant rule of the description specified for the purposes of that section).

(4)   An entry in Column 3 of the Schedule adjacent to an entry in Columns 1 and 2 specifies for the purposes of section 26(1) of the Finance Act 2003 the maximum amount of the penalty which may be imposed upon a person specified for the purposes of that section as liable for that contravention of that specified relevant rule.

(5)   Any description of a relevant rule specified in Column 1 and any description of a person prescribed in Column 2 of the Schedule is without prejudice to the effect of any directly applicable Community provision so described or description of a person responsible contained in that provision so described.

(6)   A specified relevant rule or description of a person shall be construed in accordance with the effect and scope of that directly applicable Community provision referred to in Column 1.

SCHEDULE

Column 1	Column 2	Column 3
Description of relevant Rule/Relevant Rule of a description	*Person of a description*	*Person of a description*
Report		
Section 35(1) of the Act		
To report in such form and manner containing such particulars as Customs direct.	The master.	£1,000
	Person authorised by the master.	£1,000
	Commander of the aircraft.	
Ship's Report Regulations: Regulation 3		
Completion of the forms directed by Customs under s 35(1) by the master, or a person authorised by him (as Customs permit).	The master	£1,000
	Person authorised by the master.	£1,000
Regulation 4		

Column 1	Column 2	Column 3
Description of relevant Rule/Relevant Rule of a description	*Person of a description*	*Person of a description*
Delivery of a duly completed report: (a) to a boarding officer immediately on request; (b) to the place designated within three hours of the ship having reached its place of loading or unloading; or (c) on the expiration of twenty four hours following arrival within the limits of the port when a ship has not arrived at its place of loading or unloading.	The master. Person authorised by the master.	£1,000 £1,000
Regulation 5		
To retain on board as long as the ship remains within the limits of the port a copy of the form of report for inspection by an officer.	The master.	£1,000
Aircraft Report Regulations:		
Regulation 4(1)		
Delivery to the proper officer of: (a) a General Declaration; (b) particulars of the goods on the aircraft; and (c) a list in duplicate of the stores on board the aircraft.	Commander of the aircraft.	£1,000
Section 35(6) of the Act		
To answer all such question relating to:	The master.	£1,000
(a) the ship or aircraft;	Person authorised by the master.	£1,000
(b) the goods carried therein;		
(c) the crew; and	Commander of the aircraft.	£1,000
(d) the voyage or flight as put to him by the proper officer.		
Section 35(7) of the Act		
Where prior to report:	The master.	£1,000
(a) bulk is broken;	Person authorised by the master.	£1,000
(b) stowage of any goods is altered to facilitate unloading of any part thereof before making report;	Commander of the aircraft.	£1,000
(c) any part of the goods are staved, destroyed, thrown overboard; or		
(d) a container opened		
and no proper explanation is given to the satisfaction of Customs.		
Goods brought into the customs territory of the Community (United Kingdom)		

Part II

1051

Column 1	Column 2	Column 3
Description of relevant Rule/Relevant Rule of a description	*Person of a description*	*Person of a description*
Article 38 of the Code		
To convey the goods to the customs office designated or free zone by the route specified, without delay and in accordance with the instructions of Customs.	Person bringing the goods into the Community customs territory.	£1,000
	Any person who assumes responsibility for the carriage of the goods after they have been brought into the Community customs territory.	£1,000
Article 39 of the Code		
Pursuant to Article 39, to inform without delay the Customs of:	In respect of Article 39(1) the person bringing the goods into the Community customs territory; or	£1,000
(a) the inability to comply with Article 38(1) due to unforeseen circumstances or force majeure; and	Any person who assumes responsibility for the carriage of the goods after they have been brought into the customs territory.	£1,000
(b) the precise location of the goods where the unforeseen circumstances or force majeure does not result in the total loss of the goods.	In respect of Article 39(2), the person bringing the vessel or aircraft into the customs territory, or in respect of either provision any other person acting in his place.	£1,000
Presentation of Goods to Customs		
Article 40 of the Code		
To present goods entering the United Kingdom at a customs office or other place designated.	The person who brought the goods into the customs territory of the Community.	£1,000
	The person who assumes responsibility for carriage for the goods following entry into the customs territory.	£1,000
Regulation 3 of the Importation Regulations		
To notify Customs:		

Column 1	Column 2	Column 3
Description of relevant Rule/Relevant Rule of a description	*Person of a description*	*Person of a description*
(a) of the arrival of goods in the prescribed form or where approved, by computerised record capable of being printed out; and	The person who brought the goods into the customs territory.	£1,000
(b) to make such notification within three hours of the arrival of the ship at the wharf or aircraft at the airport, or if the customs office is closed within one hour following the reopening of the office.	The person who assumes responsibility for carriage of the goods following entry.	£1,000
Article 42 of the Code		
To seek permission of the Customs before examination or sampling of goods in order that they may be assigned a customs approved treatment or use.	The person authorised to assign the goods a customs approved treatment or use.	£1,000
	Any person able to present the goods or to have them presented. A person subject to a specific obligation in relation to goods being assigned to a customs approved treatment or use.	£1,000
	Any person doing so on his behalf.	£1,000
Articles 43 and 44 of the Code and Article 183 of the Implementing Regulation and Regulation 4 of the Importation Regulations		
Upon presentation of the goods or within the period specified a signed summary declaration shall be lodged in the form prescribed. The form shall correspond to the model prescribed by the Customs.	The person who brought the goods into the customs territory.	£1,000
	Any person who assumes responsibility for carriage of the goods following entry into the customs territory.	£1,000
	The person in whose name those above acted.	£1,000
Article 46 of the Code Goods shall:		

Column 1	Column 2	Column 3
Description of relevant Rule/Relevant Rule of a description	*Person of a description*	*Person of a description*
(a) except in the event of imminent danger, only be unloaded or transhipped from the means of transport with the permission of Customs and in places designated or approved or;	The person who brought the goods into the customs territory.	£1,000
	The person who assumes responsibility for the carriage of the goods following entry into the Customs territory.	£1,000
(b) be unloaded and unpacked as required by Customs for the purposes of inspecting the goods and means of transport. Where permission is not required, Customs shall be informed forthwith of the unloading or transhipment of the goods. **Article 47 of the Code**	The person responsible for the contravention of the Importation Regulations.	£1,000
Goods shall not be removed from their original position without permission of Customs.	The person who brought the goods into the customs territory of the Community.	£1,000
	The person who assumes responsibility for the carriage of goods following entry into the customs territory.	£1,000
Articles 48 and 49 and 59 of the Code and Regulation 5 of the Importation Regulation Goods shall be assigned to a customs approved treatment or use within the period prescribed in Article 49.	The person who brought the goods into the customs territory of the Community.	
Entry to a customs approved treatment or use shall be effected by the delivery of an appropriate declaration presented to the proper officer pursuant to regulation 5.	The person who is able to present the goods to customs. The importer within the meaning of the Act	£1,000
	The importer within the meaning of the Act	£1,000
Article 51 of the Code		

Column 1	Column 2	Column 3
Description of relevant Rule/Relevant Rule of a description	*Person of a description*	*Person of a description*
Goods in temporary storage shall be stored only at places approved and under the conditions laid down by Customs.	The person bringing the goods into the customs territory of the Community	£1,000
The provision of security where required by Customs.	The person who removed the goods from customs supervision.	£1,000
	The person who participated in such removal.	£1,000
	The person required to fulfil the obligations arising from temporary storage.	£1,000
Customs Declarations **Article 59 of the Code** Goods intended to be placed under a customs procedure shall be covered by a declaration.	Any person who is able to present the goods in question together with the documents required for the application of the rules governing the procedure.	£2,500
	A specific person (where acceptance of a declaration imposes particular obligations on that specific person).	£2,500
	An agent acting on his behalf.	£2,500
Articles 62 and 77 of the Code and Article 199 of the Implementing Regulation **Section 167(3) of the Act** Declarations shall be:	By a direct agent in the case of a specific person.	£2,500

Part II

Column 1	Column 2	Column 3
Description of relevant Rule/Relevant Rule of a description	*Person of a description*	*Person of a description*
(a) made on a form corresponding to the official specimen prescribed for the purpose; (b) signed and contain all the particulars necessary for implementation of the provisions of the customs procedure; and (c) accompanied by all the documents required for implementation of the provisions of the customs procedure.	Any person who is able to present the goods in question together with the documents required for the application of the rules governing the customs procedure. A specific person (where acceptance of a declaration imposes particular obligations on that specific person).	£2,500 £2,500
	By an agent on his behalf.	£2,500
	By a direct agent in the case of a specific person.	£2,500
Simplified Procedures **Articles 6 and 7 of the Code and Articles 260 to 262 of the Implementing Regulation** To comply with a condition of an immediately enforceable binding decision of Customs, in respect of an authorisation referred to in Article 260.	The person granted permission to operate simplified procedures.	£2,500
	The declarant authorised in accordance with the conditions and in a manner laid down in Article 260 of the Implementing Regulation.	£2,500
Article 76 of the Code and Article 199 of the Implementing Regulation Simplified declaration, commercial or administrative document, or entry in the records shall contain particulars necessary for the identification of the goods.	The person granted permission to operate simplified procedures.	£2,500
Where the goods are entered for the procedure in question by means of an entry in the records, the date of such entry must be included.	The declarant authorised in accordance with the conditions and in the manner laid down in Article 260 of the Implementing Regulation.	£2,500
Furnish a supplementary declaration.		

Column 1	Column 2	Column 3
Description of relevant Rule/Relevant Rule of a description	*Person of a description*	*Person of a description*
Articles 199 and 260 of the Implementing Regulation		
To make a simplified declaration containing at least the particulars necessary for identification of the goods.	The person granted permission to operate simplified procedures.	£2,500
Where authorised by a general request for release a reference to that authorisation shall be entered on the commercial or administrative document.	The declarant authorised in accordance with the conditions and in a manner laid down in Article 260 of the Implementing Regulation.	£2,500
A simplified declaration shall be accompanied by all documents, production of which may be required to secure the release of goods for free circulation.		
Article 261 of the Implementing Regulation		
That it is possible to guarantee an effective check on compliance with provisions governing release of goods for free circulation.	The person granted permission to operate simplified procedures.	£2,500
	The declarant authorised in accordance with the conditions and in a manner laid down in Article 260 of the Implementing Regulation.	£2,500
Local Clearance Procedure		
Articles 6 and 7 of the Code and Articles 263 to 267, of the Implementing Regulation		
To comply with a condition of an immediately enforceable binding decision of Customs, in respect of an authorisation referred to in Article 263.	The person granted permission to operate simplified procedures	£2,500
	The declarant authorised in accordance with the conditions and in a manner laid down in Article 260 of the Implementing Regulation.	£2,500
Customs Procedure with Economic Impact		

Column 1	Column 2	Column 3
Description of relevant Rule/Relevant Rule of a description	*Person of a description*	*Person of a description*
Articles 6, 7, 85 to 87 and 90 of the Code and Articles 505 to 508 of the Implementing Regulation	The person to whom the authorisation for use of any customs procedure with economic impact is issued.	£2,500
To comply with a condition (including special conditions governing the procedure in question) of an immediately enforceable binding decision of Customs, in respect of an authorisation or transferred obligations for use of any customs procedure with economic impact referred to in Articles 85 to 87a	Any person to whom the conditions or obligations of a customs procedure with economic impact are transferred.	£2,500
To notify Customs of all factors arising after the authorisation is granted and which may influence its continuation or content.	Any authorised person.	£2,500
Articles 105 of the Code and Article 528 of the Implementing Regulation		
In respect of customs warehousing, the designated person shall keep stock records of all the goods placed under the customs warehousing procedure in the form approved by Customs.	The designated person.	£1,000
End Use		
Articles 6, 7, 21, 82, 85 to 87 and 90 of the Code and Article 292 and 293 of the Implementing Regulation		
To comply with a condition of an immediately enforceable binding decision of Customs in respect of an authorisation or a transferred obligation under end-use referred to in Article 21 or 82.	The person to whom the authorisation for End Use is issued.	£2,500
Free Zones		
Articles 6, 7, 167 and 172 of the Code and Articles 800 and 801 of the Implementing Regulation		
To comply with a condition of an immediately enforceable binding decision of Customs in respect of an approval for a free zone.	The person to whom the approval for a free zone has been granted.	£2,500
Article 105 of the Code and Articles 803 and 804 of the Implementing Regulation		

Column 1	Column 2	Column 3
Description of relevant Rule/Relevant Rule of a description	*Person of a description*	*Person of a description*
The person designated shall keep stock records of all the goods placed under the customs warehousing procedure in the form approved by Customs.	The designated person.	£1,000
Transit **Article 96 of the Code and The Schedule to the Transit Regulations** Obligation to: (a) produce the goods intact at the customs office of destination within the time limit prescribed;	The principal to the transit operation.	£2,500
(b) duly observe the measures adopted by Customs to ensure identification of the goods; (c) duly observe the provisions relating to the Community/common transit procedures and comply with any relevant Community provision.	A carrier or recipient of goods who accepts the goods knowing they are moving under Community transit.	£2,500
Article 94(1) of the Code To furnish a guarantee.	The principal or authorisation holder.	£2,500
Articles 6 and 7 of the Code and Articles 372 to 376 of the Implementing Regulation To comply with a condition of authorisation (including the conditions for use of simplifications and operating and control methods) of an immediately enforceable binding decision of Customs to authorise simplifications of Community transit.	The principal. The consignee.	£2,500 £2,500
Information and Records **Article 14 of the Code and section 23 of the 1994 Act** Any obligation to provide, furnish, or produce information or documents to Customs (whether subject to time limit or reasonable demand) in such form as may reasonably be required for examination, copying or making extracts or removal for such purposes and whether for a reasonable or specified period.	The person directly or indirectly involved in the customs operation concerned for the purposes of trade in goods.	£1,000

Column 1	Column 2	Column 3
Description of relevant Rule/Relevant Rule of a description	*Person of a description*	*Person of a description*
	Any person carrying on a trade or business within the meaning of section 20 of the 1994 Act.	£1,000
Article 16 of the Code and Regulations 3 to 5 and 9 of the Accounts and Records Regulations		
Any obligation for purposes of control by Customs to: (a) keep a record received or issued;	The person directly or indirectly involved in the customs operation concerned for the purposes of trade in goods.	£1,000
(b) preserve a received record and keep and preserve a copy of an issued record;		
(c) preserve a prepared or maintained record which has not been received or issued; (d) keep and preserve a copy of every supplementary declaration made (or made on behalf of the person concerned) or a record of all the information set out in that declaration; (e) keep and preserve a copy of every simplified declaration made (or made on behalf of the person concerned) or a record of all the information set out in that declaration; (f) keep and preserve such other records as Customs may specify in any case or cases in a notice published by them; (g) ensure that any record, kept or preserved which relates to a customs declaration, is so kept or preserved that it is readily apparent that it relates to that declaration; (h) preserve any record or copy of a record for a period of four years (or such lesser period as Customs may require).	A customs trader (any person carrying on a trade or business which consists of or includes any of the activities mentioned in section 20(1) of the 1994 Act).	£1,000
Assistance in Examination of goods		
Articles 241 and 243 of the Implementing Regulation		
To render Customs:	The declarant.	£1,000

Column 1	Column 2	Column 3
Description of relevant Rule/Relevant Rule of a description	*Person of a description*	*Person of a description*
(a) satisfactory assistance to facilitate examination or sampling of goods; and (b) where necessary, by a deadline set by that authority.	The person designated by the declarant to be present at the examination of the goods.	£1,000
Postal Packets **Articles 49 and 59 of the Code and Article 237(4) of the Implementing Regulation and Regulation 5a and 14 of the Postal Packets Regulations and Regulation 5 of the Importation Regulations** Where notified by Customs of a requirement to make a declaration, it shall be made in the form determined by them and shall be presented to the proper officer within 28 days.	The addressee of the packet.	£1,000
	Any other person who is, or for the time being, is the importer of the goods within the meaning of the Act.	£1,000
Regulation 9 of the Postal Packets Regulations Requirement to have affixed to the bag label a green label in the prescribed form.	The postal operator.	£1,000
	The universal service provider within the meaning of the Postal Services Act 2000.	£1,000
Regulation 11 of the Postal Packets Regulations Requirement to perform, in relation to any postal packet or the goods it contains, such duties required by virtue of the customs and excise Acts to be performed by the importer, as Customs may require.	The proper officer of the postal operator.	£1,000
Regulation 12 of the Postal Packets Regulations Requirement to: (a) produce to the proper officer postal packets arriving in the United Kingdom, (b) pen for customs examination any packets so produced.	The proper officer of the postal operator.	£1,000

Part II

Column 1	Column 2	Column 3
Description of relevant Rule/Relevant Rule of a description	*Person of a description*	*Person of a description*
Regulation 17 of the Postal Packets Regulations		
Requirement to deliver to the proper officer any postal packet upon the ground that any goods contained in it are liable to forfeiture.	The proper officer of the postal operator.	£1,000
Preference		
Section 80 of the Act		
(a) To furnish information in such form and within such time as may be specified; (b) To produce for inspection, copying or the taking of extracts, invoices, bills of lading, books or documents specified; as Customs or an officer may require for the purpose of verifying or investigating any certificate or other evidence under any Community requirement;	Any person appearing to the Customs or an officer to have been concerned in any way with the goods, or with any goods from which directly or indirectly they have been produced or manufactured, or to have been concerned with the obtaining or furnishing of the certificate or evidence.	£1,000
	The exporter	£1,000
(i) as to the origin of goods; or (ii) as to payments made or relief from duty allowed in any country or territory.		
Article 199 of the Implementing Regulation **Section 167(3) of the Act** **Community international agreements according to preferential rates of duty**		
Accurate completion of an EUR 1 or equivalent certifying Community origin for goods under any obligation of a particular international agreement entered into by the Community applying as part of the law of the United Kingdom in relation to a relevant tax or duty by virtue of directly applicable Community legislation.	The exporter.	£2,500
Community System of Duty Reliefs **Articles 7(1), 7(2) and Articles 15(1), 15(2) and Articles 37 and 38 of the Relief Regulation**		

Column 1	Column 2	Column 3
Description of relevant Rule/Relevant Rule of a description	*Person of a description*	*Person of a description*
To pre-notify the competent authorities and/or pay any unpaid duty where any of the following goods are lent, given as security, hired out, or transferred (whether for consideration or free of charge) within 12 months of acceptance of entry for free circulation, or in respect of Article 37, 36 months where that period is so extended:	In respect of Article 7, the person accorded relief from duties on the importation of the goods on the transfer of their normal place of residence.	£1,000
(a) personal property imported upon transfer of normal residence; (b) goods imported on the occasion of a marriage;	In respect of Article 15, the person accorded relief from duties on the importation of the goods on the occasion of a marriage.	£1,000
(c) capital goods and other equipment including that belonging to persons engaged in a liberal profession and to legal persons engaged in a non-profit making activity.	In respect of Articles 37 and 38, the person accorded relief from duties on the importation of capital goods and other equipment.	£1,000
As applied in relation to import VAT under the Personal Reliefs Order: (a) Parts I to IV in relation to Article 7 of the Relief Regulation; (b) Parts I to III and V in relation to Article 15 of the Relief Regulation **Article 24(1) of the Relief Regulation**		
Except where the relief continues to apply in respect of a new secondary residence and in accordance with Article 22(b) and (c), where within a two year period from the date of acceptance of the entry for free circulation of the household effects or within 10 years after of such entry, where the period is so extended in respect of valuable household effects, a secondary residence is hired or transferred to a third person, the import duties on those household effects shall be paid at the rate applicable at the time of the relevant hire or transfer. **Article 24(2) of the Relief Regulation**	The person accorded relief from duties on the importation of household effects to furnish a secondary residence.	£1,000

Part II

Column 1	Column 2	Column 3
Description of relevant Rule/Relevant Rule of a description	*Person of a description*	*Person of a description*
To pay any relevant duty where the household effects are lent, given as security, hired out, or transferred (whether for consideration or free of charge) within 2 years of acceptance of entry for free circulation or within 10 years after such entry, where the period is so extended in respect of valuable household effects and under the same conditions referred to in Article 24(1). **Article 57 Article 63b Article 68 Articles 76 and 77 of the Relief Regulation**	The person accorded relief from duties on the importation of household effects to furnish a secondary residence.	£1,000
To pre-notify the competent authorities where any: (a) educational, scientific and cultural materials, scientific instruments and apparatus identified in Articles 51, 53, 54, 56 (for the purposes of Article 57); or	The person accorded relief under Articles 51 and 52(2).	£1,000
(b) instruments or apparatus intended for medical research, establishing medical diagnosis or carrying out medical treatment referred to in Article 63a (for the purposes of Article 63b)); or	The recipient bodies accorded relief under Articles 63a(1)	£1,000
(c) goods for charitable or philanthropic organisations (for the purposes of Article 68); or	The organisation benefiting from the relief under Article 68.	£1,000
(d) articles specially designed for the educational, scientific or cultural advancement of blind or education, employment or social advancement of handicapped persons (other than blind persons) (for the purposes of Articles 76 and 77) are lent, hired out, or transferred (whether for consideration or free of charge).	The person, institute or organisation benefiting from the relief under Articles 71 and 72.	£1,000
To pre-pay import duties due, except where the goods are lent, hired out or transferred (whether for consideration or free of charge) to an establishment or organisation which is entitled to benefit from the relief pursuant to:		

Column 1	Column 2	Column 3
Description of relevant Rule/Relevant Rule of a description	*Person of a description*	*Person of a description*
(a) Articles 51 or 52(2) (for the purposes of Articles 57 and 63(b));or	The person accorded relief under Articles 51 and 52(2) who lends, hires out or transfers the goods.	£1,000
(b) Articles 65 and 67 (for the purposes of Article 68); or	The organisation benefiting from the relief under Article 68.	£1,000
(c) Article 76(2) (for the purposes of Article 76); or	The person, institute or organisation benefiting from the relief under Articles 71 and 72.	£1,000
(d) Article 77(2) (for the purposes of Article 77)	The person, institute or organisation benefiting from the relief under Articles 71 and 72.	£1,000
and uses the article, instrument or apparatus for purposes which confer such relief.		
Article 59 of the Relief Regulation		
To pre-notify the competent authorities where:		
(a) any of the equipment referred to in Article 59a is lent, hired out, or transferred (whether for consideration or free of charge);	The scientific research establishment or organisation benefiting from the relief under Article 59a.	£1,000
(b) an establishment or organisation referred to in Article 59a(1) which no longer fulfils the conditions to qualify for relief or proposes to use the equipment other than for the purposes provided for under that Article.	The scientific research establishment or organisation benefiting from the relief under Article 59a.	£1,000
Without prejudice to the application of Articles 52 and 53:		
(a) in respect of Article 59b(2), to pre-pay import duties due, except where the goods are lent, hired out, or transferred (whether for consideration or free of charge) to an establishment or organisation which is entitled to benefit from the relief pursuant to Article 59a and uses the article, instrument or apparatus for purposes which confer such relief;	The scientific research establishment or organisation benefiting from the relief under Article 59a.	£1,000

Part II

Column 1	Column 2	Column 3
Description of relevant Rule/Relevant Rule of a description	*Person of a description*	*Person of a description*
(b) in respect of Article 59b(4), for establishments or organisations which cease to fulfil the conditions, to pay import duties due;	The scientific research establishment or organisation benefiting from the relief under Article 59a.	£1,000
(c) in respect of Article 59b(4), equipment used by establishments or organisations benefiting from the relief for purposes other than those provided for under Article 59a, to pay import duties due.	The scientific research establishment or organisation benefiting from the relief under Article 59a.	£1,000
Article 78 of the Relief Regulation		
To inform the competent authorities where the organisation ceases to fulfil the conditions giving entitlement to duty free admission or proposes to use articles admitted duty free for purposes other than those provided for by Articles 71 and 72.	The institute or organisation benefiting from the relief under Articles 71 and 72.	£1,000
In respect of articles:		
(a) remaining in the possession of the institutions or organisations which cease to fulfil the conditions giving entitlement to relief; or	The institute or organisation benefiting from the relief under Articles 71 and 72.	£1,000
(b) used by the institutions or organisations for purposes other than those provided for in Articles 71 and 72	The institute or organisation benefiting from the relief under Articles 71 and 72.	£1,000
to pay any relevant import duties due.		
Article 83 of the Relief Regulation		
To pre-notify the competent authority and pre-pay import duty due where:		
(a) any of the goods referred to in Article 79(1) is lent, hired out or transferred (whether for consideration or free of charge);	The state organisation or other charitable or philanthropic organisation benefiting from the relief under Article 71(1).	£1,000
(b) an organisation referred to in Article 79(1) which no longer fulfils the conditions to qualify for relief or proposes to use the goods other than for the purposes provided for under that Article.		
Articles 100, 104 and 105 of the Relief Regulation		

Column 1	Column 2	Column 3
Description of relevant Rule/Relevant Rule of a description	*Person of a description*	*Person of a description*
1Relieved "products remaining", with the agreement and under the supervision of the competent authority upon completion of examination, analysis or testing to be (a) completely destroyed or rendered commercially valueless; or (b) surrendered to the state without causing it expense; or (c) in justified circumstances, exported outside the customs territory of the Community.	The person accorded relief under Article 100.	£1,000
2Where Article 104(1) (as set out in 1(a), (b) and (c) above) is not applied, to pay the duty due on the "products remaining".	The person accorded relief under Article 100.	£1,000

RECOVERY OF DUTIES AND TAXES ETC DUE IN OTHER MEMBER STATES (CORRESPONDING UK CLAIMS, PROCEDURE AND SUPPLEMENTARY) REGULATIONS 2004

(SI 2004/674)

Made: 9 March 2004

Authority: Finance Act 2002, Sch 39 para 3(1)–(3)

Commencement: 1 April 2004

PART 1
GENERAL

1 Citation and commencement

These Regulations may be cited as the Recovery of Duties and Taxes Etc Due in Other Member States (Corresponding UK Claims, Procedure and Supplementary) Regulations 2004 and shall come into force on 1st April 2004.

2 Interpretation

In these Regulations—

(a) "the Act" means the Finance Act 2002;

(b) "applicant authority" means an authority in a member State which makes a request for assistance under the Mutual Assistance Recovery Directive;

(c) "authorised official" means an official of an applicant authority authorised by that authority to make requests for assistance in accordance with the Mutual Assistance Recovery Directive;

(d) "the Board" means the Commissioners of Inland Revenue;

(e) "Commission" means the Commission of the European Communities;

(f) "Commissioners" means the Commissioners of Customs and Excise;

(g) "consolidated claim" means several foreign claims recoverable from the same person;

(h) "contested" means an action contesting a foreign claim or the instrument permitting enforcement brought by an interested party before the competent body of the member State in which the applicant authority is situated in accordance with the laws in force there;

(i) "a corresponding UK claim" means a claim in the United Kingdom corresponding to the foreign claim;

(j) "costs" includes fees, charges, disbursements, expenses and remuneration;

(k) "Council Directive 77/388/EEC" means that directive as amended and as last amended by [Council Directive 2004/66/EC];

(l) "the Directive" means Commission Directive 2002/94/EC [as amended by Commission Directive 2004/79/EC] laying down detailed rules for implementing certain provisions of the Mutual Assistance Recovery Directive;

(m) "electronic means" has the same meaning as in Article 2(1) of the Directive;

(n) "enforcement action" means action to enforce a foreign claim by way of legal proceedings, distress, diligence or otherwise as might be taken to enforce a corresponding UK claim;

(o) "export duties" has the same meaning as in Article 3 of the Mutual Assistance Recovery Directive;

(p) "instrument permitting enforcement" means—

  (i) any instrument issued by an applicant authority in any member State in relation to a sum claimed by that authority within the jurisdiction of that State; or

  (ii) a decision on that claim given in favour of that authority by a court or tribunal or other competent body in that State which permits recovery of that claim in that State or part thereof;

(q) "import duties" has the same meaning as in Article 3 of the Mutual Assistance Recovery Directive;

(r) "precautionary measures" means measures taken, or to be taken, in order to secure recovery of a foreign claim;

(s) "request for assistance" means a request for information, notification, recovery or precautionary measures within the meaning of the Mutual Assistance Recovery Directive.

NOTES

Words in first pair of square brackets in paras (k) and (l) substituted, and words in second pair of square brackets inserted, by the Recovery of Duties and Taxes Etc Due in Other Member States (Corresponding UK Claims, Procedure and Supplementary) (Amendment) Regulations, SI 2005/1709 art 3(1)–(3).

PART 2
CORRESPONDING UK CLAIMS

3 Corresponding UK Claims—Duties and Taxes

For the purposes of Schedule 39 to the Act, column 2 of the table in Schedule 1 prescribes the corresponding UK claim in relation to each foreign claim described in column 1.

PART 3
REQUESTS FOR ASSISTANCE

4 Requests for information

(1) A request for information shall be made in writing in the form specified in Annex I to the Directive. If the request cannot be transmitted by electronic means it shall bear the official stamp of the applicant authority and be signed by an authorised official.

(2) A request for information shall relate to—

(a) a debtor;

(b) a person liable for settlement of the debt under the law in force in the member State in which the applicant authority is situated; or

(c) any third party holding assets belonging to one of the persons mentioned in sub-paragraph (a) or (b).

(3) The relevant UK authority shall acknowledge receipt of a request for information in writing not later than seven days from the date of such receipt and as appropriate request the applicant authority to provide any additional information necessary to execute the request.

(4) The relevant UK authority shall, not later than six months from the date of acknowledgement of the request, report to the applicant authority the outcome of the investigations which it has conducted in order to obtain the information requested.

(5) The relevant UK authority shall, within a reasonable period following the date upon which that information was obtained, transmit to the applicant authority the information obtained in accordance with the request.

(6) The relevant UK authority shall not be obliged to supply information where—

(a) the request was not made in accordance with this regulation;

(b) the relevant UK authority would not be able to obtain that information for the purpose of recovery of a corresponding UK claim;

(c) the supply of the requested information would disclose any commercial, industrial or professional secret; or

(d) disclosure of the information would prejudice the security of the United Kingdom or otherwise be contrary to the law or public policy of the United Kingdom.

(7) An applicant authority may in writing at any time withdraw a request made under this regulation.

5 Requests for notification of instruments

(1) A request for notification of an instrument shall—

(a) be made in writing in duplicate in the form specified in Annex II to the Directive;

(b) bear the official stamp of the applicant authority;

(c) be signed by an authorised official of that authority;

(d) be accompanied by two copies of the instrument to be notified.

(2) A request for notification shall relate to a person specified in regulation 4(2).

(3) The relevant UK authority shall—

(a) acknowledge receipt of a request for notification in writing not later than seven days after the date of such receipt;

(b) take the necessary measures to effect notification immediately upon receipt of the request for notification in accordance with the law applicable to notification of similar instruments in that part of the UK in which notification is given;

(c) confirm to the applicant authority, as soon as reasonably practicable, the date the instrument was notified to the person concerned by returning a copy of the request form with the certificate on the reverse completed;

(d)   not question the validity of the instrument.

(4) The relevant UK authority may request additional information from the applicant authority for the purposes of effecting notification.

(5) For the purposes of this regulation "instrument" means any document or decision including those of a judicial nature which emanate from the member State in which the applicant authority is situated and which relate to a foreign claim.

6 Requests for recovery or precautionary measures

(1) A request for recovery or precautionary measures shall—

(a)   be made in writing in the form specified in Annex III to the Directive including a declaration that the conditions of the Mutual Assistance Recovery Directive for initiating a request have been fulfilled;

(b)   bear the official stamp of the applicant authority;

(c)   be signed by an authorised official of that authority;

(d)   relate to a person specified in regulation 4(2); and

(e)   be accompanied by an instrument permitting enforcement.

(2) The amount of the foreign claim stated in the request shall be stated in UK sterling and the currency of the member State in which the applicant authority is situated using the exchange rate specified in regulation 15(2).

(3) The relevant UK authority shall—

(a)   within seven days of receipt of a request for recovery or precautionary measures—

      (i)   acknowledge receipt of the request in writing to the applicant authority;

      (ii)   make a request in writing to the applicant authority to complete the request if it does not contain the full or complete information required by Article 7 of the Mutual Assistance Recovery Directive;

(b)   where it does not take any enforcement action on a request within three months of receipt, not later than seven days from the end of that period inform the applicant authority in writing of the grounds for its failure to comply with the time limit;

(c)   within a reasonable time having regard to the particular case, where all or part of the foreign claim cannot be recovered or precautionary measures cannot be taken, so inform the applicant authority, indicating the reasons therefor;

(d)   no later than at the end of each six month period following the date of acknowledgement of receipt of the request, inform the applicant authority in writing of the status or outcome of any enforcement action;

(e)   continue, save where prevented by paragraph 4 of Schedule 39 to the Act, any enforcement action or precautionary measures where a request to do so is made by the applicant authority not later than two months from the date of receipt of the notification of the outcome of that action and such request shall be subject to the provisions in these Regulations which applied to the initial request;

(f)   inform the applicant authority immediately any enforcement action has been taken on a request.

(4) For the purpose of this regulation and regulations 8 to 17 and regulations 20 to 26 a single instrument permitting enforcement which covers more than one foreign claim against a person shall be deemed to constitute a single claim.

(5) A relevant UK authority shall consult the applicant authority where in recovering a foreign claim it intends to allow the debtor time to pay by arrangement or

to make payment by instalments (whether or not interest is charged or to be charged on those arrangements).

(6)   Except where an enactment or rule of law applicable to a corresponding UK claim requires otherwise, a relevant UK authority shall not be obliged to recover a foreign claim where to do so would, because of the situation of the debtor, create serious economic or social difficulties in the United Kingdom.

7 Transfer of sums recovered

(1)   Subject to paragraph (3) the relevant UK authority shall transfer in UK sterling to the applicant authority any sum recovered in respect of a foreign claim not later than one month from the date upon which recovery was effected.

(2)   For the purposes of this regulation "sum" shall include any interest including interest charged in the UK.

(3)   The relevant UK authority and the applicant authority may agree different arrangements for the transfer of an amount where that amount is less than 1500 Euro.

(4)   For the purpose of satisfying a request for recovery any sum recovered shall be deemed to have been recovered in proportion to the foreign claim as expressed in UK sterling.

8 Contested recovery

(1)   Any enactment permitting proceedings for the recovery of or precautionary measures in relation to a corresponding UK claim shall apply to a foreign claim which is contested.

(2)   . . .

NOTES
   Para (2): revoked by the Recovery of Agricultural Levies Due in Other Member States Regulations 2004, SI 2004/800, regs 2, 3.

9 Notice of inability to take action or proceedings upon a request for recovery of a contested claim

Where, in accordance with paragraph 4 of Schedule 39 to the Act, the relevant UK authority is not permitted to take action for recovery or for a precautionary measure it shall, in writing, advise the competent authority of the reasons within one month of the receipt of the notification by the applicant authority that the foreign claim or instrument permitting enforcement is contested.

10 Notice of action contesting recovery

The relevant UK authority shall notify the applicant authority in writing of any notice of commencement of action in the UK by a person specified in regulation 4(2) for reimbursement of sums recovered or for compensation in relation to recovery of a contested claim.

11 Reimbursement of sums recovered and compensation

Where the result of contesting a foreign claim or instrument permitting enforcement is favourable to the debtor, the applicant authority shall be liable for the reimbursement of any sums recovered, together with any compensation due, in accordance with any law in force in the relevant part of the UK applicable to the corresponding UK claim.

12 Reimbursement arrangements

Where recovery of a foreign claim poses a specific problem, entails a very large amount in costs or relates to the fight against organised crime the relevant UK authority and the applicant authority may agree reimbursement arrangements specific to the case in question.

13 Notice of cancellation or payment of a claim

Where the relevant UK authority undertakes enforcement action or precautionary measures in relation to that foreign claim it shall, upon receipt of notice in writing from the applicant authority as to—

(a)   payment in satisfaction of that claim; or

(b)   cancellation or other reason for termination of that claim;

cease any enforcement action or precautionary measures in relation to that claim.

14 Adjustment of a foreign claim

(1)   This regulation applies where the amount of a foreign claim is amended for any reason.

(2)   Where the amendment leads to a reduction in the amount of the foreign claim—

(a)   the relevant UK authority shall continue the action which it has undertaken with a view to recovery or to the taking of precautionary measures, but that action shall be limited to the amount still outstanding;

(b)   if at the time the relevant UK authority is informed of the reduction in the amount of the foreign claim, an amount exceeding the amount still outstanding has already been recovered by it but the transfer procedure referred to in regulation 7 has not yet been initiated, the relevant UK authority shall repay the amount overpaid to the person entitled thereto.

(3)   Where the amendment leads to an increase in the amount of the foreign claim—

(a)   the additional request shall as far as possible be dealt with by the relevant UK authority at the same time as the original request;

(b)   where, in view of the state of progress of the existing recovery procedure, consolidation of the additional request with the original request is not possible, the relevant UK authority shall be required to comply with the additional request only if it concerns an amount not less than the threshold amount referred to in regulation 15(1).

15 Minimum amount on requests for assistance

(1)   A request for assistance shall not be entertained if the foreign claim (whether a single claim or a consolidated claim) is less than 1500 Euro or the sterling equivalent at the time of request.

(2)   The rate of exchange to be used for the purposes of these regulations shall be the latest selling rate recorded on the most representative exchange market or markets of the member State in which the applicant authority is situated on the date when the request for assistance is signed.

16 Limitation on requests for assistance

(1)   The relevant UK authority shall not be obliged to entertain a request for assistance if the foreign claim is more than five years old.

(2)   The point for commencement and calculation of a period of five years shall be—

(a)   where a foreign claim is not contested, the date the instrument permitting enforcement was established by the applicant authority in accordance with the law in force in the member State in which that authority is situated; or

(b)   where a foreign claim is contested, the date upon which the applicant authority establishes that the claim or instrument permitting recovery is no longer contested.

17 Acceptance and transmission of communications

(1) The relevant UK authority shall, as far as possible, accept and transmit all information required to be communicated in writing for the purposes of the Mutual Assistance Recovery Directive by electronic means.

(2) Paragraph (1) does not apply to requests for assistance made in accordance with regulations 5 and 6 and the instrument accompanying those requests unless the relevant UK authority and the applicant authority agree to waive paper communication.

18 Communication of documents and information

Documents and information sent to the relevant UK authority pursuant to the Mutual Assistance Recovery Directive may only be communicated by that authority to—

    (a)   the person mentioned in the request for assistance;

    (b)   those persons and authorities responsible for the recovery of the claims, and solely for that purpose; or

    (c)   the judicial authorities dealing with matters concerning the recovery of claims.

19 Language requirements

(1) Save as otherwise agreed by the relevant UK authority, requests for assistance, the instrument permitting enforcement, and any other relevant document addressed to that authority shall be accompanied by a translation of that document in the English language.

(2) All information and particulars communicated to an applicant authority by the relevant UK authority in relation to a request for assistance shall be conveyed in the English language or such other language as is agreed by that authority with the applicant authority.

20 Limitation

(1) The period of limitation or prescription in relation to any issue arising on the recovery of any foreign claim shall be that applicable under the laws in force in the member State in which the applicant authority is situated.

(2) For the purposes of paragraph (1) any step or act taken by the relevant UK authority in recovery of a foreign claim in pursuance of a request for assistance shall be deemed to have been taken in the member State in which the applicant authority is situated where that step or act would, if it had been taken by that applicant authority, have had the effect of suspending or interrupting the period of limitation or prescription in accordance with the laws in force in that member State.

21 Notice of refusal of requests for assistance

(1) Where in accordance with the Mutual Assistance Recovery Directive and the Directive or these Regulations the relevant UK authority decides not to act upon a request for assistance it shall, as soon as practicable after making its decision to refuse a request and any event within three months of the date of acknowledgement of receipt of the request, notify the applicant authority in writing of the reasons for refusal.

(2) In the cases mentioned in regulations 6(6) and 16 a copy of the reasons for refusal shall also be communicated to the Commission within the period specified in paragraph (1).

PART 4

INTEREST

22 Adaptations

Schedule 2 to these Regulations shall have effect.

23 Interest enforced by the Board

(1) A foreign claim corresponding to a UK claim for income tax, capital gains tax or corporation tax carries interest in respect of the principal and any penalty claimed at the rate applicable to the corresponding UK claim under section 178 of the Finance Act 1989 from the date of recognition until payment.

(2) In this regulation "the date of recognition" means the earlier of—

    (a)   the day following the expiry of three months from the date of receipt by the Board of the request for recovery of the foreign claim; and

    (b)   the date the instrument permitting enforcement of the foreign claim is recognised by the Board as an instrument authorising enforcement of the claim in the United Kingdom.

(3) Paragraph (1) above applies even if the date of recognition is a non-business day within the meaning of section 92 of the Bills of Exchange Act 1882.

(4) Interest is payable under this regulation without any deduction of income tax.

(5) For the purposes of this regulation, where—

    (a)   any payment is made by cheque to—

        (i)   an officer of the Board, or

        (ii)   the Board, or

        (iii) the applicant authority, and

    (b)   the cheque is paid on its first presentation to the banker on whom it is drawn;

the payment shall be treated as made on the day on which the cheque was received by the officer or the Board or the applicant authority.

(6) Interest payable under this regulation shall be recoverable as if it were interest charged under a provision of the Taxes Management Act 1970.

24 Interest enforced by the Commissioners

(1) A foreign claim corresponding to any UK claim—

    (a)   mentioned in column 2 of Part I of Schedule 1, or

    (b)   for insurance premium tax,

shall carry interest in respect of the principal and any penalty claimed at the rate applicable to the corresponding UK claim under section 197 of the Finance Act 1996 from the date of recognition until payment.

(2) In this regulation "the date of recognition" means the earlier of—

    (a)   the day following the expiry of three months from the date of receipt by the Commissioners of the request for recovery of the foreign claim; and

    (b)   the date the instrument permitting enforcement of the foreign claim is recognised by the Commissioners as an instrument authorising enforcement of the claim in the United Kingdom.

(3) Paragraph (1) above applies even if the date of recognition is a non-business day within the meaning of section 92 of the Bills of Exchange Act 1882.

(4) Interest is payable under this regulation without any deduction of income tax.

(5) For the purposes of this regulation, where—

    (a)   any payment is made by cheque to—

        (i)   an officer of Customs and Excise, or

        (ii)   the Commissioners, or

        (iii) the applicant authority, and

    (b)   the cheque is paid on its first presentation to the banker on whom it is drawn,

the payment shall be treated as made on the day on which the cheque was received by the officer or the Commissioners or the applicant authority.

(6)   Interest payable under this regulation shall be notified in writing to the person subject to enforcement action in respect of the foreign claim and may be recovered from that person as a debt due to the Crown.

PART 5
ENFORCEMENT OF CORRESPONDING CLAIMS

25 Evidence

(1)   An instrument permitting enforcement of a foreign claim recognised by the Board as an instrument authorising enforcement of the claim in the United Kingdom, together with a certificate of a collector that payment of the claim has not been made to him, or, to the best of his knowledge and belief, to any other collector, or to any person acting on his behalf or on behalf of another collector, or to the applicant authority, is sufficient evidence that the sum mentioned in the instrument is unpaid and is due to that authority.

(2)   A certificate of a collector that interest is payable under regulation 23(1) and that payment of the interest has not been made to him, or, to the best of his knowledge and belief, to any other collector, or to any person acting on his behalf or on behalf of another collector, or to the applicant authority, is sufficient evidence that the sum mentioned in the instrument is unpaid and is due to that authority.

(3)   For the purposes of this regulation, any document purporting to be such a certificate as is mentioned in paragraph (1) and (2) is deemed to be such a certificate unless the contrary is proved.

26 Enforcement in Scotland

(1)   For the purposes of enforcement in Scotland, an original, official or certified copy of a decision on a foreign claim by a court, tribunal or other competent body in the member State in which the applicant authority is situated shall be of the same force and effect as an extract of a decree of the Court of Session for the payment of money bearing a warrant for execution.

(2)   For the purposes of paragraph (1), a "decision on a foreign claim" means a decision on a foreign claim which permits recovery of that claim in the member State in which the applicant authority is situated or in part thereof.

SCHEDULES

SCHEDULE 1

CORRESPONDING CLAIMS

Regulation 3

PART 1

Column 1	Column 2
1 Foreign Claim	2 Corresponding UK Claim
Import duties and export duties charged, in any member State other than the United Kingdom	Import and export duties charged in the United Kingdom
Value added tax (howsoever described) charged in any member State other than the United Kingdom in accordance with the provisions of Council Directive 77/388/EEC	Value added tax charged, in the United Kingdom in accordance with the Value Added Tax Act 1994

Column 1	Column 2
1 Foreign Claim	2 Corresponding UK Claim
Excise duties (howsoever described) charged in any member State other than the United Kingdom upon, —manufactured tobacco, —alcohol and alcoholic beverages, —mineral oils	Excise duty charged, collected or enforced in the United Kingdom in accordance with the Tobacco Products Duty Act 1979, or the Alcoholic Liquor Duties Act 1979, or the Hydrocarbon Oil Duties Act 1979, upon the items described in column 1

(Parts 2 and 3 are outside the scope of this work).

SCHEDULE 2
ADAPTATIONS
Regulation 22

Interpretation

1.

In this Schedule—

"duties interest" means a foreign claim corresponding to a UK claim for interest on import or export duties . . .;

"IPT interest" means a foreign claim corresponding to a UK claim for interest on insurance premium tax;

"request" means a request for recovery made to the relevant UK authority in accordance with regulation 6 of these Regulations;

"VAT interest" means a foreign claim corresponding to a UK claim for interest on value added tax.

Recovery of import duties interest

2.—

(1) Subsections (2) to (4) and (6) to (8) of section 126 of the Finance Act 1999 shall not apply to duties interest.

(2) In its application to duties interest subsection (1) of section 126 shall apply as if the reference to determination and recovery of the amount of any interest charged in accordance with Article 232 of the Community Customs Code on arrears of customs duty payable to the Commissioners were a reference to the recovery by the Commissioners of an amount of duties interest for which a request has been made.

(3) For the purposes of its application to duties interest subsection (5) of section 126 shall apply as if;

(a) the reference to interest the amount of which falls to be determined in accordance with this section were a reference to duties interest to be recovered; and

(b) the reference to interest on an amount so determined were a reference to duties interest to be recovered.

Recovery of VAT interest

3.—

(1)   Subsections (1) to (8) and (10) and the expression "unless, or except to the extent that, the assessment is withdrawn or reduced" in subsection (9) of section 76 of the Value Added Tax Act 1994 shall not apply to VAT interest.

(2)   In its application to VAT interest subsection (9) of section 76 shall apply as if the reference to an amount being assessed and notified to a persons under this section were a reference to an amount of VAT interest specified in a request concerning a person specified in regulation 4(2) of these Regulations in relation to whom a request is made.

Recovery of IPT interest

4.—

(1)   Sub-paragraphs (1) to (7) and (9) and the expression "unless or except to the extent that, the assessment is withdrawn or reduced" in sub-paragraph (8) of paragraph 25 of Schedule 7 to the Finance Act 1994 shall not apply to IPT interest.

(2)   In its application to IPT interest sub-paragraph (8) of paragraph 25 shall apply as if the reference to an amount being assessed and notified to any person under this paragraph were a reference to an amount of IPT interest specified in a request concerning a person specified in regulation 4(2) of these Regulations in relation to whom a request is made.

NOTES
Para 1: in definition "duties interest" words omitted revoked by the Recovery of Agricultural Levies Due in Other Member States Regulations 2004, SI 2004/800, regs 2, 4.

CUSTOMS AND EXCISE DUTIES (TRAVELLERS' ALLOWANCES AND PERSONAL RELIEFS) (NEW MEMBER STATES) ORDER 2004

(SI 2004/1002)

NOTES
Made: 1 April 2004.
Authority: Customs and Excise Duties (General Reliefs) Act 1979, ss 7, 13(1), (3).
Commencement: 1 May 2004.

1 Citation and commencement
This Order may be cited as the Customs and Excise Duties (Travellers' Allowances and Personal Reliefs) (New Member States) Order 2004 and shall come into force on 1st May 2004.

2 Interpretation
(1)   In this Order—
  "relevant tobacco products" means, in relation to each specified country, goods of the descriptions and in the quantities shown opposite that country in Column 2 of the Schedule;
  "smoking tobacco" means hand rolling tobacco or other smoking tobacco;
  "specified country" means a country listed in Column 1 of the Schedule.
(2)   In this Order references to "cigarettes", "cigars", "hand rolling tobacco" and "other smoking tobacco" are references to the products described in the Tobacco Products (Descriptions of Products) Order 2003.

3 Relief from duty of excise

Subject to the following provisions of this Order, a person who has travelled from a specified country shall, on entering the United Kingdom, be relieved from payment of excise duty on relevant tobacco products acquired in that country and which he has transported.

NOTES

Modification: modified, in relation to goods in a control zone, by the Channel Tunnel (Alcoholic Liquor and Tobacco Products) Order 2003, SI 2003/2758, art 2(f), (g), Schedule para 12A.

4 Condition of relief

(1) The reliefs afforded under this Order are subject to the condition that the goods in question, as indicated by their nature or quantity or otherwise, are not held for a commercial purpose nor are used for such purpose; and if that condition is not complied with in relation to any goods, those goods shall, unless the non-compliance was sanctioned by the Commissioners, be liable to forfeiture.

(2) If the goods in question are not duty and tax paid in the specified country at the time of acquisition, or the duty and tax that was paid will be or has been reimbursed, refunded or otherwise dispensed with, those goods are to be regarded as being held for a commercial purpose.

5 Period in which article 3 shall have effect

Article 3 shall have effect in relation to a specified country on or before the date shown opposite that country in Column 3 of the Schedule.

6 Interpretation of The Customs and Excise Duties (Personal Reliefs for Goods Permanently Imported) Order 1992 and The Travellers' Allowances Order 1994

The references to Council Directive 77/388/EEC and Council Directive 92/12/EEC contained in—

> (a)   The Customs and Excise Duties (Personal Reliefs for Goods Permanently Imported) Order 1992; and
>
> (b)   The Travellers' Allowances Order 1994

are to be construed as references to those instruments as amended, modified or otherwise affected by the Act concerning the conditions of accession of the Czech Republic, the Republic of Estonia, the Republic of Cyprus, the Republic of Latvia, the Republic of Lithuania, the Republic of Hungary, the Republic of Malta, the Republic of Poland, the Republic of Slovenia and the Slovak Republic and the adjustments to the Treaties on which the European Union is founded.

[7

(1) The references to Council Directive 77/388/EEC and Council Directive 92/12/EEC contained in the Orders listed in article 6 above are to be construed as references to those instruments as amended, modified or otherwise affected by the Act concerning the conditions of accession of the Republic of Bulgaria and Romania and the adjustments to the treaties on which the European Union is founded.

(2) Paragraph 1 above has no effect in relation to article 21 of the Customs and Excise Duties (Personal Reliefs for Goods Permanently Imported) Order 1992.]

NOTES

Inserted by the Customs and Excise Duties (Travellers' Allowances and Personal Reliefs) (New Member States) (Amendment) Order, SI 2006/3157, arts 2, 3.

SCHEDULE

Articles 3 and 5

(1) Specified Country	(2) Relevant tobacco products	(3) Date on or before which Order shall have effect
Czech Republic	200 Cigarettes OR 50 Cigars OR 100 Cigarillos (cigars weighing no more than 3 grammes each) OR 250 grammes of smoking tobacco	31st December 2006 (in relation to relevant tobacco products other than cigarettes) 31st December 2007 (in relation to cigarettes)
Slovenia	200 Cigarettes	31st December 2007
Hungary Poland Slovakia	200 Cigarettes	31st December 2008
Estonia	200 Cigarettes OR 250 grammes of smoking tobacco	31st December 2009
Latvia Lithuania	200 Cigarettes	31st December 2009
[Bulgaria Romania	200 Cigarettes	31st December 2009]

NOTES

Entries for Bulgaria and Romania inserted by the Customs and Excise Duties (Travellers' Allowances and Personal Reliefs) (New Member States) (Amendment) Order, SI 2006/3157, arts 2, 4.

EXCISE DUTY POINTS (ETC) (NEW MEMBER STATES) REGULATIONS 2004

(SI 2004/1003)

NOTES

Made: 1 April 2004.

Authority: Customs and Excise Management Act 1979, ss 93(1), (2)(a), (fa), (fb), (3), 100G and 100H; the Tobacco Products Duty Act 1979, ss 7(1)(a), 1A(b); and the Finance (No 2) Act 1992, ss 1, 2.

Commencement: 1 May 2004.

1 Citation and commencement

These Regulations may be cited as the Excise Duty Points (Etc) (New Member States) Regulations 2004 and come into force on 1st May 2004.

Part II

2 Interpretation

(1) In these Regulations—

"cigarillo" means a cigar weighing no more than 3 grammes;

"own use" includes use as a personal gift;

"smoking tobacco" means hand rolling tobacco or other smoking tobacco.

(2) In these Regulations references to "cigarettes", "cigars", "hand rolling tobacco" and "other smoking tobacco" are references to the products described in the Tobacco Products (Descriptions of Products) Order 2003.

3 Excise duty point for tobacco products acquired in a new member State

(1) The excise duty point for tobacco products acquired in a new member State is the time when the tobacco products are charged with duty.

(2) For the purposes of paragraph (1) above, tobacco products acquired in a new member State shall mean—

    (a) cigarettes acquired by a person in a country listed in Column 1 of the Schedule for his own use and transported by him to the United Kingdom;

    (b) cigars, cigarillos or smoking tobacco acquired by a person in the Czech Republic for his own use and transported by him to the United Kingdom; and

    (c) smoking tobacco acquired by a person in Estonia for his own use and transported by him to the United Kingdom.

NOTES

Modification: modification of para (2), in relation to goods in a control zone, by the Channel Tunnel (Alcoholic Liquor and Tobacco Products) Order 2003, SI 2003/2758, art 2(f), (g), Schedule para 12A.

4 Person liable to pay the duty

The person liable to pay the duty is the person holding the tobacco products at the excise duty point.

5 Payment of the duty

(1) Subject to paragraph (2) below, the duty must be paid at the excise duty point.

(2) The Commissioners may, subject to such conditions as appear necessary for the protection of the revenue, dispense with the requirement imposed by paragraph (1).

6 Period for which regulation 3 shall apply

(1) Regulation 3(2)(a) shall have effect in relation to cigarettes transported to the United Kingdom from a country listed in Column 1 of the Schedule on or before the date shown opposite that country in Column 2 of the Schedule.

(2) Regulation 3(2)(b) shall have effect on or before 31st December 2006.

(3) Regulation 3(2)(c) shall have effect on or before 31st December 2009.

NOTES

Modification: modified, in relation to goods in a control zone, by the Channel Tunnel (Alcoholic Liquor and Tobacco Products) Order 2003, SI 2003/2758, art 2(f), (g), Schedule para 12A.

7 Interpretation of other Regulations relating to excise goods

(1) In the Regulations listed below, references to

(a)   Council Directive 92/12/EEC;

(b)   Commission Regulation (EEC) No 2719/92; and

(c)   Commission Regulation (EEC) No 2454/93

shall be treated as references to those instruments as amended, modified or otherwise affected by the Act concerning the conditions of accession of the Czech Republic, the Republic of Estonia, the Republic of Cyprus, the Republic of Latvia, the Republic of Lithuania, the Republic of Hungary, the Republic of Malta, the Republic of Poland, the Republic of Slovenia and the Slovak Republic and the adjustments to the Treaties on which the European Union is founded.

[(1A)   In the Regulations listed in sub-paragraphs (c) to (g) of paragraph (2) below, references to Council Directive 92/12/EEC shall be treated as references to that instrument as amended, modified or otherwise affected by the Act concerning the conditions of accession of the Republic of Bulgaria and Romania and the adjustments to the treaties on which the European Union is founded.]

(2)   The Regulations referred to in paragraph 1 above are—

(a)   the Excise Warehousing (Etc) Regulations 1988;

(b)   the Excise Goods (Holding, Movement, Warehousing and REDS) Regulations 1992;

(c)   the Excise Goods (Drawback) Regulations 1995;

(d)   the Excise Goods (Sales on Board Ships and Aircraft) Regulations 1999;

(e)   the Excise Goods (Export Shops) Regulations 2000;

(f)   the Excise Duty Points (Duty Suspended Movements of Excise Goods) Regulations 2001; and

(g)   the Excise Goods (Accompanying Documents) Regulations 2002.

NOTES

Para (1A): inserted by the Excise Duty Points (Etc) (New Member States) (Amendment) Regulations, SI 2006/3159, regs 2, 3.

8

(amends the Excise Goods (Holding, Movement, Warehousing and REDS) Regulations 1992, SI 1992/3135 reg 4)

9

(amends the Beer Regulations 1993, SI 1993/1228 reg 15)

10

(amends the Tobacco Products Regulations 2001, SI 2001/1712 reg 12)

SCHEDULE

Regulation 3(2)(a) and 6(1)

(1)	*(2)*
Country	*Date on or before which Regulation 3(2)(a) shall apply*
Czech Republic Slovenia	31st December 2007
Hungary Poland Slovakia	31st December 2008
Estonia Latvia Lithuania	31st December 2009

(1)	(2)
Country	Date on or before which Regulation 3(2)(a) shall apply
[Bulgaria Romania	31st December 2009]

NOTES

Entries for Bulgaria and Romania inserted by the Excise Duty Points (Etc) (New Member States) (Amendment) Regulations, SI 2006/3159, regs 2, 4.

GOODS INFRINGING INTELLECTUAL PROPERTY RIGHTS (CUSTOMS) REGULATIONS 2004

(SI 2004/1473)

NOTES

Made: 4 June 2004.

Authority: European Communities Act 1972, s 2(2).

Commencement: 1 July 2004.

1 Citation and commencement

These Regulations may be cited as the Goods Infringing Intellectual Property Rights (Customs) Regulations 2004 and shall come into force on 1st July 2004.

2 Interpretation

(1) In these Regulations—

"the 1979 Act" means the Customs and Excise Management Act 1979;

"application" means an application under Article 5 of the Council Regulation;

"the Commissioners" means the Commissioners of Customs and Excise;

"Community design" has the meaning given in Article 1(1) of Council Regulation (EC) No 6/2002 on Community designs;

"Community plant variety right" means a right of the kind provided for in Council Regulation (EC) No 2100/1994 on Community plant variety rights;

"the Council Regulation" means Council Regulation (EC) No 1383/2003 concerning customs action against goods suspected of infringing certain intellectual property rights and the measures to be taken against goods found to have infringed such rights;

"the customs and excise Acts" has the meaning given in section 1(1) of the 1979 Act;

"database rights" has the meaning given in regulation 13 of the Copyright and Rights in Databases Regulations 1997;

"decision" means a decision granting an application in accordance with Article 8 of the Council Regulation;

"declarant" has the meaning given in Article 4(18) of Council Regulation (EEC) No 2913/1992 establishing the Community Customs Code;

"design right" has the meaning given in section 213(1) of the Copyright, Designs and Patents Act 1988;

"designation of origin" has the same meaning as in Article 2(1)(c)(iv) of the Council Regulation;

"European patent (UK)" has the meaning given in section 130(1) of the Patents Act 1977;

"geographical designation" has the same meaning as in Article 2(1)(c)(v) of the Council Regulation;

"geographical indication" has the same meaning as in Article 2(1)(c)(iv) of the Council Regulation;

"goods infringing an intellectual property right" has the meaning given in Article 2(1) of the Council Regulation and related expressions shall be construed accordingly;

"patent" means a patent under the Patents Act 1977, or a European patent (UK) which is treated for the purposes of Parts 1 and 3 of the Patents Act 1977 as if it were a patent under that Act;

"plant breeders' right" means a right of the kind provided for in the Plant Varieties Act 1997;

"publication rights" has the meaning given in regulation 16 of the Copyright and Related Rights Regulations 1996;

"registered design" shall be construed in accordance with the Registered Designs Act 1949;

"right-holder" has the meaning given in Article 2(2) of the Council Regulation;

"supplementary protection certificate" has the same meaning as in Article 2(1)(c)(ii) of the Council Regulation;

"working days" has the meaning given in Article 3(1) of Council Regulation (EEC, Euratom) No 1182/1971 determining the rules applicable to periods, dates and time limits.

(2) For the purposes of these Regulations, any reference in the Council Regulation to "copyright or related right" is to be construed as a reference to "copyright, rights in performances, publication rights or database rights".

(3) These Regulations shall apply to goods which fall to be treated by virtue of Article 2(3) of the Council Regulation as being goods infringing an intellectual property right; but these Regulations shall not apply to any goods in relation to which the Council Regulation does not apply by virtue of Article 3(1) thereof.

3 Infringing goods liable to forfeiture

Subject to paragraph (2) of regulation 4, goods infringing an intellectual property right which correspond to the description of goods contained in a decision shall, during the period specified in the decision, be liable to forfeiture in any of the situations mentioned in Article 1(1) of the Council Regulation.

4 Application for action

(1) If, in the course of checks carried out in relation to goods in one of the situations referred to in Article 1(1) of the Council Regulation, and before an application has been lodged by a right-holder or, if lodged, before it has been granted, the Commissioners have sufficient grounds for suspecting that goods infringe an intellectual property right, the Commissioners may, in accordance with Article 4 of the Council Regulation—

    (a)   notify a right-holder of the nature of the items and of the actual or supposed number of items and ask a right-holder to provide any information they may need to confirm their suspicions;

    (b)   notify a right-holder and a declarant of the possible infringement of the right;

    (c)   suspend the release of, or detain, those goods; and

    (d)   if they do so suspend or detain, invite the right-holder, in the absence of an existing application, to make an application within three working days of the notification of the suspension or detention.

(2) If at any time during the period of suspension or detention under paragraph (1) an application is granted covering the goods, the decision shall, for the purposes of regulation 3, be taken to have applied at the time the goods entered any of the situations mentioned in Article 1(1) of the Council Regulation.

5 Decision to cease to have effect
A decision shall have no further effect where—

(a)   any change, following the making of the application, which takes place in the ownership or authorised use of the intellectual property right specified in the application, is not communicated in writing to the Commissioners; or

(b)   the intellectual property right specified in the application expires.

6 Samples of goods
When examining goods in accordance with Article 9(3) of the Council Regulation the Commissioners may make samples of the goods available to the right-holder at his request for the purposes of analysis and of facilitating subsequent procedures under the Council Regulation or these Regulations.

7 Detention, seizure, condemnation and forfeiture
(1)   Subject to regulation 8, section 139 of, and Schedule 3 to, the 1979 Act (provisions as to detention, seizure and condemnation of goods, etc; forfeiture) shall apply in respect of any goods liable to forfeiture by virtue of regulation 3 as they apply in respect of goods liable to forfeiture under the customs and excise Acts; and, accordingly—

(a)   section 144 of the 1979 Act (protection of officers, etc in relation to seizure and detention of goods, etc) shall apply in respect of seizure or detention effected by virtue of this regulation; and

(b)   sections 145, 146 and 152 to 155 of the 1979 Act (general provisions as to legal proceedings) shall apply in respect of condemnation proceedings brought by virtue of this regulation.

(2)   Where in any condemnation proceedings brought by virtue of paragraph (1) any question arises as to whether or not any goods are or were liable to forfeiture under regulation 3, the burden of proof shall lie upon the party alleging that they are not, or were not, so liable.

8 Detention and seizure of goods infringing specified intellectual property rights
(1)   Regulation 7 shall not apply in relation to goods as regards which the decision specifies as subsisting in those goods any one or more of the following intellectual property rights (whether or not they also appear to infringe any other intellectual property right)—

(a)   a patent;

(b)   a supplementary protection certificate;

(c)   a registered design;

(d)   a design right;

(e)   a Community design;

(f)   a plant breeders' right;

(g)   a Community plant variety right;

(h)   a designation of origin;

(i)   a geographical indication; or

(j)   a geographical designation.

(2)   A right-holder may, within 10 working days of his having been notified by the Commissioners of the suspension of release of such goods, or of such goods being detained, give notice in writing to the Commissioners waiving, for the purpose of both

the Council Regulation and these Regulations, any intellectual property right of his in the goods, being a right mentioned in sub-paragraphs (a) to (j) in paragraph (1).

(3)   The period referred to in paragraph (2) shall be 3 working days in cases where the Commissioners have suspended the release of, or detained, perishable goods.

(4)   Where notice has been given in accordance with paragraph (2)—

(a)   any right so waived shall be disregarded, as regards that right-holder, in determining whether the goods fall within paragraph (1); and

(b)   the goods shall be treated for the purposes of these Regulations as if that person did not have the right concerned in those goods.

(5)   The following provisions of the 1979 Act shall apply to any goods falling within paragraph (1) as they apply in respect of goods liable to forfeiture under the customs and excise Acts—

(a)   section 139, except subsections (5) and (6) (things seized or detained to be dealt with or disposed of as Commissioners direct; Schedule 3 to have effect); and

(b)   section 144.

(6)   Any thing seized or detained by virtue of this regulation shall be dealt with in such manner as the Commissioners may direct; but this paragraph shall apply subject to section 139(3) and (4) of the 1979 Act (detention or seizure by a constable; things retained in the custody of the police) in the cases there mentioned.

9 Initiation of proceedings

(1)   In the case of goods falling within paragraph (1) of regulation 8, the commencement of the proceedings described in paragraph (2) below, and only such proceedings, shall constitute the initiation of proceedings to determine whether an intellectual property right has been infringed for the purposes of the Council Regulation.

(2)   The proceedings mentioned in paragraph (1) above are proceedings commenced in the relevant court by a right-holder alleging that the goods infringe an intellectual property right of his and seeking relief which that court has the power to grant after a finding of such infringement.

(3)   Without prejudice to any provision of the Council Regulation, the suspension of the release of the goods, or their detention, shall cease if at any time the Commissioners—

(a)   are not satisfied, or cease to be satisfied, that the proceedings described in paragraph (2) have been commenced; or

(b)   are satisfied that such proceedings have been withdrawn or otherwise terminated without other such proceedings having been commenced.

(4)   For the purposes of this regulation proceedings shall not be taken to have been commenced before—

(a)   an originating process has been issued or, in the case of the Court of Session, signeted by the relevant court; and

(b)   that process has been served on the other party or, if more than one, all the other parties to the proceedings, in accordance with the rules of the court concerned.

(5)   In paragraph (4), the reference to an originating process is a reference to—

(a)   in England and Wales, a claim form;

(b)   in Scotland, a summons; or

(c)   in Northern Ireland, a writ.

(6)   For the purposes of this regulation the relevant court is—

(a)   in England and Wales, the High Court or any patents county court having jurisdiction by virtue of an order under section 287 of the Copyright, Designs and Patents Act 1988;

(b)   in Scotland, the Court of Session; or

(c)   in Northern Ireland, the High Court.

10 Relationship with other powers

Nothing in these Regulations shall be taken to affect—

(a)   any power of the Commissioners conferred otherwise than by any provision of these Regulations to suspend the release of, or detain, any goods; or

(b)   the power of any court to grant any relief, including any power to make an order by way of interim relief.

11 Misuse of information by a right-holder

(1)   Where the Commissioners have reasonable grounds for believing that there has been a misuse of information by a right-holder the Commissioners may suspend the decision in force at the time of the misuse of information, in relation to a relevant intellectual property right, for the remainder of its period of validity.

(2)   Where the Commissioners have reasonable grounds for believing that there has been a further misuse of information within three years of a previous misuse of information by that right-holder the Commissioners may—

(a)   suspend the decision in force at the time of the further misuse of information, in relation to a relevant intellectual property right, for the remainder of its period of validity; and

(b)   for a period of up to one year from its expiry, refuse to renew the decision in force at the time of the further misuse of information, or to accept a new application, in relation to a relevant intellectual property right.

(3)   In this regulation—

(a)   "misuse of information" means the use of information supplied to a right-holder pursuant to the first sub-paragraph of Article 9(3) of the Council Regulation other than for the purposes specified in Articles 10, 11 and 13(1) of the Council Regulation, or pursuant to an enactment or order of a court, and related expressions shall be construed accordingly;

(b)   "relevant intellectual property right" means any intellectual property right in relation to a suspected infringement of which information was supplied to a right-holder pursuant to the first sub-paragraph of Article 9(3) of the Council Regulation, and in relation to which the Commissioners have reasonable grounds for believing that there has been a misuse of that information.

12

(amends the Copyright, Designs and Patents Act 1988 s 111)

13

(amends the Trade Marks Act 1994, s 89)

14 Revocations

The Regulations listed in the Schedule are hereby revoked.

SCHEDULE

REVOCATIONS

Regulation 14

(This Schedule has not been reproduced as it contains revocations).

EXCISE WAREHOUSING (ENERGY PRODUCTS) REGULATIONS 2004

(SI 2004/2064)

NOTES

Made: 6 August 2004.

Authority: Customs and Excise Management Act 1979, ss 93, 100G(1), 100H(1)(b), (c), (d), (g), (k), (m), (2), and the Hydrocarbon Oil Duties Act 1979, ss 21(1), (2), (2A), 23C(2), (3), Sch 3 paras 3, 11, 19, 25.

Commencement: 1 September 2004.

1 Citation and commencement

These Regulations may be cited as the Excise Warehousing (Energy Products) Regulations 2004 and come into force on 1st September 2004.

2 Interpretation

In these Regulations—

"Community duty suspension arrangements" means a suspension arrangement within the meaning of Article 4(c) of Council Directive 92/12/EEC on the general arrangements for products subject to excise duty and on the holding, movement and monitoring of such products;

"duty" means any duty of excise;

"occasional importer" has the meaning given by regulation 2(1) of the REDS Regulations;

"the Oil Act" means the Hydrocarbon Oil Duties Act 1979;

"REDS" has the meaning given by regulation 2(1) of the REDS Regulations;

"the REDS Regulations" means the Excise Goods (Holding, Movement, Warehousing and REDS) Regulations 1992;

"special energy product" means a substance that is—

    (a)   petroleum gas,

    (b)   animal fat set aside for use as motor fuel or heating fuel,

    (c)   vegetable fat set aside for use as motor fuel or heating fuel,

    (d)   non-synthetic methanol set aside for use as motor fuel or heating fuel,

    (e)   biodiesel, or

    (f)   a mixture of two or more substances specified in paragraphs (a) to (e).

3 Community imports

(1) Special energy product that is imported into the United Kingdom under Community duty suspension arrangements must be warehoused in an excise warehouse as if it were a substance chargeable with duty, whether or not duty is in fact chargeable.

(2) Special energy product that is imported into the United Kingdom under Community duty suspension arrangements and which is—

    (a)   consigned under the instructions of a REDS, or

    (b)   consigned under the instructions of an occasional importer,

shall be treated as warehoused for the purposes of paragraph (1) at the time that the special energy product is received by the REDS or the occasional importer.

(3) Special energy product that is imported into the United Kingdom under Community duty suspension arrangements and which is consigned to an

ultimate destination outside the United Kingdom shall be treated as warehoused for the purposes of paragraph (1) at the time that the special energy product arrives at its ultimate destination.

4 Voluntary warehousing

Special energy product that is not chargeable with duty under the Oil Act may be warehoused in an excise warehouse as if it were a substance chargeable with duty.

5 Treatment of warehoused special energy products

(1) Special energy product that is imported into the United Kingdom under Community duty suspension arrangements shall be treated, from the time of that importation until the relevant time, for all the purposes of the customs and excise Acts, as charged with duty under the Oil Act as set out in paragraph (3).

(2) Special energy product that is warehoused (other than special energy product that falls within paragraph (1) above) shall be treated, from the time that it is put in the excise warehouse until the relevant time, for all the purposes of the customs and excise Acts, as charged with duty under the Oil Act as set out in paragraph (3).

(3) Special energy product to which paragraph (1) or (2) applies shall be treated as follows—

(a) biodiesel shall be treated as charged by section 6AA(1) of the Oil Act (biodiesel);

(b) vegetable fat, animal fat and non-synthetic methanol shall be treated as charged by section 6A(2) of the Oil Act (other fuel substitutes);

(c) petroleum gas shall be treated as charged by section 8(2) of the Oil Act (road fuel gas).

(4) In this regulation, "the relevant time" is the earlier of—

(a) the time that the special energy product is charged with duty under the Oil Act;

(b) the time that the special energy product is removed from an excise warehouse for home use;

(c) the time that the special energy product is received by the REDS or occasional importer described by regulation 3(2);

(d) the time that the special energy product reaches its ultimate destination outside the United Kingdom.

6 Distance sales of special energy products

Regulations 2(4) and 10(5) and (6) of the REDS Regulations shall apply to special energy products as if every reference in those provisions to "excise goods" were a reference to special energy products.

7

(amends the Warehousekeepers and Owners of Warehoused Goods Regulations 1999, SI 1999/1278)

BIOFUELS AND OTHER FUEL SUBSTITUTES (PAYMENT OF EXCISE DUTIES ETC) REGULATIONS 2004

(SI 2004/2065)

NOTES

Made: 6 August 2004.

Authority: Customs and Excise Management Act 1979, ss 93(1)(a), (b), (c), (2)(a), (c), (3), 100G(1), 100H(1)(b), (2), 118A(1), (2), and 127A(1), (2), (4); the Hydrocarbon Oil Duties Act

1979 ss 6AC(1)(a), (b), (2), (4), 6AF(1)(a), (b), (2), (4), 20AA(1)(a), (2)(a)–(d), (g), (h), (i), 21(1)(a), (2), 24(1), Sch 3 paras 3, 11, Sch 4 paras 3, 17, 21; and the Finance (No 2) Act 1992, ss 1(1), (3), (4)(a), (6).

Commencement: 1 September 2004.

PART 1
PRELIMINARY

1 Citation and commencement

(1)   These Regulations may be cited as the Biofuels and Other Fuel Substitutes (Payment of Excise Duties etc) Regulations 2004 and come into force on 1st September 2004.

(2)   Part 7 (relief for electricity generation) has effect in relation to any biofuel that is used as motor fuel in a generator to produce electricity on or after 1st September 2004.

2 Interpretation

(1)   In these Regulations—

"approved person" means a person approved by the Commissioners under regulation 4 of the Deferment Regulations;

"authorised person" means a person authorised by the Commissioners;

"biodiesel duty" means the duty charged on biodiesel by section 6AA(1) of the Oil Act;

"bioethanol duty" means the duty charged on bioethanol by section 6AD(1) of the Oil Act;

"biofuel" means biodiesel, bioethanol or fuel substitute;

"biofuels duty" means bioethanol duty, biodiesel duty or fuel substitute duty;

"chargeable use"—

    (a)   in relation to biodiesel, means chargeable use within the meaning of section 6AA(2) of the Oil Act,

    (b)   in relation to bioethanol, means chargeable use within the meaning of section 6AD(2) of the Oil Act, and

    (c)   in relation to fuel substitute, means chargeable use within the meaning of section 6A(2) of the Oil Act;

"the Deferment Regulations" means the Excise Duties (Deferred Payment) Regulations 1992;

"duty" means any duty of excise;

"entered premises" means premises that have been entered in accordance with [regulation 8A or 8E];

"exempt producer" means a producer who is not liable under regulation 8A or 8E to make entry of production premises;]

"fuel substitute" means a liquid that is charged with fuel substitute duty;

"fuel substitute duty" means the duty charged by section 6A of the Oil Act;

"large producer" means a producer whom the Commissioners have notified is a large producer in accordance with regulation 19A(1) (and that notification has not been withdrawn);]

"motor fuels record" has the meaning given in regulation 13;

"the Oil Act" means the Hydrocarbon Oil Duties Act 1979;

"producer" means a person who—

    (a)   sets aside biofuel for a chargeable use, or

    (b)   makes a chargeable use of biofuel,

with the consequence that biofuels duty is charged;

"production premises" means any premises in relation to which a person is a producer. . .

"quarter" means the period of three calendar months commencing on 1st January, 1st April, 1st July and 1st October in any year;

"section 108" means section 108 of the Customs and Excise Management Act 1979;]

"used as motor fuel" means used—

    (a)   as fuel for any engine, motor or other machinery, or

    (b)   as an additive or extender in any substance so used.

[(2) References to "making entry" are references to making entry under section 108 of the Customs and Excise Management Act 1979.]

NOTES

Para (1): renumbered as such by the Biofuels and Other Fuel Substitutes (Payment of Excise Duties etc) (Amendment) Regulations, SI 2007/2065, regs 2, 3(1), (2).

Para (1): words in definition of "entered premises" substituted, definitions of "exempt producer", "large producer", "quarter" and "section 108" inserted, and words in definition of "production premises" revoked, by the Biofuels and Other Fuel Substitutes (Payment of Excise Duties etc) (Amendment) Regulations, SI 2007/2065, regs 2, 3(1), (3)–(7).

Para (2): inserted by the Biofuels and Other Fuel Substitutes (Payment of Excise Duties etc) (Amendment) Regulations, SI 2007/2065, regs 2, 3(1), (8).

PART 2
EFFECT ON OTHER ENACTMENTS

3 Construction of references to hydrocarbon oil etc in the Oil Act

(1) The references to hydrocarbon oil in the following provisions of the Oil Act are to be construed as including references to biodiesel and bioethanol—

    (a)   section 15(1) (drawback of duty on exportation etc);

    (b)   section 19(3) (fuel used in lifeboats etc);

    (c)   section 20AA(1)(a) (power to allow reliefs)

    (d)   section 21(2) (regulations with respect to hydrocarbon oil);

    (e)   paragraphs 3 and 11 of Schedule 3 (subjects for regulations);

    (f)   paragraphs 17 and 21 of Schedule 4 (subjects for regulations).

(2) The references to hydrocarbon oil in the following provisions of the Oil Act are to be construed as including references to bioblend and bioethanol blend—

    (a)   section 3 (hydrocarbon oil as an ingredient in imported goods);

    (b)   section 15(1) (drawback of duty on exportation etc);

    (c)   section 19(3) (fuel used in lifeboats etc);

    (d)   section 20(1)(a) and (3)(a) (contaminated oil).

(3) The reference to the duty on hydrocarbon oil in section 15(1) of the Oil Act is to be construed as including reference to—

    (a)   biodiesel duty,

    (b)   the duty under section 6AB (bioblend) of the Oil Act,

    (c)   bioethanol duty, and

    (d)   the duty under section 6AE (bioethanol blend) of the Oil Act.

(4) The references to the duty on hydrocarbon oil in section 20AA(1)(a) of the Oil Act are to be construed as including references to biodiesel duty and bioethanol duty.

4

(revokes the Other Fuel Substitutes (Payment of Excise Duty etc) Regulations 1995, SI 1995/2717 and the Biodiesel and Bioblend Regulations, SI 2002/1928).

5

(amends the Excise Duties (Deferred Payment) Regulations 1992, SI 1992/3152)

PART 3

WAREHOUSING

6 Production in warehouse

Part 4 (production premises) does not apply where—

  (a)   the premises are an excise warehouse approved by the Commissioners under section 92 of the Customs and Excise Management Act 1979, for the production and holding of the biofuel in question, and

  (b)   the producer is an authorized warehousekeeper (within the meaning of that term in regulation 3 of the Warehousekeepers and Owners of Warehoused Goods Regulations 1999) authorised by the terms of his approval to hold biofuels of that class or description.

7 Warehousing

  (1)   Only biofuel that is—

  (a)   special energy product, or

  (b)   bioethanol for the production of bioethanol blend,

may be produced in an excise warehouse or warehoused.

  (2)   Subject to, and in accordance with, warehousing regulations—

  (a)   biofuel that is special energy product may be warehoused for any purpose,

  (b)   bioethanol may be warehoused only for the purpose of blending with hydrocarbon oil to produce bioethanol blend.

  (3)   In this regulation, "special energy product" has the same meaning as in regulation 2 of the Excise Warehousing (Energy Products) Regulations 2004.

PART 4

PRODUCTION PREMISES

[8

  (1)   Regulation 8A applies to a producer of biofuel with respect to whom either the first condition or the second condition is satisfied.

  (2)   The first condition is that at the end of any calendar month the producer has produced 2,500 litres or more of biofuel in the previous 12 months.

  (3)   The second condition is that at any time there are reasonable grounds to believe that the producer will produce 2,500 litres or more of biofuel in the following 12 months.

8A

  (1)   A producer to whom this regulation applies is liable to make entry of all premises at which he has produced or will produce biofuel, but this is subject to regulations 8B and 8C.

  (2)   A producer liable to make entry of premises must make entry of them not later than the day specified in paragraph (3).

  (3)   The specified day is—

  (a)   in the case of a producer with respect to whom the first condition is satisfied, the thirtieth day following the end of the calendar month in question;

  (b)   in the case of a producer with respect to whom the second condition is satisfied, the thirtieth day following the day on which reasonable grounds arise for believing that he will produce that quantity.

8B

A producer is not liable to make entry of production premises under regulation 8A if he has already entered the premises in accordance with section 108 for—

(a)   the purposes of that regulation; or

(b)   purposes treated as having effect under that regulation, and

that entry has not been cancelled by the Commissioners under regulation 8F.

8C

A producer who meets the first condition specified in regulation 8(2) ceases to be liable to make entry of production premises if he satisfies the Commissioners that he will produce less than 2,500 litres of biofuel in the 12 months immediately following the date he becomes liable.

8D

A producer to whom regulation 8A applies must not send out from any premises a consignment of biofuel, which is charged with biofuels duty because it is set aside for chargeable use, before he makes entry of those premises.

8E Requirement to make entry of production premises used by several producers

(1)   This regulation applies to two or more producers of biofuel with respect to whom—

(a)   the first and second conditions are satisfied; and

(b)   either the third condition or the fourth condition is satisfied.

(2)   The first condition is that the producers produce biofuel at the same premises or at the same sets of premises (those premises).

(3)   The second condition is that the producers have not previously made entry of those premises for the purpose of this regulation or the purposes specified in regulation 8(B); or, if they have made such entry, that entry has been cancelled by the Commissioners under regulation 8F.

(4)   The third condition is that at the end of any calendar month the total quantity of biofuel produced by all of those producers at all of those premises in the previous 12 months is 2,500 litres or more.

(5)   The fourth condition is that at any time there are reasonable grounds to believe that the total quantity of biofuel produced by all of those producers at all of those premises will be 2,500 litres or more in the following 12 months.

(6)   Each producer of biofuel to whom this regulation applies is liable to make entry of all those premises at which he has produced or, there are reasonable grounds to believe, will produce biofuel, but this is subject to paragraph (10).

(7)   A producer liable to make entry of those premises under paragraph (6) must make entry of them not later than the day specified in paragraph (8).

(8)   The specified day is—

(a)   in the case of a producer with respect to whom the third condition is satisfied, the thirtieth day following the end of the calendar month in question;

(b)   in the case of a producer with respect to whom the fourth condition is satisfied, the thirtieth day following the day on which reasonable grounds arise for believing that quantity will be produced.

(9)   Each producer to whom this regulation applies must not send out from any of those premises a consignment of biofuel, which is charged with biofuels duty because it is set aside for chargeable use, before he makes entry of those premises.

(10)   A producer who meets the third condition ceases to be liable to make entry of those premises if he satisfies the Commissioners that the total quantity of biofuel produced by all of those producers at all of those premises will be less than 2,500 litres of biofuel in the 12 months following the date on which he becomes liable.

8F Cancellation of an entry of production premises

(1) The Commissioners may at any time cancel an entry made by a producer in respect of production premises if the Commissioners are satisfied that the producer—

    (a)   has produced less than 2,500 litres of biofuel in the 12 months immediately preceding the proposed date of cancellation; or

    (b)   will produce less than 2,500 litres of biofuel in the 12 months immediately following the proposed date of cancellation.

(2) Where two or more producers produce biofuel at the same premises or same sets of premises and the Commissioners are satisfied that the total quantity of biofuel produced by all those producers at all those premises—

    (a)   is less than 2,500 litres in the 12 months immediately preceding the proposed date of cancellation; or

    (b)   will be less than 2,500 litres in the 12 months immediately following the proposed date of cancellation,

they may cancel the entries of those premises.

(3) The Commissioners must give a producer at least 30 days notice that they propose to cancel an entry before cancelling it.]

NOTES

Paras (8)–(8F): substituted for previous para (8) by the Biofuels and Other Fuel Substitutes (Payment of Excise Duties etc) (Amendment) Regulations, SI 2007/1640, regs 2, 4.

9 Storage of biofuels on production premises

Biofuels of different descriptions must be stored separately while on production premises, but this does not prevent biofuels from being mixed together to produce another biofuel.

10 Rights of access

(1) An authorised person may enter and inspect any production premises, other than a private dwellinghouse.

(2) An authorised person may examine any vehicle on those premises.

(3) An authorised person may inspect or sample any biofuel found on those premises.

(4) An authorised person may inspect or sample any biofuel found on or in any vehicle on those premises.

11 Provision of facilities by producers etc

Any person occupying or for the time being in charge of any premises which an authorised person enters and inspects under regulation 10 must, if required by the authorised person, give facilities for the inspection or sampling of any biofuel found—

    (a)   on those premises, or

    (b)   in or on any vehicle on those premises.

12 Removal of biofuel from production premises for warehousing

Subject to regulation 7 (warehousing), biofuel that is charged with biofuels duty while on entered premises may be removed from those premises for warehousing in an excise warehouse adjacent to the entered premises without payment of the biofuels duty.

Part II

PART 5
RECORDS AND MEASUREMENT

13 Motor fuels record

(1)   Every producer[, other than an exempt producer,] must keep and preserve at production premises a record ("the motor fuels record") in accordance with the provisions of, and containing the particulars specified in, the Schedule.

(2)   In the Schedule, a reference to "standard litres" means a litre of any liquid at a temperature of 15°C.

(3)   The motor fuels record must be preserved by the producer for a period of 6 years, or such lesser period as the Commissioners may allow, starting on the day that the record is made.

NOTES

Para (1): words in square brackets inserted by the Biofuels and Other Fuel Substitutes (Payment of Excise Duties etc) (Amendment) Regulations, SI 2007/1640, regs 2, 5.

13A

(1)   Every exempt producer must keep and preserve at production premises such records as may be specified in a notice published by the Commissioners and not withdrawn by a further notice.

(2)   The records required to be preserved by virtue of paragraph (1) must be preserved by the exempt producer for 6 years, or such lesser period as the Commissioner may allow, starting on the day the record is made.

NOTES

Inserted by the Biofuels and Other Fuel Substitutes (Payment of Excise Duties etc) (Amendment) Regulations, SI 2007/1640, regs 2, 6.

14 Fuel substitutes record and biodiesel record

(1)   This regulation applies if, before 1st September 2004, a person was obliged to keep and preserve—

  (a)   the fuel substitutes record governed by regulation 6 of the Other Fuel Substitutes (Payment of Excise Duty etc) Regulations 1995, or

  (b)   the biodiesel record governed by regulation 7 of the Biodiesel and Bioblend Regulations 2002,

(2)   Notwithstanding the revocation of the regulations described in paragraph (1), the person must continue to preserve the fuel substitutes record or the biodiesel record, as the case may be, for a period of 6 years, or such lesser period as the Commissioners may allow, starting on the day that the record is made.

15 Delivery note

(1)   This regulation applies if—

  (a)   a producer sends out from production premises a consignment of biofuel, and

  (b)   that biofuel is charged with biofuel duty because it is set aside for chargeable use when on those production premises.

(2)   The producer must, in respect of each consignment sent out from production premises, issue to the consignee a serially numbered delivery note containing the particulars specified in paragraph (3).

(3)   The particulars that are to be set out in the delivery note are as follows—

    (a)   the particulars set out in sub-paragraphs (a) to (f) of paragraph 1 of the Schedule; and

    (b)   the address from which that consignment is sent out.

16 Measurement

Where an authorised person requires the use of—

    (a)   a particular method of measurement,

    (b)   a particular method of calibration, or

    (c)   particular conversion tables,

to ascertain any quantity of biofuel at or received into, used at or sent out from a production premises or an excise warehouse, the occupier of the production premises or the excise warehouse must comply with such requirement.

PART 6
EXCISE DUTY POINTS, RETURNS AND PAYMENT

17 Excise duty points

(1) Save—

    (a)   in the case specified in paragraph (2), or

    (b)   where duty suspension arrangements apply to the biofuel,

the excise duty point for biofuel [produced by a producer liable to make entry of premises under regulation 8A or 8E(6), who has not made such entry,] is the time when it is charged with biofuels duty.

(2) The excise duty point for biofuel that is sent out from entered premises having been charged with biofuels duty when on those premises is the time that the biofuel is sent out.

(3) Where biofuel is removed from entered premises in accordance with regulation 12, but it is not deposited in an adjacent excise warehouse within a reasonable time, the excise duty point for the biofuel is the time that it was sent out from the entered premises.

(4) In this regulation, "duty suspension arrangements" means any provision made by or under the customs and excise Acts (including provision made by these Regulations) for enabling goods to be held or moved without payment of duty or any provision made by or under those Acts in connection with any provision enabling goods to be so held or moved.

NOTES

Para (1): words inserted by the Biofuels and Other Fuel Substitutes (Payment of Excise Duties etc) (Amendment) Regulations, SI 2007/1640, regs 2, 7.

---

18 Person liable

The person liable to pay the biofuels duty at an excise duty point fixed by regulation 17 is—

    (a)   in the case of biofuel that is charged to biofuels duty on production premises, the producer;

    (b)   in any other case, the person who caused the biofuel to be charged with biofuels duty.

19 Returns, time and method of payment

[(1) The requirements in paragraph (1A) apply to a producer, other than a large producer, in relation to—

    (a)   each of his entered premises, and

(b) any premises for which he is liable to make entry that have not been entered.

(1A) A producer to whom this paragraph applies must no later than the fifteenth day of each quarter—

(a) furnish a return of the quantities of biodiesel, bioethanol and fuel substitute, and

(b) pay the biofuels duty

in respect of which there was an excise duty point in the preceding quarter.]

(2) The return must be made on forms provided by the Commissioners for the purpose.

(3) The return must be furnished, and the payment made, to the Commissioners at such address as is specified in directions made by the Commissioners under section 116(1) of the Customs and Excise Management Act 1979.

(4) Where the fifteenth day of the [quarter] would fall on a day that is not a business day, the requirements of paragraph (1) must be complied with no later than the last business day before that fifteenth day.

(5) In paragraph (4), "business day" means a day that is a business day within the meaning of section 92 of the Bills of Exchange Act 1882.

(6) If the producer is an approved person who is granted deferment of the biofuels duty in accordance with regulation 5 of the Deferment Regulations, then—

(a) no information need be furnished to the Commissioners in accordance with paragraph (1) above in relation to biofuel that is subject to that deferment, and

(b) the time when the biofuels duty is to be paid shall be the payment day specified by the Deferment Regulations.

(7) In any other case for which an excise duty point is fixed by these Regulations, the biofuels duty must be paid on or before the excise duty point.

[(8) Every producer who is a producer on 30th June 2007 must, in relation to each of his entered premises, no later than 13 July 2007—

(a) furnish a return of the quantities of biodiesel, bioethanol, and fuel substitute; and

(b) pay the biofuels duty,

in respect of which there was an excise duty point in June 2007.]

NOTES

Paras (1), (1A): substituted for previous para (1) by the Biofuels and Other Fuel Substitutes (Payment of Excise Duties etc) (Amendment) Regulations, SI 2007/1640, regs 2, 8(1), (2).

Para (4): word in square brackets substituted by the Biofuels and Other Fuel Substitutes (Payment of Excise Duties etc) (Amendment) Regulations, SI 2007/1640, regs 2, 8(1), (3).

Para (8): inserted by the Biofuels and Other Fuel Substitutes (Payment of Excise Duties etc) (Amendment) Regulations, SI 2007/1640, regs 2, 8(1), (4).

[**19A Large producers**

(1) The Commissioners may at any time notify a producer that he is a large producer if—

(a) in the 12 months immediately preceding notification the producer has produced 450,000 litres or more of biofuel; or

(b) they have reasonable grounds to believe that the producer will produce 450,000 litres or more of biofuel in the 12 months following notification.

(2) The Commissioners may withdraw a notification given to a large producer under paragraph (9) if the producer satisfies them by a statement in writing that—

    (a)   he has produced less than 450,000 litres of biofuel in the 12 months immediately preceding that statement, and

    (b)   there are reasonable grounds to believe he will produce less than 450,000 litres of biofuel in the 12 months immediately following that statement.

(3)   The requirements in paragraph (4) apply to a producer who is for the time being a large producer in relation to—

    (a)   each of his entered premises, and

    (b)   any premises for which he is liable to make entry that have not been entered.

(4)   A large producer must no later than the fifteenth day of each month—

    (a)   furnish a return of the quantities of biodiesel, bioethanol and fuel substitute, and

    (b)   pay the biofuels duty

in respect of which there was an excise duty point in the preceding month.

(5)   Regulations 19(2) to 19(8) apply to large producers as they apply to producers and in the case of regulation 19(4) it so applies with the substitution of quarter for month.

NOTES

Inserted by the Biofuels and Other Fuel Substitutes (Payment of Excise Duties etc) (Amendment) Regulations, SI 2007/1640, regs 2, 9.

PART 7
RELIEF FOR ELECTRICITY GENERATION

20 Interpretation of this Part

In this Part, "qualified claimant" means a person who causes biofuel to be used as motor fuel in a generator to produce electricity.

21 Relief

(1)   Relief is afforded in accordance with this Part if a quantity of biofuel has been—

    (a)   charged with biofuels duty, and

    (b)   used as motor fuel in a generator to produce electricity,

(2)   The amount that is afforded is the amount of the biofuels duty that has been charged and paid.

(3)   Relief is allowed only upon the written application of a qualified claimant.

(4)   No relief is allowed in respect of any biofuels duty that is the subject of any other application or claim for repayment, remission or drawback.

22 Form of relief

(1)   If, at the time that the claim is made, the qualified claimant is an approved person, relief shall be in the form of an allowance to be set-off against duty payable to the Commissioners by the qualified claimant.

(2)   If, at the time that the claim is made, the qualified claimant—

    (a)   is not an approved person,

    (b)   is a producer in relation to the biofuel that is the subject of the claim for relief, and

    (c)   has entered the premises (in accordance with regulation 8) on which that biofuel was charged with biofuels duty,

Part II

relief shall be in the form of an allowance to be set-off against the biofuels duty payable to the Commissioners by the qualified claimant in respect of the biofuel that is the subject of the claim for relief.

(3) In any other case, the relief shall be in the form of a repayment by the Commissioners to the qualified claimant.

(4) If two or more qualified claimants make application for relief relating to the same fuel, the Commissioners may determine which one shall be afforded the relief.

(5) If in relation to any application for relief it appears to the Commissioners that the relief applied for exceeds the amount allowable under regulation 21, they may, in such circumstances as they see fit and notwithstanding the provisions of regulations 25(1) and 26(3), reduce the amount of the claim to such lesser sum as appears to them to be allowable.

23 Set-off

(1) In the case described by regulation 22(1) (approved persons), the qualified claimant must set-off the relief in accordance with regulation 6 of the Deferment Regulations.

(2) In the case described by regulation 22(2) (producers), the qualified claimant must set-off the relief against the biofuels duty that he is obliged to pay under regulation 19(1).

(3) In any other case, the Commissioners may set-off the amount of any repayment under regulation 22(3) against any other debt then due to them from the qualified claimant.

24 Applications

(1) Applications for relief that is set-off in accordance with regulation 23(1) must be made by submitting the claim for set-off governed by regulation 6(2) of the Deferment Regulations.

(2) Applications for relief that is set-off in accordance with regulation 23(2) must accompany the return governed by regulation 19(1) that he is obliged to furnish in respect of the biofuels duty.

(3) Applications for repayment—

    (a)   must be made no later than 3 months after the period to which they relate, and that period must not be shorter than 2 months nor longer than 3 years, and

    (b)   shall not lie where the amount to be paid is less than £50.

25 Cancellation of relief

(1) If there is a contravention of, or failure to comply with, any condition imposed by or under regulation 26 or 27, the relief allowed shall be cancelled.

(2) Where any relief is cancelled, any person who is a qualified claimant in relation to the application for relief shall, on demand, be liable to repay the amount of the relief.

26 General conditions

(1) Relief is allowed subject to the following conditions.

(2) The qualified claimant must, on being so required by the Commissioners, furnish to their satisfaction evidence that—

    (a)   the biofuel that is the subject of the application for relief has been used as motor fuel in a generator to produce electricity, and

    (b)   the biofuels duty that is the subject of the application for relief has been paid and is not the subject of any other application or claim for repayment, remission or drawback.

(3) The amount of relief applied for must not exceed the amount of relief that may be allowed by regulation 21.

27 Conditions imposed by the Commissioners
Relief is allowed subject to such conditions (if any) as the Commissioners impose on a qualified claimant.

PART 8
BIODIESEL USED OTHERWISE THAN AS ROAD FUEL

28 Applications for repayment under section 17A of the Oil Act
Applications for repayment under section 17A of the Oil Act (biodiesel used otherwise than as road fuel)—

(a)   must be made no later than 3 months after the period to which they relate, and that period must not be shorter than 2 months nor longer than 3 years, and

(b)   shall not lie where the amount to be paid is less than £50.

SCHEDULE
PARTICULARS TO BE ENTERED IN THE MOTOR FUELS RECORD
Regulation 13(1)

Charge arising on setting aside

1.
In respect of each consignment of biodiesel, bioethanol or fuel substitute that is charged with biofuels duty because it is set aside for chargeable use when on the premises from which it is sent out, the following particulars must be entered in the motor fuels record before the consignment is sent out from his premises—

(a)   the date on which the consignment is sent out;

(b)   a description of that consignment indicating whether it is biodiesel, bioethanol or fuel substitute;

(c)   in the case of a consignment of fuel substitute, a description indicating that the fuel substitute has been charged with fuel substitute duty upon being set aside as—

(i)   suitable only as fuel for a diesel engine,

(ii)   suitable only as fuel for an engine, other than a piston engine, of an aircraft,

(iii)   suitable only as fuel for a petrol engine powered by leaded petrol,

(iv)   suitable only as fuel for a petrol engine powered by unleaded petrol,

(v)   specially produced as fuel for a piston engine of an aircraft,

(vi)   fuel for an engine, motor or machinery, but not falling within sub-paragraphs (i) to (v),

(vii) suitable only as an additive or extender in fuel for a diesel engine,

(viii) suitable only as an additive or extender in fuel for an engine, other than a piston engine of an aircraft,

(ix)   suitable only as an additive or extender in fuel for a petrol engine powered by leaded petrol,

(x)   suitable only as an additive or extender in fuel for a petrol engine powered by unleaded petrol,

(xi)   a multi-purpose additive or extender (designated, made and prepared as being for use as an additive or extender in any light oil),

(xii) an additive or extender not falling within sub-paragraphs (vii) to (xi);

(d) the quantity, in standard litres, of that consignment;

(e) the name and address of the consignee to whom that consignment is sent;

(f) the address to which that consignment is consigned;

(g) the number of the delivery note (see regulation 15) that accompanied that consignment;

(h) the date upon which the entry in relation to the consignment is made in the motor fuels record; and

(j) the amount and rate of biofuels duty charged in respect of that consignment.

Charge arising on chargeable use

2.

In respect of each quantity of biodiesel, bioethanol or fuel substitute that is charged with biofuels duty because it is put to chargeable use when on his premises, the following particulars must be entered in the motor fuels record on the day of the chargeable use—

(a) the date of chargeable use;

(b) a description of the liquid indicating whether it is biodiesel, bioethanol or fuel substitute;

(c) in the case of fuel substitute, a description indicating that the fuel substitute has been charged with fuel substitute duty upon chargeable use as—

(i)   fuel for a diesel engine,

(ii) fuel for an engine, other than a piston engine, of an aircraft,

(iii) fuel for a petrol engine powered by leaded petrol,

(iv) fuel for a petrol engine powered by unleaded petrol,

(v)   fuel for a piston engine of an aircraft,

(vi) fuel for any other engine, motor or machinery not falling within sub-paragraphs (i) to (iv),

(vii) an additive or extender in fuel for a diesel engine,

(viii) an additive or extender in fuel for an engine, other than a piston engine of an aircraft,

(ix) an additive or extender in fuel for a petrol engine powered by leaded petrol,

(x)   an additive or extender in fuel for a petrol engine powered by unleaded petrol,

(xi) an additive or extender in fuel for a piston engine of an aircraft, or

(xii) an additive or extender in fuel for any engine, motor or machinery not falling within paragraphs (i) to (iv);

(d) the quantity, in standard litres, of the biofuel put to chargeable use;

(e) the date upon which the entry in relation to the consignment is made in the motor fuels record; and

(f) the amount and rate of biofuels duty charged in respect of that chargeable use.

DENATURED ALCOHOL REGULATIONS 2005

(SI 2005/1524)

NOTES

Made: 8 June 2005

Authority: the Customs and Excise Management Act 1979, s 93(1)(d) and (2)(a); the Alcoholic Liquor Duties Act 1979, s 35 and 77; the Finance (No 2) Act 1992, s 1; and the Finance Act 1995, s 5.

Commencement: 1 July 2005

PART 1
PRELIMINARY

1 Citation and commencement

These Regulations may be cited as the Denatured Alcohol Regulations 2005 and come into force on 1st July 2005.

2 Interpretation

In these Regulations—

"the Act" means the Alcoholic Liquor Duties Act 1979;

"alcohol", except in regulation 10(3), means "dutiable alcoholic liquor";

"completely denatured alcohol" has the meaning given in regulation 4;

"formulation" means the recipe or list of substances and liquids, including any proportions, quantities, standards, or other criteria relating to those substances and liquids, that a producer is to use and follow when making the class of denatured alcohol or a batch of it to which the formulation relates;

"industrial denatured alcohol" has the meaning given in regulation 4;

"producer" means—

    (a)   a person who is a distiller, rectifier or compounder, and who is authorized by the Commissioners under section 75 of the Act to denature alcohol; or

    (b)   a person who holds an excise licence granted under that section, and who denatures or intends to denature alcohol at any premises;

"trade specific denatured alcohol" has the meaning given in regulation 4.

3 Revocation

The Iso-Propyl Alcohol Regulations 1927 and the Methylated Spirits Regulations 1987 are revoked.

PART 2
CLASSES OF DENATURED ALCOHOL AND FORMULATIONS

4 Classes of denatured alcohol

(1) For the purposes of the Act, section 5 of the Finance Act 1995 and these Regulations there are the following classes of denatured alcohol—

    (a)   completely denatured alcohol;

    (b)   industrial denatured alcohol; and

    (c)   trade specific denatured alcohol.

(2) Subject to paragraphs (4), (6) and (7), completely denatured alcohol is denatured alcohol—

    (a)   that has been made in accordance with regulation 5, or

   (b)   that, if the denaturants that are employed are described in the Annex
          to Commission Regulation (EC) No 3199/93, has been made in a
          member State other than the United Kingdom in accordance with a
          formulation and other requirements of that member State.

(3) Subject to paragraphs (4) and (6), industrial denatured alcohol is denatured
alcohol—

   (a)   that has been made in accordance with regulation 6, or
   (b)   that is not completely denatured alcohol and—
          (i)   has been made in a member State other than the United Kingdom
                 in accordance with a formulation and other requirements of that
                 member State, and
          (ii)   has been incorporated into a product that is not for human
                 consumption.

(4) Denatured alcohol made in a member State other than the United Kingdom is
not denatured alcohol for the purposes of the Act, section 5 of the Finance Act 1995
or these Regulations if—

   (a)   the United Kingdom has, in accordance with Article 27(5) of Council
          Directive 92/83/EEC, advised the European Commission that it gives
          rise to evasion, avoidance or abuse, and
   (b)   it has not been determined, in accordance with the procedure laid down
          in Article 24 of Council Directive 92/12/EEC, that that denatured
          alcohol must be treated as exempt from excise duty under sub-
          paragraph (a) or (b) of Article 27(1) of Council Directive 92/83/EEC

(5) Subject to paragraph (6), trade specific denatured alcohol is denatured alcohol
that has been made in accordance with regulation 7.

(6) Denatured alcohol made outside the United Kingdom that has not been
incorporated into a product that is not for human consumption is completely
denatured alcohol, industrial denatured alcohol or trade specific denatured alcohol (as
the case may be) if, in the opinion of the Commissioners, it has been made as nearly as
is possible in accordance with one of the formulations described in the Schedule.

(7) Denatured alcohol made outside the United Kingdom and the Communities is
completely denatured alcohol if, in the opinion of the Commissioners—

   (a)   the denaturants employed are described in the Annex to Commission
          Regulation (EC) No 3199/93, and
   (b)   it has been made as nearly as is possible in accordance with a
          formulation of a member State other than the United Kingdom.

5 Completely denatured alcohol

A producer making completely denatured alcohol must—

   (a)   make it in accordance with the formulation described in paragraph 1 of
          the Schedule, and
   (b)   comply with the standards and other requirements of paragraphs 5 to
          11 of that Schedule.

6 Industrial denatured alcohol

A producer making industrial denatured alcohol must—

   (a)   make it in accordance with the formulation described in paragraph 2 of
          the Schedule, and
   (b)   comply with the standards and other requirements of paragraphs 5 to 7
          and 11 of that Schedule.

7 Trade specific denatured alcohol

(1) Subject to paragraph (2), a producer making trade specific denatured alcohol
must—

(a)   make it in accordance with a formulation described in paragraph 3 of the Schedule, and

(b)   comply with the standards and other requirements of paragraphs 4 to 6 and 11 of that Schedule (insofar as those paragraphs are applicable to the formulation he is following).

(2)   Instead of following a formulation described in paragraph 3 of the Schedule, when making a batch of trade specific denatured alcohol a producer may make that batch in accordance with a formulation that is approved by the Commissioners under this regulation.

(3)   The Commissioners may, if they think that in all the circumstances it is appropriate to do so, approve a formulation different from or as a variation on a trade specific denatured alcohol formulation described in paragraph 3 of the Schedule.

(4)   The Commissioners' approval—

(a)   may only be granted following a written application to them by a producer or other person ("the applicant"), and

(b)   may be granted subject to such conditions as the Commissioners may reasonably impose,

and those conditions may be varied by the Commissioners for reasonable cause.

(5)   The Commissioners may require for the purposes of their consideration of the application made under paragraph (4)—

(a)   a written statement containing the reasons why, in the applicant's opinion, completely denatured alcohol, industrial denatured alcohol, and a formulation of trade specific denatured alcohol described in paragraph 3 of the Schedule, would all be unsuitable or detrimental having regard to the use to which it is intended that the denatured alcohol will be put;

(b)   samples of the proposed formulation of trade specific denatured alcohol and of the ingredients of that formulation; and

(c)   any other information that the Commissioners determine to be material to their consideration of whether or not it would be appropriate for them to grant approval of the formulation in question.

PART 3
PRODUCERS AND DISTRIBUTORS OF DENATURED ALCOHOL

8 Producer's application for approval and entry of premises

(1)   A producer must, in respect of each set of premises at which he intends to make a class of denatured alcohol, make written application to the Commissioners for approval of the process he intends to employ when making that denatured alcohol.

(2)   The application must include—

(a)   the class of denatured alcohol which the producer intends to make at the premises;

(b)   the formulation which the producer intends to follow in making a batch of that class;

(c)   the process which the producer intends to employ when mixing the alcohol with the other substances specified by the formulation being followed in making the denatured alcohol;

(d)   such other information as the Commissioners may require.

(3)   No person may begin to denature alcohol until—

(a)   the Commissioners have, in accordance with this regulation, approved the process to be employed, and

Part II

    (b)   if so required by paragraph (7), entry has been made in accordance with section 108 of the Customs and Excise Management Act 1979 of each set of premises at which it is intended to make denatured alcohol.

  (4) The Commissioners' approval of the process to be employed—

    (a)   may be granted subject to such conditions as the Commissioners may reasonably impose, and

    (b)   those conditions may be varied by the Commissioners for reasonable cause.

(5)   A producer who has received the Commissioners' approval of the process to be employed must ensure that no other process is used and that the approved process is not varied without first receiving the Commissioners' approval of that other process or of that variation.

(6)   Paragraph (4) applies to any approval given under paragraph (5).

(7)   Except in the case of premises that are an excise warehouse, a producer must make entry of each set of premises at which he intends to make a class of denatured alcohol.

9 Producer's and distributor's account of goods and distributor's entry of premises

  (1) In this regulation—

"distributor" means a person who—

    (a)   holds an excise licence for the purposes of section 75 of the Act,

    (b)   does not denature alcohol at any premises on which he holds denatured alcohol, and

    (c)   deals or intends to deal wholesale in denatured alcohol;

"goods" includes—

    (a)   any alcohol, denaturants, dyes, denatured alcohol, and

    (b)   any other goods on the premises described in paragraph (2)(a) by reason of those goods having been received, held, used or produced at those premises.

  (2) A producer and a distributor must—

    (a)   control the goods on any premises on which they produce or hold denatured alcohol;

    (b)   take an account of those goods, and take an account (at the time of dispatch) of any goods dispatched from those premises in such manner and to such extent as the Commissioners may require;

    (c)   immediately record in such form and manner as the Commissioners may require any deficiency, surplus or discrepancy in their stock of goods or shown in their records, and any explanation for that deficiency, surplus or discrepancy;

    (d)   in addition to recording the details required by sub-paragraph (c), inform the Commissioners, in accordance with their instructions, of the deficiency, surplus or discrepancy;

    (e)   keep and preserve such other records relating to their business as a producer or as a distributor as the Commissioners may specify in a notice published by them and not withdrawn by a further notice.

(3)   For the purposes of paragraph (2) the Commissioners may give instructions that the stock of goods to which a deficiency, surplus or discrepancy relates must not be moved or disturbed without their permission and if they do give instructions to that effect no person may move or disturb that stock of goods without their permission.

(4)   Requirements imposed under paragraph (2) and instructions given under paragraph (3) may apply differently to different circumstances and may be varied from time to time by the Commissioners.

(5)   A distributor must make entry in accordance with section 108 of the Customs and Excise Management Act 1979 of any premises on which he holds or intends to hold denatured alcohol.

10 Receipt of alcohol for denaturing

(1)   The Commissioners may, subject to such conditions as they see fit to impose, permit alcohol to be delivered from an excise warehouse to the entered premises of a producer for denaturing without payment of excise duty.
In this paragraph "entered premises" means premises for which entry has been made in accordance with section 108 of the Customs and Excise Management Act 1979.

(2)   The power to impose conditions under paragraph (1) includes power to require such security for excise duty as the Commissioners think fit.

(3)   A producer who receives any alcohol of any description whatsoever from an excise warehouse must furnish the occupier of that excise warehouse with a receipt in such manner, within such period, and in such form, and containing such particulars, as the Commissioners may require.

11 Excise duty point

(1)   Where, in accordance with regulation 9(2)(d) a producer is required to inform the Commissioners of a deficiency in his stock of alcohol for denaturing, the time that the deficiency was discovered is the excise duty point for the missing alcohol.

(2)   The producer is liable to pay the excise duty.

(3)   This regulation does not apply to a deficiency that is attributable to evaporation or destruction of the alcohol found to be missing.

PART 4
RECEIPT, USE AND SUPPLY OF DENATURED ALCOHOL

12 Application
This Part applies to industrial denatured alcohol and trade specific denatured alcohol that has not been incorporated into a product that is not for human consumption.

13 Receipt and use of industrial denatured alcohol and trade specific denatured alcohol

(1)   No person may receive or use industrial denatured alcohol or trade specific denatured alcohol other than in accordance with the provisions of this Part.

(2)   A person may receive industrial denatured alcohol or trade specific denatured alcohol only if he is authorized in writing by the Commissioners to receive that class of denatured alcohol.

(3)   A person wishing to be authorized to receive industrial denatured alcohol or trade specific denatured alcohol must—

    (a)   apply to the Commissioners in the form and manner specified in a notice they publish that has not been withdrawn by a further notice; and

    (b)   if he wishes to receive trade specific denatured alcohol made in accordance with a formulation approved under regulation 7(2), describe the formulation in his application.

(4)   The Commissioners may authorize a person to receive industrial denatured alcohol or trade specific denatured alcohol—

    (a)   subject to restrictions on the uses to which that denatured alcohol may be put;

    (b)   subject to restrictions on the formulations of denatured alcohol that may be received; and

    (c)   subject to such conditions as they see fit to impose.

(5)   Where there has been a change in any of the particulars that were included in a person's application for authorization, before receiving any further supplies of

industrial denatured alcohol or trade specific denatured alcohol, he must give the Commissioners notice of that change in such form and manner as they require.

(6)   The Commissioners may at any time for reasonable cause vary or revoke any authorization granted or any condition or restriction imposed under this regulation.

(7)   A person may receive industrial denatured alcohol or any formulation of trade specific denatured alcohol only if, before he is supplied with that denatured alcohol, he furnishes the supplier with a copy of his authorization.

(8)   A person authorized under this regulation must keep and preserve such records relating to his use of denatured alcohol as the Commissioners may specify in a notice published by them and not withdrawn by a further notice.

(9)   A person authorized under this regulation must comply with and ensure compliance with any conditions or restrictions imposed in accordance with this regulation.

14 Supply of industrial denatured alcohol and trade specific denatured alcohol
Subject to regulation 15, industrial denatured alcohol and trade specific denatured alcohol—

    (a)   must not be sent out from any premises other than in the course of a supply to a person—

        (i)   who is authorized in accordance with these Regulations to receive denatured alcohol of that formulation, and

        (ii)   who has furnished his supplier with a copy of his authorization to receive denatured alcohol of that formulation, and

    (b)   must not be supplied for any use that contravenes the restrictions on uses to which that formulation of denatured alcohol may be put by the person supplied.

15 Supply of industrial denatured alcohol and trade specific denatured alcohol—supplementary provisions
(1)   Regulation 14 does not apply to any case where—

    (a)   the denatured alcohol is delivered to a place that is outside the United Kingdom and Isle of Man; or

    (b)   a pharmacist is sending out industrial denatured alcohol for medical use on the prescription or order of a medical or veterinary practitioner.

In this paragraph—

"pharmacist" has the meaning given in section 132(1) of the Medicines Act 1968;
"medical or veterinary practitioner" means a person entitled by law to provide medical or veterinary services in the United Kingdom;
"medical use" means any medical, veterinary, surgical or dental purpose other than administration internally.

(2)   A person is treated as authorized to receive denatured alcohol of a particular formulation in accordance with these Regulations if he receives that alcohol in the Isle of Man and is authorized in accordance with the laws of the Isle of Man to receive that alcohol.

(3)   In any case to which paragraph (2) applies the requirement contained in regulation 14(a)(ii) does not apply but the person intending to supply denatured alcohol must require the person to be supplied to provide a written statement specifying—

    (a)   the date upon which he was authorized to receive denatured alcohol of that formulation;

    (b)   the use or uses to which he intends to put that denatured alcohol;

    (c)   any conditions or restrictions imposed on him by his authorization to receive denatured alcohol; and

(d)   the uses to which he is entitled to put the received denatured alcohol.

PART 5
MISCELLANEOUS

16 Recovery of alcohol

(1)   Subject to paragraph (2), no person may by any means whatsoever recover any alcohol or remove any other substance from any denatured alcohol or from any product containing denatured alcohol.

(2)   The Commissioners may, subject to such conditions as they see fit to impose, allow a person to recover alcohol or remove any other substance from any denatured alcohol or from any product containing denatured alcohol.

(3)   Where any alcohol is recovered or any other substance is removed from any denatured alcohol or from any product containing denatured alcohol the alcohol and the product from which any other substance is removed must be kept—

(a)   under the control of the person who recovered or removed it; and

(b)   under lock or otherwise secured until disposed of or otherwise dealt with in accordance with any condition imposed under paragraph (2).

17 Disposal of stocks

(1)   A producer, a distributor or other person authorized in accordance with these Regulations to receive, use, send out or supply any class of denatured alcohol—

(a)   whose business is discontinued while he is holding stocks of denatured alcohol, or

(b)   whose authority or licence for holding stocks of any class of denatured alcohol is revoked,

must within a reasonable time and to the satisfaction of the Commissioners dispose of any of those stocks in his possession.

(2)   Where the discontinuance of a business is caused by the death of a producer, distributor or other person described in the paragraph (1), his personal representatives must dispose of any stocks of denatured alcohol in his possession at the time of his death in the manner required by the paragraph (1).

(3)   In this regulation "distributor" means a person who holds an excise licence for the purpose of section 75 of the Act whether or not he is also a producer.

18 Importing and exporting denatured alcohol

Unless it has been incorporated into a product that is not for human consumption, the Excise Goods (Accompanying Documents) Regulations 2002 shall apply to imports and exports of—

(a)   completely denatured alcohol as if it were alcohol in respect of which excise duty has been paid, and

(b)   any other denatured alcohol as if it were alcohol in respect of which excise duty has not been paid.

19 Amendment to the Spirits Regulations 1991

In regulation 20 of the Spirits Regulations 1991, omit the words "methylated spirits".

SCHEDULE
FORMULATIONS FOR THE CLASSES OF DENATURED
ALCOHOL, STANDARDS AND OTHER RELATED PROVISIONS

Regulations 5, 6 and 7

Formulation for Completely Denatured Alcohol

1.

Completely denatured alcohol must be made in accordance with the following formulation: with every 90 parts by volume of alcohol mix 9.5 parts by volume of wood naphtha or a substitute for wood naphtha and 0.5 parts by volume of crude pyridine, and to the resulting mixture add mineral naphtha (petroleum oil) in the proportion of 3.75 litres to every 1000 litres of the mixture and synthetic organic dyestuff (methyl violet) in the proportion of 1.5 grammes to every 1000 litres of the mixture.

Formulation for Industrial Denatured Alcohol

2.

Industrial denatured alcohol must be made in accordance with the following formulation: with every 95 parts by volume of alcohol mix 5 parts by volume of wood naphtha or of a substitute for wood naphtha. Where a substitute for wood naptha is used, the volume mixed with every 95 parts of alcohol may be less than 5 parts if—

    (a)   the proportion of the marker in the resulting mixture is—

        (i)   in the case of methyl alcohol, not less than 36 parts per thousand,

        (ii)   in the case of tertiary butyl alcohol, not less than one part per thousand, or

        (iii)   in the case of another marker approved by the Commissioners, not less than the proportion specified by the Commissioners when they approved that marker, and

    (b)   the resulting mixture contains the other substances that the Commissioners approved when they approved the substitute for wood naptha in the proportions that they specify.

Formulations for Trade Specific Denatured Alcohol

3.

Except in cases where the Commissioners approve an alternative formulation, trade specific denatured alcohol must be made in accordance with one of the following formulations—

    (a)   with every 999 parts by volume of alcohol (of a strength of not less than 85 per cent alcohol by volume) mix 1 part by volume of tertiary butyl alcohol, and to the resulting mixture add denatonium benzoate (of the description specified in paragraph 4) in the proportion of 10 micrograms per millilitre;

    (b)   with every 979 parts by volume of alcohol (of a strength of not less than 85 per cent alcohol by volume) mix not less than 20 parts by volume of cyclohexane and 1 part by volume of isopropyl alcohol;

    (c)   with every 979 parts by volume of alcohol (of a strength of not less than 85 per cent alcohol by volume) mix not less than 20 parts by volume of ethyl acetate and 1 part by volume of isopropyl alcohol;

    (d)   with every 975 parts by volume of alcohol (of a strength of not less than 85 per cent alcohol by volume) mix not less than 20 parts by volume of methyl alcohol and 5 parts by volume of hexane;

    (e)   with every 950 parts by volume of alcohol (of a strength of not less than 85 per cent alcohol by volume) mix not less than 50 parts by volume of benzyl benzoate;

    (f)   with every 980 parts by volume of alcohol (of a strength of not less than 85 per cent alcohol by volume) mix not less than 20 parts by volume of isopropyl alcohol, and to the resulting mixture add denatonium benzoate (of the description specified in paragraph 4), in the proportion of 10 micrograms per millilitre;

(g)   with every 950 parts by volume of alcohol (of a strength of not less than 85 per cent alcohol by volume) mix not less than 50 parts by volume of isopropyl alcohol;

(h)   with every 990 parts by volume of alcohol (of a strength of not less than 85 per cent alcohol by volume) mix 10 parts by volume of methylethylketone (consisting of 95 to 96 per cent by weight of methylethylketone, 2.5 to 3 per cent by weight of methylisopropylketone, and 1.5 to 2 per cent by weight of ethylisoamylketone), and to the resulting mixture add 1 gram of denatonium benzoate (of the description specified in paragraph 4);

(i)   with every 990 parts by volume of alcohol (of a strength of not less than 85 per cent alcohol by volume) mix 10 parts by volume of methyl alcohol and to the resulting mixture add denatonium benzoate (of the description specified in paragraph 4) in the proportion of 10 micrograms per millilitre.

Denatonium Benzoate

4.

Denatonium benzoate (mentioned in paragraph 3, and in paragraph 6) is benzyldiethyl [(2,6-xylycarbamoyl) methyl] ammonium benzoate.

Use of Water

5.

When making denatured alcohol in accordance with a formulation specified in paragraph 1, 2 or 3, water may be mixed with the alcohol before denaturing or with the denatured alcohol but the quantity of water added must not reduce the proportion or quantity of denaturing substances or dyes in the resulting mixture below the proportions or quantities specified in the formulation; and for the purpose of ascertaining the proportion or quantity of denaturing substances or dyes in any such mixture the water shall be treated as if it were alcohol.

Standards for Wood Naphtha, other Denaturing Substances and Dyes.

6.

Wood naphtha, substitute for wood naphtha, crude pyridine, mineral naphtha, tertiary butyl alcohol, denatonium benzoate, and dyes used in making denatured alcohol must conform to the respective standards and meet other respective requirements of paragraphs 7 to 11.

Wood Naphtha, and substitute for Wood Naphtha

7.—

(1)   Wood naphtha must, to the satisfaction of the Commissioners, possess such properties as to render a mixture of one part of the naphtha with 19 parts of alcohol of a strength of not less than 95 per cent alcohol by volume unfit for human consumption.

(2)   Wood naphtha must contain not less than 72 per cent by volume of methyl alcohol.

(3)   In the case of a substitute for wood naphtha—

(a)   the substitute must possess, to the satisfaction of the Commissioners, such properties as to render a mixture of one part of the substitute with 19 parts of alcohol, of a strength of not less than 95 per cent alcohol by volume, unfit for human consumption,

(b)   all the ingredients and their amounts which are to constitute the substitute must be approved by the Commissioners, and

(c)   the substitute must contain as a marker—

(i)   not less than 72 per cent by volume of methyl alcohol, or

(ii)   2 per cent by volume of tertiary butyl alcohol, or

(iii)   such other marker as may be approved by the Commissioners in the proportions specified by them.

Crude Pyridine

8.—

(1)   Crude pyridine must consist of pyridine bases and must not be more deeply coloured than a mixture of 2 millilitres of 0.05 molar iodine with one litre of water.

(2)   It must mix readily and completely with alcohol of a strength of not less than 95 per cent alcohol by volume and must give a clear or only slightly opalescent solution when mixed with twice its volume of water.

(3)   10 millilitres of a 1 per cent solution in water must produce immediately a distinct crystalline precipitate on vigorous shaking after the addition of 5 millilitres of an aqueous solution of cadmium chloride containing 5 grammes of the anhydrous fused salt in 100 millilitres, and produce an abundant separation of crystals within 10 minutes.

(4)   A white precipitate must be formed when 10 millilitres of a 1 per cent solution in water are mixed with 5 millilitres of Nessler's reagent.

(5)   1 millilitre of crude pyridine dissolved in 10 millilitres of distilled water must require not less than 9.5 millilitres of 0.5 molar sulphuric acid for neutralisation using screened methyl orange as an indicator.

(6)   100 millilitres distilled in accordance with *Determination of distillation characteristics of volatile organic liquids* (IP 195/98(2004))(BS 2000–195:1998) must give a distillate of at least 50 millilitres at a temperature of 140°C and of 90 millilitres at 160°C

Mineral Naphtha (Petroleum Oil)

9.

Mineral naphtha (petroleum oil) must be of a specific gravity of not less than 0.800 at a temperature of 15.5°C and must possess the characteristic odour and taste of commercial paraffin oil used for burning purposes.

Methyl Violet Dye (Colour Index Constitution No 42555)

10.

Methyl violet dye must be in the form of small crystals readily and completely soluble in alcohol of a strength of not less than 95 per cent alcohol by volume.

Quality

11.

All substances used in the production of denatured alcohol must be of sufficient quality to ensure that the alcohol is properly denatured.

EXCISE DUTIES (SURCHARGES OR REBATES) (HYDROCARBON OILS ETC) ORDER 2005

(SI 2005/1978)

NOTES

Revoked by the Finance Act 2006, s 6(7)(a).

...

EXCISE DUTIES (ROAD FUEL GAS) (RELIEFS) REGULATIONS 2005

(SI 2005/1979)

NOTES

Revoked by the Finance Act 2006, s 6(7)(b).

...

HYDROCARBON OIL DUTIES (RELIEFS FOR ELECTRICITY GENERATION) REGULATIONS 2005

(SI 2005/3320)

NOTES

Made: 5 December 2005.

Authority: Hydrocarbon Oil Duties Act 1979, ss 20AA(1)(a), (2)(a) to (e), (g) and (h) and (3).

Commencement: 1 January 2006.

PART 1
PRELIMINARY

1 Citation and commencement

(1)   These Regulations may be cited as the Hydrocarbon Oil Duties (Reliefs for Electricity Generation) Regulations 2005.

(2)   They come into force on 1st January 2006 and have effect in relation to any qualifying oil used to produce electricity in a generating station or combined heat and power station on or after that date.

2 Interpretation

In these Regulations—

"annual operation" means a period commencing on 1st January and finishing on 31st December;

["auto-generator" carries the meaning it would for climate change levy if that levy's taxable commodities included qualifying oil (see the Finance Act 2000 Schedule 6 paragraphs 3(1), 14(3)(a), 147, 152(1) and 152(3), and the Climate Change Levy (Electricity and Gas) Regulations 2001 regulation 6);]

"combined heat and power station" has the meaning given by paragraph 148(1) of Schedule 6 to the Finance Act 2000;

Part II

["exempt unlicensed electricity supplier" carries the meaning it would for climate change levy if that levy's taxable commodities included qualifying oil (see the Finance Act 2000 Schedule 6 paragraphs 3(1), 14(2)(a) and 14(4), and the Climate Change Levy (Electricity and Gas) Regulations 2001 regulation 5);]

"fully exempt combined heat and power station" has the meaning given by paragraph 148(2) of Schedule 6 to the Finance Act 2000;

"partly exempt combined heat and power station" has the meaning given by paragraph 148(3) of Schedule 6 to the Finance Act 2000;

"qualified claimant" means a person who causes qualifying oil to be used to produce electricity in a generating station or combined heat and power station;

"qualifying oil" means heavy [or light] oil on whose delivery for home use rebate has been allowed under section 11(1) [or 14(1)] of the Hydrocarbon Oil Duties Act 1979;

"relevant duty" means the duty charged on qualifying oil by section 6(1) of the Hydrocarbon Oil Duties Act 1979 less any rebate that has been allowed by section 11(1) [or 14(1)] of that Act.

NOTES

Definitions of "auto-generator" and "exempt unlicensed electricity supplier" substituted, and words in definitions of "qualifying oil" and "relevant duty" inserted, by the Hydrocarbon Oil Duties (Reliefs for Electricity Generation) (Amendment) Regulations, SI 2007/2191, reg 2.

PART 2
RELIEF

3 Relief

(1) Relief is allowed in accordance with these Regulations if a quantity of qualifying oil has been used to produce electricity in a—

    (a)   generating station;

    (b)   fully exempt combined heat and power station; or

    (c)   partly exempt combined heat and power station.

(2) Except where paragraph 3 [or Part 4] applies, no relief shall be allowed where qualifying oil has been used to produce electricity—

    (a)   by an auto-generator;

    (b)   by an exempt unlicensed electricity supplier.

[(3) This paragraph applies where the auto-generator or exempt unlicensed electricity supplier supplies that electricity to an electricity utility (or a person treated as such for climate change levy purposes).

In this context, "electricity utility" (or being treated as such) carries the meaning each has for climate change levy (see the Finance Act 2000 Schedule 6 paragraphs 147, 150(2), 150(4) and 151).]

(4) No relief is allowed in respect of any relevant duty that is the subject of any other application or claim for repayment, remission or drawback.

NOTES

Para (2): words in square brackets inserted by the Hydrocarbon Oil Duties (Reliefs for Electricity Generation) (Amendment) Regulations, SI 2007/2191, reg 3(2).

Para (3): substituted by the Hydrocarbon Oil Duties (Reliefs for Electricity Generation) (Amendment) Regulations, SI 2007/2191, reg 3(3).

4 Form of relief

The relief shall be in the form of a repayment by the Commissioners to the qualified claimant.

PART 3
ELECTRICITY PRODUCED IN A GENERATING STATION

5 Application of Part 3

This Part applies to relief allowed by regulation 3(1)(a).

6 Amount of relief

The amount that is allowed is the amount of relevant duty that has been charged and paid.

7 Application for relief

(1)   Relief is allowed only upon the written application of a qualified claimant.

(2)   Except as the Commissioners may otherwise allow, each application shall contain the particulars specified in paragraphs (a) to (e) of the Schedule and shall be in such form as the Commissioners may direct.

8

An application—

(a)   must be made no later than three months after the period to which they relate and that period must not be shorter than one month nor longer than three years; and

(b)   may not be made where the relief claimed is less than £50.

PART 4
ELECTRICITY PRODUCED IN A COMBINED HEAT AND POWER STATION

9 Application of Part 4

(1)   This Part applies to relief allowed by regulation 3(1)(b) or (c) above.

(2)   In this Part qualifying oil used to produce—

(a)   heat and electricity; or

(b)   heat, mechanical power and electricity

shall be treated as used to produce electricity.

10 Amount of relief

(1)   Except where paragraph (2) applies, the amount that is afforded is the amount of relevant duty that has been charged and paid on qualifying oil used to produce electricity in the annual operation to which the application relates. Where the efficiency percentage of the station is less than the threshold efficiency percentage of that station, the amount that is afforded is the relevant fraction of the relevant duty that has been charged and paid.

(2)   For the purposes of paragraph (1) the relevant fraction is the fraction—

(a)   whose numerator is the efficiency percentage for the station; and

(b)   whose denominator is the threshold efficiency percentage for that period.

(3)   For the purposes of this regulation—

(a)   A station's threshold efficiency percentage shall be 20 per cent.

(b)   A station's efficiency percentage is its power efficiency, as stated in its CHPQA certificate.

(c)   CHPQA has the meaning given in regulation 2 of the Climate Change Levy (Combined Heat and Power Stations) Regulations 2005.

(d)   CHPQA certificate means a certificate issued in respect of a combined heat and power station following assessment of the station against criteria set out in the CHPQA.

11 Application for relief

(1)   Relief is allowed only upon the written application of a qualified claimant.

(2)   Except as the Commissioners may otherwise allow, each application shall contain the particulars specified in paragraphs (a) to (g) of the Schedule and shall be in such form as the Commissioners may direct.

(3)   Applications for relief must be made in respect of an annual operation.

(4)   An application must be made no later than nine months after the annual operation to which it relates and may not be made where the amount to be paid is less than £50.

PART 5
CONDITIONS SUBJECT TO WHICH RELIEF IS ALLOWED

12 Cancellation of relief

(1)   If there is a failure to comply with any condition imposed by or under regulations 13 or 14, the relief allowed shall be cancelled.

(2)   Where any relief is cancelled, any person who is a qualified claimant in relation to the application for relief shall, on demand, be liable to repay the amount of the relief.

13 General conditions

(1)   Relief is allowed subject to the following conditions.

(2)   The qualified claimant must, if so required by the Commissioners, provide to their satisfaction evidence that—

(a)   the qualifying oil that is the subject of the application for relief has been used to produce electricity; and

(b)   the relevant duty that is the subject of the application for relief has been paid and is not the subject of any other application or claim for repayment, remission or drawback.

(3)   The qualified claimant must, if required to do so, permit an officer to inspect any generating station or combined heat and power station in which he has caused qualifying oil to be used to produce electricity.

(4)   The amount of the relief applied for must not exceed the amount of relief that may be allowed by regulation 3.

14 Conditions imposed by the Commissioners

Relief is allowed subject to such conditions (if any) as the Commissioners impose on a qualified claimant.

SCHEDULE
PARTICULARS TO BE CONTAINED IN APPLICATION

Regulations 7(2) and 11(2)

(a)   The name and address of the qualified claimant;

(b)   the period to which the application relates;

(c)   the amount of qualifying oil used in that period in each generating station, or combined heat and power station, in which the qualified claimant has caused qualifying oil to be used to produce electricity;

(d)   the address of each such station;

(e)   the amount of the claim;

(f)   a copy of the CHPQA certificate;

(g) a copy of the certificate given by the Secretary of State under paragraph 148(4) or (5) of Schedule 6 to the Finance Act 2000 (full-exemption and part-exemption certificates in respect of combined heat and power stations for the purposes of climate change levy).

DUTY STAMPS REGULATIONS 2006

(Si 2006/202)

NOTES

Made: 1 February 2006.

Authority: Customs and Excise Management Act 1979, ss 93(2)(fa), 118A(1) and (2) and 127A, and Alcoholic Liquor Duties Act 1979, Sch 2A paragraphs 1, 3, 4, and 5.

Commencement: 22 February 2006.

PART 1
PRELIMINARY

1 Citation and commencement

These Regulations may be cited as the Duty Stamps Regulations 2006 and come into force on 22nd February 2006.

2 Interpretation

(1) In these Regulations—

"alcoholic liquor" means dutiable alcoholic liquor to which Schedule 2A to the Alcoholic Liquor Duties Act 1979 applies;

"appointed contractor" means the person appointed by the Commissioners to distribute on their behalf type A stamps and the design specification for type B stamps;

"authorized warehousekeeper", subject to paragraph (4), has the meaning given in Article 4(a) of Council Directive 92/12/EEC;

"brand" includes any trademark and any visible image or words that identify the person who produced the alcoholic liquor, or the person who is responsible for marketing it;

"business day" has the meaning given in section 92 of the Bills of Exchange Act 1882;

"duty stamps representative" means a person appointed to be such a representative in accordance with regulation 13;

"export shop" has the meaning given in regulation 3 of the Excise Goods (Export Shops) Regulations 2000;

"external territory" means a place in a member State to which Council Directive 92/12/EEC does not apply, an EEA State, or a territory for whose external relations the United Kingdom or another member State is responsible, and "EEA State" means a State that is a Contracting Party to the European Economic Agreement signed at Oporto on 2nd May 1992 as adjusted by the Protocol signed at Brussels on 17th March 1993;

"irregular stamper" means a person, other than an occasional importer, who imports unstamped retail containers of alcoholic liquor into the United Kingdom and who is not authorized to hold dutiable alcoholic liquor on which excise duty has not been paid;

"merchandise" has the meaning given in regulation 2(1) of the Excise Goods (Sales on Board Ships and Aircraft) Regulations 1999;

"product type" means one of the following descriptions of alcoholic liquor, "brandy", "gin", "rum", "vodka", "whisky/whiskey", or "other product";

"occasional importer" has the meaning given in regulation 2(1) of the Excise Goods (Holding, Movement, Warehousing and REDS) Regulations 1992;

"REDS" has the meaning given in regulation 2(1) of the Excise Goods (Holding, Movement, Warehousing and REDS) Regulations 1992;

"registered mobile operator" has the meaning given in regulation 2(1) of the Excise Goods (Sales on Board Ships and Aircraft) Regulations 1999;

"registered owner" has the meaning given in regulation 2 of the Warehousekeepers and Owners of Warehoused Goods Regulations 1999;

"registered person" means a person who has been registered by the Commissioners under regulation 9, and whose registration has not ceased by virtue of regulation 12;

"tax warehouse" has the meaning given in Article 4(b) of Council Directive 92/12/EEC;

"third country" means a place that is neither a member State nor an external territory;

"unique reference number" means the number determined by the Commissioners for the purposes of regulation 4(3)(b)(i);

"unique registration number" means the number determined by the Commissioners for the purposes of regulation 9(3).

(2)   For the purposes of these Regulations, a retail container of alcoholic liquor is to be treated as stamped if—

(a)   it carries a duty stamp of a type that complies with, and has been affixed in accordance with, the laws of the Isle of Man, or

(b)   it carries a label that has been so affixed to the container, and the label incorporates a duty stamp of a type that complies with the laws of the Isle of Man.

(3)   For the purposes of these Regulations, a retail container of alcoholic liquor is to be treated as unstamped if it bears a duty stamp that has been obliterated.

A duty stamp has been obliterated if, but only if—

(a)   the words "For the UK market" have been completely removed from it,

(b)   it has been completely obscured by an indelible dye or ink, or

(c)   it has been completely covered by a label using an adhesive that prevents that label from being removed without also destroying the stamp.

(4)   For the purposes of these Regulations, a producers' collective is to be treated as an authorized warehousekeeper.

A producers' collective is a body of persons (whether incorporated or not) that—

(a)   represents and provides services to producers of alcoholic liquor of a particular description,

(b)   is, and is by law entitled to be, recognized by the authorities of the member State or external territory in which it is established as representing the interests of those producers in that State or territory, and

(c)   is by law entitled to require contributions from all producers that it is entitled to represent.

PART 2

WHEN RETAIL CONTAINERS MUST BE STAMPED OR MUST NOT BE STAMPED AND THE DESIGN AND APPEARANCE OF DUTY STAMPS

3 When a retail container must be stamped or must not be stamped

(1)   Subject to this regulation, regulation 20, and to the exceptions prescribed in Part 6, retail containers of alcoholic liquor must be stamped if the excise duty point for that alcoholic liquor falls on or after 1st October 2006.

(2)   A retail container of alcoholic liquor that is—

    (a)   entered for removal from an excise warehouse or winery for exportation or shipment as stores,

    (b)   removed from an excise warehouse or winery for exportation or shipment as stores, or

    (c)   exported otherwise than by a private individual for his own use,

must not be stamped.

(3)   A retail container of alcoholic liquor must not be stamped if the alcoholic liquor it contains is intended for consumption outside the United Kingdom and Isle of Man; but this does not apply to a retail container of alcoholic liquor exported by a private individual for his own use.

(4)   A retail container of alcoholic liquor that is exposed for retail sale outside the United Kingdom and Isle of Man must not be stamped.

(5)   A retail container filled with anything that is not alcoholic liquor must not be stamped.

(6)   Paragraphs (2), (3), and (4) do not apply to a retail container of alcoholic liquor that is merchandise or to a retail container of alcoholic liquor that is for use in an export shop.

(7)   In this regulation, "winery" has the meaning given in regulation 4 of the Wine and Made-wine Regulations 1989.

4 Design and appearance

(1)   A duty stamp is a 25mm diameter disc that has one of the appearances illustrated in the Schedule.

(2)   The dominant colour of a duty stamp is magenta.

(3)   A duty stamp includes the following in black characters—

    (a)   the words "For the UK Market", "Liable to UK excise duty", and "HM Revenue & Customs",

    (b)   in the case of a type A stamp—

        (i)   a unique alphanumeric reference determined by the Commissioners, and

        (ii)   an indication of the product type in the retail container to which the stamp will be affixed, and

    (c)   in the case of a type B stamp, an alphanumeric reference determined by the Commissioners.

(4)   A duty stamp is printed on a white background using inks that do not normally fade when exposed to sunlight for a year or more.

(5)   A duty stamp is printed using materials that are water fast and scuff resistant.

(6)   A type B stamp is—

    (a)   produced using the design specification supplied by the appointed contractor, and

    (b)   incorporated into a label that includes, in an easily legible form, a brand under which it is intended that the alcoholic liquor will be sold by retail.

Part II

PART 3
OBTAINING AND RETURNING DUTY STAMPS ETC

5 Conditions for obtaining type A stamps

(1)   A person may not obtain a type A stamp unless he is authorized to do so by this regulation.

(2)   A registered person who is not a registered owner is authorized.

(3)   A registered person who is a registered owner is authorized if he is also an authorized warehousekeeper (or a person of equivalent status in an external territory), REDS, irregular stamper, compounder, a person who bottles alcoholic liquor in the United Kingdom, the holder of an excise licence under section 54(2) or 55(2) of the Alcoholic Liquor Duties Act 1979, or he does not have a fixed establishment in the Communities or an external territory and he carries on a trade or business that consists of or includes distilling, manufacturing, or bottling, alcoholic liquor.

(4)   An occasional importer is authorized to obtain type A stamps from the Commissioners, but is not authorized to obtain them from any other person.

(5)   Subject to paragraph (6), a person who intends to affix type A stamps to retail containers on behalf of a person who is authorized to obtain type A stamps from the appointed contractor is authorized to obtain those stamps from that person.

(6)   A person is not authorized to obtain type A stamps from another person authorized to obtain those stamps, unless the registered person from whom the stamps will be obtained has given the appointed contractor the information specified in regulation 14(2)(e) and (g) and, if the case so requires, complied with regulation 14(5).

6 Conditions for obtaining authority to affix type A stamps to retail containers

(1)   A person may not affix a type A stamp to a retail container unless he is authorized to do so by this regulation.

(2)   A person authorized to obtain type A stamps is authorized to affix those stamps to retail containers himself.

(3)   A person who is not an occasional importer and who is authorized to obtain type A stamps may give another person authorization to affix those stamps to retail containers of alcoholic liquor on his behalf; but this is subject to regulation 5(6).

7 Conditions for obtaining authority to incorporate type B stamps into labels

(1)   A person may not incorporate a type B stamp into a label unless he is—

(a)   entitled to include in that label a brand required by regulation 4(6)(b), and

(b)   authorized to incorporate a type B stamp into a label by paragraph (2), (3), or (4) of this regulation.

(2)   A registered person is authorized.

(3)   A person who intends, on behalf of a registered person, to incorporate type B stamps into labels printed for that registered person is authorized; but this is subject to his particulars having first been notified to the Commissioners under regulation 9(2)(i) or 11.

(4)   If a person who intends, on behalf of a registered person, to incorporate type B stamps into labels printed for that registered person, arranges for another person to undertake this work on his behalf, that other person is authorized.

8 Conditions for obtaining authority to affix labels incorporating type B stamps to retail containers

(1)   A person may not affix a label incorporating a type B stamp to a retail container unless he is authorized to do so by this regulation.

(2)   A registered person is authorized.

(3) A person who intends, on behalf of a registered person, to affix labels incorporating type B stamps to retail containers is authorized; provided he obtains those labels from that registered person or a person acting on that registered person's behalf.

9 Registration

(1) Every person who wishes to be registered must make application to the Commissioners.

(2) An application for registration must be made in writing or by electronic communication, using a form provided by the Commissioners, and must include the following information—

(a) the applicant's name and, if different, his business name,

(b) the address of his residence or registered office and (if different) the address of his principal place of business,

(c) any registration number issued to him by the Commissioners for the purposes of value added tax,

(d) his legal status (eg individual, partnership, limited liability partnership, public limited company),

(e) the nature of his business (eg authorized warehousekeeper, REDS, registered owner, compounder, distiller, manufacturer, or bottler of alcoholic liquor),

(f) if he intends to act as a duty stamps representative, the name of his principal (and, if different, his principal's business name), the nature of his principal's business, the address of his principal's residence or registered office and (if different) the address of his principal's principal place of business, and his principal's legal status,

(g) the number of type A stamps (if any) that he expects to obtain during the twelve months following the date of his application for registration,

(h) the number of type A stamps that he would have affixed to retail containers during the twelve months preceding the date of his application for registration had he been required to affix duty stamps to retail containers during that time,

(i) whether he seeks authority to—

(i) incorporate type B stamps in labels, or

(ii) affix those labels to retail containers,

or both; and if he intends to authorize another person to incorporate type B stamps in labels on his behalf, that person's name (and, if different, his business name) and the address of that person's residence or registered office and (if different) the address of that person's principal place of business,

(j) if, in accordance with section 13(1) of the Finance Act 1994, he has been notified of an assessment to a penalty within the five years preceding the date of his application for registration, and that penalty was not withdrawn or quashed, the date that he was notified, the amount of the penalty, and the reason that he was liable to that penalty,

(k) if, in accordance with section 139(1) of the Customs and Excise Management Act 1979, he has had any thing that was in his custody or under his control seized within the five years preceding the date of his application for registration, and that thing was condemned as forfeit, the date that it was seized, the nature of the thing that was seized, and the reason that it was liable to be seized, and

(l) a declaration that he is not disqualified from being registered.

(3) A person who is not disqualified from being registered and who provides the information specified in paragraph (2) above must be registered by the Commissioners and provided with a unique registration number.

10 Disqualification from being registered

(1) A person is disqualified from being registered if he has been convicted of a relevant offence or if—

(a) in the case of a partnership, any individual partner, or

(b) in the case of a body corporate, a director, senior manager, or other person having the direction or control of that body,

has been convicted of such an offence.

(2) A person is disqualified from being registered if his conduct has made him liable to a relevant penalty or if—

(a) in the case of a partnership, any individual partner's conduct made him liable to such a penalty, or

(b) in the case of a body corporate, the conduct of a director, senior manager, or other person having the direction or control of that body, made that person liable to such a penalty.

For the purposes of this paragraph, a registered person is not disqualified from being registered until ninety days have elapsed, starting with the day on which the assessment to a relevant penalty was notified.

(3) A person is disqualified from being registered if he is an undischarged bankrupt (or has an equivalent status outside the United Kingdom).

(4) A person is disqualified from being registered if he has a fixed establishment in the Communities or an external territory, unless he is an authorized warehousekeeper (or a person of equivalent status in an external territory), REDS, irregular stamper, registered owner, compounder, a person who bottles alcoholic liquor in the United Kingdom, or the holder of an excise licence under section 54(2) or 55(2) of the Alcoholic Liquor Duties Act 1979.

(5) A person is disqualified from being registered if he does not have a fixed establishment in the Communities or an external territory, unless he carries on a trade or business that consists of or includes distilling, manufacturing, or bottling, alcoholic liquor.

(6) A person is disqualified from being registered if, in accordance with section 13(1) of the Finance Act 1994, he has been notified of an assessment to a penalty within the five years preceding the date of his application for registration, or at any time after being registered, and that penalty has not been withdrawn, quashed, or paid.

For the purposes of this paragraph, a registered person is not disqualified from being registered until ninety days have elapsed, starting with the day on which he was notified of the assessment.

(7) A relevant offence is—

(a) the common law offence of cheating the public revenue,

(b) an offence under any of the following provisions—

sections 1(1) and 5(1) of the Firearms Act 1968;

section 1(1) of the Trade Descriptions Act 1968 (but only if the goods to which the false trade description was applied were, or included, dutiable alcoholic liquor);

sections 1(1), 8(1), 9(1), 10(1), 11(1), 15(1), 15A(1), 16(1), 17(1), 19(1), 20(1) and (2), 21(1), 22(1), and 24A(1) of the Theft Act 1968;

sections 4(2) and (3), 5(2) and (3), 8, and 20 of the Misuse of Drugs Act 1971;

sections 68(2), 100(3), 129(3), 136(1), 167(1), 168(1), 169(1), 170(1) and (2), and 170B of the Customs and Excise Management Act 1979;

section 17(1) of, and paragraphs 5(1) and 6(1) of Schedule 2A to, the Alcoholic Liquor Duties Act 1979;

section 13(3) and (4) of the Hydrocarbon Oil Duties Act 1979;

sections 8G(4) and 8H(1) of the Tobacco Products Duty Act 1979;

except for sections 18 and 19, any section of the Forgery and Counterfeiting Act 1981;

section 19(2) of the Criminal Justice (International Co-operation) Act 1990;

section 72(1), (3), (8), (10), and (11) of the Value Added Tax Act 1994;

section 92(1), (2), and (3) of the Trade Marks Act 1994;

sections 327(1), 328(1), and 329(1) of the Proceeds of Crime Act 2002; and

section 144 of the Licensing Act 2003.

(c) conspiracy to commit any of the above offences.

(8) A relevant penalty is a penalty that has been assessed and notified in accordance with—

(a) section 13(1) of the Finance Act 1994 for liability to a penalty under section 8 of that Act (penalty for evasion of excise duty), or

(b) section 76(1) or 77(6) of the Value Added Tax Act 1994 for liability to a penalty under section 60 of that Act (VAT evasion: conduct involving dishonesty),

and that has not been withdrawn or quashed.

But a penalty is not a relevant penalty if it was notified more than five years before the date that an applicant makes application for registration as required by regulation 9.

11 Changes in information notified in application for registration

When there is any change in the information a registered person provided in his application for registration, or in the information that he has since provided under this regulation, he must, within 7 days of that change, notify the Commissioners in writing or by electronic communication.

12 Cessation of registration

(1) A registered person ceases to be registered if he—

(a) requests the Commissioners to remove him from their register,

(b) becomes disqualified from being registered, or

(c) has not, during the thirty-six consecutive months just passed, done any of the following—

(i) obtained duty stamps,

(ii) used his authority to incorporate duty stamps into labels, or

(iii) used his authority to affix such labels to retail containers.

(2) The Commissioners must remove a person who has ceased to be registered from their register without delay.

13 Duty stamps representative

(1) A person who—

(a) is not authorized by—

(i) regulation 5 to obtain a type A stamp,

(ii) regulation 7 to incorporate a type B stamp into a label, or

(iii) (as the case may be) regulation 8 to affix a label incorporating a type B stamp to a retail container,

> (b)   does not have a fixed establishment in the United Kingdom, and
>
> (c)   wants to obtain type A stamps, incorporate type B stamps into labels, or (as the case may be) affix labels incorporating type B stamps to retail containers,

must appoint a duty stamps representative.

(2)   Only a registered person who has a fixed establishment in the United Kingdom may be appointed as a duty stamps representative.

(3)   A duty stamps representative has the rights obligations and liabilities that his principal would have had, had that principal been a registered person.

(4)   A duty stamps representative must not act for a principal who is disqualified from being a registered person.

14   Ordering and obtaining type A stamps

(1)   To obtain type A stamps a registered person must place an order for those stamps with the appointed contractor by means of an electronic communication.

(2)   The registered person must supply the following information to the appointed contractor when an order is placed—

> (a)   his unique registration number,
>
> (b)   the number of stamps required,
>
> (c)   the product type for which they are required,
>
> (d)   the place to which the stamps should be delivered,
>
> (e)   the premises at which the stamps will be affixed to retail containers,
>
> (f)   if the registered person is—
>
> > (i)   an irregular stamper, or
> >
> > (ii)   an authorized warehousekeeper and the retail containers of alcoholic liquor were imported from an external territory or a third country,
>
> the premises at which the retail containers of alcoholic liquor will be held before the duty stamps are affixed to them, if those premises are not a tax warehouse, and
>
> (g)   if the stamps will be affixed by someone other than the registered person, that person's name (and, if different, his business name) and the address of that person's residence or registered office and (if different) the address of that person's principal place of business,

and confirm his identity by any reasonable means that the appointed contractor may require.

(3)   The appointed contractor must refuse to supply type A stamps if he is not satisfied that the person who placed the order is the registered person to whom the unique registration number given in the order relates.

(4)   A registered person may, by an electronic communication made within 24 hours of placing his order for type A stamps, amend that order by—

> (a)   reducing or increasing the number of stamps required,
>
> (b)   changing the product type for which they are required, or
>
> (c)   changing the place to which the stamps should be delivered.

(5)   If—

> (a)   the duty stamps will be affixed at premises other than those specified in the registered person's order, or
>
> (b)   the duty stamps will be affixed by a person other than the person specified in that order,

the registered person must, at least two clear business days before the stamps are affixed to retail containers, by electronic communication give the appointed contractor full particulars of the change.

(6) Without prejudice to paragraph (5), if—

(a)   the registered person is an irregular stamper or an authorized warehousekeeper,

(b)   before the duty stamps are affixed to the retail containers of alcoholic liquor, those containers are removed from the premises specified in his order ("the relevant premises"), and

(c)   the relevant premises are not a tax warehouse,

the registered person must, by the end of the first business day following the removal of the containers from the relevant premises, by electronic communication give the appointed contractor full particulars of the change of premises.

(7) To obtain type A stamps an occasional importer must place a written order for those stamps with the Commissioners at the time at which he complies with regulation 15(3)(a)(i) or (b) of the Excise Goods (Holding, Movement, Warehousing and REDS) Regulations 1992 (notification that he is expecting or has received a consignment of excise goods imported by him).

(8) The occasional importer's order must include the following information—

(a)   the number of stamps required,

(b)   the product type for which they are required,

(c)   the place to which the stamps should be delivered,

(d)   the premises at which the retail containers of alcoholic liquor will be held and at which the stamps will be affixed to those containers, and

(e)   a declaration that the retail containers of alcoholic liquor to which the stamps are to be affixed are not already stamped, and will not be stamped before he receives them.

(9) Type A duty stamps ordered from the appointed contractor or the Commissioners may only be delivered to the place of delivery specified in the order or amended order.

15 Receiving type A stamps

(1) When duty stamps are delivered to a registered person, that person, or someone specifically authorized by him, must acknowledge receipt of those stamps—

(a)   by signing a form of acknowledgement that is proffered by the person delivering those stamps, or

(b)   if no such form is proffered, by signing the form of acknowledgement enclosed with the stamps and sending it, without delay, to the appointed contractor.

If the registered person is not an individual, any individual partner, director, senior manager, or other person having the direction or control of that registered person may sign the form of acknowledgement or authorize another person to sign it.

(2) When duty stamps are delivered to an occasional importer he must acknowledge receipt of those stamps—

(a)   by signing a form of acknowledgement that is proffered by the person delivering those stamps, or

(b)   if no such form is proffered, by signing the form of acknowledgement enclosed with the stamps and sending it, without delay, to the Commissioners.

If the occasional importer is not an individual, any individual partner, director, senior manager, or other person having the direction or control of that occasional importer may sign the form of acknowledgement or authorize another person to sign it.

(3) When duty stamps are delivered to a registered person or occasional importer that person must check that the quantity and product type of the stamps delivered is in conformity with the order that he placed.

(4) If the duty stamps delivered to a registered person are not in conformity with the order that he placed, he must, by means of an electronic communication sent to the appointed contractor by the end of the first business day following the day of receipt of the stamps, give the contractor full particulars of the discrepancy between the stamps ordered and the stamps delivered.

(5) If the duty stamps delivered to an occasional importer are not in conformity with the order that he placed, he must, by means of a written communication sent to the Commissioners by the end of the first business day following the day of receipt of the stamps, give the Commissioners full particulars of the discrepancy between the stamps ordered and the stamps delivered.

16 Returning type A stamps

(1) A registered person who—

    (a)   ceases to be registered, or

    (b)   for any reason, no longer requires loose type A stamps that he holds,

must, without delay, return the loose type A stamps that he holds to the appointed contractor.

(2) A person who—

    (a)   obtained type A stamps from a registered person in order to affix them to retail containers of alcoholic liquor on behalf of that person, and

    (b)   is no longer required to affix them on that person's behalf,

must, without delay, return any loose stamps that he holds to that person (or if that is not possible, send them by secure means or give them to the appointed contractor).

(3) If some or all of the duty stamps delivered to an occasional importer are not required because—

    (a)   he did not import the retail containers of alcoholic liquor for which they were intended,

    (b)   the retail containers of alcoholic liquor for which they were intended were already stamped, or

    (c)   it turns out that the retail containers of alcoholic liquor for which they were intended must not be stamped,

he must, without delay, return those stamps by secure means to the Commissioners, giving the Commissioners written particulars of the reason for their return.

17 Ordering and obtaining the design specification for type B stamps

(1) To obtain the design specification for type B stamps a registered person must place an order for that specification with the appointed contractor by means of an electronic communication.

(2) The registered person must supply the following information to the appointed contractor when an order is placed—

    (a)   his unique registration number,

    (b)   the number of copies of the design specification required, and

    (c)   the place to which the design specification should be delivered,

and confirm his identity by any reasonable means that the contractor may require.

(3) The appointed contractor must refuse to supply the design specification for type B stamps if he is not satisfied that the person who placed the order is the registered person to whom the unique registration number given in the order relates.

(4) The design specification for type B stamps ordered from the appointed contractor may only be delivered to the place of delivery specified when the order was placed.

(5) The total number of copies of the design specification for type B stamps delivered to a registered person must not exceed the number necessary to provide one

copy to that registered person and to each of the persons notified to the Commissioners under regulation 9(2)(i) or regulation 11.

18 Receiving the design specification for type B stamps

(1) When the design specification for type B stamps is delivered to a registered person that person, or someone specifically authorized by him, must acknowledge receipt of that specification—

> (a) by signing a form of acknowledgement that is proffered by the person delivering it, or
>
> (b) if no such form is proffered, by signing the form of acknowledgement enclosed with that specification and sending it, without delay, to the appointed contractor.

If the registered person is not an individual, any individual partner, director, senior manager, or other person having the direction or control of that registered person may sign the form of acknowledgement or authorize another person to sign it.

(2) When the design specification for type B stamps is delivered to a registered person that person must check that the number of copies of the design specification delivered is in conformity with the order that he placed.

(3) If the number of copies of the design specification delivered to a registered person is not in conformity with the order that he placed, he must, by means of an electronic communication sent to the appointed contractor by the end of the first business day following the day of receipt of the specification, give that contractor full particulars of the discrepancy.

PART 4

AFFIXING DUTY STAMPS TO RETAIL CONTAINERS

19 Premises where duty stamps etc, may be affixed

(1) Duty stamps, or labels incorporating duty stamps, may only be affixed to retail containers on the following premises—

> (a) premises in a third country that are occupied by or under the control of a person who carries on a trade or business that consists of or includes distilling, manufacturing, or bottling alcoholic liquor,
>
> (b) a tax warehouse or premises having equivalent status in an external territory,
>
> (c) premises specified as those at which the duty stamps would be affixed to retail containers of alcoholic liquor when the order for those stamps was placed with the Commissioners by an occasional importer,
>
> (d) if the registered person is—
>
> > (i) an irregular stamper,
> >
> > (ii) a person who bottles alcoholic liquor in the United Kingdom, or
> >
> > (iii) an authorized warehousekeeper and the retail containers of alcoholic liquor were imported from an external territory or a third country,
>
> the premises (not a tax warehouse) specified as those at which the duty stamps would be affixed to retail containers of alcoholic liquor when the order for those stamps was placed with the appointed contractor.
>
> (e) if the registered person is a compounder, premises (not a tax warehouse)—
>
> > (i) in respect of which he made entry as required by regulation 4 of the Spirits (Rectifying, Compounding and Drawback) Regulations 1988, and

(ii)   specified as those at which the duty stamps would be affixed to retail containers of alcoholic liquor when the order for those stamps was placed with the appointed contractor.

(2)   For the purposes of this regulation, any reference to premises specified as those at which the duty stamps would be affixed to retail containers of alcoholic liquor when the order for duty stamps was placed with the appointed contractor is to be treated as including any substitute premises notified in accordance with regulation 14(5).

20 Times at which a retail container must be stamped

(1)   In the case of a retail container of alcoholic liquor held by an occasional importer, that container must be stamped within 14 days of its being imported into the United Kingdom, and in any event before it is exposed for retail sale.

(2)   In the case of a retail container of alcoholic liquor imported from an external territory or third country and held by an authorized warehousekeeper on premises that are not a tax warehouse, that container must be stamped within 14 days of its being imported into the United Kingdom.

(3)   In the case of a retail container of alcoholic liquor held by an irregular stamper, that container must be stamped within 14 days of its being imported into the United Kingdom.

(4)   In the case of a retail container of alcoholic liquor held by a compounder, that container must be stamped at the time that it is removed from the premises specified in regulation 19(1)(e), unless—

(i)   the excise duty on the alcohol in the container is to be the subject of a claim for drawback because the container is to be exported, and

(ii)   the compounder has complied with regulation 8(1) or, as the case may require, (2) of the Excise Goods (Drawback) Regulations 1995.

(5)   In the case of a retail container of alcoholic liquor held by a person who bottles alcoholic liquor on which excise duty has been paid, that container must be stamped at the time that it is removed from the premises specified in regulation 19(1)(d).

(6)   In any other case, a retail container of alcoholic liquor must be stamped before the excise duty point for the alcoholic liquor it contains.

21 Correct duty stamps

(1)   A duty stamp is the correct stamp for a retail container if it is affixed to that container in compliance with this regulation.

(2)   A type A stamp may only be affixed to a retail container if that container contains, or will contain, alcoholic liquor that may be described as the product type indicated on the stamp.

(3)   A type A stamp that includes an indication that the product type is "other product" must not be affixed to a retail container if that container contains, or will contain, alcoholic liquor that may be described as brandy, gin, rum, vodka, whisky, or whiskey.

(4)   A label incorporating a type B stamp may only be affixed to a retail container if that container contains, or will contain, alcoholic liquor that may be exposed for sale by retail under the brand or brands included in the label.

22 Correct duty stamps: supplementary provisions

(1)   Where a person discovers that he has affixed a duty stamp, or label incorporating a duty stamp, that is not the correct stamp for that retail container, he must take the following steps.

date and time when, and the address of the place at which, he intends to obliterate or remove that stamp or destroy that container; and

(b)   in the case of a type A stamp, he makes a record of the unique reference number of that stamp in his ordinary business records.

(3) A person must not export a retail container of alcoholic liquor from which a duty stamp has been removed, or that bears an obliterated duty stamp, unless by means of an electronic communication he has given the Commissioners not less than two clear business days' notice of his intention to export that container.

(4) Any record made for the purposes of this regulation must be preserved for a period of three years, starting on the day the record was made.

PART 5
RECORDS

25 Records relating to type A stamps

(1) Every registered person, and every person who affixes type A stamps to retail containers of alcoholic liquor, must ensure that his ordinary business records contain the following information—

(a)   for every stamp or batch of stamps he receives—
    (i)   the date of receipt,
    (ii)   the number of stamps received,
    (iii) the unique reference numbers shown on the stamps, and
    (iv) the product type shown on the stamps;

(b)   for each day that he affixes stamps to retail containers—
    (i)   the number of stamps affixed,
    (ii)   the unique reference numbers of those stamps, and
    (iii) the product type shown on those stamps;

(c)   if he passes stamps to another person for that person to affix to retail containers on his behalf, for each day that he does so—
    (i)   the number of stamps passed to that person,
    (ii)   the unique reference numbers of those stamps,
    (iii) the product type shown on those stamps, and
    (iv) the name of the person to whom he passed the stamps (and, if different, his business name) and the address of that person's residence or registered office and (if different) the address of that person's principal place of business;

(d)   if he is a person who affixes stamps to retail containers on behalf of another person, and that other person no longer requires the retail containers to which stamps have been affixed—
    (i)   the number of stamps affixed,
    (ii)   the unique reference numbers of those stamps,
    (iii) the product type shown on those stamps, and
    (iv) any brand or brands displayed on any label affixed, or to be affixed, to those retail containers;

(e)   the number of loose stamps held, their unique reference numbers, and the product types shown on them;

(f)   the number of loose stamps returned as required by regulation 16, their unique reference numbers, and the product types shown on them;

(g)   for stamped retail containers of alcoholic liquor that he holds, the unique reference numbers of the stamps and any brand or brands displayed on any labels affixed to those containers;

(h)   for each day that stamped retail containers of alcoholic liquor are removed from the tax warehouse in which the stamps were affixed—

(2) The first step is to ensure that, if there has been no excise duty point for any alcoholic liquor in the retail container, there is no excise duty point until the other steps have been taken.

(3) The second step is to immediately record in his ordinary business records the following information—

   (a)   the date that the duty stamp, or label incorporating the duty stamp, was affixed to the retail container,

   (b)   if more than one, the number of stamps that were affixed,

   (c)   in the case of a type A stamp, the unique reference number of that stamp, and

   (d)   any brand or brands displayed on any label affixed to the retail container.

(4) The third step is, by means of electronic communication sent by the end of the first business day following the second step, to provide the Commissioners with the information that he recorded in his ordinary business records.

(5) The fourth step is to—

   (a)   completely remove or obliterate that stamp, and affix a duty stamp that is the correct stamp for that retail container, or

   (b)   destroy that container.

(6) In the case of a retail container of alcoholic liquor for which there has been an excise duty point, the fourth step must be taken within 7 days of the discovery referred to in paragraph (1).

(7) A record made for the purposes of the second step must be preserved for a period of three years, starting on the day the record was made.

23 Affixing duty stamps to retail containers

(1) When a duty stamp, or label incorporating a duty stamp, is affixed to a retail container it must be affixed securely so that the duty stamp cannot be removed without its being obviously damaged.

(2) A type A stamp may be affixed to any surface of a retail container of alcoholic liquor other than—

   (a)   the base, or

   (b)   a part of any surface that would result in the stamp being in contact with—

      (i)   the stopper, cork, cap, or other closure of that container, or

      (ii)   any label affixed to that container.

(3) A label incorporating a type B stamp must be affixed to a surface of a retail container of alcoholic liquor that is normally visible to a purchaser when it is exposed for sale by retail, or would be visible if the container were—

   (a)   removed from any tube, box, or other packaging in which it is presented for retail sale, or

   (b)   turned through 180° on a vertical axis.

24 Notification and attendance of officers

(1) A person authorized by regulation 6 or regulation 8 must permit an officer to be present when duty stamps, or labels incorporating duty stamps, are affixed to retail containers.

(2) Except where regulation 22 applies, a person must not deliberately obliterate or remove a duty stamp or destroy a retail container of alcoholic liquor that bears a duty stamp unless—

   (a)   by means of an electronic communication, he has given the Commisioners not less than two clear business days' notice of the

Part II

      (i)   the number of stamped containers,

      (ii)   the unique reference numbers of the stamps, and

      (iii)   any brand or brands displayed on any label affixed to the retail containers; and

  (i)   if different from his principal place of business, the address of any premises at which he—

      (i)   holds duty stamps, or

      (ii)   affixes stamps to retail containers.

(2) Without prejudice to regulations 22(3) and 24(2)(b), every person who obliterates or removes stamps from retail containers must ensure that his ordinary business records contain the following information for each day upon which he undertakes any of those activities—

  (a)   the number of stamped containers,

  (b)   the unique reference numbers of the stamps,

  (c)   any brand or brands displayed on any label affixed to the retail containers, and

  (d)   whether there has been an excise duty point for any alcoholic liquor in those containers.

(3) If type A stamps are, or are discovered to have been, lost, stolen, destroyed, or damaged, or stamped retail containers of alcoholic liquor are (before the excise duty point for the alcoholic liquor they contain) destroyed or damaged so as to be unmerchantable—

  (a)   the number of stamps,

  (b)   the unique reference numbers of those stamps (or if it is impracticable to record them, the reason why it is impracticable together with any information that may help to identify the stamps concerned), and

  (c)   the product type shown on those stamps,

must be recorded in the ordinary business records of the person who had custody of those stamps or retail containers of alcoholic liquor.

26 Records relating to type B stamps

(1) Without prejudice to regulation 22(3), every person who obliterates type B stamps or labels incorporating type B stamps, or removes those stamps or labels from retail containers, must ensure that his ordinary business records contain the following information for each day upon which he undertakes any of those activities—

  (a)   the number of stamped containers,

  (b)   the brand or brands displayed on the labels incorporating the stamps, and

  (c)   whether there has been an excise duty point for the alcoholic liquor in those containers.

(2) If labels incorporating type B stamps are, or are discovered to have been, lost or stolen—

  (a)   the number of labels,

  (b)   the brand or brands displayed on those labels, and

  (c)   the circumstances and details of the occurrence,

must be recorded in the ordinary business records of the person who had custody of those labels.

(3) If the medium containing the design specification for type B stamps is, or is discovered to have been, lost or stolen, the circumstances and details of the occurrence must be recorded in the ordinary business records of the person who had custody of it.

27 Other records relating to stamped retail containers

Any person who holds or moves stamped retail containers of alcoholic liquor, and is not required to keep records under regulation 25 or, as the case may require, regulation 26, must ensure that his ordinary business records identify retail containers of alcoholic liquor that are stamped.

28 Preservation of records

A record made for the purposes of this Part must be preserved for a period of three years, starting on the day the record was made.

PART 6
EXCEPTIONS FROM REQUIREMENT THAT RETAIL CONTAINERS BE STAMPED

29 Registered mobile operators

A retail container of alcoholic liquor that is merchandise for the use of a registered mobile operator may be unstamped.

30 Export shops

Retail containers of alcoholic liquor that are for use in an export shop may be unstamped.

31 Compounders

Retail containers of alcoholic liquor that was produced on premises (not a tax warehouse) in respect of which a compounder made entry as required by regulation 4 of the Spirits (Rectifying, Compounding and Drawback) Regulations 1988 may be unstamped if—

> (a) the excise duty on the alcohol in the container is to be the subject of a claim for drawback because the container is to be exported, and
>
> (b) the compounder has complied with regulation 8(1) or, as the case may require, (2) of the Excise Goods (Drawback) Regulations 1995.

32 Diplomats and other persons enjoying immunities and privileges, and travellers from outside the United Kingdom

(1) Retail containers of alcoholic liquor acquired by private individuals for their own use, and transported by them to the United Kingdom from places that are neither external territories nor third countries, may be unstamped.

(2) Retail containers of alcoholic liquor in respect of which relief from excise duty is afforded by an Order made under section 13A(1) of the Customs and Excise Duties (General Reliefs) Act 1979 may be unstamped.

(3) Retail containers of alcoholic liquor obtained by a person in an external territory or third country, and imported into the United Kingdom by him, may be unstamped if paragraph (4) or paragraph (5) below applies.

(4) This paragraph applies if relief from excise duty on that alcoholic liquor is afforded by an Order made under section 13(1) of the Customs and Excise Duties (General Reliefs) Act 1979.

(5) This paragraph applies if relief from excise duty on that alcoholic liquor—

> (a) would have been afforded by an Order made under section 13(1) of the Customs and Excise Duties (General Reliefs) Act 1979, but for the fact that the quantity of that alcoholic liquor exceeds any limit on quantity specified in the Order,
>
> (b) the alcoholic liquor is declared as required by section 78(1) of the Customs and Excise Management Act 1979, and
>
> (c) the excise duty on that alcoholic liquor is paid.

PART 7
MISCELLANEOUS

33 Notification of lost or stolen duty stamps or design specifications

(1) If type A stamps, labels incorporating type B stamps, or the medium containing the design specification for type B stamps, are, or are discovered to have been, lost or stolen the Commissioners must be notified by electronic communication sent by the end of the first business day following the day of the occurrence or its discovery.

(2) The notification must be given by the person who had custody of the stamps, labels or medium, and must include—

    (a)   in the case of stamps or labels, the number of those stamps or labels;

    (b)   in the case of type A stamps, the unique reference numbers of the stamps and the product type shown on them;

    (c)   in the case of labels, the brand or brands displayed on those labels and the size of the retail containers to which it was intended they should be affixed; and

    (d)   in all cases, the date and time of the occurrence or its discovery.

34 Drawback of excise duty

For the purposes of any claim for drawback to which the Excise Goods (Drawback) Regulations 1995 apply, stamped retail containers of alcoholic liquor are not eligible goods unless the eligible claimant is a registered mobile operator.

35 Offence of possession, sale etc of unstamped containers

(1) A person does not commit an offence under paragraph 5(1) of Schedule 2A to the Alcoholic Liquor Duties Act 1979 in relation to any conduct of his that took place before 1 January 2007.

(2) A person does not commit an offence under paragraph 5(1) of Schedule 2A to the Alcoholic Liquor Duties Act 1979 if he is in possession of, transports or displays unstamped retail containers of alcoholic liquor that have been—

    (a)   sold by retail by a registered mobile operator,

    (b)   sold by retail in an export shop,

    (c)   acquired by private individuals for their own use, and transported by them to the United Kingdom from places that are neither external territories nor third countries,

    (d)   afforded relief from excise duty by an Order made under section 13A(1) of the Customs and Excise Duties (General Reliefs) Act 1979, or

    (e)   obtained by a person in an external territory or a third country, imported into the United Kingdom by him, and to which paragraph (4) or paragraph (5) of regulation 32 applies.

36 Prohibition on passing on type A stamps

A registered person must not pass loose type A duty stamps to a person who is not authorized by these Regulations to obtain them.

37 Prohibition on passing on design specification for type B stamps

The design specification for type B stamps must not be passed to a person who is not authorized by these Regulations to incorporate type B stamps into labels.

38 Prohibition on refilling stamped retail containers

(1) Subject to paragraphs (2) and (3), stamped retail containers must not be refilled with alcoholic liquor.

(2) A person who bottles alcoholic liquor on which excise duty has been paid may refill a stamped retail container supplied by the person to whose order the alcoholic liquor is being supplied provided that—

    (a)   excise duty has been paid on the alcoholic liquor with which the container is refilled,

    (b)   he affixes a new type A stamp to the container and complies with regulation 23 when he does so.

(3) A private individual may refill a stamped retail container with alcoholic liquor—

    (a)   from another stamped retail container, or

    (b)   from a retail container that is not required to be stamped.

39 Amendment to the Excise Warehousing (etc) Regulations 1988
In the form of United Kingdom Internal Accompanying Document, set out in Schedule 4 to the Excise Warehousing (etc) Regulations 1988, at the end of the explanatory note to Box 18a insert—

    "If alcohol or alcoholic beverages are stamped with duty stamps, a statement to this effect."

SCHEDULE
APPEARANCE OF DUTY STAMPS

Regulation 4

A type A stamp:

A type B stamp:

FUEL-TESTING PILOT PROJECTS (BIOGAS PROJECT) REGULATIONS 2006

(SI 2006/1348)

NOTES

Made: 17 May 2006.

Authority: Hydrocarbon Oil Duties Act 1979 s 20AB(1)–(3), (5), (12).

Coming into force: 10 June 1006.

1 Citation and Commencement

These Regulations may be cited as the Fuel-testing Pilot Projects (Biogas Project) Regulations 2006 and come into force on 10th June 2006.

2 Interpretation

In these Regulations—

"biogas" means a natural road fuel gas within the meaning of section 5 of the Hydrocarbon Oil Duties Act 1979 consisting as a carbon neutral liquid gas of 96% methane (CH_4) and not less than 3.75% nitrogen and containing minor trace elements;

"the project" means the project described in the Schedule to these Regulations.

3 Experimental fuel

Biogas is an experimental fuel.

4 Experimental period

The experimental period for biogas is 10th June 2006 to 28th February 2011.

5 Relief

On biogas used or to be used for the purposes of the project there shall be allowed relief in the form of a rebate of 100% of the excise duty (subject to any conditions imposed and directions given by the Commissioners).

SCHEDULE

Regulation 2

The project is that approved by the Commissioners for Her Majesty's Revenue and Customs on 17th May 2006, which approval was confirmed by their letter dated 18th May 2006 addressed to Enertech (1983) Limited the company conducting the project. The purpose of the project is to test biogas as a fuel in vehicles to evaluate the emission benefits of gas obtained from landfill sites and to provide information on the issues and problems that arise from the handling and use of such gas as an automotive fuel and the operation of gas powered vehicles. The registered office of Enertech (1983) Limited is Wentworth View, 1A Barnsley Road, Ackworth, Near Pontefract, West Yorkshire WF7 7BS.

EXCISE DUTIES (SURCHARGES OR REBATES) (HYDROCARBON OILS ETC) ORDER 2006

(SI 2006/1979)

NOTES

Revoked by the Excise Duties (Surcharges or Rebates) (Hydrocarbon Oils etc) (Revocation) Order, SI 2006/3235, art 2, with effect from 7 December 2006.

. . .

EXCISE DUTIES (ROAD FUEL GAS) (RELIEFS) REGULATIONS 2006

(SI 2006/1980)

NOTES

Revoked by the Excise Duties (Road Fuel Gas) (Reliefs) (Revocation) Regulations, SI 2006/1980, reg 2, with effect from 6 December 2006.

. . .

RELIEF FOR LEGACIES IMPORTED FROM THIRD COUNTRIES (APPLICATION) ORDER 2006

(SI 2006/3158)

NOTES

Made: 28 November 2006.

Authority: Customs and Excise Duties (General Reliefs) Act 1979 s 7.

Commencement: 1 January 2007.

1

This Order may be cited as the Relief for Legacies Imported from Third Countries (Application) Order 2006 and comes into force on 1st January 2007.

2

For the purpose of article 21 of the Customs and Excise Duties (Personal Reliefs for Goods Permanently Imported) Order 1992, the reference to Council Directive 77/388/EEC in the definition of third country in article 2 of that Order is to be construed as a reference to that instrument as amended, modified or otherwise affected by the Act concerning the conditions of accession of the Republic of Bulgaria and Romania and the adjustments to the treaties on which the European Union is founded.

HYDROCARBON OIL DUTIES (SULPHURFREE DIESEL) (HYDROGE-NATION OF BIOMASS) (RELIEFS) REGULATIONS 2006

(SI 2006/3426)

NOTES

Made: 20 December 2006.

Authority: Hydrocarbon Oil Duties Act 1979 s 20AA(1)(a) and (2)(a), (b), (c), (e), (h) and (i).

Commencement: 12 January 2007.

1 Citation and commencement

(1) These Regulations may be cited as the Hydrocarbon Oil Duties (Sulphur-free Diesel) (Hydrogenation of Biomass) (Reliefs) Regulations 2006.

(2) They come into force on 12th January 2007 and shall cease to have effect on 12th January 2009.

2 Interpretation

In these Regulations—

"biomass" has the meaning given in section 2AA(2)(c) of the Act;

"the Act" means the Hydrocarbon Oil Duties Act 1979.

3 Relief

Relief from duty charged by section 6(1) of the Act shall be allowed on sulphur-free diesel that is produced partly from the hydrogenation of biomass.

4

The relief shall take the form of a remission of duty.

5

(1) The amount of duty remitted shall be calculated in accordance with the formula

$(A - B) \times V$

where—

A is the rate of duty charged on sulphur-free diesel specified in section 6(1A) of the Act;

B is the rate of duty charged on biodiesel by section 6AA of the Act; and

V is the volume, in litres, of that proportion of the sulphur-free diesel that is produced from hydrogenated biomass.

(2) In paragraph (1) "litres" means litres of such sulphur-free diesel at a temperature of 15°C

6 Conditions imposed by the Commissioners

Relief is allowed subject to such conditions (if any) as the Commissioners impose on the person claiming relief.

7 Cancellation of relief

(1) If there is a contravention of, or failure to comply with, any condition imposed under regulation 6, the relief allowed shall be cancelled.

(2) Where any relief is cancelled, any person who claimed the relief shall, on demand, be liable to pay the amount of relief claimed.

FUEL-TESTING PILOT PROJECTS (BIOMIX PROJECT) REGULATIONS 2007

(SI 2007/314)

NOTES

Made: 7 February 2007.
Authority: Hydrocarbon Oil Duties Act 1979 s 20AB(1) to (3), (5)(a) and (12).
Commencement: 1 March 2007.

1 Citation and commencement

These Regulations may be cited as the Fuel-testing Pilot Projects (Biomix Project) Regulations 2007 and come into force on 1st March 2007.

2 Interpretation

In these Regulations—
  "the Act" means the Hydrocarbon Oil Duties Act 1979;
  "biomix" means a mixture that is produced by mixing—
    (a)   biodiesel with sulphur-free diesel, or
    (b)   biodiesel with ultra low sulphur diesel;
  the "project" means the project described in the Schedule.

3 Experimental fuel

Biomix is an experimental fuel.

4 Experimental period

The experimental period for biomix is 1st March 2007 to 31st August 2008.

5 Relief

(1)   On biomix used or to be used for the purposes of the project there shall be allowed relief from excise duty in the form specified in paragraph (2) or, as the case may be, paragraph (3) (subject to any conditions imposed and directions given by the Commissioners).

(2)   Where biomix consists of a mixture of biodiesel and sulphur-free diesel, relief shall be in the form of a rebate of excise duty less the amount per litre for the time being specified in section 11(1)(b) of the Act (rebate for gas oil which is not ultra low sulphur diesel).

(3)   Where biomix consists of a mixture of biodiesel and ultra low sulphur diesel, relief shall be in the form of a rebate of excise duty less the amount per litre for the time being specified in section 11(1)(ba) of the Act (rebate for ultra low sulphur diesel oil).

SCHEDULE

Regulation 2

The project to which these Regulations apply is that approved by the Commissioners for Her Majesty's Revenue and Customs on 8th February 2007. The project seeks to establish the extent to which biodiesel in differing proportions can be used as a substitute for corresponding proportions of ultra low sulphur diesel or sulphur-free diesel when used as fuel in sectors that currently use large amounts of rebated gas oil. Mixtures of biodiesel and ultra low sulphur diesel or biodiesel and sulphur-free diesel used in the project will benefit from a rebate of excise duty equivalent to reducing the effective rate of duty to that for rebated gas oil. The duty relief conferred by these Regulations will enable participating companies to carry out extensive tests to provide an indication of the potential environmental impacts and benefits of these mixtures in particular sorts of engines that normally would operate using only gas oil; to provide information on the issues and problems that arise from this use; and to provide information on the relative benefits of using such mixtures.

INTERNATIONAL MUTUAL ADMINISTRATIVE ASSISTANCE IN TAX MATTERS ORDER 2007

(SI 2007/2126)

NOTES

Made: 25 July 2007.

Authority: Finance Act 2006 s 173(1) to (3).

Commencement: date to be published in the London, Edinburgh and Belfast Gazettes as the date on which the Convention enters into force in respect of the UK.

1 Citation

This Order may be cited as the International Mutual Administrative Assistance in Tax Matters Order 2007.

2 Mutual administrative assistance arrangements to have effect

It is declared that—

(a)   arrangements relating to international tax enforcement that fall within the joint Council of Europe/Organisation for Economic Co-operation and Development Convention on Mutual Administrative Assistance in Tax Matters, signed on behalf of the United Kingdom on 24 May 2007, have been made in relation to the other signatory territories, and

(b)   it is expedient that those arrangements have effect.

POSTAL PACKETS (REVENUE AND CUSTOMS) REGULATIONS 2007

(SI 2007/2195)

NOTES

Made: 26 July 2007.

Authority: Postal Services Act 2000 s 105.

Commencement: 16 August 2007.

1 Citation and commencement

These Regulations may be cited as the Postal Packets (Revenue and Customs) Regulations 2007 and shall come into force on 16th August 2007.

2 Application of customs and excise enactments to certain postal packets

Section 105 of the Postal Services Act 2000 shall apply to all postal packets which are posted in the United Kingdom for transmission to any place outside it or which are brought by post into the United Kingdom, carried by a postal operator providing postal services which is not a universal service provider in connection with the provision of a universal postal service.

FUEL-TESTING PILOT PROJECTS (BIOBUTANOL PROJECT) REGULATIONS 2007

(SI 2007/3098)

NOTES

Made: 29 October 2007

Authority: Hydrocarbon Oil Duties Act 1979 s 20AB(1)–(3), (5)(a) and (12)

Commencement: 23 November 2007

1 Citation and commencement

These Regulations may be cited as the Fuel-testing Pilot Projects (Biobutanol Project) Regulations 2007 and come into force on 23rd November 2007.

2 Interpretation

(1) In these Regulations—

"the Act" means the Hydrocarbon Oil Duties Act 1979;

"the project" means the project described in the Schedule.

(2) In these Regulations "biobutanol" means a liquid—

(a) consisting of butanol produced from biomass, and

(b) capable of being used for the same purposes as light oil.

(3) In paragraph (2) "biomass" means vegetable and animal substances constituting the biodegradable fraction of-

(a) products, wastes and residues from agriculture, forestry and related activities, or

(b) industrial and municipal waste.

3 Experimental fuel

Biobutanol is an experimental fuel.

4 Experimental period

The experimental period for biobutanol is 23rd November 2007 to 1st April 2009.

5 Relief

(1) Relief from duty charged by section 6A of the Act (fuel substitutes) shall be allowed in respect of biobutanol used or to be used for the purposes of the project (subject to any conditions imposed and directions given by the Commissioners).

(2) Relief shall be in the form of a rebate of duty charged and the amount of the rebate per litre of biobutanol shall be equivalent to the difference in the rate of duty for the time being specified by section 6AD(3) of the Act (duty on bioethanol) and the rate of duty for the time being specified by article 4(2)(c) of the Other Fuel Substitutes (Rates of Excise Duty etc) Order 1995 (duty rates for fuel substitutes).

Part III

European Community Materials

COUNCIL REGULATION

(3301/74/EEC)

of 19 December 1974

on the duty-free importation of goods in small consignments of a non-commercial character within the Community

NOTES

Date of publication in OJ: OJ L 354, 31.12.74, p 55.

THE COUNCIL OF THE EUROPEAN COMMUNITIES,

Having regard to the Treaty establishing the European Economic Community, and in particular Articles 43 and 235 thereof;

Having regard to the proposal from the Commission;

Having regard to the Opinion of the European Parliament;[1]

Having regard to the Opinion of the Economic and Social Committee;[2]

Whereas Article 32(2)(c) of the Act of Accession[3] provides that duty-free entry shall, from the date of accession, apply to imports which benefit from the provisions relating to tax exemption applicable to persons travelling from one Member State to another; whereas the purpose of this provision is to facilitate personal contacts within the enlarged Community;

Whereas the exchange of small consignments of goods is a factor in cementing relationships between private persons residing in different Member States, just as is the movement of the persons themselves; whereas, because of this similarity between the situations, Council Directive No 74/651/EEC[4] of 19 December 1974 on the tax reliefs to be allowed on the importation of goods in small consignments of a non-commercial character within the Community, provides that small consignments of goods sent by a private person in one Member State to a private person in another Member State shall be relieved from turnover taxes and excise duties;

Whereas, for the same reason, relief from customs duties and charges having equivalent effect should be introduced for small consignments of goods sent between the Community as originally constituted and the new Member States or between the new Member States themselves by analogy with the arrangements for exemption provided for under Article 32(2)(c) of the Act of Accession; whereas to this end Article 235 of the Treaty should be invoked;

Whereas relief should, where appropriate, also be allowed on amounts chargeable on exchanges between Member States under the common agricultural policy and in respect of those prescribed for goods covered by Council Regulation (EEC) No 1059/69[5] of 28 May 1969, laying down the trade arrangements applicable to certain goods resulting from the processing of agricultural products, as last amended by Regulation (EEC) No 1491/73,[6]

[1] OJ C 19, 12.4.73, p 40.

[2] OJ C 69, 28.8.73, p 1.

[3] OJ L 73, 27.3.72, p 14.

[4] See [OJ L 354, 31.12.74, p 57].

[5] OJ L 141, 12.6.69, p 1.

[6] OJ L 151, 7.6.73, p 1.

HAS ADOPTED THIS REGULATION—

Article 1

1.   Goods meeting the requirements of Articles 9 and 10 of the Treaty which are sent in small consignments of a non-commercial character between the Community as originally constituted and the new Member States or between the new Member States themselves by any private person, wherever may be his permanent or usual residence or his principal place of business, to another private person, shall be relieved from customs duties and charges having equivalent effect, provided they benefit from tax relief pursuant from Council Directive No 74/651/EEC.

2.   In exchanges between Member States, relief shall be allowed, under the same conditions, in respect of amounts chargeable under the common agricultural policy and amounts prescribed for goods covered by Regulation (EEC) No 1059/69.

Article 2

This Regulation shall enter into force on 1 April 1975.

This Regulation shall be binding in its entirety and directly applicable in all Member States.

Done at Brussels, 19 December 1974.

SIXTH COUNCIL DIRECTIVE

(388/77/EEC)

of 17 May 1977

on the harmonisation of the laws of the Member States relating to turnover taxes—common system of value added tax: uniform basis of assessment

NOTES

Date of publication in OJ: OJ L145, 13.6.1977, p 1.

This Directive repealed by Council Directive of 28 November 2006 on the common system of value added tax (2006/112/EC). For correlation table, see Annex XII of that Directive.

THE COUNCIL OF THE EUROPEAN COMMUNITIES

Having regard to the Treaty establishing the European Economic Community, and in particular Articles 99 and 100 thereof,

Having regard to the proposal from the Commission,

Having regard to the opinion of the European Parliament (OJ C40, 8.4.74, p 25),

Having regard to the opinion of the Economic and Social Committee (OJ C139, 12.11.74, p 15),

Whereas all Member States have adopted a system of value added tax in accordance with the first and second Council Directives of 11 April 1967 on the harmonisation of the laws of the Member States relating to turnover taxes (OJ 71, 14.4.67, pp 1301–1367);

Whereas the Decision of 21 April 1970 on the replacement of financial contributions from Member States by the Communities' own resources (OJ L94, 28.4.70, p 19) provides that the budget of the Communities shall, irrespective of other revenue, be financed entirely from the Communities' own resources; whereas these resources are to include those accruing from value added tax and obtained by applying a common rate of tax on a basis of assessment determined in a uniform manner according to Community rules;

Whereas further progress should be made in the effective removal of restrictions on the movement of persons, goods, services and capital and the integration of national economies;

Whereas account should be taken of the objective of abolishing the imposition of tax on the importation and the remission of tax on exportation in trade between Member States; whereas it should be ensured that the common system of turnover taxes is non-discriminatory as regards the origin of goods and services, so that a common market permitting fair competition and resembling a real internal market may ultimately be achieved;

Whereas, to enhance the non-discriminatory nature of the tax, the term "taxable person" must be clarified to enable the Member States to extend it to cover persons who occasionally carry out certain transactions;

Whereas the term "taxable transaction" has led to difficulties, in particular as regards transactions treated as taxable transactions; whereas these concepts must be clarified;

Whereas the determination of the place where taxable transactions are effected has been the subject of conflicts concerning jurisdiction as between Member States, in particular as regards supplies of goods for assembly and the supply of services; whereas although the place where a supply of services is effected should in principle be defined as the place where the person supplying the services has his principal place of business, that place should be defined as being in the country of the person to whom the services are supplied, in particular in the case of certain services supplied between taxable persons where the cost of the services is included in the price of the goods;

Whereas the concepts of chargeable event and of the charge to tax must be harmonised if the introduction and any subsequent alterations of the Community rate are to become operative at the same time in all Member States;

Whereas the taxable base must be harmonised so that the application of the Community rate to taxable transactions leads to comparable results in all the Member States;

Whereas the rates applied by Member States must be such as to allow the normal deduction of the tax applied at the preceding stage;

Whereas a common list of exemptions should be drawn up so that the Communities' own resources may be collected in a uniform manner in all the Member States;

Whereas the rules governing deductions should be harmonised to the extent that they affect the actual amounts collected; whereas the deductible proportion should be calculated in a similar manner in all the Member States;

Whereas it should be specified which persons are liable to pay tax, in particular as regards services supplied by a person established in another country;

Whereas the obligations of taxpayers must be harmonised as far as possible so as to ensure the necessary safeguards for the collection of taxes in a uniform manner in all the Member States; whereas taxpayers should, in particular, make a periodic aggregate return of their transactions, relating to both inputs and outputs where this appears necessary for establishing and monitoring the basis of assessment of own resources;

Whereas Member States should nevertheless be able to retain their special schemes for small undertakings, in accordance with common provisions, and with a view to closer harmonisation; whereas Member States should remain free to apply a special scheme involving flat rate rebates of input value added tax to farmers not covered by normal schemes; whereas the basic principles of this scheme should be established and a common method adopted for calculating the value added of these farmers for the purposes of collecting own resources;

Whereas the uniform application of the provisions of this Directive should be ensured; whereas to this end a Community procedure for consultation should be laid down; whereas the setting up of a Value Added Tax Committee would enable the Member States and the Commission to co-operate closely;

Whereas Member States should be able, within certain limits and subject to certain conditions, to take or retain special measures derogating from this Directive in order to simplify the levying of tax or to avoid fraud or tax avoidance;

Whereas it might appear appropriate to authorise Member States to conclude with non-member countries or international organisations agreements containing derogations from this Directive;

Whereas it is vital to provide for a transitional period to allow national laws in specified fields to be gradually adapted,

HAS ADOPTED THIS DIRECTIVE:

TITLE I:
INTRODUCTORY PROVISIONS

Article 1

Member States shall modify their present value added tax systems in accordance with the following Articles.

They shall adopt the necessary laws, regulations and administrative provisions so that the systems as modified enter into force at the earliest opportunity and by 1 January 1978 at the latest.

NOTES

This Directive repealed by Council Directive of 28 November 2006 on the common system of value added tax (2006/112/EC).

Recast VAT Directive: see Council Directive 2006/112/EC, art 2.

TITLE II:
SCOPE

Article 2

The following shall be subject to value added tax:

(1)   the supply of goods or services effected for consideration within the territory of the country by a taxable person acting as such;

(2)   the importation of goods.

NOTES

Council Decision 93/563/EEC, art 1 allows derogation from para (1) above.

Regulations: VAT Regulations, SI 1995/2518 reg 10 (implementation of para 1 above).

This Directive repealed by Council Directive of 28 November 2006 on the common system of value added tax (2006/112/EC).

Recast VAT Directive: see Council Directive 2006/112/EC, art 2.

TITLE III:
TERRITORIAL APPLICATION

[Article 3

1.   For the purposes of this Directive—

—   "territory of a Member State" shall mean the territory of the country as defined in respect of each Member State in paragraphs 2 and 3,

—   "Community" and "territory of the Community" shall mean the territory of the Member States as defined in respect of each Member State in paragraphs 2 and 3,

—   "third territory" and "third country" shall mean any territory other than those defined in paragraphs 2 and 3 as the territory of a Member State.

2.   For the purposes of this Directive, the "territory of the country" shall be the area of application of the Treaty establishing the European Economic Community as defined in respect of each Member State in Article 227.

3.   The following territories of individual Member States shall be excluded from the territory of the country:

—   Federal Republic of Germany:
          the Island of Heligoland,
          the territory of Büsingen,
—   Kingdom of Spain:
          Ceuta,
          Melilla,
—   Republic of Italy:
          Livigno,
          Campione d'Italia,
          the Italian waters of Lake Lugano.

The following territories of individual Member States shall also be excluded from the territory of the country:

—   Kingdom of Spain:
          the Canary Islands,
—   French Republic:
          the overseas departments,
—   Hellenic Republic:
          'Аγι 'Оρζ.

[[4.   By way of derogation from paragraph 1, in view of:

—   the conventions and treaties which the Principality of Monaco and the Isle of Man have concluded respectively with the French Republic and the United Kingdom of Great Britain and Northern Ireland,
—   the Treaty concerning the Establishment of the Republic of Cyprus, the Principality of Monaco, the Isle of Man and the United Kingdom Sovereign Base Areas of Akrotiri and Dhekelia shall not be treated for the purpose of the application of this Directive as third territories.]

Member States shall take the measures necessary to ensure that transactions originating in or intended for—

—   the Principality of Monaco are treated as transactions originating in or intended for the French Republic,
—   the Isle of Man are treated as transactions originating in or intended for the United Kingdom of Great Britain and Northern Ireland.]
[—   the United Kingdom Sovereign Base Areas of Akrotiri and Dhekelia are treated as transactions originating in or intended for the Republic of Cyprus.]

5.   If the Commission considers that the provisions laid down in paragraphs 3 and 4 are no longer justified, particularly in terms of fair competition or own resources, it shall submit appropriate proposals to the Council.]

NOTES

Article 3 replaced by EEC Council Directive 91/680; OJ L376, 31.12.1991, p 1 art 1(1).

Para 4 replaced by EEC Council Directive 92/111, art 1.1; OJ L384, 30.12.92.

In para 4, words replaced and words inserted by the 2003 Act of Accession Protocol No 3 Annex Part Two (OJ L236; 23.9.2003 p 940).

This Directive repealed by Council Directive of 28 November 2006 on the common system of value added tax (2006/112/EC).

Recast VAT Directive: see Council Directive 2006/112/EC, arts 5–8.

TITLE V:
TAXABLE TRANSACTIONS

Article 7 Imports

[1. "Importation of goods" shall mean:

(a)   the entry into the Community of goods which do not fulfil the conditions laid down in Articles 9 and 10 of the Treaty establishing the European Economic Community or, where the goods are covered by the Treaty establishing the European Coal and Steel Community, are not in free circulation;

[(b)   the entry into the Community of goods from a third territory, other than the goods covered by (a).]

2.   The place of import of goods shall be the Member State within the territory of which the goods are when they enter the Community.

3.   Notwithstanding paragraph 2, where goods referred to in paragraph 1(a) are, on entry into the Community, placed under one of the arrangements referred to in Article 16(1)(B)[(a), (b), (c) and (d)], under arrangements for temporary importation with total exemption from import duty or under external transit arrangements, the place of import of such goods shall be the Member State within the territory of which they cease to be covered by those arrangements.

[Similarly, when goods referred to in paragraph 1(b) are placed, on entry into the Community, under one of the procedures referred to in Article 33a(1)(b) or (c), the place of import shall be the Member State within whose territory this procedure ceases to apply.]]

NOTES

Article 7 replaced by EEC Council Directive 91/680; OJ L376, 31.12.1991, p 1 art 1(2).

Para 1(b) replaced by EEC Council Directive 92/111, art 1.2; OJ L384, 30.12.92.

Words in para 3 added by EEC Council Directive 92/111, art 1.3, OJ L384, 30.12.92.

Words in second sub-para of para 3 replaced by EEC Council Directive 92/111, art 1.3, OJ L384, 30.12.92.

This Directive repealed by Council Directive of 28 November 2006 on the common system of value added tax (2006/112/EC).

Recast VAT Directive: see Council Directive 2006/112/EC, arts 30, 60, 61.

TITLE VII:
CHARGEABLE EVENT AND CHARGEABILITY OF TAX

Article 10

1.

(a)   "Chargeable event" shall mean the occurrence by virtue of which the legal conditions necessary for tax to become chargeable are fulfilled.

(b)   The tax becomes "chargeable" when the tax authority becomes entitled under the law at a given moment to claim the tax from the person liable to pay, notwithstanding that the time of payment may be deferred.

2.   The chargeable event shall occur and the tax shall become chargeable when the goods are delivered or the services are performed. Deliveries of goods other than those referred to in Article 5(4)(*b*) and supplies of services which give rise to successive statements of account or payments shall be regarded as being completed at the time

when the periods to which such statements of account or payments pertain expire. [Member States may in certain cases provide that continuous supplies of goods and services which take place over a period of time shall be regarded as being completed at least at intervals of one year.]

However, where a payment is to be made on account before the goods are delivered or the services are performed, the tax shall become chargeable on receipt of the payment and on the amount received.

By way of derogation from the above provisions, Member States may provide that the tax shall become chargeable, for certain transactions or for certain categories of taxable person, either:

— no later than the issue of the invoice . . ., or

— no later than receipt of the price, or

— where an invoice . . . is not issued, or is issued late, within a specified period from the date of the chargeable event.

[3. The chargeable event shall occur and the tax shall become chargeable when the goods are imported. Where goods are placed under one of the arrangements referred to in Article 7(3) on entry into the Community, the chargeable event shall occur and the tax shall become chargeable only when the goods cease to be covered by those arrangements.

However, where imported goods are subject to customs duties, to agricultural levies or to charges having equivalent effect established under a common policy, the chargeable event shall occur and the tax shall become chargeable when the chargeable event for those Community duties occurs and those duties become chargeable.

Where imported goods are not subject to any of those Community duties, Member States shall apply the provisions in force governing customs duties as regards the occurrence of the chargeable event and the moment when the tax becomes chargeable.]

NOTES

Article 10(3) replaced by EEC Council Directive 91/680; OJ L376, 31.12.1991, p 1 art 1(6).

Words in art 10(2) inserted by Council Directive 2000/65/EC art 1(1) with effect from 21 October 2000; OJ L269 p 44, 21.10.00. Member states must bring into force the measures necessary to comply with these provisions not later than 31 December 2001.

Words in art 10(2) revoked by Council Directive 2001/115/EC art 4(1) (see OJ L 015; 17.01.02).

This Directive repealed by Council Directive of 28 November 2006 on the common system of value added tax (2006/112/EC).

Recast VAT Directive: see Council Directive 2006/112/EC, arts 62–66, 70, 71.

TITLE VIII:
TAXABLE AMOUNT

Article 11

A. *Within the territory of the country*

1. The taxable amount shall be:

   (a) in respect of supplies of goods and services other than those referred to in (b), (c) and (d) below, everything which constitutes the consideration which has been or is to be obtained by the supplier from the purchaser, the customer or a third party for such supplies including subsidies directly linked to the price of such supplies;

(b)   in respect of supplies referred to in Article 5(6) and (7), the purchase price of the goods or of similar goods or, in the absence of a purchase price, the cost price, determined at the time of supply;

(c)   in respect of supplies referred to in Article 6(2), the full cost to the taxable person of providing the services;

(d)   in respect of supplies referred to in Article 6(3), the open market value of the services supplied.

"Open market value" of services shall mean the amount which a customer at the marketing stage at which the supply takes place would have to pay to a supplier at arm's length within the territory of the country at the time of the supply under the conditions of fair competition to obtain the services in question.

2.   The taxable amount shall include:

(a)   taxes, duties, levies and charges, excluding the value added tax itself;

(b)   incidental expenses such as commission, packing, transport and insurance costs charged by the supplier to the purchaser or customer. Expenses covered by a separate agreement may be considered to be incidental expenses by the Member States.

3.   The taxable amount shall not include:

(a)   price reductions by way of discount for early payment;

(b)   price discounts and rebates allowed to the customer and accounted for at the time of the supply;

(c)   the amounts received by a taxable person from his purchaser or customer as repayment for expenses paid out in the name and for the account of the latter and which are entered in his books in a suspense account. The taxable person must furnish proof of the actual amount of this expenditure and may not deduct any tax which may have been charged on these transactions.

[4.   By way of derogation from paragraphs 1, 2 and 3, Member States which, on 1 January 1993, did not avail themselves of the option provided for in the third sub-paragraph of Article 12(3)(a) may, where they avail themselves of the option provided for in Title B(6), provide that, for the transactions referred to in the second sub-paragraph of Article 12(3)(c), the taxable amount shall be equal to a fraction of the amount determined in accordance with paragraphs 1, 2 and 3.

That fraction shall be determined in such a way that the value added tax thus due is, in any event, equal to at least 5% of the amount determined in accordance with paragraphs 1, 2 and 3.]

B. Importation of goods

[1.   The taxable amount shall be the value for customs purposes, determined in accordance with the Community provisions in force; this shall also apply for the import of goods referred to in Article 7(1)(b).]

2.   . . . (repealed by Directive 91/680)

[3.   The taxable amount shall include, in so far as they are not already included:

(a)   taxes, duties, levies and other charges due outside the importing Member State and those due by reason of importation, excluding the value added tax to be levied;

(b)   incidental expenses, such as commission, packing, transport and insurance costs, incurred up to the first place of destination within the territory of the importing Member State.

"First place of destination" shall mean the place mentioned on the consignment note or any other document by means of which the goods are imported into the importing Member State. In the absence of such an indication, the first place of destination shall be taken to be the place of the first transfer of cargo in the importing Member State.

[The incidental expenses referred to above shall also be included in the taxable amount where they result from transport to another place of destination within the territory of the Community if that place is known when the chargeable event occurs.]

4. The taxable amount shall not include those factors referred to in A(3)(a) and (b).

5. When goods have been temporarily exported [from the Community] and are re-imported after having undergone abroad repair, processing or adaptation, or after having been made up or reworked [outside the Community], Member States shall take steps to ensure that the treatment of the goods for value added tax purposes is the same as that which would have applied to the goods in question had the above operations been carried out within the territory of the country.

[6. By way of derogation from paragraphs 1 to 4, Member States which, on 1 January 1993, did not avail themselves of the option provided for in the third sub-paragraph of Article 12(3)(a) may provide that for imports of the works of art, collectors' items and antiques defined in Article 26a(A)(a), (b) and (c), the taxable amount shall be equal to a fraction of the amount determined in accordance with paragraphs 1 to 4.

That fraction shall be determined in such a way that the value added tax thus due on the import is, in any event, equal to at least 5% of the amount determined in accordance with paragraphs 1 to 4.]

C. Miscellaneous provisions

1. In the case of cancellation, refusal or total or partial non-payment, or where the price is reduced after the supply takes place, the taxable amount shall be reduced accordingly under conditions which shall be determined by the Member States.

However, in the case of total or partial non-payment, Member States may derogate from this rule.

[2. Where information for determining the taxable amount on importation is expressed in a currency other than that of the Member State where assessment takes place, the exchange rate shall be determined in accordance with the Community provisions governing the calculation of the value for customs purposes.

Where information for the determination of the taxable amount of a transaction other than an import transaction is expressed in a currency other than that of the Member State where assessment takes place, the exchange rate applicable shall be the latest selling rate recorded, at the time the tax becomes chargeable, on the most representative exchange market or markets of the Member State concerned, or a rate determined by reference to that or those markets, in accordance with the. . .down by that Member State. However, for some of those transactions or for certain categories of taxable person, Member States may continue to apply the exchange rate determined in accordance with the Community provisions in force governing the calculation of the value for customs purposes.]

3. As regards returnable packing costs, Member States may:
— either exclude them from the taxable amount and take the necessary measures to see that this amount is adjusted if the packing is not returned,
— or include them in the taxable amount and take the necessary measures to see that this amount is adjusted where the packing is in fact returned.

NOTES

Some words are missing in the second paragraph of art 11(C)(2) which is reproduced above as it appears in the EEC Official Journal.

Article 11(B), (C) amended by EEC Council Directive 91/680; OJ L376, 31.12.1991, p 1, art 1(8), (9), (10).

Para (B)(1) replaced by EEC Council Directive 92/111, art 1.5; OJ L384, 30.12.92.

Para (A)(4) added by EEC Council Directive 94/5, arts 1(1), 4; OJ L60, 3.3.94. For commencement, see art 4 of the Directive.

Para (B)(6) added by EEC Council Directive 94/5, arts 1(1), 4; OJ L60, 3.3.94.

Words in para (B)(3)(b) replaced by EC Council Directive 95/7, art 1(2): OJ L102, 5.5.95, p 18 with effect from 25 May 1995.

This Directive repealed by Council Directive of 28 November 2006 on the common system of value added tax (2006/112/EC).

Recast VAT Directive: see Council Directive 2006/112/EC, arts 72–75, 77–82, 85–92.

TITLE X:
EXEMPTIONS

Article 14 Exemptions on importation

1. Without prejudice to other Community provisions, Member States shall exempt the following under conditions which they shall lay down for the purpose of ensuring the correct and straightforward application of such exemption and of preventing any possible evasion, avoidance or abuse:

(a)   final importation of goods of which the supply by a taxable person would in all circumstances be exempted within the country;

(b)   (*repealed by Directive 91/680*)

. . .

(d)   final importation of goods qualifying for exemption from customs duties other than as provided for in the Common Customs Tariff. . . However, Member States shall have the option of not granting exemption where this would be liable to have a serious effect on conditions of competition. . .; [This exemption shall also apply to the import of goods, within the meaning of Article 7(1)(b), which would be capable of benefiting from the exemption set out above if they had been imported within the meaning of Article 7(1)(a).]

(e)   reimportation by the person who exported them of goods in the state in which they were exported, where they qualify for exemption from customs duties or would qualify therefor if they were imported from a third country;

(f)   . . .

(g)   importations of goods:

— under diplomatic and consular arrangements, which qualify for exemption from customs duties . . .,

— by international organisations recognised as such by the public authorities of the host country, and by members of such organisations, within the limits and under the conditions laid down by the international conventions establishing the organisations or by headquarters agreements,

— into the territory of Member States which are parties to the North Atlantic Treaty by the armed forces of other States which are parties to that Treaty for the use of such forces or the civilian staff accompanying them or for supplying their messes or canteens where such forces take part in the common defence effort;

[— the exemptions set out in the third indent shall extend to imports by and supplies of goods and services to the forces of the United Kingdom stationed in the island of Cyprus pursuant to the Treaty of Establishment concerning the Republic of Cyprus, dated 16 August 1960, which are for the use of the forces or the civilian staff accompanying them or for supplying their messes or canteens.]

(h) importation into ports by sea fishing undertakings of their catches, unprocessed or after undergoing preservation for marketing but before being supplied;

(i) the supply of services, in connection with the importation of goods where the value of such services is included in the taxable amount in accordance with Article 11B(3)(b);

(j) importation of gold by Central Banks;

[(k) import of gas through the natural gas distribution system, or of electricity.]

2. The Commission shall submit to the Council at the earliest opportunity proposals designed to lay down Community tax rules clarifying the scope of the exemptions referred to in paragraph 1 and detailed rules for their implementation. Until the entry into force of these rules, Member States may:

— maintain their national provisions in force on matters related to the above provisions,

— adapt their national provisions to minimise distortion of competition and in particular the non-imposition or double imposition of value added tax within the Community,

— use whatever administrative procedures they consider most appropriate to achieve exemption.

Member States shall inform the Commission, which shall inform the other Member States, of the measures they have adopted and are adopting pursuant to the preceding provisions.

NOTES

Article 14(1) amended by EEC Council Directive 91/680; OJ L376, 31.12.91, p 1.

Words in para (1)(d) added by EEC Council Directive 92/111, art 1.8; OJ L384, 30.12.92.

Para (1)(c) deleted by EEC Council Directive 92/111, art 1.8; OJ L384, 30.12.92.

Para 1(k) inserted by Council Directive 2003/92/EC, art 1(3); OJ L260, 11.10.2003 p 8.

Words in para 1(g) inserted by the 2003 Act of Accession Protocol No 3 Annex Part Three para 2(a); OJ L 236; 23.9.2003 p 940.

This Directive repealed by Council Directive of 28 November 2006 on the common system of value added tax (2006/112/EC).

Recast VAT Directive: see Council Directive 2006/112/EC, arts 131, 140, 143–145.

Article 15 [Exemption of exports from the Community and like transactions and international transport]

Without prejudice to other Community provisions Member States shall exempt the following under conditions which they shall lay down for the purpose of ensuring the correct and straightforward application of such exemptions and of preventing any evasion, avoidance or abuse:

1. The supply of goods dispatched or transported to a destination [outside the Community]; by or on behalf of the vendor;

2. The supply of goods dispatched or transported to a destination [outside the Community]; by or on behalf of a purchaser not established within the territory of

Part III

the country, with the exception of goods transported by the purchaser himself for the equipping, fuelling and provisioning of pleasure boats and private aircraft or any other means of transport for private use;

[In the case of the supply of goods to be carried in the personal luggage of travellers, this exemption shall apply on condition that:

— the traveller is not established within the Community,

— the goods are transported to a destination outside the Community before the end of the third month following that in which the supply is effected,

— the total value of the supply, including value added tax, is more than the equivalent in national currency of ECU 175, fixed in accordance with Article 7(2) of Directive 69/169/EEC; however, Member States may exempt a supply with a total value of less than that amount.

For the purposes of applying the second subparagraph:

— a traveller not established within the Community shall be taken to mean a traveller whose domicile or habitual residence is not situated within the Community. For the purposes of this provision, "domicile or habitual residence" shall mean the place entered as such in a passport, identity card or other identity documents which the Member State within whose territory the supply takes place recognises as valid,

— proof of exportation shall be furnished by means of the invoice or other document in lieu thereof, endorsed by the customs office where the goods left the Community.

Each Member State shall transmit to the Commission specimens of the stamps it uses for the endorsement referred to in the second indent of the third subparagraph. The Commission shall transit this information to the tax authorities in the other Member States.]

[3.   The supply of services consisting of work on movable property acquired or imported for the purpose of undergoing such work within the territory of the Community, and dispatched or transported out of the Community by the person providing the services or by the customer if [not established within the territory of the country] or on behalf of either of them;]

4.   The supply of goods for the fuelling and provisioning of vessels:

(a)   used for navigation on the high seas and carrying passengers for reward or used for the purpose of commercial, industrial or fishing activities;

(b)   used for rescue or assistance at sea, or for inshore fishing, with the exception, for the latter, of ships' provisions;

(c)   of war, as defined in subheading 89.01 A of the Common Customs Tariff, leaving the country and bound for foreign ports or anchorages.

[The Commission shall submit to the Council as soon as possible proposals to establish Community fiscal rules specifying the scope of and practical arrangements for implementing this exemption and the exemptions provided for in (5) to (9). Until these rules come into force, Member States may limit the extent of the exemption provided for in this paragraph.]

5.   The supply, modification, repair, maintenance, chartering and hiring of the sea-going vessels referred to in paragraph 4(a) and (b) and the supply, hiring, repair and maintenance of equipment—including fishing equipment—incorporated or used therein;

6.   The supply, modification, repair, maintenance, chartering and hiring of aircraft used by airlines operating for reward chiefly on international routes, and the supply, hiring, repair and maintenance of equipment incorporated or used therein;

7.   The supply of goods for the fuelling and provisioning of aircraft referred to in paragraph 6;

8. The supply of services other than those referred to in paragraph 5, to meet the direct needs of the sea-going vessels referred to in that paragraph or of their cargoes;

9. The supply of services other than those referred to in paragraph 6, to meet the direct needs of aircraft referred to in that paragraph or of their cargoes;

10. Supplies of goods and services:
- under diplomatic and consular arrangements,
- to another Member State and intended for the forces of any Member State which is a party to the North Atlantic Treaty, other than the Member State of destination itself, for the use of those forces or of the civilian staff accompanying them, or for supplying their messes or canteens when such forces take part in the common defence effort,]
- to international organisations recognised as such by the public authorities of the host country, and to members of such organisations, within the limits and under the conditions laid down by the international conventions establishing the organisations or by headquarters agreements,
- effected within a Member State which is a party to the North Atlantic Treaty and intended either for the use of the forces of other States which are parties to that Treaty or of the civilian staff accompanying them, or for supplying their messes or canteens when such forces take part in the common defence effort.

This exemption shall be [subject to [limitations] laid down by the host Member State] until Community tax rules are adopted.

[In cases where the goods are not dispatched or transported out of the country, and in the case of services, the benefit of the exemption may be given by means of a refund of the tax.]

11. Supplies of gold to Central Banks;

12. Goods supplied to approved bodies which export them [from the Community] as part of their humanitarian, charitable or teaching activities [outside the Community]. This exemption may be implemented by means of a refund of the tax;

[13. The supply of services, including transport and ancillary operations, but excluding the supply of services exempted in accordance with Article 13, where these are directly connected with the export of goods or imports of goods covered by the provisions of Article 7(3) or Article 16(1), Title A.]

14. Services supplied by brokers and other intermediaries, acting in the name and for account of another person, where they form part of transactions specified in this Article, or of transactions carried out [outside the Community].

This exemption does not apply to travel agents who supply in the name and for account of the traveller services which are supplied in other Member States.

[15. The Portuguese Republic may treat sea and air transport between the islands making up the autonomous regions of the Azores and Madeira and between those regions and the mainland in the same way as international transport.]

NOTES

Paras 3, 14 amended by EEC Council Directive 91/680; OJ L376, 31.12.1991, p 1.

Para 15 added by the Act of Accession 1985, art 26 Annex I Part V point 2; see OJ L302, 15.11.1985, p 167.

Words in paras 3 (in inner square brackets), 4, 10 replaced by EEC Council Directive 92/111, art 1.9; OJ L384, 30.12.92.

Para 13 replaced by EEC Council Directive 92/111, art 1.9; OJ L384, 30.12.92.

Words in para 2 replaced by Council Directive 95/7, art 1.3: OJ L102, 5.5.95, p 18 with effect from 25 May 1995.

This Directive repealed by Council Directive of 28 November 2006 on the common system of value added tax (2006/112/EC).

Recast VAT Directive: see Council Directive 2006/112/EC, arts 131, 146–153.

Article 16 Special exemptions linked to international goods traffic

1. Without prejudice to other Community tax provisions, Member States may, subject to the consultations provided for in Article 29, take special measures designed to exempt all or some of the following transactions, provided that they are not aimed at final use and/or consumption and that the amount of value added tax due on cessation of the arrangements on situations referred to at A to E corresponds to the amount of tax which would have been due had each of these transactions been taxed within the territory of the country:

A   imports of goods which are intended to be placed under warehousing arrangements other than customs;

B   supplies of goods which are intended to be:

    (a)   produced to customs and, where applicable, placed in temporary storage;

    (b)   placed in a free zone or in a free warehouse;

    (c)   placed under customs warehousing arrangements or inward processing arrangements;

    (d)   admitted into territorial waters:

       —   in order to be incorporated into drilling or production platforms, for purposes of the construction, repair, maintenance, alteration or fitting-out of such platforms, or to link such drilling or production platforms to the mainland,

       —   for the fuelling and provisioning of drilling or production platforms;

    (e)   placed, within the territory of the country, under warehousing arrangements other than customs warehousing.

For the purposes of this Article, warehouses other than customs warehouses shall be taken to be:

—   for products subject to excise duty, the places defined as tax warehouses for the purposes of Article 4(b) of Directive 92/12/EEC,

—   for goods other than those subject to excise duty, the places defined as such by the Member States. However, Member States may not provide for warehousing arrangements other than customs warehousing where the goods in question are intended to be supplied at the retail stage.

Nevertheless, Member States may provide for such arrangements for goods intended for:

—   taxable persons for the purposes of supplies effected under the conditions laid down in Article 28k,

—   tax-free shops within the meaning of Article 28k, for the purposes of supplies to travellers taking flights or sea crossings to third countries, where those supplies are exempt pursuant to Article 15,

—   taxable persons for the purposes of supplies to travellers on board aircraft or vessels during a flight or sea crossing where the place of arrival is situated outside the Community,

—   taxable persons for the purposes of supplies effected free of tax pursuant to Article 15, point 10.

The places referred to in (a), (b), (c) and (d) shall be as defined by the Community customs provisions in force;

C supplies of services relating to the supplies of goods referred to in B;

D supplies of goods and of services carried out:

    (a)   in the places listed in B(a), (b), (c) and (d) and still subject to one of the situations specified therein;

    (b)   in the places listed in B(e) and still subject, within the territory of the country, to the situation specified therein.

Where they exercise the option provided for in (a) for transactions effected in customs warehouses, Member States shall take the measures necessary to ensure that they have defined warehousing arrangements other than customs warehousing which permit the provisions in (b) to be applied to the same transactions concerning goods listed in Annex J which are effected in such warehouses other than customs warehouses;

E supplies:

    —   of goods referred to in Article 7(1)(a) still subject to arrangements for temporary importation with total exemption from import duty or to external transit arrangements,

    —   of goods referred to in Article 7(1)(b) still subject to the internal Community transit procedure provided for in Article 33a,

    as well as supplies of services relating to such supplies.

By way of derogation from the first subparagraph of Article 21(1)(a), the person liable to pay the tax due in accordance with the first subparagraph shall be the person who causes the goods to cease to be covered by the arrangements or situations listed in this paragraph.

When the removal of goods from the arrangements or situations referred to in this paragraph gives rise to importation within the meaning of Article 7(3), the Member State of import shall take the measures necessary to avoid double taxation within the country.]

[1a.   Where they exercise the option provided for in paragraph 1, Member States shall take the measures necessary to ensure that intra-Community acquisitions of goods intended to be placed under one of the arrangements or in one of the situations referred to in paragraph 1(B) benefit from the same provisions as supplies of goods effected within the country under the same conditions.]

2.   Subject to the consultation provided for in Article 29, Member States may opt to exempt [intra-Community acquisitions of goods made by a taxable person and] imports for and supplies of goods to a taxable person intending to export them [outside the Community] as they are or after processing, as well as supplies of services linked with his export business, up to a maximum equal to the value of his exports during the preceding 12 months.

[When they take up this option the Member States shall, subject to the consultation provided for in Article 29, extend the benefit of this exemption to intra-Community acquisitions of goods by a taxable person, imports for and supplies of goods to a taxable person intending to supply them, as they are or after processing, under the conditions laid down in Article 28c(A), as well as supplies of services relating to such supplies, up to a maximum equal to the value of his supplies of goods effected under the conditions laid down in Article 28c(A) during the preceding twelve months.

Member States may set a common maximum amount for transactions which they exempt under the first and second subparagraphs.]

3.   The Commission shall submit to the Council at the earliest opportunity proposals concerning common arrangements for applying value added tax to the transactions referred to in paragraphs 1 and 2.

NOTES

Art 16(1) substituted, para (1A) added and para (2) amended by EC Council Directive 95/7, art 1(9): OJ L102, 5.5.95, p 18 with effect from 25 May 1995.

This Directive repealed by Council Directive of 28 November 2006 on the common system of value added tax (2006/112/EC).

Recast VAT Directive: see Council Directive 2006/112/EC, art 164, 166.

TITLE XV:
SIMPLIFICATION PROCEDURES

Article 27

[1. The Council, acting unanimously on a proposal from the Commission, may authorise any Member State to introduce special measures for derogation from the provisions of this Directive, in order to simplify the procedure for charging the tax or to prevent certain types of tax evasion or avoidance. Measures intended to simplify the procedure for charging the tax, except to a negligible extent, may not affect the overall amount of the tax revenue of the Member State collected at the stage of final consumption.]

[2. A Member State wishing to introduce the measure referred to in paragraph 1 shall send an application to the Commission and provide it with all the necessary information. If the Commission considers that it does not have all the necessary information, it shall contact the Member State concerned within two months of receipt of the application and specify what additional information is required. Once the Commission has all the information it considers necessary for appraisal of the request it shall within one month notify the requesting Member State accordingly and it shall transmit the request, in its original language, to the other Member States.]

[3. Within three months of giving the notification referred to in the last sentence of paragraph 2, the Commission shall present to the Council either an appropriate proposal or, should it object to the derogation requested, a communication setting out its objections.]

[4. In any event, the procedure set out in paragraphs 2 and 3 shall be completed within eight months of receipt of the application by the Commission.]

5. Those Member States which apply on 1 January 1977 special measures of the type referred to in paragraph 1 above may retain them providing they notify the Commission of them before 1 January 1978 and providing that where such derogations are designed to simplify the procedure for charging tax they conform with the requirement laid down in paragraph 1 above.

NOTES

Paras 1, 2, 3 replaced by Council Directive 2004/7 art 1 (OJ L 027; 30.1.2004 p 44).

This Directive repealed by Council Directive of 28 November 2006 on the common system of value added tax (2006/112/EC).

Recast VAT Directive: see Council Directive 2006/112/EC, arts 394, 395.

COUNCIL REGULATION

(918/83/EEC)

of 28 March 1983

setting up a Community system of reliefs from customs duty

NOTES

Date of publication in OJ: OJ L305, 23.04.83, p 1.

The Council of the European communities,

Having regard to the Treaty establishing the European Economic Community, and in particular Articles 28, 43 and 235 thereof,

Having regard to the proposal from the Commission,

Having regard to the opinion of the European Parliament,[1]

Having regard to the opinion of the Economic and Social Committee,[2]

Whereas, in the absence of a specific measure of derogation adopted in accordance with the provisions of the Treaty, Common Customs Tariff duties are applicable to all goods imported into the Community; whereas the same is true in the case of agricultural levies and all other import charges laid down under the common agricultural policy or the specific arrangements applicable to certain goods resulting from the processing of agricultural products;

Whereas, however, in certain well-defined circumstances, where by virtue of the special conditions under which goods are imported the usual need to protect the economy is absent, such taxation is not justified;

Whereas it is desirable that in such circumstances arrangements should be made, as they have been traditionally in most systems of customs rules, to allow goods to enjoy relief from the application of import duties to which they would normally be liable;

Whereas such relief arrangements may also be the result of multilateral international conventions to which all or some of the Member States are contracting parties; whereas, while the Community should apply such conventions, this presupposes the introduction of Community rules on reliefs from customs duties designed, in accordance with the requirements of the Customs Union, to eliminate differences in the aim, scope and conditions for application of the reliefs contained in these conventions, and to enable all those concerned to enjoy the same advantages throughout the Community;

Whereas certain reliefs currently applied in the Member States stem from specific conventions concluded with third countries or international organisations; whereas such conventions, given their purpose, concern only the signatory Member State; whereas it does not appear necessary to define, at Community level, conditions for granting such reliefs, but appears sufficient simply to authorise the Member State in question to grant these reliefs, where necessary, by means of an appropriate procedure instituted for this purpose;

Whereas the implementation of the common agricultural policy means that in certain circumstances export duties may be charged on some goods; whereas it is therefore also necessary to specify at Community level the cases in which relief from such duties may be granted;

Whereas the Council has already adopted a number of Regulations concerning reliefs from customs duties and it appears desirable, with a view to establishing a single comprehensive Community system of reliefs, to incorporate the provisions of these individual Regulations in this Regulation and to repeal, formally, the earlier Acts;

Whereas, in the interests of legal clarity, the provisions of Community acts containing certain relief measures not affected by this Regulation should be listed;

Whereas this Regulation does not preclude the application by Member States of import or export prohibitions or restrictions which are justified on grounds of public morality, public policy or public security, protection of health and life of humans, animals or plants, protection of national treasures possessing artistic, historical or archaeological value or protection of industrial or commercial property;

Whereas, with regard to the reliefs granted within the amounts fixed in ECU, rules for the conversion of such amounts into national currencies have to be drawn up;

Whereas it is necessary to ensure uniform application of the provisions of this Regulation, and hence to establish a Community procedure for the timely adoption of implementing measures; whereas a Committee making it possible to organise close and effective cooperation between the Member States and the Commission in this field should therefore be set up to replace the Committee on duty-free arrangements set up by Council Regulation (EEC) No 1798/75 of 10 July 1975 on the importation free of Common Customs Tariff duties of educational, scientific and cultural materials,[3]

---

[1] OJ C 4, 7.1.80, p 59.

[2] OJ C 72, 24.3.80, p 20.

[3] OJ L 184, 15.7.75, p 1.

Has adopted this Regulation—

Article 1

1. This Regulation sets out those cases in which, owing to special circumstances, relief from import or export duties shall be granted respectively when goods are put into free circulation or are exported from the [customs territory of the Community].

2. For the purposes of this Regulation—

(a) "import duties" means customs duties and charges having equivalent effect and also agricultural levies and other import charges provided for under the common agricultural policy or under specific arrangements applicable to certain goods resulting from the processing of agricultural products;

(b) "export duties" means agricultural levies and other export charges provided for under the common agricultural policy or under specific arrangements applicable to certain goods resulting from the processing of agricultural products;

(c) "personal property" means any property intended for the personal use of the persons concerned or for meeting their household needs.

The following, in particular, shall constitute "personal property"—
— household effects,
— cycles and motor cycles, private motor vehicles and their trailers, camping caravans, pleasure craft and private aeroplanes.

Household provisions appropriate to normal family requirements, household pets and saddle animals, as well as the portable instruments of the applied or liberal arts, required by the person concerned for the pursuit of his trade or profession, shall also constitute "personal property". Personal property must not be such as might indicate, by its nature or quantity, that it is being imported for commercial reasons;

(d) "household effects" means personal effects, household linen, furnishings and equipment intended for the personal use of the persons concerned or for meeting their household needs;

[(e) "alcoholic products" means products (beer, wine, aperitifs with a wine or alcohol base, brandies, liqueurs or spirituous beverages, etc) falling within heading Nos 2203 to 2208 of the Combined Nomenclature.]

[3. Save as otherwise provided in this Regulation for the purpose of applying Chapter I, the concept of third countries also includes those parts of Member States' territories excluded from the customs territory of the Community by virtue of Regulation (EEC) No 2151/84.][1]

---

[1] OJ L 197, 27.7.84, p 1.

Para 1: words in square brackets substituted by Council Regulation (EEC) 1315/88, Art 2, para 17.

Para 2: sub-para (e) substituted by Commission Regulation (EEC) 3691/87, Art 1, para 1.

Para 3: substituted by Council Regulation (EEC) 1315/88, Art 2, para 1.

CHAPTER I
RELIEF FROM IMPORT DUTY

TITLE I
PERSONAL PROPERTY BELONGING TO NATURAL PERSONS TRANSFERRING THEIR NORMAL PLACE OF RESIDENCE FROM A THIRD COUNTRY TO THE COMMUNITY

Article 2
Subject to Articles 3 to 10, personal property imported by natural persons transferring their normal place of residence from a third country to the customs territory of the Community shall be admitted free of import duties.

Article 3
The relief shall be limited to personal property which—

(a) except in special cases justified by the circumstances, has been in the possession of and, in the case of non-consumable goods, used by the person concerned at his former normal place of residence for a minimum of six months before the date on which he ceases to have his normal place of residence in the third country of departure;

(b) is intended to be used for the same purpose at his new normal place of residence.

In addition, Member States may make relief conditional upon such property having borne, either in the country of origin or in the country of departure, the customs and / or fiscal charges to which it is normally liable.

Article 4
Relief may be granted only to persons whose normal place of residence has been outside the [customs territory of the Community] for a continuous period of at least 12 months.

However, the competent authorities may grant exceptions to the rule in the first paragraph provided that the intention of the person concerned was clearly to reside outside the [customs territory of the Community] for a continuous period of at least 12 months.

NOTES

Words in square brackets substituted by Council Regulation (EEC) 1315/88, Art 2, para 17.

Article 5

No relief shall be granted for—

(a)   alcoholic products;

(b)   tobacco or tobacco products;

(c)   commercial means of transport;

(d)   articles for use in the exercise of a trade or profession, other than portable instruments of the applied or liberal arts.

Article 6

Except in special cases, relief shall be granted only in respect of personal property entered for free circulation within 12 months from the date of establishment, by the person concerned, of his normal place of residence in the customs territory of the Community.

The personal property may be released for free circulation in several separate consignments within the period referred to in the preceding paragraph.

Article 7

1.   Until 12 months have elapsed from the date on which its entry for free circulation was accepted, personal property which has been admitted duty-free may not be lent, given as security, hired out or transferred, whether for a consideration or free of charge, without prior notification to the competent authorities.

2.   Any loan, giving as security, hiring out or transfer before the expiry of the period referred to in paragraph 1 shall entail payment of the relevant import duties on the property concerned, at the rate applying on the date of such loan, giving as security, hiring out or transfer, on the basis of the type of property and the customs value ascertained or accepted on that date by the competent authorities.

Article 8

1.   By way of derogation from the first paragraph of Article 6, relief may be granted in respect of personal property entered for free circulation before the person concerned establishes his normal place of residence in the customs territory of the Community, provided that he undertakes actually to establish his normal place of residence there within a period of six months. Such undertaking shall be accompanied by a security, the form and amount of which shall be determined by the competent authorities.

2.   Where use is made of the provisions of paragraph 1, the period laid down in Article 3(a) shall be calculated from the date on which the personal property is brought into the customs territory of the Community.

Article 9

1.   Where, owing to occupational commitments, the person concerned leaves the third country where he had his normal place of residence without simultaneously establishing his normal place of residence in the customs territory of the Community, although having the intention of ultimately doing so, the competent authorities may authorise duty-free admission of the personal property which he transfers into the said territory for this purpose.

2.   Duty-free admission of the personal property referred to in paragraph 1 shall be granted in accordance with the conditions laid down in Articles 2 to 7, on the understanding that—

(a)   the periods laid down in Article 3(a) and the first paragraph of Article 6 shall be calculated from the date on which the personal property is brought into the customs territory of the Community;

(b)   the period referred to in Article 7(1) shall be calculated from the date when the person concerned actually establishes his normal place of residence in the customs territory of the Community.

3.   Duty-free admission shall also be subject to an undertaking from the person concerned that he will actually establish his normal place of residence in the customs territory of the Community within a period laid down by the competent authorities in keeping with the circumstances. The latter may require this undertaking to be accompanied by a security, the form and amount of which they shall determine.

Article 10

The competent authorities may derogate from Articles 3(a) and (b), 5(c) and (d) and 7, when a person has to transfer his normal place of residence from a third country to the customs territory of the Community as a result of exceptional political circumstances.

TITLE II
GOODS IMPORTED ON THE OCCASION OF A MARRIAGE

Article 11

1.   Subject to Articles 12 to 15, trousseaux and household effects, whether or not new, belonging to a person transferring his or her normal place of residence from a third country to the customs territory of the Community on the occasion of his or her marriage, shall be admitted free of import duties.

[2.   Subject to the same conditions, presents customarily given on the occasion of a marriage, which are received by a person fulfilling the conditions laid down in paragraph 1 from persons having their normal place of residence in a third country shall also be admitted free of import duties. The value of each present admitted duty-free may not, however, exceed 1 000 ECU.]

NOTES
   Para 2: substituted by Council Regulation (EEC) 1315/88, Art 2, para 2.

Article 12

The relief referred to in Article 11 may be granted only to persons—

(a)   whose normal place of residence has been outside the customs territory of the Community for a continuous period of at least 12 months. However, derogations from this rule may be granted provided that the intention of the person concerned was clearly to reside outside the customs territory of the Community for a continuous period of at least 12 months;

(b)   who produce evidence of their marriage.

Article 13

No relief shall be granted for alcoholic products, tobacco or tobacco products.

Article 14

1.   Save in exceptional circumstances, relief shall be granted only in respect of goods entered for free circulation—

—   not earlier than two months before the date fixed for the wedding (in this case the relief shall be subject to the lodging of appropriate security, the form and amount of which shall be determined by the competent authorities), and

Part III

— not later than four months after the date of the wedding.

2. The goods referred to in Article 11 may be released for free circulation in several separate consignments within the period referred to in paragraph 1 above.

Article 15

1. Until 12 months have elapsed from the date on which their entry for free circulation was accepted, goods which have been admitted duty-free under Article 11 may not be lent, given as security, hired out or transferred, whether for a consideration or free of charge, without prior notification to the competent authorities.

2. Any loan, giving as security, hiring out or transfer before the expiry of the period referred to in paragraph 1 shall entail payment of the relevant import duties on the goods concerned, at the rate applying on the date of such loan, giving as security, hiring out or transfer, on the basis of the type of goods and the customs value ascertained or accepted on that date by the competent authorities.

TITLE III
PERSONAL PROPERTY ACQUIRED BY INHERITANCE

Article 16

1. Subject to Articles 17 to 19, personal property acquired by inheritance, by a natural person having his normal place of residence in the customs territory of the Community shall be admitted free of import duties.

2. For the purposes of paragraph 1, "personal property" means all the property referred to in Article 1(2)(c) constituting the estate of the deceased.

Article 17

No relief shall be granted for—

- (a) alcoholic products;
- (b) tobacco and tobacco products;
- (c) commercial means of transport;
- (d) articles for use in the exercise of a trade or profession, other than portable instruments of the applied or liberal arts, which were required for the exercise of the trade or profession of the deceased;
- (e) stocks of raw materials and finished or semi-finished products;
- (f) livestock and stocks of agricultural products exceeding the quantities appropriate to normal family requirements.

Article 18

1. Relief shall be granted only for personal property entered for free circulation not later than two years from the date on which the person concerned becomes entitled to the property (final settlement of the inheritance).

However, this period may be extended by the competent authorities on special grounds.

2. The personal property may be imported in several separate consignments within the period referred to in paragraph 1.

Article 19

Articles 16 to 18 shall apply *mutatis mutandis* to personal property acquired by inheritance by legal persons engaged in a non-profit making activity who are established in the customs territory of the Community.

— contain goods exclusively for the personal use of the consignee or his family, which do not by their nature or quantity reflect any commercial intent,

— are sent to the consignor by the consignee free of payment of any kind.]

NOTES
Substituted, together with Arts 30, 31, by Council Regulation (EEC) 1315/88, Art 2, para 3.

[Article 30
The relief referred to in Article 29(1) shall apply to a value of 45 ECU per consignment, including the value of goods referred to in Article 31.

Where the total value per consignment of two or more items exceeds the amount referred to in the first subparagraph, relief up to that amount shall be granted for such of the items as would, if imported separately, have been granted relief, it being understood that the value of an individual item cannot be split up.]

NOTES
Substituted as noted to Art 29.

[Article 31
The relief referred to in Article 29(1) shall be limited, per consignment, to the quantities given against each of the goods listed below—

(a) tobacco products—
— 50 cigarettes, or
25 cigarillos (cigars of a maximum weight of three grams each), or
10 cigars, or
50 grams of smoking tobacco, or
a proportional assortment of these different products;

(b) alcohols and alcoholic beverages—
— distilled beverages and spirits of an alcoholic strength by volume exceeding 22% volume; non-denatured ethyl alcohol of 80% volume and over: one litre, or
— distilled beverages and spirits, and aperitifs with a wine or alcoholic base, tafia, sake or similar beverages, of an alcoholic strength by volume not exceeding 22% volume; sparkling wines, liqueur wines: one litre, or a proportional assortment of these different products and
— still wines: two litres;

(c) perfumes: 50 grams, or
toilet waters: 0,25 litre.]

NOTES
Substituted as noted to Art 29.

Part III

TITLE VIII

CAPITAL GOODS AND OTHER EQUIPMENT IMPORTED ON THE TRANSFER OF ACTIVITIES FROM A THIRD COUNTRY INTO THE COMMUNITY

Article 32

1.   Without prejudice to the measures in force in the Member States with regard to industrial and commercial policy, and subject to Articles 33 to 37, the capital goods and other equipment belonging to undertakings which definitively cease their activity in a third country and move to the customs territory of the Community in order to carry on a similar activity there, shall be admitted free of import duties.

Where the undertaking transferred is an agricultural holding, its livestock shall also be admitted free of import duties.

2.   For the purposes of paragraph 1, "undertaking" means an independent economic unit of production or of the service industry.

Article 33

Relief shall be limited to capital goods and other equipment which—

(a)   except in special cases justified by the circumstances, have actually been used in the undertaking for a minimum of 12 months before the date on which the undertaking ceased to operate in the third country from which it has transferred its activities;

(b)   are intended to be used for the same purposes after the transfer;

(c)   are appropriate to the nature and size of the undertaking in question.

Article 34

No relief shall be granted to undertakings the transfer of which into the customs territory of the Community is consequent upon or is for the purpose of merging with, or being absorbed by, an undertaking established in the customs territory of the Community, without a new activity being set up.

Article 35

No relief shall be granted for—

(a)   means of transport which are not of the nature of instruments of production or of the service industry;

(b)   supplies of all kinds intended for human consumption or for animal feed;

(c)   fuel and stocks of raw materials or finished or semi-finished products;

(d)   livestock in the possession of dealers.

Article 36

Except in special cases justified by the circumstances, the relief referred to in Article 32 shall be granted only for capital goods and other equipment entered for free circulation before the expiry of a period of 12 months from the date when the undertaking ceased its activities in the third country of departure.

Article 37

1.   Until 12 months have elapsed from the date on which their entry for free circulation was accepted, capital goods and other equipment which have been admitted duty-free may not be lent, given as security, hired out or transferred, whether for a consideration or free of charge, without prior notification to the competent authorities.

This period may be extended to up to 36 months as concerns hiring out or transfer where there is a risk of abuse.

2.   Any loan, giving as security, hiring out or transfer before the expiry of the period referred to in paragraph 1 shall entail payment of the relevant import duties on

the goods concerned, at the rate applying on the date of such loan, giving as security, hiring out or transfer, on the basis of the type of goods and the customs value ascertained or accepted on that date by the competent authorities.

Article 38

Articles 32 to 37 shall apply *mutatis mutandis* to capital goods and other equipment belonging to persons engaged in a liberal profession and to legal persons engaged in a non-profitmaking activity who transfer this activity from a third country into the customs territory of the Community.

TITLE IX
PRODUCTS OBTAINED BY COMMUNITY FARMERS ON PROPERTIES LOCATED IN A THIRD COUNTRY

Article 39

1. Subject to Articles 40 and 41, agricultural, stock-farming, bee-keeping, horticultural and forestry products from properties located in a third country adjoining the customs territory of the Community, which are operated by agricultural producers having their principal undertaking within the said customs territory and adjacent to the third country concerned shall be admitted free of import duties.

2. To benefit from the provisions of paragraph 1, stock-farming products must be derived from animals which originated in the Community or have entered into free circulation therein.

Article 40

Relief shall be limited to products which have not undergone any treatment other than that which normally follows their harvest or production.

Article 41

Relief shall be granted only for products brought into the customs territory of the Community by the agricultural producer or on his behalf.

Article 42

Articles 39 to 41 shall apply *mutatis mutandis* to the products of fishing or fish-farming activities carried out in the lakes or waterways bordering a Member State and a third country by Community fishermen and to the products of hunting activities carried out on such lakes or waterways by Community sportsmen.

TITLE X
SEEDS, FERTILISERS AND PRODUCTS FOR THE TREATMENT OF SOIL AND CROPS IMPORTED BY AGRICULTURAL PRODUCERS IN THIRD COUNTRIES FOR USE IN PROPERTIES ADJOINING THOSE COUNTRIES

Article 43

Subject to Article 44, seeds, fertilisers and products for treatment of soil and crops, intended for use on property located in the customs territory of the Community adjoining a third country and operated by agricultural producers having their principal undertaking within the said third country and adjacent to the customs territory of the Community, shall be admitted free of import duties.

Article 44

1. Relief shall be limited to the quantities of seeds, fertilisers or other products required for the purpose of operating the property.

2. It shall be granted only for seeds, fertilisers or other products imported directly into the customs territory of the Community by the agricultural producer or on his behalf.

3. Member states may make relief conditional upon the granting of reciprocal treatment.

TITLE XI
GOODS CONTAINED IN TRAVELLERS' PERSONAL LUGGAGE

Article 45

1. Subject to Articles 46 to 49, goods contained in the personal luggage of travellers coming from a third country shall be admitted free of import duties, provided such imports are of a non-commercial nature.

2. For the purposes of paragraph 1—

    (a)   "personal luggage" means the whole of the luggage which a traveller is in a position to submit to the customs authorities on his arrival in the [customs territory of the Community], as well as any luggage submitted to this same authority at a later date, provided that evidence can be produced to prove that it was registered, at the time of the traveller's departure, as accompanied luggage with the company which transported it into the [customs territory of the Community] from the third country of departure.

Without prejudice to Article 112(1)(b), portable containers holding fuel shall not constitute personal luggage;

    (b)   "imports of a non-commercial nature" means imports which—

        — are of an occasional nature, and

        — consist exclusively of goods for the personal use of the travellers or their families, or of goods intended as presents; the nature and quantity of such goods should not be such as might indicate that they are being imported for commercial reasons.

NOTES

Para 2: words in square brackets substituted by Council Regulation (EEC) 1315/88, Art 2, para 17.

Article 46

[1. The relief referred to in Article 45(1) shall, in respect of the goods listed below, apply subject to the following quantitative limits per traveller—

    (a)   tobacco products—

        200 cigarettes, or

        100 cigarillos (cigars of a maximum weight of three grams each), or

        50 cigars, or

        250 grams of smoking tobacco, or

        a proportional assortment of these different products;

    (b)   alcohols and alcoholic beverages—

        — distilled beverages and spirits of an alcoholic strength by volume exceeding 22% volume; non-denatured ethyl alcohol of 80% volume and over: one litre, or

        — distilled beverages and spirits, and aperitifs with a wine or alcoholic base, tafia, saké or similar beverages, of an alcoholic strength by volume not exceeding 22% volume; sparkling wines, liqueur wines: two litres, or a proportional assortment of these different products and

        — still wines: two litres;

    (c)   perfumes: 50 grams and

toilet waters: 0,25 litre;

(d)   medicinal products—

the quantity required to meet travellers' personal needs.]

2.   No relief for the goods referred to in paragraph 1(a) and (b) shall be granted to travellers under 17 years old.

NOTES

Para 1: substituted by Council Regulation (EEC) 1315/88, Art 2, para 4.

[Article 47

The relief referred to in Article 45 shall be granted up to a total value of ECU 175 per traveller to goods other than those listed in Article 46.

However, Member States may reduce this amount to ECU 90 for travellers under 15 years of age.]

NOTES

Substituted by Council Regulation (EC) 355/94, Art 1, para 1.

[Article 47a

1.   By way of derogation from the first subparagraph of Article 47, Spain is hereby authorised to apply, until 31 December 2000, a relief of ECU 600 for imports of the goods in question from Ceuta and Melilla entering customs territory as defined with regard to Spain in the fourth indent of Article 3(1) of Council Regulation (EEC) No 2913/92 of 12 October 1992 establishing the Community Customs Code.[1]

2.   By way of derogation from the second subparagraph of Article 47, Spain shall have the option of reducing that relief to ECU 150 for travellers under 15 years of age.]

NOTES

Inserted by Council Regulation (EC) 355/94, Art 1, para 2.

[1] OJ L 302, 19.10.92, p 1.

[Article 47b

By way of derogation from the values set out in Article 47, Finland shall be authorised until 31 December 2005 to apply a quantitative limit of not less than 6 litres for duty-free imports of beer.]

NOTES

Inserted by Council Regulation (EC) 1671/2000, Art 1.

Article 48

Where the total value per traveller of two or more items exceeds the amounts referred to in Article 47, relief up to those amounts shall be granted for such of the items as would, if imported separately, have been granted relief, it being understood that the value of an individual item cannot be split up.

Article 49

1.   Member states may reduce the value and / or the quantities of goods allowed to enter duty-free if they are imported by—

—   persons residing in the frontier zone,
—   frontier workers,
—   the crews of means of transport used between third countries and
         the Community.

These restrictions shall not apply where persons having their residence in the
frontier zone prove that they are not returning from the frontier zone of the adjacent
third country. They shall, however, still apply to frontier workers and to the crew of
means of transport used between third countries and the Community where they
import goods when travelling in the course of their work.

2.   For the purposes of applying the provisions of paragraph 1—

—   "frontier zone" means, without prejudice to existing conventions in this
         respect, a zone which, as the crow flies, does not extend more than 15
         kilometres from the frontier. The local administrative districts, part of
         whose territory lies within the zone, shall also be considered to be part
         of this frontier zone [Member States may grant exemptions therefrom.],
—   "frontier worker" means any person whose normal activities require
         that he should go to the other side of the frontier on his work days.

NOTES
   Para 2: words in square brackets inserted by Council Regulation (EEC) 1315/88, Art 2,
para 5.

TITLE XII
EDUCATIONAL, SCIENTIFIC AND CULTURAL MATERIALS; SCIENTIFIC
INSTRUMENTS AND APPARATUS

Article 50
The educational, scientific and cultural materials listed in Annex I shall be admitted
free of import duties whoever the consignee and whatever the intended use of such
materials may be.

Article 51
The educational, scientific and cultural materials listed in Annex II shall be admitted
free of import duties provided they are intended—

—   either for public educational, scientific or cultural establishments or
         organisations,
—   or for the establishments or organisations in the categories specified
         opposite each Article in column 3 of the said Annex, on condition that
         they have been approved by the competent authorities of the
         Member States to receive such articles duty-free.

[Article 52
1.   Subject to Articles 53, 54, 56, 57 and 58, scientific instruments and apparatus
which are not included in Article 51 shall be admitted free of import duties when they
are imported exclusively for non-commercial purposes.

2.   The relief referred to in paragraph 1 shall be limited to scientific instruments
and apparatus which are intended for:

—   either public establishments principally engaged in education or
         scientific research and those departments of public establishments which
         are principally engaged in education or scientific research,
—   or private establishments principally engaged in education or scientific
         research and approved by the competent authorities of the
         Member States to receive such articles duty free.]

NOTES

Substituted, together with Arts 53, 54, by Council Regulation (EEC) 3357/91, Art 1, para 2.

[**Article 53**

The relief shall also apply to:

(a) spare parts, components or accessories specifically suitable for scientific instruments or apparatus, provided that such spare parts, components or accessories are imported at the same time as such instruments or apparatus or, where they are imported subsequently, that they can be identified as being intended for instruments or apparatus:

— which have previously been admitted duty free, provided that such instruments or apparatus are still of a scientific nature at the time when relief is requested for the specific spare parts, components or accessories, or

— which would be entitled to relief at the time when such relief is requested for the specific spare parts, components or accessories;

(b) tools to be used for the maintenance, checking, calibration or repair of scientific instruments or apparatus, provided that these tools are imported at the same time as such instruments and apparatus or, where they are imported subsequently, that they can be identified as being intended for instruments or apparatus:

— which have previously been admitted duty free, provided that such instruments or apparatus are still of a scientific nature at the time when relief is requested for the tools, or

— which would be entitled to relief at the time when such relief is requested for the tools.]

NOTES

Substituted as noted to Art 52.

[**Article 54**

For the purposes of Articles 52 and 53—

— "scientific instrument or apparatus" means any instrument or apparatus which, by reason of its objective technical characteristics and the results which it makes possible to obtain, is mainly or exclusively suited to scientific activities,

— "imported for non-commercial purposes" shall be considered to apply to scientific instruments or apparatus intended to be used for non-profit-making scientific research or educational purposes.]

NOTES

Substituted as noted to Art 52.

Article 55

NOTES

Repealed by Council Regulation (EEC) 3357/91, Art 1, para 3.

[Article 56

If necessary, certain instruments or apparatus may, in accordance with the procedure laid down in Article 143(2) and (3), be excluded from entitlement to relief, where it is found that duty-free admission of such instruments or apparatus is detrimental to the interests of Community industry in the production sector concerned.]

NOTES

Substituted, together with Art 57, by Council Regulation (EEC) 3357/91, Art 1, para 4.

[Article 57

1.   The articles referred to in Article 51 and the scientific instruments or apparatus which have been admitted duty-free in accordance with the conditions laid down in Articles 53, 54 and 56 may not be lent, hired out or transferred, whether for a consideration or free of charge, without prior notification to the competent authorities.

2.   Should an article be lent, hired out or transferred to an establishment or organisation entitled to benefit from relief pursuant to Article 51 or 52(2), the relief shall continue to be granted provided the establishment or organisation uses the article, instrument or apparatus for purposes which confer the right to such relief.

In other cases, loan, hiring out or transfer shall be subject to prior payment of import duties, at the rate applying on the date of the loan, hiring out or transfer, on the basis of the type of goods and the customs value ascertained or accepted on that date by the competent authorities.]

NOTES

Substituted as noted to Art 56.

Article 58

1.   Establishments or organisations referred to in Articles 51 and 52 which cease to fulfil the conditions giving entitlement to relief, or which are proposing to use articles admitted duty-free for purposes other than those provided for by those Articles shall so inform the competent authorities.

2.   Articles remaining in the possession of establishments or organisations which cease to fulfil the conditions giving entitlement to relief shall be liable to the relevant import duties at the rate applying on the date on which those conditions cease to be fulfilled, on the basis of the type of article and the customs value ascertained or accepted on that date by the competent authorities.

Articles used by the establishment or organisation benefiting from the relief for purposes other than those provided for in Articles 51 and 52 shall be liable to the relevant import duties calculated as applicable on the date on which they are put to another use, on the basis of the type of articles and the customs value ascertained or accepted on that date by the competent authorities.

Article 59

Articles 56, 57 and 58 shall apply *mutatis mutandis* to the products referred to in Article 53.

[Article 59a

1.   Equipment imported for non-commercial purposes by or on behalf of a scientific research establishment or organisation based outside the Community shall be admitted free of import duties.

2.   The relief shall be granted provided the equipment—

(a)   is intended for use by or with the agreement of the members or representatives of the establishments and organisations referred to in paragraph 1 in the context and within the limits of scientific cooperation agreements the purpose of which is to carry out international scientific research programmes in scientific research establishments based in the Community and approved for that purpose by the competent authorities of the Member States;

(b)   remains the property of a natural or legal person resident outside the Community during its stay in the customs territory of the Community.

3.   Within the meaning of this Regulation—

— equipment is taken to mean instruments, apparatus, machines and their accessories including spare parts and tools specially designed for their maintenance, inspection, calibration or repair, used for the purpose of scientific research,

— equipment intended for use for the purpose of scientific research carried out for non-profit making purposes is considered to be 'imported for non-commercial purposes'.]

NOTES

Inserted by Council Regulation (EEC) 4235/88, Art 1.

[**Article 59b**

1.   Equipment referred to in Article 59a which has been admitted duty-free in accordance with the conditions laid down in the said Article may not be lent, hired out or transferred, whether for a consideration or free of charge, without prior notification to the competent authorities.

2.   Should equipment be lent, hired out or transferred to an establishment or organisation entitled to benefit from relief pursuant to Article 59a, the relief shall continue to be granted provided the establishment or organisation uses the equipment for purposes which confer the right to such relief.

In other cases, and without prejudice to the application of Articles 52 and 53, loan, hiring out or transfer shall be subject to prior payment of import duties, at the rate applying on the date of the loan, hiring out or transfer, on the basis of the type of equipment and the customs value ascertained or accepted on that date by the competent authorities.

3.   Establishments or organisations referred to in Article 59a(1) which no longer fulfil the conditions to qualify for relief or which are proposing to use equipment admitted duty-free for purposes other than those provided for by that Article shall so inform the competent authorities.

4.   Equipment used by establishments or organisations which cease to fulfil the conditions giving entitlement to relief shall be liable to the relevant import duties at the rate applying on the date on which those conditions cease to be fulfilled, on the basis of the type of article and the customs value ascertained or accepted on that date by the competent authorities.

Without prejudice to Articles 52 and 53, equipment used by the establishment or organisation benefiting from the relief for purposes other than those provided for in Article 59a shall be liable to the relevant import duties calculated as applicable on the date on which it is put to another use, on the basis of the type of equipment and the customs value ascertained or accepted on that date by the competent authorities.]

Part III

NOTES
Inserted by Council Regulation (EEC) 4235/88, Art 1.

TITLE XIII
LABORATORY ANIMALS AND BIOLOGICAL OR CHEMICAL SUBSTANCES INTENDED FOR RESEARCH

[Article 60

1. Relief from import duties shall be granted in respect of:
   (a)   animals specially prepared for laboratory use;
   (b)   biological or chemical substances included in a list drawn up in accordance with the procedure laid down in Article 143(2) and (3), which are imported exclusively for non-commercial purposes.
2. The relief referred to in paragraph 1 shall be limited to animals and biological or chemical substances which are intended for—
   —   either public establishments principally engaged in education or scientific research and those departments of public establishments which are principally engaged in education or scientific research, or
   —   private establishments principally engaged in education or scientific research and authorised by the competent authorities of the Member States to receive such articles duty-free.
3. The list referred to in subparagraph 1(b) may include only biological or chemical substances for which there is no equivalent production in the customs territory of the Community and which, on account of their specificity or degree of purity, are mainly or exclusively suited to scientific research.]

NOTES
Substituted by Council Regulation (EEC) 1315/88, Art 2, para 6.

TITLE XIV
THERAPEUTIC SUBSTANCES OF HUMAN ORIGIN AND BLOOD-GROUPING AND TISSUE-TYPING REAGENTS

Article 61

1. Subject to Article 62, the following shall be admitted free of import duties—
   (a)   therapeutic substances of human origin;
   (b)   blood-grouping reagents;
   (c)   tissue-typing reagents.
2. For the purposes of paragraph 1—
   —   "therapeutic substances of human origin" means human blood and its derivatives (whole human blood, dried human plasma, human albumin and fixed solutions of human plasmic protein, human immunoglobulin and human fibrinogen),
   —   "blood-grouping reagents" means all reagents, whether of human, animal, plant or other origin used for blood-type grouping and for the detection of blood incompatibilites,
   —   "tissue-typing reagents" means all reagents whether of human, animal, plant or other origin used for the determination of human tissue-types.

Article 62

Relief shall be limited to products which—

(a)   are intended for institutions or laboratories approved by the competent authorities, for use exclusively for non-commercial medical or scientific purposes;

(b)   are accompanied by a certificate of conformity issued by a duly authorised body in the third country of departure;

(c)   are in containers bearing a special label identifying them.

Article 63

Relief shall include the special packaging essential for the transport of therapeutic substances of human origin or blood-grouping or tissue-typing reagents and also any solvents and accessories needed for their use which may be included in the consignments.

[TITLE XIVA
INSTRUMENTS AND APPARATUS INTENDED FOR MEDICAL RESEARCH, ESTABLISHING MEDICAL DIAGNOSES OR CARRYING OUT MEDICAL TREATMENT

[Article 63A

1.   Instruments and apparatus intended for medical research, establishing medical diagnoses or carrying out medical treatment which are donated either by a charitable or philanthropic organisation or by a private individual to health authorities, hospital departments or medical research institutions approved by the competent authorities of the Member States to receive such articles duty free, or which are purchased by such health authorities, hospitals or medical research institutions entirely with funds supplied by a charitable or philanthropic organisation or with voluntary contributions, shall be admitted free of import duties, always provided that it is established that:

(a)   the donation of the instruments or apparatus in question does not conceal any commercial intent on the part of the donor;

and

(b)   the donor is in no way connected with the manufacturer of the instruments or apparatus for which relief is requested.

2.   The relief shall also apply, subject to the same conditions, to:

(a)   spare parts, components or accessories specifically suitable for the above instruments or apparatus, provided that these spare parts, components or accessories are imported at the same time as such instruments and apparatus or, where they are imported subsequently, that they can be identified as being intended for instruments or apparatus previously admitted duty free;

(b)   tools to be used for the maintenance, checking, calibration or repair of instruments or apparatus, provided that these tools are imported at the same time as such instruments and apparatus or, where they are imported subsequently, that they can be identified as being intended for instruments or apparatus previously admitted duty free.]

NOTES

Substituted by Council Regulation (EEC) 3357/91, Art 1, para 5 (previously inserted by Council Regulation (EEC) 1315/88, Art 2, para 7.)

[Article 63B

For the purposes of Article 63a, and in particular with regard to the instruments or apparatus and the recipient bodies referred to therein, Articles 56, 57 and 58 shall apply *mutatis mutandis*.]

NOTES

Substituted by Council Regulation (EEC) 3357/91, Art 1, para 5 (previously inserted by Council Regulation (EEC) 1315/88, Art 2, para 7.)

[TITLE XIVB
REFERENCE SUBSTANCES FOR THE QUALITY CONTROL OF
MEDICINAL PRODUCTS

Article 63C

Consignments which contain samples of reference substances approved by the World Health Organisation for the quality control of materials used in the manufacture of medicinal products and which are addressed to consignees authorised by the competent authorities of the Member States to receive such consignments free of duty shall be admitted free of import duties.]

NOTES

Inserted by Council Regulation (EEC) 1315/88, Art 2, para 7.

TITLE XV
PHARMACEUTIC PRODUCTS USED AT INTERNATIONAL SPORTS EVENTS

Article 64

Pharmaceutical products for human or veterinary medical use by persons or animals coming from third countries to participate in international sports events organised in the customs territory of the Community, shall, within the limits necessary to meet their requirements throughout their stay in that territory, be admitted free of import duties.

TITLE XVI
GOODS FOR CHARITABLE OR PHILANTHROPIC ORGANISATIONS:
ARTICLES INTENDED FOR THE BLIND AND OTHER
HANDICAPPED PERSONS

A.
FOR GENERAL PURPOSES

Article 65

1. Subject to Articles 67 and 68, the following shall be admitted free of import duties, in so far as this does not give rise to abuses or major distortions of competition—

(a)   basic necessities imported by state organisations or other charitable or philanthropic organisations approved by the competent authorities for distribution free of charge to needy persons;

(b)   goods of every description sent free of charge, by a person or an organisation established in a third country, and without any commercial intent on the part of the sender, to state organisations or other charitable or philanthropic organisations approved by the competent authorities, to be used for fund-raising at occasional charity events for the benefit of needy persons;

(c)　　　equipment and office materials sent free of charge, by a person or an organisation established outside the [customs territory of the Community], and without any commercial intent on the part of the sender, to charitable or philanthropic organisations approved by the competent authorities, to be used solely for the purpose of meeting their operating needs or carrying out their charitable or philanthropic aims.

2.　For the purposes of paragraph 1(a), "basic necessities" means those goods required to meet the immediate needs of human beings, eg food, medicine, clothing and bed-clothes.

NOTES

Para 1: words in square brackets substituted by Council Regulation (EEC) 1315/88, Art 2, para 17.

Article 66

No relief shall be granted for—
(a)　　alcoholic products;
(b)　　tobacco or tobacco products;
(c)　　coffee and tea;
(d)　　motor vehicles other than ambulances.

Article 67

Relief shall be granted only to organisations the accounting procedures of which enable the competent authorities to supervise their operations and which offer all the guarantees considered necessary.

Article 68

1.　The organisation benefiting from the relief may not lend, hire out or transfer, whether for a consideration or free of charge, the goods and equipment referred to in Article 65 for purposes other than those laid down in paragraph 1(a) and (b) of that Article without prior notification to the competent authorities.

2.　Should goods and equipment be lent, hired out or transferred to an organisation entitled to benefit from relief pursuant to Articles 65 and 67, the relief shall continue to be granted provided the latter uses the goods and equipment for purposes which confer the right to such relief.

In other cases, loan, hiring out or transfer shall be subject to prior payment of import duties, at the rate applying on the date of the loan, hiring out or transfer, on the basis of the type of goods or equipment and the customs value ascertained or accepted on that date by the competent authorities.

Article 69

1.　Organisations referred to in Article 65 which cease to fulfil the conditions giving entitlement to relief, or which are proposing to use goods and equipment admitted duty-free for purposes other than those provided for by that Article, shall so inform the competent authorities.

2.　Goods and equipment remaining in the possession of organisations which cease to fulfil the conditions giving entitlement to relief shall be liable to the relevant import duties at the rate applying on the date on which those conditions cease to be fulfilled, on the basis of the type of goods and equipment and the customs value as ascertained or accepted on that date by the competent authorities.

3.　Goods and equipment used by the organisation benefiting from the relief for purposes other than those provided for in Article 65 shall be liable to the relevant import duties at the rate applying on the date on which they are put to another use, on

Part III

the basis of the type of goods and equipment and the customs value as ascertained or accepted on that date by the competent authorities.

B.
FOR THE BENEFIT OF HANDICAPPED PERSONS

1.
Articles for the use of the blind

Article 70

Articles specially designed for the educational, scientific or cultural advancement of blind persons, as specified in Annex III, shall be admitted free of import duties.

Article 71

Articles specially designed for the educational, scientific or cultural advancement of blind persons, as specified in Annex IV, shall be admitted free of import duties provided that they are imported by—

—   either blind persons themselves for their own use,

—   or institutions or organisations concerned with the education of or the provision of assistance to the blind, approved by the competent authorities of the Member States for the purpose of duty-free entry of these articles.

The relief referred to in the first paragraph shall apply to spare parts, components or accessories specifically for the articles in question, and to the tools to be used for the maintenance, checking, calibration or repair of the said articles, provided that such spare parts, components, accessories or tools are imported at the same time as the said articles or, if imported subsequently, that they can be identified as being intended for articles previously admitted duty-free, or which would be entitled to relief at the time when such relief is requested for the specific spare parts, components or accessories and tools in question.

2.
Articles for the use of other handicapped persons

[Article 72

1.   Articles specially designed for the education, employment or social advancement of physically or mentally handicapped persons other than blind persons shall be admitted free of import duties where they are imported:

—   either by handicapped persons themselves for their own use;

—   or by institutions or organisations that are principally engaged in the education of or the provision of assistance to handicapped persons and are authorised by the competent authorities of the Member States to receive such articles duty free.

2.   The relief referred to in paragraph 1 shall apply to spare parts, components or accessories specifically for the articles in question, and to the tools to be used for the maintenance, checking, calibration or repair of the said articles provided that such spare parts, components, accessories or tools are imported at the same time as the said articles, or, where they are imported subsequently, that they can be identified as being intended for articles which were previously admitted duty free, or which would be entitled to relief at the time when such relief is requested for the specific spare parts, components or accessories and tools in question.]

NOTES

Substituted, together with Art 73, by Council Regulation (EEC) 3357/91, Art 1, para 6.

[Article 73
If necessary, certain articles may, in accordance with the procedure laid down in Article 143(2) and (3), be excluded from entitlement to relief, where it is found that duty-free admission of such articles is detrimental to the interests of Community industry in the production sector concerned.]

NOTES

Substituted as noted to Art 72.

Article 74

NOTES

Repealed by Council Regulation (EEC) 3357/91, Art 1, para 7.

3.
Common provisions

[Article 75
The direct grant of relief, for their own use, to blind persons or to other handicapped persons, as provided for in the first indent of Article 71 and the first indent of Article 72(1), shall be subject to the condition that the provisions in force in the Member States enable the persons concerned to establish their status as blind or handicapped persons entitled to such relief.]

NOTES

Substituted, together with Art 76, 77, by Council Regulation (EEC) 3357/91, Art 1, para 8.

[Article 76
  1. Articles imported duty-free by the persons referred to in Articles 71 and 72 may not be lent, hired out or transferred, whether for a consideration or free of charge, without prior notification thereof to the competent authorities.
  2. Should an article be lent, hired out or transferred to a person, institution or organisation entitled to benefit from relief pursuant to Articles 71 and 72, the relief shall continue to be granted provided the person, institution or organisation uses the article for purposes which confer the right of such relief.
  In other cases, loan, hiring out or transfer shall be subject to prior payment of import duties, at the rate applying on the date of the loan, hiring out or transfer, on the basis of the type of goods or equipment and the customs value ascertained or accepted on that date by the competent authorities.]

NOTES

Substituted as noted to Art 75.

[**Article 77**

1. Articles imported by institutions or organisations eligible for relief in accordance with the conditions laid down in Articles 71 and 72 may be lent, hired out or transferred, whether for a consideration or free of charge, by these institutions or organisations on a non-profit-making basis to the blind and other handicapped persons with whom they are concerned, without payment of the corresponding customs duties.

2. No loan, hiring out or transfer may be effected under conditions other than those provided for in paragraph 1 unless the competent authorities have first been informed.

Should an article be lent, hired out or transferred to a person, institution or organisation entitled to benefit from relief pursuant to the first paragraph of Article 71 or Article 72(1), the relief shall continue to be granted provided the person, institution or organisation uses the article for purposes which confer the right of such relief.

In other cases, loan, hiring out or transfer shall be subject to prior payment of customs duties, at the rate applying on the date of the loan, hiring out or transfer, on the basis of the type of goods or equipment and the customs value ascertained or accepted on that date by the competent authorities.]

NOTES

Substituted as noted to Art 75.

Article 78

1. Institutions or organisations referred to in Articles 71 and 72 which cease to fulfil the conditions giving entitlement to duty-free admission, or which are proposing to use articles admitted duty-free for purposes other than those provided for by those Articles shall so inform the competent authorities.

2. Articles remaining in the possession of institutions or organisations which cease to fulfil the conditions giving entitlement to relief shall be liable to the relevant import duties at the rate applying on the date on which those conditions cease to be fulfilled, on the basis of the type of goods and the customs value ascertained or accepted on that date by the competent authorities.

3. Articles used by the institution or organisation benefiting from the relief for purposes other than those provided for in Articles 71 and 72 shall be liable to the relevant import duties at the rate applying on the date on which they are put to another use, on the basis of the type of goods and the customs value ascertained or accepted on that date by the competent authorities.

C.
FOR THE BENEFIT OF DISASTER VICTIMS

Article 79

1. Subject to Articles 80 to 85, goods imported by state organisations or other charitable or philanthropic organisations approved by the competent authorities shall be admitted free of import duties where they are intended—

(a)   for distribution free of charge to victims of disasters affecting the territory of one or more Member States; or

(b)   to be made available free of charge to the victims of such disasters, while remaining the property of the organisations in question.

2. Goods imported for free circulation by disaster-relief agencies in order to meet their needs during the period of their activity shall also be granted the relief referred to in paragraph 1, under the same conditions.

Article 80

No relief shall be granted for materials and equipment intended for rebuilding disaster areas.

Article 81

Granting of the relief shall be subject to a decision by the Commission, acting at the request of the Member State or states concerned in accordance with an emergency procedure entailing the consultation of the other Member States. This decision shall, where necessary, lay down the scope and the conditions of the relief.

Pending notification of the Commission's decision, Member States affected by a disaster may authorise the suspension of any import duties chargeable on goods imported for the purposes described in Article 79, subject to an undertaking by the importing organisation to pay such duties if relief is not granted.

Article 82

Relief shall be granted only to organisations the accounting procedures of which enable the competent authorities to supervise their operations and which offer all the guarantees considered necessary.

Article 83

1. The organisations benefiting from the relief may not lend, hire out or transfer, whether for consideration or free of charge, the goods referred to in Article 79(1) under conditions other than those laid down in that Article without prior notification thereof to the competent authorities.

2. Should goods be lent, hired out or transferred to an organisation itself entitled to benefit from relief pursuant to Article 79, the relief shall continue to be granted, provided the latter uses the goods for purposes which confer the right to such relief.

In other cases, loan, hiring out or transfer shall be subject to prior payment of import duties at the rate applying on the date of the loan, hiring out or transfer, on the basis of the type of goods and the customs value ascertained or accepted on that date by the competent authorities.

Article 84

1. The goods referred to in Article 79(1)(b), after they cease to be used by disaster victims, may not be lent, hired out or transferred, whether for a consideration or free of charge, unless the competent authorities are notified in advance.

2. Should goods be lent, hired out or transferred to an organisation itself entitled to benefit from relief pursuant to Article 79 or, if appropriate, to an organisation entitled to benefit from relief pursuant to Article 65(1)(a), the relief shall continue to be granted, provided such organisations use them for purposes which confer the right to such relief.

In other cases, loan, hiring out or transfer shall be subject to prior payment of import duties at the rate applying on the date of the loan, hiring out or transfer, on the basis of the type of goods and the customs value ascertained or accepted on that date by the competent authorities.

Article 85

1. Organisations referred to in Article 79 which cease to fulfil the conditions giving entitlement to relief, or which are proposing to use the goods admitted duty-free for purposes other than those provided for by that Article, shall so inform the competent authorities.

2. In the case of goods remaining in the possession of organisations which cease to fulfil the conditions giving entitlement to relief, when these are transferred to an organisation itself entitled to benefit from relief pursuant to Article 79 or, if appropriate, to an organisation entitled to benefit from relief pursuant to Article 65(1)(a), relief shall continue to be granted, provided the organisation uses the goods

Part III

in question for purposes which confer the right to such relief. In other cases, the goods shall be liable to the relevant import duties at the rate applying on the date on which those conditions cease to be fulfilled, on the basis of the type of goods and the customs value ascertained or accepted on that date by the competent authorities.

3.   Goods used by the organisation benefiting from the relief for purposes other than those provided for in Article 79 shall be liable to the relevant import duties at the rate applying on the date on which they are put to another use, on the basis of the type of goods and the customs value ascertained or accepted on that date by the competent authorities.

TITLE XVII
HONORARY DECORATIONS OR AWARDS

Article 86

On production of satisfactory evidence to the competent authorities by the persons concerned, and provided the operations involved are not in any way of a commercial character, the following shall be admitted free of import duties—

(a)   decorations conferred by governments of third countries on persons whose normal place of residence is in the customs territory of the [customs territory of the Community];

(b)   cups, medals and similar articles of an essentially symbolic nature which, having been awarded in a third country to persons having their normal place of residence in the customs territory of the Community as a tribute to their activities in fields such as the arts, the sciences, sport or the public service or as in recognition for merit at a particular event, are imported into the [customs territory of the Community] by such persons themselves;

(c)   cups, medals and similar articles of an essentially symbolic nature which are given free of charge by authorities or persons established in a third country to be presented in the customs territory of the [customs territory of the Community] for the same purposes as those referred to in (b).

[(d)   Awards, trophies and souvenirs of a symbolic nature and of limited value intended for distribution free of charge to persons normally resident in third countries at business conferences or similar international events; their nature, unitary value or other features, must not be such as might indicate that they are being imported for commercial reasons.]

NOTES

Words in square brackets in paras (a)–(c) substituted, and para (d) inserted by Council Regulation (EEC) 1315/88, Art 2, paras 8, 17.

TITLE XVIII
PRESENTS RECEIVED IN THE CONTEXT OF INTERNATIONAL RELATIONS

Article 87

Without prejudice, where relevant, to Articles 45 to 49, and subject to Articles 88 and 89 below, relief shall be granted for goods—

(a)   imported into the customs territory of the [customs territory of the Community] by persons who have paid an official visit to a third country and who have received them on this occasion as gifts from the host authorities;

(b)   imported into the customs territory of the [customs territory of the Community] by persons coming to pay an official visit in the [customs territory of the Community] and who intend to offer them on that occasion as gifts to the host authorities;

(c)   sent as gifts, in token of friendship or goodwill, by an official body, public authority or group, carrying on an activity in the public interest which is located in a third country, to an official body, public authority or group carrying on an activity in the public interest which is located in the [customs territory of the Community] and approved by the competent authorities to receive such articles free of duty.

NOTES

Words in square brackets substituted by Council Regulation (EEC) 1315/88, Art 2, para 17.

Article 88

No relief shall be granted for alcoholic products, tobacco or tobacco products.

Article 89

Relief shall be granted only—

— where the articles intended as gifts are offered on an occasional basis,

— where they do not, by their nature, value or quantity, reflect any commercial interest,

— if they are not used for commercial purposes.

TITLE XIX
GOODS TO BE USED BY MONARCHS OR HEADS OF STATE

Article 90

The following shall be admitted free of import duties, within the limits and under the conditions laid down by the competent authorities—

(a)   gifts to reigning monarchs and heads of state;

(b)   goods to be used or consumed by reigning monarchs and heads of state of third countries, or persons officially representing them, during their official stay in the customs territory of the Community. However, relief may be made subject, by the Member State of importation, to reciprocal treatment.

The provisions of the preceding subparagraph are also applicable to persons enjoying prerogatives at international level analogous to those enjoyed by reigning monarchs or heads of state.

TITLE XX
GOODS IMPORTED FOR TRADE PROMOTION PURPOSES

A.
SAMPLES OF GOODS OF NEGLIGIBLE VALUE

Article 91

1. Without prejudice to Article 95(1)(a), samples of goods which are of negligible value and can be used only to solicit orders for goods of the type they represent with a view to their being imported into the customs territory of the Community shall be admitted free of import duties.

2. The competent authorities may require that certain articles, to qualify for relief, be rendered permanently unusable by being torn, perforated, or clearly and indelibly

Part III

marked, or by any other process, provided such operation does not destroy their character as samples.

3. For the purposes of paragraph 1, "samples of goods" means any article representing a type of goods whose manner of presentation and quantity, for goods of the same type or quality, rule out its use for any purpose other than that of seeking orders.

B.
PRINTED MATTER AND ADVERTISING MATERIAL

Article 92

Subject to Article 93, printed advertising matter such as catalogues, price lists, directions for use or brochures shall be admitted free of import duties, provided that they relate to—

(a) goods for sale or hire, or

(b) transport, commercial insurance or banking services offered

by a person established outside the customs territory of the Community.

Article 93

The relief referred to in Article 92 shall be limited to printed advertisements which fulfil the following conditions—

(a) printed matter must clearly display the name of the undertaking which produces, sells or hires out the goods, or which offers the services to which it refers;

(b) each consignment must contain no more than one document or a single copy of each document if it is made up of several documents. Consignments comprising several copies of the same document may nevertheless be granted relief, provided their total gross weight does not exceed one kilogram;

(c) printed matter may not be the subject of grouped consignments from the same consignor to the same consignee.

Article 94

Articles for advertising purposes, of no intrinsic commercial value, sent free of charge by suppliers to their customers, which, apart from their advertising function, are not capable of being used otherwise, shall also be admitted free of import duties.

C.
PRODUCTS USED OR CONSUMED AT A TRADE FAIR OR SIMILAR EVENT

Article 95

1. Subject to Articles 96 to 99, the following shall be admitted free of import duties—

(a) small representative samples of goods manufactured outside the customs territory of the Community intended for a trade fair or similar event;

(b) goods imported solely in order to be demonstrated or in order to demonstrate machines and apparatus, manufactured outside the customs territory of the Community and displayed at a trade fair or similar event;

(c) various materials of little value such as paints, varnishes, wallpaper, etc, used in the building, fitting-out and decoration of temporary stands occupied by representatives of third countries at a trade fair or similar event, which are destroyed by being used;

(d) printed matter, catalogues, prospectuses, price lists, advertising posters, calendars, whether or not illustrated, unframed photographs and other articles supplied free of charge in order to advertise goods manufactured outside the customs territory of the Community and displayed at a trade fair or similar event.

2. For the purposes of paragraph 1, " trade fair or similar event" means—

(a) exhibitions, fairs, shows and similar events connected with trade, industry, agriculture or handicrafts;

(b) exhibitions and events held mainly for charitable reasons;

(c) exhibitions and events held mainly for scientific, technical, handicraft, artistic, educational or cultural, or sporting reasons, for religious reasons or for reasons of worship, trade union activity or tourism, or in order to promote international understanding;

(d) meetings of representatives of international organisations or collective bodies;

(e) official or commemorative ceremonies and gatherings;

but not exhibitions staged for private purposes in commercial stores or premises to sell goods of third countries.

Article 96

The relief referred to in Article 95(1)(a) limited to samples which—

(a) are imported free of charge as such from third countries or are obtained at the exhibition from goods imported in bulk from those countries;

(b) are exclusively distributed free of charge to the public at the exhibition for use or consumption by the persons to whom they have been offered;

(c) are identifiable as advertising samples of low unitary value;

(d) are not easily marketable and, where appropriate, are packaged in such a way that the quantity of the item involved is lower than the smallest quantity of the same item actually sold on the market;

(e) in the case of foodstuffs and beverages not packaged as mentioned in (d), are consumed on the spot at the exhibition;

(f) in their total value and quantity, are appropriate to the nature of the exhibition, the number of visitors and the extent of the exhibitor's participation.

Article 97

The relief referred to in Article 95(1)(b) shall be limited to goods which are—

(a) consumed or destroyed at the exhibition; and

(b) are appropriate, in their total value and quantity, to the nature of the exhibition, the number of visitors and the extent of the exhibitor's participation.

Article 98

The relief referred to in Article 95(1)(d) shall be limited to printed matter and articles for advertising purposes which—

(a) are intended exclusively to be distributed free of charge to the public at the place where the exhibition is held;

(b) in their total value and quantity, are appropriate to the nature of the exhibition, the number of visitors and the extent of the exhibitor's participation.

Article 99

The relief referred to in Article 95(1)(a) and (b) shall not be granted for—

(a) alcoholic products;

(b)   tobacco or tobacco products;

(c)   fuels, whether solid, liquid or gaseous.

TITLE XXI
GOODS IMPORTED FOR EXAMINATION, ANALYSIS OR TEST PURPOSES

Article 100

Subject to Articles 101 to 106, goods which are to undergo examination, analysis or tests to determine their composition, quality or other technical characteristics for purposes of information or industrial or commercial research shall be admitted free of import duties.

Article 101

Without prejudice to Article 104, the relief referred to in Article 100 shall be granted only on condition that the goods to be examined, analysed or tested are completely used up or destroyed in the course of the examination, analysis or testing.

Article 102

Goods used in examination, analysis or tests which in themselves constitute sales promotion operations shall not enjoy relief.

Article 103

Relief shall be granted only in respect of the quantities of goods which are strictly necessary for the purpose for which they are imported. These quantities shall in each case be determined by the competent authorities, taking into account the said purpose.

Article 104

1.   The relief referred to in Article 100 shall cover goods which are not completely used up or destroyed during examination, analysis or testing, provided that the products remaining are, with the agreement and under the supervision of the competent authorities—

—   completely destroyed or rendered commercially valueless on completion of examination, analysis or testing, or

—   surrendered to the state without causing it any expense, where this is possible under national law, or

—   in duly justified circumstances, exported outside the customs territory of the Community.

2.   For the purposes of paragraph 1, "products remaining" means products resulting from the examination, analysis or tests or goods not actually used.

Article 105

Save where Article 104(1) is applied, products remaining at the end of the examinations, analyses or tests referred to in Article 100 shall be subject to the relevant import duties at the rate applying on the date of completion of the examinations, analyses or tests, on the basis of the type of goods and the customs value ascertained or accepted on that date by the competent authorities.

However, the interested party may, with the agreement and under the supervision of the competent authorities, convert products remaining to waste or scrap. In this case, the import duties shall be those applying to such waste or scrap at the time of conversion.

Article 106

The period within which the examinations, analyses or tests must be carried out and the administrative formalities to be completed in order to ensure the use of the goods for the purposes intended shall be determined by the competent authorities.

TITLE XXII
CONSIGNMENTS SENT TO ORGANISATIONS PROTECTING COPYRIGHTS OR INDUSTRIAL AND COMMERCIAL PATENT RIGHTS

Article 107

Trademarks, patterns or designs and their supporting documents, as well as applications for patents for invention or the like, to be submitted to the bodies competent to deal with the protection of copyrights or the protection of industrial or commercial patent rights, shall be admitted free of import duties.

TITLE XXIII

Tourist information literature

Article 108

Without prejudice to Articles 50 to 59, the following shall be admitted free of import duties—

(a) documentation (leaflets, brochures, books, magazines, guidebooks, posters whether or not framed, unframed photographs and photographic enlargements, maps whether or not illustrated, window transparencies, and illustrated calendars) intended to be distributed free of charge and the principal purpose of which is to encourage the public to visit foreign countries, in particular in order to attend cultural, tourist, sporting, religious or trade or professional meetings or events, provided that such literature contains not more than 25% of private commercial advertising matter, excluding all private commercial advertising for Community firms, and that the general nature of its promotional aims is evident;

(b) foreign hotel lists and yearbooks published by the official tourist agencies, or under their auspices, and timetables for foreign transport services, where such literature is intended to be distributed free of charge and contains not more than 25% of private commercial advertising, excluding all private commercial advertising for Community firms;

(c) reference material supplied to accredited representatives or correspondents appointed by official national tourist agencies and not intended for distribution, viz yearbooks, lists of telephone or telex numbers, hotel lists, fairs catalogues, specimens of craft goods of negligible value, and literature on museums, universities, spas or other similar establishments.

TITLE XXIV
MISCELLANEOUS DOCUMENTS AND ARTICLES

Article 109

The following shall be admitted free of import duties—

(a) documents sent free of charge to the public services of Member States;

(b) publications of foreign governments and publications of official international bodies intended for distribution without charge;

(c) ballot papers for elections organised by bodies set up in third countries;

(d) objects to be submitted as evidence or for like purposes to the courts or other official agencies of the Member States;

(e) specimen signatures and printed circulars concerning signatures sent as part of customary exchanges of information between public services or banking establishments;

Part III

(f)   official printed matter sent to the central banks of the Member States;

(g)   reports, statements, notes, prospectuses, application forms and other documents drawn up by companies registered in a third country and sent to the bearers or subscribers of securities issued by such companies;

(h)   recorded media (punched cards, sound recordings, microfilms, etc) used for the transmission of information sent free of charge to the addressee, in so far as duty-free admission does not give rise to abuses or to major distortions of competition;

(i)   files, archives, printed forms and other documents to be used in international meetings, conferences or congresses, and reports on such gatherings;

(j)   plans, technical drawings, traced designs, descriptions and other similar documents imported with a view to obtaining or fulfilling orders in third countries or to participating in a competition held in the customs territory of the Community;

(k)   documents to be used in examinations held in the customs territory of the Community by institutions set up in third countries;

(l)   printed forms to be used as official documents in the international movement of vehicles or goods, within the framework of international conventions;

(m)   printed forms, labels, tickets and similar documents sent by transport undertakings or by undertakings of the hotel industry in a third country to travel agencies set up in the customs territory of the Community;

(n)   printed forms and tickets, bills of lading, way-bills and other commercial or office documents which have been used;

(o)   official printed forms from third country or international authorities, and printed matter conforming to international standards sent for distribution by third country associations to corresponding associations located in the customs territory of the Community;

(p)   photographs, slides and stereotype mats for photographs, whether or not captioned, sent to press agencies or newspaper or magazine publishers.

[(q) Tax and similar stamps proving payment of charges in third countries.]

NOTES

Para (q): inserted by Council Regulation (EEC) 1315/88, Art 2, para 9.

TITLE XXV
ANCILLARY MATERIALS FOR THE STOWAGE AND PROTECTION OF GOODS DURING THEIR TRANSPORT

Article 110

The various materials such as rope, straw, cloth, paper and cardboard, wood and plastics which are used for the stowage and protection - including heat protection - of goods during their transport from a third country to the customs territory of the Community, not normally reusable, shall be admitted free of import duties.

TITLE XXVI
LITTER, FODDER AND FEEDINGSTUFFS FOR ANIMALS DURING THEIR TRANSPORT

Article 111

Litter, fodder and feedingstuffs of any description put on board the means of transport used to convey animals from a third country to the customs territory of the Community for the purpose of distribution to the said animals during the journey shall be admitted free of import duties.

TITLE XXVII
[FUEL AND LUBRICANTS PRESENT IN LAND MOTOR VEHICLES AND SPECIAL CONTAINERS]

NOTES

Heading: words substituted by Council Regulation (EEC) 1315/88, Art 2, para 10.

[Article 112

1. Subject to the provisions of Articles 113 to 115—
   (a) fuel contained in the standard tanks of—
       — private and commercial motor vehicles and motor cycles,
       — special containers,

   entering the customs territory of the Community;
   (b) fuel contained in portable tanks carried by private motor vehicles and motor cycles, with a maximum of 10 litres per vehicle and without prejudice to national provisions on the holding and transport of fuel;

   shall be admitted free of import duties.

2. For the purposes of paragraph 1—
   (a) "commercial motor vehicle" means any motorised road vehicle (including tractors with or without trailers) which by its type of construction and its equipment is designed for and capable of transporting, whether for payment or not—
       — more than nine persons including the driver,
       — goods,
       — and any road vehicle for a special purpose other than transport as such;
   (b) "private motor vehicle" means any motor vehicle not covered by the definition set out in (a);
   (c) "standard tanks" means—
       — the tanks permanently fixed by the manufacturer to all motor vehicles of the same type as the vehicle in question and whose permanent fitting enables fuel to be used directly, both for the purpose of propulsion and, where appropriate, for the operation, during transport, of refrigeration systems and other systems.
       Gas tanks fitted to motor vehicles designed for the direct use of gas as a fuel and tanks fitted to the other systems with which the vehicle may be equipped shall also be considered to be standard tanks,
       — tanks permanently fixed by the manufacturer to all containers of the same type as the container in question and whose permanent fitting enables fuel to be used directly for the operation, during

Part III

transport, of the refrigeration systems and other systems with which special containers are equipped;

(d) "special container" means any container fitted with specially designed apparatus for refrigeration systems, oxygenation systems, thermal insulation systems, or other systems.]

NOTES

Substituted by Council Regulation (EEC) 1315/88, Art 2, para 11.

[**Article 113**

As regards the fuel contained in the standard tanks of commercial motor vehicles and special containers, Member States may limit application of the relief to 200 litres per vehicle, per special container and per journey.]

NOTES

Substituted by Council Regulation (EEC) 1315/88, Art 2, para 11.

Article 114

Member States may limit the amount of duty-free fuel allowed in the case of—

— commercial motor vehicles engaged in international transport into their frontier zone to a maximum depth of 25 km as the crow flies, provided such journeys are made by persons residing in the frontier zone,

— private motor vehicles belonging to persons residing in the frontier zone specified in Article 49(2).

Article 115

Fuel admitted duty-free under Articles 112 to 114 may not be used in a vehicle other than that in which it was imported nor be removed from that vehicle and stored, except during necessary repairs to that vehicle, nor be transferred, whether for a consideration or free of charge, by the person benefiting from the relief.

Non-compliance with the preceding paragraph shall give rise to application of the import duties relating to the products in question at the rate in force on the date of such non-compliance, on the basis of the type of goods and the customs value ascertained or accepted on that date by the competent authorities.

Article 116

The relief referred to in Article 112 shall also apply to the lubricants present in the motor vehicles and required for their normal operation during the journey in question.

TITLE XXVIII
MATERIALS FOR THE CONSTRUCTION, UPKEEP OR ORNAMENTATION OF MEMORIALS TO, OR CEMETERIES FOR, WAR VICTIMS

Article 117

Goods of every description, imported by organisations authorised for this purpose by the competent authorities, to be used for the construction, upkeep or ornamentation of cemeteries and tombs of, and memorials to, war victims of third countries who are buried in the [customs territory of the Community], shall be admitted free of import duties.

NOTES

Words in square brackets substituted by Council Regulation (EEC) 1315/88, Art 2, para 17.

TITLE XXIX
COFFINS, FUNERARY URNS AND ORNAMENTAL FUNERARY ARTICLES

Article 118

    1.   The following shall be admitted free of import duties—

    (a)   coffins containing bodies and urns containing the ashes of deceased persons, as well as the flowers, funeral wreaths and other ornamental objects normally accompanying them;

    (b)   flowers, wreaths and other ornamental objects brought by persons resident in third countries attending a funeral or coming to decorate graves in the customs territory of the Community, provided these importations do not reflect, by either their nature or their quantity, any commercial intent.

CHAPTER II
RELIEF FROM EXPORT DUTIES

TITLE I
CONSIGNMENTS OF NEGLIGIBLE VALUE

Article 119

Consignments dispatched to their consignee by letter or parcel post and containing goods of a total value not exceeding 10 ECU may be exported free of export duties.

TITLE II
DOMESTICATED ANIMALS EXPORTED AT THE TIME OF TRANSFER OF AGRICULTURAL ACTIVITIES FROM THE COMMUNITY TO A THIRD COUNTRY

Article 120

    1.   Domesticated animals forming the livestock of an agricultural undertaking which has ceased to operate in the [customs territory of the Community] and transfers its activities to a third country may be exported free of export duties.

    2.   The relief referred to in paragraph 1 shall be limited to domesticated animals in numbers appropriate to the nature and size of the agricultural undertaking.

NOTES

Words in square brackets substituted by Council Regulation (EEC) 1315/88, Art 2, para 17.

TITLE III
PRODUCTS OBTAINED BY AGRICULTURAL PRODUCERS FARMING ON PROPERTIES LOCATED IN THE COMMUNITY

Article 121

    1.   Agricultural or stock-farming products obtained in the customs territory of the Community on properties adjacent to a third country, operated, in the capacity of

Part III

owner or lessee, by persons having their principal undertaking in a third country adjoining the customs territory of the Community, may be exported free of export duties.

2. To benefit from the provisions of paragraph 1, products obtained from domesticated animals must be derived from animals originating in the third country in question or satisfying the requirements for free circulation there.

Article 122

The relief referred to in Article 121(1) shall be limited to products which have not undergone any treatment other than that which normally follows their harvest or production.

Article 123

Relief shall be granted only for products brought into the third country in question by the agricultural producer or on his behalf.

TITLE IV
SEEDS EXPORTED BY AGRICULTURAL PRODUCERS FOR USE ON PROPERTIES LOCATED IN THIRD COUNTRIES

Article 124

Seeds for use on properties located in a third country adjacent to the customs territory of the Community and operated, in the capacity of owner or lessee, by persons having their principal undertaking in the said customs territory in the immediate proximity of the third country in question may be exported free of export duties.

Article 125

The relief referred to in Article 124 shall be limited to the quantities of seeds required for the purpose of operating the property.

It shall be granted only for seeds exported directly from the customs territory of the Community by the agricultural producer or on his behalf.

TITLE V
FODDER AND FEEDINGSTUFFS ACCOMPANYING ANIMALS DURING THEIR EXPORTATION

Article 126

Fodder and feedingstuffs of any description put on board the means of transport used to convey animals from the customs territory of the Community to a third country for the purpose of distribution to the said animals during the journey may be exported free of export duties.

CHAPTER III
GENERAL AND FINAL PROVISIONS

Article 127

1. Subject to paragraph 2, the provisions of Chapter I shall apply both to goods declared for free circulation coming directly from third countries and to goods declared for free circulation after having been subject to another customs procedure.

2. The cases in which duty-free admission may not be granted for goods declared for free circulation after having been subject to another customs procedure shall be determined in accordance with the procedure referred to in Article 143(2) and (3).

Article 128

Where relief from import duties is granted conditional upon goods being put to a particular use by the recipient, only the competent authorities of the Member State in whose territory the said goods are to be put to such a use may grant this relief.

Article 129

The competent authorities of the Member States shall take all appropriate measures to ensure that goods placed in free circulation, where relief from import duties is granted conditional upon goods being put to a particular use by the recipient, may not be used for other purposes without the relevant import duties being paid, unless such alternative use is in conformity with the conditions laid down by this Regulation.

Article 130

Where the same person simultaneously fulfils the conditions required for the grant of relief from import or export duties under different provisions of this Regulation the provisions in question shall apply concurrently.

Article 131

Where this Regulation provides that the granting of relief shall be subject to the fulfilment of certain conditions, the person concerned shall, to the satisfaction of the competent authorities, furnish proof that these conditions have been met.

Article 132

In the event of duty-free importation or exportation being granted within the limit of an amount determined in ECU, Member States may round-off, upwards or downwards, the sum arrived at by converting that amount into the national currency.

[Member States may also maintain unamended the exchange value in national currency of the amount determined in ECU if, at the time of the annual adjustment provided for in the first subparagraph of Article 2(2) of Regulation (EEC) No 2779/78,[1] as last amended by Regulation (EEC) No 289/84,[2] the conversion of this amount, before the rounding off provided for in the previous paragraph leads to an alteration of less than 5 % in the exchange value expressed in national currency, or to a reduction thereof.]

NOTES

Para 2: words in square brackets substituted by Council Regulation (EEC) 1315/88, Art 2, para 12.

[1] OJ L 333, 30.11.78, p 5.
[2] 2 OJ L 33, 4.2.84, p 2.]

Article 133

1. Nothing in this Regulation shall prevent the Member States from granting—
   (a) relief pursuant to the Vienna Convention on diplomatic relations of 18 April 1961, the Vienna Convention on consular relations of 24 April 1963 or other consular conventions, or the New York Convention of 16 December 1969 on special missions;
   (b) relief under the customary privileges accorded by virtue of international agreements or headquarters agreements to which either a third country or an international organisation is a contracting party, including the relief granted on the occasion of international meetings;
   (c) relief under the customary privileges and immunities accorded in the context of international agreements concluded by all the Member States and setting up a cultural or scientific institute or organisation under international law;
   (d) relief under the customary privileges and immunities accorded in the context of cultural, scientific or technical cooperation agreements concluded with third countries;

(e) special relief introduced under agreements concluded with third countries and providing for common measures for the protection of persons or of the environment;

(f) special relief introduced under agreements concluded with adjacent third countries, justified by the nature of the frontier-zone trade with the countries in question.

[(g) relief in the context of agreements entered into on the basis of reciprocity with third countries that are Contracting Parties to the Convention on International Civil Aviation (Chicago 1944) for the purpose of implementing Recommended Practices 4.42 and 4.44 in Annex 9 to the Convention (eighth edition, July 1980).]

2. Where an international convention not covered by any of the categories referred to in paragraph 1, to which a Member State intends to subscribe, provides for the grant of relief, that Member State shall submit a request to the Commission for the application of such relief, supplying the Commission with all the necessary information.

A decision shall be taken on such a request in accordance with the procedure laid down in Article 143(2) and (3).

3. The supply of information as specified in paragraph 2 shall not be required where the international convention in question provides for the grant of relief not exceeding the limits set under Community law.

NOTES

Para 1: sub-para (g) inserted by Council Regulation (EEC) 1315/88, Art 2, para 13.

Article 134

[1. Member States shall notify the Commission of the customs provisions contained in international conventions and agreements of the type referred to in Article 133(1)(b), (c), (d), (e), (f) and (g) and Article 133(3) concluded after the entry into force of this Regulation.]

2. The Commission shall forward to the other Member States the texts of the conventions and agreements notified to it in accordance with paragraph 1.

NOTES

Para 1: substituted by Council Regulation (EEC) 1315/88, Art 2, para 14.

[Article 135

This Regulation shall not preclude retention:

(a) by Greece of the special status accorded to Mount Athos as guaranteed by Article 105 of the Greek Constitution;

(b) by Spain and France, until the entry into force of arrangements governing trade relations between the Community and Andorra, of the relief resulting from the Convention of 13 July 1867 and 22 and 23 November 1867 respectively between those countries and Andorra;

(c) by the Member States and up to a limit of 210 ECU of the relief, if any, in excess of that referred to in Article 47 which they granted on 1 January 1983 to merchant-navy seamen involved in international travel.]

NOTES

Substituted by Council Regulation (EEC) 1315/88, Art 2, para 15.

[Article 136

1. Until the establishment of Community provisions in the field in question, Member States may grant special relief to armed forces not serving under their flags which are stationed on their territories in pursuance of international agreements.

2. Until the establishment of Community provisions in the field in question, this Regulation shall not preclude the retention by Member States of relief granted to workers returning to their country after having resided for at least six months outside the customs territory of the Community on account of their occupation.]

NOTES

Substituted by Council Regulation (EEC) 1315/88, Art 2, para 15.

Articles 137, 138

NOTES

Repealed by Council Regulation (EEC) 1315/88, Art 2, para 16.

Article 139

This Regulation shall apply without prejudice to—

(a) Council Regulation (EEC) No 754/76 of 25 March 1976 on the customs treatment applicable to goods returned to the customs territory of the Community;[1]

(b) the provisions in force concerning the stores of vessels, aircraft and international trains;

(c) provisions on relief introduced by other Community acts.

[1] OJ L 89, 2.4.76, p 1.

Article 140

1. The following shall be repealed with effect from the date of entry into force of this Regulation—

(a) Council Regulation (EEC) No 1544/69 of 23 July 1969 on the tariff treatment applicable to goods contained in travellers' personal luggage,[1] as last amended by Regulation (EEC) No 3313/81;[2]

(b) Council Regulation (EEC) No 1410/74 of 4 June 1974 on the tariff treatment applicable to goods imported for free circulation in the event of disasters occurring in the territory of one or more Member States;[3]

(c) Council Regulation (EEC) No 1818/75 of 10 July 1975 on the agricultural levies, compensatory amounts and other import charges applicable to agricultural products and to certain goods resulting from their processing, contained in travellers' personal baggage;[4]

(d) Regulation (EEC) No 1798/75, as last amended by Regulation (EEC) No 608/82;[5]

(e) Council Regulation (EEC) No 1990/76 of 22 July 1976 on the customs treatment applicable to goods imported for testing;[6]

(f) Council Regulation (EEC) No 3060/78 of 19 December 1978 providing exemption from import duties for goods in small consignments of a non-commercial character from third countries,[7] as amended by Regulation (EEC) No 3313/81;[8]

(g)   Council Regulation (EEC) No 1028/79 of 8 May 1979 on the importation free of Common Customs Tariff duties of articles for the use of handicapped persons.[9]

2.   References to the Regulations listed in paragraph 1 shall be construed as references to this Regulation.

[1]   OJ L 191, 5.8.69, p 1.
[2]   OJ L 334, 21.11.81, p 1.
[3]   OJ L 150, 7.6.74, p 4.
[4]   OJ L 185, 16.7.75, p 3.
[5]   OJ L 74, 18.3.82, p 4.
[6]   OJ L 219, 12.8.76, p 14.
[7]   OJ L 366, 28.12.78, p 1.
[8]   OJ L 334, 21.11.81, p 1.
[9]   OJ L 134, 31.5.79, p 8.

Articles 141–143

NOTES

Repealed by Council Regulation (EEC) 2913/92, Art 251, para 1.

Article 144

The reference made in the following Regulations to the Committee provided for in Article 7 of Regulation (EEC) No 1798/75 shall be replaced by a reference to the Committee provided for in Article 141 of this Regulation—

(a)   Article 15 of Regulation (EEC) No 754/76;
(b)   Article 25 of Council Regulation (EEC) No 1430/79 of 2 July 1979 on the repayment or remission of import or export duties;[1]
(c)   Article 10 of Council Regulation (EEC) No 1697/79 of 24 July 1979 on the post-clearance recovery of import duties or export duties which have not been required of the person liable for payment on goods entered for a customs procedure involving the obligation to pay such duties.[2]

[1]   OJ L 175, 12.7.79, p 1.
[2]   OJ L 197, 3.8.79, p 1.

Article 145

This Regulation shall enter into force on the third day following its publication in *the Official Journal of the European Communities*.

It shall apply from 1 July 1984.

This Regulation shall be binding in its entirety and directly applicable in all Member States.

Done at Brussels, 28 March 1983.

[ANNEX I

A.

BOOKS, PUBLICATIONS AND DOCUMENTS

CN code	Description
3705	Photographic plates and film, exposed and developed, other than cinematograph film—
ex 3705 20 00	—Microfilms of books, children's picture books and drawing or painting books, school exercise books (workbooks), crossword-puzzle books, newspapers and periodicals, printed documents or reports of a non-commercial character, and of loose illustrations, printed pages and reproduction proofs for the production of books
ex 3705 10 00	—Reproduction films for the production of books
ex 3705 90 10	
ex 3705 90 90	
4903 00 00	Children's picture, drawing or colouring books
4905	Maps and hydrographic or similar charts of all kinds, including atlases, wall maps, topographical plans and globes, printed— — Other—
ex 4905 99 00	— —Other— —Maps, charts and diagrams of interest in scientific fields such as geology, zoology, botany, mineralogy, palaeontology, archaeology, ethnology, meteorology, climatology and geophysics
ex 4906 00 00	Architectural, industrial or engineering plans and designs and reproductions thereof
4911	Other printed matter, including pictures and photographs—
4911 10	—Trade advertising material, commercial catalogues and the like—
ex 4911 10 90	— —Other—
	—Catalogues of books and publications, being books and publications offered for sale by publishers or booksellers established outside the territory of the European Communities —Catalogues of films, recording or other visual and auditory materials of an educational, scientific or cultural character —Posters for the promotion of tourism and tourist publications, brochures, guidebooks, timetables, pamphlets and like publications, whether or not illustrated, including those published by private concerns, designed to encourage the public to travel outside the territory of the European Communities, including microcopies of such articles —Bibliographical information material for distribution free of charge[1] —Other—
4911 99	— —Other—

CN code	Description
ex 4911 99 90	— — —Other— —Loose illustrations, printed pages and reproduction proofs to be used for the production of books, including microcopies of such articles[1] —Microcopies of books, children's picture books and drawing or painting books, school exercise books (workbooks), crossword puzzle books, newspapers and periodicals and of documents or reports of a non-commercial character[1] —Publications designed to encourage the public to study outside the territory of the European Communities, including microcopies of such publications[1] —Meteorological and geophysical diagrams
9023 00	Instruments, apparatus and models, designed for demonstrational purposes (for example, in education or exhibitions), unsuitable for other uses—
ex 9023 00 90	— Other— —Maps and charts in relief of interest in scientific fields such as geology, zoology, botany, mineralogy, palaeontology, archaeology, ethnology, meteorology, climatology and geophysics

[1] The exemption shall not, however, apply to articles in which the advertising covers more than 25 % of the surface. In the case of publications and posters for the promotion of tourism, this percentage applies only to private commercial publicity.

B.

VISUAL AND AUDITORY MATERIALS OF AN EDUCATIONAL, SCIENTIFIC OR CULTURAL CHARACTER

The articles listed in Annex II(A) produced by the United Nations or any of its specialised agencies.]

NOTES

Substituted by Commission Regulation (EEC) 3691/87, Art 1, para 2.

[ANNEX II

A.

VISUAL AND AUDITORY MATERIALS OF AN EDUCATIONAL, SCIENTIFIC OR CULTURAL CHARACTER

CN code	Description	Beneficiary establishment or organisations
3704 00	Photographic plates, film, paper, paperboard and textiles, exposed but not developed:	All organisations (including broadcasting and television organisations), institutions or associations approved by the competent authorities of the Member States for the purpose of duty-free admission of these goods

CN code	Description	Beneficiary establishment or organisations
ex 3704 00 10	—Plates and film— —Cinematograph film, positives, of an educational, scientific or cultural character	
ex 3705	Photographic plates and film, exposed and developed, other than cinematograph film— —Of an educational, scientific or cultural character	
3706	Cinematograph film, exposed and developed, whether or not incorporating sound track or consisting only of sound track—	
3706 10	—Of a width of 35 mm or more— — — Other—	
ex 3706 10 99	— — — Other positives— —Newsreels (with or without sound track) depicting events of current news value at the time of importation, and imported up to a limit of two copies of each subject for copying purposes —Archival film material (with or without sound track) intended for use in connection with newsreel films —Recreational films particularly suited for children and young people —Other films of educational, scientific or cultural character	
3706 90	— Other — — Other— — — — Other positives—	
ex 3706 90 51 ex 3706 90 91 ex 3706 90 99	—Newsreels (with or without sound track) depicting events of current news value at the time of importation, and imported up to a limit of two copies of each subject for copying purposes —Archival film material (with or without sound track) intended for use in connection with newsreel films —Recreational films particularly suited for children and young people —Other films of educational, scientific or cultural character	
4911	Other printed matter, including printed pictures and photographs— — Other	
4911 99	— — Other	

CN code	Description	Beneficiary establishment or organisations
ex 4911 99 90	— — — Other —Microcards or other information storage media required in computerised information and documentation services of an educational, scientific or cultural character —Wall charts designed solely for demonstration and education	
ex 8524	Records, tapes and other recorded media for sound or other similarly recorded phenomena including matrices and masters for the production of records, but excluding products of Chapter 37— —Of an educational, scientific or cultural character	
ex 9023 00	Instruments, apparatus and models, designed for demonstrational purposes (for example, in education or exhibitions), unsuitable for others uses— —Patterns, models and wall charts of an educational, scientific or cultural character, designed solely for demonstration and education —Mock-ups or visualisations of abstract concepts such as molecular structures or mathematical formulae	
Various	Holograms for laser projection Multi-media kits Materials for programmed instructions, including materials in kit form with the corresponding printed materials	

B.

COLLECTOR'S PIECES AND WORKS OF ART OF AN EDUCATIONAL, SCIENTIFIC OR CULTURAL CHARACTER

CN code	Description	Beneficiary establishment or organisations
Various	Collectors' pieces and works of art, not intended for sale	Galleries, museums and other institutions approved by the competent authorities of the Member States for the purpose of duty-free admission of these goods]

NOTES

Substituted by Commission Regulation (EEC) 3691/87, Art 1, para 2.

[ANNEX III

CN code	Description
4911	Other printed matter, including printed pictures and photographs—

CN code	Description
4911 10	— Trade advertising material, commercial catalogues and the like—
ex 4911 10 90	— — Other—
	— In relief for the blind and partially sighted
4911 91	Other—
	— — Pictures, prints and photographs—
	— — — Other—
ex 4911 91 91	— — — — Pictures and designs—
	—In relief for the blind and partially sighted
ex 4911 91 99	— — — — Photographs—
	—In relief for the blind and partially sighted
4911 99	— —Other—
ex 4911 99 90	— — — Other—
	—In relief for the blind and partially sighted]

NOTES

Substituted by Commission Regulation (EEC) 3691/87, Art 1, para 2.

[ANNEX IV

CN code	Description
4802	Uncoated paper and paperboard, of a kind used for writing, printing or other graphic purposes, and punch card-stock and punch tape paper, in rolls or sheets, other than paper of heading No 4801 or 4803; hand-made paper and paperboard—
	— Other paper and paperboard, not containing fibres obtained by mechanical process or of which not more than 10% by weight of the total fibre content consists of such fibres—
ex 4802 52 00	— — Weighing 40 g/m2 or more but not more than 150 g/m^2 — Braille paper
4802 53	Weighing more than 150 g/m^2—
ex 4802 53 90	— — — Other— — Braille paper
4802 60	— Other paper and paperboard of which more than 10% by weight of the total fibre content consists of fibres obtained by a mechanical process—
ex 4802 60 90	— — Other— — Braille paper
4805	Other uncoated paper and paperboard, in rolls or sheets—
4805 60	Other paper and paperboard, weighing 150 g/m^2 or less—
ex 4805 60 90	— Other— — Braille paper
4805 70	Other paper and paperboard, weighing more than 150 g/m^2 but less than 225 g/m^2—

CN code	Description
ex 4805 70 90	— Other— — Braille paper
4805 80	Other paper and paperboard, weighing 225 g/m² or more—
ex 4805 80 90	— Other— — Braille paper
4823	Other paper, paperboard, cellulose wadding and webs of cellulose fibres, cut to size or shape; other articles of paper pulp, paper, paperboard, cellulose wadding or webs of cellulose fibres— — Other paper and paperboard, of a kind used for writing, printing or other graphic purposes:
4823 59	— — Other—
ex 4823 59 90	— Other— — Braille paper
ex 6602 00 00	Walking-sticks, seat-sticks, whips, riding-crops and the like— — White canes for the blind and partially sighted
ex 8469	Typewriters and word-processing machines— Adapted for use by the blind and partially sighted
ex 8471	Automatic data-processing machines and units thereof; magnetic or optical readers, machines for transcribing data onto data media in coded form and machines for processing such data, not elsewhere specified or included— — Equipment for the mechanical production of braille and recorded material for the blind
ex 8519	Turntables (record-decks), record-players, cassette-players and other sound reproducing apparatus, not incorporating a sound recording device— — Record-players and cassette players specially designed or adapted for the blind and partially sighted
ex 8524	Records, tapes and other recorded media for sound or other similarly recorded phenomena, including matrices and masters for the production of records, but excluding products of Chapter 37— — Talking books — Magnetic tapes and cassettes for the production of Braille and talking books
9013	Liquid crystal devices not constituting articles provided for more specifically in other headings; lasers, other than laser diodes; other optical appliances and instruments, not specified or included elsewhere in this chapter—
ex 9013 80 00	Other devices, appliances and instruments— — Television enlargers for the blind and partially sighted
9021	Orthopaedic appliances, including crutches, surgical belts and trusses; splints and other fracture appliances; artificial parts of the body; hearing aids and other appliances which are worn or carried, or implanted in the body, to compensate for a defect or disability—
9021 90	— Other—
ex 9021 90 90	— — Other— —Electronic orientator and obstacle detector appliances for the blind and partially sighted —Television enlargers for the blind and partially sighted —Electronic reading machines for the blind and partially sighted
9023 00	Instruments, apparatus and models, designed for demonstrational purposes (for example, in education or exhibitions), unsuitable for other uses—

CN code	Description
ex 9023 00 90	— Other— —Teaching aids and apparatus specifically designed for the use of the blind and partially sighted
ex 9102	Wrist-watches, pocket-watches and other watches, including stop-watches, other than those of heading No 9101— —Braille watches with cases other than of precious metals
9504	Articles for funfair, table or parlour games, including pintables, billiards, special tables for casino games and automatic bowling alley equipment—
9504 90	— Other—
ex 9504 90 90	— — Other— —Tables games and accessories specially adapted for the use of the blind and partially sighted
Various	All other articles specially designed for the education, scientific or cultural advancement of the blind and partially sighted.]

NOTES

Substituted by Commission Regulation (EEC) 3691/87, Art 1, para 2.

COMMISSION REGULATION

(2288/83/EEC)

of 29 July 1983

establishing the list of biological or chemical substances provided for in Article 60(1)(b) of Council Regulation (EEC) No 918/83 setting up a Community system of reliefs from customs duty

NOTES

Date of publication in OJ: OJ L 220, 11.8.83, p 13.

THE COMMISSION OF THE EUROPEAN COMMUNITIES,

Having regard to the Treaty establishing the European Economic Community,

Having regard to Council Regulation (EEC) No 918/83 of setting up a Community system of reliefs from customs duty,[1] and in particular Article 143 thereof,

Whereas Article 60(1)(b) and (2) of Regulation (EEC) No 918/83 provides for admission with relief from import duties for biological or chemical substances imported exclusively for non-commercial purposes by public establishments, or those departments of public establishments, or by officially authorised private establishments, whose principal activity is education or scientific research; whereas such admission with relief from import duties is limited, however, to biological or chemical substances for which there is no equivalent production in the customs territory of the Community and which are included in a list drawn up in accordance with the procedure laid down in Article 143(2) and (3) of the above Regulation;

Whereas according to information obtained from the Member States there is no equivalent production in the customs territory of the Community of the biological or chemical substances listed in the Annex to this Regulation;

Whereas the measures provided for in this Regulation are in accordance with the opinion of the Committee on Duty-Free Arrangements,

[1] 1 OJ L 105, 23.4.83, p 1.

HAS ADOPTED THIS REGULATION—

Article 1

The list of biological or chemical substances eligible for admission with relief from import duty provided for in Article 60(1)(b) of Regulation (EEC) No 918/83 is set out in the Annex to this Regulation.

Article 2

This Regulation shall enter into force on 1 July 1984.

This Regulation shall be binding in its entirety and directly applicable in all Member States.

Done at Brussels, 29 July 1983.

[ANNEX

Reference No	HS heading No	Description
	2845 90 90	Helium-3
	2845 90 90	(Oxygen-18) Water
20273	2901 29 90	3-Methylpent-1-ene
20274	2901 29 90	4-Methylpent-1-ene
20275	2901 29 90	2-Methylpent-2-ene
20276	2901 29 90	3-Methylpent-2-ene
20277	2901 29 90	4-Methylpent-2-ene
25634	2902 19 10	P-Mentha-1 (7), 2-diene beta-Phellandrene
14769	2903 69 00	4,4'-Dibromobiphenyl
17305	2904 10 00	Ethyl methanesulphonate
14364	2923 90 00	Decamethonium bromide (INN)
20641	2926 90 90	1-Naphtonitrile
20642	2926 90 90	2-Naphtonitrile
22830	2936 21 00	Retinyl acetate
21887	3507 90 00	Phosphoglucomutase
		[Orcoacid Sulphurhodamine G (CN code 3204)]]

NOTES

Substituted by Commission Regulation (EEC) 3692/87, Art 1; words in square brackets inserted by Commission Regulation (EEC) 213/89, Art 1.

COMMISSION REGULATION

(2289/83/EEC)

of 29 July 1983

laying down provisions for the implementation of Articles 70 to 78 of Council Regulation (EEC) No 918/83 establishing a Community system of duty-free arrangements

NOTES

Date of publication in OJ: OJ L 220, 11.8.83, p 15.

THE COMMISSION OF THE EUROPEAN COMMUNITIES,

Having regard to the Treaty establishing the European Economic Community,

Having regard to Council Regulation (EEC) No 918/83 of 28 March 1983 establishing a Community system of duty-free arrangements,[1] and in particular Article 143 thereof,

Whereas Regulation (EEC) No 918/83 replaced, by Articles 70 to 78 thereof, Council Regulation (EEC) No 1028/79 of 8 May 1979 on the importation free of Common Customs Tariff duties of articles for the use of handicapped persons;[2] whereas it is therefore necessary to substitute for Commission Regulation (EEC) No 2783/79 of 12 December 1979 laying down provisions for the implementation of Regulation (EEC) No 1028/79[3] a new Regulation laying down provisions for the implementation of Articles 70 to 78 of Regulation (EEC) No 918/83;

Whereas the measures provided for in this Regulation are in accordance with the opinion of the Committee on Duty-Free Arrangements,

---

[1] OJ L 105, 23.4.83, p 1.

[2] OJ L 134, 31.5.79, p 8.

[3] OJ L 318, 13.12.79, p 27.

HAS ADOPTED THIS REGULATION—

Article 1

This Regulation lays down provisions for the implementation of Articles 70 to 78 of Regulation (EEC) No 918/83, hereinafter called 'basic Regulation'.

CHAPTER I
PROVISIONS APPLICABLE TO IMPORTATIONS CARRIED OUT BY INSTITUTIONS OR ORGANIZATIONS

TITLE I
GENERAL PROVISIONS

A.
Obligations on the part of the institution or organisation to which the articles are consigned

Article 2

[1. The admission free of import duties of articles referred to in Articles 71 and 72(1) and (2) of the basic Regulation shall entail the following obligations on the part of the institution or organisation to which they are consigned—]

—   to dispatch the articles in question directly to the declared place of destination,

—   to account for them in its inventory,

—   to use them exclusively for the purposes specified in the said Articles,

—   to facilitate any verification which the competent authorities consider necessary in order to ensure that the conditions for granting admission free of import duties are satisfied, or remain satisfied.

2.   The head of the institution or organisation to which the articles are consigned, or his authorised representative shall furnish the competent authorities with a statement declaring that he is aware of the various obligations listed in paragraph 1 and including an undertaking to comply with them.

The competent authorities may require that the statement referred to in the preceding subparagraph be produced for each import, or for several imports or for all the imports to be carried out by the institution or organisation to which the articles are consigned.

NOTES

Para 1: words in square brackets substituted by Commission Regulation (EEC) 735/92, Art 1, para 1.

B.

Provisions to be applied where the articles are lent, hired out or transferred

Article 3

1.   Where the provisions of the first sentence of the second subparagraph of Article 77 (2) of the basic Regulation are applied, the institution or organisation to which an article for the use of handicapped persons is lent, hired out or transferred shall, from the date of receipt of the article, comply with the same obligations as those set out in Article 2.

[[2.   Where the institution or organisation to which an article is lent, hired out or transferred is situated in a Member State other than that in which the institution or organisation that lent, hired out or transferred the article is situated, upon the dispatch of such article the competent customs office of the Member State of dispatch shall issue a Control Copy T 5 in accordance with the rules laid down in Regulation (EEC) No 2823/87 in order to ensure that such article is put to a use entitling it to continue to qualify for admission free of import duties.]

For this purpose, the said control copy shall include, in box 104 under the heading 'other', one of the following entries—

. . .

—   "Article for the handicapped: continuation of relief subject to compliance with the second subparagraph of Article 77 (2) of Regulation (EEC) No 918/83";

. . .]

3.   The provisions of paragraphs 1 and 2 shall apply mutatis mutandis to the loan, hire or transfer of spare parts, components or accessories specifically for articles for the use of handicapped persons and to tools for the maintenance, control, calibration or repair of the said articles which have been admitted free of import duties under the second subparagraph of Articles 71 and 72 (2) of the basic Regulation.

NOTES

Para 2: words in first (outer) pair of square brackets substituted by Commission Regulation (EEC) 1746/85, Art 1, para 2 (foreign language text omitted); words in second (inner) pair of square brackets substituted by Commission Regulation (EEC) 735/92, Art 1, para 2.

TITLE II
SPECIFIC PROVISIONS RELATING TO THE ADMISSION FREE OF IMPORT DUTIES OF ARTICLES REFERRED TO IN THE FIRST SUBPARAGRAPH OF ARTICLE 71 OF THE BASIC REGULATION

Article 4

1. In order to obtain admission free of import duties of an article for the use of the blind in accordance with the first subparagraph of Article 71 of the basic Regulation, the head of the institution or organisation to which the article is consigned, or his authorised representative, must submit an application to the competent authority of the Member State in which the institution or organisation is situated.

Such application must be accompanied by all information which the competent authority considers necessary for the purpose of determining whether the conditions laid down for granting admission free of import duties are fulfilled.

2. The competent authority of the Member State where the institution or organisation to which the article is consigned is situated shall give a direct ruling on the application referred to in paragraph 1.

TITLE III
SPECIFIC PROVISIONS RELATING TO THE IMPORTATION FREE OF IMPORT DUTIES OF ARTICLES REFERRED TO IN ARTICLE 72 (1) OF THE BASIC REGULATION

Article 5

NOTES
Repealed by Commission Regulation (EEC) 735/92, Art 1, para 7.

Article 6

1. In order to obtain admission free of import duties of an article for the use of handicapped persons under the provisions of Article 72 (1) of the basic Regulation the head of the institution or organisation to which the article is consigned, or his authorised representative, must submit an application to the competent authority of the Member State in which the institution or organisation is situated.

[2. The application referred to in paragraph 1 shall contain the following information relating to the article in question—

(a) the precise trade description of the article used by the manufacturer, its presumed combined nomenclature classification and the objective technical characteristics indicating that it was specially designed for the education, employment or social advancement of handicapped persons;

(b) the name or business name and address of the manufacturer and, if applicable, of the supplier;

(c) the country of origin of the article;

(d) the place of destination of the article;

(e) the precise use for which the article is intended;

(f) the price of the article or its value for customs purposes;

(g) the quantity of the article in question.

Documentary evidence providing all relevant information on the characteristics and technical specifications of the article shall be furnished with the application.]

NOTES

Para 2: substituted by Commission Regulation (EEC) 735/92, Art 1, para 3.

[Article 7

The competent authority of the Member State in which is situated the institution or organisation to which the articles are consigned shall take a direct decision on applications under Article 6.]

NOTES

Substituted by Commission Regulation (EEC) 735/92, Art 1, para 4.

Articles 8, 9

NOTES

Repealed by Commission Regulation (EEC) 735/92, Art 1, para 7.

Article 10

Authorisations for admission free of import duties shall be valid for a period of six months.

The competent authorities may, however, set a longer period in the light of the particular circumstances of each case.

Articles 11, 12

NOTES

Title IV repealed by Commission Regulation (EEC) 735/92, Art 1, para 7.

TITLE V
SPECIAL PROVISIONS RELATING TO THE ADMISSION FREE OF IMPORT DUTIES OF SPARE PARTS, COMPONENTS, SPECIFIC ACCESSORIES OR TOOLS UNDER THE SECOND SUBPARAGRAPH OF ARTICLE 71 AND ARTICLE 72 (2) OF THE BASIC REGULATION

Article 13

For the purposes of the second subparagraph of Articles 71 and 72 (2) of the basic Regulation, 'specific accessories' means items specially designed for use with a specific article for the purpose of improving its performance and scope.

Article 14

In order to obtain admission free of import duties of spare parts, components specific accessories or tools under the second subparagraph of Article 71 or 72 (2) of the basic Regulation, the head of the institution or organisation to which the articles are consigned, or his authorised representative, must submit an application to the competent authority of the Member State in which the institution or organisation is situated.

This application must be accompanied by all data deemed necessary by the competent authority for the purpose of determining whether the conditions laid down in the second subparagraph of Article 71 or in Article 72 (2) of the basic Regulation are fulfilled.

Article 15

The competent authority of the Member State in which is situated the institution or organisation to which such articles are consigned shall give a direct decision on applications under Article 14.

CHAPTER II
PROVISIONS APPLICABLE TO IMPORTATIONS CARRIED OUT BY BLIND PERSONS AND OTHER HANDICAPPED PERSONS

Article 16

Articles 4, 13, 14 and 15 shall apply mutatis mutandis to exemption from import duties of the articles referred to in the first and second subparagraphs of Article 71 of the basic Regulation imported by blind persons themselves for their own use.

[Article 17

The following shall apply mutatis mutandis to exemption from import duties of articles imported by handicapped persons themselves for their own use—

— Article 6, 7 and 10 in the case of articles referred to in Article 72 (1) of the basic Regulation,

— Articles 13, 14 and 15 in the case of articles referred to in Article 72 (2) of the basic Regulation.]

NOTES

Substituted by Commission Regulation (EEC) 735/92, Art 1, para 5.

[Article 18

The competent authorities may allow the application provided for in Articles 4 and 6 to be made in a simplified form, where it relates to items imported under the conditions referred to in Articles 16 and 17.]

NOTES

Substituted by Commission Regulation (EEC) 735/92, Art 1, para 6.

CHAPTER III
FINAL PROVISIONS

Article 19

NOTES

Repeals Council Regulation (EEC) 2783/79.

Article 20

This Regulation shall enter into force on 1 July 1984.

This Regulation shall be binding in its entirety and directly applicable in all Member States.

Done at Brussels, 29 July 1983.

Part III

[COMMISSION REGULATION

(2290/83/EEC)

of 29 July 1983

laying down provisions for the implementation of Articles 50 to 59b, 63a and 63b of Council Regulation (EEC) No 918/83 setting up a Community system of reliefs from customs duty]

NOTES

Date of publication in OJ: OJ L 220, 11.8.83, p 20.

Title substituted by Commission Regulation (EEC) 1843/89, Art 1, para 2.

THE COMMISSION OF THE EUROPEAN COMMUNITIES,

Having regard to the Treaty establishing the European Economic Community,

Having regard to Council Regulation (EEC) No 918/83 of 28 March 1983 setting up a Community system of reliefs from customs duty,[1] and in particular Article 143 thereof,

Whereas Regulation (EEC) No 918/83 replaced, by its Articles 50 to 59, Council Regulation (EEC) No 1798/75 of 10 July 1975 on the importation free of Common Customs Tariff duties of educational, scientific and cultural materials[2]; whereas it is therefore necessary to replace Commission Regulation (EEC) No 2784/79 of 12 December 1979 laying down provisions for the implementation of Regulation (EEC) No 1798/75[3] by a new Regulation laying down provisions for the implementation of Articles 50 to 59 of Regulation (EEC) No 918/83;

Whereas the measures provided for in this Regulation are in accordance with the opinion of the Committee on Duty-Free Arrangements,

---

[1] OJ L 105, 23.4.83, p 1.

[2] OJ L 184, 15.7.75, p 1.

[3] OJ L 318, 13.12.79, p 32.

HAS ADOPTED THIS REGULATION—

[Article 1

This Regulation lays down provisions for the implementation of Articles 50 to 59b, 63a and 63b of Regulation (EEC) No 918/83, hereinafter referred to as the "basic Regulation".]

NOTES

Substituted by Commission Regulation (EEC) 1843/89, Art 1, para 2.

TITLE I
GENERAL PROVISIONS

A.

Obligations on the part of the establishment or organisation to which the goods are consigned

Article 2

[1. The admission free of import duties of educational, scientific and cultural materials referred to in Article 51, 52 (1) and 53 of the basic Regulation, hereinafter referred to as "goods", shall entail the following obligations on the part of the establishment or organisation to which the goods are consigned—

— to dispatch the goods in question directly to the declared place of destination,

— to account for them in its inventory,

— to facilitate any verification which the competent authorities consider necessary in order to ensure that the conditions for granting admission free of import duties are satisfied, or remain satisfied.

In addition, in the case of goods referred to in Articles 52 (1) and 53 and the basic Regulation, it shall entail the obligation on the part of the establishment or organisation to which the goods are consigned to use the abovementioned goods exclusively for non-commercial purposes within the meaning of the second indent of Article 54 of the basic Regulation.]

2. The head of the establishment or organisation to which the goods are consigned, or his authorised representative, shall furnish the competent authorities with a statement declaring that he is aware of the various obligations listed in paragraph 1 and including an undertaking to comply with them.

The competent authorities may require that the statement referred to in the preceding subparagraph be produced for each import, or for several imports, or for all the imports to be carried out by the establishment or organisation to which the goods are consigned.

NOTES

Para 1: substituted by Commission Regulation (EEC) 734/92, Art 1, para 1.

B.

Provisions to be applied where the goods are lent, hired out or transferred

Article 3

1. Where the provisions of the first subparagraph of Article 57 (2) of the basic Regulation are applied, the establishment or organisation to which goods are lent, hired out or transferred shall, from the date of receipt of the goods, comply with the same obligations as those set out in Article 2.

[[2. Where the establishment or organisation to which the goods are lent, hired out or transferred is situated in a Member State other than that in which the establishment that lent, hired out or transferred the goods is situated, upon the dispatch of such goods the competent customs office of the Member State of dispatch shall issue a control Copy T 5 in accordance with the rules laid down in Regulation (EEC) No 2823/87 in order to ensure that such goods are put to a use entitling them to continue to qualify for admission free of import duties.]

For this purpose, the said Control Copy shall include, in box 104 under the heading "other", one of the following—

[. . .

—   "UNESCO goods: continuation of relief subject to compliance with the first subparagraph of Article 57 (2) of Regulation (EEC) No 918/83";

. . .]

3.   The provisions of paragraphs 1 and 2 shall apply mutatis mutandis to the loan, hire or transfer of spare parts, components or specific accessories for scientific instruments or apparatus, and to tools for the maintenance, control, calibration or repair of scientific instruments or apparatus, which have been admitted free of import duties under Article 53 of the basic Regulation.

NOTES

Para 2: words in first (outer) pair of square brackets substituted by Commission Regulation (EEC) 1745/85, Art 1, para 2 (foreign language text omitted); words in second (inner) pair of square brackets substituted by Commission Regulation (EEC) 734/92, Art 1, para 2.

TITLE II
SPECIFIC PROVISIONS RELATING TO THE ADMISSION FREE OF IMPORT DUTIES OF EDUCATIONAL, SCIENTIFIC OR CULTURAL MATERIALS IN ACCORDANCE WITH ARTICLE 51 OF THE BASIC REGULATION

NOTES

Title: substituted by Commission Regulation (EEC) 734/92, Art 1, para 3.

Article 4

In order to obtain admission free of import duties of goods in accordance with Article 51 of the basic Regulation, the head of the establishment or organisation to which the goods are consigned, or his authorised representative, must submit an application to the competent authority of the Member State in which the establishment or organisation is situated.

Such application must be accompanied by all information which the competent authority considers necessary for the purpose of determining whether the conditions laid down for granting admission free of import duties are fulfilled.

[TITLE III
SPECIFIC PROVISIONS RELATING TO THE IMPORTATION FREE OF IMPORT DUTIES OF SCIENTIFIC INSTRUMENTS AND APPARATUS UNDER ARTICLES 52 AND 54 OF THE BASIC REGULATION.]

[Article 5

For the purposes of the first indent of Article 54 of the basic Regulation, the objective technical characteristics of a scientific instrument or apparatus shall be understood to mean those characteristics resulting from the construction of that instrument or apparatus or from adjustments to a standard instrument or apparatus which make it possible to obtain high-level performances above those normally required for industrial or commercial use.

Where it is not possible to establish clearly on the basics of its objective technical characteristics whether an instrument or apparatus is to be regarded as a scientific instrument or apparatus, reference shall be made to the use of the instrument or apparatus for which admission free of import duties is requested. If this examination shows that the instrument or apparatus in question is used for scientific purposes, it shall be deemed to be of a scientific nature.]

Article 11

TITLE V
SPECIFIC PROVISIONS RELATING TO THE ADMISSION FREE OF IMPORT DUTIES OF SPARE PARTS, COMPONENTS, SPECIFIC ACCESSORIES AND TOOLS UNDER ARTICLE 53 OF THE BASIC REGULATION

Article 12

For the purpose of Article 53 (a) of the basic Regulation specific accessories means those articles specially designed for use with a specific scientific instrument or apparatus for the purpose of improving its performance and scope.

Article 13

In order to obtain admission free of import duties under Article 53 of the basic Regulation, either of spare parts, components or specific accessories, or of tools, the head of the establishment or organisation to which the goods are consigned, or his authorised representative, must submit an application to the competent authority of the Member State in which the establishment or organisation is situated.

This application must be accompanied by all data deemed necessary by the competent authority for the purpose of determining whether the conditions laid down in Article 53 of the basic Regulation are fulfilled.

[**Article 14**

The competent authority of the Member State in which is situated the establishment or organisation to which the goods are consigned shall take a direct decision in respect of the application referred to in Article 13.]

Article 15

The provisions of Article 8 shall apply to authorisations for admission free of import duties issued under Article 53 of the basic Regulation.

[# TITLE VA
SPECIAL PROVISIONS RELATING TO THE ADMISSION FREE OF IMPORT DUTIES OF MEDICAL INSTRUMENTS OR APPARATUS UNDER ARTICLES 63A AND 63B OF THE BASIC REGULATION

Article 15a

1. In order to obtain admission free of import duties of instruments or apparatus under Articles 63a and 63b of the basic Regulation, the head of the establishment or organisation to which the goods are consigned, or his authorised representative, must submit an application to the competent authority of the Member State in which the establishment or organisation is situated.

2. The application referred to in paragraph 1 must contain the following information relating to the instrument or apparatus in question—

[(a) the precise trade description of the instrument or apparatus used by the manufacturer, and its presumed classification in the combined nomenclature.]

Article 6

1. In order to obtain admission free of import duties of a scientific instrument or apparatus under the provisions of Article 52 (1) of the basic Regulation, the head of the establishment or organisation to which the goods are consigned, or his authorised representative, must submit an application to the competent authority of the Member State in which the establishment or organisation is situated.

[2. The application referred to in paragraph 1 must contain the following information relating to the instrument or apparatus in question:

    (a)   the precise trade description of the instrument or apparatus used by the manufacturer, its presumed combined nomenclature classification and the objective technical characteristics on the basis of which the instrument or apparatus is considered to be scientific;

    (b)   the name or business name and address of the manufacturer and, if available, of the supplier;

    (c)   the country of origin of the instrument or apparatus;

    (d)   the place where the instrument or apparatus is to be used;

    (e)   the precise use for which the instrument or apparatus is intended;

    (f)   the price of the instrument or apparatus or its value for customs purposes;

    (g)   the quantity of the instrument or apparatus in question.

Documentary evidence providing all relevant information on the characteristics and technical specifications of the instrument or apparatus must be furnished with the application.]

[Article 7

The competent authority of the Member State in which is situated the establishment or organisation to which the goods are consigned shall take a direct decision on applications under Article 6 in all cases.]

Article 8

Authorisations for admission free of import duties shall be valid for a period of six months.

The competent authorities may, however, set a longer period in the light of the particular circumstances of each case.

Articles 9–11

(b)   the name or business name and address of the manufacturer and, if available, of the supplier;

(c)   the country of origin of the instrument or apparatus;

(d)   the place where the instrument or apparatus is to be used;

(e)   the use which the instrument or apparatus is to be put.

3.   In the case of a gift, the application shall also include—

    (a)   the name of business name and address of the donor;

    (b)   a declaration by the applicant to the effect that:

        (i)   the donation of the instrument or apparatus in question does not conceal any commercial intent on the part of the donor;

        (ii)   the donor is no way associated with the manufacturer of the instruments or apparatus whose duty-free admission is requested.]

NOTES

Inserted by Commission Regulation (EEC) 3893/88, Art 1, para 5.

Para 2: sub-para (a) substituted by Commission Regulation (EEC) 734/92, Art 1, para 8.

Article 15b

NOTES

Repealed by Commission Regulation (EEC) 734/92, Art 1, para 15 (previously inserted by Commission Regulation (EEC) 3893/88, Art 1, para 5.

[Article 15c

The competent authority of the Member State in which is situated the establishment or organisation to which the goods are consigned shall take a direct decision on applications in all cases.]

NOTES

Substituted by Commission Regulation (EEC) 734/92, Art 1, para 9 (previously inserted by Commission Regulation (EEC) 3893/88, Art 1, para 5).

[Article 15d

The provisions of Articles 15a and 15c shall apply *mutatis mutandis* to spare parts, components, specific accessories and tools to be used for the maintenance, checking, calibration or repair of instruments of apparatus admitted duty-free pursuant to Article 63a (2) (a) and (b) of the basic Regulation.]

NOTES

Substituted by Commission Regulation (EEC) 734/92, Art 1, para 10 (previously inserted by Commission Regulation (EEC) 3893/88, Art 1, para 5).

[Article 15e

The provisions of Article 8 shall apply, *mutatis mutandis*.]

NOTES

Inserted by Commission Regulation (EEC) 3893/88, Art 1, para 5.

TITLE VI
COMMUNICATION OF INFORMATION TO THE COMMISSION AND THE MEMBER STATES

[Article 16

1. Each Member State shall send the Commission a list of the instruments, apparatus, spare parts, components, accessories and tools of which the price or the value for customs purposes exceeds ECU 5 000 and in respect of which it has authorised or refused admission free of import duties under Articles 7, 14 or 15c.

The list shall give the precise trade description of the goods referred to in the first subparagraph and the eight-figure combined nomenclature code. It shall also include the name of the manufacturer or manufacturers, the country or countries of origin and the price or customs value of the goods concerned.

2. The lists referred to in paragraph 1 shall be sent during the first and third quarters of each year and shall contain particulars of those goods whose admission free of import duties has been authorised or refused during the preceding six months.

3. The Commission shall forward these lists to the other Member States.]

NOTES

Substituted by Commission Regulation (EEC) 734/92, Art 1, para 11.

Article 17

NOTES

Repealed by Commission Regulation (EEC) 734/92, Art 1, para 15.

[Article 18

In order to ensure the uniform application of Community provisions, the lists referred to in Article 16 shall be examined periodically by the Committee on Duty Free Arrangements.]

NOTES

Substituted by Commission Regulation (EEC) 734/92, Art 1, para 12.

[TITLE VIA
SPECIFIC PROVISIONS RELATING TO THE ADMISSION FREE OF IMPORT DUTIES OF EQUIPMENT UNDER ARTICLES 59A AND 59B OF THE BASIC REGULATION

Article 18a

1. In order to obtain admission free of import duties of equipment under Articles 59a and 59b of the basic Regulation, the head of the scientific research establishment or organisation based outside the Community or his authorised representative shall submit an application to the competent authority of the Member State in which the scientific research establishment or organisation based in the Community is situated.

2. The application referred to in paragraph 1 shall contain the following information—

    (a)   a copy of the scientific cooperation agreement between research establishments situated in the Community and in third countries;

    [(b)   the precise trade description of the equipment as well as the quantity and value thereof and, where appropriate, its presumed classification in the combined nomenclature.]

(c)　　the country of origin and of consignment of the equipment;

(d)　　the place where the equipment is to be used;

(e)　　the use for which the equipment is intended and the duration of its use.]

NOTES

Inserted by Commission Regulation (EEC) No 1843/89, Art 1, para 3.

Para 2: sub-para (b) substituted by Commission Regulation (EEC) 734/92, Art 1, para 13.

[**Article 18b**

1. Where the competent authority of a Member State in which the establishment or organisation based in the Community is situated receives an application for the admission free of import duties of equipment as defined by Article 59a of the basic Regulation, the application and related information shall be sent to the Commission so that it can be examined within the Committee on Duty-Free Arrangements before a decision is taken by the said competent authority.

For the purposes of this examination, additional information shall be sent to the Commission on request.

2. The competent authority referred to in paragraph 1 shall inform the Commission of the decision it has taken concerning admission free of import duties.]

NOTES

Inserted by Commission Regulation (EEC) No 1843/89, Art 1, para 3.

[**Article 18c**

The provisions of Article 8 shall apply *mutatis mutandis*.]

NOTES

Substituted by Commission Regulation (EEC) 734/92, Art 1, para 14 (previously inserted by Commission Regulation (EEC) No 1843/89, Art 1, para 3).

TITLE VII
FINAL PROVISIONS

Article 19

(Repeals Commission Regulation (EEC) 2784/79.)

Article 20

This Regulation shall enter into force on 1 July 1984.

This Regulation shall be binding in its entirety and directly applicable in all Member States.

Done at Brussels, 29 July 1983.

Part III

COUNCIL REGULATION

(2658/87/EEC)

of 23 July 1987

on the tariff and statistical nomenclature and on the Common Customs Tariff

NOTES

Date of publication in OJ: OJ L 256, 7.9.87, p 1.

THE COUNCIL OF THE EUROPEAN COMMUNITIES,

[Having regard to the Treaty establishing the European Economic Community, and in particular Articles 28, 43 and 113 thereof,]

Having regard to the Act of Accession of Spain and Portugal,

Having regard to the proposal from the Commission,[1]

Having regard to the opinion of the European Parliament,[2]

Having regard to the opinion of the Economic and Social Committee,[3]

Whereas the European Economic Community is based on a customs union involving the use of a common customs tariff;

Whereas the collection and exchange of data on the statistics of external trade of the Community can best be achieved through the use of a combined nomenclature replacing the existing Common Customs Tariff and Nimexe nomenclatures, in order to meet tariff and statistical requirements simultaneously;

Whereas the Community is a signatory to the International Convention on the Harmonised Commodity Description and Coding System, known as the 'harmonised system', which is intended to replace the Convention of 15 December 1950 on Nomenclature for the Classification of Goods in Customs Tariffs;

Whereas, as a consequence, the said combined nomenclature must be established on the basis of the harmonised system;

Whereas it is appropriate to allow Member States to create national statistical subdivisions;

Whereas certain specific Community measures cannot be dealt with in the framework of the combined nomenclature; whereas it is therefore necessary to create additional Community subdivisions and to include them in an integrated tariff of the European Communities (Taric); whereas the efficient management of the Taric requires a system for immediate updating; whereas it is therefore necessary that the Commission should be empowered to manage the Taric;

Whereas Spain and Portugal will not be able to use the Taric layout in the same manner as the other Member States because of the transitional tariff arrangements provided for in the Act of Accession; whereas it is appropriate that these two Member States should be authorised not to apply the Taric for the periods during which the transitional arrangements apply;

Whereas it appears appropriate that Member States should be able to insert further subdivisions after the Taric subheadings in order to meet additional national requirements; whereas these subdivisions should be identified by appropriate code numbers in accordance with the provisions of Commission Regulation (EEC) No 2793/86 of 22 July 1986 laying down the codes to be used in the forms laid down in Regulations (EEC) No 678/85, (EEC) No 1900/85 and (EEC) No 222/77;[4]

Whereas it is essential that the combined nomenclature and any other nomenclature wholly or partly based on it, or which adds subdivisions to it, should be applied in a uniform manner by all the Member States; whereas provisions to this effect must be able to be adopted at Community level; whereas, furthermore, the Community provisions ensuring uniform application of the nomenclature of the Common Customs Tariff contained in Decision 86/98/ECSC([5]) are applicable to products falling within the province of the Treaty establishing the European Coal and Steel Community;

Whereas the preparation and application of these provisions requires close cooperation between the Member States and the Commission; whereas the implementation of these provisions must be carried out rapidly in view of the serious economic consequences that any delay might entail;

Whereas, in order to ensure uniform application of the combined nomenclature, it is necessary for the Commission to be assisted by a committee responsible for all questions relating to the combined nomenclature, to the Taric and to all other nomenclatures based on the combined nomenclature; whereas this Committee must be operational as soon as possible prior to the date of application of the combined nomenclature;

Whereas, in order to define the scope of the combined nomenclature, it is desirable to lay down preliminary provisions, additional section and chapter notes and suitable footnotes;

Whereas the Common Customs Tariff consists not only of the conventional and autonomous duties and other relevant charges fixed in Annex I to this Regulation on the basis of the combined nomenclature, but also of the tariff measures contained in the Taric and other Community legislation;

Whereas in fixing the conventional rates of duty it is appropriate to take account of GATT (General Agreement on Tariffs and Trade) negotiations;

Whereas the transition from the former nomenclature to the combined nomenclature may involve difficulties with the application of origin rules in respect of certain preference systems, in particular where the third country involved has not adopted the harmonised system; whereas it is appropriate in these circumstances to provide for suitable measures intended to remedy these difficulties;

Whereas, although the nomenclature and the rates of customs duties relating to products covered by the Treaty establishing the European Coal and Steel Community do not form part of the Common Customs Tariff, it is nevertheless appropriate to include the conventional rates for these products for information in this Regulation;

Whereas, following the setting-up of the combined nomenclature, numerous Community acts in particular in the field of the common agricultural policy must be adapted to take into account the use of this nomenclature; whereas these adaptations do not as a general rule call for any amendment of substance; whereas for purposes of simplification it is appropriate to. enable the Commission to adopt the necessary technical amendments to the acts in question;

Whereas the entry into force of this Regulation involves the repeal of Council Regulation (EEC) No 950/68 of 28 June 1968 on the Common Customs Tariff[6] and of Council Regulation (EEC) No 97/69 of 16 January 1969 on measures to be taken for the uniform application of the nomenclature of the Common Customs Tariff,[7] as last amended by Regulation (EEC) No 2055/84,[8]

NOTES

Words in square brackets substituted by Council Regulation (EEC) 3528/89, Art 1.

HAS ADOPTED THIS REGULATION—

Article 1

[1. A goods nomenclature, hereinafter called the "Combined Nomenclature", or in abbreviated form "CN", which meets at one and the same time, the requirements of the Common Customs Tariff, the external trade statistics of the Community and other Community policies concerning the importation or exportation of goods shall be established by the Commission.]

2. The combined nomenclature shall comprise—
  (a)   the harmonised system nomenclature;
  (b)   Community subdivisions to that nomenclature, referred to as 'CN subheadings' in those cases where a corresponding rate of duty is specified;
  (c)   preliminary provisions, additional section or chapter notes and footnotes relating to CN subheadings.

[3. The Combined Nomenclature is reproduced in Annex I. The rates of duty of the Common Customs Tariff and, where applicable, the supplementary statistical units as well as other necessary information are laid down in the said Annex.

The Annex comprises the conventional rates of duty.

However, whenever autonomous rates of duty are lower than the conventional rates of duty or where conventional rates of duty do not apply, the autonomous rates are also shown in the said Annex.]

NOTES

Paras 1, 3: substituted by Council Regulation (EC) 254/2000, Art 1, paras 1, 2.

[Article 2

An Integrated Tariff of the European Communities, hereinafter referred to as the "Taric", which meets the requirements of the Common Customs Tariff, external trade statistics, the commercial, agricultural and other Community policies concerning the importation or exportation of goods, shall be established by the Commission.

The tariff shall be based on the Combined Nomenclature and include—
  (a)   the measures contained in this Regulation;
  (b)   the additional Community subdivisions, referred to as "Taric subheadings", which are needed for the implementation of specific Community measures listed in Annex II;
  (c)   any other information necessary for the implementation or management of the Taric codes and additional codes as defined in Article 3(2)and (3);
  (d)   the rates of customs duty and other import and export charges, including duty exemptions and preferential tariff rates applicable to specific goods on importation or exportation;
  (e)   measures shown in Annex II applicable on the importation and exportation of specific goods.]

NOTES

Substituted by Council Regulation (EC) 254/2000, Art 1, para 3.

Article 3

1. Each CN subheading shall have an eight digit code number—

(a)   the first six digits shall be the code numbers relating to the headings and subheadings of the harmonised system nomenclature;

(b)   the seventh and eighth digits shall identify the CN subheadings. When a heading or subheading of the harmonised system is not further subdivided for Community purposes, the seventh and eighth digits shall be '00'.

[2. The Taric subheadings shall be identified by the 9th and 10th digits which, together with the code numbers referred to in paragraph 1, form the Taric code numbers. In the absence of a Community subdivision, the 9th and 10th digits shall be "00".

3. Exceptionally, additional Taric codes of four characters may be used for the application of specific Community measures which are not coded, or not entirely coded, at the 9th and 10th digit level.]

NOTES

Paras 2, 3: substituted for original paras 2–4 by Council Regulation 1969/93 of 19 July 1993, Art 1(a).

Article 4

NOTES

Repealed by Council Regulation (EC) 254/2000, Art 1, para 4.

[Article 5

1. The Taric shall be used by the Commission and the Member States for the application of Community measures concerning importation into and exportation from the Community.

2. Taric codes and Taric additional codes shall be applied to the importation and, where applicable, to the exportation of goods covered by the corresponding subheadings.

3. Member States may add subdivisions or additional codes for national purposes. Identifying codes shall be assigned to such subdivisions or additional codes in accordance with Regulation (EEC) No 2454/93.]

NOTES

Substituted by Council Regulation (EC) 254/2000, Art 1, para 5.

[Article 6

The Taric shall be established, updated, managed and disseminated by the Commission, which shall, wherever possible, use computerised means. The Commission shall, in particular, take the necessary steps to—

(a)   integrate all measures contained in this Regulation or shown in Annex II thereto into the Taric,

(b)   attribute Taric codes and Taric additional codes,

(c)   update the Taric immediately,

(d)   disseminate in electronic format changes to the Taric immediately.]

NOTES

Substituted by Council Regulation (EC) 254/2000, Art 1, para 6.

Article 7

NOTES

Repealed by Council Regulation 2913/92 of 12 October 1992, Art 252(c).

Article 8

The committee [provided for in Article 247 of the Community Customs Code] may examine any matter referred to it by its chairman, either on his own initiative or at the request of a representative of a Member State

    (a)   concerning the combined nomenclature;

    (b)   concerning the Taric nomenclature and any other nomenclature which is wholly or partly based on the combined nomenclature or which adds any subdivisions to it, and which is established by specific Community provisions with a view to the application of tariff or other measures relating to trade in goods.

NOTES

Words in square brackets inserted by Council Regulation 2913/92 of 12 October 1992, Art 252(c).

Article 9

1.   Measures relating to the matters set out below shall be adopted in accordance with the procedure defined in Article 10—

    [(a)   application of the Combined Nomenclature and the Taric, concerning in particular—

        —   the classification of goods in the nomenclatures referred to in Article 8;

        —   explanatory notes;

        —   the creation, if necessary, and for the purpose of responding to the Community's own needs, of statistical subheadings in the Taric, when to do so appears more appropriate than in the CN;]

    (b)   amendments to the combined nomenclature to take account of changes in requirements relating to statistics or to commercial policy;

    (c)   amendments to Annex II;

    (d)   amendments to the combined nomenclature and adjustments to duties in accordance with decisions adopted by the Council or the Commission;

    (e)   amendments to the combined nomenclature intended to adapt it to take account of technological or commercial developments or aimed at the alignment or clarification of texts;

    (f)   amendments to the combined nomenclature resulting from changes to the harmonised system nomenclature;

    [(g)   questions relating to the application, functioning and management of the harmonised system to be discussed within the Customs Cooperation Council, as well as their implementation by the Community.]

[2. The provisions adopted under paragraph 1 shall not amend—
— the rates of customs duties;
— agricultural duties, refunds or other amounts applicable within the framework of the common agricultural policy or within that of specific schemes applicable to certain goods resulting from the processing of agricultural products;
— quantitative restrictions laid down under Community provisions;
— nomenclatures adopted within the framework of the common agricultural policy.]

3. If necessary, amendments to CN subheadings shall be immediately included as Taric subheadings. They shall only be included in the CN under the conditions referred to in Article 12.

NOTES

Para 1: sub-paras (a), (g) substituted by Council Regulation (EC) 254/2000, Art 1, paras 7, 8.

Para 2: substituted by Council Regulation (EC) 254/2000, Art 1, para 9.

[Article 10

1. The Commission shall be assisted by the Customs Code Committee set up by Article 247 of Regulation (EEC) No 2913/92.[1]

2. Where reference is made to this paragraph, Articles 4 and 7 of Decision 1999/468/EC[2] shall apply.

The period laid down in Article 4(3) of Decision 1999/468/EC shall be set at three months.]

NOTES

Substituted by Council Regulation (EC) 254/2000, Art 1, para 10.

[1] OJ L 302, 19.10.92, p 1. Regulation as last amended by Regulation (EC) No 955/1999 (OJ L 119, 7.5.99, p 1).

[2] OJ L 184, 17.7.99, p 23.]

Article 11

NOTES

Repealed by Council Regulation 2913/92 of 12 October 1992, Art 252(c).

[Article 12

1. The Commission shall adopt each year, a regulation reproducing the complete version of the Combined Nomenclature, together with the rates of duty in accordance with Article 1, as resulting from measures adopted by the Council or the Commission. The said Regulation shall be published not later than 31 October in the *Official Journal of the European Communities* and it shall apply from 1 January of the following year.

2. Measures and information concerning the Common Customs Tariff or Taric shall, whenever possible, be disseminated in electronic format by using computerised means.

3. In order to ensure the uniform application of the Common Customs Tariff and the Taric, the Commission shall promote coordination and harmonisation of practices in Member States' customs laboratories, using wherever possible, computerised means.]

NOTES

Substituted by Council Regulation (EC) 254/2000, Art 1, para 11.

Article 13

. . . . .

NOTES

(Repealed by Council Regulation (EC) 254/2000, Art 1, para 12.)

Article 14

Where a tariff preference is granted on the basis of rules of origin derived from the nomenclature of the Customs Cooperation Council in force on 31 December 1987, those rules shall remain applicable in accordance with the Community acts in force on that date.

Article 15

1. The codes and the descriptions of goods established on the basis of the combined nomenclature shall replace those established on the basis of the nomenclatures of the Common Customs Tariff and the Nimexe, without prejudice to international agreements concluded by the Community before the entry into force of this Regulation, and to acts taken in implementation thereof, which refer to the said nomenclatures.

Community acts which include the tariff or statistical nomenclature shall be amended accordingly by the Commission.

2. References to the Nimexe in the various Community acts in force shall be deemed to refer to the combined nomenclature.

Article 16

NOTES

Repeals Council Regulation (EEC) No 950/68 and (EEC) No 97/69.

Article 17

This Regulation shall enter into force on the third day following its publication in the Official Journal of the European Communities.

Articles 1 to 5 and 12 to 16 shall not apply until 1 January 1988.

This Regulation shall be binding in its entirety and directly applicable in all Member States.

Done at Brussels, 23 July 1987.

[ANNEX I
COMBINED NOMENCLATURE

[PART ONE
PRELIMINARY PROVISIONS

SECTION I
GENERAL RULES

A.
General rules for the interpretation of the Combined Nomenclature

Classification of goods in the Combined Nomenclature shall be governed by the following principles:

1. The titles of sections, chapters and sub-chapters are provided for ease of reference only; for legal purposes, classification shall be determined according to the terms of the headings and any relative section or chapter notes and, provided such headings or notes do not otherwise require, according to the following provisions.

2. (a) Any reference in a heading to an article shall be taken to include a reference to that article incomplete or unfinished, provided that, as presented, the incomplete or unfinished article has the essential character of the complete or finished article. It shall also be taken to include a reference to that article complete or finished (or falling to be classified as complete or finished by virtue of this rule), presented unassembled or disassembled.

   (b)   Any reference in a heading to a material or substance shall be taken to include a reference to mixtures or combinations of that material or substance with other materials or substances. Any reference to goods of a given material or substance shall be taken to include a reference to goods consisting wholly or partly of such material or substance. The classification of goods consisting of more than one material or substance shall be according to the principles of rule 3.

3. When, by application of rule 2(b) or for any other reason, goods are prima facie classifiable under two or more headings, classification shall be effected as follows:

   (a)   the heading which provides the most specific description shall be preferred to headings providing a more general description. However, when two or more headings each refer to part only of the materials or substances contained in mixed or composite goods or to part only of the items in a set put up for retail sale, those headings are to be regarded as equally specific in relation to those goods, even if one of them gives a more complete or precise description of the goods;

   (b)   mixtures, composite goods consisting of different materials or made up of different components, and goods put up in sets for retail sale, which cannot be classified by reference to 3(a), shall be classified as if they consisted of the material or component which gives them their essential character, in so far as this criterion is applicable;

   (c)   when goods cannot be classified by reference to 3(a) or (b), they shall be classified under the heading which occurs last in numerical order among those which equally merit consideration.

4. Goods which cannot be classified in accordance with the above rules shall be classified under the heading appropriate to the goods to which they are most akin.

5. In addition to the foregoing provisions, the following rules shall apply in respect of the goods referred to therein:

   (a)   camera cases, musical instrument cases, gun cases, drawing-instrument cases, necklace cases and similar containers, specially shaped or fitted to contain a specific article or set of articles, suitable for long-term use and presented with the articles for which they are intended, shall be classified with such articles when of a kind normally sold therewith. This rule does not, however, apply to containers which give the whole its essential character;

(b)   subject to the provisions of rule 5(a), packing materials and packing containers [1] presented with the goods therein shall be classified with the goods if they are of a kind normally used for packing such goods. However, this provision is not binding when such packing materials or packing containers are clearly suitable for repetitive use.

6.   For legal purposes, the classification of goods in the subheadings of a heading shall be determined according to the terms of those subheadings and any related subheading notes and, *mutatis mutandis*, to the above rules, on the understanding that only subheadings at the same level are comparable. For the purposes of this rule, the relative section and chapter notes also apply, unless the context requires otherwise.

B.
General rules concerning duties

1.   The customs duties applicable to imported goods originating in countries which are Contracting Parties to the General Agreement on Tariffs and Trade or with which the European Community has concluded agreements containing the most-favoured-nation tariff clause shall be the conventional duties shown in column 3 of the schedule of duties. Unless the context requires otherwise, these conventional duties are applicable to goods, other than those referred to above, imported from any third country.

The conventional rates of duty reproduced in column 3 are applicable from 1 January 2007.

When autonomous rates of duty are lower than the conventional rates of duty, the autonomous duties, shown by means of a footnote, are applicable.

2.   Paragraph 1 shall not apply where special autonomous customs duties are provided for in respect of goods originating in certain countries or where preferential customs duties are applicable in pursuance of agreements.

3.   Paragraphs 1 and 2 shall not preclude the Member States from applying customs duties other than those of the Common Customs Tariff where the application of such other duties is justified by Community law.

4.   The duties expressed as percentage rates are ad valorem duties.

5.   The symbol "EA" indicates that the goods concerned are chargeable with an "agricultural component" fixed in accordance with Annex 1.

6.   The symbol "AD S/Z" or "AD F/M" in Chapters 17 to 19 indicates that the maximum rate of duty consists of an ad valorem duty plus an additional duty for certain forms of sugar or for flour. This additional duty is fixed in accordance with the provisions of Annex 1.

7.   In Chapter 22, the symbol " EUR /% vol/hl" means that a specific duty, expressed in euro, is to be calculated for each percentage volume of alcohol per hectolitre. Thus, a beverage having an alcohol content by volume of 40 % is to be charged as follows:

—   " EUR 1/% vol/hl" = EUR 1 × 40, giving a duty of EUR 40 per hectolitre, or

—   " EUR 1/% vol/hl + EUR 5/hl" = EUR 1 × 40 plus EUR 5, giving a duty of EUR 45 per hectolitre.

Where, in addition, a minimum (MIN) value is shown, for example " EUR 1,6/% vol/ hl MIN EUR 9/hl", it means that the duty, calculated on the basis of the abovementioned rule, is to be compared with the minimum duty, for example " EUR 9/ hl", and the higher of the two is to be applied.

C.
General rules applicable both to nomenclature and to duties

1.   Unless provided otherwise, the provisions relating to customs value shall be applied to determine, in addition to the value for the assessment of ad valorem customs duties, the values by reference to which the scope of certain headings or subheadings is defined.

2.   The dutiable weight, in the case of goods chargeable by weight, and the weights by reference to which the scope of certain headings or subheadings is defined, shall be taken to be:

(a)   in the case of a reference to "gross weight", the aggregate weight of the goods and of all the packing materials and packing containers;

(b)   in the case of a reference to "net weight" or simply to "weight" without qualification, the weight of the goods themselves without packing materials and packing containers of any kind.

3.   The equivalent in national currencies of the euro, for Member States other than participating Member States as defined in Council Regulation (EC) No 974/98 [2] (hereafter called "non-participating Member States"), shall be fixed in accordance with Article 18 of Council Regulation (EEC) No 2913/92 [3].

4.   Goods eligible for favourable tariff treatment by reason of their end-use: Where the import duty applicable under the end-use arrangements to goods for a specific end-use is not lower than that which would otherwise be applicable to the goods, the said goods shall be classified in the code referring to the end-use and Articles 291 to 300 of Regulation (EEC) No 2454/93 (OJ L 253, 11.10.1993) shall not apply.

SPECIAL PROVISIONS

A.
Goods for certain categories of ships, boats and other vessels and for drilling or production platforms

1.   Customs duties shall be suspended in respect of goods intended for incorporation in the ships, boats or other vessels listed in the following schedule, for the purposes of their construction, repair, maintenance or conversion, and in respect of goods intended for fitting to or equipping such ships, boats or other vessels.

2.   Customs duties shall be suspended in respect of:

(a)   goods intended for incorporation in drilling or production platforms:

   (1)   fixed, of subheading ex843049, operating in or outside the territorial sea of Member States, or

   (2)   floating or submersible, of subheading 890520, for the purposes of their construction, repair, maintenance or conversion, and in respect of goods intended for equipping the said platforms. Those goods such as motor fuel, lubricants and gas, which are necessary for the operation of machines and apparatus which do not affect permanently, and are not integral parts of the platforms and which are used on board for the construction, repair, maintenance, conversion or equipping of these platforms are regarded also as being used for incorporation in drilling or production platforms;

(b)   tubes, pipes, cables and their connection pieces, linking these drilling or production platforms to the mainland.

CN code	Description
8901	Cruise ships, excursion boats, ferry-boats, cargo ships, barges and similar vessels for the transport of persons or goods
890110	– Cruise ships, excursion boats and similar vessels principally designed for the transport of persons; ferry-boats of all kinds
89011010	– – Seagoing
890120	– Tankers
89012010	– – Seagoing
890130	– Refrigerated vessels, other than those of subheading 890120
89013010	– – Seagoing
890190	– Other vessels for the transport of goods and other vessels for the transport of both persons and goods
89019010	– – Seagoing
890200	Fishing vessels; factory ships and other vessels for processing or preserving fishery products
	– Seagoing
89020012	– – Of a gross tonnage exceeding 250
89020018	– – Of a gross tonnage not exceeding 250
8903	Yachts and other vessels for pleasure or sports; rowing boats and canoes
	– Other
890391	– – Sailboats, with or without auxiliary motor
89039110	– – – Seagoing
890392	– – Motorboats, other than outboard motorboats
89039210	– – – Seagoing
890400	Tugs and pusher craft
89040010	– Tugs
	– Pusher craft
89040091	– – Seagoing
8905	Light-vessels, fire-floats, dredgers, floating cranes, and other vessels the navigability of which is subsidiary to their main function; floating docks; floating or submersible drilling or production platforms
890510	– Dredgers
89051010	– – Seagoing
890590	– Other
89059010	– – Seagoing
8906	Other vessels, including warships and lifeboats other than rowing boats
89061000	– Warships
	– Other
89069010	– – Seagoing

3. The suspensions shall be subject to conditions laid down in the relevant Community provisions with a view to customs control of the use of such goods.

B.
Civil aircraft and goods for use in civil aircraft

1. Relief from customs duty is provided for:
    –   civil aircraft,
    –   certain goods for use in civil aircraft and for incorporation therein in the course of their manufacture, repair, maintenance, rebuilding, modification or conversion,
    –   ground flying-trainers and their parts, for civil use. These goods are covered by headings and subheadings listed in tables in paragraph 5.

2. For the purposes of paragraph 1, first and second indent, "civil aircraft" means aircraft other than aircraft used in military or similar services in the Member States which carry a military or non-civil registration.

3. For the purposes of paragraph 1, second indent, the expression "for use in civil aircraft" shall include goods for use in ground flying trainers for civil use.

4. The relief from customs duties shall be subject to the conditions laid down in the relevant Community provisions with a view to customs control of the use of such goods (see Articles 291 to 300 of Commission Regulation (EEC) No 2454/93 (OJ L 253, 11.10.1993, p. 1) and subsequent amendments).

5. Goods eligible to this relief of customs duties are covered by the following headings or subheadings:
391740, 401130, 401213, 401220, 681299, 732410, 732620, 830210, 830220, 830242, 830249, 830260, 840710, 840890, 840910, 8411, 841210, 841221, 841229, 841231, 841239, 84128080, 841290, 841319, 841320, 841330, 841350, 841360, 841370, 841381, 841391, 841410, 841420, 841430, 841451, 841459, 841480, 841490, 841581, 841582, 841583, 841810, 841830, 841840, 841861, 841869, 841950, 841981, 842119, 842121, 842123, 842129, 842131, 842139, 842410, 842511, 842519, 842531, 842539, 842542, 842549, 842699, 842810, 842820, 842833, 842839, 842890, 84433210, 847141, 847149, 847150, 847160, 847170, 847990, 848310, 848330, 848340, 848350, 848360, 848390, 848410, 848490, 850132, 850152, 850161, 850162, 850163, 8502, 850410, 850431, 850432, 850433, 850440, 850450, 8507, 851110, 851120, 851130, 851140, 851150, 851180, 85177011, 85177015, 85177019, 851810, 851821, 851822, 851829, 851830, 851840, 851850, 85198195, 85198990, 852110, 8526, 852841, 852851, 852861, 852910, 85311095, 853120, 853180, 853910, 854430, 8801, 880211, 880212, 880220, 880230, 880240, 880310, 880320, 880330, 880529, 900190, 900290, 901410, 901420, 9025, 9026, 90292038, 903010, 903020, 903031, 903032, 903033, 903039, 903040, 903084, 903089, 903090, 903180, 9032, 9104, 940320, 940370.
For the following subheadings, the relief of customs duties for use in civil aircraft is only granted to the goods described in column 2:

Subheading	Description
3917 21 90, 3917 22 90, 3917 23 90, 3917 29 90, 3917 31, 3917 33, 3917 39 90, 7413 00, 8307 10, 8307 90	With fittings attached
400829	Profile shapes, cut to size
400912, 400922, 400932, 400942	Suitable for conducting gases or liquids

Subheading	Description
392690, 401610, 401693, 401699	For technical uses
450490, 482390	Gaskets, washers and other seals
681280	Other than clothing, clothing accessories, footwear, headgear, paper, millboard, felt or compressed asbestos fibre jointing, in sheets or rolls
681320	With a basis of asbestos or of other mineral substances
700721	Windshields, not framed
731210, 731290	With fittings attached, or made up into articles
732290	Air heaters and hot-air distributors (excluding parts thereof)
732490	Sanitary ware (excluding parts thereof)
730431, 730439, 730441, 730449, 730451, 730459, 730490, 730630, 730640, 730650, 730661, 730669, 760810, 760820	With fittings attached, suitable for conducting gases or liquids
810890	Tubes and pipes, with fittings attached, suitable for conducting gases or liquids
841590	Of air-conditioning machines of subheading 841581, 841582 or 841583
841990	Parts of heat exchange units
847989	Hydropneumatic batteries; mechanical actuators for thrust reversers; toilet units specially designed; air humidifiers and dehumidifiers; servomechanisms, non-electric; non-electric starter motors; pneumatic starters for turbojets, turbopropellers and other gas turbines; windscreen wipers, non-electric; propeller regulators, non-electric
850120, 850140	Of an output exceeding 735 W but not exceeding 150 kW
850131	Of an output exceeding 735 W, DC generators
850133	Motors of an output not exceeding 150 kW and generators
85013492, 85013498	Generators
850151	Of an output exceeding 735 W
850153	Of an output not exceeding 150 kW
85168020	Assembled only with a simple insulated former and electrical connections, used for anti-icing or de-icing
85176931, 85176939	For radio-telephony or radio-telegraphy
851712, 851761, 851762, 85176990	Radio-telegraphic or radio-telephonic apparatus
852290	Assemblies and sub-assemblies consisting of two or more parts or pieces fastened or joined together, for apparatus of subheading 852090
852990	Assemblies and sub-assemblies consisting of two or more parts or pieces fastened or joined together, for apparatus of heading 8526
85437090	Flight recorders, electric synchros and transducers, defrosters and demisters with electric resistors

Subheading	Description
854390	Assemblies and sub-assemblies consisting of two or more parts or pieces fastened or joined together, for flight recorders
88039090	Including gliders
901490	Of instruments of subheadings 901410 or 901420
902000	Excluding parts
902910	Electric or electronic revolution counters
902990	Of revolution counters, speed indicators and tachometers
903190	Of subheading 903180
910919, 910990	Of a width or diameter not exceeding 50 mm
940110	Not leather covered
940560	Of base metal or of plastics
940592, 940599	Of the articles of subheading 940510 or 940560

6. The goods as mentioned in paragraph 5 are integrated in TARIC by subheadings with a footnote reference in the following terms "Entry under this subheading is subject to the conditions laid down in the relevant Community provisions (see Articles 291 to 300 of Commission Regulation (EEC) No 2454/93 (OJ L 253, 11.10.1993, p. 1) and subsequent amendments)".

C.
Pharmaceutical products

1. Relief from customs duty is provided for pharmaceutical products of the following categories:

(1) pharmaceutical substances which are covered by the CAS RN (chemical abstracts service registry numbers) and the international non-proprietary names (INNs) listed in Annex 3;

(2) salts, esters and hydrates of INNs which are described by combining INNs of Annex 3 with prefixes or suffixes of Annex 4, provided such products are classifiable in the same 6-digit HS-subheadings as the relevant INN;

(3) salts, esters and hydrates of INNs which are listed in Annex 5 and which are not classifiable in the same 6-digit HS-subheadings as the corresponding INNs;

(4) pharmaceutical intermediates, i.e. compounds used in the manufacture of finished pharmaceutical products which are covered by the CAS RN and the chemical names, listed in Annex 6.

2. Special cases:

(1) INNs cover only those substances described in the lists of recommended and proposed INNs published by the World Health Organisation (WHO). Where the number of substances covered by an INN is less than that covered by the CAS RN, only those substances covered by the INN will be subject to duty-free treatment;

(2) where a product of Annex 3 or Annex 6 is identified by a CAS RN corresponding to a specific isomer, only that isomer may qualify for duty-free treatment;

(3) double derivatives (salts, esters and hydrates) of INNs identified by a combination of an INN of Annex 3 with a prefix or suffix of Annex 4 qualify for duty-free treatment, provided they are classifiable in the same 6-digit HS-subheading as the relevant INN: example: alanine methyl ester, hydrochloride;

1231

(4)   where an INN of Annex 3 is a salt (or an ester), no other salt (or ester) of the acid corresponding to the INN may qualify for duty-free treatment: example: oxprenoate potassium (INN): duty-free oxprenoate sodium: not duty-free.

D.
Standard rate of duty

1.   Customs duty shall be charged at the flat rate of 3,5 % ad valorem on goods:
-      contained in consignments sent by one private individual to another, or
-      contained in travellers' personal luggage,

provided that such importations are not of a commercial nature.

This flat-rate 3,5 % customs duty shall apply, provided that the value of the goods subject to import duty does not exceed EUR 350 per consignment or per traveller.

Such flat-rate assessment shall not apply to goods of Chapter 24 which are contained in a consignment or in travellers' personal luggage in amounts exceeding those laid down in Article 31 or in Article 46 of Council Regulation (EEC) No 918/83 [OJ L 105, 23.4.83, p1].

2.   Importations shall be treated as not being of a commercial nature if:
   (a)   in the case of goods contained in consignments sent by one private individual to another, such consignments:
-      are of an occasional nature,
-      contain goods exclusively for the personal use of the consignee or his family, which do not by their nature or quantity reflect any commercial interest,
-      are sent to the consignee by the consignor free of payment of any kind;
   (b)   in the case of goods contained in travellers' personal luggage, they:
-      are of an occasional nature, and
-      consist exclusively of goods for the personal use of the travellers or their families, or of goods intended as presents; the nature and quantity of such goods must not be such as might indicate that they are being imported for commercial reasons.

3.   The flat rate of customs duty shall not apply to goods imported under the conditions set out in paragraphs 1 and 2 if the person entitled has, before the said flat rate is applied to them, requested that they be subject to the customs duties appropriate to them. All the goods making up the consignment shall then be subject to the import duties which are appropriate to them, without prejudice to the duty-free admission provided for pursuant to Articles 29 to 31 and 45 to 49 of Regulation (EEC) No 918/83.

For the purposes of the first subparagraph, import duties shall mean both customs duties and charges having equivalent effect and other import charges provided for under the common agricultural policy or under specific arrangements applicable to certain goods resulting from the processing of agricultural products.

4.   Non-participating Member States may round off the amount in national currencies resulting from the conversion of the sum of EUR 350.

5.   Non-participating Member States may maintain unchanged the equivalent in national currency of the sum of EUR 350 if, at the time of the annual adjustment provided for in Article 18(2) of Regulation (EEC) No 2913/92 the conversion of this amount, before the rounding off provided for in paragraph 4, results in a change of less than 5 % in the equivalent in national currency, or in a reduction thereof.

E.
Containers and packing materials

The following provisions are applicable to the containers and packing materials referred to in general interpretative rule 5(a) and (b) and put into free circulation at the same time as the goods which they contain or with which they are presented.

1. When the containers and packing materials are classified with the goods in accordance with the provisions of general interpretative rule 5, they shall be:

(a)　chargeable at the same rate of customs duty as the goods:

–　where such goods are subject to an ad valorem customs duty, or

–　where they are to be included in the dutiable weight of the goods;

(b)　admitted free of customs duties:

–　where the goods are free of customs duty, or

–　where the goods are dutiable otherwise than by reference to weight or value, or

–　where the weight of the containers and packing materials is not to be included in the dutiable weight of the goods.

2. Where containers and packing materials covered by the provisions of paragraph 1(a) and (b) contain or are presented with goods of several different tariff descriptions, the weight and value of the containers and packing materials shall, for the purpose of determining their dutiable weight or value, be apportioned among all the goods contained, in proportion to the weight or value of those goods.

F.
Favourable tariff treatment by reason of the nature of the goods

1. Under certain conditions, favourable tariff treatment by reason of the nature of the goods is provided for:

–　goods unfit for consumption,

–　seeds,

–　bolting cloth, not made up,

–　certain types of fresh table grapes, tobacco and nitrate.

These goods are covered by subheadings[1] with a footnote reference in the following terms: "Entry under this subheading is subject to the conditions laid down in section II, paragraph F, of the preliminary provisions."

2. Goods unfit for consumption for which favourable tariff treatment is granted by reason of their nature are listed in Annex 8 by reference to the heading under which they are classified together with the description and the quantities of the denaturants used. Such goods are presumed to be unfit for consumption when the goods to be denatured and the denaturants are homogeneously mixed and their separation is economically not viable.

3. The goods listed below shall be classified in the appropriate headings for seed or for sowing, provided that the goods comply with the relevant Community provisions:

– for sweetcorn, spelt, hybrid maize, rice and sorghum (Council Directive 66/402/EEC[2]),

– for seed potatoes (Council Directive 2002/56/EC of 13 June 2002[3]),

– for oil seeds and oleaginous fruits (Council Directive 2002/57/EC of 13 June 2002[4]).

When hybrid sweetcorn, spelt, hybrid maize, rice, hybrid sorghum or oil seeds and oleaginous fruits are of a kind to which the agricultural provisions do not apply, favourable tariff treatment by reason of their nature shall be granted, provided that it is established that the goods are actually intended for sowing.

Part III

4. Bolting cloth, not made up, is granted favourable tariff treatment on the condition that the goods are indelibly marked in a way identifying them as being intended for bolting or similar industrial purposes.

5. Fresh table grapes, tobacco and nitrate are granted favourable tariff treatment on production of a duly endorsed certificate. The particular provisions to be applied and the model of the certificates are set out at Annex 9.

---

[1] The subheadings concerned are: 0408 11 20, 0408 19 20, 0408 91 20, 0408 99 20, 0701 10 00, 0712 90 11, 0806 10 10, 1001 90 10, 1005 10 11, 1005 10 13, 1005 10 15, 1005 10 19, 1006 10 10, 1007 00 10, 1106 20 10, 1201 00 10, 1202 10 10, 1204 00 10, 1205 10 10, 1206 00 10, 1207 20 10, 1207 40 10, 1207 50 10, 1207 91 10, 1207 99 15, 2401 10 10, 2401 10 20, 2401 10 30, 2401 10 41, 2401 10 49, 2401 20 10, 2401 20 20, 2401 20 30, 2401 20 41, 2401 20 49, 2501 00 51, 3102 50 10, 3105 90 10, 3502 11 10, 3502 19 10, 3502 20 10, 3502 90 20, 5911 20 00.

[2] OJ 125, 11.7.1966, p. 2309/66. Directive as last amended by Commission Directive 2006/55/EC (OJ L 159, 13.6.2006, p. 13).

[3] OJ L 193, 20.7.2002, p. 60. Directive as last amended by Commission Decision 2005/908/EC (OJ L 329, 16.12.2005, p. 37).

[4] OJ L 193, 20.7.2002, p. 74. Directive as last amended by Council Directive 2004/117/EC (OJ L 14, 18.1.2005, p. 18).

SIGNS, ABBREVIATIONS AND SYMBOLS

★	Refers to new code numbers
▬	Refers to code numbers used the previous year but with differing coverage
AD F/M	Additional duty on flour
AD S/Z	Additional duty on sugar
b/f	Bottle flask
cm/s	Centimetre(s) per second
EA	Agricultural component
€	Euro
INN	International non-proprietary name
INNM	International non-proprietary name modified
ISO	International Organisation for Standardisation
Kbit	1024 bits
kg/br	Kilogram, gross
kg/net	Kilogram, net
kg/net eda	Kilogram drained net weight
kg/net mas	Kilogram net, of dry matter
MAX	Maximum
Mbit	1048576 bits
MIN	Minimum
ml/g	Millilitre(s) per gram
mm/s	Millimetre(s) per second

RON   Research octane number

NOTE:

A heading number placed between square brackets in column 1 of the schedule of customs duties indicates that the heading has been deleted (for example, heading [1519]).

SUPPLEMENTARY UNITS

c/k	Carats (1 metric carat = 2×10^{-4} kg)
ce/el	Number of cells
ct/l	Carrying capacity in tonnes
g	Gram
gi F/S	Gram of fissile isotopes
GT	Gross tonnage
kg $C_5H_{14}ClNO$	Kilogram of choline chloride
kg H_2O_2	Kilogram of hydrogen peroxide
kg K_2O	Kilogram of potassium oxide
kg KOH	Kilogram of potassium hydroxide (caustic potash)
kg met.am.	Kilogram of methylamines
kg N	Kilogram of nitrogen
kg NaOH	Kilogram of sodium hydroxide (caustic soda)
kg/net eda	Kilogram drained net weight
kg P_2O_5	Kilogram of diphosphorus pentaoxide
kg 90 % sdt	Kilogram of substance 90 % dry
kg U	Kilogram of uranium
1000 kWh	Thousand kilowatt hours
l	Litre
1000 l	Thousand litres
l alc. 100 %	Litre pure (100 %) alcohol
m	Metre
m2	Square metre
m3	Cubic metre
1000 m3	Thousand cubic metres
pa	Number of pairs
p/st	Number of items
100 p/st	Hundred items
1000 p/st	Thousand items
TJ	Terajoule (gross calorific value)]

* 'Carrying capacity in tonnes' (ct/l) means the carrying capacity of a vessel expressed in tonnes, not including ships' stores (fuel, equipment, food supplies, etc). Persons carried on board (crew and passengers) and their baggage are also excluded.

NOTES

Annex I substituted by Commission Regulation (EC) 1549/2006, Article 1, Annex, with effect from 1 January 2007 (OJ L 301, 31.10.06 p 1).

Annex I Part II (not reproduced) amended by Council Regulation (EC) 493/2005 (OJ L 082, 31.3.05 p 1); Council Regulation (EC) 426/2006 (OJ L 079, 16.3.06 p 1), Council Regulation (EC) 1758/2006 (OJ L 335, 1.12.2006 p 1), Council Regulation (EC) 1930/2006 (OJ L 406, 30.12.06 p 9), Council Regulation (EC) 301/2007 (OJ L 81, 22.3.07 p 11) and Council Regulation (EC) 501/2007 (OJ L 119, 9.5.07 p 1).

Annex I Part III (not reproduced) supplemented by Council Regulation (EC) 2175/2005 (OJ L 347, 30.12.05 p 9); amended by Council Regulation (EC) 683/2006 (OJ L 120, 5.5.06 p 1), Council Regulation (EC) 267/2006 (OJ L 047, 17.2.06 p 1), Council Regulation (EC) 1929/2006 (OJ L 406, 30.12.06 p 8), Council Regulation (EC) 129/2007 (OJ L 56, 23.2.07 p 1) and Council Regulation (EC) 733/2007 (OJ L 169, 29.6.07 p 1).

Annex I Parts II and III amended by Council Regulation (EC) 838/2006 (OJ L 154, 8.6.06 p 1), Council Regulation (EC) 711/2006 (OJ L 124, 11.5.06 p 1), Council Regulation (EC) 1839/2006 (OJ L 355, 15.12.06 p 1), Council Regulation (EC) 1894/2006 (OJ L 397, 30.12.06 p 1) and Council Regulation (EC) 580/2007 (OJ L 138, 30.5.07 p 1).

Annex I, Chapter 2 (not reproduced) amended by Commission Regulation (EC) 949/2006 (OJ L 174, 28.6.06 p 3).

Annex I, Chapter 17 (not reproduced) amended by Commission Regulation (EC) 996/2006 (OJ L 179, 1.7.06 p 26).

CLASSIFICATION REGULATIONS

Commission Regulation (EC) 1967/2005 (OJ L 316, 2.12.05 p 7).
Commission Regulation (EC) 2171/2005 (OJ L 346, 29.12.05 p 7).
Commission Regulation (EC) 400/2006 (OJ L 070, 9.3.06 p 9).
Commission Regulation (EC) 1114/2006 (OJ L 199, 21.07.06 p 3).
Commission Regulation (EC) 1125/2006 (OJ L 200, 22.7.06 p 3).
Commission Regulation (EC) 1578/2006 (OJ L 291, 21.10.06 p 3).
Commission Regulation (EC) 160/2007 (OJ L 51, 20.2.07 p 3).
Commission Regulation (EC) 161/2007 (OJ L 51, 20.2.07 p 5).
Commission Regulation (EC) 166/2006 (OJ L 52, 21.2.07 p 3).
Commission Regulation (EC) 652/2007 (OJ L 153, 14.6.07 p 6).
Commission Regulation (EC) 901/2007 (OJ L 196, 28.7.07 p 31).

(Remainder of Annex I and Annex II outside the scope of this work.)

COMMISSION REGULATION

(3915/88/EEC)

of 15 December 1988

laying down provisions for the implementation of Article 63c of Council Regulation (EEC) No 918/83 setting up a Community system of reliefs from customs duty

NOTES

Date of publication in OJ: OJ L 347, 16.12.88, p 55.

Title substituted by Commission Regulation (EEC) 1843/89, Art 1, para 2.

THE COMMISSION OF THE EUROPEAN COMMUNITIES,

Having regard to the Treaty establishing the European Economic Community,

Having regard to Council Regulation (EEC) No 918/83 of 28 March 1983 setting up a Community system of reliefs from customs duty,[1] as amended by Regulation (EEC) No 1315/88,[2] and in particular Article 143 thereof,

Whereas Article 63c of Regulation (EEC) No 918/83 provides for relief from import duties for consignments containing samples of reference substances approved by the World Health Organisation (WHO) which are intended for use in the quality control of materials used in the manufacture of medicinal products; whereas such consignments are addressed to consignees authorised by the competent national authorities to benefit from such relief;

Whereas the requisite conditions for the correct implementation of that provision should be laid down; whereas those conditions must be established in accordance with the procedure provided for in Article 143(2) and (3) of Regulation (EEC) No 918/83;

Whereas the measures provided for in this Regulation are in accordance with the opinion of the Committee on Duty Free Arrangements,

---

[1] OJ L 105, 23.4.83, p 1.

[2] OJ L 123, 17.5.88, p 2.

HAS ADOPTED THIS REGULATION—

Article 1

This Regulation lays down provisions for the implementation of Article 63c of Regulation (EEC) No 918/83.

Article 2

The relief referred to in Article 63c of Regulation (EEC) No 918/83 shall apply only to consignments sent by the 'WHO Collaborating Centre for Chemical Reference Substances' in Stockholm (Sweden) to consignees who are authorised by the competent national authorities to receive them duty free.

Article 3

Relief from import duties for consignments referred to in Article 63c of Regulation (EEC) No 918/83 shall be conditional on the display, on packages containing reference substances, of—

—   firstly, the stamp of the WHO Collaborating Centre referred to in Article 2 above,

—   secondly, a label, a specimen of which is shown in the Annex to this Regulation, on which the box corresponding to chemical reference substances has been clearly marked with a tick.

Article 4

Relief shall extend to any special packaging which is essential to the transportation of chemical reference substances and to any requisite accessories which the consignments may contain.

Article 5

This Regulation shall enter into force on 1 January 1989.

This Regulation shall be binding in its entirety and directly applicable in all Member States.

Done at Brussels, 15 December 1988.

ANNEX

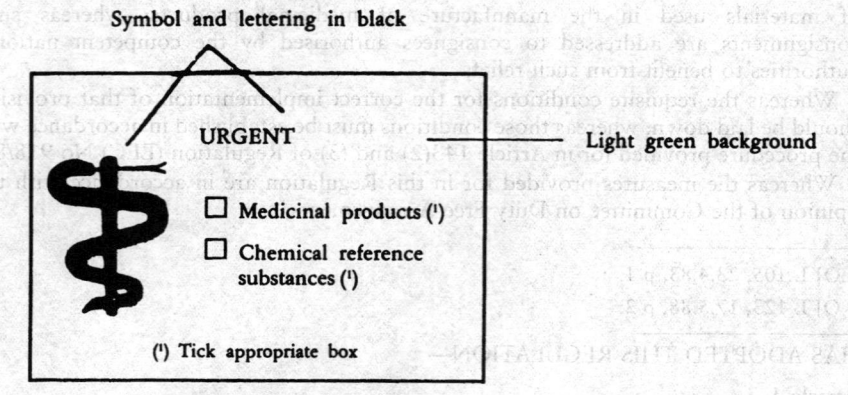

Symbol and lettering in black

URGENT

Light green background

☐ Medicinal products (¹)

☐ Chemical reference substances (¹)

(¹) Tick appropriate box

(Dimensions 62 × 44 mm)

COUNCIL DIRECTIVE

(12/92/EEC)

of 25 February 1992

on the general arrangements for products subject to excise duty and on the holding, movement and monitoring of such products

NOTES

Date of publication in OJ: OJ L 76, 23.2.92, p 1.

THE COUNCIL OF THE EUROPEAN COMMUNITIES,

Having regard to the Treaty establishing the European Economic Community, and in particular Article 99 thereof,

Having regard to the proposal from the Commission,[1]

Having regard to the opinion of the European Parliament,[2]

Having regard to the opinion of the Economic and Social Committee,[3]

Whereas the establishment and functioning of the internal market require the free movement of goods, including those subject to excise duties;

Whereas provision should be made to define the territory on which this Directive, as well as the Directive on the rates and structures of duty on products subject to excise duties, are to be applied;

Whereas the concept of products subject to excise duty should be defined; whereas only goods which are treated as such in all the Member States may be the subject of Community provisions; whereas such products may be subject to other indirect taxes for specific purposes; whereas the maintenance or introduction of other indirect taxes must not give rise to border-crossing formalities;

Whereas, in order to ensure the establishment and functioning of the internal market, chargeability of excise duties should be identical in all the Member States;

Whereas any delivery, holding with a view to delivery or supply for the purposes of a trader carrying out an economic activity independently or for the purposes of a body governed by public law, taking place in a Member State other than that in which the product is released for consumption gives rise to chargeability of the excise duty in that other Member State;

Whereas in the case of products subject to excise duty acquired by private individuals for their own use and transported by them, the duty must be charged in the country where they were acquired;

Whereas to establish that products subject to excise duty are not held for private but for commercial purposes, Member States must take account of a number of criteria;

Whereas products subject to excise duty purchased by persons who are not approved warehousekeepers or registered or non-registered traders and dispatched or transported directly or indirectly by the vendor or on his behalf must be subject to excise duty in the Member State of destination;

Whereas in order to ensure that the tax debt is eventually collected it should be possible for checks to be carried out in production and storage facilities; whereas a system of warehouses, subject to authorisation by the competent authorities, should make it possible to carry out such checks;

Whereas movement from the territory of one Member State to that of another may not give rise to checks liable to impede free movement within the Community; whereas for the purposes of chargeability it is nevertheless necessary to know of the movements of products subject to excise duty; whereas provision should therefore be made for an accompanying document for such products;

Whereas the requirements to be complied with by authorised warehousekeepers and traders without authorised warehousekeeper status should be laid down;

Whereas provision should be made, to ensure the collection of taxes at the rates laid down by Member States, for the establishment of a procedure for the movement of such goods under duty suspension;

Whereas in that respect provision should first be made for each consignment to be easily identified; whereas provision should be made for the tax status of the consignment to be immediately identifiable; whereas it is therefore necessary to provide for an accompanying document capable of meeting these needs, which may be either an administrative or commercial document; whereas the commercial document used must contain the essential elements which appear on the administrative document;

Whereas the procedure by which the tax authorities of the Member States are informed by traders of deliveries dispatched or received by means of an accompanying document should be explained;

Whereas there is no need for the accompanying document to be used when the products subject to excise duties are moved under a Community customs procedure other than release for free circulation or are placed in a free zone or a free warehouse;

Whereas in the context of national provisions, excise duty should, in the event of an offence or irregularity, be collected in principle by the Member State on whose territory the offence or irregularity has been committed, or by the Member State where the offence or irregularity was ascertained, or, in the event of non-presentation in the Member State of destination, by the Member State of departure;

Whereas the Member States may provide that products released for consumption should carry fiscal or national identification marks and whereas the use of these marks should not place any obstacle in the way of intra-Community trade;

Whereas payment of the excise duties in the Member State where the products were released for consumption must give rise to the reimbursement of those duties when the products are not intended for consumption in that Member State;

Whereas, as a result of the abolition of the principle of taxes on imports in relations between Member States, the provisions on exemptions and allowances on imports cease to apply in respect of relations between Member States; whereas these provisions should therefore be abolished and the directives concerned adapted accordingly;

Whereas a Committee on Excise Duties should be set up to examine the Community measures necessary for the implementation of the provisions on excise duties;

Whereas Article 1(2) of the Regulation concerning the elimination of controls and formalities applicable to the cabin and hold baggage of persons taking an intra-Community flight or making an intra-Community sea-crossing states that its enforcement is without prejudice to controls relating to bans or restrictions laid down by Member States, provided that they are compatible with the three Treaties establishing the European Community; whereas in that context the verifications necessary for the enforcement of the quantitative restrictions referred to in Article 26 must be considered to be such controls and, as such, to be compatible with Community legislation;

Whereas a certain period of time will be required to take the necessary measures to alleviate both the social repercussions in the sectors concerned and regional difficulties, particularly in border regions, which might arise as a result of the abolition of taxes on imports and exemptions on exports in trade between the Member States; whereas to that end the Member States should be authorised, for a period ending on 30 June 1999, to exempt products supplied, within the limits laid down, by tax-free shops in the context of passenger traffic by air or sea between the Member States;

Whereas small wine producers may be exempted from certain requirements under the general arrangements for excise duty;

Whereas, finally, Council Directive 77/799/EEC of 19 December 1977 concerning mutual assistance by the competent authorities of the Member States in the field of direct taxation and value added tax[4] should be amended in order to extend its provisions to cover excise duties,

---

[1] OJ C 322, 21.12.90, p 1; and OJ C 45, 20.8.92, p 10.

[2] OJ C 183, 15.7.91, p 131.

[3] OJ C 169, 18.3.91, p 25.

[4] OJ L 336, 27.12.77, p 15. Directive as last amended by Directive 79/1070/EEC (OJ L 331, 27.12.79, p 8).

HAS ADOPTED THIS DIRECTIVE—

TITLE I
GENERAL PROVISIONS

Article 1

1. This Directive lays down the arrangements for products subject to excise duties and other indirect taxes which are levied directly or indirectly on the consumption of such products, except for value added tax and taxes established by the Community.

2. The particular provisions relating to the structures and rates of duty on products subject to excise duty shall be set out in specific Directives.

Article 2

1. This Directive and the Directives listed in Article 1(2) shall apply in the territory of the Community as defined, for each Member State, by the Treaty establishing the European Economic Community, and in particular Article 227 thereof, except for the following national territories—

— in the case of the Federal Republic of Germany, the Island of Heligoland and the territory of Buesingen,

— in the case of the Italian Republic, Livigno, Campione d'Italia and the Italian waters of Lake Lugano,

— in the case of the Kingdom of Spain, Ceuta and Melilla.

2. Notwithstanding paragraph 1, this Directive and the Directives referred to in Article 1(2) shall not apply to the Canary Islands. However, the Kingdom of Spain may give notice, by means of a declaration, that these Directives apply to those territories in respect of all or some of the products referred to in Article 3(1) below, as from the first day of the second month following deposit of that declaration.

3. By way of derogation from paragraph 1, neither this Directive nor those referred to in Article 1(2) shall apply to the overseas departments of the French Republic.

However, the French Republic may give notice, by means of a declaration, that these Directives apply to those territories—subject to measures to adjust to their extreme remoteness—from the first day of the second month following deposit of the declaration.

4. The Member States shall take the necessary measures to ensure that transactions originating in or intended for—

— the Principality of Monaco are treated as transactions originating in or intended for the French Republic,

— Jungholz and Mittelberg (Kleines Walsertal) are treated as transactions originating in or intended for the Federal Republic of Germany,

— the Isle of Man are treated as transactions originating in or intended for the United Kingdom of Great Britain and Northern Ireland,

Part III

—   San Marino are treated as transactions originating in or intended for the Italian Republic.

5.   The provisions of this Directive shall not prevent Greece from maintaining the specific status granted to Mount Athos as guaranteed by Article 105 of the Greek Constitution.

6.   If the Commission considers that the exclusions provided for in paragraphs 1, 2, 3 and 4 are no longer justified, particularly in terms of fair competition, it shall submit appropriate proposals to the Council.

Article 3

1.   This Directive shall apply at Community level to the following products as defined in the relevant Directives—

—   mineral oils,

—   alcohol and alcoholic beverages,

—   manufactured tobacco.

2.   The products listed in paragraph 1 may be subject to other indirect taxes for specific purposes, provided that those taxes comply with the tax rules applicable for excise duty and VAT purposes as far as determination of the tax base, calculation of the tax, chargeability and monitoring of the tax are concerned.

3.   Member States shall retain the right to introduce or maintain taxes which are levied on products other than those listed in paragraph 1 provided, however, that those taxes do not give rise to border-crossing formalities in trade between Member States.

Subject to the same proviso, Member States shall also retain the right to levy taxes on the supply of services which cannot be characterised as turnover taxes, including those relating to products subject to excise duty.

Article 4

For the purpose of this Directive, the following definitions shall apply—

(a)   authorised warehousekeeper: a natural or legal person authorised by the competent authorities of a Member State to produce, process, hold, receive and dispatch products subject to excise duty in the course of his business, excise duty being suspended under tax-warehousing arrangement;

(b)   tax warehouse: a place where goods subject to excise duty are produced, processed, held, received or dispatched under duty-suspension arrangements by an authorised warehousekeeper in the course of his business, subject to certain conditions laid down by the competent authorities of the Member State where the tax warehouse is located;

(c)   suspension arrangement: a tax arrangement applied to the production, processing, holding and movement of products, excise duty being suspended;

(d)   registered trader: a natural or legal person without authorised warehousekeeper status, authorised by the competent authorities of a Member State to receive, in the course of his business, products subject to excise duty from another Member State under duty-suspension arrangements. This type of trader may neither hold nor dispatch such products under excise duty-suspension arrangements;

(e)   non-registered trader: a natural or legal person without authorised warehousekeeper status, who is entitled, in the course of his business, to receive occasionally products subject to excise duty from another Member State under duty-suspension arrangements. This type of trader may neither hold nor dispatch products under excise duty suspension arrangements. A non-registered trader must guarantee payment of excise duty to the tax authorities of the Member States of destination prior to the dispatch of the goods.

Article 5

1.   The products referred to in Article 3(1) shall be subject to excise duty at the time of their production within the territory of the Community as defined in Article 2 or of their importation into that territory.

'Importation of a product subject to excise duty' shall mean the entry of that product into the territory of the Community, including the entry of such a product from a territory covered by Article 2(1), (2) and (3) or from the Channel Islands.

However, where the product is placed under a Community customs procedure on entry into the territory of the Community, importation shall be deemed to take place when it leaves the Community customs procedure.

[2.   Without prejudice to national and Community provisions regarding customs matters, when products subject to excise duty—

[—   are coming from, or going to, third countries or territories referred to in Article 2(1), (2) and (3) or the Channel Islands and are placed under one of the customs suspensive procedures listed in Article 84(1)(a) of Regulation (EEC) No 2913/92[1] or in a free zone or a free warehouse,]

or

[—   are dispatched between Member States via EFTA countries or between a Member State and an EFTA country under the internal Community transit procedure or via one or more non-EFTA third countries under cover of a TIR or ATA carnet,]

the excise duty on them shall be deemed to be suspended.

[In cases where the single administrative document is used—]

—   box 33 of the single administrative document shall be completed with the appropriate CN code;

—   it shall be clearly indicated in box 44 of the single administrative document that a dispatch of products subject to excise duty is involved;

—   a copy of "copy 1" of the single administrative document shall be held by the consignor;

—   a duly annotated copy of "copy 5" of the single administrative document shall be sent back to the consignor by the consignee.]

[3.   Any additional details that have to be shown on the transport or commercial documents serving as transit documents and the changes that have to be made to adapt the discharge procedure where goods subject to excise duty move under a simplified internal Community transit procedure shall be established according to the procedure provided for in Article 24.]

---

[1] [OJ L 302, 19.10. 92, p 1.]

NOTES

Para 2: substituted by Council Directive 92/108/EEC, Art 1, para 1; words in square brackets substituted by Council Directive 94/74/EC, Art 1, para 1(a)–(c).

Para 3: added by Council Directive 94/74/EC, Art 1, para 1(d).

Article 6

1.   Excise duty shall become chargeable at the time of release for consumption or when shortages are recorded which must be subject to excise duty in accordance with Article 14(3).

Release for consumption of products subject to excise duty shall mean—

(a)   any departure, including irregular departure, from a suspension arrangement;

(b)   any manufacture, including irregular manufacture, of those products outside a suspension arrangement;

(c)   any importation of those products, including irregular importation, where those products have not been placed under a suspension arrangement.

2.   The chargeability conditions and rate of excise duty to be adopted shall be those in force on the date on which duty becomes chargeable in the Member State where release for consumption takes place or shortages are recorded. Excise duty shall be levied and collected according to the procedure laid down by each Member State, it being understood that Member States shall apply the same procedures for levying and collection to national products and to those from other Member States.

Article 7

1.   In the event of products subject to excise duty and already released for consumption in one Member State being held for commercial purposes in another Member State, the excise duty shall be levied in the Member State in which those products are held.

2.   To that end, without prejudice to Article 6, where products already released for consumption as defined in Article 6 in one Member State are delivered, [or intended for delivery in another Member State] or used in another Member State for the purposes of a trader carrying out an economic activity independently or for the purposes of a body governed by public law, excise duty shall become chargeable in that other Member State.

3.   Depending on all the circumstances, the duty shall be due from the person making the delivery or holding the products intended for delivery or from the person receiving the products for use in a Member State other than the one where the products have already been released for consumption, or from the relevant trader or body governed by public law.

4.   The products referred to in paragraph 1 shall move between the territories of the various Member States under cover of an accompanying document listing the main data from the document referred to in Article 18(1). The form and content of this document shall be established in accordance with the procedure laid down in Article 24 of this Directive.

5.   The person, trader or body referred to in paragraph 3 must comply with the following requirements—

(a)   before the goods are dispatched, make a declaration to the tax authorities of the Member State of destination and guarantee the payment of the excise duty;

(b)   pay the excise duty of the Member State of destination in accordance with the procedure laid down by that Member State;

(c)   consent to any check enabling the administration of the Member State of destination to satisfy itself that the goods have actually been received and that the excise duty to which they are liable has been paid.

6.   The excise duty paid in the first Member State referred to in paragraph 1 shall be reimbursed in accordance with Article 22(3).

[7.   Where products subject to excise duty and already released for consumption in a Member State are to be moved to a place of destination in that Member State via the territory of another Member State, such movements shall take place under cover of the accompanying document referred to in paragraph 4 and shall use an appropriate itinerary.

8. In the cases referred to in paragraph 7—

    (a)   the consignor shall, before the goods are dispatched, make a declaration to the tax authorities of the place of departure responsible for carrying out excise-duty checks;

    (b)   the consignee shall attest to having received the goods in accordance with the rules laid down by the tax authorities of the place of destination responsible for carrying out excise-duty checks;

    (c)   the consignor and the consignee shall consent to any check enabling their respective tax authorities to satisfy themselves that the goods have actually been received.

9. Where products subject to excise duty are moved frequently and regularly under the conditions specified in paragraph 7, Member States may agree bilaterally to authorise a simplified procedure in derogation from paragraphs 7 and 8.]

NOTES

    Para 2: words in square brackets substituted by Council Directive 92/108/EEC, Art 1, para 2.

    Paras 7–9: added by Council Directive 94/74/EC, Art 1, para 2.

Article 8

As regards products acquired by private individuals for their own use and transported by them, the principle governing the internal market lays down that excise duty shall be charged in the Member State in which they are acquired.

Article 9

1. Without prejudice to Articles 6, 7 and 8, excise duty shall become chargeable where products for consumption in a Member State are held for commercial purpose in another Member State.

In this case, the duty shall be due in the Member State in whose territory the products are and shall become chargeable to the holder of the products.

2. To establish that the products referred to in Article 8 are intended for commercial purposes, Member States must take account, inter alia, of the following—

    —   the commercial status of the holder of the products and his reasons for holding them,

    —   the place where the products are located or, if appropriate, the mode of transport used,

    —   any document relating to the products,

    —   the nature of the products,

    —   the quantity of the products.

For the purposes of applying the content of the fifth indent of the first subparagraph, Member States may lay down guide levels, solely as a form of evidence. These guide levels may not be lower than—

    (a)   Tobacco products

        cigarettes 800 items

        cigarillos (cigars weighing not more than 3 g each) 400 items

        cigars 200 items

        smoking tobacco 1,0 kg;

    (b)   Alcoholic beverages

        spirit drinks 10 l

Part III

intermediate products 20 l

wines (including a maximum of 60 l of sparkling wines) 90 l

beers 110 l.

Until 30 June 1977 Ireland shall be authorised to apply guide levels which may not be less than 45 litres for wine (including a maximum of 30 litres of sparkling wine) and 55 litres for beer.

3.   Member States may also provide that excise duty shall become chargeable in the Member State of consumption on the acquisition of mineral oils already released for consumption in another Member State if such products are transported using atypical modes of transport by private individuals or on their behalf. Atypical transport shall mean the transport of fuels other than in the tanks of vehicles or in appropriate reserve fuel canisters and the transport of liquid heating products other than by means of tankers used on behalf of professional traders.

Article 10

1.   Products subject to excise duty purchased by persons who are not authorised warehousekeepers or registered or non-registered traders and dispatched or transported directly or indirectly by the vendor or on his behalf shall be liable to excise duty in the Member State of destination. For the purposes of this Article, 'Member State of destination' shall mean the Member State of arrival of the dispatch or transport.

2.   To that end, the delivery of products subject to excise duty already released for consumption in a Member State and giving rise to the dispatch or transport of those products to a person as referred to in paragraph 1, established in another Member State, and which are dispatched or transported directly or indirectly by the vendor or on his behalf shall cause excise duty to be chargeable on those products in the Member State of destination.

3.   The duty of the Member State of destination shall be chargeable to the vendor at the time of delivery. However, Member States may adopt provisions stipulating that the excise duty shall be payable by a tax representative, other than the consignee of the products. Such tax representative must be established in the Member State of destination and approved by the tax authorities of that Member State.

The Member State in which the vendor is established must ensure that he complies with the following requirements—

— guarantee payment of excise duty under the conditions set by the Member State of destination prior to dispatch of the products and ensure that the excise duty is paid following arrival of the products,

— keep accounts of deliveries of products.

4.   In the case referred to in paragraph 2, the excise duty paid in the first Member State shall be reimbursed in accordance with Article 22(4).

5.   Subject to Community law, Member States may lay down specific rules for applying this provision to products subject to excise duty which are covered by special national distribution arrangements compatible with the Treaty.

TITLE II

PRODUCTION, PROCESSING AND HOLDING

Article 11

1.   Each Member State shall determine its rules concerning the production, processing and holding of products subject to excise duty, subject to the provisions of this Directive.

2.   Production, processing and holding of products subject to excise duty, where the latter has not been paid, shall take place in a tax warehouse.

Article 12

The opening and operation of tax warehouses shall be subject to authorisation from the competent authorities of the Member States.

Article 13

An authorised warehousekeeper shall be required to—

[(a)   provide a guarantee, if necessary, to cover production, processing and holding and a compulsory guarantee to cover movement, subject to Article 15(3), the conditions for which shall be set by the competent authorities of the Member State in which the tax warehouse is authorised;]

(b)   comply with the requirements laid down by the Member State within whose territory the tax warehouse is situated;

(c)   keep, for each warehouse, accounts of stock and product movements;

(d)   produce the products whenever so required;

(e)   consent to all monitoring and stock checks.

The requirements must respect the principle of non-discrimination between national and intra-Community transactions.

NOTES

Para (a) substituted by Council Directive 94/74/EC, Art 1, para 3.

Article 14

1.   Authorised warehousekeepers shall be exempt from duty in respect of losses occurring under suspension arrangements which are attributable to fortuitous events or force majeure and established by the authorised of the Member State concerned. They shall also be exempt, under suspension arrangements, in respect of losses inherent in the nature of the products during production and processing, storage and transport. Each Member State shall lay down the conditions under which these exemptions are granted. These exemptions shall apply equally to the traders referred to in Article 16 during the transport of products under excise duty suspension arrangements.

2.   Losses referred to in paragraph 1 occurring during the intra-Community transport of products under excise duty suspension arrangements must be established according to the rules of the Member State of destination.

3.   Without prejudice to Article 20, the duty on shortages other than the losses referred to in paragraph 1 and losses for which the exemptions referred to in paragraph 1 are not granted shall be levied on the basis of the rates applicable in the Member States concerned at the time the losses, duly established by the competent authorities, occurred, or if necessary at the time the shortage was recorded.

[4.   The shortages referred to in paragraph 3 and losses which are not exempted under paragraph 1 shall, in all cases, be indicated by the competent authorities on the reverse of the copy of the accompanying document referred to in Article 18(1) to be returned to the consignor.

The procedure shall be as follows—

—   in the case of losses or shortages occurring during intra-Community transport of products subject to excise duty that are under duty suspension arrangements, the competent authorities of the Member State in which those losses or shortages are established shall annotate the return copy of the accompanying document accordingly,

—   on the arrival of the products in the Member State of destination, the competent authorities of that Member State shall indicate whether they are granting partial exemption or no exemption in respect of the losses established.

In the cases referred to above they shall specify the basis for calculation of the excise duty to be levied in accordance with paragraph 3. The competent authorities of the Member State of destination shall send a copy of the return copy of the accompanying document to the competent authorities of the Member State in which the losses were established.]

NOTES

Para 4: added by Council Directive 94/74/EC, Art 1, para 4.

TITLE III
MOVEMENT OF GOODS

Article 15

[1. Without prejudice to Articles 5(2), 16, 19(4) and 23(1a), the movement of products subject to excise duty under suspension arrangements shall take place between tax warehouses.

The first subparagraph shall apply to the intra-Community movement of products subject to excise duty at a zero rate which have not been released for consumption.]

2. Warehousekeepers authorised by the competent authorities of a Member State in accordance with Article 13 shall be deemed to be authorised for both national and intra-Community movement.

[3. The risks inherent in intra-Community movement shall be covered by the guarantee provided by the authorised warehousekeeper of dispatch, as provided for in Article 13, or, if need be, by a guarantee jointly and severally binding on both the consignor and the transporter. The competent authorities in the Member States may permit the transporter or the owner of the products to provide a guarantee in place of that provided by the authorised warehousekeeper of dispatch. If appropriate, Member States may require the consignee to provide a guarantee.

If mineral oils subject to excise duty are transported within the Community by sea or by pipeline, Member States may relieve authorised warehousekeepers of dispatch of the obligation to provide the guarantee referred to in the first subparagraph.

The detailed rules for the guarantee shall be laid down by the Member States. The guarantee shall be valid throughout the Community.]

4. Without prejudice to the provision of Article 20, the liability of the authorised warehousekeeper of dispatch and, if the case arises, that of the transporter may only be discharged by proof that the consignee has taken delivery of the products, in particular by the accompanying document referred to in Article 18 under the conditions laid down in Article 19.

[[5. An authorised warehousekeeper of dispatch or his agent may amend the contents of boxes 4, 7, 7a, 13, 14 and/or 17 of the accompanying document to show a new consignee, who must be an authorised warehousekeeper or registered trader, or a new place of delivery. The competent authority of dispatch must be notified immediately and the new consignee or the new place of delivery shall immediately be indicated on the reverse of the accompanying document.]]

[6. In the case of intra-Community movement of mineral oils by sea or inland waterway, the authorised warehousekeeper of dispatch need not complete boxes, 4, 7, 7a, 13 and 17 on the accompanying document if, when the products are dispatched, the consignee is not definitively known, provided that—

— the competent authorities of the Member State of departure authorise the consignor in advance not to complete these boxes,

—   the same authorities are notified of the name and address of the consignee, his excise number and the country of destination as soon as they are known or at the latest when the products reach their final destination.]

NOTES

Paras 1, 3, 5: substituted by Council Directive 94/74/EC, Art 1, para 5 (para 5 previously added by Council Directive 92/108/EEC, Art 1, para 3.)

Para 6: added by Council Directive 94/74/EC, Art 1, para 5.

[Article 15a

1.   By 1 April 1993 at the latest, the competent authority of each Member State shall maintain an electronic data base which shall contain a register of persons who are authorised warehousekeepers or traders registered for excise purposes as well as a register of those premises authorised as tax warehouses.

2.   The register shall contain the following information—

(a)   the identification number issued by the competent authorities in respect of the person or premises;

(b)   the name and address of the person or premises;

(c)   the category of goods which may be held or received by the person or on the premises;

(d)   the address of the competent authorities which may be contacted for further information;

(e)   the date of issue and, where appropriate, the date of cessation of validity of the identification number.

3.   The data described in paragraphs 1 and 2(a), (b), (c) and (d) shall be communicated to the competent authority of each Member State. In those cases where the data described in paragraph 2(e) are not communicated automatically, they shall be provided at the specific request of any Member State. All data shall be used solely to identify the authorisation or registration or otherwise of a person and premises.

4.   The competent authority of each Member State shall ensure that persons involved in the intra-Community movement of products subject to excise duty are allowed to obtain confirmation of the information held under the terms of this Article.

5.   Any information communicated in whatever form pursuant to this Article shall be of a confidential nature. It shall be covered by the obligation of professional secrecy and shall enjoy the protection extended to similar information under the national law of the Member State which received it.

6.   By way of derogation from paragraph 5, the competent authority of the Member State providing the information shall permit its use for other purposes in the Member State of the applicant authority, if, under the legislation of the Member State of the requested authority, the information could be used in the Member State of the requested authority for similar purposes.]

NOTES

Inserted by Council Directive 92/108/EEC, Art 1, para 4.

[Article 15b

1.   With regard to the spot checks provided for in Article 19(6), the competent authorities in a Member State may request the competent authorities of another Member State for information in addition to that set out in Article 15a. The provisions governing data protection in Directive 77/799/EEC[1] shall apply to such exchanges of information.

2. Where information is exchanged pursuant to paragraph 1 and internal legislation in a Member State stipulates that the persons concerned by the exchange of information must be consulted, such legislation may continue to be applied.

3. The information necessary to carry out spot checks under paragraph 1 shall be exchanged by means of a uniform control document. The form and content of that document shall be established in accordance with the procedure laid down in Article 24.]

---

[1] 1 OJ L 336, 27.12.77, p 15.

NOTES

Inserted by Council Directive 94/74/EC, Art 1, para 6.

Article 16

1. Notwithstanding Article 15(1), the consignee may be a professional trader without authorised warehousekeeper status. This trader may, in the course of his business, receive products subject to excise duty from other Member States under duty-suspension arrangements. However, he may neither hold nor dispatch such products under excise duty-suspension arrangements.

Subject to Community law, Member States may lay down specific rules for applying this provision to products subject to excise duty that are covered by special national distribution arrangements compatible with the Treaty.

2. The above trader may request, prior to the receipt of goods, to be registered by the tax authorities of his Member State.

A registered trader must comply with the following requirements—

    (a)   guarantee payment of excise duty under the conditions set by the tax authorities of his Member State, without prejudice to Article 15(4) laying down the liability of the authorised warehousekeeper of dispatch and, if the case arises, of the transporter;

    (b)   keep accounts of deliveries of products;

    (c)   produce the products whenever so required;

    (d)   consent to all monitoring and stock checks.

For this type of trader excise duty shall be chargeable at the time of receipt of the goods and shall be paid in accordance with the procedure laid down by each Member State.

3. If the trader referred to in paragraph 1 above is not registered with the tax authorities of his Member State, he must comply with the following requirements—

    (a)   before the goods are dispatched, make a declaration to the tax authorities of the Member States of destination and guarantee the payment of excise duty, without prejudice to Article 15(4) laying down the liability of the authorised warehousekeeper of dispatch and, if the case arises, of the transporter;

    (b)   pay the excise duty of the Member State of destination at the time of receipt of the goods in accordance with the procedure laid down by that Member State;

    (c)   consent to any check enabling the administration of the Member State of destination to satisfy itself that the goods have actually been received and that the excise duty to which they are liable has been paid.

4. Subject to the provisions set out in paragraphs 2 and 3, the provisions of this Directive relating to the movement of products subject to excise duty under duty-suspension arrangements shall apply.

Article 17

A tax representative may be appointed by the authorised warehousekeeper of dispatch. This tax representative must be established in the Member State of destination and authorised by the tax authorities of that State. He must, instead of and in the place of the consignee without authorised warehousekeeper status, comply with the following requirements—

(a) guarantee the payment of excise duty under the conditions set by the tax authorities of the Member State of destination, without prejudice to Article 15(4) laying down the liability of the authorised warehousekeeper of dispatch and, if the case arises, the transporter;

(b) pay the excise duty of the Member State of destination at the time of receipt of the goods in accordance with the procedure laid down by the Member States of destination;

(c) keep an account of deliveries of products and advise the tax authorities of the Member States of destination of the place where the goods are delivered.

Article 18

[1. Notwithstanding the possible use of computerised procedures, all products subject to excise duty moving under duty-suspension arrangements between Member States, including those moving by sea or air directly from one Community port or airport to another, shall be accompanied by a document drawn up by the consignor. This document may be either an administrative document or a commercial document. The form and content of this document, and the procedure to be followed where its use is objectively inappropriate, shall be established in accordance with the procedure laid down in Article 24.]

2. In order to identify the goods and conduct checks, the packages should be numbered and the products described using the document referred to in paragraph 1. If need be, each container should be sealed by the consignor when the means of transport is recognised as suitable for sealing by the Member States of departure or the packages should be sealed by the consignor.

3. In cases where the consignee is not an authorised warehousekeeper or a registered trader and notwithstanding Article 17, the document referred to in paragraph 1 must be accompanied by a document certifying that excise duty has been paid in the Member State of destination or that any other procedure for collection of duty has been complied with in accordance with the conditions laid down by the competent authorities of the Member State of destination.

This document must give—

— the address of the office concerned of the tax authorities in the Member State of destination,

— the date and reference of payment or of the acceptance of the guarantee of payment by this office.

4. Paragraph 1 shall not apply when products subject to excise duty move under the conditions referred to in Article 5(2).

5. Without prejudice to Article 3(1), Member States may maintain their rules on movement and storage of raw materials used in the manufacture or preparation of products subject to excise duty.

[6. This Article shall also apply to products subject excise duty moving under duty-suspension arrangements between two tax warehouses located in the same Member State via the territory of another Member State.]

NOTES

Para 1: substituted by Council Directive 92/108/EEC, Art 1, para 5.

Para 6: added by Council Directive 94/74/EC, Art 1, para 7.

Article 19

1. The tax authorities of the Member States shall be informed by traders of deliveries dispatched or received by means of the document or a reference to the document specified in Article 18. This document shall be drawn up in quadruplicate—

— one copy to be kept by the consignor,
— one copy for the consignee,
— one copy to be returned to the consignor for discharge,
— one copy for the competent authorities of the Member State of destination.

The competent authorities of each Member State of dispatch may provide for the use of an additional copy of the document for the competent authorities of the Member State of departure.

[The competent authorities of the Member State of dispatch and destination may stipulate that the information contained in the copies of the accompanying document intended for them is to be sent by computerised means;]

The Member States of destination may stipulate that the copy to be returned to the consignor for discharge should be certified or endorsed by its national authorities. Member States applying this provision must inform the Commission which shall in turn inform the other Member States thereof.

The procedure to be followed with respect to the copy for the competent authorities of the Member States of destination shall be adopted in accordance with the procedure provided for in Article 24.

2. When products subject to excise duty move under the duty-suspension arrangements to an authorised warehousekeeper or to a registered or non-registered trader, a copy of the accompanying administrative document or a copy of the commercial document, duly annotated, shall be returned by the consignee to the consignor for discharge, at the latest within 15 days following the month of receipt by the consignee.

[Notwithstanding the above provisions, Member States of dispatch may provide for a copy of the return copy to be sent immediately to the consignor by fax so that the guarantee may be released quickly. This shall not affect the obligation to return the original pursuant to the first sentence.

Where products subject to excise duty move frequently and regularly between two Member States under duty suspension arrangements, the competent authorities of those Member States may, by mutual agreement, authorise the procedure for discharging the accompanying document to be simplified by means of summary or automated certification.]

The copy to be returned must contain the following details which are required for discharge—

(a) the address of the office of the tax authority for the consignee;
(b) the date and place of receipt of the goods;
(c) a description of the goods received in order to check whether the consignment tallies with the details contained in the document. If it does, the note 'consignment checked' must be added;
(d) the reference or registration number issued, where appropriate, by the competent authorities of the Member State of destination which use such numbering and/or the endorsement of the competent authorities of the Member State of destination if that Member State stipulates that the copy to be returned must be certified or endorsed by its authorities;
(e) the authorised signature of the consignee.

3. The duty-suspension arrangements as defined in Article 4(c) shall be discharged by the placing of the products subject to excise duty under one of the arrangements referred to in Article 5(2) and subject to the conditions referred to therein, after the consignor has received the copy to be returned of the accompanying administrative document or a copy of the commercial document, duly annotated, in which it must be noted that the products have been placed under such an arrangement.

[4. Products subject to excise duty that are dispatched by an authorised warehousekeeper established in a Member State for exportation via one or more other Member States shall be permitted to move under the duty-suspension arrangements as defined in Article 4(c). Those arrangements shall be discharged by an attestation drawn up by the customs office of departure from the Community confirming that the products have indeed left the Community. That office must send back to the consignor the certified copy of the accompanying document intended for him.]

5. If there is no discharge, the consignor shall inform the tax authorities of his Member State within a time limit to be fixed by those tax authorities. The time limit may not, however, exceed three months from the date of dispatch of the goods.

6. Member States shall cooperate to introduce spot checks which may be conducted, as necessary, by computerised procedures.

NOTES

Paras 1, 2: words in square brackets inserted by Council Directive 94/74/EC, Art 1, para 8(a), (b).

Para 4: substituted by Council Directive 94/74/EC, Art 1, para 8(a), (b).

Article 20

1. Where an irregularity or offence has been committed in the course of a movement involving the chargeability of excise duty, the excise duty shall be due in the Member State where the offence or irregularity was committed from the natural or legal person who guaranteed payment of the excise duties in accordance with Article 15(3), without prejudice to the bringing of criminal proceedings.

Where the excise duty is collected in a Member State other than that of departure, the Member State collecting the duty shall inform the competent authorities of the country of departure.

2. When, in the course of movement, an offence or irregularity has been detected without it being possible to determine where it was committed, it shall be deemed to have been committed in the Member State where it was detected.

3. Without prejudice to the provision of Article 6(2), when products subject to excise duty do not arrive at their destination and it is not possible to determine where the offence of irregularity was committed, that offence or irregularity shall be deemed to have been committed in the Member State of departure, which shall collect the excise duties at the rate in force on the date when the products were dispatched unless within a period of four months from the date of dispatch of the products evidence is produced to the satisfaction of the competent authorities of the correctness of the transaction or of the place where the offence or irregularity was actually committed. [Member States shall take the necessary measures to deal with any offence or irregularity and to impose effective penalties.]

4. If, before the expiry of a period of three years from the date on which the accompanying document was drawn up, the Member State where the offence or irregularity was actually committed is ascertained, that Member States shall collect the excise duty at the rate in force on the date when the goods were dispatched. In this case, as soon as evidence of collection has been provided, the excise duty originally levied shall be refunded.

Article 21

1. Without prejudice to Article 6(1), Member States may require that products released for consumption in their territory shall carry tax markings or national identification marks used for fiscal purposes.

2. Any Member State which requires the use of tax marking or national identification marks as set out in paragraph 1 shall be required to make them available to authorised warehousekeepers of the other Member States. However, each Member State may require that fiscal marks be made available to a tax representative authorised by the tax authority of that Member State.

[Without prejudice to any provisions they may lay down in order to ensure that this Article is implemented properly and to prevent any fraud, evasion or abuse, Member States shall ensure that these marks or markings do not create obstacles to the free movement of products subject to excise duty.]

3. Tax markings or identification marks within the meaning of paragraph 1 shall be valid in the Member State which issued them.

However, there may be mutual recognition of these markings between Member States.

4. Mineral oils may be held, transported or used in Ireland, other than in the running tanks of vehicles permitted to use rebated fuel, only where they comply with that State's control and marking requirements.

5. Intra-Community movement of products carrying a tax marking or national identification mark of a Member State within the meaning of paragraph 1 and intended for sale in that Member State, which are within the territory of another Member State, shall take place under cover of an accompanying document as provided for in Article 18(1) and (3), or if the case arises, in accordance with Article 5(2).

TITLE IV
REIMBURSEMENT

Article 22

1. In appropriate cases, products subject to excise duty which have been released for consumption may, at the request of a trader in the course of his business, be eligible for reimbursement of excise duty by the tax authorities of the Member State where they were released for consumption when they are not indented for consumption in that Member State.

However, Member States may refuse request for reimbursement where it does not satisfy the correctness criteria they lay down.

2. In the application of paragraph 1, the following provisions shall apply—

(a) before dispatch of the goods, the consignor must make a request for reimbursement from the competent authorities of his Member State and provide proof that the excise duty has been paid. However, the competent authorities may not refuse reimbursement on the sole grounds of non-presentation of the document prepared by the same authorities certifying that the initial payment had been made;

(b)   movement of the goods referred to in (a) shall take place [in accordance with the provisions of Title III];

(c)   the consignor shall submit to the competent authorities of his Member State the returned copy of the document referred to in (b) duly annotated by the consignee which must either be accompanied by a document certifying that the excise duty has been secured in the Member State of consumption or have the following details added—

— the address of the office concerned of the tax authorities in the Member State of destination,

— the date of acceptance of the declaration by this office together with the reference or registration number of that declaration;

(d)   products subject to excise duty and released for consumption in a Member State and thus bearing a tax marking or an identification mark of that Member State may be eligible for reimbursement of the excise duty due from the tax authorities of the Member States which issued the tax markings or identification marks, provided that the tax authorities of the Member State which issued them has established that such markings or marks have been destroyed.

3.   In the cases referred to in Article 7, the Member State of departure is required to reimburse the excise duty paid only where the excise duty was previously paid in the Member State of destination in accordance with the procedure laid down in Article 7(5).

However, Member States may refuse this request for reimbursement where it does not satisfy the correctness criteria they lay down.

4.   In the cases referred to in Article 8b the Member State of departure must, at the vendor's request, reimburse the excise duty paid where the vendor has followed the procedures laid down in Article 10(3).

However, Member States may refuse this request for reimbursement where it does not satisfy the correctness criteria they lay down.

Where the vendor is an authorised warehousekeeper, Member States may stipulate that the reimbursement procedure be simplified.

5.   The tax authorities of each Member State shall determine the monitoring procedures and methods applying to reimbursement made in their territory. Member States shall ensure that the reimbursement of excise duty does not exceed the sum actually paid.

NOTES

Para 2: words in square brackets substituted by Council Directive 92/108/EEC, Art 1, para 7.

TITLE V
EXEMPTIONS

Article 23

1.   Products subject to excise duty shall be exempted from payment of excise duty where they are intended—

— for delivery in the context of diplomatic or consular relations,

— for international organisations recognised as such by the public authorities of the host Member State, and by members of such organisations, within the limits and under the conditions laid down by the international conventions establishing such organisations or by headquarters agreements,

— for the armed forces of any State party to the North Atlantic Treaty other than the Member State within which the excise duty is chargeable as well as for the armed forces referred to in Article 1 of Decision 90/640/EEC[1], for the use of those forces, for the civilian staff accompanying them or for supplying their messes or canteens,

— for consumption under an agreement concluded with non-member countries or international organisations provided that such an agreement is allowed or authorised with regard to exemption from VAT.

These exemptions shall be subject to conditions and limitations laid down by the host Member State until uniform tax rules are adopted. Eligibility for exemption may be granted in accordance with a procedure for reimbursing excise duties.

[1a. The armed forces and organisations referred to in paragraph 1 shall be authorised to receive products from other Member States under excise-duty suspension arrangements under cover of the accompanying document referred to in Article 18 provided that the document is accompanied by an exemption certificate. The form and content of the exemption certificate shall be determined in accordance with the procedure laid down in Article 24.]

2. The Council, acting unanimously on a proposal from the Commission, may authorise any Member State to conclude with a non-member country or an international organisation an agreement which may contain exemptions from excise duty.

A State wishing to conclude such an agreement shall bring the matter to the notice of the Commission and provide all the background information necessary. The Commission shall inform the other Member States within one month. The Council's decision shall be deemed to have been adopted if, within two months of other Member States being informed, the matter has not been raised before the Council.

3. The provisions on excise duty laid down in the following Directives shall cease to apply on 31 December 1992—

— Directive 74/651/EEC,[2]
— Directive 83/183/EEC,[3]
— Directive 68/297/EEC.[4]

4. The provisions on excise duty laid down in Directive 69/169/EEC(9)[5] shall cease to apply on 31 December 1992 in respect of relations between Member States.

5. Until the Council, acting unanimously on a proposal from the Commission, has adopted Community provisions on stores for boats and aircraft, Member States may maintain their national provisions on the subject.

---

[1] OJ L 349, 13.12.90, p 19.

[2] OJ L 354, 30.12.74, p 6; Directive as last amended by Directive 88/663/EEC (OJ L 382, 31.12.98, p 40).

[3] OJ L 105, 23.4.83, p 64; Directive amended by Directive 89/604/EEC (OJ L 348, 29. 11.89, p 28).

[4] OJ L 175, 25.7.68, p 15; Directive as last amended by Directive 85/347/EEC (OJ L 183, 16.7.85, p 22).

[5] OJ L 135, 4.6.69, p 6. Directive as last amended by Directive 91/191/EEC (OJ L 94, 16.4.91, p 24).

NOTES

Para 1a: inserted by Council Directive 94/74/EC, Art 1, para 10.

TITLE VI
COMMITTEE ON EXCISE DUTIES

[**Article 24**

1.   The Commission shall be assisted by a committee referred to as the 'Committee on Excise Duties'.

2.   The measures necessary for the application of Articles 5, 7, 15b, 18, 19 and 23 shall be adopted in accordance with the procedure laid down in paragraph 3.

3.   Where reference is made to this paragraph, Articles 5 and 7 of Decision 1999/468/EC(112) shall apply.

The period laid down in Article 5(6) of Decision 1999/468/EC shall be set at three months.

4.   In addition to the measures referred to in paragraph 2, the Committee shall examine the matters raised by its chairman, either on his own initiative or at the request of the representative of a Member State, concerning the application of Community provisions on excise duties.

5.   The committee shall adopt its rules of procedure.]

NOTES

Substituted by Council Regulation 807/2003 art 3, Annex III para 45.

Article 25

The Member States and the Commission shall examine and assess the application of Community provisions on excise duties.

TITLE VII
FINAL PROVISIONS

[**Article 26**

1.   Without prejudice to Article 8, until 31 December 2003, Denmark and Finland shall be authorised to apply the specific arrangements laid down in the second and third subparagraphs to certain alcoholic drinks and tobacco products brought into their territory by private individuals for their own use.

From 1 January 1997, Denmark and Finland shall be authorised to continue to apply the same restrictions on the quantity of goods which may be brought into their territories without further excise duty payment as they applied on 31 December 1996. Those restrictions shall be progressively removed by these Member States. [Finland shall increase the quantitative restrictions for beer to at least 24 litres from the entry into force of the Finnish legislation transposing Article 5(9) of Directive 69/169/EEC, to at least 32 litres from 1 January 2001 and to at least 64 litres from 1 January 2003.]

Where such goods are imported by persons resident within their territories, Denmark and Finland shall be authorised to restrict the grant of admission without payment of duty to persons who have been absent from their territory for a period of more than 24 hours.

2.   Before 30 June 2000, the Commission shall report to the European Parliament and the Council on the operation of paragraph 1.

[3.   Without prejudice to Article 8, Sweden shall be authorised to apply the restrictions set out in the Annex on the quantity of alcoholic drinks and tobacco products.

The authorisation shall concern the quantity of alcoholic drinks and tobacco products which may be brought into Swedish territory by private individuals for their own use without further payment of excise duty.

It shall apply until 31 December 2003.]

Part III

4. Denmark, Finland and Sweden may collect excise duties and carry out the necessary checks with respect to the products covered by this Article.]

NOTES
Substituted by Council Directive 96/99/EC, Art 1.
Para 1: words in square brackets added by Council Directive 2000/47/EC, Art 2.
Para 3: substituted by Council Directive 2000/44/EC, Art 1, para 1.

[Article 26a

Products subject to excise duty that are under a suspension arrangement other than as specified in Articles 5(2) and 18(1) before 1 January 1993 and which has not been discharged, shall be deemed, after that date, to be under suspension of excise duty.

When the situation described in the first subparagraph involves the internal Community transit suspension arrangements, the provisions in force at the time when the products were placed under these arrangements shall continue to apply during the period when these products are under these arrangements, which shall be determined in accordance with the said provisions.

When the said situation involves national suspension arrangements, Member States shall determine the conditions and the formalities under which the suspension arrangements are discharged after 1 January 1993.]

NOTES
Inserted by Council Directive 92/108/EEC, Art 1, para 8.

Article 27

Before 1 January 1997 the Council, acting unanimously on the basis of a report from the Commission, shall re-examine the provisions of Articles 7, 8, 9 and 10 and, on the basis of a proposal from the Commission after consulting the European Parliament, adopt any necessary amendments.

Article 28

The following provisions shall apply for the period ending on 30 June 1999—

1. Member States may exempt products supplied by tax-free shops which are carried away in the personal luggage of travellers taking an intra-Community flight or sea-crossing to another Member State.

 For the purposes of this provision—

 (a) 'tax-free shop' shall mean any establishment situated within an airport or port which fulfils the conditions laid down by the competent public authorities, pursuant in particular to paragraph 3 of this Article;

 (b) 'traveller to another Member State' shall mean any passenger holding a transport document, for air or sea travel, stating that the immediate destination is an airport or port situated in another Member State;

 (c) 'intra-Community flight or sea-crossing' shall mean any transport, by air or sea, commencing within a Member State, where the actual place of arrival is situated within another Member State.

 Products supplied on board an aircraft or ship during the intra-Community passenger service shall be treated in the same way as products supplied by tax-free shops.

 This exemption shall also apply to products supplied by tax-free shops situated within one of the two access terminals to the Channel Tunnel to passengers holding transport documents which are valid for the journey between those two terminals.

2. The exemption provided for in paragraph 1 shall apply only to products in quantities which do not exceed the limits, by person and by journey, laid down by Community provisions in force in the context of the movement of travellers between third countries and the Community.

3. Member States shall take the measures necessary to ensure that the exemption provided for in this Article are applied correctly and straightforwardly, and to prevent any possible evasion, avoidance or abuse.

Article 29

1. Member States may exempt small wine producers from the requirements of Titles II and III and from the other requirements relating to movement and monitoring. Where these small producers themselves carry out intra-Community transactions, they shall inform their relevant authorities and comply with the requirements laid down by Commission Regulation No 986/89[1] of 10 April 1989 particularly as regards the register of outgoing products and the accompanying document.

'Small wine producers' should be understood to mean persons producing on average less than 1 000 hl of wine per year.

2. The tax authorities of the Member State of destination shall be informed by the consignee of wine deliveries received by means of the document referred to in paragraph 1 or by making a reference to it.

3. Member States shall take the measures necessary on a bilateral basis to introduce spot checks, which may be conducted, as necessary, by computerised procedures.

---

[1] OJ L 106, 18.4.89, p 1; Regulation as last modified by Regulation (EEC) No 592/91 (OJ L 66, 13.3.91, p 13).

Articles 30, 30a

(Art 30 amends Council Directive 77/799/EEC, title, Art 1; Art 30a amends Council Directive 76/308/EEC, title, Art 2.)

Article 31

1. Member States shall bring into force the laws, regulations and administrative provisions necessary to comply with this Directive on 1 January 1993.

However, with regard to Article 9(3) the Kingdom of Denmark is authorised to introduce the laws, regulations and administrative provisions required for complying with this provisions by 1 January 1993 at the latest.

When Member States adopt these measures, they shall contain a reference to this Directive or be accompanied by such reference on the occasion of their official publication. The methods of making such a reference shall be laid down by the Member State.

2. The Member States shall inform the Commission of the main provisions of national law which they adopt to comply with this Directive.

Article 32

This Directive is addressed to the Member States.

Done at Brussels, 25 February 1992.

[ANNEX

Article 26(3)

QUANTITY OF ALCOHOLIC DRINKS AND TOBACCO PRODUCTS WHICH
MAY BE BROUGHT INTO SWEDISH TERRITORY BY PRIVATE INDIVIDUALS
FOR THEIR OWN USE WITHOUT FURTHER PAYMENT OF EXCISE DUTY

Alcoholic drinks

	From 1 July 2000	*From 1 January 2001*	*From 1 January 2002*	*From 1 January 2003*
Spirits	1 l	1 l	2 l	5 l
Intermediate products	3 l	3 l	3 l	3 l
Wines (including sparkling wine)	20 l	26 l	26 l	52 l
Beer	24 l	32 l	32 l	64 l

Tobacco products

	From 1 July 2000
Cigarettes or	400
cigarillos or	200
cigars or	100
smoking tobacco	550g]

NOTES

Added by Council Directive 2000/44/EC, Art 1, para 2, Annex.

COMMISSION REGULATION

(2719/92/EEC)

of 11 September 1992

on the accompanying administrative document for the movement under duty-suspension arrangements of products subject to excise duty

NOTES

Date of publication in OJ: OJ L 276, 19.9.92, p 1

THE COMMISSION OF THE EUROPEAN COMMUNITIES,

Having regard to the Treaty establishing the European Economic Community,

Having regard to Council Directive 92/12/EEC of 25 February 1992 on the general arrangements for products subject to excise duty and on the holding, movement and monitoring of such products,[1] and in particular Articles 18(1) and 19(1) thereof,

Having regard to the opinion of the Committee on Excise Duties,

Whereas the movement of products subject to excise duty between tax warehouses and between a tax warehouse and a registered or non-registered operator takes place under duty-suspension arrangements; whereas it is necessary to establish in a binding manner the form and content of the accompanying document which might be either an administrative or a commercial document;

Whereas it is also necessary to determine who shall pass on the fourth copy of the accompanying document intended for the competent authorities to those authorities and how this should take place; whereas it is desirable and in line with practice to place this obligation on the consignee in the country of destination, since only he is in a position to make available to his competent authorities this document, which is important for the purposes of the tax supervision, without the danger of it being misdirected; whereas the fourth copy too should carry a certification of receipt, if this is requested by the competent authorities of the Member State of destination, which indicates to those authorities that the goods were received in the consignee's tax warehouse,

---

[1] OJ L 76, 23.3.92, p 1.

HAS ADOPTED THIS REGULATION—

[Article 1
The document shown in Annex I shall be used as the administrative document accompanying the movement under duty-suspension arrangements of products subject to excise duty within the meaning of Article 3(1) of Directive 92/12/EEC. The instructions concerning completion of the document and the procedures for its use are shown on the reverses of copy 1 of this document.]

NOTES

Substituted by Commission Regulation (EEC) 2225/93, Art 1, para 1.

Article 2

1. A commercial document may replace the administrative document provided it contains the same information required to be shown in the administrative document.

2. A commercial document which does not have the same layout as the administrative document must contain the same elements of information required by the administrative document, and the nature of the information items must be identified by a number corresponding to the relative box number on the administrative document. [The document shall be marked conspicuously with the following indication—
"Commercial accompanying document for the movement of products subject to excise duty under duty suspension".]

NOTES

Words in square brackets added by Commission Regulation (EEC) 2225/93, Art 1, para 2.

[Article 2A

1. In cases where the accompanying document is drawn up by an electronic or automatic data-processing system, the competent authorities may authorise the consignor not to sign the document but to replace the signature by the special stamp shown in Annex II. Such authorisation shall be subject to the condition that the consignor has previously given a written undertaking to those authorities that he will be liable for all risks inherent in intra-Community movements of products subject to excise duty under duty-suspension arrangements involving consignments which travel under cover of an accompanying document bearing such special stamp.

Part III

[2. Accompanying documents drawn up in accordance with paragraph 1 shall contain in that part of Box 24 which is reserved for the consignor's signature, one of the following indications:

- *(for original text, refer to Commission Regulation (EC) 1792/2006 (OJ L 362, 20.12.06, p 1))*
- Dispensa de firma
- Podpis prominut
- Fritaget for underskrift
- Freistellung von der Unterschriftsleistung
- Allkirjanõudest loobutud
- Δεν απαιτείται υπογραφή
- Signature waived
- Dispense de signature
- Dispensa dalla firma
- Dergs bez paraksta
- Parašo nereikalaujama
- Aláírás alól mentesítve
- Firma mhux metiea
- Van ondertekening vrijgesteld
- Z pominiciem podpisu
- Dispensa de assinatura
- Dispens de semntur
- Podpis sa nevyžaduje
- Opustitev podpisa]

3. The special stamp referred to in paragraph 1 shall be placed in the upper right corner of Box A of the administrative accompanying document or, plainly visible, in the corresponding Box of a commercial document. The consignor may also be authorised to pre-print the special stamp.]

NOTES

Inserted by Commission Regulation (EEC) 2225/93, Art 1, para 3.

Para 2: substituted by Commission Regulation (EC) 1792/2006, Art 1, Annex 1, Part 7(1)(a).

Article 3

Where products subject to excise duty are moved in fixed pipelines the Member States involved may, by mutual agreement, authorise the type and quantity of goods moved between the consignor tax warehouse and the consignee tax warehouse to be reported by computerised procedures which will replace the accompanying document. Such arrangement should be sufficient to ensure that all the data necessary for inventory control and for collection of duty are provided.

Article 4

The consignee, if required by the competent authorities of the Member State of destination, shall annotate the fourth copy of the accompanying document with the same certification of receipt as on the third copy (copy for return) and shall make it available to the competent authorities to which he reports in accordance with their instructions.

Article 5

This Regulation shall enter into force on 1 January 1993.

This Regulation shall be binding in its entirety and directly applicable in all Member States.

Done at Brussels, 11 September 1992.

[ANNEX I]

EUROPEAN COMMUNITY
PRODUCTS SUBJECT TO EXCISE DUTY

ADMINISTRATIVE ACCOMPANYING DOCUMENT

1 ☐ 1 Consignor	2 Consignor's excise No.	3 Reference No.
	4 Consignee's excise No.	5 Invoice No.
	6 Invoice date	
7 Consignee	8 Competent authority at dispatch	
7a Place of delivery		
	10 Guarantee	
9 Transporter		
	12 Country of dispatch	13 Country of destination
11 Other transport details	14 Tax representative	

Copy for the consignor

1 15 Place of dispatch	16 Date of dispatch	17 Journey time

18a Marks and numbers, No. and kind of packages, description of goods		19a Commodity code (CN code)
	20a Quantity	21a Gross weight (kg)
		22a Net weight (kg)
18b Marks and numbers, No. and kind of packages, description of goods		19b Commodity code (CN code)
	20b Quantity	21b Gross weight (kg)
		22b Net weight (kg)
18c Marks and numbers, No. and kind of packages, description of goods		19c Commodity code (CN code)
	20c Quantity	21c Gross weight (kg)
		22c Net weight (kg)

23 Certificates (certain wines and spirits, small breweries and distilleries)

A Record of control. For use by competent authority	24 Boxes 1–22 certified correct
	Signatory's company and telephone No.
	Name of signatory
	Place and date
	Signature

continue on reverse (copies 2, 3 and 4)

EXPLANATORY NOTES

1. General

1.1.   The Accompanying Administrative Document is required for excise purposes in accordance with the provisions of Articles 18 and 19 of Council Directive 92/12/EEC of 25 February 1992.

1.2.   The document must be completed legibly and in a manner that makes entries indelible. Information may be pre-printed. No erasures or overwriting are permitted.

Authorisation by a competent authority of a change to the place of delivery is to be shown in box B.

1.3.   The general specification of the paper to be used and the measurement of boxes is as laid down in the *Official Journal of the European Communities* No C 164/3 dated 1.7.89.

The paper is to be white for all copies with the size 210 millimetres by 297 millimetres with a maximum tolerance of 5 millimetres less or 8 millimetres more with regard to their length.

1.4.   Any unused space in boxes 18a to 22c is to be lined through so that nothing can be added. Three separate descriptions of merchandise may be entered which must be of the same excise category. The categories are mineral oils, tobacco products, and alcohol/alcoholic beverages.

1.5.   The accompanying document comprises four copies—

copy 1: to be retained by the consignor.

copy 2: to be retained by the consignee.

copy 3: to be returned by the consignor to discharge the movement with, if required, the certificate or endorsement of the fiscal authority of the Member State of destination.

copy 4: to be made available to the competent authority in the Member State of destination by the consignee.

The competent authority in the Member State of dispatch may require to be provided with an additional copy of the document.

1.6.   Copies 2, 3 and 4 must accompany the goods during the movement.

1.7.   In cases where this document is utilised for movement using fixed pipelines copies 2, 3 and 4 are to be sent to the consignee by the fastest means available to the dispatching warehousekeeper. In all cases the document is to arrive at the place of delivery within 24 hours of receipt of the goods to which it relates.

2. Headings

Box 1: Consignor: the full name, address and VAT registration number.

Box 2: Consignor's excise number: the excise registration number (if any) accorded to the consignor by his fiscal authority.

Box 3: Reference number: a reference number which identifies the consignment in the records of the consignor (for example, the invoice number may be used for this purpose).

Box 4: Consignee's excise number: in the case of an authorised warehousekeeper or a registered trader, the excise registration number (if any). In the case of a non-registered trader, the authorisation number of the consignment accorded by his fiscal authority is to be indicated.

Box 5: Invoice number: the number of the invoice relating to the goods. If the invoice has not been allocated the number of the delivery note or other transport document should be given.

Box 6: Invoice date: the date of the document shown in box 5.

Box 7: Consignee: the full name, address and VAT registration number. For goods to be exported the person acting for the consignor at the place of export or shipment should be indicated.

Box 7a: Place of delivery: the actual place of delivery if the goods have not been delivered to the address indicated in Box 7. For goods to be exported the notation 'EXPORT OUTSIDE THE COMMUNITY' is to be made together with the place of export. For goods which are subsequently to be placed under a community customs procedure (other than release for free circulation) the notation 'UNDER CUSTOMS PROCEDURE' is to be made together with the place where the goods enter customs control.

Box 8: Competent authority at dispatch: the name and address of the competent authority responsible for excise control at the place of dispatch.

Box 9: Transporter: the name and address of the person responsible for arranging the first movement, if different from the consignor.

Box 10: Guarantee: identify the party or parties responsible for arranging the guarantee. Only 'consignor', 'transporter' or 'consignee' need be entered, as appropriate.

Box 11: Other transport details: any additional information, e. g. name of any subsequent transporter, means of transport, registration number of means of transport, and the number, type and identification of any commercial seals.

Box 12: Country of dispatch: the Member State where the movement commences. An abbreviation is to be used.

> [BE Belgium
> BG Bulgaria
> CZ Czech Republic
> DK Denmark
> DE Germany
> EE Estonia
> GR Greece
> ES Spain
> FR France
> IE Ireland
> IT Italy
> CY Cyprus
> LV Latvia
> LT Lithuania
> LU Luxembourg
> HU Hungary
> MT Malta
> NL Netherlands
> AT Austria
> PL Poland
> PT Portugal
> RO Romania
> SI Slovenia
> SK Slovakia
> FI Finland
> SE Sweden
> GB United Kingdom]

Box 13: Country of destination: the final Member State of the movement. Abbreviation, as applied in box 12, are to be used.

Box 14: Tax representative: if the consignor has appointed a tax representative in the Member State of destination, his name, address, and VAT and excise registration numbers (if appropriate) are to be entered in this box.

Box 15: Place of dispatch: the authorisation number (if any) of the warehouse.

Box 16: Date of dispatch: the date, and if so required by the competent authorities at departure, the hour at which the goods leave the consignor's warehouse.

Box 17: Journey time: the normal period of time necessary for the journey taking into account the means of transport and the distance involved.

Box 18a: Packages, and description of goods: the marks and numbers of external packages, e. g. containers; the number of internal packages, e. g. cartons; and the commercial description of the goods.

> The description may be continued on a separate sheet attached to each copy. A packing list could be used for this purpose.

> Alcohol and alcoholic beverages other than beer must have the alcoholic strength shown (percentage by volume at 20°C).

> Beer is to be shown at either degrees Plato or alcohol percentage by volume at 20°C, or both, in accordance with the requirement of the Member State of destination and the Member State of dispatch. Mineral oils must show the density at 15°C.

Box 19a: Commodity code: the CN code.

Box 20a: Quantity:

- the number of items, expressed in thousands, (cigarettes)
- the net weight (cigars and cigarillos)
- litres of product at 20°C to two decimal places (alcohol and alcoholic beverages),
- litres at 15°C (mineral oils except heavy fuel oil).

Box 21a: Gross weight: the gross weight of the consignment.

Box 22a: Net weight: the weight of the excise products without packaging is to be given in respect of alcohol and alcoholic beverages, mineral oils, and for all tobacco products except cigarettes. Boxes 18b to 22b and 18c to 22c to be used when the consignment contains goods of a different description to those in boxes 18a to 22a.

Box 23: Certificates: this space is reserved for certain certificates which are required on Copy 2 only.

> 1.　In the case of certain wines, certification relating to the origin and quality of the products should, where necessary, be indicated in accordance with the relevant Community legislation.

> 2. In the case of certain spirit drinks certification relating to the place of production which is required under the relevant Community legislation should be indicated.

> 3. Beer brewed by an independent small brewery, as defined in the specific Council directive relating to the structures of excise duties on alcohol and alcoholic beverages, for which it is intended to claim a reduced rate of excise duty in the Member State of destination should be certified by the consignor in the following terms:

> *'It is hereby certified that the product described has been brewed by an independent small undertaking with a production in the previous year of . . . . . . hectolitres of beer'.*

> 4.　Ethyl alcohol produced by a small distillery, as defined in the specific Council Directive relating to the structures of excise duties

on alcohol and alcoholic beverages, for which it is intended to claim a reduced rate of excise duty in the Member State of destination should be certified by the consignor in the following terms:

'It is hereby certified that the product described has been produced by a small undertaking with a production in the previous year of . . . . . . hectolitres of pure alcohol'.

Box 24: Signatory's company, etc.: the document is to be completed by, or on behalf of, the consignor. The company of the signatory to the document is to be identified.

BOX A: Record of control: the competent authorities shall record the controls applied on Copies 2, 3 and 4. If the space is insufficient on the front of the document the record may be continued on the reverse. All comments shall be signed, dated and stamped by the responsible official. When goods enter a customs regime the controls applied are to be recorded by the responsible official.

BOX B: The consignor or his agent may request that the consignment be delivered to a place different from that indicated at box 7 or box 7a. If this request is authorised by the relevant competent authority the new place of delivery is to be indicated.

BOX C: Certificate of receipt: to be given by the consignee. In cases where there is fiscal control of receipt of goods into a warehouse, or where goods are exported or placed under a community customs procedure (other then release for free circulation), a certificate is required from the fiscal authority or customs office, as appropriate. It is recommended that the receipt of the goods should also be certified on the reverse of copy 2 which is to be retained by a consignee. Thus, in the case of an eventual loss of copy 3 on its way back to the consignor, the consignor's claim to discharge the movement could easily be fulfilled by sending a copy of the certificate on copy 2.

Part III

EUROPEAN COMMUNITY
PRODUCTS SUBJECT TO EXCISE DUTY

ADMINISTRATIVE ACCOMPANYING DOCUMENT

2	1 Consignor	2 Consignor's excise No.	3 Reference No.

4 Consignee's excise No.	5 Invoice No.

6 Invoice date

7 Consignee	8 Competent authority at dispatch

7a Place of delivery	

10 Guarantee

9 Transporter	

12 Country of dispatch	13 Country of destination

11 Other transport details	14 Tax representative

Copy for the consignee

2	15 Place of dispatch	16 Date of dispatch	17 Journey time

18a Marks and numbers, No. and kind of packages, description of goods		19a Commodity code (CN code)
		20a Quantity / 21a Gross weight (kg)
		22a Net weight (kg)

18b Marks and numbers, No. and kind of packages, description of goods		19b Commodity code (CN code)
		20b Quantity / 21b Gross weight (kg)
		22b Net weight (kg)

18c Marks and numbers, No. and kind of packages, description of goods		19c Commodity code (CN code)
		20c Quantity / 21c Gross weight (kg)
		22c Net weight (kg)

23 Certificates (certain wines and spirits, small breweries and distilleries)

A Record of control. For use by competent authority

24 Boxes 1–22 certified correct

Signatory's company and telephone No.

Name of signatory

Place and date

Signature

continue on reverse (copies 2, 3 and 4)

Reserve of copy 2

B CHANGE OF PLACE OF DELIVERY

New address:

The authorities mentioned in box 8
must be informed immediately

Name of signatory:
Place and date:

Signature

C CERTIFICATION OF RECEPTION OR EXPORTATION

☐ Goods received by consignee

Date .... Place .... Reference No. ....

Description of goods | Excess | Shortage

☐ Consignment checked

☐ Goods exported* / placed under a community
customs procedure (other then release for
free circulation)* date ....

Means of transport ....

☐ Name of signatory .... Place / date ....
Signatory's company
....

Signature ....

☐ Fiscal authority or Customs office
Name
Address

Endorsement by fiscal authority (if required) or Customs office

* delete inapplicable

A Record of control (continued)

Part III

NOTES

Substituted, together with Annex II, by Commission Regulation (EEC) 2225/93, Art 1,
para 4.

Point 2, Box 12: list substituted by Commission Regulation (EC) 1792/2006, Art 1, Annex
1, Part 7(1)(b).

ANNEX II
SPECIAL STAMP

Special Stamp

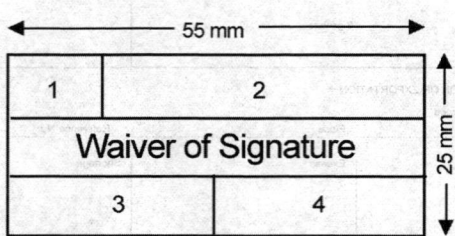

1. Coat of arms or any other signs or letters characterizing the Member State

2. Competent fiscal authority

3. Cosignor

4. No. and date of authorisation

NOTES

Substituted, together with Annex I, for original Annex II, by Commission Regulation (EEC) 2225/93, Art 1, para 4.

COUNCIL REGULATION

(2913/92/EEC)

of 12 October 1992

establishing the Community Customs Code

NOTES

Date of publication in OJ: OJ L302, 19.10.92, p 1.

Amended by: European Parliament and Council Regulation (EC) 648/2005 L 117,

04.05.2005, p 13. As to the application of these provisions, see (EC) 648/2005, Art 2.

ARRANGEMENT OF ARTICLES

Part III

TITLE IX
FINAL PROVISIONS

CHAPTER 1
CUSTOMS CODE COMMITTEE
Articles 247–249

CHAPTER 2
LEGAL EFFECTS IN A MEMBER STATE OF MEASURES TAKEN, DOCUMENTS ISSUED
AND FINDINGS MADE IN ANOTHER MEMBER STATE
Article 250

CHAPTER 3
OTHER FINAL PROVISIONS
Articles 251–253

THE COUNCIL OF THE EUROPEAN COMMUNITIES,

Having regard to the Treaty establishing the European Economic Community, and in particular Articles 28, 100a and 113 thereof,

Having regard to the proposal from the Commission[1],

In cooperation with the European Parliament[2],

Having regard to the opinion of the Economic and Social Committee[3],

Whereas the Community is based upon a customs union; whereas it is advisable, in the interests both of Community traders and the customs authorities, to assemble in a code the provisions of customs legislation that are at present contained in a large number of Community regulations and directives; whereas this task is of fundamental importance from the standpoint of the internal market;

Whereas such a Community Customs Code (hereinafter called 'the Code') must incorporate current customs legislation; whereas it is, nevertheless, advisable to amend that legislation in order to make it more consistent, to simplify it and to remedy certain omissions that still exist with a view to adopting complete Community legislation in this area;

Whereas, based on the concept of an internal market, the code must contain the general rules and procedures which ensure the implementation of the tariff and other measures introduced at Community level in connection with trade in goods between the Community and third countries; whereas it must cover, among other things, the implementation of common agricultural and commercial policy measures taking into account the requirements of these common policies;

Whereas it would appear advisable to specify that this Code is applicable without prejudice to specific provisions laid down in other fields; whereas such specific rules may exist or be introduced in the context, inter alia, of legislation relating to agriculture, statistics, commercial policy or own resources;

Whereas, in order to secure a balance between the needs of the customs authorities in regard to ensuring the correct application of customs legislation, on the one hand, and the right of traders to be treated fairly, on the other, the said authorities must be granted, inter alia, extensive powers of control and the said traders a right of appeal; whereas the implementation of a customs appeals system will require the United Kingdom to introduce new administrative procedures which cannot be effected before 1 January 1995;

Whereas in view of the paramount importance of external trade for the Community, customs formalities and controls should be abolished or at least kept to a minimum;

Whereas it is important to guarantee the uniform application of this Code and to provide, to that end, for a Community procedure which enables the procedures for its implementation to be adopted within a suitable time; whereas a Customs Code Committee should be set up in order to ensure close and effective cooperation between the Member States and the Commission in this field;

Whereas in adopting the measures required to implement this Code, the utmost care must be taken to prevent any fraud or irregularity liable to affect adversely the General Budget of the European Communities,

[1] OJ C 128, 23.5.1990, p 1.

[2] OJ C 72, 18.3.1991, p 176 and Decision of 16 September 1992 (not yet published in the Official Journal).

[3] OJ C 60, 8.3.1991, p 5.

HAS ADOPTED THIS REGULATION—

TITLE I
GENERAL PROVISIONS

CHAPTER 1
SCOPE AND BASIC DEFINITIONS

Article 1

Customs rules shall consist of this Code and the provisions adopted at Community level or nationally to implement them. The Code shall apply, without prejudice to special rules laid down in other fields

> — to trade between the Community and third countries,
> — to goods covered by the Treaty establishing the European Coal and Steel Community, the Treaty establishing the European Economic Community or the Treaty establishing the European Atomic Energy Community.

Article 2

1. Save as otherwise provided, either under international conventions or customary practices of a limited geographic and economic scope or under autonomous Community measures, Community customs rules shall apply uniformly throughout the customs territory of the Community.

2. Certain provisions of customs rules may also apply outside the customs territory of the Community within the framework of either rules governing specific fields or international conventions.

Article 3

[1. The customs territory of the Community shall comprise—

> — the territory of the Kingdom of Belgium,
> — the territory of the Kingdom of Denmark, except the Faroe Islands and Greenland,
> — the territory of the Federal Republic of Germany, except the Island of Heligoland and the territory of Busingen (Treaty of 23 November 1964 between the Federal Republic of Germany and the Swiss Confederation),
> — the territory of the Kingdom of Spain, except Ceuta and Melilla,
> [— the territory of the French Republic, except the overseas territories and Saint Pierre and Miquelon and Mayotte,]
> — the territory of the Hellenic Republic,
> — the territory of Ireland,
> — the territory of the Italian Republic, except the municipalities of Livigno and Campione d'Italia and the national waters of Lake Lugano which are between the bank and the political frontier of the area between Ponte Tresa and Porto Ceresio,

—   the territory of the Grand Duchy of Luxembourg,

—   the territory of the Kingdom of the Netherlands in Europe,

—   the territory of the Republic of Austria,

—   the territory of the Portuguese Republic,

[—   the territory of the Republic of Finland,]

—   the territory of the Kingdom of Sweden,

—   the territory of the United Kingdom of Great Britain and Northern Ireland and of the Channel Islands and the Isle of Man.]

[—   the territory of the Czech Republic,

—   the territory of the Republic of Estonia,

—   the territory of the Republic of Cyprus,

—   the territory of the Republic of Latvia,

—   the territory of the Republic of Lithuania,

—   the territory of the Republic of Hungary,

—   the territory of the Republic of Malta,

—   the territory of the Republic of Poland,

—   the territory of the Republic of Slovenia,

—   the territory of the Slovak Republic,]

[—   the territory of the Republic of Bulgaria,

—   the territory of Romania.]

[2.   Although situated outside the territory of the French Republic, the territory of the Principality of Monaco as defined in the Customs Convention signed in Paris on 18 May 1963 (*Official Journal of the French Republic* of 27 September 1963, p 8679) shall, by virtue of that Convention, also be considered to be part of the customs territory of the Community.]

3.   The customs territory of the Community shall include the territorial waters, the inland maritime waters and the airspace of the Member States, and the territories referred to in paragraph 2, except for the territorial waters, the inland maritime waters and the airspace of those territories which are not part of the customs territory of the Community pursuant to paragraph 1.

NOTES

Para 1: substituted by the 1994 Act of Accession of the Kingdom of Norway, the Republic of Austria, the Republic of Finland and the Kingdom of Sweden, Annex I(III)(B)(4), as adjusted by Council Decision 95/1(EC), Annex (XIII)(A)(I)(a), para (a); words in square brackets substituted by European Parliament and Council Regulation (EC) 82/97, Art 1, para 1. Entries inserted by the Act of Accession 2003 Annex II, art 19A(I). Entries in relation to Bulgaria and Romania inserted by Council Regulation (EC) 1791/2006, Art 1(1), Annex, Part 12.

Para 2: substituted by European Parliament and Council Regulation (EC) 82/97, Art 1, para 1.

Article 4

For the purposes of this Code, the following definitions shall apply—

(1)   'Person' means—

—   a natural person,

—   a legal person,

—   where the possibility is provided for under the rules in force, an association of persons recognised as having the capacity to perform legal acts but lacking the legal status of a legal person.

(2)   'Persons established in the Community' means—

     —   in the case of a natural person, any person who is normally resident there,

     —   in the case of a legal person or an association of persons, any person that has in the Community its registered office, central headquarters or a permanent business establishment.

(3)   'Customs authorities' means the authorities responsible *inter alia* for applying customs rules.

(4)   'Customs office' means any office at which all or some of the formalities laid down by customs rules may be completed.

[(4a)   'Customs office of entry' means the customs office designated by the customs authorities in accordance with the customs rules to which goods brought into the customs territory of the Community must be conveyed without delay and at which they will be subject to appropriate risk-based entry controls;

(4b)   'Customs office of import' means the customs office designated by the customs authorities in accordance with the customs rules where the formalities for assigning goods brought into the customs territory of the Community to a customs-approved treatment or use, including appropriate risk-based controls, are to be carried out;

(4c)   'Customs office of export' means the customs office designated by the customs authorities in accordance with the customs rules where the formalities for assigning goods leaving the customs territory of the Community to a customs-approved treatment or use, including appropriate risk-based controls, are to be completed;

(4d)   'Customs office of exit' means the customs office designated by the customs authorities in accordance with the customs rules to which goods must be presented before they leave the customs territory of the Community and at which they will be subject to customs controls relating to the completion of exit formalities, and appropriate risk-based controls.]

(5)   'Decision' means any official act by the customs authorities pertaining to customs rules giving a ruling on a particular case, such act having legal effects on one or more specific or identifiable persons; [this term covers, *inter alia*, binding information within the meaning of Article 12;]

(6)   'Customs status' means the status of goods as Community or non-Community goods.

(7)   'Community goods' means goods—

     [—   wholly obtained in the customs territory of the Community under the conditions referred to in Article 23 and not incorporating goods imported from countries or territories not forming part of the customs territory of the Community. Goods obtained from goods placed under a suspensive arrangement shall not be deemed to have Community status in cases of special economic importance determined in accordance with the committee procedure,]

     —   imported from countries or territories not forming part of the customs territory of the Community which have been released for free circulation,

     —   obtained or produced in the customs territory of the Community, either from goods referred to in the second indent alone or from goods referred to in first and second indents.

(8)   'Non-Community goods' means goods other than those referred to in subparagraph 7.

Without prejudice to Articles 163 and 164, Community goods shall lose their status as such when they are actually removed from the customs territory of the Community.

(9)   'Customs debt' means the obligation on a person to pay the amount of the import duties (customs debt on importation) or export duties (customs debt on exportation) which apply to specific goods under the Community provisions in force.

(10)   'Import duties' means—
— customs duties and charges having an effect equivalent to customs duties payable on the importation of goods,
— . . . import charges introduced under the common agricultural policy or under the specific arrangements applicable to certain goods resulting from the processing of agricultural products.

(11)   'Export duties' means—
— customs duties and charges having an effect equivalent to customs duties payable on the exportation of goods,
— . . . other export charges introduced under the common agricultural policy or under the specific arrangements applicable to certain goods resulting from the processing of agricultural products.

(12)   'Debtor' means any person liable for payment of a customs debt.

(13)   'Supervision by the customs authorities' means action taken in general by those authorities with a view to ensuring that customs rules and, where appropriate, other provisions applicable to goods subject to customs supervision are observed.

[(14)   'Customs controls' means specific acts performed by the customs authorities in order to ensure the correct application of customs rules and other legislation governing the entry, exit, transit, transfer and end-use of goods moved between the customs territory of the Community and third countries and the presence of goods that do not have Community status; such acts may include examining goods, verifying declaration data and the existence and authenticity of electronic or written documents, examining the accounts of undertakings and other records, inspecting means of transport, inspecting luggage and other goods carried by or on persons and carrying out official inquiries and other similar acts.]

(15)   'Customs-approved treatment or use of goods' means—
(a)   the placing of goods under a customs procedure;
(b)   their entry into a free zone or free warehouse;
(c)   their re-exportation from the customs territory of the Community;
(d)   their destruction;
(e)   their abandonment to the Exchequer.

(16)   'Customs procedure' means—
(a)   release for free circulation;
(b)   transit;
(c)   customs warehousing;
(d)   inward processing;
(e)   processing under customs control;
(f)   temporary admission;
(g)   outward processing;
(h)   exportation.

Part III

(17)   'Customs declaration' means the act whereby a person indicates in the prescribed form and manner a wish to place goods under a given customs procedure.

(18)   'Declarant' means the person making the customs declaration in his own name or the person in whose name a customs declaration is made.

(19)   'Presentation of goods to customs' means the notification to the customs authorities, in the manner laid down, of the arrival of goods at the customs office or at any other place designated or approved by the customs authorities.

(20)   'Release of goods' means the act whereby the customs authorities make goods available for the purposes stipulated by the customs procedure under which they are placed.

(21)   'Holder of the procedure' means the person on whose behalf the customs declaration was made or the person to whom the rights and obligations of the abovementioned person in respect of a customs procedure have been transferred.

(22)   'Holder of the authorisation' means the person to whom an authorisation has been granted.

(23)   'Provisions in force' means Community or national provisions.

[(24)   'Committee procedure' means either the procedure referred to in Articles 247 and 247a, or in Articles 248 and 248a.].

[(25)   'Risk' means the likelihood of an event occurring, in connection with the entry, exit, transit, transfer and end-use of goods moved between the customs territory of the Community and third countries and the presence of goods that do not have Community status, which

—   prevents the correct application of Community or national measures, or

—   compromises the financial interests of the Community and its Member States, or

—   poses a threat to the Community's security and safety, to public health, to the environment or to consumers.

(26)   'Risk management' means the systematic identification of risk and implementation of all measures necessary for limiting exposure to risk. This includes activities such as collecting data and information, analysing and assessing risk, prescribing and taking action and regular monitoring and review of the process and its outcomes, based on international, Community and national sources and strategies.]

NOTES

Words in square brackets in point 5 and point 7 substituted, and in points 10, 11 words omitted repealed, by European Parliament and Council Regulation (EC) 82/97, Art 1, para 2; point 24 substituted by European Parliament and Council Regulation (EC) 2700/2000, Art 1, para 1.

Points 4a–4d and 25, 26 inserted, and point 14 substituted, by European Parliament and Council Regulation (EC) 648/2005, Art 1, para 1. As to the application of these provisions, see (EC) 648/2005, Art 2.

CHAPTER 2
SUNDRY GENERAL PROVISIONS RELATING IN PARTICULAR TO THE RIGHTS AND OBLIGATIONS OF PERSONS WITH REGARD TO CUSTOMS RULES

SECTION 1
RIGHT OF REPRESENTATION

Article 5

1. Under the conditions set out in Article 64(2) and subject to the provisions adopted within the framework of Article 243(2)(b), any person may appoint a representative in his dealings with the customs authorities to perform the acts and formalities laid down by customs rules.

2. Such representation may be—

— direct, in which case the representative shall act in the name of and on behalf of another person, or

— indirect, in which case the representatives shall act in his own name but on behalf of another person.

A Member State may restrict the right to make customs declarations—

— by direct representation, or

— by indirect representation,

so that the representative must be a customs agent carrying on his business in that country's territory.

3. Save in the cases referred to in Article 64(2)(b) and (3), a representative must be established within the Community.

4. A representative must state that he is acting on behalf of the person represented, specify whether the representation is direct or indirect and be empowered to act as a representative.

A person who fails to state that he is acting in the name of or on behalf of another person or who states that he is acting in the name of or on behalf of another person without being empowered to do so shall be deemed to be acting in his own name and on his own behalf.

5. The customs authorities may require any person stating that he is acting in the name of or on behalf of another person to produce evidence of his powers to act as a representative.

[SECTION 1A
AUTHORISED ECONOMIC OPERATORS

Article 5a

1. Customs authorities, if necessary following consultation with other competent authorities, shall grant, subject to the criteria provided for in paragraph 2, the status of "authorised economic operator" to any economic operator established in the customs territory of the Community.

An authorised economic operator shall benefit from facilitations with regard to customs controls relating to security and safety and/or from simplifications provided for under the customs rules.

The status of authorised economic operator shall, subject to the rules and conditions laid down in paragraph 2, be recognised by the customs authorities in all Member States, without prejudice to customs controls. Customs authorities shall, on the basis of the recognition of the status of authorised economic operator and provided that the requirements relating to a specific type of simplification provided for in Community customs legislation are fulfilled, authorise the operator to benefit from that simplification.

2. The criteria for granting the status of authorised economic operator shall include:

- — an appropriate record of compliance with customs requirements,
- — a satisfactory system of managing commercial and, where appropriate, transport records, which allows appropriate customs controls,
- — where appropriate, proven financial solvency, and
- — where applicable, appropriate security and safety standards.

The committee procedure shall be used to determine the rules:

- — for granting the status of authorised economic operator,
- — for granting authorisations for the use of simplifications,
- — for establishing which customs authority is competent to grant such status and authorisations,
- — for the type and extent of facilitations that may be granted in respect of customs controls relating to security and safety, taking into account the rules for common risk management,
- — for consultation with, and provision of information to, other customs authorities;

and the conditions under which:

- — an authorisation may be limited to one or more Member States,
- — the status of authorised economic operator may be suspended or withdrawn, and
- — the requirement of being established in the Community may be waived for specific categories of authorised economic operator, taking into account, in particular, international agreements.

NOTES

Section 1A and Article 5a inserted by European Parliament and Council Regulation (EC) 648/2005, Art 1, para 2. As to the application of these provisions, see (EC) 648/2005, Art 2.

SECTION 2
DECISIONS RELATING TO THE APPLICATION OF CUSTOMS RULES

Article 6

1. Where a person requests that the customs authorities take a decision relating to the application of customs rules that person shall supply all the information and documents required by those authorities in order to take a decision.

2. Such decision shall be taken and notified to the applicant at the earliest opportunity.

Where a request for a decision is made in writing, the decision shall be made within a period laid down in accordance with the existing provisions, starting on the date on which the said request is received by the customs authorities. Such a decision must be notified in writing to the applicant.

However, that period may be exceeded where the customs authorities are unable to comply with it. In that case, those authorities shall so inform the applicant before the expiry of the abovementioned period, stating the grounds which justify exceeding it and indicating the further period of time which they consider necessary in order to give a ruling on the request.

3. Decisions adopted by the customs authorities in writing which either reject requests or are detrimental to the persons to whom they are addressed shall set out the grounds on which they are based. They shall refer to the right of appeal provided for in Article 243.

4. Provision may be made for the first sentence of paragraph 3 to apply likewise to other decisions.

Article 7

Save in the cases provided for in the second subparagraph of Article 244, decisions adopted shall be immediately enforceable by customs authorities.

Article 8

1. A decision favourable to the person concerned shall be annulled if it was issued on the basis of incorrect or incomplete information and—

— the applicant knew or should reasonably have known that the information was incorrect or incomplete, and

— such decision could not have been taken on the basis of correct or complete information.

2. The persons to whom the decision was addressed shall be notified of its annulment.

3. Annulment shall take effect from the date on which the annulled decision was taken.

Article 9

1. A decision favourable to the person concerned, shall be revoked or amended where, in cases other than those referred to in Article 8, one or more of the conditions laid down for its issue were not or are no longer fulfilled.

2. A decision favourable to the person concerned may be revoked where the person to whom it is addressed fails to fulfil an obligation imposed on him under that decision.

3. The person to whom the decision is addressed shall be notified of its revocation or amendment.

4. The revocation or amendment of the decision shall take effect from the date of notification. However, in exceptional cases where the legitimate interests of the person to whom the decision is addressed so require, the customs authorities may defer the date when revocation or amendment takes effect.

Article 10

Articles 8 and 9 shall be without prejudice to national rules which stipulate that decisions are invalid or become null and void for reasons unconnected with customs legislation.

SECTION 3
INFORMATION

Article 11

1. Any person may request information concerning the application of customs legislation from the customs authorities.

Such a request may be refused where it does not relate to an import or export operation actually envisaged.

2. The information shall be supplied to the applicant free of charge. However, where special costs are incurred by the customs authorities, in particular as a result of analyses or expert reports on goods, or the return of the goods to the applicant, he may be charged the relevant amount.

[Article 12

1. The customs authorities shall issue binding tariff information or binding origin information on written request, acting in accordance with the committee procedure.

2. Binding tariff information or binding origin information shall be binding on the customs authorities as against the holder of the information only in respect of the tariff classification or determination of the origin of goods.

Binding tariff information or binding origin information shall be binding on the customs authorities only in respect of goods on which customs formalities are completed after the date on which the information was supplied by them.

In matters of origin, the formalities in question shall be those relating to the application of Articles 22 and 27.

3. The holder of such information must be able to prove that—

— for tariff purposes: the goods declared correspond in every respect to those described in the information,

— for origin purposes: the goods concerned and the circumstances determining the acquisition of origin correspond in every respect to the goods and the circumstances described in the information.

4. Binding information shall be valid for a period of six years in the case of tariffs and three years in the case of origin from the date of issue. By way of derogation from Article 8, it shall be annulled where it is based on inaccurate or incomplete information from the applicant.

5. Binding information shall cease to be valid—

(a) in the case of tariff information—

(i) where a regulation is adopted and the information no longer conforms to the law laid down thereby;

(ii) where it is no longer compatible with the interpretation of one of the nomenclatures referred to in Article 20(6):

— at Community level, by reason of amendments to the explanatory notes to the combined nomenclature or by a judgment of the Court of Justice of the European Communities,

— at international level, by reason of a classification opinion or an amendment of the explanatory notes to the Nomenclature of the Harmonised Commodity Description and Coding System, adopted by the World Customs Organisation established in 1952 under the name 'the Customs Cooperation Council';

(iii) where it is revoked or amended in accordance with Article 9, provided that the revocation or amendment is notified to the holder.

The date on which binding information ceases to be valid for the cases cited in (i) and (ii) shall be the date of publication of the said measures or, in the case of international measures, the date of the Commission communication in the 'C' series of the *Official Journal of the European Communities*;

(b) in the case of origin information—

(i) where a regulation is adopted or an agreement is concluded by the Community and the information no longer conforms to the law thereby laid down;

(ii) where it is no longer compatible with—

— at Community level, the explanatory notes and opinions adopted for the purposes of interpreting the rules or with a judgment of the Court of Justice of the European Communities,

— at international level, the Agreement on Rules of Origin established in the World Trade Organisation (WTO) or with the explanatory notes or an origin opinion adopted for the interpretation of that Agreement;

(iii)   where it is revoked or amended in accordance with Article 9, provided that the holder has been informed in advance.

The date on which binding information ceases to be valid for the cases referred to in (i) and (ii) shall be the date indicated when the abovementioned measures are published or, in the case of international measures, the date shown in the Commission communication in the 'C' series of the *Official Journal of the European Communities*.

6.   The holder of binding information which ceases to be valid [pursuant to paragraph 5(a)(ii) or (iii) or (b)(ii) or (iii)] may still use that information for a period of six months from the date of publication or notification, provided that he concluded binding contracts for the purchase or sale of the goods in question, on the basis of the binding information, before that measure was adopted. However, in the case of products for which an import, export or advance-fixing certificate is submitted when customs formalities are carried out, the period of six months is replaced by the period of validity of the certificate.

In the case of paragraph 5(a)(i) and b(i), the Regulation or agreement may lay down a period within which the first subparagraph shall apply.

7.   The classification or determination of origin in binding information may be applied, on the conditions laid down in paragraph 6, solely for the purpose of—

—   determining import or export duties,

—   calculating export refunds and any other amounts granted for imports or exports as part of the common agricultural policy,

—   using import, export or advance-fixing certificates which are submitted when formalities are carried out for acceptance of the customs declaration concerning the goods in question, provided that such certificates were issued on the basis of the information concerned.

In addition, in exceptional cases where the smooth operation of the arrangements laid down under the common agricultural policy may be jeopardised, it may be decided to derogate from paragraph 6, in accordance with the procedure laid down in Article 38 of Council Regulation No 136/66/EEC of 22 September 1966 on the establishment of a common organisation of the market in oils and fats[1] and in the corresponding Articles in other regulations on the common organisation of markets.]

---

[1] OJ L 172, 30.9.66, p 3025/66. Regulation as last amended by Regulation (EC) No 3290/94 (OJ L 349, 31.12.94, p 105).

NOTES

Substituted by European Parliament and Council Regulation (EC) 82/97, Art 1, para 3.

Para 6: words substituted by Corrigendum to Council Regulation (EC) 82/97 (OJ L 179, 08.07.1997).

SECTION 4
OTHER PROVISIONS

[Article 13

1.   Customs authorities may, in accordance with the conditions laid down by the provisions in force, carry out all the controls they deem necessary to ensure that customs rules and other legislation governing the entry, exit, transit, transfer and end-use of goods moved between the customs territory of the Community and third countries and the presence of goods that do not have Community status are correctly

applied. Customs controls for the purpose of the correct application of Community legislation may be carried out in a third country where an international agreement provides for this.

2. Customs controls, other than spot-checks, shall be based on risk analysis using automated data processing techniques, with the purpose of identifying and quantifying the risks and developing the necessary measures to assess the risks, on the basis of criteria developed at national, Community and, where available, international level.

The committee procedure shall be used for determining a common risk management framework, and for establishing common criteria and priority control areas.

Member States, in cooperation with the Commission, shall establish a computer system for the implementation of risk management.

3. Where controls are performed by authorities other than the customs authorities, such controls shall be performed in close coordination with the customs authorities, wherever possible at the same time and place.

4. In the context of the controls provided for in this Article, customs and other competent authorities, such as veterinary and police authorities, may communicate data received, in connection with the entry, exit, transit, transfer and end-use of goods moved between the customs territory of the Community and third countries and the presence of goods that do not have Community status, between each other and to the customs authorities of the Member States and to the Commission where this is required for the purposes of minimising risk.

Communication of confidential data to the customs authorities and other bodies (eg security agencies) of third countries shall be allowed only in the framework of an international agreement and provided that the data protection provisions in force, in particular Directive 95/46/EC of the European Parliament and of the Council of 24 October 1995 on the protection of individuals with regard to the processing of personal data and on the free movement of such data (*) and Regulation (EC) No 45/2001 of the European Parliament and of the Council of 18 December 2000 on the protection of individuals with regard to the processing of personal data by the Community institutions and bodies and on the free movement of such data (**) are respected.]

---

* OJ L 281, 23.11.1995, p. 31. Directive as amended by Regulation (EC) No 1882/2003 (OJ L 284, 31.10.2003, p. 1).

** OJ L 8, 12.1.2001, p. 1.

NOTES

Article 13 substituted by European Parliament and Council Regulation (EC) 648/2005, Art 1, para 3. As to the application of these provisions, see (EC) 648/2005, Art 2.

Article 14

For the purposes of applying customs legislation, any person directly or indirectly involved in the operations concerned for the purposes of trade in goods shall provide the customs authorities with all the requisite documents and information, irrespective of the medium used, and all the requisite assistance at their request and by any time limit prescribed.

[Article 15

All information which is by nature confidential or which is provided on a confidential basis shall be covered by the duty of professional secrecy. It shall not be disclosed by the competent authorities without the express permission of the person or authority providing it. The communication of information shall, however, be permitted where the competent authorities are obliged to do so pursuant to the provisions in force, particularly in connection with legal proceedings. Any disclosure or communication of information shall fully comply with prevailing data protection provisions, in particular Directive 95/46/EC and Regulation (EC) No 45/2001.]

NOTES

Article 15 substituted by European Parliament and Council Regulation (EC) 648/2005, Art 1, para 4. As to the application of these provisions, see (EC) 648/2005, Art 2.

Article 16

The persons concerned shall keep the documents referred to in Article 14 for the purposes of [customs controls], for the period laid down in the provisions in force and for at least three calendar years, irrespective of the medium used. That period shall run from the end of the year in which—

- (a) in the case of goods released for free circulation in circumstances other than those referred to in (b) or goods declared for export, from the end of the year in which the declarations for release for free circulation or export are accepted;
- (b) in the case of goods released for free circulation at a reduced or zero rate of import duty on account of their end-use, from the end of the year in which they cease to be subject to customs supervision;
- (c) in the case of goods placed under another customs procedure, from the end of the year in which the customs procedure concerned is completed;
- (d) in the case of goods placed in a free zone or free warehouse, from the end of the year on which they leave the undertaking concerned.

Without prejudice to the provisions of Article 221(3), second sentence, where a check carried out by the customs authorities in respect of a customs debt shows that the relevant entry in the accounts has to be corrected, the documents shall be kept beyond the time limit provided for in the first paragraph for a period sufficient to permit the correction to be made and checked.

NOTES

Words substituted by European Parliament and Council Regulation (EC) 648/2005, Art 1, para 5. As to the application of these provisions, see (EC) 648/2005, Art 2.

Article 17

Where a period, date or time limit is laid down pursuant to customs legislation for the purpose of applying legislation, such period shall not be extended and such date or time limit shall not be deferred unless specific provision is made in the legislation concerned.

[Article 18

1. The value of the ecu in national currencies to be applied for the purposes of determining the tariff classification of goods and import duties shall be fixed once a month. The rates to be used for this conversion shall be those published in the *Official Journal of the European Communities* on the penultimate working day of the month. Those rates shall apply throughout the following month.

However, where the rate applicable at the start of the month differs by more than 5% from that published on the penultimate working day before the 15th of that same month, the latter rate shall apply from the 15th until the end of the month in question.

2. The value of the ecu in national currencies to be applied within the framework of customs legislation in cases other than those referred to in paragraph 1 shall be fixed once a year. The rates to be used for this conversion shall be those published in the *Official Journal of the European Communities* on the first working day of

October, with effect from 1 January of the following year. If no rate is available for a particular national currency, the rate applicable to that currency shall be that obtaining on the last day for which a rate was published in the *Official Journal of the European Communities*.

3. The customs authorities may round up or down the sum resulting from the conversion into their national currency of an amount expressed in ecus for purposes other than determining the tariff classification of goods or import or export duties.

The rounded-off amount may not differ from the original amount by more than 5%.

The customs authorities may retain unchanged the national-currency value of an amount expressed in ecus if, at the time of the annual adjustment provided for in paragraph 2, the conversion of that amount, prior to the abovementioned rounding-off, results in a variation of less than 5× in the national-currency value or a reduction in that value.]

NOTES

Substituted by European Parliament and Council Regulation (EC) 82/97, Art 1, para 4.

Article 19

The procedure of the Committee shall be used to determine in which cases and under which conditions the application of customs legislation may be simplified.

TITLE II
FACTORS ON THE BASIS OF WHICH IMPORT DUTIES OR EXPORT DUTIES AND THE OTHER MEASURES PRESCRIBED IN RESPECT OF TRADE IN GOODS ARE APPLIED

CHAPTER 1
CUSTOMS TARIFF OF THE EUROPEAN COMMUNITIES AND TARIFF CLASSIFICATION OF GOODS

Article 20

1. Duties legally owed where a customs debt is incurred shall be based on the Customs Tariff of the European Communities.

2. The other measures prescribed by Community provisions governing specific fields relating to trade in goods shall, where appropriate, be applied according to the tariff classification of those goods.

3. The Customs Tariff of the European Communities shall comprise—

(a) the combined nomenclature of goods;

(b) any other nomenclature which is wholly or partly based on the combined nomenclature or which adds any subdivisions to it, and which is established by Community provisions governing specific fields with a view to the application of tariff measures relating to trade in goods;

(c) the rates and other items of charge normally applicable to goods covered by the combined nomenclature as regards—

— customs duties; and,

— . . . import charges laid down under the common agricultural policy or under the specific arrangements applicable to certain goods resulting from the processing of agricultural products.

(d) the preferential tariff measures contained in agreements which the Community has concluded with certain countries or groups of countries and which provide for the granting of preferential tariff treatment;

(e)   preferential tariff measures adopted unilaterally by the Community in respect of certain countries, groups of countries or territories;

(f)   autonomous suspensive measures providing for a reduction in or relief from import duties chargeable on certain goods;

(g)   other tariff measures provided for by other Community legislation.

4.   Without prejudice to the rules on flat-rate charges, the measures referred to in paragraph 3(d), (e) and (f) shall apply at the declarant's request instead of those provided for in subparagraph (c) where the goods concerned fulfil the conditions laid down by those first-mentioned measures. An application may be made after the event provided that the relevant conditions are fulfilled.

5.   Where application of the measures referred to in paragraph 3(d), (e) and (f) is restricted to a certain volume of imports, it shall cease—

(a)   in the case of tariff quotas, as soon as the stipulated limit on the volume of imports is reached;

(b)   in the case of tariff ceilings, by ruling of the Commission.

6.   The tariff classification of goods shall be the determination, according to the rules in force, of—

(a)   the subheading of the combined nomenclature or the subheading of any other nomenclature referred to in paragraph 3(b); or

(b)   the subheading of any other nomenclature which is wholly or partly based on the combined nomenclature or which adds any subdivisions to it, and which is established by Community provisions governing specific fields with a view to the application of measures other than tariff measures relating to trade in goods,

under which the aforesaid goods are to be classified.

NOTES

Para 3: words omitted repealed by European Parliament and Council Regulation (EC) 82/97, Art 1, para 5.

Article 21

1.   The favourable tariff treatment from which certain goods may benefit by reason of their nature or end-use shall be subject to conditions laid down in accordance with the Committee procedure. Where an authorisation is required Articles 86 and 87 shall apply.

2.   For the purposes of paragraph 1, the expression 'favourable tariff treatment' means a reduction in or suspension of an import duty as referred to in Article 4(10), even within the framework of a tariff quota.

CHAPTER 2
ORIGIN OF GOODS

SECTION 1
NON-PREFERENTIAL ORIGIN

Article 22

Articles 23 to 26 define the non-preferential origin of goods for the purposes of—

(a)   applying the Customs Tariff of the European Communities with the exception of the measures referred to in Article 20(3)(d) and (e);

(b)   applying measures other than tariff measures established by Community provisions governing specific fields relating to trade in goods;

(c)   the preparation and issue of certificates of origin.

Article 23

1. Goods originating in a country shall be those wholly obtained or produced in that country.

2. The expression 'goods wholly obtained in a country' means—
   - (a) mineral products extracted within that country;
   - (b) vegetable products harvested therein;
   - (c) live animals born and raised therein;
   - (d) products derived from live animals raised therein;
   - (e) products of hunting or fishing carried on therein;
   - (f) products of sea-fishing and other products taken from the sea outside a country's territorial sea by vessels registered or recorded in the country concerned and flying the flag of that country;
   - (g) goods obtained or produced on board factory ships from the products referred to in subparagraph (f) originating in that country, provided that such factory ships are registered or recorded in that country and fly its flag;
   - (h) products taken from the seabed or subsoil beneath the seabed outside the territorial sea provided that that country has exclusive rights to exploit that seabed or subsoil;
   - (i) waste and scrap products derived from manufacturing operations and used articles, if they were collected therein and are fit only for the recovery of raw materials;
   - (j) goods which are produced therein exclusively from goods referred to in subparagraphs (a) to (i) or from their derivatives, at any stage of production.

3. For the purposes of paragraph 2 the expression 'country' covers that country's territorial sea.

Article 24

Goods whose production involved more than one country shall be deemed to originate in the country where they underwent their last, substantial, economically justified processing or working in an undertaking equipped for that purpose and resulting in the manufacture of a new product or representing an important stage of manufacture.

Article 25

Any processing or working in respect of which it is established, or in respect of which the facts as ascertained justify the presumption, that its sole object was to circumvent the provisions applicable in the Community to goods from specific countries shall under no circumstances be deemed to confer on the goods thus produced the origin of the country where it is carried out within the meaning of Article 24.

Article 26

1. Customs legislation or other Community legislation governing specific fields may provide that a document must be produced as proof of the origin of goods.

2. Notwithstanding the production of that document, the customs authorities may, in the event of serious doubts, require any additional proof to ensure that the indication of origin does comply with the rules laid down by the relevant Community legislation.

SECTION 2
PREFERENTIAL ORIGIN OF GOODS

Article 27

The rules on preferential origin shall lay down the conditions governing acquisition of origin which goods must fulfil in order to benefit from the measures referred to in Article 20(3)(d) or (e).

Those rules shall—

    (a)   in the case of goods covered by the agreements referred to in Article 20(3)(d), be determined in those agreements;

    (b)   in the case of goods benefiting from the preferential tariff measures referred to in Article 20(3)(e), be determined in accordance with the Committee procedure.

CHAPTER 3
VALUE OF GOODS FOR CUSTOMS PURPOSES

Article 28

The provisions of this Chapter shall determine the customs value for the purposes of applying the Customs Tariff of the European Communities and non-tariff measures laid down by Community provisions governing specific fields relating to trade in goods.

Article 29

1. The customs value of imported goods shall be the transaction value, that is, the price actually paid or payable for the goods when sold for export to the customs territory of the Community, adjusted, where necessary, in accordance with Articles 32 and 33, provided—

    (a)   that there are no restrictions as to the disposal or use of the goods by the buyer, other than restrictions which—

        —   are imposed or required by a law or by the public authorities in the Community,

        —   limit the geographical area in which the goods may be resold, or

        —   do not substantially affect the value of the goods;

    (b)   that the sale or price is not subject to some condition or consideration for which a value cannot be determined with respect to the goods being valued;

    (c)   that no part of the proceeds of any subsequent resale, disposal or use of the goods by the buyer will accrue directly or indirectly to the seller, unless an appropriate adjustment can be made in accordance with Article 32; and

    (d)   that the buyer and seller are not related, or, where the buyer and seller are related, that the transaction value is acceptable for customs purposes under paragraph 2.

2.—(a) In determining whether the transaction value is acceptable for the purposes of paragraph 1, the fact that the buyer and the seller are related shall not in itself be sufficient grounds for regarding the transaction value as unacceptable. Where necessary, the circumstances surrounding the sale shall be examined and the transaction value shall be accepted provided that the relationship did not influence the price. If, in the light of information provided by the declarant or otherwise, the customs authorities have grounds for considering that the relationship influenced the price, they shall communicate their grounds to the declarant and he shall be given a reasonable opportunity to respond. If the declarant so requests, the communication of the grounds shall be in writing.

Part III

(b)   In a sale between related persons, the transaction value shall be accepted and the goods valued in accordance with paragraph 1 wherever the declarant demonstrates that such value closely approximates to one of the following occurring at or about the same time—

(i)   the transaction value in sales, between buyers and sellers who are not related in any particular case, of identical or similar goods for export to the Community;

(ii)   the customs value of identical or similar goods, as determined under Article 30(2)(c);

(iii)   the customs value of identical or similar goods, as determined under Article 30(2)(d).

In applying the foregoing tests, due account shall be taken of demonstrated differences in commercial levels, quantity levels, the elements enumerated in Article 32 and costs incurred by the seller in sales in which he and the buyer are not related and where such costs are not incurred by the seller in sales in which he and the buyer are related.

(c)   The tests set forth in subparagraph (b) are to be used at the initiative of the declarant and only for comparison purposes. Substitute values may not be established under the said subparagraph.

3.—(a) The price actually paid or payable is the total payment made or to be made by the buyer to or for the benefit of the seller for the imported goods and includes all payments made or to be made as a condition of sale of the imported goods by the buyer to the seller or by the buyer to a third party to satisfy an obligation of the seller. The payment need not necessarily take the form of a transfer of money. Payment may be made by way of letters of credit or negotiable instrument and may be made directly or indirectly.

(b)   Activities, including marketing activities, undertaken by the buyer on his own account, other than those for which an adjustment is provided in Article 32, are not considered to be an indirect payment to the seller, even though they might be regarded as of benefit to the seller or have been undertaken by agreement with the seller, and their cost shall not be added to the price actually paid or payable in determining the customs value of imported goods.

Article 30

1. Where the customs value cannot be determined under Article 29, it is to be determined by proceeding sequentially through subparagraphs (a), (b), (c) and (d) of paragraph 2 to the first subparagraph under which it can be determined, subject to the proviso that the order of application of subparagraphs (c) and (d) shall be reversed if the declarant so requests; it is only when such value cannot be determined under a particular subparagraph that the provisions of the next subparagraph in a sequence established by virtue of this paragraph can be applied.

2. The customs value as determined under this Article shall be—

(a)   the transaction value of identical goods sold for export to the Community and exported at or about the same time as the goods being valued;

(b)   the transaction value of similar goods sold for export to the Community and exported at or about the same time as the goods being valued;

(c)   the value based on the unit price at which the imported goods for identical or similar imported goods are sold within the Community in the greatest aggregate quantity to persons not related to the sellers;

(d)   the computed value, consisting of the sum of—

—   the cost or value of materials and fabrication or other processing employed in producing the imported goods,

— an amount for profit and general expenses equal to that usually reflected in sales of goods of the same class or kind as the goods being valued which are made by producers in the country of exportation for export to the Community,

— the cost or value of the items referred to in Article 32(1)(e).

3. Any further conditions and rules for the application of paragraph 2 above shall be determined in accordance with the committee procedure.

Article 31

1. Where the customs value of imported goods cannot be determined under Articles 29 or 30, it shall be determined, on the basis of data available in the Community, using reasonable means consistent with the principles and general provisions of—

— the agreement on implementation of Article VII of the General Agreement on Tariffs and Trade [of 1994],

— Article VII of the General Agreement on Tariffs and Trade [of 1994],

— the provisions of this chapter.

2. No customs value shall be determined under paragraph 1 on the basis of—

(a) the selling price in the Community of goods produced in the Community;

(b) a system which provides for the acceptance for customs purposes of the higher of two alternative values;

(c) the price of goods on the domestic market of the country of exportation;

(d) the cost of production, other than computed values which have been determined for identical or similar goods in accordance with Article 30(2)(d);

(e) prices for export to a country not forming part of the customs territory of the Community;

(f) minimum customs values; or

(g) arbitrary or fictitious values.

NOTES

Para 1: words in square brackets inserted by European Parliament and Council Regulation (EC) 82/97, Art 1, para 6.

Article 32

1. In determining the customs value under Article 29, there shall be added to the price actually paid or payable for the imported goods—

(a) the following, to the extent that they are incurred by the buyer but are not included in the price actually paid or payable for the goods—

(i) commissions and brokerage, except buying commissions,

(ii) the cost of containers which are treated as being one, for customs purposes, with the goods in question,

(iii) the cost of packing, whether for labour or materials;

(b) the value, apportioned as appropriate, of the following goods and services where supplied directly or indirectly by the buyer free of charge or at reduced cost for use in connection with the production and sale for export of the imported goods, to the extent that such value has not been included in the price actually paid or payable—

(i) materials, components, parts and similar items incorporated in the imported goods,

Part III

        (ii)   tools, dies, moulds and similar items used in the production of the imported goods,

        (iii)   materials consumed in the production of the imported goods,

        (iv)   engineering, development, artwork, design work, and plans and sketches undertaken elsewhere than in the Community and necessary for the production of the imported goods;

(c)   royalties and licence fees related to the goods being valued that the buyer must pay, either directly or indirectly, as a condition of sale of the goods being valued, to the extent that such royalties and fees are not included in the price actually paid or payable;

(d)   the value of any part of the proceeds of any subsequent resale, disposal or use of the imported goods that accrues directly or indirectly to the seller;

(e)(i) the cost of transport and insurance of the imported goods, and

        (ii)   loading and handling charges associated with the transport of the imported goods

to the place of introduction into the customs territory of the Community.

2. Additions to the price actually paid or payable shall be made under this Article only on the basis of objective and quantifiable data.

3. No additions shall be made to the price actually paid or payable in determining the customs value except as provided in this Article.

4. In this Chapter, the term 'buying commissions' means fees paid by an importer to his agent for the service of representing him in the purchase of the goods being valued.

5. Notwithstanding paragraph 1(c)—

(a)   charges for the right to reproduce the imported goods in the Community shall not be added to the price actually paid or payable for the imported goods in determining the customs value; and

(b)   payments made by the buyer for the right to distribute or resell the imported goods shall not be added to the price actually paid or payable for the imported goods if such payments are not a condition of the sale for export to the Community of the goods.

Article 33

1. Provided that they are shown separately from the price actually paid or payable, the following shall not be included in the customs value—

(a)   charges for the transport of goods after their arrival at the place of introduction into the customs territory of the Community;

(b)   charges for construction, erection, assembly, maintenance or technical assistance, undertaken after importation of imported goods such as industrial plant, machinery or equipment;

(c)   charges for interest under a financing arrangement entered into by the buyer and relating to the purchase of imported goods, irrespective of whether the finance is provided by the seller or another person, provided that the financing arrangement has been made in writing and where required, the buyer can demonstrate that—

       —   such goods are actually sold at the price declared as the price actually paid or payable, and

       —   the claimed rate of interest does not exceed the level for such transactions prevailing in the country where, and at the time when, the finance was provided;

(d)   charges for the right to reproduce imported goods in the Community;

(e)   buying commissions;

(f)   import duties or other charges payable in the Community by reason of the importation or sale of the goods.

Article 34

Specific rules may be laid down in accordance with the procedure of the committee to determine the customs value of carrier media for use in data processing equipment and bearing data or instructions.

Article 35

[Where factors used to determine the customs value of goods are expressed in a currency other than that of the Member State where the valuation is made, the rate of exchange to be used shall be that duly published by the competent authorities of the Member State concerned.]

Such rate shall reflect as effectively as possible the current value of such currency in commercial transactions in terms of the currency of such Member State and shall apply during such period as may be determined in accordance with the procedure of the committee.

Where such a rate does not exist, the rate of exchange to be used shall be determined in accordance with the procedure of the committee.

NOTES

First paragraph substituted by European Parliament and Council Regulation (EC) 2700/2000, Art 1, para 2.

Article 36

1.   The provisions of this chapter shall be without prejudice to the specific provisions regarding the determination of the value for customs purposes of goods released for free circulation after being assigned a different customs-approved treatment or use.

2.   By way of derogation from Articles 29, 30 and 31, the customs value of perishable goods usually delivered on consignment may, at the request of the declarant, be determined under simplified rules drawn up for the whole Community in accordance with the committee procedure.

TITLE III

PROVISIONS APPLICABLE TO GOODS BROUGHT INTO THE CUSTOMS TERRITORY OF THE COMMUNITY UNTIL THEY ARE ASSIGNED A CUSTOMS-APPROVED TREATMENT OR USE

CHAPTER 1

ENTRY OF GOODS INTO THE CUSTOMS TERRITORY OF THE COMMUNITY

[Article 36a

1.   Goods brought into the customs territory of the Community shall be covered by a summary declaration, with the exception of goods carried on means of transport only passing through the territorial waters or the airspace of the customs territory without a stop within this territory.

2.   The summary declaration shall be lodged at the customs office of entry.

Customs authorities may allow the summary declaration to be lodged at another customs office, provided that this office immediately communicates or makes available electronically the necessary particulars to the customs office of entry.

Customs authorities may accept, instead of the lodging of the summary declaration, the lodging of a notification and access to the summary declaration data in the economic operator's computer system.

3. The summary declaration shall be lodged before the goods are brought into the customs territory of the Community.

4. The committee procedure shall be used to establish:

— the time limit by which the summary declaration is to be lodged before the goods are brought into the customs territory of the Community,

— the rules for exceptions from, and variations to, the time limit referred to in the first indent, and

— the conditions under which the requirement for a summary declaration may be waived or adapted,

in accordance with the specific circumstances and for particular types of goods traffic, modes of transport and economic operators and where international agreements provide for special security arrangements.]

NOTES

Articles 36a–36c inserted by European Parliament and Council Regulation (EC) 648/2005, Art 1, para 6. As to the application of these provisions, see (EC) 648/2005, Art 2.

[Article 36b

1. The committee procedure shall be used to establish a common data set and format for the summary declaration, containing the particulars necessary for risk analysis and the proper application of customs controls, primarily for security and safety purposes, using, where appropriate, international standards and commercial practices.

2. The summary declaration shall be made using a data processing technique. Commercial, port or transport information may be used, provided that it contains the necessary particulars.

Customs authorities may accept paper-based summary declarations in exceptional circumstances, provided that they apply the same level of risk management as that applied to summary declarations made using a data processing technique.

3. The summary declaration shall be lodged by the person who brings the goods, or who assumes responsibility for the carriage of the goods into the customs territory of the Community.

4. Notwithstanding the obligation of the person referred to in paragraph 3, the summary declaration may be lodged instead by:

(a) the person in whose name the person referred to in paragraph 3 acts; or

(b) any person who is able to present the goods in question or to have them presented to the competent customs authority; or

(c) a representative of one of the persons referred to in paragraph 3 or points (a) or (b).

5. The person referred to in paragraphs 3 and 4 shall, at his request, be authorised to amend one or more particulars of the summary declaration after it has been lodged. However, no amendment shall be possible after the customs authorities:

(a) have informed the person who lodged the summary declaration that they intend to examine the goods; or

(b) have established that the particulars in questions are incorrect; or

(c) have allowed the removal of the goods.]

NOTES

Articles 36a–36c inserted by European Parliament and Council Regulation (EC) 648/2005, Art 1, para 6. As to the application of these provisions, see (EC) 648/2005, Art 2.

[Article 36c

1. The customs office of entry may waive the lodging of a summary declaration in respect of goods for which, before expiry of the time limit referred to in Article 36a(3) or (4), a customs declaration is lodged. In such case, the customs declaration shall contain at least the particulars necessary for a summary declaration and, until such time as the former is accepted in accordance with Article 63, it shall have the status of a summary declaration.

Customs authorities may allow the customs declaration to be lodged at a customs office of import different from the customs office of entry, provided that this office immediately communicates or makes available electronically the necessary particulars to the customs office of entry.

2. Where the customs declaration is lodged other than by use of data processing technique, the customs authorities shall apply the same level of risk management to the data as that applied to customs declarations made using a data processing technique.]

NOTES

Articles 36a–36c inserted by European Parliament and Council Regulation (EC) 648/2005, Art 1, para 6. As to the application of these provisions, see (EC) 648/2005, Art 2.

Article 37

1. Goods brought into the customs territory of the Community shall, from the time of their entry, be subject to customs supervision. They may be subject to [customs controls] in accordance with the provisions in force.

2. They shall remain under such supervision for as long as necessary to determine their customs status, if appropriate, and in the case of non-Community goods and without prejudice to Article 82(1), until their customs status is changed, they enter a free zone or free warehouse or they are re-exported or destroyed in accordance with Article 182.

NOTES

Words substituted by European Parliament and Council Regulation (EC) 648/2005, Art 1, para 7. As to the application of these provisions, see (EC) 648/2005, Art 2.

Article 38

1. Goods brought into the customs territory of the Community shall be conveyed by the person bringing them into the Community without delay, by the route specified by the customs authorities and in accordance with their instructions, if any—

   (a)   to the customs office designated by the customs authorities or to any other place designated or approved by those authorities; or,

   (b)   to a free zone, if the goods are to be brought into that free zone direct—

   —   by sea or air, or

   —   by land without passing through another part of the customs territory of the Community, where the free zone adjoins the land frontier between a Member State and a third country.

2. Any person who assumes responsibility for the carriage of goods after they have been brought into the customs territory of the Community, *inter alia* as a result of transhipment, shall become responsible for compliance with the obligation laid down in paragraph 1.

3. Goods which, although still outside the customs territory of the Community, may be subject to *the control of the customs authority* of a Member State under the provisions in force, as a result of *inter alia* an agreement concluded between that

Part III

Member State and a third country, shall be treated in the same way as goods brought into the customs territory of the Community.

4. Paragraph 1(a) shall not preclude implementation of any provisions in force with respect to tourist traffic, frontier traffic, postal traffic or traffic of negligible economic importance, on condition that customs supervision and customs control possibilities are not thereby jeopardised.

[5. Paragraphs 1 to 4 and Articles 36a to 36c and 39 to 53 shall not apply to goods which temporarily leave the customs territory of the Community while moving between two points in that territory by sea or air, provided that the carriage is effected by a direct route and by regular air or shipping services without a stop outside the customs territory of the Community.]

6. Paragraph 1 shall not apply to goods on board vessels or aircraft crossing the territorial sea or airspace of the Member States without having as their destination a port or airport situated in those Member States.

NOTES

In para 3, words "customs controls by" to be substituted for words in italics by European Parliament and Council Regulation (EC) 648/2005, Art 1, para 7.

Para 5 substituted by European Parliament and Council Regulation (EC) 648/2005, Art 1, para 8. As to the application of these provisions, see (EC) 648/2005, Art 2.

Article 39

1. Where, by reason of unforeseeable circumstances or force majeure, the obligation laid down in Article 38(1) cannot be complied with, the person bound by that obligation or any other person acting in his place shall inform the customs authorities of the situation without delay. Where the unforeseeable circumstances or force majeure do not result in total loss of the goods, the customs authorities shall also be informed of their precise location.

2. Where, by reason of unforeseeable circumstances or force majeure, a vessel or aircraft covered by Article 38(6) is forced to put into port or land temporarily in the customs territory of the Community and the obligation laid down in Article 38(1) cannot be complied with, the person bringing the vessel or aircraft into the customs territory of the Community or any other person acting in his place shall inform the customs authorities of the situation without delay.

3. The customs authorities shall determine the measures to be taken in order to permit customs supervision of the goods referred to in paragraph 1 as well as those on board a vessel or aircraft in the circumstances specified in paragraph 2 and to ensure, where appropriate, that they are subsequently conveyed to a customs office or other place designated or approved by the authorities.

CHAPTER 2
PRESENTATION OF GOODS TO CUSTOMS

[**Article 40**

Goods entering the customs territory of the Community shall be presented to customs by the person who brings them into that territory or, if appropriate, by the person who assumes responsibility for carriage of the goods following such entry, with the exception of goods carried on means of transport only passing through the territorial waters or the airspace of the customs territory of the Community without a stop within this territory. The person presenting the goods shall make a reference to the summary declaration or customs declaration previously lodged in respect of the goods.]

NOTES

Article substituted by European Parliament and Council Regulation (EC) 648/2005, Art 1, para 9. As to the application of these provisions, see (EC) 648/2005, Art 2.

Article 41

Article 40 shall not preclude the implementation of rules in force relating to goods—

(a) carried by travellers;

(b) placed under a customs procedure but not presented to customs.

Article 42

Goods may, once they have been presented to customs, and with the permission of the customs authorities, be examined or samples may be taken, in order that they may be assigned a customs-approved treatment or use. Such permission shall be granted, on request, to the person authorised to assign the goods such treatment or use.

CHAPTER 3
[UNLOADING OF GOODS PRESENTED TO CUSTOMS]

NOTES

Chapter 3 heading substituted by European Parliament and Council Regulation (EC) 648/2005, Art 1, para 10. As to the application of these provisions, see (EC) 648/2005, Art 2.

Articles 43–45

. . . .

NOTES

Articles 43–45 repealed by European Parliament and Council Regulation (EC) 648/2005, Art 1, para 11. As to the application of these provisions, see (EC) 648/2005, Art 2.

Article 46

1. Goods shall be unloaded or transhipped from the means of transport carrying them solely with the permission of the customs authorities in places designated or approved by those customs authorities.

However, such permission shall not be required in the event of the imminent danger necessitating the immediate unloading of all or part of the goods. In that case, the customs authorities shall be informed accordingly forthwith.

2. For the purpose of inspecting goods and the means of transport carrying them, the customs authorities may at any time require goods to be unloaded and unpacked.

Article 47

Goods shall not be removed from their original position without the permission of the customs authorities.

CHAPTER 4
OBLIGATION TO ASSIGN GOODS PRESENTED TO CUSTOMS A CUSTOMS-APPROVED TREATMENT OR USE

Article 48

Non-Community goods presented to customs shall be assigned a customs-approved treatment or use authorised for such non-Community goods.

Article 49

1.   Where goods are covered by a summary declaration, the formalities necessary for them to be assigned a customs-approved treatment or use must be carried out within—

(a)   45 days from the date on which the summary declaration is lodged in the case of goods carried by sea;

(b)   20 days from the date on which the summary declaration is lodged in the case of goods carried otherwise than by sea.

2.   Where circumstances so warrant, the customs authorities may set a shorter period or authorise an extension of the periods referred to in paragraph 1. Such extension shall not, however, exceed the genuine requirements which are justified by the circumstances.

CHAPTER 5
TEMPORARY STORAGE OF GOODS

Article 50

Until such time as they are assigned a customs-approved treatment or use, goods presented to customs shall, following such presentation, have the status of goods in temporary storage. Such goods shall hereinafter be described as 'goods in temporary storage'.

Article 51

1.   Goods in temporary storage shall be stored only in places approved by the customs authorities under the conditions laid down by those authorities.

2.   The customs authorities may require the person holding the goods to provide security with a view to ensuring payment of any customs debt which may arise under Articles 203 or 204.

Article 52

Without prejudice to the provisions of Article 42, goods in temporary storage shall be subject only to such forms of handling as are designed to ensure their preservation in an unaltered state without modifying their appearance or technical characteristics.

Article 53

1.   The customs authorities shall without delay take all measures necessary, including the sale of the goods, to regularise the situation of goods in respect of which the formalities necessary for them to be assigned a customs-approved treatment or use are not initiated within the periods determined in accordance with Article 49.

2.   The customs authorities may, at the risk and expense of the person holding them, have the goods in question transferred to a special place, which is under their supervision, until the situation of the goods is regularised.

CHAPTER 6
PROVISIONS APPLICABLE TO NON-COMMUNITY GOODS WHICH HAVE MOVED UNDER A TRANSIT PROCEDURE

Article 54

Article 38, with the exception of paragraph 1(a) thereof, and Articles 39 to 53 shall not apply when goods already placed under a transit procedure are brought into the customs territory of the Community.

Article 55

Once non-Community goods which have moved under a transit procedure reach their destination in the customs territory of the Community and have been presented to customs in accordance with the rules governing transit, Article [42] to 53 shall apply.

NOTES

Figure in square brackets substituted by European Parliament and Council Regulation
(EC) 82/97, Art 1, para 7.

CHAPTER 7
OTHER PROVISIONS

Article 56

Where the circumstances so require, the customs authorities may have goods
presented to customs destroyed. The customs authorities shall inform the holder of the
goods accordingly. The costs of destroying the goods shall be borne by the holder.

Article 57

Where customs authorities find that goods have been brought unauthorised into the
customs territory of the Community or have been withheld from customs surveillance,
they shall take any measures necessary, including sale of the goods, in order to
regularise their situation.

TITLE IV
CUSTOMS-APPROVED TREATMENT OR USE

CHAPTER 1
GENERAL

Article 58

1. Save as otherwise provided, goods may at any time, under the conditions laid
down, be assigned any customs-approved treatment or use irrespective of their nature
or quantity, or their country of origin, consignment or destination.

2. Paragraph 1 shall not preclude the imposition of prohibitions or restrictions
justified on grounds of public morality, public policy or public security, the protection
of health and life of humans, animals or plants, the protection of national treasures
possessing artistic, historic or archaeological value or the protection of industrial and
commercial property.

CHAPTER 2
CUSTOMS PROCEDURES

SECTION 1
PLACING OF GOODS UNDER A CUSTOMS PROCEDURE

Article 59

1. All goods intended to be placed under a customs procedure shall be covered by
a declaration for that customs procedure.

2. Community goods declared for an export, outward processing, transit or
customs warehousing procedure shall be subject to customs supervision from the time
of acceptance of the customs declaration until such time as they leave the customs
territory of the Community or are destroyed or the customs declaration is invalidated.

Article 60

Insofar as Community customs legislation lays down no rules on the matter,
Member States shall determine the competence of the various customs offices situated
in their territory, account being taken, where applicable, of the nature of the goods
and the customs procedure under which they are to be placed.

Article 61

The customs declaration shall be made—

(a) in writing; or

(b) using a data-processing technique where provided for by provisions laid down in accordance with the committee procedure or where authorised by the customs authorities; or

(c) by means of a normal declaration or any other act whereby the holder of the goods expresses his wish to place them under a customs procedure, where such a possibility is provided for by the rules adopted in accordance with the committee procedure.

A.

DECLARATIONS IN WRITING

I.

Normal procedure

Article 62

1. Declarations in writing shall be made on a form corresponding to the official specimen prescribed for that purpose. They shall be signed and contain all the particulars necessary for implementation of the provisions governing the customs procedure for which the goods are declared.

2. The declaration shall be accompanied by all the documents required for implementation of the provisions governing the customs procedure for which the goods are declared.

Article 63

Declarations which comply with the conditions laid down in Article 62 shall be accepted by the customs authorities immediately, provided that the goods to which they refer are presented to customs.

Article 64

1. Subject to Article 5, a customs declaration may be made by any person who is able to present the goods in question or to have them presented to the competent customs authority, together with all the documents which are required to be produced for the application of the rules governing the customs procedure in respect of which the goods were declared.

2. However,

(a) where acceptance of a customs declaration imposes particular obligations on a specific person, the declaration must be made by that person or on his behalf;

(b) the declarant must be established in the Community.

However, the condition regarding establishment in the Community shall not apply to persons who—

— make a declaration for transit or temporary importation;

— declare goods on an occasional basis, provided that the customs authorities consider this to be justified.

3. Paragraph 2(b) shall not preclude the application by the Member States of bilateral agreements concluded with third countries, or customary practices having similar effect, under which nationals of such countries may make customs declarations in the territory of the Member States in question, subject to reciprocity.

Article 65

The declaration shall, at his request, be authorised to amend one or more of the particulars of the declaration after it has been accepted by customs. The amendment shall not have the effect of rendering the declaration applicable to goods other than those it originally covered.

However, no amendment shall be permitted where authorisation is requested after the customs authorities—

(a) have informed the declarant that they intend to examine the goods; or,

(b) have established that the particulars in question are incorrect; or,

(c) have released the goods.

Article 66

1. The customs authorities shall, at the request of the declarant, invalidate a declaration already accepted where the declarant furnishes proof that goods were declared in error for the customs procedure covered by that declaration or that, as a result of special circumstances, the placing of the goods under the customs procedure for which they were declared is no longer justified.

Nevertheless, where the customs authorities have informed the declarant of their intention to examine the goods, a request for invalidation of the declaration shall not be accepted until after the examination has taken place.

2. The declaration shall not be invalidated after the goods have been released, except in cases defined in accordance with the committee procedure.

3. Invalidation of the declaration shall be without prejudice to the application of the penal provisions in force.

Article 67

Save as otherwise expressly provided, the date to be used for the purposes of all the provisions governing the customs procedure for which the goods are declared shall be the date of acceptance of the declaration by the customs authorities.

Article 68

For the verification of declarations which they have accepted, the customs authorities may—

(a) examine the documents covering the declaration and the documents accompanying it. The customs authorities may require the declarant to present other documents for the purpose of verifying the accuracy of the particulars contained in the declaration;

(b) examine the goods and take samples for analysis or for detailed examination.

Article 69

1. Transport of the goods to the places where they are to be examined and samples are to be taken, and all the handling necessitated by such examination or taking of samples, shall be carried out by or under the responsibility of the declarant. The costs incurred shall be borne by the declarant.

2. The declarant shall be entitled to be present when the goods are examined and when samples are taken. Where they deem it appropriate, the customs authorities shall require the declarant to be present or represented when the goods are examined or samples are taken in order to provide them with the assistance necessary to facilitate such examination or taking of samples.

3. Provided that samples are taken in accordance with the provisions in force, the customs authorities shall not be liable for payment of any compensation in respect thereof but shall bear the costs of their analysis or examination.

Article 70

1.   Where only part of the goods covered by a declaration are examined, the results of the partial examination shall be taken to apply to all the goods covered by that declaration.

However, the declarant may request a further examination of the goods if he considers that the results of the partial examination are not valid as regards the remainder of the goods declared.

2.   For the purposes of paragraph 1, where a declaration form covers two or more items, the particulars relating to each item shall be deemed to constitute a separate declaration.

Article 71

1.   The results of verifying the declaration shall be used for the purposes of applying the provisions governing the customs procedure under which the goods are placed.

2.   Where the declaration is not verified, the provisions referred to in paragraph 1 shall be applied on the basis of the particulars contained in the declaration.

Article 72

1.   The customs authorities shall take the measures necessary to identify the goods where identification is required in order to ensure compliance with the conditions governing the customs procedure for which the said goods have been declared.

2.   Means of identification affixed to the goods or means of transport shall be removed or destroyed only by the customs authorities or with their permission unless, as a result of unforeseeable circumstances or force majeure, their removal or destruction is essential to ensure the protection of the goods or means of transport.

Article 73

1.   Without prejudice to Article 74, where the conditions for placing the goods under the procedure in question are fulfilled and provided the goods are not subject to any prohibitive or restrictive measures, the customs authorities shall release the goods as soon as the particulars in the declaration have been verified or accepted without verification. The same shall apply where such verification cannot be completed within a reasonable period of time and the goods are no longer required to be present for verification purposes.

2.   All the goods covered by the same declaration shall be released at the same time.

For the purposes of this paragraph, where a declaration form covers two or more items, the particulars relating to each item shall be deemed to constitute a separate declaration.

Article 74

1.   Where acceptance of a customs declaration gives rise to a customs debt, the goods covered by the declaration shall not be released unless the customs debt has been paid or secured. However, without prejudice to paragraph 2, this provision shall not apply to the temporary importation procedure with partial relief from import duties.

2.   Where, pursuant to the provisions governing the customs procedure for which the goods are declared, the customs authorities require the provision of a security, the said goods shall not be released for the customs procedure in question until such security is provided.

Article 75

Any necessary measures, including confiscation and sale, shall be taken to deal with goods which—

(a)   cannot be released because—

— it has not been possible to undertake or continue examination of the goods within the period prescribed by the customs authorities for reasons attributable to the declarant; or,

— the documents which must be produced before the goods can be placed under the customs procedure requested have not been produced; or,

— payments or security which should have been made or provided in respect of import duties or export duties, as the case may be, have not been made or provided within the period prescribed; or

— they are subject to bans or restrictions;

(b)   are not removed within a reasonable period after their release.

II.
Simplified procedures

Article 76

1.   In order to simplify completion of formalities and procedures as far as possible while ensuring that operations are conducted in a proper manner, the customs authorities shall, under conditions laid down in accordance with the committee procedure, grant permission for—

(a)   the declaration referred to in Article 62 to omit certain of the particulars referred to in paragraph 1 of that Article for some of the documents referred to in paragraph 2 of that Article not to be attached thereto;

(b)   a commercial or administrative document, accompanied by request for the goods to be placed under the customs procedure in question, to be lodged in place of the declaration referred to in Article 62;

(c)   the goods to be entered for the procedure in question by means of an entry in the records; in this case, the customs authorities may waive the requirement that the declarant presents the goods to customs.

The simplified declaration, commercial or administrative document or entry in the records must contain at least the particulars necessary for identification of the goods. Where the goods are entered in the records, the date of such entry must be included.

2.   Except in cases to be determined in accordance with the committee procedure, the declarant shall furnish a supplementary declaration which may be of a general, periodic or recapitulative nature.

3.   Supplementary declarations and the simplified declarations referred to in subparagraphs 1(a), (b) and (c), shall be deemed to constitute a single, indivisible instrument taking effect on the date of acceptance of the simplified declarations; in the cases referred to in subparagraph 1(c), entry in the records shall have the same legal force as acceptance of the declaration referred to in Article 62.

4.   Special simplified procedures for the Community transit procedure shall be laid down in accordance with the committee procedure.

B.
OTHER DECLARATIONS

Article 77

[1.]   Where the customs declaration is made by means of a data-processing technique within the meaning of Article 61(b), or by an oral declaration or any other act within the meaning of Article 61(c), Articles 62 to 76 shall apply *mutatis mutandis*without prejudice to the principles set out therein.

Part III

[2. Where the customs declaration is made by means of a data-processing technique, the customs authorities may allow accompanying documents referred to in Article 62(2) not to be lodged with the declaration. In this case the documents shall be kept at the customs authorities' disposal.]

NOTES

Para 1: numbered as such by European Parliament and Council Regulation (EC) 2700/2000, Art 1, para 3.

Para 2: added by European Parliament and Council Regulation (EC) 2700/2000, Art 1, para 3.

C.
POST-CLEARANCE EXAMINATION OF DECLARATIONS

Article 78

1. The customs authorities may, on their own initiative or at the request of the declarant, amend the declaration after release of the goods.

2. The customs authorities may, after releasing the goods and in order to satisfy themselves as to the accuracy of the particulars contained in the declaration, inspect the commercial documents and data relating to the import or export operations in respect of the goods concerned or to subsequent commercial operations involving those goods. Such inspections may be carried out at the premises of the declarant, of any other person directly or indirectly involved in the said operations in a business capacity or of any other person in possession of the said document and data for business purposes. Those authorities may also examine the goods where it is still possible for them to be produced.

3. Where revision of the declaration or post-clearance examination indicates that the provisions governing the customs procedure concerned have been applied on the basis of incorrect or incomplete information, the customs authorities shall, in accordance with any provisions laid down, take the measures necessary to regularise the situation, taking account of the new information available to them.

SECTION 2
RELEASE FOR FREE CIRCULATION

Article 79

Release for free circulation shall confer on non-Community goods the customs status of Community goods.

It shall entail application of commercial policy measures, completion of the other formalities laid down in respect of the importation of goods and the charging of any duties legally due.

Article 80

1. By way of derogation from Article 67, provided that the import duty chargeable on the goods is one of the duties referred to in the first indent of Article 4(10) and that the rate of duty is reduced after the date of acceptance of the declaration for release for free circulation but before the goods are released, the declarant may request application of the more favourable rate.

2. Paragraph 1 shall not apply where it has not been possible to release the goods for reasons attributable to the declarant alone.

Article 81

Where a consignment is made up of goods falling within different tariff classifications, and dealing with each of those goods in accordance with its tariff classification for the purpose of drawing up the declaration would entail a burden of work and expense disproportionate to the import duties chargeable, the customs authorities may, at the request of the declarant, agree that import duties be charged on the whole consignment on the basis of the tariff classification of the goods which are subject to the highest rate of import duty.

Article 82

1. Where goods are released for free circulation at a reduced or zero rate of duty on account of their end-use, they shall remain under customs supervision. Customs supervision shall end when the conditions laid down for granting such a reduced or zero rate of duty cease to apply, where the goods are exported or destroyed or where the use of the goods for purposes other than those laid down for the application of the reduced or zero rate of duty is permitted subject to payment of the duties due.

2. Articles 88 and 90 shall apply *mutatis mutandis* to the goods referred to in paragraph 1.

Article 83

Goods released for free circulation shall lose their customs status as Community goods where—

   (a)   the declaration for release for free circulation is invalidated after release . . ., or

   (b)   the imported duties payable on those goods are repaid or remitted—
       —   under the inward processing procedure in the form of the drawback system; or
       —   in respect of defective goods or goods which fail to comply with the terms of the contract, pursuant to Article 238; or
       —   in situations of the type referred to in Article 239 where repayment or remission is conditional upon the goods being exported or re-exported or being assigned an equivalent customs-approved treatment or use.

NOTES

Words omitted repealed by European Parliament and Council Regulation (EC) 82/97, Art 1, para 8.

SECTION 3
SUSPENSIVE ARRANGEMENTS AND CUSTOMS PROCEDURES WITH ECONOMIC IMPACT

A.
PROVISIONS COMMON TO SEVERAL PROCEDURES

Article 84

1. In Articles 85 to 90—
   (a)   where the term 'procedure' is used, it is understood as applying, in the case of non-Community goods, to the following arrangements—
       —   external transit;
       —   customs warehousing;
       —   inward processing in the form of a system of suspension;
       —   processing under customs control;
       —   temporary importation;
   (b)   where the term 'customs procedure with economic impact' is used, it is understood as applying to the following arrangements—

— customs warehousing;
— inward processing;
— processing under customs control;
— temporary importation;
— outward processing.

2. 'Import goods' means goods placed under a suspensive procedure and goods which, under the inward processing procedure in the form of the drawback system, have undergone the formalities for release for free circulation and the formalities provided for in Article 125.

3. 'Goods in the unaltered state' means import goods which, under the inward processing procedure or the procedures for processing under customs control, have undergone no form of processing.

Article 85

The use of any customs procedure with economic impact shall be conditional upon authorisation being issued by the customs authorities.

Article 86

Without prejudice to the additional special conditions governing the procedure in question, the authorisation referred to in Article 85 and that referred to in Article 100(1) shall be granted only—

— to persons who offer every guarantee necessary for the proper conduct of the operations;
— where the customs authorities can supervise and monitor the procedure without having to introduce administrative arrangements disproportionate to the economic needs involved.

Article 87

1. The conditions under which the procedure in question is used shall be set out in the authorisation.

2. The holder of the authorisation shall notify the customs authorities of all factors arising after the authorisation was granted which may influence its continuation or content.

[Article 87a

In the cases referred to in the second sentence of the first indent of Article 4(7), any products or goods obtained from goods placed under a suspensive arrangement shall be considered as being placed under the same arrangement.]

NOTES

Inserted by European Parliament and Council Regulation (EC) 82/97, Art 1, para 9.

Article 88

The customs authorities may make the placing of goods under a suspensive arrangement conditional upon the provision of security in order to ensure that any customs debt which may be incurred in respect of those goods will be paid.

Special provisions concerning the provision of security may be laid down in the context of a specific suspensive arrangement.

Article 89

1. A suspensive arrangement with economic impact shall be discharged when a new customs-approved treatment or use is assigned either to the goods placed under that arrangement or to compensating or processed products placed under it.

2.   The customs authorities shall take all the measures necessary to regularise the position of goods in respect of which a procedure has not been discharged under the conditions prescribed.

Article 90

The rights and obligations of the holder of a customs procedure with economic impact may, on the conditions laid down by the customs authorities, be transferred successively to other persons who fulfil any conditions laid down in order to benefit from the procedure in question.

B.

EXTERNAL TRANSIT

I.

General provisions

Article 91

1.   The external transit procedure shall allow the movement from one point to another within the customs territory of the Community of—

  (a)   non-Community goods, without such goods being subject to import duties and other charges or to commercial policy measures;

  [(b)   Community goods, in cases and on conditions determined in accordance with the committee procedure, in order to prevent products covered by or benefiting from export measures from either evading or benefiting unjustifiably from such measures].

2.   Movement as referred to in paragraph 1 shall take place—

  (a)   under the external Community transit procedure; or

  (b)   under cover of a TIR carnet (TIR Convention) provided that such movement—

    (1)   began or is to end outside the Community; or

    (2)   relates to consignments of goods which must be unloaded in the customs territory of the Community and which are conveyed with goods to be unloaded in a third country; or

    (3)   is effected between two points in the Community through the territory of a third country;

  (c)   under cover of an ATA carnet . . . used as a transit document; or

  (d)   under cover of the Rhine Manifest (Article 9 of the revised Convention for the Navigation of the Rhine); or

  (e)   under cover of the form 302 provided for in the Convention between the Parties to the North Atlantic Treaty regarding the Status of their Forces, signed in London on 19 June 1951; or

  (f)   by post (including parcel post).

3.   The external transit procedure shall apply without prejudice to the specific provisions applicable to the movement of goods placed under a customs procedure with economic impact.

NOTES

  Para 1: sub-para (b) substituted by European Parliament and Council Regulation (EC) 955/1999, Art 1, para 1.

  Para 2: words omitted repealed by European Parliament and Council Regulation (EC) 82/97, Art 1, para 10.

Part III

[Article 92

1. The external transit procedure shall end and the obligations of the holder shall be met when the goods placed under the procedure and the required documents are produced at the customs office of destination in accordance with the provisions of the procedure in question.

2. The customs authorities shall discharge the procedure when they are in a position to establish, on the basis of a comparison of the data available to the office of departure and those available to the customs office of destination, that the procedure has ended correctly.]

NOTES

Substituted by European Parliament and Council Regulation (EC) 955/1999, Art 1, para 2.

II.
Specific provisions relating to external Community transit

Article 93

The external Community transit procedure shall apply to goods passing through the territory of a third country only if—

(a)   provision is made to that effect under an international agreement; or

(b)   carriage through that country is effected under cover of a single transport document drawn up in the customs territory of the Community; in such case the operation of that procedure shall be suspended in the territory of the third country.

[Article 94

1. The principal shall provide a guarantee in order to ensure payment of any customs debt or other charges which may be incurred in respect of the goods.

2. The guarantee shall be either—

(a)   an individual guarantee covering a single transit operation; or

(b)   a comprehensive guarantee covering a number of transit operations where the principal has been authorised to use such a guarantee by the customs authorities of the Member State where he is established.

3. The authorisation referred to in paragraph 2(b) shall be granted only to persons who—

(a)   are established in the Community;

(b)   are regular users of Community transit procedures or who are known to the customs authorities to have the capacity to fulfil their obligations in relation to these procedures, and

(c)   have not committed serious or repeated offences against customs or tax laws.

4. Persons who satisfy the customs authorities that they meet higher standards of reliability may be authorised to use a comprehensive guarantee for a reduced amount or to have a guarantee waiver. The additional criteria for this authorisation shall include—

(a)   the correct use of the Community transit procedures during a given period;

(b)   cooperation with the customs authorities, and

(c)   in respect of the guarantee waiver, a good financial standing which is sufficient to fulfil the commitments of the said persons.

The detailed rules for authorisations granted under this paragraph shall be determined in accordance with the committee procedure.

5. The guarantee waiver authorised in accordance with paragraph 4 shall not apply to external Community transit operations involving goods which, as determined in accordance with the committee procedure, are considered to present increased risks.

6. In line with the principles underlying paragraph 4, recourse to the comprehensive guarantee for a reduced amount may, in the case of external Community transit, be temporarily prohibited by the committee procedure as an exceptional measure in special circumstances.

7. In line with the principles underlying paragraph 4, recourse to the comprehensive guarantee may, in the case of external Community transit, be temporarily prohibited by the committee procedure in respect of goods which, under the comprehensive guarantee, have been identified as being subject to large-scale fraud.]

NOTES

Substituted by European Parliament and Council Regulation (EC) 955/1999, Art 1, para 3.

[Article 95

1. Except in cases to be determined where necessary in accordance with the committee procedure, no guarantee need be furnished for—

    (a)   journeys by air;

    (b)   the carriage of goods on the Rhine and the Rhine waterways;

    (c)   carriage by pipeline;

    (d)   operations carried out by the railway companies of the Member States.

2. The cases in which the furnishing of a guarantee in respect of the carriage of goods on waterways other than those referred to in paragraph (b) may be waived shall be determined in accordance with the committee procedure.]

NOTES

Substituted by European Parliament and Council Regulation (EC) 955/1999, Art 1, para 4.

Article 96

1. The principal shall be the holder of the external Community transit procedure. He shall be responsible for—

    (a)   production of the goods intact at the customs office of destination by the prescribed time limit and with due observance of the measures adopted by the customs authorities to ensure identification;

    (b)   observance of the provisions relating to the Community transit procedure.

2. Notwithstanding the principal's obligations under paragraph 1, a carrier or recipient of goods who accepts goods knowing that they are moving under Community transit shall also be responsible for production of the goods intact at the customs office of destination by the prescribed time limit and with due observance of the measures adopted by the customs authorities to ensure identification.

[Article 97

1. The detailed rules for the operation of the procedure and the exemptions shall be determined in accordance with the committee procedure.

2. Provided that the implementation of Community measures applying to goods is guaranteed—

    (a)   Member States have the right, by bilateral or multilateral arrangement, to establish between themselves simplified procedures consistent with criteria to be set according to the circumstances and applying to certain types of goods traffic or specific undertakings;

(b)   each Member State shall have the right to establish simplified procedures in certain circumstances for goods not required to move in the territory of another Member State.

3.   Simplified procedures established under paragraph 2 shall be communicated to the Commission.]

NOTES

Substituted by European Parliament and Council Regulation (EC) 955/1999, Art 1, para 5.

C.
CUSTOMS WAREHOUSES

Article 98

1.   The customs warehousing procedure shall allow the storage in a customs warehouse of—

(a)   non-Community goods, without such goods being subject to import duties or commercial policy measures;

(b)   Community goods, where Community legislation governing specific fields provides that their being placed in a customs warehouse shall attract the application of measures normally attaching to the export of such goods.

2.   Customs warehouse means any place approved by and under the supervision of the customs authorities where goods may be stored under the conditions laid down.

3.   Cases in which the goods referred to in paragraph 1 may be placed under the customs warehousing procedure without being stored in a customs warehouse shall be determined in accordance with the committee procedure.

Article 99

A customs warehouse may be either a public warehouse or a private warehouse.

'Public warehouse' means a customs warehouse available for use by any person for the warehousing of goods;

'Private warehouse' means a customs warehouse reserved for the warehousing of goods by the warehousekeeper.

The warehousekeeper is the person authorised to operate the customs warehouse.

The depositer shall be the person bound by the declaration placing the goods under the customs warehousing procedure or to whom the rights and obligations of such a person have been transferred.

Article 100

1.   Operation of a customs warehouse shall be subject to the issue of an authorisation by the customs authorities, unless the said authorities operate the customs warehouse themselves.

2.   Any person wishing to operate a customs warehouse must make a request in writing containing the information required for granting the authorisation, in particular demonstrating that an economic need for warehousing exists. The authorisation shall lay down the conditions for operating the customs warehouse.

3.   The authorisation shall be issued only to persons established in the Community.

Article 101

The warehousekeeper shall be responsible for—

(a)   ensuring that while the goods are in the customs warehouse they are not removed from customs supervision;

(b)   fulfilling the obligations that arise from the storage of goods covered by the customs warehousing procedure; and

(c)   complying with the particular conditions specified in the authorisation.

Article 102

1. By way of derogation from Article 101, where the authorisation concerns a public warehouse, it may provide that the responsibilities referred to in Article 101(a) and/or (b) devolve exclusively upon the depositor.

2. The depositor shall at all times be responsible for fulfilling the obligations arising from the placing of goods under the customs warehousing procedure.

Article 103

The rights and obligations of a warehousekeeper may, with the agreement of the customs authorities, be transferred to another person.

Article 104

Without prejudice to Article 88, the customs authorities may demand that the warehousekeeper provide a guarantee in connection with the responsibilities specified in Article 101.

Article 105

The person designated by the customs authorities shall keep stock records of all the goods placed under the customs warehousing procedure in a form approved by those authorities. Stock records are not necessary where a public warehouse is operated by the customs authorities.

Subject to the application of Article 86 the customs authorities may dispense with stock records where the responsibilities referred to in Article 101(a) and/or (b) lie exclusively with the depositor and the goods are placed under that procedure on the basis of a written declaration forming part of the normal procedure or an administrative document in accordance with Article 76(1)(b).

Article 106

1. Where an economic need exists and customs supervision is not adversely affected thereby, the customs authorities may allow—

(a)   Community goods other than those referred to in Article 98(1)(b) to be stored on the premises of a customs warehouse;

(b)   non-Community goods to be processed on the premises of a customs warehouse under the inward processing procedure, subject to the conditions provided for by that procedure. The formalities which may be dispensed with in a customs warehouse shall be determined in accordance with the committee procedure;

(c)   non-Community goods to be processed on the premises of a customs warehouse under the procedure for processing under customs control, subject to the conditions provided for by that procedure. The formalities which may be dispensed with in a customs warehouse shall be determined in accordance with the committee procedure.

2. In the cases referred to in paragraph 1, the goods shall not be subject to the customs warehousing procedure.

3. The customs authorities may require the goods referred to in paragraph 1 to be entered in the stock records provided for in Article 105.

Article 107

Goods placed under the customs warehousing procedure shall be entered in the stock records provided for in Article 105 as soon as they are brought into the customs warehouse.

Article 108

1. There shall be no limit to the length of time goods may remain under the customs warehousing procedure.

However, in exceptional cases, the customs authorities may set a time limit by which the depositor must assign the goods a new customs-approved treatment or use.

2. Specific time limits for certain goods referred to in Article 98(1)(b) covered by the common agricultural policy may be laid down in accordance with the committee procedure.

Article 109

1. Import goods may undergo the usual forms of handling intended to preserve them, improve their appearance or marketable quality or prepare them for distribution or resale.

A list of cases in which those forms of handling shall be prohibited for goods covered by the common agricultural policy may be drawn up if this is necessary to ensure the smooth operation of the common organisation of markets.

2. Community goods referred to in Article 98(1)(b) which are placed under the customs warehousing procedure and are covered by the common agricultural policy may undergo only the forms of handling expressly stipulated for such goods.

3. The forms of handling provided for in the first subparagraph of paragraph 1 and in paragraph 2 must be authorised in advance by the customs authorities, which shall lay down the conditions under which they may take place.

4. The lists of the forms of handling referred to in paragraphs 1 and 2 shall be established in accordance with the committee procedure.

Article 110

Where circumstances so warrant, goods placed under the customs warehousing procedure may be temporarily removed from the customs warehouse. Such removal must be authorised in advance by the customs authorities, who shall stipulate the conditions on which it may take place.

While they are outside the customs warehouse the goods may undergo the forms of handling referred to in Article 109 on the conditions set out therein.

Article 111

The customs authorities may allow goods placed under the customs warehousing procedure to be transferred from one customs warehouse to another.

Article 112

1. Where a customs debt is incurred in respect of import goods and the customs value of such goods is based on a price actually paid or payable which includes the cost of warehousing and of preserving goods while they remain in the warehouse, such costs need not be included in the customs value if they are shown separately from the price actually paid or payable for the goods.

2. Where the said goods have undergone the usual forms of handling within the meaning of Article 109, the nature of the goods, the customs value and the quantity to be taken into account in determining the amount of import duties shall, at the request of the declarant, be those which would be taken into account for the goods, at the time referred to in Article 214, if they had not undergone such handling. However, derogations from this provision may be adopted under the committee procedure.

[3. Where import goods are released for free circulation in accordance with Article 76(1)(c), the nature of the goods, the customs value and the quantity to be taken into account for the purposes of Article 214 shall be those applicable to the goods at the time when they were placed under the customs-warehousing procedure.

The first subparagraph shall apply provided that the rules of assessment relating to those goods were ascertained or accepted at the time when the goods were placed under the customs-warehousing procedure, unless the declarant requests their application at the time when the customs debt is incurred.

The first subparagraph shall apply without prejudice to a post- clearance examination within the meaning of Article 78.]

NOTES

Para 3: substituted by European Parliament and Council Regulation (EC) 82/97, Art 1, para 11.

Article 113

Community goods referred to in Article 98(1)(b) which are covered by the common agricultural policy and are placed under the customs warehousing procedure must be exported or be assigned a treatment or use provided for by the Community legislation governing specific fields referred to in that Article.

D.

INWARD PROCESSING

I.

General

Article 114

1. Without prejudice to Article 115, the inward processing procedure shall allow the following goods to be used in the customs territory of the Community in one or more processing operations—

   (a) non-Community goods intended for re-export from the customs territory of the Community in the form of compensating products, without such goods being subject to import duties or commercial policy measures;

   (b) goods released for free circulation with repayment or remission of the import duties chargeable on such goods if they are exported from the customs territory of the Community in the form of compensating products.

2. The following expressions shall have the following meanings—

   (a) suspension system: the inward processing relief arrangements as provided for in paragraph 1(a);

   (b) drawback system: the inward processing relief arrangements as provided for in paragraph 1(b);

   (c) processing operations—

   — the working of goods, including erecting or assembling them or fitting them to other goods;

   — the processing of goods;

   — the repair of goods, including restoring them and putting them in order; and

   — the use of certain goods defined in accordance with the committee procedure which are not to be found in the compensating products, but which allow or facilitate the production of those products, even if they are entirely or partially used up in the process.

   (d) compensating products: all products resulting from processing operations;

   (e) equivalent goods: Community goods which are used instead of the import goods for the manufacture of compensating products;

(f)   rate of yield: the quantity or percentage of compensating products obtained from the processing of a given quantity of import goods.

Article 115

1. Where the conditions laid down in paragraph 2 are fulfilled, and subject to paragraph 4, the customs authorities shall allow—

(a)   compensating products to be obtained from equivalent goods;

(b)   compensating products obtained from equivalent goods to be exported from the Community before importation of the import goods.

2. Equivalent goods must be of the same quality and have the same characteristics as the import goods. However, in specific cases determined in accordance with the committee procedure, equivalent goods may be allowed to be at a more advanced stage of manufacture than the import goods.

3. Where paragraph 1 applies, the import goods shall be regarded for customs purposes as equivalent goods and the latter as import goods.

[4. Measures aimed at prohibiting, imposing certain conditions for or facilitating recourse to paragraph 1 may be adopted in accordance with the committee procedure.]

5. Where paragraph 1(b) is applied and the compensating products would be liable to export duties if they were not being exported or re-exported under an inward processing operation, the holder of the authorisation shall provide a security to ensure payment of the duties should the import goods not be imported within the period prescribed.

NOTES

Para 4: substituted by European Parliament and Council Regulation (EC) 2700/2000, Art 1, para 4.

II.
Grant of the authorisation

Article 116

The authorisation shall be issued at the request of the person who carries out processing operations or who arranges for them to be carried out.

Article 117

The authorisation shall be granted only—

(a)   to persons established in the Community. However, the authorisation may be granted to persons established outside the Community in respect of imports of a non-commercial nature;

(b)   where, without prejudice to the use of the goods referred to in the last indent of Article 114(2)(c) final indent, the import goods can be identified in the compensating products or, in the case referred to in Article 115, where compliance with the conditions laid down in respect of equivalent goods can be verified;

(c)   where the inward processing procedure can help create the most favourable conditions for the export or re-export of compensating products, provided that the essential interests of Community producers are not adversely affected (economic conditions). [The cases in which the economic conditions are deemed to have been fulfilled may be determined in accordance with the committee procedure.]

NOTES
Words in sub-para (c) added by European Parliament and Council Regulation (EC) 2700/2000, Art 1, para 5.

III.
Operation of the procedure

Article 118

1. The customs authorities shall specify the period within which the compensating products must have been exported or re-exported or assigned another customs-approved treatment or use. That period shall take account of the time required to carry out the processing operations and dispose of the compensating products.

2. The period shall run from the date on which the non-Community goods are placed under the inward processing procedure. The customs authorities may grant an extension on submission of a duly substantiated request by the holder of the authorisation.

For reasons of simplification, it may be decided that a period which commences in the course of a calendar month or quarter shall end on the last day of a subsequent calendar month or quarter respectively.

3. Where Article 115(1)(b) applies, the customs authorities shall specify the period within which the non-Community goods must be declared for the procedure. That period shall run from the date of acceptance of the export declaration relating to the compensating products obtained from the corresponding equivalent goods.

4. Specific time limits may be laid down in accordance with the committee procedure for certain processing operations or for certain import goods.

Article 119

1. The customs authorities shall set either the rate of yield of the operation or where appropriate, the method of determining such rate. The rate of yield shall be determined on the basis of the actual circumstances in which the processing operation is, or is to be, carried out.

2. Where circumstances so warrant and, in particular, in the case of processing operation customarily carried out under clearly defined technical conditions involving goods of substantially uniform characteristics and resulting in the production of compensating products of uniform quality, standard rates of yield may be set in accordance with the committee procedure on the basis of actual data previously ascertained.

Article 120

The cases in which and the conditions under which goods in the unaltered state or compensating products shall be considered to have been released for free circulation may be determined in accordance with the committee procedure.

Article 121

1. Subject to Article 122, where a customs debt is incurred, the amount of such debt shall be determined on the basis of the taxation elements appropriate to the import goods at the time of acceptance of the declaration of placing of these goods under the inward processing procedure.

2. If at the time referred to in paragraph 1 the import goods fulfilled the conditions to qualify for preferential tariff treatment within tariff quotas or ceilings, they shall be eligible for any preferential tariff treatment existing in respect of identical goods at the time of acceptance of the declaration of release for free circulation.

Part III

Article 122

By way of derogation from Article 121, compensating products—

(a)   shall be subject to the import duties appropriate to them where—

— they are released for free circulation and appear on the list adopted in accordance with the committee procedure, to the extent that they are in proportion to the exported part of the compensating products not included in that list. However, the holder of the authorisation may ask for the duty on those products to be assessed in the manual referred to in Article 121;

— they are subject to charges established under the common agricultural policy, and provisions adopted in accordance with the committee procedure so provide;

(b)   shall be subject to import duties calculated in accordance with the rules applicable to the customs procedure in question or to free zones or free warehouses where they have been placed under a suspensive arrangement or in a free zone or free warehouse;

However,

— the person concerned may request that duty be assessed in accordance with Article 121;

— in cases where the compensating products have been assigned a customs-approved treatment or use referred to above other than processing under customs control, the amount of the import duty levied shall be at least equal to the amount calculated in accordance with Article 121;

(c)   may be made subject to the rules governing assessment of duty laid down under the procedure for processing under customs control where the import goods could have been placed under that procedure;

(d)   shall enjoy favourable tariff treatment owing to the special use for which they are intended, where provision is made for such treatment in the case of identical imported goods;

(e)   shall be admitted free of import duty where such duty-free provision is made in the case of identical goods imported in accordance with Article 184.

IV.

Processing operations outside the customs territory of the Community

Article 123

1.   Some or all of the compensating products or goods in the unaltered state may be temporarily exported for the purpose of further processing outside the customs territory of the Community if the customs authority so authorises, in accordance with the conditions laid down in the outward processing provisions.

2.   Where a customs debt is incurred in respect of reimported products, the following shall be charged—

(a)   import duties on the compensating products or goods in the unaltered state referred to in paragraph 1, calculated in accordance with Articles 121 and 122; and

(b)   import duties on products reimported after processing outside the customs territory of the Community, the amount of which shall be calculated in accordance with the provisions relating to the outward processing procedure, on the same conditions as would have applied had the products exported under the latter procedure been released for free circulation before such export took place.

V.
Special provisions relating to the drawback system

[Article 124

1. The drawback system may be used for all goods. It shall not, however, be usable where, at the time the declaration of release for free circulation is accepted—

— the import goods are subject to quantitative import restrictions,
— a tariff measure within quotas is applied to the import goods,
— the import goods are subject to presentation of an import or export licence or certificate in the framework of the common agricultural policy, or
— a export refund or tax has been set for the compensating products.

2. Moreover, no reimbursement of import duties under the drawback system shall be possible if, at the time the export declaration for the compensating products is accepted, these products are subject to presentation of an import or export licence or certificate in the framework of the common agricultural policy or an export refund or tax has been set for them.

3. Derogations from paragraphs 1 and 2 may be laid down in accordance with the committee procedure.]

NOTES

Substituted by European Parliament and Council Regulation (EC) 2700/2000, Art 1, para 6.

Article 125

1. The declaration of release for free circulation shall indicate that the drawback system is being used and shall provide particulars of the authorisation.

2. At the request of the customs authorities, the said authorisation shall be attached to the declaration of release for free circulation.

Article 126

Under the drawback system, Article 115(1)(b), (3) and (5), Article 118(3), Articles 120 and 121, Article 122(a), second indent, and (c), and Article 129 shall not apply.

Article 127

Temporary exportation of compensating products carried out as provided for in Article 123(1) shall not be considered to be exportation within the meaning of Article 128 except where such products are not reimported into the Community within the period prescribed.

Article 128

[1. The holder of the authorisation may ask for the import duty to be repaid or remitted where he can establish to the satisfaction of the customs authorities that import goods released for free circulation under the drawback system in the form of compensating products or goods in the unaltered state have been either—

— exported, or
— placed, with a view to being subsequently re-exported, under the transit procedure, the customs-warehousing procedure, the temporary importation procedure or the inward-processing procedure (suspensive arrangement), or in a free zone or free warehouse,

provided that all conditions for use of the procedure have also been fulfilled.

2. For the purposes of being assigned a customs-approved treatment or use referred to in the second indent of paragraph 1, compensating products or goods in the unaltered state shall be considered to be non-Community goods.]

Part III

3.   The period within which the application for repayment must be made shall be determined in accordance with the committee procedure.

[4.   Without prejudice to point (b) of Article 122, where compensating products or goods in the unaltered state placed under a customs procedure or in a free zone or free warehouse in accordance with paragraph 1 are released for free circulation, the amount of import duties repaid or remitted shall be considered to constitute the amount of the customs debt.]

5.   For the purpose of determining the amount of import duties to be repaid or remitted, the first indent of Article 122(a) shall apply *mutatis mutandis*.

NOTES

Paras 1, 2, 4: substituted by European Parliament and Council Regulation (EC) 82/97, Art 1, para 13.

VI.
Other provisions

Article 129

The inward processing procedure, applying the suspension system shall also apply in order that the compensating products may qualify for exemption from the export duties to which identical products obtained from Community goods instead of import goods would be liable.

E.
PROCESSING UNDER CUSTOMS CONTROL

Article 130

The procedure for processing under customs control shall allow non-Community goods to be used in the customs territory of the Community in operations which alter their nature or state, without their being subject to import duties or commercial policy measures, and shall allow the products resulting from such operations to be released for free circulation at the rate of import duty appropriate to them. Such products shall be termed processed products.

[Article 131

The cases in and specific conditions under which the procedure for processing under customs control may be used shall be determined in accordance with the committee procedure.]

NOTES

Substituted by European Parliament and Council Regulation (EC) 2700/2000, Art 1, para 7.

Article 132

Authorisation for processing under customs control shall be granted at the request of the person who carries out the processing or arranges for it to be carried out.

Article 133

Authorisation shall be granted only—

   (a)   to persons established in the Community;
   (b)   where the import goods can be identified in the processed products;

(c)   where the goods cannot be economically restored after processing to their description or state as it was when they were placed under the procedure;

(d)   where use of the procedure cannot result in circumvention of the effect of the rules concerning origin and quantitative restrictions applicable to the imported goods;

(e)   where the necessary conditions for the procedure to help create or maintain a processing activity in the Community without adversely affecting the essential interests of Community producers of similar goods (economic conditions) are fulfilled. [The cases in which the economic conditions are deemed to have been fulfilled may be determined in accordance with the committee procedure.]

NOTES

Words in sub-para (e) added by European Parliament and Council Regulation (EC) 2700/2000, Art 1, para 8.

Article 134

Article 118(1), (2) and (4) and Article 119 shall apply *mutatis mutandis*.

Article 135

Where a customs debt is incurred in respect of goods in the unaltered state or of products that are at an intermediate stage of processing as compared with that provided for in the authorisation, the amount of that debt shall be determined on the basis of the items of charge elements appropriate to the import goods at the time of acceptance of the declaration relating to the placing of the goods under the procedure for processing under customs control.

Article 136

1.   Where the import goods qualified for preferential tariff treatment when they were placed under the procedure for processing under customs control, and such preferential tariff treatment is applicable to products identical to the processed products released for free circulation, the import duties to which the processed products are subject shall be calculated by applying the rate of duty applicable under that treatment.

2.   If the preferential tariff treatment referred to in paragraph 1 in respect of the import goods is subject to tariff quotas or tariff ceilings, the application of the rate of duty referred to in paragraph 1 in respect of the processed products shall also be subject to the condition that the said preferential tariff treatment is applicable to the import goods at the time of acceptance of the declaration of release for free circulation. In this case, the quantity of import goods actually used in the manufacture of the processed products released for free circulation shall be charged against the tariff quotas or ceilings in force at the time of acceptance of the declaration of release for free circulation and no quantities shall be counted against tariff quotas or ceilings opened in respect of products identical to the processed products.

F.

TEMPORARY IMPORTATION

Article 137

The temporary importation procedure shall allow the use in the customs territory of the Community, with total or partial relief from import duties and without their being subject to commercial policy measures, of non-Community goods intended for re-export without having undergone any change except normal depreciation due to the use made of them.

Article 138

Authorisation for temporary importation shall be granted at the request of the person who uses the goods or arranges for them to be used.

Article 139

The customs authorities shall refuse to authorise use of the temporary importation procedure where it is impossible to ensure that the import goods can be identified.

However, the customs authorities may authorise use of the temporary importation procedure without ensuring that the goods can be identified where, in view of the nature of the goods or of the operations to be carried out, the absence of identification measures is not liable to give rise to any abuse of the procedure.

Article 140

1.   The customs authorities shall determine the period within which import goods must have been re-exported or assigned a new customs-approved treatment or use. Such period must be long enough for the objective of authorised use to be achieved.

2.   Without prejudice to the special periods laid down in accordance with Article 141, the maximum period during which goods may remain under the temporary importation procedure shall be 24 months. The customs authorities may, however, determine shorter periods with the agreement of the person concerned.

3.   However, where exceptional circumstances so warrant, the customs authorities may, at the request of the person concerned and within reasonable limits, extend the periods referred to in paragraphs 1 and 2 in order to permit the authorised use.

Article 141

The case and the special conditions under which the temporary importation procedure may be used with total relief from import duties shall be determined in accordance with the committee procedure.

[Article 142

1.   Use of the temporary importation procedure with partial relief from import duties shall be granted in respect of goods which are not covered by the provisions adopted in accordance with Article 141 or which are covered by such provisions but do not fulfil all the conditions laid down therein for the grant of temporary importation with total relief.

2.   The list of goods in respect of which the temporary importation procedure with partial relief from import duties may not be used and the conditions subject to which the procedure may be used shall be determined in accordance with the committee procedure.]

NOTES

Substituted by European Parliament and Council Regulation (EC) 2700/2000, Art 1, para 9.

Article 143

1.   The amount of import duties payable in respect of goods placed under the temporary importation procedure with partial relief from import duties shall be set at 3%, for every month or fraction of a month during which the goods have been placed under the temporary importation procedure with partial relief, of the amount of duties which would have been payable on the said goods had they been released for free circulation on the date on which they were placed under the temporary importation procedure.

2.   The amount of import duties to be charged shall not exceed that which would have been charged if the goods concerned had been released for free circulation on the

date on which they were placed under the temporary importation procedure, leaving out of account any interest which may be applicable.

3. Transfer of the rights and obligations deriving from the temporary importation procedure pursuant to Article 90 shall not mean that the same relief arrangements must be applied to each of the periods of use to be taken into consideration.

4. Where the transfer referred to in paragraph 3 is made with partial relief for both persons authorised to use the procedure during the same month, the holder of the initial authorisation shall be liable to pay the amount of import duties due for the whole of that month.

Article 144

1. Where a customs debt is incurred in respect of import goods, the amount of such debt shall be determined on the basis of the taxation elements appropriate to those goods at the time of acceptance of the declaration of their placing under the temporary importation procedure. However, where the provisions of Article 141 so provide, the amount of the debt shall be determined on the basis of the taxation elements appropriate to the goods in question at the time referred to in Article 214.

2. Where, for a reason other than the placing of goods under the temporary importation procedure with partial relief from import duties, a customs debt is incurred in respect of goods placed under the said procedure, the amount of that debt shall be equal to the difference between the amount of duties calculated pursuant to paragraph 1 and that payable pursuant to Article 143.

G. OUTWARD PROCESSING

I. General

Article 145

1. The outward processing procedure shall, without prejudice to the provisions governing specific fields relating to the standard exchange system laid down in Articles 154 to 159 or to Article 123, allow Community goods to be exported temporarily from the customs territory of the Community in order to undergo processing operations and the products resulting from those operations to be released for free circulation with total or partial relief from import duties.

2. Temporary exportation of Community goods shall entail the application of export duties, commercial policy measures and other formalities for the exit of Community goods from the customs territory of the Community.

3. The following definitions shall apply:—

  (a)   'temporary export goods' means goods placed under the outward processing procedure;

  (b)   'processing operations' means the operations referred to in Article 114(2)(c), first, second and third indents;

  (c)   'compensating products' means all products resulting from processing operations;

  (d)   'rate of yield' means the quantity or percentage of compensating products obtained from the processing of a given quantity of temporary export goods.

Article 146

1. The outward processing procedure shall not be open to Community goods—

  —   whose export gives rise to repayment or remission of import duties,

— which, prior to export, were released for free circulation with total relief from import duties by virtue of end use, for as long as the conditions for granting such relief continue to apply,

— whose export gives rise to the granting of export refunds or in respect of which a financial advantage other than such refunds is granted under the common agricultural policy by virtue of the export of the said goods.

2. However, derogations from the second indent of paragraph 1 may be determined in accordance with the committee procedure.

II.

Grant of the authorisation

Article 147

1. Authorisation to use the outward processing procedure shall be issued at the request of the person who arranges for the processing operations to be carried out.

2. By way of derogation from paragraph 1, authorisation to use the outward processing procedure may be granted to another person in respect of goods of Community origin within the meaning of Title II, Chapter 2, Section 1, where the processing operation consists in incorporating those goods into goods obtained outside the Community and imported as compensating products, provided that use of the procedure helps to promote the sale of export goods without adversely affecting the essential interests of Community producers of products identical or similar to the imported compensating products.

The cases in which and the arrangements under which the preceding subparagraph shall apply shall be determined in accordance with the committee procedure.

Article 148

Authorisation shall be granted only—

(a)   to persons established in the Community;

(b)   where it is considered that it will be possible to establish that the compensating products have resulted from processing of the temporary export goods.

The cases in which derogations from this subparagraph may apply and the conditions under which such derogations shall apply shall be determined in accordance with the committee procedure;

(c)   where authorisation to use the outward processing procedure is not liable seriously to harm the essential interests of Community processors (economic conditions).

III.

Operation of the procedure

Article 149

1. The customs authorities shall specify the period within which the compensating products must be reimported into the customs territory of the Community. They may extend that period on submission of a duly substantiated request by the holder of the authorisation.

2. The customs authorities shall set either the rate of yield of the operation or, where necessary, the method of determining that rate.

Part III

Article 150

1. The total or partial relief from import duties provided for in Article 151(1) shall be granted only where the compensating products are declared for release for free circulation in the name of or on behalf of—

(a) the holder of the authorisation, or

(b) any other person established in the Community provided that that person has obtained the consent of the holder of the authorisation and the conditions of the authorisation are fulfilled.

2. The total or partial relief from import duties provided for in Article 151 shall not be granted where one of the conditions or obligations relating to the outward processing procedure is not fulfilled, unless it is established that the failures have no significant effect on the correct operation of the said procedure.

Article 151

1. The total or partial relief from import duties provided for in Article 145 shall be effected by deducting from the amount of the import duties applicable to the compensating products released for free circulation the amount of the import duties that would be applicable on the same date to the temporary export goods if they were imported into the customs territory of the Community from the country in which they underwent the processing operation or last processing operation.

2. The amount to be deducted pursuant to paragraph 1 shall be calculated on the basis of the quantity and nature of the goods in question on the date of acceptance of the declaration placing them under the outward processing procedure and on the basis of the other items of charge applicable to them on the date of acceptance of the declaration relating to the release for free circulation of the compensating products.

The value of the temporary export goods shall be that taken into account for those goods in determining the customs value of the compensating products in accordance with Article 32(1)(b)(i) or, if the value cannot be determined in that way, the difference between the customs value of the compensating products and the processing costs determined by reasonable means.

However,

— certain charges determined in accordance with the committee procedure shall not be taken into account in calculating the amount to be deducted;

— where, prior to being placed under the outward processing procedure, the temporary export goods were released for free circulation at a reduced rate by virtue of their end use, and for as long as the conditions for granting the reduced rate continue to apply, the amount to be deducted shall be the amount of import duties actually levied when the goods were released for free circulation.

3. Where temporary export goods could qualify on their release for free circulation for a reduced or zero rate of duty by virtue of their end use, that rate shall be taken into account provided that the goods underwent operations consistent with such an end-use in the country where the processing operation or last such operation took place.

4. Where compensating products qualify for a preferential tariff measure within the meaning of Article 20(3)(d) or (e) and the measure exists for goods falling within the same tariff classification as the temporary export goods, the rate of import duty to be taken into account in establishing the amount to be deducted pursuant to paragraph 1 shall be that which would apply if the temporary export goods fulfilled the conditions under which that preferential measure may be applied.

5. This Article shall be without prejudice to the application of provisions, adopted or liable to be adopted in the context of trade between the Community and third

countries, which provide for relief from import duties in respect of certain compensating products.

Article 152

1. Where the purpose of the processing operation is the repair of the temporary export goods, they shall be released for free circulation with total relief from import duties where it is established to the satisfaction of the customs authorities that the goods were repaired free of charge, either because of a contractual or statutory obligation arising from a guarantee or because of a manufacturing defect.

2. Paragraph 1 shall not apply where account was taken of the defect at the time when the goods in question were first released for free circulation.

Article 153

Where the purpose of the processing operation is the repair of temporary export goods and such repair is carried out in return for payment, the partial relief from import duties provided for in Article 145 shall be granted by establishing the amount of the duties applicable on the basis of the taxation elements pertaining to the compensating products on the date of acceptance of the declaration of release for free circulation of those products and taking into account as the customs value an amount equal to the repair costs, provided that those costs represent the only consideration provided by the holder of the authorisation and are not influenced by any links between that holder and the operator.

[By way of derogation from Article 151, the committee procedure may be used to determine the cases in and specific conditions under which goods may be released for free circulation following an outward-processing operation, with the cost of the processing operation being taken as the basis for assessment for the purpose of applying the Customs Tariff of the European Communities.]

NOTES

Words added by European Parliament and Council Regulation (EC) 2700/2000, Art 1, para 10.

IV. *Outward processing with use of the standard exchange system*

Article 154

1. Under the conditions laid down in this Section IV which are applicable in addition to the preceding provisions, the standard exchange system shall permit an imported product, hereinafter referred to as a 'replacement product', to replace a compensating product.

2. The customs authorities shall allow the standard exchange system to be used where the processing operation involves the repair of Community goods other than those subject to the common agricultural policy or to the specific arrangements applicable to certain goods resulting from the processing of agricultural products.

3. Without prejudice to Article 159, the provisions applicable to compensating products shall also apply to replacement products.

4. The customs authorities shall, under the conditions they lay down, permit replacement products to be imported before the temporary export goods are exported (prior importation).

In the event of prior importation of a replacement, security shall be provided to cover the amount of the import duties.

Article 155

1. Replacement products shall have the same tariff classification, be of the same commercial quality and possess the same technical characteristics as the temporary export goods had the latter undergone the repair in question.

2. Where the temporary export goods have been used before export, the replacement products must also have been used and may not be new products.

The customs authorities may, however, grant derogations from this rule if the replacement product has been supplied free of charge either because of a contractual or statutory obligation arising from a guarantee or because of a manufacturing defect.

Article 156

Standard exchange shall be authorised only where it is possible to verify that the conditions laid down in Article 155 are fulfilled.

Article 157

1. In the case of prior importation, the export goods shall be temporarily exported within a period of two months from the date of acceptance by the customs authorities of the declaration relating to the release of the replacement products for free circulation.

2. However, where exceptional circumstances so warrant, the customs authorities may, at the request of the person concerned, extend within reasonable limits the period referred to in paragraph 1.

Article 158

In the case of prior importation and where Article 151 is applied, the amount to be deducted shall be determined on the basis of the items of charge applicable to the temporary export goods on the date of acceptance of the declaration placing them under the procedure.

Article 159

Article 147(2) and Article 148(b) shall not apply in the context of standard exchange.

V.
Other provision

Article 160

The procedures provided for within the framework of outward processing shall also be applicable for the purposes of implementing non-tariff common commercial policy measures.

SECTION 4
EXPORT

Article 161

1. The export procedure shall allow Community goods to leave the customs territory of the Community.

Exportation shall entail the application of exit formalities including commercial policy measures and, where appropriate, export duties.

2. With the exception of goods placed under the outward processing procedure or a transit procedure pursuant to Article 163, and without prejudice to Article 164, all Community goods intended for export shall be placed under the export procedure.

3. Goods dispatched to Helgoland shall not be considered to be exports from the customs territory of the Community.

Part III

4. The case in which and the conditions under which goods leaving the customs territory of the Community are not subject to an export declaration shall be determined in accordance with the committee procedure.

5. The export declaration must be lodged at the customs office responsible for supervising the place where the exporter is established or where the goods are packed or loaded for export shipment. Derogations shall be determined in accordance with the committee procedure.

Article 162

Release for export shall be granted on condition that the goods in question leave the customs territory of the Community in the same condition as when the export declaration was accepted.

SECTION 5
INTERNAL TRANSIT

Article 163

1. The internal transit procedure shall, under the conditions laid down in paragraphs 2 to 4, allow the movement of Community goods from one point to another within the customs territory of the Community passing through the territory of a third country without any change in their customs status. This provision shall be without prejudice to the application of Article 91(1)(b).

2. The movement referred to in paragraph 1 may take place either—

(a) under the internal Community transit procedures provided that such a possibility is provided for in an international agreement;

(b) under cover of a TIR carnet (TIR Convention);

(c) under cover of an ATA carnet . . . used as a transit document;

(d) under cover of a Rhine Manifest (Article 9 of the Revised Convention for the Navigation of the Rhine);

(e) under cover of form 302 as provided for in the agreement between the States party to the North Atlantic Treaty on the status of their forces, signed in London on 19 June 1951, or

(f) by post (including parcel post).

3. In the case referred to in paragraph 2(a), Articles 92, 94, 95, 96 and 97 shall apply *mutatis mutandis*.

4. In the cases referred to in paragraph 2(b) to (f) goods shall keep their customs status only if that status is established under the conditions and in the form prescribed by the provisions adopted in accordance with the committee procedure.

NOTES

Para 2: words omitted repealed by European Parliament and Council Regulation (EC) 82/97, Art 1, para 14.

Article 164

The conditions under which Community goods may move, without being subject to a customs procedure, from one point to another within the customs territory of the Community and temporarily out of that territory without alteration of their customs status shall be determined in accordance with the committee procedure.

Article 165

The internal Community transit procedure shall also apply where a Community provision makes express provision for its application.

CHAPTER 3
OTHER TYPES OF CUSTOMS-APPROVED TREATMENT OR USE

SECTION 1
FREE ZONES AND FREE WAREHOUSES

A.
GENERAL

Article 166

Free zones and free warehouses shall be parts of the customs territory of the Community or premises situated in that territory and separated from the rest of it in which—

(a)   Community goods are considered, for the purpose of import duties and commercial policy import measures, as not being on Community customs territory, provided they are not released for free circulation or placed under another customs procedure or used or consumed under conditions other than those provided for in customs regulations;

(b)   Community goods for which such provision is made under Community legislation governing specific fields qualify, by virtue of being placed in a free zone or free warehouse, for measures normally attaching to the export of goods.

Article 167

1.   Member States may designate parts of the customs territory of the Community as free zones or authorise the establishment of free warehouses.

2.   Member States shall determine the area covered by each zone. Premises which are to be designated as free warehouses must be approved by Member States.

[3.   Free zones with the exception of those designated in accordance with Article 168a, shall be enclosed. The Member States shall define the entry and exit points of each free zone or free warehouse.]

4.   The construction of any building in a free zone shall require the prior approval of the customs authorities.

NOTES

Para 3: substituted by European Parliament and Council Regulation (EC) 2700/2000, Art 1, para 11.

Article 168

[1.   The perimeter and the entry and exit points of free zones, except the free zones designated in accordance with Article 168a, and of free warehouses shall be subject to supervision by the customs authorities.]

2.   Persons and means of transport entering or leaving a free zone or free warehouse may be subjected to a customs check.

3.   Access to a free zone or free warehouse may be denied to persons who do not provide every guarantee necessary for compliance with the rules provided for in this code.

4.   The customs authorities may check goods entering, leaving or remaining in a free zone or free warehouse. To enable such checks to be carried out, a copy of the transport document, which shall accompany goods entering or leaving, shall be handed to, or kept at the disposal of, the customs authority by any person designated for this purpose by such authorities. Where such checks are required, the goods shall be made available to the customs authorities.

NOTES
Para 1: substituted by European Parliament and Council Regulation (EC) 2700/2000, Art 1, para 12.

[Article 168a

1. The customs authorities may designate free zones in which customs checks and formalities shall be carried out and the provisions concerning customs debt applied in accordance with the requirements of the customs ware-housing procedure.

Articles 170, 176 and 180 shall not apply to the free zones thus designated.

2. References to free zones in Articles 37, 38 and 205 shall not apply to free zones referred to in paragraph 1.]

NOTES
Inserted by European Parliament and Council Regulation (EC) 2700/2000, Art 1, para 13.

B.
PLACING OF GOODS IN FREE ZONES OR FREE WAREHOUSES

Article 169

Both Community and non-Community goods may be placed in a free zone or free warehouse.

However, the customs authorities may require that goods which present a danger or are likely to spoil other goods or which, for other reasons, require special facilities be placed in premises specially equipped to receive them.

Article 170

1. Without prejudice to Article 168(4), goods entering a free zone or free warehouse need not be presented to the customs authorities, nor need a customs declaration be lodged.

[2. Goods shall be presented to the customs authorities and undergo the prescribed customs formalities where:

(a) they have been placed under a customs procedure which is discharged when they enter a free zone or free warehouse; however, where the customs procedure in question permits exemption from the obligation to present goods, such presentation shall not be required;

(b) they have been placed in a free zone or free warehouse on the basis of a decision to grant repayment or remission of import duties;

(c) they qualify for the measures referred to in Article 166(b);

(d) they enter a free zone or free warehouse directly from outside the customs territory of the Community.]

3. Customs authorities may require goods subject to export duties or to other export provisions to be notified to the customs department.

4. At the request of the party concerned, the customs authorities shall certify the Community or non-Community status of goods placed in a free zone or free warehouse.

in accordance with the specific circumstances and for particular types of goods traffic, modes of transport and economic operators and where international agreements provide for special security arrangements.]

NOTES

Articles 182a–182d inserted by European Parliament and Council Regulation (EC) 648/2005, Art 1, para 16. As to the application of Art 1 provisions, see (EC) 648/2005, Art 2.

[Article 182b

1. Where goods leaving the customs territory of the Community are assigned to a customs approved treatment or use for the purpose of which a customs declaration is required under the customs rules, this customs declaration shall be lodged at the customs office of export before the goods are to be brought out of the customs territory of the Community.

2. Where the customs office of export is different from the customs office of exit, the customs office of export shall immediately communicate or make available electronically the necessary particulars to the customs office of exit.

3. The customs declaration shall contain at least the particulars necessary for the summary declaration referred to in Article 182d(1).

4. Where the customs declaration is made other than by use of a data processing technique, the customs authorities shall apply the same level of risk management to the data as that applied to customs declarations made using a data processing technique.]

NOTES

Articles 182a–182d inserted by European Parliament and Council Regulation (EC) 648/2005, Art 1, para 16. As to the application of Art 1 provisions, see (EC) 648/2005, Art 2.

[Article 182c

1. Where goods leaving the customs territory of the Community are not assigned to a customs approved treatment or use for which a customs declaration is required, a summary declaration shall be lodged at the customs office of exit before the goods are to be brought out of the customs territory of the Community.

2. Customs authorities may allow the summary declaration to be lodged at another customs office, provided that this office immediately communicates or makes available electronically the necessary particulars to the customs office of exit.

3. Customs authorities may accept, instead of the lodging of a summary declaration, the lodging of a notification and access to the summary declaration data in the economic operator's computer system.]

NOTES

Articles 182a–182d inserted by European Parliament and Council Regulation (EC) 648/2005, Art 1, para 16. As to the application of Art 1 provisions, see (EC) 648/2005, Art 2.

[Article 182d

1. The committee procedure shall be used to establish a common data set and format for the summary declaration, containing the particulars necessary for risk analysis and the proper application of customs controls, primarily for security and safety purposes, using, where appropriate, international standards and commercial practices.

their temporary storage or from the use of the customs procedure under which they have been placed, or to comply with the conditions governing the placing of the goods under that procedure.

Article 205

1. A customs debt on importation shall be incurred through—

— the consumption or use, in a free zone or a free warehouse, of goods liable to import duties, under conditions other than those laid down by the legislation in force.

Where goods disappear and where their disappearance cannot be explained to the satisfaction of the customs authorities, those authorities may regard the goods as having been consumed or used in the free zone or the free warehouse.

2. The debt shall be incurred at the moment when the goods are consumed or are first used under conditions other than those laid down by the legislation in force.

3. The debtor shall be the person who consumed or used the goods and any persons who participated in such consumption or use and who were aware or should reasonably have been aware that the goods were being consumed or used under conditions other than those laid down by the legislation in force.

Where customs authorities regard goods which have disappeared as having been consumed or used in the free zone or the free warehouse and it is not possible to apply the preceding paragraph, the person liable for payment of the customs debt shall be the last person known to these authorities to have been in possession of the goods.

Article 206

1. By way of derogation from Articles 202 and 204(1)(a), no customs debt on importation shall be deemed to be incurred in respect of specific goods where the person concerned proves that the non-fulfilment of the obligations which arise from—

— the provisions of Articles 38 to 41 and the second indent of Article 177, or

— keeping the goods in question in temporary storage, or

— the use of the customs procedure under which the goods have been placed,

results from the total destruction or irretrievable loss of the said goods as a result of the actual nature of the goods or unforeseeable circumstances or *force majeure*, or as a consequence of authorisation by the customs authorities.

For the purposes of this paragraph, goods shall be irretrievably lost when they are rendered unusable by any person.

2. Nor shall a customs debt on importation be deemed to be incurred in respect of goods released for free circulation at a reduced or zero rate of import duty by virtue of their end-use, where such goods are exported or re-exported with the permission of the customs authorities.

Article 207

Where, in accordance with Article 206(1), no customs debt is deemed to be incurred in respect of goods released for free circulation at a reduced or zero rate of import duty on account of their end-use, any scrap or waste resulting from such destruction shall be deemed to be non-Community goods.

Article 208

Where in accordance with Article 203 or 204 a customs debt is incurred in respect of goods released for free circulation at a reduced rate of import duty on account of their end-use, the amount paid when the goods were released for free circulation shall be deducted from the amount of the customs debt.

This provision shall apply *mutatis mutandis* where a customs debt is incurred in respect of scrap and waste resulting from the destruction of such goods.

Article 209

1. A customs debt on exportation shall be incurred through—
   — the exportation from the customs territory of the Community, under cover of a customs declaration, of goods liable to export duties.

2. The customs debt shall be incurred at the time when such customs declaration is accepted.

3. The debtor shall be the declarant. In the event of indirect representation, the person on whose behalf the declaration is made shall also be a debtor.

Article 210

1. A customs debt on exportation shall be incurred through—
   — the removal from the customs territory of the Community of goods liable to export duties without a customs declaration.

2. The customs debt shall be incurred at the time when the said goods actually leave that territory.

3. The debtor shall be—
   — the person who removed the goods, and
   — any persons who participated in such removal and who were aware or should reasonably have been aware that a customs declaration had not been but should have been lodged.

Article 211

1. A customs debt on exportation shall be incurred through—
   — failure to comply with the conditions under which the goods were allowed to leave the customs territory of the Community with total or partial relief from export duties.

2. The debt shall be incurred at the time when the goods reach a destination other than that for which they were allowed to leave the customs territory of the Community with total or partial relief from export duties or, should the customs authorities be unable to determine that time, the expiry of the time limit set for the production of evidence that the conditions entitling the goods to such relief have been fulfilled.

3. The debtor shall be the declarant. In the event of indirect representation, the person on whose behalf the declaration is made shall also be a debtor.

Article 212

The customs debt referred to in Articles 201 to 205 and 209 to 211 shall be incurred even if it relates to goods subject to measures of prohibition or restriction on importation or exportation of any kind whatsoever. However, no customs debt shall be incurred on the unlawful introduction into the customs territory of the Community of counterfeit currency or of narcotic drugs and psychotropic substances which do not enter into the economic circuit strictly supervised by the competent authorities with a view to their use for medical and scientific purposes. For the purposes of criminal law as applicable to customs offences, the customs debt shall nevertheless be deemed to have been incurred where, under a Member State's criminal law, customs duties provide the basis for determining penalties, or the existence of a customs debt is grounds for taking criminal proceedings.

[Article 212a

Where customs legislation provides for favourable tariff treatment of goods by reason of their nature or end-use or for relief or total or partial exemption from import or export duties pursuant to Articles 21, 82, 145 or 184 to 187, such favourable tariff treatment, relief or exemption shall also apply in cases where a customs debt is incurred pursuant to Articles 202 to 205, 210 or 211, on condition that the behaviour of the person concerned involves neither fraudulent dealing nor obvious negligence

aggregation period expires. It shall be reduced by the number of days corresponding to half the number of days in the aggregation period;

(c) where payment is deferred in accordance with Article 226(c), the period shall be calculated from the day following the expiry date of the period during which the goods in question were released. It shall be reduced by the number of days corresponding to half the number of days in the period concerned.

2. Where the number of days in the periods referred to in paragraph 1(b) and (c) is an odd number, the number of days to be deducted from the 30-day period pursuant to paragraph 1(b) and (c) shall be equal to half the next lowest even number.

3. To simplify matters, where the periods referred to in paragraph 1(b) and (c) are a calendar week or a calendar month, Member States may provide that the amount of duty in respect of which payment has been deferred shall be paid—

(a) if the period is a calendar week, on the Friday of the fourth week following that calendar week;

(b) if the period is a calendar month, by the sixteenth day of the month following that calendar month.

Article 228

1. Deferment of payment shall not be granted in respect of amounts of duty which, although relating to goods entered for a customs procedure which entails the obligation to pay such duty, are entered in the accounts in accordance with the provisions in force concerning acceptance of incomplete declarations, because the declarant has not, by the time of expiry of the period set, provided the information necessary for the definitive valuation of the goods for customs purposes or has not supplied the particulars or the document missing when the incomplete declaration was accepted.

2. However, deferment of payment may be granted in the cases referred to in paragraph 1 where the amount of duty to be recovered is entered in the accounts before the expiry of a period of 30 days from the date on which the amount originally charged was entered in the accounts or, if it was not entered in the accounts, from the date on which the declaration relating to the goods in question was accepted. The duration of the deferment of payment granted in such circumstances shall not extend beyond the date of expiry of the period which, pursuant to Article 227, was granted in respect of the amount of duty originally fixed, or which would have been granted had the amount of duty legally due been entered in the accounts when the goods in question were declared.

Article 229

The customs authorities may grant the debtor payment facilities other than deferred payment.

The granting of such payment facilities shall—

(a) be conditional on the provision of security. However, such security need not be required where to require it would, because of the situation of the debtor, create serious economic or social difficulties;

(b) result in credit interest being charged over and above the amount of duty. The amount of such interest shall be calculated in such a way that it is equivalent to the amount which would be charged for this purpose on the national money or financial market of the currency in which the amount is payable.

The customs authorities may refrain from claiming credit interest where to claim it would, because of the situation of the debtor, create serious economic or social difficulties.

However, the customs authorities may also grant an application for repayment or remission in respect of a lower amount.

Article 241

1. Repayment by the competent authorities of amounts of import duties or export duties or of credit interest or interest on arrears collected on payment of such duties shall not give rise to the payment of interest by those authorities. However, interest shall be paid—

— where a decision to grant a request for repayment is not implemented within three months of the date of adoption of that decision,

— where national provisions so stipulate.

The amount of such interest shall be calculated in such a way that it is equivalent to the amount which would be charged for this purpose on the national money or financial market.

Article 242

Where a customs debt has been remitted or the corresponding amount of duty repaid in error, the original debt shall again become payable. Any interest paid under Article 241 must be reimbursed.

TITLE VIII
APPEALS

Article 243

1. Any person shall have the right to appeal against decisions taken by the customs authorities which relate to the application of customs legislation, and which concern him directly and individually.

Any person who has applied to the customs authorities for a decision relating to the application of customs legislation and has not obtained a ruling on that request within the period referred to in Article 6(2) shall also be entitled to exercise the right of appeal.

The appeal must be lodged in the Member State where the decision has been taken or applied for.

2. The right of appeal may be exercised—

(a)   initially, before the customs authorities designated for that purpose by the Member States;

(b)   subsequently, before an independent body, which may be a judicial authority or an equivalent specialised body, according to the provisions in force in the Member States.

Article 244

The lodging of an appeal shall not cause implementation of the disputed decision to be suspended.

The customs authorities shall, however, suspend implementation of such decision in whole or in part where they have good reason to believe that the disputed decision is inconsistent with customs legislation or that irreparable damage is to be feared for the person concerned.

Where the disputed decision has the effect of causing import duties or export duties to be charged, suspension of implementation of that decision shall be subject to the existence or lodging of a security. However, such security need not be required where such a requirement would be likely, owing to the debtor's circumstances, to cause serious economic or social difficulties.

Article 245

The provisions for the implementation of the appeals procedure shall be determined by the Member States.

1354

submission of an application by the person concerned within the periods laid down for submission of the application for invalidation of the customs declaration.

Article 238

1. Import duties shall be repaid or remitted in so far as it is established that the amount of such duties entered in the accounts relates to goods placed under the customs procedure in question and rejected by the importer because at the point in time referred to in Article 67 they are defective or do not comply with the terms of the contract on the basis of which they were imported.

Defective goods, within the meaning of the first subparagraph, shall be deemed to include goods damaged before their release.

2. Repayment or remission of import duties shall be granted on condition that—

(a)   the goods have not been used, except for such initial use as may have been necessary to establish that they were defective or did not comply with the terms of the contract;

(b)   the goods are exported from the customs territory of the Community.

At the request of the person concerned, the customs authorities shall permit the goods to be destroyed or to be placed, with a view to re-export, under the external transit procedure or the customs warehousing procedure or in a free zone or free warehouse, instead of being exported.

For the purposes of being assigned one of the customs-approved treatments or uses provided for in the preceding subparagraph, the goods shall be deemed to be non-Community goods.

3. Import duties shall not be repaid or remitted in respect of goods which, before being declared to customs declaration, were imported temporarily for testing, unless it is established that the fact that the goods were defective or did not comply with the terms of the contract could not normally have been detected in the course of such tests.

4. Import duties shall be repaid or remitted for the reasons set out in paragraph 1 upon submission of an application to the appropriate customs office within twelve months from the date on which the amount of those duties was communicated to the debtor.

However, the customs authorities may permit this period to be exceeded in duly justified exceptional cases.

Article 239

1. Import duties or export duties may be repaid or remitted in situations other than those referred to in Articles 236, 237, and 238—

—   to be determined in accordance with the procedure of the committee;

—   resulting from circumstances in which no deception or obvious negligence may be attributed to the person concerned. The situations in which this provision may be applied and the procedures to be followed to that end shall be defined in accordance with the committee procedure. Repayment or remission may be made subject to special conditions.

2. Duties shall be repaid or remitted for the reasons set out in paragraph 1 upon submission of an application to the appropriate customs office within 12 months from the date on which the amount of the duties was communicated to the debtor. However, the customs authorities may permit this period to be exceeded in duly justified exceptional cases.

Article 240

Import or export duties shall be repaid or remitted under the conditions laid down in this chapter only if the amount to be repaid or remitted exceeds an amount fixed in accordance with the procedure with the committee.

Part III

Article 230

Whatever the payment facilities granted to the debtor, the latter may in any case pay all or part of the amount of duty without awaiting expiry of the period he has been granted for payment.

Article 231

1. An amount of duty owed may be paid by a third person instead of the debtor.

Article 232

1. Where the amount of duty due has not been paid within the prescribed period—

(a)   the customs authorities shall avail themselves of all options open to them under the legislation in force, including enforcement, to secure payment of that amount.

Special provisions may be adopted, in accordance with Committee procedure, in respect of guarantors within the framework of the transit procedure;

(b)   interest on arrears shall be charged over and above the amount of duty. The rate of interest on arrears may be higher than the rate of credit interest. It may not be lower than that rate.

2. The customs authorities may waive collection of interest on arrears—

(a)   where, because of the situation of the debtor, it would be likely to create serious economic or social difficulties;

(b)   where the amount does not exceed a level fixed in accordance with the Committee procedure, or

(c)   if the duty is paid within five days of the expiry of the period prescribed for payment.

3. The customs authorities may fix—

(a)   minimum periods for calculation of interest;

(b)   minimum amounts payable as interest on arrears.

NOTES

The Finance Act 1999, Part VII, (Appointed Day) Order 2000, SI 2000/632 gives effect to this Article.

CHAPTER 4
EXTINCTION OF CUSTOMS DEBT

Article 233

Without prejudice to the provisions in force relating to the time-barring of a customs debt and non-recovery of such a debt in the event of the legally established insolvency of the debtor, a customs debt shall be extinguished—

(a)   by payment of the amount of duty;

(b)   by remission of the amount of duty;

(c)   where, in respect of goods declared for a customs procedure entailing the obligation to pay duties—

— the customs declaration is invalidated . . .,

— the goods, before their release, are either seized and simultaneously or subsequently confiscated, destroyed on the instructions of the customs authorities, destroyed or abandoned in accordance with Article 182, or destroyed or irretrievably lost as a result of their actual nature or of unforeseeable circumstances or *force majeure*;

(d)   where goods in respect of which a customs debt is incurred in accordance with Article 202 are seized upon their unlawful introduction and are simultaneously or subsequently confiscated.

In the event of seizure and confiscation, the customs debt shall, nonetheless for the purposes of the criminal law applicable to customs offences, be deemed not to have been extinguished where, under a Member State's criminal law, customs duties provide the basis for determining penalties or the existence of a customs debt is grounds for taking criminal proceedings.

NOTES

Words omitted repealed by European Parliament and Council Regulation (EC) 82/97, Art 1, para 19.

Article 234

A customs debt, as referred to in Article 216, shall also be extinguished where the formalities carried out in order to enable the preferential tariff treatment referred to in Article 216 to be granted are cancelled.

CHAPTER 5

REPAYMENT AND REMISSION OF DUTY

Article 235

The following definitions shall apply—

(a)   'repayment' means the total or partial refund of import duties or export duties which have been paid;

(b)   'remission' means either a decision to waive all or part of the amount of a customs debt or a decision to render void an entry in the accounts of all or part of an amount of import or export duty which has not been paid.

Article 236

1.   Import duties or export duties shall be repaid in so far as it is established that when they were paid the amount of such duties was not legally owed or that the amount has been entered in the accounts contrary to Article 220(2).

Import duties or export duties shall be remitted in so far as it is established that when they were entered in the accounts the amount of such duties was not legally owed or that the amount has been entered in the accounts contrary to Article 220(2).

No repayment or remission shall be granted when the facts which led to the payment or entry in the accounts of an amount which was not legally owed are the result of deliberate action by the person concerned.

2.   Import duties or export duties shall be repaid or remitted upon submission of an application to the appropriate customs office within a period of three years from the date on which the amount of those duties was communicated to the debtor.

That period shall be extended if the person concerned provides evidence that he was prevented from submitting his application within the said period as a result of unforeseeable circumstances or *force majeure*.

Where the customs authorities themselves discover within this period that one or other of the situations described in the first and second subparagraphs of paragraph 1 exists, they shall repay or remit on their own initiative.

Article 237

Import duties or export duties shall be repaid where a customs declaration is invalidated and the duties have been paid. Repayment shall be granted upon

Article 246

This title shall not apply to appeals lodged with a view to the annulment or revision of a decision taken by the customs authorities on the basis of criminal law.

TITLE IX
FINAL PROVISIONS

CHAPTER 1
CUSTOMS CODE COMMITTEE

[Article 247

The measures necessary for the implementation of this Regulation, including implementation of the Regulation referred to in Article 184, except for Title VIII and subject to Articles 9 and 10 of Regulation (EEC) No 2658/87[1] and to Article 248 of this Regulation shall be adopted in accordance with the regulatory procedure referred to in Article 247a(2) in compliance with the international commitments entered into by the Community.]

---

[1] OJ L256, 7.9.1987, p 1.

NOTES

Substituted, together with Arts 247a, 248, 248a, 249 for original Arts 247–249, by European Parliament and Council Regulation (EC) 2700/2000, Art 1, para 19.

[Article 247a

1. The Commission shall be assisted by a Customs Code Committee (hereinafter referred to as the Committee).

2. Where reference is made to this paragraph, Articles 5 and 7 of Decision 1999/468/EC shall apply, having regard to the provisions of Article 8 thereof.

The period laid down in Article 5(6) of Decision 1999/ 468/EC shall be set at three months.

3. The Committee shall adopt its rules of procedure.]

NOTES

Substituted, together with Arts 247, 248, 248a, 249 for original Arts 247–249, by European Parliament and Council Regulation (EC) 2700/2000, Art 1, para 19.

[Article 248

The measures necessary for implementing Articles 11, 12 and 21 shall be adopted in accordance with the management procedure referred to in Article 248a(2).]

NOTES

Substituted, together with Arts 247, 247a, 248a, 249 for original Arts 247–249, by European Parliament and Council Regulation (EC) 2700/2000, Art 1, para 19.

[Article 248a

1. The Commission shall be assisted by a Customs Code Committee, hereinafter referred to as the Committee.

2. Where reference is made to this paragraph, Articles 4 and 7 of Decision 1999/468/EC shall apply.

The period laid down in Article 4(3) of Decision 1999/ 468/EC shall be set at three months.

3. The Committee shall adopt its rules of procedure.]

NOTES

Substituted, together with Arts 247, 247a, 248, 249 for original Arts 247–249, by European Parliament and Council Regulation (EC) 2700/2000, Art 1, para 19.

[**Article 249**

The Committee may examine any question concerning customs legislation which is raised by its chairman, either on his own initiative or at the request of a Member State's representative.]

NOTES

Substituted, together with Arts 247, 247a, 248, 248a for original Arts 247–249, by European Parliament and Council Regulation (EC) 2700/2000, Art 1, para 19.

CHAPTER 2
LEGAL EFFECTS IN A MEMBER STATE OF MEASURES TAKEN,
DOCUMENTS ISSUED AND FINDINGS MADE IN ANOTHER
MEMBER STATE

Article 250

Where a customs procedure is used in several Member States,

— the decisions, identification measures taken or agreed on, and the documents issued by the customs authorities of one Member State shall have the same legal effects in other Member States as such decisions, measures taken and documents issued by the customs authorities of each of those Member States;

— the findings made at the time controls are carried out by the customs authorities of a Member State shall have the same conclusive force in the other Member States as the findings made by the customs authorities of each of those Member States.

CHAPTER 3
OTHER FINAL PROVISIONS

Article 251

1. The following Regulations and Directives are hereby repealed—

— Council Regulation (EEC) No 802/68 of 27 June 1968 on the common definition of the concept of the origin of goods[1], as last amended by Regulation (EEC) No 456/91[2];

— Council Regulation (EEC) No 754/76 of 25 March 1976 on the customs treatment applicable to goods returned to the customs territory of the Community[3], as last amended by Regulation (EEC) No 1147/86[4];

— Council Regulation (EEC) No 2779/78 of 23 November 1978 on the procedure for applying the European unit of account (EUA) to legal acts adopted in the customs sphere[5], as amended by Regulation (EEC) No 289/84[6];

— Council Regulation (EEC) No 1430/79 of 2 July 1979 on the repayment or remission of import or export duties[7], as last amended by Regulation (EEC) No 1854/89[8];

— Council Regulation (EEC) No 1697/79 of 24 July 1979 on the post-clearance recovery of import duties or export duties which have not been required of the person liable for payment on goods entered for a customs procedure involving the obligation to pay such duties[9], as last amended by Regulation (EEC) No 1854/89[10];

— Council Directive 79/695/EEC of 24 July 1979 on the harmonisation of procedures for the release of goods for free circulation[11], as last amended by Directive 90/504/EEC[12];

— Council Regulation (EEC) No 1224/80 of 28 May 1980 on the valuation of goods for customs purposes[13], as last amended by the Regulation (EEC) No 4046/89[14];

— Council Directive 81/177/EEC of 24 February 1981 on the harmonisation of procedures for the export of Community goods[15], as last amended by Regulation (EEC) No 1854/89[16];

— Council Regulation (EEC) No 3599/82 of 21 December 1982 on temporary importation arrangements[17], as last amended by Regulation (EEC) No 1620/85[18];

— Council Regulation (EEC) No 2763/83 of 26 September 1983 on arrangements permitting goods to be processed under customs control before being put into free circulation[19], as last amended by Regulation (EEC) No 720/91[20];

— Council Regulation (EEC) No 2151/84 of 23 July 1984 on the customs territory of the Community[21], as last amended by the Act of Accession of Spain and Portugal;

— Council Regulation (EEC) No 1999/85 of 16 July 1985 on inward processing relief arrangements[22];

— Council Regulation (EEC) No 3632/85 of 12 December 1985 defining the conditions under which a person may be permitted to make a customs declaration[23];

— Council Regulation (EEC) No 2473/86 of 24 July 1986 on outward processing relief arrangements and the standard exchange system[24];

— Council Regulation (EEC) No 2144/87 of 13 July 1987 on customs debt[25], as last amended by Regulation (EEC) No 4108/88[26];

— Council Regulation (EEC) No 1031/88 of 18 April 1988 determining the persons liable for payment of a customs debt[27], as last amended by Regulation (EEC) No 1716/90[28];

— Council Regulation (EEC) No 1970/88 of 30 June 1988 concerning triangular traffic under the outward processing relief arrangements and the standard exchange system[29];

— Council Regulation (EEC) No 2503/88 of 25 July 1988 on customs warehouses[30], as amended by Regulation (EEC) No 2561/90[31];

— Council Regulation (EEC) No 2504/88 of 25 July 1988 on free zones and free warehouses[32], as amended by Regulation (EEC) No 1604/92[33];

— Council Regulation (EEC) No 4151/88 of 21 December 1988 laying down the provisions applicable to goods brought into the customs territory of the Community[34];

— Council Regulation (EEC) No 1854/89 of 14 June 1989 on the entry in the accounts and terms of payment of the amounts of the import duties or export duties resulting from a customs debt[35];

— Council Regulation (EEC) No 1855/89 of 14 June 1989 on the temporary importation of means of transport[36];

— Council Regulation (EEC) No 3312/89 of 30 October 1989 on the temporary importation of containers[37];

Part III

— Council Regulation (EEC) No 4046/89 of 21 December 1989 on the security to be given to ensure payment of a customs debt[38];

— Council Regulation (EEC) No 1715/90 of 20 June 1990 on the information provided by the customs authorities of the Member States concerning the classification of goods in the customs nomenclature[39];

— Council Regulation (EEC) No 2726/90 of 17 September 1990 on Community transit[40], . . .;

— Council Regulation (EEC) No 717/91 of 21 March 1991 concerning the Single Administrative Document[41];

— Council Regulation (EEC) No 719/91 of 21 March 1991 on the use in the Community of TIR carnets and ATA carnets as transit documents[42].

2. In all Community acts where reference is made to the Regulations or Directives referred to in paragraph 1, that reference shall be deemed to refer to this Code.

---

[1] OJ L 148, 28.6.1968, p 1.

[2] OJ L 54, 28.2.1991, p 4.

[3] OJ L 89, 2.4.1976, p 1.

[4] OJ L 105, 22.4.1986, p 1.

[5] OJ L 333, 30.11.1978, p 5.

[6] OJ L 33, 4.2.1984, p 2.

[7] OJ L 175, 12.7.1979, p 1.

[8] OJ L 186, 30.6.1989, p 1.

[9] OJ L 197, 3.8.1979, p 1.

[10] OJ L 186, 30.6.1989, p 1.

[11] OJ L 205, 13.8.1979, p 19.

[12] OJ L 281, 12.10.1990, p 28.

[13] OJ L 134, 31.5.1980, p 1.

[14] OJ L 388, 30.12.1989, p 24.

[15] OJ L 83, 30.3.1981, p 40.

[16] OJ L 186, 30.6.1989, p 1.

[17] OJ L 376, 31.12.1982, p 1.

[18] OJ L 155, 14.6.1985, p 54.

[19] OJ L 272, 5.10.1985, p 1.

[20] OJ L 78, 26.3.1991, p 9.

[21] OJ L 197, 27.7.1984, p 1.

[22] OJ L 188, 20.7.1985, p 1.

[23] OJ L 350, 27.12.1985, p 1.

[24] OJ L 212, 2.8.1986, p 1.

[25] OJ L 201, 22.7.1987, p 15.

[26] OJ L 361, 29.12.1988, p 2.

[27] OJ L 102, 21.4.1988, p 5.

[28] OJ L 160, 26.6.1990, p 6.

[29] OJ L 174, 6.7.1988, p 1,

[30] OJ L 225, 15.8.1988, p 1.

[31] OJ L 246, 10.9.1990, p 1.

[32] OJ L 225, 15.8.1988, p 8.

[33] OJ L 173, 26.6.1992, p 30.

[34] OJ L 367, 31.12.1988, p 1.

[35] OJ L 186, 30.6.1989, p 1,

[36] OJ L 186, 30.6.1989, p 8.

[37] OJ L 321, 4.11.1989, p 5.

[38] OJ L 388, 30.12.1989, p 1.

[39] OJ L 160, 26.6.1990, p 1.

[40] OJ L 262, 26.9.1990, p 1.

[41] OJ L 78, 26.3.1991, p 1.

[42] OJ L 78, 26.3.1991, p 6.

NOTES

Para 1: words omitted repealed by European Parliament and Council Regulation (EC) 82/97, Art 1, para 20.

Article 252

1. Articles 141, 142 and 143 of Council Regulation (EEC) No 918/83[1] are hereby repealed.

2. Council Regulation (EEC) No 2658/87[2], as last amended by Regulation (EEC) No 3492/91[3], is hereby amended as follows—

   '(a)   Article 8 is hereby amended as follows: The following words shall be inserted after the word "committee": "provided for in Article 247 of the Community Customs Code".

   (b)   The introductory sentence in Article 10(1) is hereby amended as follows: "The representative of the Commission shall submit to the committee provided for in Article 247 of the Community Customs Code a draft . . .".

   (c)   Articles 7 and 11 are hereby repealed.'

[1] OJ L 105, 23.4.1983, p 1.

[2] OJ L 256, 7.9.1987, p 1.

[3] OJ L 328, 30.11.1991, p 80.

Article 253

This Regulation shall enter into force on the third day following that of its publication in the *Official Journal of the European Communities*.

It shall apply from 1 January 1994.

Title VIII shall not apply to the United Kingdom until 1 January 1995.

However, Article 161 and, in so far as they concern re-exportation, Articles 182 and 183 shall apply from 1 January 1993. In so far as the said Articles make reference to provisions in this Code and until such time as such provisions enter into force, the references shall be deemed to allude to the corresponding provisions in the Regulations and Directives listed in Article 251.

Before 1 October 1993, the Council shall, on the basis of a Commission progress report on discussions regarding the consequences to be drawn from the monetary conversion rate used for the application of common agricultural policy measures, review the problem of trade in goods between the Member States in the context of the internal market. This report shall be accompanied by Commission proposals if any, on which the Council shall take a decision in accordance with the provisions of the Treaty.

Before 1 January 1998, the Council shall, on the basis of a Commission report, review this Code with a view to making such adaptations as may appear necessary taking into account in particular the achievement of the internal market. This report shall be accompanied by proposals, if any, on which the Council shall take a decision in accordance with the provisions of the Treaty.

COUNCIL DIRECTIVE

(92/79/EEC)

of 19 October 1992

on the approximation of taxes on cigarettes

NOTES

Date of publication in OJ: OJ L 316, 31.10.92, p 8.

THE COUNCIL OF THE EUROPEAN COMMUNITIES,

Having regard to the Treaty establishing the European Economic Community, and in particular Article 99 thereof,

Having regard to the proposal from the Commission,[1]

Having regard to the opinion of the European Parliament,[2]

Having regard to the opinion of the Economic and Social Committee,[3]

Whereas Directive 72/464/EEC[4] lays down general provisions concerning excise duties on manufactured tobacco and special provisions concerning the structure of excise duties applicable to cigarettes;

Whereas Directive 79/32/EEC[5] laid down the definitions of the various groups of manufactured tobacco;

Whereas for the completion on 1 January 1993 of an internal market without frontiers it is necessary to establish an overall minimum excise duty for cigarettes;

Whereas it is necessary for the Kingdom of Spain to have a transitional period of two years in order to attain that overall minimum excise duty;

Whereas the Portuguese Republic should be granted the possibility of a reduced rate for cigarettes made by small-scale producers and consumed in the most remote regions of the Azores and Madeira;

Whereas a procedure should be introduced so that, as regards the overall incidence and the structure of excise duties on cigarettes, it will be possible every two years to make the adjustments necessary to take account of the proper functioning of the internal market and the wider objectives of the Treaty,

[1] OJ C 12, 18.1.90, p 4.
[2] OJ C 94, 13.4.92, p 35.
[3] OJ C 225, 10.9.90, p 56.
[4] OJ L 303, 31.12.72, p 1. Last amended by Directive 92/78/EEC.
[5] OJ L 10, 16.1.79, p 8.

HAS ADOPTED THIS DIRECTIVE—

Article 1

1. Not later than 1 January 1993, Member States shall apply to cigarettes minimum consumption taxes in accordance with the rules provided for in this Directive.

2. Paragraph 1 shall apply to the taxes which, pursuant to Directive 72/464/EEC, are levied on cigarettes and which comprise—

(a)   a specific excise duty per unit of the product;

(b)   a proportional excise duty calculated on the basis of the maximum retail selling price;

(c)   a VAT proportional to the retail selling price.

[Article 2

1.   Each Member State shall apply an overall minimum excise duty (specific duty plus *ad valorem* duty excluding VAT), the incidence of which shall be set at 57% of the retail selling price (inclusive of all taxes) and which shall not be less than EUR 60 per 1 000 cigarettes for cigarettes of the price category most in demand. As from 1 July 2006, the figure of "EUR 60" shall be replaced by "EUR 64".

2.   Member States which levy an overall minimum excise duty of at least EUR 95 per 1,000 cigarettes for cigarettes of the price category most in demand need not comply with the 57% minimum incidence requirement. As from 1 July 2006 the figure of "EUR 95" shall be replaced by "EUR 101".

3.   The overall minimum excise duty on cigarettes shall be determined on the basis of cigarettes of the price category most in demand according to data established as at 1 January of each year.

4.   Notwithstanding paragraph 1, Member States which on 1 July 2001 applied an overall minimum excise duty less than EUR 60 per 1,000 cigarettes for cigarettes of the price category most in demand, may postpone up to and including 31 December 2004 the application of an overall minimum excise duty of EUR 60 per 1,000 cigarettes for cigarettes of the price category most in demand.

5.   The value of the euro in national currencies to be applied to the amounts of the overall minimum excise duty shall be fixed once a year. The exchange rates to be applied shall be those obtained on the first working day of October and published in the *Official Journal of the European Communities* and shall have effect from 1 January of the following calendar year.

6.   By way of derogation from the preceding paragraph, Member States which have not adopted the euro shall be authorised to apply the value of the euro in national currency on the first working day of October 2000 for the conversion of the amount of EUR 95 referred to in paragraph 2.The present derogation shall be re-examined in the next report to be submitted by the Commission in accordance with Article 4.]

NOTES

Substituted by Council Directive 2002/10/EC art 1 para 1.

[Article 2A

1.   When a change in the retail selling price of cigarettes in the most popular price category occurs in a Member State, thereby bringing the incidence of the overall minimum excise duty below the level specified in the first subparagraph of Article 2, the Member State in question may refrain from adjusting the incidence of the overall minimum excise duty until not later than 1 January of the second year following that in which the change occurs.

2.   When a Member State increases the rate of value-added tax on cigarettes, it may reduce the incidence of the overall minimum excise duty up to an amount which, expressed as a percentage of the retail selling price, is equal to the incidence of the increase in the rate of value added tax, also expressed as a percentage of the retail selling price, even if such an adjustment has the effect of reducing the incidence of the overall minimum excise duty to below the level laid down in Article 2.

3.   If, in accordance with paragraph 2, a Member State reduces the incidence of the overall minimum excise duty to a level below that laid down in the first subparagraph

of Article 2, it shall raise that incidence so as to reach at least that level not later than 1 January of the second year after that in which the reduction took place.]

NOTES

Inserted by Council Directive 1999/81/EC, Art 1, para 1.

Article 3

1. The Kingdom of Spain shall have a transitional period of two years, starting on 1 January 1993, to attain the overall minimum excise duty laid down in Article 2.

2. The Portuguese Republic may apply a reduced rate of up to 50% less than that laid down in Article 2 to cigarettes consumed in the most remote regions of the Azores and Madeira, made by small-scale manufacturers each of whose annual production does not exceed 500 tonnes.

[3. Notwithstanding Article 2, the Kingdom of Sweden may postpone, up to and including 31 December 2002, the application of an overall minimum excise duty equivalent to 57% of the retail selling price (inclusive of all taxes) of cigarettes in the most popular price category. In addition, the Kingdom of Sweden may not reduce the overall excise duty below the level applied on 1 August 1998.

[4. By derogation from Article 2, from 1 January 2003 to 31 December 2009 the French Republic may continue to apply a reduced rate of excise duty to cigarettes released for consumption in Corsica. This rate shall apply solely to an annual quota of 1200 tonnes.

From 1 January 2003 to 31 December 2007 the reduced rate must equal at least 35% of the price for cigarettes in the price category most in demand in Corsica.

From 1 January 2008 to 31 December 2009 the reduced rate must equal at least 44% of the price for cigarettes in the price category most in demand in Corsica.]]

NOTES

Paras 3, 4: added by Council Directive 1999/81/EC, Art 1, para 2.

Para 4: substituted by Council Directive (EC) 2003/117 art 1.

[Article 4

Every four years, the Commission shall submit to the Council a report and, where appropriate, a proposal concerning the rates of excise duty laid down herein and the structure of excise duties as defined by Article 16 of Council Directive 95/59/EC of 27 November 1995 on taxes other than turnover taxes which affect the consumption of manufactured tobacco. The Council shall examine this report and this proposal and, acting unanimously after consulting the European Parliament, shall adopt the necessary measures. The report by the Commission and the examination by the Council shall take into account the proper functioning of the internal market, the real value of the levels of excise duty in Article 2 calculated solely in accordance with inflation and the wider objectives of the Treaty.]

NOTES

Substituted by Council Directive 2002/10/EC art 1 para 2.

Article 5

1. Member States shall bring into force the laws, regulations and administrative provisions necessary to comply with this Directive not later than 31 December 1992. They shall forthwith inform the Commission thereof.

When Member States adopt these measures, they shall contain a reference to this Directive or shall be accompanied by such reference on the occasion of their official publication. The methods of making such reference shall be laid down by the Member States.

2. Member States shall communicate to the Commission the texts of the main provisions of national law which they adopt in the field governed by this Directive.

Article 6

This Directive is addressed to the Member States.

Done at Luxembourg, 19 October 1992.

COUNCIL DIRECTIVE

(92/80/EEC)

of 19 October 1992

on the approximation of taxes on manufactured tobacco other than cigarettes

NOTES

Date of publication in OJ: OJ L 316, 31.10.92, p 10.

THE COUNCIL OF THE EUROPEAN COMMUNITIES,

Having regard to the Treaty establishing the European Economic Community, and in particular Article 99 thereof,

Having regard to the proposal from the Commission,[1]

Having regard to the opinion of the European Parliament,[2]

Having regard to the opinion of the Economic and Social Committee,[3]

Whereas Directive 72/464/EEC,[4] lays down in Title I general provisions on excise duty which are applicable to all manufactured tobacco; whereas, under Title II, special provisions have already been adopted for cigarettes; whereas special provisions have yet to be adopted for other types of manufactured tobacco;

Whereas Directive 79/32/EEC[5] laid down the definitions relating to the various groups of manufactured tobacco;

Whereas, in order to establish the internal market on 1 January 1993, it is necessary to establish minimum excise duties for manufactured tobacco other than cigarettes;

Whereas a harmonised incidence of tax should be established for all products belonging to the same group of manufactured tobacco;

Whereas the setting of an overall minimum excise duty expressed as a percentage, as an amount per kilogram or for a given number of items is the most appropriate for achieving the internal market;

Whereas the Italian Republic and the Kingdom of Spain should be granted until 31 December 1998 the possibility of a lower rate of tax on cigars and cigarillos in respect of rolls of tobacco consisting entirely of natural tobacco which are not cigarettes;

Whereas a procedure should be introduced to enable the rates or amounts laid down in this Directive to be reviewed periodically on the basis of a Commission report taking account of all the appropriate factors;

Whereas a mechanism should be set up to enable specific amounts expressed in ecu to be converted into national currency,

[1] OJ C 12, 18.1.90, p 8.

[2] OJ C 94, 13.1.92, p 38.
[3] OJ C 225, 10.9.1990, p 56.
[4] OJ L 303, 31.12.72, p 1. Last amended by Directive 92/78/EEC (see [OJ L 316, 31.10.92, p 5]).
[5] OJ L10, 16.1.79, p 8.

HAS ADOPTED THIS DIRECTIVE—

Article 1

The following groups of manufactured tobacco produced in the Community and imported from non-member countries shall be subject, in each Member State, to a minimum excise duty as laid down in Article 3—

(a)   cigars and cigarillos;

(b)   fine-cut tobacco intended for the rolling of cigarettes;

(c)   other smoking tobaccos.

Article 2

For the purposes of this Directive, the definitions of the products referred to in Article 1 shall be those laid down in Articles 2, 4 and 4a respectively of Directive 79/32/EEC.

Article 3

[1.   Member States shall apply an excise duty which may be—

(a)   either an ad valorem duty calculated on the basis of the maximum retail selling price of each product, freely determined by manufacturers established in the Community and by importers from non-member countries in accordance with Article 9 of Council Directive 95/59/EC of 27 November 1995 on taxes other than turnover taxes which affect the consumption of manufactured tobacco(8),

(b)   or a specific duty expressed as an amount per kilogram or in the case of cigars and cigarillos alternatively for a given number of items,

(c)   or a mixture of both, combining an ad valorem element and a specific element.

In cases where excise duty is either ad valorem or mixed, Member States may establish a minimum amount of excise duty.

The overall excise duty expressed as a percentage, as an amount per kilogram or for a given number of items shall be at least equivalent to the rates or minimum amounts laid down for—

—   cigars and cigarillos: 5% of the retail selling price inclusive of all taxes, or EUR 9 per 1000 items or per kilogram,

—   fine-cut smoking tobacco intended for the rolling of cigarettes: 30% of the retail selling price inclusive of all taxes, or EUR 24 per kilogram,

—   other smoking tobaccos: 20% of the retail selling price inclusive of all taxes, or EUR 18 per kilogram.

As from 1 January 2001, the amounts of EUR 9, EUR 24 and EUR 18 in the preceding three indents shall be replaced by EUR 10, EUR 25 and EUR 19 respectively.]

[As from 1 July 2002,the overall excise duty levied on fine-cut smoking tobacco intended for the rolling of cigarettes shall be at least equal to 32%of the retail selling price inclusive of all taxes, or EUR 27 per kilogram.

As from 1 July 2003,the overall excise duty shall be at least equal to the following rates or minimum amounts:

(a)   in the case of cigars or cigarillos: 5%of the retail selling price inclusive of all taxes or EUR 11 per 1,000 items or per kilogram;

(b)   in the case of fine-cut smoking tobacco intended for the rolling of cigarettes: 33% of the retail selling price inclusive of all taxes, or EUR 29 per kilogram;

(c)   in the case of other smoking tobaccos:20%of the retail selling price inclusive of all taxes, or EUR 20 per kilogram.

As from 1 July 2004,the overall excise duty levied on fine-cut smoking tobacco intended for the rolling of cigarettes shall be at least equal to 36%of the retail selling price inclusive of all taxes, or EUR 32 per kilogram.]

2.   The rates or amounts referred to in paragraph 1 shall be effective for all products belonging to the group of manufactured tobaccos concerned, without distinction within each group as to quality, presentation, origin of the products, the materials used, the characteristics of the firms involved or any other criterion.

3.   The Italian Republic and the Kingdom of Spain may until 31 December 1998 apply to rolls of tobacco consisting entirely of natural tobacco which are not cigarettes a rate or amount which may be up to 50% less than the normal national rate of excise duty for cigars and cigarillos and which may fall below the minimum rate laid down in paragraph 1.

[4. By derogation from Article 3(1), from 1 January 2003 to 31 December 2009 the French Republic may continue to apply a reduced rate of excise duty to manufactured tobaccos other than cigarettes released for consumption in Corsica. The reduced rate shall be:

(a)   for cigars and cigarillos, at least 10% of the retail selling price, inclusive of all taxes, charged in Corsica;

(b)   for fine-cut tobacco intended for the rolling of cigarettes, at least 25% of the retail selling price, inclusive of all taxes, charged in Corsica;

(c)   for other smoking tobaccos, at least 22% of the retail selling price, inclusive of all taxes, charged in Corsica.]

NOTES

Para 1: substituted by Council Directive 1999/81/EC, Art 2, para 1(a). Words in square brackets added by Council Directive 2002/10/EC art 2 para 1.

Para 4: added by Council Directive 1999/81/EC, Art 2, para 1(b). Substituted by Council Directive 2003/117 art 2.

[Article 4

Every four years, the Commission shall submit a report and, where appropriate, a proposal concerning the rates of excise duty laid down herein. The Council shall examine this report and this proposal and, acting unanimously after consulting the European Parliament, shall adopt the necessary measures. The report by the Commission and the examination by the Council shall take into account the proper functioning of the internal market, the real value of the rates of excise duty and the wider objectives of the Treaty.]

NOTES

Substituted by Council Directive 2002/10/EC art 2 para 2.

Article 5

1.   The value of the ecu in national currencies to be applied to the value of specific excise duties shall be fixed once a year. The rates to be applied shall be those obtaining on the first working day of October and published in the *Official Journal of the European Communities* and shall have effect from 1 January of the following calendar year.

2. Member States may maintain the amounts of the excise duties in force at the time of the annual adjustment provided for in paragraph 1 if the conversion of the amounts of the excise duties expressed in ecu would result in an increase of less than 5% or ECU 5, whichever is the lower amount, in the excise duty expressed in national currency.

Article 6

1. Member States shall bring into force the laws, regulations and administrative provisions necessary to comply with this Directive not later than 31 December 1992. They shall forthwith inform the Commission thereof.

When Member States adopt these measures, they shall contain a reference to this Directive or shall be accompanied by such reference on the occasion of their official publication. The methods of making such reference shall be laid down by the Member States.

2. Member States shall communicate to the Commission the texts of the main provisions of national law which they adopt in the field governed by this Directive.

Article 7

This Directive is addressed to the Member States.

Done at Luxembourg, 19 October 1992.

COUNCIL DIRECTIVE

(92/81/EEC)

of 19 October 1992

on the harmonisation of the structures of excise duties on mineral oils

. . .

NOTES

Repealed by Council Directive 2003/96 art 30.

COUNCIL DIRECTIVE

(92/82/EEC)

of 19 October 1992

on the approximation of the rates of excise duties on mineral oils

. . .

NOTES

Repealed by Council Directive 2003/96 art 30.

COUNCIL DIRECTIVE

(92/83/EEC)

of 19 October 1992

on the harmonisation of the structures of excise duties on alcohol and alcoholic beverages

NOTES

Date of publication in OJ: OJ L 316, 31.10.92, p 21.

THE COUNCIL OF THE EUROPEAN COMMUNITIES,

Having regard to the Treaty establishing the European Economic Community, and in particular Article 99 thereof,

Having regard to the proposal from the Commission,[1]

Having regard to the opinion of the European Parliament,[2]

Having regard to the opinion of the Economic and Social Committee,[3]

Whereas Directive 92/12/EEC lays down provisions on the general arrangements for products subjects subject to excise duty;[4]

Whereas Directive 92/84/EEC[5] lays down minimum rates of excise duty to be applied in the Member States to alcohol and alcoholic beverages;

Whereas it is important to the proper functioning of the internal market to determine common definitions for all the products concerned;

Whereas it is useful to base such definitions on those set out in the combined nomenclature in force at the date of the adoption of this Directive;

Whereas, in the case of beer, it is possible to permit alternative methods of calculating the duty on the finished product;

Whereas, in the case of beer, it is possible within certain limits to permit Member States to apply the duty to gravity bands of more than one degree Plato, provided always that no beer is charged at less than the Community minimum rate;

Whereas, in the case of beer produced in small independent breweries and ethyl alcohol produced in small distilleries, common solutions are required permitting Member States to apply reduced rates of duty to those products;

Whereas it is possible to permit variations in the strength at which Member States commence to subject beer to duty, provided that no unacceptable problems are caused in the internal market;

Whereas in the case of beer, wine and other fermented beverages it is advisable to permit Member States to exempt from duty home-made products which are not produced for commercial purposes;

Whereas, in principle, Member States should apply a single rate per hectolitre of finished product to all still wine and other still fermented beverages, and a single rate of duty per hectolitre of finished product to all sparkling wine and sparkling fermented beverages;

Whereas it is advisable to permit Member States to apply reduced rates of duty to all kinds of wine and other fermented beverages provided always that the actual alcoholic strength of the products does not exceed 8,5% vol.;

Whereas Member States applying a higher rate of duty to certain wines on 1 January 1992 should be permitted to continue to do so;

Whereas in principle, Member States should apply a single rate of duty per hectolitre of finished product to all intermediate products;

Whereas it is advisable to permit Member States to apply a reduced rate of the intermediate products duty, on the one hand to products of strengths not exceeding 15% vol., and on the other hand to natural sweet wines;

Whereas, in principle, Member States should apply the same rate of duty per hectolitre of pure alcohol to all ethyl alcohol as defined in this Directive;

Whereas it is possible to permit Member States to apply reduced rates or exemptions for certain products of a regional and traditional nature;

Whereas, in the cases where Member States are permitted to apply reduced rates, such reduced rates should not cause distortion of competition within the internal market;

Whereas Member States should be permitted to refund the excise duty on alcoholic drinks which have become unfit for consumption;

Whereas it is necessary to lay down at Community level the exemptions which apply to goods which are transported between Member States;

Whereas, however, it is possible to permit Member States an option to apply exemptions tied to end-uses within their territory;

Whereas it is necessary to provide for a system of notification of the denaturing requirements of each Member State for completely denatured alcohol, and for their acceptance by other Member States;

Whereas Member States should not be deprived of the means of combating any evasion, avoidance or abuse which may arise in the field of exemptions;

Whereas Member States should be permitted to give effect to the exemptions required by this Directive by way of refund;

Whereas, since certain Member States apply a higher rate of duty to 'other sparkling fermented beverages' than to intermediate products, they should be permitted to apply this higher rate to intermediate products having the characteristics of these 'other sparkling fermented beverages',

---

[1] OJ C 322, 21.12.90, p 11.

[2] OJ C 67, 16.3.92, p 165.

[3] OJ C 96, 18. 3.91, p 25.

[4] OJ L 76, 23.3.92, p 1.

[5] See [OJ L 316, 31.10.92, p 29].

HAS ADOPTED THIS DIRECTIVE—

SECTION I
BEER

Scope

Article 1

1. Member States shall apply an excise duty to beer in accordance with this Directive.

2. Member States shall fix their rates in accordance with Directive 92/84/EEC.

Article 2

For the purposes of this Directive, the term 'beer' covers any product falling within CN code 2203 or any product containing a mixture of beer with non-alcoholic drinks falling within CN code 2206, in either case with an actual alcoholic strength by volume exceeding 0,5% vol.

Establishment of the duty

Article 3

1. The excise duty levied by Member States on beer shall be fixed by reference either—

— to the number of hectolitre/degrees Plato,

or

— to the number of hectolitre/degrees of actual alcoholic strength by volume

of finished product.

2. In assessing the charge to duty on beer in accordance with the requirements of Directive 92/84/EEC, Member States may ignore fractions of a degree Plato or degree of actual alcoholic strength by volume.

In addition, Member States which levy the duty by reference to the number of hectolitre/degrees Plato may divide beer into categories consisting of no more than four degrees Plato per category and charge the same rate of duty per hectolitre on all beers falling within each category. Such rates shall invariably equal or exceed the minimum rate laid down in Article 6 of Directive 92/84/EEC, hereinafter referred to as the minimum rate.

Article 4

1. Member States may apply reduced rates of duty, which may be differentiated in accordance with the annual production of the breweries concerned, to beer brewed by independent small breweries within the following limits—

— the reduced rates shall not be applied to undertakings producing more than 200 000 hl of beer per year,

— the reduced rates, which may fall below the minimum rate, shall not be set more than 50% below the standard national rate of excise duty.

2. For the purposes of the reduced rates the term 'independent small brewery' shall mean a brewery which is legally and economically independent of any other brewery, which uses premises situated physically apart from those of any other brewery and does not operate under licence. However, where two or more small breweries cooperate, and their combined annual production does not exceed 200 000 hl, those breweries may be treated as a single independent small brewery.

3. Member States shall ensure that any reduced rates they may introduce apply equally to beer delivered into their territory from independent small breweries situated in other Member States. In particular they shall ensure that no individual delivery from another Member States ever bears more duty than its exact national equivalent.

Article 5

1. Member States may apply reduced rates, which may fall below the minimum rate, for beer with an actual alcoholic strength by volume not exceeding 2,8% vol.

2. Member States may confine the application of this Article to products containing a mixture of beer with non-alcoholic drinks falling within CN code 2206.

Article 6

Subject to such conditions as they shall lay down to ensure the straightforward application of the exemption, Member States may exempt from excise duty beer produced by a private individual and consumed by the producer, members of his family or his guests, provided that no sale is involved.

Part III

SECTION II
WINE

Scope

Article 7

1. Member States shall apply an excise duty to wine in accordance with this Directive.

2. Member States shall fix their rates in accordance with Directive 92/84/EEC.

Article 8

For the purposes of this Directive—

    1.   The term 'still wine' covers all products falling within CN codes 2204 and 2205, except sparkling wine as defined in paragraph 2 of this Article—

        — having an actual alcoholic strength by volume exceeding 1,2% vol. but not exceeding 15% vol., provided that the alcohol contained in the finished product is entirely of fermented origin,

        — having an actual alcoholic strength by volume exceeding 15% vol. and not exceeding 18% vol. provided they have been produced without any enrichment and that the alcohol contained in the finished product is entirely of fermented origin;

    2.   The term 'sparkling wine' covers all products falling within CN codes 2204 10, 2204 21 10, 2204 29 10 and 2205—

        — are contained in bottles with 'mushroom stoppers' held in place by ties or fastenings, or they have an excess pressure due to carbon dioxide in solution of three bar or more,

        — have an actual alcoholic strength by volume exceeding 1,2% vol. but not exceeding 15% vol., provided that the alcohol contained in the finished product is entirely of fermented origin.

Establishment of the duty

Article 9

1. The excise duty levied by Member States on wine shall be fixed by reference to the number of hectolitres of finished product.

2. Except as provided in paragraphs 3 and 4, Member States shall levy the same rate of excise duty on all products chargeable with the duty on still wine. Similarly, they shall levy the same rate of excise duty on products chargeable with the duty on sparkling wine. they may apply the same rate of duty to both still and sparkling wine.

3. Member States may apply reduced rates of excise duty to any type of still wine and sparkling wine of an actual alcoholic strength by volume not exceeding 8,5% vol.

4. Member States which on 1 January 1992 applied a higher rate of duty to still wines as defined in Article 8(1), second indent, may continue to apply this rate. This higher rate must not be more than the standard national rate applied to intermediate products.

Article 10

Subject to such conditions as they shall lay down to ensure the straightforward application of this Article, Member States may exempt from excise duty wine produced by a private individual and consumed by the producer, members of his family or his guests, provided no sale is involved.

SECTION III
FERMENTED BEVERAGES OTHER THAN WINE AND BEER

Scope

Article 11

1.   Member States shall apply an excise duty to fermented beverages other than beer and wine (other fermented beverages) in accordance with this Directive.

2.   Member States shall fix their rates in accordance with Directive 92/84/EEC.

Article 12

For the purposes of this Directive and without prejudice to the provisions of Article 17—

1.   The term 'other still fermented beverages' covers all products falling within CN codes 2204 and 2205 but not mentioned in Article 8 above, and products falling within CN code 2206, except other sparkling fermented beverages as defined in point 2 of this Article and any product covered by Article 2—

—   having an actual alcoholic strength by volume exceeding 1,2% vol. but not exceeding 10% vol.,

—   having an actual alcoholic strength by volume exceeding 10% but not exceeding 15% vol., provided that the alcohol contained in the product is entirely of fermented origin.

2.   The term 'other sparkling fermented beverages' covers all products falling within CN code 2206 00 91 as well as products falling within CN codes 2204 10, 2204 21 10, 2204 29 10 and 2205 not mentioned in Article 8 above which—

—   are contained in bottles with 'mushroom stoppers' held in place by ties or fastenings, or they have an excess pressure due to carbon dioxide in solution of three bar or more,

—   have an actual alcoholic strength by volume exceeding 1,2% vol., but not exceeding 13% vol.,

—   have an actual alcoholic strength by volume exceeding 13%, but not exceeding 15% vol., provided that the alcohol contained in the product is entirely of fermented origin.

Establishment of the duty

Article 13

1.   The exercise duty levied by Member States on other fermented beverages shall be fixed by reference to the number of hectolitres of finished product.

2.   Except as provided in paragraph 3, Member States shall levy the same rate of excise duty on all products chargeable with the duty on other still fermented beverages. Similarly they shall levy the same rate of excise duty on all products chargeable with the duty on other sparkling fermented beverages. They may apply the same rate of excise duty to both other still fermented beverages and other sparkling fermented beverages.

3.   Member States may apply reduced rates of excise duty to any type of other still and sparkling fermented beverages of an actual alcoholic strength by volume not exceeding 8,5% vol.

Article 14

Subject to such conditions as they shall lay down to ensure the straightforward application of this Article, Member States may exempt from excise duty other still and sparkling fermented beverages produced by a private individual and consumed by the producer, members of his family or his guests, provided no sale is involved.

Article 15

For the application of Directive 92/84/EEC and Directive 92/12/EEC, references to 'wine' shall be deemed to apply equally to other fermented beverages as defined in this section.

SECTION IV
INTERMEDIATE PRODUCTS

Scope

Article 16

1. Member States shall apply an excise duty to intermediate products in accordance with this Directive.

2. Member States shall fix their rates in accordance with Directive 92/84/EEC. Such rates shall never fall below the rates which Member States apply to the products of Articles 8(1) and 12(1) of the present Directive.

Article 17

1. For the purposes of this Directive the term 'intermediate products' covers all products of an actual alcoholic strength by volume exceeding 1,2% vol, but not exceeding 22% vol and falling within CN codes 2204, 2205 and 2206 but not covered by Articles 2, 8 and 12.

2. Notwithstanding the provisions of Article 12, Member States may treat as an intermediate product any still fermented beverage falling within the scope of Article 12(1) which has an actual alcoholic strength exceeding 5,5% vol. and which is not entirely of fermented origin, and any sparkling fermented beverage falling within the scope of Article 12(2) which has an actual alcoholic strength exceeding 8,5 vol. and which is not entirely of fermented origin.

Establishment of the duty

Article 18

1. The excise duty levied by Member States on intermediate products shall be fixed by reference to the number of hectolitres of finished product.

2. Except as provided in paragraphs 3, 4 and 5, Member States shall charge the same rate of duty on all products chargeable with the duty on intermediate products.

3. A Member State may apply a single reduced rate of duty to intermediate products with an actual alcoholic strength by volume not exceeding 15% vol. subject to the following conditions—

— the reduced rate shall not be set more than 40% below the standard national rate of excise duty,

— the reduced rate may not be less than the standard national rate applied to products covered by Articles 8(1) and 12(1) of this Directive.

4. Member States may apply a single reduced rate of duty to intermediate products which are defined in Article 13(1) and (2) of Regulation (EEC) No 4252/88. The reduced rate

— may fall below the minimum rate but shall not be set more than 50% below the standard national rate of excise duty,

or

— shall not be set below the minimum rate applied to intermediate products.

5. For intermediate products which are contained in bottles with 'mushroom stoppers' held in place by ties or fastenings, or have an excess pressure due to carbon

dioxide in solution of three bars or more, Member States may apply the same rate as provided for products falling within the scope of Article 12(2), provided that this rate is higher than the national rate for intermediate products.

SECTION V
ETHYL ALCOHOL

Scope

Article 19

1. Member States shall apply an excise duty to ethyl alcohol in accordance with this Directive.

2. Member States shall fix their rates in accordance with Directive 92/84/EEC.

Article 20

For the purposes of this Directive the term 'ethyl alcohol' covers—

— all products with an actual alcoholic strength by volume exceeding 1,2% volume which fall within CN codes 2207 and 2208, even when those products form part of a product which falls within another chapter of the CN,

— products of CN codes 2204, 2205 and 2206 which have an actual alcoholic strength by volume exceeding 22% vol.,

— potable spirits containing products, whether in solution or not.

Establishment of the duty

Article 21

The excise duty on ethyl alcohol shall be fixed per hectolitre of pure alcohol at 20°C, and shall be calculated by reference to the number of hectolitres of pure alcohol. Subject to the provisions of Article 22, Member States shall charge the same rate of duty on all products chargeable with the duty on ethyl alcohol.

Article 22

1. Member States may apply reduced rates of excise duty to ethyl alcohol produced by small distilleries within the following limits—

— the reduced rates, which may fall below the minimum rate, shall not be applied to undertakings producing more than 10 hectolitres of pure alcohol per year. However, Member States which applied reduced rates on 1 January 1992 to undertakings producing between 10 hectolitres and 20 hectolitres of pure alcohol per year may continue to do so,

— the reduced rates shall not be set more than 50% below the standard national rate of excise duty.

2. For the purposes of the reduced rates, the term 'small distillery' shall mean a distillery which is legally and economically independent of any other distillery and which does not operate under licence.

3. Member States shall ensure that any reduced rate they may introduce applies equally to ethyl alcohol delivered into their territory from independent small producers situated in other Member States.

4. Member States may lay down provisions whereby the alcohol produced by small producers shall be released for free circulation as soon as it is obtained (provided the producers have not themselves carried out any intra-Community transactions) without being subjected to the tax warehousing arrangements, and be taxed definitively on a flat-rate basis.

Part III

5. Member States may apply reduced rates of duty to products falling within CN code 2208 which have an actual alcohol strength by volume not exceeding 10% vol.

[6. Bulgaria and the Czech Republic may apply a reduced rate of excise duty, of not less than 50% of the standard national rate of excise duty on ethyl alcohol, to ethyl alcohol produced by fruit growers' distilleries producing, on an annual basis, more than 10 hectolitres of ethyl alcohol from fruit supplied to them by fruit growers' households.

The application of the reduced rate shall be limited to 30 litres of fruit spirits per producing fruit growers' household per year, destined exclusively for their personal consumption.]

[7. Hungary, Romania and Slovakia may apply a reduced rate of excise duty, of not less than 50 % of the standard national rate of excise duty on ethyl alcohol, to ethyl alcohol produced by fruit growers' distilleries producing, on an annual basis, more than 10 hectolitres of ethyl alcohol from fruit supplied to them by fruit growers' households.

The application of the reduced rate shall be limited to 50 litres of fruit spirits per producing fruit growers' household per year, destined exclusively for their personal consumption. The Commission will review this arrangement in 2015 and report to the Council on possible modifications.]

NOTES

Paras 6, 7: substituted by the 2005 Protocol concerning the conditions and arrangements for admission of the Republic of Bulgaria and Romania to the EU, Annex III(4), para 2.

Article 23

The following Member States may apply a reduced rate, which may fall below the minimum rate but not be set more than 50% below the standard national rate of duty on ethyl alcohol, to the following products—

1. the French Republic, in respect of rum as defined in Article 1(4)(a) of Regulation (EEC) No 1576/89 and produced from sugar cane harvested in the place of manufacture as set out at Article 1(3)(l) of that Regulation, having a content of volatile substances other than ethyl and methyl alcohol equal to or exceeding 225 grams per hectolitre of pure alcohol, and an actual alcoholic strength by volume equal to or exceeding 40% vol.;

2. the Hellenic Republic, in respect of those aniseed flavoured spirit drinks defined in Regulation (EEC) No 1576/89 which are colourless and have a sugar content of 50 grams or less per litre, and in which at least 20% of the alcoholic strength of the final product is composed of alcohol flavoured by distillation in traditional discontinuous copper stills with a capacity of 1 000 litres or less.

SECTION VI
MISCELLANEOUS

Article 24

1. Member States need not require that products covered by this Directive shall be manufactured in a tax warehouse from constituent alcoholic products which are held in suspension of the relevant excise duties, provided that the duty on the constituents has already been paid in advance and that the total tax payable on the constituent alcoholic products is not less than the tax payable on the product which results from their mixture.

2. The Kingdom of Spain need not consider as the manufacture of intermediate products the preparation of wines produced in the regions of Moriles-Montilla, Tarragona, Priorato and Terra Alta, to which alcohol has been added in such a way that their alcoholic strength does not increase by more than 1% vol.

Article 25

Member States may refund the excise duty on alcoholic drinks withdrawn from the market because their condition or age renders them unfit for human consumption.

Article 26

References in this Directive to CN codes shall be to those of the version of the combined nomenclature in force when this Directive is adopted.

SECTION VII
EXEMPTIONS

Article 27

1.   Member States shall exempt the products covered by this Directive from the harmonised excise duty under conditions which they shall lay down for the purpose of ensuring the correct and straightforward application of such exemptions and of preventing any evasion, avoidance or abuse—

(a)   when distributed in the form of alcohol which has been completely denatured in accordance with the requirements of any Member State, such requirements having been duly notified and accepted in accordance with paragraphs 3 and 4 of this Article. This exemption shall be conditional on the application of the provisions of Directive 92/12/EEC to commercial movements of completely denatured alcohol;

(b)   when both denatured in accordance with the requirements of any Member State and used for the manufacture of any product not for human consumption;

(c)   when used for the production of vinegar falling within CN code 2209;

(d)   when used for the production of medicines defined by Directive 65/65/EEC;

(e)   when used for the production of flavours for the preparation of foodstuffs and non-alcoholic beverages with an alcohol strength not exceeding 1,2% vol.;

(f)   when used directly or as a constituent of semi-finished products for the production of foodstuffs, filled or otherwise, provided that in each case the alcoholic content does not exceed 8,5 litres of pure alcohol per 100 kg of the product for chocolates, and 5 litres of pure alcohol per 100 kg of the product for other products.

2.   Member States may exempt the products covered by this Directive from the harmonised excise duty under conditions which they shall lay down for the purpose of ensuring the correct and straightforward application of such exemptions and of preventing any evasion, avoidance or abuse, when used—

(a)   as samples for analysis, for necessary production tests, or for scientific purposes;

(b)   for scientific research;

(c)   for medical purposes in hospitals and pharmacies;

(d)   in a manufacturing process provided that the final product does not contain alcohol;

(e)   in the manufacture of a component product which is not subject to excise duty under this Directive.

3.   Before 1 January 1993 and three months before any intended subsequent change in national law, each Member State shall communicate to the Commission, together with all relevant information, the denaturants which it intends to employ for the purposes of paragraph 1(a). The Commission shall transmit the communications to the other Member States within one month of receipt.

Part III

4. If, within two months of the other Member States being informed, neither the Commission nor any Member State has requested that the matter be raised in the Council, the Council shall be deemed to have authorised the denaturing processes notified. If an objection is raised within the time limit, a decision shall be taken in accordance with the procedure laid down in Article 24 of Directive 92/12/EEC.

5. If a Member State finds that a product which has been exempted under paragraphs 1(a) or 1(b) above gives rise to evasion, avoidance or abuse, it may refuse to grant exemption or withdraw the relief already granted. The Member State shall advise the Commission forthwith. The Commission shall transmit the communication to the other Member States within one month of receipt. A final decision shall then be taken in accordance with the procedure laid down in Article 24 of Directive 92/12/EEC. Member States shall not be obliged to give retroactive effect to such a decision.

6. Member States shall be free to give effect to the exemptions mentioned above by means of a refund of excise duty paid.

Article 28

The United Kingdom may continue to apply the exemptions which it applied on 1 January 1992 to the following products—

— concentrated malt beverage the worts of which prior to fermentation were of a specific gravity of 1 200 of Original Gravity (47° Plato) or more;

— aromatic bitters of an actual alcoholic strength from 44,2 to 49,2% vol., containing from 1,5% to 6% by weight of gentian, spices and other aromatic ingredients and from 4 to 10% by weight of sugar, delivered in containers holding 0,2 litres or less of product.

SECTION VIII
FINAL PROVISIONS

Article 29

1. Member States shall bring into force the laws, regulations and administrative provisions necessary to comply with this Directive not later than 31 December 1992. They shall forthwith inform the Commission thereof.

When Member States adopt these measures, they shall contain a reference to this Directive or shall be accompanied by such reference on the occasion of their official publication. The methods of making such reference shall be laid down by the Member States.

2. Member States shall communicate to the Commission the texts of the main provisions of national law which they adopt in the field governed by this Directive.

Article 30

This Directive is addressed to the Member States.

Done at Luxembourg, 19 October 1992.

COUNCIL DIRECTIVE

(92/84/EEC)

of 19 October 1992

on the approximation of the rates of excise duty on alcohol and alcoholic beverages

NOTES

Date of publication in OJ: OJ L 316, 31.10.92, p 29.

THE COUNCIL OF THE EUROPEAN COMMUNITIES,

Having regard to the Treaty instituting the European Economic Community, and in particular Article 99 thereof,

Having regard to the proposal from the Commission,[1]

Having regard to the opinion of the European Parliament,[2]

Having regard to the opinion of the Economic and Social Committee,[3]

Whereas Directive 92/12/EEC[4] lays down provisions on the general arrangements for products subject to excise duties;

Whereas Directive 92/83/EEC[5] lays down provisions relating to the harmonisation of the structures of excise duties on alcohol and alcoholic beverages;

Whereas Member States should apply minimum rates of excise duty on these products by 1 January 1993 if the internal market is to be achieved by that date;

Whereas the most appropriate basis for levying duty on ethyl alcohol is the volume of pure alcohol;

Whereas the most appropriate basis for levying duty on wine and intermediate products is the volume on the finished product;

Whereas the consumption pattern of sparkling wine differs from that of still wine; whereas, therefore, Member States may be allowed to charge differing rates of duty on the two products;

Whereas the methods of taxing beer within the Member States vary, and it is possible to permit this variation to continue, in particular by laying down a minimum rate expressed as a charge related both to the original gravity and to the alcoholic content of the product;

Whereas it is possible to permit certain Member States to apply reduced rates to products consumed within particular regions of their national territory;

Whereas it is necessary for the rates laid down in this Directive to be reviewed periodically on the basis of a Commission report taking account of all the appropriate factors;

Whereas a mechanism should be set up to enable specific amounts expressed in ecu to be converted into national currency,

[1] OJ C 12, 18. 1.90, p 12.

[2] OJ C 94, 13.4.92, p 46.

[3] OJ C 225, 10. 9.91, p 54.

[4] OJ L 76, 23.3.92, p 1.

[5] See [OJ L 316, 31.10.92, p 21].

HAS ADOPTED THIS DIRECTIVE—

Part III

Article 1

Not later than 1 January 1993, Member States shall apply minimum rates of excise duty in accordance with the rules laid down in this Directive.

Article 2

The products covered by this Directive are—

—   alcohol and alcoholic beverages,
—   intermediate products,
—   wine,
—   beer,

as defined in Directive 92/83/EEC.

Article 3

1.   As from 1 January 1993, the minimum rate of excise duty on alcohol and alcohol contained in beverages other than those referred to in Articles 4, 5 and 6 shall be fixed at ECU 550 per hectolitre of pure alcohol.

However, Member States which apply to alcohol and alcoholic beverages a rate of duty not exceeding ECU 1 000 per hectolitre of pure alcohol may not reduce their national rate. In addition Member States which apply to the said products a rate of duty exceeding ECU 1 000 per hectolitre of pure alcohol may not reduce their national rate below ECU 1 000.

2.   The Kingdom of Denmark may, however, maintain its existing system of taxing alcohol and the alcohol contained in other products until 30 June 1996, provided that the application of that system never results in the application of a charge which falls below that which would arise from the application of paragraph 1 in accordance with the rules laid down in Directive 92/83/EEC.

3.   The Italian Republic may, however, maintain its existing system of taxing alcohol and the alcohol contained in other products, which provides a reduced rate for some categories of alcohol, until 30 June 1996, provided that the application of that system never results in the application of a charge which falls below that which would arise from the application of paragraph 1 in accordance with the rules laid down in Council Directive 92/83/EEC.

Article 4

As from 1 January 1993, the minimum rate of excise duty on intermediate products shall be fixed at ECU 45 per hectolitre of product.

Article 5

As from 1 January 1993, the minimum rate of excise duty on wine shall be fixed—

—   for still wine at ECU 0,

and

—   for sparkling wine at ECU 0

per hectolitre of product.

Article 6

As from 1 January 1993, the minimum rate of excise duty on beer shall be fixed—

—   ECU 0,748 per hectolitre/degree Plato,

or

—   ECU 1,87 per hectolitre/degree of alcohol

of finished product.

Article 7

1.   The Hellenic Republic may apply a reduced rate of excise duty to ethyl alcohol consumed in the departments of Lesbos, Chios, Samos, the Dodecanese and the

Cyclades and on the following islands in the Aegean: Thasos, Northern Sporades, Samothrace and Skiros.

The reduced rate, which may fall below the minimum rate of duty, may not fall more than 50% below the standard national rate of duty on ethyl alcohol.

2. The Italian Republic may continue to apply the exemptions and reduced rates of excise duty, which may fall below the minimum rates, which were applied on 1 January 1992 to alcohol and alcoholic drinks consumed in the regions of Gorizia and the Aosta valley.

3. The Portuguese Republik may continue to apply, in the autonomous regions of Madeira and the Azores, reduced rates of excise duty not falling more than 50% below the national rates, on the following products—

    (a)   in Madeira
- wine obtained from the purely regional grape varieties specified in Article 15 of Regulation (EEC) No 4252/88,
- rum as defined in Article 1(4)(a) of Regulation (EEC) No 1576/89 having the geographical characteristics set out in Article 5(3) and Annex II, point 1, of that Regulation,
- liqueurs produced from sub-tropical fruit enriched with sugar cane eau-de-vie and having the characteristics and qualities defined in Article 5(3)(b) of Regulation (EEC) No 1576/89;

    (b)   in the Azores
- liqueurs as defined in Article 1(4)(r) of Regulation (EEC) No 1576/89 produced from passion fruit and pineapple,
- eau-de-vie made from wine or from grape marc having the characteristics and qualities defined in Article 1(4)(d) and (f) of Regulation (EEC) No 1576/89.

Article 8

Every two years, and for the first time not later than 31 December 1994, the Council, acting on the basis of a report and, where appropriate, a proposal from the Commission, shall examine the rates of duty laid down herein and, acting unanimously after consulting the European Parliament, shall adopt the necessary measures. The report by the Commission and the consideration by the Council shall take into account the proper functioning of the internal market, competition between the different categories of alcoholic drinks, the real value of the rates of duty and the wider objectives of the Treaty.

Article 9

1. The value of the ecu in national currencies to be applied to the value of specific excise duties shall be fixed once a year. The rates to be applied shall be those obtaining on the first working day of October and published in the *Official Journal of the European Communities* and shall have effect from 1 January of the following calendar year.

2. Member States may maintain the amounts of the excise duties in force at the time of the annual adjustment provided for in paragraph 1 if the conversion of the amounts of the excise duties expressed in ecu would result in an increase of less than 5% or less than ECU 5, whichever is the lower amount, in the excise duty expressed in national currency.

Article 10

1. Member States shall bring into force the laws, regulations and administrative provisions necessary to comply with this Directive not later than 31 December 1992. They shall forthwith inform the Commission thereof.

Part III

When Member States adopt these measures, they shall contain a reference to this Directive or shall be accompanied by such reference on the occasion of their official publication. The methods of making such a reference shall be laid down by the Member States.

2. Member States shall communicate to the Commission the texts of the main provisions of national law which they adopt in the field governed by this Directive.

Article 11

This Directive is addressed to the Member States.
Done at Luxembourg, 19 October 1992.

COMMISSION REGULATION

((EEC) No 3649/92)

of 17 December 1992

on a simplified accompanying document for the intra-Community movement of products subject to excise duty which have been released for consumption in the Member State of dispatch

NOTES

Date of publication in OJ: OJ L 369, 18.12.92, p 17.

THE COMMISSION OF THE EUROPEAN COMMUNITIES,

Having regard to the Treaty establishing the European Economic Community,

Having regard to Council Directive 92/12/EEC of 25 February 1992 on the general arrangements for products subject to excise duty and on the holding, movement and monitoring of such products (1), and in particular Article 7(4) thereof,

Having regard to the opinion of the Committee on Excise Duties,

Whereas, for excisable products being already released for consumption in a Member State, the free movement of those products shall not be restricted to the territory of that Member State; in cases where those products are destined or earmarked for commercial purposes in another Member State the excise duty shall be levied again according to the rules of the Member State of destination and thus give rise to a reimbursement of the excise duty paid in the Member State of dispatch;

Whereas to ensure fiscal control of those products, Article 7(4) of Directive 92/12/EEC provides for a simplified accompanying document listed the essential data from the accompanying document referred to in Article 18(1) of that Directive; whereas the form and the content of that document should be established;

Whereas the traders concerned should not bear any additional burden as regards transport documents, and provision should therefore be made for the use of already existing commercial documents provided they fulfil certain conditions;

Whereas it is necessary to provide a copy for the reimbursement of the excise duty paid in the Member State of dispatch;

Whereas the details of the procedure and the number of copies of the accompanying document should be established;

Whereas it is necessary to make provision for an accompanying document for commercial movements of completely denatured alcohol,

HAS ADOPTED THIS REGULATION—

Article 1

If products subject to excise duty and already released for consumption in one Member State are intended to be used in another Member State for the purposes referred to in Article 7 of Directive 92/12/EEC, the person who is responsible for the intra-Community movement must draw up a simplified accompanying document. During the movement of those products from one Member State to another Member State the document must accompany the consignment during the movement and must be made available to the competent authorities of the Member States for control purposes.

Article 2

1. The specimen shown in the Annex may be used, in accordance with the explanatory notes shown on copy 1 of the specimen, as the simplified accompanying document.

2. Commercial documents, eg invoices, delivery notes, freight documents and so on, may also be used as the simplified accompanying document provided they contain the same elements of information as the specimen document shown in the Annex, and the nature of the information is identified by a number corresponding with the relative box number of the said specimen.

Article 3

If the commercial documents referred to in Article 2 are used as the simplified accompanying document they shall be marked conspicuously with the following statement—

'Simplified accompanying document (excise goods) for fiscal control purposes'

Article 4

The simplified accompanying document shall be drawn up in three copies.

Copy 1 shall be kept by the supplier for fiscal control.

Copy 2 must accompany the goods during the movement and shall be kept by the recipient.

Copy 3 must accompany the goods and shall be returned to the supplier with a certificate of receipt which also indicates the further fiscal treatment of the goods in the Member State of destination given by the recipient if the supplier requires it in particular for reimbursement purposes. This copy shall be attached to any eventual application for reimbursement provided for in Article 22(3) of Directive 92/12/EEC.

Article 5

The simplified accompanying document shall also be used to accompany commercial intra-Community movements of completely denatured alcohol, provided for in Article 27(1)(a) of Council Directive 92/83/EEC (2).

Article 6

This Regulation shall enter into force on 1 January 1993.

This Regulation shall be binding in its entirety and directly applicable in all Member States.

Done at Brussels, 17 December 1992.

ANNEX

Commission Regulation (EEC) No 3649/92, Annex

EUROPEAN COMMUNITY EXCISE DUTIES	SIMPLIFIED ACCOMPANYING DOCUMENT INTRA-COMMUNITY MOVEMENT OF PRODUCTS WHICH HAVE BEEN RELEASED FOR CONSUMPTION

1

Copy for the supplier

1 Supplier VATNo ☐ (Name and address)	2 Transaction reference
	3 Competent authority of the country of destination (Name and address)
4 Recipient VATNo (Name and address)	

5 Transporter/means of transport	6 Reference number and date of declaration

7 Place of delivery

1

8 Marks and numbers, No and kind of packages, description of goods	9 Commodity code (CN code)
	10 Quantity / 11 Gross weight (kg)
	12 Net weight (kg)
	13 Invoice price/Commercial value

14 Certificates (certain wines and spirits, small breweries and small distilleries)

A Record of control. For use by competent authority	15 Boxes 1-13 certified correct. Return of copy 3 required yes ☐ no ☐ (*) Signatory's company and telephone No
	Name of signatory
	Place and date
	Signature

Continue on reverse (copies 2 and 3)
(*) Cross applicable

© European Communities Official Journal L 369, 18/12/1992 Annex

EXPLANATORY NOTES

(Reverse of copy 1)

INTRA-COMMUNITY MOVEMENT OF PRODUCTS SUBJECT TO EXCISE DUTY WHICH HAVE BEEN RELEASED FOR CONSUMPTION IN THE MEMBER STATE OF DISPATCH

1. General

1.1. The simplified accompanying document is required for excise purposes in accordance with the provisions of Article 7 of Council Directive 92/12/EEC of 25 February 1992.

1.2. The document must be completed legibly and in a manner that makes entries indelible. Information may be pre-printed. No erasures or overwriting is permitted.

1.3. The general specification of the paper to be used and the measurement of boxes is as laid down in the *Official Journal of the European Communities* No C 164 of 1 July 1989, page 3.

The paper is to be white for all copies with the size 210 millimetres by 297 millimetres with a maximum tolerance of 5 millimetres less or 8 millimetres more with regard to their length.

1.4. Any unused space is to be lined through so that nothing can be added.

1.5. The accompanying document comprises three copies—

copy 1 to be retained by the supplier.

copy 2 to accompany the goods and to be retained by the recipient.

copy 3 to accompany the goods and be returned to the supplier witch a certificate of receipt by the person named in box 4 if the supplier requires it in particular for reimbursement purposes.

2. Headings

Box 1   Supplier: the full name, address and VAT number (if any) of the person making the goods available in one Member State. If there is an excise number it should also be indicated.

Box 2   Transaction reference: a reference number given by the person supplying the goods which will identify the movement with his commercial records. Normally this will be the number and date of the invoice.

Box 3   Competent authority: the name and address of the authority in the Member State of destination to whom the movement has been declared in advance.

Box 4   Recipient: the full name, address and VAT number (if any) of the person receiving the goods. If there is an excise number it should also be indicated.

Box 5   Transporter: enter 'supplier', 'recipient' or the name and address of the person responsible for arranging the first movement, if different from the persons indicated in box 1 or box 4; the means of transport is also to be indicated.

Box 6   Reference number and date of the declaration: the declaration and/or authorisation which has to be given by the competent authority in the Member State of destination before the movement starts.

Box 7   Place of delivery: the address of delivery if different from the address in box 4.

Part III

Box 8   Full description of the goods, marks and numbers, and kind of packages—
the marks and numbers of external packages, eg containers; the number of internal packages, eg cartons; and the commercial description of goods.
The description may be continued on a separate sheet attached to each copy. A packing list could be used for this purpose.
Alcohol and alcoholic beverages other than beer, must have the alcoholic strength shown (percentage by volume at 20°C).
Beer is to be shown at either degrees Plato or alcohol percentage by volume at 20°C, or both, in accordance with the requirement of the Member State of destination and the Member State of dispatch.
Mineral oils must show the density at 15°C.

Box 9   Commodity code: the CN Code.

Box 10   Quantity: the number, the weight or the volume as appropriate for excise duty purposes in the Member State of destination, for example—
—cigarettes, the number of items, expressed in thousands,
—cigars and cigarillos, the net weight,
—alcohol and alcoholic beverages, litres at 20°C to two decimal places,
—mineral oils except heavy fuel oil, litres at 15°C.

Box 11   Gross weight: the gross weight of the consignment.

Box 12   Net weight: the weight of the goods without packaging.

Box 13   Invoice price or value: the sum total of the invoice excise duty included.
If there is no sale connected with the movement, the commercial value is to be entered. In that case the remark 'no sale' should be added.

Box 14   Certificates: This space is reserved for eventual certificates which are required on copy 2 only.
1.In the case of certain wines, certification relating to the origin and quality of the products should, where necessary, be indicated in accordance with the relevant Community legislation.
2.In the case of certain spirits certification relating to the place of production which is required under the relevant Community legislation should, where necessary, be indicated.
3.Beer brewed by an independent small brewery, as defined in the specific Council Directive relating to the structures of excise duties on alcohol and alcoholic beverages, for which it is intended to claim a reduced rate of excise duty in the Member State of destination should be certified in the following terms—
'It is hereby certified that the beer has been brewed by an independent small undertaking with a production in the previous year of . . . . . . hectolitres'.
4.Ethyl alcohol produced by a small distillery, as defined in the specific Council Directive relating to the structures of excise duties on alcohol and alcoholic beverages, for which it is intended to claim a reduced rate of excise duty in the Member State of destination should be certified in the following terms—
'It is hereby certified that the product described has been produced by a small undertaking with a production in the previous year of . . . . . . hectolitres of pure alcohol'.

Box 15   Signatory's company, etc: the document is to be completed by, or on behalf of, the person responsible for the movement of the goods. It can be either the supplier or the recipient. If the supplier requires copy 3 to be returned to him with a certificate of receipt this should be indicated.

Box A   Record of control: the competent authorities shall record the controls applied on copies 2 and 3. All comments shall be signed, dated and stamped by the responsible official.

Box B   Certificate of receipt: to be given by the recipient and to be returned to the supplier if he requires it in particular for reimbursement purposes.

EUROPEAN COMMUNITY EXCISE DUTIES	SIMPLIFIED ACCOMPANYING DOCUMENT INTRA-COMMUNITY MOVEMENT OF PRODUCTS WHICH HAVE BEEN RELEASED FOR CONSUMPTION

2

Copy for the recipient

1 Supplier VAT No	2 Transaction reference
(Name and address)	
	3 Competent authority of the country of destination (Name and address)
4 Recipient VAT No	
(Name and address)	
5 Transporter/means of transport	6 Reference number and date of declaration
7 Place of delivery	

2

8 Marks and numbers, No and kind of packages, description of goods	9 Commodity code (CN code)
	10 Quantity	11 Gross weight (kg)
	12 Net weight (kg)
	13 Invoice price/Commercial value

| 14 Certificates (certain wines and spirits, small breweries and small distilleries) |

A Record of control. For use by competent authority	15 Boxes 1-13 certified correct. Return of copy 3 required yes [ ] no [ ] (*)
	Signatory's company and telephone No
	Name of signatory
	Place and date
	Signature

Continue on reverse (copies 2 and 3)

(*) Cross applicable   © European Communities Official Journal L 253, 11/10/1993 Annex 31

Part III

B CERTIFICATION OF RECEIPT

Goods received by recipient

Date .... Place .... Reference No ....

The excise duty has been paid / declared to the competent authority (*)

Date .... Reference No ....

Other remarks of the recipient:

Place/date .... Name of signatory ....

Signature

(*) Delete inapplicable

A Record of control (continued)

(Copy 3 omitted.)

COMMISSION REGULATION

(2454/93/EEC)

of 2 July 1993

laying down provisions for the implementation of Council Regulation (EEC) No 2913/92 establishing the Community Customs Code

NOTES

Date of publication in OJ: OJ L 253, 11.10.93, p 1.

This Regulation is amended by Commission Regulation (EC) 1875/2006. Certain of these amendments are due to take effect from 1 July 2009. The full text of these amendments, along with the commencement details, are reproduced in full towards the end of Part III under the heading of Commission Regulation (EC) 1875/2006.

This Regulation is printed as corrected by Corrigenda, OJ L 268, 19.10.94, p 32, OJ L 180, 19.7.96, p 34, OJ L 156, 13.6.97, p 59 and OJ L 111, 29.4.99, p 88.

Amended by: Commission Regulation (EC) 3665/93, OJ L 335, 31.12.93, p 1; Commission Regulation (EC) 655/94, OJ L 82, 25.3.94, p 15; Council Regulation (EC) 2193/94, OJ L 235, 9.9.94, p 6; Commission Regulation (EC) 3254/94, OJ L 346, 31.12.94, p 1; the 1994 Act of Accession of the Kingdom of Norway, the Republic of Austria, the Republic of Finland and the Kingdom of Sweden, Annex I(III)(B)(4), as adjusted by Council Decision 95/1/EC, OJ L 1, 1.1.95, p 1; Council Regulation (EC) 1762/95, OJ L 171, 21.7.95, p 8; Commission Regulation (EC) 482/96, OJ L 70, 20.3.96, p 10; Commission Regulation (EC) 1676/96, OJ L 218, 28.8.96, p 1; Commission Regulation (EC) 2153/96, OJ L 289, 12.11.96, p 1; Commission Regulation (EC) 12/97, OJ L9, 13.1.97, p 1; Commission Regulation (EC) 89/97, OJ L 17, 21.1.97, p 28; Commission Regulation (EC) 1427/97, OJ L 196, 24.7.97, p 31; Commission Regulation (EC) 75/98, OJ L7, 13.1.98, p 3; Commission Regulation (EC) 1677/98, OJ L 212, 30.7.98, p 18; Commission Regulation (EC) 46/1999, OJ L 10, 15.01.99, p 1; Commission Regulation (EC) 502/1999, OJ L 65, 12.3.99, p1; Commission Regulation (EC) 1662/1999, OJ L 197, 29.7.99, p 25; Commission Regulation (EC) 1602/2000, OJ L 188, 26.7.00, p 1; Commission Regulation (EC) 2787/2000, OJ L 330, 27.12.00, p 1; Commission Regulation (EC) 993/2001, OJ L 141 28.05.2001, p 1; Commission Regulation (EC) 444/2002, OJ L 68, 12.03.2002, p 11; Commission Regulation (EC) 881/2003, OJ L 134, 29.5.03, p 1; Commission Regulation (EC) 1335/2003, OJ L 187, 26.7.03, p 16; Commission Regulation (EC) 2286/2003, OJ L 343, 31.12.03, p 1; and the 2003 Act of Accession, OJ L 236, 23.9.03, p 1; Council Regulation (EC) 837/2005, OJ L 139, 2.6.05, p 1; Commission Regulation (EC) 883/2005, OJ L 148, 11.6.05 p 5.

PART I
GENERAL IMPLEMENTING PROVISIONS
TITLE I
GENERAL

Part III

Part III

Part III

THE COMMISSION OF THE EUROPEAN COMMUNITIES,

Having regard to the Treaty establishing the European Economic Community,

Having regard to Council Regulation (EEC) No 2913/92 of 12 October 1992 establishing the Community Customs Code[1], hereinafter referred to as the "Code", and in particular Article 249 thereof,

Whereas the Code assembled all existing customs legislation in a single legal instrument; whereas at the same time the Code made certain modifications to this legislation to make it more coherent, to simplify it and to plug certain loopholes; whereas it therefore constitutes complete Community legislation in this area;

Whereas the same reasons which led to the adoption of the Code apply equally to the customs implementing legislation; whereas it is therefore desirable to bring together in a single regulation those customs implementing provisions which are currently scattered over a large number of Community regulations and directives;

Whereas the implementing Code for the Community Customs Code hereby established should set out existing customs implementing rules; whereas it is nevertheless necessary, in the light of experience—

—   to make some amendments in order to adapt the said rules to the provisions of the Code,

—   to extend the scope of certain provisions which currently apply only to specific customs procedures in order to take account of the Code's comprehensive application,

—   to formulate certain rules more precisely in order to achieve greater legal security in their application;

Whereas the changes made relate mainly to the provisions concerning customs debt;

Whereas it is appropriate to limit the application of Article 791(2) until 1 January 1995 and to review the subject matter in the light of experience gained before that time;

Whereas the measures provided for by this Regulation are in accordance with the opinion of the Customs Code Committee,

1 OJ L 302, 19.10.92, p 1.

HAS ADOPTED THIS REGULATION—

PART I
GENERAL IMPLEMENTING PROVISIONS

TITLE I
GENERAL

CHAPTER 1
DEFINITIONS

Article 1

For the purposes of this Regulation—

1.   Code means—

Council Regulation (EEC) No 2913/92 of 12 October 1992 establishing a Community Customs Code;

[2.   ATA carnet means—

the international customs document for temporary importation established by virtue of the ATA Convention or the Istanbul Convention;]

[3.   Committee means:

the Customs Code Committee established by Articles 247a and 248a of the Code;]

4.   Customs Cooperation Council means—

the organisation set up by the Convention establishing a Customs Cooperation Council, done at Brussels on 15 December 1950;

5.   Particulars required for identification of the goods means—

on the one hand, the particulars used to identify the goods commercially allowing the customs authorities to determine the tariff classification and, on the other hand, the quantity of the goods;

6.   Goods of a non-commercial nature means—

goods whose entry for the customs procedure in question is on an occasional basis and whose nature and quantity indicate that they are intended for the private, personal or family use of the consignees or persons carrying them, or which are clearly intended as gifts;

7.   Commercial policy measures means—

non-tariff measures established, as part of the common commercial policy, in the form of Community provisions governing the import and export of goods, such as surveillance or safeguard measures, quantitative restrictions or limits and import or export prohibitions;

Part III

8.   *Customs nomenclature means—*

one of the nomenclatures referred to in Article 20(6) of the Code;
9.   *Harmonised System means—*

the Harmonised Commodity Description and Coding System;
[10.   Treaty means:

the Treaty establishing the European Community;]
[11.   *Istanbul Convention means—*

the Convention on Temporary Admission agreed at Istanbul on 26 June 1990.]
[12.   Economic operator means:

a person who, in the course of his business, is involved in activities covered by customs legislation.]

NOTES

Definition "ATA carnet" substituted, definition "Istanbul Convention" added by Commission Regulation (EC) 1762/95, Art 1, para 1. Definitions "Committee" and "Treaty" substituted by Commission Regulation (EC) 444/2002,0. Art 1, para 1. Point 12 inserted by Commission Regulation (EC) No 1875/2006, Art 1.

[Article 1a

For the purposes of applying Articles 291 to 300, the countries of the Benelux Economic Union shall be considered as a single Member State.]

NOTES

Substituted by Commission Regulation (EC) 1602/2000, Art 1, para 1 with effect from 1 January 2001 (originally inserted by Commission Regulation (EC) 3665/93, Art 1, para 2).

CHAPTER 2
DECISIONS

Article 2

Where a person making a request for a decision is not in a position to provide all the documents and information necessary to give a ruling, the customs authorities shall provide the documents and information at their disposal.

Article 3

A decision concerning security favourable to a person who has signed an undertaking to pay the sums due at the first written request of the customs authorities, shall be revoked where the said undertaking is not fulfilled.

Article 4

A revocation shall not affect goods which, at the moment of its entry into effect, have already been placed under a procedure by virtue of the revoked authorisation.

However, the customs authorities may require that such goods be assigned to a permitted customs-approved treatment or use within the period which they shall set.

[CHAPTER 3
DATA-PROCESSING TECHNIQUES

[Article 4a

1. Under the conditions and in the manner which they shall determine, and with due regard to the principles laid down by customs rules, the customs authorities may provide that formalities shall be carried out by a data-processing technique.

For this purpose—

— "a data-processing technique" means—

(a) the exchange of EDI standard messages with the customs authorities;

(b) the introduction of information required for completion of the formalities concerned into customs data-processing systems;

— "EDI" (electronic data interchange) means, the transmission of data structured according to agreed message standards, between one computer system and another, by electronic means,

— "standard message" means a predefined structure recognised for the electronic transmission of data.

2. The conditions laid down for carrying out formalities by a data-processing technique shall include *inter alia* measures for checking the source of data and for protecting data against the risk of unauthorised access, loss, alteration or destruction.]

NOTES

Inserted, together with Art 4b, by Commission Regulation (EC) 3665/93, Art 1, para 2.

[Article 4b

Where formalities are carried out by a data-processing technique, the customs authorities shall determine the rules for replacement of the handwritten signature by another technique which may be based on the use of codes.]

NOTES

Inserted as noted to Art 4a.

[Article 4c

For test programmes using data-processing techniques designed to evaluate possible simplifications, the customs authorities may, for the period strictly necessary to carry out the programme, waive the requirement to provide the following information—

(a) the declaration provided for in Article 178(1);

(b) by way of derogation from Article 222(1), the particulars relating to certain boxes of the Single Administrative Document which are not necessary for the identification of the goods and which are not the factors on the basis of which import or export duties are applied.

However, the information shall be available on request in the framework of a control operation.

The amount of import duties to be charged in the period covered by a derogation granted pursuant to the first subparagraph shall not be lower than that which would be levied in the absence of a derogation.

Member States wishing to engage in such test programmes shall provide the Commission in advance with full details of the proposed test programme, including its intended duration. They shall also keep the Commission informed of actual implementation and results. The Commission shall inform all the other Member States.]

NOTES

Inserted by Commission Regulation (EC) 2787/2000, Art 1, para 1 with effect from 3 January 2001.

CHAPTER 4
DATA EXCHANGE BETWEEN CUSTOMS AUTHORITIES USING INFORMATION TECHNOLOGY AND COMPUTER NETWORKS

Article 4d

1. Without prejudice to any special circumstances and to the provisions of the procedure concerned, which, where appropriate, shall apply *mutatis mutandis*, where electronic systems for the exchange of information relating to a customs procedure or economic operators have been developed by Member States in co-operation with the Commission, the customs authorities shall use such systems for the exchange of information between customs offices concerned.

2. Where the customs offices involved in a procedure are located in different Member States, the messages to be used for the exchange of data shall conform to the structure and particulars defined by the customs authorities in agreement with each other.

NOTES

Inserted by Commission Regulation (EC) No 1875/2006, Art 2.

Article 4e

1. In addition to the conditions referred to in Article 4a (2), the customs authorities shall establish and maintain adequate security arrangements for the effective, reliable and secure operation of the various systems.

2. To ensure the level of system security provided for in paragraph 1 each input, modification and deletion of data shall be recorded together with information giving the reason for, and exact time of, such processing and identifying the person who carried it out. The original data and any data so processed shall be kept for at least three calendar years from the end of the year to which such data refers, unless otherwise specified.

3. The customs authorities shall monitor security regularly.

4. The customs authorities involved shall inform each other and, where appropriate, the economic operator concerned, of all suspected breaches of security.

NOTES

Inserted by Commission Regulation (EC) No 1875/2006, Art 2.

CHAPTER 5
RISK MANAGEMENT

Article 4f

1. Customs authorities shall undertake risk management to differentiate between the levels of risk associated with goods subject to customs control or supervision and to determine whether or not, and if so where, the goods will be subject to specific customs controls.

2. The determination of levels of risk shall be based on an assessment of the likelihood of the risk-related event occurring and its impact, should the event actually

materialise. The basis for the selection of consignments or declarations to be subject to customs controls shall include a random element.

NOTES
Inserted by Commission Regulation (EC) No 1875/2006, Art 2.

Article 4g

1. Risk management at Community level, referred to in Article 13(2) of the Code, shall be carried out in accordance with an electronic common risk management framework comprised of the following elements:

  (a) Community customs risk management system for the implementation of risk management, to be used for the communication among the Member States customs authorities and the Commission of any risk-related information that would help to enhance customs controls;

  (b) common priority control areas;

  (c) common risk criteria and standards for the harmonised application of customs controls in specific cases.

2. Customs authorities shall, using the system referred to in point (a) of paragraph 1, exchange risk-related information in the following circumstances:

  (a) the risks are assessed by a customs authority as significant and requiring customs control and the results of the control establish that the event, as referred to in Article 4(25) of the Code, has occurred; L 360/66 EN Official Journal of the European Union 19.12.2006;

  (b) the control results do not establish that the event, as referred to in Article 4(25) of the Code, has occurred, but the customs authority concerned considers the threat to present a high risk elsewhere in the Community.

NOTES
Inserted by Commission Regulation (EC) No 1875/2006, Art 2.

Article 4h

1. Common priority control areas shall cover particular customs-approved treatments or uses, types of goods, traffic routes, modes of transport or economic operators that are to be subject to increased levels of risk analysis and customs controls during a certain period.

2. The application of common priority control areas shall be based upon a common approach to risk analysis and, in order to ensure equivalent levels of customs controls, common risk criteria and standards for the selection of goods or economic operators for control.

3. Customs controls carried out in common priority control areas shall be without prejudice to other controls normally carried out by the customs authorities.

NOTES
Inserted by Commission Regulation (EC) No 1875/2006, Art 2.

Article 4i

1. The common risk criteria and standards referred to in Article 4g(1)(c) shall include the following elements:

  (a) a description of the risk(s);

(b)   the factors or indicators of risk to be used to select goods or economic operators for customs control;

(c)   the nature of customs controls to be undertaken by the customs authorities;

(d)   the duration of the application of the customs controls referred to in point (c).

The information resulting from the application of the elements referred to in the first subparagraph shall be distributed by use of the Community customs risk management system referred to in Article 4g(1)(a). It shall be used by the customs authorities in their risk management systems.

2.   Customs authorities shall inform the Commission of the results of customs controls carried out in accordance with paragraph 1.

NOTES

Inserted by Commission Regulation (EC) No 1875/2006, Art 2.

Article 4j

For the establishment of common priority control areas and the application of common risk criteria and standards account shall be taken of the following elements:

(a)   proportionality to the risk;

(b)   the urgency of the necessary application of the controls;

(c)   probable impact on trade flow, on individual Member States and on control resources.]

NOTES

Inserted by Commission Regulation (EC) No 1875/2006, Art 2.

[TITLE II
BINDING INFORMATION

CHAPTER 1
DEFINITIONS

Article 5

For the purpose of this Title—

1.   *binding information*—

means tariff information or origin information binding on the administrations of all Community Member States when the conditions laid down in Articles 6 and 7 are fulfilled;

2.   *applicant*—

—   tariff matters: means a person who has applied to the customs authorities for binding tariff information,

—   origin matters: means a person who has applied to the customs authorities for binding origin information and has valid reasons to do so,

3.   *holder*—

means the person in whose name the binding information is issued.]

NOTES

Substituted, together with Arts 6–14 (for original Arts 6–15) by Commission Regulation (EC) 12/97, Art 1, para 1.

[CHAPTER 2
PROCEDURE FOR OBTAINING BINDING INFORMATION—NOTIFICATION
OF INFORMATION TO APPLICANTS AND TRANSMISSION TO
THE COMMISSION

Article 6

1. Applications for binding information shall be made in writing, either to the competent customs authorities in the Member State or Member States in which the information is to be used, or to the competent customs authorities in the Member State in which the applicant is established. [Applications for binding tariff information shall be made by means of a form conforming to the specimen shown in Annex 1B.]

2. An application for binding tariff information shall relate to only one type of goods. An application for binding origin information shall relate to only one type of goods and one set of circumstances conferring origin.

3. (A) Applications for binding tariff information shall include the following particulars—

    (a)   the holder's name and address;

    (b)   the name and address of the applicant where that person is not the holder;

    (c)   the customs nomenclature in which the goods are to be classified. Where an applicant wishes to obtain the classification of goods in one of the nomenclatures referred to in Article 20(3)(b) and (6)(b) of the Code, the application for binding tariff information shall make express mention of the nomenclature in question;

    (d)   a detailed description of the goods permitting their identification and the determination of their classification in the customs nomenclature;

    (e)   the composition of the goods and any methods of examination used to determine this, where the classification depends on it;

    (f)   any samples, photographs, plans, catalogues or other documents available which may assist the customs authorities in determining the correct classification of the goods in the customs nomenclature, to be attached as annexes;

    (g)   the classification envisaged;

    (h)   agreement to supply a translation of any attached document into the official language (or one of the official languages) of the Member State concerned if requested by the customs authorities;

    (i)   any particulars to be treated as confidential;

    (j)   indication by the applicant whether, to his knowledge, binding tariff information for identical or similar goods has already been applied for, or issued in the Community;

    [(k)   acceptance that the information supplied may be stored on a database of the Commission and that the particulars of the binding tariff information, including any photograph(s), sketch(es), brochure(s) etc., may be disclosed to the public via the Internet, with the exception of the information which the applicant has marked as confidential; the provisions governing the protection of information in force shall apply.]

(B) Applications for binding origin information shall include the following particulars—

(a)   the holder's name and address;

(b)   the name and address of the applicant where that person is not the holder;

(c)   the applicable legal basis, for the purposes of Articles 22 and 27 of the Code;

(d)   a detailed description of the goods and their tariff classification;

(e)   the composition of the goods and any methods of examination used to determine this and their ex-works price, as necessary;

(f)   the conditions enabling origin to be determined, the materials used and their origin, tariff classification, corresponding values and a description of the circumstances (rules on change of tariff heading, value added, description of the operation or process, or any other specific rule) enabling the conditions in question to be met; in particular the exact rule of origin applied and the origin envisaged for the goods shall be mentioned;

(g)   any samples, photographs, plans, catalogues or other documents available on the composition of the goods and their component materials and which may assist in describing the manufacturing process or the processing undergone by the materials;

(h)   agreement to supply a translation of any attached document into the official language (or one of the official languages) of the Member State concerned if requested by the customs authorities;

(i)   any particulars to be treated as confidential, whether in relation to the public or the administrations;

(j)   indication by the applicant whether, to his knowledge, binding tariff information or binding origin information for goods or materials identical or similar to those referred to under points (d) or (f) have already been applied for or issued in the Community;

(k)   acceptance that the information supplied may be stored on a public-access database of the Commission; however, apart from Article 15 of the Code, the provisions governing the protection of information in force in the Member States shall apply.

4.   Where, on receipt of the application, the customs authorities consider that it does not contain all the particulars required to give an informed opinion, the customs authorities shall ask the applicant to supply the required information. The time limits of three months and 150 days referred to in Article 7 shall run from the moment when the customs authorities have all the information needed to reach a decision; the customs authorities shall notify the applicant that the application has been received and the date from which the said time limit will run.

5.   The list of customs authorities designated by the Member States to receive applications for or to issue binding information shall be published in the "C" series of the *Official Journal of the European Communities*.]

NOTES

Substituted as noted to Art 5.

Para 1: words added by Commission Regulation (EC) 1602/2000, Art 1, para 2 with effect from 1 January 2001.

Para 3: sub-para A(k) substituted by Commission Regulation (EC) 2286/2003, Art 1, para 1.

[**Article 7**

1. Binding information shall be notified to the applicant as soon as possible.

(a) Tariff matters: if it has not been possible to notify binding tariff information to the applicant within three months of acceptance of the application, the customs authorities shall contact the applicant to explain the reason for the delay and indicate when they expect to be able to notify the information.

(b) Origin matters: information shall be notified within a time limit of 150 days from the date when the application was accepted.

2. Binding information shall be notified by means of a form conforming to the specimen shown at Annex 1 (binding tariff information) or Annex 1A (binding origin information). The notification shall indicate what particulars will be treated as confidential. The right of appeal referred to in Article 243 of the Code shall be mentioned.]

NOTES

Substituted as noted to Art 5.

[**Article 8**

1. In the case of binding tariff information, the customs authorities of the Member States shall, without delay, transmit to the Commission the following:

(a) a copy of the application for binding tariff information (set out in Annex 1B);

(b) a copy of the binding tariff information notified (copy No 2 set out in Annex 1);

(c) the data as given on copy No 4 set out in Annex 1.

In the case of binding origin information they shall, without delay, transmit to the Commission the relevant details of the binding origin information notified.

Such transmission shall be effected by electronic means.

2. Where a Member State so requests, the Commission shall send it without delay the particulars obtained in accordance with paragraph 1. Such transmission shall be effected by electronic means.

3. The electronically transmitted data of the application for binding tariff information, the binding tariff information notified and the data as given on copy No 4 of Annex 1 shall be stored in a central database of the Commission. The data of the binding tariff information, including any photograph(s), sketch(es), brochure(s) and so forth, may be disclosed to the public via the Internet, with the exception of the confidential information contained in boxes 3 and 8 of the binding tariff information notified.]

NOTES

Substituted by Commission Regulation (EC) 2286/2003, Art 1, para 2.

[**CHAPTER 3**
PROVISIONS APPLYING IN THE EVENT OF INCONSISTENCIES IN BINDING INFORMATION

Article 9

1. Where different binding information exists—

— the Commission shall, on its own initiative or at the request of the representative of a Member State, place the item on the agenda of the Committee for discussion at the meeting to be held the following month or, failing that, the next meeting,

— in accordance with the Committee procedure, the Commission shall adopt a measure to ensure the uniform application of nomenclature or origin rules, as applicable, as soon as possible and within six months following the meeting referred to in the first indent.

2. For the purpose of applying paragraph 1, binding origin information shall be deemed to be different where it confers different origin on goods which—

— fall under the same tariff heading and whose origin was determined in accordance with the same origin rules and,

— have been obtained using the same manufacturing process.]

NOTES

Substituted as noted to Art 5.

[CHAPTER 4
LEGAL EFFECT OF BINDING INFORMATION

Article 10

1. Without prejudice to Articles 5 and 64 of the Code, binding information may be invoked only by the holder.

2. (a) Tariff matters: the customs authorities may require the holder, when fulfilling customs formalities, to inform the customs authorities that he is in possession of binding tariff information in respect of the goods being cleared through customs.

(b) Origin matters: the authorities responsible for checking the applicability of binding origin information may require the holder, when completing any formalities, to inform the said authorities that he is in possession of binding origin information covering the goods in respect of which the formalities are being completed.

3. The holder of binding information may use it in respect of particular goods only where it is established—

(a) tariff matters: to the satisfaction of the customs authorities that the goods in question conform in all respects to those described in the information presented;

(b) origin matters: to the satisfaction of the authorities referred to in paragraph 2(b) that the goods in question and the circumstances determining their origin conform in all respect to those described in the information presented.

4. The customs authorities (for binding tariff information) or the authorities referred to in paragraph 2(b) (for binding origin information) may ask for the information to be translated into the official language or one of the official languages of the Member State concerned.]

NOTES

Substituted as noted to Art 5.

[Article 11

Binding tariff information supplied by the customs authorities of a Member State since 1 January 1991 shall become binding on the competent authorities of all the Member States under the same conditions.]

NOTES

Substituted as noted to Art 5.

[**Article 12**

1. On adoption of one of the acts or measures referred to in Article 12(5) of the Code, the customs authorities shall take the necessary steps to ensure that binding information shall thenceforth be issued only in conformity with the act or measure in question.

2. (a)   For binding tariff information, for the purposes of paragraph 1 above, the date to be taken into consideration shall be as follows—

—   for the Regulations provided for in Article 12(5)(a)(i) of the Code concerning amendments to the customs nomenclature, the date of their applicability,

—   for the Regulations provided for in Article 12(5)(a)(i) of the Code and establishing or affecting the classification of goods in the customs nomenclature, the date of their publication in the "L" series of the *Official Journal of the European Communities*,

—   for the Regulations provided for in Article 12(5)(a)(ii) of the Code concerning amendments to the explanatory notes to the combined nomenclature, the date of their publication in the "C" series of the *Official Journal of the European Communities*,

—   for judgments of the Court of Justice of the European Communities provided for in Article 12(5)(a)(ii) of the Code, the date of the judgment,

—   for the measures provided for in Article 12(5)(a)(ii) of the Code concerning the adoption of a classification opinion, or amendments to the explanatory notes to the Harmonised System Nomenclature by the World Customs Organisation, the date of the Commission communication in the "C" series of the *Official Journal of the European Communities*.

(b)   For binding origin information, for the purposes of paragraph 1, the date to be taken into consideration shall be as follows—

—   for the Regulations provided for in Article 12(5)(b)(i) of the Code concerning the determination of the origin of goods and the rules provided for in Article 12(5)(b)(ii), the date of their applicability,

—   for the measures provided for in Article 12(5)(b)(ii) of the Code concerning amendments to the explanatory notes and opinions adopted at Community level, the date of their publication in the "C" series of the *Official Journal of the European Communities*,

—   for judgments of the Court of Justice of the European Communities provided for in Article 12(5)(b)(ii) of the Code, the date of the judgment,

—   for the measures provided for in Article 12(5)(b)(ii) of the Code concerning opinions on origin or explanatory notes adopted by the World Trade Organisation, the date given in the Commission communication in the "C" series of the *Official Journal of the European Communities*,

—   for the measures provided for in Article 12(5)(b)(ii) of the Code concerning the Annex to the World Trade Organisation's Agreement on rules of origin and those adopted under international agreements, the date of their applicability.

3. The Commission shall communicate the dates of adoption of the measures and acts referred to in this Article to the customs authorities as soon as possible.]

NOTES

Substituted as noted to Art 5.

[CHAPTER 5
PROVISIONS APPLYING IN THE EVENT OF EXPIRY OF
BINDING INFORMATION

Article 13

Where, pursuant to the second sentence of Article 12(4) and Article 12(5) of the Code, binding information is void or ceases to be valid, the customs authority which supplied it shall notify the Commission as soon as possible.]

NOTES

Substituted as noted to Art 5.

[Article 14

1. When a holder of binding information which has ceased to be valid for reasons referred to in Article 12(5) of the Code, wishes to make use of the possibility of invoking such information during a given period pursuant to paragraph 6 of that Article, he shall notify the customs authorities, providing any necessary supporting documents to enable a check to be made that the relevant conditions have been satisfied.

2. In exceptional cases where the Commission, in accordance with the second subparagraph of Article 12(7) of the Code, adopts a measure derogating from the provisions of paragraph 6 of that Article, or where the conditions referred to in paragraph 1 of this Article concerning the possibility of continuing to invoke binding tariff information or binding origin information have not been fulfilled, the customs authorities shall notify the holder in writing.]

NOTES

Substituted as noted to Art 5.

CHAPTER 6
TRANSITIONAL PROVISION

Article 15

NOTES

Repealed by Commission Regulation (EC) 12/97, Art 1, para 1.

[TITLE IIA
AUTHORISED ECONOMIC OPERATORS

CHAPTER 1
PROCEDURE FOR GRANTING THE CERTIFICATES

SECTION 1
GENERAL PROVISIONS

Article 14A

1. Without prejudice to the use of simplifications otherwise provided for under the customs rules, the customs authorities may, following an application by an economic operator and in accordance with Article 5a of the Code, issue the following authorised economic operators' certificates (hereinafter referred to as "AEO certificates"):

  (a)   an AEO certificate — Customs simplifications in respect of economic operators requesting to benefit from simplifications provided for under the customs rules and who fulfil the conditions laid down in Articles 14h, 14i and 14j;

  (b)   an AEO certificate — Security and safety in respect of economic operators requesting to benefit from facilitations of customs controls relating to security and safety when the goods enter the customs territory of the Community, or when the goods leave the customs territory of the Community and who fulfil the conditions laid down in Articles 14h to 14k; 19.12.2006 EN Official Journal of the European Union L 360/67

  (c)   an AEO certificate — Customs Simplifications/security and safety, in respect of economic operators requesting to benefit from the simplifications described in point (a) and from facilitations described in point (b), and who fulfil the conditions laid down in Articles 14h to 14k.

2. The customs authorities shall take due account of the specific characteristics of economic operators, in particular of small and medium-sized companies.]

NOTES

  Inserted by Commission Regulation (EC) No 1875/2006, Art 1(3) with effect from 1 January 2008.

[Article 14b

1. If the holder of an AEO certificate referred to in point (a) or (c) of Article 14a(1) applies for one or more of the authorisations referred to in Articles 260, 263, 269, 272, 276, 277, 282, 283, 313a, 313b, 324a, 324e, 372, 454a, 912g, the customs authorities shall not re-examine those conditions which have already been examined when granting the AEO certificate.

2. When an entry summary declaration has been lodged by the holder of an AEO certificate referred to in point (b) or (c) of Article 14a(1), the competent customs office may, before the arrival of the goods into the customs territory of the Community, notify the authorised economic operator when, as a result of security and safety risk analysis, the consignment has been selected for further physical control. This notice shall only be provided where it does not jeopardise the control to be carried out.

Member States may, however, carry out a physical control even where an authorised economic operator has not been notified, prior to the arrival of the goods in the customs territory of the Community, of the selection of the consignment for such control. When goods are to leave the customs territory of the Community, the first and second subparagraphs shall apply *mutatis mutandis.*

3. Holders of an AEO certificate referred to in point (b) or (c) of Article 14a(1) importing or exporting goods may lodge entry and exit summary declarations comprising the reduced data requirements set out in Section 2.5 of Annex 30A.

Carriers, freight forwarders or customs agents who are holders of an AEO certificate referred to in point (b) or (c) of Article 14a(1), and are involved in the importation or exportation of goods on behalf of holders of AEO certificate referred to in point (b) or (c) of Article 14a(1) may also lodge entry and exit summary declarations comprising the reduced data requirements set out in Section 2.5 of Annex 30A. Holders of an AEO certificate entitled to use reduced data requirements may be required to provide additional data elements in order to ensure the proper functioning of systems set out in international agreements with third countries relating to mutual recognition of AEO certificates and measures related to security.

4. The holder of an AEO certificate shall be subject to fewer physical and document-based controls than other economic operators. The customs authorities may decide otherwise in order to take into account a specific threat, or control obligations set out in other Community legislation.

Where, following risk analysis, the competent customs authority nevertheless selects for further examination a consignment covered by an entry or exit summary declaration or by a customs declaration lodged by an authorised economic operator, it shall carry out the necessary controls as a matter of priority. If the authorised economic operator so requests, and subject to agreement with the customs authority concerned, these controls may be carried out at a place which is different from the place of the customs office involved.

5. The benefits laid down in paragraphs 1 to 4 shall be subject to the economic operator concerned providing the necessary AEO certificate numbers.]

NOTES

Inserted by Commission Regulation (EC) No 1875/2006, Art 1(3). Article 14b, except for paras 2, 3, has effect from 1 January 2008. Paras 2, 3 have effect from 1 July 2009.

[SECTION 2
APPLICATION FOR AN AEO CERTIFICATE

Article 14c

1. Application for an AEO certificate shall be made in writing or in an electronic form in accordance with the specimen set out in Annex 1C.

2. Where the customs authority establishes that the application does not contain all the particulars required, the customs authority shall, within 30 calendar days of receipt of the application, ask the economic operator to supply the relevant information, stating the grounds for its request.

The time limits referred to in Articles 14l(1) and 14o(2) shall run from the date on which the customs authority receives all the necessary information to accept the application. The customs authorities shall inform the economic operator that the application has been accepted and the date from which the time limits will run.]

NOTES

Inserted by Commission Regulation (EC) No 1875/2006, Art 1(3) with effect from 1 January 2008.

[Article 14d

1. The application shall be submitted to one of the following customs authorities:

(a)   the customs authority of the Member State where the applicant's main accounts related to the customs arrangements involved are held, and where at least part of the operations to be covered by the AEO certificate are conducted;

(b)   the customs authority of the Member State where the applicant's main accounts related to the customs arrangements involved are accessible in the applicant's computer system by the competent customs authority using information technology and computer networks, and where the applicant's general logistical management activities are conducted, and where at least part of the operations to be covered by the AEO certificate are carried out.

The applicant's main accounts referred to in points (a) and (b) shall include records and documentation enabling the customs authority to verify and monitor the conditions and the criteria necessary for obtaining the AEO certificate.

2.   If the competent customs authority can not be determined under paragraph 1, the application shall be submitted to one of the following customs authorities:

(a)   the customs authority of the Member State where the applicant's main accounts related to the customs arrangements involved are held;

(b)   the customs authority of the Member State where the applicant's main accounts related to the customs arrangements involved are accessible, as referred to in paragraph 1(b), and the applicant's general logistical management activities are conducted.

3.   If a part of the relevant records and documentation is kept in a Member State other than the Member State of the customs authority to which the application has been submitted pursuant to paragraph 1 or 2, the applicant shall duly complete Boxes 13, 16, 17 and 18 of the application form set out in Annex 1C.

4.   If the applicant maintains a storage facility or other premises in a Member State other than the Member State of the customs authority to which the application has been submitted pursuant to paragraph 1 or 2, this information shall be provided by the applicant in Box 13 of the application form set out in Annex 1C, in order to facilitate the examination of the relevant conditions at the storage facility or other premises by the customs authorities of that Member State.

5.   The consultation procedure referred to in Article 14m shall apply in the cases referred to in paragraphs 2, 3 and 4 of this Article.

6.   The applicant shall provide a readily accessible central point or nominate a contact person within the administration of the applicant, in order to make available to the customs authorities all of the information necessary for proving compliance with the requirements for issuing the AEO certificate.

7.   Applicants shall, to the extent possible, submit necessary data to the customs authorities by electronic means.]

NOTES

Inserted by Commission Regulation (EC) No 1875/2006, Art 1(3) with effect from 1 January 2008.

[**Article 14e**

Member States shall communicate to the Commission a list of their competent authorities, to which applications have to be made, and any subsequent changes thereto. The Commission shall forward such information to the other Member States or make it available on the Internet.

These authorities shall also act as the issuing customs authorities of the AEO certificates.]

NOTES

Inserted by Commission Regulation (EC) No 1875/2006, Art 1(3) with effect from 1 January 2008.

[Article 14f

The application shall not be accepted in any of the following cases:

(a)   the application does not comply with Articles 14c and 14d;

(b)   the applicant has been convicted of a serious criminal offence linked to the economic activity of the applicant or is subject to bankruptcy proceedings at the time of the submission of the application;

(c)   the applicant has a legal representative in customs matters who has been convicted of a serious criminal offence related to an infringement of customs rules and linked to his activity as legal representative;

(d)   the application is submitted within three years after revocation of the AEO certificate as provided for in Article 14v(4).]

NOTES

Inserted by Commission Regulation (EC) No 1875/2006, Art 1(3) with effect from 1 January 2008.

[SECTION 3
CONDITIONS AND CRITERIA FOR GRANTING THE AEO CERTIFICATE

Article 14g

An applicant need not be established in the customs territory of the Community in the following cases:

(a)   where an international agreement between the Community and a third country in which the economic operator is established provides for mutual recognition of the AEO certificates and specifies the administrative arrangements for carrying out appropriate controls on behalf of the Member State's customs authority if required;

(b)   where an application for the granting of an AEO certificate referred to in point (b) of Article 14a(1) is made by an airline or a shipping company not established in the Community but which has a regional office there and already benefits from the simplifications laid down in Articles 324e, 445 or 448.

In the case referred to in point (b) of the first paragraph, the applicant shall be deemed to have met the conditions set out in Articles 14h, 14i and 14j, but shall be required to meet the condition set out in Article 14k(2).]

NOTES

Inserted by Commission Regulation (EC) No 1875/2006, Art 1(3) with effect from 1 January 2008.

[Article 14h

1. The record of compliance with customs requirements referred to in the first indent of Article 5a(2) of the Code shall be considered as appropriate if over the last three years preceding the submission of the application no serious infringement or repeated infringements of customs rules have been committed by any of the following persons:

(a)   the applicant;

(b)   the persons in charge of the applicant company or exercising control over its management;

(c)   if applicable, the applicant's legal representative in customs matters;

(d)   the person responsible in the applicant company for customs matters.

However, the record of compliance with customs requirements may be considered as appropriate if the competent customs authority considers any infringement to be of negligible importance, in relation to the number or size of the customs related operations, and not to create doubts concerning the good faith of the applicant.

2.   If the persons exercising control over the applicant company are established or resident in a third country, the customs authorities shall assess their compliance with customs requirements on the basis of records and information that are available to them.

3.   If the applicant has been established for less then three years, the customs authorities shall asses his compliance with customs requirements on the basis of the records and information that are available to them.]

NOTES

Inserted by Commission Regulation (EC) No 1875/2006, Art 1(3) with effect from 1 January 2008.

[Article 14i

To enable the customs authorities to establish that the applicant has a satisfactory system of managing commercial and, where appropriate, transport records, as referred to in the second indent of Article 5a(2) of the Code, the applicant shall fulfil the following requirements:

(a)   maintain an accounting system which is consistent with the generally accepted accounting principles applied in the Member State where the accounts are held and which will facilitate audit-based customs control;

(b)   allow the customs authority physical or electronic access to its customs and, where appropriate, transport records;

(c)   have a logistical system which distinguishes between Community and non-Community goods;

(d)   have an administrative organisation which corresponds to the type and size of business and which is suitable for the management of the flow of goods, and have internal controls capable of detecting illegal or irregular transactions;

(e)   where applicable, have satisfactory procedures in place for the handling of licenses and authorisations connected to commercial policy measures or to trade in agricultural products;

(f)   have satisfactory procedures in place for the archiving of the company's records and information and for protection against the loss of information;

(g)   ensure that employees are made aware of the need to inform the customs authorities whenever compliance difficulties are discovered and establish suitable contacts to inform the customs authorities of such occurrences;

(h)   have appropriate information technology security measures in place to protect the applicant's computer system from unauthorised intrusion and to secure the applicant's documentation.

An applicant requesting the AEO certificate referred to in point (b) of Article 14a(1) shall not be required to fulfil the requirement laid down in point (c) of the first paragraph of this Article.]

Part III

NOTES

Inserted by Commission Regulation (EC) No 1875/2006, Art 1(3) with effect from 1 January 2008.

[Article 14j

1. The condition relating to the financial solvency of the applicant referred to in the third indent of Article 5a(2) of the Code shall be deemed to be met if his solvency can be proven for the past three years.

For the purposes of this Article, financial solvency shall mean a good financial standing which is sufficient to fulfil the commitments of the applicant, with due regard to the characteristics of the type of the business activity.

2. If the applicant has been established for less then three years, his financial solvency shall be judged on the basis of records and information that are available.]

NOTES

Inserted by Commission Regulation (EC) No 1875/2006, Art 1(3) with effect from 1 January 2008.

[Article 14k

1. The applicant's security and safety standards referred to in the fourth indent of Article 5a(2) of the Code shall be considered to be appropriate if the following conditions are fulfilled:

(a)   buildings to be used in connection with the operations to be covered by the certificate are constructed of materials which resist unlawful entry and provide protection against unlawful intrusion;

(b)   appropriate access control measures are in place to prevent unauthorised access to shipping areas, loading docks and cargo areas;

(c)   measures for the handling of goods include protection against the introduction, exchange or loss of any material and tampering with cargo units;

(d)   where applicable, procedures are in place for the handling of import and/or export licenses connected to prohibitions and restrictions and to distinguish these goods from other goods;

(e)   the applicant has implemented measures allowing a clear identification of his business partners in order to secure the international supply chain;

(f)   the applicant conducts, in so far as legislation permits, security screening on prospective employees working in security sensitive positions and carries out periodic background checks;

(g)   the applicant ensures that its staff concerned actively participate in security awareness programmes.

2. If an airline or shipping company which is not established in the Community, but has a regional office there and benefits from the simplifications laid down in Articles 324e, 445 or 448, submits an application for an AEO certificate referred to in point (b) of Article 14a(1), it shall fulfil one of the following conditions:

(a)   be the holder of an internationally recognised security and/or safety certificate issued on the basis of the international conventions governing the transport sectors concerned;

(b)   be a regulated agent, as referred to in Regulation (EC) No 2320/2002 of the European Parliament and of the Council (*), and fulfil the requirements laid down in Commission Regulation (EC) No 622/2003 (**);

(c) be the holder of a certificate issued in a country outside of the customs territory of the Community, where a bilateral agreement concluded between the Community and the third country provides for acceptance of the certificate, subject to the conditions laid down in that agreement.

If the airline or shipping company is the holder of a certificate referred to in point (a) of this paragraph, it shall meet the criteria laid down in paragraph 1. The issuing customs authority shall consider the criteria laid down in paragraph 1 to be met, to the extent that the criteria for issuing the international certificate are identical or correspond to those laid down in paragraph 1.

3. If the applicant is established in the Community and is a regulated agent as referred to in Regulation (EC) No 2320/2002 and fulfils the requirements provided for in Regulation (EC) No 622/2003, the criteria laid down in paragraph 1 shall be deemed to be met in relation to the premises for which the economic operator obtained the status of regulated agent.

4. If the applicant, established in the Community, is the holder of an internationally recognised security and/or safety certificate issued on the basis of international conventions, of a European security and/or safety certificate issued on the basis of Community legislation, of an International Standard of the International Organisation for Standardisation, or of a European Standard of the European Standards Organisations, the criteria provided for in paragraph 1 shall be deemed to be met to the extent that the criteria for issuing these certificates are identical or correspond to those laid down in this Regulation.]

---

* OJ L 355, 30.12.2002, p. 1.
** OJ L 89, 5.4.2003, p. 9.

NOTES

Inserted by Commission Regulation (EC) No 1875/2006, Art 1(3) with effect from 1 January 2008.

SECTION 4
PROCEDURE FOR ISSUING AEO CERTIFICATES

Article 14l

1. The issuing customs authority shall communicate the application to the customs authorities of all other Member States within five working days starting from the date on which it has received the application in accordance with Article 14c using the communication system referred to in Article 14x.

2. Where the customs authority of any other Member State has relevant information which may prejudice the granting of the certificate, it shall communicate that information to the issuing customs authority within 35 calendar days starting from the date of the communication provided for in paragraph 1, using the communication system referred to in Article 14x.]

NOTES

Inserted by Commission Regulation (EC) No 1875/2006, Art 1(3) with effect from 1 January 2008.

[Article 14m

1. Consultation between the customs authorities of the Member States shall be required if the examination of one or more of the criteria laid down in Articles 14g to 14k cannot be performed by the issuing customs authority due either to a lack of information or to the impossibility of checking it. In these cases, the customs authorities of the Member States shall carry out the consultation within 60 calendar days, starting from the date of the communication of the information by the issuing customs authority, in order to allow for the issuing of the AEO certificate or the rejection of the application within the time limits set out in Article 14o(2).

If the consulted customs authority fails to respond within the 60 calendar days, the consulting authority may assume, at the responsibility of the consulted customs authority, that the criteria for which the consultation took place are met. This period may be extended if the applicant carries out adjustments in order to satisfy those criteria and communicates them to the consulted and the consulting authority.

2. Where, following the examination provided for in Article 14n, the consulted customs authority establishes that the applicant does not fulfil one or more of the criteria, the results, duly documented, shall be transferred to the issuing customs authority which shall reject the application. Article 14o(4), (5) and (6) shall apply.]

NOTES

Inserted by Commission Regulation (EC) No 1875/2006, Art 1(3) with effect from 1 January 2008.

[Article 14n

1. The issuing customs authority shall examine whether or not the conditions and criteria for issuing the certificate described in Articles 14g to 14k are met. Examination of the criteria laid down in Article 14k shall be carried out for all the premises which are relevant to the customs related activities of the applicant. The examination as well as its results shall be documented by the customs authority.

Where, in the case of a large number of premises, the period for issuing the certificate would not allow for examination of all of the relevant premises, but the customs authority has no doubt that the applicant maintains corporate security standards which are commonly used in all its premises, it may decide only to examine a representative proportion of those premises.

2. The issuing customs authority may accept conclusions provided by an expert in the relevant fields referred to in Articles 14i, 14j and 14k in respect of the conditions and criteria referred to in those Articles respectively. The expert shall not be related to the applicant.]

NOTES

Inserted by Commission Regulation (EC) No 1875/2006, Art 1(3) with effect from 1 January 2008.

[Article 14o

1. The issuing customs authority shall issue the AEO certificate in accordance with the specimen set out in Annex 1D.

2. The AEO certificate shall be issued within 90 calendar days starting from the date of receipt, in accordance with Article 14c, of the application. Where the customs authority is unable to meet the deadline, this period may be extended by one further period of 30 calendar days. In such cases, the customs authority shall, before the expiry of the period of 90 calendar days, inform the applicant of the reasons for the extension.

3.   The period provided for in the first sentence of paragraph 2 may be extended if, in the course of the examination of the criteria, the applicant carries out adjustments in order to satisfy those criteria and communicates them to the competent authority.

4.   Where the result of the examination performed in accordance with Articles 14l, 14m and 14n is likely to lead to the rejection of the application, the issuing customs authority shall communicate the findings to the applicant and provide him with the opportunity to respond within 30 calendar days, before rejecting the application. The period laid down in the first sentence of paragraph 2 shall be suspended accordingly.

5.   The rejection of an application shall not lead to the automatic revocation of any existing authorisation issued under the customs rules. 6. If the application is rejected, the customs authority shall inform the applicant of the grounds on which the decision is based. The decision to reject an application shall be notified to the applicant within the time limits laid down in paragraphs (2), (3) and (4).]

NOTES
Inserted by Commission Regulation (EC) No 1875/2006, Art 1(3) with effect from 1 January 2008.

[Article 14p
The issuing customs authority shall, within five working days, inform the customs authorities of the other Member States that an AEO certificate has been issued, using the communication system referred to in Article 14x. Information shall also be provided within the same time limit if the application is rejected.]

NOTES
Inserted by Commission Regulation (EC) No 1875/2006, Art 1(3) with effect from 1 January 2008.

[CHAPTER 2
LEGAL EFFECTS OF AEO CERTIFICATES

SECTION 1
GENERAL PROVISIONS

Article 14q
1.   The AEO certificate shall take effect on the 10th working day after the date of its issue.

2.   The AEO certificate shall be recognised in all Member States.

3.   The period of validity of the AEO certificate shall not be limited.

4.   The customs authorities shall monitor the compliance with the conditions and criteria to be met by the authorised economic operator.

5.   A re-assessment of the conditions and criteria shall be carried out by the issuing customs authority in the following cases:
   (a)   major changes to the relevant Community legislation;
   (b)   reasonable indication that the relevant conditions and criteria are not any longer met by the authorised economic operator.
In the case of an AEO certificate issued to an applicant established for less than three years, close monitoring shall take place during the first year after issue. Article 14n(2) shall apply. The results of the re-assessment shall be made available to the customs authorities of all Member States, using the communication system referred to in Article 14x.]

NOTES

Inserted by Commission Regulation (EC) No 1875/2006, Art 1(3) with effect from 1 January 2008.

[SECTION 2

SUSPENSION OF THE STATUS OF AUTHORISED ECONOMIC OPERATOR

Article 14r

1.   The status of authorised economic operator shall be suspended by the issuing customs authority in the following cases:

(a)   where non-compliance with the conditions or criteria for the AEO certificate has been detected;

(b)   the customs authorities have sufficient reason to believe that an act, which gives rise to criminal court proceedings and linked to an infringement of the customs rules, has been perpetrated by the authorised economic operator.

However, in the case referred to in point (b) of the first subparagraph, the customs authority may decide not to suspend the status of authorised economic operator if it considers an infringement to be of negligible importance in relation to the number or size of the customs related operations and not to create doubts concerning the good faith of the authorised economic operator.

Before taking a decision, the customs authorities shall communicate their findings to the economic operator concerned. The economic operator concerned shall be entitled to correct the situation and/or express his point of view within 30 calendar days starting from the date of communication.

However, where the nature or the level of the threat to citizens' security and safety, to public health or to the environment so requires, suspension shall take place immediately. The suspending customs authority shall immediately inform the customs authorities of the other Member States, using the communication system referred to in Article 14x, in order to permit them to take appropriate action.

2.   If the holder of the AEO certificate does not regularise the situation referred to in point (a) of the first subparagraph of paragraph 1 within the period of 30 calendar days referred to in the third subparagraph of paragraph 1, the competent customs authority shall notify the economic operator concerned that the status of authorised economic operator is suspended for a period of 30 calendar days, to enable the economic operator to take the required measures to regularise the situation. The notification shall also be sent to the customs authorities of the other Member States using the communication system referred to in Article 14x.

3.   If the holder of the AEO certificate has committed an act referred to in point (b) of the first subparagraph of paragraph 1, the issuing customs authority shall suspend the status of authorised economic operator for the duration of the court proceedings. It shall notify the holder of the certificate to that effect. Notification shall also be sent to the customs authorities of the other Member States, using the communication system referred to in Article 14x.

4.   Where the economic operator concerned has been unable to regularise the situation within 30 calendar days but can provide evidence that the conditions can be met if the suspension period is extended, the issuing customs authority shall suspend the status of authorised economic operator for a further 30 calendar days.]

NOTES
Inserted by Commission Regulation (EC) No 1875/2006, Art 1(3) with effect from 1 January 2008.

[Article 14s

1. The suspension shall not affect any customs procedure already started before the date of suspension and not yet completed.

2. The suspension shall not automatically affect any authorisation which has been granted without reference to the AEO certificate unless the reasons for the suspension also have relevance for that authorisation.

3. The suspension shall not automatically affect any authorisation for use of a customs simplification which has been granted on the basis of the AEO certificate and for which the conditions are still fulfilled.

4. In the case of an AEO certificate referred to in point (c) of Article 14a(1), if the economic operator concerned fails to fulfil only the conditions laid down in Article 14k, the status of authorised economic operator shall be partially suspended and a new AEO certificate, as referred to in point (a) of Article 14a(1) may be issued at his request.]

NOTES
Inserted by Commission Regulation (EC) No 1875/2006, Art 1(3) with effect from 1 January 2008.

[Article 14t

1. When the economic operator concerned has, to the satisfaction of the customs authorities, taken the necessary measures to comply with the conditions and criteria that have to be met by an authorised economic operator, the issuing customs authority shall withdraw the suspension and inform the economic operator concerned and the customs authorities of the other Member States. The suspension may be withdrawn before the expiry of the time limit laid down in Article 14r(2) or (4).

In the situation referred to in Article 14s (4), the suspending customs authority shall reinstate the suspended certificate. It shall subsequently revoke the AEO certificate referred to in point (a) of Article 14a(1).

2. If the economic operator concerned fails to take the necessary measures within the suspension period provided for in Article 14r(2) or (4), the issuing customs authority shall revoke the AEO certificate and immediately notify the customs authorities of the other Member States, using the communication system referred to in Article 14x.

In the situation referred to in Article 14s (4), the original certificate shall be revoked and only the new AEO certificate as referred to in point (a) of Article 14a(1) issued shall be valid.]

NOTES
Inserted by Commission Regulation (EC) No 1875/2006, Art 1(3) with effect from 1 January 2008.

[Article 14u

1. Where an authorised economic operator is temporarily unable to meet any of the criteria laid down in Article 14a, he may request suspension of the status of authorised economic operator. In such case, the authorised economic operator shall

notify the issuing customs authority, specifying the date when he will be able to meet the criteria again. He shall also notify the issuing customs authority of any planned measures and their timescale.

The notified customs authority shall send the notification to the customs authorities of the other Member States using the communication system referred to in Article 14x.

2. If the authorised economic operator fails to regularise the situation within the period set out in his notification, the issuing customs authority may grant a reasonable prolongation, provided that the authorised economic operator has acted in good faith. This prolongation shall be notified to the customs authorities of the other Member States using the communication system referred to in Article 14x.

In all other cases, the AEO certificate shall be revoked and the issuing customs authority shall immediately notify the customs authorities of the other Member States, using the communication system referred to in Article 14x.

3. If the required measures are not taken within the suspension period, Article 14v shall apply.]

NOTES

Inserted by Commission Regulation (EC) No 1875/2006, Art 1(3) with effect from 1 January 2008.

[SECTION 3

REVOCATION OF THE AEO CERTIFICATE

Article 14v

1. The AEO certificate shall be revoked by the issuing customs authority in the following cases:

    (a)   where the authorised economic operator fails to take the measures referred to in Article 14t(1);

    (b)   where serious infringements related to customs rules have been committed by the authorised economic operator and there is no further right of appeal;

    (c)   where the authorised economic operator fails to take the necessary measures during the suspension period referred to in Article 14u;

    (d)   upon request of the authorised economic operator.

However, in the case referred to in point (b), the customs authority may decide not to revoke the AEO certificate if it considers the infringements to be of negligible importance in relation to the number or size of the customs related operations and not to create doubts concerning the good faith of the authorised economic operator.

2. Revocation shall take effect from the day following its notification.

In the case of an AEO certificate as referred to in point (c) of Article 14a(1), where the economic operator concerned only fails to fulfil the conditions in Article 14k, the certificate shall be revoked by the issuing customs authority and a new AEO certificate as referred to in point (a) of Article 14a(1) shall be issued.

3. The issuing customs authority shall immediately inform the customs authorities of the other Member States of the revocation of an AEO certificate using the communication system referred to in Article 14x.

4. Apart from cases of revocation referred to in points (c) and (d) of paragraph 1, the economic operator shall not be permitted to submit a new application for an AEO certificate within three years from the date of revocation.]

NOTES

Inserted by Commission Regulation (EC) No 1875/2006, Art 1(3) with effect from 1 January 2008.

[CHAPTER 3
INFORMATION EXCHANGE

Article 14w

1.   The authorised economic operator shall inform the issuing customs authority of all factors arising after the certificate is granted which may influence its continuation or content.

2.   All relevant information at the disposal of the issuing customs authority shall be made available to the customs authorities of the other Member States where the authorised economic operator carries out customs related activities.

3.   If a customs authority revokes a specific authorisation granted to an authorised economic operator, on the basis of his AEO certificate, for the use of a particular customs simplification, as provided for in Articles 260, 263, 269, 272, 276, 277, 282, 283, 313a and 313b, 324a, 324e, 372, 454a, 912g, it shall so notify the customs authority which issued the AEO certificate.]

NOTES

Inserted by Commission Regulation (EC) No 1875/2006, Art 1(3) with effect from 1 January 2008.

[Article 14x

1.   An electronic information and communication system, defined by the Commission and the customs authorities in agreement with each other, shall be used for the information and communication process between the customs authorities and for information of the Commission and of the economic operators.

2.   The Commission and the customs authorities shall, using the system referred to in paragraph 1, store and have access to the following information:

(a)   the electronically transmitted data of the applications;

(b)   the AEO certificates, and where applicable, their amendment, revocation, or the suspension of the status of authorised economic operator;

(c)   all other relevant information.

3.   The issuing customs authority shall notify the risk analysis offices in its own Member State of the granting, amendment, revocation of an AEO certificate, or the suspension of the status of authorised economic operator. It shall also inform all issuing authorities of the other Member States.   4.   The list of authorised economic operators may be disclosed by the Commission to the public via the Internet with prior agreement of the authorised.]

NOTES

Inserted by Commission Regulation (EC) No 1875/2006, Art 1(3) with effect from 1 January 2008.

TITLE III
FAVOURABLE TARIFF TREATMENT BY REASON OF THE NATURE OF GOODS

Articles 16–34

. . .

NOTES

Repealed by Commission Regulation (EC) 1602/2000, Art 1, para 4.

TITLE IV
ORIGIN OF GOODS
CHAPTER 1
NON-PREFERENTIAL ORIGIN
SECTION 1
WORKING OR PROCESSING CONFERRING ORIGIN

Article 35

This chapter lays down, for textiles and textile articles falling within Section XI of the Combined Nomenclature, and for certain products other than textiles and textile articles, the working or processing which shall be regarded as satisfying the criteria laid down in Article 24 of the Code and shall confer on the products concerned the origin of the country in which they were carried out.

"Country" means either a third country or the Community as appropriate.

SUBSECTION 1
TEXTILES AND TEXTILE ARTICLES FALLING WITHIN SECTION XI OF THE COMBINED NOMENCLATURE

Article 36

For textiles and textile articles falling within Section XI of the Combined Nomenclature, a complete process, as specified in Article 37, shall be regarded as a working or processing conferring origin in terms of Article 24 of the Code.

Article 37

Working or processing as a result of which the products obtained receive a classification under a heading of the Combined Nomenclature other than those covering the various non-originating materials used shall be regarded as complete processes.

However, for products listed in Annex 10, only the specific processes referred to in column 3 of that Annex in connection with each product obtained shall be regarded as complete, whether or not they involve a change of heading.

The method of applying the rules in Annex 10 is described in the introductory notes in Annex 9.

Article 38

For the purposes of the preceding Article, the following shall in any event be considered as insufficient working or processing to confer the status of originating products whether or not there is a change of heading—

    (a)   operations to ensure the preservation of products in good condition during transport and storage (ventilation, spreading out, drying, removal of damaged parts and like operations);

(b)   simple operations consisting of removal of dust, sifting or screening, sorting, classifying, matching (including the making-up of sets of articles), washing, cutting up;

(c) (i)   changes of packing and breaking-up and assembly of consignments;

    (ii)   simple placing in bags, cases, boxes, fixing on cards or boards, etc, and all other simple packing operations;

(d)   the affixing of marks, labels or other like distinguishing signs on products or their packaging;

(e)   simple assembly of parts of products to constitute a complete product;

(f)   a combination of two or more operations specified in (a) to (e).

SUBSECTION 2
PRODUCTS OTHER THAN TEXTILES AND TEXTILE ARTICLES FALLING WITHIN SECTION XI OF THE COMBINED NOMENCLATURE

Article 39

In the case of products obtained which are listed in Annex 11, the working or processing referred to in column 3 of the Annex shall be regarded as a process or operation conferring origin under Article 24 of the Code.

The method of applying the rules set out in Annex 11 is described in the introductory notes in Annex 9.

SUBSECTION 3
COMMON PROVISIONS FOR ALL PRODUCTS

Article 40

Where the lists in Annexes 10 and 11 provide that origin is conferred if the value of the non-originating materials used does not exceed a given percentage of the ex-works price of the products obtained, such percentage shall be calculated as follows—

—   "value" means the customs value at the time of import of the non-originating materials used or, if this is not known and cannot be ascertained, the first ascertainable price paid for such materials in the country of processing,

—   "ex-works price" means the ex-works price of the product obtained minus any internal taxes which are, or may be, repaid when such product is exported,

—   "value acquired as a result of assembly operations" means the increase in value resulting from the assembly itself, together with any finishing and checking operations, and from the incorporation of any parts originating in the country where the operations in question were carried out, including profit and the general costs borne in that country as a result of the operations.

SECTION 2
IMPLEMENTING PROVISIONS RELATING TO SPARE PARTS

Article 41

[1.   Accessories, spare parts or tools delivered with any piece of equipment, machine, apparatus or vehicle which form part of its standard equipment shall be deemed to have the same origin as that piece of equipment, machine, apparatus or vehicle.]

[2].   Essential spare parts for use with any piece of equipment, machine, apparatus or vehicle put into free circulation or previously exported shall be deemed to have the same origin as that piece of equipment, machine, apparatus or vehicle provided the conditions laid down in this section are fulfilled.

NOTES

Para 1 inserted, and original text renumbered as para 2 by Commission Regulation (EC) 3665/93, Art 1, para 5.

Article 42

The presumption of origin referred to in the preceding Article shall be accepted only—

— if this is necessary for importation into the country of destination,

— if the incorporation of the said essential spare parts in the piece of equipment, machine, apparatus or vehicle concerned at the production stage would not have prevented the piece of equipment, machine, apparatus or vehicle from having Community origin or that of the country of manufacture.

Article 43

For the purposes of Article 41—

(a) "piece of equipment, machine, apparatus or vehicle" means goods listed in Sections XVI, XVII and XVIII of the Combined Nomenclature;

(b) "essential spare parts" means parts which are—

— components without which the proper operation of the goods referred to in (a) which have been put into free circulation or previously exported cannot be ensured, and

— characteristic of those goods, and

— intended for their normal maintenance and to replace parts of the same kind which are damaged or have become unserviceable.

Article 44

Where an application is presented to the competent authorities or authorised agencies of the Member States for a certificate of origin for essential spare parts within the meaning of Article 41, box 6 (Item number, marks, numbers, number and kind of packages, description of goods) of that certificate and the application relating thereto shall include a declaration by the person concerned that the goods mentioned therein are intended for the normal maintenance of a piece of equipment, machine, apparatus or vehicle previously exported, together with the exact particulars of the said piece of equipment, machine, apparatus or vehicle.

Whenever possible, the person concerned shall also give the particulars of the certificate of origin (issuing authority, number and date of certificate) under cover of which was exported the piece of equipment, machine, apparatus or vehicle for whose maintenance the parts are intended.

Article 45

Where the origin of essential spare parts within the meaning of Article 41 must be proved for their release for free circulation in the Community by the production of a certificate of origin, the certificate shall include the particulars referred to in Article 44.

Article 46

In order to ensure application of the rules laid down in this section, the competent authorities of the Member States may require additional proof, in particular—

— production of the invoice or a copy of the invoice relating to the piece of equipment, machine, apparatus or vehicle put into free circulation or previously exported,

— the contract or a copy of the contract or any other document showing that delivery is being made as part of the normal maintenance service.

SECTION 3
IMPLEMENTING PROVISIONS RELATING TO CERTIFICATES OF ORIGIN

SUBSECTION 1
PROVISIONS RELATING TO UNIVERSAL CERTIFICATES OF ORIGIN

Article 47

When the origin of a product is or has to be proved on importation by the production of a certificate of origin, that certificate shall fulfil the following conditions—

    (a)   it shall be made out by a reliable authority or agency duly authorised for that purpose by the country of issue;

    (b)   it shall contain all the particulars necessary for identifying the product to which it relates, in particular;

        — the number of packages, their nature, and the marks and numbers they bear,

        — the type of product,

        — the gross and net weight of the product; these particulars may, however, be replaced by others, such as the number or volume, when the product is subject to appreciable changes in weight during carriage or when its weight cannot be ascertained or when it is normally identified by such other particulars,

        — the name of the consignor;

    (c)   it shall certify unambiguously that the product to which it relates originated in a specific country.

Article 48

1. A certificate of origin issued by the competent authorities or authorised agencies of the Member States shall comply with the conditions prescribed by Article 47(a) and (b).

2. The certificates and the applications relating to them shall be made out on forms corresponding to the specimens in Annex 12.

3. Such certificates of origin shall certify that the goods originated in the Community.

However, when the exigencies of export trade so require, they may certify that the goods originated in a particular Member State.

If the conditions of Article 24 of the Code are fulfilled only as a result of a series of operations or processes carried out in different Member States, the goods may only be certified as being of Community origin.

Article 49

Certificates of origin shall be issued upon written request of the person concerned.

Where the circumstances so warrant, in particular where the applicant maintains a regular flow of exports, the Member States may decide not to require an application for each export operation, on condition that the provisions concerning origin are complied with.

Where the exigencies of trade so require, one or more extra copies of an origin certificate may be issued.

Such copies shall be made out on forms corresponding to the specimen in Annex 12.

Article 50

1. The certificate shall measure 210 x 297 mm. A tolerance of up to minus 5 mm or plus 8 mm in the length shall be allowed. The paper used shall be white, free of mechanical pulp, dressed for writing purposes and weigh at least 64 g/m2 or between

25 and 30 g/m2 where air-mail paper is used. It shall have a printed guilloche pattern background in sepia such as to reveal any falsification by mechanical or chemical means.

2. The application form shall be printed in the official language or in one or more of the official languages of the exporting Member State. The certificate of origin form shall be printed in one or more of the official languages of the Community or, depending on the practice and requirements of trade, in any other language.

3. Member States may reserve the right to print the certificate of origin forms or may have them printed by approved printers. In the latter case, each certificate must bear a reference to such approval. Each certificate of origin form must bear the name and address of the printer or a mark by which the printer can be identified. It shall also bear a serial number, either printed or stamped, by which it can be identified.

Article 51

The application form and the certificate of origin shall be completed in typescript or by hand in block capitals, in an identical manner, in one of the official languages of the Community or, depending on the practice and requirements of trade, in any other languages.

Article 52

Each origin certificate referred to in Article 48 shall bear a serial number by which it can be identified. The application for the certificate and all copies of the certificate itself shall bear the same number.

In addition, the competent authorities or authorised agencies of the Member States may number such documents by order of issue.

Article 53

The competent authorities of the Member States shall determine what additional particulars, if any, are to be given in the application. Such additional particulars shall be kept to a strict minimum.

Each Member State shall inform the Commission of the provisions it adopts in pursuance of the preceding paragraph. The Commission shall immediately communicate this information to the other Member States.

Article 54

The competent authorities or authorised agencies of the Member States which have issued certificates of origin shall retain the applications for a minimum of two years.

However, applications may also be retained in the form of copies thereof, provided that these have the same probative value under the law of the Member State concerned.

SUBSECTION 2
SPECIFIC PROVISIONS RELATING TO CERTIFICATES OF ORIGIN FOR CERTAIN AGRICULTURAL PRODUCTS SUBJECT TO SPECIAL IMPORT ARRANGEMENTS

Article 55

Articles 56 to 65 lay down the conditions for use of certificates of origin relating to agricultural products originating in third countries for which special non-preferential import arrangements have been established, in so far as these arrangements refer to the following provisions.

(A)

Certificates of origin

Article 56

1. Certificates of origin relating to agricultural products originating in third countries for which special non-preferential import arrangements are established shall be made out on a form conforming to the specimen in Annex 13.

2. Such certificates shall be issued by the competent governmental authorities of the third countries concerned, hereinafter referred to as the issuing authorities, if the products to which the certificates relate can be considered as products originating in those countries within the meaning of the rules in force in the Community.

3. Such certificates shall also certify all necessary information provided for in the Community legislation governing the special import arrangements referred to in Article 55.

4. Without prejudice to specific provisions under the special import arrangements referred to in Article 55 the period of validity of the certificates of origin shall be ten months from the date of issue by the issuing authorities.

Article 57

1. Certificates of origin drawn up in accordance with the provisions of this subsection shall consist only of a single sheet identified by the word "original" next to the title of the document.

If additional copies are necessary, they shall bear the designation "copy" next to the title of the document.

2. The competent authorities in the Community shall accept as valid only the original of the certificate of origin.

Article 58

1. The certificate of origin shall measure 210 x 297 mm; a tolerance of up to plus 8 mm or minus 5 mm in the length may be allowed. The paper used shall be white, not containing mechanical pulp, and shall weigh not less than 40 g/m2. The face of the original shall have a printed yellow guilloche pattern background making any falsification by mechanical or chemical means apparent.

2. The certificates shall be printed and completed in one of the official languages of the Community.

Article 59

1. The certificate shall be completed in typescript or by means of a mechanical data-processing system, or similar procedure.

2. Entries must not be erased or overwritten. Any changes shall be made by crossing out the wrong entry and if necessary adding the correct particulars. Such changes shall be initialled by the person making them and endorsed by the issuing authorities.

Article 60

1. Box 5 of the certificates of origin issued in accordance with Articles 56 to 59 shall contain any additional particulars which may be required for the implementation of the special import arrangements to which they relate as referred to in Article 56(3).

2. Unused spaces in boxes 5, 6 and 7 shall be struck through in such a way that nothing can be added at a later stage.

Article 61

Each certificate of origin shall bear a serial number, whether or not printed, by which it can be identified, and shall be stamped by the issuing authority and signed by the person or persons empowered to do so.

The certificate shall be issued when the products to which it relates are exported, and the issuing authority shall keep a copy of each certificate issued.

Article 62

Exceptionally, the certificates of origin referred to above may be issued after the export of the products to which they relate, where the failure to issue them at the time of such export was a result of involuntary error or omission or special circumstances.

The issuing authorities may not issue retrospectively a certificate of origin provided for in Articles 56 to 61 until they have checked that the particulars in the exporter's application correspond to those in the relevant export file.

Certificates issued retrospectively shall bear one of the following—

—   expedido a posteriori,
—   udstedt efterfølgende,
—   Nachträglich ausgestellt,
—   Εκδοθν εκ των υστρων,
—   Issued retrospectively,
—   Délivré a posteriori,
—   rilasciato a posteriori,
—   afgegeven a posteriori,
—   emitidio a posteriori,
[—   annettu jälkikäteen/utfärdat i efterhand,
—   utfärdat i efterhand.]
[—   Vystaveno dodatečne,
—   Välja antud tagasiulatuvalt,
—   Izsniegts retrospektvi,
—   Retrospektyvusis išdavimas,
—   Kiadva visszamenőleges hatállyal,
—   Mah-rugÿ retrospettivament,
—   Wystawione retrospektywnie,
—   Izdano naknadno,
[—   Vyhotovené dodatočne]]
[—   (for original text, refer to Commission Regulation (EC) 1792/2006 (OJ L 362, 20.12.06, p 1)),
—   eliberat ulterior]

in the "Remarks" box.

NOTES

Words inserted by the 1994 Act of Accession Annex I(III)(B)(4), as adjusted by Council Decision 95/1/EC, Annex I(XIII)(A)(b), para 5. Further words inserted by the 2003 Act of Accession Annex II(19)(A)(II), para 1.

Words "Vyhotovené dodatonče" in inner square brackets, inserted by Commission Regulation (EC) 883/2005, Art 1, OJ L 148, 11.06.05, p 5 with effect from 1 May 2004.

Last two entries inserted by Commission Regulation (EC) 1792/2006, Art 1, Annex, Part 11(A)(1).

(B)
Administrative cooperation

Article 63

1. Where the special import arrangements for certain agricultural products provide for the use of the certificate of origin laid down in Articles 56 to 62, the

entitlement to use such arrangements shall be subject to the setting up of an administrative cooperation procedure unless specified otherwise in the arrangements concerned.

To this end the third countries concerned shall send the Commission of the European Communities—

— the names and addresses of the issuing authorities for certificates of origin together with specimens of the stamps used by the said authorities,

— the names and addresses of the government authorities to which requests for the subsequent verification of origin certificates provided for in Article 64 below should be sent.

The Commission shall transmit all the above information to the competent authorities of the Member States.

2. Where the third countries in question fail to send the Commission the information specified in paragraph 1, the competent authorities in the Community shall refuse access entitlement to the special import arrangements.

Article 64

1. Subsequent verification of the certificates of origin referred to in Articles 56 to 62 shall be carried out at random and whenever reasonable doubt has arisen as to the authenticity of the certificate or the accuracy of the information it contains.

For origin matters the verification shall be carried out on the initiative of the customs authorities.

For the purposes of agricultural rules, the verification may be carried out, where appropriate, by other competent authorities.

2. For the purposes of paragraph 1, the competent authorities in the Community shall return the certificate of origin or a copy thereof to the governmental authority designated by the exporting country, giving, where appropriate, the reasons of form or substance for an enquiry. If the invoice has been produced, the original or a copy thereof shall be attached to the returned certificate. The authorities shall also provide any information that has been obtained suggesting that the particulars given on the certificates are inaccurate or that the certificate is not authentic.

Should the customs authorities in the Community decide to suspend the application of the special import arrangements concerned pending the results of the verification they shall grant release of the products subject to such precautions as they consider necessary.

Article 65

1. The results of subsequent verifications shall be communicated to the competent authorities in the Community as soon as possible.

The said results must make it possible to determine whether the origin certificates remitted in the conditions laid down in Article 64 above apply to the goods actually exported and whether the latter may actually give rise to application of the special importation arrangements concerned.

2. If there is no reply within a maximum time limit of six months to requests for subsequent verification, the competent authorities in the Community shall definitively refuse to grant entitlement to the special import arrangements.

[CHAPTER 2
PREFERENTIAL ORIGIN

Article 66

For the purposes of this Chapter—

(a) "manufacture" means any kind of working or processing including assembly or specific operations;

(b)   "material" means any ingredient, raw material, component or part, etc, used in the manufacture of the product;

(c)   "product" means the product being manufactured, even if it is intended for later use in another manufacturing operation;

(d)   "goods" means both materials and products;

(e)   "customs value" means the value as determined in accordance with the 1994 Agreement on implementation of Article VII of the General Agreement on Tariffs and Trade (WTO Agreement on customs valuation);

(f)   "ex-works price" in the list in Annex 15 means the price paid for the product ex-works to the manufacturer in whose undertaking the last working or processing is carried out, provided that the price includes the value of all the materials used, minus any internal taxes which are, or may be, repaid when the product obtained is exported;

(g)   "value of materials" in the list in Annex 15 means the customs value at the time of importation of the non-originating materials used, or, if this is not known and cannot be ascertained, the first ascertainable price paid for the materials in the Community or the beneficiary country within the meaning of Article 67(1) or in the beneficiary republic within the meaning of Article 98(1). Where the value of the originating materials used needs to be established, this subparagraph shall be applied *mutatis mutandis*;

(h)   "chapters" and "headings" mean the chapters and the headings (four-digit codes) used in the nomenclature which makes up the Harmonised System;

(i)   "classified" refers to the classification of a product or material under a particular heading;

(j)   "consignment" means products which are either sent simultaneously from one exporter to one consignee or covered by a single transport document covering their shipment from the exporter to the consignee or, in absence of such document, by a single invoice.]

NOTES

Substituted, together with Arts 67–123 (for original Arts 66–124) by Commission Regulation (EC) 1602/2000, Art 1, para 5 (originally substituted, together with Arts 67–123 (for original Arts 66–140) by Commission Regulation (EC) 12/97, Art 1, para 2).

[SECTION 1
GENERALISED SYSTEM OF PREFERENCES

SUBSECTION 1
DEFINITION OF THE CONCEPT OF ORIGINATING PRODUCTS

Article 67

1.   For the purposes of the provisions concerning generalised tariff preferences granted by the Community to products originating in developing countries (hereinafter referred to as "beneficiary countries"), the following shall be considered as originating in a beneficiary country—

(a)   products wholly obtained in that country within the meaning of Article 68;

(b)   products obtained in that country in the manufacture of which products other than those referred to in (a) are used, provided that the said products have undergone sufficient working or processing within the meaning of Article 69.

2. For the purposes of this section, products originating in the Community, within the meaning of paragraph 3, which are subject in a beneficiary country to working or processing going beyond that described in Article 70 shall be considered as originating in that beneficiary country.

3. Paragraph 1 shall apply *mutatis mutandis* in order to establish the origin of the products obtained in the Community.

4. In so far as Norway and Switzerland grant generalised tariff preferences to products originating in the beneficiary countries referred to in paragraph 1 and apply a definition of the concept of origin corresponding to that set out in this section, products originating in the Community, Norway or Switzerland which are subject in a beneficiary country to working or processing going beyond that described in Article 70 shall be considered as originating in that beneficiary country.

The provisions of the first subparagraph shall apply only to products originating in the Community, Norway or Switzerland (according to the rules of origin relative to the tariff preferences in question) which are exported direct to the beneficiary country.

The provisions of the first subparagraph shall not apply to products falling within Chapters 1 to 24 of the Harmonised System.

The Commission shall publish in the *Official Journal of the European Communities* (C series) the date from which the provisions laid down in the first and second subparagraphs shall apply.

5. The provisions of paragraph 4 shall apply on condition that Norway and Switzerland grant, by reciprocity, the same treatment to Community products.]

NOTES
Substituted as noted to Art 66.

[Article 68

1. The following shall be considered as wholly obtained in a beneficiary country or in the Community—

(a) mineral products extracted from its soil or from its seabed;
(b) vegetable products harvested there;
(c) live animals born and raised there;
(d) products from live animals raised there;
(e) products obtained by hunting or fishing conducted there;
(f) products of sea fishing and other products taken from the sea outside the territorial waters by its vessels;
(g) products made on board its factory ships exclusively from the products referred to in (f);
(h) used articles collected there fit only for the recovery of raw materials;
(i) waste and scrap resulting from manufacturing operations conducted there;
(j) products extracted from the seabed or below the seabed which is situated outside its territorial waters but where it has exclusive exploitation rights;
(k) goods produced there exclusively from products specified in (a) to (j).

2. The terms "its vessels" and "its factory ships" in paragraph 1(f) and (g) shall apply only to vessels and factory ships—

— which are registered or recorded in the beneficiary country or in a Member State,
— which sail under the flag of a beneficiary country or of a Member State,

Part III

— which are at least 50% owned by nationals of the beneficiary country or of Member States or by a company having its head office in that country or in one of those Member States, of which the manager or managers, Chairman of the Board of Directors or of the Supervisory Board, and the majority of the members of such boards are nationals of that beneficiary country or of the Member States and of which, in addition, in the case of companies, at least half the capital belongs to that beneficiary country or to the Member States or to public bodies or nationals of that beneficiary country or of the Member States,

— of which the master and officers are nationals of the beneficiary country or of the Member States, and

— of which at least 75% of the crew are nationals of the beneficiary country or of the Member States.

3. The terms "beneficiary country" and "Community" shall also cover the territorial waters of that country or of the Member States.

4. Vessels operating on the high seas, including factory ships on which the fish caught is worked or processed, shall be considered as part of the territory of the beneficiary country or of the Member State to which they belong, provided that they satisfy the conditions set out in paragraph 2.]

NOTES

Substituted as noted to Art 66.

[Article 69

For the purposes of Article 67, products which are not wholly obtained in a beneficiary country or in the Community are considered to be sufficiently worked or processed when the conditions set out in the list in Annex 15 are fulfilled.

Those conditions indicate, for all products covered by this section, the working or processing which must be carried out on non-originating materials used in manufacturing, and apply only in relation to such materials.

If a product which has acquired originating status by fulfilling the conditions set out in the list is used in the manufacture of another product, the conditions applicable to the product in which it is incorporated do not apply to it, and no account shall be taken of the non-originating materials which may have been used in its manufacture.]

NOTES

Substituted as noted to Art 66.

[Article 70

[1. Without prejudice to paragraph 2, the following operations shall be considered as insufficient working or processing to confer the status of originating products, whether or not the requirements of Article 69 are satisfied:

(a) preserving operations to ensure that the products remain in good condition during transport and storage;

(b) breaking-up and assembly of packages;

(c) washing, cleaning; removal of dust, oxide, oil, paint or other coverings;

(d) ironing or pressing of textiles;

(e) simple painting and polishing operations;

(f) husking, partial or total milling, polishing and glazing of cereals and rice;

(g) operations to colour sugar or form sugar lumps; partial or total milling of sugar;

(h)   peeling, stoning and shelling, of fruits, nuts and vegetables;

(i)   sharpening, simple grinding or simple cutting;

(j)   sifting, screening, sorting, classifying, grading, matching; (including the making-up of sets of articles);

(k)   simple placing in bottles, cans, flasks, bags, cases, boxes, fixing on cards or boards and all other simple packaging operations;

(l)   affixing or printing marks, labels, logos and other like distinguishing signs on products or their packaging;

(m)   simple mixing of products, whether or not of different kinds, where one or more components of the mixtures do not meet the conditions laid down in this section to enable them to be considered as originating in a beneficiary country or in the Community;

(n)   simple assembly of parts of articles to constitute a complete article or disassembly of products into parts;

(o)   a combination of two or more of the operations specified in points (a) to (n);

(p)   slaughter of animals.]

2.   All the operations carried out in either a beneficiary country or the Community on a given product shall be considered together when determining whether the working or processing undergone by that product is to be regarded as insufficient within the meaning of paragraph 1.]

NOTES
   Substituted as noted to Art 66.
   Para 1: substituted by Commission Regulation (EC) 881/2003 Art 1, para 1.

[Article 70a
   1.   The unit of qualification for the application of the provisions of this section shall be the particular product which is considered as the basic unit when determining classification using the nomenclature of the Harmonised System.
   Accordingly it follows that—
      (a)   when a product composed of a group or assembly of articles is classified under the terms of the Harmonised System in a single heading, the whole constitutes the unit of qualification;
      (b)   when a consignment consists of a number of identical products classified under the same heading of the Harmonised System, each product must be taken individually when applying the provisions of this section.
   2.   Where, under general rule 5 of the Harmonised System, packaging is included with the product for classification purposes, it shall be included for the purposes of determining origin.]

NOTES
   Substituted as noted to Art 66 (originally inserted by Commission Regulation (EC) 46/1999, Art 1, para 4).

[Article 71
   1.   By way of derogation from the provisions of Article 69, non-originating materials may be used in the manufacture of a given product, provided that their total value does not exceed 10% of the ex-works price of the product.
   Where, in the list, one or several percentages are given for the maximum value of non-originating materials, such percentages must not be exceeded through the application of the first subparagraph.

2. Paragraph 1 shall not apply to products falling within Chapters 50 to 63 of the Harmonised System.]

NOTES

Substituted as noted to Art 66.

[Article 72

1. By the way of derogation from Article 67, for the purposes of determining whether a product manufactured in a beneficiary country which is a member of a regional group originates therein within the meaning of that Article, products originating in any of the countries of that regional group and used in further manufacture in another country of the group shall be treated as if they originated in the country of further manufacture (regional cumulation).

2. The country of origin of the final product shall be determined in accordance with Article 72a.

[3. Regional cumulation shall apply to three separate regional groups of beneficiary countries benefiting from the generalised system of preferences:

(a)   Group I: Brunei-Darussalam, Cambodia, Indonesia, Laos, Malaysia, Philippines, Singapore, Thailand, Vietnam;

(b)   Group II: Bolivia, Colombia, Costa Rica, Ecuador, El Salvador, Guatemala, Honduras, Nicaragua, Panama, Peru, Venezuela;

(c)   Group III: Bangladesh, Bhutan, India, Maldives, Nepal, Pakistan, Sri Lanka.

4. The expression "regional group" shall be taken to mean Group I, Group II or Group III, as the case may be.]]

NOTES

Article substituted as noted to Art 66.

Paras 3, 4: substituted by Commission Regulation (EC) 881/2003 Art 1, para 2.

[Article 72a

1. When goods originating in a country which is a member of a regional group are worked or processed in another country of the same regional group, they shall have the origin of the country of the regional group where the last working or processing was carried out, provided that—

(a)   the value-added there, as defined in paragraph 3, is greater than the highest customs value of the products used originating in any one of the other countries of the regional group, and

(b)   the working or processing carried out there exceeds that set out in Article 70 and, in the case of textile products, also those operations referred to at Annex 16.

2. When the conditions of origin in paragraph 1(a) and (b) are not satisfied, the products shall have the origin of the country of the regional group which accounts for the highest customs value of the originating products coming from other countries of the regional group.

3. "Value added" means the ex-works price minus the customs value of each of the products incorporated which originated in another country of the regional group.

4. Proof of the originating status of goods exported from a country of a regional group to another country of the same group to be used in further working or processing, or to be re-exported where no further working or processing takes place, shall be established by a certificate of origin Form A issued in the first country.

5. Proof of the originating status, acquired or retained under the terms of Article 72, this Article and Article 72b, of goods exported from a country of a regional group to the Community, shall be established by a certificate of origin Form A issued or an invoice declaration made out in that country on the basis of a certificate of origin Form A issued according to the provisions of paragraph 4.

6. The country of origin shall be marked in box 12 of the certificate of origin Form A or on the invoice declaration, that country being—

—   in the case of products exported without further working or processing according to paragragh 4, the country of manufacture,

—   in the case of products exported after further working or processing, the country of origin as determined in accordance with paragraph 1.]

NOTES

Substituted as noted to Art 66.

[**Article 72b**

1. Articles 72 and 72a shall apply only where—

(a)   the rules regulating trade in the context of regional cumulation, as between the countries of the regional group, are identical to those laid down in this section;

(b)   each country of the regional group has undertaken to comply or ensure compliance with the terms of this section and to provide the administrative cooperation necessary both to the Community and to the other countries of the regional group in order to ensure the correct issue of certificates of origin Form A and the verification of certificates of origin Form A and invoice declarations.

[This undertaking shall be transmitted to the Commission through the following Secretariats, as the case may be:

(i)   Group I: the General Secretariat of the Association of South-East Asian Nations (ASEAN);

(ii)   Group II: the Andean Community – Central American Common Market and Panama Permanent Joint Committee on Origin (Comite Conjunto Permanente de Origen Comunidad Andina – Mercado Comun Centroamericano y Panama);

(iii)   Group III: the Secretariat of the South Asian Association for Regional Cooperation (SAARC).]

2. The Commission shall inform the Member States when the conditions set out in paragraph 1 have been satisfied, in the case of each regional group.

3. Article 78(1)(b) shall not apply to products originating in any of the countries of the regional group when they pass through the territory of any of the other countries of the regional group, whether or not further working or processing take place there.]

NOTES

Substituted as noted to Art 66.

Para 1: sub-paragraphs substituted by Commission Regulation (EC) 881/2003 Art 1, para 3.

[**Article 73**

Accessories, spare parts and tools dispatched with a piece of equipment, machine, apparatus or vehicle which are part of the normal equipment and included in the price thereof or which are not separately invoiced, shall be regarded as one with the piece of equipment, machine, apparatus or vehicle in question.]

NOTES

Substituted as noted to Art 66.

[Article 74

Sets, as defined in general rule 3 of the Harmonised System, shall be regarded as originating when all the component products are originating products. Nevertheless, when a set is composed of originating and non-originating products, the set as a whole shall be regarded as originating, provided that the value of the non-originating products does not exceed 15% of the ex-works price of the set.]

NOTES

Substituted as noted to Art 66.

[Article 75

In order to determine whether a product is an originating product, it shall not be necessary to determine the origin of the following which might be used in its manufacture—

    (a)   energy and fuel;

    (b)   plant and equipment;

    (c)   machines and tools;

    (d)   goods which do not enter, and which are not intended to enter, into the final composition of the product.]

NOTES

Substituted as noted to Art 66.

[Article 76

1. Derogations from the provisions of this section may be made in favour of the least-developed beneficiary countries benefiting from the generalised system of preferences when the development of existing industries or the creation of new industries justifies them. The least-developed beneficiary countries are listed in the Council Regulations and the ECSC Decision concerning the application of generalised tariff preferences. For this purpose, the country concerned shall submit to the Community a request for a derogation together with the reasons for the request in accordance with paragraph 3.

2. The examination of requests shall, in particular, take into account—

    (a)   cases where the application of existing rules of origin would affect significantly the ability of an existing industry in the country concerned to continue its exports to the Community, with particular reference to cases where this could lead to business closures;

    (b)   specific cases where it can be clearly demonstrated that significant investment in an industry could be deterred by the rules of origin and where a derogation encouraging implementation of the investment programme would enable the rules to be satisfied by stages;

    (c)   the economic and social impact of the decision to be taken especially in respect of employment in the beneficiary countries and the Community.

3. In order to facilitate the examination of requests for derogation, the country making the request shall furnish in support of its request the fullest possible information, covering in particular the points listed below—

— description of the finished product,
— nature and quantity of materials originating in a third country,
— manufacturing process,
— value-added,
— the number of employees in the enterprise concerned,
— the anticipated volume of the exports to the Community,
— other possible sources of supply for raw materials,
— reasons for the duration requested,
— other observations.

4. The Commission shall present the derogation request to the Committee. [It shall be decided on in accordance with the committee procedure.]

5. Where use is made of a derogation the following phrase must appear in box 4 of the certificate of origin Form A, or on the invoice declaration laid down in Article 89—

"Derogation—Regulation (EC) No . . . / . . .".

6. The provisions of paragraphs 1 to 5 shall apply to any prolongations.]

NOTES
Substituted as noted to Art 66.
Para 4: words substituted by Commission Regulation (EC) 881/2003 Art 1, para 4.

[Article 77
The conditions set out in this section for acquiring originating status must continue to be fulfilled at all times in the beneficiary country or in the Community.

If originating products exported from the beneficiary country or from the Community to another country are returned, they must be considered as non-originating unless it can be demonstrated to the satisfaction of the competent authorities that—

— the products returned are the same as those which were exported, and
— they have not undergone any operations beyond that necessary to preserve them in good condition while in that country or while being exported.]

NOTES
Substituted as noted to Art 66.

[Article 78
1. The following shall be considered as transported direct from the beneficiary country to the Community or from the Community to the beneficiary country—

(a) products transported without passing through the territory of any other country, except in the case of the territory of another country of the same regional group where Article 72 is applied;

(b) products constituting one single consignment transported through the territory of countries other than the beneficiary country or the Community, with, should the occasion arise, trans-shipment or temporary warehousing in those countries, provided that the products remain under the surveillance of the customs authorities in the country of transit or of warehousing and do not undergo operations other than unloading, reloading or any operation designed to preserve them in good condition;

(c) products transported through the territory of Norway or Switzerland and subsequently re-exported in full or in part to the Community or to the beneficiary country, provided that the products remain under the surveillance of the customs authorities of the country of transit or of warehousing and do not undergo operations other than unloading, reloading or any operation designed to preserve them in good condition;

(d) products which are transported by pipeline without interruption across a territory other than that of the exporting beneficiary country or of the Community.

2. Evidence that the conditions specified in paragraph 1(b) and (c) have been fulfilled shall be supplied to the competent customs authorities by the production of—

(a) a single transport document covering the passage from the exporting country through the country of transit;

(b) a certificate issued by the customs authorities of the country of transit—
— giving an exact description of the products,
— stating the dates of unloading and reloading of the products and, where applicable, the names of the ships, or the other means of transport used, and
— certifying the conditions under which the products remained in the country of transit,

(c) or, failing these, any substantiating documents.]

NOTES

Substituted as noted to Art 66.

[**Article 79**

1. Originating products sent from a beneficiary country for exhibition in another country and sold after the exhibition for importation into the Community shall benefit, on importation, from the tariff preferences referred to in Article 67, provided that the products meet the requirements of this section entitling them to be recognised as originating in the beneficiary country and provided that it is shown to the satisfaction of the competent Community customs authorities that—

(a) an exporter has consigned these products from the beneficiary country direct to the country in which the exhibition is held and has exhibited them there;

(b) the products have been sold or otherwise disposed of by that exporter to a person in the Community;

(c) the products have been consigned during the exhibition or immediately thereafter to the Community in the state in which they were sent for exhibition;

(d) the products have not, since they were consigned for exhibition, been used for any purpose other than demonstration at the exhibition.

2. A certificate of origin Form A shall be submitted to the Community customs authorities in the normal manner. The name and address of the exhibition must be indicated thereon. Where necessary, additional documentary evidence of the nature of the products and the conditions under which they have been exhibited may be required.

3. Paragraph 1 shall apply to any trade, industrial, agricultural or crafts exhibition, fair or similar public show or display which is not organised for private

purposes in shops or business premises with a view to the sale of foreign products, and during which the products remain under customs control.]

NOTES

Substituted as noted to Art 66.

[SUBSECTION 2
PROOF OF ORIGIN

Article 80

Products originating in the beneficiary country shall benefit from the tariff preferences referred to in Article 67, on submission of either—

(a)   a certificate of origin Form A, a specimen of which appears in Annex 17; or

(b)   in the cases specified in Article 89(1), a declaration, the text of which appears at Annex 18, given by the exporter on an invoice, a delivery note or any other commercial document which describes the products concerned in sufficient detail to enable them to be identified (hereinafter referred to as the "invoice declaration").]

NOTES

Substituted as noted to Art 66.

[(A)
Certificate of origin Form A

Article 81

1.   Originating products within the meaning of this section shall be eligible, on importation into the Community, to benefit from the tariff preferences referred to in Article 67, provided that they have been transported directly within the meaning of Article 78, on submission of a certificate of origin Form A, issued by the customs authorities or by other competent governmental authorities of the beneficiary country, provided that the latter country—

—   has communicated to the Commission the information required by Article 93, and

—   assists the Community by allowing the customs authorities of Member States to verify the authenticity of the document or the accuracy of the information regarding the true origin of the products in question.

2.   A certificate of origin Form A may be issued only where it can serve as the documentary evidence required for the purposes of the tariff preferences referred to in Article 67.

3.   A certificate of origin Form A shall be issued only on written application from the exporter or his authorised representative.

4.   The exporter or his authorised representative shall submit with his application any appropriate supporting documents proving that the products to be exported qualify for the issue of a certificate of origin Form A.

5.   The certificate shall be issued by the competent governmental authorities of the beneficiary country if the products to be exported can be considered as products originating in that country within the meaning of Subsection 1. The certificate shall be made available to the exporter as soon as the export has taken place or is ensured.

Part III

6. For the purposes of verifying whether the conditions set out in paragraph 5 have been met, the competent governmental authorities shall have the right to call for any documentary evidence or to carry out any check which they consider appropriate.

7. It shall be the responsibility of the competent governmental authorities of the beneficiary country to ensure that certificates and applications are duly completed.

8. The completion of box 2 of the certificate of origin Form A shall be optional. Box 12 shall be duly completed by indicating "European Community" or one of the Member States.

9. The date of issue of the certificate of origin Form A shall be indicated in box 11. The signature to be entered in that box, which is reserved for the competent governmental authorities issuing the certificate, shall be handwritten.]

NOTES

Substituted as noted to Art 66.

[Article 82

Where, at the request of the importer and on the conditions laid down by the customs authorities of the importing country, dismantled or non-assembled products within the meaning of general rule 2(a) of the Harmonised System and falling within Section XVI or XVII or heading No 7308 or 9406 of the Harmonised System are imported by instalments, a single proof of origin for such products shall be submitted to the customs authorities on importation of the first instalment.]

NOTES

Substituted as noted to Art 66.

[Article 83

Since the certificate of origin Form A constitutes the documentary evidence for the application of provisions concerning the tariff preferences referred to in Article 67, it shall be the responsibility of the competent governmental authorities of the exporting country to take any steps necessary to verify the origin of the products and to check the other statements on the certificate.]

NOTES

Substituted as noted to Art 66.

[Article 84

Proofs of origin shall be submitted to the customs authorities of the Member States of importation in accordance with the procedures laid down in Article 62 of the Code. The said authorities may require a translation of a proof of origin and may also require the import declaration to be accompanied by a statement from the importer to the effect that the products meet the conditions required for the application of this section.]

NOTES

Substituted as noted to Art 66.

[Article 85

1. By way of derogation from Article 81(5), a certificate of origin Form A may exceptionally be issued after exportation of the products to which it relates, if—

(a) it was not issued at the time of exportation because of errors or involuntary omissions or special circumstances; or

(b) it is demonstrated to the satisfaction of the competent governmental authorities that a certificate of origin Form A was issued but was not accepted at importation for technical reasons.

2. The competent governmental authorities may issue a certificate retrospectively only after verifying that the information supplied in the exporter's application agrees with that in the corresponding export file and that a certificate of origin Form A satisfying the provisions of this section was not issued when the products in question were exported.

3. Box 4 of certificates of origin Form A issued retrospectively must contain the endorsement "Issued retrospectively" or "Délivré a posteriori".]

NOTES

Substituted as noted to Art 66.

[Article 86

1. In the event of the theft, loss or destruction of a certificate of origin Form A, the exporter may apply, to the competent governmental authorities which issued it, for a duplicate to be made out on the basis of the export documents in their possession. Box 4 of a duplicate Form A issued in this way must be endorsed with the word "Duplicate" or "Duplicata", together with the date of issue and the serial number of the original certificate.

2. For the purposes of Article 90b, the duplicate shall take effect from the date of the original.]

NOTES

Substituted as noted to Art 66.

[Article 87

1. When originating products are placed under the control of a customs office in the Community, it shall be possible to replace the original proof of origin by one or more certificates of origin Form A for the purpose of sending all or some of these products elsewhere within the Community or to Switzerland or Norway. The replacement certificate(s) of origin Form A shall be issued by the customs office under whose control the products are placed.

2. The replacement certificate issued in application of paragraph 1 or Article 88 shall be regarded as the definitive certificate of origin for the products to which it refers. The replacement certificate shall be made out on the basis of a written request by the re-exporter.

3. The top right-hand box of the replacement certificate shall indicate the name of the intermediary country where it is issued.

Box 4 shall contain the words "Replacement certificate" or "Certificat de remplacement", as well as the date of issue of the original certificate of origin and its serial number.

The name of the re-exporter shall be given in box 1.

The name of the final consignee may be given in box 2.

All particulars of the re-exported products appearing on the original certificate shall be transferred to boxes 3 to 9.

References to the re-exporter's invoice shall be given in box 10.

The customs authority which issued the replacement certificate shall endorse box 11. The responsibility of the authorities is confined to the issue of the replacement

Part III

certificate. The particulars in box 12 concerning the country of origin and the country of destination shall be taken from the original certificate. This box shall be signed by the re-exporter. A re-exporter who signs this box in good faith shall not be responsible for the accuracy of the particulars entered on the original certificate.

4. The customs office which is requested to perform the operation referred to in paragraph 1 should note on the original certificate the weights, numbers and nature of the products forwarded and indicate thereon the serial numbers of the corresponding replacement certificate or certificates. It shall keep the original certificate for at least three years.

5. A photocopy of the original certificate may be annexed to the replacement certificate.

6. In the case of products which benefit from the tariff preferences referred to in Article 67, under a derogation granted in accordance with the provisions of Article 76, the procedure laid down in this Article shall apply only when such products are intended for the Community.]

NOTES
Substituted as noted to Art 66.

[Article 88
Originating products within the meaning of this section shall be eligible on importation into the Community to benefit from the tariff preferences referred to in Article 67 on production of a replacement certificate of origin Form A issued by the customs authorities of Norway or Switzerland on the basis of a certificate of origin Form A issued by the competent governmental authorities of the beneficiary country, provided that the conditions laid down in Article 78 have been satisfied and provided that Norway or Switzerland assists the Community by allowing its customs authorities to verify the authenticity and accuracy of the certificates issued. The verification procedure laid down in Article 94 shall apply *mutatis mutandis*. The time limit laid down in Article 94(3) shall be extended to eight months.]

NOTES
Substituted as noted to Art 66.

[(B)
Invoice declaration

Article 89
1. The invoice declaration may be made out—
   (a) by an approved Community exporter within the meaning of Article 90, or
   (b) by any exporter for any consignment consisting of one or more packages containing originating products whose total value does not exceed EUR 6 000, and provided that the assistance referred to in Article 81(1) shall apply to this procedure.

2. An invoice declaration may be made out if the products concerned can be considered as originating in the Community or in a beneficiary country, and fulfil the other requirements of this section.

3. The exporter making out an invoice declaration shall be prepared to submit at any time, at the request of the customs or other competent governmental authorities of the exporting country, all appropriate documents proving the originating status of the products concerned as well as the fulfilment of the other requirements of this section.

4. An invoice declaration shall be made out by the exporter in either French or English by typing, stamping or printing on the invoice, the delivery note or any other commercial document, the declaration, the text of which appears in Annex 18. If the declaration is handwritten, it shall be written in ink in printed characters.

5. Invoice declarations shall bear the original signature of the exporter in manuscript. However, an approved exporter within the meaning of Article 90 shall not be required to sign such declarations provided that he gives the customs authorities a written undertaking that he accepts full responsibility for any invoice declaration which identifies him as if it had been signed in manuscript by him.

6. In the cases referred to in paragraph 1(b), the use of an invoice declaration shall be subject to the following special conditions—

    (a)   one invoice declaration shall be made out for each consignment;

    (b)   if the goods contained in the consignment have already been subject to verification in the exporting country by reference to the definition of "originating products", the exporter may refer to this check in the invoice declaration.

The provisions of the first subparagraph shall not exempt exporters from complying with any other formalities required under customs or postal regulations.]

NOTES

Substituted as noted to Art 66.

[Article 90

1. The customs authorities of the Community may authorise any exporter, hereinafter referred to as an "approved exporter", who makes frequent shipments of products originating in the Community within the meaning of Article 67(2), and who offers, to the satisfaction of the customs authorities, all guarantees necessary to verify the originating status of the products as well as the fulfilment of the other requirements of this section, to make out invoice declarations, irrespective of the value of the products concerned.

2. The customs authorities may grant the status of approved exporter subject to any conditions which they consider appropriate.

3. The customs authorities shall grant to the approved exporter a customs authorisation number which shall appear on the invoice declaration.

4. The customs authorities shall monitor the use of the authorisation by the approved exporter.

5. The customs authorities may withdraw the authorisation at any time. They shall do so where the approved exporter no longer offers the guarantees referred to in paragraph 1, does not fulfil the conditions referred to in paragraph 2 or otherwise makes improper use of the authorisation.]

NOTES

Substituted as noted to Art 66.

[Article 90a

1. Evidence of the originating status of Community products within the meaning of Article 67(2) shall be furnished by either—

    (a)   the production of a movement certificate EUR.1, a specimen of which is set out in Annex 21; or by

    (b)   the production of a declaration as referred to in Article 89.

2. The exporter or his authorised representative shall enter "GSP beneficiary countries" and "EC" or "Pays bénéficiaires du SPG" and "CE" in box 2 of the movement certificate EUR.1.

3. The provisions of this section concerning the issue, use and subsequent verification of certificates of origin Form A shall apply *mutatis mutandis* to EUR.1 movement certificates and, with the exception of the provisions concerning their issue, to invoice declarations.]

NOTES
Substituted as noted to Art 66.

[Article 90b

1. A proof of origin shall be valid for 10 months from the date of issue in the exporting country, and shall be submitted within the said period to the customs authorities of the importing country.

2. Proofs of origin which are submitted to the customs authorities of the importing country after the final date for presentation specified in paragraph 1 may be accepted for the purpose of applying the tariff preferences referred to in Article 67, where the failure to submit these documents by the final date set is due to exceptional circumstances.

3. In other cases of belated presentation, the customs authorities of the importing country may accept the proofs of origin where the products have been submitted before the said final date.

4. At the request of the importer and having regard to the conditions laid down by the customs authorities of the importing Member State, a single proof of origin may be submitted to the customs authorities at the importation of the first consignment when the goods—

(a) are imported within the framework of frequent and continuous trade flows of a significant commercial value;

(b) are the subject of the same contract of sale, the parties of this contract established in the exporting country or in the Community;

(c) are classified in the same code (eight digits) of the Combined Nomenclature;

(d) come exclusively from the same exporter, are destined for the same importer, and are made the subject of entry formalities at the same customs office in the Community.

This procedure shall be applicable for the quantities and a period determined by the competent customs authorities. This period cannot, in any circumstances, exceed three months.

NOTES
Substituted as noted to Art 66.

[Article 90c

1. Products sent as small packages from private persons to private persons or forming part of travellers' personal luggage shall be admitted as originating products benefiting from the tariff preferences referred to in Article 67 without requiring the presentation of a certificate of origin Form A or an invoice declaration, provided that such products are not imported by way of trade and have been declared as meeting the conditions required for the application of this section and where there is no doubt as to the veracity of such a declaration.

2. Imports which are occasional and consist solely of products for the personal use of the recipients or travellers or their families shall not be considered as imports by way of trade if it is evident from the nature and quantity of the products that no commercial purpose is in view.

Furthermore, the total value of these products shall not exceed EUR 500 in the case of small packages or EUR 1 200 in the case of products forming part of travellers' personal luggage.

NOTES

Substituted as noted to Art 66.

[**Article 91**

1. When Article 67(2), (3) or (4) applies, the competent governmental authorities of the beneficiary country called on to issue a certificate of origin Form A for products in the manufacture of which materials originating in the Community, Norway or Switzerland are used shall rely on the EUR.1 movement certificate or, where necessary, the invoice declaration.

2. Box 4 of certificates of origin Form A issued in the cases set out in paragraph 1 shall contain the remark "EC cumulation", "Norway cumulation", "Switzerland cumulation", or "Cumul CE", "Cumul Norvège", "Cumul Suisse".]

NOTES

Substituted as noted to Art 66.

[**Article 92**

The discovery of slight discrepancies between the statements made in the certificate of origin Form A, in the EUR.1 movement certificate or in an invoice declaration, and those made in the documents submitted to the customs office for the purpose of carrying out the formalities for importing the products shall not *ipso facto* render the certificate or declaration null and void if it is duly established that the document does correspond to the products submitted.

Obvious formal errors such as typing errors on a certificate of origin Form A, EUR.1 movement certificate or an invoice declaration should not cause this document to be rejected if these errors are not such as to create doubts concerning the correctness of the statements made in the document.]

NOTES

Substituted as noted to Art 66.

[SUBSECTION 3
METHODS OF ADMINISTRATIVE COOPERATION

Article 93

1. The beneficiary countries shall inform the Commission of the names and addresses of the governmental authorities situated in their territory which are empowered to issue certificates of origin Form A, together with specimens of stamps used by those authorities, and the names and addresses of the relevant governmental authorities responsible for the control of the certificates of origin Form A and the invoice declarations. The stamps shall be valid as from the date of receipt by the Commission of the specimens. The Commission shall forward this information to the customs authorities of the Member States. When these communications are made within the framework of an amendment of previous communications, the Commission

shall indicate the date of entry into use of those new stamps according to the instructions given by the competent authorities of the beneficiary countries. This information is for official use; however, when goods have to be presented for free circulation, the customs authorities in question may allow the importer or his duly authorised representative to consult the specimen impressions of stamps mentioned in this paragraph.

2. The Commission shall publish in the *Official Journal of the European Communities* ("C" series) the date on which the new beneficiary countries referred to in Article 97 met the obligations referred to in paragraph 1.

3. The Commission shall send, to the beneficiary countries, specimen impressions of the stamps used by the customs authorities of the Member States for the issue of EUR.1 movement certificates.]

NOTES
  Substituted as noted to Art 66.

[**Article 93a**
For the purposes of the provisions concerning the tariff preferences referred to in Article 67, every beneficiary country shall comply or ensure compliance with the rules concerning the origin of the products, the completion and issue of certificates of origin Form A, the conditions for the use of invoice declarations and those concerning methods of administrative cooperation.]

NOTES
  Substituted as noted to Art 66.

[**Article 94**
1. Subsequent verifications of certificates of origin Form A and invoice declarations shall be carried out at random or whenever the customs authorities in the Community have reasonable doubts as to the authenticity of such documents, the originating status of the products concerned or the fulfilment of the other requirements of this section.

2. For the purposes of implementing the provisions of paragraph 1, the customs authorities in the Community shall return the certificate of origin Form A and the invoice, if it has been submitted, the invoice declaration, or a copy of these documents, to the competent governmental authorities in the exporting beneficiary country giving, where appropriate, the reasons for the enquiry. Any documents and information obtained suggesting that the information given on the proof of origin is incorrect shall be forwarded in support of the request for verification.

If the said authorities decide to suspend the granting of the tariff preferences referred to in Article 67 while awaiting the results of the verification, release of the products shall be offered to the importer subject to any precautionary measures judged necessary.

3. When an application for subsequent verification has been made in accordance with paragraph 1, such verification shall be carried out and its results communicated to the customs authorities in the Community within a maximum of six months. The results shall be such as to establish whether the proof of origin in question applies to the products actually exported and whether these products can be considered as products originating in the beneficiary country or in the Community.

4. In the case of certificates of origin Form A issued in accordance with Article 91, the reply shall include a copy (copies) of the EUR.1 movement certificate(s) or, where necessary, of the corresponding invoice declaration(s).

5. If in cases of reasonable doubt there is no reply within the six months specified in paragraph 3 or if the reply does not contain sufficient information to determine the authenticity of the document in question or the real origin of the products, a second communication shall be sent to the competent authorities. If after the second communication the results of the verification are not communicated to the requesting authorities within four months, or if these results do not allow the authenticity of the document in question or the real origin of the products to be determined, the requesting authorities shall, except in exceptional circumstances, refuse entitlement to the tariff preferences.

The provisions of the first subparagraph shall apply between the countries of the same regional group for the purposes of the subsequent verification of the certificates of origin Form A issued in accordance with this section.

6. Where the verification procedure or any other available information appears to indicate that the provisions of this section are being contravened, the exporting beneficiary country shall, on its own initiative or at the request of the Community, carry out appropriate inquiries or arrange for such inquiries to be carried out with due urgency to identify and prevent such contraventions. For this purpose, the Community may participate in the inquiries.

7. For the purposes of the subsequent verification of certificates of origin Form A, copies of the certificates, as well as any export documents referring to them, shall be kept for at least three years by the competent governmental authorities of the exporting beneficiary country.]

NOTES
Substituted as noted to Art 66.

[Article 95
Article 78(1)(c) and Article 89 shall apply only in so far as Norway and Switzerland, in the context of tariff preferences granted by them to certain products originating in developing countries, apply provisions similar to those of the Community.

The Commission shall inform the Member States' customs authorities of the adoption by Norway and Switzerland of such provisions and shall notify them of the date from which the provisions of Article 78(1)(c) and Article 88, and the similar provisions adopted by Norway and Switzerland, are applied.

These provisions shall apply on condition that the Community, Norway and Switzerland have concluded an agreement stating, among other things, that they shall provide each other with the necessary mutual assistance in matters of administrative cooperation.]

NOTES
Substituted as noted to Art 66.

[SUBSECTION 4
CEUTA AND MELILLA

Article 96
1. The term "Community" used in this section shall not cover Ceuta and Melilla. The term "products originating in the Community" shall not cover products originating in Ceuta and Melilla.

2. This Section shall apply *mutatis mutandis* in determining whether products may be regarded as originating in the exporting beneficiary country benefiting from

Part III

the generalised system of preferences when imported into Ceuta and Melilla or as originating in Ceuta and Melilla.

3. Ceuta and Melilla shall be regarded as a single territory.

4. The provisions of this section concerning the issue, use and subsequent verification of certificates of origin Form A shall apply *mutatis mutandis* to products originating in Ceuta and Melilla.

5. The Spanish customs authorities shall be responsible for the application of this section in Ceuta and Melilla.]

NOTES

Substituted as noted to Art 66.

[SUBSECTION 5
FINAL PROVISION

Article 97

When a country or territory is admitted or readmitted as a beneficiary country in respect of products referred to in the relevant Council Regulations or the ECSC Decision, goods originating in that country or territory may benefit from the generalised system of preferences on condition that they were exported from the beneficiary country or territory on or after the date referred to in Article 93(2).]

NOTES

Substituted as noted to Art 66.

[SECTION 2
[BENEFICIARY COUNTRIES OR TERRITORIES TO WHICH PREFERENTIAL TARIFF MEASURES ADOPTED UNILATERALLY BY THE COMMUNITY FOR CERTAIN COUNTRIES OR TERRITORIES APPLY]

NOTES

Heading substituted by Commission Regulation (EC) 444/2002, Art 1, para 2.

SUBSECTION 1
DEFINITION OF THE CONCEPT OF ORIGINATING PRODUCTS

Article 98

[1. For the purposes of the provisions concerning preferential tariff measures adopted unilaterally by the Community for certain countries, groups of countries or territories (hereinafter referred to as 'beneficiary countries or territories'), with the exception of those referred to in Section 1 of this Chapter and the overseas countries and territories associated with the Community, the following products shall be considered as products originating in a beneficiary country or territory—]

    (a)   products wholly obtained in that [beneficiary country or territory] with the meaning of Article 99;

    (b)   products obtained in that beneficiary republic, in the manufacture of which products other than those referred to in (a) are used, provided that the said products have undergone sufficient working or processing within the meaning of Article 100.

2. For the purposes of this section, products originating in the Community, within the meaning of paragraph 3, which are subject in a [beneficiary country or territory] to

working or processing going beyond that described in Article 101 shall be considered as originating in that beneficiary republic.

3. Paragraph 1 shall apply *mutatis mutandis* in establishing the origin of the products obtained in the Community.]

NOTES

Substituted as noted to Art 66.

Paras 1, 2 words substituted by Commission Regulation (EC) 444/2002, Art 1, paras 3, 4.

[**Article 99**

1. The following shall be considered as wholly obtained in a [beneficiary country or territory] or in the Community—

(a)   mineral products extracted from its soil or from its seabed;

(b)   vegetable products harvested there;

(c)   live animals born and raised there;

(d)   products from live animals raised there;

(e)   products obtained by hunting or fishing conducted there;

(f)   products of sea-fishing and other products taken from the sea outside the territorial waters by their vessels;

(g)   products made on board its factory ships exclusively from the products referred to in (f);

(h)   used articles collected there, fit only for the recovery of raw materials;

(i)   waste and scrap resulting from manufacturing operations conducted there;

(j)   products extracted from the seabed or below the seabed which is situated outside its territorial waters but where it has exclusive exploitation rights;

(k)   products produced there exclusively from products specified in (a) to (j).

2. The terms "its vessels" and "its factory ships" in paragraphs 1(f) and (g) shall apply only to vessels and factory ships—

—   which are registered or recorded in the [beneficiary country or territory] or in a Member State,

—   which sail under the flag of a [beneficiary country or territory] or of a Member State,

—   which are owned to the extent of at least 50% by nationals of the [beneficiary country or territory] or of Member States or by a company with its head office in that republic or in one of the Member States, of which the manager or managers, Chairman of the Board of Directors or of the Supervisory Board, and the majority of the members of such boards are nationals of that [beneficiary country or territory] or of the Member States and of which, in addition, in the case of companies, at least half the capital belongs to that [beneficiary country or territory] or to the Member States or to public bodies or nationals of that [beneficiary country or territory] or of the Member States,

—   of which the master and officers are nationals of the [beneficiary country or territory] or of the Member States, and

—   of which at least 75% of the crew are nationals of the [beneficiary country or territory] or of the Member States.

3. The terms "beneficiary republic" and "Community" shall also cover the territorial waters of that republic or territory or of the Member States.

4. Vessels operating on the high seas, including factory ships on which the fish caught is worked or processed, shall be considered as part of the territory of the

[beneficiary country or territory] or of the Member State to which they belong, provided that they satisfy the conditions set out in paragraph 2.]

NOTES
Substituted as noted to Art 66.
Paras 1, 2, 4: words substituted by Commission Regulation (EC) 444/2002, Art 1, para 4.

[**Article 100**

For the purposes of Article 98, products which are not wholly obtained in a [beneficiary country or territory] or in the Community are considered to be sufficiently worked or processed when the conditions set out in the list in Annex 15 are fulfilled.

Those conditions indicate, for all products covered by this section, the working or processing which must be carried out on non-originating materials used in manufacturing and apply only in relation to such materials.

If a product which has acquired originating status by fulfilling the conditions set out in the list is used in the manufacture of another product, the conditions applicable to the product in which it is incorporated do not apply to it, and no account shall be taken of the non-originating materials which may have been used in its manufacture.]

NOTES
Substituted as noted to Art 66.
Words substituted by Commission Regulation (EC) 444/2002, Art 1, para 4.

[**Article 101**

[1. Without prejudice to paragraph 2, the following operations shall be considered as insufficient working or processing to confer the status of originating products, whether or not the requirements of Article 100 are satisfied:

(a) preserving operations to ensure that the products remain in good condition during transport and storage;

(b) breaking-up and assembly of packages;

(c) washing, cleaning; removal of dust, oxide, oil, paint or other coverings;

(d) ironing or pressing of textiles;

(e) simple painting and polishing operations;

(f) husking, partial or total milling, polishing and glazing of cereals and rice;

(g) operations to colour sugar or form sugar lumps; partial or total milling of sugar;

(h) peeling, stoning and shelling, of fruits, nuts and vegetables;

(i) sharpening, simple grinding or simple cutting;

(j) sifting, screening, sorting, classifying, grading, matching; (including the making-up of sets of articles);

(k) simple placing in bottles, cans, flasks, bags, cases, boxes, fixing on cards or boards and all other simple packaging operations;

(l) affixing or printing marks, labels, logos and other like distinguishing signs on products or their packaging;

(m) simple mixing of products, whether or not of different kinds, where one or more components of the mixtures do not meet the conditions laid down in this section to enable them to be considered as originating in a beneficiary country or territory or in the Community;

(n) simple assembly of parts of articles to constitute a complete article or disassembly of products into parts;

(o)   a combination of two or more of the operations specified in points (a) to (n);

(p)   slaughter of animals.]

2.   All the operations carried out in either a [beneficiary country or territory] or the Community on a given product shall be considered together when determining whether the working or processing undergone by that product is to be regarded as insufficient within the meaning of paragraph 1.]

NOTES

Article substituted as noted to Art 66.
Para 1: substituted by Commission Regulation (EC) 881/2003 Art 1, para 5.
Para 2: words substituted by Commission Regulation (EC) 444/2002, Art 1, para 4.

Article 101a

1.   The unit of qualification for the application of the provisions of this section shall be the particular product which is considered as the basic unit when determining classification using the nomenclature of the Harmonised System.

Accordingly, it follows that—

(a)   when a product composed of a group or assembly of articles is classified under the terms of the Harmonised System in a single heading, the whole constitutes the unit of qualification;

(b)   when a consignment consists of a number of identical products classified under the same heading of the Harmonised System, each product must be taken individually when applying the provisions of this Section.

2.   Where, under general rule 5 of the Harmonised System, packaging is included with the product for classification purposes, it shall be included for the purposes of determining origin.

NOTES

Substituted as noted to Art 66.

[Article 102

1.   By way of derogation from the provisions of Article 100, non-originating materials may be used in the manufacture of a given product, provided that their total value does not exceed 10% of the ex-works price of the product.

Where, in the list, one or several percentages are given for the maximum value of non-originating materials, such percentages must not be exceeded through the application of the first subparagraph.

2.   Paragraph 1 shall not apply to products falling within Chapters 50 to 63 of the Harmonised System.]

NOTES

Substituted as noted to Art 66.

[Article 103

Accessories, spare parts and tools dispatched with a piece of equipment, machine, apparatus or vehicle which are part of the normal equipment and included in the price thereof or which are not separately invoiced, shall be regarded as one with the piece of equipment, machine, apparatus or vehicle in question.]

NOTES

Substituted as noted to Art 66.

[Article 104

Sets, as defined in general rule 3 of the Harmonised System, shall be regarded as originating when all the component products are originating products. Nevertheless, when a set is composed of originating and non-originating products, the set as a whole shall be regarded as originating provided that the value of the non-originating products does not exceed 15% of the ex-works price of the set.]

NOTES

Substituted as noted to Art 66.

[Article 105

In order to determine whether a product is an originating product, it shall not be necessary to determine the origin of the following which might be used in its manufacture—

(a)   energy and fuel;

(b)   plant and equipment;

(c)   machines and tools;

(d)   goods which do not enter, and which are not intended to enter, into the final composition of the product.]

NOTES

Substituted as noted to Art 66.

[Article 106

The conditions set out in this section for acquiring originating status must continue to be fulfilled at all times in the [beneficiary country or territory] or in the Community.

If originating products exported from the [beneficiary country or territory] or from the Community to another country are returned, they shall be considered as non-originating unless it can be demonstrated to the satisfaction of the competent authorities that—

— the products returned are the same as those which were exported, and

— they have not undergone any operation beyond that necessary to preserve them in good condition while in that country or while being exported.]

NOTES

Substituted as noted to Art 66.

Words substituted by Commission Regulation (EC) 444/2002, Art 1, para 4.

[Article 107

1.   The following shall be considered as transported directly from the [beneficiary country or territory] to the Community or from the Community to the beneficiary republic—

(a)   products transported without passing through the territory of any other country;

(b)   products constituting one single consignment transported through the territory of countries other than the [beneficiary country or territory] or the Community, with, should the occasion arise, trans-shipment or temporary warehousing in those countries, provided that the products remain under the surveillance of the customs authorities in the country of transit or of warehousing and do not undergo operations other than unloading, reloading or any operation designed to preserve them in good condition;

(c)   products which are transported by pipeline without interruption across a territory other than that of the exporting [beneficiary country or territory] or of the Community.

2.   Evidence that the conditions set out in paragraph 1(b) are fulfilled shall be supplied to the competent customs authorities by the production of—

(a)   a single transport document covering the passage from the exporting country through the country of transit; or

(b)   a certificate issued by the customs authorities of the country of transit—
—   giving an exact description of the products,
—   stating the dates of unloading and reloading of the products and, where applicable, the names of the ships, or the other means of transport used, and
—   certifying the conditions under which the products remained in the country of transit;

(c)   or, failing these, any substantiating documents.]

NOTES
Substituted as noted to Art 66.
Para 1: words substituted by Commission Regulation (EC) 444/2002, Art 1, para 4.

[Article 108

1.   Originating products, sent from a [beneficiary country or territory] for exhibition in another country and sold after the exhibition for importation into the Community, shall benefit on importation from the tariff preferences referred to in Article 98, provided that they meet the requirements of this section entitling them to be recognised as originating in that [beneficiary country or territory] and provided that it is shown to the satisfaction of the competent Community customs authorities that—

(a)   an exporter has consigned the products from the [beneficiary country or territory] directly to the country in which the exhibition is held and has exhibited them there;

(b)   the products have been sold or otherwise disposed of by that exporter to a person in the Community;

(c)   the products have been consigned during the exhibition or immediately thereafter to the Community in the state in which they were sent for exhibition;

(d)   the products have not, since they were consigned for exhibition, been used for any purpose other than demonstration at the exhibition.

2.   An EUR.1 movement certificate shall be submitted to the Community customs authorities in the normal manner. The name and address of the exhibition must be indicated thereon. Where necessary, additional documentary evidence of the nature of the products and the conditions under which they have been exhibited may be required.

3.   Paragraph 1 shall apply to any trade, industrial, agricultural or crafts exhibition, fair or similar public show or display which is not organised for private

Part III

purposes in shops or business premises with a view to the sale of foreign products, and during which the products remain under customs control.]

NOTES

Para 1: words substituted by Commission Regulation (EC) 444/2002, Art 1, para 4.

[SUBSECTION 2
PROOF OF ORIGIN

Article 109

Products originating in the [beneficiary countries or territories] shall benefit from the tariff preferences referred to in Article 98, on submission of either—

(a)   an EUR.1 movement certificate, a specimen of which appears at Annex 21; or

(b)   in the cases specified in Article 116(1), a declaration, the text of which appears in Annex 22, given by the exporter on an invoice, a delivery note or any other commercial document which describes the products concerned in sufficient detail to enable them to be identified (hereinafter referred to as the "invoice declaration").]

NOTES

Substituted as noted to Art 66.
Words substituted by Commission Regulation (EC) 444/2002, Art 1, para 4.

[(A)
EUR.1 movement certificate

Article 110

[1.   Originating products within the meaning of this section shall be eligible, on importation into the Community, to benefit from the tariff preferences referred to in Article 98, provided that they have been transported direct to the Community within the meaning of Article 107, on submission of an EUR.1 movement certificate issued by the customs or other competent governmental authorities of a beneficiary country or territory, on condition 87 beneficiary country or territory—]

—   have communicated to the Commission the information required by Article 121, and

—   assist the Community by allowing the customs authorities of Member States to verify the authenticity of the document or the accuracy of the information regarding the true origin of the products in question.

2.   An EUR.1 movement certificate may be issued only where it can serve as the documentary evidence required for the purposes of the tariff preferences referred to in Article 98.

3.   An EUR.1 movement certificate shall be issued only on written application from the exporter or his authorised representative. Such application shall be made on a form, a specimen of which appears in Annex 21, which shall be completed in accordance with the provisions of this subsection.

Applications for EUR.1 movement certificates shall be kept for at least three years by the competent authorities of the exporting [beneficiary country or territory] or Member State.

4.   The exporter or his authorised representative shall submit with his application any appropriate supporting documents proving that the products to be exported qualify for the issue of an EUR.1 movement certificate.

The exporter shall undertake to submit, at the request of the competent authorities, any supplementary evidence they may require for the purpose of establishing the correctness of the originating status of the products eligible for preferential treatment and shall undertake to agree to any inspection of their accounts and to any check by the said authorities on the circumstances in which the products were obtained.

5.   The EUR.1 movement certificate shall be issued by the competent governmental authorities of the [beneficiary countries or territories] or by the customs authorities of the exporting Member State, if the products to be exported can be considered as originating products within the meaning of this section.

6.   Since the EUR.1 movement certificate constitutes the documentary evidence for the application of the preferential arrangements set out in Article 98, it shall be the responsibility of the competent governmental authorities of the [beneficiary country or territory] or of the customs authorities of the exporting Member State to take any steps necessary to verify the origin of the products and to check the other statements on the certificate.

7.   For the purpose of verifying whether the conditions set out in paragraph 5 have been met, the competent governmental authorities of the [beneficiary country or territory] or the customs authorities of the exporting member State shall have the right to call for any documentary evidence or to carry out any check which they consider appropriate.

8.   It shall be the responsibility of the competent governmental authorities of the [beneficiary country or territory] or of the customs authorities of the exporting Member State to ensure that the forms referred to in paragraph 1 are duly completed.

9.   The date of issue of the EUR.1 movement certificate shall be indicated in that part of the certificate reserved for the customs authorities.

10.   An EUR.1 movement certificate shall be issued by the competent authorities of the [beneficiary country or territory] or by the customs authorities of the exporting Member State when the products to which it relates are exported. It shall be made available to the exporter as soon as the export has taken place or is ensured.]

NOTES

Substituted as noted to Art 66.

Para 1: words substituted by Commission Regulation (EC) 444/2002, Art 1, para 5.

Paras 3, 5–8, 10: words substituted by Commission Regulation (EC) 444/2002, Art 1, para 4.

[Article 111

Where, at the request of the importer and on the conditions laid down by the customs authorities of the importing country, dismantled or non-assembled products within the meaning of general rule 2(a) of the Harmonised System and falling within Section XVI or XVII or within heading No 7308 or 9406 of the Harmonised System are imported by instalments, a single proof of origin for such products shall be submitted to the customs authorities on importation of the first instalment.]

NOTES

Substituted as noted to Art 66.

Part III

[**Article 112**

Proofs of origin shall be submitted to the customs authorities of the Member State of importation in accordance with the procedures laid down in Article 62 of the Code. The said authorities may require a translation of a proof of origin and may also require the import declaration to be accompanied by a statement from the importer to the effect that the products meet the conditions required for the application of this section.]

NOTES

Substituted as noted to Art 66.

[**Article 113**

1. By way of derogation from Article 110(10), an EUR.1 movement certificate may exceptionally be issued after exportation of the products to which it relates if—

(a) it was not issued at the time of exportation because of errors or involuntary omissions or special circumstances; or

(b) it is demonstrated to the satisfaction of the customs authorities that an EUR.1 movement certificate was issued but was not accepted at importation for technical reasons.

2. The competent authorities may issue an EUR.1 movement certificate retrospectively only after verifying that the information supplied in the exporter's application agrees with that in the corresponding export file and that an EUR.1 movement certificate satisfying the provisions of this section was not issued when the products in question were exported.

3. EUR.1 movement certificates issued retrospectively shall be endorsed with one of the following phrases—

— "EXPEDIDO A *POSTERIORI*",
— "UDSTEDT EFTERFØLGENDE",
— "NACHTRÄGLICH AUSGESTELLT",
— "ΕΚΔΟΘΕΝ ΕΚ ΤΩΝ ΥΣΤΕΡΩΝ"
— "ISSUED RETROSPECTIVELY",
— "DÉLIVRÉ A POSTERIORI",
— "RILASCIATO A POSTERIORI",
— "AFGEGEVEN A POSTERIORI",
— "EMITIDO *A POSTERIORI*",
— "ANNETTU JÄLKIKÄTEEN",
— "UTFÄRDAT I EFTERHAND",
[[— VYHOTOVENÉ DODATOČNE],
— VÄLJA ANTUD TAGASIULATUVALT,
— IZSNIEGTS RETROSPEKTĪVI,
— RETROSPEKTYVUSIS IŠDAVIMAS,
— KIADVA VISSZAMENŐLEGES HATÁLLYAL,
— MARU RETROSPETTIVAMENT,
— WYSTAWIONE RETROSPEKTYWNIE,
— IZDANO NAKNADNO,
— VYDANÉ DODATONE]
[— (*for original text, refer to Commission Regulation (EC) 1792/2006 (OJ L 362, 20.12.06, p 1)*),
— ELIBERAT ULTERIOR]

4. The endorsement referred to in paragraph 3 shall be inserted in the "Remarks" box of the EUR.1 movement certificate.]

NOTES
Substituted as noted to Art 66.
Words inserted by the 2003 Act of Accession Annex II(19)(A)(II), para 3.
Words "VYHOTOVENÉ DODATOČNE" in inner square brackets, inserted by Commission Regulation (EC) 883/2005, Art 1, OJ L 148, 11.06.05, p 5 with effect from 1 May 2004.
Last two entries in para 3 inserted by Commission Regulation (EC) 1792/2006, Art 1, Annex, Part 11(A)(2).

[Article 114

1.   In the event of the theft, loss or destruction of an EUR.1 movement certificate, the exporter may apply to the competent authorities which issued it, for a duplicate to be made out on the basis of the export documents in their possession.

2.   The duplicate issued in this way shall be endorsed with one of the following words—

—   "DUPLICADO",
—   "DUPLIKAT",
—   "DUPLIKAT",
—   "ΑΝΤΙΓΡΑΦΟ",
—   "DUPLICATE",
—   "DUPLICATA",
—   "DUPLICATO",
—   "DUPLICAAT",
—   "SEGUNDA VIA",
—   "KAKSOISKAPPALE",
—   "DUPLIKAT",
[—   DUPLIKÁT,
—   DUPLIKAAT,
—   DUBLIKÄTS,
—   DUBLIKATAS,
—   MÁSODLAT,
—   DUPLIKAT,
—   DUPLIKAT,
—   DVOJNIK,
—   DUPLIKÁT]
[—   (for original text, refer to Commission Regulation (EC) 1792/2006 (OJ L 362, 20.12.06, p 1)),
—   DUPLICAT]

3.   The endorsement referred to in paragraph 2 shall be inserted in the "Remarks" box of the EUR.1 movement certificate.

4.   The duplicate, which shall bear the date of issue of the original EUR.1 movement certificate, shall take effect as from that date.]

NOTES
Substituted as noted to Art 66.
Words inserted by the 2003 Act of Accession Annex II(19)(A)(II), para 4.
Last two entries in para 3 inserted by Commission Regulation (EC) 1792/2006, Art 1, Annex, Part 11(A)(3).

[**Article 115**

When originating products are placed under the control of a customs office in the Community, it shall be possible to replace the original proof of origin by one or more EUR.1 movement certificates for the purpose of sending all or some of these products elsewhere in the Community. The replacement EUR.1 movement certificate(s) shall be issued by the customs office under whose control the products are placed.]

NOTES

Substituted as noted to Art 66.

[(B)
Invoice declaration

[**Article 116**

1.   The invoice declaration may be made out—
    (a)   by an approved Community exporter within the meaning of Article 117, or
    (b)   by any exporter for any consignment consisting of one or more packages containing originating products whose total value does not exceed EUR 6000, and on condition that the assistance referred to in Article 110(1) shall apply to this procedure.

2.   An invoice declaration may be made out if the products concerned can be considered as originating in the Community or in a [beneficiary country or territory] and fulfil the other requirements of this section.

3.   The exporter making out an invoice declaration shall be prepared to submit at any time, at the request of the customs or other competent governmental authorities of the exporting country, all appropriate documents proving the originating status of the products concerned as well as the fulfilment of the other requirements of this section.

4.   An invoice declaration shall be made out by the exporter by typing, stamping or printing on the invoice, the delivery note or any other commercial document, the declaration, the text of which appears in Annex 22, using one of the linguistic versions set out in that Annex and in accordance with the provisions of the domestic law of the exporting country. If the declaration is handwritten, it shall be written in ink, in printed characters.

5.   Invoice declarations shall bear the original signature of the exporter in manuscript. However, an approved exporter within the meaning of Article 117 shall not be required to sign such declarations provided that he gives the customs authorities a written undertaking that he accepts full responsibility for any invoice declaration which identifies him as if it had been signed in manuscript by him.

6.   In the cases referred to in paragraph 1(b), the use of an invoice declaration shall be subject to the following special conditions—
    (a)   an invoice declaration shall be made out for each consignment;
    (b)   if the goods contained in the consignment have already been subject to verification in the exporting country by reference to the definition of "originating products", the exporter may refer to this check in the invoice declaration.

The provisions of the first subparagraph shall not exempt exporters from complying with any other formalities required under customs or postal regulations.]

NOTES

Substituted as noted to Art 66.

Para 2: words substituted by Commission Regulation (EC) 444/2002, Art 1, para 4.

[Article 117

1. The customs authorities in the Community may authorise any exporter, hereinafter referred to as an "approved exporter", who makes frequent shipments of products originating in the Community within the meaning of Article 98(2), and who offers, to the satisfaction of the customs authorities, all guarantees necessary to verify the originating status of the products as well as the fulfilment of the other requirements of this section, to make out invoice declarations, irrespective of the value of the products concerned.

2. The customs authorities may grant the status of approved exporter subject to any conditions which they consider appropriate.

3. The customs authorities shall assign the approved exporter a customs authorisation number which shall appear on the invoice declaration.

4. The customs authorities shall monitor the use of the authorisation by the approved exporter.

5. The customs authorities may withdraw the authorisation at any time. They shall do so where the approved exporter no longer offers the guarantees referred to in paragraph 1, does not fulfil the conditions referred to in paragraph 2, or otherwise makes improper use of the authorisation.]

NOTES

Substituted as noted to Art 66.

[Article 118

1. A proof of origin shall be valid for four months from the date of issue in the exporting country, and shall be submitted within the said period to the customs authorities of the importing country.

2. Proofs of origin which are submitted to the customs authorities of the importing country after the final date for presentation specified in paragraph 1 may be accepted for the purpose of applying the tariff preferences referred to in Article 98, where the failure to submit these documents by the final date set is due to exceptional circumstances.

3. In other cases of belated presentation, the customs authorities of the importing country may accept the proofs of origin where the products have been submitted before the said final date.

4. At the request of the importer and having regard to the conditions laid down by the customs authorities of the importing Member State, a single proof of origin may be submitted to the customs authorities at the importation of the first consignment when the goods—

    (a)   are imported within the framework of frequent and continuous trade flows of a significant commercial value;

    (b)   are the subject of the same contract of sale, the parties of this contract established in the exporting country or in the Community;

    (c)   are classified in the same code (eight digits) of the Combined Nomenclature;

    (d)   come exclusively from the same exporter, are destined for the same importer, and are made the subject of entry formalities at the same customs office in the Community.

This procedure shall be applicable for the quantities and a period determined by the competent customs authorities. This period cannot, in any circumstances, exceed three months.]

NOTES

Substituted as noted to Art 66.

[Article 119

1. Products sent as small packages from private person to private persons or forming part of travellers' personal luggage shall be admitted as originating products benefiting from the tariff preferences referred to in Article 98 without requiring the submission of an EUR.1 movement certificate or an invoice declaration, provided that such products are not imported by way of trade and have been declared as meeting the conditions required for the application of this section, and where there is no doubt as to the veracity of such a declaration.

2. Imports which are occasional and consist solely of products for the personal use of the recipients or travellers or their families shall not be considered as imports by way of trade if it is evident from the nature and quantity of the products that no commercial purpose is in view.

Furthermore, the total value of the products shall not exceed EUR 500 in the case of small packages or EUR 1200 in the case of products forming part of traveller's personal luggage.]

NOTES

Substituted as noted to Art 66.

[Article 120

The discovery of slight discrepancies between the statements made in the proof of origin and those made in the documents submitted to the customs office for the purpose of carrying out the formalities for importing the products shall not *ipso facto* render the proof of origin null and void if it is duly established that that document does correspond to the products submitted.

Obvious formal errors such as typing errors on a proof of origin should not cause this document to be rejected if these errors are not such as to create doubts concerning the correctness of the statements made in that document.]

NOTES

Substituted as noted to Art 66.

[SUBSECTION 3
METHODS OF ADMINISTRATIVE COOPERATION

Article 121

1. The [beneficiary countries or territories] shall inform the Commission of the names and addresses of the governmental authorities situated in their territory which are empowered to issue EUR.1 movement certificates, together with specimen impressions of the stamps used by those authorities, and the names and addresses of the relevant governmental authorities responsible for the control of the EUR.1 movement certificates and the invoice declarations. The stamps shall be valid as from the date of receipt by the Commission of the specimens. The Commission shall forward this information to the customs authorities of the Member States. When these communications are made within the framework of an amendment of previous communications, the Commission shall indicate the date of entry into use of those new stamps according to the instructions given by the competent governmental authorities of the beneficiary republics. This information is for official use; however, when goods

are to be released for free circulation, the customs authorities in question may allow the importer or his duly-authorised representative to consult the specimen impressions of stamps mentioned in this paragraph.

2. The Commission shall send, to the beneficiary republics, the specimen impressions of the stamps used by the customs authorities of the Member States for the issue of EUR.1 movement certificates.]

NOTES

Substituted as noted to Art 66.

Para 1: words substituted by Commission Regulation (EC) 444/2002, Art 1, para 4.

[Article 122

1. Subsequent verifications of EUR.1 movement certificates and of invoice declarations shall be carried out at random or whenever the customs authorities in the importing Member State or the competent governmental authorities of the [beneficiary countries or territories] have reasonable doubts as to the authenticity of such documents, the originating status of the products concerned or the fulfilment of the other requirements of this section.

2. For the purposes of implementing the provisions of paragraph 1, the competent authorities in the importing Member State or [beneficiary country or territory] shall return the EUR. 1 movement certificate and the invoice, if it has been submitted, the invoice declaration, or a copy of these documents, to the competent authorities in the exporting [beneficiary country or territory] or Member State, giving, where appropriate, the reasons for the enquiry. Any documents and information obtained suggesting that the information given on the proof of origin is incorrect shall be forwarded in support of the request for verification.

If the customs authorities in the importing Member State decide to suspend the granting of the tariff preferences referred to in Article 98 while awaiting the results of the verification, release of the products shall be offered to the importer subject to any precautionary measures judged necessary.

3. When an application for subsequent verification has been made in accordance with paragraph 1, such verification shall be carried out and its results communicated to the customs authorities of the importing Member States or to the competent governmental authorities of the importing [beneficiary country or territory] within a maximum of six months. The results shall be such as to establish whether the proof of origin in question applies to the products actually exported and whether these products can be considered as originating in the [beneficiary country or territory] or in the Community.

4. If in cases of reasonable doubt there is no reply within the six months specified in paragraph 3 or if the reply does not contain sufficient information to determine the authenticity of the document in question or the real origin of the products, a second communication shall be sent to the competent authorities. If after the second communication the results of the verification are not communicated to the requesting authorities within four months, or if these results do not allow the authenticity of the document in question or the real origin of the products to be determined, the requesting authorities shall, except in exceptional circumstances, refuse entitlement to the tariff preferences.

5. Where the verification procedure or any other available information appears to indicate that the provisions of this section are being contravened, the exporting [beneficiary country or territory] shall, on its own initiative or at the request of the Community, carry out appropriate inquiries or arrange for such inquiries to be carried out with due urgency to identify and prevent such contraventions. For this purpose, the Community may participate in the inquiries.

Part III

6. For the purposes of the subsequent verification of EUR.1 movement certificates, copies of the certificates as well as any export documents referring to them shall be kept for at least three years by the competent governmental authorities of the exporting [beneficiary country or territory] or by the customs authorities of the exporting Member State.]

NOTES

Substituted as noted to Art 66.

Paras 1–3, 5, 6: words substituted by Commission Regulation (EC) 444/2002, Art 1, para 4.

[SUBSECTION 4
CEUTA AND MELILLA

Article 123

1. The term "Community" used in this section shall not cover Ceuta and Melilla. The term "products originating in the Community" shall not cover products originating in Ceuta and Melilla.

2. This section shall apply mutatis mutandis in determining whether products may be regarded as originating in the exporting [beneficiary countries or territories] benefiting from the preferences when imported into Ceuta and Melilla or as originating in Ceuta and Melilla.

3. Ceuta and Melilla shall be regarded as a single territory.

4. The provisions of this section concerning the issue, use and subsequent verification of EUR.1 movement certificates shall apply mutatis mutandis to products originating in Ceuta and Melilla.

5. The Spanish customs authorities shall be responsible for the application of this section in Ceuta and Melilla.]

NOTES

Substituted as noted to Art 66.

Para 2: words substituted by Commission Regulation (EC) 444/2002, Art 1, para 4.

Articles 125–140

. . .

NOTES

Repealed by Commission Regulation (EC) 12/97, Art 1, para 2.

TITLE V
CUSTOMS VALUE

CHAPTER 1
GENERAL PROVISIONS

Article 141

1. In applying the provisions of Articles 28 to 36 of the Code and those of this title, Member States shall comply with the provisions set out in Annex 23.

The provisions as set out in the first column of Annex 23 shall be applied in the light of the interpretative note appearing in the second column.

2. If it is necessary to make reference to generally accepted accounting principles in determining the customs value, the provisions of Annex 24 shall apply.

Article 142

1. For the purposes of this title—
    (a)   "the Agreement" means the Agreement on implementation of Article VII of the General Agreement on Tariffs and Trade concluded in the framework of the multilateral trade negotiations of 1973 to 1979 and referred to in the first indent of Article 31(1) of the Code;
    (b)   "produced goods" includes goods grown, manufactured and mined;
    (c)   "identical goods" means goods produced in the same country which are the same in all respects, including physical characteristics, quality and reputation. Minor differences in appearance shall not preclude goods otherwise conforming to the definition from being regarded as identical;
    (d)   "similar goods" means goods produced in the same country which, although not alike in all respects, have like characteristics and like component materials which enable them to perform the same functions and to be commercially interchangeable; the quality of the goods, their reputation and the existence of a trademark are among the factors to be considered in determining whether goods are similar;
    (e)   "goods of the same class or kind" means goods which fall within a group or range of goods produced by a particular industry or industry sector, and includes identical or similar goods.

2. "Identical goods" and "similar goods", as the case may be, do not include goods which incorporate or reflect engineering, development, artwork, design work, and plans and sketches for which no adjustment has been made under Article 32(1)(b)(iv) of the Code because such elements were undertaken in the Community.

Article 143

1. [For the purposes of Title II, Chapter 3 of the Code and of this Title, persons shall be deemed to be related only if—]
    (a)   they are officers or directors of one another's businesses;
    (b)   they are legally recognised partners in business;
    (c)   they are employer and employee;
    (d)   any person directly or indirectly owns, controls or holds 5% or more of the outstanding voting stock or shares of both of them;
    (e)   one of them directly or indirectly controls the other;
    (f)   both of them are directly or indirectly controlled by a third person;
    (g)   together they directly or indirectly control a third person; or
    (h)   they are members of the same family. Persons shall be deemed to be members of the same family only if they stand in any of the following relationships to one another—
    —   husband and wife,
    —   parent and child,
    —   brother and sister (whether by whole or half blood),
    —   grandparent and grandchild,
    —   uncle or aunt and nephew or niece
    —   parent-in-law and son-in-law or daughter-in-law,
    —   brother-in-law and sister-in-law.

2. For the purposes of this title, persons who are associated in business with one another in that one is the sole agent, sole distributor or sole concessionaire, however described, of the other shall be deemed to be related only if they fall within the criteria of paragraph 1.

NOTES
Para 1: words in square brackets substituted by Commission Regulation (EC) 46/1999, Art 1, para 8.

Article 144

1.   For the purposes of determining customs value under Article 29 of the Code of goods in regard to which the price has not actually been paid at the material time for valuation for customs purposes, the price payable for settlement at the said time shall as a general rule be taken as the basis for customs value.

2.   The Commission and the Member States shall consult within the Committee concerning the application of paragraph 1.

[Article 145

1.   Where goods declared for free circulation are part of a larger quantity of the same goods purchased in one transaction, the price actually paid or payable for the purposes of Article 29(1) of the Code shall be that price represented by the proportion of the total price which the quantity so declared bears to the total quantity purchased. Apportioning the price actually paid or payable shall also apply in the case of the loss of part of a consignment or when the goods being valued have been damaged before entry into free circulation.

2.   After release of the goods for free circulation, an adjustment made by the seller, to the benefit of the buyer, of the price actually paid or payable for the goods may be taken into consideration for the determination of the customs value in accordance with Article 29 of the Code, if it is demonstrated to the satisfaction of the customs authorities that:

(a)   the goods were defective at the moment referred to by Article 67 of the Code;

(b)   the seller made the adjustment in performance of a warranty obligation provided for in the contract of sale, concluded before release for free circulation of the goods;

(c)   the defective nature of the goods has not already been taken into account in the relevant sales contract.

3.   The price actually paid or payable for the goods, adjusted in accordance with paragraph 2, may be taken into account only if that adjustment was made within a period of 12 months following the date of acceptance of the declaration for entry to free circulation of the goods.]

NOTES
Substituted by Commission Regulation (EC) 444/2002, Art 1, para 6.

Article 146

Where the price actually paid or payable for the purposes of Article 29(1) of the Code includes an amount in respect of any internal tax applicable within the country of origin or export in respect of the goods in question, the said amount shall not be incorporated in the customs value provided that it can be demonstrated to the satisfaction of the customs authorities concerned that the goods in question have been or will be relieved therefrom for the benefit of the buyer.

Article 147

1.   For the purposes of Article 29 of the Code, the fact that the goods which are the subject of a sale are declared for free circulation shall be regarded as adequate indication that they were sold for export to the customs territory of the Community.

[In the case of successive sales before valuation, only the last sale, which led to the introduction of the goods into the customs territory of the Community, or a sale taking place in the customs territory of the Community before entry for free circulation of the goods shall constitute such indication.

Where a price is declared which relates to a sale taking place before the last sale on the basis of which the goods were introduced into the customs territory of the Community, it must be demonstrated to the satisfaction of the customs authorities that this sale of goods took place for export to the customs territory in question.

The provisions of Articles 178 to 181a shall apply.]

2. . . . where goods are used in a third country between the time of sale and the time of entry into free circulation the customs value need not be the transaction value.

3. The buyer need satisfy no condition other than that of being a party to the contract of sale.

NOTES

Para 1: words in square brackets substituted by Commission Regulation (EC) 1762/95, Art 1, para 2(a).

Para 2: words omitted repealed by Commission Regulation (EC) 1762/95, Art 1, para 2(b).

Article 148

Where, in applying Article 29(1)(b) of the Code, it is established that the sale or price of imported goods is subject to a condition or consideration the value of which can be determined with respect to the goods being valued, such value shall be regarded as an indirect payment by the buyer to the seller and part of the price actually paid or payable provided that the condition or consideration does not relate to either—

    (a)   an activity to which Article 29(3)(b) of the Code applies; or

    (b)   a factor in respect of which an addition is to be made to the price actually paid or payable under the provisions of Article 32 of the Code.

Article 149

1. For the purposes of Article 29(3)(b) of the Code, the term "marketing activities" means all activities relating to advertising and promoting the sale of the goods in question and all activities relating to warranties or guarantees in respect of them.

2. Such activities undertaken by the buyer shall be regarded as having been undertaken on his own account even if they are performed in pursuance of an obligation on the buyer following an agreement with the seller.

Article 150

1. In applying Article 30(2)(a) of the Code (the transaction value of identical goods), the customs value shall be determined by reference to the transaction value of identical goods in a sale at the same commercial level and in substantially the same quantity as the goods being valued. Where no such sale is found, the transaction value of identical goods sold at a different commercial level and/or in different quantities, adjusted to take account of differences attributable to commercial level and/or to quantity, shall be used, provided that such adjustments can be made on the basis of demonstrated evidence which clearly establishes the reasonableness and accuracy of the adjustment, whether the adjustment leads to an increase or a decrease in the value.

2. Where the costs and charges referred to in Article 32(1)(e) of the Code are included in the transaction value, an adjustment shall be made to take account of significant differences in such costs and charges between the imported goods and the identical goods in question arising from differences in distances and modes of transport.

3. If, in applying this Article, more than one transaction value of identical goods is found, the lowest such value shall be used to determine the customs value of the imported goods.

4. In applying this Article, a transaction value for goods produced by a different person shall be taken into account only when no transaction value can be found under paragraph 1 for identical goods produced by the same person as the goods being valued.

5. For the purposes of this Article, the transaction value of identical imported goods means a customs value previously determined under Article 29 of the Code, adjusted as provided for in paragraphs 1 and 2 of this Article.

Article 151

1. In applying Article 30(2)(b) of the Code (the transaction value of similar goods), the customs value shall be determined by reference to the transaction value of similar goods in a sale at the same commercial level and in substantially the same quantity as the goods being valued. Where no such sale is found, the transaction value of similar goods sold at a different commercial level and/or in different quantities, adjusted to take account of differences attributable to commercial level and/or to quantity, shall be used, provided that such adjustments can be made on the basis of demonstrated evidence which clearly establishes the reasonableness and accuracy of the adjustment, whether the adjustment leads to an increase or a decrease in the value.

2. Where the costs and charges referred to in Article 32(1)(e) of the Code are included in the transaction value, an adjustment shall be made to take account of significant differences in such costs and charges between the imported goods and the similar goods in question arising from differences in distances and modes of transport.

3. If, in applying this Article, more than one transaction value of similar goods is found, the lowest such value shall be used to determine the customs value for the imported goods.

4. In applying this Article, a transaction value for goods produced by a different person shall be taken into account only when no transaction value can be found under paragraph 1 for similar goods produced by the same person as the goods being valued.

5. For the purposes of this Article, the transaction value of similar imported goods means a customs value previously determined under Article 29 of the Code, adjusted as provided for in paragraphs 1 and 2 of this Article.

Article 152

1. (a) If the imported goods or identical or similar imported goods are sold in the Community in the condition as imported, the customs value of imported goods, determined in accordance with Article 30(2)(c) of the Code, shall be based on the unit price at which the imported goods or identical or similar imported goods are so sold in the greatest aggregate quantity, at or about the time of the importation of the goods being valued, to persons who are not related to the persons from whom they buy such goods, subject to deductions for the following—

    (i) either the commissions usually paid or agreed to be paid or the additions usually made for profit and general expenses (including the direct and indirect costs of marketing the goods in question) in connection with sales in the Community of imported goods of the same class or kind;

    (ii) the usual costs of transport and insurance and associated costs incurred within the Community;

    (iii) the import duties and other charges payable in the Community by reason of the importation or sale of the goods.

    [(a)a The customs value of certain perishable goods imported on consignment may be directly determined in accordance with Article 30(2)(c) of the Code. For this purpose the unit prices shall be notified to the Commission by the Member States and disseminated by the Commission via TARIC in accordance with Article 6 of Council Regulation (EEC) No 2658/87.

The unit prices shall be calculated and notified as follows:

(i) After the deductions provided for in point (a), a unit price per 100 kg net for each category of goods shall be notified by the Member States to the Commission. The Member States may fix standard amounts for the costs referred to in point (a)(ii) which shall be made known to the Commission.

(ii) The unit price may be used to determine the customs value of the imported goods for periods of 14 days, each period beginning on a Friday.

(iii) The reference period for determining the unit prices shall be the preceding period of 14 days which ends on the Thursday preceding the week during which new unit prices are to be established.

(iv) The unit prices shall be notified by the Member States to the Commission in euro not later than 12 noon on the Monday of the week in which they are disseminated by the Commission. If that day is a non-working day, notification shall be made on the working day immediately preceding that day. Unit prices shall only apply if this notification is disseminated by the Commission.

The goods referred to in the first subparagraph of this point are set out in Annex 26.]

(b) If neither the imported goods nor identical nor similar imported goods are sold at or about the time of importation of the goods being valued, the customs value of imported goods determined under this Article shall, subject otherwise to the provisions of paragraph 1(a), be based on the unit price at which the imported goods or identical or similar imported goods are sold in the Community in the condition as imported at the earliest date after the importation of the goods being valued but before the expiration of 90 days after such importation.

2. If neither the imported goods nor identical nor similar imported goods are sold in the Community in the condition as imported, then, if the importer so requests, the customs value shall be based on the unit price at which the imported goods, after further processing, are sold in the greatest aggregate quantity to persons in the Community who are not related to the persons from whom they buy such goods, due allowance being made for the value added by such processing and the deductions provided for in paragraph 1(a).

3. For the purposes of this Article, the unit price at which imported goods are sold in the greatest aggregate quantity is the price at which the greatest number of units is sold in sales to persons who are not related to the persons from whom they buy such goods at the first commercial level after importation at which such sales take place.

4. Any sale in the Community to a person who supplies directly or indirectly free of charge or at reduced cost for use in connection with the production and sale for export of the imported goods any of the elements specified in Article 32(1)(b) of the Code should not be taken into account in establishing the unit price for the purposes of this Article.

5. For the purposes of paragraph 1(b), the "earliest date" shall be the date by which sales of the imported goods or of identical or similar imported goods are made in sufficient quantity to establish the unit price.

Part III

NOTES

Para 1(a)a inserted by Commission Regulation (EC) No 215/2006, Art 1(1).

Article 153

1. In applying Article 30(2)(d) of the Code (computed value), the customs authorities may not require or compel any person not resident in the Community to produce for examination, or to allow access to, any account or other record for the purposes of determining this value. However, information supplied by the producer of the goods for the purposes of determining the customs value under this Article may be verified in a non-Community country by the customs authorities of a Member State with the agreement of the producer and provided that such authorities give sufficient advance notice to the authorities of the country in question and the latter do not object to the investigation.

2. The cost or value of materials and fabrication referred to in the first indent of Article 30(2)(d) of the Code shall include the cost of elements specified in Article 32(1)(a)(ii) and (iii) of the Code.

It shall also include the value, duly apportioned, of any product or service specified in Article 32(1)(b) of the Code which has been supplied directly or indirectly by the buyer for use in connection with the production of the imported goods. The value of the elements specified in Article 32(1)(b)(iv) of the Code which are undertaken in the Community shall be included only to the extent that such elements are charged to the producer.

3. Where information other than that supplied by or on behalf of the producer is used for the purposes of determining a computed value, the customs authorities shall inform the declarant, if the latter so requests, of the source of such information, the data used and the calculations based on such data, subject to Article 15 of the Code.

4. The "general expenses" referred to in the second indent of Article 30(2)(d) of the Code, cover the direct and indirect costs of producing and selling the goods for export which are not included under the first indent of Article 30(2)(d) of the Code.

Article 154

Where containers referred to in Article 32(1)(a)(ii) of the Code are to be the subject of repeated importations, their cost shall, at the request of the declarant, be apportioned, as appropriate, in accordance with generally accepted accounting principles.

Article 155

For the purposes of Article 32(1)(b)(iv) of the Code, the cost of research and preliminary design sketches is not to be included in the customs value.

Article 156

Article 33(c) of the Code shall apply *mutatis mutandis* where the customs value is determined by applying a method other than the transaction value.

Article 156a

1. The customs authorities may, at the request of the person concerned, authorise—

— by derogation from Article 32(2) of the Code, certain elements which are to be added to the price actually paid or payable, although not quantifiable at the time of incurrence of the customs debt,

— by derogation from Article 33 of the Code, certain charges which are not to be included in the customs value, in cases where the amounts relating to such elements are not shown separately at the time of incurrence of the customs debt, to be determined on the basis of appropriate and specific criteria.

In such cases, the declared customs value is not to be considered as provisional within the meaning of the second indent of Article 254.

2. The authorisation shall be granted under the following conditions—

(a)   the carrying out of the procedures provided for by Article 259 would, in the circumstances, represent disproportionate administrative costs;

(b)   recourse to an application of Articles 30 and 31 of the Code appears to be inappropriate in the particular circumstances;

(c)   there are valid reasons for considering that the amount of import duties to be charged in the period covered by the authorisation will not be lower than that which would be levied in the absence of an authorisation;

(d)   competitive conditions amongst operators are not distorted.]

NOTES

Inserted by Commission Regulation (EC) 1676/96, Art 1, para 1.

CHAPTER 2
PROVISIONS CONCERNING ROYALTIES AND LICENCE FEES

Article 157

1. For the purposes of Article 32(1)(c) of the Code, royalties and licence fees shall be taken to mean in particular payment for the use of rights relating—

—   to the manufacture of imported goods (in particular, patents, designs, models and manufacturing know-how), or

—   to the sale for exportation of imported goods (in particular, trade marks, registered designs), or

—   to the use or resale of imported goods (in particular, copyright, manufacturing processes inseparably embodied in the imported goods).

2. Without prejudice to Article 32(5) of the Code, when the customs value of imported goods is determined under the provisions of Article 29 of the Code, a royalty or licence fee shall be added to the price actually paid or payable only when this payment—

—   is related to the goods being valued, and

—   constitutes a condition of sale of those goods.

Article 158

1. When the imported goods are only an ingredient or component of goods manufactured in the Community, an adjustment to the price actually paid or payable for the imported goods shall only be made when the royalty or licence fee relates to those goods.

2. Where goods are imported in an unassembled state or only have to undergo minor processing before resale, such as diluting or packing, this shall not prevent a royalty or licence fee from being considered related to the imported goods.

3. If royalties or licence fees relate partly to the imported goods and partly to other ingredients or component parts added to the goods after their importation, or to post-importation activities or services, an appropriate apportionment shall be made only on the basis of objective and quantifiable data, in accordance with the interpretative note to Article 32(2) of the Code in Annex 23.

Article 159

A royalty or licence fee in respect of the right to use a trade mark is only to be added to the price actually paid or payable for the imported goods where—

— the royalty or licence fee refers to goods which are resold in the same state or which are subject only to minor processing after importation,

— the goods are marketed under the trade mark, affixed before or after importation, for which the royalty or licence fee is paid, and

— the buyer is not free to obtain such goods from other suppliers unrelated to the seller.

Article 160

When the buyer pays royalties or licence fees to a third party, the conditions provided for in Article 157(2) shall not be considered as met unless the seller or a person related to him requires the buyer to make that payment.

Article 161

Where the method of calculation of the amount of a royalty or licence fee derives from the price of the imported goods, it may be assumed in the absence of evidence to the contrary that the payment of that royalty or licence fee is related to the goods to be valued.

However, where the amount of a royalty or licence fee is calculated regardless of the price of the imported goods, the payment of that royalty or licence fee may nevertheless be related to the goods to be valued.

Article 162

In applying Article 32(1)(c) of the Code, the country of residence of the recipient of the payment of the royalty or licence fee shall not be a material consideration.

CHAPTER 3
PROVISIONS CONCERNING THE PLACE OF INTRODUCTION INTO THE COMMUNITY

Article 163

1. For the purposes of Article 32(1)(e) and Article 33(a) of the Code, the place of introduction into the customs territory of the Community shall be—

(a) for goods carried by sea, the port of unloading, or the port of transhipment, subject to transhipment being certified by the customs authorities of that port;

(b) for goods carried by sea and then, without transhipment, by inland waterway, the first port where unloading can take place either at the mouth of the river or canal or further inland, subject to proof being furnished to the customs office that the freight to the port of unloading is higher than that to the first port;

(c) for goods carried by rail, inland waterway, or road, the place where the first customs office is situated;

(d) for goods carried by other means, the place where the land frontier of the customs territory of the Community is crossed.

[2. The customs value of goods introduced into the customs territory of the Community and then carried to a destination in another part of that territory through the territories of Belarus, Russia, Switzerland, Bosnia and Herzegovina, Croatia, the Federal Republic of Yugoslavia or the former Yugoslav Republic of Macedonia shall be determined by reference to the first place of introduction into the customs territory of the Community, provided that goods are carried direct through the territories of those countries by a usual route across such territory to the place of destination.]

3. The customs value of goods introduced into the customs territory of the Community and then carried by sea to a destination in another part of that

territory shall be determined by reference to the first place of introduction into the customs territory of the Community, provided the goods are carried direct by a usual route to the place of destination.

[4. Paragraphs 2 and 3 of this Article shall also apply where the goods have been unloaded, transhipped or temporarily immobilised in the territories of Belarus, Russia, Switzerland, Bosnia and Herzegovina, Croatia, the Federal Republic of Yugoslavia or the former Yugoslav Republic of Macedonia for reasons related solely to their transport.]

5. For goods introduced into the customs territory of the Community and carried directly from one of the French overseas departments to another part of the customs territory of the Community or vice versa, the place of introduction to be taken into consideration shall be the place referred to in paragraphs 1 and 2 situated in that part of the customs territory of the Community from which the goods came, if they were unloaded or transhipped there and this was certified by the customs authorities.

6. When the conditions specified at paragraphs 2, 3 and 5 are not fulfilled, the place of introduction to be taken into consideration shall be the place specified in paragraph 1 situated in that part of the customs territory of the Community to which the goods are consigned.

NOTES

Paras 2, 4: substituted by Commission Regulation (EC) 1792/2006, Art 1, Annex, Part 11(A)(4), (5).

CHAPTER 4
PROVISIONS CONCERNING TRANSPORT COSTS

Article 164
In applying Article 32(1)(e) and 33(a) of the Code—

    (a)   where goods are carried by the same mode of transport to a point beyond the place of introduction into the customs territory of the Community, transport costs shall be assessed in proportion to the distance covered outside and inside the customs territory of the Community, unless evidence is produced to the customs authorities to show the costs that would have been incurred under a general compulsory schedule of freight rates for the carriage of the goods to the place of introduction into the customs territory of the Community;

    (b)   where goods are invoiced at a uniform free domicile price which corresponds to the price at the place of introduction, transport costs within the Community shall not be deducted from that price. However, such deduction shall be allowed if evidence is produced to the customs authorities that the free-frontier price would be lower than the uniform free domicile price;

    (c)   where transport is free or provided by the buyer, transport costs to the place of introduction, calculated in accordance with the schedule of freight rates normally applied for the same modes of transport, shall be included in the customs value.

Article 165
1. All postal charges levied up to the place of destination in respect of goods sent by post shall be included in the customs value of these goods, with the exception of any supplementary postal charge levied in the country of importation.

2. No adjustment to the declared value shall, however, be made in respect of such charges in determining the value of consignments of a non-commercial nature.

3. Paragraphs 1 and 2 are not applicable to goods carried by the express postal services known as EMS-Datapost (in Denmark, EMS-Jetpost, in Germany, EMS-Kurierpostsendungen, in Italy, CAI-Post).

Article 166
The air transport costs to be included in the customs value of goods shall be determined by applying the rules and percentages shown in Annex 25.

CHAPTER 5
VALUATION OF CERTAIN CARRIER MEDIA FOR USE IN ADP EQUIPMENT

NOTES
   Chapter repealed by Commission Regulation (EC) 444/2002, Art 1, para 7.

CHAPTER 6
PROVISIONS CONCERNING RATES OF EXCHANGE

Article 168
For the purposes of Articles 169 to 171 of this chapter—
   (a)   "rate recorded" shall mean—
      —   the latest selling rate of exchange recorded for commercial transactions on the most representative exchange market or markets of the Member State concerned, or
      —   some other description of a rate of exchange so recorded and designated by the Member State as the "rate recorded" provided that it reflects as effectively as possible the current value of the currency in question in commercial transactions;
   (b)   "published" shall mean made generally known in a manner designated by the Member State concerned;
   (c)   "currency" shall mean any monetary unit used as a means of settlement between monetary authorities or on the international market.

Article 169
   1.   Where factors used to determine the customs value of goods are expressed at the time when that value is determined in a currency other than that of the Member State where the valuation is made, the rate of exchange to be used to determine that value in terms of the currency of the Member State concerned shall be the rate recorded on the second-last Wednesday of a month and published on that or the following day.
   2.   The rate recorded on the second-last Wednesday of a month shall be used during the following calendar month unless it is superseded by a rate established under Article 171.
   3.   Where a rate of exchange is not recorded on the second-last Wednesday indicated in paragraph 1, or, if recorded, is not published on that or the following day, the last rate recorded for the currency in question published within the preceding 14 days shall be deemed to be the rate recorded on that Wednesday.

Article 170
Where a rate of exchange cannot be established under the provisions of Article 169, the rate of exchange to be used for the application of Article 35 of the Code shall be designated by the Member State concerned and shall reflect as effectively as possible the current value of the currency in question in commercial transactions in terms of the currency of that Member State.

Article 171

1. Where a rate of exchange recorded on the last Wednesday of a month and published on that or the following day differs by 5% or more from the rate established in accordance with Article 169 for entry into use the following month, it shall replace the latter rate from the first Wednesday of that month as the rate to be applied for the application of Article 35 of the Code.

2. Where in the course of a period of application as referred to in the preceding provisions, a rate of exchange recorded on a Wednesday and published on that or the following day differs by 5% or more from the rate being used in accordance with this Chapter, it shall replace the latter rate and enter into use on the Wednesday following as the rate to be used for the application of Article 35 of the Code. The replacement rate shall remain in use for the remainder of the current month, provided that this rate is not superseded due to operation of the provisions of the first sentence of this paragraph.

3. Where, in a Member State, a rate of exchange is not recorded on a Wednesday or, if recorded, is not published on that or the following day, the rate recorded shall, for the application in that Member State of paragraphs 1 and 2, be the rate most recently recorded and published prior to that Wednesday.

Article 172

When the customs authorities of a Member State authorise a declarant to furnish or supply at a later date certain details concerning the declaration for free circulation of the goods in the form of a periodic declaration, this authorisation may, at the declarant's request, provide that a single rate be used for conversion into that Member State's currency of elements forming part of the customs value as expressed in a particular currency. In this case, the rate to be used shall be the rate, established in accordance with this Chapter, which is applicable on the first day of the period covered by the declaration in question.

CHAPTER 7
SIMPLIFIED PROCEDURES FOR CERTAIN PERISHABLE GOODS

Articles 173–177

NOTES

Repealed by Commission Regulation (EC) No 215/2006, Art 1(2).

CHAPTER 8
DECLARATIONS OF PARTICULARS AND DOCUMENTS TO BE FURNISHED

Article 178

1. Where it is necessary to establish a customs value for the purposes of Articles 28 to 36 of the Code, a declaration of particulars relating to customs value (value declaration) shall accompany the customs entry made in respect of the imported goods. The value declaration shall be drawn up on a form DV1 corresponding to the specimen in Annex 28, supplemented where appropriate by one or more forms DV1 *bis* corresponding to the specimen in Annex 29.

[2. The value declaration provided for in paragraph 1 shall be made only by a person established in the Community and in possession of the relevant facts.

The second indent of Article 64(2)(b) and Article 64(3) of the Code shall apply *mutatis mutandis*.]

3. The customs authorities may waive the requirement of a declaration on the form referred to in paragraph 1 where the customs value of the goods in question cannot be determined under the provisions of Article 29 of the Code. In such cases the

person referred to in paragraph 2 shall furnish or cause to be furnished to the customs authorities such other information as may be requested for the purposes of determining the customs value under another Article of the said Code; and such other information shall be supplied in such form and manner as may be prescribed by the customs authorities.

4. The lodging with a customs office of a declaration required by paragraph 1 shall, without prejudice to the possible application of penal provisions, be equivalent to the engagement of responsibility by the person referred to in paragraph 2 in respect of—

— the accuracy and completeness of the particulars given in the declaration,

— the authenticity of the documents produced in support of these particulars, and

— the supply of any additional information or document necessary to establish the customs value of the goods.

5. This Article shall not apply in respect of goods for which the customs value is determined under the simplified procedure system established in accordance with the provisions of Articles 173 to 177.

NOTES

Para 2: substituted by Commission Regulation (EC) 1677/98, Art 1, para 1.

Article 179

1. Except where it is essential for the correct application of import duties, the customs authorities shall waive the requirement of all or part of the declaration provided for in Article 178(1)—

(a) where the customs value of the imported goods in a consignment does not exceed [EUR 10000], provided that they do not constitute split or multiple consignments from the same consignor to the same consignee; or

(b) where the importations involved are of a non-commercial nature; or

(c) where the submission of the particulars in question is not necessary for the application of the Customs Tariff of the European Communities or where the customs duties provided for in the Tariff are not chargeable pursuant to specific customs provisions.

2. The amount in ECU referred to in paragraph 1(a) shall be converted in accordance with Article 18 of the Code. The customs authorities may round-off upwards or downwards the sum arrived at after conversion.

The customs authorities may maintain unamended the exchange value in national currency of the amount determined in ECU if, at the time of the annual adjustment provided for in Article 18 of the Code, the conversion of this amount, before the rounding-off provided for in this paragraph, leads to an alteration of less than 5% in the exchange value expressed in national currency or to a reduction thereof.

3. In the case of continuing traffic in goods supplied by the same seller to the same buyer under the same commercial conditions, the customs authorities may waive the requirement that all particulars under Article 178(1) be furnished in support of each customs declaration, but shall require them whenever the circumstances change and at least once every three years.

4. A waiver granted under this Article may be withdrawn and the submission of a DV1 may be required where it is found that a condition necessary to qualify for that waiver was not or is no longer met.

NOTES
Para 1: figure substituted by Commission Regulation (EC) 444/2002, Art 1, para 8.

Article 180

Where computerised systems are used, or where the goods concerned are the subject of a general, periodic or recapitulative declaration, the customs authorities may authorise variations in the form of presentation of data required for the determination of customs value.

Article 181

1. The person referred to in Article 178(2) shall furnish the customs authorities with a copy of the invoice on the basis of which the value of the imported goods is declared. Where the customs value is declared in writing this copy shall be retained by the customs authorities.

2. In the case of written declarations of the customs value, when the invoice for the imported goods is made out to a person established in a Member State other than that in which the customs value is declared, the declarant shall furnish the customs authorities with two copies of the invoice. One of these copies shall be retained by the customs authorities; the other, bearing the stamp of the office in question and the serial number of the declaration at the said customs office shall be returned to the declarant for forwarding to the person to whom the invoice is made out.

3. The customs authorities may extend the provisions of paragraph 2 to cases where the person to whom the invoice is made out is established in the Member State in which the customs value is declared.

Article 181a

1. The customs authorities need not determine the customs valuation of imported goods on the basis of the transaction value method if, in accordance with the procedure set out in paragraph 2, they are not satisfied, on the basis of reasonable doubts, that the declared value represents the total amount paid or payable as referred to in Article 29 of the Code.

2. Where the customs authorities have the doubts described in paragraph 1 they may ask for additional information in accordance with Article 178(4). If those doubts continue, the customs authorities must, before reaching a final decision, notify the person concerned, in writing if requested, of the grounds for those doubts and provide him with a reasonable opportunity to respond. A final decision and the grounds therefor shall be communicated in writing to the person concerned.]

NOTES
Inserted by Commission Regulation (EC) 3254/94, Art 1, para 9.

TITLE VI
INTRODUCTION OF GOODS INTO THE CUSTOMS TERRITORY

CHAPTER 1
EXAMINATION OF THE GOODS AND TAKING OF SAMPLES BY THE PERSON CONCERNED

Article 182

1. Permission to examine the goods under Article 42 of the Code shall be granted to the person empowered to assign the goods a customs-approved treatment or use at

his oral request, unless the customs authorities consider, having regard to the circumstances, that a written request is required.

The taking of samples may be authorised only at the written request of the person concerned.

2.   A written request as referred to in paragraph 1 shall be signed by the person concerned and lodged with the relevant customs authorities. It shall include the following particulars—

—   name and address of the applicant,

—   the location of the goods,

—   number of the summary declaration, where it has already been presented, save where the customs office undertakes to enter such information, or indication of the previous customs procedure, or the particulars for identifying the means of transport on which the goods are located,

—   all other particulars necessary for identifying the goods.

The customs authorities shall indicate their authorisation on the request presented by the person concerned. Where the request is for the taking of samples, the said authorities shall indicate the quantity of goods to be taken.

3.   Prior examination of goods and the taking of samples shall be carried out under the supervision of the customs authorities, which shall specify the procedures to be followed in each particular case.

The person concerned shall bear the risk and the cost of unpacking, weighing, repacking and any other operation involving the goods. He shall also pay any costs in connection with analysis.

4.   The samples taken shall be the subject of formalities with a view to assigning them a customs-approved treatment or use. Where examination of the samples results in their destruction or irretrievable loss, no debt shall be deemed to have been incurred. Article 182(5) of the Code shall apply to waste and scrap.

NOTES

Chapter heading to be substituted, new Section 1 (new Articles 181a–181d) to be inserted, and Article 182 to be revoked, by Commission Regulation (EC) No 1875/2006, Art 1(4)–(6) with effect from 1 July 2009.

CHAPTER 2
SUMMARY DECLARATION

Article 183

1.   The summary declaration shall be signed by the person making it.

2.   The summary declaration shall be endorsed by the customs authorities and retained by them for the purpose of verifying that the goods to which it relates are assigned a customs-approved treatment or use within the period laid down in Article 49 of the Code.

3.   The summary declaration for goods which have been moved under a transit procedure before being presented to customs shall take the form of the copy of the transit document intended for the customs office of destination.

4.   The customs authorities may allow the summary declaration to be made in computerised form. In that case, the rules laid down [in paragraphs 1 and 2] shall be adapted accordingly.

NOTES

Para 4: words in square brackets substituted by Commission Regulation (EC) 3665/93, Art 1, para 9.

Chapter heading to be substituted, Article 183 to be substituted, and new Articles 183a–183d to be inserted by Commission Regulation (EC) No 1875/2006, Art 1(7)–(9) with effect from 1 July 2009.

Article 184

1. Goods covered by a summary declaration which have not been unloaded from the means of transport carrying them shall be re-presented intact by the person referred to in Article 183(1) whenever the customs authorities so require, until such time as the goods in question are assigned a customs-approved treatment or use.

2. Any person who holds goods after they have been unloaded in order to move or store them shall become responsible for compliance with the obligation to re-present all the goods intact at the request of the customs authorities.

NOTES

Para 1: words to be substituted by Commission Regulation (EC) No 1875/2006, Art 1(10) with effect from 1 July 2009.

New Sections 3 and 4 (new Articles 184a–184f) to be inserted by Commission Regulation (EC) No 1875/2006, Art 1(11) with effect from 1 July 2009.

CHAPTER 3
TEMPORARY STORAGE

Article 185

1. Where the places referred to in Article 51(1) of the Code have been approved on a permanent basis for the placing of goods in temporary storage, such places shall be called "temporary storage facilities".

2. In order to ensure the application of customs rules, the customs authorities may, where they do not themselves manage the temporary storage facility, require that—

(a)   temporary storage facilities be double-locked, one key being held by the said customs authorities;

(b)   the person operating the temporary storage facility keep stock accounts which enable the movements of goods to be traced.

NOTES

Heading to Chapter 3 to be substituted, by Commission Regulation (EC) No 1875/2006, Art 1(12) with effect from 1 July 2009.

Article 186

Goods shall be placed in a temporary storage facility on the basis of the summary declaration. However, the customs authorities may require the lodging of a specific declaration made out on a form corresponding to the model they have determined.

NOTES

Article 186 to be substituted, by Commission Regulation (EC) No 1875/2006, Art 1(13) with effect from 1 July 2009.

Article 187

Without prejudice to Article 56 of the Code or to the provisions applicable to the sale of goods by the customs authorities, the person who has made the summary declaration or, where such a declaration has not yet been lodged, the persons referred to in Article 44(2) of the Code, shall be responsible for giving effect to the measures taken by the customs authorities pursuant to Article 53(1) of the Code and for bearing the costs of such measures.

NOTES

Words to be substituted by Commission Regulation (EC) No 1875/2006, Art 1(14) with effect from 1 July 2009.

New Article 187a to be inserted by Commission Regulation (EC) No 1875/2006, Art 1(15) with effect from 1 July 2009.

Article 188

NOTES

Repealed by Commission Regulation (EC) 3665/93, Art 1, para 10.

CHAPTER 4
SPECIAL PROVISIONS APPLICABLE TO GOODS CONSIGNED BY SEA OR AIR

SECTION 1
GENERAL PROVISION

Article 189

Where goods are brought into the customs territory of the Community from a third country by sea or air and are consigned under cover of a single transport document by the same mode of transport, without transhipment, to another port or airport in the Community, they shall be presented to customs, within the meaning of Article 40 of the Code, only at the port or airport where they are unloaded or transhipped.

NOTES

Heading to Chapter 4 to be substituted, by Commission Regulation (EC) No 1875/2006, Art 1(16) with effect from 1 July 2009.

SECTION 2
SPECIAL PROVISIONS APPLICABLE TO THE CABIN BAGGAGE AND HOLD BAGGAGE OF TRAVELLERS

Article 190

For the purposes of this section—

(a) *Community airport* means any airport situated in Community customs territory;

(b) *international Community airport* means any Community airport which, having been so authorised by the competent authorities, is approved for air traffic with third countries;

(c) *intra-Community flight* means the movement of an aircraft between two Community airports, without any stopovers, which does not start from or end at a non-Community airport;

(d) *Community port* means any sea port situated in Community customs territory;

(e) *intra-Community sea crossing* means the movement between two Community ports without any intermediate calls, of a vessel plying regularly between two or more specified Community ports;

(f)   *pleasure craft* means private boats intended for journeys whose itinerary depends on the wishes of the user;

(g)   *tourist or business aircraft* means private aircraft intended for journeys whose itinerary depends on the wishes of the user;

(h)   *baggage* means all objects carried, by whatever means, by the person in the course of his journey.

Article 191

For the purposes of this section, in the case of air travel, baggage shall be considered as—

—   hold baggage if it has been checked in at the airport of departure and is not accessible to the person during the flight nor, where relevant, during the stopovers referred to in Articles 192(1) and (2) and 194(1) and (2) of this chapter,

—   cabin baggage if the person takes it into the cabin of the aircraft.

Article 192

Any controls and any formalities applicable to—

1.   the cabin and hold baggage of persons taking a flight in an aircraft which comes from a non-Community airport and which, after a stopover at a Community airport, continues to another Community airport, shall be carried out at this last airport provided it is an international Community airport; in this case, baggage shall be subject to the rules applicable to the baggage of persons coming from a third country when the person carrying such baggage cannot prove the Community status of the goods contained therein to the satisfaction of the competent authorities;

2.   the cabin and hold baggage of persons taking a flight in an aircraft which stops over at a Community airport before continuing to a non-Community airport, shall be carried out at the airport of departure provided it is an international Community airport; in this case, cabin baggage may be subject to control at the Community airport where the aircraft stops over, in order to ascertain that the goods it contains conform to the conditions for free movement within the Community;

3.   the baggage of persons using a maritime service provided by the same vessel and comprising successive legs departing from, calling at or terminating in a non-Community port shall be carried out at the port at which the baggage in question is loaded or unloaded as the case may be.

Article 193

Any controls and any formalities applicable to the baggage of persons on board—

1.   pleasure craft, shall be carried out in any Community port, whatever the origin or destination of these craft;

2.   tourist or business aircraft, shall be carried out—

—   at the first airport of arrival which must be an international Community airport, for flights coming from a non-Community airport, where the aircraft, after a stopover, continues to another Community airport,

—   at the last international Community airport, for flights coming from a Community airport where the aircraft, after a stopover, continues to a non-Community airport.

Article 194

1.   Where baggage arriving at a Community airport on board an aircraft coming from a non-Community airport is transferred at that Community airport, to another aircraft proceeding on an intra-Community flight—

—   any controls and any formalities applicable to hold baggage shall be carried out at the airport of arrival of the intra-Community flight, provided the latter airport is an international Community airport,

—   all controls on cabin baggage shall be carried out in the first international Community airport; additional controls may be carried out at the airport of arrival of an intra-Community flight, only in exceptional cases where they prove necessary following controls on hold baggage,

—   controls on hold baggage may be carried out at the first Community airport only in exceptional cases where they prove necessary following controls on cabin baggage.

2.   Where baggage is loaded at a Community airport onto an aircraft proceeding on an intra-Community flight for transfer at another Community airport, to an aircraft whose destination is a non-Community airport—

—   any controls and any formalities applicable to hold baggage shall be carried out at the airport of departure of the intra-Community flight, provided that airport is an international Community airport,

—   all controls on cabin baggage shall be carried out in the last international Community airport; prior controls on such baggage may be carried out in the airport of departure of an intra-Community flight only in exceptional cases where they prove necessary following controls on hold baggage,

—   additional controls on hold baggage may be carried out in the last Community airport only in exceptional cases where they prove necessary following controls on cabin baggage.

3.   Any controls and any formalities applicable to baggage arriving at a Community airport on board a scheduled or charter flight from a non-Community airport and transferred, at that Community airport, to a tourist or business aircraft proceeding on an intra-Community flight shall be carried out at the airport of arrival of the scheduled or charter flight.

4.   Any controls and any formalities applicable to baggage loaded at a Community airport onto a tourist or business aircraft proceeding on an intra-Community flight for transfer, at another Community airport, to a scheduled or charter flight whose destination is a non-Community airport, shall be carried out at the airport of departure of the scheduled or charter flight.

5.   The Member States may carry out controls at the international Community airport where the transfer of hold baggage takes place on baggage—

—   coming from a non-Community airport and transferred in an international Community airport to an aircraft bound for an international airport in the same national territory,

—   having been loaded on an aircraft in an international airport for transfer in another international airport in the same national territory to an aircraft bound for a non-Community airport.

Article 195

The Member States shall take the necessary measures to ensure that—

—   on arrival, persons cannot transfer goods before controls have been carried out on the cabin baggage not covered by Article 1 of Council Regulation (EEC) No 3925/91[1],

— on departure, persons cannot transfer goods after controls have been carried out on the cabin baggage not covered by Article 1 of Council Regulation (EEC) No 3925/91,

— on arrival, the appropriate arrangements have been made to prevent any transfer of goods before controls have been carried out on the hold baggage not covered by Article 1 of Council Regulation (EEC) No 3925/91,

— on departure, the appropriate arrangements have been made to prevent any transfer of goods after controls have been carried out on the hold baggage not covered by Article 1 of Council Regulation (EEC) No 3925/91.

------

[1] 1 OJ L 374, 31.12.91, p 4.

Article 196

Hold baggage registered in a Community airport shall be identified by a tag affixed in the airport concerned. A specimen tag and the technical characteristics are shown in Annex 30.

Article 197

Each Member State shall provide the Commission with a list of airports corresponding to the definition of "international Community airport" given in Article 190(b). The Commission shall publish this list in the *Official Journal of the European Communities*, "C" Series.

TITLE VII
CUSTOMS DECLARATIONS—NORMAL PROCEDURE

CHAPTER 1
CUSTOMS DECLARATIONS IN WRITING

SECTION 1
GENERAL PROVISIONS

Article 198

1. Where a customs declaration covers two or more articles, the particulars relating to each article shall be regarded as constituting a separate declaration.

2. Component parts of industrial plant coming under a single CN Code shall be regarded as constituting a single item of goods.

Article 199

[1]. Without prejudice to the possible application of penal provisions, the lodging with a customs office of a declaration signed by the declarant or his representative shall render him responsible under the provisions in force for—

— the accuracy of the information given in the declaration,
— the authenticity of the documents attached, and
— compliance with all the obligations relating to the entry of the goods in question under the procedure concerned.

[2. Where the declarant uses data-processing systems to produce his customs declarations, the customs authorities may provide that the handwritten signature may be replaced by another identification technique which may be based on the use of codes. This facility shall be granted only if the technical and administrative conditions laid down by the customs authorities are complied with.

The customs authorities may also provide that declarations produced using customs data-processing systems may be directly authenticated by those systems, in place of the manual or mechanical application of the customs office stamp and the signature of the competent official.

3. Under the conditions and in the manner which they shall determine, the customs authorities may allow some of the particulars of the written declaration referred to in Annex 37 to be replaced by sending these particulars to the customs office designated for that purpose by electronic means, where appropriate in coded form.]

NOTES

Para 1 numbered as such and paras 2, 3 added by Commission Regulation (EC) 3665/93, Art 1, para 11.

Article 200

Documents accompanying a declaration shall be kept by the customs authorities unless the said authorities provide otherwise or unless the declarant requires them for other operations. In the latter case the customs authorities shall take the necessary steps to ensure that the documents in question cannot subsequently be used except in respect of the quantity or value of goods for which they remain valid.

[Article 201

1. The customs declaration shall be lodged at one of the following customs offices:
    (a)   the customs office responsible for the place where the goods were or are to be presented to customs in accordance with the customs rules;
    (b)   the customs office responsible for supervising the place where the exporter is established or where the goods are packed or loaded for export shipment, except in cases provided for in Articles 789, 790, 791 and 794. The customs declaration may be lodged as soon as the goods are presented or available to the customs authorities for control.

2. The customs authorities may allow the customs declaration to be lodged before the declarant is in a position to present the goods, or make them available for control, at the customs office where the customs declaration is lodged or at another customs office or place designated by the customs authorities.

The customs authorities may set a time limit, to be determined according to the circumstances, within which the goods shall be presented or made available. If the goods are not presented or made available within this time limit, the customs declaration shall be deemed not to have been lodged.

The customs declaration may be accepted only after the goods in question have been presented to the customs authorities or have, to the satisfaction of the customs authorities, been made available for control.]

NOTES

Article substituted by Commission Regulation (EC) No 1875/2006, Art 1(17) with effect from 26 December 2006.

Article 202

1. The declaration shall be lodged with the competent customs office during the days and hours appointed for opening.

However, the customs authorities may, at the request of the declarant and at his expense, authorise the declaration to be lodged outside the appointed days and hours.

2. Any declaration lodged with the officials of a customs office in any other place duly designated for that purpose by agreement between the customs authorities and the person concerned shall be considered to have been lodged in the said office.

Article 203

The date of acceptance of the declaration shall be noted thereon.

Article 204

The customs authorities may allow or require the corrections referred to in Article 65 of the Code to be made by the lodging of a new declaration intended to replace the original declaration. In that event, the relevant date for determination of any duties payable and for the application of any other provisions governing the customs procedure in question shall be the date of the acceptance of the original declaration.

SECTION 2
FORMS TO BE USED

Article 205

1. The official model for written declarations to customs by the normal procedure, for the purposes of placing goods under a customs procedure or re-exporting them in accordance with Article 182(3) of the Code, shall be the Single Administrative Document.

2. Other forms may be used for this purpose where the provisions of the customs procedure in question permit.

3. The provisions of paragraphs 1 and 2 shall not preclude—

—   waiver of the written declaration prescribed in Articles 225 to 236 for release for free circulation, export or temporary importation,

—   waiver by the Member States of the form referred to in paragraph 1 where the special provisions laid down in Articles 237 and 238 with regard to consignments by letter or parcel-post apply,

—   use of special forms to facilitate the declaration in specific cases, where the customs authorities so permit,

—   waiver by the Member States of the form referred to in paragraph 1 in the case of existing or future agreements or arrangements concluded between the administrations of two or more Member States with a view to greater simplification of formalities in all or part of the trade between those Member States,

—   use by the persons concerned of loading lists for the completion of Community transit formalities in the case of consignments composed of more than one kind of goods,

—   printing of export, transit or import declarations and documents certifying the Community status of goods not being moved under internal Community transit procedure by means of official or private-sector data-processing systems, if necessary on plain paper, on conditions laid down by the Member States,

—   provision by the Member States to the effect that where a computerised declaration-processing system is used, the declaration, within the meaning of paragraph 1, may take the form of the Single Administrative Document printed out by that system.

4. . . .

5. Where in Community legislation, reference is made to an export, re-export or import declaration or a declaration placing goods under another customs procedure, Member States may not require any administrative documents other than those which are—

—   expressly created by Community acts or provided for by such acts,

- required under the terms of international conventions compatible with the Treaty,
- required from operators to enable them to qualify, at their request, for an advantage or specific facility,
- required, with due regard for the provisions of the Treaty, for the implementation of specific regulations which cannot be implemented solely by the use of the document referred to in paragraph 1.

NOTES

Para 4: repealed by Commission Regulation (EC) 3665/93, Art 1, para 12.

Article 206

The Single Administrative Document form shall, where necessary, also be used during the transitional period laid down in the Act of Accession of Spain and Portugal in connection with trade between the Community as constituted on 31 December 1985 and Spain or Portugal and between those two last-mentioned Member States in goods still liable to certain customs duties and charges having equivalent effect or which remain subject to other measures laid down by the Act of Accession.

For the purposes of the first paragraph, copy 2 or where applicable copy 7 of the forms used for trade with Spain and Portugal or trade between those Member States shall be destroyed.

It shall also be used in trade in Community goods between parts of the customs territory of the Community to which the provisions of Council Directive 77/388/EEC[1] apply and parts of that territory where those provisions do not apply, or in trade between parts of that territory where those provisions do not apply.

[1] 1 OJ L 145, 13.6.77, p 1.

Article 207

Without prejudice to Article 205(3), the customs administrations of the Member States may in general, for the purpose of completing export or import formalities, dispense with the production of one or more copies of the Single Administrative Document intended for use by the authorities of that Member State, provided that the information in question is available on other media.

Article 208

1. The Single Administrative Document shall be presented in subsets containing the number of copies required for the completion of formalities relating to the customs procedure under which the goods are to be placed.

2. Where the Community transit procedure or the common transit procedure is preceded or followed by another customs procedure, a subset containing the number of copies required for the completion of formalities relating to the transit procedure and the preceding or following procedure may be presented.

3. The subsets referred to in paragraphs 1 and 2 shall be taken from—
- either the full set of eight copies, in accordance with the specimen contained in Annex 31,
- or, particularly in the event of production by means of a computerised system for processing declarations, two successive sets of four copies, in accordance with the specimen contained in Annex 32.

4. Without prejudice to Articles 205(3), 222 to 224 or 254 to 289, the declaration forms may be supplemented, where appropriate, by one or more continuation forms presented in subsets containing the declaration copies needed to complete the formalities relating to the customs procedure under which the goods are to be placed.

Those copies needed in order to complete the formalities relating to preceding or subsequent customs procedures may be attached where appropriate.

The continuation subsets shall be taken from—

— either a set of eight copies, in accordance with the specimen contained in Annex 33,

— or two sets of four copies, in accordance with the specimen contained in Annex 34.

The continuation forms shall be an integral part of the Single Administrative Document to which they relate.

5. By way of derogation from paragraph 4, the customs authorities may provide that continuation forms shall not be used where a computerised system is used to produce such declarations.

Article 209

1. Where Article 208(2) is applied, each party involved shall be liable only as regards the particulars relating to the procedure for which he applied as declarant, principal or as the representative of one of these.

2. For the purposes of paragraph 1, where the declarant uses a Single Administrative Document issued during the preceding customs procedure, he shall be required, prior to lodging his declaration, to verify the accuracy of the existing particulars for the boxes for which he is responsible and their applicability to the goods in question and the procedure applied for, and to supplement them as necessary.

In the cases referred to in the first subparagraph, the declarant shall immediately inform the customs office where the declaration is lodged of any discrepancy found between the goods in question and the existing particulars. In this case the declarant shall then draw up his declaration on fresh copies of the Single Administrative Document.

Article 210

Where the Single Administrative Document is used to cover several successive customs procedures, the customs authorities shall satisfy themselves that the particulars given in the declarations relating to the various procedures in question all agree.

Article 211

The declaration must be drawn up in one of the official languages of the Community which is acceptable to the customs authorities of the Member State where the formalities are carried out.

If necessary, the customs authorities of the Member State of destination may require from the declarant or his representative in that Member State a translation of the declaration into the official language of the latter. The translation shall replace the corresponding particulars in the declaration in question.

By way of derogation from the preceding subparagraph, the declaration shall be drawn up in an official language of the Community acceptable to the Member State of destination in all cases where the declaration in the latter Member State is made on copies other than those initially presented to the customs office of the Member State.

Article 212

1. The Single Administrative Document must be completed in accordance with the explanatory note in Annex 37 and any additional rules laid down in other Community legislation.

2. The customs authorities shall ensure that users have ready access to copies of the explanatory note referred to in paragraph 1.

3. The customs administrations of each Member State may, if necessary, supplement the explanatory note.

Part III

[4. The Member States shall notify the Commission of the list of particulars they require for each of the procedures referred to in Annex 37. The Commission shall publish the list of those particulars.]

NOTES

Para 1: words to be inserted by Commission Regulation (EC) No 1875/2006, Art 1(18) with effect from 1 July 2009.

Para 4 inserted by Commission Regulation (EC) 2286/2003, Art 1, para 3 with effect from 1 January 2006. However, member states may implement the legislation before that date.

Article 213

The codes to be used in completing the forms referred to in Article 205(1) are listed in Annex 38.

[The Member States shall notify the Commission of the list of national codes used for boxes 37 (second subdivision), 44 and 47 (first subdivision). The Commission shall publish the list of those codes.]

NOTES

Second paragraph inserted by Commission Regulation (EC) 2286/2003, Art 1, para 4 with effect from 1 January 2006. However, member states may implement the legislation before that date.

Article 214

In cases where the rules require supplementary copies of the form referred to in Article 205(1), the declarant may use additional sheets or photocopies of the said form for this purpose.

Such additional sheets or photocopies must be signed by the declarant, presented to the customs authorities and endorsed by the latter under the same conditions as the Single Administrative Document. They shall be accepted by the customs authorities as if they were original documents provided that their quality and legibility are considered satisfactory by the said authorities.

Article 215

1. The forms referred to in Article 205(1) shall be printed on self-copying paper dressed for writing purposes and weighing at least 40 g/m^2. The paper must be sufficiently opaque for the information on one side not to affect the legibility of the information on the other side and its strength should be such that in normal use it does not easily tear or crease.

The paper shall be white for all copies. However, on the copies used for Community transit (1, 4 and 5), boxes 1 (first and third subdivisions), 2, 3, 4, 5, 6, 8, 15, 17, 18, 19, 21, 25, 27, 31, 32, 33 (first subdivision on the left), 35, 38, 40, 44, 50, 51, 52, 53, 55 and 56 shall have a green background.

The forms shall be printed in green ink.

2. The boxes are based on a unit of measurement of one tenth of an inch horizontally and one sixth of an inch vertically. The subdivisions are based on a unit of measurement of one-tenth of an inch horizontally.

3. A colour marking of the different copies shall be effected in the following manner—

    (a)   on forms conforming to the specimens shown in Annexes 31 and 33—

        — copies 1, 2, 3 and 5 shall have at the right hand edge a continuous margin, coloured respectively red, green, yellow and blue,

        — copies 4, 6, 7 and 8 shall have at the right hand edge a broken margin coloured respectively blue, red, green and yellow;

(b)   on forms conforming to the specimens shown in Annexes 32 and 34, copies 1/6, 2/7, 3/8 and 4/5 shall have at the right hand edge a continuous margin and to the right of this a broken margin coloured respectively red, green, yellow and blue.

The width of these margins shall be approximately 3 mm. The broken margin shall comprise a series of squares with a side measurement of 3 mm each one separated by 3 mm.

4.   The copies on which the particulars contained in the forms shown in Annexes 31 and 33 must appear by a self-copying process are shown in Annex 35.

The copies on which the particulars contained in the forms shown in Annexes 32 and 34 must appear by a self-copying process are shown in Annex 36.

5.   The forms shall measure 210 x 297 mm with a maximum tolerance as to length of 5 mm less and 8 mm more.

6.   The customs administrations of the Member States may require that the forms show the name and address of the printer or a mark enabling the printer to be identified. They may also make the printing of the forms conditional on prior technical approval.

NOTES

Para 1: words in square brackets substituted by Commission Regulation (EC) 2787/2000, Art 1, para 2.

SECTION 3
PARTICULARS REQUIRED ACCORDING TO THE CUSTOMS PROCEDURE CONCERNED

[Article 216

The list of boxes to be used for declarations for placing goods under a particular customs procedure using the single administrative document is set out in Annex 37.

NOTES

Substituted by Commission Regulation (EC) 2286/2003, Art 1, para 5 with effect from 1 January 2006. However, member states may implement the legislation before that date.

For the position before 1 January 2006, see Appendix to Part IV.

New para to be inserted by Commission Regulation (EC) No 1875/2006, Art 1(19) with effect from 1 July 2009.

Article 217

The particulars required when one of the forms referred to in Article 205(2) is used depend on the form in question. They shall be supplemented where appropriate by the provisions relating to the customs procedure in question.

SECTION 4
DOCUMENTS TO ACCOMPANY THE CUSTOMS DECLARATION

Article 218

1.   The following documents shall accompany the customs declaration for release for free circulation—

(a)   the invoice on the basis of which the customs value of the goods is declared, as required under Article 181;

(b)   where it is required under Article 178, the declaration of particulars for the assessment of the customs value of the goods declared, drawn up in accordance with the conditions laid down in the said Article;

(c) the documents required for the application of preferential tariff arrangements or other measures derogating from the legal rules applicable to the goods declared;

(d) all other documents required for the application of the provisions governing the release for free circulation of the goods declared.

2. The customs authorities may require transport documents or documents relating to the previous customs procedure, as appropriate, to be produced when the declaration is lodged.

Where a single item is presented in two or more packages, they may also require the production of a packing list or equivalent document indicating the contents of each package.

[3. Where goods qualify for the flat rate of duty referred to in Section II(D) of the preliminary provisions of the combined nomenclature or where goods qualify for relief from import duties, the documents referred to in paragraph 1(a), (b) and (c) need not be required unless the customs authorities consider it necessary for the purposes of applying the provisions governing the release of the goods in question for free circulation.]

NOTES

Para 3: substituted by Commission Regulation (EC) 482/96, Art 1, para 1.

Article 219

1. The transit declaration shall be accompanied by the transport document. The office of departure may dispense with the presentation of this document at the time of completion of the formalities. However, the transport document shall be presented at the request of the customs office or any other competent authority in the course of transport.

2. Without prejudice to any applicable simplification measures, the customs document of export/dispatch or re-exportation of the goods from the customs territory of the Community or any document of equivalent effect shall be presented to the office of departure with the transit declaration to which it relates.

3. The customs authorities may, where appropriate, require production of the document relating to the preceding customs procedure.

[Article 220

1. Without prejudice to specific provisions, the documents to accompany the declaration of entry for a customs procedure with economic impact, shall be as follows—

(a) for the customs warehousing procedure—
— type D; the documents laid down in Article 218(1)(a) and (b),
— other than type D; no documents;

(b) for the inward-processing procedure—
— drawback system; the documents laid down in Article 218(1),
— suspension system; the documents laid down in Article 218(1)(a) and (b),

and, where appropriate, the written authorisation for the customs procedure in question or a copy of the application for authorisation where [Article 508(1)] applies;

(c) for processing under customs control the documents laid down in Article 218(1)(a) and (b), and, where appropriate, the written authorisation for the customs procedure in question [or a copy of the application for authorisation where Article 508(1) applies];

(d)   for the temporary importation procedure—
- — with partial relief from import duties; the documents laid down in Article 218(1),
- — with total relief from import duties; the documents laid down in Article 218(1)(a) and (b),

and, where appropriate, the written authorisation for the customs procedure in question [or a copy of the application for authorisation where Article 508(1) applies];

(e)   for the outward-processing procedures, the documents laid down in Article 221(1) and, where appropriate, the written authorisation of the procedure or a copy of the application for authorisation where [Article 508(1)] applies.

2.   Article 218(2) shall apply to declarations of entry for any customs procedure with economic impact.

3.   The customs authorities may allow the written authorisation of the procedure or a copy of the application for authorisation to be kept at their disposal instead of accompanying the declaration.]

NOTES

Substituted by Commission Regulation (EC) 12/97, Art 1, para 3.

Para 1: words in square brackets substituted and inserted by Commission Regulation (EC) 993/2001, Art 1, para 1.

Article 221

1.   The export or re-export declaration shall be accompanied by all documents necessary for the correct application of export duties and of the provisions governing the export of the goods in question.

2.   Article 218(2) shall apply to export or re-export declarations.

[CHAPTER 2
CUSTOMS DECLARATIONS MADE USING A
DATA-PROCESSING TECHNIQUE

Article 222

1.   Where the customs declaration is made by a data-processing technique, the particulars of the written declaration referred to in Annex 37 shall be replaced by sending to the customs office designated for that purpose, with a view to their processing by computer, data in codified form or data made out in any other form specified by the customs authorities and corresponding to the particulars required for written declarations.

2.   A customs declaration made by EDI shall be considered to have been lodged when the EDI message is received by the customs authorities.

Acceptance of a customs declaration made by EDI shall be communicated to the declarant by means of a response message containing at least the identification details of the message received and/or the registration number of the customs declaration and the date of acceptance.

3.   Where the customs declaration is made by EDI, the customs authorities shall lay down the rules for implementing the provisions laid down in Article 247.

4.   Where the customs declaration is made by EDI, the release of the goods shall be notified to the declarant, indicating at least the identification details of the declaration and the date of release.

5.   Where the particulars of the customs declaration are introduced into customs data-processing systems, paragraphs 2, 3 and 4 shall apply *mutatis mutandis*.]

Part III

NOTES

Substituted, together with Arts 223, 224, by Commission Regulation (EC) 3665/93, Art 1, para 13.

[**Article 223**

Where a paper copy of the customs declaration is required for the completion of other formalities, this shall, at the request of the declarant, be produced and authenticated, either by the customs office concerned, or in accordance with the second subparagraph of Article 199(2).]

NOTES

Substituted as noted to Art 222.

[**Article 224**

Under the conditions and in the manner which they shall determine, the customs authorities may, authorise the documents required for the entry of goods for a customs procedure to be made out and transmitted by electronic means.]

NOTES

Substituted as noted to Art 222.

CHAPTER 3
CUSTOMS DECLARATIONS MADE ORALLY OR BY ANY OTHER ACT

SECTION 1
ORAL DECLARATIONS

Article 225

Customs declarations may be made orally for the release for free circulation of the following goods—

    (a)   goods of a non-commercial nature—

        — contained in travellers' personal luggage, or

        — sent to private individuals, or

        — in other cases of negligible importance, where this is authorised by the customs authorities;

    (b)   goods of a commercial nature provided—

        — the total value per consignment and per declarant does not exceed the statistical threshold laid down in the Community provisions in force, and

        — the consignment is not part of a regular series of similar consignments, and

        — the goods are not being carried by an independent carrier as part of a larger freight movement;

    (c)   the goods referred to in Article 229, where these qualify for relief as returned goods;

    (d)   the goods referred to in Article 230(b) and (c).

Article 226

Customs declarations may be made orally for the export of—

    (a)   goods of a non-commercial nature—

        —   contained in travellers' personal luggage, or

        —   sent by private individuals;

(b)   the goods referred to in Article 225(b);

(c)   the goods referred to in Article 231(b) and (c);

(d)   other goods in cases of negligible economic importance, where this is authorised by the customs authorities.

Article 227

1. The customs authorities may provide that Articles 225 and 226 shall not apply where the person clearing the goods is acting on behalf of another person in his capacity as customs agent.

2. Where the customs authorities are not satisfied that the particulars declared are accurate or that they are complete, they may require a written declaration.

Article 228

Where goods declared to customs orally in accordance with Articles 225 and 226 are subject to import or export duty the customs authorities shall issue a receipt to the person concerned against payment of the duty owing.

[The receipt shall include at least the following information—

(a)   a description of the goods which is sufficiently precise to enable them to be identified; this may include the tariff heading;

(b)   the invoice value and/or quantity of the goods, as appropriate;

(c)   a breakdown of the charges collected;

(d)   the date on which it was made out;

(e)   the name of the authority which issued it.

The Member States shall inform the Commission of any standard receipts introduced pursuant to this Article. The Commission shall forward any such information to the other Member States.]

NOTES

Words in square brackets added by Commission Regulation (EC) 12/97, Art 1, para 4.

Article 229

1. Customs declarations may be made orally for the temporary importation of the following goods, in accordance with the conditions laid down in [Article 497(3), second paragraph]—

(a)

        —   animals for transhumance or grazing or for the performance of work or transport and other goods satisfying the conditions laid down in Article 567(b), second paragraph, point (a),

        —   packings referred to in Article 571(a), bearing the permanent, indelible markings of a person established outside the customs territory of the Community,]

        —   radio and television production and broadcasting equipment and vehicles specially adapted for use for the above purpose and their equipment imported by public or private organisations established outside the customs territory of the Community and approved by the customs authorities issuing the authorisation for the procedure to import such equipment and vehicles,

        —   instruments and apparatus necessary for doctors to provide assistance for patients awaiting an organ transplant pursuant to [Article 569];

(b)   the goods referred to in Article 232;

(c)   other goods, where this is authorised by the customs authorities.

2.   The goods referred to in paragraph 1 may also be the subject of an oral declaration for re-exportation discharging a temporary importation procedure.

NOTES

Para 1: words in square brackets substituted by Commission Regulation (EC) 993/2001, Art 1, para 2.

SECTION 2
CUSTOMS DECLARATIONS MADE BY ANY OTHER ACT

Article 230

The following, where not expressly declared to customs, shall be considered to have been declared for release for free circulation by the act referred to in Article 233—

(a)   goods of a non-commercial nature contained in travellers' personal luggage entitled to relief either under Chapter I, Title XI of Council Regulation (EEC) No 918/83[1], or as returned goods;

(b)   goods entitled to relief under Chapter I, Titles IX and X of Council Regulation (EEC) No 918/83;

(c)   means of transport entitled to relief as returned goods.

(d)   goods imported in the context of traffic of negligible importance and exempted from the requirement to be conveyed to a customs office in accordance with Article 38(4) of the Code, provided they are not subject to import duty.

[1] OJ L 105, 23.4.83, p 1.

Article 231

The following, where not expressly declared to customs, shall be considered to have been declared for export by the act referred to in Article 233(b)—

(a)   goods of a non commercial nature not liable for export duty contained in travellers' personal luggage;

(b)   means of transport registered in the customs territory of the Community and intended to be re-imported;

(c)   goods referred to in Chapter II of Council Regulation (EEC) No 918/83;

(d)   other goods in cases of negligible economic importance, where this is authorised by the customs authorities.

Article 232

[1.   The following, where not declared to customs in writing or orally, shall be considered to have been declared for temporary importation by the act referred to in Article 233, subject to Article 579:

(a)   personal effects and goods for sports purposes imported by travellers in accordance with Article 563;

(b)   the means of transport referred to in Articles 556 to 561;

(c)   welfare materials for seafarers used on a vessel engaged in international maritime traffic pursuant to Article 564(a).]

2.   Where they are not declared to customs in writing or orally, the goods referred to in paragraph 1 shall be considered to have been declared for re-exportation discharging the temporary importation procedure by the act referred to in Article 233.

NOTES
Para 1: substituted by Commission Regulation (EC) 993/2001, Art 1, para 3.

Article 233

[1]. For the purposes of Articles 230 to 232, the act which is considered to be a customs declaration may take the following forms—

(a)   in the case of goods conveyed to a customs office or to any other place designated or approved in accordance with Article 38(1)(a) of the Code—

     —   going through the green or "nothing to declare" channel in customs offices where the two-channel system is in operation;

     —   going through a customs office which does not operate the two-channel system without spontaneously making a customs declaration;

     —   affixing a "nothing to declare" sticker or customs declaration disc to the windscreen of passenger vehicles where this possibility is provided for in national provisions;

(b)   in the case of exemption from the obligation to convey goods to customs in accordance with the provisions implementing Article 38(4) of the Code, in the case of export in accordance with Article 231 and in the case of re-exportation in accordance with Article 232(2)—

     —   the sole act of crossing the frontier of the customs territory of the Community.

[2. Where goods covered by point (a) of Article 230, point (a) of Article 231, point (a) of Article 232(1) or Article 232(2) contained in a passenger's baggage are carried by rail unaccompanied by the passenger and are declared to customs without the passenger being present in person, the document referred to in Annex 38a may be used within the terms and limitations set out in it.]

NOTES
Para 1 numbered as such and para 2 added by Commission Regulation (EC) 1762/95, Art 1, para 3.

Article 234

1. Where the conditions of Articles 230 to 232 are fulfilled, the goods shall be considered to have been presented to customs within the meaning of Article 63 of the Code, the declaration to have been accepted and release to have been granted, at the time when the act referred to in Article 233 is carried out.

2. Where a check reveals that the act referred to in Article 233 has been carried out but the goods imported or taken out do not fulfil the conditions in Articles 230 to 232, the goods concerned shall be considered to have been imported or exported unlawfully.

SECTION 3

PROVISIONS COMMON TO SECTIONS 1 AND 2

Article 235

The provisions of Articles 225 to 232 shall not apply to goods in respect of which the payment of refunds or other amounts or the repayment of duties is sought, or which are subject to a prohibition or restriction or to any other special formality.

Part III

Article 236

For the purposes of Sections 1 and 2, "traveller" means—

A. on import—

1   any person temporarily entering the customs territory of the Community, not normally resident there, and

2   any person returning to the customs territory of the Community where he is normally resident, after having been temporarily in a third country;

B. on export—

1   any person temporarily leaving the customs territory of the Community where he is normally resident, and

2   any person leaving the customs territory of the Community after a temporary stay, not normally resident there.

SECTION 4
POSTAL TRAFFIC

Article 237

1.   The following postal consignments shall be considered to have been declared to customs—

A.   for release for free circulation—

(a)   at the time when they are introduced into the customs territory of the Community—

—   postcards and letters containing personal messages only,

—   braille letters,

—   printed matter not liable for import duties, and

—   all other consignments sent by letter or parcel post which are exempt from the obligation to be conveyed to customs in accordance with provisions pursuant to Article 38(4) of the Code;

(b)   at the time when they are presented to customs—

—   consignments sent by letter or parcel post other than those referred to at (a), provided they are accompanied by a [CN22] and/or [CN23] declaration;

B.   for export—

(a)   at the time when they are accepted by the postal authorities, in the case of consignments by letter and parcel post which are not liable to export duties;

(b)   at the time of their presentation to customs, in the case of consignments sent by letter or parcel post which are liable to export duties, provided they are accompanied by a [CN22] and/or a [CN23] declaration.

2.   The consignee, in the cases referred to in paragraph 1A, and the consignor, in the cases referred to in paragraph 1B, shall be considered to be the declarant and, where applicable, the debtor. The customs authorities may provide that the postal administration shall be considered as the declarant and, where applicable, as the debtor.

3.   For the purposes of paragraph 1, goods not liable to duty shall be considered to have been presented to customs within the meaning of Article 63 of the Code, the customs declaration to have been accepted and release granted—

(a)   in the case of imports, when the goods are delivered to the consignee;

(b)   in the case of exports, when the goods are accepted by the postal authorities.

4.   Where a consignment sent by letter or parcel post which is not exempt from the obligation to be conveyed to customs in accordance with provisions pursuant to Article 38(4) of the Code is presented without a [CN22] and/or [CN23] declaration or where such declaration is incomplete, the customs authorities shall determine the form in which the customs declaration is to be made or supplemented.

NOTES
Paras 1, 4: words substituted by Commission Regulation (EC) 1602/2000, Art 1, para 6.

Article 238
Article 237 shall not apply—

— to consignments containing goods for commercial purposes of an aggregate value exceeding the statistical threshold laid down by the Community provisions in force; the customs authorities may lay down higher thresholds,

— to consignments containing goods for commercial purposes which form part of a regular series of like operations,

— where a customs declaration is made in writing, orally or using a data-processing technique,

— to consignments containing the goods referred to in Article 235.

TITLE VIII
EXAMINATION OF THE GOODS, FINDINGS OF THE CUSTOMS OFFICE AND OTHER MEASURES TAKEN BY THE CUSTOMS OFFICE

Article 239
1.   The goods shall be examined in the places designated and during the hours appointed for that purpose by the customs authorities.

2.   However, the customs authorities may, at the request of the declarant, authorise the examination of goods in places or during hours other than those referred to in paragraph 1.

Any costs involved shall be borne by the declarant.

Article 240
1.   Where the customs authorities elect to examine goods they shall so inform the declarant or his representative.

2.   Where they decide to examine a part of the goods only, the customs authorities shall inform the declarant or his representative which items they wish to examine. The customs authorities' choice shall be final.

Article 241
1.   The declarant or the person designated by him to be present at the examination of the goods shall render the customs authorities the assistance required to facilitate their work. Should the customs authorities consider the assistance rendered unsatisfactory, they may require the declarant to designate another person able to give the necessary assistance.

2.   Where the declarant refuses to be present at the examination of the goods or to designate a person able to give the assistance which the customs authorities consider necessary, the said authorities shall set a deadline for compliance, unless they consider that such an examination may be dispensed with.

If, on expiry of the deadline, the declarant has not complied with the requirements of the customs authorities, the latter, for the purpose of applying Article 75(a) of the Code, shall proceed with the examination of the goods, at the declarant's risk and

Part III

expense, calling if necessary on the services of an expert or any other person designated in accordance with the provisions in force.

3. The findings made by the customs authorities during the examination carried out under the conditions referred to in the preceding paragraph shall have the same validity as if the examination had been carried out in the presence of the declarant.

4. Instead of the measures laid down in paragraphs 2 and 3, the customs authorities shall have the option of deeming a declaration invalid where it is clear that the declarant's refusal to be present at the examination of the goods or to designate a person able to give the necessary assistance neither prevents, nor seeks to prevent, those authorities from finding that the rules governing the entry of the goods for the customs procedure concerned have been breached, and neither evades, nor seeks to evade, the provisions of Article 66(1) or Article 80(2) of the Code.

Article 242

1. Where the customs authorities decide to take samples, they shall so inform the declarant or his representative.

2. Samples shall be taken by the customs authorities themselves. However, they may ask that this be done under their supervision by the declarant or a person designated by him.

Samples shall be taken in accordance with the methods laid down in the provisions in force.

3. The quantities taken as samples should not exceed what is needed for analysis or more detailed examination, including possible check analysis.

Article 243

1. The declarant or the person designated by him to be present at the taking of samples shall render the customs authorities all the assistance needed to facilitate the operation.

[2. Where the declarant refuses to be present at the taking of samples or to designate a person to attend, or where he fails to render the customs authorities all the assistance needed to facilitate the operation, the provisions of the second sentence of Article 241(1) and of Article 241(2), (3) and (4) shall apply.]

NOTES

Para 2: substituted by Commission Regulation (EC) 482/96, Art 1, para 2.

Article 244

Where the customs authorities take samples for analysis or more detailed examination, they shall authorise the release of the goods in question without waiting for the results of the analysis or examination, unless there are other grounds for not doing so, and provided that, where a customs debt has been or is likely to be incurred, the duties in question have already been entered in the accounts and paid or secured.

NOTES

Modification: see the VAT Regulations 1995, SI 1995/2518 reg 121C: modification of this Article in relation to any VAT chargeable on the importation of goods from places outside the member states).

Article 245

1. The quantities taken by the customs office as samples shall not be deducted from the quantity declared.

2. Where an export or outward processing declaration is concerned, the declarant shall be authorised, where circumstances permit, to replace the quantities of goods taken as samples by identical goods, in order to make up the consignment.

Article 246

1. Unless destroyed by the analysis or more detailed examination, the samples taken shall be returned to the declarant at his request and expense once they no longer need to be kept by the customs authorities, in particular after all the declarant's means of appeal against the decision taken by the customs authorities on the basis of the results of that analysis or more detailed examination have been exhausted.

2. Where the declarant does not ask for samples to be returned, they may either be destroyed or kept by the customs authorities. In specific cases, however, the customs authorities may require the declarant to remove any samples that remain.

Article 247

1. Where the customs authorities verify the declarations and accompanying documents or examines the goods, they shall indicate, at least in the copy of the declaration retained by the said authorities, or in a document attached thereto, the basis and results of any such verification or examination. In the case of partial examination of the goods, particulars of the consignment examined shall also be given.

Where appropriate, the customs authorities shall also indicate in the declaration that the declarant or his representative was absent.

2. Should the result of the verification of the declaration and accompanying documents or examination of the goods not be in accordance with the particulars given in the declaration, the customs authorities shall specify, at least in the copy of the declaration retained by the said authorities, or in a document attached thereto, the particulars to be taken into account for the purposes of the application of charges on the goods in question and, where appropriate, calculating any refunds or other amounts payable on exportation, and for applying the other provisions governing the customs procedure for which the goods are entered.

3. The findings of the customs authorities shall indicate, where appropriate, the means of identification adopted. They shall be dated and bear the particulars needed to identify the official issuing them.

4. Where the customs authorities neither verify the declaration nor examine the goods, they need not endorse the declaration or attached document referred to in paragraph 1.

Article 248

1. The granting of release shall give rise to the entry in the accounts of the import duties determined according to the particulars in the declaration. Where the customs authorities consider that the checks which they have undertaken may enable an amount of customs duties higher than that resulting from the particulars made in the declaration to be assessed, they shall further require the lodging of a security sufficient to cover the difference between the amount according to the particulars in the declaration and the amount which may finally be payable on the goods. However, the declarant may request the immediate entry in the accounts of the amount of duties to which the goods may ultimately be liable instead of lodging this security.

2. Where, on the basis of the checks which they have carried out, the customs authorities assess an amount of import duties different from the amount which results from the particulars in the declaration, the release of the goods shall give rise to the immediate entry in the accounts of the amount thus assessed.

3. Where the customs authorities have doubts about whether or not a prohibition or restriction applies and this cannot be resolved until the results of the checks the authorities have carried out are available, the goods in question cannot be released.

[4. Notwithstanding paragraph 1, the customs authorities may refrain from taking security in respect of goods which are the subject of a drawing request on a tariff quota if they determine, at the time when the declaration for release for free circulation is accepted, that the tariff quota in question is non-critical within the meaning of Article 308c.]

NOTES

Para 4: added by Commission Regulation (EC) 1427/97, Art 1, para 1.

Modification: see the VAT Regulations 1995, SI 1995/2518 reg 121C: modification of this Article in relation to any VAT chargeable on the importation of goods from places outside the member states).

Article 249

1.   The customs authorities shall determine the form of release, taking due account of the place in which the goods are located and of the special arrangements for their supervision.

2.   Where the declaration is made in writing, a reference to the release and its date shall be made on the declaration or, where applicable, a document attached, and a copy shall be returned to the declarant.

Article 250

1.   Where the customs authorities have been unable to grant release for one of the reasons specified in the second or third indent of Article 75(a) of the Code, they shall give the declarant a time limit to regularise the situation of the goods.

2.   Where, in the circumstances referred to in the second indent of Article 75(a) of the Code, the declarant has not produced the requisite documents within the time limit referred to in paragraph 1, the declaration in question shall be deemed invalid and the customs office shall cancel it. The provisions of Article 66(3) of the Code shall apply.

3.   In the circumstances referred to in the third indent of Article 75(a) of the Code, and without prejudice to any measures taken under the first subparagraph of Article 66(1) or Article 182 of the Code, where the declarant has neither paid nor guaranteed the duties due within the time limit referred to in paragraph 1, the customs authorities may start the preliminary formalities for the sale of the goods. In this case the goods shall be sold unless the requisite conditions have been fulfilled in the interim, if necessary by forced sale where the law of the Member State of the authorities in question so permits. The customs authorities shall inform the declarant thereof.

The customs authorities may, at the risk and expense of the declarant, transfer the goods in question to special premises under their supervision.

Article 251

By way of derogation from Article 66(2) of the Code, a customs declaration may be invalidated after the goods have been released, as provided below—

1.   where it is established that the goods have been declared in error for a customs procedure entailing the payment of import duties instead of being placed under another customs procedure, the customs authorities shall invalidate the declaration if a request to that effect is made within three months of the date of acceptance of the declaration provided that—

— any use of the goods has not contravened the conditions of the customs procedure under which they should have been placed,

— when the goods were declared, they were intended to be placed under another customs procedure, all the requirements of which they fulfilled, and

— the goods are immediately entered for the customs procedure for which they were actually intended.

The declaration placing the goods under the latter customs procedure shall take effect from the date of acceptance of the invalidated declaration.

The customs authorities may permit the three-month period to be exceeded in duly substantiated exceptional cases.

[1a.   Where it is established that the goods have been declared in error, instead of other goods, for a customs procedure entailing the obligation to pay import duties, the customs authorities shall invalidate the declaration if a request to that effect is made within three months of the date of acceptance of the declaration, provided that—

— the goods originally declared—

(i)   have not been used other than as authorised in their original status; and

(ii)   have been restored to their original status;

and that

— the goods which ought to have been declared for the customs procedure originally intended;

(i)   could, when the original declaration was lodged, have been presented to the same customs office: and

(ii)   have been declared for the same customs procedure as that originally intended.

The customs authorities may allow the time limit referred to above to be exceeded in duly substantiated exceptional cases;]

[1b.   in the case of mail order goods which are returned, the customs authorities shall invalidate the declarations of release for free circulation if a request to that effect is made within three months of the date of acceptance of the declaration, provided that the goods have been exported to the original supplier's address or to another address indicated by the said supplier;]

[1c.   Where a retroactive authorisation is granted in accordance with:

— Article 294 for release for free circulation with a favourable tariff treatment or at a reduced or zero rate of duty on account of the end-use of the goods, or

— Article 508 for a customs procedure with economic impact.]

2.   where the goods have been declared for export or for the outward processing procedure, the declaration shall be invalidated provided that—

(a)   in the case of goods which are subject to export duty, to an application for the repayment of import duty, to refunds or other export amounts or to other special measures on export—

— the declarant provides the customs office of export with evidence that the goods have not left the customs territory of the Community,

— the declarant returns to the said office all copies of the customs declaration, together with any other documents issued to him on acceptance of the declaration,

— the declarant provides the customs office of export with evidence that any refunds and other amounts granted on the strength of the export declaration for the goods in question have been repaid or that the necessary measures have been taken by the departments concerned to ensure that they are not paid, and

— the declarant, in accordance with the provisions in force, complies with any other obligations laid down by the customs office of export to regularise the position of the goods.

Invalidation of the declaration shall entail cancellation of any adjustments made on an export licence or advance-fixing certificate presented in support of the declaration.

Where the goods declared for export are required to leave the customs territory of the Community by a specified time limit, failure to comply with that time limit shall entail invalidation of the relevant declaration;

[(b) in the case of other goods:

    (i) the customs office of export has been informed, in accordance with Article 792a, that the goods declared have not left the customs territory of the Community;

    (ii) after a period of 90 days from the date of release of the goods for export, the goods have not left the customs territory of the Community, or sufficient evidence of such export cannot be provided in accordance with Article 792b(2).]

3. Insofar as the re-export of the goods entails the lodging of a declaration, (2) above shall apply *mutatis mutandis*.

4. Where Community goods have been placed under the customs warehousing procedure within the meaning of Article 98(1)(b) of the Code, invalidation of the declaration of entry for that procedure may be requested and effected provided that the measures provided for in the relevant legislation in the event of failure to comply with the treatment or use prescribed have been taken.

If, on the expiry of the period laid down for the goods to remain under the customs warehousing procedure, no application has been made for their assignment to a treatment or use provided for in the relevant legislation, the customs authorities shall take the measures provided for in that legislation.

NOTES

Para 1a: inserted by Commission Regulation (EC) 3665/93, Art 1, para 15.

Para 1b: inserted by Commission Regulation (EC) 1427/97, Art 1, para 2.

Para 1c: inserted by Commission Regulation (EC) 993/2001, Art 1, para 4.

Para 2: sub-para (b) substituted by Commission Regulation (EC) No 1875/2006, Art 1(20) with effect from 26 December 2006.

[Article 252

Where the customs authorities sell Community goods in accordance with point (b) of Article 75 of the Code, this shall be done in accordance with the procedures in force in the Member States.]

NOTES

Substituted by Commission Regulation (EC) 3665/93, Art 1, para 16.

TITLE IX
SIMPLIFIED PROCEDURES

[CHAPTER 1
GENERAL PROVISIONS]

NOTES

Chapter heading: substituted by Commission Regulation (EC) 3665/93, Art 1, para 17.

Article 253

1. The procedure for incomplete declarations shall allow the customs authorities to accept, in a duly justified case, a declaration which does not contain all the particulars required, or which is not accompanied by all documents necessary for the customs procedure in question.

2. The simplified declaration procedure shall enable goods to be entered for the customs procedure in question on presentation of a simplified declaration with subsequent presentation of a supplementary declaration which may be of a general, periodic or recapitulative nature, as appropriate.

3. The local clearance procedure shall enable the entry of goods for the customs procedure in question to be carried out at the premises of the person concerned or at other places designated or approved by the customs authorities.

[Article 253a

Where a simplified procedure is applied using data-processing systems to produce customs declarations or using a data-processing technique, the provisions referred to in Articles 199(2) and (3), 222, 223 and 224 shall apply *mutatis mutandis*.]

NOTES

Inserted by Commission Regulation (EC) 3665/93, Art 1, para 18.

CHAPTER 2
DECLARATIONS FOR RELEASE FOR FREE CIRCULATION

SECTION 1
INCOMPLETE DECLARATIONS

Article 254

[Declarations for release for free circulation which the customs authorities may accept, at the declarant's request, without their containing some of the particulars referred to in Annex 37 shall contain at least the particulars referred to in boxes 1 (first and second subdivisions), 14, 21 (nationality), 31, 37, 40 and 54 of the single administrative document and:]

— a description of the goods in terms that are sufficiently precise to enable the customs authorities to determine immediately and unambiguously the Combined Nomenclature heading or subheading concerned,

— where the goods are liable to ad *valorem* duties, their value for customs purposes, or, where it appears that the declarant is not in a position to declare this value, a provisional indication of value which is considered acceptable by the customs authorities, due account being taken in particular of the information available to the declarant,

— any further particulars considered necessary by the customs authorities in order to identify the goods, implement the provisions governing their

Part III

release for free circulation and determine the amount of any security required before the goods may be released.

NOTES

Introductory wording substituted by Commission Regulation (EC) 2286/2003, Art 1, para 6 with effect from 1 January 2006. However, member states may implement the legislation before that date.

Article to be substituted by Commission Regulation (EC) No 1875/2006, Art 1(21) with effect from 1 July 2009.

Article 255

1. Declarations for release for free circulation which the customs authorities may accept at the declarant's request without their being accompanied by certain of the necessary supporting documents shall be accompanied at least by those documents which must be produced before the goods declared can be released for free circulation.

2. By way of derogation from paragraph 1, a declaration not accompanied by one or more of the documents required before the goods can be released for free circulation may be accepted once it is established to the satisfaction of the customs authorities that—

(a)   the document concerned exists and is valid;

(b)   it could not be annexed to the declaration for reasons beyond the declarant's control;

(c)   any delay in accepting the declaration would prevent the release of the goods for free circulation or make them liable to a higher rate of duty.

Data relating to missing documents shall in all cases be indicated in the declaration.

Article 256

1. The period allowed by the customs authorities to the declarant for the communication of particulars or production of documents missing at the time when the declaration was accepted may not exceed one month from the date of such acceptance.

[In the case of a document required for the application of a reduced or zero rate of import duty, where the customs authorities have good reason to believe that the goods covered by the incomplete declaration may qualify for such reduced or zero rate of duty, a period longer than that provided for in the first subparagraph may, at the declarant's request, be granted for the production of the document, if justified in the circumstances. That period may not exceed four months from the date of acceptance of the declaration. It cannot be extended.]

Where the missing particulars to be communicated or documents to be supplied concern customs value, the customs authorities may, where this proves absolutely necessary, set a longer time limit or extend the period previously set. The total period allowed shall take account of the prescribed periods in force.

[2.   Where a reduced or zero rate of import duty is applicable to goods released for free circulation within tariff quotas or, provided that the levying of normal import duties is not re-introduced, within tariff ceilings or other preferential tariff measures, the benefit of the tariff quota or preferential tariff measure shall only be granted after presentation to the customs authorities of the document on which the granting of the reduced or zero rate is conditional. The document must in any case be presented—

—   before the tariff quota has been exhausted, or

—   in other cases, before the date on which a Community measure re-introduces the levying of normal import duties.]

3. Subject to paragraphs 1 and 2, the document on whose presentation the granting of the reduced or zero rate of import duty is conditional may be produced

after the expiry date of the period for which the reduced or zero rate was set, provided the declaration in respect of the goods in question was accepted before that date.

NOTES

Para 1: words substituted by Commission Regulation (EC) 881/2003 Art 1, para 6.
Para 2: substituted by Commission Regulation (EC) 1427/97, Art 1, para 3.

Article 257

1. The customs authorities' acceptance of an incomplete declaration shall not prevent or delay the release of the goods thus declared, unless other grounds exist for so doing. Without prejudice to the provisions of Article 248, release shall take place in accordance with the conditions laid down in paragraphs 2 to 5 below.

2. Where the late production of particulars or of a supporting document missing at the time when a declaration is accepted cannot affect the amount of duties to which the goods covered by the said declaration are liable, the customs authorities shall immediately enter in the accounts the sum payable, calculated in the usual manner.

3. Where, pursuant to Article 254, a declaration contains a provisional indication of value, the customs authorities shall—

— enter immediately in the accounts the amount of duties determined on the basis of this indication,

— require, if necessary, the lodging of a security adequate to cover the difference between that amount and the amount to which the goods may ultimately be liable.

4. Where, in circumstances other than those referred to in paragraph 3, the late production of particulars or of a supporting document missing at the time when a declaration is accepted may affect the amount of duties to which the goods covered by the said declaration are liable—

(a) if late production of any missing particulars or document may lead to the application of duty at a reduced rate, the customs authorities shall—

— immediately enter in the accounts the import duties payable at the reduced rate,

— require the lodging of a security covering the difference between that sum and the sum which would be payable were the import duties on the goods in question calculated at the normal rate;

(b) if the late production of any missing particulars or document may lead to admission of the goods with total relief from duties, the customs authorities shall require the lodging of a security covering the amount which would be payable were the duties charged at the normal rate.

5. Without prejudice to any subsequent changes which may arise, particularly as a result of the final determination of the customs value, the declarant shall have the option, instead of lodging a security, of requesting the immediate entry in the accounts—

— where the second indent of paragraph 3 or the second indent of paragraph 4(a) applies, of the amount of duties to which the goods may ultimately be liable, or

— where paragraph 4(b) applies, of the amount of duties calculated at the normal rate.

NOTES

Modification: see the VAT Regulations 1995, SI 1995/2518 reg 121C: modification of this Article in relation to any VAT chargeable on the importation of goods from places outside the member states).

Article 258

If, at the expiry of the period referred to in Article 256, the declarant has not supplied the details necessary for the final determination of the customs value of the goods, or has failed to provide the missing particulars or documents, the customs authorities shall immediately enter in the accounts as duties to which the goods in question are subject the amount of the security provided in accordance with the provisions of the second indent of Article 257(3), the second indent of Article 257(4)(a) or Article 257(4)(b).

NOTES

Modification: see the VAT Regulations 1995, SI 1995/2518 reg 121C: modification of this Article in relation to any VAT chargeable on the importation of goods from places outside the member states).

Article 259

An incomplete declaration accepted under the conditions set out in Articles 254 to 257 may be either completed by the declarant or, by agreement with the customs authorities, replaced by another declaration which complies with the conditions laid down in Article 62 of the Code.

In both cases, the operative date for the fixing of any duties and the application of other provisions governing the release of goods for free circulation shall be the date of acceptance of the incomplete declaration.

SECTION 2
SIMPLIFIED DECLARATION PROCEDURE

Article 260

1. The declarant shall, upon written request containing all the necessary information, be authorised in accordance with the conditions and in the manner laid down in Articles 261 and 262, to make the declaration for release for free circulation in a simplified form when goods are presented to customs.

2. Such simplified declaration may be in the form—

— either of an incomplete declaration on a Single Administrative Document, or

— of an administrative or commercial document, accompanied by a request for release for free circulation.

It shall contain at least the particulars necessary for identification of the goods.

3. Where circumstances permit, the customs authorities may allow the request for release for free circulation referred to in the second indent of paragraph 2 to be replaced by a general request in respect of release operations to take place over a given period. A reference to the authorisation granted in response to such general request shall be entered on the commercial or administrative document presented pursuant to paragraph 1.

4. The simplified declaration shall be accompanied by all documents the production of which may be required to secure the release of the goods for free circulation. Article 255(2) shall apply.

5. This Article shall be without prejudice to Article 278.

NOTES

Para 2: to be substituted by Commission Regulation (EC) No 1875/2006, Art 1(22) with effect from 1 July 2009.

Article 261

1.   The authorisation referred to in Article 260 shall be granted to the declarant on condition that it is possible to guarantee an effective check on compliance with import prohibitions or restrictions or other provisions governing release for free circulation.

2.   Such authorisation shall in principle be refused where the person who has made the request—

—   has committed a serious infringement or repeated infringements of customs rules,

—   declares goods for release for free circulation only occasionally.

It may be refused where the person in question is acting on behalf of another person who declares goods for release for free circulation only occasionally.

3.   Without prejudice to Article 9 of the Code, the authorisation may be revoked where the cases referred to in paragraph 2 arise.

[4.   Where the person concerned holds an AEO certificate referred to in point (a) or (c) of Article 14a(1), the customs authorities in all Member States shall examine only whether the authorised economic operator declares goods for release for free circulation only occasionally. All other requirements set out in paragraphs 1 and 2 of this Article shall be deemed to be met.]

NOTES

Para 4: inserted by Commission Regulation (EC) No 1875/2006, Art 1(23) with effect from 1 January 2008.

Article 262

1.   The authorisation referred to in Article 260 shall—

—   designate the customs office(s) competent to accept simplified declarations,

—   specify the form and content of the simplified declarations,

—   specify the goods to which it applies and the particulars which must appear on the simplified declaration for the purposes of identifying the goods,

—   make reference to the security to be provided by the person concerned to cover any customs debt which may arise.

It shall also specify the form and content of the supplementary declarations, and shall set the time limits within which they must be lodged with the customs authority designated for this purpose.

2.   The customs authorities may waive the presentation of the supplementary declaration where the simplified declaration concerns goods the value of which is below the statistical threshold laid down by the Community provisions in force and the simplified declaration already contains all the information needed for release for free circulation.

NOTES

Modification: see the VAT Regulations 1995, SI 1995/2518 reg 121C: modification of this Article in relation to any VAT chargeable on the importation of goods from places outside the member states).

Para 1: to be substituted by Commission Regulation (EC) No 1875/2006, Art 1(24) with effect from 1 July 2009.

Part III

SECTION 3
LOCAL CLEARANCE PROCEDURE

Article 263

Authorisation to use the local clearance procedure shall be granted in accordance with the conditions and in the manner laid down in Articles 264 to 266 to any person wishing to have goods released for free circulation at his premises or at the other places referred to in Article 253 and who submits to the customs authorities a written request to this end containing all the particulars necessary for the grant of the authorisation—

— in respect of goods subject either to the Community or common transit procedure and for which the person referred to above is authorised to use the simplified procedures to be carried out at the office of destination in accordance with [Articles 406, 407 and 408],

— in respect of goods previously placed under a customs procedure with economic impact, without prejudice to Article 278,

— in respect of goods which, after having been presented to customs pursuant to Article 40 of the Code, are consigned to those premises or places in accordance with a transit procedure other than that referred to in the first indent,

— in respect of goods which are brought into the customs territory of the Community with an exemption from the requirement that they be presented to customs, pursuant to Article 41(b) of the Code.

NOTES

Words substituted by Commission Regulation (EC) 2787/2000, Art 1, para 3.

Article 264

1. The authorisation referred to in Article 263 shall be granted provided that—

— the applicant's records enable the customs authorities to carry out effective checks, in particular retrospective checks,

— it is possible to guarantee an effective check on compliance with import or export prohibitions or restrictions or any other provisions governing release for free circulation.

2. Authorisation shall in principle be refused where the applicant—

— has committed a serious infringement or repeated infringements of customs rules,

— declares goods for release for free circulation only occasionally.

[3. Where the person concerned holds an AEO certificate referred to in point (a) or (c) of Article 14a(1), the customs authorities in all Member States shall examine only whether the authorised economic operator declares goods for release for free circulation only occasionally. All other requirements set out in paragraphs 1 and 2 shall be deemed to be met.]

NOTES

New para 3 to be inserted by Commission Regulation (EC) No 1875/2006, Art 1(25) with effect from 1 January 2008.

Article 265

1. Without prejudice to Article 9 of the Code, the customs authorities may refrain from revoking the authorisation when—

— the holder fulfils his obligations within any time limit set by them, or

— the failure to fulfil an obligation is without any real consequence for the correct operation of the procedure.

2. An authorisation shall in principle be revoked where the case referred to in the first indent of Article 264(2) arises.

3. An authorisation may be revoked where the case referred to in the second indent of Article 264(2) arises.

Article 266

[1. To enable the customs authorities to satisfy themselves as to the proper conduct of operations, the holder of the authorisation referred to in Article 263 shall—

(a) in the cases referred to in the first and third indents of Article 263—

    (i) where the goods are released for free circulation upon their arrival at the place designated for that purpose—

        — duly notify the customs authorities of such arrival in the form and the manner specified by them, for the purpose of obtaining release of the goods, and

        — enter the goods in his records;

    (ii) where release for free circulation is preceded by temporary storage of the goods within the meaning of Article 50 of the Code at the same place, before expiry of the time-limit set under Article 49 of the Code—

        — duly notify the customs authorities, in the form and the manner specified by them, of his desire to have the goods released for free circulation, for the purpose of obtaining release of the goods, and

        — enter the goods in his records;

(b) in the cases referred to in the second indent of Article 263—

    — duly notify the customs authorities, in the form and the manner specified by them, of his desire to have the goods released for free circulation, for the purpose of obtaining release of the goods, and

    — enter the goods in his records.

    The notification referred to in the first indent shall not be required where the goods to be released for free circulation have already been placed under the customs warehousing procedure in a type D warehouse;

(c) in the cases referred to in the fourth indent of Article 263, upon arrival of the goods at the place designated for that purpose—

    — enter the goods in his records;

(d) make available to the customs authorities, from the time of the entry in the records referred to in points (a), (b) and (c), all documents, the production of which is required for the application of the provisions governing release for free circulation.]

2. On condition that checks on the proper conduct of operations are not thereby affected, the customs authorities may—

[(a) permit the notification referred to in points (a) and (b) of paragraph 1 to be effected as soon as the arrival of the goods becomes imminent;]

(b) in certain special circumstances, where the nature of the goods in question and the rapid turnover so warrant, exempt the holder of the authorisation from the requirement to notify the competent customs office of each arrival of goods, provided that he supplies the said office with all the information it considers necessary to enable it to exercise its right to examine the goods should the need arise.

In this case, entry of the goods in the records of the person concerned shall be equivalent to release.

[3. The entry in the records referred to in points (a), (b) and (c) of paragraph 1 may be replaced by any other formality offering similar guarantees stipulated by the customs authorities. The entry shall indicate the date on which it is made and the particulars necessary for identification of the goods.]

NOTES

Para 1: substituted by Commission Regulation (EC) 2193/94, Art 1, para 1.

Para 2: sub-para (a) substituted by Commission Regulation (EC) 2193/94, Art 1, para 1.

Para 3: added by Commission Regulation (EC) 2193/94, Art 1, para 1.

Para 3 to be substituted by Commission Regulation (EC) No 1875/2006, Art 1(26) with effect from 1 July 2009.

Article 267

The authorisation referred to in Article 263 shall lay down the specific rules for the operation of the procedure and in particular shall stipulate—

— the goods to which it applies,
— the form of the obligations referred to in Article 266 and the reference to the guarantee to be provided by the person concerned,
— the time of release of the goods,
— the time limit within which the supplementary declaration must be lodged with the competent customs office designated for that purpose,
— the conditions under which goods are to be covered by general, periodic or recapitulative declarations, as appropriate.

CHAPTER 3
DECLARATIONS FOR A CUSTOMS PROCEDURE WITH ECONOMIC IMPACT

SECTION 1
ENTRY FOR A CUSTOMS PROCEDURE WITH ECONOMIC IMPACT

SUBSECTION 1
ENTRY FOR THE CUSTOMS WAREHOUSING PROCEDURE

A.

Incomplete declarations

Article 268

1. Declarations for the customs warehousing procedure which the customs office of entry may accept at the declarant's request without their containing some of the particulars referred to in Annex 37 shall contain at least the particulars necessary for identification of the goods to which the declaration relates, including their quantity.

2. Articles 255, 256 and 259 shall apply *mutatis mutandis*.

3. This Article shall not apply to declarations for the procedure for the Community agricultural products referred to in [Article 524].

NOTES

Para 3: words in square brackets substituted by Commission Regulation (EC) 993/2001, Art 1, para 5.

Para 1 to be substituted by Commission Regulation (EC) No 1875/2006, Art 1(27) with effect from 1 July 2009.

B.
Simplified declaration procedure

Article 269

1. The declarant shall, upon request, be authorised, in accordance with the conditions and in the manner laid down in Article 270, to make the declaration of entry for the procedure in a simplified form when goods are presented to customs.

Such simplified declaration may be in the form—

— either of an incomplete declaration of the type referred to in Article 268, or

— of an administrative or commercial document, accompanied by a request for entry for the procedure;

It shall contain the particulars referred to in Article 268(1).

2. Where this procedure is applied in a type D warehouse the simplified declaration shall also include the nature of the goods concerned, in sufficient detail to permit their immediate and unambiguous classification, and their customs value.

[3. The procedure referred to in paragraph 1 shall not apply to Type F warehouses nor to the entry for the procedure of the Community agricultural products referred to in [Article 524] in any type of warehouse.]

[4. The procedure referred to in the second indent of paragraph 1 shall apply to Type B warehouses except that it shall not be possible to use a commercial document. Where the administrative document does not contain all the particulars shown in Annex 37, Title I(B), these should be supplied on the accompanying application.]

NOTES

Para 3: substituted by Commission Regulation (EC) 3665/93, Art 1, para 19; words in square brackets substituted by Commission Regulation (EC) 993/2001, Art 1, para 5.

Para 4 substituted by Commission Regulation (EC) 2286/2003, Art 1, para 7 with effect from 1 January 2006. However, member states may implement the legislation before that date.

Article 270

1. The application referred to in Article 269(1) shall be made in writing and contain all the particulars necessary for the grant of the authorisation.

Where circumstances permit, the application referred to in Article 269(1) may be replaced by a general request in respect of operations to take place over a given period.

In this case the application shall be made under the conditions laid down in [Articles 497, 498 and 499] and shall be submitted with the application to operate the customs warehouse or as a modification to the initial authorisation, to the customs authority which issued the authorisation for the procedure.

2. The authorisation referred to in Article 269(1) shall be granted to the person concerned provided that the proper conduct of operations is not thereby affected.

3. Such authorisation shall in principle be refused where—

— the guarantees necessary for the proper conduct of operations are not given,

— the person concerned enters goods for the procedure only occasionally,

— the person concerned has committed a serious infringement or repeated infringements of customs rules.

4. Without prejudice to Article 9 of the Code, the authorisation may be revoked where the cases referred to in paragraph 3 arise.

NOTES
Para 1: words in square brackets substituted by Commission Regulation (EC) 993/2001, Art 1, para 6.
Para 5 inserted by Commission Regulation (EC) No 1875/2006, Art 1(28) with effect from 1 January 2008.

Article 271

The authorisation referred to in Article 269(1) shall lay down the specific rules for the operation of the procedure, including—

— the office(s) of entry for the procedure,

— the form and content of the simplified declarations.

A supplementary declaration need not be provided.

NOTES
Article to be substituted by Commission Regulation (EC) No 1875/2006, Art 1(29) with effect from 1 July 2009.

C.
Local clearance procedure

Article 272

1. Authorisation to use the local clearance procedure shall be granted according to the conditions and in the manner laid down in paragraph 2 and Articles 273 and 274.

[2. The local clearance procedure shall not apply to type B and F warehouses nor to the entry of the Community agricultural products referred to in [Article 524] for the procedure in any type of warehouse.

3. Article 270 shall apply *mutatis mutandis*.]

NOTES
Paras 2, 3: substituted for original para 2 by Commission Regulation (EC) 1762/95, Art 1, para 4.
Para 2: words in square brackets substituted by Commission Regulation (EC) 993/2001, Art 1, para 7.

Article 273

1. In order to allow the customs authorities to ensure the proper conduct of operations, the holder of by the authorisation shall, upon arrival of the goods at the place designated for that purpose—

(a) duly notify such arrival to the supervising office in the form and manner specified by it;

(b) to make entries in the stock records;

(c) keep at the disposal of the supervising office all documents concerning the entry of the goods for the procedure.

The entry in the stock records referred to in (b) shall contain at least some of the particulars used to identify the goods commercially, including their quantity.

2. Article 266(2) shall apply.

Article 274

The authorisation referred to in Article 272(1) shall lay down the specific rules for the operation of the procedure and shall specify in particular—

— the goods to which it applies,
— the form of the obligations referred to in Article 273,
— the time of release of the goods.

A supplementary declaration need not be required.

SUBSECTION 2
ENTRY FOR THE INWARD PROCESSING, PROCESSING UNDER CUSTOMS CONTROL OR TEMPORARY IMPORTATION PROCEDURES

A.
Incomplete declarations

Article 275

[1. Declarations of entry for a customs procedure with economic impact other than outward processing or customs warehousing which the customs office of entry for the procedure may accept, at the declarant's request, without their containing some of the particulars referred to in Annex 37 or without their being accompanied by certain documents referred to in Article 220 shall contain at least the particulars referred to in boxes 1 (first and second subdivisions), 14, 21 (nationality), 31, 37, 40 and 54 of the single administrative document and, in box 44, a reference to the authorisation, or a reference to the application where Article 508(1) applies.]

2. Articles 255, 256 and 259 shall apply *mutatis mutandis*.

3. In cases of entry for the inward processing procedure, drawback system, Articles 257 and 258 shall also apply *mutatis mutandis*.

NOTES

Para 1 substituted by Commission Regulation (EC) 2286/2003, Art 1, para 8 with effect from 1 January 2006. However, member states may implement the legislation before that date.

Para 1 to be substituted by Commission Regulation (EC) No 1875/2006, Art 1(30) with effect from 1 July 2009.

B.
Simplified declaration and local clearance procedures

Article 276

The provisions of Articles 260 to 267 and of Article 270 shall apply *mutatis mutandis* to goods declared for the customs procedures with economic impact covered by this subsection.

SUBSECTION 3
GOODS DECLARED FOR THE OUTWARD PROCESSING PROCEDURE

Article 277

The provisions of Articles 279 to 289 applying to goods declared for export shall apply *mutatis mutandis* to goods declared for export under the outward processing procedure.

[SUBSECTION 4
COMMON PROVISIONS

Article 277a

Where two or more authorisations concerning customs procedures with economic impact are granted to the same person, and one procedure is discharged by the entry

1513

for another procedure using the local clearance procedure, a supplementary declaration need not be required.]

NOTES

Inserted by Commission Regulation (EC) 993/2001, Art 1, para 9.

SECTION 2
DISCHARGE OF A CUSTOMS PROCEDURE WITH ECONOMIC IMPACT

Article 278

1. In cases of discharge of a customs procedure with economic impact other than the outward processing and customs warehousing procedures, the simplified procedures for release for free circulation, export and re-exportation may be applied. In the case of re-exportation, the provisions of Articles 279 to 289 shall apply *mutatis mutandis*.

2. The simplified procedures referred to in Articles 254 to 267 may be applied to release of goods for free circulation under the outward processing procedure.

3. In cases of discharge of the customs warehousing procedure, the simplified procedures for release for free circulation, export or re-export may be applied.

However—

(a) for goods entered for the procedure in a type F warehouse no simplified procedure may be authorised;

(b) for goods entered for the procedure in a type B warehouse only incomplete declarations and the simplified declaration procedure shall apply;

(c) issue of an authorisation for a type D warehouse shall entail the automatic application of the local clearance procedure for release for free circulation.

However, in cases where the person concerned wishes to benefit from application of items of charge which cannot be checked without a physical examination of the goods, this procedure may not be applied. In this case, other procedures involving presentation of the goods to customs may be used;

[(d) no simplified procedure shall apply for Community agricultural goods referred to in Article 524 entered for the customs warehousing procedure.]

NOTES

Para 3: words in square brackets substituted by Commission Regulation (EC) 993/2001, Art 1, para 10.

CHAPTER 4
EXPORT DECLARATIONS

[**Article 279**

1. The formalities to be carried out at the customs office of export as provided for in Article 792 may be simplified in accordance with this Chapter.

2. Articles 792 (4), 792a, 792b, 793 to 793c and, where appropriate, Articles 796a to 796e, shall apply to this Chapter.]

NOTES
Article substituted by Commission Regulation (EC) No 1875/2006, Art 1(31) with effect from 26 December 2006.

SECTION 1
INCOMPLETE DECLARATIONS
Article 280
[1. Export declarations which the customs office may accept, at the declarant's request, without their containing some of the particulars referred to in Annex 37 shall contain at least the particulars referred to in boxes 1 (first and second subdivisions), 2, 14, 17a, 31, 33, 38, 44 and 54 of the single administrative document and any further information considered necessary in order to identify the goods, to apply the provisions governing their export or to determine the amount of any security required before the goods may be exported.

Where the goods are liable for export duties or subject to any other measures provided for under the common agricultural policy, those export declarations shall contain all the information required for the proper application of such duties or measures.

2. The customs authorities may allow the declarant not to complete boxes 17a and 33 on condition that he declares that export of the goods in question is not subject to prohibitions or restrictions and the customs authorities have no reason for doubt in this respect and that the description of the goods allows the Combined Nomenclature classification to be determined immediately and unambiguously.]

3. Copy No 3 shall include one of the following endorsements in box 44—
— Exportación simplificada
— Forenklet udførsel
— Vereinfachte Ausfuhr
— Απλουσευμ νη εξαυωνή
— Simplified exportation
— Exportation simplifiée
— Esportazione semplificata
— Vereenvoudigde uitvoer
— Exportação simplificada.
[— Yksinkertaistettu vienti/Förenklad export
— Förenklad export.]
[— Zjednodušený vývoz,
— Lihtsustatud väljavedu,
— Vienkršot izvešana,
— Supaprastintas eksportas,
— Egyszersített kivitel,
— Esportazzjoni simplifikata,
— Wywóz uproszczony,
— Poenostavljen izvoz,
— Zjednodušený vývoz]
[— *(for original text, refer to Commission Regulation (EC) 1792/2006 (OJ L 362, 20.12.06, p 1))*,
— Export simplificat]

4. Articles 255 to 259 shall apply *mutatis mutandis* to export declarations.

NOTES

Para 3: words inserted by the 1994 Act of Accession Annex I(III)(B)(4), as adjusted by Council Decision 95/1/EC, Annex I(XIII)(A)(b), para 13. Further words inserted by the 2003 Act of Accession Annex II(19)(A)(II), para 7. Last two entries in para 3 inserted by Commission Regulation (EC) 1792/2006, Art 1, Annex, Part 11(A)(6).

Paras 1, 2 substituted by Commission Regulation (EC) 2286/2003, Art 1, para 9 with effect from 1 January 2006. However, member states may implement the legislation before that date.

Articles 280 and 281 to be substituted by Commission Regulation (EC) No 1875/2006, Art 1(32) with effect from 1 July 2009.

Article 281

Where Article 789 applies, the supplementary or replacement declaration may be lodged at the customs office responsible for the place where the exporter is established. Where the sub-contractor is established in a Member State other than where the exporter is established, this possibility shall only apply on condition that agreements have been made between the administrations of the Member States concerned.

The incomplete declaration shall include the office where the supplementary declaration will be lodged. The customs office where the incomplete declaration is lodged shall send copy Nos 1 and 2 to the customs office where the supplementary declaration or replacement declaration is lodged.

NOTES

Articles 280 and 281 to be substituted by Commission Regulation (EC) No 1875/2006, Art 1(32) with effect from 1 July 2009.

SECTION 2
SIMPLIFIED DECLARATION PROCEDURE

Article 282

1. On written request containing all the information required for the authorisation to be granted, the declarant shall be authorised, under the conditions and in the manner laid down in Article 261 and 262 applied *mutatis mutandis,* to make the export declaration in a simplified form when goods are presented to customs.

2. Without prejudice to Article 288, the simplified declaration shall take the form of the incomplete Single Administrative Document containing at least the particulars necessary for identification of the goods. Paragraphs 3 and 4 of Article 280 shall apply *mutatis mutandis.*

NOTES

Para 2 to be substituted by Commission Regulation (EC) No 1875/2006, Art 1(33) with effect from 1 July 2009.

SECTION 3
LOCAL CLEARANCE PROCEDURE

Article 283

On written request, authorisation to use the local clearance procedure shall be granted under the conditions and in the manner laid down in Article 284 to any person, hereinafter referred to as an "approved exporter", wishing to carry out export procedures at his premises or at the other places designated or approved by the customs authorities.

Article 284

Articles 264 and 265 shall apply *mutatis mutandis*.

[Article 285

1. The approved exporter shall, before removal of the goods from the places referred to in Article 283, fulfil the following obligations:
   - (a)   duly inform the customs office of export of such removal by lodging a simplified export declaration, as referred to in Article 282;
   - (b)   make available to the customs authorities any documents required for the export of the goods.

2. The approved exporter may lodge a complete export declaration in place of the simplified export declaration. In this case, the requirement for a supplementary declaration, laid down in Article 76(2) of the Code, shall be waived.]

NOTES

Article substituted by Commission Regulation (EC) No 1875/2006, Art 1(34) with effect from 26 December 2006.

[Article 285a

1. The customs authorities may exempt the approved exporter from the requirement to lodge a simplified export declaration at the customs office of export for each removal of goods. This exemption shall be granted only if the approved exporter fulfils the following conditions:
   - (a)   the approved exporter informs the customs office of export of each removal, in the manner and form specified by that office;
   - (b)   the approved exporter supplies, or makes available, to the customs authorities all information they consider necessary for effective risk analysis before the removal of the goods from the places referred to in Article 283;
   - (c)   the approved exporter enters the goods in his records.

The entry referred to in point (c) of the first subparagraph may be replaced by any other formality, required by the customs authorities, which offers similar guarantees. This entry shall indicate the date on which it is made and the particulars necessary for the identification of the goods.

2. In certain particular circumstances justified by the nature of the goods in question and the rapid turnover of export operations, the customs authorities may, until 30 June 2009, exempt the approved exporter from the requirements set out in points (a) and (b) of the first subparagraph of paragraph 1, provided that he supplies the customs office of export with all the information it considers necessary to enable it to exercise its right to examine the goods, should the need arise, before the exit of the goods.

In this case, entry of the goods in the records of the approved exporter shall be equivalent to release.]

NOTES

Article inserted by Commission Regulation (EC) No 1875/2006, Art 1(35) with effect from 26 December 2006.

New Article 285b to be inserted by Commission Regulation (EC) No 1875/2006, Art 1(36) with effect from 1 July 2009.

Article 286

1. To check that the goods have actually left the customs territory of the Community, Copy No 3 of the Single Administrative Document shall be used as evidence of exit.

The authorisation shall stipulate that Copy No 3 of the Single Administrative Document be authenticated in advance.

2. Prior authentication may be effected in one of the following ways—

- (a) box A may be stamped in advance with the stamp of the competent customs office, and signed by an official from that office;
- (b) the approved exporter may stamp the declaration using a special stamp conforming to the model shown in Annex 62.

  The imprint of this stamp may be preprinted on the forms where the printing is entrusted to a printer approved for that purpose.

[3. Before the departure of the goods the approved exporter shall fulfil the following requirements:

- (a) carry out the procedures referred to in Article 285 or 285a;
- (b) indicate on any accompanying document or any other medium replacing it the following particulars:
  - (i) the reference to the entry in his records;
  - (ii) the date on which the entry referred to in point (i) was made;
  - (iii) the number of the authorisation;
  - (iv) the name of the issuing customs office.]

NOTES

Para 3: substituted for previous paras 3, 4, by Commission Regulation (EC) No 1875/2006, Art 1(37) with effect from 26 December 2006

Article 287

[The authorisation referred to in Article 283 shall specify detailed rules for the operation of the procedure and in particular the following:

- (a) the goods to which it applies;
- (b) the way the conditions laid down in Article 285a(1) are to be fulfilled;
- (c) the way and the moment the goods are released;
- (d) the content of any accompanying document or medium replacing it and the means by which it is to be validated;
- (e) the procedure for presenting the supplementary declaration and the time limit within which it must be lodged.

Where Articles 796a to 796e apply, the release referred to in point (c) of the first subparagraph shall be granted in accordance with Article 796b.]

2. The authorisation shall include an undertaking by the approved exporter to take all necessary measures to ensure the safekeeping of the special stamp or of the forms bearing the imprint of the stamp of the customs office of export or the imprint of the special stamp.

NOTES

Para 1: substituted by Commission Regulation (EC) No 1875/2006, Art 1(38) with effect from 26 December 2006

SECTION 4
PROVISIONS COMMON TO SECTIONS 2 AND 3

Article 288

1.   Instead of the Single Administrative Document, Member States may allow a commercial or administrative document or any other medium to be used where the whole of an export operation is carried out on the territory of a single Member State, or whenever this possibility is provided for by means of agreements concluded between the administrations of the Member States concerned.

2.   The document or medium referred to in paragraph 1 shall contain at least the particulars necessary for identification of the goods plus one of the endorsements referred to in Article 280(3) and it shall be accompanied by a request for export.

Where circumstances so permit, the customs authorities may allow this request to be replaced by a global request covering export operations to be carried out over a given period. A reference to the authorisation shall be made on the document or medium in question.

3.   The commercial or administrative document shall be evidence of exit from the customs territory of the Community in the same way as Copy No 3 of the Single Administrative Document. Where other media are used, the arrangements for the exit endorsement shall be defined, where appropriate, in the agreement concluded between the administrations of the Member States concerned.

NOTES

Para 2 to be substituted by Commission Regulation (EC) No 1875/2006, Art 1(39) with effect from 1 July 2009.

Article 289

Where the whole of an export operation takes place on the territory of a single Member State, that Member State may, in addition to the procedures referred to in Sections 2 and 3 and while ensuring compliance with Community policies, provide for other simplifications.
[However, the declarant shall make available to the customs authorities the necessary information for effective risk analysis and the examination of the goods before the exit of these goods.]

NOTES

Para inserted by Commission Regulation (EC) No 1875/2006, Art 1(40) with effect from 26 December 2006.

PART II
CUSTOMS-APPROVED TREATMENT OR USE

TITLE I
RELEASE FOR FREE CIRCULATION

CHAPTER 1
GENERAL PROVISIONS

Article 290

1.   Where Community goods are exported under an ATA carnet in conformity with Article 797, those goods may be released for free circulation on the basis of the ATA carnet.

2. In this case, the office where the goods are released for free circulation shall carry out the following formalities—

(a)   verify the information given in boxes A to G of the reimportation voucher;

(b)   complete the counterfoil and box H of the reimportation sheet;

(c)   retain the reimportation voucher.

3. Where the formalities discharging a temporary export operation in respect of Community goods are carried out a customs office other than the office where the goods enter the customs territory of the Community, conveyance of the goods from that office to the office where the said formalities are carried out shall require no formality.

Article 290A

Examination of bananas falling within CN code 0803 00 19 for the purposes of checking the net mass on importation shall involve a minimum of 10% of declarations per year and per customs office.

Examination of bananas shall be carried out at the time of release for free circulation, in accordance with the rules laid down in Annex 38b.]

NOTES

Inserted by Commission Regulation (EC) 89/97, Art 1, para 1.

[CHAPTER 2
END-USE

Article 291

1. This chapter applies where it is provided that goods released for free circulation with a favourable tariff treatment or at a reduced or zero rate of duty on account of their end-use are subject to end-use customs supervision.

2. For the purposes of this chapter—

(a)   "single authorisation" means: an authorisation involving different customs administrations;

(b)   "accounts" means: the holder's commercial, tax or other accounting material, or such data held on their behalf;

(c)   "records" means: the data containing all the necessary information and technical details on whatever medium, enabling the customs authorities to supervise and control operations.]

NOTES

Substituted, together with Arts 292–300 (for original Arts 291–308) by Commission Regulation (EC) 1602/2000, Art 1, para 7.

[Article 292

1. The granting of a favourable tariff treatment in accordance with Article 21 of the Code shall, where it is provided that goods are subject to end-use customs supervisions, be subject to a written authorisation.

Where goods are released for free circulation at a reduced or zero rate of duty on account of their end-use and the provisions in force require that the goods remain under customs supervision in accordance with Article 82 of the Code, a written authorisation for the purposes of end-use customs supervisions shall be necessary.

2. Applications shall be made in writing using the model set out in Annex 67. The customs authorities may permit renewal or modification to be applied for by simple written request.

3. In particular circumstances the customs authorities may allow the declaration for free circulation in writing or by means of a data-processing technique using the normal procedure to constitute an application for authorisation, provided that—

— the application only involves one customs administration,

— the applicant wholly assigns the goods to the prescribed end-use, and

— the proper conduct of operations is safeguarded.

4. Where the customs authorities consider any of the information given in the application inadequate, they may require additional details from the applicant.

In particular, in cases where an application may be made by making a customs declaration, the customs authorities shall require, without prejudice to Article 218, that the application be accompanied by a document made out by the declarant containing at least the following information, unless such information is deemed unnecessary or is entered on the customs declaration—

(a) name and address of the applicant, the declarant and the operator;

(b) nature of the end-use;

(c) technical description of the goods, products resulting from their end-use and means of identifying them;

(d) estimated rate of yield or method by which that rate is to be determined;

(e) estimated period for assigning the goods to their end-use;

(f) the place where the goods are put to the end-use.

5. Where a single authorisation is applied for, the prior agreement of the authorities shall be necessary according to the following procedure.

The application shall be submitted to the customs authorities designated for the place

— where the applicant's main accounts are kept facilitating audit-based controls, and where at least part of the operations to be covered by the authorisation are carried out; or

[— otherwise, where the applicant's main accounts are held facilitating audit-based controls of the arrangements.]

These customs authorities shall communicate the application and the draft authorisation to the other customs authorities concerned, which shall acknowledge the date of receipt within 15 days.

The other customs authorities concerned shall notify any objections within 30 days of the date on which the draft authorisation was received. Where objections are notified within the above period and no agreement is reached, the application shall be rejected to the extent to which objections were raised.

The customs authorities may issue the authorisation if they have received no objections to the draft authorisation within the 30 days.

The customs authorities issuing the authorisation shall send a copy to all customs authorities concerned.

6. Where the criteria and conditions for the granting of a single authorisation are generally agreed on between two or more customs administrations, the said administrations may also agree to replace prior consultation by simple notification. Such notification shall always be sufficient where a single authorisation is renewed or revoked.]

[7. The applicant shall be informed of the decision to issue an authorisation, or of the reasons why the application was rejected, within thirty days of the date on which the application was lodged or of the date on which any outstanding or additional information requested was received by the customs authorities.

That period shall not apply in the case of a single authorisation unless it is issued under paragraph 6.]

NOTES

Substituted as noted to Art 291.

For the purposes of para 2, Member States may continue to use their existing arrangements until Annex 67 is replaced by Commission Regulation (EC) 1602/2000, Art 2.

Para 5: second indent substituted by Commission Regulation (EC) 2286/2003, Art 1, para 10.

Para 7: added by Commission Regulation (EC) 444/2002, Art 1, para 9.

[**Article 293**

1. An authorisation using the model set out in Annex 67 shall be granted to persons established in the customs territory of the Community, provided that the following conditions are met—

    (a)   the activities envisaged are consistent with the prescribed end-use and with the provisions for the transfer of goods in accordance with Article 296 and the proper conduct of operations is ensured;

    (b)   the applicant offers every guarantee necessary for the proper conduct of operations to be carried out and will undertake the obligations—

        —   to whole or partly assign the goods to the prescribed end-use or to transfer them and to provide evidence of their assignment or transfer in accordance with the provisions in force,

        —   not to take actions incompatible with the intended purpose of the prescribed end-use,

        —   to notify all factors which may affect the authorisation to the competent customs authorities;

    (c)   efficient customs supervision is ensured and the administrative arrangements to be taken by the customs authorities are not disproportionate to the economic needs involved;

    (d)   adequate records are kept and retained;

    (e)   security is provided where the customs authorities consider this necessary.

2. For an application under Article 292(3), the authorisation shall be granted to persons established in the customs territory of the Community by acceptance of the customs declaration, under the other conditions set out in paragraph 1.

3. The authorisation shall include the following items, unless such information is deemed unnecessary—

    (a)   identification of the authorisation holder;

    (b)   where necessary Combined Nomenclature or TARIC code, type and description of the goods and of the end-use operations and provisions concerning rates of yield;

    [(c)   means and methods of identification and of customs supervision, including arrangements for:

        —   common storage, for which Article 534(2) and (3) shall apply mutatis mutandis,

        —   mixed storage of products subject to end-use supervision falling within Chapters 27 and 29 of the Combined Nomenclature or of such products with crude petroleum oils falling within CN code 2709 00.]

    (d)   the period within which the goods have to be assigned to the prescribed end-use;

(e)   the customs offices where the goods are declared for free circulation and the offices to supervise the arrangements;

(f)   the places where the goods have to be assigned to the prescribed end-use;

(g)   the security to be provided, where appropriate;

(h)   the period of validity of the authorisation;

(i)   where applicable, the possibility of transfer of the goods in accordance with Article 296(1);

(j)   where applicable, the simplified arrangements for the transfer of goods under Article 296(2), second subparagraph, and (3);

(k)   where applicable, simplified procedures authorised in accordance with Article 76 of the Code;

(l)   methods of communication.

[Where the goods referred to in the second indent of point (c) of the first subparagraph do not share the same eight-digit CN code, the same commercial quality and the same technical and physical characteristics, mixed storage may be allowed only where the whole mixture is to undergo one of the treatments referred to in Additional Notes 4 and 5 to Chapter 27 of the Combined Nomenclature.]

4.   Without prejudice to Article 294 the authorisation shall take effect on the date of issue or at any later date given in the authorisation.]

[The period of validity shall not exceed three years from the date on which the authorisation takes effect, except where there are duly substantiated good reasons.]

NOTES

Substituted as noted to Art 291.

For the purposes of para 1, Member States may continue to use their existing arrangements until Annex 67 is replaced by Commission Regulation (EC) 1602/2000, Art 2.

Para 3: Point (c) substituted, and words added, by Commission Regulation (EC) 444/2002, Art 1, para 10(a).

Para 4: Words added by Commission Regulation (EC) 444/2002, Art 1, para 10(b).

[Article 294

1.   The customs authorities may issue a retroactive authorisation.

Without prejudice to paragraphs 2 and 3, a retroactive authorisation shall take effect on the date the application was submitted.

2.   If an application concerns renewal of an authorisation for the same kind of operation and goods, an authorisation may be granted with retroactive effect from the date the original authorisation expired.

3.   In exceptional circumstances, the retroactive effect of an authorisation may be extended further, but not more than one year before the date the application was submitted, provided a proven economic need exists and—

(a)   the application is not related to attempted deception or to obvious negligence;

(b)   the applicant's accounts confirm that all the requirements of the arrangements can be regarded as having been met and, where appropriate, in order to avoid substitution the goods can be identified for the period involved, and such accounts allow the arrangements to be verified;

(c)   all the formalities necessary to regularise the situation of the goods can be carried out, including, where necessary, the invalidation of the declaration.]

NOTES

Substituted as noted to Art 291.

[Article 295
The expiry of an authorisation shall not affect goods which were in free circulation by virtue of that authorisation before it expired.]

NOTES

Substituted as noted to Art 291.

[Article 296
1. The transfer of goods between different places designated in the same authorisation may be undertaken without any customs formalities.

2. Where a transfer of goods is carried out between two authorisation holders established in different Member States and the customs authorities concerned have not agreed simplified procedures in accordance with paragraph 3, the T5 control copy provided for in Annex 63 shall be used in accordance with the following procedure—

    (a)   the transferor shall complete the T5 control copy in triplicate (one original and two copies). . ..

    (b)   the T5 control copy shall include—

— in box A ("Office of departure"), the address of the competent customs office specified in the transferor's authorisation,

— in box 2, the name or trading name, full address and authorisation number of the transferor,

— in box 8, the name or trading name, full address and authorisation number of the transferee,

— in the box "Important note" and in box B the text shall be crossed out,

— in boxes 31 and 33, respectively, the description of the goods as at the time of transfer, including the number of items, and the relevant CN code,

— in box 38, the net mass of the goods,

— in box 103, the net quantity of the goods in words

— in box 104, a tick in the box "Other (specify)", and in block capitals one of the following—

— DESTINO ESPECIAL: MERCANCÍAS RESPECTO DE LAS CUALES, LAS OBLIGACIONES SE CEDEN AL CESIONARIO (REGLAMENTO (CEE) N° 2454/93, ARTÍCULO 296)

— SÆRLIGT ANVENDELSESFORMÅL: VARER, FOR HVILKE FORPLIGTELSERNE OVERDRAGES TIL ERHVERVEREN (FORORDNING (EØF) Nr. 2454/93, ARTIKEL 296)

— BESONDERE VERWENDUNG: WAREN MIT DENEN DIE PFLICHTEN AUF DEN ÜBERNEHMER ÜBERTRAGEN WERDEN (ARTIKEL 296 DER VERORDNUNG (EWG) Nr. 2454/93)

— ΕΙΔΙΚΟΣΠΡΟΟΡΙΣΜΟΣ ΕΜΠΟΡΕГΜΑΤΑ ГΙΑ ΤΑ ΟΠΟΙΑ ΥΠΟΧΡΕΩΣΕΙΣ ΕΚΚΩΡΟΥΝΤΑΙ ΣΤΟΝ ΕΚΔΟΧΕΑ (ΑΡΘΡΟ 296 ΚΑΝΟΝΙΣΜΟΣ (ΕΟΚ) αρ

- END-USE: GOODS FOR WHICH THE OBLIGATIONS ARE TRANSFERRED TO THE TRANSFEREE (REGULATION (EEC) No 2454/93, ARTICLE 296)
- DESTINATION PARTICULIÈRE: MARCHANDISES POUR LESQUELLES LES OBLIGATIONS SONT TRANSFÉRÉES AU CESSIONNAIRE [RÈGLEMENT (CEE) No 2454/93, ARTICLE 296]
- DESTINAZIONE PARTICOLARE: MERCI PER LE QUALI GLI OBBLIGHI SONO TRASFERITI AL CESSIONARIO (REGOLAMENTO (CEE) N. 2454/93, ARTICOLO 296)
- BIJZONDERE BESTEMMING: GOEDERENWAARVOOR DE VERPLICHTINGEN AAN DE OVERNEMER WORDEN OVERGEDRAGEN (VERORDENING (EEG) Nr. 2454/93, ARTIKEL 296)
- DESTINO ESPECIAL: MERCADORIAS RELATIVAMENTE ÀS QUAIS AS OBRIGAÇÕES SÃO TRANSFERIDAS PARA O CESSIONÁRIO [REGULAMENTO (CEE) No 2454/93, ARTIGO 296.°]
- TIETTY KÄYTTÖTARKOITUS: TAVARAT, JOIHIN LIITTYVÄT VELVOITTEET SIIRRETÄÄN SIIRRONSAAJALLE (ASETUS (ETY) No. 2454/93, 296 ARTIKLA)
- ANVÄNDNING FÖR SÄRSKILDA ÄNDAMÅL: VAROR FÖR VILKA SKYLDIGHETERNA ÖVERFÖRS TILL DEN MOTTAGANDE PARTEN (ARTIKEL 296 I FÖRORDNING (EEG) nr 2454/93)
- [KONECNÉ POUŽITÍ: ZBOŽÍ, U KTERÉHO PŘECHÁZEJÍ POVINNOSTI NA PŘÍJEMCE (ČLÁNEK 296 NAŘÍZENÍ (EHS) č. 2454/93),
- EESMÄRGIPÄRANE KASUTAMINE: KAUP, MILLE KORRAL KOHUSTUSED LÄHEVAD ÜLE KAUBA SAAJALE (MÄÄRUSE ((EMÜ) NR 2454/93 ARTIKKEL 296),
- IZMANTOŠANAS MRKIS: PREČU SANMJS ATBILDGS PAR PREČU IZMANTOŠANU (REGULA (EEK) NR.2454/93, 296.PANTS),
- GALUTINIS VARTOJIMAS: PREKS, SU KURIOMIS SUSIJUSIOS PRIEVOLS PERDUOTOS J PERMJUI (REGLAMENTAS (EEB) NR. 2454/93, 296 STRAIPSNIS),
- MEGHATÁROZOTT CÉLRA TÖRTÉNŐ FELHASZNÁLÁS: AZ ÁRUKKAL KAPCSOLATOS KÖTELEZETTSÉGEK AZ ÁRUK ÁTVEVOJÉRE SZÁLLTAK ÁT (A 2454/93/EGK RENDELET 296.CIKKE),
- UU AARI: OETTI LI GALIHOM L-OBBLIGI HUMA TRASFERITI LIL MIN ISIR IT-TRASFERIMENT (REGOLAMENT (KEE) 2454/93, ARTIKOLU 296),
- PRZEZNACZENIE SZCZEGÓLNE: TOWARY, W ODNIESIENIU DO KTÓRYCH ZOBOWIZANIA SA PRZENOSZONE NA OSOB PRZEJMUJC (ROZPORZDZENIE (EWG) NR 2454/93, ART. 296),
- POSEBEN NAMEN: BLAGO, ZA KATERO SE OBVEZNOSTI PRENESEJO NA PREJEMNIKA (UREDBA (E GS) ŠT. 2454/93, Č LEN 296),

    — KONEČNÉ POUŽITIE: TOVAR, S KTORÝM PRECHÁDZAJÚ POVINNOSTI NA PRÍJEMCU (NARIADENIE (EHS) Č. 2454/93, ČLÁNOK 296),]

    [— *(for original text, refer to Commission Regulation (EC) 1792/2006 (OJ L 362, 20.12.06, p 1)),*

    — DESTINATIE FINAL: MRFURI PENTRU CARE OBLIGATIILE SUNT TRANSFERATE CESIONARULUI (REGULAMENTUL (CEE) Nr. 2454/93, ARTICOLUL 296)]

    — in box 106—

    [— the taxation elements of the goods, save where that requirement is waived by the customs authorities,].

    — the registered number and date of the declaration for release for free circulation and the name and address of the customs office where the declaration was made;

(c) the transferor shall send the complete set of T5 control copies to the transferee;

(d) the transferee shall attach the original of the commercial document showing the date of receipt of the goods to the set of T5 control copies and submit all documents to the customs office determined in his authorisation. He shall also immediately notify this customs office of any excess, shortfall, substitution or other irregularity;

(e) the customs office specified in the transferee's authorisation shall fill in box J, including the date of receipt by the transferee, in the original T5 after having verified the corresponding commercial documents and date and stamp the original in box J and the two copies in box E. The customs office shall retain the second copy in its records and return the original and the first copy to the transferee;

(f) the transferee shall retain the first T5 copy in his records and forward the original to the transferor;

(g) the transferor shall retain the original in his records.

The customs authorities concerned may agree simplified procedures in accordance with the provisions for the use of the T5 control copy.

3. Where the customs authorities concerned consider that the proper conduct of operations is safeguarded, they may agree a transfer of goods between two authorisation holders established in two different Member States to be made without using the T5 control copy.

4. Where a transfer is carried out between two authorisation holders established in the same Member States, this shall be done in accordance with national rules.

5. With the receipt of the goods the transferee shall become the holder of obligations under this chapter in respect of the transferred goods.

6. The transferor shall be discharged from his obligations where the following conditions are fulfilled—

    — the transferee has received the goods and was informed that the goods for which the obligations are transferred, are subject to end-use customs supervision;

    — customs control has been taken over by the transferee's customs authority; unless otherwise provided by the customs authorities, this shall be when the transferee has entered the goods in his records.]

NOTES

Substituted as noted to Art 291.

Para 2: words in point (a) repealed, and words in point (b) substituted, by Commission Regulation (EC) 444/2002, Art 1, para 11. Words in point (b) inserted by the 2003 Act of Accession Annex II(19)(A)(II), para 8. Entries in point (b), relating to box 104, inserted by Commission Regulation (EC) 1792/2006, Art 1, Annex, Part 11(A)(7).

[Article 297

1. In the case of the transfer of materials for the maintenance or repair of aircraft either under the terms of exchange agreements or for airlines' own needs, by airlines engaged in international traffic, an air waybill or equivalent document may be used instead of the T5 control copy.

2. The air waybill or equivalent document shall contain at least the following particulars—

(a)   the name of the consigning airline;

(b)   the name of the airport of departure;

(c)   the name of the receiving airline;

(d)   the name of the airport of destination;

(e)   the description of the materials;

(f)   the number of articles.

The particulars referred to in the first subparagraph may be given in coded form or by reference to an attached document.

3. The air waybill or equivalent document must bear on its face one of the following indications in block capitals—

— DESTINO ESPECIAL

— SÆRLIGT ANVENDELSESFORMÅL

— BESONDERE VERWENDUNG

— ΕΙΔΙΚΟΣ ΠΡΟΟΡΙΣΜΟΣ

— END-USE

— DESTINATION PARTICULIÈRE

— DESTINAZIONE PARTICOLARE

— BIJZONDERE BESTEMMING

— DESTINO ESPECIAL

— TIETTY KÄYTTÖTARKOITUS

— ANVÄNDNING FÖR SÄRSKILDA ÄNDAMÅL

[— KONEČNÉ POUŽITÍ,

— EESMÄRGIPÄRANE KASUTAMINE,

— IZMANTOŠANAS MRIS,

— GALUTINIS VARTOJIMAS,

— MEGHATÁROZOTT CÉLRA TÖRTÉNŐ FELHASZNÁLÁS,

— UU AARI,

— PRZEZNACZENIE SZCZEGÓLNE,

— POSEBEN NAMEN,

— KONEČNÉ POUŽITIE]

[— (for original text, refer to Commission Regulation (EC) 1792/2006 (OJ L 362, 20.12.06, p 1)),

— DESTINATIE FINAL]

4. The consigning airline shall retain a copy of the air waybill or equivalent document as part of its records and shall, in the manner prescribed by the customs authorities of the Member State of departure, make a further copy available to the competent customs office.

The receiving airline shall retain a copy of the air waybill or equivalent document as part of its records and shall, in the manner prescribed by the customs authorities of the

Member State of destination, make a further copy available to the competent customs office.

5. The intact materials and the copies of the air waybill or equivalent document shall be delivered to the receiving airline in the places specified by the customs authorities in the airline's Member State residence. The receiving airline shall enter the materials in its records.

6. The obligations arising under paragraphs 1 to 5 shall pass from the consigning airline to the receiving airline at the time when the intact materials and copies of the air waybill or equivalent document are delivered to the latter.]

NOTES

Substituted as noted to Art 291.

Para 3: words inserted by the 2003 Act of Accession Annex II(19)(A)(II), para 9. Last two entries in para 3, inserted by Commission Regulation (EC) 1792/2006, Art 1, Annex, Part 11(A)(8).

[**Article 298**

1. The customs authorities may, subject to conditions they shall lay down, approve the exportation of the goods or destruction of the goods.

2. Where agricultural products are exported, box 44 of the Single Administrative Document or any other document used shall bear one of the following indications in block capitals—

— ARTÍCULO 298, REGLAMENTO (CEE) N₀ 2454/93, DESTINO ESPECIAL: MERCANCÍAS DESTINADAS A LA EXPORTACINÓ — NO SE APLICAN RESTITUCIONES AGRÍCOLAS

— ART. 298 I FORORDNING (EØF) Nr. 2454/93 SÆRLIGT ANVENDELSESFORMÅL: VARER BESTEMT TIL UDFRØSEL — INGEN RESTITUTION

— ARTIKEL 298 DER VERORDNUNG (EWG) Nr.2454/93 BESONDERE VERWENDUNG: ZUR AUSFUHR VORGESEHENE WAREN — ANWENDUNG DER LANDWIRTSCHAFTLICHEN AUSFUHRERSTATTUNGEN AUSGESCHLOSSEN

— ΑΡΘΡΟ 298 ΤΟΥΚΑΝ. (ΕΟΚ) αρτθ. 2454/93 ΕΙΔΙΚΟΣΠΡΟΟΡΙΣΜΟΣ: ΕΜΠΟΡΕГΜΑΤΑ ΠΡΟΟΡΙΖΟΜΕΝΑ ГΙΑ ΕΑΞГΩГΗ — ΑΠΟΚΕΙ ΟΝΤΑΙ ΟΙГΕΩΡГΚΕΣ ΕΠΙΣΤΡΟФΕΣ

— ARTICLE 298 REGULATION (EEC) No 2454/93 END-USE: GOODS DESTINED FOR EXPORTATION — AGRICULTURAL REFUNDS NOT APPLICABLE

— ARTICLE 298, RÈGLEMENT (CEE) N₀ 2454/93 DESTINATION PARTICULIÈRE: MARCHANDISES PRVÉUES POUR L'EXPORTATION — APPLICATION DES RESTITUTIONS AGRICOLES EXCLUE

— ARTICOLO 298 (CEE) N₀ 2454/93 DESTINAZIONE PARTICOLARE: MERCI PREVISTE PER L'ESPORTAZIONE — APPLICAZIONE DELLE RESTITUZIONI AGRICOLE ESCLUSA

— ARTIKEL 298, VERORDENING (EEG) Nr. 2454/93 BIJZONDERE BESTEMMING: VOOR UITVOER BESTEMDE GOEDEREN — LANDBOUWRESTITUTIES NIET VAN TOEPASSING

— ARTIGO 298.₀ REG. (CEE) N.₀ 2454/93 DESTINO ESPECIAL: MERCADORIAS DESTINADAS À EXPORTAÇÃO — APLICAÇÃO DE RESTITUIÇÃES AGRÍCOLAS EXCLUÍDA

— 298 ART., AS. 2454/93 TIE TTYKÄYTTÖTARKOITUS: VIETÄVIKSI TARKOITETTUJA TAVAROITA — MAATALOUSTUKEA EI SOVELLETA

— ARTIKEL 298 I FÖRORDNING (EEG) nr 2454/93 AVSEENDE ANVÄNDNING FÖR SÄRSKILDA ÄNDAMÅL: VAROR AVSEDDA FÖR EXPORT — JORDBRUKSBIDRAG EJ TILLÄMPLIGA

[— CLÁNEK 298 NARÍZENÍ (EHS) č. 2454/93 KONEČNÉ POUŽITÍ: ZBOŽÍ URCENO K VÝVOZU – ZEMEDELSKÉ NÁHRADY NELZE UPLATNIT,

— MÄÄRUSE (EMÜ) NR 2454/93 ARTIKKEL 298 "EESMÄRGIPÄRANE KASUTAMINE": KAUBALE, MIS LÄHEB EKSPORDIKS, PÕLLUMAJANDUSTOETUSI EI RAKENDATA,

— REGULAS (EEK) NR. 2454/93, 298.PANTS: IZMANTOŠANAS MRKIS: PRECES PAREDZTAS IZVEŠANAI – LAUKSAIMNIECIBAS KOMPENSÁCIJU NEPIEMRO,

— REGLAMENTAS (EEB) NR. 2454/93, 298 STRAIPSNIS, GALUTINIS VARTOJIMAS: EKSPORTUOJAMOS PREKS – Ž EMS KŪIO GRŽINAMOSIOS IŠMOKOS NETAIKOMOS,

— MEGHATÁROZOTT CÉLRA TÖRTÉNO FELHASZNÁLÁS A 2454/93/EGK RENDELET 298.CIKKE SZERINT: KIVITELI RENDELTETÉSU ÁRUK – MEZOGAZDASÁGI VISSZATÉRÍTÉS NEM ALKALMAZHATÓ,

— ARTIKOLU 298 REGOLAMENT (KEE) 2454/93UU AARI: OETTI DESTINATI GHALL-ESPORTAZZJONI RIFUJONIJIET AGRIKOLI MHUX APPLIKABBLI,

— ARTYKUŁ 298 ROZPORZDZENIA (EWG) NR 2454/93 PRZEZNACZENIE SZCZEGÓLNE: TÓWARY PRZEZNACZONE DO WYWOZU – NIE STOSUJE SIE DOPŁAT ROLNYCH,

— ČLEN 298 UREDBE (EGS) ŠT. 2454/93 POSEBEN NAMEN: BLAGO DEKLARIRANO ZA IZVOZ – UPORABA KMETIJSKIH IZVOZNIH NADOMESTIL IZKLJUEČNA,

— ČLÁNOK 298 NARIADENIA (EHS) Č. 2454/93 KONEČNÉ POUŽITIE: TOVAR URČENÝ NA VÝVOZ – POI'NOHOSPODÁRSKE NÁHRADY NEMOŽNO UPLATNI]

[— (for original text, refer to Commission Regulation (EC) 1792/2006 (OJ L 362, 20.12.06, p 1)),

— ARTICOLUL 298 REGULAMENTUL (CEE) Nr. 2454/93 DESTINATIE FINAL: MRFURI DESTINATE PENTRU EXPORT — NU SE APLIC RESTITUIRI RESTITUTII AGRICOLE]

3. Where goods are exported, they shall be considered as non-Community goods from the time of acceptance of the export declaration.

4. In the case of destruction Article 182(5) of the Code shall apply.]

NOTES

Substituted as noted to Art 291.

Para 2: words inserted by the 2003 Act of Accession Annex II(19)(A)(II), para 10. Final two entries inserted by Commission Regulation (EC) 1792/2006, Art 1, Annex, Part 11(A)(9).

[Article 299

Where the customs authorities agree that the use of the goods otherwise than as provided for in the authorisation is justified, such use, other than export or destruction, shall entail the incurrence of a customs debt. Article 208 of the Code shall apply *mutatis mutandis*.]

Part III

NOTES

Substituted as noted to Art 291.

[**Article 300**

1. The goods referred to in Article 291(1) shall remain under customs supervision and liable to import duties until the are—

    (a)   first assigned to the prescribed end-use;

    (b)   exported, destroyed or used otherwise in accordance with Articles 298 and 299.

However, where the goods are suitable for repeated use and the customs authorities consider it appropriate in order to avoid abuse, customs supervision shall continue for a period not exceeding two years after the date of first assignment.

2. Waste and scrap which result from the working or processing of goods and losses due to natural wastage shall be considered as goods having been assigned to the prescribed end-use.

3. For waste and scrap which result from the destruction of goods, customs supervision shall end when they have been assigned a permitted customs-approved treatment or use.]

NOTES

Substituted as noted to Art 291.

[CHAPTER 3
MANAGEMENT OF TARIFF MEASURES

SECTION 1
MANAGEMENT OF TARIFF QUOTAS DESIGNED TO BE USED FOLLOWING
THE CHRONOLOGICAL ORDER OF DATES OF CUSTOMS DECLARATIONS

Article 308a

1. Save as otherwise provided, where tariff quotas are opened by a Community provision, those tariff quotas shall be managed in accordance with the chronological order of dates of acceptance of declarations for release for free circulation.

2. Where a declaration for release for free circulation incorporating a valid request by the declarant to benefit from a tariff quota is accepted, the Member State concerned shall draw from the tariff quota, through the Commission, a quantity corresponding to its needs.

3. Member States shall not present any request for drawing until the conditions laid down in Article 256(2) and (3) are satisfied.

4. Subject to paragraph 8, allocations shall be granted by the Commission on the basis of the date of acceptance of the relevant declaration for release for free circulation, and to the extent that the balance of the relevant tariff quota so permits. Priority shall be established in accordance with the chronological order of these dates.

5. The Member States shall communicate to the Commission all valid requests for drawing without delay. Those communications shall include the date referred to in paragraph 4, and the exact amount applied for on the relevant customs declaration.

6. For the purposes of paragraphs 4 and 5, the Commission shall fix order numbers where none are provided by the Community provision opening the tariff quota.

7. If the quantities requested for drawing from a tariff quota are greater than the balance available, allocation shall be made on a pro rata basis with respect to the requested quantities.

8. For the purposes of this Article, acceptance of a declaration by the customs authorities on 1, 2 or 3 January shall be regarded as acceptance on 3 January. However, if one of those days falls on a Saturday or a Sunday, such acceptance shall be regarded as having taken place on 4 January.

9. Where a new tariff quota is opened, drawings shall not be granted by the Commission before the 11th working day following the date of publication of the provision which created that tariff quota.

10. Member States shall immediately return to the Commission the amount of drawings which they do not use. However, where an erroneous drawing representing a customs debt of [10 euro] or less is discovered after the first month following the end of the period of validity of the tariff quota concerned, Member States need not make a return.

11. If the customs authorities invalidate a declaration for release for free circulation in respect of goods which are the subject of a request for benefit of a tariff quota, the complete request shall be cancelled in respect of those goods. The Member States concerned shall immediately return to the Commission any quantity drawn, in respect of those goods, from the tariff quota.

12. Details of drawings requested by individual Member States shall be treated by the Commission and other Member States as confidential.]

NOTES

Inserted, together with Arts 308b–308d, by Commission Regulation (EC) 1427/97, Art 1, para 4.

Para 10: words substituted by Commission Regulation (EC) No 214/2007, Art 1(1) with effect from 4 March 2007.

[Article 308b

1. The Commission shall make an allocation each working day, except—
  — days which are holidays for the Community institutions in Brussels, or
  — in exceptional circumstances, any other day, provided that the competent authorities of the Member States have been informed in advance.

2. Subject to Article 308a(8), any allocation shall take into account all unanswered requests which relate to declarations for release for free circulation accepted up to and including the second previous day, and which have been communicated to the Commission.]

NOTES

Inserted as noted to Art 308a.

[Article 308c

1. A tariff quota shall be considered as critical as soon as [90%] of the initial volume has been used, or at the discretion of the competent authorities.

2. By way of derogation from paragraph 1, a tariff quota shall be considered from the date of its opening as critical in any of the following cases:
  (a)   it is opened for less than three months;
  (b)   tariff quotas having the same product coverage and origin and an equivalent quota period as the tariff quota in question (equivalent tariff quotas) have not been opened in the previous two years;

Part III

(c)   an equivalent tariff quota opened in the previous two years had been exhausted on or before the last day of the third month of its quota period or had a higher initial volume than the tariff quota in question.

3.   A tariff quota whose sole purpose is the application, under the rules of the WTO, of either a safeguard measure or a retaliatory measure shall be considered as critical as soon as [90%] of the initial volume has been used irrespective of whether or not equivalent tariff quotas were opened in the previous two years.]

NOTES

Substituted by Commission Regulation (EC) 881/2003 Art 1, para 7.

Paras 1, 3: figures substituted by Commission Regulation (EC) No 214/2007, Art 1(2) with effect from 4 March 2007.

[SECTION 2
SURVEILLANCE OF GOODS]

NOTES

Substituted by Commission Regulation (EC) 2286/2003, Art 1, para 11 with effect from 1 January 2004.

[Article 308d

1.   Where Community surveillance is to be carried out, the Member States shall provide to the Commission at least once every week data on customs declarations for release for free circulation or on export declarations.

The Member States shall cooperate with the Commission to determine which data are required from customs declarations for release for free circulation or from export declarations.

2.   The data provided under paragraph 1 by individual Member States shall be treated as confidential.

However, aggregate data for each Member State shall be available for authorised users in all Member States.

The Member States shall cooperate with the Commission to set up the practical rules on authorised access to the aggregate data.

3.   In respect of certain goods surveillance shall be carried out on a confidential basis.

4.   Where under the simplified procedures referred to in Articles 253 to 267 and Articles 280 to 289, the data referred to in paragraph 1 of this Article are not available, the Member States shall provide to the Commission the data available at the date of acceptance of the complete or supplementary declaration.]

NOTES

Substituted by Commission Regulation (EC) No 214/2007, Art 1(3) with effect from 4 March 2007.

TITLE II
[CUSTOMS STATUS OF GOODS AND TRANSIT]

NOTES

Substituted by Commission Regulation (EC) 2787/2000, Art 1, para 4.

Chapters 1, 2 (Arts 309–312) repealed by Commission Regulation (EC) 2787/2000, Art 1, para 5.

CHAPTER 3
[CUSTOMS STATUS OF GOODS]

[SECTION 1
GENERAL PROVISIONS]

NOTES

Chapter heading: substituted by Commission Regulation (EC) 75/98, Art 1, para 3.
Sub-heading: inserted by Commission Regulation (EC) 482/96, Art 1, para 3.

[Article 313

1. Subject to Article 180 of the Code and the exceptions listed in paragraph 2 of this Article, all goods in the customs territory of the Community shall be deemed to be Community goods, unless it is established that they do not have Community status.

2. The following shall not be deemed to be Community goods unless it is established in accordance with Articles 314 to 323 that they do have Community status—

[(a) goods brought into the customs territory of the Community in accordance with Article 37 of the Code.

Nevertheless in accordance with Article 38(5) of the Code, goods brought into the customs territory of the Community shall be deemed to be Community goods unless it is established that they do not have Community status:

— where, if carried by air, the goods have been loaded or transhipped at an airport in the Community customs territory, for consignment to another airport in the Community customs territory, provided that they are carried under cover of a single transport document drawn up in a Member State, or

— where, if carried by sea, the goods have been shipped between ports in the Community customs territory by a regular shipping service authorised in accordance with Articles 313a and 313b.]

[(b) goods in temporary storage or in a free zone of control type I within the meaning of Article 799 or in a free warehouse;

(c) goods placed under a suspensive procedure or in a free zone of control type II within the meaning of Article 799.]

. . .

NOTES

Substituted by Commission Regulation (EC) 75/98, Art 1, para 4.
Para 2: sub-para (a) substituted by Commission Regulation (EC) 2787/2000, Art 1, para 6.
Sub-paras (b), (c) substituted by Commission Regulation (EC) 993/2001 Art 1, para 11.
Words repealed by Commission Regulation (EC) 2787/2000, Art 1, para 6.

[Article 313a

[1. A regular shipping service means a regular service which carries goods in vessels that ply only between ports situated in the customs territory of the Community and may not come from, go to or call at any points outside this territory or in a free zone of control type I in the meaning of Article 799 of a port in this territory.]

Part III

2. The customs authorities may require proof that the provisions on authorised shipping services have been observed.

Where the customs authorities establish that the provisions on authorised shipping services have not been observed, they shall immediately inform all the customs authorities concerned.]

NOTES

Inserted, together with Art 313b, by Commission Regulation (EC) 75/98, Art 1, para 5.

Para 1: substituted by Commission Regulation (EC) 993/2001, Art 1, para 12.

[Article 313b

[1. Where a shipping company defining its service, makes an application, the customs authorities of a Member State in whose territory that company is established may, with the agreement of the other Member States concerned, authorise the establishment of a regular shipping service.]

[2. The application shall contain the following details:

(a) the ports concerned,

(b) the names of the vessels assigned to the regular service; and

(c) any further information required by the customs authorities, in particular the shipping service's timetable.]

3. Authorisation shall be granted only to shipping companies which—

(a) are established in the Community and whose records will be available to the competent customs authorities;

[(b) have not committed any serious or repeated offences in connection with the operation of a regular shipping service]

(c) are able to satisfy the customs authorities that they operate a regular shipping service as defined in Article 313a(1); and

(d) undertake that—

[— on the routes for which authorisation is requested, no calls will be made at any port in a third country or at any free zone of control type I in the meaning of Article 799 in a port in the customs territory of the Community, and that no transhipments will be made on the high seas, and that,]

— the authorisation certificate will be carried on board the vessel and presented on request to the competent customs authorities;

[3a Where the shipping company holds an AEO certificate referred to in point (a) or (c) of Article 14a(1), the customs authorities of the Member States concerned shall examine only whether the requirements in paragraph 3(c) and (d) of this Article are met. All other requirements set out in this Article shall be deemed to be met.]

4. When they receive an application for authorisation, the customs authorities of the Member State to whom the application has been made (the authorising authorities) shall notify the customs authorities of the other Member States in whose territories the intended ports of call of the regular shipping service are situated (the corresponding authorities).

The corresponding authorities shall acknowledge receipt of the application.

Within 60 days of receipt of such notification, the corresponding authorities shall signify their agreement or refusal. Where a Member State refuses an application, it shall state the reasons. Where no reply is received, the authorising authority shall issue an authorisation which shall be accepted by the other Member States concerned.

The authorising authorities shall issue an authorisation certificate, in one or more copies as required and conforming to the model set out in Annex 42 A, and shall inform the corresponding authorities of the other Member States concerned. Each

authorisation certificate shall bear a serial number by which it can be identified. All copies of each certificate shall bear the same number.

5. Once a regular shipping service has been authorised, the shipping company concerned shall be required to use it. The shipping company shall communicate any withdrawal or change in the characteristics of the authorised service to the authorising authorities.

6. Where an authorisation is withdrawn, or a regular shipping service ceases operations, the authorising authorities shall notify the corresponding authorities of the Member States concerned. The authorising authorities shall also notify the corresponding authorities of any changes to a regular shipping service. . .. [If the details required in paragraph 2(a) change, the procedure provided for in paragraph 4 shall apply.]

[7. When a vessel of the type referred to in Article 313a(1) is forced by circumstances beyond its control to tranship at sea or temporarily put into a third-country port or a free zone of control type I in the meaning of Article 799 of a port in the customs territory of the Community, the shipping company shall immediately inform the customs authorities of the subsequent ports of call along the vessel's scheduled route.]]

NOTES

Inserted as noted to Art 313a.

Paras 1, 2: substituted by Commission Regulation (EC) 2787/2000, Art 1, para 7.

Para 3: sub-paras (a), (b) substituted by Commission Regulation (EC) 2787/2000, Art 1, para 7.

Para 3a: inserted by Commission Regulation (EC) No 1875/2006, Art 1(41) with effect from 1 January 2008.

Words in square brackets substituted by Commission Regulation (EC) 993/2001, Art 1, para 13.

Para 6: words deleted, and words in square brackets added by Commission Regulation (EC) 2787/2000, Art 1, para 7.

Para 7: substituted by Commission Regulation (EC) 993/2001, Art 1, para 13.

[Article 314

1. Where goods are not deemed to be Community goods within the meaning of Article 313, their Community status may not be established [in accordance with Article 314c[1]] unless—

(a) they have been brought from another Member State without crossing the territory of a third country on the way; or

(b) they have been brought from another Member State through the territory of a third country, and carried under cover of a single transport document issued in a Member State; or

(c) they have been transhipped in a third country on a means of transport other than that onto which they were initially loaded and a new transport document has been issued, provided that the new document is accompanied by a copy of the original document covering carriage from the Member State of departure to the Member State of destination. In line with the requirements of administrative cooperation between Member States, the customs authorities at the customs office of destination shall carry out post-clearance checks to determine the accuracy of the information entered in the copy of the original transport document.

2. . . .

3. The documents or rules referred to [in Article 314c¹] shall not be used in respect of goods for which the export formalities have been completed or which have been placed under the inward processing procedure (drawback system).

4. . . . .

¹ OJ L 276, 19.9.92, p 1.

NOTES
Substituted by Commission Regulation (EC) 75/98, Art 1, para 6.

Paras 1, 3: words in square brackets substituted by Commission Regulation (EC) 2787/2000, Art 1, para 8.

Paras 2, 4: repealed by Commission Regulation (EC) 2787/2000, Art 1, para 8.

[Articles 314a

The customs administrations of the Member States shall assist one another in checking the authenticity and accuracy of the documents and verifying that the procedures used in accordance with the provisions of this Title to prove the Community status of goods have been correctly applied.]

NOTES
Inserted by Commission Regulation (EC) 2787/2000, Art 1, para 9.

[SECTION 2
PROOF OF COMMUNITY STATUS

Article 314b

For the purposes of this Section, 'competent office' means the customs authorities responsible for certifying the Community status of goods.]

NOTES
Inserted as noted to art 314a.

[Article 314c

1. Without prejudice to goods placed under the internal Community transit procedure, proof that the goods have Community status may be established solely by one of the following means:

 (a) by one of the documents provided for in Articles 315 to 317b;

 (b) in accordance with the rules laid down in Articles 319 to 323;

 (c) by the accompanying document referred to in Commission Regulation (EEC) No 2719/92(¹);

 (d) by the document provided for in Article 325;

 (e) by the label provided for in Article 462a(2);

 (f) by the document provided for in [Article 812] certifying the Community status of the goods; or

 (g) by the T5 control copy described in Article 843.

2. Where the documents or rules referred to in paragraph 1 are used for Community goods with packaging not having Community status, the document certifying the Community status of the goods shall bear one of the following endorsements:

 — envases N

—   N-emballager
—   N-Umschlieußng
—   Συσκευασια
—   N packaging
—   emballages N
—   imballaggi N
—   N-verpakking
—   embalagens N
—   N-pakkaus
—   N förpackning.
[—   obal N,
—   N-pakendamine,
—   N iepakojums,
—   N pakuot,
—   N csomagolás,
—   ippakkjar N,
—   opakowania N,
—   N embalaža,
—   N – obal]
[—   *(for original text, refer to Commission Regulation (EC) 1792/2006 (OJ L 362, 20.12.06, p 1)),*
—   ambalaj N]

3.   Subject to the conditions for issuing the documents being met, the documents referred to in Articles 315 to 323 may be issued retroactively. Where this is the case, they shall bear one of the following phrases in red:

—   Expedido a posteriori,
—   Udstedt efterfoelgende,
—   Nachträglich ausgestellt,
—   ΕκδΟθεν εκτων υστερων
—   Issued retroactively,
—   Délivré a posteriori,
—   Rilasciato a posteriori,
—   Achteraf afgegeven,
—   Emitido a posteriori,
—   Annettu jälkiktäeen,
—   Utfärdat i efterhand.]
[[—   Vyhotovené dodatočne],
—   Välja antud tagasiulatuvalt,
—   Izsniegts retrospektvi,
—   Retrospektyvusis išdavimas,
—   Kiadva visszamenőleges hatállyal,
—   maru retrospettivament,
—   wystawione retrospektywnie,
—   Izdano naknadno,
—   Vydané dodatočne.]
[—   *(for original text, refer to Commission Regulation (EC) 1792/2006 (OJ L 362, 20.12.06, p 1)),*
—   Eliberat ulterior]

---

[1] OJ L 276, 19.9.1992, P.1.

NOTES

Inserted as noted to art 314a.

Para 1: words in point (f) substituted by Commission Regulation (EC) 444/2002, Art 1, para 12.

Para 2: words inserted by the 2003 Act of Accession Annex II(19)(A)(II), para 11. Final two entries inserted by Commission Regulation (EC) 1792/2006, Art 1, Annex, Part 11(A)(10).

Para 3: words inserted by the 2003 Act of Accession Annex II(19)(A)(II), para 12; words "Vyhotovené dodatočne" in square brackets inserted by Commission Regulation (EC) 883/2005, Art 1, OJ L 148, 11.06.05, p 5 with effect from 1 May 2004. Final two entries inserted by Commission Regulation (EC) 1792/2006, Art 1, Annex, Part 11(A)(11).

[SUBSECTION 1
T2L DOCUMENT]

NOTES

Inserted as noted to art 314a.

[Article 315

1.   Proof of the Community status of goods shall be furnished by the production of a T2L document. That document shall be drawn up in accordance with paragraphs 3 to 5.

2.   Proof of the Community status of goods consigned to or from a part of the customs territory of the Community, where Directive 77/388/EEC does not apply, shall be furnished by the production of a T2LF document.

Paragraphs 3 to 5 of this Article and Articles 316 to 324f shall apply mutatis mutandis to the T2LF document.

3.   The T2L document shall be made out on a form corresponding to Copy 4 or Copy 4/5 of the specimen in Annexes 31 and 32.

Where necessary, the said form may be supplemented by one or more continuation sheets corresponding to Copy 4 or Copy 4/5 of the specimen in Annexes 33 and 34.

Where Member States do not authorise the use of continuation sheets when a computerised system is used to produce declarations, the form shall be supplemented by one or more forms corresponding to Copy 4 or Copy 4/5 of the specimen in Annexes 31 and 32.

4.   The person concerned shall enter 'T2L' in the right-hand subdivision of box 1 of the form and 'T2Lbis' in the right-hand subdivision of box 1 of any continuation sheets used.

5.   Loading lists drawn up in accordance with the specimen in Annex 45 and made out in accordance with Annex 44a may be used instead of continuation sheets as the descriptive part of a T2L document.]

NOTES

Substituted by Commission Regulation (EC) 2787/2000, Art 1, para 10.

[Articles 315a

The customs authorities may authorise any person fulfilling the conditions of Article 373 to use as loading lists which do not comply with all the requirements of Annexes 44a and 45.

Article 385(1), second subparagraph, (2) and (3) shall apply mutatis mutandis.]

Part III

NOTES

Inserted by Commission Regulation (EC) 2787/2000, Art 1, para 11.

[Article 316

1. Subject to the provisions of Article 324f, a T2L document shall be drawn up in a single original.

2. At the request of the person concerned, T2L documents and, where necessary, any continuation sheets or loading lists used, shall be endorsed by the competent office. Such endorsements shall comprise the following, which should, as far as possible, appear in box 'C. Office of departure':

(a) in the case of T2L documents, the name and stamp of the competent office, the signature of an official of that office, the date of endorsement and either the registration number or the number of the dispatch declaration, where this is required;

(b) in the case of continuation sheets or loading lists, the number appearing on the T2L document, which shall be entered by means of a stamp including the name of the competent office, or by hand; where it is entered by hand, it shall be accompanied by the official stamp of the said office.

The documents shall be returned to the person concerned.]

NOTES

Substituted by Commission Regulation (EC) 2787/2000, Art 1, para 12.

[SUBSECTION 2
COMMERCIAL DOCUMENTS]

NOTES

Inserted by Commission Regulation (EC) 2787/2000, Art 1, para 13.

Article 317

[1. Proof of the Community status of goods shall be furnished, in accordance with the conditions set out below, by the production of the invoice or transport document relating to the goods.]

[2. The invoice or transport document referred to in paragraph 1 shall include at least the full name and address of the consignor, or of the person concerned where this is not the consignor, the number and kind, marks and reference numbers of the packages, a description of the goods, the gross mass in kilograms and, where necessary, the container numbers.

The person concerned shall mark the said document clearly with the 'T2L' symbol, accompanied by his handwritten signature.]

[3. At the request of the person concerned, the invoice or transport document duly completed and signed by him shall be endorsed by the competent office. The endorsement shall include the name and stamp of the competent office, the signature of an official of that office, the date of endorsement and either the registration number or the number of the dispatch declaration where such a declaration is required.]

[4. If the total value of the Community goods covered by the invoice or transport document, completed and signed in accordance with paragraph 2 of this Article or Article 224, does not exceed EUR 10000, the person concerned shall not be required to submit that document for endorsement by the competent office.

In that case, the invoice or transport document shall include, in addition to the information set out in paragraph 2, the particulars of the competent office.]

5. This Article shall apply only where the invoice or transport document relates exclusively to Community goods.

NOTES

Para 1: substituted by Commission Regulation (EC) 75/98, Art 1, para 8.

Paras 2–4: substituted by Commission Regulation (EC) 2787/2000, Art 1, para 14.

[Article 317a

1. Proof of the Community status of goods shall be furnished, in accordance with the conditions set out below, by the production of the shipping company's manifest relating to the goods.

2. The manifest shall include at least the following information—
- (a)   the name and full address of the shipping company;
- (b)   the name of the vessel;
- (c)   the place and date of loading;
- (d)   the place of unloading.

The manifest shall further include, for each consignment—
- (a)   the reference for the bill of lading or other commercial document;
- (b)   the number, description, marks and reference numbers of the packages;
- [(c)   the normal trade description of the goods including sufficient detail to permit their identification;]
- (d)   the gross mass in kilograms;
- (e)   the container identification numbers, where applicable; and
- [(f)   the following entries for the status of the goods:
  - —   the letter 'C' (equivalent to 'T2L') for goods whose Community status can be demonstrated,
  - —   the letter 'F' (equivalent to 'T2LF') for goods whose Community status can be demonstrated, consigned to or originating in a part of the Community customs territory where the provisions of Directive 77/388/EEC do not apply,
  - —   the letter 'N' for all other goods.]

[3.   At the request of the shipping company, the manifest it has duly completed and signed shall be endorsed by the competent office. The endorsement shall include the name and stamp of the competent office, the signature of an official at that office and the date of endorsement.]

NOTES

Inserted by Commission Regulation (EC) 75/98, Art 1, para 9.

Para 2: words in square brackets substituted by Commission Regulation (EC) 2787/2000, Art 1, para 15.

Para 3: substituted by Commission Regulation (EC) 2787/2000, Art 1, para 15.

[Article 317b

Where the simplified Community transit procedures provided for [in Articles 445 and 448] are used, proof of Community status shall be provided by entering the letter 'C' (equivalent to 'T2L') alongside the relevant items on the manifest.]

Part III

NOTES

Words substituted by Commission Regulation (EC) 444/2002, Art 1, para 13.

Article 318

. . .

NOTES

Repealed by Commission Regulation (EC) 2787/2000, Art 1, para 17.

[SUBSECTION 3
OTHER PROOF SPECIFIC TO CERTAIN OPERATIONS]

NOTES

Inserted by Commission Regulation (EC) 2787/2000, Art 1, para 17.

Article 319

1. Where goods are transported under cover of a TIR carnet or an ATA carnet, the declarant may, with a view to proving the Community status of the goods . . ., clearly enter the symbol "T2L" in the space reserved for the description of goods, together with his signature, on all the relevant vouchers of the carnet used before presenting it to the office of departure for authentication. On all the vouchers where it has been entered, the symbol "T2L" shall be authenticated with the stamp of the office of departure accompanied by the signature of the competent official.

2. Where the TIR carnet or the ATA carnet covers both Community goods and non-Community goods, those two categories of goods shall be shown separately, and the symbol "T2L" shall be entered in such a way that it clearly relates only to the Community goods.

NOTES

Para 1: words repealed by Commission Regulation (EC) 2787/2000, Art 1, para 18.

Article 320

If it is necessary to establish the Community status of motorised road vehicles registered in a Member State, such vehicles shall be considered to have Community status—

(a)   where they are accompanied by their registration plates and documents and the registration particulars shown on the said plates and documents unambiguously establish their Community status;

[(b)   in other cases, in accordance with Articles 315 to 319 and 321, 322 and 323.]

NOTES

Point (b): substituted by Commission Regulation (EC) 2787/2000, Art 1, para 19.

Article 321

If it is necessary to establish the Community status of goods wagons belonging to a railway company of a Member State, such wagons shall be considered to have Community status—

(a)   where the code number and ownership mark (distinguishing letters) displayed on them unambiguously establish their Community status;

(b)   in other cases, on presentation of one of the documents referred to in [Articles 315 to 317b].

NOTES

Words in square brackets substituted by Commission Regulation (EC) 2787/2000, Art 1, para 20.

Article 322

1. If it is necessary to establish the Community status of packaging used for the transport of goods in intra-Community trade which can be identified as belonging to a person established in a Member State and is being returned empty after use from another Member State, the packaging shall be considered to have Community status—

(a)   where they are declared as Community goods and there is no doubt as to the veracity of the declaration;

(b)   in other cases, in accordance with Articles 315 to 323.

2. The facility provided for in paragraph 1 shall be granted for receptacles, packings, pallets and other similar equipment, excluding containers . . ..

NOTES

Para 2: words repealed by Commission Regulation (EC) 993/2001, Art 1, para 14.

Article 323

If it is necessary to establish the Community status of goods in passenger-accompanied baggage the goods, provided that they are not intended for commercial use, shall be considered to have Community status—

(a)   where they are declared as Community goods and there is no doubt as to the truthfulness of the declaration;

(b)   in other cases, in accordance with Articles 315 to 322.

Articles 323A, 324

NOTES

Repealed by Commission Regulation (EC) 2787/2000, Art 1, para 21.

[SUBSECTION 4
PROOF OF COMMUNITY STATUS OF GOODS PROVIDED BY AN AUTHORISED CONSIGNOR]

NOTES

Subsection 4 inserted by Commission Regulation (EC) 2787/2000, Art 1, para 21.

[Article 324a

1. The customs authorities of each Member State may authorise any person, hereinafter referred to as the 'authorised consignor', who satisfies the requirements of Article 373 and proposes to establish the Community status of goods by means of a T2L document in accordance with Article 315, or by means of one of the documents stipulated in Articles 317 to 317b, hereinafter referred to as 'commercial documents', to use such documents without having to present them for endorsement to the competent office.

2. The provisions of Articles 374 to 378 shall apply, *mutatis mutandis*, to the authorisation referred to in paragraph 1.]

NOTES

Subsection 4 (Arts 324a–324f) is inserted by Commission Regulation (EC) 2787/2000, Art 1, para 21.

[Article 324b

The authorisation shall specify, in particular:

(a) the office assigned responsibility for pre-authenticating the forms used for drawing up the documents concerned, for the purposes of Article 324c(1)(a);

(b) the manner in which the authorised consignor shall establish that the forms have been properly used;

(c) the excluded categories or movements of goods;

(d) the period within which and the manner in which the authorised consignor shall notify the competent office in order to enable it to carry out any necessary controls before departure of the goods.]

NOTES

Inserted as noted to Art 324a.

[Article 324c

1. The authorisation shall stipulate that the front of the commercial documents concerned or box 'C. Office of departure' on the front of the forms used for the purposes of compiling T2L document and, where appropriate, the continuation sheets, must be:

(a) stamped in advance with the stamp of the office referred to in Article 324b(a) and signed by an official of that office; or

(b) stamped by the authorised consignor with a special metal stamp approved by the customs authorities and corresponding to the specimen in Annex 62. The stamp may be pre-printed on the forms where the printing is entrusted to a printer approved for that purpose.

The provisions of Article 401 shall apply mutatis mutandis.

2. Not later than on consignment of the goods, the authorised consignor shall complete and sign the form. He shall also enter in box 'D. Control by office of departure' of the T2L document, or in a clearly identifiable space on the commercial document used, the name of the competent office, the date of completion of the document, and one of the following endorsements:

— Expedidor autorizado
— Godkendt afsender
— Zugelassener Versender
— Εγκεκριμενοζ αποστολεαζ
— Authorised consignor
— Expéditeur agréé
— Speditore autorizzato
— Toegelaten afzender
— Expedidor autorizado
— Hyvksytty lähettäjä
— Godkänd avsändare,]
[— Schvláený odesílatel,

—   Volitatud kaubasaatja,
—   Atzitais nosutitajs,
—   Igaliotas siuntejas,
—   Engedélyezett felad,ó
—   Awtorizzat li jibghat,
—   Upowazniony nadawca,
—   Pooblašceni poišljatelj,
—   Schválený odosielatel.]
[—   *(for original text, refer to Commission Regulation (EC) 1792/2006 (OJ L 362, 20.12.06, p 1))*,
—   Expeditor agreat autorizat autorizat]

NOTES

Inserted as noted to Art 324a.

Para 2: words inserted by the 2003 Act of Accession Annex II(19)(A)(II), para 13. Final two entries inserted by Commission Regulation (EC) 1792/2006, Art 1, Annex, Part 11(A)(12).

[Article 324d

1.   The authorised consignor may be authorised not to sign T2L documents or commercial documents used bearing the special stamp referred to in Annex 62 which are drawn up by an electronic or automatic data processing system. Such authorisation shall be subject to the condition that the authorised consignor has previously given those authorities a written undertaking acknowledging his liability for the legal consequences arising from all T2L documents or commercial documents issued bearing the special stamp.

2.   T2L documents or commercial documents drawn up in accordance with paragraph 1 shall contain in place of the authorised consignor's signature one of the following endorsements:

—   Dispensa de firma
—   Fritaget for underskrift
—   Freistellung von der Unterschriftsleistung
—   Δєν απαατείταα υπογραφή
—   Signature waived
—   Dispense de signature
—   Dispensa dalla firma
—   Van ondertekening vrijgesteld
—   Dispensada a assinatura
—   Vapautettu allekirjoituksesta
—   Befriad från underskrift.]
[[—   Oslobodenie od podpisu],
—   allkirjanõudest loobutud,
—   derigs bez paraksta,
—   leista nepasirašyti,
—   Aláírás alól mentesítve,
—   firma mhux mehtiega,
—   zwolniony ze sladania podpisu,
—   Opustitev podpisa,
—   podpis sa nevyžaduje.]]
[—   *(for original text, refer to Commission Regulation (EC) 1792/2006 (OJ L 362, 20.12.06, p 1))*,

—   Dispens de semntur]

NOTES

Inserted as noted to Art 324a.

Para 2: words inserted by the 2003 Act of Accession Annex II(19)(A)(II), para 14; words "Oslobodenie od podpisu" in square brackets inserted by Commission Regulation (EC) 883/2005, Art 1, OJ L 148, 11.06.05, p 5 with effect from 1 May 2004. Final two entries inserted by Commission Regulation (EC) 1792/2006, Art 1, Annex, Part 11(A)(13).

[Article 324e

1. The customs authorities of the Member States may authorise shipping companies not to draw up the manifest serving to demonstrate the Community status of goods until, at the latest, the day after the departure of the vessel and, in any case, before its arrival at the port of destination.

2. The authorisation referred to in paragraph 1 shall be granted only to international shipping companies which:

(a)   fulfil the conditions of Article 373; by way of derogation from Article 373(1)(a) shipping companies need not be established in the Community if they have a regional office there, and

(b)   use electronic data interchange systems to transmit information between the ports of departure and destination in the Community, and

(c)   operate a significant number of voyages between the Member States on recognised routes.

3. On receipt of an application, the customs authorities of the Member State where the shipping company is established shall notify the other Member States in whose respective territories the ports of departure and intended destination are situated of that application.

If no objection is received within 60 days of the date of notification, the customs authorities shall authorise use of the simplified procedure described in paragraph 4.

This authorisation shall be valid in the Member States concerned and shall apply only to transit operations between the ports to which it refers.

4. The simplification shall be operated as follows:

(a)   the manifest for the port of departure shall be transmitted by electronic data interchange system to the port of destination;

(b)   the shipping company shall enter in the manifest the information indicated in Article 317a(2);

(c)   on request, a printout of the manifest transmitted by electronic data exchange system shall be presented to the customs authorities at the port of departure at the latest on the working day following the departure of the vessel and in any case before it arrives at its port of destination;

(d)   a printout of the data exchange manifest shall be presented to the customs authorities at the port of destination.

5. [Article 448(5)] shall apply mutatis mutandis.]

NOTES

Inserted as noted to Art 324a.

Para 5: words substituted by Commission Regulation (EC) 444/2002, Art 1, para 14.

[Article 324f

The authorised consignor shall make a copy of each T2L document or each commercial document issued under this subsection. The customs authorities shall specify the conditions under which the copy shall be presented for purposes of control and retained for at least two years.]

NOTES

Inserted as noted to Art 324a.

[[SUBSECTION 5]
SPECIFIC PROVISIONS CONCERNING PRODUCTS OF SEA-FISHING AND
OTHER PRODUCTS TAKEN FROM THE SEA BY BOATS]

NOTES

Heading: inserted by Commission Regulation (EC) 482/96, Art 1, para 4.

Words in square brackets substituted by Commission Regulation (EC) 2787/2000, Art 1, para 22.

[Article 325

1.   [For the purposes of this subsection]—

(a)   *Community fishing vessel* means a vessel which is listed and registered in a part of a Member State's territory forming part of the customs territory of the Community, flies the flag of a Member State, catches products of sea-fishing and, as the case may be, processes them on board;

(b)   *Community factory ship* means a vessel which is listed or registered in a part of a Member State's territory forming part of the customs territory of the Community, flies the flag of a Member State and does not catch products of sea-fishing but does process such products on board.

2.   A T2M form, made out in accordance with Articles 327 to 337, shall be produced to prove the Community status—

(a)   of the products of sea-fishing caught by a Community fishing vessel, in waters other than the territorial waters of a country or territory outside the customs territory of the Community; and

(b)   of the goods obtained from such products on board that vessel or a Community factory ship, in the production of which other products having Community status may have been used,

which may be in packaging having Community status and are to be brought into the customs territory of the Community in the circumstances set out in Article 326.

3.   Proof of the Community status of the sea-fishing products and other products taken or caught in waters other than the territorial waters of a country or territory outside the customs territory of the Community by vessels flying the flag of a Member State and listed or registered in a part of a Member State's territory forming part of the customs territory of the Community, or of such products taken or caught in territorial waters within the customs territory of the Community by vessels of a non-member country, must be provided by means of the logbook or any other means which establishes the said status.]

NOTES

Substituted by Commission Regulation (EC) 482/96, Art 1, para 5.

Para 1: words in square brackets substituted by Commission Regulation (EC) 2787/2000, Art 1, para 23.

[**Article 326**

1.   A T2M form shall be presented in respect of the products and goods referred to in Article 325(2) which are transported directly to the customs territory of the Community—

(a)   by the Community fishing vessel which caught the products and, where applicable, processed them; or

(b)   by another Community fishing vessel or by the Community factory slip which processed the products following their transhipment from the vessel referred to in point (a); or

(c)   by any other vessel onto which the said products and goods were transhipped from the vessels referred to in points (a) and (b), without any further changes being made; or

(d)   by a means of transport covered by a single transport document made out in the country or territory not forming part of the customs territory of the Community where the products or goods were landed from the vessels referred to in points (a), (b) and (c).

Thereafter the T2M form may no longer be used as proof of the Community status of the products or goods to which it refers.

2.   The customs authorities which are responsible for the port where products and/or goods are landed from a vessel referred to in point (a) of paragraph 1 may waive the application of paragraph 1 where there is no doubt about the origin of those products and/or goods, or where the attestation referred to in Article 8(1) of Council Regulation (EEC) No 2847/93[1] is applicable.]

---

[1]   OJ L 261, 20.10.93, p 1.]

NOTES

Substituted by Commission Regulation (EC) 482/96, Art 1, para 5.

Article 327

1.   The form for the T2M document shall conform to the specimen shown in Annex 43.

2.   The original shall be printed on paper without mechanical pulp, dressed for writing purposes and weighing at least 55 g/m^2. It shall have a green guilloche pattern background printed on both sides so as to reveal any falsification by mechanical or chemical means.

3.   The T2M forms shall measure 210 × 297 mm, a tolerance of −5 and +8 being allowed in the length.

4.   The form shall be printed in an official Community language specified by the competent authorities of the Member State to which the vessel belongs.

5.   The T2M forms shall be bound in booklets of 10, with one detachable original and one non detachable carbon copy of each form. Page 2 of the cover of the booklet shall contain the notes shown in Annex 44.

6.   Each T2M form shall bear an individual serial number. This number shall be the same for both original and copy.

7.   Member States may themselves print the T2M forms and assemble them in booklets, or entrust the work to printers approved by them. In the latter case, reference to the approval must appear on page 1 of the cover of each booklet and on the original of each form. Page 1 and the original of each form must also bear the name and address of the printer or a mark by which he can be identified.

8.   The T2M forms shall be completed in one of the official Community languages either in typescript or legibly by hand; if the latter, in ink and in printed characters. No erasures or alterations may be made. Corrections shall be made by crossing out the wrong words and adding any necessary particulars. Any such corrections must be initialled by the person who signed the declaration containing them.

[Article 328

The booklet of T2M forms shall be issued at the request of the appropriate person by the Community customs office responsible for supervising the base port of the Community fishing vessel for which the booklet is intended.

The booklet shall be issued only when the person concerned has completed boxes 1 and 2 in the language of the form, and has completed and signed the declaration in box 3 of all the originals and copies of the forms contained in the booklet. When issuing the booklet, the customs office shall complete box B of all the originals and copies of the forms in the booklet.

The booklet shall be valid for two years from the date of issue shown on page 2 of its cover. In addition, the validity of the forms shall be guaranteed by the presence in box A of each original and copy of a stamp applied by the authority responsible for registering the Community fishing vessel for which the booklet is issued.]

NOTES

Substituted, together with Arts 329–337, by Commission Regulation (EC) 482/96, Art 1, para 6.

[Article 329

The master of the Community fishing vessel shall complete box 4 and, if the catch has been processed on board, box 6, and shall complete and sign the declaration in box 9 of the original and copy of one of the forms in the booklet whenever he—

(a)   tranships products to one of the vessels referred to in point (b) of Article 326(1) which processes those products;

(b)   tranships products or goods to any other vessel which will not process them but take them directly either to a port in the customs territory of the Community or to another port for subsequent consignment to that territory;

(c)   without prejudice to Article 326(2), lands products or goods in a port in the customs territory of the Community;

(d)   lands products or goods in a port outside the customs territory of the Community for subsequent consignment to that territory.

Any processing of such products shall be recorded in the vessel's logbook.]

NOTES

Substituted as noted to Art 328.

[Article 330

The master of a vessel referred to in point (b) of Article 326(1) shall complete box 6 and complete and sign the declaration in box 11 of the original of the T2M form whenever he lands goods either in a port in the customs territory of the Community or in a port outside the said territory for subsequent consignment to that territory, or whenever he tranships goods onto another vessel for that purpose.

Processing of products transhipped to the vessel shall be recorded in its logbook.]

NOTES

Substituted as noted to Art 328.

[**Article 331**

When the products or goods referred to in point (a) or point (b) of Article 329 are transhipped for the first time, box 10 of the original and the copy of a T2M form shall be completed; if a further transhipment, of the type referred to in Article 330, takes place, box 12 of the original of that T2M form shall also be completed. The transhipment declaration shall be signed by both the masters concerned and the original of the T2M form shall be given to the master of the vessel to which the products or goods are transhipped. Any transhipment operation shall be recorded in the logbooks of both the vessels involved.]

NOTES

Substituted as noted to Art 328.

[**Article 332**

1.   Where products or goods covered by a T2M form go to a country or territory not forming part of the customs territory of the Community, the said form shall be valid only if the certification in box 13 of the form has been completed and endorsed by the customs authorities of that country or territory.

2.   Where some of the products or goods do not come to the customs territory of the Community, the name, kind, gross mass and treatment or use assigned to those consignments shall be entered in the "Remarks" box of the T2M form.]

NOTES

Substituted as noted to Art 328.

[**Article 333**

1.   Where products or goods covered by a T2M form go to country or territory not forming part of the customs territory of the Community for subsequent despatch in split consignments to that territory, the person concerned or his representative shall—

(a)   enter in the "Remarks" box of the initial T2M form the number of kind of packages, the gross mass, the treatment or use to which the consignment has been assigned and the number of the "Extract" referred to in point (b);

(b)   make out a T2M "Extract", using for this purpose an original form taken from a booklet of T2M forms issued in accordance with the provisions of Article 328.

Each "Extract", and its copy which shall remain in the T2M booklet, shall include a reference to the initial T2M form referred to in point (a) and shall be clearly marked with one of the following words—

—   Extracto,
—   Udskrift,
—   Auszug,
—   Α,πόσπασμα
—   Extract,
—   Extrait,
—   Estratto,
—   Uittreksel,

—   Extracto,

—   Ote,

—   Utdrag,

[—   Výpis,

—   Vläjavtõe,

—   Izraksts,

—   Išraašs,

—   Kivonat,

—   Estratt,

—   Wyciag,

—   Izpisek,

—   Výpis]

[—   (for original text, refer to Commission Regulation (EC) 1792/2006 (OJ
L 362, 20.12.06, p 1)),

—   Extras]

The T2M "Extract" accompanying the split consignment to the customs territory of the Community shall state in boxes 4, 5, 6, 7 and 8 the name, kind, CN code and quantity of products or goods making up that consignment. In addition, the certification in box 13 shall be completed and endorsed by the customs authorities of the country or territory where the products or goods remained while in transit.

2.   When all the products and goods covered by the initial T2M form referred to in point (a) of paragraph 1 have been sent to the customs territory of the Community, the certification in box 13 of the form shall be completed and endorsed by the authorities referred to in that paragraph. The form shall then be sent to the customs office referred to in Article 328.

3.   Where some of the products or goods do not come to the customs territory of the Community, the name, kind, gross mass and treatment or use assigned to the products or goods shall be entered in the "Remarks" box of the initial T2M form.]

NOTES

Substituted as noted to Art 328.

Para 1: words in sub-para (b) inserted by the 2003 Act of Accession Annex II(19)(A)(II), para 15. Final two entries inserted by Commission Regulation (EC) 1792/2006, Art 1, Annex, Part 11(A)(14).

Article 334

All T2M forms, whether initial or "Extract", shall be presented at the customs office where the products or goods to which they refer are brought into the customs territory of the Community. However, where the products or goods are brought in under a transit procedure commencing outside that territory, the forms shall be presented at the customs office of destination for that procedure.

The authorities of the office may request a translation of the form. In addition, with a view to checking the accuracy of the particulars given in the T2M form, they may require the production of all relevant documents, including the vessels' papers where necessary. The office shall complete box C of each T2M form, a copy of which shall be sent to the customs office referred to in Article 328.]

NOTES

Substituted as noted to Art 328.

[Article 335

By way of derogation from Articles 332, 333 and 334, where products or goods covered by a T2M form go to a third country that is a contracting party to the Convention on a common transit procedure, for reconsignment in full or split consignments to the customs territory of the Community under "T2" procedure, the particulars of the said procedure shall be entered in the "Remarks" box of the T2M form.

When all the products and/or goods covered by this T2M form have been sent to the customs territory of the Community, the certification in box 13 of the form shall be completed and endorsed by the customs authorities. A completed copy of the form, shall be sent to the customs office referred to in Article 328.

The provisions of Article 332(2) shall apply as appropriate.]

NOTES

Substituted as noted to Art 328.

[Article 336

The booklet containing the T2M forms shall be produced whenever the customs authorities so require.

When a vessel for which a booklet of T2M forms as referred to in Article 327 has been issued ceases to satisfy the conditions laid down, before all the forms have been used, or when all the forms in the booklet have been used or its period of validity has expired, the booklet shall be returned immediately to the customs office of issue.]

NOTES

Substituted as noted to Art 328.

Article 337

. . .

NOTES

Repealed by Commission Regulation (EC) 2787/2000, Art 1, para 24.

Articles 338–340

. . .

NOTES

Repealed by Commission Regulation (EC) 482/96, Art 1, para 7.

CHAPTER 4
COMMUNITY TRANSIT

SECTION 1
GENERAL PROVISIONS

NOTES

This Chapter (Arts 340a–387) is substituted by Commission Regulation (EC) 2787/2000, Art 1, para 25.

[Article 340a

The provisions of this Chapter shall apply to external and internal Community transit, except if provided otherwise.

The goods involving higher risk of fraud are listed in Annex 44c. When a provision of the present Regulation refers to that Annex, any measure related to goods in that Annex shall apply only when the quantity of those goods exceeds the corresponding minimum. Annex 44c shall be reviewed at least once a year.]

NOTES

Substituted by Commission Regulation (EC) 2787/2000, Art 1, para 25.

[Article 340b

For the purposes of this Chapter, the following definitions shall apply:

1. 'office of departure': means the customs office where declarations placing goods under the Community transit procedure are accepted;

2. 'office of transit' means:

(a) the customs office at the point of exit from the customs territory of the Community when the consignment is leaving that territory in the course of a transit operation via a frontier between a Member State and a third country other than an EFTA country, or

(b) the customs office at the point of entry into the customs territory of the Community when the goods have crossed the territory of a third country in the course of a transit operation;

3. 'office of destination': means the customs office where goods placed under the Community transit procedure must be presented in order to end the procedure;

4. 'office of guarantee': means the office where the customs authorities of each Member State decide that guarantees furnished by a guarantor shall be lodged;

5. 'EFTA countries': means all EFTA countries and any other country that has acceded to the Convention of 20 May 1987 on a common transit procedure[1].]

[1] OJ L 226, 13.8.1987, p 2.

NOTES

Substituted as noted to Art 340a.

[Article 340c

1. Community goods shall be placed under the internal Community transit procedure if they are consigned:

(a) from a part of the customs territory of the Community where the provisions of Directive 77/388/EEC apply, to a part of the customs territory of the Community where those provisions do not apply; or

(b) from a part of the customs territory of the Community where the provisions of Directive 77/388/EEC do not apply, to a part of the customs territory of the Community where those provisions do apply; or

(c) from a part of the customs territory of the Community where the provisions of Directive 77/388/EEC do not apply, to a part of the customs territory of the Community where those provisions do not apply either.

2. Without prejudice to paragraph 3, Community goods which are consigned from one point in the customs territory of the Community to another through the

territory of one or more EFTA countries pursuant to the Convention on a common transit procedure, shall be placed under the internal Community transit procedure. Goods covered by the first subparagraph which are carried entirely by sea or air shall not be required to be placed under the internal Community transit procedure.

3. Where Community goods are exported [to an EFTA country or where they are exported and transit the territory of one or more EFTA countries . . .] and the provisions of the Convention on a common transit procedure apply, they shall be placed under the external Community transit procedure under the following conditions:

(a)   if they have undergone customs export formalities with a view to refunds being granted on export to third countries under the common agricultural policy; or

(b)   if they have come from intervention stocks, are subject to measures of control as to use and/or destination, and have undergone customs formalities on export to third countries under the common agricultural policy; or

(c)   if they are eligible for the repayment or remission of import duties on condition that they are exported from the customs territory of the Community; or

(d)   if in the form of compensating products or goods in the unaltered state, they have undergone customs formalities on export to third countries in order to discharge the inward processing procedure, drawback system, with a view to obtaining repayment or remission of customs duty.]

NOTES

Substituted as noted to Art 340a.

Para 3: words in square brackets substituted by Corrigendum (OJ L 20, 23.1.02, p 11)

[Article 340d

Goods to which the Community transit procedure applies may be carried between two points in the Community customs territory via the territory of a third country other than an EFTA country provided that that they are carried through that third country under cover of a single transport document drawn up in a Member State. Where this is so, the effect of the transit procedure shall be suspended in the territory of the third country.]

NOTES

Substituted as noted to Art 340a.

[Article 340e

1. The Community transit procedure shall be compulsory in respect of goods carried by air only if they are loaded or reloaded at an airport in the Community.

2. Without prejudice to Article 91(1) of the Code, use of the Community transit procedure shall be compulsory for goods carried by sea if they are carried by a regular shipping service authorised in accordance with Articles 313a and 313b.]

NOTES

Substituted as noted to Art 340a.

Part III

[**Article 341**

The provisions of Chapters 1 and 2 of Title VII of the Code and the provisions of this Title shall apply *mutatis mutandis* to other charges within the meaning of Article 91(1)(a) of the Code.]

NOTES

Substituted as noted to Art 340a.

[**Article 342**

1. The guarantee furnished by the principal shall be valid throughout the Community.

2. Where the guarantee is furnished by a guarantor, the guarantor shall indicate an address for service or appoint an agent in each Member State.

3. A guarantee needs to be furnished for Community transit operations carried out by the railway companies of the Member States under a procedure other than the simplified procedure referred to in Article 372(1)(g)(i).]

NOTES

Substituted as noted to Art 340a.

[**Article 343**

Each Member State shall provide the Commission with a list, in the agreed format, of the customs offices competent to handle Community transit operations, indicating their respective identification numbers and duties and stating the days and hours when they are open. Any changes to this information shall be communicated to the Commission.

The Commission shall communicate this information to the other Member States.]

NOTES

Substituted as noted to Art 340a.

[**Article 344**

The characteristics of the forms other than the Single Administrative Document used in the Community transit system shall be set out in Annex 44b.]

NOTES

Substituted as noted to Art 340a.

[SECTION 2
PROCEDURE

SUBSECTION 1
INDIVIDUAL GUARANTEE

Article 345

[1. The individual guarantee shall cover the full amount of customs debt liable to be incurred, calculated on the basis of the highest rates applicable to goods of the same kind in the Member State of departure. For the purposes of that calculation, Community goods carried in accordance with the Convention on a common transit procedure shall be treated as non-Community goods.]

However, the rates to take into consideration for the calculation of the individual guarantee cannot be less than a minimal rate, when such a rate is mentioned in the fifth column of Annex 44c.

2. Individual guarantees in the form of a cash deposit shall be lodged at the office of departure. They shall be repaid when the procedure has been discharged.

3. An individual guarantee furnished by a guarantor may be in the form of individual guarantee vouchers for an amount of EUR 7000, issued by the guarantor to persons who intend to act as principal.

The guarantor shall be liable for up to EUR 7000 per voucher.]

NOTES

Substituted as noted to Art 340a.

Para 1: substituted by Commission Regulation (EC) 444/2002, Art 1, para 15.

[Article 346

1. An individual guarantee furnished by a guarantor shall correspond to the specimen in Annex 49.

Where the office of departure is not the office of guarantee, the latter shall keep a copy of the instrument by which it has accepted the guarantor's undertaking. The principal shall present the original at the office of departure, where it shall be retained. Where necessary this office may request a translation into the official language, or one of the official languages, of the Member State concerned.

[However, where guarantee data is exchanged between the office of guarantee and the office of departure using information technology and computer networks, the original of the guarantee instrument shall be retained at the office of guarantee and no paper copy shall be presented to the office of departure.]

2. Where required by national law, regulation or administrative provision, or by common practice, each Member State may allow the undertaking referred to in paragraph 1 to take a different form provided it has the same legal effect as the undertaking shown in the specimen.]

However, where guarantee data is exchanged between the office of guarantee and the office of departure using information technology and computer networks, the original of the guarantee instrument shall be retained at the office of departure.

NOTES

Substituted as noted to Art 340a.

Para 1: Words in square brackets added by Commission Regulation (EC) 993/2001, Art 1, para 15. Third paragraph substituted by Corrigendum (see OJ L 282, 1.9.2004, p 10).

[Article 347

1. In the case referred in Article 345(3), the individual guarantee shall correspond to the specimen in Annex 50.

Article 346(2) shall apply mutatis mutandis.

2. The individual guarantee voucher shall be drawn up on a form corresponding to the specimen in Annex 54. The guarantor shall indicate on the voucher the last date on which it may be used, which may not be later than one year from the date of issue.

3. The guarantor may issue individual guarantee vouchers which are not valid for a Community transit operation involving goods listed in Annex 44c.

To do so, the guarantor shall endorse each individual guarantee voucher diagonally with one of the following phrases:

—   Validez limitada

—   Begrænset gyldighed

—   Beschränkte Geltung
—   Περιορισμενη ισχυζ
—   Limited validity
—   Validité limitée
—   Validità limitata
—   Beperkte geldigheid
—   Validade limitada
—   Voimassa rajoitetusti
—   Begränsad giltighet,
[—   Omezená platnost,
—   Piiratud kehtivus,
—   Ierobežots dergums,
—   Galiojimas apribotas,
—   Korlátozott érvény,
—   Validità limitata,
—   Ograniczona wano,
—   Omejena veljavnost,
—   Obmedzená platnost.]
[—   *(for original text, refer to Commission Regulation (EC) 1792/2006 (OJ L 362, 20.12.06, p 1)),*
—   Validitate limitat]

[3a.   Where the office of guarantee exchanges guarantee data with the offices of departure using information technology and computer networks, the guarantor shall furnish this office with any required details about the individual guarantee vouchers that he has issued according to the modalities decided by the customs authorities.]

4.   The principal shall deliver to the office of departure the number of individual guarantee vouchers corresponding to the multiple of EUR 7000 required to cover the total amount referred to in Article 345(1). The vouchers shall be retained by the office of departure.]

NOTES

Substituted as noted to Art 340a.

Para 3: words inserted by the 2003 Act of Accession Annex II(19)(A)(II), para 16. Final two entries inserted by Commission Regulation (EC) 1792/2006, Art 1, Annex, Part 11(A)(15).

Para 3a: inserted by Commission Regulation (EC) 993/2001, Art 1, para 16.

[**Article 348**

1.   The office of guarantee shall revoke its decision accepting the guarantor's undertaking if the conditions laid down at the time of issue are no longer fulfilled.

Equally, the guarantor may cancel his undertaking at any time.

2.   The revocation or cancellation shall become effective on the 16th day following the date on which the guarantor or the office of guarantee, as appropriate, is notified.

From the date on which the revocation or cancellation becomes effective, no individual guarantee vouchers issued earlier may be used for placing goods under the Community transit procedure.

3.   The Member State responsible for the relevant office of guarantee shall notify the Commission forthwith of any revocation or cancellation and the date on which it becomes effective. The Commission shall notify the other Member States thereof.]

NOTES

Substituted as noted to Art 340a.

[SUBSECTION 2
MEANS OF TRANSPORT AND DECLARATIONS

Article 349

1.   Each transit declaration shall include only the goods loaded or to be loaded on a single means of transport for carriage from one office of departure to one office of destination.

For the purposes of this Article, the following shall be regarded as constituting a single means of transport, on condition that the goods carried are to be dispatched together:

(a)   a road vehicle accompanied by its trailer(s) or semi-trailer(s);

(b)   a set of coupled railway carriages or wagons;

(c)   boats constituting a single chain;

(d)   containers loaded on a single means of transport within the meaning of this Article.

2.   A single means of transport may be used for loading goods at more than one office of departure and for unloading at more than one office of destination.]

NOTES

Substituted as noted to Art 340a.

[Article 350

Loading lists drawn up in accordance with Annex 44a and corresponding to the specimen in Annex 45 may be used instead of the continuation sheets as the descriptive part of transit declarations, of which they shall form an integral part.]

NOTES

Substituted as noted to Art 340a.

[Article 351

In the case of consignments comprising both goods which must be placed under the external Community transit procedure and goods which must be placed under the internal Community transit procedure, the transit declaration bearing the 'T' symbol shall be supplemented by:

(a)   continuation sheets bearing the 'T1bis', 'T2bis' or 'T2Fbis' symbol, as appropriate, or

(b)   loading lists bearing the 'T1', 'T2' or 'T2F' symbol, as appropriate.]

NOTES

Substituted as noted to Art 340a.

[Article 352

Where the 'T1', 'T2' or 'T2F' symbols have been omitted from the right-hand subdivision of box 1 of the transit declaration or where, in the case of consignments containing both goods placed under the internal Community transit procedure and goods placed under the external Community transit procedure, the provisions of

Article 351 have not been complied with, the goods shall be deemed to have been placed under the external Community transit procedure.

However, for the purposes of charging export duty or implementing any of the common commercial policy export measures, such goods shall be deemed to be moving under the internal Community transit procedure.]

NOTES

Substituted as noted to Art 340a.

[Article 353

1. Transit declarations shall comply with the structure and particulars set out in Annex 37a, and shall be lodged at the office of departure using a data-processing technique.

2. The customs authorities shall accept a transit declaration made in writing on a form corresponding to the specimen set out in Annex 31 and in accordance with the procedure defined by the customs authorities in agreement with each other in the following cases:

    (a)   the customs authorities' computerised transit system is not functioning,

    (b)   the principal's application is not functioning.

3. The use of a written transit declaration under paragraph 2(b) shall be subject to the approval of the customs authorities.

4. Where the goods are transported by travellers who have no direct access to the customs' computerised system and so have no means of lodging the transit declaration using a data processing technique at the office of departure, the customs authorities shall authorise the traveller to use a transit declaration made in writing on a form corresponding to the specimen set out in Annex 31.

In this case the customs authorities shall ensure that the transit data is exchanged between customs authorities using information technology and computer networks.]

NOTES

Substituted by Council Regulation (EC) No 837/2005, Art 1 with effect from 1 July 2006. However, the customs authorities may continue to accept transit declarations made in writing until 31 December 2006 at the latest. Article, before substitution, previously read as follows—

(1)   By derogation from Article 222(1), a transit declaration lodged by means of a data-processing technique, as defined in Article 4a(1)(a), shall comply with the structure and notes set out in Annex 37a.

(2)   · · ..

Article 354

· · .

NOTES

Repealed by Council Regulation (EC) No 837/2005, Art 1 with effect from 1 July 2006. However, the customs authorities may continue to accept transit declarations made in writing until 31 December 2006 at the latest. Article, before repeal, previously read as follows—

Subject to the conditions and in the manner they shall determine, and with due regard to the principles laid down by customs rules, the customs authorities may allow transit declarations, or some of the particulars thereof, to be lodged by means of discs, magnetic tapes or other similar data media, where appropriate in coded form.

[SUBSECTION 3
FORMALITIES AT THE OFFICE OF DEPARTURE

Article 355

1. Goods placed under the Community transit procedure shall be carried to the office of destination along an economically justified route.

2. Without prejudice to Article 387, for goods on the list in Annex 44c, or when the customs authorities or the principal consider it necessary, the office of departure shall prescribe an itinerary and enter in box 44 of the transit declaration at least the Member States to be transited, taking into account any details communicated by the principal.]

NOTES

Substituted as noted to Art 340a.

[**Article 356**

1. The office of departure shall set a time limit within which the goods must be presented at the office of destination, taking into account the itinerary, any current transport or other legislation and, where appropriate, the details communicated by the principal.

2. The time limit prescribed by the office of departure shall be binding on the customs authorities of the Member States whose territory is entered during a Community transit operation and shall not be altered by those authorities.

3. Where the goods are presented at the office of destination after expiry of the time limit prescribed by the office of departure and where this failure to comply with the time limit is due to circumstances which are explained to the satisfaction of the office of destination and are not attributable to the carrier or the principal, the latter shall be deemed to have complied with the time limit prescribed.]

NOTES

Substituted as noted to Art 340a.

[**Article 357**

1. Without prejudice to paragraph 4, goods to be placed under the Community transit procedure shall not be released unless they are sealed.

2. The following shall be sealed:
   (a)   the space containing the goods, where the means of transport has been approved under other rules or recognised by the office of departure as suitable for sealing;
   (b)   each individual package, in other cases.

Seals must have the characteristics set out in Annex 46a.

3. Means of transport may be recognised as suitable for sealing on condition that:
   (a)   seals can be simply and effectively affixed to them;
   (b)   they are so constructed that no goods can be removed or introduced without leaving visible traces or without breaking the seals;
   (c)   they contain no concealed spaces where goods may be hidden;
   (d)   the spaces reserved for the load are readily accessible for inspection by the customs authorities.

Any road vehicle, trailer, semi-trailer or container approved for the carriage of goods under customs seal in accordance with an international agreement to which the European Community is a party shall be regarded as suitable for sealing.

4. The office of departure may dispense with sealing if, having regard to other possible measures for identification, the description of the goods in the transit declaration or in the supplementary documents make them readily identifiable.

A goods description shall be deemed to permit identification of the goods where it is sufficiently precise to permit easy identification of the quantity and nature of the goods.

Where the office of departure grants a waiver from sealing, it shall enter one of the following endorsements in the transit declaration, opposite the heading 'seals affixed' of box 'D. Control by office of departure':

—   Dispensa
—   Fritaget
—   Befreiung
—   Απαπαλλαγη απο την υποχρεωση τηρησηζ συγκειμενηζδιαδρομηζ
—   Waiver
—   Dispense
—   Dispensa
—   Vrijstelling
—   Dispensa
—   Vapautettu
—   Befrielse.]
[[—   Oslobodenie],
—   Loobumine,
—   Derigs bez zimoga,
—   Leista neplombuoti,
—   Mentesség,
—   Tnehhija,
—   Zwolnienie,
—   Opustitev,
—   Upustenie.]
[—   *(for original text, refer to Commission Regulation (EC) 1792/2006 (OJ L 362, 20.12.06, p 1))*,
—   Dispens]

NOTES

Substituted as noted to Art 340a.

Para 4: words inserted by the 2003 Act of Accession Annex II(19)(A)(II), para 17; word "Oslobodenie" in square brackets inserted by Commission Regulation (EC) 883/2005, Art 1, OJ L 148, 11.06.05, p 5 with effect from 1 May 2004. Final two entries inserted by Commission Regulation (EC) 1792/2006, Art 1, Annex, Part 11(A)(16).

[Article 358

1. Where a transit declaration is processed at an office of departure by a computer system, copies No 4 and No 5 of the declaration shall be replaced by a transit accompanying document corresponding to the specimen and notes in Annex 45a.

[2. Where appropriate, the transit accompanying document shall be supplemented by a list of items corresponding to the specimen and notes in Annex 45b. This list shall form an integral part of the transit accompanying document.]

3. In the circumstances referred to in paragraph 1 the office of departure shall retain the declaration and authorise release of the goods by issuing the transit accompanying document to the principal.

4. Where authorised, the transit accompanying document may be printed out from the principal's computer system.

5. Where the provisions of this Title refer to copies of the declaration accompanying a consignment, these provisions shall apply, mutatis mutandis, to the transit accompanying document.]

NOTES

Substituted as noted to Art 340a.

Para 2: substituted by Commission Regulation (EC) 881/2003 Art 1, para 11 with effect from 1 January 2005.

[SUBSECTION 4
FORMALITIES EN ROUTE

Article 359

1. Goods placed under the Community transit procedure shall be carried under cover of copies No 4 and No 5 of the transit declaration returned to the principal by the office of departure.

The consignment and copies No 4 and No 5 of the transit declaration shall be presented at each office of transit.

[2. The carrier shall present a transit advice note made out on a form corresponding to the specimen in Annex 46 to each office of transit, where the note shall be kept. However, when the transit data is exchanged between the office of departure and the office of transit using information technology and computer networks the transit advice note shall not be presented.]

[3. Where goods are carried via an office of transit other than that mentioned in Copies No 4 and No 5 of the transit declaration, the office of transit used shall send the transit advice note without delay to the office of transit initially specified, or notify the passage to the office of departure in the cases and according to the procedure mutually agreed by the customs authorities.]]

NOTES

Substituted as noted to Art 340a.

Para 2: substituted by Commission Regulation (EC) 993/2001, Art 1, para 17.

Para 3: substituted by Commission Regulation (EC) 444/2002, Art 1, para 16.

[**Article 360**

1. The carrier shall be required to make the necessary entries in copies No 4 and 5 of the transit declaration and present them with the consignment to the customs authorities of the Member State in whose territory the means of transport is located:

(a) if the prescribed itinerary is changed and the provisions of Article 355(2) apply;

(b) if seals are broken in the course of a transport operation for reasons beyond the carrier's control;

(c) if goods are transferred to another means of transport; any such transfer must be made under the supervision of the customs authorities which may, however, authorise transfers to be made without their supervision;

(d) in the event of imminent danger necessitating immediate partial or total unloading of the means of transport;

(e) in the event of any incident or accident capable of affecting the ability of the principal or the carrier to comply with his obligations.

2. Where the customs authorities consider that the Community transit operation concerned may continue in the normal way they shall take any steps that may be necessary and then endorse copies No 4 and 5 of the transit declaration.]

NOTES

Substituted as noted to Art 340a.

[SUBSECTION 5
FORMALITIES AT THE OFFICE OF DESTINATION

Article 361

1. The goods and copies No 4 and No 5 of the transit declaration shall be presented at the office of destination.

2. The office of destination shall register copies No 4 and No 5 of the transit declaration, record on them their date of arrival and enter the details of any controls carried out.

3. At the request of the principal, and to provide evidence of the procedure having ended in accordance with Article 365(2), the office of destination shall endorse an extra copy No 5 or a copy of copy No 5 of the transit declaration with one of the following phrases:

—   Prueba alternativa
—   Alternativt bevis
—   Alternativnachweis
—   Εναααλλτακτικ ααρποδεδειξη
—   Alternative proof
—   Preuve alternative
—   Prova alternativa
—   Alternatief bewijs
—   Prova alternativa
—   Vaihtoehtoinen todiste
—   Alternativt bevis,
[—   Alternativní dukaz,
—   Alternatiivsed tõendid,
—   Alternativs pieradijums,
—   Alternatyvusis irodymas,
—   Alternatív igazolás,
—   Prova alternattiva,
—   Alternatywny dowód,
—   Alternativno dokazilo,
—   Alternatívny dôkaz.]
[—   А ,
—   Prob Dovada alternativ]

4. A transit operation may end at an office other than the one entered in the transit declaration. That office shall then become the office of destination.

Where the new office of destination comes under the jurisdiction of a Member State other than the one having jurisdiction over the office originally designated, the new office of destination shall enter in box 'I. Control by office of destination' of copy No 5 of the transit declaration one of the following endorsements in addition to the usual observations it is required to make:

— Diferencias: mercancías presentadas en la oficina   nombre y país)
— Forskelle: det sted, hvor varerne blev frembudt   (navn og land)

— Unstimmigkeiten: Stelle, bei der die Gestellung erfolgte   (Name und Land)

— ΔιαφαΦεο εμρρɛεsματα ρεμπsορεμεsνεμτα στα (Ονομαμα και χωραα) τετ απεροσκομισθεντ αοτοτλ ωνειο

— Differences: office where goods were presented   (name and country)

— Diffréences: marchandises prséenteés au bureau   (nom et pays)

— Differenze: ufficio al quale sono state presentate le merci   (nome e paese)

— Verschillen: kantoor waar de goederen zijn aangebracht   (naam en land)

— Diferenças: mercadorias apresentadas na estância   (nome e país)

— Muutos: toimipaikka, jossa tavarat esitetty   (nimi ja maa)

— Avvikelse: varorna uppvisade för kontor   (namn, land).

[— Nesrovnalosti: úrad, kterméu bylo zboží předloženo   (název a zeme),

— Erinevused: asutus, kuhu kaup esitati   (nimi ja riik),

— Atškiribas: muitas iestade, kura preces tika uzraditas   (nosaukums un valsts),

— Skirtumai: istaiga, kuriai pateiktos prekes   (pavadinimas ir valstybe),

— Eltérséek: hivatal, ahol az áruk bemutatása megtörtént   (nvé sé ország),

— Differenzi: ufficcju fejn l-oggetti kienu pprezentati   (isem u pajjiz),

— Niezgodnosci: urzad w którym przedstawiono towar   (nazwa i kraj),

— Razlike: urad, pri katerem je bilo blago predloženo   (naziv in država),

[— Nezrovnalosti: úrad, ktorméu bol tovar dodaný   (názov a krajina)]]

[— *(for original text, refer to Commission Regulation (EC) 1792/2006 (OJ L 362, 20.12.06, p 1))*   (–),

— Diferente: mrfuri prezentate la biroul vamal (numebiroul unde au fost prezentate mrfurile   (denumire si tara)]

NOTES

Substituted as noted to Art 340a.

Para 3: words inserted by the 2003 Act of Accession Annex II(19)(A)(II), para 18. Final two entries inserted by Commission Regulation (EC) 1792/2006, Art 1, Annex, Part 11(A)(17).

Para 4: words inserted by the 2003 Act of Accession Annex II(19)(A)(II), para 19; words in final indent (inner square brackets) substituted by Commission Regulation (EC) 883/2005, Art 1, OJ L 148, 11.06.05, p 5 with effect from 1 May 2004. Final two entries inserted by Commission Regulation (EC) 1792/2006, Art 1, Annex, Part 11(A)(18).

[**Article 362**

1. The office of destination shall issue a receipt on request to the person presenting copies No 4 and No 5 of the transit declaration.

2. The form for the receipt shall correspond to the specimen in Annex 47. Alternatively, the receipt may be made out on specimen on the back of copy No 5 of the transit declaration.

3. The receipt shall be completed in advance by the person concerned. It may contain other particulars relating to the consignment, except in the space reserved for the office of destination. The receipt shall not be used as proof of the procedure having ended within the meaning of Article 365(2).]

Part III

NOTES

Substituted as noted to Art 340a.

[Article 363

The customs authorities of the Member State of destination shall return copy No 5 of the transit declaration to the customs authorities in the Member State of departure without delay and at most within one month of the date when the procedure ended.]

NOTES

Substituted as noted to Art 340a.

[Article 364

Each Member State shall notify the Commission of which offices have been created for the centralised receipt and transmission of documents and the types of documents involved, as well as of the responsibilities conferred on those offices. The Commission shall inform the other Member States.]

NOTES

Substituted as noted to Art 340a.

[SUBSECTION 6
CHECKING THE END OF THE PROCEDURE

Article 365

1.   If copy No 5 of the transit declaration is not returned to the customs authorities of the Member State of departure within two months of the date of acceptance of the declaration, those authorities shall inform the principal and ask him to furnish proof that the procedure has ended.

[1a.   Where the provisions of Section 2 subsection 7 apply and the customs authorities of the Member States of departure have not received the 'Arrival Advice' message by the time limit within which the goods must be presented at the office of destination those authorities shall inform the principal and ask him to furnish proof that the procedure has ended.]

2.   The proof referred to in paragraph 1 may be furnished to the satisfaction of the customs authorities in the form of a document certified by the customs authorities of the Member State of destination identifying the goods and establishing that they have been presented at the office of destination or, where Article 406 applies, to the authorised consignee.

3.   The Community transit procedure shall also be considered as having ended where the principal presents, to the satisfaction of the customs authorities, a customs document issued in a third country entering the goods for a customs-approved treatment or use, or a copy or photocopy thereof, identifying the goods. Copies or photocopies must be certified as being true copies by the body which certified the original documents, by the authorities of the third countries concerned or by the authorities of one of the Member States.]

NOTES

Substituted as noted to Art 340a.
Para 1a: inserted by Commission Regulation (EC) 993/2001, Art 1, para 18.

[Article 366

1. Where the customs authorities of the Member State of departure have not received proof within four months of the date of acceptance of the transit declaration that the procedure has ended, they shall initiate the enquiry procedure immediately in order to obtain the information needed to discharge the procedure or, where this is not possible, to establish whether a customs debt has been incurred, to identify the debtor and to determine the customs authorities responsible for entry in the accounts.

If the customs authorities receive information earlier that the transit procedure has not ended, or suspect that to be the case, the enquiry procedure shall be initiated forthwith.

[Where the provisions of Section 2 subsection 7 apply the customs authorities shall also initiate the enquiry procedure forthwith each time they have not received the 'Arrival Advice' message by the time limit within which the goods must be presented at the office of destination or the 'Control Results' message within six days after having received the 'Arrival Advice' message.]

2. The enquiry procedure shall also be initiated if it transpires subsequently that proof of the end of the procedure was falsified and the enquiry procedure is necessary to achieve the objectives of paragraph 1.

3. To initiate the enquiry procedure, the customs authorities of the Member State of departure shall send the customs authorities of the Member State of destination a request together with all the necessary information.

4. The customs authorities of the Member State of destination and, where appropriate, the offices of transit called on to act in the context of the enquiry procedure shall respond without delay.

5. Where an enquiry establishes that the transit procedure ended correctly, the customs authorities of the Member State of departure shall immediately inform the principal and, where appropriate, any customs authorities that may have initiated a recovery procedure in accordance with Articles 217 to 232 of the Code.]

NOTES

Substituted as noted to Art 340a.

Para 1: words in square brackets inserted by Commission Regulation (EC) 993/2001, Art 1, para 19.

[SUBSECTION 7
ADDITIONAL PROVISIONS APPLICABLE WHERE TRANSIT DATA IS EXCHANGED BETWEEN CUSTOMS AUTHORITIES USING INFORMATION TECHNOLOGY AND COMPUTER NETWORKS

[Article 367
This subsection shall not apply to the simplified procedures specific to the modes of transport referred to in Article 372(1)(g).]

NOTES

Article substituted by Commission Regulation (EC) No 1875/2006, Art 1(42) with effect from 26 December 2006.

Article 368
(Article revoked by Commission Regulation (EC) No 1875/2006, Art 1(43) with effect from 26 December 2006.)

Part III

[Article 368a
Where the office of guarantee and the office of departure are located in different Member States the messages to be used for the exchange of guarantee data shall conform to the structure and particulars defined by the customs authorities in agreement with each other.]

NOTES
Inserted by Commission Regulation (EC) 993/2001, Art 1, para 20.

[Article 369
On release of the goods, the office of departure shall transmit details of the community transit operation to the declared office of destination using the 'Anticipated Arrival Record' message and to each declared office of transit using the 'Anticipated Transit Record' message. These messages shall be based on data derived from the transit declaration, where the case occurs amended, and completed as appropriate. These messages shall conform to the structure and particulars defined by the customs authorities in agreement with each other.]

NOTES
Substituted by Commission Regulation (EC) 993/2001, Art 1, para 21.

[Article 369a
The office of transit shall record the passage against the 'Anticipated Transit Record' message received from the office of departure. Any inspection of the goods shall be carried out using the 'Anticipated Transit Record' message as a basis for such inspection. The passage shall be notified to the office of departure using the 'Notification Crossing Frontier' message. This message shall conform to the structure and particulars defined by the customs authorities in agreement with each other.]

NOTES
Inserted by Commission Regulation (EC) 993/2001, Art 1, para 22.

[Article 370
1. The office of destination shall keep the transit accompanying document and, using the 'Arrival advice message', notify the office of departure of the arrival of the goods on the day they are presented at the office of destination. The message may not be used as proof of the procedure having ended for the purposes of Article 365(2).

2. Except where justified, the office of destination shall forward the 'Control results' message to the office of departure at the latest on the working day following the day the goods are presented at the office of destination.

3. The messages shall conform to the structure and particulars defined by the customs authorities in agreement with each other.]

NOTES
Substituted as noted to Art 340a.

[Article 371
The examination of the goods shall be carried out using the 'Anticipated arrival record' message received from the office of departure as a basis for such examination.]

NOTES

Substituted as noted to Art 340a.

[SECTION 3
SIMPLIFICATIONS

SUBSECTION 1
GENERAL PROVISIONS CONCERNING SIMPLIFICATIONS

Article 372

1.   Following an application by the principal or the consignee, as appropriate, the customs authorities may authorise the following simplifications:

(a)   use of a comprehensive guarantee or guarantee waiver;

(b)   use of special loading lists;

(c)   use of seals of a special type;

(d)   exemption from the requirement to use a prescribed itinerary;

(e)   authorised consignor status;

(f)   authorised consignee status;

(g)   application of simplified procedures specific to goods:

(i)   carried by rail or large container;

(ii)   carried by air;

(iii)   carried by sea;

(iv)   moved by pipeline;

(h)   use of other simplified procedures based on Article 97(2) of the Code.

2.   Except where otherwise provided in this section or the authorisation, where authorisation to use the simplifications referred to in paragraph 1, points (a), (b) and (g) is granted, the simplifications shall apply in all Member States. Where authorisation to use the simplifications referred to in paragraph 1, points (c), (d), and (e) is granted, the simplifications shall apply only to Community transit operations beginning in the Member State where the authorisation was granted. Where authorisation to use the simplification referred to in paragraph 1, point (f) is granted, the simplification shall apply solely in the Member State where the authorisation was granted.]

NOTES

Substituted as noted to Art 340a.

[**Article 373**

1.   The authorisations referred to in Article 372(1) shall be granted only to persons who:

(a)   are established in the Community, with the proviso that authorisation to use a comprehensive guarantee may be granted only to persons established in the Member State where the guarantee is furnished,

(b)   regularly use the Community transit arrangements, or whose customs authorities know that they can meet the obligations under the arrangements or, in connection with the simplification referred to in Article 372(1)(f), regularly receive goods that have been entered for the Community transit procedure, and

(c)   have not committed any serious or repeated offences against customs or tax legislation.

2. To ensure the proper management of the simplifications, authorisations shall be granted only where:

(a)   the customs authorities are able to supervise the procedure and carry out controls without an administrative effort disproportionate to the requirements of the person concerned, and

(b)   the persons concerned keep records which enable the customs authorities to carry out effective controls.

[3.   Where the person concerned holds an AEO certificate referred to in point (a) or (c) of Article 14a(1), the requirements set out in paragraph 1(c) and 2(b) of this Article shall be deemed to be met.]]

NOTES

Substituted as noted to Art 340a.

Para 3: inserted by Commission Regulation (EC) No 1875/2006, Art 1(44) with effect from 1 January 2008.

[**Article 374**

1. An application for authorisation to use simplifications, hereinafter referred to as 'the application', shall be made in writing. It shall be dated and signed.

2. The application must include all the facts which will allow the customs authorities to check that the conditions subject to which use of the simplifications may be granted have been met.]

NOTES

Substituted as noted to Art 340a.

[**Article 375**

1. The application shall be lodged with the customs authorities of the Member State in which the applicant is established.

2. The authorisation shall be issued or the application rejected within three months at most of the date on which the application is lodged.]

NOTES

Substituted as noted to Art 340a.

[**Article 376**

1. The dated and signed original of the authorisation and one or more copies thereof shall be given to the holder.

2. The authorisation shall specify the conditions for use of the simplifications and lay down the operating and control methods. It shall be valid from the date of issue.

3. In the case of the simplifications referred to in Article 372(1)(c), (d) and (g), authorisations shall be presented whenever the office of departure so requires.]

NOTES

Substituted as noted to Art 340a.

[**Article 377**

1. The holder of an authorisation shall inform the customs authorities of any factor arising after the authorisation was granted which may influence its continuation or content.

2. The date on which the decision takes effect shall be indicated in a decision revoking or amending authorisation.]

NOTES
Substituted as noted to Art 340a.

[Article 378

1. The customs authorities shall keep applications and attached supporting documents, together with a copy of any authorisations issued.

2. Where an application is rejected or an authorisation is annulled or revoked, the application and the decision rejecting or annulling or revoking the application, as the case may be, and all attached supporting documents shall be kept for at least three years from the end of the calendar year in which the application was rejected or the authorisation was annulled or revoked.]

NOTES
Substituted as noted to Art 340a.

[SUBSECTION 2
COMPREHENSIVE GUARANTEE AND GUARANTEE WAIVER

Article 379

1. The principal may use a comprehensive guarantee, or guarantee waiver, up to a reference amount.

[For the application of the first subparagraph a calculation is made of the amount of the customs debt which may be incurred for each transit operation. When the necessary data is not available the amount is presumed to be 7000 euro unless other information known to the customs authorities leads to a different figure.]

2. The reference amount shall be the same as the amount of customs debt which may be incurred in respect of goods the principal places under the Community transit procedure during a period of at least one week.

The office of guarantee shall establish the amount in collaboration with the party concerned on the basis of the information on goods he has carried in the past and an estimate of the volume of intended Community transit operations as shown, inter alia, by his commercial documentation and accounts.

In establishing the reference amount, account shall be taken of the highest rates of duty and charges applicable to the goods in the Member State of the office of guarantee. [Community goods carried or to be carried in accordance with the Convention on a common transit procedure shall be treated as non-Community goods.]

3. The office of guarantee shall review the reference amount annually, particularly in the light of information obtained from the office or offices of departure, and shall adjust it if necessary.

4. The principal shall ensure that the amount at stake does not exceed the reference amount, taking into account any operations for which the procedure has not yet ended.

The principal shall inform the office of guarantee when the reference amount falls below a level sufficient to cover his Community transit operations.]

NOTES
Substituted as noted to Art 340a.

Part III

Para 1: words in square brackets added by Commission Regulation (EC) 993/2001, Art 1, para 23.

Para 2: words added by Commission Regulation (EC) 444/2002, Art 1, para 17.

[**Article 380**

1.   The amount to be covered by the comprehensive guarantee shall be the same as the reference amount referred to in Article 379.

2.   The amount to be covered by the comprehensive guarantee may be reduced:

(a)   to 50 % of the reference amount where the principal demonstrates that his finances are sound and that he has sufficient experience of the Community transit procedure;

(b)   to 30 % of the reference amount where the principal demonstrates that his finances are sound, that he has sufficient experience of the Community transit procedure and that he cooperates very closely with the customs authorities.

3.   A guarantee waiver may be granted where the principal demonstrates that he maintains the standards of reliability described in paragraph 2(b), is in command of transport operations and has sufficient financial resources to meet his obligations.

4.   For the purpose of paragraphs 2 and 3, the Member States shall take into account the criteria set out in Annex 46b.]

NOTES

Substituted as noted to Art 340a.

[**Article 381**

1.   To be authorised to furnish a comprehensive guarantee in respect of the types of goods referred to in Annex 44c, a principal must demonstrate, not only that he meets the conditions of Article 373, but also that his finances are sound, that he has sufficient experience of the Community transit procedure and either that he cooperates very closely with the customs authorities or that he is in command of transport operations.

2.   The amount to be covered by the comprehensive guarantee referred to in paragraph 1 may be reduced:

(a)   to 50% of the reference amount where the principal demonstrates that he cooperates very closely with the customs authorities and is in command of transport operations;

(b)   to 30% of the reference amount where the principal demonstrates that he cooperates very closely with the customs authorities, is in command of transport operations, and that he has sufficient financial resources to meet his obligations.

3.   For the purposes of applying paragraphs 1 and 2, the customs authorities shall take account of the criteria set out in Annex 46b.

[3a.   Paragraphs 1, 2 and 3 also apply where an application explicitly concerns the use of the comprehensive guarantee for both the types of goods referred to in Annex 44c and those not listed in that Annex under the same comprehensive guarantee certificate.]

4.   The implementing rules concerning the temporary prohibition of the use of the comprehensive guarantee for a reduced amount or the comprehensive guarantee, as provided for in Article 94(6) and (7) of the Code are set out in Annex 47a to the Regulation.]

NOTES

Substituted as noted to Art 340a.

Para 3a: inserted by Commission Regulation (EC) 444/2002, Art 1, para 18.

[**Article 382**

The comprehensive guarantee shall be furnished by a guarantor.

It shall be the subject of a guarantee document conforming to the specimen in Annex 48.

Article 346(2) shall apply *mutatis mutandis*.]

NOTES

Substituted as noted to Art 340a.

[**Article 383**

1. On the basis of the authorisation, the customs authorities shall issue the principal with one or more comprehensive guarantee certificates or guarantee waiver certificates, hereinafter referred to as certificates, drawn up as appropriate on a form corresponding to the specimen in Annex 51 or Annex 51a and supplemented in accordance with Annex 51b, to enable the principal to provide proof of the comprehensive guarantee or guarantee waiver.

2. The certificate shall be presented at the office of departure. Particulars of the certificate shall be entered on the transit declaration.

[However, where guarantee data is exchanged between the office of guarantee and the office of departure using information technology and computer networks, no certificate is presented to the office of departure.]

3. The period of validity of a certificate shall not exceed two years. That period may be extended by the office of guarantee for one further period which shall not exceed two years.]

NOTES

Substituted as noted to Art 340a.

Para 2: words in square brackets added by Commission Regulation (EC) 993/2001, Art 1, para 24.

[**Article 384**

1. Article 348(1) and the first subparagraph of Article 348(2) shall apply *mutatis mutandis* to the revocation and cancellation of the comprehensive guarantee.

2. From the effective date of revocation of an authorisation to use a comprehensive guarantee or guarantee waiver by the customs authorities, from the effective date of revocation by the office of guarantee of its acceptance of a guarantor's undertaking, or from the effective date of cancellation of an undertaking by a guarantor, certificates issued earlier may not be used to place goods under the Community transit procedure and shall be returned by the principal to the office of guarantee without delay.

3. Each Member State shall forward to the Commission the means by which certificates that remain valid and have not yet been returned may be identified. The Commission shall inform the other Member States.

4. Paragraph 3 shall also apply to certificates that have been declared as stolen, lost or falsified.]

NOTES

Substituted as noted to Art 340a.

[SUBSECTION 3
SPECIAL LOADING LISTS

Article 385

1. The customs authorities may authorise principals to use as loading lists lists which do not comply with all the requirements of Annexes 44a and 45.

Use of such lists shall be authorised only where:

    (a)   they are produced by firms which use an integrated electronic or automatic data-processing system to keep their records;

    (b)   they are designed and completed in such a way that they can be used without difficulty by the customs authorities;

    (c)   they include, for each item, the information required under Annex 44a.

2. Descriptive lists drawn up for the purposes of carrying out dispatch/export formalities may also be authorised for use as loading lists under paragraph 1, even where such lists are produced by firms not using an integrated electronic or automatic data-processing system to keep their records.

3. Firms which use an integrated electronic or automatic data-processing system to keep their records and are already authorised under paragraphs 1 and 2 to use loading lists of a special type may also be authorised to use such lists for Community transit operations involving only one type of goods if this facility is made necessary by the computer programmes of the firms concerned.]

NOTES

Substituted as noted to Art 340a.

[SUBSECTION 4
USE OF SEALS OF A SPECIAL TYPE

Article 386

1. The customs authorities may authorise principals to use special types of seals on means of transport or packages provided the customs authorities approve the seals as complying with the characteristics set out in Annex 46a.

2. Principals shall enter, opposite the heading 'seals affixed' in box 'D. Control by office of departure' of the transit declaration, the type, number and make of the seals used.

Principals shall affix seals no later than when goods are released.]

NOTES

Substituted as noted to Art 340a.

[SUBSECTION 5
EXEMPTION REGARDING PRESCRIBED ITINERARY

Article 387

1. The customs authorities may grant an exemption from the requirement to follow a prescribed itinerary to principals who ensure that the customs authorities are able to ascertain the location of the consignments concerned at all times.

2. Holders of such exemptions shall enter one of the following endorsements in box 44 of the transit declaration:

— Dispensa de itinerario obligatorio
— fritaget for bindende transportrute
— Befreiung von der verbindlichen Bef érderungsroute
— Απαλλαγηαπ ο τη ıυπ ο χ ρεω σ η τ ηρησ η ζσ υ γ κ εκρ ıμ ε ν η ζ δıα δρ oμ η ζ
— Prescribed itinerary waived
— Dispense d'itinéraire contraignant
— Dispensa dall'itinerario vincolante
— Geen verplichte route
— Dispensa de itiner ário vinculativo
— Vapautettu sitovan kuljetusreitin noudattamisesta
— Befrielse från bindande färdväg,
[— Osvobození od stanovené trasy,
— Ettenähtud marsruudist loobutud,
— Atlauts novirzities no noteikta maršruta,
— Leista nenustatyti maršruto,
— Eloírt útvonal alló mentestíve,
— Tnehhija ta 'l-itinerarju preskritt,
— Zwolniony z wiazacej trasy przewozu,
— Opustitev predpisane poti,
[— Oslobodenie od predpísanej trasy]].
[— (*for original text, refer to Commission Regulation (EC) 1792/2006 (OJ L 362, 20.12.06, p 1)*),
— Dispensa Scutit de la itinerariul obligatoriuprestabilit]

NOTES

Substituted as noted to Art 340a.

Para 2: words inserted by the 2003 Act of Accession Annex II(19)(A)(II), para 20; words "Oslobodenie od predpísanej trasy" in square brackets inserted by Commission Regulation (EC) 883/2005, Art 1, OJ L 148, 11.06.05, p 5 with effect from 1 May 2004. Final two entries inserted by Commission Regulation (EC) 1792/2006, Art 1, Annex, Part 11(A)(19).

Chapter 7 heading and section 1 heading repealed by Commission Regulation (EC) 2787/2000, Art 1, para 26.

Articles 389–396, Heading and Article 397

NOTES

Repealed by Commission Regulation (EC) 2787/2000, Art 1, para 26.

[SUBSECTION 6
AUTHORISED CONSIGNOR STATUS

Article 398

Persons wishing to carry out Community transit operations without presenting the goods and the corresponding transit declaration at the office of departure may be granted the status of authorised consignor.

This simplification shall be granted solely to persons authorised to use a comprehensive guarantee or granted a guarantee waiver.]

NOTES

Substituted by Commission Regulation (EC) 2787/2000, Art 1, para 27.

[Article 399

The authorisation shall specify in particular:

    (a)   the office or offices of departure responsible for forthcoming Community transit operations;

    (b)   how, and by when, the authorised consignor is to inform the office of departure of forthcoming Community transit operations, in order that the office may carry out any necessary controls before the departure of the goods;

    (c)   the identification measures to be taken, in which case the customs authorities may prescribe that the means of transport or the package or packages shall bear special seals, approved by the customs authorities as complying with the characteristics set out in Annex 46a and affixed by the authorised consignor;

    (d)   the excluded categories or movements of goods.]

NOTES

Substituted as noted to Art 398.

[Article 400

1.   The authorisation shall stipulate that box 'C. Office of departure' of the transit declaration forms must:

    (a)   be stamped in advance with the stamp of the office of departure and signed by an official of that office; or

    (b)   be stamped by the authorised consignor with a special metal stamp approved by the customs authorities and corresponding to the specimen in Annex 62; the stamp may be pre-printed on the forms where the printing is entrusted to a printer approved for that purpose.

The authorised consignor shall complete the box by entering the date on which the goods are consigned and shall allocate a number to the transit declaration in accordance with the rules laid down in the authorisation.

2.   The customs authorities may prescribe the use of forms bearing a distinctive mark as a means of identification.]

NOTES

Substituted as noted to Art 398.

[Article 401

1.   The authorised consignor shall take all necessary measures to ensure the safekeeping of the special stamps or forms bearing the stamp of the office of departure or a special stamp.

He shall inform the customs authorities of the security measures taken pursuant to the first subparagraph.

2.   In the event of the misuse by any person of forms stamped in advance with the stamp of the office of departure or with the special stamp, the authorised consignor shall be liable, without prejudice to any criminal proceedings, for the payment of duties and other charges payable in a particular Member State in respect of goods

carried under cover of such forms unless he can satisfy the customs authorities by whom he was authorised that he took the measures required of him under paragraph 1.]

NOTES
Substituted as noted to Art 398.

[**Article 402**
1. Not later than on consignment of the goods, authorised consignors shall complete the transit declaration and, where necessary, enter in box 44 the itinerary prescribed in accordance with Article 355(2) and, in box 'D. Control by office of departure', the period prescribed in accordance with Article 356 within which the goods must be presented at the office of destination, the identification measures applied and one of the following endorsements:

—   Expedidor autorizado
—   Godkendt afsender
—   Zugelassener Versender
—   Εγκεριμενος αποστολεαα
—   Authorised consignor
—   Expéditeur agréé
—   Speditore autorizzato
—   Toegelaten afzender
—   Expedidor autorizado
—   Hyväksytty lähettäjä
—   Godkänd avsändare,
[—   Schválený odesílatel,
—   Volitatud kaubasaatja,
—   Atzitais nosūtitjs,
—   Igaliotas siuntejas,
—   Engedélyezett feladó,
—   Awtorizzat li jibg at,
—   Upowaniony nadawca,
—   Pooblaščeni pošiljatelj,
—   Schválený odosielatel.]
[—   *(for original text, refer to Commission Regulation (EC) 1792/2006 (OJ L 362, 20.12.06, p 1)),*
—   Expeditor agreat autorizat autorizat]
2. Where the customs authorities of the Member State of departure check a consignment before its departure, they shall record the fact in box 'D. Control by office of departure' of the transit declaration.
3. Following consignment, copy No 1 of the transit declaration shall be sent without delay to the office of departure. The customs authorities may provide in the authorisation that copy No 1 be sent to the customs authorities of the Member State of departure as soon as the transit declaration is completed. The other copies shall accompany the goods.]

NOTES
Substituted as noted to Art 398.
Para 1: words inserted by the 2003 Act of Accession Annex II(19)(A)(II), para 21. Final two entries inserted by Commission Regulation (EC) 1792/2006, Art 1, Annex, Part 11(A)(20).

[Article 403

1. The authorised consignor may be authorised not to sign transit declarations bearing the special stamp referred to in Annex 62 which are made out by an integrated electronic or automatic data-processing system. This waiver shall be subject to the condition that the authorised consignor has previously given the customs authorities a written undertaking acknowledging that he is the principal for all Community transit operations carried out under cover of transit declarations bearing the special stamp.

2. Transit declarations made out in accordance with paragraph 1 shall contain, in the box reserved for the principal's signature, one of the following endorsements:

—   Dispensa de firma
—   Fritaget for underskrift
—   Freistellung von der Unterschriftsleistung
—   ΔєναπαείτΔι υπογρΔφή
—   Signature waived
—   Dispense de signature
—   Dispensa dalla firma
—   Van ondertekening vrijgesteld
—   Dispensada a assinatura
—   Vapautettu allekirjoituksesta
—   Befriad från underskrift,]
[—   podpis se nevyžaduje,
—   allkirjanõudest loobutud,
—   dergs bez paraksta,
—   leista nepasiražyti,
—   aláírás alól mentesítve,
—   firma mhux mehtiega,
—   zwolniony ze sladania podpisu,
—   opustitev podpisa,
[—   Oslobodenie od podpisu].]
[—   *(for original text, refer to Commission Regulation (EC) 1792/2006 (OJ L 362, 20.12.06, p 1))*,
—   Dispens de semntur]

NOTES

Substituted as noted to Art 398.

Para 2: words inserted by the 2003 Act of Accession Annex II(19)(A)(II), para 22;; words "Oslobodenie od podpisu" in square brackets inserted by Commission Regulation (EC) 883/2005, Art 1, OJ L 148, 11.06.05, p 5 with effect from 1 May 2004. Final two entries inserted by Commission Regulation (EC) 1792/2006, Art 1, Annex, Part 11(A)(21).

[Article 404

1. Where transit declarations are lodged at offices of departure which apply the provisions of Section 2, subsection 7, persons may be granted the status of authorised consignor if, as well as complying with the conditions set out in Articles 373 and 398, they lodge their transit declarations and communicate with the customs authorities using a data-processing technique.

2. An authorised consignor shall lodge a transit declaration at the office of departure before the release of the goods.

3. The authorisation shall indicate, inter alia, the time limit within which an authorised consignor shall lodge a transit declaration so that the customs authorities may, if necessary, carry out checks before the release of the goods.]

NOTES

Substituted as noted to Art 398.

Article 405

. . .

NOTES

Repealed by Commission Regulation (EC) 2787/2000, Art 1, para 28.

[SUBSECTION 7
AUTHORISED CONSIGNEE STATUS

Article 406

1. Persons who wish to receive at their premises or at any other specified place goods entered for the Community transit procedure without presenting them and copies No 4 and No 5 of the transit declaration at the office of destination may be granted the status of authorised consignee.

2. The principal shall have fulfilled his obligations under Article 96(1)(a) of the Code, and the Community transit procedure shall be deemed to have ended, when copies No 4 and No 5 of the transit declaration which accompanied the consignment, together with the intact goods, have been delivered within the prescribed period to the authorised consignee at his premises or at the place specified in the authorisation, the identification measures having been duly observed.

3. At the carrier's request the authorised consignee shall issue the receipt provided for in Article 362, which shall apply mutatis mutandis, in respect of each consignment delivered in accordance with paragraph 2.]

NOTES

Substituted, with Arts 407, 408, by Commission Regulation (EC) 2787/2000, Art 1, para 29.

[**Article 407**

1. The authorisation shall specify in particular:
   (a)   the office or offices of destination responsible for the goods received by the authorised consignee;
   (b)   how and by when, the authorised consignee is to inform the office of destination of the arrival of the goods in order that the office may carry out any necessary controls upon arrival of the goods;
   (c)   the excluded categories or movements of goods.

2. The customs authorities shall specify in the authorisation whether any action by the office of destination is required before the authorised consignee may dispose of goods received.]

NOTES

Substituted as noted to Art 406.

[**Article 408**

1. When the goods arrive at his premises or at the places specified in the authorisation, the authorised consignee shall:

Part III

(a)   immediately inform the office of destination, in accordance with the procedure laid down in the authorisation, of any excess quantities, deficits, substitutions or other irregularities such as broken seals;

[(b)   without delay, send to the office of destination Copies No 4 and No 5 of the transit declaration which accompanied the goods, indicating, except where communicated using a data processing technique, the date of arrival and the condition of any seals affixed.]

2.   The office of destination shall make the entries provided for in Article 361 on copies No 4 and No 5 of the transit declaration.]

NOTES
   Substituted as noted to Art 406.
   Para 1: sub-para (b) substituted by Commission Regulation (EC) 993/2001, Art 1, para 25.

[Article 408a
   1.   Where the office of destination applies the provisions of Section 2 Subsection 7, persons may be granted the status of authorised consignee if, as well as complying with the conditions set out in Article 373, they use a data processing technique to communicate with the customs authorities.
   2.   The authorised consignee shall inform the office of destination of the arrival of the goods before the unloading.
   3.   The authorisation shall indicate, in particular, how and by when the authorised consignee receives the 'Anticipate Arrival Record' data from the office of destination for the purpose of applying, *mutatis mutandis*, Article 371.]

NOTES
   Inserted by Commission Regulation (EC) 993/2001, Art 1, para 26.

Article 409, Heading, Articles 410, 411

NOTES
   Repealed by Commission Regulation (EC) 2787/2000, Art 1, para 30.

[SUBSECTION 8
SIMPLIFIED PROCEDURES FOR GOODS CARRIED BY RAIL OR IN
LARGE CONTAINERS

A.
General provisions relating to carriage by rail]

NOTES
   Headings substituted by Commission Regulation (EC) 2787/2000, Art 1, paras 31, 32.

[Article 412
   Article 359 shall not apply to the carriage of goods by rail.]

NOTES
   Substituted by Commission Regulation (EC) 2787/2000, Art 1, para 33.

Article 413

Where the Community transit procedure is applicable, formalities under that procedure shall be simplified in accordance with Articles 414 to 425, 441 and 442 for the transport of goods by railway companies under cover of a "consignment note CIM and express parcels" hereinafter referred to as the "consignment note CIM".

[Article 414

The CIM consignment note shall be equivalent to a Community transit declaration.]

NOTES
  Substituted by Commission Regulation (EC) 2787/2000, Art 1, para 34.

Article 415

The railway company of each Member State shall make the records held at their accounting offices available to the customs authorities of their country for purposes of control.

Article 416

  [1. A railway company which accepts goods for carriage under cover of a CIM consignment note serving as a Community transit declaration shall be the principal for that operation.]

  2. The railway company of the Member State through whose territory the goods enter the Community shall be the principal for operations in respect of goods accepted for transport by the railways of a third country.

NOTES
  Para 1: substituted by Commission Regulation (EC) 2787/2000, Art 1, para 35.

Article 417

The railway companies shall ensure that consignments transported under the Community transit procedure are identified by labels bearing a pictogram, a specimen of which is shown in Annex 58.

  The labels shall be affixed to the consignment note CIM and to the relevant railway wagon in the case of a full load or, in other cases, to the package or packages.

  [The label referred to in the first paragraph may be replaced by a stamp reproducing the pictogram shown in Annex 58 in green ink.]

NOTES
  Words in square brackets added by Commission Regulation (EC) 1427/97, Art 1, para 5.

Article 418

Where the contract of carriage is modified so that—
  —   a transport operation which was to end outside the customs territory of the Community ends within it,
  —   a transport operation which was to end within the customs territory of the Community ends outside it,
the railway companies shall not perform the modified contract without the prior agreement of the office of departure.

  In all other cases, the railway companies may perform the modified contract; they shall forthwith inform the office of departure of the modification made.

Part III

Article 419

1. The consignment note CIM shall be produced at the office of departure in the case of a transport operation to which the Community transit procedure applies and which starts and is to end within the customs territory of the Community.

[2. The office of departure shall clearly enter in the box reserved for customs on sheets 1, 2 and 3 of the CIM consignment note—

(a) the symbol "T1", where goods are moving under the external Community transit procedure;

(b) the symbol "T2", where goods, with the exception of those referred to in [Article 340c(1)], are moving under the internal Community transit procedure in accordance with Article 165 of the Code;

(c) the symbol "T2F", where goods are moving under the internal Community transit procedure in accordance with [Article 340c(1)].

The symbol "T2" or "T2F" shall be authenticated by the application of the stamp of the office of departure.]

3. All copies of the consignment note CIM shall be returned to the person concerned.

4. The goods referred to in [Article 340c(2)] shall be placed under the internal Community transit procedure for the whole of the journey from the Community station of departure to the station of destination in the customs territory of the Community, in accordance with arrangements determined by each Member State, without presentation at the office of departure of the consignment note CIM in respect of the goods and without affixing the labels referred to in Article 417. However, this waiver shall not apply to consignment notes CIM drawn up for goods covered by the provisions in [Article 843].

5. For the goods referred to in paragraph 2 the customs office for the station of destination shall act as the office of destination. If, however, the goods are released for free circulation or placed under another customs procedure at an intermediate station, the office responsible for that station shall act as the office of destination.

No formalities need be carried out at the office of destination with regard to the goods referred to in [Article 340c(2)].

6. For the purposes of the control referred to in Article 415, the railway companies shall, in the country of destination, make all the consignment notes CIM for the transport operations referred to in paragraph 4 available to the customs authorities, in accordance with any provisions defined by mutual agreement with those authorities.

7. When Community goods are transported by rail from a point in a Member State to a point in another Member State through the territory of a third country other than an EFTA country, the internal Community transit procedure shall apply. In this case the provisions of paragraphs 4, 5 second subparagraph and 6 shall apply *mutatis mutandis*.

NOTES

Para 2: substituted by Commission Regulation (EC) 75/98, Art 1, para 15.

Words in square brackets substituted by Commission Regulation (EC) 2787/2000, Art 1, para 36.

Para 4: words substituted by Commission Regulation (EC) 1602/2000, Art 1, para 8.

Words in square brackets substituted by Commission Regulation (EC) 2787/2000, Art 1, para 36.

Para 5: words in square brackets substituted by Commission Regulation (EC) 2787/2000, Art 1, para 36.

Article 420

As a general rule and having regard to the identification measures applied by the railway companies, the office of departure shall not seal the means of transport or the packages.

Article 421

1.   In the cases referred to in the first subparagraph of Article 419(5), the railway company of the Member State responsible for the office of destination shall forward to the latter sheets 2 and 3 of the consignment note CIM.

2.   The office of destination shall forthwith return sheet 2 to the railway company after stamping it and shall retain sheet 3.

Article 422

1.   Article 419 and 420 shall apply to a transport operation which starts within the customs territory of the Community and is to end outside it.

2.   The customs office for the frontier station through which the goods in transit leave the customs territory of the Community shall act as office of destination.

3.   No formalities need be carried out at the office of destination.

Article 423

1.   Where a transport operation starts outside the customs territory of the Community and is to end within it, the customs office for the frontier station through which the goods enter the customs territory of the Community shall act as office of departure.

No formalities need be carried out at the office of departure.

[2.   The customs office for the station of destination shall act as the office of destination. The formalities referred to in Article 421 shall be carried out at the office of destination.

3.   Where the goods are released for free circulation or placed under another customs procedure at an intermediate station, the customs office for this station shall act as the office of destination. This customs office shall stamp sheets 2 and 3 and the supplementary copy of sheet 3 forwarded by the railway company and endorse them with one of the following indications—

—	Cleared
—	Dédouané
—	Verzollt
—	Sdoganato
—	Vrijgemaakt
—	Toldbehandlet
—	Εκτελωνσμ νο
—	Despachado de aduana
—	Desalfandegado
[—	Tulliselvitetty,
—	Tullklarerat]
[—	propuštěno,
—	lõpetatud,
—	nomuitots,
—	išleista,
—	vámkezelve,
—	mgoddija,
—	odprawiony,
—	ocarinjeno,
—	prepustené.]

[— *(for original text, refer to Commission Regulation (EC) 1792/2006 (OJ L 362, 20.12.06, p 1))*,

— Vmuit]

This office shall return sheets 2 and 3, without delay, to the railway company after having stamped them and retained the supplementary copy of sheet 3.

4. The procedure referred to in paragraph 3 shall not apply to products subject to excise duty as defined in Article 3(1) and Article 5(1) of Council Directive 92/12/EEC[1].

5. In the case referred to in paragraph 3 the competent customs authorities for the office of destination may request a *posteriori* verification of the endorsements made by the competent customs authorities for the intermediate station on sheets 2 and 3.

---

[1] OJ L 76, 23.3.92, p 1.

NOTES

Para 2: substituted by Commission Regulation (EC) 2193/94, Art 1, para 2.

Paras 3–5: inserted by Commission Regulation (EC) 2193/94, Art 1, para 2.

Para 3: words inserted by Commission Regulation (EC) 444/2002, Art 1, para 19. Further words inserted by the 2003 Act of Accession Annex II(19)(A)(II), para 23. Final two entries inserted by Commission Regulation (EC) 1792/2006, Art 1, Annex, Part 11(A)(22).

Article 424

1. Where a transport operation starts and is to end outside the customs territory of the Community, the customs offices which are to act as office of departure and office of destination shall be those referred to in Articles 423(1) and 422(2) respectively.

2. No formalities need to be carried out at the offices of departure or destination.

Article 425

Goods which are transported under Articles 423(1) or 424(1) shall be considered as moving under the external Community transit procedure unless the Community status of the goods is established in accordance with Articles 313 to 340.

[B.
Provisions relating to goods carried in large containers]

NOTES

Heading substituted by Commission Regulation (EC) 2787/2000, Art 1, para 37.

[Article 426

Where the Community transit procedure is applicable, formalities under that procedure shall be simplified in accordance with Articles 427 to 442 for goods carried by the railway companies in large containers using transport undertakings as intermediaries, under cover of transfer notes referred to as "TR transfer notes". Such operations may include the dispatch of consignments by transport undertakings using modes of transport other than rail, to the nearest suitable railway station to the point of loading and from the nearest suitable railway station to the point of unloading, and any transport by sea in the course of the movement between those two stations.]

NOTES

Substituted by Commission Regulation (EC) 1427/97, Art 1, para 6.

Article 427

For the purpose of Articles 426 to 442—

1. "Transport undertaking" means an undertaking constituted by the railway companies as a corporate entity of which they are members, such undertaking being set up for the purpose of carrying goods by means of large containers under cover of TR transfer notes;

2. "Large container" means a container . . . that is—

— designed in such a way that it can be properly sealed where the application of Article 435 requires this,

— of a size such that the area bounded by the four lower external angles is not less than 7 m2.

3. "TR transfer note" means the document which comprises the contract of carriage by which the transport undertaking arranges for one or more large containers to be carried from a consignor to a consignee in international transport. The TR transfer note shall bear a serial number in the top right-hand corner by which it can be identified. This number shall be made up of eight digits preceded by the letters TR.

The TR transfer note shall consist of the following sheets, in numerical order—

— 1: sheet for the head office of the transport undertaking,

— 2: sheet for the national representative of the transport undertaking at the station of destination,

— 3A: sheet for customs,

— 3B: sheet for the consignee,

— 4: sheet for the head office of the transport undertaking,

— 5: sheet for the national representative of the transport undertaking at the station of departure,

— 6: sheet for the consignor.

Each sheet of the TR transfer note, with the exception of sheet 3A, shall have a green band approximately four centimetres wide along its right-hand edge.

4. "List of large containers", hereinafter referred to as "list", means the document attached to a TR transfer note, of which it forms an integral part, which is intended to cover the consignment of several large containers from a single station of departure to a single station of destination, at which stations the customs formalities are carried out.

The list shall be produced in the same number of copies as the TR transfer note to which it relates.

The number of lists shall be shown in the box at the top right-hand corner of the TR transfer note reserved for that purpose.

In addition, the serial number of the appropriate TR transfer note shall be entered in the top right hand corner of each list.

[5. "nearest suitable railway station" means a railway station or terminal nearest to the point of loading or unloading, which is equipped to handle the large containers defined in point 2.]

NOTES

Para 2: words repealed by Commission Regulation (EC) 993/2001, Art 1, para 27.

Para 5: added by Commission Regulation (EC) 1427/97, Art 1, para 7.

Part III

[Article 428

TR transfer notes used by transport undertakings shall have the same legal force as transit declarations.]

NOTES

Substituted by Commission Regulation (EC) 2787/2000, Art 1, para 38.

Article 429

1. In each Member State the transport undertaking shall make available to the customs authorities for control purposes, through the medium of its national representative or representatives, the records held at its accounting office or offices or at those of its national representative or representatives.

2. At the request of the customs authorities, the transport undertaking or its national representative or representatives shall communicate to them forthwith any documents, accounting records or information relating to carriage operations completed or under way which those authorities consider they should see.

3. Where, in accordance with Article 428, TR transfer notes are treated as equivalent to [Community transit declarations], the transport undertaking or its national representative or representatives shall—

  (a) inform the customs office of destination of any TR transfer note, sheet 1 of which has been sent to it without a customs endorsement;

  (b) inform the customs office of departure of any TR transfer note, sheet 1 of which has not been returned to it and in respect of which it has been unable to determine whether the consignment has been correctly presented to the customs office of destination or has been exported from the customs territory of the Community to a third country under Article 437.

NOTES

Para 3: words in square brackets substituted by Commission Regulation (EC) 2787/2000, Art 1, para 39.

Article 430

1. In the case of transport operations referred to in Article 426 accepted by the transport undertaking in a Member State, the railway company of that Member State shall be the principal.

2. In the case of transport operations referred to in Article 426 accepted by the transport undertaking in a third country, the railway company of the Member State through which the goods enter the customs territory of the Community shall be the principal.

Article 431

If customs formalities have to be carried out during carriage by means other than rail to the station of departure or from the station of destination, only one large container may be covered by each TR transfer note.

Article 432

The transport undertaking shall ensure that transport operations carried out under the Community transit procedure are identified by labels bearing a pictogram, a specimen of which is shown in Annex 58. The labels shall be affixed to the TR transfer note and to the large container or containers concerned.

[The label referred to in the first paragraph may be replaced by a stamp reproducing the pictogram shown in Annex 58 in green ink.]

NOTES

Words in square brackets added by Commission Regulation (EC) 1427/97, Art 1, para 8.

Article 433

Where a contract of carriage is modified so that—

— a transport operation which was to end outside the customs territory of the Community ends within it,

— a transport operation which was to end within the customs territory of the Community ends outside it,

the transport undertaking shall not perform the modified contract without the prior agreement of the office of departure.

In all other cases, the transport undertaking may perform the modified contract; it shall forthwith inform the office of departure of the modification made.

Article 434

1. Where a transport operation to which the Community transit procedure applies starts and is to end within the customs territory of the Community, the TR transfer note shall be presented at the office of departure.

[2. The office of departure shall clearly enter in the box reserved for customs on sheets 1, 2, 3A and 3B of the TR transfer note—

(a) the symbol "T1" where goods are moving under the external Community transit procedure;

(b) the symbol "T2", where goods, with the exception of those referred to in [Article 340c(1)], are moving under the internal Community transit procedure in accordance with Article 165 of the Code;

(c) the symbol "T2F", where goods are moving under the internal Community transit procedure in accordance with [Article 340c(1)].

The symbol "T2" or "T2F" shall be authenticated by the application of the stamp of the office of departure.

3. The office of departure shall enter in the box reserved for customs on sheets 1, 2, 3A and 3B of the TR transfer note separate references for the container(s) depending on which type of goods they contain and the symbol "T1", "T2" or "T2F", as appropriate, wherever a TR transfer note covers—

(a) containers carrying goods moving under the external Community transit procedure; and

(b) containers carrying goods, with the exception of those referred to in [Article 340c(1)], moving under the internal Community transit procedure in accordance with Article 165 of the Code;

(c) containers carrying goods moving under the internal Community transit procedure in accordance with [Article 340c(1)].

4. In cases covered by paragraph 3, where lists of large containers are used, separate lists shall be made out for each category of container and the serial number or numbers of the list or lists concerned shall be entered in the box reserved for customs on sheets 1, 2, 3A and 3B of the TR transfer note. The symbol "T1", "T2" or "T2F", as appropriate to the category of container used, shall be entered alongside the serial number(s) of the list(s).]

5. All sheets of the TR transfer note shall be returned to the person concerned.

6. The goods referred to in [Article 340c(2)] shall be placed under the internal Community transit procedure for the whole of the journey in accordance with arrangements determined by each Member State without presentation at the office of departure of the TR transfer note in respect of the goods and without affixing the

Part III

labels referred to in Article 432. However, this waiver shall not apply to the TR transfer note drawn up for goods covered by the provisions in [Article 843].

7. For the goods referred to in paragraph 2 the TR transfer note must be produced at the office of destination where the goods are declared for release for free circulation or for another customs procedure.

No formalities need be carried out at the office of destination in respect of the goods referred to in [Article 340c(2)].

8. For the purposes of the control referred to in Article 429, the transport undertaking shall in the country of destination make all TR transfer notes for the transport operations referred to in paragraph 6 available to the customs authorities in accordance with any provisions defined by mutual agreement with those authorities.

9. When Community goods are transported by rail from a point in a Member State to a point in another Member State through the territory of a third country other than an EFTA country, the internal Community transit procedure shall apply. In this case the provisions of paragraphs 6, 7 second subparagraph and 8 shall apply *mutatis mutandis*.

NOTES

Paras 2–4: substituted by Commission Regulation (EC) 75/98, Art 1, para 16.

Paras 2, 3: words in square brackets substituted by Commission Regulation (EC) 2787/2000, Art 1, para 40.

Para 6: words in square brackets substituted by Commission Regulation (EC) 1602/2000, Art 1, para 8.

Words in square brackets substituted by Commission Regulation (EC) 2787/2000, Art 1, para 40.

Para 7: words in square brackets substituted by Commission Regulation (EC) 2787/2000, Art 1, para 40.

Article 435

Identification of goods shall be ensured in accordance with [Article 357]. However, the office of departure shall not normally seal large containers where identification measures are taken by the railway companies. If seals are affixed this shall be indicated in the space reserved for customs use on sheets 3A and 3B of the TR transfer note.

NOTES

Words in square brackets substituted by Commission Regulation (EC) 2787/2000, Art 1, para 41.

Article 436

1. In the cases referred to in the first subparagraph of Article 434(7) the transport undertaking shall deliver sheets 1, 2 and 3A of the TR transfer note to the office of destination.

2. The office of destination shall forthwith endorse sheets 1 and 2 and return them to the transport undertaking and shall retain sheet 3A.

Article 437

1. Where a transport operation starts within the customs territory of the Community and is to end outside it, Article 434(1) to (5) and Article 435 shall apply.

2. The customs office responsible for the frontier station through which the goods leave the customs territory of the Community shall act as the office of destination.

3. No formalities need be carried out at the office of destination.

Article 438

1. Where a transport operation starts outside the customs territory of the Community and is to end within it, the customs office responsible for the frontier station through which the goods enter the Community shall act as the office of departure. No formalities need be carried out at the office of departure.

2. The customs office to which the goods are presented shall act as the office of destination.

The formalities laid down in Article 436 shall be carried out at the office of destination.

[3. Where the goods are released for free circulation or placed under another customs procedure at an intermediate station, the customs office for this station shall act as the office of destination. This customs office shall stamp sheets 1, 2 and 3A of the TR transfer note presented by the transport undertaking and endorse them with at least one of the following indications—

—   Despachado de aduana,
—   Toldbehandet,
—   Verzollt,
—   Εκτελωνσμ νo,
—   Cleared,
—   Dédouané,
—   Sdoganato,
—   Vrijgemaakt,
—   Desalfandegado,
—   Tulliselvitetty,
—   Tullklarerat,
[—   propušteno,
—   lõpetatud,
—   nomuitots,
—   išleista,
—   vámkezelve,
—   mgoddija,
—   odprawiony,
—   ocarinjeno,
—   prepustené.]
[—   *(for original text, refer to Commission Regulation (EC) 1792/2006 (OJ L 362, 20.12.06, p 1)),*
—   Vmuit]

This office shall return sheets 1 and 2, without delay, to the transport undertaking after having stamped them and retain sheet 3A.

4. The provisions of Article 423(4) and (5) shall apply *mutatis mutandis.*]

NOTES

Paragraphs 3, 4: inserted by Commission Regulation (EC) 1762/95, Art 1, para 5.

Para 3: words inserted by the 2003 Act of Accession Annex II(19)(A)(II), para 24. Final two entries inserted by Commission Regulation (EC) 1792/2006, Art 1, Annex, Part 11(A)(23).

Article 439

1. Where a transport operation starts and is to end outside the customs territory of the Community, the customs offices which are to act as the office of departure and

the office of destination shall be those referred to in Article 438(1) and Article 437(2) respectively.

2. No formalities need be carried out at the offices of departure or destination.

Article 440

Goods which are transported under Articles 438(1) or 439(1) shall be considered as moving under the external Community transit procedure unless the Community status of the goods is established in accordance with the provisions of Articles 313 to 340.

[C.
Other provisions]

NOTES

Heading substituted by Commission Regulation (EC) 2787/2000, Art 1, para 42.

Article 441

1. [Articles 350 and 385] shall apply to any loading lists which accompany the consignment note CIM or the TR transfer note. The number of such lists shall be shown in the box reserved for particulars of accompanying documents on the consignment note CIM or TR transfer note as the case may be.

In addition, the loading list shall include the wagon number to which the consignment note CIM refers or, where appropriate, the container number of the container containing the goods.

2. In the case of transport operations beginning within the customs territory of the Community comprising both goods moving under the external Community transit procedure and goods moving under the internal Community transit procedure, separate loading lists shall be made out; in the case of goods carried in large containers under cover of TR transfer notes, such separate lists shall be made out for each large container which contains both categories of goods.

The serial numbers of the loading lists relating to each of the two categories of goods shall be entered in the box reserved for the description of goods on the consignment note CIM or TR transfer note, as the case may be.

3. In the cases referred to in paragraphs 1 and 2 and for the purposes of the procedures provided for in Articles 413 to 442, the loading lists accompanying the consignment note CIM or the TR transfer note shall form an integral part thereof and shall have the same legal effects.

The original of such loading lists shall be stamped by the station of dispatch.

NOTES

Para 1: words in square brackets substituted by Commission Regulation (EC) 2787/2000, Art 1, para 43.

[D.
Scope of the normal procedures and the simplified procedures]

NOTES

Heading substituted by Commission Regulation (EC) 2787/2000, Art 1, para 44.

Article 442

1. Where the Community transit procedure is applicable, the provisions of Articles 412 to 441 shall not preclude the use of the procedures laid down [in Articles

NOTES

Repealed by Commission Regulation (EC) 2787/2000, Art 1, para 48.

[Article 444]

1. An airline may be authorised to use the goods manifest as a transit declaration where it corresponds in substance to the specimen in Appendix 3 of Annex 9 to the Convention on International Civil Aviation (simplified procedure — level 1).
For Community transit operations, the authorisation shall indicate the form of the manifest and the airports of departure and destination. The airline shall send the customs authorities of each of the airports concerned an authenticated copy of the authorisation.

2. Where a transport operation involves goods which must be placed under the external Community transit procedure and goods which must be placed under the internal Community transit procedure provided for in Article 340c(1), those goods shall be listed on separate manifests.

3. Each manifest shall bear an endorsement dated and signed by the airline, identifying it:

— by the 'T1' symbol where the goods are placed under the external Community transit procedure; or

— by the 'T2F' symbol where the goods are placed under the internal Community transit procedure, provided for in Article 340c(1).

4. The manifest shall also include the following information:
(a) the name of the airline transporting the goods;
(b) the flight number;
(c) the date of the flight;
(d) the name of the airport of loading (airport of departure) and unloading (airport of destination).

It shall also indicate, for each consignment:
(a) the number of the air waybill;
(b) the number of packages;
(c) the normal trade description of the goods including all the details necessary for their identification;
(d) the gross mass.

Where goods are grouped, their description shall be replaced, where appropriate, by the entry 'Consolidation', which may be abbreviated. In such cases the air waybills for consignments on the manifest shall include the normal trade description of the goods including all the details necessary for their identification.

5. At least two copies of the manifest shall be presented to the customs authorities at the airport of departure, which shall retain one copy.

6. A copy of the manifest shall be presented to the customs authorities at the airport of destination.

7. Once a month, after authenticating the list, the customs authorities at each airport of destination shall transmit to the customs authorities at each airport of departure a list drawn up by the airlines of the manifests which were presented to them during the previous month.
The description of each manifest in that list shall include the following information:
(a) the reference number of the manifest;
(b) the symbol identifying the manifest as a transit declaration in accordance with paragraph 3;
(c) the name (which may be abbreviated) of the airline which carried the goods;

344 to 362, 367 to 371 and 385], and the provisions of Articles 415 and 417 or 429 and 432 shall nevertheless apply.

2. In the cases referred to in paragraph 1, a reference to the Community transit document(s) used shall be clearly entered in the box reserved for particulars of accompanying documents at the time when the consignment note CIM or TR transfer note is made out. The reference shall include the type of document, office of issue, date and registration number of each document used.

In addition, sheet 2 of the consignment note CIM or sheets 1 and 2 of the TR transfer note shall be authenticated by the railway company responsible for the last railway station involved in the Community transit operation. This company shall authenticate the document after ascertaining that transport of the goods is covered by the Community transit document or documents referred to.

3. Where a Community transit operation is carried out under cover of a TR transfer note in accordance with Articles 426 to 440, the consignment note CIM used for the operation shall be excluded from the scope of paragraphs 1 and 2 and of Articles 413 to 425. The consignment note CIM shall bear a clear reference to the TR transfer note in the box reserved for particulars of accompanying documents. That reference shall include the words "TR transfer note" followed by the serial number.

NOTES

Para 1: words in square brackets substituted by Commission Regulation (EC) 2787/2000, Art 1, para 45.

[**Article 442a**

1. Where production of the Community transit declaration at the office of departure is not required in respect of goods which are to be dispatched under cover of a CIM consignment note or a TR transfer note in accordance with Articles 413 to 442, the customs authorities shall take the necessary measures to ensure that copies No 1, No 2 and No 3 of the CIM consignment note, or copies No 1, No 2, No 3A and No 3B of the TR transfer note bear the 'T1', 'T2' or 'T2F' symbol, as the case may be.

2. Where goods carried in accordance with Articles 413 to 442 are intended for an authorised consignee, the customs authorities may provide that, by way of derogation from Article 406(2) and Article 408(1)(b), copies No 2 and No 3 of the CIM consignment note, or copies No 1, No 2 and No 3A of the TR transfer note are to be delivered direct by the railway company or by the transport undertaking to the office of destination.]

NOTES

Inserted by Commission Regulation (EC) 2787/2000, Art 1, para 46.

[SUBSECTION 9

SIMPLIFIED PROCEDURES FOR TRANSPORT BY AIR]

NOTES

Chapter 8 heading repealed, and section heading substituted by Commission Regulation (EC) 2787/2000, Art 1, para 47.

Article 443

. . .

Part III

(d)   the flight number; and

(e)   the date of the flight.

The authorisation may also provide for the airlines themselves to transmit the information referred to in the first subparagraph.

In the event of irregularities being found in connection with the information on the manifests appearing on the said list, the customs authorities of the airport of destination shall inform the customs authorities of the airport of departure and the authority which granted the authorisation, referring in particular to the air waybills for the goods in question.]

NOTES

Substituted, together with Art 445, by Commission Regulation (EC) 2787/2000, Art 1, para 49.

[Article 445

1.   An airline may be authorised to use a manifest transmitted by data exchange systems as a transit declaration if it operates a significant number of flights between the Member States (simplified procedure — level 2).

By way of derogation from Article 373(1)(a), airlines need not be established in the Community if they have a regional office there.

2.   On receipt of an application for authorisation, the customs authorities shall notify the other Member States in whose territories the airports of departure and destination linked by electronic data interchange systems are situated.

Provided no objection is received within 60 days of the date of notification, the customs authorities shall issue the authorisation.

This authorisation shall be valid in all the Member States concerned and shall apply only to Community transit operations between the airports to which it refers.

3.   For the purposes of the simplification, the manifest drawn up at the airport of departure shall be transmitted to the airport of destination by electronic data interchange system.

The airline shall enter against the relevant items in the manifest:

(a)   the 'T1' symbol where the goods are placed under the external Community transit procedure;

(b)   the 'TF' symbol where the goods are placed under the internal Community transit procedure provided for in Article 340c(1);

(c)   the letters 'TD' for goods already placed under a transit procedure, or carried under the inward processing, customs warehouse or temporary admission procedure. In such cases, the airline shall also enter the letters 'TD' in the corresponding airway bill as well as a reference for the procedure used, the reference number and date of the transit declaration or transfer document and the name of the issuing office;

(d)   the letter 'C' (equivalent to 'T2L') for goods whose Community status may be demonstrated;

(e)   the letter 'X' for Community goods to be exported and which are not placed under a transit procedure.

The manifest must also include the information provided for in Article 444(4).

4.   The Community transit procedure shall be deemed to be [ended] when the manifest transmitted by electronic data exchange system is available to the customs authorities of the airport of destination and the goods have been presented to them.

The records kept by the airline shall contain at least the information referred to in the second subparagraph of paragraph 3.

If necessary, the customs authorities at the airport of destination shall transmit to the customs authorities at the airport of departure, for verification, the relevant details of manifests received by electronic data interchange system.

5. Without prejudice to the provisions of Articles 365 and 366, Articles 450a to 450d and Title VII of the Code:

(a)   the airline shall notify the customs authorities of all offences and irregularities;

(b)   the customs authorities at the airport of destination shall notify the customs authorities at the airport of departure and the authority which issued the authorisation of all offences and irregularities at the earliest opportunity.]

NOTES

Substituted, together with Art 444, by Commission Regulation (EC) 2787/2000, Art 1, para 49.

Para 4: word in square brackets substituted by Corrigendum (OJ L 20, 23.1.02, p 11)

[SUBSECTION 10
SIMPLIFIED PROCEDURES FOR MARITIME TRANSPORT]

NOTES

Heading substituted by Commission Regulation (EC) 2787/2000, Art 1, para 50

[Article 446

Where Articles 447 and 448 apply, it shall not be necessary to furnish a guarantee.]

NOTES

Substituted, together with Arts 447, 448, by Commission Regulation (EC) 2787/2000, Art 1, para 51.

[Article 447

1. Shipping companies may be authorised to use the goods manifest as a transit declaration (simplified procedure – level 1).

For Community transit operations, the authorisation shall indicate the form of the manifest and the ports of departure and destination. The shipping company shall send the customs authorities of each of the ports concerned an authenticated copy of the authorisation.

2. Where a transport operation involves goods which must be placed under the external Community transit procedure and goods which must be placed under the internal Community transit procedure in accordance with Article 340c(1), those goods shall be listed on separate manifests.

3. Each manifest shall bear an endorsement dated and signed by the shipping company, identifying it:

(a)   by the 'T1' symbol where the goods are placed under the external Community transit procedure; or

(b)   by the 'T2F' symbol where the goods are placed under the internal Community transit procedure in accordance with Article 340c(1).

4. The manifest shall also contain the following information:

(a)   the name and full address of the shipping company carrying the goods;

(b)   the identity of the vessel;

(c)   the place of loading;

(d)   the place of unloading.

It shall also indicate, for each consignment:

(a)   the reference for the bill of lading;

(b)   the number, kind, markings and identification numbers of the packages;

(c)   the normal trade description of the goods including all the details necessary for their identification;

(d)   the gross mass in kilograms;

(e)   where appropriate, the identifying numbers of containers.

5.   At least two copies of the manifest must be presented to the customs authorities at the port of departure, which shall keep one copy.

6.   A copy of the manifest shall be presented to the customs authorities at the port of destination.

7.   Once a month, after authenticating the list, the customs authorities at each port of destination shall transmit to the customs authorities at each port of departure a list drawn up by the shipping companies of the manifests which were presented to them during the previous month.

The description of each manifest in that list shall include the following information:

(a)   the reference number of the manifest;

(b)   the symbol identifying the manifest as a transit declaration in accordance with paragraph 3;

(c)   the name (which may be abbreviated) of the shipping company which carried the goods;

(d)   the date of the maritime transport operation.

The authorisation may also provide for the shipping companies themselves to transmit the information referred to in the first subparagraph.

In the event of irregularities being found in connection with the information on the manifests appearing on the said list, the customs authorities of the port of destination shall inform the customs authorities of the port of departure and the authority which granted the authorisation, referring in particular to the bills of lading for the goods in question.]

NOTES

Substituted, as noted to Art 446.

[Article 448

1.   A shipping company may be authorised to use a single manifest as a transit declaration if it operates a significant number of regular voyages between the Member States (simplified procedure — level 2).

By way of derogation from Article 373(1)(a), shipping companies need not be established in the Community if they have a regional office there.

2.   On receipt of an application for authorisation, the customs authorities shall notify the other Member States in whose territories the ports of departure and destination are situated.

Provided no objection is received within sixty days of the date of notification, the customs authorities shall issue the authorisation.

This authorisation shall be valid in all the Member States concerned and shall apply only to Community transit operations between the ports to which it refers.

3.   For the purposes of the simplification, the shipping company may use a single manifest for all goods carried; where it does so, it shall enter against the relevant items in the manifest:

(a)   the 'T1' symbol where the goods are placed under the external Community transit procedure;

(b)   the 'TF' symbol where the goods are placed under the internal Community transit procedure in accordance with Article 340c(1);

(c)   the letters 'TD' for goods already placed under a transit procedure, or carried under the inward processing, customs warehouse or temporary admission procedure. In such cases, the shipping company shall also enter the letters 'TD' in the corresponding bill of lading or other appropriate commercial document as well as a reference for the procedure used, the reference number and date of the transit declaration or transfer document and the name of the issuing office;

(d)   the letter 'C' (equivalent to 'T2L') for goods whose Community status may be demonstrated;

(e)   the letter 'X' for Community goods to be exported and which are not placed under a transit procedure.

The manifest must also include the information provided for in Article 447(4).

4.   The Community transit procedure shall be deemed to be concluded when the manifest and the goods are presented to the customs authorities at the port of destination.

The records kept by the shipping company in accordance with Article 373(2)(b) shall contain at least the information referred to in the first subparagraph of paragraph 3.

Where necessary, the customs authorities at the port of destination shall transmit the relevant details of manifests to the customs authorities at the port of departure for verification.

5.   Without prejudice to the provisions of Articles 365 and 366, Articles 450a to 450d and Title VII of the Code, the following notifications shall be made:

(a)   the shipping company shall notify all offences and irregularities to the customs authorities;

(b)   the customs authorities at the port of destination shall notify the customs authorities at the port of departure and the authority which issued the authorisation of all offences and irregularities at the earliest opportunity.]

NOTES

Substituted, as noted to Art 446.

Article 449

...

NOTES

Repealed by Commission Regulation (EC) 75/98, Art 1, para 20.

[SUBSECTION 11
SIMPLIFIED PROCEDURE FOR TRANSPORT BY PIPELINE]

NOTES

Heading substituted by Commission Regulation (EC) 2787/2000, Art 1, para 52.

Article 450

1. Where the Community transit procedure applies, the formalities relating to the procedure shall be adapted in accordance with paragraphs 2 to 6 for goods transported by pipeline.

2. Goods transported by pipeline shall be deemed to be placed under the Community transit procedure—

— on entry into the customs territory of the Community for those goods which enter that territory by pipeline,

— on placing into the pipeline system for those goods which are already within the customs territory of the Community.

Where necessary, the Community status of the goods shall be established in accordance with Articles 313 to 340.

3. For the goods referred to in paragraph 2, the operator of the pipeline established in the Member State through the territory of which the goods enter the customs territory of the Community or the operator of the pipeline in the Member State in which the movement starts shall be the principal.

4. For the purposes of Article 96(2) of the Code, the operator of a pipeline established in a Member State through the territory of which the goods are transported by pipeline shall be regarded as the carrier.

5. The Community transit operation shall be deemed to end when the goods transported by pipeline arrive at the consignee's plant or are accepted into the distribution network of a consignee, and are entered in his records.

6. The undertakings involved in carriage of the goods shall keep records and make them available to the customs authorities for the purpose of any controls considered necessary in connection with the Community transit operations referred to in paragraphs 2 to 4.

[SECTION 4
CUSTOMS DEBT AND RECOVERY

Article 450a

The time limit referred to in the third indent of Article 215(1) of the Code shall be 10 months from acceptance of the transit declaration.]

NOTES

This section (Arts 450a–450d) inserted by Commission Regulation (EC) 2787/2000, Art 1, para 53.

[**Article 450b**

1. Where, following initiation of recovery proceedings for other charges, the customs authorities determined in accordance with Article 215 of the Code (hereinafter referred to as 'the requesting authorities') obtain evidence by whatever means regarding the place where the events giving rise to the customs debt occurred, those authorities shall immediately send all the necessary documents, including an authenticated copy of the evidence, to the authorities competent for that place (hereinafter referred to as 'the requested authorities').

The requested authorities shall acknowledge receipt of the communication and indicate whether they are responsible for recovery. If no response is received within three months, the requesting authorities shall immediately resume the recovery proceedings they initiated.

2. Where the requested authorities are competent, they shall initiate new proceedings for recovery of other charges, where appropriate after the three months

Part III

period referred to in paragraph 1, second subparagraph, and on condition that the requesting authorities are immediately informed.

Any uncompleted proceedings for recovery of other charges initiated by the requesting authorities shall be suspended as soon as the requested authorities inform them that they have decided to take action for recovery.

As soon as the requested authorities provide proof that they have recovered the sums in question, the requesting authorities shall repay any other charges already collected or cancel the recovery proceedings.]

NOTES
Inserted as noted to Art 450a.

[Article 450c
[1. Where the procedure has not been discharged, the customs authorities of the Member State of departure shall, within 12 months of the date of acceptance of the transit declaration, notify the guarantor that the procedure has not been discharged.]

[1a. Where the procedure has not been discharged, the customs authorities, determined in accordance with Article 215 of the Code, shall, within three years of the date of acceptance of the transit declaration, notify the guarantor that he is or might be required to pay the debt for which he is liable in respect of the Community transit operation in question; the notification shall state the number and date of the declaration, the name of the office of departure, the name of the principal and the amount involved.]

[2. The guarantor shall be released from his obligations if either of the notifications provided for in paragraphs 1 and 1a have not been issued to him before the expiry of the time limit.]

3. Where either of the notifications has been issued, the guarantor shall be informed of the recovery of the debt or the discharge of the procedure.]

NOTES
Inserted as noted to Art 450a.
Paras 1, 2: substituted by Commission Regulation (EC) 444/2002, Art 1, para 20(a), (c).
Para 1a: inserted by Commission Regulation (EC) 444/2002, Art 1, para 20(b).

[Article 450d
The Member States shall assist each other in determining the authorities competent for recovery.

Those authorities shall inform the office of departure and the office of guarantee of all cases in which a customs debt was incurred in connection with Community transit declarations accepted by the office of departure, and of the action taken against the debtor to recover the sums concerned.]

NOTES
Inserted as noted to Art 450a.

CHAPTER 9
TRANSPORT UNDER THE TIR OR ATA PROCEDURE
SECTION 1
COMMON PROVISIONS

NOTES

Chapter heading: substituted by Commission Regulation (EC) 881/2003 Art 1, para 12.

Article 451

[1. Where goods are transported from one point in the customs territory of the Community to another under the procedure for the international transport of goods under cover of TIR carnets (TIR Convention) or under cover of ATA carnets (ATA Convention[/Istanbul Convention]), the customs territory of the Community shall, for the purposes of the rules governing the use of the TIR or ATA carnets for such transport, be considered to form a single territory.]

2. For the purposes of using ATA carnets as transit documents, "transit" shall mean the transport of goods from a customs office situated in the customs territory of the Community to another customs office situated within the same territory.

NOTES

Para 1: substituted by Commission Regulation (EC) 881/2003 Art 1, para 13, words in square brackets inserted by Commission Regulation (EC) 883/2005 Art 1, OJ L 148, 11.06.05, p 5, with effect from 1 October 2005.

Article 452

Where, in the course of transport from one point in the customs territory of the Community to another, goods pass through the territory of a third country, the controls and formalities associated with the TIR or ATA procedure shall be carried out at the points where the goods temporarily leave the customs territory of the Community and where they re-enter that territory.

Article 453

1. Goods transported under cover of TIR or ATA carnets within the customs territory of the Community shall be deemed to be non-Community goods, unless their Community status is duly established.

[2. The Community status of the goods referred to in paragraph 1 shall be determined in accordance with [Articles 314b to 324f], or, where appropriate, with Articles 325 to 334 within the limits laid down in Article 326.]

NOTES

Para 2: substituted by Commission Regulation (EC) 482/96, Art 1, para 14. Words substituted by Commission Regulation (EC) 881/2003 Art 1, para 14.

[SECTION 2
THE TIR PROCEDURE]

NOTES

Substituted by Commission Regulation (EC) 881/2003 Art 1, paras 15, 17.

[Article 454

The provisions of this section apply to the transport of goods under cover of TIR carnets where import duties or other charges within the Community are involved.]

NOTES

Arts 454–455a substituted for Arts 454, 455, by Commission Regulation (EC) 881/2003 Art 1, para 16.

[Article 454a

1.   Following an application by the consignee, the customs authorities may grant him the status of authorised consignee, thereby authorising him to receive at his premises or at any other specified place goods transported under the TIR procedure.

2.   The authorisation referred to in paragraph 1 shall be granted only to persons who:

(a)   are established in the Community;

(b)   regularly receive goods that have been entered for the TIR procedure, or whose customs authorities know that they can meet the obligations under that procedure;

(c)   have not committed any serious or repeated offences against customs or tax legislation.

Article 373(2) shall apply mutatis mutandis.

The authorisation shall apply solely in the Member State where the authorisation was granted.

The authorisation shall apply only to TIR operations that have as the final place of unloading the premises specified in the authorisation.

3.   Articles 374 and 375, Article 376(1) and (2), and Articles 377 and 378 shall apply mutatis mutandis to the procedure relating to the application referred to in paragraph 1.

4.   Article 407 shall apply mutatis mutandis with respect to the procedure laid down in the authorisation referred to in paragraph 1.

[5.   Where the person concerned holds an AEO certificate referred to in point (a) or (c) of Article 14a(1), the requirements set out in point (c) of the first subparagraph of paragraph 2 of this Article and in Article 373(2)(b) shall be deemed to be met.]]

NOTES

Arts 454a–454c inserted by Commission Regulation (EC) 883/2005 Art 1, OJ L 148, 11.06.05, p 5, with effect from 1 October 2005.

Para 5: inserted by Commission Regulation (EC) No 1875/2006, Art 1(45) with effect from 1 January 2008.

[Article 454b

1.   In respect of goods arriving at his premises or at the place specified in the authorisation referred to in Article 454a, the authorised consignee shall comply with the following obligations, in accordance with the procedure laid down in the authorisation:

(a)   inform the customs authorities at the office of destination of the arrival of the goods;

(b)   immediately inform the customs authorities at the office of destination of any broken seals, and of any other irregularities such as excess quantities, deficits, or substitutions;

(c)   without delay, enter the results of the unloading into his records;

(d)   without delay, present to the customs authorities at the office of destination an advice indicating the particulars and condition of any seals affixed and the date of the entry into the records.

2.   The authorised consignee shall ensure that the TIR Carnet is presented, without delay, to the customs authorities at the office of destination.

3.   The customs authorities at the office of destination shall make the necessary endorsements on the TIR Carnet and, in accordance with the procedure laid down in the authorisation, shall ensure that the TIR Carnet is returned to the TIR carnet holder or to the person acting on his behalf.

4.   The date of termination of the TIR operation shall be the date of the entry into the records referred to in point (c) of paragraph 1. However, in the cases referred to in point (b) of paragraph 1, the date of termination of the TIR operation shall be the date of the endorsement of the TIR Carnet.

5.   At the request of the TIR carnet holder, the authorised consignee shall issue a receipt, the form of which shall correspond to a copy of the advice referred to in point (d) of paragraph 1. The receipt shall not be used as proof of the termination of the TIR operation within the meaning of Article 454c(2).]

NOTES

Substituted as noted to Article 454a.

[Article 454c

1.   The TIR carnet holder shall have fulfilled his obligations under point (o) of Article 1 of the TIR Convention when the TIR carnet together with the road vehicle, the combination of vehicles or the container and the goods have been delivered intact to the authorised consignee at his premises or at the place specified in the authorisation.

2.   The termination of the TIR operation, within the meaning of point (d) of Article 1 of the TIR Convention, shall have occurred when the requirements of Article 454b(1) and (2) have been met.]

NOTES

Substituted as noted to Article 454a.

[Article 455

1.   The customs authorities of the Member State of destination or exit shall return the appropriate part of Voucher No 2 of the TIR carnet to the customs authorities of the Member State of entry or departure without delay and at most within one month of the date when the TIR operation was terminated.

2.   If the appropriate part of Voucher No 2 of the TIR carnet is not returned to the customs authorities of the Member State of entry or departure within two months of the date of acceptance of the TIR carnet, those authorities shall inform the guaranteeing association concerned, without prejudice to the notification to be made in accordance with Article 11(1) of the TIR Convention.

They shall also inform the holder of the TIR carnet, and shall invite both the latter and the guaranteeing association concerned to furnish proof that the TIR operation has been terminated.

3.   The proof referred to in the second subparagraph of paragraph 2 may be furnished to the satisfaction of the customs authorities in the form of a document certified by the customs authorities of the Member State of destination or exit identifying the goods and establishing that they have been presented at the customs office of destination or exit.

4. The TIR operation shall also be considered as having been terminated where the holder of the TIR carnet/guaranteeing association concerned presents, to the satisfaction of the customs authorities, a customs document issued in a third country entering the goods for a customs-approved treatment or use, or a copy or photocopy thereof, identifying the goods. Copies or photocopies must be certified as being true copies by the body which certified the original documents, by the authorities of the third countries concerned or by the authorities of one of the Member States.]

NOTES

Substituted as noted to Art 454.

[Article 455a

1. Where the customs authorities of the Member State of entry or departure have not received proof within four months of the date of the acceptance of the TIR carnet that the TIR operation has been terminated, they shall initiate the enquiry procedure immediately in order to obtain the information needed to discharge the TIR operation or, where this is not possible, to establish whether a customs debt has been incurred, identify the debtor and determine the customs authorities responsible for entry in the accounts.

If the customs authorities receive information earlier that the TIR operation has not been terminated, or suspect that to be the case, they shall initiate the enquiry procedure forthwith.

2. The enquiry procedure shall also be initiated if it transpires subsequently that proof of the termination of the TIR operation was falsified and the enquiry procedure is necessary to achieve the objectives of paragraph 1.

3. To initiate the enquiry procedure, the customs authorities of the Member State of entry or departure shall send the customs authorities of the Member State of destination or exit a request together with all the necessary information.

4. The customs authorities of the Member State of destination or exit shall respond without delay.

5. Where an enquiry establishes that the TIR operation was terminated correctly, the customs authorities of the Member State of entry or departure shall immediately inform the guaranteeing association and the holder of the TIR carnet and, where appropriate, any customs authorities that may have initiated a recovery procedure in accordance with Articles 217 to 232 of the Code.]

NOTES

Substituted as noted to Art 454.

[Article 456

1. When an offence or irregularity under the TIR Convention gives rise to a customs debt in the Community, the provisions of this section shall apply mutatis mutandis to the other charges mentioned in Article 91(1)(a) of the Code.

2. Articles 450a, 450b and 450d shall apply mutatis mutandis to the recovery procedure relating to the use of the TIR carnet.].

NOTES

Arts 456, 457 substituted by Commission Regulation (EC) 881/2003 Art 1, para 18.

[**Article 457**

1. For the purposes of Article 8(4) of the TIR Convention, when a TIR operation is carried out on the customs territory of the Community, any guaranteeing association established in the Community may become liable for the payment of the secured amount of the customs debt relating to the goods concerned in the TIR operation up to a limit per TIR carnet of EUR 60000 or the national currency equivalent thereof.

2. The guaranteeing association established in the Member State competent for recovery under Article 215 of the Code shall be liable for payment of the secured amount of the customs debt.

3. A valid notification of non-discharge of a TIR operation made by the customs authorities of one Member State, identified as competent for recovery under the third indent of Article 215(1) of the Code, to the guaranteeing association authorised by those authorities shall also be valid where the customs authorities of another Member State, identified as competent under the first or second indent of Article 215(1) of the Code, later proceed with recovery from the guaranteeing association authorised by those latter authorities.]

NOTES

Substituted as noted to Art 456.

[**Article 457a**

Where customs authorities of a Member State decide to exclude a person from the TIR procedure under the provisions of Article 38 of the TIR Convention, this decision shall apply throughout the customs territory of the Community.

To that end, the Member State shall communicate its decision, together with the date of application, to the other Member States and the Commission.

This decision shall apply to all TIR carnets presented to a customs office for acceptance.]

NOTES

Inserted by Commission Regulation (EC) 482/96, Art 1, para 15.

[**Article 457b**

1. Where a TIR operation concerns the same goods as those covered [by Annex 44c] or where the customs authorities consider it necessary, the office of departure/office of entry may prescribe an itinerary for the consignment. The itinerary shall be changed, on application by the holder of the TIR carnet, only by the customs authorities of the Member State in which the consignment is located in the course of its prescribed movement. The customs authorities shall record the relevant details on the TIR carnet and inform the customs authorities of the office of departure/office of entry without delay.

Member States shall take the necessary measures to deal with any offence or irregularity and to impose effective penalties.

2. In the case of force *majeure* the carrier may diverge from the prescribed itinerary. The consignment and the TIR carnet shall be presented without delay to the nearest customs authorities of the Member State in which the consignment is located. The customs authorities shall inform the office of departure/office of entry without delay and record the relevant details on the TIR carnet.]

NOTES

Inserted by Commission Regulation (EC) 12/97, Art 1, para 6.

Para 1: words in square brackets substituted by Commission Regulation (EC) 2787/2000, Art 1, para 56.

SECTION 3
[[THE ATA PROCEDURE]

NOTES

Heading: substituted by Commission Regulation (EC) 881/2003 Art 1, para 19.

[Article 457c

1. This Article shall apply without prejudice to the specific provisions of the ATA Convention [or the Istanbul Convention] concerning the liability of the guaranteeing associations when an ATA carnet is being used.

2. Where it is found that, in the course of or in connection with a transit operation carried out under cover of an ATA carnet, an offence or irregularity has been committed in a particular Member State, the recovery of duties and other charges which may be payable shall be effected by that Member State in accordance with Community or national provisions, without prejudice to the institution of criminal proceedings.

3. Where it is not possible to determine in which territory the offence or irregularity was committed, such offence or irregularity shall be deemed to have been committed in the Member State where it was detected unless, within the period referred to in Article 457d(2), proof of the regularity of the operation or of the place where the offence or irregularity was actually committed is furnished to the satisfaction of the customs authorities.

Where no such proof is furnished and the said offence or irregularity is thus deemed to have been committed in the Member State in which it was detected, the duties and other charges relating to the goods concerned shall be levied by that Member State in accordance with Community or national provisions.

If the Member State where the said offence or irregularity was actually committed is subsequently determined, the duties and other charges (apart from those levied, pursuant to the second subparagraph, as own resources of the Community) to which the goods are liable in that Member State shall be returned to it by the Member State which had originally recovered them. In that case, any overpayment shall be repaid to the person who had originally paid the charges.

Where the amount of the duties and other charges originally levied and returned by the Member State which had recovered them is smaller than that of the duties and other charges due in the Member State where the offence or irregularity was actually committed, that Member State shall levy the difference in accordance with Community or national provisions.

The customs administrations of the Member States shall take the necessary measures to deal with any offence or irregularity and to impose effective penalties.]

NOTES

Inserted by Commission Regulation (EC) 881/2003 Art 1, para 20.

Para 1: words in square brackets inserted by Commission Regulation (EC) 883/2005 Art 1, OJ L 148, 11.06.05, p 5, with effect from 1 October 2005.

[Article 457d

1. Where an offence or irregularity is found to have been committed in the course of or in connection with a transit operation carried out under cover of an ATA carnet, the customs authorities shall notify the holder of the ATA carnet and the guaranteeing

association within the period prescribed in Article 6(4) of the ATA Convention [or in Article 8(4) of Annex A to the Istanbul Convention].

2. Proof of the regularity of the operation carried out under cover of an ATA carnet within the meaning of the first subparagraph of Article 457c(3) shall be furnished within the period prescribed in Article 7(1) and (2) of the ATA Convention [or in Article 9(1)(a) and (b) of Annex A to the Istanbul Convention].

3. The proof referred to in paragraph 2 shall be furnished to the satisfaction of the customs authorities using one of the following methods:

(a)   by production of a customs or commercial document certified by the customs authorities establishing that the goods in question have been presented at the office of destination;

(b)   by the production of a customs document showing entry for a customs procedure in a third country, or a copy or photocopy thereof, certified as a true copy either by the body which endorsed the original document, or by the authorities of the third country concerned, or by the authorities of one of the Member States;

(c)   by the evidence referred to in Article 8 of the ATA Convention [or in Article 10 of Annex A to the Istanbul Convention].

The documents referred to in points (a) and (b) of the first subparagraph shall include information enabling the goods in question to be identified.]

NOTES

Inserted as noted to Art 457c.

Words in inner square brackets inserted by Commission Regulation (EC) 883/2005 Art 1, OJ L 148, 11.06.05, p 5, with effect from 1 October 2005.

Article 458

1. The customs authorities shall designate a coordinating office in each Member State for any action concerning infringements or irregularities relating to ATA carnets.

Those authorities shall inform the Commission of the designation of the coordinating offices together with their full address. A list of the offices shall be published in the *Official Journal of the European Communities*, "C" series.

2. For the purposes of determining the Member State responsible for levying the duties and other charges due, the Member State in which an offence or irregularity committed during a transit operation carried out under cover of an ATA carnet is detected within the meaning of the second subparagraph of [Article 457c(3)] shall be the Member State where the goods were found or, if they have not been found, the Member State whose coordinating office holds the most recent voucher from the carnet.

NOTES

Para 2: words substituted by Commission Regulation (EC) 881/2003 Art 1, para 21.

Article 459

1. Where the customs authorities of a Member State establish that a customs debt has been incurred, a claim shall be sent to the guaranteeing association with which that Member State is linked as soon as possible. Where the incurrence of the debt is due to the fact that the goods covered by the ATA carnet have not been re-exported or have not been assigned a customs-approved treatment or use within the periods laid down by the ATA Convention [or the Istanbul Convention], this claim shall be sent at the earliest three months after the date of expiry of the carnet.

2. The coordinating office making the claim shall at the same time, as far as possible, send to the coordinating office in the jurisdiction of which the office of temporary admission is situated, an information memo drawn up in accordance with the model shown in Annex 59.

The information memo shall be accompanied by a copy of the undischarged voucher, if the coordinating office has it in its possession. The information memo may also by used whenever this is deemed necessary.

NOTES
Para 1: words in square brackets inserted by Commission Regulation (EC) 883/2005 Art 1, OJ L 148, 11.06.05, p 5, with effect from 1 October 2005.

Article 460
1. The amount of duties and taxes arising from the claim referred to in Article 459 shall be calculated by means of the model taxation form set out in Annex 60 completed in accordance with the instructions attached to it.

The taxation form may be sent later than the claim, though not more than three months from the claim and in any event not more than six months from the date on which the customs authorities initiate the recovery proceedings.

2. In accordance with Article 461 and as provided therein, the sending of this form to a guaranteeing association by the customs administration with which that association is connected shall not release the other guaranteeing associations in the Community from an obligation to pay duties and other charges if it is found that the offence or irregularity was committed in a Member State other than the one in which the proceedings were initiated.

3. The taxation form shall be completed in duplicate or triplicate, as necessary. The first copy shall be for the guaranteeing association connected with the customs authority of the Member State in which the claim is made. The second copy shall be retained by the issuing coordinating office. Where necessary the issuing coordinating office shall send the third copy to the coordinating office in whose jurisdiction the office of temporary admission is situated.

Article 461
1. Where it is established that the offence or irregularity was committed in a Member State other than the one in which the proceedings were initiated, the coordinating office of the first Member State shall close the file as far as it is concerned.

2. For the purposes of closure it shall send to the coordinating office of the second Member State the contents of the file in its possession and if necessary shall refund to the guaranteeing association with which it is connected any sums which that association may have deposited or provisionally paid.

However, the file shall be closed only if the coordinating office of the first Member State receives a discharge from the coordinating office of the second Member State indicating that claim proceedings have been initiated in the latter Member State, in accordance with the rules of the ATA Convention [or of the Istanbul Convention]. This discharge shall be drawn up in accordance with the model in Annex 61.

3. The coordinating office of the Member State where the offence or irregularity was committed shall take over the recovery proceedings and where necessary collect from the guaranteeing association with which it is connected the amount of duties and other charges due at the rates in force in the Member State where this office is situated.

4. The proceedings must be transferred within a period of one year counting from the expiry of the carnet on condition that payment has not become definitive pursuant to Article 7(2) or (3) of the ATA Convention [or Article 9(1)(b) and (c) of Annex A to

the Istanbul Convention]. Should this time limit be exceeded the third and fourth paragraphs of [Article 457c(3)] shall apply.

NOTES

Para 2: words in square brackets inserted by Commission Regulation (EC) 883/2005 Art 1, OJ L 148, 11.06.05, p 5, with effect from 1 October 2005.

Para 4: words in first pair of square brackets inserted by Commission Regulation (EC) 883/2005 Art 1, OJ L 148, 11.06.05, p 5, with effect from 1 October 2005; words in second pair of square brackets substituted by Commission Regulation (EC) 881/2003 Art 1, para 21.

CHAPTER 10
TRANSPORT UNDER THE FORM 302 PROCEDURE

Article 462

1. Where, in accordance with Articles 91(2)(e) and 163(2)(e) of the Code, goods are transported from one point in the customs territory of the Community to another under cover of form 302 established under the Convention between the Parties to the North Atlantic Treaty on the Status of their Forces, signed in London on 19 June 1951, the customs territory of the Community shall be considered, for the purposes of the rules governing the use of the said form for such transport, to form a single territory.

2. Where, in the course of a transport operation referred to in paragraph 1, goods pass through the territory of a third country, the controls and formalities associated with form 302 shall be carried out at the points where the goods temporarily leave the customs territory of the Community and where they re-enter that territory.

3. Where it is found that, in the course of or in connection with a transport operation carried out under cover of form 302, an offence or irregularity has been committed in a particular Member State, the recovery of duties and other charges which may be payable shall be effected by that Member State in accordance with Community or national provisions, without prejudice to the institution of criminal proceedings.

4. [Article 457c(3)] shall apply *mutatis mutandis*.

NOTES

Para 4: words substituted by Commission Regulation (EC) 881/2003 Art 1, para 21.

[CHAPTER 10A
PROCEDURE FOR POSTAL CONSIGNMENTS

Article 462a

1. Where under Article 91(2)(f) of the Code, non-Community goods are carried from one point to another in the customs territory of the Community by post (including parcel post), the customs authorities of the Member State of dispatch shall be required to affix on the packaging and accompanying documents a label of the type shown in Annex 42, or have a label of this type so affixed.

2. Where Community goods are carried by post (including parcel post) to or from a part of the customs territory of the Community where Directive 77/388/EEC does not apply, the customs authorities of the Member State of dispatch shall be required to affix on the packaging and accompanying documents a label of the type shown in Annex 42b, or have a label of this type so affixed.]

NOTES

Inserted by Commission Regulation (EC) 2787/2000, Art 1, para 57.

Articles 463–495

. . . . .

Chapters 11 and 12 repealed by Commission Regulation (EC) 1602/2000, Art 1, para 9.

[TITLE III
CUSTOMS PROCEDURES WITH ECONOMIC IMPACT

CHAPTER 1
BASIC PROVISIONS COMMON TO MORE THAN ONE OF
THE ARRANGEMENTS

SECTION 1
DEFINITIONS

Article 496

For the purposes of this Title:

(a)   'arrangements' means a customs procedure with economic impact;

(b)   'authorisation' means permission by the customs authorities to use arrangements;

(c)   'single authorisation' means an authorisation involving different customs administrations covering entry for and/or discharge of the arrangements, storage, successive processing operations or uses;

(d)   'holder' means the holder of an authorisation;

(e)   'supervising office' means the customs office indicated in the authorisation as empowered to supervise the arrangements;

(f)   'office of entry' means the customs office or offices indicated in the authorisation as empowered to accept declarations entering goods for the arrangements;

(g)   'office of discharge' means the customs office or offices indicated in the authorisation as empowered to accept declarations assigning goods, following entry for the arrangements, to a new permitted customs-approved treatment or use, or, in the case of outward processing, the declaration for free circulation;

(h)   'triangular traffic' means the traffic where the office of discharge is not the same as the office of entry;

(i)   'accounts' means the holder's commercial, tax or other accounting material, or such data held on their behalf;

(j)   'records' means the data containing all the necessary information and technical details on whatever medium, enabling the customs authorities to supervise and control the arrangements, in particular as regards the flow and changing status of the goods; in the customs warehousing arrangements records are called stock records;

(k)   'main compensating products' means compensating products for the production of which the arrangements were authorised;

(l)   'secondary compensating products' means compensating products which are a necessary by-product of the processing operation other than the main compensating products specified in the authorisation;

(m)   'period for discharge' means the time by which the goods or products must have been assigned a new permitted customs-approved treatment or use including, as the case may be, in order to claim repayment of import duties after inward processing (drawback system), or in order to obtain total or partial relief from import duties upon release for free circulation after outward processing.]

NOTES

Title III (Articles 496–592) substituted for Title III (Articles 496–787) by Commission Regulation (EC) 993/2001, Art 1, para 28.

[SECTION 2
APPLICATION FOR AUTHORISATION

Article 497

1.   Application for authorisation shall be made in writing using the model set out in Annex 67.

2.   The customs authorities may permit renewal or modification of an authorisation to be applied for by simple written request.

3.   In the following cases, the application for authorisation may be made by means of a customs declaration in writing or by means of a data processing technique using the normal procedure:

(a)   for inward processing, where in accordance with Article 539 the economic conditions are deemed to be fulfilled, with the exception of applications involving equivalent goods;

(b)   for processing under customs control, where in accordance with Article 552(1), first subparagraph, the economic conditions are deemed to be fulfilled;

(c)   for temporary importation, including use of an ATA or CPD carnet;

(d)   for outward processing, where the processing operations concern repairs, including the standard exchange system without prior importation, and, after outward processing, in the following cases:

(i)   for release for free circulation after outward processing using the standard exchange system with prior importation;

(ii)   for release for free circulation after outward processing using the standard exchange system without prior importation, where the existing authorisation does not cover such a system and the customs authorities permit its modification;

(iii)   for release for free circulation after outward processing if the processing operation concerns goods of a non-commercial nature.

The application for authorisation may be made by means of an oral customs declaration for temporary importation in accordance with Article 229, subject to the presentation of a document made out in accordance with Article 499, third subparagraph.

The application for authorisation may be made by means of a customs declaration for temporary importation by any other act in accordance with Article 232(1).

4.   Applications for a single authorisation, except for temporary importation, shall be made in accordance with paragraph 1.

5.   Customs authorities may require applications for temporary importation with total relief from the import duties in accordance with Article 578 to be made in accordance with paragraph 1.]

Part III

NOTES
Substituted as noted to Art 496.

[Article 498

The application for an authorisation under Article 497 shall be submitted:

(a)   for customs warehousing: to the customs authorities designated for the place to be approved as a customs warehouse or where the applicant's main accounts are held;

(b)   for inward processing and processing under customs control: to the customs authorities designated for the place where the processing operation is to be carried out;

(c)   for temporary importation: to the customs authorities designated for the place where the goods are to be used, without prejudice to Article 580(1) second subparagraph;

(d)   for outward processing: to the customs authorities designated for the place where the goods to be declared for temporary exportation are located.]

NOTES
Substituted as noted to Art 496.

[Article 499

Where the customs authorities consider any of the information given in the application inadequate, they may require additional details from the applicant.

In particular, where an application may be made by making a customs declaration, the customs authorities shall require, without prejudice to Article 220, that the application be accompanied by a document made out by the declarant containing at least the following information, unless such information is deemed unnecessary or can be entered on the form used for the written declaration:

(a)   name and address of the applicant, the declarant and the operator;

(b)   nature of the processing or use of the goods;

(c)   technical description of the goods and compensating or processed products and means of identifying them;

(d)   codes of economic conditions in accordance with Annex 70;

(e)   estimated rate of yield or method by which that rate is to be determined;

(f)   estimated period for discharge;

(g)   proposed office of discharge;

(h)   place of processing or use;

(i)   proposed transfer formalities;

(j)   in the case of oral customs declaration, the value and quantity of the goods.

Where the document referred to in the second paragraph is presented with an oral customs declaration for temporary importation, it shall be made out in duplicate and one copy shall be endorsed by the customs authorities and given to the declarant.]

NOTES
Substituted as noted to Art 496.

[SECTION 3
SINGLE AUTHORISATION

Article 500

1. Where a single authorisation is applied for, the prior agreement of the authorities concerned shall be necessary, in accordance with the procedure set out in paragraphs 2 and 3.

2. In the case of temporary importation, the application shall be submitted to the customs authorities designated for the place of first use, without prejudice to Article 580(1), second subparagraph.

In other cases, it shall be submitted to the customs authorities designated for the place where the applicant's main accounts are held facilitating audit-based controls of the arrangements and where at least part of the storage, processing or temporary export operations to be covered by the authorisation are conducted.

[Where the competent customs authorities cannot be determined under the first or second subparagraph, the application shall be submitted to the customs authorities designated for the place where the applicant's main accounts are held facilitating audit-based controls of the arrangements.]

3. These customs authorities designated in accordance with paragraph 2 shall communicate the application and the draft authorisation to the other customs authorities concerned, which shall acknowledge the date of receipt within 15 days.

The other customs authorities concerned shall notify any objections within 30 days of the date on which the draft authorisation was received. Where objections are notified within that period and no agreement is reached, the application shall be rejected to the extent to which objections were raised.

4. The customs authorities may issue the authorisation if they have received no objections to the draft authorisation within the 30 days.

They shall send a copy of the agreed authorisation to all customs authorities concerned.]

NOTES

Substituted as noted to Art 496.
Para 2: words inserted by Commission Regulation (EC) 2286/2003, Art 1, para 13.

[**Article 501**

1. Where the criteria and conditions for the granting of a single authorisation are generally agreed upon between two or more customs administrations, the said administrations may also agree to replace prior agreement in accordance with Article 500(1) and information to be supplied in accordance with Article 500(2), second subparagraph, by simple notification.

2. Notification shall always be sufficient where:
   (a) a single authorisation is renewed, subject to modifications of a minor nature, annulled or revoked;
   (b) the application for a single authorisation concerns temporary importation and is not to be made using the model in Annex 67.

3. No notification shall be needed where:
   (a) the only element involving different customs administrations is triangular traffic under inward or outward processing, without use of recapitulative information sheets;
   (b) ATA or CPD carnets are used;
   (c) the authorisation for temporary importation is granted by accepting an oral declaration or a declaration by any other act.]

[SECTION 4
ECONOMIC CONDITIONS

Article 502

1. Except where the economic conditions are deemed to be fulfilled pursuant to Chapters 3, 4 or 6, the authorisation shall not be granted without examination of the economic conditions by the customs authorities.

2. For the inward processing arrangements (Chapter 3), the examination shall establish the economic unviability of using Community sources taking account in particular of the following criteria, the details of which are laid down in Part B of Annex 70:

    (a)   unavailability of Community-produced goods sharing the same quality and technical characteristics as the goods intended to be imported for the processing operations envisaged;

    (b)   differences in price between Community-produced goods and those intended to be imported;

    (c)   contractual obligations.

3. For the processing under customs control arrangements (Chapter 4), the examination shall establish whether the use of non-Community sources enables processing activities to be created or maintained in the Community.

4. For the outward processing arrangements (Chapter 6), the examination shall establish whether:

    (a)   carrying out processing outside the Community is likely to cause serious disadvantages for Community processors; or

    (b)   carrying out processing in the Community is economically unviable or is not feasible for technical reasons or due to contractual obligations.]

[**Article 503**

An examination of the economic conditions involving the Commission may take place:

    (a)   if the customs authorities concerned wish to consult before or after issuing an authorisation;

    (b)   if another customs administration objects to an authorisation issued;

    (c)   on the initiative of the Commission.]

[**Article 504**

1. Where an examination in accordance with Article 503 is initiated, the case shall be sent to the Commission. It shall contain the results of the examination already undertaken.

2. The Commission shall send an acknowledgement of receipt or notify the customs authorities concerned when acting on its own initiative. It shall determine in

consultation with them whether an examination of the economic conditions in the Committee is required.

3. Where the case is submitted to the Committee, the customs authorities shall inform the applicant, or holder, that such a procedure has been initiated and, if the handling of the application is not completed, that the time limits laid down in Article 506 have been suspended.

4. The Committee's conclusion shall be taken into account by the customs authorities concerned and by any other customs authorities dealing with similar authorisations or applications.

This conclusion may include its publication in the C series of the Official Journal of the European Communities.]

NOTES
Substituted as noted to Art 496.

[SECTION 5
THE DECISION ON AUTHORISATION

Article 505

The customs authorities competent to decide shall grant the authorisation as follows:

    (a)   for an application under Article 497(1), using the model set out in Annex 67;

    (b)   for an application under Article 497(3), by acceptance of the customs declaration;

    (c)   for an application for renewal or modification, by any appropriate act.]

NOTES
Substituted as noted to Art 496.

[Article 506

The applicant shall be informed of the decision to issue an authorisation, or the reasons why the application was rejected, within 30 days or 60 days in the case of the customs warehousing arrangements, of the date the application was lodged or the date any requested outstanding or additional information is received by the customs authorities.

These periods shall not apply in the case of a single authorisation unless it is issued under Article 501.]

NOTES
Substituted as noted to Art 496.

[Article 507

1. Without prejudice to Article 508, an authorisation shall take effect on the date of issue or at any later date given in the authorisation. In the case of a private warehouse, the customs authorities may exceptionally communicate their agreement to use the arrangements prior to the actual issuing of the authorisation.

2. No limit on the period of validity shall be fixed for authorisations for the customs warehousing arrangements.

3. For inward processing, processing under customs control and outward processing, the period of validity shall not exceed three years from the date the authorisation takes effect, except where there are duly justified good reasons.

4. By way of derogation from paragraph 3, for goods under inward processing covered by Annex 73, Part A, the period of validity shall not exceed six months.

In the case of milk and milk products referred to in Article 1 of Council Regulation (EC) No 1255/1999([1]), the period of validity shall not exceed three months.]

---

[1] OJ L 160, 26.6.99, p 48.

NOTES

Substituted as noted to Art 496.

[**Article 508**

1. Except for the customs warehousing arrangements, the customs authorities may issue a retroactive authorisation.

Without prejudice to paragraphs 2 and 3, a retroactive authorisation shall take effect at the earliest on the date on which the application was submitted.

2. If an application concerns renewal of an authorisation for the same kind of operation and goods, an authorisation may be granted with retroactive effect from the date the original authorisation expired.

3. In exceptional circumstances, the retroactive effect of an authorisation may be extended further, but not more than one year before the date the application was submitted, provided a proven economic need exists and:

(a)   the application is not related to attempted deception or to obvious negligence;

(b)   the period of validity which would have been granted under Article 507 is not exceeded;

(c)   the applicant's accounts confirm that all the requirements of the arrangements can be deemed to be met and, where appropriate, the goods can be identified for the period involved, and such accounts allow the arrangements to be controlled; and

(d)   all the formalities necessary to regularise the situation of the goods can be carried out, including, where necessary, the invalidation of the declaration.]

NOTES

Substituted as noted to Art 496.

[SECTION 6
OTHER PROVISIONS CONCERNING THE OPERATION OF
THE ARRANGEMENTS

SUBSECTION 1
GENERAL PROVISIONS

Article 509

1. Commercial policy measures provided for in Community acts shall be applicable on entry for the arrangements of non-Community goods only to the extent that they refer to the entry of goods into the customs territory of the Community.

2. Where compensating products other than those mentioned in Annex 75, obtained under the inward processing arrangements are released for free circulation, the commercial policy measures to be applied shall be those applicable to the release for free circulation of the import goods.

3. Where processed products, obtained under the arrangements for processing under customs control, are released for free circulation, the commercial policy measures applicable to those products shall be applied only where the import goods are subject to such measures.

4. Where Community acts provide for commercial policy measures on release for free circulation, such measures shall not apply to compensating products released for free circulation following outward processing:

— that have retained Community origin within the meaning of Articles 23 and 24 of the Code;

— involving repair, including the standard exchange system;

— following successive processing operations in accordance with Article 123 of the Code.]

NOTES
Substituted as noted to Art 496.

[Article 510
Without prejudice to Article 161(5) of the Code, the supervising office may allow the customs declaration to be presented at a customs office other than those specified in the authorisation. The supervising office shall determine how it shall be informed.]

NOTES
Substituted as noted to Art 496.

[SUBSECTION 2
TRANSFERS

Article 511
The authorisation shall specify whether and under which conditions the movement of goods or products placed under suspensive arrangements between different places or to the premises of another holder may take place without discharge of the arrangements (transfer), subject, in cases other than temporary importation, to the keeping of records.

Transfer shall not be possible where the place of departure or arrival of the goods is a type B warehouse.]

NOTES
Substituted as noted to Art 496.

[Article 512
1. Transfer between different places designated in the same authorisation may be undertaken without any customs formalities.

2. Transfer from the office of entry to the holder's or operator's facilities or place of use may be carried out under cover of the declaration for entry for the arrangements.

3. Transfer to the office of exit with a view to re-exportation may take place under cover of the arrangements. In this case, the arrangements shall not be discharged until the goods or products declared for re-exportation have actually left the customs territory of the Community.]

NOTES

Substituted as noted to Art 496.

[Article 513

Transfer from one holder to another can only take place where the latter enters the transferred goods or products for the arrangements under an authorisation to use the local clearance procedure. Notification to the customs authorities and entry in the records of the goods or products referred to in Article 266 shall take place upon their arrival at the premises of the second holder. A supplementary declaration need not be required.

In the case of temporary importation, the transfer from one holder to another may also take place where the latter enters the goods under the arrangements by means of a customs declaration in writing using the normal procedure.

The formalities to be carried out are laid down in Annex 68. Upon receipt of the goods or products, the second holder shall be obliged to enter them for the arrangements.]

NOTES

Substituted as noted to Art 496.

[Article 514

The transfer involving an increased risk as set out in Annex 44c shall be covered by a guarantee under conditions equivalent to those provided for in the transit procedure.]

NOTES

Substituted as noted to Art 496.

[SUBSECTION 3
RECORDS

Article 515

The customs authorities shall require the holder, the operator or the designated warehousekeeper to keep records, except for temporary importation or where they do not deem it necessary.

The customs authorities may approve existing accounts containing the relevant particulars as records.

The supervising office may require an inventory to be made of all or some of the goods placed under the arrangements.]

NOTES

Substituted as noted to Art 496.

[Article 516

The records referred to in Article 515 and, where they are required, under Article 581(2) for temporary imports shall contain the following information:

(a)   the information contained in the boxes of the minimum list laid down by Annex 37 for the declaration of entry for the arrangements;

(b)   particulars of the declarations by means of which the goods are assigned a customs-approved treatment or use discharging the arrangements;

(c)   the date and reference particulars of other customs documents and any other documents relating to entry and discharge;

(d)   the nature of the processing operations, types of handling or temporary use;

(e)   the rate of yield or its method of calculation where appropriate;

(f)   information enabling the goods to be monitored, including their location and particulars of any transfer;

(g)   commercial or technical descriptions necessary to identify the goods;

(h)   particulars enabling monitoring of the movements under the inward processing arrangements operating with equivalent goods.

However, the customs authorities may waive the requirement for some of this information where this does not adversely affect the control or supervision of the arrangements for the goods to be stored, processed or used.]

NOTES

Substituted as noted to Art 496.

[SUBSECTION 4
RATE OF YIELD AND CALCULATION FORMULA

Article 517

1.   Where relevant for the arrangements falling under Chapters 3, 4 and 6, a rate of yield or the method for determining a rate, including average rates, shall be established in the authorisation or at the time the goods are entered for the arrangements. Such rate is to be determined, as far as possible, on the basis of production or technical data or, where these are not available, data relating to operations of the same type.

2.   In particular circumstances the customs authorities may establish the rate of yield after the goods have been entered for the arrangements, but not later than when they are assigned a new customs-approved treatment or use.

3.   The standard rates of yield laid down for inward processing in Annex 69 shall apply to the operations mentioned therein.]

NOTES

Substituted as noted to Art 496.

[**Article 518**

1.   The proportion of import/temporary export goods incorporated in the compensating products shall be calculated in order:

—   to determine the import duties to be charged;

—   to determine the amount to be deducted when a customs debt is incurred; or

—   to apply commercial policy measures.

These calculations shall be made in accordance with the quantitative scale method, or the value scale method as appropriate, or any other method giving similar results.

For the purposes of the calculations, compensating products shall include processed products or intermediate products.

2.   The quantitative scale method shall be applicable where:

(a)   only one kind of compensating product is derived from the processing operations; in this case the quantity of import/temporary export goods deemed to be present in the quantity of compensating products for which a customs debt is incurred shall be proportional to the latter category of products as a percentage of the total quantity of compensating products;

(b)   several kinds of compensating product are derived from the processing operations and all elements of the import/temporary export goods are found in each of those compensating products; in this case the quantity of import/temporary export goods deemed to be present in the quantity of a given compensating product for which a customs debt is incurred shall be proportional to:

(i)   the ratio between this specific kind of compensating product, irrespective of whether a customs debt is incurred, and the total quantity of all compensating products, and

(ii)   the ratio between the quantity of compensating products for which a customs debt is incurred and the total quantity of compensating products of the same kind.

In deciding whether the conditions for applying the methods described in (a) or (b) are fulfilled, losses shall not be taken into account. Without prejudice to Article 862, losses means the proportion of import/temporary export goods destroyed and lost during the processing operation, in particular by evaporation, desiccation, venting as gas or leaching. In outward processing secondary compensating products that constitute waste, scrap, residues, offcuts and remainders shall be treated as losses.

3.   The value scale method shall be applied where the quantitative scale method is not applicable.

The quantity of import/temporary export goods deemed to be present in the quantity of a given compensating product incurring a customs debt shall be proportional to:

(a)   the value of this specific kind of compensating product, irrespective of whether a customs debt is incurred, as a percentage of the total value of all the compensating products; and

(b)   the value of the compensating products for which a customs debt is incurred, as a percentage of the total value of compensating products of that kind.

The value of each of the different compensating products to be used for applying the value scale shall be the recent ex-works price in the Community, or the recent selling price in the Community of identical or similar products, provided that these have not been influenced by the relationship between buyer and seller.

4.   Where the value cannot be ascertained pursuant to paragraph 3, it shall be determined by any reasonable method.]

NOTES

Substituted as noted to Art 496.

[SUBSECTION 5
COMPENSATORY INTEREST

Article 519

1.   Where a customs debt is incurred in respect of compensating products or import goods under inward processing or temporary importation, compensatory interest shall be due on the amount of import duties for the period involved.

2.   The three-month money market interest rates published in the statistical annex of the Monthly Bulletin of the European Central Bank shall apply.

The applicable rate shall be that applicable two months before the month in which the customs debt is incurred and for the Member State where the first operation or use as provided for by the authorisation took place or should have taken place.

3. Interest shall be applied on a monthly basis, starting on the first day of the month following the month in which the import goods for which a customs debt is incurred were first entered for the arrangements. The period shall close on the last day of the month in which the customs debt is incurred.

Where inward processing (drawback system) is concerned and release for free circulation is requested under Article 128(4) of the Code, the period starts from the first day of the month following the month in which the import duties were repaid or remitted.

4. Paragraphs 1, 2 and 3 shall not apply to the following cases:

(a) where the period to be taken into account is less than one month;

(b) where the amount of compensatory interest applicable does not exceed EUR 20 per customs debt incurred;

(c) where a customs debt is incurred in order to allow the application of preferential tariff treatment under an agreement between the Community and a third country on imports into that country;

(d) where waste and scrap resulting from destruction is released for free circulation;

(e) where the secondary compensating products referred to in Annex 75 are released for free circulation, provided they are in proportion to exported quantities of main compensating products;

(f) where a customs debt is incurred as a result of an application for release for free circulation under Article 128(4) of the Code, as long as the import duties payable on the products in question have not yet actually been repaid or remitted;

(g) where the holder requests release for free circulation and submits proof that particular circumstances not arising from any negligence or deception on his part make it impossible or uneconomic to carry out the re-export operation under the conditions he had anticipated and duly substantiated when applying for the authorisation;

(h) where a customs debt is incurred and to the extent a security is provided by a cash deposit in relation to this debt;

(i) where a customs debt is incurred in accordance with Article 201(1)(b) of the Code or is due to the release for free circulation of goods which were entered for the temporary importation arrangements under Articles 556 to 561, 563, 565, 568, 573(b) and 576 of this Regulation.

5. In the case of inward processing operations in which the number of import goods and/or compensating products makes it uneconomic to apply the provisions of paragraphs 2 and 3, the customs authorities, at the request of the person concerned, may allow simplified methods giving similar results to be used for the calculation of compensatory interest.]

NOTES

Substituted as noted to Art 496.

[SUBSECTION 6
DISCHARGE

Article 520

1. Where import or temporary export goods have been entered under two or more declarations for the arrangements by virtue of one authorisation:

> — in the case of a suspensive arrangement, the assignment of goods or products to a new customs-approved treatment or use shall be considered to discharge the arrangements for the import goods in question entered under the earliest of the declarations;
>
> — in the case of inward processing (drawback system) or outward processing, the compensating products shall be considered to have been obtained from the import or temporary export goods in question respectively, entered under the earliest of the declarations.

Application of the first subparagraph shall not lead to unjustified import duty advantages.

The holder may request the discharge to be made in relation to the specific import or temporary export goods.

2. Where the goods under the arrangements are placed together with other goods and there is total destruction or irretrievable loss, the customs authorities may accept evidence produced by the holder indicating the actual quantity of goods under the arrangements which was destroyed or lost. Where it is not possible for the holder to produce such evidence, the amount of goods which has been destroyed or lost shall be established by reference to the proportion of goods of that type under the arrangements at the time when the destruction or loss occurred.]

NOTES

Substituted as noted to Art 496.

[**Article 521**

1. At the latest upon expiry of the period for discharge, irrespective of whether aggregation in accordance with Article 118(2), second subparagraph, of the Code is used or not:

> — in the case of inward processing (suspension system) or processing under customs control, the bill of discharge shall be supplied to the supervising office within 30 days;
>
> — in the case of inward processing (drawback system), the claim for repayment or remission of import duties must be lodged with the supervising office within six months.

Where special circumstances so warrant, the customs authorities may extend the period even if it has expired.

2. The bill or the claim shall contain the following particulars, unless otherwise determined by the supervising office:

(a) reference particulars of the authorisation;

(b) the quantity of each type of import goods in respect of which discharge, repayment or remission is claimed or the import goods entered for the arrangements under the triangular traffic system;

(c) the CN code of the import goods;

(d) the rate of import duties to which the import goods are liable and, where applicable, their customs value;

(e) the particulars of the declarations entering the import goods under the arrangements;

(f) the type and quantity of the compensating or processed products or the goods in unaltered state and the customs-approved treatment or use to which they have been assigned, including particulars of the corresponding declarations, other customs documents or any other document relating to discharge and periods for discharge;

(g)   the value of the compensating or processed products if the value scale method is used for the purpose of discharge;

(h)   the rate of yield;

(i)   the amount of import duties to be paid or to be repaid or remitted and where applicable any compensatory interest to be paid. Where this amount refers to the application of Article 546, it shall be specified;

(j)   in the case of processing under customs control, the CN code of the processed products and elements necessary to determine the customs value.

3.   The supervising office may make out the bill of discharge.]

NOTES

Substituted as noted to Art 496.

[SECTION 7
ADMINISTRATIVE COOPERATION

Article 522

The customs authorities shall communicate to the Commission in the cases, within the time-limit and in the format set out in Annex 70 the following information:

(a)   with regard to inward processing and processing under customs control:

     (i)   authorisations issued;

     (ii)   applications refused or authorisations annulled or revoked on the grounds of economic conditions not being fulfilled;

(b)   with regard to outward processing:

     (i)   authorisations issued in accordance with Article 147(2) of the Code;

     (ii)   applications refused or authorisations annulled or revoked on the grounds of economic conditions not being fulfilled.

The Commission shall make these particulars available to the customs administrations.]

NOTES

Substituted as noted to Art 496.

[**Article 523**

In order to make pertinent information available to other customs offices involved in the application of the arrangements, the following information sheets provided for in Annex 71 may be issued at the request of the person concerned or on the initiative of the customs authorities, unless the customs authorities agree other means of exchange of information:

(a)   for customs warehousing, the information INF8, in order to communicate the elements for assessment of the customs debt applicable to the goods before usual forms of handling have taken place;

(b)   for inward processing:

     (i)   the information sheet INF1, for the communication of information on duty amounts, compensatory interest, security and commercial policy measures,

     (ii)   the information sheet INF9, for the communication of information on compensating products to be assigned another customs approved treatment or use in triangular traffic,

(iii) the information sheet INF5, for the communication to obtain duty relief for import goods, of information on prior exportation in triangular traffic,

(iv) the information sheet INF7, for the communication of information permitting repayment or remission of duties under the drawback system;

(c) for temporary importation, the information sheet INF6 in order to communicate the elements for assessment of the customs debt or of amounts of duties already levied for goods moved;

(d) for outward processing, the information sheet INF2 in order to communicate information on temporary export goods in triangular traffic, in order to obtain partial or total relief for compensating products.]

NOTES

Substituted as noted to Art 496.

[CHAPTER 2
CUSTOMS WAREHOUSING

SECTION 1
GENERAL PROVISIONS

Article 524

For the purposes of this Chapter concerning agricultural products, 'prefinanced goods' means Community goods intended for export in the unaltered state which are the subject of the payment of an amount equal to an export refund before the goods are exported, where such payment is provided for in Council Regulation (EEC) No 565/80([1]).]

---

[1] OJ L 62, 7.3.80, p 5.

NOTES

Substituted as noted to Art 496.

[**Article 525**

1. Where a customs warehouse is public, the following classification shall apply:

(a) type A, if the responsibility lies with the warehousekeeper;

(b) type B, if the responsibility lies with the depositor;

(c) type F, if the warehouse is operated by the customs authorities.

2. Where a customs warehouse is private and responsibility lies with the warehousekeeper, who is the same person as the depositor but not necessarily the owner of the goods, the following classification shall apply:

(a) type D, where release for free circulation is made by way of the local clearance procedure and may be granted on the basis of the nature, the customs value and the quantity of the goods to be taken into account at the time of their placing under the arrangements;

(b) type E, where the arrangements apply although the goods need not be stored in a place approved as a customs warehouse;

(c) type C, where neither of the special situations under points (a) and (b) applies.

3.   An authorisation for a type E warehouse may provide for the procedures laid down for type D to be applied.]

[SECTION 2
ADDITIONAL CONDITIONS CONCERNING THE GRANTING OF
THE AUTHORISATION

Article 526

1.   When granting the authorisation the customs authorities shall define the premises or any other location approved as a customs warehouse of type A, B, C or D. They may also approve temporary storage facilities as such types of warehouse or operate them as a type F warehouse.

2.   A location may not be approved as more than one customs warehouse at the same time.

3.   Where goods present a danger or are likely to spoil other goods or require special facilities for other reasons, authorisations may specify that they may only be stored in premises specially equipped to receive them.

4.   Type A, C, D and E warehouses may be approved as victualling warehouses within the meaning of Article 40 of Commission Regulation (EC) No 800/99(¹).

5.   Single authorisations may be granted only for private customs warehouses.]

¹ OJ L 102, 17.4.99, p 11.

[Article 527

1.   Authorisations may be granted only if any intended usual forms of handling, inward processing or processing under customs control of the goods do not predominate over the storage of the goods.

2.   Authorisations shall not be granted if the premises of customs warehouses or the storage facilities are used for the purpose of retail sale.

An authorisation may, however, be granted, where goods are retailed with relief from import duties:

   (a)   to travellers in traffic to third countries;
   (b)   under diplomatic or consular arrangements;
   (c)   to members of international organisations or to NATO forces.

3.   For the purposes of the second indent of Article 86 of the Code, when examining whether the administrative costs of customs warehousing arrangements are disproportionate to the economic needs involved, customs authorities shall take account, inter alia, of the type of warehouse and the procedure which may be applied therein.]

[SECTION 3
STOCK RECORDS

Article 528

1.   In warehouses of type A, C, D and E, the person designated to keep the stock records shall be the warehousekeeper.

2.   In warehouses of type F, the operating customs office shall keep the customs records in place of stock records.

3.   In type B warehouses, in place of stock records, the supervising office shall keep the declarations of entry for the arrangements.]

NOTES
   Substituted as noted to Art 496.

[Article 529

1.   The stock records shall at all times show the current stock of goods which are still under the customs warehousing arrangements. At the times laid down by the customs authorities, the warehousekeeper shall lodge a list of the said stock at the supervising office.

2.   Where Article 112(2) of the Code applies, the customs value of the goods before carrying out usual forms of handling shall appear in the stock records.

3.   Information on the temporary removal of goods and on goods in common storage in accordance with Article 534(2) shall appear in the stock records.]

NOTES
   Substituted as noted to Art 496.

[Article 530

1.   Where goods are entered for the type E warehouse arrangements, the entry in the stock records shall take place when they arrive at the holder's storage facilities.

2.   Where the customs warehouse also serves as a temporary storage facility, the entry in the stock records shall take place at the time the declaration for the arrangements is accepted.

3.   Entry in the stock records relating to discharge of the arrangements shall take place at the latest when the goods leave the customs warehouse or the holder's storage facilities.]

NOTES
   Substituted as noted to Art 496.

[SECTION 4
OTHER PROVISIONS CONCERNING THE OPERATION OF
THE ARRANGEMENTS

Article 531

Non-Community goods may undergo the usual forms of handling listed in Annex 72.]

NOTES
   Substituted as noted to Art 496.

[Article 532

Goods may be temporarily removed for a period not exceeding three months. Where circumstances so warrant, this period may be extended.]

NOTES

Substituted as noted to Art 496.

[Article 533

Applications for permission to carry out usual forms of handling or to remove goods temporarily from the customs warehouse shall be made in writing on a case by case basis to the supervising office. They must contain all particulars necessary to apply the arrangements.

Such permission may be granted as part of an authorisation to operate the warehousing arrangements. In this case the supervising office, in the manner it shall determine, shall be notified that such handling is to be carried out or the goods are to be temporarily removed.]

NOTES

Substituted as noted to Art 496.

[Article 534

1. Where Community goods are stored on the premises of a customs warehouse or the storage facilities used for goods under the warehousing arrangements, specific methods of identifying such goods may be laid down with a view, in particular, to distinguishing them from goods entered for the customs warehousing arrangements.

2. The customs authorities may permit common storage where it is impossible to identify at all times the customs status of each type of goods. Prefinanced goods shall be excluded from such permission.

Goods in common storage shall share the same eight-digit CN-code, the same commercial quality and the same technical characteristics.

3. For the purpose of being declared for a customs-approved treatment or use the goods in common storage, as well as, in particular circumstances, identifiable goods which fulfill the conditions of the second subparagraph of paragraph 2, may be deemed to be either Community goods or non-Community goods.

Application of the first subparagraph shall, however, not result in a given customs status being assigned to a quantity of goods greater than the quantity actually having that status which is stored at the customs warehouse or the storage facilities when the goods declared for a customs-approved treatment or use are removed.]

NOTES

Substituted as noted to Art 496.

[Article 535

1. Where operations of inward processing or processing under customs control are carried out on the premises of customs warehouses or in storage facilities, the provisions of Article 534 shall apply, mutatis mutandis, to the goods under these arrangements.

Where, however, these operations concern inward processing without equivalence or processing under customs control, the provisions of Article 534 on common storage shall not apply with regard to Community goods.

2. Entries in the records shall allow the customs authorities to monitor the precise situation of all goods or products under the arrangements at any time.]

NOTES

Substituted as noted to Art 496.

[CHAPTER 3
INWARD PROCESSING

SECTION 1
GENERAL PROVISION

Article 536

For the purposes of this Chapter:

(a) 'Prior exportation' means the system whereby compensating products obtained from equivalent goods are to be exported before the import goods are entered for the arrangements using the suspension system;

(b) 'Job processing' means any processing of import goods directly or indirectly placed at the disposal of the holder which is carried out according to specifications on behalf of a principal established in a third country, generally against payment of processing costs alone.]

NOTES

Substituted as noted to Art 496.

[SECTION 2
ADDITIONAL CONDITIONS CONCERNING THE GRANTING OF
THE AUTHORISATION

Article 537

An authorisation shall be granted only where the applicant has the intention of re-exporting or exporting main compensating products.]

NOTES

Substituted as noted to Art 496.

[Article 538

An authorisation may also be granted for the goods referred to in the fourth indent of Article 114(2)(c) of the Code, with the exception of:

(a) fuels and energy sources other than those needed for the testing of compensating products or for the detection of faults in import goods needing repair;

(b) lubricants other than those needed for the testing, adjustment or withdrawal of compensating products;

(c) equipment and tools.]

NOTES

Substituted as noted to Art 496.

[**Article 539**

The economic conditions shall be deemed to be fulfilled except where the application concerns import goods mentioned in Annex 73.

However, the conditions shall also be deemed to be fulfilled where an application concerns import goods mentioned in Annex 73, provided that:

(a)   the application concerns:

(i)   operations involving goods of a non-commercial nature,

(ii)   a job processing contract,

(iii)   the processing of compensating products already obtained by processing under a previous authorisation the granting of which was subject to an examination of the economic conditions,

(iv)   usual forms of handling referred to in Article 531,

(v)   repair,

(vi)   the processing of durum wheat falling within CN code 1001 10 00 to produce pasta falling within CN codes 1902 11 00 and 1902 19; or

(b)   the aggregate value of the import goods per applicant and per calendar year for each eight-digit CN code does not exceed 150000 EUR; or

(c)   in accordance with Article 11 of Council Regulation (EC) No 3448/93([1]), import goods referred to under Part A of Annex 73 are concerned and the applicant presents a document issued by a competent authority permitting the entry of those goods for the arrangements, in the limits of a quantity determined on the basis of a supply balance.]

[1] OJ L 318, 20.12.93, p 18.

NOTES

Substituted as noted to Art 496.

[**Article 540**

The authorisation shall specify the means and methods of identifying the import goods in the compensating products and lay down the conditions for the proper conduct of operations using equivalent goods.

Such methods of identification or conditions may include examination of the records.]

NOTES

Substituted as noted to Art 496.

[SECTION 3

PROVISIONS CONCERNING THE OPERATION OF ARRANGEMENTS

Article 541

1.   The authorisation shall specify whether and under which conditions equivalent goods referred to in Article 114(2)(e) of the Code and sharing the same eight-digit CN code, the same commercial quality and the same technical characteristics as the import goods may be used for the processing operations.

2.   Equivalent goods may be allowed to be at a more advanced stage of manufacture than the import goods where the essential part of the processing with

regard to these equivalent goods is carried out in the undertaking of the holder or in the undertaking where the operation is being carried out on his behalf, save in exceptional cases.

3. Special provisions, set out in Annex 74, shall apply in respect of the goods referred to in that Annex.]

NOTES

Substituted as noted to Art 496.

[Article 542

1. The authorisation shall specify the period for discharge. Where the circumstances so warrant, this period may be extended even when that originally set has expired.

2. Where the period for discharge expires on a specific date for all the goods placed under the arrangements in a given period, the authorisation may provide that the period for discharge shall be automatically extended for all goods still under the arrangements on this date. However, the customs authorities may require that such goods be assigned a new permitted customs-approved treatment or use within the period which they shall set.

3. Irrespective of whether or not aggregation is used or paragraph 2 is applied, the period for discharge for the following compensating products or goods in the unaltered state shall not exceed:

(a)   four months in the case of milk and milk products referred to in Article 1 of Regulation (EC) No 1255/1999;

(b)   two months in the case of slaughter without fattening of animals referred to in Chapter 1 of the CN;

(c)   three months in the case of fattening (including slaughter where relevant) of animals which fall under CN codes 0104 and 0105;

(d)   six months in the case of fattening (including slaughter where relevant) of other animals referred to in Chapter 1 of the CN;

(e)   six months in the case of processing of meat;

(f)   six months in the case of processing of other agricultural products of a kind eligible for advance payment of export refunds referred to in Article 1 of Regulation (EEC) No 565/80, and processed into products or goods referred to in Article 2(b) or (c) of the same Regulation.

Where successive processing operations are carried out or where exceptional circumstances so warrant, the periods may be extended on request, the total period not exceeding twelve months.]

NOTES

Substituted as noted to Art 496.

[Article 543

1. In the case of prior exportation the authorisation shall specify the period within which the non-Community goods must be declared for the arrangements, taking account of the time required for procurement and transport to the Community.

2. The period referred to in paragraph 1 shall not exceed:

(a)   three months for goods subject to a common market organisation;

(b)   six months for all other goods.

The period of six months may, however, be extended where the holder submits a reasoned request, provided that the total period does not exceed twelve months.

Where the circumstances so warrant the extension may be allowed even after the original period has expired.]

NOTES
Substituted as noted to Art 496.

[Article 544
For the purposes of discharging the arrangements or the claim for repayment of import duties, the following shall be regarded as re-exportation or exportation:

(a) the delivery of compensating products to persons who are eligible for relief from import duties pursuant to the Vienna Convention of 18 April 1961 on Diplomatic Relations, or to the Vienna Convention of 24 April 1963 on Consular Relations or other consular conventions, or the New York Convention of 16 December 1969 on Special Missions;

(b) the delivery of compensating products to the armed forces of other countries stationed in the territory of a Member State, where that Member State grants special relief from import duties in accordance with Article 136 of Regulation (EEC) No 918/83;

(c) the delivery of civil aircraft; however, the supervising office shall allow the arrangements to be discharged once import goods have been used for the first time for the manufacture, repair, modification or conversion of civil aircraft or parts thereof, on condition that the records of the holder are such as to make it possible to verify that the arrangements are being correctly applied and operated;

(d) the delivery of spacecraft and related equipment; however, the supervising office shall allow the arrangements to be discharged once import goods have been used for the first time for the manufacture, repair, modification or conversion of satellites, their launch vehicles and ground station equipment and parts thereof that are an integral part of the systems, on condition that the records of the holder are such as to make it possible to verify that the arrangements are being correctly applied and operated;

(e) disposal in accordance with the relevant provisions of secondary compensating products whose destruction under customs supervision is prohibited on environmental grounds; for these purposes, the holder shall prove that discharge of the arrangements in accordance with the normal rules is either impossible or uneconomic.]

NOTES
Substituted as noted to Art 496.

[SECTION 4
PROVISIONS CONCERNING THE OPERATION OF THE
SUSPENSION SYSTEM

Article 545
1. Use of equivalent goods for processing operations in accordance with Article 115 of the Code shall not be subject to the formalities for entry of goods for the arrangements.

2. The equivalent goods and compensating products made therefrom shall become non-Community goods and the import goods Community goods at the time of acceptance of the declaration discharging the arrangements.

Part III

However, where import goods are put on the market before the arrangements are discharged, they shall change their status at the time they are put on the market. In exceptional cases, where the equivalent goods are expected not to be present at that time, the customs authorities may allow, at the request of the holder, the equivalent goods to be present at a later time, to be determined by them and within a reasonable time.

3.   In case of prior exportation:

—   compensating products shall become non-Community goods on acceptance of the export declaration on condition that the goods to be imported are entered for the arrangements;

—   import goods shall become Community goods at the time of their entry for the arrangements.]

NOTES

Substituted as noted to Art 496.

[Article 546

The authorisation shall specify whether compensating products or goods in the unaltered state may be released for free circulation without customs declaration, without prejudice to prohibitive or restrictive measures. In this case they shall be considered to have been released for free circulation, if they have not been assigned a customs-approved treatment or use on expiry of the period for discharge.

For the purposes of the first subparagraph of Article 218(1) of the Code, the declaration for release for free circulation shall be considered to have been lodged and accepted and release granted at the time of presentation of the bill of discharge.

The products or goods shall become Community goods when they are put on the market.]

NOTES

Substituted as noted to Art 496.

[Article 547

In case of release for free circulation of compensating products, boxes 15, 16, 34, 41 and 42 of the declaration shall refer to the import goods. Alternatively, relevant information may also be supplied by information sheet INF1 or any other document accompanying the declaration.]

NOTES

Substituted as noted to Art 496.

[Article 547a

The import duties to be charged under Article 121(1)of the Code on import goods eligible, at the time when the declaration of entry for the arrangements was accepted, for favourable tariff treatment by reason of their end-use shall be calculated at the rate corresponding to such end-use. This shall be allowed only if an authorisation for such end-use could have been granted and if the conditions attaching to the granting of favourable tariff treatment would have been fulfilled.]

NOTES

Inserted by Commission Regulation (EC) 444/2002, Art 1, para 21.

[Article 548

1. The list of compensating products subject to the import duties appropriate to them in accordance with the first indent of Article 122(a) of the Code is in Annex 75.

2. Where compensating products other than those mentioned on the list referred to in paragraph 1 are destroyed, they shall be treated as if they were re-exported.]

NOTES
Substituted as noted to Art 496.

[Article 549

1. Where the compensating products or goods in the unaltered state are entered for one of the suspensive arrangements or introduced in a free zone of control type I within the meaning of Article 799 or in a free warehouse or placed in a free zone of control type II within the meaning of Article 799 enabling the arrangements to be discharged, the documents or records used for the said customs-approved treatment or use or any documents replacing them, shall contain one of the following indications:

— Mercancías PA/S,
— AF/S – varer,
— AV/S – Waren,
— Εμπορεματα ET/A
— IP/S goods,
— Marchandises PA/S,
— Merci PA/S,
— AV/S – goederen,
— Mercadorias AA/S,
— SJ/S – tavaroita,
— AF/S – varor.
[— Zboží AZS/P,
— ST/P kaup,
— IP/ATL preces,
— LP/S preks,
— AF/F áruk,
— oetti PI/S,
— towary UCz/Z,
— AO/O blago,
— AZS/PS tovar.]
[— С АУ/ОП,
— Mrfuri PA/S]

2. Where import goods entered for the arrangements are subject to specific commercial policy measures and such measures continue to be applicable at the time when the goods, either in the unaltered state or in the form of compensating products, are entered for one of the suspensive arrangements or introduced in a free zone of control type I within the meaning of Article 799 or in a free warehouse or placed in a free zone of control type II within the meaning of Article 799, the indication referred to in paragraph 1 shall be supplemented by one of the following:

— Política comercial,
— Handelspolitik,
— Handelspolitik,
— Εμπορική πολιτική
— Commercial policy,
— Politique commerciale,

- — Politica commerciale,
- — Handelspolitiek,
- — Politica comercial,
- — Kauppapolitiikka,
- — Handelspolitik,
- [— Obchodní politika,
- — Kaubanduspoliitika,
- — Tirdzniecbas politika,
- — Prekybos politika,
- — Kereskedelempolitika,
- — Politika kummerjali,
- — Polityka handlowa,
- — Trgovinska politika,
- — Obchodná politika.]
- [— *(for original text, refer to Commission Regulation (EC) 1792/2006 (OJ L 362, 20.12.06, p 1)),*
- — Politic comercial]

NOTES

Substituted as noted to Art 496.

Para 1: words inserted by the 2003 Act of Accession Annex II(19)(A)(II), para 25. Final two entries inserted by Commission Regulation (EC) 1792/2006, Art 1, Annex, Part 11(A)(24).

Para 2: words inserted by the 2003 Act of Accession Annex II(19)(A)(II), para 26. Final two entries inserted by Commission Regulation (EC) 1792/2006, Art 1, Annex, Part 11(A)(25).

[SECTION 5
PROVISION CONCERNING THE OPERATION OF THE DRAWBACK SYSTEM

Article 550

Where goods under the drawback system are assigned a customs-approved treatment or use referred to in Article 549(1), the indications required for that provision shall be the following:

- — Mercancías PA/R,
- — AF/T-varer,
- — AV/R Waren,
- — Εμπορεματα ET/E
- — IP/D goods,
- — Marchandises PA/R,
- — Merci PA/R,
- — AV/T-goederen,
- — Mercadorias AA/D,
- — SJ/T-tavaroita,
- — AF/R-varor,
- [— Zboží AZS/N,
- — ST/T kaup,
- — IP/ATM preces,
- — LP/D preks,
- — AF/V áruk,
- — oetti PI/SR,

- towary UCz/Zw,
- AO/P blago,
- AZS/SV tovar.]]
[— *(for original text, refer to Commission Regulation (EC) 1792/2006 (OJ L 362, 20.12.06, p 1)),*
- Mrfuri PA/R]

NOTES

Substituted as noted to Art 496.

Words inserted by the 2003 Act of Accession Annex II(19)(A)(II), para 27. Final two entries inserted by Commission Regulation (EC) 1792/2006, Art 1, Annex, Part 11(A)(26).

[CHAPTER 4
PROCESSING UNDER CUSTOMS CONTROL

Article 551

1. The arrangements for processing under customs control shall apply for goods the processing of which leads to products which are subject to a lower amount of import duties than that applicable to the import goods.

The arrangements shall also apply for goods which have to undergo operations to ensure their compliance with technical requirements for their release for free circulation.

2. Article 542(1) and (2) shall apply mutatis mutandis.

3. For the purposes of determining the customs value of processed products declared for free circulation, the declarant may choose any of the methods referred to in Article 30(2) (a), (b) or (c) of the Code or the customs value of the import goods plus the processing costs.]

[Processing costs means all costs incurred in making the processed products, including overheads and the value of any Community goods used.]

NOTES

Substituted as noted to Art 496.

Para 3: words inserted by Commission Regulation (EC) 881/2003 Art 1, para 22.

[**Article 552**

1. For the types of goods and operations mentioned in Annex 76, Part A, the economic conditions shall be deemed to be fulfilled.

For other types of goods and operations examination of the economic conditions shall take place.

2. For the types of goods and operations mentioned in Annex 76, Part B and not covered by Part A, the examination of the economic conditions shall take place in the Committee. Article 504(3) and (4) shall apply.]

NOTES

Substituted as noted to Art 496.

[CHAPTER 5
TEMPORARY IMPORTATION

SECTION 1
GENERAL PROVISIONS

Article 553

1. Animals, unless of negligible commercial value, born of animals placed under the arrangements are considered to be non-Community goods and placed themselves under those arrangements.

2. The customs authorities shall ensure that the total period for which the goods remain under the arrangements for the same purpose and under the responsibility of the same holder does not exceed 24 months, even where the arrangements were discharged by entry for another suspensive arrangement and subsequently entered again for temporary importation.

However, at the holder's request, they may extend this period for the time during which the goods are not used, in accordance with the conditions laid down by them.

3. For the purposes of Article 140(3) of the Code, exceptional circumstances means any event as a result of which the goods must be used for a further period in order to fulfil the purpose of the temporary importation operation.

4. Goods placed under the arrangements must remain in the same state.

Repairs and maintenance, including overhaul and adjustments or measures to preserve the goods or to ensure their compliance with the technical requirements for their use under the arrangements are admissible.]

NOTES

Substituted as noted to Art 496.

[Article 554

Temporary importation with total relief from import duties (hereinafter: 'total relief from import duties') shall only be granted in accordance with Articles 555 to 578.

Temporary importation with partial relief from import duties shall not be granted for consumable goods.]

NOTES

Substituted as noted to Art 496.

[SECTION 2
CONDITIONS FOR TOTAL RELIEF FROM IMPORT DUTIES

SUBSECTION 1
MEANS OF TRANSPORT

Article 555

1. For the purposes of this subsection:

   [(a) 'commercial use' means the use of means of transport for the transport of persons for remuneration or the industrial or commercial transport of goods, whether or not for remuneration;]

   (b) 'private use' means the use other than commercial of a means of transport;

(c)   'internal traffic' means the carriage of persons or goods picked up or loaded in the customs territory of the Community for setting down or unloading at a place within that territory.

2. Means of transport include normal spare parts, accessories and equipment accompanying them.]

NOTES

Substituted as noted to Art 496.

Para 1: sub-para (a) substituted by Commission Regulation (EC) 2286/2003, Art 1, para 14.

[Article 556

Total relief from import duties shall be granted for pallets.

The arrangements shall also be discharged when pallets of the same type and substantially the same value are exported or re-exported.]

NOTES

Substituted as noted to Art 496.

[Article 557

1. Total relief from import duties shall be granted for containers where they have been durably marked in an appropriate and clearly visible place with the following information:

(a)   the identity of the owner or operator shown by either his full name or an established identification, symbols such as emblems or flags being excluded;

(b)   with the exception of swap bodies used for combined rail-road transport, the identification marks and numbers of the container, given by the owner or operator; its tare weight, including all its permanently fixed equipment;

(c)   with the exception of containers used for transport by air, the country to which the container belongs, shown either in full or by means of the ISO alpha-2 country code provided for in International Standards ISO 3166 or 6346 or by the distinguishing initials used to indicate the country of registration of motor vehicles in international road traffic, or in numbers, in the case of swap bodies used for combined rail-road transport.

Where the application for authorisation is made in accordance with the first subparagraph of Article 497(3)(c), the containers shall be monitored by a person represented in the customs territory of the Community being able to communicate at all times their location and particulars of entry and discharge.

2. Containers may be used in internal traffic before being re-exported. However, they may be used only once during each stay in a Member State, for transporting goods loaded and intended to be unloaded within the territory of the same Member State, where the containers would otherwise have to make a journey unloaded within that territory.

3. Under the conditions of the Convention of Geneva of 21 January 1994 on Customs Treatment of Pool Containers used in International Transport, as approved by Council Decision 95/137/EC([1]), the customs authorities shall permit the arrangements to be discharged where containers of the same type or the same value are exported or re-exported.]

[1] OJ L 91, 22.4.95, p 45.

NOTES

Substituted as noted to Art 496.

[**Article 558**

1.   Total relief from import duties shall be granted for means of road, rail, air, sea and inland waterway transport where they:

(a)   are registered outside the customs territory of the Community in the name of a person established outside that territory; however, if the means of transport are not registered, the above condition may be deemed to be met where they are owned by a person established outside the customs territory of the Community;

(b)   are used by a person established outside that territory, without prejudice to Articles 559, 560 and 561; and

(c)   in the case of commercial use and with the exception of means of rail transport, are used exclusively for transport which begins or ends outside the customs territory of the Community; however, they may be used in internal traffic where the provisions in force in the field of transport, in particular those concerning admission and operations, so provide.

2.   Where the means of transport referred to in paragraph 1 are rehired by a professional hire service established in the customs territory of the Community to a person established outside that territory, they must be re-exported within eight days of entry into force of the contract.]

NOTES

Substituted as noted to Art 496.

[**Article 559**

Persons established in the customs territory of the Community shall benefit from total relief from import duties where:

(a)   means of rail transport are put at the disposal of such persons under an agreement whereby each network may use the rolling stock of the other networks as its own;

(b)   a trailer is coupled to a means of road transport registered in the customs territory of the Community;

(c)   means of transport are used in connection with an emergency situation and their use does not exceed five days; or

(d)   means of transport are used by a professional hire firm for the purpose of re-exportation within a period not exceeding five days.]

NOTES

Substituted as noted to Art 496.

[**Article 560**

1.   Natural persons established in the customs territory of the Community shall benefit from total relief from import duties where they privately use means of transport occasionally, on the instructions of the registration holder, this holder being in the customs territory at the time of use.

Such persons shall also benefit from total relief, for the private use of means of transport hired under a written contract, occasionally:

(a)   to return to their place of residence in the Community;

(b)   to leave the Community; or

(c)   where this is permitted on a general level by the customs administrations concerned.

2.   The means of transport shall be re-exported or returned to the hire service established in the customs territory of the Community within:

(a)   five days of the entry into force of the contract in the case mentioned in paragraph 1(a);

(b)   eight days of the entry into force of the contract in the case mentioned in paragraph 1(c).

The means of transport shall be re-exported within two days of the entry into force of the contract in the case mentioned under paragraph 1(b).]

NOTES

Substituted as noted to Art 496.

[**Article 561**

1.   Total relief from import duties shall be granted where means of transport are to be registered under a temporary series in the customs territory of the Community, with a view to re-exportation in the name of one of the following persons:

(a)   in the name of a person established outside that territory;

(b)   in the name of a natural person established inside that territory where the person concerned is preparing to transfer normal residence to a place outside that territory.

In the case referred to in point (b), the means of transport must be exported within three months of the date of registration.

2.   Total relief from import duties shall be granted where means of transport are used commercially or privately by a natural person established in the customs territory of the Community and employed by the owner of the means of transport established outside that territory or otherwise authorised by the owner.

Private use must have been provided for in the contract of employment.

Customs authorities may restrict the temporary importation of means of transport under this provision in the case of systematic use.

3.   Total relief from import duties may in exceptional cases be granted where means of transport are commercially used for a limited period by persons established in the customs territory of the Community.]

NOTES

Substituted as noted to Art 496.

[**Article 562**

Without prejudice to other special provisions, the periods for discharge are the following:

(a)   for means of rail transport: 12 months;

(b)   for commercially used means of transport other than rail transport: the time required for carrying out the transport operations;

(c)   for means of road transport privately used:

—   by students: the period the student stays in the customs territory of the Community for the sole purpose of pursuing their studies;

— by persons fulfilling assignments of a specified duration: the period this person stays in the customs territory of the Community for the sole purpose of fulfilling their assignment;

— in other cases, including saddle or draught animals and the vehicles drawn by them: six months;

(d)   for privately used means of air transport: six months;

(e)   for privately used means of sea and inland waterway transport: 18 months.]

NOTES

Substituted as noted to Art 496.

[SUBSECTION 2
PERSONAL EFFECTS AND GOODS FOR SPORTS PURPOSES IMPORTED BY TRAVELLERS; WELFARE MATERIAL FOR SEAFARERS

Article 563

Total relief from import duties shall be granted where personal effects reasonably required for the journey and goods for sports purposes are imported by a traveller as defined in Article 236(A)(1).]

NOTES

Substituted as noted to Art 496.

[Article 564

Total relief from import duties shall be granted for welfare materials for seafarers in the following cases:

(a)   where they are used on a vessel engaged in international maritime traffic;

(b)   where they are unloaded from such a vessel and temporarily used ashore by the crew;

(c)   where they are used by the crew of such a vessel in cultural or social establishments managed by non-profit-making organisations or in places of worship where services for seafarers are regularly held.]

NOTES

Substituted as noted to Art 496.

[SUBSECTION 3
DISASTER RELIEF MATERIAL; MEDICAL, SURGICAL AND LABORATORY EQUIPMENT; ANIMALS; GOODS FOR USE IN FRONTIER ZONES

Article 565

Total relief from import duties shall be granted for disaster relief material where it is used in connection with measures taken to counter the effects of disasters or similar situations affecting the customs territory of the Community and intended for state bodies or bodies approved by the competent authorities.]

NOTES

Substituted as noted to Art 496.

[Article 566

Total relief from import duties shall be granted where medical, surgical and laboratory equipment is dispatched on loan at the request of a hospital or other medical institution which has urgent need of such equipment to make up for the inadequacy of its own facilities and where it is intended for diagnostic or therapeutic purposes.]

NOTES

Substituted as noted to Art 496.

[Article 567

Total relief from import duties shall be granted for animals owned by a person established outside the customs territory of the Community.

It shall be granted for the following goods intended for activities in keeping with the particularities of the frontier zone as defined by the provisions in force:

(a)   equipment owned by a person established in the frontier zone adjacent to the frontier zone of temporary importation and used by a person established in that adjacent frontier zone;

(b)   goods used for the building, repair or maintenance of infrastructure in such a frontier zone under the responsibility of public authorities.]

NOTES

Substituted as noted to Art 496.

[SUBSECTION 4
SOUND, IMAGE OR DATA CARRYING MEDIA, PUBLICITY MATERIAL;
PROFESSIONAL EQUIPMENT; PEDAGOGIC MATERIAL AND
SCIENTIFIC EQUIPMENT

Article 568

Total relief from import duties shall be granted for goods:

(a)   carrying sound, image or data processing information for the purpose of presentation prior to commercialisation, or free of charge, or for provision with a sound track, dubbing or copying; or

(b)   exclusively used for publicity purposes.]

NOTES

Substituted as noted to Art 496.

[Article 569

1.   Total relief from import duties shall be granted where professional equipment is:

(a)   owned by a person established outside the customs territory of the Community;

(b)   imported either by a person established outside the customs territory of the Community or by an employee of the owner, the employee may be established in the customs territory of the Community; and

(c)   used by the importer or under their supervision, except in cases of audiovisual co-productions.

2.   Total relief shall not be granted where equipment is to be used for the industrial manufacture or packaging of goods or, except in the case of hand tools, for the

exploitation of natural resources, for the construction, repair or maintenance of buildings or for earth moving and like projects.]

NOTES
Substituted as noted to Art 496.

[Article 570
Total relief from import duties shall be granted where pedagogic material and scientific equipment are:
   (a)   owned by a person established outside the customs territory of the Community;
   (b)   imported by public or private scientific, teaching or vocational training establishments which are essentially non-profit making and exclusively used in teaching, vocational training or scientific research under their responsibility;
   (c)   imported in reasonable numbers, having regard to the purpose of the importation; and
   (d)   not used for purely commercial purposes.]

NOTES
Substituted as noted to Art 496.

[SUBSECTION 5
PACKINGS; MOULDS, DIES, BLOCKS, DRAWINGS, SKETCHES, MEASURING, CHECKING AND TESTING INSTRUMENTS AND OTHER SIMILAR ARTICLES; SPECIAL TOOLS AND INSTRUMENTS; GOODS TO CARRY OUT TESTS OR SUBJECT TO TESTS; SAMPLES; REPLACEMENT MEANS OF PRODUCTION

[Article 571
Total relief from import duties shall be granted where packings:
   (a)   if imported filled, are intended for re-exportation whether empty or filled;
   (b)   if imported empty, are intended for re-exportation filled.
  Packings are not to be used in internal traffic, except with a view to the export of goods. In the case of packings imported filled, this shall apply only from the time that they are emptied of their contents.]

NOTES
Substituted as noted to Art 496.

[Article 572
  1. Total relief from import duties shall be granted where moulds, dies, blocks, drawings, sketches, measuring, checking and testing instruments and other similar articles are:
   (a)   owned by a person established outside the customs territory of the Community; and
   (b)   used in manufacturing by a person established in the customs territory of the Community and at least 75% of the production resulting from their use is exported.

2. Total relief from import duties shall be granted for special tools and instruments where the goods are:

    (a)   owned by a person established outside the customs territory of the Community; and

    (b)   made available free of charge to a person established in the customs territory of the Community for the manufacture of goods which are to be exported in their entirety.]

NOTES

Substituted as noted to Art 496.

[**Article 573**

Total relief from import duties shall be granted for the following goods:

    (a)   goods subjected to tests, experiments or demonstrations;

    (b)   goods imported, subject to satisfactory acceptance tests in connection with a sales contract containing the provisions of the satisfactory acceptance tests and subjected to those tests;

    (c)   goods used to carry out tests, experiments or demonstrations without financial gain.

For the goods referred to in point (b), the period for discharge is six months.]

NOTES

Substituted as noted to Art 496.

[**Article 574**

Total relief from import duties shall be granted where samples are imported in reasonable quantities and solely used for being shown or demonstrated in the customs territory of the Community.]

NOTES

Substituted as noted to Art 496.

[**Article 575**

Total relief from import duties shall be granted where replacement means of production are temporarily made available to a customer by a supplier or repairer, pending the delivery or repair of similar goods.

The period for discharge is six months.]

NOTES

Substituted as noted to Art 496.

[SUBSECTION 6
GOODS FOR EVENTS OR FOR SALE

Article 576

1. Total relief from import duties shall be granted for goods to be exhibited or used at a public event not purely organised for the commercial sale of the goods, or obtained at such events from goods placed under the arrangements.

In exceptional cases, the competent customs authorities may authorise the arrangements for other events.

2.   Total relief from import duties shall be granted for goods for approval where they cannot be imported as samples and the consignor for his part wishes to sell the goods and the consignee may decide to purchase them after inspection.

The period for discharge is two months.

3.   Total relief from import duties shall be granted for the following:

(a)   works of art, collectors' items and antiques as defined in 'Annex I' of Directive 77/388/EEC, imported for the purposes of exhibition, with a view to possible sale;

(b)   goods other than newly manufactured ones imported with a view to their sale by auction.]

NOTES

Substituted as noted to Art 496.

[SUBSECTION 7
SPARE PARTS, ACCESSORIES AND EQUIPMENT; OTHER GOODS

Article 577

Total relief from import duties shall be granted where spare parts, accessories and equipment are used for repair and maintenance, including overhaul, adjustments and preservation of goods entered for the arrangements.]

NOTES

Substituted as noted to Art 496.

[Article 578

Total relief from import duties may be granted where goods other than those listed in Articles 556 to 577 or not complying with the conditions of these Articles, are imported:

(a)   occasionally and for a period not exceeding three months; or

(b)   in particular situations having no economic effect.]

NOTES

Substituted as noted to Art 496.

[SECTION 3
PROVISIONS CONCERNING THE OPERATION OF THE ARRANGEMENTS

Article 579

Where personal effects, goods imported for sports purposes or means of transport are declared orally or by any other act for entry of the arrangements, customs authorities may require a written declaration when a high amount of import duties is at stake or a serious risk of non-compliance with obligations of the arrangements exists.]

NOTES

Substituted as noted to Art 496.

[Article 580

1.   Declarations for entry for the arrangements using ATA/CPD carnets shall be accepted if they are issued in a participating country and endorsed and guaranteed by an association forming part of an international guarantee chain.

Unless otherwise provided for by bilateral or multilateral agreements, 'participating country' means a contracting party to the ATA Convention, or to the Istanbul Convention having accepted the Customs Cooperation Council recommendations of 25 June 1992 concerning acceptance of the ATA Carnet and the CPD Carnet for the temporary admission procedure.

2. Paragraph 1 shall apply only if the ATA/CPD carnets:

   (a)   relate to goods and uses covered by those Conventions or agreements;

   (b)   are certified by the customs authorities in the appropriate section of the cover page; and

   (c)   are valid throughout the customs territory of the Community.

The ATA/CPD carnet shall be presented at the office of entry into the customs territory of the Community, except where this office is unable to check the fulfilment of the conditions for the procedure.

3. Articles [Articles 457c, 457d] and 458 to 461 apply *mutatis mutandis* for goods placed under the arrangements and covered by ATA carnets.]

NOTES

Substituted as noted to Art 496.

Para 3: words in square brackets substituted by Commission Regulation (EC) 883/2005 Art 1, OJ L 148, 11.06.05, p 5, with effect from 1 October 2005.

[Article 581

1. Without prejudice to the special guarantee systems for ATA/CPD carnets, entry for the arrangements by written declaration shall be subject to the provision of security, except in the cases referred to in Annex 77.

2. In order to facilitate control of the arrangements, the customs authorities may require records to be kept.]

NOTES

Substituted as noted to Art 496.

[Article 582

1. Where goods placed under the arrangements in accordance with Article 576 are discharged by their entry for free circulation, the amount of the debt shall be determined on the basis of the elements of assessment appropriate to these goods at the moment of acceptance of the declaration for free circulation.

Where goods placed under the arrangements in accordance with Article 576 are put on the market, they shall be considered as presented to customs when they are declared for release for free circulation before the end of the period for discharge.

2. For the purposes of discharging the arrangements in respect of goods referred to in Article 576(1), their consumption, destruction or distribution free of charge to the public at the event shall be considered as re-exportation, provided their quantity corresponds to the nature of the event, the number of visitors and the extent of the holder's participation therein.

The first subparagraph shall not apply to alcoholic beverages, tobacco goods or fuels.]

NOTES

Substituted as noted to Art 496.

[**Article 583**

Where the goods placed under the arrangements are entered for one of the suspensive arrangements or introduced in a free zone of control type I within the meaning of Article 799 or in a free warehouse or placed in a free zone of control type II within the meaning of Article 799, enabling temporary importation to be discharged, the documents other than ATA/CPD carnets or records used for the said customs-approved treatment or use or any document replacing them shall contain one of the following indications:

— Mercancías IT,
— MI – varer,
— VV – Waren,
— Εμπορσματα ПE
— TA goods,
— Marchandises AT,
— Merci AT,
— TI – goederen,
— Mercadorias IT,
— VM – tavaroita,
— TI – varor,
[— Zboží DP,
— AI kaup,
— PI preces,
— LI preks,
— IB áruk,
— oetti TA,
— towary OCz,
— ZU blago,
— DP tovar.]
[— С ВВ,
— Mrfuri AT]]

NOTES

Substituted as noted to Art 496.

Words inserted by the 2003 Act of Accession Annex II(19)(A)(II), para 28. Final two entries inserted by Commission Regulation (EC) 1792/2006, Art 1, Annex, Part 11(A)(27).

[**Article 584**

For means of rail transport used jointly under an agreement, the arrangements shall also be discharged when means of rail transport of the same type or the same value as those which were put at the disposal of a person established in the customs territory of the Community are exported or re-exported.]

NOTES

Substituted as noted to Art 496.

[CHAPTER 6
OUTWARD PROCESSING

SECTION 1
ADDITIONAL CONDITIONS CONCERNING THE GRANTING OF
THE AUTHORISATION

Article 585

1. Except where indications to the contrary exist, the essential interests of Community processors shall be deemed not to be seriously harmed.

2. Where an application for authorisation is made by a person who exports the temporary export goods without arranging for the processing operations, the customs authorities shall conduct a prior examination of the conditions set out in Article 147(2) of the Code on the basis of supporting documents. Articles 503 and 504 shall apply mutatis mutandis.]

NOTES
Substituted as noted to Art 496.

[Article 586

1. The authorisation shall specify the means and methods to establish that the compensating products have resulted from processing of the temporary export goods or to verify that the conditions for using the standard exchange system are met.

Such means and methods may include the use of the information document set out in Annex 104 and the examination of the records.

2. Where the nature of the processing operations does not allow it to be established that the compensating products have resulted from the temporary export goods, the authorisation may nevertheless be granted in duly justified cases, provided the applicant can offer sufficient guarantees that the goods used in the processing operations share the same eight-digit CN code, the same commercial quality and the same technical characteristics as the temporary export goods. The authorisation shall lay down the conditions for using the arrangements.]

NOTES
Substituted as noted to Art 496.

[Article 587

Where the arrangements are requested for repair, the temporary export goods must be capable of being repaired and the arrangements shall not be used to improve the technical performance of the goods.]

NOTES
Substituted as noted to Art 496.

[SECTION 2
PROVISIONS CONCERNING THE OPERATION OF THE ARRANGEMENTS

Article 588

1. The authorisation shall specify the period for discharge. Where the circumstances so warrant, this period may be extended even when that originally set has expired.

2. Article 157(2) of the Code applies, even after the original period has expired.]

NOTES

Substituted as noted to Art 496.

[**Article 589**

1. The declaration entering the temporary export goods for the arrangements shall be made in accordance with the provisions laid down for exportation.

2. In the case of prior importation, the documents accompanying the declaration for free circulation shall include a copy of the authorisation unless such authorisation is applied for in accordance with Article 497(3)(d). Article 220(3) applies mutatis mutandis.]

NOTES

Substituted as noted to Art 496.

[SECTION 3
PROVISIONS CONCERNING THE CALCULATION OF THE DUTY RELIEF

Article 590

1. For the calculation of the amount to be deducted, no account shall be taken of anti-dumping duties and countervailing duties.

Secondary compensating products that constitute waste scrap, residues, offcuts and remainders shall be deemed to be included.

2. In determining the value of the temporary export goods in accordance with one of the methods referred to in the second subparagraph of Article 151(2) of the Code, the loading, transport, and insurance costs for the temporary export goods to the place where the processing operation or the last such operation took place shall not be included in:

(a) the value of the temporary export goods which is taken into account when determining the customs value of the compensating products in accordance with Article 32(1)(b)(i) of the Code; or

(b) the processing costs, where the value of the temporary export goods cannot be determined in accordance with Article 32(1)(b)(i) of the Code.

The loading, transport and insurance costs for the compensating products from the place where the processing operation or the last processing operation took place to the place of their entry into the customs territory of the Community shall be included in the processing costs.

Loading, transport and insurance costs shall include:

(a) commissions and brokerage, except buying commissions;

(b) the cost of containers not integral to the temporary export goods;

(c) the cost of packing, including labour and materials;

(d) handling costs incurred in connection with transport of the goods.]

NOTES

Substituted as noted to Art 496.

[**Article 591**

Partial relief from import duties by taking the cost of the processing operation as the basis of the value for duty shall be granted on request.

[Customs authorities shall refuse the calculation of partial relief from import duties under this provision if before the compensating products are released for free circulation it is established that the sole object of the release for free circulation at a zero duty rate of the temporary export goods, which are not of Community origin within the meaning of Title II, Chapter 2, Section 1, of the Code, was to benefit from partial relief under this provision.]]

NOTES

Substituted as noted to Art 496.

Second sub-para substituted by Commission Regulation (EC) 883/2005 Art 1, para 16.

[Article 592

In the case of undertakings frequently carrying out processing operations under an authorisation not covering repair, the customs authorities may, on request of the holder, set an average rate of duty applicable to all those operations (aggregated discharge).

This rate shall be determined for each period not exceeding twelve months and shall apply provisionally for compensating products released for free circulation during that period. At the end of each period, the customs authorities shall make a final calculation and, where appropriate, apply the provisions of Article 220(1) or Article 236 of the Code.

Articles 29 to 35 of the Code shall apply mutatis mutandis to the processing costs, which shall not take into account the temporary export goods.]

NOTES

Title III (Articles 496–592) substituted for Title III (Articles 496–787) by Commission Regulation (EC) 993/2001, Art 1, para 28.

TITLE IV
IMPLEMENTING PROVISIONS RELATING TO EXPORT

NOTES

Heading to Title IV to be substituted by Commission Regulation (EC) No 1875/2006, Art 1(46) with effect from 1 July 2009.

New Chapter 1 (Articles 592a–592g) to be inserted by Commission Regulation (EC) No 1875/2006, Art 1(47) with effect from 1 July 2009.

CHAPTER 1
PERMANENT EXPORTATION

NOTES

Heading to Chapter 1 to be substituted (renumbered as Chapter 2) by Commission Regulation (EC) No 1875/2006, Art 1(48) with effect from 1 July 2009.

New Article 787 to be inserted by Commission Regulation (EC) No 1875/2006, Art 1(49) with effect from 1 July 2009.

Article 788

1. The exporter, within the meaning of Article 161(5) of the Code, shall be considered to be the person on whose behalf the export declaration is made and who is the owner of the goods or has a similar right of disposal over them at the time when the declaration is accepted.

Part III

2. Where ownership or a similar right of disposal over the goods belongs to a person established outside the Community pursuant to the contract on which the export is based, the exporter shall be considered to be the contracting party established in the Community.

Article 789

In cases involving sub-contracting, the export declaration may also be lodged at the customs office responsible for the place where the sub-contractor is established.

Article 790

Where, for administrative reasons, the first sentence of Article 161(5) of the Code cannot be applied, the declaration may be lodged with any customs office, in the Member State concerned, which is competent for the operation in question.

Article 791

1. Where there are duly justified good reasons, an export declaration may be accepted—

— at a customs office other than that referred to in the first sentence of Article 161(5) of the Code, or

— at a customs office other than that referred to in Article 790.

In this case, controls relating to the application of prohibitions and restrictions shall take account of the special nature of the situation.

2. . . . .

_____

NOTES

Para 2 revoked by Commission Regulation (EC) No 1875/2006, Art 1(50) with effect from 26 December 2006.

_____

[Article 792

1. Without prejudice to Article 207, where the export declaration is made on the basis of the single administrative document, Copies 1, 2 and 3 shall be used. The customs office where the export declaration has been lodged shall stamp Box A and, where appropriate, complete Box D. On granting release of the goods, this customs office shall retain Copy 1, send Copy 2 to the statistical office of the Member State of the customs office of export and, where Articles 796a to 796e do not apply, return Copy 3 to the person concerned.

2. Where the export declaration is processed at the customs office of export using a data processing technique, Copy 3 of the single administrative document may be replaced by an accompanying document printed out from the customs authority's computerised system. This document shall contain at least the data required for the export accompanying document referred to in Article 796a. The customs authorities may authorise the declarant to print out the accompanying document from his computerised system.

3. When the entire export operation is carried out on the territory of one Member State, that Member State may waive the use of Copy 3 of the single administrative document or the export accompanying document, provided that the requirements of Article 182b(2) of the Code are met.

4. Without prejudice to Articles 796a to 796e, where the customs rules provide for another document to replace Copy 3 of the single administrative document, the provisions of this Chapter shall apply, mutatis mutandis, to that other document.]

NOTES

Article substituted by Commission Regulation (EC) No 1875/2006, Art 1(51) with effect from 26 December 2006.

[Article 792a

1. Where goods released for export do not leave the customs territory of the Community, the exporter or the declarant shall immediately inform the customs office of export. Where applicable, Copy 3 of the single administrative document shall be returned to that office. The customs office of export shall invalidate the export declaration.

2. Where, in the cases referred to in Article 793a(6) or Article 793b, a change in the transport contract has the effect of terminating inside the customs territory of the Community a transport operation which should have terminated outside it, the companies or authorities in question may only carry out the amended contract with the agreement of the customs office referred to in point (b) of the second subparagraph of Article 793(2) or, in the case of a transit operation, the office of departure. Copy 3 of the export declaration shall be returned to the customs office of export and the declaration shall be invalidated by that office.]

NOTES

Article inserted by Commission Regulation (EC) No 1875/2006, Art 1(52) with effect from 26 December 2006.

[Article 792b

1. The customs office of export may ask the exporter or declarant to provide evidence that the goods have left the customs territory of the Community.

2. Where, after a period of 90 days from the date of release of the goods for export, the goods have not left the customs territory of the Community, or sufficient evidence of such export cannot be provided, the export declaration shall be invalidated. The customs office of export shall inform the exporter or declarant accordingly.]

NOTES

Article inserted by Commission Regulation (EC) No 1875/2006, Art 1(52) with effect from 26 December 2006.

[Article 793

1. Copy 3 of the single administrative document or the accompanying document referred to in Article 792(2) and the goods released for export shall be presented together to customs at the customs office of exit.

2. The customs office of exit shall be the last customs office before the goods leave the customs territory of the Community. By way of derogation from the first subparagraph, the customs office of exit shall be one of the following:

   (a)   in the case of goods leaving by pipeline and of electrical energy, the office designated by the Member State where the exporter is established;

   (b)   the customs office competent for the place where the goods are taken over under a single transport contract for transport of the goods out of the customs territory of the Community by the railway companies, the postal authorities, the airlines or the shipping companies, provided that the following conditions are met:

    (i)   the goods are to leave the customs territory of the Community by rail, post, air or sea;

    (ii)   the declarant or his representative requests that the formalities referred to in Article 793a(2), or in Article 796e(1), be carried out at that office.]

NOTES

Article substituted by Commission Regulation (EC) No 1875/2006, Art 1(53) with effect from 26 December 2006.

[Article 793a

1.   The customs office of exit shall carry out appropriate risk-based controls prior to the exit of the goods from the customs territory of the Community, primarily to ensure that the goods presented correspond to those declared. The customs office of exit shall supervise the physical exit of the goods.

Where the export declaration has been lodged at an office other than the customs office of exit, and the particulars have been transmitted in accordance with Article 182b(2) of the Code, the customs office of exit may take account of the results of any control carried out by that other office.

2.   Where the declarant enters "RET-EXP" in Box 44, or the code 30400, or otherwise indicates his wish to have Copy 3 returned to him, the customs office of exit shall certify the physical exit of the goods by means of an endorsement on the back of that copy.

It shall give that copy to the person who presented it or to an intermediary specified in it and established in the district of the customs office of exit, for the purposes of returning it to the declarant.

The endorsement shall take the form of a stamp showing the name of the customs office of exit and the date of exit of the goods.

3.   In the case of split exportation via the same customs office of exit, the endorsement shall be given only for those goods which are actually exported.

In the case of split exportation via several different customs offices of exit, the customs office of export, or the customs office of exit where the original of Copy 3 is presented shall, upon receiving a duly substantiated request, certify a copy of Copy 3 for each part of the goods, with a view to it being presented to another customs office of exit. In the cases referred to in the first and second subparagraph, the original of Copy 3 shall be annotated accordingly.

4.   When the entire export operation is carried out on the territory of one Member State, that Member State may provide for the non-endorsement of Copy 3. In this case the Copy 3 shall not be returned to the declarant.

5.   Where the customs office of exit establishes that goods are missing, it shall annotate the copy of the export declaration presented and inform the customs office of export.

Where the customs office of exit establishes that there are goods in excess, it shall refuse exit to these goods until the export formalities have been completed.

When the customs office of exit establishes a discrepancy in the nature of the goods, it shall refuse exit to these goods until the export formalities have been completed, and shall also inform the customs office of export.

6.   In the cases referred to in point (b) of the second subparagraph of Article 793(2), the customs office of exit shall endorse Copy 3 of the export declaration in accordance with Article 793a(2) after making the endorsement "Export" on the transport document and affixing its stamp. Reference shall be made to the transport document on Copy 3 of the export declaration and vice versa.

Where, in the case of regular shipping lines or direct transport or flights to destinations outside the customs territory of the Community, the operators are able to guarantee the regularity of the operations, the endorsement "Export" and the affixing of the stamp to the transport document shall not be required.

NOTES
Article inserted by Commission Regulation (EC) No 1875/2006, Art 1(54) with effect from 26 December 2006.

[Article 793b

1.   In the case of goods brought out of the customs territory of the Community or sent to a customs office of exit under a transit procedure, the office of departure shall endorse Copy 3 in accordance with Article 793a(2) and return it to the person referred to in that Article.

Where an accompanying document is required, it shall also be endorsed with the word "Export". Reference shall be made to the accompanying document on Copy 3 of the export declaration and vice versa.

The first and second subparagraphs of this Article shall not apply where presentation of the goods at the office of departure as referred to in Article 419(4) and (7) and Article 434(6) and (9) is dispensed with.

2.   The endorsement and return of the Copy 3 referred to in the first subparagraph of paragraph 1 of this Article shall also apply to goods released for export which are not placed under a transit procedure but are sent to a customs office of exit included in a single manifest transit declaration provided for by Article 445 or Article 448 and identified in accordance with Article 445(3)(e) or Article 448(3)(e).

3.   The customs office of exit shall control the physical exit of the goods.

NOTES
Article inserted by Commission Regulation (EC) No 1875/2006, Art 1(54) with effect from 26 December 2006.

[Article 793c

1.   Where goods under excise duty suspension arrangements are brought out of the customs territory of the Community under cover of the administrative accompanying document provided for by Regulation (EEC) No 2719/92, the customs office of export shall endorse Copy 3 of the export declaration in accordance with Article 793a(2) and return it to the declarant after making the endorsement "Export" and affixing the stamp referred to in that Article on all copies of the administrative accompanying document.

Reference shall be made to the administrative accompanying document on Copy 3 of the export declaration and vice versa.

2.   The customs office of exit shall supervise the physical exit of the goods and send back the copy of the administrative accompanying document in accordance with Article 19(4) of Council Directive 92/12/EEC.

In cases provided for in Article 793a(5), the customs office of exit shall annotate the administrative accompanying document accordingly.]

NOTES
Article inserted by Commission Regulation (EC) No 1875/2006, Art 1(54) with effect from 26 December 2006.

Article 794

1. Goods not subject to prohibition or restriction and not exceeding ECU 3 000 in value per consignment and per declarant may be declared at the customs office of exit.

Member States may provide that this provision shall not apply when the person making the export declaration is acting as a professional customs agent on behalf of others.

2. Oral declarations may be made only at the customs office of exit.

Article 795

Where goods leave the customs territory of the Community without an export declaration, such declaration shall be lodged retrospectively by the exporter at the customs office competent for the place where he is established. The provisions of Article 790 shall apply in these circumstances.

Acceptance of this declaration shall be subject to presentation by the exporter, to the satisfaction of the customs authorities of the customs office concerned, of evidence concerning the nature and quantity of the goods in question and the circumstances under which they left the customs territory of the Community. That office shall also endorse Copy 3 of the Single Administrative Document.

Retrospective acceptance of the declaration shall not preclude application of the penalties in force nor the consequences which may arise as regards the Common Agricultural Policy.

NOTES

Article to be substituted by Commission Regulation (EC) No 1875/2006, Art 1(55) with effect from 1 July 2009.

Article 796

. . .

NOTES

Article revoked by Commission Regulation (EC) No 1875/2006, Art 1(56) with effect from 26 December 2006.

[CHAPTER 3
EXCHANGE OF EXPORT DATA BETWEEN CUSTOMS AUTHORITIES USING INFORMATION TECHNOLOGY AND COMPUTER NETWORKS

Article 796a

1. The customs office of export shall authorise release of the goods by issuing the export accompanying document to the declarant. The export accompanying document shall correspond to the specimen and notes in Annex 45c.

2. Where an export consignment consists of more than one item, the export accompanying document shall be supplemented by a list of items corresponding to the specimen and notes in Annex 45d. It shall form an integral part of the export accompanying document.

3. Where authorised, the export accompanying document may be printed out from the computerised system of the declarant.]

NOTES

Chapter 3 (Articles 796a–796e) inserted by Commission Regulation (EC) No 1875/2006, Art 1(57) with effect from 26 December 2006.

[**Article 796b**

1. On release of the goods, the customs office of export shall transmit particulars of the export movement to the declared customs office of exit using the "Anticipated export record" message. This message shall be based on data derived from the export declaration and supplemented as appropriate by the customs authorities.

2. Where goods are to be moved to more than one office of exit as more than one consignment, each individual consignment shall be covered by an individual "Anticipated export record" message and an individual export accompanying document.]

NOTES

Chapter 3 (Articles 796a–796e) inserted by Commission Regulation (EC) No 1875/2006, Art 1(57) with effect from 26 December 2006.

[**Article 796c**

The customs authorities may require notification of the arrival of the goods at the customs office of exit to be communicated to them electronically. In this case it shall not be necessary for the export accompanying document be physically presented to the customs authorities but shall be retained by the declarant.

Such notification shall contain the movement reference number referred to in Annex 45c.]

NOTES

Chapter 3 (Articles 796a–796e) inserted by Commission Regulation (EC) No 1875/2006, Art 1(57) with effect from 26 December 2006.

[**Article 796d**

1. The customs office of exit shall satisfy itself that the goods presented correspond to those declared.

Any examination of the goods shall be carried out by the customs office of exit using the "Anticipated export record" message received from the customs office of export as a basis for such examination.

The customs office of exit shall supervise the physical exit of the goods from the customs territory of the Community.

2. The customs office of exit shall forward the "Exit results" message to the customs office of export at the latest on the working day following the day the goods leave the customs territory of the Community. In cases justified by special circumstances the customs office of exit may forward that message at a later date.

3. In the case of split exportation, where goods covered by one "Anticipated export record" message are moved to a customs office of exit as one consignment but subsequently exit the customs territory of the Community from that office of exit as more than one consignment, the customs office of exit shall control the physical exit of the goods and send the "Exit results" message only when all of the goods have left the customs territory of the Community.

In exceptional circumstances, where goods covered by one "Anticipated export record" message are moved to a customs office of exit as one consignment but subsequently exit the customs territory of the Community as more than one consignment and through more than one customs office of exit, the customs office of exit where the consignment was first presented shall, upon receiving a duly substantiated request, certify a copy of the export accompanying document for each part of the goods.

This certification shall only be granted by the customs authorities if the data contained in the export accompanying document corresponds to the data in the "Anticipated export record" message.

The relevant copy of the export accompanying document and the goods shall be presented together to the customs office of exit concerned. Each customs office of exit shall endorse the copy of the export accompanying document with the particulars referred to in Article 793a(2) and return it to the customs office of exit where the consignment was first presented. This office shall send the "Exit results" message only when all of the goods have left the customs territory of the Community.

NOTES

Chapter 3 (Articles 796a–796e) inserted by Commission Regulation (EC) No 1875/2006, Art 1(57) with effect from 26 December 2006.

[Article 796e

1. Upon receipt of the "Exit results" message referred to in Article 796d(2), the customs office of export shall certify the physical exit of the goods for the declarant, by use of the "Export notification" message or in the form specified by that office for that purpose.

2. Where the customs office of export is informed by the exporter or the declarant, in accordance with Article 792a, that goods released for export have not left and are not to leave the customs territory of the Community, or the declaration is to be invalidated pursuant to Article 792b(2), the customs office of export shall immediately invalidate the export declaration and inform the declared customs office of exit of the invalidation, by use of the "Export cancellation notification" message.]

NOTES

Chapter 3 (Articles 796a–796e) inserted by Commission Regulation (EC) No 1875/2006, Art 1(57) with effect from 26 December 2006.

[CHAPTER 4
TEMPORARY EXPORTATION USING AN ATA CARNET]

NOTES

Heading substituted (Chapter 4 renumbered as such) by Commission Regulation (EC) No 1875/2006, Art 1(58) with effect from 26 December 2006.

Article 797

1. An ATA carnet may be used for export where the following conditions are fulfilled—

(a)   the ATA carnet shall be issued in a Member State of the Community and endorsed and guaranteed by an association established in the Community forming part of an international guarantee chain.

The Commission shall publish a list of the associations;

(b)   the ATA carnet shall be applicable only to Community goods—

—   which have not been subject on export from the customs territory of the Community to customs export formalities with a view to the payment of refunds or other export amounts under the Common Agricultural Policy,

    — in respect of which no other financial benefit has been granted under the Common Agricultural Policy, coupled with an obligation to export the said goods,

in respect of which no request for repayment has been submitted;

(c) the documents referred to in Article 221 must be presented. The customs authorities may require production of the transport document;

(d) the goods must be intended for re importation.

2. Where goods covered by an ATA carnet are entered for the purposes of temporary exportation, the customs office of export shall carry out the following formalities—

(a) verify the information given in boxes A to G of the exportation voucher against the goods under cover of the carnet;

(b) complete, where appropriate, the box on the cover page of the carnet headed "Certificate by Customs Authorities";

(c) complete the counterfoil and box H of the exportation voucher;

(d) enter its name in box H(b) of the reimportation voucher;

(e) retain the exportation voucher.

3. If the customs office of export is not the office of exit, the customs office of export shall carry out the formalities referred to in paragraph 2, but it shall not complete box 7 of the exportation counterfoil, which must be completed by the customs office of exit.

4. The time limit for reimportation of the goods laid down by the customs authorities in box H(b) of the exportation voucher may not exceed the validity of the carnet.

Article 798

Where goods which left the customs territory of the Community under cover of an ATA carnet are no longer intended to be reimported, an export declaration containing the particulars referred to in Annex 37 shall be presented to the customs office of export.

On presentation of the carnet in question, the latter shall endorse Copy 3 of the export declaration and shall invalidate the reimportation voucher and counterfoil.

TITLE V

OTHER CUSTOMS-APPROVED TREATMENTS OR USES

[CHAPTER I

FREE ZONES AND FREE WAREHOUSES

SECTION 1

PROVISIONS COMMON TO SECTIONS 2 AND 3

SUBSECTION 1

DEFINITIONS AND GENERAL PROVISIONS

Article 799

For the purposes of this Chapter:

(a) 'control type I' means controls principally based on the existence of a fence;

(b) 'control type II' means controls principally based on the formalities carried out in accordance with the requirements of the customs warehousing procedure;

(c) 'operator' means any person carrying on an activity involving the storage, working, processing, sale or purchase of goods in a free zone or a free warehouse.]

NOTES

This Chapter 1 (Articles 799–814) substituted for Arts 799–840) by Commission Regulation (EC) 993/2001, Art 1, para 29.

[Article 800

Any person may apply to the customs authorities designated by the Member States for a part of the customs territory of the Community to be designated a free zone or for a free warehouse to be set up.]

NOTES

Substituted as noted to Art 799.

[Article 801

1. The application for an authorisation to build in a free zone shall be made in writing.

2. The application referred to in paragraph 1 shall specify the activity for which the building will be used and give any other information that will enable the customs authorities designated by the Member States to evaluate the grounds for granting the authorisation.

3. The competent customs authorities shall grant authorisation in cases where the application of customs rules would not be impeded.

4. Paragraphs 1, 2 and 3 shall also apply where a building in a free zone or a building constituting a free warehouse is converted.]

NOTES

Substituted as noted to Art 799.

[Article 802

The customs authorities of the Member States shall communicate the following information to the Commission:

(a) the free zones in existence and in operation in the Community according to the classification under Article 799;

(b) the designated customs authorities to which the application referred to in Article 804 must be presented.

The Commission shall publish the information referred to in (a) and (b) in the Official Journal of the European Communities, C series.]

NOTES

Substituted as noted to Art 799.

[SUBSECTION 2
APPROVAL OF THE STOCK RECORDS

Article 803

1. The carrying on of activities by an operator shall be subject to the approval by the customs authorities of the stock records referred to:

— in Article 176 of the Code in the case of a free zone of control type I or a free warehouse;

— in Article 105 of the Code in the case of a free zone of control type II.

2. The approval shall be issued in writing. It shall be accorded only to persons offering all the necessary guarantees concerning the application of the provisions on free zones or free warehouses.]

NOTES

Substituted as noted to Art 799.

[Article 804

1. The application for approval of the stock records shall be submitted in writing to the customs authorities designated by the Member State where the free zone or free warehouse is located.

2. The application referred to in paragraph 1 shall specify which activities are envisaged, this information being considered as the notification referred to in Article 172(1) of the Code. It shall include the following:

(a)   a detailed description of the stock records kept or to be kept;

(b)   the nature and customs status of the goods to which these activities relate;

(c)   where applicable, the customs procedure under which the activities are to be carried out;

(d)   any other information needed by the customs authorities in order to ensure the proper application of the provisions.]

NOTES

Substituted as noted to Art 799.

[SECTION 2
PROVISIONS APPLICABLE TO FREE ZONES OF CONTROL TYPE I AND TO FREE WAREHOUSES

SUBSECTION 1
CONTROLS

Article 805

The fence enclosing free zones shall be such as to facilitate supervision by the customs authorities outside the free zone and prevent any goods being removed irregularly from the free zone.

The first paragraph shall also apply mutatis mutandis to free warehouses.

The area immediately outside the fence shall be such as to permit adequate supervision by the customs authorities. Access to the said area shall require the consent of the said authorities.]

NOTES

Substituted as noted to Art 799.

[Article 806

The stock records to be kept for the free zone or free warehouse shall include in particular:

(a)   particulars of marks, identifying numbers, number and kind of packages, the quantity and usual commercial description of the goods and, where relevant, the identification marks of the container;

(b)   information enabling the goods to be monitored at any time, in particular their location, the customs-approved treatment or use assigned to them after storage in the free zone or free warehouse or their re-entry into another part of the customs territory of the Community;

(c)   reference particulars of the transport document used on entry and removal of the goods;

(d)   indication of customs status and, where relevant, reference particulars of the certificate certifying this status referred to in Article 812;

(e)   particulars of usual forms of handling;

(f)   as the case may be, one of the indications referred to in Articles 549, 550 or 583;

(g)   particulars concerning goods which would not be subject upon release for free circulation or temporary importation to import duties or commercial policy measures, the use or destination of which must be checked.

The customs authorities may waive the requirement for some of this information where supervision or control of the free zone or the free warehouse is not affected.

Where records have to be kept for the purposes of a customs procedure, the information contained in those records need not appear in the stock records.]

NOTES

Substituted as noted to Art 799.

Para (h) to be inserted by Commission Regulation (EC) No 1875/2006, Art 1(59) with effect from 1 July 2009.

[Article 807

The inward processing or processing under customs control procedures shall be discharged in respect of the compensating products, processed products or goods in the unaltered state situated in a free zone or free warehouse by entry in the stock records of the free zone or free warehouse. Reference particulars of such entry shall be recorded in the records for inward processing or processing under customs control, as the case may be.]

NOTES

Substituted as noted to Art 799.

[SUBSECTION 2
OTHER PROVISIONS CONCERNING THE OPERATION OF FREE ZONE OF CONTROL TYPE I AND FREE WAREHOUSES

Article 808

Commercial policy measures provided for in Community acts shall be applicable to non-Community goods placed in a free zone or free warehouse only to the extent that they refer to the entry of goods into the customs territory of the Community.]

NOTES

Substituted as noted to Art 799.

[Article 809

Where the elements for assessment of the customs debt to be taken into consideration are those applicable before the goods have undergone usual forms of handling referred to in Annex 72, an Information Sheet INF8 may be issued in accordance with Article 523.]

NOTES

Substituted as noted to Art 799.

[Article 810

A victualling warehouse may be set up in a free zone or a free warehouse in accordance with Article 40 of Regulation (EC) No 800/1999.]

NOTES

Substituted as noted to Art 799.

[Article 811

In the case of the re-exportation of non-Community goods which are not unloaded or which are transhipped, the notification referred to in Article 182(3) of the Code shall not be required.]

NOTES

Substituted as noted to Art 799.
Article to be revoked by Commission Regulation (EC) No 1875/2006, Art 1(60) with effect from 1 July 2009.

[Article 812

Where the customs authorities certify the Community or non-Community status of the goods, in accordance with Article 170(4) of the Code, they shall use a form conforming to the model and provisions in Annex 109.

The operator shall certify the Community status of the goods by means of that form where non-Community goods are declared for release for free circulation in accordance with Article 173(a) of the Code, including where discharging the inward processing or processing under customs control procedures.]

NOTES

Substituted as noted to Art 799.

[SECTION 3
PROVISIONS APPLICABLE TO FREE ZONES OF CONTROL TYPE II

Article 813

Without prejudice to the provisions in section 1 and in Article 814, the provisions laid down for the customs warehouse arrangements shall be applicable to the free zone of control type II.]

NOTES

Substituted as noted to Art 799.

Part III

[**Article 814**]
Where non-Community goods which are not unloaded or which are only transhipped are placed under the free zone using the local clearance procedure and re-exported later using the same procedure, the customs authorities may relieve the operator from the obligation to inform the competent customs office of each arrival or departure of such goods. In this case, the control measures shall take account of the special nature of the situation.
The short-term storage of goods in connection with such transhipment shall be considered to be an integral part of the transhipment.]

NOTES
Substituted as noted to Art 799.
Article to be revoked by Commission Regulation (EC) No 1875/2006, Art 1(60) with effect from 1 July 2009.

CHAPTER 2
RE-EXPORTATION, DESTRUCTION AND ABANDONMENT

[SECTION 1]
RE-EXPORTATION

[**Article 841**]
1. Where re-exportation is subject to a customs declaration Articles 787 to 796e shall apply mutatis mutandis, without prejudice to particular provisions which may apply when the customs procedure with economic impact preceding re-exportation of the goods is discharged.'
2. Where an ATA carnet is issued for re-exportation of goods under temporary importation, the customs declaration may be lodged at a customs office other than that referred to in Article 161(5) of the Code.]

NOTES
Heading "Section 1 Re-exportation" inserted, and Article 841 substituted, by Commission Regulation (EC) No 1875/2006, Art 1(61), (62) with effect from 26 December 2006.
New Article 841a to be inserted by Commission Regulation (EC) No 1875/2006, Art 1(63) with effect from 1 July 2009.

[SECTION 2]
DESTRUCTION AND ABANDONMENT]

Article 842
1. For the purposes of Article 182(3) of the Code, notification of destruction of goods shall be made in writing and signed by the person concerned. The notification must be made in sufficient time to allow the customs authorities to supervise the destruction.
2. Where the goods in question are already the subject of a declaration accepted by the customs authorities, they shall make a reference to the destruction on the declaration and invalidate the declaration in accordance with Article 66 of the Code.
The customs authorities present when the goods are destroyed shall specify on the form or declaration the type and quantity of any waste or scrap resulting from the destruction in order to determine the items of charge applicable to them and to be used when they are assigned another customs-approved treatment or use.
3. The provisions of the first subparagraph of paragraph 2 shall apply mutatis mutandis to goods abandoned to the Exchequer.

NOTES

Heading "Section 2 Destruction and abandonment" inserted by Commission Regulation (EC) No 1875/2006, Art 1(64) with effect from 26 December 2006.

TITLE VI
GOODS LEAVING THE CUSTOMS TERRITORY OF THE COMMUNITY

NOTES

New Chapter I (Articles 842a–842e) to be inserted by Commission Regulation (EC) No 1875/2006, Art 1(65) with effect from 1 July 2009.

New heading "CHAPTER 2 Temporary export" to be inserted before Article 843, by Commission Regulation (EC) No 1875/2006, Art 1(66) with effect from 1 July 2009.

[Article 843

1. This Title lays down the conditions applicable to goods moving from one point in the customs territory of the Community to another which temporarily leave that territory, whether or not crossing the territory of a third country, whose removal or export from the customs territory of the Community is prohibited or is subject to restrictions, duties or other charges on export by a Community measure in so far as that measure so provides and without prejudice to any special provisions which it may comprise.

These conditions shall not, however, apply—

— where, on declaration of the goods for export from the customs territory of the Community, proof is furnished to the customs office at which export formalities are carried out that an administrative measure freeing the goods from restriction has been taken, that any duties, taxes or other charges due have been paid or that, in the circumstances obtaining, the goods may leave the customs territory of the Community without further formalities, or

— where the goods are transported by direct flight without stopping outside the customs territory of the Community, or by a regular shipping service within the meaning of Article 313a.

2. Where the goods are placed under a Community transit procedure, the principal shall enter on the document used for the Community transit declaration, specifically in box 44 ("Additional information") of the Single Administrative Document where that is used, one of the following phrases—

— Salida de la Comunidad sometida a restricciones o imposiciones en virtud del (de la) Reglamento/Directiva/Decisión no . . .

— Udpassage fra Fællesskabet undergivet restriktioner eller afgifter i henhold til forordning/direktiv/afgørelse nr. . . .

— Ausgang aus der Gemeinschaft — gemäß Verordnung/Richtlinie/Beschluß Nr. . . . Beschränkungen oder Abgaben unterworfen.

— Ηεξοδοζ απο την Κοινοτηα υποβαλλεται σε περιοριομουζ η σε επιβαρυνσεισ απο τον κανονισμο/την οδηγια/την αποψαση αριθ

— Exit from the Community subject to restrictions or charges under Regulation/Directive/Decision No . . .

— Sortie de la Communauté soumise à des restrictions ou à des impositions par le règlement ou la directive/décision n° . . .

— Uscita dalla Comunità soggetta a restrizioni o ad imposizioni a norma del(la) regolamento/direttiva/decisione n. . . .

—   Bij uitgang uit de Gemeenschap zijn de beperkingen of heffingen van
    Verordening/Richtlijn/Besluit nr. . . . van toepassing.

—   Saída da Comunidade sujeita a restrições ou a imposições pelo(a)
    Regulamento/Directiva/Decisão n.° . . .

—   Yhteisöstä vientiin sovelletaan asetuksen/direktiinvinl./ päätöksen N:o
    . . . mukaisia rajoituksia tai maksuja

—   Utförsel   från   gemenskapen   omfattas   i   enlighet   med
    förordning/direktiv/beslut . . . av restriktioner eller pålagor

[—   Výstup ze Společenství podléhá omezením nebo dávkám podle nařízení/
    směrnice/rozhodnutí č . . .,

—   Ühenduse territooriumilt väljumine on aluseks piirangutele ja
    maksudele vastavalt määrusele/direktiivile/otsusele nr. . .,

—   Izvešana no Kopienas, piemrojot ierobežojumus vai maksjumus
    saska ar Regulu/ Direktvu/ Lmumu Nr. . . .,

—   Išvežimui iš Bendrijos taikomi apribojimai arba mokesčiai, nustatyti
    Reglamentu/ Direktyva/ Sprendimu Nr. . .

[—   A kilépés a Közösség területéről a . . . rendelet/irányelv/határozat
    szerinti korlátozás vagy teher megfizetésének kötelezettsége alá esik

—   ru mill-Komunita' suett gall-restrizzjonijiet jew lasijiet tat
    Regola/Direttiva/Deijoni Nru . . .]

—   Wyprowadzenie ze Wspólnoty podlega ograniczeniom lub opłatom
    zgodnie z rozporzdzeniem / dyrektyw / decyzj nr . . .,

—   Iznos iz Skupnosti zavezan omejitvam ali obveznim plačilom na podlagi
    uredbe/direktive/odločbe št. . .,

—   Výstup zo spoločenstva podlieha obmedzeniam alebo platbám podľa
    nariadenia/smernice/rozhodnutia č . . .]

[—   И Ощ
    чя   ъ
    Р;/Д;/Р;ш
    № . . .,

—   Iesire din . . . Comunitate supus restrictiilor sau impozitelor prin
    Regulamentul/Directiva/Decizia Nr . . .]

3.   Where the goods are—

(a)   placed under a customs procedure other than the Community transit
      procedure, or

(b)   moved without being under a customs procedure.

The T5 control copy shall be made out in accordance with Articles 912a to 912g. In
box 104 of the T5 form a cross shall be entered in the square "Other (specify)" and
the phrase stipulated in paragraph 2 added.

In the case of goods falling within point (a) of the first subparagraph, the T5 control
copy shall be made out at the customs office at which the formalities required for
consignment of the goods are completed. In the case of goods falling within point (b)
of the first subparagraph, the T5 control copy shall be presented with the goods at the
competent customs office for the place where the goods leave the customs territory of
the Community.

Those offices shall specify the latest date by which the goods, must be presented at
the customs office of destination and, where appropriate, shall enter in the customs
document under cover of which the goods are to be transported the phrase specified in
paragraph 2.

For the purposes of the T5 control copy, the office of destination shall be either the
office of destination for the customs procedure under point (a) of the first

subparagraph or, where point (b) of the first subparagraph applies, the competent customs office for the place where the goods are brought back into the customs territory of the Community.

4. Paragraph 3 shall also apply to goods moving from one point in the customs territory of the Community to another through the territory of one or more of the EFTA countries referred to in Article 309(f) which are reconsigned from one of those countries.

5. If the Community measure referred to in paragraph 1 provides for the lodging of a guarantee, that guarantee shall be lodged in accordance with Article 912b(2).

6. Where the goods, on arrival at the office of destination, either are not immediately recognised as having Community status or do not immediately undergo the customs formalities required for goods brought into the customs territory of the Community, the office of destination shall take all the measures prescribed for them.

7. In the circumstances described in paragraph 3, the office of destination shall return the original of the T5 control copy without delay to the address shown in box B "Return to . . ." of the T5 form once all the required formalities have been completed and annotations made.

8. Where the goods are not brought back into the customs territory of the Community, they shall be deemed to have left the customs territory of the Community irregularly from the Member State where either they were placed under the procedure referred to in paragraph 2 or the T5 control copy was made out.]

NOTES

Substituted by Commission Regulation (EC) 1602/2000, Art 1, para 10.

Para 2: words in outer square brackets inserted by the 2003 Act of Accession Annex II(19)(A)(II), para 29; words in inner square brackets substituted by Commission Regulation (EC) 883/2005, Art 1, para 17, with effect from 1 May 2004. Final two entries inserted by Commission Regulation (EC) 1792/2006, Art 1, Annex, Part 11(A)(28).

Para 1: word "Chapter" to be substituted for word "Title" by Commission Regulation (EC) No 1875/2006, Art 1(67) with effect from 1 July 2009.

PART III
[PRIVILEGED OPERATIONS

TITLE I
RETURNED GOODS]

NOTES

Part and title headings substituted by Commission Regulation (EC) 75/98, Art 1, para 21.

Article 844

1. In accordance with Article 185(2)(b) of the Code, the following shall be exempt from import duties—

— goods previously exported from the customs territory of the Community, in respect of which the customs export formalities have been completed with a view to obtaining refunds or other amounts provided for on exportation under the Common Agricultural Policy, or

— goods in respect of which a financial advantage other than the said refunds or other amounts has been granted under the Common Agricultural Policy, entailing an obligation to export the said goods,

provided it is established, as appropriate, that the refunds or other amounts paid have been repaid, or that the necessary steps have been taken by the competent authorities for such sums to be withheld, or that the other financial advantages granted have been cancelled, and that the goods—

(i)   could not be entered for home use in the country to which they were sent on account of laws in force in that country;

(ii)   were returned by the consignee as being defective or not in accordance with the provisions of the contract relating to them;

(iii)   were reimported into the customs territory of the Community because they could not be used for the purposes intended owing to other circumstances outside the exporter's control.

2.   The circumstances referred to in paragraph 1(iii) shall include the following—

(a)   goods returned to the customs territory of the Community following damage occurring before delivery to the consignee, either to the goods themselves or to the means of transport on which they were carried;

(b)   goods originally exported for the purposes of consumption or sale in the course of a trade fair or similar occasion which have not been so consumed or sold;

(c)   goods which could not be delivered to the consignee on account of his physical or legal incapacity to honour the contract under which the goods were exported;

(d)   goods which, because of natural, political or social disturbances, could not be delivered to their consignee or which reached him after the mandatory delivery date stipulated in the contract under which the goods were exported;

(e)   products covered by the common organisation of the market in fruit and vegetables, exported and sent for sale on consignment, but which were not sold in the market of the third country of destination.

3.   Goods exported under the Common Agricultural Policy with an export licence or an advance fixing certificate shall not be exempt from import duties unless it is established that the relevant Community provisions have been complied with.

4.   The goods referred to in paragraph 1 shall not be exempt from import duties unless they are entered for free circulation in the customs territory of the Community within twelve months of the date of completion of the customs formalities relating to their exportation.

[However, where the goods are declared for free circulation after expiry of the period referred to in the first subparagraph, the customs authorities of the Member State of reimportation may allow the period to be exceeded where exceptional circumstances justify this. Where the customs authorities do allow the period to be exceeded, they shall send details of the case to the Commission.]

NOTES

Para 4: words in square brackets added by Commission Regulation (EC) 1677/98, Art 1, para 3.

Article 845

Returned goods shall be exempt from import duties even where they represent only a proportion of the goods previously exported from the customs territory of the Community.

The same applies where the goods consist of parts or accessories belonging to machines, instruments, apparatus or other products previously exported from the customs territory of the Community.

Article 846

1. By way of derogation from Article 186 of the Code, returned goods in one of the following situations shall be exempt from import duties—

(a) goods which, after having been exported from the customs territory of the Community, have received no treatment other than that necessary to maintain them in good condition or handling which alters their appearance only;

(b) goods which, after having been exported from the customs territory of the Community, received treatment other than that necessary to maintain them in good condition or handling other than that altering their appearance, but which proved to be defective or unsuitable for their intended use, provided that one of the following conditions is fulfilled—

— such treatment or handling was applied to the goods solely with a view to repairing them or restoring them to good condition,

— their unsuitability for their intended use became apparent only after such treatment or handling had commenced.

2. Where returned goods have undergone treatment or handling permitted under paragraph 1(b) and such treatment would have rendered them liable to import duties if they had come under outward processing arrangements, the rules in force for charging duty under the said arrangements shall apply.

However, if goods have undergone an operation consisting of repair or restoration to good condition which became necessary as a result of unforeseen circumstances which arose outside the customs territory of the Community, this being established to the satisfaction of the customs authorities, relief from import duties shall be granted provided that the value of the returned goods is not higher, as a result of such operation, than their value at the time of export from the customs territory of the Community.

3. For the purposes of the second subparagraph of paragraph 2—

(a) *repair or restoration to good condition which became necessary* means: any operation to remedy operating defects or material damage suffered by goods while they were outside the customs territory of the Community, without which the goods could no longer be used in the normal way for the purposes for which they were intended;

(b) the value of returned goods shall be considered not to be higher, as a result of the operation which they have undergone, than their value at the time of export from the customs territory of the Community, when the operation does not exceed that which is strictly necessary to enable them to continue to be used in the same way as at that time.

When the repair or restoration to good condition of goods necessitates the incorporation of spare parts, such incorporation shall be limited to those parts strictly necessary to enable the goods to be used in the same way as at the time of export.

Article 847

When completing the customs export formalities, the customs authorities shall, at the request of the person concerned, issue a document containing the information necessary for identification of the goods in the event of their being returned to the customs territory of the Community.

Article 848

1. The following shall be accepted as returned goods—

— goods for which the following documents are produced in support of the declaration for release for free circulation—

Part III

(a) the copy of the export declaration returned to the exporter by the customs authorities, or a copy of such document certified true by the said authorities; or

(b) the Information Sheet provided for in Article 850.

Where evidence available to the customs authorities at the customs office of reimportation or ascertainable by them from the person concerned indicates that the goods declared for free circulation were originally exported from the customs territory of the Community, and at that time satisfied the conditions for acceptance as returned goods, the documents referred to at (a) and (b) shall not be required.

— goods covered by an ATA carnet issued in the Community.

These goods may be accepted as returned goods, within the limits laid down by Article 185 of the Code, even when the validity of the ATA carnet has expired.

In all cases, the formalities laid down in Article 290(2) shall be carried out.

2. The first indent of paragraph 1 shall not apply to the international movement of packing materials, means of transport or certain goods admitted under specific customs arrangements where autonomous or conventional provisions lay down that customs documents are not required in these circumstances.

Nor shall it apply in cases where goods may be declared for release for free circulation orally or by any other act.

3. Where they consider it necessary, the customs authorities at the customs office of reimportation may ask the person concerned to submit additional evidence, in particular for the purposes of identification of the returned goods.

Article 849

1. A declaration for release for free circulation relating to returned goods whose export may have given rise to the completion of customs export formalities with a view to obtaining refunds or other amounts provided for on exportation under the Common Agricultural Policy, shall be supported not only by the documents referred to in Article 848, but by a certificate issued by the authorities responsible for the grant of such refunds or amounts in the Member State of exportation. Such certificate shall contain the particulars necessary to allow the customs office where the goods concerned were declared for free circulation to verify that it relates to the said goods.

2. When the export of the goods did not give rise to the completion of customs export formalities with a view to obtaining refunds or other amounts provided for on exportation under the Common Agricultural Policy, the certificate shall bear one of the following indications—

— Sin concesión de restituciones u otras cantidades a la exportación;
— Ingen restitutioner eller andre beløb ydet ved udførslen;
— Keine Ausfuhrerstattungen oder sonstige Ausfuhrvergünstigungen;
— Δεν τυχαν επιδοτήεσων ή άλλων χορηγήσεων κατά την εξαγωγή;
— No refunds or other amounts granted on exportation;
— Sans octroi de restitutions ou autres montants à l'exportation;
— Senza concessione di restituzioni o altri importi all'esportazione;
— Geen restituties of andere bij de uitvoer verleende bedragen;
— Sem concessão de restituições ou outros montantes na exportação.
[— Vietäessä ei myönetty vientitukea eikä muita määriä/Inga bidrag eller andra belopphar beviljats vid exporten;
— Inga bidrag eller andra belopp har beviljats vid exporten;]
[— Bez vývozních náhrad nebo jiných č ástek poskytovaných přI vývozu,

— Ekspordil ei makstud toetusi ega muid summasid,

— Bez kompenscijas vai citm summm, kas paredztas par prečwu izvešanu,

— Eksportas teiss gržinamsias išmokas arba kitas pinig sumas nesuteikia,

— Kivitel esetén visszatérítést vagy egyéb kedvezményt nem vettek igénybe,

— L-ebda rifujoni jew ammonti ora mogtija fuq esportazzjoni,

— Nie przyznano dopłat lub innych kwot wynikajacych z wywozu,

— Brez izvoznih nadomestil ali drugih izvoznih ugodnosti,

— Pri vývoze sa neposkytujú ž iadne náhrady alebo iné peažné čiastky.]

[— *(for original text, refer to Commission Regulation (EC) 1792/2006 (OJ L 362, 20.12.06, p 1)),*

— Fr acordarea de restituiri restitutii sau alte sume la export]

3. When the export of the goods did give rise to the completion of customs export formalities with a view to obtaining refunds or other amounts provided for on exportation under the Common Agricultural Policy, the certificate shall bear one of the following indications—

— Restituciones y otras cantidades a la exportación reintegradas por . . . (cantidad);

— De ved udførslen ydede restitutioner eller andre beløb er tilbagebetalt for . . . (mængde);

— Ausfuhrerstattungen und sonstige Ausfuhrvergünstigungen für . . . (Menge) zurückbezahlt;

— Επιδοτήσειζκαιάλλɛζχορηγήσειζ κατα την εξαγωγή επεοτράφησανγια . . . (ποσότηζ)

— Refunds and other amounts on exportation repaid for . . . (quantity);

— Restitutions et autres montants à l'exportation remboursés pour . . . (quantité);

— Restituzioni e altri importi all'esportazione rimborsati per . . . (quantità);

— Restituties en andere bedragen bij de uitvoer voor . . . (hoeveelheid) terugbetaald;

— Restituições e outras montantes na exportação reembolsados para . . . (quantidade);

[— Vývozní náhrady nebo jiné částky poskytované při vývozu vyplaceny za . . . (množství),

— Ekspordil makstud toetused ja muud summad tagastatud . . . (kogus) eest,

— Kompenscijas un citas par prečwu izvešanu paredztas summas atmakstas par . . . (daudzums),

— Gržinamosios išmokos ir kitos eksporto atveju mokamos pinig sumos išmoktos už . . . (kiekis),

— Kivitel esetén igénybevett visszatérítés vagy egyéb kedvezmény . . . (mennyiség) után visszafizetve,

— Rifujoni jew ammonti ora fuq esportazzjoni mogtija lura gal . . . (kwantita'),

— Dopłaty i inne kwoty wynikajce z wywozu wypłacono za . . . (ilo),

— Izvozna nadomestila ali zneski drugih izvoznih ugodnosti povrnjeni za . . . (količina),

— Náhrady a iné peažné čiastky pri vývoze vyplatené za . . . (množstvo)]

[— *(for original text, refer to Commission Regulation (EC) 1792/2006 (OJ L 362, 20.12.06, p 1))*,

— Restituiri si alte sume rambursate la export pentru . . . (cantitatea)]

or

[— Oikeus vientitukeen tai muihin vietäessä maksettuihin määriin peruutettu . . . (määrä) osalta/Rätt till utbetalning av bidrag och andra belopp vid exporten har annullerats för . . . (Kvantitet);

— Rätt till utbetalning av bidrag och andra belopp vid exporten har annullerats för . . . (Kvantitet);]

— Título de pago de restituciones u otras cantidades a la exportación anulado por . . . (cantidad);

— Ret til udbetaling af restituioner eller andre beløb ved udførslen er annulleret for . . . (mængde);

— Auszahlungsanordnung über die Ausfuhrerstattungen und sonstigen Ausfuhrvergünstigungen für . . . (Menge) ungültig gemacht;

— Αποδεικτικόπληρωμήζ επιδοτήσεων ή άλλων χορηγήσεων κατά την εξαγωγή ακυρωμνογια . . . (ποσότηξ)

— Entitlement to payment of refunds or other amounts on exportation cancelled for . . . (quantity);

— Títre de paiement des restitutions ou autres montants à l'exportation annulé pour . . . (quantité);

— Titolo di pagamento delle restituzioni o di altri importi all' esportazione annullato per . . . (quantità);

— Aanspraak op restituties of andere bedragen bij uitvoer vervallen voor . . . (hoeveelheid);

— Titulo de pagamento de restituições ou outros montantes na exportação anulado para . . . (quantidade);

[— Vientituki ja muut vietäessä maksetut määrät maksettu takaisin . . . (määrä) osalta/De vid exporten beviljade bidragen eller andra belopp har betalats tillbaka för . . . (kvantitet);

— De vid exporten beviljade bidragen eller andra belopp har betalats tillbaka för . . . (kvantitet);]

[— Nárok na vyplacení vývozních náhrad nebo jiných částek poskytovaných př i vývozu za . . . (množství) zanikl.

— Õigus saada toetusi või muid summasid ekspordil on . . . (kogus) eest kehtetuks tunnistatud,

— Tiesbas izmakst kompenscijas vai citas summas, kas paredztas par preču izvešanu, atceltas attiecb uz . . . (daudzums),

— Teis gržinamj išmok arba kit eksporto atveju mokam pinig sum mokjim už . . . (kiekis) panaikinta,

— Kivitel esetén . . . igénybevett visszatérítésre vagy egyéb kedvezményre való jogosultság . . . (mennyiség) után megsznt,

— Mhux intitolati gal las ta' rifujoni jew ammonti ora fuq lesportazzjoni gal . . . (kwantita'),

— Uprawnienie do otrzymania dopłat lub innych kwot wynikajcych z wywozu anulowano dla . . . (ilo),

— Upravičenost do izplačila izvoznih nadomestil ali zneskov drugih izvoznih ugodnosti razveljavljena za . . . (količina),

— Nárok na vyplatenie náhrad alebo iných peažných č iastok pri vývoze za . . . (množstvo) zanikol.]

[— *(for original text, refer to Commission Regulation (EC) 1792/2006 (OJ L 362, 20.12.06, p 1))*,

— Dreptul la plata restituirilor sau a altor sume la export a fost anulat pentru . . . (cantitatea)]

depending on whether the refunds or other amounts provided for on exportation have or have not already been paid by the competent authorities.

4. In the case referred to in subparagraph (b) of the first indent of Article 848(1), the certificate referred to in paragraph 1 shall be made out on the Information Sheet INF 3 provided for in Article 850.

5. When the customs authorities at the customs office where the goods are declared for release for free circulation have the means to satisfy themselves that no refund or other amount provided for on exportation under the Common Agricultural Policy has been granted, and cannot subsequently be granted, the certificate referred to in paragraph 1 shall not be required.

NOTES

Paras 2, 3: words inserted by the 1994 Act of Accession, Annex I(III)(B)(4), as adjusted by Council Decision 95/1/EC, Annex I(XIII)(A)(b), paras 42, 43.

Paras 2, 3: further words inserted by the 2003 Act of Accession Annex II(19)(A)(II), paras 30–32.

Paras 2, 3: final two entries inserted by Commission Regulation (EC) 1792/2006, Art 1, Annex, Part 11(A)(29)–(31).

Article 850

Information Sheet INF 3 shall be drawn up in an original and two copies on forms which conform to the specimens appearing in Annex 110.

Article 851

1. Subject to paragraph 3, Information Sheet INF 3 shall be issued at the exporter's request by the customs authorities at the customs office of exportation at the time of completion of the export formalities for the goods concerned, if the exporter declares that it is probable that these goods will be returned via a customs office other than the customs office of exportation.

2. Information Sheet INF 3 may also be issued, at the exporter's request, by the customs authorities at the customs office of exportation after completion of the export formalities for the goods concerned, provided that these authorities can establish, on the basis of the information at their disposal, that the particulars in the exporter's request relate to the goods exported.

3. In the case of the goods referred to in Article 849(1), Information Sheet INF 3 may be issued only after completion of the relevant customs export formalities, and subject to the proviso in paragraph 2.

In addition, it may be issued only on condition that—

(a) box B has been completed and endorsed by the customs authorities beforehand; and

(b) box A has been completed and endorsed by the customs authorities beforehand, where the information contained therein is required.

Article 852

1. Information Sheet INF 3 shall contain all items of information required by the customs authorities for the purpose of identifying the exported goods.

2. Where it is expected that the exported goods will be returned to the customs territory of the Community through several customs offices other than the customs office of exportation, the exporter may ask for several Information Sheets INF 3 to be issued to cover the total quantity of the goods exported.

Part III

Similarly, the exporter may ask the customs authorities which issued an Information Sheet INF 3 to replace it by several Information Sheets INF 3 covering the total quantity of goods included in the Information Sheet INF 3 initially issued.

The exporter may also ask for an Information Sheet INF 3 to be issued in respect of a proportion only of the exported goods.

Article 853

The original and one copy of Information Sheet INF 3 shall be returned to the exporter for presentation at the customs office of reimportation. The second copy shall be kept in the official files of the customs authorities who issued it.

Article 854

The customs office of re-importation shall record on the original and on the copy of Information Sheet INF 3 the quantity of returned goods exempted from import duties, retaining the original and sending the copy, bearing the reference number and the date of declaration for free circulation, to the customs authorities who issued it.

The said customs authorities shall compare this copy with the one in their possession and retain it in their official files.

Article 855

In the event of theft, loss or destruction of the original Information Sheet INF 3, the person concerned may ask the customs authorities which issued it for a duplicate. They shall comply with this request if the circumstances warrant it. A duplicate so issued shall bear one of the following indications—

—	DUPLICADO,
—	DUPLIKAT,
—	DUPLIKAT,
—	ΑΝΤΙΓΡΑΦΟ,
—	DUPLICATE,
—	DUPLICATA,
—	DUPLICATO.
—	DUPLICAAT,
—	SEGUNDA VIA.
[—	KAKSOISKAPPALE/DUPLIKAT,
—	DUPLIKAT.]
[—	DUPLIKÁT,
—	DUPLIKAAT,
—	DUBLIKĀTS,
—	DUBLIKATAS,
—	MÁSODLAT,
—	DUPLIKAT,
—	DUPLIKAT,
—	DVOJNIK,
—	DUPLIKÁT.]
[—	*(for original text, refer to Commission Regulation (EC) 1792/2006 (OJ L 362, 20.12.06, p 1)),*
—	DUPLICAT . . .]

The customs authorities shall record on the copy of Information Sheet INF 3 in their possession that a duplicate has been issued.

NOTES

Words inserted by the 1994 Act of Accession, Annex I(III)(B)(4), as adjusted by Council Decision 95/1/EC, Annex I(XIII)(A)(b), para 45.

Further words inserted by the 2003 Act of Accession Annex II(19)(A)(II), para 33.

Final two entries inserted by Commission Regulation (EC) 1792/2006, Art 1, Annex, Part 11(A)(32).

Article 856

1. At the request of the customs authorities at the customs office of reimportation, the customs authorities at the customs office of exportation shall communicate to the former all the information at their disposal to enable them to determine whether the goods meet the conditions necessary to benefit from the provisions of this part.

2. Information Sheet INF 3 may be used for the request and the transmission of the information referred to in paragraph 1.

[TITLE II
PRODUCTS OF SEA-FISHING AND OTHER PRODUCTS TAKEN FROM THE TERRITORIAL SEA OF A THIRD COUNTRY BY COMMUNITY FISHING VESSELS

Article 856a

1. Exemption from import duties for the products referred to in Article 188 of the Code shall be subject to the presentation of a certificate in support of the declaration for release for free circulation relating to those products.

2. For products to be released for free circulation in the Community, in the situations referred to in Article 329(a) to (d), the master of the Community vessel making the catch shall complete boxes 3, 4 and 5 and, if need be, box 9, of the certificate. If the catch has been processed on board, the master of the vessel shall also complete boxes 6, 7 and 8.

Articles 330, 331 and 332 shall apply to completion of the corresponding boxes on the certificate.

When the declaration is made for release for free circulation of these products, the declarant shall complete boxes 1 and 2 of the certificate.

3. The certificate must conform to the model set out in Annex 110a and be drawn up in accordance with paragraph 2.

4. Where the products are declared for release for free circulation at the port where they were unloaded from the Community fishing vessel which made the catch, the derogation referred to in Article 326(2) shall apply *mutatis mutandis*.

5. For the purposes of paragraphs 1 to 4, the meaning of "Community fishing vessel" and "Community factory vessel" shall be as defined in Article 325(1) while "products" shall be taken to mean those products and goods referred to in Articles 326 to 332, where reference is made to those provisions.

6. In order to ensure that paragraphs 1 to 5 are complied with, the Member State administrations shall accord each other mutual assistance in checking that certificates are authentic and the particulars in them accurate.]

NOTES

Inserted by Commission Regulation (EC) 75/98, Art 1, para 22.

PART IV
CUSTOMS DEBT

TITLE I
[RECOVERY OF THE AMOUNT OF THE CUSTOMS DEBT]

NOTES

Title heading: substituted by Commission Regulation (EC) 12/97, Art 1, para 11(a).

Article 857

1. The types of security other than cash deposits or guarantors, within the meaning of Articles 193, 194 and 195 of the Code, and the cash deposit or the submission of securities for which Member States may opt even if they do not comply with the conditions laid down in Article 194(1) of the Code, shall be as follows—

(a)   the creation of a mortgage, a charge on land, an antichresis or other right deemed equivalent to a right pertaining to immovable property;

(b)   the cession of a claim, the pledging, with or without surrendering possession, of goods, securities or claims or, in particular, a savings bank book or entry in the national debt register;

(c)   the assumption of joint contractual liability for the full amount of the debt by a third party approved for that purpose by the customs authorities and, in particular, the lodging of a bill of exchange the payment of which is guaranteed by such third party;

(d)   a cash deposit or security deemed equivalent thereto in a currency other than that of the Member State in which the security is given;

(e)   participation, subject to payment of a contribution, in a general guarantee scheme administered by the customs authorities.

2. The circumstances in which and the conditions under which recourse may be had to the types of security referred to in paragraph 1 shall be determined by the customs authorities.

Article 858

Where security is given by making a cash deposit, no interest thereon shall be payable by the customs authorities.

TITLE II
INCURRENCE OF THE DEBT

CHAPTER 1
FAILURES WHICH HAVE NO SIGNIFICANT EFFECT ON THE OPERATION OF TEMPORARY STORAGE OR OF THE CUSTOMS PROCEDURE

Article 859

The following failures shall be considered to have no significant effect on the correct operation of the temporary storage or customs procedure in question within the meaning of Article 204(1) of the Code, provided—

—   they do not constitute an attempt to remove the goods unlawfully from customs supervision,

—   they do not imply obvious negligence on the part of the person concerned, and

—   all the formalities necessary to regularise the situation of the goods are subsequently carried out—

1.   exceeding the time limit allowed for assignment of the goods to one of the customs-approved treatments or uses provided for under the temporary storage or customs procedure in question, where the time limit would have been extended had an extension been applied for in time;

[2   in the case of goods placed under a transit procedure, failure to fulfil one of the obligations entailed by the use of that procedure, where the following conditions are fulfilled:

(a)   the goods entered for the procedure were actually presented intact at the office of destination;

(b)   the office of destination has been able to ensure that the goods were assigned a customs-approved treatment or use or were placed in temporary storage at the end of the transit operation;

(c)   where the time limit set under Article 356 has not been complied with and paragraph 3 of that Article does not apply, the goods have nevertheless been presented at the office of destination within a reasonable time.]

3.   in the case of goods placed in temporary storage or under the customs warehousing procedure, handling not authorised in advance by the customs authorities, provided such handling would have been authorised if applied for;

4.   in the case of goods placed under the temporary importation procedure, use of the goods otherwise than as provided for in the authorisation, provided such use would have been authorised under that procedure if applied for;

5.   in the case of goods in temporary storage or placed under a customs procedure, unauthorised movement of the goods, provided the goods can be presented to the customs authorities at their request;

[6.   in the case of goods in temporary storage or entered for a customs procedure, removal of the goods from the customs territory of the Community or their introduction into a free zone of control type I within the meaning of Article 799 or into a free warehouse without completion of the necessary formalities;]

[7.   in the case of goods or products physically transferred within the meaning of Articles 296, 297 or 511,failure to fulfil one of the conditions under which the transfer takes place, where the following conditions are fulfilled—

(a)   the person concerned can demonstrate, to the satisfaction of the customs authorities, that the goods or products arrived at the specified premises or destination and, in cases of transfer based on Articles 296, 297, 512(2) or 513, that the goods or products have been duly entered in the records of the specified premises or destination, where those Articles require such entry in the records;

(b)   where a time limit set in the authorisation was not observed, the goods or products nevertheless arrived at the specified premises or destination within a reasonable time.]

[8.   in the case of goods eligible on release for free circulation for the total or partial relief from import duties referred to in Article 145 of the Code, the existence of one of the situations referred to in Article 204(1)(a) or (b) of the Code while the goods concerned are

Part III

in temporary storage or under another customs procedure before being released for free circulation;

[9.   in the framework of inward processing and processing under customs control, exceeding the time-limit allowed for submission of the bill of discharge, provided the limit would have been extended had an extension been applied for in time;]]

[10.   exceeding the time-limit allowed for temporary removal from a customs warehouse, provided the limit would have been extended had an extension been applied for in time.]

NOTES

Point 2: substituted by Commission Regulation (EC) 444/2002, Art 1, para 22.
Point 6: substituted by Commission Regulation (EC) 993/2001, Art 1, para 30.
Point 7: substituted by Commission Regulation (EC) 444/2002, Art 1, para 22.
Points 8, 9: added by Commission Regulation (EC) 1427/97, Art 1, para 11.
Point 9: substituted by Commission Regulation (EC) 993/2001, Art 1, para 30.
Point 10: added by Commission Regulation (EC) 993/2001, Art 1, para 30.

Article 860

The customs authorities shall consider a customs debt to have been incurred under Article 204(1) of the Code unless the person who would be the debtor establishes that the conditions set out in Article 859 are fulfilled.

Article 861

The fact that the failures referred to in Article 859 do not give rise to a customs debt shall not preclude the application of provisions of criminal law in force or of provisions allowing cancellation and withdrawal of authorisations issued under the customs procedure in question.

CHAPTER 2
NATURAL WASTAGE

Article 862

1.   For the purposes of Article 206 of the Code, the customs authorities shall, at the request of the person concerned, take account of the quantities missing wherever it can be shown that the losses observed result solely from the nature of the goods and not from any negligence or manipulation on the part of that person.

2.   In particular, negligence or manipulation shall mean any failure to observe the rules for transporting, storing, handling, working or processing the goods in question imposed by the customs authorities or by normal practice.

Article 863

The customs authorities may waive the obligation for the person concerned to show that the goods were irretrievably lost for reasons inherent in their nature where they are satisfied that there is no other explanation for the loss.

Article 864

The national provisions in force in the Member States concerning standard rates for irretrievable loss due to the nature of the goods themselves shall be applied where the person concerned fails to show that the real loss exceeds that calculated by application of the standard rate for the goods in question.

[CHAPTER 3
GOODS IN SPECIAL SITUATIONS]

NOTES

Chapter heading: substituted by Commission Regulation (EC) 3665/93, Art 1, para 68.

Article 865

The presentation of a customs declaration for the goods in question, or any other act having the same legal effects, and the production of a document for endorsement by the competent authorities, shall be considered as removal of goods from customs supervision within the meaning of Article 203(1) of the Code, where these acts have the effect of wrongly conferring on them the customs status of Community goods.

[However, in the case of airline companies authorised to use a simplified transit procedure with the use of an electronic manifest, the goods shall not be considered to have been removed from customs supervision if, at the initiative or on behalf of the person concerned, they are treated in accordance with their status as non-Community goods before the customs authorities find the existence of an irregular situation and if the behaviour of the person concerned does not suggest any fraudulent dealing.]

NOTES

Words in square brackets added by Commission Regulation (EC) 1677/98, Art 1, para 4.

New Article 865a to be inserted by Commission Regulation (EC) No 1875/2006, Art 1(68) with effect from 1 July 2009.

Article 866

Without prejudice to the provisions laid down concerning prohibitions or restrictions which may be applicable to the goods in question, where a customs debt on importation is incurred pursuant to Articles 202, 203, 204 or 205 of the Code and the import duties have been paid, those goods shall be deemed to be Community goods without the need for a declaration for entry into free circulation.

Article 867

The confiscation of goods pursuant to Article 233(c) and (d) of the Code shall not affect the customs status of the goods in question.

[Article 867a

1. Non-Community goods which have been abandoned to the Exchequer or seized or confiscated shall be considered to have been entered for the customs warehousing procedure.

2. The goods referred to in paragraph 1 may be sold by the customs authorities only on the condition that the buyer immediately carries out the formalities to assign them a customs-approved treatment or use.

Where the sale is at a price inclusive of import duties, the sale shall be considered as equivalent to release for free circulation, and the customs authorities themselves shall calculate the duties and enter them in the accounts.

In these cases, the sale shall be conducted according to the procedures in force in the Member States.

3. Where the administration decides to deal with the goods referred to in paragraph 1 otherwise than by sale, it shall immediately carry out the formalities to assign them one of the customs-approved treatments or uses laid down in Article 4(15)(a), (b), (c) and (d) of the Code.]

NOTE

Inserted by Commission Regulation (EC) 3665/93, Art 1, para 69.

TITLE III
ENTRY IN THE ACCOUNTS AND POST-CLEARANCE RECOVERY

Article 868

Member States need not enter in the accounts amounts of duty of less than ECU 10.

There shall be no post-clearance recovery of import duties or export duties where the amount per recovery action is less than ECU 10.

Article 869

The customs authorities shall themselves decide not to enter uncollected duties in the accounts—

(a)   in cases in which preferential tariff treatment has been applied in the context of a tariff quota, a tariff ceiling or other arrangements when entitlement to this treatment had been ended at the time of acceptance of the customs declaration without that fact having been published in the *Official Journal of the European Communities* before the release for free circulation of the goods in question or, where such fact is not published, having been made known in an appropriate manner in the Member State concerned, the person liable for payment for his part having acted in good faith and complied with all the provisions laid down by the legislation in force as regards the customs declaration;

[(b)   in cases in which they consider that the conditions laid down in Article 220(2)(b) of the Code are fulfilled, except those in which the dossier must be transmitted to the Commission pursuant to Article 871. However, where Article 871(2), second indent, is applicable, the customs authorities may not adopt a decision waiving entry in the accounts of the duties in question until the end of a procedure initiated in accordance with Articles 871 to 876.]

(c)   . . .

[Where a request is submitted for repayment or remission under Article 236 of the Code in conjunction with Article 220(2)(b) of the Code, subparagraph (b) of the first paragraph of this Article and Articles 871 to 876 shall apply *mutatis mutandis*.]

[For the purposes of applying the above paragraphs the Member States shall give each other mutual assistance, particularly where an error by the customs authorities of a Member State other than the one responsible for taking the decision is concerned.]

NOTES

Words in square brackets substituted by Commission Regulation (EC) 1677/98, Art 1, para 5.

Para (b): substituted by Commission Regulation (EC) 1335/2003 Art 1, para 1(a).

Para (c): repealed by Commission Regulation (EC) 1335/2003 Art 1, para 1(b).

Words inserted by Commission Regulation (EC) 1335/2003 Art 1, para 1(c).

[Article 870

1.   Each Member State shall hold at the disposal of the Commission a list of the cases in which the following provisions have been applied:

—   Article 869(a),

—   Article 236 of the Code in conjunction with Article 220(2)(b) of the Code, where no communication is required under paragraph 2,

— Article 869(b), where no communication is required under paragraph 2.

2. Each Member State shall communicate to the Commission a list of the cases in which the amount not collected from the operator concerned in respect of one or more import or export operations but in consequence of a single error is more than EUR 50 000, and the provisions of Article 236 of the Code in conjunction with Article 220(2)(b) of the Code or of Article 869(b) have been applied, giving a short summary of each case. This communication shall be forwarded during the first and third quarters of each year for all cases in which it was decided not to enter the uncollected duties in the accounts during the preceding half-year.]

NOTES

Substituted by Commission Regulation (EC) 1335/2003, Art 1, para 2.

[Article 871

1. The customs authority shall transmit the case to the Commission to be settled under the procedure laid down in Articles 872 to 876 where it considers that the conditions laid down in Article 220(2)(b) of the Code are fulfilled and:

— it considers that the Commission has committed an error within the meaning of Article 220(2)(b) of the Code,

— the circumstances of the case are related to the findings of a Community investigation carried out under Council Regulation (EC) No 515/97 of 13 March 1997 on mutual assistance between the administrative authorities of the Member States and co-operation between the latter and the Commission to ensure the correct application of the law on customs and agricultural matters or under any other Community legislation or any agreement concluded by the Community with countries or groups of countries in which provision is made for carrying out such Community investigations, or

— the amount not collected from the operator concerned in respect of one or more import or export operations but in consequence of a single error is EUR 500 000 or more.

2. However, the cases referred to in paragraph 1 shall not be transmitted where:

— the Commission has already adopted a decision under the procedure provided for in Articles 872 to 876 on a case involving comparable issues of fact and law,

— the Commission is already considering a case involving comparable issues of fact and law.

3. The dossier submitted to the Commission shall contain all the information required for full consideration. It shall include detailed information on the behaviour of the operator concerned, and in particular on his professional experience, good faith and diligence. This assessment shall be accompanied by all information that may demonstrate that the operator acted in good faith. The dossier shall also include a statement, signed by the applicant for repayment or remission, certifying that he has read the dossier and either stating that he has nothing to add or listing all the additional information that he considers should be included.

4. As soon as it receives the dossier the Commission shall inform the Member State concerned accordingly.

5. Should it be found that the information supplied by the Member State is not sufficient to enable a decision to be taken on the case concerned in full knowledge of the facts, the Commission may request that additional information be supplied.

6. Where one of the following situations occurs the Commission shall return the dossier to the customs authority and the procedure referred to in Articles 872 to 876 shall be deemed never to have been initiated:

— the dossier shows that there is a disagreement between the customs authority that has transmitted the dossier and the person who signed the statement referred to in paragraph 3 as regards the account of the facts,

— the dossier is obviously incomplete since it contains nothing that would justify its consideration by the Commission,

— under paragraphs 1 and 2, the dossier should not be transmitted,

— the existence of a customs debt has not been established,

— new information relating to the dossier and of a nature to alter substantially its presentation of the facts or legal assessment has been transmitted by the customs authority to the Commission while it is considering the dossier.]

NOTES

Substituted by Commission Regulation (EC) 1335/2003, Art 1, para 2.

[Article 872

The Commission shall send to the Member States a copy of the dossier referred to in Article 871(3) within 15 days of the date on which it received that dossier.

Consideration of the case in question shall be included as soon as possible on the agenda of a meeting of the group of experts provided for in Article 873.]

NOTES

Substituted by Commission Regulation (EC) 1335/2003, Art 1, para 2.

[Article 872a

Where, at any time in the procedure provided for in Articles 872 and 873, the Commission intends to take a decision unfavourable towards the person concerned by the case presented, it shall communicate its objections to him/her in writing, together with all the documents on which it bases those objections. The person concerned by the case submitted to the Commission shall express his/her point of view in writing within a period of one month from the date on which the objections were sent. If he/she does not give a point of view within that period, he/she shall be deemed to have waived the right to express a position.]

NOTES

Inserted by Commission Regulation (EC) 1677/98, Art 1, para 6.

[Article 873

After consulting a group of experts composed of representatives of all Member States, meeting within the framework of the Committee to consider the case in question, the Commission shall decide whether the circumstances under consideration are such that the duties in question need not be entered in the accounts.

That decision shall be taken within nine months of the date on which the dossier referred to in Article 871(3) is received by the Commission. However, where the declaration or detailed assessment of the operator's behaviour referred to in Article 871(3) is not included in the dossier, the nine months shall be counted only from the date of receipt of these documents by the Commission. The Commission shall notify the customs authority and the person concerned accordingly.

Where the Commission has found it necessary to ask for additional information from the Member State in order to reach its decision, the nine months shall be extended by a period equivalent to that between the date the Commission sent the request for additional information and the date it received that information. The Commission shall notify the person concerned of the extension of the procedure.

Where the Commission conducts investigations itself in order to reach a decision, the nine months shall be extended by the time necessary to complete the investigations. Such an extension shall not exceed nine months. The Commission shall notify the customs authority and the person concerned of the dates on which investigations are opened and closed.

Where the Commission has notified the person concerned of its objections in accordance with Article 872a, the period of nine months shall be extended by one month.]

NOTES

Substituted by Commission Regulation (EC) 1335/2003, Art 1, para 3.

[Article 874

The Member State concerned shall be notified of the decision referred to in Article 873 as soon as possible and in any event within one month of the expiry of the period specified in that Article.

The Commission shall notify the Member States of the decisions it has adopted in order to help customs authorities to reach decisions in situations involving comparable issues of fact and law.]

NOTES

Substituted by Commission Regulation (EC) 1335/2003, Art 1, para 3.

[Article 875

Where it is established by the decision referred to in Article 873 that the circumstances under consideration are such that the duties in question need not be entered in the accounts, the Commission may specify the conditions under which the Member States may refrain from post-clearance entry in the account in cases involving comparable issues of fact and of law.]

NOTES

Substituted by Commission Regulation (EC) 1335/2003, Art 1, para 3.

Article 876

If the Commission fails to take a decision within the period referred to in Article 873 or fails to notify a decision to the Member State concerned within the period referred to in Article 874, the customs authorities of that Member State shall not enter the duties in question in the accounts.

[Article 876a

1. The customs authorities shall suspend the debtor's obligation to pay the duties until such time as they have taken a decision on the request, provided that, where the goods are no longer under customs supervision, security is lodged for the amount of those duties, and that—

    (a)   in cases where a request for invalidation of a declaration has been presented, this request is likely to be met;

    (b)   in cases where a request has been presented for remission pursuant to Article 236 in conjunction with Article 220(2)(b) of the Code or pursuant to Article 238 or Article 239, the customs authorities consider that the conditions laid down in the relevant provision may be regarded as having been fulfilled;

(c) in cases other than those referred to under (b), a request has been presented for remission pursuant to Article 236 of the Code and the conditions referred to in the second paragraph of Article 244 of the Code have been fulfilled.

It shall not be necessary to require a security where such requirement would be likely, owing to the debtor's circumstances, to cause serious economic or social difficulties.

2. In cases where goods in one of the circumstances referred to in the second indent of Article 233(c) or in Article 233(d) of the Code are seized, the customs authorities shall suspend the debtor's obligation to pay the duties if they consider that the conditions for confiscation may be regarded as having been fulfilled.]

[3. Where a customs debt is incurred under Article 203 of the Code, the customs authorities shall suspend the obligation of the person referred to in the fourth indent of paragraph 3 of that Article to pay the duties where at least one other debtor has been identified and the amount of the duties has also been communicated to him in accordance with Article 221 of the Code.

The suspension may be granted only on the condition that the person referred to in the fourth indent of Article 203(3) of the Code is not also covered by one of the other indents of the said paragraph and has not been obviously negligent in fulfilling his obligations.

The duration of the suspension shall be limited to one year. However, this period may be extended by the customs authorities for duly justified reasons.

The suspension shall be conditional on the lodging by the person for whose benefit it is granted of a valid security for the amount of the duties at stake, except where such a security covering the whole amount of duties at stake already exists and the guarantor has not been released from his undertakings. Such security need not be required where such a requirement would be likely, owing to the debtor's circumstances, to cause serious economic or social difficulties.]

NOTES

Inserted by Commission Regulation (EC) 12/97, Art 1, para 11(c).

Para 3: inserted by Commission Regulation (EC) 881/2003 Art 1, para 24.

Modification: see the VAT Regulations 1995, SI 1995/2518 reg 121C: modification of this Article in relation to any VAT chargeable on the importation of goods from places outside the member states).

TITLE IV
REPAYMENT OR REMISSION OF IMPORT OR EXPORT DUTIES

CHAPTER 1
GENERAL PROVISIONS

Article 877

1. or the purposes of this Title—

(a) *customs office of entry in the accounts means:* the customs office where the import or export duties whose repayment or remission is requested were entered in the accounts;

(b) *decision-making customs authority means:* the customs authority competent to decide on an application for repayment or remission of import or export duties in the Member State where the duties concerned were entered in the accounts;

(c) *supervising customs office means:* the customs office having jurisdiction over the goods which gave rise to entry in the accounts of the import or export duties whose repayment or remission is requested, the said office carrying out certain checks required for appraisal of the application;

(d) *implementing customs office means:* the customs office which adopts the measures necessary to ensure that the decision to repay or remit the import or export duties is correctly implemented.

2. The functions of office of entry in the accounts, decision-making customs authority, supervising customs office and implementing customs office may be carried out wholly or in part by the same customs office.

CHAPTER 2
IMPLEMENTING PROVISIONS RELATING TO ARTICLES 236 TO 239 OF THE CODE

SECTION 1
APPLICATION

Article 878

1. Application for repayment or remission of import or export duties, hereinafter referred to as "application for repayment or remission", shall be made by the person who paid or is liable to pay those duties, or the persons who have taken over his rights and obligations.

Application for repayment or remission may also be made by the representative of the person or persons referred in the first subparagraph.

2. Without prejudice to Article 882, application for repayment or remission shall be made, in one original and one copy, on a form conforming to the specimen and provisions in Annex 111.

However, application for repayment or remission may also be made, at the request of the person or persons referred to in paragraph 1, on plain paper, provided it contains the information appearing in the said Annex.

Article 879

1. Applications for repayment or remission, accompanied by the documents referred to in Article 6(1) of the Code, must be lodged with the customs office of entry in the accounts, unless the customs authorities designate another office for this purpose; the said office shall transmit it immediately after acceptance to the decision-making customs authority if it is not itself designated as such.

2. The customs office referred to in paragraph 1 shall enter the date of receipt on the original and the copy of the application. It shall return the copy to the applicant.

Where the second subparagraph of Article 878(2) is applied, the said customs office shall acknowledge receipt in writing to the applicant.

Article 880

Without prejudice to any specific provisions adopted in this connection under the Common Agricultural Policy, an application relating to goods in respect of which an import or export licence or advance fixing certificate was produced when the relevant customs declaration was lodged must also be accompanied by certification issued by the authorities responsible for issuing such licence or certificate attesting that the necessary steps have been taken to cancel the effects of the said licence or certificate.

Such certification shall not be required, however—

— where the customs authority to which the application is submitted itself issued the licence or certificate in question,

— where the ground relied upon in support of the application is a substantive error that has no effect on the attribution of the licence or certificate in question.

Article 881

1. The customs office referred to in Article 879 may accept an application not containing all the information provided for on the form referred to in Article 878(2). However, the application must contain at least the information to be entered in boxes 1 to 3 and 7.

2. Where paragraph 1 is applied, the said customs office shall set a time limit for the supply of any missing particulars and/or documents.

3. Where the time limit set by the customs office pursuant to paragraph 2 is not observed, the application shall be considered to have been withdrawn.

The applicant shall be informed of this immediately.

Article 882

1. For returned goods on which export duties were levied at the time of their export from the customs territory of the Community, repayment or remission of these duties shall be subject to the presentation to the customs authorities of a request accompanied by—

(a) the document issued as evidence of payment, where the amounts concerned have already been collected;

(b) the original, or the copy certified by the customs office of reimportation, of the declaration for free circulation relating to the returned goods.

This document shall bear one of the following endorsements made by the customs office of re- importation—

— Mercancías de retorno en aplicación de la letra b) del apartado 2 del artículo 185 del Código

— Returvarer i henhold til kodeksens artikel 185, stk. 2, litra b)

— Rückwaren gemäß Artikel 185 Absatz 2 Buchstabe b) des ZollKodex

— Εμπορε ματα επανεισαγό μενα κατ, εφαρμγή του άρθρου185 παράγραφοζ (2) στο?χο (β) του κώ δικα

— Goods admitted as returned goods under Article 185(2)(b) of the Code

— Marchandises en retour en application de l'article 185 paragraphe 2 point b) du code

— Merci in reintroduzione in applicazione dell'articolo 185; paragrafo 2 lettera b) del codice

— Goederen die met toepassing van artikel 185, lid 2, onder b) van het Wetboek Kunnen worden toegelaten als terugkerende goederen

— Mercadorias de retorno por aplicação da alínea b) do nº 2 do artigo 185° do código

[— Yhteisön tullikoodeksin 185 artiklan 2 kohdan b alakhohdan mukaista palautustavaraa/Returvaror enligt artikel 185.2 b) i gemenskapens tullkodex

— Returvaror enligt artikel 185.2 b) i gemenskapens tullkodex]

[— Vrácené zboží podle cl. 185 odst. 2 písm. b) kodexu,

— Seadustiku artikli 185(2)(b) alusel tagasitoodud kaubaks tunnistatud kaup,

— Preces atzitas par atpakaievestam saskana ar Kodeksa 185. panta 2. punkta b) apakpšunktu,

— Prekes ivežtos kaip graižntos prekes vadovaujantis Kodekso 185 straipsnio 2 dalies b punktu,

— A Vámkódex 185. cikke (2) bekezdésének b) pontja értelmében tértiáruként behozott áruk,

— Oggetti mdahhla bhala oggetti migjuba lura taht Artikolu 185(2)(b) tal-Kodici,

— Towary dopuszczone jako towary powracajace zgodnie z art. 185 ust. 2 lit. b) Kodeksu,

— Blago se ponovno uvaaž v skladu s clenom 185(2)(b) Zakonika,

— Vrátený tovar podl'a clánku 185 ods. 2 písm. b) colného zákonnóka.]

[— (for original text, refer to Commission Regulation (EC) 1792/2006 (OJ L 362, 20.12.06, p 1)),

— Mrfuri admise ca returnate în baza Articolului 185 (2) (b) din Cod]

(c) the copy of the export declaration returned to the exporter at the time of completion of the export formalities for the goods, or a copy thereof certified by the customs office of exportation.

Where the decision-making customs authority is already in possession of the particulars contained in one or more of the declarations referred to at (a), (b) or (c) above, the declaration or declarations concerned need not be produced.

2.   The request referred to in paragraph 1 must be lodged with the customs office referred to in Article 879 within 12 months of the date of acceptance of the export declaration.

NOTES

Para 1: words in sub-para (b) inserted by the 1994 Act of Accession, Annex I(III)(B)(4), as adjusted by Council Decision 95/1/EC, Annex I(XIII)(A)(b), para 45. Final two entries in sub-para (b) inserted by Commission Regulation (EC) 1792/2006, Art 1, Annex, Part 11(A)(33).

Further words inserted by the 2003 Act of Accession Annex II(19)(A)(II), para 34.

SECTION 2
PROCEDURE FOR GRANTING REPAYMENT OR REMISSION

Article 883

The decision-making customs authority may authorise completion of the customs formalities to which any repayment or remission may be subject before it has ruled on the application for repayment or remission. Such authorisation shall be entirely without prejudice to its decision on the application.

Article 884

Without prejudice to Article 883 and until a decision has been taken on the application for repayment or remission, the goods in respect of which repayment or remission of duties has been requested may not be transferred to a location other than that specified in the said application unless the applicant notifies in advance the customs office referred to in Article 879, which shall in turn inform the decision-making customs authority.

Article 885

1.   Where an application for repayment or remission relates to a case where supplementary information must be obtained or where the goods must be examined in order to ensure that the conditions for repayment or remission laid down in the Code

and in this Title are satisfied, the decision-making customs authority shall adopt the measures necessary to that end, if necessary by requesting the assistance of the supervising customs office, specifying the nature of the information to be obtained or of the checks to be carried out.

The supervising customs office shall comply promptly with this request and shall forward the information obtained and the results of the checks carried out to the decision-making customs authority.

2. Where the application relates to goods which are situated in a Member State other than that in which the import or export duties were entered in the accounts, the provisions of Chapter 4 of this Title shall apply.

Article 886

1. When the decision-making customs authority possesses all the necessary particulars, it shall give its decision in writing on the application for repayment or remission in accordance with Article 6(2) and (3) of the Code.

2. Where the application is approved, the decision shall include all the particulars necessary for its implementation.

Depending on the circumstances, some or all of the following particulars shall appear in the decision—

(a)   the information necessary for identifying the goods to which it applies;

(b)   the grounds for repayment or remission of the import or export duties and a reference to the corresponding article of the Code and, where appropriate, the corresponding article of this Title;

(c)   the use to which the goods may be put or the destination to which they may be sent, depending on the possibilities available in the particular case under the Code and where appropriate on the basis of a specific authorisation by the decision-making customs authority;

(d)   the time limit for completion of the formalities to which repayment or remission of the import or export duties is subject;

(e)   a statement indicating that the import or export duties will not be repaid or remitted until the implementing customs office has informed the decision-making customs authority that the formalities to which repayment or remission is subject have been completed;

(f)   particulars of any requirements to which the goods remain subject pending implementation of the decision;

(g)   a notice informing the recipient that he must give the original of the decision to the implementing customs office of his choice when presenting the goods.

Article 887

1.   The implementing customs office shall take steps to ensure—

—   where appropriate, that the requirements referred to in Article 886(2)(f) are met,

—   that in all cases the goods are actually used in the manner or sent to the destination specified in the decision to repay or remit import or export duties.

2.   Where the decision specifies that the goods may be placed in a customs warehouse, a free zone or a free warehouse, and the recipient avails himself of this opportunity, the necessary formalities must be carried out with the implementing customs office.

3.   Where the decision to repay or remit duties specifies a use to which the goods are to be put or a destination to which they are to be sent which can be established only in a Member State other than that in which the implementing customs office is

located, proof of compliance shall be furnished by production of a Control Copy T5 issued and used in accordance with the provisions of [Articles 912a to 912g], and of this Article.

The Control Copy T 5 must contain the following—

(a) box 33 shall contain the Combined Nomenclature Code of the goods;

(b) box 103 shall indicate in words the net quantity of the goods;

(c) box 104 shall contain, as appropriate, either the words "exit from the customs territory of the Community", or one of the following under the heading "other"—

— Delivery free of charge to the following charity. . .. .,

— Destruction under customs supervision,

— Entry for the following customs procedure. . .. .,

— Placing in a free zone or free warehouse;

(d) box 106 shall contain reference particulars of the decision granting repayment or remission of duties;

(e) box 107 shall contain the words "Articles 877 to 912 of Regulation (EEC) No 2454/93".

4. The supervising customs office which establishes or on whose responsibility it is established that the goods have actually been used for the purpose specified or have arrived at the prescribed destination shall complete the box entitled "Control of use and/or destination" of the control document by entering a cross against "have received the use and/or destination declared overleaf" and giving the relevant date.

5. When the implementing customs office has satisfied itself that the conditions set out in paragraph 1 are fulfilled, it shall send a certificate to that effect to the decision-making customs authority.

NOTES

Para 3: words substituted by Commission Regulation (EC) 1602/2000, Art 1, para 11.

Article 888

A decision-making customs authority having approved an application for repayment or remission of duties shall repay or remit such duty only after receiving the certificate referred to in Article 887(5).

Article 889

1. Where the request for repayment or remission is based on the existence, at the time when the declaration of release for free circulation was accepted, of a reduced or zero rate of import duty on the goods under a tariff quota, a tariff ceiling or other preferential tariff arrangements, repayment or remission shall be granted only on condition that, at the time of lodging the application for repayment or remission accompanied by the necessary documents—

— in the case of a tariff quota, its volume has not been exhausted,

— in other cases, the rate of duty normally due has not been re-established.

If the conditions laid down in the preceding paragraph are not fulfilled, repayment or remission shall nevertheless be granted where the failure to apply the reduced or zero rate of duty to the goods was the result of an error on the part of the customs authorities themselves and the declaration for free circulation contained all the particulars and was accompanied by all the documents necessary for application of the reduced or zero rate.

[2. Each Member State shall keep at the disposal of the Commission a list of the cases in which the provisions of the second subparagraph of paragraph 1 have been applied.]

NOTES
Para 2: substituted by Commission Regulation (EC) 75/98, Art 1, para 24.

Article 890

[The decision-making customs authority shall grant repayment or remission when:

(a)   the request is accompanied with a certificate of origin, a movement certificate, a certificate of authenticity, an internal Community transit document or with any other appropriate document, indicating that the imported goods were eligible, at the time of acceptance of the declaration for free circulation, for Community treatment, preferential tariff treatment or favourable tariff treatment by reason of the nature of goods;

(b)   the document thus produced refers specifically to the goods in question;

(c)   all the conditions relating to acceptance of the said document are fulfilled;

(d)   all the other conditions for the granting of the Community treatment, a preferential tariff treatment or of a favourable tariff treatment by reason of the nature of goods are fulfilled.]

[Repayment or remission shall take place upon presentation of the goods. Where the goods cannot be presented to the implementing customs office, the decision-making customs authority shall grant repayment or remission only where it has information showing unequivocally that the certificate or document produced post-clearance applies to the said goods.]

NOTES
Words in first pair of square brackets substituted by Commission Regulation (EC) 881/2003 Art 1, para 25.
Words in second pair of square brackets substituted by Commission Regulation (EC) 46/1999, Art 1, para 9.

Article 891

Repayment or remission of duty shall not be granted where certificates for the advance fixing of levies are presented in support of the application.

Article 892

Import duties shall not be repaid or remitted under Article 238 of the Code where—

—   the defective nature of the goods was taken into consideration in drawing up the terms of the contract, in particular the price, under which the goods were entered for a customs procedure involving the obligation to pay import duties,

—   the goods are sold by the importer after it has been ascertained that they are defective or do not comply with the terms of the contract.

Article 893

1.   Without prejudice to Article 900(1)(c), the decision-making customs authority shall set a deadline, no later than two months from the date of notification of the decision to repay or remit import duties or export duties, for completion of the customs formalities to which the repayment or remission of duties is subject.

2.   Failure to observe the deadline referred to in paragraph 1 shall result in loss of entitlement to repayment or remission except where the person concerned by the decision proves that he was prevented from meeting this deadline by unforeseeable circumstances or *force majeure*.

Article 894

Where destruction of the goods authorised by the decision-making customs authority produces waste or scrap, such waste or scrap shall be regarded as non-Community goods once a decision has been taken accepting the application for repayment or remission.

Article 895

Where the authorisation referred to in the second subparagraph of Article 238(2)(b) of the Code is granted, the customs authorities shall take all necessary steps to ensure that goods placed in a customs warehouse, free zone or free warehouse may subsequently be recognised as non-Community goods.

Article 896

1. Goods which, under the Common Agricultural Policy, are entered for a customs procedure involving the obligation to pay import duties under an import licence or advance fixing certificate shall benefit from Articles 237, 238 and 239 of the Code only where the customs office referred to in Article 879 is satisfied that the necessary steps have been taken by the competent authorities to cancel the effects with regard to the certificate under which the importation took place.

2. Paragraph 1 shall also apply in the case of re-exportation, placing in a customs warehouse, free zone or free warehouse, or destruction of the goods.

Article 897

Where it is not the complete article that is exported, re-exported or destroyed or assigned to another authorised customs treatment or use, but one or more parts or components of that article, the amount to be repaid or remitted shall be the difference between the amount of import duties on the complete article and the amount of import duties which would have been chargeable on the remainder of the article if the latter had been entered in the unaltered state for a customs procedure involving the obligation to pay such duties on the date on which the complete article was so entered.

Article 898

The amount referred to in Article 240 of the Code is hereby set at ECU 10.

CHAPTER 3
SPECIFIC PROVISIONS RELATING TO THE APPLICATION OF ARTICLE 239 OF THE CODE

SECTION 1
DECISIONS TO BE TAKEN BY THE CUSTOMS AUTHORITIES OF THE MEMBER STATES

[Article 899

1. Where the decision-making customs authority establishes that an application for repayment or remission submitted to it under Article 239(2) of the Code:
—   is based on grounds corresponding to one of the circumstances referred to in Articles 900 to 903, and that these do not result from deception or obvious negligence on the part of the person concerned, it shall repay or remit the amount of import or export duties concerned,
—   is based on grounds corresponding to one of the circumstances referred to in Article 904, it shall not repay or remit the amount of import or export duties concerned.

2. In other cases, except those in which the dossier must be submitted to the Commission pursuant to Article 905, the decision-making customs authority shall itself decide to grant repayment or remission of the import or export duties where

there is a special situation resulting from circumstances in which no deception or obvious negligence may be attributed to the person concerned.

Where Article 905(2), second indent, is applicable, the customs authorities may not decide to authorise repayment or remission of the duties in question until the end of a procedure initiated in accordance with Articles 906 to 909.

3.   For the purposes of Article 239(1) of the Code and of this Article, "the person concerned" shall mean the person or persons referred to in Article 878(1) or their representatives, and any other person who was involved with the completion of the customs formalities relating to the goods concerned or gave the instructions necessary for the completion of these formalities.

4.   For the purposes of applying paragraphs 1 and 2 the Member States shall give each other mutual assistance, particularly where an error by the customs authorities of a Member State other than that responsible for taking the decision is concerned.]

NOTES
  Substituted by Commission Regulation (EC) 1335/2003, Art 1, para 4.

Article 900

1.   Import duties shall be repaid or remitted where—

  (a)   non-Community goods placed under a customs procedure involving total or partial relief from import duties or goods released for free circulation with favourable tariff treatment by reason of their end-use are stolen, provided that the goods are recovered promptly and placed again in their original customs situation in the state they were in when they were stolen;

  (b)   non-Community goods are inadvertently withdrawn from the customs procedure involving total or partial relief from the said duties under which they had been placed, provided that, as soon as the error is found, they are placed again in their original customs situation in the state they were in when they were withdrawn;

  (c)   it is impossible to operate the mechanism for opening the means of transport on which goods previously released for free circulation are located and accordingly to unload them on arrival at their destination, provided that they are immediately re-exported;

  (d)   goods originally released for free circulation are subsequently returned to their non-Community supplier, under the outward processing arrangements, to enable him—free of charge—to eliminate defects existing prior to the release of the goods (even if found after release of the goods) or to bring them into line with the provisions of the contract under which they were released for free circulation, and the said supplier decides to keep the goods permanently because he is unable to remedy the defects or because it would not be economic to do so;

  (e)   it is found, when the customs authorities decide on post-clearance entry in the accounts of import duties actually due on goods released for free circulation with full relief from such duties, that the goods in question have been re-exported from the customs territory of the Community without customs supervision, provided it is established that the substantive conditions laid down in the Code for the repayment or remission of such import duties would actually have been met at the time of re-exportation if the amount had been levied when the goods were released for free circulation;

  (f)   a judicial body has forbidden the marketing of an item previously entered for a customs procedure obliging the person concerned to pay import duties under normal conditions, and the said item is re-exported from the customs territory of the Community or destroyed under the control of the customs authorities, provided it is established that the item in question has not actually been used in the Community;

(g) the goods have been entered for a customs procedure involving the obligation to pay such duties by a declarant empowered to do so on his own initiative and, through no fault of the declarant, it has not been possible to deliver them to the consignee;

(h) the goods have been addressed to the consignee in error by the consignor;

(i) the goods are found to be unsuitable for the use for which the consignee intended them because of an obvious factual error in his order;

(j) after having been released for a customs procedure involving the obligation to pay import duties, the goods are found not to have complied, at the time of their release, with the rules in force concerning their use or marketing and therefore cannot be used for the purpose intended by the consignee;

(k) the use of the goods by the consignee for the purpose intended is prevented or substantially restricted as a result of measures of general scope taken, after the date of release for a customs procedure involving the obligation to pay import duties, by an authority or other body having the appropriate power of decision;

(l) total or partial import duty relief applied for by the person concerned in accordance with existing provisions cannot, through no fault of the person concerned, be granted by the customs authorities, who shall accordingly enter in the accounts the import duties which have become due;

(m) the goods reached the consignee after the binding delivery dates stipulated in the contract under which they were entered for a customs procedure involving the obligation to pay import duties;

(n) it has not been possible to sell the goods in the customs territory of the Community and they are delivered free of charge to charities—

— carrying out their activities in a third country, provided that they are represented in the Community, or

— carrying out their activities in the customs territory of the Community, provided that they are eligible for relief in the case of importation for free circulation of similar goods from third countries.

[(o) the customs debt has been incurred otherwise than under Article 201 of the Code and the person concerned is able to produce a certificate of origin, a movement certificate, an internal Community transit document or other appropriate document showing that if the imported goods had been entered for free circulation they would have been eligible for Community treatment or preferential tariff treatment, provided the other conditions referred to in Article 890 were satisfied.]

[2. Repayment or remission of import duties in the cases referred to in paragraph 1(c) and (f) to (n) shall, except where the goods are destroyed by order of a public authority or delivered free of charge to charities carrying out their activities in the Community, be conditional upon their re-export from the customs territory of the Community under the supervision of the customs authorities.

If requested, the decision-making authority shall permit re-export of the goods to be replaced by their destruction or by placing them under the external Community transit procedure, under the customs warehousing arrangements, or in a free zone or free warehouse.

Goods to be assigned one of these treatments shall be considered to be non-Community goods.

In this case, the customs authorities shall take all requisite measures to ensure that the goods placed in a customs warehouse, in a free zone or in a free warehouse may later be recognised as non-Community goods.]

3. . . .

4. In addition, the supervising customs office must be satisfied that the goods have been neither used nor sold before their re-exportation.

NOTES

Para 1: sub-para (o) inserted by Commission Regulation (EC) 3254/94, Art 1, para 29.
Para 2: substituted by Commission Regulation (EC) 881/2003 Art 1, para 26(a).
Para 3: repealed by Commission Regulation (EC) 881/2003 Art 1, para 26(b).

Article 901

1. Import duties shall be repaid or remitted where—

(a) goods entered in error for a customs procedure involving the obligation to pay import duties have been re-exported from the customs territory of the Community without having been previously entered for the customs procedure under which they should have been placed, provided the other conditions laid down in Article 237 of the Code have been met;

(b) the goods have been re-exported or destroyed in accordance with Article 238(2)(b) of the Code without customs supervision, provided the other conditions laid down in the said Article have been met;

(c) the goods have been re-exported or destroyed without customs supervision in accordance with Article 900(1)(c) and (f) to (n), provided the other conditions laid down in Article 900(2) and (4) have been met.

2. Repayment or remission of import duties in the circumstances referred to in paragraph 1 shall be conditional on—

(a) production of all the evidence needed to enable the decision-making customs authority to satisfy itself that the goods in respect of which repayment or remission is requested—

— have actually been re-exported from the customs territory of the Community, or

— have been destroyed under the supervision of authorities or persons empowered to certify such destruction officially;

(b) the return to the decision-making customs authority of any document certifying the Community status of the goods in question under cover of which the said goods may have left the customs territory of the Community, or the presentation of whatever evidence the said authority considers necessary to satisfy itself that the document in question cannot be used subsequently in connection with any importation of goods into the Community.

Article 902

1. For the purposes of Article 901(2)—

(a) the evidence needed to enable the decision-making customs authority to satisfy itself that the goods in respect of which repayment or remission is requested have actually been re-exported from the customs territory of the Community shall consist of the presentation by the applicant of—

— the original or a certified copy of the declaration for export of the goods from the customs territory of the Community, and

— certification by the customs office through which the goods actually left the customs territory of the Community.

Where such certification cannot be produced, proof that the goods have left the customs territory of the Community may be presented in the form of—

— certification by the customs office in the third country of destination confirming that the goods have arrived, or

— the original or a certified copy of the customs declaration for the goods made in the third country of destination.

These documents must be accompanied by administrative and commercial documentation enabling the decision-making customs authority to check that the goods exported from the customs territory of the Community are the same as those which had been declared for a customs procedure involving the obligation to pay import duties, namely—

— the original or a certified copy of the declaration for the said procedure, and

— where this is considered necessary by the decision-making customs authority, commercial or administrative documents (such as invoices, dispatch details, transit documents or health certificates) containing a full description of the goods (trade description, quantities, marks and other identifying particulars) which were presented with the declaration for the said procedure or with the declaration for export from the customs territory of the Community or the customs declaration made for the goods in the third country of destination, as the case may be;

(b) the evidence needed to enable the decision-making customs authority to satisfy itself that the goods in respect of which repayment or remission is requested have actually been destroyed under the supervision of authorities or persons authorised to certify officially such destruction shall consist of the presentation by the applicant of—

— a report or declaration of destruction drawn up by the authorities under whose supervision the goods were destroyed, or a certified copy thereof, or

— a certificate drawn up by the person authorised to certify destruction, accompanied by evidence of his authority.

These documents shall contain a sufficiently full description of the destroyed goods (trade description, quantities, marks and other identifying particulars) to enable the customs authorities to satisfy themselves, by means of comparison with the particulars given in the declaration for a customs procedure involving the obligation to pay import duties and the accompanying commercial documents (invoices, dispatch details, etc), that the destroyed goods are those which had been declared for the said procedure.

2. Where the evidence referred to in paragraph 1 is insufficient to allow the decision-making customs authority to take a decision on the case submitted to it in full knowledge of the facts, or where certain evidence is not available, such evidence may be supplemented or replaced by any other documents considered necessary by the said authority.

Article 903

1. For returned goods in respect of which an export duty was levied when they were exported from the customs territory of the Community, entry for free circulation shall give the right to repayment of the amounts levied.

2. Paragraph 1 shall apply only to goods which are in one of the situations referred to in Article 844.

It must be proved to the satisfaction of the customs office where the goods are declared for release for free circulation that the goods are in one of the situations referred to in Article 185(2)(b) of the Code.

3. Paragraph 1 shall apply even where the returned goods constitute only a proportion of the goods previously exported from the customs territory of the Community.

Article 904

Import duties shall not be repaid or remitted where the only grounds relied on in the application for repayment or remission are, as the case may be—

(a) re-export from the customs territory of the Community of goods previously entered for a customs procedure involving the obligation to pay import duties, for reasons other than those referred to in Article 237 or 238 of the Code or in Article 900 or 901, notably failure to sell;

(b) destruction, for any reason whatsoever, save in the cases expressly provided for by Community legislation, of goods entered for a customs procedure involving the obligation to pay import duties after their release by the customs authorities;

(c) presentation, for the purpose of obtaining preferential tariff treatment of goods declared for free circulation, of documents subsequently found to be forged, falsified or not valid for that purpose, even where such documents were presented in good faith.

[Article 904a

1. When no communication is required under paragraph 2, each Member State shall hold at the disposal of the Commission the list of the cases in which Article 899(2) was applied.

2. Each Member State shall communicate to the Commission a list of the cases in which it has applied the provisions of Article 899(2) and the amount repaid or remitted in respect of one or more import or export operations but in consequence of a single special situation is more than EUR 50 000, giving a short summary of each case. This communication shall be forwarded during the first and third quarters of each year for all cases in which it was decided to repay or remit duties during the preceding half-year.]

NOTES

Inserted by Commission Regulation (EC) 1335/2003, Art 1, para 5.

SECTION 2
DECISIONS TO BE TAKEN BY THE COMMISSION

[Article 905

1. Where the application for repayment or remission submitted under Article 239(2) of the Code is supported by evidence which might constitute a special situation resulting from circumstances in which no deception or obvious negligence may be attributed to the person concerned, the Member State to which the decision-making customs authority belongs shall transmit the case to the Commission to be settled under the procedure laid down in Articles 906 to 909 where:

— the authority considers that a special situation is the result of the Commission failing in its obligations,

— the circumstances of the case are related to the findings of a Community investigation carried out under Regulation (EC) No 515/97, or under any other Community legislation or any agreement concluded by the Community with countries or groups of countries in which provision is made for carrying out such Community investigations, or

— the amount for which the person concerned may be liable in respect of one or more import or export operations but in consequence of a single special situation is EUR 500 000 or more.

The term "the person concerned" shall be interpreted in the same way as in Article 899.

2. However, the cases referred to in paragraph 1 shall not be transmitted where:

— the Commission has already adopted a decision under the procedure provided for in Articles 906 to 909 on a case involving comparable issues of fact and of law,

— the Commission is already considering a case involving comparable issues of fact and of law.

3. The dossier submitted to the Commission shall contain all the information required for full consideration. It shall include detailed information on the behaviour of the operator concerned, and in particular on his professional experience, good faith and diligence. This assessment shall be accompanied by all information that may demonstrate that the operator acted in good faith. The dossier shall also include a statement, signed by the applicant for repayment or remission, certifying that he has read the dossier and either stating that he has nothing to add or listing all the additional information that he considers should be included.

4. As soon as it receives the dossier the Commission shall inform the Member State concerned accordingly.

5. Should it be found that the information supplied by the Member State is not sufficient to enable a decision to be taken on the case concerned in full knowledge of the facts, the Commission may request that additional information be supplied.

6. Where one of the following situations occurs the Commission shall return the dossier to the customs authority and the procedure referred to in Articles 906 to 909 shall be deemed never to have been initiated:

— the dossier shows that there is a disagreement between the customs authority that has transmitted the dossier and the person who signed the statement referred to in paragraph 3 as regards the account of the facts,

— the dossier is obviously incomplete since it contains nothing that would justify its consideration by the Commission,

— under paragraphs 1 and 2, the dossier should not be transmitted,

— the existence of a customs debt has not been established,

— new information relating to the dossier and of a nature to alter substantially its presentation of the facts or legal assessment has been transmitted by the customs authority to the Commission while it is considering the dossier.]

NOTES

Substituted by Commission Regulation (EC) 1335/2003, Art 1, para 6.

[Article 906

The Commission shall forward to the Member States a copy of the dossier referred to in Article 905(3) within 15 days of the date on which it received that dossier.

Consideration of the case in question shall be included as soon as possible on the agenda of a meeting of the group of experts provided for in Article 907.]

NOTES
  Substituted by Commission Regulation (EC) 1335/2003, Art 1, para 6.

[Article 906a

Where, at any time in the procedure provided for in Articles 906 and 907, the Commission intends to take a decision unfavourable towards the applicant for repayment or remission, it shall communicate its objections to him/her in writing, together with all the documents on which it bases those objections. The applicant for repayment or remission shall express his/her point of view in writing within a period of one month from the date on which the objections were sent. If he/she does not give his/her point of view within that period, he/she shall be deemed to have waived the right to express a position.]

NOTES
  Inserted by Commission Regulation (EC) 1677/98, Art 1, para 9.

[Article 907

After consulting a group of experts composed of representatives of all Member States, meeting within the framework of the Committee to consider the case in question, the Commission shall decide whether or not the situation which has been considered justifies repayment or remission.

That decision shall be taken within nine months of the date on which the case referred to in Article 905(3) is received by the Commission. However, where the declaration or detailed assessment of the operator's behaviour referred to in Article 905(3) is not included in the dossier, the nine months shall be counted only from the date of receipt of these documents by the Commission. The customs authority and the person applying for repayment or remission shall be notified accordingly.

Where the Commission has found it necessary to ask for additional information from the Member State in order to reach its decision, the nine months shall be extended by a period equivalent to that between the date the Commission sent the request for additional information and the date it received that information. The person applying for repayment or remission shall be notified of the extension.

Where the Commission conducts investigations itself in order to reach a decision, the nine months shall be extended by the time necessary to complete the investigations. Such an extension shall not exceed nine months. The Commission shall notify the customs authority and the person concerned of the dates on which investigations are opened and closed.

Where the Commission has notified the person applying for repayment or remission of its objections in accordance with Article 906a, the period of nine months shall be extended by one month.]

NOTES
  Substituted by Commission Regulation (EC) 1335/2003, Art 1, para 7.

[Article 908

1. The Member State concerned shall be notified of the decision referred to in Article 907 as soon as possible and in any event within one month of the expiry of the period specified in that Article.

The Commission shall notify the Member States of the decisions it has adopted in order to help customs authorities to reach decisions on cases involving comparable issues of fact and law.

2. The decision-making authority shall decide whether to grant or refuse the application made to it on the basis of the Commission's decision notified in accordance with paragraph 1.

3. Where it is established by the decision referred to in Article 907 that the circumstances under consideration justify repayment or remission, the Commission may specify the conditions under which the Member States may repay or remit duties in cases involving comparable issues of fact and of law.]

NOTES

Substituted by Commission Regulation (EC) 1335/2003, Art 1, para 7.

Article 909

If the Commission fails to take a decision within the time limit set in Article 907, or fails to notify a decision to the Member State in question within the time limit set in Article 908, the decision-making customs authority shall grant the application.

CHAPTER 4
ADMINISTRATIVE ASSISTANCE BETWEEN THE CUSTOMS AUTHORITIES OF THE MEMBER STATES

Article 910

In the cases referred to in Article 885(2), the decision-making customs authority shall send the supervising customs office two copies of its request made out in writing on a form conforming to the model in Annex 112. The request shall be accompanied by originals or copies of the application for repayment or remission and of all documents necessary to enable the supervising customs office to obtain the information or carry out the checks requested.

Article 911

1. Within two weeks of the date of receipt of the request the supervising customs office shall obtain the information or carry out the checks requested by the decision-making customs authority. It shall enter the results obtained in the portion of the original of the document referred to in Article 910 reserved for that purpose and shall return the said document to the decision-making customs authority together with all the documents forwarded to it.

2. Where it is unable to obtain the information or carry out the checks requested within the two-week period referred to in paragraph 1, the supervising customs office shall acknowledge receipt of the request submitted to it within that period by returning to the decision-making customs authority the copy of the document referred to in Article 910 duly annotated.

Article 912

The implementing customs office shall send the certificate referred to in Article 887(5) to the decision-making customs authority on a form conforming to the specimen in Annex 113.

[PART IVA
CONTROLS ON THE USE AND/OR DESTINATION OF GOODS

Article 912a

1. For purposes of this part—
  (a) "competent authorities" means: the customs authorities or any other Member State authority responsible for applying this part;
  (b) "office" means: the customs office or body responsible at local level for applying this part;

(c)   "T5 control copy" means: a T5 original and copy made out on forms corresponding to the specimen in Annex 63 accompanied where appropriate by either one or more original and copy forms T5 bis corresponding to the specimen in Annex 64 or one or more original and copy loading list T5 corresponding to the specimen in Annex 65. The forms shall be printed and completed in accordance with the explanatory note in Annex 66 and, where appropriate, any additional instructions laid down in other Community rules.

2.   Where application of Community rules concerning goods imported into, exported from, or moving within the customs territory of the Community is subject to proof of compliance with the conditions provided for or prescribed by that measure for the use and/or destination of the goods, such proof shall be furnished by production of a T5 control copy, completed and used in accordance with the provisions of this part.

3.   All goods entered on a given T5 control copy shall be loaded on a single means of transport within the meaning of the second subparagraph of [Article 349(1)], intended for a single consignee and the same use and/or destination.

The competent authorities may allow the form corresponding to the specimen in Annex 65 to be replaced by T5 loading lists made out by an integrated electronic or automatic data-processing system or by descriptive lists drawn up for the purposes of carrying out dispatch/export formalities which include all the particulars provided for in the Annex 65 specimen form, provided such lists are designed and completed in such a way that they can be used without difficulty by the authorities in question and offer all the safeguards considered appropriate by those authorities.

4.   In addition to obligations imposed under specific rules, any person who signs a T5 control copy shall be required to put the goods described in that document to the declared use and/or dispatch the goods to the declared destination.

That person shall be liable in the event of the misuse by any person of any T5 control copy which the former has drawn up.

5.   By way of derogation from paragraph 2 and unless otherwise provided in the Community rules requiring a control on the use and/or destination of the goods, each Member State shall have the right to require that the proof of goods having been assigned to the use and/or destination provided for or prescribed shall be furnished in accordance with a national procedure, provided that the goods do not leave its territory before they have been assigned to that use and/or destination.

NOTES

Inserted, together with Arts 912b to 912g by Commission Regulation (EC) 1602/2000, Art 1, para 12.

Para 3: words substituted by Commission Regulation (EC) 444/2002, Art 1, para 25.

Article 912b

1.   A T5 control copy shall be made out in one original and at least one copy. Each of their forms must bear the original signature of the person concerned and include all the particulars regarding the description of goods and any additional information required by the provisions relating to the Community rules imposing the control.

2.   Where the Community rules imposing the control provide for the lodging of a guarantee, it shall be lodged—

—   at the agency designated by those rules or, failing that, at either the office which issues the T5 control copy or another office designated for that purpose by the Member State to which that office belongs, and

—   in that manner laid down in those rules or, failing that, by the authorities of that Member State.

In that case, one of the following phrases shall be entered in box 106 of the T5 form—

— Garantía constituida por un importe de . . . euros
— Sikkerhed på . . . EUR
— Sicherheit in Höhe von . . . EURO geleistet
— Καταεθεισα εγγυηση ποσου . . . ΕΡΩ
— Guarantee of EUR . . . lodged
— Garantie d'un montant de . . . euros déposée
— Garanzia dell'importo di . . . EURO depositata
— Zekerheid voor . . . euro
— Entregue garantia num montante de . . . EURO
— Annettu . . . euron suuruinen vakuus
— Säkerhet ställd till et belopp av . . . euro;
[— Celní dluh ve výši . . . EUR zajištěn,
— Esitatud tagatis EUR . . .,
— Galvojums par EUR . . . iesniegts,
— Pateikta garantija . . . EUR sumai,
— . . . EUR vámbiztosíték letétbe helyezve,
— Garanzija fuq l-EUR . . . saret,
— Złoono zabezpieczenie w wysokoci . . . EUR,
— Položeno zavarovanje v višini . . . EUR,
— Poskytnuté zabezpečenie vo výške . . . EUR.]
[— (for original text, refer to Commission Regulation (EC) 1792/2006 (OJ L 362, 20.12.06, p 1)),
— Garantie depus în sum de . . . EUR]

3. Where the Community rules imposing the control specify a time limit for assigning the goods to a particular use and/or destination, the statement "Time limit of . . . days for completion" in box 104 of the T5 form shall be completed.

4. Where the goods are moving under a customs procedure, the T5 control copy shall be issued by the customs office where the goods are dispatched.

The document for the produce shall bear a reference to the T5 control copy issued. Similarly, box 109 of the T5 form issued shall contain a reference to the document used for the procedure.

5. Where the goods are not placed under a customs procedure, the T5 control copy shall be issued by the office where the goods are dispatched.

One of the following phrases shall be entered in box 109 of the T5 form—

— Mercancías no incluidas en un régimen aduanero
— Ingen forsendelsesprocedure
— Nicht in einem Zollverfahren befindliche Waren
— Εμπορευματα εκτοζ τελωνειακου καθεστωτοζ
— Goods not covered by a customs procedure
— Marchandises hors régime douanier
— Merci non vincolate ad un regime doganale
— Geen douaneregeling
— Mercadorias não sujeitas a regime aduaneiro
— Tullimenettelyn ulkopuolella olevat tavarat
— Varorna omfattas inte av något tullförfarande;
[— Zboží mimo celní režim,
— Kaup, millele ei rakendata tolliprotseduuri,
— Preces, kurm nav piemrota muitas procedūra,
— Preks, kurioms netaikoma muitins procedūra,

—   Vámeljárás alá nem vont áruk,
—   Oetti mhux koperti bi proedura tad-Dwana,
—   Towary nieobjete procedura celn,
—   Blago ni vključeno v carinski postopek,
—   Tovar nie je v colnom režime.]
[—   *(for original text, refer to Commission Regulation (EC) 1792/2006 (OJ L 362, 20.12.06, p 1)),*
—   Mrfuri care nu sunt acoperite de un regim vamal]

6. The T5 control copy shall be endorsed by the office referred to in paragraphs 4 and 5. Such endorsement shall comprise the following, to appear in box A (office of departure) of those documents—

(a)   in the case of the T5 form, the name and stamp of the office, the signature of the competent person, the date of authentication and a registration number which may be pre-printed;

(b)   in the case of the T5bis form or T5 loading list, the registration number appearing on the T5 form. That number shall be inserted either by means of a stamp incorporating the name of the office or by hand; in the latter case it shall be accompanied by the official stamp of the said office.

7. Unless otherwise provided in the Community rules requiring a control on the use and/or destination of the goods, [Article 357] shall apply *mutatis mutandis*. The office referred to in paragraphs 4 and 5 shall verify the consignment and shall complete and endorse box D, "Control by office of departure", on the front of the T5 form.

8. The office referred to in paragraphs 4 and 5 shall keep a copy of each T5 control copy. The originals of these documents shall be returned to the person concerned as soon as all administrative formalities have been carried out, and boxes A (Office of departure), and B (Return to . . .) of the T5 form, duly completed.

[9. Article 360 shall apply *mutatis mutandis*.]

NOTES

Inserted as noted to Art 912a.

Para 2: words inserted by the 2003 Act of Accession Annex II(19)(A)(II), para 35. Final two entries inserted by Commission Regulation (EC) 1792/2006, Art 1, Annex, Part 11(A)(34).

Para 5: words inserted by the 2003 Act of Accession Annex II(19)(A)(II), para 36. Final two entries inserted by Commission Regulation (EC) 1792/2006, Art 1, Annex, Part 11(A)(35)

Para 7: words substituted by Commission Regulation (EC) 444/2002, Art 1, para 26(a).

Para 9: substituted by Commission Regulation (EC) 444/2002, Art 1, para 26(b).

Article 912c

1. The goods and the originals of the T5 control copies shall be presented at the office of destination.

Unless otherwise provided in the Community rules requiring a control on the use and/or destination of the goods, the office of destination may allow the goods to be delivered direct to the consignee on such conditions as it shall lay down to enable it to carry out its control on or after arrival of the goods.

Any person who presents a T5 control copy and the consignment to which it relates to the office of destination may, on request, obtain a receipt made out on a form corresponding to the specimen in Annex 47. The receipt may not replace the T5 control copy.

2.   Where the Community rules require a control on the exit of goods from the customs territory of the Community—

— for goods leaving by sea, the office of destination shall be the office responsible for the port where the goods are loaded on the vessel operating a service other than a regular shipping service within the meaning of Article 313a,

— for goods leaving by air, the office of destination shall be the office responsible for the international Community airport, within the meaning of Article 190(b), at which the goods are loaded on an aircraft bound for an airport outside the Community,

[— for goods leaving by any other modes of transport, the office of destination shall be the office of exit referred to in Article 793(2).]

3.   The office of destination shall carry out controls on the use and/or destination provided for or prescribed. It shall register the particulars of the T5 control copy by keeping a copy of the said document where appropriate, and the result of the controls which have been carried out.

4.   The office of destination shall return the original of the T5 control copy to the address shown in box B ("Return to . . .") of the T5 form once all the required formalities have been completed and annotations made.

NOTES

Inserted as noted to Art 912a.

Para 2: words substituted by Commission Regulation (EC) 444/2002, Art 1, para 27.

Article 912d

1.   Where the issue of the T5 control copy calls for a guarantee under Article 912b(2), the provisions of paragraphs 2 and 3 shall apply—

2.   Where quantities of goods have not been assigned to the prescribed use and/or destination, by the expiry of a specified time limit under Article 912b(3) where applicable, the competent authorities shall take the necessary steps to enable the office referred to in Article 912b(2) to recover, where applicable from the guarantee lodged, the proportion corresponding to those quantities.

However, at the request of the person concerned, those authorities may decide to collect, where applicable from the guarantee, an amount obtained by taking the proportion of the guarantee corresponding to the amount of goods not assigned to the specified use and/or destination by the end of the prescribed time limit, and multiplying that by the quotient obtained from dividing the number of days over the time limit required for those quantities to be assigned their use and/or destination by the length, in days, of the timelimit.

This paragraph shall not apply where the person concerned can show that the goods in question have been lost through *force majeure*.

3.   If, within six months either of the date on which the T5 control copy was issued or of expiry of the time limit entered in box 104 of the T5 form under "Time limit of . . ., days for completion", as the case may be, that copy, duly endorsed by the office of destination, has not been received by the return office specified in box B of the document, the competent authorities shall take the necessary steps to require the office referred to in Article 912b(2) to recover the guarantee provided for in that Article.

This paragraph shall not apply where the delay in returning the T5 control copy was not attributable to the person concerned.

4.   The provisions of paragraphs 2 and 3 shall apply unless otherwise provided in the Community rules requiring a control on the use and/or destination of the goods and, in any event, without prejudice to the provisions concerning the customs debt.

NOTES
Inserted as noted to Art 912a.

Article 912e

1. Unless otherwise provided in the Community rules requiring a control on the use and/or destination of the goods, the T5 control copy and the consignment which it accompanies may be divided before completion of the procedure for which the form was issued. Consignments resulting from such division may themselves be further divided.

2. The office at which the division takes place shall issue, in accordance with Article 912b, an extract of the T5 control copy for each part of the divided consignment.

Each extract shall contain, inter alia, the additional information shown in boxes 100, 104, 105, 106 and 107 of the initial T5 control copy, and shall state the net mass and net quantity of the goods to which that extract applies. One of the following phrases shall be entered in box 106 of the T5 form used for each extract—

— Extracto del ejemplar de control T5 inicial (número de registro, fecha, oficina y país de expedición): . . .

— Udskrift af det oprindelige kontroleksemplar T5 (registreringsnummer, dato, sted og udstedelsesland): . . .

— Auszug aus dem ursprnüglichen Kontrollexemplar T5 (Registriernummer, Datum, ausstellende Stelle und Ausstellungsland): . . .

— Απόσπασμα του αρχικου αντιτυπου ελεγχου T5 (αριθμοζ πρωτοκολλου, ημερομηνια, τελωνειο κα ιχωρα εκδοσηζ)

— Extract of the initial T5 control copy (registration number, date, office and country of issue): . . .

— Extrait de l'exemplaire de contrôle T5 initial (numéro d'enregistrement, date, bureau et pays de délivrance): . . .

— Estratto dell'esemplare di controllo T5 originale (numero di registrazione, data, ufficio e paese di emissione): . . .

— Uittreksel van het oorspronkelijke controle-exemplaar T5 (registratienummer, datum, kantoor en land van afgifte): . . .

— Extracto do exemplar de controlo T5 inicial (número de registo, data, estância e país de emissão): . . .

— Ote alun perin annetusta T5–valvontakappaleesta (kirjaamisnumero, antamispäivämäärä, -toimipaikka ja -maa): . . .

— Utdrag ur ursprungligt kontrollexemplar T5 (registreringsnummer, datum, utfärdande kontor och land): . . .

[— Výpis z puvodního kontrolního výtisku T5 (evidenční číslo, datum, úřad a země vystavení): . . .,

— Väljavõte esialgsest T5 kontrolleksemplarist (registreerimisnumber, kuupäev, väljaandnud asutus ja riik): . . .,

— Izraksts no skotnj T5 kontroleksemplra (reg' istrcijas numurs, datums, izdevja iestde un valsts): . . .,

— Išrašas iš pirminio T5 kontrolinio egzemplioriaus (registracijos numeris, data, išdavusi istaiga ir valstyb): . . .,

— Az eredeti T5 ellenőrző példány kivonata (nyilvántartási szám, kiállítás dátuma, a kiállító ország és hivatal neve): . . .,

— Estratt tal-kopja ta' kontroll tat-T5 inizjali (numru ta' registrazzjoni, data, uffiju u pajji fejn ie marug id-dokument),

1698

— Wyciag z wyjciowej karty kontrolnej T5 (numer ewidencyjny, data, urzad i kraj wystawienia): . . .,

— Izpisek iz prvotnega kontrolnega izvoda T5 (evidenčna številka, datum, urad in država izdaje): . . .,

— Výpis z pôvodného kontrolného výtlacku T5 (registračné číslo, dátum, vydávajúci úrad a krajina vydania): . . .]

— *(for original text, refer to Commission Regulation (EC) 1792/2006 (OJ L 362, 20.12.06, p 1))*: . . .,

— Extras din exemplarul de control T5 initial (numr de înregistrare, data, biroul si tara emitente): . . .'.

Box B "Return to . . ." of the T5 form shall contain the information shown in the corresponding box of the initial T5 form.

One of the following phrases shall be entered in box J "Controls on the use and/or destination" of the initial T5 form—

— . . . (número) extractos expedidos — copias adjuntas
— . . . (antal) udstedte udskrifter — kopier vedføjet
— . . . (Anzahl) Auszüge ausgestellt — Durchschriften liegen bei
— . . .(αριθμοζ) εκδοθεν αποσματα — συνημμενα αντιγραψα
— . . . (number) extracts issued — copies attached
— . . . (nombre) extraits délivrés — copies ci-jointes
— . . . (numero) estratti rilasciati — copie allegate
— . . . (aantal) uittreksels afgegeven — kopieën bijgevoegd
— . . . (número) de extractos emitidos — cópias juntas
— Annettu . . . (lukumäärä) otetta — jäljennökset liitteenä
— . . . (antal) utdrag utfärdade — kopier bifogas;
[[— (počet) vyhotovených výpisov – kópie priložené],
— väljavõtted . . . (arv) – koopiad lisatud,
— Izsniegti . . . (skaits) izraksti – kopijas pielikum,
— Išduota . . . (skaičius) išrašu – kopijos pridedamos,
— . . . (számú) kivonat kiadva – másolatok csatolva,
— . . . (numru) estratti marua kopji mehmua,
— . . . (ilo) wydanych wyciagów – kopie załaczone,
— . . . (število) izdani izpiski – izvodi priloženi,
— . . . (počet) vydaných výpisov – kópie priložené.]
[— . . . *(for original text, refer to Commission Regulation (EC) 1792/2006 (OJ L 362, 20.12.06, p 1))*,
— . . .(numrul) de extrase emise — copii anexate]

The initial T5 control copy shall be returned without delay to the address shown in box B "Return to . . ." of the T5 form, accompanied by copies of the extracts issued.

The office where the division takes place shall keep a copy of the initial T5 control copy and extracts. The originals of the extract T5 control copies shall accompany each part of the divided consignment to the corresponding offices of destination where the provisions referred to in Article 912c shall be applied.

3. In the case of further division pursuant to paragraph 1, paragraph 2 shall be applied *mutatis mutandis.*

NOTES

Inserted as noted to Art 912a.

Para 2: words inserted by the 2003 Act of Accession Annex II(19)(A)(II), paras 37, 38; words "(počet) vyhotovených výpisov – kópie priložené" substituted by Commission Regulation 883/2005, Art 1, para 18, with effect from 1 May 2004. Final two entries in second and fourth sub-paras inserted by Commission Regulation (EC) 1792/2006, Art 1, Annex, Part 11(A)(36), (37).

Article 912f

1. The T5 control copy may be issued retrospectively on condition that—

- the person concerned is not responsible for the failure to apply for or to issue that document when the goods were dispatched or he can furnish proof that the failure is not due to any deception or obvious negligence on his part,

- the person concerned furnishes proof that the T5 control copy relates to goods in respect of which all the formalities have been completed,

- the person concerned produces the documents required for the issue of the said T5 control copy,

- it is established to the satisfaction of the competent authorities that the retrospective issue of the T5 control copy cannot give rise to the securing of financial benefits which would not be warranted in the light of the procedure used, the customs status of the goods and their use and/or destination.

Where the T5 control copy is issued retrospectively, the T5 form shall contain in red one of the following phrases—

- Expedido a *posteriori*
- Udstedt efterfølgende
- nachträglich ausgestellt
- Εκδοθν εκ των υστρων,
— Issued retrospectively
  — Délivré a posteriori
  — Rilasciato a posteriori
  — achteraf afgegeven
  — Emitido a posteriori
  — Annettu jälkikäteen
  — Utfärdat i efterhand
  [— Vystaveno dodatečně,
  — Välja antud tagasiulatuvalt,
  — Izsniegts retrospektvi,
  — Retrospektyvusis išdavimas,
  [— Kiadva visszamenőleges hatállyal],
  — Marug retrospettivament,
  — Wystawiona retrospektywnie,
  — Izdano naknadno,
  [— Vyhotovené dodatočne].]
  [—   И ,
  —   Eliberat ulteriorEmis a posteriori]

and the person concerned shall enter on it the identity of the means of transport by which the goods were dispatched, the date of departure and, if appropriate, the date on which the goods were produced at the office of destination.

2. Duplicates of T5 control copies and extract T5 control copies may be issued by the issuing office at the request of the person concerned in the event of the loss of the originals. The duplicate shall bear the stamp of the office and the signature of the competent official and in red block letters, one of the following words—

— DUPLICADO
— DUPLIKAT

— DUPLIKAT
— "ΑΝΤΙΓΡΑΦΟ",
— DUPLICATE
— DUPLICATA
— DUPLICATO
— DUPLICAAT
— SEGUNDA VIA
— KAKSOISKAPPALE
— DUPLIKAT
[— DUPLIKÁT,
— DUPLIKAAT,
— DUBLIKĀTS,
— DUBLIKATAS,
— MÁSODLAT,
— DUPLIKAT,
— DUPLIKAT,
— DVOJNIK,
— DUPLIKÁT.]
[— (*for original text, refer to Commission Regulation (EC) 1792/2006 (OJ L 362, 20.12.06, p 1)*),
— DUPLICAT]

3.   T5 control copies issued retrospectively and duplicates may be annotated by the office of destination only where that office establishes that the goods covered by the document in question have been assigned to the use and/or destination provided for or prescribed by the Community rules.

NOTES
Inserted as noted to Art 912a.
Para 1: words inserted by the 2003 Act of Accession Annex II(19)(A)(II), paras 39, 40; words "Kiadva visszamenőleges hatállyal" and "Vyhotovené dodatočne" in square brackets substituted by Commission Regulation (EC) 883/2005, Art 1, para 19, with effect from 1 May 2004. Final two entries inserted by Commission Regulation (EC) 1792/2006, Art 1, Annex, Part 11(A)(38).
Para 2: words inserted by the 2003 Act of Accession Annex II(19)(A)(II), paras 39, 40. Final two entries inserted by Commission Regulation (EC) 1792/2006, Art 1, Annex, Part 11(A)(39).

Article 912g
1.   The competent authorities of each Member State may, within the scope of their competence, authorise any person who fulfils the conditions laid down in paragraph 4 and who intends to consign goods in respect of which a T5 control copy must be made out (hereinafter referred as "the authorised consignor" not to present at the office of departure either the goods concerned or the T5 control copy covering them.
2.   With regard to the T5 control copy used by authorised consignors, the competent authorities may—
   (a)   prescribe the use of forms bearing a distinctive mark as a means of identifying the authorised consignors;
   (b)   stipulate that box A of the form, "Office of departure"—
      — be stamped in advance with the stamp of the office of departure and signed by an official of that office; or
      — be stamped by the authorised consignor with a special approved metal stamp conforming to the specimen in Annex 62, or

— be pre-printed with the imprint of the special stamp conforming to the specimen in Annex 62 if printed by a printer approved for that purpose. This imprint may also be entered by an integrated electronic or automatic data-processing system;

(c)　authorise the authorised consignor not to sign forms stamped with the special approved stamp referred to in Annex 62 which are made out by an integrated electronic or automatic data-processing system. In this event, the space reserved for the signature of the declarant in box 110 of the forms shall contain one of the following phrases—

— Dispensa de la firma, artículo 912 octavo del Reglamento (CEE) n ° 2454/93

— Underskriftsdispensation, artikel 912g i forordning (EØF) nr. 2454/93

— Freistellung von der Unterschriftsleistung, Artikel 912g der Verordnung (EWG) Nr. 2454/93

— Απαλλαγη απο την υΠοχρεωση υΠογραψηζ, αρθρο 912 ξ του κανονισμου (EOK) αρτθ. 2454/93

— Signature waived — Article 912g of Regulation (EEC) No 2454/93

— Dispense de signature, article 912 octies du règlement (CEE) n° 2454/93

— Dispensa dalla firma, articolo 912 octies del regolamento (CEE) n. 2454/93

— Vrijstelling van ondertekening — artikel 912 octies van Verordening (EEG) nr. 2454/93

— Dispensada a assinatura, artigo 912 ° —G do Regulamento (CE) n. 2454/93

— Vapautettu allekirjoituksesta —asetuksen (ETY) N:o 2454/93 912g artikla

— Befriad från underskrift, artikel 912g i förordning (EEG) nr 2454/93

[— Podpis se nevyžaduje – článek 912g nařízení (EHS) č. 2454/93,

— Allkirjanõudest loobutud – määruse (EMÜ) nr 2454/93 artikkel 912g,

— Dergs bez paraksta – Regulas (EEK) Nr.2454/93 912.g pants,

— Leista nepasirašyti – Reglamentas (EEB) Nr. 2454/93, 912g straipsnis,

— Aláírás alól mentesítve – a 2454/93/EGK rendelet 912g. cikke,

— Firma mhux metiea – Artikolu 912g tar-Regolament (KEE) 2454/93,

— Zwolniony ze skladania podpisu – art. 912g rozporzadzenia (EWG) nr 2454/93,

— Opustitev podpisa – člen 912g člen uredbe (EGS) št. 2454/93,

— [Oslobodenie od podpisu – článok 912g nariadenia (EHS) č. 2454/93].]

[— О — ч 912 Р (ЕИО) № 2454/93,

— Dispens de semntur — Articolul 912g din Regulamentul (CEE) Nr. 2454/93]

3.　The authorised consignor shall complete the T5 control copy, entering the required particulars, including—

— in box A ("Office of departure") the date on which the goods were consigned and the number allocated to the declaration, and

— in box D ("Control by office of departure)" of the T5 form one of the endorsements—

— Procedimiento simplificado, artículo 912 octavo del Reglamento (CEE) n° 2454/93

— Forenklet fremgangsmåde, artikel 912g i forordning (EØF) nr. 2454/93

— Vereinfachtes Verfahren, Artikel 912g der Verordnung (EWG) Nr. 2454/93

— Απλουστευμενη διαδικασια, αρθρο 912 ζ του κανονισμου (EOK) αρτθ. 2454/93

— Simplified procedure —Article 912g of Regulation (EEC) No 2454/93

— Procédure simplifiée, article 912 octies du règlement (CEE) n° 2454/93

— Procedura semplificata, articolo 912 octies del regolamento (CEE) n. 2454/93

— Vereenvoudigde procedure, artikel 912 octies van Verordening (EEG) nr. 2454/93

— Procedimento simplificado, artigo 912. ° —G do Regulamento (CE) n° 2454/93

— Yksinkertaistettu menettely —asetuksen (ETY) N:o 2454/93 912g artikla

— Förenklat förfarande, artikel 912g i förordning (EEG) nr 2454/93

[— Zjednodušený postup-článek 912g Nařízení (EHS) č. 2454/93,

— Lihtsustatud tolliprotseduur – määruse (EMÜ) nr 2454/93 artikkel 912g,

— Vienkršota procedūra – Regulas (EEK) Nr.2454/93 912.g pants,

— Supaprastinta procedūra – Reglamentas (EEB) Nr. 2454/93, 912g straipsnis,

— Egyszersített eljárás – a 2454/93/EGK rendelet 912g. cikke,

— Proedura simplifikata – Artikolu 912g tar-Regolament (KEE) 2454/93,

— Procedura uproszczona – art. 912g rozporzadzenia (EWG) nr 2454/93,

— Poenostavljen postopek – člen 912g uredbe (EGS) št. 2454/93,

— Zjednodušený postup – článok 912g nariadenia (EHS) č. 2454/93.]

[— (for original text, refer to Commission Regulation (EC) 1792/2006 (OJ L 362, 20.12.06, p 1)),

— Procedur simplicat – Articolul 912g din Regulamentul (CEE) Nr. 2454/93]

and, where appropriate, particulars of the period within which the goods must be presented at the office of destination, the identification measures applied and references to the dispatch document.

That copy, duly completed and, where appropriate, signed by the approved consignor, shall be deemed to have been issued by the office indicated by the stamp referred to in paragraph 2(b).

After dispatch of the goods, the authorised consignor shall without delay send the office of departure a copy of the T5 control copy, together with any document on the basis of which the T5 control copy was drawn up.

Part III

4. The authorisation referred to in paragraph 1 shall be granted only to persons who frequently consign goods, whose records enable the competent authorities to check on their operations and who have not committed serious or repeated offences against the legislation in force.

The authorisation shall specify in particular—

— the office or offices competent to act as offices of departure for consignments,

— the period within which, and the procedure by which, the authorised consignor is to inform the office of departure of the consignment to be sent, in order that the office may carry out any controls, including any required by Community rules, before the departure of the goods,

— the period within which the goods must be presented at the office of destination; this period shall be determined according to the conditions of transport or by Community rules,

— the measures to be taken to identify the goods, which may include the use of special seals approved by the competent authorities and affixed by the authorised consignor,

— the means for providing guarantees where the issue of the T5 control copy is conditional thereon.

5. The authorised consignor shall take all necessary measures to ensure the safekeeping of the special stamp or of the forms bearing the imprint of the stamp of the office of departure or the imprint of the special stamp.

The authorised consignor shall bear all the consequences, in particular the financial consequences, of any errors, omissions or other faults in the T5 control copies which he draws up or in the performance of the procedures incumbent on him under the authorisation provided for in paragraph 1.

In the event of the misuse by any person of T5 control copy forms stamped in advance with the stamp of the office of departure or with the special stamp, the authorised consignor shall be liable, without prejudice to any criminal proceedings, for the payment of duties and other charges which have not been paid and for the repayment of any financial benefits which have been wrongly obtained following such misuse, unless he can satisfy the competent authorities by whom he was authorised that he took all the measures required to ensure the safekeeping of the special stamp or of the forms bearing the imprint of the stamp of the office of departure or the imprint of the special stamp.]

NOTES

Inserted as noted to Art 912a.

Para 2: words inserted by the 2003 Act of Accession Annex II(19)(A)(II), paras 41, 42; words "Oslobodenie od podpisu – článok 912g nariadenia (EHS) č. 2454/93" substituted by Commission Regulation (EC) 883/2005, Art 1, para 20, with effect from 1 May 2004. Final two entries in sub-para (c) inserted by Commission Regulation (EC) 1792/2006, Art 1, Annex, Part 11(A)(40).

Para 3: words inserted by the 2003 Act of Accession Annex II(19)(A)(II), paras 41, 42. Final two entries inserted by Commission Regulation (EC) 1792/2006, Art 1, Annex, Part 11(A)(41).

PART V
FINAL PROVISIONS

Article 913

NOTES

Repeals Regulation (EEC) 37/70, OJ L 7, 10.1.70, p 6; Regulation (EEC) 2632/70, OJ L 279, 24.12.70, p 35; Regulation (EEC) 315/71, OJ L 36, 13.2.71, p 10; Regulation (EEC) 861/71, OJ L 95, 28.4.71, p 11; Regulation (EEC) 3103/73, OJ L 315, 16.11.73, p 34; Commission Regulation (EEC) 2945/76, OJ L 335, 4.12.76, p 1; Commission Regulation (EEC) 137/79, OJ L 20, 27.1.79, p 1; Commission Regulation (EEC) 1494/80, OJ L 154, 21.6.80, p 3; Commission Regulation (EEC) 1495/80, OJ L 154, 21.6.80, p 14; Commission Regulation (EEC) 1496/80, OJ L 154, 21.6.80, p 16; Commission Regulation (EEC) 1574/80, OJ L 161, 26.6.80, p 3; Commission Regulation (EEC) 3177/80, OJ L 335, 12.12.80, p 1; Commission Regulation (EEC) 3179/80, OJ L 335, 12.12.80, p 62; Commission Regulation (EEC) 553/81, OJ L 59, 5.3.81, p 1; Commission Regulation (EEC) 1577/81, OJ L 154, 13.6.81, p 26; Commission Directive 82/57/EEC, OJ L 28, 5.2.82, p 38; Commission Directive 82/347/EEC, OJ L 156, 7.6.82, p 1; Commission Regulation (EEC) 3040/83, OJ L 297, 29.10.83, p 13; Commission Regulation (EEC) 3158/83, OJ L 309, 10.11.83, p 19; Commission Regulation (EEC) 1751/84, OJ L 171, 29.6.84, p 1; Commission Regulation (EEC) 3548/84, OJ L 331, 19.12.84, p 5; Commission Regulation (EEC) 1766/85, OJ L 168, 28.6.85, p 21; Commission Regulation (EEC) 3787/86, OJ L 350, 12.12.86, p 14; Commission Regulation (EEC) 3799/86, OJ L 352, 13.12.86, p 19; Commission Regulation (EEC) 2458/87, OJ L 230, 17.8.87, p 1; Commission Regulation (EEC) 4128/87, OJ L 387, 31.12.87, p 1; Commission Regulation (EEC) 4129/87, OJ L 387, 31.12.87, p 9; Commission Regulation (EEC) 4130/87, OJ L 387, 31.12.87, p 16; Commission Regulation (EEC) 4131/87, OJ L 387, 31.12.87, p 22; Commission Regulation (EEC) 4132/87, OJ L 387, 31.12.87, p 36; Commission Regulation (EEC) 4133/87, OJ L 387, 31.12.87, p 42; Commission Regulation (EEC) 4134/87, OJ L 387, 31.12.87, p 48; Commission Regulation (EEC) 4135/87, OJ L 387, 31.12.87, p 54; Commission Regulation (EEC) 4136/87, OJ L 387, 31.12.87, p 60; Commission Regulation (EEC) 4137/87, OJ L 387, 31.12.87, p 63; Commission Regulation (EEC) 4138/87, OJ L 387, 31.12.87, p 67; Commission Regulation (EEC) 4139/87, OJ L 387, 31.12.87, p 70; Commission Regulation (EEC) 4140/87, OJ L 387, 31.12.87, p 74; Commission Regulation (EEC) 4141/87, OJ L 387, 31.12.87, p 76; Commission Regulation (EEC) 4142/87, OJ L 387, 31.12.87, p 82; Commission Regulation (EEC) 693/88, OJ L 77, 22.3.88, p 77; Commission Regulation (EEC) 809/88, OJ L 86, 30.3.88, p 1; Commission Regulation (EEC) 4027/88, OJ L 355, 23.12.88, p 22; Commission Regulation (EEC) 288/89, OJ L 33, 4.2.89, p 23; Commission Regulation (EEC) 597/89, OJ L 65, 9.3.89, p 11; Commission Regulation (EEC) 2071/89, OJ L 196, 12.7.89, p 24; Commission Regulation (EEC) 3850/89, OJ L 374, 22.12.89, p 8; Commission Regulation (EEC) 2561/90, OJ L 246, 10.9.90, p 1; Commission Regulation (EEC) 2562/90, OJ L 246, 10.9.90, p 33; Commission Regulation (EEC) 2883/90, OJ L 276, 6.10.90, p 13; Commission Regulation (EEC) 2884/90, OJ L 276, 6.10.90, p 14; Commission Regulation (EEC) 3561/90, OJ L 347, 12.12.90, p 10; Commission Regulation (EEC) 3620/90, OJ L 351, 15.12.90, p 25; Commission Regulation (EEC) 3672/90, OJ L 356, 19.12.90, p 30; Commission Regulation (EEC) 3716/90, OJ L 358, 21.12.90, p 48; Commission Regulation (EEC) 3796/90, OJ L 365, 28.12.90, p 17; Commission Regulation (EEC) 1364/91, OJ L 130, 25.5.91, p 18; Commission Regulation (EEC) 1365/91, OJ L 130, 25.5.91, p 28; Commission Regulation (EEC) 1593/91, OJ L 148, 13.6.91, p 11; Commission Regulation (EEC) 1656/91, OJ L 151, 16.5.91, p 39; Commission Regulation (EEC) 2164/91, OJ L 201, 24.7.91, p 16; Commission Regulation (EEC) 2228/91, OJ L 210, 31.7.91, p 1; Commission Regulation (EEC) 2249/91, OJ L 204, 27.7.91, p 31; Commission Regulation (EEC) 2365/91, OJ L 216, 3.8.91, p 24; Commission Regulation (EEC) 3717/91, OJ L 351, 20.12.91, p 23; Commission Regulation (EEC) 343/92, OJ L 38, 14.2.92, p 1; Commission Regulation (EEC) 1214/92, OJ L 132, 16.5.92, p 1; Commission Regulation (EEC) 1823/92, OJ L 185, 4.7.92, p 8; Commission Regulation (EEC) 2453/92, OJ L 249, 28.8.92, p 1; Commission Regulation (EEC) 2674/92, OJ L 271, 16.9.92, p 1; Commission Regulation (EEC) 2713/92, OJ L 18.9.92, p 11; Commission Regulation (EEC) 3269/92, OJ L 326, 12.11.92, p 11; Commission Regulation (EEC) 3566/92, OJ L 362, 11.12.92, p 11; Commission Regulation (EEC) 3689/92, OJ L 374, 22.12.92, p

14; Commission Regulation (EEC) 3691/92, OJ L 374, 22.12.92, p 25; Commission Regulation (EEC) 3710/92, OJ L 378, 23.12.92, p 9; Commission Regulation (EEC) 3903/92, OJ L 393, 31.12.92, p 1.

Article 914

References to the provisions repealed shall be understood as referring to this Regulation.

Article 915

This Regulation shall enter into force on the third day following its publication in the *Official Journal of the European Communities*.

It shall apply from 1 January 1994.

. . . .

This Regulation shall be binding in its entirety and directly applicable in all Member States.

NOTES

Words revoked by Commission Regulation (EC) No 1875/2006, Art 1(69) with effect from 26 December 2006.

ANNEXES

ANNEXES

ANNEXES

Facsimiles of forms and diagrams in these Annexes are reproduced with the permission of the Office for Official Publications of the European Communities.

ANNEX 1

Part III

▼ M24

ANNEX 1

MODEL OF TARIFF INFORMATION (BTI) NOTIFICATION FORM

EUROPEAN COMMUNITY – BINDING TARIFF INFORMATION **BTI**

1	1 Competent customs authority	2 BTI reference

3 Holder (name and address) confidential	4 Date of start of validity

COPY FOR HOLDER

Important notice

Without prejudice to the provisions of Article 12 (4) and (5) of Council Regulation (EEC) No 2913/92 this BTI remains valid for 6 years as from the date of start of validity.

The information supplied will be stored on a database of the Commission of the European Communities for the purpose of the application of Commission Regulation (EEC) No 2454/93 and the data of the BTI, including any photograph(s), sketche(s), brochure(s), etc., but with the exception of the information contained in boxes 3 and 8 may be disclosed to the public on the ...

The holder shall have the right to appeal against this BTI.

5 Date and reference of the application

6 Classification of the goods in the customs nomenclature

7 Description of the goods

SPECIMEN

8 Commercial denomination and additional information   confidential

This version of the form may not be used or submitted instead of an official form

9 Justification of the classification of the goods

10 This BTI has been issued on the basis of the following material provided by the applicant:

Description ☐   Brochures ☐   Photos ☐   Samples ☐   Other ☐

Place   Signature

Date

Stamp

© European Communities Official Journal L 253, 11/10/1993 Annex 1

(Copies 2 and 3 omitted.)

▼ M24

ANNEX 1

MODEL OF TARIFF INFORMATION (BTI) NOTIFICATION FORM

EUROPEAN COMMUNITY – BINDING TARIFF INFORMATION **BTI**

1	1 Competent customs authority	2 BTI reference

	3 **Holder** (name and address) confidential	4 Date of start of validity

Important notice

Without prejudice to the provisions of Article 12 (4) and (5) of Council Regulation (EEC) No 2913/92 this BTI remains valid for 6 years as from the date of start of validity.

The information supplied will be stored on a database of the Commission of the European Communities for the purpose of the application of Commission Regulation (EEC) No 2454/93 and the data of the BTI, including any photograph(s), sketche(s), brochure(s), etc., but with the exception of the information contained in boxes 3 and 8 may be disclosed to the public on the

The holder shall have the right to appeal against this BTI.

5 Date and reference of the application

6 Classification of the goods in the customs nomenclature

7 Description of the goods

SPECIMEN

8 Commercial denomination and additional information   confidential

This version of the form may not be used or submitted instead of an official form

9 Justification of the classification of the goods

10 This BTI has been issued on the basis of the following material provided by the applicant:

Description ▢ Brochures ▢ Photos ▢ Samples ▢ Other ▢

Place

Date

Signature

Stamp

COPY FOR HOLDER

Part III

(Copy 5 omitted.)

NOTES

Annex 1 substituted by Commission Regulation (EC) 2286/2003, Art 1, para 15, Annex I with effect from 1 February 2004.

Copies 4, 5: the letters 'CS', 'ET', 'LV', 'LT', 'HU', 'MT', 'PL, 'SK', and 'SL' inserted in Box 13 by the 2003 Act of Accession Annex II(19)(A)(II), para 43.

Copies 4, 5: the letters 'BG', 'RO' inserted in Box '13 by Commission Regulation (EC) 1792/2006, Art 1, Annex, Part 11(A)(42).

ANNEX 1A

EUROPEAN COMMUNITY	APPLICATION FOR BINDING TARIFF INFORMATION (BTI)
1. Applicant (full name and address) ☐ Telephone No: Fax No: Customs ID:	**For official use** Registration No: Place of receipt: Date of receipt: Year ☐☐☐☐ Month ☐☐ Day ☐☐ BTI application language: Images to be scanned: Yes ☐ No ... No ☐ Date of issue: Year ☐☐☐☐ Month ☐☐ Day ☐☐ Issuing officer: All samples returned: ☐
2. Holder (full name and address) (Confidential) Telephone No: Fax No: Customs ID:	**Important note** By signing the declaration the applicant accepts responsibility for the accuracy and completeness of the particulars given on this form and on any continuation sheet(s) lodged with it. The applicant accepts that this information and any photograph(s) can be stored on a database of the European Commission.
3. Agent or representative (full name and address) Telephone No: Fax No: Customs ID:	**4. Reissue of a BTI** If you are applying for the reissue of a BTI, please complete this box. BTI reference No: Valid from: Year ☐☐☐☐ Month ☐☐ Day ☐☐ Nomenclature code: ....
5. Customs nomenclature Please indicate in which nomenclature the goods are to be classified: ☐ Harmonised System (HS) ☐ Combined Nomenclature (CN) ☐ TARIC ☐ Refund nomenclature ☐ Other (specify):	**6. Type of transaction** Does this application relate to an import or export actually envisaged ? Yes ☐ No ☐ **7. Classification envisaged** Please indicate where in your view the goods are classified. Nomenclature code: ....

8. Description of the goods

Include where necessary the precise composition of the goods, the method of analysis used, the type of manufacturing process undergone, the value including the components, the use of the goods, the usual trade name and where appropriate, the packaging for retail sale in the case of sets of goods *(Please use a separate sheet if more space is required).*

NOTES

Substituted by Commission Regulation (EC) 1602/2000, Art 1, para 13, Annex I (previously inserted by Commission Regulation (EC) 12/97, Art 1, para 13, Annex I).

Box 15: letters 'CS', 'ET', 'LV', 'LT', 'HU', 'MT', 'PL', 'SK', and 'SL' inserted in Box 13 by the 2003 Act of Accession Annex II(19)(A)(II), para 44.

Box 15: letters 'BG', 'RO' inserted by Commission Regulation (EC) 1792/2006, Art 1, Annex, Part 11(A)(43).

ANNEX 1B

EUROPEAN COMMUNITY	APPLICATION FOR BINDING TARIFF INFORMATION (BTI)
1. Applicant (full name and address) Telephone No: Fax No: Customs ID:	**For official use** Registration No: Place of receipt: Date of receipt: Year ☐☐☐ Month ☐☐ Day ☐☐ BTI application language: Images to be scanned: Yes ☐ No ... No ☐ Date of Issue: Year ☐☐☐ Month ☐☐ Day ☐☐
2. Holder (full name and address) (Confidential) Telephone No: Fax No: Customs ID:	Issuing officer: All samples returned: ☐ **Important note** By signing the declaration the applicant accepts responsibility for the accuracy and completeness of the particulars given on this form and on any continuation sheet(s) lodged with it. The applicant accepts that this information and any photograph(s), sketch(es), brochure(s) etc., submitted with the application or obtained (or obtainable) by the administration, and which have not been marked in boxes 2 and 9 of the application as being confidential can be disclosed to the public via the Internet.
3. Agent or representative (full name and address) Telephone No: Fax No: Customs ID:	**4. Reissue of a BTI** If you are applying for the reissue of a BTI, please complete this box. BTI reference No: Valid from: Year ☐☐☐ Month ☐☐ Day ☐☐ Nomenclature code: ....
5. Customs nomenclature Please indicate in which nomenclature the goods are to be classified: ☐ Harmonised System (HS) ☐ Combined Nomenclature (CN) ☐ TARIC ☐ Refund nomenclature ☐ Other (specify):	**6. Type of transaction** Does this application relate to an import or export actually envisaged? Yes ☐ No ☐ **7. Classification envisaged** Please indicate where in your view the goods are classified. Nomenclature code: ....

8. Description of the goods

Include, where necessary, the precise composition of the goods, the method of analysis used, the type of manufacturing process undergone, the value (including the components), the use of the goods, the usual trade name and, where appropriate, the packaging for retail sale in the case of sets of goods *(Please use a separate sheet if more space is required)*.

9. Commercial denomination and additional information (*) (Confidential)

Please indicate which of the information, provided in accordance with box 10 of this application or obtained (or obtainable) by the administration is to be treated as confidential.

10. Samples etc.

Please indicate which, if any, of the following are enclosed with your application.

Description ☐   Brochures ☐   Photographs ☐   Samples ☐   Other ☐

Do you wish your samples to be returned?   Yes ☐   No ☐

Special costs incurred by the Customs authorities as a result of analysis, expert reports or the return of samples, may be charged to the applicant.

11. Other BTI applications and other BTI held

Please indicate if you have applied for, or been issued with, BTIs for identical or similar goods, at other Customs offices or in other Member States.

Yes ☐   No ☐   If yes, please give details and enclose a photocopy of the BTI:

Country of Application:	Country of Application:
Place of Application:	Place of Application:
Date of Application: Year ☐☐☐☐ Month ☐☐ Day ☐☐	Date of Application: Year ☐☐☐☐ Month ☐☐ Day ☐☐
BTI Reference:	BTI Reference:
Date of start of Validity: Year ☐☐☐☐ Month ☐☐ Day ☐☐	Date of start of Validity: Year ☐☐☐☐ Month ☐☐ Day ☐☐
Nomenclature Code:	Nomenclature Code:

12. BTI issued to other Holders (*)

Please indicate if you are aware of BTI for identical or similar products already issued to other holders.

Yes ☐   No ☐   If yes, please give details:

Issuing country:
BTI reference:
Date of start of validity: Year ☐☐☐☐ Month ☐☐ Day ☐☐
Nomenclature code:

13. Date and signature

Your reference:

Date: Year ☐☐☐☐ Month ☐☐ Day ☐☐

Signature:

For official use

(*) Please use a separate sheet of paper if more space is required.'

Part III

NOTES

Annex 1B substituted by Commission Regulation (EC) 2286/2003, Art 1, para 15, Annex II with effect from 1 February 2004.

[ANNEX 1C
EXPLANATORY NOTES:

1. Applicant:
Enter the full name of the applicant economic operator.

2. Legal status:
Enter the legal status as mentioned in the document of establishment.

3. Date of establishment:
Enter — with numbers — the day, month and year of establishment.

4. Address of establishment:
Enter the full address of the place where your entity was established, including the country.

5. Location of main place of business:
Enter the full address of the place of your business where the main activities are carried out.

6. Contact person:
Indicate the full name, phone and fax numbers, and e-mail address of the contact person designated by you within your company to be contacted by the customs authorities when examining the application.

7. Correspondence address:
Fill in only in case it differs from your address of establishment.

8, 9, and 10. VAT, Trader Identification and Legal registration numbers:
Enter the required numbers.
The Trader Identification Number(s) is (are) the identification number(s) registered by the customs authority(ies).
The Legal registration number is the registration number given by the company registration office.
If these numbers are the same, enter only the VAT ID number.
If the applicant has no Trader Identification Number because e.g. in the applicant's Member State this number does not exist, leave the box blank.

11. Requested type of certificate:
Make a cross in the relevant box.

12. Economic sector of activity:
Describe your activity.

13. Member States, where customs related activities are carried out:
Enter the relevant ISO alpha-2 country code(s).

14. Border crossing information:
Indicate the names of customs offices regularly used for border crossing.

15. Simplifications or facilitations already granted, certificates mentioned in Article 14k(4):
In case of simplifications already granted, indicate the type of simplification, the relevant customs procedure, and the authorisation number. The relevant customs procedure shall be entered in the form of the codes used in the second or third subdivision of Box 1 of the single administrative document.

In case of facilitations already granted, indicate the number of the certificate.

In case the applicant is the holder of one or more certificates mentioned in Article 14k(4), indicate the type and the number of the certificate(s).

16, 17 and 18.   Offices for documentations/main accounts:

Enter the full addresses of the relevant offices. If the offices have the same address, fill in only Box 16.

19.   Name, date and signature of the applicant:

Signature: the signatory should add his capacity. The signatory should always be the person who represents the applicant as a whole.

Name: name of the applicant and the stamp of the applicant.

Number of annexes: the applicant shall give the following general information:

1. Overview of the principal owners/shareholders, stating names and addresses and their proportional interests. Overview of the members of the board of directors. Are owners known by the customs authorities for previous non-compliant behaviour?

2. The person responsible in the applicant's administration for customs matters.

3. Description of the economic activities of the applicant.

4. Specification of the location details of the various sites of the applicant and brief description of the activities in each site. Specification of whether the applicant and each site acts within the supply chain in its own name and its own behalf, or acts in its own name and on behalf of another person, or acts in name of and on behalf of another person.

5. Specification of whether the goods are bought from and/or supplied to companies which are affiliated with the applicant.

6. Description of the internal structure of the organisation of the applicant. Please attach, if it exists, documentation on the functions/competencies for each department and/or function.

7. The number of the employees in total and for each division.

8. The names of the key office-holders (managing directors, divisional heads, accounting managers, head of customs division etc.). Description of the adopted routines in situations when the competent employee is not present, temporarily or permanently.

9. The names and the position within the organisation of the applicant who have specific customs expertise. Assessment of the level of knowledge of these persons in regards of the use of IT technology in customs and commercial processes and general commercial matters. 10. Agreement or disagreement with the publication of the information in the AEO certificate in the list of authorised economic operators referred to in Article 14x(4).]

NOTES

Annex 1C inserted by Commission Regulation (EC) No 1875/2006, Art 1(70), Annex I, with effect from 1 January 2008.

[ANNEX 1D
EXPLANATORY NOTES:

Certificate number

The certificate number shall always begin with the ISO alpha-2 country code of the issuing Member State, followed by one of the following letters:

AEOC for AEO certificate — Customs simplifications

AEOS for AEO certificate — Security and safety

Part III

AEOF for AEO certificate — Customs simplifications/security and safety

The letters as described above should be followed by the national authorisation number.

1. Holder of the AEO certificate

The full name of the Holder shall be mentioned, as indicated in Box 1 of the Application form in Annex 1C, as well as the VAT ID number(s) as indicated in Box 8 of the Application form, if relevant the Trader Identification Number(s) as indicated in Box 9 of the Application form, and the Legal registration number as indicated in Box 10 of the Application form.

2. Issuing authority

Signature, the name of the Member State's customs administration and the stamp.

The name of the Member State's customs administration can be mentioned on a regional level, if the customs administration organisational structure requires it.

Reference to the type of the certificate

Make a cross in the relevant box.

3. Date from which the certificate is effective

Indicate the day, the month and the year, in accordance with Article 14q(1).

NOTES

Annex 1D inserted by Commission Regulation (EC) No 1875/2006, Art 1(71), Annex II, with effect from 1 January 2008.

ANNEXES 2–8

NOTES

Annexes 2–5, 7, 8 repealed by Commission Regulation (EC) 1602/2000, Art 1, para 14; Annexes 6, 6A repealed by the 1994 Act of Accession of the Kingdom of Norway, the Republic of Austria, the Republic of Finland and the Kingdom of Sweden, Annex I(III)(B)(4), as adjusted by Council Decision 95/1/EC, Annex I(XIII)(A)(b), para 47 (Annex 6A previously inserted by Commission Regulation (EC) 3665/93, Art 1, para 70, Annex 3.

ANNEX 9

INTRODUCTORY NOTES TO THE LISTS OF WORKING OR PROCESSING OPERATIONS CONFERRING OR NON-CONFERRING ORIGINATING STATUS TO MANUFACTURED PRODUCTS WHEN THEY ARE CARRIED OUT ON NON-ORIGINATING MATERIALS

General considerations

Note 1

1.1.   The first two columns in the lists in Annexes 10 and 11 describe the product obtained. The first column gives the heading number, or the chapter number, used in the Combined Nomenclature and the second column gives the description of goods used in the Combined Nomenclature for that heading or chapter. For each entry in the first two columns, a rule is specified in column 3. Where the entry in the first column is preceded by an "ex", this signifies that the rule in column 3 only applies to the part of that heading or chapter as described in column 2.

1.2.   Where several heading numbers are grouped together in column 1 or a chapter number is given and the description of product in column 2 is therefore given in general terms, the adjacent rule in column 3 applies to all products which, under the Combined Nomenclature, are classified in headings of the chapter or in any of the headings grouped together in column 1.

1.3.   Where the lists include different rules applying to different products within one heading, each indent contains the description of that part of the heading covered by the adjacent rule in column 3.

Note 2

2.1.   The term "manufacture" covers any kind of working or processing including "assembly" or specific operations.

2.2.   The term "material" covers any "ingredient", "raw material", "component" or "part", etc, used in the manufacture of the product.

2.3.   The term "product" refers to the product being manufactured, even if it is intended for later use in another manufacturing operation.

Note 3

3.1.   The working or processing required by a rule in column 3 has to be carried out only in relation to the non-originating materials used. The restrictions contained in a rule in column 3 likewise apply only to the non-originating materials used.

3.2.   If a product, made from non-originating materials which has itself acquired originating status during manufacture, is used as a material in the process of manufacture of another product, then the list rule applicable to the product in which it is incorporated does not apply to it.

For example:

Unembroidered fabric may obtain origin by being woven from yarn. If this is then used in making embroidered bed linen, then the percentage value limit imposed on the use of unembroidered fabric does not apply in this case.

Note 4

4.1.   The rules in the lists represent the minimum amount of working or processing required and the carrying out of more working or processing also confers originating status; conversely, the carrying out of less working or processing cannot confer origin. Thus if a rule says that non-originating material at a certain level of manufacture may be used, the use of such material at an earlier stage of manufacture is allowed and the use of such material at a later stage is not.

4.2.   When a rule in a list specifies that a product may be manufactured from more than one material, this means that any one or more of the materials may be used. It does not require that all be used.

For example:

the rule for yarns says that natural fibres may be used and that chemical materials, among other materials, may also be used. This does not mean that both have to be used, one can use one or the other or both.

4.3.   When a rule in a list specifies that a product must be manufactured from a particular material, the condition obviously does not prevent the use of other materials which, because of their inherent nature, cannot satisfy the rule.

Note 5

For all products which are not mentioned in Annex 11 (other than textiles falling within Section XI), origin is determined case-by-case by evaluating any process or operation in relation to the concept of the last substantial processing or working as defined in Article 24 of the Code.

Note 6

6.1.   The term "fibres" used in the list in Annex 10 covers "natural fibres" and "man-made staple fibres" falling within CN codes 5501 to 5507, and fibres of a kind used for the manufacture of paper.

6.2. The term "natural fibres" is used in the list in Annex 10 to refer to fibres other than artificial or synthetic fibres and is restricted to the stages before spinning takes place, including waste, and unless otherwise specified, the term "natural fibres" includes fibres that have been carded, combed or otherwise processed but not spun.

6.3. The term "natural fibres" includes horsehair falling within CN code 0503, silk falling within CN codes 5002 and 5003 as well as the wool fibres, fine or coarse animal hair falling within CN codes 5101 to 5105, cotton fibres falling within CN codes 5201 to 5203 and other vegetable fibres falling within CN codes 5301 to 5305.

6.4. The term "man-made staple fibres" is used in the list in Annex 10 to refer to synthetic or artificial filament tow, staple fibres or waste, falling within CN codes 5501 to 5507.

6.5. The terms "textile pulp" and "chemical materials" are used in the list in Annex 10 to describe the non-textile materials (these are not classified in Chapters 50 to 63) which can be used to manufacture artificial or synthetic fibres or yarns, or fibres of a kind used for the manufacture of paper.

6.6. For products obtained from two or more textile materials the provisions appearing in column 3 are applicable for each of the textile materials of which the mixture is composed.

Note 7

7.1. The term "prebleached", used in the list in Annex 10 to characterise the level of manufacture required when certain non-originating materials are used, applies to certain yarns, woven fabrics and knitted or crocheted fabrics which have only been washed after the spinning or weaving operation.

Prebleached products are at an earlier stage of manufacture than bleached products, which have undergone several baths in bleaching agents (oxidising agents such as hydrogen peroxide and reducing agents).

7.2. The term "complete making-up" used in the list in Annex 10 means that all the operations following cutting of the fabric or knitting or crocheting of the fabric directly to shape have to be performed.

However, making-up shall not necessarily be considered as incomplete where one or more finishing operations have not been carried out.

The following is a list of examples of finishing operations:

—   fitting of buttons and/or other types of fastenings,

—   making of button-holes,

—   finishing off the ends of trouser legs and sleeves or the bottom hemming of skirts and dresses,

—   fitting of trimmings and accessories such as pockets, labels, badges, etc,

—   ironing and other preparations of garments for sale "ready made"

Remarks concerning finishing operations—Special cases

It is possible that in particular manufacturing operations, the accomplishment of finishing operations, especially in the case of a combination of operations, is of such importance that these operations must be considered as going beyond simple finishing.

In these particular cases, the non-accomplishing of finishing operations will deprive the making-up of its complete nature.

7.3. The term "Impregnation, coating, covering or laminating" does not cover those operations designed to bind fabrics together.

ANNEX 10
LIST OF WORKING OR PROCESSING OPERATIONS CONFERRING OR NON-CONFERRING ORIGINATING STATUS TO MANUFACTURED PRODUCTS WHEN THEY ARE CARRIED OUT ON NON-ORIGINATING MATERIALS

Textiles and textile articles falling within Section Xl

CN Code	Description of product	Working or processing carried out on non- originating materials that confers the status of originating products
(1)	(2)	(3)
ex 5101	Wool, not carded or combed: —degreased, not carbonised	Manufacture from greasy, including piece- wasted wool, the value of which does not exceed 50% of the ex-works price of the product
	—carbonised	Manufacture from degreased wool, not carbonised, the value of which does not exceed 50% of the ex-works price of the product
ex 5103	Waste of wool or of fine or coarse animal hair, carbonised	Manufacture from non-carbonised waste, the value of which does not exceed 50% of the ex-works price of the product
ex 5201	Cotton, not carded or combed,	Manufacture from raw cotton, the value of bleached which does not exceed 50% of the ex-works price of the product
5501 to 5507	Man-made staple fibres: —not carded or combed or otherwise processed for spinning	Manufacture from chemical materials or textile pulp
	—carded or combed or other	Manufacture from chemical materials or textile pulp or waste falling within CN code 5505
ex Chapters 50 to 55	Yarn, monofilament and thread, other than paper yarn:	

Part III

CN Code	Description of product	Working or processing carried out on non- originating materials that confers the status of originating products
(1)	(2)	(3)
	—printed or dyed	Manufacture from: —natural fibres not carded or combed or otherwise prepared for spinning, —grege silk or silk waste, —chemical materials or textile pulp, or —man-made staple fibres, filament tow or waste of fibres, not carded or combed or otherwise prepared for spinning or Printing or dyeing of yarn or monofilaments, unbleached or prebleached[1], accompanied by preparatory or finishing operations, twisting or texturising not being considered as such, the value of non-originating material (Including yarn), not exceeding 48% of the ex-works price of the product
	—other	Manufacture from: —natural fibres not carded or combed or otherwise prepared for spinning, —grege silk or silk waste, —chemical materials or textile pulp, or —man-made staple fibres, filament tow or waste of fibres, not carded or combed or otherwise prepared for spinning
	Woven fabrics, other than fabrics of paper yarn:	
	—printed or dyed	Manufactured from yarn or Printing or dyeing of unbleached or prebleached fabrics, accompanied by preparatory or finishing operations[1, 2]
	—other	Manufacture from yarn
5601	Wadding of textile materials and articles thereof; textile fibres not exceeding 5 mm in length (flock), textile dust and mill neps	Manufacture from fibres
5602	Felt, whether or not impregnated, coated, covered or laminated:	
	—printed or dyed	Manufacture from fibres or Printing or dyeing of unbleached or prebleached felt, accompanied by preparatory or finishing operations[1, 2]

CN Code	Description of product	Working or processing carried out on non- originating materials that confers the status of originating products
(1)	(2)	(3)
	—Impregnated, coated, covered or laminated	Impregnation, coating, covering or laminating of non-wovens, unbleached [3]
	—other	Manufacture from fibres
5603	Non-wovens, whether or not impregnated, coated, covered or laminated:	
	—printed or dyed	Manufacture from fibres or Printing or dyeing of unbleached or prebleached non-wovens, accompanied by preparatory or finishing operations [1, 2]
	—impregnated, coated, covered or laminated	Impregnation, coating, covering or laminating of non-wovens, unbleached [3]
	—other	Manufacture from fibres
5604	Rubber thread and cord, textile covered, textile yarn and strip, and the like falling within CN codes 5404 or 5405, impregnated, coated, covered or sheathed with rubber or plastics:	
	—rubber thread and cord, textile covered	Manufacture from rubber thread or cord, not textile covered
	—other	Impregnation, coating, covering or sheathing of textile yarn and strip and the like, unbleached
5607	Twine cordage, rope and cables, whether or not plaited or braided and whether or not impregnated, coated, covered or sheathed with rubber or plastics	Manufacture from fibres, coir yarn, synthetic or artificial filament yarn or monofilament
5609	Articles of yarn, strip or the like falling within CN codes 5404 or5405, twine, cordage, rope or cables, not elsewhere specified or included	Manufacture from fibres, coir yarn, synthetic or artificial filament yarn or monofilament
5704	Carpets and other textile floor coverings, of felt, not tufted or flocked, whether or not made up	Manufacture from fibres
Chapter 58	Special woven fabrics; tufted textile fabrics; lace; tapestries, trimmings; embroidery:	
	—embroidery in the piece, in strips or in motifs (CN code 5810)	Manufacture in which the value of the materials used does not exceed 50% of the ex-works price of the product

CN Code	Description of product	Working or processing carried out on non-originating materials that confers the status of originating products
(1)	(2)	(3)
	—printed or dyed	Manufacture from yarn or Printing or dyeing of unbleached or prebleached fabrics felt or non-wovens, accompanied by preparatory or finishing operations[1, 2]
	—impregnated, coated or covered	Manufacture from unbleached fabrics, felt or non-wovens
	—other	Manufacture from yarn
5901	Textile fabrics coated with gum or amylaceous substances, of a kind used for the outer covers of books or the like; tracing cloth; prepared painting canvas, buckram and similar stiffened textile fabrics of a kind for hat foundations	Manufacture from unbleached fabrics
5902	Tyre cord fabric of high tenacity yarn of nylon or other polyamides, polyesters or viscose rayon	Manufacture from yarn
5903	Textile fabrics, impregnated, coated, covered or laminated with plastics, other than those falling within CN code 5902	Manufacture from unbleached fabrics or Printing or dyeing of unbleached or prebleached fabrics, accompanied by preparatory or finishing operations[1, 2]
5904	Linoleum, whether or not cut to shape; floor coverings consisting of a coating or covering applied on a textile backing, whether or not cut to shape	Manufacture from unbleached fabrics, felt or non-wovens
5905	Textile wall coverings	Manufacture from unbleached fabrics or Printing or dyeing of unbleached or prebleached fabrics, accompanied by preparatory or finishing operations[1, 2]
5906	Rubberised textile fabrics, other than those falling within CN code 5902	Manufacture from bleached knitted or crocheted fabrics, or from other unbleached fabrics
5907	Textile fabrics otherwise impregnated, coated or covered; painted canvas being theatrical scenery, studio backcloths or the like	Manufacture from unbleached fabrics or Printing or dyeing of unbleached or prebleached fabrics, accompanied by preparatory or finishing operations[1, 2]
5908	Textile wicks, woven, plaited or knitted, for lamps, stoves, lighters, candles and the like; incandescent gas mantles and tubular knitted gas mantle fabric therefor, whether or not impregnated	Manufacture from yarn
5909	Textile hosepiping and similar textile tubing with or without lining, amour or accessories of other materials	Manufacture from yarn or fibres

CN Code	Description of product	Working or processing carried out on non- originating materials that confers the status of originating products
(1)	(2)	(3)
5910	Transmission or conveyor belts or belting, of textile material, whether or not reinforced with metal or other material	Manufacture from yarn of fibres
5911	Textile products and articles, for technical uses, specified in Note 7 to Chapter 59 of the contained nomenclature:	
	—polishing discs or rings other than of felt	Manufacture from yarn, waste fabrics or rags falling within CN code 6310
	—other	Manufacture from yarn or fibres
Chapter 60	Knitted or crocheted fabrics: —printed or dyed	Manufacture from yarn or Printing or dyeing of unbleached or prebleached fabrics, accompanied by preparatory or finishing operations[1, 2]
	—other	Manufacture from yarn
Chapter 61	Articles of apparel and clothing accessories, knitted or crocheted: —obtained by sewing together or otherwise assembling, two or more pieces of knitted or crocheted fabric which have been either cut to form or obtained directly to form	Complete making up[4]
	—other	Manufacture from yarn
ex Chapter 62	Articles of apparel and clothing accessories, not knitted or crocheted, except those falling within CN codes 6213 and 6214 for which the rules are set out below:	
	—finished or complete	Complete making up[4]
	—unfinished or incomplete	Manufacture from yarn
6213 and 6214	Handkerchiefs, shawls, scarves, mufflers, mantillas, veils and the like: —embroidered	Manufacture from yarn or
		Manufacture from unembroidered fabric, provided the value of the unembroidered fabric used does not exceed 40% of the ex- works price of the product
	—other	Manufacture from yarn

CN Code	Description of product	Working or processing carried out on non-originating materials that confers the status of originating products
(1)	*(2)*	*(3)*
6301 to ex 6306	Blankets and travelling rugs; bed linen, table linen, toilet linen and kitchen linen; curtains (including drapes) and interior blinds; curtain and bed valances; other furnishing articles (excluding those falling within CN code 9494); sacks and bags of a kind used for the packing of goods; tarpaulins, awnings, and camping goods:	
	—of felt or non-wovens:	Manufacture from fibres
	—not impregnated, coated, covered or laminated	Impregnation, coating, covering or laminating of felt or non-wovens, unbleached[4]
	—impregnated, coated, covered or laminated	Complete making up[4]
	—other:	
	—knitted or crocheted	
	—unembroidered	
	—embroidered	Complete making up[4] or Manufacture from unembroidered knitted or crocheted fabric provided the value of the unembroidered knitted or crocheted fabric used does not exceed 40% of the ex-works price of the product
	—not knitted or crocheted:	
	—unembroidered	Manufacture from yarn
	—embroidered	Manufacture from yarn or Manufacture from unembroidered fabric provided the value of the unembroidered fabric used does not exceed 40% of the ex-works price of the product
6307	Other made up textile articles (including dress patterns), except for fans and hand screens, nonmechanical, frames and handles therefore and parts of such frames and handles:	
	—floor cloths, dish cloths, dusters and the like	Manufacture from yarn
	—other	Manufacture in which the value of the materials used does not exceed 40% of the ex-works price of the product

CN Code	Description of product	Working or processing carried out on non- originating materials that confers the status of originating products
(1)	(2)	(3)
6308	Sets consisting of woven fabric and yarn, whether or not with accessories, for making up into rugs, tapestries, embroidered table cloths or serviettes or similar textile articles, put up in packings for retail sale	Incorporation in a set in which the total value of all the non-originating articles incorporated does not exceed 25%, of the ex-works price of the set
[6309	Worn clothing and other worn articles	Collection and packing for shipment]

[1] See introductory note 7.1 in Annex 9.

[2] However, to be regarded as a working or processing conferring origin, thermoprinting has to be accompanied by printing of the transfer paper.

[3] See introductory note 7.3 in Annex 9.

[4] See introductory note 7.2 in Annex 9.

NOTES

Entry for CN Code 6309 inserted by Commission Regulation (EC) 993/2001, Art 1, para 31.

ANNEX 11
LIST OF WORKING OR PROCESSING OPERATIONS CONFERRING OR NON-CONFERRING ORIGINATING STATUS TO MANUFACTURED PRODUCTS WHEN THEY ARE CARRIED OUT ON NON-ORIGINATING MATERIALS

Products other than textiles and textile articles falling within Section Xl

CN code	Description of products	Working or processing carried out on non-originating materials that confers the status of originating products
(1)	(2)	(3)
0201	Meat of bovine animals, fresh or chilled	Slaughter, preceded by a fattening period of at least three months[1]
0202	Meat of bovine animals, frozen	Slaughter, preceded by a fattening period of at least three months[1]
0203	Meat of swine, fresh, chilled or frozen	Slaughter, preceded by a fattening period of at least two months[1]
0204	Meat of sheep or goats, fresh, chilled or frozen	Slaughter, preceded by a fattening period of at least two months[1]
0205	Meat of horses, asses, mules or hinnies, fresh, chilled or frozen	Slaughter, preceded by a fattening period of at least three months[1]
0206	Edible offal of bovine animals, swine, sheep, goats, horses, asses, mules or hinnies, fresh, chilled or frozen	Slaughter, preceded by a fattening period of at least three months, or two months in the case of swine, sheep or goats[1]
Ex 0408	Birds' eggs, not in shell, dried, and egg yolks, dried	Drying (after breaking and separation, where appropriate) of:

Part III

CN code	Description of products	Working or processing carried out on non-originating materials that confers the status of originating products
(1)	(2)	(3)
		—birds' eggs, in shell, fresh or preserved, falling within CN code ex 0407
		—birds' eggs, not in shell, other than dried, falling within CN code ex 0408
		—egg whites, other than dried, falling within CN code ex 0408
Ex 1404	Cotton linters, bleaches	Manufacture from raw cotton, the value of which does not exceed 50% of the ex-works price of the product
		Working or processing carried out on non- originating materials that does not confer the status of originating products
Ex 2009	Grape juice, unfermented and not containing added spirit, whether or not containing added sugar or other sweetening matter	Manufacture from grape must
Ex 2204	Wine of fresh grapes intended for the preparation of vermouth containing added must of fresh grapes, concentrated or not, or alcohol	Manufacture from wine of fresh grapes
		Process or operation carried out on non- originating materials that confers the status of originating products
Ex 2205	Vermouth	Manufacture from wine of fresh grapes containing must of fresh grapes, concentrated or not, or alcohol, falling within CN code 2204
Ex 3401	Felt and non-wovens, impregnated, coated or covered with soap or detergent	Manufacture from felt or non-wovens
Ex 3405	Felt and non-wovens, impregnated, coated or covered with polishes and creams, for footwear, furniture, floors, coachwork, glass or metal, scouring pastes and powders and similar preparations	Manufacture from felt or non-wovens
Ex 3502	Dried egg albumin	Drying (after breaking and separation, where appropriate) of: —birds' eggs, in shell, fresh or preserved, falling within CN code ex 0407 —birds' eggs, not in shell, other than dried, falling within CN code ex 0408 or —egg whites, other than dried, falling within CN code ex 3502
Ex 4203	Articles of apparel of leather or of composition leather	Sewing or assembly of two or more pieces of leather or of composition leather

CN code	Description of products	Working or processing carried out on non-originating materials that confers the status of originating products
(1)	(2)	(3)
Ex 4910	Ceramic calendars of any kind, printed, including calendar clocks, decorated	Decoration of the ceramic article concerned, provided this decoration has resulted in the classification of the products obtained in a tariff heading other than that covering the products uses
6401 to 6405	Footwear	Manufacture from materials of any heading except for assemblies of uppers affixed to inner soles or to other sole components falling within CN code 6406
Ex 6911 to ex 6913	Ceramic tableware, kitchenware, other household articles and toilet articles; statuettes and other ornamental ceramic articles; decorated	Decoration of the ceramic article concerned, provided this decoration has resulted in the classification of the products obtained in a tariff heading other than that covering the products used
Ex 7117	Ceramic imitation jewellery, decorated	Decoration of the ceramic article concerned, provided this decoration has resulted in the classification of the products obtained in a tariff heading other than that covering the products used
Ex 8482	Ball, roller or needle roller bearings, assembled[2]	Assembly preceded by heat treatment, grinding and polishing of the inner and outer rings
Ex 8520	Magnetic tape recorders, whether or not incorporating a sound reproducing device	Manufacture where the increase in value acquired as a result of assembly operations and, if applicable, the incorporation of parts originating in the country of assembly represents at least 45% of the ex-works price of the product
		When the 45% rule is not met, the apparatus shall be treated as originating in the country of origin of parts whose ex-works price represents more than 35% of the ex-works price of the apparatus
		When the 35% rule is met in two countries, the apparatus shall be treated as originating in the country of origin of the parts representing the greater percentage value

Part III

CN code	Description of products	Working or processing carried out on non-originating materials that confers the status of originating products
(1)	(2)	(3)
[ex 8523 20 90	Unrecorded 3.5" magnetic micro diskettes, whether or not pre-formatted and with or without an analogue signal for the purposes of checking the quality of the disk's coating recorded on it	Assembly of the diskette (including insertion of the magnetic disk and assembly of the shells) plus manufacture of: either the magnetic disk (including polishing) or the upper and lower shells. If neither the disk nor upper and lower shells are manufactured in the country where assembly of the diskette takes place, the diskettes shall have the origin of the country where the components representing the highest percentage of the ex-works price originated. Assembly of the diskette (including insertion of the magnetic disk and assembly of the shells) and packing alone shall not confer origin.]
Ex 8527	Reception apparatus for radio-broadcasting whether or not combined in the same housing with sound recording or reproducing apparatus or a clock	Manufacture where the increase in value acquired as a result of assembly operations and, if applicable, the incorporation of parts originating in the country of assembly represents at least 45% of the ex-works price of the products When the 45% rule is not met, the apparatus shall be treated as originating in the country of origin of parts whose ex-works price represents more than 35% of the ex-works price of the apparatus When the 35% rule is met in two countries, the apparatus shall be treated as originating in the country of origin of the parts representing the greater percentage value
Ex 8528	Television receivers, (excluding videotuners, television projection equipment and video monitors), whether or not combined, in the same housing, with radio-broadcast receivers or sound recording or reproducing apparatus, but not with video recording or reproducing apparatus	Manufacture where the increase in value acquired as a result of assembly operations and, if applicable the incorporation of parts originating in the country of assembly represents at least 45% of the ex-works price of the products When the 45% rule is not met, the apparatus shall be treated as originating in the country of origin of parts whose ex-works price represents more than 35% of the ex-works price of the apparatus

CN code	Description of products	Working or processing carried out on non-originating materials that confers the status of originating products
(1)	(2)	(3)
		When the 35% rule is met in two countries, the apparatus shall be treated as originating in the country of origin of parts representing the greater percentage value
Ex 8542	Integrated circuits	The operation of diffusion (where integrated circuits are formed on a semi-conductor substrate by the selective introduction of an appropriate dopant)
		Working or processing carried out on non- originating materials that does not confer the status of originating products
Ex 9009	Photocopying apparatus incorporating an optical system or of the contact type	Assembly of photocopying apparatus accompanied by the manufacture of the harness, drum, rollers, side plates, roller bearings, screws and nuts
		Process or operation carried out on non- originating materials that confers the status of originating products
Ex 9113	Watch straps, watch bands and watch bracelets, and parts thereof, of textiles	Manufacture in which the value of the materials used does not exceed 40% of the ex-works price of the product
Ex 9401 and ex 9403	Ceramic seats (other than those falling within CN code 9402) whether or not convertible into beds and other furniture, and parts thereof, decorated	Decoration of the ceramic article concerned, provided this decoration has resulted in the classification of the products obtained in a tariff heading other than that covering the products used
Ex 9405	Ceramic lamps and ceramic lighting fittings, including searchlights and spotlights and parts thereof, not elsewhere specified or included decorated; illuminated ceramic signs, name-plates and the like, having a permanently fixed light source, and parts thereof, not elsewhere specified or included decorated	Decoration of the ceramic article concerned, provided this decoration has resulted in the classification of the product obtained in a tariff heading other than that covering the products used

[1] Where these conditions are not met, the meat (offal) shall be considered as originating in the country where the animals from which they where obtained were fattened or reared for the longest period.

[2] The term assembled includes partially assembled but excludes parts in their unassembled state.

NOTES

Words in square brackets inserted by Commission Regulation (EC) 12/97, Art 1, para 14, Annex II.

Part III

ANNEX 12

ANNEX 12

1 Consignor (Space reserved for translation)	No. 000000	ORIGINAL
	(Space reserved for issuing number)	(Space reserved for translation)
2 Consignee (Space reserved for translation)	**EUROPEAN COMMUNITY** (Space reserved for translation)	
	CERTIFICATE OF ORIGIN (Space reserved for translation)	
	3 Country of Origin (Space reserved for translation)	
4 Transport details (Optional) (Space reserved for translation)	5 Remarks (Space reserved for translation)	
6 Item number; marks, numbers, number and kind of packages; description of goods (Space reserved for translation)		7 Quantity (Space reserved for translation)
8 THE UNDERSIGNED AUTHORITY CERTIFIES THAT THE GOODS DESCRIBED ABOVE ORIGINATE IN THE COUNTRY SHOWN IN BOX 3 (Space reserved for translation)		
Place and date of issue, name, signature and stamp of competent authority (Space reserved for translation)		

1 Consignor *(Space reserved for translation)*	**No.** 000000 *(Space reserved for issuing number)*	**COPY** *(Space reserved for translation)*
2 Consignee *(Space reserved for translation)*	**EUROPEAN COMMUNITY** *(Space reserved for translation)* ___ **CERTIFICATE OF ORIGIN** *(Space reserved for translation)*	
	3 Country of Origin *(Space reserved for translation)*	
4 Transport details (Optional) *(Space reserved for translation)*	5 Remarks *(Space reserved for translation)*	

6 Item number; marks, numbers, number and kind of packages; description of goods *(Space reserved for translation)*	7 Quantity *(Space reserved for translation)*

8 THE UNDERSIGNED AUTHORITY CERTIFIES THAT THE GOODS DESCRIBED ABOVE ORIGINATE IN THE COUNTRY SHOWN IN BOX 3
(Space reserved for translation)

Place and date of issue, name, signature and stamp of competent authority
(Space reserved for translation)

Part III

1 Consignor (Name, or name of firm, and full address, where applicable is shown in the commercial register)	**No. 000000**	
	(Space reserved for issuing number)	**APPLICATION**
	EUROPEAN COMMUNITY	
2 Consignor (Name, or name of firm, and full address if known or mention 'to order')		
	CERTIFICATE OF ORIGIN	
	3 Country of Origin ('European Community' or country of origin concerned)	
4 Transport details (Optional)	5 Remarks	

6 Item number; marks, numbers, number and kind of packages; description of goods (For goods not packed indicate number or 'in bulk')	7 Quantity (Expressed in gross or net mass or other units of measure

8 I, the undersigned,

— APPLY for the issue of a certificate of origin indicating that the goods described above originate in the country shown in box 3,

— DECLARE that the particulars given in this application and the supporting documents and information furnished to the competent authorities with a view to the issue of this certificate are correct, that the goods to which such documents and information relate are those in respect of which this application is made, that the goods fulfill the conditions laid down by the rules concerning the common definition of the concept of the origin of goods,

— UNDERTAKE to furnish, at the respect of the competent authorities, such additional information and supporting documents as may be required for the issue of the certificate

9 Applicant (If not the cosignor)	
	Place and date
	Signature of the applicant (^{1})

(^{1}) The signature of an agent must be followed by his name in block capitals.

(Copy omitted.)

ANNEX 13

1 Consignor	CERTIFICATE OF ORIGIN for imports of agricultural products into the European Economic Community
	No ORIGINAL
2 Consignee (optional)	3 ISSUING AUTHORITY
	4 Country of origin
NOTES A. The certificate must be completed in typescript or by means of a mechanical data-processing system, or similar procedure. B. The original of the certificate must be lodged together with the declaration of release for free circulation with the relevant customs office in the Community.	5 Remarks

6 Item number — Markings and numbers — Number and kind of packages — DESCRIPTION OF GOODS	7 Gross and net mass (kg)

8 THIS IS TO CERTIFY THAT THE ABOVE PRODUCTS ORIGINATE IN THE COUNTRY INDICATED IN BOX 4 AND THAT THE INDICATIONS IN BOX 5 ARE CORRECT.

Place and date of issue   Signature   Issuing authority's stamp

9 RESERVED FOR THE CUSTOMS AUTHORITIES IN THE COMMUNITY

Part III

(Annexes 14, 15 omitted.)

ANNEX 16
WORKING EXCLUDED FROM GSP REGIONAL CUMULATION

Working such as:
—   fitting of buttons and/or other types of fastenings,
—   making of button-holes,
—   finishing off the ends of trouser legs and sleeves or the bottom hemming of skirts and dresses etc,
—   hemming of handkerchiefs, table linen etc,
—   fitting of trimmings and accessories such as pockets, labels, badges, etc,
—   ironing and other preparations of garments for sale "ready made",
—   or any combination of such working.

[ANNEX 17
CERTIFICATE OF ORIGIN FORM A

1. Certificates of origin Form A must conform to the specimen shown in this annex. The use of English or French for the notes on the reverse of the certificate shall not be obligatory. Certificates shall be made out in English or French. If completed by hand, entries must be in ink and in capital letters.

2. Each certificate shall measure 210 × 297 mm; a tolerance of up to plus 5 mm or minus 8 mm in the length may be allowed. The paper use shall be white writing paper, sized, not containing mechanical pulp and weighing not less than 25 g/m^2. It shall have a printed green guilloche-pattern background making any falsification by mechanical or chemical means apparent to the eye.

If the certificates have several copies, only the top copy which is the original shall be printed with a printed green guilloche-pattern background.

3. Each certificate shall bear a serial number, printed or otherwise, by which it can be identified.

4. Certificates, a specimen of which is shown in this annex, shall be acceptable from 1st January 1996; however certificates made out in accordance with the previous specimen, dated 1992, may be presented until 31st December 1997.

1. Goods consigned from (exporter's business name, address, country)	Reference No	A
	GENERALIZED SYSTEM OF PREFERENCES CERTIFICATE OF ORIGIN (Combined declaration and certificate) FORM A	
2. Goods consigned to (consignee's name, address, country)		
	Issued in ....
	(country)
	See notes overleaf
3. Means of transport and route (as far as known)	4. For official use	

5. Item number	6. Marks and number of packages	7. Number and kind of packages, description of goods	8. Origin criterion (see notes overleaf)	9. Gross weight or other quantity	10. Number and date of invoices

11. Certification	12. Declaration by the exporter
It is hereby certified, on the basis of control carried out, that the declaration by the exporter is correct.	The undersigned hereby declares that the above details and statement are correct; that all the goods were
	produced in ....
	(country)
	and that they comply with the origin requirements specified for those goods in the generalized system of preferences for goods exported to
	....
	(importing country)
.... Place and date, signature and stamp of certifying authority	.... Place and date, signature of authorized signatory

Part III

Notes (1996)

I. Countries which accept Form A for the purposes of the generalised system of preferences (GSP):

Australia[1]	Republic of Belarus	European Union:		
Canada	Republic of Bulgaria	Austria	Germany	Netherlands
Japan	Czech Republic	Belgium	Greece	Portugal
New Zealand[2]	Republic of Hungary	Denmark	Ireland	Spain
Norway	Republic of Poland	Finland	Italy	Sweden
Switzerland	Russian Federation	France	Luxem-bourg	United Kingdom
United States of America[3]	Slovakia			

[1] For Australia, the main requirement is the exporter's declaration on the normal commercial invoice. Form A, accompanied by the normal commercial invoice, is an acceptable alternative, but official certification is not required.

[2] Official certification is not required.

[3] The United States does not require GSP Form A. A declaration setting forth all pertinent detailed information concerning the production or manufacture of the merchandise is considered sufficient only if requested by the district collector of Customs.

Full details of the conditions covering admission to the GSP in these countries are obtainable from the designated authorities in the exporting preference-receiving countries or from the customs authorities of the preference-giving countries listed above. An information note is also obtainable from the UNCTAD secretariat.

II. General conditions

To qualify for preference, products must—

(a) fall within a description of products eligible for preference in the country of destination. The description entered on the form must be sufficiently detailed to enable the products to be identified by the customs officer examining them;

(b) comply with the rules of origin of the country of destination. Each article in a consignment must qualify separately in its own right; and,

(c) comply with the consignment conditions specified by the country of destination. In general, products must be consigned direct from the country of exportation to the country of destination but most preference-giving countries accept passage through intermediate countries subject to certain conditions. (For Australia, direct consignment is not necessary.)

III. Entries to be made in Box 8

Preference products must either be wholly obtained in accordance with the rules of the country of destination or sufficiently worked or processed to fulfil the requirements of that country's origin rules.

(a) Products wholly obtained: for export to all countries listed in Section I, enter the letter "P" in Box 8 (for Australia and New Zealand Box 8 may be left blank).

(b) Products sufficiently worked or processed: for export to the countries specified below, the entry in Box 8 should be as follows—

(1) *United States of America*: for single country shipments, enter the letter "Y" in Box 8, for shipments from recognised associations of

countries, enter the letter "Z", followed by the sum of the cost or value of the domestic materials and the direct cost of processing, expressed as a percentage of the ex-factory price of the exported products; (example "Y" 35% or "Z" 35%).

(2) Canada: for products which meet origin criteria from working or processing in more than one eligible least developed country, enter letter "G" in Box 8; otherwise "F".

(3) Japan, Norway, Switzerland and the European Union: enter the letter "W" in box 8 followed by the Harmonised Commodity Description and coding System (Harmonised System) heading at the 4-digit level of the exported product (example "W" 96.18).

(4) Bulgaria, Czech Republic, Hungary, Poland, the Russian Federation and Slovakia: for products which include value added in the exporting preference-receiving country, enter the letter "Y" in Box 8 followed by the value of imported materials and components expressed as a percentage of the fobprice of the exported products (example "Y" 45%); for products obtained in a preference-receiving country and worked or processed in one or more other such countries, enter "Pk".

(5) Australia and New Zealand: completion of Box 8 is not required. It is sufficient that a declaration be properly made in Box 12.]

(French version omitted.)

NOTES
   Substituted by Commission Regulation (EC) 12/97, Art 1, para 17, Annex V.

[ANNEX 18
INVOICE DECLARATION
The invoice declaration, the text of which is given below, must be made out in accordance with the footnotes. However, the footnotes do not have to be reproduced.

(French version omitted.)

English version

The exporter of the products covered by this document (customs authorisation No . . .[1]) declares that, except where otherwise clearly indicated, these products are of . . . preferential origin[2] according to rules of origin of the Generalised System of Preferences of the European Community.

. . . .
(place and date)[3]

. . . .
(Signature of the exporter; in addition the name of the person signing the declaration has to be indicated in clearscript)[4]

---

[1] When the invoice declaration is made out by an approved exporter within the meaning of Article 90a, the authorisation number of the approved exporter must be entered in this space. When the invoice declaration is not made out by an approved exporter, the words in brackets shall be omitted or the space left blank.

Part III

[2] Origin of products to be indicated. When the invoice declaration relates, in whole or in part, to products originating in Ceuta and Melilla within the meaning of Article 96, the exporter must clearly indicate them in the document on which the declaration is made out by means of the symbol "CM".

[3] These indications may be omitted if the information is contained on the document itself.

[4] See Article 90(5). In cases where the exporter is not required to sign, the exemption of signature also implies the exemption of the name of the signatory.]

NOTES

Substituted by Commission Regulation (EC) 12/97, Art 1, para 21, Annex IX.

(Annexes 19, 20 repealed by Commission Regulation (EC) 1602/2000, Art 1, para 17.)

ANNEX 21
MOVEMENT CERTIFICATE EUR 1 AND RELEVANT APPLICATIONS

1. Movement certificate EUR 1 shall be made out on the form of which a specimen appears in this Annex. This form shall be printed in one of the official languages of the Community. Certificates shall be made out in one of these languages and in accordance with the provisions of the domestic law of the exporting State or territory. If they are handwritten, they shall be completed in ink and in capital letters.

2. Each certificate shall measure 210 × 297 mm; a tolerance of up to minus 5 mm or plus 8 mm in the length may be allowed. The paper used must be white, sized for writing not containing mechanical pulp and weighing not less than 25 g/m2. It shall have a printed green guilloche pattern background making any falsification by mechanical or chemical means apparent to the eye.

3. The competent authorities of the exporting State or territory may reserve the right to print the certificates themselves or may have them printed by approved printers. In the latter case each certificate must include a reference to such approval. Each certificate must bear the name and address of the printer or a mark by which the printer can be identified. It shall also bear a serial number, either printed or not, by which it can be identified.

MOVEMENT CERTIFICATE

1. Exporter (Name, full address, country)	EUR. 1 No **A** 000.000
	See notes overleaf before completing this form
	2. Certificate used in preferential trade between
3. Consignee (Name, full address, country) (Optional)	
	and
	(Insert appropriate countries, groups of countries or territories)

4. Country, group of countries or territory in which the products are considered as originating	5. Country, group of countries or territory of destination

6. Transport details (Optional)	7. Remarks

(¹) If goods are not packed, indicate number of articles of state in bulk as appropriate.

8. Item number; marks and numbers; number and kind of packages (¹); description of goods	9. Gross mass(kg) or other measure (litres, m³, etc)	10. Invoices (Optional)

(²) Complete only where the regulations of the exporting country or territory require.

11. CUSTOMS ENDORSEMENT	12. DECLARATION BY THE EXPORTER
Declaration certified	I, the undersigned, declare that the goods described above meet the conditions required for the issue of this certificate.
Export document (²)	
Form .... No..............	
Customs office	
Issuing country or territory	
.... Stamp	
Place and date	Place and date ....
(Signature)	(Signature)

Part III

<table>
<tr><td>

13. REQUEST FOR VERIFICATION, to:

Verification of the authenticity and accuracy of this certificate is requested.

....
(Place and date)

Stamp

....
(Signature)

</td><td>

14. RESULT OF VERIFICATION

Verification carried out shows that this certificate(¹)

☐ was issued by the customs office indicated and that the information contained therein is accurate;

☐ does not meet the requirements as to authenticity and accuracy (see remarks appended).

....
(Place and date)

Stamp

....
(Signature)

(¹) Insert X in the appropriate box.

</td></tr>
</table>

NOTES

1. Certificates must not contain erasures or words written over one another. Any alterations must be made by deleting the incorrect particulars and adding any necessary corrections. Any such alteration must be initialed by the person who completed the certificate and endorsed by the customs authorities of the issuing country or territory.

2. No spaces must be left between the items entered on the certificate and each item must be preceded by an item number. A horizontal line must be drawn immediately bellow the last item. Any unused space must be struck through in such a manner as to make any later additions impossible.

3. Goods must be described in accordance with commercial practice and with sufficient detail to enable them to be identified.

DECLARATION BY THE EXPORTER

I, the undersigned, exporter of the goods described overleaf,

DECLARE that the goods meet the conditions required for the issue of the attached certificate;

SPECIFY as follows the circumstances which have enabled these goods to meet the above conditions:

. . . .
. . . .
. . . .

SUBMIT the following supporting documents[1]:

. . . .
. . . .
. . . .

UNDERTAKE to submit, at the request of the appropriate authorities, any supporting evidence which these authorities may require for the purpose of issuing the attached certificate, and undertake, if required, to agree to any inspection of my accounts and to any check on the processes of manufacture of the above goods, carried out by the said authorities;

REQUEST the issue of the attached certificate for these goods.

. . . .

(Place and date)

. . . .

(Signature)

---

[1] For example: import documents, movement certificates, invoices, manufacturer's declarations, etc, referring to the products used in manufacture or to the goods re-exported in the same state.

[ANNEX 22
INVOICE DECLARATION

The invoice declaration, the text of which is given below, must be made out in accordance with the footnotes. However, the footnotes do not have to be reproduced. (Non-English language versions omitted.)
English Version
The exporter of the products covered by this document (customs authorisation No . . .[1]) declares that, except where otherwise clearly indicated, these products are of . . .[2] preferential origin.

. . . .

(place and date)[3]

. . . .

(Signature of the exporter; in addition the name of the person signing the declaration has to be indicated in clearscript)[4]]

[1] When the invoice declaration is made out by an approved exporter, the authorisation number of the approved exporter must be entered in this space. When the invoice declaration is not made out by an approved exporter, the words in brackets shall be omitted or the space left blank.

[2] Origin of products to be indicated. When the invoice declaration relates, in whole or in part, to products originating in Ceuta and Melilla, the exporter must clearly indicate them in the document on which the declaration is made out by means of the symbol "CM".

[3] These indications may be omitted if the information is contained on the document itself.

[4] See Article 117(5). In cases where the exporter is not required to sign, the exemption of signature also implies the exemption of the name of the signatory.]

NOTES

Substituted by Commission Regulation (EC) 12/97, Art 1, para 21, Annex IX.

ANNEX 23
INTERPRETATIVE NOTES ON CUSTOMS VALUE

First column	Second column
Reference to provisions of the Customs Code	Notes
Article 29(1)	The price actually paid or payable refers to the price for the imported goods. Thus the flow of dividends or other payments from the buyer to the seller that do not relate to the imported goods are not part of the customs value.
Article 29(1)(a), third indent	An example of such restriction would be the case where a seller requires a buyer of automobiles not to sell or exhibit them prior to a fixed date which represents the beginning of a model year.

Part III

First column	Second column
Reference to provisions of the Customs Code	Notes
Article 29(1)(b)	Some examples of this include: (a) the seller establishes the price of the imported goods on condition that the buyer will also buy other goods in specified quantities; (b) the price of the import goods is dependent upon the price or prices at which the buyer of the imported goods sells other goods to the seller of the imported goods; (c) the price is established on the basis of a form of payment extraneous to the imported goods, such as where the imported goods are semi-finished goods which have been provided by the seller on condition. However, conditions or considerations relating to the production or marketing of the imported goods shall not result in rejection of the transaction value. For example, the fact that the buyer furnishes the seller with engineering and plans undertaken in the country of importation shall not result in rejection of the transaction value for the purposes of Article 29(1).

First column	Second column
Reference to provisions of the Customs Code	Notes
Article 29(2)	1. Paragraphs 2(a) and (b) provide different means of establishing the acceptability of a transaction value. 2. Paragraph 2(a) provides that where the buyer and the seller are related, the circumstances surrounding the sale shall be examined and the transaction value shall be accepted as the customs value provided that the relationship did not influence the price. It is not intended that there should be an examination of the circumstances in all cases where the buyer and the seller are related. Such examination will only be required where there are doubts about the acceptability of the price. Where the customs authorities have no doubts about the acceptability of the price, it should be accepted without requesting further information from the declarant. For example, the customs authorities may have previously examined the relationship, or it may already have detailed information concerning the buyer and the seller, and may already be satisfied from such examination or information that the relationship did not influence the price. 3. Where the customs authorities are unable to accept the transaction value without further inquiry, they should give the declarant an opportunity to supply such further detailed information as may be necessary to enable it to examine the circumstances surrounding the sale, in this context, the customs authorities should be prepared to examine relevant aspects of the transaction, including the way in which the buyer and seller organise their commercial relations and the way in which the price in question was arrived at, in order to determine whether the relationship influenced the price. Where it can be shown that the buyer and seller, although related under the provisions of Article 143 of this Regulation, buy from and sell to each other as if they were not related, this would demonstrate that the price had not been influenced by the relationship. As an example of this, if the price had been settled in a manner consistent with the normal pricing practices of the industry in question or with the way the seller settles prices for sales to buyers who are not related to him, this would demonstrate that the price had not been influenced by the relationship. As a further example, where it is shown that the price is adequate to ensure recovery of all costs plus a profit which is representative of the firm's overall profit realised over a representative period of time (eg on an annual basis) in sales of goods of the same class or kind, this would demonstrate that the price had not been influenced.

Part III

First column	Second column
Reference to provisions of the Customs Code	Notes
	4. Paragraph 2(b) provides an opportunity for the declarant to demonstrate that the transaction value closely approximates to a "test" value previously accepted by the customs authorities and is therefore acceptable under the provisions of Article 29. Where a test under paragraph 2(b) is met, it is not necessary to examine the question of paragraph 2(a). If the customs authorities already have sufficient information to be satisfied, without further detailed inquiries, that one of the tests provided in paragraph 2(b) has been met, there is no reason for them to require the declarant to demonstrate that the test can be met.
Article 29(2)(b)	A number of factors must be taken into consideration in determining whether one value "closely approximates" to another value. These factors include the nature of the imported goods, the nature of the industry itself, the season in which the goods are imported, and, whether the difference in values is commercially significant. Since these factors may vary from case to case, it would be impossible to apply a uniform standard such as a fixed percentage, in each case. For example, a small difference in value in a case involving one type of goods could be unacceptable while a large difference in a case involving another type of goods might be acceptable in determining whether the transaction value closely approximates to the "test" values set forth in Article 29(2)(b).
Article 29(3)(a)	An example of an indirect payment would be the settlement by the buyer, whether in whole or in part, of a debt owed by the seller.
Article 30(2)(a) Article 30(2)(b)	1. In applying these provisions, the customs authorities shall, where possible, use a sale of identical or similar goods, as appropriate, at the same commercial level and in substantially the same quantity as the goods being valued. Where no such sale is found, a sale of identical or similar goods, as appropriate, that takes place under any one of the following three conditions may by used: (a) a sale at the same commercial level but in a different quantity; (b) a sale at a different commercial level but in substantially the same quantity; or (c) a sale at a different commercial level and in a different quantity. 2. Having found a sale under any one of these three conditions adjustments will then be made, as the case may be, for: (a) quantity factors only; (b) commercial level factors or (c) both commercial level and quantity factors.

First column	Second column
Reference to provisions of the Customs Code	Notes
	3. A condition for adjustment because of different commercial levels or different quantities is that such adjustment, whether it leads to an increase or a decrease in the value, be made only on the basis of demonstrated evidence that clearly establishes the reasonableness and accuracy of the adjustment, eg valid price lists containing prices referring to different levels or different quantities. As an example of this, if the imported goods being valued consist of a shipment of 10 units and the only identical or similar imported goods, as appropriate, for which a transaction value exists involved a sale of 500 units, and it is recognised that the seller grants quantity discounts, the required adjustment may be accomplished by resorting to the seller's price list and using that price applicable to a sale of 10 units. This does not require that a sale had to have been made in quantities of 10 as long as the price list has been established as being bona fide through sales at other quantities. In the absence of such an objective measure, however, the determination of a customs value under the provisions of Article 30(2)(a) and (b) is not appropriate.
Article 30(2)(d)	1. As a general rule, customs value is determined under these provisions on the basis of information readily available in the Community. In order to determine a computed value, however, it may be necessary to examine the cost of producing the goods being valued and other information which has to be obtained from outside the Community. Furthermore, in most cases the producer of the goods will be outside the jurisdiction of the authorities of the Member States. The use of the computed value method will generally be limited to those cases where the buyer and seller are related, and the producer is prepared to supply to the authorities of the country of importation the necessary costings and to provide facilities for any subsequent verification which may be necessary. 2. The "cost or value" referred to in Article 30(2)(d), first indent, is to be determined on the basis of information relating to the production of the goods being valued supplied by or on behalf of the producer. It is to be based upon the commercial accounts of the producer, provided that such accounts are consistent with the generally accepted accounting principles applied in the country where the goods are produced. 3. The "amount for profit and general expenses" referred to in Article 30(2)(d), second indent, is to be determined on the basis of information supplied by or on behalf of the producer unless his figures are inconsistent with those usually reflected in sales of goods of the same class or kind as the goods being valued which are made by producers in the country of exportation for export to the country of importation. 4. No cost or value of the elements referred to in this Article shall be counted twice in determining the computed value.

Part III

First column	Second column
Reference to provisions of the Customs Code	Notes
	5. It should be noted in this context that the "amount for profit and general expenses" has to be taken as a whole. It follows that if, in any particular case, the producer's profit figure is low and his general expenses are high, his profit and general expenses taken together may nevertheless be consistent with that usually reflected in sales of goods of the same class or kind. Such a situation might occur, for example, if a product were being launched in the Community and the producer accepted a nil or low profit to offset high general expenses associated with the launch. Where the producer can demonstrate that he is taking a low profit on his sales of the imported goods because of particular commercial circumstances, his actual profit figures should be taken into account provided that he has valid commercial reasons to justify them and his pricing policy reflects usual pricing policies in the branch of industry concerned. Such a situation might occur, for example, where producers have been forced to lower prices temporarily because of an unforeseeable drop in demand, or where they sell goods to complement a range of goods being produced in the country of importation and accept a low profit to maintain competitivity. Where the producer's own figures for profit and general expenses are not consistent with those usually reflected in sales of goods of the same class or kind as the goods being valued which are made by producers in the country of exportation for export to the country of importation, the amount for profit and general expenses may be based upon relevant information other than that supplied by or on behalf of the producer of the goods. 6. Whether certain goods are "of the same class or kind" as other goods must be determined on a case-by-case basis with reference to the circumstances involved. In determining the usual profits and general expenses under the provisions of Article 30(2)(d), sales for export to the country of importation of the narrowest group or range of goods, which includes the goods being valued, for which the necessary information can be provided, should be examined. For the purposes of Article 30(2)(d), "goods of the same class or kind" must be from the same country as the goods being valued.

First column	Second column
Reference to provisions of the Customs Code	Notes
Article 31(1)	1. Customs values determined under the provisions of Article 31(1) should, to the greatest extent possible, be based on previously determined customs values. 2. The methods of valuation to be employed under Article 31(1) should be those laid down in Articles 29 and 30(2), but a reasonable flexibility in the application of such methods would be in conformity with the aims and provisions of Article 31(1). 3. Some examples of reasonable flexibility are as follows: (a) identical goods the requirement that the identical goods should be exported at or about the same time as the goods being valued could be flexibly interpreted; identical imported goods produced in a country other than the country of exportation of the goods being valued could be the basis for customs valuation; customs values of identical imported goods already determined under the provisions of Articles 30(2)(c) and (d) could be used; (b) similar goods the requirement that the similar goods should be exported at or about the same time as the goods being valued could be flexibly interpreted; similar imported goods produced in a country other than the country of exportation of the goods being valued could be the basis for customs valuation; customs values of similar imported goods already determined under the provisions of Articles 30(2)(c) and (d) could be used; (c) deductive method the requirement that the goods shall have been sold in the "condition as imported" in Article 152(1)(a) of this Regulation could be flexibly interpreted; the "90 days" requirement could be administered flexibly.

Part III

First column	Second column
Reference to provisions of the Customs Code	Notes
Article 32(1)(b)(ii)	1. There are two factors involved in the apportionment of the elements specified in Article 32(1)(b)(ii) to the imported goods the value of the element itself and the way in which that value is to be apportioned to the imported goods. The apportionment of these elements should be made in reasonable manner appropriate to the circumstances and in accordance with generally accepted accounting principles.
	2. Concerning the value of the element, if the buyer acquires the element from a seller not related to him at a given cost, the value of the element is that cost. If the element was produced by the buyer or by a person related to him, its value would be the cost of producing it. If the element had been previously used by the buyer, regardless of whether it had been acquired or produced by him, the original cost of acquisition or production would have to be adjusted downwards to reflect its use in order to arrive at the value of the element.
	3. Once a value has been determined for the element, it is necessary to apportion that value to the imported goods. Various possibilities exist. For example, the value might be apportioned to the first shipment, if the buyer wishes to pay duty on the entire value at one time. As another example, he may request that the value be apportioned over the number of units produced up to the time of the first shipment. As a further example, he may request that the value be apportioned over the entire anticipated production where contracts or firm commitments exist for that production. The method of apportionment used will depend upon the documentation provided by the buyer.
	4. As an illustration of the above, a buyer provides the producer with a mould to be used in the production of the imported goods and contracts with him to buy 10 000 units. By the time of arrival of the first shipment of 1 000 units, the producer has already produced 4 000 units. The buyer may request the customs authorities to apportion the value of the mould over 1 000, 4 000 or 10 000 units.

First column	Second column
Reference to provisions of the Customs Code	Notes
Article 32(1)(b)(iv)	1. Additions for the elements specified in Article 32(1)(b)(iv) should be based on objective and quantifiable data. In order to minimise the burden for both the declarant and customs authorities in determining the values to be added, data readily available in the buyer's commercial record system should be used insofar as possible. 2. For those elements supplied by the buyer which were purchased or leased by the buyer, the addition would be the cost of the purchase or the lease. No addition shall be made for those elements available in the public domain, other than the cost of obtaining copies of them. 3. The ease with which it may be possible to calculate the values to be added will depend on a particular firm's structure and management practice, as well as its accounting methods. 4. For example, it is possible that a firm which imports a variety of products from several countries maintains the records of its design centre outside the country of importation in such a way as to show accurately the costs attributable to a given product. In such cases, a direct adjustment may appropriately be made under the provisions of Article 32. 5. In another case, a firm may carry the cost of the design centre outside the country of importation as a general overhead expense without allocation to specific products. In this instance, an appropriate adjustment could be made under the provisions of Article 32 with respect to the imported goods by apportioning total design centre costs over total production benefiting from the design centre and adding such apportioned cost on a unit basis to imports. 6. Variations in the above circumstances will, of course, require different factors to be considered in determining the proper method of allocation. 7. In cases where the production of the element in question involves a number of countries and over a period of time, the adjustment should be limited to the value actually added to that element outside the Community.
Article 32(1)(c)	The royalties and licence fees referred to in Article 32(1)(c) may include, among other things, payments in respect to patents, trademarks and copyrights.

First column	Second column
Reference to provisions of the Customs Code	Notes
Article 32(2)	Where objective and quantifiable data do not exist with regard to the additions required to be made under the provisions of Article 32, the transaction value cannot be determined under the provisions of Article 29. As an illustration of this, a royalty is paid on the basis of the price in a sale in the importing country of a litre of a particular product that was imported by the kilogram and made up into a solution after importation. If the royalty is based partially on the imported goods and partially on other factors which have nothing to do with the imported goods (such as when the imported goods are mixed with domestic ingredients and are no longer separately identifiable, or when the royalty cannot be distinguished from special financial arrangements between the buyer and the seller), it would be inappropriate to attempt to make an addition for the royalty. However, if the amount of this royalty is based only on the imported goods and can be readily quantified, an addition to the price actually paid or payable can be made.
Article 143(1)(e)	One person shall be deemed to control another when the former is legally or operationally in a position to exercise restraint or direction over the latter.
Article 150(1) Article 151(1)	The expression "and/or" allows the flexibility to use the sales and make the necessary adjustments in any one of the three conditions described in paragraph 1 of the interpretative notes to Articles 30(2)(a) and (b).
Article 152(1)(a)(i)	1. The words "profit and general expenses" should be taken as a whole. The figure for the purposes of this deduction should be determined on the basis of information supplied by the declarant unless his figures are inconsistent with those obtaining in sales in the country of importation of imported goods of the same class or kind. Where the declarant's figures are inconsistent with such figures, the amount for profit and general expenses may be based upon relevant information other than that supplied by the declarant. 2. In determining either the commissions or the usual profits and general expenses under this provision, the question whether certain goods are of the same class or kind as other goods must be determined on a case-by-case basis by reference to the circumstances involved. Sales in the country of importation of the narrowest group or range of imported goods of the same class or kind, which includes the goods being valued, for which the necessary information can be provided, should be examined. For the purposes of this provision, "goods of the same class or kind" includes goods imported from the same country as the goods being valued as well as goods imported from other countries.

First column	Second column		
Reference to provisions of the Customs Code	Notes		
Article 152(2)	1. Where this method of valuation is used, deductions made for the value added by further processing shall be based on objective and quantifiable data relating to the cost of such work. Accepted industry formulas, recipes, methods of construction, and other industry practices would form the basis of the calculations. 2. This method of valuation would normally not be applicable when, as a result of the further processing, the imported goods lose their identity. However, there can be instances where, although the identity of the imported goods is lost, the value added by the processing can be determined accurately without unreasonable difficulty. On the other hand, there can also be instances where the imported goods maintain their identity but form such a minor element in the goods sold in the country of importation that the use of this valuation method would be unjustified. In view of the above, each situation of this type must be considered on a case-by-case basis.		
Article 152(3)	1. As an example of this, goods are sold from a price list which grants favourable unit prices for purchases made in larger quantities.		

Sale quantity	Unit	Number of sales	Total quantity sold at each price
1 to 10 units	100	10 sales of 5 units Five sales of 3 units	65
11 to 25 units	95	Five sales of 11 units	55
Over 25 units	90	One sale of 30 units One sale of 50 units	80

The greatest number of units sold at a price is 80; therefore, the unit price in the greatest aggregate quantity is 90.

2. As another example of this, two sales occur. In the first sale 500 units are sold at a price of 95 currency units each. In the second sale 400 units are sold at a price of 90 currency units each. In this example, the greatest number of units sold at a particular price is 500; therefore, the unit price in the greatest aggregate quantity is 95.

3. A third example would be the following situation where various quantities are sold at various prices.

Part III

First column	Second column
Reference to provisions of the Customs Code	Notes
	(a) Sales Unit price Sale 100 quantity 90 40 units 100 30 units 95 15 units 105 50 units 90 25 units 100 35 units 5 units
	(b) Total Unit price Total 90 quantity sold 95 65 100 50 105 60 25
	In this example, the greatest number of units sold at a particular price is 65; therefore, the unit price in the greatest aggregate quantity is 90.

ANNEX 24

APPLICATION OF GENERALLY ACCEPTED ACCOUNTING PRINCIPLES FOR THE DETERMINATION OF CUSTOMS VALUE

1. "Generally accepted accounting principles" refers to the recognised consensus or substantial authoritative support within a country at a particular time as to which economic resources and obligations should be recorded as assets and liabilities, which changes in assets and liabilities should be recorded, how the assets and liabilities and changes in them should be measured, what information should be disclosed and how it should be disclosed, and which financial statements should be prepared. These standards may be broad guidelines of general application as well as detailed practices and procedures.

2. For the purposes of the application of the customs valuation provisions, the customs administration concerned shall utilise information prepared in a manner consistent with generally accepted accounting principles in the country which is appropriate for the Article in question. For example, the determination of usual profit and general expenses under the provisions of Article 152(1)(a)(i) of this Regulation would be carried out utilising information prepared in a manner consistent with generally accepted accounting principles of the country of importation. On the other hand, the determination of usual profit and general expenses under the provisions of Article 30(2)(d) of the Code would be carried out utilising information prepared in a manner consistent with generally accepted accounting principles of the country of production. As a further example, the determination of an element provided for in Article 32(1)(b)(ii) of the Code undertaken in the country of importation would be carried out utilising information in a manner consistent with the generally accepted accounting principles of that country.

(Annex 25 omitted.)

ANNEX 26
LIST OF GOODS REFERRED TO IN ARTICLE 152(1)(A)A

Simplified procedure for the valuation of certain perishable goods imported on consignment in accordance with Article 30(2)(c) of the Code

CN (TARIC) Code	Description of goods	Period of validity
07019050	New potatoes	1.1. to 30.6.
07031019	Onions	1.1. to 31.12.
07032000	Garlic	1.1. to 31.12.
07082000	Beans	1.1. to 31.12.
0709200010	Asparagus: green	1.1. to 31.12.
0709200090	Asparagus: other	1.1. to 31.12.
07096010	Sweet peppers	1.1. to 31.12.
ex071420	Sweet potatoes, fresh or chilled, whole	1.1. to 31.12.
0804300090	Pineapples	1.1. to 31.12.
0804400010	Avocados	1.1. to 31.12.
08051020	Sweet oranges	1.6. to 30.11.
0805201005	Clementines	1.3. to 31.10.
0805203005	Monreales and satsumas	1.3. to 31.10.
0805205007 0805205037	Mandarins and wilkings	1.3. to 31.10.
0805207005 0805209005 0805209009	Tangerines and other	1.3. to 31.10.
0805400011	Grapefruit: white	1.1. to 31.12.
0805400019	Grapefruit: pink	1.1. to 31.12.
0805509011 0805509019	Limes (Citrus aurantifolia, Citrus latifolia)	1.1. to 31.12.
08061010	Table grapes	21.11. to 20.7.
08071100	Watermelons	1.1. to 31.12.
0807190010 0807190030	Amarillo, cuper, honey dew (including Cantalene), Onteniente, Piel de Sapo, (including Verde Liso), Rochet, Tendral, Futuro	1.1. to 31.12.
0807190091 0807190099	Other melons	1.1. to 31.12.
0808205010	Pears: Nashi (Pyrus pyrifolia)Ya (Pyrus bretscheideri)	1.5. to 30.6.
0808205090	Pears: other	1.5. to 30.6.
08091000	Apricots	1.1. to 30.5. and 1.8. to 31.12.
08093010	Nectarines	1.1. to 10.6. and 1.10. to 31.12.
08093090	Peaches	1.1. to 10.6. and 1.10. to 31.12.
08094005	Plums	1.10. to 10.6.
08101000	Strawberries	1.1. to 31.12.
08102010	Raspberries	1.1. to 31.12.
08105000	Kiwifruit	1.1. to 31.12.]

Part III

NOTES

Substituted by Commission Regulation (EC) No 215/2006, Art 1, para 3, Annex I.

ANNEX 27

MARKETING CENTRES FOR THE PURPOSE OF CALCULATING UNIT PRICES BY CLASSIFICATION HEADING

NOTES

Repealed by Commission Regulation (EC) No 215/2006, Art 1, para 4.

ANNEX 28

EUROPEAN COMMUNITY   **DECLARATION OF PARTICULARS RELATING TO CUSTOMS VALUE**   **D.V.1**

1 NAME AND ADDRESS OF SELLER (Block Letters)	FOR OFFICIAL USE
2(a) NAME AND ADDRESS OF BUYER (Block Letters)	
2(b) NAME AND ADDRESS OF DECLARANT (Block Letters)	

IMPORTANT NOTE

By signing and lodging the declaration the declarant accepts responsibility for the accuracy and completeness of the particulars given on this form and on any continuation sheet lodged with it and the authenticity of any document produced in support. The declarant also accepts responsibility to supply any additional information or document necessary to establish the customs value of the goods.

3 Terms of delivery

4 Number and date of invoice

5 Number and date of contract

---

6 Number and date of any previous Customs decision concerning boxes 7 to 9

Enter X where applicable

7(a) Are the buyer and seller RELATED in the sense of Article 143 (*) of Regulation (EEC) No 2454/93?   YES ☐ NO ☐

If 'NO', go to box 8.

(b) Did the relationship INFLUENCE the price of the imported goods?   YES ☐ NO ☐

(c) (reply optional) Does the transaction value of the imported goods CLOSELY APPROXIMATE to a value mentioned in Article 29 (2) (b) of Regulation (EEC) No 2913/92?   YES ☐ NO ☐

If 'Yes', give details:

8(a) Are there any RESTRICTIONS as to the disposition or use of the goods by the buyer, other than restrictions which:

- are imposed or required by law or by the public authorities in the Community,

- limit the geographical area in which the goods may be resold, or

- do not substantially affect the value of the goods?   YES ☐ NO ☐

(b) Is the sale or price subject to some CONDITION or CONSIDERATION for which a value cannot be determined with respect to the goods being valued?   YES ☐ NO ☐

Specify the nature of the restrictions, conditions or considerations as appropriate:

If the value of conditions or considerations can be determined, indicate the amount in box 11(b).

9(a) Are any ROYALTIES and LICENCE FEES related to the imported goods payable either directly or indirectly by the buyer as a condition of the sale?   YES ☐ NO ☐

(b) Is the sale subject to an arrangement under which part of the proceeds of any subsequent RESALE, DISPOSAL or USE accrues directly or indirectly to the seller?   YES ☐ NO ☐

If 'YES' to either of these questions, specify conditions and, if possible, indicate the amounts in boxes 15 and 16

(*) **NOTES TO BOX 7**

1. PERSONS SHALL BE DEEMED TO BE RELATED ONLY IF:
   (a) they are officers or directors of one another's businesses;
   (b) they are legally recognized partners in business;
   (c) they are employer and employee;
   (d) any person directly or indirectly owns, controls or holds 5% or more of the outstanding voting stock or shares of both of them;
   (e) one of them directly or indirectly controls the other;
   (f) both of them are directly or indirectly controlled by a third person;
   (g) together they directly or indirectly control a third person; or
   (h) they are members of the same family.

2. The fact that the buyer and the seller are related need no; preclude the use of a transaction value (see Article 29 (2) of Regulation (EEC) No 2913/92 and the Interpretative Notes on that provision in Annex 23).

10(a) Number of continuation sheets
   D.V. 1 BIS attached

10(b) **Place:**
   Date:
   Signature:

Part III

© European Communities Official Journal L 253, 11/10/1993, Annex 28

			Item	Item	Item
FOR OFFICIAL USE					
A. Basis of calculation	**11** (a) Net price in CURRENCY OF INVOICE (Price actually paid or price payable for settlement at the material time for valuation for customs purposes)				
	(b) Indirect payments – see box 8 (b)				
	(rate of exchange;)				
	12 Total A in NATIONAL CURRENCY..				
B. ADDITIONS: Costs in NATIONAL CURRENCY NOT INCLUDED in A above (*) **QUOTE BELOW previous relevant Customs decisions, if any:**	**13** Costs incurred by the buyer:				
	(a) commissions, except buying commissions				
	(b) brokerage				
	(c) containers and packing				
	14 Goods and services supplied by the buyer free of charge or at reduced cost for use in connection with the production and sale for export of the imported goods:				
	The values shown represent an apportionment where appropriate.				
	(a) materials, components, parts and similar items incorporated in the imported goods				
	(b) tools, dies, moulds and similar items used in the production of the imported goods				
	(c) materials consumed in the imported goods				
	(d) engineering, development, artwork, design work and plans and sketches undertaken elsewhere than in the Community and necessary for the production of the imported goods				
	15 Royalties and licence fees – see box 9(a)				
	16 Proceeds of any subsequent resale, disposal or use accruing to the seller – see box 9(b)				
	17 Costs of delivery to _____ (place of introduction)				
	(a) transport				
	(b) loading and handling charges				
	(c) insurance				
	18 Total B				
C. DEDUCTIONS: Costs in NATIONAL CURRENCY INCLUDED in A above (*)	**19** Costs of transport after arrival at place of introduction				
	20 Charges for construction, erection, assembly, maintenance or technical assistance undertaken after importation				
	21 Other charges (specify) _____				
	22 Customs duties and taxes payable in the Community by reason of the importation or sale of the goods				
	23 Total C				

24 VALUE DECLARED (A + B – C) ....

(*) Where amounts are payable in FOREIGN CURRENCY, indicate in this section the amount in foreign currency and the rate of exchange by reference to each relevant element and item.

Reference	Amount	Rate of exchange

ANNEX 29

| EUROPEAN COMMUNITY | | CONTINUATION SHEET | **D.V.1** | BIS |

FOR OFFICIAL USE

		Item	Item	Item
A. Basis of calculation	**11** (a) Net price in CURRENCY OF INVOICE (Price actually paid or price payable for settlement at the material time for valuation for customs purposes)			
	(b) Indirect payments – see box 8 (b)			
	(rate of exchange;)			
	12 Total A in NATIONAL CURRENCY....................................			
B. ADDI-TIONS: Costs in NATIONAL CUR-RENCY NOT IN-CLUDED in A above (*) QUOTE BELOW previous relevant Customs decisions, if any:	**13** Costs incurred by the buyer: (a) commissions, except buying commissions			
	(b) brokerage			
	(c) containers and packing			
	14 Goods and services supplied by the buyer free of charge or at reduced cost for use in connection with the production and sale for export of the imported goods: The values shown represent an apportionment where appropriate. (a) materials, components, parts and similar items incorporated in the impor-ted goods .... (b) tools, dies, moulds and similar items used in the production of the impor-ted goods .... (c) materials consumed in the production of the imported goods............ (d) engineering, development, artwork, design work and plans and sketches undertaken elsewhere than in the Community and necessary for the pro-duction of the imported goods			
	15 Royalties and licence fees – see box 9(a)			
	16 Proceeds of any subsequent resale, disposal or use accruing to the seller – see box 9(b)			
	17 Costs of delivery to _____ (place of introduction) (a) transport			
	(b) loading and handling charges			
	(c) insurance			
	18 Total B			
C. DEDUC-TIONS: Costs in NATIONAL CUR-RENCY INCLUDED in A above (*)	**19** Costs of transport after arrival at place of introduction			
	20 Charges for construction, erection, assembly, maintenance or technical assi-stance undertaken after importation			
	21 Other charges (specify) _____			
	22 Customs duties and taxes payable in the Community by reason of the impor-tation or sale of the goods			
	23 Total C			

24 VALUE DECLARED (A + B – C) ....

(*) Where amounts are payable in FOREIGN CURRENCY, indicate in this section the amount in foreign currency and the rate of exchange by reference to each relevant element and item.

Reference	Amount	Rate of exchange

Part III

FOR OFFICIAL USE			Item	Item	Item
A. Basis of calculation	**11** (a) Net price in CURRENCY OF INVOICE (Price actually paid or price payable for settlement at the material time for valuation for customs purposes)				
	(b) Indirect payments – see box 8 (b)				
	(rate of exchange;)				
	12 Total A in NATIONAL CURRENCY..................				
B. ADDI-TIONS: Costs in NATIONAL CUR-RENCY NOT IN-CLUDED in A above (*) QUOTE BELOW previous relevant Customs decisions, if any:	**13** Costs incurred by the buyer: (a) commissions, except buying commissions				
	(b) brokerage				
	(c) containers and packing				
	14 Goods and services supplied by the buyer free of charge or at reduced cost for use in connection with the production and sale for export of the imported goods: The values shown represent an apportionment where appropriate. (a) materials, components, parts and similar items incorporated in the impor-ted goods				
	(b) tools, dies, moulds and similar items used in the production of the impor-ted goods				
	(c) materials consumed in the production of the imported goods................. (d) engineering, development, artwork, design work and plans and sketches undertaken elsewhere than in the Community and necessary for the pro-duction of the imported goods				
	15 Royalties and licence fees – see box 9(a)				
	16 Proceeds of any subsequent resale, disposal or use accruing to the seller – see box 9(b)				
	17 Costs of delivery to _____ (place of introduction) (a) transport				
	(b) loading and handling charges				
	(c) insurance				
	18 Total B				
C. DEDUC-TIONS: Costs in NATIONAL CUR-RENCY INCLUDED in A above (*)	**19** Costs of transport after arrival at place of introduction				
	20 Charges for construction, erection, assembly, maintenance or technical assi-stance undertaken after importation				
	21 Other charges (specify) _____				
	22 Customs duties and taxes payable in the Community by reason of the import-tation or sale of the goods				
	23 Total C				
24 VALUE DECLARED (A + B – C)					

(*) Where amounts are payable in FOREIGN CURRENCY, indicate in this section the amount in foreign currency and the rate of exchange by reference to each relevant element and item.

Reference   Amount   Rate of exchange

ANNEX 30
TAG TO BE AFFIXED ON HOLD BAGGAGE CHECKED IN A COMMUNITY AIRPORT
(Article 196)

1.
CHARACTERISTICS

The tag referred to in Article 196 shall be designed in such a way as to prevent its re-use.

(a)   This tag shall bear a green stripe of at least 5 mm width along the full length of the two edges of its routing and identification sections.

Moreover, these green stripes may extend also to other parts of the baggage tag, with the exception of all areas showing the barcoded tag number which must be printed on an unobscured white background (See specimens at 2(a))

(b)   For 'expedite baggage', the tag shall be similar to the specified in IATA resolution No 743a with green instead of red stripes along its edges. (See specimen at 2(b))

2.
SPECIMENS

NOTES

Annex 30A to be inserted by Commission Regulation (EC) No 1875/2006, Art 1(72), Annex III, with effect from 1 July 2009.

Part III

ANNEX 31
MODEL OF SINGLE ADMINISTRATIVE DOCUMENT

NOTES

The technical provisions in respect of the forms and notably their size and colours are detailed in Article 215.

**EUROPEAN COMMUNITY
EXCISE DUTIES**

**SIMPLIFIED ACCOMPANYING DOCUMENT
INTRA-COMMUNITY MOVEMENT OF PRODUCTS WHICH HAVE BEEN RELEASED FOR CONSUMPTION**

2

Copy for the recipient

2

1 Supplier ☐ (Name and address) VAT No	2 Transaction reference
	3 Competent authority of the country of destination (Name and address)
4 Recipient VAT No (Name and address)	
5 Transporter/means of transport	6 Reference number and date of declaration
7 Place of delivery	

8 Marks and numbers, No and kind of packages, description of goods	9 Commodity code (CN code)
	10 Quantity 11 Gross weight (kg)
	12 Net weight (kg)
	13 Invoice price/Commercial value

14 Certificates (certain wines and spirits, small breweries and small distilleries)

A Record of control. For use by competent authority	15 Boxes 1-13 certified correct. Return of copy 3 required yes ☐ no ☐ (*) Signatory's company and telephone No
	Name of signatory
	Place and date
	Signature

Continue on reverse (copies 2 and 3)

(*) Cross applicable

© European Communities Official Journal L 253, 11/10/1993 Annex 31

Part III

B CERTIFICATION OF RECEIPT

Goods received by recipient

Date .... Place .... Reference No ....

The excise duty has been paid / declared to the competent authority (*)

Date .... Reference No ....

Other remarks of the recipient:

Place/date .... Name of signatory ....

Signature

(*) Delete inapplicable

A Record of control (continued)

(Forms 2, 3 omitted.)

			A OFFICE OF DISPATCH/EXPORT

EUROPEAN COMMUNITY

4

2 Consignor/Exporter	No	**1 DECLARATION**

	3 Forms	4 Loading lists

	5 Items	6 Total packages

8 Consignee   No

IMPORTANT NOTE

Where this copy is used exclusively for establishing the COMMUNITY STATUS OF GOODS NOT MOVING UNDER THE COMMUNITY TRANSIT PROCEDURE, only the information in boxes 1, 2, 3, 5, 14, 31, 32, 35, 54 and, where appropriate, 4, 33, 38, 40 and 44 is needed for that purpose.

Copy for the office of destination

14 Declarant/Representative   No

15 Country of dispatch/export

17 Country of destination

18 Identity and nationality of means of transport at departure   **19 Ctr.**

21 Identity and nationality of active means of transport crossing the border

25 Mode of transport at the border   **27 Place of loading**

4

31 Packages and description of goods

Marks and numbers - Container No(s) - Number and kind

32 Item No   **33 Commodity Code**

35 Gross mass (kg)

38 Net mass (kg)

40 Summary declaration/Previous document

44 Additional information/ Documents produced/ Certificates and authorizations

A. I. Code

Tranship- ments

Place and country:

Ident. and. nat. new means transp.:

Ctr.   (1)   Identity of new container:

(1) Enter 1 if YES or 0 if NO.

Place and country:

Ident. and. nat. new means transp.:

Ctr.   (1)   Identity of new container:

(1) Enter 1 if YES or 0 if NO.

CERTIFI- CATION BY COMPE- TENT AU- THORITIES

New seals: Number: Identity:

Signature: Stamp:

New seals: Number: Identity:

Signature: Stamp:

50 Principal   No   Signature: **C OFFICE OF DEPARTURE**

51 Intended offices of transit (and country)

represented by

Place and date:

52 Guarantee not valid for

Code   **53 Office of destination (and country)**

D CONTROL BY OFFICE OF DEPARTURE   Stamp: **54 Place and date:**

Result:

Seals affixed: Number:

   identity:

Time limit (date):

Signature:

Signature and name of declarant/representative:

Part III

(Forms 5–8 omitted.)

NOTES

This Annex substituted by Commission Regulation (EC) 2286/2003, Art 1, para 17, Annex III with effect from 1 January 2006. However, member states may implement the legislation

before that date.

ANNEX 32
MODEL OF SINGLE ADMINISTRATIVE DOCUMENT FOR PRINTING BY COMPUTERISED DECLARATION-PROCESSING SYSTEMS ON TWO SUCCESSIVE FOUR-COPY SETS

NOTES

The technical provisions in respect of the forms and notably their size and colours are detailed in Article 215.

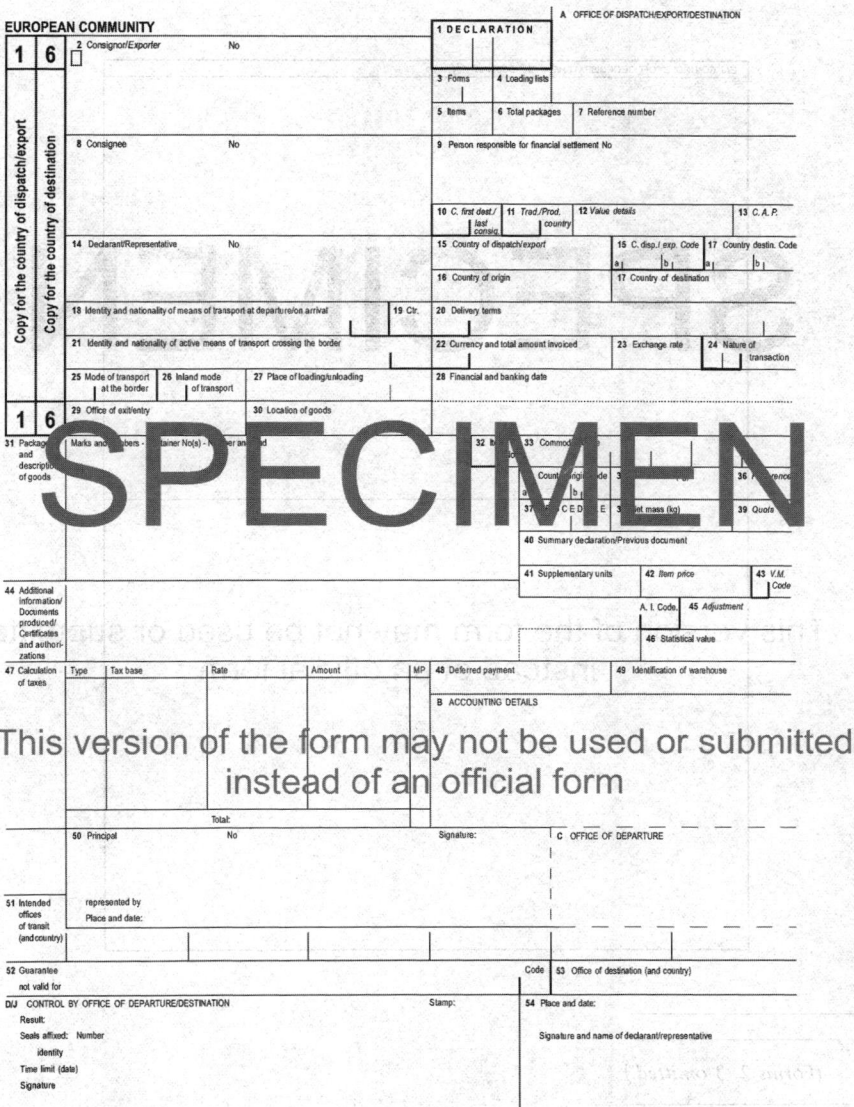

© European Communities Official Journal L 253, 11/10/1993 Annex 32

▼__B__

E/J CONTROL BY OFFICE OF DISPATCH/EXPORT/DESTINATION

SPECIMEN

This version of the form may not be used or submitted instead of an official form

(Forms 2, 3 omitted.)

EUROPEAN COMMUNITY

4 5

Copy for the office of destination
Copy for return - Community transit

2 Consignor/Exporter   No

8 Consignee   No

14 Declarant/Representative   No

18 Identity and nationality of means of transport at departure   19 Ctr.

21 Identity and nationality of active means of transport crossing the border

25 Mode of transport at the border   27 Place of loading

4 5

31 Packages and description of goods   Marks and numbers - Container No(s) - Number and kind

44 Additional information/ Documents produced/ Certificates and authorizations

55 Transhipments

F CERTIFICATION BY COMPETENT AUTHORITIES

51 Intended offices of transit (and country)

52 Guarantee not valid for

D CONTROL BY OFFICE OF DEPARTURE
Result:
Seals affixed: Number:
       identity:
Time limit (date):
Signature:

A OFFICE OF DISPATCH/EXPORT

1 DECLARATION

3 Forms   4 Loading lists

5 Items   6 Total packages

IMPORTANT NOTE

Where this copy is used exclusively for establishing the COMMUNITY STATUS OF GOODS NOT MOVING UNDER THE COMMUNITY TRANSIT PROCEDURE, only the information in boxes 1, 2, 3, 5, 14, 31, 32, 35, 54 and, where appropriate, 4, 33, 38, 40 and

15 Country of dispatch/export

17 Country of destination

Tilbagesendes til: Zurücksenden an:
En...   Return to:
Renvoyer à: Rinviare a:
Terugzenden aan: Devolver a:

32 Item No   33 Commodity Code

35 Gross mass (kg)

38 Net mass (kg)

40 Summary declaration/Previous document

A. I. Code

Place and country:
Ident. and. nat. new means transp.:
Ctr.   (1) Identity of new container:
(1) Enter 1 if YES or 0 if NO.
New seals: Number: Identity:
Signature: Stamp:

Place and country:
Ident. and. nat. new means transp.:
Ctr.   (1) Identity of new container:
(1) Enter 1 if YES or 0 if NO.
New seals: Number: Identity:
Signature: Stamp:

50 Principal   No

Signature: C OFFICE OF DEPARTURE

represented by
Place and date:

Code   53 Office of destination (and country)

Stamp: 54 Place and date:

Signature and name of declarant/representative:

© European Communities Official Journal L273, 11/10/1993 Annex 31

Part III

56 Other incidents during carriage
Details and measures taken

G CERTIFICATION BY COMPETENT AUTHORITIES

H A POSTERIOR I CONTROL (Where this copy is used for establishing the Community status of the goods)

REQUEST FOR VERIFICATION	RESULT OF VERIFICATION
Verification of the authenticity of this document and the accuracy of the information contained therein is requested.	This document (1)
	☐ was certified by the Customs office indicated and the information contained therein is accurate.
	☐ does not meet the requirements as to authenticity and regularity (see remarks below).
Place and date:	Place and date:
Signature: Stamp:	Signature: Stamp:

Remarks

(1) Enter ☒ where applicable.

I   CONTROL BY OFFICE OF DESTINATION (COMMUNITY TRANSIT)

Date of arrival:

Examination of seals:

Remarks:

Copy no 5 returned

on

after registration under

No

Signature: Stamp:

COMMUNITY TRANSIT - RECEIPT (To be completed by the person concerned before presentation to the office of destination)

This is to certify that the document _____ Issued by the Customs office at _____   Stamp of office of destination:
_____ (name and country) under No_____

has been lodged and that no irregularity has been observed to date concerning the consignment to which this document refers.

Date   Signature

NOTES

This Annex substituted by Commission Regulation (EC) 2286/2003, Art 1, para 17, Annex III with effect from 1 January 2006. However, member states may implement the legislation before that date.

ANNEX 33
MODEL OF SINGLE ADMINISTRATIVE DOCUMENT
CONTINUATION FORM

NOTES

The technical provisions in respect of the forms and notably their size and colours are detailed in Article 215.

EUROPEAN COMMUNITY

2 Consignor/*Exporter* No

1 DECLARATION

C BIS

A OFFICE OF DISPATCH/EXPORT

3 Forms 1

31 Packages and description of goods | Marks and numbers - Container No(s) - Number and kind

32 Item No

33 Commodity Code

34 Country origin Code a b

35 Gross mass (kg)

37 PROCEDURE

38 Net mass (kg)

39 *Quota*

40 Summary declaration/Previous document

41 Supplementary units

44 Additional information/ Documents produced/ Certificates and authorizations

A. I. Code

46 Statistical value

31 Packages and description of goods | Marks and numbers - Container No(s) - Number and kind

32 Item No

33 Commodity Code

34 Country origin Code a b

35 Gross mass (kg)

37 PROCEDURE

38 Net mass (kg)

39 *Quota*

40 Summary declaration/Previous document

41 Supplementary units

44 Additional information/ Documents produced/ Certificates and authorizations

A. I. Code

46 Statistical value

31 Packages and description of goods | Marks and numbers - Container No(s) - Number and kind

32 Item No

33 Commodity Code

34 Country origin Code a b

35 Gross mass (kg)

37 PROCEDURE

38 Net mass (kg)

39 *Quota*

40 Summary declaration/Previous document

41 Supplementary units

44 Additional information/ Documents produced/ Certificates and authorizations

A. I. Code

46 Statistical value

47 Calculation of taxes

Type	Tax base	Rate	Amount	MP	Type	Tax base	Rate	Amount	MP
Total first item:					Total second item:				

Type	Tax base	Rate	Amount	MP	Type	Amount	MP
Total third item:					G.T.		

← SUMMARY

1 Copy for the country of dispatch/export

C OFFICE OF DEPARTURE

© European Communities Official Journal L 253, 11/10/1993 Annex 33

(Forms 2–5 omitted.)

EUROPEAN COMMUNITY

8 Consignee   No

A OFFICE OF DESTINATION

1 DECLARATION

C | BIS

3 Forms | **6**

31 Packages and description of goods | Marks and numbers - Container No(s) - Number and kind

32 Item No

33 Commodity Code

34 Country origin Code | a | b | 35 Gross mass (kg) | 36 Preference

37 PROCEDURE | 38 Net mass (kg) | 39 Quota

40 Summary declaration/Previous document

41 Supplementary units | 42 Item price | 43 V.M. Code

A. I. Code. | 45 Adjustment

46 Statistical value

44 Additional information/ Documents produced/ Certificates and authorizations

31 Packages and description of goods | Marks and numbers - Container No(s) - Number and kind

32 Item No

33 Commodity Code

34 Country origin Code | a | b | 35 Gross mass (kg) | 36 Preference

37 PROCEDURE | 38 Net mass (kg) | 39 Quota

40 Summary declaration/Previous document

41 Supplementary units | 42 Item price | 43 V.M. Code

A. I. Code. | 45 Adjustment

46 Statistical value

44 Additional information/ Documents produced/ Certificates and authorizations

31 Packages and description of goods | Marks and numbers - Container No(s) - Number and kind

32 Item No

33 Commodity Code

34 Country origin Code | a | b | 35 Gross mass (kg) | 36 Preference

37 PROCEDURE | 38 Net mass (kg) | 39 Quota

40 Summary declaration/Previous document

41 Supplementary units | 42 Item price | 43 V.M. Code

A. I. Code. | 45 Adjustment

46 Statistical value

44 Additional information/ Documents produced/ Certificates and authorizations

47 Calculation of taxes	Type	Tax base	Rate	Amount	MP	Type	Tax base	Rate	Amount	MP
	Total first item:					Total second item:				
	Type	Tax base	Rate	Amount	MP	Type	Amount	MP		
	Total third item:						G.T.			

SUMMARY

6   **Copy for the country of dispatch/export**

C OFFICE OF DEPARTURE

© European Communities Official Journal L 273, 11/10/1993 Annex 33

(Forms 7, 8 omitted.)

NOTES

This Annex substituted by Commission Regulation (EC) 2286/2003, Art 1, para 17, Annex III with effect from 1 January 2006. However, member states may implement the legislation

Part III

before that date.

ANNEX 34

MODEL OF SINGLE ADMINISTRATIVE DOCUMENT CONTINUATION FORM FOR PRINTING BY COMPUTERISED DECLARATION-PROCESSING SYSTEMS ON TWO SUCCESSIVE FOUR-COPY SETS

NOTES

The technical provisions in respect of the forms and notably their size and colours are detailed in Article 215.

EUROPEAN COMMUNITY

A OFFICE OF DISPATCH/EXPORT/DESTINATION

2 Consignor / Exporter 8 Consignee   No

1 DECLARATION

C   BIS

3 Forms **1** **6**

31 Packages and description of goods — Marks and numbers - Container No(s) - Number and kind

32 Item No

33 Commodity Code

34 Country origin Code a | b | 35 Gross mass (kg) 36 Preference

37 PROCEDURE 38 Net mass (kg) 39 Quota

40 Summary declaration/Previous document

41 Supplementary units 42 Item price 43 V.M. Code

A.I. Code 46 Adjustment

46 Statistical value

44 Additional information/ Documents produced/ Certificates and authorizations

31 Packages and description of goods — Marks and numbers - Container No(s) - Number and kind

32 Item No

33 Commodity Code

34 Country origin Code a | b | 35 Gross mass (kg) 36 Preference

37 PROCEDURE 38 Net mass (kg) 39 Quota

40 Summary declaration/Previous document

41 Supplementary units 42 Item price 43 V.M. Code

A.I. Code 45 Adjustment

46 Statistical value

44 Additional information/ Documents produced/ Certificates and authorizations

31 Packages and description of goods — Marks and numbers - Container No(s) - Number and kind

32 Item No

33 Commodity Code

34 Country origin Code a | b | 35 Gross mass (kg) 36 Preference

37 PROCEDURE 38 Net mass (kg) 39 Quota

40 Summary declaration/Previous document

41 Supplementary units 42 Item price 43 V.M. Code

A.I. Code 45 Adjustment

46 Statistical value

44 Additional information/ Documents produced/ Certificates and authorizations

47 Calculation of taxes

Type	Tax base	Rate	Amount	MP	Type	Tax base	Rate	Amount	MP

Total first item: Total second item:

Type	Tax base	Rate	Amount	MP	Type	Amount	MP

◀ SUMMARY

1 Copy for the country of dispatch/export

6 Copy for the country of destination

C OFFICE OF DEPARTURE

Total third item: G.T.

(Forms 2–5 omitted.)

NOTES

This Annex substituted by Commission Regulation (EC) 2286/2003, Art 1, para 17, Annex III with effect from 1 January 2006. However, member states may implement the legislation

Part III

before that date.

ANNEX 35

INDICATION OF THE COPIES OF THE FORMS SHOWN IN ANNEXES 31 AND 33 ON WHICH PARTICULARS SHOULD APPEAR BY A SELF-COPYING PROCESS

(Counting copy 1)

Box number	Copies	Box number	Copies

I. BOXES FOR OPERATORS

Box number	Copies	Box number	Copies
1	1 to 8 except middle subdivision— 1 to 3	28	1 to 3
		29	1 to 3
		30	1 to 3
2	1 to 5	31	1 to 8
3	1 to 8	32	1 to 8
4	1 to 8	33	first subdivision on the left— 1 to 8 remainder: 1 to 3
5	1 to 8		
6	1 to 8		
7	1 to 3		
8	1 to 5[1]	34a	1 to 3
9	1 to 3	34b	1 to 3
10	1 to 3	35	1 to 8
11	1 to 3	36	—
12	—	37	1 to 3
13	1 to 3	38	1 to 8
14	1 to 4	39	1 to 3
15	1 to 8	40	1 to 5[1]
15a	1 to 3	41	1 to 3
15b	1 to 3	42	—
16	1, 2, 3, 6, 7 and 8	43	—
17	1 to 8	44	1 to 5[1]
17a	1 to 3	45	—
17b	1 to 3	46	1 to 3
18	1 to 5[1]	47	1 to 3
19	1 to 5[1]	48	1 to 3
20	1 to 3	49	1 to 3
21	1 to 5[1]	50	1 to 8
22	1 to 3	51	1 to 8
23	1 to 3	52	1 to 8
24	1 to 3	53	1 to 8
25	1 to 5[1]	54	1 to 4
26	1 to 3	55	—

I. BOXES FOR OPERATORS

27	1 to 5	56	—

II. ADMINISTRATIVE BOXES

A	1 to 4²	C	1 to 8²
B	1 to 3	D	1 to 4

[1] Under no circumstances may users be required to complete these boxes on copy No 5 for the purposes of transit.

[2] The Member State of dispatch can choose whether these particulars appear on the copies specified.

NOTES

Footnote 1 above substituted by Commission Regulation (EC) 2787/2000, Art 1.

ANNEX 36

INDICATION OF THE COPIES OF THE FORMS SHOWN IN ANNEXES 32 AND 34 ON WHICH PARTICULARS SHOULD APPEAR BY A SELF-COPYING PROCESS

(COUNTING COPY 1/6)

Box number	Copies	Box number	Copies

I. BOXES FOR OPERATORS

Box number	Copies	Box number	Copies
1	1 to 4 except middle subdivision: 1 to 3	28	1 to 3
		29	1 to 3
2	1 to 4	30	1 to 3
3	1 to 4	31	1 to 4
4	1 to 4	32	1 to 4
5	1 to 4	33	first subdivision on the left: 1 to 4 remainder: 1 to 3
6	1 to 4		
7	1 to 3		
8	1 to 4		
9	1 to 3	34a	1 to 3
10	1 to 3	34b	1 to 3
11	1 to 3	35	1 to 4
12	1 to 3	36	1 to 3
13	1 to 3	37	1 to 3
14	1 to 4	38	1 to 4
15	1 to 4	39	1 to 3

Part III

I. BOXES FOR OPERATORS

15a	1 to 3	40	1 to 4
15b	1 to 3	41	1 to 3
16	1 to 3	42	1 to 3
17	1 to 4	43	1 to 3
17a	1 to 3	44	1 to 4
17b	1 to 3	45	1 to 3
18	1 to 4	46	1 to 3
19	1 to 4	47	1 to 3
20	1 to 3	48	1 to 3
21	1 to 4	49	1 to 3
22	1 to 3	50	1 to 4
23	1 to 3	51	1 to 4
24	1 to 3	52	1 to 4
25	1 to 4	53	1 to 4
26	1 to 3	54	1 to 4
27	1 to 4	55	—
		56	—

II. ADMINISTRATIVE BOXES

A	1 to 4[1]	C	1 to 4
B	1 to 3	D	1 to 4

[1] The Member State of dispatch can choose whether these particulars appear on the copies specified.

[ANNEX 37
SINGLE ADMINISTRATIVE DOCUMENT EXPLANATORY NOTES[1]

TITLE I
GENERAL REMARKS

A.
GENERAL DESCRIPTION

The forms and continuation forms are to be used:

(a) where Community legislation refers to a declaration for placing goods under a customs procedure or for re-exportation;

(b) as necessary during the transitional period provided for in an act of accession to the Community, in trade between the Community as constituted prior to that accession and the new Member States, and between the latter, in respect of goods for which customs duties and charges having equivalent effect have not yet been fully eliminated or which remain subject to other measures provided for in the act of accession;

(c) where Community rules specifically provide for their use.

The forms and continuation forms used for this purpose comprise the copies needed to complete the formalities relating to one or more customs procedures, taken from a set of eight copies:

-   copy 1 is kept by the authorities of the Member State in which export (dispatch) or Community transit formalities are completed,
-   copy 2 is used for statistical purposes by the Member State of export. This copy can be used as well for statistical purposes by the Member State of dispatch in cases of trade between parts of the customs territory of the Community with a different fiscal regime,
-   copy 3 is returned to the exporter after being stamped by the customs authority,
-   copy 4 is kept by the office of destination upon completion of the Community transit operation or as the document providing evidence of Community status of the goods,
-   copy 5 is the return copy for the Community transit procedure,
-   copy 6 is kept by the authorities of the Member State in which import formalities are completed,
-   copy 7 is used for statistical purposes by the Member State of import. This copy can be used as well for statistical purposes by the Member State of import in cases of trade between parts of the customs territory of the Community with a different fiscal regime,
-   copy 8 is returned to the consignee.

Various combinations are therefore possible, such as:

-   export, outward processing or re-export: copies 1, 2 and 3,
-   Community transit: copies 1, 4 and 5,
-   customs procedures at import: copies 6, 7 and 8.

In addition, there are circumstances in which the Community status of the goods in question has to be proved at destination. In such cases copy 4 should be used as a T2L document.

Operators may, if they wish, use privately printed subsets combining the appropriate copies, provided that they conform to the official specimen.

Each subset must be designed in such a way that where boxes must contain identical information in the two Member States involved, such information can be entered directly by the exporter or the principal on copy 1 and will then appear, by means of chemical treatment of the paper, on all the copies. Where, however, for any reason (in particular where the content of the information differs according to the stage of the operation involved) the information is not to be transmitted from one Member State to another, the desensitisation of the self-copying paper must confine reproduction to the copies concerned.

Where declarations are to be processed by computer, use may be made of subsets taken from sets in which each copy has a dual function: 1/6, 2/7, 3/8, 4/5.

In this case, in each subset, the numbers of the copies being used must be shown by striking through the numbers, in the margin of the form, referring to the copies not being used.

Every such subset must be designed so that the particulars which have to appear on each copy will be reproduced by means of chemical treatment of the paper.

When, pursuant to Article 205(3) of this Regulation, declarations for placing goods under a customs procedure, for re-export, or documents certifying the Community status of goods not being moved under the internal Community transit procedure are drawn up on plain paper by means of official or private-sector data-processing systems, the format of the said declarations or documents must comply with all the conditions laid down by the Code or this Regulation, including those relating to the back of the form (in respect of copies used under the Community transit procedure), except:

- the colour used for printing,
- the use of italic characters,
- the printing of a background for the Community transit boxes.

Where a transit declaration is processed at an office of departure by a computerised system, one copy of the declaration must be lodged at that office.

B.
PARTICULARS REQUIRED

The forms contain a number of boxes only some of which will be used, depending on the customs procedure(s) in question.

Without prejudice to the application of simplified procedures, the boxes which may be completed for each procedure are set out in the following table. The specific provisions concerning each box as they are described in Title II apply without prejudice to the status of the boxes as defined in the table.

Note that the status listed below have no bearing on the fact that certain particulars are collected only where circumstances warrant it. For example, the supplementary units in box 41 (status "A") will only be collected where required by the TARIC.

Box Nos	A	B	C	D	E	F	G	H	I	J	K
1(1)	A	A	A	A	A			A	A	A	A
1(2)	A	A	A	A	A			A	A	A	A
1(3)						A	A				
2	B[1]	A	B	B	B	B	B	B	B		
2 (No)	A	A	A	A	A	B	A	B	B		
3	A[2][3]	A[2][3]	A[2][3]	A[2][3]	A[2][3]	A[2][3]	A[2][3]	A[2][3]	A[2][3]	A[2][3]	A[2][3]
4	B		B		B	A[4]	A	B	B		
5	A	A	A	A	A	A	A	A	A	A	A
6	B		B	B	B	B[4]		B	B		
7	C	C	C	C	C	A[5]		C	C	C	C
8	B	B	B	B	B	A[6]		B	B	B	B
8 (No)	B	B	B	B	B	B		A	A	A	A
12								B	B		
14	B	B	B	B	B		B	B	B	B	B
14 (No)	A	A	A	A	A		A	A	A	A	A
15						A[2]					
15a	B	B	B	B	B	A[5]		A	A	B	B
17						A[2]					
17a	A	A	A	B	A	A[5]		B	B	B	B
17b								B	B	B	B
18 (Identity)	B[1][7]		B[7]		B[7]	A[7][24]		B[7]	B[7]		
18 (Nationality)						A[8][24]					
19	A[9]	A[9]	A[9]	A[9]	A[9]	B[4]		A[9]	A[9]	A[9]	A[9]
20	B[10]		B[10]		B[10]			B[10]	B[10]		B[10]
21 (Identity)	A[1]					B[8]					

21 (Nationality)	A[8]		A[8]		A[8]	A[8]		A[8]	A[8]		
22 (Currency)	B		B		B			A	A		B
22 (Amount)	B		B		B			C	C		
23	B[11]		B[11]		B[11]			B[11]	B[11]		
24	B		B		B			B	B		
25	A	B	A	B	A	B		A	A	B	B
26	A[12]	B12]	A[12]	B[12]	A[12]	B[12]		A[13]	A[13]	B[13]	B[13]
27						B					
29	B	B	B	B	B			B	B		B
30	B	B[1]	B	B	B	B[14]		B	B	B	B
31	A	A	A	A	A	A	A	A	A	A	A
32	A[3]	A[3]	A[3]	A[3]	A[3]	A[3]	A[3]	A[3]	A[3]	A[3]	A[3]
33(1)	A	A	A	A[15]	A	A[16]	A[17]	A	A	B	A
33(2)								A	A	B	A
33(3)	A	A						A	A	B	A
33(4)	A	A						A	A	B	A
33(5)	B	B	B	B	B			B	B	B	B
34a	C[1]	A	C	C	C			A	A	A	A
34b	B		B		B						
35	B	A	B	A	B	A	A	B	B	A	A
36								A	A[17]		
37(1)	A	A	A	A	A			A	A	A	A
37(2)	A	A	A	A	A			A	A	A	A
38	A	A	A	A	A	A[17]	A[17]	A[18]	A	A	A
39								B[19]	B		
40	A	A	A	A	A	A	A	A	A	A	A
41	A	A	A	A	A			A	A	A	A
42								A	A		A
43								B	B		B
44	A	A	A	A	A	A[4]	A	A	A	A	A
45								B	B		B
46	A	B	A	B	A			A	A	B	B
47 (Type)	BC[20]		BC[20]		BC[20]			A[18][21][22]	A[18][21][22]	A[18][21][2	
47 (Tax base)	B	B	B		B			A[18][21][22]	A[18][21][22]	A[18][21][2	
47 (Rate)	BC[20]		BC[20]		BC[20]			BC[18][20][21]	BC[18][20][21]		
47 (Amount)	BC[20]		BC[20]		BC[20]			BC[18][20][21]	BC[18][20][21]		
47 (Total)	BC[20]		BC[20]		BC[20]			BC[18][20][21]	BC[18][20][21]		
47 (MP)	B	B	B	B[18][22]							
48	B		B		B			B	B		
49	B[23]	A	B[23]	A	B[23]			B[23]	B[23]	A	A
50	C		C		C	A					
51						A[4]					
52						A					
53						A					
54	A	A	A	A	A		A	A	A	A	A

55						A					
56						A					

Legend

Column headings	Codes used for box 37, 1st subdivision
A: Export/Dispatch	10, 11, 23
B: Customs warehousing of prefinanced goods for export	76, 77
C: Re-export after a customs procedure with economic impact other than the customs warehousing procedure (inward processing, temporary importation, processing under customs control)	31
D: Re-export after customs warehousing	31
E: Outward processing	21, 22
F: Transit	
G: Community status of goods	
H: Release for free circulation	01, 02, 07, 40 41, 42, 43, 45, 48, 49, 61, 63, 68
I: Placing under a customs procedure with economic impact other than the outward processing and customs warehousing procedures (inward processing (suspension system), temporary importation, processing under customs control)	51, 53, 54, 91, 92
J: Placing in type A, B, C, E and F customs warehouses (¹)	71, 78
K: Placing in a type D customs warehouse (²) (³)	71, 78

¹ Column J also covers the entry of goods into free zones subject to type II controls.

² This column is also relevant for the cases referred to in Article 525(3).

³ Column K also covers the entry of goods into free zones subject to type II controls.

SYMBOLS IN THE CELLS

A: Mandatory: Particulars required by every Member State

B: Optional for the Member States: Particulars which Member States may decide to waive

C: Optional for operators: Particulars which operators may decide to supply but which cannot be demanded by the Member States

Notes

1.   This box is mandatory for agricultural products with export refunds.

2.   This particular may only be required for non-computerised procedures.

3.   When the declaration covers only one item of goods, the Member States may provide for this box to be left empty, the figure "1" having been entered in box 5.

4.   This box is mandatory for the NCTS in the manner provided for in Annex 37a.

5.   This particular may only be required for computerised procedures.

6.   This box is optional for the Member States where the consignee is not established in the Community nor in an EFTA country.

7.   Not for use in the case of postal consignments or carriage by fixed transport installations.

8.   Not for use in the case of postal consignments or carriage by fixed transport installations or rail.

9. This particular may be required for non-computerised procedures. In the case of computerised procedures, Member States need not collect this particular if they can deduce it from information elsewhere in the declaration and so transmit it to the Commission in compliance with the provisions on the collection of external trade statistics.

10. Member States may only require completion of the third subdivision where the customs administration is calculating customs value on behalf of the economic operator.

11. Member States may only require this information in cases in which the rules on the monthly fixing of exchange rates laid down in Title V, Chapter 6 do not apply.

12. This box must not be completed when export formalities are carried out at the point of exit from the Community.

13. This box must not be completed where the import formalities are carried out at the point of entry into the Community.

14. This box may be used in the NCTS in the manner provided for in Annex 37a.

15. Mandatory in the case of re-exportation following a type D warehouse procedure.

16. This subdivision must be completed where:
    – the transit declaration is made by the same person at the same time as, or following, a customs declaration which includes a commodity code, or
    – where a transit declaration covers goods on the list in Annex 44c, or
    – where Community legislation so provides.

17. For completion only where Community legislation so provides.

18. This information is not required for goods eligible for relief from import duties, unless the customs authorities consider it necessary for the application of the provisions governing the release for free circulation of the goods concerned.

19. Member States may waive this obligation if their systems allow them to deduce this information automatically and unambiguously from information elsewhere in the declaration.

20. This information is not to be provided when customs administrations calculate duties on behalf of operators on the basis of information elsewhere in the declaration. It is otherwise optional for the Member States.

21. This information is not to be provided when customs administrations calculate duties on behalf of operators on the basis of information elsewhere in the declaration.

22. Where the declaration is accompanied by the document referred to in Article 178(1), Member States may waive completion of this box.

23. This box is to be completed where the declaration of placing of goods under a customs procedure is used to discharge a customs warehousing procedure.

[24. Where goods are carried in containers that are to be transported by road vehicles, the customs authorities may authorise the principal to leave this box blank where the logistical pattern at the point of departure may prevent the identity and nationality of the means of transport from being provided at the time of establishment of the transit declaration and where the customs authorities can ensure that the required information concerning the means of transport will be subsequently entered in box 55.]

NOTES

Footnote 24 inserted by Commission Regulation (EC) 883/2005, Art 1, para 22, Annex IB, with effect from 1 January 2006. However, member states may apply the legislation before this date.

Column G, box 2 in the table: "B" substituted for "A" by Corrigendum.

C.
INSTRUCTIONS FOR USE OF THE FORM

Whenever a particular subset contains one or more copies which may be used in a Member State other than the one in which it was first completed, the forms must be completed by typewriter or by a mechanographical or similar process. For ease of completion by typewriter the form should be inserted in the machine in such a way that the first letter of the particulars to be entered in box 2 is placed in the position box in the top left-hand corner.

Where all the copies of a subset are intended for use in the same Member State, they may be filled in legibly by hand, in ink and in block capitals, provided that this is allowed in that Member State. The same applies to the particulars to be given on the copies used for the purposes of the Community transit procedure.

The form must contain no erasures or overwriting. Any alterations must be made by crossing out the incorrect particulars and adding those required. Any alterations made in this way must be initialled by the person making them and expressly endorsed by the competent authorities. The latter may, where necessary, require a new declaration to be lodged.

In addition, the forms may be completed using an automatic reproduction process instead of any of the procedures mentioned above. They may also be produced and completed by this means on condition that the provisions concerning the specimen forms, format, language used, legibility, absence of erasures and overwriting, and amendments are strictly observed.

Only numbered boxes are to be completed, as appropriate, by operators. The other boxes, identified by a capital letter, are for administrative use.

Without prejudice to Article 205, the copies which are to remain at the office of export/dispatch or departure must bear the original signature of the persons concerned.

The lodging with a customs office of a declaration signed by the declarant or his representative shall indicate that the person concerned is declaring the goods in question for the procedure applied for and, without prejudice to the possible application of sanctions, shall be held responsible, in accordance with the provisions in force in the Member States, in respect of:

–   the accuracy of the information given in the declaration,
–   the authenticity of the documents attached,
–   the observance of all the obligations inherent in the placement of the goods in question under the procedure concerned.

The signature of the principal or, where applicable, his authorised representative commits him in respect of all particulars relating to the Community transit operation pursuant to the provisions on Community transit laid down in the Code and in this Regulation and as listed in section B above.

As regards Community transit formalities and formalities at destination, it is in the interests of each person intervening in the operation to check the contents of his declaration before signing it and lodging it with the customs office. In particular, any discrepancy found by the person concerned between the goods which he is to declare and any particulars already entered on the forms being used must immediately be reported by that person to the customs authority. In such cases the declaration must then be made out on fresh forms.

Unless Title III provides otherwise, a box that is not to be used should be left completely blank.

TITLE II
PARTICULARS TO BE ENTERED IN THE VARIOUS BOXES

A.
FORMALITIES RELATING TO EXPORT/DISPATCH, THE CUSTOMS WAREHOUSING OF PREFINANCED GOODS FOR EXPORT, RE-EXPORTATION, OUTWARD PROCESSING, COMMUNITY TRANSIT AND/OR PROVING THE COMMUNITY STATUS OF GOODS

Box 1: Declaration

In the first subdivision, enter the relevant Community code from Annex 38.

In the second subdivision, enter the type of declaration using the relevant Community code from Annex 38.

In the third subdivision, enter the relevant Community code from Annex 38.

Box 2: Consignor/Exporter

Enter the identification number assigned by the competent authorities to the person concerned for fiscal, statistical or other purposes. The structure of this number must comply with the criteria laid down in Annex 38. Where the interested party does not have such a number, the customs administration may assign him one for the declaration concerned.

For the purposes of this Annex, the definition of "exporter" is that given in Community customs legislation. In this context, "consignor" refers to an operator that acts as an exporter in the cases referred to in Article 206, [third sub-paragraph]. Enter the full name and address of the person concerned.

In the case of groupage consignments, the Member States may provide that the word various be entered in this box, and the list of consignors/exporters to be attached to the declaration.

NOTES

Words in second paragraph substituted by Corrigendum.

Box 3: Forms

Enter the number of the subset in relation to the total number of subsets of forms and continuation forms used. For example, if there is one EX form and two EX/c forms, enter 1/3 on the EX form, 2/3 on the first EX/c form and 3/3 on the second EX/c form.

Where the declaration is made up from two sets of four copies instead of one set of eight copies, the two sets are to be treated as one for the purpose of establishing the number of forms.

Box 4: Loading lists

Enter in figures the number of any loading lists attached, or of commercial descriptive lists where these are authorised by the competent authority.

Box 5: Items

Enter in figures the total number of items declared by the person concerned in all the forms and continuation forms (or loading lists or commercial lists) used. The number of items must correspond to the number of boxes 31 to be completed.

Box 6: Total packages

Enter in figures the total number of packages making up the consignment in question.

Box 7: Reference number

This entry concerns the commercial reference number assigned by the person concerned to the consignment in question. It may take the form of a Unique Consignment Reference Number (UCR)([2]).

Box 8: Consignee

Part III

Enter the full name and address of the person(s) to whom the goods are to be delivered. Where prefinanced goods for export are entered into a customs warehouse, the consignee is the person responsible for the pre-financing or the person responsible for the warehouse where the goods are stocked.

The structure of any identification number must comply with the criteria laid down in Annex 38.

In the case of groupage consignments, the Member States may provide that the word "various" be entered in this box, and the list of consignees attached to the declaration.

Box 14: Declarant/Representative

Enter the identification number assigned to the person concerned by the competent authorities for tax, statistical or other purposes. The structure of that number must comply with the criteria laid down in Annex 38. Where the interested party does not have such a number, the customs administration may assign him one for the declaration concerned.

Enter the full name and address of the person concerned.

If the declarant and the exporter/consignor are the same person, enter "exporter" or "consignor".

To designate the declarant or the status of the representative, use the relevant Community code from Annex 38.

Box 15: Country of dispatch/export

For the purposes of export formalities, the "Member State of actual export" is the Member State from which the goods were initially dispatched for the purpose of export, if the exporter is not established in the Member State of export. If no other Member State is involved, the Member State of export will be the same as the Member State of actual export.

Enter in box 15a the relevant Community code from Annex 38 for the Member State of export/dispatch of the goods. In case of transit, enter in box 15 the Member State from where the goods are dispatched.

Box 17: Country of destination

Using the relevant Community code from Annex 38, enter in box 17a the last country of destination of the goods to be exported as known at the time of export.

Box 18: Identity and nationality of means of transport at departure

Enter the identity of the means of transport on which the goods are directly loaded at the time of export or transit formalities, followed by the nationality of the means of transport (or that of the vehicle propelling the others if there are several means of transport) in the form of the relevant Community code from Annex 38. If a tractor and trailer with different registration numbers are used, enter the registration numbers of both the tractor and the trailer together with the nationality of the tractor.

Depending on the means of transport concerned, the following details concerning identity may be entered:

Means of transport	Method of identification
Sea and inland waterway transport	Name of vessel
Air transport	Number and date of flight (where there is no flight number, enter the aircraft's registration number)
Road transport	Vehicle registration number
Rail transport	Wagon number

Box 19: Container (Ctr)

Using the relevant Community code from Annex 38, enter the presumed situation when crossing the external Community frontier, based on the information available at the time of completion of the export formalities.

Box 20: Delivery terms
Using the relevant Community codes and headings from Annex 38, give particulars of the terms of the commercial contract.

Box 21: Identity and nationality of active means of transport crossing the border
Using the relevant Community code from Annex 38, enter the nationality of the active means of transport crossing the Community's external frontier as known at the time of completion of formalities.

In the case of combined transport or where several means of transport are used, the active means of transport is the one which propels the whole combination. For example, in the case of a lorry on a sea-going vessel, the active means of transport is the ship. In the case of a tractor and trailer, the active means of transport is the tractor. Depending on the means of transport concerned, the following details concerning identity may be entered:

Means of transport	Method of identification
Sea and inland waterway transport	Name of vessel
Air transport	Number and date of flight (where there is no flight number, enter the aircraft's registration number)
Road transport	Vehicle registration number
Rail transport	Wagon number

Box 22: Currency and total amount invoiced
Using the relevant code from Annex 38, enter in the first subdivision the currency in which the commercial invoice was drawn up.

Enter in the second subdivision the invoiced price for all goods declared.

Box 23: Exchange rate
This box contains the exchange rate in force between the invoice currency and the currency of the Member State concerned.

Box 24: Nature of transaction
Using the relevant Community codes and headings from Annex 38, enter the type of the transaction concerned.

Box 25: Mode of transport at the border
Using the relevant Community code from Annex 38, enter the mode of transport corresponding to the active means of transport which it is expected will be used on exit from the customs territory of the Community.

Box 26: Inland mode of transport
Using the relevant Community code from Annex 38, enter the mode of transport upon departure.

Box 27: Place of loading
Using a code where required, enter the place, as known at the time of completion of formalities, at which the goods are to be loaded onto the active means of transport on which they are to cross the Community frontier.

Box 29: Office of exit
Using the relevant Community code from Annex 38, enter the customs office by which it is intended that the goods should leave the customs territory of the Community.

Box 30: Location of goods
Enter the precise location where the goods may be examined.

Box 31: Packages and description of goods; Marks and numbers — Container No(s) — Number and kind

Enter the marks, numbers, quantity and kind of packages or, in the case of unpackaged goods, enter the number of such goods covered by the declaration together with the particulars needed to identify them. The description of the goods means the normal trade description. Where box 33 Commodity Code is to be completed, the description must be precise enough to allow the goods to be classified. This box must also contain the particulars required by any specific legislation. Using the relevant Community code from Annex 38, enter the kind of the packages.

If containers are used, their identifying marks should also be entered in this box.

Box 32: Item number

Enter the number of the item in question in relation to the total number of items declared in the forms and continuation forms used, as described in the note to box 5.

Box 33: Commodity Code

Enter the code number corresponding to the item in question, as described in Annex 38.

Box 34: Country-of-origin code

Operators completing box 34a should use the relevant Community code from Annex 38 to enter the country of origin, as defined in Title II of the Code.

Enter the region of dispatch or production of the goods in question in Box 34b.

Box 35: Gross mass (kg)

Enter the gross mass, expressed in kilograms, of the goods described in the relevant box 31. The gross mass is the aggregate mass of the goods with all their packing, excluding containers and other transport equipment.

Where a transit declaration covers several types of goods, the total gross mass needs only be entered in the first box 35, the remaining boxes 35 being left blank. Member States may extend this rule to all procedures referred to under columns A to E and G of the table in Title I, B.

Where a gross mass greater than 1 kg includes a fraction of a unit (kg), it may be rounded off in the following manner:

–   from 0.001 to 0.499: rounding down to the nearest kg,

–   from 0.5 to 0.999: rounding up to the nearest kg.

A gross mass of less than 1 kg should be entered as 0.xyz (eg 0.654 for a package of 654 grams).

Box 37: Procedure

Using the relevant Community code from Annex 38, enter the procedure for which the goods are declared.

Box 38: Net mass (kg)

Enter the net mass, expressed in kilograms, of the goods described in the relevant box 31. The net mass is the mass of the goods without any packaging.

Box 40: Summary declaration/Previous document

Using the relevant Community codes from Annex 38, enter the reference particulars of documents preceding export to a third country/dispatch to a Member State.

Where the declaration concerns goods re-exported following discharge of the customs warehousing procedure in a type B customs warehouse, enter the reference particulars of the declaration entering goods for that procedure.

In the case of a declaration entering goods for the Community transit procedure, give the reference for the previous customs destination or corresponding customs documents. Where, in the case of non-computerised transit procedures, more than one reference has to be entered, the Member States may provide that the word "various" be entered in this box and a list of the references concerned accompany the transit declaration.

Box 41: Supplementary units

Where necessary, enter the quantity of the item in question, expressed in the unit laid down in the goods nomenclature.

Box 44: Additional information/Documents produced/Certificates and authorisations

Using the relevant Community codes from Annex 38, enter the details required by any specific rules applicable together with reference particulars of the documents produced in support of the declaration, including the serial numbers of any control copies T5. The subdivision "A.I. code" (Additional information code) must not be used.

Where a re-export declaration discharging the customs warehousing procedure is lodged with a customs office other than the supervising office, enter the name and full address of the supervising office.

Declarations made in Member States which, during the transitional period for the introduction of the euro, give the opportunity to operators to opt for the use of the euro unit for the establishment of their customs declarations must include in this box, preferably in the subdivision in the bottom right-hand corner, an indicator of the currency unit, national unit or euro unit, used.

Member States may provide that this indicator be entered only in box 44 for the first item of goods of the declaration. In this case, the information will be deemed valid for all the goods items of the declaration.

This indicator will be constituted by the iso-alpha-3 currency code (ISO 4217).

Box 46: Statistical value

Enter the statistical value expressed in the currency unit the code for which may appear in box 44, or, in the absence of such a code in box 44, in the currency of the Member State where the export formalities are completed, in accordance with the Community provisions in force.

Box 47: Calculation of taxes

Enter the tax base applicable (value, weight or other). Using, where necessary, the relevant Community codes from Annex 38, the following should be shown on each line:

- the type of tax (eg excise duties),
- the tax base,
- the rate of tax applicable,
- the amount of tax payable,
- the method of payment chosen (MP).

The amounts in this box must be expressed in the currency unit the code for which may appear in box 44, or, in the absence of such a code in box 44, in the currency of the Member State where the export formalities are completed.

Box 48: Deferred payment

Enter, where applicable, the reference particulars of the authorisation in question; deferred payment here refers both to deferred payment of customs duties and to tax credit.

Box 49: Identification of warehouse

Using the relevant Community code from Annex 38, enter the reference particulars of the warehouse.

Box 50: Principal

Enter the full name (person or company) and address of the principal, together with the identification number, if any, allocated by the competent authorities. Where appropriate, enter the full name (person or company) of the authorised representative signing on behalf of the principal.

Subject to specific provisions to be adopted with regard to the use of computerised systems, the original of the handwritten signature of the person concerned must be given on the copy which is to remain at the office of departure. Where the principal is a legal person, the signatory should add his capacity after his signature and full name.

Part III

For export operations, the declarant or his representative may enter the name and address of a person established in the district of the office of exit to whom copy 3 of the declaration endorsed by the said office may be given.

Box 51: Intended offices of transit (and country)

Enter the code for the intended office of entry into each EFTA country to be crossed and the office of entry by which the goods re-enter the customs territory of the Community after having crossed the territory of an EFTA country, or, where the shipment is to cross a territory other than that of the Community or of an EFTA country, the office of exit by which the transport leaves the Community and the office of entry by which it re-enters the Community.

Using the relevant Community code from Annex 38, enter the customs offices concerned.

Box 52: Guarantee

Using the relevant Community codes from Annex 38, enter the type of guarantee or guarantee waiver used for the operation as well as, as appropriate, the number of the comprehensive guarantee certificate, the guarantee waiver certificate, or the individual guarantee voucher and the office of guarantee.

Where a comprehensive guarantee, guarantee waiver or individual guarantee is not valid for all the EFTA countries, add after not valid for the codes from Annex 38 for the EFTA country or countries concerned.

Box 53: Office of destination (and country)

Using the relevant Community code from Annex 38, enter the office where the goods are to be presented in order to complete the Community transit operation.

Box 54: Place and date, signature and name of the declarant or his representative

Enter the place and date of completion of the declaration.

Subject to specific provisions to be adopted with regard to the use of computerised systems, the original of the handwritten signature of the person concerned must be given on the copy which is to remain at the office of export/dispatch, followed by the full name of that person. Where that person is a legal person, the signatory should add his capacity after his signature and full name.

B. FORMALITIES EN ROUTE

Between the time when the goods leave the office of export and/or departure, and the time when they arrive at the office of destination, certain particulars may have to be entered on the copies of the Single Administrative Document accompanying the goods. These particulars concern the transport operation and are to be entered on the document in the course of the operation by the carrier responsible for the means of transport on which the goods are directly loaded. The particulars may be added legibly by hand; in this case, the form should be completed in ink in block capitals.

These particulars, which only appear on copies 4 and 5, concern the following boxes:

– Transhipment: Use box 55.

Box 55: Transhipments

The first three lines of this box are to be completed by the carrier where, during the operation in question, the goods are transhipped from one means of transport to another or from one container to another.

The carrier may not tranship goods without the prior authorisation of the customs authorities of the Member State in whose territory the transhipment is to be made.

Where those authorities consider that the transit operation may continue in the normal way, they shall, once they have taken any steps that may be necessary, endorse copies 4 and 5 of the transit declaration.

– Other incidents: Use box 56.

Box 56: Other incidents during carriage

Box to be completed in accordance with existing obligations under the Community transit procedure.

In addition, where the goods were loaded on a semi-trailer and only the tractor vehicle is changed during the journey (without the goods being handled or transhipped) enter in this box the registration number of the new tractor. In such cases endorsement by the competent authorities is not necessary.

C.

FORMALITIES FOR RELEASE FOR FREE CIRCULATION, INWARD PROCESSING, TEMPORARY IMPORTATION, PROCESSING UNDER CUSTOMS CONTROL, CUSTOMS WAREHOUSING AND THE ENTRY OF GOODS TO FREE ZONES SUBJECT TO TYPE II CONTROLS

Box 1: Declaration

In the first subdivision, enter the relevant Community code from Annex 38.

In the second subdivision, enter the type of declaration using the relevant Community code from Annex 38.

Box 2: Consignor/Exporter

Enter the full name and address of the last seller of the goods prior to their importation into the Community.

Where an identification number is required, the Member States may waive provision of the full name and address of the person concerned.

The structure of any identification number must comply with the criteria laid down in Annex 38.

In the case of groupage consignments, the Member States may provide that the word "various" be entered in this box, and the list of consignors/exporters attached to the declaration.

Box 3: Forms

Enter the number of the subset in relation to the total number of subsets of forms and continuation forms used. For example, if there is one IM form and two IM/c forms, enter "1/3" on the IM form, "2/3" on the first IM/c form and "3/3" on the second IM/c form.

Box 4: Loading lists

Enter in figures the number of any loading lists attached, or of commercial descriptive lists where these are authorised by the competent authority.

Box 5: Items

Enter in figures the total number of items declared by the person concerned in all the forms and continuation forms (or loading lists or commercial lists) used. The number of items must correspond to the number of boxes 31 to be completed.

Box 6: Total packages

Enter in figures the total number of packages making up the consignment in question.

Box 7: Reference number

This entry concerns the commercial reference number assigned by the person concerned to the consignment in question. It may take the form of a Unique Consignment Reference Number (UCR)([2]).

Box 8: Consignee

Enter the identification number assigned by the competent authorities to the person concerned for fiscal, statistical or other purposes. The structure of this number must comply with the criteria laid down in Annex 38. Where the interested party does not have such a number, the customs administration may assign him one for the declaration concerned.

Enter the full name and address of the person concerned.

In the case of placing of goods under the customs warehousing procedure in a private warehouse (type C, D or E), enter the full name and address of the depositor where he is not the declarant.

In the case of groupage consignments, the Member States may provide that the word "various" be entered in this box, and the list of consignees attached to the declaration.

Box 12: Value details

Enter in this box information on value, eg a reference to the authorisation whereby the customs authorities waive the requirement to produce a DV1 form in support of each declaration or details of adjustments.

Box 14: Declarant/Representative

Enter the identification number assigned to the person concerned by the competent authorities for tax, statistical or other purposes. The structure of that number must comply with the criteria laid down in Annex 38. Where the interested party does not have such a number, the customs administration may assign him one for the declaration concerned.

Enter the full name and address of the person concerned.

If the declarant and the consignee are the same person, enter the word consignee.

To designate the declarant or the status of the representative, use the relevant Community code from Annex 38.

Box 15: Country of dispatch/export

If no stoppage or judicial action unrelated to transport has taken place in an intermediate country, enter in box 15a the relevant Community code from Annex 38 for the country from which the goods were initially dispatched to the Member State of import. If such stoppages or actions have taken place, the last intermediate country is to be considered the country of dispatch/export.

Box 17: Country of destination

Enter in box 17a the Community code from Annex 38 for the Member State of final destination of the goods, as known at the time of importation.

Enter in box 17b the region of destination of the goods.

Box 18: Identity and nationality of means of transport on arrival

Enter the identity of the means of transport on which the goods are directly loaded at the time of presentation at the customs office where the destination formalities are completed. If a tractor and trailer with different registration numbers are used, enter the registration number of both the tractor and the trailer.

Depending on the means of transport concerned, the following details concerning identity may be entered:

Means of transport	Method of identification
Sea and inland waterway transport	Name of vessel
Air transport	Number and date of flight (where there is no flight number, enter the aircraft's registration number)
Road transport	Vehicle registration number
Rail transport	Wagon number

Box 19: Container (Ctr)

Using the relevant Community code from Annex 38, enter the situation when crossing the external Community frontier.

Box 20: Delivery terms

Using the relevant Community codes and headings from Annex 38, give particulars of the terms of the commercial contract.

Box 21: Identity and nationality of active means of transport crossing the border

Using the relevant Community code from Annex 38, enter the nationality of the active means of transport crossing the Communitys external frontier.

In the case of combined transport or where several means of transport are used, the active means of transport is the one which propels the whole combination. For example, in the case of a lorry on a sea-going vessel, the active means of transport is the ship. In the case of a tractor and trailer, the active means of transport is the tractor.

Box 22: Currency and total amount invoiced

Using the relevant code from Annex 38, enter in the first subdivision the currency in which the commercial invoice was drawn up.

Enter in the second subdivision the invoiced price for all goods declared.

Box 23: Exchange rate

This box contains the exchange rate in force between the invoice currency and the currency of the Member State concerned.

Box 24: Nature of transaction

Using the relevant Community codes and headings from Annex 38, enter the type of the transaction concerned.

Box 25: Mode of transport at the border

Using the relevant Community code from Annex 38, enter the mode of transport corresponding to the active means of transport with which the goods entered the customs territory of the Community.

Box 26: Inland mode of transport

Using the relevant Community code from Annex 38, enter the mode of transport upon arrival.

Box 29: Office of entry

Using the relevant Community code from Annex 38, enter the customs office by which the goods entered the customs territory of the Community.

Box 30: Location of goods

Enter the precise location where the goods may be examined.

Box 31: Packages and description of goods; Marks and numbers — Container No(s) — Number and kind

Enter the marks, numbers, quantity and kind of packages or, in the case of unpackaged goods, enter the number of such goods covered by the declaration, together with the particulars necessary to identify them. The description of the goods means the normal trade description. Except for non-Community goods placed under the customs warehousing procedure in a type A, B, C, E or F warehouse, this description must be expressed in terms sufficiently precise to enable immediate and unambiguous identification and classification. This box must also contain the particulars required by any specific rules (eg VAT, excise duties). Using the relevant Community code from Annex 38, enter the kind of the packages.

If containers are used, their identifying marks should also be entered in this box.

Box 32: Item number

Enter the number of the item in question in relation to the total number of items declared in the forms and continuation forms used, as described in the note to box 5.

Box 33: Commodity Code

Enter the code number corresponding to the item in question, as described in Annex 38. The Member States may provide for entry of a specific nomenclature concerning excise duties in the fifth subdivision.

Box 34: Country-of-origin code

Enter in box 34a the relevant Community code from Annex 38 for the country of origin, as defined in Title II of the Code.

Box 35: Gross mass (kg)

Enter the gross mass, expressed in kilograms, of the goods described in the relevant box 31. The gross mass is the aggregate mass of the goods with all their packing, excluding containers and other transport equipment.

Where a declaration covers several types of goods, Member States may decide that, for the procedures referred to under columns H to K of the table in Title I, B, the total gross mass only be entered in the first box 35, the remaining boxes 35 being left blank. Where a gross mass greater than 1 kg includes a fraction of a unit (kg), it may be rounded off in the following manner:

- from 0.001 to 0.499: rounding down to the nearest kg,
- from 0.5 to 0.999: rounding up to the nearest kg,
- a gross mass of less than 1 kg should be entered as 0.xyz (eg 0.654 for a package of 654 grams).

Box 36: Preference

This box contains information on the tariff treatment of the goods. Where its use is provided for in the matrix of Title I, section B, it must be used even when no tariff preferential treatment is requested. However, this box must not be used in the context of trade between parts of the customs territory of the Community in which the provisions of Directive 77/388/EEC are applicable and parts of that territory in which those provisions do not apply, or in the context of trade between the parts of that territory where those provisions do not apply. Enter the relevant Community code from Annex 38.

The Commission will publish at regular intervals in the C series of the *Official Journal of the European Union* the list of the combinations of codes usable together with examples and explanatory notes.

Box 37: Procedure

Using the relevant Community code from Annex 38, enter the procedure for which the goods are declared.

Box 38: Net mass (kg)

Enter the net mass, expressed in kilograms, of the goods described in the relevant box 31. The net mass is the mass of the goods without any packaging.

Box 39: Quota

Enter the order number of the tariff quota for which the declarant is applying.

Box 40: Summary declaration/Previous document

Using the relevant Community codes from Annex 38, enter the reference particulars of any summary declaration used in the Member State of import or of any previous document.

Box 41: Supplementary units

Where necessary, enter the quantity of the item in question, expressed in the unit laid down in the goods nomenclature.

Box 42: Item price

Enter the price of the item in question.

Box 43: Valuation method

Using the relevant Community code from Annex 38, enter the valuation method used.

Box 44: Additional information/Documents produced/Certificates and authorisations

Using the relevant Community codes from Annex 38, enter the details required by any specific rules applicable together with reference particulars of the documents produced in support of the declaration, including the serial numbers of any control copies T5. The subdivision "A.I. code" must not be used.

Where a declaration entering goods for the customs warehousing procedure is lodged with a customs office other than the supervising office, enter the name and full address of the supervising office.

Declarations made in Member States which, during the transitional period for the introduction of the euro, give the opportunity to operators to opt for the use of the euro unit for the establishment of their customs declarations must include in this box, preferably in the subdivision in the bottom right-hand corner, an indicator of the currency unit, national unit or euro unit, used.

Member States may provide that this indicator be entered only in box 44 for the first item of goods of the declaration. In this case, the information will be deemed valid for all the goods items of the declaration.

This indicator will be constituted by the iso-alpha-3 currency code (ISO 4217).

Box 45: Adjustment

This box contains information of any adjustments when no DV1 form is produced in support of the declaration. Any amounts to be entered in this box are to be expressed in the currency unit the code for which may appear in box 44, or, in the absence of such a code in box 44, in the currency of the Member State where the import formalities are completed.

Box 46: Statistical value

Enter the statistical value expressed in the currency unit the code for which may appear in box 44, or, in the absence of such a code in box 44, in the currency of the Member State where the import formalities are completed, in accordance with the Community provisions in force.

Box 47: Calculation of taxes

Enter the tax base applicable (value, weight or other). Using, where necessary, the relevant Community codes from Annex 38, the following should be shown on each line:

- the type of tax (eg import duty, VAT),
- the tax base,
- the rate of tax applicable,
- the amount of tax payable,
- the method of payment chosen (MP).

The amounts in this box must be expressed in the currency unit the code for which may appear in box 44, or, in the absence of such a code in box 44, in the currency of the Member State where the import formalities are completed.

Box 48: Deferred payment

Enter, where applicable, the reference particulars of the authorisation in question; deferred payment here refers both to deferred payment of customs duties and to tax credit.

Box 49: Identification of warehouse

Using the relevant Community code from Annex 38, enter the reference particulars of the warehouse.

Box 54: Place and date, signature and name of the declarant or his representative

Enter the place and date of the completion of the declaration.

Subject to specific provisions to be adopted with regard to the use of computerised systems, the original of the handwritten signature of the person concerned must be given on the copy which is to remain at the office of import, followed by the full name of that person. Where that person is a legal person, the signatory should add his capacity after his signature and full name.

TITLE III

REMARKS CONCERNING THE CONTINUATION FORMS

A.   *Continuation forms should only be used where the declaration covers more than one item (cf. box 5). They must be presented together with an IM, EX, EU or CO form.*

B.   *The instructions in Titles I and II also apply to the continuation forms.* However:

– the symbols "IM/c", "EX/c" or "EU/c" (or "CO/c" where applicable) must be entered in the first subdivision of box 1, that subdivision being left blank only where:
– the form is used for Community transit only, in which case, depending on the Community transit procedure applicable to the goods concerned, "T1bis", "T2bis", "T2Fbis" or "T2SMbis" will be entered in the third subdivision of box 1,
– the form is used solely to furnish proof of the Community status of goods, in which case, depending on the status of the goods concerned, "T2Lbis", "T2LFbis" or "T2LSMbis" will be entered in the third subdivision of the box,
– box 2/8 is for optional use by the Member States and should show only the name and identification number, if any, of the person concerned,
– the "summary" part of box 47 concerns the final summary of all the items covered by the IM and IM/c, EX and EX/c, EU and EU/c or CO and CO/c forms used. It should therefore be used only on the last of the IM/c, EX/c, EU/c or CO/c forms attached to an IM, EX, EU or CO document in order to show the total payable by type of tax.

C. *If continuation forms are used,*
– any boxes 31 (Packages and description of goods) which have not been used must be struck out to prevent later use,
– when the third subdivision of box 1 contains the symbol T, boxes 32 (Item number), 33 (Commodity code), 35 (Gross mass (kg)), 38 (Net mass (kg)), 40 (Summary declaration/previous document) and 44 (Additional information, documents produced, certificates and authorisations) of the first item of goods of the transit declaration used must be struck through and the first box 31 (Packages and description of goods) of this document may not be used to enter the marks, numbers, number and kind of packages or goods description. In the first box 31 of this document, reference will be made, as appropriate, to the number of continuation forms bearing the respective symbols T1bis, T2bis or T2Fbis.

---

[1] The term "EFTA" in this Annex refers not only to the EFTA countries but to the other non-Community contracting parties to the Conventions on a common transit procedure and on the simplification of formalities in trade in goods.

[2] Recommendation of the Customs Co-operation Council concerning the unique consignment reference number (UCR) for Customs purposes (30 June 2001).

NOTES

Annex 37 substituted by Commission Regulation 2003/2286, Art 1, para 18, Annex IV, with effect from 1 January 2006.

[ANNEX 37A

EXPLANATORY NOTE ON THE USE OF TRANSIT DECLARATIONS BY THE EXCHANGE OF EDI STANDARD MESSAGES (EDI TRANSIT DECLARATION)

TITLE I
GENERAL

The EDI transit declaration is based upon the particulars entered into the different boxes of the Single Administrative Document (SAD) as defined in Annexes 37 and 38, in association with or replaced by a code if appropriate.

This Annex contains exclusively the basic special requirements, which apply when the formalities are carried out by the exchange of the EDI standard messages. Furthermore the additional codes presented in Annex 37c are applicable. Annexes 37 and 38 apply to the EDI transit declaration unless otherwise specified in this Annex or in Annex 37c.

— GUARANTEE REFERENCE
— VALIDITY LIMITATION (EC)
— VALIDITY LIMITATION (NON-EC)

B. PARTICULARS ON THE DATA OF THE TRANSIT DECLARATION

TRANSIT OPERATION

Number: 1
The data group shall be used.

LRN
Type/Length: an ..22
The local reference number (LRN) shall be used. It is nationally defined and allocated by the user in agreement with the competent authorities to identify each single declaration.

Declaration type (box 1)
Type/Length: an ..5
The attribute shall be used.

Total number of items (box 5)
Type/Length: n ..5
The attribute shall be used.

Total number of packages (box 6)
[Type/Length: n..7]
The attribute shall be used.
The use of the attribute is optional. The total number of packages is equal to the sum of all "Number of packages", all "Number of pieces" and a value of "1" for each declared "bulk".]

Country of dispatch (box 15a)
Type/Length: a2
The attribute shall be used, if only one country of dispatch is declared. The country codes presented in Annex 37c shall be used. In this case the attribute "Country of dispatch" of the data group "GOODS ITEM" cannot be used. If more than one country of dispatch is declared, this attribute of the data group "TRANSIT OPERATION" cannot be used. In this case the attribute "Country of dispatch", of the data group "GOODS ITEM" shall be used.

Destination country (box 17a)
Type/Length: a2
The attribute shall be used, if only one country of destination is declared. The country codes presented in Annex 37c shall be used. In this case the attribute "Destination country" of the data group "GOODS ITEM" cannot be used. If more than one country of destination is declared, this attribute of the data group "TRANSIT OPERATION" cannot be used. In this case the attribute "Destination country" of the data group "GOODS ITEM" shall be used.

Identity at departure (box 18)
Type/Length: an ..27
The attribute shall be used according to Annex 37.

Identity at departure LNG
Type/Length: a2
The language code presented in Annex 37c shall be used to define the language (LNG) if the corresponding free text field is used.

Nationality at departure (box 18)
Type/Length: a2
The country code presented in Annex 37c shall be used according to Annex 37.

The detailed structure and content of the EDI transit declaration follow the technical specifications the competent authorities communicate to the principal in order to ensure the proper functioning of the system. These specifications are based upon the requirements laid down in this Annex.

This Annex describes the structure of the information exchange. The transit declaration is organised into data groups, which contain data attributes. The attributes are grouped together in such a way that they build up coherent logical blocks within the scope of the message. A data group indentation indicates that the data group depends on a lower indent data group.

When present, the appropriate number of the box on the SAD is noted.

The term "number" in the explanation of a data group indicates how many times the data group may be used in the transit declaration.

The term "type/length" in the explanation of an attribute indicates the requirements for the data type and the data length. The codes for the data types are as follows—

a alphabetic
n numeric
an alphanumeric

The number following the code indicates the admissible data length. The following applies.

The optional two dots before the length indicator mean that the data has no fixed length, but it can have up to a number of digits, as specified by the length indicator. A comma in the data length means that the attribute can hold decimals, the digit before the comma indicates the total length of the attribute, the digit after the comma indicates the maximum number of digits after the decimal point.

TITLE II
STRUCTURE OF THE EDI TRANSIT DECLARATION

A.
TABLE OF THE DATA GROUPS

TRANSIT OPERATION
TRADER consignor
TRADER consignee
GOODS ITEM
— TRADER consignor
— TRADER consignee
— CONTAINERS
— SGI CODES
— PACKAGES
— PREVIOUS ADMINISTRATIVE REFERENCES
— PRODUCED DOCUMENTS/CERTIFICATES
— SPECIAL MENTIONS
CUSTOMS OFFICE of departure
TRADER principal
REPRESENTATIVE
CUSTOMS OFFICE of transit
CUSTOMS OFFICE of destination
TRADER authorised consignee
CONTROL RESULT
SEALS INFORMATION
— SEALS ID
GUARANTEE

Part III

Container . . . . (box 19)
Type/Length: n1
The following codes shall be used
0: no
1: yes.
Nationality crossing border . . . . (box 21)
Type/Length: a2
The country code presented in Annex 37c shall be used according to Annex 37.
Identity crossing border . . . . (box 21)
Type/Length: an ..27
The use of the attribute is optional for the Member States according to Annex 37.
Identity crossing border LNG
Type/Length: a2
The language code presented in Annex 37c shall be used to define the language (LNG)
if the corresponding free text field is used.
Type of transport crossing border . . . . (box 21)
Type/Length: n ..2
The use of the attribute is optional for the Member States according to Annex 37.
Transport mode at border . . . . (box 25)
Type/Length: n ..2
The use of the attribute is optional for the Member States according to Annex 37.
Inland transport mode . . . . (box 26)
Type/Length: n ..2
The use of the attribute is optional for the Member States. It has to be used according
to the explanatory note concerning box 25 presented in Annex 38.
Loading place . . . . (box 27)
Type/Length: an ..17
The use of the attribute is optional for the Member States.
Agreed location code . . . . (box 30)
Type/Length: an ..17
The attribute cannot be used, if the data group "CONTROL RESULT" is used. If this
data group is not used the attribute is optional. If this attribute is used the precise
indication of the place in coded form where the goods can be examined is necessary.
The attributes "Agreed location of goods"/ "Agreed location code", "Authorised
location of goods" and "Customs subplace" cannot be used at the same time.
Agreed location of goods . . . . (box 30)
Type/Length: an ..35
The attribute cannot be used, if the data group "CONTROL RESULT" is used. If this
data group is not used the attribute is optional. If this attribute is used the precise
indication of the place where the goods can be examined is necessary. The attributes
"Agreed location of goods"/ "Agreed location code", "Authorised location of goods"
and "Customs subplace" cannot be used at the same time.
Agreed location of goods LNG
Type/Length: a2
The language code presented in Annex 37c shall be used to define the language (LNG)
if the corresponding free text field is used.
Authorised location of goods . . . . (box 30)
Type/Length: an ..17
The attribute is optional, if the data group "CONTROL RESULT" is used. If the
attribute is used the precise indication of the place where the goods can be examined
is necessary. If the data group "CONTROL RESULT" is not used the attribute cannot

be used. The attributes "Agreed location of goods"/ "Agreed location code", "Authorised location of goods" and "Customs subplace" cannot be used at the same time.

Customs subplace . . . . (box 30)
Type/Length: an ..17
The attribute cannot be used, if the data group "CONTROL RESULT" is used. If this data group is not used the attribute is optional. If this attribute is used the precise indication of the place where the goods can be examined is necessary. The attributes "Agreed location of goods"/ "Agreed location code", "Authorised location of goods" and "Customs subplace" cannot be used at the same time.

Total gross mass . . . . (box 35)
Type/Length: n ..11,3
The attribute shall be used.

NCTS accompanying document language code
Type/Length: a2
The language code presented in Annex 37c shall be used to define the language of the transit accompanying document (NCTS accompanying document).

Dialogue language indicator at departure
Type/Length: a2
The use of the language code presented in Annex 37c is optional. If this attribute is not used the system will use the default language of the office of departure.

Declaration date . . . . (box 50)
Type/Length: n8
The attribute shall be used.

Declaration place . . . . (box 50)
Type/Length: an ..35
The attribute shall be used.

Declaration place LNG
Type/Length: a2
The language code presented in Annex 37c shall be used to define the language (LNG) of the corresponding free text field.

TRADER consignor . . . . (box 2)
Number: 1
This data group is used, when there is only one consignor declared. In this case the data group "TRADER consignor" of the data group "GOODS ITEM" cannot be used.

Name . . . . (box 2)
Type/Length: an ..35
The attribute shall be used.

Street and number . . . . (box 2)
Type/Length: an ..35
The attribute shall be used.

Country . . . . (box 2)
Type/Length: a2
The country code presented in Annex 37c shall be used.

Postcode . . . . (box 2)
Type/Length: an ..9
The attribute shall be used.

City . . . . (box 2)
Type/Length: an ..35
The attribute shall be used.

NAD LNG

Type/Length: a2

The language code presented in Annex 37c shall be used to define the language of name and address (NAD LNG).

TIN . . . . (box 2)

Type/Length: an ..17

The use of the attribute to insert the trader identification number (TIN) is optional for the Member States.

TRADER Consignee . . . . (box 8)

Number: 1

The data group shall be used, when there is only one consignee declared and the attribute "Destination country" of the data group "TRANSIT OPERATION" contains a Member State or an EFTA country. In this case the data group "TRADER consignee" of the data group "GOODS ITEM" cannot be used.

Name . . . . (box 8)

Type/Length: an ..35

The attribute shall be used.

Street and number . . . . (box 8)

Type/Length: an ..35

The attribute shall be used.

Country . . . . (box 8)

Type/Length: a2

The country code presented in Annex 37c shall be used.

Postcode . . . . (box 8)

Type/Length: an ..9

The attribute shall be used.

City . . . . (box 8)

Type/Length: an ..35

The attribute shall be used.

NAD LNG

Type/Length: a2

The language code presented in Annex 37c shall be used to define the language of name and address (NAD LNG).

TIN . . . . (box 8)

Type/Length: an ..17

The use of this attribute to insert the trader identification number (TIN) is optional for the Member States.

GOODS ITEM

[Number: 999

The data group shall be used.]

Declaration type . . . . (ex box 1)

Type/Length: an ..5

The attribute shall be used, if the code "T-" was used for the attribute "Declaration type" of the data group "TRANSIT OPERATION". In other cases this attribute cannot be used.

Country of dispatch . . . . (ex box 15a)

Type/Length: a2

The attribute shall be used, if more than one country of dispatch is declared. The country codes presented in Annex 37c shall be used. The attribute "Country of dispatch" of the data group "TRANSIT OPERATION" cannot be used. If only one country of dispatch is declared the corresponding attribute of the data group "TRANSIT OPERATION" shall be used.

Destination country . . . . (ex box 17a)

Type/Length: a2

The attribute shall be used, if more than one country of destination is declared. The country codes presented in Annex 37c shall be used. The attribute "Destination country" of the data group "TRANSIT OPERATION" cannot be used. If only one country of destination is declared the corresponding attribute of the data group "TRANSIT OPERATION" shall be used.

Textual description . . . . (box 31)

Type/Length: an ..140

The attribute shall be used.

Textual description LNG

Type/Length: a2

The language code presented in Annex 37c shall be used to define the language (LNG) of the corresponding free text field.

Item number . . . . (box 32)

Type/Length: n ..5

The attribute shall be used, even if a number "1" was used for the attribute "Total number of items" of the data group "TRANSIT OPERATION". In this case the number "1" shall be used for this attribute. Each item number is unique throughout the declaration.

Commodity code . . . . (box 33)

Type/Length: n ..8

The attribute shall be used with at least four and up to eight digits according to Annex 37.

Gross mass . . . . (box 35)

Type/Length: n ..11,3

This attribute is optional when goods of different type covered by the same declaration are packed together in such a way that it is impossible to determine the gross mass of each type of goods.

Net mass . . . . (box 38)

Type/Length: n ..11,3

The use of the attribute is optional according to Annex 37.

TRADER consignor . . . . (ex box 2)

Number: 1

The data group "TRADER consignor" cannot be used when there is only one consignor declared. In this case the data group "TRADER consignor" on "TRANSIT OPERATION" level is used.

Name . . . . (ex box 2)

Type/Length: an ..35

The attribute shall be used.

Street and number . . . . (ex box 2)

Type/Length: an ..35

The attribute shall be used.

Country . . . . (ex box 2)

Type/Length: a2

The country code presented in Annex 37c shall be used.

Postcode . . . . (ex box 2)

Type/Length: an ..9

The attribute shall be used.

City . . . . (ex box 2)
Type/Length: an ..35
The attribute shall be used.
NAD LNG
Type/Length: a2
The language code presented in Annex 37c shall be used to define the language of
name and address (NAD LNG).
TIN . . . . (ex box 2)
Type/Length: an ..17
The use of this attribute to insert the trader identification number (TIN) is optional for
the Member States.
TRADER consignee . . . . (ex box 8)
Number: 1
The data group shall be used when more than one consignee is declared and the
attribute "Destination country" of the data group "GOODS ITEM" contains a
Member State or an EFTA country. When only one consignee is declared, the data
group "TRADER consignee" of the data group "GOODS ITEM" cannot be used.
Name . . . . (ex box 8)
Type/Length: an ..35
The attribute shall be used.
Street and number . . . . (ex box 8)
Type/Length: an ..35
The attribute shall be used.
Country . . . . (ex box 8)
Type/Length: a2
The country code presented in Annex 37c shall be used.
Postcode . . . . (ex box 8)
Type/Length: an ..9
The attribute shall be used.
City . . . . (ex box 8)
Type/Length: an ..35
The attribute shall be used.
NAD LNG
Type/Length: a2
The language code presented in Annex 37c shall be used to define the language of
name and address (NAD LNG).
TIN . . . . (ex box 8)
Type/Length: an ..17
The use of this attribute to insert the trader identification number (TIN) is optional for
the Member States.
CONTAINERS . . . . (box 31)
Number: 99
If the attribute "Container" of the data group "TRANSIT OPERATION" contains the
code "1" the data group shall be used.
Container numbers . . . . (box 31)
Type/Length: an ..11
The attribute shall be used.
SGI Codes . . . . (box 31)
Number: 9
The data group shall be used to insert the identification of sensitive goods (SGI) if the
transit declaration concerns goods of Annex 44c.

Part III

Sensitive goods code . . . . (box 31)
Type/Length: n ..2
The code presented in Annex 37c shall be used if the commodity code is not enough to uniquely identify goods of Annex 44c.
Sensitive quantity . . . . (box 31)
Type/Length: n ..11,3
The attribute shall be used when the transit declaration concerns goods of Annex 44c.
PACKAGES . . . . (box 31)
Number: 99
The data group shall be used.
Marks and numbers of packages . . . . (box 31)
Type/Length: an ..42
The attribute shall be used if the attribute "Kind of packages" contains other codes presented in Annex 37c than those for bulk (VQ, VG, VL, VY, VR or VO) or for "Unpacked" (NE). It is optional if the attribute "Kind of packages" contains one of the previous mentioned codes.
Marks and numbers of packages LNG
Type/Length: a2
The language code presented in Annex 37c shall be used to define the language (LNG) if the corresponding free text field is used.
[Kind of packages . . . . (box 31)
Type/Length: an ..2
The packaging codes listed under Box 31 of Annex 38 are used].
Number of packages . . . . (box 31)
Type/Length: n ..5
The attribute shall be used if the attribute "Kind of packages" contains other codes presented in Annex 37c than those for bulk (VQ, VG, VL, VY, VR or VO) or for "Unpacked" (NE). It cannot be used if the attribute "Kind of packages" contains one of the previous mentioned codes.
Number of pieces . . . . (box 31)
Type/Length: n ..5
The attribute shall be used if the attribute "Kind of packages" contains a code presented in Annex 37c for "Unpacked" (NE). In other cases this attribute cannot be used.
PREVIOUS ADMINISTRATIVE REFERENCES . . . . (box 40)
Number: 9
The data group shall be used according to Annex 37.
Previous document type . . . . (box 40)
Type/Length: an ..6
If the data group shall be used at least one previous document type shall be used.
Previous document reference . . . . (box 40)
Type/Length: an ..20
The reference of the previous document shall be used.
Previous document reference LNG
Type/Length: a2
The language code presented in Annex 37c shall be used to define the language (LNG) of the corresponding free text field.
Complement of information . . . . (box 40)
Type/Length: an ..26
The use of the attribute is optional for the Member States.
Complement of information LNG

Type/Length: a2

The language code presented in Annex 37c shall be used to define the language (LNG) if the corresponding free text field is used.

PRODUCED DOCUMENTS/CERTIFICATES .... (box 44)

Number: 99

The data group shall be used according to Annex 37. If the data group is used at least one of the following attributes shall be used.

Document type .... (box 44)

Type/Length: an ..3

The code presented in Annex 37c shall be used.

Document reference .... (box 44)

Type/Length: an ..20

Document reference LNG

Type/Length: a2

The language code presented in Annex 37c shall be used to define the language (LNG) if the corresponding free text field is used.

Complement of information .... (box 44)

Type/Length: an ..26

Complement of information LNG

Type/Length: a2

The language code presented in Annex 37c shall be used to define the language (LNG) if the corresponding free text field is used.

SPECIAL MENTIONS .... (box 44)

Number: 99

The data group shall be used according to Annex 37. If the data group is used either the attribute "Additional information id" or "Text" shall be used.

Additional information id .... (box 44)

Type/Length: an ..3

The code presented in Annex 37c shall be used to insert the identification (id) of the additional information.

Export from EC .... (box 44)

Type/Length: n1

If the attribute "Additional information id" contains the code "DG0" or "DG1" the attribute "Export from EC" or "Export from country" shall be used. Both attributes cannot be used at the same time. In other cases the attribute cannot be used. If this attribute is used the following codes are to be used:

0 = no

1 = yes.

Export from country .... (box 44)

Type/Length: a2

If the attribute "Additional information id" contains the code "DG0" or "DG1" the attribute "Export from EC" or "Export from country" shall be used. Both attributes cannot be used at the same time. In other cases the attribute cannot be used. If this attribute is used the country code presented in Annex 37c shall be used.

Text .... (box 44)

Type/Length: an ..70

Text LNG

Type/Length: a2

The language code presented in Annex 37c shall be used to define the language (LNG) if the corresponding free text field is used.

CUSTOMS OFFICE of departure .... (box C)

Number: 1

The data group shall be used.

Reference number .... (box C)

Type/Length: an8

The code presented in Annex 37c shall be used.

TRADER principal .... (box 50)

Number: 1

The data group shall be used.

TIN .... (box 50)

[Type/Length: an ..17

The attribute shall be used where the data group "CONTROL RESULT" contains the code A3 or where the attribute "GRN" is used.]

Name .... (box 50)

Type/Length: an ..35

The attribute shall be used if the attribute "TIN" is used and the other attributes of this data group are not already known by the system.

Street and number .... (box 50)

Type/Length: an ..35

The attribute shall be used if the attribute "TIN" is used and the other attributes of this data group are not already known by the system.

Country .... (box 50)

Type/Length: a2

The country code presented in Annex 37c shall be used if the attribute "TIN" is used and the other attributes of this data group are not already known by the system.

Postcode .... (box 50)

Type/Length: an ..9

The attribute shall be used if the attribute "TIN" is used and the other attributes of this data group are not already known by the system.

City .... (box 50)

Type/Length: an ..35

The attribute shall be used if the attribute "TIN" is used and the other attributes of this data group are not already known by the system.

NAD LNG

Type/Length: a2

The language code presented in Annex 37c shall be used to define the language of name and address (NAD LNG) if the corresponding free text fields are used.

REPRESENTATIVE .... (box 50)

Number: 1

The data group shall be used if the principal makes use of an authorised representative.

Name .... (box 50)

Type/Length: an ..35

The attribute shall be used.

Representative capacity .... (box 50)

Type/Length: a ..35

The use of this attribute is optional.

Representative capacity LNG

Type/Length: a2

The language code presented in Annex 37c shall be used to define the language (LNG) if the corresponding free text field is used.

CUSTOMS OFFICE of transit .... (box 51)

Number: 9

The data group shall be used according to Annex 37.

Reference number . . . . (box 51)

Type/Length: an8

The code presented in Annex 37c shall be used.

CUSTOMS OFFICE of destination . . . . (box 53)

Number: 1

The data group shall be used.

Reference number . . . . (box 53)

Type/Length: an8

The code presented in Annex 37c shall be used.

TRADER authorised consignee . . . . (box 53)

Number: 1

The data group can be used to indicate that the goods will be delivered to an authorised consignee.

TIN authorised consignee . . . . (box 53)

Type/Length: an ..17

The attribute shall be used to insert the trader identification number (TIN).

CONTROL RESULT . . . . (box D)

Number: 1

The data group shall be used if an authorised consignor lodges the declaration.

Control result code . . . . (box D)

Type/Length: an2

The code A3 shall be used.

Date limit . . . . (box D)

Type/Length: n8

The attribute shall be used.

SEALS INFORMATION . . . . (box D)

Number: 1

The data group shall be used if an authorised consignor lodges a declaration for which his authorisation requires the use of seals or a principal is granted the use of seals of a special type.

Seals number . . . . (box D)

Type/Length: n4

The attribute shall be used.

SEALS ID . . . . (box D)

Number: 99

The data group shall be used for the identification (id) of seals.

Seals identity . . . . (box D)

Type/Length: an ..20

The attribute shall be used.

Seals identity LNG

Type/Length: a2

The language code (LNG) presented in Annex 37c shall be used.

GUARANTEE

Number: 9

The data group shall be used.

Guarantee type . . . . (box 52)

[Type/Length: an 1]

The code presented in Annex 38 shall be used.

GUARANTEE REFERENCE .... (box 52)
[Number: 99

The data group shall be used if the attribute "Guarantee type" contains the code "0", "1", "2", "4" or "9".]

GRN .... (box 52)
[[Type/Length: an24]

The attribute shall be used to insert the guarantee reference number (GRN) if the attribute "Guarantee type" contains the code "0", "1", "2", "4" or "9". In this case the attribute "Other guarantee reference" can not be used.]

[The Guarantee Reference number (GRN) is allocated by the office of guarantee to identify each single guarantee and it is structured as follows:

Field	Content	Field type	Examples
1	Last two digits of the year at which the guarantee was accepted (YY)	Numeric 2	97
2	Identifier of the country where the guarantee is lodged (ISO alpha 2 country code)	Alphabetic 2	IT
3	Unique identifier for the acceptance given by the Office of Guarantee per year and country	Alphanumeric 12	1234AB788966
4	Check digit	Alphanumeric 1	8
5	Identifier of the individual guarantee by means of voucher (1 letter + 6 digits) or NULL for other guarantee types	Alphanumeric 7	A001017

Field 1 and 2 as explained above.

Field 3 has to be filled with a unique identifier per year and country for the acceptance of the guarantee given by the office of guarantee. National Administrations which want to have the Customs Office Reference Number of the office of guarantee included in the GRN, could use up to the first 6 characters to insert the national number of the office of guarantee.

Field 4 has to be filled with a value that is a check digit for the fields 1 to 3 of the GRN. This field allows to detect an error when capturing the first four fields of the GRN.

Field 5 is only used when the GRN is related to an individual guarantee by means of vouchers registered in the computerised transit system. In that case, this field has to be filled with the identifier of the voucher.]

Other guarantee reference .... (box 52)
[Type/Length: an ..35

This attribute shall be used if the attribute "Guarantee type" contains other codes than "0", "1", "2", "4" or "9". In this case the attribute "GRN" can not be used.]

Access code
[Type/Length: an4

The attribute shall be used when the attribute "GRN" is used, otherwise this attribute is optional for the Member States. Depending on the type of guarantee, it is issued by the office of guarantee, the guarantor or the principal and used to secure a specific guarantee.]

VALIDITY LIMITATION (EC)
Number: 1

Not valid for EC .... (box 52)
Type/Length: n1

The code 0 = no shall be used for Community transit.

VALIDITY LIMITATION (NON-EC)

Number: 99
Not valid for other contracting parties .... (box 52)
Type/Length: a2
The country code presented in Annex 37c shall be used to indicate the EFTA country concerned.]

This Annex was previously omitted from the handbook. It is substituted by Commission Regulation (EC) 2787/2000, Art 1, para 60, Annex II.

Title II, para B: words in square brackets in the data group "Guarantee Reference" substituted by Commission Regulation (EC) 993/2001, Art 1, para 33, Annex I. Attribute "Number of loading lists" and explanatory text repealed; explanatory text of attribute "Total number of packages" substituted; and explanatory text of data group "GOODS ITEM" substituted; by Commission Regulation (EC) 881/2003 Art 1, para 30, Annex IV with effect from 1 January 2005; in data group "PACKAGES", words in square brackets substituted by Commission Regulation 883/2005, Art 1, para 23, with effect from 1 July 2005; in data groups "TRADER principal", "GUARANTEE" words in square brackets substituted by Commission Regulation 883/2005, Art 1, para 24, with effect from 1 May 2004; in data group "GUARANTEE REFERENCE", words in square brackets in attributes "GRN (box 52) substituted by Commission Regulation 883/2005, Art 1, para 24, with effect from 1 May 2004.

ANNEX 37B

NOTE
This Annex was repealed by Commission Regulation (EC) 2787/2000, Art 1, para 61.

[ANNEX 37C
ADDITIONAL CODES FOR THE COMPUTERISED TRANSIT SYSTEM

1. Country codes (CNT)

Field	Content	Field type	Example
1	ISO alpha 2 country code.	Alphabetic 2	IT

The ISO alpha 2 country code is used (see Annex 38).

2. Language code
ISO alpha 2 codification as specified in ISO — 639: 1988 shall apply.

3. Commodity code (COM)

Field		Content	Field type	Examples
1	HS6		Numeric 6 (left aligned)	010290

The six digits of the Harmonised System have to be entered (HS6). The commodity code may be expanded to eight digits for national use.

4. Sensitive goods code

Field	Content	Field type	Examples
1	Additional identifier for sensitive goods	Numeric ..2	2

The code is used in extension to HS6, as shown in Annex 44c, where a sensitive good cannot sufficiently be identified with HS6.

5. Package code

NOTES

Repealed by Commission Regulation (EC) 883/2005, Art 1, para 25, with effect from 1 July 2005.

6. Produced documents/certificates code
(numeric codes extracted from the 1997b UN Directories for electronic data interchange for administration, commerce and transport: List of code for data element 1001, Document/message name, coded.)

Certificate of conformity	2
Certificate of quality	3
Movement certificate A.TR.1	18
Container list	235
Packing list	271
Proforma invoice	325
Commercial invoice	380
House waybill	703
Master bill of lading	704
Bill of lading	705
House bill of lading	714
Road list-SMGS	722
Road consignment note	730
Air waybill	740
Master air waybill	741
Dispatch note (post parcels)	750
Multimodal/combined transport document (generic)	760
Cargo manifest	785
Bordereau	787
Dispatch note model T	820
Dispatch note model T1	821
Dispatch note model T2	822
Control document T5	823
Dispatch note model T2L	825
Goods declaration for exportation	830
Phytosanitary certificate	851
Sanitary certificate	852
Veterinary certificate	853
Certificate of origin	861
Declaration of origin	862
Preference certificate of origin	864
Certificate of origin form GSP	865
Import licence	911

Cargo declaration (arrival)	933
Embargo permit	941
TIF form	951
TIR carnet	952
EUR 1 certificate of origin	954
ATA carnet	955
Other	zzz

7. Additional information/Special indication code

The codes applicable are as follows—

DG0 = Export from one EFTA country subject to restriction or export from EC subject to restriction.

DG1 = Export from one EFTA country subject to duties or export from EC subject to duties.

DG2 = Export.

Additional special indication codes can also be defined at national domain level.

8. Customs office reference number (COR)

Field	Content	Field type	Example
1	Identifier of the country to which the customs office belongs (see CNT)	Alphabetic 2	IT
2	National number of the customs office	Alphanumeric 6	0830AB

Field 1 as explained above.

Field 2 has to be freely filled with a 6-character alphanumeric code. The 6 characters allow national administrations, where necessary, to define a hierarchy of customs offices.]

This Annex was previously omitted from the handbook. It is substituted by Commission Regulation (EC) 2787/2000, Art 1, para 62, Annex III.

[ANNEX 38

CODES TO BE USED IN THE FORMS [1], [2]

TITLE I

GENERAL REMARKS

This Annex contains only the specific basic requirements applicable when using paper forms. Where transit formalities are completed by the exchange of EDI messages, the instructions contained in this Annex apply unless Annexes 37a or 37c provide otherwise.

In some cases, the requirements for the type and length of entries are specified. The codes for the different types of data are:

a alphabetic

n numeric

an alphanumeric

The number after the code indicates the authorised length of the data entry. Two points before the indication of the length means that the data entry is not of a determined length, but that it may include a number of characters up to the number indicated.

TITLE II
CODES

Box 1: Declaration

First subdivision

The codes applicable (a2) are given below:

EX For trade with countries and territories situated outside of the customs territory of the Community other than the EFTA countries

> For placing goods under a customs procedure referred to in columns A and E of the table in Annex 37, Title I, B)

> To confer on goods a customs-approved treatment or use referred to in columns C and D of the table in Annex 37, Title I, B)

> For dispatch of non-Community goods in the context of trade between Member States

IM For trade with countries and territories situated outside of the customs territory of the Community other than the EFTA

> For placing goods under a customs procedure referred to in columns H to K of the table in Annex 37, Title I, B)

> For placing non-Community goods under a customs procedure in the context of trade between Member States

EU In the context of trade with EFTA countries

> For placing goods under a customs procedure referred to in columns A, E and H to K of the table in Annex 37, Title I, B)

> To confer on goods a customs-approved treatment or use referred to in columns C and D of the table in Annex 37, Title I, B)

CO In respect of Community goods subject to specific measures during the transitional period following the accession of new Member States

Placing of pre-financed goods in a customs warehouse or free zone

In respect of Community goods in the context of trade between parts of the customs territory of the Community to which the provisions of Directive 77/388/EEC are applicable and parts of that territory to which those provisions do not apply, or in the context of trade between parts of that territory where those provisions do not apply.

---

[1] The use, in this Annex, of the words export, re-export, importation and re-importation equally cover dispatch, re-dispatch, introduction and re-introduction.

[2] The term 'EFTA' in this Annex refers not only to the EFTA countries but to the other non-Community contracting parties to the Conventions on a common transit procedure and on the simplification of formalities in trade in goods.

Second subdivision

The codes applicable (a1) are given below:

A for a normal declaration (normal procedure under Article 62 of the Code)

B for an incomplete declaration (simplified procedure under Article 76(1)(a) of the Code)

C for a simplified declaration (simplified procedure under Article 76(1)(b) of the Code)

D For lodging a normal declaration (such as referred to under code A) before the declarant is in a position to present the goods.

E For lodging an incomplete declaration (such as referred to under code B) before the declarant is in a position to present the goods.

F For lodging a simplified declaration (such as referred to under code C) before the declarant is in a position to present the goods.

X for a supplementary declaration under a simplified procedure covered by B

Y for a supplementary declaration under a simplified procedure covered by C

Z for a supplementary declaration under a simplified procedure under Article 76(1)(c) of the Code (entry of the goods in the records)

Codes D, E and F can only be used in the framework of the procedure provided for in Article 201(2) where customs authorities authorise the lodging of a declaration before the declarant is in a position to present the goods.

Third subdivision

The codes applicable (an 5) are given below:

T1 Goods required to move under the external Community transit procedure

T2 Goods required to move under the internal Community transit procedure in accordance with Article 163 or 165 of the Code, unless Article 340c(2) applies

T2F Goods required to move under the internal Community transit procedure, in accordance with Article 340c(1)

T2SM Goods placed under the internal Community transit procedure, in application of Article 2 of Decision 4/92 of the EEC-San Marino Co-operation Committee of 22 December 1992.

T Mixed consignments covered by Article 351, in which case the space following the 'T' must be scored through

T2L Form establishing the Community status of goods

T2LF Form establishing the Community status of goods consigned to, or from, a part of the customs territory of the Community where the provisions of Directive 77/388/EEC do not apply

T2LSM Form establishing the status of goods destined for San Marino in application of Article 2 of Decision 4/92 of the EEC-San Marino Cooperation Committee of 22 December 1992.

NOTES

Amended by Corrigendum.

Box 2: Consignor/Exporter

Where identification numbers are used, the code takes the following form:

On import: Country code (a2); code UN/EDIFACT 3055 (an..3); exporter's identification code (an..13)

On export: Country code (a2); exporter's identification code (an..16)

Country code: The Community's alphabetical codes for countries and territories are based on the current ISO alpha 2 (a2) in so far as they are compatible with the requirements of Community law. The legal basis for these codes is Council Regulation (EC) No 1172/95 of 22 May 1995 on the statistics relating to the trading of goods by the Community and its Member States with non-member countries (OJ L 118, 25.5.1995). The Commission regularly publishes regulations updating the list of country codes.

UN/EDIFACT 3055: With regard to the coding of the operators in the third countries mentioned in boxes 2 and 8, Member States use a list issued and updated by an agency or another institution which defines the interested parties' codes. The selected agency will be identified in the list of the agencies published by the UN under the heading UN/EDIFACT 3055 (Electronic Data Interchange for Administration, Commerce and Transport) which contains a list of the agencies responsible for the development of such lists of economic operators.

Example: 'JP1511234567890' for a Japanese exporter (country code: JP) whose identification number with Japanese customs (agency code 151 in the list of codes for UN/EDIFACT data element 3055) is 1234567890.

Box 8: Consignee

Where identification numbers are used, the code takes the following form:

On import: Country code (a2); consignee's identification code (an..16)

Part III

On export: Country code (a2); code UN/EDIFACT 3055 (an..3); importer's identification code (an..13).

Use the country codes entered in box 2.

Example: 'JP1511234567890' for a Japanese importer (country code: JP) whose identification number with Japanese customs (agency code 151 in the list of codes for UN/EDIFACT data element 3055) is 1234567890.

Box 14: Declarant/Representative

(a) Insert one of the following codes (n1) before the full name and address to designate the declarant or the status of the representative:

1 Declarant

2 Representative (direct representation within the meaning of the first indent of Article 5(2) of the Code)

3 Representative (indirect representation within the meaning of the second indent of Article 5(2) of the Code).

Where this data element is printed on a paper document, it will be in square brackets (Ex: [1], [2] or [3])

(b) Where identification numbers are used, the code takes the following form: Country code (a2); identification code of the declarant/representative (an..16).

Use the country codes entered in box 2.

NOTES

Amended by Corrigendum.

Box 15a: Country of dispatch/export code
Use the country codes entered in box 2.

Box 17a: Country-of-destination code
Use the country codes entered in box 2.

Box 17b: Region-of-destination code
Use the codes to be adopted by the Member States.

Box 18: Nationality of means of transport at departure
Use the country codes entered in box 2.

Box 19: Container (Ctr)
The relevant codes (n1) are given below:

0 Goods not transported in containers

1 Goods transported in containers.

Box 20: Delivery terms
The codes and statements to be entered, as appropriate, in the first two subdivisions of this box are as follows:

First subdivision	Meaning	Second subdivision
Incoterm code	Incoterms — ICC/ECE	Place to be specified
EXW	Ex works	Named place
FCA	Free carrier	Named place
FAS	Free alongside ship	Named port of shipment
FOB	Free on board	Named port of shipment
CFR	Cost and freight	Named port of destination
CIF	Cost, insurance and freight	Named port of destination

First subdivision	Meaning	Second subdivision
CPT	Carriage paid to	Named place of destination
CIP	Carriage and insurance paid to	Named place of destination
DAF	Delivered at frontier	Named place
DES	Delivered ex-ship	Named port of destination
DEQ	Delivered ex-quay	Named port of destination
DDU	Delivered duty unpaid	Named port of destination
DDP	Delivered duty paid	Named port of destination
XXX	Delivery terms other than those listed above	Narrative description of delivery terms given in the contract

The Member States may require the following coded particulars (n1) in the third subdivision:

1   Place situated in the territory of the Member State concerned
2   Place situated in the territory of another Member State
3   Other (place situated outside the Community).

NOTES

Amended by Corrigendum.

Box 21: Nationality of active means of transport crossing the border
Use the country codes entered in box 2.

Box 22: Invoice currency
The invoice currency is to be entered by means of the ISO alpha-3 currency code (Codes ISO 4217 for the representation of currencies and funds).

[Box 24: Nature of the transaction
The Member States which require this item of information must use the single digit codes listed in column A of the table provided for under Article 13(2) of Commission Regulation (EC) No 1917/2000 (excluding, where appropriate, code 9), this digit being entered in the left-hand side of the box. They may also provide for a second digit from the list in column B of that table to be entered in the right-hand side of the box.]

Column A	Column B
1 Transactions involving actual or intended transfer of ownership against payment or other consideration (other than the transactions listed under 2, 7 and 8(1)(2)(3))	1 Final purchase/sale (2) 2 Goods dispatched for viewing, trial samples, goods dispatched with right of return and transactions involving commission 3 Transactions involving payment in kind 4 Sale to foreign travellers for their personal use 5 Financial leasing (3)
2 Return of goods already recorded under code 1 (4); replacement of goods free of charge (4)	1 Return of goods 2 Replacement for returned goods 3 Replacement (eg under terms of guarantee) for goods not returned

Part III

Column A	Column B
3 Transactions (not temporary in nature) involving transfer of ownership but without consideration (financial or otherwise)	1 Deliveries of goods under programmes wholly or partly financed by the European Community 2 Other government-aid deliveries 3. Other aid deliveries (individuals and non-governmental organisations) 4 Other
4 Transactions with a view to processing (5) or contractor repair (6) (other than the transactions recorded under 7)	1 Processing 2 Repair and maintenance against payment 3 Repair and maintenance free of charge
5 Transactions after processing (5) or contractor repair (6) (other than the transactions recorded under 7)	1 Processing 2 Repair and maintenance against payment 3 Repair and maintenance free of charge
6 Transactions not involving transfer of ownership, eg hire, loan, operational leasing (7) and other temporary uses (8), with the exception of processing under contract or repair (delivery and return)	1 Hire, loan, operational leasing 2 Other temporary uses
7 Transactions in connection with a joint defence programme or another intergovernmental production programme (eg Airbus)	
8 Delivery of building material and equipment in connection with construction or civil engineering activities constituting part of a general contract (9)	
9 Other transactions	

Notes

1 This item covers most exports and imports, ie transactions in respect of which:
- ownership is transferred from resident to non-resident or vice versa,
- payment or other compensation (payment in kind) is or will be made.

It should be noted that this applies to goods sent between entities of a same enterprise or of a same group of enterprises and to goods sent from/to central distribution depots, unless no payment or other compensation is made in respect of these transactions (in which case such transactions shall be listed under code 3).

2 Including spare parts and other replacement deliveries made against payment.

3 Including financial leasing: the lease instalments are calculated in such a way as to cover all or virtually all the value of the goods.

The benefits and risks of ownership are transferred to the lessee. At the end of the contract, the lessee becomes the legal owner.

4 Return and replacement dispatches of goods originally recorded under headings 3 to 9 of column A should be recorded under the corresponding headings.

5 Processing operations (whether or not under customs supervision) should be recorded under headings 4 and 5 of column A. Own account processing operations are not covered by these headings and should be recorded under heading 1 of column A.

6 Repair entails the restoration of goods to their original function; this may involve some structural alterations or improvements.

7   Operational leasing: all lease contracts other than financial leasing (see note3).

8   This item covers goods exported/imported with the intention of subsequent reimport/re-export without any change of ownership taking place.

9   The transactions recorded under heading 8 of column A involve goods which are not separately invoiced but for which a single invoice is made covering the total collective value. Where this is not the case, the transactions should be recorded under heading 1.

NOTES

Amended by Corrigendum.

Note to Box 24 substituted by Commission Regulation (EC) No 215/2006, Art 1, para 5, Annex II.

Box 25: Mode of transport at the border
The codes applicable (n1) are given below:

Code	Description
1	Sea transport
2	Rail transport
3	Road transport
4	Air transport
5	Postal consignment
7	Fixed transport installations
8	Inland waterway transport
9	Own propulsion

Box 26: Inland mode of transport
The codes listed for box 25 are applicable.

Box 29: Office of exit/entry
Use (an8) codes structured as follows:

– the first two characters (a2) serve to identify the country by means of the country code entered in box 2,

– the next six characters (an6) stand for the office concerned in that country. It is suggested that the following structure be adopted:

The first three characters (a3) would be taken up by the UN/LOCODE and the last three by a national alphanumeric subdivision (an3). If this subdivision is not used, the characters '000' should be inserted.

Example: BEBRU000: BE = ISO 3166 for Belgium, BRU = UN/LOCODE for the city of Brussels, 000 for the unused subdivision.

[Box 31: Packages and description of goods; Marks and numbers — Container No(s) — Number and kind

Kind of packages

Use the following codes.

(UN/ECE Recommendation No 21/REV. 4, May 2002)

Aerosol	AE
Ampoule, non-protected	AM
Ampoule, protected	AP
Atomizer	AT
Bag	BG

Part III

Bag, flexible container	FX
Bag, large	ZB
Bag, multiply	MB
Bag, paper	5M
Bag, paper, multi-wall	XJ
Bag, paper, multi-wall, water resistant	XK
Bag, plastic	EC
Bag, plastics film	XD
Bag, super bulk	43
Bag, textile	5L
Bag, textile, sift proof	XG
Bag, textile, water resistant	XH
Bag, textile, without inner coat/liner	XF
Bag, woven plastic	5H
Bag, woven plastic, sift proof	XB
Bag, woven plastic, water resistant	XC
Bag, woven plastic, without inner coat/liner	XA
Bale, compressed	BL
Bale, non-compressed	BN
Balloon, non-protected	BF
Balloon, protected	BP
Bar	BR
Barrel	BA
Barrel, wooden	2C
Barrel, wooden, bung type	QH
Barrel, wooden, removable head	QJ
Bars, in bundle/bunch/truss	BZ
Basin	BM
Basket	BK
Basket, with handle, cardboard	HC
Basket, with handle, plastic	HA
Basket, with handle, wooden	HB
Bin	BI
Board	BD
Board, in bundle/bunch/truss	BY
Bobbin	BB
Bolt	BT
Bottle, gas	GB
Bottle, non-protected, bulbous	BS
Bottle, non-protected, cylindrical	BO
Bottle, protected bulbous	BV
Bottle, protected cylindrical	BQ
Bottlecrate/bottlerack	BC
Box	BX
Box, aluminium	4B

Box, Commonwealth Handling Equipment Pool (CHEP), Eurobox	DH
Box, fibreboard	4G
Box, for liquids	BW
Box, natural wood	4C
Box, plastic	4H
Box, plastic, expanded	QR
Box, plastic, solid	QS
Box, plywood	4D
Box, reconstituted wood	4F
Box, steel	4A
Box, wooden, natural wood, ordinary	QP
Box, wooden, natural wood, with sift proof walls	QQ
Bucket	BJ
Bulk, gas (at 1031 mbar and 15 °C)	VG
Bulk, liquefied gas (at abnormal temperature/pressure)	VQ
Bulk, liquid	VL
Bulk, solid, fine particles (powders)	VY
Bulk, solid, granular particles (grains)	VR
Bulk, solid, large particles (nodules)	VO
Bunch	BH
Bundle	BE
Butt	BU
Cage	CG
Cage, Commonwealth Handling Equipment Pool (CHEP)	DG
Cage, roll	CW
Can, cylindrical	CX
Can, rectangular	CA
Can, with handle and spout	CD
Canister	CI
Canvas	CZ
Capsule	AV
Carboy, non-protected	CO
Carboy, protected	CP
Card	CM
Carton	CT
Cartridge	CQ
Case	CS
Case, isothermic	EI
Case, skeleton	SK
Case, steel	SS
Case, with pallet base	ED
Case, with pallet base, cardboard	EF
Case, with pallet base, metal	EH
Case, with pallet base, plastic	EG

Case, with pallet base, wooden	EE
Cask	CK
Chest	CH
Churn	CC
Clamshell	AI
Coffer	CF
Coffin	CJ
Coil	CL
Composite packaging, glass receptacle	6P
Composite packaging, glass receptacle in aluminium crate	YR
Composite packaging, glass receptacle in aluminium drum	YQ
Composite packaging, glass receptacle in expandable plastic pack	YY
Composite packaging, glass receptacle in fibre drum	YW
Composite packaging, glass receptacle in fibreboard box	YX
Composite packaging, glass receptacle in plywood drum	YT
Composite packaging, glass receptacle in solid plastic pack	YZ
Composite packaging, glass receptacle in steel crate box	YP
Composite packaging, glass receptacle in steel drum	YN
Composite packaging, glass receptacle in wickerwork hamper	YV
Composite packaging, glass receptacle in wooden box	YS
Composite packaging, plastic receptacle	6H
Composite packaging, plastic receptacle in aluminium crate	YD
Composite packaging, plastic receptacle in aluminium drum	YC
Composite packaging, plastic receptacle in fibre drum	YJ
Composite packaging, plastic receptacle in fibreboard box	YK
Composite packaging, plastic receptacle in plastic drum	YL
Composite packaging, plastic receptacle in plywood box	YH
Composite packaging, plastic receptacle in plywood drum	YG
Composite packaging, plastic receptacle in solid plastic box	YM
Composite packaging, plastic receptacle in steel crate box	YB
Composite packaging, plastic receptacle in steel drum	YA
Composite packaging, plastic receptacle in wooden box	YF
Cone	AJ
Container, not otherwise specified as transport equipment	CN
Cover	CV
Crate	CR
Crate, beer	CB
Crate, bulk, cardboard	DK
Crate, bulk, plastic	DL
Crate, bulk, wooden	DM
Crate, framed	FD
Crate, fruit	FC

Crate, milk	MC
Crate, multiple layer, cardboard	DC
Crate, multiple layer, plastic	DA
Crate, multiple layer, wooden	DB
Crate, shallow	SC
Creel	CE
Cup	CU
Cylinder	CY
Demijohn, non-protected	DJ
Demijohn, protected	DP
Dispenser	DN
Drum	DR
Drum, aluminium	1B
Drum, aluminium, non-removable head	QC
Drum, aluminium, removable head	QD
Drum, fibre	1G
Drum, iron	DI
Drum, plastic	IH
Drum, plastic, non-removable head	QF
Drum, plastic, removable head	QG
Drum, plywood	1D
Drum, steel	1A
Drum, steel, non-removable head	QA
Drum, steel, removable head	QB
Drum, wooden	1W
Envelope	EN
Envelope, steel	SV
Filmpack	FP
Firkin	FI
Flask	FL
Foodtainer	FT
Footlocker	FO
Frame	FR
Girder	GI
Girders, in bundle/bunch/truss	GZ
Hamper	HR
Hogshead	HG
Ingot	IN
Ingots, in bundle/bunch/truss	IZ
Intermediate bulk container	WA
Intermediate bulk container, aluminium	WD
Intermediate bulk container, aluminium, liquid	WL
Intermediate bulk container, aluminium, pressurised 10 kPa	WH
Intermediate bulk container, composite	ZS

Intermediate bulk container, composite, flexible plastic, liquids	ZR
Intermediate bulk container, composite, flexible plastic, pressurised	ZP
Intermediate bulk container, composite, flexible plastic, solids	ZM
Intermediate bulk container, composite, rigid plastic, liquids	ZQ
Intermediate bulk container, composite, rigid plastic, pressurised	ZN
Intermediate bulk container, composite, rigid plastic, solids	ZL
Intermediate bulk container, fibreboard	ZT
Intermediate bulk container, flexible	ZU
Intermediate bulk container, metal	WF
Intermediate bulk container, metal, liquid	WM
Intermediate bulk container, metal, other than steel	ZV
Intermediate bulk container, metal, pressure 10 kPa	WJ
Intermediate bulk container, natural wood	ZW
Intermediate bulk container, natural wood, with inner liner	WU
Intermediate bulk container, paper, multi-wall	ZA
Intermediate bulk container, paper, multi-wall, water resistant	ZC
Intermediate bulk container, plastic film	WS
Intermediate bulk container, plywood	ZX
Intermediate bulk container, plywood, with inner liner	WY
Intermediate bulk container, reconstituted wood	ZY
Intermediate bulk container, reconstituted wood, with inner liner	WZ
Intermediate bulk container, rigid plastic	AA
Intermediate bulk container, rigid plastic, freestanding, liquids	ZK
Intermediate bulk container, rigid plastic, freestanding, pressurised	ZH
Intermediate bulk container, rigid plastic, freestanding, solids	ZF
Intermediate bulk container, rigid plastic, with structural equipment, solids	ZD
Intermediate bulk container, rigid plastic, with structural equipment, liquids	ZJ
Intermediate bulk container, rigid plastic, with structural equipment, pressurised	ZG
Intermediate bulk container, steel	WC
Intermediate bulk container, steel, liquid	WK
Intermediate bulk container, steel, pressurised 10 kPa	WG
Intermediate bulk container, textile without coat/liner	WT
Intermediate bulk container, textile, coated	WV
Intermediate bulk container, textile, coated and liner	WX
Intermediate bulk container, textile, with liner	WW

Intermediate bulk container, woven plastic, coated	WP
Intermediate bulk container, woven plastic, coated and liner	WR
Intermediate bulk container, woven plastic, with liner	WQ
Intermediate bulk container, woven plastic, without coat/liner	WN
Jar	JR
Jerry-can, cylindrical	JY
Jerry-can, plastic	3H
Jerry-can, plastic, non-removable head	QM
Jerry-can, plastic, removable head	QN
Jerry-can, rectangular	JC
Jerry-can, steel	3A
Jerry-can, steel, non-removable head	QK
Jerry-can, steel, removable head	QL
Jug	JG
Jute bag	JT
Keg	KG
Lift van	LV
Log	LG
Logs, in bundle/bunch/truss	LZ
Lot	LT
Mat	MT
Matchbox	MX
Mutually defined	ZZ
Nest	NS
Net	NT
Net, tube, plastic	NU
Net, tube, textile	NV
Not available	NA
Package	PK
Package, cardboard, with bottle grip-holes	IK
Package, display, cardboard	IB
Package, display, metal	ID
Package, display, plastic	IC
Package, display, wooden	IA
Package, flow	IF
Package, paper-wrapped	IG
Package, show	IE
Packet	PA
Pail	PL
Pallet	PX
Pallet, 100 cm × 110 cm	AH
Pallet, box	PB
Pallet, modular, collars 80 cm × 100 cm	PD
Pallet, modular, collars 80 cm × 120 cm	PE

Part III

Pallet, modular, collars 80 cm × 60 cm	AF
Pallet, shrink-wrapped	AG
Parcel	PC
Pen	PF
Pipe	PI
Pipes, in bundle/bunch/truss	PV
Pitcher	PH
Plank	PN
Planks, in bundle/bunch/truss	PZ
Plate	PG
Plates, in bundle/bunch/truss	PY
Pot	PT
Pouch	PO
Punnet	PJ
Rack	RK
Rack, clothing hanger	RJ
Receptacle, fibre	AB
Receptacle, glass	GR
Receptacle, metal	MR
Receptacle, paper	AC
Receptacle, plastic	PR
Receptacle, plastic-wrapped	MW
Receptacle, wooden	AD
Rednet	RT
Reel	RL
Ring	RG
Rod	RD
Rods, in bundle/bunch/truss	RZ
Roll	RO
Sachet	SH
Sack	SA
Sack, multi-wall	MS
Sea-chest	SE
Set	SX
Sheet	ST
Sheet, plastic wrapping	SP
Sheet metal	SM
Sheets, in bundle/bunch/truss	SZ
Shrink-wrapped	SW
Skid	SI
Slab	SB
Sleeve	SY
Slip-sheet	SL
Spindle	SD
Spool	SO

Suitcase	SU
Tank, cylindrical	TY
Tank, rectangular	TK
Tea-chest	TC
Tierce	TI
Tin	TN
Tray	PU
Tray, one layer no cover, cardboard	DV
Tray, one layer no cover, plastic	DS
Tray, one layer no cover, polystyrene	DU
Tray, one layer no cover, wooden	DT
Tray, two layers no cover, cardboard	DY
Tray, two layers no cover, plastic tray	DW
Tray, two layers no cover, wooden	DX
Trunk	TR
Truss	TS
Tub	TB
Tub, with lid	TL
Tube	TU
Tube, collapsible	TD
Tube, with nozzle	TV
Tubes, in bundle/bunch/truss	TZ
Tun	TO
Uncaged	UC
Unpacked or unpackaged	NE
Unpacked or unpackaged, multiple units	NG
Unpacked or unpackaged, single unit	NF
Vacuum-packed	VP
Vanpack	VK
Vat	VA
Vial	VI
Wicker bottle	WB]

NOTES

Text for Box 31 substituted by Commission Regulation (EC) 883/2005, Art 1, para 27, Annex IV, with effect from 1 January 2006. However, member states may apply the legislation before this date.

Box 33: Commodity Code

First subdivision (8 digits)

To be completed using the headings of the Combined Nomenclature.

Where the form is used for Community transit procedure purposes, the commodity code made up of at least the six digits of the Harmonised Commodity Description and Coding System shall be entered in this subdivision. However, where Community legislation so requires, the Combined Nomenclature heading shall be used.

Second subdivision (two characters)

Part III

To be completed in accordance with the Taric code (two characters for the application of specific Community measures in respect of formalities to be completed at destination).

Third subdivision (four characters)

To be completed in accordance with the Taric code (first additional code).

Fourth subdivision (four characters)

To be completed in accordance with the Taric code (second additional code).

Fifth subdivision (four characters)

Codes to be adopted by the Member States concerned.

Box 34a: Country-of-origin code

Use the country codes entered in box 2.

Box 34b: Region-of-origin/-production code

Codes to be adopted by the Member States.

Box 36: Preference

This box is for three-digit codes comprising a single-digit component from 1). and a two-digit component from 2).

The relevant codes are given below:

1. First digit of the code

1 Tariff arrangement erga omnes

    2   Generalised System of Preferences (GSP)

3 Tariff preferences other than those mentioned under code 2

    4   Non-imposition of customs duties under the provisions of customs union agreements concluded by the Community

2. Next two digits

00 None of the following

   10 Tariff suspension

    15   Tariff suspension with specified end-use

   18   Tariff suspension with certificate confirming the special nature of the product

   19   Temporary suspension for products imported with a certificate of airworthiness

   20   Tariff quota ([1])

   23   Tariff quota with specified end-use ([1])

   25   Tariff quota with certificate confirming the special nature of the product ([1])

   28   Tariff quota following outward processing ([1])

   40   Special end-use resulting from the Common Customs Tariff

   50   Certificate confirming the special nature of the product

Box 37: Procedure

  A. First subdivision

The codes to be entered in this subdivision are four-digit codes, composed of a two-digit code representing the procedure requested, followed by a second two-digit code representing the previous procedure. The list of two-digit codes is given below.

'Previous procedure' means the procedure under which the goods were placed before being placed under the procedure requested.

It should be noted that where the previous procedure is a warehousing procedure or temporary importation, or where the goods have come from a free zone, the relevant code should be used only where the goods have not been placed under a customs procedure with economic impact (inward processing, outward processing or processing under customs control).

For example: re-export of goods imported under the customs inward processing procedure (suspension system) and subsequently placed under the customs warehousing procedure = 3151 (not 3171). (First operation =5100; second operation =7151: re-export =3151).

Similarly, where goods previously temporarily exported are re-imported, placing under one of the abovementioned suspensive procedures is to be regarded as simple importation under that procedure. Indication of the 'reimportation' aspect is to be given only when the goods are released for free circulation.

For example: entry for home use with simultaneous entry for free circulation of goods exported under the customs outward processing procedure and placed under a customs warehousing procedure on re-importation = 6121 (not 6171). (First operation: temporary export for outward processing = 2100; second operation: storage in customs warehouse = 7121; third operation: entry for home use + entry for free circulation = 6121).

The codes marked in the list below with the letter (a) cannot be used as the first two digits of the procedure code, but only to indicate the previous procedure.

For example: 4054 = entry for free circulation and home use of goods previously placed under the IP — suspension system in another Member State.

List of procedures for coding purposes

Two of these basic elements must be combined to produce a four-digit code.

00 This code is used to indicate that there is no previous procedure (a)

01 Free circulation of goods simultaneously redispatched in the context of trade between parts of the customs territory of the Community in which the provisions of Directive 77/388/EEC are applicable and parts of that territory in which these provisions do not apply, or in the context of trade between the parts of that territory where these provisions do not apply.

Free circulation of goods simultaneously redispatched in the context of trade between the Community and the countries with which it has formed a customs union.

¹ Where the requested tariff quota is exhausted, Member States may allow the request to be valid for any other existing preference.

Example: Goods arriving from a third country, released for free circulation in France and sent on to the Channel Islands.

02 Free circulation of goods with a view to applying the inward processing procedure (drawback system).

Explanation: Inward processing (drawback system) in accordance with Article 114(1)(b) of the Code.

07 Free circulation with simultaneous placing of goods under a warehousing procedure other than a customs warehousing procedure.

Explanation: This code is to be used where the goods are released for free circulation but where VAT and possibly excise duties have not been paid.

Examples: Imported machines are released for free circulation but VAT has not been paid. While the goods are placed in a tax warehouse or approved area, payment of the VAT is suspended.

Imported cigarettes are released for free circulation but VAT and excise duties have not been paid. While the goods are stored in a tax warehouse or approved area, payment of the VAT and excise duties is suspended.

10 Permanent export.

Example: Normal export of Community goods to a third country, but also export of Community goods to parts of the customs territory of the Community to which the provisions of Council Directive 77/388/EEC do not apply (OJ L 145, 13.6.1977, p.1).

Part III

11 Export of compensating products obtained from equivalent goods under the inward processing procedure (suspension system) before entering import goods for the procedure.

Explanation: Prior export (EX-IM) in accordance with Article 115(1)(b) of the Code.

Example: Export of cigarettes manufactured from Community tobacco leaves before placing of tobacco leaves from a third country under the inward processing procedure.

21 Temporary export under the outward processing procedure.

Explanation: Outward processing procedure under Articles 145 to 160 of the Code.

See also code 22.

22 Temporary export other than that referred to under code 21.

Example: The simultaneous application to textile products of the outward processing procedure and the economic outward processing procedure (Council Regulation (EC) No 3036/94).

23 Temporary export for return in the unaltered state.

Example: Temporary export for exhibitions of articles such as samples, professional equipment, etc.

31 Re-export.

Explanation: Re-export of non-Community goods following a suspensive arrangement with economic impact.

Example: Goods are placed under a customs warehousing procedure and subsequently declared for re-export.

40 Simultaneous release for free circulation and home use of goods which are not subject of a VAT-exempt supply.

Example: Goods coming from a third country with payment of the customs duties and VAT.

41 Simultaneous release for free circulation and home use of goods placed under the inward processing procedure (drawback system).

Example: Inward processing procedure with payment of customs duties and national taxes on import.

42 Simultaneous release for free circulation and home use of goods which are the subject of a VAT-exempt supply to another Member State.

Example: Import of goods with exemption from VAT through a tax representative.

43 Simultaneous release for free circulation and home use of goods subject to specific measures connected with the collection of an amount during the transitional period following the accession of new Member States.

Example: Release for free circulation of agricultural products subject, during a special transitional period following the accession of new Member States, to a special customs procedure or special measures between the new Member States and the rest of the Community of the kind applied in their time to ES and PT.

45 Release of goods for free circulation and home use for either VAT or excise duties and their placing under the tax warehouse procedure.

Explanation: VAT or excise exemption by placing the goods under a fiscal warehouse procedure.

Example: Cigarettes imported from a third country are released for free circulation and VAT has been paid. While the goods are in the tax warehouse or approved area, the payment of excise duties is suspended.

Cigarettes imported from a third country are released for free circulation and excise duties are paid. While the goods are in the tax warehouse or approved area the payment of VAT is suspended.

48 Entry for home use with simultaneous release for free circulation of replacement goods under the customs outward processing procedure prior to the export of the temporary export goods.

Explanation: Standard exchange system (IM-EX), prior importation in accordance with Article 154(4) of the Code.

49 Entry for home use of Community goods in the context of trade between parts of the customs territory of the Community in which the provisions of Directive 77/388/EEC are applicable and parts of that territory in which those provisions do not apply, or in the context of trade between the parts of that territory where these provisions do not apply.

Entry for home use of goods in the context of trade between the Community and the countries with which it has formed a customs union.

Explanation: Import with entry for home use of goods from parts of the Community to which the Sixth VAT Directive (77/388/ EEC) does not apply. The use of the SAD is laid down in Article 206.

Examples: Goods arriving from Martinique and entered for home use in Belgium.

Goods coming from Turkey and entered for home use in Germany.

51 Inward processing procedure (suspension system).

Explanation: Inward processing (suspension system) in accordance with Article 114(1)(a) and (2)(a) of the Code.

53 Import under temporary import procedure.

Example: Temporary importation, eg for an exhibition.

54 Inward processing (suspension system) in another Member State (without their being released for free circulation in that Member State).(a)

Explanation: This code is used to record the operation for the purposes of statistics on intra-Community trade.

Example: Goods from a third country are placed under inward processing in Belgium (5100). After undergoing inward processing, they are dispatched to Germany for release for free circulation (4054) or further processing (5154).

61 Re-importation with simultaneous release for free circulation and home use of goods which are not the subject of a VAT-exempt supply.

63 Re-importation with simultaneous release for free circulation and home use of goods which are the subject of a VAT-exempt supply to another Member State.

Example: Re-importation after outward processing or temporary export, with any VAT debt being charged to a tax representative.

68 Re-importation with partial entry for home use and simultaneous entry for free circulation and placing of goods under a warehousing procedure other than a customs warehousing procedure.

Example: Processed alcoholic beverages are re-imported and placed in an excise warehouse.

71 Placing of goods under the customs warehousing procedure.

Explanation: Placing of goods under the customs warehousing procedure. This in no way precludes the simultaneous placement of goods in, say, an excise or VAT warehouse.

76 Placing under the customs warehousing procedure or in a free zone with advance payment of export refunds of products or goods intended for export without further processing.

Example: Storage of goods intended for export with advance payment of export refunds. (Article 5(2) of Council Regulation (EEC) No 565/80 of 4 March 1980 on the advance payment of export refunds in respect of agricultural products (OJ L 62, 7. 3. 1980, p. 5)).

77 Placing in an export warehouse, free zone or free warehouse with advance payment of export refunds of processed products or goods intended for export after processing.

Example: Storage of processed products and goods obtained from basic products intended for export with advance payment of export refunds. (Article 4(2) of Regulation (EEC) No 565/80.

78 Entry of goods for a free zone subject to type II controls.

91 Placing of goods under processing under customs control.

92 Processing under customs control in another Member State (without release for free circulation in that Member State).(a)

Explanation: This code is used to record the operation for the purposes of statistics on intra-Community trade.

Example: Goods from a third country are processed under customs control in Belgium (9100). After undergoing processing, they are dispatched to Germany for release for free circulation (4092) or further processing (9192).

B. *Second subdivision*

1. Where this box is used to specify a Community procedure, a code composed of an alphabetic character followed by two alpha-numeric characters must be used, the first character of which identifies a category of measures in the following manner:

Inward processing	Axx
Outward processing	Bxx
Relief	Cxx
Temporary import	Dxx
Agricultural products	Exx
Other	Fxx

Inward processing (IP)
(Article 114 of the Code)

Procedure	Code
Goods entered for an IP procedure (suspension system) after prior export of compensating products obtained from milk and milk products	A01
Goods placed under an IP procedure (suspension system) and intended for military use abroad	A02
Goods placed under an IP procedure (suspension system) and intended for re-export to the continental shelf	A03
Goods placed under an IP procedure (suspension system) (VAT only)	A04
Goods placed under an IP procedure (suspension system) (VAT only) and intended for re-export to the continental shelf	A05
Goods placed under an IP procedure (drawback system) and intended for military use abroad	A06
Goods placed under an IP procedure (drawback system) and intended for re-export to the continental shelf	A07
Goods which are placed under an IP procedure (suspension system) without suspension of excise duties.	A08
Export	
Compensating products obtained from milk and milk products	A51
Compensating products placed under an IP procedure (suspension system) (VAT only)	A52
Compensating products placed under an IP procedure and intended for military use abroad	A53

Outward processing (OP)
(Article 145 of the Code)

Procedure	Code
Import	
Compensating products returning to the Member State in which duties were paid	B01
Compensating products returning after repair under guarantee	B02
Compensating products returning after replacement under guarantee	B03
Compensating products returning after outward processing and VAT suspension in case of end-use.	B04
Compensating products returning with partial relief of customs duties when the cost of the processing operation is used for calculation (article 591)	B05
Export	
Goods imported for IP exported for repair under OP	B51
Goods imported for IP exported for replacement under guarantee	B52
OP under agreements with third countries, possibly combined with VAT OP	B53
VAT OP only	B54

Relief

(Regulation (EEC) No 918/83)

	Article No	Code
Relief from import duties		
Personal property belonging to natural persons transferring their normal place of residence to the Community	2	C01
Goods imported on the occasion of a marriage (trousseaux and household effects)	11.1	C02
Goods imported on the occasion of a marriage (presents customarily given on the occasion of a marriage)	11.2	C03
Personal property acquired by inheritance	16	C04
Household effects for furnishing a secondary residence	20	C05
School outfits, scholastic materials and other scholastic household effects	25	C06
Consignments of negligible value	27	C07
Consignments sent from one private individual to another	29	C08
Capital goods and other equipment imported on the transfer of activities from a third country into the Community	32	C09
Capital goods and other equipment belonging to persons engaged in a liberal profession and to legal persons engaged in a non-profit making activity	38	C10
Educational, scientific and cultural materials; scientific instruments and apparatus as listed in Annex I	50	C11

Part III

	Article No	Code
Educational, scientific and cultural materials; scientific instruments and apparatus as listed in Annex II	51	C12
Educational, scientific and cultural materials; scientific instruments and apparatus (spare parts, components, accessories and tools)	53	C13
Equipment imported for non-commercial purposes by or on behalf of a scientific research establishment or organisation based outside the Community	59a	C14
Laboratory animals and biological or chemical substances intended for research	60	C15
Therapeutic substances of human origin and blood-grouping and tissue-typing reagents	61	C16
Instruments and apparatus used in medical research, establishing medical diagnoses or carrying out medical treatment	63a	C17
Reference substances for the quality control of medicinal products	63c	C18
Pharmaceutical products used at international sports events	64	C19
Goods for charitable or philanthropic organisations	65	C20
Articles in Annex III intended for the blind	70	C21
Articles in Annex IV intended for the blind imported by blind persons themselves for their own use.	71, 1st indent	C22
Articles in Annex IV intended for the blind imported by certain institutions or organisations	71, 2nd indent	C23
Articles intended for other handicapped persons (other than blind persons) imported by handicapped persons themselves for their own use	72, 74	C24
Articles intended for other handicapped persons (other than blind persons) imported by certain institutions or organisations	72, 74	C25
Goods imported for the benefit of disaster victims	79	C26
Honorary decorations or awards	86	C27
Presents received in the context of international relations	87	C28
Goods to be used by monarchs or heads of state	90	C29
Samples of goods imported for trade promotion purposes	91	C30
Printed matter and advertising material imported for trade promotion purposes	92	C31
Products used or consumed at a trade fair or similar event	95	C32
Goods imported for examination, analysis or test purposes	100	C33

	Article No	Code
Consignments sent to organisations protecting copyrights or industrial and commercial patent rights	107	C34
Tourist information literature	108	C35
Miscellaneous documents and articles	109	C36
Ancillary materials for the stowage and protection of goods during their transport	110	C37
Litter, fodder and feedingstuffs for animals during their transport	111	C38
Fuel and lubricants present in land motor vehicles	112	C39
Materials for cemeteries for, and memorials to, war victims	117	C40
Coffins, funerary urns and ornamental funerary articles	118	C41
Relief from export duties		
Domesticated animals exported at the time of transfer of agricultural activities from the Community to a third country	120	C51
Fodder and feedingstuffs accompanying animals during their exportation	126	C52

Temporary import

(The Code and this Regulation)

Procedure	Article of this Regulation	Code
Pallets	556	D01
Containers	557	D02
Means of transport	558	D03
Personal effects and goods for sports purposes imported by travellers	563	D04
Welfare material for seafarers	564	D05
Disaster relief material	565	D06
Medical, surgical and laboratory equipment	566	D07
Animals	567	D08
Goods intended for activities in keeping with the particularities of the frontier zone	567	D09
Sound, image or data carrying media	568	D10
Publicity material	568	D11
Professional equipment	569	D12
Pedagogic material and scientific equipment	570	D13
Packings, full	571	D14
Packings, empty	571	D15
Moulds, dies, blocks, drawings, sketches, measuring, checking and testing instruments and other similar articles	572	D16
Special tools and instruments	572	D17
Goods to be subjected to tests	573(a)	D18

Procedure	Article of this Regulation	Code
Goods imported, subject to satisfactory acceptance tests, in connection with a sales contract	573(b)	D19
Goods used to carry out tests	573(c)	D20
Samples	574	D21
Replacement means of production	575	D22
Goods to be exhibited or used at a public event	576(1)	D23
Goods for approval (two months)	576(2)	D24
Works of art, collectors' items and antiques	576(3a)	D25
Goods imported with a view to their sale by auction	576(3b)	D26
Spare parts, accessories and equipment	577	D27
Goods imported in particular situations having no economic effect	578(b)	D28
Goods imported occasionally and for a period not exceeding three months	578(a)	D29
	Article of the Code	Code
Temporary importation with partial relief from duties	142	D51

Agricultural products

Procedure	Code
Import	
Use of the unit values for the determination of the customs value for certain perishable goods (Articles 173 — 177)	E01
Standing import values (for example: Regulation (EC) No 3223/94)	E02
Export	
Agricultural products for which a refund is requested, subject to an export certificate (Annex I goods).	E51
Agricultural products for which a refund is requested, not requiring an export certificate (Annex I goods).	E52
Agricultural products for which a refund is requested, exported in small quantities, not requiring an export certificate (Annex I goods).	E53
Agricultural products for which a refund is requested, subject to a refund certificate (non-Annex I goods).	E61
Agricultural products for which a refund is requested, not requiring a refund certificate (non-Annex I goods)	E62
Agricultural products for which a refund is requested, exported in small quantities, without a refund certificate (non-Annex I goods)	E63
Agricultural products for which a refund is requested, exported in small quantities disregarded for the calculation of minimum rates of checks.	E71

Other

Procedure	Code
Import	
Relief from import duties for returned goods (Article 185 of the Code)	F01
Relief from import duties for returned goods (Special circumstances provided for in Article 844, 1: agriculture goods)	F02
Relief from import duties for returned goods (Special circumstances provided for in Article 846, 2: repair or restoration)	F03
Compensatory products which return to the Community after having been previously exported or re-exported (Article187 of the Code)	F04
Processing under customs control where the economic conditions are deemed to be fulfilled (Article 552, 1, first subparagraph)	F11
Exemption from import duties of products of sea-fishing and other products taken from the territorial sea of a third country by vessels registered or recorded in a Member State and flying the flag of the state	F21
Exemption from import duties of products obtained from products of sea-fishing and other products taken from the territorial sea of a third country on board factory-ships registered or recorded in a Member State and flying the flag of the state	F22
Goods which, after having been under an outward-processing procedure, are placed under a warehousing procedure without suspension of excise duties	F31
Goods which, after having been under an inward-processing procedure, are placed under a warehousing procedure without suspension of excise duties	F32
Goods which, after having been in a free zone subject to type-II controls, are placed under a warehousing procedure without suspension of excise duties	F33
Goods which, after having been subject to processing under customs control, are placed under a warehousing procedure without suspension of excise duties	F34
Release for free circulation of goods for events or for sale placed under temporary importation, applying the elements of calculation in force at the moment of acceptance of the declaration for free circulation	F41
Release for free circulation of compensating products when their own customs duties are to be applied (Article 122(a) of the Code)	F42
Release for free circulation of goods placed under an IP procedure, or release for free circulation of compensating products without compensatory interests (Article 519, paragraph 4)	F43
Export	
Exports for military use	F51
Victualling	F61
Victualling of goods eligible for refunds	F62
Entry in victualling warehouse (Articles 40-43 Regulation (EEC) No 800/99)	F63
Exit from victualling warehouse of goods intended for victualling	F64

2. Codes exclusively for national use must be composed of a numeric character followed by two alphanumeric characters according to that Member State's own nomenclature.

Box 40: Summary declaration/Previous document

This box is for alphanumeric (an..26) codes.

Each code has three components, which are separated by dashes (-). The first component (a1) consists of three different letters and is used to distinguish between the three categories mentioned below. The second component (an..3), which consists of a combination of digits and/or letters, serves to identify the type of document. The third component (an..20) represents the particulars needed to recognise the document, either its identification number or another recognisable reference.

   1. *The first component (a1):*

      the summary declaration, represented by 'X',

      the initial declaration, represented by 'Y'

      the previous document, represented by 'Z',

   2. *The second component (an..3):*

      Choose the abbreviation for the document from the 'list of abbreviations for documents'.

      This list includes the code 'CLE', which stands for 'date and reference of the entry of the goods in the records'. (Article 76(1)(c) of the Code). The date is coded as follows: yyyymmdd.

   3. *The third component (an..20):*

The identification number or another recognisable reference of the document is inserted here.

Examples:

     –   The previous document is a T1 transit document to which the office of destination has assigned the number '238544'. The code will therefore be 'Z-821-238544'. ('Z' for previous document, '821' for the transit procedure and '238544' for the document's registration number (or the MRN for the NCTS operations))

     –   A cargo manifest bearing the number '2222' is used as a summary declaration. The code will be 'X-785-2222'. ('X' for the summary declaration, '785' for the cargo manifest and '2222' for the manifest's identification number).

     –   Goods were entered in the records on 14 February 2002. The code will therefore be 'Y-CLE-20020214-5' ('Y' to show there was an initial declaration, 'CLE' for 'entry in the records', '20020214' for the date of entry, '2002' being the year, '02' the month, '14' the day and '5' for the reference of the entry in the records).

List of abbreviations for documents	
Container list	235
Loading list (delivery note)	270
Packing list	271
Proforma invoice	325
Commercial invoice	380
House waybill	703
Master bill of lading	704
Bill of lading	705
CIM consignment note (rail)	720

List of abbreviations for documents	
Road list SMGS	722
Road consignment note	730
Air waybill	740
Master air waybill	741
Despatch note (post parcels)	750
Multimodal/combined transport document	760
Cargo manifest	785
Bordereau	787
Community transit Declaration — Mixed consignments (T)	820
External Community transit Declaration (T1)	821
Internal Community transit Declaration (T2)	822
Control copy T5	823
TIR carnet	952
ATA carnet	955
Reference/date of entry of the goods in the records	CLE
Information sheet INF3	IF3
Information sheet INF8	IF8
Cargo manifest — simplified procedure	MNS
Internal Community transit Declaration — Article 340 c, 1)	T2F
T2M	T2M
Other	ZZZ

If the above document is drawn up using the SAD, the abbreviation will comprise the codes specified for the first subdivision of box 1. (IM, EX, CO and EU)

Box 43: Valuation method

The provisions used to determine the customs value of imported goods are to be coded as follows:

Code	Relevant Article of the Code	Method
1	29(1)	Transaction value of the imported goods
2	30(2)(a)	Transaction value of identical goods
3	30(2)(b)	Transaction value of similar goods
4	30(2)(c)	Deductive value method
5	30(2)(d)	Computed value method
6	31	Value based on the data available ('fall-back' method)

Box 44: Additional information/Documents produced/Certificates and authorisations

  1. *Additional information*

A five-digit code is used to encode additional information of a customs nature. This code follows the additional information unless Community law provides for the code to be used in place of the text.

Example: In a simplified export procedure, copy 3 must contain the information 'simplified export procedure'. (Article 280(3). 'Simplified exportation — 30100' should therefore be entered in box 44.

Community law provides for certain additional information to be entered in boxes other than box 44. However, such additional information should be coded according to the same rules as the information to be specifically entered in box 44. Furthermore, where Community law fails to specify the box in which information is to be entered, that information is to be entered in box 44.

All types of additional information are listed at the end of this Annex.

Member States may provide for the use of national additional information provided that their codification presents a structure different to the codes for Community additional information.

   2.   *Documents produced, certificates and authorisations*

     (a)   Documents, certificates and Community or international authorisations produced in support of the declaration must be entered in the form of a code composed of 4 alpha-numeric characters, followed either by an identification number or another recognisable reference. The list of documents, certificates and authorisations and their respective codes can be found in the Taric database.

     (b)   National documents, certificates and authorisations produced in support of the declaration must be entered in the form of a code composed of an numeric character followed by 3 alpha-numeric characters (Ex: 2123, 34d5), possibly followed either by an identification number or another recognisable reference. The four characters represent codes based on that Member State's own nomenclature.

Box 47: Calculation of taxes

First column: Type of tax

   (a)   The codes applicable are given below:

Customs duties on industrial products	A00
Customs duties on agricultural products	A10
Additional duties	A20
Definitive antidumping duties	A30
Provisional antidumping duties	A35
Definitive countervailing duties	A40
Provisional countervailing duties	A45
VAT	B00
Compensatory interest (VAT)	B10
Interest on arrears (VAT)	B20
Export taxes	C00
Export taxes on agricultural products	C10
Interest on arrears	D00
Compensatory interest (I.e. Inward processing)	D10
Duties collected on behalf of other countries	E00

   (b)   Codes exclusively for national use must be composed of a numeric character followed by two alphanumeric characters according to that Member State's own nomenclature.

Last column: Method of payment

The following codes may be used by the Member States:

A Payment in cash

B Payment by credit card

C Payment by cheque

D Other (e. g. direct debit to agent's cash account)

E Deferred or postponed payment

F Deferred payment — customs system

G Postponed payment — VAT system (Article 23 Sixth VAT Directive)
H: Electronic credit transfer
J: Payment through post office administration (postal consignments) or other public sector or government department
K Excise credit or rebate
M Security, including cash deposit
P From agent's cash account
R Guarantee
S Individual guarantee account
T From agents' guarantee account
U From agent's guarantee — standing authority
V From agent's guarantee — individual authority
O Guarantee lodged with Intervention Agency.

NOTES
Amended by Corrigendum.

Box 49: Identification of warehouse
The code to be entered has the following three-part structure:
- the letter identifying the type of warehouse in accordance with the descriptions contained in Article 525 (a1). For warehouses other than those mentioned in Article 525, the following codes should be used:

Y for a non-customs warehouse
Z for a free zone or free warehouse
- the identification number allocated by the Member State when issuing the authorisation (an..14)
- the country code for the authorising Member State, as defined in box 2 (a2).

Box 51: Intended offices of transit (and country)
Use the codes entered in box 29.

NOTES
"BG" and "RO" added to the note on Box 51 by Commission Regulation (EC) 1792/2006, Art 1, Annex, Part 11(A)(47).

Box 52: Guarantee
Guarantee codes
The codes applicable (n1) are given below:

Situation	Code	Other entries
[For guarantee waiver (Articles 94(4) of the Code and 380(3) of this Regulation)	0	— guarantee waiver certificate number
For comprehensive guarantee	1	— comprehensive guarantee certificate number— office of guarantee
For individual guarantee by a guarantor	2	— reference for the guarantee undertaking— office of guarantee
For individual guarantee in cash	3	

Situation	Code	Other entries
For individual guarantee in the form of vouchers	4	— individual guarantee voucher number
For guarantee waiver where secured amount does not exceed EUR 500 (Article 189(5) of the Code)	5	
For guarantee not required (Article 95 of the Code)	6	
For guarantee not required for certain public bodies	8	
For individual guarantee of the type under point 3 of Annex 47a	9	— reference to the guarantee undertaking— office of guarantee]

NOTES

Text of the applicable codes in Box 52 substituted by Commission Regulation (EC) 883/2005, Art 1, para 29, Annex IV, with effect from 1 January 2006. However, member states may apply the legislation before this date.

Entering countries under the heading 'not valid for':

Use the country codes entered in box 2.

Box 53: Office of destination (and country)

Use the codes entered in box 29.

Additional information — code XXXXX

General category — Code 0xxxx

Legal basis	Subject	Additional information	Box	Code
Article 497 § 3	Application for authorisation on the declaration for a customs procedure with economic impact	'Simplified authorisation'	44	00100
Annex 37	Several exporters, consignees or previous documents	other	2, 8 and 40	00200
Annex 37	Identity between declarant and consignor	'Consignor'	14	00300
Annex 37	Identity between declarant and exporter	'Exporter'	14	00400
Annex 37	Identity between declarant and consignee	'Consignee'	14	00500

On import: Code 1xxxx

Article	Subject	Additional information	Box	Code
2 paragraph 1 of Regulation No 1147/2002	Temporarily suspension of the autonomous duties	'Import with airworthiness certificate'	44	10100
549 Paragraph 1	Discharge of inward processing (suspension system)	IP/S goods	44	10200
549 Paragraph 2	Discharge of inward processing (suspension system) (specific commercial policy measures)	IP/S goods, Commercial policy	44	10300
550	Discharge of inward processing (drawback)	IP/D goods	44	10400
583	Temporary admission	'TA goods'	44	10500

On export: Code 3xxxx

Article	Subject	Additional information	Box	Code
280(3)	Incomplete export declaration	'Simplified exportation'		30100
286(4)	Local clearance procedure	'Simplified exportation' with the number of the authorisation and the name of the customs office of issue		30200
298	Export of agricultural goods subject to end-use	Article 298 Regulation (EEC) No 2454/93 End-use: Goods destined for exportation — agricultural refunds not applicable		30300
793(3)	The desire to have copy 3 returned	'RET-EXP'		30400

[ANNEX 38A

CUSTOMS DECLARATION FOR REGISTERED BAGGAGE

Part III

ANNEX 38a

CUSTOMS DECLARATION FOR REGISTERED BAGGAGE

1. I HEREBY DECLARE

    (a) that the baggage referred to below contains only articles of personal use normally used when travelling, such as clothing, household linen, toiletries, books and sports equipment, and that these articles are not being imported for commercial purposes;

    (b) that the baggage does not contain:

    — foodstuffs, tobacco, alcoholic beverages, anethol, firearms, sidearm, ammunition, explosives, drugs, live animals, plants, radio transmitters or transmitter-receivers, currency, species and products obtained from species protected under the Washington Convention of 3 March 1973 on International Trade in Endangered Species of Wild Flora and Fauna; articles forbidden by the laws of the country of destination on the protection public decency and morality,

    — goods intended for distribution free of charge or otherwise or for professional or commercial purposes,

    — goods bought or received by myself outside the customs territory of my country and not yet declared to the customs authorities of my country of normal residence (this restriction applies only when returning to the country of normal residence).

2. I HEREBY AUTHORISE the railway authorities to carry out all customs formalities.

3. I KNOW that making a false statement renders me liable to prosecution and seizure of my goods.

Country of destination: .... Place of destination: ....

Number of items		Number of persons accompanying the passenger	

IN BLOCK LETTERS

SURNAME: OTHER NAMES:

....

Normal residence: Street: .... No: ....

Town: .... Country: ....

Signature of passenger:

Date-stamp of
departure station
                                        ....

Consignment note No

NOTES

Inserted by Commission Regulation (EC) 1762/95, Art 1, para 16, Annex IV.

[ANNEX 38B

1. For the purposes of the application of Article 290a, the customs authorities of the customs office at which the declaration for free circulation of fresh bananas is lodged shall determine the net mass, based on a sample of units of packaging for each type of packaging and for each place of origin.

2. The units of packaging weighed should constitute a representative sample of the declaration. It shall involve at least the quantities indicated below—

Number of units of packaging declared (by type of packing and by origin)	Number of units of packaging to be examined
—up to 400	5
—from 401 to 700	7
—from 701 to 1 000	10
—from 1 001 to 2 000	13
—more than 2 000	15

Where a whole cargo load is covered by a single declaration, the customs office may, unless fraud is suspected, base the calculation of the net mass on a minimum sample of 15 units of packaging (of the same type of packaging and from the same place of origin).

The net mass shall be determined as follows—

— opening at least one unit of packaging, then calculating the mass of the packaging,

— the mass of the packaging shall be accepted for all packaging of the same type and shall be deducted from the mass of all the units of packaging weighed,

— the average mass per unit of packaging of bananas thus established, based on the mass of the sample checked, shall be accepted as the basis for determining the net mass of the bananas covered by the declaration.]

NOTES

Inserted by Commission Regulation (EC) 89/97, Art 1, para 2.

ANNEXES 39–41

NOTES

Annexes 39–41 repealed by Commission Regulation (EC) 1602/2000, Art 1, para 20.

ANNEX 42

YELLOW LABEL

Part III

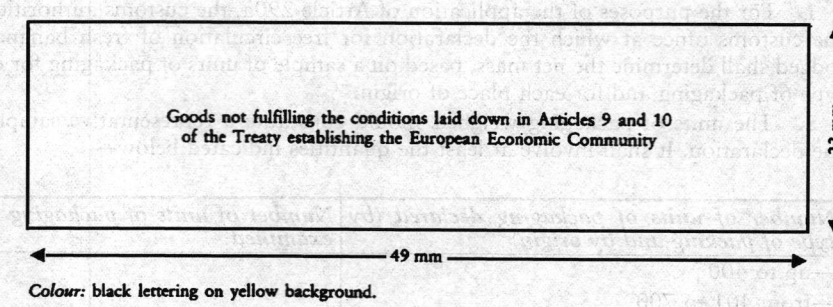

Goods not fulfilling the conditions laid down in Articles 9 and 10
of the Treaty establishing the European Economic Community

← 49 mm →

↕ 23 mm

Colour: black lettering on yellow background.

[ANNEX 42A

EUROPEAN COMMUNITY

1. Applicant (name of the shipping company, or its representative, and full address)	Serial number:
☐	**CERTIFICATE OF** **REGULAR SHIPPING SERVICES** — Article 313a of Regulation (EEC) No 2454/93

2. Ports concerned (route, with ports of call in order of calling)

3. Vessels of the shipping service

4. Other information

5. Declaration by the shipping company

I, the undersigned, hereby declare that the vessels forming part of the regular service in respect of which this application is made:
1. ply solely between ports in Community customs territory;
2. do not call at any points outside Community customs territory or at any free zone of a port in Community customs territory; and
3. do not tranship cargo on the high seas.

Date: .... (Signature) ....

A. Customs authority which issued the certificate authorizing the regular service: ....
Date: .... Stamp

Name:
Address:

Member State:
(Signature)

© European Communities Official Journal L 253, 11/10/1993 Annex 42A

Part III

NOTES

Inserted by Commission Regulation (EC) 75/98, Art 1, para 27, Annex III.

ANNEX 42B
YELLOW LABEL

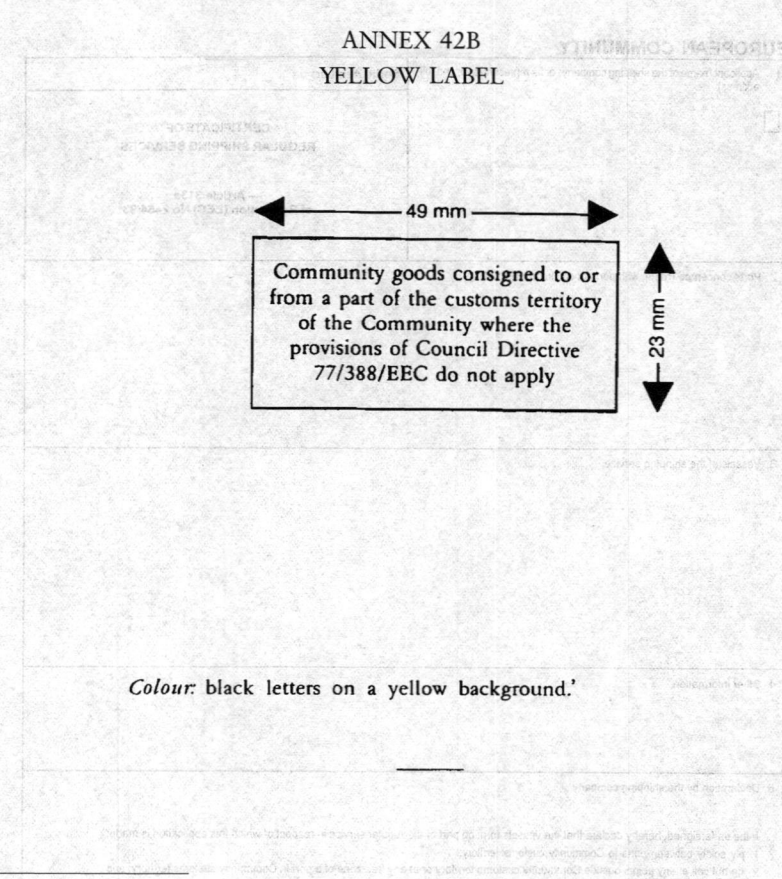

← 49 mm →

Community goods consigned to or
from a part of the customs territory
of the Community where the
provisions of Council Directive
77/388/EEC do not apply

23 mm

Colour: black letters on a yellow background.'

NOTES
Inserted by Commission Regulation (EC) 75/98, Art 1, para 27, Annex III.

ANNEX 43
FORM T2M

EUROPEAN COMMUNITY

1

1. Applicant (full name or name of company or business and full address)	**T2M**		No A 000000

2. Community fishing vessel
Name: ....
Recorded number: ....
Base port: ....
Flag: ....

3. Declaration by the operator

I the undersigned, hereby declare that the products and goods to be showed in boxes 4 and 6 have Community status.

Date: ....

(Signature)

A. Stamp of the fishing vessel registration authority

Authority: .... Stamp

Date: ....

4. Products of sea-fishing (Name and type)	5. Gross mass (kg)

1

6. Goods obtained from the products referred to above (Kind)	7. CN Code	8. Gross mass (kg)

9. Declaration by the master of the Community fishing vessel

I the undersigned,_____ (full name), master of the vessel shown in box 2, declare that the products referred to in box 4:
— Were caught by my vessel in waters other than the territorial waters of a country or territory outside Community customs territory;
— have undergone on board my vessel processing which has been recorded on page ......of the logbook and that the goods obtained are described in box 6(3)

Date: Signature:

10. Declaration in event of a first transshipment from a Community fishing vessel

The products and/or goods described in this document were transshipped onto the following vessel:

(a) Name: ....   (b) Registration number: ....

(c) Flag: ....   (d) Full name of master: ....

The transshipment has been recorded on page ...... of the logbook of the Community fishing vessel.

The transhipment has been recorded on page.............of the logbook of the vessel onto which the products and/or goods were transhipped.

Date: ....

....
(Signature of the master of the Community fishing vessel)   (Signature of the master of the receiving vessel)

B. Office which issued the T2M form
Customs office: ....
Address: ....
Member State: ....   Stamp
Date: ....
Signature: ....

Part III

11. **Declaration when processing takes place on board the vessel onto which the catch has been transported**

The products referred to in box 4 have undergone on board the vessel shown in box 10 processing which has been recorded on page .... of the logbook and the resulting goods are shown in box 6.

Date: ....

....
(Signature of master)

12. **Declaration in the event of a second transhipment without further processing**

The products and/or goods referred to in this document have been transhipped onto the folowing vessel:

(a) Name: ....   (c) Registration number: ....

(b) Flag: ....   (d) Full name of master: ....

The transhipment has been recorded on page .... of the logbook of the vessel from which the products and/or goods were transhipped.   The transhipment has been recorded on page .... of the logbook of the vessel onto which the products and/or goods were transhipped

Date: ....

....
(Signature of the master of the transhipping vessel)   (Signature of the master of the receiving vessel)

13. **Certification by the customs authority of the country or territory not forming part of Community territory**

The undersigned customs authority, hereby certifies that the products and/or goods referred to in boxes 4 and/or 6 were under customs supervision throughout their stay and have undergone no handlnig other than the necessary for their preservation.

Date of arrival of the products/goods: ....

Date of departure of the products/goods: ....

Means of transport used for reconsignments to Community territory: ....

Full address of the customs office: ....

Stamp

Country or territory: ....

Date: ....

....
(Signature)

C. **Stamp of the customs office where the products and/or goods were brought into the Community customs territory**

Customs office: ....

Member state: ....

Date: ....

Stamp

A copy of this form must be sent to the customs office indicated in box B

REMARKS

(1)   If this authority is the same as the customs office indicated in Box B, then the impression of the stamp is sufficient for completion of Box A.

(2)   Approximate figure.

(3)   Delete when no processing takes place on board.

(4)   Community fishing vessel or Community factory ship.]

(Copy omitted.)

NOTES
Substituted by Commission Regulation (EC) 482/96, Art 1, para 25, Annex III.

[ANNEX 44
NOTES
(to be added to the booklet containing the T2M forms)

I. General considerations

1. The purpose of a T2M form is to prove the Community status, upon entry into Community customs territory, of a catch made by a Community fishing vessel outside the territorial waters of a country or territory not forming part of Community customs territory and/or of goods obtained from such catches by processing carried out on board the Community fishing vessel which made the catch, another Community fishing vessel, or a Community factory ship.

2. The Community fishing vessel is a vessel which is registered and listed in a part of a Member State's territory forming part of Community customs territory, flies the flag of a Member State, makes the catch and may process it on board. The Community factory ship is a vessel, similarly registered or listed, which processes only transhipped catches.

3. This booklet contains 10 forms, each consisting of an original and a copy. The copies must not be separated from the booklet.

4. The booklet must be produced whenever the customs authorities so require.

5. It must be returned to the customs authorities by which it was issued when the vessel for which it was issued ceases to fulfil the conditions laid down, when all the forms contained in the booklet have been used or when the period of validity of the booklet expires.

II. Authentication of T2M forms

6. The forms must be completed in typescript or legibly by hand; if the latter, in ink and in printed characters. No erasures or alterations may be made. Amendments must be made by striking out the incorrect particulars and adding those required where appropriate. Any such amendments must be initialled by the person who signed the declaration containing them.

7. Boxes 1 to 3 of the form must be completed by the person indicated, in the language in which the form is printed. Boxes 4 to 12 of the form must be completed in one of the official Community languages.

8. The validity of the T2M forms contained in a booklet is guaranteed by the presence, in box A of both originals and copies, of an endorsement by the authority responsible for registering the Community fishing vessel for which the booklet was issued. The booklet is valid for two years from the date shown on page 2 of its cover.

III. Use of T2M forms

9. The master of the Community fishing vessel must complete boxes 4, 5 and/or boxes 6, 7, 8 and complete and sign the declaration in box 9, of the original and the copy of a T2M form whenever—
- a catch and/or the goods resulting from on-board processing of a catch are landed either in a port in Community customs territory, or in another part from which they will leave for that territory,
- the catch and/or goods are transhipped onto another Community fishing vessel, a Community factory ship—where the catch undergoes on-board processing—or any other vessel which transports the catch and/or goods without processing them, either directly to a port

Part III

within Community customs territory or to a port not in Community customs territory from where they will leave for that territory. In this case the master of the Community fishing vessel and the master of the vessel onto which the catch and/or goods are transhipped must complete and sign box 10 of the original and the copy.

10. Where appropriate, the master of the vessel onto which a Community fishing vessel's catch has been transhipped to undergo on-board processing must complete boxes 6, 7 and 8, and complete and sign the declaration in box 11 of the original whenever—

— goods resulting from on-board processing are landed either in a port in Community customs territory, or in a port not in Community customs territory from which they will leave for that territory,

— the goods are transhipped onto any other vessel which transports them without processing, either directly to a port in Community customs territory or to a port not in Community customs territory from where they will leave for that territory. In this case, the master of the processing vessel and the master of the vessel onto which the goods are transhipped must complete and sign box 12 of the original.

11. Where catch or goods have gone to a country or territory not forming part of Community customs territory before being shipped to Community customs territory, box 13 of the form must be completed and signed by the customs authorities of the country or territory. If a part of the catch or goods does not go to Community customs territory, the name, kind, gross mass and treatment or use assigned to the consignments concerned must be entered in the "Remarks" box of the form.

12. Whenever catch and/or goods are transhipped for carriage to Community customs territory, they must be accompanied by the original of a T2M form.

IV. Use of "Extracts" of T2M forms

Where catch and/or goods have been transported to a country or territory not forming part of Community customs territory for later reconsignment to that territory in split consignments—

13. A number of original T2M forms equal to the number of split consignments must be taken from the booklet issued to the fishing vessel which made the catch and/or processed it into goods, and clearly marked with the word "Extract" and particulars of the T2M form for the initial consignment. This information must also be entered in the copies of the "Extracts" which must remain in the booklet.

14. For each split consignment—

— boxes 4, 5 and/or 6, 7, 8 of the T2M "Extract" form must be completed, stating the quantities of catch and/or goods consigned,

— box 13 of the original of the "Extract" form must be completed, endorsed and signed by the customs authorities of the country or territory concerned,

— the number and kind of packages, the gross mass, the treatment or use assigned to the consignment and the number and date of the "Extract" form must be entered in the "Remarks" box of the initial T2M form,

— the "Extract" form must accompany the consignment of catch and/or goods.

15. When all the catch and/or goods covered by the initial T2M form have been shipped to Community customs territory, box 13 of the form must be completed, endorsed and signed by the customs authorities of the country or territory concerned. This form must be sent to the office which issued the T2M booklet. If a part of the catch or goods does not go to Community customs territory, the name, kind and gross mass of the consignments concerned, and the treatment or use assigned, must be entered in the "Remarks" box on the form.

V. Discharge of T2M forms

16. All original T2M forms (initial or "Extract") must be presented to the customs office where the catch or goods to which it refers have been brought into Community customs territory. However, where such catch or goods are brought into Community customs territory under a transit procedure and the corresponding operation began outside that territory, the T2M forms must be presented to the customs office of destination for that procedure.]

NOTES

Substituted by Commission Regulation (EC) 482/96, Art 1, para 25, Annex IV.

[ANNEX 44A

EXPLANATORY NOTE ON THE LOADING LIST

TITLE I
GENERAL

1. Definition

The loading list means a document having the characteristics described in this Annex.

2. Loading list form

2.1. Only the front of the form may be used as a loading list.

2.2. The features of a loading list are—
- (a) the heading "Loading list";
- (b) a 70 × 55 millimetre box divided into an upper part of 70 by 15 millimetres and a lower part of 70 by 40 millimetres;
- (c) columns with the following headings in the following order—
  - — serial number,
  - — marks, numbers, number and kind of packages, goods description,
  - — country of dispatch/export,
  - — gross mass in kilograms,
  - — reserved for the administration.

Users may adjust the width of the columns to their needs. However, the column headed "reserved for the administration" must always be at least 30 millimetres wide. Users may also decide for themselves how to use the spaces other than those referred to in points (a), (b) and (c).

2.3. A horizontal line must be drawn immediately under the last entry and any spaces not used must be scored through to prevent later additions.

TITLE II
PARTICULARS TO BE ENTERED IN THE DIFFERENT HEADINGS

1. Box

1.1. Upper part

Where a loading list accompanies a transit declaration, the principal must enter "T1", "T2" or "T2F" in the upper part of the box.

Where a loading list accompanies a T2L document, the person concerned must enter "T2L" or "T2LF" in the upper part of the box.

1.2. Upper part

The particulars listed in paragraph 4 of Title III below must be entered in this part of the box.

2. Columns

2.1. Serial number

Every item shown on the loading list must be preceded by a serial number.

Part III

2.2. Marks, numbers, number and kind of packages, goods description

The particulars required shall be given in accordance with Annexes 37 and 38.

[Where a loading list accompanies a transit declaration, the list must include the information entered in boxes 31 (Packages and description of goods), 40 (Summary declaration/previous document) 44 (Additional information, documents produced, certificates and authorisations) and, where appropriate, 33 (Commodity code) and 38 (Net mass (kg)) of the transit declaration.]

2.3. Country of dispatch/export

Enter the name of the Member State from which the goods are being consigned or exported.

Do not use this column where a loading list accompanies a T2L document.

2.4. Gross mass (kg)

Enter the details entered in box 35 of the SAD (see Annex 37).

TITLE III
USE OF LOADING LISTS

1. A transit declaration may not have both a loading list and one or more continuation sheets attached to it.

2. [Where a loading list is used, boxes 15 (Country of dispatch/export), 32 (Item number), 33 (Commodity code), 35 (Gross mass (kg)), 38 (Net mass (kg)), 40 (Summary declaration/previous document) and, where appropriate, 44 (Additional information, documents produced, certificates and authorisations) of the transit declaration form must be struck through and box 31 (Packages and description of goods) may not be used to enter the marks, numbers, number and kind of packages or goods description.]

(Gross mass (kg)), 38 (Net mass (kg)) and, where appropriate, 44 (Additional information, documents produced, certificates and authorisations) of the transit declaration form must be struck through and box 31 (Packages and goods description) may not be used to enter the marks, numbers, number and kind of packages or goods description. A reference to the serial number and the symbol of the different loading lists shall be entered in box 31 (Packages and goods description) of the transit declaration form used.

3. The loading list must be produced in the same number of copies as the form to which it relates.

. . .

4. When a transit declaration is registered the loading list must be given the same registration number as the form to which it relates. This number must be entered by using a stamp which includes the name of the office of departure, or by hand. If entered by hand, it must be endorsed by the official stamp of the office of departure.

It is not obligatory for an official of the office of departure to sign the forms.

5. Where several loading lists are attached to one form used for the purpose of Community transit, the lists must bear a serial number allocated by the principal, and the number of loading lists attached must be entered in box 4 (Loading lists) of the said form.

6. The provisions of paragraphs 1 to 5 apply, as appropriate, where a loading list is attached to a T2L or T2LF document.]

NOTES

Inserted by Commission Regulation (EC) 2787/2000, Art 1, para 64, Annex V.

Title II, para 2.2: words substituted by Commission Regulation (EC) 444/2002, Art 29, Annex II.

Title III, para 2: words substituted by Commission Regulation (EC) 444/2002, Art 1, para 29, Annex II.

Title III, para 3: second paragraph repealed by Commission Regulation (EC) 881/2003 Art 1, para 32, Annex VI with effect from 1 January 2005.

[ANNEX 44B
PROVISIONS CONCERNING FORMS USED IN COMMUNITY TRANSIT

This Annex sets out the characteristics of forms other than the single administrative document used in Community transit.

1. Loading lists

1.1.   The forms shall be printed on paper dressed for writing purposes, weighing at least 40 g/m2 and sufficiently strong to prevent easy tearing or creasing in normal use. The colour may be decided by those concerned.

1.2.   The format of the forms shall be 210 by 297 millimetres, with a maximum tolerance of 5 millimetres less and 8 millimetres more on the length.

2. Transit advice note

2.1.   The forms shall be printed on paper dressed for writing purposes, weighing at least 40 g/m_2 and sufficiently strong to prevent easy tearing or creasing in normal use. The paper shall be white.

2.2.   The format of the forms shall be 210 by 148 millimetres.

3. Receipt

3.1.   The forms shall be printed on paper dressed for writing purposes, weighing at least 40 g/m2 and sufficiently strong to prevent easy tearing or creasing in normal use. The paper shall be white.

3.2.   The format of the forms shall be 148 by 105 millimetres.

4. Individual guarantee

4.1.   The forms shall be printed on paper free of mechanical pulp, dressed for writing purposes and weighing at least 55 g/m2. It shall have a printed guilloche pattern background in red so as to reveal any falsification by mechanical or chemical means. The paper shall be white.

4.2.   The format of the forms shall be 148 by 105 millimetres.

4.3.   The forms shall show the name and address of the printer, or a mark by which he may be identified, and a serial identification number.

5. Comprehensive guarantee and guarantee waiver certificates

5.1.   The forms for comprehensive guarantee of guarantee waiver certificates, hereinafter referred to as "certificates", shall be printed on white paper free of mechanical pulp and weighing at least 100 g/m_2. Both sides shall have a printed guilloche pattern background so as to reveal any falsification by mechanical or chemical means. The printing shall be—

—   in green for guarantee certificates,

—   in pale blue for guarantee waiver certificates.

5.2.   The format of the forms shall be 210 by 148 millimetres.

5.3.   The Member States shall be responsible for printing the forms or having them printed. Each certificate shall bear a serial identification number.

6. Provisions common to all of Title II

6.1.   Forms must be completed using a typewriter or other mechanographical or similar process. Loading list, transit advice and receipt forms may also be completed legibly in manuscript, in which case they shall be completed in ink and in block letters.

6.2. Forms must be drawn up in one of the official languages of the Member States which is acceptable to the customs authorities of the Member State of departure. This provision shall not apply to flat-rate guarantee vouchers.

6.3. The customs authorities of a Member State in which the forms must be produced may if necessary require a translation into the official language, or one of the official languages, of that Member State.

6.4. The language to be used for the comprehensive guarantee and guarantee waiver certificates shall be designated by the customs authorities of the Member State responsible for the office of guarantee.

6.5. No erasures or alterations shall be made. Amendments shall be made by striking out the incorrect particulars and, where appropriate, adding those required. Any such amendments shall be initialled by the person making the amendment and expressly endorsed by the customs authorities.]

NOTES

Inserted by Commission Regulation (EC) 2787/2000, Art 1, para 65, Annex VI.

[ANNEX 44C

GOODS INVOLVING GREATER RISK OF FRAUD

1	2	3	4	5
HS code	Description of the goods	Minimum quantities	Sensitive goods code ($_1$)	Minimum rate of indi-vidual guarantee
ex 0102 90	Other live animals, of the bovine do-mestic species	4 000 kg	1	1 500 EUR/t
0201 10 0201 20 0201 30	Meat of bovine ani-mals, fresh or chilled	3 000 kg		2 700 EUR/t 2 900 EUR/t 5 200 EUR/t
0202 10 0202 20 0202 30	Meat of bovine ani-mals, frozen	3 000 kg		2 700 EUR/t 2 900 EUR/t 3 900 EUR/t
0402 10 0402 21 0402 29 0402 91 0402 99	Milk and cream, concentrated or containing added sugar or other sweetening matter	2 500 kg		1 600 EUR/t 1 900 EUR/t 2 500 EUR/t 1 400 EUR/t 1 600 EUR/t
0405 10 0405 90	Butter and other fats and oils derived from milk	3 000 kg		2 600 EUR/t 2 800 EUR/t
ex 0803 00	Fresh bananas, ex-cluding plantains	8 000 kg	1	800 EUR/t
1701 11 1701 12 1701 91 1701 99	Cane or beet sugar and chemically pure sucrose, in solid form	7 000 kg		— — — —
2207 10	Undenatured ethyl alcohol of an alco-holic strength by volume of 80 % vol or higher	3 hl		2 500 EUR/hl pure alcohol

1	2	3	4	5
HS code	Description of the goods	Minimum quantities	Sensitive goods code (₁)	Minimum rate of individual guarantee
2208 20 2208 30 2208 40 2208 50 2208 60	Spirits, liquors and other spirituous beverages	5 hl	1	2 500 EUR/hl pure alcohol
2208 70 ex 2208 90				
2402 20	Cigarettes containing tobacco	35 000 pieces		120 EUR/1 000 pieces

(1)   Where the provisions of Part II, Title II, Chapter 4, section 2, subsection 7 apply and the HS code is not enough to identify without ambiguity the goods listed in column 2, both the sensitive goods code given in column 4 and the HS code given in column 1 must be used.]

NOTES

Inserted by Commission Regulation (EC) 2787/2000, Art 1, para 66, Annex VII.
Figure "1" in row 11, column 4 added by Corrigendum (OJ L 20, 23.1.02, p 11).

ANNEX 45
LOADING LIST

No	Marks, numbers, number and kind of packages; description of goods	Country of dispatch/export	Gross mass (kg)	Reserved for official use
				(Signature)

ANNEX 45A

CHAPTER I

Specimen of transit accompanying document]

EUROPEAN COMMUNITY

A	**A**	**TRANSIT – ACCOMPANYING DOCUMENT**

2 Consignor/Exporter   No

1 REGIME   **MRN**

3 Forms	**4** Loading lists
5 Items	**6** Total packages

8 Consignee   No

Return copy has to be sent to the Office:

15 Country of dispatch/export

17 Country of destination

18 Identity and nationality of means of transport at departure

56 Other incidents during carriage
Details and measures taken

G CERTIFICATION BY COMPETENT AUTHORITIES

31 Packages and description of goods   Marks and numbers –Container No(s) – Number and kind

32 Item   No

33 Commodity Code

35 Gross mass (kg)

36 Net mass (kg)

40 Summary declaration/Previous document

44 Additional information/ Documents produced/ Certificates and authorisations

55 Transhipments   Place and country:

Identity and nationality of new means of transport:

Ctr. ☐   (1) Identity of new container:

(1) Enter 1 if YES or 0 if NO.

Place and country:

Identity and nationality of new means of transport:

Ctr. ☐   (1) Identity of new container:

(1) Enter 1 if YES or 0 if NO.

F CERTIFICATION BY COMPETENT AUTHORITIES

New seals: Number: Identity:

Signature: Stamp:

☐ Data already recorded into the system

New seals: Number: Identity:

Signature: Stamp:

☐ Data already recorded into the system

50 Principal   No

C OFFICE OF DEPARTURE

51 Intended offices of transit (and country)

52 Guarantee not valid for   Code

53 Office of destination (and country)

D CONTROL BY OFFICE OF DEPARTURE

Result:

Seals affixed: Number:

identity:

Time limit (date):

I CONTROL BY OFFICE OF DESTINATION

Date of arrival:

Examination of seals:

Remarks

Return copy sent

on

after registration under

No

Signature: Stamp:

© European Communities Official Journal L 253, 11/10/1993 Annex 45a

EUROPEAN COMMUNITY

B

TRANSIT – RETURN COPY

2 Consignor/Exporter	No

1 REGIME		MRN
3 Forms	4 Loading lists	
5 Items	6 Total packages	

8 Consignee   No

Return copy has to be sent to the Office:

15 Country of dispatch/export

17 Country of destination

18 Identity and nationality of means of transport at departure

56 Other incidents during carriage Details and measures taken

G CERTIFICATION BY COMPETENT AUTHORITIES

B

31 Packages and description of goods	Marks and numbers –Container No(s) – Number and kind	32 Item No	33 Commodity Code
			35 Gross mass (kg)
			36 Net mass (kg)
			40 Summary declaration/Previous document

44 Additional information/ Documents produced/ Certificates and authorisations

55 Transhipments	Place and country:	Place and country:
	Identity and nationality of new means of transport:	Identity and nationality of new means of transport:
	Ctr. ☐ (1) Identity of new container:	Ctr. ☐ (1) Identity of new container:
	(1) Enter 1 if YES or 0 if NO.	(1) Enter 1 if YES or 0 if NO.
F CERTIFICATION BY COMPETENT AUTHORITIES	New seals: Number: identity:	New seals: Number: identity:
	Signature: Stamp:	Signature: Stamp:
	☐ Data already recorded into the system	☐ Data already recorded into the system

50 Principal	No	C OFFICE OF DEPARTURE

51 Intended offices of transit (and country)	

52 Guarantee not valid for	Code	53 Office of destination (and country)

D CONTROL BY OFFICE OF DEPARTURE	I CONTROL BY OFFICE OF DESTINATION	
Result:	Date of arrival:	Return copy sent
Seals affixed: Number:	Examination of seals:	on
identity:		after registration under
Time limit (date):	Remarks	No
		Signature: Stamp:

(Section B omitted.)

[CHAPTER II

Explanatory notes and particulars (data) for the Transit Accompanying Document

A. Explanatory notes for completing the transit accompanying document

The transit accompanying document shall be printed based on data derived from the transit declaration, where the case occurs amended by the principal and/or verified by the office of departure, and completed with—

1. MRN (movement reference number)

The information is given alphanumerically with 18 digits on the following specimen—

Field	Content	Field type	Examples
1	Last two digits of year of formal acceptance of transit movement (YY)	Numeric 2	97
2	Identifier of the country from which movement originates. (ISO alpha 2 country code)	Alphabetic 2	IT
3	Unique identifier for transit movement per year and country	Alphanumeric 13	9876AB8890123
4	Check digit	Alphanumeric 1	5

Fields 1 and 2 as explained above.

Field 3 has to be filled in with an identifier for the transit transaction. The way that field is used is under the responsibility of national administrations but each transit transaction handled during one year within the given country must have a unique number. National administrations that want to have the office reference number of the competent authorities included in the MRN, could use up to the first 6 characters to insert the national number of the office.

Field 4 has to be filled with a value that is a check digit for the whole MRN. This field allows for detection of an error when capturing the whole MRN.

[The "MRN" shall also be printed in bar code mode using the standard "code 128", character set "B".]

2. Box 3—
   — first subdivision: serial number of the current printed sheet,
   — second subdivision: total number of sheets printed (including list of items),
   — hall not be used when only one item.

3. In the space to the right of box 8—

Name and address of the customs office to which the return copy of the transit accompanying document has to be returned.

4. Box C—
   — the name of the office of departure,
   — reference number of the office of departure,
   — acceptance date of the transit declaration,
   — the name and the authorisation number of the authorised consignor (if any).

5. Box D—
   — control results,
   — the indication "Binding itinerary", where appropriate.

The transit accompanying document shall not be modified nor shall any addition or deletion be made thereto unless otherwise specified in this regulation.

[B. **Explanatory notes for printing**
The following possibilities exist for the printing of the transit accompanying document:
1. the declared office of destination is linked to the computerised transit system:
— print only copy A (Accompanying Document);
2. the declared office of destination is not linked to the computerised transit system:
— print copy A (Accompanying Document), and
— print copy B (Return Copy).]

[C. **Explanatory notes for the return of the control results from the office of destination**
The following possibilities exist for the return of the control results from the office of destination:
1. the actual office of destination is the declared one and it is linked to the computerised transit system:
— the control results shall be sent to the office of departure by electronic means;
2. the actual office of destination is the declared one and it is not linked to the computerised transit system:
— the control results shall be sent to the office of departure using return copy B of the transit accompanying document (including list of items, if any);
3. the declared office of destination is linked to the computerised transit system but the actual office of destination is not linked to the computerised transit system (change of office of destination):
— the control results shall be sent to the office of departure using a photocopy of the transit accompanying document, copy A (including list of items, if any);
4. the declared office of destination is not linked to the computerised transit system but the actual office of destination is linked to the computerised transit system (change of office of destination):
— the control results shall be sent to the office of departure by electronic means.]

. . .]

NOTES
Inserted by Commission Regulation (EC) 502/1999, Art 1, para 12.
Chapter I substituted; in Chapter II, points B, C substituted, and point D repealed, by Commission Regulation (EC) 881/2003 Art 1, para 33, Annex VII with effect from 1 January 2005.
Chapter II: substituted by Commission Regulation (EC) 2787/2000, Art 1, para 67, Annex VIII.
Chapter II, para A: words in square brackets in sub-para 1 added by Commission Regulation (EC) 993/2001, Art 1, para 35, Annex III.

ANNEX 45B

LIST OF ITEMS

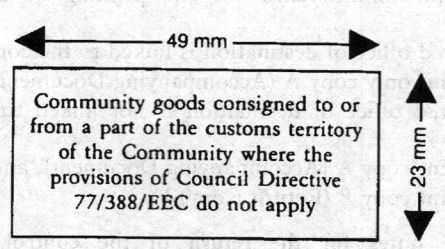

Colour: black letters on a yellow background.'

(Copy omitted.)

[CHAPTER II

Explanatory notes and the particulars (data) for the List of Items

When a movement consists of more than one item, then the sheet A of the list of items shall always be printed by the computer system and shall be attached to the copy A of the transit accompanying document.

Where the transit accompanying document is printed in the two copies, A and B, then also the sheet B of the list of items shall be printed and attached to the copy B of the transit accompanying document.

The boxes of the list of items are vertically expandable.

Particulars have to be printed as follows—

    1. In the identification box (upper left corner)—
        (a)   list of items;
        (b)   sheet A/B;
        (c)   serial number of the current sheet and the total number of the sheets (including the transit accompanying document).
    2. OoDep — name of the office of departure.
    3. Date — acceptance date of the transit declaration.
    4. MRN — movement reference number as defined in Annex 45a.

5. The particulars of the different boxes at item level have to be printed as follows—

    (a)   item No — serial number of the current item;

    (b)   regime — if the status of the goods for the whole declaration is uniform, the box is not used;

    (c)   if mixed consignment, the actual status, T1, T2 or T2F, is printed;

    (d)   the remaining boxes are completed as described in Annex 37, if appropriate in coded form.]]

NOTES

Inserted by Commission Regulation (EC) 502/1999, Art 1, para 13.

Chapter II: substituted by Commission Regulation (EC) 2787/2000, Art 1, para 68, Annex IX.

[ANNEX 45C
EXPORT ACCOMPANYING DOCUMENT

CHAPTER I
SPECIMEN OF THE EXPORT ACCOMPANYING DOCUMENT

Form   reproduced   at:
http://eur-lex.europa.eu/LexUriServ/site/en/oj/2006/l_360/l_36020061219en00640125.pdf

CHAPTER II
EXPLANATORY NOTES AND PARTICULARS (DATA) FOR THE EXPORT ACCOMPANYING DOCUMENT

The export accompanying document shall be printed based on data derived from the export declaration, where the case occurs amended by the declarant/representative and/or verified by the office of export, and completed with:

1. MRN (movement reference number)

The information is given alphanumerically with 18 digits on the following specimen:

	Content	Field type	Examples
1	Last two digits of year of formal acceptance of the export declaration (YY)	Numeric 2	06
2	Identifier of the country of export (alpha 2 code as provided for Box 2 of the single administrative document in Annex 38)	Alphabetic 2	PL
3	Unique identifier for export operation per year and country	Alphanumeric 13	9876AB8890123
4	Check digit	Alphanumeric 1	5

Fields 1 and 2 as explained above.

Field 3 has to be filled in with an identifier for the export control system transaction. The way that field is used is under the responsibility of national administrations but each export transaction handled during one year within the given country must have a unique number. National administrations that want to have the office reference number of the competent authorities included in the MRN, could use up to the first 6 characters to insert the national number of the office.

Field 4 has to be filled with a value that is a check digit for the whole MRN. This field allows for detection of an error when capturing the whole MRN.

The "MRN" shall also be printed in bar code mode using the standard "code 128", character set "B".

2. *Customs office*

Reference number of the office of export.

The export accompanying document shall not be modified nor shall any addition or deletion be made thereto unless otherwise specified in this regulation.]

NOTES

Annex inserted by Commission Regulation (EC) 1875/2006, Art 73, Annex IV, with effect from 26 December 2006.

[ANNEX 45D
EXPORT LIST OF ITEMS

CHAPTER I
SPECIMEN OF THE EXPORT LIST OF ITEMS

Form reproduced at:
http://eur-lex.europa.eu/LexUriServ/site/en/oj/2006/l_360/l_36020061219en00640125.pdf

CHAPTER II
EXPLANATORY NOTES AND THE PARTICULARS (DATA) FOR THE LIST
OF ITEMS

When an export consists of more than one item, then the list of items shall always be printed by the computer system and shall be attached to the export accompanying document.

The boxes of the list of items are vertically expandable.

Particulars have to be printed as follows:

1. MRN — movement reference number as defined in Annex 45c.
2. The particulars of the different boxes at item level have to be printed as follows:
   (a)   Item No — serial number of the current item;
   (b)   The remaining boxes are completed in accordance with the requirements in the explanatory notes in Annex 37, if appropriate in coded form.]

NOTES

Annex inserted by Commission Regulation (EC) 1875/2006, Art 74, Annex V, with effect from 26 December 2006.

ANNEX 46

TC 10 – TRANSIT ADVICE NOTE

Identification of means of transport: ....

TRANSIT DECLARATION		OFFICE OF TRANSIT INTENDED (AND COUNTRY):
Type (T1, T2 or T2F) and number	Office of departure	
		FOR OFFICIAL USE
		Date of transit:
		(Signature)
		Official stamp

NOTES

Substituted by Commission Regulation (EC) 2787/2000, Art 1, para 69, Annex X.

[ANNEX 46A

CHARACTERISTICS OF SEALS

The seals referred to in Article 357 shall have at least the following characteristics and comply with the following technical specifications—

    (a)   Essential characteristics—

Seals must—

    1.   remain secure in normal use;

    2.   be easily checkable and recognisable;

    3.   be so manufactured that any breakage or removal leaves traces visible to the naked eye;

4. be designed for single use or, if intended for multiple use, be so designed that they can be given a clear, individual identification mark each time they are re-used.

5. bear identification marks.

(b) Technical specifications—

1. the form and dimensions of seals may vary with the sealing method used but the dimensions must be such as to ensure that identification marks are easy to read;

2. the identification marks of seals must be impossible to falsify and difficult to reproduce;

3. the material used must be resistant to accidental breakage and such as to prevent undetectable falsification or reuse.]

NOTES

Inserted by Commission Regulation (EC) 2787/2000, Art 1, para 70, Annex XI.

[ANNEX 46B

CRITERIA REFERRED TO IN ARTICLES 380 AND 381

Criterion	Observations
1. Sufficient experience	Proof of sufficient experience is provided by the correct use of the Community transit procedure, in the capacity of principal, over one of the following periods, prior to re-questing a reduction— — one year, for the application of Article 380(2)(a) and Article 381(1), — two years for the application of Article 380(2)(b) and Article 381(2)(a), — three years for the application of Article 380(3) and Article 381(2)(b). These periods shall be reduced by one year for applicants who use data-processing methods for lodging transit declarations.
2. High level of cooperation with the customs authorities	A principal achieves a high level of cooperation with the customs authorities by incorporating in the management of his operations specific measures which thereby make it easier for the authorities to carry out checks and protect the interests involved. Providing they satisfy the customs authorities, such measures may relate to, *inter alia*— — particular methods of completing transit declarations (in particular the use of data processing methods), or — the content of such declarations, with the principal providing additional information, even where this is not mandatory, or — methods of completing the formalities for placing goods under the procedure (for example the principal always presenting his declarations at the same customs office).

Part III

Criterion	Observations
3. Being in command of transport operations	The principal demonstrates that he is in command of transport operations, *inter alia*— (a) by carrying out the transport operation himself and applying high standards of security, or (b) using a carrier with whom he has had long-standing contractual relations and who provides a service which meets high standards of security, or (c) using an intermediary contractually bound to a carrier who provides a service which meets high standards of security.
4. Sufficient financial resources to cover obligations	The principal demonstrates that he has the financial resources to cover his obligations by providing the customs authorities with evidence to show that he has the means to pay the customs debt likely to be incurred in connection with the goods concerned.]

NOTES

Inserted by Commission Regulation (EC) 2787/2000, Art 1, para 71, Annex XII.

[ANNEX 47]

TC 11 - RECEIPT

The office of destination at ....

hereby certifies that document T1, T2, T2F(¹)

.... control copy T5 (¹)

registered on .... under No ....

by the office at ....

has been lodged

At.. , , on ....

Official
stamp

(Signature)

(¹) Delete as necessary'.

NOTES

Substituted by Commission Regulation (EC) 2787/2000, Art 1, para 72, Annex XIII.

In the third line, "declaration" substituted for "document" by Corrigendum (OJ L 20, 23.1.02, p 11).

Form substituted by Corrigendum (OJ L 20, 23.1.02, p 11).

[ANNEX 47A

APPLICATION OF ARTICLE 94(6) AND (7) OF THE CODE
TEMPORARY PROHIBITION OF THE USE OF THE COMPREHENSIVE
GUARANTEE FOR A REDUCED AMOUNT OR THE
COMPREHENSIVE GUARANTEE

1.   Situations where use of the comprehensive guarantee for a reduced amount or the comprehensive guarantee may be prohibited temporarily

1.1.   Temporary prohibition of the use of the comprehensive guarantee for a reduced amount

The "special circumstances" referred to in Article 94(6) of the Code mean a situation in which it has been established, in a significant number of cases involving more than one principal and putting at risk the smooth functioning of the procedure that, in spite of the application of Article 384 and Article 9 of the Code, the comprehensive guarantee for a reduced amount referred to in Article 94(4) of the Code is no longer sufficient to ensure payment, within the prescribed time limit, of the customs debt arising when any of the goods listed in Annex 44c are removed from the Community transit procedure.

1.2.   Temporary prohibition of the use of a comprehensive guarantee

The "large-scale fraud" referred to in Article 94(7) means a situation where it is established that, in spite of the application of Article 384, Article 9 of the Code and, where appropriate, Article 94(6) of the Code, the comprehensive guarantee referred to in Article 94(2)(b) of the Code is no longer sufficient to ensure payment, within the time limit prescribed, of the customs debt arising when any of the goods listed in Annex 44c are removed from the Community transit procedure. In this connection account should be taken of the volume of goods removed and the circumstances of their removal, particularly if these result from internationally organised criminal activities.

2.   Effect of the decision

2.1.   The effect of the decision temporarily prohibiting use of the comprehensive guarantee for a reduced amount or the comprehensive guarantee shall be limited to a period of 12 months unless the Commission decides to extend the period or repeal the decision in accordance with the committee procedure.

2.2.   The following measures shall apply to transit operations involving goods which are subject to decisions prohibiting use of the comprehensive guarantee—

—   one of the following endorsements, measuring at least 100 × 10 mm and printed in red, shall be affixed diagonally to all copies of the transit declaration—

—   GARANTÍA GLOBAL PROHIBIDA
—   FORBUD MOD SAMLET KAUTION
—   GESAMTBRÜGSCHAFT UNTERSAGT
—   AπAGOPEYETAIHΣΣYNOΛIKHEGGYHΣH
—   COMPREHENSIVE GUARANTEE PROHIBITED
—   GARANTIE GLOBALE INTERDITE
—   GARANZIA GLOBALE VIETATA
—   DOORLOPENDE ZEKERHEID VERBODEN
—   GARANTIA GLOBAL PROIBIDA
—   YLEISVAKUUDEN KYÄTTÖKIELLETTY
—   SAMLAD SKÄERHET FRÖBJUDEN
[—   ZÁKAZ GLOBÁLNÍ ZÁRUKY,

> — ÜLDTAGATISE KASUTAMINE KEELATUD,
> — VISPĀRJS GALVOJUMS AIZLIEGTS,
> — NAUDOTI BENDRJ GARANTIJ UŽDRAUSTA,
> — ÖSSZKEZESSÉG TILALMA,
> — MHUX PERMESSA GARANZIJA KOMPRENSIVA,
> — ZAKAZ KORZYSTANIA Z GWARANCJI GENERALNEJ,
> — PREPOVEDANO SKUPNO ZAVAROVANJE,
> [— ZÁKAZ CELKOVEJ ZÁRUKY].]
> [— (for original text, refer to Commission Regulation (EC) 1792/2006 (OJ L 362, 20.12.06, p 1)),
> — GARANTIA GLOBAL INTERZIS']

— by way of derogation from Article 363, the office of destination shall return Copy No 5 of any transit declaration endorsed with this phrase no later than on the working day following that on which the consignment and the requisite copies of the declaration were presented at that office. Where such a consignment is presented to an authorised consignee within the meaning of Article 406, he shall transmit the copy No 5 to his local office of destination no later than on the working day following that on which he took receipt of the consignment.

3. Measures to alleviate the financial consequences of the prohibition on using the comprehensive guarantee

When the use of the comprehensive guarantee has been prohibited temporarily for Annex 44c goods, holders of comprehensive guarantees may, upon request, use an individual guarantee. However, the following special conditions shall apply—

— the individual guarantee shall be put up in the form of a specific guarantee document which includes a reference to this Annex and covers only the goods referred to in the decision,

[— except where guarantee data is exchanged between the office of guarantee and the office of departure using information technology and computer networks, this individual guarantee may be used only at the office of departure identified in the guarantee document;]

— it may be used to cover several simultaneous or successive operations provided that the sum of the amounts involved in current operations for which the procedure has not yet been discharged does not exceed the amount of the individual guarantee,

— each time the procedure is discharged for a Community transit operation covered by this individual guarantee, the amount corresponding to that operation shall be released and may be reused to cover another operation up to the maximum amount of the guarantee.

4. Derogation from the decision temporarily prohibiting use of the comprehensive guarantee for a reduced amount or the comprehensive guarantee

4.1. Principals may be authorised to use a comprehensive guarantee for a reduced amount or a comprehensive guarantee to place under the Community transit procedure goods to which the decision temporarily prohibiting such use applies if they can show that no customs debt has arisen in respect of the goods in question in the course of Community transit operations which they have undertaken in the two years preceding the decision or, where customs debts have arisen during that period, if they can show that these were fully paid up by the debtor or debtors or the guarantor within the time limit prescribed.

To obtain authorisation to use a temporarily prohibited comprehensive guarantee, the principal must also meet the conditions set out in Article 381(2)(b).

4.2. Articles 374 to 378 shall apply *mutatis mutandis* to applications and authorisations for the derogations referred to in point 4.1.

Part III

4.3.   When the customs authorities grant a derogation they shall endorse box 8 of the comprehensive guarantee certificate with one of the following phrases—
—   UTILIZACIÓN NO LIMITADA
—   UBEGRÆNSET ANVENDELSE
—   UNBESCHRÄNKTE VERWENDUNG
—   AπΕΡΙΟΡΙΣΤΗΧΡΗΣΗ
—   UNRESTRICTED USE
—   UTILISATION NON LIMITEE
—   UTILIZZAZIONE NON LIMITATA
—   GEBRUIK ONBEPERKT
—   UTILIZAÇÃO ILIMITADA
—   KÄYTTÖÄ EI RAJOITETTU
—   OBEGRÄNSAD ANVÄNDNING]
[—   NEOMEZENÉ POUŽITÍ,
—   PIIRAMATU KASUTAMINE,
—   NEIEROBEŽOTS IZMANTOJUMS,
—   NEAPRIBOTAS NAUDOJIMAS,
—   KORLÁTOZÁS ALÁ NEM ESŐ HASZNÁLAT,
—   UU MHUX RISTRETT,
—   NIEOGRANICZONE KORZYSTANIE,
—   NEOMEJENA UPORABA,
—   NEOBMEDZENÉ POUŽITIE.]
—   *(for original text, refer to Commission Regulation (EC) 1792/2006 (OJ L 362, 20.12.06, p 1))*
—   UTILIZARE NELIMITATANERESTRICTIONAT'.

NOTES
Inserted by Commission Regulation (EC) 2787/2000, Art 1, para 73, Annex XIV.
Point 2: words inserted by the 2003 Act of Accession Annex II(19)(A)(II), para 48(a); words "ZÁKAZ CELKOVEJ ZÁRUKY" in square brackets substituted by Commission Regulation (EC) 883/2005, Art 1, para 30, with effect from 1 May 2004. Final two entries inserted by Commission Regulation (EC) 1792/2006, Art 1, Annex, Part 11(A)(48)(a).
Point 3: words substituted by Commission Regulation (EC) 993/2001, Art 1, para 36, Annex IV.
Point 4: words inserted by the 2003 Act of Accession Annex II(19)(A)(II), para 48(b). Final two entries inserted by Commission Regulation (EC) 1792/2006, Art 1, Annex, Part 11(A)(48)(b).

[ANNEX 48
COMMON / COMMUNITY TRANSIT PROCEDURE
COMPREHENSIVE GUARANTEE
    I.   Undertaking by the guarantor
    1.   The undersigned (¹) resident at (²)
hereby jointly and severally guarantees, at the office of guarantee of   . . . .
up to a maximum amount of, ...
being 100% / 50%/ 30% (³) of the reference amount,
[in favour of the European Community comprising the Kingdom of Belgium, the Republic of Bulgaria, the Czech Republic, the Kingdom of Denmark, the Federal Republic of Germany, the Republic of Estonia, the Hellenic Republic, the Kingdom of Spain, the French Republic, Ireland, the Italian Republic, the Republic of Cyprus, the Republic of Latvia, the Republic of Lithuania, the Grand Duchy of Luxembourg, the

Republic of Hungary, the Republic of Malta, the Kingdom of the Netherlands, the Republic of Austria, the Republic of Poland, the Portuguese Republic, Romania, the Republic of Slovenia, the Slovak Republic, the Republic of Finland, the Kingdom of Sweden, the United Kingdom of Great Britain and Northern Ireland, and the Republic of Iceland, the Kingdom of Norway, the Swiss Confederation, the Principality of Andorra and the Republic of San Marino ([4]), any amount of principal [5] . . .]

. . . .

may be or become liable to the abovementioned countries for debt in the form of duty and other charges applicable to the goods placed under the Community or common transit procedure.

2.   The undersigned undertakes to pay upon the first application in writing by the competent authorities of the countries referred to in paragraph 1 and without being able to defer payment beyond a period of 30 days from the date of application the sums requested up to the limit of the above mentioned maximum amount, unless he or she or any other person concerned establishes before the expiry of that period, to the satisfaction of the competent authorities, that [the operation has ended.].

At the request of the undersigned and for any reasons recognised as valid, the competent authorities may defer beyond a period of 30 days from the date of application for payment the period within which he or she is obliged to pay the requested sums. The expenses incurred as a result of granting this additional period, in particular any interest, must be so calculated that the amount is equivalent to what would be charged under similar circumstances on the money market or financial market in the country concerned.

This amount may not be reduced by any sums already paid under the terms of this undertaking unless the undersigned is called upon to pay a debt arising during a Community or common transit operation commenced before the preceding demand for payment was received or within 30 days thereafter.

3.   This undertaking shall be valid from the day of its acceptance by the office of guarantee. The undersigned shall remain responsible for payment of any debt arising during the Community or common transit operations covered by this undertaking and commenced before the date on which any revocation or cancellation the guarantee took effect, even if the demand for payment is made after that date.

4.   For the purposes of this undertaking the undersigned gives his or her address for service in each of the other countries referred to in paragraph 1 as ([6])—

Country	Surname and forenames, or name of firm, and full address
. . . .	. . . .
. . . .	. . . .
. . . .	. . . .
. . . .	. . . .

The undersigned acknowledges that all correspondence and notices and any formalities or procedures relating to this undertaking addressed to or effected in writing at one of his or her addresses for service shall be accepted as duly delivered to him or her.

The undersigned acknowledges the jurisdiction of the courts of the places where he or she has an address for service.

The undersigned undertakes not to change his or her addresses for service or, if he or she has to change one or more of those addresses, to inform the office of guarantee in advance.

Done at . . . . on . . . .
. . . .
(Signature) (^{7})

II. Acceptance by the office of guarantee

Office of guarantee . . . .

Guarantor's undertaking accepted on . . . .

. . . .

(Stamp and signature)

---

^{1} Surname and forenames, or name of firm.

^{2} Full address.

^{3} Delete what does not apply.

^{4} Delete the name of the Contracting Party or Parties or States (Andorra or San Marino) whose territory is not transited. The references to the Principality of Andorra and the Republic of San Marino shall apply solely to Community transit operations.

^{5} Surname and forenames, or name of firm, and full address of the principal.

^{6} If, in the law of the country, there is no provision for address for service the guarantor shall appoint, in this country, an agent authorised to receive any communications addressed to him and the acknowledgement in the second subparagraph and the undertaking in the fourth subparagraph of paragraph 4 must be made to correspond. The courts of the places in which the addresses for service of the guarantor or of his agents are situated shall have jurisdiction in disputes concerning this guarantee.

^{7} The person signing the document must enter the following by hand before his or her signature: "Guarantee for the amount of . . . . ", the amount being written out in letters.]

NOTES

Substituted by Commission Regulation (EC) 2787/2000, Art 1, para 74, Annex XV.

Para I(1): words substituted by Commission Regulation (EC) 1792/2006, Art 1, Annex, Part 11(A)(49).

Para I(2): words substituted by Corrigendum (OJ L 20, 23.1.02, p 11).

[ANNEX 49

COMMON / COMMUNITY TRANSIT PROCEDURE

Individual guarantee

I. Undertaking by the guarantor

1. The undersigned (^{1}) . . . .

resident at (^{2}) . . . .

hereby jointly and severally guarantees, at the office of guarantee of . . . .

up to a maximum amount of . . . .

[in favour of the European Community comprising the Kingdom of Belgium, the Republic of Bulgaria, the Czech Republic, the Kingdom of Denmark, the Federal Republic of Germany, the Republic of Estonia, the Hellenic Republic, the Kingdom of Spain, the French Republic, Ireland, the Italian Republic, the Republic of Cyprus, the Republic of Latvia, the Republic of Lithuania, the Grand Duchy of Luxembourg, the Republic of Hungary, the Republic of Malta, the Kingdom of the Netherlands, the Republic of Austria, the Republic of Poland, the Portuguese Republic, Romania, the Republic of Slovenia, the Slovak Republic, the Republic of Finland, the Kingdom of Sweden, the United Kingdom of Great Britain and Northern Ireland, and the Republic of Iceland, the Kingdom of Norway, the Swiss Confederation, the Principality of Andorra and the Republic of San Marino (^{3}), any amount of principal . . .^{4}]

. . . .
may be or become liable to the abovementioned countries for debt in the form of duty and other charges applicable to the goods described below placed under the Community or common transit procedure from the office of departure of . . . . to the office of destination of . . . .
Goods description: . . . .
. . . .

2. The undersigned undertakes to pay upon the first application in writing by the competent authorities of the countries referred to in point 1 and without being able to defer payment beyond a period of 30 days from the date of application the sums requested unless he or she or any other person concerned establishes before the expiry of that period, to the satisfaction of the competent authorities, that [the operation has ended.].

At the request of the undersigned and for any reasons recognised as valid, the competent authorities may defer beyond a period of 30 days from the date of application for payment the period within which he or she is obliged to pay the requested sums. The expenses incurred as a result of granting this additional period, in particular any interest, must be so calculated that the amount is equivalent to what would be charged under similar circumstances on the money market or financial market in the country concerned.

3. This undertaking shall be valid from the day of its acceptance by the office of guarantee. The undersigned shall remain liable for payment of any debt arising during the Community or common transit operation covered by this undertaking and commenced before any revocation or cancellation of the guarantee took effect, even if the demand for payment is made after that date.

4. For the purpose of this undertaking, the undersigned gives his or her address for service in each of the other countries referred to in paragraph 1 as (^{5})—

Country	Surname and forenames, or name of firm, and full address
. . . .	. . . .
. . . .	. . . .
. . . .	. . . .
. . . .	. . . .
. . . .	. . . .

The undersigned acknowledges that all correspondence and notices and any formalities or procedures relating to this undertaking addressed to or effected in writing at one of his or her addresses for service shall be accepted as duly delivered to him or her.

The undersigned acknowledges the jurisdiction of the courts of the places where he or she has an address for service.

The undersigned undertakes not to change his or her addresses for service or, if he or she has to change one or more of those addresses, to inform the office of guarantee in advance.

Done at . . . . on . . . .
. . . .
(Signature) (^{6})
II. Acceptance by the office of guarantee
Office of guarantee . . . .

Guarantor's undertaking accepted on . . to cover the Community/common transit operation effected under transit declaration No . . . . of . . . .(^{7})
(Stamp and signature)

---

^{1} Surname and forename or name of firm.

^{2} Full address.

^{3} Delete the name of the Contracting Party or Parties or States (Andorra or San Marino) whose territory is not transited. The references to the Principality of Andorra and the Republic of San Marino shall apply solely to Community transit operations.

^{4} Surname and forename, or name of firm and full address of the principal.

^{5} If, in the law of the country, there is no provision for address for service the guarantor shall appoint, in this country, an agent authorised to receive any communications addressed to him and the acknowledgement in the second subparagraph and the undertaking in the fourth subparagraph of paragraph 4 must be made to correspond. The courts of the places in which the addresses for service of the guarantor or of his agents are situated shall have jurisdiction in disputes concerning this guarantee.

^{6} The person signing the document must enter the following by hand before his or her signature: "Guarantee for the amount of . .", the amount being written out in letters.

^{7} To be completed by the office of departure.]

NOTES

Substituted by Commission Regulation (EC) 2787/2000, Art 1, para 74, Annex XVI.

Para I(1): words substituted by Commission Regulation (EC) 1792/2006, Art 1, Annex, Part 11(A)(50).

Para I(2): words substituted by Corrigendum (OJ L 20, 23.1.02, p 11).

[ANNEX 50

COMMON / COMMUNITY TRANSIT PROCEDURE

Individual guarantee in the form of vouchers

  I. Undertaking by the guarantor

  1. The undersigned (^{1}) . . . .
resident at (^{2}) . . . .
hereby jointly and severally guarantees, at the office of guarantee of . . . .
[in favour of the European Community comprising the Kingdom of Belgium, the Republic of Bulgaria, the Czech Republic, the Kingdom of Denmark, the Federal Republic of Germany, the Republic of Estonia, the Hellenic Republic, the Kingdom of Spain, the French Republic, Ireland, the Italian Republic, the Republic of Cyprus, the Republic of Latvia, the Republic of Lithuania, the Grand Duchy of Luxembourg, the Republic of Hungary, the Republic of Malta, the Kingdom of the Netherlands, the Republic of Austria, the Republic of Poland, the Portuguese Republic, Romania, the Republic of Slovenia, the Slovak Republic, the Republic of Finland, the Kingdom of Sweden, the United Kingdom of Great Britain and Northern Ireland, and the Republic of Iceland, the Kingdom of Norway, the Swiss Confederation, the Principality of Andorra and the Republic of San Marino (^{3}), any amount of principal (^{4}). . .]

  2. The undersigned undertakes to pay upon the first application in writing by the competent authorities of the countries referred to in paragraph 1 and without being able to defer payment beyond a period of 30 days from the date of application the sums requested, up to EUR 7 000 per individual guarantee voucher, unless he or she or any other person concerned establishes before the expiry of that period, to the satisfaction of the competent authorities, that [the operation has ended.]

At the request of the undersigned and for any reasons recognised as valid, the competent authorities may defer beyond a period of 30 days from the date of application for payment the period within which he or she is obliged to pay the requested sums. The expenses incurred as a result of granting this additional period, in particular any interest, must be so calculated that the amount is equivalent to what would be charged under similar circumstances on the money market or financial market in the country concerned.

3.   This undertaking shall be valid from the day of its acceptance by the office of guarantee. The undersigned shall remain liable for payment of any debt arising during any Community or common transit operations covered by this undertaking and commenced before any revocation or cancellation of the guarantee took effect, even if the demand for payment is made after that date.

4.   For the purpose of this undertaking the undersigned gives his or her address for service ([4]) in each of the other countries referred to in paragraph 1 as—

Country	Surname and forenames, or name of firm, and full address
. . . .	. . . .
. . . .	. . . .
. . . .	. . . .
. . . .	. . . .
. . . .	. . . .

The undersigned acknowledges that all correspondence and notices and any formalities or procedures relating to this undertaking addressed to or effected in writing at one of his or her addresses for service shall be accepted as duly delivered to him or her.

The undersigned acknowledges the jurisdiction of the courts of the places where he or she has an address for service.

The undersigned undertakes not to change his or her addresses for service or, if he or she has to change one or more of those addresses, to inform the office of guarantee in advance.

Done at . . . . on . . . .
. . . .

(Signature) ([5])

II.   Acceptance by the office of guarantee

Office of guarantee . . . .

Guarantor's undertaking accepted on . . . .
. . . .

(Stamp and signature)

---

[1] Surname and forenames, or name of firm.

[2] Full address.

[3] Only for Community transit operations

[4] If, in the law of the country, there is no provision for address for service the guarantor shall appoint, in this country, an agent authorised to receive any communications addressed to him and the acknowledgement in the second subparagraph and the undertaking in the fourth subparagraph of paragraph 4 must be made to correspond. The courts of the places in which the addresses for service of the guarantor or of his agents are situated shall have jurisdiction in disputes concerning this guarantee.

[5] The signature must be preceded by the following in the signatory's own handwriting: "Valid as guarantee voucher.]

Part III

NOTES

Substituted by Commission Regulation (EC) 2787/2000, Art 1, para 74, Annex XVII.

Paras I.(1), I.(2): Words substituted by Corrigendum (OJ L 20, 23.1.02, p 11).

Para I.(1): words substituted by Commission Regulation (EC) 1792/2006, Art 1, Annex, Part 11(A)(51).

[ANNEX 51]

TC 31 — COMPREHENSIVE GUARANTEE CERTIFICATE

(Front)

1. Valid until	Day	Month	Year	2. Number
3. Principal (surname and forename, or name of company, full address and country)				
4. Guarantor (surname and forename, or name of company, full address and country)				
5. Office of guarantee (name, full address and country)				
6. Reference amount Currency code	in figures:		in letters:	

7. The office of guarantee certifies that the principal named above has furnished a comprehensive guarantee which is valid for Community/common transit operations through the customs territory of those countries listed below whose names have not been crossed out:

EUROPEAN COMMUNITY, HUNGARY, ICELAND, NORWAY, POLAND, SLOVAKIA, SWITZERLAND, CZECH REPUBLIC, ANDORRA (*), SAN MARINO (*)

8. Special observations

9. Period of validity extended until

Day	Month	Year

inclusive

Done at ...., on ....
(place) (date)

(Signature and stamp of office of guarantee)

Done at ...., on ....
(place) (date)

(Signature and stamp of office of guarantee)

(*) Only for Community transit operations.

10. Persons authorised to sign Community/common transit declarations on behalf of the principal

(Back)

11. Surname, forename and specimen signature of authorised person	12. Signature of principal (¹)	11. Surname, forename and specimen signature of authorised person	12. Signature of principal (¹)

(¹) Where the principal is a legal person, the person whose signature appears in box 12 must add to his signature his surname, forename and the capacity in which he is signing.'

NOTES

Substituted by Commission Regulation (EC) 2787/2000, Art 1, para 75, Annex XVIII: the previous form was not reproduced.

Box 7: words "the customs territories listed below" substituted for "the customs territory of those countries listed below" by Corrigendum (OJ L 20, 23.1.02, p 11). Words 'CZECH REPUBLIC', 'HUNGARY', 'POLAND', 'SLOVAKIA', repealed by the 2003 Act of Accession Annex II(19)(A)(II), para 52.

[ANNEX 51A]

TC 33 — GUARANTEE WAIVER CERTIFICATE

(Front)

1. Valid until	Day	Month	Year	2. Number

3. Principal (surname and forename, or name of company, full address and country)	

4. Office of guarantee (name, full address and country)	

5. Reference amount Currency code	in figures:	in letters:

6. The office of guarantee hereby certifies that the principal named above has been granted a guarantee waiver in respect of his Community/common transit operations through the customs territory of those countries listed below whose names have not been crossed out:

     EUROPEAN COMMUNITY, HUNGARY, ICELAND, NORWAY, POLAND, SLOVAKIA, SWITZERLAND, CZECH REPUBLIC, ANDORRA (*), SAN MARINO (*)

7. Special observations

8. Period of validity extended until

Day	Month	Year	
			inclusive

Done at ...., on ....
       (place)   (date)

(Signature and stamp of office of guarantee)

Done at ...., on ....
       (place)   (date)

(Signature and stamp of office of guarantee)

(*) Only for Community transit operations.

9. Persons authorised to sign Community/common transit declarations on behalf of the principal

(Back)

10. Surname, forename and specimen signature of authorised person	11. Signature of principal (¹)	10. Surname, forename and specimen signature of authorised person	11. Signature of principal (¹)

(¹) Where the principal is a legal person, the person whose signature appears in box 11 must add to his signature his surname, forename and the capacity 'in which he is signing.'

NOTES

Inserted by Commission Regulation (EC) 2787/2000, Art 1, para 76, Annex XIX.

Box 6: words "the customs territories listed below" substituted for "the customs territory of those countries listed below" by Corrigendum (OJ L 20, 23.1.02, p 11).

Words 'CZECH REPUBLIC', 'HUNGARY', 'POLAND', 'SLOVAKIA' repealed by the 2003 Act of Accession Annex II(19)(A)(II), para 53.

[ANNEX 51B

EXPLANATORY NOTE ON COMPREHENSIVE GUARANTEE CERTIFICATES AND GUARANTEE WAIVER CERTIFICATES

1. Particulars to be entered on the front of a certificate

Once issued, there shall be no amendment, addition or deletion to the remarks in boxes 1 to 8 of the comprehensive guarantee certificate or boxes 1 to 7 of the guarantee waiver certificate.

1.1. Currency code

Member States shall enter in box 6 of the comprehensive guarantee certificate and box 5 of the guarantee waiver certificate the ISO ALPHA 3 (ISO 4217) code of the currency used.

1.2. Endorsements

1.2.1. Where a comprehensive guarantee may not be used because the goods are listed in Annex 44C, one of the following must be entered in box 8 of the certificate—

— Validez limitada
— Begrænset gyldighed
— Beschränkte Geltung
— Περιορισμενη ισXυς
— Limited validity

—	Validité limitée
—	Validità limitata
—	Beperkte geldigheid
—	Validade limitada
—	Voimassa rajoitetusti
—	Begränsad giltighet
[—	Omezená platnost,
—	Piiratud kehtivus,
—	Ierobežots dergums,
—	Galiojimas apribotas,
—	Korlátozott érvényü,
—	Validita' limitata,
—	Ograniczona wano,
—	Omejena veljavnost,
—	Obmedzená platnost.]
—	*(for original text, refer to Commission Regulation (EC) 1792/2006 (OJ L 362, 20.12.06, p 1)),*
—	Validitate limitat]

1.2.2.   Where a principal has undertaken to lodge all his transit declarations at a specific office of departure, the name of the office must be entered in capitals in box 8 of the comprehensive guarantee certificate or box 7 of the guarantee waiver certificate, as appropriate.

1.3.   Endorsement of certificates in the event of their validity being extended
Where the period of validity of a certificate is extended, the office of guarantee must endorse box 9 of the comprehensive guarantee certificate or box 8 of the guarantee waiver certificate, as appropriate.

2.   Particulars to be entered on the back of a certificate. Persons authorised to sign transit declarations

2.1.   When a certificate is issued, or at any time during its period of validity, the principal must enter on the back the names of the persons he authorises to sign transit declarations. Each of these entries must comprise the surname and first name of the authorised person and a specimen of his signature and each must be countersigned by the principal. The principal has the option of striking through any boxes he does not wish to use.

2.2.   The principal may revoke such authorisations at any time.

2.3.   Any person whose name has been entered on the back of a certificate of this kind which is presented at an office of departure is the authorised representative of the principal.

3.   Use of such certificates where use of a comprehensive guarantee is prohibited
For procedure, see point 4 of Annex 47A.]

NOTES

Inserted by Commission Regulation (EC) 2787/2000, Art 1, para 77, Annex XX.

Item 1.2.1: words inserted by the 2003 Act of Accession Annex II(19)(A)(II), para 54. Final two entries inserted by Commission Regulation (EC) 1792/2006, Art 1, Annex, Part 11(A)(52).

(Annex 52 repealed by Commission Regulation (EC) 2000/2787, Art 1, para 78.)

(Annex 53 repealed by Commission Regulation (EC) 3254/94, Art 1, para 37.)

[ANNEX 54

(Front)

TC 32 – INDIVIDUAL GUARANTEE VOUCHER   A 000
                                                                    000

A 000 000 Issued by: ....
....
                    (Name and address of individual or
                    firm)
(undertaking of the guarantor accepted on .. by the guarantee office of ..)This
voucher, issued on . is valid for an amount of up to 7 000 euro for a Community
transit/common transit operation beginning not later than .... and in respect of
which the principal is ....
....
                    (Name and address of individual or
                    firm)

(Signature of the principal)[1]   (Signature and stamp of guarantor)

---

[1] Signature
optional.

(Back)

To be completed by the office of departure
Transit operation effected under document T1, T2, T2F[1],
registered on .... under No ....
by the office at ....

....
(Official stamp)   (Signature)

---

[1] Delete as
necessary.]

NOTES

Substituted by Commission Regulation (EC) 2787/2000, Art 1, para 79, Annex XXI.
(Annex 55 repealed by Commission Regulation (EC) 2000/2787, Art 1, para 80.)
(Annex 56 repealed by Commission Regulation (EC) No 75/98, Art 1, para 32.)
(Annex 57 repealed by Commission Regulation (EC) 2000/2787, Art 1, para 80.)

ANNEX 58

Label (Articles 417 and 432)

Colour: black on green

Colour: **black on green.**

ANNEX 59

MODEL OF THE INFORMATION MEMO REFERRED TO IN ARTICLE 459

Letter heading of the coordinating office initiating the dispute

Addressee: coordinating office covering the office of temporary importation, or other coordinating office

SUBJECT: ATA CARNET—SUBMISSION OF CLAIM

Be informed that a claim for payment of duties and taxes under the ATA Convention[1] was sent on . . .[2] to our guaranteeing association in respect of:

1. ATA carnet No:
2. Issued by the Chamber of Commerce of:

City:
   Country:
3. On behalf of:
   Holder:
   Address:
4. Expiry date of the carnet:
5. Date set for re-exportation[3]:
6. Number of transit/import voucher[4]:
7. Date of endorsement of voucher:

Signature and stamp of the issuing coordinating office.

---

[1] Article 7 of the ATA Convention, Brussels, 6 December 1991

[2] Enter date of dispatch.

[3] Details obtained from the undischarged transit or temporary importation voucher or, if no voucher is available, from the information available to the issuing coordinating office.

[4] Delete whichever is not applicable.

ANNEX 60

TAXATION FORM

No . . . . of . . . .

The following particulars must be given in the order shown:

1. ATA carnet No: . . . .
2. Number of transit/import voucher[1] . . . .
3. Date of endorsement of voucher: . . . .
4. Holder and address: . . . .
. . . .
. . . .

. . . .
5. Chamber of commerce: . . . .
6. Country of origin: . . . .
7. Date of expiry of carnet: . . . .
8: Date set for the re-exportation of goods: . . . .
9. Customs office of entry: . . . .
10. Customs office of temporary admission: . . . .
11. Trade description of goods: . . . .
. . . .
12. CN code: . . . .
13. Number of pieces: . . . .
14. Weight or volume: . . . .
15. Value: . . . .
16. Breakdown of duties and taxes: . . . .

Type	Taxable amount	Rate	Amount	Exchange rate
			Total:	

Total: . . . .

(Total in
words:)

17.Customs office: . . . .
Place and date: . . . .
Signature   Stamp

_____

_____

¹ Delete whichever is inapplicable.

TAXATION FORM A

No . . . . of . . . .
11. Trade description of goods: . . . .
12. CN code . . . .
13. Number of pieces: . . . .
14. Weight or volume: . . . .
15. Value: . . . .
16. Breakdown of duties and taxes: . . . .

Type	Taxable amount	Rate	Amount	Exchange rate
			Total:	

Total:
(Total in words: . . . .
11. Trade description of goods: . . . .
12. CN code . . . .
13. Number of pieces: . . . .
14. Weight or volume: . . . .
15. Value: . . . .
16. Breakdown of duties and taxes: . . . .

Type	Taxable amount	Rate	Amount	Exchange rate
			Total:	

(Total in words: ....)

Summary

Type	Taxable amount	Rate	Amount	Exchange rate
			Total:	

Total: ....

(Total in words: ....)

PROVISIONS GOVERNING THE INFORMATION TO BE ENTERED ON THE TAXATION FORM

I. General

The taxation form shall bear the following letters, indicating the Member State issuing the form:

[AT = Austria]	IT = Italy
BE = Belgium	[LT = Lithuania]
[BG = Bulgaria]	LU = Luxembourg
[CY = Cyprus]	[LV = Latvia]
[CZ = the Czech Republic]	[MT = Malta]
DK = Denmark	NL = Netherlands
DE = Germany	[PL = Poland]
[EE = Estonia]	PT = Portugal
EL = Greece	[RO = Romania]
ES = Spain	[SE = Sweden]
[FI = Finland]	[SI = Slovenia]
FR = France	[SK = Slovakia]
[HU = Hungary]	UK = United Kingdom
IE = Ireland	

The taxation form must include the following information under the appropriate headings. It must be completed legibly by the coordinating office referred to in Article 458(1) of this Regulation.

Headings 1, 2, 3, 4, 5, 6, 7, 8, 11, 13 and 14: Enter the same information as appears on the transit voucher or the import voucher at the bottom of the voucher, at the bottom of the space reserved for customs and in boxes A, G(a), overleaf column G(c), H(b), overleaf column 1, overleaf column 2, overleaf column 3 and overleaf column 4 respectively. If the coordinating office is not in possession of a voucher the information is entered according to the coordinating office's information. Where more than one kind of goods have to be entered on the form they are to be included on taxation form A, the headings on which are to be completed in accordance with these instructions.

Heading 9: State the name of the customs office which completed box H(a) to (e) of the transit voucher, or box H of the import voucher, as the case may be. Failing this, the customs office of entry is entered according to the coordinating office's knowledge of it.

Heading 10: State the name of the customs office which appears in box H(e) of the transit voucher or which completed box H of the import voucher, as the case may be. Failing this, the customs office of entry is entered according to the coordinating office's knowledge of it.

*Heading 15:*State the amount, in the currency laid down by the Member State in which the claim was made, of the value for customs.

Heading 16: State on the taxation form the amounts of duty and other taxes claimed. The amounts are shown in such a way as to make clear customs duties and taxes (using the Community codes provided for the purpose), the surcharge referred to in Article 6 of the ATA Convention [/Article 8 of Annex A to the Istanbul Convention], expressed in both figures and words. The amounts have to be paid in the currency of the Member State issuing the form, the code for which is entered at the top of the second column:

BEF = Belgian francs	FRF = French francs
DEM = German marks	ITL = Italian lire
ESP = Spanish pesetas	NLG = Dutch guilders GBP = Pounds
IEP = Irish pounds	[ATS = Austrian schillings
LUF = Luxembourg francs	FIM = Finnish markkas
PTE = Portuguese escudos	SEK = Swedish kronor]
DKK = Danish kroner	[CZK = Czech koruna]
GRD = Greek drachmas	[EEK = Estonian kroon]
	[CYP = Cyprus pound]
	[LVL = Latvian lats]
	[LTL = Lithuanian litas]
	[HUF = Hungarian forint]
	[MTL = Maltese lira]
	[PLN = Polish zloty]
	[SIT = Slovenian tolar]
	[SKK = Slovak koruna]
	[BGN = Bulgarian Lev]
	[RON = New Romanian LeiLe

Heading 17: State the name of the coordinating office and the date of completion of the form; place the stamp of the office and the signature of the authorised official in the appropriate places.

II. Remarks on Form A

A. Form A is to be used only where several articles are being taxed. It must be submitted in conjunction with a principal form. Total duties etc from the principal form and form A are entered under the heading "Summary".

B. The general remarks under I also apply to form A.

NOTES

Para I: words in square brackets inserted by the 1994 Act of Accession, Annex I(III)(B)(4), as adjusted by Council Decision 95/1/EC, Annex I(XIII)(A)(b), para 59. Further entries inserted by the 2003 Act of Accession Annex II(19)(A)(II), para 55. Words in square brackets in general remarks relating to Heading 16, inserted by Commission Regulation (EC) 883/2005, Art 1, para 32, with effect from 1 October 2005. Entries in both tables relating to Bulgaria and Romania inserted by Commission Regulation (EC) 1792/2006, Art 1, Annex, Part 11(A)(53).

Part III

ANNEX 61
MODEL OF DISCHARGE

Letter heading of the coordinating office of the second Member State submitting the claim

Addressee: coordinating office of the first Member State submitting the original claim.

Subject: ata carnet—discharge

Be informed that a claim for payment of duties and taxes under the ATA Convention[1] was sent on . . .[2] to our guaranteeing association in respect of:

1. ATA carnet No:
2. Issued by the Chamber of Commerce of:
   City:
   Country:
3. On behalf of:
   Holder:
   Address:
4. Expiry date of the carnet:
5. Date set for re-exportation[3]:
6. Number of transit/import voucher[4]:
7. Date of endorsement of voucher:

The present note discharges your responsibility in this file.

Signature and stamp of issuing coordinating office.

---

[1] Article 7 of the ATA Convention, Brussels, 6 December 1991.

[2] Enter date of dispatch.

[3] Details obtained from the undischarged transit or temporary importation voucher or, if no voucher is available, from the information available to the issuing coordinating office.

[4] Delete whichever is not applicable.

ANNEX 62

1. Member State's coat of arms or other sign or letters characterising the Member State

2. Customs office[1]

3. Number of document

4. Date

5. Authorised consignor[2]

6. Authorisation

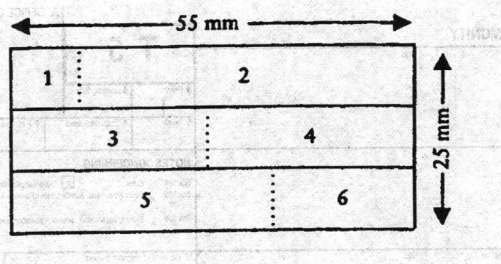

¹ Where this stamp is used in the framework of [Article 912g] of this Regulation, it concerns the office of departure.

² Where this stamp is used in the framework of Article 286 of this Regulation, it concerns the authorised exporter.

NOTE

Reference to Article 912g below substituted by Commission Regulation (EC) 1602/2000, Art 1, para 21.

ANNEX 63

A OFFICE OF DEPARTURE

EUROPEAN COMMUNITY

1

2 Consignor/Exporter   No

T 5

| 3 Forms | 4 Loading lists |
| 5 Items | 6 Total packages | 7 Reference number |

8 Consignee

NOTES CONCERNING

Box 104: Enter [X] when applicable
Box 105: Enter type, serial number, date of issue and name of issuing authority
Box 106: Enter type, number, date of registration and name of customs office.

14 Declarant/Representative   No

15 Country of dispatch/export

18 Identity and nationality of means of transport at departure   19 Ctr.

B Tilbagesendes til:
Zurücksenden an:
Επιστρεπτέον εις:
Return to:
Devolver a:
Palautusosoite:
Renvoyer à:
Da rispedire a:
Terugzenden aan:
Áter till:

17 Country of destination

IMPORTANT NOTE
This original must accompany the goods and be lodged:
- in the case of goods to be exported, with the Customs office of exit from the customs territory of the Community.
- in other cases, with the competent office in the Member State of destination.

1

31

Packages and description of goods

Marks and numbers - Container No(s) - Number and kind

32 Item No   33 Commodity Code   X X X X X / X X X X X

X X X X X X X X X   35 Gross mass (kg)   X X X X X
X X X X X X X X X   X X X X X
X X X X X X X X X   38 Net mass (kg)   X X X X X
X X X X X X X X X   X X X X X

40 Previous document

41 Supplementary units   X X X X X X X X X X X X X X X
                        X X X X X X X X X X X X X X X

ADDITIONAL INFORMATION

100 (For national use)

103 Net quantity (kg, litres or in other units) in words

104 USE AND/OR DESTINATION

☐ Exit from the customs territory of the Community

☐ Supply to the following international organisation:

☐ Other (specify):

☐ Supply for victualling

☐ Supply to the .... (nationality)

forces in .... (Member State)

Time limit of .... days for completion

105 Licences

106 Further Particulars

107 Legislation applicable

108 attached documents

109 Administrative or customs document

D CONTROL BY OFFICE OF DEPARTURE
Result:
Seals affixed: No:
identity:
Time limit (date):
Signature:

Stamp:

110 Place and date:

Signature and name of declarant/representative

See Notice before completing this form

ORIGINAL OF CONTROL COPY

E   FOR USE BY MEMBER STATE OF DEPARTURE

F   CONTROL OF USE AND/OR DESTINATION

The goods described in this declaration (enter ☒ where applicable)

☐   have received the use and/or destination declared overleaf on ....
                                                                                    (date)

☐   have not received the use and/or destination declared overleaf.

☐   have received the use and/or destination declared overleaf only as regards the quantities and at the dates entered below:

Remarks :

Place and date :   Signature :   Returned after registration under
                                                                      No.

                                                                                              Stamp :

Part III

(Copy omitted.)

Front page of form substituted by Commission Regulation (EC) 1602/2000, Art 1, para 22, Annex VI. Forms in use prior to 2 August 2000 may continue to be used until stocks are exhausted, and in any case no later than 31 December 2001, provided that the necessary editorial changes are made.

Copy 1: in Box B, words 'Vrat'te', 'Tagastada', 'Nosūtt atpaka', 'Graz¡inti i', 'Visszaküldeni', 'Ibgatlura lil', 'Odesłac' do', 'Vrnjeno', 'Vrátit' inserted by the 2003 Act of Accession Annex II(19)(A)(II), para 56. In Box B, words 'Въ ', 'Returnat la' inserted by Commission Regulation (EC) 1792/2006, Art 1, Annex, Part 11(A)(54).

ANNEX 64

A OFFICE OF DEPARTURE

EUROPEAN COMMUNITY

T 5

See Notice before completing this form

ORIGINAL OF CONTROL COPY

1

2 Consignor/Exporter	No

3 Forms
4 Loading lists
5 Items
6 Total packages
7 Reference number

8 Consignee

NOTES CONCERNING

Box 104: Enter [x] where applicable
Box 105: Enter type, serial number, date of issue and name of issuing authority
Box 106: Enter type, number, date of registration and name of customs office.

14 Declarant/Representative	No

15 Country of dispatch/export

B Tilbagesendes til:
Zurücksenden an:
Επιστρεπτεο εις:
Return to:
Devolver a:
Palautusosoite:
Renvoyer à:
Da rispedire a:
Terugzenden aan:
Åter till:

17 Country of destination

18 Identity and nationality of means of transport at departure
19 Ctr.

IMPORTANT NOTE
This original must accompany the goods and be lodged:
- in the case of goods to be exported, with the Customs office of exit from the customs territory of the Community,
- in other cases, with the competent office in the Member State of destination.

1

31 Packages and description of goods

Marks and numbers - Container No(s) - Number and kind

32 Item No
33 Commodity Code

XXXXX
XXXXX

X X X X X X X X X **35** Gross mass (kg)
X X X X X X X X X
X X X X X X X X X **38** Net mass (kg)
X X X X X X X X X

XXXXX
XXXXX
XXXXX
XXXXX

40 Previous document

41 Supplementary units

X X X X X X X X X X X X X X X
X X X X X X X X X X X X X X X X

ADDITIONAL INFORMATION

109 (For national use)

103 Net quantity (kg, litres or in other units) in words

104 USE AND/OR DESTINATION

☐ Exit from the customs territory of the Community
☐ Supply to the following international organisation:

☐ Supply for victualling
☐ Supply to the .... (nationality)
forces in .... (Member State)

☐ Other (specify):

Time limit of .... days for completion

105 Licences

106 Further Particulars

107 Legislation applicable
108 attached documents
109 Administrative or customs document

D CONTROL BY OFFICE OF DEPARTURE
Result:
Seals affixed: No:
identity:
Time limit (date):
Signature:

Stamp:

110 Place and date:

Signature and name of declarant/representative:

© European Communities Official Journal L 253, 11/10/1993 Annex 63

Part III

(Copy omitted.)

NOTE

Form amended by Commission Regulation (EC) 482/96, Art 1, para 26, Annex V.

ANNEX 65

EUROPEAN COMMUNITY

IMPORTANT NOTES

1. A loading list may be used only when the goods to which it relates are for the same use and/or destination which is to be shown in box 104 of the Control Copy T 5 to which it is attached.
2. Agricultural products for exportation must be described in accordance with the nomenclature used for refund purposes.
3. Details of licences or advance fixing certificates instead of being shown in box 105 of Control Copy T 5 must be shown on the loading list following the description of goods to which they relate.

LOADING LIST

T 5 ORIGINAL

attached to Control Copy T 5 bearing the registration number shown opposite.

OFFICE OF DEPARTURE

Item number	Marks and numbers - Number and kind of packages - Description of goods and, where appropriate, particulars of their composition	Commodity	Gross mass (kg)	Net mass (kg)	Net quantity (kg, litres or in other units) in words	RESERVED FOR OFFICIAL USE

Total number of packages (in figures)

Total (kg) | Total (kg)

Place and date:

Signature of declarant/representative

© European Communities Official Journal L 273, 11/10/1993 Annex 65

(Copy omitted.)

NOTE
Form amended by Commission Regulation (EC) 482/96, Art 1, para 26, Annex V.

[ANNEX 66
INSTRUCTIONS FOR USE OF THE FORMS REQUIRED TO DRAW UP
CONTROL COPY T5

A.
GENERAL REMARKS

1.   The T5 control copy is a document drawn up on a T5 form accompanied, where appropriate, either by one or more T5*bis* forms or by one or more T5 loading lists.

2.   The T5 control copy is intended to supply proof that the goods in respect of which it was issued have either been used in the way, or have reached the destination provided for by the specific Community provisions governing their use, it being the responsibility of the competent office of destination to be satisfied either directly or through persons acting on its behalf as to the use and/or destination of the goods concerned. In some cases, the T5 control copy is also used to inform the competent authorities of destination that the goods which it covers are subject to special measures. The procedure thus instituted is a framework procedure, to be put into effect only if specific Community legislation expressly so provides. It can apply even where the goods are not moving under a customs procedure.

3.   The T5 control copy must be drawn up in one original and at least one copy, each of which must bear an original signature.

When goods are transported under a customs procedure, the original and the copy or copies of the T5 control copy must be submitted together to the customs office of departure or consignment, which retains one copy while the original accompanies the goods and must be presented with them at the customs office of destination.

Where the goods are not placed under a customs procedure, the T5 control copy shall be issued by the office of consignment, which shall keep a copy. The words "Goods not covered by a customs procedure" shall be entered in box 109 of the T5 form. The original of the T5 control copy must be presented together with the goods to the competent office of destination.

4.   If T5*bis* forms are used, the T5 form and the T5*bis* forms must be completed.

If T5 loading lists are used, the T5 form must be completed but boxes 31, 32, 33, 35, 38, 100, 103 and 105 must be struck through and the information concerned must be entered only on the T5 loading list or lists.

5.   A T5 form may not be accompanied both by T5*bis* and by T5 loading lists.

6.   The forms must be printed on pale blue paper, dressed for writing purposes and weighing at least 40 g/m^2. The paper must be sufficiently opaque for the information on one side not to affect the legibility of the information on the other side and its strength should be such that in normal use it does not easily tear or crease.

The forms must measure 210 × 297 mm for T5 forms and T5*bis* and 297 × 420 mm for T5 loading lists, a tolerance in the length of between $^-$5 and +8 mm being allowed.

The address for return and the important note on the front of the form may be printed in red.

The competent authorities of the Member States may require that control copy T5 forms show the name and address of the printer, or a symbol enabling the printer to be identified.

7. The T5 control copy shall be made out in an official language of the Community which is acceptable to the competent authorities of the Member State of departure.

The competent authorities of another Member State in which such a document is presented may, as necessary, require a translation into the official language, or one of the official languages, of that Member State.

8. T5 forms and any T5*bis* forms or T5 loading lists must be completed in typescript or by a mechanographical or similar process. They may also be filled in legibly by hand, in ink and in block letters. To make it easier to complete T5 forms in typescript, they should be inserted in such a way that the first letter to be entered in box 2 is located in the small positioning box in the top left hand corner.

Forms must contain no erasures or overwriting. Alterations must be made by crossing out incorrect particulars and adding those required. Any such amendments must be initialled by the person making the amendment and authenticated by the competent authorities, who may require a new form to be lodged.

In addition, forms may be completed using an automatic reproduction process instead of any of the processes mentioned above. They may also be produced and completed by that means provided that the rules relating to the specimens, paper, size of forms, language to be used, legibility, prohibition of erasures and overwriting and alterations are strictly observed.

B.
PROVISIONS RELATING TO T5 FORMS

Only boxes marked with a serial number need be completed, as appropriate. The other boxes, marked with a capital letter, are for official use only except in cases provided for in specific regulations or in the provisions relating to authorised consignors.

BOX 2:   CONSIGNOR/EXPORTER

Enter the full name and address of the person or company concerned. Instructions regarding the identification number can be added by the Member States (identification number allocated to the person concerned by the competent authorities for tax, statistical or other purposes).

BOX 3:   FORMS

Enter the number of the form in relation to the total number of T5 and T5*bis* forms used. For example, if there is one T5 form and two T5*bis* forms, indicate in the T5 form "1/3", on the first T5*bis* form "2/3" and on the second T5 form "3/3".

Where the consignment consists of only one item, ie only one "Description of goods" box, has to be completed, do not enter anything in box 3, but enter the figure 1 in box 5.

BOX 4:   LOADING LISTS

Enter in figures the total number of T5 loading lists attached, if any.

BOX 5:   ITEMS

Enter in figures the total number of items declared by the person concerned on the T5 forms and on all T5*bis* forms or T5 loading lists used. The number of items must be 1 if there is only the T5 form or correspond on the total number of goods indicated in box 31 of the T5*bis* forms or in the T5 loading lists.

BOX 6:   TOTAL PACKAGES

Enter the total number of packages making up the consignment in question.

BOX 7:   REFERENCE NUMBER

Optional item for users to indicate any reference number allocated by the person concerned to the consignment in question.

BOX 8:   CONSIGNEE

Enter the full name and address of the person(s) or company(ies) concerned to whom the goods are to be delivered.

BOX 14:   DECLARANT/REPRESENTATIVE

Enter the full name and address of the person or company concerned in accordance with the provisions in force. If the declarant and the consignor/exporter are the same person, enter "consignor/exporter". Instructions regarding the identification number can be added by the Member States (identification number allocated to the person concerned by the competent authorities for tax, statistical or other purposes).

BOX 15:   COUNTRY OF DISPATCH/EXPORT

Enter the name of the country from which the goods are dispatched/exported.

BOX 17:   COUNTRY OF DESTINATION

Enter name of the country concerned.

BOX 18:   IDENTITY AND NATIONALITY OF MEANS OF TRANSPORT AT DEPARTURE

Enter the identity, e.g. registration number(s) or name of the means of transport (lorry, ship, railway wagon, aircraft) on which the goods are or were directly loaded when the consignment formalities were completed, followed (except in the case of rail transport) by the nationality of the means of transport (or that of the vehicle propelling the others if there are several means of transport), using the appropriate Community codes.

BOX 19:   CONTAINER (Ctr)

Using the appropriate Community codes ("0"—Goods not transported in containers or "1"—Goods transported in containers), indicate the situation at departure.

BOX 31:   PACKAGES AND DESCRIPTION OF GOODS—MARKS AND NUMBERS—CONTAINER No(s)—NUMBER AND KIND

Enter the marks, numbers, number and kind of packages or, in the case of unpackaged goods, the number of goods covered by the declaration, or the work "bulk", as appropriate, together with the particulars necessary to identify the goods. The description of the goods means the normal trade description expressed in sufficiently precise terms to allow their identification and classification.

Where the Community rules applicable to the goods concerned provide for particular procedures in this respect, the description of the goods must conform to those rules.

All additional information required by the said rules must also be entered in this box. The description of agricultural products must be in accordance with the Community provisions in force in the agricultural sector.

If containers are used, the identifying marks of the container must also be entered in this box. The unused space in this box must be crossed through.

BOX 32: ITEM NUMBER

Enter the number of the item in question in relation to the total number of articles declared in the T5 and T5*bis* forms used, as described in the note to box 5.

Where the consignment consists of only one item (a single T5 form), do not complete this box but enter the figure 1 in box 5.

BOX 33: COMMODITY CODE

Enter the code number corresponding to the item in question, using that of the nomenclature for export refunds where appropriate.

BOX 35: GROSS MASS

Enter the gross mass of the goods described in the corresponding box 31, expressed in kilograms. The gross mass is the aggregate mass of the goods with all their packagings, excluding containers and other transport equipment.

BOX 38: NET MASS

Where Community rules so require, enter the net mass of the goods described in the corresponding box 31, expressed in kilograms. The net mass is the mass of the goods themselves without any packaging.

BOX 40: PREVIOUS DOCUMENT

Box for optional use by the Member States (reference numbers of documents relating to the administrative procedure preceding dispatch/export).

BOX 41: SUPPLEMENTARY UNITS

For use as necessary in accordance with the goods nomenclature (enter the quantity of the item in question, expressed in the unit laid down in the goods nomenclature).

BOX 100: FOR NATIONAL USE

To be completed in accordance with the rules of the Member State of dispatch/export.

BOX 103: NET QUANTITY (kg, litres or other units) IN WORDS

To be completed in accordance with Community rules.

BOX 104: USE AND/OR DESTINATION

Indicate the use and/or destination intended or prescribed for the goods by placing an X in the appropriate box or, failing that, place an X in the box marked "Other" and specify the use and/or destination.

Where Community rules fix a time limit by which the goods must be assigned to a use and/or destination, complete the phrase "time limit of . . . days for completion", by inserting the number of days.

BOX 105: LICENCES

To be completed in accordance with Community rules.

Enter the type, serial number, date of issue and issuing authority.

BOX 106: FURTHER PARTICULARS

To be completed in accordance with Community rules and the rules on the application of Article 912(b)(9).

BOX 107: LEGISLATION APPLICABLE

Enter the number of any Community regulation, directive or decision concerning the measure providing for or prescribing control of the use and/or destination of the goods.

BOX 108: ATTACHED DOCUMENTS

List the accompanying documents attached to the control copy T5, which are to accompany it to its destination.

BOX 109: ADMINISTRATIVE OR CUSTOMS DOCUMENT

Enter the type, number and date of registration of the document relating to the procedure used for the transport of the goods, and the issuing office or, where appropriate, the words "Goods not covered by a customs procedure".

BOX 110: PLACE AND DATE; SIGNATURE AND NAME OF DECLARANT/REPRESENTATIVE

Subject to any specific provisions adopted with regard to the use of computerised systems, the original of the hand-written signature of the person concerned must appear both on the original and on the copy or copies of the T5 form. Where the person concerned is a legal person, the signatory must add his full name and capacity after his signature.

C.

PROVISIONS RELATING TO USE OF T5BIS FORMS

See notes in Section B.

Subject to any special provisions adopted on the use of automatic data-processing techniques, the original and copy or copies of the T5*bis* form must bear the original signature of the person who signed the corresponding T5 form.

Boxes headed "Packages and descriptions of goods" which have not been used must be struck through to prevent subsequent entries.

D.

PROVISIONS RELATING TO THE USE OF T5 LOADING LISTS FORMS

Every column in the loading lists, except that reserved for official use, must be completed. Only the front of the T5 loading list form may be used.

The registration number of the T5 control copy must be shown in the box for registration particulars of the T5 loading list.

The goods shown on the T5 loading list must be serially numbered in the column headed "item number" (see item number, box 32) in such a way that the last of these is the total given in box 5 of the T5 form.

The particulars normally entered in boxes 31, 33, 35, 38, 100, 103 and 105 of the form T5 must be entered on the T5 loading list.

Particulars relating to boxes 100 (national use) and 105 (licences) must be entered in the column for the description of the goods, immediately after the information concerning the goods to which those particulars refer.

A horizontal line must be drawn after the last entry and the spaces not used must be crossed through to prevent later additions being made.

The total number of packages containing the goods listed and the total gross and net mass of those goods must be shown at the foot of the appropriate columns.

Subject to any specific provisions adopted with regard to the use of computerised systems, the original signature of the signatory of the corresponding T5 form must appear both on the original and on the copy or copies of the T5 loading list.]

Substituted by Commission Regulation (EC) 1602/2000, Art 1, para 23, Annex VII.

[ANNEX 67]

APPLICATION AND AUTHORISATION FORMS

(Articles 292, 293, 497 and 505)

General remarks

1. The layout of the models is not binding; e.g. instead of boxes the Member States may provide for forms with a line structure or if required the space of the boxes may be extended.

However the order numbers and the appropriate text are obligatory.

2. The Member States may provide for boxes or lines for national purposes. These boxes or lines shall be indicated by an order number plus a capital letter (e.g. 5A).

3. In principle boxes with a bold order number must be completed. The explanatory note refers to exceptions. The customs administrations may provide for the completion of box 5 as mandatory only where a single authorisation is applied for.

4. The Appendix of the notes shall contain the IPR economic-condition-codes according to Annex 70.

(Forms omitted)

EXPLANATORY NOTES

TITLE I

PARTICULARS TO BE ENTERED IN THE VARIOUS BOXES OF THE APPLICATION FORM

General note:

References are to the Implementing Provisions of the Customs Code unless otherwise stated.

1 Applicant

Enter the full name and address of the applicant. The applicant is the person to whom the authorisation should be issued.

2 Customs procedure(s)

Enter the customs procedure(s) under which the goods listed in box 7 are intended to be placed. The relevant customs procedures are given below—

- free circulation with end-use
- customs warehousing
- inward processing – suspension system
- inward processing – drawback system
- processing under customs control
- temporary importation
- outward processing

Note—

If the applicant applies for an authorisation to use more than one customs procedure (integrated authorisation) and the form does not fit the requirements (e.g. because the goods which should be placed under the customs procedures are not the same for each procedure) separate forms should be used.

3 Type of application

Type of application must be entered in this box by using at least one of the following codes:

1 = first application

2 = application for modified or renewed authorisation (also indicate the appropriate authorisation number)

3 = application for a single authorisation

4 = application for successive authorisation (inward processing)

4 Continuation forms

Enter the number of continuation forms attached.

Note—

Continuation forms are provided for the following customs procedures—

customs warehousing, inward processing (where necessary) and outward processing (where necessary)

5 Place and kind of accounts/records

Enter the place of accounts. This is the place where the applicant's commercial, tax or other accounting material, or such data held on his behalf, is located. Specify also the kind of accounts by giving details about the system used.

State also the kind of records (stock records) to be used for the customs procedure. Records means: the data containing all the necessary information and technical details, enabling the customs authorities to supervise and control the customs procedure.

Note—

If it is intended to use a **customs warehouse type B,** box 5 is not to be completed.

In case of **temporary importation** box 5 need be completed only where required by customs authorities.

In case of application for a **single authorisation** indicate the place and kind of main accounts.

6 Period of validity of the authorisation

a		b

Indicate in box 6a the requested date on which the authorisation should take effect (day month year). In principle the authorisation takes effect on the date of issue at the earliest. In this case enter "date of issue". The date of expiry of the authorisation may be suggested in box 6b.

7 Goods to be placed under the customs procedure

	CN code	Description	Quantity	Value

CN code

Complete according to the Combined Nomenclature (CN code = 8 digits).

Description

The description of the goods means the trade and/or technical description.

Quantity

Enter the estimated quantity of the goods intended to be placed under the customs procedure.

Part III

Value

Enter the estimated value in euro or in other currency of the goods intended to be placed under the customs procedure.

Notes regarding
end-use—

1. If the application concerns goods other than those under (2) below, you should enter in sub-box "CN code" —where appropriate—the Taric Code (10 digits or 14 digits).

2. If the application concerns goods under the special provisions (Part A and B) contained in the Preliminary Provisions of the Combined Nomenclature (goods for certain categories of ships, boats and other vessels and for drilling or production platforms/civil aircraft and goods for use in civil aircraft) CN codes are not required. Applicants should state in sub-box "Description" for instance: "Civil aircraft and parts thereof/special provisions, part B of the CN". Furthermore it is then not necessary to give details about the CN code, quantity and the value of the goods;

customs warehousing: if the application covers a number of items of different goods, you may enter the word "various" in sub-box "CN code". In this case describe the nature of goods to be stored in sub-box "Description". It is not necessary to give details about the CN code, quantity and value of the goods;

inward and outward processing—

CN code: The four-digit code may be indicated. However the eight-digit code must be given where—

—   equivalent goods or the standard exchange system are to be used,
—   Article 586(2) is applied,
[—   the economic conditions are identified by codes 01, 10, 11, 31 or 99,
—   milk and milk products referred to in Article 1 of Council Regulation (EC) No 1255/1999 are concerned and code 30 is used in relation with the situations referred to under subdivisions 2, 5 and 7 of this code, or]
—   the customs authorities require this in accordance with Article 499, first paragraph.

Description: The trade and/or technical description should be sufficiently clear and detailed to enable a decision to be taken on the application. Where it is planned to use equivalent goods or the standard exchange system give details about commercial quality and technical characteristics of the goods.

Quantity: This information need not be entered with regard to inward processing where the code used to refer to the economic conditions is 30 in so far as it is not intended to use equivalent goods. However the quantity must be indicated where processing of durum wheat to produce pasta is involved or where the eight-digit code must be given for milk and milk products.

Value: This information need not be given where the quantity is not required unless the applicant intends to avail himself of Code 30 (de minimis value).

8 Compensating or processed products		
CN code	Description	Rate of yield

General remark—

Enter details of all compensating products resulting from the operations indicating Main Compensating Product (MCP) or Secondary Compensating Product (SCP) as appropriate.

CN code and Description

See comments on box 7.

Rate of yield

Indicate the estimated rate of yield or method by which that rate is to be determined. In case of standard rates of yield refer to Annex 69 and indicate the appropriate numerical order.

9 Details of the planned activities

Describe the nature of the planned activities (e.g. details of the operations under a job-processing contract or kind of usual forms of handling) to be carried out on the goods within the customs procedure. Indicate also the appropriate place(s).

If more than one customs procedure is applied for in box 2, the description must clearly show whether the goods are to be placed under the customs procedures alternatively or successively.

If more than one customs administration is involved, indicate the name(s) of the Member State(s) as well as the places.

Note—

In the case of "end-use" enter the intended end-use and the place(s) where the goods will be assigned to the prescribed end-use.

Where appropriate enter name, address and function of other operators involved.

If a transfer of rights and obligations is intended (Articles 82 (2) and 90 of the Code), enter in box 9, if possible, details about the transferee.

10 Economic conditions

The applicant must give reasons for the fulfilment of the economic conditions.

In particular for

— customs warehousing that an economic need for warehousing exists,

—inward processing by using at least one of the two-digit codes set out in the appendix for each CN code which has been indicated in box 7,

— processing under customs control that the use of non-Community sources enables processing activities to be created or maintained in the Community.

Note—

In the case of

end-use box 10 is not to be completed;

temporary importation it is necessary to indicate the Article(s) under which authorisation is applied for and to give details about the owner of the goods described in box 7;

outward processing complete box 10 only if required by the customs authorities pursuant to Article 585(1).

11 Customs office(s)	
a	of entry
b	of discharge
c	Supervising office(s)

Indicate the suggested customs office(s).

Note—

In case of end-use box 11b is not to be completed.

12 Identification

Enter in box 12 the intended means of identification by using at least one of the following codes:

1 = serial or manufacturer's number

Part III

2 = affixing of plumbs, seals, clip-marks or other distinctive marks

3 = information sheet INF

4 = taking of samples, illustrations or technical descriptions

5 = carrying out of analyses

6 = information document set out in Annex 104 (only suitable for **outward processing**)

7 = other means of identification (explain in box 16 "additional information")

8 = without identification measures according to

Article 139 second subparagraph of the Code (only suitable for **temporary importation**)

Note—

In the case of **customs warehousing** completion is necessary only if prefinanced goods are involved or if this is required by the customs authorities.

Box 12 is not to be completed in the case of **inward processing with equivalent goods, outward processing with standard exchange system** or where **Article 586 (2)** is applied. Box 18 of the continuation form "inward processing" or boxes 19 or 21 of the continuation form "outward processing" shall be completed instead.

---

13 Period for discharge (months)

Enter the estimated period needed for the operations to be carried out or use within the customs procedure(s) applied for (box 2). The period starts when the goods are placed under the customs procedure. This period ends when the goods or products have been assigned a new permitted customs-approved treatment or use including, as the case may be, in order to claim repayment of import duties after inward processing (drawback system), or in order to obtain total or partial relief from import duties upon release for free circulation after outward processing.

Note—

— In the case of **end-use** state the period which will be needed to assign the goods to the prescribed end-use or to transfer the goods to another holder of authorisation.

— In the case of **customs warehousing** the period is unlimited; therefore leave blank.

— In the case of **inward processing:** where the period for discharge expires on a specific date for all the goods placed under the arrangements in a given period, the authorisation may provide that the period for discharge shall be automatically extended for all goods still under the arrangements on this date. If this simplification is required enter: "Article 542(2)" and give the details in box 16.

---

14 Simplified procedures

a		b	

Box 14 a—

If it is intended to use a simplified entry procedure specify using at least one of the following codes—

1 = Incomplete declaration (Article 253 (1))

2 = Simplified declaration procedure (Article 253 (2))

3 = Local clearance procedure with presentation (Article 253 (3))

4 = Local clearance procedure without presentation (Article 253 (3))

Box 14 b—

If it is intended to use a simplified discharge procedure specify using at least one of the following codes—

The same as for box 14 a.

Note—

In the case of **end-use** procedure box 14 b is not to be completed.

---

15 Transfer

If a transfer of goods or products is intended state the proposed transfer formalities using at least one of the following codes:

1 = **without customs formalities between different places designated in the authorisation applied for**

2 = transfer from the office of entry to the applicant's or operator's facilities or place of use under cover of the declaration for entry for the customs procedure

3 = transfer to the office of exit with a view to re-exportation should take place under cover of the customs procedure

4 = transfer from one holder to another in accordance with Annex 68

Note—

Indicate in box 16 the suggested procedure

5 = control copy T 5 (only suitable for **end-use**)

6 = other documents (only suitable for **end-use**; describe in box 16).

Note—

Transfer is not possible where the place of departure or arrival of the goods is a **type B warehouse**.

---

16 Additional information

Indicate all additional information considered useful.

17
Signed   **Name**
Date

If a continuation form is used complete only the appropriate box (22, 23 or 26) instead.

TITLE II
REMARKS CONCERNING THE CONTINUATION FORMS
CONTINUATION FORM "CUSTOMS WAREHOUSING"

---

18 Warehouse type

Indicate one of the following types—

Type A, B, C, D or E.

---

19 Warehouse or storage facilities (type E)

Enter the precise place intended to be used as the customs warehouse or, where the application relates to a type E warehouse, as storage facilities.

---

20 Deadline for lodging
inventory of goods

You can make a suggestion for the deadline for lodging inventory of goods.

21 Loss rate

Give details –where appropriate- of loss rate(s).

22 Storage of goods not under the arrangements		
CN code	Description	Category/customs procedure

CN code and Description

Where it is planned to use common storage state the eight-digit CN code, commercial quality and technical characteristics of the goods. In all other cases the trade and/or technical description is sufficient or if the storage of goods not under the arrangements covers a number of items of different goods, you may enter the word "various" in sub-box "CN code". In this case describe the nature of goods to be stored in sub-box "Description".

Category/customs procedure

Indicate in column "Category/customs procedure" the appropriate code(s)—

    1 = Community agricultural goods
    2 = Community industrial goods
    3 = Non-Community agricultural goods
    4 = Non-Community industrial goods

and specify the customs procedure if any to which the goods are subject.

23 Usual forms of handling

Complete if usual forms of handling are envisaged.

24 Temporary removal. Purpose:

Complete if temporary removal is envisaged.

25 Additional information

Indicate all additional information considered useful with regard to boxes 18 to 24.

CONTINUATION FORM "INWARD PROCESSING"

18 Equivalent goods	
CN code	Description

Where it is planned to use equivalent goods, state the eight-digit CN code, commercial quality and technical characteristics of the equivalent goods to enable the customs authorities to make the necessary comparison between import goods and equivalent goods. The Codes provided for box 12 may be used to suggest supporting means, which might be useful for this comparison. If the equivalent goods are at a more advanced stage of manufacture than the import goods give appropriate information in box 21.

19 Prior exportation

Where it is planned to use the prior exportation system indicate the period within which the non-Community goods should be declared for the arrangements taking account of the time required for procurement and transport to the Community.

20 Release for free circulation without customs declaration?

Where it is requested that the compensating products or goods in the unaltered state will be released for free circulation without formalities, enter "YES".

21 Additional information

Indicate all additional information considered useful with regard to boxes 18 to 20.

CONTINUATION FORM "OUTWARD PROCESSING"

18 System

Where intended enter the appropriate code(s)—

1 = standard exchange system without prior importation
2 = standard exchange system with prior importation

19 Replacement products	
CN code	Description

Where it is planned to use the standard exchange system (only possible in case of repair), state the eight-digit CN code, commercial quality and technical characteristics of the replacement products to enable the customs authorities to make the necessary comparison between temporary export goods and the replacement products. The Codes provided for box 12 may be used to suggest supporting means, which might be useful for this comparison.

20 Article 147(2) of the Code?

Where the applicant is not the person who arranges for the processing operations to be carried out, authorisation may be granted (only for goods of Community origin) in accordance with Article 147(2) of the Code. Enter in box 20 "YES" and give the appropriate details.

21 Article 586(2)?

Where the nature of the processing operations does not allow it to be established that the compensating products have resulted from the temporary export goods, the authorisation may nevertheless be granted in duly justified cases, provided the applicant can offer sufficient guarantees that the goods used in the processing operations share the same eight-digit CN code, the same commercial quality and the same technical characteristics as the temporary export goods. The Codes provided for box 12 may be used to suggest supporting means, which might be useful for this purpose. If such an authorisation is applied for enter in box 21 "YES" and give the appropriate details.

22 Additional information

Indicate all additional information considered useful with regard to boxes 18 to 21.

Part III

APPENDIX
(IPR ECONOMIC-CONDITION-CODES ACCORDING TO ANNEX 70)]

Annexes 67–77 substituted for Annexes 67–103 by Commission Regulation (EC) 993/2001, Art 1, para 37, Annex V.

Explanatory notes, Title I, Box 7, inward and outward processing: words in square brackets substituted by Commission Regulation (EC) 881/2003 Art 1, para 34, Annex VIII.

[ANNEX 68

TRANSFER OF GOODS OR PRODUCTS COVERED BY THE
ARRANGEMENTS FROM ONE HOLDER TO ANOTHER
(Article 513)

A.

Normal procedure (3 SAD copies)

1. Where goods or products are transferred from one holder to another without discharge of the arrangements, a form corresponding to the model drawn up in accordance with Articles 205 to 215 shall be completed on copies 1, 4 and an additional identical copy to copy 1.

2. Before a transfer takes place, the supervising office dealing with the first holder shall be notified of the proposed transfer, in a manner which that office shall determine, in order to enable the performance of any checks considered necessary.

3. Additional copy 1 shall be retained by the first holder (the sender of the goods or products), and copy 1 forwarded to his supervising office.

4. Copy 4 shall accompany the goods or products and be retained by the second holder.

5. The supervising office of the first holder shall forward copy 1 to the supervising office of the second holder.

6. The second holder shall issue the first holder a receipt for the transferred goods or products specifying the date of their entry into the records (acceptance of the written customs declaration in the case of temporary importation) which the latter shall retain.

B.

Simplified procedures—

I. Using 2 SAD copies—

1. Where goods or products are transferred from one holder to another without discharge of the arrangements only copies 1 and 4 of the document referred to in paragraph 1 of Part A shall be completed.

2. Before the goods or products are transferred, the supervising offices shall be informed of the intended transfer in the manner which they shall stipulate, to enable them to carry out any controls they consider necessary.

3. The first holder (the sender of the goods or products) shall retain copy 1.

4. Copy 4 may accompany the goods or products and be retained by the second holder.

5. Paragraph 6 of Part A shall apply.

II. *Using other methods instead of the SAD where the necessary information is provided:*
— data processing,
— commercial or administrative documents, or
— any other document.

APPENDIX

Where the SAD copies are used, the boxes indicated must contain the following information—

2. *Consignor*: Give the name and address of the first holder, the name and address of his supervising office, followed by the authorisation number and the issuing customs authority.

3. *Forms*: Indicate the order number of the set of forms among the total number of sets used.

Where the declaration relates to a single item (i.e. where only one "description of goods" box needs to be filled in), leave box 3 blank but enter the figure 1 in box 5.

5. *Items*: State the total number of items declared in all the forms or supplementary forms used. The number of items is equal to the number of "description of goods" boxes which need to be filled in.

8. *Consignee*: Give the name of the second holder, the name and address of his supervising office and the address where the goods or products are to be stored, used or processed followed by the authorisation number and the issuing customs authority.

15. *Dispatching country*: Indicate the Member State from which the goods are dispatched.

31. *Packages and description of goods; marks and numbers — container No(s) — number and kind*: Enter the marks, (identifying) numbers, number and kind of packages or, in the case of unpacked goods, the number of goods covered by the declaration or the indication "in bulk", as appropriate, plus the details needed to identify them.

The goods should be described using their usual commercial description, in sufficient detail to allow the goods to be identified. Where a container is used, the identification marks of the container should also be indicated in this box.

32. *Item No*: State the order number of the item in question among the total number of items declared in the forms or supplementary forms used, as defined in box 5.

Where the declaration relates to a single item, the customs authorities may stipulate that nothing should be entered in this box.

33. *Commodity code*: Enter the CN code for the item in question.[1]

35. *Gross mass*: Where necessary, state the gross mass in kilograms of the goods described in the corresponding box 31. The gross mass is the aggregate mass of the goods with all their packing, excluding containers and other transport equipment.

38. *Net mass*: State the net mass in kilograms of the goods described in the corresponding box 31. The net mass is the mass of the goods stripped of all packaging.

41. *Supplementary Units*: Where necessary, indicate the quantity in the units laid down in the Combined Nomenclature.

44. *Additional information; documents produced, certificates and authorisation:* Enter the date of the first entry into the arrangements and "Transfer" in capital letters followed by, as appropriate—
 - "CW"-
 - "IP/S"-
 - "PCC"-
 - "TI"-.

When the import goods are subject to specific commercial policy measures and when these measures are still to be applied at the moment of transfer, the words "Commercial Policy" should be added to this entry.

47. Calculation of taxes: Enter the tax base (value, weight or other).[1]

54. *Place and date; signature and name of the declarant or his representative:* Enter the original hand-written signature of the person indicated in box 2 followed by his name. Where the person concerned is a legal person, the person signing the form should state his capacity after his signature and name.]

---

[1] Box not mandatory in the case of the customs warehousing arrangements.

NOTE

Substituted as noted to Annex 67.

[ANNEX 69

STANDARD RATES OF YIELD

(Article 517 (3))

General remark:

The standard rates of yield shall apply only to import goods of sound, genuine and merchantable quality which conform to any standard quality laid down in Community legislation and on condition that the compensating products are not obtained by special processing methods in order to meet specific quality requirements.

Import goods		Nu-merical or-der	Compensating products		Quantity of com-pensating products for each 100 kg of im-ported goods (kg)[2]
CN code	Description		Code[1]	Description	
(1)		(2)	(3)	(4)	(5)
0407 00 30	Eggs in shell	1	ex 0408 99 80	a) Eggs, not in shell, liquid or frozen	86,00
			ex 0511 99 90	b) Shells	12,00
		2	0408 19 81	a) Egg yolks, liquid or frozen	33,00
			ex 0408 19 89	b) Egg albumin, liquid or frozen	53,00
			ex 3502 19 90	c) Shells	12,00
			ex 0511 99 90		
		3	0408 91 80	a) Eggs, not in shell, dried	22,10
			ex 0511 99 90	b) Shells	12,00

		16	1108 11 00	a) Wheat starch	45,46
			1109 00 00	b) Wheat gluten	7,50
			ex 2302 30 10	c) Bran	25,50
			ex 2303 10 90	d) Residues of starch manufacture	12,00
1001 10 00	Durum wheat	17	ex 1103 11 10	a) Cereal meal 'Couscous'(4)	50,00
			1103 11 10	b) Cereal groats and cereal meal with an ash content, referred to dry matter, of 0,95% or more but less than 1,30% by weight	17,00
				c) Flour	
			1101 00 11	d) Bran	8,00
			ex 2302 30 10		20,00
		18	ex 1103 11 10	a) Cereal groats and cereal meal with an ash content, referred to dry matter, of less than 0,95% by weight	60,00
			1101 00 11	b) Flour	15,00
			ex 2302 30 10	c) Bran	20,00
		19	ex 1103 11 10	a) Cereal groats and cereal meal with an ash content, referred to dry matter, of 0,95% or more but less than 1,30% by weight	67,00
				b) Flour	
			1101 00 11	c) Bran	8,00
			ex 2302 30 10		20,00
		20	ex 1103 11 10	a) Cereal groats and cereal meal with an ash content, referred to dry matter, of 1,30% or more by weight	75,00
			ex 2302 30 10	b) Bran	20,00
		21	ex 1902 19 10	a) Pasta, containing no eggs and no common wheat flour or meal, with an ash content in the dry matter not exceeding 0,95% by weight	62,50
			1101 00 11	b) Flour	13,70
			ex 2302 30 10	c) Bran	18,70
		22	ex 1902 19 10	a) Pasta, containing no eggs and no common wheat flour or meal, with an ash content in the dry matter of more than 0,95% but not exceeding 1,10% by weight	66,67
			1101 00 11	b) Flour	8,00
			ex 2302 30 10	c) Bran	20,00
		23	ex 1902 19 10	a) Pasta, containing no eggs and no common wheat flour or meal, with an ash content in the dry matter of more than 1,10% but not exceeding 1,30% by weight	71,43
			1101 00 11	b) Flour	3,92
			ex 2302 30 10	c) Bran	19,64
		24	ex 1902 19 10	a) Pasta, containing eggs and no common wheat flour or meal, with an ash content, in the dry matter, of more than 1,30% by weight	79,36
			ex 2302 30 10	b) Bran	15,00

		4	0408 11 80	a) Egg yolks, dried	15,40
			ex 3502 11 90	b) Egg albumin, dried (in crystals)	7,40
			ex 0511 99 90	c) Shells	12,00
		5	0408 11 80	a) Egg yolks, dried	15,40
			ex 3502 11 90	b) Egg albumin, dried (in another form)	6,50
			ex 0511 99 90	c) Shells	
					12,00
ex 0408 99 80	Eggs, not in shell, liquid or frozen	6	0408 91 80	Eggs, not in shell, dried	25,70
0408 19 81 and ex 0408 19 89	Egg yolks, liquid or frozen	7	0408 11 80	Egg yolks, dried	46,60
ex 1001 90 99	Common wheat	8	ex 1101 00 15(100)	a) Common wheat flour having by weight on the dry product an ash content not exceeding 0,60%	73,00
			ex 2302 30 10	b) Bran	
			ex 2302 30 90	c) Sharps	22,50
					2,50
		9	ex 1101 00 15 (130)	a) Common wheat flour having by weight on the dry product an ash content exceeding 0,60% but not exceeding 0,90%	78,13
			ex 2302 30 10	b) Bran	20,00
		10	1101 00 15 (150)	a) Common wheat flour having by weight on the dry product an ash content exceeding 0,90% but not exceeding 1,10%	84,75
			ex 2302 30 10	b) Bran	13,25
		11	1101 00 15 (170)	a) Common wheat flour having by weight on the dry product an ash content exceeding 1,10% but not exceeding 1,65%	91,75
			ex 2302 30 10	b) Bran	6,25
		12	1101 00 15 (180)	Common wheat flour having by weight on the dry product an ash content exceeding 1,65% but not but not exceeding 1,90%	98,03
		13	1104 29 11	Hulled wheat (shelled or husked) whether or not sliced or kibbled (3)	°
		14	1107 10 11	a) Malt, unroasted, obtained from wheat, in the form of flour	°
			ex 1001 90 99 ex 2302 30 10	b) Not-germinated common wheat	1,00
			. . .	c) Bran	19,00
			or ex 2303 30 00	d) Rootlets	3,50
		15	1107 10 19	a) Malt, unroasted, obtained from wheat, in a form other than of flour	°
			ex 1001 90 99	b) Not-germinated common wheat	0,95
			. . .		
			or ex 2303 30 00	c) Rootlets	3,33

		25	ex 1902 11 00	a) Pasta, containing eggs but no common wheat flour or meal, with an ash content, in the dry matter, not exceeding 0,95% by weight[5]	[5]
			1101 00 11	b) Flour	13,70
			ex 2302 30 10	c) Bran	18,70
		26	ex 1902 11 00	a) Pasta, containing eggs but no common wheat flour or meal, with an ash content, in the dry matter of more than 0,95% but not exceeding 1,10% by weight[5]	[5]
			1101 00 11	b) Flour	8,00
			ex 2302 30 10	c) Bran	20,00
		27	ex1902 11 00	a) Pasta, containing eggs but no common wheat flour or meal, with an ash content, in the dry matter, of more than 1,10% but not exceeding 1,30% by weight[5]	[5]
			1101 00 11	b) Flour	3,92
			ex 2302 30 10	c) Bran	19,64
		28	ex 1902 11 00	a) Pasta, containing eggs but no common wheat flour or meal, with an ash content, in the dry matter of 1,30% or more by weight[5]	[5]
				b) Bran	
			ex 2302 30 10		15,00
1003 00 90	Barley	29	ex 1102 90 10 (100)	a) Barley flour, or an ash content, referred to dry matter, not exceeding 0,9% by weight and of a crude fibre content, referred to dry matter, not exceeding 0,9% by weight b) Bran	66,67
			ex 2302 40 10	c) Sharps	10,00
			ex 2302 40 90		21,50
		30	ex 1103 19 30 (100)	a) Barley groats and meal, of an ash content, referred to dry matter, not exceeding 1% by weight and of a crude fibre content, referred to dry matter, not exceeding 0,9% by weight	*
			1102 90 10	b) Barley flour	2,00
			ex 2302 40 10	c) Bran	10,00
			ex 2302 40 90	d) Sharps	21,50
		31	ex 1104 21 10 (100)	a) Hulled (shelled or husked) barley, of an ash content, referred to dry matter, not exceeding 1% by weight and of a crude fibre content, referred to dry matter, not exceeding 0,9% by weight (3)	*
			ex 2302 40 10	b) Bran	10,00
			ex 2302 40 90	c) Sharps	21,50
		32	ex 1104 21 30 (100)	a) Hulled and sliced or kibbled barley, of an ash content, referred to dry matter, not exceeding 1% by weight and of a crude fibre content, referred to dry matter, not exceeding 0,9% by weight ('Grütze' or 'Grutten') (3)	*
			ex 2302 40 10	b) Bran	10,00
			ex 2302 40 90	c) Sharps	21,50

Part III

		33	ex 1104 21 50 (100)	a) Pearled barley (6), of an ash content, referred to dry matter, not exceeding 1% by weight (without talc) — First category	50,00
			ex 2302 40 10	b) Bran	20,00
			ex 2302 40 90	c) Sharps	27,50
		34	ex 1104 21 50 (300)	a) Pearled barley (6), of an ash content, referred to dry matter, not exceeding 1% by weight (without talc) — Second category	*
			ex 2302 40 10	b) Bran	20,00
			ex 2302 40 90	c) Sharps	15,00
		35	ex 1104 11 90	a) Flaked barley, of an ash content, referred to dry matter, not exceeding 1% by weight and a crude fibre content, referred to dry matter, not exceeding 0,9% by weight	66,67
			ex 2302 40 10	b) Bran	10,00
			ex 2302 40 90	c) Sharps	21,33
		36	ex 1107 10 91	a) Barley malt, unroasted, in the form of flour	*
				b) Barley, not germinated	
			ex 1003 00 90	c) Bran	1,00
			ex 2302 40 10	d) Rootlets	19,00
			. . . ex 2303 30 00		3,50
		37	ex 1107 10 99	a) Barley malt, unroasted	*
			ex 1003 00 90	b) Barley, not germinated	0,98
			. . . ex 2303 30 00	c) Rootlets	3,42
		38	1107 20 00	a) Malt, roasted	*
			ex 1003 00 90	b) Barley, not germinated	0,96
			. . .. ex 2303 30 00	c) Rootlets	3,36
1004 00 00	Oats	39	ex 1102 90 30 (100)	a) Oat flour, of an ash content, referred to dry matter, not exceeding 2,3% by weight, of a crude fibre content, referred to dry matter, not exceeding 1,8% by weight, of a moisture content not exceeding 11% by weight and of which the peroxydase is virtually inactivated	55,56
			ex 2302 40 10	b) Bran	33,00
			ex 2302 40 90	c) Sharps	7,50
		40	ex 1103 12 00 (100)	a) Oat groats and meal, of an ash content, referred to dry matter, not exceeding 2,3% by weight, of a tegument content not exceeding 0,1% by weight, of a moisture content not exceeding 11% by weight and of which the peroxydase is virtually inactivated	*
				b) Flour	
			ex 1102 90 30	c) Bran	2,00
			ex 2302 40 10	d) Sharps	33,00
			ex 2302 40 90		7,50
		41	ex 1104 22 98	Clipped oats	98,04

		42	ex 1104 22 20 (100)	a) Hulled (shelled or husked) oats, of an ash content, referred to dry matter, not exceeding 2,3% by weight, of a tegument content not exceeding 0,5% by weight, of a moisture content not exceeding 11% by weight and of which the peroxydase is virtually in-activated (3)	*
			ex 2302 40 10	b) Bran	33,00
		43	ex 1104 22 30 (100)	a) Hulled and sliced or kibbled oats, of an ash content, referred to dry matter, not exceeding 2,3% by weight, of a tegument content not exceeding 0,1% by weight of a mois-ture content not exceeding 11% by weight and of which the peroxydase is virtually inactivated ('Grütze' or 'Grutten')(3)	*
			ex 2302 40 10	b) Bran	33,00
			ex 2302 40 90	c) Sharps	3,50
		44	ex 1104 12 90 (100)	a) Flaked oats, of an ash content, re-ferred to dry matter, not exceeding 2,3% by weight, of a tegument con-tent not exceeding 0,1% by weight, of a moisture content not exceeding 12% by weight and of which the per-oxydase is virtually inactivated	50,00
				b) Bran	
			ex 2302 40 10	c) Sharps	33,00
			ex 2302 40 90		13,00
		45	ex 1104 12 90 (300)	a) Flaked oats, of an ash content, re-ferred to dry matter, not exceeding 2,3% by weight, of a tegument con-tent exceeding 0,1% but not exceed-ing 1,5% by weight, of a moisture content not exceeding 12% by weight and of which the peroxydase is virtu-ally inactivated	62,50
				b) Bran	
			ex 2302 40 10		33,00
1005 90 00	Maize, other	46	ex 1102 20 10 (100)	a) Maize flour, of a fat content, re-ferred to dry matter, not exceeding 1,3% by weight and of a crude fibre content, referred to dry matter, not exceeding 0,8% by weight	71,43
			ex 1104 30 90	b) Maize germ	12,00
			ex 2302 10 10	c) Bran	14,00
		47	ex 1102 20 10 (200)	a) Maize flour, of a fat content ex-ceeding 1,3% but not exceeding 1,5% by weight and of a crude fibre con-tent, referred to dry matter, not ex-ceeding 0,8% by weight	*
			ex 1104 30 90	b) Maize germ	8,00
			ex 2302 10 10	c) Bran	6,50
		48	ex 1102 20 90 (100)	a) Maize flour, of a fat content ex-ceeding 1,5% but not exceeding 1,7% by weight and of a crude fibre con-tent, referred to dry matter, not ex-ceeding 1% by weight	83,33
			ex 1104 30 90	b) Maize germ	8,00
			ex 2302 10 10	c) Bran	6,50

Part III

49	ex 1103 13 10 (100)	a) Maize groats and meal, of a fat content not exceeding 0,9% by weight and of a crude fibre content, referred to dry matter, not exceeding 0,6% by weight[7]	55,56
	1102 20 10 or	b) Maize flour	16,00
	1102 20 90	c) Maize germ	12,00
	ex 1104 30 90	d) Bran	14,00
	ex 2302 10 10		
50	ex 1103 13 10 (300)	a) Maize groats and meal, of a fat content not exceeding 1,3% by weight and of a crude fibre content, referred to dry matter, not exceeding 0,8% by weight[7]	71,43
	ex 1104 30 90	b) Maize germ	12,00
	ex 2302 10 10	c) Bran	14,00
51	ex 1103 13 10 (500)	a) Maize groats and meal, of a fat content exceeding 1,3% by weight but not exceeding 1,5% by weight and of a crude fibre content, referred to dry matter, not exceeding 1% by weight[7]	*
	ex 1104 30 90	b) Maize germ	8,00
	ex 2302 10 10	c) Bran	6,50
52	ex 1103 13 90 (100)	a) Maize groats and meal, of a fat content exceeding 1,5% by weight but not exceeding 1,7% by weight and of a crude fibre content, referred to dry matter, not exceeding 1% by weight[7]	*
	ex 1104 30 90	b) Maize germ	8,00
	ex 2302 10 10	c) Bran	6,50
53	ex 1104 19 50 (110)	a) Flaked maize, of a fat content, referred to dry matter, not exceeding 0,9% by weight and of a crude fibre content, referred to dry matter, not exceeding 0,7% by weight	62,50
		b) Bran	
	ex 2302 10 10		35,50
54	ex 1104 19 50 (130)	a) Flaked maize, of a fat content, referred to dry matter, not exceeding 1,3% by weight and of a crude fibre content, referred to dry matter, not exceeding 0,8% by weight	76,92
	ex 2302 10 10	b) Bran	21,08
55	ex 1104 19 50 (150)	a) Flaked maize, of a fat content, referred to dry matter, exceeding 1,3% by but not exceeding 1,7% by weight and of a crude fibre content, referred to dry matter, not exceeding 1% by weight	90,91
	ex 2302 10 10	b) Bran	7,09
56	1108 12 00	a) Maize starch	*
		b) The products shown under numerical order No 62	29,91

			ex 2303 10 19	feed						
			or ex 2309 90 20	Gluten feed containing residues of maize oil	23,85	19,38	23,85	1938	22,56	27,03
				Maize germ oil-cake			3,18	3,18		
			ex 2306 70 00		29,91	29,91	29,91	29,91	29,91	29,91
		63		Complementary products to the compensating products found under numerical order Nos 59 to 61[12] Maize germ						
			ex 1104 30 90	Maizen oil						
			ex 1515	Maize gluten	6,10	6,10				
			ex 2303 10 11	Corn-gluten			2,90	2,90	2,90	2,90
			ex 2303 10 19	feed		4,50		4,50	4,50	
				Gluten feed containing residues of maize oil						
			or ex 2309 90 20	Maize germ oil-cake	23,85	18,50	23,00	18,50	21,70	26,20
							3,20	3,20		
			ex 2307 70 00		29,10	29,10	29,10	29,10	29,10	29,10

57	ex 1702 30 51or	a) Glucose, in the form of white crystalline powder, whether or not agglomerated (8)	*
	ex 1702 30 91	b) The products shown under numerical order No 62	29,91
	ex 1702 30 99	c) Glucose waste	9,95
58	ex 1702 30 59 or ex 1702 30 99	a) Glucose, other than glucose in the form of white crystalline powder, whether or not agglomerared[9]	*
		b) The products shown under numerical order No 62	29,91
59	ex 2905 44 11or	a) D-Glucitol (sorbitol) in aqueous solution containing 2% or less by weight of D-mannitol, calculated on the D-glucitol content[10]	59,17
	ex 3824 60 11	b) The products shown under numerical order No 63	29,10
60	ex 2905 44 19 or ex 3824 60 19	a) D-Glucitol (sorbitol) in aqueous solution containing more than 2% by weight of D-mannitol, calculated on the D-glucitol content[11]	67,56
		b) The products shown under numerical order No 63	29,10
61	ex 2905 44 91 or ex 2905 44 99 or ex 3824 60 91 or ex 3824 60 99	a) D-Glucitol (sorbitol), relative to 100 kg of the dry matter	41,32
		b) The products shown under numerical order No 63	29,10

Import goods		Numerical order	Compensating products		Quantity of compensating products for each 100 kg of imported goods (kg)[2]					
CN code	Description		Code[1]	Description						
(1)		(2)	(3)	(4)	(5)					
					a)	b)	c)	d)	e)	f)
1005 90 00(cont'd)		62		Complementary products to the compensating products found under numerical order Nos 56 to 58[12] Maize germ						
			ex 1104 30 90	Maize oils	6,06	6,06				
			ex 1515	Maize gluten			2,88	2,88	2,88	2,88
			ex 2303 10 11	Corn-gluten		4,47		4,47	4,47	

Part III

| Import goods | | Numerical order | Compensating products | | Quantity of compensating products for each 100 kg of imported goods (kg)[2] |
CN code	Description		Code[1]	Description	
(1)		(2)	(3)	(4)	(5)
1006 10 21	Rice in the husk (paddy or Rough),	64	1006 20 11	a) Husked (brown) rice parboiled, round grain	80.00
			ex 1213 00 00	b) Husks	20.00
	Parboiled, round grain	65	1006 30 21 1102 30 00 or	a) Semi-milled rice, whether or not polished or glazed, parboiled, round grain	71.00
			ex 2302 20 10 or ex 2302 20 90 1006 40 00	b) Rice flour or bran	6.00
			ex 1213 00 00	c) Broken rice	3.00
				d) Husks	20.00
		66	1006 30 61 1102 30 00	a) Wholly milled rice, whether or not polished or glazed, parboiled, round grain	65.00
			or ex 2302 20 10 or	b) Rice flour or bran	8.00
			ex 2302 20 90 1006 40 00 ex 1213 00 00	c) Broken rice d) Husks	7.00 20.00
1006 10 23	Rice in the husk (paddy or rough), parboiled, medium grain	67	1006 20 13	a) Husked (brown) rice, parboiled, medium grain	8.00
			ex 1213 00 00	b) Husks	20.00

Part III

		68	1006 30 23	a) Semi-milled rice, whether or not polished or glazed, parboiled, medium grain	71.00
				b) Rice flour or bran	6.00
			1102 30 00 or		
			ex 2302 20 10	c) Broken rice	
			or	d) Husks	
			ex 2302 20 90		3.00
			1006 40 00		20.00
			ex 1213 00 00		
		69	1006 30 63	a) Wholly milled rice, whether or not polished or glazed, parboiled, medium grain	65.00
				b) Rice flour or bran	
			1102 30 00 or		8.00
			ex 2302 20 10 or		
			ex 2302 20 90	c) Broken rice	
			1006 40 00	d) Husks	7.00
			ex 1213 00 00		20.00
1006 10 25	Rice in the husk (paddy or rough), parboiled, long grain, of a length/width ratio greater than 2 but less than 3	70	1006 20 15	a) Husked (brown) rice, parboiled, long grain of a length/width ratio greater than 2 but less than 3	80.00
			ex 1213 00 00	b) Husks	20.00

		71	1006 30 25	a) Semi-milled rice, whether or not polished or glazed, parboiled, long grain of a length/width ratio greater than 2 but less than 3	71.00
				b) Rice flour or bran	
			1102 30 00 or		6.00
			ex 2302 20 10 or		
			ex 2302 20 90	c) Broken rice	
			1006 40 00	d) Husks	3.00
			ex 1213 00 00		20.00
		72	1006 30 65	a) Wholly milled rice, whether or not polished or glazed, parboiled, long grain of a length/width ratio greater than 2 but less than 3	65.00
			1102 30 00 or ex 2302 20 10 or ex 2302 20 90	b) Rice flour or bran	8.00
			1006 40 00	c) Broken rice	7.00
			ex 1213 00 00	d) Husks	20.00
1006 10 27	Rice in the husk (paddy or rough), parboiled, long grain, of a length/width ratio equal to or greater than 3	73	1006 20 17	a) Husked (brown) rice, parboiled, long grain, of a length/width ratio equal to or greater than 3	80.00
			ex 1213 00 00	b) Husks	20.00

		74	1006 30 27	a) Semi-milled rice, whether or not polished or glazed, parboiled, long grain, of a length/width ratio equal to or greater than 3	68.00
			1102 30 00 or ex 2302 20 10 or ex 2302 20 90		
			1006 40 00	c) Broken rice	6.00
			ex 1213 00 00	d) Husks	20.00
			1006 30 67	a) Wholly milled rice, whether or not polished or glazed, parboiled, long grain, of a length/width ratio equal to or greater than 3	62.00
				b) Rice flour or bran	
			1102 30 00 or ex 2302 20 10		8.00
			ex 2302 20 90	c) Broken rice	
			1006 40 00		
			ex 1213 00 00	d) Husks	10.00
		75			20.00
1006 10 92	Rice in the husk (paddy or rough), round grain	76	1006 20 11	a) Husked (brown) rice, parboiled, round grain	80.00
				b) Husks	
			ex 1213 00 00		20.00
			1006 20 92	a) Husked (brown) rice, round grain	80.00
		77	ex 1213 00 00	b) Husks	20.00

			1006 30 21	a) Semi-milled rice, whether or not polished or glazed, par-boiled, round grain	71.00
			0102 30 00 or ex 2302 20 10 or ex 2302 20 90	b) Rice flour or bran	6.00
				c) Broken rice	3.00
			1006 40 00 ex 1213	
		78	00 00	d) Husks	20.00
			1006 30 42	a) Semi-milled rice, whether or not polished or glazed, round grain	65.00
			1102 30 00 or ex 2302 20 10 or ex 2302 20 90	b) Rice flour or bran	5.00
			1006 40 00	c) Broken rice	10.00
		79	ex 1213 00 00	d) Husks	20.00
			1006 30 61	a) Wholly milled rice, whether or not polished or glazed, par-boiled, round grain	65.00
			1102 30 00 or ex 2302 20 10 or ex 2302 20 90	b) Rice flour or bran	8.00
			1006 40 00	c) Broken rice	7.00
		80	ex 1213 00 00	d) Husks	20.00

Part III

		1006 30 92	a) Wholly milled rice, whether or not polished or glazed, round grain	60.00
		1102 30 00 or	b) Rice flour or bran	8.00
		ex 2302 20 10 or ex 2302 20 90		
		1006 40 00	c) Broken rice	12.00
	81	ex 1213 00 00	d) Husks	20.00
1006 10 94	Rice in the husk (paddy or rough), medium grain	1006 20 13	a) Husked (brown) rice, parboiled, medium grain	80.00 20.00
	82	ex 1213 00 00	b) Husks	20.00
		1006 20 94	a) Husked (brown) rice, medium grain	80.00
	83	ex 1213 00 00	b) Husks	20.00
		1006 30 23	a) Semi-milled rice, whether or not polished or glazed, parboiled, medium grain	71.00
		1102 30 00 or ex 2302 20 10 or ex 2302 20 90	b) Rice flour or bran	6.00
		1006 40 00	c) Broken rice	3.00
	84	ex 1213 00 00	d) Husks	20.00
		1006 30 44	a) Semi-milled rice, whether or not polished or glazed, medium grain	65.00
		1102 30 00 or ex 2302 20 10 or ex 2302 20 90	b) Rice flour or bran	5.00
		1006 40 00	c) Broken rice	10.00
	85	ex 1213 00 00	d) Husks	20.00

		1006 30 63	a) Wholly milled rice, whether or not polished or glazed, par-boiled, medium grain	65.00
		1102 30 00 or	b) Rice flour or bran	8.00
		ex 2302 20 10 or		
		ex 2302 20 90	c) Broken rice	
		1006 40 00	d) Husk	7.00
	86	ex 1213 00 00		20.00
		a) Wholly milled rice, whether or not polished or glazed, medium grain	60.00	
		1102 30 00	b) Rice flour or bran	8.00
		or ex 2302 20 10 orex 2302 20 90		
		1006 40 00	c) Broken rice	12.00
	87	ex 1213 00 00	d) Husks	20.00
Rice in the husk (paddy or rough) long grain, of a length/width	88	1006 20 15	a) Husked (brown) rice par-boiled, long grain of a length/width ratio greater than 2 but less than 3	80.00
		ex 1213 00 00	b) Husks	20.00
ratio greater than 2 but less than 3	89	1006 20 96	a) Husked (brown) rice, long grain of a length/width ratio of more than 2, but less than 3	80.00
		ex 1213 00 00	b) Husks	20.00

			1006 30 25 or ex 2302 20 10 or ex 2302 20 90 1006 40 00 ex 1213 00	a) Semi-milled rice, whether or not polished or glazed parboiled, long grain of a length/width ratio greater than 2 but less than 3	6.00
		90	00	c) Broken rice d) Husks	3.00 20.00
		91	1006 30 46 1102 30 00 or ex 2302 20 10 or ex 2302 20 90 1006 40 00 ex 1213 00 00	a) Semi-milled rice, whether or not polished or glazed, long grain of a length/width ratio greater than 2 but less than 3 b) Rice flour or bran c) Broken rice d) Husks	65.00 5.00 10.00 20.00
		92	1006 30 65 1102 30 00 or ex 2302 20 10 or ex 2302 20 90 1006 40 00 ex 1213 00 00	a) Wholly milled rice, whether or not polished or glazed, parboiled, long grain of a length/width ratio greater than 2 but less than 3 b) Rice flour or bran c) Broken rice d) Husks	65.00 8.00 7.00 20.00

		93	1006 30 96 1102 30 00 or ex 2302 20 10 or ex 2302 20 90 1006 40 00 ex 1213 00 00	a) Wholly milled rice, whether or not polished or glazed, long grain, of a length/width ratio greater than 2 but less than 3 b) Rice flour or bran c) Broken rice d) Husks	60.00 8.00 12.00 20.00
		94	1006 20 17 ex 1213 00 00	a) Husked (brown) rice parboiled, long grain, of a length/width ratio equal to or greater than 3 b) Husks	80.00 20.00
		95	1006 20 98 ex 1213 00 00	a) Husked (brown) rice, long grain of a length/width ratio greater than 3 b) Husks	80.00 20.00
		96	1006 30 27 1102 30 00 or ex 2302 20 10 or ex 2302 20 90 1006 40 00 ex 1213 00 00	a) Semi-milled rice, whether or not polished or glazed, parboiled, of a length/width ratio equal to or greater than 3 b) Rice flour or bran c) Broken rice d) Husks	68.00 6.00 6.00 20.00
1006 10 98	Rice in the husk (paddy or rough), long grain, of a length/width ratio equal to or greater than 3	97	1006 30 48 1102 30 00 or ex 2302 20 10 or ex 2302 20 90 1006 40 00 ex 1213 00 00	a) Semi-milled rice, whether or not polished or glazed, of a length/width ratio greater than 3 b) Rice flour or bran c) Broken rice d) Husks	58.00 7.00 15.00 20.00

Part III

			1006 30 67 1102 30 00 or ex 2302 20 10 or ex 2302 20 90 1006 40 00 ex 1213 00 00	a) Wholly milled rice, whether or not polished or glazed, par-boiled, long grain, of a length/width ratio equal to or greater than 3 b) Rice flour or bran c) Broken rice d) Husks	62.00 8.00 10.00 20.00
		98			
			1006 30 98 1102 30 00 or ex 2302 20 10 or ex 2302 20 90 1006 40 00 ex 1213 00 00	a) Wholly milled rice, whether or not polished or glazed, long grain, of a length/width ratio equal to or greater than 3 b) Rice flour or bran c) Broken rice d) Husks	55.00 9.00 16.00 20.00
		99			
1006 20 11	Husked (brown) rice, par-boiled, round grain	100	1006 30 21 1102 30 00 or ex 2302 20 10 or ex 2302 20 90 1006 40 00	a) Semi-milled rice, whether or not polished or glazed, par-boiled, round grain b) Rice flour or bran c) Broken rice	93.00 5.00 2.00
		101	1006 30 61 1102 30 00 or ex 2302 20 10 or ex 2302 20 90 1006 40 00	a) Wholly milled rice, whether or not polished or glazed, par-boiled, round grain b) Rice flour or bran c) Broken rice	88.00 10.00 2.00

	Husked (brown) rice, long grain, of a length/width ratio equal to or greater than 3	114	1006 30 48 1102 30 00 or ex 2302 20 10 or ex 2302 20 90 1006 40 00	a) Semi-milled rice, whether or not polished or glazed, long grain, of a length/width ratio equal to of greater than 3 — 78.00 b) Rice flour or bran — 10.00 c) Broken rice — 12.00
		115	1006 30 98 1102 30 00 or ex 2302 20 10 or ex 2302 20 90 1006 40 00	a) Wholly-milled rice, whether or not polished or glazed, long grain, of a length/width ratio equal to or greater than 3 — 73.00 b) Rice flour or bran — 12.00 c) Broken rice — 15.00
1006 30 21	Semi-milled rice, whether or not polished or glazed, parboiled, round grain	116	1006 30 61 1102 30 00 or ex 2302 20 10 or ex 2302 20 90 1006 40 00	a) Wholly milled rice, whether or not polished or glazed, parboiled, round grain — 96.00 b) Rice flour or bran — 2.00 c) Broken rice — 2.00
1006 30 23	Semi-milled rice, whether or not polished or glazed, parboiled, medium grain,	117	1006 30 63 1102 30 00 or ex 2302 20 10 or ex 2302 20 90 1006 40 00	a) Wholly milled rice, whether or not polished or glazed, parboiled, medium grain — 96.00 b) Rice flour or bran — 2.00 c) Broken rice — 2.00

1006 20 94	Husked (brown) rice, medium grain	110	1006 30 44 1102 30 00 or ex 2302 20 10 or ex 2302 20 90 1006 40 00	a) Semi-milled rice, whether or not polished or glazed, medium grain b) Rice flour or bran c) Broken rice	84.00 6.00 10.00
		111	1006 30 94 1102 30 00 or ex 2302 20 10 or ex 2302 20 90 1006 40 00	a) Wholly milled rice, whether or not polished or glazed, medium grain b) Rice flour or bran c) Broken rice	77.00 12.00 11.00
1006 20 96	Husked (brown) rice, long grain, of a length/width ratio greater than 2 but less than 3	112	1006 30 46 1102 30 00 or ex 2302 20 10 or ex 2302 20 90 1006 40 00	a) Semi-milled rice, whether or not polished or glazed, long grain, of a length/width ratio greater than 2 but less than 3 b) Rice flour or bran c) Broken rice	84.00 6.00 10.00
		113	1006 30 96 1102 30 00 or ex 2302 20 10 or ex 2302 20 90 1006 40 00	a) Wholly milled rice, whether or not polished or glazed, long grain, of a length/width ratio greater than 2 but less than 3 b) Rice flour or bran c) Broken rice	77.00 12.00 11.00

Part III

1006 20 17	Husked (brown) rice, par-boiled, long grain of a length/width ratio equal to or greater than 3	106	1006 30 27 1102 30 00 or ex 2302 20 10 or ex 2302 20 90 1006 40 00	a) Semi-milled rice, whether or not polished or glazed, par-boiled, long grain, of a length/width ratio equal to or greater than 3 93.00 b) Rice flour or bran 5.00 c) Broken rice 2.00
		107	1006 30 67 1102 30 00 or ex 2302 20 10 or ex 2302 20 90 1006 40 00	a) Wholly milled rice, whether or not polished or glazed, par-boiled, long grain, of a length/width ratio equal to or greater than 3 88.00 b) Rice flour or bran 10.00 c) Broken rice 2.00
1006 20 92	Husked (brown) rice, round grain	108	1006 30 42 1102 30 00 or ex 2302 20 10 or ex 2302 20 90 1006 40 00	a) Semi-milled rice, whether or not polished or glazed, round grain 84.00 b) Rice flour or bran 6.00 c) Broken rice 10.00
		109	1006 30 92 1102 30 00 or ex 2302 20 10 or ex 2302 20 90 1006 40 00	a) Wholly milled rice, whether or not polished or glazed, round grain 77.00 b) Rice flour or bran 12.00 c) Broken rice 11.00

1006 20 13	Husked (brown) rice, par-boiled, medium grain	102	1006 30 23 1102 30 00 or ex 2302 20 10 or ex 2302 20 90 1006 40 00	a) Semi-milled rice, whether or not polished or glazed, par-boiled, medium grain b) Rice flour or bran c) Broken rice	93.00 5.00 2.00
		103	1006 30 63 1102 30 00 or ex 2302 20 10 or ex 2302 20 90 1006 40 00	a) Wholly milled rice, whether or not polished or glazed, par-boiled, medium grain b) Rice flour or bran c) Broken rice	88.00 10.00 2.00
1006 20 15	Husked (brown) rice, par-boiled, long grain of a length/width ratio greater than 2 but less than 3	104	1006 30 25 1102 30 00 or ex 2302 20 10 or ex 2302 20 90 1006 40 00	a) Semi-milled rice, whether or not polished or glazed, par-boiled, long grain, of a length/width ratio greater than 2 but less than 3 b) Rice flour or bran c) Broken rice	93.00 5.00 2.00
		105	1006 30 65 1102 30 00 or ex 2302 20 10 or ex 2302 20 90 1006 40 00	a) Wholly milled rice, whether or not polished or glazed, par-boiled, long grain, of a length/width ratio greater than 2 but less than 3 b) Rice flour or bran c) Broken rice	88.00 10.00 2.00

Part III

	Semi-milled rice, whether or not polished or glazed, parboiled, long grain, of a length/width ratio greater than 2 but less than 3	118	1006 30 65 1102 30 00 or ex 2302 20 10 or ex 2302 20 90 1006 40 00	a) Wholly milled rice, whether or not polished or glazed, parboiled, long grain, of a length/width ratio greater than 2 but less than 3 — 96.00 b) Rice flour or bran — 2.00 c) Broken rice — 2.00
1006 30 27	Semi-milled rice, whether or not polished or glazed, parboiled, long grain, of a length/width ratio equal to or greater than 3	119	1006 30 67 1102 30 00 or ex 2302 20 10 or ex 2302 20 90 1006 40 00	a) Wholly milled rice, whether or not polished or glazed, parboiled, long grain, of a length/width ratio equal to or greater than 3 — 96.00 b) Rice flour or bran — 2.00 c) Broken rice — 2.00
1006 30 42	Semi-milled rice, whether or not polished or glazed, round grain	120	1006 30 92 1102 30 00 or ex 2302 20 10 or ex 2302 20 90 1006 40 00	a) Wholly milled rice, whether or not polished or glazed, round grain — 94.00 b) Rice flour or bran — 2.00 c) Broken rice — 4.00
1006 30 44	Semi-milled rice, whether or not polished or glazed, medium grain	121	1006 30 94 1102 30 00 or ex 2302 20 10 or ex 2302 20 90 1006 40 00	a) Wholly milled rice, whether or not polished or glazed, medium grain — 94.00 b) Rice flour or bran — 2.00 c) Broken rice — 4.00

Part III

1006 30 46	Semi-milled rice, whether or not polished or glazed, long grain of a length/width ratio greater than 2 but less than 3	122	1006 30 96 1102 30 00 or 2302 20 10 or 2302 20 90 1006 40 00	a) Wholly milled rice, whether or not polished or glazed, long grain, of a length/width ratio greater than 2 but less than 3 b) Rice flour or bran c) Broken rice	94.00 2.00 4.00
1006 30 48	Semi-milled rice, whether or not polished or glazed, long grain of a length/width ratio equal to or greater than 3	123	1006 30 98 1102 30 00 or 2302 20 10 or 2302 20 90 1006 40 00	a) Wholly milled rice, whether or not polished or glazed, long grain, of a length/width ratio equal to or greater than 3 b) Rice flour or bran c) Broken rice	93.00 2.00 5.00
1006 30 61 to 1006 30 98	Wholly milled rice	124	ex 1006 30 61 to ex 1006 30 98	Wholly milled rice, polished, glazed or pre-packed[13]	100.00
1006 30 92 1006 30 94 1006 30 96 1006 30 98	Wholly milled rice, other	125	ex 1904 10 30	Puffed rice	60.61
1006 30 61 1006 3063 1006 30 65 1006 30 67	Wholly milled rice, par-boiled	126	ex 1904 90 10	Pre-cooked rice[14]	80,00
1006 30 92 1006 30 94 1006 30 96 1006 30 98	Wholly milled rice, other	127	ex 1904 90 10	Pre-cooked rice[14]	70,00 60,00 60,00 50,00

1006 40 00	Broken rice	128	1102 30 00	Rice flour	*
		129	1103 14 00	Rice groats and meal	*
		130	1104 19 91	Rice, flaked	*
1509 10 10	Lampante virgin olive oil	131	ex 1509 90 00 ex 3823 19 90	a) Olive oil, refined, or olive oil b) Acid oils from refining[15]	98,00
ex 1510 00 10	Unrefined olive-pomace oil	132	ex 1510 00 90 ex 1522 00 39 ex 3823 19 90	a) Olive-pomace oil, refined, or olive-pomace oil b) Stearin c) Acid oils from refining[15a]	95,00 3,00
ex 1801 00 00	Cocoa beans, whole or broken, raw	133	ex 1801 00 00 1802 00 00	a) Cocoa beans, whole or broken, shelled and roasted b) Cocoa shells, husks, skins and waste	76,3 16,7
1801 00 00	Cocoa beans, whole or broken, raw or	134	1803 1802 00 00	a) Cocoa paste~ b) Cocoa shells, husks, skins and waste	76,3 16,7
	roasted	135	ex 1803 20 00 ex 1804 00 00 1802 00 00	a) Cocoa paste, containing not more than 14% of fats b) Cocoa butter c) Cocoa shells, husks, skins and waste	40,3 36,0 16,7
		136	ex 1803 20 00 ex 1804 00 00 1802 00 00	a) Cocoa paste, containing more than 14% but not more than 18% of fats b) Cocoa butter c) Cocoa shells, husks, skins and waste	42,7 33,6 16,7
		137	ex 1803 20 00 ex 1804 00 00 1802 00 00	a) Cocoa paste, containing more than 18% of fats b) Cocoa butter c) Cocoa shells, husks, skins and waste	44,8 31,5 16,7
		138	ex 1804 00 00 ex 1805 00 00 1802 00 00	a) Cocoa butter b) Cocoa powder, containing not more than 14% of fats[16] c) Cocoa shells, husks, skins and waste	36,0 40,3 16,7
1801 00 00 (cont'd)		139	ex 1804 00 00 ex 1805 00 00 1802 00 00	a) Cocoa butter b) Cocoa powder, containing more than 14% but not more than 18% of fats[16] c) Cocoa shells, husks, skins and waste	33,6 42,7 16,7

Part III

		140	ex 1804 00 00 ex 1805 00 00 1802 00 00	a) Cocoa butter b) Cocoa powder, containing more than 18% of fats[16] c) Cocoa shells, husks, skins and waste	31,5 44,8 16,7
1803 10 00	Cocoa paste not defatted	141	ex 1804 00 00 ex 1803 20 00	a) Cocoa butter b) Cocoa paste, containing not more than 14% of fats	46,7 52,2
		142	ex 1804 00 00 ex 1803 20 00	a) Cocoa butter b) Cocoa paste, containing more than 14% but not more than 18% of fats	43,6 55,3
		143	ex 1804 00 00 ex 1803 20 00	a) Cocoa butter b) Cocoa paste, containing more than 18% of fats	40,8 58,1
		144	ex 1804 00 00 ex 1805 00 00	a) Cocoa butter b) Cocoa powder, containing not more than 14% of fats[16]	46,7 52,2
		145	ex 1804 00 00 ex 1805 00 00	a) Cocoa butter b) Cocoa powder, containing more than 14% but not more than 18% of fats[16]	43,6 55,3
1803 10 00 (cont'd)		146	ex 1804 00 00 ex 1805 00 00	a) Cocoa butter b) Cocoa paste, containing more than 18% of fats[16]	40,8 58,1
1803 20 00	Cocoa paste, defatted	147	1805 00 00	Cocoa powder	99,0
1701 99 10	White sugar	148	2905 44 19 or 2905 44 91 2905 44 99 3824 60 19 3824 60 91 3824 60 99 2905 43 00	a) D-Glucitol (sorbitol) relative to 100 kg of the dry matter b) D-Mannitol (mannitol)	73,53 24,51
1703	Molasses	149	2102 10 31	Dried bakers' yeasts[17]	23,53
		150	2102 10 39	Other bakers' yeasts[17][18]	80,00]

* The standard rate of yield shall be calculated on the basis of the corresponding conversion coefficient set out in Annex E of Commission Regulation (EC) No 1520/2000 (OJ No L 177, 15.7.2000, p.1).

[1] The subheadings in this column correspond to those in the combined nomenclature. When further subdivision has been necessary this is shown in parentheses(). These subdivisions correspond to those used in the regulations fixing export refunds.

[2] Losses are calculated by subtracting from 100 the sum of the quantities shown in this column.

[3] Hulled grains are grains corresponding to the definition given in Annex to Regulation (EEC) No 821/68 (OJ No L 149, 29.6.1968, p. 46).

[4] Cereal meal with an ash content, referred to dry matter, of less than 0,95% by weight and a rate of passage through a sieve with an aperture of 0,25 mm of less than 10% by weight.

[5] The standard rate of yield to be applied is based on the number of eggs used per kg of pasta produced, using the following formula—

[5]

$$\text{Numerical order25: } T = \frac{100}{160 - (X \times 1.6)} \times 100$$

[5] >

$$\text{Numerical order25: } T = \frac{100}{150 - (X \times 1.6)} \times 100$$

[5]

$$\text{Numerical order25: } T = \frac{100}{140 - (X \times 1.6)} \times 100$$

[5]

$$\text{Numerical order25: } T = \frac{100}{126 - (X \times 1.6)} \times 100$$

[5] X represents the number of eggs in shell (or the 50th of their weight expressed in grams of their equivalent in other egg products) uses per kg of pasta produced, the result being given to two decimal points.

[6] Pearled grains are grains corresponding to the definition given in the Annex to Regulation (EEC) No 821/68 (OJ No L 149, 29.6.1968, p. 46).

[7] This concerns maize groats and meal—

— of which a percentage not exceeding 30% by weight passes through a sieve with an aperture of 315 micrometers, or

— of which a percentage not exceeding 5% by weight passes through a sieve with an aperture of 150 micrometers.

[8] For glucose in the form of white crystalline powder, of a concentration other than 92%, the quantity to be shown is 43,81 kilograms of D-glucitol anhydrate per 100 kilograms of maize.

[9] For glucose other than in the form of white crystalline powder, of a concentration other than 82%, the quantity to be shown is 50,93 kilograms of D-glucitol anhydrate per 100 kilograms of maize.

[10] For D-glucitol, of a concentration other than 70%, the quantity to be shown is 41,4 kilograms of D-glucitol per 100 kilograms of maize.

[11] For D-glucitol, of a concentration other than 70%, the quantity to be shown is 47,3 kilograms of D-glucitol anhydrate per 100 kilograms of maize.

[12] For the application of the alternatives (a) to (f), the real results from the operations have to be taken into account.

[13] For the purposes of completing the arrangements, the quantity of broken rice obtained shall correspond to the quantity of broken rice as determined at the time of importation for processing of rice under CN codes 1006 30 61 to 1006 30 98. In the case of polishing, this quantity shall be increased by 2% of the imported rice excluding the broken rice as determined at importation.

[14] Pre-cooked rice is constituted by bleached rice in grains undergoing a pre-cooking and partial dehydration intended to facilitate final cooking.

[15] Twice the percentage expressed as oleic acid of the lampante virgin olive oil shall be deducted from the quantity of product shown in column 5 for refined olive oil/olive oil and shall constitute the quantity of acid oil of refining.

Part III

[15a] Twice the percentage expressed as oleic acid of the unrefined olive-residue oil shall be deducted from the quantity of product shown in column 5 for refined olive-residue oil/olive-residue oil and shall constitute the quantity of acid oil of refining.

[16] In the case of soluble cocoa, add 1,5% alkaline to the quantity shown in column 5.

[17] Yield fixed for bakers' yeast, with a content in the dry matter of 95%, obtained from beet molasses brought to 48% of total sugar, or of cane molasses brought to 52% of total sugar. For bakers' yeasts with a different content in the dry matter, the quantity to be shown is 22,4 kilograms of yeast anhydrate per 100 kilograms of beet molasses brought to 48% of total sugar, or of cane molasses brought to 52% of total sugar.

[18] Yield fixed for bakers' yeast, with a content in the dry matter of 28%, obtained from beet molasses brought to 48% of total sugar, or of cane molasses brought to 52% of total sugar. For bakers' yeasts with a different content in the dry matter, the quantity to be shown is 22,4 kilograms of yeast anhydrate per 100 kilograms of beet molasses brought to 48% of total sugar, or of cane molasses brought to 52% of total sugar.

NOTES

Substituted as noted to Annex 67.

Figures substituted, and words repealed, by Commission Regulation (EC) 444/2002, Art 1, para 30, Annex III.

Annex amended by Corrigendum (see OJ L 175, 28.6.2001, p 27).

[ANNEX 70
ECONOMIC CONDITIONS AND ADMINISTRATIVE CO-OPERATION
(Articles 502 and 522)

1. GENERAL PROVISIONS

This annex deals on the one hand with the detailed criteria for economic conditions applicable to the inward processing arrangements and on the other hand with information to be exchanged in the framework of the administrative co-operation.

The cases, the format and the time limit within which information must be provided in accordance with Article 522 are indicated for each of the arrangements concerned. Information must also be communicated where the information concerning authorisations granted is modified.

2. DETAILED CRITERIA FOR ECONOMIC CONDITIONS APPLICABLE TO THE INWARD PROCESSING ARRANGEMENTS

Codes and detailed criteria

[01: Where import goods not mentioned in Annex 73 are concerned and Code 30 does not apply.]

10: unavailability of goods produced in the Community falling within the same eight-digit CN code, being of the same commercial quality and having the same technical characteristics (comparable goods) as the import goods referred to in the application.

The unavailability covers the total absence of Community production of comparable goods, the unavailability of a sufficient quantity of those goods in order to carry out the processing operations envisaged or the fact that comparable Community goods cannot be made available to the applicant in time for the proposed commercial operation to be carried out, despite a request having been made in good time.

11: although available, comparable goods can not be used because their price would make the proposed commercial operation economically unviable.

In deciding whether the price of comparable goods produced in the Community would make the proposed commercial operation economically unviable, it shall be necessary to take account *inter alia* of the impact that the use of Community-produced goods would have on the cost price of the compensating product and hence on the disposal of the product on the third-country market, having regard to—

The information intended to complete the columns 2 to 10 of the form reproduced in the appendix is communicated electronically to the Commission. This information may only be communicated using the form reproduced in the appendix where technical problems make its electronic communication temporarily impossible.

Communication time limit

Information are communicated as soon as possible. If the form reproduced in the appendix is used, the information is communicated within the time limit indicated thereon.

1.2.Processing under customs control

Information shall be communicated where types of goods and operations other than those mentioned in Annex 76 Part A are concerned.

Information shall be communicated using the form reproduced in the appendix within the time indicated thereon.

1.3.Outward processing

Column (8) and (9) "Authorisations granted" are only to be filled in where an authorisation is granted in accordance with Article 147 (2) of the Code.

In column (10) "Reason", it shall be also mentioned if the rejection of the application, annulment or revocation of the authorisation concern an application submitted or an authorisation granted in accordance with Article 147 (2) of the Code.

Information shall be communicated using the form reproduced in the appendix within the time indicated thereon.

---

[1] The value is the value for customs purposes of the goods estimated on the basis of the known particulars and on the basis of the documents submitted at the time of the submission of the request.

APPENDIX TO ANNEX 70

Part III

— the price before duty of the goods for processing and the price of comparable goods produced in the Community less domestic taxes refunded or refundable on export, taking into account the conditions of sale and any refunds or other amounts applying under common agricultural policy,

— the price obtainable for the compensating products on the third-country market, as ascertained from commercial correspondence or other information.

12: comparable goods do not conform to the expressly stated requirements of the third-country purchaser of the compensating products or the compensating products must be obtained from import goods in order to comply with provisions concerning the protection of industrial or commercial property rights (contractual obligations).

30:
1. operations involving import goods of a non-commercial nature;
2. operations carried out under a job-processing contract;
3. usual forms of handling referred to in Article 531;
4. repair;
5. processing operations on compensating products obtained under a previous inward processing authorisation the granting of which was subject to an examination of the economic conditions;
6. processing of durum wheat falling within CN code 1001 10 00 to produce pasta falling within CN codes 1902 11 00 and 1902 19;
7. operations in which the value[1] of the import goods, by eight-digit CN code, does not exceed 150 000 euro for goods listed in Annex 73 or 500 000 euro for other goods, per applicant and per calendar year (de minimis value); [or]
8. [building, modification or conversion of civil aircraft or satellites or parts of them.]

[31: Where, according to Article 11 of Council Regulation (EC) 3448/93, import goods referred to under part A of Annex 73 are concerned and the applicant presents a document issued by a competent authority permitting the entry for the arrangements for those goods, in the limits of a quantity determined with the aid of a supply balance.]

99: the applicant considers the economic conditions to be fulfilled for reasons other than those corresponding to the previous codes. The said reasons are indicated in his application.

[Note: The Codes 10, 11, 12, 31 and 99 may be used only, where the goods mentioned in Annex 73 are concerned.]

3. INFORMATION TO BE PROVIDED TO THE COMMISSION FOR EACH ARRANGEMENT CONCERNED

The information to be communicated to the Commission corresponds to the boxes of the form the model of which is reproduced in the appendix.

1.1.Inward processing

The information concerning the economic conditions shall be provided by using one or more of the codes laid down under part B.

The reason for the rejection of the application or for annulment or revocation of the authorisation for non-observance of the economic conditions is indicated by using code(s). The same codes as those used to identify the economic conditions are used, preceded by the sign of negation (for example: — 10).

Cases in which information is mandatory

[Where the economic conditions are identified by codes 01, 10, 11, 31 or 99.]

[For milk and milk products referred to in Article 1 of Council Regulation (EC) No 1255/1999 information is also mandatory where code 30 is used in relation with the situations referred to under subdivisions 2, 5 and 7 of this code.]

Communication of information

NOTES

Substituted as noted to Annex 67.

Part 2, Code 01: inserted by Commission Regulation (EC) 881/2003 Art 1, para 35, Annex IX para (a).

Part 2, Code 30: word after para (7) inserted, para (8) substituted, and para (9) repealed, by Commission Regulation (EC) 881/2003 Art 1, para 35, Annex IX paras (b)–(d).

Part 2, Code 31: inserted by Commission Regulation (EC) 881/2003 Art 1, para 35, Annex IX para (e).

Part 2, Note: inserted by Commission Regulation (EC) 881/2003 Art 1, para 35, Annex IX para (f).

Part 3, para 1.1: words substituted by Commission Regulation (EC) 881/2003 Art 1, para 35, Annex IX para (g).

Appendix: words in columns 3, 4 substituted, and footnote (d) substituted, by Commission Regulation (EC) 881/2003 Art 1, para 35, Annex IX para (h)–(j).

[ANNEX 71

INFORMATION SHEETS

(Article 523)

EUROPEAN COMMUNITY

Part III

Member State ....

(Information to be provided before the end of the month following the month during which the decision is taken)

Arrangements concerned^a
[ ] Inward processing
[ ] Processing under customs control
[ ] Outward processing

MONTH (number/year) ..../.........

Order Number	Goods to be processed/transformed			Main compensating/ processed products	Economic conditions^b Code(s)	Equivalence^c	Authorisations granted		Application rejected Authorisations annulled/revoked
	CN Code	[Value]	[Quantity]^d	CN code			Date of beginning of authorisation	Date of expiry of authorisation	Reason
(1)	(2)	(3)	(4)	(5)	(6)	(7)	(8)	(9)	(10)

a A separate form must be filled for each one of the arrangements concerned. Put a cross in the corresponding box.

b To be filled in only for the inward processing arrangements. Indicate the economic conditions by using the codes in accordance with part B of the Annex.

c To be filled in only for inward processing authorisations for import goods referred to in Article 1 of Council Regulation (EC) No 1255/99. Indicate "yes" or "no".

[d Quantity: UN/CEFACT codes, for ex. (a) weight in tonnes (TNE), (b) number of articles (NAR), (c) volume in hectolitre (HLT), (d) length in metre (MTR).]

EUROPEAN COMMUNITY

1. Declarant:	**INF8** ORIGINAL	INFORMATION SHEET No / 0 0 0 0 0 0 **CUSTOMS WAREHOUSES / FREE ZONES / FREE WAREHOUSES** **USUAL FORMS OF HANDLING**

| 2. Customs office to which application is made: | |

| 4. Customs office to which the information is addressed: | 3. APPLICATION |

The undersigned requests determination of the nature, customs value and quantity of the goods referred to in box 9 which would be taken into consideration if the goods concerned had not undergone the handling referred to in box 8.

Place:

Date: | | | | | | |
day month year

5. Holder of the authorisation/approval:

Signature:

6. Identification number:	7. Document with which goods are removed from the customs warehouse or the free zone or free warehouse:
8. Nature of the handling:	Nature: No: Date: Customs office:
Date on which it took place:	

9. Marks and numbers; number and kind of packages. Description of goods:	10. Net quantity:

Particulars to be taken into consideration for determination of the customs debt in respect of the goods referred to in box 9, if they had not undergone the usual forms of handling referred to in box 8:

11. Nature:	12. Customs value:	13. Quantity:

14. Stamp of the customs office where the declaration for release for free circulation is lodged (see box 4) Place and date: Signature and stamp:	15. Stamp of the customs office which provided the information (see box 2) Place and Date: Signature and stamp:

Part III

© European Communities Official Journal L 273, 11/10/1993 Annex 71

NOTES

A. **General notes**

The form must be completed legibly and indelibly, preferably by typewriter. It must not contain any erasures or overwritten words. Corrections should be made by crossing out the wrong words and adding any necessary particulars. Corrections must be initialled by the person completing the sheet and endorsed by the customs office.

Boxes 1 to 10 of the sheet must be completed in by the person declaring the goods, which have undergone usual forms of handling, for free circulation or another procedure which could imply the creation of a customs debt or, where the sheet is drawn up at the time of removal of the goods from the customs warehouse or from the free zone or free warehouse, for another customs procedure.

B. **Special notes referring to the relevant box numbers**

1. Give the name and address

2. and 4. Give the name, address of the customs office. Box 4 is not to be completed where the form is made out when goods are removed from the customs warehouse, free zone or free warehouse;

5. Give the name and address:

 — of the holder, or

 — of the holder of the approval of stock records in the free zone or the free warehouse where the usual forms of handling were carried out

6. Give the identification number of the customs warehouse or reference particulars of the approval of stock records in a free zone or free warehouse, as appropriate.

7. Box 7 is not to be completed where the form is made out before the goods are removed from the customs warehouse, free zone or free warehouse

NOTES

A. General notes

1. The form must be filled in legibly and indelibly, preferably by typewriter. It must not contain any erasures or overwritten words. Corrections should be made by crossing out the wrong words and adding any necessary particulars. Corrections must be initialled by the person filling in the sheet and endorsed by the customs office.

2. Boxes 1 to 10 of the sheet must be filled in by the person declaring the goods, which have undergone usual forms of handling, for free circulation or another procedure which could imply the creation of a customs debt or, where the sheet is drawn up at the time of removal of the goods from the customs warehouse or from the free zone or free warehouse, for another customs procedure.

B. Special notes referring to the relevant box numbers.

1. give the name and address;

2./4. give the name, address of the customs office. Box 4 is not to be filled in where the form is made out at

when goods are removed from the customs warehouse, free zone or free warehouse;

5. give the name and address;

– of the holder, or

 – of the holder of the approval of stock records in the free zone or the free warehouse where the usual forms of handling were carried out;

6. give the identification number of the customs warehouse or reference particulars of the approval of stock records in a free zone or free warehouse, as appropriate.

7. Box 7 not to be filled in where the form is made out before the goods are removed from the customs warehouse, free zone or free warehouse.

EUROPEAN COMMUNITY

EUROPEAN COMMUNITY

1. Holder:	**INF 1**	INFORMATION SHEET No / 0 0 0 0 0 0 INWARD PROCESSING

3. APPLICATION (¹)

The undersigned holder requests:

☐ transfer

2. Application to be made to:

The customs office shown in box 4 requests:

☐ that the amount of imports duties and of compensatory interest applicable to the goods entered for the arrangements in the event of the authorised release for free circulation of the goods or products specified in box 5 be ascertained and indicated

☐ commercial policy measures be indicated

☐ that the amount of the security be indicated.

4. Information to be supplied to:

Date: |__|__|__|__|__|__| Stamp
    day month year

Signature:

5. Marks and numbers – Number and kind of packages. Description of products or goods:	6. Net quantity:	7. CN code:

INFORMATION SUPPLIED BY THE CUSTOMS OFFICE

8. Particulars necessary for application of specific commercial policy measures:

9. Liability to:

(a) Import duties	(b) Compensatory interest	(c) Other charges (²)	(d) Currency

10. Remarks:

11. Date (¹):

☐ for the first entering for the arrangements or

☐ where the import duties have been repaid or remitted in accordance with Article 128(1) of the Code:

|__|__|__|__|__|__|
day month year

(¹) Mark ☒ in the appropriate box.
(²) Specify as appropriate in box 10.

12. Place:

Date: |__|__|__|__|__|__| Stamp
    day month year

Signature:

© European Communities Official Journal L 273, 11/10/1993 Annex 71

Part III

▼ M20

---

13. Request for post-clearance verification

The customs authorities shown below request that the authenticity of this information sheet and the accuracy of the information it contains be verified.

Place:

Date: | | | | | | Stamp:
day   month   year

Signature:

Name and address of the custom authorities:

---

14. Results of verification

The check carried out by the customs authorities shown below confirm that this information sheet ([1]):

☐ has been stamped by the customs office indicated and the information it contains is accurate.

☐ gives rise to the remarks given below.

Place:

Date: | | | | | | Stamp:
day   month   year

Signature:

Name and address of the custom authorities:

---

15. Remarks

([1]) Mark ☒ in the appropriate box.

NOTES

A. General notes

1. The part of the sheet requesting information (boxes 1 to 7) shall be completed either by the holder or by the office requesting the information.

2. The form must be completed so that it is legible and indelible, preferably using a typewriter. It shall not contain any erasures or overwritten words. Corrections should be made by crossing out the wrong words and adding further particulars, if necessary. Corrections must be initialled by the person completing in the sheet and endorsed by the customs office.

B. Special notes referring to the relevant box numbers

1. Give the name, address and the name of the Member State. This item may be left blank when the application is made by the customs office of the member state requesting the information.

2. Give the name, address and the name of the Member State of the customs office to whom the application is made

4. Give the name, address and the name of the Member State of the customs office requesting the information. This item is left blank when the application is made by the holder.

5. Give the number, kind, marks and numbers of packages. In the case of unpackaged goods or products, give the number of objects, or, if appropriate, insert 'in bulk'.

   Give the usual trade description of the products or goods or their tariff description.

6. The net quantity must be expressed in units of the metric system: kg, litres, m^2, etc.

9. The amounts shall be entered in euro or national currency.

   Where appropriate, the Member State where the products are released for free circulation shall convert the amount shown on the information sheet at the rate used for calculating the customs value.

   Currencies are to be indicated as follows:

   — EUR for euro
   — GBP for pound sterling
   — CYP for Cyprus pounds
   — HUF for Hungarian forint
   — SIT for Slovenian tolars

   — DKK for Danish krone
   — CZK for Czech koruna
   — LVL for Latvian lati
   — MTL for Maltese lira
   — SKK for Slovak koruny

   — SEK for Swedish krona
   — EEK for Estonian kroons
   — LTL for Lithuanian litaї
   — PLN for Polish zloty

10. Fiscal changes may, for instance, be specified.

NOTES

A. General notes

1. The part of the sheet requesting information (boxes 1 to 7) shall be filled in either by the holder or by the office requesting the information.

EUROPEAN COMMUNITY

1. Holder:	INFORMATION SHEET **INF 9** No/000000 Original	INWARD PROCESSING TRIANGULAR TRAFFIC IM/EX

	Person to be contacted:

2. Person authorised to discharge the arrangements:	3. Authorisation issued
Person to be contacted:	at on
	day month year
	under No:
	and valid until inclusive
	day month year

4. Description of import goods:	5. CN code:	6. Net quantity:

7. Description of compensating products:	8. CN code:

9. Name and address of supervising office:	10. Name and address of office of discharge:

INFORMATION TO BE SUPPLIED UPON ENTRY FOR THE ARRANGEMENTS

11. The declaration of entry was accepted:
day month year

Stamp:

Last day for discharge:
day month year

Identification measures or measures to control the use of equivalent goods:

Office of entry:

INFORMATION TO BE SUPPLIED UPON DISCHARGE

12. The declaration of discharge was accepted:	13. Net quantity:	14. Customs value:	15. Currency:
day month year			

Remarks:

Office of discharge:

Stamp:

© European Communities Official Journal L 273, 11/10/1993 Annex 71

1946

2. The form must be filled in so that it is legible and indelible, preferably using a typewriter. It shall not contain any erasures or overwritten words. Corrections should be made by crossing out the wrong words and adding further particulars, if necessary. Corrections must be initialled by the person filling in the sheet and endorsed by the customs office.

B. Special notes referring to the relevant box numbers

1. Give the name, address and the name of the Member State. This item may be left blank when the application is made by the customs office of the Member State requesting the information.

2. Give the name, address and the name of the Member State, of the customs office requesting the information.

4. Give the name, address and the name of the Member State of the customs office to whom the application is made. This item is left blank when the application is made by the holder.

5. Give the number, kind, marks and numbers of packages. In the case of unpackaged goods or products, give the number of objects, or, if appropriate, insert 'bulk'.

Give the usual trade description of the products or goods or their tariff description.

6. The net quantity must be expressed in units of the metric system: kg, litres, m², etc.

9. The amounts shall be entered in Euro or national currency.

Where appropriate, the Member State where the products are released for free circulation shall convert the amount shown on the information sheet at the rate used for calculating the customs value.

Currencies are to be indicated as follows—

— EUR for Euro
— DKK for Danish Krone
— SEK for Swedish Krona
— GBP for Pound Sterling
[— CZK for Czech koruna
— EEK for Estonian kroons
— CYP for Cyprus pounds
— LVL for Latvian lati
— LTL for Lithuanian litai
— HUF for Hungarian forint
— MTL for Maltese lira
— PLN for Polish zloty
— SIT for Slovenian tolars
— SKK for Slovak koruny],
[— BGN for Bulgarian Lev
— RON for New Romanian Leu]

10. Fiscal charges may, for instance, be specified.

EUROPEAN COMMUNITY

▼ **M20**

16. Request for post-clearance verification	
The customs authorities shown below request that the authenticity of this information sheet and the accuracy of the information it contains be verified.	
Place:	Stamp:
Date: [day	month	year]	
Signature:	Name and address of the customs authorities:

17. Results of verification	
The verification carried out by the customs authorities shown below confirm that this information sheet ([1]) was stamped by the customs office indicated and the information it contains	
☐ is accurate	
☐ gives rise to the remarks given below.	
Place:	Name and address of the customs authorities
Date: [day	month	year] Stamp:	
Signature:	

18. Discharge of compensating products

Indicate the quantity available in boxes A and the quantity discharged in boxes B.

Quantities	Type, number and date of the declaration of discharge	Quantities (continuation)	Type, number and date of the declaration of discharge	Quantities (continuation)	Type, number and date of the declaration of discharge
A		A		A	
B		B		B	

19. Remarks:

([1]) Place a cross ☒ in the appropriate box.

NOTES

A. **General notes**

1. Boxes 1 to 8 are to be completed by the holder.

2. The form must be completed legibly and indelibly, preferably by typewriter. It must not contain any erasures or overwritten words. Corrections should be made by crossing out the wrong words and adding any necessary particulars. Corrections must be initialled by the person completing the sheet and endorsed by the customs office which issued it.

B. **Special notes referring to the relevant box numbers**

1. and 2. Give the name, address and the name of the Member State. In the case of a legal person the name of the person responsible should also be given

6. and 13. The net quantity must be expressed in units of the metric system: kg, litres, m^2, etc.

14. Currencies are to be indicated as follows:

— EUR for euro	— DKK for Danish krone	— SEK for Swedish krona
— GBP for pound sterling	— CZK for Czech koruna	— EEK for Estonian kroons
— CYP for Cyprus pounds	— LVL for Latvian lati	— LTL for Lithuanian litaï
— HUF for Hungarian forint	— MTL for Maltese lira	— PLN for Polish zloty
— SIT for Slovenian tolars	— SKK for Slovak koruny	

NOTES

A. General notes

1. Boxes 1 to 8 are to be filled in by the holder.

2. The form must be filled in legibly and indelibly, preferably by typewriter. It must not contain any erasures or overwritten words. Corrections should be made by crossing out the wrong words and adding any necessary particulars. Corrections must

be initialled by the person filling in the sheet and endorsed by the customs office which issued it.

B. Special notes referring to the relevant box numbers:

1/2.   Give the name, address and the name of the Member State. In the case of a legal person the name of the person responsible should also be given.

6/13.   The net quantity must be expressed in units of the metric system: kg, litres, m2, etc.

15.   Currencies are to be indicated as follows—

— EUR for Euro
— DKK for Danish Krone
— SEK for Swedish Krona
— GBP for Pound Sterling
[— CZK for Czech koruna
— EEK for Estonian kroons
— CYP for Cyprus pounds
— LVL for Latvian lati
— LTL for Lithuanian litai
— HUF for Hungarian forint
— MTL for Maltese lira
— PLN for Polish zloty
— SIT for Slovenian tolars
— SKK for Slovak koruny.]
[— BGN for Bulgarian Lev
— RON for New Romanian Leu]

EUROPEAN COMMUNITY

▼ <u>M20</u>

EUROPEAN COMMUNITY

1. Holder:	**INF5**	INFORMATION SHEET
		No / 0 0 0 0 0 0
Person to be contacted:		INWARD PROCESSING
		TRIANGULAR TRAFFIC (EX/IM)

2. Importer authorised to enter the goods described in box 4 for the arrangements:

3. Authorisation issued:

at

on | | | | | |
 day month year

under No

Person to be contacted:

and valid until | | | | | | inclusive
 day month year

4. Description of import goods to be entered for the arrangements:

5. CN code:

6. Net quantity:

7. Name and address of supervising office:

8. Name and address of the office of entry:

INFORMATION TO BE SUPPLIED ON EXPORT

9. The declaration for prior export of the compensating products corresponding to the goods described in box 4 was accepted:

| | | | | |
day month year

Last day for import: | | | | | |
 day month year

Identification measures taken:

Customs office of export:

Stamp:

10. The compensating products left the customs territory of the Community:

| | | | | |
day month year

Remarks:

Customs office of exit:

Stamp:

INFORMATION TO BE SUPPLIED ON IMPORT

| 11. The declaration of entry was accepted: | 12. Net quantity: | 13. Customs value: | 14. Currency: |
| | | | |

| | | | |
day month year

Remarks:

Office of entry:

Stamp:

Part III

▼ **M20**

15. Request for post-clearance verification

The customs authorities shown below request that the authenticity of this information sheet and the accuracy of the information it contains be verified.

Place:

Date: |_|_|_|_|_|_| Stamp:
     day month year

| | Name and address of the customs authorities: |

Signature:

16. Results of verification

The verification check carried out by the customs authorities shown below confirm that this information sheet ([1]):

☐ was stamped by the customs office indicated and the information it contains is accurate

☐ gives rise to the remarks given below

Place:

Date: |_|_|_|_|_|_| Stamp:
     day month year

| | Name and address of the customs authorities: |

Signature:

15. Entry of non-Community goods into the arrangements

Indicate the quantity available in boxes A and the quantity placed under the arrangements in boxes B.

Quantities	Type, number and date of the declaration of entry	Quantities (continuation)	Type, number and date of the declaration of entry	Quantities (continuation)	Type, number and date of the declaration of entry
A		A		A	
B		B		B	

18. Remarks

([1]) Place a cross ☒ in the appropriate box.

NOTES

A. **General notes**

1. Boxes 1 to 8 are to be completed by the holder.

2. The form must be completed legibly and indelibly, preferably by typewriter. It must not contain any erasures or overwritten words. Corrections should be made by crossing out the wrong words and adding any necessary particulars. Corrections must be initialled by the person completing the sheet and endorsed by the customs office which issued it.

B. **Special notes referring to the relevant box numbers**

1. and 2. Give the name, address and the name of the Member State. In the case of a legal person the name of the person responsible should also be given

6. and 12. The net quantity must be expressed in units of the metric system: kg, litres, m^2, etc.

14. Currencies are to be indicated as follows:

— EUR for euro	— DKK for Danish krone	— SEK for Swedish krona
— GBP for pound sterling	— CZK for Czech koruna	— EEK for Estonian kroons
— CYP for Cyprus pounds	— LVL for Latvian lati	— LTL for Lithuanian litaï
— HUF for Hungarian forint	— MTL for Maltese lira	— PLN for Polish zloty
— SIT for Slovenian tolars	— SKK for Slovak koruny	

NOTES

A. **General notes**

1. Boxes 1 to 8 are to be filled in by the holder.

2. The form must be filled in legibly and indelibly, preferably by typewriter. It must not contain any erasures or overwritten words. Corrections should be made by crossing out the wrong words and adding any necessary particulars. Corrections must

---

EUROPEAN COMMUNITY

1 Holder:	**INF7**	INFORMATION SHEET
		No / 0 0 0 0 0 0
Person to be contacted:		INWARD PROCESSING

2 Declarant:	3 Customs office of issue:

4 Inward processing authorisation reference:	Notes:
5 Number and date of previous authorisation and issuing Member State:	

6 Compensating Products

7 Description:	8 Net quantity (¹):

9 Customs-approved treatment or use and document references.

10 Goods entered for the arrangements:

11 Description:	12 Net quantity (¹):

11 Description:	12 Net quantity (¹):

11 Description:	12 Net quantity (¹):

STAMP OF ISSUING CUSTOMS OFFICE	13 Place and date:
Information certified correct	Declarant's signature:
Place and date: Signature and stamp:	

(¹) Kilograms, litres, number of pieces.   © European Communities Official Journal L 273, 11/10/1993 Annex 71

be initialled by the person filling in the sheet and endorsed by the customs office which issued it.

B.   Special notes referring to the relevant box numbers:

1./2.   Give the name, address and the name of the Member State. In the case of a legal person the name of the person responsible should also be given.

6./12.   The net quantity must be expressed in units of the metric system: kg, litres, m2, etc.

14.   Currencies are to be indicated as follows—

—	EUR for Euro
—	DKK for Danish Krone
—	SEK for Swedish Krona
—	GBP for Pound Sterling
[—	CZK for Czech koruna
—	EEK for Estonian kroons
—	CYP for Cyprus pounds
—	LVL for Latvian lati
—	LTL for Lithuanian litai
—	HUF for Hungarian forint
—	MTL for Maltese lira
—	PLN for Polish zloty
—	SIT for Slovenian tolars
—	SKK for Slovak koruny.]
[—	BGN for Bulgarian Lev
—	RON for New Romanian Leu]

EUROPEAN COMMUNITY

EUROPEAN COMMUNITY

1. Holder:	**INF6** INFORMATION SHEET No / 0 0 0 0 0 0 TEMPORARY IMPORTATION

2. Customs office to which application is made:	3. Application (¹) The undersigned, ☐ holder ☐ representative of the holder

requests the issue of this information sheet
☐ Transit
☐ Transfer

4. Customs office to which information is addressed:	Place: Date: ⌊_⌊_⌊_⌊_⌊_⌊_⌋ day month year

5. Date on which goods were entered for the arrangements: ⌊_⌊_⌊_⌊_⌊_⌊_⌋ day month year	Signature:

6. Latest date for re-exportation ⌊_⌊_⌊_⌊_⌊_⌊_⌋ day month year	7. Under which article of Regulation:

	8. Marks and numbers; number and kind of packages. Description of goods:	9. CN code:
A		10. Net quantity:
		11. Customs value:
	8. Marks and numbers; number and kind of packages. Description of goods:	9. CN code:
B		10. Net quantity:
		11. Customs value:

INFORMATION SUPPLIED BY THE CUSTOMS OFFICE

12. Identification measures taken:

13. Amount of duties collected (in the currency of the Member State supplying the information)

A ⌊_⌊_⌊_⌊_⌊_⌊_⌊_⌊_⌋   B ⌊_⌊_⌊_⌊_⌊_⌊_⌊_⌊_⌋

14. Period taken into account for collection: month(s)	Office of discharge Place:
15. Remarks Authentification office: Place: Date: ⌊_⌊_⌊_⌊_⌊_⌊_⌋ day month year	Date: ⌊_⌊_⌊_⌊_⌊_⌊_⌋ day month year Signature: ☐ Re-exportation (¹) ☐ Release for free circulation (¹) ☐ Other customs arrangements allowed (¹)
Signature: Stamp:	Stamp:

(¹) Place a cross ☒ in the appropriate box.

EUROPEAN COMMUNITY

Part III

14. **Request for post-clearance verification**

The customs authorities shown below request that the authenticity of this information sheet and the accuracy of the information it contains be verified.

Name and address of the customs authorities:	Place and date:
	Signature and stamp:

15. **Results of verification**

The check carried out by the customs authorities shown below confirm that this information sheet (¹):

☐ has been stamped by the customs office indicated and the information it contains is accurate.

☐ gives rise to the remarks given below.

Name and address of the customs authorities:	Place and date:
	Signature and stamp:

16. **Remarks:**

(¹) Place a cross ☒ in the appropriate box.

▼M20

16. **Request for post-clearance verification**

The customs authorities shown below request that the authenticity of this information sheet and the accuracy of the information it contains be verified.

Place:

Date: | | | | | | Stamp:
    day   month   year

Name and address of the customs authorities:

Signature:

17. **Result of verification**

The verification check carried out by the customs authorities shown below confirm that this information sheet (¹):

☐ has been stamped by the customs office indicated and the information it contains is accurate,

☐ gives rise to the remarks given below.

Place:

Date: | | | | | | Stamp:
    day   month   year

Name and address of the customs authorities:

Signature:

18. **Remarks:**

(¹) Place a cross ☒ in the appropriate box.

NOTES

A. **General notes**

1. The application (boxes 1 to 11) is to be completed by the holder or his representative.

2. The form must be completed legibly and indelibly, preferably by typewriter. It must not contain any erasures or overwritten words. Corrections should be made by crossing out the wrong words and adding any necessary particulars. Corrections must be initialled by the person completing the sheet and endorsed by the customs office.

B. **Special notes referring to the relevant box numbers**

1. Give the name, address and the Member State.

2. Give the name, address and the Member State of the customs office to which the application is sent.

4. Give the name, address and the Member State of the customs office to which the information is supplied.

8. Give the marks and numbers, the number and the kind of packages. In the case of unpackaged goods, give the number of objects or enter the words "in bulk", as appropriate.

   Give the usual commercial description of the products or goods or their tariff description.

10. The net quantity must be expressed in units of the metric system: kg, litres, m², etc.

13. Currencies are to be indicated as follows:

— EUR for euro	— DKK for Danish krone	— SEK for Swedish krona
— GBP for pound sterling	— CZK for Czech koruna	— EEK for Estonian kroons
— CYP for Cyprus pounds	— LVL for Latvian lati	— LTL for Lithuanian litaï
— HUF for Hungarian forint	— MTL for Maltese lira	— PLN for Polish zloty
— SIT for Slovenian tolars	— SKK for Slovak koruny	

NOTES

A. **General notes**

1. The application (boxes 1 to 11) is to be filled in by the holder or his representative.

2. The form must be filled in legibly and indelibly, preferably by typewriter. It must not contain any erasures or overwritten words. Corrections should be made by crossing out the wrong words and adding any necessary particulars. Corrections must be initialled by the person filling in the sheet and endorsed by the customs office which issued it.

B. **Special notes referring to the relevant box numbers—**

1. Give the name, address and the Member State.

2. Give the name, address and the Member State of the customs office to which the application is sent.

4. Give the name, address and the Member State of the customs office to which the information is supplied.

8. Give the marks and numbers, the number and the kind of packages. In the case of unpackaged goods, give the number of objects or enter the words "in bulk", as appropriate.

Give the usual commercial description of the goods or their tariff description.

10. The net quantity must be expressed in units of the metric system: kg, litres, m_2, etc.

13. Currencies are to be indicated as follows—

— EUR for Euro
— DKK for Danish Krone
— SEK for Swedish Krona
— GBP for Pound Sterling
[— CZK for Czech koruna
— EEK for Estonian kroons
— CYP for Cyprus pounds
— LVL for Latvian lati
— LTL for Lithuanian litai
— HUF for Hungarian forint
— MTL for Maltese lira
— PLN for Polish zloty
— SIT for Slovenian tolars
— SKK for Slovak koruny.]
[— BGN for Bulgarian Lev
— RON for New Romanian Leu]

EUROPEAN COMMUNITY

EUROPEAN COMMUNITY

1. Holder of outward processing authorization Person responsible	**INF 2** INFORMATION SHEET No / 000000 ORIGINAL OUTWARD PROCESSING TRIANGULAR TRAFFIC
3. Customs office to which application is made	2. APPLICATION The undersigned requests certification of the information on the goods referred to in box 12 with a view to their reimportation into the Community. Place: Signature: Date: |__|__|__|__|__|__| day month year
4. Intended Member State of reimportation	5. Country of processing or destination
6. Outward processing authorization	7. Rate of yield
8. Autorized processing operations	9. Other details of the authorization
10. Description of compensating products to be reimported	11. CN code

12. Description of temporary export goods	13. CN code:	14. Net quantity:	15. Statistical value:

INFORMATION TO BE SUPPLIED AT THE TIME OF TEMPORARY EXPORT

16. STAMP OF CUSTOMS OFFICE OF ENTRY

Information certified correct   Stamp:

Temporary exportation document number   Last day for reimportation of compensating products:

dated: \|__\|__\|__\|__\|__\|__\| dated: \|__\|__\|__\|__\|__\|__\|
     day   month   year   day   month   year

Means of identification used

Observations:

Customs office (name and Member State):

17. STAMP OF CUSTOMS OFFICE OF EXIT

The goods described in box 12 left the Customs territory of the Community   Stamp:

on \|__\|__\|__\|__\|__\|__\|
   day   month   year

Observations:

Customs office (name and Member State):

Part III

18. REQUEST FOR POST-CLEARANCE VERIFICATION

The customs authority indicated below requests verification of the authenticity of this information sheet and the accuracy of the particulars which it contains.

Place:

Date: |__|__|__|__|__|__| Stamp:
      day month year

Signature: Name and full address of customs authority

19. RESULT OF VERIFICATION

This information sheet (^{1})

☐ was stamped by the customs office indicated in box 16 and the particulars which it contains are correct,

☐ gives rise to the following observations

Place:

Date: |__|__|__|__|__|__| Stamp:
      day month year

Signature: Name and full address of customs authority

20. REIMPORTATION OF COMPENSATING PRODUCTS

Indicate the quantity available in boxes A and the quantity reimported in boxes B.

Quantity	Type, number and date of document for release for free circulation, stamp of customs office	Quantity (continuation)	Type, number and date of document for release for free circulation, stamp of customs office
A			
B			
A			
B			

21. Remarks:

(^{1}) Place a cross ☒ in the appropriate box.

NOTES

A. General Notes

1. The form must be completed legibly and indelibly, preferably by typewriter. It must not contain any erasures or overwritten words, Corrections should be made by crossing out wrong entries and if necesary adding the correct particulars. Corrections must be initialled by the person completing the form and endorsed by the customs office which completes box 16.

2. Boxes 1 to 15 must be completed by the holder.

B. Special notes referring to box numbers:

1. Give the name, address and the name of the Member State. In the case of a legal person, the name of the person responsible should also be given.

3. Give the name, address, and the Member State.

6. Give the number and date of autorisation and the name of the customs authorities which issued it.

10. Give an exact description of the compensating products using the normal commercial description or the tariff description.

11. Give the tariff heading or subheading of the compensating products as shown on the authorisation.

12. Give an exact description of the goods using the normal commercial description or the tariff description. The description must correspond with that given in the export document. If the goods are subject to the inward processing procedure enter 'IP goods' and give the number of the information sheet INF 1 if used.

14. Give the net quantity expressed in units of themetric system (kg, litres, m^2, etc.).

15. Give the statistical value at the time the export declaration was lodged, preceded by one of the following currency abbreviations:

− EUR for euro	− DKK for Danish krone	− SEK for Swedish krona
− GBP for punds sterling	(^{1}) − CZK for Czech koruna	− EEK for Estonian kroons
− CYP for Cyprus pounds	− LVL for Latvian lati	− LTL for Lithuanian litaï
− HUF for Hungarian forint	− MTL for Maltese lira	− PLN for Polish zloty
− SIT for Slovenian tolars	− SKK for Slovak koruny	

NOTES

A. General notes

1. The form must be filled in legibly and indelibly, preferably by typewriter. It must not contain any erasures or overwritten words. Corrections should be made by crossing out wrong entries and if necessary adding the correct particulars. Corrections must be initialled by the person filling in the form and endorsed by the customs office which completes box 16.

2. Boxes 1 to 15 must be filled in by the holder.

B. Special notes referring to box numbers—

1. Give the name, address and the name of the Member State. In the case of a legal person, the name of the person responsible should also be given.

3. Give the name, address and the Member State.

6. Give the number and date of the authorisation and the name of the customs authorities which issued it.

10. Give an exact description of the compensating products using the normal commercial description or the tariff description.

11. Give the tariff heading or subheading of the compensating products as shown on the authorisation.

12. Give an exact description of the goods using the normal commercial description or the tariff description. The description must correspond with that given in the export document. If the goods are subject to the inward processing procedure enter "IP goods" and give the number of the information sheet INF1 if used—

14. Give the net quantity expressed in units of the metric system (kg, litres, m_2, etc).

15. Give the statistical value at the time the export declaration was lodged, preceded by one of the following currency abbreviations—

- EUR for Euro
- DKK for Danish Krone
- SEK for Swedish Krona
- GBP for Pound Sterling
- [— CZK for Czech koruna
- EEK for Estonian kroons
- CYP for Cyprus pounds
- LVL for Latvian lati
- LTL for Lithuanian litai
- HUF for Hungarian forint
- MTL for Maltese lira
- PLN for Polish zloty
- SIT for Slovenian tolars
- SKK for Slovak koruny.]
- [— BGN for Bulgarian Lev
- RON for New Romanian Leu]

APPENDIX

1. General Notes

1.1. The information sheets shall comply with the model set out in this Annex and be printed on white paper without mechanical pulp, dressed for writing purposes and weighing between 40 and 65 g/m².

1.2. The form shall measure 210 × 297 mm.

1.3. The customs administrations shall be responsible for having the form printed. Each form shall bear the initials of the issuing Member State in accordance with the ISO-Norm Alpha 2, followed by an individual serial number.

1.4.   The form shall be printed and the boxes shall be filled in an official language of the Community. The customs office requested to provide the information or make use of it may ask for the information contained in the form presented to it to be translated into the official language, or one of the official languages, of the customs administration.

2.   Use of the Information sheets

2.1.   Common provisions

(a)   Where the customs office issuing the information sheet considers that additional information to that appearing on the information sheet is required, it shall enter such particulars. Where not enough space remains, an additional sheet shall be annexed. It shall be mentioned on the original.

(b)   The customs office which endorsed the information sheet may be asked to carry out post-clearance verification of the authenticity of the sheet and the accuracy of the particulars which its contains.

(c)   In the case of successive consignments, the requisite number of information sheets may be made out for the quantity of goods or products entered for the arrangements. The initial information sheet may also be replaced with further information sheets or, where only one information sheet is used, the customs office to which the sheet is endorsed may note on the original the quantities of goods or products. Where not enough space remains, an additional sheet shall be annexed which shall be mentioned on the original.

(d)   The customs authorities may permit the use of recapitulative information sheets for triangular traffic trade flows involving a large number of operations which cover the total quantity of imports/exports over a given period.

(e)   In exceptional circumstances, the information sheet may be issued a posteriori but not beyond the expiry of the period required for keeping documents.

(f)   In the event of theft, loss or destruction of the information sheet, the operator may ask the customs office which endorsed it for a duplicate to be issued.

The original and copies of the information sheet so issued shall bear one of the following indications—

—   DUPLICADO,
—   DUPLIKAT,
—   DUPLIKAT,
—   ΑΝΤΙφΡΑFO,
—   DUPLICATE,
—   DUPLICATA,
—   DUPLICATO,
—   DUPLICAAT,
—   SEGUNDA VIA,
—   KAKSOISKAPPALE,
—   DUPLIKAT,
[—   DUPLIKÁT,
—   DUPLIKAAT,
—   DUBLIKATS,
—   DUBLIKATAS,
—   MÁSODLAT,
—   DUPLIKAT,

original and copies 1 and 2 of the INF5 the quantity of import goods entered for the arrangements and the date of acceptance of the declaration. It shall send copy 2 to the supervising office, returning the original to the declarant and retaining copy 1.

2.2.5. INFORMATION SHEET INF7 (INWARD PROCESSING)

(a) The information sheet INF7 (hereafter: INF7) may be used where the compensating products or the goods in the unaltered state under the drawback system are assigned one of the customs approved treatments or uses permitting repayment or remission, in accordance with Article 128(1) of the Code, without a repayment claim being lodged.

Where the holder has given the consent to transfer the right to claim repayment to another person in accordance with Article 90 of the Code, this information shall appear on the INF7.

(b) The INF7 shall be made out in an original and two copies.

(c) The customs office accepting the declaration of discharge shall endorse the INF7, return the original and one copy to the holder and retain the other copy.

(d) When the repayment claim is lodged, it shall be accompanied by the duly endorsed original of the INF7.

2.2.6. INFORMATION SHEET INF6 (TEMPORARY IMPORTATION)

(a) The information sheet INF6 (hereafter: INF6) may be used to communicate elements for assessment of the customs debt or of amounts of duties already levied where import goods are moved within the customs territory of the Community.

(b) The INF6 shall comprise all the information needed to show the customs authorities—

— the date on which the import goods were entered for the temporary importation arrangements,

— the elements for assessment of the customs debt ascertained on that date,

— the amount of any import duties already levied under partial relief arrangements and the period taken into account for that purpose.

(c) The INF6 shall be made out of an original and two copies.

(d) The INF6 shall be endorsed either when the goods are placed under the external transit procedure, at the beginning of the transfer operation or at an earlier moment.

(e) One copy shall be retained by the customs office which endorsed it. The original and the other copy shall be returned to the person concerned giving this copy to the office of discharge. After endorsement this copy shall be returned by the person concerned to the customs office which initially endorsed it.

2.2.7. INFORMATION SHEET INF2 (OUTWARD PROCESSING)

(a) The information sheet INF2 (hereafter: INF2) may be used, where compensating or replacement products are imported under triangular traffic.

(b) The INF2 shall be made out in an original and one copy for the quantity of goods entered for the procedure.

(c) The request for the issue of the INF2 shall constitute the consent of the holder to transfer the right of the total or partial relief from the import duties to another person importing the compensating or replacement products under triangular traffic.

Part III

(d)   The office of entry shall endorse the original and the copy of the INF2. It shall retain the copy and return the original to the declarant.

It shall indicate in box 16 the means used to identify the temporary export goods.

Where samples are taken or illustrations or technical descriptions are used, this office shall authenticate such samples, illustrations or technical descriptions by affixing its customs seal either on the goods, where their nature permits it, or on the packaging, in such a way that it cannot be tampered with.

A label bearing the stamp of the office and reference particulars of the export declaration shall be attached to the samples, illustrations or technical descriptions in a manner which prevents substitution.

The samples, illustrations or technical descriptions, authenticated and sealed shall be returned to the exporter, who shall present them with the seals intact when the compensating or replacement products are re-imported.

Where an analysis is required and the results will not be known until after the office of entry has endorsed the INF2, the document containing the results of the analysis shall be given to the exporter in a sealed tamper-proof envelope.

(e)   The office of exit shall certify on the original that the goods have left the customs territory of the Community and shall return it to the person presenting it.

(f)   The importer of the compensating or replacement products shall present the original of the INF2 and, where appropriate, the means of identification to the office of discharge.]

NOTES

Substituted as noted to Annex 67.

Words inserted by the 2003 Act of Accession Annex II(19)(A)(II), para 57.

Words relating to Bulgaria and Romania inserted by Commission Regulation (EC) 1792/2006, Art 1, Annex, Part 11(A)(55).

[ANNEX 72

LIST OF USUAL FORMS OF HANDLING REFERRED TO IN ARTICLE 531 AND ARTICLE 809

Unless otherwise specified, none of the following forms of handling may give rise to a different eight-digit CN code.

Usual forms of handling listed below shall not be granted if, in the opinion of the customs authorities, the operation is likely to increase the risk of fraud.

1.   ventilation, spreading-out, drying, removal of dust, simple cleaning operations, repair of packing, elementary repairs of damage incurred during transport or storage insofar as it concerns simple operations, application and removal of protective coating for transport;

2.   reconstruction of the goods after transport;

3.   stocktaking, sampling, sorting, sifting, mechanical filtering and weighing of the goods;

4.   removal of damaged or contaminated components;

5.   conservation, by means of pasteurisation, sterilisation, irradiation or the addition of preservatives;

6.   treatment against parasites;

7.   anti-rust treatment;

8. treatment—
    —   by simple raising of the temperature, without further treatment or distillation process; or,
    —   by simple lowering of the temperature;
even if this results in a different eight-digit CN code

9. electrostatic treatment, uncreasing or ironing of textiles;

10. treatment consisting in—
    —   stemming and/or pitting of fruits, cutting up and breaking down of dried fruits or vegetables, rehydration of fruits; or,
    —   dehydration of fruits even if this results in a different eight-digit CN code;

11. desalination, cleaning and butting of hides;

12. addition of goods or addition or replacement of accessory components as long as this addition or replacement is relatively limited or is intended to ensure compliance with technical standards and does not change the nature or improve the performances of the original goods, even if this results in a different eight-digit CN code for the added or replacement goods;

13. dilution or concentration of fluids, without further treatment or distillation process, even if this results in a different eight-digit CN code;

14. mixing between them of the same kind of goods, with a different quality, in order to obtain a constant quality or a quality which is requested by the customer, without changing the nature of the goods;

15. dividing or size cutting out of goods if only simple operations are involved;

16. packing, unpacking, change of packing, decanting and simple transfer into containers, even if this results in a different eight-digit CN code; affixing, removal and altering of marks, seals, labels, price tags or other similar distinguishing signs;

17. testing, adjusting, regulating and putting into working order of machines, apparatus and vehicles, in particular in order to control the compliance with technical standards, if only simple operations are involved.

18. dulling of pipe fittings to prepare the goods for certain markets.]

[19. Any usual forms of handling, other than the abovementioned, intended to improve the appearance or marketable quality of the import goods or to prepare them for distribution or resale, provided that these operations do not change the nature or improve the performance of the original goods. Where costs for usual forms of handling have been incurred, such costs or the increase in value shall not be taken into account for the calculation of the import duty where satisfactory proof of these costs is provided by the declarant. However, the customs value, nature and origin of non-Community goods used in the operations shall be taken into account for the calculation of the import duties.]

NOTES

Substituted as noted to Annex 67.

Point 19 added by Commission Regulation (EC) 883/2005, Art 1, para 34.

Part III

[ANNEX 73

IMPORT GOODS FOR WHICH THE ECONOMIC CONDITIONS ARE
DEEMED NOT TO BE FULFILLED BY VIRTUE OF ARTICLE 539,
FIRST PARAGRAPH

PART A:

Agricultural products covered by Annex I to the Treaty

1.   The following products falling under one of the following common market
organisations—

Cereals sector:Products referred to in Article 1(1) of Council Regulation (EEC)
No 1766/92[1],

Rice sector:Products referred to in Article 1(1) of Council Regulation (EC) No
3072/95[2],

Sugar sector:Products referred to in Article 1(1) of Council Regulation (EC) No
2038/99[3],

Olive oil sector:Products referred to in Article 1 (2) (c) of Council Regulation
(EEC) No 136/66[4],

Milk and milk products sector:Products referred to in Article 1 of Council
Regulation (EC) No 1255/99,

Wine sector:Products referred to in Article 1 (2) of Council Regulation (EC) No
1493/99[5] and falling under CN codes—

08 06 10 90
20 09 60
22 04 21 (quality wine excepted)
22 04 29 (quality wine excepted)
22 04 30

2.   Following products falling under CN codes—

02 04 10 to 02 04 43
22 07 10
22 07 20
22 08 90 91
22 08 90 99

3.   Products other than those under points 1 and 2, for which agricultural export
refunds equal to or higher than zero are fixed.

PART B:

*Goods not covered by Annex I to the Treaty resulting from the processing of
agricultural products*

Goods resulting from the processing of agricultural products and listed in the
following annexes of Regulations on the common organisation of markets in the
agricultural sector or concerning production refunds—

Annex B to Council Regulation (EEC) No 1766/92 (cereals sector),

Annex B to Council Regulation (EC) No 3072/95 (rice sector),

Annex I to Council Regulation (EC) No 2038/99 (sugar sector),

Annex II to Council Regulation (EC) No 1255/99 (milk and milk products
sector),

Annex I to Council Regulation (EEC) No 2771/75[6] (eggs sector),

Annex to Council Regulation (EEC) No 1010/86[7] (production refunds on certain
sugar products used in the chemical industry) and

Annex I to Commission Regulation (EEC) No 1722/93[8] (production refunds in the cereals and rice sectors).

PART C:

Fishery products

Fishery products listed in Annexes I, II and V to Council Regulation (EC) No 104/2000[9] on the common organisation of the markets in fishery and aquaculture products and products listed in Annex VI to this Regulation subject to a partial autonomous suspension.

All fishery products subject to an autonomous quota.]

---

[1] OJ L181, 1.7.92, p 21.

[2] OJ L329, 30.12.95, p 18.

[3] OJ L252, 25.9.99, p 1.

[4] OJ L172, 30.9.66, p 3025/66.

[5] OJ L179, 14.7.99, p 1.

[6] OJ L282, 1.11.75, p 49.

[7] OJ L94, 9.4.86, p 9.

[8] OJ L159, 1.7.93, p 112.

[9] OJ L17, 21.1.2000, p 22.

NOTE

Substituted as noted to Annex 67.

[ANNEX 74
SPECIAL PROVISIONS CONCERNING EQUIVALENT GOODS
(Article 541)

1. Rice

Rice classified under CN code 1006 shall not be deemed equivalent unless it falls within the same eight-digit CN code of the combined nomenclature. Nevertheless, for rice with a length not exceeding 6,0 mm and a length/width ratio equal to or more than 3 and for rice with a length equal to or less than 5,2 mm and a length/width ratio equal to or more than 2, equivalence shall be established by determination of the length/width ratio only. The measurement of the grains shall be done in accordance with Annex A(2)(d) to Council Regulation (EC) No 3072/95 of 22 December 1995 on the common organisation of the market in rice[1].

The use of equivalent goods shall be prohibited where inward processing operations consist of the "usual forms of handling" listed in Annex 72 to this Regulation.

---

[1] OJ No L 329, 30.12.1995, p.18.

---

2. Wheat

Equivalent goods may be used only between wheat harvested in a third country and already released for free circulation and non-Community wheat, of the same eight-digit CN code, having the same commercial quality and the same technical characteristics.

However—

Part III

— derogations from the ban on use of equivalent goods may be adopted in respect of wheat on the basis of a communication from the Commission to the Member States, after examination by the Committee;

— the use of equivalent goods is permitted between Community durum wheat and durum wheat of third-country origin provided it is for the production of pasta falling within CN codes 1902 11 00 and 1902 19.

3. Sugar

Recourse to the use of equivalent goods is permitted between raw cane sugar falling within CN code 1701 11 90 and raw beet sugar within CN code 1701 12 90 under the condition that compensating products falling within CN code 1701 99 10 (white sugar) are obtained.

4. Live animals and meat

Equivalent goods may not be used for inward processing operations on live animals or meat.

Derogation from the ban on the use of equivalent goods can be made for meat which has been made subject of a communication by the Commission to the Member States, after an examination carried out by the Customs Code Committee if the applicant can prove that equivalence is economically necessary and if the customs authorities transmit the draft of the procedures foreseen to control the operation.

5. Maize

Recourse to the use of equivalent goods between Community and non-Community maize is possible only in the following cases and subject to the following conditions—

1. In the case of maize for use in animal feed, the use of equivalent goods is possible provided that a customs control system is set up to ensure that the non-Community maize is in fact used for processing into animal feed.

2. In the case of maize used in the manufacture of starch and starch products, the use of equivalent goods is possible between all varieties with the exception of maizes rich in amylopectin (wax-like maize or "waxy" maize) which are only equivalent between themselves.

3. In the case of maize used in the manufacture of meal products, the use of equivalent goods is possible between all varieties with the exception of maizes of the vitreous type ("Plata" maize of the "Duro" type, "Flint" maize) which are only equivalent between themselves.

6. Olive oil

A. Recourse to the use of equivalent goods is permitted only in the following cases and under the following conditions—

1. Virgin olive oil

(a) Between Community extra virgin olive oil falling within CN code 1509 10 90 which corresponds to the description in point 1(a) of the Annex to Council Regulation No 136/66/EEC[1], as last amended by Regulation (EC) No 1581/96[2], and non-Community extra virgin olive oil of the same CN code, provided that the processing operation produces extra virgin olive oil falling within the same CN code and satisfying the requirements of the said point 1(a).

(b) Between Community virgin olive oil falling within CN code 1509 10 90 which corresponds to the description in point 1(b) of the Annex to Regulation No 136/66/EEC and non-Community virgin olive oil of the same CN code, provided that the processing operation produces virgin olive oil falling within the same CN code and satisfying the requirements of the said point 1(b).

(c) Between Community ordinary virgin olive oil falling within CN code 1509 10 90 which corresponds to the description in point 1(c) of the

Annex to Regulation No 136/66/EEC and non-Community ordinary virgin olive oil of the same CN code, provided that the compensating product is—

— refined olive oil falling within CN code 1509 90 00 which corresponds to the description in point 2 of the above mentioned Annex,

— olive oil falling within CN code 1509 90 00 which corresponds to the description in point 3 of the said Annex and is obtained by blending with Community virgin olive oil falling within CN code 1509 10 90.

(d) Between Community lampante virgin olive oil falling within CN code 1509 10 10 which corresponds to the description in point 1 (d) of the Annex to Regulation No 136/66/EEC and non-Community lampante virgin olive oil of the same CN code, provided that the compensating product is—

— refined olive oil falling within CN code 1509 90 00 which corresponds to the description in point 2 of the above mentioned Annex, or

— olive oil falling within CN code 1509 90 00 which corresponds to the description in point 3 of the said Annex and is obtained by blending with Community virgin olive oil falling within CN code 1509 10 90.

2. Olive-pomace oil

Between Community unrefined olive-pomace oil falling within CN code 1510 00 10 which corresponds to the description in point 4 of the Annex to Regulation No 136/66/EEC and non-Community unrefined olive-pomace oil of the same CN code, provided that the olive-pomace oil compensating product falling within CN code 1510 00 90 and corresponding to the description in point 6 of the said Annex is obtained by blending with Community virgin olive oil falling within CN code 1509 10 90.

B. The blending referred to in point A.1(c) second indent and (d) second indent and point A.2, with non-Community virgin olive oil, used in an identical manner, are authorized only where the arrangements for supervision of the procedure are organized in a manner that makes it possible to identify the proportion of non-Community virgin olive oil in the total quantity of blended oil exported.

C. The compensating products must be put into immediate packaging of 220 litres or less. By way of derogation, in the case of agreed containers of 20 tonnes maximum, the customs authorities may allow the exportation of the oils found in the preceding points on condition that there is systematic control of the quality and quantity of the exported product.

D. Equivalence shall be checked by using commercial records to verify the quantity of oils used for blending and, for the purpose of verifying the quality concerned, by comparing the technical characteristics of samples of the non-Community oil taken when it was entered for the procedure with the technical characteristics of the samples of the Community oil used taken when the compensating product concerned was processed against the technical characteristics of the samples taken at the time of actual exportation of the compensating product at the point of exit. Samples shall be taken in accordance with international standards EN ISO 5555 (sampling) and EN ISO 661 (sending of samples to laboratories and preparation of samples for tests). The analysis shall be carried out with reference to the parameters in Annex I to Commission Regulation (EEC) No 2568/91[3], as last amended by Regulation (EC) No 2527/95[4].

[1] OJ L 172, 30.9.66, p 3025.

[2] OJ L 206, 16.8.96, p 11.

[3] OJ L 248, 5.9.91, p 1.

[4] OJ L 258, 28.10.95, p 49.

[7.   Milk and milk products

Recourse to the use of equivalence is permitted under the following conditions:

The weight of each component of milk dry matter, milk fat matter and milk protein of the import goods shall not exceed the weight of each of these components in the equivalent goods. However, where the economic value of the import goods is determined by only one or two of the above mentioned components, the weight may be calculated on the basis of this or these component(s). The authorisation shall specify the details, notably the reference period for which the total weight has to be calculated. The reference period shall not exceed 4 months.

The weight of the relevant component(s) of the import goods and of the equivalent goods shall be entered on the customs declarations and on any information sheet INF9 or INF5, to enable the customs authorities to control the equivalence on the basis of those elements.

Physical checks shall be carried out on at least 5% of the declarations for entry of import goods for the arrangements and the export declaration (IM/EX) and cover the import goods as well as the equivalent goods concerned.

Physical checks shall be carried out on at least 5% of the prior export declarations and the declarations for entry for the arrangements (EX/IM). These checks shall cover the equivalent goods that shall be checked before the processing operations start as well as the concerned import goods at the moment they are entered for the arrangements.

Physical checks imply the verification of the declaration and the documents attached thereto, and representative samples shall be taken for analysis of the ingredients by a competent laboratory.

If the Member State applies a system of risk analysis, a lower percentage of physical checks may be permitted.

Each physical check shall be the subject of a detailed report by the official who has carried out this check. These reports shall be centralised by the customs authorities designated in each Member State.]

NOTE

Substituted by Commission Regulation (EC) 2286/2003, Art 1, para 19, Annex V.

[ANNEX 75
LIST OF COMPENSATING PRODUCTS SUBJECT TO THE IMPORT DUTIES
APPROPRIATE TO THEM

(Article 548 (1))

Description of the secondary compensating products	Processing operations from which they result
(1)	(2)
Waste, scrap, residues, offcuts and remainders	Any working or processing]

NOTE

Substituted by Commission Regulation (EC) 2286/2003, Art 1, para 20, Annex VI.

[ANNEX 76

ECONOMIC CONDITIONS IN THE FRAMEWORK OF THE ARRANGEMENTS FOR PROCESSING UNDER CUSTOMS CONTROL

(Article 551(1), second paragraph)

PART A

The economic conditions shall be deemed to be fulfilled for the following types of goods and operations:

	Column 1	*Column 2*
Order No	Goods	Processing
1	Goods of any kind	Processing into samples presented as such or put up into sets
2	Goods of any kind	Reduction to waste and scrap or destruction
3	Goods of any kind	Denaturing
4	Goods of any kind	Recovery of parts or components
5	Goods of any kind	Separation and/or destruction of damaged parts
6	Goods of any kind	Processing to correct the effects of damage to the goods
7	Goods of any kind	Usual forms of handling permitted in customs warehouses or free zones
8	Goods of any kind	Processing into products of a kind to be incorporated in or used for civil aircraft for which an airworthiness certificate is issued by a company authorised for such operations by the European aviation authorities or the aviation authorities of a third country
[8a	Goods of any kind	Processing into products which may benefit from the autonomous suspension of import duties on certain weapons and military equipment.]
9	Goods covered by Article 551(1) second indent	Any form of processing
10	Goods of any kind not subject to a(n) agricultural—or commercial policy measure or provisional or definitive antidumping—or provisional or definitive countervailing duty	Any form of processing, where the import duty advantage resulted by using the arrangements does not exceed the value of 50 000 euro per applicant and per calendar year.
11	Any electronic type of components, parts, assemblies (including sub-assemblies), or materials (whether or not electronic), which are vital to the electronic working performance of the processed product Processing into information technology products:	1. covered by the Agreement on trade in information technology products which has been approved by Council Decision 97/359/EC[1], where a duty exemption operates on the date of authorisation, or 2. falling within a CN code provided for in Articles 1, 2 or 3 of Council Regulation (EC) No 2216/97[2], where a duty exemption operates on the date of authorisation

12	Solid fractions of palm oil falling within CN code 1511 90 19 or Fluid fractions of palm oil falling within CN code 1511 90 91 or Coconut oil falling within CN code 1513 11 10 or Fluid fractions of coconut oil falling within CN code ex 1513 19 30 or Palm kernel oil falling within CN code 1513 21 11 or Fluid fractions of palm kernel oil falling within CN code ex 1513 29 30 or Babassu oil falling within CN code 1513 21 19.	Processing into— —Mixtures of fatty acids falling within CN codes 3823 11 00, 3823 12 00, ex 3823 19 10, ex 3823 19 30 and ex 3823 19 90 —Fatty acids falling within CN codes 2915 70 15, 2915 70 25, 2915 90 10, ex 2915 90 80, ex 2916 15 00 and ex 2916 19 80 —Mixture of methyl esters of fatty acids falling within CN code ex 3824 90 95 —Methyl esters of fatty acids falling within CN codes ex 2915 70 20, ex 2915 70 80, ex 2915 90 80, ex 2916 15 00 and ex 2916 19 80 —Mixture of fatty alcohols falling within CN code 3823 70 00 —Fatty alcohols falling within CN codes 2905 16 80, 2905 17 00 and 2905 19 00 —glycerol falling within CN code 1520 00 00
13	Castor oil falling within CN code 1515 30 90	Processing into— —hydrogenated castor oil ("opal-wax";) of CN code 1516 20 10 —12-12-hydrostearic acid (purity less than 90%) of CN code ex 3823 19 10 —12-12-hydrostearic acid (purity 90% or more) of CN code ex 2918 19 99 —glycerol of CN code 2905 45 00
14	Tobaccos falling within Chapter 24 of the CN	Processing into "homogenised"; or "reconstituted"; tobacco falling within CN code 2403 91 00 and/or tobacco powder falling within CN code ex 2403 99 90
15	Raw or unmanufactured tobacco falling within CN code 2401 10 Raw or unmanufactured tobacco partly stemmed/ stripped falling within CN code ex 2401 20	Processing into partly or wholly stemmed/stripped tobaccos falling within CN code 2401 20 and into tobacco refuse falling within CN code 2401 30 00
16	Products falling within CN codes— 2707 10, 2707 20, 2707 30, 2707 50, 2707 91 00, 2707 99 30, 2707 99 91, 2707 99 99 and 2710 00	Processing into products falling within CN codes— 2710 00 71 or 2710 00 72
17	Crude oils falling within CN codes 2707 99 11	Processing into products falling within CN codes 2707 10 90, 2707 20 90, 2707 30 90, 2707 50 90, 2707 99 30, 2707 99 99, 2902 20 90, 2902 30 90, 2902 41 00, 2902 42 00, 2902 43 00, 2902 44 90

18	Gas oils with a sulphur content exceeding 0.2% by weight falling within CN code 2710 00 68 Kerosene falling within CN code 2710 00 55 White spirit falling within CN code 2710 00 21	Mixture of the goods in column 1 or a mixture of one and/or other of the goods in column 1 with gas oil with a sulphur content not exceeding 0.2% by weight falling within CN code 2710 00 66 or 2710 00 67 to obtain a gas oil with a sulphur content not exceeding 0.2% by weight falling within CN code 2710 00 66 or 2710 00 67
19	PVC material falling within CN code 3921 90 60	Processing into filmscreens falling within CN code 9010 60 00
20	Skating boots without skates attached of CN code 6402 19 00 Skating boots without skates attached of CN code 6403 19 00	Processing into— Ice skates of CN code 9506 70 10 Roller skates of CN code 9506 70 30
21	Motor chassis fitted with cabs, of CN code 8704 21 31	Processing into fire engines fitted with integral fire fighting and/ or life saving equipment, of CN code 8705 30 00

PART B

The economic conditions shall be examined in the Committee for the following types of goods and operations, which are not covered by Part A—

	Column 1	*Column 2*
	Goods	Processing
	All goods subject to a(n) agricultural measure or provisional or definitive antidumping – or provisional or definitive countervailing duty	Any form of processing]

[1] OJ L155, 12.6.97, p 1 (the Information Technology Agreement).

[2] OJ L305, 8.11.97, p 1.

NOTES

Substituted as noted to Annex 67.

Part A, Order No 8a: inserted by Commission Regulation (EC) 881/2003 Art 1, para 36, Annex X.

[ANNEX 77

CASES WHERE THE ENTRY OF GOODS FOR TEMPORARY IMPORTATION BY WRITTEN DECLARATION IS NOT SUBJECT TO THE PROVISION OF A SECURITY

(Article 581)

1. Materials belonging to airline, shipping or railway companies or postal services and used by them in international traffic, subject to them being distinctively marked;

2. Packings imported empty, carrying indelible non-removable markings;

3. Disaster relief material intended for state or approved bodies;

4. Medical, surgical and laboratory equipment intended for a hospital or medical institution which has urgent need of such equipment.

5. Entry for temporary importation of goods transferred in the meaning of Article 513, where the previous holder entered the goods for temporary importation in accordance with Articles 229 or 232.]

NOTE

Annexes 67–77 substituted for Annexes 67–103 by Commission Regulation (EC) 993/2001, Art 1, para 37, Annex V.

ANNEX 104
INFORMATION DOCUMENT TO FACILITATE THE TEMPORARY EXPORTATION OF GOODS SENT FROM ONE COUNTRY FOR MANUFACTURE, PROCESSING OR REPAIR IN ANOTHER

INFORMATION DOCUMENT TO FACILITATE THE TEMPORARY EXPORTATION OF GOODS SENT FROM ONE COUNTRY FOR MANUFACTURE, PROCESSING OR REPAIR IN ANOTHER

Before completing this form please read note on page 4

I

TO BE COMPLETED AT EXPORTATION (*)

(*) Unused lines or cages must be struck out or the word 'Nil' written across them.
(**) Delete if inapplicable.

A The goods described below, intended for manufacture – processing – repair (**) in ....

Customs administration of ....

Customs office of ....

have been entered for exportation { by (**) / on behalf of } ....
(Name of exporter in block capitals)

of ....
(Address in block capitals)

Specification of goods

B Number, type, marks and numbers of packages	Tariff ref. No	Commercial description	Quantity		Value	Remarks
			Gross weight	Net weight, number, volume, measurements, etc.		
– 1 –	– 2 –	– 3 –	– 4 –	– 5 –	– 6 –	– 7 –

C Nature of proposed operations:

D Particulars of examinations carried out:

E Means of identification used:

F Certified to correspond with the particulars shown on ....

.... (Customs document)

No .... dated ....

.... (Place) .... (Date)

.... (Signature)

(Customs office stamp)

Part III

II

TO BE COMPLETED AT IMPORTATION (*)

(*) Unused lines or cages must be struck out or the word 'Nil' written across them.
(**) Delete if inapplicable.

A The goods described { in Part I (**) intended for manufacture – processing – repair (**)
{ below

were entered { by
{ on behalf of (**) ....
(Name of importer in block capitals)

of ....
(Address in block capitals)

Customs administration of
....

Customs office of ....
....

Specification of goods

B

Number, type, marks and numbers of packages	Tariff ref. No	Commercial description	Quantity		Value	Remarks
			Gross weight	Net weight, number, volume, measurements etc.		
– 1 –	– 2 –	– 3 –	– 4 –	– 5 –	– 6 –	– 7 –

C Nature of proposed operations:
....
....
....

D Particulars of examinations carried out:
....
....

E Means of identification used:
....
....

F Certified to correspond with the particulars shown on ....
(Customs document)

No .... dated ....

....
(Place)   (Date)

....   (Customs office stamp)
(Signature)

②

III

TO BE COMPLETED AT RE-EXPORTATION (*)

(*) Unused lines or cages must be struck out or the word 'Nil' written across them.
(**) Delete if inapplicable.

A   The goods described { below / in Part II (**) } { resulting from the manufacture or processing of the goods described in part II (**) / which have been repaired } were entered for re-exportation { by / on behalf of (**) } ....

of .... (Name of re-exporter in block capitals)

.... (Address in block capitals)

B Specification of goods

Number, type, marks and numbers of packages	Tariff ref. No	Commercial description	Quantity		Value	Remarks
			Gross weight	Net weight, number, volume, measurements, etc.		
– 1 –	– 2 –	– 3 –	– 4 –	– 5 –	– 6 –	– 7 –

C   Nature of operations: (Include particulars of any parts added and/or any manufacturing waste):

D   Particulars of examinations carried out:

E   It { has / has not (**) } been established that the re-exported goods { are those which were imported / have been made or obtained from the goods imported (**) }

Means of identification used:

G   Split re-exportation No ....

No .... dated ....
(Customs document)

....
(Customs office)

} Particulars as in Part I Cage F

F   Certified to correspond with the particulars shown on

....
(Customs document)

No .... dated ....

....
(Place)   (Date)

....
(Signature)   (Customs office stamp)

③

Part III

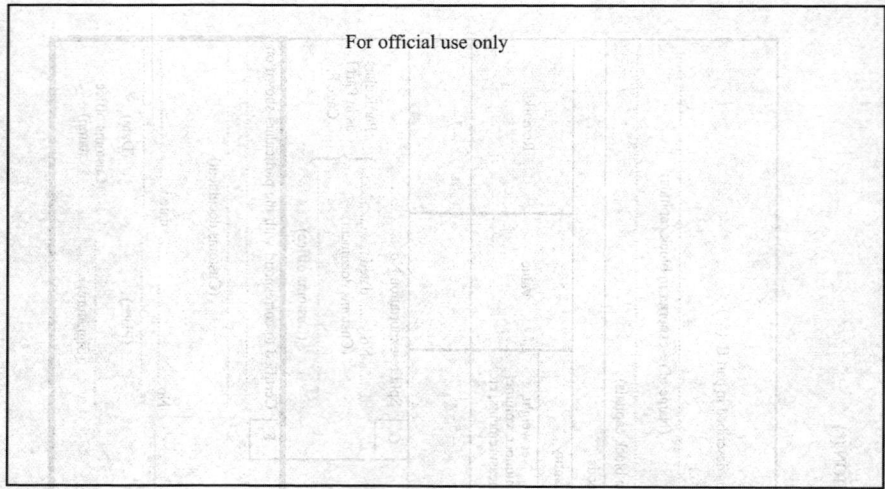

For official use only

NOTE FOR THE USE OF THE INFORMATION DOCUMENT

1. The exporter must ensure that, subject to any conditions they may lay down, the Customs authorities of the country of temporary importation are in a position to establish the identity of the goods.

2. The duly completed Information Document (I. D.) must be presented to the Customs authorities whenever the goods are cleared.

3. If the goods are to be re-imported in split consignements the following procedure applies:

   (a) Temporary exportation:

   The exporter produces the I. D. in duplicate. The Customs certify both copies (Part I) and return them to the exporter who sends the original I. D. to the importer who keeps it until the last split re-exportation. The exporter keeps the duplicate I.D.

   (b) Temporary importation:

   The importer produces the original I.D. to the Customs who certify Part II and return the I.D. to him.

   (c) Split re-exportation:

   The re-exporter completes an additional Part III (including Cage G) and produces it to the Customs together with the original I. D. The Customs certify the additional Part III after checking it against the I. D. The re-exporter sends the additional Part III to re-importer.

   (d) Split re-importation:

   The re-importer produces the additional Part III and his copy of the I.D. to the Customs for checking against each other.

   (e) Last split re-exportation:

   The re-exporter completes Part III of the original I. D. including Cage G. The Customs certify the original I. D. and return it to the re-exporter who sends it to the re-importer.

   (f) Last split re-importation:

   The re-importer produces both copies of the I. D. to the Customs.

④

For official use only

NOTE FOR THE USE OF THE INFORMATION DOCUMENT

1.   The exporter must ensure that, subject to any conditions they may lay down, the Customs authorities of the country of temporary importation are in a position to establish the identity of the goods.

2.   The duly completed Information Document (ID) must be presented to the Customs authorities whenever the goods are cleared.

3.   If the goods are to be re-imported in split consignments the following procedure applies.

(a)   Temporary exportation:

The exporter produces the ID in duplicate. The Customs certify both copies (Part I) and return them to the exporter who sends the original ID to the importer who keeps it until the last split re-exportation. The exporter keeps the duplicate ID.

(b)   Temporary importation.

The importer produces the original ID to the Customs who certify Part II and return the ID to him.

(c)   Split re-exportation:

The re-exporter completes an original Part III (including Cage G) and produces it to the Customs together with the original ID. The Customs certify the additional Part III after checking it against the ID. The re-exporter sends the original Part III to re-emporter.

(d)   Split re-importation

The re-importer produces the additional Part III and his copy of the ID to the Customs for checking against each other.

(e)   Last split re-exportation:

The re-exporter completes Part III of the original ID including Cage G. The Customs certify the original ID and return it to the re-exporter who sends it to the re-importer.

(f)   Last split re-importation:

The re-importer produces both copies of the ID to the Customs.

NOTES
Annexes 105–107 repealed by Commission Regulation (EC) 993/2001, Art 1, para 38.
Annex 108 repealed by Commission Regulation (EC) 1427/97, Art 1, para 17

Part III

ANNEX 109

EUROPEAN COMMUNITY | CERTIFICATE OF CUSTOMS STATUS

| 1. | 1. Holder (full name and address): | Certificate of the customs status of goods in a FREE ZONE or CUSTOMS WAREHOUSE |
| | | No: Date: |

H O L D E R

2. Issuing customs office: (full name and address):	3. The goods described in box 4 are (¹):
	☐ Community goods
	☐ non-Community goods

(¹) Delete as appropriate so that no subsequent change is possible.

4. Order number — Marks, identifying numbers, number and kind of packages — Quantity and description of the goods

5. Place:

Date: Signature:

Stamp of issuing office

(Copy omitted.)

PROVISIONS REGARDING THE CERTIFICATE OF THE CUSTOMS STATUS OF GOODS ENTERED IN A FREE ZONE OR FREE WAREHOUSE

1.   The form for the certificate of the customs status of goods entered in a free zone or free warehouse shall be printed on white paper without mechanical pulp, dressed for writing purposes and weighing between 40 and 65 g/m$_2$.

2.   The form shall measure 210 by 297 mm.

3.   Member States shall be responsible for having the form printed. Each form shall bear an individual serial number.

4.   The form shall be printed in one of the official languages of the Community designated by the customs authorities of the Member State in which the certificate is issued. The boxes shall be filled in with an official language of the Community designated by the customs authorities of the Member States in which the certificate is issued.

5.   The form must not contain erasures or insertions. Any changes must be made by crossing out the incorrect particulars and adding, where appropriate, the correct particulars. Any such changes must be endorsed by the person making out the certificate and by the customs authorities.

6.   The articles referred to in the certificate must be listed in single spacing and each article must be preceded by a serial number. A horizontal line must be drawn immediately under the last article. Unused spaces must be crossed through in such a way as to prevent any subsequent addition.

7.   The original and one copy of the form duly completed shall be lodged with the competent customs office when the goods enter the free zone or free warehouse or when the customs declaration is lodged, as appropriate.

The customs authorities shall endorse the form and keep the copy of the certificate.

8.   Where the operator makes out the certificate pursuant to Article 819(2), box 5 may be

—   stamped by the customs office and signed by an official of that office in advance, or

—   stamped by the operator with a special metal stamp accepted by the customs authorities.

The operator shall keep the copy of the certificate with his stock records.

ANNEX 110

Part III

EUROPEAN COMMUNITY

1. Exporter	**INF 3**	No
	ORIGINAL	

2. Consignee at time of exportation	RETURNED GOODS INFORMATION SHEET

	3. Country to which goods consigned at time of exportation
IMPORTANT	

1. Before completing this form the person concerned must refer to the provisions relating to returned goods as well as to the notes appearing on the reverse of this form.

2. The person concerned must complete by typewriter or by hand in block letters boxes 1 to 11 of this form.

3. When this information sheet is completed for goods whose exportation has been effected, within the framework of the common agricultural policy, under an export licence or advance fixing certificate or for goods liable to the benefit or refunds or other amounts provided for on exportation, it is valid only if box B, and where necessary box A, below, have been endorsed by the competent authorities.

4. This information sheet must be presented to the customs office of reimportation.

4. Number, kind, marks and numbers of packages and description of goods exported	5. Gross weight
	6. Net weight	7. Statistical value

8. Quantity for which information sheet is required

(a) in figures:	(b) in words:	9. CN code

A. ENDORSEMENT BY COMPETENT AUTHORITIES FOR EXPORT LICENCES OR ADVANCE FIXING CERTIFICATES	B. ENDORSEMENT BY COMPETENT AUTHORITIES FOR GRANT OF REFUNDS OR OTHER AMOUNTS PROVIDED FOR ON EXPORTATION	10. Additional information relating to the goods
— Regulations or licences or certificates observed	— No refunds or other amounts granted on exportation (¹) — Refunds and other amounts on exportation repaid for .... (quantity) (¹) — Entitlement to payment of refunds or other amounts on exportation cancelled for .... (quantity) (¹)	(a) export document type Ref. No dated (b) goods exported in completion of an inward processing operation (¹) (c) goods which have been released for free circulation for a specific use (¹) (d) goods in one of the situations referred to in Article 9 (2) of the Treaty (¹)
At .... , on	At .... , on	
(Signature) (Stamp)	(Signature) (Stamp)	

C. ENDORSEMENT BY THE OFFICE COMPLETING THE CUSTOMS EXPORT FORMALITIES	11. REQUEST OF EXPORTER
Information given in boxes 1 to 10 certified exact Identification measures taken	The undersigned, being the exporter (¹) on behalf of the exporter(¹) requests the issue of this information sheet for the purposes of the reimportation of the goods described therein
At .... , on	At .... , on ....
(Signature) (Stamp)	(Signature)

(¹) Delete as necessary.

FULL NAME AND ADDRESS OF CUSTOMS OFFICE OF EXPORTATION

NOTES

Box 1:	Give the name or trade name and full address including Member State.
Box 4:	Give exact details of the goods according to their normal commercial description or according to their tariff description. The description must correspond with that used in the export document.
Boxes 5 and 6:	Give the quantity appearing in the export document.
Box 7:	Give the statistical value at the time of exportation in the currency of the Member State of exportation.
Box 8:	Give details of net weight, volume, etc. which the person concerned wishes to reimport.
Box 10 (c):	This item relates to goods which have been released for free circulation in the Community, benefiting from total or partial relief from import duties by reason of their use for specific purposes.
Box 10 (d):	This item relates to the situation of goods at the time of their exportation.

REQUEST BY THE OFFICE OF REIMPORTATION

The office of reimportation indicated below requests:
— verification of the authenticity of this information sheet and the correctness of the information therein (')
— the following information to be supplied ('):

(') Delete as necessary.

Full name and address of office of reimportation	At .... , on ....
	(Signature) (Stamp)

REPLY OF THE COMPETENT AUTHORITIES

This information sheet is authentic and the details contained therein are exact (').
This information sheet gives rise to the following comments ('):

Other information required ('):

(') Delete as necessary.

Full name and address of the competent authorities	At .... , on ....
	(Signature) (Stamp)

REIMPORTATION

Quantity reimported	Reference number, date and type of reimportation document Signature and stamp of office of reimportation

(Copy omitted.)

NOTE CONCERNING INFORMATION SHEET INF 3

1. The forms shall be printed on white paper, free of mechanical pulp, dressed for writing purposes and shall weigh at least 40 g/m^2.

2. The size of the forms shall be 210 × 297 mm, a maximum tolerance in the length of between - 5 and 8 mm being allowed; the layout of the forms must be strictly observed, except in respect of the size of boxes 6 and 7.

Part III

3.   Member States shall be responsible for taking the necessary steps to have the forms printed. Each form shall bear the individual serial number, which may be pre-printed.

4.   The forms shall be printed in one of the official languages of the Community accepted by the competent authorities of the Member State of exportation. They shall be completed in the same language as that in which they are printed. Where necessary, the competent authorities of the customs office of reimportation in which information sheet INF 3 is required to be produced may request its translation into its official language or one of its official languages.

ANNEX 110A

EUROPEAN COMMUNITY

1. **Declarant** (full name or name of company or business and full address)	**CERTIFICATE** **on fishery products caught by Community fishing vessels in the territorial waters of a third country**

2. **Certification by the declarant** I, the undersigned, hereby declare that the products and goods shown in boxes 4 and 6 fulfill the conditions referred to in Article 188 of the Community Customs Code Date: (Signature)	3. **Community fishing vessel** Name: Recorded number: Base port: Flag:

4. **Products of sea-fishing** (name and type)	5. **Gross mass** (kg) (¹)
Container number(s):	

6. **Goods obtained from the products referred to above** (kind)	7. **CN code**	8. **Gross mass** (kg)
Container number(s):		

9. **Declaration by the master of the Community fishing vessel**

I, the undersigned, ... (full name),
master of the vessel shown in box 3, declare that the products referred to in box 4:
— were caught by my vessel in the territorial waters of .... (country or territory)
— have undergone on board my vessel processing which has been recorded on page .... of the logbook and that the goods obtained are described in box 6 (²).

Date: Signature:

10. **Declaration in the event of a first transhipment from a Community fishing vessel**

The products and/or goods described in this document were transhipped onto the following vessel:

(a) name: (b) registration number:

(c) flag: (d) full name of master:

The transhipment has been recorded on page .... of the logbook of the Community fishing vessel.   The transhipment has been recorded on page .... of the logbook of the vessel onto which the products and/or goods were transhipped.

Date:

(Signature of the master of the Community fishing vessel)   (Signature of the master of the receiving vessel)

(¹) Approximate figure.
(²) Delete when no processing takes place on board.

© European Communities Official Journal L 253, 11/10/1993 Annex 110A

Part III

11. **Declaration when processing takes place on board the vessel onto which that catch has been transhipped (¹)**

The products referred to in box 4 have undergone on board the vessel shown in box 10 processing which has been recorded on page .... of the logbook and the resulting goods are shown in box 6.

Date: (Signature of master)

12. **Declaration in the event of a second transhipment without further processing**

The products and/or goods referred to in this document have been transhipped onto the following vessel:

(a) name: (b) registration number:

(c) flag: (d) full name of master:

The transhipment has been recorded on page........of the logbook of the vessel from which the products and/or goods were transhipped.   The transhipment has been recorded on page .... of the logbook of the vessel onto which the products and/or goods were transhipped.

Date:

               (Signature of the master of the transhipping vessel)   (Signature of the master of the receiving vessel)

13. **Certification by the customs authority of the country or territory not forming part of Community customs territory**

The undersigned customs authority, hereby certifies that the products and/or goods referred to in boxes 4 and/or 6 were under customs supervision throughout their stay and have undergone no handling other than that necessary for their preservation.

Date of arrival of the products/goods:

Date of departure of the products/goods:

Means of transport used for reconsignment to Community customs territory:

Full address of the customs office: Stamp

Country or territory:

Date: (Signature)

Remarks

(¹) Community fishing vessel or Community factory ship.

NOTES

Inserted by Commission Regulation (EC) No 75/98, Art 1, para 33, Annex X.

ANNEX 111

ANNEX III

	EUROPEAN COMMUNITY	APPLICATION FOR REPAYMENT / REMISSION (*)

1 — ORIGINAL for the customs authority

1. Applicant or his representative (name and address)	2. Application for repayment / remission
□	
	Reference to the customs declaration
3. Customs office of entry in the accounts (name and address)	4. Supervising customs office (name and address)
5. Location of the goods	6. Comments of the supervising customs office
7. Destination of the goods (request for prior assignment)	

1

8. Description of the goods, number and type	9. CN code
	10. Net quantity / 11. Customs value
	12. Amount of repayment / remission of duties applied for in national currency
	Number of annexes

13. Application for repayment / remission

The undersigned hereby applies for the repayment / remission (¹) of import / export (¹) duties under the following Article of the Code (²)

□ 236

14. Acknowledgement of receipt of the application by the customs office of entry in the accounts

□ 237

Place and date

□ 238

Signature   Stamp

□ 239

15. Comments

16. Place and date

Signature of the applicant

(*) Read the notes on the back of the copy before completing the form.
(¹) Delete as appropriate
(²) Make a cross in the appropriate box thus – (X)

© European Communities Official Journal L 253, 11/10/1993 Annex 111

EUROPEAN COMMUNITY

APPLICATION FOR REPAYMENT / REMISSION (*)

2

1. Applicant or his representative (name and address)	2. Application for repayment / remission
	Reference to the customs declaration
3. Customs office of entry in the accounts (name and address)	4. Supervising customs office (name and address)
5. Location of the goods	6. Comments of the supervising customs office
7. Destination of the goods (request for prior assignment)	

2

8. Description of the goods, number and type	9. CN code
	10. Net quantity / 11. Customs value
	12. Amount of repayment / remission of duties applied for in national currency
	Number of annexes

13. Application for repayment / remission
The undersigned hereby applies for the repayment / remission (^{1}) of import / export (^{1}) duties under the following Article of the Code (^{2})

☐ 236

14. Acknowledgement of receipt of the application by the customs office of entry in the accounts

☐ 237

Place and date

☐ 238

Signature   Stamp

☐ 239

15. Comments

16. Place and date

Signature of the applicant

(*) Read the notes on the back of the copy before completing the form.
(^{1}) Delete as appropriate
(^{2}) Make a cross in the appropriate box thus – (X)

Part III

NOTES

A. General note

The part of the form constituting the application (boxes 1 to 13) shall be filled in by the applicant so that it is legible and indelible, preferably using a typewriter. It shall not contain any erasures or overwritten words. Correction should be made by crossing out the wrong words and adding further particulars, as necessary. Corrections must be initialed by the applicant and endorsed by the customs authority.

B. Special notes referring to the relevant box numbers

1. Give the name or business name and full address, including the postal code if any, of the applicant or of his representative.

   Where the applicant is not the person who paid or is liable to pay the duties to which the application refers, indicate the capacity in which the applicant is acting.

2. Give particulars of the customs declaration which gave rise to entry in the accounts of the duties the repayment or remission of which is requested.

3. Give the name and full address, including postal code if any, of the customs office where the import or export duties to which the application refers were entered in the accounts.

4. This box must be filled in where the goods are under the jurisdiction of a customs office other than the one referred to in box 3. In this case, give the name and full address, including postal code if any, of the customs office concerned.

5. Give the full address including postal code if any.

6. This box must be filled in where Article 897 of Regulation (EEC) No 2454/93 is applied. In this case, give the quantity, nature and value of the goods which are to remain in the Community.
   Where the goods are for delivery to a charity, give the name or business name and full address, including postal code if any.

7. Except in the cases referred to in Article 236 of the Code, give the customs-approved use or treatment to which the applicant wishes to assign the goods, depending on the possibilities available in the particular case under the Community Customs code (re-export from the customs territory of the Community, entry for another customs procedure, placing in a free zone or free warehouse, destruction, or delivery to a charity). Where the new customs treatment is subject to authorisation, give particulars of such authorisation.

   Indicate if prior assignment to the treatment or use in question is requested.

8. Give the usual trade description of the goods or their tariff description. The description must correspond to that used in the customs declaration referred to in box 2.

   State the number, kind, marks and identification numbers of packages. In the case of unpackaged goods, state the number of objects or indicate 'in bulk'.

9. Give the combined nomenclature code.

10. The quantity must be expressed in units of the metric system kilograms, litres, square metres, etc.

11. Indicate the customs value of the goods.

12. Amounts should be entered in national currency indicated as follows:

    — EUR: euro
    — DKK: Danish kroner
    — SEK: Swedish kronor
    — GBP: Pound sterling
    — CZK: Czech koruna
    — EEK: Estonian kroons
    — CYP: Cyprus pounds
    — LVL: Latvian lati
    — LTL: Lithuanian litai
    — HUF: Hungarian forint
    — MTL: Maltese lira
    — PLN: Polish zloty
    — SLT: Slovenian tolars
    — SKK: Slovak koruny

13. List of circumstances which may give rise to repayment / remission (for guidance):

    Article 236: No customs debt / amount fixed at a level higher than that lawfully due;

    Article 237: Goods entered in error for a customs procedure involving the obligation to pay duties;

    Article 238: Goods refused because they are defective or do not comply with the contract;

    Article 239: Special situations resulting from circumstances in which no deception or obvious negligence may be attributed to the person concerned.

    Where the application is based on Article 239 of the Code, the special situation must be described in detail in an annex to the application.

    NB: Where the application is based on an Article of the Code other than Article 239 an explanatory annex may likewise be attached where necessary.

    When an annex is attached indicate the number of pages.

C. Technical provisions regarding the application form for repayment or remission

1. The form on which the application for repayment or remission is to be drawn up shall be printed on self copying white paper free of mechanical pulp and dressed for writing purposes and shall weigh between 40 and 65 g/m2.

2. The size of the form shall be 210 x 297 mm.

3. Member states shall be responsible for having the form printed. The form shall bear an individual serial number.

4. The form shall be printed in one of the official languages of the European Communities designated by the customs authorities of the Member State in which the application for repayment or remission is made.

(Copy omitted.)

NOTES

A. General note

The part of the form constituting the application (boxes 1 to 13) shall be filled in by the applicant so that it is legible and indelible, preferably using a typewriter. It shall not contain any erasures or overwritten words. Correction should be made by crossing out the wrong words and adding further particulars, as necessary. Corrections must be initialled by the applicant and endorsed by the customs authority.

B. Special notes referring to the relevant box numbers

1. Give the name or business name and address, including the postal code if any, of the applicant or of his representative.

Where the applicant is not the person who paid or is liable to pay the duties to which the application refers, indicate the capacity in which the applicant is acting.

2. Give particulars of the customs declaration which gave rise to entry in the accounts of the duties the repayment or remission of which is requested.

3. Give the name and full address, including postal code if any, of the customs office where the import or export duties to which the application refers were entered in the accounts.

4. This box must be filled in where the goods are under the jurisdiction of a customs office other than the one referred to in box 3. In this case, give the name and full address, including postal code if any, of the customs office concerned.

5. Give the full address, including postal code if any.

6. This box must be filled in where Article 897 of Regulation (EEC) No 2454/93 is applied. In this case, give the quantity, nature and value of the goods which are to remain in the Community.

Where the goods are for delivery to a charity, give the name or business name and full address, including postal code if any.

7. Except in the cases referred to in Article 236 of the Code, give the customs-approved use or treatment to which the applicant wishes to assign the goods, depending on the possibilities available in the particular case under the Community Customs Code (re-export from the customs territory of the Community, entry for another customs procedure, placing in a free zone or free warehouse, destruction, or delivery to a charity). Where the new customs treatment is subject to authorisation, give particulars of such authorisation.

Indicate if prior assignment to the treatment or use in question is requested.

8. Give the usual trade description of the goods or their tariff description. The description must correspond to that used in the customs declaration referred to in box 2.

State the number, kind, marks and identification numbers of packages. In the case of unpackaged goods, state the number of objects or indicate "in bulk".

9. Give the Combined Nomenclature code.

10. The quantity must be expressed in units of the metric system, kilogrammes, litres, square metres, etc.

11. Indicate the customs value of the goods.

12. Amounts should be entered in national currency as indicated as follows:

— BEF for Belgian francs

— FRF for French francs

— LUF for Luxembourg francs

— DKK for Danish kroner

— GBP for pounds sterling

— ESP for Spanish pesetas

— PTE for Portuguese escudos

[— CZK: Czech koruna,

— EEK: Estonian kroons,

— CYP: Cyprus pounds,

— LVL: Latvian lati,

— LTL: Lithuanian litai,

— ITL for Italian lire

— NLG for Dutch guilders

— IEP for Irish pounds

— GRD for Greek drachmas

— [ATS for Austrian schillings

— FIM for Finnish markkas

— SEK for Swedish kronor]

— DEM for German marks

— HUF: Hungarian forint,

— MTL: Maltese lira,

— PLN: Polish zloty,

— SIT: Slovenian tolars,

— SKK: Slovak koruny.]

[—BGN: Bulgarian Lev

— RON: New Romanian Leu]

13. List of circumstances which may give rise to repayment/remission (for guidance):

Article 236: No customs debt/amount fixed at a level higher than that lawfully due;

Article 237: Goods entered in error for a customs procedure involving the obligation to pay duties.

Article 238: Goods refused because they are defective or do not comply with the contract.

Article 239: Special situations resulting from circumstances in which no deception or obvious negligence may be attributed to the person concerned.

Where the application is based on Article 239 of the Code, the special situation must be described in detail in an annex to the application.

NB: Where the application is based on an Article of the Code other than Article 239 an explanatory annex may likewise be attached where necessary.

When an annex is attached, indicate the number of pages.

C. Technical provisions regarding the application form for repayment or remission

1. The form on which the application for repayment or remission is to be drawn up shall be printed on self copying white paper free of mechanical pulp and dressed for writing purposes and shall weigh between 40 and 65 g/m².

2. The size of the form shall be 210 × 297 mm.

3. Member States shall be responsible for having the form printed. The form shall bear an individual serial number.

4. The form shall be printed in one of the official languages of the European Communities designated by the customs authorities of the Member State in which the application for repayment or remission is made.

NOTES

Notes: words in para 12 inserted by the 1994 Act of Accession, Annex I(XIII)(A)(b), para 68. Further words inserted by the 2003 Act of Accession Annex II(19)(A)(II), para 58.

Words relating to Bulgaria and Romania inserted by Commission Regulation (EC) 1792/2006, Art 1, Annex, Part 11(A)(56).

ANNEX 112

EUROPEAN COMMUNITY | **REQUEST FOR EXAMINATION**

1	1. Name and address of decision making authority ☐	2. Repayment / remission of duties
		File reference of decision-making customs authority
ORIGINAL	3. Name and address of supervising customs office	4. Application of Article 885 of Regulation (EEC) No. 2454/93
	5. Location of goods (¹)	6. Name and full address of person from whom the information requested may be obtained or who can assist the supervising customs office
		7. List of documents attached
1		

8. Purpose of the request

– that the following be obtained:

– that the following examination be carried out:

9. Decision-making customs authority

Place and date:

Signature:

Stamp

(¹) Complete only when applicable.

© European Communities Official Journal L 253, 11/10/1993 Annex 112

Part III

REPLY OF SUPERVISING CUSTOMS OFFICE (¹)   **ACKNOWLEDGEMENT OF RECEIPT (¹)**

10. Information obtained

11. Result of examination carried out

12. Place and date:

13. Signature and official stamp:

The supervising customs office shall give an acknowledgement of receipt only if it is unable to give effect to the request within two weeks of the date of receipt thereof. Acknowledgement of receipt shall be made as a copy of this document.

(Copy omitted.)

ANNEX 113

EUROPEAN COMMUNITY   **REPAYMENT OF REMISSION OF DUTY**

1. Name and address of the person concerned	2. Application of Article 912 of Regulation (ECC) No 2454/93
3. Name and address of customs office of entry in the accounts	4. Reference to the decision granting repayment or remission
	5. Name and address of implementing customs office

6. Description of the goods, number and type	7. CN code
	8. Quantity or net mass 9. Customs value

10. Implementing customs office

Certification for the granting of repayment or remission of duties

This is to certify that in accordance with the decision referred to in Box 4 the goods described above were

on ☐☐ | ☐☐ | ☐☐
    (date)

☐ exported from the Community   ☐ destroyed under customs supervisions

☐ placed in a customs warehouse   ☐ placed in free zone or free warehouse

☐ delivered free of charge to a charity specified in the decision   ☐ entered under the customs procedure specified in the decision

Customs declaration references, if any: ....

On this date the goods fulfilled the conditions laid down for repayment or remission of duty (1).

11. Place and date	Stamp
Signature	

(1) Where the Implementation customs office finds that the goods no longer satisfy those conditions it shall delete this sentence and record its findings overleaf under the heading 'Observations'.

Part III

OBSERVATIONS

(Copy omitted.)

COUNCIL DIRECTIVE

(95/59/EC)

of 27 November 1995

on taxes other than turnover taxes which affect the consumption of manufactured tobacco

NOTES

Date of publication in OJ: OJ L 55, 11.3.95, p 42.

THE COUNCIL OF THE EUROPEAN UNION,

Having regard to the Treaty establishing the European Community, and in particular Article 99 thereof,

Having regard to the proposal from the Commission,

Having regard to the opinion of the European Parliament,[1]

Having regard to the opinion of the Economic and Social Committee,[2]

(1) Whereas Council Directive 72/464/EEC of 19 December 1972 on taxes other than turnover taxes which affect the consumption of manufactured tobacco[3] and Second Council Directive 79/32/EEC of 18 December 1978 on taxes other than turnover taxes which affect the consumption of manufactured tobacco[4] have been amended substantially and on a number of occasions; whereas for reasons of rationality and clarity the said Directives should be consolidated in a single text;

(2) Whereas the objective of the Treaty is to establish an economic union within which there is healthy competition and whose characteristics are similar to those of a domestic market; and, as regards manufactured tobacco, achievement of this aim presupposes that the application in the Member States of taxes affecting the consumption of products in this sector does not distort conditions of competition and does not impede their free movement within the Community;

(3) Whereas, as far as excise duties are concerned, harmonisation of structures must, in particular, result in competition in the different categories of manufactured tobacco belonging to the same group not being distorted by the effects of the charging of the tax and, consequently, in the opening of the national markets of the Member States;

(4) Whereas the structure of the excise duty on cigarettes must include, in addition to a specific component calculated per unit of the product, a proportional component based on the retail selling price, inclusive of all taxes; whereas the turnover tax on cigarettes has the same effect as a proportional excise duty and this fact should be taken into account when the ratio between the specific component of the excise duty and the total tax burden is being established;

(5) Whereas, as regards cigarettes, the abovementioned objective is best achieved by a system which provides for a degression in the incidence of the tax and whereas for this purpose, the tax imposed on these products should consist of a proportional excise duty combined with a specific excise duty, the amount of which is fixed by each Member State in accordance with Community criteria;

(6) Whereas the structures for excise duties on manufactured tobacco should be harmonised by stages;

(7) Whereas the imperative needs of competition imply a system of freely formed prices for all groups of manufactured tobacco;

(8) Whereas there are several types of manufactured tobacco, distinguished by their characteristics and by the way in which they are used;

(9) Whereas these different types of manufactured tobacco should be defined;

(10) Whereas, for economic reasons, temporary derogations should be provided for certain Member States;

(11) Whereas a distinction needs to be made between fine-cut tobacco for the rolling of cigarettes and other smoking tobacco;

(12) Whereas a manufacturer needs to be defined as a natural or legal person who actually prepares tobacco products and sets the maximum retail selling price for each of the Member States for which the products in question are to be released for consumption;

(13) Whereas a majority of Member States grant exemptions from excise duty or make refunds of excise duty in respect of certain types of manufactured tobacco depending on the use which is made of them, and whereas the exemptions or refunds for particular uses need to be specified in this Directive;

(14) Whereas rolls of tobacco capable of being smoked as they are after simple handling should also be deemed to be cigarettes for the purposes of uniform taxation of these products;

(15) Whereas the Federal Republic of Germany should be authorised to tax rolls at least at the rate or amount applicable to fine-cut tobacco for the rolling of cigarettes until 31 December 1998 at the latest;

(16) Whereas this Directive must not affect the obligations of Member States concerning the deadlines for implementation of the Directives set out in Annex I, Part B,

---

[1] OJ C 56, 6.3.95, p 164.

[2] OJ C 133, 31.5.95, p 1.

[3] OJ L 303, 31.12.1972, p 1. Directive as last amended by Directive 92/78/EEC (OJ L 316, 31.10.92, p 5).

[4] OJ L 10, 16.1.79, p 8. Directive as last amended by Directive 92/78/EEC.

HAS ADOPTED THIS DIRECTIVE—

TITLE I
GENERAL PRINCIPLES

Article 1

1. The structure of the excise duty to which the Member States subject manufactured tobacco shall be harmonised in several stages.

2. This Directive lays down general principles for this harmonisation, as well as the special criteria applicable during the stages of harmonisation.

3. The transition from one stage of harmonisation to the next shall be decided on by the Council on a proposal from the Commission, taking into account the effects produced during the stage in progress by the measures introduced by the Member States into their system of excise duties in order to comply with the provisions applicable during that stage. The transition from one stage to the next may be deferred especially if it is likely to involve disproportionate losses of revenue for a Member State.

Article 2

1. The following shall be considered to be manufactured tobacco—
   (a)   cigarettes;
   (b)   cigars and cigarillos;
   (c)   smoking tobacco
   —   fine-cut tobacco for the rolling of cigarettes,
   —   other smoking tobacco;
as defined in Articles 3 to 7.

2. The Council shall, on a proposal from the Commission, adopt the provisions necessary to determine the way in which manufactured tobacco should be defined and classified in groups.

3. Notwithstanding existing Community provisions, the definitions referred to in Articles 3 to 7 shall be without prejudice to the choice of system or the level of taxation which shall apply to the different groups of products referred to in these Articles.

Article 3

The following shall be deemed to be cigars or cigarillos if they can be smoked as they are—

1.   rolls of tobacco made entirely of natural tobacco;
2.   rolls of tobacco with an outer wrapper of natural tobacco;
[3.   rolls of tobacco with a threshed blend filler and with an outer wrapper of the normal colour of a cigar covering the product in full, including where appropriate the filter but not in the case of tipped cigars, the tip, and a binder, both being of reconstituted tobacco, where the unit weight, not including filter or mouth-piece, is not less than 1,2 g and where the wrapper is fitted in spiral form with an acute angle of at least 30° to the longitudinal axis of the cigar;]
[4.   rolls of tobacco with a threshed blend filler and with an outer wrapper of the normal colour of a cigar, of reconstituted tobacco, covering the product in full, including where appropriate the filter but not, in the case of tipped cigars, the tip, where the unit weight, not including filter or mouth-piece, is not less than 2,3 g and the circumference over at least one third of the length is not less than 34 mm.]

NOTES

Points 3, 4: substituted by Council Directive 2002/10/EC art 3 para 1.

Article 4

1. The following shall be deemed to be cigarettes—
   (a)   rolls of tobacco capable of being smoked as they are and which are not cigars or cigarillos within the meaning of Article 3;
   (b)   rolls of tobacco which, by simple non-industrial handling, are inserted into cigarette-paper tubes;
   (c)   rolls of tobacco which, by simple non-industrial handling, are wrapped in cigarette paper.

[Up to and including 31 December 2001], the Federal Republic of Germany shall be authorised to tax the rolls of tobacco referred to in (b) at least at the rate or amount applicable to fine-cut tobacco for the rolling of cigarettes.

2. A roll of tobacco referred to in paragraph 1 shall, for excise duty purposes, be considered as two cigarettes where, excluding filter or mouth piece, it is longer than 9 cm but not longer than 18 cm, as three cigarettes where, excluding filter or mouthpiece, it is longer than 18 cm but not longer than 27 cm, and so on.

NOTES

Para 1: words in square brackets substituted by Council Directive 1999/81/EC, Art 3, para 1.

Article 5

The following shall be deemed to be smoking tobacco—

Part III

1.   tobacco which has been cut or otherwise split, twisted or pressed into blocks and is capable of being smoked without further industrial processing;

2.   tobacco refuse put up for retail sale which does not fall under Articles 3 and 4 and which can be smoked.

Article 6

Smoking tobacco as defined in Article 5 in which more than 25 % by weight of the tobacco particles have a cut width of less than 1 millimetre shall be deemed to be fine-cut tobacco for the rolling of cigarettes. Member States which do not apply this cut width of 1 millimetre on 1 January 1993 shall have until 31 December 1997 to comply with this provision.

Member States may also deem smoking tobacco in which more than 25 % by weight of the tobacco particles have a cut width of more than 1 millimetre and which was sold or intended to be sold for the rolling of cigarettes to be fine-cut tobacco for the rolling of cigarettes.

Article 7

1.   Products consisting in part of substances other than tobacco but otherwise conforming to the criteria set out in Article 3 shall be treated as cigars and cigarillos provided they have respectively—

—   a wrapper of natural tobacco,

—   a wrapper and binder of tobacco, both of reconstituted tobacco,

—   a wrapper of reconstituted tobacco.

2.   Products consisting in whole or in part of substances other than tobacco but otherwise conforming to the criteria set out in Article 4 or 5 shall be treated as cigarettes and smoking tobacco.

Notwithstanding the first subparagraph, products containing no tobacco and used exclusively for medical purposes shall not be treated as manufactured tobacco.

Article 8

1.   Cigarettes manufactured in the Community and those imported from non-member countries shall be subject to a proportional excise duty calculated on the maximum retail selling price, including customs duties, and also to a specific excise duty calculated per unit of the product.

2.   The rate of the proportional excise duty and the amount of the specific excise duty must be the same for all cigarettes.

3.   At the final stage of harmonisation of structures, the same ratio shall be established for cigarettes in all Member States between the specific excise duty and the sum of the proportional excise duty and the turnover tax, in such a way that the range of retail selling prices reflects fairly the difference in the manufacturers' delivery prices.

4.   Where necessary, the excise duty on cigarettes may include a minimum tax component, the ceiling for which shall be determined for each stage by the Council on a proposal from the Commission.

Article 9

1.   A natural or legal person established in the Community who converts tobacco into manufactured products prepared for retail sale shall be deemed to be a manufacturer.

Manufacturers, or, where appropriate, their representatives or authorised agents in the Community and importers of tobacco from non-member countries shall be free to determine the maximum retail selling price for each of their products for each Member State for which the products in question are to be released for consumption.

The second paragraph may not, however, hinder implementation of national systems of legislation regarding the control of price levels or the observance of imposed prices, provided that they are compatible with Community legislation.

2.   In order to facilitate the levying of the excise duty, Member States may, for each group of manufactured tobacco, fix a scale of retail selling prices on condition that each scale has sufficient scope and variety to correspond in fact with the variety of Community products. Each scale shall be valid for all the products belonging to the group of manufactured tobacco which it concerns, without distinction on the basis of quality, presentation, the origin of the products or of the materials used, the characteristics of the undertakings or of any other criterion.

Article 10

1.   At the final stage at the latest the rules for collecting the excise duty shall be harmonised. During the preceding stages the excise duty shall, in principle, be collected by means of tax stamps. If they collect the excise duty by means of tax stamps, Member States shall be obliged to make these stamps available to manufacturers and dealers in other Member States. If they collect the excise duty by other means, Member States shall ensure that no obstacle, either administrative or technical, affects trade between Member States on that account.

2.   Importers and national manufacturers of manufactured tobacco shall be subject to the system set out in paragraph 1 as regards the detailed rules for levying and paying the excise duty.

Article 11

The following may be exempted from excise duty or excise duty already paid on them may be refunded—

   (a)   denatured manufactured tobacco used for industrial or horticultural purposes;

   (b)   manufactured tobacco which is destroyed under administrative supervision;

   (c)   manufactured tobacco which is solely intended for scientific tests and for tests connected with product quality;

   (d)   manufactured tobacco which is reworked by the producer.

Member States shall determine the conditions and formalities to which the abovementioned exemptions or refunds are subject.

TITLE II
SPECIAL PROVISIONS APPLICABLE DURING THE FIRST STAGE OF HARMONIZATION

Article 12

1.   Subject to Article 1(3), the first stage of harmonisation of the structures of the excise duty on manufactured tobacco shall cover a period of sixty months from 1 July 1973.

2.   During the first stage of harmonisation Articles 13 and 14 shall be applicable.

Article 13

1.   The amount of the specific excise duty levied on cigarettes shall be established for the first time by reference to cigarettes in the most popular price category according to the data available on 1 January 1973.

2.   Without prejudice to the solution to be finally adopted regarding the ratio between the specific component and the proportional component, the amount referred to in paragraph 1 may not be lower than 5 % or higher than 75 % of the aggregate amount of the proportional excise duty and the specific excise duty levied on these cigarettes.

Part III

3. If the excise duty on the price category referred to in paragraph 1 is amended after 1 January 1973, the amount of the specific excise duty shall be established by reference to the new tax burden on the cigarettes referred to in paragraph 1.

Article 14

Notwithstanding Article 8(1), each Member State may exclude customs duties from the basis for calculating the proportional excise duty on cigarettes.

TITLE III
SPECIAL PROVISIONS APPLICABLE DURING THE SECOND STAGE OF HARMONIZATION

Article 15

1. The second stage of harmonisation of the structures of the excise duty on manufactured tobacco shall run from 1 July 1978.

2. During the second stage of harmonisation Article 16 shall apply.

Article 16

1. The amount of the specific excise duty on cigarettes shall be established by reference to cigarettes in the most popular price category according to the information available at 1 January each year, beginning 1 January 1978.

2. The specific component of the excise duty may not be less than 5 % or more than 55 % of the amount of the total tax burden resulting from the aggregation of the proportional excise duty, the specific excise duty and the turnover tax levied on these cigarettes.

[2a. By way of derogation from paragraph 2, where a change in the retail selling price of cigarettes in the most popular price category occurs in a Member State, thereby bringing the specific component of the excise duty, expressed as a percentage of the total tax burden, below 5 % or above 55 % of the total tax burden, the Member State in question may refrain from adjusting the amount of the specific excise duty until not later than 1 January of the second year following that in which the change occurs.]

3. [If the excise duty levied] on the price category referred to in paragraph 1 is amended after 1 January 1978, the amount of the specific excise duty shall be established by reference to the new total tax burden on the cigarettes referred to in paragraph 1.

4. Notwithstanding Article 8(1), each Member State may exclude customs duties from the basis for calculating the proportional excise duty on cigarettes.

[5. Member States may levy a minimum excise duty on cigarettes sold at a price lower than the retail selling price for cigarettes of the price category most in demand, provided that such excise duty does not exceed the amount of the excise duty levied on cigarettes of the price category most in demand.]

NOTES

Para 2a: inserted by Council Directive 1999/81/EC, Art 3, para 2(a).

Para 3: words in square brackets substituted by Council Directive 1999/81/EC, Art 3, para 2(b).

Para 5: substituted by Council Directive 2002/10/EC art 3 para 2.

TITLE IV
FINAL PROVISIONS

Article 17

Where necessary, the Council shall, on a proposal from the Commission, adopt provisions for the application of this Directive.

Article 18

Member States shall communicate to the Commission the text of the main provisions of national law which they adopt in the field covered by this Directive.

Article 19

1. The Directives listed in Annex 1, Part A shall be repealed, without prejudice to the obligations of the Member States concerning the time-limits for implementation set out in Annex I, Part B.

2. References to the repealed Directives shall be construed as references to this Directive and shall be read in accordance with the correlation table set out in Annex II.

Article 20

This Directive shall enter into force on the twentieth day following its publication in the *Official Journal of the European Communities*.

Article 21

This Directive is addressed to the Member States.
Done at Brussels, 27 November 1995.

ANNEX I
(Article 19)

PART A
REPEALED DIRECTIVES

1. Directive 72/464/EEC
2. Directive 79/32/EEC and their successive amendments—
   — Directive 74/318/EEC
   — Directive 75/786/EEC
   — Directive 76/911/EEC
   — Directive 77/805/EEC
   — Directive 80/369/EEC
   — Directive 80/1275/EEC
   — Directive 81/463/EEC
   — Directive 82/2/EEC
   — Directive 82/877/EEC
   — Directive 84/217/EEC
   — Directive 86/246/EEC
   — Directive 92/78/EEC.

Part III

PART B

Directive	Time-limits for transposition
—72/464/EEC	1.7.1973[1]
—79/32/EEC	1.1.1980
—74/318/EEC	1.1.1986
—75/786/EEC	31.12.1992
—76/911/EEC	
—77/805/EEC	
—80/369/EEC	
—80/1275/EEC	
—81/463/EEC	
—82/2/EEC	
—82/877/EEC	
—84/217/EEC	
—86/246/EEC	
—92/78/EEC	

ANNEX II
CORRELATION TABLE

This Directive	Directive 72/464/EEC	Directive 79/32/EEC
Title I	Title I	
Article 1, (1) and (2)	Article 1, (1) and (2)	
Article 1, (3)	Article 1, (4)	
Article 2, (1) and (2)	Article 3, (1) and (2)	Article 1, (1)
Article 2, (3)		Article 1, (2)
Article 3		Article 2
Article 4		Article 3
Article 5		Article 4
Article 6		Article 4a
Article 7		Article 7
Article 8	Article 4	
Article 9	Article 5	
Article 10	Article 6	
Article 11	Article 6a	
Title II	Title II	
Article 12	Article 7	
Article 13	Article 8	
Article 14	Article 9	
Title III	Title III	
Article 15	Article 10a	
Article 16	Article 10b	
Title IV	Title III	
Article 17	Article 11	
Article 18	Article 12, (2)	
Article 19	—	—
Article 20	—	—

This Directive	Directive 72/464/EEC	Directive 79/32/EEC
Article 21	Article 13	Article 10

[1] 1 The United Kingdom and Ireland were allowed to postpone this time-limit until 31 December 1977.

COMMISSION REGULATION

(2388/2000/EC)

of 13 October 2000

amending Annex I to Council Regulation (EEC) No 2658/87 on the tariff and statistical nomenclature and on the Common Customs Tariff

NOTES

Date of publication in OJ: OJ L 264, 18.10.2000, p 1.

THE COMMISSION OF THE EUROPEAN COMMUNITIES,

Having regard to the Treaty establishing the European Community,

Having regard to Council Regulation (EEC) No 2658/87 of 23 July 1987[1] and in particular Articles 9 and 12 thereof,

Whereas—

(1) Regulation (EEC) No 2658/87 established a goods nomenclature, hereinafter called the "Combined Nomenclature", to meet, at one and the same time, the requirements of the Common Customs Tariff, the external trade statistics of the Community and other Community policies concerning the importation or exportation of goods.

(2) The combined Nomenclature is reproduced in Annex I to Regulation (EEC) No 2658/87 together with the autonomous and the conventional duty rates and the statistical supplementary units.

(3) It is appropriate to modernise and to simplify Annex I as envisaged by the SLIM initiative (Simpler legislation for the internal market).

(4) It is necessary to amend the Combined Nomenclature to take account of—

1. changes in requirements relating to statistics and commercial policy;
2. the need for alignment or clarification of texts.

(5) Following the adoption of Council Regulation (EC) No 254/2000[2] amending Regulation (EEC) No 2658/87 on the tariff and statistical nomenclature and the Common Customs Tariff, and in particular Article 1 thereof, the presentation of Annex I has been rationalised and simplified by having one column reflecting the conventional duty rates with an indication in a footnote of the autonomous duty rate whenever such a rate is lower than the conventional duty rate.

(6) Annex I includes adjustments of duty rates resulting from measures adopted by the Council, including Decision 94/800/EC of 22 December 1994 concerning the conclusion on behalf of the European Community, as regards matters within its competence, of the agreements reached in the Uruguay Round multilateral negotiations (1986 to 1994), Council Regulation (EC) 3093/95 of 22 December 1995 laying down the rates of duty to be applied by the Community resulting from negotiations under GATT Article XXIV:6 (consequent upon the accession of Austria, Finland and Sweden to the European Union) as well as measures adopted by the Council or the Commission[3].

(7) In accordance with Article 12 the Commission shall adopt a regulation reproducing the complete version of the Combined Nomenclature, together with the autonomous and conventional duty rates, as resulting from measures adopted by

the Council or the Commission. The said Regulation shall published not later than 31 October in the *Official Journal of the European Communities* and it shall apply from 1 January of the following year.[4]

(8) The measures provided for in this Regulation are in accordance with the opinion of the Customs Code Committee,

---

[1] OJ L 256, 7.9.87, p 1, as last amended by Regulation (EC) No 1264/2000, OJ L 144, 17.6.2000, p 6).

[2] OJ L 28, 3.2.2000, p 16.

[3] Incorporated in Annex I to this Regulation are amendments resulting from the adoption of the following measures—

— Council Decision (EC) No 96/611 of 16 September 1996 (OJ L 271, 24.10.96, p 31),
— Council Decisions 97/359/EC and 97/360/EC of 24 March 1997 (OJ L 155, 12.6.97, p 1),
— Council Regulation (EC) No 2216/97 of 3 November 1997 (OJ L 305, 8.11.97, p 1),
— Commission Regulation (EC) No 2472/97 of 11 December 1997 (OJ L 341, 12.12.97, p 25),
— Council Regulation (EC) No 1110/1999 of 10 May 1999 (OJ L 135, 29.5.99, p 1).
— Commission Regulation (EC) No 2626/1999 of 14 December 1999 (OJ L 321, 14.12.99, p 3),
— Commission Regulation (EC) No 1264/1999 of 8 June 2000 (OJ L 144, 17.6.2000, p 6).

[4] Title substituted by Corrigendum (see OJ L276 28.10.2000 P 92).

HAS ADOPTED THIS REGULATION—

Article 1

(Introduces Annex I which substitutes Council Regulation (EEC) 2658/87, Annex I.)

Article 2

This Regulation shall enter into force on 1 January 2001.

This Regulation shall be binding in its entirety and directly applicable in all Member States.

Done at Brussels, 13 October 2000.

(Annex substitutes Council Regulation (EEC) 2658/87, Annex I.)

COMMISSION REGULATION

(2787/2000/EC)

of 15 December 2000

amending Regulation (EEC) No 2454/93 laying down provisions for the implementation of Council Regulation (EEC) No 2913/92 establishing the Community Customs Code

THE COMMISSION OF THE EUROPEAN COMMUNITIES,

Having regard to the Treaty establishing the European Community,

Having regard to Council Regulation (EEC) No 2913/92 of 12 October 1992 establishing the Community Customs Code[1], as last amended by Regulation (EC) No 2700/2000 of the European Parliament and of the Council[2], (hereinafter referred to as "the Code"), and in particular Article 249 thereof,

Whereas—

(1) Member States may wish to engage in simplification test programmes to evaluate initiatives taken in particular at international level, to harmonise and simplify customs procedures. Without prejudice to the application of Council Regulation (EC) No 1172/95 of 22 May 1995 on the statistics relating to the trading of goods by the Community and its Member States with non-member countries[3], as last amended by Regulation (EC) No 374/98[4], this type of initiative may require derogations from the application of Commission Regulation (EEC) No 2454/93[5], as last amended by Regulation (EC) No 1602/2000[6], for the period necessary to carry out such test programmes.

(2) Experience has shown that some of the provisions on authorising the operation of regular shipping services should be adjusted.

(3) Simpler and clearer Community transit rules would benefit business and customs services alike.

(4) The problems encountered in recent years in connection with the transit procedures have caused significant losses for the budgets of the Member States and the Community and have represented a constant threat to European business and traders.

(5) These procedures should therefore be modernised to make them more business-oriented while still ensuring effective protection of the public interests of the Member States and the Community.

(6) The circumstances in which use of the Community transit procedure is mandatory should be defined more clearly.

(7) A clear distinction should also be made between a standard procedure applicable to all traders and simplifications applicable only to traders complying with certain conditions. This calls for a balanced approach which takes risk into account and benefits reliable traders by specifically authorising them to use simplifications while maintaining the principle of free access to the basic transit procedure.

(8) To ensure uniform application of Article 94(4) of the Code, rules and conditions should be laid down for reducing the amount of a comprehensive guarantee and waiving guarantees. The rules and conditions should take into account both an operator's reliability and the risks attaching to the goods.

(9) The circumstances in which use of a lower comprehensive guarantee or a comprehensive guarantee may be prohibited for goods involving greater risks should also be set out.

(10) Pending the coming on stream of the full computerised transit system, the administration of and controls on the Community transit procedures could be improved by incorporating in the provisions a number of rules clearly stating the procedures to be applied and the time limits to be observed to ensure a quality service for transit users.

(11) New provisions should be added to Community transit legislation to facilitate and speed up debt recovery.

(12) Certain corrections should be made to the content with regard to references to the TIR Convention.

(13) In view of technical progress in the production of malt, the standard rates of yield with regard to unroasted and roasted malt should be adjusted.

(14) Commission Regulation (EC) No 2513/98[7] updates Annex I to Regulation (EEC) No 1501/95[8] which sets out the processing coefficients for the production of unroasted and roasted malt used in order to calculate the export refunds on processed products. The standard rates of yield should therefore be calculated on the basis of those coefficients.

(15) To avoid disadvantages in terms of the advance payment of export refunds in accordance with Council Regulation (EEC) No 565/80[9], as last amended by Regulation (EC) No 2026/83[10], provision should be made to the new standard rates of yield for prefinanced goods to apply with effect from 1 September 1998.

(16) Regulation (EEC) No 2454/93 should be amended accordingly.

(17) Certain transitional provisions of the present Regulation should replace those in Article 2 of Commission Regulation (EC) No 502/1999[11]. For reasons of clarity, the latter should therefore be deleted.

(18) The measures provided for in this Regulation are in accordance with the opinion of the Customs Code Committee,

---

[1] OJ L 302, 19.10.1992, p 1.
[2] OJ L 311, 12.12.2000, p 17.
[3] OJ L 118, 25.5.1995, p 10.
[4] OJ L 48, 19.2.1998, p 6.
[5] OJ L 253, 11.10.1993, p 1.
[6] OJ L 188, 26.7.2000, p 1.
[7] OJ L 313, 21.11.1998, p 16.
[8] OJ L 147, 30.6.1995, p 7.
[9] OJ L 62, 7.3.1980, p 5.
[10] OJ L 199, 22.7.1983, p 12.
[11] OJ L 65, 12.3.1999, p 1.

HAS ADOPTED THIS REGULATION—

Article 1

(Amends Regulation (EEC) No 2454/93).

Article 2

Any of the forms referred to in Article 1(69), (72), (75) and (79) in use before the date of the entry into force of this Regulation may continue to be used, subject to the necessary editorial changes being made, until stocks run out or until 31 December 2002.

Subject to the conditions set out in the first subparagraph, the TC32 form (flat-rate guarantee voucher) may be used as an individual guarantee voucher within the meaning of Article 347(2) of Regulation (EEC) No 2454/93. Where it is so used, the word "flat-rate" at the top of the front of the form shall be crossed out and replaced by the word "individual".

Article 3

Before 1 January 2003, on the basis of a report drawn up in consultation with the bodies which represent the operators involved, the Commission shall review the provision concerning the furnishing of the HS code to identify goods. If appropriate, the Commission shall define when and subject to what conditions the obligation to use this Code and, possibly, other information to identify goods placed under the Community transit procedure might be extended to the widest possible range of Community transit operations. The review shall take into account the computerisation of the Community transit procedure.

Article 4

1. This Regulation shall enter into force on the seventh day following that of its publication in the *Official Journal of the European Communities*.

2. Points 2 to 80 of Article 1 shall apply from 1 July 2001.

However, from 1 January 2001 Community transit operations on goods listed in Annex 44C to Regulation (EEC) No 2454/93 may only be carried out under cover of a comprehensive guarantee if it has been authorised in accordance with Articles 372 to 384 of that Regulation.

Article 404 of Regulation (EEC) No 2454/93, as well as the transitional provision set out in the second subparagraph of paragraph 5 of this Article shall be applicable from 1 January 2001.

For the purposes of Article 4(3) of Regulation (EEC) No 565/80, point 81 of Article 1 shall apply with effect from 1 September 1998.

3. The provisions of this Regulation shall not apply to goods placed under the Community transit procedure before its date of application.

4. Article 358(1) of Regulation (EEC) No 2454/93 shall apply to offices of departure no later than when they apply the provisions of Articles 367 to 371 of that Regulation.

5. As regards the authorisations provided for in Part II, Title II, Chapter 4, Section 3 of Regulation (EEC) No 2454/93, authorisations which are valid at the date of application of this Regulation may remain applicable until 31 December 2001 at the latest.

Each authorisation granting the status of authorised consignor must comply with Article 404 of Regulation (EEC) No 2454/93 as soon as the office of departure concerned applies the provisions of Articles 367 to 371 of that Regulation. However, authorisations valid prior to 31 March 1999 shall comply with Article 404 by a date as decided by the customs authorities and by 31 March 2004 at the latest. [This subparagraph does not apply to transit operations carried out by the authorised consignor using simplified procedures referred to in Article 372(1)(g).]

The simplifications referred to in Article 372(1)(g)(i) and (iv) will require an authorisation as from a date and subject to conditions to be determined by the committee procedure.

6. The second sentence of the second subparagraph and the third subparagraph of Article 2 of Regulation (EC) No 502/1999 are deleted.

This Regulation shall be binding in its entirety and directly applicable in all Member States.

NOTES

Para 5: words added by Commission Regulation (EC) 444/2002, Art 2.

Done at Brussels, 15 December 2000.

(Annexes amend and substitute Annexes to Regulation (EEC) 2454/93.)

COMMISSION REGULATION

(993/2001/EC)

of May 2001

amending Regulation (EEC) No 2454/93 laying down provisions for the implementation of Council Regulation (EEC) No 2913/92 establishing the Community Customs Code

NOTES

Date of publication in OJ: OJ L 141, 28.5.01, p 1.

THE COMMISSION OF THE EUROPEAN COMMUNITIES,

Having regard to the Treaty establishing the European Community,

Having regard to Council Regulation (EEC) No 2913/92 of 12 October 1992 establishing the Community Customs Code[1], as last amended by European Parliament and Council Regulation (EC) No 2700/2000[2], and in particular Article 247 thereof,

Whereas—

(1) Legal provisions serving to develop, complete and where appropriate to update the existing legal framework for the computerised transit system, to ensure the homogenous and reliable operation of the full computerised transit procedure, should be introduced into Commission Regulation (EEC) No 2454/93[3], as last amended by Regulation (EC) No 2787/2000[4].

(2) The exchange of information between the customs authorities at offices of departure and offices of transit using information technology and computer networks will follow a more effective control on the transit operations, whilst at the same time relieving carriers from the formality of presenting the transit advice note to each office of transit.

(3) For the monitoring of the use of the comprehensive guarantee and guarantee waiver it is necessary to establish a presumed amount of duties and other charges involved in each transit operation in the cases where the data needed for this calculation is not available. However the customs authorities should be empowered to assess a different figure on the basis of other information that may be known to them.

(4) For guarantees monitored by the computerised transit system it should be possible to dispense with the presentation of paper guarantee documents to the office of departure.

(5) For the computerised control of the individual guarantee by means of vouchers it is appropriate oblige the guarantor to provide the office of guarantee with any required information on vouchers issued.

(6) To maximise the benefits attainable from the computerised transit system by the customs authorities and economic operators it is appropriate to extend also to the authorised consignee the obligation to exchange information with the office of destination using a data-processing technique.

(7) The computerised environment will allow a considerable shortening of the current time-limits for launching the enquiry procedure.

(8) Access to the electronic transit data will be facilitated by printing the Movement Reference Number (MRN) as a standard bar code on the Transit Accompanying Document, making the procedure quicker and more efficient.

(9) Title III of Part II of Regulation (EEC) No 2454/93, concerning customs warehousing, inward processing, processing under customs control, temporary importation and outward processing, should be simplified and rationalised. Chapter I of Title V, which covers free Zones and free warehouses, should be replaced.

(10) Regulation (EEC) No 2913/92 (hereinafter: "the Code"), as amended by Regulation (EC) No 2700/2000, provides the basis for making the conditions for access

to certain procedures more flexible, by replacing the positive list by an examination of the economic conditions in the case of processing under customs control, by concentrating the examination of economic conditions prior to issuing inward processing authorisations on sensitive goods and, in outward processing, increasing the application of the taxation method based on the cost of the process.

(11) The interaction between the inward processing arrangements and the export refund system in the agricultural products and goods sector requires more detailed rules following the reduction in export subsidies agreed within the World Trade Organisation.

(12) The whole body of rules on the customs procedures with economic impact should be rationalised taking into account the fact that in each of the five customs procedures with economic impact a number of identical provisions apply. In order to avoid repetition in the rules, provisions common to two or more procedures should be contained in a single chapter. This part concerns in particular authorisations – including those involving several administrations – and simplified authorisation arrangements, stock records, rates of yield, compensatory interest, methods of discharge, transfers and administrative cooperation as well as a harmonised structure for the application and authorisation forms. In order to introduce more flexibility into procedural rules, the possibility of granting a retroactive authorisation for a period of one year under certain conditions should be provided for.

(13) The Code, as amended by Regulation (EC) No 2700/2000, also provides the basis for allowing the Member States to designate free zones in which customs checks and formalities shall be carried out and the provisions concerning customs debt applied in accordance with the requirements of the customs warehousing procedure. Free zones should therefore be distinguished according to the type of control to which they are submitted.

(14) The transparency of all the rules should be improved by a more rigorous structure and greater concision in the provisions and by avoiding as far as possible overlapping of customs and agricultural rules.

(15) The number of annexes should be significantly reduced. Some should be incorporated in the text itself (Nos 69a, 74, 95); others should be combined (67 and 68; 70, 75a, 81, 82, 84, 98 and 106; 71, 72 and 83; 85, 86, 88, 89 and 107); finally, another group should be deleted, the content of these annexes having rather an explanatory, illustrative or exemplary nature. Two new annexes should be created (70 and 73).

(16) The international trade in worn and packed clothing is experiencing a rapid growth. In order to facilitate such trade, it is opportune to specify the origin rule applicable for worn clothing and other worn articles which have been collected and packed. The rule adopted by the WTO Committee on Rules of Origin in the context of the international harmonisation of non-preferential rules of origin (WTO Agreement on Rules of Origin) bases the determination of the origin of worn clothing and other worn articles on the concept of last substantial transformation.

(17) Regulation (EEC) No 2454/93 should therefore be amended accordingly.

(18) The measures provided for by this Regulation are in accordance with the opinion of the Customs Code Committee,

---

[1] OJ L302, 19.10.92, p 1.

[2] OJ L311, 12.12.2000, p 17.

[3] OJ L253, 11.10.93, p 1.

[4] OJ L330, 27.12.2000, p 1.

HAS ADOPTED THIS REGULATION—

Article 1

(Amends Regulation (EEC) No 2454/93).

Part III

Article 2

1. This Regulation shall enter into force on the seventh day following that of its publication in the *Official Journal of the European Communities*.

2. Points 1 to 30 and 32 to 38 of Article 1 shall apply from 1 July 2001.

3. Each authorisation granting the status of authorised consignee shall comply with Article 408a of Regulation (EEC) No 2454/93 by a date decided by the customs authorities, and at the latest by 31 March 2004. [This subparagraph does not apply to transit operations where the authorised consignee receives goods using simplified procedures referred to in Article 372(1)(g).]

Before 1 January 2004, the Commission shall evaluate the implementation of Article 408a of Regulation (EEC) No 2454/93 in relation to Articles 367 to 371 of that Regulation. The evaluation will be based on a report drawn up from contributions of the Member States. The Commission may decide on this basis and in accordance with the committee procedure if and subject to what conditions a deferral of the date mentioned in first subparagraph is necessary.

This Regulation shall be binding in its entirety and directly applicable in all Member States.

NOTES

Para 3: words added by Commission Regulation (EC) 444/2002, Art 3.

Done at Brussels, 4 May 2001.

(Annexes amend and substitute Annexes to Regulation (EEC) 2454/93.)

[COUNCIL REGULATION

(1207/2001/EC)

of 11 June 2001

on procedures to facilitate the issue or the making out in the Community of proofs of origin and the issue of certain approved exporter authorisations under the provisions governing preferential trade between the European Community and certain countries]

NOTES

Date of publication in OJ: L 165, 21.06.2001, p 1.

Heading substituted by Council Regulation (EC) 1617/2006, Art 1(1) (see OJ L 300, 31.10.06 p 5).

THE COUNCIL OF THE EUROPEAN UNION,

Having regard to the Treaty establishing the European Community, and in particular Article 133 thereof,

Having regard to the proposal from the Commission,

Whereas:

(1) Council Regulation (EEC) No 3351/83 of 14 November 1983 on the procedure to facilitate the issue of movement certificates EUR.1 and the making-out of forms EUR.2 under the provisions governing preferential trade between the European Economic Community and certain countries[1] provided for the correct application of

the preferential origin rules in relation to exports from the Community to certain third countries.

(2) Many changes have taken place in the customs field since Regulation (EEC) No 3351/83 was adopted.

(3) In the context of the single market, it has been found that firms exporting goods from one or more Member States other than the one in which they are established and wishing to use simplified procedures for the issue of proof of origin, sometimes have to apply for a separate authorisation for each Member State of export. It is desirable to simplify this situation, while ensuring that the machinery of the preferential arrangements can continue to operate properly.

(4) The authorities responsible for issuing or verifying proofs of origin should be in a position to fulfil the Community's commitments under the preferential agreements within the requisite deadlines.

(5) In the interests of clarity, Regulation (EEC) No 3351/83 should be repealed and replaced by this Regulation,

---

[1] OJ L 339, 5.12.1983, p. 19.

HAS ADOPTED THIS REGULATION—

Article 1 Scope
This Regulation lays down rules intended to facilitate—

    (a)   [the issue or the making-out in the Community of proofs of origin under the provisions governing preferential trade between the Community and certain countries;]

    (b)   the issue of approved-exporter authorisations valid in several Member States;

    (c)   the functioning of the methods of administrative cooperation between the Member States.

NOTES
Para (a): substituted by Council Regulation (EC) 1617/2006, Art 1(2) (see OJ L 300, 31.10.06 p 5).

Article 2 Supplier's declarations and their use
1. Suppliers shall provide, by means of a declaration, information concerning the status of products with regard to the Community's preferential rules of origin.

2. [Supplier's declarations shall be used by exporters as evidence, in particular in support of applications for the issue or the making-out in the Community of proofs of origin under the provisions governing preferential trade between the Community and certain countries.]

NOTES
Para 2: substituted by Council Regulation (EC) 1617/2006, Art 1(3) (see OJ L 300, 31.10.06 p 5).

Article 3 Making of supplier's declarations
Except in the cases provided for in Article 4, the supplier shall furnish a separate declaration for each consignment of goods.

The supplier shall include that declaration on the commercial invoice relating to that consignment or on a delivery note or any other commercial document which describes the goods concerned in sufficient detail to enable them to be identified.

Part III

The supplier may furnish the declaration at any time, even after the goods have been delivered.

Article 4 Long-term supplier's declarations

1. When a supplier regularly supplies a particular customer with goods whose status in respect of the rules of preferential origin is expected to remain constant for considerable periods of time, he may provide a single declaration to cover subsequent shipments of those goods, hereinafter referred to as "a long-term supplier's declaration". A long-term supplier's declaration may be issued for a period of up to one year from the date of issue of the declaration.

2. A long-term supplier's declaration may be issued with retroactive effect. In such cases, its validity may not exceed the period of one year from the date on which it came into effect.

3. The supplier shall inform the buyer immediately when the long-term supplier's declaration is no longer valid in relation to the goods supplied.

Article 5 Form and making-out of supplier's declarations

1. For products having obtained preferential originating status, the supplier's declaration shall be given in the form prescribed in Annex I or, for long-term suppliers' declarations, in that prescribed in Annex II.

2. For products which have undergone working or processing in the Community without having obtained preferential originating status, the supplier's declaration shall be given in the form prescribed in Annex III or, for long-term supplier's declarations, in that prescribed in Annex IV.

3. The supplier's declaration shall bear the original signature of the supplier in manuscript and may be made out on a pre-printed form. However, where the invoice and supplier's declaration are drawn up by computer, the declaration need not be signed in manuscript provided that the supplier gives the client a written undertaking accepting complete responsibility for every supplier's declaration which identifies him as if it had been signed in manuscript by him.

Article 6 Information certificates INF 4

1. To verify the accuracy or authenticity of a supplier's declaration, the customs authorities may call upon on the exporter to obtain from the supplier an information certificate INF 4, using the form shown in Annex V.

2. The information certificate INF 4 shall be issued by the customs authorities of the Member State in which the supplier is established. The said authorities shall have the right to call for any evidence and to carry out any inspection of the supplier's accounts or any other check that they consider necessary.

3. The customs authorities shall issue the information certificate INF 4 within three months of receipt of the application submitted to them by the suppliers, indicating whether or not the declaration given by the supplier was correct.

4. The completed certificate shall be given to the supplier to forward to the exporter for transmission to the relevant customs authority.

Article 7 Preservation of declarations and supporting documents

1. A supplier who makes out a supplier's declaration shall keep all the documentary evidence proving the correctness of the declaration for at least three years.

2. A customs authority to which an application for the issue of an information certificate INF 4 has been made shall keep the application form for at least three years.

Article 8 Approved-exporter authorisation

1.   An exporter who frequently exports goods from a Member State other than the one in which he is established may obtain approved exporter status covering such exports.

For that purpose, he shall submit an application to the competent customs authorities of the Member State in which he is both established and keeps the records containing the evidence of origin.

2.   When the authorities referred to in paragraph 1 are satisfied that the conditions set out in the origin Protocols to the relevant Agreements or in the Community legislation concerning the autonomous preferential regimes are fulfilled, and issue the authorisation, they shall notify the Customs administrations of the Member States concerned.

Article 9 Mutual administrative assistance

The Member States' customs authorities shall assist each other in checking the accuracy of the information given in suppliers' declarations and in ensuring that the system of approved exporter authorisations operates correctly.

Article 10 Checking supplier's declarations

1.   Where an exporter is unable to present an information certificate INF 4 within four months of the request of the customs authorities, the customs authorities of the Member State of export may directly ask the authorities of the Member State where the supplier is established to confirm the status of the products concerned in respect of the rules of preferential origin.

2.   For the purposes of paragraph 1, the customs authorities of the Member State of export shall send the customs authorities of the Member State to whom the request is addressed all information available to them and give the reasons of form or substance for their enquiry.

In support of their request, they shall provide all documents or information they have obtained which suggest that the supplier's declaration is inaccurate.

3.   The verification shall be carried out by the customs authorities of the Member State in which the supplier's declaration has been issued. The authorities in question may call for any evidence, carry out any inspection of the producer's accounts or conduct any other verification considered appropriate.

4.   The customs authorities requesting the verification shall be informed of the results as soon as possible by means of the information certificate INF 4.

5.   [Where there is no reply within five months of the date of the verification request or where the reply does not contain sufficient information to demonstrate the real origin of the products, the customs authorities of the country of export shall declare invalid the proof of origin established on the basis of the documents in question.]

NOTES

Para 5: substituted by Council Regulation (EC) 1617/2006, Art 1(4) (see OJ L 300, 31.10.06 p 5).

Article 11 Repeal

Regulation (EEC) No 3351/83 is hereby repealed.

References to the repealed Regulation shall be construed as references being made to this Regulation.

Article 12 Transitional provisions

1. Supplier's declarations, including long-term suppliers' declarations made before the date of entry into force of this Regulation shall remain valid.

2. Supplier's declarations conforming to the specimens in Regulation (EEC) No 3351/83 may continue to be issued for a period of 12 months from the entry into force of this Regulation.

3. Information certificate INF 4 forms of the type shown in Annex V to Regulation (EEC) No 3351/83 may continue to be used for a period of 12 months from the date of entry into force of this Regulation.

Article 13 Entry into force

This Regulation shall enter into force on the 20th day following that of its publication in the Official Journal of the European Communities.

This Regulation shall be binding in its entirety and directly applicable in all Member States.

Done at Luxembourg, 11 June 2001.

(Annexes I to V are not reproduced)

COMMISSION REGULATION

(444/2002/EC)

of 11 March 2002

amending Regulation (EEC) No 2454/93 laying down provisions for the implementation of Council Regulation (EEC) No 2913/92 establishing the Community Customs Code and Regulations (EC) No 2787/2000 and (EC) No 993/2001

NOTES

Date of publication in OJ: L 68, 12.03.2002, p 11.

THE COMMISSION OF THE EUROPEAN COMMUNITIES,

Having regard to the Treaty establishing the European Community,

Having regard to Council Regulation (EEC) No 2913/92 of 12 October 1992 establishing the Community Customs Code[1], as last amended by European Parliament and Council Regulation (EC) No 2700/2000[2] (hereinafter: "the Code"), and in particular Article 247 thereof,

Whereas:

(1) Certain definitions set out in Commission Regulation (EEC) No 2454/93[3], as last amended by Regulation (EC) No 993/2001[4], require updating.

(2) Under the common commercial policy it is frequently necessary to amend the list of countries and territories qualifying for autonomous Community tariff preferences and consequently to amend the list in Section 2 of Part I, Title IV, Chapter 2, of Regulation (EEC) No 2454/93.

(3) The heading and wording of Section 2 should therefore be based not on an exhaustive list of those countries and territories, but on a general reference to "beneficiary countries or territories", since the latter are duly listed in the Council regulations granting the preferences.

(4) In certain circumstances it is possible to have defective goods repaired outside the

customs territory of the Community without incurring a customs debt on reimportation.

(5) After release for free circulation, the price agreed between buyer and seller can be subject in certain cases to modification in order to take account of the defective nature of goods.

(6) Consequently, the rules in force should expressly allow a transaction value under Article 29 of the Code to take account of those special circumstances, with appropriate safeguards and subject to the application of reasonable time limits.

(7) The purpose of Article 167(1) of Regulation (EEC) No 2454/93 was to avoid the levying of customs duties on software imported on carrier media. That objective has since been achieved by the Agreement on trade in information technology products (ITA), approved by Council Decision 97/359/EC[5]. Without prejudice to the application of GATT Decision 4.1 of 12 May 1995, it is therefore no longer necessary to provide special implementing provisions for the determination of the customs value of carrier media.

(8) The threshold limit, specified in Article 179(1)(a) of Regulation (EEC) No 2454/93, for presentation of the declaration of particulars relating to customs value (value declaration) should be raised to EUR 10000 to take into account monetary changes and to simplify import formalities.

(9) Certain adjustments and corrections are required to the provisions on end-use, in particular to clarify them and to align them with the rules for the customs procedures with economic impact.

(10) The provisions on Community transit laid down in Regulation (EEC) No 2454/93 have been the subject of a complete and thorough review that has led to the revision of a substantial part of the provisions. Since then, it has been found that the amended provisions contain certain inadequacies and inaccuracies, which need to be remedied.

(11) For the protection of the financial interests of the other Contracting Parties to the Convention on a common transit procedure, approved by Council Decision 87/415/EEC[6], it should be ensured that an appropriate guarantee is furnished where a transit operation concerning Community goods involves their territory. The guarantee should be calculated as if the goods were non-Community goods.

(12) Where the principal wishes to use the comprehensive guarantee certificate for all goods, the criteria concerning the use of the comprehensive guarantee for goods involving higher risk of fraud should apply to all goods.

(13) In order to ensure the uniform application of the customs rules within the Community, provisions should be inserted concerning the import duties to be charged on import goods which receive a favourable tariff treatment by reason of their end-use. This should be done for clarification reasons. The insertion should have retroactive effect because similar provisions already existed until 30 June 2001, notably in Article 52 of Commission Regulation (EEC) No 2228/91[7], which was repealed by Regulation (EEC) No 2454/93, and in Article 585a of Regulation (EEC) No 2454/93, before it was amended by Regulation (EC) No 993/2001.

(14) Article 859 of Regulation (EEC) No 2454/93 contains a list of cases in which no customs debt is incurred, even in one of the situations referred to in Article 204(1)(a) or (b) of the Code.

(15) That list should be adapted so that it covers cases of non-compliance with certain obligations applicable to goods under a Community transit procedure, where those goods are presented intact at the office of destination.

(16) The list should also cover cases of non-compliance with certain rules on transfers, applicable to goods placed under a suspensive procedure or to goods benefiting from a favourable treatment on account of their end-use, where those goods arrive at the specified destination.

(17) Since the amendment of Article 859 is linked to the provisions of Regulation (EC) No 993/2001, which has applied since 1 July 2001, it is appropriate to make that amendment applicable from the same date.

Part III

(18) In order to rationalise management of the deadlines for examining applications for waiver of post-clearance entry in the accounts under Article 220(2)(b) of the Code or for repayment or remission of duty under Article 239 thereof, the suspension of the period for examining such applications where the person concerned is consulted in accordance with Articles 872a or 906a of Regulation (EEC) No 2454/93 should be fixed at one month in all cases.

(19) In order to ensure a consistent interpretation of the provisions concerning the designation of the office of destination for the control of the use and/or destination of goods, it is necessary to specify the office at which the goods should be presented for the control of the exit of goods from the customs territory of the Community.

(20) The standard rates of yield should be calculated for certain main compensating products on the basis of the corresponding coefficients set out in Annex E to Commission Regulation (EC) No 1520/2000 of 13 July 2000 laying down common detailed rules for the application of the system of granting export refunds on certain agricultural products exported in the form of goods not covered by Annex I to the Treaty, and the criteria for fixing the amount of such refunds[8] as last amended by Regulation (EC) No 1563/2001[9] Corollary changes should be made for certain secondary compensating products.

(21) Annex 111 to Regulation (EEC) No 2454/93 should be amended to take account of the introduction of the single currency from 1 January 2002.

(22) The transitional provisions on the computerised transit system, laid down in Article 4 of Commission Regulation (EC) No 2787/2000[10] and in Article 2 of Regulation (EC) No 993/2001, should not apply to authorisations granting the status of authorised consignor or authorised consignee in connection with simplifications for certain modes of transport.

(23) Regulation (EEC) No 2454/93 as well as Regulations (EC) No 2787/2000 and (EC) No 993/2001 should therefore be amended accordingly.

(24) The measures provided for in this Regulation are in accordance with the opinion of the Customs Code Committee,

---

[1] OJ L 302, 19.10.1992, p. 1.
[2] OJ L 311, 12.12.2000, p. 17.
[3] OJ L 253, 11.10.1993, p. 1.
[4] OJ L 141, 28.5.2001, p. 1.
[5] OJ L 155, 12.6.1997, p. 1.
[6] OJ L 226, 13.8.1987, p. 1.
[7] OJ L 210, 31.7.1991, p. 1.
[8] OJ L 177, 15.7.2000, p. 1.
[9] OJ L 208, 1.8.2001, p. 8.
[10] OJ L 330, 27.12.2000, p. 1.

HAS ADOPTED THIS REGULATION:

Article 1

(Amends Regulation (EEC) No 2454/93)

Article 2

(Amends Regulation (EC) No 2787/2000)

Article 3

(Amends Regulation (EC) No 993/2001)

Article 4

1. This Regulation shall enter into force on the seventh day following its publication in the Official Journal of the European Communities.

2. Points 21 and 22 of Article 1 shall apply with effect from 1 July 2001.

3. Points 12 to 20 and 25 to 29 of Article 1 and Articles 2 and 3 shall apply from 1 April 2002.

The provisions referred to in the first subparagraph shall not apply to Community transit operations for which the transit declaration has been presented before 1 April 2002.

This Regulation shall be binding in its entirety and directly applicable in all Member States.

Done at Brussels, 11 March 2002.

(Annexes amend annexes to Regulation (EEC) No 2454/93)

COMMISSION REGULATION

(No 881/2003/EC)
of 21 May 2003

amending Regulation (EEC) No 2454/93 laying down provisions for the implementation of Council Regulation (EEC) No 2913/92 establishing the Community Customs Code

NOTES

Date of publication in OJ: L 134, 29.05.2003, p 1.

THE COMMISSION OF THE EUROPEAN COMMUNITIES,

Having regard to the Treaty establishing the European Community,

Having regard to Council Regulation (EEC) No 2913/92 of 12 October 1992 establishing the Community Customs Code[1], as last amended by Regulation (EC) No 2700/2000 of the European Parliament and of the Council[2], and in particular Article 247 thereof,

Whereas:

(1) Council Regulation (EC) No 2501/2001 of 10 December 2001 applying a scheme of generalised tariff preferences for the period from 1 January 2002 to 31 December 2004[3] incorporates the "Everything But Arms" principle laid down in Council Regulation (EC) No 2820/98 of 21 December 1998 applying a multiannual scheme of generalised tariff preferences for the period 1 July 1999 to 31 December 2001[4], as amended by Regulation (EC) No 416/2001[5], so as to extend duty-free access without any quantitative restrictions to products originating in the least developed countries.

(2) In order to ensure that such access benefits only the least developed countries and to avoid diversions of trade through certain of those countries in the framework of regional cumulation of origin, certain minimal, low value-added operations in the rice and sugar sectors that currently suffice to confer the status of originating product for the purposes of the scheme of generalised tariff preferences in accordance with Article 70 of Commission Regulation (EEC) No 2454/93[6], as last amended by Regulation (EC) No 444/2002[7], should no longer be considered as sufficient working or processing to confer the status of originating product.

(3) Consequently, the list set out in Article 70 of Regulation (EEC) No 2454/93 of operations considered as insufficient working or processing should be amended accordingly. Moreover, in the interests of consistency, the same amendments should be made to Article 101 of that Regulation, which concerns the countries or territories to which preferential tariff measures adopted unilaterally by the Community apply.

Part III

(4) The amendments to the harmonised system nomenclature entered into effect on 1 January 2002. The list of working or processing required to be carried out on non-originating products to confer originating status should be updated to take account of those changes, as should its introductory notes. Certain corrections are also required. In the interests of clarity, those texts should be republished in their entirety.

(5) The Andean Community and the Central American Common Market, which, pursuant to Article 72 of Regulation (EEC) No 2454/93, have benefited separately from regional cumulation of origin within the framework of the generalised system of preferences, have requested that, in order to foster industrial development in those regions, they be allowed to benefit jointly from the regional cumulation provisions. They have formed a common secretariat for this purpose, the Andean Community - Central American Common Market and Panama Permanent Joint Committee on Origin. All the countries of this new group have met the requirements of Article 72b of Regulation (EEC) No 2454/93, in particular as regards the submission of undertakings to comply with the rules in force and to provide the necessary administrative cooperation. It should therefore be made possible for that group to benefit from the regional cumulation provisions.

(6) Proofs of origin issued under the arrangements previously applicable for the Andean Community and the Central American Common Market should continue to be accepted within the limits of their validity.

(7) In order to avoid confusion, given that entitlement to regional cumulation does not always coincide with membership of regional groups, the names of regional groups should no longer be used to indicate the countries which may benefit from regional cumulation.

(8) The opportunity should be taken to make a correction in Article 76 of Regulation (EEC) No 2454/93.

(9) The time-limits for the production of a document showing that goods covered by an incomplete declaration qualify for a reduced or zero rate of import duty should be made more flexible.

(10) The management system for tariff quotas provides, as a measure to reduce the administrative burden and costs at importation and to promote uniformity of treatment, that certain tariff quotas are to be considered as critical. Experience with the system has demonstrated that the criteria used in determining the critical status can be further relaxed without a risk for the Community's own resources.

(11) The system of surveillance of preferential imports has proved to be suitable also for the surveillance of non-preferential imports and should therefore be extended to those imports.

(12) The state of implementation of the computerised transit system no longer justifies allowing traders to use the loading list as the descriptive part of transit declarations lodged by means of a data processing technique. That possibility should therefore be removed.

(13) It is appropriate to introduce provisions designed to develop, supplement and, where necessary, update the existing rules so that the provisions resulting from the recent reform of the Community/common transit procedure, and in particular those concerning termination of the operation, alternative proof and the enquiry procedure, can be used in conjunction with the TIR procedure.

(14) Regulation (EEC) No 2454/93 should also be aligned with the TIR Convention.

(15) With a view to improving the effectiveness and transparency of the procedure, provision should be made for the recovery procedure also to apply when the TIR carnet is used.

(16) The maximum amount that the guaranteeing associations in the Community are required to pay when they incur liability should be expressed in euro and set at EUR 60000 per TIR carnet.

(17) In order to uphold the financial interests of the Community and of its Member States, provision should be made for a non-discharge notification, issued validly within a year by the competent customs administration to a guaranteeing association established in the Community, to be legally enforceable against other

guaranteeing associations established in the Community if it transpires that they are liable under the first or second indent of Article 215(1) of Regulation (EEC) No 2913/92, hereinafter "the Code".

(18) Although there is no change in the rules laid down for the ATA procedure, the relevant provisions should be adapted in consequence of the amendment of the TIR rules.

(19) In accordance with Article 551(3) of Regulation (EEC) No 2454/93, for the purposes of determining the customs value of processed products declared for free circulation, the declarant may choose the customs value of the import goods plus the processing costs. In order to ensure that the import duties are levied in a uniform manner, the notion of processing costs should be clarified.

(20) Article 841 of that Regulation should be amended in order to allow the formalities for re-exportation to be carried out at the office of exit where goods are moved by ATA carnet under the temporary importation arrangements.

(21) Pursuant to Article 222(2) of the Code, it is appropriate, in cases where a customs debt is incurred by the removal of goods from customs supervision and there is more than one debtor, to lay down the conditions in which the obligation of certain debtors to pay duty is to be suspended. The duration of the suspension should be limited to one year but it should be possible to extend it in particular where debtors who are not benefiting from the suspension have contested the customs debt before the competent judicial authorities.

(22) Article 890 of Regulation (EEC) No 2454/93 provides that duties are to be repaid or remitted on imports eligible for Community treatment or preferential tariff treatment where a customs debt has been incurred as a result of release for free circulation of the goods and where the importer can produce a post-clearance document showing entitlement to such treatments at the time of the release for free circulation. That possibility should be extended to cases where a document showing entitlement to a favourable tariff treatment by reason of the nature of goods is produced after clearance. Indeed, the obligation to pay duty in such cases, where no deception or obvious negligence is involved, is disproportionate to the need for protection which the Common Customs Tariff is intended to provide.

(23) To avoid problems with interpretation, Article 900(2) and (3) of Regulation (EEC) No 2454/93 should be re-drafted. The new version should also be adapted to the current economic climate of vigorous competition. Accordingly, Article 900(2) should not automatically require the re-export of goods entitled to repayment or remission under Article 900(1) and should permit the goods to be destroyed or to be placed under the Community external transit procedure or the customs warehousing procedure or in a free zone or free warehouse, instead of being re-exported.

(24) Annex 25 to Regulation (EEC) No 2454/93, laying down the percentages of air transport costs to be included in the customs value, should be simplified and adjusted to take account of the enlarged customs territory of the Community following the accession of the new Member States.

(25) Annex 38 to Regulation (EEC) No 2454/93 contains in box 36 of the Single Administrative Document (SAD) the codes for the Tariff arrangements under which products are placed for free circulation.

(26) In the interests of clarity, it is necessary to add a specific code to be used for the temporary suspension on goods destined for civil aircraft and in respect of which an airworthiness certificate has been issued.

(27) Annex 67 to Regulation (EEC) No 2454/93 should be adapted to reflect the amendments to Annex 70.

(28) Annex 70 to Regulation (EEC) No 2454/93 should be amended in order to allow the use of an existing system for communication of information concerning processed agricultural products. Furthermore, the benefits resulting from the simplification of the "Information system – processing procedures (ISPP)" should be extended to those products. Finally, a specific economic reason code should be introduced for applications for inward processing authorisation involving non-sensitive goods.

(29) It is desirable to simplify the use of the customs procedure "processing under

Part III

customs control" in the case of import goods which are processed into products which may benefit from the autonomous suspension of import duties on certain weapons and military equipment.

(30) Regulation (EEC) No 2454/93 should therefore be amended accordingly.

(31) The measures provided for in this Regulation are in accordance with the opinion of the Customs Code Committee,

---

¹ OJ L 302, 19.10.1992, p. 1.
² OJ L 311, 12.12.2000, p. 17.
³ OJ L 346, 31.12.2001, p. 1.
⁴ OJ L 357, 30.12.1998, p. 1.
⁵ OJ L 60, 1.3.2001, p. 43.
⁶ OJ L 253, 11.10.1993, p. 1.
⁷ OJ L 68, 12.3.2002, p. 11.

HAS ADOPTED THIS REGULATION:

Article 1
(Amends Regulation (EEC) No 2454/93)

Article 2
The Commission shall, before 1 July 2004, evaluate the degree of implementation of the computerised transit system by traders. That evaluation shall be based on a report drawn up from information contributed by the Member States.

Article 3
1. This Regulation shall enter into force on the third day following that of its publication in the Official Journal of the European Union.

2. Points (2) and (3) of Article 1 shall apply from 1 June 2003.
Proofs of origin issued in accordance with the provisions applicable before 1 June 2003 shall continue to be accepted after that date within the limits of their validity.

3. Points (10), (11), (30), (32) and (33) of Article 1 shall apply from 1 January 2005.
However, on the basis of the evaluation provided for in Article 2, that date may be deferred by decision adopted in accordance with the committee procedure.

4. Points (12) to (21) of Article 1 shall apply from 1 September 2003.

5. Point (29) of Article 1 shall apply from 1 May 2004.

This Regulation shall be binding in its entirety and directly applicable in all Member States.

Done at Brussels, 21 May 2003.

(Annexes amend annexes to Regulation (EEC) No 2454/93)

COUNCIL DIRECTIVE

((EC) No 2003/96)

of 27 October 2003

restructuring the Community framework for the taxation of energy products and electricity

NOTES

Date of publication in OJ: L 283, 31.10.2003, p 51.

THE COUNCIL OF THE EUROPEAN UNION,

Having regard to the Treaty establishing the European Community, and in particular Article 93 thereof,

Having regard to the proposal from the Commission,

Having regard to the opinion of the European Parliament,

Having regard to the opinion of the European Economic and Social Committee,

Whereas:

(1) The scope of Council Directive 92/81/EEC of 19 October 1992 on the harmonisation of the structures of excise duties on mineral oils and of Council Directive 92/82/EEC of 19 October 1992 on the approximation of the rates of excise duties on mineral oils is restricted to mineral oils.

(2) The absence of Community provisions imposing a minimum rate of taxation on electricity and energy products other than mineral oils may adversely affect the proper functioning of the internal market.

(3) The proper functioning of the internal market and the achievement of the objectives of other Community policies require minimum levels of taxation to be laid down at Community level for most energy products, including electricity, natural gas and coal.

(4) Appreciable differences in the national levels of energy taxation applied by Member States could prove detrimental to the proper functioning of the internal market.

(5) The establishment of appropriate Community minimum levels of taxation may enable existing differences in the national levels of taxation to be reduced.

(6) In accordance with Article 6 of the Treaty, environmental protection requirements must be integrated into the definition and implementation of other Community policies.

(7) As a party to the United Nations Framework Convention on Climate Change, the Community has ratified the Kyoto Protocol. The taxation of energy products and, where appropriate, electricity is one of the instruments available for achieving the Kyoto Protocol objectives.

(8) The Council needs to examine the exemptions and reductions and the minimum levels of taxation periodically, taking into consideration the proper functioning of the internal market, the real value of the minimum levels of taxation, the competitiveness of Community businesses in the international framework and the wider objectives of the Treaty.

(9) Member States should be given the flexibility necessary to define and implement policies appropriate to their national circumstances.

(10) Member States wish to introduce or retain different types of taxation on energy products and electricity. To that end, Member States should be permitted to comply with the Community minimum taxation levels by taking into account the total charge levied in respect of all indirect taxes which they have chosen to apply (excluding VAT).

(11) Fiscal arrangements made in connection with the implementation of this Com-

munity framework for the taxation of energy products and electricity are a matter for each Member State to decide. In this regard, Member States might decide not to increase the overall tax burden if they consider that the implementation of such a principle of tax neutrality could contribute to the restructuring and the modernisation of their tax systems by encouraging behaviour conducive to greater protection of the environment and increased labour use.

(12) Energy prices are key elements of Community energy, transport and environment policies.

(13) Taxation partly determines the price of energy products and electricity.

(14) The minimum levels of taxation should reflect the competitive position of the different energy products and electricity. It would be advisable in this connection to base the calculation of these minimum levels as far as possible on the energy content of the products.

However, this method should not be applied to motor fuels.

(15) The possibility of applying differentiated national rates of taxation to the same product should be allowed in certain circumstances or permanent conditions, provided that Community minimum levels of taxation and internal market and competition rules are respected.

(16) As heat is only subject to very limited intra-Community trade, output taxation of heat should remain outside the scope of this Community framework.

(17) It is necessary to establish different Community minimum levels of taxation according to the use of the energy products and electricity.

(18) Energy products used as a motor fuel for certain industrial and commercial purposes and those used as heating fuel are normally taxed at lower levels than those applicable to energy products used as a propellant.

(19) The taxation of diesel motor fuel used by hauliers, notably those engaging in intra-Community activities, requires a possibility for a specific treatment, including measures to allow for the introduction of a system of road user charges, in order to limit the distortion of competition operators might be confronted with.

(20) Member States may need to differentiate between commercial and non-commercial diesel. Member States may use this possibility to reduce the gap between the taxation of non-commercial gas oil used as propellant and petrol.

(21) Business use and non-business use of energy products and electricity may be treated differently for tax purposes.

(22) Energy products should essentially be subject to a Community framework when used as heating fuel or motor fuel. To that extent, it is in the nature and the logic of the tax system to exclude from the scope of the framework dual uses and non-fuel uses of energy products as well as mineralogical processes. Electricity used in similar ways should be treated on an equal footing.

(23) Existing international obligations and the maintaining of the competitive position of Community companies make it advisable to continue the exemptions of energy products supplied for air navigation and sea navigation, other than for private pleasure purposes, while it should be possible for Member States to limit these exemptions.

(24) Member States should be permitted to apply certain other exemptions or reduced levels of taxation, where that will not be detrimental to the proper functioning of the internal market and will not result in distortions of competition.

(25) In particular, combined heat and power generation and, in order to promote the use of alternative energy sources, renewable forms of energy may qualify for preferential treatment.

(26) It is desirable to establish a Community framework to allow Member States to exempt or reduce excise duties so as to promote biofuels, thereby contributing to the better functioning of the internal market and affording Member States and economic operators a sufficient degree of legal certainty. Distortions of competition should be limited and the incentive of a reduction in the basic costs for producers and distributors of biofuels should be maintained through, inter alia, the adjustments by Member States

taking into account changes in raw material prices.

(27) This Directive shall be without prejudice to the application of the relevant provisions of Council Directive 92/12/EEC of 25 February 1992 on the general arrangements for products subject to excise duty and on the holding, movement and monitoring of such products, and Council Directive 92/83/EEC of 19 October 1992 on the harmonization of the structures of excise duties on alcohol and alcoholic beverages, when the product intended for use, offered for sale or used as motor fuel or fuel additive is ethyl alcohol as defined in Directive 92/83/EEC.

(28) Certain exemptions or reductions in the tax level may prove necessary; notably because of the lack of a stronger harmonisation at Community level, because of the risks of a loss of international competitiveness or because of social or environmental considerations.

(29) Businesses entering into agreements to significantly enhance environmental protection and energy efficiency deserve attention; among these businesses, energy intensive ones merit specific treatment.

(30) Transitional periods and arrangements may be required in order to allow Member States to smoothly adapt to the new levels of taxation, thus limiting possible negative side effects.

(31) It is necessary to provide for a procedure authorising the introduction by Member States, for a set period, of other exemptions or reduced levels of taxation. Such exemptions or reductions should be under regular review.

(32) Provision should be made for the Member States to notify the Commission of certain national measures. Such notification does not release Member States from the obligation, laid down in Article 88(3) of the Treaty, to notify certain national measures. This Directive does not prejudice the outcome of any future State aid procedure that may be undertaken in accordance with Articles 87 and 88 of the Treaty.

(33) The scope of Directive 92/12/EEC should, where appropriate, be extended to the products and indirect taxes covered by this Directive.

(34) The measures necessary for the implementation of this Directive should be adopted in accordance with Council Decision 1999/468/EC of 28 June 1999 laying down the procedures for the exercise of implementing powers conferred on the Commission,

HAS ADOPTED THIS DIRECTIVE:

Article 1

Member States shall impose taxation on energy products and electricity in accordance with this Directive.

Article 2

1. For the purposes of this Directive, the term 'energy products' shall apply to products:

    (a)   falling within CN codes 1507 to 1518, if these are intended for use as heating fuel or motor fuel;

    (b)   falling within CN codes 2701, 2702 and 2704 to 2715;

    (c)   falling within CN codes 2901 and 2902;

    (d)   falling within CN code 2905 11 00, which are not of synthetic origin, if these are intended for use as heating fuel or motor fuel;

    (e)   falling within CN code 3403;

    (f)   falling within CN code 3811;

    (g)   falling within CN code 3817;

    (h)   falling within CN code 3824 90 99 if these are intended for use as heating fuel or motor fuel.

2. This Directive shall also apply to:

Electricity falling within CN code 2716.

3. When intended for use, offered for sale or used as motor fuel or heating fuel, energy products other than those for which a level of taxation is specified in this Directive shall be taxed according to use, at the rate for the equivalent heating fuel or motor fuel.

In addition to the taxable products listed in paragraph 1, any product intended for use, offered for sale or used as motor fuel, or as an additive or extender in motor fuels, shall be taxed at the rate for the equivalent motor fuel.

In addition to the taxable products listed in paragraph 1, any other hydrocarbon, except for peat, intended for use, offered for sale or used for heating purposes shall be taxed at the rate for the equivalent energy product.

4. This Directive shall not apply to:

(a)   output taxation of heat and the taxation of products falling within CN-codes 4401 and 4402;

(b)   the following uses of energy products and electricity:

— energy products used for purposes other than as motor fuels or as heating fuels,

— dual use of energy products

An energy product has a dual use when it is used both as heating fuel and for purposes other than as motor fuel and heating fuel. The use of energy products for chemical reduction and in electrolytic and metallurgical processes shall be regarded as dual use,

— electricity used principally for the purposes of chemical reduction and in electrolytic and metallurgical processes,

— electricity, when it accounts for more than 50 % of the cost of a product. 'Cost of a product' shall mean the addition of total purchases of goods and services plus personnel costs plus the consumption of fixed capital, at the level of the business, as defined in Article 11. This cost is calculated per unit on average. 'Cost of electricity' shall mean the actual purchase value of electricity or the cost of production of electricity if it is generated in the business,

— mineralogical processes

'Mineralogical processes' shall mean the processes classified in the NACE nomenclature under code DI 26 'manufacture of other non-metallic mineral products' in Council Regulation (EEC) No 3037/90 of 9 October 1990 on the statistical classification of economic activities in the European Community.

However, Article 20 shall apply to these energy products.

5. References in this Directive to codes of the combined nomenclature shall be to those of Commission Regulation (EC) No 2031/2001 of 6 August 2001, amending Annex I to Council Regulation (EEC) No 2658/87 on the tariff and statistical nomenclature and on the Common Customs Tariff.

A Decision to update the codes of the combined nomenclature for the products referred to in this Directive shall be taken once every year in accordance with the procedure laid down in Article 27. The Decision must not result in any changes in the minimum tax rates applied in this Directive or to the addition or removal of any energy products and electricity.

Article 3

References in Directive 92/12/EEC to 'mineral oils' and 'excise duty', insofar as it applies to mineral oils, shall be interpreted as covering all energy products, electricity and national indirect taxes referred to respectively in Articles 2 and 4(2) of this Directive.

Article 4

1. The levels of taxation which Member States shall apply to the energy products and electricity listed in Article 2 may not be less than the minimum levels of taxation prescribed by this Directive.

2. For the purpose of this Directive 'level of taxation' is the total charge levied in respect of all indirect taxes (except VAT) calculated directly or indirectly on the quantity of energy products and electricity at the time of release for consumption.

Article 5

Provided that they respect the minimum levels of taxation prescribed by this Directive and that they are compatible with Community law, differentiated rates of taxation may be applied by Member States, under fiscal control, in the following cases:

— when the differentiated rates are directly linked to product quality;

— when the differentiated rates depend on quantitative consumption levels for electricity and energy products used for heating purposes;

— for the following uses: local public passenger transport (including taxis), waste collection, armed forces and public administration, disabled people, ambulances;

— between business and non-business use, for energy products and electricity referred to in Articles 9 and 10.

Article 6

Member States shall be free to give effect to the exemptions or reductions in the level of taxation prescribed by this Directive either:

(a)   directly,

(b)   by means of a differentiated rate, or

(c)   by refunding all or part of the amount of taxation.

Article 7

1. As from 1 January 2004 and from 1 January 2010, the minimum levels of taxation applicable to motor fuels shall be fixed as set out in Annex I Table A.

Not later than 1 January 2012, the Council, acting unanimously after consulting the European Parliament, shall, on the basis of a report and a proposal from the Commission, decide upon the minimum levels of taxation applicable to gas oil for a further period beginning on 1 January 2013.

2. Member States may differentiate between commercial and non-commercial use of gas oil used as propellant, provided that the Community minimum levels are observed and the rate for commercial gas oil used as propellant does not fall below the national level of taxation in force on 1 January 2003, notwithstanding any derogations for this use laid down in this Directive.

3. 'Commercial gas oil used as propellant' shall mean gas oil used as propellant for the following purposes:

(a)   the carriage of goods for hire or reward, or on own account, by motor vehicles or articulated vehicle combinations intended exclusively for the carriage of goods by road and with a maximum permissible gross laden weight of not less than 7,5 tonnes;

(b)   the carriage of passengers, whether by regular or occasional service, by a motor vehicle of category M2 or category M3, as defined in Council Directive 70/156/EEC of 6 February 1970 on the approximation of the laws of the Member States relating to the type-approval of motor vehicles and their trailers.

4. Notwithstanding paragraph 2, Member States which introduce a system of road user charges for motor vehicles or articulated vehicle combinations intended exclusively for the carriage of goods by road may apply a reduced rate on gas oil used

by such vehicles, that goes below the national level of taxation in force on 1 January 2003, as long as the overall tax burden remains broadly equivalent, provided that the Community minimum levels are observed and that the national level of taxation in force on 1 January 2003 for gas oil used as propellant is at least twice as high as the minimum level of taxation applicable on 1 January 2004.

Article 8

1. As from 1 January 2004, notwithstanding Article 7, the minimum levels of taxation applicable to products used as motor fuel for the purposes set out in paragraph 2 shall be fixed as set out in Annex I Table B.

2. This Article shall apply to the following industrial and commercial purposes:
    (a)   agricultural, horticultural or piscicultural works, and in forestry;
    (b)   stationary motors;
    (c)   plant and machinery used in construction, civil engineering and public works;
    (d)   vehicles intended for use off the public roadway or which have not been granted authorisation for use mainly on the public roadway.

Article 9

1. As from 1 January 2004, the minimum levels of taxation applicable to heating fuels shall be fixed as set out in Annex I Table C.

2. Member States, which on 1 January 2003 are authorised to apply a monitoring charge for heating gas oil, may continue to apply a reduced rate of EUR 10 per 1 000 litres for that product. This authorisation shall be repealed on 1 January 2007 if the Council, acting unanimously on the basis of a report and a proposal from the Commission, so decides, having noted that the level of the reduced rate is too low to avoid problems of trade distortion between the Member States.

Article 10

1. As from 1 January 2004, the minimum levels of taxation applicable to electricity shall be fixed as set out in Annex I Table C.

2. Above the minimum levels of taxation referred to in paragraph 1, Member States will have the option of determining the applicable tax base provided that they respect Directive 92/12/EEC.

Article 11

1. In this Directive, 'business use' shall mean the use by a business entity, identified in accordance with paragraph 2, which independently carries out, in any place, the supply of goods and services, whatever the purpose or results of such economic activities.

The economic activities comprise all activities of producers, traders and persons supplying services including mining and agricultural activities and activities of the professions.

States, regional and local government authorities and other bodies governed by public law shall not be considered as business entities in respect of the activities or transactions in which they engage as public authorities. However, when they engage in such activities or transactions, they shall be considered as a business in respect of these activities or transactions where treatment as non-business would lead to significant distortions of competition.

2. With respect to this Directive, the business entity cannot be considered as smaller than a part of an enterprise or a legal body that from an organisational point of view constitutes an independent business, that is to say an entity capable of functioning by its own means.

3. Where mixed use takes place, taxation shall apply in proportion to each type of use, although where either the business or non-business use is insignificant, it may be treated as nil.

4. Member States may limit the scope of the reduced level of taxation for business use.

Article 12

1. Member States may express their national levels of taxation in units other than those specified in Articles 7 to 10 provided that the corresponding levels of taxation, following conversion into those units, are not below the minimum levels specified in this Directive.

2. For energy products specified in Articles 7, 8 and 9, with levels of taxation based on volumes, the volume shall be measured at a temperature of 15° C.

Article 13

1. For Member States that have not adopted the euro, the value of the euro in national currencies to be applied to the value of the levels of taxation shall be fixed once a year. The rates to be applied shall be those obtaining on the first working day of October and published in the Official Journal of the European Union and shall have effect from 1 January of the following calendar year.

2. Member States may maintain the amounts of taxation in force at the time of the annual adjustment provided for in paragraph 1 if the conversion of the amounts of the level of taxation expressed in euro would result in an increase of less than 5 % or EUR 5, whichever is the lower amount, in the level of taxation expressed in national currency.

Article 14

1. In addition to the general provisions set out in Directive 92/12/EEC on exempt uses of taxable products, and without prejudice to other Community provisions, Member States shall exempt the following from taxation under conditions which they shall lay down for the purpose of ensuring the correct and straightforward application of such exemptions and of preventing any evasion, avoidance or abuse:

(a) energy products and electricity used to produce electricity and electricity used to maintain the ability to produce electricity.

However, Member States may, for reasons of environmental policy, subject these products to taxation without having to respect the minimum levels of taxation laid down in this Directive. In such case, the taxation of these products shall not be taken into account for the purpose of satisfying the minimum level of taxation on electricity laid down in Article 10;

(b) energy products supplied for use as fuel for the purpose of air navigation other than in private pleasure-flying.

For the purposes of this Directive 'private pleasure-flying' shall mean the use of an aircraft by its owner or the natural or legal person who enjoys its use either through hire or through any other means, for other than commercial purposes and in particular other than for the carriage of passengers or goods or for the supply of services for consideration or for the purposes of public authorities.

Member States may limit the scope of this exemption to supplies of jet fuel (CN code 2710 19 21);

(c) energy products supplied for use as fuel for the purposes of navigation within Community waters (including fishing), other than private pleasure craft, and electricity produced on board a craft.

For the purposes of this Directive 'private pleasure craft' shall mean any craft used by its owner or the natural or legal person who enjoys its use either

Part III

through hire or through any other means, for other than commercial purposes and in particular other than for the carriage of passengers or goods or for the supply of services for consideration or for the purposes of public authorities.

2. Member States may limit the scope of the exemptions provided for in paragraph 1(b) and (c) to international and intra-Community transport. In addition, where a Member State has entered into a bilateral agreement with another Member State, it may also waive the exemptions provided for in paragraph 1(b) and (c). In such cases, Member States may apply a level of taxation below the minimum level set out in this Directive.

Article 15

1. Without prejudice to other Community provisions, Member States may apply under fiscal control total or partial exemptions or reductions in the level of taxation to:

(a)   taxable products used under fiscal control in the field of pilot projects for the technological development of more environmentally-friendly products or in relation to fuels from renewable resources;

(b)   electricity:
— of solar, wind, wave, tidal or geothermal origin;
— of hydraulic origin produced in hydroelectric installations;
— generated from biomass or from products produced from biomass;
— generated from methane emitted by abandoned coalmines;
— generated from fuel cells;

(c)   energy products and electricity used for combined heat and power generation;

(d)   electricity produced from combined heat and power generation, provided that the combined generators are environmentally friendly. Member States may apply national definitions of 'environmentally-friendly' (or high efficiency) cogeneration production until the Council, on the basis of a report and a proposal from the Commission, unanimously adopts a common definition;

(e)   energy products and electricity used for the carriage of goods and passengers by rail, metro, tram and trolley bus;

(f)   energy products supplied for use as fuel for navigation on inland waterways (including fishing) other than in private pleasure craft, and electricity produced on board a craft;

(g)   natural gas in Member States in which the share of natural gas in final energy consumption was less than 15 % in 2000;

The total or partial exemptions or reductions may apply for a maximum period of ten years after the entry into force of this Directive or until the national share of natural gas in final energy consumption reaches 25 %, whichever is the sooner. However, as soon as the national share of natural gas in final energy consumption reaches 20 %, the Member States concerned shall apply a strictly positive level of taxation, which shall increase on a yearly basis in order to reach at least the minimum rate at the end of the period referred to above.

The United Kingdom of Great Britain and Northern Ireland may apply the total or partial exemptions or reductions for natural gas separately for Northern Ireland;

(h)   electricity, natural gas, coal and solid fuels used by households and/or by organisations recognised as charitable by the Member State concerned. In the case of such charitable organisations, Member States may confine the exemption or reduction to use for the purpose of non-business activities.

Where mixed use takes place, taxation shall apply in proportion to each type of use. If a use is insignificant, it may be treated as nil;

(i) natural gas and LPG used as propellants;

(j) motor fuels used in the field of the manufacture, development, testing and maintenance of aircraft and ships;

(k) motor fuels used for dredging operations in navigable waterways and in ports;

(l) products falling within CN code 2705 used for heating purposes.

2. Member States may also refund to the producer some or all of the amount of tax paid by the consumer on electricity produced from products specified in paragraph 1(b).

3. Member States may apply a level of taxation down to zero to energy products and electricity used for agricultural, horticultural or piscicultural works, and in forestry.

On the basis of a proposal from the Commission, the Council shall before 1 January 2008 examine if the possibility of applying a level of taxation down to zero shall be repealed.

Article 16

1. Member States may, without prejudice to paragraph 5, apply an exemption or a reduced rate of taxation under fiscal control on the taxable products referred to in Article 2 where such products are made up of, or contain, one or more of the following products:

— products falling within CN codes 1507 to 1518;

— products falling within CN codes 3824 90 55 and 3824 90 80 to 3824 90 99 for their components produced from biomass;

— products falling within CN codes 2207 20 00 and 2905 11 00 which are not of synthetic origin;

— products produced from biomass, including products falling within CN codes 4401 and 4402.

Member States may also apply a reduced rate of taxation under fiscal control on the taxable products referred to in Article 2 where such products contain water (CN codes 2201 and 2851 00 10).

'Biomass' shall mean the biodegradable fraction of products, waste and residues from agriculture (including vegetal and animal substances), forestry and related industries, as well as the biodegradable fraction of industrial and municipal waste.

2. The exemption or reduction in taxation resulting from the application of the reduced rate laid down in paragraph 1 may not be greater than the amount of taxation payable on the volume of the products referred to in paragraph 1 present in the products eligible for the reduction.

The levels of taxation applied by Member States on the products made up of or containing the products referred to in paragraph 1 may be lower than the minimum levels specified in Article 4.

3. The exemption or reduction in taxation applied by Member States shall be adjusted to take account of changes in raw material prices to avoid over-compensating for the extra costs involved in the manufacture of the products referred to in paragraph 1.

4. Until 31 December 2003, Member States may exempt or continue to exempt products solely or almost solely made up of the products referred to in paragraph 1.

5. The exemption or reduction provided for the products referred to in paragraph 1 may be granted under a multiannual programme by means of an authorisation issued by an administrative authority to an economic operator for more than one calendar year. The exemption or reduction authorised may not be applied for a period of more than six consecutive years. This period may be renewed.

As part of a multiannual programme authorised by an administrative authority prior to 31 December 2012, Member States may apply the exemption or reduction under paragraph 1 after 31 December 2012 and until the end of the multiannual programme. The period may not be renewed.

6. Should Member States be required by Community law to comply with legally binding obligations to place on their markets a minimum proportion of the products referred to in paragraph 1, paragraphs 1 to 5 shall cease to apply as from the date when such obligations become binding on the Member States.

7. Member States shall communicate to the Commission the schedule of tax reductions or exemptions applied in accordance with this Article by 31 December 2004 and every 12 months thereafter.

8. No later than 31 December 2009, the Commission shall report to the Council on the fiscal, economic, agricultural, energy, industrial and environmental aspects of the reductions granted in accordance with this Article.

Article 17

1. Provided the minimum levels of taxation prescribed in this Directive are respected on average for each business, Member States may apply tax reductions on the consumption of energy products used for heating purposes or for the purposes of Article 8(2)(b) and (c) and on electricity in the following cases:

(a) in favour of energy-intensive business

An 'energy-intensive business' shall mean a business entity, as referred to in Article 11, where either the purchases of energy products and electricity amount to at least 3,0 % of the production value or the national energy tax payable amounts to at least 0,5 % of the added value. Within this definition, Member States may apply more restrictive concepts, including sales value, process and sector definitions.

'Purchases of energy products and electricity' shall mean the actual cost of energy purchased or generated within the business. Only electricity, heat and energy products that are used for heating purposes or for the purposes of Article 8(2)(b) and (c) are included. All taxes are included, except deductible VAT.

'Production value' shall mean turnover, including subsidies directly linked to the price of the product, plus or minus the changes in stocks of finished products, work in progress and goods and services purchased for resale, minus the purchases of goods and services for resale.

'Value added' shall mean the total turnover liable to VAT including export sales minus the total purchases liable to VAT including imports.

Member States, which currently apply national energy tax systems in which energy-intensive businesses are defined according to criteria other than energy costs in comparison with production value and national energy tax payable in comparison with value added, shall be allowed a transitional period until no later than 1 January 2007 to adapt to the definition set out in point (a) first subparagraph;

(b) where agreements are concluded with undertakings or associations of undertakings, or where tradable permit schemes or equivalent arrangements are implemented, as far as they lead to the achievement of environmental protection objectives or to improvements in energy efficiency.

2.   Notwithstanding Article 4(1), Member States may apply a level of taxation down to zero to energy products and electricity as defined in Article 2, when used by energy-intensive businesses as defined in paragraph 1 of this Article.

3.   Notwithstanding Article 4(1), Member States may apply a level of taxation down to 50 % of the minimum levels in this Directive to energy products and electricity as defined in Article 2, when used by business entities as defined in Article 11, which are not energy-intensive as defined in paragraph 1 of this Article.

4.   Businesses that benefit from the possibilities referred to in paragraphs 2 and 3 shall enter into the agreements, tradable permit schemes or equivalent arrangements as referred to in paragraph 1(b). The agreements, tradable permit schemes or equivalent arrangements must lead to the achievement of environmental objectives or increased energy efficiency, broadly equivalent to what would have been achieved if the standard Community minimum rates had been observed.

Article 18

1.   [By way of derogation from the provisions of the present Directive, the Member States specified in Annex II are authorised to continue to apply the reductions in the levels of taxation or the exemptions set out in that Annex.]
Subject to a prior review by the Council, on the basis of a proposal from the Commission, this authorisation shall expire on 31 December 2006 or on the date specified in Annex II.

2.   Notwithstanding the periods set out [in paragraphs 3 to 13] and provided that this does not significantly distort competition, Member States with difficulties in implementing the new minimum levels of taxation will be allowed a transitional period of until 1 January 2007, particularly in order to avoid jeopardising price stability.

3.   The Kingdom of Spain may apply a transitional period until 1 January 2007 to adjust its national level of taxation on gas oil used as propellant to the new minimum level of EUR 302 and until 1 January 2012 to reach EUR 330. Until 31 December 2009, it may furthermore apply a special reduced rate on commercial use of gas oil used as propellant, provided that this does not result in taxation at below EUR 287 per 1 000 l and that the national levels of taxation in force on 1 January 2003 are not reduced. From 1 January 2010 until 1 January 2012, it may apply a differentiated rate on commercial use of gas oil used as propellant, provided that it does not result in taxation at below EUR 302 per 1 000 l and that the national levels of taxation in force on 1 January 2010 are not reduced. The special reduced rate on commercial use of gas oil used as propellant may also be applied for taxis until 1 January 2012. With respect to Article 7(3)(a), it may apply, until 1 January 2008, a maximum permissible gross laden weight of not less than 3,5 tonnes in the definition of commercial purposes.

4.   The Republic of Austria may apply a transitional period until 1 January 2007 to adjust its national level of taxation on gas oil used as propellant to the new minimum level of EUR 302 and until 1 January 2012 to reach EUR 330. Until 31 December 2009, it may furthermore apply a special reduced rate on commercial use of gas oil used as propellant, provided that this does not result in taxation at below EUR 287 per 1 000 l and that the national levels of taxation in force on 1 January 2003 are not reduced. From 1 January 2010 until 1 January 2012, it may apply a differentiated rate on commercial use of gas oil used as propellant, provided that it does not result in taxation at below EUR 302 per 1 000 l and that the national levels of taxation in force on 1 January 2010 are not reduced.

5.   The Kingdom of Belgium may apply a transitional period until 1 January 2007 to adjust its national level of taxation on gas oil used as propellant to the new

Part III

minimum level of EUR 302 and until 1 January 2012 to reach EUR 330. Until 31 December 2009, it may furthermore apply a special reduced rate on commercial use of gas oil used as propellant, provided that this does not result in taxation at below EUR 287 per 1 000 l and that the national levels of taxation in force on 1 January 2003 are not reduced. From 1 January 2010 until 1 January 2012, it may apply a differentiated rate on commercial use of gas oil used as propellant, provided that it does not result in taxation at below EUR 302 per 1 000 l and that the national levels of taxation in force on 1 January 2010 are not reduced.

6. The Grand Duchy of Luxembourg may apply a transitional period until 1 January 2009 to adjust its national level of taxation on gas oil used as propellant to the new minimum level of EUR 302 and until 1 January 2012 to reach EUR 330. Until 31 December 2009, it may furthermore apply a special reduced rate on commercial use of gas oil used as propellant, provided that this does not result in taxation at below EUR 272 per 1 000 l and that the national levels of taxation in force on 1 January 2003 are not reduced. From 1 January 2010 until 1 January 2012, it may apply a differentiated rate on commercial use of gas oil used as propellant, provided that this does not result in taxation at below EUR 302 per 1 000 l and that the national levels of taxation in force on 1 January 2010 are not reduced.

7. The Portuguese Republic may apply levels of taxation on energy products and electricity consumed in the Autonomous Regions of the Azores and Madeira lower than the minimum levels of taxation laid down in this Directive in order to compensate for the transport costs incurred as a result of the insular and dispersed nature of these regions.

The Portuguese Republic may apply a transitional period until 1 January 2009 to adjust its national level of taxation on gas oil used as propellant to the new minimum level of EUR 302 and until 1 January 2012 to reach EUR 330. Until 31 December 2009, it may furthermore apply a differentiated rate on commercial use of gas oil used as propellant, provided that this does not result in taxation at below EUR 272 per 1 000 l and that the national levels of taxation in force on 1 January 2003 are not reduced. From 1 January 2010 until 1 January 2012, it may apply a differentiated rate on commercial use of gas oil used as propellant, provided that this does not result in taxation at below EUR 302 per 1000 l and that the national levels of taxation in force on 1 January 2010 are not reduced.

The differentiated rate on commercial use of gas oil used as propellant may also be applied for taxis until 1 January 2012.

With respect to Article 7(3)(a) it may apply, until 1 January 2008, a maximum permissible gross laden weight of not less than 3,5 tonnes in the definition of commercial purposes.

The Portuguese Republic may apply total or partial exemptions in the level of taxation of electricity until 1 January 2010.

8. The Hellenic Republic may apply levels of taxation up to in this Directive on gas oil used as propellant and on petrol consumed in the departments of Lesbos, Chios, Samos, the Dodecanese and the Cyclades and on the following islands in the Aegean: Thasos, North Sporades, Samothrace and Skiros.

The Hellenic Republic may apply a transitional period until 1 January 2010 to convert its current input electricity taxation system into an output taxation system and to reach the new minimum level of taxation for petrol.

The Hellenic Republic may apply a transitional period until 1 January 2010 to adjust its national level of taxation on gas oil used as propellant to the new minimum level of EUR 302 per 1 000 l and until 1 January 2012 to reach EUR 330. Until 31 December 2009 it may furthermore apply a differentiated rate on commercial use of gas oil used as propellant, provided that this does not result in taxation at below EUR 264 per 1 000 l and that the national levels of taxation in force on 1 January 2003 are not reduced. From 1 January 2010 until 1 January 2012, it may apply a differentiated rate on commercial use of gas oil used as propellant, provided that this does not result in taxation at below EUR 302 per 1 000 l and that the national levels of taxation in force on 1 January 2010 are not reduced.

The differentiated rate on commercial use of gas oil used as propellant may also be applied for taxis until 1 January 2012.

With respect to Article 7(3)(a) it may apply, until 1 January 2008, a maximum permissible gross laden weight of not less than 3,5 tonnes in the definition of commercial purposes.

9. Ireland may apply total or partial exemptions or reductions in the level of taxation of electricity until 1 January 2008.

10. The French Republic may apply total or partial exemptions or reductions for energy products and electricity used by the State, regional and local government authorities or other bodies governed by public law, in respect of the activities or transactions in which they engage as public authorities until 1 January 2009.

The French Republic may apply a transitional period until 1 January 2009 to adapt its current electricity taxation system to the provisions set out in this Directive. During this period, the global average level of the current local electricity taxation is to be taken into account to assess whether the minimum rates set out in this Directive are respected.

11. The Italian Republic may apply, until 1 January 2008, a maximum permissible gross laden weight of not less than 3,5 tonnes in the definition of commercial purposes as given in Article 7(3)(a).

12. The Federal Republic of Germany may apply, until 1 January 2008, a maximum permissible gross laden weight of 12 tonnes in the definition of commercial purposes as given in Article 7(3)(a).

13. The Kingdom of the Netherlands may apply, until 1 January 2008, a maximum permissible gross laden weight of 12 tonnes in the definition of commercial purposes as given in Article 7(3)(a).

14. Within the transitional periods established, Member States shall progressively reduce their respective gaps with respect to the new minimum levels of taxation. However, when the difference between the national level and the minimum level does not exceed 3 % of that minimum level, the Member State concerned may wait until the end of the period to adjust its national level.

NOTES

Para 1: first sub-paragraph substituted by Council Directive 2004/74, Art 1 para 1(a). The Directive is itself amended by Corrigendum (see OJ L 195, 2.6.2004).

Para 2: words substituted by Council Directive 2004/74, Art 1 para 1(b). The Directive is itself amended by Corrigendum (see OJ L 195, 2.6.2004).

[Article 18A

1. By way of derogation from the provisions of the present Directive, the Member States specified in Annex III are authorised to apply the reductions in the levels of taxation or the exemptions set out in that Annex.

Subject to a prior review by the Council, on the basis of a proposal from the Commission, this authorisation shall expire on 31 December 2006 or on the date specified in Annex III.

2. Notwithstanding the periods set out in paragraphs 3 to 11 and provided that this does not significantly distort competition, Member States with difficulties in implementing the new minimum levels of taxation shall be allowed a transitional period until 1 January 2007, particularly in order to avoid jeopardising price stability.

3. The Czech Republic may apply total or partial exemptions or reductions in the level of taxation of electricity, solid fuels and natural gas until 1 January 2008.

4.   The Republic of Estonia may apply a transitional period until 1 January 2010 to adjust its national level of taxation on gas oil used as propellant to the new minimum level of EUR 330 per 1000 l. However, the level of taxation on gas oil used as propellant shall be no less than EUR 245 per 1000 l as from 1 May 2004.

The Republic of Estonia may apply a transitional period until 1 January 2010 to adjust its national level of taxation on unleaded petrol used as propellant to the new minimum level of EUR 359 per 1000 l. However, the level of taxation on unleaded petrol shall be no less than EUR 287 per 1000 l as from 1 May 2004.

The Republic of Estonia may apply a total exemption from taxation of oil shale until 1 January 2009. Until 1 January 2013, it may furthermore apply a reduced rate in the level of taxation of oil shale, provided that it does not result in taxation at below 50 % of the relevant Community minimum rate as from 1 January 2011.

The Republic of Estonia may apply a transitional period until 1 January 2010 to adjust its national level of taxation on shale oil used for district heating purposes to the minimum level of taxation.

The Republic of Estonia may apply a transitional period until 1 January 2010 to convert its current input electricity taxation system into an output electricity taxation system.

5.   The Republic of Latvia may apply a transitional period until 1 January 2011 to adjust its national level of taxation on gas oil and kerosene used as propellant to the new minimum level of EUR 302 per 1000 l and until 1 January 2013 to reach EUR 330. However, the level of taxation on gas oil and kerosene shall be no less than EUR 245 per 1000 l as from 1 May 2004 and no less than EUR 274 per 1000 l as from 1 January 2008.

The Republic of Latvia may apply a transitional period until 1 January 2011 to adjust its national level of taxation on unleaded petrol used as propellant to the new minimum level of EUR 359 per 1000 l. However, the level of taxation on unleaded petrol cannot be less than EUR 287 per 1000 l as from 1 May 2004 and no less than EUR 323 per 1000 l as from 1 January 2008.

The Republic of Latvia may apply a transitional period until 1 January 2010 to adjust its national level of taxation on heavy fuel oil used for district heating purposes to the minimum level of taxation.

The Republic of Latvia may apply a transitional period until 1 January 2010 to adjust its national level of taxation on electricity to the relevant minimum levels of taxation. However, the level of taxation on electricity shall be no less than 50 % of the relevant Community minimum rates as from 1 January 2007.

The Republic of Latvia may apply a transitional period until 1 January 2009 to adjust its national level of taxation on coal and coke to the relevant minimum levels of taxation. However, the level of taxation on coal and coke shall be no less than 50 % of the relevant Community minimum rates as from 1 January 2007.

6.   The Republic of Lithuania may apply a transitional period until 1 January 2011 to adjust its national level of taxation on gas oil and kerosene used as propellant to the new minimum level of EUR 302 per 1000 l and until 1 January 2013 to reach EUR 330. However, the level of taxation on gas oil and kerosene shall be no less than EUR 245 per 1000 l as from 1 May 2004 and no less than EUR 274 per 1000 l as from 1 January 2008.

The Republic of Lithuania may apply a transitional period until 1 January 2011 to adjust its national level of taxation on unleaded petrol used as propellant to the new minimum level of EUR 359 per 1000 l. However, the level of taxation on unleaded petrol shall be no less than EUR 287 per 1000 l as from 1 May 2004 and no less than EUR 323 per 1000 l as from 1 January 2008.

7.   The Republic of Hungary may apply a transitional period until 1 January 2010 to adjust its national level of taxation on electricity, natural gas, coal and coke, used for district heating purposes, to the relevant minimum levels of taxation.

8. The Republic of Malta may apply a transitional period until 1 January 2010 to adjust its national level of taxation on electricity. However, the levels of taxation on electricity shall be no less than 50 % of the relevant Community minimum rates as from 1 January 2007.

The Republic of Malta may apply a transitional period until 1 January 2010 to adjust its national level of taxation on gas oil and kerosene used as propellant to the minimum levels of EUR 330 per 1000 l. However, the levels of taxation on gas oil and kerosene used as propellant shall be no less than EUR 245 per 1000 l as from 1 May 2004.

The Republic of Malta may apply a transitional period until 1 January 2010 to adjust its national level of taxation on unleaded petrol and leaded petrol used as propellant to the relevant minimum levels of taxation. However, the levels of taxation on unleaded petrol and leaded petrol shall be no less than EUR 287 per 1000 l and EUR 337 per 1000 l respectively as from 1 May 2004.

The Republic of Malta may apply a transitional period until 1 January 2010 to adjust its national level of taxation on natural gas used as heating fuel to the relevant minimum levels of taxation. However, the effective tax rates applied to natural gas shall be no less than 50 % of the relevant Community minimum rates as from 1 January 2007.

The Republic of Malta may apply a transitional period until 1 January 2009 to adjust its national level of taxation on solid fuel to the relevant minimum levels of taxation. However, the effective tax rates applied to the energy products concerned shall be no less than 50 % of the relevant Community minimum rates as from 1 January 2007.

9. The Republic of Poland may apply a transitional period until 1 January 2009 to adjust its national level of taxation on unleaded petrol used as propellant to the new minimum level of EUR 359 per 1000 l. However, the level of taxation on unleaded petrol shall be no less than EUR 287 per 1000 l as from 1 May 2004.

The Republic of Poland may apply a transitional period until 1 January 2010 to adjust its national level of taxation on gas oil used as propellant to the new minimum level of EUR 302 per 1000 l and until 1 January 2012 to reach EUR 330. However, the level of taxation on gas oil shall be no less than EUR 245 per 1000 l as from 1 May 2004 and no less than EUR 274 per 1000 l as from 1 January 2008.

The Republic of Poland may apply a transitional period until 1 January 2008 to adjust its national level of taxation on heavy fuel oil to the new minimum level of EUR 15 per 1000 kg. However, the level of taxation on heavy fuel oil shall be no less than EUR 13 per 1000 kg as from 1 May 2004.

The Republic of Poland may apply a transitional period until 1 January 2012 to adjust its national level of taxation on coal and coke used for district heating to the relevant minimum level of taxation.

The Republic of Poland may apply a transitional period until 1 January 2012 to adjust its national level of taxation on coal and coke used for heating purposes other than district heating to the relevant minimum levels of taxation.

The Republic of Poland may, until 1 January 2008, apply total or partial exemptions or reductions for gas oil used as heating fuel by schools, nursery schools and other public utilities, in respect of the activities or transactions in which they engage as public authorities.

The Republic of Poland may apply a transitional period until 1 January 2006 to align its electricity taxation system with the Community framework.

10. The Republic of Slovenia may, under fiscal control, total or partial exemption from or reduction in the level of taxation to natural gas. The total or partial exemption or reduction may apply until May 2014 or until the national share of natural gas in final energy consumption reaches 25 %, whichever is the sooner. However, as soon as the national share of natural gas in final energy consumption

reaches 20 %, it shall apply a strictly positive level of taxation, which shall increase on a yearly basis in order to reach at least the minimum rate at the end of the period referred to above.

11. The Slovak Republic may apply a transitional period until 1 January 2010 to adjust its national level of taxation on electricity and natural gas used as heating fuel to the relevant minimum levels of taxation. However, the level of taxation on electricity and natural gas used as heating fuel shall be no less than 50 % of the relevant Community minimum rates as from 1 January 2007.

The Slovak Republic may apply a transitional period until 1 January 2009 to adjust its national level of taxation on solid fuels to the relevant minimum levels of taxation. However, the level of taxation on solid fuels shall be no less than 50 % of the relevant Community minimum rates as from 1 January 2007.

12. Within the transitional periods established, Member States shall progressively reduce their respective gaps with regard to the new minimum levels of taxation. However, where the difference between the national level and the minimum level does not exceed 3 % of that minimum level, the Member State concerned may wait until the end of the period to adjust its national level.]

NOTES

Art 18a inserted by Council Directive 2004/74, Art 1 para 2. The Directive is itself amended by Corrigendum (see OJ L 195, 2.6.2004).

[Article 18b

1. Notwithstanding the periods set out in paragraph 2 and provided that this does not significantly distort competition, Member States with difficulties in implementing the new minimum levels of taxation shall be allowed a transitional period until 1 January 2007, particularly in order to avoid jeopardising price stability.

2. The Republic of Cyprus may apply a transitional period until 1 January 2008 to adjust its national level of taxation on gas oil and kerosene used as propellant to the new minimum level of EUR 302 per 1000 l and until 1 January 2010 to reach EUR 330. However, the level of taxation on gas oil and kerosene used as propellant shall be not less than EUR 245 per 1000 l as from 1 May 2004.

The Republic of Cyprus may apply a transitional period until 1 January 2010 to adjust its national level of taxation on unleaded petrol used as propellant to the new minimum level of EUR 359 per 1000 l. However, the level of taxation on unleaded petrol shall be not less than EUR 287 per 1000 l as from 1 May 2004.

3. Within the transitional periods established, Member States shall progressively reduce their respective gaps with respect to the new minimum levels of taxation. However, where the difference between the national level and the minimum level does not exceed 3% of that minimum level, the Member State concerned may wait until the end of the period to adjust its national level.]

NOTES

Art 18b inserted by Council Directive 2004/75/EC, Art 1 para 1. The Directive is itself amended by Corrigendum (see OJ L 195, 2.6.04, p 31).

Article 19

1. In addition to the provisions set out in the previous Articles, in particular in Articles 5, 15 and 17, the Council, acting unanimously on a proposal from the Commission, may authorise any Member State to introduce further exemptions or reductions for specific policy considerations.

A Member State wishing to introduce such a measure shall inform the Commission accordingly and shall also provide the Commission with all relevant and necessary information.

The Commission shall examine the request, taking into account, *inter alia*, the proper functioning of the internal market, the need to ensure fair competition and Community health, environment, energy and transport policies.

Within three months of receiving all relevant and necessary information, the Commission shall either present a proposal for the authorisation of such a measure by the Council or, alternatively, shall inform the Council of the reasons why it has not proposed the authorisation of such a measure.

2. The authorisations referred to in paragraph 1 shall be granted for a maximum period of 6 years, with the possibility of renewal in accordance with the procedure set out in paragraph 1.

3. If the Commission considers that the exemptions or reductions provided for in paragraph 1 are no longer sustainable, particularly in terms of fair competition or distortion of the operation of the internal market, or in terms of Community policy in the areas of health, protection of the environment, energy and transport, it shall submit appropriate proposals to the Council. The Council shall take a unanimous decision on these proposals.

Article 20

1. Only the following energy products shall be subject to the control and movement provisions of Directive 92/12/EEC:

   (a) products falling within CN codes 1507 to 1518, if these are intended for use as heating fuel or motor fuel;

   (b) products falling within CN codes 2707 10, 2707 20, 2707 30 and 2707 50;

   (c) products falling within CN codes 2710 11 to 2710 19 69.

   However, for products falling within CN codes 2710 11 21, 2710 11 25 and 2710 19 29, the control and movement provisions shall only apply to bulk commercial movements;

   (d) products falling within CN codes 2711 (except 2711 11, 2711 21 and 2711 29);

   (e) products falling within CN code 2901 10;

   (f) products falling within CN codes 2902 20, 2902 30, 2902 41, 2902 42, 2902 43 and 2902 44;

   (g) products falling within CN code 2905 11 00, which are not of synthetic origin, if these are intended for use as heating fuel or motor fuel;

   (h) products falling within CN code 3824 90 99 if these are intended for use as heating fuel or motor fuel.

2. If a Member State finds that energy products other than those referred to in paragraph 1 are intended for use, offered for sale or used as heating fuel, motor fuel or are otherwise giving rise to evasion, avoidance or abuse, it shall advise the Commission forthwith. This provision shall also apply for electricity.

The Commission shall transmit the communication to the other Member States within one month of receipt. A Decision as to whether the products in question should be made subject to the control and movement provisions of Directive 92/12/EEC shall then be taken in accordance with the procedure laid down in Article 27(2).

3. Member States may, pursuant to bilateral arrangements, dispense with some or all of the control measures set out in Directive 92/12/EEC in respect of some or all of the products referred to in paragraph 1, insofar as they are not covered by Articles 7 to 9 of this Directive. Such arrangements shall not affect Member States which are not

party to them. All such bilateral arrangements shall be notified to the Commission, which shall inform the other Member States.

Article 21

1. In addition to the general provisions defining the chargeable event and the provisions for payment set out in Directive 92/12/EEC, the amount of taxation on energy products shall also become due on the occurrence of one of the chargeable events mentioned in Article 2(3).

2. For the purpose of this Directive, the word 'production' in Article 4(c) and 5(1) of Directive 92/12/EEC shall be deemed to include 'extraction', when appropriate.

3. The consumption of energy products within the curtilage of an establishment producing energy products shall not be considered as a chargeable event giving rise to taxation, if the consumption consist of energy products produced within the curtilage of the establishment. Member States may also consider the consumption of electricity and other energy products not produced within the curtilage of such an establishment and the consumption of energy products and electricity within the curtilage of an establishment producing fuels to be used for generation of electricity as not giving rise to a chargeable event.

Where the consumption is for purposes not related to the production of energy products and in particular for the propulsion of vehicles, this shall be considered a chargeable event, giving rise to taxation.

4. Member States may also provide that taxation on energy products and electricity shall become due when it is established that a final use condition laid down in national rules for the purpose of a reduced level of taxation or exemption is not, or is no longer, fulfilled.

5. For the purpose of applying Articles 5 and 6 of Directive 92/12/EEC, electricity and natural gas shall be subject to taxation and shall become chargeable at the time of supply by the distributor or redistributor. Where the delivery to consumption takes place in a Member State where the distributor or redistributor is not established, the tax of the Member States of delivery shall be chargeable to a company that has to be registered in the Member State of delivery. Tax shall in all cases be levied and collected according to procedures laid down by each Member State.

Notwithstanding the first subparagraph, Member States have the right to determine the chargeable event, in the case where there are no connections between their gas pipe lines and those of other Member States.

An entity producing electricity for its own use is regarded as a distributor. Notwithstanding Article 14(1)(a), Member States may exempt small producers of electricity provided that they tax the energy products used for the production of that electricity.

For the purpose of applying Articles 5 and 6 of Directive 92/12/EEC, coal, coke and lignite shall be subject to taxation and shall become chargeable at the time of delivery by companies, which have to be registered for that purpose by the relevant authorities. Those authorities may allow the producer, trader, importer or fiscal representative to substitute the registered company for the fiscal obligations imposed upon it. Tax shall be levied and collected according to procedures laid down by each Member State.

6. Member States need not treat as 'production of energy products':

    (a)   operations during which small quantities of energy products are obtained incidentally;

    (b)   operations by which the user of an energy product makes its reuse possible in his own undertaking provided that the taxation already paid on such product is not less than the taxation which would be due if the reused energy product were again to be liable to taxation;

(c)   an operation consisting of mixing, outside a production establishment or a tax warehouse, energy products with other energy products or other materials, provided that:

(i)   taxation on the components has been paid previously; and

(ii)   the amount paid is not less than the amount of the tax which would be chargeable on the mixture.

The condition under (i) shall not apply where the mixture is exempted for a specific use.

Article 22

When taxation rates are changed, stocks of energy products already released for consumption may be subject to an increase in, or a reduction of, the tax.

Article 23

Member States may refund the amounts of taxation already paid on contaminated or accidentally mixed energy products sent back to a tax warehouse for recycling.

Article 24

1.   Energy products released for consumption in a Member State, contained in the standard tanks of commercial motor vehicles and intended to be used as fuel by those same vehicles, as well as in special containers, and intended to be used for the operation, during the course of transport, of the systems equipping those same containers shall not be subject to taxation in any other Member State.

2.   For the purposes of this Article,

'standard tanks' shall mean:

—   the tanks permanently fixed by the manufacturer to all motor vehicles of the same type as the vehicle in question and whose permanent fitting enables fuel to be used directly, both the purpose of propulsion and, where appropriate, for the operation, during transport, of refrigeration systems and other systems. Gas tanks fitted to motor vehicles designed for the direct use of gas as a fuel and tanks fitted to the other systems with which the vehicle may be equipped shall also be considered to be standard tanks;

—   the tanks permanently fixed by the manufacturer to all containers of the same type as the container in question and whose permanent fitting enables fuel to be used directly for the operation, during transport, of the refrigeration systems and other systems with which special containers are equipped.

'Special container' shall mean any container fitted with specially designed apparatus for refrigeration systems, oxygenation systems, thermal insulation systems or other systems.

Article 25

1.   Member States shall inform the Commission of the levels of taxation which they apply to the products listed in Article 2 on 1 January each year and following each change in national law.

2.   Where the levels of taxation applied by the Member States are expressed in units of measurement other than those specified for each product in Articles 7 to 10, Member States shall also notify the corresponding levels of taxation following conversion into these units.

Article 26

1.   Member States shall inform the Commission of measures taken pursuant to Articles 5, 14(2), 15 and 17.

2. Measures such as tax exemptions, tax reductions, tax differentiation and tax refunds within the meaning of this Directive might constitute State aid and in those cases have to be notified to the Commission pursuant to Article 88(3) of the Treaty.

Information provided to the Commission on the basis of this Directive does not free Member States from the notification obligation pursuant to Article 88(3) of the Treaty.

3. The obligation to inform the Commission pursuant to paragraph 1 of measures taken pursuant to Article 5 does not free Member States from any notification obligations pursuant to Directive 83/189/EEC.

Article 27

1. The Commission shall be assisted by the Committee on Excise Duties set up by Article 24(1) of Directive 92/12/EEC.

2. Where reference is made to this paragraph, Article 5 and 7 of Decision 1999/468/EC shall apply.

The period laid down in Article 5(6) of Decision 1999/468/EC shall be set at three months.

3. The Committee shall adopt its Rules of Procedure.

Article 28

1. Member States shall adopt and publish the laws, regulations and administrative provisions necessary to comply with this Directive not later than 31 December 2003. They shall forthwith inform the Commission thereof.

2. They shall apply these provisions from 1 January 2004, except the provisions laid down in Articles 16 and 18(1), which may be applied by the Member States from 1 January 2003.

3. When Member States adopt these measures, they shall contain a reference to this Directive or shall be accompanied by such reference on the occasion of their official publication.

The methods of making such reference shall be laid down by the Member States.

4. Member States shall communicate to the Commission the texts of the main provisions of national law which they adopt in the field governed by this Directive.

Article 29

The Council, acting on the basis of a report and, where appropriate, a proposal from the Commission, shall periodically examine the exemptions and reductions and the minimum levels of taxation laid down in this Directive and, acting unanimously after consulting the European Parliament, shall adopt the necessary measures. The report by the Commission and the consideration by the Council shall take into account the proper functioning of the internal market, the real value of the minimum levels of taxation and the wider objectives of the Treaty.

Article 30

Notwithstanding Article 28(2), Directives 92/81/EEC and 92/82/EEC shall be repealed as from 31 December 2003.

[References to the repealed directives shall be construed as references to this Directive.]

NOTES

Paragraph inserted by Council Directive 2004/75/EC, Art 1 para 2. The Directive is itself amended by Corrigendum (see OJ L 195, 2.6.04, p 31).

Article 31

This Directive shall enter into force on the day of its publication in the Official Journal of the European Union.

Article 32

This Directive is addressed to the Member States.

Done at Luxembourg, 27 October 2003.

ANNEX I

TABLE A—MINIMUM LEVELS OF TAXATION APPLICABLE TO MOTOR FUELS

	1 January 2004	*1 January 2010*
Leaded petrol (in euro per 1 000 l) CN codes 2710 11 31, 2710 11 51 and 2710 11 59	421	421
Unleaded petrol (in euro per 1 000 l) CN codes 2710 11 31, 2710 11 41, 2710 11 45 and 2710 11 49	359	359
Gas oil (in euro per 1 000 l) CN codes 2710 19 41 to 2710 19 49	302	330
Kerosene (in euro per 1 000 l) CN codes 2710 19 21 and 2710 19 25	302	330
LPG (in euro per 1 000 kg) CN codes 2711 12 11 to 2711 19 00	125	125
Natural gas (in euro per gigajoule gross calorific value) CN codes 2711 11 00 and 2711 21 00	2,6	2,6

TABLE B—MINIMUM LEVELS OF TAXATION APPLICABLE TO MOTOR FUELS USED FOR THE PURPOSE SET OUT IN ARTICLE 8(2)

Gas oil (in euro per 1 000 l) CN codes 2710 19 41 to 2710 19 49	21
Kerosene (in euro per 1 000 l) CN codes 2710 19 21 and 2710 19 25	21
LPG (in euro per 1 000 kg) CN codes 2711 12 11 to 2711 19 00	41
Natural gas (in euro per gigajoule gross calorific value) CN codes 2711 11 00 and 2711 21 00	0,3

Part III

TABLE C—MINIMUM LEVELS OF TAXATION APPLICABLE TO HEATING FUELS AND ELECTRICITY

	Business use	*Non-business use*
Gas oil (in euro per 1 000 l) CN codes 2710 19 41 to 2710 19 49	21	21
Heavy fuel oil (in euro per 1 000 kg) CN codes 2710 19 61 to 2710 19 69	15	15
Kerosene (in euro per 1 000 l) CN codes 2710 19 21 and 2710 19 25	0	0
LPG (in euro per 1 000 kg) CN codes 2711 12 11 to 2711 19 00	0	0
Natural gas (in euro per gigajoule gross calorific value) CN codes 2711 11 00 and 2711 21 00	0,15	0,3
Coal and coke (in euro per gigajoule gross calorific value) CN codes 2701, 2702 and 2704	0,15	0,3
Electricity (in euro per MWh) CN code 2716	0,5	1,0

ANNEX II

REDUCED RATES OF TAXATION AND EXEMPTIONS FROM SUCH TAXATION REFERRED TO IN ARTICLE 18(1)

1. BELGIUM:
   — for liquid petroleum gas (LPG), natural gas and methane;
   — for local public passenger transport vehicles;
   — for air navigation other than that covered by Article 14(1)(b) of this Directive;
   — for navigation in private pleasure craft;
   — for a reduction in the rate of excise duty on heavy fuel oil to encourage the use of more environmentally friendly fuels. Such reduction shall be specifically linked to sulphur content and in no case can the reduced rate fall below EUR 6,5 per tonne;
   — for waste oils which are reused as fuel, either directly after recovery or following a recycling process for waste oils, and where the reuse is subject to duty;
   — for a differentiated rate of excise duty on low-sulphur (50 ppm) and low-aromatic (35 %) unleaded petrol;
   — for a differentiated rate of excise duty on low-sulphur (50 ppm) diesel.
2. DENMARK:

— for a differentiated rate of excise duty, from 1 February 2002 to 31 January 2008, to heavy fuel oil and heating oil used by energy-intensive firms to produce heating and hot water. The maximum amount of the authorised differentiation in the excise duty is EUR 0,0095 per kg on heavy fuel oil and EUR 0,008 per litre on heating oil. The reductions in excise duty must comply with the terms of this Directive, and in particular the minimum rates;

— for a reduction in the rate of duty on diesel to encourage the use of more environmentally friendly fuels, provided that such incentives are linked to established technical characteristics including specific gravity, sulphur content, distillation point, cetane number and index and provided that such rates are in accordance with the obligations laid down in this Directive;

— for the application of differentiated rates of excise duty between petrol distributed from petrol stations equipped with a return system for petrol fumes and petrol distributed from other petrol stations, provided that the differentiated rates are in accordance with the obligations laid down in this Directive, and in particular the minimum rates of excise duty;

— for differentiated rates of excise duties on petrol, provided that the differentiated rates are in accordance with the obligations laid down in this Directive, and in particular the minimum levels of taxation provided for in Article 7 thereof;

— for local public passenger transport vehicles;

— for differentiated rates of excise duties on gas oil, provided that the differentiated rates are in accordance with the obligations laid down in this Directive, and in particular the minimum levels of taxation provided for in Article 7 thereof;

— for partial reimbursement to the commercial sector, provided that the taxes concerned are in conformity with Community law and provided that the amount of the tax paid and not reimbursed at all times respects the minimum rates of duty or monitoring charge on mineral oils as provided for in Community law;

— for air navigation other than that covered by Article 14(1)(b) of this Directive;

— for the application of a reduced rate of excise duty of a maximum of DKK 0,03 per litre on petrol distributed from petrol stations meeting more stringent standards of equipment and operation designed to reduce leakage of methyl tertiary butyl ether into ground water, provided that the differentiated rates are in accordance with the obligations laid down in this Directive, and in particular the minimum rates of excise duty.

3. GERMANY:

— for a differentiated rate on excise duty on fuels with a maximum sulphur content of 10 ppm from 1 January 2003 until 31 December 2005;

— for the use of waste hydrocarbon gases as heating fuel;

— for a differentiated rate of excise duty on mineral oils used as fuel in local public passenger transport vehicles, subject to compliance with the obligations laid down in Directive 92/82/EEC;

— for samples of mineral oils intended for analysis, tests on production or for other scientific purposes;

— for a differentiated rate of excise duty on heating oils used by manufacturing industries, provided that the differentiated rates are in accordance with the obligations laid down in this Directive;

— for waste oils which are reused as fuel, either directly after recovery or following a recycling process for waste oils, and where the reuse is subject to duty.

4. GREECE:

— for use by national armed forces;

— to grant relief from the excise duties on mineral oils for fuels intended to be used to power the official vehicles of the Ministry of the Presidency and the national police force;

— for local public passenger transport vehicles;

— for differentiated rates of tax on unleaded petrol to reflect different environmental categories, provided that the differentiated rates are in accordance with the obligations laid down in this Directive, and in particular the minimum levels of taxation provided for in Article 7 thereof;

— for LPG and methane used for industrial purposes.

5. SPAIN:

— for LPG used as fuel in local public transport vehicles;

— for LPG used as fuel in taxis;

— for differentiated rates of tax on unleaded petrol to reflect different environmental categories, provided that the differentiated rates are in accordance with the obligations laid down in this Directive, and in particular the minimum levels of taxation provided for in Article 7 thereof;

— for waste oils which are reused as fuel, either directly after recovery or following a recycling process for waste oils, and where the reuse is subject to duty.

6. FRANCE:

— for differential rates of tax on diesel used in commercial vehicles, until 1 January 2005, which cannot be less than EUR 380 per 1 000 l as from 1 March 2003;

— in the framework of certain policies aimed at assisting areas suffering from depopulation;

— for consumption on the island of Corsica, provided that the reduced rates at all times respect the minimum rates of duty on mineral oils as provided for under Community law;

— for a differentiated rate of excise duty on a new fuel composed of a water-and-antifreeze/diesel emulsion stabilised by surfactants, provided that the differentiated rates are in accordance with the obligations laid down in this Directive, and in particular the minimum rates of excise duty;

— for a differentiated rate of excise duty for premium-grade unleaded petrol containing a potassium-based additive to improve resistance to valve burn-out (or any other additive of equivalent effect);

— for fuel used in taxis, within the limits of an annual quota;

— for exemption from excise duty on gases used as fuel for public transport subject to an annual quota;

— for an exemption from excise duties for gases used as engine fuels in gas-powered refuse collection vehicles;

— for a reduction in the rate of taxation on heavy fuel oil to encourage the use of more environmentally friendly fuels; this reduction shall be specifically linked to sulphur content and the rate of duty charged on heavy fuel oil must correspond to the minimum rate of taxation on heavy fuel oil as provided for in Community law;

— for an exemption for heavy fuel oil used as fuel for the production of alumina in the region of Gardanne;

— for air navigation other than that covered by Article 14(1)(b) of this Directive;

— for gasoline delivered from the harbours of Corsica to private pleasure craft;

— for waste oils which are reused as fuel, either directly after recovery or following a recycling process for waste oils, and where the reuse is subject to duty;

— for local public passenger transport vehicles until 31 December 2005;

— for the granting of permits for the application of a differentiated rate of excise duty to the fuel mixture 'petrol/ethyl alcohol derivatives whose alcohol component is of agricultural origin' and for the application of a differentiated rate of excise duty to the fuel mixture 'diesel/vegetable oil esters'. To allow a reduction in excise duty on blends incorporating vegetable oil esters and ethyl alcohol derivatives which are used as fuel within the meaning of this Directive, the French authorities must issue the necessary permits to the biofuel production units concerned by 31 December 2003 at the latest. The authorisations will be valid for a maximum of six years from the date of issue. The reduction specified in the authorisation may be applied after 31 December 2003 until the expiry of the authorisation. The reductions in excise duties shall not exceed EUR 35,06/hl or EUR 396,64/t for vegetable oil esters and EUR 50,23/hl or EUR 297,35/t for ethyl alcohol derivatives used in the mixtures referred to. The reductions in excise duties shall be adjusted to take account of changes in the price of raw materials to avoid overcompensating for the extra costs involved in the manufacture of biofuels. This Decision shall apply with effect from 1 November 1997. It shall expire on 31 December 2003;

— for the granting of permits for the application of a differentiated rate of excise duty to the mixture 'domestic heating fuel/vegetable oil esters'. To allow a reduction in excise duty on mixtures incorporating vegetable oil esters and used as fuel within the meaning of this Directive, the French authorities must issue the necessary permits to the biofuel production units concerned by 31 December 2003 at the latest. The authorisations will be valid for a maximum of six years from the date of issue. The reduction specified in the authorisation may be applied after 31 December 2003 until the expiry of the authorisation, but may not be extended. The reductions in excise duties shall not exceed EUR 35,06/hl or EUR 396,64/t for the vegetable oil esters used in the mixtures referred to. The reductions in excise duty shall be adjusted to take account of changes in the price of raw materials to avoid overcompensating for the extra costs involved in the manufacture of biofuels. This Decision shall apply with effect from 1 November 1997. It shall expire on 31 December 2003.

7. IRELAND:

— for LPG, natural gas and methane used as motor fuel;

— in motor vehicles used by the disabled;

— for local public passenger transport vehicles;

— for differentiated rates of tax on unleaded petrol to reflect different environmental categories, provided that the differentiated rates are in accordance with the obligations laid down in this Directive, and in particular the minimum levels of taxation provided for in Article 7 thereof;

Part III

—   for a differentiated rate of excise on low-sulphur diesel;

—   for the production of alumina in the Shannon region;

—   for air navigation other than that covered by Article 14(1)(b) of this Directive;

—   for navigation in private pleasure craft;

—   for waste oils which are reused as fuel, either directly after recovery or following a recycling process for waste oils, and where the reuse is subject to duty.

8.   ITALY:

—   for differentiated rates of excise duty on mixtures used as motor fuels containing 5 % or 25 % of biodiesel until 30 June 2004. The reduction in excise duty may not be greater than the amount of excise duty payable on the volume of biofuels present in the products eligible for the reduction. The reduction in excise duty shall be adjusted to take account of changes in the price of raw materials to avoid overcompensating for the extra costs involved in the manufacture of biofuels;

—   for a reduction in the rate of excise duty used as fuel by road transport operators, until 1 January 2005, which cannot be less than EUR 370 per 1 000 l as from 1 January 2004;

—   for waste hydrocarbon gases used as fuel;

—   for a reduced rate of excise duty to water/diesel emulsions and water/heavy fuel oil emulsions from 1 October 2000 until 31 December 2005 provided that the reduced rate is in accordance with the obligations laid down in this Directive, and in particular with the minimum rates of excise duty;

—   for methane used as fuel in motor vehicles;

—   for the national armed forces;

—   for ambulances;

—   for local public passenger transport vehicles;

—   for fuel used in taxis;

—   in certain particularly disadvantaged geographical areas, for reduced rates of excise duty on domestic fuel and LPG used for heating and distributed through the networks of such areas, provided that the rates are in accordance with the obligations laid down in this Directive, and in particular the minimum rates of excise duty;

—   for consumption in the regions of Val d'Aosta and Gorizia;

—   for a reduction in the rate of excise duty on petrol consumed on the territory of Friuli-Venezia Giulia, provided that the rates are in accordance with the obligations laid down in this Directive, and in particular the minimum rates of excise duty;

—   for a reduction in the rate of excise duty on mineral oils consumed in the regions of Udine and Trieste, provided that the rates are in accordance with the obligations laid down in this Directive;

—   for an exemption from excise duty on mineral oils used as fuel for alumina production in Sardinia;

—   for a reduction in the rate of excise duty on fuel oil, for the production of steam, and for gas oil, used in ovens for drying and 'activating' molecular sieves in Reggio Calabria, provided that the rates are in accordance with the obligations laid down in this Directive;

—   for air navigation other than that covered by Article 14(1)(b) of this Directive;

—   for waste oils which are reused as fuel, either directly after recovery or following a recycling process for waste oils, and where the reuse is subject to duty.

9. LUXEMBOURG:
—   for LPG, natural gas and methane;
—   for local public passenger transport vehicles;
—   for a reduction in the rate of excise duty on heavy fuel oil to encourage the use of more environmentally friendly fuels. Such reduction shall be specifically linked to sulphur content and in no case can the reduced rate fall below EUR 6,5 per tonne;
—   for waste oils which are reused as fuel, either directly after recovery or following a recycling process for waste oils, and where the reuse is subject to duty.

10. NETHERLANDS:
—   for LPG, natural gas and methane;
—   for samples of mineral oils intended for analysis, tests on production or for other scientific purposes;
—   for use by the national armed forces;
—   for the application of differentiated rates of excise duty on LPG used as fuel in public transport;
—   for a differentiated rate of excise duty on LPG used as fuel for waste-collection, drain suction and by streetcleaning vehicles;
—   for a differentiated rate of excise duty on low sulphur (50 ppm) diesel to 31 December 2004;
—   for a differentiated rate of excise duty on low sulphur (50 ppm) petrol to 31 December 2004.

11. AUSTRIA:
—   for natural gas and methane;
—   for LPG used as fuel by local public transport vehicles;
—   for waste oils which are reused as fuel, either directly after recovery or following a recycling process for waste oils, and where the reuse is subject to duty.

12. PORTUGAL:
—   for differentiated rates of tax on unleaded petrol to reflect different environmental categories, provided that the differentiated rates are in accordance with the obligations laid down in this Directive, and in particular the minimum levels of taxation provided for in Article 7 thereof;
—   for exemption from excise duty on LPG, natural gas and methane used as fuel in local public passenger transport;
—   for a reduction in the rate of excise duty on fuel oil consumed in the autonomous region of Madeira; this reduction may not be greater than the additional costs incurred in transporting the fuel oil to that region;
—   for a reduction in the rate of excise duty on heavy fuel oil to encourage the use of more environmentally friendly fuels; this reduction shall be specifically linked to sulphur content and the rate of duty charged on heavy fuel oil must correspond to the minimum rate of duty on heavy fuel oil as provided for in Community law;
—   for air navigation other than that covered by Article 14(1)(b) of this Directive;
—   for waste oils which are reused as fuel, either directly after recovery or following a recycling process for waste oils, and where the reuse is subject to duty.

Part III

13. FINLAND:
—   for natural gas used as fuel;
—   for an exemption from excise duty for methane and LPG for all purposes;
—   for reduced excise duty rates on diesel fuel and heating gas oil, provided that the rates are in accordance with the obligations laid down in this Directive, and in particular the minimum levels of taxation provided for in Articles 7 to 9;
—   for reduced excise duty rates on reformulated unleaded and leaded petrol, provided that the rates are in accordance with the obligations laid down in this Directive, and in particular the minimum levels of taxation provided for in Article 7 thereof;
—   for air navigation other than that covered by Article 14(1)(b) of this Directive;
—   for navigation in private pleasure craft;
—   for waste oils which are reused as fuel, either directly after recovery or following a recycling process for waste oils, and where the reuse is subject to duty.

14. SWEDEN:
—   for reduced tax rates for diesel in accordance with environmental classifications;
—   for differentiated rates of tax on unleaded petrol to reflect different environmental categories, provided that the differentiated rates are in accordance with the obligations laid down in this Directive, and in particular the minimum rates of excise duty;
—   for a differentiated rate of energy tax to alkylate-based petrol for two-stroke engines, until 30 June 2008, provided that the total excise duty applicable comply with the terms of this Directive;
—   for an exemption from excise duty for biologically produced methane and other waste gases;
—   for a reduced rate of excise duty on mineral oils used for industrial purposes, provided that the rates are in accordance with the obligations laid down in this Directive;
—   for a reduced rate of excise duty on mineral oils used for industrial purposes by introducing both a rate which is lower than the standard rate and a reduced rate for energy-intensive enterprises, provided that the rates are in accordance with the obligations laid down in this Directive, and do not give rise to distortions of competition;
—   for air navigation other than that covered by Article 14(1)(b) of the present Directive.

15. UNITED KINGDOM:
—   for differentiated rates of excise duty for road fuel containing biodiesel and biodiesel used as pure road fuel, until 31 March 2007. Community minimum rates have to be respected and no overcompensation for the extra costs involved in the manufacture of biofuels can take place;
—   for LPG, natural gas and methane used as motor fuel;
—   for a reduction in the rate of excise duty on diesel to encourage the use of more environmentally friendly fuels;
—   for differentiated rates of tax on unleaded petrol to reflect different environmental categories, provided that the differentiated rates are in accordance with the obligations laid down in this Directive, and in particular the minimum levels of taxation provided for in Article 7 thereof;

—   for local public passenger transport vehicles;
—   for a differentiated rate of excise duty on water/diesel emulsion provided that the differentiated rates are in accordance with the obligations laid down in this Directive, and in particular the minimum rates of excise duty;
—   for air navigation other than that covered by Article 14(1)(b) of this Directive;
—   for navigation in private pleasure craft;
—   for waste oils which are reused as fuel, either directly after recovery or following a recycling process for waste oils, and where the reuse is subject to duty.

[ANNEX III
REDUCED RATES OF TAXATION AND EXEMPTIONS FROM SUCH TAXATION REFERRED TO IN ARTICLE 18A(1).

1. Latvia
—   for energy products and electricity used in local public passenger transport vehicles;

2. Lithuania
—   for coal, coke and lignite, until 1 January 2007,
—   for natural gas and electricity, until 1 January 2010,
—   for orimulsion used for purposes other than to produce electricity or heat until 1 January 2010;

3. Hungary
—   for coal and coke, until 1 January 2009;

4. Malta
—   for navigation in private pleasure craft,
—   for air navigation other than that covered by Article 14(1)(b) of Directive 2003/96/EC;

5. Poland
—   for aviation fuel and turbo-combustion engine fuels and engine oils for aviation engines, sold by the producer of such fuels on the order of the Minister of National Defence or the competent minister for internal affairs, for purposes of the aviation industry, or the Agency of Material Reserves to supplement State reserves, or organisational units of sanitary aviation for purposes of such units,
—   gas oil for ship engines and engines for sea technology and engine oils for ship engines and for sea technology, sold by the producer of such fuel on the order of the Agency of Stock Reserves to supplement State reserves, or on the order of the Minister of National Defence to be used for purposes of the navy, or on the order of the competent minister for internal affairs to be used for sea engineering,
—   aviation fuel, turbo-combustion engine fuel and gas oil for ship engines and engines for sea technology and oils for aviation engines, ship engines and engines for sea technology, sold by the Agency of Stock Reserves on the order of the Minister of National Defence or the competent minister for internal affairs.]

NOTES
Annex III inserted by Council Directive 2004/74, Art 1 para 3. The Directive is itself amended by Corrigendum (see OJ L 195, 2.6.2004).

Part III

COMMISSION REGULATION

((EC) No 2286/2003)

of 18 December 2003

amending Regulation (EEC) No 2454/93 laying down provisions for the implementation of Council Regulation (EEC) No 2913/92 establishing the Community Customs Code

NOTES

Date of publication in OJ: L 343, 31.12.2003, p 1.

THE COMMISSION OF THE EUROPEAN COMMUNITIES,

Having regard to the Treaty establishing the European Community,

Having regard to Council Regulation (EEC) No 2913/92 of 12 October 1992 establishing the Community Customs Code(1), and in particular Article 247 thereof,

Whereas:

(1) Binding tariff information, issued by Member States for economic operators and containing both confidential and non-confidential data, is transmitted to the Commission in accordance with Commission Regulation (EEC) No 2454/93(2) and stored in a central database managed by the Commission and accessible to all national administrations. In the past, the Commission made publicly available a CD-ROM containing extracts from the database, which did not show confidential data. Currently, the issue of this CD-ROM has been suspended, for technical and financial reasons.

(2) Since both the public and the candidate countries urgently need access to that information, the Commission should be able to grant such access by publishing on its website an extract from the database for binding tariff information which does not show confidential data such as data on the holder or confidential information about the composition of the goods. Unlike the CD-ROM, that extract should also include images, if available.

(3) The economic operators who apply for binding tariff information should be informed about the use of the data stored in the database and it is therefore necessary to adjust the "Important notice" on the related application form and on the form for setting out binding tariff information.

(4) In addition, it is appropriate in the interests of clarity to rephrase the wording of Article 8(1) and (2) of Regulation (EEC) No 2454/93. At the same time, the opportunity should be taken to simplify the system for communicating binding origin information. The transmission of such information should therefore be limited to those elements that are strictly necessary.

(5) Since the introduction of the single administrative document on 1 January 1988, customs legislation has undergone fundamental changes, in particular as a result of the introduction of the single market on 1 January 1993 and of Regulation (EEC) No 2913/92 on 1 January 1994. Technological progress, and in particular the increasingly widespread use of computer-based clearance methods, has also made it necessary to amend the provisions governing use of the single administrative document.

(6) It is also necessary to bring together those provisions and to republish the forms for the single administrative document, which have been amended since they were first introduced. That update entails the replacement of Annexes 31 to 34, 37 and 38 to Regulation (EEC) No 2454/93.

(7) In order to guarantee the Community's economic operators and customs administrations the most harmonised and simplified documentation possible, it also seems necessary to conduct, in due consultation with the representatives of the business circles concerned, a regular review of the requirements connected with the use of the

form, in the light of developments in business practices and the activities of international fora in this area.

(8) In order to enable Member States to make adequate preparation for the implementation of the new rules concerning the single administrative document, provision should be made for those rules to apply with effect from 1 January 2006. However, since some Member States wish to introduce the new measures as soon as possible, it is necessary to allow an early implementation.

(9) It will be necessary to evaluate Member States' plans for implementation of the measures concerned and, on this basis, to provide for the possibility of agreeing, subject to certain conditions, on a deferral of the date of implementation.

(10) Articles 292(5) and 500(2) of Regulation (EEC) No 2454/93 determine the competent authorities to whom applications for single authorisations are to be submitted. Except in the case of temporary importation, those applications have to be submitted to the customs authorities designated for the place where the applicant's main accounts are held and where at least part of the operations to be covered by the authorisation are conducted. Experience in practice has shown that the current criteria for determining the competent authorities are not sufficient to cover all cases which might occur in practice. It is therefore appropriate to provide that, if the competent authorities cannot be determined on the basis of the existing rules, the application is to be submitted to the customs authorities designated for the place where the applicant's main accounts are held.

(11) A surveillance system for imports was introduced in 1997 in Regulation (EEC) No 2454/93. The significant and rapid increase of exports of certain products for which refunds are granted, on the one hand, and the level of preferential imports for the same products, on the other hand, seems sometimes to be highly artificial. Surveillance, which is currently confined to products put into free circulation, should also be made possible for exports in order to combat abuses associated with such flows of goods.

(12) Regulation (EEC) No 2454/93 lays down provisions on the use of means of transport under the temporary importation procedure. The transport of persons without remuneration in the framework of the economic activity of an enterprise is defined as a "commercial use" of means of transport. However, under the Istanbul Convention, "commercial use" means exclusively the transport of persons for remuneration. The different definitions of the term "commercial use" are not justified. That definition should therefore be amended.

(13) Regulation (EEC) No 2454/93 lays down special provisions on the use of equivalent goods in the dairy sector. The application of those provisions has led to certain problems in practice. Therefore, it is desirable to simplify recourse to the use of equivalent goods in the dairy sector.

(14) Where a customs debt is incurred under the arrangements for inward processing, in certain cases, for the purposes of determining that customs debt, the compensating products are subject to the import duties appropriate to them. Those cases are mentioned in Article 548(1) of Regulation (EEC) No 2454/93 in conjunction with Annex 75 to that Regulation. In accordance with a general remark preceding the list set out in Annex 75, the supervising office may allow Article 548(1) to be applied also to waste, scrap, residues, offcuts and remainders other than those in that list. Member States need no longer inform the Commission of such additional cases. It is therefore appropriate to simplify Annex 75.

(15) Regulation (EEC) No 2454/93 should therefore be amended accordingly.

(16) The measures provided for in this Regulation are in accordance with the opinion of the Customs Code Committee,

HAS ADOPTED THIS REGULATION:

Article 1

(Amends Regulation (EEC) 2454/93. However, Art 1(3)–(9), (17), (18), Annexes III and IV amend that Regulation with effect from 1 January 2006, although member states may implement the legislation before that date).

3. In Article 212, the following paragraph 4 is added:

"4. The Member States shall notify the Commission of the list of particulars they require for each of the procedures referred to in Annex 37.

The Commission shall publish the list of those particulars."

4. In Article 213, the following second subparagraph is added: "The Member States shall notify the Commission of the list of national codes used for boxes 37 (second subdivision), 44 and 47 (first subdivision). The Commission shall publish the list of those codes."

5. Article 216 is replaced by the following:

"Article 216

The list of boxes to be used for declarations for placing goods under a particular customs procedure using the single administrative document is set out in Annex 37."

6. In Article 254, the introductory wording is replaced by the following: "Declarations for release for free circulation which the customs authorities may accept, at the declarant's request, without their containing some of the particulars referred to in Annex 37 shall contain at least the particulars referred to in boxes 1 (first and second subdivisions), 14, 21 (nationality), 31, 37, 40 and 54 of the single administrative document and:"

7. Article 269(4) is replaced by the following:

"4. The procedure referred to in the second indent of paragraph 1 shall apply to Type B warehouses except that it shall not be possible to use a commercial document. Where the administrative document does not contain all the particulars shown in Annex 37, Title I(B), these should be supplied on the accompanying application."

8. Article 275(1) is replaced by the following:

"1. Declarations of entry for a customs procedure with economic impact other than outward processing or customs warehousing which the customs office of entry for the procedure may accept, at the declarant's request, without their containing some of the particulars referred to in Annex 37 or without their being accompanied by certain documents referred to in Article 220 shall contain at least the particulars referred to in boxes 1 (first and second subdivisions), 14, 21 (nationality), 31, 37, 40 and 54 of the single administrative document and, in box 44, a reference to the authorisation, or a reference to the application where Article 508(1) applies."

9. Article 280(1) and (2) are replaced by the following:

"1. Export declarations which the customs office may accept, at the declarant's request, without their containing some of the particulars referred to in Annex 37 shall contain at least the particulars referred to in boxes 1 (first and second subdivisions), 2, 14, 17a, 31, 33, 38, 44 and 54 of the single administrative document and any further information considered necessary in order to identify the goods, to apply the provisions governing their export or to determine the amount of any security required before the goods may be exported.

Where the goods are liable for export duties or subject to any other measures provided for under the common agricultural policy, those export declarations shall contain all the information required for the proper application of such duties or measures.

2. The customs authorities may allow the declarant not to complete boxes 17a and 33 on condition that he declares that export of the goods in question is not subject to prohibitions or restrictions and the customs authorities have no reason for doubt in this respect and that the

description of the goods allows the Combined Nomenclature classification to be determined immediately and unambiguously."

. . .

17. Annexes 31 to 34 are replaced by the text in Annex III to this Regulation.

18. Annexes 37 and 38 are replaced by the text in Annex IV to this Regulation.

. . .

NOTES

Para 4: words in square brackets substituted by Corrigendum (see OJ L 360, 7.12.04, p 33).

Article 2

Before 1 January 2005, the Commission shall evaluate Member States' plans for implementation of the measures provided for in Article 1(3) to (9), (17) and (18). That evaluation shall be based on a report drawn up from contributions of the Member States.

Article 3

[1. This Regulation shall enter into force on the seventh day following that of its publication in the Official Journal of the European Union.]

2. Article 1(11) and (12) shall apply with effect from 1 January 2004.

3. Article 1(1), (2), (15) and (16) shall apply with effect from 1 February 2004.

[4. Article 1(3) to (9), (17) and (18) shall apply from 1 January 2006. However, Member States may implement these provisions before that date.

In addition, Member States having difficulty adapting their customs clearance computer systems may defer the adaptation of these systems until 1 January 2007. In such cases, Member States shall notify the Commission of the method by which and the date on which they implement Article 1(3) to (9), (17) and (18). The Commission shall publish that information.]

NOTES

Para 1: substituted by Commission Regulation (EC) No 215/2006, Art 2 (see OJ L 038, 9.2.06, p 11).

This Regulation shall be binding in its entirety and directly applicable in all Member States.

Done at Brussels, 18 December 2003.

ANNEXES I, II

(substitute Regulation (EEC) No 2454/93 Annexes 1, 1B)

ANNEX III

(the text in this Annex replaces that in Regulation (EEC) 2454/93 Annex 31).

ANNEX IV

(not reproduced. The text in this Annex replaces that in Regulation (EEC) 2454/93 Annexes 37 and 38. The substitution takes effect from 1 January 2006, although member states may implement the legislation before that date).

ANNEXES V, VI

(amend Regulation (EEC) 2454/93 Annexes 74, 75).

Part III

EUROPEAN PARLIAMENT AND COUNCIL REGULATION

((EC) No 648/2005)

of 13 April 2005

amending Council Regulation (EEC) No 2913/92 establishing the Community Customs Code

NOTES

Date of publication in OJ: L 117, 04.05.2005, p 13.

THE EUROPEAN PARLIAMENT AND THE COUNCIL OF THE EUROPEAN UNION,

Having regard to the Treaty establishing the European Community, and in particular Articles 26, 95, 133 and 135 thereof,

Having regard to the proposal from the Commission,

Having regard to the opinion of the European Economic and Social Committee[1],

Acting in accordance with the procedure laid down in Article 251 of the Treaty[2],

Whereas:

(1) Council Regulation (EEC) No 2913/92[3] lays down the rules for the customs treatment of goods that are imported or to be exported.

(2) It is necessary to establish an equivalent level of protection in customs controls for goods brought into or out of the customs territory of the Community. In order to achieve this objective, it is necessary to establish an equivalent level of customs controls in the Community and to ensure a harmonised application of customs controls by the Member States, which have principal responsibility for applying these controls. Such controls should be based upon commonly agreed standards and risk criteria for the selection of goods and economic operators in order to minimise the risks to the Community and its citizens and to the Community's trading partners. Member States and the Commission should therefore introduce a Community-wide risk management framework to support a common approach so that priorities are set effectively and resources are allocated efficiently with the aim of maintaining a proper balance between customs controls and the facilitation of legitimate trade. Such a framework should also provide for common criteria and harmonised requirements for authorised economic operators and ensure a harmonised application of such criteria and requirements. The establishment of a risk management framework common to all Member States should not prevent Member States from controlling goods by spot-checks.

(3) Member States should grant the status of authorised economic operator to any economic operator that meets common criteria relating to the operator's control systems, financial solvency and compliance record. The status of authorised economic operator, once granted by one Member State, should be recognised by the other Member States, but does not confer the right to benefit automatically in the other Member States from simplifications provided for in the customs rules. However, the other Member States should allow the use of simplifications by authorised economic operators provided they meet all the specific requirements for use of the particular simplifications. In considering a request to use simplifications, the other Member States need not repeat the evaluation of the operator's control systems, financial solvency or compliance record, which will already have been completed by the Member State that granted the operator the status of authorised economic operator, but should ensure that any other specific requirements for use of the particular simplification are met. The use of simplifications in other Member States may also be coordinated by agreement between the customs authorities concerned.

(4) Simplifications under the customs rules should continue to be without prejudice to customs controls as defined within the Community Customs Code, notably relating

to safety and security. Such controls are the responsibility of the customs authorities and, while the status of authorised economic operator should be recognised by those authorities as a factor during risk analysis and in the granting of any facilitation to the economic operator with regard to controls relating to safety and security, the right to control should remain.

(5) Risk-related information on import and export goods should be shared between the competent authorities of the Member States and the Commission. To this end, a common, secure system should be set up, enabling the competent authorities to access, transfer and exchange this information in a timely and effective manner. Such information may also be shared with third countries where an international agreement so provides.

(6) The conditions under which information provided by economic operators to customs may be disclosed to other authorities in the same Member State, other Member States, to the Commission, or to authorities in third countries should be specified. For this purpose, it should be clearly indicated that Directive 95/46/EC of the European Parliament and of the Council of 24 October 1995 on the protection of individuals with regard to the processing of personal data and on the free movement of such data[4] and Regulation (EC) No 45/2001 of the European Parliament and of the Council of 18 December 2000 on the protection of individuals with regard to the processing of personal data by the Community institutions and bodies and on the free movement of such data[5] apply to the processing of personal data by the competent authorities as well as by any other authority receiving data pursuant to the Community Customs Code.

(7) In order to allow for appropriate risk-based controls, it is necessary to establish the requirement of pre-arrival or pre-departure information for all goods brought into or out of the customs territory of the Community, except for goods passing through by air or ship without a stop within this territory. Such information should be available before the goods are brought into or out of the customs territory of the Community. Different timeframes and rules may be set according to the type of goods, of transport or of economic operator or where international agreements provide for special security arrangements. In order to avoid security loopholes, this requirement should also be introduced with regard to goods brought into or out of a free zone.

(8) Regulation (EEC) No 2913/92 should therefore be amended accordingly,

---

[1] OJ C 110, 30.4.2004, p. 72.

[2] Opinion of the European Parliament of 20 April 2004 (not yet published in the Official Journal), Council Common Position of 29 November 2004 (OJ C 38 E, 15.2.2005, p. 36) and Position of the European Parliament of 23 February 2005 (not yet published in the Official Journal).

[3] OJ L 302, 19.10.1992, p. 1. Regulation as last amended by the 2003 Act of Accession.

[4] OJ L 281, 23.11.1995, p. 31. Directive as amended by Regulation (EC) No 1882/2003 (OJ L 284, 31.10.2003, p. 1).

[5] OJ L 8, 12.1.2001, p. 1.

HAVE ADOPTED THIS REGULATION

Article 1
(amends Council Regulation (EEC) 2913/93 establishing the Community Customs Code.)

Article 2
This Regulation shall enter into force on the seventh day following its publication in the Official Journal of the European Union.

Article 5a(2), Article 13(2) 2nd subparagraph, Article 36a(4), Article 36b(1), Article 182a(2) and Article 182d(1) shall be applicable from 11 May 2005.

All other provisions shall be applicable once the implementing provisions on the basis of the Articles referred to in the second subparagraph have entered into force.

However, electronic declaration and automated systems for the implementation of risk management and for the electronic exchange of data between customs offices of entry, import, export and exit, as stipulated in Articles 13, 36a, 36b, 36c, 182b, 182c and 182d, shall be in place three years after these Articles have become applicable.

Not later than two years after these Articles have become applicable, the Commission shall evaluate any request from Member States for an extension of the three-year period referred to in the third subparagraph for electronic declaration and automated systems for the implementation of risk management and for the electronic exchange of data between customs offices. The Commission shall submit a report to the European Parliament and to the Council and propose, where appropriate, an extension of the three-year period referred to in the third subparagraph.

This Regulation shall be binding in its entirety and directly applicable in all Member States.

Done at Strasbourg, 13 April 2005.

COMMISSION REGULATION

((EC) No 883/2005)

of 10 June 2005

amending Regulation (EEC) No 2454/93 laying down provisions for the implementation of Council Regulation (EEC) No 2913/92 establishing the Community Customs Code (Text with EEA relevance)

NOTES

Date of publication in OJ: L 148, 11.6.05, p 5.

THE COMMISSION OF THE EUROPEAN COMMUNITIES,

Having regard to the Treaty establishing the European Community,

Having regard to Council Regulation (EEC) No 2913/92 of 12 October 1992 establishing the Community Customs Code[1], and in particular Article 247 thereof,

Whereas:

(1) The Customs Convention on the international transport of goods under cover of TIR carnets (TIR Convention) of 14 November 1975 was approved on behalf of the Community by Council Regulation (EEC) No 2112/78[2] and entered into force in the Community on 20 June 1983[3]. Given the importance of international trade for the Community it is necessary to modernise the customs formalities concerning the TIR procedure. Article 49 of the TIR Convention envisages the application of greater facilities for the benefit of economic operators provided such facilities do not impede the application of the provisions of the Convention. Currently the Community rules concerning the TIR procedure do not provide for the status of authorised consignee. In order to meet the needs of economic operators and to facilitate international trade it is desirable to develop provisions, based on the existing Community/common transit rules, allowing the status of authorised consignee to be used in conjunction with the TIR procedure.

(2) The Convention on Temporary Admission of 26 June 1990 (the Istanbul Convention) and the Annexes thereto were approved by the European Community by Council Decision 93/329/EEC[4]. Annex A to the Istanbul Convention replaces the Customs Convention on the ATA carnet for the temporary admission of goods of 6 December 1961 (the ATA Convention) with regard to relations between countries which have accepted the Istanbul Convention and its Annex A. It is therefore necessary to amend the provisions relating to the ATA procedure to include references

to the Istanbul Convention. However, in order to facilitate international trade between the Community and those countries that have not accepted Annex A to the Istanbul Convention, it is appropriate to maintain the references to the ATA Convention.

(3) In the framework of the outward processing procedure, Commission Regulation (EEC) No 2454/93[5] has, since 2001, permitted partial relief from import duty after outward processing to be calculated on the basis of the costs of the processing operation, in accordance with the "value-added method". However, this method is not allowed if the temporary export goods which are not of Community origin have been released for free circulation at a zero duty rate. Those restrictive conditions for goods which are not of Community origin should be modified in order to promote the use of the value-added method.

(4) However, in order to avoid an abuse of the system it is desirable to provide that this method of duty relief may be refused if it is established that the sole object of the release for free circulation of the temporary export goods had been to benefit from this relief.

(5) The identity and nationality of means of transport at departure is regarded as mandatory information that has to be entered in box 18 of a transit declaration. At container terminals that have high levels of traffic it may occur that the details of the road means of transport to be used are unknown at the time when the transit formalities are carried out. Nevertheless, the identification of the container in which the goods subject to transit declaration will be carried is available and is already indicated in box 31 of the transit declaration. Given that the goods can be controlled on this basis, it is appropriate to allow box 18 of the transit declaration to be left blank, provided that it can be ensured that the proper details will be subsequently entered in the relevant box.

(6) Annex 37c and Annex 38 to Regulation (EEC) No 2454/93 both contain lists of packaging codes based on Annex V to Recommendation No 21 of the United Nations Economic Commission for Europe, Rev. 1, of August 1994, hereinafter "the UN/ECE Recommendation". Annex V to the UN/ECE Recommendation, which contains the list of codes, has been revised several times since its introduction in order to adapt it to practice in commerce and transport, the last time being in May 2002 (Revision 4). To enable traders to use the most widely accepted standard and thus to harmonise commercial and administrative practice within the Community as far as possible, it is necessary to provide that the packaging codes used in customs declarations are to reflect the latest version of Annex V to the UN/ECE Recommendation.

(7) In the interests of clarity and rationality, the list of packaging codes should be published solely in Annex 38, to which reference should be made when the list is mentioned in other customs legislation.

(8) The packaging codes are closely linked to the provisions applicable to transit operations as referred to in Articles 367 to 371 and to the new rules on the single administrative document, or form part of them. The new provisions must therefore be applicable for all customs procedures.

(9) A list of the numerical codes used in connection with the transit guarantee, for use on the single administrative document forms, was established by Regulation (EEC) No 2454/93. It is necessary to complete that list, in order to take into account all the situations relating to the guarantee waivers.

(10) As a consequence of the modification of the numerical codes of the transit guarantees, it is also necessary to adapt the corresponding data concerning the New Computerised Transit System.

(11) Given that the Convention of 20 May 1987 on a common transit procedure provides that the numerical codes of the transit guarantees are to apply from 1 May 2004, the new codes should apply with effect from that date.

(12) In view of the foregoing, Annexes 37 and 38 to Regulation (EEC) No 2454/93, as amended by Regulation (EC) No 2286/2003, should be amended. It is necessary, however, to make similar amendments also to Annex 37 to Regulation (EEC) No 2454/93, as amended by Commission Regulation (EC) No 444/2002[6], and Annex 38 to Regulation (EEC) No 2454/93, as amended by Commission Regulation (EC) No 881/2003[7], since they both remain in force until 1 January 2006.

(13) Article 531 of Regulation (EEC) No 2454/93 defines the usual forms of handling which are allowed under the customs warehousing procedure. The framework of the permitted activities is established by Article 109(1) of Regulation (EEC) No 2913/92. The usual forms of handling which non-Community goods may undergo are exhaustively listed in Annex 72 to Regulation (EEC) No 2454/93. However, the restrictive scope of this Annex has led to certain problems in practice. Therefore, it is desirable to provide for more flexibility.

(14) Some endorsements on customs documents expressed in the language of certain new Member States are not consistent with the terminology relating to customs matters already used in the languages concerned and adjustments are therefore necessary.

(15) Since the 2003 Act of Accession took effect on 1 May 2004, those endorsements should be applicable on the same date.

(16) Regulation (EEC) No 2454/93 should therefore be amended accordingly.

(17) The measures provided for in this Regulation are in accordance with the opinion of the Customs Code Committee,

---

[1] OJ L 302, 19.10.1992, p. 1. Regulation as last amended by the 2003 Act of Accession.

[2] OJ L 252, 14.9.1978, p. 1.

[3] OJ L 31, 2.2.1983, p. 13.

[4] OJ L 130, 27.5.1993, p. 1.

[5] OJ L 253, 11.10.1993, p. 1. Regulation as last amended by Regulation (EC) No 2286/2003 (OJ L 343, 31.12.2003, p. 1).

[6] OJ L 68, 12.3.2002, p. 11.

[7] OJ L 134, 29.5.2003, p. 1.

HAS ADOPTED THIS REGULATION:

Article 1

(Amends Commission Regulation (EEC) 2454/93.)

Article 2

1. This Regulation shall enter into force on the third day following its publication in the Official Journal of the European Union.

2. Points 1 to 8, 17 to 20, 24, 28 and 30 of Article 1 shall apply with effect from 1 May 2004.

3. Points 9 to 15, 31, 32 and 33 of Article 1 shall apply with effect from 1 October 2005.

4. Points 23, 25 and 26 of Article 1 shall apply with effect from 1 July 2005.

5. Points 22, 27 and 29 of Article 1 shall apply with effect from 1 January 2006. However, the Member States may apply those points before that date. In such cases, the Member States shall notify the Commission of the date of application. The Commission shall publish this information.

This Regulation shall be binding in its entirety and directly applicable in all Member States.

Done at Brussels, 10 June 2005.

COUNCIL REGULATION

(1777/2005/EC)

of 17 October 2005

laying down implementing measures for Directive 77/388/EEC on the common system of value added tax

NOTES

Date of publication in OJ: L 288, 29.10.05, p 1

THE COUNCIL OF THE EUROPEAN UNION,

Having regard to the Treaty establishing the European Community,

Having regard to the Sixth Council Directive 77/388/EEC of 17 May 1977 on the harmonisation of the laws of the Member States relating to turnover taxes — Common system of value added tax: uniform basis of assessment[1], hereinafter referred to as "Directive 77/388/EEC", and in particular Article 29a thereof,

Having regard to the proposal from the Commission,

Whereas:

(1) Directive 77/388/EEC contains rules on value added tax which, in some cases, are subject to interpretation by the Member States. The adoption of common provisions implementing Directive 77/388/EEC should ensure that application of the value added tax system complies more fully with the objective of the internal market, in cases where divergences in application have arisen or may arise which are incompatible with the proper functioning of the said market. These implementing measures are legally binding only from the date of the entry into force of this Regulation and are without prejudice to the validity of the legislation and interpretation previously adopted by the Member States.

(2) It is necessary for the achievement of the basic objective of ensuring a more uniform application of the current value added tax system to lay down rules implementing Directive 77/388/EEC, in particular in respect of taxable persons, the supply of goods and services, and the place of their supply. In accordance with the principle of proportionality as set out in the third subparagraph of Article 5 of the Treaty, this Regulation does not go beyond what is necessary in order to achieve the objective pursued. Since it is binding and directly applicable in all Member States, uniformity of application will be best ensured by a Regulation.

(3) These implementing provisions contain specific rules in response to selective questions of application and are designed to bring uniform treatment throughout the Community to those specific circumstances only. They are therefore not conclusive for other cases and, in view of their formulation, are to be applied restrictively.

(4) The further integration of the internal market has led to an increased need for cooperation by economic operators established in different Member States across internal borders and the development of European economic interest groupings (EEIGs), constituted in accordance with Regulation (EEC) No 2137/85[2], it should therefore be provided that such EEIGs are also taxable persons where they supply goods or services for consideration.

(5) The sale of an option as a financial instrument should be treated as a supply of services separate from the underlying transactions to which the option relates.

(6) It is necessary, on the one hand, to establish that a transaction which consists solely of assembling the various parts of a machine provided by a customer must be considered as a supply of services, and, on the other hand, to establish the place of such supply.

(7) Where various services supplied in the framework of organising a funeral form a part of a single service, the rule on the place of supply should also be determined.

(8) Certain specific services such as the assignment of television broadcasting rights in respect of football matches, the translation of texts, services for claiming value added tax refunds, certain services as an agent, the hiring of means of transport and certain electronic services involve cross-border scenarios or even the participation of economic operators established in third countries. The place of supply of these services needs to be clearly determined in order to create greater legal certainty. It should be noted that the services identified as electronic services or otherwise do not constitute a definitive, exhaustive list.

(9) In certain specific circumstances a credit or debit card handling fee which is paid in connection with a transaction should not reduce the taxable amount for the latter.

(10) Vocational training or retraining should include instruction relating directly to a trade or profession as well as any instruction aimed at acquiring or updating knowledge for vocational purposes, regardless of the duration of a course.

(11) "Platinum nobles" should be treated as being excluded from the exemptions for currency, bank notes and coins.

(12) Goods transported outside the Community by the purchaser thereof and used for the equipping, fuelling or provisioning of means of transport used for non-business purposes by persons other than natural persons, such as bodies governed by public law and associations, should be excluded from the exemption for export transactions.

(13) To guarantee uniform administrative practices for the calculation of the minimum value for exemption on exportation of goods carried in the personal luggage of travellers, the provisions on such calculations should be harmonised.

(14) Electronic import documents should also be admitted to exercise the right to deduct, where they fulfil the same requirements as paper-based documents.

(15) Weights for investment gold which are definitely accepted by the bullion market should be named and a common date for establishing the value of gold coins be determined to ensure equal treatment of economic operators.

(16) The special scheme for taxable persons not established in the Community, supplying electronic services to non-taxable persons established or resident within the Community is subject to certain conditions. Where those conditions are no longer fulfilled, the consequences thereof should, in particular, be made clear.

(17) In the case of intra-Community acquisition of goods, the right of the Member State of acquisition to tax the acquisition should remain unaffected by the value added tax treatment of the transaction in other Member States.

(18) Rules should be established to ensure the uniform treatment of supplies of goods once a supplier has exceeded the distance selling threshold for supplies to another Member State,

---

[1] OJ L 145, 13.6.1977, p. 1. Directive as last amended by Directive 2004/66/EC (OJ L 168, 1.5.2004, p. 35).

[2] OJ L 199, 31.7.1985, p. 1.

HAS ADOPTED THIS REGULATION:

CHAPTER IV
TAXABLE AMOUNT

(Article 11 of Directive 77/388/EEC)

Article 13

Where a supplier of goods or services, as a condition of accepting payment by credit or debit card, requires the customer to pay an amount to himself or another undertaking, and where the total price payable by that customer is unaffected irrespective of how payment is accepted, that amount shall constitute an integral part of the taxable amount for the supply of the goods or services, under Article 11 of Directive 77/388/EEC.

SECTION 2

(Article 15 of directive 77/388/EEC)

Article 16

"Means of transport for private use" as referred to in the first subparagraph of Article 15(2) of Directive 77/388/EEC shall include means of transport used for non-business purposes by persons other than natural persons, such as bodies governed by public law within the meaning of Article 4(5) of that Directive and associations.

Article 17

In order to determine whether the threshold set by a Member State in accordance with the third indent of the second subparagraph of Article 15(2) of Directive 77/388/EEC has been exceeded, the calculation shall be based on the invoice value. The aggregate value of several goods may be used only if all those goods are included on the same invoice issued by the same taxable person supplying goods to the same customer.

CHAPTER IX
FINAL PROVISIONS

Article 23

This Regulation shall enter into force on 1 July 2006.

Article 13 shall be applicable from 1 January 2006.

This Regulation shall be binding in its entirety and directly applicable in all Member States.

Done at Luxembourg, 17 October 2005.

Part III

COUNCIL DIRECTIVE

(2006/112/EC)

of 28 November 2006

on the common system of value added tax

NOTE

This Directive repeals Council Directives 67/227/EEC (First Council Directive of 11 April 1967) and 77/388 (Sixth Council Directive of 17 May 1977).

THE COUNCIL OF THE EUROPEAN UNION,

Having regard to the Treaty establishing the European Community, and in particular Article 93 thereof,

Having regard to the proposal from the Commission,

Having regard to the Opinion of the European Parliament,

Having regard to the Opinion of the European Economic and Social Committee,

Whereas:

(1)   Council Directive 77/388/EEC of 17 May 1977 on the harmonisation of the laws of the Member States relating to turnover taxes — Common system of value added tax: uniform basis of assessment [1] has been significantly amended on several occasions. Now that new amendments are being made to the said Directive, it is desirable, for reasons of clarity and rationalisation that the Directive should be recast.

(2)   The recast text should incorporate all those provisions of Council Directive 67/227/EEC of 11 April 1967 on the harmonisation of legislation of Member States concerning turnover taxes [2] which are still applicable. That Directive should therefore be repealed.

(3)   To ensure that the provisions are presented in a clear and rational manner, consistent with the principle of better regulation, it is appropriate to recast the structure and the wording of the Directive although this will not, in principle, bring about material changes in the existing legislation. A small number of substantive amendments are however inherent to the recasting exercise and should nevertheless be made. Where such changes are made, these are listed exhaustively in the provisions governing transposition and entry into force.

(4)   The attainment of the objective of establishing an internal market presupposes the application in Member States of legislation on turnover taxes that does not distort conditions of competition or hinder the free movement of goods and services. It is therefore necessary to achieve such harmonisation of legislation on turnover taxes by means of a system of value added tax (VAT), such as will eliminate, as far as possible, factors which may distort conditions of competition, whether at national or Community level.

(5)   A VAT system achieves the highest degree of simplicity and of neutrality when the tax is levied in as general a manner as possible and when its scope covers all stages of production and distribution, as well as the supply of services. It is therefore in the interests of the internal market and of Member States to adopt a common system which also applies to the retail trade.

Part III

(6) It is necessary to proceed by stages, since the harmonisation of turnover taxes leads in Member States to alterations in tax structure and appreciable consequences in the budgetary, economic and social fields.

(7) The common system of VAT should, even if rates and exemptions are not fully harmonised, result in neutrality in competition, such that within the territory of each Member State similar goods and services bear the same tax burden, whatever the length of the production and distribution chain.

(8) Pursuant to Council Decision 2000/597/EC, Euratom, of 29 September 2000 on the system of the European Communities' own resources [3], the budget of the European Communities is to be financed, without prejudice to other revenue, wholly from the Communities' own resources. Those resources are to include those accruing from VAT and obtained through the application of a uniform rate of tax to bases of assessment determined in a uniform manner and in accordance with Community rules.

(9) It is vital to provide for a transitional period to allow national laws in specified fields to be gradually adapted.

(10) During this transitional period, intra-Community transactions carried out by taxable persons other than exempt taxable persons should be taxed in the Member State of destination, in accordance with the rates and conditions set by that Member State.

(11) It is also appropriate that, during that transitional period, intra-Community acquisitions of a certain value, made by exempt persons or by non-taxable legal persons, certain intra-Community distance selling and the supply of new means of transport to individuals or to exempt or non-taxable bodies should also be taxed in the Member State of destination, in accordance with the rates and conditions set by that Member State, in so far as such transactions would, in the absence of special provisions, be likely to cause significant distortion of competition between Member States.

(12) For reasons connected with their geographic, economic and social situation, certain territories should be excluded from the scope of this Directive.

(13) In order to enhance the non-discriminatory nature of the tax, the term 'taxable person' should be defined in such a way that the Member States may use it to cover persons who occasionally carry out certain transactions.

(14) The term 'taxable transaction' may lead to difficulties, in particular as regards transactions treated as taxable transactions. Those concepts should therefore be clarified.

(15) With a view to facilitating intra-Community trade in work on movable tangible property, it is appropriate to establish the tax arrangements applicable to such transactions when they are carried out for a customer who is identified for VAT purposes in a Member State other than that in which the transaction is physically carried out.

(16) A transport operation within the territory of a Member State should be treated as the intra-Community transport of goods where it is directly linked to a transport operation carried out between Member States, in order to simplify not only the principles and arrangements for taxing those domestic transport services but also the rules applicable to ancillary services and to services supplied by intermediaries who take part in the supply of the various services.

(17)   Determination of the place where taxable transactions are carried out may engender conflicts concerning jurisdiction as between Member States, in particular as regards the supply of goods for assembly or the supply of services. Although the place where a supply of services is carried out should in principle be fixed as the place where the supplier has established his place of business, it should be defined as being in the Member State of the customer, in particular in the case of certain services supplied between taxable persons where the cost of the services is included in the price of the goods.

(18)   It is necessary to clarify the definition of the place of taxation of certain transactions carried out on board ships, aircraft or trains in the course of passenger transport within the Community.

(19)   Electricity and gas are treated as goods for VAT purposes. It is, however, particularly difficult to determine the place of supply. In order to avoid double taxation or non taxation and to attain a genuine internal market free of barriers linked to the VAT regime, the place of supply of gas through the natural gas distribution system, or of electricity, before the goods reach the final stage of consumption, should therefore be the place where the customer has established his business. The supply of electricity and gas at the final stage, that is to say, from traders and distributors to the final consumer, should be taxed at the place where the customer actually uses and consumes the goods.

(20)   In the case of the hiring out of movable tangible property, application of the general rule that supplies of services are taxed in the Member State in which the supplier is established may lead to substantial distortion of competition if the lessor and the lessee are established in different Member States and the rates of taxation in those States differ. It is therefore necessary to establish that the place of supply of a service is the place where the customer has established his business or has a fixed establishment for which the service has been supplied or, in the absence thereof, the place where he has his permanent address or usually resides.

(21)   However, as regards the hiring out of means of transport, it is appropriate, for reasons of control, to apply strictly the general rule, and thus to regard the place where the supplier has established his business as the place of supply.

(22)   All telecommunications services consumed within the Community should be taxed to prevent distortion of competition in that field. To that end, telecommunications services supplied to taxable persons established in the Community or to customers established in third countries should, in principle, be taxed at the place where the customer for the services is established. In order to ensure uniform taxation of telecommunications services which are supplied by taxable persons established in third territories or third countries to non-taxable persons established in the Community and which are effectively used and enjoyed in the Community, Member States should, however, provide for the place of supply to be within the Community.

(23)   Also to prevent distortions of competition, radio and television broadcasting services and electronically supplied services provided from third territories or third countries to persons established in the Community, or from the Community to customers established in third territories or third countries, should be taxed at the place of establishment of the customer.

(24)   The concepts of chargeable event and of the chargeability of VAT should be harmonised if the introduction of the common system of VAT and of

any subsequent amendments thereto are to take effect at the same time in all Member States.

(25) The taxable amount should be harmonised so that the application of VAT to taxable transactions leads to comparable results in all the Member States.

(26) To prevent loss of tax revenues through the use of connected parties to derive tax benefits, it should, in specific limited circumstances, be possible for Member States to intervene as regards the taxable amount of supplies of goods or services and intra-Community acquisitions of goods.

(27) In order to combat tax evasion or avoidance, it should be possible for Member States to include within the taxable amount of a transaction which involves the working of investment gold provided by a customer, the value of that investment gold where, by virtue of being worked, the gold loses its status of investment gold. When they apply these measures, Member States should be allowed a certain degree of discretion.

(28) If distortions are to be avoided, the abolition of fiscal controls at frontiers entails, not only a uniform basis of assessment, but also sufficient alignment as between Member States of a number of rates and rate levels.

(29) The standard rate of VAT in force in the various Member States, combined with the mechanism of the transitional system, ensures that this system functions to an acceptable degree. To prevent divergences in the standard rates of VAT applied by the Member States from leading to structural imbalances in the Community and distortions of competition in some sectors of activity, a minimum standard rate of 15 % should be fixed, subject to review.

(30) In order to preserve neutrality of VAT, the rates applied by Member States should be such as to enable, as a general rule, deduction of the VAT applied at the preceding stage.

(31) During the transitional period, certain derogations concerning the number and the level of rates should be possible.

(32) To achieve a better understanding of the impact of reduced rates, it is necessary for the Commission to prepare an assessment report on the impact of reduced rates applied to locally supplied services, notably in terms of job creation, economic growth and the proper functioning of the internal market.

(33) In order to tackle the problem of unemployment, those Member States wishing to do so should be allowed to experiment with the operation and impact, in terms of job creation, of a reduction in the VAT rate applied to labour-intensive services. That reduction is also likely to reduce the incentive for the businesses concerned to join or remain in the black economy.

(34) However, such a reduction in the VAT rate is not without risk for the smooth functioning of the internal market and for tax neutrality. Provision should therefore be made for an authorisation procedure to be introduced for a period that is fixed but sufficiently long, so that it is possible to assess the impact of the reduced rates applied to locally supplied services. In order to make sure that such a measure remains verifiable and limited, its scope should be closely defined.

(35) A common list of exemptions should be drawn up so that the Communities' own resources may be collected in a uniform manner in all the Member States.

(36) For the benefit both of the persons liable for payment of VAT and the competent administrative authorities, the methods of applying VAT to certain supplies and intra-Community acquisitions of products subject to excise duty should be aligned with the procedures and obligations concerning the duty to declare in the case of shipment of such products to another Member State laid down in Council Directive 92/12/EEC of 25 February 1992 on the general arrangements for products subject to excise duty and on the holding, movement and monitoring of such products [4].

(37) The supply of gas through the natural gas distribution system, and of electricity is taxed at the place of the customer. In order to avoid double taxation, the importation of such products should therefore be exempted from VAT.

(38) In respect of taxable operations in the domestic market linked to intra-Community trade in goods carried out during the transitional period by taxable persons not established within the territory of the Member State in which the intra-Community acquisition of goods takes place, including chain transactions, it is necessary to provide for simplification measures ensuring equal treatment in all the Member States. To that end, the provisions concerning the taxation system and the person liable for payment of the VAT due in respect of such operations should be harmonised. It is however, necessary to exclude in principle from such arrangements goods that are intended to be supplied at the retail stage.

(39) The rules governing deductions should be harmonised to the extent that they affect the actual amounts collected. The deductible proportion should be calculated in a similar manner in all the Member States.

(40) The scheme which allows the adjustment of deductions for capital goods over the lifetime of the asset, according to its actual use, should also be applicable to certain services with the nature of capital goods.

(41) It is appropriate to specify the persons liable for payment of VAT, particularly in the case of services supplied by a person who is not established in the Member State in which the VAT is due.

(42) Member States should be able, in specific cases, to designate the recipient of supplies of goods or services as the person liable for payment of VAT. This should assist Member States in simplifying the rules and countering tax evasion and avoidance in identified sectors and on certain types of transactions.

(43) Member States should be entirely free to designate the person liable for payment of the VAT on importation.

(44) Member States should be able to provide that someone other than the person liable for payment of VAT is to be held jointly and severally liable for its payment.

(45) The obligations of taxable persons should be harmonised as far as possible so as to ensure the necessary safeguards for the collection of VAT in a uniform manner in all the Member States.

(46) The use of electronic invoicing should allow tax authorities to carry out their monitoring activities. It is therefore appropriate, in order to ensure the internal market functions properly, to draw up a list, harmonised at Community level, of the particulars that must appear on invoices and to establish a number of common arrangements governing the use of electronic invoicing and the electronic storage of invoices, as well as for self-billing and the outsourcing of invoicing operations.

(47) Subject to conditions which they lay down, Member States should allow certain statements and returns to be made by electronic means, and may require that electronic means be used.

(48) The necessary pursuit of a reduction in the administrative and statistical formalities to be completed by businesses, particularly small and medium-sized enterprises, should be reconciled with the implementation of effective control measures and the need, on both economic and tax grounds, to maintain the quality of Community statistical instruments.

(49) Member States should be allowed to continue to apply their special schemes for small enterprises, in accordance with common provisions, and with a view to closer harmonisation.

(50) Member States should remain free to apply a special scheme involving flat rate rebates of input VAT to farmers not covered by the normal scheme. The basic principles of that special scheme should be established and a common method adopted, for the purposes of collecting own resources, for calculating the value added by such farmers.

(51) It is appropriate to adopt a Community taxation system to be applied to second-hand goods, works of art, antiques and collectors' items, with a view to preventing double taxation and the distortion of competition as between taxable persons.

(52) The application of the normal VAT rules to gold constitutes a major obstacle to its use for financial investment purposes and therefore justifies the application of a special tax scheme, with a view also to enhancing the international competitiveness of the Community gold market.

(53) The supply of gold for investment purposes is inherently similar to other financial investments which are exempt from VAT. Consequently, exemption appears to be the most appropriate tax treatment for supplies of investment gold.

(54) The definition of investment gold should cover gold coins the value of which primarily reflects the price of the gold contained. For reasons of transparency and legal certainty, a yearly list of coins covered by the investment gold scheme should be drawn up, providing security for the operators trading in such coins. That list should be without prejudice to the exemption of coins which are not included in the list but which meet the criteria laid down in this Directive.

(55) In order to prevent tax evasion while at the same time alleviating the financing burden for the supply of gold of a degree of purity above a certain level, it is justifiable to allow Member States to designate the customer as the person liable for payment of VAT.

(56) In order to facilitate compliance with fiscal obligations by operators providing electronically supplied services, who are neither established nor required to be identified for VAT purposes within the Community, a special scheme should be established. Under that scheme it should be possible for any operator supplying such services by electronic means to non-taxable persons within the Community, if he is not otherwise identified for VAT purposes within the Community, to opt for identification in a single Member State.

(57) It is desirable for the provisions concerning radio and television broadcasting and certain electronically supplied services to be put into place on a temporary basis only and to be reviewed in the light of experience within a short period of time.

(58)   It is necessary to promote the uniform application of the provisions of this Directive and to that end an advisory committee on value added tax should be set up to enable the Member States and the Commission to cooperate closely.

(59)   Member States should be able, within certain limits and subject to certain conditions, to introduce, or to continue to apply, special measures derogating from this Directive in order to simplify the levying of tax or to prevent certain forms of tax evasion or avoidance.

(60)   In order to ensure that a Member State which has submitted a request for derogation is not left in doubt as to what action the Commission plans to take in response, time-limits should be laid down within which the Commission must present to the Council either a proposal for authorisation or a communication setting out its objections.

(61)   It is essential to ensure uniform application of the VAT system. Implementing measures are appropriate to realise that aim.

(62)   Those measures should, in particular, address the problem of double taxation of cross-border transactions which can occur as the result of divergences between Member States in the application of the rules governing the place where taxable transactions are carried out.

(63)   Although the scope of the implementing measures would be limited, those measures would have a budgetary impact which for one or more Member States could be significant.

Accordingly, the Council is justified in reserving to itself the right to exercise implementing powers.

(64)   In view of their limited scope, the implementing measures should be adopted by the Council acting unanimously on a proposal from the Commission.

(65)   Since, for those reasons, the objectives of this Directive cannot be sufficiently achieved by the Member States and can therefore be better achieved by at Community level, the Community may adopt measures, in accordance with the principle of subsidiarity as set out in Article 5 of the Treaty. In accordance with the principle of proportionality, as set out in that Article, this Directive does not go beyond what is necessary in order to achieve those objectives.

(66)   The obligation to transpose this Directive into national law should be confined to those provisions which represent a substantive change as compared with the earlier Directives. The obligation to transpose into national law the provisions which are unchanged arises under the earlier Directives.

(67)   This Directive should be without prejudice to the obligations of the Member States in relation to the time-limits for transposition into national law of the Directives listed in Annex XI, Part B,

---

[1] OJ L 145, 13.6.1977, p. 1. Directive as last amended by Directive 2006/98/EC (OJ L 221, 12.8.2006, p. 9).

[2] OJ 71, 14.4.1967, p. 1301. Directive as last amended by Directive 69/ 463/EEC (OJ L 320 of 20.12.1969, p. 34).

[3] OJ L 253, 7.10.2000, p. 42.

[4] OJ L 76, 23.3.1992, p. 1. Directive as last amended by Directive 2004/106/EC (OJ L 359, 4.12.2004, p. 30).

HAS ADOPTED THIS DIRECTIVE:

ARRANGEMENT OF CONTENTS

Part III

TITLE I
SUBJECT MATTER AND SCOPE

Article 1

1.   This Directive establishes the common system of value added tax (VAT).

2.   The principle of the common system of VAT entails the application to goods and services of a general tax on consumption exactly proportional to the price of the goods and services, however many transactions take place in the production and distribution process before the stage at which the tax is charged.

On each transaction, VAT, calculated on the price of the goods or services at the rate applicable to such goods or services, shall be chargeable after deduction of the amount of VAT borne directly by the various cost components.

The common system of VAT shall be applied up to and including the retail trade stage.

Article 2

1.   The following transactions shall be subject to VAT:

(*a*)   the supply of goods for consideration within the territory of a Member State by a taxable person acting as such;

(*b*)   the intra-Community acquisition of goods for consideration within the territory of a Member State by:

(i)   a taxable person acting as such, or a non-taxable legal person, where the vendor is a taxable person acting as such who is not eligible for the exemption for small enterprises provided for in Articles 282 to 292 and who is not covered by Articles 33 or 36;

(ii)   in the case of new means of transport, a taxable person, or a non-taxable legal person, whose other acquisitions are not subject to VAT pursuant to Article 3(1), or any other non-taxable person;

(iii)   in the case of products subject to excise duty, where the excise duty on the intra-Community acquisition is chargeable, pursuant to Directive 92/12/EEC, within the territory of the Member State, a taxable person, or a non-taxable legal person, whose other acquisitions are not subject to VAT pursuant to Article 3(1);

(*c*)   the supply of services for consideration within the territory of a Member State by a taxable person acting as such;

(*d*)   the importation of goods.

2. (*a*) For the purposes of point (ii) of paragraph 1(*b*), the following shall be regarded as 'means of transport', where they are intended for the transport of persons or goods:

   (i)   motorised land vehicles the capacity of which exceeds 48 cubic centimetres or the power of which exceeds 7,2 kilowatts;

   (ii)   vessels exceeding 7,5 metres in length, with the exception of vessels used for navigation on the high seas and carrying passengers for reward, and of vessels used for the purposes of commercial, industrial or fishing activities, or for rescue or assistance at sea, or for inshore fishing;

   (iii) aircraft the take-off weight of which exceeds 1 550 kilograms, with the exception of aircraft used by airlines operating for reward chiefly on international routes.

(*b*) These means of transport shall be regarded as 'new' in the cases:

   (i)   of motorised land vehicles, where the supply takes place within six months of the date of first entry into service or where the vehicle has travelled for no more than 6 000 kilometres;

   (ii)   of vessels, where the supply takes place within three months of the date of first entry into service or where the vessel has sailed for no more than 100 hours;

   (iii) of aircraft, where the supply takes place within three months of the date of first entry into service or where the aircraft has flown for no more than 40 hours.

(*c*)   Member States shall lay down the conditions under which the facts referred to in point (*b*) may be regarded as established.

3.   'Products subject to excise duty' shall mean energy products, alcohol and alcoholic beverages and manufactured tobacco, as defined by current Community legislation, but not gas supplied through the natural gas distribution system or electricity.

Article 3

1.   By way of derogation from Article 2(1)(*b*)(i), the following transactions shall not be subject to VAT:

   (*a*)   the intra-Community acquisition of goods by a taxable person or a non-taxable legal person, where the supply of such goods within the territory of the Member State of acquisition would be exempt pursuant to Articles 148 and 151;

   (*b*)   the intra-Community acquisition of goods, other than those referred to in point (*a*) and Article 4, and other than new means of transport or products subject to excise duty, by a taxable person for the purposes of his agricultural, forestry or fisheries business subject to the common flat-rate scheme for farmers, or by a taxable person who carries out only supplies of goods or services in respect of which VAT is not deductible, or by a non-taxable legal person.

2.   Point (*b*) of paragraph 1 shall apply only if the following conditions are met:

   (*a*)   during the current calendar year, the total value of intra-Community acquisitions of goods does not exceed a threshold which the Member States shall determine but which may not be less than EUR 10 000 or the equivalent in national currency;

   (*b*)   during the previous calendar year, the total value of intra-Community acquisitions of goods did not exceed the threshold provided for in point (*a*).

The threshold which serves as the reference shall consist of the total value, exclusive of VAT due or paid in the Member State in which dispatch or transport of the goods began, of the intra-Community acquisitions of goods as referred to under point (b) of paragraph 1.

3. Member States shall grant taxable persons and non-taxable legal persons eligible under point (*b*) of paragraph 1 the right to opt for the general scheme provided for in Article 2(1)(*b*)(i).

Member States shall lay down the detailed rules for the exercise of the option referred to in the first subparagraph, which shall in any event cover a period of two calendar years.

TITLE II
TERRITORIAL SCOPE

Article 5

For the purposes of applying this Directive, the following definitions shall apply:

(1) 'Community' and 'territory of the Community' mean the territories of the Member States as defined in point (2);

(2) 'Member State' and 'territory of a Member State' mean the territory of each Member State of the Community to which the Treaty establishing the European Community is applicable, in accordance with Article 299 of that Treaty, with the exception of any territory referred to in Article 6 of this Directive;

(3) 'third territories' means those territories referred to in Article 6;

(4) 'third country' means any State or territory to which the Treaty is not applicable.

Article 6

1. This Directive shall not apply to the following territories forming part of the customs territory of the Community:

(*a*) Mount Athos;

(*b*) the Canary Islands;

(*c*) the French overseas departments;

(*d*) the Åland Islands;

(*e*) the Channel Islands.

2. This Directive shall not apply to the following territories not forming part of the customs territory of the Community:

(*a*) the Island of Heligoland;

(*b*) the territory of Büsingen;

(*c*) Ceuta;

(*d*) Melilla;

(*e*) Livigno;

(*f*) Campione d'Italia;

(*g*) the Italian waters of Lake Lugano.

Article 7

1. In view of the conventions and treaties concluded with France, the United Kingdom and Cyprus respectively, the Principality of Monaco, the Isle of Man and the United Kingdom Sovereign Base Areas of Akrotiri and Dhekelia shall not be regarded, for the purposes of the application of this Directive, as third countries.

2. Member States shall take the measures necessary to ensure that transactions originating in or intended for the Principality of Monaco are treated as transactions originating in or intended for France, that transactions originating in or intended for the Isle of Man are treated as transactions originating in or intended for the United Kingdom, and that transactions originating in or intended for the United Kingdom

Sovereign Base Areas of Akrotiri and Dhekelia are treated as transactions originating in or intended for Cyprus.

Article 8

If the Commission considers that the provisions laid down in Articles 6 and 7 are no longer justified, particularly in terms of fair competition or own resources, it shall present appropriate proposals to the Council.

TITLE IV
TAXABLE TRANSACTIONS

CHAPTER 4
IMPORTATION OF GOODS

Article 30

'Importation of goods' shall mean the entry into the Community of goods which are not in free circulation within the meaning of Article 24 of the Treaty.

In addition to the transaction referred to in the first paragraph, the entry into the Community of goods which are in free circulation, coming from a third territory forming part of the customs territory of the Community, shall be regarded as importation of goods.

TITLE V
PLACE OF TAXABLE TRANSACTIONS

CHAPTER 4
PLACE OF IMPORTATION OF GOODS

Article 60

The place of importation of goods shall be the Member State within whose territory the goods are located when they enter the Community.

Article 61

By way of derogation from Article 60, where, on entry into the Community, goods which are not in free circulation are placed under one of the arrangements or situations referred to in Article 156, or under temporary importation arrangements with total exemption from import duty, or under external transit arrangements, the place of importation of such goods shall be the Member State within whose territory the goods cease to be covered by those arrangements or situations.

Similarly, where, on entry into the Community, goods which are in free circulation are placed under one of the arrangements or situations referred to in Articles 276 and 277, the place of importation shall be the Member State within whose territory the goods cease to be covered by those arrangements or situations.

TITLE VI
CHARGEABLE EVENT AND CHARGEABILITY OF VAT

CHAPTER 1
GENERAL PROVISIONS

Article 62

For the purposes of this Directive:

(1)   'chargeable event' shall mean the occurrence by virtue of which the legal conditions necessary for VAT to become chargeable are fulfilled;

(2)   VAT shall become 'chargeable' when the tax authority becomes entitled under the law, at a given moment, to claim the tax from the person liable to pay, even though the time of payment may be deferred.

CHAPTER 2
SUPPLY OF GOODS OR SERVICES

Article 63

The chargeable event shall occur and VAT shall become chargeable when the goods or the services are supplied.

Article 64

1.   Where it gives rise to successive statements of account or successive payments, the supply of goods, other than that consisting in the hire of goods for a certain period or the sale of goods on deferred terms, as referred to in point (b) of Article 14 (2), or the supply of services shall be regarded as being completed on expiry of the periods to which such statements of account or payments relate.

2.   Member States may provide that, in certain cases, the continuous supply of goods or services over a period of time is to be regarded as being completed at least at intervals of one year.

Article 65

Where a payment is to be made on account before the goods or services are supplied, VAT shall become chargeable on receipt of the payment and on the amount received.

Article 66

By way of derogation from Articles 63, 64 and 65, Member States may provide that VAT is to become chargeable, in respect of certain transactions or certain categories of taxable person at one of the following times:

    (a)   no later than the time the invoice is issued;

    (b)   no later than the time the payment is received;

    (c)   where an invoice is not issued, or is issued late, within a specified period from the date of the chargeable event.

CHAPTER 4
IMPORTATION OF GOODS

Article 70

The chargeable event shall occur and VAT shall become chargeable when the goods are imported.

Article 71

1.   Where, on entry into the Community, goods are placed under one of the arrangements or situations referred to in Articles 156, 276 and 277, or under temporary importation arrangements with total exemption from import duty, or under external transit arrangements, the chargeable event shall occur and VAT shall become chargeable only when the goods cease to be covered by those arrangements or situations.

However, where imported goods are subject to customs duties, to agricultural levies or to charges having equivalent effect established under a common policy, the chargeable event shall occur and VAT shall become chargeable when the chargeable event in respect of those duties occurs and those duties become chargeable.

2.   Where imported goods are not subject to any of the duties referred to in the second subparagraph of paragraph 1, Member States shall, as regards the chargeable event and the moment when VAT becomes chargeable, apply the provisions in force governing customs duties.

TITLE VII
TAXABLE AMOUNT

CHAPTER 4
IMPORTATION OF GOODS

Article 72

For the purposes of this Directive, 'open market value' shall mean the full amount that, in order to obtain the goods or services in question at that time, a customer at the same marketing stage at which the supply of goods or services takes place, would have to pay, under conditions of fair competition, to a supplier at arm's length within the territory of the Member State in which the supply is subject to tax.

Where no comparable supply of goods or services can be ascertained, 'open market value' shall mean the following:

    (1)   in respect of goods, an amount that is not less than the purchase price of the goods or of similar goods or, in the absence of a purchase price, the cost price, determined at the time of supply;

    (2)   in respect of services, an amount that is not less than the full cost to the taxable person of providing the service.

CHAPTER 2
SUPPLY OF GOODS OR SERVICES

Article 73

In respect of the supply of goods or services, other than as referred to in Articles 74 to 77, the taxable amount shall include everything which constitutes consideration obtained or to be obtained by the supplier, in return for the supply, from the customer or a third party, including subsidies directly linked to the price of the supply.

Article 74

Where a taxable person applies or disposes of goods forming part of his business assets, or where goods are retained by a taxable person, or by his successors, when his taxable economic activity ceases, as referred to in Articles 16 and 18, the taxable amount shall be the purchase price of the goods or of similar goods or, in the absence of a purchase price, the cost price, determined at the time when the application, disposal or retention takes place.

Article 75

In respect of the supply of services, as referred to in Article 26, where goods forming part of the assets of a business are used for private purposes or services are carried out free of charge, the taxable amount shall be the full cost to the taxable person of providing the services.

Article 76

In respect of the supply of goods consisting in transfer to another Member State, the taxable amount shall be the purchase price of the goods or of similar goods or, in the absence of a purchase price, the cost price, determined at the time the transfer takes place.

Article 77

In respect of the supply by a taxable person of a service for the purposes of his business, as referred to in Article 27, the taxable amount shall be the open market value of the service supplied.

Article 78

The taxable amount shall include the following factors:

    (a)   taxes, duties, levies and charges, excluding the VAT itself;

(b)   incidental expenses, such as commission, packing, transport and insurance costs, charged by the supplier to the customer.

For the purposes of point (b) of the first paragraph, Member States may regard expenses covered by a separate agreement as incidental expenses.

Article 79

The taxable amount shall not include the following factors:

(a)   price reductions by way of discount for early payment;

(b)   price discounts and rebates granted to the customer and obtained by him at the time of the supply;

(c)   amounts received by a taxable person from the customer, as repayment of expenditure incurred in the name and on

behalf of the customer, and entered in his books in a suspense account.

The taxable person must furnish proof of the actual amount of the expenditure referred to in point (c) of the first paragraph and may not deduct any VAT which may have been charged.

Article 80

1.   In order to prevent tax evasion or avoidance, Member States may in any of the following cases take measures to ensure that, in respect of the supply of goods or services involving family or other close personal ties, management, ownership, membership, financial or legal ties as defined by the Member State, the taxable amount is to be the open market value:

(a)   where the consideration is lower than the open market value and the recipient of the supply does not have a full right of deduction under Articles 167 to 171 and Articles 173 to 177;

(b)   where the consideration is lower than the open market value and the supplier does not have a full right of deduction under Articles 167 to 171 and Articles 173 to 177 and the supply is subject to an exemption under Articles 132, 135, 136, 371, 375, 376, 377, 378(2), 379(2) or Articles 380 to 390;

(c)   where the consideration is higher than the open market value and the supplier does not have a full right of deduction under Articles 167 to 171 and Articles 173 to 177.

For the purposes of the first subparagraph, legal ties may include the relationship between an employer and employee or the employee's family, or any other closely connected persons.

2.   Where Member States exercise the option provided for in paragraph 1, they may restrict the categories of suppliers or recipients to whom the measures shall apply.

3.   Member States shall inform the VAT Committee of national legislative measures adopted pursuant to paragraph 1 in so far as these are not measures authorised by the Council prior to 13 August 2006 in accordance with Article 27 (1) to (4) of Directive 77/388/EEC, and which are continued under paragraph 1 of this Article.

Article 81

Member States which, at 1 January 1993, were not availing themselves of the option under Article 98 of applying a reduced rate may, if they avail themselves of the option under Article 89, provide that in respect of the supply of works of art, as referred to in Article 103(2), the taxable amount is to be equal to a fraction of the amount determined in accordance with Articles 73, 74, 76, 78 and 79.

The fraction referred to in the first paragraph shall be determined in such a way that the VAT thus due is equal to at least 5% of the amount determined in accordance with Articles 73, 74, 76, 78 and 79.

Article 82

Member States may provide that, in respect of the supply of goods and services, the taxable amount is to include the value of exempt investment gold within the meaning of Article 346, which has been provided by the customer to be used as basis for working and which as a result, loses its VAT exempt investment gold status when such goods and services are supplied. The value to be used is the open market value of the investment gold at the time that those goods and services are supplied.

CHAPTER 4
IMPORTATION OF GOODS

Article 85

In respect of the importation of goods, the taxable amount shall be the value for customs purposes, determined in accordance with the Community provisions in force.

Article 86

1. The taxable amount shall include the following factors, in so far as they are not already included:

  (a)   taxes, duties, levies and other charges due outside the Member State of importation, and those due by reason of importation, excluding the VAT to be levied;

  (b)   incidental expenses, such as commission, packing, transport and insurance costs, incurred up to the first place of destination within the territory of the Member State of importation as well as those resulting from transport to another place of destination within the Community, if that other place is known when the chargeable event occurs.

2. For the purposes of point (b) of paragraph 1, 'first place of destination' shall mean the place mentioned on the consignment note or on any other document under which the goods are imported into the Member State of importation. If no such mention is made, the first place of destination shall be deemed to be the place of the first transfer of cargo in the Member State of importation.

Article 87

The taxable amount shall not include the following factors:

  (a)   price reductions by way of discount for early payment;

  (b)   price discounts and rebates granted to the customer and obtained by him at the time of importation.

Article 88

Where goods temporarily exported from the Community are reimported after having undergone, outside the Community, repair, processing, adaptation, making up or re-working, Member States shall take steps to ensure that the tax treatment of the goods for VAT purposes is the same as that which would have been applied had the repair, processing, adaptation, making up or re-working been carried out within their territory.

Article 89

Member States which, at 1 January 1993, were not availing themselves of the option under Article 98 of applying a reduced rate may provide that in respect of the importation of works of art, collectors' items and antiques, as defined in points (2), (3) and (4) of Article 311(1), the taxable amount is to be equal to a fraction of the amount determined in accordance with Articles 85, 86 and 87.

The fraction referred to in the first paragraph shall be determined in such a way that the VAT thus due on the importation is equal to at least 5% of the amount determined in accordance with Articles 85, 86 and 87.

CHAPTER 5
MISCELLANEOUS PROVISIONS

Article 90

1.   In the case of cancellation, refusal or total or partial nonpayment, or where the price is reduced after the supply takes place, the taxable amount shall be reduced accordingly under conditions which shall be determined by the Member States.

2.   In the case of total or partial non-payment, Member States may derogate from paragraph 1.

Article 91

1.   Where the factors used to determine the taxable amount on importation are expressed in a currency other than that of the Member State in which assessment takes place, the exchange rate shall be determined in accordance with the Community provisions governing the calculation of the value for customs purposes.

2.   Where the factors used to determine the taxable amount of a transaction other than the importation of goods are expressed in a currency other than that of the Member State in which assessment takes place, the exchange rate applicable shall be the latest selling rate recorded, at the time VAT becomes chargeable, on the most representative exchange market or markets of the Member State concerned, or a rate determined by reference to that or those markets, in accordance with the rules laid down by that Member State.

However, for some of the transactions referred to in the first subparagraph or for certain categories of taxable persons, Member States may use the exchange rate determined in accordance with the Community provisions in force governing the calculation of the value for customs purposes.

Article 92

As regards the costs of returnable packing material, Member States may take one of the following measures:

(a)   exclude them from the taxable amount and take the measures necessary to ensure that this amount is adjusted if the packing material is not returned;

(b)   include them in the taxable amount and take the measures necessary to ensure that this amount is adjusted if the packing material is in fact returned.

TITLE IX
EXEMPTIONS

CHAPTER 1
GENERAL PROVISIONS

Article 131

The exemptions provided for in Chapters 2 to 9 shall apply without prejudice to other Community provisions and in accordance with conditions which the Member States shall lay down for the purposes of ensuring the correct and straightforward application of those exemptions and of preventing any possible evasion, avoidance or abuse.

CHAPTER 4
EXEMPTIONS FOR INTRA-COMMUNITY TRANSACTIONS

SECTION 1
Exemptions related to the supply of goods

Article 138

1.   Member States shall exempt the supply of goods dispatched or transported to a destination outside their respective territory but within the Community, by or on behalf of the vendor or the person acquiring the goods, for another taxable person, or for a non-taxable legal person acting as such in a Member State other than that in which dispatch or transport of the goods began.

2.   In addition to the supply of goods referred to in paragraph 1, Member States shall exempt the following transactions:

(a)   the supply of new means of transport, dispatched or transported to the customer at a destination outside their respective territory but within the Community, by or on behalf of the vendor or the customer, for taxable persons, or non-taxable legal persons, whose intra-Community acquisitions of goods are not subject to VAT pursuant to Article 3(1), or for any other non-taxable person;

(b)   the supply of products subject to excise duty, dispatched or transported to a destination outside their respective territory but within the Community, to the customer, by or on behalf of the vendor or the customer, for taxable persons, or non-taxable legal persons, whose intra-Community acquisitions of goods other than products subject to excise duty are not subject to VAT pursuant to Article 3(1), where those products have been dispatched or transported in accordance with Article 7(4) and (5) or Article 16 of Directive 92/12/EEC;

(c)   the supply of goods, consisting in a transfer to another Member State, which would have been entitled to exemption under paragraph 1 and points (a) and (b) if it had been made on behalf of another taxable person.

Article 139

1.   The exemption provided for in Article 138(1) shall not apply to the supply of goods carried out by taxable persons who are covered by the exemption for small enterprises provided for in Articles 282 to 292.

Nor shall that exemption apply to the supply of goods to taxable persons, or non-taxable legal persons, whose intra-Community acquisitions of goods are not subject to VAT pursuant to Article 3(1).

2.   The exemption provided for in Article 138(2)(b) shall not apply to the supply of products subject to excise duty by taxable persons who are covered by the exemption for small enterprises provided for in Articles 282 to 292.

3.   The exemption provided for in Article 138(1) and (2)(b) and (c) shall not apply to the supply of goods subject to VAT in accordance with the margin scheme provided for in Articles 312 to 325 or the special arrangements for sales by public auction.

The exemption provided for in Article 138(1) and (2)(c) shall not apply to the supply of second-hand means of transport, as defined in Article 327(3), subject to VAT in accordance with the transitional arrangements for second-hand means of transport.

Part III

SECTION 2

Exemptions for intra-community acquisitions of goods

Article 140

Member States shall exempt the following transactions:

(a)   the intra-Community acquisition of goods the supply of which by taxable persons would in all circumstances be exempt within their respective territory;

(b)   the intra-Community acquisition of goods the importation of which would in all circumstances be exempt under points (a), (b) and (c) and (e) to (l) of Article 143;

(c)   the intra-Community acquisition of goods where, pursuant to Articles 170 and 171, the person acquiring the goods would in all circumstances be entitled to full reimbursement of the VAT due under Article 2(1)(b).

Article 141

Each Member State shall take specific measures to ensure that VAT is not charged on the intra-Community acquisition of goods within its territory, made in accordance with Article 40, where the following conditions are met:

(a)   the acquisition of goods is made by a taxable person who is not established in the Member State concerned but is identified for VAT purposes in another Member State;

(b)   the acquisition of goods is made for the purposes of the subsequent supply of those goods, in the Member State concerned, by the taxable person referred to in point (a);

(c)   the goods thus acquired by the taxable person referred to in point (a) are directly dispatched or transported, from a Member State other than that in which he is identified for VAT purposes, to the person for whom he is to carry out the subsequent supply;

(d)   the person to whom the subsequent supply is to be made is another taxable person, or a non-taxable legal person, who is identified for VAT purposes in the Member State concerned;

(e)   the person referred to in point (d) has been designated in accordance with Article 197 as liable for payment of the VAT due on the supply carried out by the taxable person who is not established in the Member State in which the tax is due.

SECTION 3

Exemptions for certain transport services

Article 142

Member States shall exempt the supply of intra-Community transport of goods to and from the islands making up the autonomous regions of the Azores and Madeira, as well as the supply of transport of goods between those islands.

CHAPTER 5

EXEMPTIONS ON IMPORTATION

Article 143

Member States shall exempt the following transactions:

(a)   the final importation of goods of which the supply by a taxable person would in all circumstances be exempt within their respective territory;

(b)   the final importation of goods governed by Council Directives 69/169/EEC [1], 83/181/EEC [2] and 2006/79/ EC [3];

(c)   the final importation of goods, in free circulation from a third territory forming part of the Community customs territory, which would be entitled to exemption under point (b) if they had been imported within the meaning of the first paragraph of Article 30;

(d)   the importation of goods dispatched or transported from a third territory or a third country into a Member State other than that in which the dispatch or transport of the goods ends, where the supply of such goods by the importer designated or recognised under Article 201 as liable for payment of VAT is exempt under Article 138;

(e)   the reimportation, by the person who exported them, of goods in the state in which they were exported, where those goods are exempt from customs duties;

(f)   the importation, under diplomatic and consular arrangements, of goods which are exempt from customs duties;

(g)   the importation of goods by international bodies recognised as such by the public authorities of the host Member State, or by members of such bodies, within the limits and under the conditions laid down by the international conventions establishing the bodies or by headquarters agreements;

(h)   the importation of goods, into Member States party to the North Atlantic Treaty, by the armed forces of other States party to that Treaty for the use of those forces or the civilian staff accompanying them or for supplying their messes or canteens where such forces take part in the common defence effort;

(i)   the importation of goods by the armed forces of the United Kingdom stationed in the island of Cyprus pursuant to the Treaty of Establishment concerning the Republic of Cyprus, dated 16 August 1960, which are for the use of those forces or the civilian staff accompanying them or for supplying their messes or canteens;

(j)   the importation into ports, by sea fishing undertakings, of their catches, unprocessed or after undergoing preservation for marketing but before being supplied;

(k)   the importation of gold by central banks;

(l)   the importation of gas through the natural gas distribution system, or of electricity.

---

[1] Council Directive 69/169/EEC of 28 May 1969 on the harmonisation of provisions laid down by Law, Regulation or Administrative Action relating to exemption from turnover tax and excise duty on imports in international travel (OJ L 133, 4.6.1969, p. 6). Directive as last amended by Directive 2005/93/EC (OJ L 346, 29.12.2005, p. 16).

[2] Council Directive 83/181/EEC of 28 March 1983 determining the scope of Article 14(1)(d) of Directive 77/388/EEC as regards exemption from value added tax on the final importation of certain goods (OJ L 105, 23.4.1983, p. 38). Directive as last amended by the 1994 Act of Accession.

[3] Council Directive 2006/79/EC of 5 October 2006 on the exemption from taxes of imports of small consignments of goods of a non-commercial character from third countries (codified version) (OJ L 286, 17.10.2006, p. 15).

Article 144

Member States shall exempt the supply of services relating to the importation of goods where the value of such services is included in the taxable amount in accordance with Article 86(1)(b).

Article 145

1. The Commission shall, where appropriate, as soon as possible, present to the Council proposals designed to delimit the scope of the exemptions provided for in Articles 143 and 144 and to lay down the detailed rules for their implementation.

2. Pending the entry into force of the rules referred to in paragraph 1, Member States may maintain their national provisions in force.

Member States may adapt their national provisions so as to minimise distortion of competition and, in particular, to prevent non-taxation or double taxation within the Community.

Member States may use whatever administrative procedures they consider most appropriate to achieve exemption.

3. Member States shall notify to the Commission, which shall inform the other Member States accordingly, the provisions of national law which are in force, in so far as these have not already been notified, and those which they adopt pursuant to paragraph 2.

CHAPTER 6
EXEMPTIONS ON EXPORTATION

Article 146

1. Member States shall exempt the following transactions:

- (a) the supply of goods dispatched or transported to a destination outside the Community by or on behalf of the vendor;
- (b) the supply of goods dispatched or transported to a destination outside the Community by or on behalf of a customer not established within their respective territory, with the exception of goods transported by the customer himself for the equipping, fuelling and provisioning of pleasure boats and private aircraft or any other means of transport for private use;
- (c) the supply of goods to approved bodies which export them out of the Community as part of their humanitarian, charitable or teaching activities outside the Community;
- (d) the supply of services consisting in work on movable property acquired or imported for the purpose of undergoing such work within the Community, and dispatched or transported out of the Community by the supplier, by the customer if not established within their respective territory or on behalf of either of them;
- (e) the supply of services, including transport and ancillary transactions, but excluding the supply of services exempted in accordance with Articles 132 and 135, where these are directly connected with the exportation or importation of goods covered by Article 61 and Article 157(1)(a).

2. The exemption provided for in point (c) of paragraph 1 may be granted by means of a refund of the VAT.

Article 147

1. Where the supply of goods referred to in point (b) of Article 146(1) relates to goods to be carried in the personal luggage of travellers, the exemption shall apply only if the following conditions are met:

- (a) the traveller is not established within the Community;
- (b) the goods are transported out of the Community before the end of the third month following that in which the supply takes place;
- (c) the total value of the supply, including VAT, is more than EUR 175 or the equivalent in national currency, fixed annually by applying the

conversion rate obtaining on the first working day of October with effect from 1 January of the following year.

However, Member States may exempt a supply with a total value of less than the amount specified in point (c) of the first subparagraph.

2. For the purposes of paragraph 1, 'a traveller who is not established within the Community' shall mean a traveller whose permanent address or habitual residence is not located within the Community. In that case 'permanent address or habitual residence' means the place entered as such in a passport, identity card or other document recognised as an identity document by the Member State within whose territory the supply takes place.

Proof of exportation shall be furnished by means of the invoice or other document in lieu thereof, endorsed by the customs office of exit from the Community.

Each Member State shall send to the Commission specimens of the stamps it uses for the endorsement referred to in the second subparagraph. The Commission shall forward that information to the tax authorities of the other Member States.

CHAPTER 7
EXEMPTIONS RELATED TO INTERNATIONAL TRANSPORT

Article 148

Member States shall exempt the following transactions:

(a) the supply of goods for the fuelling and provisioning of vessels used for navigation on the high seas and carrying passengers for reward or used for the purpose of commercial, industrial or fishing activities, or for rescue or assistance at sea, or for inshore fishing, with the exception, in the case of vessels used for inshore fishing, of ships' provisions;

(b) the supply of goods for the fuelling and provisioning of fighting ships, falling within the combined nomenclature (CN) code 8906 10 00, leaving their territory and bound for ports or anchorages outside the Member State concerned;

(c) the supply, modification, repair, maintenance, chartering and hiring of the vessels referred to in point (a), and the supply, hiring, repair and maintenance of equipment, including fishing equipment, incorporated or used therein;

(d) the supply of services other than those referred to in point (c), to meet the direct needs of the vessels referred to in point (a) or of their cargoes;

(e) the supply of goods for the fuelling and provisioning of aircraft used by airlines operating for reward chiefly on international routes;

(f) the supply, modification, repair, maintenance, chartering and hiring of the aircraft referred to in point (e), and the supply, hiring, repair and maintenance of equipment incorporated or used therein;

(g) the supply of services, other than those referred to in point (f), to meet the direct needs of the aircraft referred to in point (e) or of their cargoes.

Article 149

Portugal may treat sea and air transport between the islands making up the autonomous regions of the Azores and Madeira and between those regions and the mainland as international transport.

Article 150

1. The Commission shall, where appropriate, as soon as possible, present to the Council proposals designed to delimit the scope of the exemptions provided for in Article 148 and to lay down the detailed rules for their implementation.

2. Pending the entry into force of the provisions referred to in paragraph 1, Member States may limit the scope of the exemptions provided for in points (*a*) and (*b*) of Article 148.

CHAPTER 8
EXEMPTIONS RELATING TO CERTAIN TRANSACTIONS TREATED AS EXPORTS

Article 151

1. Member States shall exempt the following transactions:

(*a*) the supply of goods or services under diplomatic and consular arrangements;

(*b*) the supply of goods or services to international bodies recognised as such by the public authorities of the host Member State, and to members of such bodies, within the limits and under the conditions laid down by the international conventions establishing the bodies or by headquarters agreements;

(*c*) the supply of goods or services within a Member State which is a party to the North Atlantic Treaty, intended either for the armed forces of other States party to that Treaty for the use of those forces, or of the civilian staff accompanying them, or for supplying their messes or canteens when such forces take part in the common defence effort;

(*d*) the supply of goods or services to another Member State, intended for the armed forces of any State which is a party to the North Atlantic Treaty, other than the Member State of destination itself, for the use of those forces, or of the civilian staff accompanying them, or for supplying their messes or canteens when such forces take part in the common defence effort;

(*e*) the supply of goods or services to the armed forces of the United Kingdom stationed in the island of Cyprus pursuant to the Treaty of Establishment concerning the Republic of

Cyprus, dated 16 August 1960, which are for the use of those forces, or of the civilian staff accompanying them, or for supplying their messes or canteens.

Pending the adoption of common tax rules, the exemptions provided for in the first subparagraph shall be subject to the limitations laid down by the host Member State.

2. In cases where the goods are not dispatched or transported out of the Member State in which the supply takes place, and in the case of services, the exemption may be granted by means of a refund of the VAT.

Article 152

Member States shall exempt the supply of gold to central banks.

CHAPTER 9
EXEMPTIONS FOR THE SUPPLY OF SERVICES BY INTERMEDIARIES

Article 153

Member States shall exempt the supply of services by intermediaries, acting in the name and on behalf of another person, where they take part in the transactions referred to in Chapters 6, 7 and 8, or of transactions carried out outside the Community.

The exemption referred to in the first paragraph shall not apply to travel agents who, in the name and on behalf of travellers, supply services which are carried out in other Member States.

CHAPTER 10
EXEMPTIONS FOR TRANSACTIONS RELATING TO
INTERNATIONAL TRADE

SECTION 2
*Transactions exempted with a view to export and in the framework of trade between
the Member States*

Article 164

1. Member States may, after consulting the VAT Committee, exempt the following transactions carried out by, or intended for, a taxable person up to an amount equal to the value of the exports carried out by that person during the preceding 12 months:

    (*a*)   intra-Community acquisitions of goods made by the taxable person, and imports for and supplies of goods to the taxable person, with a view to their exportation from the Community as they are or after processing;

    (*b*)   supplies of services linked with the export business of the taxable person.

2. Where Member States exercise the option of exemption under paragraph 1, they shall, after consulting the VAT Committee, apply that exemption also to transactions relating to supplies carried out by the taxable person, in accordance with the conditions specified in Article 138, up to an amount equal to the value of the supplies carried out by that person, in accordance with the same conditions, during the preceding 12 months.

Article 165

Member States may set a common maximum amount for transactions which they exempt pursuant to Article 164.

SECTION 3
Provisions common to Sections 1 and 2

Article 166

The Commission shall, where appropriate, as soon as possible, present to the Council proposals concerning common arrangements for applying VAT to the transactions referred to in Sections 1 and 2.

TITLE XI
OBLIGATIONS OF TAXABLE PERSONS AND CERTAIN
NON-TAXABLE PERSONS

CHAPTER 8
OBLIGATIONS RELATING TO CERTAIN IMPORTATIONS
AND EXPORTATIONS

SECTION 1
Importation

Article 274

Articles 275, 276 and 277 shall apply to the importation of goods in free circulation which enter the Community from a third territory forming part of the customs territory of the Community.

Article 275

The formalities relating to the importation of the goods referred to in Article 274 shall be the same as those laid down by the Community customs provisions in force for the importation of goods into the customs territory of the Community.

Article 276

Where dispatch or transport of the goods referred to in Article 274 ends at a place situated outside the Member State of their entry into the Community, they shall circulate in the Community under the internal Community transit procedure laid down by the Community customs provisions in force, in so far as they have been the subject of a declaration placing them under that procedure on their entry into the Community.

Article 277

Where, on their entry into the Community, the goods referred to in Article 274 are in one of the situations which would entitle them, if they were imported within the meaning of the first paragraph of Article 30, to be covered by one of the arrangements or situations referred to in Article 156, or by a temporary importation arrangement with full exemption from import duties, Member States shall take the measures necessary to ensure that the goods may remain in the Community under the same conditions as those laid down for the application of those arrangements or situations.

SECTION 2
Exportation

Article 278

Articles 279 and 280 shall apply to the exportation of goods in free circulation which are dispatched or transported from a Member State to a third territory forming part of the customs territory of the Community.

Article 279

The formalities relating to the exportation of the goods referred to in Article 278 from the territory of the Community shall be the same as those laid down by the Community customs provisions in force for the exportation of goods from the customs territory of the Community.

Article 280

In the case of goods which are temporarily exported from the Community, in order to be reimported, Member States shall take the measures necessary to ensure that, on reimportation into the Community, such goods may be covered by the same provisions as would have applied if they had been temporarily exported from the customs territory of the Community.

TITLE XIII
DEROGATIONS

CHAPTER 2
DEROGATIONS SUBJECT TO AUTHORISATION

SECTION 1
Simplification measures and measures to prevent tax evasion or avoidance

Article 394

Member States which, at 1 January 1977, applied special measures to simplify the procedure for collecting VAT or to prevent certain forms of tax evasion or avoidance may retain them provided that they have notified the Commission accordingly before

1 January 1978 and that such simplification measures comply with the criterion laid down in the second subparagraph of Article 395(1).

Article 395

1. The Council, acting unanimously on a proposal from the Commission, may authorise any Member State to introduce special measures for derogation from the provisions of this Directive, in order to simplify the procedure for collecting VAT or to prevent certain forms of tax evasion or avoidance.

Measures intended to simplify the procedure for collecting VAT may not, except to a negligible extent, affect the overall amount of the tax revenue of the Member State collected at the stage of final consumption.

2. A Member State wishing to introduce the measure referred to in paragraph 1 shall send an application to the Commission and provide it with all the necessary information. If the Commission considers that it does not have all the necessary information, it shall contact the Member State concerned within two months of receipt of the application and specify what additional information is required.

Once the Commission has all the information it considers necessary for appraisal of the request it shall within one month notify the requesting Member State accordingly and it shall transmit the request, in its original language, to the other Member States.

3. Within three months of giving the notification referred to in the second subparagraph of paragraph 2, the Commission shall present to the Council either an appropriate proposal or, should it object to the derogation requested, a communication setting out its objections.

4. The procedure laid down in paragraphs 2 and 3 shall, in any event, be completed within eight months of receipt of the application by the Commission.

SECTION 2
International agreements

Article 396

1. The Council, acting unanimously on a proposal from the Commission, may authorise any Member State to conclude with a third country or an international body an agreement which may contain derogations from this Directive.

2. A Member State wishing to conclude an agreement as referred to in paragraph 1 shall send an application to the Commission and provide it with all the necessary information. If the Commission considers that it does not have all the necessary information, it shall contact the Member State concerned within two months of receipt of the application and specify what additional information is required.

Once the Commission has all the information it considers necessary for appraisal of the request it shall within one month notify the requesting Member State accordingly and it shall transmit the request, in its original language, to the other Member States.

3. Within three months of giving the notification referred to in the second subparagraph of paragraph 2, the Commission shall present to the Council either an appropriate proposal or, should it object to the derogation requested, a communication setting out its objections.

4. The procedure laid down in paragraphs 2 and 3 shall, in any event, be completed within eight months of receipt of the application by the Commission.

Part III

TITLE XIV
MISCELLANEOUS

CHAPTER 4
OTHER TAXES, DUTIES AND CHARGES

Article 401

Without prejudice to other provisions of Community law, this Directive shall not prevent a Member State from maintaining or introducing taxes on insurance contracts, taxes on betting and gambling, excise duties, stamp duties or, more generally, any taxes, duties or charges which cannot be characterised as turnover taxes, provided that the collecting of those taxes, duties or charges does not give rise, in trade between Member States, to formalities connected with the crossing of frontiers.

TITLE XV
FINAL PROVISIONS

CHAPTER 2
TRANSITIONAL MEASURES APPLICABLE IN THE CONTEXT OF ACCESSION TO THE EUROPEAN UNION

Article 405

For the purposes of this Chapter, the following definitions shall apply:

(1)   'Community' means the territory of the Community as defined in point (1) of Article 5 before the accession of new Member States;

(2)   'new Member States' means the territory of the Member States which acceded to the European Union after 1 January 1995, as defined for each of those Member States in point (2) of Article 5;

(3)   'enlarged Community' means the territory of the Community as defined in point (1) of Article 5 after the accession of new Member States.

Article 406

The provisions in force at the time the goods were placed under temporary importation arrangements with total exemption from import duty or under one of the arrangements or situations referred to in Article 156, or under similar arrangements or situations in one of the new Member States, shall continue to apply until the goods cease to be covered by these arrangements or situations after the date of accession, where the following conditions are met:

(a)   the goods entered the Community or one of the new Member States before the date of accession;

(b)   the goods were placed, on entry into the Community or one of the new Member States, under these arrangements or situations;

(c)   the goods have not ceased to be covered by these arrangements or situations before the date of accession.

Article 407

The provisions in force at the time the goods were placed under customs transit arrangements shall continue to apply until the goods cease to be covered by these arrangements after the date of accession, where the following conditions are met:

(a)   the goods were placed, before the date of accession, under customs transit arrangements;

(b)   the goods have not ceased to be covered by these arrangements before the date of accession.

Article 408

1.   The following shall be treated as an importation of goods where it is shown that the goods were in free circulation in one of the new Member States or in the Community:

(a)   the removal, including irregular removal, of goods from temporary importation arrangements under which they were placed before the date of accession under the conditions provided for in Article 406;

(b)   the removal, including irregular removal, of goods either from one of the arrangements or situations referred to in Article 156 or from similar arrangements or situations under which they were placed before the date of accession under the conditions provided for in Article 406;

(c)   the cessation of one of the arrangements referred to in Article 407, started before the date of accession in the territory of one of the new Member States, for the purposes of a supply of goods for consideration effected before that date in the territory of that Member State by a taxable person acting as such;

(d)   any irregularity or offence committed during customs transit arrangements started under the conditions referred to in point (c).

2.   In addition to the case referred to in paragraph 1, the use after the date of accession within the territory of a Member State, by a taxable or non-taxable person, of goods supplied to him before the date of accession within the territory of the Community or one of the new Member States shall be treated as an importation of goods where the following conditions are met:

(a)   the supply of those goods has been exempted, or was likely to be exempted, either under points (a) and (b) of Article 146(1) or under a similar provision in the new Member States;

(b)   the goods were not imported into one of the new Member States or into the Community before the date of accession.

Article 409

In the cases referred to in Article 408(1), the place of import within the meaning of Article 61 shall be the Member State within whose territory the goods cease to be covered by the arrangements or situations under which they were placed before the date of accession.

Article 410

1.   By way of derogation from Article 71, the importation of goods within the meaning of Article 408 shall terminate without the occurrence of a chargeable event if one of the following conditions is met:

(a)   the imported goods are dispatched or transported outside the enlarged Community;

(b)   the imported goods within the meaning of Article 408(1)(a) are other than means of transport and are redispatched or transported to the Member State from which they were exported and to the person who exported them;

(c)   the imported goods within the meaning of Article 408(1)(a) are means of transport which were acquired or imported before the date of accession in accordance with the general conditions of taxation in force on the domestic market of one of the new Member States or of one of the Community or which have not been subject, by reason of their exportation, to any exemption from, or refund of, VAT.

2.   The condition referred to in paragraph 1(c) shall be deemed to be fulfilled in the following cases:

(a)   when the date of first entry into service of the means of transport was more than eight years before the accession to the European Union.

(b)   when the amount of tax due by reason of the importation is insignificant.

CHAPTER 3
TRANSPOSITION AND ENTRY INTO FORCE

Article 411

1. Directive 67/227/EEC and Directive 77/388/EEC are repealed, without prejudice to the obligations of the Member States concerning the time-limits, listed in Annex XI, Part B, for the transposition into national law and the implementation of those Directives.

2. References to the repealed Directives shall be construed as references to this Directive and shall be read in accordance with the correlation table in Annex XII.

Article 412

1. Member States shall bring into force the laws, regulations and administrative provisions necessary to comply with Article 2 (3), Article 44, Article 59(1), Article 399 and Annex III, point (18) with effect from 1 January 2008. They shall forthwith communicate to the Commission the text of those provisions and a correlation table between those provisions and this Directive.

When Member States adopt those provisions, they shall contain a reference to this Directive or be accompanied by such a reference on the occasion of their official publication. Member States shall determine how such reference is to be made.

2. Member States shall communicate to the Commission the text of the main provisions of national law which they adopt in the field covered by this Directive.

Article 413

This Directive shall enter into force on 1 January 2007.

Article 414

This Directive is addressed to the Member States.

Done at Brussels, 28 November 2006.

For the Council
The President
E. HEINÄLUOMA

ANNEX XI

PART A

REPEALED DIRECTIVES WITH THEIR SUCCESSIVE AMENDMENTS

(1) Directive 67/227/EEC (OJ 71, 14.4.1967, p. 1301)

Directive 77/388/EEC

(2) Directive 77/388/EEC (OJ L 145, 13.6.1977, p. 1)

Directive 78/583/EEC (OJ L 194, 19.7.1978, p. 16)

Directive 80/368/EEC (OJ L 90, 3.4.1980, p. 41)

Directive 84/386/EEC (OJ L 208, 3.8.1984, p. 58)

Directive 89/465/EEC (OJ L 226, 3.8.1989, p. 21)

Directive 91/680/EEC (OJ L 376, 31.12.1991, p. 1) — (except for Article 2)

Directive 92/77/EEC (OJ L 316, 31.10.1992, p. 1)

Directive 92/111/EEC (OJ L 384, 30.12.1992, p. 47)

Directive 94/4/EC (OJ L 60, 3.3.1994, p. 14) — (only Article 2)

Directive 94/5/EC (OJ L 60, 3.3.1994, p. 16)

Directive 94/76/EC (OJ L 365, 31.12.1994, p. 53)
Directive 95/7/EC (OJ L 102, 5.5.1995, p. 18)
Directive 96/42/EC (OJ L 170, 9.7.1996, p. 34)
Directive 96/95/EC (OJ L 338, 28.12.1996, p. 89)
Directive 98/80/EC (OJ L 281, 17.10.1998, p. 31)
Directive 1999/49/EC (OJ L 139, 2.6.1999, p. 27)
Directive 1999/59/EC (OJ L 162, 26.6.1999, p. 63)
Directive 1999/85/EC (OJ L 277, 28.10.1999, p. 34)
Directive 2000/17/EC (OJ L 84, 5.4.2000, p. 24)
Directive 2000/65/EC (OJ L 269, 21.10.2000, p. 44)
Directive 2001/4/EC (OJ L 22, 24.1.2001, p. 17)
Directive 2001/115/EC (OJ L 15, 17.1.2002, p. 24)
Directive 2002/38/EC (OJ L 128, 15.5.2002, p. 41)
Directive 2002/93/EC (OJ L 331, 7.12.2002, p. 27)
Directive 2003/92/EC (OJ L 260, 11.10.2003, p. 8)
Directive 2004/7/EC (OJ L 27, 30.1.2004, p. 44)
Directive 2004/15/EC (OJ L 52, 21.2.2004, p. 61)
Directive 2004/66/EC (OJ L 168, 1.5.2004, p. 35) — (only Point V of the Annex)
Directive 2005/92/EC (OJ L 345, 28.12.2005, p. 19)
Directive 2006/18/EC (OJ L 51, 22.2.2006, p. 12)
Directive 2006/58/EC (OJ L 174, 28.6.2006, p. 5)
Directive 2006/69/EC (OJ L 221, 12.8.2006, p. 9 — (only Article 1)
Directive 2006/98/EC (OJ L . . ., . . ., p. . . . (*) — (only point 2 of the Annex)

PART B

TIME LIMITS FOR TRANSPOSITION INTO NATIONAL LAW (REFERRED TO
IN ARTICLE 411)

Directive	Deadline for transposition
Directive 67/227/EEC	1 January 1970
Directive 77/388/EEC	1 January 1978
Directive 78/583/EEC	1 January 1979
Directive 80/368/EEC	1 January 1979
Directive 84/386/EEC	1 July 1985
Directive 89/465/EEC	1 January 1990
	1 January 1991
	1 January 1992
	1 January 1993
	1 January 1994 for Portugal
Directive 91/680/EEC	1 January 1993
Directive 92/77/EEC	31 December 1992

Directive 92/111/EEC	1 January 1993 1 January 1994 1 October 1993 for Germany
Directive 94/4/EC	1 April 1994
Directive 94/5/EC	1 January 1995
Directive 94/76/EC	1 January 1995
Directive 95/7/EC	1 January 1996 1 January 1997 for Germany and Luxembourg
Directive 96/42/EC	1 January 1995
Directive 96/95/EC	1 January 1997
Directive 98/80/EC	1 January 2000
Directive 1999/49/EC	1 January 1999
Directive 1999/59/EC	1 January 2000
Directive 1999/85/CE	—
Directive 2000/17/EC	—
Directive 2000/65/EC	31 December 2001
Directive 2001/4/EC	1 January 2001
Directive 2001/115/EC	1 January 2004
Directive 2002/38/EC	1 July 2003
Directive 2002/93/EC	—
Directive 2003/92/EC	1 January 2005
Directive 2004/7/EC	30 January 2004
Directive 2004/15/EC	—
Directive 2004/66/EC	1 May 2004
Directive 2005/92/EC	1 January 2006
Directive 2006/18/EC	—
Directive 2006/58/EC	1 July 2006
Directive 2006/69/EC	1 January 2008

COMMISSION REGULATION

(1875/2006/EC)

of18 December 2006

amending Regulation (EEC) No 2454/93 laying down provisions for the implementation of Council Regulation (EEC) No 2913/92 establishing the Community Customs Code

THE COMMISSION OF THE EUROPEAN COMMUNITIES,

Having regard to the Treaty establishing the European Community,

Having regard to Council Regulation (EEC) No 2913/92 of 12 October 1992 establishing the Community Customs Code (^{1}), and in particular Article 247 thereof,

Whereas:

(1)   The amendments to Regulation (EEC) No 2913/92, hereinafter 'the Code', laid down in Regulation (EC) No 648/2005, introduce a number of measures to tighten security for goods entering or leaving the Community. Those measures should produce faster and better targeted customs controls, and consist in the analysis and electronic exchange of risk information between customs authorities and between those authorities and the Commission under a common risk management framework, the requirement for pre-arrival and predeparture information to be provided to the customs authorities on all goods entering or leaving the customs territory of the Community, and the granting of the status of authorised economic operator to reliable economic operators who meet certain criteria and who are to benefit from simplifications provided for under the customs rules and/or facilitations with regard to customs controls.

(2)   In order to ensure effective and expeditious implementation of those measures, it is necessary that data exchange between customs authorities is carried out through information technology and computer networks, using agreed standards and common data sets.

(3)   Given the progress in Member States' computerised customs clearance systems, as well as the use by the Member States and the Commission of information technology and computer networks, the common use of such systems should be extended beyond the existing computerised transit system, starting with the introduction of an computerised system for the control of exports.

(4)   For the purposes of a common risk management framework and the establishment of an equivalent level of customs controls throughout the Community, risk analysis should be based upon data processing techniques using common criteria. The risk information should therefore be exchanged among customs authorities and the Commission using, without prejudice to national or international obligations, a Community customs risk management system, common priority control areas, and common risk criteria and standards for the harmonised application of customs controls in specific cases.

(5)   Economic operators who fulfil the conditions for obtaining the status of authorised economic operator, thus distinguishing themselves positively from other economic operators, should be considered as reliable partners in the supply chain. Authorised economic operators should therefore be able to benefit not only from simplifications provided for under the customs rules but also, where they fulfil certain safety and security conditions, from facilitations with regard to customs controls.

Part III

(6) It is necessary to establish common conditions and criteria in all Member States for the granting, amendment or revocation of authorised economic operators' certificates, or for suspension of the status of authorised economic operator, as well as rules on the application for and issuing of authorised economic operators' certificates. In order to ensure that a high level of security is maintained, customs authorities should continuously monitor the compliance of authorised economic operators with the relevant requirements.

(7) It is necessary to establish and maintain a common electronic information and communication system to store and exchange information regarding authorised economic operators.

(8) In order to enable proper risk analysis and appropriate risk-based controls, it is necessary to establish the time limits and detailed rules governing the obligation of economic operators to provide pre-arrival and predeparture information to the customs authorities for all goods brought into or out of the customs territory of the Community. In keeping with similar measures adopted at international level as part of the Framework of Standards to Secure and Facilitate Global Trade, endorsed by the World Customs Organisation, and in accordance with other special arrangements provided for in international agreements, it is appropriate to take into account different means of transport, as well as different types of goods or economic operators.

(9) In order to enable customs authorities to carry out effective risk analysis, it is necessary for pre-arrival and pre-departure information to be lodged electronically. Paper-based declarations or notifications should be permitted only in certain exceptional circumstances.

(10) The data to be required in entry and exit summary declarations should be harmonised so as to ensure a common basis for risk analysis throughout the Community and to enable the effective exchange of information between customs authorities. Although for those purposes account should be taken of the type of traffic by which the goods are carried and of the status of authorised economic operator, security and safety measures should not be jeopardised. Furthermore, although a waiver of the requirement for summary declarations can be justified for goods moved under the rules of the Universal Postal Union, due to the particular circumstances that surround this type of traffic, it is nevertheless necessary to provide for a technical framework for data to be provided to customs authorities by electronic means in respect of this traffic, for mutual benefit.

(11) In the event of a positive risk analysis, an equivalent level of preventive control should be applied throughout the Community. In that context, the trader or carrier should be notified accordingly.

(12) The rules governing the presentation and temporary storage of goods brought into the customs territory of the Community should incorporate the changes in data requirements.

(13) Accordingly, for cases in which the customs declaration is used as an entry or exit summary declaration, it is also appropriate to adjust the general rules governing the method, time and place of lodging customs declarations for placing goods under a customs procedure.

(14) In order to enable a more efficient control of the export procedure and outward processing, as well as re-exportation, for the purposes of security and safety as well as customs controls, the customs authorities should replace the current paper-based procedure with an electronic

exchange of data between the customs office of export and the customs office of exit.

(15) The computerised system for the control of exports should operate in parallel with the paper-based export procedure for a transitional period. The paper-based export procedure should also be used as a fallback arrangement for the electronic system both during and after the transitional period. Specific provisions should apply where export data is exchanged between customs offices under the computerised system for the control of exports. In order to ensure the proper functioning of that system, the existing provisions of the paper-based export procedure should also be amended.

(16) In order to maintain the simplifications possible under the export rules, without affecting the benefits offered to economic operators by the computerised system for the control of exports, exporters should be able to choose whether to use the provisions relating to goods leaving the customs territory of the Community under a single transport contract.

(17) The provisions relating to the granting of the status of authorised economic operator should apply from 1 January 2008, in order to allow Member States to set up the necessary administrative structures.

(18) However, in order to allow reasonable time for Member States and economic operators to adapt their electronic systems, the provisions laid down in this Regulation relating to the definition of data requirements and the electronic lodging of pre-arrival and pre-departure information should apply from 1 July 2009.

(19) Commission Regulation (EEC) No 2454/93 (²) should therefore be amended accordingly.

(20) The measures provided for in this Regulation are in accordance with the opinion of the Customs Code Committee,

---

¹ OJ L 302, 19.10.1992, p. 1. Regulation as last amended by Regulation (EC) No 648/2005 of the European Parliament and of the Council (OJ L 117, 4.5.2005, p. 13).

² OJ L 253, 11.10.1993, p. 1. Regulation as last amended by Regulation (EC) No 402/2006 (OJ L 70, 9.3.2006, p. 35).

HAS ADOPTED THIS REGULATION:

Article 1

Regulation (EEC) No 2454/93 is amended as follows:

1. In Article 1, the following point is added:

'12. Economic operator means: a person who, in the course of his business, is involved in activities covered by customs legislation.'

4. In Part I, Title VI, the heading of Chapter 1 is replaced by the following:

'CHAPTER 1 Entry summary declaration'

5. In Part I, Title VI, Chapter 1, the following Section 1 is inserted:

'Section 1

Scope

Article 181b

Except where otherwise provided for in this Regulation, all goods brought into the customs territory of the Community shall be covered by a summary declaration in accordance with Article 36a of the Code, hereinafter referred to as an "entry summary declaration".

Article 181c

An entry summary declaration shall not be required in respect of the following goods:

(a)   electrical energy;

(b)   goods entering by pipeline;

(c)   letters, postcards and printed matter, including on electronic medium;

(d)   goods moved under the rules of the Universal Postal Union Convention;

(e)   goods covered by customs declarations made by any other act in accordance with Articles 230, 232 and 233;

(f)   goods contained in travellers' personal luggage;

(g)   goods for which an oral customs declaration is permitted, in accordance with Articles 225, 227 and 229(1);

(h)   goods covered by ATA and CPD Carnets;

(i)   goods moved under cover of the form 302 provided for in the Convention between the Parties to the North Atlantic Treaty regarding the Status of their Forces, signed in London on 19 June 1951;

(j)   goods carried on board vessels of regular shipping services, duly certified in accordance with Article 313b;

(k)   goods entitled to relief pursuant to the Vienna Convention on diplomatic relations of 18 April 1961, the Vienna Convention on consular relations of 24 April 1963 or other consular conventions, or the New York Convention of 16 December 1969 on special missions.

However, in the cases covered by points (e), (f) and (g) of the first subparagraph, an entry summary declaration shall be required where the goods are to be placed in temporary storage. The first subparagraph of Article 184c shall apply. Article 181d If an international agreement between the Community and a third country provides for the recognition of security checks carried out in the country of export, the conditions set out in that agreement shall apply.'

6.   Article 182 is deleted.

7.   In Part I, Title VI, the heading of Chapter 2 is replaced by the following:
'Section 2

Lodging of an entry summary declaration'

8.   Article 183 is replaced by the following:
'*Article 183*

1.   The entry summary declaration shall be made electronically. It shall contain the particulars laid down for such declaration in Annex 30A and shall be completed in accordance with the explanatory notes in that Annex. The entry summary declaration shall be authenticated by the person making it. Article 199(1) shall apply mutatis mutandis.

2.   The customs authorities shall allow the lodgement of a paper-based entry summary declaration only in one of the following circumstances:

(a)   the customs authorities' computerised system is not functioning;

(b)   the electronic application of the person lodging the entry summary declaration is not functioning.

Such paper-based entry summary declarations shall be accompanied, where necessary, by loading lists or other appropriate lists, and shall contain the particulars laid down for entry summary declarations in Annex 30A.

3.   The customs authorities shall establish, in agreement with each other, the procedure to be followed in the cases referred to in point (a) of the first subparagraph of paragraph 2.

4. The use of a paper-based entry summary declaration referred to in point (b) of the first subparagraph of paragraph 2 shall be subject to the approval of the customs authorities. The paper-based entry summary declaration shall be signed by the person making it.

5. Entry summary declarations shall be registered by the customs authorities immediately upon their receipt.'

9. The following Articles 183a to 183d are inserted:

'*Article 183a*

1. The data provided under a transit procedure may be used as an entry summary declaration if the following conditions are met:
(a) the goods are brought into the customs territory of the Community under a transit procedure;
(b) the transit data is exchanged using information technology and computer networks;
(c) the data comprises all of the particulars required for an entry summary declaration.

2. Provided the transit data containing the required particulars is exchanged by the relevant time limit laid down in Article 184a, the requirements of Article 183 shall be deemed to have been met, even where the goods have been released for transit outside the customs territory of the Community.

Article 183b

In case of combined transportation, where the active means of transport entering the customs territory of the Community is only transporting another active means of transport, the obligation to lodge the entry summary declaration shall lie with the operator of that other means of transport.

The time limit for lodging the entry summary declaration shall correspond to the time limit applicable to the active means of transport crossing the border, as specified in Article 184a.

Article 183c

In the case of maritime or air traffic where a vessel sharing or contracting arrangement is in place, the obligation to lodge the entry summary declaration shall lie with the person who has undertaken a contract, and issued a bill of lading or air waybill, for the actual carriage of the goods on the vessel or aircraft subject to the arrangement.

Article 183d

1. In the cases referred to in Articles 183b and 183c, the operator of the active means of transport entering the customs territory of the Community shall lodge a pre-arrival notification at the customs office of entry listing all consignments carried on that means of transport.

The pre-arrival notification shall specify the active means of transport entering the customs territory of the Community. For each consignment, it shall contain the following information:
(a) the identity of the person responsible for carriage of the goods at the entry into the customs territory;
(b) the identity of the person lodging the entry summary declaration;
(c) the place of loading;
(d) the place of unloading;
(e) the unique consignment reference number, transport document number or reference for the bill of lading/air waybill;
(f) where appropriate, the identity of the means of transport or, if containerised, the equipment identification number.

The pre-arrival notification shall be lodged in the same format and by the same means as the entry summary declaration, or in the form of a commercial, port or transport manifest or loading list, provided that it contains the necessary particulars and is lodged in a manner acceptable to the customs authorities of the customs office of entry.

2. In cases other than those referred to in Articles 183b and 183c, where an entry summary declaration for goods carried on a means of transport entering the customs territory of the Community is to be lodged by a person other than the operator of that means of transport, that operator may lodge a pre-arrival notification with the customs authorities at the customs office of entry.

The pre-arrival notification shall specify the identity of the means of transport crossing the border. For each consignment, it shall contain the following information:

(a) the identity of the person lodging the entry summary declaration;

(b) the place of loading;

(c) the place of unloading;

(d) the unique consignment reference number, transport document number or reference for the bill of lading/air waybill;

(e) if containerised, the equipment identification number.

3. The notification referred to in paragraphs 1 and 2 shall be lodged by the time limit applicable to the means of transport set out in Article 184a.

However in the case of the traffic referred to in point (a) of Article 184a(1) the notification shall be lodged at least 24 hours before the goods are brought into the customs territory of the Community.

4. Article 183 shall apply, *mutatis mutandis*, to pre-arrival notifications.'

10. In Article 184(1), 'Article 183(1)' is replaced by 'Article 183(1) and(2)'.

11. In Part 1, Title VI, Chapter 1, the following Sections 3 and 4 are added:

'Section 3
Time limits

Article 184a

1. In the case of maritime traffic the entry summary declaration shall be lodged at the customs office of entry by the following deadlines:

(a) for containerised cargo, other than where point (c) or (d) applies, at least 24 hours before loading at the port of departure;

(b) for bulk/break bulk cargo, at least four hours before arrival at the first port in the customs territory of the Community;

(c) for movement between Greenland, the Faeroe Islands, Ceuta, Melilla, Norway, Iceland or ports on the Baltic Sea, the North Sea, the Black Sea or the Mediterranean, all ports of Morocco, and the customs territory of the Community with the exception of the French overseas departments, the Azores, Madeira and the Canary Islands, at least two hours before arrival at the first port in the customs territory of the Community;

(d) for movement, other than where point (c) applies, between a territory outside the customs territory of the Community and the French overseas departments, the Azores, Madeira or the Canary Islands, where the duration of the voyage is less than 24 hours, at least two hours before arrival at the first port in the customs territory of the Community;

2. In the case of air traffic the entry summary declaration shall be lodged at the customs office of entry by the following deadlines:

(a) for short haul flights, at least by the time of the actual take off of the aircraft;

(b)   for long haul flights, at least four hours prior to arrival at the first airport in the customs territory of the Community;

For the purposes of this paragraph, "short haul flight" means a flight the duration of which is less than four hours from the last airport of departure in a third country till the arrival to the first Community airport. All other flights are considered to be long haul flights.

3.   In the case of rail and inland waters traffic, the entry summary declaration shall be lodged at the customs office of entry at least two hours prior to arrival at the customs office of entry in the customs territory of the Community.

4.   In the case of road traffic, the entry summary declaration shall be lodged at the customs office of entry at least one hour prior to arrival at the customs office of entry in the customs territory of the Community.

5.   Where the entry summary declaration is not lodged by use of a data processing technique, the time limit laid down in points (c) and (d) of paragraph 1, point (a) of paragraph 2 and in paragraphs 3 and 4 shall be at least four hours.

6.   If the customs authorities' computerised system is temporarily not functioning, the deadlines provided for in paragraphs 1 to 4 shall still apply.

Article 184b

The deadlines referred to in Article 184a(1) to (4) shall not apply in the following cases:

(a)   where international agreements between the Community and third countries provide for the recognition of security checks as referred to in Article 181d;

(b)   where international agreements between the Community and third countries require the exchange of declaration data by deadlines different from those referred to in Article 184a(1) to (4);

(c)   cases of force majeure.

Article 184c

Where it is found that goods presented to customs requiring the lodging of an entry summary declaration are not covered by such a declaration, the person who brought the goods, or who assumed responsibility for the carriage of the goods, into the customs territory of the Community shall lodge an entry summary declaration immediately.

If an economic operator lodges the entry summary declaration after the deadlines provided for in Article 184a, this shall not preclude the application of the penalties laid down in the national legislation.

Section 4

Risk analysis

Article 184d

1.   The customs office of entry shall, upon receipt of the information contained in the entry summary declaration, carry out appropriate risk analysis, primarily for security and safety purposes, prior to arrival of the goods in the customs territory of the Community. Where the entry summary declaration has been lodged at a customs office other than the customs office of entry, and the particulars have been made available in accordance with Article 36a(2) and the second subparagraph of Article 36c(1) of the Code, the customs authorities at the customs office of entry shall either accept the results of any risk analysis carried out by that other customs office, or take into consideration the results when carrying out their own risk analysis.

2. The customs authorities shall complete the risk analysis prior to the arrival of the goods, provided that the relevant deadline set out in Article 184a is met.

However, for goods carried by the type of traffic referred to in point (a) of Article 184a(1), the customs authorities shall complete the risk analysis within 24 hours of the receipt of the entry summary declaration. Where that analysis provides reasonable grounds for the customs authorities to consider that the introduction of the goods into the customs territory of the Community would pose such a serious threat to the safety and security of the Community that immediate intervention is required, the customs authorities shall notify the person who lodged the entry summary declaration and, where different, the person responsible for the carriage of the goods into the customs territory of the Community, that the goods are not to be loaded. The notification shall be made within 24 hours of receipt of the entry summary declaration.

3. Where goods not covered by an entry summary declaration, in accordance with Article 181c(a) to (i), are brought into the customs territory of the Community, risk analysis shall be carried out upon presentation of the goods, on the basis of the customs declaration covering the goods.

4. Goods presented to customs may be released for a customs-approved treatment or use as soon as the risk analysis has been carried out and the results allow such a release.

Article 184e

Where a vessel or aircraft is to call at more than one port or airport in the customs territory of the Community, provided that it moves between those ports without calling at any port or airport outside the customs territory of the Community, an entry summary declaration shall be lodged at the first Community port or airport for all the goods carried. The customs authorities at this first port or airport of entry shall carry out the risk analysis for security and safety purposes for all the goods carried. Additional risk analysis may be carried out for those goods at the port or airport at which they are discharged.

Where a risk is identified, the customs office of the first port or airport of entry shall, dependent upon the level of threat, either take prohibitive action in the case of consignments identified as posing a threat of such a serious nature that immediate intervention is required, or pass on the results of the risk analysis to the subsequent ports or airports.

At subsequent ports or airports in the customs territory of the Community, an entry summary declaration shall only be required for goods to be discharged at that port or airport. The time limit laid down in Article 184a(1) and (2) shall not apply.

Article 184f

Where goods are loaded at a port in the customs territory of the Community for discharge at another Community port and are carried on a vessel moving between those ports without calling at any port outside the customs territory of the Community, an entry summary declaration shall only be required for those goods at the Community port at which they are to be discharged. The time limit laid down in Article 184a(1) shall not apply.'

12. In Part I, Title VI, the heading of Chapter 3 is replaced by the following:
'CHAPTER 2

Temporary storage'

13. Article 186 is replaced by the following:
'*Article 186*

1. When goods are presented to customs in accordance with Article 40 of the Code, they shall be deemed to have been placed under temporary

storage and the entry summary declaration shall be kept by the customs authorities for the purpose of verifying that the goods to which it relates are assigned a customs-approved treatment or use. For the purposes of Article 49 of the Code, the entry summary declaration shall be deemed to have been lodged on the date of presentation of the goods.

2. When a customs declaration has been lodged at the customs office of entry as an entry summary declaration, in accordance with Article 36c of the Code, the customs authorities shall accept the declaration immediately upon the presentation of the goods and the goods shall be placed directly under the declared procedure subject to the conditions laid down for that procedure.

3. For the purposes of paragraphs 1 and 2, where non- Community goods moved from the customs office of departure under a transit procedure are presented to customs at an office of destination within the customs territory of the Community, the transit declaration intended for the customs authorities at the office of destination is deemed to be the entry summary declaration for the purposes of temporary storage.'

14. In Article 187, 'Article 44(2)' is replaced by 'Article 36b(3)'.

15. The following Article 187a is added:

'*Article 187a*

1. The customs authorities may grant permission to examine the goods under Article 42 of the Code to the person who, under the customs rules, may assign the goods a customs-approved treatment or use, at that person's oral request. The customs authorities may, however, consider, having regard to the circumstances, that a written request is required.

2. The customs authorities may authorise the taking of samples only at the written request of the person referred to in paragraph 1.

3. The written request may be paper-based or electronic. It shall be signed or authenticated by the person concerned and lodged with the competent customs authorities. It shall include the following particulars:

   (a) name and address of the applicant;

   (b) location of the goods;

   (c) reference to one of the following:

      (i)   the entry summary declaration;

      (ii) the previous customs procedure;

      (iii) the means of transport;

   (d) all other particulars necessary for identifying the goods.

4. The customs authorities shall communicate their decision to the person concerned. Where the request is for the taking of samples, the decision shall specify the quantity of goods to be taken.

5. Examination of goods and the taking of samples shall be carried out under the supervision of the customs authorities, which shall specify the procedures to be followed.

The person concerned shall bear all risks and costs related to the examination, taking of samples and analysis of the goods.

6. The samples taken shall be subject to formalities with a view to assigning them a customs-approved treatment or use. Where examination of the samples results in their destruction or irretrievable loss, no customs debt shall be deemed to have been incurred.

Any waste or scrap resulting from the examination shall be assigned a customs-approved treatment or use prescribed for non-Community goods.' 19.12.2006 EN Official Journal of the European Union L 360/81

16. In Part I, Title VI, the heading of Chapter 4 is replaced by the following:
'CHAPTER 3
Special provisions applicable to goods consigned by sea or air'
18. In Article 212(1), the following subparagraph is added:
'Where a customs declaration is used as an entry summary declaration, in accordance with Article 36c(1) of the Code, that declaration shall, in addition to the particulars required for the specific procedure set out in Annex 37, include the particulars for an entry summary declaration set out in Annex 30A.'
19. In Article 216, the following paragraph is added:
'Where a customs declaration is required for goods to be brought out of the customs territory of the Community, in accordance with Article 182b of the Code, that declaration shall, in addition to the particulars required for the specific procedure set out Annex 37, include the particulars for an exit summary declaration set out in Annex 30A.'
Article 254 is replaced by the following:
'Article 254 If the declarant so requests, the customs authorities may accept declarations for release for free circulation which do not contain all the particulars set out in Annex 37.
However, those declarations shall contain at least the particulars for an incomplete declaration set out in Annex 30A.'
22. In Article 260, paragraph 2 is replaced by the following:
'2. Such simplified declaration shall contain at least the particulars for a simplified import declaration set out in Annex 30A.'
24. In Article 262, paragraph 1 is replaced by the following:
'1. The authorisation referred to in Article 260 shall contain the following particulars:
        (a)   the customs office(s) competent to accept simplified declarations;
        (b)   the goods to which it applies; and
        (c)   a reference to the guarantee to be provided by the person concerned to cover any customs debt which may arise.
It shall also specify the form and content of the supplementary declarations, and shall set the time-limits within which they must be lodged with the customs authority designated for this purpose.'
26. In Article 266, paragraph 3 is replaced by the following:
'3. The entry in the records referred to in points (a), (b) and (c) of paragraph 1 may be replaced by any other formality offering similar guarantees requested by the customs authorities. This entry shall indicate the date on which it is made and contain at least the particulars for a declaration under the local clearance procedure set out in Annex 30A.'
27. In Article 268, paragraph 1 is replaced by the following:
'1. If the declarant so requests the customs office of entry may accept declarations for the customs warehousing procedure which do not contain all the particulars set out in Annex 37.
However, those declarations shall contain at least the particulars for an incomplete declaration set out in Annex 30A.'
29. Article 271 is replaced by the following:
'*Article 271*
The authorisation referred to in Article 269(1) shall lay down the specific rules for the operation of the procedure, including the customs office(s) of entry for the procedure.
It shall not be necessary to provide a supplementary declaration.'
30. In Article 275, paragraph 1 is replaced by the following:

'1. If the declarant so requests the customs office of entry may accept declarations for placing goods under a customs procedure with economic impact other than outward processing or customs warehousing which do not contain all the particulars set out in Annex 37 or which are not accompanied by certain documents referred to in Article 220.

However, those declarations shall contain at least the particulars for an incomplete declaration set out in Annex 30A.'

32. Articles 280 and 281 are replaced by the following:

'*Article 280*

1. If the declarant so requests, the customs office of export may accept export declarations which do not contain all the particulars set out in Annex 37.

However, those declarations shall contain at least the particulars for an incomplete declaration set out in Annex 30A.

Where the goods are liable for export duties or subject to any other measures provided for under the common agricultural policy, the export declarations shall contain all the information required for the application of such duties or measures.

2. Articles 255 to 259 shall apply mutatis mutandis to export declarations.

Article 281

1. Where Article 789 applies, the supplementary declaration may be lodged at the customs office responsible for the place where the exporter is established.

2. Where the subcontractor is established in a Member State other than that where the exporter is established, paragraph 1 shall only apply where the required data is exchanged electronically in accordance with Article 4d.

3. The incomplete export declaration shall specify the customs office where the supplementary declaration shall be lodged. The customs office which receives the incomplete export declaration shall communicate the particulars of the incomplete export declaration to the customs office where the supplementary declaration is to be lodged as provided for in paragraph 1.

4. In the cases referred to in paragraph 2, the customs office which has received the supplementary declaration shall immediately communicate the particulars of the supplementary declaration to the customs office where the incomplete export declaration has been lodged.'

33. In Article 282, paragraph 2 is replaced by the following:

'2. The simplified declaration shall contain at least the particulars for a simplified declaration set out in Annex 30A.

Articles 255 to 259 shall apply mutatis mutandis.'

36. The following Article 285b is inserted:

'*Article 285b*

1. The information referred to in point (a) of the first subparagraph of Article 285a(1) shall be given to the customs office of export by the deadlines provided for in Articles 592b and 592c.

2. The entry in the records referred to in point (c) of the first subparagraph of Article 285a(1) shall include the particulars for the local clearance procedure set out in Annex 30A.

3. The customs authorities shall ensure that the requirements of Articles 796a to 796e are met.'

39. In Article 288, paragraph 2 is replaced by the following:

'2. The document or medium referred to in paragraph 1 shall contain at least the particulars set out in Annex 30A for the procedure to be used. This document or medium shall be accompanied by a request for export.

The customs authorities may authorise the replacement of this request by a global request under condition that the economic operator has provided the customs authorities with the information they consider necessary for effective risk analysis and the examination of the goods. The global request shall cover export operations to be carried out over a given period. The declarant shall refer to the authorisation on the document or medium used for export.'

46.   In Part II, the heading of Title IV is replaced by the following:

'IMPLEMENTING PROVISIONS RELATING TO EXPORTATION'

47.   In Part II, Title IV, the following Chapter 1 is inserted:

'CHAPTER 1

General provisions for customs declarations

Article 592a

Articles 592b to 592f shall not apply to the following goods:

(a)   electrical energy;

(b)   goods leaving by pipeline;

(c)   letters, postcards, printed matter, including on electronic medium;

(d)   goods moved under the rules of the Universal Postal Union Convention;

(e)   goods covered by customs declarations made by any other act in accordance with Articles 231 and 233;

(f)   goods contained in travellers' personal luggage;

(g)   goods for which an oral declaration is permitted in accordance with Articles 226, 227 and 229(2);

(h)   goods covered by ATA and CPD Carnets;

(i)   goods moved under cover of the form 302 provided for under the Convention between the Parties to the North Atlantic Treaty regarding the Status of their Forces, signed in London on 19 June 1951;

(j)   goods carried on board vessels of regular shipping services, duly certified in accordance with Article 313b.

Article 592b

1.   Whenever goods leaving the customs territory of the Community are covered by a customs declaration, this customs declaration shall be lodged at the competent customs office by the following deadlines:

(a)   in the case of maritime traffic:

(i)   for containerised cargo, other than where point (iii) or (iv) applies, at least 24 hours before the goods are loaded onto the vessel on which they are to leave the customs territory of the Community;

(ii)   for bulk/break bulk cargo, at least four hours before leaving the port in the customs territory of the Community;

(iii)   for movement between the customs territory of the Community with the exception of the French overseas departments, the Azores, Madeira or the Canary Islands and Greenland, the Faeroe Islands, Ceuta, Melilla, Norway, Iceland, ports on the Baltic Sea, the North Sea, the Black Sea, the Mediterranean or all ports of Morocco, at least two hours before leaving the port in the customs territory of the Community;

(iv) for movement, in cases other than those covered under point (iii), between the French overseas departments, the Azores, Madeira, the Canary Islands and territories outside the customs territory of the Community, where the duration of the voyage is less than 24 hours, at least two hours before leaving the port in the customs territory of the Community.

(b) in the case of air traffic, at least 30 minutes prior to departure from an airport in the customs territory of the Community;

(c) in the case of rail and inland waters traffic, at least two hours prior to departure from the customs office of exit;

(d) in the case of road traffic, at least one hour prior to departure from the customs office of exit;

(e) in the case of suppliers of spare and repair parts, intended for incorporation in ships and aircraft for the purpose of their repair and maintenance, of motor fuels, lubricants and gas which are necessary for the operation of machines and apparatus used on board, and foodstuff used for consumption on board, at least 15 minutes prior to departure of the means of transport from the port or airport in the customs territory of the Community;

(f) in cases where Regulation (EC) No 800/1999 applies, according to the rules of that Regulation.

2. Where the customs declaration is not lodged by use of data processing technique, the time limit laid down in points (a)(iii) and (iv), (b), (c), (d) and (e) of paragraph 1 shall be at least four hours.

3. If the customs authorities' computerised system is temporarily not functioning, the deadlines provided for in paragraph 1 shall still apply.

Article 592c

1. In the case of inter-modal transportation, where goods are transferred from one means of transport to another for transport out of the customs territory of the Community, the time limit for submission of the declaration shall correspond to the time limit applicable to the means of transport leaving the customs territory of the Community, as specified in Article 592b.

2. In the case of combined transportation, where the active means of transport crossing the border is only transporting another active means of transport, the time limit for the lodging of the declaration shall correspond to the time limit applicable to the active means of transport crossing the border, as specified in Article 592b.

Article 592d

1. The deadlines laid down in Articles 592b and 592c shall not apply where international agreements between the Community and third countries require the exchange of customs declaration data by deadlines different from those referred to in those Articles.

2. The time limit shall not, in any event, be reduced below the period required for completion of risk analysis before the goods leave the customs territory of the Community.

Article 592e

1. The competent customs office shall, upon receipt of the customs declaration, carry out appropriate risk analysis and customs controls, prior to release of the goods for exportation.

2. Goods may be released as soon as the risk analysis has been carried out and the results allow such a release.

Article 592f

Part III

1. Where it is found that goods presented to customs are not covered by a customs declaration containing the particulars necessary for the exit summary declaration, the person who brings the goods, or who assumes responsibility for the carriage of the goods out of the customs territory of the Community, shall lodge a customs declaration or an exit summary declaration immediately.

2. If the declarant lodges a customs declaration after the deadlines provided for in Articles 592b and 592c, this shall not preclude application of penalties laid down in the national legislation.

Article 592g

Where goods covered by an exemption, under Article 592a(d) to (j), from the requirement to lodge a customs declaration by the time limits set out in Articles 592b and 592c, are brought out of the customs territory of the Community, risk analysis shall be carried out upon presentation of the goods, on the basis of the customs declaration covering these goods.'

48. In Part II, Title IV, the heading of Chapter 1 is replaced by the following:

'CHAPTER 2

Permanent exportation'

49. In Part II, Title IV, Chapter 2, the following Article 787 is inserted:

'Article 787

1. Export declarations shall comply with the provisions relating to structure and particulars set out in this Chapter, Articles 279 to 289, Annex 37 and Annex 30A. They shall be lodged at the competent customs office using a dataprocessing technique.

2. The customs authorities shall accept a paper-based export declaration made on a form corresponding to the specimen set out in Annexes 31 to 34, which shall contain the minimum list of data set out in Annex 37 and Annex 30A for the export procedure, only in one of the following circumstances:

(a) the customs authorities' computerised system is not functioning;

(b) the electronic application of the person lodging the export declaration is not functioning.

3. The customs authorities shall establish, in agreement with each other, the procedure to be followed in the cases referred to in point (a) of paragraph 2.

4. The use of a paper-based export declaration referred to in paragraph 2(b) shall be subject to the approval of the customs authorities.

5. Where the goods are exported by travellers who have no direct access to the customs' computerised system and so have no means of lodging the export declaration using a data processing technique at the office of export, the customs authorities shall authorise the traveller to use a paper-based customs declaration made on a form corresponding to the specimen set out in Annexes 31 to 34 and containing the minimum list of data set out in Annex 37 and Annex 30A for the export procedure.

6. In the cases referred to in paragraphs 4 and 5 of this Article, the customs authorities shall ensure that the requirements of Articles 796a to 796e are met.'

55. Article 795 is replaced by the following:

'Article 795

1. Where goods have left the customs territory of the Community without an export declaration, such declaration shall be lodged retrospectively

by the exporter at the customs office competent for the place where he is established.

Article 790 shall apply.

Acceptance of this declaration by the customs authorities shall be subject to provision by the exporter of one of the following:

 (a) reference to the exit summary declaration;

 (b)) sufficient evidence concerning the nature and quantity of the goods, and the circumstances under which they left the customs territory of the Community.

That office shall also, if the declarant so requests, provide the exit certification referred to in Article 793a(2) or in Article 796e(1).

 2. Retrospective acceptance of the export declaration by the customs authorities shall not preclude the application of either of the following:

  (a) penalties under national legislation;

  (b) the consequences of measures under the common agricultural or commercial policy.'

59. In Article 806, the following point (h) is added:

'(h) any additional particulars required for an exit summary declaration, set out in Annex 30A, when required under Article 182c of the Code.'

60. Articles 811 and 814 are deleted.

63. The following Article 841a is inserted:

'*Article 841a*

Where re-exportation is not subject to a customs declaration, an exit summary declaration shall be lodged in accordance with Articles 842a to 842e.

Provided that an entry summary declaration is lodged at the time when the goods are brought into the customs territory of the Community, an exit summary declaration shall not be required for re-exportation of non-Community goods in one of the following cases:

 (a) the goods are not unloaded from the means of transport which carried them into the customs territory of the Community;

 (b) the goods are transhipped at the place where they are unloaded from the means of transport which carried them into the customs territory of the Community.

The short term storage of goods in connection with such transhipment shall be considered to be an integral part of the transhipment. The control measures shall take account of the special nature of the situation.'

65. In Part II, Title VI, the following Chapter 1 is inserted:

'CHAPTER 1

Exit summary declaration

Article 842a

Where goods to be brought out of the customs territory of the Community are not covered by a customs declaration, a summary declaration, hereinafter referred to as "an exit summary declaration", shall be lodged at the customs office of exit, as defined in Article 793(2) of this Regulation, in accordance with Article 182c of the Code.

An exit summary declaration shall not be required in the following cases:

 (a) the cases listed in Article 592a(a) to (j);

 (b) where Community goods are loaded in the customs territory of the Community for discharge at another port or airport in the customs territory of the Community and are carried on a vessel or aircraft moving between those ports or airports without calling at any port or airport outside the customs territory of the Community;

(c) goods entitled to relief pursuant to the Vienna Convention on diplomatic relations of 18 April 1961, the Vienna Convention on consular relations of 24 April 1963 or other consular conventions, or the New York Convention of 16 December 1969 on special missions.

Article 842b

1. The exit summary declaration shall be made using a data processing technique. It shall contain the particulars for such declaration set out in Annex 30A and shall be completed in accordance with the explanatory note in that Annex.

The exit summary declaration shall be authenticated by the person making it.

2. Exit summary declarations which comply with the conditions set out in paragraph 1 shall be registered by the customs authorities immediately upon their receipt.

Article 199(1) shall apply mutatis mutandis.

3. The customs authorities shall allow the lodging of a paper-based exit summary declaration only in one of the following circumstances:

(a) the customs authorities' computerised system is not functioning;

(b) the electronic application of the person lodging the exit summary declaration is not functioning.

Such paper-based summary declarations shall be accompanied, where necessary, by loading lists or other commercial documents, and shall contain the information required for summary declarations in Annex 30A.

4. The customs authorities shall establish, in agreement with each other, the procedure to be followed in the cases referred to in point (a) of the first subparagraph of paragraph 3.

5. The use of a paper-based exit summary declaration referred to in point (b) of the first subparagraph of paragraph 3 shall be subject to the approval of the customs authorities.

The paper-based exit summary declaration shall be signed by the person making it.

Article 842c

1. In the case of inter-modal transportation, where goods are transferred from one means of transport to another for transport out of the customs territory of the Community, the time limit for lodging the exit summary declaration shall correspond to the time limit applicable to the means of transport leaving the customs territory of the Community, as specified in Article 842d(1).

2. In the case of combined transportation, where the active means of transport crossing the border is only transporting another active means of transport, the obligation to lodge the exit summary declaration shall lie with the operator of that other means of transport.

The time limit for lodging the declaration shall correspond to the time limit applicable to the active means of transport crossing the border, as specified in Article 842d(1).

Article 842d

1. The exit summary declaration shall be lodged at the office of exit by the relevant time limit specified in Article 592b(1).

Article 592b(2) and (3) shall apply mutatis mutandis.

2. The competent customs office shall, upon lodgement of the exit summary declaration, carry out appropriate risk based controls, primarily for safety and security purposes, prior to release of the goods for exit from the Community, within a period corresponding to that

> between the deadline for lodgement of the declaration laid down in Article 592b for the particular type of traffic and the loading or departure of the goods.

Where goods covered by one of the exemptions laid down in Article 592a(a) to (i) from the requirement for an exit summary declaration are brought out of the customs territory of the Community, risk analysis shall be carried out upon presentation of the goods, on the basis of the documentation or other information covering the goods.

Goods may be released for exit as soon as the risk analysis has been carried out.

> 3.   Where it is found that goods intended to be brought out of the customs territory of the Community and for which an exit summary declaration is required are not covered by such a declaration, the person who brings the goods, or who assumes responsibility for the carriage of the goods, out of the customs territory of the Community shall lodge an exit summary declaration immediately.

If the person lodges an exit summary declaration after the deadlines specified in Articles 592b and 592c, this shall not preclude application of penalties laid down in the national legislation.

> 4.   Where, on the basis of the checks which they have carried out, the customs authorities are unable to grant release of the goods for exit, the competent customs office shall notify the person who lodged the exit summary declaration and, where different, the person responsible for the carriage of the goods out of the customs territory of the Community, that the goods are not to be released.

Such notification shall be given within a reasonable time after risk analysis has been finalised for these goods.

> *Article 842e*
>
> 1.   The deadlines referred to in Article 842d(1) shall not apply where international agreements between the Community and third countries require the exchange of customs declaration data by deadlines different from those referred to in that Article.
>
> 2.   The time limit shall not, in any event, be reduced below the period required for completion of the risk analysis before the goods leave the customs territory of the Community.'

66.   The following heading is inserted before Article 843:

> 'CHAPTER 2
>
> **Temporary export**'

67.   In Article 843(1), the word 'Title' is replaced by the word 'chapter'.

68.   The following Article 865a is inserted:

> '*Article 865a*
>
> Where the entry summary declaration has been amended and the behaviour of the person concerned does not suggest any fraudulent dealing, no customs debt shall be incurred on the basis of Article 202 of the Code as a result of the unlawful introduction of the goods which, prior to the amendment of the declaration, were not correctly declared.'

72.   Annex 30A as set out in Annex III to this Regulation is inserted.

Article 2

During a transitional period of 24 months starting from 1 January 2008, the period for issuing the AEO certificate referred to in the first sentence of Article 14o(2) shall be extended to 300 calendar days, the period for communication of the application referred to in Article 14l(1) shall be extended to 10 working days, the period for information referred to in Article 14l(2) shall be extended to 70 calendar days, and the period for consultation referred to in Article 14m(1) shall be extended to 120 calendar days.

Article 3

1. This Regulation shall enter into force on the seventh day following that of its publication in the Official Journal of the European Union.

2. Point (3), except insofar as it relates to paragraphs 2 and 3 of Article 14b, and points (23), (25), (28), (41), (44), (45), (70) and (71) of Article 1 shall apply from 1 January 2008.

3. Point (3), insofar as it relates to paragraphs 2 and 3 of Article 14b, and points (4) to (16), (18), (19), (21), (22), (24), (26), (27), (29), (30), (32), (33), (36), (39), (46) to (49), (55), (59), (60), (63), (65) to (68), (72) of Article 1 shall apply from 1 July 2009.

This Regulation shall be binding in its entirety and directly applicable in all Member States.

Done at Brussels, 18 December 2006. For the Commission László KOVÁCS Member of the Commission

ANNEX III

'ANNEX 30A

1. Introductory notes to the tables

Note 1. Generalities

1.1 The summary declaration that must be lodged for goods entering or leaving the customs territory of the Community contains the information detailed in Tables 1 to 5 for each of the situations or modes of transport concerned.

1.2 Tables 1 to 6 include all data elements necessary for the procedures and declarations concerned. They provide comprehensive views of the requirements necessary for the various procedures and declarations.

1.3 The headings of the columns are self-explanatory and refer to these procedures and declarations. In case of temporary storage, data in the column "Entry summary declaration" of Table 1 shall be used.

1.4 An "X" in a given cell of the tables indicates that the data element concerned is requested for the procedure or declaration described in the title of the relevant column at the declaration item of goods level. An "Y" in a given cell of the tables indicates that the data element concerned is requested for the procedure or declaration described in the title of the relevant column at declaration header level. A "Z" in a given cell of the tables indicates that the data element concerned is requested for the procedure or declaration described in the title of the relevant column at the conveyance report level. Any combination of these symbols "X", "Y" and "Z" means that the data element concerned can be requested for the procedure or declaration described in the title of the relevant column at any of the levels concerned.

1.5 The use within this annex of the words entry and exit summary declarations refer respectively to the summary declarations provided for under Articles 36a(1) and 182a(1) of the Code.

1.6 The descriptions and notes contained in Section 4 in respect of entry and exit summary declarations and of simplified procedures apply to the data elements referred to in Tables 1 to 6.

Note 2. Customs declaration used as an entry summary declaration

2.1 Where a customs declaration, as referred to in Article 62(1) of the Code, is used as a summary declaration, in accordance with Article 36c(1) of the Code, that declaration must, in addition to the particulars required for the specific procedure under Annex 37 or Annex 37A, include the particulars set out in column "Entry summary declaration" of Tables 1 to 4.

Where a customs declaration, as referred to in Article 76(1) of the Code, is used as a summary declaration, in accordance with Article 36c(1) of the Code, that declaration must, in addition to the particulars required for the specific procedure in Table 6, include the particulars set out in column "Entry summary declaration" of Tables 1 to 4.

2.2 When Article 14b(3) applies and where a customs declaration, as referred to in Article 62(1) of the Code, is used as a summary declaration, in accordance with Article 36c(1) of the Code, that declaration must, in addition to the particulars required for the specific procedure under Annex 37 or Annex 37A, include the particulars set out in column "AEO Entry summary declaration" of Table 5.

When Article 14b(3) applies and where a customs declaration, as referred to in Article 76(1) of the Code, is used as a summary declaration, in accordance with Article 36c(1) of the Code, that declaration must, in addition to the particulars required for the specific procedure in Table 6, include the particulars set out in column "AEO Entry summary declaration" of Table 5.

Note 3. Customs declaration at export

3.1 Where a customs declaration, as referred to in Article 62(1) of the Code, is required, in accordance with Article 182b of the Code, that declaration must, in addition to the particulars required for the specific procedure under Annex 37 or Annex 37A, include the particulars set out in column "Exit summary declaration" of Tables 1 and 2.

Where a customs declaration, as referred to in Article 76(1) of the Code, is required, in accordance with Article 182b of the Code, that declaration must, in addition to the particulars required for the specific procedure in Table 6, include the particulars set out in column "Exit summary declaration" of Tables 1 and 2.

3.2 When Article 14b(3) applies and where a customs declaration, as referred to in Article 62(1) of the Code, is required, in accordance with Article 182b of the Code, that declaration must, in addition to the particulars required for the specific procedure under Annex 37 or Annex 37A, include the particulars set out in column "AEO Exit summary declaration" of Table 5.

When Article 14b (3) applies and where a customs declaration, as referred to in Article 76(1) of the Code, is required, in accordance with Article 182b of the Code, that declaration must, in addition to the particulars required for the specific procedure in Table 6, include the particulars set out in column "AEO Exit summary declaration" of Table 5.

Note 4. Other specific circumstances in respect of exit and entry summary declarations and particular types of goods traffic. Note to Tables 2 to 4

4.1 The columns "Exit summary declaration — postal and express consignments" and "Entry summary declaration — postal and express consignments" of Table 2 cover the required data which may be provided electronically to Customs authorities for risk-analysis purposes prior to departure or arrival of postal and express consignments.

4.2 For the purpose of this annex, a postal consignment means an individual item of a maximum weight of 50 kg, conveyed via the postal system in accordance with the rules of the Universal Postal Union Convention, when the goods are carried by or on behalf of holders of rights and obligations under such rules.

4.3 For the purpose of this annex, an express consignment means an individual item carried via an integrated service of expedited/time-definite collection, transport, customs clearance and delivery of parcels whilst tracking the location of, and maintaining control over such items throughout the supply of the service.

4.4 The column "Exit — ship and aircraft supplies" of Table 2 covers the data requirements in respect of exit summary declarations for ship and aircraft supplies.

4.5 Tables 3 and 4 contain the information necessary for entry summary declarations in the context of road and rail modes of transport.

4.6 Table 3 for road mode of transport applies also in case of multimodal transport, unless otherwise provided in Section 4.

Note 5. Simplified procedures

5.1 The declarations for simplified procedures referred to in Articles 254, 260, 266, 268, 275, 280, 282, 285, 285a, 288 and 289 contain the information detailed in Table 6.

5.2 The reduced format for certain data elements provided for simplified procedures does not limit or influence the requirements set out in Annexes 37 and 38, notably in respect of the information to be provided in supplementary declarations.

2. Requirements for entry and exit summary declarations

2.1 Situation for air, sea, inland waterways and other modes of transport or situations not referred to under Tables 2 to 4 — Table 1

Name	Exit summary declaration (See note 3.1)	Entry summary declaration (See note 2.1)
Number of items	Y	Y
Unique consignment reference number	X/Y	X/Y
Transport document number	X/Y	X/Y
Consignor	X/Y	X/Y
Person lodging the summary declaration	Y	Y
Consignee	X/Y	X/Y
Carrier		Z
Notify party		X/Y
Identity and nationality of active means of transport crossing the border		Z
Conveyance reference number		Z
First place of arrival code		Z
Date and time of arrival at first place of arrival in Customs territory		Z
Country(ies) of routing codes	Y	Y
Customs office of exit	Y	

Name	Exit summary declaration (See note 3.1)	Entry summary declaration (See note 2.1)
Location of goods	Y	
Place of loading		X/Y
Place of unloading code		X/Y
Goods description	X	X
Type of packages (code)	X	X
Number of packages	X	X
Shipping marks	X/Y	X/Y
Equipment identification number, if containerised	X/Y	X/Y
Goods item number	X	X
Commodity code	X	X
Gross mass (kg)	X/Y	X/Y
UN Dangerous Goods code	X	X
Seal number	X/Y	X/Y
Transport charges method of payment code	X/Y	X/Y
Declaration date	Y	Y
Signature/Authentication	Y	Y
Other specific circumstance indicator	Y	Y

2.2   Postal and express consignments, ship and aircraft supplies — Table 2

Name	Exit summary declaration — postal and express consignments (See notes 3.1 and 4.1 to 4.3)	Exit summary declaration — ship and aircraft supplies (See notes 3.1 and 4.4)	Entry summary declaration — postal and express consignments (See notes 2.1 and 4.1 to 4.3)
Unique consignment reference number		X/Y	
Transport document number		X/Y	
Consignor	X/Y	X/Y	X/Y
Person lodging the summary declaration	Y	Y	Y
Consignee	X/Y	X/Y	X/Y
Carrier			Z
Country(ies) of routing codes	Y		Y

Name	Exit summary declaration — postal and express consignments (See notes 3.1 and 4.1 to 4.3)	Exit summary declaration — ship and aircraft supplies (See notes 3.1 and 4.4)	Entry summary declaration — postal and express consignments (See notes 2.1 and 4.1 to 4.3)
Customs office of exit	Y	Y	
Location of goods	Y	Y	
Place of loading			Y
Place of unloading code			X/Y
Goods description	X	X	X
Equipment identification number, if containerised		X/Y	
Goods item number	X	X	X
Commodity code	X	X	X
Gross mass (kg)	X/Y	X/Y	X/Y
UN Dangerous Goods Code	X		X
Transport charges method of payment code	X/Y	X/Y	X/Y
Declaration date	Y	Y	Y
Signature/Authentication	Y	Y	Y
Other specific circumstance indicator	Y	Y	Y

2.3   Road mode of transport — Entry summary declaration information — Table 3

Name	Road — Entry summary declaration (See note 2.1)
Number of items	Y
Unique consignment reference number	X/Y
Transport document number	X/Y
Consignor	X/Y
Person lodging the summary declaration	Y
Consignee	X/Y
Carrier	Z
Identity and nationality of active means of transport crossing the border	Z
First place of arrival code	Z

Name	Road — Entry summary declaration (See note 2.1)
Date and time of arrival at first place of arrival in Customs territory	Z
Countries of routing codes	Y
Place of loading	X/Y
Place of unloading code	X/Y
Goods description	X
Type of packages code	X
Number of packages	X
Equipment identification number if containerised	X/Y
Goods item number	X
Commodity code	X
Gross mass (kg)	X/Y
Transport charges method of payment code	X/Y
UN Dangerous Goods Code	X
Seal number	X/Y
Declaration date	Y
Signature/Authentication	Y
Other specific circumstance indicator	Y

2.4   Rail mode of transport — Entry summary declaration information — Table 4

Name	Rail — Entry summary declaration (See note 2.1)
Number of items	Y
Unique consignment reference number	X/Y
Transport document number	X/Y
Consignor	X/Y
Person lodging the entry summary declaration	Y
Consignee	X/Y
Carrier Z	Z
Identity and nationality of active means of transport crossing the border	Z
Conveyance reference number	Z
First place of arrival code	Z
Date and time of arrival at first place of arrival in Customs territory	Z
Countries of routing codes	Y
Place of loading	X/Y
Place of unloading code	X/Y
Goods description	X

Part III

Name	Rail — Entry summary declaration (See note 2.1)
Type of packages code	X
Number of packages	X
Equipment identification number, if containerised	X/Y
Goods item number	X
Commodity code	X
Gross mass (kg)	X/Y
Transport charges method of payment code	X/Y
UN Dangerous Goods Code	X
Seal number	X/Y
Declaration date	Y
Signature/Authentication	Y
Other specific circumstance indicator	Y

2.5   Authorised economic operators — reduced data requirements for exit and entry summary declarations — Table 5

Name	Exit summary declaration (See note 3.2)	Entry summary declaration (See note 2.2)
Unique consignment reference number	X/Y	X/Y
Transport document number	X/Y	X/Y
Consignor	X/Y	X/Y
Person lodging the summary declaration	Y	Y
Consignee	X/Y	X/Y
Carrier		Z
Notify party		X/Y
Identity and nationality of active means of transport crossing the border		Z
Conveyance reference number		Z
First place of arrival code		Z
Date and time of arrival at first place of arrival in Customs territory		Z
Country(ies) of routing codes	Y	Y
Customs office of exit	Y	
Place of loading		X/Y
Goods description	X	X
Number of packages	X	X
Equipment identification number, if containerised	X/Y	X/Y
Commodity code	X	X

Name	Exit summary declaration (See note 3.2)	Entry summary declaration (See note 2.2)
Declaration date	y	y
Signature/Authentication	y	y
Other specific circumstance indicator	y	y

3. Requirements for simplified procedures — Table 6

Name	Local clearance export (See note 3.1)	Simplified declaration export (See note 3.1)	Incomplete declaration export (See note 3.1)	Local clearance import (See note 2.1)	Simplified declaration import (See note 2.1)	Incomplete declaration import (See note 2.1)
Declaration		Y	Y		Y	Y
Number of items		Y	Y		Y	Y
Unique consignment reference number	X	X	X	X	X	X
Transport document number	X/Y	X/Y	X/Y	X/Y	X/Y	X/Y
Consignor/exporter	X/Y	X/Y	X/Y			
Consignee				X/Y	X/Y	X/Y
Declarant/representative	Y	Y	Y	Y	Y	Y
Declarant/representative status code	Y	Y	Y	Y	Y	Y
Currency code				X	X	X
Customs office of exit	Y	Y	Y			
Customs office for supplementary declaration			Y			
Goods description	X	X	X	X	X	X
Type of packages (code)	X	X	X	X	X	XX
Number of packages	X	X	X	X	X	X
Shipping marks	X/Y	X/Y	X/Y	X/Y	X/Y	X/Y
Equipment identification number, if containerised				X/Y	X/Y	X/Y
Goods item number		X	X		X	X
Commodity code	X	X	X	X	X	X
Gross mass (kg)				X	X	X
Procedure	X	X	X	X	X	X
Net mass (kg)	X	X	X	X	X	X
Item amount				X	X	X
Reference number for simplified procedures	X			X		
Number of the authorisation	X	X		X	X	
Additional information				X	X	X

Part III

Name	Local clearance export (See note 3.1)	Simpli-fied dec-laration export (See note 3.1)	Incom-plete declara-tion ex-port (See note 3.1)	Local clearance import (See note 2.1)	Simpli-fied dec-laration import (See note 2.1)	Incom-plete declara-tion im-port (See note 2.1)
Declaration date	Y	Y	Y	Y	Y	Y
Signature/Authentication	Y	Y	Y	Y	Y	Y

4. Data elements explanatory notes.

Declaration

Enter the codes provided for in Annex 38 for SAD Box 1, 1st and 2nd subdivisions.

Number of items ([1])

Total number of items declared in the declaration or in the summary declaration.

[Ref.: SAD Box 5]

Unique consignment reference number

Unique number assigned to goods, for entry, import, exit and export. WCO (ISO15459) codes or equivalent shall be used.

Summary declarations: it is an alternative to the transport document number when the latter is not available.

Simplified procedures: the information can be provided where available.

This element provides a link to other useful sources of information.

[Ref.: SAD Box 7]

Transport document number

Reference of the transport document that covers the transport of goods into or out of the customs territory.

This includes the code for the type of transport document as provided for in Annex 38, followed by the identification number of the document concerned.

This element is an alternative to the unique consignment reference number [UCR] when the latter is not available. It provides a link to other useful sources of information.)

Exit ship and aircraft supplies summary declarations: invoice or loading list number.

Entry road mode of transport summary declarations: this information shall be provided to the extent available and may include both references to TIR carnet and to CMR.

[Ref.: SAD Box 44]

Consignor ([2])

Party consigning goods as stipulated in the transport contract by the party ordering transport.

Exit summary declarations: this element must be provided when different from the person lodging the summary declaration.

Consignor/exporter ([3])

Party who makes or on whose behalf the export declaration is made and who is the owner of the goods or has similar right of disposal over them at the time when the declaration is accepted.

[Ref.: SAD Box 2]

---

[1] Automatically generated by computer systems.

[2] Coded version, where available.

Person lodging the summary declaration ([1])

Entry summary declarations: one of the persons mentioned in Article 36b(3) and (4) of the Code.

Exit summary declarations: party defined in Article 182d(3) of the Code. This information shall not be provided where, in accordance with Article 182a(1) of the Code, the goods are covered by a customs declaration.

Note: This information is necessary to identify the person responsible for presenting the declaration.

Consignee ([1])

Party to whom goods are actually consigned.

Entry summary declarations: this element must be provided when different from the person lodging the summary declaration. Where the goods are carried under a negotiable bill of lading that is "to order blank endorsed", the consignee is unknown and his particulars shall be replaced by the following code 10600.

Legal basis	Subject	Box	Code
Annex 30A	Situations where negotiable bills of lading that are "to order blank endorsed" are concerned, in the case of entry summary declarations, where the consignee particulars are unknown.	44	10600

Exit summary declarations: In cases referred to in Article 789, this information shall be provided where available.

[Ref.: SAD Box 8]

Declarant/representative (¹)

To be required if different from the consignor/exporter at export/the consignee at import.

[Ref.: SAD Box 14]

Declarant/representative status code

Code representing the declarant or the status of the representative. The codes to be used are those provided for in Annex 38 for Box 14 of the SAD.

Carrier (¹)

Party that transports the goods at entry into the customs territory. This information shall be provided where it is different from the person lodging the summary declaration. This information does not need to be provided where it can be deduced automatically and unambiguously from other data elements provided by the trader.

Notify party (¹)

Party to be notified at entry of the arrival of the goods. This information needs to be provided where applicable. Where the goods are carried under a negotiable bill of lading that is "to order blank endorsed", in which case the consignee is not mentioned and code 10600 is entered, the notify party shall always be provided.

Identity and nationality of active means of transport crossing the border

Identity and nationality of active means of transport crossing the border of the EU Customs territory. The definitions provided for in Annex 37 for SAD Box 18 shall be used for identity. The codes provided for in Annex 38 for SAD Box 21 shall be used for nationality.

Rail mode of transport: the wagon number shall be provided.

---

¹ Coded version, where available.

Conveyance reference number (¹)

Identification of the journey of the means of transport, for example voyage number, flight number, trip number, if applicable.

Rail mode of transport: the train number shall be provided. This data element shall be provided in case of multimodal transport, where applicable.

First place of arrival code

Identification of the first arrival location in the Customs territory. This would be a port for sea, airport for air and border post for land crossing.

The code shall adhere to the following pattern: UN/LOCODE (an..5) + national code (an..6).

Road and rail modes of transport: the code shall follow the pattern provided for customs offices in Annex 38.

Date and time of arrival at first place of arrival in Customs territory

Date and time/scheduled date and time of arrival of means of transport at (for air) first airport, (land) arrival at first border post and (sea) arrival at first port, code. n12 (CCYYMMDDHHMM) shall be used. Local time of first place of arrival shall be provided.

Country(ies) of routing codes

Identification in a chronological order of the countries through which goods are routed between the country of original departure and final destination. This comprises the countries of original departure and of final destination of the goods. Codes provided for in Annex 38 for SAD Box 2 shall be used. This information is to be provided to the extent known.

Exit postal and express consignments summary declarations: only the country of final destination of the goods shall be provided.

Entry postal and express consignments summary declarations: only the country of original departure of the goods shall be provided.

Currency code

Code provided for in Annex 38 for SAD Box 22 for the currency in which the commercial invoice was drawn up.

This information is used in conjunction with "Item amount" where it is necessary for the calculation of import duties.

Member States may waive this requirement for simplified declarations and local clearance procedures at import where the conditions prescribed in the authorisations associated with these procedures allow them to defer the collection of this data element in the supplementary declaration. [Ref.: SAD Boxes 22 and 44]

Customs office of exit

Code provided for in Annex 38 for SAD Box 29 for the customs office of exit, in accordance with Article 793(2).

Exit postal and express consignments summary declarations: this element does not need to be provided where it can be deduced automatically and unambiguously from other data elements provided by the trader.

Customs office for supplementary declaration

Export incomplete declarations: this element may only be used in cases referred to under Article 281(3).

Location of goods (¹)

Precise location where the goods may be examined.

[Ref.: SAD Box 30]

---

¹ Information to be produced where appropriate.

Place of loading (¹)

Name of a seaport, airport, freight terminal, rail station or other place at which goods are loaded onto the means of transport being used for their carriage, including the country where it is located.

Entry postal and express consignments summary declarations: this element does not need to be provided where it can be deduced automatically and unambiguously from other data elements provided by the trader.

Road and rail modes of transport: this can be the place where goods were taken over according to the transport contract or the TIR customs office of departure.

Place of unloading ([1])

Name of the seaport, airport, freight terminal, rail station or other place at which the goods are unloaded from the means of transport having been used for their carriage, including the country where it is located.

Road and rail modes of transport: where the code is not available, the name of the place shall be provided, with the maximum level of precision available.

Note: This element provides useful information for procedure management.

Goods description

Summary declarations: it is a plain language description that is precise enough for Customs services to be able to identify the goods. General terms (i.e. "consolidated", "general cargo" or "parts") cannot be accepted. A list of such general terms will be published by the Commission. It is not necessary to provide this information where the Commodity code is provided.

Simplified procedures: it is a description for tariff purposes.

[Ref.: SAD Box 31]

Type of packages (code)

Code specifying the type of package as provided for in Annex 38 for SAD Box 31 (UN/ECE Recommendation 21 Annex VI)

Number of packages

Number of individual items packaged in such a way that they cannot be divided without first undoing the packing, or number of pieces, if unpackaged. This information shall not be provided where goods are in bulk.

[Ref.: SAD Box 31]

Shipping marks

Free form description of the marks and numbers on transport units or packages. This information shall only be provided for packaged goods where applicable. Where goods are containerised, the container number can replace the shipping marks, which can however be provided by the trader where available. A UCR or the references in the transport document that allows for the unambiguous identification of all packages in the consignment may replace the shipping marks.

Note: This element helps to identify consignments.

[Ref.: SAD Box 31]

Equipment identification number, if containerised

Marks (letters and/or numbers) which identify the container.

[Ref.: SAD Box 31]

---

[1] Coded version, where available.

Goods item number ([1])

Number of the item in relation to the total number of items contained in the declaration or the summary declaration.

To be used only where there is more than one item of goods.

Note: This element, which is automatically generated by computer systems, helps to identify the item of goods concerned within the declaration.

[Ref.: SAD Box 32]

Commodity code

Code number corresponding to the item in question;

<u>Entry summary declarations:</u> first four digits of the CN code; It is not necessary to provide this information where the goods description is provided.

<u>Import simplified procedures:</u> 10-digit TARIC code. Traders may supplement this information, where appropriate, with additional TARIC codes. Member States may waive this requirement for simplified declarations and local clearance procedures at import where the conditions prescribed in the authorisations associated with these procedures allow them to defer the collection of this data element in the supplementary declaration.

<u>Exit summary declarations:</u> first four digits of the CN code. It is not necessary to provide this information where the goods description is provided.

<u>Exit ship and aircraft supplies summary declarations:</u> a specific simplified goods nomenclature will be published by the Commission.

<u>Export simplified procedures:</u> 8-digit CN code. Traders may complement this information, where appropriate, with additional TARIC codes. Member States may waive this requirement for simplified declarations and local clearance procedures at export where the conditions prescribed in the authorisations associated with these procedures allow them to defer the collection of this data element in the supplementary declaration.

[Ref.: SAD Box 33]

Gross mass (kg)

Weight (mass) of goods including packaging but excluding the carrier's equipment for the declaration.

Where possible, the trader can provide that weight at declaration item level.

<u>Import simplified procedures:</u> this information shall be provided only where it is necessary for the calculation of import duties.

Member States may waive this requirement for simplified declarations and local clearance procedure at import where the conditions prescribed in the authorisations associated with these procedures allow them to defer the collection of this data element in the supplementary declaration.

[Ref.: SAD Box 35]

Procedure

Procedure code as provided for in Annex 38 for SAD Box 37, 1st and 2nd subdivisions.

Member States may waive the obligation to provide the codes as defined in Annex 38 for Box 37, 2nd subdivision of the SAD for simplified declarations and local clearance procedures at import and export where the conditions prescribed in the authorisations associated with these procedures allow them to defer the collection of this data element in the supplementary declaration.

---

[1] Automatically generated by computer systems.

Net mass (kg)

Weight (mass) of the goods themselves without any packing.

Member States may waive this requirement for simplified declarations and local clearance procedures at import and export where the conditions prescribed in the authorisations associated with these procedures allow them to defer the collection of this data element in the supplementary declaration.

[Ref.: SAD Box 38]

Item amount

Price of the goods for the declaration item concerned. This information is used in conjunction with "Currency code" where it is necessary for the calculation of import duties.

Member States may waive this requirement for simplified declarations and local clearance procedures at import where the conditions prescribed in the authorisations associated with these procedures allow them to defer the collection of this data element in the supplementary declaration.

[Ref.: SAD Box 42]

Reference number for simplified procedures

It is the reference number of entry into the records for the procedures described in Articles 266 and 285a. Member States may waive this requirement where other satisfactory consignments tracing systems are in place.

Additional information

Enter code 10100 where Article 2 paragraph 1 of Regulation (EC) No 1147/2002 (1) applies (goods imported with airworthiness certificates).

[Ref.: SAD Box 44]

Number of the authorisation

Number of the authorisation for simplified procedures. Member States may waive this requirement where they are satisfied that their computer systems are able to derive this information without ambiguity from other elements of the declaration, such as the trader identification.

UN Dangerous Goods code

The United Nations Dangerous Goods Identifier (UNDG) is the unique serial number (n4) assigned within the United Nations to substances and articles contained in a list of the dangerous goods most commonly carried.

This element shall only be provided where it is relevant.

Seal number (²)

The identification numbers of the seals affixed to the transport equipment, where applicable.

Transport charges method of payment code

The following codes shall be used:

A	Payment in cash
B	Payment by credit card
C	Payment by cheque
D	Other (e.g. direct debit to cash account)
H	Electronic credit transfer
Y	Account holder with carrier
Y	Not pre-paid

This information is to be provided only where available.

---

¹ OJ L 170, 29.6.2002 p. 8.

² Information to be produced where appropriate.

Declaration date (¹)

Date at which the respective declarations were issued and when appropriate, signed or otherwise authenticated.

For local clearance procedures pursuant to Articles 266 and 285a, this is the date of entry into the records.

[Ref.: SAD Box 54]

Signature/Authentication (²)

[Ref.: SAD Box 54]

Other specific circumstance indicator

Coded element that indicates the special circumstance the benefit of which is claimed by the trader concerned.

A	Postal and express consignments

B	Ship and aircraft supplies
C	Road mode of transport
D	Rail mode of transport
E	Authorised economic operators

This element needs to be provided only where the benefit of a special circumstance other than those referred to under Table 1 is requested by the person lodging the summary declaration.

This element does not need to be provided where it can be deduced automatically and unambiguously from other data elements provided by the trader.

CONVENTION ON MUTUAL ADMINISTRATIVE ASSISTANCE IN TAX MATTERS

(CETS 127)

Strasbourg, 25 January 1988

NOTES

Subordinate legislation: International Mutual Administrative Assistance in Tax Matters Order 2007, SI 2007/2126.

Preamble

The member States of the Council of Europe and the member countries of the Organisation for Economic Co-operation and Development (OECD), signatories of this Convention,

Considering that the development of international movement of persons, capital, goods and services – although highly beneficial in itself – has increased the possibilities of tax avoidance and evasion and therefore requires increasing co-operation among tax authorities;

Welcoming the various efforts made in recent years to combat tax avoidance and tax evasion on an international level, whether bilaterally or multilaterally;

Considering that a co-ordinated effort between States is necessary in order to foster all forms of administrative assistance in matters concerning taxes of any kind whilst at the same time ensuring adequate protection of the rights of taxpayers;

Recognising that international co-operation can play an important part in facilitating the proper determination of tax liabilities and in helping the taxpayer to secure his rights;

Considering that fundamental principles entitling every person to have his rights and obligations determined in accordance with a proper legal procedure should be recognised as applying to tax matters in all States and that States should endeavour to protect the legitimate interests of taxpayers, including appropriate protection against discrimination and double taxation;

Convinced therefore that States should not carry out measures or supply information except in conformity with their domestic law and practice, having regard to the necessity of protecting the confidentiality of information, and taking account of international instruments for the protection of privacy and flows of personal data;

Desiring to conclude a convention on mutual administrative assistance in tax matters,

Have agreed as follows:

Part III

CHAPTER I
SCOPE OF THE CONVENTION

Article 1 Object of the Convention and persons covered

1. The Parties shall, subject to the provisions of Chapter IV, provide administrative assistance to each other in tax matters. Such assistance may involve, where appropriate, measures taken by judicial bodies.

2. Such administrative assistance shall comprise:

    a.   exchange of information, including simultaneous tax examinations and participation in tax examinations abroad;

    b.   assistance in recovery, including measures of conservancy; and

    c.   service of documents.

3. A Party shall provide administrative assistance whether the person affected is a resident or national of a Party or of any other State.

Article 2 Taxes covered

1. This Convention shall apply:

    a.   to the following taxes:

        i.   taxes on income or profits;

        ii.   taxes on capital gains which are imposed separately from the tax on income or profits;

        iii.   taxes on net wealth;

    imposed on behalf of a Party; and

    b.   to the following taxes:

        i.   taxes on income, profits, capital gains or net wealth which are imposed on behalf of political divisions or local authorities of a Party;

        ii.   compulsory social security contributions payable to general government or to social security institutions established under public law;

        iii.   taxes in other categories, except customs duties, imposed on behalf of a Party, namely:

           A.   estate, inheritance or gift taxes;

           B.   taxes on immovable property;

           C.   general consumption taxes, such as value-added or sales taxes;

           D.   specific taxes on goods and services such as excise taxes;

           E.   taxes on the use or ownership of motor vehicles;

           F.   taxes on the use or ownership of movable property other than motor vehicles;

           G.   any other taxes.

        iv.   taxes in categories referred to in sub-paragraph iii above which are imposed on behalf of political subdivisions or local authorities of a Party.

2. The existing taxes to which the Convention shall apply are listed in Annex A in the categories referred to in paragraph 1.

3. The Parties shall notify the Secretary General of the Council of Europe or the Secretary General of OECD (hereinafter referred to as the "Depositaries") of any change to be made to Annex A as a result of a modification of the list mentioned in paragraph 2. Such change shall take effect on the first day of the month following the expiration of a period of three months after the date of receipt of such notification by the Depositary.

4. The Convention shall also apply, as from their adoption, to any identical or substantially similar taxes which are imposed in a Contracting State after the entry into force of the Convention in respect of that Party in addition to or in place of the existing taxes listed in Annex A and, in that event, the Party concerned shall notify one of the Depositaries of the adoption of the tax in question.

CHAPTER II
GENERAL DEFINITIONS

Article 3 Definitions

1. For the purposes of this Convention, unless the context otherwise requires:
   (a)   the terms "applicant State" and "requested State" mean respectively any Party applying for administrative assistance in tax matters and any Party requested to provide such assistance;
   (b)   the term "tax" means any tax or social security contribution to which the Convention applies pursuant to Article 2;
   (c)   the term "tax claim" means any amount of tax, as well as interest thereon, related administrative fines and costs incidental to recovery, which are owed and not yet paid;
   (d)   the term "competent authority" means the persons and authorities listed in Annex B;
   (e)   the term "nationals" in relation to a Party means:
       i.   all individuals possessing the nationality of that Party, and
       ii.   all legal persons, partnerships, associations and other entities deriving their status as such from the laws in force in that Party.

For each Party that has made a declaration for that purpose, the terms used above will be understood as defined in Annex C.

2. As regards the application of the Convention by a Party, any term not defined therein shall, unless the context otherwise requires, have the meaning which it has under the law of that Party concerning the taxes covered by the Convention.

3. The Parties shall notify one of the Depositaries of any change to be made to Annexes B and C. Such change shall take effect on the first day of the month following the expiration of a period of three months after the date of receipt of such notification by the Depositary in question.

CHAPTER III
FORMS OF ASSISTANCE

SECTION I
EXCHANGE OF INFORMATION

Article 4 General provisions

1. The Parties shall exchange any information, in particular as provided in this section, that is foreseeably relevant to:
   a.   the assessment and collection of tax, and the recovery and enforcement of tax claims, and
   b.   the prosecution before an administrative authority or the initiation of prosecution before a judicial body.

Information which is unlikely to be relevant to these purposes shall not be exchanged under this Convention.

2. A Party may use information obtained under this Convention as evidence before a criminal court only if prior authorisation has been given by the Party which has supplied the information. However, any two or more Parties may mutually agree to waive the condition of prior authorisation.

3. Any Party may, by a declaration addressed to one of the Depositories, indicate that, according to its internal legislation, its authorities may inform its resident or national before transmitting information concerning him, in conformity with Articles 5 and 7.

Article 5 Exchange of information on request

1. At the request of the applicant State, the requested State shall provide the applicant State with any information referred to in Article 4 which concerns particular persons or transactions.

2. If the information available in the tax files of the requested State is not sufficient to enable it to comply with the request for information, that State shall take all relevant measures to provide the applicant State with the information requested.

Article 6 Automatic exchange of information

With respect to categories of cases and in accordance with procedures which they shall determine by mutual agreement, two or more Parties shall automatically exchange the information referred to in Article 4.

Article 7 Spontaneous exchange of information

1. A Party shall, without prior request, forward to another Party information of which it has knowledge in the following circumstances:

a. the first-mentioned Party has grounds for supposing that there may be a loss of tax in the other Party;

b. a person liable to tax obtains a reduction in or an exemption from tax in the first-mentioned Party which would give rise to an increase in tax or to liability to tax in the other Party;

c. business dealings between a person liable to tax in a Party and a person liable to tax in another Party are conducted through one or more countries in such a way that a saving in tax may result in one or the other Party or in both;

d. a Party has grounds for supposing that a saving of tax may result from artificial transfers of profits within groups of enterprises;

e. information forwarded to the first-mentioned Party by the other Party has enabled information to be obtained which may be relevant in assessing liability to tax in the latter Party.

2. Each Party shall take such measures and implement such procedures as are necessary to ensure that information described in paragraph 1 will be made available for transmission to another Party.

Article 8 Simultaneous tax examinations

1. At the request of one of them, two or more Parties shall consult together for the purposes of determining cases and procedures for simultaneous tax examinations. Each Party involved shall decide whether or not it wishes to participate in a particular simultaneous tax examination.

2. For the purposes of this Convention, a simultaneous tax examination means an arrangement between two or more Parties to examine simultaneously, each in its own territory, the tax affairs of a person or persons in which they have a common or related interest, with a view to exchanging any relevant information which they so obtain.

Article 9 Tax examinations abroad

1. At the request of the competent authority of the applicant State, the competent authority of the requested State may allow representatives of the competent authority of the applicant State to be present at the appropriate part of a tax examination in the requested State.

Part III

2. If the request is acceded to, the competent authority of the requested State shall, as soon as possible, notify the competent authority or official of the applicant State about the time and place of the examination, the authority or official designated to carry out the examination and the procedures and conditions required by the requested State for the conduct of the examination. All decisions with respect to the conduct of the tax examination shall be made by the requested State.

3. A Party may inform one of the Depositaries of its intention not to accept, as a general rule, such requests as are referred to in paragraph 1. Such a declaration may be made or withdrawn at any time.

Article 10 Conflicting information

If a Party receives from another Party information about a person's tax affairs which appears to it to conflict with information in its possession, it shall so advise the Party which has provided the information.

SECTION II
ASSISTANCE IN RECOVERY

Article 11 Recovery of tax claims

1. At the request of the applicant State the requested State shall, subject to the provisions of Articles 14 and 15, take the necessary steps to recover tax claims of the first-mentioned State as if they were its own tax claims.

2. The provision of paragraph 1 shall apply only to tax claims which form the subject of an instrument permitting their enforcement in the applicant State and, unless otherwise agreed between the Parties concerned, which are not contested. However, where the claim is against a person who is not a resident of the applicant State, paragraph 1 shall only apply, unless otherwise agreed between the Parties concerned, where the claim may no longer be contested.

3. The obligation to provide assistance in the recovery of tax claims concerning a deceased person or his estate, is limited to the value of the estate or of the property acquired by each beneficiary of the estate, according to whether the claim is to be recovered from the estate or from the beneficiaries thereof.

Article 12 Measures of conservancy

At the request of the applicant State the requested State shall, with a view to the recovery of an amount of tax, take measures of conservancy even if the claim is contested or is not yet the subject of an instrument permitting enforcement.

Article 13 Documents accompanying the request

1. The request for administrative assistance under this section shall be accompanied by:

a. a declaration that the tax claim concerns a tax covered by the Convention and, in the case of recovery that, subject to paragraph 2 of Article 11, the tax claim is not or may not be contested;

b. an official copy of the instrument permitting enforcement in the applicant State; and

c. any other document required for recovery or measures of conservancy.

2. The instrument permitting enforcement in the applicant State shall, where appropriate and in accordance with the provisions in force in the requested State, be accepted, recognised, supplemented or replaced as soon as possible after the date of the receipt of the request for assistance, by an instrument permitting enforcement in the latter State.

Article 14 Time limits

1. Questions concerning any period beyond which a tax claim cannot be enforced shall be governed by the law of the applicant State. The request for assistance shall give particulars concerning that period.

2. Acts of recovery carried out by the requested State in pursuance of a request for assistance, which, according to the laws of that State, would have the effect of suspending or interrupting the period mentioned in paragraph 1, shall also have this effect under the laws of the applicant State. The requested State shall inform the applicant State about such acts.

3. In any case the requested State is not obliged to comply with a request for assistance which is submitted after a period of 15 years from the date of the original instrument permitting enforcement.

Article 15 Priority

The tax claim in the recovery of which assistance is provided shall not have in the requested State any priority specially accorded to the tax claims of that State even if the recovery procedure used is the one applicable to its own tax claims.

Article 16 Deferral of payment

The requested State may allow deferral of payment or payment by instalments if its laws or administrative practice permit it to do so in similar circumstances but shall first inform the applicant State.

SECTION III
SERVICE OF DOCUMENTS

Article 17 Service of documents

1. At the request of the applicant State the requested State shall serve upon the addressee documents, including those relating to judicial decisions, which emanate from the applicant State and which relate to a tax covered by this Convention.

2. The requested State shall effect service of documents:

   a. by a method prescribed by its domestic laws for the service of documents of a substantially similar nature;

   b. to the extent possible, by a particular method requested by the applicant State or the closest to such method available under its own laws.

3. A Party may effect service of documents directly through the post on a person within the territory of another Party.

4. Nothing in the Convention shall be construed as invalidating any service of documents by a Party in accordance with its laws.

5. When a document is served in accordance with this article it need not be accompanied by a translation. However, where it is satisfied that the addressee cannot understand the language of the document the requested State shall arrange to have it translated into or a summary drafted in its or one of its official languages. Alternatively, it may ask the applicant State to have the document either translated into or accompanied by a summary in one of the official languages of the requested State, the Council of Europe or OECD.

CHAPTER IV
PROVISIONS RELATING TO ALL FORMS OF ASSISTANCE

Article 18 Information to be provided by the applicant state

1. A request for assistance shall indicate where appropriate:

   a. the authority or agency which initiated the request made by the competent authority;

b.   the name, address and any other particulars assisting in the identification of the person in respect of whom the request is made;

c.   in the case of a request for information, the form in which the applicant State wishes the information to be supplied in order to meet its needs;

d.   in the case of a request for assistance in recovery or measures of conservancy, the nature of the tax claim, the components of the tax claim and the assets from which the tax claim may be recovered;

e.   in the case of a request for service of documents, the nature and the subject of the document to be served;

f.   whether it is in conformity with the law and administrative practice of the applicant State and whether it is justified in the light of the requirements of Article 19.

2.   As soon as any other information relevant to the request for assistance comes to its knowledge, the applicant State shall forward it to the requested State.

Article 19 Possibility of declining a request

The requested State shall not be obliged to accede to a request if the applicant State has not pursued all means available in its own territory, except where recourse to such means would give rise to disproportionate difficulty.

Article 20 Response to the request for assistance

1.   If the request for assistance is complied with, the requested State shall inform the applicant State of the action taken and of the result of the assistance as soon as possible.

2.   If the request is declined, the requested State shall inform the applicant State of that decision and the reason for it as soon as possible.

3.   If, with respect to a request for information, the applicant State has specified the form in which it wishes the information to be supplied and the requested State is in a position to do so, the requested State shall supply it in the form requested.

Article 21 Protection of persons and limits to the obligation to provide assistance

1.   Nothing in this Convention shall affect the rights and safeguards secured to persons by the laws or administrative practice of the requested State.

2.   Except in the case of Article 14 the provisions of this Convention shall not be construed so as to impose on the requested State the obligation:

a.   to carry out measures at variance with its own laws or administrative practice or the laws or administrative practice of the applicant State;

b.   to carry out measures which it considers contrary to public policy (ordre public) or to its essential interests;

c.   to supply information which is not obtainable under its own laws or its administrative practice or under the laws of the applicant State or its administrative practice;

d.   to supply information which would disclose any trade, business, industrial, commercial or professional secret, or trade process, or information the disclosure of which would be contrary to public policy (ordre public) or to its essential interests;

e.   to provide administrative assistance if and insofar as it considers the taxation in the applicant State to be contrary to generally accepted taxation principles or to the provisions of a convention for the avoidance of double taxation, or of any other convention which the requested State has concluded with the applicant State;

Part III

f.   to provide assistance if the application of this Convention would lead to discrimination between a national of the requested State and nationals of the applicant State in the same circumstances.

Article 22 Secrecy

1.   Any information obtained by a Party under this Convention shall be treated as secret in the same manner as information obtained under the domestic laws of that Party, or under the conditions of secrecy applying in the supplying Party if such conditions are more restrictive.

2.   Such information shall in any case be disclosed only to persons or authorities (including courts and administrative or supervisory bodies) involved in the assessment, collection or recovery of, the enforcement or prosecution in respect of, or the determination of appeals in relation to, taxes of that Party. Only the persons or authorities mentioned above may use the information and then only for such purposes. They may, notwithstanding the provisions of paragraph 1, disclose it in public court proceedings or in judicial decisions relating to such taxes, subject to prior authorisation by the competent authority of the supplying Party. However, any two or more Parties may mutually agree to waive the condition of prior authorisation.

3.   If a Party has made a reservation provided for in sub-paragraph a of paragraph 1 of Article 30, any other Party obtaining information from that Party shall not use it for the purpose of a tax in a category subject to the reservation. Similarly the Party making such a reservation shall not use information obtained under this Convention for the purpose of a tax in a category subject to the reservation.

4.   Notwithstanding the provisions of paragraphs 1, 2 and 3, information received by a Party may be used for other purposes when such information may be used for such other purposes under the laws of the supplying Party and the competent authority of that Party authorises such use. Information provided by a Party to another Party may be transmitted by the latter to a third Party, subject to prior authorisation by the competent authority of the first-mentioned Party.

Article 23 Proceedings

1.   Proceedings relating to measures taken under this Convention by the requested State shall be brought only before the appropriate body of that State.

2.   Proceedings relating to measures taken under this Convention by the applicant State, in particular those which, in the field of recovery, concern the existence or the amount of the tax claim or the instrument permitting its enforcement, shall be brought only before the appropriate body of that State. If such proceedings are brought, the applicant State shall inform the requested State which shall suspend the procedure pending the decision of the body in question.

However, the requested State shall, if asked by the applicant State, take measures of conservancy to safeguard recovery. The requested State can also be informed of such proceedings by any interested person. Upon receipt of such information the requested State shall consult on the matter, if necessary, with the applicant State.

3.   As soon as a final decision in the proceedings has been given, the requested State or the applicant State, as the case may be, shall notify the other State of the decision and the implications which it has for the request for assistance.

CHAPTER V
SPECIAL PROVISIONS

Article 24 Implementation of the Convention

1.   The Parties shall communicate with each other for the implementation of this convention through their respective competent authorities. The competent authorities may communicate directly for this purpose and may authorise subordinate authorities

to act on their behalf. The competent authorities of two or more Parties may mutually agree on the mode of application of the Convention among themselves.

2. Where the requested State considers that the application of this Convention in a particular case would have serious and undesirable consequences, the competent authorities of the requested and of the applicant State shall consult each other and endeavour to resolve the situation by mutual agreement.

3. A co-ordinating body composed of representatives of the competent authorities of the Parties shall monitor the implementation and development of this Convention, under the aegis of OECD. To that end, the co-ordinating body shall recommend any action likely to further the general aims of the Convention. In particular it shall act as a forum for the study of new methods and procedures to increase international co-operation in tax matters and, where appropriate, it may recommend revisions or amendments to the Convention. States which have signed but not yet ratified, accepted or approved the Convention are entitled to be represented at the meetings of the co-ordinating body as observers.

4. A Party may ask the co-ordinating body to furnish opinions on the interpretation of the provisions of the Convention.

5. Where difficulties or doubts arise between two or more Parties regarding the implementation or interpretation of the Convention, the competent authorities of those Parties shall endeavour to resolve the matter by mutual agreement. The agreement shall be communicated to the co-ordinating body.

6. The Secretary General of OECD shall inform the Parties, and the Signatory States which have not yet ratified, accepted or approved the Convention, of opinions furnished by the co-ordinating body according to the provisions of paragraph 4 above and of mutual agreements reached under paragraph 5 above.

Article 25 Language
Requests for assistance and answers thereto shall be drawn up in one of the official languages of OECD and of the Council of Europe or in any other language agreed bilaterally between the Contracting States concerned.

Article 26 Costs
Unless otherwise agreed bilaterally by the Parties concerned:
  a. ordinary costs incurred in providing assistance shall be borne by the requested State;
  b. extraordinary costs incurred in providing assistance shall be borne by the applicant State.

CHAPTER VI
FINAL PROVISIONS

Article 27 Other international agreements or arrangements
1. The possibilities of assistance provided by this Convention do not limit, nor are they limited by, those contained in existing or future international agreements or other arrangements between the Parties concerned or other instruments which relate to co-operation in tax matters.

2. Notwithstanding the rules of the present Convention, those Parties which are members of the European Economic Community shall apply in their mutual relations the common rules in force in that Community.

Article 28 Signature and entry into force of the Convention
1. This Convention shall be open for signature by the member States of the Council of Europe and the member countries of OECD. It is subject to ratification, acceptance or approval. Instruments of ratification, acceptance or approval shall be deposited with one of the Depositaries.

Part III

2. This Convention shall enter into force on the first day of the month following the expiration of a period of three months after the date on which five States have expressed their consent to be bound by the Convention in accordance with the provisions of paragraph 1.

3. In respect of any member State of the Council of Europe or any member country of OECD which subsequently expresses its consent to be bound by it, the Convention shall enter into force on the first day of the month following the expiration of a period of three months after the date of the deposit of the instrument of ratification, acceptance or approval.

Article 29 Territorial application of the Convention

1. Each State may at the time of signature, or when depositing its instrument of ratification, acceptance or approval, specify the territory or territories to which this Convention shall apply.

2. Any State may, at any later date, by a declaration addressed to one of the Depositaries, extend the application of this Convention to any other territory specified in the declaration. In respect of such territory the Convention shall enter into force on the first day of the month following the expiration of a period of three months after the date of receipt of such declaration by the Depositary.

3. Any declaration made under either of the two preceding paragraphs may, in respect of any territory specified in such declaration, be withdrawn by a notification addressed to one of the Depositaries. The withdrawal shall become effective on the first day of the month following the expiration of a period of three months after the date of receipt of such notification by the Depositary.

Article 30 Reservations

1. Any State may, at the time of signature or when depositing its instrument of ratification, acceptance or approval or at any later date declare that it reserves the right:

a. not to provide any form of assistance in relation to the taxes of other Parties in any if the categories listed in sub-paragraph b of paragraph 1 of Article 2, provided that it has not included any domestic tax in that category under Annex A of the Convention;

b. not to provide assistance in the recovery of any tax claim, or in the recovery of an administrative fine, for all taxes or only for taxes in one or more of the categories listed in paragraph 1 of Article 2;

c. not to provide assistance in respect of any tax claim, which is in existence at the date of entry into force of the Convention in respect of that State or, where a reservation has previously been made under sub-paragraph a or b above, at the date of withdrawal of such a reservation in relation to taxes in the category in question;

d. not to provide assistance in the service of documents for all taxes or only for taxes in one or more of the categories listed in paragraph 1 of Article 2;

e. not to permit the service of documents through the post as provided for in paragraph 3 of Article 17.

2. No other reservation may be made.

3. After the entry into force of the Convention in respect of a Party, that Party may make one or more of the reservations listed in paragraph 1 which it did not make at the time of ratification, acceptance or approval. Such reservations shall enter into force on the first day of the month following the expiration of a period of three months after the date of receipt of the reservation by one of the Depositaries.

4. Any Party which has made a reservation under paragraphs 1 and 3 may wholly or partly withdraw it by means of a notification addressed to one of the Depositaries.

The withdrawal shall take effect on the date of receipt of such notification by the Depositary in question.

5. A Party which has made a reservation in respect of a provision of this Convention may not require the application of that provision by any other Party; it may, however, if its reservation is partial, require the application of that provision insofar as it has itself accepted it.

Article 31 Denunciation

1. Any Party may at any time denounce this Convention by means of a notification addressed to one of the Depositaries.

2. Such denunciation shall become effective on the first day of the month following the expiration of a period of three months after the date of receipt of the notification by the Depositary.

3. Any Party which denounces the Convention shall remain bound by the provisions of Article 22 for as long as it retains in its possession any documents or information obtained under the Convention.

Article 32 Depositaries and their functions

1. The Depositary with whom an act, notification or communication has been accomplished, shall notify the member States of the Council of Europe and the member countries of OECD of:

a. any signature;

b. the deposit of any instrument of ratification, acceptance or approval;

c. any date of entry into force of this Convention in accordance with the provisions of Articles 28 and 29;

d. any declaration made in pursuance of the provisions of paragraph 3 of Article 4 or paragraph 3 of Article 9 and the withdrawal of any such declaration;

e. any reservation made in pursuance of the provisions of Article 30 and the withdrawal of any reservation effected in pursuance of the provisions of paragraph 4 of Article 30;

f. any notification received in pursuance of the provisions of paragraph 3 or 4 of Article 2, paragraph 3 of Article 3, Article 29 or paragraph 1 of Article 31;

g. any other act, notification or communication relating to this Convention.

2. The Depositary receiving a communication or making a notification in pursuance of the provisions of paragraph 1 shall inform the other Depositary thereof. In witness whereof the undersigned, being duly authorised thereto, have signed the Convention.

Done at Strasbourg, the 25th day of January 1988 in English and French, both texts being equally authentic, in two copies of which one shall be deposited in the archives of the Council of Europe and the other in the archives of OECD. The Secretaries General of the Council of Europe and of OECD shall transmit certified copies to each member State of the Council of Europe and of the member countries of OECD.

ANNEXES

ANNEX A
TAXES TO WHICH THE CONVENTION WOULD APPLY
AZERBAIJAN

Article 2, paragraph 1.a.i:

Part III

Income tax from individuals;

Profit tax from legal persons (with the exception of entities and enterprises that are the property of municipalities);

Tax withheld at the source of payment on income of non-residents;

Tax withheld from the net profit of a permanent establishment.

Article 2, paragraph 1.b.i:

Profit tax from entities and enterprises that are the property of municipalities.

Article 2, paragraph 1.b.ii:

Payments to the State Social Protection Fund.

Article 2, paragraph 1.b.iii.A:

Property tax from legal persons.

Article 2, paragraph 1.b.iii.B:

Land tax from legal persons.

Article 2, paragraph 1.b.iii.C:

Value added tax.

Article 2, paragraph 1.b.iii.D:

Excise tax.

Article 2, paragraph 1.b.iii.E:

Road tax.

Article 2, paragraph 1.b.iii.G:

Mining tax,

Tax under simplified system,

Duties withheld according to the "Law of state duties".

Article 2, paragraph 1.b.iv:

Land tax from individuals,

Property tax from individuals,

Mining tax on the exploitation of constructions materials produced in certain regions.

BELGIUM

I. Article 2, paragraph 1.a.i:

Personal tax,

Corporation tax,

Tax on legal persons,

Tax on non-residents,

Withholding tax on income from movable assets (tax on capital incomes), income tax reduced at source

Special surcharge on tax on non-residents

II. Article 2, paragraph 1.b.i:

Special surcharge on personal tax,

Withholding tax on income from immovable assets (property tax) and surcharge.

III. Article 2, paragraph 1.b.iii:

Under category A: Registration duties on gifts inter vivos.

Under category C: Value added tax.

Under category D:

Excise duties,

Special excise duties,

Annual tax on insurance policies,

Annual tax on profit sharing.

IV. Article 2, paragraph 1.b.iv:

Under category A: Death duties and duties on transfers following death

DENMARK

Danish taxes

Article 2, paragraph 1.a.i:
income taxes to the State (*indkomstskatter til staten*).

Article 2, paragraph 1.a.ii: . .

Article 2, paragraph 1.a.iii:
capital tax to the State (*formueskat til staten*) – repealed as of 1 January 1997, enforceable and collectible until 1 January 2002 (in cases of fraud until 1 January 2017).

Article 2, paragraph 1.b.i:
income tax to the municipalities (*kommunal indkomstskat*),
income tax to the county municipalities (*amtskommunal indkomstskat*),
tax on immovable property (*ejendomsskat*);
tax on assessed value of immovable property (*vdiskat*),
church tax (*kirkeskat*).

Article 2, paragraph 1.b.ii:
labour market contribution (*arbejdsmarkedsbidrag*),
special pension contribution (*srligt pensionsbidrag*).

Article 2, paragraph 1.b.iii.A:
tax on inheritance and gifts (*afgift af dødsboer og gaver*).

Article 2, paragraph 1.b.iii.B: . .

Article 2, paragraph 1.b.iii.C:
value added tax (*merværdiafgift*).

Article 2, paragraph 1.b.iii.D:
excise duties imposed by the State (*forbrugsafgifter, som pålægges af staten*).

Article 2, paragraph 1.b.iii.E:
registration tax on motor vehicles (*registreringsafgift af motorkøretøjer*),
weight tax on motor vehicles and other taxes on the ownership or use of motor vehicles (*vægtafgift af motorkøretøjer og andre afgifter på eje eller brug af motorkøretøjer*).

Article 2, paragraph 1.b.iii.F:
tax on insurances for yachts (*afgift af lystfartøjsforsikringer*).

Article 2, paragraph 1.b.iii.G:
payroll tax (*lønsumsafgift*),
taxes on betting, on casinos and on lottery prizes (*afgift af totalisatorspil, spillekasinoer og gevinster ved lotterispil*),
tax on registration of rights in real property etc. (*afgift af tinglysning og registrering af cíer- og panterettigheder*),
stamp duty (*stempelafgift*).

Article 2, paragraph 1.b.iv:
service charge on business property (*dækningsafgift af forretningsejendom*),
property release tax (*frigørelsesafgift*).

Greenlandic taxes

Article 2, paragraph 1.a.i:
income tax to the Greenlandic home rule Government (*landsskat*,
særlig landsskat),
dividend tax (*udbytteskat*),
company tax (*selskabsskat*).

Article 2, paragraph 1.b.i:

municipal tax (*kommuneskat*),
common municipal tax (*fælleskommunal ska*),
dividend tax (*udbytteskat*);
company tax (*selskabsskat*).

Article 2, paragraph 1.b.ii:

employer's contributions to vocational training (*arbejdsgivernes erhvervsuddannelsesbidrag*).

Article 2, paragraph 1.b.iii.A:

tax on inheritance and gifts (*afgift af arv og gave*).

Article 2, paragraph 1.b.iii.C:

import duty (*indførselsafgift*).

Article 2, paragraph 1.b.iii.D:

tax on gambling machines (*afgift af automatspil*),
harbour duty (*havneafgift*),
tax on sea transport of goods to, from and within Greenland (*afgift på søtransport af gods til, fra og I Grønland*),
tax on shrimps (*afgift på rejer*).

Article 2, paragraph 1.b.iii.E:

tax on motor vehicles (*afgift af motorkøretøjer*).

Article 2, paragraph 1.b.iii.G:

tax on lottery (*lotteriafgift*),
stamp duty (*stempelafgift*).

Faroese taxes

Article 2, paragraph 1.a.i:

income taxes to the Faroese home rule Government (*landsskattur*),
royalty taxes (*skattur av nýtslugjaldi*),
taxes levied under the Hydrocarbon Tax Act (*skattur eftier kolvetnisskattalógini*);
taxes levied under the Tonnage Tax Act (*skattur eftir tonnsaskattalógini*).

Article 2, paragraph 1.a.ii:

taxes levied under the Act on Taxation of Capital Gains (*kapitalvinningsskattur*).

Article 2, paragraph 1.b.i:

income taxes to the municipalities (*komunuskattur*);
church tax (*kirkjuskattur*).

Article 2, paragraph 1.b.ii:

labour market contribution (*ALS-gjald*),
special pension contribution (*arbeiðsmarknareftirlønargjald*).

Article 2, paragraph 1.b.iii.C:

value added tax (*meirvirðisgjald*).

Article 2, paragraph 1.b.iii.D:

import and excise duties (*tollur*).

Article 2, paragraph 1.b.iii.E:

registration tax on motor vehicles (*skrásetingargjald*),
weight tax on motor vehicles and other taxes on the ownership or use of motor vehicles (*veggjald*).

Article 2, paragraph 1.b.iii.G:

Tax on registration of rights in real property (*tinglýsingargjald*).

FINLAND

Article 2, paragraph 1 (a)(i):

the state income taxes *(valtion tuloverot; de statliga inkomstskatterna)*,

the corporate income tax *(yhteisöjen tulovero; inkomstskatten för samfund)*,

the tax withheld at source from non-residents' income *(rajoitetusti verovelvollisen lähdevero; källskatten för begränsat skattskyldig)*,

the tax withheld at source from interest *(korkotulon lähdevero; källskatten på ränteinkomst)*

the tax withheld at source from interest *(korkotulon lähdevero; källstkatten på ränteinkomst)*

the withholding tax for foreign employees *(ulkomailta tulevan palkansaajan lähdevero; källskatt för löntagare från utlandet)*

Article 2, paragraph 1 (a)(ii):

. . .

Article 2, paragraph 1 (a)(iii):

the state capital tax *(valtion varallisuusvero; den statliga förmögenhetsskatten)*

Article 2, paragraph 1 (b) (i):

the communal tax *(kunnallisvero; kommunalskatten)*,

the church tax *(kirkollisvero; kyrkoskatten)*,

the forestry duty *(metsänhoitomaksu; skogsvårdsavgiften)*

Article 2, paragraph 1 (b) (ii):

the national pension insurance contribution *(vakuutetun kansaneläkevakuutusmaksu; försäkrads folkpensionsförsäkringspremie)*,

the health insurance contribution *(vakuutetun sairausvakuutusmaksu; försäkrads sjukförsäkringspremie)*,

the employer's social security contribution *(työnantajan sosiaaliturvamaksu; arbetsgivares socialskyddsavgift)*

Article 2, paragraph 1 (b) (iii) A:

the inheritance tax and the gift tax *(perintövero ja lahjavero; arvsskatten och gåvoskatten)*

Article 2, paragraph 1 (b) (iii) B:

. . .

Article 2, paragraph 1 (b) (iii) C:

the value added tax *(arvonlisävero; mervärdesskatten)*

Article 2, paragraph 1 (b) (iii) D:

the excise duty on tobacco *(tupakkavero; tobaksaccisen)*,

the excise duty on soft drinks *(virvoitusjuomavero; läskedrycksaccisen)*,

the excise duty on liquid fuels *(nestemäisten polttoaineiden valmistevero; accisen på flytande bränslen)*,

the excise duty on electricity and certain energy sources *(sähkön ja eräiden polttoaineiden valmistevero; accis på elström och vissa bränslen)*,

the excise duty on alcohol and alcoholic beverages (*alkoholi- ja alkoholijuomavero; accisen på alkohol och alkoholdrycker)*,

the tax on certain insurance premiums *(eräistä vakuutusmaksuista suoritettava vero; skatten på vissa försäkringspremier)*,

the oil waste duty *(öljyjätemaksu; oljeavfallsavgiften)*,

the motor-car tax *(autovero; bilskatten)*

Article 2, paragraph 1 (b) (iii) E:

the tax on specific motor vehicles *(moottoriajoneuvovero; motorfordonsskatten)*,

the fuel fee *(polttoainemaksu; bränsleavgift)*,

the vehicle tax *(ajoneuvovero; fordonsskatt)*

Article 2, paragraph 1 (b) (iii) F: . . .

Article 2, paragraph 1 (b) (iii) G:

Part III

the stamp duty (*leimavero; stämpelskatten*),
the oil damage duty (*öljysuojamaksu, oljeskyddsavgiften*),
the transfer tax (*varallisuudensiirtovero; överlåtelseskatt*),
the tax on lottery prizes (*arpajaisvero; lotteriskatt*),
the tax on waste (*jätevero; avfallsskatt*)

Article 2, paragraph 1 (b) (iv):
the municipal tax on real property (*kiinteistövero; fastighetsskatten*)

ITALY

Article 2, paragraph 1 (a) (i)
— Personal Income Tax (*Imposta sul reddito delle persone fisiche - IRPEF*)
— Corporate Income Tax (*Imposta sul reddito delle società – IRES* and the former *Imposta sul reddito delle persone giuridiche –IRPEG*).

Article 2, paragraph 1 (a) (ii)
— Substitute Income Taxes, irrespective of their denomination.

Article 2, paragraph 1 (b) (i)
— Regional Tax on Productive Activities (*Imposta regionale sulle attività produttive – IRAP*).

Article 2, paragraph 1 (b) (iii)
Under category C: Value Added Tax (*Imposta sul valore aggiunto – IVA*).
Under category G:
Registration Tax (*Imposta di registro*);
Mortgage and Cadastral Taxes (*Imposte ipotecaria e catastale*).

Article 2, paragraph 1 (b) (iv)
— Local Property Tax (*Imposta comunale sugli immobili – ICI*).

THE NETHERLANDS

Article 2, paragraph 1 (a)
— Income Tax (*Inkomstenbelasting*)
— Salaries Tax (*Loonbelasting*)
— Corporation Tax (*Vennootschapsbelasting*)
— Dividend Tax (*Dividendbelasting*)
— Wealth Tax (*Vermogensbelasting*)

Article 2, paragraph 1 (b)
— Social Security Contributions (*Premies sociale verzekering*)

Article 2, paragraph 1 (c)
— Inheritance, Transfer or Gift Tax (*Rechten van successie, overgang of schenking*)

THE NETHERLANDS ANTILLES

Article 2, paragraph 1 (a)
— Income Tax (*Inkomstenbelasting*)
— Salaries Tax (*Loonbelasting*)
— Corporation Tax (*Winstbelasting*)

ARUBA

Article 2, paragraph 1 (a)
— Income Tax (*Inkomstenbelasting*)
— Salaries Tax (*Loonbelasting*)
— Corporation Tax (*Winstbelasting*)

NORWAY

Article 2, paragraph 1.a:
1. the national tax on income (*inntektsskatt til staten*)
the national dues on remuneration to non-resident artists (*avgift til staten av honorarer som tilfaller kunstnere bosatt i utlandet*)

2.   the national tax on capital gains from the alienation of shares (*skatt til staten av gevinst ved avhendelse av aksjer*)

3.   the national tax on capital (*formuesskatt til staten*)

Article 2, paragraph 1.b:

1.   the county municipal tax on income (*inntektsskat til fylkeskommunen*)
the municipal tax on income (*inntektsskat til kommunen*)
the municipal tax on capital (*formuesskatt til kommunen*)
the national contributions to the Tax Equalisation Fund (*fellesskatt til Skattefordelingsfondet*)

2.   contributions to the National Insurance Scheme (*folketrygdavgift*)

3. A.   tax on inheritance and certain gifts (*avgift på arv og visse gaver*)

3. B.   . . .

3. C.   value added tax (*merverdiavgift*)
investment tax (*investeringsavgift*)

3. D.   taxes and excises on:
     alcoholic beverages (*brennevin og vin m.v.*)
     alcohol in imported essences (*alkohol i essenser som innføres*)
     beer (*øl*)
     tobacco (*tobakksvarer*)
     petrol (*bensin*)
     petroleum (*mineralolje*)
     lubricants (*smøreolje*)
     marine engines (*båtmotorer*)
     electric power (*elektrisk kraft*)
     chocolates and sweets (*sjokolade*)
     sugar (*sukker*)
     non-alcoholic beverages (*alkoholfrie drikkevarer*)
     air-charter travel (*charterreiser med fly*)
     cosmetic toiletries (*kosmetiske toalettmidler*)
     equipment for recording and reproduction of sound and pictures etc. (*utstyr for opptak og gjengivelse av lyd og bilde m.v.*)
     unrecorded audiotapes as well as recorded and unrecorded videotapes (*uinnspilte lydkassettbånd og innspilte og uinnspilte videokassettbånd*)
     radio and television equipment (*radio og televisjonsmateriell*)
     non-returnable bottles (*engangsflasker*)
     batteries hazardous to the environment (*miljøskadelige batterier*)

3. E.   annual tax on motor vehicles (*årsavgift på motorvogner*)
tax on motor vehicles etc. (*engangsavgift på motorvogner m.v.*)
mileage tax on the use of diesel-powered vehicles (*kilometeravgift*)
reregistration tax (*omregistreringsavgift*)
tax on assembled motor vehicles (*oppbyggingsavgift*)

3. F.   tax on the registration of caravans (*avgift på førstegangs registrering av campingtilhengere*)
annual tax on caravans (*årsavgift på campingtilhengere*)

3. G.   tax on documents transferring title to real property (*avgift på dokument som overfører hjemmel til fast eiendom*)
tax on the transfer of ownership rights and rights of use to real property etc. abroad (*avgift på overføring av eiendomsrett og bruksrett til fast eiendom m.v. i utlandet*)

4.   municipal tax on real property (*eiendomsskatt til kommunen*)

Part III

POLAND

For the Republic of Poland, the Convention shall apply to the taxes referred to in sub-paragraphs (a)(i)–(iii) and (b) (ii)–(iii) of paragraph 1 of Article 2.

SWEDEN

Article 2, paragraph 1.a:

i. The State income tax (*den statliga inkomstskatten*)
the sailors' tax (*sjömansskatten*)
the coupon tax (*kupongskatten*)
the tax on public entertainers (*bevillningsavgiften för särskilda förmåner och rättigheter*)
the tax on the undistributed profits of companies (*ersättningsskatten*)
the tax on distribution in connection with reduction of share capital or the winding up of a company (*utskiftningsskatten*), and
the profit sharing tax (*vinstdelningsskatten*).

iii. The State capital tax (*den statliga förmögenhetsskatten*)

Article 2, paragraph 1.b:

i. The communal income tax (*den kommunala inkomstskatten*)

ii. Charges according to:
— the Act (1981:691) on Social Security Contributions [*lagen (1981:691) om socialavgifter*]
— the Act (1982:423) on General Payroll Fee [*om allmän löneavgift*]
— the Act (1984:668) on the Collection of Social Security Contributions from Employers [*om uppbörd av socialavgifter från arbetsgivare*], and
— the Act (1989:484) on Work Environment Fee [*om arbetsmiljöavgift*].

iii. A. The inheritance tax and the gift tax (*arvsskatten och gåvoskatten*).

iii. B. The State tax on real estate (*den statliga fastighetsskatten*).

iii. C. Taxes according to the Act (1968:430) on Value Added Tax [*om mervärdeskatt*].

iii. D. Taxes according to the Act (1978:144) on Tax on certain travels [*lagen (1978:144) om skatt på vissa resor*], and
the Act (1983:1053) on turnover tax on certain securities [*om skatt på omsättning av vissa värdepapper*].

iii. E. Charges and taxes according to:
— the Road Traffic Tax Act (1973:601) *vägtrafikskattelagen (1973:601)]*
— the Act (1976:338) on Road Traffic Tax on Vehicles which are not registered in Sweden [*(1976:388) om vägtrafikskatt på vissa fordon som inte är registrerade här i riket*]
— the Act (1976:339) on Tax on Cars for Sale [*lagen (1976:339) om saluvagnsskatt*]
— the Road Traffic Tax Act (1988:327) [*vägtrafikskattelagen (1988:327)*], and
— the Road Traffic Tax Act (1988:328) on foreign vehicles [*lagen (1988:328) om vägtrafikskatt på utländska fordon*].

iii. G. Charges according to the Act (1972:435) on Fee on Excess Freight [*lagen (1972:435) om överlastavgift*].

UNITED STATES OF AMERICA

For the United States, this Convention shall apply to taxes imposed under Title 26 of the United States Code (the Internal Revenue Code of 1986), as amended, which correspond to the taxes in the categories referred to in paragraph 1.A and 1.B II and III of Article 2 of the Convention.

ANNEX B
COMPETENT AUTHORITIES
AZERBAIJAN

Ministry of taxes,
State Customs Committee,
Ministry of Labour and Social Protection of Population,
Ministry of Finance.

BELGIUM

Minister for Finance or an authorised representative.

DENMARK

(except for Greenland)
The Minister for Taxation of his authorised representative,

GREENLAND

The Local Government or its authorised representative.

FINLAND

The National Board of Taxes.

ITALY

The Ministry of Economy and Finance – Tax Policy Department.

THE NETHERLANDS

— For tax purposes: the Minister of Finance or his authorised representative;
— For Social security purposes: the State Secretary for Social Affairs and Employment or his authorised representative.

THE NETHERLANDS ANTILLES

The Minister of Finance or his authorised representative.

ARUBA

The Minister of Finance or his authorised representative.

NORWAY

The Minister of Finance and Customs or his authorised representative.

POLAND

For the Republic of Poland, the term "competent authority" means the Minister of Finance or his authorized representative.

SWEDEN

The Minister of Finance or the National Tax Board.

UNITED STATES OF AMERICA

For the United States, the term "competent authority" means the Secretary of the Treasury or his designee.

ANNEX C

DEFINITION OF THE WORD "NATIONAL" FOR THE FOR THE PURPOSE OF THE CONVENTION
AZERBAIJAN

— all individuals possessing the nationality of the Republic of Azerbaijan;
— all legal persons (including partnership and joint venture), companies, associations and other organisations deriving their status as such from the legislation of the Republic of Azerbaijan.

BELGIUM

None.

THE NETHERLANDS

1. all individuals possessing the Dutch nationality;

2. all legal persons, companies and associations deriving their status as such from the laws in force in the Netherlands.

THE NETHERLANDS ANTILLES

1. all individuals possessing the Dutch nationality;

2. all legal persons, companies and associations deriving their status as such from the laws in force in the Netherlands Antilles.

ARUBA

1. all individuals possessing the Dutch nationality and having a legally valid title of residence for Aruba;

2. all legal persons, companies and associations deriving their status as such from the laws in force in Aruba.

Extra Statutory Concessions

Part VI

Part IV

Part IV
Extra Statutory Concessions

NOTICE 48
EXTRA-STATUTORY CONCESSIONS

(March 2002)

This notice cancels and replaces Notice 48 (December 1999). Details of any changes to the previous version can be found in paragraph 1.1 of this notice. Update 1 (June 2002) and Update 2 (August 2002) are included in this notice. Update 3 (March 2003) is not relevant to this publication.

1 INTRODUCTION

1.1 What is this notice about?

This notice gives details of all Customs and Excise extra-statutory concessions (ESCs) in force at the time of going to print. It replaces Notice 48 (December 1999) and Update 1 to Notice 48 (October 2000).

This Notice has been re-written to include details of ESCs that have been granted, or become obsolete, since the last edition. New ESCs are shown in paragraphs 2.7 [and] 6.4 . . .. Where possible, the numbering of ESCs that have become obsolete have been reused.

This notice is available both on paper and on our Internet website at www.hmce.gov.uk.

1.2 What is an extra-statutory concession?

In certain circumstances where remission or repayment of revenue is not provided for by law, the Department may allow relief on an extra-statutory basis. Extra-Statutory Concessions (ESCs) are remissions of revenue that allow relief in specific sets of circumstances to all businesses falling within the relevant conditions. They are authorised when strict application of the law would create a disadvantage or the effect would not be the one intended.

1.3 How are ESCs applied?

Customs and Excise ESCs are of general application. That is, a concession may be exercised by anyone to whom the circumstances set out in the concession apply without reference to C&E. However, where an attempt is made to use an ESC for tax avoidance, the Commissioners may withdraw or restrict its application.

1.4 Agreements with trade bodies

In certain trades, particular arrangements for applying VAT and other charges have been agreed with the appropriate trade association. These are not ESCs and are listed in Notice 700/57 *Administrative agreements entered into with trade bodies.*

1.5 Inland Revenue ESCs

Inland Revenue ESCs are published in their notice IR1 Extra-Statutory Concessions.

2 INTERNATIONAL FIELD

2.1 VAT, excise and customs duties—Goods and services

Duty (which includes all import and excise duties) and VAT are remitted or refunded in accordance with agreements with the authorities concerned on—

(a) goods and services imported by or supplied to visiting forces and their instrumentalities, for the official use of the force, or their instrumentalities;

(b) goods and services imported by or supplied to NATO military headquarters, organisations or agencies, for their official use;

(c) United States and Canadian Government expenditure on mutual defence or mutual aid contracts; and

(d) temporary importations of equipment required by contractors for fulfilling NATO infrastructure contracts or in connection with the provision and maintenance of US forces defence facilities in the United Kingdom.

2.2 VAT, excise and customs duties—UK-manufactured alcoholic liquor and tobacco products purchased by diplomats

Duty and VAT are remitted on alcoholic liquor and tobacco products of UK manufacture imported by, or supplied to, diplomatic representatives of foreign states in the United Kingdom who are entitled to similar privileges in respect of imported products of foreign manufacture under the Diplomatic Privileges Act 1964.

2.3 VAT, excise and customs duties—United States Air Force

Relief from VAT and/or excise duty is allowed, in accordance with conditions agreed with the United States Air Force, on—

(a) charges for admission to air shows and open days; and

(b) goods sold by US forces organisations during air shows and open days to persons not entitled to receive/consume them unless customs charges have been paid.

2.4 VAT and customs duty—Gifts

Duty and VAT are remitted on gifts (whether imported or purchased in the United Kingdom) from United States forces to charitable organisations.

2.5

(Outside scope of this work.)

2.7 VAT and customs duty—Certain aircraft ground and security equipment

The Convention on International Civil Aviation (Chicago Convention) allows relief from duty and VAT for certain ground and security equipment imported into the territory of one Contracting State by an airline of another Contracting State operating an international service. The United Kingdom is a signatory to the Chicago Convention.

Additionally, the United Kingdom has concluded a number of Air Service Agreements which allow, on a reciprocal basis, the various reliefs detailed in the Convention, including the one mentioned above.

We have become aware that end-use relief may be being claimed erroneously in these cases. Aircraft ground and security equipment does not qualify for end-use relief. We are in the process of drawing up a new procedure to enable the relief to be correctly claimed.

In the interim period an extra-statutory concession has been agreed to allow relief for ground and security equipment to be claimed. The following list details those goods which qualify for relief and who is eligible to claim it.

Qualifying goods—The following ground and security equipment for aircraft—

(a)   Repair, maintenance and servicing equipment—
— material for airframes, engines and instruments;
— specialised aircraft repair kits;
— starter batteries and carts;
— maintenance platforms and steps;
— test equipment for aircraft, aircraft engines, and instruments;
— aircraft engine heaters and coolers; and
— ground radio equipment.
(b)   Passenger-handling equipment—
— passenger—loading steps;
— specialised passenger-weighing devices; and
— specialised catering equipment.
(c)   Cargo-loading equipment—
— vehicles for moving or loading of baggage, cargo, equipment or supplies;
— specialised cargo-loading devices; and
— specialised cargo-weighing devices.
(d)   Component parts for incorporation into ground equipment including the items listed above.
(e)   Security equipment—
— weapon-detecting devices;
— explosives-detecting devices; and
— intrusion detecting devices.
(f)   Component parts for incorporation into security equipment.

Claims for relief of duty and VAT under this concession should be addressed to the Entry Processing Unit where the goods will be cleared with a copy of this advice.

2.8 Relief from UK excise duty on alcoholic drinks supplied duty-paid in another Member State for consumption on Eurostar trains which are in UK territory

The measure provides a scheme to tax alcohol supplied for consumption on Eurostar trains. The basis for the scheme is that alcoholic drinks loaded in France or Belgium duty paid on journeys commencing from those Member States and destined for the UK will not incur a liability to UK duty when entering the UK. Conversely, such goods loaded for journeys commencing from the UK will be UK duty paid, but will not attract reimbursement when consumed outside UK territory. The revenue effect will therefore be broadly neutral.

Part IV

3 VAT—CONCESSIONS DESIGNED TO REMOVE INEQUITIES OR ANOMALIES IN ADMINISTRATION

3.1–3.12

(Outside scope of this work.)

3.13 VAT—Repayment of import VAT to shipping agents and freight forwarders

Import VAT may be paid directly to shipping agents and freight forwarders where importers go into liquidation, or where an administrator or administrative receiver has been appointed who certifies that, in his or her opinion, ordinary unsecured creditors would receive nothing in a liquidation, leaving the agents unable to recover VAT paid on their behalf. The importers must have gone into a formal state of insolvency or receivership within 6 months of the date of lodgement of the Customs entry, and the goods must have remained under the agents' control throughout their stay in the UK and have been re-exported unused from the European Community.

3.14 VAT—Zero-rating of certain supplies of free zone goods

From 1 August 1991 the supply of goods subject to import VAT which are free zone goods in the UK may be zero-rated on condition that there is an agreement between the supplier and the customer that the customer will clear the goods for removal from the zone and will take responsibility for payment of the import VAT.

3.15–3.38

(Outside scope of this work.)

6 EXCISE DUTIES—CONCESSIONS DESIGNED TO REMOVE INEQUITIES OR ANOMALIES IN ADMINISTRATION

6.1 Excise—hydrocarbon oil duty—Duty-paid deliveries for bonded users/distributors

When the Commissioners are satisfied that duty-paid oil has been delivered to a person approved to receive duty-free oil of the same description under the provisions of the Hydrocarbon Oil Duties Act 1979, they may repay to the supplier the duty which they are satisfied has been paid, and not repaid, on the quantity of oil so delivered subject to the conditions which would apply if the oil had been delivered without payment of duty.

6.2 Excise—hydrocarbon oil duty—Duty-paid deliveries for refinery boilers

When the Commissioners are satisfied that unused, duty-paid, hydrocarbon oil has been delivered to any premises approved as a refiners for use as fuel for the production of energy they may repay to the supplier the duty which they are satisfied has been paid, and not repaid, on the quantity of oil delivered.

6.3 Excise—hydrocarbon oil duty—Relief of duty on recovered motor spirit vapour

From 15 April 1993 duty relief may be allowed on motor spirit vapour recovered, during duty-paid deliveries of motor spirit from bonded mineral oil installations to service stations, and returned to bonded installations for conversion to liquid motor spirit.

6.4 Excise Duty—hydrocarbon oil duty: Fuel substitutes, additives and extenders

The rate of duty applicable where a duty of excise is charged under section 6A of the Hydrocarbon Oils Duties Act 1979 ('HODA') is prescribed by the Other Fuel Substitutes (Rates of Excise Duty etc) Order 1995, SI 1995/2716 ('the 1995 Order'). The Other Fuel Substitutes (Payment of Excise Duty etc) Regulations 1995, SI 1995/2717 ('the 1995 Regulations') make various provisions regarding the payment of duty, making of returns and keeping and preservation of the fuel substitutes record.

By way of concession:

Fuel substitutes

(1)   Where a liquid is—
   (a)   entered in the fuel substitutes record as being suitable only as a fuel for a diesel engine, (see article 4(2)(a) of the 1995 Order); or
   (b)   used as fuel in such an engine (see article 4(5) of the 1995 Order).

The rate of duty shall be that specified in section 6(1A) HODA in respect of ultra sulphur diesel and not that for heavy oil.

(1)   Where the liquid is–
   (a)   entered in the fuel substitutes record as being suitable only as a fuel for a petrol engine powered by unleaded petrol (see article 4(2)(c) of the 1995 Order); or
   (b)   used as a fuel in such an engine (see article 4(5) of the 1995 Order),
   the rate of duty shall be that specified in section 6(1A) HODA in respect of ultra sulphur petrol and not the effective rate for unleaded petrol.

Liquid suitable for use as a fuel, or as an additive or extender in fuel, for any petrol engine

(1)   Where a liquid is suitable for use both as fuel, or as an additive or extender in fuel, for both:
   (a)   a petrol engine powered by unleaded petrol; and
   (b)   a petrol engine powered by leaded petrol,
   it may be entered in the fuel substitutes record, and accounted for, as if the liquid were suitable only as a fuel, or as an additive or extender in fuel (as the case may be), for a petrol engine powered by unleaded petrol.

(2)   Where paragraph (3) above apples, the rate of duty shall be that specified in section 6(1A) HODA in respect of ultra low sulphur and not that for light oil.

Additives or extenders in fuels

(1)   Where a liquid is:
   (a)   entered in the fuel substitutes record as being suitable only as an additive or extender in fuel for a diesel engine, (see article 5(2) of the Order); or
   (b)   used as an additive or extender in fuel used is such an engine (see article 5(5)(a) of the 1995 Order),
   the rate of duty shall be that specified in section 6(1A) HODA in respect of ultra sulphur diesel and not that for heavy oil.

(2)   Where a liquid is:

    (a)   entered in the fuel substitutes record as being suitable only as an additive or extender in fuel for a petrol engine powered by unleaded petrol (see article 5(2) of the 1995 Order); or

    (b)   used as an additive or extender in fuel used in such an engine (see article 5(5)(a) of the 1995 Order,

the rate of duty shall be that specified in section 6(1A) HODA in respect of ultra low petrol and not the effective rate for unleaded petrol.

6.5 Excise—spirits duty—The Alcoholic Liquor Duties Act 1979—application of sections 18 and 21 to the recovery of spirits by authorised duty-free spirits users

Persons authorised to receive duty-free spirits under section 8 or 10 of the Alcoholic Liquor Duties Act 1979 may recover spirits by distillation provided a licence to rectify is taken out under section 18(1) of that Act. The requirements of section 21 of the Act and Part II of the Spirits (Rectifying, Compounding and Drawback) Regulations 1988 will be waived.

6.6 Excise—spirits duty—The Methylated Spirits Regulations 1987—application of regulations 14 and 15 to the production and distribution of trade specific denatured alcohol

The denatured ethanol grade of spirits described in the Methylated Spirits Regulations 1987 regulation 14(1)(c) will be interpreted as including grades of denatured ethanol other than the statutory formulation of regulation 15(1)(c) provided—

— it is demonstrated than an alternative formulation for denatured ethanol is required; and
— that such a formulation is approved by the Commissioners following evaluation of the denaturant properties of the product.

6.7 Excise—spirits duty: The Beer Regulations 1993: Amendment to Part IX, Regulations 26–33, to make provision for repayment of duty on beer that is not of satisfactory quality in the case of beer that is not currently eligible for repayment of duty

This concession provides for the brewing industry to assume the practical control of beer of unsatisfactory quality, subject to the following conditions being observed:

— there is a complete audit trail which confirms the beer has been destroyed and that is was duty paid;
— the destruction of the beer is supervised by a responsible representative of the brewery; and
— the requirements of other regulatory authorities are observed.

6.8 Excise—spirits duty: Deregulating the proportion of duty-free spirits that may be mixed with wine or made-wine in an excise warehouse

Sections 57 and 58 of the ALDA enables the Commissioners of Customs and Excise to permit, and impose conditions on, the mixing in an excise warehouse of duty-free spirits with the wine or made-wine in a proportion not exceeding 12 litres of alcohol to 1 hectolitre (100 litres) of wine or made-wine.

That proportion may be disregarded under this concession so long as the resultant mixture does not assume the essential characteristics of a spirit (as defined in the Integrated Tariff of the United Kingdom).

However, the requirements in ALDA that the mixtures in question must not by virtue of the relevant provisions be raised to strengths greater than 22 per cent remain unaffected.

This concession has been amended with effect from 27 April 2002.

6.9 Excise—warehoused goods: Requirement for revenue traders to register

The Warehousekeepers and Owners of Warehoused Goods Regulations 1999 (SI 1999/1278) require revenue traders who wish to deposit dutiable goods other than hydrocarbon oil ('relevant goods') in an excise warehouse, or purchase warehoused relevant goods, to be approved as registered owners.

As a concession, from 1 October 1999 the Commissioners will treat the definition of 'relevant goods' in regulation 2 as if it were amended so as to exclude wine and made-wine so that wine and made-wine will be treated in the same way as hydrocarbon oil is treated for the purposes of the Regulations. (Wine and made-wine are defined in sections 1(4) and 1(5) respectively of the Alcohol Liquor Duties Act 1979, which Act, by section 4(2), is to be construed as one Act with the Customs and Excise Management Act 1979).

6.10 Excise—duty-free successor regime: Goods in transit through the UK

From 18 June 2001 the requirement that excise goods imported as merchandise on board aircraft from other EU Member States in accordance with the simplified procedure must be exported from the UK not later than twenty-four hours after the time of importation is relaxed. That requirement (imposed by regulation 25(5)(c) of the Excise Goods (Sales on Board Ships and Aircraft) Regulations 1999) will be treated as having been complied with if the excise goods are exported no later than 15 days after importation.

8 FACILITATION OF EXPORTS

8.1 VAT—Sailaway boats

Under regulation 129 of the Value Added Tax Regulations 1995, the supply of a sailaway boat to an overseas resident outside the VAT territory of the Member States may be zero-rated provided the boat is exported to a place outside the Member States within 6 months of the date of delivery, and the supplier obtains satisfactory proof of its eventual export.

As a concession and to prevent loss of UK trade, the supply of a boat to a UK resident may also be zero-rated provided—

(a) the supplier has evidence that the UK resident intends to keep the boat outside the VAT territory of the Member States for a continuous period of at least 12 months; and

(b) the boat is exported, within 2 months of the date of delivery, to a place outside the VAT territory of the Member States; and

(c) the boat is not used for any commercial purposes between the time of supply and exportation; and

(d) the supplier obtains and holds satisfactory evidence of export of the boat directly to a place outside the VAT territory of the Member States on copy 3 of the Form C88 (Single Administrative Document).

The above conditions apply to boats supplied both to UK residents who intend to keep them abroad and to UK residents intending to emigrate.

Part IV

9 NON-COMMERCIAL TRANSACTIONS

9.1, 9.2

(Outside scope of this work.)

9.3 VAT and excise duties—Personal reliefs for goods permanently imported from third countries

Where property (including motor vehicles) which has been purchased in accordance with the terms of Article 15/10 of Directive 77/388/EEC and which otherwise qualifies for relief from payment of customs charges under Article 11 of the Customs and Excise Duties (Personal Reliefs for Goods Permanently Imported) Order 1992, relief is not to be refused solely by reason of Article 11.2 of that Order.

9.4 VAT and excise duties—Personal reliefs for goods permanently imported from third countries

Where property (including motor vehicles) which has been purchased by members of UK forces (or by the civilian staff accompanying them) in countries outside the area of the European Community and which otherwise qualifies for relief from payment of customs charges under Article 11 of the Customs and Excise Duties (Personal Reliefs for Goods Permanently Imported) Order 1992, relief is not to be refused solely by reason of Article 11.2 of that Order.

9.5 VAT and excise duties—Personal reliefs for goods permanently imported from third countries

Where property (including motor vehicles) which has been purchased under a UK export scheme by members of the UK diplomatic service, by members of UK forces or by the civilian staff accompanying them or by members of international organisations and which otherwise qualifies for relief from payment of customs charges under Article 11 of the Customs and Excise Duties (Personal Reliefs for Goods Permanently Imported) Order 1992, relief is not to be refused solely by reason of Article 11.2 of that Order.

9.6 VAT and excise duties—Personal reliefs for goods permanently imported from third countries

Where personal belongings otherwise qualify for relief under Article 11 of the Customs and Excise Duties (Personal Reliefs for Goods Permanently Imported) Order 1992 save only that the property has not been possessed and used for the specified period, then just as relief can be granted from customs duties as 'special cases justified by the circumstances' under Article 3 of Council Regulation 918/83, similar consideration shall apply in respect of VAT and excise duties and relief may be granted accordingly.

9.7 VAT and excise duties—Personal reliefs for goods permanently imported from third countries

Where personal belongings otherwise qualify for relief under Article 11 of the Customs and Excise Duties (Personal Reliefs for Goods Permanently Imported) Order 1992 save only that the property is declared for relief outside the specific periods, then just as relief can be granted from customs duties as special cases under Article 6, or under Article 9 of Council Regulation 918/83, similar consideration shall apply in respect of VAT and excise duties and relief may be granted accordingly.

10 CONCESSIONS OBSOLETE SINCE LAST EDITION OF UPDATE 1 TO NOTICE 48 (PUBLISHED IN OCTOBER 2000)

(Outside scope of this work.)

INDEX

CUSTOMS AND EXCISE DUTIES – *cont.*

hydrocarbon oil, on. *See*
HYDROCARBON OIL

imported goods, on. *See* IMPORTATION
OF GOODS

new or altered, addition or deduction in
case of contract, FA 1901 s 10

overpaid interest, repayment of, FA 1999
s 129

overpaid, recovery of, CEMA 1979 s 137A

personal reliefs. *See* RELIEFS

products subject to excise duties. *See*
EXCISE GOODS

recovery of, CEMA 1979 s 137

relevant rule, contravention of, SI
2003/3113

remission. *See* REMISSION OF DUTY

repayment. *See* REPAYMENT OF DUTY

resolutions not having statutory effect,
provisions for securing, PCTA 1968
s 3

revenues, protection of, F(No 2)A 1992
s 3

temporary tax
payments and deductions made on
account, PCTA 1968 s 2
provisional effect, resolutions
giving, PCTA 1968 s 5
resolutions not having statutory effect,
provisions for securing, PCTA
1968 s 3

tobacco products, on. *See* TOBACCO
PRODUCTS

unpaid, handling goods subject to, CEMA
1979 s 170A

CUSTOMS AND EXCISE ENACTMENTS

postal packets, application to, POA 1953
s 16

CUSTOMS DEBT

entry in accounts, 2454/93/EEC
arts 868–876a

extinction of, 2913/92/EEC arts 233, 234

incurring, 2913/92/EEC arts 201–216
failures having no significant effect on
temporary storage or customs
procedure, 2454/93/EEC
arts 859–861
natural wastage, 2454/93/EEC
arts 862–864
special situations, goods in,
2454/93/EEC arts 865–867a

joint and several liability for, 2913/92/EEC
art 213

recovery of
communication to debtor, 2913/92/EEC
arts 217–221
deferment, 2913/92/EEC arts 224–229

CUSTOMS DEBT – *cont.*

recovery of – *cont.*
enforcement, 2913/92/EEC art 232
entry in accounts, 2913/92/EEC
arts 217–221
post-clearance, 2454/93/EEC
arts 868–876a
procedures for, 2913/92/EEC
arts 222–232
third person, payment by, 2913/92/EEC
art 231
time limit. 2913/92/EEC art 222

security, 2913/92/EEC arts 189–200,
2454/93/EEC arts 857, 858

unpaid, interest on, FA 1999 s 126

CUSTOMS DECLARATIONS

acts considered to be, 2454/93/EEC
arts 230–236

data-processing technique, using,
2913/92/EEC art 77, 2454/93/EEC
arts 222–224, Annex 32

deemed, 2454/93/EEC arts 230–236

economic impact, procedure with
customs control, processing under,
2454/93/EEC arts 275, 276
customs warehousing procedure,
2454/93/EEC arts 268–274
discharge, 2454/93/EEC arts 277a, 278
incomplete, 2454/93/EEC art 268
inward processing, for, 2454/93/EEC
arts 275, 276
local procedure, 2454/93/EEC
arts 272–274, 276
outward processing, for, 2454/93/EEC
art 277
simplified, 2454/93/EEC arts 269–271,
276
temporary importation, 2454/93/EEC
arts 275, 276

export
documents, 2454/93/EEC art 288
formalities, simplified, 2454/93/EEC
art 279
incomplete, 2454/93/EEC arts 282, 281
local procedure, 2454/93/EEC
arts 283–287
simplified, 2454/93/EEC art 282
single member State, operation in,
2454/93/EEC art 289

incomplete, 2454/93/EEC art 253

invalidation, 2454/93/EEC art 251

oral, 2913/92/EEC art 77, 225–229, 235,
236

permanent export, on, 2454/93/EEC
arts 788–796

post-clearance examination, 2913/92/EEC
art 78

EXCISE GOODS. *See also* **ALCOHOLIC LIQUOR, ETC** – *cont.*
ships and aircraft, sales on – *cont.*
registered mobile operators – *cont.*
registration, SI 1999/1565 reg 3
simplified procedures, notice of, SI 1999/1565 regs 24, 25
simplified procedures
application of regulations, SI 1999/1565 reg 23
notice, SI 1999/1565 reg 24
procedure, SI 1999/1565 reg 25
transitional provisions, SI 1999/1565 reg 28
suspension of duty. *See* DUTY-SUSPENSION ARRANGEMENTS
tariffs. *See* TARIFFS
transitional provisions, 92/12/EEC art 28
EXCISE LICENCE
entry of premises
new or further, CEMA 1979 s 109
offences, CEMA 1979 s 111
proof as to, CEMA 1979 s 110
requirement, CEMA 1979 s 108
form and content of, CEMA 1979 s 101
licence year, definition, CEMA 1979 s 1
payments by cheque, CEMA 1979 s 102
removal of, CEMA 1979 s 104
renewal, CEMA 1979 s 103
sets of premises, for, CEMA 1979 s 101
trade
definition, CEMA 1979 s 1
sets of premises, on, CEMA 1979 s 101
sign, requirement to display, CEMA 1979 s 107
transfer and removal of, CEMA 1979 s 104
transfer of, CEMA 1979 s 104
EXPLOSIVES
movement of, CEMA 1979 s 75
EXPORTATION OF GOODS
Channel Tunnel. *See* CHANNEL TUNNEL
customs procedures, 2913/92/EEC arts 161, 162
departing aircraft, loading of goods on, SI 1981/1259 reg 7
information, provision of, CEMA 1979 ss 77, 77A
local export control, CEMA 1979 ss 58A, 58B
movement certificates, 1207/2001/EC
offences
agricultural levies, as to, CEMA 1979 s 68A
generally, CEMA 1979 s 67

EXPORTATION OF GOODS – *cont.*
offences – *cont.*
penalties, SI 2003/3102
prohibited or restricted goods, as to, CEMA 1979 s 68
origin of goods evidenced
under Community law or practice, information as to, CEMA 1979 s 80
outward entry and clearance
aircraft, of
clearance, CEMA 1979 s 64
refusal or cancellation of clearance, CEMA 1979 s 65
Community customs documents, authentication, CEMA 1979 s 58E
correction and cancellation of entry, CEMA 1979 s 55
date for Community purposes, CEMA 1979 s 58D
delivery of entry, CEMA 1979 s 53
dutiable or restricted goods
meaning, CEMA 1979 s 52
restrictions, CEMA 1979 s 60
failure to export, CEMA 1979 s 56
incomplete entry, acceptance of, CEMA 1979 s 54
information and documentation, CEMA 1979 s 62
local export control, CEMA 1979 s 58A
owner of exporting ship, delivery of entry by, CEMA 1979 s 57
putting goods alongside for loading, restriction on, CEMA 1979 s 59
ships, of
clearance, CEMA 1979 s 64
entry outwards, CEMA 1979 s 63
refusal or cancellation of clearance, CEMA 1979 s 65
simplified clearance procedure, CEMA 1979 ss 58, 58B
outward processing. *See* OUTWARD PROCESSING
permanent
declarations, 2454/93/EEC arts 788–796
Single Administrative Document, 2454/93/EEC arts 792, 793
pipe-line, by, CEMA 1979 s 58C
presentation for export
definitions, SI 2003/467 reg 2
documentary means, by, SI 2003/467 reg 3, Schs 1, 2
electronic communication, SI 2003/467 regs 4, 5
records, CEMA 1979 s 75A
regulations, power to make, CEMA 1979 s 66

FREE ZONES – *cont.*

certificate of customs status, 2454/93/EEC Annex 109

commercial policy measures, application of, 2454/93/EEC art 808

communication of information to Commission, 2454/93/EEC art 802

construction in, 2913/92/EEC art 167

controls, 2454/93/EEC arts 805–814

customs status of goods, certificate of, 2454/93/EEC Annex 109

customs territory, part of, 2913/92/EEC art 166

definitions, SI 1984/1177 reg 2, SI 1991/2727 reg 2

designation, CEMA 1979 s 100A, 2913/92/EEC arts 167, 168a

enclosure, 2913/92/EEC art 167

goods

agricultural levy, charge of, SI 1984/1177 reg 19

chargeable operation on, SI 1984/1177 reg 19

Community status

acknowledgement of, SI 1984/1177 reg 7

proof of, 2454/93/EEC arts 314b–336

customs duty on, SI 1984/1177 reg 25

destruction of, SI 1984/1177 reg 21

detention, seizure and condemnation, SI 1991/2727 reg 7

duty deemed to have been paid on, SI 1984/1177 reg 20

entry before removal for home use, SI 1984/1177 reg 11

excise goods becoming, SI 1984/1177 reg 5

goods becoming, SI 1984/1177 reg 6

information, provision of, SI 1984/1177 reg 24

movement of, VATA 1994 s 17

operations on, SI 1984/1177 reg 9

other customs procedure, subject to, SI 1984/1177 reg 8

procedure for entering, SI 1984/1177 reg 10

production of, SI 1984/1177 reg 22

records, keeping, SI 1984/1177 reg 24

remaining in

entry of, SI 1984/1177 reg 17

payment of duty on, SI 1984/1177 reg 18

removal of, 2913/92/EEC arts 177–181

after entry, SI 1984/1177 reg 13

export, for, SI 1984/1177 reg 14

FREE ZONES – *cont.*

goods – *cont.*

remaining in – *cont.*

removal of, 2913/92/EEC arts 177–181 – *cont.*

payment of duty before, SI 1984/1177 reg 16

restriction on, SI 1984/1177 reg 15

without entry, SI 1984/1177 reg 12

segregation, SI 1984/1177 reg 23

supply to non-VAT registered person, relief from import tax, SI 1984/1177 reg 27

zero-rating, ESC 48 3.14

information sheets, 2454/93/EEC Annex 71

meaning, CEMA 1979 s 100A

offences, penalties and forfeiture, SI 1991/2727 reg 6

operation of, 2913/92/EEC arts 171–176

operator, meaning, 2454/93/EEC art 799

placing of goods in, 2913/92/EEC arts 169, 170

powers of search, CEMA 1979 s 100F

relevant Community provisions, SI 1991/2727 Sch

repealed provisions, SI 1991/2727 reg 3

residence not permitted in, SI 1984/1177 reg 4

security and recovery of expenditure, SI 1984/1177 reg 3

stock records, approval of, 2454/93/EEC arts 803, 804

supervision, 2913/92/EEC art 168

FREIGHT FORWARDER

import VAT, repayment of, ESC 48 3.13

GAME

licences, CEMA 1979 s 176

GAMING DUTY

rates of, FA 2005 s 6

GOODS

control of movement of

accidents, SI 1984/1176 reg 18

application of regulations, SI 1984/1176 reg 4

completion of removals, SI 1984/1176 reg 16

definitions, SI 1984/1176 reg 3

goods, vehicles and container, security of, SI 1984/1176 regs 14, 15

local export control, SI 1984/1176 reg 9

removal document, requirement for, SI 1984/1176 reg 11

restrictions on movement, SI 1984/1176 regs 5–8

RELIEFS – *cont.*
Community system of – *cont.*
import duty relief – *cont.*
organisations protecting copyrights or patent rights, consignments sent to, 918/83/EEC art 107
personal luggage, goods in, 918/83/EEC arts 45–49
pharmaceutical products used at international sporting events, 918/83/EEC art 64
place of normal residence, transfer of, 918/83/EEC arts 2–10
present received in context of international relations, 918/83/EEC arts 87–89
reference substances for quality control of medicinal products, 918/83/EEC art 63c
scholastic effects, 918/83/EEC arts 25, 26
scientific instruments and apparatus, 918/83/EEC arts 50–59, 2290/83/EEC arts 5–8, 2290/83/EEC arts 18a–18c
secondary residence, household effects for furnishing, 918/83/EEC arts 20–24
seeds, fertilisers and products for treatment of soil and crops, 918/83/EEC arts 43, 44
spare parts, components, accessories and tools, 2290/83/EEC arts 12–15
stowage and protection of goods, materials for, 918/83/EEC art 110
therapeutic substances or human origin, 918/83/EEC arts 61–63
tourist information literature, 918/83/EEC art 108
trade promotion purposes, goods imported for, 918/83/EEC arts 91–99
transfer of activities from third country, capital goods and equipment for, 918/83/EEC arts 32–38
war victims, materials for upkeep of cemeteries etc for, 918/83/EEC art 117
information, communication of, 2290/83/EEC arts 16, 18
intention, fulfilment of, SI 1984/719 art 6
normal residence, rules for determining, SI 1984/719 art 3

RELIEFS – *cont.*
Community system of – *cont.*
visual and auditory materials of educational, scientific or cultural nature, 918/83/EEC Annex II
continental shelf, produce of, CED(GR)A 1979 s 14
customs duties, from
annual report, CED(GR)A 1979 s 16
Community obligations, conformity with, CED(GR)A 1979 s 1
Community practices, referable to, CED(GR)A 1979 s 2
false statements relating to, CED(GR)A 1979 s 15
international obligations, conformity with, CED(GR)A 1979 s 1
excise duties, from
foreign goods re-imported, for, CED(GR)A 1979 s 11
testing, goods imported for, CED(GR)A 1979 s 11A
UK goods re-imported, for, CED(GR)A 1979 s 10
giving of, FA 1994 s 12B
goods permanently imported, for
declaration of goods, SI 1992/3193 art 8
definitions, SI 1992/3193 art 2
disposal without authorisation, restriction on, SI 1992/3193 art 7
enforcement, SI 1992/3193 art 10
gifts of official visitors, SI 1992/3193 arts 18, 19
honorary decorations and awards, SI 1992/3193 art 17
inheritance, goods acquired by, SI 1992/3193 art 21
intention, condition of fulfilment, SI 1992/3193 art 9
marriage, import on from third country, SI 1992/3193 arts 13–15
place of normal residence, determining, SI 1992/3193 arts 3, 4
pupils and students, equipment of, SI 1992/3193 art 16
security, SI 1992/3193 art 6
separate consignments, in, SI 1992/3193 art 5
transfer of normal residence from third country, SI 1992/3193 arts 11, 12
grant of, 2913/92/EEC art 184
Her Majesty's ships, supplies to, CED(GR)A 1979 s 12
importation, on
application for, SI 1958/1965 art 2
application of, SI 1958/1965 art 1